MARTIN'S
ANNUAL CRIMINAL CODE
=== 2017 ===

Special Edition
In Memory of The Honourable
Mr. Justice Marc Rosenberg

CANADA LAW BOOK

MARTIN'S
ANNUAL CRIMINAL CODE
2017

With Annotations by

MARIE HENEIN, LL.B., LL.M.

In Memory and Acknowledgement of his valued
contributions from 1997 to 2015:
The Honourable Mr. Justice
MARC ROSENBERG

In Memory and Acknowledgement of his valued
contributions from 1978 to 2014:
EDWARD L. GREENSPAN, Q.C.

THOMSON REUTERS®

A cataloguing record for this publication is available from Library and Archives Canada

ISBN: 978-0-88804-933-9; 978-0-88804-934-6 (judicial); 978-0-88804-935-3 (police); 978-0-88804-936-0 (student)

Printed in the United States by Thomson Reuters

TELL US HOW WE'RE DOING
Scan the QR code to the right with your smartphone to send your comments regarding our products and services.
Free QR Code Readers are available from your mobile device app store.
You can also email us at carswell.feedback@thomsonreuters.com

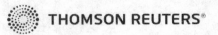

THOMSON REUTERS®

THOMSON REUTERS CANADA, A DIVISION OF THOMSON REUTERS CANADA LIMITED

One Corporate Plaza
2075 Kennedy Road
Toronto, ON
M1T 3V4

Customer Relations
Toronto 1-416-609-3800
Elsewhere in Canada/U.S. 1-800-387-5164
Fax 1-416-298-5082
www.carswell.com
E-mail www.carswell.com/email

TABLE OF CONTENTS

IN MEMORY OF
The Honourable Justice Marc Rosenberg
(1950-2015)

It is with great sadness that we commemorate the passing of The Honourable Justice Marc Rosenberg.

Justice Rosenberg was a highly regarded appellate advocate, judge and one of our greatest legal minds. His tireless commitment to legal judicial education, both nationally and internationally, was a great contribution. The Honourable Justice Rosenberg was a long-standing co-author and co-editor of *Martin's Annual Criminal Code, Martin's Criminal Code (Counsel Edition), Martin's Related Criminal Statutes, Martin's Ontario Criminal Practice, Martin's Pocket Criminal Code, Martin's Online Criminal Code*, the *Dominion Law Reports* and the *Canadian Criminal Cases*.

It was a great honour to work with him and be the beneficiary, like so many in his profession, of his knowledge, compassion and great wisdom. He will be greatly missed.

Marie Henein

IN MEMORY OF
Edward L. Greenspan, Q.C.
(1944-2014)

It is with great sadness that we acknowledge the passing of Edward L. Greenspan, Q.C., one of the most celebrated criminal defence lawyers in Canada.

A tireless and passionate advocate, speaker and writer, Mr. Greenspan was a long-standing co-author of *Martin's Annual Criminal Code*, *Martin's Criminal Code (Counsel Edition)*, *Martin's Related Criminal Statutes*, *Martin's Ontario Criminal Practice*, *Martin's Pocket Criminal Code*, *Martin's Online Criminal Code*, *Canadian Charter of Rights Annotated*, and *Dubin Lectures on Advocacy 1998-2002*. He was, in addition, on the Editorial Boards for the *Canadian Criminal Cases* law report series from 1972 and the *Weekly Criminal Bulletin* from 1976.

It was a privilege and a pleasure to work with him on these career-long projects that he cared so deeply about. We are filled with great sadness at the loss of our colleague and dear friend.

Marc Rosenberg
Marie Henein

CRIMINAL CODE CONCORDANCE

This Table sets out all sections of the *Criminal Code*, R.S.C. 1970, c. C-34, as amended to December, 1988, and the corresponding numbering in R.S.C. 1985, c. C-46, as amended to May, 2016. References to subsections, paragraphs and subparagraphs appear only when the numbering has been changed in the R.S.C. 1985 Code. The numbers listed under the heading "R.S.C. 1985" reflect the numbering scheme set out in the main volumes of the Revised Statutes of Canada, 1985, the First, Second, Third and Fourth Supplements and amendments.

Locate the number under the heading R.S.C. 1970, c. C-34, and cross-refer to the number that appears in the opposite column under the heading R.S.C. 1985, c. C-46. Where a case cites provisions from the 1970 Code, consult the R.S.C. 1985 column for the corresponding 1985 Code section numbers. Where contemporary cases cite the 1985 Code, consult the R.S.C. 1970 column for the corresponding 1970 Code numbers.

Note: Users should bear in mind, however, that the Concordance is not a citator and has been assembled only as a guide to the numbering of the 1985 Code.

R.S.C. 1970, c. C-34	R.S.C. 1985, c. C-46	R.S.C. 1970, c. C-34	R.S.C. 1985, c. C-46
1	1	—	2 "radioactive material" [en. 2013, c. 13, s. 2(2)]
2	2		
—	2 "associated personnel" [en. 2001, c. 41, s. 2(2)]	—	2 "street racing" [en. 2006, c. 14, s. 1]
—	2 "common-law partner" [en. 2000, c. 12, s. 91]	2 "superior court of criminal jurisdiction"	2 "superior court of criminal jurisdiction"
—	2 "criminal organization" [en. 1997, c. 23, s. 1]	—	2 "terrorism offence" [en. 2001, c. 41, s. 2(2)]
—	2 "criminal organization offence" [en. 1997, c. 23, s. 1]	—	2 "terrorist activity" [en. 2001, c. 41, s. 2(2)]
—	2 "environment" [en. 2013, c. 13, s. 2(2)]	—	2 "terrorist group" [en. 2001, c. 41, s. 2(2)]
—	2 "government or public facility" [en. 2001, c. 41, s. 2(2)]	—	2 "United Nations operation" [en. 2001, c. 41, s. 2(2)]
—	2 "justice system participant" [en. 2001, c. 41, s. 2(2)]	—	2 "United Nations personnel" [en. 2001, c. 41, s. 2(2)]
—	2 "nuclear facility" [en. 2013, c. 13, s. 2(2)]	—	2 "valuable mineral" [en. 1999, c. 5, s. 1]
—	2 "nuclear material" [en. 2013, c. 13, s. 2(2)]	2(d)	2(e)
		2(e)	2(d)
—	2 "offence-related property" [en. 1997, c. 23, s. 1]	2(f)	2(f)
		2(g)	2(g)
—	2 "magistrate" [rep. R.S.C. 1985, c. 27 (1st Supp.), s. 2(4)]	—	2.1 [en. 2009, c. 22, s. 1]
		—	2.2 [en. 2015, c. 13, s. 4]
2 "peace officer"	2 "peace officer"	2.1	3
2(d.1)	2(e)	—	3 (3.71) to (3.75) [en. 2001, c. 41, s. 126(2)]
2(e)	2(f)		
2(f)	2(g)	—	3.1 [en. 2002, c. 13, s. 2]

R.S.C. 1970, c. C-34	R.S.C. 1985, c. C-46	R.S.C. 1970, c. C-34	R.S.C. 1985, c. C-46
Part I	Part I	8	9
3	4	9	10
3(1)	repealed	10	11
3(2)	4(1)	11	12
3(3)	4(2)	12	13
3(4)	4(3)	13	repealed
3(5)	4(4)	14-33	14-33
3(6)	4(5)	—	25.1 to 25.4 [en.
3(7)	4(6)		2001, c. 32, s. 2]
3(8)	4(7)	—	27.1 [en. 2004, c. 12,
—	4(8) [en. 2014, c. 31,		s. 2]
	s. 2]	—	33.1 [en. 1995, c. 32,
4	5		s. 1]
5	6	34	34
6	7	35	35
6(1.1)	7(2)	36-42	36-42 [rep. 2012, c.
—	7(2.01)-(2.02) [en.		9, s. 2]
	2005, c. 40, s. 2]	43	43
	7(2.21) [en. 2013, c.	44	44 [rep. 2001, c. 26,
	13, s. 3(1)]		s. 294]
6(1.2)	7(3)	45	45
6(1.3)	7(3.1)	Part II	Part II
6(1.4)	7(3.2) [rep. 2013, c.	46-55	46-55
	13, s. 3(2)]	56	repealed
6(1.5)	7(3.3) [rep. 2013, c.	57	56
	13, s. 3(2)]	—	56.1 [en. 2009, c. 28,
6(1.6)	7(3.4) [rep. 2013, c.		s. 1]
	13, s. 3(2)]	58	57
6(1.7)	7(3.5) [rep. 2013, c.	59	58
	13, s. 3(2)]	60	59
6(1.8)	7(3.6) [rep. 2013, c.	61	60
	13, s. 3(2)]	62	61
6(1.9)	7(3.7)	63	62
6(1.91)	7(3.71)	64	63
6(1.92)	7(3.72)	65	64
6(1.93)	7(3.73)	66	65 [renumbered as
6(1.94)	7(3.74)		(1) and (2) en.
6(1.95)	7(3.75)		2013, c. 15, s. 2]
6(1.96)	7(3.76)	67	66 [renumbered as
6(1.97)	7(3.77)		(1) and (2) en.
6(2)	7(4)		2013, c. 15, s. 3]
—	7(4.2) [rep. 2002, c.	68	67
	13, s. 3(2)]	69	68
6(3)	7(5)	70	69
6(3.1)	7(5.1)	71	70
6(4)	7(6)	72	71
6(5)	7(7)	73	72
6(6)	7(8)	74	73
6(7)	7(9)	75	74
6(8)	7(10)	76	75
6(9)	7(11)	76.1	76
7	8	76.2	77
7(1)(a)	8(1)(b)	76.3	78
7(1)(b)	8(1)(a)		

R.S.C. 1970, c. C-34	R.S.C. 1985, c. C-46	R.S.C. 1970, c. C-34	R.S.C. 1985, c. C-46
—	78.1 [en 1993, c. 7, s. 4]	90	—
		91	—
77	79	92	—
78	80	93	—
79	81	—	—
80	82	94	—
—	82.1 [en. 1997, c. 23, s. 2]	95	—
		96	—
—	82.2 [en. 2013, c. 13, s. 5]	97	—
		98	—
—	82.3 [en. 2013, c. 13, s. 5]	98(11) "appeal court"	—
		98(11)(a)	—
—	82.4 [en. 2013, c. 13, s. 5]	98(11)(b)	—
		98(11)(b.1)	—
—	82.5 [en. 2013, c. 13, s. 5]	98(11)(c)	—
		98(11)(d)	—
—	82.6 [en. 2013, c. 13, s. 5]	98(11)(e)	—
		98(11)(f)	—
—	82.7 [en. 2013, c. 13, s. 5]	99	—
81	83	100	—
—	Part II.1 (ss. 83.01 to 83.33) [en. 2001, c. 41, s. 4]	101	—
		102	—
		103	—
—	83.181 [en. 2013, c. 9, c. 6]	104	—
—	83.191 [en. 2013, c. 9, c. 7]	104 [1976-77, c. 53, s. 47(3)]	—
—	83.201 [en. 2013, c. 9, c. 8]	104(3)	—
—	83.202 [en. 2013, c. 9, c. 8]	104(4)	—
		104(5)	—
—	83.221 [en. 2015, c. 20, c. 16]	104(6)	—
		104(7)	—
—	83.222 [en. 2015, c. 20, c. 16]	104(8)	—
		104(9)	—
—	83.223 [en. 2015, c. 20, c. 16]	104(10)	—
		104(11)	—
—	83.231 [en. 2004, c. 15, s. 32]	104(12)	—
		105	—
—	83.3(7.1), (7.2), (8.1), (11.1) and (11.2) [en. 2015, c. 20, c. 17]	106	—
		106.1	—
		106.2	—
		—	—
Part II.1	Part III (replaced 1995, c. 39, s. 139)	106.3	—
82	—	106.4	—
83	—	106.5	—
84	—	106.6	—
85	—	106.7	—
86	—	106.8	—
87	—	106.9	—
88	—	—	84
—	—	—	85
89	—	—	86
—	—	—	87
		—	88

R.S.C. 1970, c. C-34	R.S.C. 1985, c. C-46	R.S.C. 1970, c. C-34	R.S.C. 1985, c. C-46
—	89	108	119
—	90	109	120
—	91	110	121
—	92	—	121.1 [en. 2014, c. 23, s. 3]
—	93		
—	94	111	122
—	95	112	123
—	96	113	124
—	97 [not yet in force]	114	125
—	98	115	126
—	99	116	127
—	100	117	128
—	101	118	129
—	102	119	130
—	103	—	130.1 [en. 2014, c. 10, s. 1]
—	104		
—	105	120	131
—	106	121	132
—	107	122	133
—	108	122.1	134
—	109	123	135 [rep. R.S.C. 1985, c. 27 (1st Supp.), s. 17]
—	110		
—	110(2.1) [en. 2015, c. 27, s. 31]		
—	110.1 [en. 2015, c. 27, s. 32]	124	136
		125	137
—	111	126	138
—	112	127	139
—	113	128	140
—	114	129	141
—	115	130	142
—	116	131	143
—	117	132	144
—	117.01	133	145
—	117.011	—	145(5.1) [en. 1997, c. 18, s. 3(2)]
—	117.02		
—	117.03	133(7)	145(7) [rep. R.S.C. 1985, c. 27 (1st Supp.), s. 20(2)]
—	117.04		
—	117.05		
—	117.06	134	146
—	117.07	135	147
—	117.08	136	148
—	117.09	137	149
—	117.1	Part IV	Part V
—	117.11	138	150
—	117.12	139	150.1
—	117.13	—	150.1(2.3) [en. 2015, c. 29, s. 6]
—	117.14		
—	117.15	140	151
—	117.15(3) and (4) [en. 2015, c. 27, s. 34]	141	152
		142-145	repealed
Part III	Part IV	146	153
107	118	—	153(1.1) and (1.2) [en. 2005, c. 32, s. 4(2)]

R.S.C. 1970, c. C-34	R.S.C. 1985, c. C-46	R.S.C. 1970, c. C-34	R.S.C. 1985, c. C-46
147	154 [rep. R.S.C. 1985, c. 19 (3rd Supp.), s. 1]	168(2)	172(2) [rep. R.S.C. 1985, c. 19 (3rd Supp.), s. 6]
148 and 149	repealed	—	172.1 [en. 2002, c. 13, s. 8]
150	155		
151-153	156-158 [rep. R.S.C. 1985, c. 19 (3rd Supp.), s. 2]	169	173
		170	174
—	153.1 [en. 1998, c. 9, s. 2]	171	175
		172	176
154	159	173	177
155	160	174	178
156	repealed	175	179
157 and 158	161 and 162 [rep. R.S.C. 1985, c. 19 (3rd Supp.), s. 4]	175(1)(a) to (c)	repealed
		175(1)(d)	179(1)(a)
		175(1)(e)	179(1)(b)
—	161 [en. 1993, c. 45, s. 1]	175(2)	179(2)
		175(3)	repealed
—	161(1.1) [en. 2005, c. 32, s. 5(2)]	176	180
		177	181
—	162 [en. 2005, c. 32, s. 6]	178	182
		Part IV.1	Part VI
—	162.1 [en. 2014, c. 31, s. 3]	178.1	183
—	162.2 [en. 2014, c. 31, s. 3]	—	183.1 [en. 1993, c. 40, s. 2]
159	163	178.11	184
159(6)	163(6) [rep. 1993, c. 46, s. 1(2)]	—	184(2)(e) [en. 2004, c. 12, s. 4(1)]
—	163.1 [en. 1993, c. 46, s. 2]	178.11(3)	184(3) [rep. 1993, c. 40, s. 3(3); re-en. 2004, c. 12, s. 4(2)]
—	163.1(4.1) and (4.2) [en. 2002, c. 13, s. 5(3)]	—	184.1 [en. 1993, c. 40, s. 4]
160	164	—	184.2 [en. 1993, c. 40, s. 4]
160(8) "court"	164(8) "court"	—	184.2(5) [en. 2014, c. 31, s. 8]
160(8)(a)	164(8)(a)	—	184.3 [en. 1993, c. 40, s. 4]
160(8)(a.1)	164(8)(b)		
160(8)(b)	164(8)(c)	—	184.4 [en. 1993, c. 40, s. 4]
160(8)(c)	164(8)(d)	—	184.5 [en. 1993, c. 40, s. 4]
—	164.1 [en. 2002, c. 13, s. 7]	—	184.6 [en. 1993, c. 40, s. 4]
—	164.2 [en. 2002, c. 13, s. 7]	178.12	185
—	164.3 [en. 2002, c. 13, s. 7]	178.12(1)(e.1)	185(1)(f)
161	165	178.12(1)(f)	185(1)(g)
162	166 [rep. 1994, c. 44, s. 9]	178.12(1)(g)	185(1)(h)
163	167	—	185(1.1) [en. 1997, c. 23, s. 4]
164	168	178.13	186
165	169	—	186(1.1) [en. 1997, c. 23, s. 5]
166	170		
167	171	178.13(1.1)	186(2)
168	172	178.13(1.2)	186(3)

R.S.C. 1970, c. C-34	R.S.C. 1985, c. C-46
178.13(2)	186(4)
178.13(2.1)	186(5)
—	186(5.1) [en. 1999, c. 5, s. 5]
—	186(5.2) [en. 1999, c. 5, s. 5]
178.13(3)	186(6)
178.13(4)	186(7)
—	186(8) [en. 2014, c. 31, s. 9]
—	186.1 [en. 1997, c. 23, s. 6]
178.14	187
—	187(8) [en. 2014, c. 31, s. 10]
178.15	188
178.15(3)	188(3) [rep. 1993, c. 40, s. 8(3)]
178.15(4)(a), (b)	188(4)(a), (b)
178.15(4)(b.1)	188(4)(e.1)
178.15(4)(c)	188(4)(f.1)
178.15(4)(c.1)	188(4)(d)
178.15(4)(c.2)	188(4)(c)
178.15(4)(d)	188(4)(e)
178.15(4)(e)	188(4)(f)
178.15(4)(f)	188(4)(g)
178.15(4)(g)	188(4)(h)
—	188(6) [en. 2014, c. 31, s. 11]
—	188.1 [en. 1993, c. 40, s. 9]
—	188.2 [en. 1993, c. 40, s. 9]
178.16	189
178.16(1)-(3)	189(1)-(3) [rep. 1993, c. 40, s. 10(1)]
178.16(3.1)	189(4) [rep. 1993, c. 40, s. 10(1)]
178.16(4)	189(5)
178.16(5)	189(6)
178.17	190
178.18	191
178.19	192
178.2	193
—	193(2)(d)(iii) [en. 2004, c. 12, s. 5]
—	193.1 [en. 1993, c. 40, s. 12]
178.21	194
178.22	195
178.22(2)(g.1)	195(2)(h)
178.22(2)(h)	195(2)(i)
178.22(2)(i)	195(2)(j)
178.22(2)(j)	195(2)(k)
178.22(2)(k)	195(2)(l)
178.22(2)(l)	195(2)(m)
178.22(2)(m)	195(2)(n)
—	195(2.1) [en. 2013, c. 8, s. 5(3)]
178.23	196
178.23(2)	—
178.23(3)	196(2)
178.23(4)	196(3)
178.23(5)	196(4)
—	196(5) [en. 1997, c. 23, s. 7]
—	196.1 [en. 2013, c. 8, s. 6]
Part V	Part VII
179	197
180	198
181	199
182 and 183	repealed
184	200 [rep. R.S.C. 1985, c. 27 (1st Supp.), s. 30]
185	201
186	202
187	203
188	204
188(6.1)	204(7)
188(6.2)	204(8)
188(6.3)	204(8.1)
188(7)	204(9)
188(7.1)	204(9.1)
188(8)	204(10)
188.1	205 [rep. R.S.C. 1985, c. 52 (1st Supp.), s. 1]
189	206
190	207
—	207(4.1) [en. 2014, s. 171]
—	207.1 [en. 1999, c. 5, s. 7]
191	208 [rep. R.S.C. 1985, c. 27 (1st Supp.), s. 32]
192	209
193	210
194	211
195	212 [rep., with heading, 2014, c. 25, s. 13]
—	212(5) [rep. 1999, c. 5, s. 8]
195.1	213
—	213(1.1) [en. 2014, c. 25, s. 15(3)]
Part VI	Part VIII

R.S.C. 1970, c. C-34	R.S.C. 1985, c. C-46	R.S.C. 1970, c. C-34	R.S.C. 1985, c. C-46
196	214	—	249.1 [en. 2000, c. 2, s. 1]
197	215		
198	216	—	249.2 [en. 2006, c. 14, s. 2]
199	217		
200	218	—	249.3 [en. 2006, c. 14, s. 2]
201	repealed		
202	219	—	249.4 [en. 2006, c. 14, s. 2]
203	220		
204	221	234	250
205	222	235	251
206	223	236	252
207	224	237	253(1)
208	225	—	253(2) [en. 2008, c. 6, s. 18]
209	226		
210	227 [rep. 1999, c. 5, s. 9(1)]	238	254
		—	254(1) "evaluating officer" [en. 2008, c. 6, s. 19]
211	228		
212	229	—	254.1 [en. 2008, c. 6, s. 20]
213	230		
214	231	239	255
214(6)	231(6) [rep. R.S.C. 1985, c. 27 (1st Supp.), s. 35]	—	255(2.1) [en. 2008, c. 6, s. 21]
	231(6.01) [en. 2001, c. 41, s. 9]	—	255(2.2) [en. 2008, c. 6, s. 21]
—	231(6.1) [en. 1997, c. 23, s. 8]	—	255(3.1) [en. 2008, c. 6, s. 21]
—	231(6.2) [en. 2001, c. 32, s. 9(2)]	—	255(3.2) [en. 2008, c. 6, s. 21]
		—	255.1 [en. 1999, c. 32, s. 4]
215	232		
216	233	240	256
217	234	240.1	257
218	235	241	258
219	236	—	258(1)(d.01) [en. 2008, c. 6, s. 24(5)]
220	237		
221	238	—	258(1)(d.1) [en. 1997, c. 18, s. 10(2)]
222	239		
223	240	—	258(1)(f.1) [en. 2008, c. 6, s. 24(6)]
224	241		
225	repealed	—	258.1 [en. 2008, c. 6, s. 25]
226	242		
227	243	242	259
228	244 [en. 1995, c. 39, s. 144]	—	259(1.2) to (1.4) [en. 2001, c. 37, s. 1]
—	244.1 [en. 1995, c. 39, s. 144]	—	259(3.1) to (3.4) [en. 2006, c. 14, s. 3(2)]
—	244.2 [en. 2009, c. 22, s. 8]	243	260
229	245	243.1	261
230	246	243.2	262
231	247	243.3	263
232	248	243 [old provision]	264 [rep. R.S.C. 1985, c. 27 (1st Supp.), s. 37]
233	249		

R.S.C. 1970, c. C-34	R.S.C. 1985, c. C-46	R.S.C. 1970, c. C-34	R.S.C. 1985, c. C-46
—	264 [en. 1993, c. 45, s. 2]	250	281
		250.1	282
243.4	264.1	250.2	283
244	265	250.3	284
245	266	250.4	285
245.1	267	250.5	286
245.2	268	—	286.1 [en. 2014, c. 25, s. 20]
245.3	269		
—	269.01 [en. 2015, c. 1, s. 1]	—	286.2 [en. 2014, c. 25, s. 20]
245.4	269.1	—	286.3 [en. 2014, c. 25, s. 20]
246	270		
—	270.01 [en. 2009, c. 22, s. 9]	—	286.4 [en. 2014, c. 25, s. 20]
—	270.02 [en. 2009, c. 22, s. 9]	—	286.5 [en. 2014, c. 25, s. 20]
—	270.03 [en. 2015, c. 34, s. 2]	251	287
—	270.1 [en. 2002, c. 13, s. 11]	251(6) "Minister of Health"	287(6) "Minister of Health"
246.1	271	251(6)(a)	287(6)(a)
246.1(2)	271(2) [rep. R.S.C. 1985, c. 19 (3rd Supp.), s. 10]	251(6)(a.1)	287(6)(d)
		251(6)(b)	287(6)(c)
		251(6)(c)	287(6)(b)
246.2	272	251(6)(d)	287(6)(e)
246.3	273	252	288
—	273.1 [en. 1992, c. 38, s. 1]	253	289 [rep. R.S.C. 1985, c. 27 (1st Supp.), s. 41]
—	273.2 [en. 1992, c. 38, s. 1]	254	290
		255	291
—	273.3 [en. 1992, c. 38, s. 1]	256	292
		257	293
246.4	274	—	293.1 [en. 2015, c. 29, s. 9]
246.5	275		
246.6	276	—	293.2 [en. 2015, c. 29, s. 9]
—	276.1 [en. 1992, c. 38, s. 2]	258	294
246.7	277	259	295
246.8	278	260	296
—	278.1 to 278.91 [en. 1997, c. 30, s. 1]	261	297
		262	298
247	279	263	299
—	279(1.21) [en. 2013, c. 32, s. 1]	264	300
		265	301
—	279.01 [en. 2005, c. 43, s. 3]	266	302
		267	303
—	279.02 [en. 2005, c. 43, s. 3]	268	304
		269	305
—	279.03 [en. 2005, c. 43, s. 3]	270	306
—	279.04 [en. 2005, c. 43, s. 3]	271	307
		272	308
247.1	279.1	273	309
248	repealed	274	310
249	280	275	311

R.S.C. 1970, c. C-34	R.S.C. 1985, c. C-46	R.S.C. 1970, c. C-34	R.S.C. 1985, c. C-46
276	312	301.2	342.1
277	313	—	342.1(1)(d) [en. 1997, c. 18, s. 18(1)]
278	314		
279	315		
280	316	—	342.1(2) "computer data" [en. 2014, c. 31, s. 16(4)]
281	317		
281.1	318		
281.2	319	—	342.1(2) "computer password" [en. 1997, c. 18, s. 18(2)]
281.3	320		
281.3(8) "court"	320(8) "court"		
281.3(8)(a)	320(8)(a)	—	342.1(2) "traffic" [en. 1997, c. 18, s. 18(2)]
281.3(8)(a.1)	320(8)(b)		
281.3(8)(b)	320(8)(c)	—	342.2 [en. 1997, c. 18, s. 19]
281.3(8)(c)	320(8)(d)		
—	320.1 [en. 2001, c. 41, s. 10]	—	342.2(4) [en. 2014, c. 31, s. 17(2)]
Part VII	Part IX		
282	321	302	343
283	322	303	344
284	323	304	345
285	324	305	346
286	325	305.1	347
287	326 [rep. 2014, c. 31, s. 14(2)]	—	347.1 [en. 2007, c. 9, s. 2]
287.1	327	306	348
288	328	—	348.1 [en. 2002, c. 13, s. 15]
289	329 [rep. 2000, c. 12, s. 94]	306(3)	repealed
290	330	306(4)	348(3)
291	331	307	349
292	332	308	350
293	333	309	351
—	333.1 [en. 2010, c. 14, s. 3]	310	352
294	334	311	353
295	335	—	353(1.1) [en. 1997, c. 18, s. 22(1)]
—	335(1.1) [en. 1997, c. 18, s. 15]	—	353(2.1) [en. 1997, c. 18, s. 22(2)]
296	336	—	353.1 [en. 2010, c. 14, s. 4]
297	337		
298	338	312	354
298(1.1)	338(2)	—	354(4) [en. 1997, c. 18, s. 23]
298(2)	338(3)	313	355
298(3)	338(4)	—	355.1 [en. 2010, c. 14, s. 5]
299	339	—	355.2 [en. 2010, c. 14, s. 5]
300	340		
301	341	—	355.3 [en. 2010, c. 14, s. 5]
301.1	342	—	355.4 [en. 2010, c. 14, s. 5]
—	342(3) [en. 1997, c. 18, s. 16(2)]	—	355.5 [en. 2010, c. 14, s. 5]
—	342(4) [en. 1997, c. 18, s. 16(2)]	314	356
—	342.01 [en. 1997, c. 18, s. 17]		

R.S.C. 1970, c. C-34	R.S.C. 1985, c. C-46	R.S.C. 1970, c. C-34	R.S.C. 1985, c. C-46
315	357	339	381
316	358	340	382
317	359	341	383
318	360	342	384
319	361	343	385
320	362	344	386
321	363	345	387
322	364	346	388
323	365	347	389
324	366	348	390
—	366(5) [en. 2009, c. 28, s. 7]	349	391
		350	392
325	367	351	393
—	367(2) [rep. 1994, c. 44, s. 24]	352	394
326	368	—	394.1 [en. 1999, c. 5, s. 10]
—	368(1)(c) [en. 1997, c. 18, s. 25]	353	395
		354	396
—	368(1)(d) [en. 1997, c. 18, s. 25]	355	397
		356	398
—	368(1.1) [en. 2009, c. 28, s. 8]	357	399
—	368.1 [en. 2009, c. 28, s. 9]	358	400
		359	401
—	368.2 [en. 2009, c. 28, s. 9]	360	402
		—	402.1 [en. 2009, c. 28, s. 10]
327	369		
328	370	—	402.2 [en. 2009, c. 28, s. 10]
329	371		
330	372	361	403
331	373 [rep. R.S.C. 1985, c. 27 (1st Supp.), s. 53]	362	404
		363	405
		364	406
332	374	365	407
333	375	366	408
334	376	367	409
335	377	368	410
336	378	369	411
Part VIII	Part X	370	412
337	379	371	413
338	380	372	414
—	380(1.1) [en. 2011, c. 6, s. 2]	373	415
		374	416
—	380.1 [en. 2004, c. 3, s. 3]	375	417
		376	418
—	380.01(1.1) [en. 2011, c. 6, s. 3(5)]	377	419
		378	420
—	380.2 [en. 2011, c. 6, s. 4]	379	421
		380	422
—	380.3 [en. 2011, c. 6, s. 4; rep. 2015, c. 13, s. 11]	381	423
		—	423.1 [en. 2001, c. 32, s. 11]
—	380.4 [en. 2011, c. 6, s. 4; rep. 2015, c. 13, s. 11]	—	423.1(2) [rep. 2015, c. 13, s. 12(2)]
		381.1	424

R.S.C. 1970, c. C-34	R.S.C. 1985, c. C-46
—	424.1 [en. 2001, c. 41, s. 11]
382	425
383	426
384	427
Part IX	Part XI
385	428
386	429
387	430
—	430(4.1) [en. 2001, c. 41, s. 12]
—	430(4.11) [en. 2014, c. 9, s. 1]
—	430(4.2) [en. 2005, c. 40, s. 3]
387.1	431
—	431.1 [en. 2001, c. 41, s. 13]
—	431.2 [en. 2001, c. 41, s. 13]
388	432 [rep. R.S.C. 1985, c. 27 (1st Supp.), s. 58]
389	433
390	434
—	434.1 [en. 1990, c. 15, s. 1]
391	435
392	436
—	436.1 [en. 1990, c. 15, s. 1]
393	437
394	438
395	439
396	440
397	441
398	442
399	443
400	444
401	445
—	445.01 [en. 2015, c. 34, s. 3]
—	445.1 [en. 2008, c. 12, s. 1]
402	446
403	447
—	447.1 [en. 2008, c. 12, s. 1]
404 and 405	repealed
Part X	Part XII
406	448
407	449
408	450
409	451
410	452

R.S.C. 1970, c. C-34	R.S.C. 1985, c. C-46
411	453
412	454
413	455
414	456
415	457
416	458
417	459
418	460
419	461
420	462
Part X.1	Part XII.1
420.1	462.1
420.2	462.2
Part X.1	Part XII.2
420.1	462.3
—	462.3 "designated drug offence" [rep. 1996, c. 19, s. 68(1)]
—	462.3 "designated substance offence" [rep. 2001, c. 32, s. 12(3)]
—	462.3 "designated offence" [en. 2001, c. 32, s. 12(6)]
—	462.3 "enterprise crime offence" [rep. 2001, c. 32, s. 12(2)]
—	462.3(2)-(4) [en. 2001, c. 32, s. 12(7)]
420.11	462.31
—	462.31(3) [en. 1997, c. 18, s. 28(2)]
420.12	462.32
—	462.32(4.1) [en. 2001, c. 41, s. 14(2)]
420.13	462.33
—	462.33(2)(e) [en. 1997, c. 18, s. 30(1)]
—	462.33(3.01) [en. 1997, c. 18, s. 30(3)]
—	462.331 [en. 2001, c. 32, s. 16]
420.14	462.34
—	462.34(5.1) [en. 1997, c. 18, s. 31(2)]
—	462.34(5.2) [en. 1997, c. 18, s. 31(2)]

R.S.C. 1970, c. C-34	R.S.C. 1985, c. C-46	R.S.C. 1970, c. C-34	R.S.C. 1985, c. C-46
—	462.341 [en. 1997, c. 18, s. 32]	428	470
		429	471
420.15	462.35	429.1	472 [rep. R.S.C.
420.16	462.36		1985, c. 27 (1st
420.17	462.37		Supp.), s. 63]
—	462.37(2.01)-(2.07)	430	473
	[en. 2005, c. 44, s.	431	474
	6]	431.1	475
—	462.37(2.1) [en.	432	476
	2001, c. 32, s. 19]	433	477
—	462.371 [en. 1997, c.	—	477.1 [rep. 1996, c.
	18, s. 34]		31, s. 8]
420.18	462.38	—	477.2 [en. 1990, c.
—	462.38(2.1) [en.		44, s. 15]
	2001, c. 32, s.	—	477.3 [en. 1990, c.
	20(3)]		44, s. 15]
420.19	462.39	—	477.4 [en. 1990, c.
420.2	462.4		44, s. 15]
420.21	462.41	434	478
420.22	462.42	435	479
420.23	462.43	436	480
—	462.43(2) [en. 2001,	437	481
	c. 32, s. 24]	—	481.1 [en. 1996, c.
420.24	462.44		31, s. 72]
420.25	462.45	—	481.2 [en. 1996, c.
420.26	462.46		31, s. 72]
420.27	462.47	—	481.3 [en. 1996, c.
420.28	462.48		31, s. 72]
—	462.48(1)(c) [en.	438	482
	1997, c. 23, s. 10]	438(1.1)	482(2)
420.29	462.49	438(2)	482(3)
420.3	462.5	438(3)	not consolidated
Part XI	Part XIII	438(4)	482(4)
421	463	438(5)	482(5)
422	464	—	482.1 [en. 2002, c.
423	465		13, s. 18]
423(1)(c)	repealed	Part XIII	Part XV
423(1)(d)	465(1)(c)	439	483
423(1)(e)	465(1)(d)	440	484
423(2)	465(2) [rep. R.S.C.	440.1	485
	1985, c. 27 (1st	—	485(1.1) [en. 1997, c.
	Supp.), s. 61(3)]		18, s. 40]
424	466	440.2	485.1
425	467	441	repealed
—	467.1 [en. 1997, c.	442	486
	23, s. 11]	—	486(1.5) [en. 2001, c.
—	467.11 to 467.14 [en.		32, s. 29(1)]
	2001, c. 32, s. 27]	442(2.1)	486(2.1)
—	467.111 [en. 2014, c.	442(2.2)	486(2.2)
	17, s. 9]	442(3)	486(3)
—	467.2 [en. 1997, c.	442(3.1) [re-en. 1987, c.	486(4)
	23, s. 11]	24, s. 14(1)]; 1988, c. 30,	
Part XII	Part XIV	s. 1	
426	468	442(4)	486(5)
427	469		

R.S.C. 1970, c. C-34	R.S.C. 1985, c. C-46	R.S.C. 1970, c. C-34	R.S.C. 1985, c. C-46
442(5)	486(6) [rep. R.S.C. 1985, c. 19 (3rd Supp.), s. 14(2)]	—	487.11 [en. 1997, c. 18, s. 46]
—	486.1 to 486.6 [en. 2005, c. 32, s. 15]	443.2	487.2
—	486.2(7) and (8) [rep. 2015, c. 13, s. 15]	—	487.2(2) [rep. 2005, c. 32, s. 16(2)]
—	486.31 [en. 2015, c. 13, s. 17]	—	487.3 [en. 1997, c. 23, s. 14]
—	486.5(2.1) [en. 2015, c. 13, s. 19(1)]	444	488
—	486.7 [en. 2015, c. 20, s. 22]	444.1	488.1
		445	489
443	487	445.1	489.1
—	487(1)(c.1) [en. 1997, c. 23, s. 12]	446	490
—	487(2.1) [en. 1997, c. 18, s. 40]	—	490(1.1) [en. 2001, c. 41, s. 18; rep. 2001, c. 41, s. 130(7.1)]
—	487(2.2) [en. 1997, c. 18, s. 40]	—	490(3.1) [en. 1997, c. 18, s. 50(1)]
—	487.01 [en. 1993, c. 40, s. 15]	—	490(18) [en. 1997, c. 18, s. 50(4)]
—	487.01(5.1) [en. 1997, c. 23, s. 13]	—	490.01 [en. 1997, c. 18, s. 5; am. 1999, c. 5, s. 17]
—	487.01(5.2) [en. 1997, c. 23, s. 13]	—	490.011 to 490.032 [en. 2004, c. 10, c. 20]
—	487.01(7) [en. 1997, c. 18, s. 49(2)]	—	490.016(3) [en. 2007, c. 5, s. 16(2)]
—	487.018 to 487.0199 [en. 2014, c. 31, s. 20]	—	490.017(2) [en. 2007, c. 5, s. 17]
—	487.02 [en. 1993, c. 40, s. 15]	—	490.023(1.1) [en. 2007, c. 5, s. 23]
—	487.021 [en. 2014, c. 31, s. 20]	—	490.027(3) [en. 2007, c. 5, s. 25(2)]
—	487.03 [en. 1993, c. 40, s. 15]	—	490.02901 to 490.02915 [en. 2010, c. 17, s. 19]
—	487.04 [en. 1995, c. 27, s. 1]	—	490.03111 [en. 2007, c. 5, s. 29]
—	487.05(3) [en. 1997, c. 18, s. 44]	—	490.0312 [en. 2010, c. 17, s. 23]
—	487.051 to 487.058 [en. 1998, c. 37, s. 17]	—	490.1 to 490.9 [en. 1997, c. 23, s. 15]
—	487.06 to 487.09 [en. 1995, c. 27, s. 1]	—	490.2(4.1) [en. 2001, c. 32, s. 31(4)]
—	487.071 [en. 1998, c. 7, s. 20]	—	490.41 [en. 2001, c. 32, s. 33]
—	487.091 [en. 1998, c. 37, s. 23]	—	490.8(3.1) [en. 2001, c. 32, s. 35(2)]
—	487.092 [en. 1997, c. 18, s. 45; renum. 1998, c. 37, s. 23]	—	490.81 [en. 2001, c. 32, s. 36]
		446.1	491
		446.2	491.1
		446.3	491.2
443.1	487.1	447	492
		—	492.1 [en. 1993, c. 40, s. 18]

R.S.C. 1970, c. C-34	R.S.C. 1985, c. C-46	R.S.C. 1970, c. C-34	R.S.C. 1985, c. C-46
—	492.1(5) [en. 1999, c. 5, s. 18(2)]	457(2)(d)	515(2)(e)
		457(2.1)	515(2.1)
—	492.2 [en. 1993, c. 40, s. 18]	457(3)	515(3)
		457(4)	515(4)
Part XIV	Part XVI	—	515(4.1)(b.1) [en. 2001, c. 32, s. 37(1)]
448	493		
449	494	—	515(4.3) [en. 2001, c. 41, s. 19(3)]
—	494(4) [en. 2012, c. 9, s. 3(2)]	457(5)	515(5)
450	495	457(5.1)	515(6)
451	496	457(5.2)	515(7)
452	497	457(5.3)	515(8)
453	498	457(6)	515(9)
453.1	499	—	515(9.1) [en. 2009, c. 29, s. 2]
—	499(2)(e) to (g) [en. 1997, c. 18, s. 53(1)]	457(7)	515(10)
		457(8)	515(11)
—	499(4) [en. 1997, c. 18, s. 53(2)]	—	515(13) and (14) [en. 2015, c. 13, s. 20]
453.2	500 [rep. 1999, c. 25, s. 6]	—	515.1 [en. 1997, c. 18, s. 60]
453.3	501	457.1	516
453.4	502	—	516(2) [en. 1999, c. 5, s. 22]
454	503		
454(1.1)	503(2)	457.2	517
—	503(2.1)(e) to (g) [en. 1997, c. 18, s. 55(1)]	—	517(3) [rep. 2005, c. 32, s. 17(2)]
—	503(2.3) [en. 1997, c. 18, s. 55(2)]	457.3	518
		457.4	519
454(2)	503(3)	457.5	520
454(2.1)	503(3.1)	457.6	521
454(3)	503(4)	457.7	522
454(4)	503(5)	457.7(2.1)	522(3)
455	504	457.7(2.2)	522(4)
455.1	505	457.7(3)	522(5)
455.2	506	457.7(4)	522(6)
455.3	507	457.8	523
—	507.1 [en. 2002, c. 13, s. 22]	—	523(1.2) [en. 2011, c. 16, s. 2(1)]
455.4	508	458	524
—	508.1 [en. 1997, c. 18, s. 56]	458(4.1)	524(5)
		458(4.2)	524(6)
455.5	509	458(4.3)	524(7)
455.6	510	458(5)	524(8)
456	511	458(5.1)	524(9)
—	511(3) [en. 1997, c. 18, s. 57]	458(6)	524(10)
		458(7)	524(11)
—	511(4) [en. 1997, c. 18, s. 57]	458(8)	524(12)
456.1	512	458(9)	524(13)
456.2	513	459	525
456.3	514	459.1	526
457	515	460	527
457(2)(c.1)	515(2)(d)	461	528

R.S.C. 1970, c. C-34	R.S.C. 1985, c. C-46	R.S.C. 1970, c. C-34	R.S.C. 1985, c. C-46
462	529 [rep. 1994, c. 44, s. 52]	469	541
		470	542
—	529 to 529.5 [en. 1997, c. 39, s. 2]	—	542(3) [rep. 2005, c. 32, s. 19(2)]
Part XIV.1	Part XVII	471	543
462.1	530	471.1	544
—	530.01 [en. 2008, c. 18, s. 19]	472	545
		473	546
462.11	530.1	474	547
—	530.2 [en. 2008, c. 18, s. 21]	474.1	547.1
		475	548
462.2	531	476	549
462.3	532	477	550
462.4	533	478	551
—	534 [rep. 1997, c. 18, s. 63]	479 — 481	repealed
		—	Part XVIII.1 [en. 2011, c. 16, s. 4]
Part XV	Part XVIII	—	551.1 [en. 2011, c. 16, s. 4]
463	535		
464	536	—	551.2 [en. 2011, c. 16, s. 4]
—	536.1 [en. 1999, c. 3, s. 35]	—	551.3 [en. 2011, c. 16, s. 4]
—	536.2 [en. 2002, c. 13, s. 27]	—	551.4 [en. 2011, c. 16, s. 4]
—	536.3 [en. 2002, c. 13, s. 27]	—	551.5 [en. 2011, c. 16, s. 4]
—	536.4 [en. 2002, c. 13, s. 27]	—	551.6 [en. 2011, c. 16, s. 4]
—	536.5 [en. 2002, c. 13, s. 27]	—	551.7 [en. 2011, c. 16, s. 4]
465	537	Part XVI	Part XIX
465(1)(a)	repealed	482	552
465(1)(b)	537(1)(a)	482 "judge"	552 "judge"
465(1)(c)	537(1)(b)	482(b)	552(b)
465(1)(d)	537(1)(c)	482(c.1)	552(d)
465(1)(e)	537(1)(d)	482(d)	552(g)
465(1)(f)	537(1)(e)	482(e)	552(e)
465(1)(g)	repealed	482(f)	552(h)
465(1)(h)	537(1)(f)	482(g)	552(f)
465(1)(i)	537(1)(g)	482(h)	552(i)
465(1)(j)	537(1)(h)	482 "magistrate"	552 "magistrate" [rep. R.S.C. 1985, c. 27 (1st Supp.), s. 103(2)]
465(1)(k)	537(1)(i)		
—	537(1)(j.1) [en. 2002, c. 13, s. 28]		
—	537(1)(k) [en. 1997, c. 18, s. 64(1)]	483	553
—	537(1.1) [en. 2002, c. 13, s. 28]	—	553(c)(viii.1) [en. 1997, c. 18, s. 66]
—	537(2) [en. 1997, c. 18, s. 64(2)] [new provision]	—	553(c)(x) and (xi) [en. 1997, c. 19, s. 72]
466	538	484	554
467	539	484(2)-(4)	554(2)-(4) [rep. R.S.C. 1985, c. 27 (1st Supp.), s. 105]
—	539(4) [rep. 2005, c. 32, s. 18(2)]		
468	540		

R.S.C. 1970, c. C-34	R.S.C. 1985, c. C-46	R.S.C. 1970, c. C-34	R.S.C. 1985, c. C-46
—	554(2) [en. 1999, c. 3, s. 38]	505	575 [rep. R.S.C. 1985, c. 27 (1st Supp.), s. 113]
485	555		
—	555.1 [en. 1999, c. 3, s. 39]	506	576
		507	577
486	556	507.1	578
487	557	508	579
488	558	—	579.01 [en. 2002, c. 13, s. 47]
489	559		
490	560	—	579.1 [en. 1994, c. 44, s. 60]
490(5)	560(5) [rep. R.S.C. 1985, c. 27 (1st Supp.), s. 109(2)]	509	580
		510	581
491	561	511	582
—	561.1 [en. 1999, c. 3, s. 43]	512	583
		513	584
492	562	514	585
—	562.1 [en. 1999, c. 3, s. 44]	515	586
		516	587
493	563	517	588
—	563.1 [en. 1999, c. 3, s. 45]	518	589
		519	590
494	564 [rep. R.S.C. 1985, c. 27 (1st Supp.), s. 110]	520	591
		—	591(4.1) [en. 2011, c. 16, s. 5]
495	565	521	592
—	565(1.1) [en. 1999, c. 3, s. 46]	522	593
		523-525	594-596 [rep. R.S.C. 1985, c. 27 (1st Supp.), s. 120]
496	566		
—	566.1 [en. 1999, c. 3, s. 47]	526	597
		—	597(4) [en. 1997, c. 18, s. 68]
497	567	—	597(5) [en. 1997, c. 18, s. 68]
—	567.1 [en. 1999, c. 3, s. 48]		
498	568	526.1	598
499	569 [rep. R.S.C. 1985, c. 27 (1st Supp.), s. 111]	527	599
		527(1.1)	599(2) [rep. R.S.C. 1985, c. 1 (4th Supp.), s. 16]
—	569 [en. 1999, c. 3, s. 49]		
500	570	527(2)	599(3)
501	571	527(3)	599(4)
502	572	527(4)	599(5)
503	573 [rep. R.S.C. 1985, c. 27 (1st Supp.), s. 113]	528	600
		529	601
—	Part XIX.1	530	602
—	573 [en. 1999, c. 3, s. 50]	531	603
		532	604 [rep. 1997, c. 18, s. 69]
—	573.1 [en. 1999, c. 3, s. 50]		
		533	605
—	573.2 [en. 1999, c. 3, s. 50]	534	606
Part XVII	Part XX	—	606(1.1), (1.2) and (5) [en. 2002, c. 13, s. 49(1)]
504	574		

R.S.C. 1970, c. C-34	R.S.C. 1985, c. C-46	R.S.C. 1970, c. C-34	R.S.C. 1985, c. C-46
—	606(4.1), (4.2), (4.3) and (4.4) [en. 2015, c. 13, s. 21]	565	636 [rep. 1992, c. 41, s. 2]
535	607	566	637 [rep. 1992, c. 41, s. 2]
535(6)	607(6)	567	638
536	608	—	638(3) and (4) [rep. 1997, c. 18, s. 74]
537	609	568	639
538	610	569	640
539	611	570	641
540	612	571	642
541	613	—	642.1 [en. 2002, c. 13, s. 57]
542	614	572	643
543	615	—	643(1.1) [en. 2002, c. 13, s. 58]
543(2.1)	615(3)	573	644
543(3)	615(4)	—	644(1.1) [en. 1997, c. 18, s. 75]
543(4)	615(5)	574	645
543(5)	615(6)	575	646
543(6)	615(7)	576	647
543(7)	615(8)	576.1	648
543(8)	615(9)	—	648(3) [rep. 2005, c. 32, s. 21(2)]
544	616	576.2	649
545	617	577	650
546	618	—	650(1.2) [en. 1997, c. 18, s. 77]
547	619	—	650.01 [en. 2002, c. 13, s. 61]
548	620	—	650.02 [en. 2002, c. 13, s. 61]
549	621	—	650.1 [en. 1997, c. 18, s. 78]
550	622	578	651
551	623	579	652
552	624	—	652.1 [en. 2011, c. 16, s. 13]
553	625	580	653
553.1	625.1	—	653.1 [en. 2011, c. 16, s. 14]
554	626	581	654
—	626.1 [en. 2002, c. 13, s. 51]	582	655
555	627 [en. 1998, c. 9, s. 4]	583	656
556	repealed	584	657
557 [rep. 1985, c. 19, s. 129]	628 [rep. R.S.C. 1985, c. 27 (1st Supp.) s. 129]	584.1	657.1
558	629	—	657.1(2)(c.1) [en. 1997, c. 18, s. 79]
559	630	—	657.2 [en. 1997, c. 18, s. 80]
560	631	—	657.3 [en. 1997, c. 18, s. 80]
—	631(2.2) [en. 2011, c. 16, s. 7]	—	657.3(3) to (7) [en. 2002, c. 13, s. 62]
561	632		
562	633		
563	634		
—	634(2.01) [en. 2011, c. 16, s. 8]		
—	634(2.1) [en. 2002, c. 13, s. 54(2)]		
564	635		

R.S.C. 1970, c. C-34	R.S.C. 1985, c. C-46	R.S.C. 1970, c. C-34	R.S.C. 1985, c. C-46
585	658	—	672.5(5.2) [en. 2014, c. 6, s. 7(2)]
586	659 [rep. R.S.C. 1985, c. 19 (3rd Supp.), s. 15]	—	672.5(8.1) and (8.2) [en. 1997, c. 18, s. 84(1)]
—	659 [en. 1993, c. 45, s. 9]	—	672.5(13) [en. 1997, c. 18, s. 84(2)]
587	660	—	672.5(13.1) and (13.2) [en. 2005, c. 22, s. 16(2)]
588	661		
589	662	—	672.5(13.3) [en. 2014, c. 6, s. 7(3)]
590	663		
591	664	—	672.5(15.1), (15.2) and (15.3) [en. 2005, c. 22, s. 16(3)]
592	665 [rep. 1995, c. 22, s. 3]		
593	666		
594	667	—	672.501 [en. 2005, c. 22, s. 17]
594(3.1)	667(4)		
594(4)	667(5)	—	672.54 [en. 1999, c. 25, s. 12]
595	668 [rep. 1995, c. 22, s. 4]	—	672.5401 [en. 2014, c. 6, s. 10]
596	669 [rep. 1995, c. 22, s. 4]	—	672.541 [en. 2014, c. 6, s. 10]
597	669.1	—	672.542 [en. 2014, c. 6, s. 10]
597.1	669.2		
—	669.3 [en. 1994, c. 44, s. 66]	—	672.55(2) [rep. 2005, c. 22, s. 22]
598	670	—	672.56(1.1) [en. 2014, c. 6, s. 11(2)]
599	671		
600	672	—	672.64-672.66 and heading [rep. 2005, c. 22, s. 24]
—	Part XX.1		
—	672.1-672.95 [en. 1991, c. 43, s. 4]	—	672.64 [re-en. 2014, c. 6, s. 12]
—	672.1(2) [en. 2005, c. 22, s. 1(3)]	—	672.79 [rep. 2005, c. 22, s. 26]
—	672.121 [en. 2005, c. 22, s. 3]	—	672.8 [rep. 2005, c. 22, s. 25]
—	672.16(1.1) and (1.2) [en. 2005, c. 22, s. 7(2)]	—	672.83(2) [rep. 2005, c. 22, s. 29]
—	672.191 [en. 1997, c. 18, s. 81]	—	672.84 [rep. 2005, c. 22, s. 30; re-en. 2014, c. 6, s. 16]
—	672.21(3)(c) [rep. 2005, c. 22, s. 12]	—	Schedule to Part XXI [rep. 2005, c. 22, s. 37]
—	672.24(2) and (3) [en. 1997, c. 18, s. 82]	—	672.851 [en. 2005, c. 22, s. 33]
—	672.33(1.1) [en. 2005, c. 22, s. 13]	—	672.852 [en. 2005, c. 22, s. 33]
—	672.38(3) [en. 1997, c. 18, s. 83]	Part XVIII	Part XXI
—	672.45(1.1) [en. 2005, c. 22, s. 14]	601	673
—	672.47(4) and (5) [en. 2014, c. 6, s. 6(2)]	—	673 "sentence" (d) [en. 1996, c. 19, s. 74]
—	672.5(5.1) [en. 2005, c. 22, s. 16(1)]		

R.S.C. 1970, c. C-34	R.S.C. 1985, c. C-46	R.S.C. 1970, c. C-34	R.S.C. 1985, c. C-46
602	674	622.1	694.1
603	675	622.2	694.2
—	675(1.1) [en. 1997, c. 18, s. 92(1)]	623	695
		—	695(2) [rep. 1999, c. 3, s. 27]
603(1.1)	675(2)	624	696
—	675(2.1) [en. 1997, c. 18, s. 92(2)]	—	Part XXI.1 [en. 2002, c. 13, s. 71]
—	675(2.3) [en. 2011, c. 5, s. 2]	625	697
603(2)	675(3)	626	698
603(3)	675(4)	627	699
604	repealed	—	699(5.1) [en. 1997, c. 30, s. 2]
605	676		
—	676(1.1) [en. 1997, c. 18, s. 93(2)]	—	699(7) [en. 1997, c. 30, s. 2]
—	676(6) [en. 2011, c. 5, s. 3]	628	700
		—	700.1 [en. 1999, c. 18, s. 94]
—	676.1 [en. 1997, c. 18, s. 94]	629	701
606	677	—	701.1 [en. 1997, c. 18, s. 100]
607	678		
607.1	678.1	630	702
608	679	631	703
—	679(7.1) [en. 1997, c. 18, s. 95]	631.1	703.1
		631.2	703.2
608.1	680	632	704
608.2	681	633	705
609	682	634	706
610	683	635	707
—	683(2.1) amd (2.2) [en. 2002, c. 13, s. 68]	636	708
		—	708.1 [en. 1997, c. 18, s. 101]
—	683(5)(e) [en. 1997, c. 18, s. 97(2)]	637	709
		638	710
—	683(5.1) [en. 2008, c. 18, s. 29(1)]	639	711
		640	712
—	683(7) [en. 2008, c. 18, s. 29(2)]	640(3)	712(3) [rep. R.S.C. 1985, c. 27 (1st Supp.), s. 153(2)]
611	684		
612	685	641	713
613	686	—	713.1 [en. 1994, c. 44, s. 76]
—	686(5.1) [en. 1997, c. 18, s. 98]		
		642	714
614	687	—	714.1 [en. 1999, c. 18, s. 95]
615	688		
—	688(2.1) [en. 2002, c. 13, s. 68]	—	714.2 [en. 1999, c. 18, s. 95]
		—	714.3 [en. 1999, c. 18, s. 95]
616	689		
617	690 [rep. 2002, c. 13, s. 70]	—	714.4 [en. 1999, c. 18, s. 95]
		—	714.5 [en. 1999, c. 18, s. 95]
618	691		
619	repealed	—	714.6 [en. 1999, c. 18, s. 95]
620	692		
621	693		
622	694		

R.S.C. 1970, c. C-34	R.S.C. 1985, c. C-46	R.S.C. 1970, c. C-34	R.S.C. 1985, c. C-46
—	714.7 [en. 1999, c. 18, s. 95]	—	739.1 [en. 2015, c. 13, s. 30]
—	714.8 [en. 1999, c. 18, s. 95]	—	742.3(1.1), (1.2), (1.3) [en. 2014, c. 21, s. 3]
643	715	—	742.3(4) [en. 2008, c. 18, s. 40]
643.1	715.1	—	742.3(5)-(10) [en. 2011, c. 7, s. 5(2)]
—	715.2 [en. 1998, c. 9, s. 8]	—	742.31 [en. 2011, c. 7, s. 6]
Part XX	Part XXIII	—	743.21 [en. 2008, c. 28, s. 42]
ss. 644 to 686	ss. 716 to 751.1, as amended. *Please note: this Part was replaced as a whole by 1995, c. 22, s. 6. For in force information, see the list of amendments to the Code starting on page CC/1.	—	743.4 [rep. 2002, c. 1, s. 184]
		—	743.6(1.1) [en. 1997, c. 23, s. 18]
		—	743.6(1.2) [en. 2001, c. 41, s. 21]
		—	745.1
—	718.01 [en. 2005, c. 32, s. 24]	—	745.01 [en. 1999, c. 25, s. 21]
—	718.02 [en. 2009, c. 22, s. 18]	—	745.01(2) [en. 2011, c. 2, s. 2]
—	718.03 [en. 2015, c. 34, s. 4]	—	745.2
—	718.3(5), (6) and (7) [en. 2015, c. 23, s. 17]	—	745.21 [en. 2011, c. 5, s. 4]
—	720(2) [en. 2008, c. 18, s. 35]	—	745.3
—	722.1 [rep. 1999, c. 25, s. 18]	—	745.4
—	722.2 [en. 1999, c. 25, s. 18]	—	745.5
—	722.2(3), (4) and (5) [en. 2015, c. 13, s. 26]	—	745.51 [en. 2011, c. 5, s. 5]
—	729.1 [en. 2011, c. 7, s. 2]	—	745.6
—	731(3.1) [en. 1997, c. 17, s. 1]	—	745.6 (2.1) to (2.8) [en. 2011, c. 2, s. 3]
—	732(6) [en. 2008, c. 18, s. 37]	—	745.61
—	732.1 [en. 1995, c. 22, s. 6]	—	745.62
—	732.1(2.1), (2.2) [en. 2014, c. 21, s. 2]	—	745.63
—	732.1(7)-(12) [en. 2011, c. 7, s. 3(2)]	—	745.64
—	732.11 [en. 2011, c. 7, s. 4]	Part XXI	Part XXIV
—	737	—	747 to 747.8 and heading [rep. 2005, c. 22, s. 39]
—	737.1 [en. 2015, c. 13, s. 29]	687	752
—	738(1)(d) [en. 2009, c. 28, s. 11]	—	752 "designated offence" [en. 2008, c. 6, ss. 40, 61]
		—	752 "long-term supervision" [en. 2008, c. 6, s. 40]
		—	752 "primary designated offence" [en. 2008, c. 6, s. 40]
		—	752.01 [en. 2008, c. 6, s. 41]

R.S.C. 1970, c. C-34	R.S.C. 1985, c. C-46	R.S.C. 1970, c. C-34	R.S.C. 1985, c. C-46
—	752.1 [en. 1997, c. 17, s. 4]	703	769
		704	770
688	753	705	771
—	753(1.1) [en. 2008, c. 6, s. 42(2)]	706	772
		707	773
—	753(4.1) [en. 1997, c. 17, s. 4]	Part XXIII	Part XXVI
		708	774
—	753(4.2) [en. 2008, c. 6, s. 42(4)]	—	774.1 [en. 2002, c. 13, s. 77]
—	753(6) [rep. 2008, c. 6, s. 42(5)]	709	775
		710	776
—	753.01 [en. 2008, c. 6, s. 43]	711	777
		712	778
—	753.02 [en. 2008, c. 6, s. 43]	713	779
		714	780
—	753.1 [en. 1997, c. 17, s. 4]	715	781
		716	782
—	753.1(4), (5) [rep. 2008, c. 6, s. 44(2)]	717	783
		718	repealed
—	753.2 [en. 1997, c. 17, s. 4]	719	784
—	753.3 [en. 1997, c. 17, s. 4]	Part XXIV	Part XXVII
		720	785
—	753.4 [en. 1997, c. 17, s. 4]	—	785 "sentence" (d) [en. 1997, c. 19, s. 76]
689	754		
690	755 [rep. 1997, c. 17, s. 5; re-en. 2008, c. 6, s. 49]	721	786
		722	787
		723	788
691	756 [rep. 1997, c. 17, s. 5]	724	789
		725	790
692	757	725(3) and (4)	790(3) and (4) [rep. R.S.C. 1985, c. 27 (1st Supp.), s. 172]
693	758		
694	759	725(5)	repealed
—	759(1.1) [en. 1997, c. 17, s. 6]	726	791 [rep. R.S.C. 1985, c. 27 (1st Supp.), s. 173]
—	759(3.1) [en. 1997, c. 17, s. 6]	727	repealed
—	759(3.2) [en. 1997, c. 17, s. 6]	728	792 [rep. R.S.C. 1985, c. 27 (1st Supp.), s. 174]
—	759(4.1) [en. 1997, c. 17, s. 6]	729	793 [rep. R.S.C. 1985, c. 27 (1st Supp.), s. 175]
—	759(4.2) [en. 1997, c. 17, s. 6]		
695	760	730	794
695.1	761	731	795
Part XXII	Part XXV	732	796 [rep. R.S.C. 1985, c. 27 (1st Supp.), s. 176]
696	762		
697	763		
698	764	732.1	797 [rep. R.S.C. 1985, c. 27 (1st Supp.), s. 176]
699	765		
700	766		
701	767	733	798
701.1	767.1	734	799
702	768	735	800

R.S.C. 1970, c. C-34	R.S.C. 1985, c. C-46
—	800(2.1) [en. 1997, c. 18, s. 111]
736	801
736(4) and (5)	801(4) and (5) [rep. R.S.C. 1985, c. 27 (1st Supp.), s. 177(2)]
737	802
—	802.1 [en. 2002, c. 13, s. 79]
738	803
738(2)	repealed
738(3)	803(2)
738(3.1)	803(3)
739	804
740	805 [rep. R.S.C. 1985, c. 27 (1st Supp.), s. 179]
741	806
742	807
743	808
744	809
745	810
—	810(3.01), (3.02) [en. 2011, c. 7, s. 7]
—	810.01 [en. 1997, c. 23, s. 19]
—	810.01(3.1), (4.1) [en. 2009, c. 22, s. 19]
—	810.011 [en. 2015, c. 20, s. 25]
—	810.02 [en. 2015, c. 29, s. 11]
—	810.1 [en. 1993, c. 45, s. 11]
—	810.1(3.01) to (3.05) [en. 2008, c. 6, ss. 52, 62]
—	810.1(3.1) [en. 1997, c. 18, s. 113(2)]
—	810.2 [en. 1997, c. 17, s. 9]
—	810.2(3.1) [en. 2008, c. 6, s. 53(1)]
—	810.2(4.1) [en. 2008, c. 6, s. 53(2)]
—	810.21 [en. 2015, c. 20, s. 26]
—	810.22 [en. 2015, c. 20, s. 26]
—	810.3 [en. 2011, c. 7, s. 11]
—	810.4 [en. 2011, c. 7, s. 11]
746	811

R.S.C. 1970, c. C-34	R.S.C. 1985, c. C-46
—	811.1 [en. 2011, c. 7, s. 12]
747	812
747 "appeal court"	812 "appeal court"
747(a)	812(1)(f)
747(b)	812(1)(g)
747(c)	812(1)(c)
747(d)	812(1)(b)
747(e)	812(1)(a)
747(f)	812(1)(d)
747(g)	repealed
747(h)	812(1)(e) [rep. 1992, c. 51, s. 43(2)]
747(i)	812(1)(h)
—	812(1)(i) [en. 1999, c. 3, s. 55]
—	812(2) [en. 1999, c. 3, s. 55]
748	813
749	814
750	815
751	repealed
752	816
752.1	817
752.2	818
752.3	819
753	820
754	821
755	822
755.1	823
756	824
757	825
758	826
759	827
760	828
761	829
—	829(2) [en. 1999, c. 3, s. 56]
762	830
763	831
764	832
765	833
766	834
767	835
768	836
769	837
770	838
771	839
—	839(1.1) [en. 1999, c. 3, s. 57]
772	840
Part XXV	Part XXVIII [replaced 2002, c. 13, s. 84]

R.S.C. 1970, c. C-34	R.S.C. 1985, c. C-46	R.S.C. 1970, c. C-34	R.S.C. 1985, c. C-46
773	841 [replaced 2002, c. 13, s. 84]	—	Form 28.1 [en. 2000, c. 10, s. 24; rep. 2007, c. 22, s. 26]
773(3)	841(3)	Form 25.1	Form 29
—	842 to 849 [en. 2002, c. 13, s. 84]	Form 26	Form 30
Forms 1 and 2	Forms 1 and 2	Form 27	Form 31
Form 3	Form 3 [rep. R.S.C. 1985, c. 27 (1st Supp.), s. 184(2)]	Form 28	Form 32
		Form 29	Form 33
Forms 4 to 5.2	Forms 4 to 5.2	Form 30	Form 34
—	Forms 5.01 to 5.09 [en. 1998, c. 37, s. 24]	—	Form 34.1 [en. 2011, c. 6, s. 5]
—	Forms 5.001 to 5.0091 [en. 2014, c. 31, s. 26]	—	Form 34.2 [en. 2015, c. 13, s. 35]
		—	Form 34.3 [en. 2015, c. 13, s. 35]
—	Form 5.041 [en. 2005, c. 25, s. 12; 2007, c. 22, s. 23]	Form 31	Form 35
		Form 32	Form 36
—	Form 5.061 [en. 2005, c. 25, s. 12; 2007, c. 22, s. 23]	Form 33	Form 37
		Form 34	Form 38
Form 5.3	Form 5.3	Form 35	Form 39
Forms 6 and 7	Forms 6 and 7	Form 36	Form 40
Form 8	Form 7.1 [en. 1997, c. 39, s. 3]	Form 37	Form 41
		Form 38	Form 42
—	Form 8	Form 39	Form 43
Form 8.1	Form 9	Forms 40 and 41	repealed
Form 8.2	Form 10	Form 42	Form 44
Form 8.3	Form 11	Form 43	Form 45
—	Form 11.1 [en. 1994, c. 44, s. 84]	Form 44	Form 46
		Form 45	Form 47
Form 9	Form 12	774	repealed
Form 9.1	Form 13	—	Form 48 [en. 1991, c. 43, s. 8]
Form 9.2	Form 14	—	Form 48.1 [en. 2005, c. 22, s. 40]
Form 10	Form 15		
Form 11	Form 16	—	Form 48.2 [en. 2015, c. 13, s. 36]
—	Form 16.1 [en. 1997, c. 30, s. 3]	—	Form 49 [en. 1991, c. 43, s. 8]
Form 12	Form 17	—	Form 50 [en. 1991, c. 43, s. 8]
Form 13	Form 18	—	Form 51 [en. 1991, c. 43, s. 8; rep. 2005, c. 22, s. 41; en. 2011, c. 7, s. 13]
Form 14	Form 19		
Form 15	repealed		
Form 16	Form 20		
Form 17	repealed	—	Form 52 [en. 2004, c. 10, s. 21]
Form 18	Form 21		
Form 19	Form 22	—	Form 53 [en. 2004, c. 10, s. 2]
Form 20	Form 23		
Form 21	Form 24	—	Form 54 [en. 2010, c. 17, s. 27]
Form 22	Form 25		
Form 23	Form 26		
Form 24	Form 27		
Form 25	Form 28		

TABLE OF CASES

Available in PDF

Images of reported decisions (as they appear in the law reports) and original judgments are available as PDF files. To request PDF files, please contact Customer Relations at www.carswell.com/email or 1-800-387-5164.

References are to section numbers of the *Criminal Code* except where preceded by one of the following:

CE   Canada Evidence Act
CH   Canadian Charter of Rights and Freedoms
CD   Controlled Drugs and Substances Act
WC   Crimes Against Humanity and War Crimes Act
YC   Youth Criminal Justice Act

Sections

Sections

THE
CRIMINAL CODE
R.S.C. 1985, Chap. C-46

Amended R.S.C. 1985, c. 2 (1st Supp.); brought into force January 1, 1990, as provided by R.S.C. 1985, c. 27 (1st Supp.), s. 188

Amended R.S.C. 1985, c. 11 (1st Supp.); proclaimed in force December 12, 1988

Amended R.S.C. 1985, c. 27 (1st Supp.); originally proclaimed in force as follows: ss. 1 to 35, 37 to 93, 96 to 126, 128 to 186, 188 and 203 to 208 proclaimed in force December 4, 1985; parts of s. 36 enacting ss. 249 to 253, 254(1), (3) to (6), 255(1) to (4) and 256 to 261 with the exception of s. 258(1)(*c*)(i) and (*g*)(iii)(A) of the *Criminal Code* proclaimed in force December 4, 1985; s. 258(1)(*c*)(i) and (*g*)(iii)(A) to come into force on proclamation (repealed before coming into force 2008, c. 20, s. 3); part of s. 36 enacting s. 254(2) of the *Criminal Code* proclaimed in force December 4, 1985 in each of the provinces; part of s. 36 enacting s. 255(5) of the *Criminal Code* proclaimed in force December 4, 1985 in New Brunswick, Manitoba, Prince Edward Island, Alberta, Saskatchewan, Yukon Territory and Northwest Territories, proclaimed in force January 1, 1988 in Nova Scotia, and to come into force on proclamation in the remaining provinces; s. 94 in force June 20, 1985 in New Brunswick, Manitoba, Ontario, Yukon Territory, Northwest Territories, proclaimed in force September 1, 1987 in Nova Scotia, P.E.I. and Saskatchewan and with respect to indictable offences in Saskatchewan, into force on proclamation in the remaining provinces; and s. 127 proclaimed in force September 1, 1988

Amended R.S.C. 1985, c. 31 (1st Supp.), s. 61; proclaimed in force December 12, 1988

Amended R.S.C. 1985, c. 47 (1st Supp.); proclaimed in force December 12, 1988

Amended R.S.C. 1985, c. 51 (1st Supp.); in force December 12, 1988

Amended R.S.C. 1985, c. 52 (1st Supp.); proclaimed in force December 12, 1988

Amended R.S.C. 1985, c. 1 (2nd Supp.), s. 213; proclaimed in force December 12, 1988

Amended R.S.C. 1985, c. 24 (2nd Supp.), ss. 45 to 47; proclaimed in force December 12, 1988

Amended R.S.C. 1985, c. 27 (2nd Supp.), s. 10, Sch. item 6(1) to (16); proclaimed in force December 12, 1988 (but see s. 11)

Amended R.S.C. 1985, c. 35 (2nd Supp.), s. 34; proclaimed in force December 12, 1988

Amended R.S.C. 1985, c. 10 (3rd Supp.); proclaimed in force May 1, 1989

Amended R.S.C. 1985, c. 19 (3rd Supp.), ss. 1 to 16; proclaimed in force May 1, 1989 (but see s. 19)

Amended R.S.C. 1985, c. 30 (3rd Supp.), ss. 1 and 2; proclaimed in force May 1, 1989

Amended R.S.C. 1985, c. 34 (3rd Supp.), ss. 9 to 13; proclaimed in force May 1, 1989

Amended R.S.C. 1985, c. 1 (4th Supp.), ss. 13 to 17; originally in force February 4, 1988

Amended R.S.C. 1985, c. 23 (4th Supp.); originally ss. 1 to 3 and 7 proclaimed in force October 1, 1988, ss. 4, 5 and that part of s. 6 which enacts s. 727.9 proclaimed in force July 31, 1989, s. 8 proclaimed in force November 1, 1989; that part of s. 6 which enacts ss. 725 to 727.8 repealed by 1995, c. 22, s. 11 (in force September 3, 1996)

Amended R.S.C. 1985, c. 29 (4th Supp.), s. 17; proclaimed in force November 1, 1989

Amended R.S.C. 1985, c. 30 (4th Supp.), s. 45; proclaimed in force November 1, 1989

Amended R.S.C. 1985, c. 31 (4th Supp.), ss. 94 to 97; s. 96 proclaimed in force September 15, 1988, s. 97 proclaimed in force February 1, 1989, remainder in force as noted

Amended R.S.C. 1985, c. 32 (4th Supp.), ss. 55 to 62; proclaimed in force November 1, 1989

Amended R.S.C. 1985, c. 40 (4th Supp.), s. 2; proclaimed in force November 1, 1989

Amended R.S.C. 1985, c. 42 (4th Supp.), ss. 1 to 8; proclaimed in force November 1, 1989

Amended R.S.C. 1985, c. 50 (4th Supp.); proclaimed in force November 1, 1989

Amended 1989, c. 2, s. 1; in force June 29, 1989

Amended 1990, c. 15; brought into force July 1, 1990 by SI/90-83, *Can. Gaz., Part II*, July 4, 1990

Amended 1990, c. 16, ss. 2 to 7; brought into force July 1, 1990 by SI/90-90, *Can. Gaz., Part II*, July 18, 1990 (but see s. 24)

Amended 1990, c. 17, ss. 7 to 15; brought into force September 1, 1990 by SI/90-106, *Can. Gaz., Part II*, August 29, 1990 (but see s. 45)

Amended 1990, c. 44, s. 15; brought into force February 4, 1991 by SI/91-18, *Can. Gaz., Part II*, February 13, 1991 (but see s. 20)

Amended 1991, c. 1, s. 28; in force January 17, 1991

Amended 1991, c. 4; in force January 17, 1991

Amended 1991, c. 28, ss. 6 to 12; brought into force October 3, 1991 by SI/91-136, *Can. Gaz., Part II*, October 23, 1991

Amended 1991, c. 40, ss. 1 to 20, 21(2) and 22 to 41; s. 28 brought into force March 26, 1992, remainder, except ss. 3, 5(1) and (2), 8, 10(1), 14, 18, 19(1) to (7), 20, 22, 23, 39, 40 and 42, brought into force August 1, 1992 by SI/92-138, *Can. Gaz., Part II*, July 29, 1992, *however*, by SI/92-144, *Can. Gaz., Part II*, August 12, 1992, s. 2(3) and that part of s. 2(6) which enacts s. 84(1.2) are brought into force July 27, 1992; ss. 5(1) and (2), 10(1), 23(1), (2), (3), (5) and 42 brought into force October 1, 1992; that part of s. 3 which enacts s. 86(3), ss. 14, 18, 19(1), (2), (5) to (7), 20, 22, 23(4), 39 (except s. 39(4)(*a*)) and 40 in force January 1, 1993; s. 19(3) and (4) were to come into force July 1, 1993 (see SI/92-156) but amended by P.C. 1993-1446, so that s. 19(3) and (4) came into force January 1, 1994 (see SI/94-7), s. 106(2)(*c*) as enacted by s. 19(3) in force (*a*), in Alberta, British Columbia, Ontario, Prince Edward Island, Quebec and the Yukon Territory on January 1, 1994, and (*b*), in Manitoba, New Brunswick, Newfoundland, Nova Scotia and Saskatchewan on April 1, 1994, however, the coming into force in Saskatchewan was deferred to September 1, 1994, the coming into force in the Northwest Territories was repealed by SI/98-80, *Can. Gaz., Part II*, July 8, 1998; the order bringing ss. 8 and 39(4)(*a*) into force on January 1, 1993 was amended so that s. 8 now in force as of January 1, 1995 and s. 39(4)(*a*) is to come into force on some future, unspecified date; that part of s. 3 which enacts s. 86(2) to come into force by order of the Governor in Council; however, s. 86(2) as enacted by s. 3 repealed by 1995, c. 39, s. 163 (brought into force December 1, 1998 by SI/98-93, *Can. Gaz., Part II*, September 30, 1998 (in force date amended by SI/98-95, *Can. Gaz., Part II*, September 30, 1998)); s. 34 repealed by 1995, c. 39, s. 162 (brought into force December 1, 1998 by SI/98-93, *Can. Gaz., Part II*, September 30, 1998 (in force date amended by SI/98-95, *Can. Gaz., Part II*, September 30, 1998)); s. 105(4) of the *Criminal Code* as enacted by s. 39(4) repealed by 1995, c. 39, s. 164 (brought into force December 1, 1998 by SI/98-93, *Can. Gaz., Part II*, September 30, 1998 (in force date amended by SI/98-95, *Can. Gaz., Part II*, September 30, 1998))

Amended 1991, c. 43, ss. 1 to 10; brought into force, except that part of s. 4 which enacts ss. 672.64 to 672.66, ss. 5, 6 and 10(8), February 4, 1992 by SI/92-9, *Can. Gaz., Part II*, February 12, 1992; ss. 5 and 6 repealed by 1995, c. 22, s. 12 (in force September 3, 1996); that part of s. 4 which enacts ss. 672.64 to 672.66 and 10(8) to come into force by order of the Governor in Council (repealed before coming into force by 2005, c. 22, ss. 24, 43(3) (in force January 2, 2006))

Amended 1992, c. 1, ss. 58 and 59; in force February 28, 1992

Amended 1992, c. 11, ss. 14 to 17; in force May 15, 1992

Amended 1992, c. 20, ss. 199 to 204, 215, 216, 228 and 229; brought into force, except s. 204, November 1, 1992; s. 204 repealed by 1995, c. 42, s. 61 (in force January 24, 1996)

Amended 1992, c. 21, s. 9; brought into force June 30, 1992 by SI/92-126, *Can. Gaz., Part II*, July 15, 1992

Amended 1992, c. 22, s. 12; brought into force July 24, 1992 by SI/92-134, *Can. Gaz., Part II*, July 29, 1992

Amended 1992, c. 27, s. 90(1)(*i*); brought into force November 30, 1992

Amended 1992, c. 38; brought into force August 15, 1992 by SI/92-136, *Can. Gaz., Part II*, July 29, 1992

Amended 1992, c. 41; in force July 23, 1992 (but see s. 7)

Amended 1992, c. 47, ss. 68 to 72; brought into force August 1, 1996 by SI/96-56, *Can. Gaz., Part II*, July 1, 1996

Amended 1992, c. 51, ss. 32 to 43; brought into force January 30, 1993

Amended 1993, c. 7; brought into force September 1, 1993

Amended 1993, c. 25, ss. 93 to 95; s. 93 deemed in force January 1, 1993; ss. 94 and 95 in force June 10, 1993

Amended 1993, c. 28, Sch. III, ss. 25 to 37; however, s. 27 repealed by 1995, c. 39, s. 192 and s. 35 replaced by 1998, c. 15, s. 20 (in force June 11, 1998); in force April 1, 1999; however, ss. 25(2), 28, 29, 31, 32, 34, 35.1 to 36 repealed 1999, c. 3, s. 12 (in force March 11, 1999)

Amended 1993, c. 34, s. 59(1); in force on the day after the day on which 1993, c. 34, s. 142 is brought into force (1993, c. 34, s. 59(1) in force December 15, 1994)

Amended 1993, c. 37, ss. 21 and 32; brought into force September 1, 1993

Amended 1993, c. 40, ss. 1 to 18; brought into force August 1, 1993

Amended 1993, c. 45, ss. 1 to 14 and 16 to 19; brought into force August 1, 1993 by SI/94-137

Amended 1993, c. 46, ss. 1 to 5; brought into force August 1, 1993

Amended 1994, c. 12, s. 1; brought into force July 1, 1994

Amended 1994, c. 13, s. 7(1)(*b*); in force May 12, 1994

Amended 1994, c. 38, ss. 14 and 25(1)(*g*); brought into force January 12, 1995 by SI/95-9, *Can. Gaz., Part II*, January 25, 1995

Amended 1994, c. 44, ss. 1 to 84 and 103; brought into force, except ss. 8(2), 39 to 43 and 84, February 15, 1995; ss. 8(2), 39 to 43 and 84 brought into force April 1, 1995

Amended 1995, c. 5, s. 25(1)(*g*); brought into force May 13, 1995 by SI/95-65, *Can. Gaz., Part II*, May 31, 1995

Amended 1995, c. 19, ss. 37 to 41; brought into force December 1, 1995 by SI/95-116, *Can. Gaz., Part II*, November 29, 1995

Amended 1995, c. 22, ss. 1 to 12, 14, 15, 18 to 24 and 26; brought into force September 3, 1996 by SI/96-79, *Can. Gaz., Part II*, August 21, 1996, except that part of s. 6 that enacts ss. 718.3(5) and 747 to 747.8 (to come into force by order of the Governor in Council (that part of s. 6 that enacts s. 718.3(5) repealed before coming into force by 1999, c. 5, s. 30 (in force July 1, 1999); that part of s. 6 that enacts ss. 747-747.8 repealed before coming into force by 2005, c. 22, s. 39 (in force January 2, 2006); s. 7(2) repealed before conditions were satisfied by 2005, c. 22, s. 44 (in force January 2, 2006)); that part of s. 6 that enacted ss. 745.6 to 745.64 re-enacted 1996, c. 34, s. 2(2); brought into force January 9, 1997 by SI/97-12, *Can. Gaz., Part II*, January 22, 1997

Amended 1995, c. 27, ss. 1 and 3; in force July 13, 1995

Amended 1995, c. 29, ss. 39 and 40; brought into force November 1, 1995 by SI/95-115, *Can. Gaz., Part II*, November 15, 1995

Amended 1995, c. 32, s. 1; brought into force September 15, 1995 by SI/95-101, *Can. Gaz.*, *Part II*, September 20, 1995

Amended 1995, c. 39, ss. 138 to 157, 163, 164, 188(*a*) and (*b*), 189(*e*) and 190; that part of s. 139 which replaces s. 85 and ss. 141 to 150 brought into force January 1, 1996, by SI/96-2, *Can. Gaz., Part II*, January 10, 1996; ss. 138, 139 (except to the extent that it replaces ss. 85 and 97 of the *Criminal Code*), 140, 151 to 157, 163, 164, 188(*a*) and (*b*), 189(*e*), 190 brought into force December 1, 1998 by SI/98-93, *Can. Gaz., Part II*, September 30, 1998 (in force date amended by SI/98-95, *Can. Gaz., Part II*, September 30, 1998); that part of s. 139 which replaces s. 97 to come into force by order of the Governor in Council; however, repealed before coming into force

Amended 1995, c. 42, ss. 73 to 76, 86 and 87; brought into force January 24, 1996 by SI/96-10, *Can. Gaz., Part II*, February 7, 1996 (see ss. 86 and 87)

Amended 1996, c. 7, s. 38; brought into force July 31, 1996 by SI/96-57, Can. Gaz., Part II, July 10, 1996

Amended 1996, c. 8, s. 32(1)(*d*); brought into force July 12, 1996 by SI/96-69, *Can. Gaz., Part II*, July 24, 1996

Amended 1996, c. 16, s. 60(1)(*d*); brought into force July 12, 1996 by SI/96-67, *Can. Gaz., Part II*, July 24, 1996

Amended 1996, c. 19, ss. 65 to 76 and 93.3; ss. 65 to 76 brought into force May 14, 1997 by SI/97-47, *Can. Gaz., Part II*, May 14, 1997; s. 93.3 in force December 1, 1998 as provided by that section

Amended 1996, c. 31, ss. 67 to 72; brought into force January 31, 1997 by SI/97-21, *Can. Gaz., Part II*, February 5, 1997

Amended 1996, c. 34, ss. 1 and 2(2); s. 2(2) in force January 1, 1997; s. 1 to come into force by order of the Governor in Council (repealed before coming into force 2008, c. 20, s. 3)

Amended 1997, c. 16, s. 2; brought into force May 26, 1997 by SI/97-66, *Can. Gaz.*, *Part II*

Amended 1997, c. 17, ss. 1 to 10; brought into force August 1, 1997 by SI/97-84, *Can. Gaz., Part II*, July 23, 1997

Amended 1997, c. 18, ss. 1 to 115; ss. 107.1 and 139.1 in force May 2, 1997 by SI/97-60, *Can. Gaz., Part II*, May 14, 1997; ss. 1, 23, 27 to 39, 99, 100, 109 and 140 in force May 14, 1997 by SI/97-62, *Can. Gaz., Part II*, May 28, 1997; ss. 2 to 22, 24 to 26, 40 to 98, 101 to 105, 108, 110 to 115 and 141 in force June 16, 1997 by SI/97-68, *Can. Gaz., Part II*, June 25, 1997; ss. 106 and 107 to come into force by order of the Governor in Council (repealed before coming into force 2008, c. 20, s. 3)

Amended 1997, c. 23, ss. 1 to 20 and 26; ss. 1 to 20 in force May 2, 1997 by SI/97-61, *Can. Gaz., Part II*, May 14, 1997; s. 26 brought into force December 1, 1998

Amended 1997, c. 30; brought into force May 12, 1997 by SI/97-63, *Can. Gaz., Part II*, May 28, 1997

Amended 1997, c. 39, ss. 1 to 3; in force December 18, 1997

Amended 1998, c. 7, ss. 2, 3; brought into force May 1, 2000 by SI/2000-25, *Can. Gaz., Part II*, April 26, 2000

Amended 1998, c. 9, ss. 2 to 8; brought into force June 30, 1998 by SI/98-79, *Can. Gaz., Part II*, June 24, 1998

Amended 1998, c. 30, ss. 14(*d*) and 16 (and see ss. 10 and 11); brought into force April 19, 1999 by SI/99-37, *Can. Gaz., Part II*, April 28, 1999

Amended 1998, c. 34, ss. 8, 9 and 11; ss. 8 and 9 brought into force February 14, 1999 by SI/99-13, *Can. Gaz., Part II*, March 3, 1999; s. 11 in force September 1, 1999 (as provided by s. 11)

Amended 1998, c. 35, ss. 119 to 121; brought into force September 1, 1999 by SI/99-75, *Can. Gaz., Part II*, July 21, 1999

Amended 1998, c. 37, ss. 15 to 24; brought into force June 30, 2000 by SI/2000-60, *Can. Gaz., Part II*, July 19, 2000

Amended 1999, c. 2, s. 47; brought into force March 18, 1999 by SI/99-25, *Can. Gaz., Part II*, March 31, 1999

Amended 1999, c. 3, ss. 12, 25 to 58; s. 12 in force March 11, 1999; ss. 25 to 58 in force April 1, 1999

Amended 1999, c. 5, ss. 1 to 47; s. 9 in force March 11, 1999; s. 51 in force July 1, 1999 (as provided by 1999, c. 5, s. 51); s. 52 in force March 18, 1999 (as provided by 1999, c. 5, s. 52); ss. 6 and 7 brought into force March 15, 1999 by para. (*a*) of SI/99-24, *Can. Gaz., Part II*, March 31, 1999; ss. 1 to 5, 8, 10 to 24, 26 to 28 and 43 to 47 brought into force May 1, 1999 by para. (*b*) of SI/99-24, *Can. Gaz., Part II*, March 31, 1999; ss. 25 and 29 to 42 brought into force July 1, 1999 by para. (*c*) of SI/99-24, *Can. Gaz., Part II*, March 31, 1999

Amended 1999, c. 17, s. 120; brought into force November 1, 1999 by SI/99-111, *Can. Gaz., Part II*, October 13, 1999

Amended 1999, c. 18, ss. 92 to 95; in force June 17, 1999

Amended 1999, c. 25, ss. 1 to 27, 30, 31(3) and (5); ss. 1 to 27, 31(3) and (5) brought into force December 1, 1999 by SI/99-135, *Can. Gaz., Part II*, December 8, 1999; s. 30 brought into force May 1, 2000 as provided by s. 30; (s. 29(2) repealed before conditions were satisfied by 2005, c. 22, s. 46 (in force January 2, 2006))

Amended 1999, c. 28, ss. 155 and 156; brought into force June 28, 1999 by SI/99-70, *Can. Gaz., Part II*, July 7, 1999

Amended 1999, c. 31, ss. 67 to 69; in force June 17, 1999

Amended 1999, c. 32, ss. 1 to 6; brought into force July 1, 1999 by SI/99-73, *Can. Gaz., Part II*, July 21, 1999

Amended 1999, c. 33, s. 346; brought into force March 31, 2000 by SI/2000-15, *Can. Gaz., Part II*, March 29, 2000

Amended 1999, c. 35, s. 11; brought into force May 1, 2000 by SI/2000-27, *Can. Gaz., Part II*, April 26, 2000

Amended 2000, c. 1, s. 9; brought into force August 1, 2000 by SI/2000-73, *Can. Gaz., Part II*, August 16, 2000

Amended 2000, c. 2, ss. 1 to 3; in force March 30, 2000

Amended 2000, c. 10, ss. 13 to 24; brought into force June 30, 2000 by SI/2000-61, *Can. Gaz., Part II*, July 19, 2000

Amended 2000, c. 12, ss. 91 to 95; brought into force July 31, 2000 by SI/2000-76, *Can. Gaz., Part II*, August 16, 2000

Amended 2000, c. 17, s. 89; brought into force October 28, 2001 by SI/2001-88, *Can. Gaz., Part II*, September 12, 2001

Amended 2000, c. 24, ss. 42 to 46; brought into force October 23, 2000 by SI/2000-95, *Can. Gaz., Part II*, November 8, 2000 (however, s. 43 later replaced 2001, c. 34, s. 36, in force December 18, 2001)

Amended 2000, c. 25, ss. 2 to 4; brought into force March 15, 2001 by SI/2001-42, *Can. Gaz., Part II*, March 28, 2001

Amended 2001, c. 26, s. 294; brought into force July 1, 2007 by SI/2007-65, *Can. Gaz., Part II*, June 27, 2007

Amended 2001, c. 27, ss. 244 to 247; ss. 244, 246 and 247 brought into force June 28, 2002 by paras. (*f*) and (*g*) of SI/2002-97, *Can. Gaz., Part II*, June 14, 2002 (however, s. 246 since repealed 2001, c. 32, s. 81(3)(*d*) in force June 28, 2002 as provided by the section); s. 245 to come into force by order of the Governor in Council (repealed before coming into force 2004, c. 15, s. 110)

Amended 2001, c. 32, ss. 1(1) to (5), 2, 4 to 8, 9(1), 10, 11, 12(1) to (4), (6), (7), 13 to 30, 31(1), (2), (4), 32 to 42, 45 and 46; ss. 1(1) to (5), 4 to 8, 9(1), 10, 11, 16, 24, 27 to 30, 31(1), (2), (4), 32 to 42, 45 and 46 brought into force January 7, 2002 by para. (*a*) of SI/2002-17, *Can. Gaz.*, *Part II*, January 16, 2002; ss. 2, 12(1) to (4), (6), (7), 13 to 15, 17 to 23, 25 and 26 brought into force February 1, 2002 by part (*b*) of SI/2002-17, *Can. Gaz.*, *Part II*, January 16, 2002

Amended 2001, c. 37, s. 1; in force December 18, 2001

Amended 2001, c. 41, ss. 2 to 23, 31 to 34, 80, 126(2), (3), 130(7.1), 131(2), 133(2), (5), (8) to (11), (13), (14) to (19), (21) and 143; ss. 80, 133(21) in force December 18, 2001; ss. 2 to 23, 31 to 34 brought into force December 24, 2001 by SI/2002-16; s. 131(2) in force December 24, 2001 (as provided by this section); ss. 130(7.1), 133(2), (5), (8) to (10), (13) to (19) in force January 7, 2002 (as provided by these sections); s. 133(11) in force February 1, 2002 (as provided by this section); s. 126(2), (3) in force June 28, 2002 (as provided by these sections); s. 143 in force July 2, 2003 (as provided by this section)

Amended 2002, c. 1, ss. 175 to 177, 179 and 181 to 186 brought into force April 1, 2003 by SI/2002-91, *Can. Gaz.*, *Part II*, June 19, 2002

Amended 2002, c. 7, ss. 137 to 150 brought into force April 1, 2003 by SI/2003-48, *Can. Gaz.*, *Part II*, April 9, 2003

Amended 2002, c. 13, ss. 2 to 4, 5(2), (3), (4), 6 to 15 and 17 to 85; ss. 2 to 4, 5(2), (3), (4), 6 to 15, 17 to 23, 47, 50 to 58, 60, 61, 63 to 65, 67 to 69, 73 to 78, 80 to 86 brought into force July 23, 2002 by para. (*b*) of SI/2002-106, *Can. Gaz.*, *Part II*, July 31, 2002; ss. 49 and 62 brought into force September 23, 2002 by para. (*c*) of SI/2002-106, *Can. Gaz.*, *Part II*, July 31, 2002; ss. 66, 70, 71 brought into force November 25, 2002 by para. (*d*) of SI/2002-106, *Can. Gaz.*, *Part II*, July 31, 2002; ss. 24 to 46, 48, 59 and 72 brought into force June 1, 2004 as provided by para. (*b*) of SI/2003-182, *Can. Gaz.*, *Part II*, December 3, 2003; s. 79 brought into force July 23, 2003 by para. (*b*) of SI/2003-127, *Can. Gaz.*, *Part II*, July 2, 2003

Amended 2002, c. 22, ss. 324 to 327 and 409(2)(*b*); s. 409(2)(*b*) in force June 13, 2002 as provided by this section; ss. 324 to 327 brought into force July 1, 2003 by SI/2003-47, *Can. Gaz.*, *Part II*, April 9, 2003 [Note: ss. 326 and 327 since repealed by 2002, c. 22, s. 409(2)(*a*) and (6) as provided in the section, in force June 13, 2002.]

Amended 2003, c. 8, ss. 2 to 8; s. 2(1) brought into force May 30, 2003 by SI/2003-114, *Can. Gaz.*, *Part II*, June 18, 2003; ss. 2(2) and 3 to 7 brought into force August 15, 2003 by SI/2003-144, *Can. Gaz.*, August 27, 2003; s. 8 to come into force by order of the Governor in Council (repealed before coming into force 2012, c. 1, s. 47)

Amended 2003, c. 21, ss. 1 to 21; brought into force March 31, 2004 by SI/2004-22, *Can. Gaz.*, *Part II*, February 25, 2004; s. 22 in force June 1, 2004, as provided by that section

Amended 2003, c. 22, s. 224(*z*.23), brought into force April 6, 2005 by SI/2005-24, *Can. Gaz.*, *Part II*, April 6, 2005

Amended 2004, c. 3, ss. 1 to 8; ss. 2 to 8 brought into force September 15, 2004 by SI/2004-119, *Can. Gaz.*, *Part II*, September 22, 2004; s. 1 brought into force September 15, 2005 by SI/2005-60, *Can. Gaz.*, *Part II*, June 29, 2005

Amended 2004, c. 10, ss. 20 and 21 brought into force December 15, 2004 by SI/2004-157, *Can. Gaz.*, *Part II*, December 15, 2004

Amended 2004, c. 12, ss. 1 to 7 and 9 to 17; ss. 1 to 7 and 9 to 16 in force on Royal Assent, April 22, 2004; s. 17 brought into force October 1, 2004 by SI/2004-131, *Can. Gaz.*, *Part II*, October 20, 2004

Amended 2004, c. 14, ss. 1 and 2, in force on Royal Assent, April 29, 2004

Amended 2004, c. 15, ss. 32 and 108; brought into force December 1, 2004 by SI/2004-158, *Can. Gaz.*, *Part II*, December 15, 2004

Amended 2005, c. 10, ss. 18 to 25 and 34(1)(*f*), brought into force April 4, 2005 by SI/2005-29, *Can. Gaz.*, *Part II*, April 20, 2005

Amended 2005, c. 22, ss. 1 to 8, 10 to 26, 27(2), 28 to 34, 36 to 41 and 64(2); ss. 1 to 7, 10, 11, 33 and 40 brought into force June 30, 2005 by para. (*a*) of SI/2005-56, *Can. Gaz.*, *Part II*, June 15, 2005; ss. 8, 12 to 26, 27(2), 28 to 32, 34, 36 to 39 and 41, brought into force January 2, 2006 by para. (*b*) of SI/2005-56, *Can. Gaz.*, *Part II*, June 15, 2005; s. 64(2) in force January 2, 2006 as provided by the section

Amended 2005, c. 25, ss. 1 and 3 to 13; s. 5 in force on Royal Assent, May 19, 2005; ss. 1, 3, 4 and 6 to 13 brought into force January 1, 2008 by SI/2007-108, *Can. Gaz.*, *Part II*, December 12, 2007

Amended 2005, c. 32, ss. 1 to 7, 8(2) to (5) and 9 to 25; ss. 1 to 7, 8(2) to (5), 9 to 12, 24 and 25 brought into force November 1, 2005 by para. (*a*) of SI/2005-104, *Can. Gaz.*, *Part II*, November 16, 2005; ss. 13 to 23 brought into force January 2, 2006 by para. (*b*) of SI/2005-104, *Can. Gaz.*, *Part II*, November 16, 2005

Amended 2005, c. 38, ss. 58, 138(*e*) and 140(*b*); brought into force December 12, 2005 by SI/2005-119, *Can. Gaz.*, *Part II*, December 14, 2005

Amended 2005, c. 40, ss. 1 to 3 and 7; ss. 1 to 3 in force November 24, 2005; s. 7 in force November 24, 2005 as provided by the section

Amended 2005, c. 43, ss. 1 to 7 and 8(3); ss. 1 to 7 in force November 25, 2005; s. 8(3) in force November 25, 2005 as provided by the section

Amended 2005, c. 44, ss. 1, 3 to 12; in force November 25, 2005

Amended 2006, c. 9, s. 246; brought into force March 1, 2007 by SI/2007-15, *Can. Gaz.*, *Part II*, February 21, 2007

Amended 2006, c. 14, ss. 1, 2, 3(2) and (3), and 4 to 7, in force on Royal Assent, December 14, 2006

Amended 2007, c. 5, ss. 11 to 20, 21(2), 22 to 29, 30(2), (3) and 31; brought into force September 12, 2008 by SI/2008-93, *Can. Gaz.*, *Part II*, September 4, 2008

Amended 2007, c. 9, ss. 1 and 2; in force on Royal Assent, May 3, 2007

Amended 2007, c. 12, ss. 1 and 2; in force December 1, 2007, as provided by s. 2 (received Royal Assent May 31, 2007)

Amended 2007, c. 13, ss. 1 to 11; in force on Royal Assent, May 31, 2007

Amended 2007, c. 20, s. 1; in force on Royal Assent, June 22, 2007

Amended 2007, c. 22, ss. 2 to 4, 7 to 26; ss. 2 to 4, 8(2) to (5), 9, 11(1), 13(1), 18, 19, 20(1) to (3), 21, 23 and 25 in force June 22, 2007; ss. 7, 8(1), 10, 11(2) to (4), 12, 13(2), 14 to 17, 20(4), 22, 24 and 26 brought into force January 1, 2008 by SI/2007-108, *Can. Gaz.*, *Part II*, December 12, 2007

Amended 2007, c. 28, s. 1; in force on Royal Assent, June 22, 2007

Amended 2008, c. 6, ss. 2 to 44, 45(1), (2), 46, 47, 48(1) and 49 to 54; ss. 2 to 17, 28 to 38 and 54 brought into force May 1, 2008 by SI/2008-34, *Can. Gaz.*, *Part II*, April 2, 2008; remainder brought into force July 2, 2008, by SI/2008-34, *Can. Gaz.*, *Part II*, April 2, 2008

Amended 2008, c. 12, s. 1; in force on Royal Assent, April 17, 2008

Amended 2008, c. 18, ss. 1 to 26, and 28 to 45.2; ss. 1 to 6, 9 to 17, 22 to 26, 28, 30 to 34, 36, 41, 43, 45 and 45.2 in force on Royal Assent, May 29, 2008; remainder in force October 1, 2008 by SI/2008-71, *Can. Gaz.*, *Part II*, June 25, 2008

Amended 2009, c. 2, s. 442; in force March 12, 2010 by s. 444 of the Act

Amended 2009, c. 22, ss. 1 to 19; brought into force October 2, 2009 by SI/2009-92, *Can. Gaz.*, *Part II*, September 30, 2009

Amended 2009, c. 28, ss. 1 to 11; brought into force January 8, 2010 by SI/2009-120, *Can. Gaz.*, *Part II*, December 23, 2009

Amended 2009, c. 29, ss. 2 to 5; brought into force February 22, 2010 by SI/2010-9, *Can. Gaz., Part II*, February 17, 2010

Amended 2010, c. 3, ss. 1 to 8; in force June 29, 2010

Amended 2010, c. 14, ss. 2 to 11; brought into force April 29, 2011 by SI/2011-23, *Can. Gaz., Part II*, April 13, 2011

Amended 2010, c. 17, ss. 2 to 27; brought into force April 15, 2011 by SI/2011-35, April 13, 2011

Amended 2010, c. 19, s. 1; brought into force November 30, 2011 by SI/2011-99, *Can. Gaz., Part II*, December 7, 2011

Amended 2010, c. 20, s. 1; in force on Royal Assent, December 15, 2010

Amended 2011, c. 2, ss. 2 to 5; brought into force December 2, 2011 by SI/2011-108, *Can. Gaz., Part II*, December 21, 2011

Amended 2011, c. 5, ss. 2 to 5; brought into force December 2, 2011 by SI/2011-107, *Can. Gaz., Part II*, December 21, 2011

Amended 2011, c. 6, ss. 2 to 5; brought into force November 1, 2011 by SI/2011-82, *Can. Gaz., Part II*, October 12, 2011

Amended 2011, c. 7, ss. 2 to 13; brought into force March 31, 2015 by SI/2014-105, *Can. Gaz., Part II*, December 31, 2014

Amended 2011, c. 16, ss. 2, and 4 to 16; ss. 2, 4 to 6, 7(2) and (4), 10, 11 and 14 to 16 brought into force August 15, 2011 by SI/2011-62, *Can. Gaz., Part II*, August 17, 2011; remainder bought into force October 24, 2011 by SI/2011-62, *Can. Gaz., Part II*, August 17, 2011

Amended 2012, c. 1, ss. 10 to 38, 47, 141(2) and (3), 143 to 146, 160(c), 200; s. 32(2), 141(2) and (3), 143 to 146 in force March 13, 2012; s. 147 brought into force June 13, 2012 by SI/2012-40 *Can. Gaz., Part II*, June 20, 2012; ss. 10 to 31 and 35 to 38 brought into force August 9, 2012 by SI/2012-48, *Can. Gaz., Part II*, July 4, 2012; ss. 32(1), 33 and 47 brought into force November 6, 2012 by SI/2012-48, *Can. Gaz., Part II*, July 4, 2012; s. 34 brought into force November 20, 2012 by SI/2012-48, *Can. Gaz., Part II*, July 4, 2012; s. 200 brought into force October 23, 2012 by SI/2012/48, *Can. Gaz., Part II*, July 4, 2012; s. 160(c) brought into force February 28, 2013 by SI/2013-13, *Can. Gaz., Part II*, February 27, 2013

Amended 2012, c. 6, ss. 2 to 8; brought into force April 5, 2012 by SI/2012-28, *Can. Gaz., Part II*, April 25, 2012

Amended 2012, c. 9, ss. 2 and 3; brought into force March 11, 2013, by SI/2013-5, *Can. Gaz., Part II*, September 12, 2012

Amended 2012, c. 15, ss. 1 and 2; in force on Royal Assent, June 28, 2012

Amended 2012, c. 19, s. 371; brought into force August 20, 2012 by *Can. Gaz., Part II*, SI/2012-68, September 12, 2012

Amended 2012, c. 29, s. 2; brought into force January 13, 2013

Amended 2013, c. 8, ss. 2 to 6; s. 5 in force September 27, 2013; remainder in force March 27, 2013

Amended 2013, c. 9, ss. 2, 3(2) and 4 to 16; in force July 15, 2013 by SI/2013-67, *Can. Gaz., Part II*, June 19, 2013

Amended 2013, c. 11, ss. 2 to 4; brought into force October 24, 2013 by SI/2013-112, *Can. Gaz., Part II*, October 23, 2013

Amended 2013, c. 13, ss. 2 to 9; brought into force November 1, 2013 by SI/2013-108, *Can. Gaz., Part II*, October 9, 2013

Amended 2013, c. 15, ss. 2 and 3; in force on Royal Assent, June 19, 2013

Amended 2013, c. 19, s. 1; in force on Royal Assent, June 19, 2013

Amended 2013, c. 32, s. 1; in force June 26, 2013

Amended 2013, c. 40, s. 174; in force on Royal Assent, December 12, 2013

Amended 2014, c. 6, ss. 2 to 20; in force July 11, 2014, three months after Royal Assent, April 11, 2014

Amended 2014, c. 9, s. 1; in force on Royal Assent, June 19, 2014

Amended 2014, c. 10, s. 1; in force on Royal Assent, June 19, 2014

Amended 2014, c. 17, ss. 1 to 16; in force on Royal Assent, June 19, 2014

Amended 2014, c. 21, ss. 1 to 4; in force September 19, 2014

Amended 2014, c. 23, ss. 2 and 3; brought into force April 10, 2015 by SI/2015-26, *Can. Gaz., Part II*, April 8, 2015

Amended 2014, c. 25, ss. 2 to 33, 46(2) to (7) and 48(5) and (6); ss. 2 to 33 in force December 6, 2014; s. 46(2) to (7) in force March 9, 2015; s. 48(5) and (6) in force July 23, 2015

Amended 2014, c. 31, ss. 2 to 13, 14(2), 15 to 26; in force March 9, 2015

Amended 2014, c. 32, s. 59 in force on Royal Assent, December 9, 2014

Amended 2014, c. 39, s. 171 in force on Royal Assent, December 16, 2014

Amended 2015, c. 1, s. 1; in force on Royal Assent, February 25, 2015

Amended 2015, c. 3, ss. 44 to 59; in force on Royal Assent, February 26, 2015

Amended 2015, c. 13, ss. 3 to 36; in force July 23, 2015, 90 days after Royal Assent, April 23, 2015; ss. 5(1), 18(3) repealed 2014, c. 25, s. 48(3), (8)

Amended 2015, c. 16, ss. 1, 3, 4; to come into force by order of the Governor in Council

Amended 2015, c. 20, ss. 15-28, 34(2)-(4), 35, 38; ss. 15(1), 16, 19-23, 35 in force on Royal Assent, June 18, 2015; ss. 15(2), 17, 18, 24, 25-28 in force July 18, 2015, 30 days after Royal Assent, June 18, 2015; s. 27(2) repealed 2015, c. 20, s. 37(3); s. 38 in force July 23, 2015

Amended 2015, c. 23, ss. 2-19, 30, 31, 33; ss. 2-19, 33 brought into force July 17, 2015 by SI/2015-68, *Can. Gaz., Part II*, July 17, 2015; ss. 30, 31; to come into force by order of the Governor in Council

Amended 2015, c. 27, ss. 18-34; in force on Royal Assent, June 18, 2015

Amended 2015, c. 29, ss. 6-12; brought into force July 17, 2015 by SI/2015-67, *Can. Gaz., Part II*, July 17, 2015

Amended 2015, c. 34; in force on Royal Assent, June 23, 2015

An Act respecting the Criminal Law

SHORT TITLE

SHORT TITLE.

1. This Act may be cited as the *Criminal Code*. R.S., c. C-34, s. 1.

INTERPRETATION

DEFINITIONS / "Act" / "Associated personnel" / "Attorney General" / "Bank-note" / "Bodily harm" / "Canadian Forces" / "Cattle" / "Clerk of the court" / "Common-law partner" / "Complainant" / "Counsel" / "Count" / "Court of appeal" / "Court of criminal jurisdiction" / "Criminal organization" / "Criminal organization offence" / "Day" / "Document of title to goods" / "Document of title to lands" / "Dwelling-house" / "Every one", "person", "owner" / "Explosive substance" / "Firearm" / "Government or public facility" / "Her Majesty's Forces" / "Highway" / "Indictment" / "Internationally protected person" / "Justice" / "Justice system participant" / "Mental disorder" / "Military" / "Military law" / "Motor vehicle" / "Municipality" / "Newly-born child" /

"Night" / "Offence-related property" / "Offender" / "Offensive weapon" / "Organization" / "Peace officer" / "Prison" / "Property" / "Prosecutor" / "Provincial court judge" / "Public department" / "Public officer" / "Public stores" / "Railway equipment" / "Representative" / "Senior officer" / "Serious offence" / "Steal" / "Street racing" / "Superior court of criminal jurisdiction" / "Territorial division" / "Terrorism offence" / "Terrorist activity" / "Terrorist group" / "Testamentary Instrument" / "Trustee" / "Unfit to stand trial" / "United Nations operation" / "United Nations personnel" / "Valuable mineral" / "Valuable security" / "Victim" / "Weapon" / "Wreck" / "Writing".

2. In this Act,

"Act" includes

- (*a*) an Act of Parliament,
- (*b*) an Act of the legislature of the former Province of Canada,
- (*c*) an Act of the legislature of a province, and
- (*d*) an Act or ordinance of the legislature of a province, territory or place in force at the time that province, territory or place became a province of Canada;

"associated personnel" means persons who are

- (*a*) assigned by a government or an intergovernmental organization with the agreement of the competent organ of the United Nations,
- (*b*) engaged by the Secretary-General of the United Nations, by a specialized agency of the United Nations or by the International Atomic Energy Agency, or
- (*c*) deployed by a humanitarian non-governmental organization or agency under an agreement with the Secretary-General of the United Nations, by a specialized agency of the United Nations or by the International Atomic Energy Agency,

to carry out activities in support of the fulfilment of the mandate of a United Nations operation;

"Attorney General"

- (*a*) subject to paragraphs (*b*.1) to (*g*), with respect to proceedings to which this Act applies, means the Attorney General or Solicitor General of the province in which those proceedings are taken and includes his or her lawful deputy,
- (*b*) with respect to Yukon, the Northwest Territories and Nunavut, or with respect to proceedings commenced at the instance of the Government of Canada and conducted by or on behalf of that Government in respect of a contravention of, a conspiracy or attempt to contravene, or counselling the contravention of, any Act of Parliament other than this Act or any regulation made under such an Act, means the Attorney General of Canada and includes his or her lawful deputy,
- (*b*.1) with respect to proceedings in relation to an offence under subsection 7(2.01), means either the Attorney General of Canada or the Attorney General or Solicitor General of the province in which those proceedings are taken and includes the lawful deputy of any of them,
- (*c*) with respect to proceedings in relation to a terrorism offence or to an offence under section 57, 58, 83.12, 424.1 or 431.1 or in relation to an offence against a member of United Nations personnel or associated personnel under section 235, 236, 266, 267, 268, 269, 269.1, 271, 272, 273, 279 or 279.1, means either the Attorney General of Canada or the Attorney General or Solicitor General of the province in which those proceedings are taken and includes the lawful deputy of any of them,
- (*d*) with respect to proceedings in relation to an offence referred to in subsection 7(3.71), or in relation to an offence referred to in paragraph (*a*) of the definition "terrorist activity" in subsection 83.01(1) if the act or omission was committed outside Canada but is deemed under any of subsections 7(2), (2.1) to (2.21), (3),

(3.1), (3.72) and (3.73) to have been committed in Canada, means either the Attorney General of Canada or the Attorney General or Solicitor General of the province in which those proceedings are taken and includes his or her lawful deputy,

(e) with respect to proceedings in relation to an offence where the act or omission constituting the offence

   (i) constitutes a terrorist activity referred to in paragraph (b) of the definition "terrorist activity" in subsection 83.01(1), and

   (ii) was committed outside Canada but is deemed by virtue of subsection 7(3.74) or (3.75) to have been committed in Canada,

means either the Attorney General of Canada or the Attorney General or Solicitor General of the province in which those proceedings are taken and includes the lawful deputy of any of them,

(f) with respect to proceedings under section 83.13, 83.14, 83.222, 83.223, 83.28, 83.29 or 83.3, means either the Attorney General of Canada or the Attorney General or Solicitor General of the province in which those proceedings are taken and includes the lawful deputy of any of them, and

(g) with respect to proceedings in relation to an offence referred to in sections 121.1, 380, 382, 382.1 and 400, means either the Attorney General of Canada or the Attorney General or Solicitor General of the province in which those proceedings are taken and includes the lawful deputy of any of them;

Note: Subparagraph (b)(i) of the definition "Attorney General" had been replaced by 2002, c. 7, s. 137(1); however, before it came into force, the definition was replaced by 2001, c. 41, s. 2, and as such, there was no longer a subpara. (b)(i).

"bank-note" includes any negotiable instrument

(a) issued by or on behalf of a person carrying on the business of banking in or out of Canada, and

(b) issued under the authority of Parliament or under the lawful authority of the government of a state other than Canada,

intended to be used as money or as the equivalent of money, immediately on issue or at some time subsequent thereto, and includes bank bills and bank post bills;

"bodily harm" means any hurt or injury to a person that interferes with the health or comfort of the person and that is more than merely transient or trifling in nature;

"Canadian Forces" means the armed forces of Her Majesty raised by Canada;

"cattle" means neat cattle or an animal of the bovine species by whatever technical or familiar name it is known, and includes any horse, mule, ass, pig, sheep or goat;

"clerk of the court" includes a person, by whatever name or title he may be designated, who from time to time performs the duties of a clerk of the court;

"common-law partner", in relation to an individual, means a person who is cohabiting with the individual in a conjugal relationship, having so cohabited for a period of at least one year;

"complainant" means the victim of an alleged offence;

"counsel" means a barrister or solicitor, in respect of the matters or things that barristers and solicitors, respectively, are authorized by the law of a province to do or perform in relation to legal proceedings;

"count" means a charge in an information or indictment;

"court of appeal" means, in all provinces, the Court of Appeal;

"court of criminal jurisdiction" means

(a) a court of general or quarter sessions of the peace, when presided over by a superior court judge,

> (*a*.1) in the Province of Quebec, the Court of Quebec, the municipal court of Montreal and the municipal court of Quebec,
>
> (*b*) a provincial court judge or judge acting under Part XIX, and
>
> (*c*) in the Province of Ontario, the Ontario Court of Justice;

"criminal organization" has the same meaning as in subsection 467.1(1);

"criminal organization offence" means

> (*a*) an offence under section 467.11, 467.111, 467.12 or 467.13, or a serious offence committed for the benefit of, at the direction of, or in association with, a criminal organization, or
>
> (*b*) a conspiracy or an attempt to commit, being an accessory after the fact in relation to, or any counselling in relation to, an offence referred to in paragraph (*a*);

"day" means the period between six o'clock in the forenoon and nine o'clock in the afternoon of the same day;

"document of title to goods" includes a bought and sold note, bill of lading, warrant, certificate or order for the delivery or transfer of goods or any other valuable thing, and any other document used in the ordinary course of business as evidence of the possession or control of goods, authorizing or purporting to authorize, by endorsement or by delivery, the person in possession of the document to transfer or receive any goods thereby represented or therein mentioned or referred to;

"document of title to lands" includes any writing that is or contains evidence of the title, or any part of the title, to real property or to any interest in real property, and any notarial or registrar's copy thereof and any duplicate instrument, memorial, certificate or document authorized or required by any law in force in any part of Canada with respect to registration of titles that relates to title to real property or to any interest in real property;

"dwelling-house" means the whole or any part of a building or structure that is kept or occupied as a permanent or temporary residence, and includes

> (*a*) a building within the curtilage of a dwelling-house that is connected to it by a doorway or by a covered and enclosed passageway, and
>
> (*b*) a unit that is designed to be mobile and to be used as a permanent or temporary residence and that is being used as such a residence;

"environment" means the components of the Earth and includes

> (*a*) air, land and water,
>
> (*b*) all layers of the atmosphere,
>
> (*c*) all organic and inorganic matter and living organisms, and
>
> (*d*) the interacting natural systems that include components referred to in paragraphs (*a*) to (*c*);

"every one", "person" and "owner", and similar expressions, include Her Majesty and an organization;

"explosive substance" includes

> (*a*) anything intended to be used to make an explosive substance,
>
> (*b*) anything, or any part thereof, used or intended to be used, or adapted to cause, or to aid in causing an explosion in or with an explosive substance, and
>
> (*c*) an incendiary grenade, fire bomb, molotov cocktail or other similar incendiary substance or device and a delaying mechanism or other thing intended for use in connection with such a substance or device;

"feeble-minded person" [*Repealed*, 1991, c. 43, s. 9.]

"firearm" means a barrelled weapon from which any shot, bullet or other projectile can be discharged and that is capable of causing serious bodily injury or death to a person, and includes any frame or receiver of such a barrelled weapon and anything that can be adapted for use as a firearm;

"government or public facility" means a facility or conveyance, whether permanent or temporary, that is used or occupied in connection with their official duties by representatives of a state, members of a government, members of a legislature, members of the judiciary, or officials or employees of a state or of any other public authority or public entity, or by officials or employees of an intergovernmental organization;

"Her Majesty's Forces" means the naval, army and air forces of Her Majesty wherever raised, and includes the Canadian Forces;

"highway" means a road to which the public has the right of access, and includes bridges over which or tunnels through which a road passes;

"indictment" includes

    (a) information or a count therein,

    (b) a plea, replication or other pleading, and

    (c) any record;

"internationally protected person" means

    (a) a head of state, including any member of a collegial body that performs the functions of a head of state under the constitution of the state concerned, a head of a government or a minister of foreign affairs, whenever that person is in a state other than the state in which he holds that position or office,

    (b) a member of the family of a person described in paragraph (a) who accompanies that person in a state other than the state in which that person holds that position or office,

    (c) a representative or an official of a state or an official or agent of an international organization of an intergovernmental character who, at the time when and at the place where an offence referred to in subsection 7(3) is committed against his person or any property referred to in section 431 that is used by him, is entitled, pursuant to international law, to special protection from any attack on his person, freedom or dignity, or

    (d) a member of the family of a representative, official or agent described in paragraph (c) who forms part of his household, if the representative, official or agent, at the time when and at the place where any offence referred to in subsection 7(3) is committed against the member of his family or any property referred to in section 431 that is used by that member, is entitled, pursuant to international law, to special protection from any attack on his person, freedom or dignity;

"justice" means a justice of the peace or a provincial court judge, and includes two or more justices where two or more justices are, by law, required to act or, by law, act or have jurisdiction;

"justice system participant" means

    (a) a member of the Senate, of the House of Commons, of a legislative assembly or of a municipal council, and

    (b) a person who plays a role in the administration of criminal justice, including

        (i) the Minister of Public Safety and Emergency Preparedness and a Minister responsible for policing in a province,

        (ii) a prosecutor, a lawyer, a member of the Chambre des notaires du Québec and an officer of a court,

        (iii) a judge and a justice,

        (iv) a juror and a person who is summoned as a juror,

        (v) an informant, a prospective witness, a witness under subpoena and a witness who has testified,

    (vi) a peace officer within the meaning of any of paragraphs (*b*), (*c*), (*d*), (*e*) and (*g*) of the definition "peace officer",

   (vii) a civilian employee of a police force,

  (viii) a person employed in the administration of a court,

(viii.1) a public officer within the meaning of subsection 25.1(1) and a person acting at the direction of such an officer,

    (ix) an employee of the Canada Revenue Agency who is involved in the investigation of an offence under an Act of Parliament,

  (ix.1) an employee of the Canada Border Services Agency who is involved in the investigation of an offence under an Act of Parliament,

    (x) an employee of a federal or provincial correctional service, a parole supervisor and any other person who is involved in the administration of a sentence under the supervision of such a correctional service and a person who conducts disciplinary hearings under the *Corrections and Conditional Release Act*, and

   (xi) an employee and a member of the Parole Board of Canada and of a provincial parole board; and

 (*c*) a person who plays a role in respect of proceedings involving

    (i) security information,

   (ii) criminal intelligence information,

  (iii) information that would endanger the safety of any person if it were disclosed,

  (iv) information that is obtained in confidence from a source in Canada, the government of a foreign state, an international organization of states or an institution of such a government or international organization, or

   (v) potentially injurious information or sensitive information as those terms are defined in section 38 of the *Canada Evidence Act*;

"magistrate" [*Repealed*, R.S.C. 1985, c. 27 (1st Supp.), s. 2(4).]

"mental disorder" means a disease of the mind;

"military" shall be construed as relating to all or any of the Canadian Forces;

"military law" includes all laws, regulations or orders relating to the Canadian Forces;

"motor vehicle" means a vehicle that is drawn, propelled or driven by any means other than muscular power, but does not include railway equipment;

"municipality" includes the corporation of a city, town, village, county, township, parish or other territorial or local division of a province, the inhabitants of which are incorporated or are entitled to hold property collectively for a public purpose;

"newly-born child" means a person under the age of one year;

"night" means the period between nine o'clock in the afternoon and six o'clock in the forenoon of the following day;

"nuclear facility" means

 (*a*) any nuclear reactor, including a reactor installed on a vessel, vehicle, aircraft or space object for use as an energy source in order to propel the vessel, vehicle, aircraft or space object or for any other purpose, and

 (*b*) any plant or conveyance used for the production, storage, processing or transport of nuclear material or radioactive material;

"nuclear material" means

 (*a*) plutonium, except plutonium with an isotopic concentration of plutonium-238 that is greater than 80%,

 (*b*) uranium-233,

 (*c*) uranium containing uranium-233 or uranium-235 or both in an amount such that the abundance ratio of the sum of those isotopes to the isotope uranium-238 is greater than 0.72%, (*d*) uranium with an isotopic concentration equal to that occurring in nature, except uranium in the form of ore or ore-residue, and

(*e*) any substance containing any material described in paragraphs (*a*) to (*d*);

"offence-related property" means any property, within or outside Canada,

(*a*) by means or in respect of which an indictable offence under this Act or the *Corruption of Foreign Public Officials Act* is committed,

(*b*) that is used in any manner in connection with the commission of such an offence, or

(*c*) that is intended to be used for committing such an offence;

"offender" means a person who has been determined by a court to be guilty of an offence, whether on acceptance of a plea of guilty or on a finding of guilt;

"offensive weapon" has the same meaning as "weapon";

"organization" means

(*a*) a public body, body corporate, society, company, firm, partnership, trade union or municipality, or

(*b*) an association of persons that
  (i) is created for a common purpose,
  (ii) has an operational structure, and
  (iii) holds itself out to the public as an association of persons;

"peace officer" includes

(*a*) a mayor, warden, reeve, sheriff, deputy sheriff, sheriff's officer and justice of the peace,

(*b*) a member of the Correctional Service of Canada who is designated as a peace officer pursuant to Part I of the *Corrections and Conditional Release Act*, and a warden, deputy warden, instructor, keeper, jailer, guard and any other officer or permanent employee of a prison other than a penitentiary as defined in Part I of the *Corrections and Conditional Release Act*,

(*c*) a police officer, police constable, bailiff, constable, or other person employed for the preservation and maintenance of the public peace or for the service or execution of civil process,

(*c*.1) a designated officer as defined in section 2 of the *Integrated Cross-border Law Enforcement Operations Act*, when
  (i) participating in an integrated cross-border operation, as defined in section 2 of that Act, or
  (ii) engaging in an activity incidental to such an operation, including travel for the purpose of participating in the operation and appearances in court arising from the operation;

(*d*) an officer within the meaning of the *Customs Act*, the *Excise Act* or the *Excise Act, 2001*, or a person having the powers of such an officer, when performing any duty in the administration of any of those Acts,

(*d*.1) an officer authorized under subsection 138(1) of the *Immigration and Refugee Protection Act*,

(*e*) a person designated as a fishery guardian under the *Fisheries Act* when performing any duties or functions under that Act and a person designated as a fishery officer under the *Fisheries Act* when performing any duties or functions under that Act or the *Coastal Fisheries Protection Act*,

(*f*) the pilot in command of an aircraft
  (i) registered in Canada under regulations made under the *Aeronautics Act*, or
  (ii) leased without crew and operated by a person who is qualified under regulations made under the *Aeronautics Act* to be registered as owner of an aircraft registered in Canada under those regulations,
  while the aircraft is in flight, and

(*g*) officers and non-commissioned members of the Canadian Forces who are

(i) appointed for the purposes of section 156 of the *National Defence Act*, or

(ii) employed on duties that the Governor in Council, in regulations made under the *National Defence Act* for the purposes of this paragraph, has prescribed to be of such a kind as to necessitate that the officers and non-commissioned members performing them have the powers of peace officers;

"prison" includes a penitentiary, common jail, public or reformatory prison, lock-up, guard-room or other place in which persons who are charged with or convicted of offences are usually kept in custody;

"property" includes

(a) real and personal property of every description and deeds and instruments relating to or evidencing the title or right to property, or giving a right to recover or receive money or goods,

(b) property originally in the possession or under the control of any person, and any property into or for which it has been converted or exchanged and anything acquired at any time by the conversion or exchange, and

(c) any postal card, postage stamp or other stamp issued or prepared for issue under the authority of Parliament or the legislature of a province for the payment to the Crown or a corporate body of any fee, rate or duty, whether or not it is in the possession of the Crown or of any person;

"prosecutor" means the Attorney General or, where the Attorney General does not intervene, means the person who institutes proceedings to which this Act applies, and includes counsel acting on behalf of either of them;

"provincial court judge" means a person appointed or authorized to act by or pursuant to an Act of the legislature of a province, by whatever title that person may be designated, who has the power and authority of two or more justices of the peace and includes the lawful deputy of that person;

"public department" means a department of the Government of Canada or a branch thereof or a board, commission, corporation or other body that is an agent of Her Majesty in right of Canada;

"public officer" includes

(a) an officer of customs or excise,

(b) an officer of the Canadian Forces,

(c) an officer of the Royal Canadian Mounted Police, and

(d) any officer while the officer is engaged in enforcing the laws of Canada relating to revenue, customs, excise, trade or navigation;

"public stores" includes any personal property that is under the care, supervision, administration or control of a public department or of any person in the service of a public department;

"radioactive material" means any material that emits one or more types of ionizing radiation, such as alpha or beta particles, neutrons and gamma rays, and that is capable of, owing to its radiological or fissile properties, causing death, serious bodily harm or substantial damage to property or the environment;

"railway equipment" means

(a) any machine that is constructed for movement exclusively on lines of railway, whether or not the machine is capable of independent motion, or

(b) any vehicle that is constructed for movement both on and off lines of railway while the adaptations of that vehicle for movement on lines of railway are in use;

"representative", in respect of an organization, means a director, partner, employee, member, agent or contractor of the organization;

"senior officer" means a representative who plays an important role in the establishment of an organization's policies or is responsible for managing an important aspect of the organization's activities and, in the case of a body corporate, includes a director, its chief executive officer and its chief financial officer;

"serious offence" has the same meaning as in subsection 467.1(1);

"steal" means to commit theft;

"street racing" means operating a motor vehicle in a race with at least one other motor vehicle on a street, road, highway or other public place;

"superior court of criminal jurisdiction" means

    (a) in the Province of Ontario, the Court of Appeal or the Superior Court of Justice,

    (b) in the Province of Quebec, the Superior Court,

    (c) in the Provinces of Nova Scotia, British Columbia and Prince Edward Island, the Court of Appeal or the Supreme Court,

    (d) in the Provinces of New Brunswick, Manitoba, Saskatchewan and Alberta, the Court of Appeal or the Court of Queen's Bench,

    (e) in the Province of Newfoundland and Labrador, Yukon and the Northwest Territories, the Supreme Court, and

    (f) in Nunavut, the Nunavut Court of Justice;

    (g) [*Repealed*, 2015, c. 3, s. 44(3)]

    (h) [*Repealed*, 2015, c. 3, s. 44(3)]

"territorial division" includes any province, county, union of counties, township, city, town, parish or other judicial division or place to which the context applies;

"terrorism offence" means

    (a) an offence under any of sections 83.02 to 83.04 or 83.18 to 83.23,

    (b) an indictable offence under this or any other Act of Parliament committed for the benefit of, at the direction of or in association with a terrorist group,

    (c) an indictable offence under this or any other Act of Parliament where the act or omission constituting the offence also constitutes a terrorist activity, or

    (d) a conspiracy or an attempt to commit, or being an accessory after the fact in relation to, or any counselling in relation to, an offence referred to in paragraph (a), (b) or (c);

"terrorist activity" has the same meaning as in subsection 83.01(1);

"terrorist group" has the same meaning as in subsection 83.01(1);

"testamentary instrument" includes any will, codicil or other testamentary writing or appointment, during the life of the testator whose testamentary disposition it purports to be and after his death, whether it relates to real or personal property or to both;

"trustee" means a person who is declared by any Act to be a trustee or is, by the law of the province, a trustee, and without restricting the generality of the foregoing, includes a trustee on an express trust created by deed, will or instrument in writing, or by parol;

"unfit to stand trial" means unable on account of mental disorder to conduct a defence at any stage of the proceedings before a verdict is rendered or to instruct counsel to do so, and, in particular, unable on account of mental disorder to

    (a) understand the nature or object of the proceedings,

    (b) understand the possible consequences of the proceedings, or

    (c) communicate with counsel;

"United Nations operation" means an operation that is established by the competent organ of the United Nations in accordance with the Charter of the United Nations and is conducted under United Nations authority and control, if the operation is for the purpose of maintaining or restoring international peace and security or if the Security Council or the General Assembly of the United Nations has declared, for the purposes of the Convention on the Safety of United Nations and Associated Personnel, that there exists an exceptional risk to the safety of the personnel participating in the operation. It does not include an operation authorized by the Security Council as an enforcement action under Chapter VII of the Charter of the United Nations in which any of the personnel are engaged as combatants against organized armed forces and to which the law of international armed conflict applies;

"United Nations personnel" means

  (*a*) persons who are engaged or deployed by the Secretary-General of the United Nations as members of the military, police or civilian components of a United Nations operation, or

  (*b*) any other officials or experts who are on mission of the United Nations or one of its specialized agencies or the International Atomic Energy Agency and who are present in an official capacity in the area where a United Nations operation is conducted;

"valuable mineral" means a mineral of a value of at least $100 per kilogram, and includes precious metals, diamonds and other gemstones and any rock or ore that contains those minerals;

"valuable security" includes

  (*a*) an order, exchequer acquittance or other security that entitles or evidences the title of any person

   (i) to a share or interest in a public stock or fund or in any fund of a body corporate, company or society, or

   (ii) to a deposit in a financial institution,

  (*b*) any debenture, deed, bond, bill, note, warrant, order or other security for money or for payment of money,

  (*c*) a document of title to lands or goods wherever situated,

  (*d*) a stamp or writing that secures or evidences title to or an interest in a chattel personal, or that evidences delivery of a chattel personal, and

  (*e*) a release, receipt, discharge or other instrument evidencing payment of money;

"victim" means a person against whom an offence has been committed, or is alleged to have been committed, who has suffered, or is alleged to have suffered, physical or emotional harm, property damage or economic loss as the result of the commission or alleged commission of the offence and includes, for the purposes of sections 672.5, 722 and 745.63, a person who has suffered physical or emotional harm, property damage or economic loss as the result of the commission of an offence against any other person;

"weapon" means any thing used, designed to be used or intended for use

  (*a*) in causing death or injury to any person, or

  (*b*) for the purpose of threatening or intimidating any person

and, without restricting the generality of the foregoing, includes a firearm and, for the purposes of sections 88, 267 and 272, any thing used, designed to be used or intended for use in binding or tying up a person against their will;

"wreck" includes the cargo, stores and tackle of a vessel and all parts of a vessel separated from the vessel, and the property of persons who belong to, are on board or have quitted a vessel that is wrecked, stranded or in distress at any place in Canada;

"writing" includes a document of any kind and any mode in which, and any material on which, words or figures, whether at length or abridged, are written, printed or otherwise expressed, or a map or plan is inscribed. R.S., c. C-34, s. 2; 1972, c. 13, s. 2, c. 17, s. 2; 1973-74, c. 17, s. 9; 1974-75-76, c. 19, ss. 1, 2, c. 48, s. 24, c. 93, s. 2; 1976-77, c. 35, s. 21; 1978-79, c. 11, s. 10; 1980-81-82-83, c. 125, s. 1; R.S.C. 1985, c. 11 (1st Supp.), s. 2, c. 27 (1st Supp.), s. 2, c. 31 (1st Supp.), s. 61; c. 1 (2nd Supp.), s. 213(4), c. 27 (2nd Supp.), s. 10, c. 35 (2nd Supp.), s. 34; c. 32 (4th Supp.), s. 55; c. 40 (4th Supp.), s. 2; 1990, c. 17, s. 7; 1991, c. 1, s. 28; 1991, c. 43, ss. 1, 9; 1991, c. 40, s. 1; 1992, c. 20, s. 216; 1992, c.

51, s. 32; 1993, c. 28, Sch. III, s. 25(1), (2) **(repealed by 1999, c. 3, s. 12)**; 1994, c. 44, s. 2; 1995, c. 29, ss. 39, 40, c. 39, s. 138; 1997, c. 23, s. 1; 1998, c. 30, s. 14(*d*); 1999, c. 3, ss. 12, 25; c. 5, s. 1; c. 25, s. 1; c. 28, s. 155; 2000, c. 12, s. 91; 2001, c. 32, s. 1; 2001, c. 41, s. 2 and 131(2); 2002, c. 7, s. 137(2); 2002, c. 22, s. 324; 2003, c. 21, s. 1; 2004, c. 3, s. 1; 2005, c. 10, s. 34(1)(*f*)(i); 2005, c. 38, s. 58; 2005, c. 40, ss 1 and 7; 2006, c. 14, s. 1; 2007, c. 13, s. 1; 2012, c. 1, s. 160(*c*)(i); 2012, c. 19, s. 371; 2013, c. 13, s. 2; 2014, c. 17, s. 1; 2014, c. 23, s. 2; 2014, c. 25, s. 2; 2015, c. 3, s. 44; 2015, c. 13, s. 3; c. 20, s. 15.

CROSS-REFERENCES

In addition to the definitions set out in this section which are applicable to the *Criminal Code* as a whole, certain provisions contain their own definitions of particular words or phrases. Some Parts of the *Criminal Code* also contain definition sections as follows: Part III, firearms and other offensive weapons, s. 84; Part IV, offences against the administration of law and justice; Part V, sexual offences, public morals and disorderly conduct, s. 150; Part VI, invasion of privacy, s. 183; Part VII, disorderly houses, gaming and betting, s. 197; Part VIII, offences against the person and reputation, ss. 214, 254; Part IX, offences against rights of property, s. 321; Part X, fraudulent transactions relating to contracts and trade, s. 379; Part XI, wilful and forbidden acts in respect of certain property, s. 428; Part XII, offences relating to currency, s. 448; Part XII.1, instruments and literature for illicit drug use, s. 462.1; Part XII.2, proceeds of crime, s. 462.3; Part XVI, compelling appearance of accused before a justice and interim release, s. 493; Part XIX, indictable offences — trial without jury, s. 552; Part XXI, appeals — indictable offences, s. 673; Part XXIII, punishment, fines, forfeitures, costs and restitution of property, s. 716; Part XXIV, dangerous and long-term offenders, s. 752; Part XXV, effect and enforcement of recognizances, s. 762; Part XXVII, summary convictions, s. 785.

Refer also to Part XX.1 of the *Criminal Code* containing definitions for the following: accused, assessment, chairperson, court, justice, dual status offender, hospital, medical practitioner, party, placement decision, prescribed, Review Board and verdict of not criminally responsible on account of mental disorder, s. 672.1; protected statements, s. 672.21; psychosurgery, s. 672.61(2); electro-convulsive therapy, s. 672.61(2); Minister, s. 672.68(1).

Reference should also be made to the *Interpretation Act*, R.S.C. 1985, c. I-21, which, pursuant to s. 3(1) of that Act, applies to every federal enactment, "unless a contrary intention appears". That Act, in addition to codifying certain rules of interpretation, also defines certain terms in s. 35. Other federal enactments may also contain definitions of words or phrases which are applicable to the *Criminal Code* by virtue of s. 4(4) of the Code and s. 15(2) of the *Interpretation Act* which provides that, "where an enactment contains an interpretation section or provision, it shall be read and construed . . . as being applicable to all other enactments relating to the same subject-matter unless a contrary intention appears". Throughout the *Criminal Code* in the note of related sections, an attempt has been made to identify these related sections in other enactments.

ANNOTATIONS

"Attorney General" / *also see definition of prosecutor, infra* – It is clear that Parliament may constitutionally vest exclusive jurisdiction in the Attorney General of Canada to prosecute offences which do not depend for their validity on s. 91(27) of the *Constitution Act, 1867*: *R. v. Hauser*, [1979] 1 S.C.R. 984, 46 C.C.C. (2d) 481 (5:2). It would also seem that Parliament may vest prosecutorial authority in the federal Attorney General under this section even where the offence depends for its validity on the criminal law power in s. 91(27): *Canada (Attorney General) v. Canadian National Transportation, Ltd.; Canada (Attorney General) v. Canadian Pacific Transport Co.*, [1983] 2 S.C.R. 206, 7 C.C.C. (3d) 449 (the court splitting 4:3 on the issue) with respect to the *Combines Investigation Act*, R.S.C. 1970, c. C-23; and *R. v. Wetmore*, [1983] 2 S.C.R. 161, 7 C.C.C. (3d) 507 (6:1) with respect to the *Food and Drugs Act*, R.S.C. 1970, c. F-27.

Where the Attorney General of Canada does not intervene in a prosecution, such as for an offence under the *Fisheries Act*, R.S.C. 1970, c. F-14, then counsel for the provincial

Attorney General may conduct the prosecution: *R. v. Sacobie and Paul* (1979), 51 C.C.C. (2d) 430, 28 N.B.R. (2d) 288 (C.A.), affd [1983] 1 S.C.R. 241, 1 C.C.C. (3d) 446*n* (7:0).

It was open to the Crown Attorney by letter to appoint a federal prosecutor as an *ad hoc* counsel or agent for the provincial Attorney General to prosecute an offence under the *Criminal Code* which was jointly charged with an offence under the former *Narcotic Control Act: R. v. Luz* (1988), 5 O.R. (3d) 52 (H.C.J.).

Proceedings under the former *Narcotic Control Act* are commenced at the instance of the Government of Canada if charges are laid pursuant to agreed procedures which confer general authority on officers of a municipal police force to institute or commence proceedings on behalf of the Government of Canada. It is not necessary that counsel for the Attorney General of Canada be consulted specifically with respect to each particular charge or that there be specific authority to lay that charge: *R. v. King* (1987), 40 C.C.C. (3d) 359 (Ont. C.A.).

Reference should also be made to s. 467.2 respecting the authority of the Attorney General of Canada to conduct proceedings in respect of a criminal organization offence where the offence arises out of contravention of an Act of Parliament other than the *Criminal Code*.

"bank-note" – Most offences relating to currency are found in Part XII which also defines certain terms in s. 448. Under s. 35(1) of the *Interpretation Act*, R.S.C. 1985, c. I-21, "bank" means a bank to which the *Bank Act*, R.S.C. 1985, c. B-1, applies.

"Canadian Forces" – Note definition of "peace officer" in this section. Reference may also be made to *National Defence Act*, R.S.C. 1985, c. N-5.

"cattle" – The principal offences relating to injury to cattle and other animals are in ss. 444 to 447.

An information charging the accused with wilfully killing a "heifer" properly charged the offence contrary to s. 444 of wilfully killing "cattle", heifer" being the familiar name for a young cow: *R. v. Allen* (1974), 17 C.C.C. (2d) 549 (N.B.C.A.).

"clerk of the court" – The definition of this position is wide enough to include a person describing himself as a deputy clerk: *Ex p. Leclerc* (1972), 7 C.C.C. (2d) 346 (Que. Q.B.).

"counsel" – In light of this definition, reference must be made to the applicable provincial legislation which will define the matters which barristers and solicitors are required to do. Note also s. 10(*b*) of the *Charter of Rights and Freedoms* giving a person arrested or detained the right to "counsel".

"day" – "Day" as defined in this section refers to "day" as distinguished from "night" and has no application to provisions which, for example, require that a notice be served within seven clear days: *R. ex rel. McLearn v. Meagher* (1956), 117 C.C.C. 198 (N.S.S.C.). Thus, this definition would apply where there is a requirement that a certain act be done "by day" as in execution of a search warrant in s. 488. For other definitions relating to periods of time, see *Interpretation Act*, R.S.C. 1985, c. I-21, s. 35: "local time", "month", "standard time", s. 37: "year". As to calculation of time periods, see ss. 26, 27, 28 and 29 of the *Interpretation Act*, especially s. 27 relating to calculation of number of days where the time is expressed in terms of "clear days" or "at least" a number of days.

"dwelling-house" – A motel unit is a dwelling-house: *R. v. Henderson*, [1975] 1 W.W.R. 360 (B.C. Prov. Ct.).

"Curtilage" is not a term of normal usage in Canada, but has been extensively considered in the United States because of the Fourth Amendment protection against unreasonable search and seizure. In *United States v. Potts*, 297 F. 2d 68 (6th Cir. 1961), curtilage was defined to include all buildings in close proximity to a dwelling, which are continually used for carrying on domestic employment; or such place as is necessary and convenient to a dwelling and is habitually used for family purposes.

Detached buildings on an accused's property fall outside "dwelling-house": *R. v. M. (N.)* (2007), 223 C.C.C. (3d) 417 (Ont. S.C.J.).

Explosive substance – The definition is met whether or not a device functions properly and "explodes": *R. v. A. (K.D.S.)* (2010), 253 C.C.C. (3d) 556 (N.B.C.A.).

Liability of the Crown and Crown corporations – In determining the liability of the Crown or a Crown corporation for alleged criminal acts, reference must be made to s. 17 of the *Interpretation Act*, R.S.C. 1985, c. I-21, which provides that, "No enactment is binding on Her Majesty or affects Her Majesty or Her Majesty's rights or prerogatives in any manner, except as mentioned or referred to in the enactment."

The definitions of "person" and "every one" in this section were held to apply to the C.B.C. which was charged with broadcasting an obscene film contrary to s. 163, although the corporation, as a Crown corporation, is an agent of Her Majesty. It is only when the C.B.C. is lawfully executing the powers entrusted to it by the *Broadcasting Act*, R.S.C. 1985, c. B-9, that it is deemed to be a Crown agent and entitled to Crown immunity. When the corporation exercises its powers in a manner inconsistent with the purposes of the *Broadcasting Act*, it steps outside its agency role: *R. v. Canadian Broadcasting Corporation*, [1983] 1 S.C.R. 339, 3 C.C.C. (3d) 1 (7:0).

The Crown was held to be immune from prosecution under the former *Combines Investigation Act*. This immunity also extends to Crown corporations who are agents of the Crown for all their purposes, acting within their authorized purposes: *R. v. Eldorado Nuclear Ltd.-Eldorado Nucleaire Ltée; R. v. Uranium Canada Ltd.-Uranium Canada Ltée*, [1983] 2 S.C.R. 551, 8 C.C.C. (3d) 449 (5:2).

Where, from an examination of the statute as a whole, it is apparent that Parliament's intention was that the Crown be bound then, notwithstanding the Crown is not expressly referred to, it will be bound by the statute. Thus it was apparent from the provisions of the *Criminal Code* with respect to costs in summary conviction appeal matters that both the Crown and the defendant were to be treated equally with respect to costs and accordingly the court had power to award costs against the Crown in summary conviction appeals notwithstanding the applicable provisions of the *Criminal Code* did not expressly mention the Crown: *R. v. Ouellette*, [1980] 1 S.C.R. 568, 52 C.C.C. (2d) 336.

"explosive substance" – The principle provisions relating to liability for the handling of explosives are found in ss. 79 to 82.1.

"firearm" – This definition includes not only a barrelled weapon that is actually capable of causing serious bodily injury or death, but also anything that has the potential of becoming a firearm through an adaptation. The acceptable amount of adaptation, and the time required therefor, for something still to remain within the definition is dependent upon the nature of the offence where the definition is involved. The purpose of each section must be identified and the amount, nature and time spent for adaptation determined so as to give effect to Parliament's intention when enacting the particular section: *R. v. Covin and Covin*, [1983] 1 S.C.R. 725, 8 C.C.C. (3d) 240 (5:0).

There is no burden on the Crown to negative what theoretically might be a defence, that the pistol was not a firearm in the sense that it was incapable of firing bullets or missiles, but has no foundation in the evidence. "If there is evidence on the record either *viva voce* or based upon an examination of the exhibit itself from which it can be reasonably inferred that the alleged firearm is, because of some physical defect or inadequacy, incapable of being fired then, depending on the circumstances, it might be that it is something less than a firearm": *R. v. Marchesani*, [1970] 1 C.C.C. 350 (Ont. H.C.J.) at p. 351.

An inoperative handgun can constitute a firearm if it can be converted into an operating weapon in a relatively short period of time and with relative ease: *R. v. Sinclair* (2005), 207 C.C.C. (3d) 80 (Alta. C.A.).

Barrelled objects that meet the definition of "firearm" in s. 2 need not also meet the definition of "weapon" in paras. (*a*) or (*b*) to be deemed firearms and hence weapons for the various weapons offences in the Code. Therefore, a handgun that fires BBs propelled by compressed air is a weapon for these purposes: *R. v. Dunn* (2013), 305 C.C.C. (3d) 372 (Ont. C.A.), affirmed [2014] S.C.J. No. 69 (S.C.C.).

However, a pellet gun lacking a magazine and a CO2 canister was held not to qualify as a firearm: *R. v. Crawford* (2015), 322 C.C.C. (3d) 528 (Alta. C.A.).

"highway" – A road in a company town, owned by the company but which the public have a *de facto* right to use, was held to constitute a highway for the purposes of the intimidation offence in s. 423: *R. v. Stockley* (1977), 36 C.C.C. (2d) 387 (Nfld. C.A.).

A logging road, however, built and maintained by the company which controls access to the road by means of a permit system, is not a highway: *R. v. Sahonovitch* (1969), 69 W.W.R. 674 (B.C.S.C.).

"indictment" – See definition of "count" above. As to provisions respecting sufficiency of indictments and informations, see ss. 581 to 601.

"mental disorder" – The definition of "mental disorder" as a disease of the mind clearly imports the terminology used to define insanity under the previous provisions of s. 16. Therefore, see the notes under s. 16.

"military" and **"military law"** – See definition of "Canadian Forces" above. Reference may also be made to *National Defence Act*, R.S.C. 1985, c. N-5, and the regulations made thereunder, especially the Queen's Regulations.

"motor vehicle" – This definition contemplates a kind of vehicle, not whether the vehicle is actually operable or effectively functionable: *R. v. Saunders*, [1967] 3 C.C.C. 278, [1967] S.C.R. 284. Thus, an automobile which is out of gas is still a motor vehicle: *R. v. Lloyd*, [1988] 4 W.W.R. 423, 66 Sask. R. 100 (C.A.).

"night" – See notes under "day", *supra*.

"offence-related property" – This term extends to proceeds of sale of offence-related property: *Scotia Mortgage Corp. v. Leung* (2007), 221 C.C.C. (3d) 505 (B.C.C.A.), leave to appeal to S.C.C. refused 223 C.C.C. (3d) vi.

"offensive weapon" – See notes under "weapon", *infra*.

"peace officer" / *municipal enforcement officers* – A municipal by-law enforcement officer was not entitled to enforce the provisions of the *Criminal Code*: *R. v. Laramee* (1972), 9 C.C.C. (2d) 433 (N.W.T. Mag. Ct.). Folld: *R. v. Wright*, [1973] 6 W.W.R. 687 (Sask. D.C.).

In *R. v. Jones and Huber* (1975), 30 C.R.N.S. 127, [1975] 5 W.W.R. 97 (Y.T. Mag. Ct.), it was held that an animal control officer appointed under a municipal by-law enacted pursuant to the Municipal Ordinance, R.O.Y.T. 1971, c. M-12, is a peace officer within the Code as is a poundkeeper appointed under a municipal by-law: *R. v. Moore*, [1983] 5 W.W.R. 176, 21 Man. R. (2d) 77 (Co. Ct.).

First Nations constables appointed pursuant to the *Police Services Act* (Ont.) are peace officers within the meaning of this section: *R. v. Stephens* (1995), 102 C.C.C. (3d) 416 (Ont. C.A.).

Bailiff refers to a Crown-appointed officer or court and does not include a person employed by a private bailiff company: *R. v. Burns* (2002), 170 C.C.C. (3d) 288 (Man. C.A.).

Territorial limits – A peace officer is limited territorially by the authority which appoints him: *R. v. Soucy* (1975), 23 C.C.C. (2d) 561 (N.B.S.C. App. Div.).

Military Police – A military police officer is not a peace officer within the meaning of para. (*g*)(i) when exercising authority over persons not subject to the Code of Service Discipline. He is, however, a peace officer within the meaning of para. (*g*)(ii) if the circumstances fall within s. 22.01(2) of the Queen's Regulations which sets out duties of a kind as to necessitate the officers and members performing them to have the powers of peace officers, including duties performed as a result of established military action or practice related to the maintenance of law and order, protection of property and persons, and the arrest or custody of persons. This would include the detection and arrest of an impaired driver and making of a breathalyzer demand after the driver, a civilian, was stopped, albeit on a public highway, for breach of a traffic regulation on an armed forces base: *R. v. Nolan*, [1987] 1 S.C.R. 1212, 34 C.C.C. (3d) 289 (7:0).

A military police officer, appointed pursuant to s. 156 of the *National Defence Act*, R.S.C. 1985, c. N-5, is a peace officer within the meaning of this section when exercising authority over a person, such as a regular member of the armed forces, who is subject to the Code of Service Discipline even where the offence was committed by that person off a military establishment: *R. v. Courchene* (1989), 52 C.C.C. (3d) 375 (Ont. C.A.).

Game wardens and wildlife enforcement officers – A wildlife officer appointed under the *Wildlife Act*, 1979 (Sask.), c. W-13.1 is a peace officer: *R. v. Rutt* (1981), 59 C.C.C. (2d) 147 (Sask. C.A.), as is a game warden appointed under the *Fish and Wildlife Act*, 1980 (N.B.), c. F-14: *R. v. Rushton* (1981), 62 C.C.C. (2d) 403 (N.B.C.A.); and a conservation officer appointed under the *Game and Fish Act*, R.S.O. 1970, c. 186; *R. v. Renz* (1972), 10 C.C.C. (2d) 250 (Ont. C.A.).

Band constable / Indian reserve – A band constable on an Indian reserve appointed as a special constable to enforce certain provisions of the *Indian Act*, such as s. 97 which involves drunkenness on the reserve, is a person "employed for the preservation and maintenance of the public peace" and thus within the definition of "peace officer": *R. v. Whiskeyjack and Whiskeyjack* (1984), 17 C.C.C. (3d) 245 (Alta. C.A.).

First Nations Constables are "peace officers" within the meaning of this section and are empowered to discharge their duties outside the reserve in relation to the First Nations communities they were primarily employed to serve: *R. v. Decorte*, [2005] 1 S.C.R. 133, 192 C.C.C. (3d) 441.

in flight – This term is defined in s. 7(8).

"prison" – This definition would override the narrower definition of "prison" in the *Prisons and Reformatories Act*, R.S.C. 1985, c. P-20. The term "penitentiary" is defined in s. 2 of the *Corrections and Conditional Release Act*, S.C. 1992, c. 20.

"property" – A promissory note falls within this definition and is also "anything" capable of being stolen within the meaning of s. 322: *R. v. Cinq-Mars* (1989), 51 C.C.C. (3d) 248 (Que. C.A.).

"prosecutor" – Notwithstanding the accused elects trial by provincial court judge, where the offence charged is an indictable offence he is tried under the provisions of Part XIX and it is the definition of "prosecutor" in this section which applies rather than the definition in Part XXVII. Accordingly, a police officer who is neither the informant nor counsel may not conduct the prosecution: *R. v. Edmunds*, [1981] 1 S.C.R. 233, 58 C.C.C. (2d) 485 (4:1).

However, a police officer, as agent of the Attorney General, may communicate to the court the Attorney General's decision as to whether or not to proceed by indictment on a Crown option offence and the officer is not at that stage a prosecutor: *R. v. Parsons* (1984), 14 C.C.C. (3d) 490 (Nfld. C.A.), leave to appeal to S.C.C. refused 51 Nfld. & P.E.I.R. 90*n*, 57 N.R. 77*n*.

Absent flagrant impropriety, the Attorney General has the right to intervene in any private prosecution: *R. v. Kowalski* (1990), 57 C.C.C. (3d) 168 (Alta. Prov. Ct.).

"public officer" – This definition is not exhaustive and therefore an officer who reports to a provincial or municipal government such as a municipally appointed agricultural inspector is a public officer for the purposes of the offence contrary to s. 129 of the *Criminal Code: R. v. Cartier; R. v. Libert* (1978), 43 C.C.C. (2d) 553 (Que. S.C.).

Also see definition in s. 35 of the *Interpretation Act*, R.S.C. 1985, c. I-21.

"unfit to stand trial" – The definition of "unfit to stand trial" statutorily entrenches the extensive case law in the area. Any individual who is unable to understand either the nature or object of the proceedings, the possible consequences or to communicate with counsel as a result of a mental disorder is rendered "unfit to stand trial". The terminology provides clarification of the conflicting case-law by requiring the issue of fitness to be raised solely in the context of a mental disorder and at any stage in the proceedings prior to the rendering of a verdict. Reference should also be made to ss. 672.22 to 672.33 relating to the trial of the issue of fitness.

"valuable security" – A travellers cheque is a valuable security, its value being the amount paid for it by the owner: *R. v. Pennell*, [1966] 1 C.C.C. 258 (B.C.C.A); *R. v. Zinck* (1986), 32 C.C.C. (3d) 150 (N.B.C.A.).

"weapon" – A firearm will always fall within the definition of weapon. It is not necessary to prove that the accused used it or intended to use it for causing death or injury or for a purpose of threatening or intimidation: *R. v. Felawka*, [1993] 4 S.C.R. 199, 85 C.C.C. (3d) 248.

Barrelled objects that meet the definition of "firearm" in s. 2 need not also meet the definition of "weapon" in paras. (*a*) or (*b*) to be deemed firearms and hence weapons for the various weapons offences in the Code. Therefore, a handgun that fires BBs propelled by compressed air is a weapon for these purposes: *R. v. Dunn* (2013), 305 C.C.C. (3d) 372 (Ont. C.A.), affd [2014] 3 S.C.R. 490.

The expression "injury" in para. (*a*) of the definition is not synonymous with "bodily harm". In contrast to the design, the use or the intended use of an object to threaten or intimidate in para. (*b*), when an object is actually used in causing death or injury, there is no requirement that the object be used "for the purpose" of killing or injuring, but merely "in causing" death or injury. When an accused sexually assaults the complainant, by using force against her without her consent, and causes her injuries by the use of such force which includes forcible penetration with an object (here a dildo), that object falls squarely within this definition being an object used in causing injury, thereby constituting a weapon: *R. v. Lamy*, [2002] 1 S.C.R. 860, 162 C.C.C. (3d) 353.

FURTHER DEFINITIONS — FIREARMS.

2.1 In this Act, "ammunition", "antique firearm", "automatic firearm", "cartridge magazine", "cross-bow", "handgun", "imitation firearm", "prohibited ammunition", "prohibited device", "prohibited firearm", "prohibited weapon", "replica firearm", "restricted firearm" and "restricted weapon", as well as "authorization", "licence" and "registration certificate" when used in relation to those words and expressions, have the same meaning as in subsection 84(1). 2009, c. 22, s. 1.

ACTING ON VICTIM'S BEHALF / Exception.

2.2 (1) For the purposes of sections 606, 672.5, 722, 737.1 and 745.63, any of the following individuals may act on the victim's behalf if the victim is dead or incapable of acting on their own behalf:

    (*a*) **the victim's spouse, or if the victim is dead, their spouse at the time of death;**

    (*b*) **the victim's common-law partner, or if the victim is dead, their common-law partner at the time of death;**

    (*c*) **a relative or dependant of the victim;**

    (*d*) **an individual who has in law or fact custody, or is responsible for the care or support, of the victim; and**

    (*e*) **an individual who has in law or fact custody, or is responsible for the care or support, of a dependant of the victim.**

(2) An individual is not entitled to act on a victim's behalf if the individual is an accused in relation to the offence or alleged offence that resulted in the victim suffering harm or loss or is an individual who is found guilty of that offence or who is found not criminally

responsible on account of mental disorder or unfit to stand trial in respect of that offence. 2015, c. 13, s. 4.

DESCRIPTIVE CROSS-REFERENCES.

3. Where, in any provision of this Act, a reference to another provision of this Act or a provision of any other Act is followed by words in parenthesis that are or purport to be descriptive of the subject-matter of the provision referred to, the words in parenthesis form no part of the provision in which they occur but shall be deemed to have been inserted for convenience of reference only. 1976-77, c. 53, s. 2.

CROSS-REFERENCES

Other rules of interpretation may be found in the *Interpretation Act*, R.S.C. 1985, c. I-21. See especially s. 14 relating to marginal notes and historical references.

SYNOPSIS

This section is designed to avoid confusion arising from the use of *descriptive cross-references* within sections. It states that such words, which appear in parentheses, are not intended to have any interpretative value and are solely added for ease of cross-reference. (For an example of a descriptive cross-reference, see s. 183 – definition section within the "wiretap" section of the *Criminal Code*.)

EFFECT OF JUDICIAL ACTS.

3.1 Unless otherwise provided or ordered, anything done by a court, justice or judge is effective from the moment it is done, whether or not it is reduced to writing. 2002, c. 13, s. 2.

CROSS-REFERENCES

With respect to commencement of sentence, see s. 719.

Part I / GENERAL

POSTCARD A CHATTEL, VALUE / Value of valuable security / Possession / Expressions taken from other Acts / Sexual intercourse / Proof of notifications and service of documents / Proof of service in accordance with provincial laws / Attendance for examination / Means of telecommunication.

4. (1) For the purposes of this Act, a postal card or stamp referred to in paragraph (c) of the definition "property" in section 2 shall be deemed to be a chattel and to be equal in value to the amount of the postage, rate or duty expressed on its face.

(2) For the purposes of this Act, the following rules apply for the purpose of determining the value of a valuable security where value is material:

    (a) where the valuable security is one mentioned in paragraph (a) or (b) of the definition "valuable security" in section 2, the value is the value of the share, interest, deposit or unpaid money, as the case may be, that is secured by the valuable security;

    (b) where the valuable security is one mentioned in paragraph (c) or (d) of the definition "valuable security" in section 2, the value is the value of the lands, goods, chattel personal or interest in the chattel personal, as the case may be; and

    (c) where the valuable security is one mentioned in paragraph (e) of the definition "valuable security" in section 2, the value is the amount of money that has been paid.

(3) For the purposes of this Act,

    (*a*) **a person has anything in possession when he has it in his personal possession or knowingly**

        (i) **has it in the actual possession or custody of another person, or**

        (ii) **has it in any place, whether or not that place belongs to or is occupied by him, for the use or benefit of himself or of another person; and**

    (*b*) **where one of two or more persons, with the knowledge and consent of the rest, has anything in his custody or possession, it shall be deemed to be in the custody and possession of each and all of them.**

(4) Where an offence that is dealt with in this Act relates to a subject that is dealt with in another Act, the words and expressions used in this Act with respect to that offence have, subject to this Act, the meaning assigned to them in that other Act.

(5) For the purposes of this Act, sexual intercourse is complete on penetration to even the slightest degree, notwithstanding that seed is not emitted.

(6) For the purposes of this Act, the service of documents and the giving or sending of any notice may be proved

    (*a*) **by oral evidence given under oath by, or by the affidavit or solemn declaration of, the person claiming to have served, given or sent it; or**

    (*b*) **in the case of a peace officer, by a statement in writing certifying that the document was served or the notice was given or sent by the peace officer, and such a statement is deemed to be a statement made under oath.**

(6.1) Despite subsection (6), the service of documents may be proved in accordance with the laws of a province relating to offences created by the laws of that province.

(7) Despite subsection (6) or (6.1), the court may require the person who appears to have signed an affidavit, a solemn declaration or a statement in accordance with that subsection to appear before it for examination or cross-examination in respect of the issue of proof of service or of the giving or sending of any notice.

(8) For greater certainty, for the purposes of this Act, if the elements of an offence contain an explicit or implicit element of communication without specifying the means of communication, the communication may also be made by a means of telecommunication. R.S., c. C-34, s. 3; 1980-81-82-83, c. 125, s. 2; R.S.C. 1985, c. 27 (1st Supp.), s. 3; 1994, c. 44, s. 3; 1997, c. 18, s. 2; 2008, c. 18, s. 1; 2014, c. 31, s. 2.

CROSS-REFERENCES

Subsection (1) – "property" is defined in s. 2.

Subsection (2) – "valuable security" is defined in s. 2.

Subsection (3) – The definition of possession in this subsection is applicable to all offences. However, s. 358 enacts a special provision relating to possession for the purposes of ss. 342, 354 and 356(1)(*b*). Also note the rule in s. 588 respecting deemed ownership of property.

Subsection (4) – Also see similar rule in s. 15(2) of the *Interpretation Act*, R.S.C. 1985, c. I-21, and note under s. 2, *supra*.

Subsection (5) – With the gradual amendment to the sexual offences, sexual intercourse as an element of an offence is now rare. However, it is still relevant to the incest offence in s. 156.

Subsections (6), (7) – As to service of subpoena, see ss. 509(2) and 701.

  As to service of summons, see s. 509.

Note: This section formerly provided the formula for determining when a person gained a certain age. Resort must now be had to s. 30 of the *Interpretation Act*, R.S.C. 1985, c. I-21. The effect of that provision is that, for example, a person attains the age of 16 years on the day of the anniversary of her birthday rather than the following day as was the effect of the former Code provision.

SYNOPSIS

This section contains several general statements of criminal law. The first two subsections provide interpretative assistance in determining the value to be ascribed to "postal cards or stamps" and "valuable security" if the value is material. The former phrase is part of the s. 2 definition of "property" and the latter is a defined term in the same section.

Subsection (3) deals with the often contentious subject of what constitutes "possession". Determining when an accused is in possession of an item arises in many types of property offences and is also pivotal in many drug cases. The first definition states that *personal possession includes actual possession or knowingly* having an item in the possession of another *with* some measure of *control* over the item. The possessor must *know* the *nature of the item*. It does not matter if the accused owns or occupies the place where the goods are as long as the elements of knowledge and control are satisfied and the goods are for the benefit of the accused or another.

Subsection (4) provides that interpretive assistance may be gained from referring to other Acts which deal with the same subject, unless the *Criminal Code* modifies the meaning otherwise applicable.

Subsection (5) was created to avoid technical arguments about what amount of penile penetration constitutes sexual intercourse.

Subsections (6), (6.1) and (7) set out simple methods of proving service of a document and notice, and permit a court to order the person who did the service to testify, if necessary.

Subsection (8) sets out a general rule that, if an offence contains an element of communication, it is deemed to include telecommunication.

ANNOTATIONS

Subsection (3) / personal possession – To constitute possession for purposes of the criminal law, in a case of manual handling of the object, there must also be knowledge of what that thing is; and both these elements must be co-existent with some act of control (outside public duty): *R. v. Beaver*, [1957] S.C.R. 531, 118 C.C.C. 129.

There can exist circumstances where there is no possession in law notwithstanding there is a right of control with knowledge of the presence and character of the thing if there is no intent to exercise control over it, as where the accused manually handles the thing to destroy it or turn it over to the police: *R. v. Christie* (1978), 41 C.C.C. (2d) 282, 21 N.B.R. (2d) 261 (App. Div.).

Whether or not the inference of possession from the presence of fingerprints on the contraband can be drawn is not subject to a hard and fast rule. It is a question of fact which depends on all of the circumstances of the case and all of the evidence adduced: *R. v. Lepage*, [1995] 1 S.C.R. 654, 95 C.C.C. (3d) 385.

Constructive possession – Constructive possession is complete where the accused: (i) has knowledge of the character of the object; (ii) knowingly puts or keeps the object in a particular place whether or not that place belongs to him; and (iii) intends to have the object in the particular place for his use or benefit or that of another person: *R. v. Morelli*, [2010] 1 S.C.R. 253, 252 C.C.C. (3d) 273.

In dealing with virtual objects, such as computer images, the mere fact that an image has been accessed by or displayed in a Web browser does not, without more, constitute possession. Previous access and the possibility of again accessing a website that contains digital images, located on a distant server over which the viewer has no control, do not constitute, either alone or together, constructive possession. Furthermore, the automatic caching of a file to the hard drive does not, without more, constitute possession. The cached file might be a place over which the computer user has control but, in order to establish possession, it is necessary to satisfy the *mens rea* or fault requirement as well by showing that the file was knowingly stored and retained through the cache: *R. v. Morelli, supra.*

In *R. v. Terrence*, [1983] 1 S.C.R. 357, 4 C.C.C. (3d) 193 (7:0), the court held that for para. (*b*) to apply there must be evidence of a measure of control on the part of the accused. In upholding the acquittal of the accused, a passenger in the stolen motor vehicle, the court noted that there was no such evidence and no evidence that he was a party to the offence of the person actually in possession (the driver) pursuant to s. 21.

The requisite element of control can be found in the fact that the contraband was in the accused's room and she had the right to grant or withhold her consent to the contraband being stored there: *R. v. Chambers* (1985), 20 C.C.C. (3d) 440 (Ont. C.A.).

Innocent possession – This doctrine applies to circumstances in which the accused exercises control over the contraband, but with the absence of intent to exercise control beyond that needed to destroy it or otherwise put it permanently beyond one's control: *R. v. Chalk* (2007), 227 C.C.C. (3d) 141 (Ont. C.A.); *R. v. Farmer* (2014), 318 C.C.C. (3d) 322 (Ont. C.A.).

Application – The definition of "possession" in this subsection is applicable to all proceedings under the *Criminal Code* and is not limited to possession offences. Possession of certain articles may link the accused to pieces of evidence in respect of a crime, such as robbery, in which their possession is not, otherwise, a material element: *R. v. Lovis*, [1975] 2 S.C.R. 294, 17 C.C.C. (2d) 481, 47 D.L.R. (3d) 732 (8:0).

An accused may be found in possession as a party by virtue of s. 21. The accused's liability is not confined to this subsection: *R. v. Zanini,* [1967] S.C.R. 715, [1968] 2 C.C.C. 1 (5:0).

Subsection (5) – When intercourse "complete": "for the purposes of [s. 4(5)] of the Code sexual intercourse is complete upon the penetration of the labia, either labia majora or labia minora, no matter how little, even though the hymen is never touched nor is there any penetration of the vagina": *R. v. Johns* (1956), 116 C.C.C. 200, 25 C.R. 153, 20 W.W.R. 92 (B.C. Co. Ct.).

Subsection (6) – A certificate of analysis under s. 258 is a document within the meaning of this section and therefore proof of service may be made by way of affidavit: *R. v. Spreen* (1987), 40 C.C.C. (3d) 190, 8 M.V.R. (2d) 148, 82 A.R. 318 (C.A.).

CANADIAN FORCES NOT AFFECTED.

5. Nothing in this Act affects any law relating to the government of the Canadian Forces. R.S., c. C-34, s. 4.

CROSS-REFERENCES
The terms "Canadian Forces", "Her Majesty's Forces", "military" and "military law" are defined in s. 2. In addition, in certain circumstances, members of the armed forces come within the definition of "peace officer" in s. 2 and officers of the Canadian Forces are within the definition of "public officer" in s. 2. As to offences involving the military, see ss. 46, 50, 52, 53, 62, 269.1, 419, 420. As to immunity of armed forces personnel from firearms and weapons provisions, see ss. 92, 98.

SYNOPSIS
This section states that the *Criminal Code* does not affect other laws relating to the *Canadian Forces*. The *National Defence Act* and its regulations set out a full Code of Service Discipline and it also provides that a breach of an offence under the *Criminal Code* may be tried by court martial. However, neither this section of the *Criminal Code* nor the *National Defence Act* exempt members of the armed forces from trial by a civilian court for a *Criminal Code* offence committed in Canada.

PRESUMPTION OF INNOCENCE / Offences outside Canada / Definition of "enactment".

6. (1) Where an enactment creates an offence and authorizes a punishment to be imposed in respect of that offence,

    (*a*) a person shall be deemed not to be guilty of the offence until he is convicted or discharged under section 730 of the offence; and

    (*b*) a person who is convicted or discharged under section 730 of the offence is not liable to any punishment in respect thereof other than the punishment prescribed by this Act or by the enactment that creates the offence.

(2) Subject to this Act or any other Act of Parliament, no person shall be convicted or discharged under section 730 of an offence committed outside Canada.

(3) In this section, "enactment" means

    (*a*) an Act of Parliament, or

    (*b*) an Act of the legislature of a province that creates an offence to which Part XXVII applies,

or any regulation made thereunder. R.S., c. C-34, s. 5; R.S.C. 1985, c. 27 (1st Supp.), s. 4; 1995, c. 22, s. 10.

CROSS-REFERENCES

Subsection (1) – As to presumption of innocence, see s. 11(*d*) of the *Canadian Charter of Rights and Freedoms*.

Subsection (2) – For offences committed on territorial sea or inland waters of Canada, see s. 477. As to definition of territorial sea, see *Territorial Sea and Fishing Zones Act*, R.S.C. 1985, c. T-8.

Those sections providing for trial in Canada of offences committed outside Canada are as follows: s. 7(1), offence committed on Canadian aircraft; s. 7(2), hijacking and offences relating to aircraft where accused found in Canada; s. 7(3), certain offences against internationally protected person committed on Canadian aircraft or ships, by Canadian citizen or against internationally protected person performing duties on behalf of Canada; s. 7(3.1), hostage taking in certain circumstances; s. 7(3.2) to (3.6), offences involving nuclear material; s. 7(3.7), torture; s. 7(3.71) to (3.77), war crimes and crimes against humanity; s. 7(4), indictable offences by employee within meaning of *Public Service Employment Act*; s. 57, passport offences; s. 58, offences in relation to certificate of citizenship or naturalization; s. 74, piracy; s. 75, piratical acts; s. 290, bigamy; s. 342, possession in Canada of credit card obtained by crime outside Canada; s. 354, possession in Canada of goods obtained by crime outside Canada; s. 357, bringing into Canada property obtained by crime; s. 462.31, laundering proceeds of offences committed outside Canada; s. 465(1)(*a*), conspiracy to commit murder outside Canada; s. 465(4), conspiracy outside Canada to commit offence inside Canada.

SYNOPSIS

Subsection (1)(*a*) provides a legislative statement of the *presumption of innocence*, first articulated in the common law and now enshrined in the *Canadian Charter of Rights and Freedoms*. If the accused is convicted, or found guilty and discharged under s. 736, subsec. (1)(*b*) states that the only punishment which can be imposed is that set out in the enactment creating the offence. The enactment, as defined in subsec. (3), may be either the *Criminal Code*, another federal statute or a provincial statute creating a summary conviction offence.

Subsection (2) states the rule limiting the *territorial application* of Canadian criminal law to those offences committed in Canada, unless Canadian jurisdiction is specifically extended by federal law. For an example of such a provision, see s. 7. If the relevant legislation does not extend jurisdiction, it will be necessary to show that there is a *real and substantial link* between the offence and Canada.

ANNOTATIONS

Subsection (1)(*a*) – In *R. v. Negridge* (1980), 54 C.C.C. (2d) 304, 17 C.R. (3d) 14 (Ont. C.A.), reference was made to this subsection when the Court held that an accused was not liable to the increased minimum penalties for a second or subsequent "offence" when the second or subsequent offence was committed before the earlier conviction although after the commission of the offence that led to the earlier conviction.

Subsection (1)(*b*) – Where the offence with which the accused was charged has been repealed and new offences created which would apply to the accused's conduct, had it occurred after enactment of these new offences, then the accused is entitled to the benefit of the lesser maximum punishment prescribed for the new offences. This results not from s. 11(*i*) of the *Charter of Rights and Freedoms* but s. 44(*c*) of the *Interpretation Act*, R.S.C. 1985, c. I-21: *R. v. B.(J.W.)* (1989), 51 C.C.C. (3d) 35 (P.E.I.S.C.).

Subsection (2) – All that is necessary to make an offence subject to the jurisdiction of Canadian courts is that a significant portion of the activities constituting that offence take place in Canada. It is sufficient that there is a real and substantial link between the offence and this country. For this purpose, the court must take into account all relevant facts that take place in Canada that may legitimately give this country an interest in prosecuting the offence. The court must then consider whether there is anything in those facts that offends international comity and it may be that the outer limits of the test of a real and substantial link are coterminous with the requirements of international comity. Where the evidence with respect to charges of fraud and conspiracy was that the fraudulent inducements were made by persons in Canada, albeit over the telephone, to residents of the United States, and that some of the proceeds found their way back to Canada, then the charges were properly tried in Canada: *R. v. Libman*, [1985] 2 S.C.R. 178, 21 C.C.C. (3d) 206 (7:0).

Whether there is a "real and substantial link" to Canada is assessed having regard to the circumstances and the importance of the elements of the offence linked to Canada, the relevant facts which arose in Canada and the harmful consequences which were caused or which could have been caused in Canada. In this case, the victim had suffered the injury in another country, but had died in Canada. In addition, the harmful consequences of the offence occurred in Canada as both the victim, the accused and their families were resident in Canada. The accused's interest in being tried in Canada is also a relevant factor in determining whether Canadian courts have jurisdiction: *R. v. Ouellette* (1998), 126 C.C.C. (3d) 219 (Que. S.C.).

A Canadian court has the jurisdiction to try an accused for breach of a probation order even if the breaching acts occurred in a foreign country. There is no rule of international law depriving a judge of jurisdiction to make a probation order binding on the conduct of a probationer abroad. There was a "real and substantial link" between the commission of the offence and Canada where the accused and his companion had travelled from Canada abroad where he assaulted her: *R. v. Greco* (2001), 159 C.C.C. (3d) 146 (Ont. C.A.), leave to appeal to S.C.C. refused [2002] 2 S.C.R. vi, 162 C.C.C. (3d) vi.

See also *R. v. Rattray* (2008), 229 C.C.C. (3d) 496 (Ont. C.A.), to the same effect in respect of an extra-territorial breach of a recognizance.

In *Chowdhury v. Canada* (2014), 309 C.C.C. (3d) 447 (Ont. S.C.J.), the court applied the above principles to hold that Canada lacked territorial jurisdiction to try a foreign national who had never been to Canada for offences under the *Corruption of Foreign Public Officials Act*, S.C. 1998, c. 34.

OFFENCES COMMITTED ON AIRCRAFT / Idem / Offences in relation to cultural property / Definition of "Convention" / Offences against fixed platforms or international maritime navigation / Offences against fixed platforms or navigation in the internal waters or territorial sea of another state / Nuclear terrorism offence committed outside Canada / Space Station — Canadian crew members / Space Station

— crew members of Partner States / Proceedings by Attorney General of Canada / Consent of Attorney General of Canada / Definitions / Offence against internationally protected person / Offence of hostage taking / Offences involving nuclear material / Idem / Idem / Idem / Definition of "nuclear material" / Jurisdiction / Offence against United Nations or associated personnel / Offence involving explosive or other lethal device / Offence relating to financing of terrorism / Terrorism offence committed outside Canada / Terrorist activity committed outside Canada / Offences by Public Service employees / Offence in relation to sexual offences against children / Offence in relation to trafficking in persons / Consent of Attorney General / Jurisdiction / Appearance of accused at trial / Where previously tried outside Canada / If accused not Canadian citizen / Definition of "flight" and "in flight" / Definition of "in service" / Certificate as evidence / Idem.

7. (1) Notwithstanding anything in this Act or any other Act, every one who

(*a*) on or in respect of an aircraft

(i) registered in Canada under regulations made under the *Aeronautics Act*, or

(ii) leased without crew and operated by a person who is qualified under regulations made under the *Aeronautics Act* to be registered as owner of an aircraft registered in Canada under those regulations,

while the aircraft is in flight, or

(*b*) on any aircraft, while the aircraft is in flight if the flight terminated in Canada,

commits an act or omission in or outside Canada that if committed in Canada would be an offence punishable by indictment shall be deemed to have committed that act or omission in Canada.

(2) Notwithstanding this Act or any other Act, every one who

(*a*) on an aircraft, while the aircraft is in flight, commits an act or omission outside Canada that if committed in Canada or on an aircraft registered in Canada under regulations made under the *Aeronautics Act* would be an offence against section 76 or paragraph 77(*a*),

(*b*) in relation to an aircraft in service, commits an act or omission outside Canada that if committed in Canada would be an offence against any of paragraphs 77(*c*), (*d*) or (*g*),

(*c*) in relation to an air navigation facility used in international air navigation, commits an act or omission outside Canada that if committed in Canada would be an offence against paragraph 77(*e*),

(*d*) at or in relation to an airport serving international civil aviation, commits an act or omission outside Canada that if committed in Canada would be an offence against paragraph 77(*b*) or (*f*), or

(*e*) commits an act or omission outside Canada that if committed in Canada would constitute a conspiracy or an attempt to commit an offence referred to in this subsection, or being an accessory after the fact or counselling in relation to such an offence,

shall be deemed to have committed that act or omission in Canada if the person is, after the commission thereof, present in Canada.

(2.01) Despite anything in this Act or any other Act, a person who commits an act or omission outside Canada that if committed in Canada would constitute an offence under section 322, 341, 344, 380, 430 or 434 in relation to cultural property as defined in Article 1 of the Convention, or a conspiracy or an attempt to commit such an offence, or being an accessory after the fact or counselling in relation to such an offence, is deemed to have committed that act or omission in Canada if the person

(*a*) is a Canadian citizen;

(*b*) is not a citizen of any state and ordinarily resides in Canada; or

(*c*) is a permanent resident within the meaning of subsection 2(1) of the *Immigration and Refugee Protection Act* and is, after the commission of the act or omission, present in Canada.

(2.02) For the purpose of subsection (2.01), "Convention" means the Convention for the Protection of Cultural Property in the Event of Armed Conflict, done at The Hague on May 14, 1954. Article 1 of the Convention is set out in the schedule to the *Cultural Property Export and Import Act*.

(2.1) Notwithstanding anything in this Act or any other Act, every one who commits an act or omission outside Canada against or on board a fixed platform attached to the continental shelf of any state or against or on board a ship navigating or scheduled to navigate beyong the territorial sea of any state, that if committed in Canada would constitute an offence against, a conspiracy or an attempt to commit an offence against, or being an accessory after the fact or counselling in relation to an offence against, section 78.1, shall be deemed to commit that act or omission in Canada if it is committed

   (*a*) against or on board a fixed platform attached to the continental shelf of Canada;
   (*b*) against or on board a ship registered or licensed, or for which an identification number has been issued, pursuant to any Act of Parliament;
   (*c*) by a Canadian citizen;
   (*d*) by a person who is not a citizen of any state and who ordinarily resides in Canada;
   (*e*) by a person who is, after the commission of the offence, present in Canada;
   (*f*) in such a way as to seize, injure or kill, or threaten to injure or kill, a Canadian citizen; or
   (*g*) in an attempt to compel the Government of Canada to do or refrain from doing any act.

(2.2) Notwithstanding anything in this Act or any other Act, every one who commits an act or omission outside Canada against or on board a fixed platform not attached to the continental shelf of any state or against or on board a ship not navigating or scheduled to navigate beyond the territorial sea of any state, that if committed in Canada would constitute an offence against, a conspiracy or an attempt to commit an offence against, or being an accessory after the fact or counselling in relation to an offence against, section 78.1, shall be deemed to commit that act or omission in Canada

   (*a*) if it is committed as described in any of paragraphs (2.1)(*b*) to (*g*); and
   (*b*) if the offender is found in the territory of a state, other than the state in which the act or omission was committed, that is
      (i) a party to the Convention for the Suppression of Unlawful Acts against the Safety of Maritime Navigation, done at Rome on March 10, 1988, in respect of an offence committed against or on board a ship, or
      (ii) a party to the Protocol for the Suppression of Unlawful Acts against the Safety of Fixed Platforms Located on the Continental Shelf, done at Rome on March 10, 1988, in respect of an offence committed against or on board a fixed platform.

(2.21) Despite anything in this Act or anyother Act, everyone who commits an act or omission outside Canada that if committed in Canada would constitute an offence under any of sections 82.3 to 82.6, or a conspiracy or attempt to commit such an offence, or being an accessory after the fact or counselling in relation to such an offence, is deemed to have committed that act or omission in Canada if

   (*a*) the act or omission is committed on a ship that is registered or licensed, or for which an identification number has been issued, under any Act of Parliament;
   (*b*) the act or omission is committed on an aircraft that
      (i) is registered in Canada under regulations made under the *Aeronautics Act*, or
      (ii) is leased without crew and operated by a person who is qualified under regulations made under the *Aeronautics Act* to be registered as owner of an aircraft in Canada under those regulations;
   (*c*) the person who commits the act or omission is a Canadian citizen; or

(*d*) the person who commits the act or omission is, after the commission of the act or omission, present in Canada.

(2.3) Despite anything in this Act or any other Act, a Canadian crew member who, during a space flight, commits an act or omission outside Canada that if committed in Canada would constitute an indictable offence is deemed to have committed that act or omission in Canada, if that act or omission is committed

    (*a*) on, or in relation to, a flight element of the Space Station; or

    (*b*) on any means of transportation to or from the Space Station.

(2.31) Despite anything in this Act or any other Act, a crew member of a Partner State who commits an act or omission outside Canada during a space flight on, or in relation to, a flight element of the Space Station or on any means of transportation to and from the Space Station that if committed in Canada would constitute an indictable offence is deemed to have committed that act or omission in Canada, if that act or omission

    (*a*) threatens the life or security of a Canadian crew member; or

    (*b*) is committed on or in relation to, or damages, a flight element provided by Canada.

(2.32) Despite the definition "Attorney General" in section 2, the Attorney General of Canada may conduct proceedings in relation to an offence referred to in subsection (2.3) or (2.31). For that purpose, the Attorney General of Canada may exercise all the powers and perform all the duties and functions assigned to the Attorney General by or under this Act.

(2.33) No proceedings in relation to an offence referred to in subsection (2.3) or (2.31) may be instituted without the consent of the Attorney General of Canada.

(2.34) The definitions in this subsection apply in this subsection and in subsections (2.3) and (2.31).

"Agreement" has the same meaning as in section 2 of the *Civil International Space Station Agreement Implementation Act.*

"Canadian crew member" means a crew member of the Space Station who is

    (*a*) a Canadian citizen; or

    (*b*) a citizen of a foreign state, other than a Partner State, who is authorized by Canada to act as a crew member for a space flight on, or in relation to a flight element.

"crew member of a Partner State" means a crew member of the Space Station who is

    (*a*) a citizen of a Partner State; or

    (*b*) a citizen of a state, other than that Partner State, who is authorized by that Partner State to act as a crew member for a space flight on, or in relation to, a flight element.

"flight element" means a Space Station element provided by Canada or by a Partner State under the Agreement and under any memorandum of understanding or other implementing arrangement entered into to carry out the Agreement.

"Partner State" means a State, other than Canada, who contracted to enter into the Agreement and for which the Agreement has entered into force in accordance with article 25 of the Agreement.

"space flight" means the period that begins with the launching of a crew member of the Space Station, continues during their stay in orbit and ends with their landing on earth.

"Space Station" means the civil international Space Station that is a multi-use facility in low-earth orbit, with flight elements and dedicated ground elements provided by, or on behalf of, the Partner States.

(3) Notwithstanding anything in this Act or any other Act, every one who, outside Canada, commits an act or omission against the person of an internationally protected person or against any property referred to in section 431 used by that person that, if

committed in Canada, would be an offence against any of sections 235, 236, 266, 267, 268, 269, 269.1, 271, 272, 273, 279, 279.1, 280 to 283, 424 and 431 is deemed to commit that act or omission in Canada if

> (a) the act or omission is committed on a ship that is registered or licensed, or for which an identification number has been issued, pursuant to any Act of Parliament;
> (b) the act or omission is committed on an aircraft
>> (i) registered in Canada under regulations made under the *Aeronautics Act*, or
>> (ii) leased without crew and operated by a person who is qualified under regulations made under the *Aeronautics Act* to be registered as owner of an aircraft in Canada under those regulations;
> (c) the person who commits the act or omission is a Canadian citizen or is, after the act or omission has been committed, present in Canada; or
> (d) the act or omission is against
>> (i) a person who enjoys the status of an internationally protected person by virtue of the functions that person performs on behalf of Canada, or
>> (ii) a member of the family of a person described in subparagraph (i) who qualifies under paragraph (b) or (d) of the definition "internationally protected person" in section 2.

(3.1) Notwithstanding anything in this Act or any other Act, every one who, outside Canada, commits an act or omission that if committed in Canada would be an offence against section 279.1 shall be deemed to commit that act or omission in Canada if

> (a) the act or omission is committed on a ship that is registered or licensed, or for which an identification number has been issued, pursuant to any Act of Parliament;
> (b) the act or omission is committed on an aircraft
>> (i) registered in Canada under regulations made under the *Aeronautics Act*, or
>> (ii) leased without crew and operated by a person who is qualified under regulations made under the *Aeronautics Act* to be registered as owner of an aircraft in Canada under such regulations;
> (c) the person who commits the act or omission
>> (i) is a Canadian citizen, or
>> (ii) is not a citizen of any state and ordinarily resides in Canada;
> (d) the act or omission is committed with intent to induce Her Majesty in right of Canada or of a province to commit or cause to be committed any act or omission;
> (e) a person taken hostage by the act or omission is a Canadian citizen; or
> (f) the person who commits the act or omission is, after the commission thereof, present in Canada.

(3.2) [*Repealed*, 2013, c. 13, s. 3(2).]

(3.3) [*Repealed*, 2013, c. 13, s. 3(2).]

(3.4) [*Repealed*, 2013, c. 13, s. 3(2).]

(3.5) [*Repealed*, 2013, c. 13, s. 3(2).]

(3.6) [*Repealed*, 2013, c. 13, s. 3(2).]

(3.7) Notwithstanding anything in this Act or any other Act, every one who, outside Canada, commits an act or omission that, if committed in Canada, would constitute an offence against, a conspiracy or an attempt to commit an offence against, being an accessory after the fact in relation to an offence against, or any counselling in relation to an offence against, section 269.1 shall be deemed to commit that act or omission in Canada if

> (a) the act or omission is committed on a ship that is registered or licensed, or for which an identification number has been issued, pursuant to any Act of Parliament;

(*b*) the act or omission is committed on an aircraft
   (i) registered in Canada under regulations made under the *Aeronautics Act*, or
   (ii) leased without crew and operated by a person who is qualified under regulations made under the *Aeronautics Act* to be registered as owner of an aircraft in Canada under those regulations;
(*c*) the person who commits the act or omission is a Canadian citizen;
(*d*) the complainant is a Canadian citizen; or
(*e*) the person who commits the act or omission is, after the commission thereof, present in Canada.

(3.71) Notwithstanding anything in this Act or any other Act, every one who, outside Canada, commits an act or omission against a member of United Nations personnel or associated personnel or against property referred to in section 431.1 that, if committed in Canada, would constitute an offence against, a conspiracy or an attempt to commit an offence against, or being an accessory after the fact or counselling in relation to an offence against, section 235, 236, 266, 267, 268, 269, 269.1, 271, 272, 273, 279, 279.1, 424.1 or 431.1 is deemed to commit that act or omission in Canada if
(*a*) the act or omission is committed on a ship that is registered or licensed, or for which an identification number has been issued, under an Act of Parliament;
(*b*) the act or omission is committed on an aircraft
   (i) registered in Canada under regulations made under the *Aeronautics Act*, or
   (ii) leased without crew and operated by a person who is qualified under regulations made under the *Aeronautics Act* to be registered as owner of an aircraft in Canada under those regulations;
(*c*) the person who commits the act or omission
   (i) is a Canadian citizen, or
   (ii) is not a citizen of any state and ordinarily resides in Canada;
(*d*) the person who commits the act or omission is, after the commission of the act or omission, present in Canada;
(*e*) the act or omission is committed against a Canadian citizen; or
(*f*) the act or omission is committed with intent to compel the Government of Canada or of a province to do or refrain from doing any act.

(3.72) Notwithstanding anything in this Act or any other Act, every one who, outside Canada, commits an act or omission that, if committed in Canada, would constitute an offence against, a conspiracy or an attempt to commit an offence against, or being an accessory after the fact or counselling in relation to an offence against, section 431.2 is deemed to commit that act or omission in Canada if
(*a*) the act or omission is committed on a ship that is registered or licensed, or for which an identification number has been issued, under any Act of Parliament;
(*b*) the act or omission is committed on an aircraft
   (i) registered in Canada under regulations made under the *Aeronautics Act*,
   (ii) leased without crew and operated by a person who is qualified under regulations made under the *Aeronautics Act* to be registered as owner of an aircraft in Canada under those regulations, or
   (iii) operated for or on behalf of the Government of Canada;
(*c*) the person who commits the act or omission
   (i) is a Canadian citizen, or
   (ii) is not a citizen of any state and ordinarily resides in Canada;
(*d*) the person who commits the act or omission is, after the commission of the act or omission, present in Canada;
(*e*) the act or omission is committed against a Canadian citizen;
(*f*) the act or omission is committed with intent to compel the Government of Canada or of a province to do or refrain from doing any act; or
(*g*) the act or omission is committed against a Canadian government or public facility located outside Canada.

(3.73) Notwithstanding anything in this Act or any other Act, every one who, outside Canada, commits an act or omission that, if committed in Canada, would constitute an offence against, a conspiracy or an attempt to commit an offence against, or being an accessory after the fact or counselling in relation to an offence against, section 83.02 is deemed to commit the act or omission in Canada if

   (a) the act or omission is committed on a ship that is registered or licensed, or for which an identification number has been issued, under an Act of Parliament;

   (b) the act or omission is committed on an aircraft

        (i)   registered in Canada under regulations made under the *Aeronautics Act*, or

        (ii) leased without crew and operated by a person who is qualified under regulations made under the *Aeronautics Act* to be registered as the owner of an aircraft in Canada under those regulations;

   (c) the person who commits the act or omission

        (i)   is a Canadian citizen, or

        (ii) is not a citizen of any state and ordinarily resides in Canada;

   (d) the person who commits the act or omission is, after its commission, present in Canada;

   (e) the act or omission is committed for the purpose of committing an act or omission referred to in paragraph 83.02(a) or (b) in order to compel the Government of Canada or of a province to do or refrain from doing any act;

   (f) the act or omission is committed for the purpose of committing an act or omission referred to in paragraph 83.02(a) or (b) against a Canadian government or public facility located outside Canada; or

   (g) the act or omission is committed for the purpose of committing an act or omission referred to in paragraph 83.02(a) or (b) in Canada or against a Canadian citizen.

(3.74) Notwithstanding anything in this Act or any other Act, every one who commits an act or omission outside Canada that, if committed in Canada, would be a terrorism offence, other than an offence under section 83.02 or an offence referred to in paragraph (a) of the definition "terrorist activity" in subsection 83.01(1), is deemed to have committed that act or omission in Canada if the person

   (a) is a Canadian citizen;

   (b) is not a citizen of any state and ordinarily resides in Canada; or

   (c) is a permanent resident within the meaning of subsection 2(1) of the *Immigration and Refugee Protection Act* and is, after the commission of the act or omission, present in Canada.

(3.75) Notwithstanding anything in this Act or any other Act, every one who commits an act or omission outside Canada that, if committed in Canada, would be an indictable offence and would also constitute a terrorist activity referred to in paragraph (b) of the definition "terrorist activity" in subsection 83.01(1) is deemed to commit that act or omission in Canada if

   (a) the act or omission is committed against a Canadian citizen;

   (b) the act or omission is committed against a Canadian government or public facility located outside Canada; or

   (c) the act or omission is committed with intent to compel the Government of Canada or of a province to do or refrain from doing any act.

(3.76) [*Repealed*, 2000, c. 24, s. 42.]

(3.77) [*Repealed*, 2000, c. 24, s. 42.]

(4) Every one who, while employed as an employee within the meaning of the *Public Service Employment Act* in a place outside Canada, commits an act or omission in that place that is an offence under the laws of that place and that, if committed in Canada, would be an offence punishable by indictment shall be deemed to have committed that act or omission in Canada.

(4.1) Notwithstanding anything in this Act or any other Act, every one who, outside Canada, commits an act or omission that if committed in Canada would be an offence against section 151, 152, 153, 155 or 159, subsection 160(2) or (3), section 163.1, 170, 171, 171.1, 172.1, 172.2 or 173 or subsection 286.1(2) shall be deemed to commit that act or omission in Canada if the person who commits the act or omission is a Canadian citizen or a permanent resident within the meaning of subsection 2(1) of the *Immigration and Refugee Protection Act*.

(4.11) Notwithstanding anything in this Act or any other Act, every one who, outside Canada, commits an act or omission that if committed in Canada would be an offence against section 279.01, 279.011, 279.02 or 279.03 shall be deemed to commit that act or omission in Canada if the person who commits the act or omission is a Canadian citizen or a permanent resident within the meaning of subsection 2(1) of the *Immigration and Refugee Protection Act*.

(4.2) [*Repealed*, 2002, c. 13, s. 3(2).]

(4.3) Proceedings with respect to an act or omission deemed to have been committed in Canada under subsection (4.1) may only be instituted with the consent of the Attorney General.

(5) Where a person is alleged to have committed an act or omission that is an offence by virtue of this section, proceedings in respect of that offence may, whether or not that person is in Canada, be commenced in any territorial division in Canada and the accused may be tried and punished in respect of that offence in the same manner as if the offence had been committed in that territorial division.

(5.1) For greater certainty, the provisions of this Act relating to
   (*a*) requirements that an accused appear at and be present during proceedings, and
   (*b*) the exceptions to those requirements,
apply to proceedings commenced in any territorial division pursuant to subsection (5).

(6) Where a person is alleged to have committed an act or omission that is an offence by virtue of this section and that person has been tried and dealt with outside Canada in respect of the offence in such a manner that, if that person had been tried and dealt with in Canada, he would be able to plead *autrefois acquit, autrefois convict* or pardon, that person shall be deemed to have been so tried and dealt with in Canada.

(7) If the accused is not a Canadian citizen, no proceedings in respect of which courts have jurisdiction by virtue of this section shall be continued unless the consent of the Attorney General of Canada is obtained not later than eight days after the proceedings are commenced.

(8) For the purposes of this section, of the definition "peace officer" in section 2 and of sections 27.1, 76 and 77, "flight" means the act of flying or moving through the air and an aircraft is deemed to be in flight from the time when all external doors are closed following embarkation until the later of
   (*a*) the time at which any such door is opened for the purpose of disembarkation, and
   (*b*) where the aircraft makes a forced landing in circumstances in which the owner or operator thereof or a person acting on behalf of either of them is not in control of the aircraft, the time at which control of the aircraft is restored to the owner or operator thereof or a person acting on behalf of either of them.

(9) For the purposes of this section and section 77, an aircraft shall be deemed to be in service from the time when pre-flight preparation of the aircraft by ground personnel or the crew thereof begins for a specific flight until
   (*a*) the flight is cancelled before the aircraft is in flight,
   (*b*) twenty-four hours after the aircraft, having commenced the flight, lands, or
   (*c*) the aircraft, having commenced the flight, ceases to be in flight,
whichever is the latest.

(10) In any proceedings under this Act, a certificate purporting to have been issued by or under the authority of the Minister of Foreign Affairs is admissible in evidence without proof of the signature or authority of the person appearing to have signed it and, in the absence of evidence to the contrary, is proof of the facts it states that are relevant to the question of whether any person is a member of United Nations personnel, a member of associated personnel or a person who is entitled under international law to protection from attack or threat of attack against his or her person, freedom or dignity.

(11) A certificate purporting to have been issued by or under the authority of the Minister of Foreign Affairs stating

- (a) that at a certain time any state was engaged in an armed conflict against Canada or was allied with Canada in an armed conflict,
- (b) that at a certain time any convention, treaty or other international agreement was or was not in force and that Canada was or was not a party thereto, or
- (c) that Canada agreed or did not agree to accept and apply the provisions of any convention, treaty or other international agreement in an armed conflict in which Canada was involved,

is admissible in evidence in any proceedings without proof of the signature or authority of the person appearing to have issued it, and is proof of the facts so stated. R.S., c. C-34, s. 6; 1972, c. 13, s. 3; 1974-75-76, c. 93, s. 3; 1980-81-82-83, c. 125, s. 3; R.S.C. 1985, c. 27 (1st Supp.), s. 5; R.S.C. 1985, c. 10 (3rd Supp.), s. 1, c. 30 (3rd Supp.), s. 1; 1992, c. 1, s. 58; 1993, c. 7, s. 1; 1995, c. 5, s. 25; 1997, c. 16, s. 1; 1999, c. 35, s. 11; 2000, c. 24, s. 42; 2001, c. 41, ss. 3, 126(1) and (2); 2002, c. 13, s. 3; 2004, c. 12, s. 1; 2005, c. 40, s. 2; 2012, c. 1, s. 10; 2012, c. 15, s. 1; 2013, c. 9, s. 2; 2013, c. 13, s. 3; 2014, c. 25, s. 3.

CROSS-REFERENCES

This section deals with some, but not all, of the circumstances where offences may be tried in Canada although the act may have been committed outside Canada. Thus, see note of related sections under s. 6, *supra*. As to other terms referred to in this section, see the following s. 2, definitions of "Attorney General", "internationally protected person", "United Nations personnel", "associated personnel", "terrorism offence", "territorial division"; *Citizenship Act*, R.S.C. 1985, c. C-29, definition of Canadian citizen; s. 465, definition and punishment of conspiracy; s. 24, definition of attempt; s. 463, punishment for attempt; s. 23, definition of accessory after fact; s. 463, punishment of accessory after fact; s. 22, definition of counselling; s. 464, punishment of counselling; s. 21, parties generally; s. 2, definition of "territorial divisions"; Part XVI, commencement of proceedings and compelling appearance; ss. 607 to 610, *autrefois* pleas, especially limitation on plea of *autrefois* in s. 607(6). As to place of trial, see ss. 481.1 to 481.3.

Although "ship" and "fixed platform" are not defined in this section, reference may be made to the definition of those terms in s. 78.1. For war crimes and crimes against humanity, now see *Crimes Against Humanity and War Crimes Act*, S.C. 2000, c. 24.

SYNOPSIS

This section extends Canadian criminal law jurisdiction to cover a number of offences which often have international law implications such as air piracy, offences against diplomats, terrorist offences, protection of nuclear material and torture. A number of the offences referred to in this section, such as torture (s. 269.1), crimes against internationally protected persons (s. 431), and terrorism offences (Part II.1), were created to fulfil Canada's obligations under international treaties aimed at preventing and suppressing certain types of offences.

Section 7 permits such offences to be tried in Canada as if the offence had occurred here. The bulk of the section contains definitions and deeming provisions to facilitate the trial within Canada of these offences when they have occurred largely or entirely outside Canada.

Subsections (2.3) to (2.34) extend Canadian jurisdiction to offences committed in some circumstances in relation to the International Space Station. No proceedings in relation to such offences may be instituted without the consent of the Attorney General of Canada. Subsections (3) to (3.75) extend Canadian jurisdiction to offences committed in the defined circumstances relating to *inter alia* internationally protected persons, United Nations personnel and terrorism offences.

Subsection (4) extends Canadian jurisdiction to permit the trial in Canada of offences committed outside Canada by *public service employees*, while so employed, as long as the conduct would be an indictable offence if it had occurred here. Subsections (4.1) to (4.3) allow for the trial of certain sexual offences when committed outside Canada by Canadian citizens or permanent residents.

To preserve defences otherwise available if the accused had been tried elsewhere, s. 7(6) makes the *special pleas* of *autrefois acquit, convict* and pardon applicable. This means that, if an accused had previously been tried and acquitted, convicted or pardoned elsewhere in connection with the same conduct which led to the Canadian prosecution, the accused could rely on the special plea as if the prior trial had been in Canada.

Section 7(7) prevents the institution of proceedings under this section against *non-citizens without the consent* of the federal Attorney General.

Subsection (4.1) does not violate s. 7 of the *Charter of Rights and Freedoms* as evidence obtained through extra-territorial investigations may be excluded if its admission would render the trial unfair: *R. v. Klassen* (2008), 240 C.C.C. (3d) 328 (B.C.S.C.).

APPLICATION TO TERRITORIES / Application of criminal law of England / Common law principles continued.

8. (1) The provisions of this Act apply throughout Canada except
    (a) in Yukon, in so far as they are inconsistent with the *Yukon Act*;
    (b) in the Northwest Territories, in so far as they are inconsistent with the *Northwest Territories Act*, and
    (c) in Nunavut, in so far as they are inconsistent with the *Nunavut Act*.

(2) The criminal law of England that was in force in a province immediately before April 1, 1955 continues in force in the province except as altered, varied, modified or affected by this Act or any other Act of the Parliament of Canada.

(3) Every rule and principle of the common law that renders any circumstance a justification or excuse for an act or a defence to a charge continues in force and applies in respect of proceedings for an offence under this Act or any other Act of Parliament except in so far as they are altered by or are inconsistent with this Act or any other Act of Parliament. R.S., c. C-34, s. 7; 1993, c. 28, Sch. III, s. 26; 2002, c. 7, s. 138.

CROSS-REFERENCES
Subsection (1) – Definition of "Attorney General" for the Territories is the Attorney General of Canada pursuant to s. 2.

Subsections (2), (3) – The combined effect of this section and s. 9 is to abolish criminal liability, except as provided in a Canadian statute. The only common law crime which has been preserved is contempt of court. On the other hand, this section preserves any common law defence, except as it may be inconsistent with a statutory provision. The purpose of preserving the criminal law of England was to provide for gaps in procedure or rules of evidence not provided for in the *Criminal Code*. However, it should be noted that it is the criminal law of England which was in force in the province in 1955 and this varies somewhat between provinces because of the different dates of reception of the law of England. [See 1955 *Martin's* at p. 34.] As far as procedure, this can have little practical effect since the *Criminal Code*, to a large extent, codifies the procedure and renders obsolete the criminal procedure in England. On the other hand, very recently it was held in *R. v. Jacobson*, noted under s. 672, *infra*, that a trial judge had jurisdiction to exercise the common law power to arrest judgment where it was discovered after conviction, but prior to sentence, that the accused had been convicted of an offence unknown to law. As regards the rules of evidence, these are largely a creature of common law which is declared by the various courts in Canada from time to time. The most important effect of this section is to preserve the common law defences and excuses. These, of course, are not tied to any date and will continue to evolve with the common law. Thus, the Supreme Court of Canada has recognized a common law "defence" of entrapment although, as noted below, the House of Lords has clearly rejected such a defence.

Many defences and excuses of general application have been at least partially codified as follows: s. 15, obedience to *de facto* law; s. 16, insanity; ss. 17, 18, compulsion by threats; s. 19, ignorance of the law is no excuse; s. 25, use of force in administration or enforcement of law; s. 27, use of force to prevent commission of certain offences; s. 28, execution of warrant; ss. 30, 31, detention or arrest for breach of peace; s. 32, use of force to suppress riot; s. 33.1, intoxication; ss. 34, 35, 37, self-defence; s. 37, use of force to defend person under accused's protection; ss. 38 to 42, defence of property; s. 43, correction of child or pupil; s. 44, use of force by ship's master; s. 45, reasonable surgical operation.

As to the so-called *Kienapple* defence, see notes under ss. 12 and 613, *infra*. As to double jeopardy, including *res judicata* and *issue estoppel*, see notes under s. 613, *infra*. The pleas of *autrefois* are dealt with in ss. 607 to 610. As to abuse of process, see notes under s. 579. As to mistake of fact and mistake of law, see notes under s. 19, *infra*.

SYNOPSIS

This section explains where within Canada the *Criminal Code* applies and its relationship to the common law. Section 8(1) makes the *Criminal Code* applicable throughout Canada except that, in the Yukon, Northwest Territories and Nunavut, it has no effect if it is inconsistent with the Acts creating those jurisdictions.

Section 8(2) permits the English criminal law which was in force before the major *1953-54 Criminal Code* revision came into force to continue, *except* as changed by the *Criminal Code* or other federal legislation.

The key aspect of this section is s. 8(3) which retains all common law defences, excuses and justifications, except as altered by or to the extent that they are inconsistent with the *Criminal Code* or other federal enactments. It is under this provision that defences such as necessity, due diligence, intoxication, mistake of fact and entrapment have remained an uncodified part of our criminal law. Recently, s. 7 of the Charter has also been used to interpret the scope of these defences.

ANNOTATIONS

Necessity defence – The common law defence of necessity is preserved by s. 8(3): *R. v. Morgentaler*, [1976] 1 S.C.R. 616, 20 C.C.C. (2d) 449.

In *R. v. Perka*, [1984] 2 S.C.R. 232, 14 C.C.C. (3d) 385 (5:0), Dickson J., for the majority, set out the elements of the necessity defence as follows:

(1) necessity is an excuse rather than a justification and operates by virtue of this subsection;

(2) the criterion is the moral involuntariness of the wrongful action;

(3) this involuntariness is measured on the basis of society's expectation of appropriate and normal resistance to pressure;

(4) negligence or involvement in criminal or immoral activity does not disentitle the actor to the excuse of necessity;

(5) actions or circumstances which indicate that the wrongful deed was not truly involuntary do disentitle;

(6) the existence of a reasonable legal alternative similarly disentitles; to be involuntary the act must be inevitable, unavoidable and afford no reasonable opportunity for an alternative course of action that does not involve a breach of the law;

(7) the defence only applies in circumstances of imminent risk where the action was taken to avoid a direct and immediate peril;

(8)   the defence cannot excuse the infliction of a greater harm so as to allow the actor to avert a lesser evil; and

(9)   where the accused places before the court sufficient evidence to raise the issue, the onus is on the Crown to meet it beyond a reasonable doubt.

There are three elements to the defence of necessity: (1) imminent peril or danger; (2) the absence of a reasonable legal alternative; and (3) proportionality between the harm inflicted and the harm avoided. The first two elements must be evaluated on a modified objective standard that involves an objective evaluation that takes into account the situation and characteristics of the particular accused person. The proportionality requirement must be assessed on an objective standard: *R. v. Latimer*, [2001] 1 S.C.R. 3, 150 C.C.C. (3d) 129.

The defence of necessity was not made out to a charge of "over 80" contrary to s. 253 where the accused, although believing an attacker was pursuing her, was not in immediate danger and had other options available besides getting into her car and driving away. Her act of driving while intoxicated was not realistically unavoidable: *R. v. Berriman* (1987), 62 Nfld. & P.E.I.R. 239, 45 M.V.R. 165 (Nfld. C.A.).

The common law defence of necessity was not available to accused charged with contempt of court as result of their violation of a court order against interfering with the operation of an abortion services clinic. The defence of necessity is only available to those whose wrongful acts are committed under pressure which no reasonable person could withstand. The accused's genuine belief that abortion is immoral could not change the fact that it could not be said that no reasonable person could withstand the pressure to defy the court order: *R. v. Bridges* (1989), 48 C.C.C. (3d) 535, 61 D.L.R. (4th) 126 (B.C.S.C.), affd (1990), 62 C.C.C. (3d) 455, 78 D.L.R. (4th) 529 (B.C.C.A.).

Entrapment defence – In *R. v. Mack*, [1988] 2 S.C.R. 903, 44 C.C.C. (3d) 513 (7:0), the court laid down both the elements of the entrapment defence and the procedure to be followed. The important holdings may be summarized as follows:

1.   Entrapment arises either when the authorities provide an opportunity to persons to commit an offence without reasonable suspicion or acting *mala fides* for dubious motives unrelated to the investigation and repression of crime or, having a reasonable suspicion or acting in the course of a *bona fide* inquiry, they go beyond providing an opportunity and induce the commission of an offence;

2.   As regards the latter form of entrapment the court should consider whether an average person in the position of the accused would have been induced to commit the offence;

3.   As far as possible an objective assessment is to be made of the conduct of the police and their agents;

4.   The pre-disposition of the accused is relevant only in considering whether the authorities were justified in providing the accused an opportunity to commit the offence;

5.   In considering whether the police have used means which go further than providing an opportunity the court will consider a number of factors such as the following:

   (a)   the type of crime being investigated and the availability of other investigative techniques;

   (b)   whether an average person with both the strengths and weaknesses in the position of the accused would be induced into the commission of a crime;

   (c)   the persistence and number of attempts made by the police;

   (d)   the type of inducement used by the police including deceit, fraud, trickery or reward;

   (e)   the timing of the police conduct;

   (f)   whether the police conduct involved an exploitation of human characteristics such as friendship;

   (g)   whether the police appear to have exploited a particular vulnerability of a person such as mental handicap or substance addiction;

   (h)   the proportionality between the police involvement as compared to the accused;

    (i)   the existence of any threats implied or expressed made to the accused by the police or their agents; and

    (j)   whether the police conduct is directed at undermining other constitutional values;

6.   The entrapment issue is to be tried by the judge after the Crown has proved beyond a reasonable doubt that the accused is guilty;

7.   In a jury case the jury determines guilt or innocence and then the judge determines the entrapment issue;

8.   The burden of proof of entrapment is on the accused on a balance of probabilities and while he need not show that the police conduct shocks the community the defence will only be made out in the clearest of cases;

9.   Where the defence is made out the appropriate remedy is a stay of proceedings, not an acquittal.

In *R. v. Barnes*, [1991] 1 S.C.R. 449, 63 C.C.C. (3d) 1 (8:1), the court considered the defence of entrapment based on the fact that the officer was not engaged in a *bona fide* inquiry, but rather so-called "random virtue testing". While the basic rule is that the police may only present the opportunity to commit a particular crime to an individual who arouses a suspicion of involvement in that crime, there is an exception when the police undertake a *bona fide* investigation directed in an area where it is reasonably suspected that criminal activity is occurring. When such location is defined with sufficient precision, the police may present any person associated with the area with the opportunity to commit the particular offence. Random virtue testing only arises when an officer presents a person with the opportunity to commit an offence without a reasonable suspicion that the person is already engaged in a particular activity or that the physical location with which the person is associated is a place where the particular criminal activity is likely occurring. In this case, the court approved an investigation which included offering to persons anywhere within a six-block pedestrian mall the opportunity to sell drugs to an undercover officer. The mall as a whole was responsible for a substantial number of the drug offences in the city.

Where the police, pursuant to a "dial-a-dope" operation, had obtained the accused's cell phone number from a contact list compiled from tips received from various sources, the defence of entrapment was available. Although the police were operating *bona fides* to the extent that they were conducting their operation with the genuine goal of pursuing serious crime and without ulterior motive, they overstepped their bound by proceeding with only a mere suspicion and the hope that their unknown targets would provide the additional support which was a necessary precursor to the invitation to traffic drugs: *R. v. Swan* (2009), 244 C.C.C. (3d) 108, 65 C.R. (6th) 240 (B.C.C.A.).

Entrapment may be made out where the police provided the accused an opportunity to commit an offence and did so without reasonable suspicion. Merely asking an accused "Can you hook me up" with drugs does not make out the defence: *R. v. Imoro* (2010), 251 C.C.C. (3d) 131, 72 C.R. (6th) 292 (Ont. C.A.), affd [2010] 3 S.C.R. 62, 263 C.C.C. (3d) 296.

The defence of entrapment is available to an accused who had no contact with the undercover officer, if the officer was at the time engaged in impermissible random virtue testing: *R. v. Kenyon* (1990), 61 C.C.C. (3d) 538 (B.C.C.A.).

Due diligence defence – In *R. v. Sault Ste. Marie (City)*, [1978] 2 S.C.R. 1299, 40 C.C.C. (2d) 353 (9:0), the court in considering provincial pollution legislation held that there are three categories of offences created by statute distinguished as follows: (1) full *mens rea* offences requiring proof by the prosecution of a positive state of mind such as intent, knowledge or recklessness; (2) strict liability offences in which there is no necessity for the prosecution to prove *mens rea* but which leave it open to the accused to avoid liability by proving that he took all reasonable care; and (3) offences of absolute liability where it is not open to the accused to exculpate himself by showing that he was free of fault. Offences which are criminal in the true sense fall in the first category. "Public welfare offences" are *prima facie* in the second category unless the statute includes the words such as "wilfully" evidencing an intent that the offence be placed in the first category. Offences in the third category would be those in respect of which the legislature has made it clear that guilt would follow proof merely of the proscribed act.

Shifting the burden to the defendant, charged with a regulatory offence, to prove on a balance of probabilities that it acted with due diligence is a reasonable limit on the guarantee to the presumption of innocence: *R. v. Wholesale Travel Group Inc.*, [1991] 3 S.C.R. 154, 67 C.C.C. (3d) 193.

Intoxication defence – See notes under s. 33.1.

Alibi Defence – Where the accused fails to disclose the alibi defence to the Crown in advance of the trial, the trier of fact may draw an adverse inference when weighing the alibi evidence heard at trial. Improper disclosure can, however, only weaken alibi evidence, but cannot exclude the alibi. The alibi need not be disclosed at the time of arrest or at the first possible opportunity. It is sufficient if it was disclosed at a time and in a manner which would permit a meaningful investigation. Furthermore, there is no requirement that the alibi be disclosed by the accused himself: *R. v. Cleghorn*, [1995] 3 S.C.R. 175, 100 C.C.C. (3d) 393 (3:2).

An alibi which is disbelieved does not have any evidentiary value whereas an alibi which is proven to be false can be evidence of consciousness of guilt. If the evidence adduced by the Crown is capable of supporting the inference that an accused concocted a false alibi, an alibi notice professing an intention to advance that alibi at trial would be relevant in that it would tend to support the inference of consciousness of guilt. Before this inference is available, however, there must be evidence from which a reasonable jury could infer that the alibi was deliberately fabricated and that the accused was a party to that fabrication. Mere rejection of an alibi as untruthful or unreliable does not constitute affirmative evidence of guilt: *R. v. Witter* (1996), 105 C.C.C. (3d) 44, 27 O.R. (3d) 579 (C.A.). See also *R. v. Carey* (1996), 113 C.C.C. (3d) 74 (Que. C.A.).

Where the issue had been raised by the testimony of the accused and the rebuttal evidence went to the context and essential fabric of the alibi defence, the Crown was entitled to adduce rebuttal evidence that, contrary to the accused's testimony, the accused had not disclosed his alibi to the witness: *R. v. Lawes*, [1997] 3 S.C.R. 694, 119 C.C.C. (3d) 289, affg 119 C.C.C. (3d) 289 at p. 290 (Alta. C.A.).

CRIMINAL OFFENCES TO BE UNDER LAW OF CANADA.

9. Notwithstanding anything in this Act or any other Act, no person shall be convicted or discharged under section 730

    (*a*) **of an offence at common law,**

    (*b*) **of an offence under an Act of the Parliament of England, or of Great Britain, or of the United Kingdom of Great Britain and Ireland, or**

    (*c*) **of an offence under an Act or ordinance in force in any province, territory or place before that province, territory or place became a province of Canada,**

but nothing in this section affects the power, jurisdiction or authority that a court, judge, justice or provincial court judge had, immediately before April 1, 1955, to impose punishment for contempt of court. R.S., c. C-34, s. 8; R.S.C. 1985, c. 27 (1st Supp.), s. 6; 1995, c. 22, s. 10.

CROSS-REFERENCES
Rights of appeal from finding of contempt of court and from sentence are set out in s. 10. The notes under s. 10 deal with procedural issues relating to contempt of court.

As noted under s. 8, the only common law offence for which a person may now be convicted is the offence of criminal contempt of court. This is not to say that contempt of court is wholly a common law offence. Certain aspects of contempt of court have been codified as offences or the court's power to deal with the misconduct has been codified, thus see: ss. 119, 120, offences relating to bribery of judicial officers; s. 127, disobeying lawful order of court; ss. 131 to 137, perjury and related offences; s. 139, attempt to obstruct justice; s. 484, preserving order in court; s. 545, witness at preliminary inquiry refusing to be sworn or testify; s. 605(2), failing to comply with order respecting testing of exhibits; ss. 648 to 649, offences relating to juries; s. 708, witness failing to attend.

SYNOPSIS

This section prohibits prosecution for common law offences, offences under British law or the law in force in the provinces before they joined Canada. The only exception is the retention of the common law power of judges to punish for contempt of court.

The common law offence of contempt of court can be divided into two broad categories of civil and criminal contempt. The former lies essentially in disobeying the order of a court or a judgment in civil proceedings. However, as the case of *Poje v. A.-G. B.C.*, [1953] 1 S.C.R. 516, illustrates, even disobedience of a civil injunction can amount to criminal contempt if the conduct of the accused in disobeying the order amounts to a public challenge to the court's authority. In general, criminal contempt can be described as conduct likely to obstruct the administration of justice or to bring discredit onto the administration of justice. As a common law crime, contempt of court suffers from lack of clarity of definition of procedure and of the elements of the offence. Criminal contempt can, however, be subdivided into two types, contempt in the face of the court [*in facie*], for example, disruption of the proceedings in the courtroom, failure of counsel to attend court as required, or refusal of a witness to be sworn or to answer questions, and contempt out of the face of the court [*ex facie*].

The most troublesome aspect of criminal contempt is contempt out of the face of the court. It involves essentially three different types of conduct: (1) breach of the *sub judice* rule, *e.g.*, publication of material likely to interfere with the fair trial of the case; (2) obstruction of justice, *e.g.*, interfering with a witness or a juror; and (3) scandalizing the court, *i.e.*, criticism of a court or a judge. While the elements of these three types of contempt are not well-defined, it is suggested that case law supports the following propositions:

Breach of the *sub judice* rule – Until recently, this has been considered a strict liability offence if not virtually an absolute liability offence, the offence being described as requiring proof only that the words were calculated to interfere with the course of justice in the sense that they had that tendency. It was not necessary to find either that the words were intended to have that effect or that they did in fact interfere with the course of justice. Moreover, liability has been attributed to persons such as the editor or publisher on a vicarious basis, if they were responsible for the publication of the newspaper, for example, even if they had no prior knowledge of the contemptuous remarks. It is not sufficient, however, that there be a mere possibility of interference with the due administration of justice, the conduct must present a real risk to the due administration of justice. [A somewhat lesser standard adopted by the House of Lords in the *Times Newspapers* case, [1974] A.C. 273, probably does not represent the law in Canada.] It is suggested that, in light of the *Charter of Rights and Freedoms* and in particular the fundamental justice guarantee in s. 7 as interpreted by the Supreme Court of Canada in *Reference re Section 94(2) of the Motor Vehicle Act (B.C.)*, [1985] 2 S.C.R. 486, 23 C.C.C. (3d) 289, it can no longer be confidently stated that liability can be imposed on a vicarious basis or that no intent to interfere with the administration of justice is required. At least the accused should probably be able to defend the case by demonstrating that they were without fault, perhaps through the exercise of due diligence or was operating under an honest (and perhaps reasonable) mistake of fact. Finally, it would seem that a contempt can be made out even if there was no real risk of interference in the due administration of justice by the particular publication, if the accused intended to produce such prejudice. Perhaps such conduct is more accurately described as an attempt but the cases do not make any such distinction.

Obstruction of justice – The elements of this offence are similar to those for breach of the *sub judice* rule, and, in fact, the former may be considered simply a special example of this form of contempt which has been described as anything done that is calculated to obstruct or interfere with the due course of justice or the lawful process of the courts. Again "calculated" does not mean intended but merely "fixed, suited, apt". In *B.C.G.E.U. v. British Columbia (Attorney General)*, [1988] 2 S.C.R. 214, 44 C.C.C. (3d) 289, Chief Justice Dickson adopted the following list of acts which could fall into this category: victimizing jurors, witnesses and other persons; obstructing person officially connected with court or its process; interference with person under the special protective jurisdiction of the court; breach of duty by persons officially connected with the court or its process; forging; altering or abusing the process of the court; divulging the confidences of the jury-room; preventing access by the public to courts of law, service of process in the precinct of the court and disclosing the identity of witnesses. Again, the Charter may have implications for the *mens rea* of the offence, bearing in mind, however, that it could be argued that some limits on Charter guarantees may be upheld under s. 1 because of the close connection of this form of contempt to the fundamental principle of the rule of law.

Scandalizing the court – This is the one form of contempt which does not bear a clear, direct relationship to the administration of justice. It has been defined as any act done or writing published, calculated to bring a court into contempt or lower its authority. Thus, conduct which could have no possible effect on any particular case may nevertheless come within this definition. The difficulty with this form of contempt has always been to distinguish between contemptuous comment and fair criticism of the courts and the judiciary. The basis for this form of contempt lies in the assumption that public confidence in the administration of justice would be undermined by comments that tend to lower the authority of the court. Perhaps the clearest examples of this form of contempt would be comments attributing improper motives to a court or allegations of corruption, partiality and attempts to pervert the course of justice by a judge. It is equally clear that reasonable argument or expostulation offered against any judicial act as contrary to law or the public good is not contempt. [*Re Duncan*, [1958] S.C.R. 41]. The impact of the *Charter of Rights and Freedoms* has been felt in relation to this form of contempt, a majority of the Ontario Court of Appeal holding in *R. v. Kopyto, infra* that, as presently framed, contempt by scandalizing the court is not a reasonable limit on the guarantee to freedom of expression. The defect in the common law definition appeared to lie in the fact that there was no requirement of proof of any real danger, present or future, to the fair and effective administration of justice. Interestingly, the dissenting members of the court would be prepared to uphold the constitutionality of this form of contempt because, in their view, it required proof of an intent to bring the administration of justice into disrepute and truth would be a defence. Further, the *actus reus* of the offence requires proof that, by reason of the statement, there was a serious risk that the administration of justice would be interfered with.

ANNOTATIONS

Grounds for finding contempt of court / Violation of court orders – An unincorporated union is capable of being found in criminal contempt of court for violation of a court order. The fact that criminal contempt is not codified does not result in a violation of ss. 7 or 11(*a*) or (*g*) of the Charter. To establish criminal contempt, the Crown must prove beyond a reasonable doubt that the accused defied or disobeyed a court order in a public way (the *actus reus*), with intent, knowledge or recklessness as to the fact that the public disobedience will tend to depreciate the authority of the court (the *mens rea*). The necessary *mens rea* may however be inferred from the circumstances and since an open and public defiance of a court order will tend to depreciate the authority of the court, when it is clear that the accused must have known her act of defiance would be public, it may be inferred that she was at least reckless as to whether the authority of the court would be brought into contempt. While publicity is required for the offence, a civil contempt is not converted to a criminal contempt merely because it attracts publicity, but rather because it constitutes a public act of defiance of the court in circumstances where the accused knew, intended or was reckless as to the fact that the act would publicly bring the court into contempt. While it would seem that a judge entertaining a motion for contempt of an order made by a judge of the court, as opposed to an inferior tribunal, would not have the power to go behind the order. The validity of the order is not an issue on the contempt hearing. Unless the order has been set aside for want of jurisdiction, the judge hearing the motion on criminal contempt must accept it as valid: *U.N.A. v. Alberta (Attorney General)*, [1992] 1 S.C.R. 901, 71 C.C.C. (3d) 225 (4:3).

The accused were properly found in contempt of court for their flagrant disobedience of an injunction. While the accused sought to argue that the injunction was overbroad and infringed their rights under the Charter, the injunction was valid until set aside and the accused had taken no steps to challenge the injunction: *Everywoman's Health Centre Society (1988) v. Bridges* (1990), 62 C.C.C. (3d) 455, 78 D.L.R. (4th) 529 (B.C.C.A.), supp. reasons 54 B.C.L.R. (2d) 294 (C.A.). Also see: *R. v. Toth* (1991), 63 C.C.C. (3d) 273 (B.C.C.A.), leave to appeal to S.C.C. refused 7 W.A.C. 23*n*, 136 N.R. 404*n*.

The defence of necessity was not available to accused charged with violating a court injunction prohibiting obstruction of logging crews. The necessity defence cannot operate to excuse conduct which has been specifically enjoined. An application to the court, which could be heard on short notice, would have determined whether the circumstances were sufficient to engage the defence of necessity. In addition, the defence of necessity can never operate to avoid a peril that is lawfully authorized by the law. Similarly, s. 27 of the *Criminal Code* was not available. Section 27 does not contemplate the justification of force or other conduct which the court has already specifically enjoined: *MacMillan Bloedel Ltd. v. Simpson* (1994), 89 C.C.C. (3d) 217, 113 D.L.R. (4th) 368 (B.C.C.A.), leave to appeal to S.C.C. refused 23 C.R.R. (2d) 192*n* (Pulker app'n granted).

An allegation of contempt of court is criminal, or at least *quasi*-criminal, in character and therefore the elements of the offence must be proved beyond a reasonable doubt. Where the allegation is based on failure to comply with a court order, there must be proof of knowledge of the order alleged to have been breached. Service of a court order on the solicitor for a Minister of the Crown did not fix the Minister with actual knowledge in the absence of evidence from which that knowledge could be inferred as where there were circumstances which reveal a special reason for bringing the order to the Minister's attention. Further, the Minister could not be held liable for contempt of court on the basis of the doctrine of vicarious liability, delegation or the identification theory: *Bhatnager v. Canada (Minister of Employment and Immigration)*, [1990] 2 S.C.R. 217, 71 D.L.R. (4th) 84 (9:0).

Even though the conduct may involve a breach of the criminal law, contempt will remain civil where the conduct falls short of public defiance: *Wightman v. Walmsley* (1997), 117 C.C.C. (3d) 470, [1998] 4 W.W.R. 459 (B.C.C.A.).

Interference with access to courts – Any action to prevent, impede or obstruct access to the courts runs counter to the rule of law and constitutes a criminal contempt of court: *N.A.P.E. v. Newfoundland (Attorney General)*, [1988] 2 S.C.R. 204, 44 C.C.C. (3d) 186 (6:0); *B.C.G.E.U. v. British Columbia (Attorney General)*, [1988] 2 S.C.R. 214, 44 C.C.C. (3d) 289 (6:0).

Scandalizing the court – In determining contempt scandalizing a court or judge it is not the effect that the author intended his article to have but the effect the article itself was calculated to have: *R. v. Murphy*, [1969] 4 C.C.C. 147, 6 C.R.N.S. 353 (N.B.S.C. App. Div.).

It is *prima facie* legitimate to criticize a judge's conduct in a particular case or to criticize any particular decision given by the courts if done without casting any aspersions on the motives of a judge or court, and without abuse: *R. v. Dalke* (1981), 59 C.C.C. (2d) 477, 21 C.R. (3d) 380 (B.C.S.C.).

It was held in *R. v. Kopyto* (1987), 39 C.C.C. (3d) 1, 61 C.R. (3d) 209 (Ont. C.A.) (3:2), that the offence of contempt of court by scandalizing the court, as presently understood, is unconstitutional by reason of the guarantee of freedom of expression in s. 2(*b*) of the Charter. It would seem, however, that if the offence were redefined to require proof that the accused's remarks created a real, significant, and present or imminent danger to the fair and effective administration of justice then the offence might be valid. The dissenting members of the court held that properly understood the offence did not violate s. 2(*b*) but that the Crown would have to prove an intention to bring the administration of justice into disrepute and that by reason of the statement made there was a serious risk that the administration of justice would be interfered with. As well, truth would be a defence.

It was held in *R. v. Edmonton Sun Publishing Ltd.* (1981), 62 C.C.C. (2d) 318 (Alta. Q.B.), that for the court to find that an editorial cartoon concerning a court case was a contempt of court it must be proved that it tended to obstruct or defeat the administration of justice or that it showed disrespect of the court process or that it tended to bring the court into disrepute.

Publicity – In *R. v. Carocchia* (1973), 15 C.C.C. (2d) 175, 43 D.L.R. (3d) 427 (Que. C.A.), the publication of a police press release which was of such a nature as to influence the result of a non-jury criminal case was held to be an interference of the administration of justice and a contempt of court.

A broadcaster was properly found in contempt of court for broadcasting during the accused's trial details of other criminal conduct by the accused, even though in the end the same information was placed before the jury through evidence called during the defence. The issue in every case is whether there has been a real risk of prejudice to the course of justice, not simply to the accused. Thus, substantial interference with the trial process by causing undue delay and expense or by creating an appearance of substantial unfairness at any stage of the proceedings may result in a conviction for contempt, regardless of prejudice to the accused. Finally, it was also not improper for the trial judge to base the amount of the fine on the costs thrown away as a result of contempt: *R. v. CHEK TV Ltd.* (1987), 33 C.C.C. (3d) 24, 30 B.C.L.R. (2d) 36 (C.A.).

The public's vital interest in knowing the facts as protected by freedom of expression, including freedom of the press in s. 2(*b*) of the Charter, will be assessed differently in the context of an accused who is in custody awaiting trial than it will be where a dangerous suspect is at large and public assistance may be required to apprehend the suspect. Publication of the criminal record of an accused who is not at large and who does not constitute a danger to the community is *prima facie* a contempt of court: *Alberta (Attorney General) v. Interwest Publications Ltd.* (1990), 58 C.C.C. (3d) 114, 73 D.L.R. (4th) 83 (Alta. Q.B.).

Although a contempt of court charge brought as a result of violation of the *sub judice* rule infringes a publisher's freedom of expression as guaranteed by s. 2(*b*) of the Charter of Rights, the *sub judice* is a reasonable limit on freedom of expression, being required to ensure the fair trial of the accused. Contempt of court will lie only where there is proof of either a clear intent to influence the fair trial of an accused or where the publication presents a real risk that the article will prejudice the fair hearing of the accused, and the *sub judice* rule only delays publication until completion of the trial: *R. v. Robinson-Blackmore Printing & Publishing Co.* (1989), 47 C.C.C. (3d) 366, 73 Nfld. & P.E.I.R. 46 (Nfld. S.C.).

The test for publication contempt is whether having regard to all the circumstances, including the effectiveness of alternative means, the court is satisfied beyond a reasonable doubt that the publication created a real and substantial risk to the administration of justice. This test does not violate ss. 2(*b*) or 7 of the Charter as it is neither void for vagueness nor an unconstitutional limit on the freedom of the press: *R. v. Edmonton Sun* (2003), 170 C.C.C. (3d) 455 (Alta. C.A.).

The *actus reus* of contempt is made out where a publication impairs the right of an accused to a fair trial or the publication otherwise deprecates the authority of the court: *R. v. Edmonton Sun, supra.*

While publication contempt requires proof of a real risk of prejudice, the enactment of the Charter has not changed the *mens rea* for publication contempt, which is the intention to publish words that, on an objective basis, are calculated to interfere with the course of justice: *R. v. CHBC Television* (1999), 132 C.C.C. (3d) 390, 23 C.R. (5th) 135 (B.C.C.A.).

Publication of a summary of the evidence given on the preliminary issue of the accused's fitness to stand trial, in violation of the trial judge's order that it not be published was held to constitute contempt of court: *R. v. Southam Press (Ontario) Ltd.* (1976), 31 C.C.C. (2d) 205 (Ont. C.A.).

Counsel's failure to attend court – In *R. v. Hill* (1976), 33 C.C.C. (2d) 60, 73 D.L.R. (3d) 621 (B.C.C.A.), affg 25 C.C.C. (2d) 348, 62 D.L.R. (3d) 692 (Co. Ct.), it was held that conduct, in this case by a lawyer, which is calculated to delay, disrupt and bring the judicial process into contempt will constitute criminal contempt and it need not be further proved that the accused intended to disrupt, hinder or delay the course of justice.

In considering whether or not a lawyer is guilty of contempt the court must consider the apology tendered by the lawyer at the contempt hearing: *R. v. Kopyto* (1981), 60 C.C.C. (2d) 85, 21 C.R. (3d) 276 (Ont. C.A.), leave to appeal to S.C.C. refused 38 N.R. 540*n*.

However, the lawyer's apology did not negative his contempt where his conduct in failing to appear at court showed a serious indifference to his obligation to the court and to his client and when he again failed to attend court on the following day as directed by the judge: *R. v. Anders* (1982), 67 C.C.C. (2d) 138, 136 D.L.R. (3d) 316 (Ont. C.A.).

The *actus reus* of criminal contempt is conduct which seriously interferes with, or obstructs, the administration of justice or would cause a serious risk of that occurring. While the failure, of a lawyer who has undertaken to appear in court, to attend is capable of constituting contempt, the court should consider the consequences of failing to appear. Conduct that had little or no effect on the administration of justice could not support a conviction for contempt. The *mens rea* of contempt requires proof of deliberate or intentional conduct, or indifference akin to recklessness: *R. v. Glasner* (1994), 93 C.C.C. (3d) 226, 119 D.L.R. (4th) 113, 19 O.R. (3d) 739 (C.A.).

Before an absent lawyer may be found in contempt he must first be brought before the court and given the right to make full answer and defence which at a minimum requires that he be given notice that he is facing a charge of contempt of court: *R. v. Pinx* (1979), 50 C.C.C. (2d) 65, 105 D.L.R. (3d) 143 (Man. C.A.).

While the deliberate failure of counsel who has undertaken to represent an accused to appear when the case is called, or even failure to attend in circumstances showing indifference, may constitute contempt of court, failure to attend due to mere inadvertence even if due to negligence, but falling short of indifference, does not necessarily constitute contempt of court: *R. v. Jones* (1978), 42 C.C.C. (2d) 192 (Ont. C.A.).

Counsel withdrawing from case – In contempt proceedings against a lawyer a distinction must be drawn between the lawyer who deliberately frustrates the due carrying on of court proceedings by the wilful act of non-attendance, an act which may constitute contempt of court, and the act of a lawyer who impulsively reacts to an adverse ruling by the court by attempting to withdraw, which is at worst an error of judgment: *R. v. Swartz* (1977), 34 C.C.C. (2d) 477, [1977] 2 W.W.R. 751 (Man. C.A.).

A trial judge has no right in law to order counsel to continue in the defence of an accused after counsel has advised that he has decided that he will no longer represent the accused. While the judge may urge counsel to reconsider and to try to reconcile any differences with his client, should counsel stand firm then he cannot properly be cited for contempt for refusing to comply with an order by the trial judge that he continue to act: *Leask v. Cronin* (1985), 18 C.C.C. (3d) 315, [1985] 3 W.W.R. 152 (B.C.S.C.).

Conduct of counsel in court – Language by a lawyer attributing dishonourable or disgraceful conduct to the judge trying a case and suggesting that the judge acted dishonestly, is capable of constituting contempt of court: *R. v. Doz* (1985), 19 C.C.C. (3d) 434 (Alta. C.A.), revd on other grounds [1987] 2 S.C.R. 463, 38 C.C.C. (3d) 479, 55 Alta. L.R. (2d) 289.

There is a distinction between conduct by a barrister which though open to censure is merely discourteous and conduct which constitutes contempt of court: *R. v. Fox* (1976), 30 C.C.C. (2d) 330, 70 D.L.R. (3d) 577 (Ont. C.A.).

Mere discourtesy or use of uncomplimentary remarks to the court is not always to be taken as contempt. On the other hand where there has been a proper question put to counsel by the presiding judge the repeated refusal by counsel to answer the question will normally constitute contempt: *R. v. Barker* (1980), 53 C.C.C. (2d) 322, [1980] 4 W.W.R. 202 (Alta. C.A.).

A charge of contempt of court, arising out of a lawyer's submissions in the course of a trial, requires proof of a serious, real imminent risk of obstruction of the administration of justice. It must be shown that he had a dishonest intention or acted in bad faith in that he intentionally discredited or attempted to discredit the administration of justice: *R. v. Bertrand* (1989), 49 C.C.C. (3d) 397, 70 C.R. (3d) 362 (Que. S.C.).

Conduct of other persons in court – Words or actions directed at other persons besides the judge such as jurors, counsel or other officers of the court may also be regarded as contempt where such words or acts interfere or tend to interfere with the administration of justice. Thus, in *R. v. Paul* (1978), 44 C.C.C. (2d) 257, 6 C.R. (3d) 272 (Ont. C.A.), it was held (2:1) that the deliberately false allegation in open court by an unrepresented accused that the charges laid against him were the work of a "corrupt" Crown Attorney, constituted contempt of court. The decision of the Court of Appeal was affirmed, [1980] 2 S.C.R. 169, 52 C.C.C. (2d) 331, 15 C.R. (3d) 219 (5:0), where it was held that the trial judge did not err in dealing with the contempt summarily rather than requiring the Crown Attorney to take the matter to the Attorney General.

An accused's voluntary act in consuming a large quantity of alcohol shortly before his trial well-knowing the effect this would have on him and which would result in the court being unable to proceed with the trial constitutes contempt of court notwithstanding the accused did not intend to obstruct the course of justice: *R. v. Perkins* (1980), 51 C.C.C. (2d) 369, [1980] 4 W.W.R. 763 (B.C.C.A.).

It was held by the majority in *R. v. Flamand* (1980), 57 C.C.C. (2d) 366 (Que. C.A.), that remarks by an accused to the trial judge that he was not fit to try the case because the judge's son was a police officer and that he (the accused) no longer had confidence in the judge constituted contempt of court being deliberately calculated to bring the trial judge into contempt, lower his authority, cast discredit on the administration of justice and impede its normal course. Mayrand J.A. dissenting would have quashed the conviction on the basis that an expressed lack of confidence in a judge, if a genuinely held belief, even if not justified on a rational basis, does not constitute contempt of court. His Lordship also considered the summary manner in which the proceedings were conducted by the trial judge deprived the accused of an opportunity to present a full and complete defence. On further appeal [1982] 1 S.C.R. 337, 65 C.C.C. (2d) 192*n*, 42 N.R. 87 (7:0), the dissenting judgment of Mayrand J.A. was approved and the conviction quashed.

Abusive language by an accused attributing gross insensitivity to the trial judge could be viewed as calculated to lower his authority and thus capable of constituting contempt of court: *R. v. Martin* (1985), 19 C.C.C. (3d) 248, 15 C.R.R. 231 (Ont. C.A.).

Conduct outside of court – Notwithstanding the accused's conduct may also have constituted the offence of attempting to obstruct justice contrary to s. 139 [R.S.C. 1985], the Crown may proceed by way of contempt of court: *R. v. Vermette*, [1987] 1 S.C.R. 577, 32 C.C.C. (3d) 519, 57 C.R. (3d) 340 (4:0).

Refusal of witness to be sworn or answer questions – On an appeal from conviction for contempt of court in the face of the court based on a refusal to answer a question in a criminal case if it is not shown that the question was relevant then the conviction cannot stand. However, at the trial itself it is the judge not the witness who must decide whether or not the question is relevant and a witness who disagrees with the judge's ruling on relevancy nevertheless must abide by it or risk being cited for contempt. On the other hand where the witness objects to the question the trial judge ought to inquire into and determine its relevancy: *R. v. Fields* (1986), 28 C.C.C. (3d) 353, 53 C.R. (3d) 260, 56 O.R. (2d) 213 (C.A.).

APPEAL / Idem / Part XXI applies.

10. (1) Where a court, judge, justice or provincial court judge summarily convicts a person for a contempt of court committed in the face of the court and imposes punishment in respect thereof, that person may appeal

(*a*) **from the conviction; or**

(*b*) **against the punishment imposed.**

(2) Where a court or judge summarily convicts a person for a contempt of court not committed in the face of the court and punishment is imposed in respect thereof, that person may appeal

(*a*) **from the conviction; or**

(*b*) **against the punishment imposed.**

(3) An appeal under this section lies to the court of appeal of the province in which the proceedings take place, and, for the purposes of this section, the provisions of Part XXI apply, with such modifications as the circumstances require. R.S., c. C-34, s. 9; 1972, c. 13, s. 4.

CROSS-REFERENCES

Section 9 preserves the common law power to punish for contempt and the notes under that section relate to the grounds of contempt of court. The notes under this section relate to procedural issues, including rights of appeal. Procedure on appeal and powers of the Court of Appeal, in appeals from summary contempt proceedings, is governed by Part XXI: procedure on appeal by indictment [notwithstanding the contempt finding was made in the course of a summary conviction proceeding]. This section would not apply to an accused convicted in summary conviction proceedings of a summary conviction offence such as the offence in s. 648 of publishing proceedings in the absence of the jury.

SYNOPSIS

This section creates the right to have an appeal from a conviction for contempt of court heard in accordance with the procedure for appeals in cases which have proceeded by indictment, even if the conviction for contempt of court was summary. The appeal is to be heard by the provincial court of appeal, with such modifications to the procedure on appeals from convictions on indictable offences as may be necessary.

The forms of contempt of court are discussed in a comment under s. 9, *supra*. This comment is meant to draw attention to certain procedural problems. It is first necessary to distinguish between contempt in the face of the court [*in facie*], for example, disruption of the proceedings in the courtroom, failure of counsel to attend court as required, or refusal of a witness to be sworn or to answer questions; and contempt out of the face of the court [*ex facie*], such as interference with a witness, or publication of material calculated to interfere with the fair trial of an accused. The distinction is important because, while a superior court can punish both types of contempt, an inferior court can only punish contempts committed in the face of the court. The line between the two types of contempt can be exceedingly fine. Consider the failure of counsel to appear at a criminal trial as required. While the act of non-appearance is committed in the face of the court, the reasons why counsel failed to attend court may be, and usually would be, completely outside the personal knowledge of the presiding judge. Nevertheless, since the decision in *R. v. McKeown*, [1971] S.C.R. 446, there can be little doubt that this conduct constitutes contempt *in facie* and is punishable by the presiding judge.

A second problem concerns the procedure by which the contempt is initiated. For contempt *in facie*, it would seem that no particular form of notice is required and even verbal notice to a person disrupting the proceedings would be sufficient, provided the alleged contemnor is sufficiently advised of the act said to constitute contempt. On the other hand, the presiding judge can leave it to some other party such as the Attorney General to initiate proceedings through some more formal process. Where the contempt is out of the face of the court and thus triable only by the superior court, some form of written notice would ordinarily be required to secure the person's attendance. The usual notice is by way of originating notice of motion served upon the alleged contemnor and returnable in the superior court and is referred to as the summary procedure. However, it would also seem that a more formal process is available by preferring a direct indictment in the superior court. This latter form of process has fallen almost entirely into disuse, but the Supreme Court of Canada in *R. v. Vermette, infra*, recognized that it was still available.

It seems clear that the *Charter of Rights and Freedoms* applies to the trial of the contempt charge whether *ex facie* or *in facie* and that, unless very unusual circumstances arise, the person must be given a reasonable opportunity to prepare a defence and to consult counsel. Further, it would seem that proof of contempt must be made out on the criminal standard and the accused would have the right to call witnesses, be represented by counsel if he wished and the right not to be compelled to be a witness. Authority is unanimous that the constitutional right to jury trial does not apply. On the other hand, it may be that, where the unusual direct indictment procedure were resorted to, the trial would have to be by jury, which was the manner of trying such contempts before use of the summary process was widely resorted to. A particular concern relates to the constitutional guarantee to trial by an independent and impartial tribunal. Some forms of contempt *in facie* involve insulting or abusive behaviour towards the presiding judge. Once the judge has restored order, which may include removal of the person from the court and citing the person for contempt, it is probably best that the actual contempt be tried by some other judge in order to preserve the appearance of fairness. It should be noted, however, that, in light of *R. v. Doz*, [1987] 2 S.C.R. 463, 38 C.C.C. (3d) 479, 82 A.R. 394, one judge of an inferior court has no jurisdiction to try a contempt committed in the face of the court of another inferior court judge. Accordingly, if fairness requires that the inferior court judge not deal with the contempt himself then the proceedings for contempt of court would have to be taken in the superior court.

ANNOTATIONS

Contempt of court: Procedure / Jurisdiction of courts to try contempt of court – At common law, superior courts have an inherent and exclusive jurisdiction to punish for contempt not committed in the face of the court while inferior courts have only a limited inherent jurisdiction to punish for contempt in the face of court. Inferior courts which are not courts of record have no power to punish for contempt unless such power is conferred by statute. Violation of an order of the Quebec Police Commission prohibiting publication of the photograph of a witness is contempt out of the face of the court and therefore punishable only by the superior court: *Canadian Broadcasting Corp. v. Cordeau*, [1979] 2 S.C.R. 618, 48 C.C.C. (2d) 289, 101 D.L.R. (3d) 24 (9:0).

A judge presiding at a preliminary hearing has no power to punish summarily for contempt of court a witness who refuses to answer relevant questions without reasonable excuse. The power of the judge is limited to the procedure under s. 545: *R. v. Bubley* (1976), 32 C.C.C. (2d) 79, [1976] 6 W.W.R. 179 (Alta. S.C. App. Div.).

Section 484 of this Act, however, gives the judge power to commit for contempt in the face of court in order to preserve order in his court-room: *R. v. Barker* (1980), 53 C.C.C. (2d) 322, [1980] 4 W.W.R. 202 (Alta. C.A.).

A provincial court judge exercising the jurisdiction to try an indictable offence under Part XIX does have an inherent jurisdiction to punish for contempt committed in the face of the court, such as the wilful refusal of a witness to testify: *R. v. Dunning* (1979), 50 C.C.C. (2d) 296 (Ont. C.A.); *R. v. Layne* (1984), 14 C.C.C. (3d) 149, [1984] 6 W.W.R. 108 (B.C.S.C.). *Contra: R. v. Heer* (1982), 68 C.C.C. (2d) 333, 38 B.C.L.R. 176 (S.C.).

Similarly a provincial court judge presiding at a trial of an accused for a summary conviction offence under Part XXVII constitutes a court of record and has power to punish for contempt of court committed in the face of the court, such as the refusal of a witness to answer relevant questions: *R. v. Fields* (1986), 28 C.C.C. (3d) 353, 53 C.R. (3d) 260, 56 O.R. (2d) 213 (C.A.).

It was held in *R. v. Vaillancourt*, [1981] 1 S.C.R. 69, 58 C.C.C. (2d) 31, 19 C.R. (3d) 178 (5:0), that a judge presiding in the criminal courts has power to punish summarily as a contempt in the face of the court the refusal of a juvenile witness to testify. It was held that such a contempt is not a delinquency which could only be tried under the former *Juvenile Delinquents Act* but rather was the exercise of the court's inherent power which is preserved by this section. It would seem that in light of s. 15(3) of the *Youth Criminal Justice Act* this jurisdiction in the ordinary courts is retained but the Youth Court also has jurisdiction to try the contempt. In either case the penalty is determined by the provisions of the *Youth Criminal Justice Act* (see s. 15(4) of that Act).

Initiation of contempt proceedings – Although rarely employed, procedure by indictment for punishment of contempt *ex facie* is preserved by this section. However, the offence is triable only by the superior court and the provisions of Part IX do not apply to the trial of such offence so as to permit the accused to elect trial by provincial court judge. Finally, it would seem that where an indictment for criminal contempt is employed it would have to be by direct indictment to the superior court: *R. v. Vermette*, [1987] 1 S.C.R. 577, 32 C.C.C. (3d) 519, 57 C.R. (3d) 340 (4:0).

Even where the court initiates summary procedure for contempt out of the face of the court, in a matter of interference with the administration of justice the Attorney General has the responsibility to present the evidence and if he chooses not to adduce any evidence on the show cause hearing then the charge should be dismissed: *R. v. Hamel and Lesage* (1978), 9 C.R. (3d) 214 (Que. C.A.).

Criminal contempt proceedings may be brought at the instance of an individual: *Letourneau-Belanger v. Société de Publication Merlin Ltée*, [1969] 4 C.C.C. 313, 6 C.R.N.S. 308 (Que. Q.B., App. Side) or any interested party: *R. v. Froese (No. 1)* (1979), 50 C.C.C. (2d) 105, [1980] 1 W.W.R. 667 (B.C.S.C.).

The initiation of the summary process by way of an originating notice of motion for a contempt *ex facie curiae* is appropriate where the accused has broadcast inflammatory and prejudicial material at the opening of a criminal trial. Further, the hearing of the contempt motion may then be properly adjourned until the conclusion of the criminal trial so as not to further prejudice that trial. In the interim should there be any repetition of the contempt the currency of the notice of motion ensures that the accused can be immediately controlled: *R. v. Froese and British Columbia Television Broadcasting System Ltd. (No. 3)* (1980), 54 C.C.C. (2d) 315, 18 C.R. (3d) 75 *sub nom. R. v. Bengert; R. v. Froese and British Columbia Television Broadcasting System Ltd. (No. 3)* (B.C.C.A.).

In *Cotroni v. Quebec Police Commission and Brunet*, [1978] 1 S.C.R. 1048, 38 C.C.C. (2d) 56, a conviction for contempt of the Commissioners was quashed because of the vagueness of the charge. It was held that where testimony is false in its entirety, a charge of perjury, and consequently of contempt, is specific enough if it simply states that. However, where as in this case the objection is not to the testimony as a whole, the charge must specify which part of the testimony is complained of. Where the complaint is the evasiveness of some of the witnesses' answers it was necessary to specify what was considered evasive.

Procedure on trial of contempt – As developed at common law, the summary procedure for dealing with the contempt of a witness refusing to testify at a criminal trial, does not offend the principles guaranteed by s. 7 or s. 11. Those principles include the right to be presumed innocent until proven guilty beyond a reasonable doubt, to be informed without unreasonable delay of the specific offence with which he is charged, to have counsel, to have a reasonable time to prepare a defence, to call witnesses and not to be compelled to give evidence. He also has the right to be tried by an independent and impartial tribunal and where the contempt alleged consists of insolent or contemptuous behaviour or other disorderly conduct or behaviour which reflects adversely upon the character, integrity or reputation of the initiating judge, the charge should be tried by another judge. However, there may be very exceptional cases where the circumstances are so compelling and the need for action on the part of the presiding judge so urgent to preserve the order and protect the authority of the court that some limitation on such rights, particularly with respect to time, may be justified: *R. v. Cohn* (1984), 15 C.C.C. (3d) 150, 42 C.R. (3d) 1 (Ont. C.A.), leave to appeal to S.C.C. refused [1985] 1 S.C.R. vii, 9 O.A.C. 160, 58 N.R. 160*n*.

However, the fact that the witness was the last witness for the Crown was not such a compelling circumstance as required infringement of the accused's rights, particularly an opportunity to consult counsel and prepare the defence to a charge of contempt for refusing to testify. The major inducement to a recalcitrant witness to give evidence is the knowledge that his actions may constitute contempt of court, and if found in contempt he may be sentenced to a substantial term of imprisonment. In those cases where a witness refuses to be sworn or to testify, the trial judge is always in a position to threaten that he will cite the proposed witness for contempt and to warn him that if he is found in contempt he may be sentenced to imprisonment. If, however, after repeated appearances and repeated warnings, the witness still refuses to testify it is most unlikely that a finding of contempt by the trial judge would induce such witness to testify. Once he has been sentenced, there is no longer any effective inducement as the court cannot vary a sentence once it is imposed: *R. v. Ayres* (1984), 15 C.C.C. (3d) 208, 42 C.R. (3d) 33 (Ont. C.A.).

While *instanter* summary contempt procedures may be justified in some exceptional cases, in most circumstances, natural justice requires the usual steps of putting the witness on notice that he or she must show cause why they should not be found in contempt of court, followed by an adjournment which need be no longer than that required to offer the witness an opportunity to be advised by counsel and, if he or she chooses, to be represented by counsel. In addition, upon a finding of contempt, there should be an opportunity to have representations made as to the appropriate sentence: *R. v. K. (B.)*, [1995] 4 S.C.R. 186, 102 C.C.C. (3d) 18, 43 C.R. (4th) 123.

A contempt citation is not a finding of contempt but rather notice to the accused that he has been contemptuous and would have to show cause why he should not be held in contempt. Contempt may be dealt with two ways: the ordinary procedure which provides the same procedural guarantees of a criminal trial, or the summary procedure which allows a judge to avoid the formalities of a criminal trial, even *instanter*, in some cases. The summary procedure can only be justified where it is urgent and imperative to act immediately. Other than in exceptional circumstances where the *instanter* summary proceeding is justified, the power to punish summarily is subject to the requirements of natural justice. While citing for contempt may take place at any time, including in the presence of the jury, conviction and sentence where it is not urgent and imperative to act immediately is an error of law that is reviewable by the appellate court. In some cases, it may be appropriate to convict an accused of contempt of court *instanter* in the presence of the jury, but in so doing, the trial judge must ensure that the jury is not given the impression that the judge is making a determination as to the credibility of the accused. Accordingly, in this case the accused's refusal to answer questions constituted contempt of court but the circumstances did not justify recourse to the *instanter* proceedings: *R. v. Arradi* (2003), 173 C.C.C. (3d) 1, 9 C.R. (6th) 207, 224 D.L.R. (4th) 301 (S.C.C.).

A person cited for civil contempt who is liable to be imprisoned for up to one year cannot be compelled to testify at the contempt proceedings: *Vidéotron Ltée v. Industries Microlec Produits Electroniques Inc.*, [1992] 2 S.C.R. 1065, 76 C.C.C. (3d) 289, 96 D.L.R. (4th) 376.

Proceedings for contempt of court arising out of abusive remarks by the accused to the trial judge after he convicted her, having made adverse findings of credibility, ought not to have been tried by that same judge. In the circumstances, the accused could have a reasonable apprehension of bias and her rights under s. 11(*d*) of the Charter were infringed: *R. v. Martin* (1985), 19 C.C.C. (3d) 248 (Ont. C.A.).

Where there are contradicted facts relating to matters essential to a decision as to whether or not a party is in contempt of court, those facts cannot be found by an assessment of the credibility of deponents of affidavits who have not been seen or heard by the trier of fact: *R.*

v. Jetco Manufacturing Ltd. and Alexander (1987), 31 C.C.C. (3d) 171, 57 O.R. (2d) 776 (C.A.).

While the same sentencing provisions are available in respect of the offence of contempt, the victim fine surcharge pursuant to s. 737 of the *Criminal Code*, however, has no application as it does not apply to common law offences: *R. v. Puddester* (2003), 174 C.C.C. (3d) 453, 226 Nfld. & P.E.I.R. 1 *sub nom. R. v. Puddister* (Nfld. C.A.).

Right to jury trial – A witness cited for contempt of court is "charged with an offence" within the meaning of s. 11 of the *Charter of Rights and Freedoms* and therefore is entitled to the rights guaranteed by that section as well as to fundamental justice under s. 7. However, the summary procedure is not an unconstitutional derogation from the right to a jury trial as guaranteed by s. 11(*f*) since the offender is subject only to a punishment of less than five years' imprisonment: *R. v. Cohn* (1984), 15 C.C.C. (3d) 150, 42 C.R. (3d) 1 (Ont. C.A.); *R. v. Robinson-Blackmore Printing & Publishing Co.* (1989), 47 C.C.C. (3d) 366, 73 Nfld. & P.E.I.R. 46 (Nfld. S.C.). Similarly: *MacMillan Bloedel Ltd. v. Simpson* (1994), 89 C.C.C. (3d) 217 (B.C.C.A.).

A person before the superior court on a summary motion to have him cited for contempt is not "charged with an offence" within the meaning of s. 11(*f*) of the *Canadian Charter of Rights and Freedoms* so as to have the benefit of a jury trial as guaranteed by that provision: *Quebec (Attorney General) v. Laurendeau* (1982), 3 C.C.C. (3d) 250 (Que. S.C.); *Manitoba (Attorney General) v. Groupe Quebecor Inc.* (1987), 37 C.C.C. (3d) 421 (Man. C.A.).

The summary procedure for trying contempt of court is a reasonable limitation on the right to a jury trial as provided for in s. 11(*f*) of the Charter: *R. v. Layne, supra*.

Appeal – Where the trial judge made an order for costs against defence counsel personally, there was a right of appeal. The jurisdiction to impose such a penalty could only be consequent upon a finding of contempt and therefore, the trial judge was effectively exercising contempt powers: *R. v. McCullough* (1995), 24 O.R. (3d) 239, 82 O.A.C. 63 (C.A.). [Also, now see s. 676.1.]

CIVIL REMEDY NOT SUSPENDED.

11. No civil remedy for an act or omission is suspended or affected by reason that the act or omission is a criminal offence. R.S., c. C-34, s. 10.

SYNOPSIS

This section states that parties may pursue civil remedies notwithstanding the fact that the same act or omission giving rise to the civil proceeding is also a criminal offence. Courts retain their inherent jurisdiction to protect their process and may, in an exceptional case, stay the civil proceedings until the conclusion of the criminal trial, to protect the accused's right to a fair trial.

ANNOTATIONS

In *British Acceptance Corporation Ltd. v. Belzberg* (1962), 36 D.L.R. (2d) 587, 39 C.R. 72 (Alta. S.C.), it was held that there was no general principle in Canada preventing the simultaneous trial of criminal and civil proceedings. A stay may be granted for either of the proceedings if simultaneous action would be vexatious but that is entirely discretionary.

Concurrent criminal and civil proceedings against a person is not in itself an exceptional cause for staying the latter proceedings: *Stickney v. Trusz* (1973), 16 C.C.C. (2d) 25, 25 C.R.N.S. 257 (Ont. H.C.J.), affd 17 C.C.C. (2d) 478*n*, 28 C.R.N.S. 125 (Div. Ct.), affd 17 C.C.C. (2d) 480*n*, 46 D.L.R. (3d) 82*n* (C.A.).

OFFENCE PUNISHABLE UNDER MORE THAN ONE ACT.

12. Where an act or omission is an offence under more than one Act of Parliament, whether punishable by indictment or on summary conviction, a person who does the act or makes the omission is, unless a contrary intention appears, subject to proceedings under any of those Acts, but is not liable to be punished more than once for the same offence. R.S., c. C-34, s. 11.

CROSS-REFERENCES

As to an *autrefois* plea, see ss. 7(6), 607 to 610 of the Code and s. 11(*h*) of the *Charter of Rights and Freedoms*. As to the abuse of process generally, see notes following s. 579. As to the common law rule precluding multiple convictions for same *delict*, the "*Kienapple*" rule and common law principles of *res judicata* and issue estoppel, see notes following s. 613.

SYNOPSIS

This provision *prevents* the *punishment* of an accused *more than once* for the same conduct where such conduct is an offence under more than one Act of Parliament. However, Parliament can make specific exceptions to this general rule (see, for example, s. 85).

ANNOTATIONS

This section does not modify the scope of *res judicata* which precludes multiple convictions for the same delict, although the matter is the basis of two separate offences: *R. v. Kienapple*, [1975] 1 S.C.R. 729, 15 C.C.C. (2d) 524, 26 C.R.N.S. 1 (5:4) Folld: *Dore v. Canada (Attorney General) (No. 2)*, [1975] 1 S.C.R. 756, 17 C.C.C. (2d) 359, 27 C.R.N.S. (8:1).

Also see notes under s. 613, *infra*.

CHILD UNDER TWELVE.

13. No person shall be convicted of an offence in respect of an act or omission on his part while that person was under the age of twelve years. R.S., c. C-34, s. 12; 1980-81-82-83, c. 110, s. 72.

CROSS-REFERENCES

Note that s. 23.1 provides that an accused may be convicted as a party, or accessory after the fact under ss. 21 to 23, notwithstanding that the person whom the accused aids or abets, counsels or procures or receives, comforts or assists, cannot be convicted of the offence.

Trial of offences committed by young persons aged 12 to 17 years is governed by the *Youth Criminal Justice Act*.

A person's age is determined by s. 30 of the *Interpretation Act*, R.S.C. 1985, c. I-21.

SYNOPSIS

No child under 12 years of age may be held criminally accountable. The age of 12 represents a relatively recent increase from the common law rule which established age seven as the start of accountability. Below this age, provincial child welfare legislation may apply to children who are involved in criminal activity.

ANNOTATIONS

The reference to age in this section is to chronological age not "mental age". Thus, this section does not bar the trial of a mentally retarded adult, nor do such proceedings violate s. 15 of the Charter: *R. v. Sawchuk* (1991), 66 C.C.C. (3d) 255, [1991] 5 W.W.R. 381, 6 W.A.C. 311 (Man. C.A.), leave to appeal to S.C.C. refused 67 C.C.C. (3d) vi, 137 N.R. 385*n*.

CONSENT TO DEATH.

14. No person is entitled to consent to have death inflicted on him, and such consent does not affect the criminal reponsibility of any person by whom death may be inflicted on the person by whom consent is given. R.S., c. C-34, s. 14.

CROSS-REFERENCES

For the offences of murder and manslaughter see ss. 222 to 240. The offence of counselling or aiding suicide is set out in s. 241.

SYNOPSIS

This section states that *no* one has the *right to consent* to have death inflicted on him. In addition, if a person causes the death of another, the consent of the deceased does not provide the person who caused the death a defence to criminal responsibility.

ANNOTATIONS

Notwithstanding this section, in the case of a genuine suicide pact, the surviving party should have a defence to murder. This defence will only be available when the parties are in such a mental state that they have formed a common and irrevocable intent to commit suicide together simultaneously and by the same act where the risk of death is identical and equal for both. The survivor may, however, be liable to be convicted of the offence contrary to s. 241: *R. v. Gagnon* (1993), 84 C.C.C. (3d) 143, 24 C.R. (4th) 369, [1993] R.J.Q. 1716 (C.A.).

OBEDIENCE TO *DE FACTO* LAW.

15. No person shall be convicted of an offence in respect of an act or omission in obedience to the laws for the time being made and enforced by persons in *de facto* possession of the sovereign power in and over the place where the act or omission occurs. R.S., c. C-34, s. 15.

CROSS-REFERENCES

This provision does not apply to trials of war crimes and crimes against humanity: *Crimes Against Humanity and War Crimes Act*, s. 13. Note also the provisions of s. 269.1(3) which limit the availability of the defence of obedience to superior orders, etc., to the offence of torture. This provision is of quite limited application and provisions similar to it were originally enacted in England to protect persons serving the King *de facto* who might turn out to be on the wrong side of a civil war, and to make it clear that it was not treason to the successful claimant to the throne to have faithfully served the then reigning monarch.

In present times, a more relevant defence may be the emerging defence of officially induced error noted under s. 19, *infra*.

SYNOPSIS

This provision states that obedience to the laws, for the time being, made and enforced by those who are *de facto* in possession of the sovereign power in and over the place where the acts or omissions occur will prevent a conviction – unless a specific exception is made in the provision creating the offence.

ANNOTATIONS

This section does not afford a defence to a movie theatre, that, in compliance with provincial legislation, received approval for public showing of a film later alleged by the Crown to be obscene: *R. v. Daylight Theatre Company Ltd.* (1973), 13 C.C.C. (2d) 524, 41 D.L.R. (3d) 236 (Sask. C.A.). Folld: *R. v. McFall* (1975), 26 C.C.C. (2d) 181 (B.C.C.A.), although evidence of the provincial censor as to why he approved the film is relevant to the issue of whether in fact the film was obscene. Similarly, on a charge of distributing obscene publications, this section has no application notwithstanding the offending publications were first cleared through customs: *R. v. 294555 Ontario Ltd.* (1978), 39 C.C.C. (2d) 352, 61 D.L.R. (4th) 85, 69 O.R. (2d) 557 (C.A.).

DEFENCE OF MENTAL DISORDER / Presumption / Burden of proof.

16. (1) No person is criminally responsible for an act committed or an omission made while suffering from a mental disorder that rendered the person incapable of appreciating the nature and quality of the act or omission or of knowing that it was wrong.

(2) Every person is presumed not to suffer from a mental disorder so as to be exempt from criminal responsibility by virtue of subsection (1), until the contrary is proved on the balance of probabilities.

(3) The burden of proof that an accused was suffering from a mental disorder so as to be exempt from criminal responsibility is on the party that raises the issue. R.S. c. C-34, s. 16; 1991, c. 43, s. 2.

CROSS-REFERENCES

This section deals with the defence of mental disorder. Where that defence is made out, the trier of fact is required to deliver a verdict of not criminally responsible on account of mental disorder: s. 672.34. As to the disposition hearing subsequent to a verdict of not criminally responsible on account of mental disorder or unfit to stand trial, see. ss. 672.45 to 672.52. As to dispositions by a court or review board, see ss. 672.54 to 672.63. As to review of dispositions, see ss. 672.81 to 672.85. As to remand for assessment, see ss. 672.11 to 672.2. As to trial of issue of fitness to stand trial, see ss. 672.22 to 672.33. As to review boards, see ss. 672.38 to 672.44. As to dual status offender, see ss. 672.67 to 672.71. As to appeals, see ss. 672.72 to 672.8. As to interprovincial transfers, see ss. 672.86 to 672.89. As to application of Part XX.1 to young offenders, see s. 141 of the *Youth Criminal Justice Act*. Mental disorder is defined in s. 2. The report of an expert may be admitted under s. 657.3.

SYNOPSIS

These provisions are effectively identical to the previous s. 16 except for terminology which replaces the concept of insanity with the phraseology "mental disorder". The new terminology, however, still codifies the common law test of insanity, now termed mental disorder. Subsection (1) sets out the long-standing principle of criminal law that no person who committed an offence while suffering a mental disorder may be convicted. Subsection (1) also restates, with one significant modification, the common law rule developed in nineteenth century England in the *McNaughten* case. This is a legal and not a medical test although expert psychiatric and psychological evidence is almost invariably used to assist in making the determination. Subsection (2) sets out the presumption of sanity until the contrary is proven on the balance of probabilities and subsec. (3) requires the party raising the issue of mental disorder to bear the burden of proof.

The first arm of the test is that the accused is proved to be suffering from a mental disorder which replaces the concepts of "natural imbecility" and "disease of the mind" contained in the prior definition of insanity. These principles, however, are incorporated by virtue of the generic term "mental disorder". To be found to be suffering from a mental disorder, the accused must meet one of two tests: the mental disorder must have rendered them incapable (1) of appreciating the nature and quality of the act or omission or (2) of knowing that an act or omission is wrong.

Subsection (3) of the previous legislation which stated that a person "who has specific delusions, but is in other respects sane, shall not be acquitted on the ground of insanity unless the delusions caused that person to believe in the existence of a state of things that, if it existed, would have justified or excused the act or omission of that person" is now subsumed under the definition of "mental disorder" contained in subsec. (1). Consequently, a person who suffers from a delusion to the point where it renders them incapable of appreciating the nature and quality of the act or omission or of knowing that it was wrong will be characterized as suffering from a "mental disorder".

Subsections (2) and (3) of the new provisions speak to the presumption of sanity and the burden of proof on the balance of probability which must be borne by the party raising the issue.

ANNOTATIONS

Note: Most of the cases below were decided under the predecessor legislation. The two significant changes to the legislation are to replace the term "insane" with the term "not criminally responsible" and to replace the term "state of natural imbecility or has disease of the mind" with the term "mental disorder". However, "mental disorder" is defined in s. 2 as meaning a "disease of the mind" and so it is believed that much of the case-law decided under the predecessor legislation is applicable to the new provision.

General – In determining whether an accused has met the evidential burden necessary to leave the issue with the jury, the trial judge must assume the truth of the evidence that tends to support the defence and leave questions of reliability, credibility and weight to be determined by the jury. In this case, the trial judge erred in refusing to leave the defence of mental disorder on the basis that the defence psychiatrist's opinion had been based on facts recounted by the accused, that the evidence was contradicted by other psychiatrists and that the accused's testimony contained significant inconsistencies. It is not necessary that the relevant evidence be believed in order for the defence to succeed, as an accused is entitled to be acquitted on the basis of exculpatory evidence that the jury does not reject but either accepts or about which it is undecided: *R. v. Fontaine*, [2004] 1 S.C.R. 702, 183 C.C.C. (3d) 1, 18 C.R. (6th) 203.

A malfunctioning of the mind exclusively from the voluntary consumption of drugs is not a disease of the mind in the legal sense, since it is not a product of the individual's inherent psychological make-up but rather voluntary activity: *R. v. Bouchard-Lebrun*, [2011] 3 S.C.R. 575, 275 C.C.C. (3d) 145.

Meaning of "disease of the mind" – The term "disease of the mind" is a legal concept and it is therefore a question of law for the trial judge what mental conditions are included within the term. Any malfunctioning of the mind, or mental disturbance having its source primarily in some subjective condition or weakness internal to the accused (whether fully understood or not), may be a disease of the mind if it prevents the accused from knowing what he is doing, but transient disturbances of consciousness due to certain specific external factors do not fall within the concept. In particular, the ordinary stresses and disappointments of life, though they may bring about malfunctioning of the mind such as a dissociative state, do not constitute an external cause constituting an explanation for a malfunctioning of the mind which takes it out of the category of a disease of the mind and could not form the basis of a defence of non-insane automatism: *R. v. Rabey* (1977), 37 C.C.C. (2d) 461, 79 D.L.R. (3d) 414 (Ont. C.A.), affd [1980] 2 S.C.R. 513, 54 C.C.C. (2d) 1, 15 C.R. (3d) 225 (4:3). [Also see *R. v. Stone*, *infra*, under "Automatism".]

The term "disease of the mind" embraces any illness, disorder or abnormal condition which impairs the human mind and its functioning, excluding, however, self-induced states caused by alcohol or drugs, as well as transitory mental states such as hysteria or concussion. Thus personality disorders may constitute disease of the mind. The word "appreciates" imports a requirement beyond mere knowledge of the physical quality of the act and requires a capacity to apprehend the nature of the act and its consequences: *R. v. Cooper*, [1980] 1 S.C.R. 1149, 51 C.C.C. (2d) 129, 13 C.R. (3d) 97 and 18 C.R. (3d) 138 (5:2), where the decisions of the Ontario Court of Appeal in *R. v. Rabey, supra*, and *R. v. Simpson* (1977), 35 C.C.C. (2d) 337, 77 D.L.R. (3d) 507, were referred to with approval.

The syndrome known as delirium tremens, brought about by prolonged and chronic, albeit voluntary, consumption of alcohol, is a "disease of the mind". Delirium tremens is not self-induced in the way of drunkenness, but is the supervening result of abuse of alcohol over an extended period of time: *R. v. Malcolm* (1989), 50 C.C.C. (3d) 172 (Man. C.A.).

"Mental disorder" includes mental retardation: *R. v. R. (M.S.)* (1996), 112 C.C.C. (3d) 406 (Ont. Ct. (Gen. Div.)).

A mental disorder may still constitute a disease of the mind even if it is not prone to recur. "Disease of the mind" includes any medically recognized mental disorder or mental illness that could render a person incapable of appreciating the nature and quality of his act, or of knowing that it is wrong, save for transient mental disturbances caused by external factors such as violence or drugs: *R. v. Oakley* (1986), 24 C.C.C. (3d) 351 (Ont. C.A.).

Automatism – The determination of whether non-insane [more properly non-mental disorder] automatism should be left to the jury involves a two-step procedure. The trial judge must first determine whether the accused has satisfied the evidentiary burden for the defence of automatism and then whether the condition alleged by the accused is mental disorder or non-mental disorder automatism. Since the law presumes that people act voluntarily, the accused bears the legal burden of proving involuntariness by reason of automatism on a balance of probabilities. Accordingly, to meet the evidentiary burden, the accused must satisfy the trial judge that there is evidence upon which a properly instructed jury could find that the accused acted involuntarily on a balance of probabilities. To meet this burden the accused must claim that he acted involuntarily at the relevant time and this assertion must be confirmed by expert psychiatric evidence. With respect to automatism alleged to have been caused by a psychological blow, the defence will generally have to provide evidence of a trigger equivalent to a "shock" to satisfy the evidentiary burden. Other evidence that should be considered is the accused's appearance at the time, a history of similar involuntary conduct and whether there was a motive for the crime. If the crime is explicable without reference to the alleged automatism, this will generally tell against the existence of automatism. Assuming the defence can meet the first step, the judge must then consider the question of mixed law and fact as to whether the condition the accused claims to have suffered from satisfied the legal test for disease of the mind. In making this determination the trial judge starts from the proposition that the condition the accused claims to have suffered from is a disease of the mind and that therefore only the defence of mental disorder under this section should be put to the jury. In making the mental disorder determination the trial judge should consider a number of factors. One factor is the internal cause factor, namely, that the defence of non-mental disorder automatism is limited to cases involving triggers that a normal person, similarly situated, would find extremely shocking. Involuntariness caused by any less severe shock or mere stress is presumed to be triggered by a factor internal to the accused and thus a disease of the mind. Another factor is whether the accused presents a recurring danger to the public. If so, this favours a finding that a mental disorder is involved. In considering this factor the judge will take into account the accused's psychiatric history and the likelihood that the trigger will recur. There may as well be other policy factors: *R. v. Stone*, [1999] 2 S.C.R. 290, 134 C.C.C. (3d) 353. As to the burden on the accused to read sufficient evidence to require that the automatism defence be left to the jury, also see *R. v. Fontaine*, *supra*.

In charging the jury on non-mental disorder automatism, the trial judge should thoroughly review the serious policy factors that surround automatism including concerns about feignability and the repute of the administration of justice. The judge should also refer specifically to evidence relevant to the issue of involuntariness: *R. v. Stone*, *supra*.

Where the accused is in a state of automatism to which a disease of the mind is a contributing factor then his defence is insanity, not non-insane automatism, even if there were other factors such as consumption of alcohol and a physical illness which were contributing factors: *R. v. Revelle* (1979), 48 C.C.C. (2d) 267 (Ont. C.A.), affd [1981] 1 S.C.R. 576, 61 C.C.C. (2d) 575 (9:0).

Automatism is not a defence but rather a denial of the commission of the *actus reus* of the crime. A person who is unable to decide whether to perform an act and unable to control the performance of the act cannot be said to have committed the act. If an accused's automatism is rooted in a mental disorder, the accused should be found not criminally responsible on account of mental disorder rather than acquitted. Such a finding would require a post-verdict disposition hearing before either the trial judge or review board. The distinction between non-mental disorder automatism and mental disorder automatism depends on whether the automatistic state is the product of a mental disorder as defined within s. 2 of the *Criminal Code*. In deciding whether to characterize the automatism as "mental disorder" or "non-mental disorder", the trial judge has to assess the danger that the accused's condition poses to the public, including not only the risk of further violence while in an automatistic state, but also the risk of recurrence of the factors or events that triggered that state. In this case, the hereditary nature of the parasomnia and the accused's history of sexomania were particularly relevant to the likelihood of the recurrence of triggering circumstances, which support the characterization of the accused's condition as a mental disorder: *R. v. Luedecke* (2008), 236 C.C.C. (3d) 317 (Ont. C.A.).

Meaning of "appreciating" and "knowing" – In using the two words "appreciating" and "knowing", Parliament clearly intended that different tests be used. The verb "know" has a positive connotation requiring a base awareness while "appreciate" involves a further step of analysis of knowledge or experience: *R. v. Barnier*, [1980] 1 S.C.R. 1124, 51 C.C.C. (2d) 193 (7:0), affg 37 C.C.C. (2d) 508 (B.C.C.A.). And see: *R. v. Baltzer* (1979), 27 C.C.C. (2d) 118 (N.S.S.C. App. Div.), and *R. v. Simpson, infra.*

Appreciation of the nature and quality of the act refers to an incapacity by reason of disease of the mind to appreciate the physical consequences of the act. Thus, an accused could not rely on this branch of the insanity defence where he was aware that he was killing the victim and knew that killing was a crime, although he believed that the victim was "Satan" and that in killing the deceased he was acting on divine orders. On the other hand, an accused, who by reason of disease of the mind was acting under such a delusion, would be entitled to a finding of insanity on the basis that he did not know the act was wrong in view of the expanded definition given the term "wrong" in *R. v. Chaulk, infra*: *R. v. Landry*, [1991] 1 S.C.R. 99, 62 C.C.C. (3d) 117 (7:0).

An accused's personal sense of justifiability is never sufficient to ground the defence. Rather, the accused's mental disorder must also render him or her incapable of knowing that the act in question is morally wrong as measured against societal standards, and therefore incapable of making the choice to act in accordance with those standards: *R. v. Campione* (2015), 321 C.C.C. (3d) 63 (Ont. C.A.).

Although personality disorders or psychopathic personalities are capable of constituting a disease of the mind the defence of insanity is not made out where the accused has the necessary understanding of the nature, character and consequences of the act, but merely lacks appropriate feelings for the victim or lacks feelings of remorse or guilt for what he has done, even though such lack of feeling stems from disease of the mind: *R. v. Simpson* (1977), 35 C.C.C. (2d) 337 (Ont. C.A.).

This part of the judgment in *R. v. Simpson, supra*, was approved in *R. v. Kjeldsen*, [1981] 2 S.C.R. 617, 64 C.C.C. (2d) 161 (9:0).

A delusion which renders the accused incapable of appreciating that the penal sanctions attaching to the commission of the crime are applicable to him does not render him incapable of appreciating the nature and quality of the act within the meaning of this section so as to give rise to the insanity defence. While the concept of appreciating the nature and quality of an act requires an understanding of the consequences of the act, this refers to the physical consequences of the act: *R. v. Abbey*, [1982] 2 S.C.R. 24, 68 C.C.C. (2d) 394 (9:0).

This provision has no application where the accused understands society's views as to what is right and wrong but because of a delusion chooses to act in contravention of society's view: *R. v. W. (J.M.)* (1998), 123 C.C.C. (3d) 245 (B.C.C.A.).

In *R. v. Wolfson*, [1965] 3 C.C.C. 304 (Alta. S.C. App. Div.), it was held that evidence of an irresistible impulse is not, by itself, enough to support a finding of insanity under this section.

Meaning of "wrong" – The term "wrong" in subsec. (2) means "morally wrong" and not simply "legally wrong". The court must determine whether the accused, because of a disease of the mind, was rendered incapable of knowing that the act committed was something that he ought not to have done. Thus, the inquiry cannot terminate with the discovery that the accused knew that the act was contrary to the formal law. A person may know that the act was contrary to law and yet, by reason of a disease of the mind, be incapable of knowing that the act is morally wrong in the circumstances according to the moral standards of society: *R. v. Chaulk*, [1990] 3 S.C.R. 1303, 62 C.C.C. (3d) 193.

The inquiry under this section focuses not on a general capacity to know right from wrong, but rather on the ability to know that a particular act was wrong in the cirumstances. The accused must not only possess the intellectual ability to know right from wrong in an abstract sense but must possess the ability to apply that knowledge in a rational way to the alleged criminal act. The crux of the inquiry is whether the accused lacks the capacity to rationally decide whether the act is right or wrong and hence to make a rational choice of whether to do it or not. The accused would not be criminally responsible where, by reason of delusions, he perceives an act which is wrong as right or justifiable, and the disordered condition of his mind deprives the accused of the ability to rationally evaluate what he is doing. It is not necessary to show that, if the delusions were true, a specific defence such as self-defence would also apply: *R. v. Oommen*, [1994] 2 S.C.R. 507, 91 C.C.C. (3d) 8.

Mental illness short of insanity – Our *Criminal Code* does not recognize the defence of diminished responsibility and even though the accused may have been ill at the time of the offence he is technically sane if he was able to distinguish between right and wrong: *R. v. Chartrand*, [1977] 1 S.C.R. 314, 26 C.C.C. (2d) 417 (8:0).

Nevertheless where the accused is charged with an offence which requires proof of a specific intent, evidence that the accused was suffering from mental illness or mental disorder, though falling short of proof of insanity, may negative the requisite specific intent, as in the case of murder reduce the charge to manslaughter: *R. v. Baltzer, supra*. And to the same effect: *R. v. Hilton* (1977), 34 C.C.C. (2d) 206 (Ont. C.A.); *R. v. Meloche* (1975), 34 C.C.C. (2d) 184 (Que. C.A.); *R. v. Lechasseur* (1977), 38 C.C.C. (2d) 319 (Que. C.A.); *R. v. Browning* (1976), 34 C.C.C. (2d) 200 (Ont. C.A.); *R. v. Leblanc* (1991), 4 C.R. (4th) 98, [1991] R.J.Q. 686 (C.A.); *R. v. Wright* (1979), 48 C.C.C. (2d) 334, 11 C.R. (3d) 257 (Alta. S.C. App. Div.), leave to appeal to S.C.C. refused 48 C.C.C. (2d) 334*n*; *R. v. Bailey* (1996), 111 C.C.C. (3d) 122, 133 W.A.C. 105 (B.C.C.A.).

Where evidence is adduced in support of a defence of insanity to a charge of first degree murder, the jury is to be directed to first consider that defence. If that defence fails, then the jury should consider all the evidence in the case, including relevant evidence which was adduced in support of the insanity defence to determine whether the accused had the relevant intent for murder and, if so, whether the killing was planned and deliberate: *R. v. Allard* (1990), 57 C.C.C. (3d) 397, 78 C.R. (3d) 228 (Que. C.A.).

Procedure – Where the accused seeks to introduce evidence to support a defence of automatism, whether insane or non-insane automatism, a *voir dire* should not be resorted to where the evidence is relevant and not subject to rejection on any recognized legal ground. The evidence should be led before the jury and at the end of the case it will be for the trial judge to instruct the jury whether there is any evidence which will support the particular defence: *R. v. Sproule* (1975), 26 C.C.C. (2d) 92 (Ont. C.A.).

The accused may raise the defence of insanity at any time during the trial and in fact may raise the defence after the trier of fact has found the accused guilty but prior to conviction. If, during the course of the trial, prior to the finding of guilt, evidence is led which does not satisfy the trier of fact of insanity under this section, such evidence may nevertheless be considered on the issue of whether the accused had the requisite *mens rea*: *R. v. Swain*, [1991] 1 S.C.R. 933, 63 C.C.C. (3d) 481 (6:1).

Section 650(3) which gives the accused the right "after the close of the case for the prosecution" to make full answer and defence must apply to evidence given by way of rebuttal as well as to that given during the Crown's case in chief. Accordingly, it was held in *R. v. Ewert* (1989), 52 C.C.C. (3d) 280 (B.C.C.A.), that the rules regarding the permissible scope of surrebuttal must be applied liberally in favour of the accused, where the accused relied on the defence of insanity and evidence to rebut that defence was first given by the Crown in rebuttal.

Where the trial judge is of the view that there is no evidence to support the defence of insanity, he should so inform counsel prior to their making their jury addresses: *R. v. Charest* (1990), 57 C.C.C. (3d) 312 (Que. C.A.).

Even where the Crown has notice that the accused intends to rely on the insanity defence as provided in this section, the Crown need not adduce evidence in chief to challenge that defence. The Crown was therefore properly permitted to adduce its evidence with respect to sanity in rebuttal. The accused suffered no prejudice as he was given the opportunity for surrebuttal: *R. v. Chaulk, supra.*

Expert evidence – The placing of the crucial question of the accused's state of mind to the expert witness, while ordinarily framed as a hypothetical question may, if the facts are uncontradicted be put in direct form. This discretion of the trial judge was confirmed in *R. v. Bleta*, [1964] S.C.R. 561, [1965] 1 C.C.C. 1 (5:0), *per* Ritchie J., at p. 6 C.C.C., p. 198 C.R.: "Provided that the questions are so phrased as to make clear what the evidence is on which an expert is being asked to found his conclusion, the failure of counsel to put such questions in hypothetical form does not of itself make the answers inadmissible. It is within the competence of the trial judge in any case to insist upon the foundation for the expert opinion being laid by way of hypothetical question if he feels this to be the best way in which he can be assured of the matter being fully understood by the jury, but this does not, in my opinion, mean that the judge is necessarily precluded in the exercise of his discretion in the conduct of the trial from permitting the expert's answer to go before the jury if the nature and foundation of his opinion has been clearly indicated by other means."

While an expert opinion based on second-hand evidence is admissible, if relevant, the facts asserted in this second-hand evidence are not admissible for their truth. Thus, while medical experts are entitled to take into consideration all possible information in forming their opinions, "this in no way removes from the party tendering such evidence the obligation of establishing, through properly admissible evidence, the factual basis on which such opinions are based." *R. v. Abbey, supra.*

Provided there is some admissible evidence to establish the foundation for the expert opinion, a trial judge cannot subsequently instruct the jury to completely ignore the testimony. Where the factual basis of an expert opinion is a mixture of admissible and second-hand (hearsay) evidence the duty of the trial judge is to caution the jury that the weight attributable to the expert testimony is directly related to the amount and quality of admissible evidence on which the opinion depends: *R. v. Lavallee*, [1990] 1 S.C.R. 852, 55 C.C.C. (3d) 97 (7:0). See also *R. v. Skrzydlewski* (1995), 103 C.C.C. (3d) 467 (Ont. C.A.).

On the other hand, not all "second-hand" evidence is hearsay and thus, statements of a preposterous nature by an accused may be relevant to the issue of insanity and may be original evidence on that issue. For example, utterances by the accused manifesting a delusion or hallucination are not used to prove any fact asserted in them, but as circumstantial evidence to support an inference that the accused suffers from delusions or hallucinations. While such statements may be feigned, whether they indicate an actual mental state must be determined by the court, usually with the assistance of experts: *R. v. Kirkby* (1985), 21 C.C.C. (3d) 31 (Ont. C.A.), leave to appeal to S.C.C. refused [1986] 2 S.C.R. vii.

An expert may be cross-examined to determine what the expert considered relevant, whether there are matters relevant that were not considered and whether the expert might have arrived at his conclusion as a result of considerations irrelevant to his particular expertise. Since an expert cannot take into account facts that are not subject to his professional expert assessment, he cannot be cross-examined and asked to take such facts into account. Further, it is not open to the cross-examiner or examiner to put as a fact or even a hypothetical fact, that which is not and will not become part of the case as admissible evidence: *R. v. Howard*, [1989] 1 S.C.R. 1337, 48 C.C.C. (3d) 38 (3:1).

Where counsel requires the services of an expert in order to assist him in preparing the defence, communications between the accused and the expert are covered by solicitor-client privilege. There is no requirement that counsel be present during the examination. Where defence counsel, however, subsequently calls the expert, he may be required to disclose his communications with the accused. This is because the accused, by calling as a witness in his defence a psychiatrist, whose opinion was based at least in part on what the accused has confided in him, thereby waived privilege: *R. v. Perron* (1990), 54 C.C.C. (3d) 108 (Que. C.A.).

Where statements by the accused are adduced through cross-examination of defence experts or through examination of experts retained by the Crown solely for their bearing on the expert opinion and not as evidence of their truth on which the jury could act independently, then no issue of voluntariness arises: *R. v. Stevenson* (1990), 58 C.C.C. (3d) 464 (Ont. C.A.).

Also see notes under s. 150.1 re expert evidence.

Confession of "insane" accused – While the correct test for admissibility of the confession of an insane accused may be framed *per R. v. Ward*, [1979] 2 S.C.R. 30, 44 C.C.C. (2d) 498, as to whether it represents the "operating mind" of the accused, this is not the only word formula for testing the admissibility of an insane accused's statements to the police. Thus in *R. v. Nagotcha*, [1980] 1 S.C.R. 714, 51 C.C.C. (2d) 353 (9:0), the trial judge's ruling admitting the statements was upheld where he found that the accused, who at the time of the making of the statements was a paranoid schizophrenic and unfit to stand trial, was not "so devoid of rationality and understanding, or so replete with psychotic delusions that his uttered words could not be fairly be said to be his statements at all". Also see: *R. v. Whittle*, [1994] 2 S.C.R. 914, 92 C.C.C. (3d) 11, noted under s. 10 of the Charter, *infra*.

Subsection (3) – It was held in *R. v. Chaulk, supra*, that the former s. 16(4) which also placed the burden on the accused to prove the defence on a balance of probabilities while infringing the presumption of innocence guarantee in s. 11(*d*) of the Charter was a reasonable limit and therefore valid.

Adverse inference from failure to submit to examination – Where the accused relies on the defence of insanity, although he is not required to submit to psychiatric examination by a psychiatrist retained by the Crown, evidence of such refusal is admissible and an inference adverse to the accused may be drawn from such refusal: *R. v. Sweeney (No. 2)* (1977), 35 C.C.C. (2d) 245 (Ont. C.A.).

Further, the drawing of the adverse inference does not infringe the accused's right to fundamental justice under s. 7 of the Charter: *R. v. Worth* (1995), 98 C.C.C. (3d) 133 (Ont. C.A.), leave to appeal to S.C.C. refused 109 C.C.C. (3d) vi, application for extension of time granted per S.C.C. bull. 11/08/96, pp. 1877-8.

The defence decision to permit access to the accused by a Crown psychiatrist is imbued with a use limitation restricted by the character of the disclosure impelled by the principle that an accused, who raises an issue of diminished intent or mental disorder and refuses to see a Crown psychiatrist, may suffer an adverse inference. The Crown may not lead evidence from its psychiatrist in-chief to prove the identity of the accused by virtue of statements made by the accused during the interview: *R. v. Brunczlik* (1995), 103 C.C.C. (3d) 131 (Ont. Ct. (Gen. Div.)).

Where the accused, who relied on a defence of lack of specific intent, relied upon the evidence of psychiatrists retained by the defence, it was open to the Crown to adduce evidence that the accused refused to discuss details of the offence with a psychiatrist who examined the accused on behalf of the Crown. This evidence was admissible to explain why the Crown's expert's evidence may not have been as complete as that of the defence experts. The trial judge ought however to have instructed the jury that, in not discussing the circumstances of the offence, the accused was exercising his right to remain silent and that no inference of guilt could be drawn against him on this account: *R. v. Stevenson, supra.*

Right of Crown to adduce evidence of insanity – The Crown may lead evidence of insanity only in two circumstances: (1) where the accused's own defence, in the opinion of the trial judge, has somehow put the accused's mental capacity for criminal intent in issue, in which case the trial judge will be entitled to charge on the insanity defence; and (2) after the trier of fact had concluded that the accused was otherwise guilty of the offence charged. Where the Crown is required to adduce its evidence only after the accused has been found guilty, then the jury should be instructed that the Crown does so only because this is what the law requires, not because the Crown has chosen to conduct its case in this manner: *R. v. Swain, supra.*

COMPULSION BY THREATS.

17. A person who commits an offence under compulsion by threats of immediate death or bodily harm from a person who is present when the offence is committed is excused for committing the offence if the person believes that the threats will be carried out and if the person is not a party to a conspiracy or association whereby the person is subject to compulsion, but this section does not apply where the offence that is committed is high treason or treason, murder, piracy, attempted murder, sexual assault, sexual assault with a weapon, threats to a third party or causing bodily harm, aggravated sexual assault, forcible abduction, hostage taking, robbery, assault with a weapon or causing bodily harm, aggravated assault, unlawfully causing bodily harm, arson or an offence under sections 280 to 283 (abduction and detention of young persons). R.S., c. C-34, s. 17; 1974-75-76, c. 105, s. 29; 1980-81-82-83, c. 125, s. 4; R.S.C. 1985, c. 27 (1st Supp.), s. 40(2).

CROSS-REFERENCES

The offences excepted from the defence created by this section are defined in the following sections: ss. 46, 47, high treason or treason; ss. 229, 230, murder; s. 74, piracy; s. 239, attempted murder; ss. 271 to 273, sexual assault; s. 279(2), forcible abduction; s. 279.1, hostage taking; s. 343, robbery; s. 267(*a*), assault with weapon; s. 267(*b*), assault causing bodily harm; s. 268, aggravated assault; s. 269, unlawfully causing bodily harm; s. 433, arson.

SYNOPSIS

Subject to the application of the Charter (see *R. v. Ruzic, infra*), this section defines the scope of the defence of *duress* as it affects those who personally commit an offence. For reasons of public policy many *serious offences involving personal violence* (*e.g.*, murder, sexual assault) or threats to public safety (*e.g.*, arson, high treason) are exempted from the operation of this section and therefore duress will afford *no defence* to a *principal* charged with the listed offences. Cases have held that a *party may rely* on the defence of duress, notwithstanding that they were a party to one of the exempted offences listed in s. 17.

ANNOTATIONS

Constitutional Considerations – The requirements of immediacy (threat of immediate death or bodily harm) and presence (threat from a person who is present when the offence is committed) infringe s. 7 of the *Canadian Charter of Rights and Freedoms* and must be struck down as unconstitutional. It would seem that an accused, even a principal offender, may rely upon the common law defence of duress: *R. v. Ruzic*, [2001] 1 S.C.R. 687, 153 C.C.C. (3d) 1.

The exclusion of robbery and assault with a weapon from the statutory defence of duress is contrary to s. 7 of the Charter because it does not comply with the requirement of moral voluntariness recognized in *Ruzic, supra.* By way of remedy, the court severed the words "robbery" and "assault with a weapon" from s. 17: *R. v. Allen* (2014), 318 C.C.C. (3d) 335 (Sask. Q.B.).

In *R. v. Aravena* (2015), 323 C.C.C. (3d) 54 (Ont. C.A.), leave to appeal to S.C.C. refused 2016 CarswellOnt 5410, the constitutionality of the murder exception to the duress defence in s. 17 was not before the court. However, as a result of its analysis of the common law defence as applied to parties, the court observed that, subject to any s. 1 argument the Crown might advance justifying the exception as it applies to perpetrators, the exception must be found unconstitutional.

Elements of statutory defence – The statutory defence of duress applies to principals and the common law to parties. Nonetheless, both forms share the following common elements: there must be an explicit or implicit threat of present or future death or bodily harm (this threat can be directed at the accused or a third party); the accused must reasonably believe that the threat will be carried out; there must be no safe avenue of escape, evaluated on a modified objective standard; there must be a close temporal connection between the threat and the harm threatened; there must be proportionality between the harm threatened and the harm inflicted by the accused, also evaluated on a modified objective standard; and the accused cannot be a party to a conspiracy or association whereby he or she is subject to compulsion and actually knew that threats and coercion to commit an offence were a possible result of this criminal activity, conspiracy or association: *R. v. Ryan*, [2013] 1 S.C.R. 14, 290 C.C.C. (3d) 477.

There was no evidence to support a defence of duress to a charge of perjury where the accused could have informed the police of the threats he received prior to testifying and thus obtained police protection. A threat of death, from which the accused could have easily escaped and that he could have rendered unenforceable when he gave his evidence, does not give rise to the defence under this section: *R. v. Hebert*, [1989] 1 S.C.R. 233, 49 C.C.C. (3d) 59, affg 3 Q.A.C. 251, C.C.C. *loc. cit.* (C.A.).

The defence of duress to a charge of perjury was rejected where although the persons who threatened the accused were present in court at the time the false testimony was given the accused had the opportunity to seek official protection: *R. v. Falkenberg* (1973), 13 C.C.C. (2d) 562 (Ont. Co. Ct.), revd on other grounds 16 C.C.C. (2d) 525 (C.A.). *Cf. R. v. Hudson and Taylor* (1971), 56 Cr. App. R. 1 (C.A.).

The offence of "forcible abduction" is not the equivalent of kidnapping. The latter offence is defined by s. 279 and therefore this section does offer a defence to a person charged with kidnapping. However, a threat that the accused's own children would be kidnapped and taken to another country is not a threat of death of grievous bodily harm so as to give the accused a defence under this section: *R. v. Robins* (1982), 66 C.C.C. (2d) 550 (Que. C.A.).

Availability of common law defence – The common law defence of duress is available to a party to an offence such as murder or robbery. While that defence, if made out, excuses the commission of the offence, the existence of threats does not negate the *mens rea* of the party: *R. v. Hibbert*, [1995] 2 S.C.R. 973, 99 C.C.C. (3d) 193; *R. v. Paquette*, [1977] 2 S.C.R. 189, 30 C.C.C. (2d) 417.

The common law defence remains available to persons charged as parties to murder. Duress is an excuse, not a justification. The availability of the defence cannot be settled by giving automatic priority to the right to life of the victim over that of an accused. Instead, the right to life of the victim must be factored into the proportionality assessment as part of the broader moral involuntariness inquiry: *R. v. Aravena* (2015), 323 C.C.C. (3d) 54 (Ont. C.A.), leave to appeal to S.C.C. refused 2016 CarswellOnt 5410.

The common law defence of duress is similar to the defence of necessity and, like necessity, can only be invoked where there is no legal way out of the situation of duress the accused faces. Accordingly, the defence is unavailable if a safe avenue of escape was available to the accused. The question of whether or not a safe avenue of escape existed is to be determined according to an objective standard. When considering the perceptions of a reasonable person, however, the personal circumstances of the accused are relevant and important and should be taken into account: *R. v. Hibbert, supra.*

Where the accused relies upon the common law defence of duress, the trial judge should instruct the jury on *inter alia* the need for a close temporal connection between the threat and the harm threatened. The jury should also be instructed on the need for the application of an objective-subjective assessment of whether there was an obvious safe avenue of escape. However, the law does not require an accused to seek the official protection of the police in all cases before the defence can succeed. The objective requirement must take into consideration the special circumstances where the accused found herself as well as her perception of them. Once the duress defence has been raised and there is some evidence to support it, the burden is on the Crown to show beyond a reasonable doubt that the accused did not act under duress: *R. v. Ruzic, supra.*

While threat of death or serious physical injury is necessary that threat may be express or implied, provided that where an implied threat is relied upon to constitute duress there must be evidence from the acts, conduct or words of the person alleged to have made the threat which could reasonably be construed as a threat of the required kind. *R. v. Mena* (1987), 34 C.C.C. (3d) 304 (Ont. C.A.).

The proviso in this section that the defence is unavailable where the accused was party to a conspiracy whereby he was subject to compulsion also exists at common law and therefore participation in such a conspiracy would similarly prevent an accused from relying on the common law duress defence: *R. v. Logan* (1988), 46 C.C.C. (3d) 354 (Ont. C.A.), affd on other grounds [1990] 2 S.C.R. 731, 58 C.C.C. (3d) 391.

The defence of duress is unavailable where the accused voluntarily joined a criminal organization that he knew might pressure him to engage in criminal acts: *R. v. Li* (2002), 162 C.C.C. (3d) 360 (Ont. C.A.).

The defence of duress is only available when a person commits an offence while under compulsion of a threat made for the purpose of compelling him or her to commit the offence. Accordingly, duress was not available to a battered spouse who tried to hire a hit man to kill her abusive husband: *R. v. Ryan* (2013), 290 C.C.C. (3d) 477 (S.C.C.).

COMPULSION OF SPOUSE.

18. No presumption arises that a married person who commits an offence does so under compulsion by reason only that the offence is committed in the presence of the spouse of that married person. R.S., c. C-34, s. 18; 1980-81-82-83, c. 125, s. 4.

CROSS-REFERENCES
The defence of compulsion by threats is found in s. 17.

SYNOPSIS
At common law there was an outdated presumption that a woman who committed an offence in the presence of her husband was presumed to have been coerced by him. This section abolishes this presumption.

ANNOTATIONS
This section has abolished the antiquated common law defence of marital coercion: *R. v. Robins* (1982), 66 C.C.C. (2d) 550 (Que. C.A.).

IGNORANCE OF THE LAW.

19. Ignorance of the law by a person who commits an offence is not an excuse for committing that offence. R.S., c. C-34, s. 19.

CROSS-REFERENCES

Notwithstanding the apparent breadth of this section, certain offences by their definition allow for a colour of right defence which would include at least mistake as to the civil law, for example: s. 322, theft; s. 429, mischief and arson; s. 72, forcible entry.

SYNOPSIS

This provision codifies the common law rule that *ignorance of the law is no excuse* for the commission of a criminal offence. This section does not affect the common law defence of mistake of fact which is preserved by s. 8. In addition, there may be a defence of officially induced error if an accused relies upon incorrect legal advice from governmental officials but the scope of this defence remains uncertain.

ANNOTATIONS

Ignorance of the law – By virtue of this section, ignorance, whether of the existence of the law or of its meaning, scope or application, is no defence. Thus, an accused's ignorance that a certain drug had been added to [former] Sch. H to the *Food and Drugs Act*, R.S.C. 1985, c. F-27, by regulation which was published in the *Canada Gazette,* was no defence to a charge of trafficking in that drug contrary to [former] s. 48(1) of that Act: *R. v. Molis*, [1980] 2 S.C.R. 356, 55 C.C.C. (2d) 558 (7:0).

Where, on the trial for a provincial offence, the only possible defence an accused can put forward is his ignorance of the fact that his licence had been suspended by the provisions of the provincial statute, which constitutes a mistake of law and is therefore not available as a defence, the accused is effectively denied the defence of due diligence. In those circumstances, the offence must be characterized as absolute liability: *R. v. Pontes*, [1995] 3 S.C.R. 44, 100 C.C.C. (3d) 353.

Officially induced error – By virtue of this section an accused's honest belief based on reasonable inquiries of customs authorities that certain gambling devices were legal in Canada is no defence to a charge contrary to s. 202(1)(*b*) of the *Criminal Code: R. v. Potter* (1978), 39 C.C.C. (2d) 538 (P.E.I.S.C.).

However, in *R. v. MacDougall*, [1982] 2 S.C.R. 605, 1 C.C.C. (3d) 65 (7:0), the court in dealing with a provincial offence referred to this section as "no more than a codification of the common law rule" and applicable to the provincial prosecution. Ritchie J., for the court then continued: "It is not difficult to envisage a situation in which an offence could be committed under mistake of law arising because of, and therefore induced by, "officially induced error' and if there was evidence in the present case to support such a situation existing it might well be an appropriate vehicle for applying the reasoning adopted by Mr. Justice Macdonald". Macdonald J.A. had held at 60 C.C.C. (2d) 137, 46 N.S.R. (2d) 47 (C.A.), that officially induced error was a defence to the charge, in this case driving while suspended contrary to the *Motor Vehicle Act*, R.S.N.S. 1967, c. 191.

In *R. v. Cancoil Thermal Corp. and Parkinson* (1986), 27 C.C.C. (3d) 295, 52 C.R. (3d) 188 (Ont. C.A.), the court considered officially induced error as a defence to a provincial offence. It was held that the defence is available as a defence to a "regulatory" offence where the accused reasonably relied upon the erroneous legal opinion or advice of an official who is responsible for the administration or enforcement of the particular law.

An accused must demonstrate the objective reasonableness of the advice given and the reliance on the advice. The issue must be considered from the perspective of a reasonable person in a situation similar to that of the accused: *Lévis (City) v. Tétreault; Lévis (City) v. 2629-4470 Québec Inc.*, [2006] 1 S.C.R. 420, 207 C.C.C. (3d) 1.

Mistake of fact – Unless the statute otherwise provides, as in s. 150.1, a mistake of fact is made out if the belief is honestly, *i.e.*, genuinely held. The reasonableness or unreasonableness of the belief is merely evidence from which the trier of fact may determine whether the mistake was genuine: *R. v. Pappajohn*, [1980] 2 S.C.R. 120, 52 C.C.C. (2d) 481; *R. v. Rees*, [1956] 2 S.C.R. 640, 115 C.C.C. 1.

Closely related to the defence of mistake of fact is the concept of wilful blindness. The doctrine of wilful blindness is "justified by the accused's fault in deliberately failing to inquire when he knows there is reason for inquiry" and the defence of mistake will not be available if the accused's mistake or ignorance falls within this doctrine: *R. v. Sansregret*, [1985] 1 S.C.R. 570, 18 C.C.C. (3d) 223.

Where, on the facts as he believed them to be, the accused was in fact committing a more serious offence than the offence with which he is charged then he is properly convicted of the offence, the *actus reus*, of which he committed: *R. v. Ladue*, [1965] 4 C.C.C. 264 (Y.T.C.A.).

Mistake of fact is available as a defence where the belief under which the accused claimed to have acted involved both fact and law. Mistakes of mixed fact and law were, for the purpose of the defence, considered mistakes of fact and not in conflict with this provision: *R. v. Manuel* (2008), 231 C.C.C. (3d) 468 (B.C.C.A.), leave to appeal to S.C.C. refused 233 C.C.C. (3d) vi.

A mistaken belief as to the type of narcotic being imported would not be a defence, but a mere belief by the accused that he was importing something illegal would not be sufficient *mens rea*: *R. v. Blondin* (1970), 2 C.C.C. (2d) 118 (B.C.C.A.).

On the other hand, the accused's mistake as to the nature of the drug in his possession is no defence provided that the drug is proscribed either by the [former] *Food and Drugs Act* or *Narcotic Control Act*: *R. v. Couture* (1976), 33 C.C.C. (2d) 74 (Ont. C.A.); *R. v. Futa* (1976), 31 C.C.C. (2d) 568 (B.C.C.A.).

It has been held that a provision of the Code [former s. 146, now repealed], which removed the defence of mistake of fact, was to that extent inconsistent with s. 7 of the *Charter of Rights and Freedoms* and that part of the provision was struck out: *R. v. Nguyen*, [1990] 2 S.C.R. 906, 59 C.C.C. (3d) 161 (5:2) [noted under the Charter, s. 7].

CERTAIN ACTS ON HOLIDAYS VALID.

20. A warrant or summons that is authorized by this Act or an appearance notice, promise to appear, undertaking or recognizance issued, given or entered into in accordance with Part XVI, XXI or XXVII may be issued, executed, given or entered into, as the case may be, on a holiday. R.S., c. C-34, s. 20; c. 2 (2nd Supp.), s. 2.

CROSS-REFERENCES

Definition of "holiday", see s. 35 of the *Interpretation Act*, R.S.C. 1985, c. I-21. Where the time limited for doing of a thing expires or falls on a holiday, the thing may be done on the day next following that is not a holiday . . . s. 26 of the *Interpretation Act*. The jury's verdict may be taken on Sunday or on a holiday, see s. 654.

SYNOPSIS

Warrants, summons and other forms of process created by the *Criminal Code* (*e.g.*, a promise to appear) may be validly issued, given or entered into on holidays. This section reverses a common law rule that prohibited the issuance and execution of process on holidays.

Parties to Offences

PARTIES TO OFFENCE / Common intention.

21. (1) Every one is a party to an offence who
    (a) **actually commits it;**

(*b*) does or omits to do anything for the purpose of aiding any person to commit it; or

(*c*) abets any person in committing it.

(2) Where two or more persons form an intention in common to carry out an unlawful purpose and to assist each other therein and any one of them, in carrying out the common purpose, commits an offence, each of them who knew or ought to have known that the commission of the offence would be a probable consequence of carrying out the common purpose is a party to that offence. R.S., c. C-34, s. 21.

CROSS-REFERENCES

This section defines the liability of a person for the offence actually committed by the principal. Pursuant to s. 22, an accused is also rendered liable for offences committed by a person whom he counselled to commit an offence. Liability of an organization as a party to an offence is defined in ss. 22.1 and 22.2. A series of related provisions concern other forms of liability as follows: ss. 23, 463, accessory after the fact; ss. 24, 463, attempt; s. 465, conspiracy; s. 464, counselling offence not committed; s. 23.1, as to liability of party notwithstanding person who actually commits offence cannot be convicted.

Certain provisions deal specifically with the liability of a secondary party. For example: s. 46, treason; s. 50, failing to report treason or high treason; s. 54, assisting Canada Forces deserters; s. 56, assisting R.C.M.P. deserters; s. 129(*b*), failing to assist peace officer; s. 146, assisting escape; s. 147, permitting rescue of prisoner; s. 148, assisting prisoner of war; s. 160(2), compelling person to commit bestiality; s. 167, assisting in immoral performance; ss. 170, 171, procuring or permitting sexual activity of minors; s. 201, gaming house offences; s. 210, bawdy house offences; s. 212, procuring; s. 240, accessory after the fact to murder; s. 241, counselling or aiding suicide; s. 272, party to sexual assault.

SYNOPSIS

Section 21 sets out the *liability of principals and parties* to an offence.

Section 21(1)(*a*) holds an accused liable for the role as principal (or perpetrator) if the accused personally committed that offence.

Section 21(1)(*b*) makes an accused liable as a party for acts or omissions which are done *for the purpose* of aiding a principal to commit an offence. It is not sufficient that the acts had the effect of aiding in the commission of the offence – the purpose must be proven.

Section 21(1)(*c*) makes an accused liable as a party to the offence if that accused *abetted* the principal. Abetting simply means encouraging. Merely being present is not enough, unless presence is accompanied by such additional factors as the prior knowledge that the principal was going to commit the offence.

Section 21(2) extends the liability of the principal and parties beyond the wrongful act originally intended. It encompasses other offences which are committed while carrying out the original intention if the additional offence is a *probable consequence* of carrying out the original *unlawful purpose*. The key to establishing liability for the party is proving that the accused foresaw that the resulting offence was a probable consequence of carrying out the unlawful purpose agreed to. The phrase, referring to the liability of a party, "or ought to have known" has been the subject of attack under the *Canadian Charter of Rights and Freedoms*. See the notes below under heading "Application of Charter of Rights".

ANNOTATIONS

Subsection (1) / *Liability of party generally* – Mere presence at the scene of an offence is not sufficient to ground liability under this subsection. There must be more: encouragement of the principal; an act which facilitates the commission of the offence; or an act which tends to prevent or hinder interference with accomplishment of the criminal act. Passive acquiescence is not sufficient. Presence at the scene of an offence can be evidence of aiding and abetting only if accompanied by other factors such as prior knowledge of the principal's intention to commit the offence or attendance for the purpose of encouragement: *R. v. Dunlop and Sylvester*, [1979] 2 S.C.R. 881, 47 C.C.C. (2d) 93 (4:3). And see the earlier appellate court decisions in *R. v. Salajko*, [1970] 1 C.C.C. 352 (Ont. C.A.); *R. v. Clow* (1975), 25 C.C.C. (2d) 97, 8 Nfld. & P.E.I.R. 96 (P.E.I.S.C.), and *R. v. Black*, [1970] 4 C.C.C. 251, 10 C.R.N.S. 17 (B.C.C.A.).

Where there is evidence that the offence was committed by one or more persons then it is appropriate to direct the jury as to the application of this section even on the trial of a single accused and although the identity of the other person is unknown as is the precise part played by each person. However, where there is no evidence to support the proposition that more than one person was involved then it is misdirection to charge the jury on this section: *R. v. Sparrow* (1979), 51 C.C.C. (2d) 443 (Ont. C.A.); *R. v. Isaac*, [1984] 1 S.C.R. 74, 9 C.C.C. (3d) 289 (7:0); *R. v. Thatcher*, [1987] 1 S.C.R. 652, 32 C.C.C. (3d) 481 (7:0).

The words "actually commits it" in subsec. (1)(*a*) include the case of an accused who commits an offence by means of an innocent agent: *R. v. Berryman* (1990), 57 C.C.C. (3d) 375 (B.C.C.A.).

To render a person liable as a party to attempted murder under this subsection, it is not sufficient that it be shown merely that the accused knew the principal offender intended to commit some act of violence. While the party need not necessarily have knowledge of the details of the specific crime committed by the principal, he must have some knowledge of the essential nature of the offence committed by the principal. Thus, on a charge of attempted murder, the accused must know of the principal's intention to kill: *R. v. Adams* (1989), 49 C.C.C. (3d) 100 (Ont. C.A.).

The *actus reus* of aiding or abetting is doing or omitting to do something that assists or encourages the perpetrator to commit the offence. The concepts of aiding and abetting are distinct. Aiding means to assist or help the actor. To abet includes encouraging, instigating, promoting or procuring the crime to be committed. The *mens rea* reflected in "purpose" under para. (*b*) is synonymous with intention. The Crown must prove that the accused intended to assist the principal in the commission of the offence. However, the accused need not have desired that the offence be successfully committed. In order to have the intention to assist in the commission of an offence, the aider must know that the perpetrator intends to commit the crime although he or she does not need to know precisely how it will be committed. *R. v. Kirkness*, [1990] 3 S.C.R 74, should not be read as requiring that the aider and abettor of a murder have the same *mens rea* as the actual killer. It is sufficient that, armed with the knowledge of the perpetrator's intention to commit the crime, the accused acts with the intention of assisting the perpetrator in its commission. Willful blindness can substitute for actual knowledge whenever knowledge is a component of *mens rea*. The doctrine of willful blindness imputes knowledge to an accused whose suspicion is aroused to the point where he or she sees the need for further inquiries but deliberately chooses not to make those inquiries. This is distinct from recklessness and involves no departure from the subjective inquiry into the accused's state of mind. Willful blindness is not simply a failure to inquire but deliberate ignorance: *R. v. Briscoe*, [2010] 1 S.C.R. 411, 253 C.C.C. (3d) 140.

A person may be convicted of manslaughter who aids and abets another in the offence of murder, where a reasonable person in all the circumstances would have appreciated that bodily harm was the foreseeable consequence of the dangerous act which was being undertaken; *R. v. Jackson*, [1993] 4 S.C.R. 573, 86 C.C.C. (3d) 385.

The term "for the purpose of" is essentially synonymous with "intention" and does not require proof that the accused also desired the commission of the offence: *R. v. Hibbert*, [1995] 2 S.C.R. 973, 99 C.C.C. (3d) 193.

The charge "or omitted to do anything which assisted the rape" is incorrect, it should be "or omitted to do anything for the purpose of aiding such person to commit the rape": *R. v. Cosgrove* (1975), 29 C.C.C. (2d) 169 (Ont. C.A.), leave to appeal to S.C.C. refused February 21, 1977.

A failure to act where there is a legal duty to do so can constitute an act of aiding and abetting. Any act or omission that occurs before or during the commission of the crime and which somehow and to some extent furthers, facilitates, promotes, assists or encourages the perpetrator in the commission of the crime will suffice, irrespective of any causative role in the commission of the crime: *R. v. Dooley* (2009), 249 C.C.C. (3d) 449 (Ont. C.A.), leave to appeal to S.C.C. refused [2010] 2 S.C.R. vi, 258 C.C.C. (3d) iv.

Self-induced intoxication is a defence to a charge of a general intent offence where the accused's liability depends on his being a party under para. (*b*) or para. (*c*): *R. v. Fraser* (1984), 13 C.C.C. (3d) 292 (B.C.C.A.).

The *mens rea* required is proof of actual knowledge or willful blindness but does not include recklessness: *R. v. Roach* (2004), 192 C.C.C. (3d) 557 (Ont. C.A.).

Abetting – "Abets" means to encourage and while it is common to speak of "aiding and abetting", the two concepts are not the same and either activity constitutes a sufficient basis of liability: *R. v. Meston* (1975), 28 C.C.C. (2d) 497 (Ont. C.A.).

Although subsec. (1)(*c*) does not provide that the words or actions must be for the purpose of abetting the person nevertheless the Crown must prove that the accused intended that the words or acts would encourage the principal: *R. v. Curran* (1977), 38 C.C.C. (2d) 151 (Alta. S.C. App. Div.), motion for leave to appeal to S.C.C. dismissed 20 N.R. 180*n*.

An accused who is present at the scene of the offence and who carries out no act to aid or encourage the commission of the offence may, nevertheless, be convicted as a party, if his purpose in failing to act was to aid in the commission of the offence and the accused was under a duty to act. Thus, a police officer who was the officer in charge of the lock-up could be convicted as a party to an assault committed by another officer on a prisoner. The accused was under a statutory and common law duty to protect the prisoner and his failure to act to prevent the assault may be found to have encouraged the commission of the offence: *R. v. Nixon* (1990), 57 C.C.C. (3d) 97 (B.C.C.A.).

Involvement of party undetermined – This section precludes a requirement of jury unanimity as to the particular nature of the accused's participation in the offence, whether he personally committed the offence or aided or abetted someone else to commit the offence: *R. v. Thatcher*, [1987] 1 S.C.R. 652, 32 C.C.C. (3d) 481.

Where, on a charge of murder, evidence shows that the accused acted in concert pursuant to a common motive, there is no requirement that the jury be instructed that if it could not decide which of the accused had administered the fatal beating to the deceased then all must be acquitted. In such circumstances, it is open to the jury to convict all accused as aiders or abettors although the extent of individual participation in the violence is unclear: *R. v. Wood* (1989), 51 C.C.C. (3d) 201 (Ont. C.A.).

Two persons may both be actual committers of an offence even though each has not performed every act which constitutes the *actus reus* of the offence. Where co-perpetrators engaged in a deadly assault, the Crown is not required to prove which attacker struck the fatal blow. For the purpose of subsec. (1)(*a*), agreement to carry out a common purpose is not necessary. The issue is whether there was an indication of common participation. In this case, where the death occurred in the context of a swarming of two individuals, it did not matter that each attacker did not lay a hand on each person assaulted: *R. v. Ball* (2011), 267 C.C.C. (3d) 532 (B.C.C.A.), leave to appeal to S.C.C. refused November 24, 2011.

Liability as a party to a conspiracy is limited to cases where the accused aids or abets the initial formation of the agreement, or aids or abets a new member to join a pre-existing agreement. Aiding or abetting the furtherance of the unlawful object does not establish aiding or abetting the principal with any element of the offence of conspiracy, and thus cannot ground party liability for conspiracy. However, where a person, with knowledge of a conspiracy, does or omits to do something for the purpose of furthering the unlawful object, with the knowledge and consent of one or more of the existing conspirators, this provides powerful circumstantial evidence from which membership in the conspiracy can be inferred: *R. v. F. (J.)*, [2013] 1 S.C.R. 565, 293 C.C.C. (3d) 377. See also: *R. v. Trieu* (2008), 429 A.R. 200 (C.A.). The broader approach to party liability proposed in *R. v. McNamara (No. 1)* (1981), 56 C.C.C. (2d) 193 (Ont. C.A.), affd [1985] 1 S.C.R. 662, *sub nom. Canadian*

Dredge & Dock Co. v. R., 19 C.C.C. (3d) 1, must now be read in light of *R. v. F. (J.)*, *supra*.

Relationship to corporate liability – The fact that the acts of an individual accused were at law those of his corporation, which was also charged, for the purpose of imposing liability on the corporation, does not prevent the conviction of the individual accused either as a principal or as a party under this subsection: *R. v. Fell* (1981), 64 C.C.C. (2d) 456, 131 D.L.R. (3d) 105 (Ont. C.A.).

Subsection (2) | *Application of Charter of Rights* – If the offence with which the accused is charged is one of the few for which s. 7 of the Charter requires a minimum degree of *mens rea*, then Parliament is precluded from providing for the conviction of a party to that offence on the basis of a degree of *mens rea* below the constitutionally required minimum. Thus, since it has been determined that as a constitutional requirement no one can be convicted of murder unless the Crown proves that the person had subjective foresight of the death of the victim, then a party cannot be convicted on the basis of any lesser *mens rea*. Similarly, the constitutionally required minimum for attempted murder is subjective foresight of the consequences and so the party to a charge of attempted murder cannot be convicted on any lesser *mens rea*. To the extent that subsec. (2) would allow for the conviction of a party to the offence of attempted murder or murder on the basis of objective foresight, it is of no force and effect. Accordingly, the words "or ought to have known" in subsec. (2) must be declared inoperative in such a case: *R. v. Logan*, [1990] 2 S.C.R. 731, 58 C.C.C. (3d) 391; *R. v. Rodney*, [1990] 2 S.C.R. 687, 58 C.C.C. (3d) 408.

Since there is no constitutional requirement of foresight of death for the offence of manslaughter, liability for that offence may be based on objective liability and the words "or ought to have known" are operative: *R. v. Jackson* (1991), 68 C.C.C. (3d) 385 (Ont. C.A.), affd [1993] 4 S.C.R. 573, 86 C.C.C. (3d) 385. *Contra*: *R. v. Haché* (2007), 227 C.C.C. (3d) 162 (N.B.C.A.).

Application of subsection generally – This subsection has no application where the unlawful purpose is the same as the offence charged. This subsection covers the case where, in the absence of aiding and abetting, a person may become a party to an offence committed by another which he knew or ought to have known was a probable consequence of carrying out the unlawful purpose: *R. v. Simpson and Ochs*, [1988] 1 S.C.R. 3, 38 C.C.C. (3d) 481.

This subsection may be resorted to on a possession charge. The liability of the accused is not confined to s. 4(3): *R. v. Zanini*, [1967] S.C.R. 715, [1968] 2 C.C.C. 1 (5:0), where it was also held that an accused may be convicted as a party to the offence committed by his companions notwithstanding the charge against them had been withdrawn.

In a "gang rape" situation it was held that the trial judge erred in leaving this subsection to the jury where there was no evidence that the accused, although present at the scene, were part of a plan to lure the victim there as part of the motorcycle gang's initiation rites: *R. v. Dunlop and Sylvester*, [1979] 2 S.C.R. 881, 47 C.C.C. (2d) 93 (4:3).

The expression "intention in common" means only that the party and principal must have in mind the same unlawful purpose and does not require proof of a mutuality of motives and desires between them: *R. v. Hibbert*, [1995] 2 S.C.R. 973, 99 C.C.C. (3d) 193.

Where three accused were charged with a murder committed in the course of a robbery, the judge was required to make clear to the jury that guilt could only be found under this section if each accused had actual foresight or knowledge that another accused would stab the deceased with intent to kill in carrying out the robbery: *R. v. Laliberty* (1997), 117 C.C.C. (3d) 97 (Ont. C.A.).

This provision is applicable to render a party guilty of second degree murder where the common unlawful purpose is assault and the accused knew that murder would be a probable consequence of carrying out that assault: *R. v. Rochon* (2003), 173 C.C.C. (3d) 321 (Ont. C.A.), leave to appeal to S.C.C. refused [2004] 3 S.C.R. xii, 188 C.C.C. (3d) vi; *R. v. Young* (2009), 246 C.C.C. (3d) 417 (Ont. C.A.), leave to appeal to S.C.C. refused 251 C.C.C. (3d) vii.

Liability of party for offence committed by principal – In *R. v. Jackson*, [1993] 4 S.C.R. 573, 86 C.C.C. (3d) 385, the court held that the wording of this subsection did not preclude the conviction of the party of manslaughter although the principal offender was convicted of murder. If the accused party did not foresee the probability of murder by the principal offender, but a reasonable person in all the circumstances would have foreseen at least a risk of harm to another as a result of carrying out the common intention, the party could be found guilty of manslaughter. Liability of manslaughter under this subsection does not depend upon proof that a reasonable person would have foreseen the risk of death. [Note: The holding that the party could be convicted of a different offence than the principal appears to have been based, in part, on the theory that the words "the offence" and "that offence" in subsec. (2) refer not only to the actual offence committed by the principal offender but encompass all included offences. The court had no occasion to consider the reverse situation where it is sought to render the party liable for a more serious offence than the principal. On this latter issue, see the earlier decision in *R. v. Hebert* (1986), 51 C.R. (3d) 264, 68 N.B.R. (2d) 379 (C.A.), leave to appeal to S.C.C. refused 76 N.B.R. (2d) 360*n*, 72 N.R. 79*n*, holding that where the principal was convicted of manslaughter the party could not be convicted of murder under this subsection.]

Liability for first degree murder under s. 231(5) can be made out pursuant to s. 21(2). While liability for first degree murder under s. 231(5) is premised on active participation in the murder, that liability flows from the participant's acts, not any additional mental element. Provided the participant's conduct was a substantial cause of the death and the other elements of s. 231(5) are made out including liability for murder and the underlying crime, the accused can be found guilty of murder as a party. Liability under s. 231(5) would also flow if the party, while not intending to kill the victim, knew that the principal offender would probably commit murder in carrying out the unlawful purpose. The participation by the party is the same whether the party intended to kill or merely knew that the principal offender would probably commit murder: *R. v. Ferrari* (2012), 287 C.C.C. (3d) 503 (Ont. C.A.).

An accused's conviction as a party to first degree murder where the principal was only convicted of second degree murder does not violate s. 7 of the *Charter of Rights and Freedoms*: *R. v. Huard* (2013), 302 C.C.C. (3d) 469 (Ont. C.A.), leave to appeal to S.C.C. refused 2014 CarswellOnt 4229.

Abandonment – For the defence of abandonment there must be evidence of timely and reasonable unequivocal notice by the accused to his co-accused of his intention to abandon the common criminal purposes before the crime was committed: *R. v. Miller and Cockriell*, [1977] 2 S.C.R. 680, 31 C.C.C. (2d) 177 (9:0).

Under either s. 21(1) or (2), the defence of abandonment requires: (1) an intention to abandon or withdraw from the unlawful purpose; (2) timely communication of abandonment or withdrawal from the person in question to those who wished to continue; (3) the communication served unequivocal notice upon those who wished to continue; and (4) that the accused took reasonable steps in the circumstances either to neutralize or otherwise cancel out the effects of his participation or to prevent the commission of the offence. There will be circumstances in which timely and unequivocal communication by the accused of his intention to abandon the unlawful purpose will be sufficient to neutralize the effects of his participation in the crime. But there will be other circumstances, primarily where a person has aided in the commission of the offence, in which it is hard to see how timely communication to the principal offender of the person's intention to withdraw from the unlawful purpose would, on its own, be considered reasonable and sufficient: *R. c. Gauthier*, [2013] 2 S.C.R. 403, 298 C.C.C. (3d) 277.

The accused was charged with another with murder. The evidence indicated that the co-accused sexually assaulted the victim after he and the accused broke into her house, and then the co-accused strangled and suffocated the victim. In the course of the strangulation the accused told the co-accused to stop as he would kill her. This statement to the co-accused constituted timely notice that the co-accused was from that point on acting on his own and that the accused was not a party to the strangulation and suffocation. Thus even if the accused could be considered a party to the earlier sexual assault by the time of the attempted strangulation he had clearly resiled from any agreement or arrangement with the co-accused and was not party to the suffocation of the victim: *R. v. Kirkness*, [1990] 3 S.C.R. 74, 60 C.C.C. (3d) 97 (5:2).

Evidence – In *R. v. Vetrovec; R. v. Gaja*, [1982] 1 S.C.R. 811, 67 C.C.C. (2d) 1 (9:0) (affirming *R. v. Vetrovec* (1980), 58 C.C.C. (2d) 537 (B.C.C.A.)), the Supreme Court of Canada had occasion to re-examine the question of the mandatory accomplice warning. The court held that it is no longer a rule of law that a trial judge must direct the jury that it is dangerous to act on the uncorroborated evidence of an accomplice. An accomplice is to be treated like any other witness testifying at a criminal trial and the judge's conduct if he chooses to give his opinion, is governed by the general rules. Thus a judge may properly consider that he should instruct the jury that in the circumstances the jury should, as a matter of prudence, look for evidence which confirms the story of such a witness. A clear and sharp warning to attract the attention of the juror to the risks of adopting, without more, the evidence of the witness, may be appropriate. The judge may, as well, properly illustrate from the evidence the kind of evidence which might be drawn upon by the juror in confirmation of the witness' testimony or some important part thereof. This common sense approach applies to other kinds of witnesses such as a disreputable witness of demonstrated moral lack or other situations where corroboration was required at common law. It does not of course apply where corroboration is required by statute as in s. 133.

In providing a *Vetrovec* warning, the court should draw the attention of the jury to the testimonial evidence requiring special scrutiny, explain why this evidence is subject to special scrutiny, caution the jury that it is dangerous to convict on unconfirmed evidence of this sort though the jury is entitled to do so if satisfied that the evidence is true, and instruct the jury that, in determining the veracity of the suspect evidence, it should look for evidence from another source tending to show that the untrustworthy witness is telling the truth as to the guilt of the accused. Not all evidence presented at trial is capable of confirming the testimony of an impugned witness. The attribute of independence defines the kind of evidence that is capable of constituting confirmation. Where evidence is tainted by connection to the *Vetrovec* witness, it cannot serve to confirm his or her testimony. While individual items of confirmatory evidence need not implicate the accused, when looked at in the context of the case as a whole, the items of confirmatory evidence should give comfort to the jury that the witness can be trusted in his assertion that the accused is the person who committed the offence. Confirmatory evidence must be capable of restoring the trier's faith in the relevant aspects of the witness' evidence. Accordingly, where the only issue in dispute is whether the accused committed the offence, the trier must be comforted that the impugned witness is telling the truth in that regard before convicting on the strength of the witness' evidence: *R. v. Khela*, [2009] 1 S.C.R. 104, 238 C.C.C. (3d) 489.

There is no requirement that the jury be instructed to make separate and distinct assessments of an accomplice's credibility as it related to each accused, as it is inevitable that the assessment of the overall credibility of the accomplice would be influenced by the totality of the evidence heard at trial, including that relating solely to one accused: *R. v. Rojas*, [2008] 3 S.C.R. 111, 236 C.C.C. (3d) 153.

Independent evidence to be confirmatory does not have to implicate the accused. The evidence should, however, be capable of restoring the trier's faith in the relevant aspects of the witness's evidence, although not necessarily a disputed aspect of the witness's evidence. Where a particular risk attaches to one critical element of the evidence of a disreputable witness, the trier of fact must be satisfied that the potentially unreliable evidence of the witness can be relied upon as truthful in that regard. Such a risk may arise where there is any basis in the record for suggesting that the unsupported evidence of an accomplice, though evidently truthful as to his own participation in the offence charged, is for any reason subject to particular caution as regards his implication of the accused: *R. v. Kehler*, [2004] 1 S.C.R. 328, 181 C.C.C. (3d) 1.

The trial judge has a discretion to determine whether the evidence of any witness is for some reason untrustworthy to such an extent that a warning to the jury is necessary. However, if a warning is given regarding a particular witness it is not the case that the trial judge must always go on to point out in detail evidence which is capable of corroborating that witnesses testimony. While an instruction of that nature may be given in tandem with the clear sharp warning, it is not a requirement in all cases. The extent to which the trial judge should refer to potentially corroborative evidence depends upon the circumstances of the case, although it is not required, nor would it be appropriate, that the potentially corroborative evidence be reviewed exhaustively: *R. v. Bevan*, [1993] 2 S.C.R. 599, 82 C.C.C. (3d) 310.

Also see *R. v. Brooks*, [2000] 1 S.C.R. 237, 141 C.C.C. (3d) 321, holding that the prosecutorial use of jailhouse informants generally calls for special caution. Whether a warning should be given for a particular witness depends upon the credibility of the witness and the importance of the evidence to the Crown's case. In this case, a majority of the court held that a *Vetrovec* warning should have been given in relation to the two informants to whom the accused allegedly confessed. (A different majority upheld the accused's conviction although no warning had been given.)

Collusion among "*Vetrovec*" witnesses does not necessarily prevent the evidence of one such witness from confirming the evidence of another. Whether the witness's evidence is so tainted by collusion that it loses its required independence and cannot reasonably be used as confirmation is a matter for the jury to decide: *R. v. Magno* (2015), 321 C.C.C. (3d) 554 (Ont. C.A.), leave to appeal to S.C.C. refused 2015 CarswellOnt 10830.

The so-called co-conspirators exception to the hearsay rule that acts or declarations done in furtherance of a common criminal design are admissible against all the parties thereto applies in all situations where one person is talking or acting on behalf of another and not just when the charge is one of conspiracy: *R. v. Koufis*, [1941] S.C.R. 481, 76 C.C.C. 161.

PERSON COUNSELLING OFFENCE / Idem / Definition of "counsel".

22. (1) Where a person counsels another person to be a party to an offence and that other person is afterwards a party to that offence, the person who counselled is a party to that offence, notwithstanding that the offence was committed in a way different from that which was counselled.

(2) Every one who counsels another person to be a party to an offence is a party to every offence that the other commits in consequence of the counselling that the person who counselled knew or ought to have known was likely to be committed in consequence of the counselling.

(3) For the purposes of this Act, "counsel" includes procure, solicit or incite. R.S., c. C-34, s. 22; R.S.C. 1985, c. 27 (1st Supp.), s. 7(1).

CROSS-REFERENCES

Section 464, where the offence counselled is not committed; s. 23.1, as to liability of accused notwithstanding, person counselled cannot be convicted of the offence; s. 53(*b*), inciting mutiny; s. 56(*a*), counselling R.C.M.P. member to desert or go absent without leave; s. 62(1)(*c*), counselling disloyalty, mutiny, etc., of member of military forces. As to terrorism offences, see s. 83.01(1), definition of "terrorist activity".

SYNOPSIS

This section, like s. 21, defines when a person is party to an offence as a result of counselling commission of an offence.

Subsection (3) provides a non-exhaustive definition of *counsel* stating that it includes procure, solicit or incite.

Subsection (1) requires proof that the person who was *counselled* by the accused *actually was a party to* the offence counselled. If that is established, the accused is a *party* to that offence, even if it is committed in a different way than that suggested by the accused.

Subsection (2) applies when the person counselled commits an additional offence as a consequence of committing the offence originally counselled by the accused. It must be shown that the accused (counsellor) *knew or ought to have known* that the additional offence was the consequence of counselling the original offence. If the liability of the counselled accused for the additional offence is based on proof of a subjective mental element, it is doubtful that the phrase "or ought to have known" can be relied upon as a basis of liability, as it would impose liability for an objective intent upon the counsellor, which would likely be a violation of the accused's rights under ss. 7 and 11(*d*) of the Charter.

ANNOTATIONS

The *mens rea* for counseling a specific offence is the same whether or not the offence counseled is actually committed. The requisite mental element requires that the counselor intend the commission of the offence counseled be committed or that the result of his conduct was that the offence would actually be committed. Recklessness is insufficient as it may attach liability to instances of counseling that are casual or accidental: *R. v. Janeteas* (2003), 172 C.C.C. (3d) 97, 11 C.R. (6th) 330 (Ont. C.A.).

The offence of counseling to commit the offence of inciting genocide or hatred requires that the statements, viewed objectively, actively promote, advocate, or encourage the commission of the offence described in them. The criminal act will be made out where the statements are likely to incite and are made with a view to inciting the commission of the offence. An intention to bring about the criminal result, in that the counselor intended the commission of the offence, will satisfy the requisite *mens rea* for the offence of counseling: *Mugesera v. Canada (Minister of Citizenship and Immigration)*, [2005] 2 S.C.R. 100, 197 C.C.C. (3d) 233.

OFFENCES OF NEGLIGENCE / Organizations.

22.1 In respect of an offence that requires the prosecution to prove negligence, an organization is a party to the offence if
> (*a*) **acting within the scope of their authority**
>> (i) **one of its representatives is a party to the offence, or**
>> (ii) **two or more of its representatives engage in conduct, whether by act or omission, such that, if it had been the conduct of only one representative, that representative would have been a party to the offence; and**
> (*b*) **the senior officer who is responsible for the aspect of the organization's activities that is relevant to the offence departs — or the senior officers, collectively, depart — markedly from the standard of care that, in the circumstances, could reasonably be expected to prevent a representative of the organization from being a party to the offence. 2003, c. 21, s. 2.**

CROSS-REFERENCES

The terms "organization", "representative" and "senior officer" are defined in s. 2. Section 22.2 defines the liability of an organization as a party to the offence where the offence requires proof of fault other than negligence. Section 21 sets out the liability of a party to an offence.

SYNOPSIS

This section defines the liability of an organization as a party to an offence, where the offence is one that only requires proof of negligence. The prosecution must prove two elements to render the organization liable for the negligence of a representative of the organization. The first element, in effect, requires proof that a representative or representatives acting within the scope of their authority were parties to the offence, which would be determined in accordance with normal party liability principles, for example, as set out in s. 21. Second, there must be proof that a senior officer who is responsible for the aspect of the organization's activities that is relevant to the offence departs markedly from the standard of care that could reasonably be expected to prevent the representative from being a party to the offence.

ANNOTATIONS

Note: The following case was decided before the enactment of this section and s. 22.2 and therefore must be applied with care to cases involving liability of organizations.

In *R. v. Sault Ste. Marie (City)*, [1978] 2 S.C.R. 1299, 40 C.C.C. (2d) 353, Dickson J., for the court, considered the issue of corporate responsibility with respect to a strict liability offence for which proof of due diligence would be a defence. Dickson J. pointed out that, where an employer is charged in respect of an act committed by an employee acting in the course of employment, the question will be whether the act took place without the accused's direction or approval, thus negating wilful involvement of the accused, and whether the accused exercised all reasonable care by establishing a proper system to prevent commission of the offence and by taking reasonable steps to ensure the effective operation of the system. The availability of the defence to a corporation will depend on whether such due diligence was taken by those who are the directing mind and will of the corporation, whose acts are therefore in law the acts of the corporation itself.

OTHER OFFENCES / Organizations.

22.2 In respect of an offence that requires the prosecution to prove fault — other than negligence — an organization is a party to the offence if, with the intent at least in part to benefit the organization, one of its senior officers

    (a) acting within the scope of their authority, is a party to the offence;

    (b) having the mental state required to be a party to the offence and acting within the scope of their authority, directs the work of other representatives of the organization so that they do the act or make the omission specified in the offence; or

    (c) knowing that a representative of the organization is or is about to be a party to the offence, does not take all reasonable measures to stop them from being a party to the offence. 2003, c. 21, s. 2.

CROSS-REFERENCES

The terms "organization", "representative" and "senior officer" are defined in s. 2. Section 22.1 defines the liability of an organization as a party to the offence where the offence only requires proof of negligence. Section 21 sets out the liability of a party to an offence.

SYNOPSIS

This section defines the liability of an organization as a party to an offence, where the offence is one that requires proof of fault other than negligence. The prosecution must prove that one of the senior officers at least had the intent in part to benefit the organization. In addition, the prosecution must prove one of three alternatives bases for liability: one of the senior officer acting within the scope of their authority was a party to the office; the senior officer had the *mens rea* for the offence, was acting within the scope of authority and directed the work of other representatives to perform the *actus reus* of the offence; or the senior officer did not take reasonable measures to stop the commission of the offence by a representative.

ANNOTATIONS

Note: The following cases were decided before the enactment of this section and s. 22.2 and therefore must be applied with care to cases involving liability of organizations.

In the case of true criminal offences requiring proof of *mens rea*, liability is attributed to the corporate accused through the identification theory of liability. This theory produces the element of *mens rea* in the corporate entity. The theory establishes the identity between the directing mind and the corporation that results in the corporation being found guilty for the act of the natural person, the employee. The identity of the directing mind and the corporation coincide and the corporation is liable so long as the actions of the directing mind are performed by the manager within the sector of operation assigned to him by the corporation. The sector may be functional or geographic or may embrace the entire undertaking of the corporation. The act in question must be done by the directing force of the company when carrying out his assigned function in the corporation. Acts of the ego of a corporation taken within the assigned managerial area may give rise to corporate criminal responsibility whether or not there is formal delegation; whether or not there is awareness of the activity in the board of directors or the officers of the company, and whether or not there is express prohibition from the board of directors. The identity doctrine merges the board of directors, the managing director, the superintendent, the manager or anyone else to whom the board of directors has delegated the governing executive authority of the corporation, and the conduct of any of the merged entities is thereby attributed to the corporation. Accordingly, a corporation may have more than one directing mind. However, the outer limit of the delegation doctrine is reached and exceeded when the directing mind ceases completely to act, in fact or in substance, in the interests of the corporation. The identification doctrine, accordingly, only operates where the Crown demonstrates that the action taken by the directing mind was within the field of operation assigned to him, was not totally in fraud of the corporation and was by design or result partly for the benefit of the company: *R. v. Canadian Dredge & Dock Co.*, [1985] 1 S.C.R. 662, 19 C.C.C. (3d) 1 (8:0). Also see *"Rhone" (The) v. "Peter A.B. Widener" (The)*, [1993] 1 S.C.R. 497, 101 D.L.R. (4th) 188.

ACCESSORY AFTER THE FACT.

23. (1) An accessory after the fact to an offence is one who, knowing that a person has been a party to the offence, receives, comforts or assists that person for the purpose of enabling that person to escape. R.S., c. C-34, s. 23; 1974-75-76, c. 66, s. 7; 2000, c. 12, s. 92.

(2) [*Repealed*, 2000, c. 12, s. 92.]

CROSS-REFERENCES

The punishment and classification of the offence of accessory after the fact is found in s. 463, except for accessory after the fact to murder, see s. 240. The effect of s. 463 is that the accessory's liability depends on the nature of the offence to which he or she is an accessory. For example, an accessory after the fact to the indictable offence of robbery which has a maximum punishment of life imprisonment is by virtue of s. 463(*a*) guilty of an indictable offence and liable to imprisonment for 14 years. The mode of trial will be determined by the nature of the offence. For example, an accessory after the fact to robbery will have an election under s. 536(2). Certain offences are, however, within the absolute jurisdiction of a provincial court judge pursuant to s. 553(*b*). For example, accessory after the fact to theft of goods of a value not exceeding one thousand dollars where the prosecution elects to proceed by way of indictment is pursuant to s. 553(*b*) within the absolute jurisdiction of a provincial court judge. Note as well that, by virtue of s. 469(*b*), the offences of accessory after the fact to high treason, treason or murder may be tried only by the superior court of criminal jurisdiction (defined in s. 2).

Section 23.1, liability of accessory after the fact although person assisted cannot be convicted.

Section 592, indictment of accessory after the fact, whether or not the principal has been indicted, convicted or is amenable to justice. Under s. 657.2(2), where an accused is charged with being an accessory after the fact, evidence of the conviction or discharge of another person of the offence is admissible against the accused and, in the absence of evidence to the contrary, is proof that the offence was committed.

Section 54, specific offence for assisting, harbouring, etc., deserter or absentee without leave from Canadian Forces and s. 56(*b*), deserter or absentee without leave of member of R.C.M.P. As to terrorism offences, see s. 83.01(1), definition of "terrorist activity".

SYNOPSIS

It is an offence under this section to be an *accessory* after the commission of a crime.

The *actus reus* of the offence is described as *receiving, comforting or assisting* another after that person has committed an offence. The mental element requires that the accused *knew that the person assisted* has been a party to an offence and that the acts were done *for the purpose* of assisting that person to escape. Proof that the acts had the effect of assisting the party to the prior offence to escape is not sufficient.

ANNOTATIONS

Elements of offence – Mere failure to disclose the fact that an offence has been committed in his presence does not make the accused an accessory after the fact: *R. v. Dumont* (1921), 37 C.C.C. 166, 64 D.L.R. 128 (Ont. C.A.); nor does the mere failure to aid in the apprehension of the principal: *R. v. Young* (1950), 98 C.C.C. 195, 10 C.R. 142 (Que. C.A.).

The charge must allege the commission of a specific offence and the Crown must prove that the alleged accessory knew that the person assisted was a party to that offence. This burden will be met if it is proven that the accused had actual knowledge of the offence committed or actual suspicion combined with a conscious decision not to make inquiries which could confirm that suspicion. Where the accused chooses to make no inquiries, speculation as to what the accused would have learned if the inquiries had been made is irrelevant to the determination of the blameworthiness of that accused's state of mind: *R. v. Duong* (1998), 124 C.C.C. (3d) 392, 15 C.R. (5th) 209 (Ont. C.A.).

Trial of accessory after the fact although no conviction of principal offender – In *R. v. S. (F.J.)* (1997), 115 C.C.C. (3d) 450, 159 N.S.R. (2d) 285 (C.A.), affd [1998] 1 S.C.R. 88, 121 C.C.C. (3d) 223, 165 N.S.R. (2d) 160, Jones J.A., for the court, held that in light of ss. 23.1 and 592, it is not necessary to convict a principal in order to convict an accessory. Further, while the language does not refer to the acquittal of the principal, the words, "whether or not the principal or any other party to the offence has been indicted or convicted", in s. 592, are broad enough to encompass the acquittal of the principal. On appeal by the accused, the Supreme Court of Canada, "substantially for the reasons of Jones J.A.", dismissed the appeal. This would appear to overrule the earlier decision in *R. v. Vinette*, [1975] 2 S.C.R. 222, 19 C.C.C. (2d) 1, 50 D.L.R. (3d) 697, where the court held that an accessory after the fact may not be tried or tender a valid plea of guilty until the principal is convicted, so that if the latter is acquitted, the accessory must of necessity be discharged.

The decision in *R. v. S. (F.J.)*, *supra*, would also appear to confirm the correctness of these earlier decisions: In *R. v. Anderson* (1980), 57 C.C.C. (2d) 255, 26 A.R. 172 (C.A.), leave to appeal to S.C.C. refused 28 A.R. 498*n*, 35 N.R. 356*n*, the court held that an accessory after the fact can be convicted, notwithstanding there is no evidence the principal was convicted, if the Crown proves that the principal committed the offence. Further, in tendering such proof, any evidence that is admissible against the principal is admissible against the accessory. A similar conclusion was reached in *R. v. McAvoy* (1981), 60 C.C.C. (2d) 95, 21 C.R. (3d) 305 (Ont. C.A.). Similarly, in *R. v. Camponi* (1993), 82 C.C.C. (3d) 506, 22 C.R. (4th) 348 (B.C.C.A.), it was held that, especially in light of s. 23.1, the accessory could be convicted although the charge against the principal offender has been stayed.

WHERE ONE PARTY CANNOT BE CONVICTED.

23.1 For greater certainty, sections 21 to 23 apply in respect of an accused notwithstanding the fact that the person whom the accused aids or abets, counsels or procures or receives, comforts or assists cannot be convicted of the offence. R.S.C. 1985, c. 24 (2nd Supp.), s. 45.

CROSS-REFERENCES
Section 592, indictment of accessory after the fact, whether or not the principal has been indicted, convicted or is amenable to justice.

SYNOPSIS
This section has been recently added to the *Criminal Code* to clarify that an accused may be convicted under ss. 21 to 23 even if the principal whom the accused aids, abets, counsels or in relation to whose offence the accused is an accessory after the fact cannot be convicted. Examples of circumstances under which the other accused may not be convicted would be if the person is under 12 years or is not guilty by reason of insanity.

ANNOTATIONS
An accessory after the fact may be convicted even if the principal is acquitted: *R. v. S. (F.J.)* (1997), 115 C.C.C. (3d) 450, 159 N.S.R. (2d) 285 (C.A.), affd [1998] 1 S.C.R. 88, 121 C.C.C. (3d) 223, 165 N.S.R. (2d) 160.

ATTEMPTS / Question of law.

24. (1) Every one who, having an intent to commit an offence, does or omits to do anything for the purpose of carrying out his intention is guilty of an attempt to commit the offence whether or not it was possible under the circumstances to commit the offence.

(2) The question whether an act or omission by a person who has an intent to commit an offence is or is not mere preparation to commit the offence, and too remote to constitute an attempt to commit the offence, is a question of law. R.S., c. C-34, s. 24.

CROSS-REFERENCES
The punishment and classification of the offence of attempt is found in s. 463, except for certain offences such as attempted murder, see s. 239 and certain terrorist offences, see s. 83.01(1), definition of "terrorist activity". Certain other substantive offences resemble attempts such as treason and high treason, s. 46, 47; mutiny, s. 53; attempt to influence municipal official, s. 123; bribery of judicial officers, members of Parliament or the legislature, s. 119; bribery of other officers, s. 120; obstruct justice, s. 139. These provisions set out the classification and punishment for the offence. The effect of s. 463 for other attempt offences is that the accused's liability depends on the nature of the offence which he attempted to commit. For example, robbery has a maximum punishment of life imprisonment and, thus, by virtue of s. 463(*a*), a person convicted of attempted robbery is guilty of an indictable offence and liable to imprisonment for 14 years. The mode of trial will be determined by the nature of the offence. For example, an accused charged with attempted robbery will have an election under s. 536(2). Certain offences are, however, within the absolute jurisdiction of a provincial court judge pursuant to s. 553(*b*). For example, attempted theft of goods of a value not exceeding one thousand dollars where the prosecution elects to proceed by way of indictment is pursuant to s. 553(*b*) within the absolute jurisdiction of a provincial court judge. Note as well that, by virtue of s. 469(*d*), an attempt to commit the offences in ss. 47, 49, 51, 53, 61, 74, and 75 may be tried only by the superior court of criminal jurisdiction (defined in s. 2). Thus, attempted murder is not within the exclusive jurisdiction of the superior court of criminal jurisdiction and the accused has his election as to mode of trial pursuant to s. 536(2). The offence described by s. 119 which includes attempt to obtain a bribe (subsec.

(1)(*a*)(iii)) where the accused is the holder of a judicial office, can only be tried by the superior court of criminal jurisdiction by virtue of s. 469(*c*).

Sections 660 and 661 make provision for conviction of an accused for attempt where the full offence is charged, and conviction of the accused for the attempt charged although the full offence is proved.

SYNOPSIS

This section creates liability for attempting to commit an offence regardless of whether it was factually possible to commit.

Subsection (1) sets out that it must be proven that the accused intended to commit an offence and did or attempted to do anything for the purpose of committing that offence. The *mens rea* for the offence of attempt will vary with the mental element required to commit the full offence attempted.

A vexing aspect of this section is determining whether the acts of the accused have progressed beyond mere preparation to commit the offence to an attempt to commit it. It is not necessary to show that the accused's acts were unlawful. Subsection (2) states that whether the acts done by an accused proven to have the requisite *mens rea*, constitutes an attempt or mere preparation is a question of law and is therefore to be determined by a judge. However, it is no defence, if the acts were done with intention, that the offence could not be committed only because the would-be victim of the offence (for example in a case of fraud or public mischief) was not deceived by the acts.

ANNOTATIONS

Distinction between preparation and attempt – In *R. v. Cline* (1956), 115 C.C.C. 18, 24 C.R. 58 (Ont. C.A.), the court substituted a conviction of an attempt to commit the offence charged. The court said that there can be no general test to distinguish attempt from preparation, but laid down the following propositions:

1. There must be both *mens rea* and an *actus reus* to constitute a criminal attempt, but the criminality of misconduct lay mainly in the intention of the accused.
2. Evidence of similar acts done by the accused before the offence with which he is charged, and also afterwards, if not too remote in time, was admissible to establish a pattern of conduct from which the court might properly find *mens rea*.
3. Such evidence might be advanced in the case for the prosecution without waiting for the defence to raise a specific issue.
4. It was not essential that the *actus reus* be a crime or a tort or even a moral wrong or social mischief.
5. The *actus reus* must be more than mere preparation to commit a crime.
6. But when the preparation was fully complete and ended, the next step done by the accused for the purpose and with the intention of committing a specific crime constituted an *actus reus* sufficient in law to establish a criminal attempt to commit that crime.

Where the accused's intention is otherwise proved, acts which on the face are equivocal may none the less be sufficiently proximate to constitute an attempt. However, where there is no such extrinsic evidence as to the accused's intent acts which on the face are equivocal may be insufficient to show the acts were done with intent to commit the crime charged: *R. v. Sorrell and Bondett* (1978), 41 C.C.C. (2d) 9 (Ont. C.A.).

No satisfactory general criterion can be formulated for drawing a line between preparation and attempt. The application of the distinction to the facts of a particular case must be left to common-sense judgment. The distinction is essentially a qualitative one, involving the relationship between the nature and quality of the act in question and the nature of the complete offence, although consideration must necessarily be given, in making that qualitative distinction, to the relative proximity of the act in question to what would have been the completed offence, in terms of time, location and acts under the control of the accused remaining to be accomplished. While relative proximity may give an act which might otherwise appear to be mere preparation the quality of an attempt, an act which on its face is an act of commission, does not lose its quality as the *actus reus* of attempt because further acts were required or because a significant period of time may have to elapse before the completion of the offence: *R. v. Deutsch*, [1986] 2 S.C.R. 2, 27 C.C.C. (3d) 385 (5:0). See also *R. v. Root* (2008), 241 C.C.C. (3d) 125 (Ont. C.A.), leave to appeal to S.C.C. refused 247 C.C.C. (3d) vi.

"Impossible" attempt – Canadian law does not recognize the distinction between legal impossibility and factual impossibility. Subsection (1) draws no distinction between attempts to do the possible but by inadequate means, attempts to do the physically impossible, and attempts to do something that turns out to be impossible following completion. All are varieties of attempts to do the factually impossible and all are crimes. Only attempts to commit imaginary crimes fall outside the scope of this subsection: *United States of America v. Dynar*, [1997] 2 S.C.R. 462, 115 C.C.C. (3d) 481.

It is no bar to a conviction for an attempt that the acts went beyond mere preparation and were fully carried out although in circumstances which did not amount to the full offence, as on a charge of fraud where proof of the full offence failed because the "victim" was not in fact deceived by the accused's act: *R. v. Detering*, [1982] 2 S.C.R. 583, 70 C.C.C. (2d) 321 (7:0).

Attempting to conspire to commit a substantive offence is not a crime in Canadian law: *R. v. Déry*, [2006] 2 S.C.R. 669, 213 C.C.C. (3d) 289.

Protection of Persons Administering and Enforcing the Law

PROTECTION OF PERSONS ACTING UNDER AUTHORITY / Idem / When not protected / When protected / Power in case of escape from penitentiary.

25. (1) Every one who is required or authorized by law to do anything in the administration or enforcement of the law

  (*a*) as a private person,
  (*b*) as a peace officer or public officer,
  (*c*) in aid of a peace officer or public officer, or
  (*d*) by virtue of his office,

is, if he acts on reasonable grounds, justified in doing what he is required or authorized to do and in using as much force as is necessary for that purpose.

(2) Where a person is required or authorized by law to execute a process or to carry out a sentence, that person or any person who assists him is, if that person acts in good faith, justified in executing the process or in carrying out the sentence notwithstanding that the process or sentence is defective or that it was issued or imposed without jurisdiction or in excess of jurisdiction.

(3) Subject to subsections (4) and (5), a person is not justified for the purposes of subsection (1) in using force that is intended or is likely to cause death or grievous bodily harm unless the person believes on reasonable grounds that it is necessary for the self-preservation of the person or the preservation of any one under that person's protection from death or grievous bodily harm.

(4) A peace officer, and every person lawfully assisting the peace officer, is justified in using force that is intended or is likely to cause death or grievous bodily harm to a person to be arrested, if

  (*a*) the peace officer is proceeding lawfully to arrest, with or without warrant, the person to be arrested;
  (*b*) the offence for which the person is to be arrested is one for which that person may be arrested without warrant;
  (*c*) the person to be arrested takes flight to avoid arrest;
  (*d*) the peace officer or other person using the force believes on reasonable grounds that the force is necessary for the purpose of protecting the peace officer, the

person lawfully assisting the peace officer or any other person from imminent or future death or grievous bodily harm; and

(e) the flight cannot be prevented by reasonable means in a less violent manner.

(5) A peace officer is justified in using force that is intended or is likely to cause death or grievous bodily harm against an inmate who is escaping from a penitentiary within the meaning of subsection 2(1) of the *Corrections and Conditional Release Act*, if

(a) the peace officer believes on reasonable grounds that any of the inmates of the penitentiary poses a threat of death or grievous bodily harm to the peace officer or any other person; and

(b) the escape cannot be prevented by reasonable means in a less violent manner. R.S., c. C-34, s. 25; 1994, c. 12, s. 1.

CROSS-REFERENCES

Definition of "peace officer" and "public officer", s. 2.

As to power of arrest by private citizen, see s. 494, and peace officer, s. 495.

The following provisions also define circumstances where a person is required or authorized to use force: s. 27, use of force to prevent commission of certain offences; s. 30, use of force to prevent breach of peace; s. 31, arrest by peace officer of person in breach of peace; s. 32, 33, use of force to suppress riot; ss. 34, 35, 37, self-defence; s. 37, defence of persons under protection; ss. 38 to 42, defence of property; s. 43, use of force by way of correction; s. 44, use of force by master of ship.

Also see the following: s. 25.1, defence to commission of certain offences by public officer where authorized by a competent authority; s. 26, liability of person for excessive force; s. 28, protection of persons executing and assisting in execution of warrant; s. 29, also note requirement that person have possession of the warrant or other process; s. 45, protection from liability for surgical operations.

Section 31 of the *Interpretation Act*, R.S.C. 1985, c. I-21, gives persons, authorized to exercise a power to do or enforce the doing of any act or thing, ancillary powers necessary to do the act or thing. Section 31 has, however, been strictly construed where the statutory power would encroach on the common law rights of the property owner. Thus, a former provision of the *Criminal Code*, which authorized police officers to seize firearms in certain circumstances, did not imply the right to enter and search private property: *R. v. Colet*, [1981] 1 S.C.R. 2, 57 C.C.C. (2d) 105, 19 C.R. (3d) 84. However, compare *R. v. Lyons*, [1984] 2 S.C.R. 633, 15 C.C.C. (3d) 417, where reference was made to s. 31 as confirmation that the authority to intercept private communications included the power to enter private premises to install the electronic device where such entry was necessary to implement the authorization granted under Part VI. Section 24 of the *Interpretation Act* provides for the exercise of powers by a successor in office. Also see *Crimes Against Humanity and War Crimes Act*, s. 14.

SYNOPSIS

This section establishes protection from liability for certain persons acting under authority.

Subsection (1) provides justification for the actions of any of the persons listed in paras. (a) to (d), if the additional requirements of the subsection are met. The person must be either *required or authorized by law* to do anything in relation to the *administration* or *enforcement* of the law. The requirement or authorization may be found in either statute or common law. In addition, it must be shown that the specified person acted on *reasonable grounds* and used *only as much force as was necessary* to achieve that purpose. If the actions of the person exceed the scope of activities authorized or required by law or the force used was more than that which was necessary to achieve that protected purpose, this subsection will not apply to exclude liability. However, to understand the scope of the provision as it applies to peace officers, it must be read together with subsecs. (3) and (4).

Subsection (2) protects a person acting *in good faith* who was executing process or carrying out a sentence, if authorized or required to do so. This protection will apply, even if the sentence or the process is determined to have been defective or without effect for any of the reasons noted in the subsection. The protection also extends to those who assist the authorized person in carrying out these functions.

Subsection (3) both provides an exception to the scope of protection conferred by the section and is itself subject to an exception in subsecs. (4) and (5). It limits the type of harm which may be inflicted under the protection of the section, by excluding the use of force *intended to or likely to cause death* or *grievous bodily harm unless the person believes, on reasonable grounds*, that such force must be used to protect himself or a person under his protection from death or grievous bodily harm. The application of the subsection is to take account of the circumstances in which the force is used and it is not required that a person in such a situation weigh the force used with precision. The phrase "grievous bodily harm" has been held to mean serious hurt or pain.

Subsection (4) permits a peace officer and persons lawfully assisting the officer to use force, that is intended or likely to cause death or grievous bodily harm, to prevent flight from a lawful arrest provided that the conditions in the subsection are met. Those conditions include that the arrest is lawful, the offence is one for which the person can be arrested without a warrant, the flight cannot be prevented by reasonable means in a less violent manner and the peace officer or person assisting believes on reasonable grounds that the force is necessary for the purpose of protecting the peace officer, the person assisting the officer or any other person from "imminent or future death or grievous bodily harm".

Subsection (5) is a special provision permitting use of force that is intended or likely to cause death or grievous bodily harm to prevent an escape from a penitentiary. However, the officer must believe on reasonable grounds that any of the inmates poses a threat of death or grievous bodily harm to the officer or any other person and the escape cannot be prevented by reasonable means in a less violent manner.

ANNOTATIONS

Use of force in enforcement or administration of law – An analysis of the justification of a peace officer's apprehension of a citizen who he has been informed was going to commit a crime is found in *Kennedy v. Tomlinson* (1959), 126 C.C.C. 175, 20 D.L.R. (2d) 273 (Ont. C.A.).

The exemption from liability under subsec. (1) has no application to negligent conduct: *Green v. Lawrence* (1998), 127 C.C.C. (3d) 416, 163 D.L.R. (4th) 115 (Man. C.A.).

This provision protects against civil liability for reasonable mistakes of fact but not for mistakes of law. Accordingly, the police were not protected from a claim for trespass in entering the plaintiff's home to execute a warrantless arrest. Subsec. (2) has no application because this was not a case in which the law or process under which the officers were operating was later found to be defective: *Hudson v. Brantford Police Services Board* (2001), 158 C.C.C. (3d) 390, 48 C.R. (5th) 69, 204 D.L.R. (4th) 645 (C.A.).

However, in *Tymkin v. Ewatski* (2014), 306 C.C.C. (3d) 24 (Man. C.A.), leave to appeal to S.C.C. refused 2014 CarswellMan 301, a police officer entering a dwelling house without a warrant to effect an arrest was entitled to the protection of subsec. (2) because the officer sought and obtained consent to enter from a person with ostensible authority to grant it.

This section does not permit a police officer to use as much force as necessary to generally carry out the lawful execution of his duty. Thus, while an officer has a duty to investigate crimes and question citizens, this section does not give him the right to detain the person or to use force for that purpose short of arrest: *R. v. O'Donnell; R. v. Cluett* (1982), 3 C.C.C. (3d) 333, 55 N.S.R. (2d) 6 (C.A.), reversed, with respect to *Cluett*, on other grounds [1985] 2 S.C.R. 216, 21 C.C.C. (3d) 318, 21 D.L.R. (4th) 306 (7:0).

In the absence of a specific statutory exemption, a police officer, pursuing a person suspected of committing a criminal offence, is not insulated from liability for the offence of failing to stop at a stop sign contrary to the *Highway Traffic Act* (Ont.). Assuming that this section could apply, the issue is not whether the officer was required or authorized by law to apprehend the suspect but, rather, whether he was required or authorized by law to drive through the stop sign without stopping. There is no common law authority in a constable which would give him immunity wider than that provided by this section: *R. v. Brennan* (1989), 52 C.C.C. (3d) 366, 75 C.R. (3d) 38, 18 M.V.R. (2d) 161 (Ont. C.A.).

While a search warrant authorizes a search of the premises for the items referred to in the warrant, the existence of the warrant does not determine whether the officers acted reasonably in the manner in which they executed the warrant. In a civil action, the officers had to prove on a balance of probabilities that it was reasonable, in the circumstances, to execute the warrant in the aggressive manner that they did in this case. The bald statement by one of the officers that he believed the occupants might be armed was not sufficient to meet this onus, there being no evidence to allow the trial judge to evaluate the objective reasonableness of the officer's belief. As the information to obtain the warrant was sealed, the police defendants should have applied under s. 487.3 to lift the sealing order if they needed this material to make out the defence under this section: *Crampton v. Walton* (2005), 194 C.C.C. (3d) 207, 250 D.L.R. (4th) 292, [2005] 6 W.W.R. 414 (Alta. C.A.).

A peace officer's honest belief in the legality of his conduct must be founded on reasonable grounds. This provision was applicable, therefore, where a peace officer forcibly returned a prisoner to his cell due to the prisoner's refusal to sign a property release form. The officer honestly believed that he had the authority to detain the complainant as a result of the applicability of operation procedures of the prison: *R. v. Devereaux* (1996), 112 C.C.C. (3d) 243, 147 Nfld. & P.E.I.R. 108 (Nfld. C.A.).

Subsection (2) – In *R. v. Finta*, [1994] 1 S.C.R. 701, 88 C.C.C. (3d) 417, 28 C.R. (4th) 265, the court considered this subsection in the context of a prosecution for war crimes under now repealed provisions of this Act. The court held that the defence under this subsection is distinct from the defence of obedience to or in conformity with the law in force at the time and in the place of commission of the offence and was therefore available to a person charged with war crimes or crimes against humanity. Unless the law was manifestly illegal, the police officer must obey and implement that law and, if it turns out that the officer has followed an illegal order, he may plead the defence under this subsection just as a military officer may properly put forth the defence of obedience to superior orders under certain limited conditions. However, an officer acting pursuant to a manifestly unlawful order or law would not be able to defend his actions on the grounds they were justified under this subsection. The holding in *Finta* must now be read with care when applied to prosecutions for war crimes and crimes against humanity having regard to the codification of the defence of obedience to superior orders in s. 14 of the *Crimes Against Humanity and War Crimes Act*.

Subsection (3) – The use of force is to be judged on a subjective-objective basis. Police actions should not be judged against a standard of perfection. Regard must be had to the circumstances as they existed at the time that the force was used: *R. v. Nasogaluak*, [2010] 1 S.C.R. 206, 251 C.C.C. (3d) 293.

The words "grievous bodily harm" in subsec. (3) mean serious hurt or pain. Moreover, in determining the availability of the defence under this section the jury must be directed to have regard to the circumstances as they existed at the time the force was used, keeping in mind that the officer could not be expected to measure the force used with exactitude: *R. v. Bottrell* (1981), 60 C.C.C. (2d) 211, 22 C.R. (3d) 371 (B.C.C.A.).

Use of force where person takes flight / subsec. (4) – **Note:** The case noted below was decided under the predecessor to this section which allowed the use of as much force as necessary to prevent the escape, unless the escape could not be prevented by reasonable means in a less violent manner.

A peace officer who had lawful authority to arrest a person in one province under s. 495 and is in fresh pursuit of that person retains for the purposes of subsec. (4) his status of a peace officer even where the pursuit takes him into an adjoining province: *R. v. Roberge*, [1983] 1 S.C.R. 312, 4 C.C.C. (3d) 304, 33 C.R. (3d) 289 (7:0).

DEFINITIONS / "Competent authority" / "Public officer" / "Senior official" / Principle / Designation of public officers / Considerations / Designation of senior officials / Emergency designation / Conditions / Justification for acts or omissions / Requirements for certain acts / Person acting at direction of public officer / Limitation / Protection, defences and immunities unaffected / Compliance with requirements Exception: offences under *Controlled Drugs and Substances Act.*

25.1 (1) The following definitions apply in this section and sections 25.2 to 25.4.

"competent authority" means, with respect to a public officer or a senior official,

    (*a*) in the case of a member of the Royal Canadian Mounted Police, the Minister of Public Safety and Emergency Preparedness, personally;

    (*b*) in the case of a member of a police service constituted under the laws of a province, the Minister responsible for policing in the province, personally; and

    (*c*) in the case of any other public officer or senior official, the Minister who has responsibility for the Act of Parliament that the officer or official has the power to enforce, personally.

"public officer" means a peace officer, or a public officer who has the powers of a peace officer under an Act of Parliament.

"senior official" means a senior official who is responsible for law enforcement and who is designated under subsection (5).

(2) It is in the public interest to ensure that public officers may effectively carry out their law enforcement duties in accordance with the rule of law and, to that end, to expressly recognize in law a justification for public officers and other persons acting at their direction to commit acts or omissions that would otherwise constitute offences.

(3) A competent authority may designate public officers for the purposes of this section and sections 25.2 to 25.4.

(3.1) A competent authority referred to in paragraph (*a*) or (*b*) of the definition of that term in subsection (1) may not designate any public officer under subsection (3) unless there is a public authority composed of persons who are not peace officers that may review the public officer's conduct.

(3.2) The Governor in Council or the lieutenant governor in council of a province, as the case may be, may designate a person or body as a public authority for the purposes of subsection (3.1), and that designation is conclusive evidence that the person or body is a public authority described in that subsection.

(4) The competent authority shall make designations under subsection (3) on the advice of a senior official and shall consider the nature of the duties performed by the public officer in relation to law enforcement generally, rather than in relation to any particular investigation or enforcement activity.

(5) A competent authority may designate senior officials for the purposes of this section and sections 25.2 to 25.4.

(6) A senior official may designate a public officer for the purposes of this section and sections 25.2 to 25.4 for a period of not more than 48 hours if the senior official is of the opinion that

    (*a*) by reason of exigent circumstances, it is not feasible for the competent authority to designate a public officer under subsection (3); and

    (*b*) in the circumstances of the case, the public officer would be justified in committing an act or omission that would otherwise constitute an offence.

The senior official shall without delay notify the competent authority of the designation.

(7) A designation under subsection (3) or (6) may be made subject to conditions, including conditions limiting

    (*a*) the duration of the designation;

(*b*) the nature of the conduct in the investigation of which a public officer may be justified in committing, or directing another person to commit, acts or omissions that would otherwise constitute an offence; and

(*c*) the acts or omissions that would otherwise constitute an offence and that a public officer may be justified in committing or directing another person to commit.

(8) A public officer is justified in committing an act or omission — or in directing the commission of an act or omission under subsection (10) — that would otherwise constitute an offence if the public officer

(*a*) is engaged in the investigation of an offence under, or the enforcement of, an Act of Parliament or in the investigation of criminal activity;

(*b*) is designated under subsection (3) or (6); and

(*c*) believes on reasonable grounds that the commission of the act or omission, as compared to the nature of the offence or criminal activity being investigated, is reasonable and proportional in the circumstances, having regard to such matters as the nature of the act or omission, the nature of the investigation and the reasonable availability of other means for carrying out the public officer's law enforcement duties.

(9) No public officer is justified in committing an act or omission that would otherwise constitute an offence and that would be likely to result in loss of or serious damage to property, or in directing the commission of an act or omission under subsection (10), unless, in addition to meeting the conditions set out in paragraphs (8)(*a*) to (*c*), he or she

(*a*) is personally authorized in writing to commit the act or omission — or direct its commission — by a senior official who believes on reasonable grounds that committing the act or omission, as compared to the nature of the offence or criminal activity being investigated, is reasonable and proportional in the circumstances, having regard to such matters as the nature of the act or omission, the nature of the investigation and the reasonable availability of other means for carrying out the public officer's law enforcement duties; or

(*b*) believes on reasonable grounds that the grounds for obtaining an authorization under paragraph (*a*) exist but it is not feasible in the circumstances to obtain the authorization and that the act or omission is necessary to

(i) preserve the life or safety of any person,

(ii) prevent the compromise of the identity of a public officer acting in an undercover capacity, of a confidential informant or of a person acting covertly under the direction and control of a public officer, or

(iii) prevent the imminent loss or destruction of evidence of an indictable offence.

(10) A person who commits an act or omission that would otherwise constitute an offence is justified in committing it if

(*a*) a public officer directs him or her to commit that act or omission and the person believes on reasonable grounds that the public officer has the authority to give that direction; and

(*b*) he or she believes on reasonable grounds that the commission of that act or omission is for the purpose of assisting the public officer in the public officer's law enforcement duties.

(11) Nothing in this section justifies

(*a*) the intentional or criminally negligent causing of death or bodily harm to another person;

(*b*) the wilful attempt in any manner to obstruct, pervert or defeat the course of justice; or

(*c*) conduct that would violate the sexual integrity of an individual.

(12) Nothing in this section affects the protection, defences and immunities of peace officers and other persons recognized under the law of Canada.

(13) Nothing in this section relieves a public officer of criminal liability for failing to comply with any other requirements that govern the collection of evidence.

(14) Nothing in this section justifies a public officer or a person acting at his or her direction in committing an act or omission — or a public officer in directing the commission of an act or omission — that constitutes an offence under a provision of Part I of the *Controlled Drugs and Substances Act* or of the regulations made under it. 2001, c. 32, s. 2; 2005, c. 10, s. 34(1)(*f*)(ii).

CROSS-REFERENCES
"Peace officer" is defined in s. 2. Section 25 sets out the circumstances where the use of force is justified. Also see: s. 26, respecting use of excessive force; s. 27, use of force to prevent commission of offence; ss. 30 and 31 preventing and arrest for breach of the peace. Under s. 25.2 every public officer who commits or directs commission of an act or omission under subsec. (9) must file a written report as soon as feasible. Section 25.3 provides for publication of an annual report by a competent authority concerning the use of this section. Section 25.4 provides for the notification of any person whose property was lost or seriously damaged as a result of acts or omissions undertaken in accordance with subsec. (9). By its terms, this section does not apply to offences committed by public officers under Part I of the *Controlled Drugs and Substances Act*. However, s. 55(2) and (2.1) of the *Controlled Drugs and Substances Act* and the *Controlled Drugs and Substances Act (Police Enforcement) Regulations*, SOR/97-234 provide a similar defence.

ANNOTATIONS
In *R. v. Campbell*, [1999] 1 S.C.R. 565, 133 C.C.C. (3d) 257, 24 C.R. (5th) 365, *sub nom. R. v. Shirose*, the court considered whether an illegal "reverse sting operation" conducted in the course of a drug investigation would amount to an abuse of process and thus entitle an accused caught up in such an investigation to a stay of proceedings. That investigation was carried out before the enactment of this provision. The decision will still be of assistance where the police conduct an investigation involving commission of crimes without proper designation under this section. Authorization for the type of investigation undertaken in that case would now be governed by ss. 55(2) and (2.1) of the *Controlled Drugs and Substances Act* and the regulations made thereunder, especially *Controlled Drugs and Substances Act (Police Enforcement) Regulations*, SOR/97-234.

PUBLIC OFFICER TO FILE REPORT.

25.2 Every public officer who commits an act or omission — or directs the commission by another person of an act or omission — under paragraph 25.1(9)(*a*) or (*b*) shall, as soon as is feasible after the commission of the act or omission, file a written report with the appropriate senior official describing the act or omission. 2001, c. 32, s. 2.

CROSS-REFERENCES
"Public officer" and "senior official" are defined in s. 25.1.

ANNUAL REPORT / Limitation.

25.3 (1) Every competent authority shall publish or otherwise make available to the public an annual report for the previous year that includes, in respect of public officers and senior officials designated by the competent authority,

(*a*) the number of designations made under subsection 25.1(6) by the senior officials;

(*b*) the number of authorizations made under paragraph 25.1(9)(*a*) by the senior officials;

(*c*) the number of times that acts and omissions were committed in accordance with paragraph 25.1(9)(*b*) by the public officers;

(*d*) the nature of the conduct being investigated when the designations referred to in paragraph (*a*) or the authorizations referred to in paragraph (*b*) were made or when the acts or omissions referred to in paragraph (*c*) were committed; and

(*e*) the nature of the acts or omissions committed under the designations referred to in paragraph (*a*), under the authorizations referred to in paragraph (*b*) and in the manner described in paragraph (*c*).

(2) The annual report shall not contain any information the disclosure of which would

(*a*) compromise or hinder an ongoing investigation of an offence under an Act of Parliament;

(*b*) compromise the identity of a public officer acting in an undercover capacity, of a confidential informant or of a person acting covertly under the direction and control of a public officer;

(*c*) endanger the life or safety of any person;

(*d*) prejudice a legal proceeding; or

(*e*) otherwise be contrary to the public interest. 2001, c. 32, s. 2.

CROSS-REFERENCES

"Competent authority", "public officer" and "senior official" are defined in s. 25.1.

WRITTEN NOTIFICATION TO BE GIVEN / Limitation.

25.4 (1) When a public officer commits an act or omission — or directs the commission by another person of an act or omission — under paragraph 25.1(9)(*a*) or (*b*), the senior official with whom the public officer files a written report under section 25.2 shall, as soon as is feasible after the report is filed, and no later than one year after the commission of the act or omission, notify in writing any person whose property was lost or seriously damaged as a result of the act or omission.

(2) The competent authority may authorize the senior official not to notify the person under subsection (1) until the competent authority is of the opinion that notification would not

(*a*) compromise or hinder an ongoing investigation of an offence under an Act of Parliament;

(*b*) compromise the identity of a public officer acting in an undercover capacity, of a confidential informant or of a person acting covertly under the direction and control of a public officer;

(*c*) endanger the life or safety of any person;

(*d*) prejudice a legal proceeding; or

(*e*) otherwise be contrary to the public interest. 2001, c. 32, s. 2.

Transitional provision

2001, c. 32, s. 46.1 provides as follows:

46.1 Within three years after this section comes into force, a review of sections 25.1 to 25.4 of the *Criminal Code* and their operation shall be undertaken by any committee of the Senate, of the House of Commons or of both Houses of Parliament that is designated or established for that purpose.

CROSS-REFERENCES

"Competent authority", "public officer" and "senior official" are defined in s. 25.1.

EXCESSIVE FORCE.

26. Every one who is authorized by law to use force is criminally responsible for any excess thereof according to the nature and quality of the act that constitutes the excess. R.S., c. C-34, s. 26.

CROSS-REFERENCES

A number of provisions authorize the use of force in carrying out duties under the law, to prevent commission of offences or in defence of oneself or others, such as the following: s. 25, use of force by person required or authorized by law to do anything in the administration or enforcement of the law [*e.g.*, to effect an arrest under s. 494 or s. 495]; s. 27, use of force to prevent commission of certain offences; s. 30, use of force to prevent breach of peace; s. 31, arrest by peace officer of person in breach of peace; ss. 32, 33, use of force to suppress riot; ss. 34, 35, 37, self-defence; s. 37, defence of persons under protection; ss. 38 to 42, defence of property; s. 43, use of force by way of correction; s. 44, use of force by master of ship. Also see s. 25.1 authorizing commission of certain otherwise illegal acts by designated public officers.

SYNOPSIS

This section imposes criminal liability for the use of force in excess of that authorized by law. Thus, it has been held that if one exceeds the force permitted by s. 27 or the force permitted as self-defence under s. 34, the excess force which results in death will be murder and not considered reduced to manslaughter.

ANNOTATIONS

It now seems clear as a result of a series of cases in the Supreme Court of Canada: *R. v. Gee*, [1982] 2 S.C.R. 286, 68 C.C.C. (2d) 516, 29 C.R. (3d) 347, *R. v. Faid*, [1983] 1 S.C.R. 265, 2 C.C.C. (3d) 513, 33 C.R. (3d) 1, *R. v. Brisson*, [1982] 2 S.C.R. 227, 69 C.C.C. (2d) 97, 29 C.R. (3d) 289, and *R. v. Reilly*, [1984] 2 S.C.R. 396, 15 C.C.C. (3d) 1, 42 C.R. (3d) 154 (6:0), that there does not exist in Canada a qualified defence of excessive force in self-defence or in preventing the commission of an offence which would have the effect of reducing murder to manslaughter. If the accused has used excessive force so that the defence provided by s. 34 or s. 27 is not available, then absent any other defence, the accused is liable to be convicted of murder. The evidence led in self-defence may however support a defence of provocation or negative the specific intent for murder in which case the proper verdict would be manslaughter.

In *R. v. Bayard* (1988), 29 B.C.L.R. (2d) 366, 92 N.R. 376 (C.A.), the majority of the court ordered a new trial on a Crown appeal from the accused's acquittal on murder and conviction for manslaughter on the basis, *inter alia*, that the trial judge had misdirected the jury as to the effect of excessive force in self defence. Lambert J.A., dissenting, was of the view that the impugned instructions related solely to s. 34(1) which could not apply if the accused had the intent for murder. If, however, he did not have the intent to kill and used no more force than necessary, then, pursuant to that subsection, the accused would be acquitted. If, however, he did use more force than was necessary then, in fact, the verdict should be manslaughter. On appeal by the accused to the Supreme Court of Canada, [1989] 1 S.C.R. 425, 70 C.R. (3d) 95, [1989] 5 W.W.R. 121, the appeal was allowed and the accused's conviction for manslaughter restored substantially for the dissenting reasons of Lambert J.A.

USE OF FORCE TO PREVENT COMMISSION OF OFFENCE.

27. Every one is justified in using as much force as is reasonably necessary
    (*a*) to prevent the commission of an offence
        (i) for which, if it were committed, the person who committed it might be arrested without warrant, and

    (ii) **that would be likely to cause immediate and serious injury to the person or property of anyone; or**

  (*b*) **to prevent anything being done that, on reasonable grounds, he believes would, if it were done, be an offence mentioned in paragraph (*a*). R.S., c. C-34, s. 27.**

CROSS-REFERENCES

In most cases, the determination of whether or not the person, "might be arrested without warrant", will be determined by reference to ss. 494 and 495 which authorizes warrantless arrest by anyone and by a peace officer, respectively. The most important power is that provided by s. 494(1)(*a*) which authorizes the arrest of a person found committing an indictable offence. Virtually all offences which would be likely to cause immediate and serious injury to person or property will constitute indictable offences, bearing in mind that even Crown-option offences are deemed to be indictable offences by s. 34(1)(*a*) of the *Interpretation Act*, R.S.C. 1985, c. I-21.

In many circumstances, the use of force will be authorized not only by this section but the self-defence and defence of property provisions set out in ss. 34 to 42.

Section 26 renders the person liable for any excessive use of force. The use of force to prevent commission of an offence on aircraft in flight in Canadian airspace or in respect of any aircraft registered in Canada is found in s. 27.1.

SYNOPSIS

This section provides authorization for the use of force to prevent the commission of specified types of offences or to prevent anything that might lead to the commission of such offences.

Section 27(*a*) permits the use of such *force* by *any one* as is *reasonably necessary* to *prevent the commission of certain types of offences* under the circumstances outlined in s. 27(*a*)(i) and (ii). This paragraph may be applied to any person, as contrasted with provisions such as s. 28 which can be relied upon only by a person authorized to execute process. In addition, it should be noted that the amount of force used will be judged by an objective standard as denoted by the term "reasonably necessary". Section 27(*a*)(i) limits the type of offence to those for which a person may be arrested without warrant. The criteria in s. 27(*a*)(ii) must also be met, namely that the offence, if committed, would be *likely* to cause *immediate* and *serious* injury to either a person or property. Again, it should be noted that the likelihood of the result is to be judged on an objective basis and the harm feared must be immediate and serious.

Section 27(*b*) permits an element of the accused's subjective beliefs to be incorporated but only if those beliefs are *reasonable* on an objective basis.

ANNOTATIONS

A personal assault against the accused does not trigger the application of this provision: *R. v. Hebert*, [1996] 2 S.C.R. 272, 107 C.C.C. (3d) 42, 135 D.L.R. (4th) 577.

USE OF FORCE ON BOARD AN AIRCRAFT / Application of this section.

27.1 (1) Every person on an aircraft in flight is justified in using as much force as is reasonably necessary to prevent the commission of an offence against this Act or another Act of Parliament that the person believes on reasonable grounds, if it were committed, would be likely to cause immediate and serious injury to the aircraft or to any person or property therein.

(2) This section applies in respect of any aircraft in flight in Canadian airspace and in respect of any aircraft registered in Canada in accordance with the regulations made under the *Aeronautics Act* in flight outside Canadian airspace. 2004, c. 12, s. 2.

CROSS-REFERENCES

"Flight" is defined in s. 7(8). The general defence of use of force to prevent commission of an offence is found in s. 27.

ARREST OF WRONG PERSON / Person assisting.

28. (1) Where a person who is authorized to execute a warrant to arrest believes, in good faith and on reasonable grounds, that the person whom he arrests is the person named in the warrant, he is protected from criminal responsibility in respect thereof to the same extent as if that person were the person named in the warrant.

(2) Where a person is authorized to execute a warrant to arrest,

(a) every one who, being called on to assist him, believes that the person in whose arrest he is called on to assist is the person named in the warrant, and

(b) every keeper of a prison who is required to receive and detain a person who he believes has been arrested under the warrant,

is protected from criminal responsibility in respect thereof to the same extent as if that person were the person named in the warrant. R.S., c. C-34, s. 28.

CROSS-REFERENCES

This provision, in and of itself, does not authorize the use of force but merely deals with the case of mistake in execution of the warrant. The use of force to arrest is dealt with primarily under s. 25 and see notes under that section. Section 29 requires the person executing a warrant to have it with him where feasible and prescribes other duties. In addition, s. 10 of the *Canadian Charter of Rights and Freedoms* requires a police officer to inform the arrestee of the reason for the arrest and of his right to counsel. See notes under s. 10 of the Charter, *infra*. As to where an arrest warrant may be exercised, see ss. 514, 703 and 528. An accused who was illegally arrested and in the course of the arrest killed the person attempting to effect the arrest, may, in some circumstances, have a defence of provocation under s. 232(4) or self-defence under s. 34. The offence of resisting or obstructing a peace officer, public officer, or person in the lawful execution of process is found in s. 129. The offences of assault with intent to resist arrest and assault of an officer in the execution of duty are in s. 270. The offence of misconduct by officers executing process is found in s. 128.

SYNOPSIS

Section 28 creates a limited exemption from criminal liability for persons who are *authorized* to execute arrest warrants and mistakenly arrest the wrong person or keep such wrongfully arrested person in custody.

It must be shown that the mistake of identity was made *in good faith and on reasonable grounds*.

Section 28(2) provides protection for those who *assist the person making the mistaken arrest* or *detain* such wrongfully arrested person on the same basis as if the person arrested was the person sought. As with s. 28(1), the person making the arrest must have been authorized to execute an arrest warrant. Section 28(2)(a) deals with the person who assists in the arrest after being *called upon to do so*. The assistant must believe that the person whom he is asked to help arrest is the person sought. This is a much lower standard of belief than that applied in s. 28(1); it need not be based on reasonable and probable grounds. Section 28(2)(b) protects the keeper of a prison, if the keeper has a subjective belief that the person he is asked to detain has been arrested under a warrant.

DUTY OF PERSON ARRESTING / Notice / Failure to comply.

29. (1) It is the duty of every one who executes a process or warrant to have it with him, where it is feasible to do so, and to produce it when requested to do so.

(2) It is the duty of every one who arrests a person, whether with or without a warrant, to give notice to that person, where it is feasible to do so, of
- (*a*) **the process or warrant under which he makes the arrest; or**
- (*b*) **the reason for the arrest.**

(3) Failure to comply with subsection (1) or (2) does not of itself deprive a person who executes a process or warrant, or a person who makes an arrest, or those who assist them, of protection from criminal responsibility. R.S., c. C-34, s. 29.

CROSS-REFERENCES

Subsection (1) – This provision, in and of itself, does not authorize the use of force. The use of force to arrest is dealt with primarily under s. 25 and see notes under that section. Section 28 deals with the case of mistake in execution of an arrest warrant. As to where an arrest warrant may be exercised, see ss. 514, 703 and 528. As to execution of a search warrant, see s. 487, search warrant; s. 487.1, tele-warrants; s. 488, time of execution; s. 488.1, execution of warrant at lawyer's office; s. 489, seizure of other items; s. 462.32, proceeds of crime. As to search warrants for weapons etc., see s. 103. An accused who was illegally arrested and, in the course of the arrest, killed the person attempting to effect the arrest may, in some circumstances, have a defence of provocation under s. 232(4) or self-defence under s. 34. The offence of misconduct by officers executing process is found in s. 128.

Subsection (2) – In addition to the duties prescribed by this subsection, s. 10 of the Charter requires a police officer to inform the arrestee of the reason for the arrest and of his right to counsel. See notes under s. 10 of the Charter, *infra*. The power of arrest is also circumscribed by other provisions of the Charter, see especially notes under s. 9 of the Charter. Arrest without warrant is authorized by a number of sections: s. 31, breach of the peace; s. 33, arrest of rioters; s. 117.02, arrest for weapons offences; s. 199(2), arrest of inmates of disorderly house; s. 494, arrest by any person for certain criminal offences; s. 495, arrest by peace officer for criminal offences; s. 524(2), arrest by peace officer of accused on interim release. The offence of resisting or obstructing a peace officer, public officer, or person in the lawful execution of process is found in s. 129. The offences of assault with intent to resist arrest and assault of an officer in the execution of duty are in s. 270.

SYNOPSIS

This section outlines the duties imposed upon those who execute process or make an arrest, and states the effect of non-compliance with the section.

Section 29(1) states that it is the duty of a person *executing a process or warrant* to have a copy of such document with him. In addition, such document must be shown if a request is made to see it. Both requirements apply only if it is *feasible* to comply with them.

Section 29(2) sets out the *duty of a person making an arrest* with or without warrant. The requirements are that the person being arrested is to be told of the process or warrant permitting the arrest *or* the reason for the arrest. As with s. 29(1), the duties apply only *when feasible*. These duties are supplemented by the requirements in s. 10 of the Charter.

Section 29(3) spells out that *non-compliance* with either of the foregoing subsections does not *by itself* deprive the person making the arrest, executing process, or those who assist such persons, of the protection from criminal responsibility conferred elsewhere under the *Criminal Code* (see, for example, s. 28).

ANNOTATIONS

Subsection (1) – A search is not presumptively unreasonable because the initial team first entering did not have the warrant. The purpose of the provision is to allow the occupant to know why the search is being carried out, to allow an assessment of his or her legal position and to know that there is a color of authority for the search making forcible resistance improper. This requirement is met if the warrant is in the possession of at least one member of the team executing the warrant: *R. v. Cornell*, [2010] 2 S.C.R. 142, 258 C.C.C. (3d) 429.

An officer executing a search warrant is required to have the warrant with her. Where, however, the officer forgot to bring the warrant through inadvertence and the accused consented to the search commencing while the warrant was being brought to his home, then it was not shown that the search was unlawful: *R. v. B. (J.E.)* (1989), 52 C.C.C. (3d) 224 (N.S.C.A.).

The failure to produce a search warrant when requested in relation to the search of a dwelling house constitutes a breach of s. 8 of the *Canadian Charter of Rights and Freedoms*: *R. v. Bohn* (2000), 145 C.C.C. (3d) 320, 33 C.R. (5th) 265 (B.C.C.A.).

The failure to comply with this provision does not, by itself, give rise to a breach of s. 8 of the Charter: *R. v. Patrick* (2007), 227 C.C.C. (3d) 525 (Alta. C.A.), affd 242 C.C.C. (3d) 158 (S.C.C.).

Subsection (2) – The provisions of this subsection are to be read disjunctively, so that when an arrest is being made without possession of a warrant, but pursuant thereto, the duty of the arresting officer is fully discharged by telling the arrested person that the reason for his arrest is the existence of an outstanding warrant. The arresting officer is under no duty to obtain the warrant or ascertain its contents to tell the accused: *R. v. Gamracy*, [1974] S.C.R. 640, 12 C.C.C. (2d) 209 (3:2), where Ritchie J., writing the major decision also held that the leading British case in this area, *Christie v. Leachinsky*, [1947] 1 All E.R. 567 (H.L.), was of no assistance in interpreting s. 29.

PREVENTING BREACH OF PEACE.

30. Every one who witnesses a breach of the peace is justified in interfering to prevent the continuance or renewal thereof and may detain any person who commits or is about to join in or to renew the breach of the peace, for the purpose of giving him into the custody of a peace officer, if he uses no more force than is reasonably necessary to prevent the continuance or renewal of the breach of the peace or than is reasonably proportioned to the danger to be apprehended from the continuance or renewal of the breach of the peace. R.S., c. C-34, s. 30.

CROSS-REFERENCES

Section 31 authorizes a peace officer to receive into custody a person detained under this section. This section does not itself create an offence, however, a provincial court judge would appear to still have a common law power to bind a person over to keep the peace. See notes under s. 810, *infra*. There are also other provisions of the *Criminal Code* which may apply to conduct amounting to breach of the peace. See s. 49, breach of the peace in presence of Her Majesty; s. 175, causing a disturbance. A breach of the peace may escalate into an unlawful assembly or a riot, in which case see ss. 32, 33 and 63 to 69.

SYNOPSIS

This section empowers *anyone who witnesses a breach of the peace* to do a number of things, including using force, to stop it or prevent its continuation or renewal.

A person described above may *detain another* who *is committing* such a breach or *is about to*, if the *purpose* of the detention is to turn the person over to a peace officer. In addition, it must be shown on an objective standard, *either* that the *force used did not exceed that required* to prevent the continuation of the breach of the peace, or its renewal, *or* that it is *proportionate to the danger feared* from such activity.

ARREST FOR BREACH OF PEACE / Giving person in charge.

31. (1) Every peace officer who witnesses a breach of the peace and every one who lawfully assists the peace officer is justified in arresting any person whom he finds

committing the breach of the peace or who, on reasonable grounds, he believes is about to join in or renew the breach of the peace.

(2) Every peace officer is justified in receiving into custody any person who is given into his charge as having been a party to a breach of the peace by one who has, or who on reasonable grounds the peace officer believes has, witnessed the breach of the peace. R.S., c. C-34, s. 31.

CR. CODE

CROSS-REFERENCES

"Peace officer" is defined in s. 2. Section 30 authorizes a citizen to detain a person for breach of the peace. Neither this section nor s. 30 create an offence, however, a provincial court judge would appear to still have a common law power to bind a person over to keep the peace. See notes under s. 810, *infra*. There are also other provisions of the *Criminal Code* which may apply to conduct amounting to breach of the peace. See s. 49, breach of the peace in presence of Her Majesty; s. 175, causing a disturbance. A breach of the peace may escalate into an unlawful assembly or a riot, in which case see ss. 32, 33 and 63 to 69. As to use of force in effecting an arrest, see s. 25 and notes thereunder. As to duty of peace officer when effecting an arrest, see s. 29. The offence of resisting or obstructing a peace officer is found in s. 129. The offences of assault with intent to resist arrest and assault of an officer in the execution of duty are in s. 270.

SYNOPSIS

Section 31 empowers peace officers to arrest and detain persons involved in a breach of the peace.

Section 31(1) applies only to peace officers and anyone *lawfully assisting* a peace officer. It is a requirement that the officer *witness* the breach of the peace. The subsection authorizes the arrest of a person committing the breach *or* a person the officer believes is about to join or renew the breach. In the latter circumstance, it must be shown that the officer's belief was based on *reasonable grounds*. This objective requirement modifies the standard to be applied to the officer's beliefs.

Section 31(2) justifies a peace officer in receiving into custody anyone who has been detained by another who either has witnessed that person commit a breach of the peace or the officer believes has witnessed the breach. In the latter case, it must be shown that the officer had *reasonable grounds for the belief* that the person who turned over the suspect witnessed the breach.

ANNOTATIONS

Subsection (1) – In *Blanchard v. Galbraith* (1966), 10 Crim. L.Q. 122 (Man. Q.B.), the plaintiff claimed damages for false imprisonment when in a belligerent and defiant manner he accepted gaol on being given the alternative of returning to his hotel room by an R.C.M.P. constable who was endeavouring to disperse a group of loiterers outside a location that was a known town trouble spot. Hall J. dismissed the action with costs for the defendant R.C.M.P. officers, holding that it was the plain duty of peace officers to act in anticipation of, and thereby prevent breaches of the peace, and the plaintiff's refusal by inviting arrest amounted to obstruction in the discharge of the arresting officer's duty.

Although there is no offence in Canada of breach of the peace, this section does give the police officer a power to arrest anyone for breach of the peace and resisting such an arrest may be the basis for a charge under s. 129. This section is a form of preventive remedy either through arrest for not more than 24 hours or a peace bond at common law: *R. v. Lefebvre* (1982), 1 C.C.C. (3d) 241 (B.C. Co. Ct.), affd 15 C.C.C. (3d) 503 (B.C.C.A.). See also *R. v. Januska* (1996), 106 C.C.C. (3d) 183 (Ont. Ct. (Gen. Div.)).

Although this subsection is confined to breaches of the peace that have actually taken place, there is a common law power for a peace officer to arrest without a warrant where the officer honestly and reasonably believes that such a breach will be committed in the immediate future: *Hayes v. Thompson* (1985), 18 C.C.C. (3d) 254, 44 C.R. (3d) 316 (B.C.C.A.).

The police were justified in making an arrest under this subsection where the accused persisted in interfering with attempts by the officers to shut down a noisy house party. The officers were engaged in the preservation of the peace arising from the continuance of the large and noisy party: *R. v. Khatchadorian* (1998), 127 C.C.C. (3d) 565, 178 W.A.C. 264 (B.C.C.A.).

Subsection (2) – The word "justified" in subsec. (2) gives lawful sanction to the actions of an officer who receives into his custody any person who is given into his charge as having been a party to a breach of the peace by a person who he reasonably believes has witnessed a breach of the peace. The officer is then in the execution of his duty and an accused may be convicted of the offence under s. 129(*a*) if he resists this officer notwithstanding his acquittal on the charge for which he was originally arrested: *R. v. Biron*, [1976] S.C.R. 56, 23 C.C.C. (2d) 513 (5:3).

Suppression of Riots

USE OF FORCE TO SUPPRESS RIOT / Person bound by military law / Obeying order of peace officer / Apprehension of serious mischief / Question of law.

32. **(1) Every peace officer is justified in using or in ordering the use of as much force as the peace officer believes, in good faith and on reasonable grounds,**

(*a*) **is necessary to suppress a riot; and**

(*b*) **is not excessive, having regard to the danger to be apprehended from the continuance of the riot.**

(2) Every one who is bound by military law to obey the command of his superior officer is justified in obeying any command given by his superior officer for the suppression of a riot unless the order is manifestly unlawful.

(3) Every one is justified in obeying an order of a peace officer to use force to suppress a riot if

(*a*) **he acts in good faith; and**

(*b*) **the order is not manifestly unlawful.**

(4) Every one who, in good faith and on reasonable grounds, believes that serious mischief will result from a riot before it is possible to secure the attendance of a peace officer is justified in using as much force as he believes in good faith and on reasonable grounds,

(*a*) **is necessary to suppress the riot; and**

(*b*) **is not excessive, having regard to the danger to be apprehended from the continuance of the riot.**

(5) For the purposes of this section, the question whether an order is manifestly unlawful or not is a question of law. R.S., c. C-34, s. 32.

CROSS-REFERENCES

"Peace officer" and "military law" are defined by s. 2. Section 33 sets out the duties of peace officers and others, where rioters do not disperse after a proclamation has been read under s. 67 or an offence committed under s. 68. The offence of resisting or obstructing a peace officer is found in s. 129. The offences of assault with intent to resist arrest and assault of an officer in the execution of duty are in s. 270. Section 26 makes a person liable for excessive force. Also see s. 25 as to use of force generally in acting to enforce the law.

SYNOPSIS

This section and s. 33 have the combined effect of protecting specified categories of persons who seek to suppress a riot.

Section 32(1) applies only to peace officers. It justifies the use of force, or ordering others to use it to suppress a riot. The officer will be protected if he had both *good faith* and *reasonable grounds* for believing that the other requirements of the subsection were met. They are that the force used was necessary to suppress a riot *and* that it was *not excessive* considering the *danger* perceived if the riot continued.

Section 32(2) applies to those who are bound by *military law* to obey the orders of a superior officer. It justifies obeying an order by such superior to suppress a riot. However, the protection is removed if the order was *manifestly unlawful*.

Section 32(3) justifies the actions of *anyone obeying the orders of a peace officer* to suppress a riot, if the other conditions of the section are met. It must be shown that the person obeying the order acts in good faith. In addition, the subsection limits protection to those circumstances in which the order of the peace officer is not manifestly unlawful.

Section 32(5) states that the determination of whether an order was manifestly unlawful is a question of law.

Section 32(4) permits a person to act to suppress a riot under certain stringent conditions. It must be shown that the person believes *in good faith and on reasonable grounds* that a peace officer cannot be brought to the scene in time to prevent *serious mischief* from a riot. The remaining requirements of this subsection are the same as those imposed upon peace officers under s. 32(1).

ANNOTATIONS

It was held in *Hebert v. Martin*, [1931] S.C.R. 145, 54 C.C.C. 257, that the taking of life can only be justified by the necessity to disperse a riotous crowd which is dangerous unless dispersed and a police officer was not liable civilly for the death of a person when he had good reason to fear danger to his own life.

The defence under subsec. (1) is made out where the peace officer: (1) believed that the force used was necessary to suppress the riot; (2) believed that the force used was not excessive having regard to the danger to be apprehended from the continuance of the riot; (3) had reasonable grounds for the belief that the force used was necessary to suppress the riot; and (4) had reasonable grounds for the belief that the force was not excessive having regard to the danger apprehended from the continuance of the riot. The determination of "reasonable grounds" requires a consideration of the peace officer's training, experience and the orders of the day. It is not an element of the defence that the person injured by the use of force unlawfully assaulted the police officer or anyone else: *Berntt v. Vancouver (City)* (1999), 135 C.C.C. (3d) 353, 174 D.L.R. (4th) 403, supplementary reasons 139 C.C.C. (3d) 139, 179 D.L.R. (4th) 380 (B.C.C.A.).

DUTY OF OFFICERS IF RIOTERS DO NOT DISPERSE / Protection of officers / Section not restrictive.

33. (1) Where the proclamation referred to in section 67 has been made or an offence against paragraph 68(*a*) or (*b*) has been committed, it is the duty of a peace officer and of a person who is lawfully required by him to assist, to disperse or to arrest persons who do not comply with the proclamation.

(2) No civil or criminal proceedings lie against a peace officer or a person who is lawfully required by a peace officer to assist him in respect of any death or injury that by reason of resistance is caused as a result of the performance by the peace officer or that person of a duty that is imposed by subsection (1).

(3) Nothing in this section limits or affects any powers, duties or functions that are conferred or imposed by this Act with respect to the suppression of riots. R.S., c. C-34, s. 33.

CROSS-REFERENCES

"Peace officer" is defined in s. 2. This section is complementary to ss. 67 to 69 which deal with providing for the reading of a proclamation to disperse a riotous assembly. The unlawful assembly offences and riot offences are found in ss. 63 to 66. Section 32 authorizes the use of force to suppress a riot. The offence of resisting or obstructing a peace officer is found in s. 129. The offences of assault with intent to resist arrest and assault of an officer in the execution of duty are in s. 270. Section 26 makes a person liable for excessive force. Also see s. 25 as to use of force generally in acting to enforce the law.

SYNOPSIS

Section 33 states the duties of peace officers and those lawfully required to assist them if a crowd fails to disperse following the reading of the proclamation under s. 67 of the *Criminal Code* (the "riot act") or if an offence under s. 68 is committed (which relates to the prevention of or interference with the reading of the "riot act" or the failure to disperse after it is read). In addition, subsec. (3) explicitly provides that this section does not limit any powers conferred elsewhere in the *Criminal Code* in relation to the suppression of riots.

Section 33(1) imposes a duty upon peace officers or those lawfully required to assist them to disperse or arrest those who fail to disperse after the proclamation is read or an offence under s. 68 is committed.

Section 33(2) protects persons carrying out the duties imposed by subsec. (1) from civil or criminal liability if death or injury results from the resistance to the carrying out of those duties.

Self-induced Intoxication

WHEN DEFENCE NOT AVAILABLE / Criminal fault by reason of intoxication / Application.

33.1 (1) It is not a defence to an offence referred to in subsection (3) that the accused, by reason of self-induced intoxication, lacked the general intent or the voluntariness required to commit the offence, where the accused departed markedly from the standard of care as described in subsection (2).

(2) For the purposes of this section, a person departs markedly from the standard of reasonable care generally recognized in Canadian society and is thereby criminally at fault where the person, while in a state of self-induced intoxication that renders the person unaware of, or incapable of consciously controlling, their behaviour, voluntarily or involuntarily interferes or threatens to interfere with the bodily integrity of another person.

(3) This section applies in respect of an offence under this Act or any other Act of Parliament that includes as an element an assault or any other interference or threat of interference by a person with the bodily integrity of another person. 1995, c. 32, s. 1.

CROSS-REFERENCES

For notes on other defences generally, see s. 8. For intoxication as a defence to murder, see s. 229. While the term "bodily integrity" is not defined in this Act, reference might be made to *R. v. McCraw*, [1991] 3 S.C.R. 72, 66 C.C.C. (3d) 517, 7 C.R. (4th) 314, where the court considered the term "serious bodily harm" in the former s. 264.1, and held that the phrase includes any hurt or injury, whether physical or psychological, that interferes in a substantial way with the physical or psychological integrity, health or well-being of the complainant.

SYNOPSIS

This section was enacted in response to the decision of the Supreme Court of Canada in *R. v. Daviault*, [1994] 3 S.C.R. 63, 93 C.C.C. (3d) 21, 33 C.R. (4th) 165, noted below, where the court held that self-induced intoxication can be a defence to a general intent offence, including an offence involving assault, such as sexual assault. This section now places limits on the defence. The defence recognized in *Daviault* will not be available for any of the offences referred to in subsec. (3) if the accused departed markedly from the standard of care described in subsec. (2). The effect of subsec. (2) is to deem a certain level of fault in an accused who departs markedly from the standard of care set out in that subsection. Subsection (3) would probably include most of the personal injury offences since even a threat of interference with the complainant's bodily integrity is sufficient to trigger the limits set down in this section.

ANNOTATIONS

Classification of general and specific intent offences – The analysis starts with determining the mental element of the offence by way of statutory interpretation. The next question is whether the crime is one of general or specific intent. There are two main considerations: the importance of the mental element and the social policy underlying the offence. The importance of the mental element refers to the complexity of the thought and reasoning processes that are required. For general intent offences, the mental element simply relates to the performance of the illegal act. These crimes involve such minimal mental acuity that intoxication short of automatism could not deprive the accused of the low level of intent required. In contrast, specific intent offences involve a heightened mental element which may take the form of an ulterior purpose or may entail actual knowledge of circumstances or consequences. When this analysis fails to yield a clear answer, one should turn to policy considerations. This assessment will generally focus on whether alcohol consumption is habitually associated with the crime in question. If it is, then allowing an accused to rely on intoxication as a defence is likely inappropriate: *R. v. Tatton*, [2015], 2 S.C.R. 574, 323 C.C.C. (3d) 166.

Intoxication defence (specific intent offences) – The rules in *D.P.P. v. Beard*, [1920] A.C. 479, 14 Cr. App. R. 159 (H.L.), violate ss. 7 and 11(*d*) of the Charter because they limit the defence of intoxication to the capacity of an accused to form the specific intent. Before a trial judge charges a jury on the issue of intoxication, the judge must be satisfied that the effect of the intoxication was such that it might have impaired the accused's foresight of consequences sufficient to raise a reasonable doubt. Once this threshold test is met, the judge must make clear to the jury that the issue is whether the Crown has satisfied them beyond a reasonable doubt that the accused had the requisite intent. In most circumstances, a one-step charge which omits any reference to "capacity" or "capability" and focuses the jury on the question of "intent in fact" is appropriate. Consequently, the jury must consider whether the accused possessed the requisite specific intent having regard to the evidence of intoxication, along with all of the other evidence in the case. In certain cases, however, in light of the facts of the case and/or the admission of expert evidence, a two-step charge may be appropriate. In this case, the jury is charged both with regard to the capacity to form the requisite intent and with regard to the need to determine in all of the circumstances whether the requisite intent was in fact formed by the accused. In these circumstances, the jury might be instructed that their overall duty is to determine whether or not the accused possessed the requisite intent for the crime. If, on the basis of the expert evidence, the jury is left with a reasonable doubt as to whether, as a result of the consumption of the alcohol, the accused had the capacity to form the requisite intent, that ends the inquiry and the accused must be acquitted of the offence and consideration must then be given to any included lesser offences. If the jury is not left with a reasonable doubt as a result of the expert evidence as to the capacity to form the intent, they must consider and take into account all the surrounding circumstances and the evidence pertaining to those circumstances in determining whether or not the accused possessed the requisite intent for the offence. Furthermore, the presumption that a person intends the natural consequences of their act refers only to a common-sense and logical inference that the jury can, but is not compelled, to make. Where there is some evidence of intoxication, the trial judge must link the instructions on intoxication with the instruction on the common-sense inference so that the jury is specifically instructed that evidence of intoxication can rebut the inference: *R. v. Robinson*, [1996] 1 S.C.R. 683, 105 C.C.C. (3d) 97. See also *R. v. McMaster*, [1996] 1 S.C.R. 740, 105 C.C.C. (3d) 193; and *R. v. Seymour*, [1996] 2 S.C.R. 252, 106 C.C.C. (3d) 520.

The threshold for putting the intoxication defence to the jury on a charge of murder must be evidence sufficient to permit a reasonable inference that the accused did not in fact foresee those consequences. The defence of intoxication is available in circumstances in which evidence falls short of establishing that the accused lacked capacity to form the intent but may still leave the jury with a reasonable doubt that when the offence was committed, the accused in fact foresaw the likelihood of death: *R. v. Lemky*, [1996] 1 S.C.R. 757, 105 C.C.C. (3d) 137.

Where the accused not only understood the nature and quality of his or her acts and knew that they were wrong but had formed the specific intent required for the offence, the fact that, by reason of consumption of drugs, he or she had entered a psychotic state which had caused a loss of self-control or an irresistible impulse, did not constitute a defence of self-induced intoxication: *R. v. Courville* (1982), 2 C.C.C. (3d) 118 (Ont. C.A.), affd [1985] 1 S.C.R. 847, 19 C.C.C. (3d) 97 (7:0).

Intoxication defence (general intent offences) – Extreme drunkenness inducing a state akin to insanity or automatism is a defence to a general intent offence. However, the burden is on the accused to prove the defence on a balance of probabilities and the accused's testimony would have to be supported by expert evidence: *R. v. Daviault*, [1994] 3 S.C.R. 63, 93 C.C.C. (3d) 21. [Note: this case was decided prior to the enactment of this section and, thus, while its holding may apply to certain other general intent offences, this section now limits the availability of the drunkenness defence for the offence considered by the court in *Daviault*, *i.e.*, sexual assault.]

The Crown need not prove that the substance was illegal, that the accused knew precisely what the substance was, or that the accused's purpose in taking the substance was to experience its effects. Voluntary intoxication means the consuming of a substance where the person knew or had reasonable grounds for believing such might cause him to be impaired. The accused need not contemplate the extent of the intoxication or intend a certain level of intoxication. The test for self-induced intoxication requires that the accused voluntarily consumed a substance which he knew or ought to have known was an intoxicant, and the risk of becoming intoxicated was or should have been within his contemplation: *R. v. Chaulk* (2007), 223 C.C.C. (3d) 174 (N.S.C.A.).

Application of subsec. (1) – This section did not apply where the Crown failed to prove that the intoxication was self-induced in the sense that the accused intended to become intoxicated, either by voluntarily ingesting a substance knowing or having reasonable grounds to know it might be dangerous, or by recklessly ingesting the substance, in this case, prescription medication: *R. v. Vickberg* (1998), 16 C.R. (5th) 164 (B.C.S.C.).

Constitutional considerations – Section 7 of the Charter does not require that the intoxication defence be available for all offences and, thus, it was open to Parliament to create an offence such as impaired care or control as defined in s. 253 for which intoxication is no defence: *R. v. Penno*, [1990] 2 S.C.R. 865, 59 C.C.C. (3d) 344.

Although this section violates ss. 7 and 11(*d*) of the *Canadian Charter of Rights and Freedoms*, it is a reasonable limit within the meaning of s. 1 and is therefore valid: *R. v. Vickberg* (1998), 16 C.R. (5th) 164 (B.C.S.C.). See also *R. v. Dow* (2010), 261 C.C.C. (3d) 399 (Que. S.C.).

Defence of Person

DEFENCE — USE OR THREAT OF FORCE / Factors / No defence.

34. (1) A person is not guilty of an offence if

  (*a*) they believe on reasonable grounds that force is being used against them or another person or that a threat of force is being made against them or another person;

  (*b*) the act that constitutes the offence is committed for the purpose of defending or protecting themselves or the other person from that use or threat of force; and

  (*c*) the act committed is reasonable in the circumstances.

(2) In determining whether the act committed is reasonable in the circumstances, the court shall consider the relevant circumstances of the person, the other parties and the act, including, but not limited to, the following factors:

  (*a*) the nature of the force or threat;

  (*b*) the extent to which the use of force was imminent and whether there were other means available to respond to the potential use of force;

  (*c*) the person's role in the incident;

  (*d*) whether any party to the incident used or threatened to use a weapon;

  (*e*) the size, age, gender and physical capa- bilities of the parties to the incident;

  (*f*) the nature, duration and history of any relationship between the parties to the incident, including any prior use or threat of force and the nature of that force or threat;

  (*f*.1) any history of interaction or communication between the parties to the incident;

  (*g*) the nature and proportionality of the person's response to the use or threat of force; and

  (*h*) whether the act committed was in response to a use or threat of force that the person knew was lawful.

(3) Subsection (1) does not apply if the force is used or threatened by another person for the purpose of doing something that they are required or authorized by law to do in the administration or enforcement of the law, unless the person who commits the act that constitutes the offence believes on reasonable grounds that the other person is acting unlawfully. R.S., c. C-34, s. 34; 2012, c. 9, s. 2.

CROSS-REFERENCES

The defence of property is dealt with in s. 35. As to use of force in administration or enforcement of the law, see s. 25.

SYNOPSIS

This section codifies the defence of use of force in defence of one's self or another person. It replaces a number of sections that had created a complex web of overlapping and confusing provisions. For ease of reference, the person using the force in self-defence is referred to here as the accused. Under this section, the accused is justified in acting in defence of themselves or another person if the following three basic conditions are met: (1) they must believe on reasonable grounds that force is being used against them or another person or that a threat of force is being used against them or another person; (2) the accused's act is committed for the purpose of defending or protecting themselves or the other person from that use or threat of force; and (3) the accused's act was reasonable in the circumstances. Note that, unlike the predecessor sections, the use of force in defence of another is not limited to a person under the accused's protection. However, a factor to be considered in subsec. (2) is the nature of the relationship between the parties to the incident (para. (*f*)).

As under the predecessor provisions, this section incorporates a subjective and objective test. The accused's belief lies at the core of the defence but that belief in the need to resort to force must be based on reasonable grounds and the justifiable amount of force must be reasonable. Subsection (2) is of great importance because it contains a list of non-exhaustive factors that the trier of fact must consider in determining whether the amount of force was reasonable. Unlike the predecessor sections, this section does not explicitly distinguish between deadly force and other types of force in defence. The issue is whether the resort to this amount of force was reasonable in the circumstances. Subsection (2) avoids hard and fast rules such as a duty to retreat before responding with use of force or that the force used be proportionate to the attack defended against. But the subsection does incorporate common sense considerations such as the availability of other means (para. (*b*)) in measuring the reasonableness of the need to resort to force and the amount of force and the need to take into account proportionality (para. (*g*)). Similarly, the section does not expressly distinguish between cases where the resort to force in defence was provoked and unprovoked by the accused. But, subsec. (2) does require the trier of fact to consider the accused's role in the incident (para. (*c*)) and the history of the interaction or communication between the parties to the incident (para. (*f*.1)).

Finally, subsec. (3) incorporates an important limit on the use of the defence under this section. The defence is not available if the victim used force or the threat of force for the purpose of doing something that they are required or authorized by law to do in the administration or enforcement of the law, unless the accused believed on reasonable grounds that the victim was acting unlawfully.

ANNOTATIONS

Editors' Note: We have removed most of the annotations from ss. 34 to 42 which previously dealt with self-defence and related defences. The remaining annotations, although decided under the predecessor sections, were thought to be of some assistance but they must be read with considerable care given the wholesale revisions of the provisions of the Code dealing with the justifiable use of force in defence of person or property.

Application of new provisions – The dominant view is that the amendments to the self-defence provisions effected a substantive change in the law and should be applied purely prospectively: *R. v. Evans* (2015), 321 C.C.C. (3d) 130 (B.C.C.A.); *R. v. Bengy* (2015), 325 C.C.C. (3d) 22 (Ont. C.A.); *R. v. Carriere* (2013), [2014] 1 W.W.R. 117 (Alta. Q.B.). Other cases have held that the provisions should apply retrospectively to charges pre-dating enactment of the new provisions: *R. v. Pandurevic* (2013), 298 C.C.C. (3d) 504 (Ont. S.C.J.); *R. v. Paskimin* (2014), 440 Sask. R. 152 (Q.B.). Still others have held that a judge sitting alone should give the accused the benefit of both regimes: *R. v. Parker* (2013), 107 W.C.B. (2d) 10, [2013] O.J. No. 1755 (C.J.); *R. v. Rothgordt* (2014), 114 W.C.B. (2d) 623, [2014] B.C.J. No. 1398 (S.C.).

Subsection (1) – The issue is not whether the accused was, in fact, unlawfully assaulted but rather whether she reasonably believed in the circumstances that she was being unlawfully assaulted. Further, there is no requirement that the danger be imminent. The imminence of apprehended danger is only one factor that the jury should weigh in determining whether the accused had a reasonable apprehension of danger and a reasonable belief that she could not extricate herself otherwise than by killing the attacker: *R. v. Pétel*, [1994] 1 S.C.R. 3, 87 C.C.C. (3d) 97. Also see *R. v. Nelson* (1992), 71 C.C.C. (3d) 449 (Ont. C.A.); and *R. v. Proulx* (1998), 127 C.C.C. (3d) 511 (B.C.C.A.).

While a trial judge has a duty to put to the jury any defence for which there is an air of reality, the judge also has a duty not to put defences for which there is no air of reality. A defence possesses an air of reality if a properly instructed jury acting reasonably could acquit the accused on the basis of the defence. In applying the air of reality test, a trial judge considers the totality of the evidence, and assumes the evidence relied upon by the accused to be true. The evidential foundation can be indicated by evidence emanating from the examination-in-chief or cross-examination of the accused, of defence witnesses, or of Crown witnesses. It can also rest upon the factual circumstances of the case or from any other evidential source on the record. There is no requirement that the evidence be adduced by the accused. This requires an assessment of whether the evidence relied upon is reasonably capable of supporting the inferences required for the defence to succeed: *R. v. Cinous*, [2002] 2 S.C.R. 3, 162 C.C.C. (3d) 129.

The air of reality test applies to affirmative defences such as self-defence, but it is never the function of the trial judge in a jury trial to assess the evidence and make a determination that the Crown has proven one or more of the essential elements of the offence and direct the jury accordingly. It does not matter how obvious the judge may believe the answer to be or that the judge may be of the view that any other conclusion would be perverse. The trial judge may give an opinion on the matter but never a direction: *R. v. Gunning*, [2005] 1 S.C.R. 627, 196 C.C.C. (3d) 123.

Subsection (2) – To avail himself of this defence, the accused is not necessarily required to retreat and certainly when he is in his own home is not required to retreat and give up his home to his adversary: *R. v. Deegan* (1979), 49 C.C.C. (2d) 417 (Alta. C.A.). Similarly, in *R. v. Docherty* (2012), 292 C.C.C. (3d) 465, the Ontario Court of Appeal held that the jury was not entitled to consider whether the accused could have retreated from his own home in the face of an attack by the deceased.

A person need not be reduced to a state of frenzy in resisting the attack before self-defence is available to him as a defence to a charge of assault: *R. v. Antley* (1963), [1964] 2 C.C.C. 142 (Ont. C.A.).

Subsection (3) – Where physical resistance is offered to an illegal search by peace officers this defence will lie: *R. v. Larlham*, [1971] 4 W.W.R. 304 (B.C.C.A.).

Evidence to support self-defence – Expert psychiatric evidence as to the "battered wife syndrome" was admissible where the accused relied upon the defence under former subsec. (2), which justified the use of deadly force in certain circumstances. Such evidence, relating to the ability of the accused to perceive danger from the deceased, went to the issue of whether she reasonably apprehended death or grievous bodily harm, on the occasion in question, from a threat by the deceased to kill the accused at some later time. While subsec. (2) does not actually stipulate that the accused apprehend imminent danger before acting in self-defence, there is an assumption that it is inherently unreasonable to apprehend death or grievous bodily harm unless and until the physical assault is actually in progress, at which point the victim can reasonably gauge the requisite amount of force needed to repel the attack and act accordingly. Expert testimony can cast doubt on these assumptions as they applied in the context of the battered wife's efforts to repel an assault. Such evidence can explain the heightened sensitivity of a battered woman to her partner's acts. The issue is not what an outsider would have reasonably perceived but what the accused reasonably perceived given her situation and experience. The expert evidence would also be of assistance to the jury on the issue of whether the accused believed on reasonable grounds that it was not otherwise possible to preserve herself from death or grievous bodily harm. The question the jury must ask itself is whether, given the history, circumstances and perception of the accused, her belief that she could not preserve herself from being killed by the deceased later that night except by killing the spouse first was reasonable. This evidence would explain, for example, why the accused could not flee: *R. v. Lavallee*, [1990] 1 S.C.R. 852, 55 C.C.C. (3d) 97 (7:0). See also *R. v. McConnell*, [1996] 1 S.C.R. 1075, affg the dissenting judgment of Conrad J.A. (1995), 169 A.R. 321 (C.A.).

An unlawful assault includes an honest but reasonable mistake as to the existence of an assault. To the extent that expert evidence respecting battered woman syndrome may assist a jury in assessing the reasonableness of an accused's perception, it is relevant to the issue of unlawful assault. A jury must be charged that evidence regarding battered woman syndrome is relevant to the issue of self-defence in respect of the following: why an abused woman might remain in an abusive relationship; the nature and extent of the violence that may exist in an abusive relationship; the accused's ability to perceive danger from her abuser; and whether the accused believed on reasonable grounds that she could not otherwise preserve herself from death or grievous bodily harm: *R. v. M. (M.A.)*, [1998] 1 S.C.R. 123, 121 C.C.C. (3d) 456.

On the trial of a charge of murder where the accused relies on self-defence, evidence of the deceased's character or disposition for violence is admissible to show the probability of the deceased having been the aggressor and to support the accused's evidence that he was attacked by the deceased. This disposition may be evidenced by proof of specific acts of violence unknown to the accused at the time of the incident, by evidence of reputation and by psychiatric evidence, if the question falls within the proper sphere of expert evidence. However, to be admissible, the specific acts of violence unknown to the accused must have sufficient probative value that they will legitimately and reasonably assist the jury and there must exist some other appreciable evidence of the deceased's aggression on the occasion in question. This latter evidence may emanate from the accused himself: *R. v. Scopelliti* (1981), 63 C.C.C. (2d) 481 (Ont. C.A.).

In assessing the admissibility of prior acts of violence by the deceased, its prejudicial impact in arousing feelings of hostility towards the deceased must be weighed against its probative value within the context of affording a fair trial to the accused. On the other hand, where the evidence was of acts of violence against the accused and her relatives, it was no objection to admission that some of these acts had taken place sometime in the past. Even prior acts of destruction of property can be admitted in proper circumstances where, as here, in light of the deceased's history of violence, it would not be unreasonable for the accused to fear that anger directed for the moment towards property would be expanded to assaults upon the person. Further, in light of defence counsel's statement that the evidence was essential for the defence of self-defence to which the accused would be testifying, it may be elicited by counsel through cross-examination of Crown witnesses: *R. v. Ryan* (1989), 49 C.C.C. (3d) 490 (Nfld. C.A.).

The mere fact that the accused raised the defence of self-defence in his evidence, here evidence that the deceased pointed a gun at him, did not permit the Crown to lead evidence of the deceased's peaceable character in rebuttal: *R. v. Dejong* (1998), 125 C.C.C. (3d) 302 (B.C.C.A.).

The evidence of the prior acts of violence unknown to the accused must have sufficient probative value for the purpose for which it is tendered to justify its admission. Evidence which is logically relevant may still be excluded because of the costs or risks associated with its admission: *R. v. Yaeck* (1991), 68 C.C.C. (3d) 545 (Ont. C.A.), leave to appeal to S.C.C. refused [1992] 1 S.C.R. xii, 71 C.C.C. (3d) vii.

Defence of Property

DEFENCE — PROPERTY / No defence / No defence.

35. (1) A person is not guilty of an offence if
- **(*a*) they either believe on reasonable grounds that they are in peaceable possession of property or are acting under the authority of, or lawfully assisting, a person whom they believe on reasonable grounds is in peaceable possession of property;**
- **(*b*) they believe on reasonable grounds that another person**
  - **(i) is about to enter, is entering or has entered the property without being entitled by law to do so,**
  - **(ii) is about to take the property, is doing so or has just done so, or**
  - **(iii) is about to damage or destroy the property, or make it inoperable, or is doing so;**
- **(*c*) the act that constitutes the offence is committed for the purpose of**

     (i) **preventing the other person from entering the property, or removing that person from the property, or**

     (ii) **preventing the other person from taking, damaging or destroying the property or from making it inoperative, or retaking the property from that person; and**

  (*d*) **the act committed is reasonable in the circumstances.**

(2) Subsection (1) does not apply if the person who believes on reasonable grounds that they are, or who is believed on reasonable grounds to be, in peaceable possession of the property does not have a claim of right to it and the other person is entitled to its possession by law.

(3) Subsection (1) does not apply if the other person is doing something that they are required or authorized by law to do in the administration or enforcement of the law, unless the person who commits the act that constitutes the offence believes on reasonable grounds that the other person is acting unlawfully. R.S.C. 1970, c. C-34, s. 35; 2012, c. 9, s. 2.

CROSS-REFERENCES

The defence of use of force to protect persons is dealt with in s. 34. As to use of force in administration or enforcement of the law, see s. 25.

SYNOPSIS

This section codifies the defence of use of force in defence of property. It replaces a number of sections that had created a complex web of overlapping and confusing provisions. The section also avoids terms such as trespasser and trespassing. While the former provisions dealt separately with real and personal property, this section deals with both types of property. Subsection (1) sets out four essential requirements. For the sake of convenience, the person seeking to avail themselves of the defence will be referred to as the accused. First, the accused must believe that they are in peaceable possession of the property or they are acting under the authority of, or lawfully assisting, the person who they believe is in peaceable possession. The belief must be on reasonable grounds. Second, the accused must believe on reasonable grounds that the other person is entering or has entered the property without being entitled by law, is about to take the property, is doing so, or has just done so or is about to damage or destroy the property or make it inoperative or is doing so. Third, the act constituting the offence must be committed for the purpose of prevent the other person from entering the property or removing the person from the property or preventing the other person from taking, damaging, or destroying the property or from making it inoperative, or retaking the property from that person. Finally, the act committed by the accused must be reasonable in the circumstances.

    Under subsec. (2), the defence in this section is not available if the accused does not have a claim of right and the other person is entitled to possession by law. The defence is also not available if victim is doing something that they are required or authorized by law to do in the administration or enforcement of the law, unless the accused believes on reasonable grounds that the victim is acting unlawfully.

ANNOTATIONS

Editors' Note: We have removed most of the annotations from ss. 34 to 42 which previously dealt with self-defence, related defences and defence of property. The remaining annotations, although decided under the predecessor sections, were thought to be of some assistance but they must be read with considerable care give the wholesale revisions of the provisions of the Code dealing with the justifiable use of force in defence of person or property.

    While the firing of a gun at a person to prevent him from taking movable property may not be justified, the mere pointing of the firearm to scare the person off may, depending on the circumstances, be justified: *R. v. Weare* (1983), 4 C.C.C. (3d) 494 (N.S.C.A.).

A private licensed bailiff may re-acquire possession of movable property for his principal peacefully, but he cannot oppose resistance by another person entitled by law to its possession: *R. v. Doucette* (1960), 129 C.C.C. 102 (Ont. C.A.).

"Claim of right" includes an honest although mistaken belief in entitlement to the property, even though the mistake of fact is based on an error of law or fact: *R. v. Lei* (1997), 120 C.C.C. (3d) 441 (Man. C.A.), leave to appeal to S.C.C. refused (1998), 123 C.C.C. vi, *sub nom. R. v. Kwan.*

On a prosecution for obstructing a peace officer in the execution of his duty arising out of an attempt by the accused to prevent the warrantless entry of the officer into the accused's home, the onus of establishing justification is a severe one. Where the Crown failed to establish either a statutory or common law right of entry, the accused was entitled to resist the entry by force: *R. v. Kephart* (1988), 44 C.C.C. (3d) 97 (Alta. C.A.).

36. [*Repealed, 2012, c. 9, s. 2.*]

37. [*Repealed, 2012, c. 9, s. 2.*]

38. [*Repealed, 2012, c. 9, s. 2.*]

39. [*Repealed, 2012, c. 9, s. 2.*]

40. [*Repealed, 2012, c. 9, s. 2.*]

41. [*Repealed, 2012, c. 9, s. 2.*]

42. [*Repealed, 2012, c. 9, s. 2.*]

Protection of Persons in Authority

CORRECTION OF CHILD BY FORCE.

43. Every schoolteacher, parent or person standing in the place of a parent is justified in using force by way of correction toward a pupil or child, as the case may be, who is under his care, if the force does not exceed what is reasonable under the circumstances. R.S., c. C-34, s. 43.

CROSS-REFERENCES

The terms "schoolteacher", "child", "pupil" and "parent" are not defined, but case-law has provided meaning to those terms. See especially *R. v. Ogg-Moss*, and *R. v. Nixon, infra.* As to liability for excessive force, see s. 26.

SYNOPSIS

This section justifies the use of *force* by certain persons *to correct a child or pupil.*

The persons who may rely upon this section are *schoolteachers, parents or those standing in the place of a parent.* The child or pupil must be *under the care of the person using the force,* and the force must be applied for the *purpose of correcting the child.* Thus, if the child is too young to learn from the correction or is incapable due to mental disability, the use of force will not be justified by s. 43. The force applied cannot exceed what is *reasonable* in the circumstances. This would appear to be an objective standard, although the reference to "in the circumstances" permits some element of subjectivity to be considered.

ANNOTATIONS

This provision does not violate ss. 7, 12, or 15 of the *Canadian Charter of Rights and Freedoms* due to vagueness or overbreadth: *Canadian Foundation for Children, Youth, and the Law v. Canada (Attorney General)*, [2004] 1 S.C.R. 76, 180 C.C.C. (3d) 353.

The person applying the force must have intended it to be for educative or corrective purposes and the child must be capable of benefiting from the correction. "Reasonable under the circumstances" requires the application of an objective test in the context and in light of all of the circumstances of the case. The gravity of the precipitating event is not a relevant consideration. Only minor corrective force of a transitory and trifling nature is exempt from criminal sanction. The provision does not apply to children under two or teenagers as they are not capable of benefiting from such correction. Similarly, children suffering from a disability or as a result of some other contextual factor may not be capable of learning from the force and in such circumstances, the force cannot be said to be corrective. Degrading, inhuman or harmful conduct is not protected. Discipline by the use of objects or blows or slaps to the head is unreasonable. Teachers may reasonably apply force to remove a child from a classroom or secure compliance with instructions but not merely as corporal punishment. Conduct stemming from the caregiver's frustration, loss of temper or abusive personality is not reasonable: *Canadian Foundation for Children, Youth, and the Law v. Canada (Attorney General)*, supra.

A mentally retarded adult at a residential centre is neither a "child" nor a "pupil" within the meaning of this section. A "pupil" is limited to a child taking instruction. Further, a mental retardation counsellor at such a centre is not a person standing in the place of a parent, having only temporary care of the adult, not being responsible for the adult's pecuniary needs and by express direction not the delegate of the Minister for the purpose of using force for correction. As well, such counsellor having functions related to personal care of the patient rather than *teaching was not a "schoolteacher"*: *R. v. Ogg-Moss*, [1984] 2 S.C.R. 173, 14 C.C.C. (3d) 116 (5:0); *R. v. Nixon*, [1984] 2 S.C.R. 197, 14 C.C.C. (3d) 257 (5:0).

A babysitter in charge of a child is a person standing in the place of a parent for the purpose of this section: *R. v. Murphy* (1996), 108 C.C.C. (3d) 414, 49 C.R. (4th) 321 (B.C.C.A.).

In determining whether the force used was reasonable under the circumstances the court must consider the customs of the contemporary Canadian community, not the customs of the accused's former country where corporal punishment may have greater acceptance: *R. v. Baptiste and Baptiste* (1980), 61 C.C.C. (2d) 438 (Ont. Prov. Ct.).

Religious beliefs cannot be used to expand the constitutionally accepted scope of this provision: *R. v. Poulin* (2002), 169 C.C.C. (3d) 378, 7 C.R. (6th) 369, 218 Nfld. & P.E.I.R. 68 (P.E.I.S.C.T.D.).

The trial judge erred by stating that the spanking should not have gone on to the point that an onlooker called police. This wrongly applied a subjective standard that effectively delegated the determination of reasonableness to the onlooker: *R. v. S. (S.)* (2011), 277 C.C.C. (3d) 169 (N.B.C.A.).

---

44. [*Repealed*, 2001, c. 26, s. 294.]

SURGICAL OPERATIONS.

45. Every one is protected from criminal responsibility for performing a surgical operation on any person for the benefit of that person if
   (a) the operation is performed with reasonable care and skill; and
   (b) it is reasonable to perform the operation, having regard to the state of health of the person at the time the operation is performed and to all the circumstances of the case. R.S., c. C-34, s. 45.

CROSS-REFERENCES

As to duty to use reasonable knowledge, skill and care in administering surgical care, see s. 216. This section is complementary to the criminal negligence provisions in ss. 219 to 221.

SYNOPSIS

This section sets forth the circumstances in which a person performing surgery for the benefit of a patient is protected from criminal responsibility. They are where: (1) the surgery was done with reasonable care and skill; and (2) it was demonstrably reasonable to perform the operation. In assessing whether these circumstances existed, the relevant factors are the state of the patient's health when the surgery was performed and all other circumstances of the case.

ANNOTATIONS

The conduct of a physician in stopping the respiratory support treatment of his patient, at the freely given and informed request of the patient so that nature may take its course, is not unreasonable within the meaning of this section and would not attract criminal liability: *Nancy B. v. Hôtel-Dieu de Québec* (1992), 69 C.C.C. (3d) 450, 86 D.L.R. (4th) 385, [1992] R.J.Q. 361 (S.C.).

Part II / OFFENCES AGAINST PUBLIC ORDER

Treason and other Offences against the Queen's Authority and Person

HIGH TREASON / Treason / Canadian citizen / Overt act.

46. (1) Every one commits high treason who, in Canada,

   (a) kills or attempts to kill Her Majesty, or does her any bodily harm tending to death or destruction, maims or wounds her, or imprisons or restrains her;

   (b) levies war against Canada or does any act preparatory thereto; or

   (c) assists an enemy at war with Canada, or any armed forces against whom Canadian Forces are engaged in hostilities, whether or not a state of war exists between Canada and the country whose forces they are.

(2) Every one commits treason who, in Canada,

   (a) uses force or violence for the purpose of overthrowing the government of Canada or a province;

   (b) without lawful authority, communicates or makes available to an agent of a state other than Canada, military or scientific information or any sketch, plan, model, article, note or document of a military or scientific character that he knows or ought to know may be used by that state for a purpose prejudicial to the safety or defence of Canada;

   (c) conspires with any person to commit high treason or to do anything mentioned in paragraph (a);

   (d) forms an intention to do anything that is high treason or that is mentioned in paragraph (a) and manifests that intention by an overt act; or

   (e) conspires with any person to do anything mentioned in paragraph (b) or forms an intention to do anything mentioned in paragraph (b) and manifests that intention by an overt act.

(3) Notwithstanding subsection (1) or (2), a Canadian citizen or a person who owes allegiance to Her Majesty in right of Canada,

   (a) commits high treason if, while in or out of Canada, he does anything mentioned in subsection (1); or (*b*) **commits treason if, while in or out of Canada, he does anything mentioned in subsection (2).**

(4) Where it is treason to conspire with any person, the act of conspiring is an overt act of treason. R.S., c. C-34, s. 46; 1974-75-76, c. 105, s. 2.

CROSS-REFERENCES

Punishment for high treason, see ss. 47(1), 745(*a*). Punishment for treason, see s. 47(2). Limitation period for treason, see s. 48. Limitation as to admission of evidence of overt acts in treason trials, see s. 55. Section 581(4) requires that every overt act that is to be relied on shall be stated in the indictment and by s. 601(9) the indictment may not be amended so as to add to the overt acts. Indictments in case of high treason, see s. 582. Section 604 enacts special provisions for delivery of the indictment, list of witnesses and jury panel to the accused prior to trial of treason or high treason, with some exceptions, as, for example, the offence described by subsec. (1)(*a*). Unavailability of defence of compulsion by threats, see s. 17. The offences in this section are triable only by the superior court of criminal jurisdiction (defined in s. 2) by virtue of ss. 468 and 469. By virtue of s. 522, only a judge of the superior court of criminal jurisdiction may release an accused charged with this offence. This offence may be the basis for constructive murder under s. 230 and the basis for an application for an authorization to intercept private communications by reason of s. 183.

Related offences: s. 49, acts intended to alarm Her Majesty or cause her bodily harm; s. 50(1)(*a*), assisting enemy alien; s. 51, intimidating Parliament or legislature; s. 52, sabotage; s. 53, inciting mutiny; s. 54, assisting deserter from Canadian Forces; s. 56, assisting deserter from R.C.M.P. It is also an offence to fail to report the fact that a person is about to commit treason or high treason, s. 50(1)(*b*). Reference should also be made to the *Official Secrets Act*, R.S.C. 1985, c. O-5.

SYNOPSIS

This section creates the offences of treason and high treason. It also prohibits certain activities by persons outside of Canada.

The elements of high treason are set out in s. 46(1). It includes specified violent actions against the Queen, levying war (or preparing to do so) against Canada or assisting an enemy at war with Canada or whose armed forces are engaged in hostilities with our armed forces.

The offence of treason is created by s. 46(2). Section 46(2)(*a*) states that treason is committed if a person uses force to overthrow the government of Canada or of a province. Section 46(2)(*d*) provides that if a person forms the intention to commit the acts described in s. 46(1)(*a*) and shows that intention by doing an overt act, this is also the full offence of treason. It is also treason to conspire to do the acts described in s. 46(1)(*a*) or to conspire to commit high treason.

An alternative basis for liability is found in s. 46(2)(*b*), stemming from making available any of a specified class of documents to a foreign agent or state which the accused *knows or ought to know* could be used for a purpose prejudicial to the *safety or defence of Canada*. This paragraph specifies that the accused must have no lawful authority for communicating or making available such material. A conspiracy to do so or the intention to do so if accompanied by an overt act constitutes treason under s. 46(2)(*e*).

Section 46(4) provides that conspiring is an overt act of treason in circumstances in which it is treason to conspire with another person.

Section 46(3) imposes liability for either high treason or treason, as the case may be, upon Canadians or those who owe allegiance to Her Majesty in right of Canada for doing the things *inside or outside of Canada* described in s. 46(1) or (2).

PUNISHMENT FOR HIGH TREASON / Punishment for treason / Corroboration / Minimum punishment.

47. (1) Every one who commits high treason is guilty of an indictable offence and shall be sentenced to imprisonment for life.

(2) **Every one who commits treason is guilty of an indictable offence and liable**

   (*a*) **to be sentenced to imprisonment for life if he is guilty of an offence under paragraph 46(2)(*a*), (*c*) or (*d*);**

   (*b*) **to be sentenced to imprisonment for life if he is guilty of an offence under paragraph 46(2)(*b*) or (*e*) committed while a state of war exists between Canada and another country; or**

   (*c*) **to be sentenced to imprisonment for a term not exceeding fourteen years if he is guilty of an offence under paragraph 46(2)(*b*) or (*e*) committed while no state of war exists between Canada and another country.**

(3) **No person shall be convicted of high treason or treason on the evidence of only one witness, unless the evidence of that witness is corroborated in a material particular by evidence that implicates the accused.**

(4) **For the purposes of Part XXIII, the sentence of imprisonment for life prescribed by subsection (1) is a minimum punishment. R.S., c. C-34, s. 47; 1974-75-76, c. 105, s. 2.**

CROSS-REFERENCES
Definition of treason and high treason, see s. 46. Punishment for high treason, parole ineligibility, see s. 745(*a*).

Limitation period in treason, see s. 48; Limitation as to admission of evidence of overt acts in treason trials, see s. 55. Section 581(4) requires that every overt act that is to be relied on shall be stated in the indictment and, by s. 601(9), the indictment may not be amended so as to add to the overt acts. Indictments in case of high treason, see s. 582. Unavailability of defence of compulsion by threats, see s. 17. Trial of these offences is by the superior court of criminal jurisdiction (defined in s. 2) by virtue of ss. 468 and 469. By virtue of s. 522, only a judge of the superior court of criminal jurisdiction may release an accused charged with these offences. This offence may be the basis for constructive murder under s. 230 and the basis for an application for an authorization to intercept private communications by reason of s. 183.

SYNOPSIS
This section sets out the punishment for high treason and treason as well as providing for an evidentiary rule applicable to such cases.

The *punishment for high treason is life imprisonment* and this is the *minimum* mandatory punishment. Subsection (2) defines a number of different circumstances under which the sentence for treason varies from 14 years to life.

Section 47(3) provides that no one may be convicted of either offence on the evidence of a sole witness unless that evidence is corroborated in a material particular by evidence implicating the accused.

ANNOTATIONS
In *R. v. B.(G.)*, [1990] 2 S.C.R. 3, 56 C.C.C. (3d) 161, 77 C.R. (3d) 327 (5:0), the court considered the effect of now repealed s. 586, which provided that no person shall be convicted on the unsworn evidence of a child "unless the evidence of the child is corroborated in a material particular by evidence that implicates the accused". The wording is thus almost identical to subsec. (3) of this section. It was there held that the requirement that the corroborating evidence implicate the accused requires only that the evidence confirm in some material particular the story of the witness giving the evidence which required corroboration. The confirming evidence need not also itself implicate the accused.

LIMITATION / Information for treasonable words.
48. (1) No proceedings for an offence of treason as defined by paragraph 46(2)(*a*) shall be commenced more than three years after the time when the offence is alleged to have been committed.

(2) No proceedings shall be commenced under section 47 in respect of an overt act of treason expressed or declared by open and considered speech unless

    (*a*) **an information setting out the overt act and the words by which it was expressed or declared is laid under oath before a justice within six days after the time when the words are alleged to have been spoken; and**

    (*b*) **a warrant for the arrest of the accused is issued within ten days after the time when the information is laid. R.S., c. C-34, s. 48; 1974-75-76, c. 105, s. 29.**

CROSS-REFERENCES

The term "year" is defined in s. 37 of the *Interpretation Act*, R.S.C. 1985, c. I-21, and, by reason of that definition, calculation of the three year period would be pursuant to s. 28 of the same Act as a number of months. Calculation of the periods of time set out in subsec. (2) is pursuant to the rules in s. 27 of the *Interpretation Act*. In particular, subsec. (5) which provides that where anything is to be done "within" a time after a specified day, the time does not include that day. Also see s. 26 for when time limited expires on a holiday (defined in s. 35 of the same Act). For other provisions relating to treason, see notes under ss. 46 and 47.

SYNOPSIS

This section imposes certain time limits within which prosecutions for particular types of treason may be commenced.

Section 48(1) states that a three-year time-limit applies from the date of the offence if the allegation is based upon the use of force to overthrow the government of Canada or of a province (s. 46(2)(*a*)).

Section 48(2) requires that in order for a prosecution on an allegation of treason based on words spoken in open speech to proceed, the information must be placed before a justice within six days of the words being said and a warrant for the arrest of the accused issued within 10 days thereafter. The information alleging the offence must specify the words which are said to constitute treason.

Prohibited Acts

ACTS INTENDED TO ALARM HER MAJESTY OR BREAK PUBLIC PEACE.

49. Every one who wilfully, in the presence of Her Majesty,

    (*a*) **does an act with intent to alarm Her Majesty or to break the public peace, or**

    (*b*) **does an act that is intended or is likely to cause bodily harm to Her Majesty, is guilty of an indictable offence and liable to imprisonment for a term not exceeding fourteen years. R.S., c. C-34, s. 49.**

CROSS-REFERENCES

Limitation on admission of evidence of overt acts, see s. 55. Section 581(4) requires that every overt act that is to be relied on shall be stated in the indictment and, by s. 601(9), the indictment may not be amended so as to add to the overt acts. This offence is triable only by the superior court of criminal jurisdiction (defined in s. 2) pursuant to ss. 468 and 469. By virtue of s. 522, only a judge of the superior court of criminal jurisdiction may release an accused charged with this offence.

Related offences: s. 46(1)(*a*), high treason includes killing, attempting to kill or causing certain forms of bodily harm to, or imprisoning or restraining Her Majesty. Conviction for these offences will, in certain circumstances, require imposition of an order prohibiting possession of firearms, ammunition or explosive substance under s. 109.

SYNOPSIS

This section creates indictable offences punishable by a maximum of 14 years for doing an act *in the presence of Her Majesty* which is likely to cause her bodily harm or is intended to do so, or for doing an act *with the intention* of either *alarming* her or breaching the public peace. In addition to the elements of the offence already noted, such acts must be proven to be *wilful.*

ASSISTING ALIEN ENEMY TO LEAVE CANADA, OR OMITTING TO PREVENT TREASON / Punishment.

50. (1) Every one commits an offence who
  (a) **incites or wilfully assists a subject of**
    (i) **a state that is at war with Canada, or**
    (ii) **a state against whose forces Canadian Forces are engaged in hostilities, whether or not a state of war exists between Canada and the state whose forces they are,**
  to leave Canada without the consent of the Crown, unless the accused establishes that assistance to the state referred to in subparagraph (i) or the forces of the state referred to in subparagraph (ii), as the case may be, was not intended thereby; or
  (b) **knowing that a person is about to commit high treason or treason does not, with all reasonable dispatch, inform a justice of the peace or other peace officer thereof or make other reasonable efforts to prevent that person from committing high treason or treason.**

(2) Every one who commits an offence under subsection (1) is guilty of an indictable offence and liable to imprisonment for a term not exceeding fourteen years. R.S., c. C-34, s. 50; 1974-75-76, c. 105, s. 29.

CROSS-REFERENCES

The terms "Canadian forces", "justice" and "peace officer" are defined in s. 2. Treason and high treason are defined in s. 46. Limitation on admission of evidence of overt acts, see s. 55. The accused has an election as to mode of trial pursuant to s. 536(2). Release of the accused pending trial is governed by s. 515. Section 581(4) requires that every overt act that is to be relied on shall be stated in the indictment and, by s. 601(9), the indictment may not be amended so as to add to the overt acts. Section 7(11) provides for admission of a certificate of the Secretary of State for External Affairs stating that, at a certain time, any state was engaged in an armed conflict against Canada. The term "wilfully" does not have a fixed meaning and must take its meaning from the context. Generally speaking, however, it connotes an intention to bring about a proscribed consequence. See: *R. v. Buzzanga and Durocher* (1979), 49 C.C.C. (2d) 369 (Ont. C.A.).

SYNOPSIS

This section sets out the indictable offences of assisting an enemy alien to leave Canada or omitting to prevent treason. Both offences are punishable by a maximum sentence of 14 years imprisonment.

The offence created by s. 50(1)(a) is committed by either *inciting or wilfully assisting* a person who is a subject of a country with whom Canada is at war or with whom our armed forces are engaged in hostilities (regardless of whether war has been declared) to leave Canada. It must be shown that the accused did not have the consent of the Crown for the impugned actions or incitement. The accused may rely upon the defence that there was no intention to assist the foreign government or forces but the *onus is upon the accused* to establish that no such intention existed.

Section 50(1)(b) creates one of the few offences in the *Criminal Code* in which liability is established by an omission to report to the authorities the *knowledge that another is about to commit* an offence. The offence is based on the omission of the accused to advise a justice of the peace or peace officer that another person is about to commit *treason or high treason* or to make other reasonable efforts to prevent the commission of either offence.

INTIMIDATING PARLIAMENT OR LEGISLATURE.

51. Every one who does an act of violence in order to intimidate Parliament or the legislature of a province is guilty of an indictable offence and liable to imprisonment for a term not exceeding fourteen years. R.S., c. C-34, s. 51.

CROSS-REFERENCES

Limitation on admission of evidence of overt acts, see s. 55. Section 581(4) requires that every overt act that is to be relied on shall be stated in the indictment and, by s. 601(9), the indictment may not be amended so as to add to the overt acts. This offence is triable only by the superior court of criminal jurisdiction (defined in s. 2) pursuant to ss. 468 and 469. By virtue of s. 522, only a judge of the superior court of criminal jurisdiction may release an accused charged with this offence. This offence may be the basis for an application for an authorization to intercept private communications by reason of s. 183.

SYNOPSIS

This section spells out the indictable offence of intimidating Parliament or a provincial legislature. It must be shown that the accused did an act of violence with the *intention* of creating such intimidation. The maximum sentence upon conviction is 14 years.

SABOTAGE / Definition of "prohibited act" / Saving / Idem.

52. (1) Every one who does a prohibited act for a purpose prejudicial to

    (*a*) **the safety, security or defence of Canada, or**

    (*b*) **the safety or security of the naval, army or air forces of any state other than Canada that are lawfully present in Canada,**

is guilty of an indictable offence and liable to imprisonment for a term not exceeding ten years.

(2) In this section, "prohibited act" means an act or omission that

    (*a*) **impairs the efficiency or impedes the working of any vessel, vehicle, aircraft, machinery, apparatus or other thing; or**

    (*b*) **causes property, by whomever it may be owned, to be lost, damaged or destroyed.**

(3) No person does a prohibited act within the meaning of this section by reason only that

    (*a*) **he stops work as a result of the failure of his employer and himself to agree on any matter relating to his employment;**

    (*b*) **he stops work as a result of the failure of his employer and a bargaining agent acting on his behalf to agree on any matter relating to his employment; or**

    (*c*) **he stops work as a result of his taking part in a combination of workmen or employees for their own reasonable protection as workmen or employees.**

(4) No person does a prohibited act within the meaning of this section by reason only that he attends at or near or approaches a dwelling-house or place for the purpose only of obtaining or communicating information. R.S., c. C-34, s. 52.

CROSS-REFERENCES

"Dwelling-house" is defined in s. 2.

Limitation on admission of evidence of overt acts, see s. 55. Section 581(4) requires that every overt act that is to be relied on shall be stated in the indictment. Note, however, that unlike, for example, on the trial of an offence under s. 53, s. 601(9), which provides that the indictment may not be amended so as to add to the overt acts, does not apply to the trial of this offence. The accused has an election as to mode of trial pursuant to s. 536(2). Release of the accused pending trial is governed by s. 515. This offence may be the basis for an application for an authorization to intercept private communications by reason of s. 183 or a warrant to conduct video surveillance under s. 487.01(5).

SYNOPSIS

This section creates the indictable offence of sabotage and provides exceptions from liability for certain acts or omissions.

The offence is set out in s. 52(1) and consists of doing one of the *prohibited acts* specified in subsec. (2) *for a purpose prejudicial* to the safety, security or defence of the nation, or to the armed forces of another nation which are lawfully within Canada. The maximum sentence for this offence is 10 years.

Subsections (3) and (4) set out the exceptions to the application of this section. Subsection (3) details a number of reasons why an accused may have stopped work (relating primarily to labour disputes and safety concerns) and provides that *these actions alone* do not constitute a prohibited act (see subsec. (2)). Subsection (4) exempts those who go near a place or house *for the purpose only* of obtaining or communicating information.

INCITING TO MUTINY.

53. Every one who
- **(a) attempts, for a traitorous or mutinous purpose, to seduce a member of the Canadian Forces from his duty and allegiance to Her Majesty, or**
- **(b) attempts to incite or to induce a member of the Canadian Forces to commit a traitorous or mutinous act,**

is guilty of an indictable offence and liable to imprisonment for a term not exceeding fourteen years. R.S., c. C-34, s. 53.

CROSS-REFERENCES

"Canadian Forces" is defined in s. 2. Attempt is defined in s. 24.

Limitation on admission of evidence of overt acts, see s. 55. Section 581(4) requires that every overt act that is to be relied on shall be stated in the indictment and, by s. 601(9), the indictment may not be amended so as to add to the overt acts. This offence is triable only by the superior court of criminal jurisdiction (defined in s. 2) pursuant to ss. 468 and 469. By virtue of s. 522, only a judge of the superior court of criminal jurisdiction may release an accused charged with this offence. Other provisions also deal with offences concerning the military, see, for example, s. 54, assisting deserter; s. 62, offences in relation to military forces; ss. 419, 420, offences in relation to military uniforms and certificates and military stores.

Reference should also be made to the *National Defence Act*, R.S.C. 1985, c. N-5.

SYNOPSIS

This section prohibits attempting to *incite* members of the armed forces *to mutiny*. Paragraph (*a*) requires proof that the accused had a *traitorous or mutinous purpose* for attempting to seduce a member of the forces from his duty and allegiance to the Queen. Paragraph (*b*) prohibits the accused from attempting to induce or incite a member of the armed forces to a mutinous or traitorous act. In neither case is it necessary to show that the attempt was successful. The maximum sentence upon conviction for this indictable offence is 14 years.

ASSISTING DESERTER.

54. Every one who aids, assists, harbours or conceals a person who he knows is a deserter or absentee without leave from the Canadian Forces is guilty of an offence

punishable on summary conviction, but no proceedings shall be instituted under this section without the consent of the Attorney General of Canada. R.S., c. C-34, s. 54.

CROSS-REFERENCES

"Canadian Forces" and "Attorney General" are defined in s. 2. As to consent of Attorney General, see s. 583(*h*). Trial of this offence is by a summary conviction court pursuant to Part XXVII. The punishment for this offence is set out in s. 787. The limitation period is set out in s. 786(2). Release pending trial is governed by s. 515, although the accused is eligible for release by a peace officer or the officer in charge, pursuant to ss. 496, 497 and 498. Other provisions also deal with offences concerning the military, see for example: s. 53, inciting to mutiny; s. 62, offences in relation to military forces; ss. 419, 420, offences in relation to military uniforms and certificates and military stores and s. 120, bribery of public officer [note *officers* of the Canadian Forces are within the definition of public officer in s. 2]; s. 122, breach of trust by official; s. 129(*a*), obstructing public officer; s. 129(*b*), refusing to aid public officer; s. 399, false return by public officer.

SYNOPSIS

Section 54 creates an offence punishable on summary conviction for *aiding, assisting, harbouring,* or *concealing* a *deserter* or person who is absent without leave from the armed forces. The accused *must know the status* of the forces member. The federal Attorney General must consent to the commencement of any prosecution under this section.

EVIDENCE OF OVERT ACTS.

55. In proceedings for an offence against any provision in section 47 or sections 49 to 53, no evidence is admissible of an overt act unless that overt act is set out in the indictment or unless the evidence is otherwise relevant as tending to prove an overt act that is set out therein. R.S., c. C-34, s. 55.

CROSS-REFERENCES

Section 581(4) also requires that every overt act that is to be relied on shall be stated in the indictment and except in the case of the offence of sabotage under s. 52, by s. 601(9), the indictment may not be amended so as to add to the overt acts.

SYNOPSIS

This section sets out a rule of criminal procedure which imposes particular requirements upon the wording of an indictment in prosecutions under ss. 47 and 49 to 53. The indictment (which includes an information pursuant to s. 2) must specify the overt act alleged in order for such evidence to be received against the accused. This section mirrors the contents of s. 581(3), in that the substance of the overt act alleged in prosecutions under the aforementioned sections must be specified in the indictment. However, if the evidence is otherwise relevant as tending to prove an overt act alleged in the indictment it may be admitted.

OFFENCES IN RELATION TO MEMBERS OF R.C.M.P.

56. Every one who wilfully

    (*a*) **persuades or counsels a member of the Royal Canadian Mounted Police to desert or absent himself without leave,**

    (*b*) **aids, assists, harbours or conceals a member of the Royal Canadian Mounted Police who he knows is a deserter or absentee without leave, or**

    (*c*) **aids or assists a member of the Royal Canadian Mounted Police to desert or absent himself without leave, knowing that the member is about to desert or absent himself without leave,**

is guilty of an offence punishable on summary conviction. R.S., c. C-34, s. 57; R.S.C. 1985, c. 27 (1st Supp.), s. 8.

CROSS-REFERENCES

"Counsel" is defined in s. 22(3). Trial of this offence is by a summary conviction court pursuant to Part XXVII. The punishment for this offence is set out in s. 787. The limitation period is set out in s. 786(2). Release pending trial is governed by s. 515 although the accused is eligible for release by a peace officer or the officer in charge pursuant to ss. 496, 497 and 498. Other provisions also deal with offences concerning the R.C.M.P., see for example: s. 120, bribery of public officer [note *officers* of the R.C.M.P. are within the definition of public officer in s. 2]; s. 122, breach of trust by official; s. 129(*a*), obstructing public officer; s. 129(*b*), refusing to aid public officer; s. 399, false return by public officer.

SYNOPSIS

Section 56 creates a number of summary conviction offences in relation to members of the R.C.M.P. who are deserters or unlawfully absent without leave. The section specifies a number of prohibited activities which may occur prior to the action by the member or after the member has deserted or is absent without leave. The actions must be done *wilfully* and the assistance be given to the member about to improperly leave the force must be done either *with the knowledge* that the member of the force *is about to desert* or be absent without leave (s. 56(*c*)), or *knowing* that the member has already done so (s. 56(*b*)). It is also an offence to counsel to persuade a member to desert or to be absent without leave. It is not necessary to prove that the accused succeeded in convincing the member to leave the force improperly.

Official Documents

IDENTITY DOCUMENTS / For greater certainty / Definition of "identity document" / Punishment.

56.1 (1) Every person commits an offence who, without lawful excuse, procures to be made, possesses, transfers, sells or offers for sale an identity document that relates or purports to relate, in whole or in part, to another person.

(2) For greater certainty, subsection (1) does not prohibit an act that is carried out

> **(*a*) in good faith, in the ordinary course of the person's business or employment or in the exercise of the duties of their office;**
>
> **(*b*) for genealogical purposes;**
>
> **(*c*) with the consent of the person to whom the identity document relates or of a person authorized to consent on behalf of the person to whom the document relates, or of the entity that issued the identity document; or**
>
> **(*d*) for a legitimate purpose related to the administration of justice.**

(3) For the purposes of this section, "identity document" means a Social Insurance Number card, a driver's licence, a health insurance card, a birth certificate, a death certificate, a passport as defined in subsection 57(5), a document that simplifies the process of entry into Canada, a certificate of citizenship, a document indicating immigration status in Canada, a certificate of Indian status or an employee identity card that bears the employee's photograph and signature, or any similar document, issued or purported to be issued by a department or agency of the federal government or of a provincial or foreign government.

(4) Every person who commits an offence under subsection (1)

> **(*a*) is guilty of an indictable offence and liable to imprisonment for a term of not more than five years; or**
>
> **(*b*) is guilty of an offence punishable on summary conviction. 2009, c. 28, s. 1.**

```
  440              555        4692
 x  4             x 2        1273
-----           -----       -----
 1760            1110        3419
 1110
-----             440
 2870            x 5
                -----
3300.50           00
2354.89
-------                      3300
1045.61                       227
 227.70                     -----
-------                      3527
1273 31  ✳      ✳.
                             4692
                             3527
   cancel                   -----
                             1175
   CIBC m/c
   —

Lois Ann Burney
Re Reh @ Church
_____

Dionne      CIBC
            519 539 55 44
Fred rc tables        ) x226
```

Youtube . com

World Trade Centre
History
8.55

8.52
Toronto 18 videos

Oklahoma bombing
news footage from
Oklahoma building
4 17

How OKC bombing
unfolded
Domestic terrorist
bombing, ships
vessel

CROSS-REFERENCES

Related offences are: s. 57, offences in relation to passports; s. 130, personating a peace officer; s. 340, destroying identity documents; s. 342, unauthorized use of credit cards; s. 342.01, possession of instrument for copying credit cards; s. 362, obtaining by false pretences; s. 367, forgery; s. 368, use and trafficking in a forged document; s. 368.1, possession of instruments for purpose of committing forgery; s. 374, drawing a false document; s. 380, fraud; ss. 402.1-403, identity theft and fraud; s. 404, personation at an examination.

SYNOPSIS

This section, part of Bill S-4, a comprehensive scheme for dealing with identity theft and related offences, makes it an offence, without lawful excuse, to procure to be made, possess, transfer, sell or offer for sale identity documents as defined in subsec. (3) that relate or purport to relate, in whole or in part, to another person. For greater certainty, subsec. (2) makes clear that certain activities do not come within the offence, such as a person who creates such documents as part of their ordinary business or employment, or has the consent of the other person, or for a legitimate purpose related to the administration of justice.

FORGERY OF OR UTTERING FORGED PASSPORT / False statement in relation to passport / Possession of forged, etc., passport / Special provisions applicable / Definition of "passport" / Jurisdiction / Appearance of accused at trial.

57. (1) Every one who, while in or out of Canada,

   (*a*) forges a passport, or

   (*b*) knowing that a passport is forged

      (i) uses, deals with or acts on it, or

      (ii) causes or attempts to cause any person to use, deal with, or act on it, as if the passport were genuine,

is guilty of an indictable offence and liable to imprisonment for a term not exceeding fourteen years.

(2) Every one who, while in or out of Canada, for the purpose of procuring a passport for himself or any other person or for the purpose of procuring any material alteration or addition to any such passport, makes a written or an oral statement that he knows is false or misleading

   (*a*) is guilty of an indictable offence and liable to imprisonment for a term not exceeding two years; or

   (*b*) is guilty of an offence punishable on summary conviction.

(3) Every one who without lawful excuse, the proof of which lies on him, has in his possession a forged passport or a passport in respect of which an offence under subsection (2) has been committed is guilty of an indictable offence and liable to imprisonment for a term not exceeding five years.

(4) For the purposes of proceedings under this section,

   (*a*) the place where a passport was forged is not material; and

   (*b*) the definition "false document" in section 321, and section 366, apply with such modifications as the circumstances require.

(5) In this section, "passport" has the same meaning as in section 2 of the *Canadian Passport Order*.

(6) Where a person is alleged to have committed, while out of Canada, an offence under this section, proceedings in respect of that offence may, whether or not that person is in Canada, be commenced in any territorial division in Canada and the accused may be tried and punished in respect of that offence in the same manner as if the offence had been committed in that territorial division.

(7) For greater certainty, the provisions of this Act relating to (*a*) **requirements that an accused appear at and be present during proceedings, and**

    (*b*) **the exceptions to those requirements,**

apply to proceedings commenced in any territorial division pursuant to subsection (6).
R.S., c. C-34, s. 58; R.S.C. 1985, c. 27 (1st Supp.), s. 9; 1994, c. 44, s. 4; 1995, c. 5, s. 25; 2013, c. 19, s. 1.

CROSS-REFERENCES

The general offence of forgery is set out in ss. 366 and 367 and of uttering in s. 368. For the offences prescribed by subsec. (1) and (3) the accused has an election as to mode of trial pursuant to s. 536(2). For the offence prescribed by subsec. (2), where the prosecution proceeds by way of summary conviction, then the trial is conducted by a summary conviction court pursuant to Part XXVII. The punishment for the offence is then as set out in s. 787 and the limitation period is set out in s. 786(2). Where the prosecution proceeds by way of indictment, then the accused has an election as to mode of trial pursuant to s. 536(2). In any event, release pending trial is governed by s. 515, except that, for the offence in subsec. (2), the accused is eligible for release by a peace officer or the officer in charge pursuant to ss. 496, 497 and 498 and, in the case of the offence in subsec. (3), by the officer in charge pursuant to s. 498. The reference in subsec. (7) to requirements as to presence of the accused is to s. 650. The term "territorial division" is defined in s. 2. The offences in this section may be the basis for an application for an authorization to intercept private communications by reason of s. 183.

The related offence of fraudulent use of a certificate of citizenship and similar documents is found in s. 58. Reference may also be made to the personation offence in s. 403.

SYNOPSIS

This section creates offences relating to the creation of forged passports and their subsequent use or possession.

Section 57(5) provides a definition of passport for the purpose of this section. Section 57(4)(*b*) provides that the definitions of "false document" in ss. 321 and 366 apply to this section with whatever modifications are required. Section 57(6) extends the normal concept of jurisdiction to facilitate prosecution in any territorial division of Canada for an offence under this section which was committed outside the country. Section 57(7) provides that provisions which normally govern when the accused must be present at trial (and when there are exceptions to that rule) apply to any prosecution brought using the special jurisdictional provisions in s. 57(6). The section states that it does not matter where the passport was forged (s. 57(4)(*a*)).

Section 57(1) creates an indictable offence punishable by a maximum of 14 years if the accused *forges the passport personally* or for specified acts relating to either using, dealing with it or acts on it personally or causes another to do so when the accused *knows* that it is forged. The subsection applies regardless of whether these acts occur in Canada.

Section 57(2) creates an offence which turns on the accused making *false or misleading statements* in connection with passports. It must be shown that these statements were made *for the purpose* of either obtaining a passport initially or getting one altered or added to in some *material* way. This offence states that the accused may be in or out of Canada when the statements are made. This offence may be tried by summary conviction proceeding or by way of indictment. If prosecuted by indictment the maximum sentence is two years.

Section 57(3) makes it an offence to possess a passport resulting from the commission of the offence described in subsec. (2). This is an indictable offence punishable by a maximum sentence of five years. The accused may rely upon a lawful excuse but must prove such excuse. As with all burdens placed upon the accused, this provision is likely to attract scrutiny under the *Canadian Charter of Rights and Freedoms.*

ANNOTATIONS

An accused may be convicted of the offence under subsec. (1)(*a*) where she caused another person to actually make the false passport, although the other person was unaware that the statements provided by the accused were false. While the accused could not be convicted of aiding or abetting the other person, who committed no offence, she could be convicted as a principal by application of the common law doctrine of innocent agent, a doctrine preserved in s. 21(1)(*a*): *R. v. Berryman* (1990), 57 C.C.C. (3d) 375, 78 C.R. (3d) 376 (B.C.C.A.).

An accused could be convicted of the offences under both subsec. (1)(*a*) and subsec. (2), although both charges arose out of the same circumstances. The elements of the two offences are quite different and, in this case, there were other acts beside the providing of the false statements which were instrumental in the forging of the passport: *R. v. Berryman, supra.*

FRAUDULENT USE OF CERTIFICATE OF CITIZENSHIP / Definition of "certificate of citizenship" and "certificate of naturalization".

58. (1) Every one who, while in or out of Canada,

   (*a*) **uses a certificate of citizenship or a certificate of naturalization for a fraudulent purpose, or**

   (*b*) **being a person to whom a certificate of citizenship or a certificate of naturalization has been granted, knowingly parts with the possession of that certificate with intent that it should be used for a fraudulent purpose,**

is guilty of an indictable offence and liable to imprisonment for a term not exceeding two years.

(2) In this section, "certificate of citizenship" and "certificate of naturalization", respectively, mean a certificate of citizenship and a certificate of naturalization as defined by the *Citizenship Act*. R.S., c. C-34, s. 59; 1974-75-76, c. 108, s. 41.

CROSS-REFERENCES

The accused has an election as to mode of trial pursuant to s. 536(2). Release pending trial is governed by s. 515, except that the accused is eligible for release by the officer in charge pursuant to s. 498.

The related offences of forgery of or uttering a forged passport are found in s. 57. Reference may also be made to the personation offence in s. 403.

SYNOPSIS

This section creates the indictable offence of *fraudulently using* a certificate of naturalization or citizenship. It also prohibits *parting with* a certificate of citizenship or naturalization, *knowing and intending* that it will be used fraudulently. The offence is committed whether the improper activities involving these certificates occur inside or outside Canada. The certificates referred to in the section are to be given the meaning set out in the *Citizenship Act*. The maximum sentence for this offence is two years.

Sedition

SEDITIOUS WORDS / Seditious libel / Seditious conspiracy / Seditious intention.

59. (1) Seditious words are words that express a seditious intention.

(2) A seditious libel is a libel that expresses a seditious intention.

(3) A seditious conspiracy is an agreement between two or more persons to carry out a seditious intention.

(4) Without limiting the generality of the meaning of the expression "seditious intention", every one shall be presumed to have a seditious intention who

   (*a*) **teaches or advocates, or**

(*b*) **publishes or circulates any writing that advocates,**

the use, without the authority of law, of force as a means of accomplishing a governmental change within Canada. R.S., c. C-34, s. 60.

CROSS-REFERENCES
Defence of good faith, see s. 60.

Punishment for sedition, see s. 61.

Special provisions for indictment of seditious libel and for proof of the libel, see s. 584. The sedition offences are triable only by the superior court of criminal jurisdiction (defined in s. 2) by virtue of ss. 468 and 469. By virtue of s. 522, only a judge of the superior court of criminal jurisdiction may release an accused charged with this offence. The offences in this section may be the basis for an application for an authorization to intercept private communications by reason of s. 183. The offence of blasphemous libel is in s. 296, of defamatory libel in ss. 297 to 317 and advocating genocide and hate propaganda in ss. 318 to 320.

SYNOPSIS
This section sets out the essential elements of offences relating to sedition which are created in s. 61. Section 59(4) provides two examples of what is *presumed to demonstrate a seditious intention*, but it is expressly stated that this subsection is not intended to exhaustively define what is encompassed by the phrase *seditious intention*. This presumption may be subject to attack under the *Canadian Charter of Rights and Freedoms*. The heart of the examples given in this subsection is advocating, without legal authority, the use of *force to achieve governmental change within Canada.*

Section 59(1) to (3) defines what is meant by seditious words, seditious libel and seditious conspiracy, all of which have, as the cornerstone, the concept of expressing or agreeing to carry out a seditious intention.

ANNOTATIONS
The leading case on this section is *R. v. Boucher*, [1951] S.C.R. 265, 99 C.C.C. 1, [1951] 2 D.L.R. 369 (after rehearing ordered from 96 C.C.C. 48, [1950] 1 D.L.R. 657, 9 C.R. 127) decided under s. 133 of the 1927 Code which was essentially worded the same as this section. The court was divided on whether a "seditious intention" required proof in all cases of an intention to incite acts of violence or public disorder. Kerwin, Rand, Kellock and Estey JJ. were of the view that it did. Taschereau, Cartwright, Fauteux and (*semble*) Locke JJ. were of the view that it did in all cases except those related to the administration of justice which required only proof of an intention to bring the administration of justice into hatred or contempt or incite disaffection against it. Rinfret C.J.C. did not come to a firm conclusion on the matter but merely pointed out that the advocating of force was not the only instance in which there could be a "seditious intention".

EXCEPTION.
60. Notwithstanding subsection 59(4), no person shall be deemed to have a seditious intention by reason only that he intends, in good faith,
   (*a*) **to show that Her Majesty has been misled or mistaken in her measures;**
   (*b*) **to point out errors or defects in**
      (i) **the government or constitution of Canada or a province,**
      (ii) **Parliament or the legislature of a province, or**
      (iii) **the administration of justice in Canada;**
   (*c*) **to procure, by lawful means, the alteration of any matter of government in Canada; or**
   (*d*) **to point out, for the purpose of removal, matters that produce or tend to produce feelings of hostility and ill-will between different classes of persons in Canada. R.S., c. C-34, s. 61.**

CROSS-REFERENCES

The sedition offences are defined in s. 59.

Punishment for sedition offences is in s. 61.

The sedition offences are triable only by the superior court of criminal jurisdiction (defined in s. 2) by virtue of ss. 468 and 469. By virtue of s. 522 only a judge of the superior court of criminal jurisdiction may release an accused charged with this offence. The sedition offences may be the basis for an application for an authorization to intercept private communications by reason of s. 183.

SYNOPSIS

This section sets out several specific exceptions protecting what might otherwise be said to come within the phrase *seditious intention* as expressed in s. 59(4). The focus of the exceptions is to permit legitimate criticism of the Queen or government policies or to procure change in the government by lawful means. In addition, s. 60(*d*) permits a person to point out matters which may produce ill will among the people of Canada if this is done with the intention of their removal.

PUNISHMENT OF SEDITIOUS OFFENCES.

61. Every one who

  (*a*) **speaks seditious words,**

  (*b*) **publishes a seditious libel, or**

  (*c*) **is a party to a seditious conspiracy,**

is guilty of an indictable offence and liable to imprisonment for a term not exceeding fourteen years. R.S., c. C-34, s. 62.

CROSS-REFERENCES

The sedition offences are defined in s. 59. Note the good faith exception in s. 60.

Special provision for indictment of seditious libel, see s. 584.

Special provisions for indictment of seditious libel and for proof of the libel, see s. 584.

The sedition offences are triable only by the superior court of criminal jurisdiction (defined in s. 2) by virtue of ss. 468 and 469. By virtue of s. 522, only a judge of the superior court of criminal jurisdiction may release an accused charged with this offence. The offences referred to in this section may be the basis for an application for an authorization to intercept private communications by reason of s. 183.

SYNOPSIS

This section creates indictable offences relating to sedition and provides for a maximum sentence upon conviction of 14 years. The gravamen of these offences is expressing a seditious intention, either through speaking words evincing such intention or publishing such words. The third offence also involves seditious intention and prohibits conspiring to carry out this intention.

OFFENCES IN RELATION TO MILITARY FORCES / Definition of "member of a force".

62. (1) Every one who wilfully

  (*a*) **interferes with, impairs or influences the loyalty or discipline of a member of a force,**

  (*b*) **publishes, edits, issues, circulates or distributes a writing that advises, counsels or urges insubordination, disloyalty, mutiny or refusal of duty by a member of a force, or**

  (*c*) **advises, counsels, urges or in any manner causes insubordination, disloyalty, mutiny or refusal of duty by a member of a force,**

is guilty of an indictable offence and liable to imprisonment for a term not exceeding five years.

(2) In this section, "member of a force" means a member of

    (a) **the Canadian Forces; or**

    (b) **the naval, army or air forces of a state other than Canada that are lawfully present in Canada. R.S., c. C-34, s. 63.**

CROSS-REFERENCES

"Canadian Forces" is defined in s. 2. "Counsels" is defined in s. 22(3). The term "wilfully" does not have a fixed meaning and must take its meaning from the context. Generally speaking, however, it connotes an intention to bring about a proscribed consequence. See: *R. v. Buzzanga and Durocher* (1979), 49 C.C.C. (2d) 369 (Ont. C.A.). The accused has an election as to mode of trial pursuant to s. 536(2). Release pending trial is governed by s. 515 except that the accused is eligible for release by the officer in charge pursuant to s. 498.

Other provisions also deal with offences concerning the military, see, for example, s. 53, inciting to mutiny; s. 54, assisting deserter; ss. 419, 420, offences in relation to military uniforms and certificates and military stores.

Reference should also be made to the *National Defence Act*, R.S.C. 1985, c. N-5.

SYNOPSIS

This section prohibits activity designed to create disloyalty, insubordination, mutiny or refusal of duty by military forces in Canada. Subsection (2) expands the section to apply to both Canadian forces and the armed forces of any other nation which are lawfully present in Canada. Section 62(1)(a) spells out a variety of activities which are prohibited, including interfering with the loyalty or discipline of a member of the forces. Section 62(1)(b) focuses on participation in activities such as the publication, circulation and distribution of written material advocating such insubordination, disloyalty, mutiny or refusal of duty. Section 62(1)(c) prohibits urging, counselling, *or in any way causing* the same range of improper activities by a member of a force as is set out in s. 62(1)(b).

The maximum sentence for this indictable offence is five years.

Unlawful Assemblies and Riots

UNLAWFUL ASSEMBLY / Lawful assembly becoming unlawful / Exception.

63. (1) An unlawful assembly is an assembly of three or more persons who, with intent to carry out any common purpose, assemble in such a manner or so conduct themselves when they are assembled as to cause persons in the neighbourhood of the assembly to fear, on reasonable grounds, that they

    (a) **will disturb the peace tumultuously; or**

    (b) **will by that assembly needlessly and without reasonable cause provoke other persons to disturb the peace tumultuously.**

(2) Persons who are lawfully assembled may become an unlawful assembly if they conduct themselves with a common purpose in a manner that would have made the assembly unlawful if they had assembled in that manner for that purpose.

(3) Persons are not unlawfully assembled by reason only that they are assembled to protect the dwelling-house of any one of them against persons who are threatening to break and enter it for the purpose of committing an indictable offence therein. R.S., c. C-34, s. 64.

CROSS-REFERENCES

Arrest powers for breach of the peace, see ss. 30, 31.

Being a member of an unlawful assembly is a summary conviction offence pursuant to s. 66. The trial is conducted by a summary conviction court pursuant to Part XXVII. The punishment for the offence is then as set out in s. 787 and the limitation period is set out in s. 786(2).

Related provisions concerning riots, including procedure for reading of proclamation to disperse rioters and offences relating to riots, see ss. 64, 65, 67, 68, 69. Use of force to suppress a riot and the duty of officers to disperse rioters, see ss. 32 and 33. The offence of causing a disturbance is in s. 175.

SYNOPSIS

Section 63 sets out what constitutes an *unlawful assembly*, and also provides for certain exceptions. Stripped to its essentials, s. 63(1) requires that three or more persons be involved, and that they assemble in a way, or behave in such a way after assembling, that causes others in the neighbourhood to be afraid that the assembly will either disturb the peace tumultuously or provoke others to do so. Tumultuous means chaotic, disorderly, clamourous or uproarious. It must be shown that the assembly has gathered together *with the intention to carry out a common purpose*, and that the *fears* of those in the area of the assembly are *based on reasonable grounds*. If the offence lies under s. 63(1)(b) (provoking others), the accused have the defence of reasonable cause.

Simplified, s. 63(2) provides that any assembly, which was initially lawful may become an unlawful assembly if the people assembled conduct themselves in a manner which would have brought them within s. 63(1), had they done so at the outset of the assembly. Again, it must be shown that there was a common purpose for the assembly under this paragraph.

Subsection (3) exempts persons from criminal liability if they have assembled for the *purpose of protecting the dwelling house* of any of those assembled from others who wish to break and enter this dwelling with the intention of committing therein an indictable offence.

ANNOTATIONS

Subsection (1)(a) does not violate ss. 2(b), (c), (d) or 7 of the Charter: *R. v. Lecompte* (2000), 149 C.C.C. (3d) 185 (Que. C.A.), leave to appeal to S.C.C. refused 151 C.C.C. (3d) vi.

An individual member of an assembly is not guilty if he is unaware that the other individuals assembled for the purpose of disturbing the peace or that some individuals conducted themselves in the neighbourhood of the assembly in a manner as to cause fear, on reasonable grounds, that they will disturb the peace tumultuously: *R. v. Lecompte, supra*.

A grievance against the authorities does not provide a legal right to occupy a roadway, which is a public highway over which all members of the public are entitled to traverse: *R. v. Thomas* (1971), 2 C.C.C. (2d) 514, [1971] 2 W.W.R. 734 (B.C. Co. Ct.).

Provided that the accused is part of the assembly which has become unlawful through the conduct of its members then it is no defence that he was passively acquiescent: *R. v. Paulger and Les* (1982), 18 C.C.C. (3d) 78 (B.C. Co. Ct.).

RIOT.

64. A riot is an unlawful assembly that has begun to disturb the peace tumultuously.
R.S., c. C-34, s. 65.

CROSS-REFERENCES

Section 63, definition of "unlawful assembly"; s. 65, punishment of rioters; s. 67, procedure for reading of proclamation to disperse rioters; s. 68, offences relating to reading of proclamation; s. 69, offence for failure of peace officer to suppress riot; ss. 32 and 33, use of force to suppress a riot and the duty of officers to disperse rioters.

ANNOTATIONS

It is essential to proof of a riot that there be actual or threatened force and violence, in addition to public disorder, confusion and uproar. Moreover, even if a tumultuous disturbance of the peace breaks out during an assembly, the accused must be shown first to have taken some part in that disturbance in one way or another. In addition, the requirement that the persons in the neighbourhood of the assembly fear "on reasonable grounds" that the members of the assembly will disturb the peace tumultuously requires that these grounds be manifest to any reasonable person within the assembly. What is required is at least objective foresight of the consequences set out in s. 63. Finally, the accused must be shown not only to have acted as a participant, but also to have intended to take part in the riot or to have been so reckless as to have acted as if he did so intend. The offence therefore requires proof of a guilty intent, does not impose absolute liability and therefore does not violate s. 7 of the Charter: *R. v. Brien* (1993), 86 C.C.C. (3d) 550, [1994] N.W.T.R. 59 (S.C.).

A tumultuous disturbance requires an air or atmosphere of actual or constructive force of violence. This provision does not violate s. 7 of the Charter as it is neither vague nor overbroad: *R. v. Berntt* (1997), 120 C.C.C. (3d) 344, 11 C.R. (5th) 131 (B.C.C.A.).

PUNISHMENT OF RIOTER / Concealment of identity.

65. (1) Every one who takes part in a riot is guilty of an indictable offence and liable to imprisonment for a term not exceeding two years.

(2) Every person who commits an offence under subsection (1) while wearing a mask or other disguise to conceal their identity without lawful excuse is guilty of an indictable offence and liable to imprisonment for a term not exceeding 10 years. R.S., c. C-34, s. 66; 2013, c. 15, s. 2.

CROSS-REFERENCES

Definition of "riot", see s. 64. The accused has an election as to mode of trial pursuant to s. 536(2). Release pending trial is governed by s. 515 except that the accused is eligible for release by the officer in charge pursuant to s. 498. Conviction for this offence may, in certain circumstances, attract imposition of an order prohibiting possession of firearms, ammunition or explosive substance under s. 110. Procedure for reading of proclamation to disperse rioters, see s. 67 and offences relating to reading of proclamation, see s. 68. Offence for failure of peace officer to suppress riot, see s. 69. Use of force to suppress a riot and the duty of officers to disperse rioters, see ss. 32 and 33.

PUNISHMENT FOR UNLAWFUL ASSEMBLY / Concealment of identity.

66. Every one who is a member of an unlawful assembly is guilty of an offence punishable on summary conviction.

(2) Every person who commits an offence under subsection (1) while wearing a mask or other disguise to conceal their identity without lawful excuse is guilty of

> **(a) an indictable offence and liable to imprisonment for a term not exceeding five years; or**
>
> **(b) an offence punishable on summary conviction. R.S., c. C-34, s. 67; 2013, c. 15, s. 3.**

CROSS-REFERENCES

Definition of "unlawful assembly", see s. 63. The trial is conducted by a summary conviction court pursuant to Part XXVII. The punishment for the offence is set out in s. 787 and the limitation period is set out in s. 786(2). Release pending trial is governed by s. 515, except that the accused is eligible for release by a peace officer or the officer in charge pursuant to ss. 496, 497 and 498. Arrest powers for breach of the peace, see ss. 30, 31. Related provisions concerning riots, including procedure for reading of proclamation to disperse rioters and offences relating to riots, see ss. 64, 65, 67, 68, 69. Use of force to suppress a riot and the duty of officers to disperse rioters, see ss. 32 and 33. The offence of causing a disturbance is in s. 175.

ANNOTATIONS

This provision does not violate ss. 2(*b*), (*c*), (*d*) or 7 of the Charter: *R. v. Lecompte* (2000), 149 C.C.C. (3d) 185 (Que. C.A.), leave to appeal to S.C.C. refused 151 C.C.C. (3d) vi.

The actions of only a few members can turn the assembly into an unlawful one as defined in s. 63 and thereby render all members of the assembly liable to be convicted of the offence under this section: *R. v. Kalyn* (1980), 52 C.C.C. (2d) 378 (Sask. Prov. Ct.).

READING PROCLAMATION.

67. A person who is
> (*a*) **a justice, mayor or sheriff, or the lawful deputy of a mayor or sheriff,**
> (*b*) **a warden or deputy warden of a prison, or**
> (*c*) **the institutional head of a penitentiary, as those expressions are defined in subsection 2(1) of the *Corrections and Conditional Release Act*, or that person's deputy,**

who receives notice that, at any place within the jurisdiction of the person, twelve or more persons are unlawfully and riotously assembled together shall go to that place and, after approaching as near as is safe, if the person is satisfied that a riot is in progress, shall command silence and thereupon make or cause to be made in a loud voice a proclamation in the following words or to the like effect:

Her Majesty the Queen charges and commands all persons being assembled immediately to disperse and peaceably to depart to their habitations or to their lawful business on the pain of being guilty of an offence for which, on conviction, they may be sentenced to imprisonment for life. GOD SAVE THE QUEEN. R.S., c. C-34, s. 68; 1994, c. 44, s. 5.

CROSS-REFERENCES

Definition of "justice", see s. 2. Definition of riot, see s. 64. The definition of sheriff or mayor will be found in the relevant provincial legislation. A justice, sheriff and mayor are peace officers as defined by s. 2. Offences of obstructing a peace officer, see s. 129 and assaulting a peace officer in execution of duty, see s. 270. The offence of taking part in a riot is in s. 65. Punishment of offences in relation to reading of proclamation, see s. 68. Offence by peace officer in failing to suppress riot, see s. 69. Use of force to suppress a riot and the duty of officers to disperse rioters, see ss. 32 and 33.

SYNOPSIS

Section 67 provides for what is commonly referred to as "*reading the riot act*" by a justice, mayor or sheriff (or lawful deputy of the latter two officials) or the head of a prison or penitentiary. The prerequisites for reading the proclamation are that there be *12 or more people* who are unlawfully and riotously assembled and that the official is satisfied that a riot is in progress. The official must then command silence, and shall read, or cause another to read, the "riot act" in a loud voice from as close to those assembled as is safe. The precise words set out in the *Criminal Code* need not be used, so long as the words are "of like effect".

ANNOTATIONS

The trial judge erred in instructing Crown witnesses to omit reference to imprisonment "for life" when testifying about the proclamation, as the evidence did not convey the same message as the proclamation referred to in this provision: *R. v. Thorne* (2004), 192 C.C.C. (3d) 424, 27 C.R. (6th) 366 (N.B.C.A.).

OFFENCES RELATED TO PROCLAMATION.

68. Every one is guilty of an indictable offence and liable to imprisonment for life who

   (*a*) opposes, hinders or assaults, wilfully and with force, a person who begins to make or is about to begin to make or is making the proclamation referred to in section 67 so that it is not made;

   (*b*) does not peaceably disperse and depart from a place where the proclamation referred to in section 67 is made within thirty minutes after it is made; or

   (*c*) does not depart from a place within thirty minutes when he has reasonable grounds to believe that the proclamation referred to in section 67 would have been made in that place if some person had not opposed, hindered or assaulted, wilfully and with force, a person who would have made it. R.S., c. C-34, s. 69.

CROSS-REFERENCES

Procedure for reading proclamation, see s. 67 and cross-references noted under that section. The accused has an election as to mode of trial pursuant to s. 536(2). Release pending trial is governed by s. 515. Conviction for these offences will, in certain circumstances, require imposition of an order prohibiting possession of firearms, ammunition or explosive substance under s. 109.

SYNOPSIS

Section 68 creates a number of indictable offences which flow from the reading of the "riot act" pursuant to s. 67, or an effort to do so. The maximum punishment for these offences is imprisonment for life.

Section 68(*a*) sets out a number of different means of obstructing the efforts of the person who is about to begin, or who has begun, to read the "riot act". The actions of the accused must prevent the completion or the reading of the proclamation. There is no intention specified in the paragraph beyond the intention to do the specified acts *wilfully and with force* to thwart the reading of the proclamation.

Section 68(*b*) makes it an offence not to leave the location where the "riot act" was read and to disperse peacefully within 30 minutes of it being read.

Section 68(*c*) imposes liability for failing to depart and disperse in similar terms to that described in para. (*b*) if the accused had *reasonable grounds to believe* that the proclamation, although not read, would have been, had the official not been thwarted from doing so.

NEGLECT BY PEACE OFFICER.

69. A peace officer who receives notice that there is a riot within his jurisdiction and, without reasonable excuse, fails to take all reasonable steps to suppress the riot is guilty of an indictable offence and liable to imprisonment for a term not exceeding two years. R.S., c. C-34, s. 70.

CROSS-REFERENCES

"Peace officer" is defined in s. 2. Definition of "riot", see s. 64. Procedure for reading proclamation to disperse rioters, see s. 67 and see cross-references noted under that section. Use of force to suppress a riot and the duty of officers to disperse rioters, see ss. 32 and 33. The accused has an election as to mode of trial pursuant to s. 536(2). Release pending trial is governed by s. 515 except that the accused is eligible for release by the officer in charge pursuant to s. 498.

SYNOPSIS

This section creates an offence applicable *only to peace officers* who fail to take all reasonable steps to suppress a riot. It must be shown that the peace officer had notice of the riot within the officer's jurisdiction, and that there was no reasonable excuse for the failure to take steps. This is an indictable offence with a maximum sentence of two years.

ANNOTATIONS

An action against a police officer for damages as the result of the killing of a person taking part in a riot by the officer was dismissed where the officer was found to be acting lawfully within the scope of his duty imposed by this section and s. 32: *Herbert v. Martin*, [1931] S.C.R. 145, 54 C.C.C. 257.

Unlawful Drilling

ORDERS BY GOVERNOR IN COUNCIL / General or special order / Punishment.

70. (1) The Governor in Council may, by proclamation, make orders
   (*a*) **to prohibit assemblies, without lawful authority, of persons for the purpose**
      (i) **of training or drilling themselves,**
      (ii) **of being trained or drilled to the use of arms, or**
      (iii) **of practising military exercises; or**
   (*b*) **to prohibit persons when assembled for any purpose from training or drilling themselves or from being trained or drilled.**

(2) An order that is made under subsection (1) may be general or may be made applicable to particular places, districts or assemblies to be specified in the order.

(3) Every one who contravenes an order made under this section is guilty of an indictable offence and liable to imprisonment for a term not exceeding five years. R.S., c. C-34, s. 71.

CROSS-REFERENCES

"Proclamation" is defined in s. 35 of the *Interpretation Act*, R.S.C. 1985, c. I-21, and procedure for issuing proclamations in s. 18 of that Act. Publication of proclamations is governed by the *Statutory Instruments Act*, R.S.C. 1985, c. S-22.

The accused has an election as to mode of trial pursuant to s. 536(2).

Release pending trial is governed by s. 515 except that the accused is eligible for release by the officer in charge pursuant to s. 498.

SYNOPSIS

Section 70 authorizes the Governor in Council (Cabinet) to make orders which prohibit various types of assemblies for the purpose of activities such as the training or drilling of groups, practising military exercises or arms training. The section only applies if the assembly is without lawful authority. It also prohibits persons who are assembled *for any purpose* from undertaking any of the prohibited activities.

Subsection (2) states that an order made under s. 70(1) may be general or made specifically applicable at a particular area, assembly and so on. One example of the latter would be an order prohibiting a particular private paramilitary training school from being run within Canada.

If the accused contravenes an order proclaimed under s. 70(1), s. 70(3) makes this an indictable offence punishable by up to five years' imprisonment. Basic principles of criminal responsibility (and s. 7 of the *Canadian Charter of Rights and Freedoms*) would require that there be proof that the accused knew of the existence of the relevant order.

Duels

DUELLING.

71. Every one who
   (*a*) **challenges or attempts by any means to provoke another person to fight a duel,**
   (*b*) **attempts to provoke a person to challenge another person to fight a duel, or**

(c) **accepts a challenge to fight a duel,**
is guilty of an indictable offence and liable to imprisonment for a term not exceeding two years. R.S., c. C-34, s. 72.

CROSS-REFERENCES
The accused has an election as to mode of trial for this offence, pursuant to s. 536(2). Release pending trial is governed by s. 515 except that the accused is eligible for release by the officer in charge pursuant to s. 498. Conviction for this offence may in some circumstances attract imposition of an order prohibiting possession of firearms, ammunition or explosive substance under s. 110.

SYNOPSIS
Section 71 prohibits duelling and makes it an indictable offence subject to a maximum sentence of two years.
   The section bans all aspects of duelling including making the challenge personally, attempting to provoke another to make a challenge for a duel or accepting such a challenge. The duel need not take place for any of the offences to be made out.

ANNOTATIONS
The act of the accused in loading a gun and carrying it out to the street in acceptance of a challenge by the deceased constitutes an unlawful act within this section which will support a charge of manslaughter notwithstanding the shot which killed the deceased was fired accidentally: *R. v. Lelievre* (1962), 132 C.C.C. 288, 32 D.L.R. (2d) 723 (Ont. C.A.).

Forcible Entry and Detainer

FORCIBLE ENTRY / Matters not material / Forcible detainer / Questions of law.
72. (1) A person commits forcible entry when that person enters real property that is in the actual and peaceable possession of another in a manner that is likely to cause a breach of the peace or reasonable apprehension of a breach of the peace.

(1.1) For the purposes of subsection (1), it is immaterial whether or not a person is entitled to enter the real property or whether or not that person has any intention of taking possession of the real property.

(2) A person commits forcible detainer when, being in actual possession of real property without colour of right, he detains it in a manner that is likely to cause a breach of the peace or reasonable apprehension of a breach of the peace, against a person who is entitled by law to possession of it.

(3) The questions whether a person is in actual and peaceable possession or is in actual possession without colour of right are questions of law. R.S., c. C-34, s. 73; R.S.C. 1985, c. 27 (1st Supp.), s. 10.

CROSS-REFERENCES
Punishment for this offence is prescribed by s. 73 and see cross-references under that section as to mode of trial. There are a number of related provisions as follows: ss. 30 and 31, arrest and detention for breach of the peace; s. 40, defence of dwelling against person forcibly breaking or entering dwelling house; ss. 41 and 42, defence of real property.
   The offence of break and enter with intent to commit an indictable offence is defined by s. 348. The term "colour of right" is not defined, but likely embraces an honest, although mistaken, belief of entitlement to the property although the mistake is based on a mistake of law or fact. [See discussion of colour of right in relation to theft in *R. v. Howson*, [1966] 3 C.C.C. 348 (Ont. C.A.).]

SYNOPSIS

Section 72 sets out what constitutes forcible entry or detainer.

Section 72(1) states that *forcible entry* requires proof that the accused entered real property that was actually peacefully possessed by another. It must be further shown that the accused did so in a manner that is *likely to produce either a breach of the peace* or a *reasonable apprehension* of a breach of the peace. Section 72(1.1) provides the clarification that it is irrelevant whether the accused is entitled to enter the property or whether the accused intends to try to take possession of it. Section 72(3) specifies that the issue of whether a person is in actual and peaceable possession is a question of law.

Section 72(2) spells out what comprises *forcible detainer*. It focuses upon the *improper retention of real property* by an accused who does *not have a colour of right* for doing so against the person who has a lawful right to possess this property. The accused must be in actual possession of the real property. It must be shown that the manner of detaining the property is likely to cause a breach of the peace or the reasonable apprehension of this occurring. Subsection (3) provides that the question of whether the accused is in actual possession without colour of right is a question of law. This means that the judge will determine these issues.

ANNOTATIONS

Forcible entry requires taking possession in the sense of some interference with the peaceable possession of the person in actual possession of the real property at the time of entry. The possession must be done in a manner likely to cause a breach of the peace or a reasonable apprehension of a breach of the peace. The breach or apprehended breach must flow from the manner in which possession of the real property is taken, not from the subsequent events. Accordingly, where the accused, while being pursued by the police, was allowed into the home of an acquaintance, there was no interference with peaceable possession and no actual or apprehended breach of the peace. *R. v. D. (J.)* (2002), 171 C.C.C. (3d) 188, 11 C.R. (6th) 396 (Ont. C.A.).

PUNISHMENT.

73. Every person who commits forcible entry or forcible detainer is guilty of
   (a) an offence punishable on summary conviction; or
   (b) an indictable offence and liable to imprisonment for a term not exceeding two years. R.S., c. C-34, s. 74; R.S.C. 1985, c. 27 (1st Supp.), s. 11; 1992, c. 1, s. 58.

CROSS-REFERENCES

Where the prosecution proceeds by way of summary conviction, the trial is conducted by a summary conviction court pursuant to Part XXVII. The punishment for the offence is then as set out in s. 787 and the limitation period is set out in s. 786(2). Where the prosecution proceeds by way of indictment, then the accused has an election as to mode of trial pursuant to s. 536(2), except that the accused is eligible for release by the peace officer and officer in charge pursuant to ss. 496, 497 and 498. Conviction for this offence may in some circumstances attract imposition of an order prohibiting possession of firearms, ammunition or explosive substance under s. 110.

SYNOPSIS

This section sets out the punishment for offences committed under s. 72 (forcible entry or detainer). The offence may be prosecuted by way of summary conviction or by indictment. In the latter case, the maximum sentence is two years imprisonment.

Piracy

PIRACY BY LAW OF NATIONS / Punishment.

74. (1) Every one commits piracy who does any act that, by the law of nations, is piracy.

(2) Every one who commits piracy while in or out of Canada is guilty of an indictable offence and liable to imprisonment for life. R.S., c. C-34, s. 75; 1974-75-76, c. 105, s. 3.

CROSS-REFERENCES

There is no definition of piracy in the *Criminal Code*, apparently because there was no internationally recognized definition of piracy when the Code was first enacted. In their text, *Canadian Criminal Law, International and Transnation Aspects* (Butterworths, 1981), Williams and Castel suggest that the 1958 Geneva Convention on the High Seas, to which Canada is not a party, is generally declaratory of established principles relating to piracy. Articles 15 and 16 of that Convention are as follows:

> Article 15
>
> Piracy consists of any of the following acts:
>
> (1) Any illegal acts of violence, detention or any act of depredation, committed for private ends by the crew or the passengers of a private ship or a private aircraft, and directed:
>
> (a)   On the high seas, against another ship or aircraft, or against persons or property on board such ship or aircraft;
>
> (b)   Against a ship, aircraft, persons or property in a place outside the jurisdiction of any state;
>
> (2) Any act of voluntary participation in the operation of a ship or of an aircraft with knowledge of facts making it a pirate ship or aircraft;
>
> (3) Any act of inciting or of intentionally facilitating an act described in sub-paragraph 1 or sub-paragraph 2 of this article.
>
> Article 16
>
> The acts of piracy, as defined in Article 15, committed by a warship, government ship or government aircraft whose crew has mutinied and taken control of the ship or aircraft are assimilated to acts committed by a private ship.

As to unavailability of defence of compulsion by threats, see s. 17. The offence in this section is triable only by the superior court of criminal jurisdiction (defined in s. 2) by virtue of ss. 468 and 469. By virtue of s. 522, only a judge of the superior court of criminal jurisdiction may release an accused charged with this offence. Where the offence is committed on the territorial sea or on internal waters, see s. 477. Conviction for this offence will require imposition of an order prohibiting possession of firearms, ammunition or explosive substance under s. 109.

SYNOPSIS

Section 74 makes it an indictable offence to commit any act which is defined by the law of nations as *piracy*.

Subsection (2) provides for a maximum sentence of imprisonment for life regardless of whether the act of piracy takes place in or out of Canada.

PIRATICAL ACTS.

75. Every one who, while in or out of Canada,

    (*a*)   **steals a Canadian ship,**

    (*b*)   **steals or without lawful authority throws overboard, damages or destroys anything that is part of the cargo, supplies or fittings in a Canadian ship,**

    (*c*)   **does or attempts to do a mutinous act on a Canadian ship, or**

    (*d*)   **counsels a person to do anything mentioned in paragraph (*a*), (*b*) or (*c*),** is guilty of an indictable offence and liable to imprisonment for a term not exceeding fourteen years. R.S., c. C-34, s. 76; R.S.C. 1985, c. 27 (1st Supp.), s. 7(3).

CROSS-REFERENCES

"Counsels" is defined in s. 22(3). "Steal" is defined in s. 2 as theft. Theft is defined in s. 322. Inciting to mutiny is also an offence under s. 53.

The offences in this section are triable only by the superior court of criminal jurisdiction (defined in s. 2) by virtue of ss. 468 and 469. By virtue of s. 522, only a judge of the superior court of criminal jurisdiction may release an accused charged with this offence. Where the offence is committed on the territorial sea or on internal waters, see s. 477. Conviction for this offence may, in some circumstances, require imposition of an order prohibiting possession of firearms, ammunition or explosive substance under s. 109.

SYNOPSIS

This indictable offence deals with *piracy*, but is limited to such acts committed in relation to a *Canadian ship*. The maximum sentence upon conviction for any of the offences created by this section is 14 years.

Paragraph (*a*) prohibits stealing a Canadian ship. Paragraph (*b*) prohibits, *without lawful authority*, throwing anything overboard, stealing, or damaging either the cargo of the ship or any part of supplies or fittings of the ship. Paragraph (*c*) states that doing or attempting to do a mutinous act on a Canadian ship is an offence. Finally, para. (*d*) makes it an offence to counsel any one to do any of the acts in the aforementioned paragraphs.

Offences against Air or Maritime Safety 1993, c. 7, s. 2.

HIJACKING.

76. Every one who, unlawfully, by force or threat thereof, or by any other form of intimidation, seizes or exercises control of an aircraft with intent
  (*a*) to cause any person on board the aircraft to be confined or imprisoned against his will,
  (*b*) to cause any person on board the aircraft to be transported against his will to any place other than the next scheduled place of landing of the aircraft,
  (*c*) to hold any person on board the aircraft for ransom or to service against his will, or
  (*d*) to cause the aircraft to deviate in a material respect from its flight plan,
is guilty of an indictable offence and liable to imprisonment for life. 1972, c. 13, s. 6.

CROSS-REFERENCES

Definition of "flight", see s. 7(8).

This offence, if committed outside Canada, is deemed to have been committed in Canada where the accused is found in Canada (s. 7(2)). As to place of trial, see s. 7(5). Availability of plea of *autrefois*, see s. 7(6). Requirement of consent of Attorney General of Canada where offence committed outside Canada and accused is not a Canadian citizen, see s. 7(7). As to territorial jurisdiction where offence committed in Canada, see s. 476(*d*). The accused has an election as to mode of trial pursuant to s. 536(2). Release pending trial is governed by s. 515. This offence may be the basis for first degree murder under s. 231(5)(*a*), and the basis for an application for an authorization to intercept private communications by reason of s. 183 or a warrant to conduct video surveillance under s. 487.01(5). Conviction for this offence will require imposition of an order prohibiting possession of firearms, ammunition or explosive substance under s. 109.

SYNOPSIS

Section 76 prohibits, as an indictable offence, hijacking of aircraft and provides that a person is liable to life imprisonment upon conviction.

It must be shown that the accused acted unlawfully and used either *force or the threat* thereof, or any other form of intimidation *with the intention* of procuring one of the results described in paras. (*a*) to (*d*). Briefly stated, the prohibited acts relate to confining any one against their will on a plane, holding such persons for ransom, transporting any person on a plane against their will, or causing a plane to be diverted from its scheduled flight plan. Also prohibited is forcing any person on the plane from serving against their will.

ENDANGERING SAFETY OF AIRCRAFT OR AIRPORT.

77. Every one who

  (*a*) **on board an aircraft in flight, commits an act of violence against a person that is likely to endanger the safety of the aircraft,**

  (*b*) **using a weapon, commits an act of violence against a person at an airport serving international civil aviation that causes or is likely to cause serious injury or death and that endangers or is likely to endanger safety at the airport,**

  (*c*) **causes damage to an aircraft in service that renders the aircraft incapable of flight or that is likely to endanger the safety of the aircraft in flight,**

  (*d*) **places or causes to be placed on board an aircraft in service anything that is likely to cause damage to the aircraft, that will render it incapable of flight or that is likely to endanger the safety of the aircraft in flight,**

  (*e*) **causes damage to or interferes with the operation of any air navigation facility where the damage or interference is likely to endanger the safety of an aircraft in flight,**

  (*f*) **using a weapon, substance or device, destroys or causes serious damage to the facilities of an airport serving international civil aviation or to any aircraft not in service located there, or causes disruption of services of the airport, that endangers or is likely to endanger safety at the airport, or**

  (*g*) **endangers the safety of an aircraft in flight by communicating to any other person any information that the person knows to be false,**

is guilty of an indictable offence and liable to imprisonment for life. 1972, c. 13, s. 6; 1993, c. 7, s. 3.

CROSS-REFERENCES

Definition of "flight", see s. 7(8). Aircraft deemed to be in service, see s. 7(9). Assault is defined in s. 265.

This offence, if committed outside Canada, is deemed to have been committed in Canada where the accused is found in Canada (s. 7(2)). As to place of trial, see s. 7(5). Availability of plea of *autrefois*, see s. 7(6). Requirement of consent of Attorney General of Canada where offence committed outside Canada and accused is not a Canadian citizen, see s. 7(7). As to territorial jurisdiction where offence committed in Canada, see s. 476(*d*). The accused has an election as to mode of trial pursuant to s. 536(2). Release pending trial is governed by s. 515. This offence may be the basis for an application for an authorization to intercept private communications by reason of s. 183. Conviction for this offence may in some circumstances require imposition of an order prohibiting possession of firearms, ammunition or explosive substance under s. 109.

SYNOPSIS

Section 77 creates five indictable offences relating to endangering aircraft safety while in flight or rendering an aircraft incapable of flight. Upon conviction under s. 77, a person is liable to imprisonment for life.

Paragraphs (*a*) and (*e*) involve actions by the accused *during flight*. The former makes it an offence to commit an assault that is *likely to endanger* the safety of the aircraft. Paragraph (*e*) imposes criminal liability upon any one who *communicates* any information to another that the *accused knows is false* and *endangers the safety* of the aircraft. Note that, unlike the other paragraphs in this section, para. (*e*) requires actual danger to result from the accused's action.

Paragraphs (*b*) and (*c*) prohibit activities which either result in damage to the aircraft so that it is *likely to endanger the safety* of the aircraft or make it incapable of flight. Paragraph (*d*) prohibits interference with air navigation facilities which is likely to endanger aircraft in flight. The doing of an action specified in one of these paragraphs which has the likelihood of producing the endangerment is sufficient to make out the offence.

OFFENSIVE WEAPONS AND EXPLOSIVE SUBSTANCES / Definition of "civil aircraft".

78. (1) Every one, other than a peace officer engaged in the execution of his duty, who takes on board a civil aircraft an offensive weapon or any explosive substance

    (*a*) **without the consent of the owner or operator of the aircraft or of a person duly authorized by either of them to consent thereto, or**

    (*b*) **with the consent referred to in paragraph (*a*) but without complying with all terms and conditions on which the consent was given,**

is guilty of an indictable offence and liable to imprisonment for a term not exceeding fourteen years.

(2) For the purposes of this section, "civil aircraft" means all aircraft other than aircraft operated by the Canadian Forces, a police force in Canada or persons engaged in the administration or enforcement of the *Customs Act*, the *Excise Act* or the *Excise Act, 2001*. 1972, c. 13, s. 6; R.S.C. 1985, c. 1 (2nd Supp.), s. 213(3); 2002, c. 22, s. 325.

CROSS-REFERENCES

Definitions of "Canadian Forces", "peace officers", "offensive weapon", "explosive substance", see s. 2.

Pursuant to s. 7(1), offences, whether inside or outside Canada, in relation to aircraft registered in Canada, or on any aircraft in flight, if the flight terminates in Canada, are deemed to be committed in Canada. Requirement of consent of Attorney General of Canada where proceedings instituted under s. 7 and accused is not a Canadian citizen, see s. 7(7). As to territorial jurisdiction where offence committed in Canada, see s. 476(*d*). The accused has an election as to mode of trial pursuant to s. 536(2). Release pending trial is governed by s. 515. This offence may be the basis for an application for an authorization to intercept private communications by reason of s. 183. Conviction for this offence may attract the imposition of an order prohibiting possession of firearms, ammunition or explosive substance under s. 109.

SYNOPSIS

This section makes it an indictable offence, subject to a number of exceptions, to take an *offensive weapon or explosive device on board a civilian aircraft*. Subsection (2) provides a definition of "civil aircraft".

Peace officers, engaged in the lawful execution of their duty, are exempted from the operation of the section. Also exempt are persons who have the consent of the owner or operator of the aircraft or a duly authorized representative of either. If conditions are imposed as part of such an agreement, it is still an offence to take explosives or offensive weapons on the aircraft *unless the accused acts in compliance with all of the terms and conditions imposed* upon the consent. The maximum sentence for an offence under this section is 14 years.

SEIZING CONTROL OF SHIP OR FIXED PLATFORM / Endangering safety of ship or fixed platform / False communication / Threats causing death or injury/ Definitions / "fixed platform" / "ship".

78.1 (1) Every one who seizes or exercises control over a ship or fixed platform by force or threat of force or by any other form of intimidation is guilty of an indictable offence and liable to imprisonment for life.

(2) Every one who

- (*a*) commits an act of violence against a person on board a ship or fixed platform,
- (*b*) destroys or causes damage to a ship or its cargo or to a fixed platform,
- (*c*) destroys or causes serious damage to or interferes with the operation of any maritime navigational facility, or
- (*d*) places or causes to be placed on board a ship or fixed platform anything that is likely to cause damage to the ship or its cargo or to the fixed platform,

where that act is likely to endanger the safe navigation of a ship or the safety of a fixed platform, is guilty of an indictable offence and liable to imprisonment for life.

(3) Every one who communicates information that endangers the safe navigation of a ship, knowing the information to be false, is guilty of an indictable offence and liable to imprisonment for life.

(4) Every one who threatens to commit an offence under paragraph (2)(*a*), (*b*) or (*c*) in order to compel a person to do or refrain from doing any act, where the threat is likely to endanger the safe navigation of a ship or the safety of a fixed platform, is guilty of an indictable offence and liable to imprisonment for life.

(5) In this section,

"fixed platform" means an artificial island or a marine installation or structure that is permanently attached to the seabed for the purpose of exploration or exploitation of resources or for other economic purposes;

"ship" means every description of vessel not permanently attached to the seabed, other than a warship, a ship being used as a naval auxiliary or for customs or police purposes or a ship that has been withdrawn from navigation or is laid up; 1993, c. 7, s. 4.

CROSS-REFERENCES

Section 7(2.2), (2.3), (3.5) and (3.7) deems certain offences to have been committed in Canada where they were committed on board a fixed platform or a ship in the circumstances set out in those subsections. Reference should be made to ss. 477 to 477.2, which set out special rules for Canadian courts assuming jurisdiction over certain offences committed in the exclusive economic zone of Canada, the continental shelf of Canada and on a ship. Section 477.3 sets out powers of arrest, entry, search or seizure or other powers of investigation in relation to such offences. Section 477.4 provides for proof by way of certificate of certain jurisdictional facts. Where a firearm is used in relation to these offences, the accused may be liable to be convicted of the offence under s. 85. The accused may also be liable to the mandatory firearm prohibition in s. 109. This offence may be the basis for an application for an authorization to intercept private communications by reason of s. 183.

The related offences of interfering with marine signals are found in s. 439.

SYNOPSIS

This section creates a number of offences in relation to a ship or fixed platform as defined in subsec. (5). While this section creates the offences, jurisdiction to try the offences will be determined in accordance with the rules set out in s. 7 and ss. 477 to 477.2. Subsection (1) creates an offence similar to the offence of hijacking aircraft. Subsection (2) creates offences where the acts of the accused endanger the safe navigation of a ship or the safety of a fixed platform. Subsection (3) makes it an offence to knowingly communicate false information that endangers the safe navigation of a ship. Subsection (4) makes it an offence to threaten to commit one of the offences set out in subsec. (2)(*a*) to (*c*) to compel a person to do or refrain from doing any act, where the threat is likely to endanger the safe navigation of a ship or the safety of the fixed platform. All offences are indictable offences for which the maximum penalty is life imprisonment.

Dangerous Materials and Devices 2013, c. 13, s. 4.

DUTY OF CARE RE EXPLOSIVE.

79. Every one who has an explosive substance in his possession or under his care or control is under a legal duty to use reasonable care to prevent bodily harm or death to persons or damage to property by that explosive substance. R.S., c. C-34, s. 77.

CROSS-REFERENCES

Definition of "explosive substance", see s. 2. Definition of "possession", see s. 4(3).

Offences for breach of duty of care re explosives, see s. 80. Note that it would seem the criminal negligence offences would also apply, see ss. 219, 220, 221.

Other offences in relation to explosives: s. 78 (take explosives aboard civil aircraft); s. 81 (using explosive); s. 82 (unlawful possession of explosives).

Although "bodily harm" is not defined in this Part, reference might be made to the definition of that term in the assault section, s. 2.

SYNOPSIS

Section 79 imposes a legal duty upon anyone, who has possession, care or control over an *explosive substance*, to use *reasonable care to prevent bodily harm, death or property damage* arising from the substance.

BREACH OF DUTY.

80. Every one who, being under a legal duty within the meaning of section 79, fails without lawful excuse to perform that duty, is guilty of an indictable offence and, if as a result an explosion of an explosive substance occurs that
  (*a*) causes death or is likely to cause death to any person, is liable to imprisonment for life; or
  (*b*) causes bodily harm or damage to property or is likely to cause bodily harm or damage to property, is liable to imprisonment for a term not exceeding fourteen years. R.S., c. C-34, s. 78.

CROSS-REFERENCES

Definition of "explosive substance", see s. 2. Although "bodily harm" is not defined for this Part, reference might be made to s. 2. The accused has an election as to mode of trial pursuant to s. 536(2). Release pending trial is governed by s. 515. This offence may be the basis for an application for an authorization to intercept private communications by reason of s. 183. Conviction for this offence may, in some circumstances, require imposition of an order prohibiting possession of firearms, ammunition or explosive substance under s. 109.

Other offences in relation to explosives: s. 78 (taking explosives aboard civil aircraft); s. 81 (using explosives); s. 82 (unlawful possession).

SYNOPSIS

Section 80 makes it an indictable offence for anyone upon whom a legal duty regarding explosives was imposed by the terms of s. 79 to breach that duty. It provides for punishment upon conviction which varies depending on the harm which was likely to result or did result from the failure of the accused to perform that duty. Note that there must be an actual explosion for this section to come into operation. The accused may rely upon a lawful excuse for the failure.

If death resulted or was likely to result, the accused is liable to life imprisonment. For lesser potential or actual harm, the punishment is a maximum of 14 years.

ANNOTATIONS

This section does not contain an included offence of failing to discharge the duty to take reasonable care under s. 79 when no explosion results: *R. v. Yanover and Gerol* (1985), 20 C.C.C. (3d) 300 (Ont. C.A.).

USING EXPLOSIVES / Punishment.

81. (1) Every one commits an offence who

  (*a*) **does anything with intent to cause an explosion of an explosive substance that is likely to cause serious bodily harm or death to persons or is likely to cause serious damage to property;**

  (*b*) **with intent to do bodily harm to any person**

   (i) **causes an explosive substance to explode,**

   (ii) **sends or delivers to a person or causes a person to take or receive an explosive substance or any other dangerous substance or thing, or**

   (iii) **places or throws anywhere or at or on a person a corrosive fluid, explosive substance or any other dangerous substance or thing;**

  (*c*) **with intent to destroy or damage property without lawful excuse, places or throws an explosive substance anywhere; or**

  (*d*) **makes or has in his possession or has under his care or control any explosive substance with intent thereby**

   (i) **to endanger life or to cause serious damage to property, or**

   (ii) **to enable another person to endanger life or to cause serious damage to property.**

(2) Every one who commits an offence under subsection (1) is guilty of an indictable offence and liable

  (*a*) **for an offence under paragraph (1)(*a*) or (*b*), to imprisonment for life; or**

  (*b*) **for an offence under paragraph (1)(*c*) or (*d*), to imprisonment for a term not exceeding fourteen years. R.S., c. C-34, s. 79.**

CROSS-REFERENCES

Definition of "explosive substance", see s. 2. Definition of possession, see s. 4(3).

The accused has an election as to mode of trial pursuant to s. 536(2). Release pending trial is governed by s. 515. This offence may be the basis for an application for an authorization to intercept private communications by reason of s. 183 and a warrant to conduct video surveillance by reason of s. 487.01(5). Conviction for this offence may, in some circumstances, require imposition of an order prohibiting possession of firearms, ammunition or explosive substance under s. 109. Under s. 231(6.1) murder is first degree murder where death is caused while committing or attempting to commit this offence for the benefit etc. of a "criminal organization".

Other offences in relation to explosives: s. 78 (taking explosive aboard civil aircraft); s. 80 (breach of duty of care in relation to explosives); s. 82 (possession without lawful excuse); s. 431.2 (placing explosives in place of public use, government or public facility or public transportation system).

SYNOPSIS

This section makes certain actions relating to dangerous substances into indictable offences and provides for the punishment of such actions.

Section 81(1)(*a*) and (*b*) prohibit actions done which may result in bodily harm to another or, in the case of para. (*a*), either bodily harm or serious damage to property. Violations of either paragraph carry a maximum sentence of life imprisonment. Section 81(1)(*a*) requires that the accused did the action with the intention of causing the explosion of an explosive device. Section 81(1)(*b*) requires that the accused intended to cause bodily harm to another by doing one of the things specified in subparas. (i) to (iii). Note that para. (*a*) requires the *likelihood* of *serious* bodily harm or death, but not the *intent* to cause such harm. On the other hand, para. (*b*) requires the intent to harm but no likelihood that such harm result.

Section 81(1)(*c*) makes it an offence to place or throw an explosive device. However, it must be shown that the accused did the act with the intention of damaging or destroying property without lawful excuse.

Section 81(1)(*d*) relates to the possession, care or control over such a device. To make out the offence under this paragraph, it must be shown that the accused had the intention by the possession, etc., of the device to either endanger life, cause serious property damage or to enable another to do so.

The maximum sentence for offences under s. 81(1)(*c*) and (*d*) is 14 years.

ANNOTATIONS
A conspiracy to violate subsec. (1)(*a*) may be based on possession of explosives where the requisite intent is shown, notwithstanding the existence of the specific possession offence in subsec. (1)(*d*): *R. v. Musitano* (1985), 24 C.C.C. (3d) 65, 53 O.R. (2d) 321 (C.A.).

POSSESSION WITHOUT LAWFUL EXCUSE / Possession in association with criminal organization.
82. (1) Every person who, without lawful excuse, the proof of which lies on the person, makes or has in the possession or under the care or control of the person any explosive substance is guilty of an indictable offence and liable to imprisonment for a term not exceeding five years.

(2) Every person who, without lawful excuse, the proof of which lies on the person, makes or has in the possession or under the care or control of the person any explosive substance for the benefit of, at the direction of or in association with a criminal organization is guilty of an indictable offence and liable to imprisonment for a term not exceeding fourteen years. R.S., c. C-34, s. 80; R.S.C. 1985, c. 27 (1st Supp.), s. 12; 1997, c. 23, s. 2.

CROSS-REFERENCES
Definition of "explosive substance" and "criminal organization", see s. 2. Definition of possession, see s. 4(3).

The accused has an election as to mode of trial pursuant to s. 536(2). Release pending trial is governed by s. 515. This offence may be the basis for an application for an authorization to intercept private communications by reason of s. 183.

Other offences in relation to explosives: s. 78 (taking explosive aboard civil aircraft); s. 80 (breach of duty of care in relation to explosives); s. 81 (using explosives).

SYNOPSIS
This section makes it an indictable offence to make, possess or have care or control of an *explosive substance*. The section permits the accused to rely upon a lawful excuse, but places the onus on the accused to establish it. The punishment upon conviction for this offence is a maximum of five years, except if the possession is for the benefit etc., of a criminal organization, in which case the maximum is 14 years and any sentence is to be served consecutively pursuant to s. 82.1.

ANNOTATIONS

The burden imposed on the accused by this section does not apply until the Crown proves beyond a reasonable doubt that the accused had possession of the explosives: *R. v. Mongeau* (1957), 25 C.R. 195 (Que. C.A.).

An accused can be guilty of possession of an explosive substance even if the device he built did not in fact explode when tested by the police. The words "explosive device" are broad enough to encompass devices that fail to function as intended: *R. v. A. (K.D.S.)* (2010), 253 C.C.C. (3d) 556 (N.B.C.A.).

SENTENCES TO BE SERVED CONSECUTIVELY

82.1 A sentence imposed on a person for an offence under subsection 82(2) shall be served consecutively to any other punishment imposed on the person for an offence arising out of the same event or series of events and to any other sentence to which the person is subject at the time the sentence is imposed on the person for an offence under subsection 82(2). 1997, c. 23, s. 2.

DEFINITION OF "DEVICE".

82.2 For the purposes of sections 82.3 to 82.5, "device" means any of the following:
　　(*a*) **a nuclear explosive device;**
　　(*b*) **a device that disperses radioactive material;**
　　(*c*) **a device that emits ionizing radiation and that is capable of causing death, serious bodily harm or substantial damage to property or the environment;**
　　(*d*) **a device that emits ionizing radiation and that is capable of causing death, serious bodily harm or substantial damage to property or the environment. 2013, c. 13, s. 5.**

CROSS-REFERENCES

The terms "environment", "nuclear facility", "nuclear material" and "radioactive material" are defined in s. 2. Section 7(2.21) allows for the prosecution in Canada of the offences in ss. 82.3 to 82.6, or a conspiracy or attempt to commit, accessory after the fact or counselling those offences although the acts or omissions were committed outside Canada if the conditions in s. 7(2.21)(*a*), (*b*), (*c*) or (*d*) are met. The definition of "terrorist activity" in s. 83.01 encompasses the offences referred to in s. 7(2.21) that implement the international instruments referred to in s. 83.01(1)(*a*)(v).

SYNOPSIS

The offences in ss. 82.3 to 82.6 were added to this Act to implement the amendments to the Convention on the Physical Protection of Nuclear Material and the International Convention for the Suppression of Acts of Nuclear Terrorism. This section defines "device" for the purpose of ss. 82.3 to 82.5. These three offences are all punishable by life imprisonment. The s. 82.3 offence deals with making a device or possessing, using or otherwise dealing with nuclear material, radioactive material or a device with intent to cause death, serious bodily harm or substantial damage to property or the environment. The section also creates offences in relation to acts against a nuclear facility. Section 82.4 in effect creates offences where nuclear material, radioactive material or a device are used for purposes of extortion. The section makes it an offence to use or alter nuclear material, radioactive material or a device to compel a person, government or international organization to do or refrain from doing any act. The section also makes it an offence to commit an act against a nuclear facility or an act that causes serious interference with or serious disruption of the facility's operation. Section 82.5 makes it an offence to commit an indictable offence with intent to obtain nuclear material, radioactive material or a device or to obtain access to a nuclear facility. Under s.

82.6, a threat to commit any of the offences under ss. 82.3 to 82.5 is itself an offence punishable by 14 years' imprisonment.

Section 82.7 confirms that these offences are not committed where the acts are committed during an armed conflict in accordance with customary or conventional international law or to activities undertaken by military forces in the circumstances set out in that section.

POSSESSION, ETC., OF NUCLEAR MATERIAL, RADIOACTIVE MATERIAL OR DEVICE.

82.3 Everyone who, with intent to cause death, serious bodily harm or substantial damage to property or the environment, makes a device or possesses, uses, transfers, exports, imports, alters or disposes of nuclear material, radioactive material or a device or commits an act against a nuclear facility or an act that causes serious interference with or serious disruption of its operations, is guilty of an indictable offence and liable to imprisonment for life. 2013, c. 13, s. 5.

CROSS-REFERENCES
See CROSS-REFERENCES under s. 82.2.

SYNOPSIS
See SYNOPSIS under s. 82.2.

USE OR ALTERATION OF NUCLEAR MATERIAL, RADIOACTIVE MATERIAL OR DEVICE.

82.4 Everyone who, with intent to compel a person, government or international organization to do or refrain from doing any act, uses or alters nuclear material, radioactive material or a device or commits an act against a nuclear facility or an act that causes serious interference with or serious disruption of its operations, is guilty of an indictable offence and liable to imprisonment for life. 2013, c. 13, s. 5.

CROSS-REFERENCES
See CROSS-REFERENCES under s. 82.2.

SYNOPSIS
See SYNOPSIS under s. 82.2.

COMMISSION OF INDICTABLE OFFENCE TO OBTAIN NUCLEAR MATERIAL, ETC.

82.5 Everyone who commits an indictable offence under this or any other Act of Parliament, with intent to obtain nuclear material, radioactive material or a device or to obtain access to a nuclear facility, is guilty of an indictable offence and is liable to imprisonment for life. 2013, c. 13, s. 5.

CROSS-REFERENCES
See CROSS-REFERENCES under s. 82.2.

SYNOPSIS
See SYNOPSIS under s. 82.2.

THREATS.

82.6 Everyone who threatens to commit an offence under any of sections 82.3 to 82.5 is guilty of an indictable offence and is liable to imprisonment for a term of not more than 14 years. 2013, c. 13, s. 5.

CROSS-REFERENCES

See CROSS-REFERENCES under s. 82.2.

SYNOPSIS

See SYNOPSIS under s. 82.2.

ARMED FORCES.

82.7 For greater certainty, sections 82.3 to 82.6 do not apply to an act that is committed during an armed conflict and that, at the time and in the place of its commission, is in accordance with customary international law or conventional international law applicable to the conflict, or to activities undertaken by military forces of a state in the exercise of their official duties, to the extent that those activities are governed by other rules of international law. 2013, c. 13, s. 5.

CROSS-REFERENCES

See CROSS-REFERENCES under s. 82.2.

SYNOPSIS

See SYNOPSIS under s. 82.2.

Prize Fights

ENGAGING IN PRIZE FIGHT / Definition of "prize fight".

83. (1) Every one who
    (a) engages as a principal in a prize fight,
    (b) advises, encourages or promotes a prize fight, or
    (c) is present at a prize fight as an aid, second, surgeon, umpire, backer or reporter,
is guilty of an offence punishable on summary conviction.

(2) In this section, "prize fight" means an encounter or fight with fists, hands or feet between two persons who have met for that purpose by previous arrangement made by or for them, but does not include
    (a) a contest between amateur athletes in a combative sport with fists, hands or feet held in a province if the sport is on the programme of the International Olympic Committee or the International Paralympic Committee and, in the case where the province's lieutenant governor in council or any other person or body specified by him or her requires it, the contest is held with their permission;
    (b) a contest between amateur athletes in a combative sport with fists, hands or feet held in a province if the sport has been designated by the province's lieutenant governor in council or by any other person or body specified by him or her and, in the case where the lieutenant governor in council or other specified person or body requires it, the contest is held with their permission;
    (c) a contest between amateur athletes in a combative sport with fists, hands or feet held in a province with the permission of the province's lieutenant governor in council or any other person or body specified by him or her; and

(*d*) a boxing contest or mixed martial arts contest held in a province with the permission or under the authority of an athletic board, commission or similar body established by or under the authority of the province's legislature for the control of sport within the province. R.S., c. C-34, s. 81; R.S.C. 1985, c. 27 (1st Supp.), s. 186; 2013, c. 19, s. 1.

CROSS-REFERENCES

The trial of this offence is conducted by a summary conviction court pursuant to Part XXVII. The punishment for the offence is set out in s. 787 and the limitation period is set out in s. 786(2). Release pending trial is determined by s. 515, although the accused is eligible for release by a peace officer under ss. 496, 497 or by the officer in charge under s. 498.

SYNOPSIS

This section prohibits *prize fights* as defined by s. 83(2). The definition is tailored to exclude sanctioned bouts and amateur boxing if the match meets one of the criteria in subsec. (2).

This summary conviction offence may be committed by being one of the pugilists, advising or encouraging others to fight or by promoting the fight. The presence of certain persons is also an offence if the person is there to act in one of the specific capacities which are prohibited, including that of surgeon, second, reporter, umpire, aid or backer.

Part II.1 / TERRORISM

Note: Part II.1 (ss. 83.01 to 83.33) enacted by 2001, c. 41, s. 4 (in force January 17, 2002).

Interpretation

DEFINITIONS / For greater certainty / For greater certainty / Facilitation.

83.01 (1) The following definitions apply in this Part.

"Canadian" means a Canadian citizen, a permanent resident within the meaning of subsection 2(1) of the *Immigration and Refugee Protection Act* or a body corporate incorporated and continued under the laws of Canada or a province.

"entity" means a person, group, trust, partnership or fund or an unincorporated association or organization.

"listed entity" means an entity on a list established by the Governor in Council under section 83.05.

"terrorist activity" means

(*a*) an act or omission that is committed in or outside Canada and that, if committed in Canada, is one of the following offences:

(i) the offences referred to in subsection 7(2) that implement the Convention for the Suppression of Unlawful Seizure of Aircraft, signed at The Hague on December 16, 1970,

(ii) the offences referred to in subsection 7(2) that implement the Convention for the Suppression of Unlawful Acts against the Safety of Civil Aviation, signed at Montreal on September 23, 1971,

(iii) the offences referred to in subsection 7(3) that implement the Convention on the Prevention and Punishment of Crimes against Internationally Protected Persons, including Diplomatic Agents, adopted by the General Assembly of the United Nations on December 14, 1973,

(iv) the offences referred to in subsection 7(3.1) that implement the International Convention against the Taking of Hostages, adopted by the General Assembly of the United Nations on December 17, 1979,

   (v) the offences referred to in subsection 7(2.21) that implement the Convention on the Physical Protection of Nuclear Material, done at Vienna and New York on March 3, 1980, as amended by the Amendment to the Convention on the Physical Protection of Nuclear Material, done at Vienna on July 8, 2005 and the International Convention for the Suppression of Acts of Nuclear Terrorism, done at New York on September 14, 2005,

   (vi) the offences referred to in subsection 7(2) that implement the Protocol for the Suppression of Unlawful Acts of Violence at Airports Serving International Civil Aviation, supplementary to the Convention for the Suppression of Unlawful Acts against the Safety of Civil Aviation, signed at Montreal on February 24, 1988,

   (vii) the offences referred to in subsection 7(2.1) that implement the Convention for the Suppression of Unlawful Acts against the Safety of Maritime Navigation, done at Rome on March 10, 1988,

   (viii) the offences referred to in subsection 7(2.1) or (2.2) that implement the Protocol for the Suppression of Unlawful Acts against the Safety of Fixed Platforms Located on the Continental Shelf, done at Rome on March 10, 1988,

   (ix) the offences referred to in subsection 7(3.72) that implement the International Convention for the Suppression of Terrorist Bombings, adopted by the General Assembly of the United Nations on December 15, 1997, and

   (x) the offences referred to in subsection 7(3.73) that implement the International Convention for the Suppression of the Financing of Terrorism, adopted by the General Assembly of the United Nations on December 9, 1999, or

  (*b*) an act or omission, in or outside Canada,

   (i) that is committed

    (A) in whole or in part for a political, religious or ideological purpose, objective or cause, and

    (B) in whole or in part with the intention of intimidating the public, or a segment of the public, with regard to its security, including its economic security, or compelling a person, a government or a domestic or an international organization to do or to refrain from doing any act, whether the public or the person, government or organization is inside or outside Canada, and

   (ii) that intentionally

    (A) causes death or serious bodily harm to a person by the use of violence,

    (B) endangers a person's life,

    (C) causes a serious risk to the health or safety of the public or any segment of the public,

    (D) causes substantial property damage, whether to public or private property, if causing such damage is likely to result in the conduct or harm referred to in any of clauses (A) to (C), or

    (E) causes serious interference with or serious disruption of an essential service, facility or system, whether public or private, other than as a result of advocacy, protest, dissent or stoppage of work that is not intended to result in the conduct or harm referred to in any of clauses (A) to (C),

and includes a conspiracy, attempt or threat to commit any such act or omission, or being an accessory after the fact or counselling in relation to any such act or omission, but, for greater certainty, does not include an act or omission that is committed during an armed conflict and that, at the time and in the place of its commission, is in accordance with customary international law or conventional international law applicable to the conflict, or the activities undertaken by military forces of a state in the exercise of their official duties, to the extent that those activities are governed by other rules of international law.

"terrorist group" means

(*a*) an entity that has as one of its purposes or activities facilitating or carrying out any terrorist activity, or

(*b*) a listed entity,

and includes an association of such entities.

(1.1) For greater certainty, the expression of a political, religious or ideological thought, belief or opinion does not come within paragraph (*b*) of the definition "terrorist activity" in subsection (1) unless it constitutes an act or omission that satisfies the criteria of that paragraph.

(1.2) For greater certainty, a suicide bombing is an act that comes within paragraph (*a*) or (*b*) of the definition "terrorist activity" in subsection (1) if it satisfies the criteria of that paragraph.

(2) For the purposes of this Part, facilitation shall be construed in accordance with subsection 83.19(2). 2001, c. 41, ss. 4, 126(3); 2010, c. 19, s. 1; 2013, c. 13, s. 6.

CROSS-REFERENCES

Expanded jurisdiction to try offences committed outside Canada that, if committed in Canada would be an indictable offence and would also constitute terrorist activity as defined in para. (*b*) of the definition of terrorist activity in this section, is set out in s. 7(3.75). As to the place of trial in such circumstances, see s. 7(5); procuring attendance of accused, see s. 7(5.1); defences of *autrefois acquit* and *autrefois convict* and pardon, see s. 7(6); consent of the Attorney General of Canada for trial in such cases of non-citizens, see s. 7(7).

ANNOTATIONS

The "motive clause" in s. 83.01(1)(*b*)(i)(A) does not infringe freedom of expression under s. 2(*b*) of the Charter. While the activities targeted by the terrorism offences are in a sense expressive activities, most of the conduct caught by the provisions concerns acts or threats of violence, which are excluded from the scope of the s. 2(*b*) guarantee. Further, it is impossible to infer, without evidence, that the motive clause will have a chilling effect on the exercise of s. 2 freedoms: *R. v. Khawaja* (2012), 290 C.C.C. (3d) 361 (S.C.C.), affg 273 C.C.C. (3d) 415 (Ont. C.A.).

The mental component of the definition of "terrorist activity" has three components: (i) the act or omission must be done with the intention of bringing about one of the consequences described in sub-paras. (A) through (E); (ii) the act or omission must be done with the further intention of bringing about one of the consequences described in subsec. (1)(*b*)(i)(B), namely the intimidation of the public or a segment of the public with respect to its security or compelling a person, government or domestic or international organization to do or refrain from doing any act; and (iii) the act must be done for political, religious or ideological purpose, objective or cause: *R. v. Khawaja, supra.*

Financing of Terrorism

PROVIDING OR COLLECTING PROPERTY FOR CERTAIN ACTIVITIES.

83.02 Every one who, directly or indirectly, wilfully and without lawful justification or excuse, provides or collects property intending that it be used or knowing that it will be used, in whole or in part, in order to carry out (*a*) **an act or omission that constitutes an offence referred to in subparagraphs (*a*)(i) to (ix) of the definition of "terrorist activity" in subsection 83.01(1), or**

    (*b*) **any other act or omission intended to cause death or serious bodily harm to a civilian or to any other person not taking an active part in the hostilities in a situation of armed conflict, if the purpose of that act or omission, by its nature or context, is to intimidate the public, or to compel a government or an international organization to do or refrain from doing any act,**

is guilty of an indictable offence and is liable to imprisonment for a term of not more than 10 years. 2001, c. 41, s. 4.

CROSS-REFERENCES

Expanded jurisdiction to try offences committed outside Canada that, if committed in Canada would be an offence under this section or a conspiracy, an attempt, being an accessory after or counselling the offence under this section, is set out in s. 7(3.73). As to the place of trial in such circumstances, see s. 7(5); procuring attendance of accused, see s. 7(5.1); defences of *autrefois acquit* and *autrefois convict* and pardon, see s. 7(6); consent of the Attorney General of Canada for trial in such cases of non-citizens, see s. 7(7).

The offence under this section cannot be commenced without the consent of the Attorney General, s. 83.24.

Procedure for freezing terrorist property, see ss. 83.08 to 83.17.

Proceedings may be commenced at instance of Government of Canada and conducted by Attorney General of Canada where the offence was alleged to have occurred outside the province in which the proceedings are commenced, whether or not proceedings have previously been commenced elsewhere in Canada and whether or not the person is in Canada, s. 83.25.

The sentence imposed under this section is to be served consecutively to any other punishment in accordance with s. 83.26. As to parole ineligibility, see s. 743.6(1.2).

A wiretap authorization may be obtained for the offence under this section in accordance with Part VI. Special provisions apply to such authorizations, thus see ss. 185(1.1)(*c*), 186(1.1)(*c*), 186.1(*c*).

Special protections for victims or witnesses in proceedings against an accused for this offence are set out in s. 486. See ss. 37 to 39 of the *Canada Evidence Act*, respecting Crown privilege and disclosure of information injurious to national security, national defence and foreign relations.

PROVIDING, MAKING AVAILABLE, ETC., PROPERTY OR SERVICES FOR TERRORIST PURPOSES.

83.03 Every one who, directly or indirectly, collects property, provides or invites a person to provide, or makes available property or financial or other related services

    (*a*) **intending that they be used, or knowing that they will be used, in whole or in part, for the purpose of facilitating or carrying out any terrorist activity, or for the purpose of benefiting any person who is facilitating or carrying out such an activity, or**

    (*b*) **knowing that, in whole or part, they will be used by or will benefit a terrorist group,**

is guilty of an indictable offence and is liable to imprisonment for a term of not more than 10 years. 2001, c. 41, s. 4.

CROSS-REFERENCES

Expanded jurisdiction to try offences committed outside Canada that, if committed in Canada would be an offence under this section, is set out in s. 7(3.74). As to the place of trial in such circumstances, see s. 7(5); procuring attendance of accused, see s. 7(5.1); defences of *autrefois acquit* and *autrefois convict* and pardon, see s. 7(6); consent of the Attorney General of Canada for trial in such cases of non-citizens, see s. 7(7).

"Terrorist activity" and "terrorist group" are defined in s. 83.01. Section 83.05 sets out the process for listing entities, which then fall within the definition of terrorist group. Procedure for freezing terrorist property, see ss. 83.08 to 83.17.

The offence under this section cannot be commenced without the consent of the Attorney General, s. 83.24

Proceedings may be commenced at instance of Government of Canada and conducted by Attorney General of Canada where the offence was alleged to have occurred outside the province in which the proceedings are commenced, whether or not proceedings have previously been commenced elsewhere in Canada and whether or not the person is in Canada, s. 83.25.

The sentence imposed under this section is to be served consecutively to any other punishment in accordance with s. 83.26. As to parole ineligibility, see s. 743.6(1.2).

A wiretap authorization may be obtained for the offence under this section in accordance with Part VI. Special provisions apply to such authorizations, thus see ss. 185(1.1)(*c*), 186(1.1)(*c*), 186.1(*c*).

Special protections for victims or witnesses in proceedings against an accused for this offence are set out in s. 486. See ss. 37 to 39 of the *Canada Evidence Act*, respecting Crown privilege and disclosure of information injurious to national security, national defence and foreign relations.

USING OR POSSESSING PROPERTY FOR TERRORIST PURPOSES.

83.04 Every one who
 (*a*) **uses property, directly or indirectly, in whole or in part, for the purpose of facilitating or carrying out a terrorist activity, or**
 (*b*) **possesses property intending that it be used or knowing that it will be used, directly or indirectly, in whole or in part, for the purpose of facilitating or carrying out a terrorist activity,**
is guilty of an indictable offence and is liable to imprisonment for a term of not more than 10 years. 2001, c. 41, s. 4.

CROSS-REFERENCES

Expanded jurisdiction to try offences committed outside Canada that, if committed in Canada would be an offence under this section, is set out in s. 7(3.74). As to the place of trial in such circumstances, see s. 7(5); procuring attendance of accused, see s. 7(5.1); defences of *autrefois acquit* and *autrefois convict* and pardon, see s. 7(6); consent of the Attorney General of Canada for trial in such cases of non-citizens, see s. 7(7).

"Terrorist activity" is defined in s. 83.01.

Procedure for freezing terrorist property, see ss. 83.08 to 83.17.

The offence under this section cannot be commenced without the consent of the Attorney General, s. 83.24

Proceedings may be commenced at instance of Government of Canada and conducted by Attorney General of Canada where the offence was alleged to have occurred outside the province in which the proceedings are commenced, whether or not proceedings have previously been commenced elsewhere in Canada and whether or not the person is in Canada, s. 83.25.

The sentence imposed under this section is to be served consecutively to any other punishment in accordance with s. 83.26. As to parole ineligibility, see s. 743.6(1.2).

A wiretap authorization may be obtained for the offence under this section in accordance with Part VI. Special provisions apply to such authorizations, thus see ss. 185(1.1)(*c*), 186(1.1)(*c*), 186.1(*c*).

Special protections for victims or witnesses in proceedings against an accused for this offence are set out in s. 486. See ss. 37 to 39 of the *Canada Evidence Act*, respecting Crown privilege and disclosure of information injurious to national security, national defence and foreign relations.

List of Entities

ESTABLISHMENT OF LIST / Recommendation / Application to Minister / Deeming / Notice of the decision to the applicant / Judicial review / Reference / Evidence / Publication / New application / Review of list / Completion of review / Definition of "judge".

83.05 (1) The Governor in Council may, by regulation, establish a list on which the Governor in Council may place any entity if, on the recommendation of the Minister of Public Safety and Emergency Preparedness, the Governor in Council is satisfied that there are reasonable grounds to believe that

- (a) **the entity has knowingly carried out, attempted to carry out, participated in or facilitated a terrorist activity; or**
- (b) **the entity is knowingly acting on behalf of, at the direction of or in association with an entity referred to in paragraph (a).**

(1.1) The Minister may make a recommendation referred to in subsection (1) only if he or she has reasonable grounds to believe that the entity to which the recommendation relates is an entity referred to in paragraph (1)(a) or (b).

(2) On application in writing by a listed entity, the Minister shall decide whether there are reasonable grounds to recommend to the Governor in Council that the applicant no longer be a listed entity.

(3) If the Minister does not make a decision on the application referred to in subsection (2) within 60 days after receipt of the application, he or she is deemed to have decided to recommend that the applicant remain a listed entity.

(4) The Minister shall give notice without delay to the applicant of any decision taken or deemed to have been taken respecting the application referred to in subsection (2).

(5) Within 60 days after the receipt of the notice of the decision referred to in subsection (4), the applicant may apply to a judge for judicial review of the decision.

(6) When an application is made under subsection (5), the judge shall, without delay

- (a) **examine, in private, any security or criminal intelligence reports considered in listing the applicant and hear any other evidence or information that may be presented by or on behalf of the Minister and may, at his or her request, hear all or part of that evidence or information in the absence of the applicant and any counsel representing the applicant, if the judge is of the opinion that the disclosure of the information would injure national security or endanger the safety of any person;**
- (b) **provide the applicant with a statement summarizing the information available to the judge so as to enable the applicant to be reasonably informed of the reasons for the decision, without disclosing any information the disclosure of which would, in the judge's opinion, injure national security or endanger the safety of any person;**
- (c) **provide the applicant with a reasonable opportunity to be heard; and**
- (d) **determine whether the decision is reasonable on the basis of the information available to the judge and, if found not to be reasonable, order that the applicant no longer be a listed entity.**

(6.1) The judge may receive into evidence anything that, in the opinion of the judge, is reliable and appropriate, even if it would not otherwise be admissible under Canadian law, and may base his or her decision on that evidence.

(7) The Minister shall cause to be published, without delay, in the *Canada Gazette* notice of a final order of a court that the applicant no longer be a listed entity.

(8) A listed entity may not make another application under subsection (2), except if there has been a material change in its circumstances since the time when the entity

made its last application or if the Minister has completed the review under subsection (9).

(9) Two years after the establishment of the list referred to in subsection (1), and every two years after that, the Minister shall review the list to determine whether there are still reasonable grounds, as set out in subsection (1), for an entity to be a listed entity and make a recommendation to the Governor in Council as to whether the entity should remain a listed entity. The review does not affect the validity of the list.

(10) The Minister shall complete the review as soon as possible and in any event, no later than 120 days after its commencement. After completing the review, he or she shall cause to be published, without delay, in the *Canada Gazette* notice that the review has been completed.

(11) In this section, "judge" means the Chief Justice of the Federal Court or a judge of the Trial Division of that Court designated by the Chief Justice. 2001, c. 41, s. 4; 2005, c. 10, ss. 18 and 34(1)(*f*)(iii).

CROSS-REFERENCES

"Terrorist activity" is defined in s. 83.01. Once an entity becomes a listed entity under this section it falls within the definition of "terrorist group" in s. 83.01. Specific offences relating to terrorist groups include collecting, providing, making available, etc. property or services for use or benefit of a terrorist group, s. 83.03. As to freezing property of terrorist groups see ss. 83.08, 83.1, 83.12; freezing property of listed entity, see s. 83.11, 83.12. As to forfeiture of property owned controlled by or on behalf of terrorist group, see ss. 83.13 to 83.17. Offence of participating in activity of terrorist group, s. 83.18; committing offence for terrorist group, s. 83.2; instructing persons to carry out activity for benefit etc. of terrorist group, s. 83.21; harbouring or concealing persons known to have or likely to commit terrorist activity, s. 83.24.

Special provision for receiving foreign confidential information, see s. 83.06. Also see generally ss. 37 to 39 of the *Canada Evidence Act*, respecting Crown privilege and disclosure of information injurious to national security, national defence and foreign relations.

Under s. 83.07, an entity may apply to the Solicitor General of Canada for a certificate stating that it is not a listed entity.

ADMISSION OF FOREIGN INFORMATION OBTAINED IN CONFIDENCE / Return of information / Use of information.

83.06 (1) For the purposes of subsection 83.05(6), in private and in the absence of the applicant or any counsel representing it,

(*a*) the Minister of Public Safety and Emergency Preparedness may make an application to the judge for the admission of information obtained in confidence from a government, an institution or an agency of a foreign state, from an international organization of states or from an institution or an agency of an international organization of states; and

(*b*) the judge shall examine the information and provide counsel representing the Minister with a reasonable opportunity to be heard as to whether the information is relevant but should not be disclosed to the applicant or any counsel representing it because the disclosure would injure national security or endanger the safety of any person.

(2) The information shall be returned to counsel representing the Minister and shall not be considered by the judge in making the determination under paragraph 83.05(6)(*d*), if

(*a*) the judge determines that the information is not relevant;

(*b*) the judge determines that the information is relevant but should be summarized in the statement to be provided under paragraph 83.05(6)(*b*); or

(*c*) the Minister withdraws the application.

(3) If the judge decides that the information is relevant but that its disclosure would injure national security or endanger the safety of persons, the information shall not be disclosed in the statement mentioned in paragraph 83.05(6)(*b*), but the judge may base the determination under paragraph 83.05(6)(*d*) on it. 2001, c. 41, s. 4; 2005, c. 10, s. 19.

CROSS-REFERENCES

See cross-references under s. 83.05.

MISTAKEN IDENTITY / Issuance of certificate.

83.07 (1) An entity claiming not to be a listed entity may apply to the Minister of Public Safety and Emergency Preparedness for a certificate stating that it is not a listed entity.

(2) The Minister shall, within 15 days after receiving the application, issue a certificate if he or she is satisfied that the applicant is not a listed entity. 2001, c. 41, s. 4; 2005, c. 10, s. 20.

CROSS-REFERENCES

"Listed entity" is defined in s. 83.01 as an entity listed in accordance with s. 83.05. For other cross-references, see s. 83.05.

Freezing of Property

FREEZING OF PROPERTY / No civil liability.

83.08 (1) No person in Canada and no Canadian outside Canada shall knowingly

   (*a*) deal directly or indirectly in any property that is owned or controlled by or on behalf of a terrorist group;

   (*b*) enter into or facilitate, directly or indirectly, any transaction in respect of property referred to in paragraph (*a*); or

   (*c*) provide any financial or other related services in respect of property referred to in paragraph (*a*) to, for the benefit of or at the direction of a terrorist group.

(2) A person who acts reasonably in taking, or omitting to take, measures to comply with subsection (1) shall not be liable in any civil action arising from having taken or omitted to take the measures, if they took all reasonable steps to satisfy themselves that the relevant property was owned or controlled by or on behalf of a terrorist group. 2001, c. 41, s. 4; 2013, c. 9, s. 3(2).

CROSS-REFERENCES

"Terrorist group" and "Canadian" are defined in s. 83.01. In accordance with s. 83.09 the Solicitor General of Canada or a person designated by the Solicitor General may exempt persons from activity otherwise prohibited by this section. Contravention of this section is an offence under s. 83.12. As to procedures for seizure and forfeiture of property owned or controlled by or on behalf of a terrorist group, see ss. 83.13 to 83.17.

EXEMPTIONS / Ministerial authorization / Existing equities maintained / Third party involvement.

83.09 (1) The Minister of Public Safety and Emergency Preparedness, or a person designated by him or her, may authorize any person in Canada or any Canadian outside Canada to carry out a specified activity or transaction that is prohibited by section 83.08, or a class of such activities or transactions.

(2) The Minister, or a person designated by him or her, may make the authorization subject to any terms and conditions that are required in their opinion and may amend, suspend, revoke or reinstate it.

(3) All secured and unsecured rights and interests in the frozen property that are held by persons, other than terrorist groups or their agents, are entitled to the same ranking that they would have been entitled to had the property not been frozen.

(4) If a person has obtained an authorization under subsection (1), any other person involved in carrying out the activity or transaction, or class of activities or transactions, to which the authorization relates is not subject to sections 83.08, 83.1 and 83.11 if the terms or conditions of the authorization that are imposed under subsection (2), if any, are met. 2001, c. 41, s. 4; 2005, c. 10, s. 21.

CROSS-REFERENCES

"Terrorist group" is defined in s. 83.01. Under s. 83.11, certain entities, such as banks, have additional obligations to determine whether they are in possession or control of property owned or controlled by or on behalf of listed entities (see ss. 83.01 and 83.05).

DISCLOSURE / Immunity.

83.1 (1) Every person in Canada and every Canadian outside Canada shall disclose without delay to the Commissioner of the Royal Canadian Mounted Police or to the Director of the Canadian Security Intelligence Service

(*a*) the existence of property in their possession or control that they know is owned or controlled by or on behalf of a terrorist group; and

(*b*) information about a transaction or proposed transaction in respect of property referred to in paragraph (*a*).

(2) No criminal or civil proceedings lie against a person for disclosure made in good faith under subsection (1). 2001, c. 41, s. 4; 2013, c. 9, s. 4.

CROSS-REFERENCES

"Terrorist group" and "Canadian" are defined in s. 83.01. Contravention of this section is an offence under s. 83.12. As to procedures for seizure and forfeiture of property owned or controlled by or on behalf of a terrorist group, see ss. 83.13 to 83.17.

AUDIT / Monthly report / Immunity / Regulations.

83.11 (1) The following entities must determine on a continuing basis whether they are in possession or control of property owned or controlled by or on behalf of a listed entity:

(*a*) authorized foreign banks within the meaning of section 2 of the *Bank Act* in respect of their business in Canada, or banks to which that Act applies;

(*b*) cooperative credit societies, savings and credit unions and caisses populaires regulated by a provincial Act and associations regulated by the *Cooperative Credit Associations Act*;

(*c*) foreign companies within the meaning of subsection 2(1) of the *Insurance Companies Act* in respect of their insurance business in Canada;

(*c*.1) companies, provincial companies and societies within the meaning of subsection 2(1) of the *Insurance Companies Act*;

(*c*.2) fraternal benefit societies regulated by a provincial Act in respect of their insurance activities, and insurance companies and other entities engaged in the business of insuring risks that are regulated by a provincial Act;

(*d*) companies to which the *Trust and Loan Companies Act* applies;

(*e*) trust companies regulated by a provincial Act;

    (*f*) **loan companies regulated by a provincial Act; and**

    (*g*) **entities authorized under provincial legislation to engage in the business of dealing in securities, or to provide portfolio management or investment counselling services.**

(2) Subject to the regulations, every entity referred to in paragraphs (1)(*a*) to (*g*) must report, within the period specified by regulation or, if no period is specified, monthly, to the principal agency or body that supervises or regulates it under federal or provincial law either

    (*a*) **that it is not in possession or control of any property referred to in subsection (1), or**

    (*b*) **that it is in possession or control of such property, in which case it must also report the number of persons, contracts or accounts involved and the total value of the property.**

(3) No criminal or civil proceedings lie against a person for making a report in good faith under subsection (2).

(4) The Governor in Council may make regulations

    (*a*) **excluding any entity or class of entities from the requirement to make a report referred to in subsection (2), and specifying the conditions of exclusion; and**

    (*b*) **specifying a period for the purposes of subsection (2). 2001, c. 41, s. 4.**

CROSS-REFERENCES

"Listed entity" is defined in s. 83.01 as an entity listed in accordance with s. 83.05. Contravention of this section is an offence under s. 83.12. As to procedures for seizure and forfeiture of property owned or controlled by or on behalf of a terrorist group, see ss. 83.13 to 83.17.

OFFENCES — FREEZING OF PROPERTY, DISCLOSURE OR AUDIT / No contravention.

83.12 (1) Every one who contravenes any of sections 83.08, 83.1 and 83.11 is guilty of an offence and liable

    (*a*) **on summary conviction, to a fine of not more than $100,000 or to imprisonment for a term of not more than one year, or to both; or**

    (*b*) **on conviction on indictment, to imprisonment for a term of not more than 10 years. 2001, c. 41, s. 4; 2013, c. 9, c. 5.**

(2) [*Repealed*, 2013, c. 9, s. 5.]

CROSS-REFERENCES

Proceedings for an offence under this section cannot be commenced without the consent of the Attorney General, s. 83.24.

    Proceedings may be commenced at instance of Government of Canada and conducted by Attorney General of Canada where the offence was alleged to have occurred outside the province in which the proceedings are commenced, whether or not proceedings have previously been commenced elsewhere in Canada and whether or not the person is in Canada, s. 83.25.

    As to procedures for seizure and forfeiture of property owned or controlled by or on behalf of a terrorist group, see ss. 83.13 to 83.17.

    See ss. 37 to 39 of the *Canada Evidence Act*, respecting Crown privilege and disclosure of information injurious to national security, national defence and foreign relations.

Seizure and Restraint of Property

SEIZURE AND RESTRAINT OF ASSETS / Contents of application / Appointment of manager / Appointment of Minister of Public Works and Government Services / Power to manage / Application for destruction order / Notice / Manner of giving notice / Order / When management order ceases to have effect / Application to vary / Procedure / Procedure.

83.13 (1) Where a judge of the Federal Court, on an *ex parte* application by the Attorney General, after examining the application in private, is satisfied that there are reasonable grounds to believe that there is in any building, receptacle or place any property in respect of which an order of forfeiture may be made under subsection 83.14(5), the judge may issue

(a) if the property is situated in Canada, a warrant authorizing a person named therein or a peace officer to search the building, receptacle or place for that property and to seize that property and any other property in respect of which that person or peace officer believes, on reasonable grounds, that an order of forfeiture may be made under that subsection; or

(b) if the property is situated in or outside Canada, a restraint order prohibiting any person from disposing of, or otherwise dealing with any interest in, that property other than as may be specified in the order.

(1.1) An affidavit in support of an application under subsection (1) may be sworn on information and belief, and, notwithstanding the *Federal Court Rules, 1998*, no adverse inference shall be drawn from a failure to provide evidence of persons having personal knowledge of material facts.

(2) On an application under subsection (1), at the request of the Attorney General, if a judge is of the opinion that the circumstances so require, the judge may

(a) appoint a person to take control of, and to manage or otherwise deal with, all or part of the property in accordance with the directions of the judge; and

(b) require any person having possession of that property to give possession of the property to the person appointed under paragraph (a).

(3) When the Attorney General of Canada so requests, a judge appointing a person under subsection (2) shall appoint the Minister of Public Works and Government Services.

(4) The power to manage or otherwise deal with property under subsection (2) includes

(a) in the case of perishable or rapidly depreciating property, the power to sell that property; and

(b) in the case of property that has little or no value, the power to destroy that property.

(5) Before a person appointed under subsection (2) destroys property referred to in paragraph (4)(b), he or she shall apply to a judge of the Federal Court for a destruction order.

(6) Before making a destruction order in relation to any property, a judge shall require notice in accordance with subsection (7) to be given to, and may hear, any person who, in the opinion of the judge, appears to have a valid interest in the property.

(7) A notice under subsection (6) shall be given in the manner that the judge directs or as provided in the rules of the Federal Court.

(8) A judge may order that property be destroyed if he or she is satisfied that the property has little or no financial or other value.

(9) A management order ceases to have effect when the property that is the subject of the management order is returned to an applicant in accordance with the law or forfeited to Her Majesty.

(10) The Attorney General may at any time apply to a judge of the Federal Court to cancel or vary an order or warrant made under this section, other than an appointment made under subsection (3).

(11) Subsections 462.32(4) and (6), sections 462.34 to 462.35 and 462.4, subsections 487(3) and (4) and section 488 apply, with such modifications as the circumstances require, to a warrant issued under paragraph (1)(*a*).

(12) Subsections 462.33(4) and (6) to (11) and sections 462.34 to 462.35 and 462.4 apply, with such modifications as the circumstances require, to an order issued under paragraph (1)(*b*). 2001, c. 41, s. 4.

CROSS-REFERENCES

"Attorney General" is defined in s. 2. Sections 462.42(6), 462.43 and 462.46 (which deal with disposal of seized property) apply with necessary modifications to property subject to a warrant or restraint order issued under this section, see s. 83.15. An appeal from an order under this section presumably lies to the Federal Court of Appeal under s. 27 of the *Federal Courts Act*.

Forfeiture of Property

APPLICATION FOR ORDER OF FORFEITURE / Contents of application / Respondents / Notice / Granting of forfeiture order / Use of proceeds / Regulations / Order refusing forfeiture / Notice / Third party interests / Dwelling-house / Motion to vary or set aside / No extension of time.

83.14 (1) The Attorney General may make an application to a judge of the Federal Court for an order of forfeiture in respect of

    (*a*) property owned or controlled by or on behalf of a terrorist group; or

    (*b*) property that has been or will be used, in whole or in part, to facilitate or carry out a terrorist activity.

(2) An affidavit in support of an application by the Attorney General under subsection (1) may be sworn on information and belief, and, notwithstanding the *Federal Court Rules, 1998,* no adverse inference shall be drawn from a failure to provide evidence of persons having personal knowledge of material facts.

(3) The Attorney General is required to name as a respondent to an application under subsection (1) only those persons who are known to own or control the property that is the subject of the application.

(4) The Attorney General shall give notice of an application under subsection (1) to named respondents in such a manner as the judge directs or as provided in the rules of the Federal Court.

(5) If a judge is satisfied on a balance of probabilities that property is property referred to in paragraph (1)(*a*) or (*b*), the judge shall order that the property be forfeited to Her Majesty to be disposed of as the Attorney General directs or otherwise dealt with in accordance with the law.

(5.1) Any proceeds that arise from the disposal of property under subsection (5) may be used to compensate victims of terrorist activities and to fund anti-terrorist initiatives in accordance with any regulations made by the Governor in Council under subsection (5.2).

(5.2) The Governor in Council may make regulations for the purposes of specifying how the proceeds referred to in subsection (5.1) are to be distributed.

(6) Where a judge refuses an application under subsection (1) in respect of any property, the judge shall make an order that describes the property and declares that it is not property referred to in that subsection.

(7) On an application under subsection (1), a judge may require notice to be given to any person who, in the opinion of the Court, appears to have an interest in the property, and any such person shall be entitled to be added as a respondent to the application.

(8) If a judge is satisfied that a person referred to in subsection (7) has an interest in property that is subject to an application, has exercised reasonable care to ensure that the property would not be used to facilitate or carry out a terrorist activity, and is not a member of a terrorist group, the judge shall order that the interest is not affected by the forfeiture. Such an order shall declare the nature and extent of the interest in question.

(9) Where all or part of property that is the subject of an application under subsection (1) is a dwelling-house, the judge shall also consider

(a) the impact of an order of forfeiture on any member of the immediate family of the person who owns or controls the dwelling-house, if the dwelling-house was the member's principal residence at the time the dwelling-house was ordered restrained or at the time the forfeiture application was made and continues to be the member's principal residence; and

(b) whether the member appears innocent of any complicity or collusion in the terrorist activity.

(10) A person who claims an interest in property that was forfeited and who did not receive notice under subsection (7) may bring a motion to the Federal Court to vary or set aside an order made under subsection (5) not later than 60 days after the day on which the forfeiture order was made.

(11) The Court may not extend the period set out in subsection (10). 2001, c. 41, s. 4.

CROSS-REFERENCES

"Attorney General" is defined in s. 2. "Terrorist activity" and "terrorist group" are defined in s. 83.01. Sections 462.42(6), 462.43 and 462.46 (which deal with disposal of seized property) apply with necessary modifications to property ordered forfeited under this section, see s. 83.15. The property is to be preserved pending any appeal from an order made under this section, see s. 83.16. Section 83.16(2) incorporates with necessary modifications the provisions in s. 462.34 to an appeal from refusal to make a forfeiture order. The provisions of this Part do not affect other provisions under this Act order other federal legislation relating to forfeiture of property (s. 83.17). Thus, for example see Part XX.2. An appeal from an order under this section presumably lies to the Federal Court of Appeal under s. 27 of the *Federal Courts Act*.

DISPOSITION OF PROPERTY.

83.15 Subsection 462.42(6) and sections 462.43 and 462.46 apply, with such modifications as the circumstances require, to property subject to a warrant or restraint order issued under subsection 83.13(1) or ordered forfeited under subsection 83.14(5). 2001, c. 41, s. 4.

INTERIM PRESERVATION RIGHTS / Appeal of refusal to grant order.

83.16 (1) Pending any appeal of an order made under section 83.14, property restrained under an order issued under section 83.13 shall continue to be restrained, property seized under a warrant issued under that section shall continue to be detained, and any person appointed to manage, control or otherwise deal with that property under that section shall continue in that capacity.

(2) Section 462.34 applies, with such modifications as the circumstances require, to an appeal taken in respect of a refusal to grant an order under subsection 83.14(5). 2001, c. 41, s. 4.

CROSS-REFERENCES

Presumably, the appeal referred to in this section is an appeal taken to the Federal Court of Appeal in accordance with s. 27 of the *Federal Courts Act*.

OTHER FORFEITURE PROVISIONS UNAFFECTED / Priority for restitution to victims of crime.

83.17 (1) This Part does not affect the operation of any other provision of this or any other Act of Parliament respecting the forfeiture of property.

(2) Property is subject to forfeiture under subsection 83.14(5) only to the extent that it is not required to satisfy the operation of any other provision of this or any other Act of Parliament respecting restitution to, or compensation of, persons affected by the commission of offences. 2001, c. 41, s. 4.

Participating, Facilitating, Instructing and Harbouring

PARTICIPATION IN ACTIVITY OF TERRORIST GROUP / Prosecution / Meaning of participating or contributing / Factors.

83.18 (1) Every one who knowingly participates in or contributes to, directly or indirectly, any activity of a terrorist group for the purpose of enhancing the ability of any terrorist group to facilitate or carry out a terrorist activity is guilty of an indictable offence and liable to imprisonment for a term not exceeding ten years.

(2) An offence may be committed under subsection (1) whether or not
- **(a) a terrorist group actually facilitates or carries out a terrorist activity;**
- **(b) the participation or contribution of the accused actually enhances the ability of a terrorist group to facilitate or carry out a terrorist activity; or**
- **(c) the accused knows the specific nature of any terrorist activity that may be facilitated or carried out by a terrorist group.**

(3) Participating in or contributing to an activity of a terrorist group includes
- **(a) providing, receiving or recruiting a person to receive training;**
- **(b) providing or offering to provide a skill or an expertise for the benefit of, at the direction of or in association with a terrorist group;**
- **(c) recruiting a person in order to facilitate or commit**
  - **(i) a terrorism offence, or**
  - **(ii) an act or omission outside Canada that, if committed in Canada, would be a terrorism offence;**
- **(d) entering or remaining in any country for the benefit of, at the direction of or in association with a terrorist group; and**
- **(e) making oneself, in response to instructions from any of the persons who constitute a terrorist group, available to facilitate or commit**
  - **(i) a terrorism offence, or**
  - **(ii) an act or omission outside Canada that, if committed in Canada, would be a terrorism offence.**

(4) In determining whether an accused participates in or contributes to any activity of a terrorist group, the court may consider, among other factors, whether the accused
- **(a) uses a name, word, symbol or other representation that identifies, or is associated with, the terrorist group;**
- **(b) frequently associates with any of the persons who constitute the terrorist group;**
- **(c) receives any benefit from the terrorist group; or**
- **(d) repeatedly engages in activities at the instruction of any of the persons who constitute the terrorist group. 2001, c. 41, s. 4.**

CR. CODE

CROSS-REFERENCES

"Terrorist activity" and "terrorist group" are defined in s. 83.01. "Terrorism offence" is defined in s. 2. Expanded jurisdiction to try offences committed outside Canada that, if committed in Canada would be an offence under this section, is set out in s. 7(3.74). As to the place of trial in such circumstances, see s. 7(5); procuring attendance of accused, see s. 7(5.1); defences of *autrefois acquit* and *autrefois convict* and pardon, see s. 7(6); consent of the Attorney General of Canada for trial in such cases of non-citizens, see s. 7(7).

The offence under this section cannot be commenced without the consent of the Attorney General, s. 83.24.

Proceedings may be commenced at instance of Government of Canada and conducted by Attorney General of Canada where the offence was alleged to have occurred outside the province in which the proceedings are commenced, whether or not proceedings have previously been commenced elsewhere in Canada and whether or not the person is in Canada, s. 83.25.

The sentence imposed under this section is to be served consecutively to any other punishment in accordance with s. 83.26. As to parole ineligibility, see s. 743.6(1.2).

As to freezing of assets of terrorist groups, see ss. 83.08 to 83.12 and seizure and forfeiture of terrorist property, see ss. 83.13 to 83.17. Offences relating to terrorist property, see ss. 83.01 to 83.04.

A wiretap authorization may be obtained for the offence under this section in accordance with Part VI. Special provisions apply to such authorizations, thus see ss. 185(1.1)(*c*), 186(1.1)(*c*), 186.1(*c*).

Special protections for victims or witnesses in proceedings against an accused for this offence are set out in s. 486. See ss. 37 to 39 of the *Canada Evidence Act*, respecting Crown privilege and disclosure of information injurious to national security, national defence and foreign relations.

ANNOTATIONS

This provision is not overbroad and does not violate s. 7 of the Charter. A purposive inter-pretation of the *actus reus* and *mens rea* excludes convictions for: (1) innocent or socially useful conduct that is undertaken absent any intent to enhance the abilities of a terrorist group to facilitate or carry out a terrorist activity; and (2) conduct that a reasonable person would not view as capable of materially enhancing the abilities of a terrorist group to facilitate or carry out a terrorist activity. To convict under s. 83.18, a judge must be satisfied beyond a reasonable doubt that the accused specifically intended to enhance the ability of a terrorist group to facilitate or carry out a terrorist activity: *R. v. Khawaja* (2012), 290 C.C.C. (3d) 361 (S.C.C.), affg 273 C.C.C. (3d) 415 (Ont. C.A.).

LEAVING CANADA TO PARTICIPATE IN ACTIVITY OF TERRORIST GROUP.

83.181 Everyone who leaves or attempts to leave Canada, or goes or attempts to go on board a conveyance with the intent to leave Canada, for the purpose of committing an act or omission outside Canada that, if committed in Canada, would be an offence under subsection 83.18(1) is guilty of an indictable offence and liable to imprisonment for a term of not more than 10 years. 2013, c. 9, c. 6.

CROSS-REFERENCES

"Terrorism offence" is defined in s. 2. Expanded jurisdiction to try offences committed outside Canada that, if committed in Canada would be an offence under this section, is set out in s. 7(3.74). As to the place of trial in such circumstances, see s. 7(5); procuring attendance of accused, see s. 7(5.1); defences of *autrefois acquit* and *autrefois convict* and pardon, see s. 7(6); consent of the Attorney General of Canada for trial in such cases of non-citizens, see s. 7(7).

The offence under this section cannot be commenced without the consent of the Attorney General, s. 83.24.

Proceedings may be commenced at instance of Government of Canada and conducted by Attorney General of Canada where the offence was alleged to have occurred outside the province in which the proceedings are commenced, whether or not proceedings have previously been commenced elsewhere in Canada and whether or not the person is in Canada, s. 83.25.

The sentence imposed under this section is to be served consecutively to any other punishment in accordance with s. 83.26. As to parole ineligibility, see s. 743.6(1.2).

As to freezing of assets of terrorist groups, see ss. 83.08 to 83.12 and seizure and forfeiture of terrorist property, see ss. 83.13 to 83.17. Offences relating to terrorist property, see ss. 83.01 to 83.04.

A wiretap authorization may be obtained for the offence under this section in accordance with Part VI. Special provisions apply to such authorizations, thus see ss. 185(1.1)(*c*), 186(1.1)(*c*), 186.1(*c*).

Special protections for victims or witnesses in proceedings against an accused for this offence are set out in s. 486. See ss. 37 to 39 of the *Canada Evidence Act*, respecting Crown privilege and disclosure of information injurious to national security, national defence and foreign relations.

FACILITATING TERRORIST ACTIVITY / Facilitation.

83.19 (1) Every one who knowingly facilitates a terrorist activity is guilty of an indictable offence and liable to imprisonment for a term not exceeding fourteen years.

(2) For the purposes of this Part, a terrorist activity is facilitated whether or not
  (*a*) the facilitator knows that a particular terrorist activity is facilitated;
  (*b*) any particular terrorist activity was foreseen or planned at the time it was facilitated; or
  (*c*) any terrorist activity was actually carried out. 2001, c. 41, s. 4.

CROSS-REFERENCES

"Terrorist activity" is defined in s. 83.01. Expanded jurisdiction to try offences committed outside Canada that, if committed in Canada would be an offence under this section, is set out in s. 7(3.74). As to the place of trial in such circumstances, see s. 7(5); procuring attendance of accused, see s. 7(5.1); defences of *autrefois acquit* and *autrefois convict* and pardon, see s. 7(6); consent of the Attorney General of Canada for trial in such cases of non-citizens, see s. 7(7).

The offence under this section cannot be commenced without the consent of the Attorney General, s. 83.24

Proceedings may be commenced at instance of Government of Canada and conducted by Attorney General of Canada where the offence was alleged to have occurred outside the province in which the proceedings are commenced, whether or not proceedings have previously been commenced elsewhere in Canada and whether or not the person is in Canada, s. 83.25.

The sentence imposed under this section is to be served consecutively to any other punishment in accordance with s. 83.26. As to parole ineligibility, see s. 743.6(1.2).

As to freezing of assets of terrorist groups, see ss. 83.08 to 83.12 and seizure and forfeiture of terrorist property, see ss. 83.13 to 83.17. Offences relating to terrorist property, see ss. 83.01 to 83.04.

A wiretap authorization may be obtained for the offence under this section in accordance with Part VI. Special provisions apply to such authorizations, thus see ss. 185(1.1)(*c*), 186(1.1)(*c*), 186.1(*c*).

Special protections for victims or witnesses in proceedings against an accused for this offence are set out in s. 486. See ss. 37 to 39 of the *Canada Evidence Act*, respecting Crown privilege and disclosure of information injurious to national security, national defence and foreign relations.

ANNOTATIONS

The fault requirement of the offence in this section is consistent with s. 7 of the *Canadian Charter of Rights and Freedoms*: *R. v. Khawaja* (2006), 214 C.C.C. (3d) 399, 42 C.R. (6th) 348 (Ont. S.C.J.), leave to appeal to S.C.C. refused [2007] 1 S.C.R. x, 216 C.C.C. (3d) vi.

LEAVING CANADA TO FACILITATE TERRORIST ACTIVITY.

83.191 Everyone who leaves or attempts to leave Canada, or goes or attempts to go on board a conveyance with the intent to leave Canada, for the purpose of committing an act or omission outside Canada that, if committed in Canada, would be an offence under subsection 83.19(1) is guilty of an indictable offence and liable to imprisonment for a term of not more than 14 years. 2013, c. 9, s. 7.

CROSS-REFERENCES

"Terrorism offence" is defined in s. 2. Expanded jurisdiction to try offences committed outside Canada that, if committed in Canada would be an offence under this section, is set out in s. 7(3.74). As to the place of trial in such circumstances, see s. 7(5); procuring attendance of accused, see s. 7(5.1); defences of *autrefois acquit* and *autrefois convict* and pardon, see s. 7(6); consent of the Attorney General of Canada for trial in such cases of non-citizens, see s. 7(7).

The offence under this section cannot be commenced without the consent of the Attorney General, s. 83.24.

Proceedings may be commenced at instance of Government of Canada and conducted by Attorney General of Canada where the offence was alleged to have occurred outside the province in which the proceedings are commenced, whether or not proceedings have previously been commenced elsewhere in Canada and whether or not the person is in Canada, s. 83.25.

The sentence imposed under this section is to be served consecutively to any other punishment in accordance with s. 83.26. As to parole ineligibility, see s. 743.6(1.2).

As to freezing of assets of terrorist groups, see ss. 83.08 to 83.12 and seizure and forfeiture of terrorist property, see ss. 83.13 to 83.17. Offences relating to terrorist property, see ss. 83.01 to 83.04.

A wiretap authorization may be obtained for the offence under this section in accordance with Part VI. Special provisions apply to such authorizations, thus see ss. 185(1.1)(c), 186(1.1)(c), 186.1(c).

Special protections for victims or witnesses in proceedings against an accused for this offence are set out in s. 486. See ss. 37 to 39 of the *Canada Evidence Act*, respecting Crown privilege and disclosure of information injurious to national security, national defence and foreign relations.

COMMISSION OF OFFENCE FOR TERRORIST GROUP.

83.2 Every one who commits an indictable offence under this or any other Act of Parliament for the benefit of, at the direction of or in association with a terrorist group is guilty of an indictable offence and liable to imprisonment for life. 2001, c. 41, s. 4.

CROSS-REFERENCES

"Terrorist group" is defined in s. 83.01. Expanded jurisdiction to try offences committed outside Canada that, if committed in Canada would be an offence under this section, is set out in s. 7(3.74). As to the place of trial in such circumstances, see s. 7(5); procuring attendance of accused, see s. 7(5.1); defences of *autrefois acquit* and *autrefois convict* and pardon, see s. 7(6); consent of the Attorney General of Canada for trial in such cases of non-citizens, see s. 7(7).

The offence under this section cannot be commenced without the consent of the Attorney General, s. 83.24

Proceedings may be commenced at instance of Government of Canada and conducted by Attorney General of Canada where the offence was alleged to have occurred outside the province in which the proceedings are commenced, whether or not proceedings have previously been commenced elsewhere in Canada and whether or not the person is in Canada, s. 83.25.

The sentence imposed under this section is to be served consecutively to any other punishment in accordance with s. 83.26. As to parole ineligibility, see s. 743.6(1.2).

As to freezing of assets of terrorist groups, see ss. 83.08 to 83.12 and seizure and forfeiture of terrorist property, see ss. 83.13 to 83.17. Offences relating to terrorist property, see ss. 83.01 to 83.04.

A wiretap authorization may be obtained for the offence under this section in accordance with Part VI. Special provisions apply to such authorizations, thus see ss. 185(1.1)(c), 186(1.1)(c), 186.1(c).

Special provisions for protecting witnesses on trials of this offence are set out in s. 486. See ss. 37 to 39 of the *Canada Evidence Act*, respecting Crown privilege and disclosure of information injurious to national security, national defence and foreign relations.

LEAVING CANADA TO COMMIT OFFENCE FOR TERRORIST GROUP.

83.201 Everyone who leaves or attempts to leave Canada, or goes or attempts to go on board a conveyance with the intent to leave Canada, for the purpose of committing an act or omission outside Canada that, if committed in Canada, would be an indictable offence under this or any other Act of Parliament for the benefit of, at the direction of or in association with a terrorist group is guilty of an indictable offence and liable to imprisonment for a term of not more than 14 years. 2013, c. 9, s. 8.

CROSS-REFERENCES

"Terrorism offence" is defined in s. 2. Expanded jurisdiction to try offences committed outside Canada that, if committed in Canada would be an offence under this section, is set out in s. 7(3.74). As to the place of trial in such circumstances, see s. 7(5); procuring attendance of accused, see s. 7(5.1); defences of *autrefois acquit* and *autrefois convict* and pardon, see s. 7(6); consent of the Attorney General of Canada for trial in such cases of non-citizens, see s. 7(7).

The offence under this section cannot be commenced without the consent of the Attorney General, s. 83.24.

Proceedings may be commenced at instance of Government of Canada and conducted by Attorney General of Canada where the offence was alleged to have occurred outside the province in which the proceedings are commenced, whether or not proceedings have previously been commenced elsewhere in Canada and whether or not the person is in Canada, s. 83.25.

The sentence imposed under this section is to be served consecutively to any other punishment in accordance with s. 83.26. As to parole ineligibility, see s. 743.6(1.2).

As to freezing of assets of terrorist groups, see ss. 83.08 to 83.12 and seizure and forfeiture of terrorist property, see ss. 83.13 to 83.17. Offences relating to terrorist property, see ss. 83.01 to 83.04.

A wiretap authorization may be obtained for the offence under this section in accordance with Part VI. Special provisions apply to such authorizations, thus see ss. 185(1.1)(c), 186(1.1)(c), 186.1(c).

Special protections for victims or witnesses in proceedings against an accused for this offence are set out in s. 486. See ss. 37 to 39 of the *Canada Evidence Act*, respecting Crown privilege and disclosure of information injurious to national security, national defence and foreign relations.

LEAVING CANADA TO COMMIT OFFENCE THAT IS TERRORIST ACTIVITY.

83.202 Everyone who leaves or attempts to leave Canada, or goes or attempts to go on board a conveyance with the intent to leave Canada, for the purpose of committing an act or omission outside Canada that, if committed in Canada, would be an indictable offence under this or any other Act of Parliament if the act or omission constituting the offence also constitutes a terrorist activity is guilty of an indictable offence and liable to imprisonment for a term of not more than 14 years. 2013, c. 9, s. 8.

CROSS-REFERENCES

"Terrorism offence" is defined in s. 2. Expanded jurisdiction to try offences committed outside Canada that, if committed in Canada would be an offence under this section, is set out in s. 7(3.74). As to the place of trial in such circumstances, see s. 7(5); procuring attendance of accused, see s. 7(5.1); defences of *autrefois acquit* and *autrefois convict* and pardon, see s. 7(6); consent of the Attorney General of Canada for trial in such cases of non-citizens, see s. 7(7).

The offence under this section cannot be commenced without the consent of the Attorney General, s. 83.24.

Proceedings may be commenced at instance of Government of Canada and conducted by Attorney General of Canada where the offence was alleged to have occurred outside the province in which the proceedings are commenced, whether or not proceedings have previously been commenced elsewhere in Canada and whether or not the person is in Canada, s. 83.25.

The sentence imposed under this section is to be served consecutively to any other punishment in accordance with s. 83.26. As to parole ineligibility, see s. 743.6(1.2).

As to freezing of assets of terrorist groups, see ss. 83.08 to 83.12 and seizure and forfeiture of terrorist property, see ss. 83.13 to 83.17. Offences relating to terrorist property, see ss. 83.01 to 83.04.

A wiretap authorization may be obtained for the offence under this section in accordance with Part VI. Special provisions apply to such authorizations, thus see ss. 185(1.1)(*c*), 186(1.1)(*c*), 186.1(*c*)

Special protections for victims or witnesses in proceedings against an accused for this offence are set out in s. 486. See ss. 37 to 39 of the *Canada Evidence Act*, respecting Crown privilege and disclosure of information injurious to national security, national defence and foreign relations.

INSTRUCTING TO CARRY OUT ACTIVITY FOR TERRORIST GROUP / Prosecution.

83.21 (1) Every person who knowingly instructs, directly or indirectly, any person to carry out any activity for the benefit of, at the direction of or in association with a terrorist group, for the purpose of enhancing the ability of any terrorist group to facilitate or carry out a terrorist activity, is guilty of an indictable offence and liable to imprisonment for life.

(2) An offence may be committed under subsection (1) whether or not

   (*a*) the activity that the accused instructs to be carried out is actually carried out;

   (*b*) the accused instructs a particular person to carry out the activity referred to in paragraph (*a*);

   (*c*) the accused knows the identity of the person whom the accused instructs to carry out the activity referred to in paragraph (*a*);

   (*d*) the person whom the accused instructs to carry out the activity referred to in paragraph (*a*) knows that it is to be carried out for the benefit of, at the direction of or in association with a terrorist group;

   (*e*) a terrorist group actually facilitates or carries out a terrorist activity;

   (*f*) the activity referred to in paragraph (*a*) actually enhances the ability of a terrorist group to facilitate or carry out a terrorist activity; or

   (*g*) the accused knows the specific nature of any terrorist activity that may be facilitated or carried out by a terrorist group. 2001, c. 41, s. 4.

CROSS-REFERENCES

"Terrorist activity" and "terrorist group" are defined in s. 83.01. Expanded jurisdiction to try offences committed outside Canada that, if committed in Canada would be an offence under this section, is set out in s. 7(3.74). As to the place of trial in such circumstances, see s. 7(5); procuring attendance of accused, see s. 7(5.1); defences of *autrefois acquit* and *autrefois convict* and pardon, see s. 7(6); consent of the Attorney General of Canada for trial in such cases of non-citizens, see s. 7(7).

The offence under this section cannot be commenced without the consent of the Attorney General, s. 83.24.

Proceedings may be commenced at instance of Government of Canada and conducted by Attorney General of Canada where the offence was alleged to have occurred outside the province in which the proceedings are commenced, whether or not proceedings have previously been commenced elsewhere in Canada and whether or not the person is in Canada, s. 83.25.

The sentence imposed under this section is to be served consecutively to any other punishment in accordance with s. 83.26. As to parole ineligibility, see s. 743.6(1.2).

As to freezing of assets of terrorist groups, see ss. 83.08 to 83.12 and seizure and forfeiture of terrorist property, see ss. 83.13 to 83.17. Offences relating to terrorist property, see ss. 83.01 to 83.04.

A wiretap authorization may be obtained for the offence under this section in accordance with Part VI. Special provisions apply to such authorizations, thus see ss. 185(1.1)(*c*), 186(1.1)(*c*), 186.1(*c*).

Special protections for victims or witnesses in proceedings against an accused for this offence are set out in s. 486. See ss. 37 to 39 of the *Canada Evidence Act*, respecting Crown privilege and disclosure of information injurious to national security, national defence and foreign relations.

ANNOTATIONS
The fault requirement of the offence in this section is consistent with s. 7 of the *Canadian Charter of Rights and Freedoms*: *R. v. Khawaja* (2006), 214 C.C.C. (3d) 399 (Ont. S.C.J.), leave to appeal to S.C.C. refused [2007] 1 S.C.R. x, 216 C.C.C. (3d) vi.

INSTRUCTING TO CARRY OUT TERRORIST ACTIVITY / Prosecution.
83.22 (1) Every person who knowingly instructs, directly or indirectly, any person to carry out a terrorist activity is guilty of an indictable offence and liable to imprisonment for life.

(2) An offence may be committed under subsection (1) whether or not
> **(*a*) the terrorist activity is actually carried out;**
> **(*b*) the accused instructs a particular person to carry out the terrorist activity;**
> **(*c*) the accused knows the identity of the person whom the accused instructs to carry out the terrorist activity; or**
> **(*d*) the person whom the accused instructs to carry out the terrorist activity knows that it is a terrorist activity. 2001, c. 41, s. 4.**

CROSS-REFERENCES

"Terrorist activity" is defined in s. 83.01. Expanded jurisdiction to try offences committed outside Canada that, if committed in Canada would be an offence under this section, is set out in s. 7(3.74). As to the place of trial in such circumstances, see s. 7(5); procuring attendance of accused, see s. 7(5.1); defences of *autrefois acquit* and *autrefois convict* and pardon, see s. 7(6); consent of the Attorney General of Canada for trial in such cases of non-citizens, see s. 7(7).

The offence under this section cannot be commenced without the consent of the Attorney General, s. 83.24

Proceedings may be commenced at instance of Government of Canada and conducted by Attorney General of Canada where the offence was alleged to have occurred outside the province in which the proceedings are commenced, whether or not proceedings have previously been commenced elsewhere in Canada and whether or not the person is in Canada, s. 83.25.

The sentence imposed under this section is to be served consecutively to any other punishment in accordance with s. 83.26. As to parole ineligibility, see s. 743.6(1.2).

As to freezing of assets of terrorist groups, see ss. 83.08 to 83.12 and seizure and forfeiture of terrorist property, see ss. 83.13 to 83.17. Offences relating to terrorist property, see ss. 83.01 to 83.04.

A wiretap authorization may be obtained for the offence under this section in accordance with Part VI. Special provisions apply to such authorizations, thus see ss. 185(1.1)(*c*), 186(1.1)(*c*), 186.1(*c*).

Special protections for victims or witnesses in proceedings against an accused for this offence are set out in s. 486. See ss. 37 to 39 of the *Canada Evidence Act*, respecting Crown privilege and disclosure of information injurious to national security, national defence and foreign relations.

CR. CODE

ADVOCATING OR PROMOTING COMMISSION OF TERRORISM OFFENCES / Definitions.

83.221 (1) Every person who, by communicating statements, knowingly advocates or promotes the commission of terrorism offences in general — other than an offence under this section — while knowing that any of those offences will be committed or being reckless as to whether any of those offences may be committed, as a result of such communication, is guilty of an indictable offence and is liable to imprisonment for a term of not more than five years.

(2) The following definitions apply in this section.

"communicating" has the same meaning as in subsection 319(7).

"statements" has the same meaning as in subsection 319(7). 2015, c. 20, s. 16.

CROSS-REFERENCES

"Terrorism offence" is defined in s. 2. Expanded jurisdiction to try offences committed outside Canada that, if committed in Canada, would be an offence under this section, is set out in s. 7(3.74). As to the place of trial in such circumstances, see s. 7(5); procuring attendance of accused, see s. 7(5.1); defences of *autrefois acquit* and *autrefois convict* and pardon, see s. 7(6); consent of Attorney General for trial in such cases of non-citizens, see s. 7(7).

The offence under this section cannot be commenced without the consent of the Attorney General, s. 83.24.

Proceedings may be commenced at the instance of the Government of Canada and conducted by the Attorney General of Canada where the offence was alleged to have occurred outside the province in which the proceedings are commenced, whether or not proceedings have previously been commenced elsewhere in Canada and whether or not the person is in Canada, s. 83.25.

The sentence imposed under this section is to be served consecutively to any other punishment in accordance with s. 83.26. As to parole ineligibility, see s. 743.6(1.2.).

As to freezing of assets of terrorist groups, see ss. 83.08 to 83.12 and seizure and forfeiture of terrorist property, see ss. 83.13 to 83.17.

A wiretap authorization may be obtained for the offence under this section in accordance with Part VI. Special provisions apply to such authorizations, thus see ss. 185(1.1)(*c*), 186(1.1)(*c*), and 186(1)(*c*).

Special protections for victims or witnesses in proceedings against an accused for this offence are set out in s. 486. See ss. 37 to 39 of the *Canada Evidence Act*, respecting Crown privilege and disclosure of information injurious to national security, national defence and foreign relations.

WARRANT OF SEIZURE / Summons to occupier / Owner and author may appear / Order of forfeiture / Disposal of matter / Appeal / Consent / Definitions.

83.222 (1) A judge who is satisfied by information on oath that there are reasonable grounds to believe that any publication, copies of which are kept for sale or distribution in premises within the court's jurisdiction, is terrorist propaganda may issue a warrant authorizing seizure of the copies.

(2) Within seven days after the day on which the warrant is issued, the judge shall issue a summons to the premises' occupier requiring the occupier to appear before the court and to show cause why the matter seized should not be forfeited to Her Majesty.

(3) The owner and the author of the matter seized and alleged to be terrorist propaganda may appear and be represented before the court in order to oppose the making of an order for the forfeiture of the matter.

(4) If the court is satisfied, on a balance of probabilities, that the publication is terrorist propaganda, it may make an order declaring that the matter be forfeited to Her Majesty, for disposal as the Attorney General may direct.

(5) If the court is not satisfied that the publication is terrorist propaganda, it may order that the matter be restored to the person from whom it was seized without delay after the time for final appeal has expired.

(6) An appeal lies from an order made under subsection (4) or (5) by any person who appeared before the court, on any ground of appeal that involves a question of law or fact alone, or a question of mixed law and fact, as if it were an appeal against conviction or against a judgment or verdict of acquittal, as the case may be, on a question of law alone under Part XXI, and sections 673 to 696 apply with any modifications that the circumstances require.

(7) No proceeding under this section shall be instituted without the Attorney General's consent.

(8) The following definitions apply in this section.

"court" has the same meaning as in subsection 320(8).

"judge" has the same meaning as in subsection 320(8).

"terrorist propaganda" means any writing, sign, visible representation or audio recording that advocates or promotes the commission of terrorism offences in general — other than an offence under subsection 83.221(1) — or counsels the commission of a terrorism offence. 2015, c. 20, s. 16.

CROSS-REFERENCES

A similar procedure for *in rem* seizure of proscribed materials is provided by s. 164.1 (child pornography) and s. 320 (hate propaganda).

Section 83.223 provides for an *in rem* proceeding to shut down terrorist propaganda sites on a computer system.

"Attorney General" is defined in s. 2.

ORDER TO COMPUTER SYSTEM'S CUSTODIAN / Notice to person who posted material / Person who posted material may appear / Non-appearance / Order of deletion / Destruction of electronic copy / Return of material / Appeal / Consent / When order takes effect / Definitions.

83.223 (1) If a judge is satisfied by information on oath that there are reasonable grounds to believe that there is material — that is terrorist propaganda or computer data that makes terrorist propaganda available — stored on and made available to the public through a computer system that is within the court's jurisdiction, the judge may order the computer system's custodian to

    (*a*) give an electronic copy of the material to the court;

    (*b*) ensure that the material is no longer stored on and made available through the computer system; and

    (*c*) provide the information that is necessary to identify and locate the person who posted the material.

(2) Within a reasonable time after receiving the information referred to in paragraph (1)(*c*), the judge shall cause notice to be given to the person who posted the material, giving that person the opportunity to appear and be represented before the court and to show cause why the material should not be deleted. If the person cannot be identified or located or does not reside in Canada, the judge may order the computer system's custodian to post the text of the notice at the location where the material was previously stored and made available, until the time set for the appearance.

(3) The person who posted the material may appear and be represented before the court in order to oppose the making of an order under subsection (5).

(4) If the person who posted the material does not appear before the court, the court may proceed to hear and determine the proceedings in the absence of the person as fully and effectually as if the person had appeared.

(5) If the court is satisfied, on a balance of probabilities, that the material is available to the public and is terrorist propaganda or computer data that makes terrorist propaganda available, it may order the computer system's custodian to delete the material.

(6) When the court makes the order for the deletion of the material, it may order the destruction of the electronic copy in the court's possession.

(7) If the court is not satisfied that the material is available to the public and is terrorist propaganda or computer data that makes terrorist propaganda available, the court shall order that the electronic copy be returned to the computer system's custodian and terminate the order under paragraph (1)(*b*).

(8) An appeal lies from an order made under subsection (5) or (6) by any person who appeared before the court, on any ground of appeal that involves a question of law or fact alone, or a question of mixed law and fact, as if it were an appeal against conviction or against a judgment or verdict of acquittal, as the case may be, on a question of law alone under Part XXI, and sections 673 to 696 apply with any modifications that the circumstances require.

(9) No proceeding under this section shall be instituted without the Attorney General's consent.

(10) No order made under any of subsections (5) to (7) takes effect until the time for final appeal has expired.

(11) The following definitions apply in this section.

"computer data" has the same meaning as in subsection 342.1(2).

"computer system" has the same meaning as in subsection 342.1(2).

"court" has the same meaning as in subsection 320(8).

"data" [Repealed 2015, c. 20, s. 35(d).]

"judge" has the same meaning as in subsection 320(8).

"terrorist propaganda" has the same meaning as in subsection 83.222(8). 2015, c. 20, ss. 16, 35.

CROSS-REFERENCES

A similar *in rem* procedure for shutting down sites on a computer system is provided by s. 164.1 (child pornography).

Section 83.222 provides a procedure for the seizure of terrorist propaganda and *in rem* forfeiture proceedings.

"Attorney General" is defined in s. 2.

CONCEALING PERSON WHO CARRIED OUT TERRORIST ACTIVITY / Concealing person who is likely to carry out terrorist activity.

83.23 (1) Everyone who knowingly harbours or conceals any person whom they know to be a person who has carried out a terrorist activity, for the purpose of enabling the person to facilitate or carry out any terrorist activity, is guilty of an indictable offence and liable to imprisonment

   (*a*) for a term of not more than 14 years, if the person who is harboured or concealed carried out a terrorist activity that is a terrorism offence for which that person is liable to imprisonment for life; and (*b*) **for a term of not more than 10 years, if the person who is harboured or concealed carried out a terrorist activity that is a terrorism offence for which that person is liable to any other punishment.**

(2) Everyone who knowingly harbours or conceals any person whom they know to be a person who is likely to carry out a terrorist activity, for the purpose of enabling the person to facilitate or carry out any terrorist activity, is guilty of an indictable offence and liable to imprisonment for a term of not more than 10 years. 2001, c. 41, s. 4; 2013, c. 9, s. 9.

CROSS-REFERENCES

"Terrorist activity" is defined in s. 83.01. Expanded jurisdiction to try offences committed outside Canada that, if committed in Canada would be an offence under this section, is set out in s. 7(3.74). As to the place of trial in such circumstances, see s. 7(5); procuring attendance of accused, see s. 7(5.1); defences of *autrefois acquit* and *autrefois convict* and pardon, see s. 7(6); consent of the Attorney General of Canada for trial in such cases of non-citizens, see s. 7(7).

The offence under this section cannot be commenced without the consent of the Attorney General, s. 83.24.

Proceedings may be commenced at instance of Government of Canada and conducted by Attorney General of Canada where the offence was alleged to have occurred outside the province in which the proceedings are commenced, whether or not proceedings have previously been commenced elsewhere in Canada and whether or not the person is in Canada, s. 83.25.

The sentence imposed under this section is to be served consecutively to any other punishment in accordance with s. 83.26. As to parole ineligibility, see s. 743.6(1.2).

As to freezing of assets of terrorist groups, see ss. 83.08 to 83.12 and seizure and forfeiture of terrorist property, see ss. 83.13 to 83.17. Offences relating to terrorist property, see ss. 83.01 to 83.04.

A wiretap authorization may be obtained for the offence under this section in accordance with Part VI. Special provisions apply to such authorizations, thus see ss. 185(1.1)(*c*), 186(1.1)(*c*), 186.1(*c*).

Special protections for victims or witnesses in proceedings against an accused for this offence are set out in s. 486. See ss. 37 to 39 of the *Canada Evidence Act*, respecting Crown privilege and disclosure of information injurious to national security, national defence and foreign relations.

Hoax Regarding Terrorist Activity

HOAX — TERRORIST ACTIVITY / Punishment / Causing bodily harm / Causing death.

83.231 (1) Every one commits an offence who, without lawful excuse and with intent to cause any person to fear death, bodily harm, substantial damage to property or serious interference with the lawful use or operation of property,

(*a*) **conveys or causes or procures to be conveyed information that, in all the circumstances, is likely to cause a reasonable apprehension that terrorist activity is occurring or will occur, without believing the information to be true; or**

(*b*) **commits an act that, in all the circumstances, is likely to cause a reasonable apprehension that terrorist activity is occurring or will occur, without believing that such activity is occurring or will occur.**

(2) Every one who commits an offence under subsection (1) is guilty of

(*a*) **an indictable offence and liable to imprisonment for a term not exceeding five years; or**

(*b*) **an offence punishable on summary conviction.**

(3) Every one who commits an offence under subsection (1) and thereby causes bodily harm to any other person is guilty of

(*a*) an indictable offence and liable to imprisonment for a term not exceeding ten years; or

(*b*) an offence punishable on summary conviction and liable to imprisonment for a term not exceeding eighteen months.

(4) Every one who commits an offence under subsection (1) and thereby causes the death of any other person is guilty of an indictable offence and liable to imprisonment for life. 2004, c. 15, s. 32.

CROSS-REFERENCES

"Bodily harm" is defined in s. 2. "Terrorist activity" is defined in s. 83.01.

SYNOPSIS

This section creates two types of offences relating to terrorist activity hoaxes. The offence defined in subsec. (1)(*a*) is committed where the person without lawful excuse and with intent to cause a person to fear death, bodily harm, substantial damage to property or serious interference with the lawful use or operation of property conveys, causes or procures to be conveyed information that is likely to cause a reasonable apprehension that terrorist activity is occurring or will occur, without believing the information is true. The subsec. (1)(*b*) offence has a similar intent but is based on the commission by the accused of an act that is likely to cause a reasonable apprehension of terrorist activity. The penalty imposed depends on the consequences of the offence as set out in subsecs. (2), (3) and (4).

Proceedings and Aggravated Punishment

ATTORNEY GENERAL'S CONSENT.

83.24 Proceedings in respect of a terrorism offence or an offence under section 83.12 shall not be commenced without the consent of the Attorney General. 2001, c. 41, s. 4.

CROSS-REFERENCES

"Attorney General" and "terrorism offence" are defined in s. 2.

JURISDICTION / Trial and punishment.

83.25 (1) Where a person is alleged to have committed a terrorism offence or an offence under section 83.12, proceedings in respect of that offence may, whether or not that person is in Canada, be commenced at the instance of the Government of Canada and conducted by the Attorney General of Canada or counsel acting on his or her behalf in any territorial division in Canada, if the offence is alleged to have occurred outside the province in which the proceedings are commenced, whether or not proceedings have previously been commenced elsewhere in Canada.

(2) An accused may be tried and punished in respect of an offence referred to in subsection (1) in the same manner as if the offence had been committed in the territorial division where the proceeding is conducted. 2001, c. 41, s. 4.

CROSS-REFERENCES

"Territorial division" is defined in s. 2. For special provisions respecting territorial jurisdiction for offences under this Part committed outside Canada see ss. 7(3.73) to (3.75).

SENTENCES TO BE SERVED CONSECUTIVELY.

83.26 A sentence, other than one of life imprisonment, imposed on a person for an offence under any of sections 83.02 to 83.04 and 83.18 to 83.23 shall be served consecutively to

(a) any other punishment imposed on the person, other than a sentence of life imprisonment, for an offence arising out of the same event or series of events; and

(b) any other sentence, other than one of life imprisonment, to which the person is subject at the time the sentence is imposed on the person for an offence under any of those sections. 2001, c. 41, s. 4.

ANNOTATIONS

This provision does not oust the application of the totality principle in sentencing for terrorism offences. The fact that sentences of over 20 years may be imposed more often in terrorism cases is not inconsistent with the totality principle. It merely attests to the particular gravity of terrorist offences and the moral culpability of those who commit them. Denunciation and deterrence, both specific and general, are inevitably important principles in the sentencing of terrorism offences: *R. v. Khawaja* (2012), 290 C.C.C. (3d) 361 (S.C.C.), affg 273 C.C.C. (3d) 415 (Ont. C.A.).

PUNISHMENT FOR TERRORIST ACTIVITY / Offender must be notified.

83.27 (1) Notwithstanding anything in this Act, a person convicted of an indictable offence, other than an offence for which a sentence of imprisonment for life is imposed as a minimum punishment, where the act or omission constituting the offence also constitutes a terrorist activity, is liable to imprisonment for life.

(2) Subsection (1) does not apply unless the prosecutor satisfies the court that the offender, before making a plea, was notified that the application of that subsection would be sought. 2001, c. 41, s. 4.

CROSS-REFERENCES

"Terrorist activity" is defined in s. 83.01. For proof of notice, see s. 4(6), (7).

Investigative Hearing

DEFINITION OF "JUDGE" / Order for gathering information /Attorney General's consent / Making of order / Contents of order / Execution of order / Variation of order / Obligation to answer questions and produce things / Judge to rule / No person excused from complying with subsection (8) / Right to counsel / Order for custody of thing.

83.28 (1) In this section and section 83.29, "judge" means a provincial court judge or a judge of a superior court of criminal jurisdiction.

(2) Subject to subsection (3), a peace officer may, for the purposes of an investigation of a terrorism offence, apply ex parte to a judge for an order for the gathering of information.

(3) A peace officer may make an application under subsection (2) only if the Attorney General's prior consent was obtained.

(4) The judge to whom the application is made may make an order for the gathering of information if they are satisfied that the Attorney General's consent was obtained as required by subsection (3), and

(a) that there are reasonable grounds to believe that

      (i) a terrorism offence has been committed,

      (ii) information concerning the offence, or information that may reveal the whereabouts of a person suspected by the peace officer of having committed the offence, is likely to be obtained as a result of the order, and

     (iii) reasonable attempts have been made to obtain the information referred to in subparagraph (ii) by other means; or

   (*b*) that

      (i) there are reasonable grounds to believe that a terrorism offence will be committed,

      (ii) there are reasonable grounds to believe that a person has direct and material information that relates to the offence referred to in subparagraph (i), or that may reveal the whereabouts of an individual who the peace officer suspects may commit the offence referred to in that subparagraph, and

     (iii) reasonable attempts have been made to obtain the information referred to in subparagraph (ii) by other means.

(5) An order made under subsection (4) shall order the examination, on oath or not, of the person named in the order and require the person to attend at the place fixed by the judge, or by the judge designated under paragraph (*b*), as the case may be, for the examination and to remain in attendance until excused by the presiding judge, and may

   (*a*) order the person to bring to the examination any thing in their possession or control, and produce it to the presiding judge;

   (*b*) designate another judge as the judge before whom the examination is to take place; and

   (*c*) include any other terms or conditions that the judge considers desirable, including terms or conditions for the protection of the interests of the person named in the order and of third parties or for the protection of any ongoing investigation.

(6) The order may be executed anywhere in Canada.

(7) The judge who made the order, or another judge of the same court, may vary its terms and conditions.

(8) A person named in an order made under subsection (4) shall answer questions put to them by the Attorney General or the Attorney General's agent, and shall produce to the presiding judge things that the person was ordered to bring, but may refuse if answering a question or producing a thing would disclose information that is protected by any law relating to privilege or to disclosure of information.

(9) The presiding judge shall rule on any objection or other issue relating to a refusal to answer a question or to produce a thing.

(10) No person shall be excused from answering a question or producing a thing under subsection (8) on the ground that the answer or thing may tend to incriminate them or subject them to any proceeding or penalty, but

   (*a*) no answer given or thing produced under subsection (8) shall be used or received against the person in any criminal proceedings against them, other than a prosecution under section 132 or 136; and

   (*b*) no evidence derived from the evidence obtained from the person shall be used or received against the person in any criminal proceedings against them, other than a prosecution under section 132 or 136.

(11) A person has the right to retain and instruct counsel at any stage of the proceedings.

(12) The presiding judge, if satisfied that any thing produced during the course of the examination will likely be relevant to the investigation of any terrorism offence, may order that the thing be given into the custody of the peace officer or someone acting on the peace officer's behalf. 2001, c. 41, s. 4; 2013, c. 9, s. 10.

CROSS-REFERENCES

"Attorney General", "peace officer", "provincial court judge", "superior court of criminal jurisdiction", and "terrorism offence" are defined in s. 2. A judge may issue a warrant for the arrest of the person named in the order if the circumstances set out in s. 83.29.

The Attorney General of Canada is to report to Parliament on the operation of this section annually in accordance with s. 83.31. This provision is subject to the "sunset provision" in s. 83.32.

ANNOTATIONS

Note: The cases noted below were decided before the repeal and re-enactment of this section, which came into force on July 15, 2013. The section was re-enacted in almost identical terms.

This provision does not violate ss. 7 or 11(*d*) of the Charter: *R. v. Bagri*, [2004] 2 S.C.R. 248, 184 C.C.C. (3d) 449.

This provision is procedural and accordingly, applies retrospectively to incidents that occurred prior to its enactment: *R. v. Bagri, supra.*

The purpose of this legislation is the prosecution and prevention of terrorism offences. The role of counsel for the named person should be broadly defined to include objections not only on the specified grounds based on the application of law related to non-disclosure of information or privilege, but also objections on the basis of abusive or irrelevant questioning. The investigative hearing is governed by Part I of the *Canada Evidence Act* which affords the named person the protections of spousal privilege, procedures concerning cross-examination of adverse witnesses and cross-examination in relation to prior statements. In addition, the common rule of relevance applies to the hearing. The boundaries of relevance will be dictated in large measure by the supporting materials for the s. 83.28 order for the gathering of information, as well as by the investigatory nature of the proceeding. While the nature of the proceeding may increase the scope of allowable questioning, it must be kept within reasonable bounds by the judicial nature of the investigative hearing and all of the procedural protections that the oversight of a judge implies: *R. v. Bagri, supra.*

Subsection (10) provides both use and derivative use immunity. The protection in para. (*b*) provides absolute derivative use immunity such that evidence derived from the evidence provided at the judicial investigative hearing may not be presented in evidence against the witness in another prosecution, even if the Crown is able to establish, on a balance of probabilities, that it would have inevitably discovered the same evidence through alternative means. These procedural safeguards must be extended to extradition and deportation proceedings. Where there is the potential for the use by the state of the evidence gathered in deportation or extradition proceedings against the named person, the hearing judge must make and, if necessary, vary the terms of an order to properly provide use and derivative use immunity in extradition or deportation proceedings: *R. v. Bagri, supra.*

ARREST WARRANT / Execution of warrant / Person to be brought before judge / Application of section 707.

83.29 (1) The judge who made the order under subsection 83.28(4), or another judge of the same court, may issue a warrant for the arrest of the person named in the order if the judge is satisfied, on an information in writing and under oath, that the person

   (*a*) is evading service of the order;

   (*b*) is about to abscond; or

   (*c*) did not attend the examination, or did not remain in attendance, as required by the order.

(2) The warrant may be executed at any place in Canada by any peace officer having jurisdiction in that place.

CR. CODE

(3) A peace officer who arrests a person in the execution of the warrant shall, without delay, bring the person, or cause them to be brought, before the judge who issued the warrant or another judge of the same court. The judge in question may, to ensure compliance with the order, order that the person be detained in custody or released on recognizance, with or without sureties.

(4) Section 707 applies, with any necessary modifications, to persons detained in custody under this section. 2001, c. 41, s. 4; 2013, c. 9, s. 10.

CROSS-REFERENCES

The Attorney General of Canada is to report to Parliament on the operation of this section annually in accordance with s. 83.31. This provision is subject to the "sunset provision" in s. 83.32.

Recognizance with Conditions

ATTORNEY GENERAL'S CONSENT / Terrorist activity / Appearance / Arrest without warrant / Duty of peace officer / When person to be taken before judge / How person dealt with / Adjournment under subparagraph (7)(*b*)(ii) / Adjournment under paragraph (7.1)(*b*) / Hearing before judge / Duration extended / Refusal to enter into recognizance / Conditions — firearms / Surrender, etc. / Condition — passport / Condition — specified geographic area / Reasons / Variance of conditions / Other provisions to apply.

83.3 (1) The Attorney General's consent is required before a peace officer may lay an information under subsection (2).

(2) Subject to subsection (1), a peace officer may lay an information before a provincial court judge if the peace officer

  (*a*) believes on reasonable grounds that a terrorist activity may be carried out; and

  (*b*) suspects on reasonable grounds that the imposition of a recognizance with conditions on a person, or the arrest of a person, is likely to prevent the carrying out of the terrorist activity.

(3) The judge who receives the information may cause the person to appear before any provincial court judge.

(4) Despite subsections (2) and (3), a peace officer may arrest a person without a warrant and cause the person to be detained in custody, in order to bring them before a provincial court judge in accordance with subsection (6), if

  (*a*) either

    (i) the grounds for laying an information referred to in paragraphs (2)(*a*) and (*b*) exist but, by reason of exigent circumstances, it would be impracticable to lay an information under subsection (2), or

    (ii) an information has been laid under subsection (2) and a summons has been issued; and

  (*b*) the peace officer suspects on reasonable grounds that the detention of the person in custody is likely to prevent a terrorist activity.

(5) If a peace officer arrests a person without a warrant in the circumstance described in subparagraph (4)(*a*)(i), the peace officer shall, within the time prescribed by paragraph (6)(*a*) or (*b*),

  (*a*) lay an information in accordance with subsection (2); or

  (*b*) release the person.

(6) Unless a peace officer, or an officer in charge as defined in Part XVI, is satisfied that a person should be released from custody unconditionally before their appearance before a provincial court judge in accordance with the rules in paragraph (*a*) or (*b*), and

so releases the person, the person detained in custody shall be taken before a provincial court judge in accordance with the following rules:

(*a*) if a provincial court judge is available within 24 hours after the person has been arrested, the person shall be taken before a provincial court judge without unreasonable delay and in any event within that period; and

(*b*) if a provincial court judge is not available within 24 hours after the person has been arrested, the person shall be taken before a provincial court judge as soon as feasible.

(7) When a person is taken before a provincial court judge under subsection (6),

(*a*) if an information has not been laid under subsection (2), the judge shall order that the person be released; or

(*b*) if an information has been laid under subsection (2),

(i) the judge shall order that the person be released unless the peace officer who laid the information shows cause why the person's detention in custody is justified on one or more of the following grounds:

(A) the detention is necessary to ensure the person's appearance before a provincial court judge in order to be dealt with in accordance with subsection (8),

(B) the detention is necessary for the protection or safety of the public, including any witness, having regard to all the circumstances including

(I) the likelihood that, if the person is released from custody, a terrorist activity will be carried out, and

(II) any substantial likelihood that the person will, if released from custody, interfere with the administration of justice, and

(C) the detention is necessary to maintain confidence in the administration of justice, having regard to all the circumstances, including the apparent strength of the peace officer's grounds under subsection (2), and the gravity of any terrorist activity that may be carried out, and

(ii) the judge may adjourn the matter for a hearing under subsection (8) but, if the person is not released under subparagraph (i), the adjournment may not exceed 48 hours.

(7.1) If a judge has adjourned the matter under subparagraph (7)(*b*)(ii) and the person remains in custody at the end of the period of adjournment, the person shall be taken before a provincial court judge who

(*a*) shall order that the person be released unless a peace officer shows cause why the person's detention in custody is justified on one or more of the grounds set out in clauses (7)(*b*)(i)(A) to (C) and satisfies the judge that the investigation in relation to which the person is detained is being conducted diligently and expeditiously; and

(*b*) may adjourn the matter for a hearing under subsection (8) but, if the person is not released under paragraph (*a*), the adjournment may not exceed 48 hours.

(7.2) If a judge has adjourned the matter under paragraph (7.1)(*b*) and the person remains in custody at the end of the period of adjournment, the person shall be taken before a provincial court judge who

(*a*) shall order that the person be released unless a peace officer shows cause why the person's detention in custody is justified on one or more of the grounds set out in clauses (7)(*b*)(i)(A) to (C) and satisfies the judge that the investigation in relation to which the person is detained is being conducted diligently and expeditiously; and

(*b*) may adjourn the matter for a hearing under subsection (8) but, if the person is not released under paragraph (*a*), the adjournment may not exceed 48 hours.

(8) The judge before whom the person appears in accordance with subsection (3)

CR. CODE

(*a*) may, if the judge is satisfied by the evidence adduced that the peace officer has reasonable grounds for the suspicion, order that the person enter into a recognizance, with or without sureties, to keep the peace and be of good behaviour for a period of not more than 12 months and to comply with any other reasonable conditions prescribed in the recognizance, including the conditions set out in subsections (10), (11.1) and (11.2), that the judge considers desirable for preventing the carrying out of a terrorist activity; and

(*b*) if the person was not released under subparagraph (7)(*b*)(i) or paragraph (7.1)(*a*) or (7.2)(*a*), shall order that the person be released, subject to the recognizance, if any, ordered under paragraph (*a*).

(8.1) However, if the judge is also satisfied that the person was convicted previously of a terrorism offence, the judge may order that the person enter into the recognizance for a period of not more than two years.

(9) The judge may commit the person to prison for a term not exceeding 12 months if the person fails or refuses to enter into the recognizance.

(10) Before making an order under paragraph (8)(*a*), the judge shall consider whether it is desirable, in the interests of the safety of the person or of any other person, to include as a condition of the recognizance that the person be prohibited from possessing any firearm, crossbow, prohibited weapon, restricted weapon, prohibited device, ammunition, prohibited ammunition or explosive substance, or all of those things, for any period specified in the recognizance, and if the judge decides that it is so desirable, they shall add the condition to the recognizance.

(11) If the judge adds the condition described in subsection (10) to a recognizance, they shall specify in it the manner and method by which

(*a*) the things referred to in that subsection that are in the person's possession shall be surrendered, disposed of, detained, stored or dealt with; and

(*b*) the authorizations, licences and registration certificates that are held by the person shall be surrendered.

(11.1) The judge shall consider whether it is desirable, to prevent the carrying out of a terrorist activity, to include in the recognizance a condition that the person deposit, in the specified manner, any passport or other travel document issued in their name that is in their possession or control. If the judge decides that it is desirable, the judge shall add the condition to the recognizance and specify the period during which it applies.

(11.2) The judge shall consider whether it is desirable, to prevent the carrying out of a terrorist activity, to include in the recognizance a condition that the person remain within a specified geographic area unless written permission to leave that area is obtained from the judge or any individual designated by the judge. If the judge decides that it is desirable, the judge shall add the condition to the recognizance and specify the period during which it applies.

(12) If the judge does not add a condition described in subsection (10), (11.1) or (11.2) to a recognizance, the judge shall include in the record a statement of the reasons for not adding it.

(13) The judge, or any other judge of the same court, may, on application of the peace officer, the Attorney General or the person, vary the conditions fixed in the recognizance.

(14) Subsections 810(4) and (5) apply, with any necessary modifications, to proceedings under this section. 2001, c. 41, s. 4; 2013, c. 9, s. 10; 2015, c. 20, s. 17.

CROSS-REFERENCES

"Attorney General", "peace officer", "provincial court judge" and "terrorism offence" are defined in s. 2.

"Terrorist activity" is defined in s. 83.01.

With respect to the grounds for detention in subsec. (7)(*b*)(i)(A) to (C), reference should be had to the analogous grounds in s. 515(10)(*a*) to (*c*) and the case law developed thereunder.

The Attorney General of Canada is to report to Parliament on the operation of this section annually in accordance with s. 83.31. This section is subject to the "sunset provision" in s. 83.32.

ANNUAL REPORT (SECTIONS 83.28 AND 83.29) / Attorney General's opinion / Annual report (section 83.3) / Annual report (section 83.3) / Opinions / Limitation.

83.31 (1) The Attorney General of Canada shall prepare and cause to be laid before Parliament and the Attorney General of every province shall publish or otherwise make available to the public an annual report for the previous year on the operation of sections 83.28 and 83.29 that includes

  (*a*) the number of consents to make an application that were sought, and the number that were obtained, by virtue of subsections 83.28(2) and (3);

  (*b*) the number of orders for the gathering of information that were made under subsection 83.28(4); and

  (*c*) the number of arrests that were made with a warrant issued under section 83.29.

(1.1) The Attorney General of Canada shall include in the annual report under subsection (1) his or her opinion, supported by reasons, on whether the operation of sections 83.28 and 83.29 should be extended.

(2) The Attorney General of Canada shall prepare and cause to be laid before Parliament and the Attorney General of every province shall publish or otherwise make available to the public an annual report for the previous year on the operation of section 83.3 that includes

  (*a*) the number of consents to lay an information that were sought, and the number that were obtained, by virtue of subsections 83.3(1) and (2);

  (*b*) the number of cases in which a summons or a warrant of arrest was issued for the purposes of subsection 83.3(3);

  (*c*) the number of cases in which a person was not released under subsection 83.3(7), (7.1) or (7.2) pending a hearing;

  (*d*) the number of cases in which an order to enter into a recognizance was made under paragraph 83.3(8)(*a*), and the types of conditions that were imposed;

  (*e*) the number of times that a person failed or refused to enter into a recognizance, and the term of imprisonment imposed under subsection 83.3(9) in each case; and

  (*f*) the number of cases in which the conditions fixed in a recognizance were varied under subsection 83.3(13).

(3) The Minister of Public Safety and Emergency Preparedness shall prepare and cause to be laid before Parliament and the Minister responsible for policing in every province shall publish or otherwise make available to the public an annual report for the previous year on the operation of section 83.3 that includes

  (*a*) the number of arrests without warrant that were made under subsection 83.3(4) and the period of the arrested person's detention in custody in each case; and

  (*b*) the number of cases in which a person was arrested without warrant under subsection 83.3(4) and was released

    (i) by a peace officer under paragraph 83.3(5)(*b*), or

    (ii) by a judge under paragraph 83.3(7)(*a*), (7.1)(*a*) or (7.2)(*a*).

(3.1) The Attorney General of Canada and the Minister of Public Safety and Emergency Preparedness shall include in their annual reports under subsections (2) and (3), respectively, their opinion, supported by reasons, on whether the operation of section 83.3 should be extended.

(4) The annual report shall not contain any information the disclosure of which would
- (*a*) compromise or hinder an ongoing investigation of an offence under an Act of Parliament;
- (*b*) endanger the life or safety of any person;
- (*c*) prejudice a legal proceeding; or
- (*d*) otherwise be contrary to the public interest. 2001, c. 41, s. 4; 2005, c. 10, s. 35(1)(*f*)(iv); 2013, c. 9, s. 11; 2015, c. 20, s. 18.

SUNSET PROVISION / Review / Report / Order in Council / Rules / Subsequent extensions / Definition of "sitting day of Parliament".

83.32 (1) Sections 83.28, 83.29 and 83.3 cease to have effect at the end of the 15th sitting day of Parliament after the fifth anniversary of the coming into force of this subsection unless, before the end of that day, the operation of those sections is extended by resolution — whose text is established under subsection (2) — passed by both Houses of Parliament in accordance with the rules set out in subsection (3).

(1.1) A comprehensive review of sections 83.28, 83.29 and 83.3 and their operation shall be undertaken by any committee of the Senate, of the House of Commons or of both Houses of Parliament that may be designated or established by the Senate or the House of Commons, or by both Houses of Parliament, as the case may be, for that purpose.

(1.2) The committee referred to in subsection (1.1) shall, within a year after a review is undertaken under that subsection or within any further time that may be authorized by the Senate, the House of Commons or both Houses of Parliament, as the case may be, submit a report on the review to Parliament, including its recommendation with respect to extending the operation of section 83.28, 83.29 or 83.3.

(2) The Governor in Council may, by order, establish the text of a resolution that provides for the extension of the operation of section 83.28, 83.29 or 83.3 and that specifies the period of the extension, which may not exceed five years from the first day on which the resolution has been passed by both Houses of Parliament.

(3) A motion for the adoption of the resolution may be debated in both Houses of Parliament but may not be amended. At the conclusion of the debate, the Speaker of the House of Parliament shall immediately put every question necessary to determine whether or not the motion is concurred in.

(4) The operation of section 83.28, 83.29 or 83.3 may be further extended in accordance with the procedure set out in this section, but the reference to "the fifth anniversary of the coming into force of this subsection" in subsection (1) is to be read as a reference to "the expiry of the most recent extension under this section".

(5) In subsection (1), "sitting day of Parliament" means a day on which both Houses of Parliament sit. 2001, c. 41, s. 4; 2013, c. 9, s. 12.

TRANSITIONAL PROVISION — SECTIONS 83.28 AND 83.29 / Transitional provision — section 83.3.

83.33 (1) In the event that sections 83.28 and 83.29 cease to have effect in accordance with section 83.32, proceedings commenced under those sections shall be completed if the hearing before the judge of the application made under subsection 83.28(2) began before those sections ceased to have effect.

(2) In the event that section 83.3 ceases to have effect in accordance with section 83.32, a person detained in custody under section 83.3 shall be released when that section ceases to have effect, except that subsections 83.3(7) to (14) continue to apply to a person who was taken before a judge under subsection 83.3(6) before section 83.3 ceased to have effect. 2001, c. 41, s. 4; 2013, c. 9, s. 13.

Part III / FIREARMS AND OTHER WEAPONS

Note: Part III (ss. 84, 86 to 96, 98 to 117) replaced 1995, c. 39, s. 139 (brought into force December 1, 1998) (s. 85 in force January 1, 1996) (s. 97 in force January 1, 2003):

Interpretation

DEFINITIONS / "Ammunition" / "Antique firearm" / "Authorization" / "Automatic firearm" / "Cartridge magazine" / "Chief firearms officer" / "Commissioner of firearms" / "Cross-bow" / "Export" / "Firearms officer" / "Handgun" / "Imitation firearm" / "Import" / "Licence" / "Non-restricted firearm" / "Prescribed" / "Prohibited ammunition" / "Prohibited device" / "Prohibited firearm" / "Prohibited weapon" / "Prohibition order" / "Registrar" / "Registration certificate" / "Replica firearm" / "Restricted firearm" / "Restricted weapon" / "Superior court" / "Transfer" / Barrel length / Certain weapons deemed not to be firearms / Exception / antique firearms / Meaning of "holder" / Subsequent offences / Sequence of convictions only.

84. (1) In this Part,

"ammunition" means a cartridge containing a projectile designed to be discharged from a firearm and, without restricting the generality of the foregoing, includes a caseless cartridge and a shot shell;

"antique firearm" means

    (*a*) any firearm manufactured before 1898 that was not designed to discharge rim-fire or centre-fire ammunition and that has not been redesigned to discharge such ammunition, or

    (*b*) any firearm that is prescribed to be an antique firearm;

"authorization" means an authorization issued under the *Firearms Act*;

"automatic firearm" means a firearm that is capable of, or assembled or designed and manufactured with the capability of, discharging projectiles in rapid succession during one pressure of the trigger;

"cartridge magazine" means a device or container from which ammunition may be fed into the firing chamber of a firearm;

"chief firearms officer" means a chief firearms officer as defined in subsection 2(1) of the *Firearms Act*;

"Commissioner of Firearms" means the Commissioner of Firearms appointed under section 81.1 of the *Firearms Act*.

"cross-bow" means a device with a bow and a bowstring mounted on a stock that is designed to propel an arrow, a bolt, a quarrel or any similar projectile on a trajectory guided by a barrel or groove and that is capable of causing serious bodily injury or death to a person;

"export" means export from Canada and, for greater certainty, includes the exportation of goods from Canada that are imported into Canada and shipped in transit through Canada;

"firearms officer" means a firearms officer as defined in subsection 2(1) of the *Firearms Act*;

"handgun" means a firearm that is designed, altered or intended to be aimed and fired by the action of one hand, whether or not it has been redesigned or subsequently altered to be aimed and fired by the action of both hands;

"imitation firearm" means any thing that imitates a firearm, and includes a replica firearm;

"import" means import into Canada and, for greater certainty, includes the importation of goods into Canada that are shipped in transit through Canada and exported from Canada;

"licence" means a licence issued under the *Firearms Act*;

"non-restricted firearm" means

(*a*) a firearm that is neither a prohibited firearm nor a restricted firearm, or

(*b*) a firearm that is prescribed to be a non-restricted firearm;

"prescribed" means prescribed by the regulations;

"prohibited ammunition" means ammunition, or a projectile of any kind, that is prescribed to be prohibited ammunition;

"prohibited device" means

(*a*) any component or part of a weapon, or any accessory for use with a weapon, that is prescribed to be a prohibited device,

(*b*) a handgun barrel that is equal to or less than 105 mm in length, but does not include any such handgun barrel that is prescribed, where the handgun barrel is for use in international sporting competitions governed by the rules of the International Shooting Union,

(*c*) a device or contrivance designed or intended to muffle or stop the sound or report of a firearm,

(*d*) a cartridge magazine that is prescribed to be a prohibited device, or

(*e*) a replica firearm;

"prohibited firearm" means

(*a*) a handgun that

(i) has a barrel equal to or less than 105 mm in length, or

(ii) is designed or adapted to discharge a 25 or 32 calibre cartridge,

but does not include any such handgun that is prescribed, where the handgun is for use in international sporting competitions governed by the rules of the International Shooting Union,

(*b*) a firearm that is adapted from a rifle or shotgun, whether by sawing, cutting or any other alteration, and that, as so adapted,

(i) is less than 660 mm in length, or

(ii) is 660 mm or greater in length and has a barrel less than 457 mm in length,

(*c*) an automatic firearm, whether or not it has been altered to discharge only one projectile with one pressure of the trigger, or

(*d*) any firearm that is prescribed to be a prohibited firearm;

"prohibited weapon" means

(*a*) a knife that has a blade that opens automatically by gravity or centrifugal force or by hand pressure applied to a button, spring or other device in or attached to the handle of the knife, or

(*b*) any weapon, other than a firearm, that is prescribed to be a prohibited weapon;

"prohibition order" means an order made under this Act or any other Act of Parliament prohibiting a person from possessing any firearm, cross-bow, prohibited weapon, restricted weapon, prohibited device, ammunition, prohibited ammunition or explosive substance, or all such things;

"Registrar" means the Registrar of Firearms appointed under section 82 of the *Firearms Act*;

"registration certificate" means a registration certificate issued under the *Firearms Act*;

"replica firearm" means any device that is designed or intended to exactly resemble, or to resemble with near precision, a firearm, and that itself is not a firearm, but does not include any such device that is designed or intended to exactly resemble, or to resemble with near precision, an antique firearm;

"restricted firearm" means

    (*a*) a handgun that is not a prohibited firearm,

    (*b*) a firearm that

        (i) is not a prohibited firearm,

        (ii) has a barrel less than 470 mm in length, and

        (iii) is capable of discharging centre-fire ammunition in a semi-automatic manner,

    (*c*) a firearm that is designed or adapted to be fired when reduced to a length of less than 660 mm by folding, telescoping or otherwise, or

    (*d*) a firearm of any other kind that is prescribed to be a restricted firearm;

"restricted weapon" means any weapon, other than a firearm, that is prescribed to be a restricted weapon;

"superior court" means

    (*a*) in Ontario, the Superior Court of Justice, sitting in the region, district or county or group of counties where the relevant adjudication was made,

    (*b*) in Quebec, the Superior Court,

    (*c*) in New Brunswick, Manitoba, Saskatchewan and Alberta, the Court of Queen's Bench,

    (*d*) in Nova Scotia, British Columbia, Prince Edward Island and a territory, the Supreme Court, and

    (*e*) in Newfoundland and Labrador, the Trial Division of the Supreme Court;

"transfer" means sell, provide, barter, give, lend, rent, send, transport, ship, distribute or deliver.

(2) For the purposes of this Part, the length of a barrel of a firearm is

    (*a*) in the case of a revolver, the distance from the muzzle of the barrel to the breach end immediately in front of the cylinder, and

    (*b*) in any other case, the distance from the muzzle of the barrel to and including the chamber,

but does not include the length of any component, part or accessory including any component, part or accessory designed or intended to suppress the muzzle flash or reduce recoil.

(3) For the purposes of sections 91 to 95, 99 to 101, 103 to 107 and 117.03 of this Act and the provisions of the *Firearms Act*, the following weapons are deemed not to be firearms:

    (*a*) any antique firearm;

    (*b*) any device that is

        (i) designed exclusively for signalling, for notifying of distress, for firing blank cartridges or for firing stud cartridges, explosive-driven rivets or other industrial projectiles, and

        (ii) intended by the person in possession of it to be used exclusively for the purpose for which it is designed;

    (*c*) any shooting device that is

        (i) designed exclusively for the slaughtering of domestic animals, the tranquilizing of animals or the discharging of projectiles with lines attached to them, and

        (ii) intended by the person in possession of it to be used exclusively for the purpose for which it is designed; and

    (*d*) any other barrelled weapon, where it is proved that the weapon is not designed or adapted to discharge

        (i) a shot, bullet or other projectile at a muzzle velocity exceeding 152.4 m per second or at a muzzle energy exceeding 5.7 Joules, or

        (ii) a shot, bullet or other projectile that is designed or adapted to attain a velocity exceeding 152.4 m per second or an energy exceeding 5.7 Joules.

(3.1) Notwithstanding subsection (3), an antique firearm is a firearm for the purposes of regulations made under paragraph 117(*h*) of the *Firearms Act* and subsection 86(2) of this Act.

(4) For the purposes of this Part, a person is the holder of
- (*a*) an authorization or a licence if the authorization or licence has been issued to the person and the person continues to hold it; and
- (*b*) a registration certificate for a firearm if
  - (i) the registration certificate has been issued to the person and the person continues to hold it, or
  - (ii) the person possesses the registration certificate with the permission of its lawful holder.

(5) In determining, for the purpose of subsection 85(3), 95(2), 99(2), 100(2) or 103(2), whether a convicted person has committed a second or subsequent offence, if the person was earlier convicted of any of the following offences, that offence is to be considered as an earlier offence:
- (*a*) an offence under section 85, 95, 96, 98, 98.1, 99, 100, 102 or 103 or subsection 117.01(1);
- (*b*) an offence under section 244 or 244.2; or
- (*c*) an offence under section 220, 236, 239, 272 or 273, subsection 279(1) or section 279.1, 344 or 346 if a firearm was used in the commission of the offence.

However, an earlier offence shall not be taken into account if 10 years have elapsed between the day on which the person was convicted of the earlier offence and the day on which the person was convicted of the offence for which sentence is being imposed, not taking into account any time in custody.

(6) For the purposes of subsection (5), the only question to be considered is the sequence of convictions and no consideration shall be given to the sequence of commission of offences or whether any offence occurred before or after any conviction. 1995, c. 39, s. 139; 1998, c. 30, s. 16; 2003, c. 8, s. 2; 2008, c. 6, s. 2; 2009, c. 22, s. 2; 2015, c. 3, s. 45; 2015, c. 27, s. 18.

CROSS-REFERENCES

"Firearm" and "weapon" are defined in s. 2. Section 117.15 gives the Governor in Council power to make regulations prescribing anything that may be prescribed under this part, for example prohibited and restricted firearms and weapons, provided those things are not reasonably for use for hunting and sporting purposes.

SYNOPSIS

Subsection (1) sets out the definitions for use in this part and certain other specified sections of the Code. In particular, these definitions apply to ss. 491 [forfeiture of weapons and ammunition], 515(4.1), (4.11) [condition of release pending trial prohibiting possession of weapons], 810(3.1), (3.11) [condition of peace bond prohibiting possession of weapons]. Subsection (2) determines the length of the barrel of a firearm for the purposes of the definitions of prohibited devices and firearms and restricted firearms. Subsection (3) deems certain types of weapons not to be firearms for the purposes of provisions of this part dealing with firearms, except that pursuant to subsec. (3) antique firearms are still deemed to be firearms for certain purposes. Subsection (4) defines who is the "holder" of an authorization or licence or a firearm registration certificate. Subsection (5) defines what are earlier offences of the purpose of determining if the offender is liable to the increased punishment in ss. 85, 95, 99, 100 and 103, by reason of having committed a second or subsequent offence. Subsection (6) provides that the sequence of convictions is the only relevant consideration, not the sequence in which the offences were committed.

ANNOTATIONS

Note: The following cases were decided under the predecessor legislation but were thought to be of some assistance in applying these provisions.

"Automatic firearm" – It was held, considering the slightly different definition of prohibited weapon under the former legislation, that firearms that in their original condition were capable of firing bullets in rapid succession during one pressure of the trigger and of being converted to fire automatically, by use of hand tools and without replacement of any part in about 10 minutes, fell within the definition: *R. v. Barnes* (1996), 104 C.C.C. (3d) 374, 27 O.R. (3d) 626 (C.A.).

"Handgun" – It was held, considering the slightly different definition of restricted weapon under the former legislation, that a pistol, although lacking a magazine when found in the possession of the accused, comes within this definition, notwithstanding that in this state two hands would be required to fire. Once the magazine was loaded, it could be fired with one hand and was thus "designed" to be aimed and fired by the action of one hand: *R. v. Watkins and Graber* (1987), 33 C.C.C. (3d) 465 (B.C.C.A.).

"Prohibited weapon" – A knife may come within para. (*a*) whether or not it comes within the ordinary meaning of weapon and whether or not it was designed to be used as a prohibited weapon if in fact its blade, through wear and tear or alteration, can be fully opened for use by applying centrifugal force or gravity to the blade. It is the capability and not the design of the knife that determines whether or not it is a prohibited weapon. The words "any knife that has a blade that opens automatically by . . . centrifugal force" should be interpreted as meaning one that opens by means of a centrifugal force applied to the blade and not to the handle. The word "open" in the definition means open with the capacity for use as a weapon. Any knife which, when held in a position where the handle is above the blade and the blade drops open at or about a 90-degree angle to the handle and by gravity continues to open fully, available for use, when the handle is placed in a vertical position or when centrifugal force is applied to a partially opened blade, is a knife having a blade that opens automatically by gravity or centrifugal force and is therefore a prohibited weapon: *R. v. Richard and Walker* (1981), 63 C.C.C. (2d) 333, 24 C.R. (3d) 373 (N.B.C.A.).

A knife that will only open by holding the blade and applying centrifugal force to the handle is not within the definition. However, a knife although not originally so designed, which through long use opens by application of centrifugal force to the blade, is a prohibited weapon: *R. v. Archer* (1983), 6 C.C.C. (3d) 129 (Ont. C.A.).

The fact that an additional manual operation had to be performed before the knife, a so-called "butterfly knife", was in a position to be opened automatically by centrifugal force, and that some skill was required to perform the operation, did not prevent the knife from being a prohibited weapon: *R. v. Vaughan*, [1991] 3 S.C.R. 691, 69 C.C.C. (3d) 576*n* (5:0).

In *R. v. Vokac* (1978), 42 C.C.C. (2d) 201, [1978] 5 W.W.R. 397 (B.C.C.A.), it was held that where the prohibited weapon was defined under [former] Prohibited Weapons Order No. 1, SOR/74-297 [now see Part 3 of the Regulation], as "any device designed to be used for the purpose of injuring, immobilizing or otherwise incapacitating any person by the discharge therefrom of . . . (b) any liquid, spray, powder or other substance that is capable of injuring, immobilizing or otherwise incapacitating any person", the label on the spray canister was admissible as proof of the purpose for which it was designed although the label could not prove the capability of the spray. This latter element was proved by *viva voce* evidence of a police officer who experimented with the spray seized from the accused.

In order to constitute a prohibited weapon it was held not to be sufficient that the device falls within the description set out in a Prohibited Weapons Order. The device must also come within the definition of "weapon" in s. 2: *R. v. Murray* (1985), 24 C.C.C. (3d) 568, 7 O.A.C. 127 (C.A.). *Contra: R. v. K. (A.)* (1991), 68 C.C.C. (3d) 135, 9 C.R. (4th) 269 (B.C.C.A.), leave to appeal to S.C.C. refused 70 C.C.C. (3d) vi, 17 W.A.C. 79*n*, where it was held that the word "weapon" in [former] para. (*e*) [now para. (*b*)] should be given a broader meaning than as defined in s. 2 to encompass any article or device that can on occasion be used to inflict injury, harm or death to a person whether used offensively or defensively. Thus, in the absence of a challenge to the power of the Governor in Council to designate the device as a prohibited weapon on the basis that it does not fall within this normal everyday meaning of weapon, a prohibited weapon under s. 84 is simply what the Governor in Council has declared [now prescribed] to be a prohibited weapon.

If the accused knew he possessed an object that met the description of brass knuckles prescribed under subsec. (1) (whether or not he knew it was prescribed by regulation to be a "prohibited weapon"), then he possessed an object that was "designed to be used" as a weapon within the meaning of s. 2. The amendment to s. 2 has removed the concern of the court in *K.(A.)*, *supra*, that the interpretation of s. 84(1)(*e*) in *Murray*, *supra*, imposed a completely subjective element: *R. v. Strong* (2012), 288 C.C.C. (3d) 357 (B.C.C.A.).

"Cartridge magazine" – An accused was convicted of an offence for possessing several magazine casings with a 30-round capacity. His argument that he intended to alter the casings in order to bring them within the requirement that magazines have no more than a 5-round capacity was rejected. Even though an expert testified that the casings would require the installation of a number of parts before they could be functional as magazines, the court concluded that they were prohibited devices because they were capable of becoming operable with the addition of readily available parts: *R. v. Cancade* (2011), 270 C.C.C. (3d) 536 (B.C.C.A.).

Exemptions (subsec. (3)) – This provision had no application where the accused stole a starter pistol knowing that the purchaser intended to drill out the gun to accommodate the firing of live ammunition: *R. v. Goswami* (2002), 164 C.C.C. (3d) 378 (Ont. C.A.).

REGULATIONS PRESCRIBING CERTAIN FIREARMS AND OTHER WEAPONS, COMPONENTS AND PARTS OF WEAPONS, ACCESSORIES, CARTRIDGE MAGAZINES, AMMUNITION AND PROJECTILES AS PROHIBITED, RESTRICTED OR NON-RESTRICTED

Interpretation

1. In these Regulations, "semi-automatic", in respect of a firearm, means a firearm that is equipped with a mechanism that, following the discharge of a cartridge, automatically operates to complete any part of the reloading cycle necessary to prepare for the discharge of the next cartridge.

Prescription

2. The firearms listed in Part 1 of the schedule are prohibited firearms for the purposes of paragraph (*d*) of the definition "prohibited firearm" in subsection 84(1) of the *Criminal Code*.

3. The firearms listed in Part 2 of the schedule are restricted firearms for the purposes of paragraph (*d*) of the definition "restricted firearm" in subsection 84(1) of the *Criminal Code*, except for those firearms that are prohibited firearms within the meaning of paragraph (*b*) or (*c*) of the definition "prohibited firearm" in that subsection.

3.1 The firearms listed in Part 2.1 of the schedule that have a barrel that is less than 470 mm in length, and firearms listed in items 3, 4, 6, 7, 9 and 10 of that Part that do not have a barrel, are restricted firearms for the purposes of paragraph (*d*) of the definition "restricted firearm" in subsection 84(1) of the *Criminal Code*, except for those firearms that

(a) discharge projectiles in rapid succession during one pressure of the trigger; or

(b) are prohibited firearms within the meaning of paragraph (*b*) of the definition "prohibited firearm" in subsection 84(1) of the *Criminal Code*.

3.2 The firearms listed in Part 2.1 of the schedule that have a barrel that is at least 470 mm in length, and the firearms listed in items 1, 2, 5, 8 and 11 to 15 of that Part that do not have a barrel, are non-restricted firearms for the purposes of paragraph (*b*) of the definition "non-restricted firearm" in subsection 84(1) of the *Criminal Code*, except for those firearms that

(a) discharge projectiles in rapid succession during one pressure of the trigger; or

(b) are prohibited firearms within the meaning of paragraph (*b*) of the definition "prohibited firearm" in subsection 84(1) of the *Criminal Code*.

4. The weapons listed in Part 3 of the schedule are prohibited weapons for the purposes of paragraph (*b*) of the definition "prohibited weapon" in subsection 84(1) of the *Criminal Code*.

5. The components and parts of weapons, accessories, and cartridge magazines listed in Part 4 of the schedule are prohibited devices for the purposes of paragraphs (*a*) and (*d*) of the definition "prohibited device" in subsection 84(1) of the *Criminal Code*.

6. The ammunition and projectiles listed in Part 5 of the schedule are prohibited ammunition for the purposes of the definition "prohibited ammunition" in subsection 84(1) of the *Criminal Code*.

Coming into Force

7. These Regulations come into force on December 1, 1998.

Schedule

(Sections 2 to 6)

PART 1
Prohibited Firearms

Former Prohibited Weapons Order, No. 3

1. Any firearm capable of discharging a dart or other object carrying an electrical current or substance, including the firearm of the design commonly known as the Taser Public Defender and any variant or modified version of it.

Former Prohibited Weapons Order, No. 8

2. The firearm known as the SSS-1 Stinger and any similar firearm designed or of a size to fit in the palm of the hand.

Former Prohibited Weapons Order, No. 11

3. The firearm of the design commonly known as the Franchi SPAS 12 shotgun, and any variant or modified version of it, including the Franchi LAW 12 shotgun.

4. The firearm of the design commonly known as the Striker shotgun, and any variant or modified version of it, including the Striker 12 shotgun and the Streetsweeper shotgun.

5. The firearm of the design commonly known as the USAS-12 Auto Shotgun, and any variant or modified version of it.

6. The firearm of the design commonly known as the Franchi SPAS-15 shotgun, and any variant or modified version of it.

7. The firearms of the designs commonly known as the Benelli M1 Super 90 shotgun and the Benelli M3 Super 90 shotgun, and any variants or modified versions of them, with the exception of the

(a) M1 Super 90 Field;

(b) M1 Super 90 Sporting Special;

(c) Montefeltro Super 90;

(d) Montefeltro Super 90 Standard Hunter;

(e) Montefeltro Super 90 Left Hand;

(f) Montefeltro Super 90 Turkey;

(g) Montefeltro Super 90 Uplander;

(h) Montefeltro Super 90 Slug;

(i) Montefeltro Super 90 20 Gauge;

(j) Black Eagle;

(k) Black Eagle Limited Edition;

(l) Black Eagle Competition;

(m) Black Eagle Slug Gun;

(n) Super Black Eagle; and

(o) Super Black Eagle Custom Slug.

8. The firearms of the designs commonly known as the Bernardelli B4 shotgun and the Bernardelli B4/B shotgun, and any variants or modified versions of them.

9. The firearm of the design commonly known as the American 180 Auto Carbine, and any variant or modified version of it, including the AM-180 Auto Carbine and the Illinois Arms Company Model 180 Auto Carbine.

10. The firearms of the designs commonly known as the Barrett "Light Fifty" Model 82A1 rifle and the Barrett Model 90 rifle, and any variants or modified versions of them.

11. The firearm of the design commonly known as the Calico M-900 rifle, and any variant or modified version of it, including the M-951 carbine, M-100 carbine and M-105 carbine.

12. The firearm of the design commonly known as the Iver Johnson AMAC long-range rifle, and any variant or modified version of it.

13. The firearm of the design commonly known as the McMillan M87 rifle, and any variant or modified version of it, including the McMillan M87R rifle and the McMillan M88 carbine.

14. The firearms of the designs commonly known as the Pauza Specialties P50 rifle and P50 carbine, and any variants or modified versions of them.

15. The firearm of the design commonly known as the Encom MK-IV carbine, and any variant or modified version of it.

16. The firearms of the designs commonly known as the Encore MP-9 and MP-45 carbines, and any variants or modified versions of them.

17. The firearm of the design commonly known as the FAMAS rifle, and any variant or modified version of it, including the MAS 223, FAMAS Export, FAMAS Civil and Mitchell MAS/22.

18. The firearm of the design commonly known as the Feather AT-9 Semi-Auto Carbine, and any variant or modified version of it, including the Feather AT-22 Auto Carbine.

19. The firearm of the design commonly known as the Federal XC-450 Auto Rifle, and any variant or modified version of it, including the Federal XC-900 rifle and Federal XC-220 rifle.

20. The firearm of the design commonly known as the Gepard long-range sniper rifle, and any variant or modified version of it.

21. The firearm of the design commonly known as the Heckler and Koch (HK) Model G11 rifle, and any variant or modified version of it.

22. The firearm of the design commonly known as the Research Armament Industries (RAI) Model 500 rifle, and any variant or modified version of it.

23. The firearm of the design commonly known as the Spectre Auto Carbine, and any variant or modified version of it.

24. The firearm of the design commonly known as the US Arms PMAI "Assault" 22 rifle, and any variant or modified version of it.

25. The firearm of the design commonly known as the Weaver Arms Nighthawk Carbine, and any variant or modified version of it.

26. The firearm of the design commonly known as the A.A. Arms AR9 Semi-Automatic Rifle, and any variant or modified version of it.

27. The firearms of the designs commonly known as the Claridge HI-TEC c. LEC-9 and ZLEC-9 carbines, and any variants or modified versions of them.

28. The firearm of the design commonly known as the Kimel Industries AR-9 rifle or carbine, and any variant or modified version of it.

29. The firearm of the design commonly known as the Grendel R-31 Auto Carbine, and any variant or modified version of it.

30. The firearms of the designs commonly known as the Maadi Griffin Rifle and the Maadi Griffin Carbine, and any variants or modified versions of them.

31. The firearm of the design commonly known as the AA Arms Model AR-9 carbine, and any variant or modified version of it.

32. The firearm of the design commonly known as the Bushmaster Auto Pistol, and any variant or modified version of it.

33. The firearm of the design commonly known as the Calico M-950 Auto Pistol, and any variant or modified version of it, including the M-110 pistol.

34. The firearm of the design commonly known as the Encom MK-IV assault pistol, and any variant or modified version of it.

35. The firearms of the designs commonly known as the Encom MP-9 and MP-45 assault pistols, and any variants or modified versions of them, including the Encom MP-9 and MP-45 mini pistols.

36. The firearm of the design commonly known as the Federal XP-450 Auto Pistol, and any variant or modified version of it, including the XP-900 Auto Pistol.

37. The firearm of the design commonly known as the Heckler and Koch (HK) SP89 Auto Pistol, and any variant or modified version of it.

38. The firearms of the designs commonly known as the Intratec Tec-9 Auto Pistol, and any variant or modified version of it, including the Tec-9S, Tec-9M, Tec-9MS, and any semi-automatic variants of them, including the Tec-DC9, Tec-DC9M, Tec-9A, Tec-Scorpion, Tec-22T and Tec-22TN.

39. The firearms of the designs commonly known as the Iver Johnson Enforcer Model 3000 Auto Pistol and the Iver Johnson Plainfield Super Enforcer Carbine, and any variants or modified versions of them.

40. The firearm of the design commonly known as the Skorpion Auto Pistol, and any variant or modified version of it.

41. The firearm of the design commonly known as the Spectre Auto Pistol, and any variant or modified version of it.

42. The firearm of the design commonly known as the Sterling Mk 7 pistol, and any variant or modified version of it, including the Sterling Mk 7 C4 and Sterling Mk 7 C8.

43. The firearm of the design commonly known as the Universal Enforcer Model 3000 Auto Carbine, and any variant or modified version of it, including the Universal Enforcer Model 3010N, Model 3015G, Model 3020TRB and Model 3025TCO Carbines.

44. The firearm of the design commonly known as the US Arms PMAIP "Assault" 22 pistol, and any variant or modified version of it.

45. The firearm of the design commonly known as the Goncz High-Tech Long Pistol, and any variant or modified version of it, including the Claridge Hi-Tec models s. L, T, ZL-9 and ZT-9 pistols.

46. The firearm of the design commonly known as the Leader Mark 5 Auto Pistol, and any variant or modified version of it.

47. The firearm of the design commonly known as the OA-93 assault pistol, and any variant or modified version of it.

48. The firearm of the design commonly known as the A.A. Arms AP9 Auto Pistol, and any variant or modified version of it.

49. The firearm of the design commonly known as the Patriot pistol, and any variant or modified version of it.

50. The firearm of the design commonly known as the XM 231S pistol, and any variant or modified version of it, including the A1, A2 and A3 Flattop pistols.

51. The firearm of the design commonly known as the AA Arms Model AP-9 pistol, and any variant or modified version of it, including the Target AP-9 and the Mini AP-9 pistols.

52. The firearm of the design commonly known as the Kimel Industries AP-9 pistol, and any variant or modified version of it.

53. The firearms of the designs commonly known as the Grendel P-30, P-30 M, P-30 L and P-31 pistols, and any variants or modified versions of them.

54. The firearms of the designs commonly known as the Claridge HI-TEC ZL-9, HI-TEC S. HI-TEC L, HI-TEC T, HI-TEC ZT-9 and HI-TEC ZL-9 pistols, and any variants or modified versions of them.

55. The firearm of the design commonly known as the Steyr SPP Assault Pistol, and any variant or modified version of it.

56. The firearm of the design commonly known as the Maadi Griffin Pistol, and any variant or modified version of it.

57. The firearm of the design commonly known as the Interdynamics KG-99 Assault Pistol, and any variant or modified version of it.

Former Prohibited Weapons Order, No. 12

58. The firearm of the design commonly known as the Sterling Mk 6 Carbine, and any variant or modified version of it.

59. The firearm of the design commonly known as the Steyr AUG rifle, and any variant or modified version of it.

60. The firearm of the design commonly known as the UZI carbine, and any variant or modified version of it, including the UZI Model A carbine and the Mini-UZI carbine.

61. The firearms of the designs commonly known as the Ingram M10 and M11 pistols, and any variants or modified versions of them, including the Cobray M10 and M11 pistols, the RPB M10, M11, SM10 and SM11 pistols and the SWD M10, M11, SM10 and SM11 pistols.

62. The firearm of the design commonly known as the Partisan Avenger Auto Pistol, and any variant or modified version of it.

63. The firearm of the design commonly known as the UZI pistol, and any variant or modified version of it, including the Micro-UZI pistol.

Former Prohibited Weapons Order, No. 13

64. The firearm of the design commonly known as the AK-47 rifle, and any variant or modified version of it except for the Valmet Hunter, the Valmet Hunter Auto and the Valmet M78 rifles, but including the

(a) AK-74;

(b) AK Hunter;

(c) AKM;

(d) AKM-63;

(e) AKS-56S;

(f) AKS-56S-1;

(g) AKS-56S-2;

(h) AKS-74;

(i) AKS-84S-1;

(j) AMD-65;

(k) AR Model .223;

(l) Dragunov;

(m) Galil;

(n) KKMPi69;

(o) M60;

(p) M62;

(q) M70B1;

(r) M70AB2;

(s) M76;

(t) M77B1;

(u) M78;

(v) M80;

(w) M80A;

(x) MAK90;

(y) MPiK;

(z) MPiKM;

(z.1) MPiKMS-72;

(z.2) MPiKS;

(z.3) PKM;

(z.4) PKM-DGN-60;

(z.5) PMKM;

(z.6) RPK;

(z.7) RPK-74;

(z.8) RPK-87S;

(z.9) Type 56;

(z.10) Type 56-1;

(z.11) Type 56-2;

(z.12) Type 56-3;

(z.13) Type 56-4;

(z.14) Type 68;

(z.15) Type 79;

(z.16) American Arms AKY39;

(z.17) American Arms AKF39;

(z.18) American Arms AKC47;

(z.19) American Arms AKF47;

(z.20) MAM70WS762;

(z.21) MAM70FS762;

(z.22) Mitchell AK-22;

(z.23) Mitchell AK-47;

(z.24) Mitchell Heavy Barrel AK-47;

(z.25) Norinco 84S;

(z.26) Norinco 84S AK;

(z.27) Norinco 56;

(z.28) Norinco 56-1;

(z.29) Norinco 56-2;

(z.30) Norinco 56-3;

(z.31) Norinco 56-4;

(z.32) Poly Technologies Inc. AK-47/S;

(z.33) Poly Technologies Inc. AKS-47/S;

(z.34) Poly Technologies Inc. AKS-762;

(z.35) Valmet M76;

(z.36) Valmet M76 carbine;

(z.37) Valmet M78/A2;

(z.38) Valmet M78 (NATO) LMG;

(z.39) Valmet M82; and

(z.40) Valmet M82 Bullpup.

65. The firearm of the design commonly known as the Armalite AR-180 Spotter carbine, and any variant or modified version of it.

66. The firearm of the design commonly known as the Beretta AR70 assault rifle, and any variant or modified version of it.

67. The firearm of the design commonly known as the BM 59 rifle, and any variant or modified version of it, including

(a) the Beretta

(i) BM 59,

(ii) BM 59R,

(iii) BM 59GL,

(iv) BM 59D,

(v) BM 59 Mk E,

(vi) BM 59 Mk I,

(vii) BM 59 Mk Ital,

(viii) BM 59 Mk II,

(ix) BM 59 Mk III,

(x) BM 59 Mk Ital TA,

(xi) BM 59 Mk Ital Para,

(xii) BM 59 Mk Ital TP, and

(xiii) BM 60CB; and

(b) the Springfield Armory

(i) BM 59 Alpine,

(ii) BM 59 Alpine Paratrooper, and

(iii) BM 59 Nigerian Mk IV.

68. The firearm of the design commonly known as the Bushmaster Auto Rifle, and any variant or modified version of it.

69. The firearm of the design commonly known as the Cetme Sport Auto Rifle, and any variant or modified version of it.

70. The firearm of the design commonly known as the Daewoo K1 rifle, and any variant or modified version of it, including the Daewoo K1A1, K2, Max 1, Max 2, AR-100, AR 110C, MAXI-II and KC-20.

71. The firearm of the design commonly known as the Demro TAC-1M carbine, and any variant or modified version of it, including the Demro XF-7 Wasp Carbine.

72. The firearm of the design commonly known as the Eagle Apache Carbine, and any variant or modified version of it.

73. The firearm of the design commonly known as the FN-FNC rifle, and any variant or modified version of it, including the FNC Auto Rifle, FNC Auto Paratrooper, FNC-11, FNC-22 and FNC-33.

74. The firearm of the design commonly known as the FN-FAL (FN-LAR) rifle, and any variant or modified version of it, including the FN 308 Model 44, FN-FAL (FN-LAR) Competition Auto, FN-FAL (FN-LAR) Heavy Barrel 308 Match, FN-FAL (FN-LAR) Paratrooper 308 Match 50-64 and FN 308 Model 50-63.

75. The firearm of the design commonly known as the G3 rifle, and any variant or modified version of it, including the Heckler and Koch

(a) HK 91;
(b) HK 91A2;
(c) HK 91A3;
(d) HK G3 A3;
(e) HK G3 A3 ZF;
(f) HK G3 A4;
(g) HK G3 SG/1; and
(h) HK PSG1.

76. The firearm of the design commonly known as the Galil assault rifle, and any variant or modified version of it, including the AP-84, Galil ARM, Galil AR, Galil SAR, Galil 332 and Mitchell Galil/22 Auto Rifle.

77. The firearm of the design commonly known as the Goncz High-Tech Carbine, and any variant or modified version of it.

78. The firearm of the design commonly known as the Heckler and Koch HK 33 rifle, and any variant or modified version of it, including the

(a) HK 33A2;
(b) HK 33A3;
(c) HK 33KA1;
(d) HK 93;
(e) HK 93A2; and
(f) HK 93A3.

79. The firearm of the design commonly known as the J & R Eng M-68 carbine, and any variant or modified version of it, including the PJK M-68 and the Wilkinson Terry carbine.

80. The firearm of the design commonly known as the Leader Mark Series Auto Rifle, and any variant or modified version of it.

81. The firearms of the designs commonly known as the MP5 submachine gun and MP5 carbine, and any variants or modified versions of them, including the Heckler and Koch

(a) HK MP5;
(b) HK MP5A2;
(c) HK MP5A3;
(d) HK MP5K;
(e) HK MP5SD;
(f) HK MP5SD1;
(g) HK MP5SD2;
(h) HK MP5SD3;
(i) HK 94;
(j) HK 94A2; and
(k) HK 94A3.

82. The firearm of the design commonly known as the PE57 rifle, and any variant or modified version of it.

83. The firearms of the designs commonly known as the SG-550 rifle and SG-551 carbine, and any variants or modified versions of them.

84. The firearm of the design commonly known as the SIG AMT rifle, and any variant or modified version of it.

85. The firearm of the design commonly known as the Springfield Armory SAR-48 rifle, and any variant or modified version of it, including the SAR-48 Bush, SAR-48 Heavy Barrel, SAR-48 Para and SAR-48 Model 22.

86. The firearm of the design commonly known as the Thompson submachine gun, and any variant or modified version of it, including the

(a) Thompson Model 1921;
(b) Thompson Model 1927;
(c) Thompson Model 1928;
(d) Thompson Model M1;
(e) Auto-Ordnance M27A-1;
(f) Auto-Ordnance M27A-1 Deluxe;
(g) Auto-Ordnance M1927A-3;
(h) Auto-Ordnance M1927A-5;
(i) Auto-Ordnance Thompson M1;
(j) Commando Arms Mk I;
(k) Commando Arms Mk II;
(l) Commando Arms Mk III;
(m) Commando Arms Mk 9; and
(n) Commando Arms Mk 45.

PART 2
Restricted Firearms

Former Restricted Weapons Order

1. The firearms of the designs commonly known as the High Standard Model 10, Series A shotgun and the High Standard Model 10, Series B shotgun, and any variants or modified versions of them.

2. The firearm of the design commonly known as the M-16 rifle, and any variant or modified version of it, including the

(a) Colt AR-15;
(b) Colt AR-15 SPI;
(c) Colt AR-15 Sporter;
(d) Colt AR-15 Collapsible Stock Model;
(e) Colt AR-15 A2;
(f) Colt AR-15 A2 Carbine;
(g) Colt AR-15 A2 Government Model Rifle;
(h) Colt AR-15 A2 Government Model Target Rifle;
(i) Colt AR-15 A2 Government Model Carbine;
(j) Colt AR-15 A2 Sporter II;
(k) Colt AR-15 A2 H-BAR;
(l) Colt AR-15 A2 Delta H-BAR;
(m) Colt AR-15 A2 Delta H-BAR Match;
(n) Colt AR-15 9mm Carbine;
(o) Armalite AR-15;
(p) AAI M15;
(q) AP74;
(r) EAC J-15;

(s) PWA Commando;
(t) SGW XM15A;
(u) SGW CAR-AR;
(v) SWD AR-15; and
(w) any 22-calibre rimfire variant, including the
(i) Mitchell M-16A-1/22,
(ii) Mitchell M-16/22,
(iii) Mitchell CAR-15/22, and
(iv) AP74 Auto Rifle.

PART 2.1
Firearms for the Purpose of Sections 3.1 and 3.2M

1. Ceská Zbrojovka (CZ) Model CZ858 Tactical-2P rifle
2. Ceská Zbrojovka (CZ) Model CZ858 Tactical-2V rifle
3. Ceská Zbrojovka (CZ) Model CZ858 Tactical-4P rifle
4. Ceská Zbrojovka (CZ) Model CZ858 Tactical-4V rifle
5. SAN Swiss Arms Model Classic Green rifle
6. SAN Swiss Arms Model Classic Green carbine
7. SAN Swiss Arms Model Classic Green CQB rifle
8. SAN Swiss Arms Model Black Special rifle
9. SAN Swiss Arms Model Black Special carbine
10. SAN Swiss Arms Model Black Special CQB rifle
11. SAN Swiss Arms Model Black Special Target rifle
12. SAN Swiss Arms Model Blue Star rifle
13. SAN Swiss Arms Model Heavy Metal rifle
14. SAN Swiss Arms Model Red Devil rifle
15. SAN Swiss Arms Model Swiss Arms Edition rifle

PART 3
Prohibited Weapons

Former Prohibited Weapons Order, No. 1

1. Any device designed to be used for the purpose of injuring, immobilizing or otherwise incapacitating any person by the discharge therefrom of

(a) tear gas, Mace or other gas; or
(b) any liquid, spray, powder or other substance that is capable of injuring, immobilizing or otherwise incapacitating any person.

Former Prohibited Weapons Order, No. 2

2. Any instrument or device commonly known as "nunchaku", being hard non-flexible sticks, clubs, pipes, or rods linked by a length or lengths of rope, cord, wire or chain, and any similar instrument or device.

3. Any instrument or device commonly known as "shuriken", being a hard non-flexible plate having three or more radiating points with one or more sharp edges in the shape of a polygon, trefoil, cross, star, diamond or other geometrical shape, and any similar instrument or device.

4. Any instrument or device commonly known as "manrikigusari" or "kusari", being hexagonal or other geometrically shaped hard weights or hand grips linked by a length or lengths of rope, cord, wire or chain, and any similar instrument or device.

5. Any finger ring that has one or more blades or sharp objects that are capable of being projected from the surface of the ring.

Former Prohibited Weapons Order, No. 3

6. Any device that is designed to be capable of injuring, immobilizing or incapacitating a person or an animal by discharging an electrical charge produced by means of the amplification or accumulation of the electrical current generated by a battery, where the device is designed or altered so that the electrical charge may be discharged when the device is of a length of less than 480 mm, and any similar device.

7. A crossbow or similar device that

(a) is designed or altered to be aimed and fired by the action of one hand, whether or not it has been redesigned or subsequently altered to be aimed and fired by the action of both hands; or
(b) has a length not exceeding 500 mm.

Former Prohibited Weapons Order, No. 4

8. The device known as the "Constant Companion", being a belt containing a blade capable of being withdrawn from the belt, with the buckle of the belt forming a handle for the blade, and any similar device.

9. Any knife commonly known as a "push-dagger" that is designed in such a fashion that the handle is placed perpendicular to the main cutting edge of the blade and any other similar device other than the aboriginal "ulu" knife.

10. Any device having a length of less than 30 cm and resembling an innocuous object but designed to conceal a knife or blade, including the device commonly known as the "knife-comb", being a comb with the handle of the comb forming a handle for the knife, and any similar device.

Former Prohibited Weapons Order, No. 5

11. The device commonly known as a "Spiked Wristband", being a wristband to which a spike or blade is affixed, and any similar device.

Former Prohibited Weapons Order, No. 6

12. The device commonly known as "Yaqua Blowgun", being a tube or pipe designed for the purpose of shooting arrows or darts by the breath, and any similar device.

Former Prohibited Weapons Order, No. 7

13. The device commonly known as a "Kiyoga Baton" or "Steel Cobra" and any similar device consisting of a manually triggered telescoping spring-loaded steel whip terminated in a heavy calibre striking tip.

14. The device commonly known as a "Morning Star" and any similar device consisting of a ball of metal or other heavy material, studded with spikes and connected to a handle by a length of chain, rope or other flexible material.

Former Prohibited Weapons Order, No. 8

15. The device known as "Brass Knuckles" and any similar device consisting of a band of metal with one or more finger holes designed to fit over the fingers of the hand.

PART 4
Prohibited Devices

Former Prohibited Weapons Order, No. 9

1. Any electrical or mechanical device that is designed or adapted to operate the trigger mechanism of a semi-automatic firearm for the purpose of causing the firearm to discharge cartridges in rapid succession.

2. Any rifle, shotgun or carbine stock of the type known as the "bull-pup" design, being a stock that, when combined with a firearm, reduces the overall length of the firearm such that a substantial part of the reloading action or the magazine-well is located behind the trigger of the firearm when it is held in the normal firing position.

Former Cartridge Magazine Control Regulations

3. (1) Any cartridge magazine

(a) that is capable of containing more than five cartridges of the type for which the magazine was originally designed and that is designed or manufactured for use in

(i) a semi-automatic handgun that is not commonly available in Canada,

(ii) a semi-automatic firearm other than a semi-automatic handgun,

(iii) an automatic firearm whether or not it has been altered to discharge only one projectile with one pressure of the trigger,

(iv) the firearms of the designs commonly known as the Ingram M10 and M11 pistols, and any variants or modified versions of them, including the Cobray M10 and M11 pistols, the RPB M10, M11 and SM11 pistols and the SWD M10, M11, SM10 and SM11 pistols,

(v) the firearm of the design commonly known as the Partisan Avenger Auto Pistol, and any variant or modified version of it, or

(vi) the firearm of the design commonly known as the UZI pistol, and any variant or modified version of it, including the Micro-UZI pistol; or

(b) that is capable of containing more than 10 cartridges of the type for which the magazine was originally designed and that is designed or manufactured for use in a semi-automatic handgun that is commonly available in Canada.

(2) Paragraph (1)(*a*) does not include any cartridge magazine that

(a) was originally designed or manufactured for use in a firearm that

(i) is chambered for, or designed to use, rimfire cartridges,

(ii) is a rifle of the type commonly known as the "Lee Enfield" rifle, where the magazine is capable of containing not more than 10 cartridges of the type for which the magazine was originally designed, or

(iii) is commonly known as the U.S. Rifle M1 (Garand) including the Beretta M1 Garand rifle, the Breda M1 Garand rifle and the Springfield Armoury M1 Garand rifle;

(b) is not a reproduction and was originally designed or manufactured for use in a firearm that

(i) is commonly known as the Charlton Rifle,

(ii) is commonly known as the Farquhar-Hill Rifle, or

(iii) is commonly known as the Huot Automatic Rifle;

(c) is of the "drum" type, is not a reproduction and was originally designed or manufactured for use in a firearm commonly known as

(i) the .303 in. Lewis Mark 1 machine-gun, or any variant or modified version of it, including the Lewis Mark *, Mark 2, Mark 2*, Mark 3, Mark 4, Lewis SS and .30 in. Savage-Lewis,

(ii) the .303 in. Vickers Mark 1 machine-gun, or any variant or modified version of it, including the Mark 1*, Mark 2, Mark 2*, Mark 3, Mark 4, Mark 4B, Mark 5, Mark 6, Mark 6* and Mark 7, or

(iii) the Bren Light machine-gun, or any variant or modified version of it, including the Mark 1, Mark 2, Mark 2/1, Mark 3 and Mark 4;

(d) is of the "metallic-strip" type, is not a reproduction and was originally designed or manufactured for use in conjunction with the firearm known as the Hotchkiss machine-gun, Model 1895 or Model 1897, or any variant or modified version of it, including the Hotchkiss machine-gun, Model 1900, Model 1909, Model 1914 and Model 1917, and the Hotchkiss machine-gun (Enfield), Number 2, Mark 1 and Mark 1*;

(e) is of the "saddle-drum" type (doppeltrommel or satteltrommel), is not a reproduction and was originally designed or manufactured for use in the automatic firearms known as the MG-13, MG-15, MG-17, MG-34, T6-200 or T6-220, or any variant or modified version of it; or

(f) is of the "belt" type consisting of a fabric or metal belt, is not a reproduction and was originally designed or manufactured for the purpose of feeding cartridges into a automatic firearm of a type that was in existence before 1945.

(3) Paragraph (1)(b) does not include any cartridge magazine that

(a) is of the "snail-drum" type (schneckentrommel) that was originally designed or manufactured for use in a firearm that is a handgun known as the Parabellum-Pistol, System Borchardt-Luger, Model 1900, or "Luger", or any variant or modified version of it, including the Model 1902, Model 1904 (Marine), Model 1904/06 (Marine), Model 1904/08 (Marine), Model 1906, Model 1908 and Model 1908 (Artillery) pistols;

(b) was originally designed or manufactured for use in a firearm that is a semi-automatic handgun, where the magazine was manufactured before 1910;

(c) was originally designed or manufactured as an integral part of the firearm known as the Mauser Selbstladepistole C/96 ("broomhandle"), or any variant or modified version of it, including the Model 1895, Model 1896, Model 1902, Model 1905, Model 1912, Model 1915, Model 1930, Model 1931, M711 and M712; or

(d) was originally designed or manufactured for use in the semi-automatic firearm that is a handgun known as the Webley and Scott Self-Loading Pistol, Model 1912 or Model 1915.

(4) A cartridge magazine described in subsection (1) that has been altered or re-manufactured so that it is not capable of containing more than five or ten cartridges, as the case may be, of the type for which it was originally designed is not a prohibited device as prescribed by that subsection if the modification to the magazine cannot be easily removed and the magazine cannot be easily further altered so that it is so capable of containing more than five or ten cartridges, as the case may be.

(5) For the purposes of subsection (4), altering or re-manufacturing a cartridge magazine includes

(a) the indentation of its casing by forging, casting, swaging or impressing;

(b) in the case of a cartridge magazine with a steel or aluminum casing, the insertion and attachment of a plug, sleeve, rod, pin, flange or similar device, made of steel or aluminum, as the case may be, or of a similar material, to the inner surface of its casing by welding, brazing or any other similar method; or

(c) in the case of a cartridge magazine with a casing made of a material other than steel or aluminum, the attachment of a plug, sleeve, rod, pin, flange or similar device, made of steel or of a material similar to that of the magazine casing, to the inner surface of its casing by welding, brazing or any other similar method or by applying a permanent adhesive substance, such as a cement or an epoxy or other glue.

PART 5
Prohibited Ammunition

Former Prohibited Weapons Order, No. 10

1. Any cartridge that is capable of being discharged from a commonly available semi-automatic handgun or revolver and that is manufactured or assembled with a projectile that is designed, manufactured or altered so as to be capable of penetrating body armour, including KTW, THV and 5.7 x 28 mm P-90 cartridges.

2. Any projectile that is designed, manufactured or altered to ignite on impact, where the projectile is designed for use in or in conjunction with a cartridge and does not exceed 15 mm in diameter.

3. Any projectile that is designed, manufactured or altered so as to explode on impact, where the projectile is designed for use in or in conjunction with a cartridge and does not exceed 15 mm in diameter.

4. Any cartridge that is capable of being discharged from a shotgun and that contains projectiles known as "fléchettes" or any similar projectiles. **SOR/98-462; SOR/98-472; SOR/2015-213.**

Use Offences

USING FIREARM IN COMMISSION OF OFFENCE / Using imitation firearm in commission of offence / Punishment / Sentences to be served consecutively.

85. (1) Every person commits an offence who uses a firearm, whether or not the person causes or means to cause bodily harm to any person as a result of using the firearm,

   (*a*) **while committing an indictable offence, other than an offence under section 220 (criminal negligence causing death), 236 (manslaughter), 239 (attempted murder), 244 (discharging firearm with intent), 244.2 (discharging firearm — recklessness), 272 (sexual assault with a weapon) or 273 (aggravated sexual assault), subsection 279(1) (kidnapping) or section 279.1 (hostage taking), 344 (robbery) or 346 (extortion);**

   (*b*) **while attempting to commit an indictable offence; or**

   (*c*) **during flight after committing or attempting to commit an indictable offence.**

(2) Every person commits an offence who uses an imitation firearm

   (*a*) **while committing an indictable offence,**

   (*b*) **while attempting to commit an indictable offence, or**

   (*c*) **during flight after committing or attempting to commit an indictable offence,**

whether or not the person causes or means to cause bodily harm to any person as a result of using the imitation firearm.

(3) Every person who commits an offence under subsection (1) or (2) is guilty of an indictable offence and liable

    (*a*) in the case of a first offence, except as provided in paragraph (*b*), to imprisonment for a term not exceeding fourteen years and to a minimum punishment of imprisonment for a term of one year; and

    (*b*) in the case of a second or subsequent offence, to imprisonment for a term not exceeding 14 years and to a minimum punishment of imprisonment for a term of three years.

    (*c*) [*Repealed*, 2008, c. 6, s. 3(2).]

(4) A sentence imposed on a person for an offence under subsection (1) or (2) shall be served consecutively to any other punishment imposed on the person for an offence arising out of the same event or series of events and to any other sentence to which the person is subject at the time the sentence is imposed on the person for an offence under subsection (1) or (2). R.S., c. C-34, s. 83; 1976-77, c. 53, s. 3; 1995, c. 39, s. 139; 2003, c. 8, s. 3; 2008, c. 6, s. 3; 2009, c. 22, s. 3.

CROSS-REFERENCES

"Firearm" is defined in s. 2. "Imitation firearm" is defined in s. 84.

    A person convicted of this offence is subject to the mandatory prohibition order prescribed by s. 109.

    An accused charged with this offence may elect his mode of trial pursuant to s. 536(2) and release pending trial is determined by s. 515.

    Note provision for forfeiture of weapons used in commission of an offence in s. 491.

    The prosecutor must give notice under s. 727 where it seeks the greater punishment pursuant to subsec. (3)(*c*).

    Upon conviction, the accused is liable to the mandatory prohibition order under s. 109.

    For the purpose of determining whether a person has committed a second or subsequent offence, see s. 84(5) and (6).

SYNOPSIS

This offence was created by Parliament for the purpose of imposing an additional punishment upon those accused who use firearms or imitation firearms while committing or fleeing from the commission of indictable offences (or the attempt to do either). It is important to note that s. 85(1)(a) does not apply in respect of certain indictable offences which already impose an additional penalty for the use of a firearm during the commission of the offence. It is not necessary that the accused intend to harm anyone with the firearm nor that it be proven to be loaded at the time it is used. There were several early challenges to the constitutional validity of the preceding s. 85 alleging violations of ss. 11(*h*) and 7 of the Charter. These efforts were unsuccessful but may need to be re-assessed as the case law continues to evolve, setting out the constitutionally permissible minimum level of intention in the criminal law.

    This section carries a maximum punishment of 14 years' imprisonment and a minimum period of imprisonment upon a first conviction of one year, and upon a second (or subsequent) conviction of three years. For the purpose of determining whether a person has committed a second or subsequent offence, see s. 84(5) and (6). Subsection (4) requires that the sentence for this offence must be consecutive to any other sentence imposed in connection with the same events.

ANNOTATIONS

Underlying offences which may found liability – An accused may be convicted of attempted robbery, specified as an attempt to commit the offence under s. 343(*d*), and the offence under this section. Further, conviction of both offences does not violate the principles of fundamental justice as guaranteed by s. 7 of the *Canadian Charter of Rights and Freedoms*: *R. v. Krug*, [1985] 2 S.C.R. 255, 21 C.C.C. (3d) 193 (7:0).

An accused cannot be convicted of the offence under this section where the "indictable offence" referred to in subsec. (1) by its definition in the Code required the use of a firearm as a constituent element of the offence, for example, pointing a firearm under s. 86(1): *R. v. Langevin* (1979), 47 C.C.C. (2d) 138 (Ont. C.A.); *R. v. Krug, supra*.

An accused may also be convicted of this offence and the offence of possession of a weapon for a purpose dangerous to the public peace contrary to s. 87 where the evidence showed that the accused discharged the firearm: *R. v. Yurkiv* (1980), 18 C.R. (3d) 287 (Ont. C.A.).

An accused may be convicted of this offence and aggravated assault contrary to s. 268: *R. v. Switzer* (1987), 32 C.C.C. (3d) 303 (Alta. C.A.); *R. v. Osbourne* (1994), 94 C.C.C. (3d) 435 (Ont. C.A.); *R. v. Griffin* (1996), 111 C.C.C. (3d) 567 (B.C.C.A.).

A conviction under s. 88(1) for possession of a weapon for a purpose dangerous to the public peace cannot constitute the predicate indictable offence necessary for a conviction under this section: *R. v. Andrade* (2015), 326 C.C.C. (3d) 507 (Ont. C.A.), leave to appeal to S.C.C. refused 2016 CarswellOnt 5734.

Requirement of conviction for underlying offence – To render the accused guilty of the offence under this section, there must be a distinct conviction for the underlying indictable offence and not merely a finding of fact that the accused had committed an indictable offence in the course of which he used a firearm. Further, the count charging the offence under this section should clearly indicate the offence during which the accused allegedly used the firearm: *R. v. Pringle*, [1989] 1 S.C.R. 1645, 48 C.C.C. (3d) 449 (5:0).

Proof of "use" of firearm – A person may be convicted of this offence although he does not use the firearm himself but is merely a party to the offence by virtue of s. 21: *R. v. McGuigan*, [1982] 1 S.C.R. 284, 66 C.C.C. (2d) 97.

An offender "uses" a firearm where, to facilitate the commission of an offence or escape, the offender reveals by words or conduct the actual presence or immediate availability of the firearm. The weapon must be in the physical possession of the offender or readily at hand. In this case, although the weapon was not seen by the victims, the offenders repeatedly referred to a firearm in their physical possession or readily at hand during the break and enter, such that the firearm was "used" within the meaning of this provision: *R. v. Steele*, [2007] 3 S.C.R. 3, 221 C.C.C. (3d) 14.

The use of the firearm must be connected to the commission of an indictable offence for which a conviction has been entered. If it were otherwise, an accused could be convicted under s. 85 for conduct that is merely coincidental to the commission of the indictable offence. This would open the door for prohibited convictions under s. 85 based on uncharged conduct or charges that do not result in conviction: *R. v. Andrade, supra*.

Neither the Charter nor the "*Kienapple*" rule against multiple convictions bar a conviction under this provision where the predicate offence is accosting someone while "openly wearing or carrying a weapon" under s. 265(1)(c). For a conviction to be registered under the use firearm provisions of s. 85(1), it is simply necessary to prove that the accused did something beyond what is required to establish the predicate offence. The element of "use" is an additional and distinguishing element from that required for a conviction for assault under s. 265(1)(c): *R. v. Meszaros* (2013), 309 C.C.C. (3d) 392 (Ont. C.A.).

The one-year minimum sentence imposed by subsec. (3)(a) does not constitute cruel and unusual punishment within the meaning of s. 12 of the Charter: *R. v. Meszaros, supra*.

A separate offence contrary to this section is committed by the accused each time he uses a firearm in the commission of a separate indictable offence notwithstanding the indictable offences take place within a short time of each other and involve the same firearm: *R. v. Woods* (1982), 65 C.C.C. (2d) 554 (Ont. C.A.).

Meaning of "firearm" – To constitute a firearm within the meaning of this section, whatever is used on the scene of the crime must be proven by the Crown as capable either at the outset or through adaptation or assembly of being loaded and fired so as to have the potential for causing serious bodily harm during the commission of the offence or during the flight after the commission of that main offence. An operable but unloaded revolver or air pistol is a firearm because it is capable, during the commission of the offence when loaded and fired, of causing bodily injury. There is no requirement that the Crown prove that the accused was in possession of ammunition. If, however, the weapon is inoperable, then it is a firearm if, given the nature of the repairs or modifications required and the availability of parts on the scene, whatever was used could, during the commission of the offence, have been adapted by an ordinary person or by the accused, if possessing special skills, so as to be capable of firing and of causing serious injury: *R. v. Covin and Covin*, [1983] 1 S.C.R. 725, 8 C.C.C. (3d) 240 (5:0).

Thus, a pistol which lacked the magazine was a firearm for the purposes of this section, although without the magazine the safety disconnector was also engaged. The Crown is not required to prove that the accused at the time of the offence was in possession of ammunition and any of the paraphernalia, including the magazine, by which the ammunition is loaded into the weapon: *R. v. Watkins and Graver* (1987), 33 C.C.C. (3d) 465 (B.C.C.A.).

The Crown may prove that the weapon used is a "firearm" by establishing that the weapon was fired during the offence; adducing expert evidence that the weapon was operable at the time of the offence and capable of causing bodily injury or death, or where the weapon is not available for examination, calling a witness who is knowledgeable about guns and may be able to satisfy the court that the weapon was an operable firearm: *R. v. Osiowy* (1997), 113 C.C.C. (3d) 117 (Alta. C.A.).

Meaning of "imitation" – Imitation firearm includes a real firearm. Imitation may be read to include an object that appears to be a firearm whether or not that object is in fact a firearm: *R. v. Scott* (2000), 145 C.C.C. (3d) 52 (B.C.C.A.), affd [2001] 3 S.C.R. 425, 159 C.C.C. (3d) 319.

Imposition of sentence – It was held in *R. v. MacLean* (1979), 49 C.C.C. (2d) 552 (N.S.S.C. App. Div.); *R. v. Goforth* (1986), 24 C.C.C. (3d) 573 (B.C.C.A.); *R. v. Cochrane* (1994), 88 C.C.C. (3d) 570 (B.C.C.A.); *R. v. Herrell* (1994), 88 C.C.C. (3d) 412 (Ont. C.A.), that in view of the language of subsec. (2) where the accused is convicted of several offences under subsec. (1) the sentences imposed for those offences must not only be consecutive to the indictable offence but consecutive to each other. The court in *R. v. MacLean* did not appear to consider the further question whether where all convictions for the offence under subsec. (1) occur after the commission of the last offence the three-year minimum rather than the one-year minimum applies to all but the first conviction under this section. In *R. v. Boucher*, [1986] 1 S.C.R. 750 (5:0), the court in a brief judgment indicated that it essentially agreed with the interpretation of this section by the Court of Appeal in *R. v. MacLean*, supra.

The mandatory minimum of one consecutive year does not violate s. 12 of the *Canadian Charter of Rights and Freedoms*: *R. v. Stewart* (2010), 253 C.C.C. (3d) 301 (B.C.C.A.).

Former subsec. (1)(*d*) [now subsec. (3)(*b*)] applies even where the accused did not actually use the firearm himself in the prior non-s. 85 offence and was merely a party to its use: *R. v. Nicholson*, [1981] 2 S.C.R. 600, 64 C.C.C. (2d) 116, 24 C.R. (3d) 284 (7:0).

Notwithstanding the wording of subsec. (2), the sentence for the offence under this section cannot be made consecutive to a life sentence: *R. v. Cochrane* (1994), 88 C.C.C. (3d) 570, 67 W.A.C. 315 (B.C.C.A.).

The totality principle is considered in determining the fitness for the underlying offence only and should not take into account the consequences of adding the required consecutive sentence to the sentence for the underlying offence: *R. v. Brewer* (1999), 141 C.C.C. (3d) 290, 182 Nfld. & P.E.I.R. 14 (Nfld. C.A.).

Where it was unclear whether the nature of an object used in the commission of a robbery was a firearm, an imitation firearm or an offensive weapon, the trial judge should have convicted on the offence not carrying a mandatory consecutive sentence and stayed the charge of use of a firearm in the commission of an indictable offence: *R. v. Delage* (2001), 154 C.C.C. (3d) 85 (Que. C.A.), remanded to the Que. C.A. [2002] 1 S.C.R. ix.

CARELESS USE OF FIREARM, ETC. / Contravention of storage regulations, etc. / Punishment.

86. (1) Every person commits an offence who, without lawful excuse, uses, carries, handles, ships, transports or stores a firearm, a prohibited weapon, a restricted weapon, a prohibited device or any ammunition or prohibited ammunition in a careless manner or without reasonable precautions for the safety of other persons.

(2) Every person commits an offence who contravenes a regulation made under paragraph 117(*h*) of the *Firearms Act* respecting the storage, handling, transportation, shipping, display, advertising and mail-order sales of firearms and restricted weapons.

(3) Every person who commits an offence under subsection (1) or (2)

   (*a*) is guilty of an indictable offence and liable to imprisonment

   (i) in the case of a first offence, for a term not exceeding two years, and

   (ii) in the case of a second or subsequent offence, for a term not exceeding five years; or

   (*b*) is guilty of an offence punishable on summary conviction. 1995, c. 39, s. 139.

CROSS-REFERENCES

"Firearm" and "weapon" are defined in s. 2. "Prohibited weapon", "restricted weapon", "prohibited device", "ammunition" and "prohibited ammunition" are defined in s. 84(1). Section 117.13 allows for the admission into evidence of a certificate of an analyst who has examined the weapon, prohibited device, ammunition, prohibited ammunition, explosive substance, or any part or component of such a thing.

Where the prosecution seeks the higher penalty prescribed by subsec. (3)(*a*)(ii), it must comply with the provisions of s. 727. Section 667 provides one method of proof of the prior conviction. Note that no reference to the prior conviction may be made in the indictment, by virtue of s. 664.

Where the prosecution elects to proceed by way of summary conviction, then the trial of this offence is conducted by a summary conviction court pursuant to Part XXVII. The punishment for the offence is then as set out in s. 787 and the limitation period is set out in s. 786(2). In either case, release pending trial is determined by s. 515, although the accused is eligible for release by a peace officer under ss. 496, 497 or by the officer in charge under s. 498.

A person found guilty of the offences in this section is liable to the discretionary prohibition order prescribed by s. 110, unless the accused was prohibited from possessing weapons or other regulated items at the time of the offence, in which case the mandatory prohibition order in s. 109 applies.

Note provision for forfeiture of weapons used in commission of an offence in s. 491.

SYNOPSIS

This section creates two offences: subsec. (1) relates to the careless storage, use etc. of a firearm, prohibited weapon, restricted weapon, prohibited device or ammunition or prohibited ammunition; subsec. (2) deals with breach of regulations.

Subsection (1) requires that it be proven that the care used to deal with the weapon fell below the reasonable standard of care required to ensure that no person is endangered by the firearm, weapon etc. In addition, it must be shown that there is no lawful excuse for the apparent carelessness. Case law has established that the offence is proven if only a single person is endangered, notwithstanding the use of the words "other persons" in the section.

Subsection (2) makes it an offence to breach *Firearms Act* regulations on storage, handling, transportation, shipping, display, advertising and mail-order sales of firearms and restricted weapons.

Subsection (3) sets out the penalty for these offences. Note the increased maximum punishment in the case of a second or subsequent offence.

ANNOTATIONS

Subsection (1) – This offence requires proof of conduct showing a marked departure from the standard of care of a reasonably prudent person in the circumstances. So interpreted this provision does not violate s. 7 of the *Canadian Charter of Rights and Freedoms*. This offence can also constitute the underlying or predicate offence for the unlawful act of manslaughter: *R. v. Gosset*, [1993] 3 S.C.R. 76, 83 C.C.C. (3d) 494, 23 C.R. (4th) 280; *R. v. Finlay*, [1993] 3 S.C.R. 103, 83 C.C.C. (3d) 513, 23 C.R. (4th) 321.

The offence of use of a firearm in a careless manner was made out where the accused intentionally discharged a firearm over the head of another hunter in order to scare him: *R. v. Zimmer* (1981), 60 C.C.C. (2d) 190 (B.C.C.A.).

The offence under this subsection is not included in the offence of pointing a firearm under [now] s. 87: *R. v. Morrison* (1991), 66 C.C.C. (3d) 257, 7 W.A.C. 73 (B.C.C.A.).

In a series of cases, the Supreme Court of Canada had occasion to explore the fault element in cases of so-called "penal negligence" apparently as distinguished from criminal negligence. Careless use of a firearm would be one of these offences. In *R. v. Creighton*, [1993] 3 S.C.R. 3, 83 C.C.C. (3d) 346, 23 C.R. (4th) 189, McLachlin J., writing for a majority of the court, suggested the following approach to proof of such offences. The first question is whether the *actus reus* is established. This requires that the negligence constitute a marked departure from the standards of a reasonable person in all the circumstances of the case. The next question is whether the *mens rea* is established. Normally the *mens rea* for objective foresight of risk of harm is inferred from the facts. The standard is that of the reasonable person in the circumstances of the accused. The normal inference that a person who committed a manifestly dangerous act failed to direct their mind to the risk and the need to take care may be negated by evidence raising a reasonable doubt as to the incapacity to appreciate the risk. Short of incapacity, personal factors are not relevant whether those factors might indicate, for example, either a lack of experience or a special experience. Also see: *R. v. Naglik*, [1993] 3 S.C.R. 122, 83 C.C.C. (3d) 526, 23 C.R. (4th) 335; *R. v. Finlay, supra*; and *R. v. Gosset, supra*.

A finding of careless storage cannot be based upon the personal opinion of a police officer. Where existing regulations dealing with the storage of firearms and ammunition were not relevant, as in the instant case, it was incumbent upon the Crown to adduce expert evidence to establish that the storage of the firearms and ammunition was careless: *R. v. Halliday* (1995), 100 C.C.C. (3d) 574, 82 O.A.C. 150 (C.A.), leave to appeal to S.C.C. refused 103 C.C.C. (3d) vi, 93 O.A.C. 79*n*. In considering carelessness, the federal firearm storage regulations are relevant in determining the appropriate standard for those who are transporting or storing guns: *R. v. Blanchard* (1994), 103 C.C.C. (3d) 360 (Y.T. Terr. Ct.).

There is no requirement under this section that the accused plan a long-term or permanent storage. The accused having deposited a loaded .357 Magnum in an ill-planned temporary hiding spot was guilty of the careless storage offence under subsec. (1). While a short interruption in the use or handling of firearms would still constitute use or handling rather that storage, in this case the accused took steps to put away and hide his weapons such that the proper characterization of his actions was that he stored them, albeit temporarily, rather than continue his use and handling of the firearms in plain view of the police. Similarly, the temporary placing of the two loaded handguns inside a locked safe in violation of the regulations constituted the offence under subsec. (2): *R. v. Carlos*, [2002] 2 S.C.R. 411, 163 C.C.C. (3d) 449, 1 C.R. (6th) 1.

The defence under s. 41 (defence of property) is available on a charge under subsec. (1) and thus to the offence of unlawful act manslaughter where the unlawful act relied upon by the Crown is the offence under subsec. (1): *R. v. Gunning*, [2005] 1 S.C.R. 627, 196 C.C.C. (3d) 123, 29 C.R. (6th) 17.

Subsection (2) – It was held under the predecessor to subsec. (2) that the Crown need only prove beyond a reasonable doubt that the accused stored firearms in a manner contrary to the regulations and need not prove that the accused was negligent. The defence may raise a reasonable doubt with respect to mistake of fact or by raising the defence of due diligence in complying with the regulation. The provision did not violate s. 7 of the *Canadian Charter of Rights and Freedoms*: *R. v. Smillie* (1998), 129 C.C.C. (3d) 414, 20 C.R. (5th) 179 (B.C.C.A.).

This provision creates an offence of strict liability: *R. v. Porter* (2004), 193 C.C.C. (3d) 254 (B.C.S.C.), affd 221 C.C.C. (3d) 309 (B.C.C.A.), leave to appeal to S.C.C. refused [2007] 2 S.C.R. vii, 374 N.R. 393*n*.

Risk is not an essential element in the *mens rea* required under this provision: *R. v. Porter*, *supra* (B.C.C.A.).

Editor's Note: Regulations respecting the *Storage, Display, Transportation and Handling of Firearms by Individuals Regulations*, SOR/98-209, enacted under the *Firearms Act*, may be found in *Martin's Related Criminal Statutes*.

POINTING A FIREARM / Punishment.

87. (1) Every person commits an offence who, without lawful excuse, points a firearm at another person, whether the firearm is loaded or unloaded.

(2) Every person who commits an offence under subsection (1)

    (a) **is guilty of an indictable offence and liable to imprisonment for a term not exceeding five years; or**

    (b) **is guilty of an offence punishable on summary conviction. 1995, c. 39, s. 139.**

CROSS-REFERENCES

"Firearm" is defined in s. 2. Where the prosecution elects to proceed by way of summary conviction then the trial of this offence is conducted by a summary conviction court pursuant to Part XXVII. The punishment for the offence is then as set out in s. 787 and the limitation period is set out in s. 786(2). In either case, release pending trial is determined by s. 515, although the accused is eligible for release by a peace officer under ss. 496, 497 or by the officer in charge under s. 498.

A person found guilty of the offences in this section is liable to the discretionary prohibition order prescribed by s. 110, unless the accused was prohibited from possessing weapons or other regulated items at the time of the offence, in which case the mandatory prohibition order in s. 109 applies.

Note mandatory forfeiture of weapons used in commission of an offence in s. 491.

SYNOPSIS

This section creates the offence of pointing a firearm at another person without lawful excuse. The offence is committed whether or not the firearm was loaded.

ANNOTATIONS

The offence created by this section is one of general intent for the purpose of the self-induced intoxication defence: *R. v. Kelly* (1984), 13 C.C.C. (3d) 203, 50 Nfld. & P.E.I.R. 106 (Nfld. Dist. Ct.).

Possession Offences

POSSESSION OF WEAPON FOR DANGEROUS PURPOSE / Punishment.

88. (1) Every person commits an offence who carries or possesses a weapon, an imitation of a weapon, a prohibited device or any ammunition or prohibited ammunition for a purpose dangerous to the public peace or for the purpose of committing an offence.

(2) Every person who commits an offence under subsection (1)

(*a*) **is guilty of an indictable offence and liable to imprisonment for a term not exceeding ten years; or**

(*b*) **is guilty of an offence punishable on summary conviction. 1995, c. 39, s. 139.**

CROSS-REFERENCES

"Weapon" is defined in s. 2. "Prohibited device", "ammunition" and "prohibited ammunition" are defined in s. 84(1). "Possession" is defined in s. 4(3). Section 117.13 allows for the admission into evidence of a certificate of an analyst who has examined the weapon, prohibited device, ammunition, prohibited ammunition, explosive substance, or any part or component of such a thing.

An accused charged with this offence may elect the mode of trial pursuant to s. 536(2) where the Crown proceeds by way of indictment. Where the prosecution elects to proceed by way of summary conviction then the trial of this offence is conducted by a summary conviction court pursuant to Part XXVII. The punishment for the offence is then as set out in s. 787 and the limitation period is set out in s. 786(2). In either case, release pending trial is determined by s. 515, although the accused is eligible for release by a peace officer under ss. 496, 497 or by the officer in charge under s. 498.

A person found guilty of the offences in this section is liable to the discretionary prohibition order prescribed by s. 110, unless the accused was prohibited from possessing weapons or other regulated items at the time of the offence, in which case the mandatory prohibition order in s. 109 applies.

Note mandatory forfeiture of weapons used in commission of an offence in s. 491.

SYNOPSIS

The crucial element in this offence is the purpose for which the accused has the weapon. Merely using the weapon in a way which is in fact dangerous will not make out the charge unless it is proven that this was the accused's purpose for possessing the weapon or other specified thing. All circumstances surrounding the possession of the weapon, or specified thing including its use, if any, will be considered to determine the accused's purpose.

ANNOTATIONS

Note: The following cases were decided under the predecessor to this section which while similarly worded applied only to weapons and imitations of weapons.

Elements of offence – The offence contrary to this section requires proof of possession and proof that the purpose of that possession was one dangerous to the public peace. There must, at some time, be a meeting of these two elements and generally the purpose will have been formed prior to the taking of possession and will continue as possession is taken. However, the elements of the offence must be distinguished from the evidentiary problems which can arise as demonstrated by cases such as *R. v. Proverbs, infra*, where the proof of the unlawful purpose is only through the actual use of the weapon. In this case, *R. v. Cassidy*, [1989] 2 S.C.R. 345, 50 C.C.C. (3d) 193, 71 C.R. (3d) 350 (7:0), the court held that it did not have to determine whether the accused could never be convicted if the actual use was the only evidence of the purpose since there was evidence adduced of formation of the unlawful purpose prior to use of the weapon.

The purpose for which the accused had possession of the weapon must be determined at an instant of time that precedes its use. The use of the weapon in a manner dangerous to the public peace does not constitute the offence although the formation of the unlawful purpose may be inferred from the circumstances in which the weapon was used. Thus, if the accused, in fear of harm to himself in his own home loaded, on the sudden, a weapon that he had not had for a purpose dangerous to the public peace and only intended to use it to defend himself in the event that his premises were broken into, unaware that it was the police seeking entry to execute a warrant, the offence was not made out: *R. v. Proverbs* (1983), 9 C.C.C. (3d) 249, 2 O.A.C. 98 (C.A.).

Relevance of self-defence – The subjective purpose, *i.e.*, self-defence, of a person carrying an offensive weapon is only a factor that should be considered in determining whether an offence has been committed. Therefore, notwithstanding the explanation given by the possessor of the weapon, the trial judge may still convict if the other circumstances in the evidence prove a purpose dangerous to the public peace: *R. v. Nelson* (1972), 8 C.C.C. (2d) 29, [1972] 3 O.R. 174 (C.A.) (4:1).

    This section does not prohibit persons arming themselves for self-protection and, in the absence of other circumstances, the offence under this section is not committed if the accused carries for self-defence a weapon that is an appropriate instrument with which to repel, in a lawful manner, the type of attack reasonably apprehended and if the accused is competent to handle the weapon and likely to use it responsibly: *R. v. Sulland* (1982), 2 C.C.C. (3d) 68, 41 B.C.L.R. 167 (C.A.).

Meaning of "weapon" – A broken beer bottle was held to be a weapon so as to support a conviction under this section: *R. v. Allan* (1971), 4 C.C.C. (2d) 521, 4 N.B.R. (2d) 6 (Q.B.). As also was sulphuric acid where the accused intended to inflict injury, albeit to himself in a suicide attempt. The further element of the purpose dangerous to the public peace was established where the accused exposed others to danger, namely those whom he knew would attempt to frustrate his suicide: *R. v. Dugan* (1974), 21 C.C.C. (2d) 45 (Ont. Prov. Ct.). Similarly, *R. v. Pelly*, [1980] 1 W.W.R. 120 (Sask. Prov. Ct.).

Proof of offence – The possession by the accused of weapons in his own home does not preclude a finding of a purpose dangerous to the public peace: *R. v. Stavroff*, [1980] 1 S.C.R. 411, 101 D.L.R. (3d) 193, 48 C.C.C. (2d) 353 (7:0).

CARRYING WEAPON WHILE ATTENDING PUBLIC MEETING / Punishment.

89. (1) Every person commits an offence who, without lawful excuse, carries a weapon, a prohibited device or any ammunition or prohibited ammunition while the person is attending or is on the way to attend a public meeting.

(2) Every person who commits an offence under subsection (1) is guilty of an offence punishable on summary conviction. 1995, c. 39, s. 139.

CROSS-REFERENCES

"Weapon" is defined in s. 2. "Prohibited device", "ammunition" and "prohibited ammunition" are defined in s. 84(1).

    The trial of this offence is conducted by a summary conviction court pursuant to Part XXVII. The punishment for the offence is set out in s. 787 and the limitation period is set out in s. 786(2). Release pending trial is determined by s. 515, although the accused is eligible for release by a peace officer under ss. 496, 497 or by the officer in charge under s. 498.

    Under s. 117.11, the onus is on the accused to prove that he or she is the holder of a licence, authorization or registration certificate. Section 117.12 provides for admission into evidence of copies of such documents and the evidentiary value of the original and copies. Section 117.13 allows for the admission into evidence of a certificate of an analyst who has examined the weapon, prohibited device, ammunition, prohibited ammunition, explosive substance, or any part or component of such a thing.

    A person found guilty of the offences in this section is liable to the discretionary prohibition order prescribed by s. 110, unless the accused was prohibited from possessing weapons or other regulated items at the time of the offence, in which case the mandatory prohibition order in s. 109 applies.

    Note mandatory forfeiture of weapons used in commission of an offence in s. 491.

SYNOPSIS

This section focuses on the circumstances under which the accused carries a weapon, prohibited device, ammunition or prohibited ammunition. If the accused has it while attending or on the way to a public meeting, the accused is guilty unless there is a lawful excuse for the possession of the weapon. An example of such an excuse would be that the accused is a peace officer armed in the line of duty (see s. 117.07). No additional intention, such as the intention to use the weapon, is required.

CARRYING CONCEALED WEAPON / Punishment.

90. (1) Every person commits an offence who carries a weapon, a prohibited device or any prohibited ammunition concealed, unless the person is authorized under the *Firearms Act* **to carry it concealed.**

(2) Every person who commits an offence under subsection (1)
   (a) is guilty of an indictable offence and liable to imprisonment for a term not exceeding five years; or
   (b) is guilty of an offence punishable on summary conviction. 1995, c. 39, s. 139.

CROSS-REFERENCES

"Weapon" is defined in s. 2. "Prohibited device" and "prohibited ammunition" are defined in s. 84(1). Under s. 117.11, the onus is on the accused to prove that he or she is the holder of a licence, authorization or registration certificate. Section 117.12 provides for admission into evidence of copies of such documents and the evidentiary value of the original and copies. Section 117.13 allows for the admission into evidence of a certificate of an analyst who has examined the weapon, prohibited device, ammunition, prohibited ammunition, explosive substance, or any part or component of such a thing.

An accused charged with this offence may elect the mode of trial pursuant to s. 536(2) where the Crown proceeds by way of indictment. Where the prosecution elects to proceed by way of summary conviction then the trial of this offence is conducted by a summary conviction court pursuant to Part XXVII. The punishment for the offence is then as set out in s. 787 and the limitation period is set out in s. 786(2).

A person found guilty of the offences in this section is liable to the discretionary prohibition order prescribed by s. 110, unless the accused was prohibited from possessing weapons or other regulated items at the time of the offence, in which case the mandatory prohibition order in s. 109 applies.

Note mandatory forfeiture of weapons used in commission of an offence in s. 491.

SYNOPSIS

The intentional concealment of a weapon, prohibited device or prohibited ammunition is the central element of this offence. The weapon may be concealed on the accused's person or in a vehicle under the control of the accused. A defence is provided if the person is authorized under the *Firearms Act* to carry it concealed.

ANNOTATIONS

Note: The following cases were decided under the predecessor to this section which while similarly worded applied only to weapons.

Meaning of "carries" – A person carries a weapon if it is in an automobile of which he has care and control and it was not necessary that the accused have the weapon on his person: *R. v. Hanabury* (1970), 1 C.C.C. (3d) 438, 13 C.R.N.S. 378 (P.E.I.S.C.).

Meaning of "concealed" – To prove concealment it must be established that the accused took steps to hide an object that he knew to be a weapon so that it would not be observed or come to the notice of others. On the other hand, a gun that is carried in a gun case will not be considered concealed. In most cases the gun carrying case will resemble the firearm itself so that it cannot be considered to be hidden. Wrapping a firearm in a blanket or canvass and securing it with a rope as required by some provincial regulations should also not be considered to be concealing the weapon. In most cases the wrapped weapon will still resemble a firearm and not be considered to be concealed. Finally placing of a firearm in a locked trunk in a locked and unattended vehicle in compliance with federal regulations must be considered an exception to the carrying a concealed weapon offence: *R. v. Felawka*, [1993] 4 S.C.R. 199 , 85 C.C.C. (3d) 248, 25 C.R. (4th) 70.

Meaning of "weapon" – In the absence of evidence to the contrary, the concealment of certain objects such as a handgun, switch-blade knife or brass knuckles fall within this provision because the unlawful purpose of the object may be assumed or implied. Where the object could be used for a peaceful purpose, such as a hunting knife or steak knife, the prosecution must establish that the object is being concealed for an unlawful purpose in that the object was intended to be used as a weapon: *R. v. Constantine* (1996), 46 C.R. (4th) 105, 137 Nfld. & P.E.I.R. 85 (Nfld. C.A.).

UNAUTHORIZED POSSESSION OF FIREARM / Unauthorized possession of prohibited weapon or restricted weapon / Punishment / Exceptions / Borrowed firearm for sustenance.

91. (1) Subject to subsection (4), every person commits an offence who possesses a prohibited firearm, a restricted firearm or a non-restricted firearm without being the holder of

    (a) a licence under which the person may possess it; and

    (b) in the case of a prohibited firearm or a restricted firearm, a registration certificate for it.

(2) Subject to subsection (4), every person commits an offence who possesses a prohibited weapon, a restricted weapon, a prohibited device, other than a replica firearm, or any prohibited ammunition, without being the holder of a licence under which the person may possess it.

(3) Every person who commits an offence under subsection (1) or (2)

    (a) is guilty of an indictable offence and liable to imprisonment for a term not exceeding five years; or

    (b) is guilty of an offence punishable on summary conviction.

(4) Subsections (1) and (2) do not apply to

    (a) a person who possesses a prohibited firearm, a restricted firearm, a non-restricted firearm, a prohibited weapon, a restricted weapon, a prohibited device or any prohibited ammunition while the person is under the direct and immediate supervision of a person who may lawfully possess it, for the purpose of using it in a manner in which the supervising person may lawfully use it; or

    (b) a person who comes into possession of a prohibited firearm, a restricted firearm, a non-restricted firearm, a prohibited weapon, a restricted weapon, a prohibited device or any prohibited ammunition by the operation of law and who, within a reasonable period after acquiring possession of it,

        (i) lawfully disposes of it, or

        (ii) obtains a licence under which the person may possess it and, in the case of a prohibited firearm or a restricted firearm, a registration certificate for it. **1995, c. 39, s. 139; 2008, c. 6, s. 4; 2012, c. 6, s. 2; 2015, c. 27, s. 19.**

(5) *[Repealed, 2012, c. 1, s. 2(3).]*

CROSS-REFERENCES

"Firearm" is defined in s. 2. "Possession" is defined in s. 4(3). "Prohibited firearm", "restricted firearm", "non-restricted firearm", "prohibited weapon", "restricted weapon", "prohibited device", "replica firearm", "prohibited ammunition", "licence" and "registration certificate" are defined in s. 84(1).

An accused charged with this offence may elect the mode of trial pursuant to s. 536(2) where the Crown proceeds by way of indictment. Where the prosecution elects to proceed by way of summary conviction, then the trial of this offence is conducted by a summary conviction court pursuant to Part XXVII. The punishment for the offence is then as set out in s. 787 and the limitation period is set out in s. 786(2).

A person found guilty of the offences in this section is liable to the discretionary prohibition order prescribed by s. 110, unless the accused was prohibited from possessing weapons or other regulated items at the time of the offence, in which case the mandatory prohibition order in s. 109 applies.

Note mandatory forfeiture of weapons used in commission of an offence in s. 491.

Under s. 117.11, the onus is on the accused to prove that he or she is the holder of a licence, authorization or registration certificate. Section 117.12 provides for admission into evidence of copies of such documents and the evidentiary value of the original and copies. Section 117.13 allows for the admission into evidence of a certificate of an analyst who has examined the weapon, prohibited device, ammunition, prohibited ammunition, explosive substance, or any part or component of such a thing.

Section 92 creates the related offence of possession of prohibited firearm, restricted firearm, non-restricted firearm, prohibited weapon, restricted weapon, prohibited device and prohibited ammunition knowing its possession is unauthorized.

Sections 117.07 to 117.09 exempt certain persons such as police officers from the operation of this section, provided that the person is not subject to a prohibition order (see s. 117.1).

SYNOPSIS

This section creates two offences relating to the simple possession of firearms and other weapons. Under subsec. (1), it is an offence to have possession of a firearm without a licence and, in the case of prohibited and restricted firearms, a registration certificate. Subsection (2) creates the similar offence of possession of a prohibited weapon, restricted weapon, prohibited device, or prohibited ammunition without being the holder of a licence. By virtue of subsec. (4)(*a*), no offence is committed if the person is under the direct and immediate supervision of someone who is authorized to have the weapon, provided that they are using the weapon in a manner in which the supervising person is authorized. Under subsec. (4)(*b*), the offence does not apply to a person who comes into possession by operation of law and who, within a reasonable time, lawfully disposes of it or obtains a licence and registration certificate, if necessary.

ANNOTATIONS

Constitutional considerations – The licensing and registration provisions of the *Firearms Act* are *intra vires* Parliament even to the extent that they regulate the ownership of an ordinary firearm: *Reference re: Firearms Act (Canada)* (1998), 128 C.C.C. (3d) 225, 164 D.L.R. (4th) 513 (Alta. C.A.), affd [2000] 1 S.C.R. 783, 144 C.C.C. (3d) 385.

Note: The following annotations were decided under the previous legislation.

Elements of offence/*mens rea* – *Mens rea* is an element of this offence and where the prohibited weapon is a knife "that opens automatically by gravity or centrifugal force" as defined in [now] para. (*a*) of the definition "prohibited weapon" in s. 84(1), ignorance by the accused that the knife possessed this quality is a defence to a charge under this section: *R. v. Phillips* (1978), 44 C.C.C. (2d) 548 (Ont. C.A.).

The requisite *mens rea* is supplied by either knowledge or recklessness with respect to the characteristics of the knife which, in fact, make it a prohibited weapon: *R. v. Archer* (1983), 6 C.C.C. (3d) 129 (Ont. C.A.).

However, in *R. v. Richard* (1981), 63 C.C.C. (2d) 333, 24 C.R. (3d) 373 (N.B.C.A.), it was held that the offence was one of strict liability but it was open to the accused to avoid liability by proof that he did not know that the blade would open by the application of centrifugal force to the blade.

Provided the accused was aware of the characteristics that make the weapon a prohibited weapon, it is no defence that he was unaware that such a weapon was prohibited. The accused's mistake is one of law: *R. v. Baxter* (1982), 6 C.C.C. (3d) 447 (Alta. C.A.). Similarly, *R. v. Williams* (1988), 44 C.C.C. (3d) 58 (Y.T. Terr. Ct.).

Exemption for possession by operation of law – The exemption in former s. 91(4)(*c*) [now subsec. (4)(*b*)] did not apply to police officers who did not have registration certificates and took possession of restricted weapons at the scene of an investigation with the intention of keeping the weapons for themselves. The officers had attended at the scene of a suicide and, at the insistence of a relative of the deceased, had removed all the firearms from the home. The officers treated the firearms as gifts and only turned them in to the police when their superior learned of the "gift". The term "by operation of law" refers to a situation where the person, from the outset, was justified in acquiring the weapon without first having obtained a certificate: *R. v. Bibeau* (1990), 61 C.C.C. (3d) 339, 1 C.R. (4th) 397 (Que. C.A.).

POSSESSION OF FIREARM KNOWING ITS POSSESSION IS UNAUTHORIZED / Possession of prohibited weapon, device or ammunition knowing its possession is unauthorized / Punishment / Exceptions / Borrowed firearm for sustenance / Evidence for previous conviction.

92. (1) Subject to subsection (4), every person commits an offence who possesses a prohibited firearm, a restricted firearm or a non-restricted firearm knowing that the person is not the holder of

(*a*) a licence under which the person may possess it; and

(*b*) in the case of a prohibited firearm or a restricted firearm, a registration certificate for it.

(2) Subject to subsection (4), every person commits an offence who possesses a prohibited weapon, a restricted weapon, a prohibited device, other than a replica firearm, or any prohibited ammunition knowing that the person is not the holder of a licence under which the person may possess it.

(3) Every person who commits an offence under subsection (1) or (2) is guilty of an indictable offence and liable

(*a*) in the case of a first offence, to imprisonment for a term not exceeding ten years;

(*b*) in the case of a second offence, to imprisonment for a term not exceeding ten years and to a minimum punishment of imprisonment for a term of one year; and

(*c*) in the case of a third or subsequent offence, to imprisonment for a term not exceeding ten years and to a minimum punishment of imprisonment for a term of two years less a day.

(4) Subsections (1) and (2) do not apply to

(*a*) a person who possesses a prohibited firearm, a restricted firearm, a non-restricted firearm, a prohibited weapon, a restricted weapon, a prohibited device or any prohibited ammunition while the person is under the direct and immediate supervision of a person who may lawfully possess it, for the purpose of using it in a manner in which the supervising person may lawfully use it; or

(*b*) a person who comes into possession of a prohibited firearm, a restricted firearm, a non-restricted firearm, a prohibited weapon, a restricted weapon, a prohibited device or any prohibited ammunition by the operation of law and who, within a reasonable period after acquiring possession of it,

(i) lawfully disposes of it, or

(ii) obtains a licence under which the person may possess it and, in the case of a prohibited firearm or a restricted firearm, a registration certificate for it.

1995, c. 39, s. 139; 2008, c. 6, s. 5; 2012, c. 6, s. 3; 2015, c. 27, s. 20.

(5) and (6) [*Repealed,* 2012, c. 6, s. 3(3).]

CROSS-REFERENCES

"Firearm" is defined in s. 2. "Possession" is defined in s. 4(3). "Prohibited firearm", "restricted firearm", "non-restricted firearm", "prohibited weapon", "restricted weapon", "prohibited device", "prohibited firearm", "restricted firearm", "replica firearm", "prohibited ammunition", "licence" and "registration certificate" are defined in s. 84(1). Section 117.12 provides for admission into evidence of copies of any licence, registration certificate or authorization and the evidentiary value of the original and copies of such documents. Section 117.13 allows for the admission into evidence of a certificate of an analyst who has examined the weapon, prohibited device, ammunition, prohibited ammunition, explosive substance, or any part or component of such a thing.

Where the prosecution seeks the higher penalty prescribed by subsec. (3)(*b*) or (*c*), it must comply with the provisions of s. 727. Section 667 provides one method of proof of the prior conviction. Note that no reference to the prior conviction may be made in the indictment, by virtue of s. 664. A person found guilty of the offences in this section is liable to the discretionary prohibition order prescribed by s. 110, unless the accused was prohibited from possessing weapons or other regulated items at the time of the offence, in which case the mandatory prohibition order in s. 109 applies.

Note mandatory forfeiture of weapons used in commission of an offence in s. 491.

Section 91 creates the related offence of simple unauthorized possession of a firearm, prohibited weapon, restricted weapon, prohibited device and prohibited ammunition. Sections 117.07 to 117.09 exempt certain persons such as police officers from the operation of this section, provided that the person is not subject to a prohibition order (see s. 117.1).

SYNOPSIS

This section creates two offences relating to the possession of firearms and other weapons. Under subsec. (1), it is an offence to have possession of a prohibited firearm, restricted firearm, or non-restricted firearm knowing that one is not the holder of a licence or, in the case of prohibited and restricted firearms, a registration certificate. Subsection (2) creates the similar offence of possession of a prohibited weapon, restricted weapon, prohibited device, or prohibited ammunition knowing one is not the holder of a licence. By virtue of subsec. (4)(*a*), no offence is committed if the person is under the direct and immediate supervision of someone who is authorized to have the weapon, provided that they are using the weapon in a manner in which the supervising person is authorized. Under subsec. (4)(*b*), the offence does not apply to a person who comes into possession by operation of law and who, within a reasonable time, lawfully disposes of it or obtains a licence and registration certificate, if necessary.

ANNOTATIONS

Constitutional considerations – The licensing and registration provisions of the *Firearms Act* are *intra vires* Parliament even to the extent that they regulate the ownership of an ordinary firearm: *Reference re: Firearms Act (Canada)* (1998), 128 C.C.C. (3d) 225, 19 C.R. (5th) 63 (Alta. C.A.), affd [2000] 1 S.C.R. 783, 144 C.C.C. (3d) 385.

Exemption for possession by operation of law – The exemption in former s. 91(4)(*c*) [now subsec. (4)(*b*)] did not apply to police officers who did not have registration certificates and took possession of restricted weapons at the scene of an investigation with the intention of keeping the weapons for themselves. The officers had attended at the scene of a suicide and, at the insistence of a relative of the deceased, had removed all the firearms from the home. The officers treated the firearms as gifts and only turned them in to the police when their superior learned of the "gift". The term "by operation of law" refers to a situation where the person, from the outset, was justified in acquiring the weapon without first having obtained a certificate: *R. v. Bibeau* (1990), 61 C.C.C. (3d) 339, 1 C.R. (4th) 397 (Que. C.A.).

POSSESSION AT UNAUTHORIZED PLACE / Punishment / Exception.

93. (1) Subject to subsection (3), every person commits an offence who, being the holder of an authorization or a licence under which the person may possess a prohibited firearm, a restricted firearm, a non-restricted firearm, a prohibited weapon, a restricted weapon, a prohibited device or prohibited ammunition, possesses them at a place that is

- (*a*) **indicated on the authorization or licence as being a place where the person may not possess it;**
- (*b*) **other than a place indicated on the authorization or licence as being a place where the person may possess it; or**
- (*c*) **other than a place where it may be possessed under the *Firearms Act*.**

(2) Every person who commits an offence under subsection (1)

- (*a*) **is guilty of an indictable offence and liable to imprisonment for a term not exceeding five years; or**
- (*b*) **is guilty of an offence punishable on summary conviction.**

(3) Subsection (1) does not apply to a person who possesses a replica firearm. 1995, c. 39, s. 139; 2008, c. 6, s. 6; 2015, c. 27, s. 21.

CROSS-REFERENCES

"Firearm" is defined in s. 2. "Prohibited firearm", "restricted firearm", "non-restricted firearm", "prohibited weapon", "restricted weapon", "prohibited device", "replica firearm", "prohibited ammunition", "licence" and "authorization" are defined in s. 84(1). "Possession" is defined in s. 4(3).

An accused charged with this offence may elect the mode of trial pursuant to s. 536(2) where the Crown proceeds by way of indictment. Where the prosecution elects to proceed by way of summary conviction then the trial of this offence is conducted by a summary conviction court pursuant to Part XXVII. The punishment for the offence is then as set out in s. 787 and the limitation period is set out in s. 786(2).

A person found guilty of the offences in this section is liable to the discretionary prohibition order prescribed by s. 110, unless the accused was prohibited from possessing weapons or other regulated items at the time of the offence, in which case the mandatory prohibition order in s. 109 applies.

Note mandatory forfeiture of weapons used in commission of an offence in s. 491.

Under s. 117.11, the onus is on the accused to prove that he or she is the holder of a licence, authorization or registration certificate. Section 117.12 provides for admission into evidence of copies of such documents and the evidentiary value of the original and copies. Section 117.13 allows for the admission into evidence of a certificate of an analyst who has examined the weapon, prohibited device, ammunition, prohibited ammunition, explosive substance, or any part or component of such a thing. Section 98 of the Code and ss. 120 to 135 of the *Firearms Act* provide transitional provisions relating to registration and licensing.

The related offence of unauthorized possession of a weapon in a motor vehicle is in s. 94.

SYNOPSIS

Subsection (1) creates an offence relating to the possession of a prohibited firearm, restricted firearm, non-restricted firearm, prohibited weapon, restricted weapon, prohibited device, or prohibited ammunition in places not authorized by the authorization or licence or in a place where they may not be possessed under the *Firearms Act*. The offence may be committed in three different ways: (1) possession in a place prohibited by the authorization or licence; (2) possession in a place other than the places permitted by the authorization or licence; or (3) possession in a place where it may not be possessed under the *Firearms Act*. Section 98 allows for a transitional period for licences and registration of firearms. The offence under this section does not apply to a replica of a firearm [subsec. (3)].

UNAUTHORIZED POSSESSION IN MOTOR VEHICLE / Punishment / Exception / Exception.

94. (1) Subject to subsections (3) and (4), every person commits an offence who is an occupant of a motor vehicle in which the person knows there is a prohibited firearm, a restricted firearm, a non-restricted firearm, a prohibited weapon, a restricted weapon, a prohibited device, other than a replica firearm, or any prohibited ammunition, unless

  (*a*) in the case of a prohibited firearm, a restricted firearm or a non-restricted firearm,

   (i) the person or any other occupant of the motor vehicle is the holder of

    (A) a licence under which the person or other occupant may possess the firearm, and

    (B) in the case of a prohibited firearm or a restricted firearm, an authorization and a registration certificate for it,

   (ii) the person had reasonable grounds to believe that any other occupant of the motor vehicle was the holder of

    (A) a licence under which that other occupant may possess the firearm, and

    (B) in the case of a prohibited firearm or a restricted firearm, an authorization and a registration certificate for it, or

   (iii) the person had reasonable grounds to believe that any other occupant of the motor vehicle was a person who could not be convicted of an offence under this Act by reason of sections 117.07 to 117.1 or any other Act of Parliament; and

  (*b*) in the case of a prohibited weapon, a restricted weapon, a prohibited device or any prohibited ammunition,

   (i) the person or any other occupant of the motor vehicle is the holder of an authorization or a licence under which the person or other occupant may transport the prohibited weapon, restricted weapon, prohibited device or prohibited ammunition, or

   (ii) the person had reasonable grounds to believe that any other occupant of the motor vehicle was

    (A) the holder of an authorization or a licence under which the other occupant may transport the prohibited weapon, restricted weapon, prohibited device or prohibited ammunition, or

    (B) a person who could not be convicted of an offence under this Act by reason of sections 117.07 to 117.1 or any other Act of Parliament.

(2) Every person who commits an offence under subsection (1)

  (*a*) is guilty of an indictable offence and liable to imprisonment for a term not exceeding ten years; or

  (*b*) is guilty of an offence punishable on summary conviction.

(3) Subsection (1) does not apply to an occupant of a motor vehicle who, on becoming aware of the presence of the firearm, weapon, device or ammunition in the motor vehicle, attempted to leave the motor vehicle, to the extent that it was feasible to do so, or actually left the motor vehicle.

(4) Subsection (1) does not apply to an occupant of a motor vehicle when the occupant or any other occupant of the motor vehicle is a person who came into possession of the firearm, weapon, device or ammunition by the operation of law. 1995, c. 39, s. 139; 2008, c. 6, s. 7; 2012, c. 6, s. 4; 2015, c. 27, s. 22.

(5) [*Repealed*, 2012, c. 6, s. 4(3).]

CROSS-REFERENCES
"Firearm" and "motor vehicle" are defined in s. 2. "Possession" is defined in s. 4(3). "Prohibited firearm", "restricted firearm", "non-restricted firearm", "prohibited weapon", "restricted weapon",

"prohibited device", "prohibited firearm", "restricted firearm", "replica firearm", "prohibited ammunition", "licence", "registration certificate" and "authorization" are defined in s. 84(1).

An accused charged with this offence may elect the mode of trial pursuant to s. 536(2) where the Crown proceeds by way of indictment. Where the prosecution elects to proceed by way of summary conviction, then the trial of this offence is conducted by a summary conviction court pursuant to Part XXVII. The punishment for the offence is then as set out in s. 787 and the limitation period is set out in s. 786(2).

A person found guilty of the offences in this section is liable to the discretionary prohibition order prescribed by s. 110, unless the accused was prohibited from possessing weapons or other regulated items at the time of the offence, in which case the mandatory prohibition order in s. 109 applies. Sections 117.07 to 117.09 exempt certain persons such as police officers from the operation of this section, provided that the person is not subject to a prohibition order (see s. 117.1).

Note mandatory forfeiture of weapons used in commission of an offence in s. 491.

Section 117.13 allows for the admission into evidence of a certificate of an analyst who has examined the weapon, prohibited device, ammunition, prohibited ammunition, explosive substance, or any part of component of such a thing.

The related offence of unauthorized possession of a weapon in an unauthorized place is in s. 93.

SYNOPSIS

This somewhat complex provision in essence makes it an offence to be an occupant in a motor vehicle knowing that possession of the weapon in that place is not authorized. The scheme of the section is to make it an offence to be an occupant of a motor vehicle knowing that there is a prohibited firearm, restricted firearm, non-restricted firearm, prohibited weapon, restricted weapon, prohibited device, other than a replica firearm, or prohibited ammunition in the motor vehicle. Subsection (1)(*a*) and (*b*) then provide for exemptions from liability if some person in the vehicle is entitled to possess and transport the weapon and, in the case of a prohibited or restricted firearm, the person has a registration certificate. The accused will also be exempt from liability if he or she had "reasonable grounds" to believe that another occupant had the requisite authorization, licence or registration certificate. Subsection (3) also creates a type of due diligence defence for an occupant who attempts to leave the vehicle when he or she learned of the presence of the weapon. Subsection (4) provides a defence for an occupant who came into possession of the weapon by operation of law.

POSSESSION OF PROHIBITED OR RESTRICTED FIREARM WITH AMMUNITION / Punishment / Exception.

95. (1) Subject to subsection (3), every person commits an offence who, in any place, possesses a loaded prohibited firearm or restricted firearm, or an unloaded prohibited firearm or restricted firearm together with readily accessible ammunition that is capable of being discharged in the firearm, without being the holder of

  (*a*) **an authorization or a licence under which the person may possess the firearm in that place; and**

  (*b*) **the registration certificate for the firearm.**

(2) Every person who commits an offence under subsection (1)

  (*a*) **is guilty of an indictable offence and liable to imprisonment for a term not exceeding 10 years and to a minimum punishment of imprisonment for a term of**

   (i) **in the case of a first offence, three years, and**

   (ii) **in the case of a second or subsequent offence, five years; or**

  (*b*) **is guilty of an offence punishable on summary conviction and liable to imprisonment for a term not exceeding one year.**

(3) Subsection (1) does not apply to a person who is using the firearm under the direct and immediate supervision of another person who is lawfully entitled to possess it and is using the firearm in a manner in which that other person may lawfully use it. 1995, c. 39, s. 139; 2008, c. 6, s. 8; 2012, c. 6, s. 5.

CROSS-REFERENCES

"Possession" is defined in s. 4(3). "Prohibited firearm", "restricted firearm", "ammunition", "licence", "registration certificate" and "authorization" are defined in s. 84(1).

An accused charged with this offence may elect the mode of trial pursuant to s. 536(2) where the Crown proceeds by way of indictment. Where the prosecution elects to proceed by way of summary conviction then the trial of this offence is conducted by a summary conviction court pursuant to Part XXVII. The maximum punishment for the offence is then one year imprisonment, rather than the punishment as set out in s. 787, and the limitation period is set out in s. 786(2). A person convicted of this offence is subject to the mandatory prohibition orders provided for in s. 109. For the purpose of determining whether a person has committed a second or subsequent offence, see s. 84(5) and (6).

Section 117.13 allows for the admission into evidence of a certificate of an analyst who has examined the weapon, prohibited device, ammunition, prohibited ammunition, explosive substance, or any part or component of such a thing.

SYNOPSIS

This section creates an offence to have a prohibited or restricted firearm that is either loaded or together with readily accessible ammunition capable of being discharged in that firearm, unless the person has an authorization or a licence that allows possession of the firearm at that particular place and a registration certificate for that firearm. By virtue of subsec. (3), no offence is committed if the person is under the direct and immediate supervision of someone who is authorized to have the weapon provided that they are using the weapon in a manner that the supervising person is authorized.

ANNOTATIONS

The *mens rea* is satisfied where the accused had knowledge that he was in possession of a loaded firearm. Knowledge of the length of the handgun's barrel is immaterial to the *mens rea*: *R. v. Williams* (2009), 244 C.C.C. (3d) 138 (Ont. C.A.).

This section creates two offences: possession of a loaded firearm and possession of an unloaded firearm with readily accessible ammunition. The latter is *not* a lesser included offence of the former: *R. v. Wong* (2012), 289 C.C.C. (3d) 38 (Ont. C.A.).

The Crown is not required to prove that the accused knew his possession and acquisition licence and authorization to transport the firearm did not extend to the place where he unlawfully had it in his possession. Ignorance of the law is no excuse. Knowledge that one possesses a loaded restricted firearm, together with an intention to possess the loaded firearm in that place, is enough: *R. v. MacDonald*, [2014] 1 S.C.R. 37, 303 C.C.C. (3d) 113.

The three-year mandatory minimum sentence for a first offender violates s. 12 of the Charter and cannot be justified under s. 1: *R. v. Nur*, [2015] 1 S.C.R. 773, 322 C.C.C. (3d) 149.

The five-year mandatory minimum sentence for a repeat offender also violates s. 12 of the Charter and cannot be justified under s. 1: *R. v. Nur*, *supra*.

See also *R. v. Adamo* (2013), 300 C.C.C. (3d) 515 (Man. Q.B.), holding that the mandatory minimum sentences violate ss. 7 and 12, as well as s. 15 of the Charter on the ground that it perpetuated and worsened the accused's disadvantage arising from his mental disability.

POSSESSION OF WEAPON OBTAINED BY COMMISSION OF OFFENCE / Punishment / Exception.

96. (1) Subject to subsection (3), every person commits an offence who possesses a firearm, a prohibited weapon, a restricted weapon, a prohibited device or any prohibited ammunition that the person knows was obtained by the commission in Canada of an offence or by an act or omission anywhere that, if it had occurred in Canada, would have constituted an offence.

(2) Every person who commits an offence under subsection (1)

   (*a*) is guilty of an indictable offence and liable to imprisonment for a term not exceeding ten years and to a minimum punishment of imprisonment for a term of one year; or

   (*b*) is guilty of an offence punishable on summary conviction and liable to imprisonment for a term not exceeding one year.

(3) Subsection (1) does not apply to a person who comes into possession of anything referred to in that subsection by the operation of law and who lawfully disposes of it within a reasonable period after acquiring possession of it. 1995, c. 39, s. 139.

CROSS-REFERENCES

"Firearm" is defined in s. 2. "Possession" is defined in s. 4(3). "Prohibited weapon", "restricted weapon", "prohibited device" and "prohibited ammunition" are defined in s. 84(1). An accused charged with this offence may elect the mode of trial pursuant to s. 536(2) where the Crown proceeds by way of indictment. Where the prosecution elects to proceed by way of summary conviction then the trial of this offence is conducted by a summary conviction court pursuant to Part XXVII. The maximum punishment for the offence is then one year imprisonment, rather than the punishment as set out in s. 787, and the limitation period is set out in s. 786(2).

A person found guilty of the offences in this section is liable to the discretionary prohibition order prescribed by s. 110, unless the accused was prohibited from possessing weapons or other regulated items at the time of the offence, in which case the mandatory prohibition order in s. 109 applies.

Note mandatory forfeiture of weapons used in commission of an offence in s. 491.

Section 117.13 allows for the admission into evidence of a certificate of an analyst who has examined the weapon, prohibited device, ammunition, prohibited ammunition, explosive substance, or any part or component of such a thing.

An authorization to intercept private communications may be obtained in relation to an offence under this section by virtue of ss. 183 and 186.

The related offence of possession of property obtained by crime is found in s. 354.

SYNOPSIS

This offence is similar to the offence of property obtained by crime under s. 354, except that this offence relates specifically to firearms, prohibited weapons, restricted weapons, prohibited devices and prohibited ammunition. As with the offence under s. 354, the prosecution must prove that the accused had possession of the item with knowledge that it had been obtained by the commission in Canada of an offence or by an act of omission anywhere that, if it had occurred in Canada, would have constituted an offence. Subsection (3) provides a defence for a person who comes into possession of the item by operation of law and who lawfully disposes of it within a reasonable period.

ANNOTATIONS

Note: The following cases were decided under s. 354 and may be of assistance in applying this section.

Doctrine of recent possession – The most recent review of the elements of the "doctrine" of recent possession that, in part, permits the trier of fact to infer the requisite guilty knowledge from possession of recently stolen goods is found in *R. v. Kowlyk*, [1988] 2 S.C.R. 59, 43 C.C.C. (3d) 1 (4:1). Those elements, as set out in that case and distilled from the various decisions as approved in *Kowlyk*, may be summarized as follows:

1. No adverse inference may be drawn against an accused from the fact of possession alone unless it was recent: *R. v. Graham*, [1974] S.C.R. 206, 7 C.C.C. (2d) 93;
2. If a pre-trial explanation of such possession were given by the accused, and if it possessed that degree of contemporaneity with the possession making evidence of it admissible, no adverse inference could be drawn on the basis of recent possession alone if the explanation were one which could reasonably be true: *R. v. Graham, supra*;
3. Where the accused does not testify, a jury instruction as to the inference arising from unexplained possession does not constitute a "comment" within the meaning of s. 4(6) of the *Canada Evidence Act*: *R. v. Newton*, [1977] 1 S.C.R. 399, 28 C.C.C. (2d) 286;
4. Where an explanation which could reasonably be true is given for the possession, no inference of guilt on the basis of recent possession alone may be drawn, even if the trier of fact is not satisfied as to the truth of the explanation and thus, to obtain a conviction in the face of such an explanation, the prosecution must establish by other evidence the guilt of the accused beyond a reasonable doubt.

In *Saieva v. Canada*, [1982] 1 S.C.R. 897, 68 C.C.C. (2d) 97 (7:0), the court, in considering whether possession was sufficiently "recent" to entitle reliance on the doctrine of recent possession, approved the statement in *R. v. Killam* (1973), 12 C.C.C. (2d) 114 (B.C.C.A.), that the criteria to be used are the nature of the object, "its rareness, the readiness in which it can, and is likely to, pass from hand to hand, the ease of its identification and the likelihood of transferability".

For other notes on recent possession, see s. 354.

Proof that goods obtained by crime – An admission by the accused is admissible for its truth, even if the admission itself contains hearsay, provided that the accused indicates a belief in the acceptance of the truth of the hearsay statement. If, however, the accused merely reports a hearsay statement without either adopting it or indicating a belief in its truth then the statement is not admissible for the truth of its contents. Thus, out of court statements by an accused, charged with the offence under this section, that he did not know the origin of the goods but his friend had stolen the goods and he knew they were "hot", made in circumstances indicating he believed the statements were true, were admissible not only to prove guilty knowledge but that, in fact, the goods were stolen: *R. v. Streu*, [1989] 1 S.C.R. 1521, 48 C.C.C. (3d) 321 (5:0).

Constitutional considerations – Application of the doctrine of recent possession does not offend the guarantees in s. 11(*c*) and (*d*) of the *Canadian Charter of Rights and Freedoms*: *R. v. Russell* (1983), 4 C.C.C. (3d) 460 (N.S.S.C.A.D.).

---

97. [Enacted 1995, c. 39, s. 139; however, repealed before coming into force]

BREAKING AND ENTERING TO STEAL FIREARM / Definitions of "break" and "place" / Entrance / Punishment.

98. (1) Every person commits an offence who
  (*a*) **breaks and enters a place with intent to steal a firearm located in it;**
  (*b*) **breaks and enters a place and steals a firearm located in it; or**
  (*c*) **breaks out of a place after**
    (i) **stealing a firearm located in it, or**
    (ii) **entering the place with intent to steal a firearm located in it.**

(2) In this section, "break" has the same meaning as in section 321, and "place" means any building or structure — or part of one — and any motor vehicle, vessel, aircraft, railway vehicle, container or trailer.

(3) For the purposes of this section,

  (*a*) a person enters as soon as any part of his or her body or any part of an instrument that he or she uses is within any thing that is being entered; and

  (*b*) a person is deemed to have broken and entered if he or she

   (i) obtained entrance by a threat or an artifice or by collusion with a person within, or

   (ii) entered without lawful justification or excuse by a permanent or temporary opening.

(4) Every person who commits an offence under subsection (1) is guilty of an indictable offence and liable to imprisonment for life. 1995, c. 39, s. 139, 2008, c. 6, s. 9.

CROSS-REFERENCES

"Firearm" and "steal" are defined in s. 2. The other break and enter offences are defined in s. 348. Section 350 enacts a deeming provision similar to subsec. (3) of this section. Section 98.1 creates a specific robbery offence where the object of the robbery is a firearm. Section 662(6) provides that a person charged with the offence under subsec. (1)(*b*), may be convicted of the offence under subsec. (1)(*a*), where the evidence does not prove the former offence but does prove the latter. Being unlawfully in a dwelling house is an offence under s. 349. Possession of break-in instruments is an offence under s. 351(1). Defence of property is dealt with in ss. 38 to 42. Section 494 gives the owner of property or person in possession and persons authorized by them a power to arrest, without warrant, a person found committing a criminal offence on or in relation to that property. This offence may be the basis for an application for an authorization to intercept private communications by reason of s. 183.

Pursuant to s. 348.1, if a person is convicted of the offence under this section in relation to a dwelling-house, it is an aggravating factor in sentencing that the dwelling-house was occupied at the time and the offender knew or was reckless as to whether the dwelling-house was occupied and used violence or threats of violence to a person or property.

SYNOPSIS

This section creates offences that are virtually identical to the offences in s. 348 of the *Criminal Code* except that the target of the break and enter is theft of a firearm. Unlike s. 348, this section does not distinguish between places as far as penalty; the offender is liable to life imprisonment even though the premises are not a dwelling-house.

ANNOTATIONS

Note: For notes on the meaning of break and enter and the application of the deeming provision in subsec. (3), see ss. 348 and 350.

ROBBERY TO STEAL FIREARM.

98.1 Every person who commits a robbery within the meaning of section 343 with intent to steal a firearm or in the course of which he or she steals a firearm commits an indictable offence and is liable to imprisonment for life. 2008, c. 6, s. 9.

CROSS-REFERENCES

"Firearm" is defined in s. 2. The similar break and enter offence, where the object of the theft is a firearm, is created by s. 98. This offence may be the basis for an application for an authorization to intercept private communications by reason of s. 183.

Trafficking Offences

WEAPONS TRAFFICKING / Punishment — firearm / Punishment — other cases.

99. (1) Every person commits an offence who

(a) manufactures or transfers, whether or not for consideration, or

(b) offers to do anything referred to in paragraph (a) in respect of

a prohibited firearm, a restricted firearm, a non-restricted firearm, a prohibited weapon, a restricted weapon, a prohibited device, any ammunition or any prohibited ammunition knowing that the person is not authorized to do so under the *Firearms Act* or any other Act of Parliament or any regulations made under any Act of Parliament.

(2) Every person who commits an offence under subsection (1) when the object in question is a prohibited firearm, a restricted firearm, a non-restricted firearm, a prohibited device, any ammunition or any prohibited ammunition is guilty of an indictable offence and liable to imprisonment for a term not exceeding 10 years and to a minimum punishment of imprisonment for a term of

(a) in the case of a first offence, three years; and

(b) in the case of a second or subsequent offence, five years.

(3) In any other case, a person who commits an offence under subsection (1) is guilty of an indictable offence and liable to imprisonment for a term not exceeding 10 years and to a minimum punishment of imprisonment for a term of one year. 1995, c. 39, s. 139; 2008, c. 6, s. 10; 2015, c. 27, s. 23.

CROSS-REFERENCES

"Firearm" is defined in s. 2. "Prohibited firearm", "restricted firearm", "non-restricted firearm", "prohibited weapon", "restricted weapon", "prohibited device", "ammunition", "prohibited ammunition" and "transfer" are defined in s. 84(1). The accused may elect the mode of trial pursuant to s. 536(2). A person convicted of this offence is subject to the mandatory prohibition order under s. 109. For the purpose of determining whether a person has committed a second or subsequent offence, see s. 84(5) and (6).

Note mandatory forfeiture of weapons used in commission of an offence in s. 491.

Section 117.13 allows for the admission into evidence of a certificate of an analyst who has examined the weapon, prohibited device, ammunition, prohibited ammunition, explosive substance, or any part of component of such a thing.

An authorization to intercept private communications may be obtained in relation to an offence under this section by virtue of ss. 183 and 186.

Section 101 creates the related offence of unauthorized transfer of weapons and s. 100 creates the offence of possession of weapons for the purpose of trafficking. Section 104 creates the offence of unauthorized importing and exporting of weapons. Section 105 creates the offence of smuggling weapons into and out of Canada.

SYNOPSIS

This section creates the offence of trafficking in weapons. This offence requires proof that the accused knew that he or she was not authorized to manufacture or transfer, or offer to do so, under the *Firearms Act* or regulations or any other federal legislation or regulations.

Subsection (2) creates a special penalty regime where the offence is committed in relation to a prohibited firearm, restricted firearm, non-restricted firearm, prohibited device, any ammunition or any prohibited ammunition. The maximum penalty is 10 years and the minimum punishment for a first offence is three years and is five years for a second or subsequent offence, as determined in accordance with the rules set out in s. 84(5) and (6). In any other case, the minimum punishment is one year.

POSSESSION FOR PURPOSE OF WEAPONS TRAFFICKING / Punishment — firearm / Punishment — other cases.

100. (1) Every person commits an offence who possesses a prohibited firearm, a restricted firearm, a non-restricted firearm, a prohibited weapon, a restricted weapon, a prohibited device, any ammunition or any prohibited ammunition for the purpose of

    (*a*) transferring it, whether or not for consideration, or

    (*b*) offering to transfer it,

knowing that the person is not authorized to transfer it under the *Firearms Act* or any other Act of Parliament or any regulations made under any Act of Parliament.

(2) Every person who commits an offence under subsection (1) when the object in question is a prohibited firearm, a restricted firearm, a non-restricted firearm, a prohibited device, any ammunition or any prohibited ammunition is guilty of an indictable offence and liable to imprisonment for a term not exceeding 10 years and to a minimum punishment of imprisonment for a term of

    (*a*) in the case of a first offence, three years; and

    (*b*) in the case of a second or subsequent offence, five years.

(3) In any other case, a person who commits an offence under subsection (1) is guilty of an indictable offence and liable to imprisonment for a term not exceeding 10 years and to a minimum punishment of imprisonment for a term of one year. 1995, c. 39, s. 139; 2008, c. 6, s. 11; 2015, c. 27, s. 24.

CROSS-REFERENCES

"Firearm" is defined in s. 2. "Possession" is defined in s. 4(3). "Prohibited firearm", "restricted firearm", "non-restricted firearm", "prohibited weapon", "restricted weapon", "prohibited device", "ammunition", "prohibited ammunition" and "transfer" are defined in s. 84(1). The accused may elect the mode of trial pursuant to s. 536(2). A person convicted of this offence is subject to the mandatory prohibition order under s. 109. For the purpose of determining whether a person has committed a second or subsequent offence, see s. 84(5) and (6).

Note mandatory forfeiture of weapons used in commission of an offence in s. 491.

Section 117.13 allows for the admission into evidence of a certificate of an analyst who has examined the weapon, prohibited device, ammunition, prohibited ammunition, explosive substance, or any part or component of such a thing.

An authorization to intercept private communications may be obtained in relation to an offence under this section by virtue of ss. 183 and 186.

Section 99 creates the related offence of trafficking in weapons and s. 101 creates the basic offence of unauthorized transfer of weapons. Section 104 creates the offence of unauthorized importing and exporting of weapons. Section 105 creates the offence of smuggling weapons into and out of Canada.

SYNOPSIS

This section creates the offence of possession of weapons for the purpose of trafficking in weapons. This offence requires proof that the accused had possession of the prohibited firearm, restricted firearm, non-restricted firearm, prohibited weapon, restricted weapon, prohibited device, ammunition or prohibited ammunition for the purpose of transferring it, or offering to do so, knowing that he or she was not authorized to transfer it under the *Firearms Act* or regulations or any other federal legislation or regulations.

Subsection (2) creates a special penalty regime where the offence is committed in relation to a prohibited firearm, restricted firearm, non-restricted firearm, prohibited device, any ammunition or any prohibited ammunition. The maximum penalty is 10 years and the minimum punishment for a first offence is three years and is five years for a second or subsequent offence, as determined in accordance with the rules set out in s. 84(5) and (6). In any other case, the minimum punishment is one year.

ANNOTATIONS

This provision does not apply to the mere movement of a firearm from one place to another. A contextual reading of s. 100 and the related provisions reveals that Parliament intended to reserve the stiffest penalties for transfers that amount to weapons trafficking, not for the mere movement of a firearm from place to place. Since the trial judge did not find that the accused was in possession of the gun for the purpose of transferring it to another person, the s. 100(1) conviction cannot stand. There are other provisions, such as s. 86(2) that capture conduct falling short of trafficking: *R. v. Grant* (2009), 245 C.C.C. (3d) 1 (S.C.C.).

TRANSFER WITHOUT AUTHORITY / Punishment.

101. (1) Every person commits an offence who transfers a prohibited firearm, a restricted firearm, a non-restricted firearm, a prohibited weapon, a restricted weapon, a prohibited device, any ammunition or any prohibited ammunition to any person otherwise than under the authority of the *Firearms Act* or any other Act of Parliament or any regulations made under an Act of Parliament.

(2) Every person who commits an offence under subsection (1)

> **(*a*) is guilty of an indictable offence and liable to imprisonment for a term not exceeding five years; or**
>
> **(*b*) is guilty of an offence punishable on summary conviction. 1995, c. 39, s. 139; 2015, c. 27, s. 25.**

CROSS-REFERENCES

"Firearm" is defined in s. 2. "Prohibited firearm", "restricted firearm", "non-restricted firearm", "prohibited weapon", "restricted weapon", "prohibited device", "ammunition", "prohibited ammunition" and "transfer" are defined in s. 84(1). An accused charged with this offence may elect the mode of trial pursuant to s. 536(2) where the Crown proceeds by way of indictment. Where the prosecution elects to proceed by way of summary conviction then the trial of this offence is conducted by a summary conviction court pursuant to Part XXVII. The punishment for the offence is then as set out in s. 787 and the limitation period is set out in s. 786(2). In either case, release pending trial is determined by s. 515, although the accused is eligible for release by a peace officer under ss. 496, 497 or by the officer in charge under s. 498.

A person found guilty of the offences in this section is liable to the discretionary prohibition order prescribed by s. 110, unless the accused was prohibited from possessing weapons or other regulated items at the time of the offence, in which case the mandatory prohibition order in s. 109 applies.

Note mandatory forfeiture of weapons used in commission of an offence in s. 491.

Under s. 117.11, where any question arises as to whether a person is the holder of an authorization, a licence or a registration certificate, the onus is on the accused to prove that the person is the holder of the authorization, licence or registration certificate. Section 117.12 provides for admission into evidence of copies of such documents and the evidentiary value of the original and copies. Section 117.13 allows for the admission into evidence of a certificate of an analyst who has examined the weapon, prohibited device, ammunition, prohibited ammunition, explosive substance, or any part or component of such a thing.

Section 99 creates the related offence of trafficking in weapons and s. 100 creates the offence of possession of weapons for the purpose of trafficking.

SYNOPSIS

This section makes it an offence to transfer a prohibited firearm, restricted firearm, non-restricted firearm, prohibited weapon, restricted weapon, prohibited device, ammunition and prohibited ammunition to any person except under the authority of the *Firearms Act* or regulations or any other federal legislation or regulations. "Transfer" is broadly defined in s. 84(1) to mean "sell, provide, barter, give, lend, rent, send, transport, ship, distribute or deliver".

ANNOTATIONS

The Crown must prove that the accused knew, was wilfully blind to or reckless as to the fact that the recipient of the ammunition was unlicensed: *R. v. Hault* (2004), 201 C.C.C. (3d) 375 (Alta. Q.B.).

Assembling Offence

MAKING AUTOMATIC FIREARM / Punishment.

102. (1) **Every person commits an offence who, without lawful excuse, alters a firearm so that it is capable of, or manufactures or assembles any firearm that is capable of, discharging projectiles in rapid succession during one pressure of the trigger.**

(2) **Every person who commits an offence under subsection (1)**

  (*a*) **is guilty of an indictable offence and liable to imprisonment for a term not exceeding ten years and to a minimum punishment of imprisonment for a term of one year; or**

  (*b*) **is guilty of an offence punishable on summary conviction and liable to imprisonment for a term not exceeding one year. 1995, c. 39, s. 139.**

CROSS-REFERENCES

"Firearm" is defined in s. 2. "Automatic firearm" is defined in s. 84(1). An accused charged with this offence may elect the mode of trial pursuant to s. 536(2) where the Crown proceeds by way of indictment. Where the prosecution elects to proceed by way of summary conviction then the trial of this offence is conducted by a summary conviction court pursuant to Part XXVII. The maximum punishment for the offence is then one year imprisonment, rather than the punishment as set out in s. 787, and the limitation period is set out in s. 786(2). Where the Crown proceeds by indictment, this offence carries a minimum punishment of one year imprisonment. A person convicted of this offence is subject to the mandatory prohibition order under s. 109.

Note mandatory forfeiture of weapons used in commission of an offence in s. 491.

Section 117.13 allows for the admission into evidence of a certificate of an analyst who has examined the weapon, prohibited device, ammunition, prohibited ammunition, explosive substance, or any part or component of such a thing.

An authorization to intercept private communications may be obtained in relation to an offence under this section by virtue of ss. 183 and 186.

SYNOPSIS

This offence, in effect, prohibits, without lawful excuse, the alteration of a firearm into an automatic firearm. It also prohibits, without lawful excuse, the manufacture or assembly of such firearms. Note the minimum punishment of one year imprisonment where the Crown proceeds by way of indictment.

Export and Import Offences

IMPORTING OR EXPORTING KNOWING IT IS UNAUTHORIZED / Punishment — firearm / Punishment — other cases / Attorney General of Canada may act.

103. (1) **Every person commits an offence who imports or exports**

  (*a*) **a prohibited firearm, a restricted firearm, a non-restricted firearm, a prohibited weapon, a restricted weapon, a prohibited device or any prohibited ammunition, or**

  (*b*) **any component or part designed exclusively for use in the manufacture of or assembly into an automatic firearm,** knowing that the person is not authorized to do so under the *Firearms Act* or any other Act of Parliament or any regulations made under an Act of Parliament.

(2) Every person who commits an offence under subsection (1) when the object in question is a prohibited firearm, a restricted firearm, a non-restricted firearm, a prohibited device or any prohibited ammunition is guilty of an indictable offence and liable to imprisonment for a term not exceeding 10 years and to a minimum punishment of imprisonment for a term of

   (*a*) in the case of a first offence, three years; and

   (*b*) in the case of a second or subsequent offence, five years.

(2.1) In any other case, a person who commits an offence under subsection (1) is guilty of an indictable offence and liable to imprisonment for a term not exceeding 10 years and to a minimum punishment of imprisonment for a term of one year.

(3) Any proceedings in respect of an offence under subsection (1) may be commenced at the instance of the Government of Canada and conducted by or on behalf of that government. 1995, c. 39, s. 139; 2008, c. 6, s. 12; 2015, c. 27, s. 26.

CROSS-REFERENCES

"Firearm" is defined in s. 2. "Prohibited firearm", "restricted firearm", "non-restricted firearm", "prohibited weapon", "restricted weapon", "prohibited device", "automatic firearm", "prohibited ammunition", "import" and "export" are defined in s. 84(1). The accused may elect the mode of trial pursuant to s. 536(2). A person convicted of this offence is subject to the mandatory prohibition order under s. 109. For the purpose of determining whether a person has committed a second or subsequent offence, see s. 84(5) and (6).

Section 117.13 allows for the admission into evidence of a certificate of an analyst who has examined the weapon, prohibited device, ammunition, prohibited ammunition, explosive substance, or any part or component of such a thing.

An authorization to intercept private communications may be obtained in relation to an offence under this section by virtue of ss. 183 and 186. The related offence of simple unauthorized importing or exporting of weapons is found in s. 104.

SYNOPSIS

This section makes it an offence to import or export a prohibited firearm, restricted firearm, non-restricted firearm, prohibited weapon, restricted weapon, prohibited device or any prohibited ammunition, or any component or part designed exclusively for use in the manufacture of or assembly into an automatic firearm knowing that one is not authorized to do so under the authority of the *Firearms Act* and regulations or some other federal legislation or regulations. If prosecuted by indictment, the offence carries a minimum punishment of one year imprisonment. Offences under this section may be prosecuted at the instance of the federal government.

Subsection (2) creates a special penalty regime where the offence is committed in relation to a prohibited firearm, restricted firearm, non-restricted firearm, prohibited device, or any prohibited ammunition. The maximum penalty is 10 years and the minimum punishment for a first offence is three years and is five years for a second or subsequent offence, as determined in accordance with the rules set out in s. 84(5) and (6). In any other case, the minimum punishment is one year.

UNAUTHORIZED IMPORTING OR EXPORTING / Punishment / Attorney General of Canada may act.

104. (1) Every person commits an offence who imports or exports

   (*a*) a prohibited firearm, a restricted firearm, a non-restricted firearm, a prohibited weapon, a restricted weapon, a prohibited device or any prohibited ammunition, or (*b*) any component or part designed exclusively for use in the manufacture of or assembly into an automatice firearm,

otherwise than under the authority of the *Firearms Act* or any other Act of Parliament or any regulations made under an Act of Parliament.

(2) Every person who commits an offence under subsection (1)

    (*a*) is guilty of an indictable offence and liable to imprisonment for a term not exceeding five years; or

    (*b*) is guilty of an offence punishable on summary conviction.

(3) Any proceedings in respect of an offence under subsection (1) may be commenced at the instance of the Government of Canada and conducted by or on behalf of that government. 1995, c. 39, s. 139; 2015, c. 27, s. 27.

CROSS-REFERENCES

"Firearm" is defined in s. 2. "Prohibited firearm", "restricted firearm", "non-restricted firearm", "prohibited weapon", "restricted weapon", "prohibited device", "automatic firearm", "prohibited ammunition", "import" and "export" are defined in s. 84(1). An accused charged with this offence may elect the mode of trial pursuant to s. 536(2) where the Crown proceeds by way of indictment. Where the prosecution elects to proceed by way of summary conviction then the trial of this offence is conducted by a summary conviction court pursuant to Part XXVII. The punishment for the offence is then as set out in s. 787 and the limitation period is set out in s. 786(2).

A person found guilty of the offences in this section is liable to the discretionary prohibition order prescribed by s. 110, unless the accused was prohibited from possessing weapons or other regulated items at the time of the offence, in which case the mandatory prohibition order in s. 109 applies.

Note mandatory forfeiture of weapons used in commission of an offence in s. 491.

Under s. 117.11, where any question arises as to whether a person is the holder of an authorization, a licence or a registration certificate, the onus is on the accused to prove that the person is the holder of the authorization, licence or registration certificate. Section 117.12 provides for admission into evidence of copies of such documents and the evidentiary value of the original and copies. Section 117.13 allows for the admission into evidence of a certificate of an analyst who has examined the weapon, prohibited device, ammunition, prohibited ammunition, explosive substance, or any part of component of such a thing.

An authorization to intercept private communications may be obtained in relation to an offence under this section by virtue of ss. 183 and 186.

The related offence of smuggling weapons is found in s. 104. Unauthorized transfer of weapons is an offence under s. 101, and trafficking in weapons is an offence under s. 99.

SYNOPSIS

This section makes it an offence to import or export a prohibited firearm, restricted firearm, non-restricted firearm, prohibited weapon, restricted weapon, prohibited device or any prohibited ammunition, or any component or part designed exclusively for use in the manufacture of or assembly into an automatic firearm otherwise than under the authority of the *Firearms Act* and regulations or some other federal legislation or regulations. Offences under this section may be prosecuted at the instance of the federal government.

Offences relating to Lost, Destroyed or Defaced Weapons, etc.

LOSING OR FINDING / Punishment.

105. (1) Every person commits an offence who

    (*a*) having lost a prohibited firearm, a restricted firearm, a non-restricted firearm, a prohibited weapon, a restricted weapon, a prohibited device, any prohibited ammunition, an authorization, a licence or a registration certificate, or having had it stolen from the person's possession, does not with reasonable despatch report the loss to a peace officer, to a firearms officer or a chief firearms officer; or

(b) **on finding a prohibited firearm, a restricted firearm, a non-restricted firearm, a prohibited weapon, a restricted weapon, a prohibited device or any prohibited ammunition that the person has reasonable grounds to believe has been lost or abandoned, does not with reasonable despatch deliver it to a peace officer, a firearms officer or a chief firearms officer or report the finding to a peace officer, a firearms officer or a chief firearms officer.**

(2) **Every person who commits an offence under subsection (1)**

(a) **is guilty of an indictable offence and liable to imprisonment for a term not exceeding five years; or**

(b) **is guilty of an offence punishable on summary conviction. 1995, c. 39, s. 139; 2015, c. 27, s. 28.**

CROSS-REFERENCES

"Firearm" and "peace officer" are defined in s. 2. "Prohibited firearm", "restricted firearm", "non-restricted firearm", "prohibited weapon", "restricted weapon", "prohibited device", "prohibited ammunition", "firearms officer", "chief firearms officer, "licence", "registration certificate" and "authorization" are defined in s. 84(1). An accused charged with this offence may elect the mode of trial pursuant to s. 536(2) where the Crown proceeds by way of indictment. Where the prosecution elects to proceed by way of summary conviction then the trial of this offence is conducted by a summary conviction court pursuant to Part XXVII. The punishment for the offence is then as set out in s. 787 and the limitation period is set out in s. 786(2). A person found guilty of the offences in this section is liable to the discretionary prohibition order prescribed by s. 110, unless the accused was prohibited from possessing weapons or other regulated items at the time of the offence, in which case the mandatory prohibition order in s. 109 applies.

Note mandatory forfeiture of weapons used in commission of an offence in s. 491.

Under s. 117.11, where any question arises as to whether a person is the holder of an authorization, a licence or a registration certificate, the onus is on the accused to prove that the person is the holder of the authorization, licence or registration certificate. Section 117.12 provides for admission into evidence of copies of such documents and the evidentiary value of the original and copies. Section 117.13 allows for the admission into evidence of a certificate of an analyst who has examined the weapon, prohibited device, ammunition, prohibited ammunition, explosive substance, or any part or component of such a thing.

The related offence of failing to report the destruction of weapons is found in s. 106. It is also an offence under s. 107 to make a false report concerning the loss or theft of a weapon or an authorization, licence or registration certificate.

SYNOPSIS

This section creates two offences of omission concerning firearms, weapons and documents. Under subsec. (1)(a), it is an offence to fail with reasonable despatch to report the loss or theft of a prohibited firearm, restricted firearm, non-restricted firearm, prohibited weapon, restricted weapon, prohibited device, any prohibited ammunition, an authorization, a licence or a registration certificate. Similarly, it is an offence under subsec. (1)(b) to fail to report or deliver with reasonable despatch any prohibited firearm, restricted firearm, non-restricted firearm, prohibited weapon, restricted weapon, prohibited device, or any prohibited ammunition that the person reasonably believes to have been abandoned or lost. The report or delivery, as the case may be, is to be made to a peace officer, firearms officer or chief firearms officer.

DESTROYING / Punishment.

106. (1) Every person commits an offence who

    (*a*) **after destroying any prohibited firearm, restricted firearm, prohibited weapon, restricted weapon, prohibited device or prohibited ammunition, or**

    (*b*) **on becoming aware of the destruction of any prohibited firearm, restricted firearm, prohibited weapon, restricted weapon, prohibited device or prohibited ammunition that was in the person's possession before its destruction,**

does not with reasonable despatch report the destruction to a peace officer, firearms officer or chief firearms officer.

(2) Every person who commits an offence under subsection (1)

    (*a*) **is guilty of an indictable offence and liable to imprisonment for a term not exceeding five years; or**

    (*b*) **is guilty of an offence punishable on summary conviction. 1995, c. 39, s. 139; 2012, c. 6, s. 6.**

CROSS-REFERENCES

"Firearm" and "peace officer" are defined in s. 2. "Possession" is defined in s. 4(3). "Prohibited weapon", "restricted weapon", "prohibited device", "prohibited ammunition", "restricted firearm", "prohibited firearm", "firearms officer", "chief firearms officer", "licence", "registration certificate" and "authorization" are defined in s. 84(1). An accused charged with this offence may elect the mode of trial pursuant to s. 536(2) where the Crown proceeds by way of indictment. Where the prosecution elects to proceed by way of summary conviction then the trial of this offence is conducted by a summary conviction court pursuant to Part XXVII. The punishment for the offence is then as set out in s. 787 and the limitation period is set out in s. 786(2). A person found guilty of the offences in this section is liable to the discretionary prohibition order prescribed by s. 110, unless the accused was prohibited from possessing weapons or other regulated items at the time of the offence, in which case the mandatory prohibition order in s. 109 applies.

Note mandatory forfeiture of weapons used in commission of an offence in s. 491.

Section 117.13 allows for the admission into evidence of a certificate of an analyst who has examined the weapon, prohibited device, ammunition, prohibited ammunition, explosive substance, or any part or component of such a thing.

The related offence of failing to report the loss or theft of weapons is found in s. 105. It is also an offence under s. 107 to make a false report concerning the destruction of weapons.

SYNOPSIS

This section makes it an offence to fail with reasonable despatch to report destroying any prohibited or restricted firearm, prohibited weapon, restricted weapon, prohibited device, and any prohibited ammunition. It is also an offence to fail to report the destruction of such items that were in the person's possession before their destruction on becoming aware of the destruction. The report may be made to a peace officer, firearms officer or chief firearms officer.

FALSE STATEMENTS / Punishment / Definition of "report" or "statement".

107. (1) Every person commits an offence who knowingly makes, before a peace officer, firearms officer or chief firearms officer, a false report or statement concerning the loss, theft or destruction of a prohibited firearm, a restricted firearm, a non-restricted firearm, a prohibited weapon, a restricted weapon, a prohibited device, any prohibited ammunition, an authorization, a licence or a registration certificate.

(2) Every person who commits an offence under subsection (1)

    (*a*) **is guilty of an indictable offence and liable to imprisonment for a term not exceeding five years; or**

    (*b*) **is guilty of an offence punishable on summary conviction.**

CR. CODE

(3) In this section, "report" or "statement" means an assertion of fact, opinion, belief or knowledge, whether material or not and whether admissible or not. 1995, c. 39, s. 139; 2015, c. 27, s. 29.

CROSS-REFERENCES

"Firearm" and "peace officer" are defined in s. 2. "Possession" is defined in s. 4(3). "Prohibited firearm", "restricted firearm", "non-restricted firearm", "prohibited weapon", "restricted weapon", "prohibited device", "prohibited ammunition", "firearms officer", "chief firearms officer", "licence", "registration certificate" and "authorization" are defined in s. 84(1). An accused charged with this offence may elect the mode of trial pursuant to s. 536(2) where the Crown proceeds by way of indictment. Where the prosecution elects to proceed by way of summary conviction then the trial of this offence is conducted by a summary conviction court pursuant to Part XXVII. The punishment for the offence is then as set out in s. 787 and the limitation period is set out in s. 786(2).

The offence of failing to report the loss or theft of weapons and documents is found in s. 105. The offence of failing to report the destruction of weapons is found in s. 106. There are a number of related offences under the *Firearms Act*. See, for example, s. 106 of that Act, which makes it an offence to provide false information for the purpose of obtaining a licence, registration certificate or authorization.

SYNOPSIS

This section creates the offence of knowingly making a false report or statement about the loss, theft or destruction of a prohibited firearm, restricted firearm, non-restricted firearm, prohibited weapon, restricted weapon, prohibited device, any prohibited ammunition, authorization, licence or registration certificate. The terms "report" and "statement" are defined in subsec. (3).

TAMPERING WITH SERIAL NUMBER / Punishment / Exception / Evidence.

108. (1) Every person commits an offence who, without lawful excuse, the proof of which lies on the person,

> **(a) alters, defaces or removes a serial number on a firearm; or**
> **(b) possesses a firearm knowing that the serial number on it has been altered, defaced or removed.**

(2) Every person who commits an offence under subsection (1)

> **(a) is guilty of an indictable offence and liable to imprisonment for a term not exceeding five years; or**
> **(b) is guilty of an offence punishable on summary conviction.**

(3) No person is guilty of an offence under paragraph (1)(b) by reason only of possessing a prohibited firearm or restricted firearm the serial number on which has been altered, defaced or removed, if that serial number has been replaced and a registration certificate in respect of the firearm has been issued setting out a new serial number for the firearm.

(4) In proceedings for an offence under subsection (1), evidence that a person possesses a firearm the serial number on which has been wholly or partially obliterated otherwise than through normal use over time is, in the absence of evidence to the contrary, proof that the person possesses the firearm knowing that the serial number on it has been altered, defaced or removed. 1995, c. 39, s. 139; 2012, c. 6, s. 7.

CROSS-REFERENCES

"Firearm" is defined in s. 2. "Possession" is defined in s. 4(3). "Registration certificate", "restricted firearm" and "prohibited firearm" are defined in s. 84(1). An accused charged with this offence may elect the mode of trial pursuant to s. 536(2) where the Crown proceeds by way of indictment.

Where the prosecution elects to proceed by way of summary conviction, then the trial of this offence is conducted by a summary conviction court pursuant to Part XXVII. The punishment for the offence is then as set out in s. 787 and the limitation period is set out in s. 786(2). A person found guilty of the offences in this section is liable to the discretionary prohibition order prescribed by s. 110, unless the accused was prohibited from possessing weapons or other regulated items at the time of the offence, in which case the mandatory prohibition order in s. 109 applies.

Note mandatory forfeiture of weapons used in commission of an offence in s. 491.

SYNOPSIS

It is an offence under this section to, without lawful excuse, alter, deface or remove a firearm's serial number or to possess a firearm knowing that the serial number has been altered, defaced or removed. The onus is on the accused to show a lawful excuse. Subsection (3) provides a defence where the serial number on a restricted or prohibited firearm has been replaced and a registration certificate has been issued setting out the new serial number. Under subsec. (4), evidence that the accused possesses a firearm, the serial number on which has been wholly or partially obliterated otherwise than through normal use over time, is, in the absence of evidence to the contrary, proof that the accused knew that the serial number had been altered, defaced or removed.

Prohibition Orders

MANDATORY PROHIBITION ORDER / Duration of prohibition order — first offence / Duration of prohibition order — subsequent offences / Definition of "release from imprisonment" / Application of ss. 113 to 117.

109. (1) Where a person is convicted, or discharged under section 730, of

   (*a*) an indictable offence in the commission of which violence against a person was used, threatened or attempted and for which the person may be sentenced to imprisonment for ten years or more,

   (*a*.1) an indictable offence in the commission of which violence was used, threatened or attempted against

   (i) the person's current or former intimate partner,

   (ii) a child or parent of the person or of anyone referred to in subparagraph (i), or

   (iii) any person who resides with the person or with anyone referred to in subparagraph (i) or (ii),

   (*b*) an offence under subsection 85(1) (using firearm in commission of offence), subsection 85(2) (using imitation firearm in commission of offence), 95(1) (possession of prohibited or restricted firearm with ammunition), 99(1) (weapons trafficking), 100(1) (possession for purpose of weapons trafficking), 102(1) (making automatic firearm), 103(1) (importing or exporting knowing it is unauthorized) or section 264 (criminal harassment),

   (*c*) an offence relating to the contravention of subsection 5(1) or (2), 6(1) or (2) or 7(1) of the *Controlled Drugs and Substances Act*, or

   (*d*) an offence that involves, or the subject-matter of which is, a firearm, a cross-bow, a prohibited weapon, a restricted weapon, a prohibited device, any ammunition, any prohibited ammunition or an explosive substance and, at the time of the offence, the person was prohibited by any order made under this Act or any other Act of Parliament from possessing any such thing,

the court that sentences the person or directs that the person be discharged, as the case may be, shall, in addition to any other punishment that may be imposed for that offence or any other condition prescribed in the order of discharge, make an order prohibiting the person from possessing any firearm, cross-bow, prohibited weapon, restricted

weapon, prohibited device, ammunition, prohibited ammunition and explosive substance during the period specified in the order as determined in accordance with subsection (2) or (3), as the case may be.

(2) An order made under subsection (1) shall, in the case of a first conviction for or discharge from the offence to which the order relates, prohibit the person from posssessing

- (a) any firearm, other than a prohibited firearm or restricted firearm, and any cross-bow, restricted weapon, ammunition and explosive substance during the period that
  - (i) begins on the day on which the order is made, and
  - (ii) ends not earlier than ten years after the person's release from imprisonment after conviction for the offence or, if the person is not then imprisoned or subject to imprisonment, after the person's conviction for or discharge from the offence; and
- (b) any prohibited firearm, restricted firearm, prohibited weapon, prohibited device and prohibited ammunition for life.

(3) An order made under subsection (1) shall, in any case other than a case described in subsection (2), prohibit the person from possessing any firearm, cross-bow, restricted weapon, ammunition and explosive substance for life.

(4) In subparagraph (2)(a)(ii), "release from imprisonment" means release from confinement by reason of expiration of sentence, commencement of statutory release or grant of parole.

(5) Sections 113 to 117 apply in respect of every order made under subsection (1). 1995, c. 39, ss. 139, 188(a), 190(d); 1996, c. 19, s. 65.1; 2003, c. 8, s. 4; 2015, c. 27, s. 30.

CROSS-REFERENCES

"Intimate partner" is defined in s. 110.1. "Firearm", " explosive substance" and "weapon" are defined in s. 2. "Prohibition order", "prohibited weapon", "restricted weapon", "prohibited device", "cross-bow", "ammunition" and "prohibited ammunition" are defined in s. 84(1). Possession is defined in s. 4(3). This is one of four provisions in this part that mandate or permit the imposition of orders prohibiting the possession of weapons and other articles such as explosive substances. There are, as well, other provisions of the Code authorizing various forms of prohibition orders. Thus see: s. 110 [discretionary prohibition order upon conviction of certain offences]; s. 111 [preventative prohibition order]; s. 117.05 [preventative prohibition order after seizure]; s. 515(4.1) [condition of bail]; s. 732.1 [condition of probation]; and s. 742.3 [conditional sentence], ss. 810(3.1), 810.01(5), 810.2(5) [condition of recognizance (peace bond)]. A prohibition order shall also be made under subsecs. 51(1) and (2) of the *Youth Criminal Justice Act.*

Section 117.01 creates the offences of possessing a firearm, cross-bow, prohibited weapon, restricted weapon, prohibited device, ammunition, prohibited ammunition or explosive substance while prohibited from doing so and wilfully failing to surrender an authorization, licence or registration certificate when the person was required to surrender it by any order made under the Code.

Under s. 113, the judge may lift the prohibition order for sustenance or employment purposes. Section 114 permits the court that makes a prohibition order to order the person to surrender anything the possession of which is prohibited by the order and every authorization, licence and registration certificate relating to anything the possession of which is prohibited by the order. The person must be given a reasonable time to comply with the order and during that period the offence under s. 117.01 does not apply. Under s. 115, unless the prohibition order specifies otherwise, everything the possession of which is prohibited by the order is forfeited to the Crown. However, on application under s. 117, the judge may order the return of articles to the person who is lawfully entitled to possess it provided that the owner had no reasonable grounds to believe that the thing would or might be used in the commission of the offence in respect of which the prohibition order was made. Pursuant to s. 116, every authorization, licence and registration certificate relating to anything the possession of which is prohibited by a prohibition order and issued to a person against whom the prohibition order is made is, on the commencement of the prohibition order, revoked, or amended, as the case may be, to the extent of the prohibitions in the order. Section 117.011 allows for an application to a provincial court judge for a limitation on access order against a person who is an associate of, or cohabits with, a person subject to a prohibition order.

Section 89 of the *Firearms Act* requires a court that makes, varies or revokes a prohibition order to have the chief firearms officer informed of the order or its variation or revocation.

An order made under this section falls within the definition of "sentence" in s. 673 and therefore may be appealed as a sentence appeal under Part XXI.

SYNOPSIS

This section sets out the circumstances in which a prohibition order relating to weapons and other articles such as ammunition and explosive substances is mandatory. The order is mandatory in four circumstances: subsec. (1)(*a*), an indictable offence in the commission of which violence against a person was used, threatened or attempted and for which the person may be sentenced to imprisonment for 10 years or more; para. (*a*.1), an indictable offence in the commission of which violence is used, threatened or attempted against a current or former intimate partner, child or parent of a current or former intimate partner, or any person residing with any such individuals; paras. (*b*) and (*c*), an offence under certain specified offences in this part, under s. 264 [criminal harrassment] and under certain provisions of the *Controlled Drugs and Substances Act*; and para. (*d*), an offence that involves, or the subject-matter of which is, a firearm, a cross-bow, a prohibited weapon, a restricted weapon, a prohibited device, any ammunition, any prohibited ammunition or an explosive substance and, at the time of the offence, the person was prohibited by any order made under the Code any other Act of Parliament from possessing any such thing. Where the circumstances do not fit within one of these categories, reference should be made to s. 110.

The section envisages two types of orders. The offender will be subject to a lifetime prohibition in relation to prohibited firearms, restricted firearms, prohibited weapons, prohibited devices and prohibited ammunition. The offender will be subject to a 10-year prohibition with respect to other firearms, restricted weapons, cross-bows, ammunition and explosive substances in the case of a first offence to which the order relates. For second and subsequent offences the order for these articles is for life. As to other conditions that may be included in the order, see ss. 113 to 116. The 10-year period is calculated in accordance with subsec. (4) from the date the offender is released from confinement after conviction for the offence or the date of the conviction or discharge if no term of imprisonment is imposed.

ANNOTATIONS

Note: Some of the following cases were decided under the predecessor legislation but were thought to be of some assistance in applying this section.

Constitutional Considerations – The mandatory firearms prohibition under subsec. (1)(*c*) for a conviction for the production of cannabis does not violate s. 12 of the *Canadian Charter of Rights and Freedoms* as the provision has a legitimate connection to s. 7 offences pursuant to the *Controlled Drugs and Substances Act*: *R. v. Wiles* (2005), 203 C.C.C. (3d) 161 (S.C.C.).

Circumstances in which order must be made – An order was to be made under former s. 100(1) [similar to present subsec. (1)(*a*)] whether or not a firearm was used in the commission of the offence: *R. v. Savard* (1979), 55 C.C.C. (2d) 286 (Que. C.A.); *R. v. Broome* (1981), 63 C.C.C. (2d) 426 (Ont. C.A.).

Further, the order must be made even where the commission of violence is not an essential element of the offence (as in break and enter with intent to commit an indictable offence under s. 348), it being sufficient that violence occurred in a manner which was closely related to the commission of the offence: *R. v. Howard* (1981), 60 C.C.C. (2d) 344 (B.C.C.A.).

Sex with a child always involves a violent assault notwithstanding that, in this case, other than pleading with the child, the accused did not use any other form of coercion or force. No other form of violence or threat is required where a child's sexual integrity has been compromised: *R. v. Bossé* (2005), 201 C.C.C. (3d) 77 (N.B.C.A.).

The phrase "against a person" refers to a person other than the accused and thus this subsection does not apply where the offence arises out of a suicide attempt and violence was not used against any other person: *R. v. Vandermeulen* (1986), 33 C.C.C. (3d) 286 (B.C.C.A.).

In ordering a weapons prohibition, reasons should be given specifying clearly the weapons to which the prohibition extends, whether the basis of a prohibition for life is under subsec. (2)(*b*) or (3) and, if the prohibition is under subsec. (3), the court must be satisfied that the notice to the accused has been given by the Crown. The failure to provide reasons constitutes an error of law: *R. v. Friesen* (2004), 192 C.C.C. (3d) 67 (Man. C.A.).

The prohibition under subsec. (1) is mandatory, notwithstanding the prosecutor's failure to apply for an order: *R. v. Goguen* (2006), 208 C.C.C. (3d) 181 (N.B.C.A.).

Making of order where previous conviction – The mandatory prohibition is to be imposed even where the previous conviction for an offence, in the commission of which violence was used, threatened or attempted was registered prior to the proclamation of the section: *R. v. Keays* (1983), 10 C.C.C. (3d) 229 (Ont. C.A.).

Where the Crown seeks the longer prohibition for a subsequent conviction, it must give notice as required by former s. 665 [now s. 727]: *R. v. Jobb* (1988), 43 C.C.C. (3d) 476 (Sask. C.A.); *R. v. Ellis* (2001), 143 O.A.C. 43 (C.A.).

DISCRETIONARY PROHIBITION ORDER / Duration of prohibition order / Exception / Reasons / Definition of "release from imprisonment" / Application of ss. 113 to 117.

110. (1) Where a person is convicted, or discharged under section 730, of

> **(*a*) an offence, other than an offence referred to in any of paragraphs 109(1)(*a*) to (*c*), in the commission of which violence against a person was used, threatened or attempted, or**

> **(*b*) an offence that involves, or the subject-matter of which is, a firearm, a cross-bow, a prohibited weapon, a restricted weapon, a prohibited device, ammunition, prohibited ammunition or an explosive substance and, at the time of the offence, the person was not prohibited by any order made under this Act or any other Act of Parliament from possessing any such thing,**

the court that sentences the person or directs that the person be discharged, as the case may be, shall, in addition to any other punishment that may be imposed for that offence or any other condition prescribed in the order of discharge, consider whether it is desirable, in the interests of the safety of the person or of any other person, to make an order prohibiting the person from possessing any firearm, cross-bow, prohibited weapon, restricted weapon, prohibited device, ammunition, prohibited ammunition or explosive substance, or all such things, and where the court decides that it is so desirable, the court shall so order.

(2) An order made under subsection (1) against a person begins on the day on which the order is made and ends not later than ten years after the person's release from imprisonment after conviction for the offence to which the order relates or, if the person is not then imprisoned or subject to imprisonment, after the person's conviction for or discharge from the offence.

(2.1) Despite subsection (2), an order made under subsection (1) may be imposed for life or for any shorter duration if, in the commission of the offence, violence was used, threatened or attempted against

> **(*a*) the person's current or former intimate partner;**

> **(*b*) a child or parent of the person or of anyone referred to in paragraph (*a*); or**

(*c*) **any person who resides with the person or with anyone referred to in paragraph (*a*) or (*b*).**

(3) Where the court does not make an order under subsection (1), or where the court does make such an order but does not prohibit the possession of everything referred to in that subsection, the court shall include in the record a statement of the court's reasons for not doing so.

(4) In subsection (2), "release from imprisonment" means release from confinement by reason of expiration of sentence, commencement of statutory release or grant of parole.

(5) Sections 113 to 117 apply in respect of every order made under subsection (1). 1995, c. 39, ss. 139, 190(*e*); 2015, c. 27, s. 31.

CROSS-REFERENCES

"Intimate partner" is defined in s. 110.1. "Firearm", "explosive substance" and "weapon" are defined in s. 2. "Prohibition order", "prohibited weapon", "restricted weapon", "prohibited device", "cross-bow", "ammunition" and "prohibited ammunition" are defined in s. 84(1). Possession is defined in s. 4(3). This is one of four provisions in this part that mandate or permit the imposition of orders prohibiting the possession of weapons and other articles such as explosive substances. There are, as well, other provisions of the Code authorizing various forms of prohibition orders. Thus see: s. 109 (mandatory prohibition order upon conviction of certain offences); s. 111 (preventative prohibition order); s. 117.05 (preventative prohibition order after seizure); s. 515(4.1) (condition of bail); s. 732.1 (condition of probation); s. 742.3 (conditional sentence), ss. 810(3.1), 810.01(5), 810.2(5) (condition of recognizance (peace bond)). A prohibition order may also be made under subsecs. 51(3) and (4) of the *Youth Criminal Justice Act*.

Section 117.01 creates the offences of possessing a firearm, cross-bow, prohibited weapon, restricted weapon, prohibited device, ammunition, prohibited ammunition or explosive substance while prohibited from doing so and wilfully failing to surrender an authorization, licence or registration certificate when the person was required to surrender it by any order made under the Code. Under s. 113, the judge may lift the prohibition order for sustenance or employment purposes. Section 114 permits the court that makes a prohibition order to require the person to surrender anything the possession of which is prohibited by the order and every authorization, licence and registration certificate relating to anything the possession of which is prohibited by the order. The person must be given a reasonable time to comply with the order and during that period the offence under s. 117.01 does not apply. Under s. 115, unless the prohibition order specifies otherwise, everything the possession of which is prohibited by the order is forfeited to the Crown. However, on application under s. 117, the judge may order the return of articles to the person who is lawfully entitled to possess it provided that the owner had no reasonable grounds to believe that the thing would or might be used in the commission of the offence in respect of which the prohibition order was made. Pursuant to s. 116, every authorization, licence and registration certificate relating to anything the possession of which is prohibited by a prohibition order and issued to a person against whom the prohibition order is made is, on the commencement of the prohibition order, revoked, or amended, as the case may be, to the extent of the prohibitions in the order. Section 117.011 allows for an application to a provincial court judge for a limitation on access order against a person who is an associate of, or cohabits with, a person subject to a prohibition order.

Section 89 of the *Firearms Act* requires a court that makes, varies or revokes a prohibition order to have the chief firearms officer informed of the order or its variation or revocation.

An order made under this section falls within the definition of "sentence" in ss. 673 and 785 and therefore may be appealed as a sentence appeal under Part XXI [indictable offence] or Part XXVII [summary conviction offence], as the case may be.

SYNOPSIS

This section gives a court a discretion to impose a prohibition against possession of firearms, weapons and other articles such as explosive substances where the accused has been convicted or discharged of an offence in circumstances not covered by the mandatory order under s. 109. Unlike s. 109, which involves a blanket order, the order under this section may prohibit the person from possessing any firearm, cross-bow, prohibited weapon, restricted weapon, prohibited device, ammunition, prohibited ammunition or explosive substance, or all such things. The maximum length of the order is 10 years calculated from the date of the conviction or discharge or the date from which the person was released from confinement as defined in subsec. (4), except in the case of an order made in the circumstances described in s. 110(2.1) (violence used, threatened or attempted against an intimate partner or relation thereof), which may be imposed for life. As to other conditions that may be included in the order, see ss. 113 to 116.

The prerequisite for making the prohibition order is the determination that the order is desirable in the interests of the safety of the offender or any other person. Where the court does not make the order or does not make a blanket order, the court must include reasons in the record.

ANNOTATIONS

This provision does not require actual violence or force and could operate where violence was merely threatened. In this case, breaching a no contact term of a recognizance could constitute an implied threat of violence: *R. v. Samery* (2007), 219 C.C.C. (3d) 435 (Ont. S.C.J.).

Before a weapons prohibition is imposed under this section, there must be some evidence of a safety concern. In some cases, the nature of the offence itself will be sufficient to raise a safety concern and justify a discretionary prohibition: *R. v. Wauer* (2014), 315 C.C.C. (3d) 170 (Alta. C.A.).

Sentencing principles such as proportionality apply to weapons prohibition orders: *R. v. Levesque* (2010), 264 C.C.C. (3d) 531 (P.E.I.C.A.).

DEFINITION OF "INTIMATE PARTNER".

110.1 In sections 109 and 110, "intimate partner" includes a spouse, a common-law partner and a dating partner. 2015, c. 27, s. 32.

CROSS-REFERENCES

"Common-law partner" is defined in s. 2.

APPLICATION FOR PROHIBITION ORDER / Date for hearing and notice / Hearing of application / Where hearing may proceed *ex parte* / Prohibition order / Reasons / Application of ss. 113 to 117 / Appeal by person or Attorney General / Appeal by Attorney General / Application of Part XXVII to appeals / Definition of "provincial court judge".

111. (1) A peace officer, firearms officer or chief firearms officer may apply to a provincial court judge for an order prohibiting a person from possessing any firearm, cross-bow, prohibited weapon, restricted weapon, prohibited device, ammunition, prohibited ammunition or explosive substance, or all such things, where the peace officer, firearms officer or chief firearms officer believes on reasonable grounds that it is not desirable in the interests of the safety of the person against whom the order is sought or of any other person that the person against whom the order is sought should possess any such thing.

(2) On receipt of an application made under subsection (1), the provincial court judge shall fix a date for the hearing of the application and direct that notice of the hearing be given, in such manner as the provincial court judge may specify, to the person against whom the order is sought.

(3) Subject to subsection (4), at the hearing of an application made under subsection (1), the provincial court judge shall hear all relevant evidence presented by or on behalf of the applicant and the person against whom the order is sought.

(4) A provincial court judge may proceed *ex parte* to hear and determine an application made under subsection (1) in the absence of the person against whom the order is sought in the same circumstances as those in which a summary conviction court may, under Part XXVII, proceed with a trial in the absence of the defendant.

(5) Where, at the conclusion of a hearing of an application made under subsection (1), the provincial court judge is satisfied that the circumstances referred to in that subsection exist, the provincial court judge shall make an order prohibiting the person from possessing any firearm, cross-bow, prohibited weapon, restricted weapon, prohibited device, ammunition, prohibited ammunition or explosive substance, or all such things, for such period, not exceeding five years, as is specified in the order, beginning on the day on which the order is made.

(6) Where a provincial court judge does not make an order under subsection (1), or where a provincial court judge does make such an order but does not prohibit the possession of everything referred to in that subsection, the provincial court judge shall include in the record a statement of the court's reasons.

(7) Sections 113 to 117 apply in respect of every order made under subsection (5).

(8) Where a provincial court judge makes an order under subsection (5), the person to whom the order relates, or the Attorney General, may appeal to the superior court against the order.

(9) Where a provincial court judge does not make an order under subsection (5), the Attorney General may appeal to the superior court against the decision not to make an order.

(10) The provisions of Part XXVII, except sections 785 to 812, 816 to 819 and 829 to 838, apply in respect of an appeal made under subsection (8) or (9), with such modifications as the circumstances require and as if each reference in that Part to the appeal court were a reference to the superior court.

(11) In this section and sections 112, 117.011 and 117.012, "provincial court judge" means a provincial court judge having jurisdiction in the territorial division where the person against whom the application for an order was brought resides. 1995, c. 39, s. 139.

CROSS-REFERENCES

"Attorney General", "firearm", "explosive substance", "peace officer" and "weapon" are defined in s. 2. "Superior court", "chief firearms officer", "prohibition order", "prohibited weapon", "restricted weapon", "prohibited device", "cross-bow", "ammunition" and "prohibited ammunition" are defined in s. 84(1). "Possession" is defined in s. 4(3). This is one of four provisions in this part that mandate or permit the imposition of orders prohibiting the possession of weapons and other articles such as explosive substances. There are, as well, other provisions of the Code authorizing various forms of prohibition orders. Thus see: s. 109 [mandatory prohibition order upon conviction of certain offences]; s. 110 [discretionary prohibition order upon conviction of certain offences]; s. 117.05 [preventative prohibition order after seizure]; s. 515(4.1) [condition of bail]; s. 732.1 [condition of probation]; s. 742.3 [conditional sentence], ss. 810(3.1), 810.01(5), 810.2(5) [condition of recognizance (peace bond)]. A prohibition order is also available under s. 51 of the *Youth Criminal Justice Act*.

Section 117.01 creates the offences of possessing a firearm, cross-bow, prohibited weapon, restricted weapon, prohibited device, ammunition, prohibited ammunition or explosive substance while prohibited from doing so and wilfully failing to surrender an authorization, licence or registration certificate when the person was required to surrender it by any order made under the Code. Under s. 113, the judge may lift the prohibition order for sustenance or employment purposes. Section 114 permits the court that makes a prohibition order to require the person to surrender anything the possession of which is prohibited by the order and every authorization, licence and registration certificate relating to anything the possession of which is prohibited by the order. The person must be given a reasonable time to comply with the order and during that period the offence under s. 117.01 does not apply. Under s. 115, unless the prohibition order specifies otherwise, everything the possession of which is prohibited by the order is forfeited to the Crown. However, on application under s. 117, the judge may order the return of articles to the person who is lawfully entitled to possess it. Pursuant to s. 116, every authorization, licence and registration certificate relating to anything the possession of which is prohibited by a prohibition order and issued to a person against whom the prohibition order is made is, on the commencement of the prohibition order, revoked, or amended, as the case may be, to the extent of the prohibitions in the order. Section 117.011 allows for an application to a provincial court judge for a limitation on access order against a person who is an associate of, or cohabits with, a person subject to a prohibition order.

As to the circumstances in which the judge can proceed *ex parte*, see s. 803(2).

Section 89 of the *Firearms Act* requires a court that makes, varies or revokes a prohibition order to have the chief firearms officer informed of the order or its variation or revocation.

Under s. 112, a provincial court judge may revoke an order made under subsec. (5).

SYNOPSIS

This section allows a peace officer, firearms officer or chief firearms officer to apply to a provincial court judge for a preventative prohibition order, *i.e.*, where the person has not committed an offence that would allow or require a prohibition order under either of s. 109 or s. 110. The grounds for making the application under subsec. (1) and the making of the order under subsec. (5) are that there are reasonable grounds to believe that it is not desirable in the interests of the safety of the person against whom the order is sought or of any other person that the person against whom the order is sought should possess any firearm, cross-bow, prohibited weapon, restricted weapon, prohibited device, ammunition, prohibited ammunition or explosive substance, or all such things. The maximum period of the order is five years. Subsection (2) requires the provincial court judge to fix a date for hearing the application and the manner in which the person is to be given notice of the hearing. The judge is to hear all relevant evidence adduced by the parties and may proceed *ex parte* if the same circumstances exist that would have permitted a judge to have proceeded with a summary conviction trial in the absence of the defendant. Where the judge does not make the order requested, or does not make a blanket order prohibiting possession of all the things referred to in subsec. (1), the judge must include reasons in the record. As to other conditions that may be included in the order, see ss. 113 to 116.

The decision of the judge may be appealed by the person against whom the order was made or the Attorney General to the superior court in accordance with the summary conviction appeal procedure in Part XXVII.

ANNOTATIONS

Note: Some of the following cases were decided under the predecessor to this section but may be of assistance in applying this section.

It was held that the predecessor legislation is *intra vires* Parliament: *R. v. Motiuk* (1981), 60 C.C.C. (2d) 161, 127 D.L.R. (3d) 146 (B.C.S.C.); *R. v. Anderson* (1981), 59 C.C.C. (2d) 439 (Ont. Co. Ct.), leave to appeal refused 1 C.C.C. (3d) 267 (Ont. C.A.).

The scheme of the pre-emptive prohibition is that a peace officer, acting on reasonable grounds, may apply to a provincial court judge for an order prohibiting a particular person from possessing a firearm. The peace officer is not required to act solely on the basis of evidence that would be admissible at trial. At the subsequent hearing, the provincial court judge must be satisfied that there are reasonable grounds to believe that it is not desirable, in the interests of the safety of the person or of others, that the subject of the prohibition application should possess a firearm. The provincial court judge thus confirms the existence of the reasonable grounds that led the peace officer to launch the application. It was not intended that the judge strictly applies the rules of evidence. Rather, the judge must simply be satisfied that the peace officer had reasonable grounds to believe as he did, that is, that there was an objective basis for the reasonable grounds on which the peace officer acted. Accordingly, hearsay evidence is admissible at a firearm prohibition hearing under this section. Frailties in the evidence are a matter of weight. In considering what weight to attach to hearsay evidence, the judge should take into account the explanation, if any, for not making the best evidence available. Further, the Crown bears the burden of proof and, in considering the weight of the evidence, a judge must scrutinize the evidence to ensure that it is credible and trustworthy: *R. v. Zeolkowski*, [1989] 1 S.C.R. 1378, 50 C.C.C. (3d) 566, 69 C.R. (3d) 281 (5:0).

A judge conducting a hearing under this provision is not limited to considering only the three criteria set out in s. 5(2) of the *Firearms Act*, S.C. 1995, c. 39: *Christiansen (Re)* (2006), 208 C.C.C. (3d) 154 (B.C.C.A.).

REVOCATION OF PROHIBITION ORDER UNDER S. 111(5).

112. A provincial court judge may, on application by the person against whom an order is made under subsection 111(5), revoke the order if satisfied that the circumstances for which it was made have ceased to exist. 1995, c. 39, s. 139.

CROSS-REFERENCES

"Provincial court judge" is defined in s. 111. Section 111(5) allows a provincial court judge to make a preventative prohibition order for a period not exceeding five years where the judge is satisfied that there are reasonable grounds to believe that it is not desirable in the interests of the safety of the person against whom the order is sought or of any other person that the person against whom the order is sought should possess any firearm, cross-bow, prohibited weapon, restricted weapon, prohibited device, ammunition, prohibited ammunition or explosive substance, or all such things. Section 89 of the *Firearms Act* requires a court that makes, varies or revokes a prohibition order to have the chief firearms officer informed of the order or its variation or revocation.

LIFTING OF PROHIBITION ORDER FOR SUSTENANCE OR EMPLOYMENT / Factors / Effect of order / When order can be made / Meaning of "competent authority".

113. (1) Where a person who is or will be a person against whom a prohibition order is made establishes to the satisfaction of a competent authority that

> **(a) the person needs a firearm or restricted weapon to hunt or trap in order to sustain the person or the person's family, or**
>
> **(b) a prohibition order against the person would constitute a virtual prohibition against employment in the only vocation open to the person,**

the competent authority may, notwithstanding that the person is or will be subject to a prohibition order, make an order authorizing a chief firearms officer or the Registrar to issue, in accordance with such terms and conditions as the competent authority considers appropriate, an authorization, a licence or a registration certificate, as the case may be, to the person for sustenance or employment purposes.

(2) A competent authority may make an order under subsection (1) only after taking the following factors into account:

> **(a) the criminal record, if any, of the person;**
>
> **(b) the nature and circumstances of the offence, if any, in respect of which the prohibition order was or will be made; and**
>
> **(c) the safety of the person and of other persons.**

(3) Where an order is made under subsection (1),

(*a*) an authorization, a licence or a registration certificate may not be denied to the person in respect of whom the order was made solely on the basis of a prohibition order against the person or the commission of an offence in respect of which a prohibition order was made against the person; and

(*b*) an authorization and a licence may, for the duration of the order, be issued to the person in respect of whom the order was made only for sustenance or employment purposes and, where the order sets out terms and conditions, only in accordance with those terms and conditions, but, for greater certainty, the authorization or licence may also be subject to terms and conditions set by the chief firearms officer that are not inconsistent with the purpose for which it is issued and any terms and conditions set out in the order.

(4) For greater certainty, an order under subsection (1) may be made during proceedings for an order under subsection 109(1), 110(1), 111(5), 117.05(4) or 515(2), paragraph 732.1(3)(*d*) or subsection 810(3).

(5) In this section, "competent authority" means the competent authority that made or has jurisdiction to make the prohibition order. 1995, c. 39, ss. 139, 190(*f*).

CROSS-REFERENCES

"Firearm" is defined in s. 2. "Possession" is defined in s. 4(3). "Prohibition order", "restricted weapon", "Registrar", "chief firearms officer, "licence", "registration certificate" and "authorization" are defined in s. 84(1).

SYNOPSIS

This section permits the justice or judge who made or had jurisdiction to make a prohibition order to lift the prohibition order for the purposes of sustenance hunting and trapping or for employment where the prohibition order would constitute a virtual prohibition against employment in the only vocation open to the person. The entire order is not lifted, rather the Registrar and chief firearms officer are required to issue an authorization, licence or registration certificate, as the case may be, for the purposes specified in the order and on the conditions and terms specified by the court. However, the chief firearms officer may also impose terms and conditions not inconsistent with the purpose for which the authorization or licence was issued. The order may only be made after the court has taken into account the person's criminal record, the nature and circumstances of the offence, if any, that led to the prohibition order and the safety of that person or any other person. While subsec. (4) specifies "for greater certainty" that an order may be made under this section during proceedings for a prohibition order under certain specified provisions, the term "prohibition order" is broadly defined in s. 84(1), and thus this section likely applies to other weapons prohibition orders made under the Code.

REQUIREMENT TO SURRENDER.

114. A competent authority that makes a prohibition order against a person may, in the order, require the person to surrender to a peace officer, a firearms officer or a chief firearms officer

(*a*) any thing the possession of which is prohibited by the order that is in the possession of the person on the commencement of the order, and

(*b*) every authorization, licence and registration certificate relating to any thing the possession of which is prohibited by the order that is held by the person on the commencement of the order,

and where the competent authority does so, it shall specify in the order a reasonable period for surrendering such things and documents and during which section 117.01 does not apply to that person. 1995, c. 39, s. 139.

CROSS-REFERENCES

"Peace officer" is defined in s. 2. "Prohibition order, "firearms officer", "chief firearms officer", "licence", "registration certificate" and "authorization" are defined in s. 84(1). "Competent authority" is defined in s. 113(5). Section 117.01 creates the offences of possessing a firearm, cross-bow, prohibited weapon, restricted weapon, prohibited device, ammunition, prohibited ammunition or explosive substance while prohibited from doing so and wilfully failing to surrender an authorization, licence or registration certificate when the person was required to surrender it by any order made under the Code. A person may be prohibited from possessing weapons under several sections of the Code including: s. 109 [mandatory prohibition order upon conviction of certain offences]; s. 110 [discretionary prohibition order upon conviction of certain offences]; s. 111 [preventative prohibition order]; s. 117.05 [preventative prohibition order after seizure]; s. 515(4.1) [condition of bail]; s. 732.1 [condition of probation]; s. 742.3 [conditional sentence], ss. 810(3.1), 810.01(5), 810.2(5) [condition of recognizance (peace bond)]. A prohibition order is also available under s. 51 of the *Youth Criminal Justice Act*.

SYNOPSIS

This section allows the "competent authority", which could include a justice or judge, that makes a prohibition order to include conditions requiring the surrender of anything the possession of which is prohibited by the order and to surrender any authorization, licence or registration certificate relating to any such thing. The order is to give the person a reasonable period for surrendering such things and documents and no offence contrary to s. 117.01 is committed during that time. Prohibition order is broadly defined in s. 84(1), and thus would include not only orders made under this part but orders under ss. 515(4.1), 732.1, 810(3.1) and 810.2(5).

FORFEITURE / Disposal.

115. (1) Unless a prohibition order against a person specifies otherwise, every thing the possession of which is prohibited by the order that, on the commencement of the order, is in the possession of the person is forfeited to Her Majesty.

(1.1) Subsection (1) does not apply in respect of an order made under section 515.

(2) Every thing forfeited to Her Majesty under subsection (1) shall be disposed of or otherwise dealt with as the Attorney General directs. 1995, c. 39, s. 139; 2003, c. 8, s. 5.

CROSS-REFERENCES

"Prohibition order" is defined in s. 84(1). "Attorney General" is defined in s. 2.

ANNOTATIONS

While a term of probation made under s. 732.1(3)(*d*) of the Code was a prohibition order for the purpose of this section and s. 84, this provision did not apply as the accused could not be said to be in possession of the firearms at the commencement of the order as they were in the possession of the police. The appropriate procedure is for the Crown to seek a forfeiture order under s. 491: *Roggie v. Ontario* (2012), 293 C.C.C. (3d) 46 (Ont. C.A.).

AUTHORIZATIONS REVOKED OR AMENDED / Duration of revocation or amendment — orders under s. 115.

116. (1) Subject to subsection (2), every authorization, licence and registration certificate relating to any thing the possession of which is prohibited by a prohibition order and issued to a person against whom the prohibition order is made is, on the commencement of the prohibition order, revoked, or amended, as the case may be, to the extent of the prohibitions in the order.

(2) An authorization, a licence and a registration certificate relating to a thing the possession of which is prohibited by an order made under section 515 is revoked, or amended, as the case may be, only in respect of the period during which the order is in force. 1995, c. 39, s. 139; 2003, c. 8, s. 6.

CROSS-REFERENCES

"Authorization", "licence", "registration certificate" and "prohibition order" are defined in s. 84(1). Possession is defined in s. 4(3). Failure to surrender a licence, registration certificate or authorization that is revoked is an offence contrary to s. 114 of the *Firearms Act*.

SYNOPSIS

This section deems any authorization, licence or registration certificate relating to anything the possession of which is prohibited by a prohibition order and issued to a person against whom the prohibition order is made, is to be revoked, or amended, as the case may be, to the extent of the prohibitions in the order.

RETURN TO OWNER.

117. Where the competent authority that makes a prohibition order or that would have had jurisdiction to make the order is, on application for an order under this section, satisfied that a person, other than the person against whom a prohibition order was or will be made,

> **(a) is the owner of any thing that is or may be forfeited to Her Majesty under subsection 115(1) and is lawfully entitled to possess it, and**
>
> **(b) in the case of a prohibition order under subsection 109(1) or 110(1), had no reasonable grounds to believe that the thing would or might be used in the commission of the offence in respect of which the prohibition order was made,**

the competent authority shall order that the thing be returned to the owner or the proceeds of any sale of the thing be paid to that owner or, if the thing was destroyed, that an amount equal to the value of the thing be paid to the owner. 1995, c. 39, s. 139.

CROSS-REFERENCES

"Prohibition order" is defined in s. 84(1).

SYNOPSIS

The true owner of articles subject to a prohibition order may apply to a judge or justice who made a prohibition order, or who would have had jurisdiction to make the order for return of the articles. The applicant cannot be the person against whom the order was made and must show that he or she is the owner and is lawfully entitled to possess it. Further, in the case of the prohibition orders made under ss. 109 and 110 as a result of the commission of an offence, the applicant must show that he or she had no reasonable grounds to believe that the article would or might be used in the commission of the offence. If the article has been sold, the owner is entitled to the proceeds of the sale. If it has been destroyed, the owner is entitled to an amount equal to its value.

POSSESSION CONTRARY TO ORDER / Failure to surrender authorization, etc. / Punishment / Exception.

117.01 (1) Subject to subsection (4), every person commits an offence who possesses a firearm, a cross-bow, a prohibited weapon, a restricted weapon, a prohibited device, any ammunition, any prohibited ammunition or an explosive substance while the person is prohibited from doing so by any order made under this Act or any other Act of Parliament.

(2) Every person commits an offence who wilfully fails to surrender to a peace officer, a firearms officer or a chief firearms officer any authorization, licence or registration certificate held by the person when the person is required to do so by any order made under this Act or any other Act of Parliament.

(3) Every person who commits an offence under subsection (1) or (2)

    (*a*) is guilty of an indictable offence and liable to imprisonment for a term not exceeding ten years; or

    (*b*) is guilty of an offence punishable on summary conviction.

(4) Subsection (1) does not apply to a person who possessed a firearm in accordance with an authorization or licence issued to the person as the result of an order made under subsection 113(1). 1995, c. 39, s. 139.

CROSS-REFERENCES

"Firearm", "explosive substance" and "peace officer" are defined in s. 2. "Possession" is defined in s. 4(3). "Prohibited weapon", "restricted weapon", "prohibited device", "prohibited ammunition", "cross-bow", "firearms officer", "chief firearms officer, "licence", "registration certificate" and "authorization" are defined in s. 84(1). "Provincial court judge" is defined in s. 2. An accused charged with this offence may elect the mode of trial pursuant to s. 536(2) where the Crown proceeds by way of indictment. Where the prosecution elects to proceed by way of summary conviction then the trial of this offence is conducted by a summary conviction court pursuant to Part XXVII. The punishment for the offence is then as set out in s. 787 and the limitation period is set out in s. 786(2). Weapons that are the subject-matter of the offence must be forfeited pursuant to s. 491. An accused convicted of the offence under subsec. (2) is subject to the mandatory prohibition order under s. 109.

A person may be prohibited from possessing weapons under several sections of the Code including: s. 109 [mandatory prohibition order upon conviction of certain offences]; s. 110 [discretionary prohibition order upon conviction of certain offences]; s. 111 [preventative prohibition order]; s. 117.05 [preventative prohibition order after seizure]; s. 515(4.1) [condition of bail]; s. 732.1 [condition of probation]; s. 742.3 [conditional sentence]; and ss. 810(3.1), 810.01(5), 810.2(5) [condition of recognizance (peace bond)]. A prohibition order is also available under s. 51 of the *Youth Criminal Justice Act*. Section 114 permits the court that makes a prohibition order to require the person to surrender anything the possession of which is prohibited by the order and every authorization, licence and registration certificate relating to anything the possession of which is prohibited by the order. The person must be given a reasonable time to comply with the order and during that period this section does not apply. Section 113 allows the court to lift the prohibition order for sustenance or employment purposes. The related offence of failing to surrender a licence, authorization or registration certificate that has been revoked is found in s. 114 of the *Firearms Act*.

SYNOPSIS

This section creates two offences to deal with persons who fail to comply with the terms of a prohibition order made under the Code or other federal legislation. Subsection (1) makes it an offence to possess any firearm, cross-bow, prohibited weapon, restricted weapon, prohibited device, ammunition, prohibited ammunition or explosive substance while prohibited from doing so. No offence is committed under this subsection if the person has possession of a firearm in accordance with an authorization or licence issued pursuant to an order made under s. 113 for sustenance or employment purposes. Subsection (2) makes it an offence to wilfully fail to surrender an authorization, licence or registration certificate when the person was required to surrender it by any order made under the Code (such as s. 114) or other federal legislation.

ANNOTATIONS

In the absence of evidence of present operability through firing, by virtue of missing or broken parts or modifications, expert evidence is required to establish that the gun is a firearm: *R. v. Stacey* (2009), 249 C.C.C. (3d) 389, 292 Nfld. & P.E.I.R. 140 (Nfld. & Lab. C.A.).

Limitations on Access

APPLICATION FOR ORDER / Date for hearing and notice / Hearing of application / Where hearing may proceed *ex parte* / Order / Terms and conditions / Appeal by person or Attorney General / Appeal by Attorney General / Application of Part XXVII to appeals.

117.011 (1) A peace officer, firearms officer or chief firearms officer may apply to a provincial court judge for an order under this section where the peace officer, firearms officer or chief firearms officer believes on reasonable grounds that

    (*a*) **the person against whom the order is sought cohabits with, or is an associate of, another person who is prohibited by any order made under this Act or any other Act of Parliament from possessing any firearm, cross-bow, prohibited weapon, restricted weapon, prohibited device, ammunition, prohibited ammunition or explosive substance, or all such things; and**

    (*b*) **the other person would or might have access to any such thing that is in the possession of the person against whom the order is sought.**

(2) On receipt of an application made under subsection (1), the provincial court judge shall fix a date for the hearing of the application and direct that notice of the hearing be given, in such manner as the provincial court judge may specify, to the person against whom the order is sought.

(3) Subject to subsection (4), at the hearing of an application made under subsection (1), the provincial court judge shall hear all relevant evidence presented by or on behalf of the applicant and the person against whom the order is sought.

(4) A provincial court judge may proceed *ex parte* to hear and determine an application made under subsection (1) in the absence of the person against whom the order is sought in the same circumstances as those in which a summary conviction court may, under Part XXVII, proceed with a trial in the absence of the defendant.

(5) Where, at the conclusion of a hearing of an application made under subsection (1), the provincial court judge is satisfied that the circumstances referred to in that subsection exist, the provincial court judge shall make an order in respect of the person against whom the order was sought imposing such terms and conditions on the person's use and possession of anything referred to in subsection (1) as the provincial court judge considers appropriate.

(6) In determining terms and conditions under subsection (5), the provincial court judge shall impose terms and conditions that are the least intrusive as possible, bearing in mind the purpose of the order.

(7) Where a provincial court judge makes an order under subsection (5), the person to whom the order relates, or the Attorney General, may appeal to the superior court against the order.

(8) Where a provincial court judge does not make an order under subsection (5), the Attorney General may appeal to the superior court against the decision not to make an order.

(9) The provisions of Part XXVII, except sections 785 to 812, 816 to 819 and 829 to 838, apply in respect of an appeal made under subsection (7) or (8), with such modifications

as the circumstances require and as if each reference in that Part to the appeal court were a reference to the superior court. 1995, c. 39, s. 139.

CROSS-REFERENCES

"Attorney General", "firearm", "explosive substance", "peace officer" and "weapon" are defined in s. 2. "Superior court", "chief firearms officer", "prohibition order", "prohibited weapon", "restricted weapon", "prohibited device", "cross-bow", "ammunition" and "prohibited ammunition" are defined in s. 84(1). Possession is defined in s. 4(3). This section should be read with the provisions of the Code that permit a court to make a prohibition order. Thus see: s. 109 [mandatory prohibition order upon conviction of certain offences]; s. 110 [discretionary prohibition order upon conviction of certain offences]; s. 111 [preventative prohibition order]; s. 117.05 [preventative prohibition order after seizure]; s. 515(4.1) [condition of bail]; s. 732.1 [condition of probation]; s. 742.3 [conditional sentence]; and ss. 810(3.1), 810.01(5), 810.2(5) [condition of recognizance (peace bond)]. A prohibition order is also available under s. 51 of the *Youth Criminal Justice Act*.

Under s. 117.012, a provincial court judge may revoke an order made under subsec. (5).

SYNOPSIS

This section allows a peace officer, firearms officer or chief firearms officer to apply to a provincial court judge for a limitation on access order, *i.e.*, where the respondent cohabits or associates with a person who is subject to a prohibition order. The grounds for making the application under subsec. (1) and the making of the order under subsec. (5) are that there are reasonable grounds to believe that the person against whom the order is sought, cohabits with, or is an associate of, another person who is prohibited by any order made under the Code or any other Act of Parliament from possessing any firearm, cross-bow, prohibited weapon, restricted weapon, prohibited device, ammunition, prohibited ammunition or explosive substance, or all such things, and that the other person would or might have access to any such thing that is in the possession of the person against whom the order is sought. Subsection (2) requires the provincial court judge to fix a date for hearing the application and the manner in which the person is to be given notice of the hearing. The judge is to hear all relevant evidence adduced by the parties and may proceed *ex parte* if the same circumstances exist that would have permitted a judge to have proceeded with a summary conviction trial in the absence of the defendant.

If the judge decides to make the order, he or she shall impose terms and conditions on the respondent's use and possession of his weapons and other things referred to in subsec. (1). The judge is required by subsec. (6) to impose the least intrusive terms and conditions.

The decision of the judge may be appealed by the person against whom the order was made, or by the Attorney General, to the superior court in accordance with the summary conviction appeal procedure in Part XXVII.

REVOCATION OF ORDER UNDER S. 117.011.

117.012 A provincial court judge may, on application by the person against whom an order is made under subsection 117.011(5), revoke the order if satisfied that the circumstances for which it was made have ceased to exist. 1995, c. 39, s. 139.

CROSS-REFERENCES

"Provincial court judge" is defined in s. 111.

SYNOPSIS

This section allows a person who has been the subject of a limitation on access order to apply to have the order revoked. The judge may revoke the order if the circumstances have changed, in that the circumstances for which it was originally made under s. 117.011

have ceased to exist. This is not an appeal section. An appeal of s. 117.011 must be taken to the superior court in accordance with s. 117.011(7).

Search and Seizure

SEARCH AND SEIZURE WITHOUT WARRANT WHERE OFFENCE COMMITTED / Disposition of seized things.

117.02 (1) Where a peace officer believes on reasonable grounds

    (*a*) **that a weapon, an imitation firearm, a prohibited device, any ammunition, any prohibited ammunition or an explosive substance was used in the commission of an offence, or**

    (*b*) **that an offence is being committed, or has been committed, under any provision of this Act that involves, or the subject-matter of which is, a firearm, an imitation firearm, a cross-bow, a prohibited weapon, a restricted weapon, a prohibited device, ammunition, prohibited ammunition or an explosive substance,**

and evidence of the offence is likely to be found on a person, in a vehicle or in any place or premises other than a dwelling-house, the peace officer may, where the conditions for obtaining a warrant exist but, by reason of exigent circumstances, it would not be practicable to obtain a warrant, search, without warrant, the person, vehicle, place or premises, and seize any thing by means of or in relation to which that peace officer believes on reasonable grounds the offence is being committed or has been committed.

(2) Any thing seized pursuant to subsection (1) shall be dealt with in accordance with sections 490 and 491. 1995, c. 39, s. 139.

CROSS-REFERENCES

The terms "imitation firearm", "prohibited weapon", "restricted weapon", "prohibited device", "cross-bow", "ammunition" and "prohibited ammunition" are defined in s. 84(1). "Dwelling house", "peace officer", "explosive substance", "weapon" and "firearm" are defined in s. 2. Search of a dwelling house would have to be pursuant to a warrant as authorized by s. 487 or s. 487.1. Section 117.04 provides for the issuance of a search warrant or for a warrantless search where there are grounds for believing that it is not desirable in the interests of safety for a person to have possession, custody or control of a firearm, offensive weapon, ammunition or explosive substance. Seizure of weapons and other regulated articles is also authorized in certain circumstances under s. 117.03. Reference should also be made to s. 8 of the *Canadian Charter of Rights and Freedoms*. A person searched pursuant to this section would be detained within the meaning of s. 10 of the Charter and, therefore, see the notes under that section. Use of force in enforcement of the law is principally dealt with in s. 25. Obstructing a peace officer in the execution of his or her duty is an offence under s. 129 and assaulting a peace officer in the execution of his or her duty is an offence under s. 270.

SYNOPSIS

This section authorizes a search without warrant of persons, vehicles or places, other than dwelling houses, in two different circumstances where the peace officer has reasonable grounds to believe: subsec. (1)(*a*), that a weapon, an imitation firearm, a prohibited device, any ammunition, any prohibited ammunition or an explosive substance was used in the commission of an offence; and subsec. (1)(*b*), an offence is being committed, or has been committed under the Code that involves, or the subject-matter of which is, a firearm, an imitation firearm, a cross-bow, a prohibited weapon, a restricted weapon, a prohibited device, ammunition, prohibited ammunition or an explosive substance. This section applies if the peace officer has reasonable grounds to believe that evidence of the offence is likely to be found but exigent circumstances make the obtaining of a warrant impracticable.

Subsection (2) states that the usual procedures making a return before a justice after the search and the restitution or forfeiture of property seized apply to this type of search.

ANNOTATIONS

This provision does not require reasonable grounds to make an arrest but merely requires a reasonable belief that an offence has been committed and that the evidence is likely to be found in the search: *R. v. V. (T.A.)* (2001), 48 C.R. (5th) 366, (Alta. C.A.).

SEIZURE ON FAILURE TO PRODUCE AUTHORIZATION / Return of seized thing on production of authorization / Forfeiture of seized thing.

117.03 (1) Despite section 117.02, a peace officer who finds

  (*a*) **a person in possession of a prohibited firearm, a restricted firearm or a non-restricted firearm who fails, on demand, to produce, for inspection by the peace officer, an authorization or a licence under which the person may lawfully possess the firearm and, in the case of a prohibited firearm or a restricted firearm, a registration certificate for it, or**

  (*b*) **a person in possession of a prohibited weapon, a restricted weapon, a prohibited device or any prohibited ammunition who fails, on demand, to produce, for inspection by the peace officer, an authorization or a licence under which the person may lawfully possess it,**

may seize the firearm, prohibited weapon, restricted weapon, prohibited device or prohibited ammunition unless its possession by the person in the circumstances in which it is found is authorized by any provision of this Part, or the person is under the direct and immediate supervision of another person who may lawfully possess it.

(2) If a person from whom any thing is seized under subsection (1) claims the thing within 14 days after the seizure and produces for inspection by the peace officer by whom it was seized, or any other peace officer having custody of it,

  (*a*) **a licence under which the person is lawfully entitled to possess it, and**

  (*b*) **in the case of a prohibited firearm or a restricted firearm, an authorization and registration certificate for it,**

the thing shall without delay be returned to that person.

(3) Where any thing seized pursuant to subsection (1) is not claimed and returned as and when provided by subsection (2), a peace officer shall forthwith take the thing before a provincial court judge, who may, after affording the person from whom it was seized or its owner, if known, an opportunity to establish that the person is lawfully entitled to possess it, declare it to be forfeited to Her Majesty, to be disposed of or otherwise dealt with as the Attorney General directs. 1995, c. 39, s. 139; 2012, c. 6, s. 8; 2015, c. 27, s. 33.

CROSS-REFERENCES

"Attorney General", "firearm", "provincial court judge" and "peace officer" are defined in s. 2. "Possession" is defined in s. 4(3). "Authorization", "licence", "registration certificate", "restricted firearm", "prohibited firearm", "non-restricted firearm", "prohibited weapon", "restricted weapon", "prohibited device" and "prohibited ammunition" are defined in s. 84(1). This section deals only with seizure. Other provisions under this part and in the Code, as well as the common law, provide for the search of persons and places. See, in particular, s. 117.02, which provides for a warrantless search and seizure power. As well, s. 117.04 provides for the issuance of a search warrant or for a warrantless search where there are grounds for believing that it is not desirable in the interests of safety for a person to have possession, custody or control of a weapon and other articles. Reference should also be made to s. 8 of the *Canadian Charter of Rights and Freedoms*.

SYNOPSIS

This provision permits the warrantless seizure of certain types of weapons, firearms and other regulated items where the person fails to produce the authorization, licence or registration certificate that allows the person to lawfully possess the article upon demand, unless possession of the article in the circumstances in which it is found is authorized under this part, or the person is under the direct and immediate supervision of another person who may lawfully possess it. Subsection (2) requires the return of the article if the requisite authorization, licence or registration certificate is produced within 14 days after the seizure.

If the weapon or firearm is not returned pursuant to subsec. (2), the police shall bring the article to a provincial court judge for forfeiture. The person from whom the article is seized, or the owner of the weapon, has the opportunity to establish that he or she had lawful possession of the weapon.

APPLICATION FOR WARRANT TO SEARCH AND SEIZE / Search and seizure without warrant / Return to justice / Authorizations, etc., revoked.

117.04 (1) Where, pursuant to an application made by a peace officer with respect to any person, a justice is satisfied by information on oath that there are reasonable grounds to believe that the person possesses a weapon, a prohibited device, ammunition, prohibited ammunition or an explosive substance in a building, receptacle or place and that it is not desirable in the interests of the safety of the person, or of any other person, for the person to possess the weapon, prohibited device, ammunition, prohibited ammunition or explosive substance, the justice may issue a warrant authorizing a peace officer to search the building, receptacle or place and seize any such thing, and any authorization, licence or registration certificate relating to any such thing, that is held by or in the possession of the person.

(2) Where, with respect to any person, a peace officer is satisfied that there are reasonable grounds to believe that it is not desirable, in the interests of the safety of the person or any other person, for the person to possess any weapon, prohibited device, ammunition, prohibited ammunition or explosive substance, the peace officer may, where the grounds for obtaining a warrant under subsection (1) exist but, by reason of a possible danger to the safety of that person or any other person, it would not be practicable to obtain a warrant, search for and seize any such thing, and any authorization, licence or registration certificate relating to any such thing, that is held by or in the possession of the person.

(3) A peace officer who executes a warrant referred to in subsection (1) or who conducts a search without a warrant under subsection (2) shall forthwith make a return to the justice who issued the warrant or, if no warrant was issued, to a justice who might otherwise have issued a warrant, showing

(a) in the case of an execution of a warrant, the things or documents, if any, seized and the date of execution of the warrant; and

(b) in the case of a search conducted without a warrant, the grounds on which it was concluded that the peace officer was entitled to conduct the search, and the things or documents, if any, seized.

(4) Where a peace officer who seizes any thing under subsection (1) or (2) is unable at the time of the seizure to seize an authorization or a licence under which the person from whom the thing was seized may possess the thing and, in the case of a seized firearm, a registration certificate for the firearm, every authorization, licence and registration certificate held by the person is, as at the time of the seizure, revoked. 1995, c. 39, s. 139; 2004, c. 12, s. 3.

CROSS-REFERENCES

"Firearm", "explosive substance", "justice", "weapon" and "peace officer" are defined in s. 2. "Possession" is defined in s. 4(3). "Prohibited device", "ammunition", "prohibited ammunition", "licence", "registration certificate" and "authorization" are defined in s. 84(1). As to other cross-references respecting seizure of weapons and other regulated articles, see s. 117.02. Failing to surrender a licence, authorization or registration certificate that has been revoked is an offence under s. 114 of the *Firearms Act*. Application for the disposition of the seized things is made under s. 117.05. If no application is made, the things are dealt with under s. 117.06.

SYNOPSIS

This section deals primarily with the issuance of a warrant to seize firearms, etc., and the procedure for the disposition of the things so seized. Subsection (1) permits a peace officer to make an application to a justice for a warrant to search for and seize any weapon, prohibited device, ammunition, prohibited ammunition or explosive substance, and any authorization, licence or registration certificate relating to any such thing that is held by or in the possession of the person. It must be shown that there are reasonable grounds to believe that the weapon, prohibited device, ammunition, prohibited ammunition or explosive substance is in the place to be searched and that it is against the interests of the safety of the person in possession, control or custody of the weapons, etc., or any other person, for such possession to continue. Subsection (2) permits a warrantless search and seizure by a peace officer in the same circumstances as subsec. (1), if it is impractical, for reasons of safety, to obtain a warrant.

Subsection (3) requires a return to the justice after a seizure is made under either subsec. (1) or (2). If the search is made without warrant, the officer must also set out the grounds upon which the search was made and why the seizure of the objects is justified. Subsection (4) deems any licence, authorization and registration certificate relating to seized articles and which could not be seized at the time of the search to be revoked.

ANNOTATIONS

Note: The following case was decided under the predecessor legislation but may be of assistance in applying this provisions.

Subsection (1) – The bare, unsupported allegation that the persons were members of a motorcycle gang shown to be involved in violent criminal activity was not a sufficient basis for the issuance of a search warrant under this section. On the other hand, it may be that if it were shown that the persons wore the gang "colours" or insignia and thus were identified with the gang then there would be a basis for issuing the warrant: *R. v. Conrad* (1989), 51 C.C.C. (3d) 311, 72 C.R. (3d) 364 (Alta. C.A.).

Subsection (2) – It was impracticable to obtain a warrant because of a possible danger to the safety of the accused, notwithstanding that she was detained in a psychiatric facility under the authority of a Form 1. The accused could have been released from the hospital at any time. The police are not required to speculate upon the timing of the release from hospital before seizing the firearms without a warrant: *R. v. Peacock-McDonald* (2007), 218 C.C.C. (3d) 257, 46 C.R. (6th) 163 (Ont. C.A.).

APPLICATION FOR DISPOSITION / *Ex parte* hearing / Hearing of application / Forfeiture and prohibition order on finding / Reasons / Application of ss. 113 to 117 / Appeal by person / Appeal by Attorney General / Application of part XXVII to appeals.

117.05 (1) Where any thing or document has been seized under subsection 117.04(1) or (2), the justice who issued the warrant authorizing the seizure or, if no warrant was issued, a justice who might otherwise have issued a warrant, shall, on application for an order for the disposition of the thing or document so seized made by a peace officer within thirty days after the date of execution of the warrant or of the seizure without a warrant, as the case may be, fix a date for the hearing of the application and direct that notice of the hearing be given to such persons or in such manner as the justice may specify.

(2) A justice may proceed *ex parte* to hear and determine an application made under subsection (1) in the absence of the person from whom the thing or document was seized in the same circumstances as those in which a summary conviction court may, under Part XXVII, proceed with a trial in the absence of the defendant.

(3) At the hearing of an application made under subsection (1), the justice shall hear all relevant evidence, including evidence respecting the value of the thing in respect of which the application was made.

(4) Where, following the hearing of an application made under subsection (1), the justice finds that it is not desirable in the interests of the safety of the person from whom the thing was seized or of any other person that the person should possess any weapon, prohibited device, ammunition, prohibited ammunition and explosive substance, or any such thing, the justice shall

(*a*) order that any thing seized be forfeited to Her Majesty or be otherwise disposed of; and

(*b*) where the justice is satisfied that the circumstances warrant such an action, order that the possession by that person of any weapon, prohibited device, ammunition, prohibited ammunition and explosive substance, or of any such thing, be prohibited during any period, not exceeding five years, that is specified in the order, beginning on the making of the order.

(5) Where a justice does not make an order under subsection (4), or where a justice does make such an order but does not prohibit the possession of all of the things referred to in that subsection, the justice shall include in the record a statement of the justice's reasons.

(6) Sections 113 to 117 apply in respect of every order made under subsection (4).

(7) Where a justice makes an order under subsection (4) in respect of a person, or in respect of any thing that was seized from a person, the person may appeal to the superior court against the order.

(8) Where a justice does not make a finding as described in sbusection (4) following the hearing of an application under subsection (1), or makes the finding but does not make an order to the effect described in paragraph (4)(*b*), the Attorney General may appeal to the superior court against the failure to make the finding or to make an order to the effect so described.

(9) The provisions of Part XXVII, except sections 785 to 812, 816 to 819 and 829 to 838, apply in respect of an appeal made under subsection (7) or (8) with such modifications as the circumstances require and as if each reference in that Part to the appeal court were a reference to the superior court. 1995, c. 39, s. 139.

CROSS-REFERENCES

"Justice", "peace officer", "weapon", "explosive substance" and "Attorney General" are defined in s. 2. "Superior court", "prohibited device", "ammunition" and "prohibited ammunition" are defined in s. 84(1).

This is one of several provisions in this part and in the Code that authorize the making of a prohibition order. Thus see: s. 109 [mandatory prohibition order upon conviction of certain offences]; s. 110 [discretionary prohibition order upon conviction of certain offences]; s. 111 [preventative prohibition order]; s. 515(4.1) [condition of bail]; s. 732.1 [condition of probation]; s. 742.3 [conditional sentence]; and ss. 810(3.1), 810.01(5), 810.2(5) [condition of recognizance (peace bond)]. A prohibition order is also available under s. 51 of the *Youth Criminal Justice Act*.

Section 117.01 creates the offences of possessing a firearm, cross-bow, prohibited weapon, restricted weapon, prohibited device, ammunition, prohibited ammunition or explosive substance while prohibited from doing so and wilfully failing to surrender an authorization, licence or registration certificate when the person was required to surrender it by any order made under the Code. Under s. 113, the judge may lift the prohibition order for sustenance or employment purposes. Section 114 permits the court that makes a prohibition order to require the person to surrender anything the possession of which is prohibited by the order and every authorization, licence and registration certificate relating to anything the possession of which is prohibited by the order. The person must be given a reasonable time to comply with the order and during that period the offence under s. 117.01 does not apply. Under s. 115, unless the prohibition order specifies otherwise, everything the possession of which is prohibited by the order is forfeited to the Crown. However, on application under s. 117, the judge may order the return of articles to the person who is lawfully entitled to possess it. Pursuant to s. 116, every authorization, licence and registration certificate relating to anything the possession of which is prohibited by a prohibition order and issued to a person against whom the prohibition order is made is, on the commencement of the prohibition order, revoked, or amended, as the case may be, to the extent of the prohibitions in the order. Section 117.011 allows for an application to a provincial court judge for a limitation on access order against a person who is an associate of, or cohabits with, a person subject to a prohibition order.

Section 89 of the *Firearms Act* requires a court that makes, varies or revokes a prohibition order to have the chief firearms officer informed of the order or its variation or revocation.

This section sets out the procedure for disposition of items seized for public safety concerns under s. 117.04. Where no application is made under this section or the justice does not find that the seized things should be forfeited, they are dealt with in accordance with s. 117.06. As to the circumstances in which the judge can proceed *ex parte*, see s. 803(2).

SYNOPSIS

This section sets out the procedure for dealing with things seized either with or without warrant for public safety reasons under s. 117.04. The section contemplates two types of orders based on a finding that it is not desirable in the interests of safety that the person should possess any weapon, prohibited device, ammunition, prohibited ammunition or explosive substance, namely: subsec. (4)(*a*), forfeiture of the things seized; and subsec. (4)(*b*), an order prohibiting the person from possessing any weapon, prohibited device, ammunition, prohibited ammunition or explosive substance. The peace officer is required to make an application for an order under this section within 30 days of the seizure. The justice will then fix a date for the hearing and direct notice be given to persons and in the manner as the justice specifies. The judge is to hear all relevant evidence adduced by the parties and may proceed *ex parte* if the same circumstances exist that would have permitted a judge to have proceeded with a summary conviction trial in the absence of the defendant. Where the justice does not make the order requested, or does not make a blanket order prohibiting possession of all the things referred to in subsec. (4), the justice must include reasons in the record. The maximum period of the prohibition order is five years. As to other conditions that may be included in the order, see ss. 113 to 116.

The decision of the justice may be appealed by the person against whom the order was made or the Attorney General to the superior court in accordance with the summary conviction appeal procedure in Part XXVII.

ANNOTATIONS

It was held, considering the predecessor to this section [former s. 103(4)] that the warrant having been quashed, it was not open to the Crown to proceed with a disposition hearing and the firearms must be returned to their owners: *R. v. Merchant*, (1991), 64 C.C.C. (3d) 316 (Alta. C.A.).

As to the conduct of the hearing, see *R. v. Zeolkowski*, [1989] 1 S.C.R. 1378, 50 C.C.C. (3d) 566, noted under s. 111.

The public safety assessment under subsec. (4) is to be made from the perspective of the present day, not the time of the events giving rise to the application: *R. v. Douglas* (2013), 304 C.C.C. (3d) 318 (Ont. C.J.).

WHERE NO FINDING OR APPLICATION / Restoration of authorizations.

117.06 (1) Any thing or document seized pursuant to subsection 117.04(1) or (2) shall be returned to the person from whom it was seized if

    (*a*) no application is made under subsection 117.05(1) within thirty days after the date of execution of the warrant or of the seizure without a warrant, as the case may be; or

    (*b*) an application is made under subsection 117.05(1) within the period referred to in paragraph (*a*), and the justice does not make a finding as described in subsection 117.05(4).

(2) Where, pursuant to subsection (1), any thing is returned to the person from whom it was seized and an authorization, a licence or a registration certificate, as the case may be, is revoked pursuant to subsection 117.04(4), the justice referred to in paragraph (1)(*b*) may order that the revocation be reversed and that the authorization, licence or registration certificate be restored. 1995, c. 39, s. 139.

CROSS-REFERENCES

"Authorization", "licence" and "registration certificate" are defined in s. 84(1).

SYNOPSIS

Where no application is made under s. 117.05 following a seizure under s. 117.04, the things or documents are to be returned to the person from whom they were seized. They are also to be returned if an application is made but the judge does not find that it is not desirable in the interests of the safety of the person from whom the thing was seized or of any other person that the person should possess any weapon, prohibited device, ammunition, prohibited ammunition and explosive substance, or any such thing. In the latter case, the judge may also reverse the revocation of any licence, authorization or registration certificate and order that the documents be restored.

Exempted Persons

PUBLIC OFFICERS / Definition of "public officer".

117.07 (1) Notwithstanding any other provision of this Act, but subject to section 117.1, no public officer is guilty of an offence under this Act or the *Firearms Act* by reason only that the public officer

    (*a*) possesses a firearm, a prohibited weapon, a restricted weapon, a prohibited device, any prohibited ammunition or an explosive substance in the course of or for the purpose of the public officer's duties or employment;

    (*b*) manufactures or transfers, or offers to manufacture or transfer, a firearm, a prohibited weapon, a restricted weapon, a prohibited device, any ammunition or any prohibited ammunition in the course of the public officer's duties or employment;

    (*c*) exports or imports a firearm, a prohibited weapon, a restricted weapon, a prohibited device or any prohibited ammunition in the course of the public officer's duties or employment;

    (*d*) exports or imports a component or part designed exclusively for use in the manufacture of or assembly into an automatic firearm in the course of the public officer's duties or employment;

    (*e*) in the course of the public officer's duties or employment, alters a firearm so that it is capable of, or manufactures or assembles any firearm with intent to produce a firearm that is capable of, discharging projectiles in rapid succession during one pressure of the trigger;

(f) fails to report the loss, theft or finding of any firearm, prohibited weapon, restricted weapon, prohibited device, ammunition, prohibited ammunition or explosive substance that occurs in the course of the public officer's duties or employment or the destruction of any such thing in the course of the public officer's duties or employment; or

(g) alters a serial number on a firearm in the course of the public officer's duties or employment.

(2) In this section, "public officer" means

(a) a peace officer;

(b) a member of the Canadian Forces or of the armed forces of a state other than Canada who is attached or seconded to any of the Canadian forces;

(c) an operator of a museum established by the Chief of the Defence Staff or a person employed in any such museum;

(d) a member of a cadet organization under the control and supervision of the Canadian Forces;

(e) a person training to become a police officer or a peace officer under the control and supervision of

(i) a police force, or

(ii) a police academy or similar institution designated by the Attorney General of Canada or the lieutenant governor in council of a province;

(f) a member of a visiting force, within the meaning of section 2 of the *Visiting Forces Act*, who is authorized under paragraph 14(a) of that Act to possess and carry explosives, ammunition and firearms;

(g) a person, or member of a class of persons, employed in the federal public administration or by the government of a province or municipality who is prescribed to be a public officer; or

(h) the Commissioner of Firearms, the Registrar, a chief firearms officer, any firearms officer and any person designated under section 100 of the *Firearms Act*. 1995, c. 39, s. 139; 2003, c. 8, s. 7; c. 22, s. 224(z.23).

CROSS-REFERENCES

"Peace officer", "Canadian forces", "firearm" and "weapon" are defined in s. 2. "Possession" is defined in s. 4(3). "Prohibited weapon", "restricted weapon", "prohibited device", "ammunition", "prohibited ammunition", "import", "export", "transfer", "automatic firearm", "chief firearms officer" and "firearms officer" are defined in s. 84(1).

Pursuant to s. 117.1, the exemption in this section does not apply where the person is subject to a prohibition order and the person acts contrary to the order or to an authorization or a licence issued under the authority of a sustenance or hunting order made under s. 113. Section 117.08 exempts persons who supply the weapons and other regulated items to police forces, the Canadian Forces and visiting forces.

SYNOPSIS

This section acts as an exception to liability otherwise triggered by the offences under the Code or the *Firearms Act*. Subsections (1) and (2) exempt wide categories of law enforcement and armed forces personnel acting in the course of their duties or employment.

REGULATIONS PRESCRIBING PUBLIC OFFICERS

1. (1) A member of any of the following classes of persons, if employed in the public service of Canada or by the government of a province or municipality, is a public officer for the purposes of paragraph 117.07(2)(g) of the *Criminal Code*:

(a) employees who are responsible for the examination, inventory, storage, maintenance or transportation of court exhibits and evidence;

(b) employees of police forces or other public service agencies who are responsible for the acquisition, examination, inventory, storage, maintenance, issuance or transportation of firearms, prohibited weapons, restricted weapons, prohibited devices, prohibited ammunition or explosive substances;

(c) technicians, laboratory analysts and scientists who work at forensic or research laboratories;

(d) armourers and firearms instructors who work at police academies or similar institutions designated under subparagraph 117.07(2)(e)(ii) of the *Criminal Code*, or are employed by a federal or provincial department of natural resources, fisheries, wildlife, conservation or the environment, or by Revenue Canada;

(e) park wardens and other employees of a federal or provincial department who are responsible for the enforcement of laws and regulations dealing with natural resources, fisheries, wildlife, conservation or the environment;

(f) immigration officers;

(g) security personnel employed by the House of Commons or the Senate or by the Service, as defined in section 79.51 of the *Parliament of Canada Act*; and

(h) aircraft pilots employed by the Department of Transport or other public service agencies.

(2) For the purposes of subsection (1), the expression "public service agencies" has the same meaning as in section 1 of the Public Agents Firearms Regulations.

Coming into Force

2. These Regulations come into force on December 1, 1998. **SOR/98-466; SOR/98-472; SOR/2011-68; SOR/2015-166, s. 1.**

INDIVIDUALS ACTING FOR POLICE FORCE, CANADIAN FORCES AND VISITING FORCES.

117.08 Notwithstanding any other provision of this Act, but subject to section 117.1, no individual is guilty of an offence under this Act or the *Firearms Act* by reason only that the individual

(a) **possesses a firearm, a prohibited weapon, a restricted weapon, a prohibited device, any prohibited ammunition or an explosive substance,**

(b) **manufactures or transfers, or offers to manufacture or transfer, a firearm, a prohibited weapon, a restricted weapon, a prohibited device, any ammunition or any prohibited ammunition,**

(c) **exports or imports a firearm, a prohibited weapon, a restricted weapon, a prohibited device or any prohibited ammunition,**

(d) **exports or imports a component or part designed exclusively for use in the manufacture of or assembly into an automatic firearm,**

(e) **alters a firearm so that it is capable of, or manufactures or assembles any firearm with intent to produce a firearm that is capable of, discharging projectiles in rapid succession during one pressure of the trigger,**

(f) **fails to report the loss, theft or finding of any firearm, prohibited weapon, restricted weapon, prohibited device, ammunition, prohibited ammunition or explosive substance or the destruction of any such thing, or**

(g) **alters a serial number on a firearm,**

if the individual does so on behalf of, and under the authority of, a police force, the Canadian Forces, a visiting force, within the meaning of section 2 of the *Visiting Forces Act*, or a department of the Government of Canada or of a province. 1995, c. 39, s. 139.

CROSS-REFERENCES

"Peace officer", "Canadian forces", "firearm" and "weapon" are defined in s. 2. "Possession" is defined in s. 4(3). "Prohibited weapon", "restricted weapon", "prohibited device", "ammunition", "prohibited ammunition", "import", "export", "transfer", "automatic firearm", "chief firearms officer" and "firearms officer" are defined in s. 84(1).

Pursuant to s. 117.1, the exemption in this section does not apply where the person is subject to a prohibition order and the person acts contrary to the order or to an authorization or a licence issued under the authority of a sustenance or hunting order made under s. 113. Pursuant to s. 117.1, the exemption in this section does not apply where the person is subject to a prohibition order and the person acts contrary to the order or to an authorization or a licence issued under the authority of a sustenance or hunting order made under s. 113.

SYNOPSIS

This section, in effect, exempts persons from liability under this Act and the *Firearms Act* who supply or deal with the weapons and other regulated items on behalf of and under the authority of the police, Canadian forces and a visiting armed force. The person's acts must come within one of the activities covered by this section to take advantage of the exemption.

EMPLOYEES OF BUSINESS WITH LICENCE / Employees of business with licence / Employees of carriers / Employees of museums handling functioning imitation antique firearm / Employees of museums handling firearms generally / Public safety / Conditions.

117.09 (1) Notwithstanding any other provision of this Act, but subject to section 117.1, no individual who is the holder of a licence to possess and acquire restricted firearms and who is employed by a business as defined in subsection 2(1) of the *Firearms Act* that itself is the holder of a licence that authorizes the business to carry out specified activities in relation to prohibited firearms, prohibited weapons, prohibited devices or prohibited ammunition is guilty of an offence under this Act or the *Firearms Act* by reason only that the individual, in the course of the individual's duties or employment in relation to those specified activities,

  (*a*) **possesses a prohibited firearm, a prohibited weapon, a prohibited device or any prohibited ammunition;**

  (*b*) **manufactures or transfers, or offers to manufacture or transfer, a prohibited weapon, a prohibited device or any prohibited ammunition;**

  (*c*) **alters a firearm so that it is capable of, or manufactures or assembles any firearm with intent to produce a firearm that is capable of, discharging projectiles in rapid succession during one pressure of the trigger; or**

  (*d*) **alters a serial number on a firearm.**

(2) Notwithstanding any other provision of this Act, but subject to section 117.1, no individual who is employed by a business as defined in subsection 2(1) of the *Firearms Act* that itself is the holder of a licence is guilty of an offence under this Act or the *Firearms Act* by reason only that the individual, in the course of the individual's duties or employment, possesses, manufactures or transfers, or offers to manufacture or transfer, a partially manufactured barrelled weapon that, in its unfinished state, is not a barrelled weapon from which any shot, bullet or other projectile can be discharged and that is capable of causing serious bodily injury or death to a person.

(3) Notwithstanding any other provision of this Act, but subject to section 117.1, no individual who is employed by a carrier, as defined in subsection 2(1) of the *Firearms Act*, is guilty of an offence under this Act or that Act by reason only that the individual, in the course of the individual's duties or employment, possesses any firearm, cross-bow, prohibited weapon, restricted weapon, prohibited device, ammunition or prohibited ammunition or transfers, or offers to transfer any such thing.

(4) Notwithstanding any other provision of this Act, but subject to section 117.1, no individual who is employed by a museum as defined in subsection 2(1) of the *Firearms Act* that itself is the holder of a licence is guilty of an offence under this Act or the *Firearms Act* by reason only that the individual, in the course of the individual's duties or employment, possesses or transfers a firearm that is designed or intended to exactly resemble, or to resemble with near precision, an antique firearm if the individual has been trained to handle and use such a firearm.

(5) Notwithstanding any other provision of this Act, but subject to section 117.1, no individual who is employed by a museum as defined in subsection 2(1) of the *Firearms Act* that itself is the holder of a licence is guilty of an offence under this Act or the *Firearms Act* by reason only that the individual possesses or transfers a firearm in the course of the individual's duties or employment if the individual is designated, by name, by a provincial minister within the meaning of subsection 2(1) of the *Firearms Act*.

(6) A provincial minister shall not designate an individual for the purpose of subsection (5) where it is not desirable, in the interests of the safety of any person, to designate the individual.

(7) A provincial minister may attach to a designation referred to in subsection (4) any reasonable condition that the provincial minister considers desirable in the particular circumstances and in the itnerests of the safety of any person. 1995, c. 39, s. 139.

CROSS-REFERENCES

"Firearm" and "weapon" are defined in s. 2. "Possession" is defined in s. 4(3). "Prohibited weapon", "prohibited firearm", "restricted weapon", "prohibited device", "ammunition", "prohibited ammunition", "import", "export", "transfer", "automatic firearm", "replica firearm", "licence", "chief firearms officer" and "firearms officer" are defined in s. 84(1). "Provincial Minister", although not defined in this part, probably bears the meaning assigned to that term in s. 2(1) of the *Firearms Act*.

Pursuant to s. 117.1, the exemption in this section does not apply where the person is subject to a prohibition order and the person acts contrary to the order or to an authorization or a licence issued under the authority of a sustenance or hunting order made under s. 113. The exemption in this section does not apply where the person is subject to a prohibition order and the person acts contrary to the order or to an authorization or a licence issued under the authority of a sustenance or hunting order made under s. 113.

SYNOPSIS

This section exempts from liability for offences under this Act and the *Firearms Act* certain classes of persons who perform the specified acts in the course of their duties in dealing with weapons and other regulated things. This section is important for persons engaged in the business of dealing in or manufacturing such things, common carriers and employees of museums designated by a provincial Minister. Subsection (5) provides that the Minister shall not designate a museum employee where it is not in the interests of the safety of any person that the individual be designated.

RESTRICTION.

117.1 Sections 117.07 to 117.09 do not apply if the public officer or the individual is subject to a prohibition order and acts contrary to that order or to an authorization or a licence issued under the authority of an order made under subsection 113(1). 1995, c. 39, s. 139.

CROSS-REFERENCES

"Prohibition order", "authorization" and licence" are defined in s. 84(1). The reference to "public officer" is a public officer as defined in s. 117.07(2). Section 113(1) gives the court the power to lift a prohibition order for sustenance hunting or trapping or for purposes of employment.

General

ONUS ON THE ACCUSED.

117.11 Where, in any proceedings for an offence under any of sections 89, 90, 91, 93, 97, 101, 104 and 105, any question arises as to whether a person is the holder of an authorization, a licence or a registration certificate, the onus is on the accused to prove that the person is the holder of the authorization, licence or registration certificate. 1995, c. 39, s. 139.

CROSS-REFERENCES

"Authorization", "licence" and "registration certificate" are defined in s. 84(1).

SYNOPSIS

This section places the onus on the accused to prove that the person is the holder of an authorization, licence or registration certificate where that is an issue on a prosecution for any of the offences listed in this section.

ANNOTATIONS

It was held that the predecessor to this section, at least as it applied to the offence of unlawful possession of restricted weapons, contrary to [former] s. 91(1) was not unconstitutional by reason of the guarantee to the presumption of innocence in s. 11(*d*) of the *Canadian Charter of Rights and Freedoms*: *R. v. Schwartz*, [1988] 2 S.C.R. 443, 45 C.C.C. (3d) 97.

AUTHORIZATIONS, ETC., AS EVIDENCE / Certified copies.

117.12 (1) In any proceedings under this Act or any other Act of Parliament, a document purporting to be an authorization, a licence or a registration certificate is evidence of the statements contained therein.

(2) In any proceedings under this Act or any other Act of Parliament, a copy of any authorization, licence or registration certificate is, if certified as a true copy by the Registrar or a chief firearms officer, admissible in evidence and, in the absence of evidence to the contrary, has the same probative force as the authorization, licence or registration certificate would have had if it had been proved in the ordinary way. 1995, c. 39, s. 139.

CROSS-REFERENCES

"Authorization", "licence", "registration certificate", "Registrar" and "chief firearms officer" are defined in s. 84(1).

SYNOPSIS

This section deals with the evidentiary value of an authorization, licence or registration certificate. Subsection (1) abrogates the hearsay rule by making the statements in the documents admissible for their truth. Subsection (2) gives a certified copy of any authorization, licence or registration certificate the same evidentiary value as the original, in the absence of evidence to the contrary.

CERTIFICATE OF ANALYST / Attendance of analyst / Notice of intention to produce certificate.

117.13 (1) A certificate purporting to be signed by an analyst stating that the analyst has analyzed any weapon, prohibited device, ammunition, prohibited ammunition or explosive substance, or any part or component of such a thing, and stating the results of the analysis is evidence in any proceedings in relation to any of those things under this Act or under section 19 of the *Export and Import Permits Act* in relation to subsection 15(2) of that Act without proof of the signature or official character of the person appearing to have signed the certificate.

(2) The party against whom a certificate of an analyst is produce may, with leave of the court, require the attendance of the analyst for the purposes of cross-examination.

(3) No certificate of an analyst may be admitted in evidence unless the party intending to produce it has, before the trial, given to the party against whom it is intended to be produced reasonable notice of that intention together with a copy of the certificate. 1995, c. 39, s. 139; 2008, c. 18, s. 2.

(4) and (5) [*Repealed*, 2008, c. 18, s. 2.]

CROSS-REFERENCES

"Weapon" and "explosive substance" are defined in s. 2. "Prohibited device", "ammunition", "prohibited ammunition", "authorization", "licence" and "registration certificate" are defined in s. 84(1).

SYNOPSIS

This section permits the evidence of an analyst to be presented by way of certificate. The results of an analysis of a weapon, prohibited device, ammunition, prohibited ammunition or explosive substance, or any part or component of such a thing as set out in the certificate is admissible as evidence, without proof of the signature, if the certificate purports to be signed by the analyst. The party intending to introduce the certificate must give the opposite party reasonable notice of such intention together with a copy of the certificate. Proof of service of the certificate may be made by way of affidavit. The party against whom the certificate is produced may apply for leave to have the analyst and the person who signed the affidavit attend for the purposes of cross-examination.

AMNESTY PERIOD / Purposes of amnesty period / Reliance on amnesty period / Proceedings are a nullity.

117.14 (1) The Governor in Council may, by order, declare for any purpose referred to in subsection (2) any period as an amnesty period with respect to any weapon, prohibited device, prohibited ammunition, explosive substance or component or part designed exclusively for use in the manufacture of or assembly into an automatic firearm.

(2) An order made under subsection (1) may declare an amnesty period for the purpose of

    (*a*) permitting any person in possession of any thing to which the order relates to do anything provided in the order, including, without restricting the generality of the foregoing, delivering the thing to a peace officer, a firearms officer or a chief firearms officer, registering it, destroying it or otherwise disposing of it; or

    (*b*) permitting alterations to be made to any prohibited firearm, prohibited weapon, prohibited device or prohibited ammunition to which the order relates so that it no longer qualifies as a prohibited firearm, a prohibited weapon, a prohibited device or prohibited ammunition, as the case may be.

(3) No person who, during an amnesty period declared by an order made under subsection (1) and for a purpose described in the order, does anything provided for in the order, is, by reason only of the fact that the person did that thing, guilty of an offence under this Part.

(4) Any proceedings taken under this Part against any person for anything done by the person in reliance of this section are a nullity. 1995, c. 39, s. 139.

CROSS-REFERENCES

"Weapon", "peace officer" and "explosive substance" are defined in s. 2. "Prohibited device", "ammunition", "prohibited ammunition", "prohibited weapon", "prohibited firearm", "automatic firearm", "firearms officer", "chief firearms officer", "authorization", "licence" and "registration certificate" are defined in s. 84(1). "Possession" is defined in s. 4(3).

SYNOPSIS

This section permits the Governor in Council to declare amnesty periods to permit a person to deliver anything to which the order relates for destruction, or to permit alterations to be made to the thing so that it no longer qualifies as a prohibited firearm, prohibited weapon, prohibited device, or prohibited ammunition. See, for example, SOR/98-467 as amended by SOR/98-472.

ORDER DECLARING AN AMNESTY PERIOD (2015)

Definition non-restricted firearm

1. In this Order, "non-restricted firearm"means a firearm other than a prohibited firearm or a restricted firearm.

Amnesty

2. (1) The amnesty period set out in subsection (3) is declared under section 117.14 of the *Criminal Code* for an individual who, at any time during the amnesty period, is in possession of a non-restricted firearm and who holds or held a licence to possess firearms or a licence to possess and acquire firearms
    (*a*) that expired during the period beginning on January 1, 2004 and ending on May 16, 2015; or
    (*b*) that expires during the period beginning on May 17, 2015 and ending on May 16, 2017.

Purpose

(2) The purpose of the amnesty period is to permit the individual to
    (*a*) obtain the licence;
    (*b*) deactivate the firearm so that it is no longer a firearm;
    (*c*) export the firearm in accordance with all applicable legal requirements, including the legal requirements of the country to which the firearm is exported;
    (*d*) turn in the firearm to a police officer or a firearms officer for destruction or other disposal;
    (*e*) sell or give the firearm to a public service agency, as defined in section 1 of the *Public Agents Firearms Regulations*, to a business, including a museum, that holds a licence authorizing the acquisition of firearms or to an individual who holds a licence to possess and acquire firearms; or
    (*f*) possess the firearm before doing one of the things described in paragraphs (*a*) to (*e*).

Amnesty period

(3) The amnesty period begins on May 17, 2015 and ends on May 16, 2017.

Coming into force

3. This Order comes into force on the day on which it is registered. **SOR/2015-105**.

REGULATIONS / Restriction/ Non-restricted firearm / Restricted firearm.

117.15 (1) Subject to subsection (2), the Governor in Council may make regulations prescribing anything that by this Part is to be or may be prescribed.

(2) In making regulations, the Governor in Council may not prescribe any thing to be a prohibited firearm, a restricted firearm, a prohibited weapon, a restricted weapon, a prohibited device or prohibited ammunition if, in the opinion of the Governor in Council, the thing to be prescribed is reasonable for use in Canada for hunting or sporting purposes.

(3) Despite the definitions "prohibited firearm" and "restricted firearm" in subsection 84(1), a firearm that is prescribed to be a non-restricted firearm is deemed not to be a prohibited firearm or a restricted firearm.

(4) Despite the definition "prohibited firearm" in subsection 84(1), a firearm that is prescribed to be a restricted firearm is deemed not to be a prohibited firearm.1995, c. 39, s. 139; 2015, c. 27, s. 34.

CROSS-REFERENCES

"Prohibited firearm", "restricted firearm", "non-restricted firearm", "prohibited weapon", "restricted weapon", "prohibited device" and "prohibited ammunition" are defined in s. 84(1). Publication of regulations is governed by the *Statutory Instruments Act*, R.S.C. 1985, c. S-22. A much wider regulation power is included in s. 117 of the *Firearms Act*.

SYNOPSIS

This section gives the Governor in Council the power to make regulations prescribing anything that may be prescribed under this part, for example, prohibited ammunition, prohibited device, prohibited firearm, prohibited weapon, restricted firearm and restricted weapon. However, subsec. (2) prevents the Governor in Council from prescribing anything as prohibited ammunition, prohibited device, prohibited firearm, prohibited weapon, restricted firearm and restricted weapon if the thing to be prescribed is reasonable for use in Canada for hunting or sporting purposes. Subsections (3) and (4), respectively, entail that, notwithstanding the definitions given in s. 84(1), no firearm prescribed to be a non-restricted firearm can be considered to be a prohibited firearm or a restricted firearm, and that no firearm prescribed to be a restricted firearm can be considered to be a prohibited firearm.

Part IV / OFFENCES AGAINST THE ADMINISTRATION OF LAW AND JUSTICE

Interpretation

DEFINITIONS / "Evidence" or "statement" / "Government" / "Judicial proceeding" / "Office" / "Official" / "Witness".

118. In this Part

"evidence" or "statement" means an assertion of fact, opinion, belief or knowledge, whether material or not and whether admissible or not;

"government" means

    (*a*) the Government of Canada,

    (*b*) the government of a province, or

    (*c*) Her Majesty in right of Canada or a province;

"judicial proceeding" means a proceeding

    (*a*) in or under the authority of a court of justice,

(*b*) before the Senate or House of Commons or a committee of the Senate or House of Commons, or before a legislative council, legislative assembly or house of assembly or a committee thereof that is authorized by law to administer an oath,

(*c*) before a court, judge, justice, provincial court judge or coroner,

(*d*) before an arbitrator or umpire, or a person or body of persons authorized by law to make an inquiry and take evidence therein under oath, or

(*e*) before a tribunal by which a legal right or legal liability may be established, whether or not the proceeding is invalid for want of jurisdiction or for any other reason;

"office" includes

(*a*) an office or appointment under the government,

(*b*) a civil or military commission, and

(*c*) a position or an employment in a public department;

"official" means a person who

(*a*) holds an office, or

(*b*) is appointed or elected to discharge a public duty;

"witness" means a person who gives evidence orally under oath or by affidavit in a judicial proceeding, whether or not he is competent to be a witness, and includes a child of tender years who gives evidence but does not give it under oath, because, in the opinion of the person presiding, the child does not understand the nature of an oath. R.S., c. C-34, s. 107; R.S.C. 1985, c. 27 (1st Supp.), s. 15; 2007, c. 13, s. 2.

CROSS-REFERENCES

In addition to the definitions set out in this section, applicable to offences created by this Part, reference should also be made to s. 2 and in particular the definitions of "justice", "provincial court judge", "peace officer", "public department", "public officer" and "Attorney General".

SYNOPSIS

This contains definitions which apply to this Part of the Code.

ANNOTATIONS

"evidence" – This definition, which has appeared in slightly different forms since the 1982 Code, was intended to avoid the difficulty at common law that, to prove perjury, it was necessary to show that the statement was material in the sense that, unless it related to the exact issue which was under consideration then the offence was not made out: *R. v. Drew* (1902), 6 C.C.C. 241 (Que. K.B., App. Side), affd 6 C.C.C. 424, 33 S.C.R. 228.

"judicial proceeding" – While it had been held in several earlier cases, notably *R. v. Kohel* (1926), 46 C.C.C. 279, [1926] 3 W.W.R. 478 (Sask. K.B.); *R. v. Rulofson* (1908), 14 C.C.C. 253 (B.C.S.C.), and *R. v. Allen* (1924), 43 C.C.C. 118, [1925] 1 D.L.R. 57 (Man. K.B.), that a civil examination for discovery is not a judicial proceeding where the official who administered the oath was not present during the examination, the Saskatchewan Court of Appeal has now held to the contrary in *R. v. Foster and Walton-Ball* (1982), 69 C.C.C. (2d) 484, and overruled *R. v. Kohel*. The absence of the official, in this case the deputy local registrar, was held not to invalidate the proceedings.

Properly interpreted, the relevant provision of the provincial *Securities Act* authorized the Registrar to require a person to submit to an examination under oath before him and, accordingly, such proceedings fell within para. (*d*) of this definition: *Re M.C. Shumiatcher*, [1962] S.C.R. 38, 131 C.C.C. 259 (Judson J. in chambers).

Although they were not entitled to make a final decision, persons, appointed under the provincial *Securities Act* to conduct an investigation and question witnesses under oath, were authorized by law to make an "inquiry" within the meaning of para. (*d*) and, accordingly, the proceeding was a judicial proceeding: *R. v. Thomson* (1974), 2 O.R. (2d) 644 (Co. Ct.).

"office" – This definition does not apply to an office under a municipal government so as to determine liability for the offence, contrary to s. 123, of offering a benefit to a municipal official [defined in s. 123(3), *inter alia*, as a person who holds an office under a municipal government]. The court, therefore, properly applied the dictionary definition of "office" as, *inter alia*, "A position to which certain duties are attached, esp. a place of trust, authority, or service under constituted authority.": *R. v. Belzberg*, [1962] S.C.R. 254, 131 C.C.C. 281 (5:0).

"Office" is not confined to provincial or federal governments and may include a position of duty, trust or authority, especially in the public service or in some corporation society or the like. Accordingly, a Health Director and Chief of the Siksika Nation held "office" and was an "official" within the meaning of this provision: *R. v. Yellow Old Woman (No. 2)* (2003), 181 C.C.C. (3d) 439, [2004] 10 W.W.R. 276 (Alta. C.A.), leave to appeal to S.C.C. refused [2004] 2 S.C.R. vii, 184 C.C.C. (3d) vi.

"official" – The expression "means" used in this definition is of an explanatory and restrictive nature and in contradistinction to the expression "includes", used in the definition of "office", *supra*, which is of an extensive nature. It follows that, the definition in this subsection being governed by the definition of "office", an official is a person who holds an office either within the meaning in para. (*a*), (*b*) or (*c*) of that definition, or within the usual meaning of the word office, which can be ascertained by reference to dictionaries, meaning in part, a "position of duty, trust, or authority, esp., in the public service, or in some corporation, society or the like" or a "position to which certain duties are attached, esp. a place of trust, authority, or service under constituted authority." An elected member of a municipal council was, therefore, an official holding an office within the meaning of para. (*a*) and was also within the definition in para. (*b*). As regards the latter, while the term "appointed" is often used in contrast to the word "elected", Parliament could not have intended any such distinction: *R. v. Sheets*, [1971] S.C.R. 614, 1 C.C.C. (2d) 508 (9:0). **Note**: It would appear that this meaning has now been codified by a 2007 amendment to include the term "elected".

A member of the Legislative Council of Quebec appointed by the Lieutenant Governor in the name of The Queen is an official within the meaning of subpara. (ii): *R. v. Martineau*, [1966] S.C.R. 103, [1966] 4 C.C.C. 327 (5:0).

A director of public security for a municipality is an official: *R. v. Boulanger*, [2006] 2 S.C.R. 49, 210 C.C.C. (3d) 1.

A paramedic is not an "official". Despite the public importance of a paramedic's job, he or she owes no duty to the public at large and holds no public "office": *R. v. Cosh* (2015), 327 C.C.C. (3d) 410 (N.S.C.A.).

"witness" – The reference to a "child of tender years" in this definition is apparently a reference to former s. 16 of the *Canada Evidence Act*, which provided for the taking of the unsworn evidence of such a child. Section 16 has now been amended to provide for the taking of unsworn evidence of a "person under fourteen years of age or a person whose mental capacity is challenged", who does not understand the nature of an oath or a solemn affirmation, but is able to communicate the evidence and who promises to tell the truth.

Section 14(2) of the *Canada Evidence Act* provides that evidence by a person, who makes a solemn affirmation in accordance with s. 14(1), has the same effect as if taken under oath and by s. 15(2), a person, who makes a solemn affirmation under s. 14(1), is liable to indictment and punishment for perjury in all respects as if he had been sworn. The form of the solemn affirmation is prescribed by s. 14(1).

While s. 13 of the *Canada Evidence Act* authorizes the administering of an oath, neither the *Criminal Code* nor the *Canada Evidence Act* prescribe a form of oath and no particular form was prescribed at common law. The essential element of an oath is that it be in a form which binds the conscience of the witness as a solemn appeal to the witness' deity: *R. v. Lee Tuck and Lung Tung* (1912), 19 C.C.C. 471, 5 D.L.R. 629 (Alta. S.C.).

A witness who takes a certain form of oath, without objection, in the form generally administered to persons of his faith, agreeing that it binds his conscience, cannot thereafter be heard to say that he was not sworn: *R. v. Shajoo Ram (No. 2)* (1915), 51 S.C.R. 392, 25 C.C.C. 69 (5:0).

Corruption and Disobedience

BRIBERY OF JUDICIAL OFFICERS, ETC. / Consent of Attorney General.

119. (1) Every one is guilty of an indictable offence and liable to imprisonment for a term not exceeding fourteen years who

> (a) **being the holder of a judicial office, or being a member of Parliament or of the legislature of a province, directly or in-directly, corruptly accepts, obtains, agrees to accept or attempts to obtain, for themselves or another person, any money, valuable consideration, office, place or employment in respect of anything done or omitted or to be done or omitted by them in their official capacity, or**

> (b) **directly or indirectly, corruptly gives or offers to a person mentioned in paragraph (a), or to anyone for the benefit of that person, any money, valuable consideration, office, place or employment in respect of anything done or omitted or to be done or omitted by that person in their official capacity.**

(2) No proceedings against a person who holds a judicial office shall be instituted under this section without the consent in writing of the Attorney General of Canada. R.S., c. C-34, s. 108; 2007, c. 13, s. 3.

CROSS-REFERENCES

The term "office" is defined in s. 118. The term "corruptly" is not defined in this Part but has been considered by the courts in relation to the secret commission offence in s. 426 where it was held not to mean wickedly or dishonestly but to refer to an act done *mala fides*, designed wholly or partially for the purpose of bringing about the effect forbidden by the section: *R. v. Brown* (1956), 116 C.C.C. 287 (Ont. C.A.).

This offence may be the basis for an application for an authorization to intercept private communications by reason of s. 183. Conviction for this offence may, in some circumstances, result in loss of the office by virtue of s. 748(1) and other disabilities as prescribed by s. 748(2).

Where the accused is the holder of a judicial office, the consent in writing of the Attorney General of Canada is required (subsec. (2)) and the offence may only be tried by a superior court of criminal jurisdiction (defined in s. 2) by virtue of ss. 468 and 469. [Note, attempt and conspiracy to commit the offence by the holder of a judicial office would not fall within the exclusive jurisdiction of the superior court.] It would also seem that, by virtue of s. 522, only a judge of a superior court can release on bail in such circumstances.

In all other cases, the accused has an election as to mode of trial under s. 536(2) and release pending trial is dealt with under s. 515.

SYNOPSIS

Sections 119 to 130 deal generally with corruption and disobedience of court orders. Section 119 creates *offences* which apply both to the person who directly or indirectly *accepts a bribe* and to the person who *offers a bribe*. The *offer,* the *acceptance,* the *agreement to accept* or the *attempt to obtain* make out the full offence. It is an element of both offences that the offer, acceptance or solicitation must be done *corruptly* and there must be an attempt to influence the office-holder *in his or her official capacity.*

The seriousness of this offence is recognized by the maximum sentence of 14 years imprisonment.

Subsection (2) requires the consent of the federal Attorney General before a prosecution can be launched against a judge.

ANNOTATIONS

The corrupt act of a Member of Parliament does not have to be in connection with his legislative duties, it may be in connection with his participation in an administrative act of government: *R. v. Bruneau*, [1964] 1 C.C.C. 97, 42 C.R. 93 (Ont. C.A.).

In *R. v. Arseneau*, [1979] 2 S.C.R. 136, 45 C.C.C. (2d) 321 (7:2), the majority of the court rejected the proposition that a member of the Legislature who is also a Minister of the Crown is to be taken not to be acting in his official capacity as a member in respect of acts and decisions which he makes in the administration of his ministry. In the absence of evidence to the contrary it must be accepted that it was as a member that he was appointed a Minister it being the generally accepted practice that a Minister participate in the process of obtaining legislative authority for implementing his policies and approving expenditures. Thus, his capacity as a member cannot be so severed from his functions as a Minister as to make it an offence under this section to bribe him as a member but no offence to bribe the same person in his capacity as Minister.

On a charge under this section the use to be made of the money received is irrelevant. Thus, it is no defence that the member used the money for non-reimbursable expenses he incurred as a Member of Parliament: *R. v. Yanakis* (1981), 64 C.C.C. (2d) 374 (Que. C.A.).

BRIBERY OF OFFICERS.

120. Every one is guilty of an indictable offence and liable to imprisonment for a term not exceeding fourteen years who

   (*a*) **being a justice, police commissioner, peace officer, public officer or officer of a juvenile court, or being employed in the administration of criminal law, directly or indirectly, corruptly accepts, obtains, agrees to accept or attempts to obtain, for themselves or another person, any money, valuable consideration, office, place or employment with intent**

   (i) **to interfere with the administration of justice,**

   (ii) **to procure or facilitate the commission of an offence, or**

   (iii) **to protect from detection or punishment a person who has committed or who intends to commit an offence; or**

   (*b*) **directly or indirectly, corruptly gives or offers to a person mentioned in paragraph (*a*), or to anyone for the benefit of that person, any money, valuable consideration, office, place or employment with intent that the person should do anything mentioned in subparagraph (*a*)(i), (ii) or (iii). R.S., c. C-34, s. 109; 2007, c. 13, s. 4.**

CROSS-REFERENCES

The terms "justice", "peace officer" and "public officer" are defined in s. 2. The term "office" is defined in part in s. 118; see notes of that term under that section. The term "juvenile court" would appear to refer to an officer of the "juvenile court" as defined in s. 2 of the *Juvenile Delinquents Act*, R.S.C. 1970, c. J-3 (now repealed). The *Youth Criminal Justice Act* now only contains definitions of "youth justice court" and "youth worker". The term "corruptly" is not defined in this Part but has been considered by the courts in relation to the secret commission offence in s. 426 where it was held not to mean wickedly or dishonestly, but to refer to an act done *mala fides* designed wholly or partially for the purpose of bringing about the effect forbidden by the section: *R. v. Brown* (1956), 116 C.C.C. 287 (Ont. C.A.).

This offence may be the basis for an application for an authorization to intercept private communications by reason of s. 183 and falls within the definition of "enterprise crime offence" in

s. 462.3 for the purposes of Part XII.2. Conviction for this offence may, in some circumstances, result in loss of the office by virtue of s. 748(1) and other disabilities as prescribed by s. 748(2).

The accused has an election as to mode of trial pursuant to s. 536(2). Release pending trial is governed by s. 515.

SYNOPSIS

This section parallels s. 119 in many ways, creating offences both relating to the *person offering* the bribe and the *person* who *accepts* or agrees to accept it. The group of public officers is different from those captured by s. 119, with this section targeting *police officers, justices* and others involved in the *administration of the criminal law*. Again, as with s. 119, the offer or acceptance must be done *corruptly* directly or indirectly. The maximum punishment for this offence is 14 years imprisonment.

The acts need not involve the officers in their public capacity. However, the *intent* must be to interfere with justice, making it easier for another person to commit an offence or to protect an offender from detection or punishment. There is no need to obtain the consent of the Attorney General to prosecute under this section.

ANNOTATIONS

"administration of justice" – It was held, considering the predecessor of this section, that the "administration of justice" is not limited to apprehended proceedings in respect of crimes in the strict sense but extends to proceedings in respect of provincial offences. Further it was immaterial whether the police officer actually intended to institute a prosecution; it sufficed if the accused was apprehensive of a prosecution and gave the bribe to prevent it: *R. v. Kalick* (1920), 61 S.C.R. 175, 35 C.C.C. 159 (5:1).

The term "the administration of justice" in this section refers to events leading up to the imposition of sentence and does not cover the administrative structure that governs convicts after they have been sentenced: *R. v. Smalbrugge* (1984), 19 C.C.C. (3d) 283 (B.C. Co. Ct.).

"an offence" – "Offence" in para. (*a*)(vi) includes the contravention of a valid provincial statute: *R. v. Sommerville*, [1963] 3 C.C.C. 240, 40 C.R. 384 (Sask. C.A.).

mens rea – The offence contrary to para. (*b*) is a specific intent offence for which drunkenness is a defence. Further, evidence of good character adduced by the accused may not only serve to support the accused's credibility but must be considered from the standpoint of whether the accused as a person of good character was likely to have committed this offence unless he was so drunk as to lack the capacity to form the requisite intent: *R. v. Dees* (1978), 40 C.C.C. (2d) 58 (Ont. C.A.).

FRAUDS ON THE GOVERNMENT / Contractor subscribing to election fund / Punishment.

121. (1) Every one commits an offence who
   (*a*) directly or indirectly
      (i) gives, offers or agrees to give or offer to an official or to any member of his family, or to any one for the benefit of an official, or
      (ii) being an official, demands, accepts or offers or agrees to accept from any person for himself or another person,
   a loan, reward, advantage or benefit of any kind as consideration for cooperation, assistance, exercise of influence or an act or omission in connection with
      (iii) the transaction of business with or any matter of business relating to the government, or
      (iv) a claim against Her Majesty or any benefit that Her Majesty is authorized or is entitled to bestow,

whether or not, in fact, the official is able to cooperate, render assistance, exercise influence or do or omit to do what is proposed, as the case may be;

(b) having dealings of any kind with the government, directly or indirectly pays a commission or reward to or confers an advantage or benefit of any kind on an employee or official of the government with which the dealings take place, or to any member of the employee's or official's family, or to anyone for the benefit of the employee or official, with respect to those dealings, unless the person has the consent in writing of the head of the branch of government with which the dealings take place;

(c) being an official or employee of the government, directly or indirectly demands, accepts or offers or agrees to accept from a person who has dealings with the government a commission, reward, advantage or benefit of any kind for themselves or another person, unless they have the consent in writing of the head of the branch of government that employs them or of which they are an official;

(d) having or pretending to have influence with the government or with a minister of the government or an official, directly or in-directly demands, accepts or offers or agrees to accept, for themselves or another person, a reward, advantage or benefit of any kind as consideration for cooperation, assistance, exercise of influence or an act or omission in connection with

(i) anything mentioned in subparagraph (a)(iii) or (iv), or

(ii) the appointment of any person, including themselves, to an office;

(e) directly or indirectly gives or offers, or agrees to give or offer, to a minister of the government or an official, or to anyone for the benefit of a minister or an official, a reward, advantage or benefit of any kind as consideration for cooperation, assistance, exercise of influence, or an act or omission, by that minister or official, in connection with

(i) anything mentioned in subparagraph (a)(iii) or (iv), or

(ii) the appointment of any person, including themselves, to an office; or

(f) having made a tender to obtain a contract with the government,

(i) directly or indirectly gives or offers, or agrees to give or offer, to another person who has made a tender, to a member of that person's family or to another person for the benefit of that person, a reward, advantage or benefit of any kind as consideration for the withdrawal of the tender of that person, or

(ii) directly or indirectly demands, accepts or offers or agrees to accept from another person who has made a tender a reward, advantage or benefit of any kind for themselves or another person as consideration for the withdrawal of their own tender.

(2) Every one commits an offence who, in order to obtain or retain a contract with the government, or as a term of any such contract, whether express or implied, directly or indirectly subscribes or gives, or agrees to subscribe or give, to any person any valuable consideration

(a) for the purpose of promoting the election of a candidate or a class or party of candidates to Parliament or the legislature of a province; or

(b) with intent to influence or affect in any way the result of an election conducted for the purpose of electing persons to serve in Parliament or the legislature of a province.

(3) Every one who commits an offence under this section is guilty of an indictable offence and liable to imprisonment for a term not exceeding five years. R.S., c. C-34, s. 110; 2007, c. 13, s. 5.

CROSS-REFERENCES

The terms "official" and "government" are defined in s. 118. The term "office" is defined, in part, in s. 118; see notes of that term under that section. The term "person" is defined in s. 2. With respect to the offences set out in subsec. (1)(*f*), also see "bid-rigging" offence in s. 47 of the *Competition Act*, R.S.C. 1985, c. C-34.

This offence may be the basis for an application for an authorization to intercept private communications by reason of s. 183 and falls within the definition of "enterprise crime offence" in s. 462.3 for the purposes of Part XII.2. Conviction for this offence bars the accused from contracting with Her Majesty or from receiving any benefit under a contract between Her Majesty and any other person or to hold office under Her Majesty, by virtue of s. 750(3), unless the capacity is restored by the Governor in Council under s. 750(4).

The accused has an election as to mode of trial pursuant to s. 536(2). Release pending trial is determined by s. 515, although the accused is eligible for release by the officer in charge under s. 498.

SYNOPSIS

Section 121 creates a number of offences relating to *frauds upon government* and is aimed, in part, at what is known as *influence peddling*. As with ss. 119 and 120, offences are created to catch both the government officials (or a family member of such officials) and the person offering the bribe. The offence is committed if the act is done directly or indirectly.

Section 121(1)(*a*), which deals specifically with influence peddling, catches a wide range of activities, including offers of *loans or benefits offered* for the *purpose* of *obtaining an advantage* in government business or benefits which the government may confer. There is no requirement that the official be actually able to be of assistance to bring about the result sought to be obtained. As with most offences created by this section, it is broad enough to encompass situations in which the intended recipient of the benefit is a *family member* of the government official.

Section 121(1)(*b*) creates an offence applicable to the *person who confers* an advantage or *benefit* upon an employee or an official of the government, by a *person who has any kind of dealings with the government*. The person offering the benefit must do so with *the intention* of conferring a benefit, however, no offence is committed where he has the *consent in writing* of the head of the branch of government, with which he deals, to do so. The accused must prove the existence of such consent.

Section 121(1)(*c*) creates a companion offence to the previous paragraph, and is aimed at the *employee* or official who *receives the reward* or benefit. The broad scope of this paragraph extends to benefits to *family members* of the accused official. As with the previous paragraph, the defence of consent by senior officials is provided and the onus is on the accused to demonstrate their consent.

Section 121(1)(*d*) and (*e*) create companion offences aimed at the *person demanding and the person accepting a reward* and the person offering the reward for the same *purposes* as in subsec. (1)(*a*) or to obtain the *appointment of any person to an office*. This offence requires the *intention* on the part of the person agreeing to accept the benefit of influencing, or pretending to do so, a minister or other employee of the government. The offence requires more than merely seeking access to governmental officials; the gravamen of the offence is attempting to *influence decisions*.

Section 121(1)(*f*) is aimed at the attempted *influencing* of *government tendering processes*. This paragraph creates offences for both sides of this type of corrupt deal-making. The key aspect of this offence is to offer or accept, the reward, advantage and so on, for the *purpose* of having *competing tenders withdrawn* from consideration.

Subsection (2) deals with attempts to curtail improper ties between those who have or seek to obtain government contracts and those who seek (or who wish to retain) elected office in the federal or provincial legislatures. The subsection is aimed at the intention to promote one or more candidate or to influence such elections to attain or retain government contracts. This offence prohibits *valuable consideration* being given, or promised, for such purpose directly or indirectly. The maximum punishment for the breach of this subsection is, by virtue of subsec. (3), five years' imprisonment.

ANNOTATIONS

Note: The cases noted below were decided before the amendment to this section adding the phrase "directly or indirectly".

Subsection (1) – In *R. v. Giguere*, [1983] 2 S.C.R. 448, 8 C.C.C. (3d) 1 (4:1), it was held by three of the five judges (including Wilson J., dissenting) that "influence" as used in this section refers to actually affecting a decision such as awarding a contract. However, co-operation and assistance are not so limited and would include opening doors or arranging meetings as the first step in an effort by another to secure a government contract. While the mere arranging of a meeting, for example, is not itself a crime it becomes so when a benefit is given, offered or demanded for the arranging of the meeting respecting the matters listed in this subsection and the person who receives or demands it is an official or one having or pretending to have influence in the relevant sense. A person having influence in the government in this sense is one who could affect, for example, a decision by the government to award a contract and similarly a person who pretends to have influence is a person who pretends he could affect such a government decision.

Subsection (1)(*a*) – The application of this subsection is not confined to a person who holds office or has responsibility for the administration of law or justice but is also aimed at a person who exercises legislative functions and thus the offence may be committed by an appointed member of the Legislative Council of Quebec. The gist of the offence is influence peddling and the section is aimed at the improper use, actual or pretended, of the real or pretended influence that the official enjoys. It is not necessary to prove that the prohibited conduct was committed by the person in his official capacity: *R. v. Martineau*, [1966] S.C.R. 103, [1966] 4 C.C.C. 327.

"Corruption" is not a required element of the *actus reus* or the *mens rea*. There is no requirement that the Crown prove that a benefit was conferred because of a person's position and, correspondingly, that the recipient knew that it was given because of his or her employment status. The Crown need only prove that the accused intentionally committed the prohibited act with a knowledge of the circumstances that are necessary elements of the offence. Accordingly, the accused must know that he is an official; he must intentionally demand or accept a loan, reward, advantage or benefit of any kind for himself or another person; and the accused must know that the reward is in consideration for co-operation, assistance or exercise of influence in connection with the transaction of business with or relating to the government: *R. v. Cogger*, [1997] 2 S.C.R. 842, 116 C.C.C. (3d) 322.

Subsection (1)(*b*) – It was held in *R. v. Cooper*, [1978] 1 S.C.R. 860, 34 C.C.C. (2d) 18, that the offence is not one of strict liability, but is one requiring proof of *mens rea* of the intention to confer a benefit with respect to dealings with the Government. It was also held (4:3) that the jury was not misdirected by the judge directing them that the offence was committed if the funds were conferred "directly or indirectly" in relation to the dealings. [**Note:** The use of that phrase has been codified by a 2007 amendment that added the words "directly or indirectly".]

In *R. v. Achtem* (1979), 52 C.C.C. (2d) 240, 13 C.R. (3d) 199 (Alta. C.A.), leave to appeal to S.C.C. refused C.C.C. *loc. cit.*, it was held that the accused had dealings with the "government" where his dealings were with the Alberta Housing Corporation, a corporation created by provincial statute whose board of directors was appointed by the Executive Council and consisted of Deputy Ministers and performed the functions designated by the Lieutenant Governor in Council. Where, as in this case, the statute does not specifically provide whether or not the corporation is a Crown corporation the test is the nature and degree of control exercised by the Crown over it.

The offence is made out if a gift is given for an ulterior purpose, even if no return is ultimately given and even if there is no acceptance by the official: *R. v. Pilarinos* (2002), 167 C.C.C. (3d) 97, 216 D.L.R. (4th) 680 (B.C.S.C.).

Subsection (1)(c) – This section is not limited to situations where the gift was motivated by the recipient's position in government. "Dealings", as used in this section, are limited to conduct whereby persons are in the process of having commercial dealings with the government at the time of the offence. The phrase "commission, reward, advantage or benefit of any kind" requires the beneficiary to have secured a material or tangible gain before falling into the parameters of the provision. It is important to consider the relationship between the parties as well as the scope of the benefit. The closer the relationship, the less likely the gift should be perceived as an advantage or benefit to the recipient. Whether a gift is a true "benefit" is a question of fact. To prove the requisite *mens rea*, it must be shown that the accused knew of the conduct and the circumstances in which it occurred. The crown is required to prove: (*a*) an employee's conscious decision to accept what in all of the circumstances is found to be a "commission, reward, advantage or benefit of any kind" and (*b*) knowledge (or wilful blindness) at the time of the receipt that the giver was having dealings with the government and that the employee's superior had not consented to his or her receipt of the "commission, reward, advantage or benefit of any kind": *R. v. Hinchey*, [1996] 3 S.C.R. 1128, 111 C.C.C. (3d) 353.

The offence under this subsection is committed even where the accused has received only the true value of services rendered outside his working hours where the compensation was received from a person who has dealings with the Government and the accused did not have the consent of his department head: *Dore v. Canada (Attorney General)*, [1975] 1 S.C.R. 756, 15 C.C.C. (2d) 542, reheard in part [1975] 1 S.C.R. at p. 784, 17 C.C.C. (2d) 359.

A government employee receives an "advantage" or "benefit" within the meaning of this paragraph when the employee receives something of value which, in all of the circumstances, the trier of fact concludes constitutes a profit to the employee (or a family member) derived, in part at least, because the employee is a government employee or because of the nature of the work done by the employee for the government. Thus, this would include not only arrangements involving a *quid pro quo* but also where the employee gets something because he is a government employee, even though the giver expects nothing in return and the employee has done nothing to earn the thing given. In making the determination of whether or not there has been an advantage or benefit, an objective assessment of all the relevant evidence must be made and not exclusively by reference to the employee's subjective state of mind. Once the prosecution has proved receipt of a benefit or advantage, there is no need for proof of any intent by the employee to exercise some undue influence in favour of the person giving the benefit. It is sufficient that there is proof that the employee decided to accept the thing offered with knowledge of the relevant circumstances: *R. v. Greenwood* (1991), 67 C.C.C. (3d) 435 (Ont. C.A.).

The fact that this paragraph does not set out the mental element required for proof of the offence or that the section is extremely broad does not render it so vague as to be unconstitutional and infringe the principles of fundamental justice as guaranteed by s. 7 of the Charter. However, the placing of the burden on the accused to prove the existence of written consent from the head of the department violates the guarantee to the presumption of innocence in s. 11(*d*) of the Charter. Accordingly, the words "the proof of which lies on him" must be deleted: *R. v. Fisher* (1994), 88 C.C.C. (3d) 103, 28 C.R. (4th) 63, 17 O.R. (3d) 295 (C.A.), leave to appeal to S.C.C. refused 94 C.C.C. (3d) vii, 119 D.L.R. (4th) vi, 25 C.R.R. (2d) 188*n*.

It is not a defence that the accused's family received a benefit but the accused did not. The words "for his benefit" modify the words "through anyone" and do not modify the words "through a member of his family". The phrase "through a member of his family" deems a benefit to a family member to be a benefit to the accused: *R. v. Mathur* (2010), 256 C.C.C. (3d) 97 (Ont. C.A.).

Subsection (1)(d) – This subsection is limited to persons who have, or pretend to have, a significant nexus with government. This means someone who could or pretends he could affect, for example, a decision by government to award a contract. It is not directed at persons who are merely able to arrange a meeting with government officials: *R. v. Giguere*, [1983] 2 S.C.R. 448, 8 C.C.C. (2d) 1, 37 C.R. (3d) 1.

In light of the wide definition of "person" in s. 2 an unincorporated political association such as the Nova Scotia Liberal Association may constitute a "person", within the meaning of this paragraph: *R. v. Barrow*, [1987] 2 S.C.R. 694, 38 C.C.C. (3d) 193.

SELLING ETC., OF TOBACCO PRODUCTS AND RAW LEAF TOBACCO / Exceptions — subsections 30(2) and 32(2) and (3) of *Excise Act, 2001* / Exception — section 31 of *Excise Act, 2001* / Punishment / Subsequent offences.

121.1 (1) No person shall sell, offer for sale, transport, deliver, distribute or have in their possession for the purpose of sale a tobacco product, or raw leaf tobacco that is not packaged, unless it is stamped. The terms "tobacco product", "raw leaf tobacco", "packaged" and "stamped" have the same meanings as in section 2 of the *Excise Act, 2001*.

(2) Subsection (1) does not apply in any of the circumstances described in any of subsections 30(2) and 32(2) and (3) of the *Excise Act, 2001*.

(3) A tobacco grower does not contravene subsection (1) by reason only that they have in their possession raw leaf tobacco described in paragraph 31(*a*), (*b*) or (*c*) of the *Excise Act, 2001*.

(4) Every person who contravenes subsection (1)

    (*a*) is guilty of an indictable offence and liable to imprisonment for a term of not more than five years and, if the amount of tobacco product is 10,000 cigarettes or more or 10 kg or more of any other tobacco product, or the amount of raw leaf tobacco is 10 kg or more,

        (i) in the case of a second offence, to a minimum punishment of imprisonment for a term of 90 days,

        (ii) in the case of a third offence, to a minimum punishment of imprisonment for a term of 180 days, and

        (iii) in the case of a fourth or subsequent offence, to a minimum punishment of imprisonment for a term of two years less a day; or

    (*b*) is guilty of an offence punishable on summary conviction and liable to imprisonment for a term of not more than six months.

(5) For the purpose of determining whether a convicted person has committed a second or subsequent offence, an offence under this section for which the person was previously convicted is considered to be an earlier offence whether it was prosecuted by indictment or by way of summary conviction proceedings. 2014, c. 23, s. 3.

CROSS-REFERENCES

Definitions and exceptions to liability relevant to this offence are found in the *Excise Act, 2001*, S.C. 2002, c. 22.

SYNOPSIS

Section 121.1 creates an offence in relation to the unauthorized sale of tobacco. The regulatory scheme enacted in the *Excise Act, 2001* is incorporated by reference in subsecs. (2) and (4), such that authorized selling, etc. is not caught by the provision. Subsection (4) distinguishes the indictable from the summary conviction offence based on the amount of tobacco involved, and provides for escalating penalties on subsequent offences.

BREACH OF TRUST BY PUBLIC OFFICER.

122. Every official who, in connection with the duties of his office, commits fraud or a breach of trust is guilty of an indictable offence and liable to imprisonment for a term not exceeding five years, whether or not the fraud or breach of trust would be an offence if it were committed in relation to a private person. R.S., c. C-34, s. 111.

CROSS-REFERENCES

The term "official" is defined in s. 118. The term "office" is defined, in part, in s. 118; see notes of that term under that section. Breach of trust by a trustee is an offence under s. 336. The secret commission offence is found in s. 426.

This offence may be the basis for an application for an authorization to intercept private communications by reason of s. 183 and falls within the definition of "enterprise crime offence" in s. 462.3 for the purposes of Part XII.2.

The accused has an election as to mode of trial pursuant to s. 536(2). Release pending trial is determined by s. 515, although the accused is eligible for release by the officer in charge under s. 498.

SYNOPSIS

Section 122 creates offences relating to *fraud* or *breach of trust* by a *public officer*. The offences are limited to activities in connection with the duties of the public office-holder. This section specifically imposes broader liability upon public officials than that which would apply to private persons who were involved in the same activities. This indictable offence is punishable by a maximum period of imprisonment of five years.

ANNOTATIONS

Breach of trust – In *R. v. Boulanger*, [2006] 2 S.C.R. 49, 210 C.C.C. (3d) 1, the Supreme Court of Canada held that the offence is made out where the Crown establishes the following elements beyond a reasonable doubt: (1) the accused is an official; (2) the accused was acting in connection with the duties of his or her office; (3) the accused breached the standard of responsibility and conduct demanded of him or her by the nature of the office; (4) the conduct of the accused represented a serious and marked departure from the standards expected of an individual in the accused's position of public trust; and (5) the accused acted with the intention to use his or her public office for a purpose other than the public good, for example, for a dishonest, partial, corrupt or oppressive purpose. Not every breach of the appropriate standard of conduct, however, will constitute an offence under this provision. The conduct must be sufficiently serious to move it from the realm of administrative fault to that of criminal behaviour. The *mens rea* turns on the intention to use one's public office for purposes other than the benefit of the public. An attempt to conceal his or her actions or the receipt of a significant personal benefit may provide evidence of the requisite *mens rea*. The receipt of a benefit, however, is not conclusive of a culpable *mens rea*. In this case, the accused, a director of public security for a municipality, did not commit a breach of trust when he directed a police officer to produce a supplementary report regarding a motor vehicle accident involving his daughter. While the accused knew that he would benefit from a further police report, it is not misconduct to make a decision knowing it furthers one's personal interests if the decision is made honestly and in the belief that it is a proper exercise of the public power of the official. The accused's private purpose did not seek to undermine the public good, nor could the conduct be said to constitute a marked departure from the course of action that should have been taken.

The use of the phrase "breach of trust" does not render this provision unconstitutionally vague. Breach of trust can be interpreted by courts in part as a function of social norms of tolerance and community standards: *R. v. Lippé* (1996), 111 C.C.C. (3d) 187, 2 C.R. (5th) 32 (Que. C.A.).

The accused, the town's mayor, was properly convicted upon evidence that he misled a constituent as to the value of the constituent's land and endeavoured to procure it for himself for personal profit. The work of a public servant must be a real service in which no concealed pecuniary self-interest should bias the judgment of the officer and in which the substantial truth of every transaction should be made to appear: *R. v. McKitka* (1982), 66 C.C.C. (2d) 164, 35 B.C.L.R. 116 (C.A.), citing *R. v. Arnoldi* (1892), 23 O.R. 201 (H.C.J.).

"Official" / *Also see note under s. 118* – Despite s. 123 an elected municipal official is an official holding office under this section: *R. v. Sheets*, [1971] S.C.R. 614, 1 C.C.C. (2d) 508, 15 C.R.N.S. 232 (9:0).

MUNICIPAL CORRUPTION / Influencing municipal official / Definition of "municipal official".

123. (1) Every one is guilty of an indictable offence and liable to imprisonment for a term not exceeding five years who directly or indirectly gives, offers or agrees to give or offer to a municipal official or to anyone for the benefit of a municipal official — or, being a municipal official, directly or indirectly demands, accepts or offers or agrees to accept from any person for themselves or another person — a loan, reward, advantage or benefit of any kind as consideration for the official

    (*a*) to abstain from voting at a meeting of the municipal council or a committee of the council;

    (*b*) to vote in favour of or against a measure, motion or resolution;

    (*c*) to aid in procuring or preventing the adoption of a measure, motion or resolution; or

    (*d*) to perform or fail to perform an official act.

(2) Every one is guilty of an indictable offence and liable to imprisonment for a term not exceeding five years who influences or attempts to influence a municipal official to do anything mentioned in paragraphs (1)(*a*) to (*d*) by

    (*a*) suppression of the truth, in the case of a person who is under a duty to disclose the truth;

    (*b*) threats or deceit; or

    (*c*) any unlawful means.

(3) In this section, "municipal official" means a member of a municipal council or a person who holds an office under a municipal government. R.S., c. C-34, s. 112; R.S.C. 1985, c. 27 (1st Supp.), s. 16; 2007, c. 13, s. 6.

CROSS-REFERENCES

A municipal official may also be convicted of the offence under s. 122. Bribery, etc., of other officials is dealt with in ss. 119 and 120.

This offence may be the basis for an application for an authorization to intercept private communications by reason of s. 183.

The accused has an election as to mode of trial pursuant to s. 536(2). Release pending trial is determined by s. 515, although the accused is eligible for release by the officer in charge under s. 498.

SYNOPSIS

This section is aimed at *municipal officials* who seek out or accept *benefits to be influenced* and those who offer such benefits. The section contains its own expanded definitions of the class of person included within the term "municipal official". The prohibited activities are limited to efforts at influencing such officials in the performance of *job related responsibilities,* including voting for a resolution, or doing (or not doing) an official act. Also, it is an offence to enlist the assistance of an official (or for the official to offer) to influence others to vote for or against any resolution.

Subsection (2) is aimed at the party seeking to influence officials in those actions outlined above (*i.e.*, voting for or against a resolution, or doing or not doing an official act) by a variety of means, including using threats, unlawful means or by the suppression of the truth by those who have a duty to tell the truth. This indictable offence has a maximum punishment of five years' imprisonment.

ANNOTATIONS

In *R. v. Belzberg*, [1962] S.C.R. 254, 131 C.C.C. 281, 36 C.R. 368, it was held that the chief building inspector in Calgary held office under a municipal government and that, if he had complied with the requests made to him, he would have failed to perform an official act. Note that the word "office" in subsec. (3) was interpreted by reference to dictionaries and that it was held that the definition in s. 118 does not apply to this section.

SELLING OR PURCHASING OFFICE.

124. Every one who
   (*a*) **purports to sell or agrees to sell an appointment to or a resignation from an office, or a consent to any such appointment or resignation, or receives or agrees to receive a reward or profit from the purported sale thereof, or**
   (*b*) **purports to purchase or gives a reward or profit for the purported purchase of any such appointment, resignation or consent, or agrees or promises to do so,**
is guilty of an indictable offence and liable to imprisonment for a term not exceeding five years. R.S., c. C-34, s. 113.

CROSS-REFERENCES

The term "office" is defined, in part, in s. 118; see notes with respect to that term under that section. Similar offences, relating to attempting to influence appointments to offices, are dealt with in s. 125.

Conviction for this offence bars the accused from contracting with Her Majesty or from receiving any benefit under a contract between Her Majesty and any other person or to hold office under Her Majesty, by virtue of s. 748(3), unless the capacity is restored by the Governor in Council under s. 748(4).

The accused has an election as to mode of trial pursuant to s. 536(2). Release pending trial is determined by s. 515, although the accused is eligible for release by the officer in charge under s. 498.

SYNOPSIS

This section creates the offence of *agreeing to sell or purchase a public office,* to arrange the resignation from such office or to arrange the appointment of a person to such office. No sale need take place; the agreement to carry out one side of transaction of the proposed buying, selling, purchasing, etc., establishes the criminal liability. This indictable offence carries a five year maximum punishment.

INFLUENCING OR NEGOTIATING APPOINTMENTS OR DEALING IN OFFICES.

125. Every one who
   (*a*) **receives, agrees to receive, gives or procures to be given, directly or indirectly, a reward, advantage or benefit of any kind as consideration for cooperation, assistance or exercise of influence to secure the appointment of any person to an office,**
   (*b*) **solicits, recommends or negotiates in any manner with respect to an appointment to or resignation from an office, in expectation of a direct or indirect reward, advantage or benefit, or**

(*c*) **keeps without lawful authority, the proof of which lies on him, a place for transacting or negotiating any business relating to**
  (i) **the filling of vacancies in offices,**
  (ii) **the sale or purchase of offices, or**
  (iii) **appointments to or resignations from offices,**
is guilty of an indictable offence and liable to imprisonment for a term not exceeding five years. R.S., c. C-34, s. 114.

CROSS-REFERENCES
The term "office" is defined, in part, in s. 118; see notes with respect to that term under that section. Similar offences, relating to purchasing or sale of offices, are dealt with in s. 125.

The accused has an election as to mode of trial pursuant to s. 536(2). Release pending trial is determined by s. 515, although the accused is eligible for release by the officer in charge under s. 498.

SYNOPSIS
Section 125 prohibits attempts to influence or negotiate appointments to, or resignations from, office. Paragraphs (*a*) and (*b*) create criminal liability for a person who agrees to receive any benefit and the person who offers such benefit, respectively. The expansive language includes *indirect benefits of any kind.*

Paragraph (*c*) prohibits keeping a place for the purpose of business relating to the resignation from or appointments to offices or sales or purchases of offices. This paragraph permits the *defence of lawful authority* but the accused has the burden of proof of establishing it. This indictable offence has a maximum punishment of five years' imprisonment.

ANNOTATIONS
Proof of corrupt intent is not an element of this offence: *R. v. Auger* (1942), 78 C.C.C. 136 (Que. Ct. Sess.). *Contra: R. v. Melnyk* (1938), 71 C.C.C. 362 (Alta. S.C.).

DISOBEYING A STATUTE / Attorney General of Canada may act.

126. (1) Every one who, without lawful excuse, contravenes an Act of Parliament by wilfully doing anything that it forbids or by wilfully omitting to do anything that it requires to be done is, unless a punishment is expressly provided by law, guilty of an indictable offence and liable to imprisonment for a term not exceeding two years.

(2) Any proceedings in respect of a contravention of or conspiracy to contravene an Act mentioned in subsection (1), other than this Act, may be instituted at the instance of the Government of Canada and conducted by or on behalf of that Government. R.S., c. C-34, s. 115; 1974-75-76, c. 93, s. 4.

CROSS-REFERENCES
Conspiracy is defined in s. 465.

The term "wilfully" does not have a fixed meaning and must take its meaning from the context. Generally speaking, however, it connotes an intention to bring about a proscribed consequence. See: *R. v. Buzzanga and Durocher* (1979), 49 C.C.C. (2d) 369 (Ont. C.A.).

The accused has an election as to mode of trial pursuant to s. 536(2). Release pending trial is determined by s. 515, although the accused is eligible for release by the officer in charge under s. 498.

SYNOPSIS
This section creates the offence of contravening any federal Act by *wilfully doing* any act prohibited thereby or *wilfully failing to do* any act required to be done by that Act. Such acts

or omissions are punishable by a term of imprisonment not exceeding two years, *if the Act does not create its own punishment*. Up to two years is the minimum punishment created by the *Criminal Code* for indictable offences.

The section permits the defence of lawful excuse but, unlike many other sections in this Part of the Criminal Code, the onus of proving the lawful excuse is not shifted to the accused.

For offences covered by subsec. (1), other than those created by the *Criminal Code*, the *federal government may commence prosecution* for the offence, or conspiracy to commit the offence.

ANNOTATIONS

Subsection (1) – An accused's mistaken belief as to his legal obligations as imposed by the Act of Parliament does not constitute a lawful excuse within the meaning of this subsection: *R. v. Parrot* (1979), 51 C.C.C. (2d) 539 (Ont. C.A.), leave to appeal to S.C.C. refused *loc. cit.* C.C.C.

Subsection (2) – This subsection is *intra vires* Parliament: *R. v. Parrot, supra.* [Also see notes under definition of "Attorney General" in s. 2.]

DISOBEYING ORDER OF COURT / Attorney General of Canada may act.

127. (1) Every one who, without lawful excuse, disobeys a lawful order made by a court of justice or by a person or body of persons authorized by any Act to make or give the order, other than an order for the payment of money, is, unless a punishment or other mode of proceeding is expressly provided by law, guilty of

    (*a*) **an indictable offence and liable to imprisonment for a term not exceeding two years; or**

    (*b*) **an offence punishable on summary conviction.**

(2) Where the order referred to in subsection (1) was made in proceedings instituted at the instance of the Government of Canada and conducted by or on behalf of that Government, any proceedings in respect of a contravention of or conspiracy to contravene that order may be instituted and conducted in like manner. R.S., c. C-34, s. 116; 1974-75-76, c. 93, s. 5; 2005, c. 32, s. 1.

CROSS-REFERENCES

The term "Act" is defined in s. 2.

SYNOPSIS

The hybrid offence created by this section is disobeying an order of a court or other person or body established by legislation to give orders if there is no other penalty specified for such disobedience. Orders to pay money are specifically excluded from the operation of the section. The maximum punishment for this offence is two years' imprisonment where the Crown proceeds by way of indictment and six months' imprisonment where the Crown proceeds by way of summary conviction.

As with s. 126, the federal government may prosecute if the order disobeyed was made by proceedings commenced by and prosecuted by (or on behalf of) the federal government.

ANNOTATIONS

The words "lawful order" apply to an order of a court either criminal or civil in nature, such as an order enjoining one party to a matrimonial dispute from molesting the other. Further, the inherent power of the court to punish for contempt is not a mode of proceeding expressly provided by law within the meaning of the exception so as to bar a conviction under subsec. (1): *R. v. Clement*, [1981] 2 S.C.R. 468, 61 C.C.C. (2d) 449 (7:0).

It was not open to an accused who had breached a non-publication order in respect of criminal proceedings to collaterally attack the validity of that order as a defence to a charge under this provision: *R. v. Domm* (1996), 111 C.C.C. (3d) 449 (Ont. C.A.), leave to appeal to S.C.C. refused 114 C.C.C. (3d) vi.

The "other mode of proceeding expressly provided by law" exception will be triggered where Parliament or a legislature has provided a legal foundation for the court's power to issue contempt orders, defined the circumstances in which a person will be found in contempt, and provided a specific punishment or mode of proceeding. The fact that rules of court address contempt proceedings is not sufficient to trigger the exception if the order was issued pursuant to the court's inherent common law power. Here, even though Ontario rules 60.11 and 60.12 set out in considerable detail the procedure to be followed on a motion for a contempt order, in light of the court's reasoning in *Clement, supra*, this alone is insufficient to trigger the exception: *R. v. Gibbons*, [2012] 2 S.C.R. 92, 283 C.C.C. (3d) 295.

Similarly, the provisions in the *Alberta Rules of Court* governing contempt of court flow from the court's inherent jurisdiction and do not trigger the "other mode of proceeding" exception: *R. v. Nielsen* (2015), 322 C.C.C. (3d) 457 (Alta. C.A.).

The weight of authority holds that breach of a common law peace bond may be prosecuted pursuant to this section: *R. v. Musoni* (2009), 243 C.C.C. (3d) 17 (Ont. S.C.J.), affirmed (2009), 248 C.C.C. (3d) 487 (Ont. C.A.), leave to appeal to S.C.C. refused (2010), 251 C.C.C. (3d) vii; *R. v. Petre* (2013), 299 C.C.C. (3d) 246 (Ont. S.C.J.); *R. v. Pope* (2013), 107 W.C.B. (2d) 750, 2013 YKTC 47; *R. v. Palosaari* (2012), 100 W.C.B. (2d) 827, [2012] B.C.J. No. 723 (Prov. Ct.). A minority view holds that breach of a common law peace bond results in monetary liability but not a criminal offence that can be prosecuted under this provision: *R. v. Mousseau* (2011), 273 C.C.C. (3d) 109 (Ont. C.J.).

MISCONDUCT OF OFFICERS EXECUTING PROCESS.

128. Every peace officer or coroner who, being entrusted with the execution of a process, wilfully

　　(*a*) misconducts himself in the execution of the process, or

　　(*b*) makes a false return to the process,

is guilty of an indictable offence and liable to imprisonment for a term not exceeding two years. R.S., c. C-34, s. 117.

CROSS-REFERENCES

The term "peace officer" is defined in s. 2. The term "wilfully" does not have a fixed meaning and must take its meaning from the context. Generally speaking, however, it connotes an intention to bring about a proscribed consequence. See: *R. v. Buzzanga and Durocher* (1979), 49 C.C.C. (2d) 369 (Ont. C.A.). Section 29 imposes certain duties on anyone executing a process. The use of force in enforcement of the law is principally dealt with under s. 25. Personating a peace officer is an offence under s. 130.

The accused has an election as to mode of trial pursuant to s. 536(2). Release pending trial is determined by s. 515, although the accused is eligible for release by the officer in charge under s. 498.

SYNOPSIS

Section 128 is limited in its application to offences committed by *peace officers* or *coroners* in connection with their duties to *execute process*. It is a criminal offence for such persons to *wilfully* engage in *misconduct* in the execution of this process or to make a *false return* to the process. Section 128 creates an indictable offence punishable by a maximum sentence of two years' imprisonment.

OFFENCES RELATING TO PUBLIC OR PEACE OFFICER.

129. Every one who

    (*a*) resists or wilfully obstructs a public officer or peace officer in the execution of his duty or any person lawfully acting in aid of such an officer,

    (*b*) omits, without reasonable excuse, to assist a public officer or peace officer in the execution of his duty in arresting a person or in preserving the peace, after having reasonable notice that he is required to do so, or

    (*c*) resists or wilfully obstructs any person in the lawful execution of a process against lands or goods or in making a lawful distress or seizure,

is guilty of

    (*d*) an indictable offence and is liable to imprisonment for a term not exceeding two years, or

    (*e*) an offence punishable on summary conviction. R.S., c. C-34, s. 118; 1972, c. 13, s. 7.

CROSS-REFERENCES

The terms "peace officer" and "public officer" are defined in s. 2. The term "wilfully" does not have a fixed meaning and must take its meaning from the context. Generally speaking, however, it connotes an intention to bring about a proscribed consequence. See: *R. v. Buzzanga and Durocher* (1979), 49 C.C.C. (2d) 369 (Ont. C.A.) where, however, reference was made to *Rice v. Connolly*, [1966] 2 Q.B. 414 (C.A.), a case of wilfully obstructing a constable in the execution of his duty. In that case, "wilful" was held to mean not only intentional but "something which is done without lawful excuse".

Offence of assaulting a peace officer in execution of duty, see s. 270 and see also, notes under that section for further discussion of meaning of "execution of his duty". The offence of attempting to obstruct justice is in s. 139, of public mischief in s. 140 and escape offences in ss. 144 to 147. Misconduct by a peace officer in executing process is an offence under s. 128. Section 29 imposes certain duties on anyone executing a process. The use of force in enforcement of the law is principally dealt with under s. 25 and see notes under that section. Sections 494 and 495 deal specifically with warrantless arrest powers. Additional duties are imposed and powers given under other provisions of the Code, especially in Parts I and II, respecting breach of the peace and more serious disorders. Personating a peace officer is an offence under s. 130. As to power to enter dwelling house, see ss. 529-529.3.

Where the prosecution elects to proceed by way of summary conviction then the trial of this offence is conducted by a summary conviction court pursuant to Part XXVII. The punishment for the offence is then as set out in s. 787 and the limitation period is set out in s. 786(2). In either case, release pending trial is determined by s. 515, although the accused is eligible for release by a peace officer under ss. 496, 497 or by the officer in charge under s. 498.

A person found guilty of the offences in this section is, in certain circumstances, liable to the discretionary prohibition order prescribed by s. 110 for possession of firearms, ammunition and explosives.

SYNOPSIS

This section creates an offence of *wilfully obstructing* or resisting a peace or *public officer*, or a person assisting that officer in the execution of his duties.

As a precondition to conviction under para. (*a*), it must be shown that the *purpose* of the accused's actions was to *obstruct the officer and* that the officer was *engaged in the execution of his duties.*

Paragraphs (*a*) and (*c*) require proof that the accused either *resisted* or *wilfully obstructed* the carrying out of these duties. Section 129(*b*) dictates that the accused receive *reasonable notice* that the accused's *assistance* is required to arrest a person or to preserve the peace and the accused has *no reasonable excuse* for refusing to assist.

These offences are punishable by summary conviction proceedings or by way of indictment. In the latter case, the maximum punishment is two years' imprisonment.

ANNOTATIONS

Conduct amounting to obstruction of peace officer – The wilful obstruction of a police officer is a general intent offence. The conduct of an accused lawyer who instructed his client to leave the courtroom after a bench warrant for the client had been issued satisfied the *mens rea* requirement despite the accused's belief that the client's arrest was illegal: *R. v. Gunn* (1997), 113 C.C.C. (3d) 174 (Alta. C.A.), leave to appeal to S.C.C. refused 115 C.C.C. (3d) vi.

Paragraph (*a*) does not create two separate offences of "resisting" and "obstructing" an officer, but rather a single offence. The gravamen of the offence is interference with a peace officer engaged in the execution of his duty by resisting or by wilful obstruction. The concept of resisting has been subsumed in the larger concept of obstructing. It is a general intent offence: *R. v. Glowach* (2011), 277 C.C.C. (3d) 89 (B.C.S.C.).

Although the accused, a bicyclist, committed no provincial offence by refusing to identify himself to a police officer who had found him committing the summary conviction offence of going through a red light contrary to the *Motor Vehicle Act* (B.C.), since the officer had no power to arrest the accused under s. 495(2) (applicable to provincial offences by virtue of the *Summary Convictions Act* (B.C.) except if arrest was necessary to, *inter alia*, "establish the identity of the person", the officer by requesting the accused to identify himself was carrying out the duty of enforcing the law and when the accused refused to accede to the officer's request he was obstructing the officer in the performance of his duties: *R. v. Moore*, [1979] 1 S.C.R. 195, 43 C.C.C. (2d) 83 (5:2).

However, no charge lay under this section where the accused refused to identify herself in circumstances where the officer had no evidence that she had committed any offence: *R. v. Guthrie* (1982), 69 C.C.C. (2d) 216 (Alta. C.A.).

A person is not guilty of obstructing a peace officer merely by doing nothing, unless there is a legal duty to act arising at common law or by statute. The refusal of a motorist to hand over a radar detecting device could not constitute obstruction. The police officer had the right to arrest the accused if necessary to search him, but the refusal did not amount to obstruction. Willful obstruction of a police officer requires either some positive act, such as concealment of evidence, or an omission to do something which one is legally obliged to do: *R. v. Lavin* (1992), 76 C.C.C. (3d) 279 (Que. C.A.).

An accused could not be convicted of this offence for failing to comply with the order of a police officer to comply with a municipal by-law where the by-law was later held to be *ultra vires*. Moreover, even if the by-law were valid, since the applicable provincial legislation provided other means of enforcement such as ticketing the offender, and since the accused did not interfere with that procedure, the accused could not be charged with this offence merely for disobeying the officer's order: *R. v. Sharma*, [1993] 1 S.C.R. 650, 79 C.C.C. (3d) 142.

In *R. v. Long*, [1970] 1 C.C.C. 313 (B.C.C.A.), it was held that the exercise of the right of the prisoner or someone speaking for him to know the reason for arrest does not *per se* amount to obstruction.

Any privilege which a person placed under arrest may have to resist that arrest where he is not informed of the reason for the arrest does not extend to a friend of the person and will not constitute a defence to a charge of obstructing a police officer where the friend interferes with the arrest: *R. v. Saunders* (1977), 34 C.C.C. (2d) 243 (N.S.C.A.).

In *R. v. Westlie* (1971), 2 C.C.C. (2d) 315 (B.C.C.A.), the accused was convicted of wilfully obstructing a peace officer where on several occasions he stopped people in the "skid row" area of the city and pointed out to those people that the officer, who was in plain clothes for the purpose of detecting and arresting beggars, was a police officer. The members of the court in three separate opinions were of the view that the officer was in the execution of his duty at the time and that the accused's conduct constituted a wilful obstruction of that duty in that it completely frustrated him in the duty in which he was engaged.

It is the purpose of the wilful obstruction, not its result, that goes to the offence and accordingly the fact that the assault did not prevent the peace officer from executing his duty is not a defence: *R. v. Tortolano, Kelly and Cadwell* (1975), 28 C.C.C. (2d) 562 (Ont. C.A.), overruling *R. v. Bakin* (1973), 14 C.C.C. (2d) 541 (Ont. Co. Ct.).

Furthermore, the lawfulness of the accused's arrest is not dependent on whether the accused is convicted of the underlying offence of obstruction: *R. v. Anderson* (1996), 111 C.C.C. (3d) 540 (B.C.C.A.), leave to appeal to S.C.C. refused 114 C.C.C. (3d) vi.

Section 254(3) places a duty on a motorist to remain in the presence of the officer until he has completed the duties imposed on the officer by the section. Thus, an accused may be convicted of the offence contrary to this section where he flees the scene before the officer has had an opportunity to make a demand that he provide breath samples for analysis in the breathalyzer: *R. v. Quist* (1981), 61 C.C.C. (2d) 207, 11 Sask. R. 28 (C.A.).

However, in *R. v. Gall* (1984), 35 Sask. R. 138, 28 M.V.R. 91 (Q.B.), the accused was acquitted of the offence under this section where he took flight after he had registered a "fail" on the roadside screening device and *after* the officer had given him the breathalyzer demand. The accused's identity was known and the officer had completed his duties under the section. The accused should have been charged with failing or refusing to comply with the breathalyzer demand.

Conduct amounting to resisting – A charge of resisting an officer in the execution of his duty will lie under this section where the accused resists an officer to whom he has been delivered by other officers even when the accused is arrested for a summary conviction offence and is ultimately acquitted of that charge. Although s. 495(1)(*b*) of the Code limits the power of arrest to where an officer "finds [the accused] committing" the offence the validity of the arrest is to be determined in relation to the circumstances which were apparent to the officer at the time the arrest was made. In any event an officer who receives an accused into custody from other officers is in the execution of his duty pursuant to s. 31(2) of the Code: *R. v. Biron*, [1976] 2 S.C.R. 56, 23 C.C.C. (2d) 513 (5:3).

Execution of his duty / *Also see notes under s. 270* – An officer would be in the execution of his duty in forcibly entering private premises where he believes on reasonable and probable grounds that he is confronted with an emergency situation involving the preservation of life of a person in the dwelling-house, or the prevention of serious injury to that person, and if a proper announcement is made prior to entry: *R. v. Custer* (1984), 12 C.C.C. (3d) 372, [1984] 4 W.W.R. 133 (Sask. C.A.). Also see notes under s. 529.3.

There is an implied authority for a person to proceed from the gate to the front door of a house and police officers on premises by invitation may, as well, have a reasonable time to leave following revocation of an invitation to enter. Thereafter, however, in the absence of common law or statutory authority, the officer is no longer in the execution of his duty if he remains on the premises. A mere failure to keep the peace does not of itself empower the police to enter private premises: *R. v. Thomas* (1991), 67 C.C.C. (3d) 81, 91 Nfld. & P.E.I.R. 341 (Nfld. C.A.), affd [1993] 1 S.C.R. 835, 78 C.C.C. (3d) 575*n*; *R. v. Evans*, [1996] 1 S.C.R. 8, 104 C.C.C. (3d) 23.

An officer is not in the execution of his duty where he is seeking to enforce a law which has been repealed even though he honestly and reasonably believes that the law exists: *R. v. Houle* (1985), 24 C.C.C. (3d) 57, 48 C.R. (3d) 284 (Alta. C.A.).

A police officer who uses his powers associated with provincial highway safety legislation to detain an accused for an unrelated purpose is not acting in the execution of his duty: *R. v. Guénette* (1999), 136 C.C.C. (3d) 311, 2 M.V.R. (4th) 81 (Que. C.A.). In *R. v. Waugh* (2010), 251 C.C.C. (3d) 139, however, the Ontario Court of Appeal held that, by causing an uninsured vehicle to be impounded and towed to safety, the police were acting in the exercise of their common law duty to protect the life and property of the public (leave to appeal to S.C.C. refused [2010] 2 S.C.R. ix, 255 C.C.C. (3d) vi).

The police were not acting in lawful execution of their duty in unlawfully trespassing on private property at the time of the accused's arrest: *R. v. Lauda* (1999), 136 C.C.C. (3d) 358, 25 C.R. (5th) 320 (Ont. C.A.).

A peace officer need not be involved in the investigation of a specific crime, with an identifiable suspect, in order to be "in execution of his duty". The officer will be engaged "in execution of his duty" if, at any given time while on duty, a peace officer's activities fall within the duties and responsibilities of a peace officer described by statute or common law. However, something more than merely being "on duty" or "at work" is required before a peace officer will be "in the execution of his duty". Further, while the accused cannot be convicted unless he knew that the officer was engaged in the execution of a duty, the accused need not know the specifics of that duty in detail: *R. v. Noel* (1995), 101 C.C.C. (3d) 183 (B.C.C.A.).

Failing to assist officer / para. (b) – It is no defence to a charge under para. (*b*) that the person whom the officer sought to arrest was the accused's son. The assistance contemplated by para. (*b*) may be either verbal or physical depending on the circumstances but if the verbal assistance is obviously ineffectual then it is incumbent on the person to whom the request has been made to offer such physical assistance as may be required: *R. v. Foster* (1981), 65 C.C.C. (2d) 388, 27 C.R. (3d) 187 (Alta Q.B.).

The accused pawnbroker's conduct fell within the purview of para. (*b*) where he returned a pawned item to the holder of a pawnticket whom the accused knew or had reason to suspect was not the rightful owner. The accused's conduct could not be properly characterized as an omission because despite being advised by the police to retain possession of the item, the accused had deliberately committed an act intended to obstruct the police in the course of their investigation by rendering the item inaccessible to the police by returning it to the holder of the pawnticket. Furthermore, the existence of provincial legislation stating that the holder of a pawnticket is entitled to the item is not a defence to a charge under this provision as the provincial legislation cannot empower the return of a pledged item where to do so would constitute a criminal offence: *R. v. Akrofi* (1997), 113 C.C.C. (3d) 201, 96 O.A.C. 306 (C.A.).

Obstructing execution of process / para. (c) – It is no defence to a charge under this section arising out of the obstructing of a sheriff attempting to levy a distress pursuant to a warrant valid on its face, that the warrant may have been a nullity due to some procedural irregularity: *R. v. Fritz* (1979), 58 C.C.C. (2d) 285 (B.C.C.A.).

PERSONATING PEACE OFFICER / Punishment.

130. (1) Everyone commits an offence who

    (*a*) **falsely represents himself to be a peace officer or a public officer; or**

    (*b*) **not being a peace officer or public officer, uses a badge or article of uniform or equipment in a manner that is likely to cause persons to believe that he is a peace officer or a public officer, as the case may be.**

(2) Everyone who commits an offence under subsection (1)

    (*a*) **is guilty of an indictable offence and liable to imprisonment for a term of not more than five years; or**

    (*b*) **is guilty of an offence punishable on summary conviction. R.S., c. C-34, s. 119; 2009, c. 28, s. 2.**

CROSS-REFERENCES

The terms "peace officer" and "public officer" are defined in s. 2. The offence of obstructing a peace officer is in s. 129 and see notes under that section. Misconduct by a peace officer in executing process is an offence under s. 128. Other personation offences are dealt with in ss. 402.1 to 405.

SYNOPSIS

The final section in this group of offences creates the hybrid offence of *personating a peace officer*. The offence may be committed by a person either by actually *representing himself as a peace officer* or public officer, or by using a *badge or other equipment* which is likely to cause others to believe that he is such an officer.

ANNOTATIONS

Mens rea is an essential element of this offence and where a municipality-licensed bailiff mistakenly believes that he is a peace officer, he must be acquitted of impersonation: *R. v. Wallace, R. v. Hall, R. v. Leach* (1959), 125 C.C.C. 72 (Ont. Mag. Ct.).

The offence under para. (*a*) of this section requires proof of a misrepresentation as a peace officer or public officer as defined in s. 2, which implicitly means a person vested with powers within Canada. Thus, it would not be an offence under para. (*a*) for the accused to falsely represent that he was a United States Sheriff's officer: *R. v. Saleman* (1984), 19 C.C.C. (3d) 526 (Ont. Co. Ct.).

A peace officer as used in s. 2 of the *Criminal Code* does not include a person employed by a private bailiff company: *R. v. Burns* (2002), 170 C.C.C. (3d) 288, [2003] 2 W.W.R. 638 (Man. C.A.).

AGGRAVATING CIRCUMSTANCE.

130.1 If a person is convicted of an offence under section 130, the court imposing the sentence on the person shall consider as an aggravating circumstance the fact that the accused personated a peace officer or a public officer, as the case may be, for the purpose of facilitating the commission of another offence. 2014, c. 10, s. 1.

Misleading Justice

PERJURY / Video links, etc. / Idem / Application.

131. (1) Subject to subsection (3), every one commits perjury who, with intent to mislead, makes before a person who is authorized by law to permit it to be made before him a false statement under oath or solemn affirmation, by affidavit, solemn declaration or deposition or orally, knowing that the statement is false.

(1.1) Subject to subsection (3), every person who gives evidence under subsection 46(2) of the *Canada Evidence Act*, or gives evidence or a statement pursuant to an order made under section 22.2 of the *Mutual Legal Assistance in Criminal Matters Act*, commits perjury who, with intent to mislead, makes a false statement knowing that it is false, whether or not the false statement was made under oath or solemn affirmation in accordance with subsection (1), so long as the false statement was made in accordance with any formalities required by the law of the place outside Canada in which the person is virtually present or heard.

(2) Subsection (1) applies whether or not a statement referred to in that subsection is made in a judicial proceeding.

(3) Subsections (1) and (1.1) do not apply to a statement referred to in either of those subsections that is made by a person who is not specially permitted, authorized or required by law to make that statement. R.S., c. C-34, s. 120; R.S.C. 1985, c. 27 (1st Supp.), s. 17; 1999, c. 18, s. 92.

CROSS-REFERENCES

The terms "statement", and "judicial proceeding" are defined in s. 118. As to oath and solemn affirmation, see the notes concerning "witness" under s. 118 and ss. 13 to 16 of the *Canada Evidence Act*. Perjury is created an indictable offence by s. 132, which also prescribes the punishment. The requirement for corroboration is set out in s. 133. The related offence for cases excepted by the proviso in subsec. (3) is found in s. 134. The offence of giving contradictory evidence is in s. 136. The offence of fabricating evidence is in s. 137 and offences relating to affidavits in s. 138. The offence of attempting to obstruct justice is in s. 139. Note that s. 13 of the *Canadian Charter of Rights and Freedoms*, which otherwise protects against the use of prior testimony, does not apply to prosecutions for the offences of perjury and giving contradictory evidence. Section 5 of the *Canada Evidence Act*, which also protects against use of prior testimony, does not apply in a prosecution for perjury in the giving of that evidence.

Section 585 provides that no count charging perjury is insufficient by reason only that it does not state the nature of the authority of the tribunal before which the statement was made, or the subject of the inquiry, or the words used, or that it does not expressly negative the words used. However, s. 587(1)(*a*) provides for the furnishing of particulars in perjury cases.

The accused has an election as to mode of trial pursuant to s. 536(2). Release pending trial is determined by s. 515. This offence may be the basis for an application for an authorization to intercept private communications by reason of s. 183.

SYNOPSIS

This section spells out the parameters of the offence of *perjury*. It requires proof of several discrete elements, including that the *statement* made must be *false* and that the *accused knew that it was false*. There must also be an *intent to mislead*. The false statement may have been made *under oath or solemn affirmation,* orally, by affidavit or solemn declaration. Section 131 has been amended to encompass the contents of two earlier sections: one related to perjury committed in judicial proceedings, and the other to extra-judicial proceedings. Pursuant to subsec. (1.1), this provision applies to evidence given under s. 46(2) of the *Canada Evidence Act* and s. 22.2 of the *Mutual Legal Assistance in Criminal Matters Act*. Section 131(2) removes this distinction by stating that the offence may be committed regardless of whether the false statement was made in a judicial proceeding. Another element of the offence is that the person before whom the statement is sworn, affirmed or declared must be authorized to receive such statements, and includes persons such as a judge at trial, a commissioner for the taking of oaths and a notary public.

Subsection (3) excludes liability under this section if the person making the false statement was not specially authorized or required by law to make a statement.

ANNOTATIONS

Relationship to other offences – It would appear that the effect of the amendments to this section and former s. 122 are to create a single offence of perjury which may be committed either by making false statements in a judicial proceeding (former s. 120) or in extrajudicial proceedings (former s. 122). This would overcome the problems encountered in cases such as *R. v. Wilson* (1977), 33 C.C.C. (2d) 383, [1977] 2 W.W.R. 520 (Alta. C.A.), and *R. v. Hewson* (1977), 35 C.C.C. (2d) 407 (Ont. C.A.), where the accused who swore a false affidavit was held to have been improperly charged with the former s. 122 offence since the affidavit, being intended for use in judicial proceedings, civil or criminal, the offence, if any, was perjury as defined by the former s. 120.

Elements of offence generally – In *R. v. Calder*, [1960] S.C.R. 892, 129 C.C.C. 202 (9:0), Cartwright J. summarized the elements of this offence as requiring proof beyond a reasonable doubt that the evidence specified in the indictment was false in fact, that the accused when he gave it knew that it was false, and that he gave it with intent to mislead the court. Judson J. pointed out that where the most that can be found against the accused is that evidence he gave was in error then this affords no basis for the inference of the requisite knowledge and intent.

Mere carelessness or even recklessness in giving testimony on collateral matters, without any intent to mislead and give false evidence, does not amount to the offence of perjury: *R. v. Besner* (1975), 33 C.R.N.S. 122 (Que. C.A.).

Where the accused had given a complete statement to the police which he confirmed and then gave evidence at the preliminary inquiry that he knew to be false when he testified that he did not remember either being beaten or seeing at that time the two men who were charged with assaulting him, the argument that he could not be said to have had any intent to mislead the court when there was no other evidence before it against which his failure of recollection could be measured was rejected. It was held that those non-recollections were "evidence" as defined under this Part of the *Criminal Code*, and the fact that a court could or would not be misled does not alone preclude a finding that the accused intended to mislead it, for in the absence of other evidence as to the accused's intention the inference could properly be drawn that in so doing what he did he intended to mislead the court: *R. v. Wolf*, [1975] 2 S.C.R. 107, 17 C.C.C. (2d) 425 (9:0).

For there to be perjury, there has to be more than a deliberate false statement. The statement must also have been made with intent to mislead. In an exceptional case, an accused may be able to show that while he deliberately lied, he did not do so with intent to mislead: *R. v. Hebert*, [1989] 1 S.C.R. 233, 49 C.C.C. (3d) 59.

In assessing whether or not perjury has occurred, the trier of fact must have all of the evidence of the accused bearing on the impugned testimony. However, an outright confession to prior perjury in testimony given several weeks earlier in the same proceeding cannot qualify as an explanatory statement to show that there was no intent to mislead: *R. v. Zazulak* (1993), 84 C.C.C. (3d) 303 (Alta. C.A.), affd [1994] 25 S.C.R. 5*n*, 88 C.C.C. (3d) 415*n*.

Proof that testimony false – In *R. v. Farris*, [1965] 3 C.C.C. 245, [1965] 2 O.R. 396 (C.A.), it was held that it is no defence if the accused's statement is literally true if he well knew and intended that the statement should be taken in another sense.

It is no defence to say that the perjured evidence was so preposterous that it could not possibly be expected to mislead the court, and that the accused could therefore not have had an "intent to mislead". The accused's decision to withhold his evidence from the court was done with an intent to lead the court astray in the sense of not assisting the trier to arrive at a correct view of the facts: *R. v. Wilson* (2011), 272 C.C.C. (3d) 35 (Ont. S.C.J.).

In attempting to prove that the accused's sworn statement was knowingly false, the Crown may lead evidence that other people said similar things that were untrue in similar ways. The hearsay rule is not infringed because the probative value of multiple erroneous similarities arises from the unlikelihood of coincidence: *R. v. Bentley* (2013), 300 C.C.C. (3d) 273 (B.C.S.C.).

Proof of record – Proof of the record of proceedings in a civil action was made by exemplification, relying on s. 23 of the *Canada Evidence Act*. While s. 28 of the *Canada Evidence Act* requires at least 7 days notice where a "copy" of the record is produced, that requirement does not apply to exemplifications, being a "certified transcript under the great seal or under the seal of a particular court": *R. v. Kobold* (1927), 48 C.C.C. 290 (Man. C.A.). In *R. v. Tatomir* (1989), 51 C.C.C. (3d) 321 (Alta. C.A.), the court considered the admissibility of a certified copy of a driving prohibition to prove an offence under s. 259. The court held that, at common law, judicial documents could be proved by the production of the original record or an exemplification under the seal of the court to which the record belongs without notice.

Requirement of oath or solemn affirmation – A witness who takes a certain form of oath, without objection, in the form generally administered to persons of his faith, agreeing that it binds his conscience, cannot thereafter be heard to say that he was not sworn: *R. v. Shajoo Ram (No. 2)* (1915), 51 S.C.R. 392, 25 C.C.C. 69 (5:0).

There is no statutory requirement as to the method of proof of the fact of a witness being sworn and thus, evidence of the court reporter and the instructing police officer that they both heard the oath being administered to the accused was sufficient proof of the administration of the oath. That the proof might have been made by other or different means, such as by the official record of the court or the testimony of the official who administered the oath, did not render the evidence of these witnesses inadmissible: *R. v. Pfahler*, [1963] 2 C.C.C. 289 (Ont. C.A.).

There is no specific set of words required for an oath to be properly administered. Accordingly, even though the commissioner was unsure whether she employed the standard practice for swearing affidavit or whether she used a modified procedure, there was sufficient evidence to allow the judge to conclude that the accused appreciated that he had assumed a moral obligation to tell the truth: *R. v. Seath* (2000), 147 C.C.C. (3d) 133 (Alta. C.A.).

Effect of s. 5 of *Canada Evidence Act* – Where the accused had testified on a trial under the protection of s. 5 of the *Canada Evidence Act* that certain statements he had made at an earlier inquest and preliminary inquiry were false, his trial evidence could not later be used on prosecution for perjury in respect of his testimony at the inquest and preliminary inquiry. The provision in s. 5 applies only to perjury in the giving of "that evidence", *i.e.*, the evidence which it is alleged is false: *R. v. Kruchkovski* (1925), 43 C.C.C. 299, [1925] 2 D.L.R. 167 (Sask. C.A.).

Double jeopardy | *Also see notes under s. 613* – As long as it does not amount to a retrial of the original offence and particularly where the Crown is able to rely upon his subsequent contrary testimony an acquitted accused may be tried for his prior perjured denial of his commission of the original offence: *R. v. Gushue* (1976), 32 C.C.C. (2d) 189 (Ont. C.A.), affd [1980] 1 S.C.R. 798, 50 C.C.C. (2d) 417 (7:0), holding that this principle applies to a prosecution under s. 124 [now s. 136] as well. Also see *R. v. Grdic*, [1985] 1 S.C.R. 810, 19 C.C.C. (3d) 289, noted under s. 613, *infra*.

Permitted, authorized or required by law (subsec. (3)) | *Also see notes under s. 134* – An affidavit which the legislator has not permitted, authorized or required, in short, an affidavit which has no legal meaning or scope is exempted from the perjury offence: *R. v. Boisjoly*, [1972] S.C.R. 42, 5 C.C.C. (2d) 309 (5:0). [Considering former s. 122 of R.S.C. 1970, c. C-34 which made it an offence for a person being permitted, authorized or required by law to make a statement by affidavit, knowing it to be a false statement.]

Where the accused provided an affidavit merely as a witness for a party to matrimonial proceedings, the Crown had satisfied the criteria in subsec. (3). That statement was permitted, authorized or required by law. The affidavit in this case was never filed nor was the accused ever examined on it. However, the oath given in the context of matrimonial proceedings pursuant to the *Divorce Act* was required or authorized by the laws of Canada and Alberta and whether the affidavit was filed or not, it was intended to be relied upon: *R. v. Seath, supra*.

PUNISHMENT.

132. Every one who commits perjury is guilty of an indictable offence and liable to imprisonment for a term not exceeding fourteen years. R.S., c. C-34, s. 121; R.S.C. 1985, c. 27 (1st Supp.), s. 17; 1998, c. 35, s. 119.

CROSS-REFERENCES

The offence of perjury is defined in s. 131. The requirement for corroboration is set out in s. 133. As to related offences, see notes under s. 131. The accused has an election as to mode of trial pursuant to s. 536(2). Release pending trial is determined by s. 515. This offence may be the basis for an application for an authorization to intercept private communications by reason of s. 183.

SYNOPSIS

Section 132 states the punishment for the indictable offence of perjury. The maximum sentence is 14 years' imprisonment.

CORROBORATION.

133. No person shall be convicted of an offence under section 132 on the evidence of only one witness unless the evidence of that witness is corroborated in a material particular by evidence that implicates the accused. R.S., c. C-34, s. 122; R.S.C. 1985, c. 27 (1st Supp.), s. 17.

CROSS-REFERENCES

The offence of perjury is defined in s. 131 and punishment is set out in s. 132. For related offences, see notes under s. 131.

SYNOPSIS

This section deals with an evidentiary requirement in a perjury prosecution. Before an accused may be convicted of perjury, there must be *corroboration* of a *material particular* if there is only one witness to the offence giving evidence.

ANNOTATIONS

Application to party to offence – Although this section also applies to the offence of subornation of perjury as laid down under s. 21, where the charge is inciting [now counselling] to commit perjury that was not in fact committed this section does not apply to the proof of the lesser s. 464 offence: *R. v. Kyling*, [1970] S.C.R. 953, 2 C.C.C. (2d) 79 (5:0).

Evidence amounting to corroboration – While corroboration may be required on a charge of suborning perjury, it is only the perjury that requires corroboration not the accused's participation in the perjury and his knowledge of the falsity of the witness' evidence: *R. v. Doz* (1984), 12 C.C.C. (3d) 200 (Alta. C.A.).

There is a conflict in the authorities as to what element of the offence must be corroborated. Thus, it was held in *R. v. Nash* (1914), 23 C.C.C. 38 (Alta. C.A.), that it was sufficient to show corroboration of the element of the offence that the testimony was false. *R. v. Pattyson* (1973), 12 C.C.C. (2d) 174 (Sask. C.A.), seems to be to the same effect. However, in *R. v. Boisjoly* (1970), 11 C.R.N.S. 265 (Que. C.A.), it was held that there must be corroboration of the accused's knowledge of the falsity of the evidence.

While corroboration is required of a material particular it need not be with respect to a contested issue: *R. v. Van Straten* (1994), 89 C.C.C. (3d) 470 (Alta. C.A.). Also see *R. v. Kehler*, [2004] 1 S.C.R. 328, 181 C.C.C. (3d) 1.

In *R. v. B. (G.)*, [1990] 2 S.C.R. 3, 56 C.C.C. (3d) 161 (5:0), the court considered the effect of now repealed s. 586, which provided that no person shall be convicted on the unsworn evidence of a child "unless the evidence of the child is corroborated in a material particular by evidence that implicates the accused". The wording is thus almost identical to this section. It was there held that the requirement that the corroborating evidence implicate the accused requires only that the evidence confirm, in some material particular, the story of the witness giving the evidence which required corroboration. The confirming evidence need not also itself implicate the accused.

However, in *R. v. Thind* (1991), 64 C.C.C. (3d) 301 (B.C.C.A.), the court refused to apply *R. v. B. (G.), supra,* and held that, to be capable of corroboration under this section, the evidence from the other witness must be in contradiction to what has been sworn to by the accused in the previous proceeding. The requirement of more than one witness must be as to the falsity of the statement alleged to be perjured and it is not sufficient that the evidence simply confirms the reliability or trustworthiness of the other prosecution witness. Similarly, in *R. v. Neveu* (2004), 184 C.C.C. (3d) 18, the Quebec Court of Appeal held that where only one witness testifies, the corroboration must be more than evidence that strengthens the credibility of a witness whose credibility is not impugned. The corroboration must be of a material particular which implicates the accused. The corroboration requirement does not apply where the case against the accused is wholly circumstantial. See also *R. v. Evans* (1995), 101 C.C.C. (3d) 369 (Man. C.A.).

On the trial of two accused on a charge of perjury arising out of testimony given at a judicial inquiry a statement given by one accused to the police several months before the inquiry is capable of constituting corroboration against his co-accused if it was made in furtherance of a conspiracy to hide the truth with respect to a matter dealt with at the inquiry even if it was not made in furtherance of a conspiracy to testify falsely at the inquiry: *R. v. Zappia and Luppino* (1975), 27 C.C.C. (2d) 448 (Ont. C.A.).

Corroboration not required – As indicated above, corroboration is not required on a charge contrary to s. 464, counselling perjury which is not in fact committed: *R. v. Kyling, supra.* Nor is it required on a charge of conspiracy to commit perjury: *R. v. Fergusson and Petrie*, [1969] 1 C.C.C. 353 (B.C.C.A.).

In *R. v. Bouchard* (1982), 66 C.C.C. (2d) 338 (Man. C.A.), the court was divided as to whether corroboration was required where the perjury charge was proved by the accused's own confession to a police officer that he had lied at the original trial. O'Sullivan J.A. was of the view that this section nevertheless required corroboration. Matas J.A. allowed the accused's appeal on another ground and therefore did not consider the point. Monnin J.A., dissenting, was of the view that this section had no application in such circumstances. Also see *R. v. Evans, supra.*

The falsity of a statement by an accused as to his criminal record may be proved by production of a certificate of a fingerprint examiner as authorized by s. 667. Proof in such a manner must be considered an exception to the corroboration requirements of this section: *R. v. Predy* (1983), 17 C.C.C. (3d) 379 (Alta. C.A.).

Corroboration is not required where the case involves the contradictory statements of the accused: *R. v. Eriksen* (2006), 213 C.C.C. (3d) 374 (Y.T.C.A.). See also: *R. v. Wilson* (2011), 272 C.C.C. (3d) 35 (Ont. S.C.J.).

IDEM / Application.

134. (1) Subject to subsection (2), every one who, not being specially permitted, authorized or required by law to make a statement under oath or solemn affirmation, makes such a statement, by affidavit, solemn declaration or deposition or orally before a person who is authorized by law to permit it to be made before him, knowing that the statement is false, is guilty of an offence punishable on summary conviction.

(2) Subsection (1) does not apply to a statement referred to in that subsection that is made in the course of a criminal investigation. 1974-75-76, c. 93, s. 6; R.S.C. 1985, c. 27 (1st Supp.), s. 17.

CROSS-REFERENCES

The term "statement" is defined in s. 118. As to oath and solemn affirmation, see the notes concerning "witness" under s. 118 and ss. 13 to 16 of the *Canada Evidence Act*. This section covers most of the circumstances excepted from the perjury offence by s. 131(3). Other related offences are as follows: The offence of giving contradictory evidence is in s. 136. The offence of fabricating evidence is in s. 137 and other offences relating to affidavits in s. 138. The offence of attempting to obstruct justice is in s. 139. Note that subsec. (2), while exempting from liability statements made in the course of a criminal investigation, would not protect against conduct amounting to public mischief under s. 140. The trial of this offence is conducted by a summary conviction court pursuant to Part XXVII. The punishment for the offence is then as set out in s. 787 and the limitation period is set out in s. 786(2). Release pending trial is determined by s. 515, although the accused is eligible for release by a peace officer under ss. 496, 497 or by the officer in charge under s. 498.

Section 585 provides that no count charging the making of a false statement is insufficient by reason only that it does not state the nature of the authority of the tribunal before which the statement was made, or the subject of the inquiry, or the words used, or that it does not expressly negative the words used. However, s. 587(1)(*a*) provides for the furnishing of particulars in such cases.

SYNOPSIS

This section creates an offence covering the conduct excepted from the main offence of perjury by s. 131(3). This summary conviction offence prohibits the making of false statements before a person authorized to receive statements when the *accused was not specially required* or authorized to make the statement under oath or affirmation. Like s. 131, this section applies to false statements made under oath or solemn affirmation orally, by affidavit or solemn declaration. While there is a requirement that the accused know that the statement is false, there is no requirement of an intent to mislead.

This section also contains an exception which is found in subsec. (2) which removes from its ambit statements made during a criminal investigation.

ANNOTATIONS

Permitted, authorized or required by law – An affidavit which the legislator has not permitted, authorized or required, in short, an affidavit which has no legal meaning or scope is one which is not permitted, authorized or required by law: *R. v. Boisjoly*, [1972] S.C.R. 42, 5 C.C.C. (2d) 309 (5:0). [Considering former s. 122 of R.S.C. 1970, c. C-34, which made it an offence for a person being permitted, authorized or required by law to make a statement by affidavit, knowing it to be a false statement.]

There being no law which specifically required or authorized the use of an affidavit on a bail review hearing, until that affidavit was actually filed or used at the bail review, it had no legal significance and was thus not one permitted, authorized or required by law: *R. v. Hewson* (1977), 35 C.C.C. (2d) 407 (Ont. C.A.) (considering former s. 122).

Authorized by law to permit it to be made – Where the patent of the commissioner before whom the affidavits were sworn was limited to work in connection with a particular law firm and that firm had nothing whatever to do with the proceedings in which those affidavits were sworn then the commissioner had no authorization to take the oath of the accused and the offence is not made out: *R. v. Edwards* (1974), 20 C.C.C. (2d) 112 (Ont. C.A.) [considering former s. 122 of R.S.C. 1970, c. C-34 which contained a similar phrase].

135. [*Repealed*, R.S.C. 1985, c. 27 (1st Supp.), s. 17.]

WITNESS GIVING CONTRADICTORY EVIDENCE / Evidence in specific cases / Definition of "evidence" / Proof of former trial / Consent required.

136. (1) Every one who, being a witness in a judicial proceeding, gives evidence with respect to any matter of fact or knowledge and who subsequently, in a judicial proceeding, gives evidence that is contrary to his previous evidence is guilty of an indictable offence and liable to imprisonment for a term not exceeding fourteen years, whether or not the prior or later evidence or either is true, but no person shall be convicted under this section unless the court, judge or provincial court judge, as the case may be, is satisfied beyond a reasonable doubt that the accused, in giving evidence in either of the judicial proceedings, intended to mislead.

(1.1) Evidence given under section 714.1, 714.2, 714.3 or 714.4 or under subsection 46(2) of the *Canada Evidence Act* or evidence or a statement given pursuant to an order made under section 22.2 of the *Mutual Legal Assistance in Criminal Matters Act* is deemed to be evidence given by a witness in a judicial proceeding for the purposes of subsection (1).

(2) Notwithstanding the definition "evidence" in section 118, "evidence", for the purposes of this section, does not include evidence that is not material.

(2.1) Where a person is charged with an offence under this section, a certificate specifying with reasonable particularity the proceeding in which that person is alleged to have given the evidence in respect of which the offence is charged, is evidence that it was given in a judicial proceeding, without proof of the signature or official character of the person by whom the certificate purports to be signed if it purports to be signed by the clerk of the court or other official having the custody of the record of that proceeding or by his lawful deputy.

(3) No proceedings shall be instituted under this section without the consent of the Attorney General. R.S., c. C-34, s. 124; R.S.C. 1985, c. 27 (1st Supp.), s. 18; 1999, c. 18, s. 93.

CROSS-REFERENCES

The terms "witness", and "judicial proceeding" are defined in s. 118. "Attorney General" is defined in s. 2. Note that s. 13 of the *Canadian Charter of Rights*, which otherwise protects against the use of prior testimony, does not apply to prosecutions for the offences of perjury and giving contradictory evidence. Section 5 of the *Canada Evidence Act*, which also protects against use of prior testimony, does not apply in a prosecution for perjury in the giving of that evidence. Thus, statements made under the protection of s. 5 could not be used in a prosecution under this section. Related offences are found in: s. 131, perjury; s. 134, false statements under oath; s. 137, fabricating evidence; s. 138, offences relating to affidavits; s. 139, attempting to obstruct justice; s. 140, public mischief.

Section 585 provides that no count charging the making of a false statement is insufficient by reason only that it does not state the nature of the authority of the tribunal before which the statement was made, or the subject of the inquiry, or the words used, or that it does not expressly negative the words used. However, s. 587(1)(*a*) provides for the furnishing of particulars in such cases. These provisions may apply to the charging of the offence under this section. Section 583(*h*) provides that a count is not insufficient by reason only that it does not state that the consent has been obtained. As to proof of that consent, see notes under that section.

The accused has an election as to mode of trial pursuant to s. 536(2). Release pending trial is determined by s. 515.

SYNOPSIS

Section 136 is limited to *witnesses* who give *evidence* in a *judicial proceeding* and then give *contradictory evidence* in a judicial proceeding. Pursuant to subsec. (1.1), "judicial proceeding" includes evidence given under ss. 46(2), and 714.1 to 714.4 of the *Canada Evidence Act* and pursuant to an order under s. 22.2 of the *Mutual Legal Assistance in Criminal Matters Act*. The issue on which the impugned evidence is given may be either about facts or knowledge. It is not necessary to prove which of the contradictory statements is false. However, it is an element of the offence that the accused *intended to mislead* by giving the evidence in either of the judicial proceedings. The seriousness of this indictable offence is reflected in its maximum penalty of 14 years.

Subsection (2) narrows the *definition* of *evidence* which would otherwise apply in this Part (see s. 118) by excluding *evidence* which is *not material*.

The proof of this offence is facilitated by subsec. (2.1) which permits the use of a certificate signed by a court clerk or other court official who has control of the record. The certificate can be used as proof that the evidence was given in a judicial proceeding, and the signature of the official character of the person signing need not be proved.

The availability of this section is further limited by a prerequisite under subsec. (3) that the Attorney General consent to all prosecutions under this section.

ANNOTATIONS

Elements of offence – Motive and intention are two separate matters and once the intention to mislead is established, even though it may have been for the highest motive, the offence, except for raising the successful defence of duress, is established: *R. v. Falkenberg* (1973), 13 C.C.C. (2d) 562 (Ont. Co. Ct.), revd on other grounds 16 C.C.C. (2d) 525 (C.A.), *infra*.

Double jeopardy / *Also see notes under ss. 131 and 613* – As long as it does not amount to a retrial of the original offence an acquitted accused may be tried under this section for his prior perjured denial of his commission of the original offence: *R. v. Gushue*, [1980] 1 S.C.R. 798, 50 C.C.C. (2d) 417 (7:0).

Consent of Attorney General / *Also see notes under s. 583(1)(h)* – A count for an offence for which the statutory consent of the Attorney-General to institute proceedings has been obtained cannot be amended if the amended count alleges another offence: *R. v. Falkenberg* (1974), 16 C.C.C. (2d) 525, 25 C.R.N.S. 374 (Ont. C.A.), quashing his conviction in 13 C.C.C. (2d) 562, *supra*.

FABRICATING EVIDENCE.

137. Every one who, with intent to mislead, fabricates anything with intent that it shall be used as evidence in a judicial proceeding, existing or proposed, by any means other than perjury or incitement to perjury is guilty of an indictable offence and liable to imprisonment for a term not exceeding fourteen years. R.S., c. C-34, s. 125.

CROSS-REFERENCES

The term "judicial proceeding" is defined in s. 118. Perjury is defined by s. 131. "Incite" is within the definition of "counsel" in s. 22(3). By s. 22(1), a person is party to the offence counselled.

Related offences are found in s. 131, perjury; s. 134, false statements under oath; s. 136, giving contradictory evidence; s. 138, offences relating to affidavits; s. 139, attempting to obstruct justice; s. 140, public mischief.

Section 585 provides that no count charging the fabricating of evidence is insufficient by reason only that it does not state the nature of the authority of the tribunal before which the statement was made, or the subject of the inquiry, or the evidence fabricated, or that it does not expressly negative the words used. However, s. 587(1)(*a*) provides for the furnishing of particulars in such cases.

Note that s. 25(1) of the *Interpretation Act*, R.S.C. 1985, c. I-21, provides, in effect, that a document, such as one produced under subsec. (2.1), is admissible in evidence and the fact is deemed to be established in the absence of evidence to the contrary.

The accused has an election as to mode of trial pursuant to s. 536(2). Release pending trial is determined by s. 515.

SYNOPSIS

Section 137 creates the indictable offence of *fabricating* anything which the accused *intends* to use in a *judicial proceeding*. This section is broadly worded to apply to circumstances in which such proceedings are either in existence or are proposed at the time that the fabrication occurs. It is an element of the offence that the accused did the act with the *intention to mislead*.

The maximum punishment under this section is 14 years' imprisonment.

ANNOTATIONS

An accused could not be convicted of this offence, by reason of her having signed notes alleging that she had been kidnapped by a certain person, since the notes would not be admissible in evidence at the trial of the person alleged to have committed the kidnapping: *R. v. Boyko* (1945), 83 C.C.C. 295 (Sask. C.A.).

OFFENCES RELATING TO AFFIDAVITS.

138. Every one who

(*a*) signs a writing that purports to be an affidavit or statutory declaration and to have been sworn or declared before him when the writing was not so sworn or declared or when he knows that he has no authority to administer the oath or declaration,

(*b*) uses or offers for use any writing purporting to be an affidavit or statutory declaration that he knows was not sworn or declared, as the case may be, by the affiant or declarant or before a person authorized in that behalf, or

(*c*) signs as affiant or declarant a writing that purports to be an affidavit or statutory declaration and to have been sworn or declared by him, as the case may be, when the writing was not so sworn or declared,

is guilty of an indictable offence and liable to imprisonment for a term not exceeding two years. R.S., c. C-34, s. 126.

CROSS-REFERENCES

Section 15 of the *Canada Evidence Act* provides for the form of solemn affirmation in the case of an affidavit or deposition. No particular form of oath is prescribed by law and see notes under "witness" in s. 118. A form of statutory declaration under the *Canada Evidence Act* is prescribed by s. 41 of that Act, but reference may also be made to the various provincial *Evidence Acts*.

Related offences are found in s. 131, perjury; s. 134, false statements under oath; s. 136, giving contradictory evidence; s. 137, fabricating evidence; s. 139, attempting to obstruct justice; s. 140, public mischief.

Section 585 provides that no count charging the making of a false oath is insufficient by reason only that it does not state the nature of the authority of the tribunal before which the oath was taken, or the subject of the inquiry. However, s. 587(1)(*a*) provides for the furnishing of particulars in such cases.

The accused has an election as to mode of trial pursuant to s. 536(2). Release pending trial is determined by s. 515, although the accused is eligible for release by the officer in charge under s. 498.

SYNOPSIS

This section creates offences relating to what may be referred to generally as "phoney affidavits" and it prohibits the use of such documents. It prohibits the accused, who may be either the affiant or the supposed witness, from signing a document saying that it is an affidavit or statutory declaration when the document was not so sworn or declared *or* if the accused *knows* that he is without authority to administer the oath or declaration. It also prohibits the use or offer for use of such documents if the person offering the document *knows* that the writing was not properly sworn or declared. It is not necessary to prove that the contents of such writings is false, only that it is not what it appears to be, namely a properly sworn or declared document.

The maximum punishment for this indictable offence is two years.

ANNOTATIONS

Paragraph (*a*) – The offence contrary to this paragraph requires proof of *mens rea* and the accused's mistaken belief as to the formalities requisite to constitute the ceremony of swearing and justify his completing the jurat is a defence to the charge: *R. v. Chow* (1978), 41 C.C.C. (2d) 143 (Sask. C.A.).

Paragraph (*b*) – The word "uses" in this paragraph simply means "employs for a purpose" and the offence contrary to this paragraph does not require proof that the use of the affidavit had as its purpose the misleading of justice. A use intended to bring about a result, which would adversely affect another's legal position was clearly within this paragraph. Finally, making use of a photocopy of the sham affidavit was using the original within the meaning of this paragraph: *R. v. Stevenson and McLean* (1980), 57 C.C.C. (2d) 526 (Ont. C.A.).

OBSTRUCTING JUSTICE / Idem / Idem.

139. (1) Every one who wilfully attempts in any manner to obstruct, pervert or defeat the course of justice in a judicial proceeding,

    (*a*) **by indemnifying or agreeing to indemnify a surety, in any way and either in whole or in part, or**

    (*b*) **where he is a surety, by accepting or agreeing to accept a fee or any form of indemnity whether in whole or in part from or in respect of a person who is released or is to be released from custody,**

is guilty of

    (*c*) **an indictable offence and is liable to imprisonment for a term not exceeding two years, or**

    (*d*) **an offence punishable on summary conviction.**

(2) Every one who wilfully attempts in any manner other than a manner described in subsection (1) to obstruct, pervert or defeat the course of justice is guilty of an indictable offence and liable to imprisonment for a term not exceeding ten years.

(3) Without restricting the generality of subsection (2), every one shall be deemed wilfully to attempt to obstruct, pervert or defeat the course of justice who in a judicial proceeding, existing or proposed,

    (*a*) **dissuades or attempts to dissuade a person by threats, bribes or other corrupt means from giving evidence;**

    (*b*) **influences or attempts to influence by threats, bribes or other corrupt means a person in his conduct as a juror; or**

    (*c*) **accepts or obtains, agrees to accept or attempts to obtain a bribe or other corrupt consideration to abstain from giving evidence, or to do or to refrain from doing anything as a juror. R.S., c. C-34, s. 127; R.S., c. 2 (2nd Supp.), s. 3; 1972, c. 13, s. 8.**

CROSS-REFERENCES

The term "judicial proceeding" is defined in s. 118. Several provisions of the *Criminal Code* refer to sureties, see ss. 515, 679, 810, 816, 817. The responsibilities of sureties and procedure for rendering the accused into custody by his sureties are dealt with in ss. 762 to 773. The term "wilfully" does not have a fixed meaning and must take its meaning from the context. Generally speaking, however, it connotes an intention to bring about a proscribed consequence. See: *R. v. Buzzanga and Durocher* (1979), 49 C.C.C. (2d) 369 (Ont. C.A.). Section 649, which prohibits disclosure of jury proceedings, provides an exemption for the purposes of an investigation of an alleged offence under subsec. (2) of this section in relation to a juror, and for giving evidence in relation to such offence.

    Related offences are as follows: s. 129, obstructing peace officer; s. 130, personation of peace officer; s. 131, perjury; s. 136, giving contradictory evidence; s. 137, fabricating evidence; s. 140, public mischief; s. 141, compounding indictable offence; s. 143, advertising reward and immunity. Also, see notes respecting contempt of court under ss. 9 and 10.

    Where the prosecution elects to proceed by way of summary conviction on the charge contrary to subsec. (1) then the trial of this offence is conducted by a summary conviction court pursuant to Part XXVII. The punishment for the offence is then as set out in s. 787 and the limitation period is set out in s. 786(2). Where the Crown proceeds by way of indictment then the accused has an election as to mode of trial under s. 536(2). In either case, release pending trial is determined by s. 515, although the accused is eligible for release by a peace officer under s. 496, 497 or by the officer in charge under s. 498.

    An accused charged with the offence under subsec. (2) has an election as to mode of trial under s. 536(2) and release pending trial is governed by s. 515.

This offence may be the basis for an application for an authorization to intercept private communications by reason of s. 183.

SYNOPSIS

Section 139 spells out the elements of the offence of *attempting to obstruct justice*.

The first group of offences relates to *sureties* and is found in subsec. (1). It prohibits anyone from indemnifying a surety (or agreeing to do so) for any loss arising from acting as surety ("signing bail") and also prohibits a surety from accepting or agreeing to accept an offer of a fee for so acting. The requisite *intention* is that the accused *wilfully* attempted to *obstruct, pervert or defeat the course of justice* in a judicial proceeding. This offence can be prosecuted by way of summary conviction or by way of indictment, and, in the latter case, is punishable by two years imprisonment.

Subsection (2) creates the offence of attempting to obstruct, pervert or defeat the course of justice in a manner apart from those described in s. 139(1). The actions of the accused must be proven to be *wilful*. The maximum sentence for this indictable offence is 10 years.

Section 139(3) provides a number of examples of how the offence created by subsec. (2) may be committed in the context of a *judicial proceeding*, either existing or proposed. This section is merely *illustrative not exhaustive*.

ANNOTATIONS

Course of justice – In *R. v. Hoggarth* (1957), 119 C.C.C. 234 (B.C.C.A.), a conviction for attempting to obstruct the course of justice was quashed. The court did not undertake to define "the course of justice" but held that, as no investigation of a possible crime was under way at the time nor had any charge been laid, there was nothing in the circumstances surrounding the making of the false statement in question that fell within that term.

The expression "the course of justice" in subsec. (2) includes judicial proceedings existing or proposed but is not limited to such proceedings. The offence under this subsection also includes attempts by a person to obstruct, prevent or defeat a prosecution which he contemplates may take place, notwithstanding that no decision to prosecute has been made: *R. v. Spezzano* (1977), 34 C.C.C. (2d) 87 (Ont. C.A.).

The term "the course of justice" includes the investigatory stage. The term is, as well, applicable to disciplinary proceedings of the law society. The course of justice includes all the judicial proceedings defined in s. 118. Any decision-making body would come within the phrase "the course of justice" if it was a body which judged; its authority to do so was derived from a statute; and the body, by the terms of its empowering statute, was required to act in a judicial manner: *R. v. Wijesinha*, [1995] 3 S.C.R. 422, 100 C.C.C. (3d) 410. Accordingly, a parole board hearing determining whether parole should be revoked is a judicial proceeding within the meaning of s. 118: *R. v. Heater* (1996), 111 C.C.C. (3d) 445 (Ont. C.A.).

Mens rea of offence – In *R. v. Savinkoff*, [1963] 3 C.C.C. 163 (B.C.C.A.), the accused was charged under this section with attempting to persuade other persons to make statements connected with other offences. There was no proof that the accused knew the statements he was suggesting were false. It was held (2:1) that *mens rea* was a necessary element requiring proof of the knowledge of the falsity of the statement.

It is no defence that the accused believed that the evidence that he sought to suppress was false evidence: *R. v. Walker* (1972), 7 C.C.C. (2d) 270 (Ont. Prov. Ct.).

However, where the accused approached a witness who had testified against his friend and told the witness he should tell the truth, he was acquitted. The court found that his purpose was to protest an injustice, not to obstruct justice: *R. v. Belliveau* (1978), 42 C.C.C. (2d) 243 (N.B.S.C. App. Div.).

Attempts in any manner (subsec. (2)) – In *R. v. Balsdon*, [1968] 2 C.C.C. 164 (Ont. Co. Ct.), it was held, following the two doctrines *nemo tenetur seipsum accusare* — no man can be compelled to incriminate himself — and *nemo tenetur prodere seipsum* — no one is bound to betray himself, that, although attempts at service of warrants of committal following convictions for summary conviction offences is a part of the course of justice, deliberate misidentification of himself by the accused to police officers endeavouring to serve him is not obstruction of justice.

In *R. v. Spezzano, supra*, the court, without passing on the correctness of *R. v. Balsdon, supra*, distinguished it on the basis that whatever protection the common law right to remain silent confers on a person, it will not protect him when he not only denies his identity but gives the police a false name in order to protect himself. The court, however, pointed out that it is not every false statement to the police, such as a false denial of guilt, which will be capable of supporting a charge under this provision.

It would seem that subsec. (2) is wide enough to include a threat by an accused to cause bodily harm to the complainant who was present in court, notwithstanding at the time of the threat the accused had been convicted and sentenced for the offence which the complainant had initially reported: *R. v. Vermette* (1983), 6 C.C.C. (3d) 97 (Alta. C.A.), affd on other grounds [1987] 1 S.C.R. 577, 32 C.C.C. (3d) 519.

A charge under this subsection could be made out if the accused approached a police officer with a request that certain charges not be laid in exchange for a payment to the officer, even if the officer did not in fact attempt to obstruct justice: *R. v. Rousseau*, [1985] 2 S.C.R. 38, 21 C.C.C. (3d) 1 (7:0).

Any attempt to pay compensation in any form to a witness that has, as its purpose, a direct tendency to influence a witness not to give evidence in a judicial proceeding, irrespective of the motive for doing so, is a corrupt attempt to obstruct justice. Similarly, an attempt to pay compensation to the complainant in order to influence the proceeding by, for example, persuading the Crown to withdraw the charge is capable of amounting to an offence. The offence would not, however, cover a *bona fide* negotiation for the withholding, withdrawal or reduction of a given charge that is conducted with a law officer of the Crown. Nor would honestly approaching a witness who has made a false or mistaken statement and by reasoned arguments supported by material facts, trying to dissuade him from giving perjured or erroneous testimony constitute an offence: *R. v. Kotch* (1990), 61 C.C.C. (3d) 132 (Alta. C.A.). [Also, note s. 141(2).]

Subsection (2) of this section, although framed in the language of an attempt, in fact creates a substantive offence, the gist of which is the doing of an act which has a tendency to prevent or obstruct the course of justice and which is done for that purpose: *R. v. May* (1984), 13 C.C.C. (3d) 257 (Ont. C.A.), leave to appeal to S.C.C. refused [1984] 2 S.C.R. viii. It is not necessary to establish that the tendency materialized. Thus, an accused who sent a letter from jail requesting his brother to intimidate a witness could be convicted of this offence although the letter was intercepted by the jail authorities and never reached the brother. The acts of the accused went beyond an intention or even expression of an intention: *R. v. Graham* (1985), 20 C.C.C. (3d) 210 (Ont. C.A.), affd [1988] 1 S.C.R. 214, 38 C.C.C. (3d) 574 (5:0).

An attempt to dissuade someone from reporting an incident to the police may amount to an obstruction of justice: *R. v. Whalen* (1974), 17 C.C.C. (2d) 217 (Ont. Co. Ct.).

False courtroom testimony is a possible mode of committing this offence as s. 13 of the Charter provides no protection where the testimony is the *actus reus* of the offence: *R. v. Schertzer* (2015), 325 C.C.C. (3d) 202 (Ont. C.A.), leave to appeal to S.C.C. refused 2015 CarswellOnt 16494.

A lawyer is under a duty not to mislead the court and may be convicted of this offence where he participates in the client's deception by arranging for the client's friend to attend in court to answer a charge against the client, who had previously given the friend's name to the police as his own upon arrest: *R. v. Doz* (1984), 12 C.C.C. (3d) 200 (Alta. C.A.).

A police officer cannot be convicted of this offence solely because he improperly exercised his discretion not to charge someone, here a fellow officer, with a criminal offence. Rather, it must first be determined whether the conduct in issue can be regarded as a proper exercise of police discretion. If not, it must then be determined whether the offence of obstructing justice has been committed in the sense that the act tended to defeat or obstruct the course of justice. If the *actus reus* is established, the Crown must then prove that the accused did in fact intend to act in a way tending to obstruct, pervert or defeat the course of justice. A simple error in judgment will not be enough. An accused who acted in good faith has not committed the offence even if the conduct cannot be characterized as a legitimate exercise of discretion: *R. v. Beaudry*, [2007] 1 S.C.R. 190, 216 C.C.C. (3d) 353.

The offence of attempting to obstruct justice requires the specific intention to obstruct justice. Thus, in the case of a charge based on an attempt by the accused to obtain a false affidavit from a client, the accused's honest belief that the affidavit was true would constitute a defence: *R. v. Charbonneau* (1992), 74 C.C.C. (3d) 49 (Que. C.A.).

The gravamen of the offence under subsec. (2) is the wilful attempt to obstruct justice and it does not matter that the attempt was not only unsuccessful but could not have succeeded. Thus, it was no defence that the accused attempted to procure a witness to give false evidence on an issue which in law was irrelevant: *R. v. Hearn* (1989), 48 C.C.C. (3d) 376 (Nfld. C.A.), affd [1989] 2 S.C.R. 1180, 53 C.C.C. (3d) 352n.

"Other corrupt means" (subsec. (3)(a)) – Suggesting that a witness avoid testifying at the accused's preliminary inquiry by presenting a false doctor's certificate to the court amounted to "dissuading" the witness from testifying through "other corrupt means". Recommending a deceitful way of accomplishing the desired objective is just as much a part of the persuasion package as providing the incentive to carry out the desired objective in the first place: *R. v. Reynolds*, [2011] 1 S.C.R. 693, 268 C.C.C. (3d) 35.

Witness at preliminary inquiry – Where the procedure under s. 545 has been resorted to by the justice presiding at a preliminary inquiry then a charge will not lie under this section for the same conduct – the witness' refusal to be sworn and testify. However, if the justice did not act under s. 545 or if the conduct were repeated after an initial resort to s. 545, then a charge under this section or of contempt of court would lie: *R. v. Mercer* (1988), 43 C.C.C. (3d) 347 (Alta. C.A.); *R. v. Poulin* (1998), 127 C.C.C. (3d) 115 (Que. C.A.).

Procedure and evidence – Statements by the accused police officers, which were part of a plan to cover up the commission of a criminal offence by one of them, were part of the *actus reus* of the offence under this section and need not be proved voluntary on a *voir dire*: *R. v. Hanneson* (1989), 49 C.C.C. (3d) 467 (Ont. C.A.).

The words "attempts in any manner" in subsec. (2) include perjury as a means of committing this offence notwithstanding that by charging the accused with this offence rather than the offence under s. 131 the requirement of corroboration (s. 133) is avoided. Under this section, corroboration is not required either at law or as a matter of practice, although the conduct involves an allegation of perjury: *R. v. Simon* (1979), 45 C.C.C. (2d) 510 (Ont. C.A.); *R. v. Moore* (1980), 52 C.C.C. (2d) 202 (B.C.C.A.).

PUBLIC MISCHIEF / Punishment.

140. (1) Every one commits public mischief who, with intent to mislead, causes a peace officer to enter on or continue an investigation by
   (*a*) **making a false statement that accuses some other person of having committed an offence;**
   (*b*) **doing anything intended to cause some other person to be suspected of having committed an offence that the other person has not committed, or to divert suspicion from himself;**
   (*c*) **reporting that an offence has been committed when it has not been committed; or**
   (*d*) **reporting or in any other way making it known or causing it to be made known that he or some other person has died when he or that other person has not died.**

(2) Every one who commits public mischief

(a) **is guilty of an indictable offence and liable to imprisonment for a term not exceeding five years; or**

(b) **is guilty of an offence punishable on summary conviction. R.S., c. C-34, s. 128; 1972, c. 13, s. 8; R.S.C. 1985, c. 27 (1st Supp.), s. 19.**

CROSS-REFERENCES

The term "statement" is defined in s. 118. The term "peace officer" is defined in s. 2. Section 585 provides that no count charging the making of a false statement is insufficient by reason only that it does not state the nature of the authority of the tribunal before which the statement was made, or the subject of the inquiry, or the words used, or that it does not expressly negative the truth of the words used. However, s. 587(1)(a) provides for the furnishing of particulars in such cases.

Related offences are as follows: s. 129, obstructing peace officer; s. 130, personation of peace officer; s. 137, fabricating evidence; s. 139, attempting to obstruct justice; s. 141, compounding indictable offence; s. 143, advertising reward and immunity; s. 403, personation. This offence is to be contrasted to the property offences also referred to as mischief, in s. 430.

Where the prosecution elects to proceed by way of summary conviction then the trial of this offence is conducted by a summary conviction court pursuant to Part XXVII. The punishment for the offence is then as set out in s. 787 and the limitation period is set out in s. 786(2). Where the Crown proceeds by way of indictment then the accused has an election as to mode of trial under s. 536(2). In either case, release pending trial is determined by s. 515, although the accused is eligible for release by a peace officer under s. 496, 497 or by the officer in charge under s. 498.

SYNOPSIS

This section creates the offence of *public mischief* which involves causing peace officers to *begin*, or to *continue* an investigation with the *intention of misleading them*. The ways in which the offence may be committed are specified in subsec. (1). Among these are *falsely accusing another* of committing a criminal offence or *falsely reporting that an offence has occurred*. When public mischief is committed by either of these methods, the false report by the accused is the *actus reus* of the offence.

This offence is punishable by summary conviction or by way of indictment. If prosecuted by way of indictment, the maximum punishment is five years.

ANNOTATIONS

Meaning of "offence" – An "offence" referred to in this section is not restricted to only a *Criminal Code* offence but pertains to any breach of the law whether federal, provincial or otherwise that involves penal sanction: *R. v. Howard* (1972), 7 C.C.C. (2d) 211 (Ont. C.A.).

Meaning of "report – "Reporting" need not be directly to the police and can include a report to an entity such as the CAS, who may in turn report to the police: *R. v. Delacruz* (2009), 249 C.C.C. (3d) 501 (Ont. S.C.J.).

Attempt to commit offence – On a charge of public mischief the accused may be convicted of an attempt to commit the offence where because the officer did not believe the accused he did not embark upon an investigation and was not misled: *R. v. Whalen* (1977), 34 C.C.C. (2d) 557 (B.C. Prov. Ct.).

Evidence – The statement by the accused to the police reporting the offence is the *actus reus* of the offence contrary to para. (c) and no *voir dire* is required to determine the voluntariness of such a statement: *R. v. Stapleton* (1982), 66 C.C.C. (2d) 231 (Ont. C.A.).

A similar result was reached in considering a statement taken from a young person, it being held that the special conditions for taking of statements as prescribed by [former] s. 56 of the *Young Offenders Act* were intended to apply only to young persons accused of committing crimes and not to a young person who provided a statement as a victim of the offence. Thus, on a charge under this section based on such a statement, the Crown need not prove compliance with s. 56. As in the case of an adult, the complaint is the *actus reus* of the offence and admissible without proof of voluntariness: *R. v. J.(J.)* (1988), 43 C.C.C. (3d) 257 (Ont. C.A.), leave to appeal to S.C.C. refused 101 N.R. 231*n*.

COMPOUNDING INDICTABLE OFFENCE / Exception for diversion agreements.

141. (1) Every one who asks for or obtains or agrees to receive or obtain any valuable consideration for himself or any other person by agreeing to compound or conceal an indictable offence is guilty of an indictable offence and liable to imprisonment for a term not exceeding two years.

(2) No offence is committed under subsection (1) where valuable consideration is received or obtained or is to be received or obtained under an agreement for compensation or restitution or personal services that is

    (*a*) entered into with the consent of the Attorney General; or

    (*b*) made as part of a program, approved by the Attorney General, to divert persons charged with indictable offences from criminal proceedings. R.S., c. C-34, s. 129; R.S.C. 1985, c. 27 (1st Supp.), s. 19.

CROSS-REFERENCES

The term "Attorney General" is defined in s. 2. An "indictable offence" would include a Crown option offence by virtue of s. 34 of the *Interpretation Act*, R.S.C. 1985, c. I-21. The term "compound" is not defined but may be taken to refer to the element of the common law offence of compounding a felony being an agreement not to prosecute or inform on a person who has committed an offence. See *R. v. Burgess* (1885), 15 Cox, C.C. 779 (C.A.). The reference to programmes in subsec. (2) presumably refers to restitution orders under s. 726 to 727.8, s. 737(2), a fine option programme under s. 718.1 and extrajudicial measures under ss. 4 to 10 of the *Youth Criminal Justice Act*.

Related offences are as follows: s. 23, accessory after the fact; s. 137, fabricating evidence; s. 139, attempting to obstruct justice; s. 140, public mischief; s. 142, corruptly taking reward; s. 143, advertising reward and immunity; s. 346, extortion. In addition it should be noted that courts will on occasion stay proceedings as an abuse of process where it is shown that the criminal proceedings were launched to collect a debt or realize on a civil claim, or following a threat to swear out an information to obtain payment of a debt. See *R. v. Leroux* (1928), 50 C.C.C. 52 (Ont. C.A.). Also see notes following s. 579.

The accused has an election as to mode of trial pursuant to s. 536(2). Release pending trial is determined by s. 515, although the accused is eligible for release by the officer in charge under s. 498.

SYNOPSIS

Section 141(1) creates an indictable offence applicable if a person asks for, obtains, or *agrees to accept* any form of *valuable consideration* in exchange for agreeing to compound or *conceal an indictable offence*. The maximum sentence for this offence is two years.

Subsection (2) provides two exceptions to the liability which would otherwise result from subsec. (1). Section 141(2)(*a*) excludes cases in which the valuable consideration is obtained (or will be so in the future) by virtue of an agreement made with the consent of the Attorney General. Section 141(2)(*b*) provides an exemption covering agreements made as part of a program for the diversion of persons from indictable criminal proceedings. To come within this paragraph, the diversion program must be approved by the Attorney General.

ANNOTATIONS

The Crown need not prove that an indictable offence was actually committed, it being sufficient to prove that the accused believed that an indictable offence had been committed: *R. v. H.L.* (1987), 57 C.R. (3d) 136 (Que. Ct. Sess.).

CORRUPTLY TAKING REWARD FOR RECOVERY OF GOODS.

142. Every one who corruptly accepts any valuable consideration, directly or indirectly, under pretence or on account of helping any person to recover anything obtained by the commission of an indictable offence is guilty of an indictable offence and liable to imprisonment for a term not exceeding five years. R.S., c. C-34, s. 130.

CROSS-REFERENCES

An "indictable offence" would include a Crown option offence by virtue of s. 34 of the *Interpretation Act*, R.S.C. 1985, c. I-21. The term "corruptly" is not defined in this Part but has been considered by the courts in relation to the secret commission offence in s. 426, where it was held not to mean wickedly or dishonestly, but to refer to an act done *mala fides*, designed wholly or partially for the purpose of bringing about the effect forbidden by the section: *R. v. Brown* (1956), 116 C.C.C. 287 (Ont. C.A.).

Related offences are as follows: s. 23, accessory after the fact; s. 137, fabricating evidence; s. 139, attempting to obstruct justice; s. 140, public mischief; s. 141, compounding indictable offence; s. 143, advertising reward and immunity; s. 346, extortion; ss. 354 and 355, possession of property obtained by crime; s. 462.31, laundering proceeds of crime.

The accused has an election as to mode of trial pursuant to s. 536(2). Release pending trial is determined by s. 515, although the accused is eligible for release by the officer in charge under s. 498.

SYNOPSIS

This section creates the indictable offence of *corruptly accepting valuable consideration* for the *recovery* of goods which were obtained by the commission of an indictable offence. It must be proven that the accused accepted the valuable consideration *corruptly* (directly or indirectly) and its receipt flowed from the pretence of helping or as the result of actually helping recover the goods. The maximum punishment for this offence is five years.

ANNOTATIONS

In *R. v. Butler* (1975), 26 C.C.C. (2d) 445 (Ont. Co. Ct.), the trial judge adopted the definition of the word "corruptly" given by Cussen J., in *R. v. Worthington*, [1921] V.L.R. 660, as "an act done by a man knowing that he is doing what is wrong, and doing it with an evil object" and found that in the factual circumstances the accused's acceptance of reward for obtaining the return of stolen goods was corrupt.

ADVERTISING REWARD AND IMMUNITY.

143. Every one who
    (*a*) **publicly advertises a reward for the return of anything that has been stolen or lost, and in the advertisement uses words to indicate that no questions will be asked if it is returned,**
    (*b*) **uses words in a public advertisement to indicate that a reward will be given or paid for anything that has been stolen or lost, without interference with or inquiry about the person who produces it,**
    (*c*) **promises or offers in a public advertisement to return to a person who has advanced money by way of loan on, or has bought, anything that has been stolen or lost, the money so advanced or paid, or any other sum of money for the return of that thing, or**
    (*d*) **prints or publishes any advertisement referred to in paragraph (*a*), (*b*) or (*c*),**
is guilty of an offence punishable on summary conviction. R.S., c. C-34, s. 131.

CROSS-REFERENCES

The term "steal" is defined in s. 2 as theft and accordingly see s. 322.

Related offences are as follows: s. 23, accessory after the fact; s. 139, attempting to obstruct justice; s. 140, public mischief; s. 141, compounding indictable offence; s. 142, corruptly taking reward; s. 346, extortion; ss. 354 and 355, possession of property obtained by crime. In addition, it should be noted that courts will, on occasion, stay proceedings as an abuse of process where it is shown that the criminal proceedings were launched to collect a debt or realize on a civil claim, or following a threat to swear out an information to obtain payment of a debt. See *R. v. Leroux* (1928), 50 C.C.C. 52 (Ont. C.A.). Also see notes following s. 579.

The trial of this offence is conducted by a summary conviction court pursuant to Part XXVII. The punishment for the offence is as set out in s. 787 and the limitation period is set out in s. 786(2). Release pending trial is determined by s. 515 although the accused is eligible for release by a peace officer under s. 496, 497 or by the officer in charge under s. 498.

SYNOPSIS

This section creates the summary conviction offence of *publicly advertising* for the return of *lost or stolen goods* with a promise of reward and immunity. Paragraph (*a*) prohibits public advertisements which offer a reward and state that no questions will be asked if the item is returned. Paragraph (*b*) prohibits similar advertisements if they state that no inquiry will be made of the person who returns the item, nor will there be efforts to interfere with such persons. Finally, para. (*c*) creates the offence of publicly offering to indemnify anyone who has advanced money on the security of the lost or stolen thing, or who had purported to buy it, in exchange for the return of the item.

Section 143(*d*) states that it is an offence to publish or print any of the types of advertisements described above.

Escapes and Rescues

PRISON BREACH.

144. Every one who

  (*a*) **by force or violence breaks a prison with intent to set at liberty himself or any other person confined therein, or**

  (*b*) **with intent to escape forcibly breaks out of, or makes any breach in, a cell or other place within a prison in which he is confined,**

is guilty of an indictable offence and liable to imprisonment for a term not exceeding ten years. R.S., c. C-34, s. 132; 1976-77, c. 53, s. 5.

CROSS-REFERENCES

"Prison" is defined in s. 2. Section 149 provides an exception to the normal rule as set out in s. 743.1 that a sentence of less than two years is served in a reformatory. The court has the power to order that a sentence for escape may be served in a penitentiary. Escape is defined in s. 149 to include the offence under this section. Under s. 719(2), any time during which a convicted person is unlawfully at large does not count as part of any term of imprisonment. A finding of guilt in relation to the offence under para. (*a*) will require the court to impose an order prohibiting possession of firearms, ammunition or explosive substances under s. 109.

The related offence of escaping lawful custody and being unlawfully at large is in s. 145. Other related offences are as follows: s. 146, permitting or assisting escape; s. 147, rescue from lawful custody or officer permitting escape; s. 148, assisting prisoner of war to escape.

Murder of a warden, deputy warden, instructor, keeper, jailer, guard or other officer or permanent employee of a prison, acting in the course of his duties, is first degree murder by virtue of s. 231(4). This offence may be the basis for an application for an authorization to intercept private communications by reason of s. 183 or for a warrant to conduct video surveillance under s. 487.01(5).

The accused has an election as to mode of trial under s. 536(2). Release pending trial is determined by s. 515. However, by virtue of s. 519, the accused would not be released pursuant to any release order until the accused was not required to be detained in custody in respect of any other matter.

SYNOPSIS

This section sets out what constitutes prison breach and specifies that it is an indictable offence carrying a maximum sentence of 10 years.

The *actus reus* of the offence in s. 144(*a*) is the use of force or violence to break out of a prison. The mental element of this offence is the *intention* of the accused to set himself or another free.

The *actus reus* of the offence created in s. 144(*b*) is the action of *forcibly breaking* out or making a *breach* in a *cell* or any other part of a prison in which the *accused is incarcerated*. It must be shown that the accused did the act with the intention of *escaping*.

ESCAPE AND BEING AT LARGE WITHOUT EXCUSE / **Failure to attend court** / **Failure to comply with condition of undertaking or recognizance** / **Failure to appear or to comply with summons** / **Failure to comply with appearance notice or promise to appear** / **Failure to comply with conditions of undertaking** / **Idem** / **Election of Crown under Contraventions Act** / **Proof of certain facts by certificate** / **Attendance and right to cross-examination** / **Notice of intention to produce.**

145. (1) Every one who

    (*a*) **escapes from lawful custody, or**

    (*b*) **is, before the expiration of a term of imprisonment to which he was sentenced, at large in or out of Canada without lawful excuse, the proof of which lies on him,**

is guilty of an indictable offence and liable to imprisonment for a term not exceeding two years or is guilty of an offence punishable on summary conviction.

(2) Every one who,

    (*a*) **being at large on his undertaking or recognizance given to or entered into before a justice or judge, fails, without lawful excuse, the proof of which lies on him, to attend court in accordance with the undertaking or recognizance, or**

    (*b*) **having appeared before a court, justice or judge, fails, without lawful excuse, the proof of which lies on him, to attend court as thereafter required by the court, justice or judge,**

or to surrender himself in accordance with an order of the court, justice or judge, as the case may be, is guilty of an indictable offence and liable to imprisonment for a term not exceeding two years or is guilty of an offence punishable on summary conviction.

(3) Every person who is at large on an undertaking or recognizance given to or entered into before a justice or judge and is bound to comply with a condition of that undertaking or recognizance, and every person who is bound to comply with a direction under subsection 515(12) or 522(2.1) or an order under subsection 516(2), and who fails, without lawful excuse, the proof of which lies on them, to comply with the condition, direction or order is guilty of

    (*a*) **an indictable offence and is liable to imprisonment for a term not exceeding two years; or**

    (*b*) **an offence punishable on summary conviction.**

(4) Every one who is served with a summons and who fails, without lawful excuse, the proof of which lies on him, to appear at a time and place stated therein, if any, for the purposes of the *Identification of Criminals Act* or to attend court in accordance therewith, is guilty of

    (*a*) **an indictable offence and liable to imprisonment for a term not exceeding two years; or**

    (*b*) **an offence punishable on summary conviction.**

(5) Every person who is named in an appearance notice or promise to appear, or in a recognizance entered into before an officer in charge or another peace officer, that has been confirmed by a justice under section 508 and who fails, without lawful excuse, the proof of which lies on the person, to appear at the time and place stated therein, if any, for the purposes of the *Identification of Criminals Act*, or to attend court in accordance therewith, is guilty of

    (*a*) an indictable offence and is liable to imprisonment for a term not exceeding two years; or

    (*b*) an offence punishable on summary conviction.

(5.1) Every person who, without lawful excuse, the proof of which lies on the person, fails to comply with any condition of an undertaking entered into pursuant to subsection 499(2) or 503(2.1)

    (*a*) is guilty of an indictable offence and is liable to imprisonment for a term not exceeding two years; or

    (*b*) is guilty of an offence punishable on summary conviction.

(6) For the purposes of subsection (5), it is not a lawful excuse that an appearance notice, promise to appear or recognizance states defectively the substance of the alleged offence.

(7) [*Repealed*, R.S.C. 1985, c. 27 (1st Supp.), s. 20(2).]

(8) For the purposes of subsections (3) to (5), it is a lawful excuse to fail to comply with a condition of an undertaking or recognizance or to fail to appear at a time and place stated in a summons, an appearance notice, a promise to appear or a recognizance for the purposes of the *Identification of Criminals Act* if before the failure the Attorney General, within the meaning of the *Contraventions Act*, makes an election under section 50 of that Act.

(9) In any proceedings under subsection (2), (4) or (5), a certificate of the clerk of the court or a judge of the court before which the accused is alleged to have failed to attend or of the person in charge of the place at which it is alleged the accused failed to attend for the purposes of the *Identification of Criminals Act* stating that,

    (*a*) in the case of proceedings under subsection (2), the accused gave or entered into an undertaking or recognizance before a justice or judge and failed to attend court in accordance therewith or, having attended court, failed to attend court thereafter as required by the court, justice or judge or to surrender in accordance with an order of the court, justice or judge, as the case may be,

    (*b*) in the case of proceedings under subsection (4), a summons was issued to and served on the accused and the accused failed to attend court in accordance therewith or failed to appear at the time and place stated therein for the purposes of the *Identification of Criminals Act*, as the case may be, and

    (*c*) in the case of proceedings under subsection (5), the accused was named in an appearance notice, a promise to appear or a recognizance entered into before an officer in charge or another peace officer, that was confirmed by a justice under section 508, and the accused failed to appear at the time and place stated therein for the purposes of the *Identification of Criminals Act*, failed to attend court in accordance therewith or, having attended court, failed to attend court thereafter as required by the court, justice or judge, as the case may be,

is evidence of the statements contained in the certificate without proof of the signature or the official character of the person appearing to have signed the certificate.

(10) An accused against whom a certificate described in subsection (9) is produced may, with leave of the court, require the attendance of the person making the certificate for the purposes of cross-examination.

(11) No certificate shall be received in evidence pursuant to subsection (9) unless the party intending to produce it has, before the trial, given to the accused reasonable notice of his intention together with a copy of the certificate. R.S., c. C-34, s. 133; R.S., c. 2 (2nd Supp.), s. 4; 1974-75-76, c. 93, s. 7; R.S.C. 1985, c. 27 (1st Supp.), s. 20; 1992, c. 47, s. 68; 1994, c. 44, s. 8; 1996, c. 7, s. 38; 1997, c. 18, s. 3; 2008, c. 18, s. 3.

CROSS-REFERENCES

The term "justice" is defined in s. 2. The terms "undertaking" and "recognizance" principally refer to forms of release authorized by Part XVI. In addition, pending appeal in indictable and summary conviction matters, an accused may be released on an undertaking or recognizance pursuant to ss. 679 and 816. The term "summons" refers to a form of process issued under Part XVI, while the terms "promise to appear" and "appearance notice" refer to process issued by a peace officer. Reference should also be made to the following provisions: ss. 494 and 495, warrantless arrest power; s. 510, issue of warrant for failing to comply with term of summons to appear for purposes of *Identification of Criminals Act*; s. 512, issuing of arrest warrant; s. 524, arrest of accused for misconduct while on a form of release; s. 475, accused absconding during trial; s. 544, accused absconding during preliminary inquiry; s. 598, accused failing to attend for jury trial; Part XXV, procedure for forfeiture of recognizances and for rendering of accused by sureties. Note that by virtue of s. 803(3), where the summary conviction court proceeds to try the accused *ex parte* then no proceedings may be taken under this section arising out of the failure of the accused to appear for trial except with the consent of the Attorney General.

Section 149 provides an exception to the normal rule as set out in s. 743.1 that a sentence of less than two years is served in a reformatory. The court has the power to order that a sentence for escape may be served in a penitentiary. "Escape" is defined in s. 149 to include the offence under subsec. (1) of this section. Under s. 719(2), any time during which a convicted person is unlawfully at large does not count as part of any term of imprisonment. A finding of guilt in relation to this offence may, in certain circumstances, give the court discretion to impose an order prohibiting possession of firearms, ammunition or explosive substances under s. 110.

The related offence of prison breach is in s. 145. Other related offences are as follows: s. 146, permitting or assisting escape; s. 147, rescue from lawful custody or officer permitting escape; s. 148, assisting prisoner of war to escape; s. 405, acknowledging bail in name of another person.

Murder of a peace officer, warden, deputy warden, instructor, keeper, jailer, guard or other officer or permanent employee of a prison, acting in the course of his duties, is first degree murder by virtue of s. 231(4). This offence in subsec. (1) may be the basis for an application for an authorization to intercept private communications by reason of s. 183 or a warrant to conduct video surveillance under s. 487.01(5).

The offences in this section are all Crown option offences. Where the prosecution elects to proceed by way of summary conviction then the trial of this offence is conducted by a summary conviction court pursuant to Part XXVII. The punishment for the offence is then as set out in s. 787 and the limitation period is set out in s. 786(2). Where the Crown proceeds by way of indictment then the accused has an election as to mode of trial under s. 536(2). In either case, release pending trial is determined by s. 515, although the accused is eligible for release by a peace officer under ss. 496 and 497 or by the officer in charge under s. 498. However, note s. 515(6) which puts the burden of proof on the accused to show why he should be released in certain circumstances, including the case where the accused is charged with an offence under subsecs. (2) to (5) of this section, or is charged with an indictable offence while at large after being released in respect of another indictable offence. Further, by virtue of s. 519, the accused would not be released pursuant to any release order until the accused was not required to be detained in custody in respect of any other matter.

SYNOPSIS

This section creates the offences of *escaping, being unlawfully at large,* and offences relating to *failing to comply* with various forms of process or judicial interim release. It also facilitates the prosecution of charges of failing to comply by authorizing the use of certificates to prove some aspects of these offences.

Subsection (1) deals with escapes and being unlawfully at large. Under s. 145(1)(*a*), it must be proven that the accused was in *lawful custody* at the time of the escape. Section 145(1)(*b*) states the elements of the offence of being unlawfully at large inside or outside of Canada before the expiration of the custodial portion of a sentence.

Section 145(2) creates offences pertaining to those who *fail to attend court* as required by the terms of an order of judicial interim release, or to appear subsequently as required by a court, judge or justice after initially appearing in court.

Subsection (3) creates the offence of failing to comply with a condition in a judicial interim release order and with directions or orders in detention orders or remand orders that the detainee not communicate with a victim, witness or other person identified in the order or direction.

Subsection (4) creates the offence of *failing to comply* with a requirement in a *summons* to attend court or at the specified place for fingerprinting as required by the *Identification of Criminals Act*.

Subsection (5) spells out the offence of *failing to comply* with a requirement in a *release order* entered into before the officer in charge of the station that the accused attend court or at the specified place for fingerprinting as required by the *Identification of Criminals Act*. This subsection only applies if the appearance notice, promise to appear or recognizance has been confirmed by a justice of the peace.

Subsections (2) to (5) permit the accused to rely upon a *lawful excuse,* but the onus is upon the accused to establish such excuse. As with other provisions placing a burden upon the accused, this aspect of the section is likely to be attacked as violating ss. 7 and 11(*d*) of the Charter. Subsection (6) specifically excludes from what might otherwise be a "lawful excuse" reliance upon a defect in the way in which the substance of the alleged offence is stated in the release documents described in subsec. (5).

The offences created in subsecs. (2) to (5) are punishable by way of summary conviction procedure or by indictment. In the latter event, the maximum punishment is two years.

Section 145(8) provides that for the sole purpose of the *Identification of Criminals Act,* an accused charged with or convicted of what is a summary conviction offence under this section, shall be deemed to have been charged with or convicted of an indictable offence.

Subsection (9) permits a *certificate* to be used to prove that an accused charged under s. 145(2), (4) or (5) *did fail* to attend court or for fingerprints as required. The certificate is to be provided by the clerk of the court or the person who is in charge of the place in which the accused was to have attended for fingerprints. It is proof of the statements contained in it without the need to prove the signature or the official character of the person who appears to have signed it.

Section 145(10) permits the cross-examination of the person who made the certificate in subsec. (9) but leave of the court is required. Subsection (11) provides that unless the accused is given notice of the intention to use a certificate along with a copy of it, a certificate made under subsec. (9) cannot be used as evidence.

ANNOTATIONS

Subsection (1) / Meaning of lawful custody – In *R. v. Piper*, [1965] 3 C.C.C. 135, 51 D.L.R. (2d) 534 (Man. C.A.), the accused was found guilty where he had escaped from the penitentiary confines but was still on penitentiary property.

In *R. v. Whitfield*, [1970] S.C.R. 46, [1970] 1 C.C.C. 129, it was held (5:2) that arrest is an undivided act that defies separation into "custodial" or "symbolic" arrest.

An arrest stated to be for one described offence cannot be validated by a later reliance upon another offence for which it might have been, but was not, made: *R. v. Huff* (1979), 50 C.C.C. (2d) 324, 17 A.R. 499 (C.A.).

Where an accused is informed at least of the general nature of the charge for which he was apprehended, his arrest is lawful: *R. v. Boughton* (1975), 23 C.C.C. (2d) 395, [1975] W.W.D. 79 (Alta. S.C. App. Div.).

Notwithstanding the applicable provincial legislation only permits the arrest of a person "found" to be intoxicated in a public place an accused may be convicted of escaping lawful custody provided he was apparently intoxicated when arrested even if the Judge finds as a fact he was not intoxicated: *R. v. Robertson* (1978), 42 C.C.C. 78, [1978] 5 W.W.R. 289 (B.C.C.A.).

A conviction under this section was imposed on an accused who was present in court when a sentence of incarceration was imposed but then left the court after a recess when the officer in charge briefly left the room. He was in custody within the meaning of the section as he was present when sentence was pronounced and submitted to arrest by asking permission of the officer to do various things, notwithstanding he was never placed in a prisoner's dock, handcuffed or otherwise physically placed under arrest: *R. v. Zajner* (1977), 36 C.C.C. (2d) 417 (Ont. C.A.).

An inmate of a transition house who leaves the house with permission of the management but fails to return to prison as required does not commit the offence under para. (*a*). A person cannot be convicted of escaping custody where his initial physical liberty was legally obtained. In such circumstances his offence, if any, is that created by para. (*b*): *R. v. Folchito* (1986), 26 C.C.C. (3d) 253, [1986] R.J.Q. 563 (C.A.).

Unlawfully at large – An inmate, when released on a temporary pass, could be unlawfully at large immediately if at that moment he decided not to return to the institution when required: *R. v. MacCaud* (1975), 22 C.C.C. (2d) 445 (Ont. H.C.J.).

It is not every breach of a condition of a temporary absence permit which operates to deprive the inmate of a lawful excuse under this subsection, but rather only a wilful breach of a condition which shows an intention by the inmate to withdraw himself from the control, in the sense of the custody, of the correctional authorities even where the permit itself provided that apparent breach of the conditions rendered it null and void and deemed the inmate to be unlawfully at large: *R. v. Seymour* (1980), 52 C.C.C. (2d) 305 (Ont. C.A.).

Secure and open custody imposed pursuant to the [former] *Young Offenders Act* constitutes a form of imprisonment. Thus an offender who fails to return after expiry of a day pass may be convicted of the offence under para. (*b*): *R. v. McKay* (1985), 21 C.C.C. (3d) 191 (Man. C.A.); *R. v. B.D.* (1986), 24 C.C.C. (3d) 187, 49 C.R. (3d) 283 (Ont. C.A.). Similarly, *R. v. C.A.* (1986), 25 C.C.C. (3d) 133 (Sask. C.A.).

Proof of lawful custody – A calendar of sentence is sufficient proof that the accused is in lawful custody: *R. v. Ouellette* (1978), 39 C.C.C. (2d) 278 (B.C.C.A.).

In *R. v. Adams* (1978), 45 C.C.C. (2d) 459, 6 C.R. (3d) 257 (B.C.C.A.), two of the three members of the court held that it is not open to an accused to go behind a warrant of committal valid on its face.

Subsection (2) – An accused charged with a summary conviction offence and released on an undertaking to appear in court complies with that undertaking by appearing either personally or by counsel or agent, as permitted by s. 800(2), and where counsel appears on the court date the accused may not be charged with the offence under this section: *R. v. Okanee* (1981), 59 C.C.C. (2d) 149, 9 Sask. R. 10 (C.A.).

The *mens rea* requirement is largely objective. Lawful excuse requires the accused to establish due diligence, which includes an honest and reasonable belief in a state of facts that would excuse non-attendance. The defence was, however, made out where the accused did not attend because he was incorrectly advised by the complainant that the charge had been dropped: *R. v. Ludlow* (1999), 136 C.C.C. (3d) 460, 27 C.R. (5th) 46 (B.C.C.A.).

Failure to appear on a return date subsequent to the issuance of an arrest warrant marked "with discretion" cannot support a charge of failure to appear: *R. v. Bowen* (1999), 139 C.C.C. (3d) 131, 28 C.R. (5th) 162 (Ont. C.J.).

This provision creates one offence with subsections that describe three different methods of committing the offence: (1) being at large on an undertaking or recognizance and failing to attend court; (2) having appeared before a court and failing to attend thereafter as required by the court; and (3) having appeared before a court and failing to surrender in accordance with an order of the court. Accordingly, an information need not specify whether the offence was committed under para. (*a*) or (*b*): *R. v. Charles* (2006), 210 C.C.C. (3d) 289, 391 A.R. 269 (C.A.).

Subsection (3) – This is a true criminal offence and mere carelessness or failure to take the precautions that a reasonable person would take will not support a conviction. The Crown must prove that the accused had the requisite *mens rea* before any issue of lawful excuse arises: *R. v. Legere* (1995), 95 C.C.C. (3d) 555, 22 O.R. (3d) 89 (C.A.). Not folld: *R. v. Ludlow, supra.*

The *mens rea* of this offence requires proof that the accused knowingly or recklessly infringed the conditions of the undertaking. However, a mistake of law cannot negative *mens rea*. In this case, the accused was ordered to reside at a named apartment. When he could not obtain entry to the apartment, he decided to sleep in his car in the building's parking lot. The accused's mistaken belief that he was complying with the term of the undertaking was a mistake of law and no defence. The accused also failed to make out a lawful excuse by a showing of due diligence to satisfy the obligation: *R. v. Custance* (2005), 194 C.C.C. (3d) 225, 28 C.R. (6th) 357 (Man. C.A.), leave to appeal to S.C.C. refused 198 C.C.C. (3d) vi.

It is not a defence that the conviction which gave rise to the undertaking is subsequently set aside. Court orders must be obeyed until set aside or modified regardless of doubts or challenges as to their validity: *R. v. Gaudreault* (1996), 105 C.C.C. (3d) 270 (Que. C.A.), leave to appeal to S.C.C. refused 108 C.C.C. (3d) vi.

The Crown is required to prove beyond a reasonable doubt that the accused was bound by a recognizance condition on the date in question and it is only after this that the onus shifts to the accused to provide a lawful excuse: *R. v. Truong* (2008), 235 C.C.C. (3d) 547 (B.C.S.C.).

Subsection (5) – *Mens rea* is an element of the offence of failing to appear and accordingly the accused may raise the defence of honest mistake: *R. v. Bender* (1976), 30 C.C.C. (2d) 496, [1976] W.W.D. 84 (B.C.S.C.).

Thus where an accused honestly forgot the date of his court appearance he has a defence to the charge even if he forgot due to his own negligence: *R. v. Stuart* (1981), 58 C.C.C. (2d) 203 (B.C.S.C.). Folld: *R. v. Neal* (1982), 67 C.C.C. (2d) 92, 136 D.L.R. (3d) 86 (Ont. Co. Ct.). See also: *R. v. Loutitt* (2011), 284 C.C.C. (3d) 518 (Alta. Q.B.).

Where the accused appeared pursuant to the first appearance notice but not for her trial date, the Crown had the option of proceeding under subsecs. (2) or (5). Subsection (5) applies not only to the "time and place stated" in the appearance notice, but also to attendance "in accordance therewith", which includes appearances "thereafter as required by the court": *R. v. Hubek* (2011), 277 C.C.C. (3d) 550 (Alta. C.A.).

Subsection (9) – A certificate under this subsection may be evidence not only that the accused failed to appear but that, for example, he was named in an appearance notice which was confirmed by a justice: *R. v. Dorigo* (1982), 69 C.C.C. (2d) 141 (B.C.S.C.).

PERMITTING OR ASSISTING ESCAPE.

146. Every one who
    (*a*) **permits a person whom he has in lawful custody to escape, by failing to perform a legal duty,**
    (*b*) **conveys or causes to be conveyed into a prison anything, with intent to facilitate the escape of a person imprisoned therein, or**
    (*c*) **directs or procures, under colour of pretended authority, the discharge of a prisoner who is not entitled to be discharged,**
is guilty of an indictable offence and liable to imprisonment for a term not exceeding two years. R.S., c. C-34, s. 134.

CROSS-REFERENCES
The term "prison" is defined in s. 2.

The related offences of escaping lawful custody and being unlawfully at large are in s. 145. Other related offences are as follows: s. 144, prison breach; s. 147, rescue from lawful custody or officer permitting escape; s. 148, assisting prisoner of war to escape.

Murder of a peace officer, warden, deputy warden, instructor, keeper, jailer, guard or other officer or permanent employee of a prison, acting in the course of his duties, is first degree murder by virtue of s. 231(4).

The accused has an election as to mode of trial pursuant to s. 536(2). Release pending trial is determined by s. 515, although the accused is eligible for release by the officer in charge under s. 498.

SYNOPSIS

Section 146 creates an indictable offence of *permitting* or *assisting* a prisoner to *escape lawful custody* or *prison*.

Section 146(*a*) makes the *failure* to *perform* a *legal duty* which *permits* another to *escape* an offence. The principal in the offence must have *lawful custody* of the escapee.

Section 146(*b*) applies when a person takes anything into a prison or causes anything to be brought with the *intention* of *facilitating* an escape.

Section 146(*c*) spells out the offence of discharging a prisoner when the person who directs or procures such release does so under *pretended authority*. The accused must *know* that he or she does not have proper authority and that the *prisoner* is *not entitled* to be discharged.

The maximum punishment upon conviction is two years.

RESCUE OR PERMITTING ESCAPE.

147. Every one who
>   (*a*) **rescues any person from lawful custody or assists any person in escaping or attempting to escape from lawful custody,**
>   (*b*) **being a peace officer, wilfully permits a person in his lawful custody to escape, or**
>   (*c*) **being an officer of or an employee in a prison, wilfully permits a person to escape from lawful custody therein,**

is guilty of an indictable offence and liable to imprisonment for a term not exceeding five years. R.S., c. C-34, s. 135.

CROSS-REFERENCES

The terms "prison" and "peace officer" are defined in s. 2.

The related offence of escaping lawful custody and being unlawfully at large is in s. 145. Other related offences are as follows: s. 144, prison breach; s. 146, permitting or assisting escape; s. 148, assisting prisoner of war to escape.

Murder of a peace officer, warden, deputy warden, instructor, keeper, jailer, guard or other officer or permanent employee of a prison, acting in the course of his duties, is first degree murder by virtue of s. 231(4).

The accused has an election as to mode of trial pursuant to s. 536(2). Release pending trial is determined by s. 515, although the accused is eligible for release by the officer in charge under s. 498.

SYNOPSIS

Section 147 sets out three indictable offences of rescuing a person from lawful custody and prohibits actions of peace officers or prison employees which permit a person to escape.

Section 147(*a*) creates offences of assisting anyone to *escape* (or attempting to do so) or rescuing anyone from lawful custody.

Section 147(*b*) applies to peace officers and s. 147(*c*) to officers or employees of prisons who *wilfully permit* a person to escape from *lawful custody*.

The maximum sentence for these offences is five years.

ANNOTATIONS

A prisoner was still "escaping" within the meaning of this section although at the time the accused assisted him, he was in an area of the province which was landlocked and his flight from the authorities could only be transitory: *R. v. Stutt; R. v. Claussen* (1979), 52 C.C.C. (2d) 53 (B.C.C.A.).

In the absence of evidence to the contrary a police officer's testimony that he was transporting the prisoner in custody from police jail cells to court to set a trial date at the time he escaped was sufficient proof that the prisoner was in lawful custody and the Crown was not required to produce the actual warrant under which the prisoner was being held: *R. v. Stutt; R. v. Claussen, supra.*

Assistance is provided if the act of the accused joins in the enterprise of escape even if the act does not materially contribute to the escape: *R. v. Harrer* (1998), 124 C.C.C. (3d) 368, 172 W.A.C. 311 (B.C.C.A.).

ASSISTING PRISONER OF WAR TO ESCAPE.

148. Every one who knowingly and wilfully

> (*a*) **assists a prisoner of war in Canada to escape from a place where he is detained, or**
>
> (*b*) **assists a prisoner of war, who is permitted to be at large on parole in Canada, to escape from the place where he is at large on parole,**

is guilty of an indictable offence and liable to imprisonment for a term not exceeding five years. R.S., c. C-34, s. 136.

CROSS-REFERENCES

Related offences include the following: s. 50, assisting enemy alien; s. 54, assisting deserter; s. 55, assisting deserter from R.C.M.P.

Murder of a peace officer, warden, deputy warden, instructor, keeper, jailer, guard or other officer or permanent employee of a prison, acting in the course of his duties, is first degree murder by virtue of s. 231(4).

A finding of guilt in relation to this offence may, in certain circumstances, give the court a discretion to impose an order prohibiting possession of firearms, ammunition or explosive substances under s. 110.

The accused has an election as to mode of trial pursuant to s. 536(2). Release pending trial is determined by s. 515, although the accused is eligible for release by the officer in charge under s. 498.

SYNOPSIS

Section 148 creates the offence of assisting a *prisoner of war to escape*. Section 148(*a*) and (*b*) spell out the details of the prisoner of war's status at the time of the offence. Both offences require that the accused *know* of the status of the prisoner of war and *wilfully* assist in the escape. The maximum sentence for this indictable offence is five years' imprisonment.

SERVICE OF TERM FOR ESCAPE / Definition of "escape".

149. (1) Notwithstanding section 743.1, a court that convicts a person for an escape committed while undergoing imprisonment may order that the term of imprisonment be served in a penitentiary, even if the time to be served is less than two years.

(2) In this section, "escape" means breaking prison, escaping from lawful custody or, without lawful excuse, being at large before the expiration of a term of imprisonment to

which a person has been sentenced. R.S., c. C-34, s. 137; 1972, c. 13, s. 9; 1976-77, c. 53, s. 6; 1992, c. 20, s. 199; 1995, c. 22, ss. 1 and 10.

CROSS-REFERENCES

"Penitentiary" is defined in s. 2 of the *Corrections and Conditional Release Act*, S.C. 1992, c. 20. Under s. 719(2), any time during which a convicted person is unlawfully at large does not count as part of any term of imprisonment.

SYNOPSIS

This section provides an exception to the normal rule as set out in s. 743.1 that a sentence of less than two years is served in a reformatory. The court has the power to order that a sentence for escape, as defined in subsec. (2), may be served in a penitentiary. Subsection (2) contains a broad definition of "escape" so that it includes prison breach (s. 144) and escaping or being unlawfully at large (s. 145(1)).

Part V / SEXUAL OFFENCES, PUBLIC MORALS AND DISORDERLY CONDUCT

Interpretation

DEFINITIONS / "Guardian" / "Public place" / "Theatre".

150. In this Part

"guardian" includes any person who has in law or in fact the custody or control of another person;

"public place" includes any place to which the public have access as of right or by invitation, express or implied;

"theatre" includes any place that is open to the public where entertainments are given, whether or not any charge is made for admission. R.S., c. C-34, s. 138.

CROSS-REFERENCES

In addition to the definitions in this section, see s. 2 and notes to that section. Despite the heading of this Part, in fact, many of the sexual offences are found in Part VIII and many of the offences dealing with public disorder are found in Part II.

SYNOPSIS

Section 150 provides definitions of the terms "guardian", "public place" and "theatre" which are used in a number of sections within Part V of the *Criminal Code*.

ANNOTATIONS

Public place – As the definitive words preceded by the word "includes" were not intended to be exhaustive and to exclude the ordinary dictionary meaning of those words, private property, frequented by members of the public with no objection by the owner, is a public place: *R. v. Lavoie*, [1968] 1 C.C.C. 265 (N.B.C.A.).

To constitute a public place it is not necessary that all segments of the public have a right of access thereto and accordingly a beverage room, from which a portion of the public may be excluded by law or by choice, is a public place under this section: *R. v. Tegstrom*, [1971] 1 W.W.R. 147 (Sask. D.C.).

"Public place" in this section was not meant to cover private places exposed to public view. The definition requires physical access to the place in which the impugned act was committed; visual access is not sufficient: *R. v. Clark*, [2005] 1 S.C.R. 6, 193 C.C.C. (3d) 289.

Sexual Offences

CONSENT NO DEFENCE / Exception — complainant aged 12 or 13 / Exception — complainant aged 14 or 15 / Exception for transitional purposes / Exception for transitional purposes / Exemption for accused aged twelve or thirteen / Mistake of age / Idem / Idem.

150.1 (1) Subject to subsections (2) to (2.2), when an accused is charged with an offence under section 151 or 152 or subsection 153(1), 160(3) or 173(2) or is charged with an offence under section 271, 272 or 273 in respect of a complainant under the age of 16 years, it is not a defence that the complainant consented to the activity that forms the subject-matter of the charge.

(2) When an accused is charged with an offence under section 151 or 152, subsection 173(2) or section 271 in respect of a complainant who is 12 years of age or more but under the age of 14 years, it is a defence that the complainant consented to the activity that forms the subject-matter of the charge if the accused

   (*a*) is less than two years older than the complainant; and

   (*b*) is not in a position of trust or authority towards the complainant, is not a person with whom the complainant is in a relationship of dependency and is not in a relationship with the complainant that is exploitative of the complainant.

(2.1) If an accused is charged with an offence under section 151 or 152, subsection 173(2) or section 271 in respect of a complainant who is 14 years of age or more but under the age of 16 years, it is a defence that the complainant consented to the activity that forms the subject-matter of the charge if the accused

   (*a*) is less than five years older than the complainant; and

   (*b*) is not in a position of trust or authority towards the complainant, is not a person with whom the complainant is in a relationship of dependency and is not in a relationship with the complainant that is exploitative of the complainant.

(2.2) When the accused referred to in subsection (2.1) is five or more years older than the complainant, it is a defence that the complainant consented to the activity that forms the subject matter of the charge if, on the day on which this subsection comes into force,

   (*a*) the accused is the common-law partner of the complainant, or has been cohabiting with the complainant in a conjugal relationship for a period of less than one year and they have had or are expecting to have a child as a result of the relationship; and

   (*b*) the accused is not in a position of trust or authority towards the complainant, is not a person with whom the complainant is in a relationship of dependency and is not in a relationship with the complainant that is exploitative of the complainant.

(2.3) If, immediately before the day on which this subsection comes into force, the accused referred to in subsection (2.1) is married to the complainant, it is a defence that the complainant consented to the activity that forms the subject-matter of the charge.

(3) No person aged twelve or thirteen years shall be tried for an offence under section 151 or 152 or subsection 173(2) unless the person is in a position of trust or authority towards the complainant, is a person with whom the complainant is in a relationship of dependency or is in a relationship with the complainant that is exploitative of the complainant.

(4) It is not a defence to a charge under section 151 or 152, subsection 160(3) or 173(2), or section 271, 272 or 273 that the accused believed that the complainant was 16 years of age or more at the time the offence is alleged to have been committed unless the accused took all reasonable steps to ascertain the age of the complainant.

(5) It is not a defence to a charge under section 153, 159, 170, 171 or 172 or subsection 286.1(2), 286.2(2) or 286.3(2) that the accused believed that the complainant was eighteen years of age or more at the time the offence is alleged to have been committed unless the accused took all reasonable steps to ascertain the age of the complainant.

(6) An accused cannot raise a mistaken belief in the age of the complainant in order to invoke a defence under subsection (2) or (2.1) unless the accused took all reasonable steps to ascertain the age of the complainant. R.S.C. 1985, c. 19 (3rd Supp.), s. 1; 2005, c. 32, s. 2; 2008, c. 6, ss. 13, 54(*a*); 2014, c. 25, s. 4; 2015, c. 29, s. 6.

CROSS-REFERENCES

The term "complainant" is defined in s. 2. The terms "position of trust or authority" and "relationship of dependency" are not defined. Section 153(1.2) sets out circumstances from which a judge may infer that a person is in an exploitative relationship with a young person.

In effect, this section attempts to define the circumstances in which a child may legally consent to sexual activity and the parameters of the "defence" of mistake of fact where the mistake is as to the age of the complainant. As to other notes concerning the mistake defence generally, see notes following s. 19 and, with respect to consent in particular, the notes following s. 265.

Age is determined by s. 30 of the *Interpretation Act*, R.S.C. 1985, c. I-21. Section 658 provides means of proving the age of a child.

Special evidentiary and procedural provisions – Section 274 provides that no corroboration is required for a conviction for any of the offences in ss. 151 to 153.1, 155, 159, 160 and 170 to 173 and the judge shall not instruct the jury that it is unsafe to find the accused guilty in the absence of corroboration. That provision, in effect, reverses the common law rule of practice that required the trial judge to direct the jury as to the need for corroboration for most sexual offences, especially those involving children. Section 275 provides that the rule relating to evidence of recent complaint is abrogated respecting ss. 151 to 153.1, 155, 159, 160(2) and (3) and 170 to 173. Sections 276 to 276.4 enact special rules limiting the circumstances in which the complainant may be questioned with respect to his or her prior sexual conduct with persons other than the accused in proceedings under ss. 151 to 153.1, 155, 159, 160(2) and (3) and 170 to 173. Section 277 provides that evidence of sexual reputation is inadmissible in proceedings under ss. 151 to 153.1, 155, 159, 160(2) and (3) and 170 to 173. Production of records containing personal information for use by the accused at the trial of these offences is governed by ss. 278.1 to 278.9.

Section 486(1) and (2) provide that the judge may make an order excluding all or any members of the public where such order is in the interest of public morals, the maintenance of order or the proper administration of justice or is necessary to prevent injury to international relations or national defence or national security. The proper administration of justice includes safeguarding the interests of witnesses under the age of 18 years. Where the accused is charged with an offence in ss. 151 to 153.1, 155, 159, 160, 170 to 173 or 279.01 to 279.03 and the application by the accused or the prosecutor for the exclusion order is dismissed, the judge shall state the reason for not making the order. Section 486.1 sets out the circumstances in which the judge shall or may order a support person to be present and close to a witness while the witness testifies. Where the witness is under the age of 18 years or has a mental or physical disability, the order is to be made upon request, unless the judge is of the opinion that the order would interfere with the proper administration of justice. In the case of other witnesses, the order is to be made if necessary to obtain a full and candid account from the witness of the matters complained of. The application for this order may be made during the proceedings or before they begin to the judge who is to preside at the proceedings.

Similarly, s. 486.2 sets out the circumstances in which the judge shall or may order a witness to testify outside the courtroom or behind a screen or other device that would not allow the witness to see the accused. Where the witness is under the age of 18 years or may have difficulty communicating the evidence by reason of a mental or physical disability, the judge shall make the order unless the judge is of the opinion that the order would interfere with the proper administration of justice. In all other cases, the order may be made if the judge is of the opinion that the order is necessary to obtain a full and candid account from the witness of the acts complained of. Similarly, s. 486.3 provides that, on application by the prosecutor or a witness under the age of 18 years, the accused shall not personally cross-examine the witness unless the judge is of the opinion that the proper administration of justice requires the accused to personally conduct the cross-examination. In other cases, the judge may make an order that the accused not personally cross-examine the witness if the judge is of the opinion that the order is necessary to obtain a full and candid account from the witness of the acts complained of. The judge will appoint counsel to conduct the cross-examination.

Under s. 486.4, the judge may make an order directing that the identity of the complainant or a witness not be disclosed in any publication, broadcast or transmitted in any way. The order is mandatory where the complainant or a witness under the age of 18 years or the prosecutor applies for the order. Section 486.5 also gives the judge a discretion respecting non-publication orders in proceedings under these provisions in other circumstances.

Section 659 abrogates any rule requiring a warning about convicting the accused on the evidence of a child.

Where the accused is found guilty of the offences under ss. 151, 152, 155 or 159, 160(2) or (3), 163.1, 170, 171, 172.1, 173(2), 271, 272, 273 or 281 and the offence is in respect of a person who is under 16 years of age, then the court has the discretion to impose an order of prohibition under s. 161 prohibiting the accused from attending certain public areas and facilities or taking certain employment which will bring him into contact with persons under 16 years of age.

Section 715.1 provides that, in proceedings against the accused in which the victim (defined in s. 2) or other witness was under the age of 18 years at the time the offence is alleged to have been committed, a video recording made within a reasonable time after the alleged offence, in which the victim or witness describes the acts complained of, is admissible in evidence if the victim or witness, while testifying, adopts its contents, unless the judge is of the opinion that the admission of the video recoding would interfere with the proper administration of justice. Section 715.2 provides for a similar procedure where the victim or another witness may have difficulty communicating the evidence by reason of a mental or physical disability. Under s. 4(2) of the *Canada Evidence Act*, the spouse of an accused charged with an offence under ss. 151 to 153.1, 155, 159, 160(2), (3), 170 to 173, or 177 is a compellable witness at the instance of the prosecution. Sections 16 and 16.1 of the *Canada Evidence Act* deal with the competency of witnesses under the age of 14 years.

Section 718.01 provides that, in imposing a sentence for an offence involving the abuse of a person under the age of 18 years, the court shall give primary consideration to the objectives of denunciation and deterrence. Further, under s. 718.2, evidence that the offender, in committing the offence, abused a person under the age of 18 years is an aggravating circumstance.

SYNOPSIS

This section provides a series of rules that apply to enumerated sections to prevent an accused from relying on the consent of a complainant under a specified age. It also spells out when a mistake by the accused may be a defence.

Subsection (1) provides that the consent of the complainant, who is less than 16 years old, is no defence to the sexual assault offences (ss. 271 to 273) and no defence at all, no matter what the age of the complainant, to the other enumerated offences, such as sexual exploitation (s. 153(1)).

Subsection (2) provides an exception to subsec. (1) and permits the defence of consent to be raised to the offences of sexual interference (s. 151), invitation to sexual touching (s. 152), indecent exposure to a person under 16 (s. 173(2)), or sexual assault (s. 271) if the complainant is at least 12 but less than 14 years old and the additional requirements of the subsection are met. The further conditions which must be met for the exception to apply are as follows: (a) the accused is less than two years older than the complainant; (b) the accused is not in a position of trust or authority towards the complainant, the complainant is not in a relationship of dependency with the accused and the accused is not in a relationship with the complainant that is exploitative of the complainant.

Subsection (2.1) provides for a similar exception where the complainant is 14 years of age or more but under the age of 16 years. The conditions which must be met are as follow: (a) the accused is less than five years older than the complainant; and (b) the accused is not in a position of trust or authority towards the complainant, the complainant is not in a relationship of dependency with the accused and the accused is not in a relationship with the complainant that is exploitative of the complainant.

Importantly, subsec. (6) provides that mistake of fact cannot be invoked under subsecs. (2) or (2.1) unless the accused took all reasonable steps to ascertain the age of the complainant.

Subsection (2.2) provides a form of transitional provision for cases where the accused is five or more years older than the complainant when this section came into force (May 1, 2008) and (a) the accused and the complainant are either in a common-law relationship or cohabiting in a conjugal relationship and have or are expecting a child; and (b) the accused is not in a position of trust or authority towards the complainant, the complainant is not in a relationship of dependency with the accused and the accused is not in a relationship with the complainant that is exploitative of the complainant.

Subsection (2.3) provides a transitional provision that allows accused persons referred to in subsec. (2.1) who were married to the complainant when this subsection came into force to rely on the defence that the complainant consented to the activity that forms the subject-matter of the charge.

Subsection (3) prohibits the prosecution of a 12 or 13-year-old unless the accused comes within condition (b) noted above.

Under subsecs. (4) and (5), for the offences listed in this section, it is not an excuse that the accused believed the complainant was over 16 years or 18 years, as the case may be, unless the accused took all reasonable steps to ascertain the age of the complainant.

ANNOTATIONS

Note: The cases noted below were decided when the age of consent was 14 years.

Application of Charter of Rights – It has been held that former s. 246.1(2), which also limited the consent defence where the complainant was under fourteen years of age, did not constitute an unconstitutional violation of the equality rights guaranteed by s. 15 of the Charter: *R. v. Bearhead* (1986), 27 C.C.C. (3d) 546, 22 C.R.R. 211 (Alta. Q.B.); *R. v. Le Gallant* (1986), 29 C.C.C. (3d) 291, 54 C.R. (3d) 46 (B.C.C.A.); *R. v. Perkins* (1987), 59 C.R. (3d) 56, [1987] N.W.T.R. 308 (S.C.); *R. v. Halleran* (1989), 39 C.C.C. (3d) 177 (Nfld. C.A.). *Contra: R. v. Black* (1990), 11 W.C.B. (2d) 557 (B.C.S.C.), where it was held that former s. 246.1(2) infringed s. 7 of the Charter and was not a reasonable limit.

Elimination of the defence of consent by subsec. (1) where the complainant is under 14 years of age does not infringe s. 7 of the Charter: *R. v. M. (R.S.)* (1991), 69 C.C.C. (3d) 223, 10 C.R. (4th) 121 (P.E.I.C.A.).

The removal of the defence of consent to a charge contrary to s. 153 violates neither s. 7 nor s. 15 of the Charter: *R. v. Hann* (1992), 75 C.C.C. (3d) 355, 15 C.R. (4th) 355 (Nfld. C.A.).

Trial of child (Subsec. (3)) – It was held, considering a predecessor to subsec. (3) in relation to the former offence of rape, that the section merely enacted a rule of immunity not incapacity and therefore an accused who is over fourteen years of age may be convicted as a party although the principal being under fourteen years of age is immune from prosecution: *R. v. Cardinal* (1982), 3 C.C.C. (3d) 376, [1983] 1 W.W.R. 689 (Alta. C.A.), affd [1984] 2 S.C.R. 523, 18 C.C.C. (3d) 96 (7:0).

The fact that subsec. (3) does not extend immunity from prosecution to the offence of sexual assault under s. 271 does not violate an offender's rights under s. 7 of the Charter.

Nevertheless, the discretion as to whether the accused should be charged with sexual assault must be exercised in a proper manner and for a proper motive and it would be for the Crown to ensure that a 12- or 13-year-old offender, who did not use force in circumstances which would only amount to an offence under s. 151 or s. 152, was not charged under s. 271 merely to avoid the immunity provisions of subsec. (3): *R. v. V. (K.S.)* (1994), 89 C.C.C. (3d) 477, 119 Nfld. & P.E.I.R. 290 (Nfld. C.A.), leave to appeal to S.C.C. refused 95 C.C.C. (3d) vi.

Mistake as to age – It was held in *R. v. Brooks* (1989), 47 C.C.C. (3d) 276, [1989] 3 W.W.R. 1 (Alta. C.A.), that the defence of honest belief provided by subsec. (4) should be given retrospective effect so as to give an accused charged with the offence under s. 271, in relation to a complainant under the age of 14 years, the benefit of that subsection, although the offence was committed prior to enactment of this subsection but after proclamation of the *Charter of Rights and Freedoms*. It would be contrary to the fundamental guarantee in s. 7 to deprive the accused of a defence of reasonable mistake of fact in such circumstances. [Also see note: *R. v. Nguyen*, [1990] 2 S.C.R. 906, 59 C.C.C. (3d) 161 (5:2) under the Charter, s. 7.]

The accused, in order to rely on the defence of mistake, need only raise a reasonable doubt. The accused must, however, have made an earnest inquiry or there should be some compelling factor that obviates the need for such an inquiry. Thus, the accused must show what steps he took and those steps were all that could be reasonably required of him in the circumstances: *R. v. Osborne* (1992), 17 C.R. (4th) 350, 102 Nfld. & P.E.I.R. 194 (Nfld. C.A.).

Where the accused raises the defence of honest but mistaken belief in the complainant's age, the Crown must prove beyond a reasonable doubt that the accused did not take all reasonable steps to ascertain the complainant's age or did not have an honest belief as to the complainant's age. The issue to be determined is what steps would have been reasonable for the accused to take in the circumstances. While in certain circumstances a visual observation may suffice, where it does not, further reasonable steps should be considered having regard to the complainant's physical appearance, her behaviour, the ages and appearance of those in whose company the complainant was found, the activities engaged in, the times, places and other circumstances in which the accused observes the complainant and her conduct. The accused's subjective belief is relevant but not conclusive of this determination: *R. v. P. (L.T.)* (1997), 113 C.C.C. (3d) 42, 142 W.A.C. 20 (B.C.C.A.).

Subsection (4) is not concerned with the accused's belief as to the complainant's age; it assumes that the accused believed the complainant to be old enough to give legal consent. This provision mandates an inquiry akin to a due diligence inquiry by the trier of fact, albeit with the onus of proof on the Crown. It was therefore an error of law for the trial judge to limit his analysis to the accused's own state of mind with no consideration of what steps were taken to confirm that belief: *R. v. Saliba* (2013), 304 C.C.C. (3d) 133 (Ont. C.A.). See also: *R. v. Dragos* (2012), 291 C.C.C. (3d) 350 (Ont. C.A.).

Where the circumstances in which the accused and the complainant met — including the complainant's appearance, her behaviour, and the apparent ages of the other partygoers — all indicated that she was at least 16 years old, subsec. (4) did not mandate any further inquiry: *R. v. Tannas* (2015), 324 C.C.C. (3d) 93 (Sask. C.A.).

Subsection (5) does not create a reverse onus as the Crown must prove beyond a reasonable doubt that the accused did not take all reasonable steps or that he did not have an honest belief that the complainant was 18 years of age or more. However, where an accused does not lead any evidence other than through the Crown's case, his ability to obtain an acquittal on subsec. (5) may be compromised. Section 212(4) does not require the Crown to prove that a victim appeared to be less than 18 years of age in order to meet an argument that an accused who does not provide evidence has taken all reasonable steps to ascertain the victim's age merely on the basis of appearance: *R. v. Slater* (2005), 201 C.C.C. (3d) 85, 269 Sask. R. 42 (C.A.).

Consent defence – The burden is on the accused to prove the consent defence provided by age proximity in subsec. (2)(*a*): *R. v. Thompson* (1992), 76 C.C.C. (3d) 142 (Alta. C.A.).

Whether the accused took "all reasonable steps" will depend on the circumstances. In order to rely on this provision, the accused need not necessarily directly ask the victim her age or ask collateral questions that would disclose her age. The age differential between the accused and the victim may be considered in determining whether the steps taken were reasonable and the greater the disparity in ages, the more inquiry will be required: *R. v. K. (R.A.)* (1996), 106 C.C.C. (3d) 93 (N.B.C.A.).

Whether the accused is in a position of trust for the purpose of subsec. (2)(*c*) must be considered with respect to the accused's position toward the complainant. While the position of the accused as viewed by other individuals, such as family members, may be relevant, it is not determinative. It will be an infrequent case in which the accused, who is a young person close in age to the complainant, will have been entrusted with sufficient responsibility to have been considered to have been in a position of trust toward the complainant, although such cases may arise where the accused was the complainant's baby-sitter, camp counsellor, lifeguard or tutor: *R. v. L. (D.B.)* (1995), 101 C.C.C. (3d) 406, 43 C.R. (4th) 252 (Ont. C.A.).

Expert evidence respecting child abuse – Evidence adduced solely for the purpose of bolstering the credibility of a witness is excluded by virtue of the rule against oath-helping: *R. v. Kyselka* (1962), 133 C.C.C. 103, 37 C.R. 391 (Ont. C.A.). Thus, the opinion of a child witness' teacher that she was a trustworthy witness is inadmissible: *R. v. Hill* (1986), 32 C.C.C. (3d) 314 (Ont. C.A.). Further the opinion of a psychologist that children rarely lie about sexual abuse is inadmissible: *R. v. Kostuck* (1986), 29 C.C.C. (3d) 190, 43 Man. R. (2d) 84 (C.A.). Expert evidence is admissible even if it relates directly to the ultimate question which the trier of fact must answer. In *R. v. R. (D.)*, [1996] 2 S.C.R. 291, 107 C.C.C. (3d) 289, therefore, the expert in child abuse who testified for the defence about the nature of the child complainant's memory was also entitled to also testify about conclusions on the reliability of the child's memory.

While expert evidence on the ultimate credibility of a witness is not admissible, expert evidence on human conduct and the psychological and physical factors which may lead to certain behaviour relevant to credibility is admissible, provided that the testimony goes beyond the ordinary experience of the trier of fact. Where such evidence is admitted, the jury must be carefully instructed as to its function and duty in making the final decision without being unduly influenced by the expert evidence: *R. v. Marquard*, [1993] 4 S.C.R. 223, 85 C.C.C. (3d) 193.

It did not violate the rule against "oath-helping" to ask an expert on child sexual abuse whether, as far as he was aware, the complainant had told him something that was untrue. The expert's evidence was directed to legitimate purposes having nothing to do with whether the complainant was truthful or not. The question and answer admissible for the purpose of supporting the opinion of the expert expressed on other matters, such as his diagnosis of the complainant's condition and his explanation of her behaviour. His conclusions were based, in large part, on what the complainant had told him and those conclusions would be weakened if not invalidated if the expert did not believe what she had told him. It was therefore relevant to determine whether he believed her or not: *R. v. Burns*, [1994] 1 S.C.R. 656, 89 C.C.C. (3d) 193.

In *R. v. Beliveau* (1986), 30 C.C.C. (3d) 193 (B.C.C.A.), it was held that, while an expert could not be asked whether a child witness was truthful, the expert could give an opinion that certain observed behaviour, demeanour and other facts were consistent with the child having been sexually abused. Similarly *R. v. H. (E.L.)* (1990), 2 C.R. (4th) 187, 100 N.S.R. (2d) 1 (C.A.). In *R. v. J. (F.E.)* (1990), 53 C.C.C. (3d) 64, 74 C.R. (3d) 269 (Ont. C.A.), it was held that a psychologist and social worker could give expert evidence to the effect that a letter written by the child complainant, recanting the allegations of sexual abuse by her father, was typical of the recantations commonly seen among children who have been sexually abused when they realize the problems that their revelations have caused. However, the further opinion by the expert, that he had not found one case in which a child was being truthful when recanting, was inadmissible.

Expert evidence from a clinical psychologist, specializing in the treatment of young victims and perpetrators of sexual offences, that several behavioural characteristics noticed in the young victim were similar to those experienced by young victims of sexual offences is admissible on the trial of a charge of sexual assault and such evidence will often prove invaluable: *R. v. B. (G.)*, [1990] 2 S.C.R. 3, 56 C.C.C. (3d) 161 (5:0). However, expert evidence was not required to explain evidence from the complainant's mother regarding behavioural changes around the time of the offence. The trial judge was entitled to rely on common sense and experience in evaluating these behavioural changes: *R. v. N. (R.A.)* (2001), 152 C.C.C. (3d) 464, 277 A.R. 288 (C.A.).

On the trial of charges of sexual assault by the accused on his stepsons, expert evidence from a sexual abuse therapist was properly admitted to explain why the victims continued to associate with the accused, why the child did not immediately complain to the other parent, but did complain to outsiders, and why the memory of the events could improve as the self-protective mechanism of involuntary forgetting is overcome by the child being required to repeat the story on many occasions. This kind of evidence could be helpful to the jury on the issues of credibility by tending to show that the inferences which might well be drawn on the basis of common sense and common experience should not be drawn as a matter of course in cases of sexual abuse. The jury must, however, be warned as to the dangers in utilizing this kind of evidence, especially the danger of giving undue weight to the expert opinion: *R. v. C. (R.A.)* (1990), 57 C.C.C. (3d) 522, 78 C.R. (3d) 390 (B.C.C.A.).

In *R. v. D. (D.)*, [2000] 2 S.C.R. 275, 148 C.C.C. (3d) 41, the Supreme Court of Canada held that expert evidence regarding delayed disclosure was inadmissible as the expert's evidence was simply a statement of the law that the failure to make a timely complaint must not be the subject of a presumptive adverse inference against the complainant. Where there is an issue of delayed disclosure, the trial judge should instruct the jury that there is no inviolable rule relating to how people who are the victims of trauma like a sexual assault will behave. Some will make an immediate complaint, some will delay disclosure and some will not ever disclose the abuse. The reasons for delay are many and may include embarrassment, fear, guilt or a lack of understanding and knowledge. In assessing credibility, the timing of the complaint is simply one circumstance to consider the context of the case. Delayed disclosure, standing alone, will never give rise to an adverse inference against the credibility of the complainant.

In a case involving alleged physical abuse of a child, the opinion of an expert is admissible as to whether certain injuries were caused accidentally or intentionally; whether it is usual or rare to find injuries of a particular kind in a child of a particular age; the kind and degree of force required to cause the injuries; the age of the injuries; and the consistency or inconsistency of the injuries with explanations given for them. However, it is within the discretion of the trial judge to rule that the evidence be given in a less emotional but just as accurate form, for example, by use of the term "intentional force" rather than "child abuse". The judge may also require that a conclusory statement be excluded where opinion evidence can be given just as accurately in less conclusory terms, for example, in terms of the degree of likelihood of the injuries being caused in a particular manner, provided that this does not affect the honesty or accuracy of the opinion. Further, in a jury case, the trial judge must give a careful direction to the jury as to the manner in which this evidence must be analyzed and applied by the jury: *R. v. Millar* (1989), 49 C.C.C. (3d) 193, 71 C.R. (3d) 78 (Ont. C.A.).

Before an expert's opinion is admissible on behalf of the defence to show that the accused by reason of his disposition could not have been the perpetrator of the offence, the trial judge must be satisfied, as a matter of law, that either the perpetrator of the crime or the accused has a distinctive behavioural characteristic such that a comparison of one with the other will be of material assistance in determining innocence or guilt. The court must consider whether the scientific community has developed a standard profile for the offender who commits this type of crime: *R. v. Mohan*, [1994] 2 S.C.R. 9, 89 C.C.C. (3d) 402. See, however, *R. v. S.*

(J.T.) (1996), 47 C.R. (4th) 240, 181 A.R. 181 *sub. nom R. v. Somers* (C.A.), in which expert evidence that there are three recognized psychological profiles of men who abuse young women and that the accused did not fit any of these profiles was admitted.

Where the Crown seeks to adduce expert evidence in respect of the accused, the condition for admission is that either the accused must be shown to be a member of a distinctive group capable of diagnosis by a psychiatrist or it must be shown that the perpetrator of the offence must have been a member of such a group. In this case, while expert evidence that the accused was a homosexual paedophile was relevant to determining the intent of the accused in touching the complainants, in the absence of a useful behavioural profile of the accused or homosexual paedophiles in general from which the jury could make its own judgment as to the accused's purpose at the time of the touching incidents, it was merely evidence of propensity or disposition: *R. v. Pascoe* (1997), 113 C.C.C. (3d) 126, 32 O.R. (3d) 37 (C.A.).

An expert may not testify that, based upon "statement validity analysis", the allegation by the complainant is credible. Evidence tendered for the specific purpose of bolstering the credibility of a witness is inadmissible and, in any event, this theory has not been shown to be scientifically valid: *R. v. Jmieff* (1994), 94 C.C.C. (3d) 157, 84 W.A.C. 213 (B.C.C.A.).

Similar fact evidence respecting child abuse – It was held in *R. v. D. (L.E.)*, [1989] 2 S.C.R. 111, 50 C.C.C. (3d) 142 (4:1), that testimony from the complainant, the accused's daughter, as to much more serious acts of sexual assault than those alleged in the charges, was inadmissible. This similar fact evidence bore nearly the entire burden of proving the Crown's case against the accused on the acts charged and its probative value was not sufficient to overcome its prejudicial effect. However, evidence from the complainant of other conduct, similar to the acts charged and more proximate in time, was properly admitted. Where similar fact evidence is admitted, the jury must be specifically warned that it is not to rely on the evidence as proof that the accused is the sort of person who would commit the offence charged and, on that basis, infer that the accused is in fact guilty of the offence charged.

In *R. v. B. (C.R.)*, [1990] 1 S.C.R. 717, 55 C.C.C. (3d) 1 (5:2), it was held that, on the trial of charges of sexual assault of the accused's natural daughter, evidence was admissible of sexual assaults by the accused upon the daughter of a woman with whom he had lived several years before. While there were differences between the conduct alleged by the complainant and by the similar fact witness it was open to the trial judge to conclude that the probative value of the similar fact evidence with respect to the credibility of the complainant outweighed its prejudicial effect.

On a charge of manslaughter involving the death of an infant, evidence was admissible of other injuries, suffered by the child in the weeks prior to his death, where there was evidence from which the jury could find that these other injuries were intentionally inflicted by the accused: *R. v. Millar* (1989), 49 C.C.C. (3d) 193, 71 C.R. (3d) 78 (Ont. C.A.).

As to similar fact evidence generally, see *R. v. Handy*, [2002] 2 S.C.R. 908, 164 C.C.C. (3d) 481.

Credibility of children – While the court must carefully assess the credibility of child witnesses the standard of a reasonable adult is not necessarily appropriate in assessing the credibility of young children. Young children may not be able to recount precise details and communicate the when and where of an event with exactitude, but this does not mean that they have misconceived what happened to them or who did it: *R. v. B. (G.)*, *supra*.

There have been major changes in recent years with respect to the treatment of evidence of children. While, in a proper case, a child's evidence may be treated with caution, there is no assumption that children's evidence is always less reliable than the evidence of adults. Thus, if a court proceeds to discount a child's evidence automatically, without regard to the circumstances of the particular case, it will have fallen into error. It is also wrong to apply adult tests for credibility to the evidence of children. This does not mean that the evidence of children should not be subject to the same standard of proof as evidence of adult witnesses in criminal cases, but only that the evidence of children must not be approached from the perspective of rigid stereotypes but on the basis of common sense, taking into account the strengths and weaknesses which characterize the evidence offered in the particular case. The credibility of every witness of whatever age must be assessed by reference to criteria appropriate to her mental development, understanding and ability to communicate. In general, however, where an adult is testifying as to events which occurred when she was a child, her credibility should be assessed according to criteria applicable to her as an adult witness bearing in mind that the presence of inconsistencies, particularly as to peripheral matters such as time and location, should be considered in the context of the age of the witness at the time of the events to which she was testifying: *R. v. W. (R)*, [1992] 2 S.C.R. 122, 74 C.C.C. (3d) 134.

Hearsay exception – Reference should also be made to annotations found under s. 9 of the *Canada Evidence Act*.

It is open to the courts to create new hearsay exceptions where the circumstances meet the requirements for necessity, meaning "reasonably necessary", and reliability. In the case of out of court statements by children, necessity may be created where the child is found not to be competent to testify or where there is expert evidence that testimony in court might be traumatic for the child or harm the child. The requirement of necessity will probably mean that, in most cases, children will be called to give *viva voce* evidence. As regards the reliability requirement, the court would have to take into consideration many facts such as timing, demeanour, personality of the child, the intelligence and understanding of the child and the absence of any reason to expect fabrication. The trial judge might also attach conditions to the admission of the evidence in order to safeguard the interests of the accused. This might include the right to cross-examine the child, where the judge thinks it is possible and fair in all the circumstances: *R. v. Khan*, [1990] 2 S.C.R. 531, 59 C.C.C. (3d) 92 (5:0).

The necessity requirement includes a diverse number of circumstances ranging from total testimonial incompetence to traumatic consequences of the witness testifying. Necessity may be established on the basis of what has happened at trial or on the basis of extrinsic evidence. While expert evidence will often be required, evidence does not have to be called to establish necessity. Necessity may be established from the facts and circumstances of the case or from evidence called by the Crown. If the child cannot give evidence in a meaningful way, the trial judge may conclude that it is self-evident from the proceedings that out-of-court statements are necessary. In this case, it was open to the trial judge to find necessity had been established by the child's inability to respond in any way to questions about events: *R. v. F. (W.J.)*, [1999] 3 S.C.R. 569, 138 C.C.C. (3d) 1. See also *R. v. Rockey*, [1996] 3 S.C.R. 829, 110 C.C.C. (3d) 481; *R. v. Dubois* (1997), 118 C.C.C. (3d) 544 (Que. C.A.).

In a case where the child testifies, her hearsay statement will be admissible if reasonably necessary and if there are *indicia* of reliability present. Reasonable necessity in this context refers to the need to obtain an accurate and frank rendition of the child's version of events pertaining to the alleged assault: *Khan v. College of Physicians and Surgeons of Ontario* (1992), 76 C.C.C. (3d) 10 (Ont. C.A.).

In *R. v. Khelawon*, [2006] 2 S.C.R. 787, 215 C.C.C. (3d) 161, the Supreme Court of Canada considered the issue of threshold reliability. While at the threshold stage, the trial judge does not determine whether the statement will be relied upon as true, the truthfulness of the statement may be a concern in some cases at this initial stage. It might be appropriate to consider the presence of corroborating or conflicting evidence. In determining admissibility, courts should adopt a functional approach and focus on the particular danger raised by the hearsay evidence sought to be introduced, and on those attributes or circumstances relied upon by the proponent to overcome those dangers.

In *R. v. A. (S.)* (1992), 76 C.C.C. (3d) 522 (Ont. C.A.), the court set out guidelines to assist the trial judge in directing the jury as to the use to be made of a hearsay complaint. The court recommended that the jury be told they must determine whether the statement was made and, if it was, its contents; that the statement cannot be placed on the same footing as a statement made by a witness in the course of her testimony since out-of-court statements made by persons who do not testify, offered for the truth of their contents, are subject to frailties which warrant a cautious approach; and that the weight to be given to the statement will be affected by the other evidence which may support or undermine the reliability of the statement.

SEXUAL INTERFERENCE.

151. Every person who, for a sexual purpose, touches, directly or indirectly, with a part of the body or with an object, any part of the body of a person under the age of 16 years

- (*a*) **is guilty of an indictable offence and is liable to imprisonment for a term of not more than 14 years and to a minimum punishment of imprisonment for a term of one year; or**
- (*b*) **is guilty of an offence punishable on summary conviction and is liable to imprisonment for a term of not more than two years less a day and to a minimum punishment of imprisonment for a term of 90 days. R.S.C. 1985, c. 19 (3rd Supp.), s. 1; 2005, c. 32, s. 3; 2008, c. 6, s. 54(b); 2012, c. 1, s. 11; 2015, c. 23, s. 2.**

CROSS-REFERENCES

Age is determined by s. 30 of the *Interpretation Act*, R.S.C. 1985, c. I-21. Section 658 provides means of proving the age of a child. The term "sexual purpose" is not defined. The defences of consent and mistaken belief as to the age of the complainant are defined in s. 150.1. Under s. 150.1(3), a young offender aged 12 or 13 years may not be tried for an offence under subsec. (2) unless he is in a position of trust or authority. Section 170 creates an offence for a parent or guardian to procure a person under the age of 18 years for the purpose of engaging in any sexual activity prohibited by the Code. Section 171 creates an offence for a householder and other similarly situated persons to permit a person under the age of 18 years to resort to premises for the purpose of engaging in any sexual activity prohibited by the Code. Section 171.1 makes it an offence to transmit, make available, distribute or sell sexually explicit material to a person who is, or who the accused believes is under the age of 16 years for purpose of facilitating the commission of the offence created by this section. Section 172.1 makes it an offence to communicate by means of telecommunication with a person who is or who the accused believes is under the age of 16 years for the purpose of facilitating the commission of the offence under this section. Section 172.2 makes it an offence to agree with a person or make an arrangement with a person by means of telecommunication to commit an offence under this section with a person who is or who the accused believes is under the age of 16 years.

A person, found guilty of the offence in this section, may, depending on the circumstances, be liable to either the mandatory prohibition order in s. 109 or to the discretionary prohibition order prescribed by s. 110 for possession of weapons, ammunition and explosives. Where the accused is found guilty of this offence in respect of a person who is under 16 years of age, the court has the discretion to impose an order of prohibition under s. 161 prohibiting the accused from attending certain public areas and facilities or taking certain employment which will bring him into contact with persons under 16 years of age or using a computer system for the purpose of communicating with a person under the age of 16 years.

Special evidentiary and procedural provisions: see cross-references under s. 150.1.

As to cases concerning admissibility of evidence in child abuse cases, see notes under s. 150.1.

Section 718.01 provides that, in imposing a sentence for an offence involving the abuse of a person under the age of 18 years, the court shall give primary consideration to the objectives of denunciation and deterrence. Further, under s. 718.2, evidence that the offender, in committing the offence, abused a person under the age of 18 years is an aggravating circumstance.

The offence in this section is a primary designated offence for the purpose of making a forensic DNA data bank order. Under s. 490.012, on application by the prosecutor, where an offender is convicted of this offence, the judge shall make an order requiring the offender to comply with the *Sex Offender Information Registration Act*, S.C. 2004, c. 10.

SYNOPSIS

This section creates the offence of sexual interference with a person under 16 years and spells out the sentence for it. The offence may be committed by touching the complainant's body, directly or indirectly, with either a part of the accused's body or an object. It must be proven that the accused had a sexual purpose for the touching. This offence is punishable by way of summary conviction or by way of indictment. In the latter case, it is punishable by a maximum sentence of 14 years and to a minimum punishment of one year imprisonment. If the Crown proceeds by way of summary conviction, the offence is punishable by a maximum of two years less a day and a minimum of 90 days' imprisonment. Section 718.01 provides that, in imposing a sentence for an offence involving the abuse of a person under the age of 18 years, the court shall give primary consideration to the objectives of denunciation and deterrence. Further, under s. 718.2, evidence that the offender, in committing the offence, abused a person under the age of 18 years is an aggravating circumstance.

ANNOTATIONS

An accused who intends sexual interaction of any kind with a child and with that intent makes contact with the body of a child, "touches" the child within the meaning of this section, even where the sexual interaction is suggested by the child: *R. v. Sears* (1990), 58 C.C.C. (3d) 62 (Man. C.A.).

While the different minimum sentences applicable depending on Crown election violates s. 9 of the Charter, it is a reasonable limit pursuant to s. 1: *R. v. Lonegren* (2009), 250 C.C.C. (3d) 377 (B.C.S.C.), supp. reasons 260 C.C.C. (3d) 367 (B.C.S.C.).

The mandatory minimum sentence in para. (*b*) does not violate s. 15 of the Charter, as it does not perpetuate discrimination in the justice system against Aboriginal offenders: *R. v. B. (T.M.)* (2013), 299 C.C.C. (3d) 493 (Ont. S.C.J.).

INVITATION TO SEXUAL TOUCHING.

152. Every person who, for a sexual purpose, invites, counsels or incites a person under the age of 16 years to touch, directly or indirectly, with a part of the body or with an object, the body of any person, including the body of the person who so invites, counsels or incites and the body of the person under the age of 16 years,

   (*a*) is guilty of an indictable offence and is liable to imprisonment for a term of not more than 14 years and to a minimum punishment of imprisonment for a term of one year; or

   (*b*) is guilty of an offence punishable on summary conviction and is liable to imprisonment for a term of not more than two years less a day and to a minimum punishment of imprisonment for a term of 90 days. R.S.C. 1985, c. 19 (3rd Supp.), s. 1; 2005, c. 32, s. 3; 2008, c. 6, s. 54(*b*); 2012, c. 1, s. 12; 2015, c. 23, s. 3.

CROSS-REFERENCES

Age is determined by s. 30 of the *Interpretation Act*, R.S.C. 1985, c. I-21. Section 658 provides means of proving the age of a child. The term "counsels" is defined in s. 22 and in fact includes "incite". The term "sexual purpose" is not defined. The defences of consent and mistaken belief as to the age of the complainant are defined in s. 150.1. Under s. 150.1(3), a young offender aged 12 or 13 years may not be tried for an offence under subsec. (2) unless he is in a position of trust or authority. Section 170 creates an offence for a parent or guardian to procure a person under the age of 18 years for the purpose of engaging in any sexual activity prohibited by the Code. Section 171 creates an offence for a householder and other similarly situated persons to permit a person under the age of 18 years to resort to premises for the purpose of engaging in any sexual activity prohibited by the Code. Section 171.1 makes it an offence to transmit, make available, distribute or sell sexually explicit material to a person who is, or who the accused believes is under the age of 16 years for purpose of facilitating the commission of the offence created by this section. Section

172.1 makes it an offence to communicate by means of telecommunication with a person who is or who the accused believes is under the age of 16 years for the purpose of facilitating the commission of the offence under this section. Section 172.2 makes it an offence to agree with a person or make an arrangement with a person by means of telecommunication to commit an offence under this section with a person who is or who the accused believes is under the age of 16 years.

A person, found guilty of the offence in this section, may, depending on the circumstances, be liable to either the mandatory prohibition order in s. 109 or to the discretionary prohibition order prescribed by s. 110 for possession of weapons, ammunition and explosives. Where the accused is found guilty of this offence in respect of a person who is under 16 years of age, the court has the discretion to impose an order of prohibition under s. 161 prohibiting the accused from attending certain public areas and facilities or taking certain employment which will bring him into contact with persons under 16 years of age or using a computer system for the purpose of communicating with a person under the age of 16 years.

Special evidentiary and procedural provisions: see cross-references under s. 150.1.

As to cases concerning admissibility of evidence in child abuse cases, see notes under s. 150.1.

Section 718.01 provides that, in imposing a sentence for an offence involving the abuse of a person under the age of 18 years, the court shall give primary consideration to the objectives of denunciation and deterrence. Further, under s. 718.2, evidence that the offender, in committing the offence, abused a person under the age of 18 years is an aggravating circumstance.

The offence in this section is a primary designated offence for the purpose of making a forensic DNA data bank order. Under s. 490.012, on application by the prosecutor, where an offender is convicted of this offence, the judge shall make an order requiring the offender to comply with the *Sex Offender Information Registration Act*, S.C. 2004, c. 10.

SYNOPSIS

This section provides for the offence of inviting, counselling or inciting a person under 16 years of age to touch, directly or indirectly, any person's body. The touching may be with a part of the body or with an object. The person inviting the touching must do so for a sexual purpose. The section applies regardless of whether the accused invites the touching of his or herself or another person or incites the person under 16 to touch their own body. The offence is punishable by indictment or by way of summary conviction. In the former case, it is punishable by a maximum sentence of 14 years and to a minimum punishment of one year imprisonment. If the Crown proceeds by way of summary conviction, the offence is punishable by a maximum of two years less a day and a minimum of 90 days' imprisonment.

ANNOTATIONS

This offence does not require proof of actual physical contact between body parts or an invitation to engage in that level of contact. This section covers not only actual touching but "indirect" touching and thus includes an invitation by the accused to the complainant to hold a tissue onto which the accused ejaculated: *R. v. Fong* (1994), 92 C.C.C. (3d) 171 (Alta. C.A.), leave to appeal to S.C.C. refused 94 C.C.C. (3d) vii.

Incitement is more than mere passive acquiescence and requires some positive act by the accused to cause the complainant to engage in sexual touching. Failure to resist, therefore, is not inciting: *R. v. Rhynes* (2004), 186 C.C.C. (3d) 29 (P.E.I.S.C.), leave to appeal refused 2004 PESCAD 15 (P.E.I.C.A.).

SEXUAL EXPLOITATION / Punishment / Inference of sexual exploitation / Definition of "young person".

153. (1) Every person commits an offence who is in a position of trust or authority towards a young person, who is a person with whom the young person is in a relationship of dependency or who is in a relationship with a young person that is exploitative of the young person, and who

(*a*) for a sexual purpose, touches, directly or indirectly, with a part of the body or with an object, any part of the body of the young person; or

(*b*) for a sexual purpose, invites, counsels or incites a young person to touch, directly or indirectly, with a part of the body or with an object, the body of any person, including the body of the person who so invites, counsels or incites and the body of the young person.

(1.1) Every person who commits an offence under subsection (1)

(*a*) is guilty of an indictable offence and is liable to imprisonment for a term of not more than 14 years and to a minimum punishment of imprisonment for a term of one year; or

(*b*) is guilty of an offence punishable on summary conviction and is liable to imprisonment for a term of not more than two years less a day and to a minimum punishment of imprisonment for a term of 90 days.

(1.2) A judge may infer that a person is in a relationship with a young person that is exploitative of the young person from the nature and circumstances of the relationship, including

(*a*) the age of the young person;

(*b*) the age difference between the person and the young person;

(*c*) the evolution of the relationship; and

(*d*) the degree of control or influence by the person over the young person.

(2) In this section, "young person" means a person 16 years of age or more but under the age of eighteen years. R.S.C. 1985, c. 19 (3rd Supp.), s. 1; 2005, c. 32, s. 4; 2008, c. 6, s. 54(*c*); 2012, c. 1, s. 13; 2015, c. 23, s. 4.

CROSS-REFERENCES

Age is determined by s. 30 of the *Interpretation Act*, R.S.C. 1985, c. I-21. Section 658 provides means of proving the age of a child or young person. The term "counsels" is defined in s. 22 and in fact includes "incite". The term "sexual purpose" is not defined. The terms "position of trust or authority" and "relationship of dependency" are not defined. The Report of the Committee on Sexual Offences Against Children and Youths [The "Badgley" Report], released in 1984, contained many recommendations concerning the treatment of sexual offences against children and appears to have been the origin of many of the offences now found in this Part. That report, in its Recommendation 9, had suggested a definition of person in position of trust as including parent; step-parent; adoptive parent; foster parent; legal guardian; common-law partner of child's parent, step-parent, adoptive parent, foster parent, or legal guardian; grandparent; uncle, aunt; boarder in young person's home; teacher; baby-sitter, group home worker; youth group worker; and employer. The defences of consent and mistaken belief as to the age of the complainant are defined in s. 150.1. Section 170 creates an offence for a parent or guardian to procure a person under the age of 18 years for the purpose of engaging in any sexual activity prohibited by the Code. Section 171 creates an offence for a householder and other similarly situated persons to permit a person under the age of 18 years to resort to premises for the purpose of engaging in any sexual activity prohibited by the Code. Section 171.1 makes it an offence to transmit, make available, distribute or sell sexually explicit material to a person who is, or who the accused believes is under the age of 18 years for purpose of facilitating the commission of the offence created by this section. Section 172.1 makes it an offence to communicate by means of telecommunication with a person who is or who the accused believes is under the age of 18 years for the purpose of facilitating the commission of the offence under this section. Section 172.2 makes it an offence to agree with a person or make an arrangement with a person by means of telecommunication to commit an offence under this section with a person who is or who the accused believes is under the age of 18 years.

A person found guilty of the offence in this section, may, depending on the circumstances, be liable to the discretionary prohibition order prescribed by s. 110 for possession of weapons, ammunition and explosives.

Special evidentiary and procedural provisions: see cross-references under s. 150.1.

As to cases concerning admissibility of evidence in child abuse cases, see notes under s. 150.1.

Section 718.01 provides that, in imposing a sentence for an offence involving the abuse of a person under the age of 18 years, the court shall give primary consideration to the objectives of denunciation and deterrence. Further, under s. 718.2, evidence that the offender, in committing the offence, abused a person under the age of 18 years is an aggravating circumstance.

The offence in this section is a primary designated offence for the purpose of making a forensic DNA data bank order under s. 487.051. Under s. 490.012, on application by the prosecutor, where an offender is convicted of this offence, the judge shall make an order requiring the offender to comply with the *Sex Offender Information Registration Act*, S.C. 2004, c. 10.

SYNOPSIS

This section creates the hybrid offence of sexual exploitation of a young person. Subsection (2) provides a definition of "young person", namely a person between 16 and 17 years old inclusive. The offence is predicated upon either the accused being in a position of trust toward the young complainant, or the young person being in a relationship of dependency with the accused, or being in a relationship with a young person that is exploitative of the young person. If one of those relationships exist and the accused commits acts amounting to either sexual interference (s. 151) or invitation to sexual touching (s. 152), then the offence is committed. (Note that it must be shown that the accused had a sexual purpose.) The maximum sentence upon conviction for the indictable offence of sexual exploitation is 14 years and the minimum punishment is one year imprisonment. Where the Crown proceeds by way of summary conviction, the offence is punishable by a maximum of two years less a day imprisonment and not less than 90 days.

ANNOTATIONS

Note: Some of these cases were decided before the amendment to this section adding subsec. (1.2).

Sexual assault, as defined by s. 271, is not an included offence to the offence created by this section: *R. v. Nelson* (1989), 51 C.C.C. (3d) 150 (Ont. H.C.J.).

Unlike sexual assault, as defined by s. 271, the offence created by this section is a specific intent offence: *R. v. Nelson, supra.*

The Crown need not prove that the accused actually abused or exploited his position of trust or authority towards the young person: *R. v. Audet*, [1996] 2 S.C.R. 171, 106 C.C.C. (3d) 481.

The combined effect of this section and s. 150.1(1) does not result in violation of the equality provisions of s. 15 of the Charter, although some professions, such as teachers, are treated differently since the defence that the complainant consented is denied them. Nor does the denial of the consent defence violate s. 7 of the Charter: *R. v. Hann* (1992), 75 C.C.C. (3d) 355 (Nfld. C.A.).

"Authority" is not restricted to cases in which the relationship of authority stems from a role of the accused but extends to any relationship in which the accused actually exercises such a power. The word "trust" as used in this provision must be interpreted in accordance with its primary meaning of confidence or reliance. In considering whether the accused was in a "position of authority" or "position of trust", the age difference between the accused, the evolution of the relationship and the status of the accused in relation to the young person are relevant considerations. Teachers will usually be in a position of trust and authority towards their students: *R. v. Audet, supra.*

The Crown is required to prove a relationship that is exploitative of the young person independent of proof of the sexual conduct. Proof of consensual sexual relations between an accused and a young person is not by itself proof of a relationship that was exploitative of the young person. The scope of the meaning of an exploitative relationship should be determined to some extent by the scope of the other types of relationships set out in this section. There must be a power imbalance in favour of an accused person in circumstances other than where the accused is in a position of trust or authority, or circumstances where the young person has developed a reliance on the accused who has assumed a position of power over the young person. The evidence must demonstrate, or it must be possible for the court to draw, the inference from all of the circumstances that the young person is, as the result of this power imbalance, vulnerable to the actions and conduct of the accused who is taking advantage of the young person for his or her own benefit: *R. v. Anderson* (2009), 241 C.C.C. (3d) 432 (P.E.I.C.A.).

The accused's subjective belief that he was not in a position of trust or authority in relation to the complainant does not, in itself, provide a defence to a charge under subsec. (1): *R. v. R. (L.V.)* (2014), 316 C.C.C. (3d) 120 (B.C.C.A.), leave to appeal to S.C.C. refused 2015 CarswellBC 554.

The trial judge erred in relying on a school directive to conclude that a teaching assistant was presumptively in a position of trust. The determination of a relationship of trust or authority requires a factual consideration of the characteristics of the relationship in issue: *R. v. S. (J.S.)* (2010), 257 C.C.C. (3d) 403 (N.B.C.A.).

Although the accused was physically bigger than the complainant and ran the arcade where the complainant was employed, it was not shown that the accused was in a position of trust or authority or that the young person was in a relationship of dependency: *R. v. Caskenette* (1993), 80 C.C.C. (3d) 439 (B.C.C.A.).

It was a question of fact whether the accused was in a position of trust or authority towards the 17-year-old daughter of his common-law wife and whether she was in a relationship of dependency although they lived in the same house. The relationship of trust or authority on the part of the man or dependency on the part of the complainant could not be conclusively presumed to exist as a matter of law: *R. v. J. (R.H.)* (1993), 86 C.C.C. (3d) 354 (B.C.C.A.), leave to appeal to S.C.C. refused 87 C.C.C. (3d) vi.

The term "dependency" is to be read *ejusdem generis* with two other categories of trust or authority and contemplates a relationship in which there is a *de facto* reliance by a young person on a figure who has assumed a position of power, such as trust or authority over the young person along non-traditional lines. The disentitling condition of dependency must exist independently of a sexual relationship: *R. v. Galbraith* (1994), 90 C.C.C. (3d) 76 (Ont. C.A.), leave to appeal to S.C.C. refused 92 C.C.C. (3d) vi.

The Crown need only prove that the purpose of the touching was sexual in nature and need not prove that the accused touched the complainant for his own sexual gratification: *R. v. B. (G.)* (2009), 244 C.C.C. (3d) 185 (B.C.C.A.).

SEXUAL EXPLOITATION OF PERSON WITH DISABILITY / Definition of "consent" / When no consent obtained / Subsection (3) not limiting / When belief in consent not a defence / Accused's belief as to consent.

153.1 (1) Every person who is in a position of trust or authority towards a person with a mental or physical disability or who is a person with whom a person with a mental or physical disability is in a relationship of dependency and who, for a sexual purpose, counsels or incites that person to touch, without that person's consent, his or her own body, the body of the person who so counsels or incites, directly or indirectly, with a part of the body or with an object, the body of any person, including the body of the person who so invites, counsels or incites and the body of the person with the disability, is guilty of

> **(a) an indictable offence and liable to imprisonment for a term not exceeding five years; or**

> **(b) an offence punishable on summary conviction and liable to imprisonment for a term not exceeding eighteen months.**

(2) Subject to subsection (3), "consent" means, for the purposes of this section, the voluntary agreement of the complainant to engage in the sexual activity in question.

(3) No consent is obtained, for the purposes of this section, if

    (a) **the agreement is expressed by the words or conduct of a person other than the complainant;**

    (b) **the complainant is incapable of consenting to the activity;**

    (c) **the accused counsels or incites the complainant to engage in the activity by abusing a position of trust, power or authority;**

    (d) **the complainant expresses, by words or conduct, a lack of agreement to engage in the activity; or**

    (e) **the complainant, having consented to engage in sexual activity, expresses, by words or conduct, a lack of agreement to continue to engage in the activity.**

(4) Nothing in subsection (3) shall be construed as limiting the circumstances in which no consent is obtained.

(5) It is not a defence to a charge under this section that the accused believed that the complainant consented to the activity that forms the subject-matter of the charge if

    (a) **the accused's belief arose from the accused's**

        (i) **self-induced intoxication, or**

        (ii) **recklessness or wilful blindness; or**

    (b) **the accused did not take reasonable steps, in the circumstances known to the accused at the time, to ascertain that the complainant was consenting.**

(6) If an accused alleges that he or she believed that the complainant consented to the conduct that is the subject-matter of the charge, a judge, if satisfied that there is sufficient evidence and that, if believed by the jury, the evidence would constitute a defence, shall instruct the jury, when reviewing all the evidence relating to the determination of the honesty of the accused's belief, to consider the presence or absence of reasonable grounds for that belief. 1998, c. 9, s. 2.

CROSS-REFERENCES

Section 153 creates the related offence of sexual exploitation of a young person. Pursuant to s. 274, no corroboration is required for a conviction of the offence under this section and the judge shall not instruct the jury that it is unsafe to find the accused guilty in the absence of corroboration. Pursuant to s. 275, the rules relating to recent complaint are abrogated with respect to this offence. Sections 276 and 277, which limit cross-examination on prior sexual conduct of the complainant, apply to a prosecution for the offence under this section. Section 273.1 gives a similar definition of "consent" as in subsecs. (2) to (4) of this section, for the purposes of the sexual assault offences in ss. 271 to 273. Sections 278.1 to 278.9 govern the production of records containing personal information of the complainant or a witness. Section 273.2 gives a similar definition for the defence of belief in consent as in subsecs. (5) and (6) of this section, for the purposes of the sexual assault offences in ss. 271 to 273. Section 486(2.1) provides that, where an accused is charged with this offence and the complainant is, at the time of the trial or preliminary inquiry, under the age of 18 years or may have difficulty communicating the evidence by reason of a mental or physical disability, the judge may order that the complainant testify outside the courtroom or behind a screen where such procedure is necessary to obtain a full and candid account of the acts complained of. Section 627 provides that the judge may permit a juror with a physical disability who is otherwise qualified to serve as a juror to have technical, personal, interpretative or other support services. Sections 709 and 711 provide for the taking of commission evidence from a witness who is, by reason of physical disability arising out of illness not likely to be able to attend at the time the trial. Section 715.2 provides that, in proceedings under this section, a videotape, made within a reasonable time after the alleged offence, in which the complainant describes the acts complained of is admissible in evidence if the complainant adopts its contents and if the complainant may have difficulty communicating the evidence by reason of a mental or physical disability. Section 6 of the *Canada Evidence Act* provides that the court may order that a witness who has difficulty communicating, by reason of a physical or mental disability, be permitted to give evidence by any means that enables the evidence to be intelligible. Under s. 6.1 of the Act, a witness may give evidence as to the identity of an accused whom the witness is able to identify visually or in any other sensory manner.

The offence in this section is a primary designated offence for the purpose of making a forensic DNA data bank order under s. 487.051. Under s. 490.012, on application by the prosecutor, where an offender is convicted of this offence, the judge shall make an order requiring the offender to comply with the *Sex Offender Information Registration Act*, S.C. 2004, c. 10.

SYNOPSIS

This section creates the hybrid offence of sexual exploitation of a person with a mental or physical disability. The offence is predicated upon either the accused being in a position of trust toward the young complainant or the young person being in a relationship of dependency with the accused. If either relationship exists and the accused for a sexual purpose incites or counsels the complainant to touch any person's body directly or indirectly with an object or a part of the body, the offence is made out. Note that unlike the similar offences involving children it must be shown that the touching is without the complainant's consent. Consent is defined in subsecs. (2) to (4). Subsection (5) limits the availability of the defence of belief in consent and subsec. (6) sets out a mandatory jury instruction where such a defence is available. The maximum sentence upon conviction for the indictable offence of sexual exploitation is five years.

ANNOTATIONS

The definition of consent in this section and the limits of the defence of belief in consent are similar to the provisions of ss. 273.1 and 273.2 (respecting sexual assault) and therefore reference should be made to the notes under those sections. See in particular *R. v. Ewanchuk*, [1999] 1 S.C.R. 330, 131 C.C.C. (3d) 481, noted under both sections.

---

154. [*Repealed*, R.S.C. 1985, c. 19 (3rd Supp.), s. 1.]

INCEST / Punishment / Defence / Definition of "brother" and "sister".

155. (1) Every one commits incest who, knowing that another person is by blood relationship his or her parent, child, brother, sister, grandparent or grandchild, as the case may be, has sexual intercourse with that person.

(2) Everyone who commits incest is guilty of an indictable offence and is liable to imprisonment for a term of not more than 14 years and, if the other person is under the age of 16 years, to a minimum punishment of imprisonment for a term of five years.

(3) No accused shall be determined by a court to be guilty of an offence under this section if the accused was under restraint, duress or fear of the person with whom the accused had the sexual intercourse at the time the sexual intercourse occurred.

(4) In this section, "brother" and "sister", respectively, include half-brother and half-sister. R.S., c. C-34, s. 150; 1972, c. 13, s. 10; R.S.C. 1985, c. 27 (1st Supp.), s. 21; 2012, c. 1, s. 14.

CROSS-REFERENCES

Section 4(5) sets out a definition for sexual intercourse. Section 171.1 makes it an offence to transmit, make available, distribute or sell sexually explicit material to a person who is, or who the accused believes is under the age of 18 years for purpose of facilitating the commission of the offence created by this section. Section 172.1 makes it an offence to communicate by means of telecommunication with a person who is or who the accused believes is under the age of 18 years for the purpose of facilitating the commission of the offence under this section. Section 172.2 makes it an offence to agree with a person or make an arrangement with a person by means of telecommunication to commit an offence under this section with a person who is or who the accused believes is under the age of 18 years.

The accused may elect his mode of trial pursuant to s. 536(2) and release pending trial is determined by s. 515. Section 170 creates an offence for a parent or guardian to procure a person under the age of 18 years for the purpose of engaging in any sexual activity prohibited by the Code. Section 171 creates an offence for a householder and other similarly situated persons to permit a person under the age of 18 years to resort to premises for the purpose of engaging in any sexual activity prohibited by the Code.

A person, found guilty of the offence in this section, may, depending on the circumstances, be liable to the mandatory prohibition order prescribed by s. 109 for possession of certain weapons, ammunition and explosives. Where the accused is found guilty of this offence in respect of a person who is under 16 years of age, the court has the discretion to impose an order of prohibition under s. 161 prohibiting the accused from attending certain public areas and facilities or taking certain employment which will bring him into contact with persons under 16 years of age or using a computer system for the purpose of communicating with a person under the age of 16 years.

Special evidentiary and procedural provisions: see cross-references under s. 150.1.

As to cases concerning admissibility of evidence in child abuse cases, see notes under s. 150.1.

The offence in this section is a primary designated offence for the purpose of making a forensic DNA data bank order under s. 487.051. Under s. 490.012, on application by the prosecutor, where an offender is convicted of this offence, the judge shall make an order requiring the offender to comply with the *Sex Offender Information Registration Act*, S.C. 2004, c. 10.

SYNOPSIS

This section prohibits incest and provides for a maximum sentence for this indictable offence of 14 years' imprisonment and a minimum sentence of 5 years if the other person is under the age of 16 years.

The offence requires that *sexual intercourse* occur between the accused and another person whom the accused *knows* is one of the *blood relations* specified in subsec. (1). In addition, subsec. (4) expands the definitions of "brother" and "sister" to include half-siblings.

Section 155(3) prevents a finding of guilt in circumstances in which the *accused was in fear* of the relation involved, or under restraint or duress *when* intercourse took place.

ANNOTATIONS

This provision does not violate s. 7 of the Charter. In addition, the denial of the defence of consent does not violate s. 7: *R. v. F. (R.P.)* (1996), 105 C.C.C. (3d) 435 (N.S.C.A.). Nor does this provision violate ss. 2(*a*), 2(*d*) and 15 of the Charter: *R. v. S. (M.)* (1996), 111 C.C.C. (3d) 467 (B.C.C.A.), leave to appeal to S.C.C. refused 113 C.C.C. (3d) vii.

Incest is a general intent offence requiring no more than an intent to commit the *actus reus*: *R. v. B. (S.J.)* (2002), 166 C.C.C. (3d) 537 (Alta. C.A.).

Sexual assault and sexual interference are not included offences of this offence where the information simply charges that the accused committed incest with his daughter, even though the complainant was, to the accused's knowledge, under 14 years of age and thus incapable of consenting. Neither lack of consent, nor age of the complainant are elements of the offence under this section: *R. v. R. (G.)*, [2005] 2 S.C.R. 371, 198 C.C.C. (3d) 161.

---

156. [*Repealed*, R.S.C. 1985, c. 19 (3rd Supp.), s. 2.]

---

157. [*Repealed*, R.S.C. 1985, c. 19 (3rd Supp.), s. 2.]

---

158. [*Repealed*, R.S.C. 1985, c. 19 (3rd Supp.), s. 2.]

ANAL INTERCOURSE / Exception / Idem.

159. (1) Every person who engages in an act of anal intercourse is guilty of an indictable offence and liable to imprisonment for a term not exceeding ten years or is guilty of an offence punishable on summary conviction.

(2) Subsection (1) does not apply to any act engaged in, in private, between

    (a) husband and wife, or

    (b) any two persons, each of whom is eighteen years of age or more,

both of whom consent to the act.

(3) For the purposes of subsection (2),

    (a) an act shall be deemed not to have been engaged in in private if it is engaged in in a public place or if more than two persons take part or are present; and

    (b) a person shall be deemed not to consent to an act

        (i) if the consent is extorted by force, threats or fear of bodily harm or is obtained by false and fraudulent misrepresentations respecting the nature and quality of the act, or

        (ii) if the court is satisfied beyond a reasonable doubt that that person could not have consented to the act by reason of mental disability. R.S.C. 1985, c. 19 (3rd Supp.), s. 3.

SYNOPSIS

Section 159 creates the offence of *anal intercourse* and also sets out a number of exemptions from its application. Section 159(1) sets out the prohibition against anal intercourse and provides for prosecution by way of summary conviction procedure or by indictment. In the latter case the maximum sentence is 10 years.

Section 159(2) provides an exemption from liability if the acts were done in *private,* with the *mutual consent* of those involved, by either *husband and wife* or by two persons both of whom are at least 18 years old.

Section 159(3) limits the scope of the exceptions in subsec. (2) in two ways. First, the meaning of "private" excludes acts done in a public place, or with more than two persons present. Second, s. 159(3)(*b*) limits what is meant by "consent". The accused cannot rely upon consent if it is proven beyond a reasonable doubt that the other person was unable to consent due to mental disability. In addition, consent is rendered invalid if it was obtained by force, threats, fear or fraud.

Two appellate courts have held this section to be unconstitutional.

ANNOTATIONS

Application of the Charter of Rights – It was held in *R. v. M. (C.)* (1995), 98 C.C.C. (3d) 481, 41 C.R. (4th) 134 (Ont. C.A.), that this section discriminates on the basis of age contrary to s. 15 of the Charter and is therefore of no force and effect.

Similarly, in *R. v. Roy* (1998), 125 C.C.C. (3d) 442, 161 D.L.R. (4th) 148 (Que. C.A.), it was held that this section infringes s. 15 of the Charter as it discriminates on the basis of age, sexual orientation and marital status and is therefore of no force and effect.

BESTIALITY / Compelling the commission of bestiality / Bestiality in presence of or by child.

160. (1) Every person who commits bestiality is guilty of an indictable offence and liable to imprisonment for a term not exceeding ten years or is guilty of an offence punishable on summary conviction.

(2) Every person who compels another to commit bestiality is guilty of an indictable offence and liable to imprisonment for a term not exceeding ten years or is guilty of an offence punishable on summary conviction.

(3) Despite subsection (1), every person who commits bestiality in the presence of a person under the age of 16 years, or who incites a person under the age of 16 years to commit bestiality, (*a*) is guilty of an indictable offence and is liable to imprisonment for a term of not more than 14 years and to a minimum punishment of imprisonment for a term of one year; or

(*b*) is guilty of an offence punishable on summary conviction and is liable to imprisonment for a term of not more than two years less a day and to a minimum punishment of imprisonment for a term of six months. R.S.C. 1985, c. 19 (3rd Supp.), s. 3; 2008, c. 6, s. 54(*d*); 2012, c. 1, s. 15; 2015, c. 23, s. 5.

CROSS-REFERENCES

Age is determined by s. 30 of the *Interpretation Act*, R.S.C. 1985, c. I-21. The term "incites" is within the definition of "counsels" in s. 22(3). A person convicted of the offence under subsec. (2) or (3), who is found to be loitering in or near a school ground, playground, public park or bathing area, is liable to be convicted of the vagrancy offence under s. 179. Section 170 creates an offence for a parent or guardian to procure a person under the age of 18 years for the purpose of engaging in any sexual activity prohibited by the Code. Section 171 creates an offence for a householder and other similarly situated persons to permit a person under the age of 18 years to resort to premises for the purpose of engaging in any sexual activity prohibited by the Code. Section 171.1 makes it an offence to transmit, make available, distribute or sell sexually explicit material to a person who is, or who the accused believes is under the age of 16 years for purpose of facilitating the commission of the offence created by subsec. (3). Section 172.1 makes it an offence to communicate by means of telecommunication with a person who is or who the accused believes is under the age of 16 years for the purpose of facilitating the commission of the offence under subsec. (3). Section 172.2 makes it an offence to agree with a person or make an arrangement with a person by means of telecommunication to commit an offence under subsec. (3) with a person who is or who the accused believes is under the age of 18 years.

Where the prosecution elects to proceed by indictment on this offence then the accused may elect his mode of trial pursuant to s. 536(2). Where the prosecution elects to proceed by way of summary conviction then the trial of this offence is conducted by a summary conviction court pursuant to Part XXVII. The punishment for the offence is then as set out in s. 787 and the limitation period is set out in s. 786(2). In either case, release pending trial is determined by s. 515, although the accused is eligible for release by a peace officer under s. 496, 497 or by the officer in charge under s. 498.

A person, found guilty of the offence in this section, may, depending on the circumstances, be liable to either the mandatory prohibition order under s. 109 or the discretionary prohibition order prescribed by s. 110 for possession of firearms, ammunition and explosives. Where the accused is found guilty of the offence under subsec. (2) or (3) in respect of a person who is under 16 years of age, the court has the discretion to impose an order of prohibition under s. 161 prohibiting the accused from attending certain public areas and facilities or taking certain employment which will bring him into contact with persons under 16 years of age or using a computer system for the purpose of communicating with a person under the age of 16 years.

Section 150.1(4) deals with the defence of mistake of age for the offence under subsec. (3).

Special evidentiary and procedural provisions: see cross-references under s. 150.1.

Section 486(1) and (2) provide that the judge may make an order excluding all or any members of the public where such order is in the interest of public morals, the maintenance of order or the proper administration of justice, or is necessary to prevent injury to international relations or national defence or national security. The proper administration of justice includes safeguarding the interests of witnesses under the age of 18 years. Section 486.1 sets out the circumstances in which the judge shall or may order a support person to be present and close to a witness while the witness testifies. Where the witness is under the age of 18 years or has a mental or physical disability, the order is to be made upon request unless the judge is of the opinion that the order would interfere with the proper administration of justice. In the case of other witnesses, the order is to be made if necessary to obtain a full and candid account from the witness of the matters complained of. The application for this order may be made during the proceedings or before they begin to the judge who is to preside at the proceedings.

Similarly, s. 486.2 sets out the circumstances in which the judge shall or may order a witness to testify outside the courtroom or behind a screen or other device that would not allow the witness to see the accused. Where the witness is under the age of 18 years or may have difficulty communicating the evidence by reason of a mental or physical disability, the judge shall make the order unless the judge is of the opinion that the order would interfere with the proper administration of justice. In all other cases, the order may be made if the judge is of the opinion that the order is necessary to obtain a full and candid account from the witness of the acts complained of. Similarly, s. 486.3 provides that, on application by the prosecutor or a witness under the age of 18 years, the accused shall not personally cross-examine the witness unless the judge is of the opinion that the proper administration of justice requires the accused to personally conduct the cross-examination. In other cases, the judge may make an order that the accused not personally cross-examine the witness if the judge is of the opinion that the order is necessary to obtain a full and candid account from the witness of the acts complained of. The judge will appoint counsel to conduct the cross-examination.

Under s. 486.4, the judge may make an order directing that the identity of a witness not be disclosed in any publication, broadcast or transmitted in any way. The order is mandatory where the complainant or a witness under the age of 18 years or the prosecutor applies for the order. Section 486.5 also gives the judge a discretion respecting non-publication orders in proceedings under these provisions in other circumstances.

Under s. 490.012, on application by the prosecutor, where an offender is convicted of the offence in subsec. (3), the judge shall make an order requiring the offender to comply with the *Sex Offender Information Registration Act*, S.C. 2004, c. 10.

SYNOPSIS

Section 160 prohibits *bestiality* and provides for its punishment.

Section 160(1) states the basic prohibition against the accused committing bestiality. Section 160(2) creates a parallel offence which applies if the accused *compels another* to commit bestiality. Section 160(3) creates criminal liability when the accused commits bestiality in the *presence* of another person who is *less than 16* years old or *incites* a person under 16 to commit the act.

All three offences created by this section may be prosecuted by way of summary conviction procedure or by indictment. The maximum sentence for the offences in subsecs. (1) and (2) where the Crown proceeds by way of indictment is 10 years. For the offence created by subsec. (3), the maximum sentence is 14 years and the minimum sentence is one year imprisonment, where the Crown proceeds by way of indictment. Where the Crown proceeds by way of summary conviction for the subsec. (3) offence, the maximum sentence is two years less one day and the minimum is six months' imprisonment.

ANNOTATIONS

This offence being one of "general intent" drunkenness is no defence to either the full offence or an attempt: *R. v. Triller* (1980), 55 C.C.C. (2d) 411 (B.C. Co. Ct.).

Penetration is an essential element of the offence of bestiality: *R. v. W. (D.L.)* (2015), 325 C.C.C. (3d) 73 (B.C.C.A.) (2:1).

---

161. (old provision) [*Repealed*, R.S.C. 1985, c. 19 (3rd Supp.), s. 4.]

ORDER OF PROHIBITION / Offences / Duration of prohibition / Court may vary order / Offence.

161. (1) When an offender is convicted, or is discharged on the conditions prescribed in a probation order under section 730, of an offence referred to in subsection (1.1) in respect of a person who is under the age of 16 years, the court that sentences the offender or directs that the accused be discharged, as the case may be, in addition to any other punishment that may be imposed for that offence or any other condition

prescribed in the order of discharge, shall consider making and may make, subject to the conditions or exemptions that the court directs, an order prohibiting the offender from

(a) attending a public park or public swimming area where persons under the age of 16 years are present or can reasonably be expected to be present, or a daycare centre, schoolground, playground or community centre;

(a.1) being within two kilometres, or any other distance specified in the order, of any dwelling-house where the victim identified in the order ordinarily resides or of any other place specified in the order;

(b) seeking, obtaining or continuing any employment, whether or not the employment is remunerated, or becoming or being a volunteer in a capacity, that involves being in a position of trust or authority towards persons under the age of 16 years;

(c) having any contact — including communicating by any means — with a person who is under the age of 16 years, unless the offender does so under the supervision of a person whom the court considers appropriate; or

(d) using the Internet or other digital network, unless the offender does so in accordance with conditions set by the court.

(1.1) The offences for the purpose of subsection (1) are

(a) an offence under section 151, 152, 155 or 159, subsection 160(2) or (3), section 163.1, 170, 171, 171.1, 172.1 or 172.2, subsection 173(2), section 271, 272, 273 or 279.011, subsection 279.02(2) or 279.03(2), section 280 or 281 or subsection 286.1(2), 286.2(2) or 286.3(2);

(b) an offence under section 144 (rape), 145 (attempt to commit rape), 149 (indecent assault on female), 156 (indecent assault on male) or 245 (common assault) or subsection 246(1) (assault with intent) of the *Criminal Code*, chapter C-34 of the Revised Statutes of Canada, 1970, as it read immediately before January 4, 1983;

(c) an offence under subsection 146(1) (sexual intercourse with a female under 14) or section 153 (sexual intercourse with step-daughter), 155 (buggery or bestiality), 157 (gross indecency), 166 (parent or guardian procuring defilement) or 167 (householder permitting defilement) of the *Criminal Code*, chapter C-34 of the Revised Statutes of Canada, 1970, as it read immediately before January 1, 1988; or

(d) an offence under subsection 212(1) (procuring), 212(2) (living on the avails of prostitution of person under 18 years), 212(2.1) (aggravated offence in relation to living on the avails of prostitution of person under 18 years) or 212(4) (prostitution of person under 18 years) of this Act, as it read from time to time before the day on which this paragraph comes into force.

(2) The prohibition may be for life or for any shorter duration that the court considers desirable and, in the case of a prohibition that is not for life, the prohibition begins on the later of

(a) the date on which the order is made; and

(b) where the offender is sentenced to a term of imprisonment, the date on which the offender is released from imprisonment for the offence, including release on parole, mandatory supervision or statutory release.

(3) A court that makes an order of prohibition or, where the court is for any reason unable to act, another court of equivalent jurisdiction in the same province, may, on application of the offender or the prosecutor, require the offender to appear before it at any time and, after hearing the parties, that court may vary the conditions prescribed in the order if, in the opinion of the court, the variation is desirable because of changed circumstances after the conditions were prescribed.

(4) Every person who is bound by an order of prohibition and who does not comply with the order is guilty of

  (*a*) an indictable offence and is liable to imprisonment for a term of not more than four years; or

  (*b*) an offence punishable on summary conviction and is liable to imprisonment for a term of not more than 18 months. 1993, c. 45, s. 1; 1995, c. 22, s. 18 (Sched. IV, item 26); 1997, c. 18, s. 4; 1999, c. 31, s. 67; 2002, c. 13, s. 4; 2005, c. 32, s. 5; 2008, c. 6, s. 54(*e*); 2012, c. 1, s. 16; 2014, c. 21, s. 1; 2014, c. 25, s. 5; 2015, c. 23, s. 6.

CROSS-REFERENCES

Age is determined by s. 30 of the *Interpretation Act*, R.S.C. 1985, c. 1-21. Section 658 provides means of proving the age of a child.

By virtue of s. 42(2)(*j*) of the *Youth Criminal Justice Act*, an order cannot be made under this section with respect to a young person. Under s. 810.1, a person may apply to a provincial court judge for an order requiring the defendant to enter into a recognizance including conditions resembling the conditions which can be imposed as part of a prohibition order under this section.

SYNOPSIS

This provision permits the court to make an order prohibiting the offender from attending near certain public places and other facilities where persons under 16 years of age may be present, from obtaining employment which may involve the offender being in a position of trust or authority over persons under 16 years of age, having any contact with a person who is under the age of 16 years, unless the offender does so under the supervision of a person whom the court considers appropriate, and using the Internet or other digital network, unless the offender does so in accordance with conditions set by the court. The order may be made where the offender is found guilty of a specified sexual offence and the complainant was under 16 years of age. The order may be for life or some shorter period and its terms may be varied upon application of the offender or the prosecutor. Failure to comply with the prohibition order is a Crown option offence. It would seem that this section will now be resorted to rather than s. 179(1)(*b*) which has been held to be unconstitutional by the Supreme Court of Canada.

ANNOTATIONS

"Public park" is a defined or discrete location that is accessible to the public for recreational use that involves or is reasonably likely to involve children under a specified age. In particular cases, other factors may be relevant, such as the presence of greenery or the public designation of the location as a park, but are not definitive: *R. v. Perron* (2009), 244 C.C.C. (3d) 369 (Ont. C.A.).

"Public swimming area" includes a swimming pool open to members of a building complex: *R. v. D'Angelo* (2002), 8 C.R. (6th) 386 (Ont. C.A.).

"Playground" is an outdoor area the purpose of which is to accommodate play by children. A carnival was not a playground, but rather a commercial operation intended for the amusement of the public including children. Children's play was not its main object or purpose: *R. v. Lachapelle* (2009), 247 C.C.C. (3d) 59 (B.C.C.A.).

---

162. (old provision) [*Repealed*, R.S.C. 1985, c. 19 (3rd Supp.), s. 4.]

VOYEURISM / Definition of "visual recording" / Exemption / Printing, publication, etc., of voyeuristic recordings / Punishment / Defence / Question of law, motives

162. (1) Every one commits an offence who, surreptitiously, observes — including by mechanical or electronic means — or makes a visual recording of a person who is in circumstances that give rise to a reasonable expectation of privacy, if

(*a*) the person is in a place in which a person can reasonably be expected to be nude, to expose his or her genital organs or anal region or her breasts, or to be engaged in explicit sexual activity;

(*b*) the person is nude, is exposing his or her genital organs or anal region or her breasts, or is engaged in explicit sexual activity, and the observation or recording is done for the purpose of observing or recording a person in such a state or engaged in such an activity; or

(*c*) the observation or recording is done for a sexual purpose.

(2) In this section, "visual recording" includes a photographic, film or video recording made by any means.

(3) Paragraphs (1)(*a*) and (*b*) do not apply to a peace officer who, under the authority of a warrant issued under section 487.01, is carrying out any activity referred to in those paragraphs.

(4) Every one commits an offence who, knowing that a recording was obtained by the commission of an offence under subsection (1), prints, copies, publishes, distributes, circulates, sells, advertises or makes available the recording, or has the recording in his or her possession for the purpose of printing, copying, publishing, distributing, circulating, selling or advertising it or making it available.

(5) Every one who commits an offence under subsection (1) or (4)

(*a*) is guilty of an indictable offence and liable to imprisonment for a term not exceeding five years; or

(*b*) is guilty of an offence punishable on summary conviction.

(6) No person shall be convicted of an offence under this section if the acts that are alleged to constitute the offence serve the public good and do not extend beyond what serves the public good.

(7) For the purposes of subsection (6),

(*a*) it is a question of law whether an act serves the public good and whether there is evidence that the act alleged goes beyond what serves the public good, but it is a question of fact whether the act does or does not extend beyond what serves the public good; and

(*b*) the motives of an accused are irrelevant. 2005, c. 32, s. 6.

CROSS-REFERENCES

"Peace officer" is defined in s. 2. The offence of trespassing by night is defined in s. 177. Criminal harassment is defined in s. 264.

SYNOPSIS

This section creates the offence of voyeurism that is committed by surreptitiously observing a person in circumstances that give rise to a reasonable expectation of privacy if the person is in certain places defined in subsec. (1)(*a*), or the person is actually nude or exposing genital organs, anal region or a woman's breasts, or engaging in explicit sexual activity and the observation or recording is done for the purpose of observing or recording a person in such a state or engaged in the sexual activity (subsec. (1)(*b*)), or the observation or recording is done for a sexual purpose (subsec. (1)(*c*)). The offence is committed whether the observation is direct or done by mechanical or electronic means or through making a visual recording (defined in subsec. (2)). The offence is not committed by a peace officer acting under the authority of a general warrant issued under s. 487.01. This section also creates an offence in subsec. (4) of, in effect, trafficking or possessing for the purpose of trafficking recordings, if the accused knows that the recording was obtained by the commission of the offence under subsec. (1). The subsec. (4) offence is committed in any of the ways set out such as printing, copying, publishing or distributing. Subsection (6) provides for a defence where the alleged acts serve the public good. Subsection (7) provides that it is a question of law whether the act serves the public good and whether there is any evidence that the act alleged goes beyond what serves the public good. It is a question of fact whether or not the act does extend beyond what serves the public good. The accused's motives are irrelevant in determining the public good offence.

PUBLICATION ETC., OF AN INTIMATE IMAGE WITHOUT CONSENT / Definition of "intimate image" / Defence / Question of fact and law, motives.

162.1 (1) Everyone who knowingly publishes, distributes, transmits, sells, makes available or advertises an intimate image of a person knowing that the person depicted in the image did not give their consent to that conduct, or being reckless as to whether or not that person gave their consent to that conduct, is guilty

- **(a) of an indictable offence and liable to imprisonment for a term of not more than five years; or**
- **(b) of an offence punishable on summary conviction.**

(2) In this section, "intimate image" means a visual recording of a person made by any means including a photographic, film or video recording,

- **(a) in which the person is nude, is exposing his or her genital organs or anal region or her breasts or is engaged in explicit sexual activity;**
- **(b) in respect of which, at the time of the recording, there were circumstances that gave rise to a reasonable expectation of privacy; and**
- **(c) in respect of which the person depicted retains a reasonable expectation of privacy at the time the offence is committed.**

(3) No person shall be convicted of an offence under this section if the conduct that forms the subject-matter of the charge serves the public good and does not extend beyond what serves the public good.

(4) For the purposes of subsection (3),

- **(a) it is a question of law whether the conduct serves the public good and whether there is evidence that the conduct alleged goes beyond what serves the public good, but it is a question of fact whether the conduct does or does not extend beyond what serves the public good; and**
- **(b) the motives of an accused are irrelevant. 2014, c. 31, s. 3.**

CROSS-REFERENCES

For notes on the "public good" defence provided by subsec. (3), see the notes under s. 163.

Section 164 enacts an alternative procedure, *in rem* proceedings, for the seizure, forfeiture and restoration of intimate images. Where an order has been made under s. 164, no proceedings may be taken under this section except with the consent of the Attorney General.

Section 164.1 sets out an *in rem* procedure for removal of intimate images from computer systems.

Section 164.2 provides that a court that convicts a person of an offence under this section may order that any thing, other than real property, be forfeited to the Crown if the court is satisfied that the thing was used in the commission of the offence and is the property of the offender, another person who was a party to the offence, or a person who acquired the thing from such a person in circumstances giving rise to a reasonable inference that it was transferred to avoid a forfeiture order.

This offence may be the basis for an application for an authorization to intercept private communications by reason of s. 183, or a video surveillance warrant under s. 487.01(5).

Where the victim of an offence under this section has incurred expenses to have the intimate image removed from the Internet, restitution of such expenses may be ordered pursuant to s. 738(1)(*e*) when sentence is imposed.

A "peace bond" is available under s. 810 where a person fears on reasonable grounds that another person will commit an offence under this section.

SYNOPSIS

This provision creates an offence in relation to the non-consensual distribution of intimate images. Under subsec. (1), the *actus reus* is satisfied if the person depicted did not consent to the image being distributed (or transmitted, etc.), and the *mens rea* is made out if the accused knows of or is reckless as to the person's non-consent. The subject matter of the offence ("intimate image") is defined in subsec. (2). The key concept is a "reasonable expectation of privacy" on the part of the person depicted, which must be present both at the time the recording was made and at the time the offence is committed. For guidance on "reasonable expectation of privacy", reference may be had to the annotations under s. 8 of the Charter.

Subsection (3) provides a "public good" defence, which is subject to subsec. (4). For guidance on this defence, see notes under s. 163.

PROHIBITION ORDER / Duration of prohibition / Court may vary order / Offence.

162.2 (1) When an offender is convicted, or is discharged on the conditions prescribed in a probation order under section 730, of an offence referred to in subsection 162.1(1), the court that sentences or discharges the offender, in addition to any other punishment that may be imposed for that offence or any other condition prescribed in the order of discharge, may make, subject to the conditions or exemptions that the court directs, an order prohibiting the offender from using the Internet or other digital network, unless the offender does so in accordance with conditions set by the court.

(2) The prohibition may be for any period that the court considers appropriate, including any period to which the offender is sentenced to imprisonment.

(3) A court that makes an order of prohibition or, if the court is for any reason unable to act, another court of equivalent jurisdiction in the same province may, on application of the offender or the prosecutor, require the offender to appear before it at any time and, after hearing the parties, that court may vary the conditions prescribed in the order if, in the opinion of the court, the variation is desirable because of changed circumstances after the conditions were prescribed.

(4) Every person who is bound by an order of prohibition and who does not comply with the order is guilty of

> **(a) an indictable offence and is liable to imprisonment for a term of not more than four years; or**
>
> **(b) an offence punishable on summary conviction and is liable to imprisonment for a term of not more than 18 months. 2014, c. 31, s. 3; 2015, c. 23, s. 33.**

CROSS-REFERENCES

Section 161(1)(*d*) provides for a similar prohibition order available in respect of other sexual offences.

SYNOPSIS

This provision creates a new form of prohibition order that may be imposed on a person convicted or discharged of an offence in relation to intimate images under s. 162.1. It allows the court to prohibit the offender from using the Internet or other digital network except in accordance with conditions set by the court. The prohibition can be for any period deemed appropriate, and may be varied on application of the offender or the Crown. Subsection (4) creates a separate offence of failing to comply with such a prohibition.

Offences Tending to Corrupt Morals

CORRUPTING MORALS / Idem / Defence of public good / Question of law and question of fact / Motives irrelevant / Ignorance of nature no defence / Definition of "crime comic" / Obscene publication.

163. (1) Every one commits an offence who

    (a) makes, prints, publishes, distributes, circulates, or has in his possession for the purpose of publication, distribution or circulation any obscene written matter, picture, model, phonograph record or other thing whatever; or

    (b) makes, prints, publishes, distributes, sells or has in his possession for the purposes of publication, distribution or circulation a crime comic.

(2) Every one commits an offence who knowingly, without lawful justification or excuse,

    (a) sells, exposes to public view or has in his possession for such a purpose any obscene written matter, picture, model, phonograph record or other thing whatever;

    (b) publicly exhibits a disgusting object or an indecent show;

    (c) offers to sell, advertises or publishes an advertisement of, or has for sale or disposal, any means, instructions, medicine, drug or article intended or represented as a method of causing abortion or miscarriage; or

    (d) advertises or publishes an advertisement of any means, instructions, medicine, drug or article intended or represented as a method for restoring sexual virility or curing venereal diseases or diseases of the generative organs.

(3) No person shall be convicted of an offence under this section if the public good was served by the acts that are alleged to constitute the offence and if the acts alleged did not extend beyond what served the public good.

(4) For the purposes of this section, it is a question of law whether an act served the public good and whether there is evidence that the act alleged went beyond what served the public good, but it is a question of fact whether the acts did or did not extend beyond what served the public good.

(5) For the purposes of this section, the motives of an accused are irrelevant.

(6) [*Repealed*, 1993, c. 46, s. 1.]

(7) In this section, "crime comic" means a magazine, periodical or book that exclusively or substantially comprises matter depicting pictorially

    (a) the commission of crimes, real or fictitious; or

    (b) events connected with the commission of crimes, real or fictitious, whether occurring before or after the commission of the crime.

(8) For the purposes of this Act, any publication a dominant characteristic of which is the undue exploitation of sex, or of sex and any one or more of the following subjects, namely, crime, horror, cruelty and violence, shall be deemed to be obscene. R.S., c. C-34, s. 159; 1993, c. 46, s. 1.

CROSS-REFERENCES

Possession is defined by s. 4(3). The punishment for this offence is set out in s. 169. Where the prosecution elects to proceed by indictment on this offence then the accused may elect his mode of trial pursuant to s. 536(2). Where the prosecution elects to proceed by way of summary conviction then the trial of this offence is conducted by a summary conviction court pursuant to Part XXVII. The punishment for the offence is then as set out in s. 787 [although note the maximum fine for a corporation is determined by s. 735(1)(*b*)] and the limitation period is set out in s. 786(2). In either case, release pending trial is determined by s. 515, although the accused is eligible for release by a peace officer under s. 496, 497 or by the officer in charge under s. 498. This offence is an enterprise crime offence for the purposes of Part XII.2 and the offence in subsec. (1)(*a*) may be the basis for an application for an authorization to intercept private communications by reason of s. 183 and a warrant for video surveillance by reason of s. 487.01(5). Section 584 deals with the sufficiency of an indictment in relation to obscene written material and s. 587(1)(*d*) provides for the ordering of particulars in such cases.

Section 164 enacts an alternative procedure, "*in rem*" proceedings, for determination of whether or not a publication is obscene or a crime comic. Where an order has been made under s. 164 then no proceedings may be taken under this section except with the consent of the Attorney General. Section 583(*h*) provides that a count in an indictment is not insufficient by reason only that it does not state that the required consent has been obtained. Section 165 makes it an offence to refuse to supply publications to a person because he refuses to purchase or acquire publications which he believes to be obscene or a crime comic. Section 166 makes it an offence to publish certain material calculated to injure public morals or in relation to marital and similar proceedings. Section 167 makes it an offence to take part in immoral theatrical performances. Section 168 makes it an offence to use the mail for the purpose of transmitting obscene material. Wilfully doing an indecent act is an offence under s. 173. Public nudity is an offence under s. 174. Exposing an indecent exhibition is an offence under s. 175(1)(*b*). Child pornography is dealt with in s. 163.1.

SYNOPSIS

Section 163 makes it an offence to produce, publish or distribute *obscene things or crime comics.*

Section 163(1)(*a*) is very broadly worded to prohibit all phases of the making, printing, publication, distribution and circulation, and the possession of *obscene things,* with the intention of doing any of the prohibited activities. The prohibited class of obscene things is expansive, covering written material, pictures, models, records or "any other thing whatsoever". Section 163(8) provides the sole definition of what is deemed to be obscene. It states that if a dominant characteristic of the publication is the *undue exploitation of sex,* or the combination of sex and at least one of crime, horror, cruelty or violence. The acts described within the section have received a broad interpretation, as reflected, for example, by a decision stating that the display of such objects in plain view within a store amounts to publication.

Section 163(1)(*b*), which deals with *crime comics,* prohibits many aspects of the publication process including the distribution and sale of crime comics, or their possession for such purposes. Section 163(7) defines what constitutes a crime comic.

Section 163(5) makes the accused's motives irrelevant. Subsection (6) purports to state that it is *no defence* that the accused was ignorant of the nature or presence of obscene content of the thing or of the crime comic. However, decisions made under the *Canadian Charter of Rights and Freedoms* have held that this subsection is unconstitutional and have established that it is a defence if the accused made an *honest* and *reasonable mistake of fact.* A mistake of law, which causes the accused to believe that the material he or she knows the nature or presence of is not obscene or a crime comic, is not a defence.

Section 163(2) makes it an offence to *knowingly* and *without lawful justification or excuse* engage in any of the acts listed in this subsection, which relate to obscenity, indecent objects, drugs and other things used to induce (or said to be useful to induce) abortions or miscarriages, and a number of other specified sex related materials.

Section 163(3) provides a defence if the accused *establishes* that the acts which make out the offence under this section *served the public good,* and extended no further than was required to achieve that objective. Subsection (4) states that whether an act served the public good, and whether there is any evidence that the act extended beyond what was required to achieve that end, are questions of law. That means that in a jury trial these issues would be determined by the trial judge. However, the subsection also provides that if it is determined that there is some evidence, the decision as to whether the act actually extended beyond what was needed to achieve the public good is a question of fact and will, therefore, be determined by the trier of fact.

ANNOTATIONS

Subsection (1) / Elements of offence generally / *Distinction between subsecs. (1) and (2)* – There is a difference between selling or having in possession for the purpose of selling contrary to subsec. (2) and distributing contrary to subsec. (1): *R. v. Fraser*, [1967] S.C.R. 38, [1967] 2 C.C.C. 43 (5:0).

In *R. v. Dorosz* (1971), 4 C.C.C. (2d) 203 (Ont. C.A.), the evidence upon conviction of possession of obscene matter for the purpose of distribution was simply the display for sale in a variety store of certain obscene publications. It was held (2:1) that Parliament had drawn a line in the chain from production to consumption of such material by virtue of mutually exclusive subsecs. (1) and (2), with the result that although the omission of proof of knowledge of obscenity is directed against the maker, circulator and distributor, that element must be proven against the person through whose hands the publication must finally pass before public consumption. Furthermore, it was the unanimous view of the Court that in any event the retail store clerk is not a distributor. Also see *R. v. Sudbury News Service Ltd.* (1978), 39 C.C.C. (2d) 1 (Ont. C.A.).

Meaning of "circulates" and "distributes" – A private showing of obscene films in the accused's home does not constitute circulation: *R. v. Rioux*, [1969] S.C.R. 599, [1970] 3 C.C.C. 149.

The rental of video movie cassettes comes within the meaning of distribution or circulation in this subsection: *R. v. Video Movieshop* (1982), 67 C.C.C. (2d) 87 (Nfld. S.C. T.D.). *Contra: R. v. Householders T.V. and Appliances Ltd.* (1984), 20 C.C.C. (3d) 561 (Ont. Co. Ct.), affd 20 C.C.C. (3d) 571 (C.A.).

While the mere renting of video movie cassettes may not constitute the offence under this paragraph, the offence was made out where the accused copied tapes for rental to other persons: *R. v. Harris and Lighthouse Video Centres Ltd.* (1987), 35 C.C.C. (3d) 1 (Ont. C.A.), leave to appeal to S.C.C. refused [1986] 2 S.C.R. vii, 38 C.C.C. (3d) vi.

Mens rea and mistake of fact – While an intent to publish is not an element of all the offences created by this subsection, such as the offence of making, where the crown has framed its information to allege making an obscene publication, the allegation of publication cannot be said to be mere surplusage and the accused was entitled to be discharged where there was no evidence of publication or intent to publish: *R. v. Hawkshaw*, [1986] 1 S.C.R. 668, 26 C.C.C. (3d) 129 (7:0).

In *R. v. Metro News Ltd.* (1986), 29 C.C.C. (3d) 35 (Ont. C.A.), leave to appeal to S.C.C. refused C.C.C. *loc. cit.*, while the court held that subsec. (6) was unconstitutional as it had the effect of making the offences under this subsection absolute liability offences, nevertheless this holding did not have the effect of requiring the crown to prove *mens rea*. Rather, the act of distributing matter which is in fact obscene *prima facie* imports the offence, but it is open to an accused to avoid criminal liability by raising a reasonable doubt that he acted under an honest and reasonable belief in a state of facts which, if it had been as he believed them to be, would make his act innocent. However an accused's belief that the magazine did not exceed the community standards of tolerance and was not obscene did not constitute a reasonable mistake of fact nor give rise to a defence of due diligence. Whether a publication unduly exploits sex under subsec. (8) or whether the allegedly obscene matter exceeded the community's standard of tolerance constitutes a value judgment to which the doctrine of mistake of fact is inapplicable. An accused's belief that the publication was not legally obscene is not a defence.

Subsection (2) / Meaning of "knowingly" – The offence of "knowingly" selling obscene material requires proof of knowledge with respect to all aspects of the *actus reus*. It is not sufficient that the accused was aware that the dominant characteristic of the material was the exploitation of sex as the sale of such material is lawful. The Crown must show that the seller of the obscene material was aware of the relevant facts that made the material obscene. In the case of pornographic films and videos, it cannot easily be inferred that those selling the materials know their contents. While it may be inferred that the retailer is aware that the materials are erotic or pornographic and deal with the exploitation of sex, selling films dealing with the exploitation of sex is not illegal unless the material is obscene. Not only must the dominant characteristic of the material be the exploitation of sex, but the exploitation of sex must be undue. To prove knowledge, the Crown must prove beyond a reasonable doubt that the accused knew that the materials being sold have the qualities or contain the specific scenes which render such material obscene in law. This does not require proof that the retailer actually viewed the tapes. Knowledge can be proven by circumstantial evidence. In addition, in proper circumstances, the Crown can rely upon the principles of willful blindness. Where the accused knew of the presence of the ingredients of the subject-matter which rendered the exploitation of sex undue and thus obscene, the fact that the material had been approved by the provincial film review board does not constitute a lawful justification or excuse nor negative the necessary *mens rea*: *R. v. Jorgensen*, [1995] 4 S.C.R. 55, 102 C.C.C. (3d) 97.

Expose to public view – An obscene film was not exposed to public view within the meaning of this subsection where it was only shown to friends and relatives of the groom attending a private "stag party". The hall in which the film was shown was, at the time, not open to the public, but rather, was used for a private gathering. In this respect, the definition of "private" in the *Oxford English Dictionary* as "kept or removed from public view . . . not within the cognizance of people generally . . . not open to the public; intended only for the use of particular and privileged persons" accurately described the circumstances in which the film was shown: *R. v. Harrison* (1973), 12 C.C.C. (2d) 26 (Alta. Dist. Ct.).

On the other hand, where an obscene film was shown not only to invited guests but to others who merely paid an admission charge then there was an exposure to public view: *R. v. Vigue*, 13 C.C.C. (2d) 381 (B.C. Prov. Ct.).

Disgusting object, indecent show (para. (*b*)) – The offence created by para. (*b*) of exhibiting an indecent show is not so vague as to be an unconstitutional infringement of freedom of expression as guaranteed by s. 2(*b*) of the *Canadian Charter of Rights and Freedoms*. The test to be applied in determining indecency is that of the community standard of tolerance. A relevant consideration in applying that test is the nature of the audience, the issue being whether the show is inappropriate according to Canadian standards of tolerance because of the context in which it takes place: *R. v. Pelletier* (1985), 27 C.C.C. (3d) 77 (Que. C.A.).

The word "disgusting" was held to have a known dictionary as well as judicial meaning and, therefore, not to violate the due process guarantee under the *Canadian Bill of Rights*: *R. v. Isaacs' Gallery Ltd.* (1975), 19 C.C.C. (2d) 570 (Ont. C.A.), leave to appeal refused [1975] 1 S.C.R. ix.

The offence of exhibiting a disgusting object is unconstitutionally vague and violates ss. 2(*b*) and 7 of the *Canadian Charter of Rights and Freedoms* and is of no force and effect: *R. v. Glassman and Bogyo* (1986), 53 C.R. (3d) 164 (Ont. Prov. Ct.).

Note: Also see notes under ss. 174 and 175.

Subsection (3) (public good) – Where, although the book has certain literary merit particularly for the more sophisticated reader, it was available for the general public to whom the book was neither symbolism nor a psychological study the accused cannot rely on the defence of public good: *R. v. Delorme* (1973), 15 C.C.C. (2d) 350 (Que. C.A.) (2:1).

In *R. v. American News Co.* (1957), 118 C.C.C. 152 (Ont. C.A.), Laidlaw J.A. adopted as a definition of the words "public good" a formula used in Stephen's *Digest of Criminal Law*, namely, "necessary or advantageous to religion or morality to the administration of justice, the pursuit of science, literature or art, or other objects of general interest".

Subsection (6) – This subsection is of no force and effect by reason of its inconsistency with s. 7 of the *Canadian Charter of Rights and Freedoms*: *R. v. Metro News Ltd.* (1986), 29 C.C.C. (3d) 35 (Ont. C.A.), leave to appeal to S.C.C. refused C.C.C. *loc. cit.*; *R. v. Saint John News Co.* (1984), 17 C.C.C. (3d) 234 (N.B.Q.B.). *Contra*: *R. v. Red Hot Video Ltd.*

(1984), 11 C.C.C. (3d) 389 (B.C. Co. Ct.), affd on other grounds 18 C.C.C. (3d) 1 (C.A.), leave to appeal to S.C.C. refused [1985] 2 S.C.R. x.

Subsection (8) [definition of obscenity] / Test for obscenity – In *R. v. Butler*, [1992] 1 S.C.R. 452, 70 C.C.C. (3d) 129, the court laid down a new comprehensive interpretation of subsec. (8). It would appear that this test is to be applied in two stages. The first stage involves a determination of whether the particular material involves the undue exploitation of sex. The second stage requires application of a test of "internal necessities". For the purposes of this definition, the court referred to three categories of pornography: (1) explicit sex with violence; (2) explicit sex without violence but which subjects people to treatment that is degrading or dehumanizing; and (3) explicit sex without violence that is neither degrading nor dehumanizing. Violence in this context includes both actual physical violence and threats of physical violence. In applying the definition to the three categories, the courts must determine what the community would tolerate others being exposed to on the basis of the degree of harm that may flow from such exposure. Harm in this context means that it predisposes persons to act in an anti-social manner as, for example, the physical or mental mistreatment of women by men or possibly the reverse. Anti-social conduct for this purpose is conduct which society formally recognizes as incompatible with its proper functioning. The stronger the inference of risk of harm, the lesser the likelihood of tolerance. Material falling in the first category will almost always constitute the undue exploitation of sex. Explicit sex which is degrading or dehumanizing may be undue if the risk of harm is substantial. Explicit sex that is not violent and neither degrading nor dehumanizing is generally tolerated and will not fall within the definition unless it employs children in its production. If material is not obscene under this framework, it does not become so by reason of the person to whom it is or may be shown or exposed nor by reason of the place or manner in which it is shown. Even if the work contains sexually explicit material that, by itself, would constitute the undue exploitation of sex, the portrayal of sex must then be viewed in context to determine whether that is the dominant theme of the work as a whole [the "internal necessities" test]. In other words, is undue exploitation of sex the main object of the work or is this portrayal of sex essential to a wider artistic, literary, or other similar purpose? Again, the community standards test applies at this stage, the court having to determine whether the sexually explicit material, when viewed in the context of the whole work, would be tolerated by the community as a whole. Since artistic expression rests at the heart of freedom of expression values, any doubt in this regard must be resolved in favour of freedom of expression.

Videotapes which merely display a large number of explicit sexual acts in a non-violent consensual manner, although devoid of any loving or affectionate relationship or any plot of meaningful value, are not necessarily degrading or dehumanizing. Further, even if the material could be found to be degrading or dehumanizing, it will not necessarily be found to be obscene. The material must also create a substantial risk of harm to society. Like any element of criminal allegation, it must be proved beyond a reasonable doubt and that proof must be found in the evidence adduced at trial. It does not follow from proof of portrayal of sexually explicit acts in a degrading or dehumanizing manner that the films are harmful and therefore obscene. It is open to the court to find that the harm component of the offence is not established. Where the participants appear as fully willing participants occupying substantially equal roles in a setting devoid of violence, bondage or bestiality or sex associated with crime, horror, cruelty, coercion or children, the risk of societal harm may not be evident. Further evidence may be required to prove that exposure to the impugned material will create a substantial risk of an identifiable harm that may cause persons to act in a manner inimical to the proper functioning of society. The question is essentially one of degree but the onus remains on the Crown to prove that the offence is made out: *R. v. Hawkins* (1993), 86 C.C.C. (3d) 246 (Ont. C.A.), leave to appeal to S.C.C. refused 87 C.C.C. (3d) vi.

In considering the requirement of proof of harm, reference may be made to *R. v. Labaye*, [2005] 3 S.C.R. 728, 203 C.C.C. (3d) 170; *R. v. Kouri*, [2005] 3 S.C.R. 798, 203 C.C.C. (3d)

217, noted under s. 197 and concerned with the related term of "indecency" in the definition of common bawdy house.

In determining whether the material depicts explicit sex, the trier of fact must consider the circumstances and context of the material. Even where no sexual act is depicted, material may still depict explicit sex. The trier of fact must consider whether a reasonable person viewing the material would consider whether the material was explicitly sexual in nature, taking into account the part of the body depicted; the nature of the depiction; the context; the accompanying dialogue, words, or gestures; and all other surrounding circumstances. However, so-called "sexualized nudity" would not itself be sufficient to constitute depiction of explicit sex. Explicit sex captures portrayals at the far end of the spectrum: *R. v. Smith* (2005), 198 C.C.C. (3d) 499 (Ont. C.A.), leave to appeal to S.C.C. refused 198 C.C.C. (3d) 499*n*.

Effect of audience to which publication directed – The audience viewing a publication is not relevant in determining whether the publication is obscene. Thus, the fact that articles were for sale in a store restricted to adults did not prevent a finding that the articles were obscene: *R. v. Germain*, [1985] 2 S.C.R. 241, 21 C.C.C. (3d) 289 (9:0); *R. v. Butler, supra*.

Application of subsection to articles other than publications – It was held in *R. v. Hawkshaw*, [1986] 1 S.C.R. 668, 26 C.C.C. (3d) 129 (7:0), that this subsection sets out the sole test for obscenity in charges under the *Criminal Code* whether based on publication or not, thus clearing up the issue left open in several earlier cases such as *R. v. Dechow*, [1978] 1 S.C.R. 951, 35 C.C.C. (2d) 22, and *Germain, supra*.

Application of Charter of Rights – The prohibition on obscene material as defined by subsec. (8) infringes freedom of expression but constitutes a reasonable limit prescribed by law within the meaning of s. 1: *R. v. Butler, supra*.

DEFINITION OF "CHILD PORNOGRAPHY" / Making child pornography / Distribution, etc. of child pornography / Possession of child pornography / Accessing child pornography / Interpretation / Aggravating factor / Defence / Defence / Question of law.

163.1 (1) In this section, "child pornography" means

  (*a*) **a photographic, film, video or other visual representation, whether or not it was made by electronic or mechanical means,**

   (i) **that shows a person who is or is depicted as being under the age of eighteen years and is engaged in or is depicted as engaged in explicit sexual activity, or**

   (ii) **the dominant characteristic of which is the depiction, for a sexual purpose, of a sexual organ or the anal region of a person under the age of eighteen years;**

  (*b*) **any written material, visual representation or audio recording that advocates or counsels sexual activity with a person under the age of eighteen years that would be an offence under this Act;**

  (*c*) **any written material whose dominant characteristic is the description, for a sexual purpose, of sexual activity with a person under the age of eighteen years that would be an offence under this Act; or**

  (*d*) **any audio recording that has as its dominant characteristic the description, presentation or representation, for a sexual purpose, of sexual activity with a person under the age of eighteen years that would be an offence under this Act.**

(2) Every person who makes, prints, publishes or possesses for the purpose of publication any child pornography is guilty of an indictable offence and liable to imprisonment for a term of not more than 14 years and to a minimum punishment of imprisonment for a term of one year.

(3) Every person who transmits, makes available, distributes, sells, advertises, imports, exports or possesses for the purpose of transmission, making available, distribution, sale, advertising or exportation any child pornography is guilty of an indictable offence and liable to imprisonment for a term of not more than 14 years and to a minimum punishment of imprisonment for a term of one year.

(4) Every person who possesses any child pornography is guilty of

    (*a*) an indictable offence and is liable to imprisonment for a term of not more than 10 years and to a minimum punishment of imprisonment for a term of one year; or

    (*b*) an offence punishable on summary conviction and is liable to imprisonment for a term of not more than two years less a day and to a minimum punishment of imprisonment for a term of six months.

(4.1) Every person who accesses any child pornography is guilty of

    (*a*) an indictable offence and is liable to imprisonment for a term of not more than 10 years and to a minimum punishment of imprisonment for a term of one year; or

    (*b*) an offence punishable on summary conviction and is liable to imprisonment for a term of not more than two years less a day and to a minimum punishment of imprisonment for a term of six months.

(4.2) For the purposes of subsection (4.1), a person accesses child pornography who knowingly causes child pornography to be viewed by, or transmitted to, himself or herself.

(4.3) If a person is convicted of an offence under this section, the court that imposes the sentence shall consider as an aggravating factor the fact that the person committed the offence with intent to make a profit.

(5) It is not a defence to a charge under subsection (2) in respect of a visual representation that the accused believed that a person shown in the representation that is alleged to constitute child pornography was or was depicted as being eighteen years of age or more unless the accused took all reasonable steps to ascertain the age of that person and took all reasonable steps to ensure that, where the person was eighteen years of age or more, the representation did not depict that person as being under the age of eighteen years.

(6) No person shall be convicted of an offence under this section if the act that is alleged to constitute the offence

    (*a*) has a legitimate purpose related to the administration of justice or to science, medicine, education or art; and

    (*b*) does not pose an undue risk of harm to persons under the age of eighteen years.

(7) For greater certainty, for the purposes of this section, it is a question of law whether any written material, visual representation or audio recording advocates or counsels sexual activity with a person under the age of eighteen years that would be an offence under this Act. 1993, c. 46. s. 2; 2002, c. 13, s. 5; 2005, c. 32, s. 7; 201, c. 1, s. 17; 2015, c. 23, s. 7.

CROSS-REFERENCES

Possession is defined by s. 4(3). For notes on procedure on arrest and trial for this offence, see the notes under s. 163.

Section 164 enacts an alternative procedure, *in rem* proceedings, for determination of whether or not the representation or written material is child pornography. The offences in this section may be the basis for obtaining an authorization to intercept private communications or a warrant for video surveillance. Section 164.1 sets out an *in rem* procedure for removal of child pornography from a computer system. Section 164.2 provides that a court that convicts a person of an offence under this section may order that any thing, other than real property, be forfeited to the Crown if the court is satisfied that the thing was used in the commission of the offence and is the property of the offender, another person who was a party to the offence or a person who acquired the thing from such a person in circumstances giving rise to a reasonable inference that it was transferred to avoid a forfeiture order.

If the accused is found guilty of this offence in respect of a person who is under 16 years of age, the court may impose an order of prohibition under s. 161 prohibiting the accused from attending certain public areas and facilities or taking certain employment that will bring him into contact with persons under the age of 16 years. Section 171.1 makes it an offence to transmit, make available, distribute or sell sexually explicit material to a person who is, or who the accused believes is under the age of 18 years for purpose of facilitating the commission of the offence created by this section. Section 172.1 makes it an offence to communicate by means of telecommunication with a person who is or who the accused believes is under the age of 18 years for the purpose of facilitating the commission of the offence under this section. Section 172.2 makes it an offence to agree with a person or make an arrangement with a person by means of telecommunication to commit an offence under this section with a person who is or who the accused believes is under the age of 18 years.

Section 486(1) and (2) provide that the judge may make an order excluding all or any members of the public where such order is in the interest of public morals, the maintenance of order or the proper administration of justice, or is necessary to prevent injury to international relations or national defence or national security. The proper administration of justice includes safeguarding the interests of witnesses under the age of 18 years. Section 486.1 sets out the circumstances in which the judge shall or may order a support person to be present and close to a witness while the witness testifies. Where the witness is under the age of 18 years or has a mental or physical disability, the order is to be made upon request unless the judge is of the opinion that the order would interfere with the proper administration of justice. In the case of other witnesses, the order is to be made if necessary to obtain a full and candid account from the witness of the matters complained of. The application for this order may be made during the proceedings or before they begin to the judge who is to preside at the proceedings.

Similarly, s. 486.2 sets out the circumstances in which the judge shall or may order a witness to testify outside the courtroom or behind a screen or other device that would not allow the witness to see the accused. Where the witness is under the age of 18 years or may have difficulty communicating the evidence by reason of a mental or physical disability, the judge shall make the order unless the judge is of the opinion that the order would interfere with the proper administration of justice. In all other cases, the order may be made if the judge is of the opinion that the order is necessary to obtain a full and candid account from the witness of the acts complained of. Similarly, s. 486.3 provides that, on application by the prosecutor or a witness under the age of 18 years, the accused shall not personally cross-examine the witness unless the judge is of the opinion that the proper administration of justice requires the accused to personally conduct the cross-examination. In other cases, the judge may make an order that the accused not personally cross-examine the witness if the judge is of the opinion that the order is necessary to obtain a full and candid account from the witness of the acts complained of. The judge will appoint counsel to conduct the cross-examination.

Under s. 486.4, the judge may make an order directing that the identity of a witness not be disclosed in any publication, broadcast or transmitted in any way. The order is mandatory where the complainant or a witness under the age of 18 years or the prosecutor applies for the order. Under s. 486.4(3), the judge shall make an order directing that the identity of a witness who is under the age of 18 years and any person who is the subject of a representation, written material or recording that constitutes child pornography not be disclosed in any publication, broadcast or transmitted in any way. Section 486.5 also gives the judge a discretion respecting non-publication orders in proceedings under these provisions in other circumstances.

Section 718.01 provides that, in imposing a sentence for an offence involving the abuse of a person under the age of 18 years, the court shall give primary consideration to the objectives of denunciation and deterrence. Further, under s. 718.2, evidence that the offender, in committing the offence, abused a person under the age of 18 years is an aggravating circumstance.

The offence in this section is a primary designated offence for the purpose of making a forensic DNA data bank order under s. 487.051. Under s. 490.012, where an offender is convicted of this offence, the judge shall make an order requiring the offender to comply with the *Sex Offender Information Registration Act*, S.C. 2004, c. 10.

Bill C-22, *An Act respecting the mandatory reporting of Internet child pornography by persons who provide an Internet service*, in force as of December 8, 2011, requires Internet service providers to report tips they receive regarding Web sites where child pornography, as defined by this section, may be publicly available, to the Canadian Centre for Child Protection; and, to notify the police and safeguard evidence for 21 days (or longer pursuant to a court order) if they have reasonable grounds to believe that a child pornography offence has been or is being committed using an Internet service that they provide.

SYNOPSIS

This section creates various offences relating to child pornography, which is defined in subsec. (1). To determine whether the material offends para. (*b*) of the definition, resort will have to be made to the various sexual offences of the Code: ss. 151, 152, 153, 155, 159, 160, 170, 171, 172, and 271 to 273. Subsections (2) and (3) correspond to the similar offences under s. 163 and notes under that section should be referred to in determining whether the material has, for example, been published. Pursuant to subsec. (7), it is a question of law whether the written material, visual representation or audio recording advocates or counsels sexual activity with a person under the age of 18 years that would be an offence under the Code. The offences of making and distributing child pornography in subsecs. (2) and (3) are punishable by a maximum of 14 years and a minimum of one year imprisonment. Subsection (4) creates an offence of simple possession of child pornography. Where the Crown proceeds by way of indictment, the offence is punishable by a maximum of 10 years and a minimum of one year imprisonment. Where the Crown proceeds by way of summary conviction, the offence is punishable by two years less a day and a minimum of six months' imprisonment. Subsection (4.1) creates the offence of accessing any child pornography. Accessing is defined in subsec. (4.2). Where the Crown proceeds by way of indictment, the offence is punishable by a maximum of 10 years and a minimum of one year imprisonment. Where the Crown proceeds by way of summary conviction, the offence is punishable by two years less a day and a minimum of six months' imprisonment. In addition, the fact that the person committed the offence with intent to make a profit is a deemed aggravating factor under subsec. (4.3).

Subsections (5) to (7) set out certain defence. Subsection (5) allows for a limited defence of reasonable mistake of fact as to the age of the persons depicted. Subsection (6) recognizes a defence where the accused has a legitimate purpose related to the administration of justice or to science, medicine, education or art, provided the act does not pose an undue risk of harm to persons under the age of 18 years.

ANNOTATIONS

Note: Some of the cases noted under this section were decided prior to the revisions to this section that came into force on November 1, 2005 and should be read with that in mind and, in particular, in light of the expansion of the definition of child pornography in subsec. (1)(*c*) and (*d*) and the addition of subsec. (6)(*b*) that limits the legitimate purpose defence by providing that the act must not pose an undue risk of harm to persons under the age of 18 years.

Subsections (1)(*a*), (*b*) and (4) violate s. 2(*b*) of the Charter but are justified under s. 1: *R. v. Sharpe*, [2001] 1 S.C.R. 45, 150 C.C.C. (3d) 321.

Subsection (1) – "Person" includes both actual and imaginary human beings: *R. v. Sharpe*, *supra*.

"Advocates or counsels" concerns material that, viewed objectively, sends the message that sex with children could and should be pursued: *R. v. Sharpe, supra*.

Active inducement or encouragement may come from a message that is implicit in the stories themselves. Material that describes sex with children as enjoyable, normal, and beneficial, and the children as willing, may send the message that sex with children can and should be pursued and therefore falls within the definition in para. (*b*), even though the author does not expressly advocate the commission of criminal sexual acts with children: *R. v. Beattie* (2005), 201 C.C.C. (3d) 533 (Ont. C.A.), leave to appeal to S.C.C. refused 201 C.C.C. (3d) 533*n*.

Subsection (2) – This provision does not include private recordings of lawful sexual activity which includes any visual recording that did not depict unlawful sexual activity and was held by the accused exclusively for private use: *R. v. Sharpe, supra*.

The private use exception has three requirements: (1) the recording must depict lawful sexual activity; (2) the persons depicted must consent to the recording; and (3) the recording must be held for private use. There is no additional "exploitation" inquiry, as exploitation is already captured under lawfulness. Section 153 of the Code makes sexual exploitation of a young person a crime. Thus, where the Crown seeks to rely on s. 153 to negate the legality of the sexual activity depicted, the judge must consider whether it occurred in the context of an exploitative relationship. If so, the sexual activity is not lawful, and the private use exception does not apply: *R. v. Barabash*, [2015] 2 S.C.R. 522, 322 C.C.C. (3d) 287.

Constructive possession is complete where the accused: (i) has knowledge of the character of the object; (ii) knowingly puts or keeps the object in a particular place whether or not that place belongs to him; and (iii) intends to have the object in the particular place for his use or benefit, or that of another person. In dealing with virtual objects, such as computer images, the mere fact that an image has been accessed by or displayed in a Web browser does not, without more, constitute possession of that image. Previous access and the possibility of again accessing a website that contains digital images, located on a distant server over which the viewer has no control, do not constitute, either alone or together, constructive possession. Furthermore, the automatic caching of a file to the hard drive does not, without more, constitute possession. The cached file might be a place over which the computer user has control but in order to establish possession, it is necessary to satisfy the *mens rea* or fault requirement as well by showing that the file was knowingly stored and retained through the cache: *R. v. Morelli*, [2010] 1 S.C.R. 253, 252 C.C.C. (3d) 273.

Possession requires knowledge of the criminal character of the items in issue. Accordingly, the Crown must prove that the accused had knowledge of the contents of the videos in issue, although it is irrelevant whether the accused knew that the contents constituted child pornography. In addition, the Crown must also prove that an accused with the requisite knowledge had a measure of control over the item in issue, in that he had power or authority over the item whether it was exercised or not. There are circumstances of innocent possession where an individual has the requisite control and knowledge, but cannot be said to be in possession for the purpose of imposing criminal liability. Such circumstances include taking control of contraband exclusively for the purpose of immediately destroying it or otherwise placing it permanently beyond that person's ability to exercise any control over the contraband. In such cases, the intention is solely to divest oneself of control rather than to possess: *R. v. Chalk* (2007), 227 C.C.C. (3d) 141 (Ont. C.A.).

Wilful blindness was not present where the accused was merely "suspicious" that his partner had viewed child pornography on a computer owned by the accused and used by both men: *R. v. Farmer* (2014), 318 C.C.C. (3d) 322 (Ont. C.A.).

The accused had requested that clearly identified child pornography files be downloaded but aborted the downloading process. No images of child pornography were in fact found on the computer. The accused was in constructive possession of the files even though the images were not on the computer screen as he had knowledge of the nature of the materials, the intention or consent to have possession and the necessary control over the material by virtue of the ability to permit the files to be downloaded or to abort the process. It is the element of control, including deciding what will be done with the material, that is essential to possession. It is not necessary for the individual to have viewed the material. Once the downloading of the transmission commenced, the material was in a place over which the accused had control: *R. v. Daniels* (2004), 191 C.C.C. (3d) 393 (Nfld. & Lab. C.A.).

Where child pornography was discovered on a non-password protected computer belonging to the accused, and the Crown led no other evidence to establish who had access to the computer or how it was typically used, a properly instructed jury could not reasonably conclude that possession had been established beyond a reasonable doubt: *R. v. Villaroman* (2015), 320 C.C.C. (3d) 50 (Alta. C.A.), leave to appeal to S.C.C. allowed 2015 CarswellAlta 1620.

Subsection (3) – There is no requirement that the accused take a "positive step" to make child pornography available in order to be guilty of the offence. A possessor of child pornography who uses a file sharing program and passively acquiesces in the program making the material available (or is willfully blind to it) has committed the offence of making available: *R. v. Spencer*, [2014] 2 S.C.R. 212, 312 C.C.C. (3d) 215. See also: *R. v. Smith* (2011), 282 C.C.C. (3d) 494 (B.C.S.C.). *Contra*: *R. v. Pressacco* (2010), 352 Sask. R. 276 (Q.B.); *R. v. Lamb* (2010), 92 W.C.B. (2d) 408 (B.C.S.C.), requiring "actual intent" to make available.

Subsection (6) – The defences in this section should be liberally construed and based on an objective test. The accused can raise the defences by pointing to facts capable of supporting them and the Crown must disprove them beyond a reasonable doubt. The artistic merit defence includes any expression that might reasonably be viewed as art. Any objectively established artistic value, however small, can support the defence. The defences of medical, educational and scientific purpose should also be liberally construed and include possession by people in the justice system for purposes associated with prosecution, researchers studying the effects of child pornography and by those in possession of works for the purpose of addressing the political or philosophical aspects of child pornography: *R. v. Sharpe*, *supra*.

In order for a purpose to be "legitimate" under s. 163.1(6)(*a*), there must be: (1) an objective connection between the accused's actions and his or her purpose; and (2) an objective relationship between the accused's purpose and one or more of the protected activities (administration of justice, science, medicine, education, or art). However, this objective assessment does not involve the court in any assessment of the *value* of the particular scientific or artistic activity in question. "Undue risk of harm" under s. 163.1(6)(*b*) means a significant risk of objectively ascertainable harm as required by the law of obscenity, rather than the former "moral views of the community" approach: *R. v. Katigbak*, [2011] 3 S.C.R. 326, 276 C.C.C. (3d) 1.

Sentence – The minimum penalty in subsec. (3)(*a*) does not violate s. 12 of the Charter: *R. v. Schultz* (2008), 239 C.C.C. (3d) 535 (Alta. Q.B.).

WARRANT OF SEIZURE / Summons to occupier / Owner and maker may appear / Order of forfeiture / Disposal of matter / Appeal / Consent / Definitions / "Advertisement of sexual services" / "Court" / "Crime comic" / "Judge" / "Voyeuristic recording".

164. (1) A judge may issue a warrant authorizing seizure of copies of a recording, a publication, a representation or any written material, if the judge is satisfied by information on oath that there are reasonable grounds to believe that

    (*a*) **the recording, copies of which are kept for sale or distribution in premises within the jurisdiction of the court, is a voyeuristic recording;**

    (*b*) **the recording, copies of which are kept for sale or distribution in premises within the jurisdiction of the court, is an intimate image;**

    (*c*) **the publication, copies of which are kept for sale or distribution in premises within the jurisdiction of the court, is obscene or a crime comic, as defined in section 163;**

   (*d*) the representation, written material or recording, copies of which are kept in premises within the jurisdiction of the court, is child pornography as defined in section 163.1; or

   (*e*) the representation, written material or recording, copies of which are kept in premises within the jurisdiction of the court, is an advertisement of sexual services.

(2) Within seven days of the issue of the warrant under subsection (1), the judge shall issue a summons to the occupier of the premises requiring him to appear before the court and show cause why the matter seized should not be forfeited to Her Majesty.

(3) The owner and the maker of the matter seized under subsection (1), and alleged to be obscene, a crime comic, child pornography, a voyeuristic recording, an intimate image or an advertisement of sexual services, may appear and be represented in the proceedings to oppose the making of an order for the forfeiture of the matter.

(4) If the court is satisfied, on a balance of probabilities, that the publication, representation, written material or recording referred to in subsection (1) is obscene, a crime comic, child pornography, a voyeuristic recording, an intimate image or an advertisement of sexual services, it may make an order declaring the matter forfeited to Her Majesty in right of the province in which the proceedings take place, for disposal as the Attorney General may direct.

(5) If the court is not satisfied that the publication, representation, written material or recording referred to in subsection (1) is obscene, a crime comic, child pornography, a voyeuristic recording, an intimate image or an advertisement of sexual services, it shall order that the matter be restored to the person from whom it was seized without delay after the time for final appeal has expired.

(6) An appeal lies from an order made under subsection (4) or (5) by any person who appeared in the proceedings

   (*a*) on any ground of appeal that involves a question of law alone,

   (*b*) on any ground of appeal that involves a question of fact alone, or

   (*c*) on any ground of appeal that involves a question of mixed law and fact,

as if it were an appeal against conviction or against a judgment or verdict of acquittal, as the case may be, on a question of law alone under Part XXI and sections 673 to 696 apply with such modifications as the circumstances require.

(7) If an order is made under this section by a judge in a province with respect to one or more copies of a publication, a representation, written material or a recording, no proceedings shall be instituted or continued in that province under section 162, 162.1, 163, 163.1 or 286.4 with respect to those or other copies of the same publication, representation, written material or recording without the consent of the Attorney General.

(8) In this section,

"advertisement of sexual services" means any material — including a photographic, film, video, audio or other recording, made by any means, a visual representation or any written material — that is used to advertise sexual services contrary to section 286.4.

"court" means

   (*a*) in the Province of Quebec, the Court of Quebec, the municipal court of Montreal and the municipal court of Quebec,

  (*a*.1) in the Province of Ontario, the Superior Court of Justice,

   (*b*) in the Provinces of New Brunswick, Manitoba, Saskatchewan and Alberta, the Court of Queen's Bench,

   (*c*) in the Province of Newfoundland and Labrador, the Trial Division of the Supreme Court,

  (*c*.1) [*Repealed.* 1992, c. 51, s. 34.]

(*d*) **in the Provinces of Nova Scotia, British Columbia and Prince Edward Island, in Yukon and in the Northwest Territories, the Supreme Court, and**
(*e*) **in Nunavut, the Nunavut Court of Justice;**

"crime comic" has the same meaning as it has in section 163;

"intimate image" has the same meaning as in subsection 162.1(2).

"judge" means a judge of a court.

"voyeuristic recording" means a visual recording within the meaning of subsection 162(2) that is made as described in subsection 162(1). R.S., c. C-34, s. 160; 1974-75-76, c. 48, s. 25; 1978-79, c. 11, s. 10; R.S.C. 1985, c. 27 (2nd Supp.), s. 10; c. 40 (4th Supp.), s. 2; 1990, c. 16, s. 3; 1990, c. 17, s. 9; 1992, c. 1, s. 58; 1992, c. 51, s. 34; 1993, c. 28, Sch. III, s. 28 (repealed by 1999, c. 3, s. 12); 1993, c. 46, s. 3; 1997, c. 18, s. 5; 1998, c. 30, s. 14(*d*); 1999, c. 3, ss. 12, 27; 2002, c. 7, s. 139; c. 13, s. 6; 2005, c. 32, s. 8; 2014, c. 25, s. 6; 2014, c. 31, s. 4; 2015, c. 3, s. 46.

CROSS-REFERENCES

The definition of obscenity is in s. 163(8) and of child pornography in s. 163.1(1). The voyeurism offence is defined in s. 162. The offence of advertising sexual services is set out in s. 286.4. "Attorney General" is defined in s. 2. An ordinary search warrant to search for evidence of the obscenity, child pornography and voyeurism offences under other sections of the *Criminal Code* may be obtained under ss. 487 and 487.1. (See *R. v. Video Movies Ltd.* (1984), 16 C.C.C. (3d) 351, 59 N.B.R. (2d) 82 (Q.B.).) The procedure in this section relates only to the *in rem* proceedings.

SYNOPSIS

This provision authorizes special search and seizure powers in relation to obscene publications, crime comics, child pornography, voyeuristic recordings, intimate images and advertisements of sexual services, and for the restoration or forfeiture of seized items.

Section 164(1) permits a judge to issue a warrant to seize obscene publications, crime comics, child pornography, voyeuristic recordings, intimate images and advertisements of sexual services kept within the jurisdiction of the court.

The procedure is like that usually employed in the issuance of warrants. It requires that, after receiving information on oath, the judge is to be satisfied that there are reasonable grounds to believe there are copies of any publication kept for sale or distribution at the place to be searched or, in the case of child pornography and advertisements of sexual services, simply that the materials are kept in the premises to be searched. Subsection (8) provides definitions of "advertisements of sexual services", "court", "crime comic", "intimate image", "judge" and "voyeuristic recording" for the purposes of this section.

Section 164(2) commences the forfeiture proceedings, the details of which are set out in the rest of this section. The judge shall issue a summons within seven days of the issuance of the search warrant, to the occupier of the searched premises, requiring that person to show cause why the items should not be forfeited. Despite the wording of this subsection, it has been determined that the onus remains on the Crown.

Section 164(3) permits the owner and author of the seized items to be represented in the forfeiture proceedings and oppose the proposed forfeiture.

Section 164(4) provides that, if the court is satisfied on a balance of probabilities that the material is one of the listed items, it may make a forfeiture order. However, if the court is not satisfied that the items come within the prohibited categories, then the items shall be restored to the person from whom they were seized (subsec. (5)). An order under this subsection will not be made until the time for launching an appeal has passed. Subsection (6) provides for a right of appeal to any one who appeared in the proceedings as if it was an indictable appeal under Part XXI with such modifications as are required. The grounds of appeal are the broadest possible, ranging from questions of fact to questions of law, or a mixture of the two.

The incorporation of the sections relating to indictable appeals specified in this subsection also incorporates an appeal to the Supreme Court of Canada, but only on the usual ground, *i.e.*, a question of law, and not the broader grounds permitted in the initial level of appeal.

Section 164(7) provides that if a judge has made an order of restoration or forfeiture under this section, no prosecution under s. 162 (voyeurism), s. 163 (which prohibits possessing obscene items or crime comics for certain purposes), s. 162.1 (publication of an intimate image without consent), s. 163.1 (child pornography) and s. 286.4 (advertising sexual services) may be brought in relation to the same publication, representation, written material or recording unless the Attorney General consents.

ANNOTATIONS

Sufficiency of warrant – The warrant under this subsection must specify the publications and the phrase "and others" following certain titles will be severed from the warrant as being too indefinite: *R. v. Laborde* (1972), 7 C.C.C. (2d) 86 (Sask. Q.B.).

For the purposes of this section a video tape is not a "publication": *R. v. Video Movies Ltd., supra. Contra: R. v. Nicols* (1984), 17 C.C.C. (3d) 555 (Ont. Co. Ct.).

Procedure on *in rem* proceedings – The summons must be returnable before the court and not a judge in chambers: *R. v. Belding* (1976), 37 C.R.N.S. 229, 16 N.B.R. (2d) 8 (C.A.).

Despite the wording of this subsection calling for the owner to "show cause" why the matter should not be forfeited, the burden of proof is on the Crown to show that the material is obscene and the ordinary rules of evidence apply: *R. v. Penthouse Magazine* (1977), 37 C.C.C. (2d) 376 (Ont. Co. Ct.). [An appeal by the owner to the Ont. C.A. was dismissed 46 C.C.C. (2d) 111 without reference to these issues.] Similarly, *R. v. H. H. Marshall Ltd.* (1982), 69 C.C.C. (2d) 197 (N.S.C.A.).

The burden on the Crown is to prove beyond a reasonable doubt that the publication is obscene: *R. v. Benjamin News (Montreal) Reg'd* (1978), 48 C.C.C. (2d) 399 (Que. C.A.).

The Superior Court has an inherent jurisdiction to quash a warrant issued under this section, where no show cause hearing has ever been held, even where the warrant is originally issued, as in Prince Edward Island, by another judge of the Superior Court: *R. v. Shama's Clover Farm* (1982), 1 C.C.C. (3d) 119 (P.E.I.S.C.).

Appeal procedure – This subsection only provides for an appeal to an appellate court and does not apply to a further appeal to the Supreme Court of Canada: *R. v. Provincial News Co.*, [1976] 1 S.C.R. 89, 20 C.C.C. (2d) 385 (3:2).

WARRANT OF SEIZURE / Notice to person who posted the material / Person who posted the material may appear / Non-appearance / Order / Destruction of copy / Return of material / Other provisions to apply / When order takes effect.

164.1 (1) If a judge is satisfied by information on oath that there are reasonable grounds to believe that there is material — namely, child pornography as defined in section 163.1, a voyeuristic recording, an intimate image or an advertisement of sexual services as defined in 164(8) or computer data as defined in subsection 342.1(2) that makes child pornography, a voyeuristic recording, an intimate image or an advertisement of sexual services available — that is stored on and made available through a computer system as defined in subsection 342.1(2) that is within the jurisdiction of the court, the judge may order the custodian of the computer system to

(*a*) give an electronic copy of the material to the court;

(*b*) ensure that the material is no longer stored on and made available through the computer system; and

(*c*) provide the information necessary to identify and locate the person who posted the material.

(2) Within a reasonable time after receiving the information referred to in paragraph (1)(*c*), the judge shall cause notice to be given to the person who posted the material,

giving that person the opportunity to appear and be represented before the court, and show cause why the material should not be deleted. If the person cannot be identified or located or does not reside in Canada, the judge may order the custodian of the computer system to post the text of the notice at the location where the material was previously stored and made available, until the time set for the appearance.

(3) The person who posted the material may appear and be represented in the proceedings in order to oppose the making of an order under subsection (5).

(4) If the person who posted the material does not appear for the proceedings, the court may proceed *ex parte* to hear and determine the proceedings in the absence of the person as fully and effectually as if the person had appeared.

(5) If the court is satisfied, on a balance of probabilities, that the material is child pornography as defined in section 163.1, a voyeuristic recording, an intimate image or an advertisement of sexual services as defined in subsection 164(8) or computer data as defined in subsection 342.1(2) that makes child pornography, the voyeuristic recording, the intimate image or the advertisement of sexual services available, it may order the custodian of the computer system to delete the material.

(6) When the court makes the order for the deletion of the material, it may order the destruction of the electronic copy in the court's possession.

(7) If the court is not satisfied that the material is child pornography as defined in 163.1, a voyeuristic recording, an intimate image or an advertisement of sexual services as defined in subsection 164(8) or computer data as defined in subsection 342.1(2) that makes child pornography, the voyeuristic recording, the intimate image or the advertisement of sexual services available, the court shall order that the electronic copy be returned to the custodian of the computer system and terminate the order under paragraph (1)(*b*).

(8) Subsections 164(6) to (8) apply, with any modifications that the circumstances require, to this section.

(9) No order made under subsections (5) to (7) takes effect until the time for final appeal has expired. 2002, c. 13, s. 7; 2005, c. 32, s. 9; 2014, c. 25, s. 7; 2014, c. 31, s. 5.

CROSS-REFERENCES

"Judge" is defined in s. 164(8). Section 164 provides a procedure for the seizure of child pornography and voyeuristic recordings and *in rem* forfeiture proceedings. Section 164.2 provides for the forfeiture of any thing, other than real property, used in the commission of the offence under s. 163.1 (child pornography). Section 172.1 creates the offence of using a computer system to communicate with a child for the purpose of committing various sexual offences.

SYNOPSIS

This section provides a procedure for shutting down sites hosting child pornography, voyeuristic recordings, intimate images or advertisements of sexual services. The procedure begins with an order made under subsec. (1) directing the custodian of the computer system to provide a copy of the material to the court, ensure that the material is no longer stored on and made available through the computer system (para. (*b*)) and provide information necessary to identify and locate the person who posted the material. Under subsec. (2), the judge is then to cause notice to be given to the person who posted the material to show cause why the material should not be deleted. Following a hearing, if the judge is satisfied on a balance of probabilities that the material is one of the items in question, the court may order the custodian to delete the material. If not so satisfied, the judge shall order that the electronic copy be returned to the custodian and the order under subsec. (1)(*b*) is terminated. An appeal from an order made under this section lies to the court of appeal in accordance with s. 164(6).

FORFEITURE AFTER CONVICTION / Third party rights / Right of appeal — third party / Right of appeal — Attorney General / Application of Part XXI.

164.2 (1) On application of the Attorney General, a court that convicts a person of an offence under section 162.1, 163.1, 172.1 or 172.2, in addition to any other punishment that it may impose, may order that anything — other than real property — be forfeited to Her Majesty and disposed of as the Attorney General directs if it is satisfied, on a balance of probabilities, that the thing

> (*a*) **was used in the commission of the offence; and**
>
> (*b*) **is the property of**
>
> > (i) **the convicted person or another person who was a party to the offence, or**
> >
> > (ii) **a person who acquired the thing from a person referred to in subparagraph (i) under circumstances that give rise to a reasonable inference that it was transferred for the purpose of avoiding forfeiture.**

(2) Before making an order under subsection (1), the court shall cause notice to be given to, and may hear, any person whom it considers to have an interest in the thing, and may declare the nature and extent of the person's interest in it.

(3) A person who was heard in response to a notice given under subsection (2) may appeal to the court of appeal against an order made under subsection (1).

(4) The Attorney General may appeal to the court of appeal against the refusal of a court to make an order under subsection (1).

(5) Part XXI applies, with any modifications that the circumstances require, with respect to the procedure for an appeal under subsections (3) and (4). 2002, c. 13, s. 7; 2008, c. 18, s. 4; 2012, c. 1, s. 18; 2014, c. 31, s. 6.

CROSS-REFERENCES

"Attorney General" is defined in s. 164.2. Section 164 provides for *in rem* forfeiture proceeding of *inter alia* child pornography. Section 164.1 provides for *in rem* proceedings for shutting down child pornography and other sites on a computer system. Section 164.3 provides a procedure for relief from a forfeiture order made under this section. An order made under this section falls within the definition of "sentence" for the purpose of appeal under Parts XXI and XXVII.

SYNOPSIS

This section sets out the procedure, following conviction of a child pornography offence under s. 163.1, the intimate image offence under s. 162.1, the child luring offence under s. 172.1 and the offence under s. 172.2 of making an arrangement to commit certain sexual offences by means of telecomminiction, for forfeiture of anything, other than real property, used in the commission of the offence. The court that convicts the person may make the forfeiture order if satisfied, on a balance of probabilities, that the thing was used in commission of the offence and is the property of the convicted person, or of a person to whom the property was transferred to avoid forfeiture. The court shall cause notice to be given to any person with an interest in the thing and may declare the nature and extent of the person's interest. A person to whom notice was given may appeal to the Court of Appeal, as may the Attorney General.

RELIEF FROM FORFEITURE / Hearing of application / Notice to Attorney General / Order / Appeal to court of appeal / Powers of Attorney General.

164.3 (1) Within thirty days after an order under subsection 164.2(1) is made, a person who claims an interest in the thing forfeited may apply in writing to a judge for an order under subsection (4).

(2) The judge shall fix a day — not less than thirty days after the application is made — for its hearing.

(3) At least fifteen days before the hearing, the applicant shall cause notice of the application and of the hearing day to be served on the Attorney General.

(4) The judge may make an order declaring that the applicant's interest in the thing is not affected by the forfeiture and declaring the nature and extent of the interest if the judge is satisfied that the applicant

(*a*) was not a party to the offence; and

(*b*) did not acquire the thing from a person who was a party to the offence under circumstances that give rise to a reasonable inference that it was transferred for the purpose of avoiding forfeiture.

(5) A person referred to in subsection (4) or the Attorney General may appeal to the court of appeal against an order made under that subsection. Part XXI applies, with any modifications that the circumstances require, with respect to the procedure for an appeal under this subsection.

(6) On application by a person who obtained an order under subsection (4), made after the expiration of the time allowed for an appeal against the order and, if an appeal is taken, after it has been finally disposed of, the Attorney General shall direct that

(*a*) the thing be returned to the person; or

(*b*) an amount equal to the value of the extent of the person's interest, as declared in the order, be paid to the person. 2002, c. 13, s. 7.

CROSS-REFERENCES

"Attorney General" is defined in s. 164.2. Section 164 provides for *in rem* forfeiture proceeding of *inter alia* child pornography. Section 164.1 provides for *in rem* proceedings for shutting down child pornography sites on a computer system.

SYNOPSIS

This section provides the procedure for a person claiming an interest in things forfeited under s. 164.2 to obtain an order declaring that the person's interest is not affected by the forfeiture order. Under subsec. (4) the order will be made if the judge is satisfied that the applicant was not a party to the offence under s. 163.1 and did not acquire the thing from a person who was a party to the offence under circumstances giving rise to a reasonable inference that it was transferred to the applicant for the purpose of avoiding forfeiture. Both the applicant and the Attorney General may appeal to the court of appeal in accordance with Part XXI.

TIED SALE.

165. Every one commits an offence who refuses to sell or supply to any other person copies of any publication for the reason only that the other person refuses to purchase or acquire from him copies of any other publication that the other person is apprehensive may be obscene or a crime comic. R.S., c. C-34, s. 161.

CROSS-REFERENCES

The definitions of obscenity and crime comic are in s. 163. The punishment for this offence is set out in s. 169. Where the prosecution elects to proceed by indictment on this offence then the accused may elect his mode of trial pursuant to s. 536(2). Where the prosecution elects to proceed by way of summary conviction then the trial of this offence is conducted by a summary conviction court pursuant to Part XXVII. The punishment for the offence is then as set out in s. 787 [although, note the maximum fine for a corporation is determined by s. 735] and the limitation period is set out in s. 786(2). In either case, release pending trial is determined by s. 515, although the accused is eligible for release by a peace officer under s. 496, 497 or by the officer in charge under s. 498.

SYNOPSIS

This section prohibits tying the sale or supply of a publication to the purchase or acquisition of any other publication under particular circumstances.

The key to the section is that the seller/supplier refuses to provide another publication to the person based *solely* on the refusal of the would-be recipient to also purchase or receive a publication which that person is *apprehensive may be either obscene or a crime comic*.

166. [*Repealed, 1994, c. 44, s. 9.*]

IMMORAL THEATRICAL PERFORMANCE / Person taking part.

167. (1) Every one commits an offence who, being the lessee, manager, agent or person in charge of a theatre, presents or gives or allows to be presented or given therein an immoral, indecent or obscene performance, entertainment or representation.

(2) Every one commits an offence who takes part or appears as an actor, a performer or an assistant in any capacity, in an immoral, indecent or obscene performance, entertainment or representation in a theatre. R.S., c. C-34, s. 163.

CROSS-REFERENCES

The term "theatre" is defined in s. 150. The definition of obscenity is in s. 163(8). In addition to the obscenity offences in s. 163, related offences are: s. 173, wilfully doing an indecent act; s. 174, public nudity; s. 175(1)(*b*), exposing an indecent exhibition.

The punishment for this offence is set out in s. 169. Where the prosecution elects to proceed by indictment on this offence then the accused may elect his mode of trial pursuant to s. 536(2). Where the prosecution elects to proceed by way of summary conviction then the trial of this offence is conducted by a summary conviction court pursuant to Part XXVII. The punishment for the offence is then as set out in s. 787 [although, note the maximum fine for a corporation is determined by s. 735] and the limitation period is set out in s. 786(2). In either case, release pending trial is determined by s. 515, although the accused is eligible for release by a peace officer under s. 496, 497 or by the officer in charge under s. 498.

SYNOPSIS

Section 167 makes it an offence to either take part in an *immoral, indecent or obscene performance,* or to permit such a performance in a theatre.

Section 167(1) prohibits the lessee, manager, agent, or person in charge of the theatre, to give any of the forms of permission or acquiescence listed in the subsection for such a performance. Section 167(2) creates liability for those performing or assisting in such a performance. The determination of what is immoral, indecent or obscene is to be made with reference to Canadian contemporary community standards.

ANNOTATIONS

Relationship to public nudity offence – The fact that Parliament has made it an offence to be nude in a public place under s. 174 is irrelevant to a charge under this section. A performance is not rendered "immoral" solely because it is performed in the nude: *R. v. Johnson*, [1975] 2 S.C.R. 160, 13 C.C.C. (2d) 402 (6:3).

Application of obscenity definition – The definition of "obscenity" in s. 163(8) applies to a charge under this section of presenting an obscene entertainment where the entertainment is a movie and thus a "publication" within the meaning of s. 163(8): *R. v. Towne Cinema Theatres Ltd.*, [1985] 1 S.C.R. 494, 18 C.C.C. (3d) 193 (7:0).

So-called "lap dancing" constitutes an indecent performance within the meaning of this section. A performance is indecent if the social harm engendered by the performance, having reference to the circumstances in which it took place, is such that the community would not tolerate it taking place. While the tolerance basis of the community standards test is the same in indecency cases as in obscenity cases, indecency requires an assessment of the surrounding circumstances in applying the community standards test. What the community will tolerate will vary with the placed in which the acts take place and the composition of the audience. The social harm to be considered is the attitudinal harm on those watching the performance as perceived by the community as a whole. In this case, the conduct was harmful in many ways because it de-humanized women and publicly portrayed them n a servile and humiliating manner. Furthermore, it predisposes persons to act in an anti-social manner as if the treatment of women in this way was socially acceptable and normal conduct: *R. v. Mara*, [1997] 2 S.C.R. 630, 115 C.C.C. (3d) 539.

This is a full *mens rea* offence and thus to prove that the accused owner or manager allowed the indecent performance the Crown must prove either concerted acquiescence or wilful blindness. If the owner delegates responsibility in bad faith in an attempt to gain protection from the law rather than ensure compliance with the law, then in certain circumstances this would amount to wilful blindness: *R. v. Mara, supra.*

Charter Considerations – Sexual activity involving physical contact between performers and patrons and between performers is not a form of expression but rather physical activity not intended to convey meaning and consequently, s. 2(*b*) of the Charter is not engaged. Even if such activity could be characterized as a form of expression, the provision is saved by s. 1 of the Charter: *R. v. Ludacka* (1996), 105 C.C.C. (3d) 565 (Ont. C.A.).

MAILING OBSCENE MATTER / Exceptions.

168. (1) Every one commits an offence who makes use of the mails for the purpose of transmitting or delivering anything that is obscene, indecent, immoral or scurrilous.

(2) Subsection (1) does not apply to a person who

    (*a*) **prints or publishes any matter for use in connection with any judicial proceedings or communicates it to persons who are concerned in the proceedings;**

    (*b*) **prints or publishes a notice or report under the direction of a court; or**

    (*c*) **prints or publishes any matter**

        (i) **in a volume or part of a genuine series of law reports that does not form part of any other publication and consists solely of reports of proceedings in courts of law, or**

        (ii) **in a publication of a technical character that is intended, in good faith, for circulation among members of the legal or medical profession. R.S., c. C-34, s. 164; 1999, c. 5, s. 2.**

CROSS-REFERENCES

The punishment for this offence is set out in s. 169. Where the prosecution elects to proceed by indictment on this offence then the accused may elect his mode of trial pursuant to s. 536(2). Where the prosecution elects to proceed by way of summary conviction then the trial of this offence is conducted by a summary conviction court pursuant to Part XXVII. The punishment for the offence is then as set out in s. 787 [although, note the maximum fine for a corporation is determined by s. 735(1)(*b*)] and the limitation period is set out in s. 786(2). In either case, release pending trial is determined by s. 515, although the accused is eligible for release by a peace officer under s. 496, 497 or by the officer in charge under s. 498. With respect to territorial jurisdiction of a mail in the course of the door-to-door delivery of the mail, see s. 476(*e*). As to definition of "mail", see s. 2 of the *Canada Post Corporation Act*, R.S.C. 1985, c. C-10.

SYNOPSIS

This section makes it an offence to *use the mails* to transmit, or deliver anything that is *obscene, scurrilous, immoral or indecent*. The accused must intend to use the mail for this purpose.

ANNOTATIONS

A private letter intended only for the recipient may fall under this section: *R. v. Lambert* (1965), 47 C.R. 12, 53 W.W.R. 186 (B.C.S.C.).

Where the matter involved is a magazine or newspaper, it is not necessary that the entire publication is found to be indecent, immoral or scurrilous. As with other offences under this Part the determination of what is immoral or indecent is judged by an objective standard, namely the community standard of tolerance of indecency or immorality. Evidence of such standards while sometimes helpful is not required: *R. v. Popert* (1981), 58 C.C.C. (2d) 505 (Ont. C.A.), affg 51 C.C.C. (2d) 485 *sub nom. R. v. Pink Triangle Press* (Ont. Co. Ct.).

PUNISHMENT.

169. Every one who commits an offence under section 163, 165, 167 or 168 is guilty of
- **(a) an indictable offence and liable to imprisonment for a term not exceeding two years; or**
- **(b) an offence punishable on summary conviction. R.S., c. C-34, s. 165; 1999, c. 5, s. 3.**

CROSS-REFERENCES

Where the prosecution elects to proceed by indictment on the offences set out in this section then the accused may elect his mode of trial pursuant to s. 536(2). Where the prosecution elects to proceed by way of summary conviction then the trial of the offence is conducted by a summary conviction court pursuant to Part XXVII. The punishment for the offence is then as set out in s. 787 [although, note the maximum fine for a corporation is determined by s. 735(1)(b)] and the limitation period is set out in s. 786(2). In either case, release pending trial is determined by s. 515, although the accused is eligible for release by a peace officer under s. 496, 497 or by the officer in charge under s. 498.

PARENT OR GUARDIAN PROCURING SEXUAL ACTIVITY.

170. Every parent or guardian of a person under the age of 18 years who procures the person for the purpose of engaging in any sexual activity prohibited by this Act with a person other than the parent or guardian is guilty of an indictable offence and liable to imprisonment for a term of not more than 14 years and to a minimum punishment of imprisonment for a term of one year. R.S.C. 1985, c. 19 (3rd Supp.), s. 5; 2005, c. 32, s. 9.1; 2008, c. 6, s. 54(f); 2012, c. 1, s. 19; 2015, c. 23, s. 8.

CROSS-REFERENCES

The term "guardian" is defined in s. 150. "Procures" is part of the definition of "counsels" in s. 22(3). Age is determined by reference to s. 30 of the *Interpretation Act*, R.S.C. 1985, c. I-21. The defence of mistake as to age is set out in s. 150.1(5). Section 658 provides means of proving the age of a child or young person. Sexual activity prohibited by this Act would refer to, *inter alia*, the offences in ss. 151 to 153, 155, 159, 160, the various forms of sexual assault in ss. 217 to 273 and may also refer to the prostitution offences in ss. 210 to 213. Where the accused is found guilty of this offence in respect of a person who is under 16 years of age, the court has the discretion to impose an order of prohibition under s. 161 prohibiting the accused from attending certain public areas and facilities or taking certain employment which will bring him into contact with persons under 16 years of age or using a computer system for the purpose of communicating with a person under the age of 16 years. Section 171.1 makes it an offence to transmit, make available, distribute or sell sexually explicit material to a person who is, or who the accused believes is under the age of 18 years for purpose of facilitating the commission of the offence created by this section. Section 172.1 makes it an offence to communicate by means of telecommunication with a person who is or who the accused believes is under the age of 18 years for the purpose of facilitating the commission of the offence under this section. Section 172.2 makes it an offence to agree with a person or make an arrangement with a person by means of telecommunication to commit an offence under this section with a person who is or who the accused believes is under the age of 18 years.

The accused has an election as to mode of trial pursuant to s. 536(2). Release pending trial is determined by s. 515, although the accused is eligible for release by the officer in charge under s. 498.

Special evidentiary and procedural provisions: see cross-references under s. 150.1.

As to cases concerning admissibility of evidence in child abuse cases, see notes under s. 150.1.

Section 718.01 provides that, in imposing a sentence for an offence involving the abuse of a person under the age of 18 years, the court shall give primary consideration to the objectives of denunciation and deterrence. Further, under s. 718.2, evidence that the offender, in committing the offence, abused a person under the age of 18 years is an aggravating circumstance.

The offence in this section is a primary designated offence for the purpose of making a forensic DNA data bank order under s. 487.051. Under s. 490.012, on application by the prosecutor, where an offender is convicted of this offence, the judge shall make an order requiring the offender to comply with the *Sex Offender Information Registration Act*, S.C. 2004, c. 10.

SYNOPSIS

This section creates an indictable offence for every parent or guardian of a person under the age of 18 to procure that person for the purpose of engaging in any sexual activity prohibited by the Code with a person other than the parent or guardian. The maximum sentence is 14 years and the minimum punishment is one year imprisonment. Thus, a conditional sentence is not available for this offence.

HOUSEHOLDER PERMITTING PROHIBITED SEXUAL ACTIVITY.

171. Every owner, occupier or manager of premises, or any other person who has control of premises or assists in the management or control of premises, who knowingly permits a person under the age of 18 years to resort to or to be in or on the premises for the purpose of engaging in any sexual activity prohibited by this Act is guilty of an indictable offence and liable to imprisonment for a term of not more than 14 years and to a minimum punishment of imprisonment for a term of one year. R.S.C. 1985, c. 19 (3rd Supp.), s. 5; 2005, c. 32, s. 9.1; 2008, c. 6, s. 54(g); 2012, c. 1, s. 20; 2015, c. 23, s. 9.

CROSS-REFERENCES

Age is determined by reference to s. 30 of the *Interpretation Act*, R.S.C. 1985, c. I-21. Section 658 provides means of proving the age of a child or young person. The defence of mistake as to age is set out in s. 150.1(5). Sexual activity prohibited by this Act would refer to, *inter alia*, the offences in ss. 151 to 153, 155, 159, 160, the various forms of sexual assault in ss. 217 to 273 and presumably the prostitution offences in ss. 210 to 213. Where the accused is found guilty of this offence in respect of a person who is under 16 years of age, the court has the discretion to impose an order of prohibition under s. 161 prohibiting the accused from attending certain public areas and facilities or taking certain employment which will bring him into contact with persons under 16 years of age or using a computer system for the purpose of communicating with a person under the age of 16 years. Section 171.1 makes it an offence to transmit, make available, distribute or sell sexually explicit material to a person who is, or who the accused believes is under the age of 18 years for purpose of facilitating the commission of the offence created by this section. Section 172.1 makes it an offence to communicate by means of telecommunication with a person who is or who the accused believes is under the age of 18 years for the purpose of facilitating the commission of the offence under this section. Section 172.2 makes it an offence to agree with a person or make an arrangement with a person by means of telecommunication to commit an offence under this section with a person who is or who the accused believes is under the age of 18 years.

The accused has an election as to mode of trial pursuant to s. 536(2). Release pending trial is determined by s. 515, although the accused is eligible for release by the officer in charge under s. 498.

Special evidentiary and procedural provisions: see cross-references under s. 150.1.

As to cases concerning admissibility of evidence in child abuse cases, see notes under s. 150.1.

Section 718.01 provides that, in imposing a sentence for an offence involving the abuse of a person under the age of 18 years, the court shall give primary consideration to the objectives of denunciation and deterrence. Further, under s. 718.2, evidence that the offender, in committing the offence, abused a person under the age of 18 years is an aggravating circumstance.

SYNOPSIS

This section is aimed at a householder who permits the premises to be used for sexual activities involving persons under the age of 18.

The class of accused is described as the owner, occupier, manager or other person with control over the premises, or a person who assists in its management and control. It is an indictable offence for an accused who comes within one of these categories of persons to knowingly permit a person under 18 to be in, or to resort to, the relevant premises for the purpose of engaging in any sexual act prohibited by the Act. The maximum sentence is 14 years and the minimum punishment is one year imprisonment.

MAKING SEXUALLY EXPLICIT MATERIAL AVAILABLE TO CHILD / Punishment / Presumption / No defence / Definition of "sexually explicit material".

171.1 (1) Every person commits an offence who transmits, makes available, distributes or sells sexually explicit material to

- (*a*) **a person who is, or who the accused believes is, under the age of 18 years, for the purpose of facilitating the commission of an offence with respect to that person under subsection 153(1), section 155, 163.1, 170, 171 or 279.011 or subsection 279.02(2), 279.03(2), 286.1(2), 286.2(2) or 286.3(2);**
- (*b*) **a person who is, or who the accused believes is, under the age of 16 years, for the purpose of facilitating the commission of an offence under section 151 or 152, subsection 160(3) or 173(2) or section 271, 272, 273 or 280 with respect to that person; or**
- (*c*) **a person who is, or who the accused believes is, under the age of 14 years, for the purpose of facilitating the commission of an offence under section 281 with respect to that person.**

(2) Every person who commits an offence under subsection (1)

- (*a*) **is guilty of an indictable offence and is liable to imprisonment for a term of not more than 14 years and to a minimum punishment of imprisonment for a term of six months; or**
- (*b*) **is guilty of an offence punishable on summary conviction and is liable to imprisonment for a term of not more than two years less a day and to a minimum punishment of imprisonment for a term of 90 days.**

(3) Evidence that the person referred to in paragraph (1)(*a*), (*b*) or (*c*) was represented to the accused as being under the age of 18, 16 or 14 years, as the case may be, is, in the absence of evidence to the contrary, proof that the accused believed that the person was under that age.

(4) It is not a defence to a charge under paragraph (1)(*a*), (*b*) or (*c*) that the accused believed that the person referred to in that paragraph was at least 18, 16 or 14 years of age, as the case may be, unless the accused took reasonable steps to ascertain the age of the person.

(5) In subsection (1), "sexually explicit material" means material that is not child pornography, as defined in subsection 163.1(1), and that is

- (*a*) **a photographic, film, video or other visual representation, whether or not it was made by electronic or mechanical means,**

CR. CODE

> (i) that shows a person who is engaged in or is depicted as engaged in explicit sexual activity, or
>
> (ii) the dominant characteristic of which is the depiction, for a sexual purpose, of a person's genital organs or anal region or, if the person is female, her breasts;
>
> (*b*) written material whose dominant characteristic is the description, for a sexual purpose, of explicit sexual activity with a person; or
>
> (*c*) an audio recording whose dominant characteristic is the description, presentation or representation, for a sexual purpose, of explicit sexual activity with a person. 2012, c. 1, s. 21; 2014, c. 25, s. 8; 2015, c. 23, s. 10.

CROSS-REFERENCES

Related offences are offences in relation to child pornography, s. 163.1, child luring in s. 172.1 and making an arrangement by means of telecommunication to commit various child sexual offences. For further references, see Cross-References under s. 172.1.

SYNOPSIS

This section creates the hybrid offence of transmitting, making available, distributing or selling sexually explicit material for the purpose of facilitating the commission of the various sexual offences involving children. The offence is punishable by 14 years' imprisonment and a minimum punishment of six months where the Crown proceeds by indictment and by two years less a day imprisonment and a minimum punishment of 90 days where the Crown proceeds by way of summary conviction. Subsection (3) creates a rebuttable presumption that the accused believed that the person was under the age of 18, 16 or 14 years as the case may be if the person was represented to the accused as being under that age. By virtue of subsec. (4), it is no defence that the accused believed that the person was under the age of 18, 16 or 14 years as the case may be, unless the accused took reasonable steps to ascertain the age of the person. Subsection (5) defines "sexually explicit material".

CORRUPTING CHILDREN / Limitation / Definition of "child" / Who may institute prosecutions.

172. (1) Every one who, in the home of a child, participates in adultery or sexual immorality or indulges in habitual drunkenness or any other form of vice, and thereby endangers the morals of the child or renders the home an unfit place for the child to be in, is guilty of an indictable offence and liable to imprisonment for a term not exceeding two years.

(2) [*Repealed*, R.S.C. 1985, c. 19 (3rd Supp.), s. 6.]

(3) For the purposes of this section, "child" means a person who is or appears to be under the age of eighteen years.

(4) No proceedings shall be commenced under subsection (1) without the consent of the Attorney General, unless they are instituted by or at the instance of a recognized society for the protection of children or by an officer of a juvenile court. R.S., c. C-34, s. 168; R.S.C. 1985, c. 19 (3rd Supp.), s. 6.

CROSS-REFERENCES

Attorney General is defined in s. 2. The term "officer of a juvenile court" is not defined and presumably referred to an officer of the "juvenile court" as defined in s. 2(1) of the former *Juvenile Delinquents Act*, R.S.C. 1970, c. J-3. This section was not amended when that Act was repealed and the former *Young Offenders Act* proclaimed. Nor was it amended when the *Young Offenders Act* was repealed and the *Youth Criminal Justice Act* proclaimed. Section 583(*h*) provides that a count in an indictment is not insufficient by reason only that it does not state that the required consent has been obtained. Section 658 provides means of proving the age of a child. The defence of mistake as to age is set out in s. 150.1(5).

The accused has an election as to mode of trial of the offence described in subsec. (1) pursuant to s. 536(2). Release pending trial is determined by s. 515, although the accused is eligible for release by the officer in charge under s. 498.

Special evidentiary and procedural provisions: see cross-references under s. 150.1.

As to cases concerning admissibility of evidence in child abuse cases, see notes under s. 150.1.

SYNOPSIS

This section makes it an indictable offence to indulge in behaviour, in a *child's home*, which corrupts children. Children are defined in s. 172(3) as being *under or apparently under* the age of *18*. The prohibited activities listed in the section are expansively defined by adultery, sexual immorality, habitual drunkenness, or *any other form of vice*. However, it must be shown that the *result* of this behaviour is to *endanger the morals* of a child or to make the house unfit for a child to live in. It does not appear to be necessary that the accused intend that the conduct indulged in will have this result, only that the accused intended to behave in the proscribed way and certain results flowed from those actions. Conviction for this offence makes the accused liable to imprisonment for two years.

Prosecution under this section may only be undertaken with the Attorney General's consent, unless the prosecution is by a recognized society for the protection of children (such as a Children's Aid Society) or by an officer of a juvenile court.

ANNOTATIONS

Although the offence of engaging in sexual immorality in the home of a child violates s. 2(*b*) of the Charter, it is a reasonable limit within the meaning of s. 1 and is therefore valid: *R. v. E. (B.)* (1999), 139 C.C.C. (3d) 100 (Ont. C.A.).

The offence of engaging in sexual immorality in the home of a child requires proof that the accused intentionally engaged in the prohibited conduct including knowledge or at least wilful blindness that the children were aware of the sexually immoral conduct. "Sexual immorality" requires an objective consideration of conduct by reference to community standards of tolerance that are tied directly to the harm caused or threatened by the conduct. "Participation" requires proof of some form of conduct. "Morals" refers to those core values that are central to the maintenance of a free and democratic society. The morals of a child will be endangered by sexual immorality where: (1) the sexual conduct presents a real risk that the child will not develop an understanding that exploitive or non-consensual sexual activity is wrong; (2) the conduct degrades or dehumanizes women such that the child will not develop an understanding that all persons are equal and worthy of respect regardless of gender; (3) the conduct imperils the child's understanding of parents' responsibilities to protect and nurture their children; and (4) to the extent that the conduct actively involves the child, it may endanger the child's morals by leaving him or her without a proper sense of his or her own self-worth or autonomy: *R. v. E.(B.), supra.*

LURING A CHILD / Punishment / Presumption re age / No defence.

172.1 (1) Every person commits an offence who, by a means of telecommunication, communicates with

    (*a*) a person who is, or who the accused believes is, under the age of 18 years, for the purpose of facilitating the commission of an offence with respect to that person under subsection 153(1), section 155, 163.1, 170, 171 or 279.011 or subsection 279.02(2), 279.03(2), 286.1(2), 286.2(2) or 286.3(2);

    (*b*) a person who is, or who the accused believes is, under the age of 16 years, for the purpose of facilitating the commission of an offence under section 151 or 152, subsection 160(3) or 173(2) or section 271, 272, 273 or 280 with respect to that person; or

(c) a person who is, or who the accused believes is, under the age of 14 years, for the purpose of facilitating the commission of an offence under section 281 with respect to that person.

(2) Every person who commits an offence under subsection (1)

(a) is guilty of an indictable offence and is liable to imprisonment for a term of not more than 14 years and to a minimum punishment of imprisonment for a term of one year; or

(b) is guilty of an offence punishable on summary conviction and is liable to imprisonment for a term of not more than two years less a day and to a minimum punishment of imprisonment for a term of six months.

(3) Evidence that the person referred to in paragraph (1)(a), (b) or (c) was represented to the accused as being under the age of eighteen years, sixteen years or fourteen years, as the case may be, is, in the absence of evidence to the contrary, proof that the accused believed that the person was under that age.

(4) It is not a defence to a charge under paragraph (1)(a), (b) or (c) that the accused believed that the person referred to in that paragraph was at least eighteen years of age, sixteen years or fourteen years of age, as the case may be, unless the accused took reasonable steps to ascertain the age of the person. 2002, c. 13, s. 8; 2007, c. 20, s. 1; 2008, c. 6, s. 14; 2012, c. 1, s. 22; 2014, c. 25, s. 9; 2015, c. 23, s. 11.

CROSS-REFERENCES

Section 164.1 provides for *in rem* proceedings for shutting down child pornography sites on a computer system. If the accused is found guilty of this offence in respect of a person who is under 16 years of age, the court may impose an order of prohibition under s. 161 prohibiting the accused from attending certain public areas and facilities or taking certain employment that will bring him into contact with persons under the age of 16 years. Section 164.2 allows the Attorney General to apply to the court that convicts the accused of this offence for an order that any thing, other than real property, be forfeited to the Crown, if the thing was used in the commission of the offence and the property is the property of the offender, or another person who was a party to the offence, or from a third party who acquired the thing under circumstances giving rise to a reasonable inference that it was transferred for the purpose of avoiding forfeiture. The term "telecommunication" is defined in s. 35 of the *Interpretation Act*. Related offences are offences in relation to child pornography, s. 163.1, making sexually explicit material available to children for the purpose of committing various child sexual offences under s. 171.1 and making an arrangement by means of telecommunication to commit various child sexual offences under s. 172.2.

Section 486(1) and (2) provide that the judge may make an order excluding all or any members of the public where such order is in the interest of public morals, the maintenance of order or the proper administration of justice or is necessary to prevent injury to international relations or national defence or national security. The proper administration of justice includes safeguarding the interests of witnesses under the age of 18 years. Section 486.1 sets out the circumstances in which the judge shall or may order a support person to be present and close to a witness while the witness testifies. Where the witness is under the age of 18 years or has a mental or physical disability, the order is to be made upon request unless the judge is of the opinion that the order would interfere with the proper administration of justice. In the case of other witnesses, the order is to be made if necessary to obtain a full and candid account from the witness of the matters complained of. The application for this order may be made during the proceedings or before they begin to the judge who is to preside at the proceedings.

Similarly, s. 486.2 sets out the circumstances in which the judge shall or may order a witness to testify outside the courtroom or behind a screen or other device that would not allow the witness to see the accused. Where the witness is under the age of 18 years or may have difficulty communicating the evidence by reason of a mental or physical disability, the judge shall make the order unless the judge is of the opinion that the order would interfere with the proper administration of justice. In all other cases, the order may be made if the judge is of the opinion that the order is necessary to obtain a full and candid account from the witness of the acts complained of. Similarly, s. 486.3 provides that, on application by the prosecutor or a witness under the age of 18 years, the accused shall not personally cross-examine the witness unless the judge is of the opinion that the proper administration of justice requires the accused to personally conduct the cross-examination. In other cases, the judge may make an order that the accused not personally cross-examine the witness if the judge is of the opinion that the order is necessary to obtain a full and candid account from the witness of the acts complained of. The judge will appoint counsel to conduct the cross-examination.

Under s. 486.4, the judge may make an order directing that the identity of a witness not be disclosed in any publication, broadcast or transmitted in any way. The order is mandatory where the complainant or a witness under the age of 18 years or the prosecutor applies for the order. Section 486.5 also gives the judge a discretion respecting non-publication orders in proceedings under these provisions in other circumstances.

The offence in this section is a primary designated offence for the purpose of making a forensic DNA data bank order under s. 487.051. Under s. 490.012, on application by the prosecutor, where an offender is convicted of this offence, the judge shall make an order requiring the offender to comply with the *Sex Offender Information Registration Act*, S.C. 2004, c. 10.

SYNOPSIS

This section creates the offence of using means of telecommunication to communicate with children for the purpose of facilitating the commission of certain sexual offences. Paragraphs (1)(*a*), (*b*) and (*c*) set out the various sexual offences depending on the age of the child. The offence is committed if the person was under the particular age specified or if the accused believed the person to be under that age. Subsection (3) sets up a rebuttable presumption that the accused believed the person was under the relevant age if there is evidence that the person was represented to the accused as being under that age. Under subsec. (4), it is no defence that the accused believed that the person was over the relevant age unless the accused took reasonable steps to ascertain the age of the person. The offence is punishable by 14 years' imprisonment and a minimum punishment of one year imprisonment where the Crown proceeds by indictment and by two years less a day imprisonment and a minimum punishment of six months where the Crown proceeds by way of summary conviction.

ANNOTATIONS

Subsection (1)(*c*) creates an inchoate offence requiring proof of: (i) an intentional communication by computer; (ii) with a person who the accused knows or believes to be under 14 years of age; (iii) for the specific purpose of facilitating the commission of a specified secondary offence with respect to the underage person. Intention must be determined subjectively. Sexually explicit comments may be sufficient to establish the criminal purpose of the accused but the content of the communication is not necessarily determinative. "Facilitating" includes helping to bring about and making easier or more probable. It is not necessarily sufficient for the impugned acts of the accused to be objectively capable of facilitating the commission of the specified secondary offence. The court must be satisfied beyond a reasonable doubt that the accused communicated by computer with an underage person for the purpose of facilitating the commission of a specified secondary offence. Given the drafting of the section, it is not helpful to characterize the essential elements of the offence as either part of the *actus reus* or the *mens rea*: R. v. Legare, [2009] 3 S.C.R. 551, 249 C.C.C. (3d) 129.

Where it has been communicated to the accused that the person with whom he or she is communicating is underage, the accused is presumed to have believed that the individual was underage. This is a rebuttable presumption by evidence to the contrary which must include evidence that the accused took steps to ascertain the real age of the other person. Objectively considered, the steps taken must be reasonable in the circumstances. The evidential burden is on the accused but the persuasive burden remains on the Crown. Such evidence will constitute both "evidence to the contrary" within the meaning of subsec. (3) and "reasonable steps" evidence under subsec. (4). Where the evidential burden of the accused has been discharged, he or she must be acquitted if the trier of fact is left with a reasonable doubt whether the accused in fact believed that his or her interlocutor was not underage: *R. v. Levigne*, [2010] 2 S.C.R. 3, 257 C.C.C. (3d) 1.

The offence in subsec. (1)(*c*) has three elements: (i) the accused must communicate by means of a computer; (ii) the communication must be with a person under 14 years of age or with a person who the accused believes is under the age of 14; and (iii) the accused's purpose in making the communication must be to facilitate the commission of one of the designated offences with the person with whom the communication is made. If the person to whom the communication is made is under 14, his or her age is a condition or circumstance that must be proven to complete the *actus reus*. If the person is over 14 but the accused believes that he or she is under the age of 14, the accused's belief is the circumstance or condition that the Crown must prove to establish the prohibited act. If the Crown proves the culpable *mens rea* existed, that is that the communication was for the purpose of the facilitation of the commission of a designated offence, the offence under this section is made out regardless of whether the designated crime is ever committed, attempted or is even factually possible. It is the belief that the person is under 14, not their actual age, that is relevant to the accused's purpose in engaging in the communication: *R. v. Alicandro* (2009), 246 C.C.C. (3d) 1 (Ont. C.A.), leave to appeal to S.C.C. refused [2010] 2 S.C.R. v, 255 C.C.C. (3d) vi.

Text messaging via cellular telephones satisfies the *actus reus* of communicating "by means of a computer system": *R. v. Woodward* (2011), 276 C.C.C. (3d) 86 (Ont. C.A.).

AGREEMENT OR ARRANGEMENT — SEXUAL OFFENCE AGAINST CHILD / Punishment / Presumption / No defence / No defence.

172.2 (1) Every person commits an offence who, by a means of telecommunication, agrees with a person, or makes an arrangement with a person, to commit an offence
  - (*a*) **under subsection 153(1), section 155, 163.1, 170, 171 or 279.011 or subsection 279.02(2), 279.03(2), 286.1(2), 286.2(2) or 286.3(2) with respect to another person who is, or who the accused believes is, under the age of 18 years;**
  - (*b*) **under section 151 or 152, subsection 160(3) or 173(2) or section 271, 272, 273 or 280 with respect to another person who is, or who the accused believes is, under the age of 16 years; or**
  - (*c*) **under section 281 with respect to another person who is, or who the accused believes is, under the age of 14 years.**

(2) Every person who commits an offence under subsection (1)
  - (*a*) **is guilty of an indictable offence and is liable to imprisonment for a term of not more than 14 years and to a minimum punishment of imprisonment for a term of one year; or**
  - (*b*) **is guilty of an offence punishable on summary conviction and is liable to imprisonment for a term of not more than two years less a day and to a minimum punishment of imprisonment for a term of six months.**

(3) Evidence that the person referred to in paragraph (1)(*a*), (*b*) or (*c*) was represented to the accused as being under the age of 18, 16 or 14 years, as the case may be, is, in the absence of evidence to the contrary, proof that the accused believed that the person was under that age.

(4) It is not a defence to a charge under paragraph (1)(*a*), (*b*) or (*c*) that the accused believed that the person referred to in that paragraph was at least 18, 16 or 14 years of age, as the case may be, unless the accused took reasonable steps to ascertain the age of the person.

(5) It is not a defence to a charge under paragraph (1)(*a*), (*b*) or (*c*)
  - (*a*) **that the person with whom the accused agreed or made an arrangement was a peace officer or a person acting under the direction of a peace officer; or**

(b) **that, if the person with whom the accused agreed or made an arrangement was a peace officer or a person acting under the direction of a peace officer, the person referred to in paragraph (1)(a), (b) or (c) did not exist. 2012, c. 1, s. 23; 2014, c. 25, s. 10; 2015, c. 23, s. 12.**

CROSS-REFERENCES
Related offences are offences in relation to child pornography, s. 163.1, making sexually explicit material available to children for the purpose of facilitating sexual offences in relation to children under s. 171.1, and child luring in s. 172.1 Section 164.2 provides that a court that convicts a person of an offence under this section may order that any thing, other than real property, be forfeited to the Crown if the court is satisfied that the thing was used in the commission of the offence and is the property of the offender, another person who was a party to the offence or a person who acquired the thing from such a person in circumstances giving rise to a reasonable inference that it was transferred to avoid a forfeiture order. This offence is a designated offence for the purposes of s. 752. For further Cross-References, see notes under s. 172.1.

SYNOPSIS
This section creates an offence of agreeing with a person or making an arrangement with a person by means of telecommunications to commit various sexual offences. Paragraphs (1)(a), (b) and (c) set out the various sexual offences depending on the age of the child. The offence is committed if the person was under the particular age specified or if the accused believed the person to be under that age. Subsection (3) sets up a rebuttable presumption that the accused believed the person was under the relevant age if there is evidence that the person was represented to the accused as being under that age. Under subsec. (4), it is no defence that the accused believed that the person was over the relevant age unless the accused took reasonable steps to ascertain the age of the person. It is also no defence that the person with whom the accused agreed or made the arrangement was a peace officer or someone acting under the direction of a peace officer or that the "victim" did not exist, if the person with whom the accused agreed or made an arrangement was a peace officer or acting under the direction of a peace officer. The offence is punishable by 14 years' imprisonment and a minimum punishment of one year imprisonment where the Crown proceeds by indictment and by two years less a day imprisonment and a minimum punishment of six months where the Crown proceeds by way of summary conviction.

Disorderly Conduct

INDECENT ACTS / Exposure.

173. (1) **Everyone who wilfully does an indecent act in a public place in the presence of one or more persons, or in any place with intent to insult or offend any person,**

    (a) **is guilty of an indictable offence and is liable to imprisonment for a term of not more than two years; or**

    (b) **is guilty of an offence punishable on summary conviction and is liable to imprisonment for a term of not more than six months.**

(2) **Every person who, in any place, for a sexual purpose, exposes his or her genital organs to a person who is under the age of 16 years**

    (a) **is guilty of an indictable offence and is liable to imprisonment for a term of not more than two years and to a minimum punishment of imprisonment for a term of 90 days; or**

    (b) **is guilty of an offence punishable on summary conviction and is liable to imprisonment for a term of not more than six months and to a minimum punishment of imprisonment for a term of 30 days. R.S., c. C-34, s. 169; R.S.C. 1985, c. 19 (3rd Supp.), s. 7; 2008, c. 6, s. 54(h); 2010, c. 17, s. 2; 2012, c. 1, s. 23.**

CROSS-REFERENCES

The term "public place" is defined in s. 150. Age is determined by reference to s. 30 of the *Interpretation Act*, R.S.C. c. I-21. Section 658 provides means of proving the age of a child or young person. The defence of mistake as to the age of the victim is set out in s. 150.1(4). A limited defence of consent to the subsec. (2) offence is set out in s. 150.1(2). Under s. 150.1(3) a young offender aged 12 or 13 years may not be tried for an offence under subsec. (2) unless he is in a position of trust or authority. A person convicted of the offence under subsec. (2), who is found to be loitering in or near a school ground, playground, public park or bathing area, is liable to be convicted of the vagrancy offence under s. 179. Section 171.1 makes it an offence to transmit, make available, distribute or sell sexually explicit material to a person who is, or who the accused believes is under the age of 16 years for purpose of facilitating the commission of the offence created by subsec. (2). Section 172.1 makes it an offence to communicate by means of telecommunication with a person who is or who the accused believes is under the age of 16 years for the purpose of facilitating the commission of the offence under subsec. (2). Section 172.2 makes it an offence to agree with a person or make an arrangement with a person by means of telecommunication to commit an offence under subsec. (2) with a person who is or who the accused believes is under the age of 16 years.

The trial of these offences is conducted by a summary conviction court pursuant to Part XXVII. The punishment for the offence is then as set out in s. 787 and the limitation period is set out in s. 786(2). Release pending trial is determined by s. 515, although the accused is eligible for release by a peace officer under s. 496, 497 or by the officer in charge under s. 498.

Special evidentiary and procedural provisions: see cross-references under s. 150.1.

SYNOPSIS

This section creates offences for doing indecent acts or exposing oneself in certain circumstances.

Section 173(1) creates the offence of committing an indecent act in two ways. The first way requires that the indecent act be done in a public place in the presence of one or more other persons. It has been held that, if the place is one in which the public could witness the acts complained of, then it is public for the purposes of this section. Alternatively, the offence may be committed by doing an indecent act with the intention of insulting or offending another person. There must be proof that the accused acted wilfully. The hybrid offence is punishable by indictment or summary conviction. The maximum punishment by indictment is two years and the maximum punishment by way of summary conviction is six months.

Section 173(2) makes it an offence to expose one's genitals to a person under the age of 16, wherever the act occurs if the accused does so for a sexual purpose. Where the Crown proceeds by indictment, the maximum punishment is two years and the minimum punishment is 90 days. If the Crown proceeds by way of summary conviction, the maximum punishment is six months and the minimum punishment is 30 days.

ANNOTATIONS

Proof of intent – A presumption of intent to do the indecent act wilfully arises where it is seen by another person: *R. v. Parsons*, [1963] 3 C.C.C. 92 (B.C.S.C.). Folld *R. v. Dalen* (1978), 44 C.C.C. (2d) 228 (Sask. Dist. Ct.).

In *R. v. Sloan* (1994), 89 C.C.C. (3d) 97, 30 C.R. (4th) 156 (Ont. C.A.), leave to appeal to S.C.C. refused 91 C.C.C. (3d) vi, 77 O.A.C. 399*n*, the members of the court disagreed as to the elements of the offence. Galligan J.A. was of the view that the gravamen of the offence is the wilful commission of an indecent act in the presence of one or more persons and where there was no intention on the part of the accused to perform a sexual act in the presence of any person other than her "client" the surreptitious surveillance by police cannot turn what is essentially an act done in private into one which takes place in public. Goodman J.A. held that it was not necessary to determine whether the term "wilfully" applies both to the doing of the act and to the requirement that the act be done in the presence of one or more persons since the motor vehicle in the cirumstances of this case was not a public place. The mere fact that a vehicle is parked in a lot to which the public has access is not in itself sufficient to make that vehicle a public place, considering that the vehicle was parked late at night at the edge of the lot considerable distance from any other vehicle and where the activity could only be discerned by someone looking into the vehicle from a short distance. Since the place in which the act was done in this case was a private place, subsec. (1)(a) did not apply. Osborne J.A. dissenting held that the Crown need only prove that the indecent act was done wilfully and since the act was done in a car parked in a public place the offence was made out.

In *R. v. Mailhot* (1996), 108 C.C.C. (3d) 376 (Que. C.A.), the court held that conviction under subsec. (1)(a) of this provision required proof that the accused (1) wilfully committed an indecent act and (2) wilfully committed the act in a public place in the presence of one or more persons, excluding those who participated in the activity. In this case, the accused lacked the necessary intent where he mistakenly believed that an undercover police officer who observed him masturbate would participate in the act if only by looking at him and by getting emotional or sexual satisfaction from it.

An accused who walked down the streets with her breasts uncovered did not commit an indecent act. An indecent act need not have sexual context and may relate to other objectionable behaviour. The test of indecency is the community standard of tolerance. In applying this test, the court must consider what harm will accrue from exposure to the allegedly obscene act or material. The greater the harm, the less that the community will tolerate others being exposed to it: *R. v. Jacob* (1996), 112 C.C.C. (3d) 1, 142 D.L.R. (4th) 411 (Ont. C.A.).

Public place – In *R. v. McEwen*, [1980] 4 W.W.R. 85 (Sask. Prov. Ct.), the court, distinguishing *R. v. Hutt*, [1978] 2 S.C.R. 476, 38 C.C.C. (2d) 418, held that an accused did an indecent act in a "public place" where he exposed his private parts to pedestrians at a crosswalk although he was inside his own car at the time. Similarly, *R. v. Figliuzzi* (1981), 59 C.C.C. (2d) 144, 21 C.R. (3d) 326 (Alta. Q.B.); *R. v. Wise* (1982), 67 C.C.C. (2d) 231, [1982] 4 W.W.R. 658 (B.C. Co. Ct.). Also see note on *R. v. Sloan, supra*.

"Public place" within the meaning of subsec. (1)(a) and as defined in s. 150 means a place to which one is invited or where one has a right to be as in entering, visiting or using that place. It does not include simply access by way of looking or listening in from the outside. Thus, the accused could not be convicted of the offence under subsec. (1)(a) where he performed the indecent act in the living room of his own private home, even if he could be observed by people outside the home: *R. v. Clark*, [2005] 1 S.C.R. 6, 193 C.C.C. (3d) 289.

Subsection (2) applies to images sent over the internet. The victim and the perpetrator need not be in the same physical place for an offence to be committed: *R. v. Alicandro* (2009), 246 C.C.C. (3d) 1 (Ont. C.A.), leave to appeal to S.C.C. refused [2010] 2 S.C.R. v, 255 C.C.C. (3d) vi.

The requirement in subsec. (1)(a) that the act be performed in the presence of one or more persons is not made out where the act is merely observed by an unmonitored video camera nor by the fact that there was another participant in the act: *R. v. Follett* (1994), 91 C.C.C. (3d) 435, 120 Nfld. & P.E.I.R. 230 (Nfld. S.C.), affd 98 C.C.C. (3d) 493 (Nfld. C.A.), leave to appeal to S.C.C. refused 101 C.C.C. (3d) vi, 42 C.R. (4th) 408n.

NUDITY / Nude / Consent of Attorney General.

174. (1) Every one who, without lawful excuse,
   (a) **is nude in a public place, or**
   (b) **is nude and exposed to public view while on private property, whether or not the property is his own,**
is guilty of an offence punishable on summary conviction.

(2) For the purposes of this section, a person is nude who is so clad as to offend against public decency or order.

CR. CODE

(3) No proceedings shall be commenced under this section without the consent of the Attorney General. R.S., c. C-34, s. 170.

CROSS-REFERENCES

The term "public place" is defined in s. 150. Attorney General is defined in s. 2. Section 583(*h*) provides that a count in an indictment is not insufficient by reason only that it does not state that the required consent has been obtained. Related offences are: s. 163(2)(*b*), publicly exhibiting an indecent show; s. 167, immoral theatrical performance; s. 173, wilfully doing an indecent act; s. 175(1)(*b*), exposing an indecent exhibition.

The trial of this offence is conducted by a summary conviction court pursuant to Part XXVII. The punishment for the offence is then as set out in s. 787 and the limitation period is set out in s. 786(2). Release pending trial is determined by s. 515, although the accused is eligible for release by a peace officer under s. 496, 497 or by the officer in charge under s. 498.

SYNOPSIS

This section prohibits nudity in a public place, or a place which is exposed to the public, even if the accused is on private property. The accused may rely upon a lawful excuse for the behaviour.

Section 174(2) expands the usual definition of nudity to include being clothed so as to offend against public decency or order. In the absence of any greater specificity as to what offends public decency the courts have resorted to the standard used for obscenity, namely, contemporary Canadian standards of tolerance.

By virtue of subsec. (3), no one may be prosecuted for this summary conviction offence unless the Attorney General consents.

ANNOTATIONS

Application of provision – Where the accused is completely naked in a public place without lawful excuse the offence under this section is committed whether or not the nudity offends against public decency or order. Subsection (2) covers the situation where the accused is partially clothed, by creating the legal fiction that such a person is "nude" when clad as to offend public decency or order, but this subsection does not import the requirement of proof of offence against public decency or order where the accused is totally naked: *R. v. Verrette*, [1978] 2 S.C.R. 838, 40 C.C.C. (2d) 273, 85 D.L.R. (3d) 1 (9:0).

Notwithstanding the provision in s. 167 of the Code for the separate offence of appearing in an immoral or indecent performance in a theatre, an accused may be charged under this section since "public place" includes a theatre: *R. v. McCutcheon* (1977), 40 C.C.C. (2d) 555, 1 C.R. (3d) 39 (Que. C.A.).

This offence is not aimed at conduct such as swimming nude at an isolated beach, even where the accused misjudges the loneliness of the beach: *R. v. Benolkin* (1977), 36 C.C.C. (2d) 206 (Sask. Q.B.).

The mere fact that a female dancer is nude does not mean that her performance cannot be legitimate entertainment and therefore constitute a lawful excuse. The trial judge must, however, make this factual assessment in each case and a finding by the trial judge that the accused's dancing offended against public decency and order does not determine the issue of lawful excuse: *R. v. Zikman* (1990), 56 C.C.C. (3d) 430, 37 O.A.C. 277 (C.A.).

Offending against public decency or order (subsec. (2)) – The requirement of offence against public decency or order in subsec. (2) applies where the accused is partially, albeit lightly, dressed as where she wears only a transparent veil since such person is not "nude" in the dictionary sense of wearing no clothes: *R. v. McCutcheon* (1977), 40 C.C.C. (2d) 555, 1 C.R. (3d) 39 (Que. C.A.). [Note: this case was decided before *R. v. Verrette, supra*, and portions of it must therefore be read subject to that case.]

Although the accused is partially clad so that subsec. (2) applies, the Crown need not adduce evidence as to what offends public decency. Rather, the trial judge may make the finding that the manner of dress did offend public decency without such evidence: *R. v. Sidey* (1980), 52 C.C.C. (2d) 257 (Ont. C.A.).

The test of public decency in subsec. (2) is one of the community standard of tolerance to and for the actions of the accused in the circumstances in which they occur: *R. v. Giambalvo* (1982), 70 C.C.C. (2d) 324, 39 O.R. (2d) 588 (C.A.).

Attorney General's consent (subsec. 3) – In exercising the power under subsec. (3) the Attorney General is under no duty that can be enforced by the courts to act fairly and is not required to afford the accused a hearing before deciding whether or not to consent to the prosecution: *R. v. Warren* (1981), 61 C.C.C. (2d) 65, 22 C.R. (3d) 58 (Ont. H.C.J.).

The consent required by subsec. (3) may be endorsed on the face of the information and if done in that manner need not recite particulars of the charge: *R. v. Willard* (1984), 15 C.C.C. (3d) 350 (Ont. H.C.J.).

CAUSING DISTURBANCE, INDECENT EXHIBITION, LOITERING, ETC. / Evidence of peace officer.

175. (1) Every one who
- **(a) not being in a dwelling-house, causes a disturbance in or near a public place,**
  - **(i) by fighting, screaming, shouting, swearing, singing or using insulting or obscene language,**
  - **(ii) by being drunk, or**
  - **(iii) by impeding or molesting other persons,**
- **(b) openly exposes or exhibits an indecent exhibition in a public place,**
- **(c) loiters in a public place and in any way obstructs persons who are in that place, or**
- **(d) disturbs the peace and quiet of the occupants of a dwelling-house by discharging firearms or by other disorderly conduct in a public place or who, not being an occupant of a dwelling-house comprised in a particular building or structure, disturbs the peace and quiet of the occupants of a dwelling-house comprised in the building or structure by discharging firearms or by other disorderly conduct in any part of a building or structure to which, at the time of such conduct, the occupants of two or more dwelling-houses comprised in the building or structure have access as of right or by invitation, express or implied,**

is guilty of an offence punishable on summary conviction.

(2) In the absence of other evidence, or by way of corroboration of other evidence, a summary conviction court may infer from the evidence of a peace officer relating to the conduct of a person or persons, whether ascertained or not, that a disturbance described in paragraph (1)(a) or (d) or an obstruction described in paragraph (1)(c) was caused or occurred. R.S., c. C-34, s. 171; 1972, c. 13, s. 11; 1974-75-76, c. 93, s. 9; 1997, c. 18, s. 6.

CROSS-REFERENCES

The terms "dwelling house" and "peace officer" are defined in s. 2, "public place" in s. 150. Section 84 contains a definition of "firearm" for Part III which, however, may be a useful reference for this section. Related offences are: ss. 63 to 69, offences in relation to unlawful and riotous assemblies; s. 163(2)(b), exhibiting an indecent show; s. 167, indecent theatrical performances; s. 173, wilfully doing indecent act; s. 174, public nudity; s. 179, vagrancy; s. 180, common nuisance. Sections 30 and 31 authorize the use of force to prevent a breach of the peace and arrest for breach of the peace. The offence of discharging a firearm with intent is in s. 244.

The trial of this offence is conducted by a summary conviction court pursuant to Part XXVII. The punishment for the offence is then as set out in s. 787 and the limitation period is set out in s. 786(2). Release pending trial is determined by s. 515, although the accused is eligible for release by a peace officer under s. 496, 497 or by the officer in charge under s. 498.

SYNOPSIS

This section creates summary conviction offences in relation to a variety of activities which cause a disturbance, including fighting, exposing an indecent exhibition, loitering and other public-nuisance activities.

Under s. 175(1)(*a*) it must be shown that the accused did one of the listed acts, that the accused was not in a dwelling-house and that the accused's acts resulted in a disturbance. The resulting disturbance must be at or near a public place. Paragraphs (*b*) and (*c*) contain straightforward prohibitions against certain types of actions in public. Paragraph (*d*) prohibits certain types of conduct which disrupt persons in a dwelling-house. First, liability may be shown by proving that the accused discharged a firearm, or engaged in other disorderly conduct in a public place which resulted in disturbing the peace and quiet of those occupying a dwelling-house. Second, liability may be shown by proving that the accused, who was not an occupant of the dwelling-house, disturbed the peace and quiet of those in the dwelling by discharging a firearm or engaging in other disorderly conduct within any part of the building or structure comprising the dwelling. An additional element for this second type of liability is the necessity to prove that the occupants of two or more units of the dwelling had a right or invitation to have access to that portion of the structure within which the accused created the disturbance. An example of the latter situation would be a disturbance created in the garage of an apartment building.

To facilitate the proof of these offences s. 175(2) permits the trial court to draw an inference, from the evidence of a peace officer who may testify as to the reactions of the members of the public who observed the accused's conduct, as proof that a disturbance did result from the accused's acts. Such evidence is permitted even if the peace officer did not know the identity of the members of the public whose reactions he observed.

ANNOTATIONS

Causing disturbance (subsec. (1)(*a*)) / Proof of disturbance – Subsection (1)(*a*)(i) requires proof of an externally manifested disturbance of the public peace, in the sense of interference with the ordinary or customary use of the premises by the public. There may be direct evidence of such an effect or interference, or it may be inferred by the evidence of a police officer as to the conduct of a person or persons under subsec. (2). The disturbance may consist of the impugned act itself, as in the case of a fight, interfering with the peaceful use of a barroom, or it may flow as a consequence of the impugned act, as where shouting and swearing produce a scuffle. An interference with the ordinary and customary conduct in or near the public place may consist of something as small as being distracted from one's work, but this interference must be present and must be externally manifested. The disturbance must be one which may reasonably have been foreseen in the particular circumstances of time and place: *R. v. Lohnes*, [1992] 1 S.C.R. 167, 69 C.C.C. (3d) 289.

Proof of disturbance requires that someone was affected or disturbed by the activity. Accordingly, where the accused engaged in a fight in a secluded laneway that was observed by his friends, there was no evidence of anyone being disturbed: *R. v. V.B. (J.G.)* (2002), 165 C.C.C. (3d) 494, 205 N.S.R. (2d) 391 *sub nom. R. v. B. (J.G.V.)* (C.A.).

One may be convicted of an attempt to cause a disturbance: *R. v. Kennedy* (1973), 11 C.C.C. (2d) 263, 21 C.R.N.S. 251 (Ont. C.A.).

"Swear" should be given its modern meaning of "to use bad or profane or obscene language" and is not limited to invoking the Deity or something sacred in condemnation of a person or object: *R. v. Clothier* (1975), 13 N.S.R. (2d) 141 (S.C. App. Div.) *Contra: R. v. Enns* (1968), 5 C.R.N.S. 115, 66 W.W.R. 318 (Sask. Dist. Ct.).

In *R. v. Berry* (1980), 56 C.C.C. (2d) 99 (Ont. C.A.), the court overruled *R. v. Goddard* (1971), 4 C.C.C. (2d) 396, [1971] 3 O.R. 517 (H.C.J.), and held that the offence under subsec. (1)(*a*)(iii) "by impeding" does not require proof of an affray, riot or unlawful assembly. The word "disturbance" is to be given its ordinary dictionary meaning.

It would seem that speaking normally into an electronic megaphone can constitute shouting within the meaning of para. (*a*)(i): *R. v. Reed* (1992), 76 C.C.C. (3d) 204 (B.C.C.A.).

A "public disturbance" requires more than a crowd observing — or even shouting anti-police sentiments at — police officers in the course of arrest. In order to satisfy the *actus reus* of causing a public disturbance by using obscene language, the offending language must *cause* an externally manifested disturbance: *R. v. Swinkels* (2010), 263 C.C.C. (3d) 49 (Ont. C.A.).

Exposing or exhibiting indecent exhibition (subsec. (1)(*b*)) – The words "openly" and "exhibits" in subsec. (1)(*b*) should be given meanings consistent with Parliament's intention in enacting the entire section, that is, to prevent acts which disturb the peace or interfere with the peaceful enjoyment of the street. Thus "openly" may be defined as "in an open manner without concealment so that all may see, hear or take cognizance in public" and "exhibit" may be defined as "to submit or to expose to view, to show, to display": *R. v. Bagu* (1981), 61 C.C.C. (2d) 355 (Ont. Prov. Ct.).

Loitering (subsec. (1)(*c*)) – The offence in subsec. (1)(*c*) is directed at a nuisance. To constitute the offence there must be evidence of obstruction in the sense of rendering impassable or difficult of passage. As well, the ordinary meaning of "loiter" is to hang idly about a place and does not embrace purposeful activity such as the conduct of a prostitute attempting to attract customers in circumstances falling short of soliciting as defined in s. 213: *R. v. Munroe* (1983), 5 C.C.C. (3d) 217, 34 C.R. (3d) 268 (Ont. C.A.). Similarly, *R. v. Gauvin* (1984), 11 C.C.C. (3d) 229 (Ont. C.A.), leave to appeal to S.C.C. refused November 13, 1984.

Meaning of "dwelling-house" – A beer parlour in a hotel is not part of a "dwelling-house" for the purposes of subsec. (1)(*a*). It is only those parts of the hotel kept or occupied as a residence which fall within the definition of dwelling-house in s. 2: *R. v. Garnot* (1979), 47 C.C.C. (2d) 355 (B.C.S.C.).

Although the patients' rooms in a hospital may constitute dwelling places, the television rooms and hallways to which the public have access are public places within the meaning of subsec. (1)(*a*): *R. v. Campbell* (1980), 22 C.R. (3d) 219 (Alta. Q.B.).

Constitutional considerations – The offence of causing a disturbance by swearing, although an infringement of freedom of expression under s. 2(*b*) of the Charter, is a reasonable limit on that freedom and the provision is therefore valid: *R. v. Lawrence* (1992), 74 C.C.C. (3d) 495, [1992] 5 W.W.R. 659 (Alta. Q.B.), affd without reference to the point 81 C.C.C. (3d) 159, 9 Alta. L.R. (3d) 347 (C.A.).

OBSTRUCTING OR VIOLENCE TO OR ARREST OF OFFICIATING CLERGYMAN / Disturbing religious worship or certain meetings / Idem.

176. (1) Every one who

(*a*) by threats or force, unlawfully obstructs or prevents or endeavours to obstruct or prevent a clergyman or minister from celebrating divine service or performing any other function in connection with his calling, or

(*b*) knowing that a clergyman or minister is about to perform, is on his way to perform or is returning from the performance of any of the duties or functions mentioned in paragraph (*a*)

(i) assaults or offers any violence to him, or

(ii) arrests him on a civil process, or under the pretence of executing a civil process,

is guilty of an indictable offence and liable to imprisonment for a term not exceeding two years.

(2) Every one who wilfully disturbs or interrupts an assemblage of persons met for religious worship or for a moral, social or benevolent purpose is guilty of an offence punishable on summary conviction.

(3) Every one who, at or near a meeting referred to in subsection (2), wilfully does anything that disturbs the order or solemnity of the meeting is guilty of an offence punishable on summary conviction. R.S., c. C-34, s. 172.

CROSS-REFERENCES
The accused has an election as to mode of trial of the offence described in subsec. (1) pursuant to s. 536(2). Release pending trial is determined by s. 515, although the accused is eligible for release by the officer in charge under s. 498. The trial of the offences in subsecs. (2) and (3) is conducted by a summary conviction court pursuant to Part XXVII. The punishment for the offence is then as set out in s. 787 and the limitation period is set out in s. 786(2). Release pending trial is determined by s. 515, although the accused is eligible for release by a peace officer under s. 496, 497 or by the officer in charge under s. 498.

SYNOPSIS
This section makes it an offence to interfere with religious services or worship and provides for punishment upon conviction for these offences.

Section 176(1) creates the indictable offence of obstructing or preventing *a clergyman* or minister from performing religious services or other religious functions. Subsection (1)(*a*) prohibits the use of *threats or force* to attempt to achieve this aim.

Section 176(1)(*b*) creates a similar offence. The elements consist of doing one of the acts listed in sub-para. (i) or (ii), together with proof that the accused intended to do the act alleged and that the accused *knew* that the clergyman or minister was on the way to or from, or was about to perform religious duties. The maximum sentence for this offence is two years' imprisonment.

Subsections (2) and (3) create summary conviction offences involving *intentional disruption of religious worship* or meetings assembled for one of the purposes stated in subsec. (2). To prove the offence, it must be shown that the accused *wilfully* did actions which were disruptive or which were productive of disorder or interruption, and not merely that the acts caused upset among the assembled.

ANNOTATIONS
Constitutional issues – This section does not violate the guarantee to freedom of speech and religion in s. 2 of the *Charter of Rights and Freedoms*: *R. v. Reed* (1983), 8 C.C.C. (3d) 153 (B.C. Co. Ct.), affd 10 C.C.C. (3d) 573 (C.A.), and *R. v. Reed* (1985), 19 C.C.C. (3d) 180 (B.C.C.A.). [It should be noted that while the question of the inconsistency of subsec. (3) with the guarantees to religious freedom in the *Bill of Rights* and the *Charter of Rights and Freedoms* was raised in *R. v. Skoke-Graham, infra*, the court having entered an acquittal on other grounds declined to deal with these issues.]

The offence created by subsec. (3) is *intra vires* Parliament being validly enacted under the criminal law power: *R. v. Skoke-Graham*, [1985] 1 S.C.R. 106, 17 C.C.C. (3d) 289 (6:0).

Subsection (2) – Where members of a congregation have assembled at the place of worship for Sunday service they have "met for religious worship" within the meaning of subsec. (2) although the service has not yet begun and an accused who at that time is using a loud hailer outside the place to condemn the beliefs of the worshippers may be convicted of the offence described in that subsection: *R. v. Reed, supra*.

Subsection (3) – The offence under subsec. (3) requires proof of some activity in the nature of a disorder. The conduct must either be disorderly in itself or productive of disorder. It is not sufficient that the accused's conduct produced annoyance, anxiety or emotional upset among the members of the assemblage meeting for religious worship, where the impugned acts, here kneeling to accept communion in violation of a diocesan directive, are brief, essentially passive and peaceful in nature and voluntarily desisted from upon request: *R. v. Skoke-Graham, supra*.

Two people are an assemblage of persons within the meaning of subsec. (2) and a meeting for the purpose of subsec. (3) occurs when people meet for religious worship and includes the period prior to the formal ceremony: *R. v. Reed* (1994), 91 C.C.C. (3d) 481, 24 C.R.R. (2d) 163 (B.C.C.A.), leave to appeal to S.C.C. refused 95 C.C.C. (3d) vi, 26 C.R.R. (2d) 188n.

While brief temporary annoyance would not be sufficient, the requisite element of "disturbs" is made out by deliberate continued annoyance constituting obstruction or partial obstruction of entrance to the place of worship: *R. v. Reed, supra*.

TRESPASSING AT NIGHT.

177. Every one who, without lawful excuse, the proof of which lies on him, loiters or prowls at night on the property of another person near a dwelling-house situated on that property is guilty of an offence punishable on summary conviction. R.S., c. C-34, s. 173.

CROSS-REFERENCES

The terms "dwelling-house" and "night" are defined in s. 2. While the term "property" is also defined in s. 2, the very broad definition in that provision appears unsuited to the context of this offence. Under s. 494(2), a property owner or person in lawful possession of property and anyone authorized by such person may arrest, without warrant, a person whom he finds committing a criminal offence on or in relation to that property. Reference should also be made to ss. 40 to 42 relating to use of force in defence of dwelling-house and other real property.

The trial of this offence is conducted by a summary conviction court pursuant to Part XXVII. The punishment for the offence is then as set out in s. 787 and the limitation period is set out in s. 786(2). Release pending trial is determined by s. 515, although the accused is eligible for release by a peace officer under s. 496, 497 or by the officer in charge under s. 498.

Section 162 creates the voyeurism offence.

SYNOPSIS

This section makes it a summary conviction offence to *loiter* or *prowl by night* near a dwelling house on another person's property. The accused may raise a lawful excuse but the burden of proving it is upon the accused. As with all sections which place a burden upon the accused, this aspect of the section is likely to attract scrutiny under the *Canadian Charter of Rights and Freedoms*.

ANNOTATIONS

This section creates two offences of prowling and loitering. The essence of loitering is the conduct of someone who is wandering about apparently without precise destination and is conduct which essentially has nothing reprehensible about it, if it does not take place on private property where the loiterer has no business. Prowling, on the other hand, involves some notion of evil. The prowler does not act without a purpose: *R. v. Cloutier* (1991), 66 C.C.C. (3d) 149 (Que. C.A.).

"Prowls" means to traverse stealthily in the sense of furtively, secretly, clandestinely or moving by imperceptible degrees. The Crown need not prove that the accused was looking for an opportunity to carry out an unlawful purpose. It is not a lawful excuse within the meaning of this section that the accused was trying to conceal himself following commission of a criminal offence: *R. v. Willis* (1987), 37 C.C.C. (3d) 184 (B.C. Co. Ct.).

The accused commits an offence under this section by intentionally loitering or prowling at night near a residence on another person's property unless the accused establishes a lawful excuse for his or her conduct. The Crown is not required to prove that the accused also had an intention to commit a specific evil act: *R. v. Priestap* (2006), 207 C.C.C. (3d) 490, 79 O.R. (3d) 561, 208 O.A.C. 351 (C.A.).

This section does not create an unconstitutional reverse onus provision inconsistent with the guarantee to the presumption of innocence in s. 11(*d*) of the *Canadian Charter of Rights and Freedoms*: *R. v. Tassou* (1984), 16 C.C.C. (3d) 567 (Alta. Prov. Ct.).

OFFENSIVE VOLATILE SUBSTANCE.

178. Every one other than a peace officer engaged in the discharge of his duty who has in his possession in a public place or who deposits, throws or injects or causes to be deposited, thrown or injected in, into or near any place,

    (*a*) **an offensive volatile substance that is likely to alarm, inconvenience, discommode or cause discomfort to any person or to cause damage to property, or**

    (*b*) **a stink or stench bomb or device from which any substance mentioned in paragraph (*a*) is or is capable of being liberated,**

is guilty of an offence punishable on summary conviction. R.S., c. C-34, s. 174.

CROSS-REFERENCES

The term "peace officer" is defined in s. 2, "public place" in s. 150 and possession is defined in s. 4(3).

The trial of this offence is conducted by a summary conviction court pursuant to Part XXVII. The punishment for the offence is then as set out in s. 787 and the limitation period is set out in s. 786(2). Release pending trial is determined by s. 515, although the accused is eligible for release by a peace officer under s. 496, 497 or by the officer in charge under s. 498.

The related offence of common nuisance is in s. 180.

SYNOPSIS

This section makes it a summary conviction offence to do certain things with an offensive *volatile substance or a stink* or stench *bomb*.

It prohibits the accused from having in his possession any of the items described in paras. (*a*) or (*b*), in a *public place*, or depositing, throwing or injecting such items into, or near, any place (or causing this to occur).

The section expressly exempts actions of a peace officer engaged in the discharge of his or her duties.

VAGRANCY / Punishment.

179. (1) Every one commits vagrancy who

    (*a*) **supports himself in whole or in part by gaming or crime and has no lawful profession or calling by which to maintain himself; or**

    (*b*) **having at any time been convicted of an offence under section 151, 152 or 153, subsection 160(3) or 173(2) or section 271, 272 or 273, or of an offence under a provision referred to in paragraph (*b*) of the definition "serious personal injury offence" in section 687 of the *Criminal Code*, chapter C-34 of the Revised Statutes of Canada, 1970, as it read before January 4, 1983, is found loitering in or near a school ground, playground, public park or bathing area.**

(2) Every one who commits vagrancy is guilty of an offence punishable on summary conviction. R.S., c. C-34, s. 175; 1972, c. 13, s. 12; 1984, c. 40, s. 20; R.S.C. 1985, c. 27 (1st Supp.), s. 22; c. 19 (3rd Supp.), s. 8.

CROSS-REFERENCES

"Gaming" is not defined in this section but presumably refers to the offences described by Part VII.

Section 687 of the *Criminal Code*, R.S.C. 1970, c. C-34, as it read prior to January 4, 1983 defined "serious personal injury offence" as follows:

> "(b) an offence mentioned in section 144 (rape) or 145 (attempted rape) or an offence or attempt to commit an offence mentioned in section 146 (sexual intercourse with a female under fourteen or between fourteen and sixteen), 149 (indecent assault on a female), 156 (indecent assault on a male) or 157 (gross indecency)"

Now also see s. 161 which makes it an offence to violate a prohibition order made against a sex offender.

The trial of this offence is conducted by a summary conviction court pursuant to Part XXVII. The punishment for the offence is then as set out in s. 787 and the limitation period is set out in s. 786(2). Release pending trial is determined by s. 515, although the accused is eligible for release by a peace officer under s. 496, 497 or by the officer in charge under s. 498.

Under s. 4(2) of the *Canada Evidence Act*, the spouse of an accused charged with this offence is a compellable witness at the instance of the prosecution. Section 16 of the Canada Evidence Act deals with the competency of witnesses under the age of 14 years.

SYNOPSIS

This section creates the summary conviction offence of *vagrancy*.

Section 179(1)(*a*) states that a person is guilty of vagrancy if that person has no visible, lawful means of support and the accused supports himself in part, or entirely, by gaming or crime.

Section 179(1)(*b*) states that a person is guilty of vagrancy if that person has been *convicted* of one of the offences specified in the paragraph and is found *loitering* in one of the listed *public places*. Loitering connotes hanging around for no valid purpose. It need not be shown that the accused had any particular intention beyond loitering in the prohibited location nor that the accused did any other act beyond being present.

ANNOTATIONS

Subsection (1)(*b*) of this section violates s. 7 of the Charter and is of no force and effect: *R. v. Heywood*, [1994] 3 S.C.R. 761, 94 C.C.C. (3d) 481, 34 C.R. (4th) 133.

Nuisances

COMMON NUISANCE / Definition.

180. (1) Every one who commits a common nuisance and thereby
    (*a*) endangers the lives, safety or health of the public, or
    (*b*) causes physical injury to any person,
is guilty of an indictable offence and liable to imprisonment for a term not exceeding two years.

(2) For the purposes of this section, every one commits a common nuisance who does an unlawful act or fails to discharge a legal duty and thereby
    (*a*) endangers the lives, safety, health, property or comfort of the public; or
    (*b*) obstructs the public in the exercise or enjoyment of any right that is common to all the subjects of Her Majesty in Canada. R.S., c. C-34, s. 176.

CROSS-REFERENCES

The accused has an election as to mode of trial pursuant to s. 536(2). Release pending trial is determined by s. 515, although the accused is eligible for release by the officer in charge under s. 498.

Related offences may be found in Part XI [wilful and forbidden act in relation to property]. Also note the intimidation offence in s. 423, explosive offences and duty in handling explosives in ss.

79 to 82, offences in relation to aircraft in ss. 76 to 78, sabotage in s. 52, careless handling of firearm in s. 86, duty to provide necessaries in s. 215 and duty of person undertaking dangerous acts in ss. 216, 217.

SYNOPSIS

The section creates the indictable offence of creating a *common nuisance*.

Subsection (2) sets out *what constitutes a common nuisance*. First, it must be proven that the accused either did an unlawful act or failed to discharge a legal duty. Secondly, it must be proven that the accused's act or omission resulted in one of the ill-effects described in s. 180(2)(a) or (b).

The offence created in subsec. (1) requires that, in addition to establishing proof that a *common nuisance* occurred, it must be shown that the nuisance *resulted in the harm* described in s. 180(1)(a) or (b). The maximum sentence for this offence is two years' imprisonment. As there is a substantial overlap between the two subsections, the "additional" elements set out in subsec. (1) may be satisfied by the same evidence that brought the accused within the definition of common nuisance under subsec. (2).

ANNOTATIONS

A common nuisance must be directed to the public generally and a conviction under this section cannot be supported where the acts were directed to three individuals: *R. v. Schula* (1956), 115 C.C.C. 382, 23 C.R. 403 (Alta. S.C. App. Div.).

Section 216 imposed a legal duty on the accused, who knew he was infected with the AIDS virus, to not donate blood to the Red Cross and breach of this duty may found a conviction under this section: *R. v. Thornton*, [1993] 2 S.C.R. 445, 82 C.C.C. (3d) 530, 21 C.R. (4th) 215 (9:0).

SPREADING FALSE NEWS.

181. Every one who wilfully publishes a statement, tale or news that he knows is false and that causes or is likely to cause injury or mischief to a public interest is guilty of an indictable offence and liable to imprisonment for a term not exceeding two years. R.S., c. C-34, s. 177.

ANNOTATIONS

This section violates the guarantee of freedom of expression under s. 2(b) of the Charter and is of no force and effect: *R. v. Zundel*, [1992] 2 S.C.R. 731, 75 C.C.C. (3d) 449, 16 C.R. (4th) 1.

DEAD BODY.

182. Every one who
  (a) neglects, without lawful excuse, to perform any duty that is imposed on him by law or that he undertakes with reference to the burial of a dead human body or human remains, or
  (b) improperly or indecently interferes with or offers any indignity to a dead human body or human remains, whether buried or not,
is guilty of an indictable offence and liable to imprisonment for a term not exceeding five years. R.S., c. C-34, s. 178.

CROSS-REFERENCES

The duty imposed by law, referred to in this section, presumably refers to provincial legislation which governs the burial of human remains.

The accused has an election as to mode of trial pursuant to s. 536(2). Release pending trial is determined by s. 515, although the accused is eligible for release by the officer in charge under s. 498.

A related offence is found in s. 243 which makes it an offence to dispose of the dead body of a child with intent to conceal the fact that its mother has been delivered of it.

SYNOPSIS

This rarely used section creates two indictable offences relating to the *neglect or improper interference with a dead body*. The first offence is *neglecting* to perform a *duty* imposed by law *or* which the accused agrees to undertake in connection with burying a dead person. The prosecution must prove that the accused did not have a *lawful excuse* for such neglect of the body.

The second offence is committed when an accused treats a dead body, buried or not, improperly, indecently or improperly interferes with it. Both offences under this section require proof that the accused knew that the body was dead. The maximum sentence is five years' imprisonment.

ANNOTATIONS

Paragraph (b) – Although it would be a defence to this charge if the accused did not know that the body was dead if on the facts as he believed them he was acting lawfully and innocently, such a defence is not open to an accused who believing the person is alive is attempting to have intercourse with the body because if, as he thought, the woman was alive he was raping her there being no suggestion he thought he had her consent to the act: *R. v. Ladue*, [1965] 4 C.C.C. 264, 45 C.R. 287 (Y.T.C.A.).

A physical interference with the human remains is not a necessary element of the offence under para. (b) and it applies to offering indignities to monuments that mark human remains because to offer indignities to such monuments is to offer indignities to the remains themselves: *R. v. Moyer*, [1994] 2 S.C.R. 899, 92 C.C.C. (3d) 1, 32 C.R. (4th) 232.

Part VI / INVASION OF PRIVACY

Definitions

DEFINITIONS / "authorization" / "electro-magnetic, acoustic, mechanical or other device" / "intercept" / "offence" / "police officer" / "private communication" / "public switched telephone network" / "radio-based telephone communication" / "sell" / "solicitor".

183. In this Part,

"authorization" means an authorization to intercept a private communication given under section 186 or subsection 184.2(3), 184.3(6) or 188(2);

"electro-magnetic, acoustic, mechanical or other device" means any device or apparatus that is used or is capable of being used to intercept a private communication, but does not include a hearing aid used to correct subnormal hearing of the user to not better than normal hearing;

"intercept" includes listen to, record or acquire a communication or acquire the substance, meaning or purport thereof;

"offence" means an offence contrary to, any conspiracy or attempt to commit or being an accessory after the fact in relation to an offence contrary to, or any counselling in relation to an offence contrary to

    (a) any of the following provisions of this Act, namely,

        (i) section 47 (high treason),

        (ii) section 51 (intimidating Parliament or a legislature),

        (iii) section 52 (sabotage),

      (iii.1) section 56.1 (identity documents),

(iv) section 57 (forgery, etc.),
(v) section 61 (sedition),
(vi) section 76 (hijacking),
(vii) section 77 (endangering safety of aircraft or airport),
(viii) section 78 (offensive weapons, etc., on aircraft),
(ix) section 78.1 (offences against maritime navigation or fixed platforms),
(x) section 80 (breach of duty),
(xi) section 81 (using explosives),
(xii) section 82 (possessing explosives),
(xii.01) section 82.3 (possession, etc., of nuclear material, radioactive material or device),
(xii.02) section 82.4 (use or alteration of nuclear material, radioactive material or device),
(xii.03) section 82.5 (commission of indictable offence to obtain nuclear material, etc.),
(xii.04) section 82.6 (threats),
(xii.1) section 83.02 (providing or collecting property for certain activities),
(xii.2) section 83.03 (providing, making available, etc., property or services for terrorist purposes),
(xii.3) section 83.04 (using or possessing property for terrorist purposes),
(xii.4) section 83.18 (participation in activity of terrorist group),
(xii.41) section 83.181 (leaving Canada to participate in activity of terrorist group),
(xii.5) section 83.19 (facilitating terrorist activity),
(xii.51) section 83.191 (leaving Canada to facilitate terrorist activity),
(xii.6) section 83.2 (commission of offence for terrorist group),
(xii.61) section 83.201 (leaving Canada to commit offence for terrorist group),
(xii.62) section 83.202 (leaving Canada to commit offence that is terrorist activity),
(xii.7) section 83.21 (instructing to carry out activity for terrorist group),
(xii.8) section 83.22 (instructing to carry out terrorist activity),
(xii.81) subsection 83.221(1) (advocating or promoting commission of terrorism offences),
(xii.9) section 83.23 (harbouring or concealing),
(xii.91) section 83.231 (hoax — terrorist activity),
(xiii) section 96 (possession of weapon obtained by commission of offence),
(xiii.1) section 98 (breaking and entering to steal firearm),
(xiii.2) section 98.1 (robbery to steal firearm),
(xiv) section 99 (weapons trafficking),
(xv) section 100 (possession for purpose of weapons trafficking),
(xvi) section 102 (making automatic firearm),
(xvii) section 103 (importing or exporting knowing it is unauthorized),
(xviii) section 104 (unauthorized importing or exporting),
(xix) section 119 (bribery, etc.),
(xx) section 120 (bribery, etc.),
(xxi) section 121 (fraud on government),
(xxii) section 122 (breach of trust),
(xxiii) section 123 (municipal corruption),
(xxiv) section 132 (perjury),
(xxv) section 139 (obstructing justice),
(xxvi) section 144 (prison breach),
(xxvii) subsection 145(1) (escape, etc.),
(xxvii.1) section 162 (voyeurism),
(xxvii.2) section 162.1 (intimate image),
(xxviii) paragraph 163(1)(a) (obscene materials),
(xxix) section 163.1 (child pornography),

(xxix.1) section 170 (parent or guardian procuring sexual activity),
(xxix.2) section 171 (householder permitting sexual activity),
(xxix.3) section 171.1 (making sexually explicit material available to child),
(xxix.4) section 172.1 (luring a child),
(xxix.5) section 172.2 (agreement or arrangement — sexual offence against child),
(xxx) section 184 (unlawful interception),
(xxxi) section 191 (possession of intercepting device),
(xxxii) subsection 201(1) (keeping gaming or betting house),
(xxxiii) paragraph 202(1)(e) (pool-selling, etc.),
(xxxiv) subsection 210(1) (keeping common bawdy house),
(xxxv) [*Repealed*, 2014, c. 25, s. 11(1).]
(xxxvi) [*Repealed*, 2014, c. 25, s. 11(1).]
(xxxvii) [*Repealed*, 2014, c. 25, s. 11(1).]
(xxxviii) [*Repealed*, 2014, c. 25, s. 11(1).]
(xxxix) section 235 (murder),
(xxxix.1) section 244 (discharging firearm with intent),
(xxxix.2) section 244.2 (discharging firearm — recklessness),
(xl) section 264.1 (uttering threats),
(xli) section 267 (assault with a weapon or causing bodily harm),
(xlii) section 268 (aggravated assault),
(xliii) section 269 (unlawfully causing bodily harm),
(xliii.1) section 270.01 (assaulting peace officer with weapon or causing bodily harm),
(xliii.2) section 270.02 (aggravated assault of peace officer),
(xliv) section 271 (sexual assault),
(xlv) section 272 (sexual assault with a weapon, threats to a third party or causing bodily harm),
(xlvi) section 273 (aggravated sexual assault),
(xlvii) section 279 (kidnapping),
(xlvii.1) section 279.01 (trafficking in persons),
(xlvii.11) section 279.011 (trafficking of a person under the age of eighteen years),
(xlvii.2) section 279.02 (material benefit),
(xlvii.3) section 279.03 (withholding or destroying documents),
(xlviii) section 279.1 (hostage taking),
(xlix) section 280 (abduction of person under sixteen),
(l) section 281 (abduction of person under fourteen),
(li) section 282 (abduction in contravention of custody order),
(lii) section 283 (abduction),
(lii.1) 286.1 (obtaining sexual services for consideration),
(lii.2) 286.2 (material benefit from sexual services),
(lii.3) 286.3 (procuring),
(lii.4) 286.4 (advertising sexual services),
(liii) section 318 (advocating genocide),
(liv) section 327 (possession of device to obtain telecommunication facility or service),
(liv.1) section 333.1 (motor vehicle theft),
(lv) section 334 (theft),
(lvi) section 342 (theft, forgery, etc., of credit card),
(lvi.1) section 342.01 (instruments for copying credit card data or forging or falsifying credit cards),
(lvii) section 342.1 (unauthorized use of computer),
(lviii) section 342.2 (possession of device to obtain unauthorized use of computer system or to commit mischief),
(lix) section 344 (robbery),

(lx)   section 346 (extortion),
(lxi)   section 347 (criminal interest rate),
(lxii)   section 348 (breaking and entering),
(lxii.1)   section 353.1 (tampering with vehicle identification number),
(lxiii)   section 354 (possession of property obtained by crime),
(lxiii.1)   section 355.2 (trafficking in property obtained by crime),
(lxiii.2)   section 355.4 (possession of property obtained by crime — trafficking),
(lxiv)   section 356 (theft from mail),
(lxv)   section 367 (forgery),
(lxvi)   section 368 (use, trafficking or possession of forged document),
(lxvi.1)   section 368.1 (forgery instruments),
(lxvii)   section 372 (false information),
(lxviii)   section 380 (fraud),
(lxix)   section 381 (using mails to defraud),
(lxx)   section 382 (fraudulent manipulation of stock exchange transactions),
(lxx.1)   subsection 402.2(1) (identity theft),
(lxx.2)   subsection 402.2(2) (trafficking in identity information),
(lxx.3)   section 403 (identity fraud),
(lxxi)   section 423.1 (intimidation of justice system participant or journalist),
(lxxii)   section 424 (threat to commit offences against internationally protected person),
(lxxii.1)   section 424.1 (threat against United Nations or associated personnel),
(lxxiii)   section 426 (secret commissions),
(lxxiv)   section 430 (mischief),
(lxxv)   section 431 (attack on premises, residence or transport of internationally protected person),
(lxxv.1)   section 431.1 (attack on premises, accommodation or transport of United Nations or associated personnel),
(lxxv.2)   subsection 431.2(2) (explosive or other lethal device),
(lxxvi)   section 433 (arson),
(lxxvii)   section 434 (arson),
(lxxviii)   section 434.1 (arson),
(lxxix)   section 435 (arson for fraudulent purpose),
(lxxx)   section 449 (making counterfeit money),
(lxxxi)   section 450 (possession, etc., of counterfeit money),
(lxxxii)   section 452 (uttering, etc., counterfeit money),
(lxxxiii)   section 462.31 (laundering proceeds of crime),
(lxxxiv)   subsection 462.33(11) (acting in contravention of restraint order),
(lxxxv)   section 467.11 (participation in criminal organization),
(lxxxv.1)   section 467.111 (recruitment of members — criminal organization),
(lxxxvi)   section 467.12 (commission of offence for criminal organization), or
(lxxxvii)   section 467.13 (instructing commission of offence for criminal organization),
(*b*)   section 198 (fraudulent bankruptcy) of the *Bankruptcy and Insolvency Act,*
(*b*.1)   any of the following provisions of the *Biological and Toxin Weapons Convention Implementation Act,* namely,
(i)   section 6 (production, etc., of biological agents and means of delivery), or
(ii)   section 7 (unauthorized production, etc., of biological agents),
(*c*)   any of the following provisions of the *Competition Act,* namely,
(i)   section 45 (conspiracies, agreements or arrangements between competitors),
(ii)   section 47 (bid-rigging), or
(iii)   subsection 52.1(3) (deceptive telemarketing),

    (*d*) any of the following provisions of the *Controlled Drugs and Substances Act*, namely,

        (i) section 5 (trafficking),

       (ii) section 6 (importing and exporting), or

     (iii) section 7 (production),

  (*d*.1) section 42 (offences related to infringement of copyright) of the *Copyright Act*,

    (*e*) section 3 (bribing a foreign public official) of the *Corruption of Foreign Public Officials Act*,

  (*e*.1) the *Crimes Against Humanity and War Crimes Act*,

    (*f*) either of the following provisions of the *Customs Act*, namely,

        (i) section 153 (false statements), or

       (ii) section 159 (smuggling),

    (*g*) any of the following provisions of the *Excise Act, 2001*, namely,

        (i) section 214 (unlawful production, sale, etc., of tobacco or alcohol),

       (ii) section 216 (unlawful possession of tobacco product),

     (iii) section 218 (unlawful possession, sale, etc., of alcohol),

    (iv) section 219 (falsifying or destroying records),

     (v) section 230 (possession of property obtained by excise offences), or

    (vi) section 231 (laundering proceeds of excise offences),

    (*h*) any of the following provisions of the *Export and Import Permits Act*, namely,

        (i) section 13 (export or attempt to export),

       (ii) section 14 (import or attempt to import),

     (iii) section 15 (diversion, etc.),

    (iv) section 16 (no transfer of permits),

     (v) section 17 (false information), or

    (vi) section 18 (aiding and abetting),

    (*i*) any of the following provisions of the *Immigration and Refugee Protection Act*, namely,

        (i) section 117 (organizing entry into Canada),

       (ii) section 118 (trafficking in persons),

     (iii) section 119 (disembarking persons at sea),

    (iv) section 122 (offences related to documents),

     (v) section 126 (counselling misrepresentation), or

    (vi) section 129 (offences relating to officers),

    (*j*) any offence under the *Security of Information Act*, or

    (*k*) section 51.01 (offences related to goods, labels, packaging or services) of the *Trademarks Act*,

and includes any other offence that there are reasonable grounds to believe is a criminal organization offence or any other offence that there are reasonable grounds to believe is an offence described in paragraph (*b*) or (*c*) of the definition "terrorism offence" in section 2;

Note: Definition "offence" amended by 2001, c. 27, s. 245 (to come into force by order of the Governor in Council; however, repealed before coming into force, 2004, c. 15, s. 110).

"police officer" means any officer, constable or other person employed for the preservation and maintenance of the public peace;

"private communication" means any oral communication, or any telecommunication, that is made by an originator who is in Canada or is intended by the originator to be received by a person who is in Canada and that is made under circumstances in which it is reasonable for the originator to expect that it will not be intercepted by any person other than the person intended by the originator to receive it, and includes any radio-based telephone communication that is treated electronically or otherwise for the purpose of preventing intelligible reception by any person other than the person intended by the originator to receive it;

"**public switched telephone network**" means a telecommunication facility the primary purpose of which is to provide a land line-based telephone service to the public for compensation;

"**radio-based telephone communication**" means any radiocommunication within the meaning of the *Radiocommunication Act* that is made over apparatus that is used primarily for connection to a public switched telephone network;

"**sell**" includes offer for sale, expose for sale, have in possession for sale or distribute or advertise for sale;

"**solicitor**" means, in the Province of Quebec, an advocate or notary and, in any other province, a barrister or solicitor. 1973-74, c. 50, s. 2; 1976-77, c. 53, s. 7; 1980-81-82-83, c. 125, s. 10; 1984, c. 21, s. 76; 1985, c. 27 (1st Supp.), ss. 7(2)(*a*), 23; R.S.C. 1985, c. 1 (2nd Supp.), s. 213; R.S.C. 1985, c. 1 (4th Supp.), s. 13; c. 29 (4th Supp.), s. 17; c. 42 (4th Supp.), s. 1; 1991, c. 28, s. 12; 1992, c. 27, s. 90; 1993, c. 7, s. 5; 1993, c. 25, s. 94; 1993, c. 40, s. 1; 1993, c. 46, s. 4; 1995, c. 39, s. 140; 1996, c. 19, s. 66; 1997, c. 18, s. 7; 1997, c. 23, s. 3; 1998, c. 34, s. 8; 1999, c. 2, s. 47; c. 5, s. 4; 2000, c. 24, s. 43; 2001, c. 32, s. 4; 2001, c. 41, ss. 5, 31, 133(2) and (5); 2002, c. 22, s. 409(2)(*b*); 2004, c. 15, s. 108; 2005, c. 32, s. 10; 2005, c. 43, s. 1; 2008, c. 6, s. 15; 2009, c. 22, s. 4; 2009, c. 28, s. 3; 2010, c. 3, s. 1; 2010, c. 17, s. 2; 2012, c. 1, s. 24; 2013, c. 8, s. 2; 2013, c. 9, s. 14; 2013, c. 13, s. 7; 2014, c. 17, s. 2; 2014, c. 25, s. 11; 2014, c. 31, s. 7; 2014, c. 32, s. 59; 2015, c. 20, s. 19.

CROSS-REFERENCES

In addition to the definitions in this section, see s. 2 and notes to that section. The term "telecommunication" is defined in s. 35 of the *Interpretation Act*, R.S.C. c. I-21, as "any transmission, emission or reception of signs, signals, writing, images or sounds or intelligence of any nature by wire, radio, visual or other electromagnetic system". "Radio" is also defined in s. 35. Note that s. 3 provides that a description in parenthesis after a section number is inserted for convenience of reference only and is no part of the provision.

Related offences may be found in s. 326, theft of telecommunication service and s. 327, unlawful possession of device to obtain telecommunication facility.

This Part is just one aspect of a more or less comprehensive scheme for regulating surreptitious use of electronic devices by agents of the state. Also see s. 487.01 which provides for a general warrant which would cover surreptitious electronic surveillance, s. 492.1 which regulates the use of tracking devices and s. 492.2 which regulates the use of telephone number recorders. In addition, provision is made in s. 487.02 for the making of an assistance order to require persons to co-operate in the carrying out of orders made under this Part.

The interception of private communications by the state constitutes a search or seizure for the purposes of s. 8 of the *Charter of Rights and Freedoms* and, therefore, in addition to the notes in this Part, see notes under s. 8 of the Charter.

At the time this Part was enacted, certain amendments to other federal statutes were made, in particular to the *Crown Liability and Proceedings Act*, R.S.C. 1985, c. C-50. Reference should also be made to the *Canadian Security Intelligence Service Act*, R.S.C. 1985, c. C-23, which provides authority for authorizations in national security matters.

SYNOPSIS

This section provides definitions which are used throughout Part VI of the *Criminal Code* dealing with intercepted private communications. The definition of "offence" contained in this section is pivotal because the offences contained in this list are the only offences which may form the basis of an application for an authorization to intercept private communications and a warrant for video surveillance under s. 487.01(5).

ANNOTATIONS

"Intercept" *[Also see notes under s. 189(1), "Intercepted".]* – Surreptitious electronic surveillance constitutes a search or seizure within the meaning of s. 8 of the *Charter of Rights and Freedoms*: *R. v. Duarte*, [1990] 1 S.C.R. 30, 53 C.C.C. (3d) 1.

The term "intercept", at least as used in s. 189, which deals with the admissibility of evidence, must be interpreted in context and in accordance with its primary dictionary meaning as an interference between the place of origination and the place of destination of the communication. Thus, there is no interception where the originator was simply mistaken as to the identity of the person to whom he was talking: *R. v. McQueen* (1975), 25 C.C.C. (2d) 262 (Alta. S.C.); *R. v. Singh* (1998), 127 C.C.C. (3d) 429 (B.C.C.A.).

This part has no application to a communication which is merely overheard by a third party without the use of any mechanical or other device: *R. v. Beckner* (1978), 43 C.C.C. (2d) 356 (Ont. C.A.). *Contra*: *R. v. Boutilier and Melnick* (1976), 35 C.C.C. (2d) 555, 77 D.L.R. (3d) 291 (N.S.S.C.).

"Private communication" – For the purposes of this definition the "originator" of the private communication is the person who makes the remarks or series of remarks which the Crown seeks to adduce in evidence. Thus, if a person with a reasonable expectation of privacy, speaking in an electronically intercepted conversation, makes statements which the Crown seeks to use against him he has the protection of this Part: *R. v. Goldman*, [1980] 1 S.C.R. 976, 51 C.C.C. (2d) 1 (8:1).

An obscene or threatening phone call is a private communication even where it is that call which forms the substance of the charge: *R. v. Dunn* (1975), 28 C.C.C. (2d) 538, 33 C.R.N.S. 299 (N.S. Co. Ct.).

A telephone call to a police switchboard in which the accused threatened the life of a member of that force is not a private communication. It would not be reasonable to expect that such a communication would not be listened to or recorded by a person other than the switchboard operator: *R. v. Monachan* (1981), 60 C.C.C. (2d) 286, 22 C.R. (3d) (Ont. C.A.), affd [1985] 1 S.C.R. 176, 16 C.C.C. (3d) 576 (7:0).

To a similar effect is *R. v. Lubovac* (1989), 52 C.C.C. (3d) 551 (Alta. C.A.), where it was held that pager messages were not private communications, since the pager simply broadcast a message to those who may happen to hear or overhear it. It was also held that retrieval, by the police, of messages left by the accused's accomplice at a computer message centre was not a violation of s. 8 of the Charter. The police had obtained a number from an informer which enabled them to retrieve any messages which had been left by the accomplice. The informer had, in turn, been given the number from the accomplice. The accomplice had no reasonable expectation that his messages would be sent out or received in confidence. Also see *R. v. Nin* (1985), 34 C.C.C. (3d) 89 (Que. Ct. Sess.).

However, it was held in *R. v. Solomon* (1996), 110 C.C.C. (3d) 354, 139 D.L.R. (4th) 625 (Que. C.A.), affd [1997] 3 S.C.R. 696, 118 C.C.C. (3d) 351, that even assuming that a conversation made from a cellular telephone is not a "private communication" within the meaning of this section, there is an expectation of privacy in the use of a cellular phone and therefore s. 8 of the Charter is violated unless the interceptions are authorized.

It was held in *R. v. Cheung* (1995), 100 C.C.C. (3d) 441 (B.C.S.C.), that, at least in 1990, conversations over a cellular telephone were private communications. While a person sending or receiving a call on a cellular telephone did face some risk of being overheard by someone who just happened to meet the combination of factors which matched a scanner to a call, the chance of someone, who set out to intercept the calls of a particular individual by scanner, to succeed in that venture was very small.

Use of a dial number recorder does not involve interception of a private communication. Communication in this section contemplates an exchange of information between persons: *R. v. Fegan* (1993), 80 C.C.C. (3d) 356, 21 C.R. (4th) 65 (Ont. C.A.). *Contra*: *R. v. Kutsak* (1993), 108 Sask. R. 241 (Q.B.). [Note that a warrant may now be obtained to install a dial number recorder pursuant to s. 492.2.]

CONSENT TO INTERCEPTION.

183.1 Where a private communication is originated by more than one person or is intended by the originator thereof to be received by more than one person, a consent to the interception thereof by any one of those persons is sufficient consent for the purposes of any provision of this Part. 1993, c. 40, s. 2.

CROSS-REFERENCES

Consent to interception is relevant to s. 184 which creates the offence of interception of private communications and ss. 184.1 and 184.2 which authorize interception of private communications where one of the parties consents to the interception.

Interception of Communications

INTERCEPTION / Saving provision / Use or retention.

184. (1) Every one who, by means of any electro-magnetic, acoustic, mechanical or other device, wilfully intercepts a private communication is guilty of an indictable offence and liable to imprisonment for a term not exceeding five years.

(2) Subsection (1) does not apply to

    (*a*) a person who has the consent to intercept, express or implied, of the originator of the private communication or of the person intended by the originator thereof to receive it;

    (*b*) a person who intercepts a private communication in accordance with an authorization or pursuant to section 184.4 or any person who in good faith aids in any way another person who the aiding person believes on reasonable grounds is acting with an authorization or pursuant to section 184.4;

    (*c*) a person engaged in providing a telephone, telegraph or other communication service to the public who intercepts a private communication,

        (i) if the interception is necessary for the purpose of providing the service,

        (ii) in the course of service observing or random monitoring necessary for the purpose of mechanical or service quality control checks, or

        (iii) if the interception is necessary to protect the person's rights or property directly related to providing the service;

    (*d*) an officer or servant of Her Majesty in right of Canada who engages in radio frequency spectrum management, in respect of a private communication intercepted by that officer or servant for the purpose of identifying, isolating or preventing an unauthorized or interfering use of a frequency or of a transmission; or

    (*e*) a person, or any person acting on their behalf, in possession or control of a computer system, as defined in subsection 342.1(2), who intercepts a private communication originating from, directed to or transmitting through that computer system, if the interception is reasonably necessary for

        (i) managing the quality of service of the computer system as it relates to performance factors such as the responsiveness and capacity of the system as well as the integrity and availability of the system and data, or

        (ii) protecting the computer system against any act that would be an offence under subsection 342.1(1) or 430(1.1).

(3) A private communication intercepted by a person referred to in paragraph (2)(*e*) can be used or retained only if

    (*a*) it is essential to identify, isolate or prevent harm to the computer system; or

    (*b*) it is to be disclosed in circumstances referred to in subsection 193(2). 1973-74, c. 50, s. 2; 1993, c. 40, s. 3; 2004, c. 12, s. 4.

CROSS-REFERENCES

The terms "electro-magnetic, acoustic, mechanical or other device", "intercept", "private communication" and "authorization" are defined in s. 183. The term "radio" is defined in s. 35 of the *Interpretation Act*, R.S.C. c. I-21. The term "wilfully" does not have a fixed meaning and must take its meaning from the context. Generally, however, it connotes an intention to bring about a proscribed consequence. See *R. v. Buzzanga and Durocher* (1979), 49 C.C.C. (2d) 369 (Ont. C.A.).

Consent to interception is given an expanded meaning in s. 183.1.

This provision is fundamental to the scheme enacted by this Part. It makes unlawful the interception of private communications by the devices defined in s. 183, subject to certain narrow exceptions in subsec. (2). Those exceptions are interceptions pursuant to a normal "60-day" authorization obtained under s. 186, interceptions under the emergency "36-hour" authorization obtained under s. 188, unauthorized interceptions in exceptional circumstances as set out in s. 184.4 and consent interceptions. The other exceptions listed essentially concern interceptions incidental to the providing of the telephone service. An important incentive to compliance with the law, in addition to the penalties under this section, is that if the interception is not lawfully made by agents of the state then it is probably a violation of s. 8 of the Charter and therefore subject to exclusion under s. 24(2) of the Charter.

Separate offences have been created for interception of cellular telephone communications under ss. 184.5 and 193.1.

It is an offence under s. 191 to unlawfully have possession of any device designed primarily for the surreptitious interception of private communications. Under s. 193, it is an offence to unlawfully disclose an intercepted private communication.

Pursuant to s. 192, any device, by means of which the offence under this section was committed, may be ordered forfeited. As well, pursuant to s. 194, the court that convicts the accused of the offence under this section may make an order for punitive damages. The offence in this section can itself be the basis for an authorization to intercept private communications, by virtue of the definition of "offence" in s. 183. Under s. 195(3), the annual reports of the Solicitor General and Attorneys General are to set out the number of prosecutions under this section of officers or servants of the Crown.

The accused has an election as to mode of trial pursuant to s. 536(2) and release pending trial is determined by s. 515, although the accused is eligible for release by the officer in charge under s. 498.

SYNOPSIS

This section makes it an *offence*, subject to a number of exceptions, *to intercept private communications by means of a specified device*, and provides for punishment upon conviction for this offence.

Subsection (1) creates the *indictable offence of unlawful interception*. The *device* used to intercept the private communication must be one listed in this section, as elaborated in the definition of such devices found in s. 183. The communication must be *private*, and this term is also defined in s. 183. The communication, must be *intercepted*, a defined term in s. 183. The act of the accused must be done *wilfully*, but no specific purpose beyond the interception need be shown. A person convicted under this subsection is liable to imprisonment for five years.

Subsection (2) provides a number of *exceptions to subsec. (1)*. Subsection (2)(*a*) states that subsec. (1) does not apply if one obtains the *consent* of either the *originator or the intended recipient* of the communication. The consent may be explicit or implied.

Section 184(2)(*b*) creates an exception to liability under subsec. (1) if the communication was intercepted *in accordance with an authorization* or pursuant to s. 184.4. It also exempts a person acting in good faith who assists another in the interception in any way, if that person believes, on reasonable grounds, that the person doing the interception is acting in accordance with an authorization.

Section 184(2)(*c*) and (*d*) permit certain types of interceptions required to provide or maintain the *service*, or quality control of a communication service or which are otherwise necessarily incidental to managing radio frequencies, if the interception is made by one of the specified categories of worker.

Subsection (2)(*e*) permits interceptions through a computer system by persons in control of a computer system if the interception is necessary to manage the quality of service of the system or to protect the system from unauthorized use as described in s. 342.1(1) or interfering with the use of the system as described in s. 430(1.1). However, subsec. (3) places limits on the use or retention of the intercepted communication.

ANNOTATIONS

Subsection (2)(*a*) – The consent contemplated by this section is one which is voluntary in the sense that it is free from coercion and made knowingly in that the consentor must be aware of what he is doing and aware of the significance of his act and the use which the police may be able to make of the consent. However, the test employed in determining the admissibility of a confession made by an accused to a person in authority has no application. If the consent which the person gives is the one he intended and given as a result of his own decision and not under external coercion the fact that his motives for so doing are selfish and even reprehensible will not vitiate it. Coercion in this context means the use of intimidating conduct or force or threats of force by the police, but coercion does not arise merely because the consent is given as a result of promised or expected leniency or immunity from prosecution: *R. v. Goldman*, [1980] 1 S.C.R. 976, 51 C.C.C. (2d) 1 (8:1).

A consent given by a police informer is valid and renders the interception lawful notwithstanding that the informer testifies at trial that he expected to be paid for his co-operation: *R. v. Playford* (1984), 17 C.C.C. (3d) 454 (Ont. H.C.J.), revd on other grounds 40 C.C.C. (3d) 142, 61 C.R. (3d) 101 (Ont. C.A.).

The Charter does not apply, where the interception was made by Bell Canada on its own in an attempt to identify the person who was using its services to make obscene and harassing telephone calls to its subscribers. Bell Canada was not an agent of the state: *R. v. Fegan* (1993), 80 C.C.C. (3d) 356, 21 C.R. (4th) 65 (Ont. C.A.).

An accused has standing to raise the violation of s. 8 of the *Charter of Rights and Freedoms* by reason of a consent interception between an alleged co-conspirator and an undercover police officer. The accused was entitled to have the evidence of this communication excluded pursuant to s. 24(2) of the Charter if to admit the evidence would bring the administration of justice into disrepute: *R. v. Montoute* (1991), 62 C.C.C. (3d) 481, 113 A.R. 95 (C.A.).

In using a dial number recorder, Bell Canada was not intercepting a "private communication". In any event, such conduct undertaken in an attempt to identify a person making obscene and harassing telephone calls, was lawful within the meaning of this paragraph, Bell Canada being the intended recipient of the signal caused by the originator in dialing a particular telephone number: *R. v. Fegan, supra. Contra: R. v. Kutsak* (1993), 108 Sask. R. 241 (Q.B.). [**Note:** An authorization to use a dial number recorder may now be obtained under s. 492.2.]

Subsection (2)(*c*) – In using a dial number recorder, Bell Canada was not intercepting a "private communication". In any event, such conduct, undertaken in an attempt to identify a person making obscene and harassing telephone calls, was lawful within the meaning of this paragraph, being necessary to protect the person's rights or property directly related to providing the telephone service within the meaning of subpara. (iii). The term "person" can refer to both the subscribers and Bell Canada: *R. v. Fegan, supra. Contra: R. v. Kutsak, supra.*

INTERCEPTION TO PREVENT BODILY HARM / Admissibility of intercepted communication / Destruction of recordings and transcripts / Definition of "agent of the state".

184.1 (1) An agent of the state may intercept, by means of any electro-magnetic, acoustic, mechanical or other device, a private communication if

(*a*) either the originator of the private communication or the person intended by the originator to receive it has consented to the interception;

(*b*) the agent of the state believes on reasonable grounds that there is a risk of bodily harm to the person who consented to the interception; and

(*c*) the purpose of the interception is to prevent the bodily harm.

(2) The contents of a private communication that is obtained from an interception pursuant to subsection (1) are inadmissible as evidence except for the purpose of proceedings in which actual, attempted or threatened bodily harm is alleged, including proceedings in respect of an application for an authorization under this Part or in respect of a search warrant or a warrant for the arrest of any person.

(3) The agent of the state who intercepts a private communication pursuant to subsection (1) shall, as soon as is practicable in the circumstances, destroy any recording of the private communication that is obtained from an interception pursuant to subsection (1), any full or partial transcript of the recording and any notes made by that agent of the private communication if nothing in that private communication suggests that bodily harm, attempted bodily harm or threatened bodily harm has occurred or is likely to occur.

(4) For the purposes of this section, "agent of the state" means

(*a*) a peace officer; and

(*b*) a person acting under the authority of, or in cooperation with, a peace officer. **1993, c. 40, s. 4.**

CROSS-REFERENCES

Consent to interception is given an expanded meaning in s. 183.1. Although "bodily harm" is not defined in this Part, reference might be made to the definition in s. 267. The terms "electro-magnetic, acoustic, mechanical or other device", "intercept", "private communication" are defined in s. 183. The term "peace officer" is defined in s. 2.

Since the interception under this section is made with consent of one of the parties, no offence is committed under s. 184. The purpose of this section is to make lawful, interceptions by agents of the state even though the interception is made without court authorization. Since the exception is relatively narrowly drawn, the expectation would be that the evidence would not be rendered inadmissible by ss. 8 and 24(2) of the Charter. In normal circumstances, the police would be required to obtain an authorization under s. 184.2. In the limited circumstances where evidence which was obtained under this section is sought to be admitted at a trial, the Crown must comply with the provisions of s. 189. Section 188.2 provides protection against civil or criminal liability for a person acting under this section.

SYNOPSIS

This section permits interception of private communications by agents of the state [defined in subsec. (2)], although there is no court authorization. The section is narrowly focused and applies only where a party to the communication consents to the interception, the agent of the state believes on reasonable grounds that there is a risk of bodily harm to the person who consented, and the purpose of the interception is to prevent bodily harm. Thus, unlike the normal authorization provisions such as s. 186, the purpose of this section is not to obtain evidence. Thus, any evidence which is obtained is only admissible in certain limited circumstances set out in subsec. (2). Any recordings or notes which do not meet the requirements of subsec. (2) are to be destroyed.

INTERCEPTION WITH CONSENT / Application for authorization / Judge to be satisfied / Content and limitation of authorization / Related warrant or order.

184.2 (1) A person may intercept, by means of any electro-magnetic, acoustic, mechanical or other device, a private communication where either the originator of the private communication or the person intended by the originator to receive it has consented to the interception and an authorization has been obtained pursuant to subsection (3).

(2) An application for an authorization under this section shall be made by a peace officer, or a public officer who has been appointed or designated to administer or enforce any federal or provincial law and whose duties include the enforcement of this or any other Act of Parliament, *ex parte* and in writing to a provincial court judge, a judge of a superior court of criminal jurisdiction or a judge as defined in section 552, and shall be accompanied by an affidavit, which may be sworn on the information and belief of that peace officer or public officer or of any other peace officer or public officer, deposing to the following matters:

- (*a*) that there are reasonable grounds to believe that an offence against this or any other Act of Parliament has been or will be committed;
- (*b*) the particulars of the offence;
- (*c*) the name of the person who has consented to the interception;
- (*d*) the period for which the authorization is requested; and
- (*e*) in the case of an application for an authorization where an authorization has previously been granted under this section or section 186, the particulars of the authorization.

(3) An authorization may be given under this section if the judge to whom the application is made is satisfied that

- (*a*) there are reasonable grounds to believe that an offence against this or any other Act of Parliament has been or will be committed;
- (*b*) either the originator of the private communication or the person intended by the originator to receive it has consented to the interception; and
- (*c*) there are reasonable grounds to believe that information concerning the offence referred to in paragraph (*a*) will be obtained through the interception sought.

(4) An authorization given under this section shall

- (*a*) state the offence in respect of which private communications may be intercepted;
- (*b*) state the type of private communication that may be intercepted;
- (*c*) state the identity of the persons, if known, whose private communications are to be intercepted, generally describe the place at which private communications may be intercepted, if a general description of that place can be given, and generally describe the manner of interception that may be used;
- (*d*) contain the terms and conditions that the judge considers advisable in the public interest; and
- (*e*) be valid for the period, not exceeding sixty days, set out therein.

(5) A judge who gives an authorization under this section may, at the same time, issue a warrant or make an order under any of sections 487, 487.01, 487.014 to 487.018, 487.02, 492.1 and 492.2 if the judge is of the opinion that the requested warrant or order is related to the execution of the authorization. 1993, c. 40, s. 4; 2014, c. 31, s. 8.

CROSS-REFERENCES
Consent to interception is given an expanded meaning in s. 183.1. The terms "electro-magnetic, acoustic, mechanical or other device", "intercept", "private communication" are defined in s. 183. The terms "peace officer" and "public officer" "provincial court judge" and "superior court judge" are defined in s. 2.

Since the interception under this section is made with consent of one of the parties and under an authorization, no offence is committed under s. 184. The purpose of this section is to deal with the implications of the decision of the Supreme Court of Canada in *R. v. Duarte*, [1990] 1 S.C.R. 30, 53 C.C.C. (3d) 1, 74 C.R. (3d) 281, which had held that a consent interception by agents of the state, although not unlawful under s. 184, was still a violation of s. 8 of the Charter, unless there was prior judicial authorization. Where evidence which was obtained through execution of the authorization is sought to be admitted at a trial, the Crown must comply with the provisions of s. 189.

Note that provision is made for obtaining the authorization through means of telecommunication under s. 184.3 in much the same way that a telewarrant may be obtained for seizure of things by search warrant. By virtue of s. 187, the material used on the application is to be kept secret and only disclosed in the circumstances set out in that section. The authorization may be executed anywhere in Canada in accordance with s. 188.1. Section 188.2 provides protection against civil or criminal liability for a person acting in accordance with an authorization. Provision is made in s. 487.02 for the making of an assistance order to require persons to co-operate in the carrying out of orders made under this section.

SYNOPSIS

This section permits the police to obtain a court authorization where one of the parties to the communication consents to the interception. Because one of the parties has consented, the requirements for obtaining the authorization are not as strict as for obtaining an authorization for surreptitious interceptions under ss. 185 and 186. The grounds for obtaining the authorization under this section more closely resemble the grounds for obtaining an ordinary search warrant under s. 487 and the authorization may be obtained for any federal offence, not just those specified in s. 183. Subsection (4) sets out the terms of the authorization and provides *inter alia* that the authorization be valid only for a period not exceeding 60 days. The time limit provided in subsec. (4)(*e*) does not apply in the case of criminal organizations, in which case the authorization may be valid for a period not exceeding one year.

ANNOTATIONS

Prior to the enactment of this section, the Supreme Court held that interception of private communications without a court authorization, even if with the consent of one of the parties to the communication, was an unreasonable search and seizure under s. 8 of the Charter: *R. v. Duarte*, [1990] 1 S.C.R. 30, 53 C.C.C. (3d) 1, 74 C.R. (3d) 281.

The absence of a requirement that other investigative means have been tried and failed does not violate s. 8 of the *Canadian Charter of Rights and Freedoms*: *R. v. Bordage* (2000), 146 C.C.C. (3d) 549 (Que. C.A.); *R. v. Largie* (2010), 258 C.C.C. (3d) 297 (Ont. C.A.), leave to appeal to S.C.C. refused 242 N.S.R. 400*n*.

This provision also applies to future crimes: *R. v. Bordage, supra.*

APPLICATION BY MEANS OF TELECOMMUNICATION / Application / Recording / Oath / Alternative to oath / Authorization / Giving authorization / Giving authorization where telecommunication produces writing.

184.3 (1) Notwithstanding section 184.2, an application for an authorization under subsection 184.2(2) may be made *ex parte* to a provincial court judge, a judge of a superior court of criminal jurisdiction or a judge as defined in section 552, by telephone or other means of telecommunication, if it would be impracticable in the circumstances for the applicant to appear personally before a judge.

(2) An application for an authorization made under this section shall be on oath and shall be accompanied by a statement that includes the matters referred to in paragraphs 184.2(2)(*a*) to (*e*) and that states the circumstances that make it inpracticable for the applicant to appear personally before a judge.

(3) The judge shall record, in writing or otherwise, the application for an authorization made under this section and, on determination of the application, shall cause the writing or recording to be placed in the packet referred to in subsection 187(1) and sealed in that packet, and a recording sealed in a packet shall be treated as if it were a document for the purposes of section 187.

(4) For the purposes of subsection (2), an oath may be administered by telephone or other means of telecommunication.

(5) An applicant who uses a means of telecommunication that produces a writing may, instead of swearing an oath for the purposes of subsection (2), make a statement in writing stating that all matters contained in the application are true to the knowledge or belief of the applicant and such a statement shall be deemed to be a statement made under oath.

(6) Where the judge to whom an application is made under this section is satisfied that the circumstances referred to in paragraphs 184.2(3)(*a*) to (*c*) exist and that the circumstances referred to in subsection (2) make it impracticable for the applicant to appear personally before a judge, the judge may, on such terms and conditions, if any, as are considered advisable, given an authorization by telephone or other means of telecommunication for a period of up to thirty-six hours.

(7) Where a judge gives an authorization by telephone or other means of telecommunication, other than a means of telecommunication that produces a writing,

>   (*a*) the judge shall complete and sign the authorization in writing, noting on its face the time, date and place at which it is given;
>   (*b*) the applicant shall, on the direction of the judge, complete a facsimile of the authorization in writing, noting on its face the name of the judge who gave it and the time, date and place at which it was given; and
>   (*c*) the judge shall, as soon as is practicable after the authorization has been given, cause the authorization to be placed in the packet referred to in subsection 187(1) and sealed in that packet.

(8) Where a judge gives an authorization by a means of telecommunication that produces a writing, the judge shall

>   (*a*) complete and sign the authorization in writing, noting on its face the time, date and place at which it is given;
>   (*b*) transmit the authorization by the means of telecommunication to the applicant, and the copy received by the applicant shall be deemed to be a facsimile referred to in paragraph (7)(*b*); and
>   (*c*) as soon as is practicable after the authorization has been given, cause the authorization to be placed in the packet referred to in subsection 187(1) and sealed in that packet. 1993, c. 40, s. 4.

CROSS-REFERENCES

This section supplements s. 184.2 and allows for the obtaining of an authorization to intercept private communications with the consent of one of the parties by means of telecommunications. The procedure is similar to the telewarrant procedure in s. 487.1 and thus see notes under that section. The material used in the application is to be kept secret in accordance with the provisions of s. 187. Provision is made in s. 487.02 for the making of an assistance order to require persons to co-operate in the carrying out of orders made under this section.

IMMEDIATE INTERCEPTION — IMMINENT HARM.

184.4 A police officer may intercept, by means of any electro-magnetic, acoustic, mechanical or other device, a private communication if the police officer has reasonable grounds to believe that

(*a*) **the urgency of the situation is such that an authorization could not, with reasonable diligence, be obtained under any other provision of this Part;**

(*b*) **the interception is immediately necessary to prevent an offence that would cause serious harm to any person or to property; and**

(*c*) **either the originator of the private communication or the person intended by the originator to receive it is the person who would commit the offence that is likely to cause the harm or is the victim, or intended victim, of the harm. 1993, c. 40, s. 4; 2013, c. 8, s. 3**

CROSS-REFERENCES

The terms "electro-magnetic, acoustic, mechanical or other device", "intercept", "private communication" are defined in s. 183. The term "peace officer" is defined in s. 2. An interception under this section is not unlawful by virtue of s. 184. The Crown must give notice of evidence obtained pursuant to this section in accordance with s. 189. Section 188.2 provides protection against civil or criminal liability for a person acting under this section.

SYNOPSIS

This section authorizes warrantless interception of private communications in exigent circumstances where an authorization could not be obtained with reasonable diligence, there are reasonable grounds to believe that the interception is necessary to prevent an unlawful act that would cause serious harm and one of the parties to the communication is the person who would commit the unlawful act or is the intended victim.

ANNOTATIONS

To the extent that the power to intercept private communications without judicial authorization is available only in exigent circumstances to prevent serious harm, this section strikes an appropriate balance. However, this provision violates s. 8 of the Charter because it does not provide a mechanism for oversight, and more particularly, notice to persons whose private communications have been intercepted. This breach cannot be saved under s. 1 of the Charter. This declaration of invalidity was suspended for 12 months to allow Parliament to redraft a constitutionally compliant provision: *R. v. Tse*, [2012] 1 S.C.R. 531, 280 C.C.C. (3d) 423.

INTERCEPTION OF RADIO-BASED TELEPHONE COMMUNICATIONS / Other provisions to apply.

184.5 (1) Every person who intercepts, by means of any electro-magnetic, acoustic, mechanical or other device, maliciously or for gain, a radio-based telephone communication, if the originator of the communication or the person intended by the originator of the communication to receive it is in Canada, is guilty of an indictable offence and liable to imprisonment for a term not exceeding five years.

(2) Section 183.1, subsection 184(2) and sections 184.1 to 190 and 194 to 196 apply, with such modifications as the circumstances require, to interceptions of radio-based telephone communications referred to in subsection (1). 1993, c. 40, s. 4.

CROSS-REFERENCES

The terms "electro-magnetic, acoustic, mechanical or other device", "intercept", and "radio-based telephone communication" are defined in s. 183. Under s. 193.1 it is an offence to disclose the contents of radio-based telephone communications subject to certain exceptions.

SYNOPSIS

This section helps to fill the gap created by several cases which had held under the predecessor legislation that cellular telephone conversations were not private communications. This section now creates an offence to intercept such communications where the interception was made for gain or maliciously. Subsection (2) then integrates such communications with the rest of this Part of the Code, allowing for the obtaining of authorizations and warrantless interceptions in the same way as for private communications.

ONE APPLICATION FOR AUTHORIZATION SUFFICIENT.

184.6 For greater certainty, an application for an authorization under this Part may be made with respect to both private communications and radio-based telephone communications at the same time. 1993, c. 40, s. 4.

SYNOPSIS

This section makes clear that applications may be made at the same time for authorization to intercept private communications and radio-based telephone [i.e. cellular] communications. Such authorizations might be obtained under s. 184.2 where one of the parties consent or under s. 186 where there is no consent by any of the parties. It is unclear whether the authorization to intercept both types of communications can be contained in the same document, although there is no apparent reason why it could not. One limitation on the scope of this section is that the ordinary s. 186 authorization cannot be obtained through the telewarrant procedure in s. 184.3.

APPLICATION FOR AUTHORIZATION / Exception for criminal organizations and terrorist groups / Extension of period for notification / Where extension to be granted / Where extension not granted.

185. (1) An application for an authorization to be given under section 186 shall be made *ex parte* and in writing to a judge of a superior court of criminal jurisdiction or a judge as defined in section 552 and shall be signed by the Attorney General of the province in which the application is made or the Minister of Public Safety and Emergency Preparedness or an agent specially designated in writing for the purposes of this section by

> **(a)** **the Minister personally or the Deputy Minister of Public Safety and Emergency Preparedness personally, if the offence under investigation is one in respect of which proceedings, if any, may be instituted at the instance of the Government of Canada and conducted by or on behalf of the Attorney General of Canada, or**
>
> **(b)** **the Attorney General of a province personally or the Deputy Attorney General of a province personally, in any other case,**

and shall be accompanied by an affidavit, which may be sworn on the information and belief of a peace officer or public officer deposing to the following matters:

> **(c)** **the facts relied upon to justify the belief that an authorization should be given together with particulars of the offence,**
>
> **(d)** **the type of private communication proposed to be intercepted,**
>
> **(e)** **the names, addresses and occupations, if known, of all persons, the interception of whose private communications there are reasonable grounds to believe may assist the investigation of the offence, a general description of the nature and location of the place, if known, at which private communications are proposed to be intercepted and a general description of the manner of interception proposed to be used,**
>
> **(f)** **the number of instances, if any, on which an application has been made under this section in relation to the offence and a person named in the affidavit pursuant to paragraph (e) and on which the application was withdrawn or no authorization was given, the date on which each application was made and the name of the judge to whom each application was made,**
>
> **(g)** **the period for which the authorization is requested, and**

    (*h*) whether other investigative procedures have been tried and have failed or why it appears they are unlikely to succeed or that the urgency of the matter is such that it would be impractical to carry out the investigation of the offence using only other investigative procedures.

(1.1) Notwithstanding paragraph (1)(*h*), that paragraph does not apply where the application for an authorization is in relation to

    (*a*) an offence under section 467.11, 467.111, 467.12 or 467.13;

    (*b*) an offence committed for the benefit of, at the direction of or in association with a criminal organization; or

    (*c*) a terrorism offence.

(2) An application for an authorization may be accompanied by an application, personally signed by the Attorney General of the province in which the application for the authorization is made or the Minister of Public Safety and Emergency Preparedness if the application for the authorization is made by him or on his behalf, to substitute for the period mentioned in subsection 196(1) such longer period not exceeding three years as is set out in the application.

(3) Where an application for an authorization is accompanied by an application referred to in subsection (2), the judge to whom the applications are made shall first consider the application referred to in subsection (2) and where, on the basis of the affidavit in support of the application for the authorization and any other affidavit evidence submitted in support of the application referred to in subsection (2), the judge is of the opinion that the interests of justice warrant the granting of such application, he shall fix a period, not exceeding three years, in substitution for the period mentioned in subsection 196(1).

(4) Where the judge to whom an application for an authorization and an application referred to in subsection (2) are made refuses to fix a period in substitution for the period mentioned in subsection 196(1) or where the judge fixes a period in substitution therefor that is less than the period set out in the application referred to in subsection (2), the person appearing before the judge on the application for the authorization may withdraw the application for the authorization and thereupon the judge shall not proceed to consider the application for the authorization or to give the authorization and shall return to the person appearing before him on the application for the authorization both applications and all other material pertaining thereto. 1973-74, c. 50, s. 2; 1976-77, c. 53, s. 8; 1993, c. 40, s. 5; 1997, c. 18, s. 8; 1997, c. 23, s. 4; 2001, c. 32, s. 5; 2001, c. 41, s. 6 and 133(8); 2005, c. 10, ss. 22 and 34(1)(*f*)(v); 2014, c. 17, s. 3.

CROSS-REFERENCES

The terms "criminal organization", "superior court of criminal jurisdiction", "terrorism offences", "peace officer" and "public officer" are defined in s. 2. The terms "offence", and "private communication" are defined in s. 183. While the term "authorization" is defined in s. 183 to include an authorization under s. 186 and 188, it seems from the context that this section concerns an application for an authorization granted under s. 186. Prerequisites for applications for renewals of authorizations are set out in s. 186(6) and for emergency "36-hour" authorizations in s. 188. However, certain of the prerequisites in this section will be imported to the application under s. 188, in view of the lack of detail in the latter section. In addition, constitutional imperatives may require that some of the conditions in this section be imported into s. 188. By virtue of s. 187, the documents relating to an application under this section are confidential and placed in a sealed packet, which is kept in the custody of the court and not opened except pursuant to a judge's order or for the purpose of dealing with an application for a renewal. Other related provisions are as follows: s. 184, offence to unlawfully intercept private communications; s. 189, admissibility of evidence obtained through interceptions; s. 191, unlawful possession of devices for surreptitious interception; s. 193, unlawful disclosure of intercepted private communication; s. 194, provision for damages for unlawful interceptions; s. 195, report by Solicitor General of Canada and provincial Attorney General concerning applications for authorizations under this section.

Also see sections which provide for obtaining the following authorizations: s. 184.2 (consent interceptions); s. 487.01 (general warrant including video surveillance); s. 492.1 (tracking device); s. 492.2 (dial number recorder).

SYNOPSIS

This section sets out the *procedure and criteria for granting authorization* to intercept private communications, and *permits extensions* of the period within which *notice* must be given to the person whose communications are intercepted (see s. 196(1)).

The introductory words in 185(1) set out certain procedural matters which apply to an application for an authorization. It provides that the application shall be made *ex parte* and *in writing*. The only judges who may grant such authorizations are of the *superior court of criminal jurisdiction* or a *judge as defined in s. 552*. Only the Attorney General, the Solicitor General or their *agents specially designated in writing* for the purpose may sign such applications. Section 185(1)(*a*) and (*b*) set out the offences, in respect of which the Solicitor General, the Attorney General or their respective deputies may make such designations.

The written application must be accompanied by an *affidavit*, which may be *sworn* on *information and belief* by a peace officer or public officer. *Section 185(1)(c) to (h) specifies* the information the affidavit must contain.

Section 185(1)(*c*) dictates that the affidavit set out the *facts* which the application is based upon, including the *particulars of the offence*. Section 185(1)(*d*) requires that the affidavit state the *type of private communication* to be intercepted.

Section 185(1)(*e*) requires that the affidavit contain the following information: the identity of the *known persons* whose private communications are to be intercepted, a *general description* of the nature and location of the *place, if known*, where the private communications are to be intercepted and a *general description* of the *proposed manner of interception*. Note that, unlike the previous two requirements which must be satisfied only if known, the *description of the manner* of the interception *must* be given. The *person* whose private communications are to be intercepted is generally referred to as the *object of the interception*.

Section 185(1)(*f*) provides for the affidavit to give the *history of any prior applications*, including the details of any unsuccessful applications or applications which were withdrawn. Section 185(1)(*g*) states that the *period* for which the *authorization is sought* must be set out in the affidavit.

The final requirement is that the affidavit must state if *other investigative procedures have been tried and failed* or why they appear *unlikely to succeed* or why the matter is so *urgent* that it is *impractical* to pursue other means of investigation. However, this requirement does not apply in relation to an offence under ss. 467.11 to 467.13 or an offence committed for the benefit, etc., of a criminal organization, or a terrorism offence.

Pursuant to subsec. (1.1), the investigative necessity requirement is not a constitutional requirement. Accordingly, where the wiretap authorization relates to a criminal organization, the provision allowing the authorization without the need for investigative necessity does not violate s. 8 of the Charter. In addition, there is no constitutional requirement that an authorization be time-limited to 60 days. In this case, the extension of the wiretap authorization for a one-year period was not unreasonable or contrary to s. 8 of the Charter: *R. v. Doiron* (2007), 221 C.C.C. (3d) 97 (N.B.C.A.), leave to appeal to S.C.C. refused 223 C.C.C. (3d) vi.

Section 185(2) to (5) provides that the *notice period* within which the object of the interception is to be notified (s. 196(1)) may be *extended on application* of the Attorney General or Solicitor General. It permits a judge issuing an authorization to grant such an extension. Section 185(2) requires that either the Attorney General or Solicitor General must *personally sign* the application for this extension. The extension may be for up to *three years*. Subsection (3) requires that the judge considering the application for the authorization must first consider the application to extend notice under subsec. (2). The test to be applied by the judge, in granting the extension of notice, is that the *interests of justice* warrant the granting of it. However, subsec. (4) provides that, if the judge *declines to grant the application under subsection (2)*, the *applicant for the authorization* may *withdraw* it, in which event the judge shall not consider the application for an authorization and must return all *materials* relating to the application for the extension of the notice period under subsec. (2) and to the application for authorization to the applicant.

By virtue of s. 487.01(5), this section applies to general warrants to do video surveillance.

ANNOTATIONS

Jurisdiction of judge – As offences under the [former] *Narcotic Control Act* are ones in respect of which proceedings may be validly instituted at the instance of the Government of Canada and conducted by or on behalf of the Attorney General of Canada (in view of *R. v. Hauser*, [1979] 1 S.C.R. 984, 46 C.C.C. (2d) 481, 8 C.R. (3d) 89) an agent designated by the Solicitor General of Canada may apply for an authorization in respect of such offences: *R. v. Cordes*, [1979] 1 S.C.R. 1062, 47 C.C.C. (2d) 46 (7:0).

Since the definition of Attorney General of Canada in s. 2, *supra*, is in respect *inter alia* to both proceedings under other Federal Acts and a conspiracy under this Act to commit an offence under another Federal Act, only the provincial Attorney General has the power under para. (*b*) to designate an agent for applications in connection with the *Criminal Code* offences enumerated under this Part: *R. v. Hancock and Proulx* (1976), 30 C.C.C. (2d) 544 (B.C.C.A.).

The grounds for the application (subsec. (1)(*c*)) – An affidavit supporting an authorization must be full, frank, clear and concise. The use of boiler-plate language, which may be misleading, should be avoided. Although there is no legal requirement to do so, consideration should be given to obtaining affidavits directly from those with the best firsthand knowledge of the facts: *R. v. Araujo*, [2000] 2 S.C.R. 992, 149 C.C.C. (3d) 449. The prerequisite for the granting of the authorization, as set out in s. 186(1)(*a*), that the granting of the authorization be in the best interest of the administration of justice imports as a minimum requirement, consistent with s. 8 of the *Charter of Rights and Freedoms*, that the judge be satisfied that there are reasonable and probable grounds to believe that a particular offence or a conspiracy, attempt or incitement to commit it has been, or is being committed and that the authorization sought will afford evidence of that offence: *R. v. Duarte*, [1990] 1 S.C.R. 30, 53 C.C.C. (3d) 1.

The failure of the officer to swear that he had reasonable and probable grounds to support his belief was not a fatal defect. What is required is disclosure of the facts relied upon to justify the belief that an authorization should be granted: *R. v. Bicknell* (1988), 41 C.C.C. (3d) 545 (B.C.C.A.).

The failure of an explicit statement attesting to belief in the informer's reliability is not fatal to the authorization: *R. v. Al-Maliki* (2005), 201 C.C.C. (3d) 96 (B.C.C.A.).

Type of communication to be intercepted (subsec. (1)(*c*)) – The affidavit must comply frankly, fully and fairly with the provisions of this section and the authorities must not try to conceal their true intention from the authorizing judge. In *R. v. Gill* (1980), 56 C.C.C. (2d) 169 (B.C.C.A.), it was held that the affidavit by "obfuscation" concealed or failed to reveal the clear intention of the police to intercept the face-to-face oral communications between certain persons who were to be placed in the same gaol cell and as a consequence failed to comply with subsec. (1)(*c*) and (*e*).

Identification of "known" persons (subsec. (1)(*e*)) – A person is known within the meaning of subsec. (1)(*e*), if the police know of the existence of such person and have reasonable and probable grounds to believe that interception of her communications *may* assist. If the person meets both of those requirements then interception of her private communications cannot be lawfully made under a "basket clause" for unknown persons: *R. v. Chesson*, [1988] 2 S.C.R. 148, 43 C.C.C. (3d) 353 (4:0).

In the subsequent case of *R. v. Duarte, supra*, the court accepted that the prerequisite that the granting of the authorization be in the best interest of the administration of justice in s. 186(1)(*a*) imported as a minimum requirement, consistent with s. 8 of the *Charter of Rights and Freedoms*, that the judge be satisfied that there are reasonable and probable grounds to believe that an offence has been or is being committed and that the authorization sought *will* afford evidence of that offence. Care should therefore be taken in the drafting of the affidavit to ensure that, in simply following the wording of subsec. (1)(*e*), the authorities do not adopt too low a test in setting out the grounds required by subsec. (1)(*c*) upon which the authorization may be granted.

An application may be made to intercept, pursuant to a "basket clause", private communications of persons who are both unknown and unidentified at the time of the application: *R. v. Samson* (1983), 9 C.C.C. (3d) 194 (Ont. C.A.).

This provision does not distinguish between categories of "principal" known persons and "other" known persons: *R. v. Mahal* (2012), 292 C.C.C. (3d) 252 (Ont. C.A.), application for judicial review refused 2013 CarswellOnt 4853 (S.C.C.), leave to appeal to S.C.C. refused 2013 CarswellOnt 4853.

Necessity requirement (subsec. (1)(*h*)) – Investigative necessity requires that, practically speaking, there are no other reasonable means of investigation in the particular circumstances of the case: *R. v. Araujo*, [2000] 2 S.C.R. 992, 149 C.C.C. (3d) 449, 193 D.L.R. (4th) 440.

An authorization cannot be granted to prevent criminal activity in the future or to uncover evidence of unknown crimes. In this case, an authorization should not have been granted where the police were not investigating any specific crime known to them but were simply attempting to stop what they believed to be a continuing criminal activity by named individuals: *R. v. Grant* (1998), 130 C.C.C. (3d) 53 (Man. C.A.).

The fact that the police have enough information to lay a charge is not a bar to obtaining an authorization where there are grounds for permitting the investigation to continue by means of intercepted communications as where there is a reasonable expectation that evidence of a further offence might also be obtained: *R. v. Paulson* (1995), 97 C.C.C. (3d) 344 (B.C.C.A.).

Prior authorizations (subsec. (1)(*f*)) | *Also see cases noted under s. 186(6)* – On an application for a subsequent authorization in the same investigation there must be full and frank disclosure, but the requirements set out in s. 186(6) need not be complied with: *R. v. Moore; R. v. Bogdanich* (1993), 81 C.C.C. (3d) 161 (B.C.C.A.), affd [1995] 1 S.C.R. 756, 95 C.C.C. (3d) 288.

JUDGE TO BE SATISFIED / Exception for criminal organizations and terrorism offences / Where authorization not to be given / Terms and conditions / Content and limitation of authorization / Persons designated / Installation and removal of device / Removal after expiry of authorization / Renewal of authorization / Renewal / Related warrant or order.

186. (1) An authorization under this section may be given if the judge to whom the application is made is satisfied

    (*a*) that it would be in the best interests of the administration of justice to do so; and

    (*b*) that other investigative procedures have been tried and have failed, other investigative procedures are unlikely to succeed or the urgency of the matter is such that it would be impractical to carry out the investigation of the offence using only other investigative procedures.

(1.1) Notwithstanding paragraph (1)(*b*), that paragraph does not apply where the judge is satisfied that the application for an authorization is in relation to

   (*a*) an offence under section 467.11, 467.111, 467.12 or 467.13;

   (*b*) an offence committed for the benefit of, at the direction of or in association with a criminal organization; or

   (*c*) a terrorism offence.

(2) No authorization may be given to intercept a private communication at the office or residence of a solicitor, or at any other place ordinarily used by a solicitor and by other solicitors for the purpose of consultation with clients, unless the judge to whom the application is made is satisfied that there are reasonable grounds to believe that the solicitor, any other solicitor practising with him, any person employed by him or any other such solicitor or a member of the solicitor's household has been or is about to become a party to an offence.

(3) Where an authorization is given in relation to the interception of private communications at a place described in subsection (2), the judge by whom the authorization is given shall include therein such terms and conditions as he considers advisable to protect privileged communications between solicitors and clients.

(4) An authorization shall

   (*a*) state the offence in respect of which private communications may be intercepted;

   (*b*) state the type of private communication that may be intercepted;

   (*c*) state the identity of the persons, if known, whose private communications are to be intercepted, generally describe the place at which private communications may be intercepted, if a general description of that place can be given, and generally describe the manner of interception that may be used;

   (*d*) contain such terms and conditions as the judge considers advisable in the public interest; and

   (*e*) be valid for the period, not exceeding sixty days, set out therein.

(5) The Minister of Public Safety and Emergency Preparedness or the Attorney General, as the case may be, may designate a person or persons who may intercept private communications under authorizations.

(5.1) For greater certainty, an authorization that permits interception by means of an electro-magnetic, acoustic, mechanical or other device includes the authority to install, maintain or remove the device covertly.

(5.2) On an *ex parte* application, in writing, supported by affidavit, the judge who gave an authorization referred to in subsection (5.1) or any other judge having jurisdiction to give such an authorization may give a further authorization for the covert removal of the electro-magnetic, acoustic, mechanical or other device after the expiry of the original authorization

   (*a*) under any terms or conditions that the judge considers advisable in the public interest; and

   (*b*) during any specified period of not more than sixty days.

(6) Renewals of an authorization may be given by a judge of a superior court of criminal jurisdiction or a judge as defined in section 552 on receipt by him or her of an *ex parte* application in writing signed by the Attorney General of the province in which the application is made or the Minister of Public Safety and Emergency Preparedness — or an agent specially designated in writing for the purposes of section 185 by the Minister or the Attorney General, as the case may be — accompanied by an affidavit of a peace officer or public officer deposing to the following matters:

   (*a*) the reason and period for which the renewal is required, (*b*) full particulars, together with times and dates, when interceptions, if any, were made or attempted under the authorization, and any information that has been obtained by any interception, and

(*c*) the number of instances, if any, on which, to the knowledge and belief of the deponent, an application has been made under this subsection in relation to the same authorization and on which the application was withdrawn or no renewal was given, the date on which each application was made and the name of the judge to whom each such application was made,

and supported by such other information as the judge may require.

(7) A renewal of an authorization may be given if the judge to whom the application is made is satisfied that any of the circumstances described in subsection (1) still obtain, but no renewal shall be for a period exceeding sixty days.

(8) A judge who gives an authorization under this section may, at the same time, issue a warrant or make an order under any of sections 487, 487.01, 487.014 to 487.018, 487.02, 492.1 and 492.2 if the judge is of the opinion that the requested warrant or order is related to the execution of the authorization. 1973-74, c. 50, s. 2; 1976-77, c. 53, s. 9; 1993, c. 40, s. 6; 1997, c. 23, s. 5; 1999, c. 5, s. 5; 2001, c. 32, s. 6; 2001, c. 41, s. 6.1 and 133(8.1); 2005, c. 10, ss. 23 and 34(1)(*f*)(vi); 2014, c. 17, s. 4; 2014, c. 31, s. 9.

CROSS-REFERENCES

The reference to "judge" is a judge referred to in s. 185, being a judge of the superior court of criminal jurisdiction or a judge as defined in s. 552. The terms "solicitor", "intercept", "private communication" and "offence" are defined in s. 183. "Attorney General", "terrorism offence", and "criminal organization" are defined in s. 2. Procedure for obtaining an emergency "36-hour" authorization is set out in s. 188. The documents used on an application are confidential and must be dealt with in accordance with s. 187. Other related provisions are as follows: s. 184, offence to unlawfully intercept private communications [*i.e., inter alia*, not in accordance with an authorization]; s. 189, admissibility of evidence obtained through interceptions; s. 191, unlawful possession of devices for surreptitious interception; s. 193, unlawful disclosure of intercepted private communication; s. 194, provision for damages for unlawful interceptions; s. 195, reports by Solicitor General of Canada and provincial Attorney General concerning applications for authorizations under this section.

As to the impact of the Charter on the admissibility of evidence, also see notes under s. 189.

Provision is made in s. 487.02 for the making of an assistance order to require persons to co-operate in the carrying out of orders made under this section. The interception of "consent" interceptions may be authorized under s. 184.2. Also see s. 487.01 which makes this section applicable to obtaining a general warrant to conduct surreptitious video surveillance, s. 492.1 which regulates the use of tracking devices and s. 492.2 which regulates the use of telephone number recorders.

Authorizations may be executed anywhere in Canada in accordance with s. 188.1.

As to renewals of authorizations relating to "criminal organizations" see s. 186.1.

Section 188.2 provides protection against civil or criminal liability for a person acting in accordance with an authorization.

SYNOPSIS

This section sets out the *criteria which a judge is to apply* when considering whether to *grant a request for an authorization to intercept private communications*. It also sets out what must be *contained in an authorization*, and *who may intercept* private communications pursuant to an authorization. In addition, it provides for the *renewal of an authorization*.

Subsection (1) provides two conditions which must be met before a judge may issue an authorization. The first condition is that the interception must be in the *best interests of the administration of justice*. In addition, s. 186(1)(*b*) requires that the judge be satisfied of the *necessity of this means of investigation*. This requirement parallels the contents of the affidavit in support of the application as set out in s. 185(1)(*h*). As with s. 185, this requirement does not apply where the authorization is in relation to an offence under ss. 467.11 to 467.13 or an offence committed for the benefit, etc., of a criminal organization, or a terrorism offence.

Subsections (2) and (3) impose *strict limits* on when an authorization may be given in connection with the *home or office of a solicitor* or any *other place ordinarily used by solicitors for the purpose of consulting with their clients.* Before such an authorization may be issued, the judge must be satisfied that there are *reasonable grounds to believe* that the *solicitor*, or any of the other categories of people specified in subsec. (2) (generally those who have a close personal or business tie to the lawyer), *has been or is about to be a party to an offence.* As with all references to "offence" in this Part, it is limited to those offences listed in s. 183. Subsection (3) provides that, if such an authorization is granted, the judge *must impose terms and conditions to protect privileged conversations* between solicitors and clients. A typical condition which is imposed is that such authorizations be "live monitored", *i.e.*, listened to by an officer whenever communications are intercepted to ensure that no solicitor-client communications are unintentionally intercepted.

Subsection (4) sets out the *terms which must appear in all authorizations* and also provides a general power, in s. 186(4)(*d*), to impose *other terms and conditions* which the judge considers advisable *in the public interest.* Section 186(4)(*a*) requires that the *offence* in respect of which the authorization is given be stated. Section 186(4)(*b*) mandates that the *type of private communication that may be intercepted* be stated. Section 186(4)(*c*) parallels the requirements for the affidavit in support of the application set out in s. 185(1)(*e*) which deal with the *identity* of the *persons* whose communications are to be intercepted and a *description* of the *place and manner* of the interception. The final condition which must appear in the authorization is the *period for which it is valid, not exceeding 60 days.*

Section 186(5) permits the Solicitor General or the Attorney General to designate *who may make the authorized intercept.* Subsection (5.1) provides that an authorization includes the authority to install, maintain and remove the device covertly. Subsection (5.2) gives a judge authority to authorize covert removal of a device after the authorization has expired.

Subsection (6) deals with *renewal of authorizations.* The procedure set out for renewals parallels that in s. 185 dealing with initial applications, including that they be made *ex parte* and be supported by an *affidavit.* Section 186(6)(*c*) parallels s. 185(1)(*f*). The additional requirements relate to full disclosure of the reasons for the renewal and the interceptions made to date under the original authorization. In addition, the applicant must provide whatever other information the judge hearing the application may require. The *criteria* to be applied in deciding whether to *grant a renewal* are set out in subsec. (7). If the conditions set out in subsec. (1) still obtain, the judge *may* grant the *renewal* for *no more than 60 days.*

The time limit provided in subsecs. (4)(*e*) and (7) does not apply in the case of criminal organizations, in which case the authorization or renewal may be valid for a period not exceeding one year.

ANNOTATIONS

Unlawful interception – Evidence of private communications, intercepted by the police with the consent of one of the parties to the communication but without an authorization, violates s. 8 of the *Canadian Charter of Rights and Freedoms* and the evidence will be inadmissible if its admission would bring the administration of justice into disrepute within the meaning of s. 24(2) of the Charter. Where, however, the police acted in good faith, in reasonable reliance on what they understood the law to be as set out in s. 184(2)(*a*), then the evidence should be admitted: *R. v. Duarte*, [1990] 1 S.C.R. 30, 53 C.C.C. (3d) 1.

Where the evidence of the intercepted communication was inadmissible against the co-conspirator by reason of a violation of the Charter then it was not admissible against the accused. Where the Crown seeks to rely on the co-conspirators exception to the hearsay rule, there is a threshold condition that the tendered evidence be admissible against the person who actually made the statements in question: *R. v. Montoute* (1991), 62 C.C.C. (3d) 481 (Alta. C.A.).

Conversations between the accused and the co-accused were admissible only against the co-accused because the accused's rights under s. 8 of the Charter were violated. The authorization named the co-accused but did not name the accused and did not include a basket clause: *R. v. Mooring* (1999), 137 C.C.C. (3d) 324 (B.C.C.A.).

Where there is a clear dividing line between the good and bad parts of an authorization so that they are not so interwoven that they cannot be separated but are actually separate authorizations given in the same order, the court can divide the order, preserve the valid portion which then forms the authorization: *R. v. Grabowski*, [1985] 2 S.C.R. 434, 22 C.C.C. (3d) 449 (7:0).

Subsection (1)(*a*) – Surreptitious electronic surveillance constitutes a search or seizure within the meaning of s. 8 of the Charter: *R. v. Duarte, supra*.

In *R. v. Duarte, supra*, the court accepted that the prerequisite that the granting of the authorization be in the best interest of the administration of justice imported as a minimum requirement, consistent with s. 8 of the Charter, that the judge be satisfied that there are reasonable and probable grounds to believe that an offence has been, or is being, committed and that the authorization sought will afford evidence of that offence.

Hearsay statements of an informer may provide reasonable and probable grounds to justify the granting of an authorization to intercept private communications. A tip from an informer by itself, however, is insufficient to establish reasonable and probable grounds. The reliability of the tip is to be assessed by recourse to the totality of the circumstances. The court will look to a variety of factors including the degree of detail of the tip, the informer's source of knowledge, and any *indicia* of the informer's reliability such as past performance or confirmation from other investigative sources. The results of the interception cannot, however, *ex post facto* provide evidence of the reliability of the information: *R. v. Garofoli*, [1990] 2 S.C.R. 1421, 60 C.C.C. (3d) 161 (5:2).

Subsection (1)(*b*) – See notes under heading **Necessity requirement (subsec. (1)(*h*))** in s. 185.

Subsection (1.1) – The investigative necessity requirement is not a constitutional requirement. Accordingly, where the wiretap authorization relates to a criminal organization, the provision allowing the authorization without the need for investigative necessity does not violate s. 8 of the Charter. In addition, there is no constitutional requirement that an authorization be time-limited to 60 days. In this case, the extension of the wiretap authorization for a one-year period was not unreasonable or contrary to s. 8 of the Charter: *R. v. Doiron* (2007), 221 C.C.C. (3d) 97 (N.B.C.A.), leave to appeal to S.C.C. refused 223 C.C.C. (3d) vi (S.C.C.). See also: *R. v. Lucas* (2014), 313 C.C.C. (3d) 159 (Ont. C.A.), leave to appeal to S.C.C. refused 2015 CarswellOnt 639.

Subsections (2), (3) / *Interception of solicitor-client communications* – In seeking to admit private communications intercepted pursuant to an authorization there is no burden on the Crown to prove this subsection has not been breached: *R. v. Lyons* (1979), 52 C.C.C. (2d) 113 (B.C. Co. Ct.).

A police cell block where lawyers were permitted to consult with their clients was nevertheless held not to be a place ordinarily used by a solicitor for the purpose of consultation with clients. Use of the cells in this manner constituted an unusual or extraordinary use: *R. v. Johnny and Billy* (1981), 62 C.C.C. (2d) 33 (B.C.S.C.), affd 5 C.C.C. (3d) 538 (C.A.).

A jail telephone is not a "place" where a solicitor ordinarily consults with clients. Accordingly, the imposition of a live monitoring condition requiring the recording to be stopped when the accused was speaking to a solicitor struck the appropriate balance: *R. v. Blais* (2003), 182 C.C.C. (3d) 39 (Ont. C.A.).

In *R. v. Taylor* (1997), 121 C.C.C. (3d) at p. 353 (B.C.C.A.), affd [1998] 1 S.C.R. 26, 121 C.C.C. (3d) 353, the court held that a term in an authorization prohibiting interceptions "at" the office of a solicitor was not violated where the interception was of the communication by a named target while using his cellular phone, even though the recipient was at a law office. The place of interception was not at the office but at the distribution centre for cellular calls.

A practicing solicitor can be named in an authorization as a known person in limited circumstances even though the provisions of this section had not been established — for instance, where there is a credibly based probability that a non-privileged communication of potential investigative assistance would occur between a practicing solicitor and another at a location other than a solicitor's home or office: *R. v. Mastop* (2012), 296 C.C.C. (3d) 205 (B.C.S.C.).

Subsection (3) – This subsection does not require that the judge impose conditions if he does not consider them advisable: *R. v. Chambers* (1983), 9 C.C.C. (3d) 132 (B.C.C.A.), affd [1986] 2 S.C.R. 29, 26 C.C.C. (3d) 353.

Subsection (4) / Contents of authorization / The offence (para. (*a*)) – The purpose of this requirement is to demonstrate, on the face of the authorization, that the judge has exercised his jurisdiction within the limits described in s. 183 and thus a simple generic statement of the offence, in this case "murder" and "conspiracy to commit murder", is sufficient: *R. v. Mathurin* (1978), 41 C.C.C. (2d) 263 (Que. C.A.).

Basket clause (para. (*c*)) – In a case involving consideration of the former s. 178.13(2)(*c*) it was held that an authorization providing for the interception of the private communications of a certain named person and that "such interceptions" may be made at certain addresses does not authorize the interception of the communications of other unnamed persons at those addresses. It was clear from the wording of the clause that it was not intended to operate as a "basket clause" so as to authorize the interception of conversations of unknown persons at those addresses: *R. v. Douglas* (1977), 33 C.C.C. (2d) 395 (Ont. C.A.).

An authorization simply authorizing the interception of conversations of certain named persons and "other persons as yet unknown who may become identified within the time limit of this authorization" did not sufficiently comply with the former s. 178.13(2) in so far as it purported to authorize the interception of private communications of unknown persons. Nor was this defect cured by inclusion in the authorization of the standard clause authorizing the installation of electromagnetic and other devices. This clause was not a description of the manner of interception within the meaning of that subsection: *R. v. Badovinac* (1977), 34 C.C.C. (2d) 65 (Ont. C.A.).

A "basket clause" must identify the class of persons who are to be intercepted and may not simply delegate that function to the police by identifying the unknown persons who may be intercepted as persons of whom there are reasonable and probable grounds to believe that the interception of their private communications may assist the investigation of any of the offences named in the order. This wording, virtually identical to s. 185(1)(*e*) simply vests a discretion in the police to determine who may be intercepted: *R. v. Paterson* (1985), 18 C.C.C. (3d) 137 (Ont. C.A.), affd [1987] 2 S.C.R. 291, 39 C.C.C. (3d) 575 (7:0).

To be named in the authorization as a known person, the existence of that person must be known to the police and must be one the interception of whose private communications there are reasonable grounds to believe may assist the investigation of the offence. If at the time the police apply for an authorization a person meets these criteria she will be a known person and therefore if her communications are to be admitted, she must be named in the authorization as a target for interception: *R. v. Chesson*, [1988] 2 S.C.R. 148, 43 C.C.C. (3d) 353 (4:0).

This provision does not distinguish between categories of "principal" known persons and "other" known persons: *R. v. Mahal* (2012), 292 C.C.C. (3d) 252 (Ont. C.A.), application for judicial review refused 2013 CarswellOnt 4853 (S.C.C.), leave to appeal to S.C.C. refused 2013 CarswellOnt 4853.

A new authorization does not have to be obtained for each unknown person as soon as he becomes known during the duration of an authorization: *R. v. Gray* (1998), 132 C.C.C. (3d) 565 (N.B.C.A.).

Place of interception (para. (c)) – A clause in an authorization purporting to authorize the interception of a named person's communications without any limitation as to place is invalid: *R. v. Ritch* (1982), 69 C.C.C. (2d) 289 (Alta. C.A.) affd [1984] 2 S.C.R. 333 *sub nom. R. v. Brese* 16 C.C.C. (3d) 191*n* (7:0). Similarly, *R. v. Grabowski*, [1985] 2 S.C.R. 434, 22 C.C.C. (3d) 449 (7:0), where it was held that a clause was invalid which authorized interception of the private communications of named persons and unknown persons provided for by the "basket clause" at any place where such persons could be found. As it stood, the authorization contained no limitations as to persons or place or interception. However, the authorization was severable and the offending clause relating to interception at unspecified locations could be excluded.

A clause in an authorization may validly provide for interception of private communications at places resorted to by the named targets. Inclusion of such a clause does not, *per se,* infringe s. 8 of the Charter. The judge can properly find that there are reasonable and probable grounds for believing that evidence will be obtained as to the commission of the offence with respect to certain classes of places. Further, there is no requirement that the authorization include the most specific description possible, and thus a general resort to a clause was sufficient to include pay telephones resorted to by the targets. However, in some circumstances interceptions at pay telephones may violate s. 8. Thus, in this case, although prior to seeking the first of several authorizations, it was known to the police that the named targets resorted to public telephones, there was nothing in the authorizations to indicate that such telephones were to be wire-tapped nor that the slightest consideration was given to protection of the public interest by imposing conditions as contemplated by para. (*d*). At a minimum, where it is intended to intercept pay telephones pursuant to a resort to a clause, the authorization should provide that conversations at a public telephone not be intercepted unless there are reasonable and probable grounds for believing that the target was using the telephone at the time that the device was activated: *R. v. Thompson*, [1990] 2 S.C.R. 1111, 59 C.C.C. (3d) 225 (4:2).

An automobile is a "place" within the meaning of this subsection: *R. v. Papalia*, [1988] 2 S.C.R. 137, 43 C.C.C. (3d) 129 (4:0).

An authorization to intercept private communications of the accused and his parents at any place resorted to or used by the named persons did not extend to the interception of a communication where the accused was detained and the police provided a room for the accused and his parents to talk. *R. v. Mojtahedpour* (2003), 171 C.C.C. (3d) 428 (B.C.C.A.).

Where the authorization fails to describe the place at which the private communication of named persons may be intercepted, where such a description must be given as required by s. 186(4)(*c*), then interceptions made pursuant to such an authorization are not lawfully made: *R. v. Blacquiere* (1980), 57 C.C.C. (2d) 330, 28 Nfld. & P.E.I.R. 336 (P.E.I.S.C.).

Interceptions of private communications pursuant to an authorization which permits installation of a device in a motor vehicle is not rendered unlawful by reason of the fact that the device used is attached to the vehicle's battery: *R. v. Chesson*, [1988] 2 S.C.R. 148, 43 C.C.C. (3d) 353.

Description of manner of interception (para. (c)) – It was held in *R. v. Glesby* (1982), 66 C.C.C. (2d) 332, 135 D.L.R. (3d) 524 (Man. Q.B.), affd 70 C.C.C. (2d) 148, [1982] 5 W.W.R. 351, *sub nom. R. v. Diamond* (C.A.), that an authorization complied with the present subsec. (2)(*c*) as to generally describing the manner of interception where it authorized the police to "intercept or cause to be intercepted private communications as hereunder specified and for such purposes to take all steps as are reasonably necessary to install, make use of, monitor and remove any electro-magnetic, acoustic, mechanical and other device as may be required to implement this authorization".

An authorization complies with the requirement in para. (*c*) as to description of the manner of interception although that description authorizes the use of any electromagnetic, accoustic, mechanical or other device which in the opinion of the police is required to investigate the offence: *R. v. Lawrence*, [1988] 1 S.C.R. 619, 40 C.C.C. (3d) 192*n*.

Surreptitious entry – It is implied in the authorization that the police officer may make a surreptitious entry into private premises to install a device such as a radio transmitter where such entry is necessary to implement the authorization and the authorizing judge has not included in the authorization any limitations on or prohibition of such entry. However, the judge in the exercise of his supervisory jurisdiction should designate the procedures, devices and conditions which are necessary in the public interest: *R. v. Lyons*, [1984] 2 S.C.R. 633, 15 C.C.C. (3d) 417 (4:2); *Reference re an Application for an Authorization*, [1984] 2 S.C.R. 697, 15 C.C.C. (3d) 466 (4:2). [Also, now see subsecs. (5.1) and (5.2).]

However, the guarantee to protection against unreasonable search and seizure in s. 8 of the Charter requires that, with respect to private residences, the authorizing judge should consider what conditions, if any, are required in the public interest. In order to ensure that the authorizing judge has at least considered these matters, the authorization should, at minimum, refer specifically to each place that is a private residence and designate the type of devices that may be employed. In the absence of express mention of a private residence in the authorization, and hence this minimal protection, the safeguards provided by the judicial role are illusory. Surreptitious entry of a private dwelling which has not been specifically mentioned in the authorization is unreasonable and contrary to s. 8 of the Charter. Evidence obtained pursuant to such an entry may be excluded under s. 24(2) of the Charter: *R. v. Thompson, supra.* [However, now see subsec. (5.1).]

Constitutional considerations – "Public interest" as used in subsec. (4)(*d*) is not so vague so as to violate s. 7 of the *Canadian Charter of Rights and Freedoms*: *R. v. Shalala* (2000), 224 N.B.R. (2d) 118 (C.A.), leave to appeal to S.C.C. refused 262 N.R. 400*n*.

Other terms and conditions (para. (*d*)) – Failure to include a clause in an authorization imposing a duty on police to minimize interception of irrelevant conversations is not a violation of the guarantee to protection against unreasonable search or seizure in s. 8 of the Charter: *R. v. Garofoli*, [1990] 2 S.C.R. 1421, 60 C.C.C. (3d) 161 (5:2).

Period of time (para. (*e*)) – The authorization to comply with para. (*e*) may state merely that it is valid for a period not exceeding a certain number of days commencing on a specified date. It need not set out a specific number of identifiable days to be valid: *R. v. Murphy and Holme* (1982), 69 C.C.C. (2d) 152 (B.C.C.A.), leave to appeal to S.C.C. refused 43 N.R. 450*n*.

A statement in the preamble of the authorization to the effect that interception was to be by "electronic" means was an adequate description of the manner of interception: *R. v. Rowbotham* (1988), 41 C.C.C. (3d) 1, 63 C.R. (3d) 113 (Ont. C.A.).

Severance – An authorization is severable and an offending clause relating to interception at unspecified locations, a clause which was never resorted to, may be severed and the balance of the authorization upheld: *R. v. Grabowski, supra.*

Where, however, the good and bad parts of the authorization are so interwoven that they cannot be separated, then it is not possible to sever the valid portions of the authorization from the invalid portion and the trial court has no power to amend the authorization so as to place a limit on the places where the interception of communications of unknown persons could have been made: *R. v. Braithwaite* (1986), 30 C.C.C. (3d) 348, 72 A.R. 227 (C.A.).

Review of validity of authorization – Since a wiretap constitutes a search or seizure within the meaning of s. 8 of the Charter, statutory provisions authorizing interception of private communications must conform to the minimum constitutional requirements demanded by s. 8 of the Charter. Thus, before granting an authorization, a judge must be satisfied that the granting of the authorization is in the best interests of the administration of justice. This requires that the judge be satisfied by affidavit that there are reasonable and probable grounds to believe that a specified crime has been or is being committed and that the interception of the private communications in question will afford evidence of the crime. In addition, the applicant must meet the requirements of subsec. (1)(*b*) with respect to the unavailability of other investigative procedures. The statutory requirements of subsec. (1)(*a*) are identical to the constitutional requirements. The review to determine compliance with the statutory minimum requirements and hence the minimum constitutional requirements is to be conducted by the trial judge rather than a judge of the court which granted the authorization. The judge conducting the review must hear evidence and submissions as to whether the interception constitutes an unreasonable search and seizure. Since this is an issue as to the admissibility of evidence, it is an issue which may be raised at trial. Applications for review should be made to the trial judge. If the judge concludes that the minimum statutory conditions set out in subsec. (1)(*a*) have not been complied with then the search is not authorized by law and is unlawful. The judge should not, however, review the authorization *de novo* and should not substitute his view for that of the authorizing judge. If based on the record which was before the authorizing judge as amplified on the review, the trial judge concludes that the authorizing judge could have granted the authorization then he should not interfere. In this process, the existence of fraud, non-disclosure, misleading evidence and new evidence are not prerequisites to a review but merely relevant factors, their sole impact being to determine whether there continues to be any basis for the decision of the authorizing judge: *R. v. Garofoli, supra.*

Even though the accused may not have been directly incriminated by conversations recorded pursuant to an authorization, where incriminating remarks made by other individuals during the conversations would be admissible as evidence against the accused under the co-conspirators exception to the rule against hearsay, then it would seem that the accused has standing to challenge the validity of the authorization: *R. v. Durette*, [1994] 1 S.C.R. 469, 88 C.C.C. (3d) 1, 28 C.R. (4th) 1.

While an accused has standing to challenge the validity of an authorization to intercept the private communications of a third party if the accused's communications were also intercepted, he has no standing to challenge the legality of the interception of conversations of co-conspirators where he was not a party to those conversations: *R. v. Rendon* (1999), 140 C.C.C. (3d) 12, 33 C.R. (5th) 311 (Que. C.A.), affd [2001] 1 S.C.R. 997, 156 C.C.C. (3d) 222 *sub nom. R. v. Peters.*

Errors in the information presented to the authorizing judge, whether advertent or even fraudulent, are only factors to be considered in deciding whether or not to set aside the authorization. The trial judge should examine the information in the affidavit which was independent of the evidence found to be misleading to determine whether there was sufficient reliable information to support an authorization: *R. v. Bisson*, [1994] 3 S.C.R. 1097, 94 C.C.C. (3d) 94, 65 Q.A.C. 241.

Where the information filed in support of the authorization included a reference to a Crime Stoppers tip which was subject to the police informer privilege, the Crown should have been entitled to withdraw the reference to the tip from the information and to defend the authorization without reference to this information: *R. v. Leipert*, [1997] 1 S.C.R. 281, 112 C.C.C. (3d) 385, 4 C.R. (5th) 259.

An affidavit supporting an authorization must be full, frank, clear and concise. The use of boiler-plate language, which may be misleading, should be avoided. Although there is no legal requirement to do so, consideration should be given to obtaining affidavits directly from those with the best firsthand knowledge of the facts. Where the reliability of the content of the affidavit is challenged, the question is whether there was at least some evidence that might reasonably be believed on the basis of which the authorization could have been granted. The question is not whether in the opinion of the reviewing judge, the application should have been granted at all by the authorizing judge. In engaging in this analysis, the reviewing judge must exclude erroneous information. If the police acted in good faith, then the reviewing judge may consider the amplification of the record on the review.

Amplification, however, must not become a means of circumventing the prior authorization requirement. Amplification is permissible where the police had the requisite reasonable and probable grounds and demonstrated investigative necessity but have, in good faith, made some minor, technical error in the drafting of their affidavit material: *R. v. Araujo*, [2000] 2 S.C.R. 992, 149 C.C.C. (3d) 449, 193 D.L.R. (4th) 440.

In *R. v. Araujo, supra*, the court referred with apparent approval to the decision in *R. v. Morris* (1998), 134 C.C.C. (3d) 539, 23 C.R. (5th) 354 (N.S.C.A.), where it was held that while even fraudulent errors do not automatically invalidate the warrant, this does not mean that errors, particularly deliberate ones, are irrelevant in the review process. While not leading to automatic vitiation of the warrant, there remains the need to protect the prior authorization process. In appropriate circumstances the reviewing judge may conclude on the totality of the circumstances that the conduct of the police in seeking prior authorization was so subversive of that process that the resulting warrant must be set aside to protect the process and the preventive function it serves.

Where the wiretap authorization has been granted but evidence has not yet been obtained pursuant to it, an application to review the granting of the authorization may be brought before the authorizing judge. In any other case, there will necessarily be an issue to the admissibility of the evidence obtained, which should be determined by the trial judge: *R. v. Santos*, [2000] W.W.R. 103 (Man. Q.B.).

Cross-examination of deponent of affidavit – While the accused has no right to cross-examine the deponent of the affidavit, the trial judge should grant leave to cross-examine where satisfied that cross-examination is necessary to enable the accused to make full answer and defence. A basis must be shown by the accused for the view that the cross-examination will elicit testimony tending to discredit the existence of one of the preconditions to the authorization, as, for example, the existence of reasonable and probable grounds. The test previously applied by most of the lower courts, refusing to permit counsel for the accused to cross-examine the deponent of the affidavit unless there was *prima facie* proof of a deliberate falsehood or reckless disregard for the truth in respect of statements in the affidavit and that this false statement is necessary to the finding that there were grounds for granting the authorization, was too strict. Cross-examination will be limited by the trial judge to questions that are directed to establish that there was no basis upon which the authorization could have been granted. With respect to confidential informers, there is no right to cross-examine. The informer is not a witness and cannot be identified, unless the accused brings himself within the exception which permits disclosure of the informer's identity where the accused's innocence is at stake: *R. v. Garofoli, supra*.

In *R. v. Pires; R. v. Lising*, [2005] 3 S.C.R. 343, 201 C.C.C. (3d) 449, 33 C.R. (6th) 241, the Supreme Court of Canada held that subsequent Charter jurisprudence did not result in the abolition or relaxation of the *Garofoli, supra*, leave requirement. The *Garofoli* threshold was consistent with Charter principles. The review hearing was not intended to test the merits of the Crown's allegations in respect of the offence charged, but only the sufficiency of the information supporting the wiretap authorization. Accordingly, cross-examination could not be permitted where there was no reasonable likelihood that it would impact on the admissibility of the evidence, particularly having regard to the concern over the prolixity of proceedings and the need to protect informants.

Where the actual deponent of the affidavit had only a limited role in the investigation, the accused should be permitted to cross-examine the sub-affiant police officers who were actively involved in the investigation and provided the deponent with the information used for the affidavit: *R. v. Pasaluko* (1992), 77 C.C.C. (3d) 190 (B.C.S.C.).

A judge presiding at a preliminary inquiry has jurisdiction to grant leave to the accused to cross-examine police witnesses on affidavits used to obtain an authorization: *R. v. Dawson* (1998), 123 C.C.C. (3d) 385, 15 C.R. (5th) 201 (Ont. C.A.).

Subsection (5) / *[Designation of persons who may intercept]* – A designation by the provincial Attorney General is valid notwithstanding it is not expressly limited to offences within provincial jurisdiction (*i.e.*, Code offences). A designation in general terms will be construed as being so limited: *R. v. Miller and Thomas (No. 2)* (1975), 28 C.C.C. (2d) 115 (B.C. Co. Ct.). Furthermore, this subsection does not mean that interceptions may only be made by designated interceptors: *R. v. Miller and Thomas (No. 3)* (1975), 28 C.C.C. (2d) 118 (B.C. Co. Ct.).

If an interceptor is named in the authorization and described as a person designated by the Attorney General, the presumption of regularity applies and the Crown is not required to prove the designation in the absence of evidence to indicate some irregularity: *R. v. Shaw* (1983), 4 C.C.C. (3d) 348, 45 N.B.R. (2d) 21 (C.A.).

Where authority to intercept was given to a particular commanding officer or persons acting under his authority then the right to intercept would include a person acting within the scope or ambit of the general authority conferred upon him by his commanding officer. Such person need not be specifically and personally authorized by the commanding officer: *R. v. Vrany, Zikan and Dvorak* (1979), 46 C.C.C. (2d) 14 (Ont. C.A.).

Where the authorization names a certain interceptor and "any person acting under his authority" it is incumbent on the Crown to establish that the persons participating in the interceptions were in fact acting under his authority. On the other hand, interceptions recorded automatically at times when the equipment was not being monitored are admissible: *R. v. Shaw, supra.*

Subsections (6), (7) / [Renewals] – A renewal may only extend the time of the original authorization. It may not extend or modify the terms of the original authorization by including, for example, a person not provided for in the original authorization: *R. v. Badovinac, supra.* Nor may the renewal change the address of the place of interception: *R. v. Dass* (1979), 47 C.C.C. (2d) 194, 8 C.R. (3d) 224 (Man. C.A.), leave to appeal to S.C.C. refused 4 Man. R. (2d) 86n, 30 N.R. 609n.

Where, however, it is apparent that the second order was intended to be both a renewal of the original authorization and a new authorization it may properly include persons not included in the original authorization: *R. v. Vrany* (1979), 46 C.C.C. (2d) 14 (Ont. C.A.), application for leave to appeal to S.C.C. dismissed May 6, 1980.

Where the authorities seek to intercept the private communications of more targets then they may apply for a fresh authorization with respect to all of the proposed targets. There is no requirement that a renewal be obtained with respect to the persons named in the original authorization: *R. v. Thompson, supra.*

Further, where the authorities do obtain a second authorization, which includes additional persons and places, they do not have to comply with the provisions of subsec. (6) and thus do not have to disclose all of the details of each and every piece of incriminating evidence known to the authorities. The material in support of the fresh authorization should, however, include a full, fair and frank disclosure of relevant intercepted private communications obtained up to the time of the second authorization: *R. v. Moore: R. v. Bogdanich* (1993), 81 C.C.C. (3d) 161, 21 C.R. (4th) 387 (B.C.C.A.), affd [1995] 1 S.C.R. 756, 95 C.C.C. (3d) 288, 38 C.R. (4th) 44.

TIME LIMITATION IN RELATION TO CRIMINAL ORGANIZATIONS AND TERRORISM OFFENCES.

186.1 Notwithstanding paragraphs 184.2(4)(*e*) and 186(4)(*e*) and subsection 186(7), an authorization or any renewal of an authorization may be valid for one or more periods specified in the authorization exceeding sixty days, each not exceeding one year, where the authorization is in relation to

- (*a*) **an offence under section 467.11, 467.111, 467.12 or 467.13;**
- (*b*) **an offence committed for the benefit of, at the direction of or in association with a criminal organization; or**
- (*c*) **a terrorism offence. 1997, c. 23, s. 6; 2001, c. 32, s. 7; 2001, c. 41, s. 7 and 133(9); 2014, c. 17, s. 5.**

CROSS-REFERENCES

The terms "criminal organization" and "terrorism offence" are defined in s. 2. Sections 467.11 to 467.13 create offences with respect to criminal organizations. Section 184.2 provides for an authorization to intercept communications with the consent of one of the participants. Section 186 provides for the granting of an authorization to surreptitiously intercept private communications. Section 196(5) also gives a judge power to extend the notification required under that section in case of criminal organization investigations.

MANNER IN WHICH APPLICATION TO BE KEPT SECRET / Exception / Opening for further application / Opening on order of judge / Opening on order of trial judge / Order for destruction of documents / Order of judge / Idem / Editing of copies / Accused to be provided with copies / Original documents to be returned / Deleted parts / Documents to be kept secret — related warrant or order.

187. (1) All documents relating to an application made pursuant to any provision of this Part are confidential and, subject to subsection (1.1), shall be placed in a packet and sealed by the judge to whom the application is made immediately on determination of the application, and that packet shall be kept in the custody of the court in a place to which the public has no access or in such other place as the judge may authorize and shall not be dealt with except in accordance with subsections (1.2) to (1.5).

(1.1) An authorization given under this Part need not be placed in the packet except where, pursuant to subsection 184.3(7) or (8), the original authorization is in the hands of the judge, in which case that judge must place it in the packet and the facsimile remains with the applicant.

(1.2) The sealed packet may be opened and its contents removed for the purpose of dealing with an application for a further authorization or with an application for renewal of an authorization.

(1.3) A provincial court judge, a judge of a superior court of criminal jurisdiction or a judge as defined in section 552 may order that the sealed packet be opened and its contents removed for the purpose of copying and examining the documents contained in the packet.

(1.4) A judge or provincial court judge before whom a trial is to be held and who has jurisdiction in the province in which an authorization was given may order that the sealed packet be opened and its contents removed for the purpose of copying and examining the documents contained in the packet if

(*a*) any matter relevant to the authorization or any evidence obtained pursuant to the authorization is in issue in the trial; and

(*b*) the accused applies for such an order for the purpose of consulting the documents to prepare for trial.

(1.5) Where a sealed packet is opened, its contents shall not be destroyed except pursuant to an order of a judge of the same court as the judge who gave the authorization.

(2) An order under subsection (1.2), (1.3), (1.4) or (1.5) made with respect to documents relating to an application made pursuant to section 185 or subsection 186(6) or 196(2) may only be made after the Attorney General or the Minister of Public Safety and Emergency Preparedness by whom or on whose authority the application for the authorization to which the order relates was made has been given an opportunity to be heard.

(3) An order under subsection (1.2), (1.3), (1.4) or (1.5) made with respect to documents relating to an application made pursuant to subsection 184.2(2) or section 184.3 may only be made after the Attorney General has been given an opportunity to be heard.

(4) Where a prosecution has been commenced and an accused applies for an order for the copying and examination of documents pursuant to subsection (1.3) or (1.4), the judge shall not, notwithstanding those subsections, provide any copy of any document to the accused until the prosecutor has deleted any part of the copy of the document that the prosecutor believes would be prejudicial to the public interest, including any part that the prosecutor believes could

(*a*) compromise the identity of any confidential informant;

(*b*) compromise the nature and extent of ongoing investigations;

(*c*) endanger persons engaged in particular intelligence-gathering techniques and thereby prejudice future investigations in which similar techniques would be used; or

(*d*) prejudice the interests of innocent persons.

(5) After the prosecutor has deleted the parts of the copy of the document to be given to the accused under subsection (4), the accused shall be provided with an edited copy of the document.

(6) After the accused has received an edited copy of a document, the prosecutor shall keep a copy of the original document, and an edited copy of the document and the original document shall be returned to the packet and the packet resealed.

(7) An accused to whom an edited copy of a document has been provided pursuant to subsection (5) may request that the judge before whom the trial is to be held order that any part of the document deleted by the prosecutor be made available to the accused, and the judge shall order that a copy of any part that, in the opinion of the judge, is required in order for the accused to make full answer and defence and for which the provision of a judicial summary would not be sufficient, be made available to the accused.

(8) The rules provided for in this section apply to all documents relating to a request for a related warrant or order referred to in subsection 184.2(5), 186(8) or 188(6) with any necessary modifications. 1973-74, c. 50, s. 2, R.S.C. 1985, c. 27 (1st Supp.), s. 24; 1993, c. 40, s. 7; 2005, c. 10, s. 24; 2014, c. 31, s. 10.

CROSS-REFERENCES

Note that s. 24 of the *Access to Information Act*, R.S.C. 1985, c. A-1, provides that the head of a government institution shall refuse to disclose any record requested under that Act that contains information, the disclosure of which is restricted by or pursuant to this section.

SYNOPSIS

This section sets out the manner in which certain documents relating to applications under this Part are to be kept confidential. Subject to subsec. (1.1), all documents are to be placed in a sealed packet and kept in the custody of the court. By virtue of subsec. (1.1), the authorization itself is not placed in the packet except in the case of the telecommunication procedure under s. 184.3 in which case the authorization is placed in the sealed packet and the facsimile remains with the applicant.

The other provisions of this section deal with the circumstances in which the sealed packet can be opened and the material used on the application disclosed. Under subsec. (1.2), the packet may be opened for the purpose of a renewal or further authorization. Under subsec. (1.3), a judge may permit the packet to be opened and the contents copied and examined. Similarly, the trial judge, under subsec. (1.4), may permit the packet to be opened and the contents copied and examined where application is made by the accused for the purpose of preparing for trial and any matter relevant to the authorization or any evidence obtained pursuant to the authorization is "in issue" in the trial. These applications must be made upon notice to the Attorney General.

Subsections (4) to (7) then set out the editing procedure. In summary Crown counsel will first edit the material to remove information, the disclosure of which would be prejudicial to the public interest. The accused is then provided with the edited copy. The accused, however, may apply to the trial judge for an order that portions which were deleted be disclosed to the accused. The further disclosure order will be made where the judge is of the opinion that the additional material is necessary in order for the accused to make full answer and defence and where provision of a "judicial summary" of the deleted material would not be sufficient. This process roughly tracks the decisions of the Supreme Court of Canada in *Dersch v. Canada (Attorney General)*, [1990] 2 S.C.R. 1505, 60 C.C.C. (3d) 132, 80 C.R. (3d) 299, and *R. v. Garofoli*, [1990] 2 S.C.R. 1421, 60 C.C.C. (3d) 161, 80 C.R. (3d) 317. The former decision had held under the predecessor legislation that, as a result of the enactment of the *Charter of Rights and Freedoms*, the accused had the right to access to the sealed packet in order to make full answer and defence. The latter decision had laid out a procedure for editing the affidavit and is noted below and noted under s. 186 in reference to the right to cross-examine the deponent of the affidavit.

ANNOTATIONS

Note: The cases noted under this section were decided under the predecessor legislation but were considered to be of assistance in applying this legislation.

Access to sealed packet – An application for access to the sealed packet may be made to a superior court judge prior to the preliminary inquiry. That judge may also edit the affidavit. Where, however, the accused claims that he needs access to the identity of a secret informer then that issue will probably have to be determined by the trial judge: *R. v. Giannakopoulos* (1991), 66 C.C.C. (3d) 541, 82 Alta. L.R. (2d) 243 (Q.B.).

The right to full disclosure requires that an accused, against whom wiretap evidence is to be adduced, have access to an edited copy of the affidavit in the sealed packet prior to electing his mode of trial. At this initial stage, the affidavit is to be edited by Crown counsel since only the trial judge has the power to make the final determination as to what material should be edited from the affidavit: *R. v. Aranda* (1992), 69 C.C.C. (3d) 420 (Ont. Ct. (Gen. Div.)).

Where there is likely no affidavit in the sealed packet because the application was brought on an emergency basis pursuant to s. 188 the accused is entitled to cross-examine the person upon whose submissions the order was granted: *R. v. Graves* (1987), 31 C.C.C. (3d) 552 (N.S.S.C.).

A non-accused target may apply pursuant to subsec. (1.3) to examine the contents of the packet. Different considerations, however, apply to a non-accused target who does not face the threat of imprisonment. The non-accused target's substantive constitutional rights do not compel absolute access to confidential information held by the state where the applicant does not face the jeopardy of the criminal process. In the balancing process, the state's pressing interests in the confidentiality of the package is the dominant consideration in the exercise of this discretion. A judge should normally only exercise discretion in favour of granting access to the packet to a non-accused target on the presentation of some evidence that law enforcement officials engaged in fraud or wilful non-disclosure in obtaining the authorization although such a judicial order may be justified in other cases. If the target is successful in securing access to the packet, he may only then seek access to the recording materials upon a new motion in a subsequent proceeding: *Michaud v. Quebec (Attorney General)*, [1996] 3 S.C.R. 3, 109 C.C.C. (3d) 289, 1 C.R. (5th) 1.

Editing of affidavit – If the Crown can support the authorization on the basis of the material as edited then the authorization is confirmed. If, however, the editing renders the authorization insupportable then the Crown may apply to have the trial judge consider as much of the excised material as is necessary to support the authorization. The trial judge should accede to such a request only if satisfied that the accused is sufficiently aware of the nature of the excised material to challenge it in argument or by evidence. In this respect, a judicial summary of the excised material should be provided if it will fulfil that function: *R. v. Garofoli*, [1990] 2 S.C.R. 1421, 60 C.C.C. (3d) 161, 80 C.R. (3d) 317 (5:2).

When determining whether the contents of a wiretap affidavit should be disclosed to an accused, full disclosure should be the rule, subject to certain exceptions based upon overriding public interests which may justify non-disclosure. It was improper to edit out material which had already been disclosed in earlier proceedings arising out of the same investigation. Since it is only confidential information that should be edited, the affidavits as edited at the earlier trial should have been the starting point in this case. It was also an error to excise not only information which might tend to identify informers but information obtained from informers and others and material characterized merely as commentary, summary or opinion. The discretion to determine what editing is required to ensure that the public interest is protected does not include the power to edit material whose continued confidentiality clearly is not justified by any of the public interest concerns: *R. v. Durette*, [1994] 1 S.C.R. 469, 88 C.C.C. (3d) 1, 28 C.R. (4th) 1.

Cross-examination of deponent of affidavit – See notes under s. 186 above.

Appeal or review of decision refusing or granting access – No appeal lies to the Court of Appeal from the decision of the authorizing judge refusing an application to open the sealed packet so as to prepare to review and set aside the authorization: *R. v. Meltzer* (1986), 29 C.C.C. (3d) 266 (B.C.C.A.), affd on other grounds [1989] 1 S.C.R. 1764, 49 C.C.C. (3d) 453, 70 C.R. (3d) 383; *R. v. Kumar* (1987), 35 C.C.C. (3d) 477 (Sask. C.A.), leave to appeal to S.C.C. refused [1987] 1 S.C.R. ix, 79 N.R. 395, 58 Sask. R. 80*n*.

Similarly, where the Director of Civil Forfeiture brought a civil action seeking forfeiture of property and a judge made an order unsealing wiretap affidavits under subsec. (1.3), the Director's appeal of that order to the Court of Appeal was quashed. The court held (2:1) that the unsealing order was criminal in nature, despite having taken place in the context of a civil proceeding: *British Columbia (Director of Civil Forfeiture) v. Hells Angels Motorcycle Corp.* (2014), 314 C.C.C. (3d) 229 (B.C.C.A.).

APPLICATIONS TO SPECIALLY APPOINTED JUDGES / Authorizations in emergency / Certain interceptions deemed not lawful / Definition of "Chief Justice" / Inadmissibility of evidence / Related warrant or order.

188. (1) Notwithstanding section 185, an application made under that section for an authorization may be made *ex parte* to a judge of a superior court of criminal jurisdiction, or a judge as defined in section 552, designated from time to time by the Chief Justice, by a peace officer specially designated in writing, by name or otherwise, for the purposes of this section by

(*a*) the Minister of Public Safety and Emergency Preparedness, if the offence is one in respect of which proceedings, if any, may be instituted by the Government of Canada and conducted by or on behalf of the Attorney General of Canada, or

(*b*) the Attorney General of a province, in respect of any other offence in the province,

if the urgency of the situation requires interception of private communications to commence before an authorization could, with reasonable diligence, be obtained under section 186.

(2) Where the judge to whom an application is made pursuant to subsection (1) is satisfied that the urgency of the situation requires that interception of private communications commence before an authorization could, with reasonable diligence, be obtained under section 186, he may, on such terms and conditions, if any, as he considers advisable, give an authorization in writing for a period of up to thirty-six hours.

(3) [*Repealed*, 1993, c. 40, s. 8.]

(4) In this section, "Chief Justice" means

(*a*) in the Province of Ontario, the Chief Justice of the Ontario Court;

(*b*) in the Province of Quebec, the Chief Justice of the Superior Court;

  (c) in the Provinces of Nova Scotia, British Columbia and Prince Edward Island, the Chief Justice of the Supreme Court;

  (d) in the Provinces of New Brunswick, Manitoba, Saskatchewan and Alberta, the Chief Justice of the Court of Queen's Bench;

  (e) in the Province of Newfoundland and Labrador, the Chief Justice of the Supreme Court, Trial Division; and

  (f) in Yukon, the Northwest Territories and Nunavut, the senior judge within the meaning of subsection 22(3) of the *Judges Act.*

(5) The trial judge may deem inadmissible the evidence obtained by means of an interception of a private communication pursuant to a subsequent authorization given under this section, where he finds that the application for the subsequent authorization was based on the same facts, and involved the interception of the private communications of the same person or persons, or related to the same offence, on which the application for the original authorization was based.

(6) A judge who gives an authorization under this section may, at the same time, issue a warrant or make an order under any of sections 487, 487.01, 487.014 to 487.018, 487.02, 492.1 and 492.2 if the judge is of the opinion that the requested warrant or order is related to the execution of the authorization, that the urgency of the situation requires the warrant or the order and that it can be reasonably executed or complied with within 36 hours. 1973-74, c. 50, s. 2; 1974-75-76, c. 19, s. 1; 1978-79, c. 11, s. 10; R.S.C. 1985, c. 27 (1st Supp.), s. 25; c. 27 (2nd Supp.), s. 10; 1990, c. 17, s. 10; 1992, c. 1, s. 58; 1992, c. 51, s. 35; 1993, c. 28, Sch. III, s. 29 (repealed by 1999, c. 3, s. 12); 1993, c. 40, s. 8; 1999, c. 3, ss. 12, 28; 2002, c. 7, s. 140; 2005, c. 10, s. 34(1)(f)(vii); 2014, c. 31, s. 11; 2015, c. 3, s. 47.

CROSS-REFERENCES

The terms "intercept", "offence" and "private communication" are defined in s. 183. "Peace officer" and "superior court of criminal jurisdiction" are defined in s. 2.

The procedure for applying for and granting of a normal "60-day" authorization is dealt with in ss. 185 and 186. Admissibility of evidence obtained as a result of execution of the authorization is dealt with in s. 189. The unlawful interception offence in s. 184 would not apply to a person acting under an authorization granted under this section by virtue of s. 184(2)(b).

Authorizations may be executed anywhere in Canada in accordance with s. 188.1. Provision is made in s. 487.02 for the making of an assistance order to require persons to co-operate in the carrying out of orders made under this section. Section 188.2 provides protection against civil or criminal liability for a person acting in accordance with an authorization.

SYNOPSIS

This section authorizes *emergency applications* for *authorizations to be issued to a designated judge* and sets out an *evidentiary rule* regarding the *admission of such evidence* at trial.

Section 188(1) permits such applications to be made *ex parte* by a peace officer to a judge designated by the Chief Justice of a province, if the *urgency of the situation* requires that an *interception be made before* one could, *with reasonable diligence,* bring an application in accordance with s. 186. "Chief Justice" is defined in s. 188(4). The *peace officer* bringing the application must be *designated in writing* by either the Attorney General or the Solicitor General (depending on whose behalf the application is made) *for the purpose of this section.* Subsection (2) provides that, if the *judge is satisfied* that the *urgency* of the situation requires that the interception should begin before a conventional application could, with reasonable diligence, be made, he *may* issue a written authorization. This type of authorization can *last for a maximum of 36 hours* and may contain whatever *terms and conditions* the judge deems advisable.

Subsection (5) gives a *trial judge* the *discretion to exclude* evidence of private communications intercepted under a *subsequent emergency authorization* under certain circumstances. The circumstances triggering the discretion are that the *judge finds* that the *subsequent authorization* was based on the *same facts*, and involved the *same targeted persons or the same offence*, as the *first application* for an authorization was based upon.

ANNOTATIONS
To comply with the requirements of s. 8 of the Charter, the information which forms the basis for the application under this section must be made on oath or affirmation, or *semble*, the informant must undertake to confirm the information under oath. It may also be that s. 8 requires that the process relating to the obtaining of the authorization includes some form of memorializing or recording the gist of the sworn allegations: *R. v. Galbraith* (1989), 49 C.C.C. (3d) 178, 70 C.R. (3d) 392 (Alta. C.A.). Folld: *R. v. Laudicina* (1990), 53 C.C.C. (3d) 281, 41 C.R.R. 142 (Ont. H.C.J.).

The certificate referred to in subsec. (3) may be given at the same time as the authorization is granted and based on the same material: *R. v. Laudicina, supra.*

EXECUTION OF AUTHORIZATIONS / Execution in another province.

188.1 (1) Subject to subsection (2), the interception of a private communication authorized pursuant to section 184.2, 184.3, 186 or 188 may be carried out anywhere in Canada.

(2) Where an authorization is given under section 184.2, 184.3, 186 or 188 in one province but it may reasonably be expected that it is to be executed in another province and the execution of the authorization would require entry into or upon the property of any person in the other province or would require that an order under section 487.02 be made with respect to any person in that other province, a judge in the other province may, on application, confirm the authorization and when the authorization is so confirmed, it shall have full force and effect in that other province as though it had originally been given in that other province. 1993, c. 40, s. 9.

CROSS-REFERENCES
The various orders referred to in this section are the authorizations to intercept with consent of one of the parties [ss. 184.2 and 184.3]; the normal 60-day order for surreptitious interception [s. 186] and the emergency 36-hour authorization [s. 188]. This section also applies to general warrants to conduct video surveillance under s. 487.01(5).

SYNOPSIS
This section reverses case law under the predecessor legislation which had held that a judge in one province could not grant an authorization to intercept private communications in another province. By virtue of subsec. (1), the authorization may be carried out anywhere in Canada. The only caveat is that, pursuant to subsec. (2), if it will be necessary to enter private property in the other province or to obtain an assistance order under s. 487.02, then the authorization must be confirmed in the other province. It is unclear what material, other than the authorization, needs to be placed before the judge in the other province.

ANNOTATIONS
A confirmation order was not required to effect an interception obtained in one province where the telephone company employees in the other province voluntarily assisted the police by re-routing calls to equipment in the police interception room. Neither of the two circumstances set out in this section that require a confirmation order existed: *R. v. Pham* (1997), 122 C.C.C. (3d) 90, 164 W.A.C. 55 (B.C.C.A.), leave to appeal to S.C.C. refused 128 C.C.C. (3d) vi.

This provision is permissive rather than mandatory. Accordingly, there is no requirement for an authorization made in one province but executed in another province to be confirmed by a judge in the province of execution: *R. v. Doiron* (2007), 221 C.C.C. (3d) 97 (N.B.C.A.), leave to appeal to S.C.C. refused 223 C.C.C. (3d) vi (S.C.C.).

NO CIVIL OR CRIMINAL LIABILITY.

188.2 No person who acts in accordance with an authorization or under section 184.1 or 184.4 or who aids, in good faith, a person who he or she believes on reasonable grounds is acting in accordance with an authorization or under one of those sections incurs any criminal or civil liability for anything reasonably done further to the authorization or to that section. 1993, c. 40, s. 9.

CROSS-REFERENCES

"Authorization" is defined in s. 183. This section would therefore apply to persons executing authorizations granted under ss. 184.2, 184.3, 186 and 188, in addition to persons acting under ss. 184.1 [interception without authorization but with consent of party to communication where risk of bodily harm] and s. 184.4 [interception without authorization in exigent circumstances].

NOTICE OF INTENTION TO PRODUCE EVIDENCE / Privileged evidence.

189. (1) to (4) [*Repealed*, 1993, c. 40, s. 10.]

(5) The contents of a private communication that is obtained from an interception of the private communication pursuant to any provision of, or pursuant to an authorization given under, this Part shall not be received in evidence unless the party intending to adduce it has given to the accused reasonable notice of the intention together with

　　(a) a transcript of the private communication, where it will be adduced in the form of a recording, or a statement setting out full particulars of the private communication, where evidence of the private communication will be given *viva voce*; and

　　(b) a statement respecting the time, place and date of the private communication and the parties thereto, if known.

(6) Any information obtained by an interception that, but for the interception, would have been privileged remains privileged and inadmissible as evidence without the consent of the person enjoying the privilege. 1973-74, c. 50, s. 2; 1976-77, c. 53, s. 10; 1993, c. 40, s. 10.

CROSS-REFERENCES

The terms "intercept" and "private communication" are defined in s. 183. Section 190 makes provision for the giving of further particulars of the private communication that is intended to be adduced in evidence. The notice requirement in subsec. (5) of this section is distinct from the requirements of s. 196 which requires the Attorney General or Solicitor General to give notice to a person who has been the target of an interception pursuant to an authorization.

SYNOPSIS

This section imposes *notice and disclosure requirements* which must be complied *with before evidence* of lawfully intercepted private communications *may be received* in evidence. The accused must receive *reasonable notice of the intention to introduce* such evidence along with either a *transcript* of the intercepted private communications or a statement setting out the full particulars of the communication (depending on how it is intended that the evidence be adduced) *and* details of the place, date, time of, and parties to, the communication (if known).

Subsection (6) *protects the character* of intercepted otherwise *privileged communications* by providing that such evidence is inadmissible without the consent of the person who enjoys the privilege.

ANNOTATIONS

Many of the annotations under this section have been removed, consequent upon the amendment of this section to remove the automatic exclusionary rule for unlawfully intercepted private communications. Nevertheless, where private communications have been unlawfully intercepted then there will likely be a violation of s. 8 of the Charter. It has previously been held that a search will be reasonable if it is authorized by law, if the law itself is reasonable and if the manner in which the search was carried out is reasonable: *R. v. Collins*, [1987] 1 S.C.R. 265, 33 C.C.C. (3d) 1, 56 C.R. (3d) 193. In considering whether the particular interception was lawful, reference should be made to the notes under ss. 184 to 186 which authorize interceptions and to the notes under this section which deal with circumstances in which the interception has been lawfully made. If the search or seizure of the evidence is unlawful and unreasonable then the evidence is subject to exclusion if the conditions in s. 24(2) of the Charter have been fulfilled. Reference should also be made to the notes under ss. 8 and 24(2) of the Charter, *infra*.

The amendment to this section removing the automatic rule of exclusion where the interception was not lawfully made applies retrospectively. Thus, admission of the evidence at the accused's trial is to be determined under s. 24(2) of the *Canadian Charter of Rights and Freedoms*, and not under the provisions of this section as they stood at the time the accused was charged: *R. v. Rendon* (1999), 140 C.C.C. (3d) 12, 33 C.R. (5th) 311 (Que. C.A.), leave to appeal to S.C.C. granted 143 C.C.C. (3d) vi.

Intercepted private communications are not "conscriptive" evidence for the purpose of analysis under s. 24(2) of the Charter as explained in *R. v. Stillman*, [1997] 1 S.C.R. 607, 113 C.C.C. (3d) 321, 5 C.R. (5th) 1 [noted under s. 24 of the Charter, *infra*]: *R. v. Fliss*, [2002] 1 S.C.R. 535, 161 C.C.C. (3d) 225, 49 C.R. (5th) 395.

Meaning of "intercepted" – "Intercepted" means an interference by a third party between the place of origin and the place of destination of the communication and does not include the situation where there are only two people involved although the originator is mistaken as to the identity of the party receiving the communication: *R. v. McQueen* (1975), 25 C.C.C. (2d) 262, [1975] 6 W.W.R. 604 (Alta. S.C. App. Div.); *R. v. Singh* (1998), 127 C.C.C. (3d) 429, 178 W.A.C. 198 (B.C.C.A.).

Eavesdropping by a police officer as to the private conversation between two accused in a prison cell constitutes the interception of a private communication within the meaning of this section: *R. v. Boutilier and Melnick* (1976), 35 C.C.C. (2d) 555, 76 D.L.R. (3d) 291 (N.S. T.D.). *Contra: R. v. Beckner* (1978), 43 C.C.C. (2d) 356 (Ont. C.A.), where it was held that Part VI has no application where the conversation is merely overheard by a third party without the use of any mechanical or other device. Similarly, where the recipient of the conversation testifies as to its contents, the provisions of this Part have no application: *R. v. Gamble and Nichols* (1978), 40 C.C.C. (2d) 415 (Alta. S.C. App. Div.).

Subsection (5) [Notice] / Persons entitled to notice – On a joint trial all the accused must be served with the notice prescribed by this subsection not merely those accused who were the subject of the interception: *R. v. Viscount* (1977), 37 C.C.C. (2d) 533 (Ont. Co. Ct.).

A co-accused has the right to notice of another accused's intention to adduce the contents of intercepted communications during the course of their joint trial: *R. v. Proudfoot* (1995), 102 C.C.C. (3d) 260, 102 W.A.C. 241 *sub nom. R. v. Steel*, 34 Alta. L.R. (3d) 426 (C.A.).

It was held in *R. v. Nygaard*, [1989] 2 S.C.R. 1074, 51 C.C.C. (3d) 417, 72 C.R. (3d) 257 (8:1), that this section applies where Crown counsel sought to cross-examine a defence witness on intercepted private communications which she had with the accused. The effect of the cross-examination substantially undermined the alibi evidence given by this witness and in reality the private communications were used as evidence against the accused. Accordingly it was necessary for the Crown to prove that subsec. (5) has been complied with.

Notice given at preliminary inquiry – A notice given prior to the preliminary inquiry remains valid for all subsequent proceedings including a trial on a preferred indictment where the accused is discharged at the preliminary hearing: *R. v. Welsh and Iannuzzi (No. 6), supra.*

The fact that the intercepted private communication was introduced at the accused's preliminary hearing does not satisfy the specific notice provisions of this subsection: *R. v. Dunn* (1975), 28 C.C.C. (2d) 538, 33 C.R.N.S. 299 (N.S. Co. Ct.).

Transcript (para. (*a*)) – A "transcript" within the meaning of this subsection need not be absolutely word perfect nor need it be certified by a Court stenographer: *R. v. Dunn* (1977), 36 C.C.C. (2d) 495, 38 C.R.N.S. 383 (Sask. C.A.), affd 52 C.C.C. (2d) 127*n*, [1979] 2 S.C.R. 1012 *sub nom. R. v. Yee.*

This subsection is complied with where the transcript is in one of the official languages even where the conversation was in another language: *R. v. Ma, Ho and Lai* (1975), 28 C.C.C. (2d) 16 (B.C. Co. Ct.); *R. v. Johnny and Billy* (1981), 62 C.C.C. (2d) 33 (B.C.S.C.), affd 5 C.C.C. (3d) 538, 149 D.L.R. (3d) 710 (C.A.).

The requirement of a "transcript" is satisfied by giving the accused a copy of the actual tape recording: *R. v. Dass* (1977), 39 C.C.C. (2d) 465 (Man. Q.B.).

While it is the tapes themselves which constitute the evidence which should be and must be considered by the jury, it is nonetheless appropriate, in many instances, that transcripts not only be read while the tapes are being played but also be retained by the jury during their deliberations. Examples of cases where the trial judge might properly exercise his discretion are where the tape is in a foreign language or where the communications are lengthy or numerous. Where, however, the jury is permitted to retain the transcripts, there must be instructions by the trial judge that it is the tapes which constitute the evidence and the necessary equipment must be made available so that the jury may listen to the tapes during their deliberations. A police officer who has listened to the tapes may give evidence as to the identification of the voices reproduced and may, as well, tender a transcript which he has prepared and which he testifies accurately represents the conversations heard on the tape. The officer can, of course, be cross-examined both on voice identification and accuracy of the transcripts and it would be open to the defence to tender a witness who also has listened to the tapes and prepared a transcript setting out an alternate interpretation. The two transcripts could then go to the jury: *R. v. Rowbotham* (1988), 41 C.C.C. (3d) 1, 63 C.R. (3d) 113, 25 O.A.C. 321 (C.A.).

Whether the tapes of communications in a foreign language will be played for the jury during the course of the trial and whether the tapes should be left with the jury during its deliberations are matters within the trial judge's discretion. Where the communications are in a foreign language, secondary opinion evidence in the form of a translation will be essential to the trier of fact. If the translation is in the form of a transcript, the transcript should be filed but the extent to which the transcripts are read during the course of the trial and left with the jury during deliberations falls within the discretion of the trial judge: *R. v. Shayesteh* (1996), 111 C.C.C. (3d) 225, 31 O.R. (3d) 161 (C.A.).

While a police officer who has prepared a transcript of the conversations may not be an "expert" on voice identification, it was open to the trial judge to point out to the jury the greater opportunities the officer had for identification, provided the jury was clearly told that they were not bound to accept the officer's opinion: *R. v. Rowbotham* (1988), 41 C.C.C. (3d) 1, 63 C.R. (3d) 113 (Ont. C.A.).

Contents of notice (para. (*b*)) – This subsection was complied with where the accused was served with copies of the transcripts showing time, date, telephone number and parties to the conversation and told that the transcripts could be used at trial, and where his solicitor was given written notice of intention which also contained details of the date, place and parties to the conversations: *R. v. Schmitke and Mudry* (1981), 60 C.C.C. (2d) 180 (B.C.C.A.).

The words "if known" in subpara. (*b*) modify the entire phrase "time, place and date of the private communication and the parties thereto" and therefore only if the time, place and date are known need those particulars be given. Where, however, the evidence establishes that the police did have this information but did not supply it to the accused, the taped conversation is inadmissible: *R. v. Allen (No. 4)* (1979), 47 C.C.C. (2d) 55 (Ont. H.C.J.).

Identification of the place of the interception requires the prosecution to inform the accused of the location of the two telephones at the opposite ends of the communication, where they are known. Thus, where the police knew the location of the pay telephone from which a call was made it should have been identified in the notice: *R. v. Morello* (1987), 40 C.C.C. (3d) 278, 83 A.R. 75 (C.A.).

Subsection (6) / Privilege – This subsection renders inadmissible intercepted private communications between the accused husband and his wife where the wife could not be a competent or compellable witness at the instance of the Crown. The privilege attaching to husband and wife communications is not destroyed where the communication is obtained by an interception within the meaning of this Part: *R. v. Jean and Piesinger* (1979), 46 C.C.C. (2d) 176, 7 C.R. (3d) 338 (Alta. S.C. App. Div.), affd [1980] 1 S.C.R. 400, 51 C.C.C. (2d) 192*n*, 20 A.R. 360; *R. v. Lloyd and Lloyd*, [1981] 2 S.C.R. 645, 64 C.C.C. (2d) 169, 31 C.R. (3d) 157 (6:3).

While this subsection preserves privileges which are recognized at law, although the conversations have been intercepted pursuant to an authorization, the police informer privilege had no application so as to exclude conversations between the accused, a former police informer, and his co-accused a police officer. To be protected by the privilege, the actions of the informer must relate to his function as a police informer. On the evidence accepted by the trial judge in this case, the conduct and communications between the accused and other parties had nothing to do with the accused's function as an informer. The evidence showed that the accused was acting in his own interests and that of his co-accused. The fact that the accused was a police informer did not give him licence to commit criminal offences solely in his own interests: *R. v. Hiscock; R. v. Sauvé* (1992), 46 Q.A.C. 263 (C.A.).

There is no class privilege for communications between parent and child that would render intercepted communications inadmissible at the trial of the child (a young offender): *R. v. E. (T.K.)* (2005), 194 C.C.C. (3d) 496, 28 C.R. (6th) 366, 281 N.B.R. (2d) 360 (C.A.), leave to appeal to S.C.C. refused 198 C.C.C. (3d) vi. [Also see note of this case under s. 146 of the *Youth Criminal Justice Act*.]

FURTHER PARTICULARS.

190. Where an accused has been given notice pursuant to subsection 189(5), any judge of the court in which the trial of the accused is being or is to be held may at any time order that further particulars be given of the private communication that is intended to be adduced in evidence. 1973-74, c. 50, s. 2.

CROSS-REFERENCES

The term "private communication" is defined in s. 183.

The particulars referred to in this section should not be confused with particulars ordered by a court under s. 587 to supplement an information or indictment.

SYNOPSIS

This section permits a *judge of the trial court* to order that *additional particulars pertaining to private communications* be provided to an *accused who has received a notice* under s. 189(5) that the actual private communications (*i.e.*, primary evidence) will be introduced as evidence against him.

POSSESSION, ETC. / Exemptions / Terms and conditions of licence.

191. **(1) Every one who possesses, sells or purchases any electromagnetic, acoustic, mechanical or other device or any component thereof knowing that the design thereof renders it primarily useful for surreptitious interception of private communications is guilty of an indictable offence and liable to imprisonment for a term not exceeding two years.**

(2) Subsection (1) does not apply to

   (*a*) a police officer in possession of a device or component described in subsection (1) in the course of his employment;

   (*b*) a person in possession of such a device or component for the purpose of using it in an interception made or to be made in accordance with an authorization;

   (*b*.1) a person in possession of such a device or component under the direction of a police officer in order to assist that officer in the course of his duties as a police officer;

   (*c*) an officer or a servant of Her Majesty in right of Canada or a member of the Canadian Forces in possession of such a device or component in the course of his duties as such an officer, servant or member, as the case may be; and

   (*d*) any other person in possession of such a device or component under the authority of a licence issued by the Minister of Public Safety and Emergency Preparedness.

(3) A licence issued for the purpose of paragraph (2)(*d*) may contain such terms and conditions relating to the possession, sale or purchase of a device or component described in subsection (1) as the Minister of Public Safety and Emergency Preparedness may prescribe. 1973-74, c. 50, s. 2; R.S.C. 1985, c. 27 (1st Supp.), s. 26; 2005, c. 10, s. 34(1)(*f*)(viii); 2013, c. 8, s. 4.

CROSS-REFERENCES

The terms "authorization", "electro-magnetic, acoustic, mechanical or other device", "intercept", "private communication" and "sell" are defined in s. 183. Possession is defined in s. 4(3). "Canadian Forces" is defined in s. 2 and police officer and police constable are within the definition of "peace officer" in s. 2. Under s. 193 it is an offence to unlawfully disclose an intercepted private communication.

Pursuant to s. 192, any device by means of which the offence under this section was committed may be ordered forfeited. The offence in this section can itself be the basis for an authorization to intercept private communications, by virtue of the definition of "offence" in s. 183. Related offences are the interception offence in s. 184 and the disclosure offence in s. 193.

The accused has an election as to mode of trial of the offence described in subsec. (1) pursuant to s. 536(2). Release pending trial is determined by s. 515, although the accused is eligible for release by the officer in charge under s. 498.

Note: By virtue of s. 487.01(5) the offence and exceptions in this section also apply to video surveillance in circumstances where persons have a reasonable expectation of privacy.

SYNOPSIS

Section 191 makes it an *indictable offence* to do any of the specified things in relation to *any of the devices* listed (which may be used to *surreptitiously intercept private communications*). The prohibited devices include not only any electromagnetic, acoustic, mechanical device, but extend also to *any other device or component* thereof, if *its design makes it useful primarily* for the *surreptitious interception of private communications*. It must be shown that the accused *knew* of the *nature or abilities* of the device or component. The wide-ranging description of the prohibited activities with such devices is *possessing, selling, or purchasing*. The penalty upon conviction is a maximum of two years' imprisonment.

Subsection (2) provides a series of *exceptions to liability under subsec. (1)*. Subsection (2)(*a*) to (*c*) exclude the operation of subsec. (1) to certain *classes of persons*, generally police officers, those carrying out lawful interceptions, those working under the direction of the police, or members of the Canadian forces. Such possession by the police or Canadian forces members must generally be in the course of their employment. Section 191(2)(*d*) exempts those who *hold licences to possess such devices* from criminal liability under subsec. (1). These licences are *issued by the federal Solicitor General* and may contain, pursuant to subsec. (3), terms and conditions.

ANNOTATIONS

A radio receiver tuned to a police band is not a device prohibited by this section where the evidence shows that the police are aware that members of the public have receivers capable of intercepting their communications. In such circumstances it could not be said that the device was intercepting "private communications" as those words are defined by s. 183: *R. v. Pitts* (1975), 29 C.C.C. (2d) 150 (Ont. Co. Ct.).

Similarly, *R. v. Comeau* (1984), 11 C.C.C. (3d) 61, 37 C.R. (3d) 286 (N.B.C.A.), where it was held that the use of codes by the police to disguise the broadcasts while showing an intention that they only be understood by the police was insufficient to produce any reasonable expectation that the broadcasts would not be intercepted. The originators would still expect many persons to continue to "listen" to the broadcasts.

FORFEITURE / Limitation.

192. (1) Where a person is convicted of an offence under section 184 or 191, any electro-magnetic, acoustic, mechanical or other device by means of which the offence was committed or the possession of which constituted the offence, on the conviction, in addition to any punishment that is imposed, may be ordered forfeited to Her Majesty whereupon it may be disposed of as the Attorney General directs.

(2) No order for forfeiture shall be made under subsection (1) in respect of telephone, telegraph or other communication facilities or equipment owned by a person engaged in providing telephone, telegraph or other communication service to the public or forming part of the telephone, telegraph or other communication service or system of that person by means of which an offence under section 184 has been committed if that person was not a party to the offence. 1973-74, c. 50, s. 2.

CROSS-REFERENCES

The terms "electro-magnetic, acoustic, mechanical or other device", are defined in s. 183. "Attorney-General" is defined in s. 2. A party to an offence is defined by ss. 21 and 22.

In addition to the penalties set out in ss. 184 and 191 and the order under this section, a court that convicts an accused of the s. 184 offence or an offence under s. 193 may make an award of punitive damages under s. 194.

SYNOPSIS

This section authorizes the *forfeiture of any device* which was the *means of committing an offence* for which the accused has been convicted under s. 184 (unlawful interception of private communications) or s. 191 (unlawful possession, etc., of such devices). Such an order may be made *upon sentencing, in addition* to any other punishment. The section provides that the device is to be turned over to Her Majesty, and the Attorney General may then direct how it will be disposed of.

Subsection (2) *exempts* from such order, the *listed equipment owned by a person who is involved in providing telephone* services (and other specified lawful activities) to the public. However, the exception only applies if the owner was *not a party to the offence*.

DISCLOSURE OF INFORMATION / Exemptions / Publishing of prior lawful disclosure.

193. (1) Where a private communication has been intercepted by means of an electromagnetic, acoustic, mechanical or other device without the consent, express or implied, of the originator thereof or of the person intended by the originator thereof to receive it, every one who, without the express consent of the originator thereof or of the person intended by the originator thereof to receive it, wilfully

    (*a*) uses or discloses the private communication or any part thereof or the substance, meaning or purport thereof or of any part thereof, or

    (*b*) discloses the existence thereof,

is guilty of an indictable offence and liable to imprisonment for a term not exceeding two years.

(2) Subsection (1) does not apply to a person who discloses a private communication or any part thereof or the substance, meaning or purport thereof or of any part thereof or who discloses the existence of a private communication

    (*a*) in the course of or for the purpose of giving evidence in any civil or criminal proceedings or in any other proceedings in which the person may be required to give evidence on oath;

    (*b*) in the course of or for the purpose of any criminal investigation if the private communication was lawfully intercepted;

    (*c*) in giving notice under section 189 or furnishing further particulars pursuant to an order under section 190;

    (*d*) in the course of the operation of

        (i) a telephone, telegraph or other communication service to the public,

        (ii) a department or an agency of the Government of Canada, or

        (iii) services relating to the management or protection of a computer system, as defined in subsection 342.1(2),

    if the disclosure is necessarily incidental to an interception described in paragraph 184(2)(*c*), (*d*) or (*e*);

    (*e*) where disclosure is made to a peace officer or prosecutor in Canada or to a person or authority with responsibility in a foreign state for the investigation or prosecution of offences and is intended to be in the interests of the administration of justice in Canada or elsewhere; or

    (*f*) where the disclosure is made to the Director of the Canadian Security Intelligence Service or to an employee of the Service for the purpose of enabling the Service to perform its duties and functions under section 12 of the *Canadian Security Intelligence Service Act*.

(3) Subsection (1) does not apply to a person who discloses a private communication or any part thereof or the substance, meaning or purport thereof or of any part thereof or who discloses the existence of a private communication where that which is disclosed by him was, prior to the disclosure, lawfully disclosed in the course of or for the purpose of giving evidence in proceedings referred to in paragraph (2)(*a*). 1973-74, c. 50, s. 2; 1976-77, c. 53, s. 11; 1984, c. 21, s. 77; R.S.C. 1985, c. 30 (4th Supp.), s. 45; 1993, c. 40, s. 11; 2004, c. 12, s. 5.

CROSS-REFERENCES

The terms "authorization", "electro-magnetic, acoustic, mechanical or other device", "intercept", "private communication" and "sell" are defined in s. 183. "Peace officer" is defined in s. 2. As to cases on the meaning of consent, see notes under s. 184. As to the meaning of "lawfully intercepted", reference should be made to the exception in s. 184(2) to the unlawful interception offence. The term "wilfully" does not have a fixed meaning and must take its meaning from the context. Generally, however, it connotes an intention to bring about a proscribed consequence. See *R. v. Buzzanga and Durocher* (1979), 49 C.C.C. (2d) 369 (Ont. C.A.).

Pursuant to s. 194, the court that convicts the accused of the offence under this section may make an order for punitive damages. Under s. 195(3), the annual report of the Solicitor General and Attorneys General are to set out the number of prosecutions under this section of officers or servants of the Crown.

The accused has an election as to mode of trial pursuant to s. 536(2) and release pending trial is determined by s. 515, although the accused is eligible for release by the officer in charge pursuant to s. 498.

Note that s. 24 of the *Access to Information Act*, R.S.C. 1985, c. A-1, provides that the head of a government institution shall refuse to disclose any record requested under that Act that contains information, the disclosure of which is restricted by or pursuant to this section.

SYNOPSIS

This section makes it an indictable offence to *disclose* certain information *pertaining to intercepted private communications*, subject to certain exceptions.

The offence created by subsec. (1) contains three elements. First, the interception must have been *made by one of the devices* listed, and it must have been done *without the consent* of either the originator or the person intended to receive it. (Thus, only interceptions made lawful pursuant to s. 183.1 are excluded by this aspect of s. 193.) Second, there must be *no express consent* of such persons to use information or disclose its contents or meaning as set out in s. 193(1)(*a*) or to disclose its existence. Third, the *actions of the accused* must be proven to be *wilful*. The maximum punishment for this offence is two years.

Section 193(2)(*a*) and (*c*) and subsec. (3) are *exceptions* to subsec. (1) and apply generally to the use of such information in relation to *evidence being given in proceedings or procedural matters* in relation to such proceedings. Section 193(2)(*c*) complements ss. 189 and 190, which require certain information to be disclosed in order to provide additional information to the accused. Section 193(2)(*b*) and (*e*) relate to *law enforcement and prosecutorial needs* and permit *disclosure of lawfully intercepted private communications* to assist in the investigation or prosecution of offences. In the case of the exception under s. 193(2)(*e*), there is the additional requirement that the disclosure be intended to be *in the interests of the administration of justice*. As this paragraph also authorizes disclosure to foreign police and prosecutors, the reference to the administration of justice may refer to its benefit in Canada or elsewhere. Section 193(2)(*d*) complements s. 184(2)(*c*) and (*d*) and exempts disclosure which is necessarily incidental to interceptions described in those paragraphs which basically relate to running and servicing public telephone or other communications services or monitoring them. Disclosure to *employees of the Canadian Security Intelligence Service (CSIS)* for the purpose of carrying out its duties as specified is also exempted from liability under subsection (1). Subsection (3) exempts persons who disclose information which has already been lawfully disclosed in court proceedings.

ANNOTATIONS

Subsection (1) – The essence of this offence is the making known to another person the existence of an unlawfully intercepted private communication. It is irrelevant that the tape recordings given to the other person were of such poor quality that the voices on it were not discernible, so long as the existence of the unlawful interception was revealed: *R. v. Simm* (1976), 31 C.C.C. (2d) 322 (Alta. S.C.T.D.).

In one of the few successful prosecutions under this section the court held that the system which the accused had installed in his office and adjoining boardroom fell under the prohibition in subsec. (1). The system allowed for the surreptitious interception of private conversations in both rooms through use of hidden microphones and interception of private conversations of anyone using the accused's telephone. The accused's own testimony that he wished to use the devices to ascertain if unauthorized persons were making use of his office or boardroom constituted an admission that they would be used for surreptitious interceptions: *R. v. McLelland* (1986), 30 C.C.C. (3d) 134 (Ont. C.A.).

Subsection (2) – A witness required to testify at a public inquiry established by the provincial Government and to disclose the contents of an intercepted private communication comes within the exception in this subsection: *Re Royal Commission of Inquiry into Activities of Royal American Shows Inc.* (1977), 39 C.C.C. (2d) 22 (Laycraft J. Com'r).

A party to a civil proceeding can request the disclosure of recordings of private communications intercepted by the state in the course of a criminal investigation. Nothing in the words of para. (2)(*a*) limits its application to the time when evidence is being given at trial. The documents requested at the discovery stage of any civil proceeding may be requested "for the purpose" of testifying at the hearing. However, this section creates neither an actual disclosure mechanism nor a right of access. Recourse must be had to the applicable rules of civil procedure: *Imperial Oil v. Jacques*, [2014] 3 S.C.R. 287, 316 C.C.C. (3d) 1.

The protection afforded by this subsection also extends to civil proceedings over which the province has jurisdiction and the words "for the purpose of giving evidence" would protect the production of the tape recording prior to trial: *Tide Shore Logging Ltd. v. Commonwealth Ins. Co.* (1979), 47 C.C.C. (2d) 215 (B.C.S.C.).

Either para. (*a*) or (*b*) of this subsection permits defence counsel to cross-examine a Crown witness on intercepted private communications even if the lawfulness of the interception has not been established. In particular, as regards para. (*b*), the phrase "any criminal investigation" is not limited to a police investigation but would include the investigation carried out by counsel in the course of cross-examination at a trial: *R. v. Lessard (No. 3)* (1986), 33 C.C.C. (3d) 569 (Que. S.C.).

Paragraph (2)(*e*) does not offend s. 8 of the Charter. It reasonably limits the scope of disclosure of the products of wiretap authorizations, requiring that the disclosing party must subjectively believe that disclosure will further the interests of justice in Canada or the foreign state. A disclosing party who knows little or nothing about the justice system in the foreign state or for what purpose the state intends to use the information will have a hard time satisfying a court that this burden has been met. The same holds true for a disclosing party who has reason to believe that the information will be used in relation to torture or other human rights violations. The section incentivizes disclosing parties to proceed cautiously: *United States of America v. Wakeling*, [2014] 3 S.C.R. 549, 318 C.C.C. (3d) 134.

DISCLOSURE OF INFORMATION RECEIVED FROM INTERCEPTION OF RADIO-BASED TELEPHONE COMMUNICATIONS / Other provisions to apply.

193.1 (1) Every person who wilfully uses or discloses a radio-based telephone communication or who wilfully discloses the existence of such a communication is guilty of an indictable offence and liable to imprisonment for a term not exceeding two years, if

(*a*) **the originator of the communication or the person intended by the originator of the communication to receive it was in Canada when the communication was made;**

(*b*) **the communciation was intercepted by means of an electromagnetic, acoustic, mechanical or other device without the consent, express or implied, of the originator of the communication or of the person intended by the originator to receive the communication; and**

(*c*) **the person does not have the express or implied consent of the originator of the communication or of the person intended by the originator to receive the communication.**

(2) Subsections 193(2) and (3) apply, with such modifications as the circumstances require, to disclosures of radio-based telephone communications. 1993, c. 40, s. 12.

CROSS-REFERENCES

The terms "electro-magnetic, acoustic, mechanical or other device", "intercept", and "radio-based telephone communication" are defined in s. 183. The interception of radio-based telephone communications is itself an offence under s. 184.5 if the interception was done maliciously or for gain. No such limitation applies to the offence created by this section. Disclosure is permitted, however, with the consent of one of the parties or if any of the exemptions in s. 193(2) or (3) apply. Thus, see the synopsis and notes under s. 193.

SYNOPSIS

This section makes it an indictable offence to disclose certain information pertaining to intercepted radio-based telephone communications [*e.g.*, cellular phones] if one of the parties to the communication was in Canada, the communication was intercepted by means of an electro-magnetic, acoustic, mechanical or other device without the consent of one of the parties and the disclosure was not consented to. Disclosure is permitted where any of the conditions set out in s. 193(2) or (3) apply.

DAMAGES / No damages where civil proceedings commenced / Judgment may be registered / Moneys in possession of accused may be taken.

194. (1) Subject to subsection (2), a court that convicts an accused of an offence under section 184, 184.5, 193 or 193.1 may, on the application of a person aggrieved, at the time sentence is imposed, order the accused to pay to that person an amount not exceeding five thousand dollars as punitive damages.

(2) No amount shall be ordered to be paid under subsection (1) to a person who has commenced an action under Part II of the *Crown Liability Act.*

(3) Where an amount that is ordered to be paid under subsection (1) is not paid forthwith, the applicant may, by filing the order, enter as a judgment, in the superior court of the province in which the trial was held, the amount ordered to be paid, and that judgment is enforceable against the accused in the same manner as if it were a judgment rendered against the accused in that court in civil proceedings.

(4) All or any part of an amount that is ordered to be paid under subsection (1) may be taken out of moneys found in the possession of the accused at the time of his arrest, except where there is a dispute respecting ownership of or right of possession to those moneys by claimants other than the accused. 1973-74, c. 50, s. 2; 1993, c. 40, s. 13.

CROSS-REFERENCES

In addition to an order under this section, where a person is convicted of an offence under s. 184 or 191, any electro-magnetic, acoustic, mechanical or other device, by means of which the offence was committed or the possession of which constituted the offence, may be ordered forfeited to the Crown.

An order under this section may be appealed under Part XXI as a sentence appeal.

SYNOPSIS

This section permits a *court, which convicts a person* of an offence under s. 184 (unlawful interception) or s. 193 (unlawful possession, etc., of devices), to order *punitive damages* be awarded to a person aggrieved by the offence. The order is only to be made *on application by the aggrieved person* and must be made at the *time of sentencing.* The *maximum amount* of such an order is *$5000*. If there is no dispute about the ownership or right of possession (by persons other than the accused), funds located in the possession of the accused at the time of his arrest may be used to satisfy an order made under subsec. (1). If the amount of damages awarded is not paid forthwith, subsec. (3) permits the order to be *treated as if it were a civil judgment* for enforcement purposes.

Subsection (2) prohibits money being paid under this section to a person who has begun an action under Part II of the *Crown Liability Act.*

ANNUAL REPORT / Information respecting authorizations — sections 185 and 188 / Information respecting interceptions — section 184.4 / Other information / Report to be laid before Parliament / Report by Attorneys General.

195. (1) The Minister of Public Safety and Emergency Preparedness shall, as soon as possible after the end of each year, prepare a report relating to

(a) authorizations for which that Minister and agents specially designated in writing by that Minister for the purposes of section 185 applied and the interceptions made under those authorizations in the immediately preceding year;

(b) authorizations given under section 188 for which peace officers specially designated by that Minister for the purposes of that section applied and the interceptions made under those authorizations in the immediately preceding year; and

(c) interceptions made under section 184.4 in the immediately preceding year if the interceptions relate to an offence for which proceedings may be commenced by the Attorney General of Canada.

(2) The report shall, in relation to the authorizations and interceptions referred to in paragraphs (1)(a) and (b), set out

(a) the number of applications made for authorizations;

(b) the number of applications made for renewal of authorizations;

(c) the number of applications referred to in paragraphs (a) and (b) that were granted, the number of those applications that were refused and the number of applications referred to in paragraph (a) that were granted subject to terms and conditions;

(d) the number of persons identified in an authorization against whom proceedings were commenced at the instance of the Attorney General of Canada in respect of

   (i) an offence specified in the authorization,

   (ii) an offence other than an offence specified in the authorization but in respect of which an authorization may be given, and

   (iii) an offence in respect of which an authorization may not be given;

(e) the number of persons not identified in an authorization against whom proceedings were commenced at the instance of the Attorney General of Canada in respect of

   (i) an offence specified in such an authorization,

   (ii) an offence other than an offence specified in such an authorization but in respect of which an authorization may be given, and

   (iii) an offence other than an offence specified in such an authorization and for which no such authorization may be given,

and whose commission or alleged commission of the offence became known to a peace officer as a result of an interception of a private communication under an authorization;

(f) the average period for which authorizations were given and for which renewals thereof were granted;

(g) the number of authorizations that, by virtue of one or more renewals thereof, were valid for more than sixty days, for more than one hundred and twenty days, for more than one hundred and eighty days and for more than two hundred and forty days;

(h) the number of notifications given pursuant to section 196;

(i) the offences in respect of which authorizations were given, specifying the number of authorizations given in respect of each of those offences;

(j) a description of all classes of places specified in authorizations and the number of authorizations in which each of those classes of places was specified;

(*k*) a general description of the methods of interception involved in each interception under an authorization;

(*l*) the number of persons arrested whose identity became known to a peace officer as a result of an interception under an authorization;

(*m*) the number of criminal proceedings commenced at the instance of the Attorney General of Canada in which private communications obtained by interception under an authorization were adduced in evidence and the number of those proceedings that resulted in a conviction; and

(*n*) the number of criminal investigations in which information obtained as a result of the interception of a private communication under an authorization was used although the private communication was not adduced in evidence in criminal proceedings commenced at the instance of the Attorney General of Canada as a result of the investigations.

(2.1) The report shall, in relation to the interceptions referred to in paragraph (1)(*c*), set out

(*a*) the number of interceptions made;

(*b*) the number of parties to each intercepted private communication against whom proceedings were commenced in respect of the offence that the police officer sought to prevent in intercepting the private communication or in respect of any other offence that was detected as a result of the interception;

(*c*) the number of persons who were not parties to an intercepted private communication but whose commission or alleged commission of an offence became known to a police officer as a result of the interception of a private communication, and against whom proceedings were commenced in respect of the offence that the police officer sought to prevent in intercepting the private communication or in respect of any other offence that was detected as a result of the interception;

(*d*) the number of notifications given under section 196.1;

(*e*) the offences in respect of which interceptions were made and any other offences for which proceedings were commenced as a result of an interception, as well as the number of interceptions made with respect to each offence;

(*f*) a general description of the methods of interception used for each interception;

(*g*) the number of persons arrested whose identity became known to a police officer as a result of an interception;

(*h*) the number of criminal proceedings commenced in which private communications obtained by interception were adduced in evidence and the number of those proceedings that resulted in a conviction;

(*i*) the number of criminal investigations in which information obtained as a result of the interception of a private communication was used even though the private communication was not adduced in evidence in criminal proceedings commenced as a result of the investigations; and

(*j*) the duration of each interception and the aggregate duration of all the interceptions related to the investigation of the offence that the police officer sought to prevent in intercepting the private communication.

(3) The report shall, in addition to the information referred to in subsections (2) and (2.1), set out

(*a*) the number of prosecutions commenced against officers or servants of Her Majesty in right of Canada or members of the Canadian Forces for offences under section 184 or 193; and

(*b*) a general assessment of the importance of interception of private communications for the investigation, detection, prevention and prosecution of offences in Canada.

(4) The Minister of Public Safety and Emergency Preparedness shall cause a copy of each report prepared by him under subsection (1) to be laid before Parliament forthwith on completion thereof, or if Parliament is not then sitting, on any of the first fifteen days next thereafter that Parliament is sitting.

(5) The Attorney General of each province shall, as soon as possible after the end of each year, prepare and publish or otherwise make available to the public a report relating to

    (*a*) authorizations for which the Attorney General and agents specially designated in writing by the Attorney General for the purposes of section 185 applied and to the interceptions made under those authorizations in the immediately preceding year;

    (*b*) authorizations given under section 188 for which peace officers specially designated by the Attorney General for the purposes of that section applied and to the interceptions made under those authorizations in the immediately preceding year; and

    (*c*) interceptions made under section 184.4 in the immediately preceding year, if the interceptions relate to an offence not referred to in paragraph (1)(*c*).

The report must set out, with any modifications that the circumstances require, the information described in subsections (2) to (3). 1973-74, c. 50, s. 2; 1976-77, c. 53, s. 11.1; R.S.C. 1985, c. 27 (1st Supp.), s. 27; 2005, c. 10, s. 34(1)(*f*)(ix) and (x); 2013, c. 8, s. 5; 2015, c. 20, s. 20.

CROSS-REFERENCES

The term "authorization" is defined in s. 183. "Peace officer", "Canadian Forces", and "Attorney General" are defined in s. 2.

SYNOPSIS

This section imposes a number of *annual reporting requirements upon the Solicitor General of Canada and the Attorneys General of the provinces*, relating to *activity under this Part* of the *Criminal Code*. Subsections (1) to (4), require the Solicitor General to cause a report to be prepared annually and *presented to Parliament*. The details of what must be in the report are set out in subsecs. (2) and (3). In broad terms, the report must provide detailed information relating to applications for authorization (whether successful or not), and the contents of authorizations which were given under the normal powers in s. 185 or emergency orders made under ss. 184.4 and 188. In addition, the results of the authorizations (for example, the number of cases in which such evidence was used and if the prosecution resulted in a conviction) must be set out. Attorneys General have similar duties imposed upon them under subsec. (5).

WRITTEN NOTIFICATION TO BE GIVEN / Extension of period for notification / Where extension to be granted / Application to be accompanied by affidavit / Exception for criminal organization and terrorist groups.

196. (1) The Attorney General of the province in which an application under subsection 185(1) was made or the Minister of Public Safety and Emergency Preparedness if the application was made by or on behalf of that Minister shall, within 90 days after the period for which the authorization was given or renewed or within such other period as is fixed pursuant to subsection 185(3) or subsection (3) of this section, notify in writing the person who was the object of the interception pursuant to the authorization and shall, in a manner prescribed by regulations made by the Governor in Council, certify to the court that gave the authorization that the person has been so notified.

(2) The running of the 90 days referred to in subsection (1), or of any other period fixed pursuant to subsection 185(3) or subsection (3) of this section, is suspended until any application made by the Attorney General or the Minister to a judge of a superior court of criminal jurisdiction or a judge as defined in section 552 for an extension or a

subsequent extension of the period for which the authorization was given or renewed has been heard and disposed of.

(3) Where the judge to whom an application referred to in subsection (2) is made, on the basis of an affidavit submitted in support of the application, is satisfied that

(*a*) the investigation of the offence to which the authorization relates, or

(*b*) a subsequent investigation of an offence listed in section 183 commenced as a result of information obtained from the investigation referred to in paragraph (*a*),

is continuing and is of the opinion that the interests of justice warrant the granting of the application, the judge shall grant an extension, or a subsequent extension, of the period, each extension not to exceed three years.

(4) An application pursuant to subsection (2) shall be accompanied by an affidavit deposing to

(*a*) the facts known or believed by the deponent and relied on to justify the belief that an extension should be granted; and

(*b*) the number of instances, if any, on which an application has, to the knowledge or belief of the deponent, been made under that subsection in relation to the particular authorization and on which the application was withdrawn or the application was not granted, the date on which each application was made and the judge to whom each application was made.

(5) Notwithstanding subsections (3) and 185(3), where the judge to whom an application referred to in subsection (2) or 185(2) is made, on the basis of an affidavit submitted in support of the application, is satisfied that the investigation is in relation to

(*a*) an offence under section 467.11, 467.111, 467.12 or 467.13,

(*b*) an offence committed for the benefit of, at the direction of, or in association with, a criminal organization, or

(*c*) a terrorism offence.

and is of the opinion that the interests of justice warrant the granting of the application, the judge shall grant an extension, or a subsequent extension, of the period, but no extension may exceed three years. 1973-74, c. 50, s. 2; 1976-77, c. 53, s. 12; R.S.C. 1985, c. 27 (1st Supp.), s. 28; 1993, c. 40, s. 14; 1997, c. 23, s. 7; 2001, c. 32, s. 8; 2001, c. 41, s. 8 and 133(10); 2005, c. 10, s. 25; 2014, c. 17, s. 6.

REGULATIONS: PROTECTION OF PRIVACY REGULATIONS

2. For the purposes of subsection [196(1)] of the *Criminal Code*, the Attorney General of a province who gave a notice required to be given by that subsection, or the Solicitor General of Canada where the notice was given by him, shall certify to the court that issued the authorization that such notice was given by filing with a judge of the court a certificate signed by the person who gave the notice specifying

(*a*) the name and address of the person who was the object of the interception;

(*b*) the date on which the authorization and any renewal thereof expired;

(*c*) if any delay for the giving of notice was granted under section [196] or subsection [185(3)] of the *Criminal Code*, the period of such delay; and

(*d*) the date, place and method of the giving of the notice.

3. [*Revoked.* SOR/81-859, s. 2.]

4. A certificate filed pursuant to section 2 shall be treated as a confidential document, shall be placed in a packet, sealed by the judge with whom it is filed and kept with the packet sealed pursuant to section [187] of the *Criminal Code* that relates to the authorization to which the certificate relates. **C.R.C. 1978, c. 440; SOR/81-859,** *Can. Gaz., Part II,* **26/10/ 81, p. 3153.**

CROSS-REFERENCES

The terms "Attorney General", "criminal organization", "peace officer", "public officer" and "superior court of criminal jurisdiction" are defined in s. 2. The documents relating to an application under subsec. (2) are to be kept confidential in accordance with s. 187.

SYNOPSIS

Section 196 provides that those persons, whose private communications have been intercepted pursuant to an authorization, be *notified that they have been the object of such an interception.*

Subsection (1) requires the Attorney General or the Solicitor General (depending on who made the application for the authorization) to provide the notification *within 90 days* after the period for which the authorization was given or renewed, unless an order was made varying such period; (the period of time for giving notice may be altered by an order under s. 185(3) or 196(3). The notice must be *in writing* but it need not tell the person the contents or the details of the authorization. After notice is given, the person who gave the notice must *certify to the court issuing the authorization* that the *notice has been given.* The Governor in Council may pass regulations providing for the contents of such certification.

Subsections (2) to (4) permit an *application to be made to a judge, before the period for the giving of notice has run, to extend the period for up to three years.* A subsequent application for the extension of such period may be made. The application may be brought by either the Attorney General or the Solicitor General, depending on whose behalf the application for the authorization is made. The same types of judges, who are authorized by this Part to grant authorizations under s. 185, may extend the notice. An application to extend the time for notice must be accompanied by an *affidavit sworn on the basis of information and belief of a peace or public officer.* The running of the 90 days or any other period is suspended once the application for an extension is made, until the application can be heard and disposed of. Subsection (4) sets out the required contents of such an affidavit which include (in addition to information regarding prior applications for authorization — whether successful, withdrawn or refused) the *facts which the deponent relies upon* for support that the notice period should be extended. Subsection (3) spells out the *criteria to be applied by the judge* hearing such an application. The affidavit must first satisfy the judge that either: (a) the *investigation of an offence* to which the authorization relates; or (b) subsequent investigation for an offence listed in s. 183, obtained as a result of the investigation noted in (a), *is continuing.* Finally, the judge must be of the opinion that the *interests of justice warrant* the granting of the application. If these conditions are met, the judge *must* fix an extended period, of *less than three years,* for the notice to be given.

Subsection (5) sets out special provisions relating to "criminal organizations".

ANNOTATIONS

Subsection (1) is complied with merely by notifying the person that he was the object of an interception. The person has no right to any wider notification such as receipt of a copy of the authorization: *R. v. Zaduk* (1978), 38 C.C.C. (2d) 349 (Ont. H.C.J.), affd (1979), 46 C.C.C. (2d) 327, 98 D.L.R. (3d) 133 (Ont. C.A.).

The Crown, having informed the accused that they were not the targets of any wiretap investigation in relation to the charges for which they were then being tried, had no obligation to disclose whether or not the accused were named as targets in any other authorizations. Before the Crown would be required to disclose this information, the defence must meet a threshold test of showing some basis which would enable the presiding judge to conclude that there is in existence material which is potentially relevant: *R. v. Chaplin,* [1995] 1 S.C.R. 727, 96 C.C.C. (3d) 225, 36 C.R. (4th) 201.

WRITTEN NOTICE — INTERCEPTION IN ACCORDANCE WITH SECTION 184.4 / Extension of period for notification / Where extension to be granted / Application to be accompanied by affidavit / Exception — criminal organization or terrorism offence.

196.1 (1) Subject to subsections (3) and (5), the Attorney General of the province in which a police officer intercepts a private communication under section 184.4 or, if the interception relates to an offence for which proceedings may be commenced by the Attorney General of Canada, the Minister of Public Safety and Emergency Preparedness shall give notice in writing of the interception to any person who was the object of the interception within 90 days after the day on which it occurred.

(2) The running of the 90-day period or of any extension granted under subsection (3) or (5) is suspended until any application made by the Attorney General of the province or the Minister to a judge of a superior court of criminal jurisdiction or a judge as defined in section 552 for an extension or a subsequent extension of the period has been heard and disposed of.

(3) The judge to whom an application under subsection (2) is made shall grant an extension or a subsequent extension of the 90-day period — each extension not to exceed three years — if the judge is of the opinion that the interests of justice warrant granting the application and is satisfied, on the basis of an affidavit submitted in support of the application, that one of the following investigations is continuing:

　(*a*)　the investigation of the offence to which the interception relates; or

　(*b*)　a subsequent investigation of an offence commenced as a result of information obtained from the investigation referred to in paragraph (*a*).

(4) An application shall be accompanied by an affidavit deposing to

　(*a*)　the facts known or believed by the deponent and relied on to justify the belief that an extension should be granted; and

　(*b*)　the number of instances, if any, on which an application has, to the knowledge or belief of the deponent, been made under subsection (2) in relation to the particular interception and on which the application was withdrawn or the application was not granted, the date on which each application was made and the judge to whom each application was made.

(5) Despite subsection (3), the judge to whom an application under subsection (2) is made shall grant an extension or a subsequent extension of the 90-day period — each extension not to exceed three years — if the judge is of the opinion that the interests of justice warrant granting the application and is satisfied, on the basis of an affidavit submitted in support of the application, that the interception of the communication relates to an investigation of

　(*a*)　an offence under section 467.11, 467.12 or 467.13;

　(*b*)　an offence committed for the benefit of, at the direction of or in association with a criminal organization; or

　(*c*)　a terrorism offence. 2013, c. 8, s. 6.

Part VII / DISORDERLY HOUSES, GAMING AND BETTING

Interpretation

DEFINITIONS / "bet" / "common bawdy-house" / "common betting house" / "common gaming house" / "disorderly house" / "game" / "gaming equipment" / "keeper" / "place" / "public place" / Exception / Onus / Effect when game partly played on premises.

197. (1) In this Part

"bet" means a bet that is placed on any contingency or event that is to take place in or out of Canada, and without restricting the generality of the foregoing, includes a bet that is placed on any contingency relating to a horse-race, fight, match or sporting event that is to take place in or out of Canada;

"common bawdy-house" means for the practice of acts of indecency, a place that is kept or occupied or resorted to by one or more persons;

"common betting house" means a place that is opened, kept or used for the purpose of
- (a) enabling, encouraging or assisting persons who resort thereto to bet between themselves or with the keeper, or
- (b) enabling any person to receive, record, register, transmit or pay bets or to announce the results of betting;

"common gaming house" means a place that is
- (a) kept for gain to which persons resort for the purpose of playing games, or
- (b) kept or used for the purpose of playing games
  - (i) in which a bank is kept by one or more but not all of the players,
  - (ii) in which all or any portion of the bets on or proceeds from a game is paid, directly or indirectly, to the keeper of the place,
  - (iii) in which, directly or indirectly, a fee is charged to or paid by the players for the privilege of playing or participating in a game or using gaming equipment, or
  - (iv) in which the chances of winning are not equally favourable to all persons who play the game, including the person, if any, who conducts the game;

"disorderly house" means a common bawdy-house, a common betting house or a common gaming house;

"game" means a game of chance or mixed chance and skill;

"gaming equipment" means anything that is or may be used for the purpose of playing games or for betting;

"keeper" includes a person who
- (a) is an owner or occupier of a place,
- (b) assists or acts on behalf of an owner or occupier of a place,
- (c) appears to be, or to assist or act on behalf of an owner or occupier of a place,
- (d) has the care or management of a place, or
- (e) uses a place permanently or temporarily, with or without the consent of the owner or occupier thereof;

"place" includes any place, whether or not
- (a) it is covered or enclosed,
- (b) it is used permanently or temporarily, or
- (c) any person has an exclusive right of user with respect to it;

"prostitute" [*Repealed*, 2014, c. 25, s. 12(1).]

"public place" includes any place to which the public have access as of right or by invitation, express or implied.

(2) A place is not a common gaming house within the meaning of paragraph (a) or subparagraph (b)(ii) or (iii) of the definition "common gaming house" in subsection (1) while it is occupied and used by an incorporated genuine social club or branch thereof, if
- (a) the whole or any portion of the bets on or proceeds from games played therein is not directly or indirectly paid to the keeper thereof; and
- (b) no fee is charged to persons for the right or privilege of participating in the games played therein other than under the authority of and in accordance with the terms of a licence issued by the Attorney General of the province in which the place is situated or by such other person or authority in the province as may be specified by the Attorney General thereof.

(3) The onus of proving that, by virtue of subsection (2), a place is not a common gaming house is on the accused.

(4) A place may be a common gaming house notwithstanding that

- (*a*) it is used for the purpose of playing part of a game and another part of the game is played elsewhere;
- (*b*) the stake that is played for is in some other place; or
- (*c*) it is used on only one occasion in the manner described in paragraph (*b*) of the definition "common gaming house" in subsection (1), if the keeper or any person acting on behalf of or in concert with the keeper has used another place on another occasion in the manner described in that paragraph. R.S., c. C-34, s. 179; 1972, c. 13, s. 13; 1980-81-82-83, c. 125, s. 11; R.S.C. 1985, c. 27 (1st Supp.), s. 29; 2014, c. 25, s. 12.

CROSS-REFERENCES

In addition to the definitions in this section, see s. 2 and notes to that section. The gaming, betting and lottery offences are found in ss. 201 to 209; bawdy house and prostitution offences in ss. 210 to 213.

SYNOPSIS

Section 197(1) provides exhaustive definitions for a number of terms which are used in several sections throughout Part VII of the *Criminal Code*. The definition of "common gaming house" in subsec. (1) must be read together with subsec. (2) which provides a number of exceptions to the definition.

Section 197(3) provides that the onus of proving that the house comes within one of the exclusions within s. 197(2) is upon the accused.

Section 197(4) clarifies and extends the meaning of *common gaming house*. It is aimed at foreclosing methods of avoiding conviction by the use of techniques such as using a number of different locations for a "floating crap game".

ANNOTATIONS

"bet" – "Bets" or "betting" under the *Criminal Code* do not have the same connotation as found in civil law of contract, and there are other considerations in determining illegal betting: *R. v. Benwell* (1972), 9 C.C.C. (2d) 158, [1972] 3 O.R. 906 (C.A.) (2:1), affd [1973] S.C.R. v, 10 C.C.C. (2d) 503.

"common bawdy-house" / *[Also see notes under s. 210]* – Note: the following cases were decided under a previous version of this section in which "prostitution" was part of the definition of "common bawdy house" and should be read with caution in light of the amended language which focuses solely on "indecency".

The words "kept or occupied" or "resorted to" connote a frequent or habitual use of the premises for the purpose of prostitution: *R. v. Patterson*, [1968] S.C.R. 157, [1968] 2 C.C.C. 247 (5:0). In that case Spence J., summarized the type of evidence from which the court has found that the prohibited nature of the premises was established, as follows:

first, there has been actual evidence of the continued and habitual use of the premises for prostitution . . .

secondly, there has been evidence of the reputation in the neighbourhood of the premises as a common bawdy-house, or,

thirdly, there has been evidence of such circumstances as to make the inference that the premises were resorted to habitually as a place of prostitution, a proper inference for the Court to draw from such evidence.

"Acts of indecency" and "prostitution" are not vague so as to violate s. 7 of the Charter: *R. v. DiGiuseppe* (2002), 161 C.C.C. (3d) 424, 155 O.A.C. 62 (C.A.), leave to appeal to S.C.C. refused [2002] 3 S.C.R. vii, 167 C.C.C. 93d) vi.

Indecency requires proof beyond a reasonable doubt of two elements: (1) that, by its nature, the conduct at issue causes harm or presents a significant risk of harm to individuals or society in a way that undermines or threatens to undermine a value reflected in, and thus formally endorsed through, the Constitution or similar fundamental laws by, for example: (a) confronting members of the public with conduct that significantly interferes with their autonomy and liberty; (b) predisposing others to anti-social behaviour; or (c) physically or psychologically harming persons involved in the conduct; and (2) that the harm or risk of harm is of a degree that is incompatible with the proper functioning of society.

The first requirement is not based on individual notions of harm, nor on the teachings of a particular ideology, but on what society, through its fundamental laws, has recognized as essential. Views about the harm that the sexual conduct at issue may produce, however widely held, do not suffice to ground a conviction. Unlike the community standard of tolerance test, the requirement of formal recognition inspires confidence that the values upheld by judges and jurors are truly those of Canadian society. Autonomy, liberty, equality and human dignity are among these values. The list of harms is not closed. Bad taste does not suffice and moral views, even if strongly held, do not suffice. Similarly, the fact that most members of the community might disapprove of the conduct does not suffice. The second requirement requires proof that the conduct, not only by its nature but also in degree, rises to the level of threatening the proper functioning of our society. If the harm is based on the threat to autonomy and liberty arising from unwanted confrontation by a particular kind of sexual conduct, the Crown must establish a real risk that the way people live will be significantly and adversely affected by the conduct. If the only people involved in or observing the conduct were willing participants, indecency on the basis of this harm will not be made out. If the harm is based on predisposing others to antisocial behaviour, a real risk that the conduct will have this effect must be proved. Vague generalizations that the sexual conduct at issue will lead to attitudinal changes and hence antisocial behaviour will not suffice. The causal link between images of sexuality and antisocial behaviour cannot be assumed. Attitudes in themselves are not crimes, however deviant they may be or disgusting they may appear. What is required is proof of links, first between the sexual conduct at issue and the formation of negative attitudes, and second between those attitudes and real risk of antisocial behaviour. Finally, if the harm is based on physical or psychological injury to participants, it must be shown that the harm has occurred or that there is a real risk that this will occur. Witnesses may testify as to actual harm. Expert witnesses may give evidence on the risks of potential harm. In considering psychological harm, care must be taken to avoid substituting disgust for the conduct involved, for proof of harm to the participants. In the case of vulnerable participants, it may be easier to infer psychological harm than in cases where participants operate on an equal and autonomous basis. As a general rule, these are matters that can and should be established by evidence. In most cases, expert evidence will be required to establish that the nature and degree of the harm makes it incompatible with the proper functioning of society: *R. v. Labaye*, [2005] 3 S.C.R. 728, 203 C.C.C. (3d) 170; *R. v. Kouri*, [2005] 3 S.C.R. 789, 203 C.C.C. (3d) 217.

"common betting house" / *[Also see notes under s. 201]* – Use of a hotel room on only one occasion will not come within this definition which requires proof that the activity is frequent or habitual in nature. While the word "opened" may have a very wide meaning it must take its meaning from the context, in this case the words "kept or used" which have been held to require proof of a frequent or habitual use: *R. v. Grainger* (1978), 42 C.C.C. (2d) 119 (Ont. C.A.).

"common gaming house" / *[Also see notes under s. 201]* – In *R. v. Rockert*, [1978] 2 S.C.R. 704, 38 C.C.C. (2d) 438 (7:2), it was held that premises which are used on only one occasion do not fall within either para. (*a*) or (*b*) of this definition. The words "kept" and "resort" in para. (*a*) connote frequent or habitual activity, as does "kept" in para. (*b*). The word "used" in para. (*b*) means "that is made use of" and requires a practice of employing the premises in the prohibited manner or at least a practice consisting of more than one use or occasion.

Following this decision, subsec. (4) was amended to add para. (*c*) to that subsection with the result that, in some cases, in the circumstances therein described, a single use of premises may nevertheless suffice to constitute the premises a common gaming house.

A place to which persons who have paid a membership fee resort nightly to play rummy and at which the accused sells refreshments comes within para. (*a*) of the definition notwithstanding the membership fee is devoted to a *bona fide* soccer club (which however was not incorporated under subsec. (2)) where the accused kept the proceeds from the refreshment sales and was clearly carrying on a business for gain: *R. v. Karavasilis* (1980), 54 C.C.C. (2d) 530 (Ont. C.A.).

In addition to proof of the elements in the definition in para. (*a*) the Crown must prove as an element of the offence of gaming that the participants had the chance of both winning and losing money or money's worth. Thus, possible outcomes must be a result, direct or indirect, of wagering or hazarding a stake prior to or during the game. Where no money changed hands between the players, this element of gaming is not made out merely because it is customary for the loser of the card game to pay for the refreshments. The players in such circumstances were not putting up a stake on the outcome of the game but had merely found a convenient way for taking turns at who would purchase drinks which would normally be consumed: *R. v. Di Pietro and Di Pietro*, [1986] 1 S.C.R. 250, 25 C.C.C. (3d) 100 (7:0), approving *R. v. Irwin* (1982), 1 C.C.C. (3d) 212, 39 O.R. (2d) 314 (C.A.).

In this case, a scheme devised by the accused, in which persons purchased memberships in a club which purchased provincial government lottery tickets, constituted keeping a common gaming house. A portion of the fee was used to pay the accused's expenses and the other portion was used to purchase the tickets. The accused guaranteed that each group would have a certain number of winning combinations or he would give a refund. This was more than a group of persons getting together to purchase tickets and play a lottery. Rather, it was a new game of chance. It was a game played for a consideration and in accordance with rules developed by the accused. Under the accused's scheme, he and each of the members stood the chance of both winning and losing money or money's worth. The requisite element of wagering was therefore made out:*R. v. Herger* (1991), 4 O.R. (3d) 359 (C.A.).

"gain" – As used in para. (*a*), "gain" can include direct winnings. Consequently, where the accused was an exceptionally skilled professional gambler who supported the commercial gambling establishment and paid employees out of his large winnings, the premises fell within the meaning of "common gaming house": *R. v. Turmel* (1996), 109 C.C.C. (3d) 162 (Ont. C.A.).

"game" – In *R. v. Ross, Banks and Dyson*, [1968] S.C.R. 786, [1969] 1 C.C.C. 1, it was held (by four judges to one) following the rule of literal interpretation in the absence of ambiguity that the word "mixed" in this definition implies no indication of the proportions of chance and skill and therefore bridge is a game within this subsection.

A carnival operation where the patrons toss coins at glasses and other vessels, winning the glass or vessel on which the coin lands, is a game within the meaning of this definition: *R. v. Touzin and Touzin* (1979), 49 C.C.C. (2d) 183 (Que. C.A.).

In *R. v. Riesberry*, [2015] 3 S.C.R. 1167, 331 C.C.C. (3d) 23, the trial judge erred in entering an acquittal on a charge under s. 209 without considering evidence that a horse race is a game with a systematic resort to chance to determine outcomes. There was evidence that post position is determined at random and that certain post positions are more advantageous than others, leading to a possible conclusion that a horse race qualifies as a "game" under this definition.

"keeper" – It was held in *R. v. Kerim*, [1963] S.C.R. 124, [1963] 1 C.C.C. 233 (3:2), that not every person who falls within this definition as a "keeper" keeps a common gaming house. Rather, there must be some act of participation in the wrongful use of the place. Presumably, this reasoning would apply to the other keeping offences, keeping a common betting house and keeping a common bawdy house. [Note: While this decision would seem to render this definition redundant, it is suggested that, in any of the keeping offences, it must be proved as a minimum that the person fell within the definition of keeper in this section and also committed some act as indicated by the court in *Kerim*. Some of the difficulty in interpretation of this section appears to be as a result of its derivation from s. 229(3) of the 1927 Code, which enacted a presumption that a person was a keeper of a disorderly house if he or she "appears, acts or behaves" as, *inter alia*, the person having the care, government, or management of the premises.]

While it has been held that, for premises to be considered a common gaming house, there must be evidence of frequent or habitual use: *R. v. Rockert, supra*, it is not necessary to prove that the person charged with keeping the common gaming house acted as such frequently or habitually, particularly in light of para. (*e*) of this definition which refers to a permanent or temporary use of the place: *R. v. Lamolinara* (1989), 53 C.C.C. (3d) 250 (Que. C.A.).

Social club exemption [subsec. (2)] – It was held in *R. v. MacDonald*, [1966] S.C.R. 3, [1966] 2 C.C.C. 307 (5:0), that a branch of the Royal Canadian Legion was not entitled to the social club exemption where bingo was carried out on a large scale and on a daily basis. The court held that this was not an "occupation and use by a *bona fide* social club". However, following that decision, this subsection was substantially amended so that the activities carried on in that case might fall within this exemption, provided that the requisite licence was obtained and complied with.

A gaming house, which falls within the definition of "common gaming house" in para. (*b*)(i), being a place kept or used for the purpose of playing games in which a bank is kept by one or more but not all of the players, is not entitled to the exemption in this subsection: *R. v. Pon Chung and Mow Chong Social Club*, [1965] 2 C.C.C. 331 (Ont. C.A.).

The social club's "*bona fides*" is not lost merely because some of the avowed objects of the club were not carried out: *R. v. Pon Chung and Mow Chong Social Club, supra*.

Presumptions

PRESUMPTIONS / Conclusive presumption from slot machine / Definition of "slot machine".

198. (1) In proceedings under this Part,

   (*a*) **evidence that a peace officer who was authorized to enter a place was wilfully prevented from entering or was wilfully obstructed or delayed in entering is, in the absence of any evidence to the contrary, proof that the place is a disorderly house;**

   (*b*) **evidence that a place was found to be equipped with gaming equipment or any device for concealing, removing or destroying gaming equipment is, in the absence of any evidence to the contrary, proof that the place is a common gaming house or a common betting house, as the case may be;**

   (*c*) **evidence that gaming equipment was found in a place entered under a warrant issued pursuant to this Part, or on or about the person of anyone found therein, is, in the absence of any evidence to the contrary, proof that the place is a common gaming house and that the persons found therein were playing games, whether or not any person acting under the warrant observed any persons playing games therein; and**

   (*d*) **evidence that a person was convicted of keeping a disorderly house is, for the purpose of proceedings against any one who is alleged to have been an inmate or to have been found in that house at the time the person committed the offence of which he was convicted, in the absence of any evidence to the contrary, proof that the house was, at that time, a disorderly house.**

(2) For the purpose of proceedings under this Part, a place that is found to be equipped with a slot machine shall be conclusively presumed to be a common gaming house.

(3) In subsection (2), "slot machine" means any automatic machine or slot machine

   (*a*) that is used or intended to be used for any purpose other than vending merchandise or services, or

   (*b*) that is used or intended to be used for the purpose of vending merchandise or services if

      (i) the result of one of any number of operations of the machine is a matter of chance or uncertainty to the operator,

      (ii) as a result of a given number of successive operations by the operator the machine produces different results, or

      (iii) on any operation of the machine it discharges or emits a slug or token,

but does not include an automatic machine or slot machine that dispenses as prizes only one or more free games on that machine. R.S., c. C-34, s. 180; 1974-75-76, c. 93, s. 10.

CROSS-REFERENCES

The terms "gaming equipment", "disorderly house", "common gaming house" and "common betting house" are defined in s. 197. The term "peace officer" is defined in s. 2. The offences relating to gaming house, betting house and bawdy house are set out in ss. 201 and 210 respectively. The warrant referred to in para. (1)(*c*) is issued under s. 199.

Wilful obstruction of a peace officer in the execution of duty is an offence under s. 129(*a*).

SYNOPSIS

Section 198 creates a number of presumptions relating to a number of different offences under this Part.

Section 198(3) exhaustively defines "slot machines". Section 198(2) creates an *irrebuttable presumption* that a place found to contain a slot-machine shall be presumed to be a common gaming house.

ANNOTATIONS

Subsection (1)(*a*) – The bare fact that the officer was delayed in entering the premises is not sufficient to invoke this presumption: *R. v. McEwan and Lee* (1932), 59 C.C.C. 75, [1933] 1 D.L.R. 398 (Alta. S.C. App. Div.), distinguishing *R. v. Theirlynck*, [1931] S.C.R. 478, 56 C.C.C. 156 (5:0).

Subsection (1)(*b*) – Evidence that a place is found to be equipped with "gaming equipment" which, however, is not, or may not, be used for betting is not proof that the place was a "common betting house", notwithstanding the definition of "gaming equipment" in s. 197 as anything that is or may be used for the purpose of playing games or for betting: *R. v. Ruskoff, Marbella and Damore* (1979), 45 C.C.C. (2d) 504 (Ont. C.A.).

Twenty-five cent pieces being used to play the game "heads or tails" came within the definition of "gaming equipment" in s. 197 and thus the presumption in this subsection is applicable: *R. v. Lefrancois* (1981), 63 C.C.C. (2d) 380 (Que. C.A.).

Subsection (1)(*d*) – The presumption in this subsection infringes ss. 7 and 11(*d*) of the Charter and is of no force and effect: *R. v. Janoff* (1991), 68 C.C.C. (3d) 454, [1991] R.J.Q. 2427 (Que. C.A.).

Subsection (2) – While the courts have held that where a charge although laid under s. 201 could have been laid under s. 206(1)(*f*) or (*g*) the accused may nevertheless rely on the exhibition or fair exemption in s. 206(3), the special relationship which slot-machines bear to common gaming houses by virtue of this subsection must make s. 201 the governing section where such machines are involved and an accused is not entitled to invoke the provisions of s. 206(3): *R. v. Cross* (1978), 40 C.C.C. (2d) 505, [1978] 4 W.W.R. 644 (Alta. S.C. App. Div.).

It was held in *R. v. Shisler* (1990), 53 C.C.C. (3d) 531 (Ont. C.A.), that the conclusive presumption created by this subsection is of no force and effect being inconsistent with the presumption of innocence as guaranteed by s. 11(*d*) of the Charter.

Subsection (3) – While the amendment of this subsection, so as to deprive the Crown of reliance on the presumption in a case involving a slot machine such as a pinball machine which only gives free games or prizes, would not necessarily foreclose a conviction under s. 201 if the operation otherwise came within the definition of "common gaming house" in s. 197, it was held in *R. v. Zippilli* (1980), 54 C.C.C. (2d) 481 (Ont. C.A.), that a place equipped with such games is not within that definition. "Gaming" requires an element of wagering which is absent in the mere playing of a pinball game for amusement.

A "pull-ticket" vending machine falls within the definition in para. (*b*) where although it always dispenses a ticket it is a matter of chance or uncertainty whether the operator of the machine receives a valuable or worthless ticket: *Charity Vending Ltd. v. Alberta (Gaming Commission)* (1988), 45 C.C.C. (3d) 455 (Alta. C.A.).

Search

WARRANT TO SEARCH / Search without warrant, seizure and arrest / Disposal of property seized / When declaration or direction may be made / Conversion into money / Telephones exempt from seizure / Exception.

199. (1) A justice who is satisfied by information on oath that there are reasonable grounds to believe that an offence under section 201, 202, 203, 206, 207 or 210 is being committed at any place within the jurisdiction of the justice may issue a warrant authorizing a peace officer to enter and search the place by day or night and seize anything found therein that may be evidence that an offence under section 201, 202, 203, 206, 207 or 210, as the case may be, is being committed at that place, and to take into custody all persons who are found in or at that place and requiring those persons and things to be brought before that justice or before another justice having jurisdiction, to be dealt with according to law.

(2) A peace officer may, whether or not he is acting under a warrant issued pursuant to this section, take into custody any person whom he finds keeping a common gaming house and any person whom he finds therein, and may seize anything that may be evidence that such an offence is being committed and shall bring those persons and things before a justice having jurisdiction, to be dealt with according to law.

(3) Except where otherwise expressly provided by law, a court, judge, justice or provincial court judge before whom anything that is seized under this section is brought may declare that the thing is forfeited, in which case it shall be disposed of or dealt with as the Attorney General may direct if no person shows sufficient cause why it should not be forfeited.

(4) No declaration or direction shall be made pursuant to subsection (3) in respect of anything seized under this section until

  (*a*) it is no longer required as evidence in any proceedings that are instituted pursuant to the seizure; or

  (*b*) the expiration of thirty days from the time of seizure where it is not required as evidence in any proceedings.

(5) The Attorney General may, for the purpose of converting anything forfeited under this section into money, deal with it in all respects as if he were the owner thereof.

(6) Nothing in this section or in section 489 authorizes the seizure, forfeiture or destruction of telephone, telegraph or other communication facilities or equipment that may be evidence of or that may have been used in the commission of an offence under section 201, 202, 203, 206, 207 or 210 and that is owned by a person engaged in

providing telephone, telegraph or other communication service to the public or forming part of the telephone, telegraph or other communication service or system of that person.

(7) Subsection (6) does not apply to prohibit the seizure, for use as evidence, of any facility or equipment described in that subsection that is designed or adapted to record a communication. R.S., c. C-34, s. 181; 1994, c. 44, s. 10.

CROSS-REFERENCES

The terms "justice", "peace officer", "day", "night" and "Attorney General" are defined in s. 2.

Section 29 sets out duties of persons executing a warrant and, *inter alia*, the officer must have it with him, where it is feasible to do so, and produce it when requested to do so.

As to the use of force generally in enforcement of the law, see ss. 25, 26, 27 and 31.

Warrants in relation to the offences described in this section could also be obtained pursuant to ss. 487 and 487.1. The declaration of forfeiture under subsec. (3) may be appealed as a sentence appeal under Part XXI or Part XXVII, as the case may be.

SYNOPSIS

Section 199 creates search, seizure and forfeiture provisions relating to the offences within Part VII listed in s. 199(1). In addition it authorizes taking into custody persons found within the places searched.

Section 199(1) permits a justice who is satisfied by information on oath that there are reasonable grounds to believe that one of the offences listed in the subsection (all "vice"-type offences) is being committed at a place, to issue a warrant authorizing the search of the place. It allows the search to take place day or night and gives the police authority to detain any person or thing found on the premises and then to bring them before a justice.

Section 199(2) permits a police officer who enters a *common gaming house* to detain the *keeper* of the house and all those who are *found in* the house, and to seize all things within the house. There is no requirement that the police have a warrant to enter or seize property from the *common gaming house* at the time the seizures are made under this subsection.

It should be noted that s. 199(6) adds certain restrictions to what may be seized by warrant under this section or s. 489. These restrictions deal basically with communication facilities and equipment.

Section 199(7) permits the seizure of items otherwise included within subsec. (6) if the item is designed or adapted to record conversations and it is seized for evidentiary purposes.

Section 199(3) creates a broad discretion in judicial officers to direct that whatever is seized be forfeited. It appears that the onus is upon the person who seeks to avoid forfeiture to "show sufficient cause" why it *should not be forfeited*. The Attorney General controls how items ordered seized are to be dealt with, including requiring that they be disposed of as directed. Section 199(5) gives the Attorney General the same powers as the owner to convert a forfeited item into money. Section 199(4) provides certain time-limits within which an item seized is not to be the subject of a declaration or direction.

ANNOTATIONS

Constitutional considerations – This provision meets the constitutional requirement of prior judicial authorization: *R. v. Huynh* (2009), 249 C.C.C. (3d) 569 (Alta. Q.B.).

Forfeiture – For forfeiture of seized funds it is not necessary that the Crown prove their identity with the specific proven offence: *R. v. Owens* (1971), 5 C.C.C. (2d) 125, [1972] 1 O.R. 341 (C.A.).

A declaration for forfeiture may be made only after a hearing in conformity with the provisions of this section, notice of which has been given to all interested parties: *R. v. Tobin* (1982), 69 C.C.C. (2d) 137, 37 Nfld. & P.E.I.R. 182 (Nfld. S.C.T.D.).

A forfeiture order may be made under this section at the conclusion of the trial of an accused for an offence under s. 201. Subsection (4) does not require that the court await the outcome of any appeal proceedings before making the declaration: *R. v. Anderson and Blackie* (1983), 10 C.C.C. (3d) 183 (B.C.C.A.).

Items, such as money, which may be evidence of the gaming-house offence may be seized from the keeper under subsec. (2) and declared forfeited under subsec. (3) although he is not on the premises at the time of the execution of the warrant: *R. v. Anderson and Blackie*, *supra*.

A forfeiture order may be made under subsec. (3), where the gaming equipment was seized pursuant to a search warrant issued under s. 487: *R. v. Harb* (1994), 88 C.C.C. (3d) 204 (N.S.C.A.).

200. [*Repealed*, R.S.C. 1985, c. 27 (1st Supp.), s. 30.]

Gaming and Betting

KEEPING GAMING OR BETTING HOUSE / Person found in or owner permitting use.

201. **(1) Every one who keeps a common gaming house or common betting house is guilty of an indictable offence and liable to imprisonment for a term not exceeding two years.**

(2) Every one who

    (a) is found, without lawful excuse, in a common gaming house or common betting house, or

    (b) as owner, landlord, lessor, tenant, occupier or agent, knowingly permits a place to be let or used for the purposes of a common gaming house or common betting house,

is guilty of an offence punishable on summary conviction. R.S., c. C-34, s. 185.

CROSS-REFERENCES

The terms "keeper", "common gaming house" and "common betting house" are defined in s. 197(1) and (4). The exemptions for genuine social clubs is set out in s. 197(2). Section 198 sets out certain presumptions which aid in proof that premises are a common gaming house or common betting house. In particular, note s. 198(2) and (3) respecting slot machines. Sections 204 and 207 enact certain exemptions respecting gaming and betting. While s. 206 enacts exemptions for certain kinds of gaming and lotteries, those sections do not in specific terms exempt an accused from liability under this section. Accordingly, the reach of those exemptions is uncertain, see cases below in particular respecting the Agricultural fair exemption. Related offences are found in s. 203, placing bets on behalf of others; s. 206, lotteries and games of chance; s. 209, cheating at play.

The offence in subsec. (1) may be the basis for an application for an authorization to intercept private communications by reason of s. 183 or a warrant for video surveillance under s. 487.01(5) and falls within the definition of "enterprise crime offence" in s. 462.3 for the purposes of Part XII.2. As regards special search and seizure powers in relation to gaming houses and betting houses, see s. 199.

The offence in subsec. (1) is a pure indictable offence, but, by virtue of s. 553, it is an offence over which a provincial court judge has absolute jurisdiction and does not depend on the consent of the accused. That is, the accused does not have an election as to mode of trial, although the provincial court judge may, by virtue of s. 555(1), elect to continue the proceedings as a preliminary inquiry, in which case the accused is deemed to have elected trial by judge and jury pursuant to s. 565(1)(a). The trial of the offences in subsec. (2) are conducted by a summary conviction court pursuant to Part XXVII. The punishment for the offences in subsec. (2) are as set out in s. 787 and the limitation period is set out in s. 786(2). For all offences under this section, release pending trial is determined by s. 515, although the accused is eligible for release by a peace officer under s. 496, 497 or by the officer in charge under s. 498.

SYNOPSIS

This section creates offences in relation to *keeping a common gaming or betting house.*

Section 201(1) makes it an indictable offence to *keep* such a premises. The maximum punishment upon conviction is two years' imprisonment.

Section 201(2) creates two summary conviction offences. Paragraph (2)(*a*) makes it an offence for an accused to be a *found in* at a *common gaming house* or *common betting house.* It must be shown that the accused had *no lawful excuse* for being present in such a premises.

Section 201(2)(*b*) prohibits *permitting* a place to be used as a *common gaming house* or a *common betting house* if the accused is in the capacity of an owner, landlord, tenant, occupier or agent. It must be shown that the accused *knew* the use being made of the place and permitted it to occur.

ANNOTATIONS

Meaning of "keeps" / *Also see notes under heading "Keeper" in s. 197* – Not every person who falls within the definition of "keeper" within s. 197 "keeps" a common gaming house. To constitute that offence there must be some act of participation in the wrongful use of the place. Thus the accused who was the owner of the premises and rented them out to various charitable organizations but who in no way participated in the promotion, organization or operation of the games was acquitted of this charge. The fact that he operated a refreshment stand for the patrons of the games which was entirely independent of the activities of the organization renting the premises is immaterial. The accused in such circumstances may, however, come within the offence in subsec. (2)(*b*): *R. v. Kerim*, [1963] S.C.R. 124, [1963] 1 C.C.C. 233, 39 C.R. 390 (3:2).

R. v. Kerim, supra, was distinguished and the accused's conviction upheld where the accused leased the premises, provided cards and score pads and sold refreshments, notwithstanding there was no "rake-off". The accused had involved himself in the use of the premises to such an extent that he was participating in the illegal use. His own activities in providing the accommodation and facilities and selling the refreshments made the premises a common gaming house: *R. v. Karavasilis* (1980), 54 C.C.C. (2d) 530 (Ont. C.A.).

Where the game's rules do not preclude some or all of its players from having equal opportunity to becoming its banker and that position does not confer some advantage over the players then the banker cannot be said to be the keeper of a common gaming house: *R. v. Monroe* (1970), 1 C.C.C. (2d) 68, 74 W.W.R. 373 (B.C.C.A.).

Mere participation in an illegal gaming activity, for example through employment at a bingo hall, does not render an individual a party to the offence of keeping a common gaming house: *R. v. Bragdon* (1996), 112 C.C.C. (3d) 91, 3 C.R. (5th) 156 (N.B.C.A.).

Common gaming house / *Also see notes under s. 197* – In *R. v. Rockert*, [1978] 2 S.C.R. 704, 38 C.C.C. (2d) 438, 2 C.R. (3d) 97 (7:2), it was held that premises which are used on only one occasion do not fall within either para. (*a*) or para. (*b*) of the definition of common gaming house in s. 197(1). However, following this decision, subsec. (4) of s. 197 was amended to add para. (*c*) to that subsection with the result that in some cases, in the circumstances therein described, a single use of premises may nevertheless suffice to constitute the premises a common gaming house.

Common betting house / *Also see notes under s. 197* – Use of premises on one occasion will not constitute such premises a common betting house as defined in s. 197: *R. v. Grainger* (1978), 42 C.C.C. (2d) 119 (Ont. C.A.).

The recording of bets, let alone proof of the method of recording, is not an ingredient of keeping a common betting house and there need not even be direct evidence of the accused having received a bet. It is enough that premises were kept by the accused for the purpose of enabling any person to receive bets: *R. v. Silvestro*, [1965] S.C.R. 155, [1965] 2 C.C.C. 253 (3:2).

First Nations gambling – The accused members of the Shawanaga First Nations failed to adduce evidence to demonstrate that gambling, or the regulation of gambling, was an integral part of their distinctive cultures. They therefore failed to demonstrate that the high stakes bingo and other gambling activities in which they were engaged, and their Band's regulation of those activities, took place pursuant to an aboriginal right recognized and affirmed by s. 35(1) of the *Constitution Act, 1982*. The accused were properly convicted of offences under this section: *R. v. Gardner; R. v. Jones*, [1996] 2 S.C.R. 821, 109 C.C.C. (3d) 275, 138 D.L.R. (4th) 204, *sub nom. R. v. Pamajewon*.

Agricultural fair exemptions – Notwithstanding there is no exemption clause for offences charged under this section, if the charge could have been laid under s. 206(1)(*f*) or (*g*) and the accused can bring himself within the exemption clause in s. 206(3) (games operated at an exhibition or fair) the accused is entitled to the protection of any exemption set out in that subsection: *R. v. Andrews and five others* (1975), 28 C.C.C. (2d) 450, 32 C.R.N.S. 358 (Sask. C.A.). Also see *R. v. Beasley* (1936), 65 C.C.C. 337, [1936] 2 D.L.R. 377 (Ont. C.A.). But see: *R. v. Cross* (1978), 40 C.C.C. (2d) 505, [1978] 4 W.W.R. 644 (Alta. S.C. App. Div.) where slot machines are involved; noted under s. 198(2), *supra*.

BETTING, POOL-SELLING, BOOK-MAKING, ETC. / Punishment.

202. (1) Every one commits an offence who

   (*a*) **uses or knowingly allows a place under his control to be used for the purpose of recording or registering bets or selling a pool;**

   (*b*) **imports, makes, buys, sells, rents, leases, hires or keeps, exhibits, employs or knowingly allows to be kept, exhibited or employed in any place under his control any device or apparatus for the purpose of recording or registering bets or selling a pool, or any machine or device for gambling or betting;**

   (*c*) **has under his control any money or other property relating to a transaction that is an offence under this section;**

   (*d*) **records or registers bets or sells a pool;**

   (*e*) **engages in book-making or pool-selling, or in the business or occupation of betting, or makes any agreement for the purchase or sale of betting or gaming privileges, or for the purchase or sale of information that is intended to assist in book-making, pool-selling or betting;**

   (*f*) **prints, provides or offers to print or provide information intended for use in connection with book-making, pool-selling or betting upon any horse-race, fight, game or sport, whether or not it takes place in or outside of Canada or has or has not taken place;**

   (*g*) **imports or brings into Canada any information or writing that is intended or is likely to promote or be of use in gambling, book-making, pool-selling or betting on a horse-race, fight, game or sport, and where this paragraph applies it is immaterial**

      (i) **whether the information is published before, during or after the race, fight, game or sport, or**

      (ii) **whether the race, fight, game or sport takes place in Canada or elsewhere, but this paragraph does not apply to a newspaper, magazine or other periodical published in good faith primarily for a purpose other than the publication of such information;**

   (*h*) **advertises, prints, publishes, exhibits, posts up, or otherwise gives notice of any offer, invitation or inducement to bet on, to guess or to foretell the result of a contest, or a result of or contingency relating to any contest;**

   (*i*) **wilfully and knowingly sends, transmits, delivers or receives any message that conveys any information relating to book-making, pool-selling, betting or** wagering, or that is intended to assist in book-making, poolselling, betting or wagering; or

(*j*) aids or assists in any manner in anything that is an offence under this section.

(2) Every one who commits an offence under this section is guilty of an indictable offence and liable

(*a*) for a first offence, to imprisonment for not more than two years;

(*b*) for a second offence, to imprisonment for a term not more than two years and not less than fourteen days; and

(*c*) for each subsequent offence, to imprisonment for not more than two years and not less than three months. R.S., c. C-34, s. 186; 1974-75-76, c. 93, s. 11; 2008, c. 18, s. 5.

CROSS-REFERENCES

The terms "bet", "gaming equipment", and "place" are defined in s. 197.

The offence in para. (1)(*e*) may be the basis for an application for an authorization to intercept private communications by reason of s. 183 or a warrant for video surveillance by reason of s. 487.01(5), and the offences in this section fall within the definition of "enterprise crime offence" in s. 462.3 for the purposes of Part XII.2. As regards special search and seizure powers in relation to gaming houses and betting houses, see s. 199. Sections 204 and 207 enact certain exemptions respecting gaming and betting. While s. 206 enacts exemptions for certain kinds of gaming and lotteries, that section does not, in specific terms, exempt an accused from liability under this section. Accordingly, the reach of those exemptions is uncertain, see cases noted under heading **Agricultural fair exemption**, under s. 201.

The offence in subsec. (2) is a pure indictable offence, but by virtue of s. 553 it is an offence over which a provincial court judge has absolute jurisdiction and does not depend on the consent of the accused. That is, the accused does not have an election as to mode of trial, although the provincial court judge may, by virtue of s. 555(1), elect to continue the proceedings as a preliminary inquiry, in which case, the accused is deemed to have elected trial by judge and jury pursuant to s. 565(1)(*a*). Release pending trial is determined by s. 515, although the accused is eligible for release by a peace officer under s. 496, 497 or by the officer in charge under s. 498.

Where the prosecution seeks the higher penalty prescribed by subsec. (2)(*b*) or (*c*), it must comply with the provisions of s. 665. Section 667 provides one method of proof of the prior conviction. Note that no reference to the prior conviction may be made in the information by virtue of s. 664.

Related offences are: s. 201, keeping common gaming or betting house; s. 203, placing bets on behalf of others; s. 206, offences in relation to lotteries and games of chance; s. 209, cheating at play.

SYNOPSIS

This section creates indictable offences prohibiting betting, pool selling, bookmaking, importing equipment to engage in any of these activities, and other similar illicit gambling activities. It also provides for punishment upon conviction for such offences. To determine the scope of liability under this section it is necessary to read it together with s. 204 which provides for a number of exemptions.

Section 202(1) creates a number of specific prohibitions set out in paras. (*a*), (*b*), (*d*) to (*i*), which spell out the prohibited acts and in the case of certain paragraphs also spell out the mental element. One such paragraph is para. (*i*) which specifies certain actions such as sending, transmitting, delivering or receiving any message by one of the means specified in the paragraph which is related to bookmaking, pool-selling, or wagering, or that is intended to *assist* in such activity. It must be shown that the accused's actions were both wilful and done knowingly.

Section 202(1)(*c*) and (*j*) create broad offences which extend the liability created by the more specific paragraphs. Section 202(1)(*c*) makes it an offence for the accused to have *control* over any *money* or property relating to a transaction prohibited by this subsection. Similarly subsec. (1)(*j*) makes it an offence to *aid or assist in any manner* anything which is otherwise an offence under subsec. (1). It must be shown that the accused *knew* that the acts assisted in the commission of the other offence created by the subsection but it does not appear that it must be shown that the accused's *purpose was to assist.*

Section 202(2) creates an escalating punishment scale based on the number of prior offences for which the accused has been convicted.

ANNOTATIONS

Constitutional Considerations: This offence is a valid exercise of Parliament's criminal law power: *R. v. J.B.L. Amusements Ltd.* (1998), 123 C.C.C. (3d) 419 (Nfld. C.A.).

Subsection (1)(*b*) – The accused's honest but mistaken belief that the devices were legal even where such belief is the result of reasonable inquiries made of Customs officials is no defence to this charge, by virtue of s. 19: *R. v. Potter* (1978), 39 C.C.C. (2d) 538, 3 C.R. (3d) 154 (P.E.I.S.C.).

To obtain a conviction for the offence under subsec. (1)(*b*), the Crown was required to prove that the accused kept devices in a place under her control, that the devices were gambling devices, and that the accused knew that the devices were gambling devices and knowingly kept them. Gambling or gaming must, as well, involve a chance of gain and a risk of loss. The Crown, however, was not required to show that the machines were actually used for the purpose of gambling: *R. v. Kent*, [1994] 3 S.C.R. 133, 92 C.C.C. (3d) 344.

The offence of keeping a device for gambling or betting constitutes a valid exercise of Parliament's criminal law power: *R. v. J.B.L. Amusements Ltd.* (1998), 123 C.C.C. (3d) 419, 161 Nfld. & P.E.I.R. 181 (Nfld. C.A.).

Subsection (1)(*d*) – The registering or recording must be of the bookmaker's, not the bettor's, record of bets: *R. v. Michael* (1974), 18 C.C.C. (2d) 282, [1974] 5 W.W.R. 749 (Alta. S.C. App. Div.).

Subsection (1)(*e*) – The keeper of a common betting house is one who does something for the purpose of aiding and abetting other persons to engage in the business or occupation of betting and thus he may be convicted of the offence under this section: *R. v. Silvestro*, [1965] S.C.R. 155, [1965] 2 C.C.C. 253 (3:2).

The term "bookmaking" is not limited to horse races. A bookmaker is one who engages in the occupation of taking bets or negotiating bets and the keeping of accounts, regardless of whether the bet is on a horse-race or is more general in scope. Thus, bookmaking describes an enterprise, the business of taking bets and of keeping accounts: *R. v. Decome* (1991), 63 C.C.C. (3d) 460, [1991] R.J.Q. 618 (C.A.).

The accused's scheme in which persons purchased memberships in a club which purchased provincial government lottery tickets did not amount to pool-selling or selling a pool. The scheme was not one in which the participants or members bet with one another and one or more of the members or participants won, as is usually the case in pool-betting or pool-selling. Rather the members shared equally in the winnings: *R. v. Herger* (1991), 4 O.R. (3d) 359 (C.A.).

Subsection (1)(*f*) – The Crown was not required to prove that the British football pools, which were the source of the information provided or conveyed by the accused, were illegal pools in England: *R. v. Ede* (1993), 84 C.C.C. (3d) 447*n*, 63 O.A.C. 319 (C.A.).

Lotteries constitute a form of gaming and betting: *R. v. World Media Brokers Inc.* (1998), 132 C.C.C. (3d) 180 (Ont. Ct. (Prov. Div.)), affd 174 C.C.C. (3d) 385, 171 O.A.C. 99 (C.A.).

PLACING BETS ON BEHALF OF OTHERS.

203. Every one who

   (*a*) places or offers or agrees to place a bet on behalf of another person for a consideration paid or to be paid by or on behalf of that other person,

   (*b*) engages in the business or practice of placing or agreeing to place bets on behalf of other persons, whether for a consideration or otherwise, or

   (*c*) holds himself out or allows himself to be held out as engaging in the business or practice of placing or agreeing to place bets on behalf of other persons, whether for a consideration or otherwise,

is guilty of an indictable offence and liable

   (*d*) for a first offence, to imprisonment for not more than two years,

   (*e*) for a second offence, to imprisonment for not more than two years and not less than fourteen days, and

   (*f*) for each subsequent offence, to imprisonment for not more than two years and not less than three months. R.S., c. C-34, s. 187; 1974-75-76, c. 93, s. 11.

CROSS-REFERENCES

The term "bet" is defined in s. 197.

Section 204 enacts certain exemptions respecting betting, for offences under ss. 201 and 202, but not this section. Section 206 enacts exemptions for certain kinds of gaming but does not, in specific terms, exempt an accused from liability under this section. Accordingly, the reach of those exemptions is uncertain, see cases noted under heading **Agricultural fair exemption**, under s. 201. The exemption in s. 207 would, however, apply to conduct otherwise within this section.

The offences under this section are pure indictable offences, but, by virtue of s. 553, are offences over which a provincial court judge has absolute jurisdiction and does not depend on the consent of the accused. That is, the accused does not have an election as to mode of trial, although the provincial court judge may, by virtue of s. 555(1), elect to continue the proceedings as a preliminary inquiry, in which case, the accused is deemed to have elected trial by judge and jury pursuant to s. 565(1)(*a*). Release pending trial is determined by s. 515, although the accused is eligible for release by a peace officer under s. 496, 497 or by the officer in charge under s. 498.

Where the prosecution seeks the higher penalty prescribed by para. (*e*) or (*f*), it must comply with the provisions of s. 665. Section 667 provides one method of proof of the prior conviction. Note that no reference to the prior conviction may be made in the information by virtue of s. 664.

SYNOPSIS

Section 203 prohibits the activities of the actions of "bookies" and other off-track betting schemes and sets out a schedule of available sentences based on whether the accused is a repeat offender.

Section 203(*a*) makes it an indictable offence to *place* a *bet* for another in exchange for *consideration*. The offence is also stated to encompass *offers* or *agreements* to place the bet. The consideration may be received either at the time of the act described or it may be agreed that the consideration may be received at a later time.

Section 203(*b*) makes it an indictable offence to engage in the business or practice of either placing or agreeing to place bets, whether or not for consideration.

Section 203(*c*) makes it an indictable offence to hold oneself out to be a "bookie", or allow oneself to be so held out.

ANNOTATIONS

This section, which was first introduced following the decision of the Ontario Court of Appeal in *R. v. Gruhl and Brennan*, [1970] 1 C.C.C. 104, 4 D.L.R. (3d) 583, has been amended from time to time and liability extended as various off-track betting schemes have come before the courts. Thus, cases such as *R. v. Williams and Adams* (1970), 2 C.C.C. (2d) 476, [1971] 1 W.W.R. 722 (Alta. S.C. App. Div.), affd [1971] S.C.R. vi, 3 C.C.C. (2d) 91*n*

(5:0), and *R. v. Benwell* (1972), 9 C.C.C. (2d) 158, [1972] 3 O.R. 906 (2:1) (C.A.), affd [1973] S.C.R. vi, 10 C.C.C. (2d) 503 (9:0), decided before the enactment of subsecs. (*b*) and (*c*) must be read with care.

EXEMPTION / Exception / Presumption / Operation of pari-mutuel system / Supervision of pari-mutuel system / Percentage that may be deducted and retained / Percentage that may be deducted and retained / Stopping of betting / Regulations / Approvals / Idem / 900 metre zone / Contravention / Definition of "association".

204. (1) Sections 201 and 202 do not apply to

(*a*) any person or association by reason of his or their becoming the custodian or depository of any money, property or valuable thing staked, to be paid to
  (i) the winner of a lawful race, sport, game or exercise,
  (ii) the owner of a horse engaged in a lawful race, or
  (iii) the winner of any bets between not more than ten individuals;

(*b*) a private bet between individuals not engaged in any way in the business of betting;

(*c*) bets made or records of bets made through the agency of a pari-mutuel system on running, trotting or pacing horse-races if
  (i) the bets or records of bets are made on the race-course of an association in respect of races conducted at that race-course or another race-course in or out of Canada, and, in the case of a race conducted on a race-course situated outside Canada, the governing body that regulates the race has been certified as acceptable by the Minister of Agriculture and Agri-Food or a person designated by that Minister pursuant to subsection (8.1) and that Minister or person has permitted pari-mutuel betting in Canada on the race pursuant to that subsection, and
  (ii) the provisions of this section and the regulations are complied with.

(1.1) For greater certainty, a person may, in accordance with the regulations, do anything described in section 201 or 202, if that person does it for the purposes of legal pari-mutuel betting.

(2) For the purposes of paragraph (1)(*c*), bets made, in accordance with the regulations, in a betting theatre referred to in paragraph (8)(*e*), or by any means of telecommunication to the racecourse of an association or to such a betting theatre, are deemed to be made on the racecourse of the association.

(3) No person or association shall use a pari-mutuel system of betting in respect of a horse-race unless the system has been approved by and its operation is carried on under the supervision of an officer appointed by the Minister of Agriculture and Agri-Food.

(4) Every person or association operating a pari-mutuel system of betting in accordance with this section in respect of a horse-race, whether or not the person or association is conducting the race-meeting at which the race is run, shall pay to the Receiver General in respect of each individual pool of the race and each individual feature pool one-half of one per cent, or such greater fraction not exceeding one per cent as may be fixed by the Governor in Council, of the total amount of money that is bet through the agency of the pari-mutuel system of betting.

(5) Where any person or association becomes a custodian or depository of any money, bet or stakes under a pari-mutuel system in respect of a horse-race, that person or association shall not deduct or retain any amount from the total amount of money, bets or stakes unless it does so pursuant to subsection (6).

(6) An association operating a pari-mutuel system of betting in accordance with this section in respect of a horse-race, or any other association or person acting on its behalf, may deduct and retain from the total amount of money that is bet through the agency of the pari-mutuel system, in respect of each individual pool of each race or each

individual feature pool, a percentage not exceeding the percentage prescribed by the regulations plus any odd cents over any multiple of five cents in the amount calculated in accordance with the regulations to be payable in respect of each dollar bet.

(7) Where an officer appointed by the Minister of Agriculture and Agri-Food is not satisfied that the provisions of this section and the regulations are being carried out in good faith by any person or association in relation to a race-meeting, he may, at any time, order any betting in relation to the race-meeting to be stopped for any period that he considers proper.

(8) The Minister of Agriculture and Agri-Food may make regulations

   (*a*) prescribing the maximum number of races for each race-course on which a race meeting is conducted, in respect of which a pari-mutuel system of betting may be used for the race meeting or on any one calendar day during the race meeting, and the circumstances in which the Minister of Agriculture and Agri-Food or a person designated by him for that purpose may approve of the use of that system in respect of additional races on any race-course for a particular race meeting or on a particular day during the race meeting;

   (*b*) prohibiting any person or association from using a pari-mutuel system of betting for any race-course on which a race meeting is conducted in respect of more than the maximum number of races prescribed pursuant to paragraph (*a*) and the additional races, if any, in respect of which the use of a pari-mutuel system of betting has been approved pursuant to that paragraph;

   (*c*) prescribing the maximum percentage that may be deducted and retained pursuant to subsection (6) by or on behalf of a person or association operating a pari-mutuel system of betting in respect of a horse-race in accordance with this section and providing for the determination of the percentage that each such person or association may deduct and retain;

   (*d*) respecting pari-mutuel betting in Canada on horse-races conducted on a race-course situated outside Canada; and

   (*e*) authorizing pari-mutuel betting and governing the conditions for pari-mutuel betting, including the granting of licences therefor, that is conducted by an association in a betting theatre owned or leased by the association in a province in which the Lieutenant Governor in Council, or such other person or authority in the province as may be specified by the Lieutenant Governor in Council thereof, has issued a licence to that association for the betting theatre.

(8.1) The Minister of Agriculture and Agri-Food or a person designated by that Minister may, with respect to a horse-race conducted on a race-course situated outside Canada,

   (*a*) certify as acceptable, for the purposes of this section, the governing body that regulates the race; and

   (*b*) permit pari-mutuel betting in Canada on the race.

(9) The Minister of Agriculture and Agri-Food may make regulations respecting

   (*a*) the supervision and operation of pari-mutuel systems related to race meetings, and the fixing of the dates on which and the places at which an association may conduct such meetings;

   (*b*) the method of calculating the amount payable in respect of each dollar bet;

   (*c*) the conduct of race-meetings in relation to the supervision and operation of pari-mutuel systems, including photo-finishes, video patrol and the testing of bodily substances taken from horses entered in a race at such meetings, including, in the case of a horse that dies while engaged in racing or immediately before or after the race, the testing of any tissue taken from its body;

   (*d*) the prohibition, restriction or regulation of

    (i) the possession of drugs or medicaments or of equipment used in the administering of drugs or medicaments at or near race-courses, or

    (ii) the administering of drugs or medicaments to horses participating in races run at a race meeting during which a pari-mutuel system of betting is used; and

  (*e*) the provision, equipment and maintenance of accommodation, services or other facilities for the proper supervision and operation of pari-mutuel systems related to race meetings, by associations conducting those meetings or by other associations.

(9.1) For the purposes of this section, the Minister of Agriculture and Agri-Food may designate, with respect to any race-course, a zone that shall be deemed to be part of the race-course, if

  (*a*) the zone is immediately adjacent to the race-course;

  (*b*) the farthest point of that zone is not more than 900 metres from the nearest point on the race track of the race-course; and

  (*c*) all real property situated in that zone is owned or leased by the person or association who owns or leases the race-course.

(10) Every person who contravenes or fails to comply with any of the provisions of this section or of any regulations made under this section is guilty of

  (*a*) an indictable offence and liable to imprisonment for a term not exceeding two years; or

  (*b*) an offence punishable on summary conviction.

(11) For the purposes of this section, "association" means an association incorporated by or pursuant to an Act of Parliament or of the legislature of a province that owns or leases a race-course and conducts horse-races in the ordinary course of its business and, to the extent that the applicable legislation requires that the purposes of the association be expressly stated in its constating instrument, having as one of its purposes the conduct of horse-races. R.S., c. C-34, s. 188; 1980-81-82-83, c. 99, s. 1; R.S.C. 1985, c. 47 (1st Supp.), s. 1; 1989, c. 2, s. 1; 1994, c. 38, ss. 14, 25; 2008, c. 18, s. 6.

CROSS-REFERENCES

Where the prosecution elects to proceed by indictment on the offence under subsec. (10) then the accused may elect his mode of trial pursuant to s. 536(2). Where the prosecution elects to proceed by way of summary conviction then the trial of this offence is conducted by a summary conviction court pursuant to Part XXVII. The punishment for the offence is then as set out in s. 787 and the limitation period is set out in s. 786(2). In either case, release pending trial is determined by s. 515, although the accused is eligible for release by a peace officer under s. 496, 497 or by the officer in charge under s. 498.

SYNOPSIS

Section 204 creates *exemptions* from liability which would otherwise arise under s. 201 or 202, and it also creates a system of legalized *pari-mutuel betting*.

Section 204(1) creates *three types* of exemptions. Section 204(1)(*a*) exempts the *custodian* or the *stakeholder of moneys* when such person pays out the stakes or money to one of the class of persons described in subparas. (i) to (iii).

Section 204(1)(*c*) excludes bets made or records of bets made through the *pari-mutuel system* if the conditions in subparas. (i) and (ii) are satisfied. Subsection (2) deems bets made in accordance with the regulations in a betting theatre, or by means of telecommunication to the race-course or betting theatre, to have been made at the race-course.

Section 204(3) to (9.1) permit the setting of and functioning of a pari-mutuel betting operation for *horse races*. It provides for regulations to be made dealing with many aspects of system described in subsec. (8). Subsection (1.1) states that if the person does an act described in ss. 201 to 202 for the *purpose of legal pari-mutuel* betting it is exempt from liability if the acts are done in accordance with the regulations.

Section 204(11) provides an exhaustive *definition* of the word *association* for the purposes of the section.

Section 204(10) creates the *offence* of contravening the section or the regulations made under it. In addition it provides for punishment by way of summary conviction procedure or by way of indictment. In the latter case the maximum sentence is two years.

205. [*Repealed*, R.S.C. 1985, c. 52 (1st Supp.), s. 1.]

OFFENCE IN RELATION TO LOTTERIES AND GAMES OF CHANCE / Definition of "three-card monte" / Exemption for fairs / Definition of "fair or exhibition" / Offence / Lottery sale void / *Bona fide* exception / Foreign lottery included / Saving.

206. (1) Every one is guilty of an indictable offence and liable to imprisonment for a term not exceeding two years who

(*a*) makes, prints, advertises or publishes, or causes or procures to be made, printed, advertised or published, any proposal, scheme or plan for advancing, lending, giving, selling or in any way disposing of any property by lots, cards, tickets or any mode of chance whatever;

(*b*) sells, barters, exchanges or otherwise disposes of, or causes or procures, or aids or assists in, the sale, barter, exchange or other disposal of, or offers for sale, barter or exchange, any lot, card, ticket or other means or device for advancing, lending, giving, selling or otherwise disposing of any property by lots, tickets or any mode of chance whatever;

(*c*) knowingly sends, transmits, mails, ships, delivers or allows to be sent, transmitted, mailed, shipped or delivered, or knowingly accepts for carriage or transport or conveys any article that is used or intended for use in carrying out any device, proposal, scheme or plan for advancing, lending, giving, selling or otherwise disposing of any property by any mode of chance whatever;

(*d*) conducts or manages any scheme, contrivance or operation of any kind for the purpose of determining who, or the holders of what lots, tickets, numbers or chances, are the winners of any property so proposed to be advanced, lent, given, sold or disposed of;

(*e*) conducts, manages or is a party to any scheme, contrivance or operation of any kind by which any person, on payment of any sum of money, or the giving of any valuable security, or by obligating himself to pay any sum of money or give any valuable security, shall become entitled under the scheme, contrivance or operation to receive from the person conducting or managing the scheme, contrivance or operation, or any other person, a larger sum of money or amount of valuable security than the sum or amount paid or given, or to be paid or given, by reason of the fact that other persons have paid or given, or obligated themselves to pay or give any sum of money or valuable security under the scheme, contrivance or operation;

(*f*) disposes of any goods, wares or merchandise by any game of chance or any game of mixed chance and skill in which the contestant or competitor pays money or other valuable consideration;

(*g*) induces any person to stake or hazard any money or other valuable property or thing on the result of any dice game, three-card monte, punch board, coin table or on the operation of a wheel of fortune;

(*h*) for valuable consideration carries on or plays or offers to carry on or to play, or employs any person to carry on or play in a public place or a place to which the public have access, the game of three-card monte;

(*i*) receives bets of any kind on the outcome of a game of three-card monte; or

433

    (*j*) being the owner of a place, permits any person to play the game of three-card monte therein.

(2) In this section "three-card monte" means the game commonly known as three-card monte and includes any other game that is similar to it, whether or not the game is played with cards and notwithstanding the number of cards or other things that are used for the purpose of playing.

(3) Paragraphs (1)(*f*) and (*g*), in so far as they do not relate to a dice game, three-card monte, punch board or coin table, do not apply to the board of an annual fair or exhibition, or to any operator of a concession leased by that board within its own grounds and operated during the fair or exhibition on those grounds.

(3.1) For the purposes of this section, "fair or exhibition" means an event where agricultural or fishing products are presented or where activities relating to agriculture or fishing take place.

(4) Every one who buys, takes or receives a lot, ticket or other device mentioned in subsection (1) is guilty of an offence punishable on summary conviction.

(5) Every sale, loan, gift, barter or exchange of any property, by any lottery, ticket, card or other mode of chance depending on or to be determined by chance or lot, is void, and all property so sold, lent, given, bartered or exchanged is forfeited to Her Majesty.

(6) Subsection (5) does not affect any right or title to property acquired by any *bona fide* purchaser for valuable consideration without notice.

(7) This section applies to the printing or publishing, or causing to be printed or published, of any advertisement, scheme, proposal or plan of any foreign lottery, and the sale or offer for sale of any ticket, chance or share, in any such lottery, or the advertisement for sale of such ticket, chance or share, and the conducting or managing of any such scheme, contrivance or operation for determining the winners in any such lottery.

(8) This section does not apply to
    (*a*) the division by lot or chance of any property by joint tenants or tenants in common, or persons having joint interests in any such property; or
    (*b*) [*Repealed*, 1999, c. 28, s. 156.]
    (*c*) bonds, debentures, debenture stock or other securities recallable by drawing of lots and redeemable with interest and providing for payment of premiums on redemption or otherwise. R.S., c. C-34, s. 189; R.S.C. 1985, c. 52 (1st Supp.), s. 2; 1999, c. 28, s. 156.

CROSS-REFERENCES

The term "bet" is defined in s. 197 and "property" and "valuable security" in s. 2. The game of "three-card monte", referred to in subsec. (2), was described in *Re Rosen* (1920), 37 C.C.C. 381 (Que. C.A.), as "a game played with three cards, say, two black ones and a red one, shuffled or manipulated by the dealer and placed face down and the opponent backs his ability to spot the position of a particular card. By sleight of hand or quickness of movement, the dealer endeavours to induce the person backing his opinion to put his hand on the wrong card."

    The offences under subsec. (1) are pure indictable offences, but by virtue of s. 553 are offences over which a provincial court judge has absolute jurisdiction and does not depend on the consent of the accused. That is, the accused does not have an election as to mode of trial, although the provincial court judge may by virtue of s. 555(1) elect to continue the proceedings as a preliminary inquiry, in which case, the accused is deemed to have elected trial by judge and jury pursuant to s. 565(1)(*a*). The trial of the offence in subsec. (4) is conducted by a summary conviction court pursuant to Part XXVII. The punishment for the offence in subsec. (4) is as set out in s. 787 and the limitation period is set out in s. 787(2). For all offences under this section, release pending trial is determined by s. 515, although the accused is eligible for release by a peace officer under s. 496, 497 or by the officer in charge under s. 498. As regards special search and seizure powers in relation to offences under this section, see s. 199.

Section 207 provides for certain types of permitted lotteries. As regards pyramid selling and similar schemes, reference should be made to ss. 55 and 56 of the *Competition Act*, R.S.C. 1985, c. C-34, and respecting the conduct of promotional contests involving a lottery or other game, see s. 59 of the same Act. Section 207.1 authorizes lotteries on international cruise ships.

Related offences are: s. 201, keeping common gaming or betting house; s. 203, placing bets on behalf of others; s. 209, cheating at play.

The offence in s. 206(1)(*e*) is an enterprise crime offence pursuant to s. 462.3.

SYNOPSIS

Sections 206, 207 and 207.1, when read together, create liability for acts in relation to *lotteries and games of chance* and create *exceptions* to such liability.

Section 206(1) creates the indictable offence of doing the acts specified on paras. (*a*) to (*j*). No purpose beyond the doing of the acts described need be proven. The maximum sentence upon imprisonment is two years.

Section 206(2) defines "three-card monte" for the purposes of this section.

Section 204(3) creates an exception from s. 206(1)(*f*) to (*g*) for the use of a board located at an *annual fair or exhibition* or the operator of such a board. However, the exemption does not include dice games, three-card monte, punch board or coin tables. Subsection (3.1) sets out an exhaustive definition of the phrase "fair or exhibition" – see where it is used in subsec. (3).

Section 206(4) creates a summary conviction offence applicable to any one who takes or receives a lot, ticket or other item mentioned in subsec. (1).

Section 206(5) provides that any right of property involved in the specified acts relating to lotteries and games of chance is void and is forfeited to the Crown. However, s. 206(6) is a saving provision which states that if a person acquires the property as a *bona fide purchaser for valuable consideration* without notice their rights are protected.

Section 206(7) sets out that application of this section to a foreign lottery.

Section 206(8) sets out additional general exemptions to the operation of this section.

ANNOTATIONS

Subsection (1)(*a*) – A conviction was upheld where the scheme was that 20 ticket holders would be chosen by chance and then those 20 would compete in a potato-peeling contest to see who would win the 10 cars which were offered as prizes. The court held that the whole scheme was one of chance determining the result, as "the twenty drawn to enter the contest might well be without any real skill in paring a potato, and the cars would go to the ten least unskilful or inefficient . . . or what is also important, if any of the twenty should prove skilful, they were chosen as contestants by chance": *R. v. Wallace* (1954), 109 C.C.C. 351, 20 C.R. 39 (Alta. S.C. App. Div.). This case was distinguished in *R. v. Young* (1957), 119 C.C.C. 389, 27 C.R. 226 (B.C.C.A.), where it was held that the selection by chance of the persons entitled to participate in the contest of skill did not render the whole scheme a lottery.

The burden is on the Crown to prove that the proposed disposition of property was by mode of chance alone, involving the absence of any genuine skill and if the "skill testing question" constitutes an exercise of skill then the scheme is not a prohibited lottery. Where the police halt the lottery before the draw is held there is no burden on the accused to prove that the intended question would be a genuine test of skill: *R. v. Young* (1978), 45 C.C.C. (2d) 565, [1979] 2 W.W.R. 231 (Alta. S.C. App. Div.).

This provision prohibits the sale of a share of lottery tickets: *R. v. Stromberg* (1999), 131 C.C.C. (3d) 546, 192 W.A.C. 182 (B.C.C.A.), leave to appeal to S.C.C. refused 140 C.C.C. (3d) vi, 252 N.R. 396*n*.

Furthermore, a new element of risk or chance in addition to that already implicit in the lottery itself need not be established in relation to a scheme for the sale of shares in a lottery: *R. v. World Media Brokers Inc.* (1998), 132 C.C.C. (3d) 180 (Ont. Ct. (Prov. Div.)), affd 174 C.C.C. (3d) 385, 171 O.A.C. 99 (C.A.).

Subsection (1)(d) – Where the lucky draw and skill-testing scheme was found to simply be a device to attempt to avoid prosecution, a conviction for operating a lottery was affirmed: *R. v. Robert Simpson (Regina) Limited* (1958), 121 C.C.C. 39 (Sask. C.A.).

A scheme which is one of skill or mixed skill and chance does not contravene this subsection: *R. v. Roe*, [1949] S.C.R. 652, 94 C.C.C. 273.

The Montreal voluntary tax plan was reviewed under appeal in *Montreal (City) v. Quebec (Attorney General)*, [1970] 2 C.C.C. 1, 10 D.L.R. (3d) 315 (S.C.C.). The court, agreeing that the prize offering of silver ingots was a cash prize and that the scheme was based essentially on chance, held (7:0) that the plan was a lottery.

The accused's belief that the *Criminal Code* lottery provisions did not apply to bingo games held on an Indian Reserve was a mistake of law and, thus, no defence to the charge under this paragraph: *R. v. Jones*, [1991] 3 S.C.R. 110, 66 C.C.C. (3d) 512, 8 C.R. (4th) 137 (7:0).

The accused members of the Eagle Lake First Nations failed to adduce evidence to demonstrate that gambling, or the regulation of gambling, was an integral part of their distinctive cultures. They therefore failed to demonstrate that the bingo operation in which they were engaged, and their Band's regulation of that activity, took place pursuant to an aboriginal right recognized and affirmed by s. 35(1) of the *Constitution Act, 1982*. The accused were therefore properly convicted of offences under this section: *R. v. Gardner; R. v. Jones*, [1996] 2 S.C.R. 821, 109 C.C.C. (3d) 275, 138 D.L.R. (4th) 204, *sub nom. R. v. Pamajewon.*

Any aboriginal rights the First Nations may have in relation to economic activity on the reserves did not include the right to regulate high-stakes gambling on the reserve. By the valid exercise of the criminal law power, Parliament has made such activities a criminal offence: *R. v. Gardner; R. v. Jones* (1994), 95 C.C.C. (3d) 97, 120 D.L.R. (4th) 475, 21 O.R. (3d) 385 (C.A.).

Subsection (1)(e) – Chance and skill are not factors in the offence of conducting a lottery as the offence is committed if a purchaser stands to receive back a larger amount than he contributed because other persons have contributed. Further, the offence was committed even where the accused deposited with the trust company running the contest sufficient funds to pay for the prize even if only one ticket was sold. The deposit of the funds with the trust company was only made by the accused by reason of the fact that it was part of a scheme by which contestants would pay money to enter the contest and such contest clearly contemplated, at its inception and throughout, that the prize would be awarded at the conclusion of the contest by reason of the payments for tickets of all the non-successful contestants: *R. v. Dream Home Contests (Edmonton) Ltd.; R. v. Hodges*, [1960] S.C.R. 414, 126 C.C.C. 241 (5:0). Folld: *R. v. Canus Of North America Ltd.*, [1965] 1 C.C.C. 91, 43 C.R. 321 (Sask. C.A.).

The legitimacy of a business is not a factor to be considered if a part of its operation is a lottery scheme. Furthermore, the key to this offence is that a participant shall become entitled to receive from others under the scheme an amount larger than his investment, and accordingly it does not matter whether that larger amount was in existence in the scheme before or after he joined it: *R. v. Golden Canada Products* (1973), 15 C.C.C. (2d) 1, 43 D.L.R. (3d) 251 (Alta. C.A.).

The essential element of this offence is the scheme and it is not necessary that money has been paid by the new recruits so long as it is contemplated that it will be payable and that a participant will receive a larger sum than he paid in as a result of the participation of others. It is not a requisite of the scheme that there be a banker: *R. v. Mackenzie, Ennis and Meilleur* (1982), 66 C.C.C. (2d) 528, 135 D.L.R. (3d) 374, 36 O.R. (2d) 562 (C.A.); *R. v. Fehr* (1983), 4 C.C.C. (3d) 382 (B.C.C.A.).

The value of the product in relation to the price for which it is sold is one of many relevant factors in determining whether a multi-marketing scheme violates this provision. The entire scheme must be examined to determine whether it is a recruitment scheme which will inevitably lead to loss by some who have paid into it by way of contribution in the expectation of receiving a larger amount from amounts paid in by subsequent recruits: *R. v. Friskie* (2003), 177 C.C.C. (3d) 72, 299 D.L.R. (4th) 670, [2004] 4 W.W.R. 223 (Sask. C.A.).

The Crown is not required to prove that at the time of the alleged offence other people had already paid money so that one of the persons in the scheme had already been paid a sum greater than what he had earlier paid. It is sufficient that the Crown establishes that the scheme whereby that result could obtain was in existence: *R. v. Stead* (1981), 60 C.C.C. (2d) 397 (Sask. Prov. Ct.).

Where a significant part of the scheme operated in the province it is no defence that part of the scheme, such as the actual payment of the money, also operated in the United States: *R. v. Stead, supra.*

Subsection 1(*f*) – Simply because there is an increased level of difficulty or because some elements of the game are out of the player's control does not necessarily render the game one of mixed chance and skill. In this case, however, a "crane machine" in which the player operates a joystick to move the crane to a location and uses the claw to obtain toys and novelties was a game of mixed chance and skill as virtually all of the elements of the game were out of the control of the player: *R. v. Balance Group International Trading Inc.* (2002), 162 C.C.C. (3d) 126, 155 O.A.C. 357 (C.A.).

Subsection (1)(*g*) – A wheel of fortune is a gambling device bearing some resemblance to a revolving wheel with sections indicating chances taken or bets placed: *R. v. Andrews and five others* (1975), 28 C.C.C. (2d) 450, 32 C.R.N.S. 358 (Sask. C.A.).

Subsection (3) – An accused who can bring himself within this subsection is entitled to its protection even on a charge of keeping a common gaming house under s. 201: *R. v. Andrews and five others, supra.*

However, this principle does not apply where the games involved are slot machines: *R. v. Cross* (1978), 40 C.C.C. (2d) 505, [1978] 4 W.W.R 644 (Alta. S.C. App. Div.).

Subsection (7) – This section is not unconstitutionally vague: *R. v. Stromberg, infra.*

Subsection (8) – The exemption in para. (*a*) does not apply to a bingo game where, although all participants must be members of the sponsoring association, the prize money is derived from the sale of the bingo cards: *R. v. Gladue and Kirby* (1986), 30 C.C.C. (3d) 308 (Alta. Prov. Ct.).

PERMITTED LOTTERIES / Terms and conditions of licence / Offence / Definition of "lottery scheme" / Exception — charitable or religious organization / Exception re: pari-mutuel betting.

207. (1) Notwithstanding any of the provisions of this Part relating to gaming and betting, it is lawful

    (*a*) **for the government of a province, either alone or in conjunction with the government of another province, to conduct and manage a lottery scheme in that province, or in that and the other province, in accordance with any law enacted by the legislature of that province;**

    (*b*) **for a charitable or religious organization, pursuant to a licence issued by the Lieutenant Governor in Council of a province or by such other person or authority in the province as may be specified by the Lieutenant Governor in Council thereof, to conduct and manage a lottery scheme in that province if the proceeds from the lottery scheme are used for a charitable or religious object or purpose;**

    (*c*) **for the board of a fair or of an exhibition or an operator of a concession leased by that board, to conduct and manage a lottery scheme in a province where the Lieutenant Governor in Council of the province or such other person or authority in the province as may be specified by the Lieutenant Governor in Council thereof has**

       (i) designated that fair or exhibition as a fair or exhibition where a lottery scheme may be conducted and managed, and

       (ii) issued a licence for the conduct and management of a lottery scheme to that board or operator;

  (d) for any person, pursuant to a licence issued by the Lieutenant Governor in Council of a province or by such other person or authority in the province as may be specified by the Lieutenant Governor in Council thereof, to conduct and manage a lottery scheme at a public place of amusement in that province if

       (i) the amount or value of each prize awarded does not exceed five hundred dollars, and

       (ii) the money or other valuable consideration paid to secure a chance to win a prize does not exceed two dollars;

  (e) for the government of a province to agree with the government of another province that lots, cards or tickets in relation to a lottery scheme that is by any of paragraphs (a) to (d) authorized to be conducted and managed in that other province may be sold in the province;

  (f) for any person, pursuant to a licence issued by the Lieutenant Governor in Council of a province or such other person or authority in the province as may be designated by the Lieutenant Governor in Council thereof, to conduct and manage in the province a lottery scheme that is authorized to be conducted and managed in one or more other provinces where the authority by which the lottery scheme was first authorized to be conducted and managed consents thereto;

  (g) for any person, for the purpose of a lottery scheme that is lawful in a province under any of paragraphs (a) to (f), to do anything in the province, in accordance with the applicable law or licence, that is required for the conduct, management or operation of the lottery scheme or for the person to participate in the scheme; and

  (h) for any person to make or print anywhere in Canada or to cause to be made or printed anywhere in Canada anything relating to gaming and betting that is to be used in a place where it is or would, if certain conditions provided by law are met, be lawful to use such a thing, or to send, transmit, mail, ship, deliver or allow to be sent, transmitted, mailed, shipped or delivered or to accept for carriage or transport or convey any such thing where the destination thereof is such a place.

(2) Subject to this Act, a licence issued by or under the authority of the Lieutenant Governor in Council of a province as described in paragraph (1)(b), (c), (d) or (f) may contain such terms and conditions relating to the conduct, management and operation of or participation in the lottery scheme to which the licence relates as the Lieutenant Governor in Council of that province, the person or authority in the province designated by the Lieutenant Governor in Council thereof or any law enacted by the legislature of that province may prescribe.

(3) Every one who, for the purposes of a lottery scheme, does anything that is not authorized by or pursuant to a provision of this section

  (a) in the case of the conduct, management or operation of that lottery scheme,

       (i) is guilty of an indictable offence and liable to imprisonment for a term not exceeding two years, or

       (ii) is guilty of an offence punishable on summary conviction; or

  (b) in the case of participating in that lottery scheme, is guilty of an offence punishable on summary conviction.

(4) In this section, "lottery scheme" means a game or any proposal, scheme, plan, means, device, contrivance or operation described in any of paragraphs 206(1)(a) to (g), whether or not it involves betting, pool selling or a pool system of betting other than

  (a) three-card monte, punch board or coin table;

(*b*) **bookmaking, pool selling or the making or recording of bets, including bets made through the agency of a pool or pari-mutuel system, on any race or fight, or on a single sport event or athletic contest; or**

(*c*) **for the purposes of paragraphs (1)(*b*) to (*f*), a game or proposal, scheme, plan, means, device, contrivance or operation described in any of paragraphs 206(1)(*a*) to (*g*) that is operated on or through a computer, video device or slot machine, within the meaning of subsection 198(3), or a dice game.**

(4.1) The use of a computer for the sale of a ticket, selection of a winner or the distribution of a prize in a raffle, including a 50/50 draw, is excluded from paragraph (4)(*c*) in so far as the raffle is authorized under paragraph (1)(*b*) and the proceeds are used for a charitable or religious object or purpose.

(5) For greater certainty, nothing in this section shall be construed as authorizing the making or recording of bets on horse-races through the agency of a pari-mutuel system other than in accordance with section 204. R.S., c. C-34, s. 190; 1974-75-76, c. 93, s. 12; R.S.C. 1985, c. 27 (1st Supp.), s. 31, c. 52 (1st Supp.), s. 3; 1999, c. 5, s. 6; 2014, c. 39, s. 171.

CROSS-REFERENCES

The terms "bet" and "game" are defined in s. 197. Pari-mutuel systems are dealt with in s. 204. The game of "three-card monte", referred to in subsec. (4), was described in *Re Rosen* (1920), 37 C.C.C. 381 (Que. C.A.), as a "a game played with three cards, say, two black ones and a red one, shuffled or manipulated by the dealer and placed face down and the opponent backs his ability to spot the position of a particular card. By sleight of hand or quickness of movement, the dealer endeavours to induce the person backing his opinion to put his hand on the wrong card".

Where the Crown elects to proceed by indictment on the offence described in subsec. (3)(*a*) then the accused has an election as to mode of trial under s. 536(2). Where the Crown elects to proceed by way of summary conviction for the offence under subsec. (3)(*a*) and for any case under subsec. (3)(*b*), the trial is conducted by a summary conviction court pursuant to Part XXVII. The punishment for these summary conviction offences is as set out in s. 787 and the limitation period is set out in s. 786(2). For all offences under this section, release pending trial is determined by s. 515, although the accused is eligible for release by a peace officer under ss. 496, 497 or by the officer in charge under s. 498. As regards special search and seizure powers in relation to offences under this section, see s. 199.

As regards pyramid selling and similar schemes, reference should be made to ss. 55 and 56 of the *Competition Act*, R.S.C. 1985, c. C-34, and respecting the conduct of promotional contests involving a lottery or other game, see s. 59 of the same Act. Section 207.1 authorizes lotteries on international cruise ships.

Related offences are: s. 201, keeping common gaming or betting house; s. 203, placing bets on behalf of others; s. 209, cheating at play.

SYNOPSIS

Section 207 legalizes the *creation* and *operation* of *lotteries* run by any of the bodies specified in s. 207(1)(*a*) to (*d*). In addition it provides for the *regulation* of such schemes and creates an offence of operating or participating in a lottery not created or run in accordance with s. 207.

Section 207(1) permits lotteries to be created by a *province*, or *under licence* by charitable or religious organizations, by a board of a fair or exhibition or by any other person to whom a licence has been issued. The last-mentioned category only applies to lotteries in which the ticket cost no more than two dollars and the prize does not exceed $500.

Section 207(1)(*e*) to (*h*) permits persons to do specified activities required to carry out the operation of lawful lotteries under this section.

Section 207(4) *exhaustively defines* the term *lottery scheme* for the purposes of this section and also specifically excludes the activities noted in s. 207(4)(*a*) to (*c*) which are dealt with (either by way of prohibition or regulation) in ss. 202 to 206.

Section 207(4.1) clarifies that the use of a computer in a raffle or 50/50 draw does not place it within the exemption in subsec. (4)(*c*).

Section 207(5) clarifies the scope of the exclusion in s. 207(4)(*b*) in relation to pari-mutuel schemes.

Section 207(2) permits *terms and conditions* to be imposed in a *licence* under this section to regulate the conduct, management, and operation or participation in a lottery scheme.

Section 207(3) makes it an offence to do anything not authorized by this section if the act is done for the purpose of a lottery scheme. It is a summary conviction offence or an indictable offence punishable by up to two years imprisonment if the act is done in relation to the conduct, management or operation of such scheme. It is a summary conviction offence to participate in an unlawful scheme.

ANNOTATIONS

Since a "pull-ticket" vending machine falls within the definition of a slot machine in s. 198(3) the provincial gaming commission acts properly in refusing to issue licenses to charities or religious organizations seeking to use such machines: *Charity Vending Ltd. v. Alberta (Gaming Commission)* (1988), 45 C.C.C. (3d) 455 (Alta. C.A.).

The statutory scheme established by this section and s. 206 which, in effect, decriminalizes certain forms of gambling and creates a regulated industry does not constitute an unconstitutional delegation to the province, although the power to impose terms and conditions on licenses is delegated to the Lieutenant Governor: *R. v. Furtney*, [1991] 3 S.C.R. 89, 66 C.C.C. (3d) 498, 8 C.R. (4th) 121 (7:0).

EXEMPTION — LOTTERY SCHEME ON AN INTERNATIONAL CRUISE SHIP / Paragraph 207(1)(*h*) and subsection 207(5) apply / Offence / Definitions.

207.1 (1) Despite any of the provisions of this Part relating to gaming and betting, it is lawful for the owner or operator of an international cruise ship, or their agent, to conduct, manage or operate and for any person to participate in a lottery scheme during a voyage on an international cruise ship when all of the following conditions are satisfied:

(*a*) **all the people participating in the lottery scheme are located on the ship;**

(*b*) **the lottery scheme is not linked, by any means of communication, with any lottery scheme, betting, pool selling or pool system of betting located off the ship;**

(*c*) **the lottery scheme is not operated within five nautical miles of a Canadian port at which the ship calls or is scheduled to call; and**

(*d*) **the ship is registered**

   (i) **in Canada and its entire voyage is scheduled to be outside Canada, or**

   (ii) **anywhere, including Canada, and its voyage includes some scheduled voyaging within Canada and the voyage**

   (A) **is of at least forty-eight hours duration and includes some voyaging in international waters and at least one non-Canadian port of call including the port at which the voyage begins or ends, and**

   (B) **is not scheduled to disembark any passengers at a Canadian port who have embarked at another Canadian port, without calling on at least one non-Canadian port between the two Canadian ports.**

(2) For greater certainty, paragraph 207(1)(*h*) and subsection 207(5) apply for the purposes of this section.

(3) Every one who, for the purpose of a lottery scheme, does anything that is not authorized by this section

(*a*) in the case of the conduct, management or operation of the lottery scheme,

   (i) is guilty of an indictable offence and liable to imprisonment for a term of not more than two years, or

   (ii) is guilty of an offence punishable on summary conviction; and

(*b*) in the case of participating in the lottery scheme, is guilty of an offence punishable on summary conviction.

(4) The definitions in this subsection apply in this section.

"international cruise ship" means a passenger ship that is suitable for continuous ocean voyages of at least forty-eight hours duration, but does not include such a ship that is used or fitted for the primary purpose of transporting cargo or vehicles.

"lottery scheme" means a game or any proposal, scheme, plan, means, device, contrivance or operation described in any of paragraphs 206(1)(*a*) to (*g*), whether or not it involves betting, pool selling or a pool system of betting. It does not include

(*a*) three-card monte, punch board or coin table; or

(*b*) bookmaking, pool selling or the making or recording of bets, including bets made through the agency of a pool or pari-mutuel system, on any race or fight, or on a single sporting event or athletic contest. 1999, c. 5, s. 7.

CROSS-REFERENCES

For other exemptions from liability for lottery schemes, see ss. 206(3), (7) and 207.

SYNOPSIS

This section creates an exemption from liability for the gaming and betting offences created by this Part for lottery schemes conducted on international cruise ships. To take advantage of the exemption the operator must comply with all of the conditions set out in subsec. (1). Subsection (4) defines "international cruise ship" and "lottery scheme". Subsection (2) makes it clear that it is lawful to make or print items for use in a scheme authorized by this section and that this section does not authorize the making or recording of bets on horse-races through the agency of a pari-mutuel system other than in accordance with s. 204. Subsection (3) creates two offences: para. (*a*) for a person conducting, managing or operating the lottery scheme not authorized by this section and para. (*b*) participating in an unauthorized lottery scheme. The former is a hybrid offence. The latter is a summary conviction offence.

ANNOTATIONS

Paragraph (*b*) prohibits either extra-provincial or international sales of lottery tickets and accordingly, charitable lottery tickets marketed via the Internet were not lawful: *Reference re: Earth Future Lottery and Criminal Code s. 207* (2002), 166 C.C.C. (3d) 373, 215 D.L.R. (4th) 656, 211 Nfld. & P.E.I.R. 311 (P.E.I.C.A.), affd [2003] 1 S.C.R. 123, 171 C.C.C. (3d) 225, 222 D.L.R. (4th) 383.

---

208. [*Repealed*, R.S.C. 1985, c. 27 (1st Supp.), s. 32.]

CHEATING AT PLAY.

209. Every one who, with intent to defraud any person, cheats while playing a game or in holding the stakes for a game or in betting is guilty of an indictable offence and liable to imprisonment for a term not exceeding two years. R.S., c. C-34, s. 192.

CROSS-REFERENCES

The terms "game" and "bet" are defined in s. 197.

   This offence is a pure indictable offence, but, by virtue of s. 553, it is an offence over which a provincial court judge has absolute jurisdiction and does not depend on the consent of the accused.

That is, the accused does not have an election as to mode of trial, although the provincial court judge may, by virtue of s. 555(1), elect to continue the proceedings as a preliminary inquiry, in which case, the accused is deemed to have elected trial by judge and jury pursuant to s. 565(1)(*a*). Release pending trial is determined by s. 515, although the accused is eligible for release by a peace officer under s. 496, 497 or by the officer in charge under s. 498.

Related offences are: s. 201, keeping common gaming or betting house; s. 202, offences in relation to betting, pool-selling and book-making, etc.; s. 203, placing bets on behalf of others; s. 380, fraud.

SYNOPSIS

This section makes it an indictable offence to *cheat at play*. The *actus reus* of the offence is to cheat while doing any of the following: playing a game; holding the stakes; or betting. The requisite mental element is the *intention of defrauding* any person. The maximum sentence upon conviction is two years.

ANNOTATIONS

In *R. v. McGarey*, [1974] S.C.R. 278, 6 C.C.C. (2d) 525, 26 D.L.R. (3d) 231, the booth operator was convicted in the operation of a midway milk bottle toss game where the unsuspecting patron was unaware that the bottom bottles of each pyramid were heavily weighted. It was held (5:0) that in this game of mixed chance and skill the booth operator was a player and the surreptitious weighting of the bottom bottles constituted his intent to defraud the patron player by creating a false visual impression of the game, which false impression in itself was the ill-practice of cheating.

However, simple measures taken to increase the degree of skill required for success are not improper: *R. v. Reilly* (1979), 48 C.C.C. (2d) 286 (Ont. C.A.).

Bawdy-houses

KEEPING COMMON BAWDY-HOUSE / Landlord, inmate, etc. / Notice of conviction to be served on owner / Duty of landlord on notice.

210. (1) Every one who keeps a common bawdy-house is guilty of an indictable offence and liable to imprisonment for a term not exceeding two years.

(2) Every one who
> **(a) is an inmate of a common bawdy-house,**
> **(b) is found, without lawful excuse, in a common bawdy-house, or**
> **(c) as owner, landlord, lessor, tenant, occupier, agent or otherwise having charge or control of any place, knowingly permits the place or any part thereof to be let or used for the purposes of a common bawdy-house,**

is guilty of an offence punishable on summary conviction.

(3) Where a person is convicted of an offence under subsection (1), the court shall cause a notice of the conviction to be served on the owner, landlord or lessor of the place in respect of which the person is convicted or his agent, and the notice shall contain a statement to the effect that it is being served pursuant to this section.

(4) Where a person on whom a notice is served under subsection (3) fails forthwith to exercise any right he may have to determine the tenancy or right of occupation of the person so convicted, and thereafter any person is convicted of an offence under subsection (1) in respect of the same premises, the person on whom the notice was served shall be deemed to have committed an offence under subsection (1) unless he proves that he has taken all reasonable steps to prevent the recurrence of the offence. R.S., c. C-34, s. 193.

CROSS-REFERENCES

The terms "keeper", "common bawdy-house" and "place" are defined in s. 197. Section 198(1)(*a*) and (*d*) set out certain presumptions which aid in proof that premises are a common bawdy-house.

As regards special search and seizure powers in relation to bawdy-houses, see s. 199.

The offence in subsec. (1) is a pure indictable offence, but, by virtue of s. 553, it is an offence over which a provincial court judge has absolute jurisdiction and does not depend on the consent of the accused. That is, the accused does not have an election as to mode of trial, although the provincial court judge may, by virtue of s. 555(1), elect to continue the proceedings as a preliminary inquiry, in which case, the accused is deemed to have elected trial by judge and jury pursuant to s. 565(1)(*a*). The trial of the offences in subsec. (2) are conducted by a summary conviction court pursuant to Part XXVII. The punishment for the offences in subsec. (2) are as set out in s. 787 and the limitation period is set out in s. 786(2). For all offences under this section, release pending trial is determined by s. 515, although the accused is eligible for release by a peace officer under s. 496, 497 or by the officer in charge under s. 498.

This offence falls within the definition of "enterprise crime offence" in s. 462.3 for the purposes of Part XII.2.

Other offences related to prostitution may be found in ss. 211 to 213.

As to production of records containing personal information of the complainant or a witness, see ss. 278.1 to 278.9.

Section 486(1) and (2) provide that the judge may make an order excluding all or any members of the public where such order is in the interest of public morals, the maintenance of order or the proper administration of justice, or is necessary to prevent injury to international relations or national defence or national security. The proper administration of justice includes safeguarding the interests of witnesses under the age of 18 years. Section 486.1 sets out the circumstances in which the judge shall or may order a support person to be present and close to a witness while the witness testifies. Where the witness is under the age of 18 years or has a mental or physical disability, the order is to be made upon request unless the judge is of the opinion that the order would interfere with the proper administration of justice. In the case of other witnesses, the order is to be made if necessary to obtain a full and candid account from the witness of the matters complained of. The application for this order may be made during the proceedings or before they begin to the judge who is to preside at the proceedings.

Similarly, s. 486.2 sets out the circumstances in which the judge shall or may order a witness to testify outside the courtroom or behind a screen or other device that would not allow the witness to see the accused. Where the witness is under the age of 18 years or may have difficulty communicating the evidence by reason of a mental or physical disability, the judge shall make the order unless the judge is of the opinion that the order would interfere with the proper administration of justice. In all other cases, the order may be made if the judge is of the opinion that the order is necessary to obtain a full and candid account from the witness of the acts complained of. Similarly, s. 486.3 provides that, on application by the prosecutor or a witness under the age of 18 years, the accused shall not personally cross-examine the witness unless the judge is of the opinion that the proper administration of justice requires the accused to personally conduct the cross-examination. In other cases, the judge may make an order that the accused not personally cross-examine the witness if the judge is of the opinion that the order is necessary to obtain a full and candid account from the witness of the acts complained of. The judge will appoint counsel to conduct the cross-examination.

Under s. 486.4, the judge may make an order directing that the identity of the complainant or a witness not be disclosed in any publication, broadcast or transmitted in any way. The order is mandatory where the complainant or a witness under the age of 18 years or the prosecutor applies for the order. Section 486.5 also gives the judge a discretion respecting non-publication orders in proceedings under these provisions in other circumstances.

SYNOPSIS

This section creates a number of offences in relation to a common bawdy-house.

Section 210(1) makes it an indictable offence to *keep a common bawdy-house*. The maximum sentence upon conviction is two years.

Section 210(2) creates three summary conviction offences. Section 210(2)(*a*) makes it an offence to be an *inmate* in a common bawdy-house. "Inmate" is not defined in the *Criminal Code* but would include a resident or regular occupant of the premises. Section 210(2)(*b*) makes it an offence to be *found in* a common bawdy-house. It must be shown that there was no lawful excuse for the accused's presence. The term "found in" is not defined. Section 210(2)(*c*) makes it an offence for any of the named persons to *knowingly permit* any part of a premises to be used or let for the *purposes* of a common bawdy-house. The category of persons who are caught by this paragraph are those who have actual control or charge over the premises. To demonstrate that the conduct satisfies the necessary mental element of having *knowingly permitted* the use, it must be shown that the accused was aware of the use of the premises and either acquiesced or encouraged its continued use for the illicit purposes.

Subsections (3) and (4) must be read together and create a duty upon the owner, landlord or lessor of the premises which was the subject of a conviction under subsec. (1) (keeping a common bawdy-house). Subsection (3) provides for a notice to be served upon such person or his agent advising of the conviction, and upon receipt of the notice the landlord, owner or lessor must either *forthwith* attempt to terminate the tenancy or other arrangement permitting the keeper to be on the premises or face possible later prosecution. If there is a conviction under subsec. (1) in relation to the same premises after the notice has served upon the owner (or other person mentioned in the subsection) the person who had received the notice *shall be deemed* to also be a keeper pursuant to subsec. (1). To accord with fundamental fairness, at the least it must be shown that the later conviction involving the same premises related to activity which occurred after the notice has been served. The effect of the deeming provision may be ousted if the accused establishes that all reasonable steps were taken to prevent the reoccurrence of the offence under subsec. (1).

ANNOTATIONS

Note: The following cases were decided with reference to a former version of s. 197 in which "prostitution" was part of the definition of "common bawdy house". The amendment was in response to the Supreme Court's decision in *Canada (Attorney General) v. Bedford*, [2013] 3 S.C.R. 1101, 303 C.C.C. (3d) 146, which struck the word "prostitution" from the former definition. The following cases should be read with caution in light of the amended definition which focuses solely on "indecency".

Common bawdy-house / *Also see notes under s. 197* – Any defined space is capable of being a common bawdy-house, even a parking lot, if there is localization of a number of acts of prostitution within its specified boundaries. However, mere presence by prostitutes in the parking lot on a number of occasions, where they did not exercise any control or management over the lot and had no right or interest in the lot as owners, tenants or licensees, is not sufficient to establish them as keeping a common bawdy-house: *R. v. Pierce* (1982), 66 C.C.C. (2d) 388 (Ont. C.A.).

That the premises are a common bawdy-house may be proved by evidence of the general reputation of the house in the community: *R. v. Theirlynck*, [1931] S.C.R. 478, 56 C.C.C. 156.

As well, where there is evidence that the place has the reputation as a common bawdy-house, evidence was admissible as to the accused's reputation as a prostitute. Such evidence is not admitted to show that the accused was the keeper but that the place is occupied by a person whose reputation is consistent with the reputation which it is said the place bears: *R. v. West* (1950), 96 C.C.C. 349 (Ont. C.A.).

"Acts of indecency" and "prostitution" are not vague so as to violate s. 7 of the Charter: *R. v. DiGiuseppe* (2002), 161 C.C.C. (3d) 424 (Ont. C.A.), leave to appeal to S.C.C. refused [2002] 3 S.C.R. vii, 167 C.C.C. (3d) vi.

As to the meaning of acts of indecency, see *R. v. Labaye*, [2005] 3 S.C.R. 728, 203 C.C.C. (3d) 170; *R. v. Kouri*, [2005] 3 S.C.R. 789, 203 C.C.C. (3d) 217, noted under s. 197.

Keeps (subsec. (1)) – As not every "keeper" as defined in s. 197 "keeps" a common bawdy-house, an information charging that the accused "were the keepers of a common bawdy-house" does not charge an offence known to law: *R. v. Catalano* (1977), 37 C.C.C. (2d) 255 (Ont. C.A.).

Thus the offence requires proof of provision of accommodation by the accused. A prostitute who on several occasions over a two-week period resorted to the same hotel must be acquitted of this offence where there is no evidence she was given any particular room, or had rented a particular room or even that she had paid the rent on the room: *R. v. McLellan* (1980), 55 C.C.C. (2d) 543 (B.C.C.A.).

To establish the offence of keeping there must be proof that the accused had some degree of control over the care and management of the premises, and that the accused participated to some extent in the illicit activities of the common bawdy-house. This element of participation does not, however, require personal participation in the sexual acts which occur in the house. It is sufficient that the accused participated in the use of the house as a common bawdy-house. Thus, a person who satisfies the definition of "keeper" in s. 197(1) does not necessarily commit the offence under subsec. (1): *R. v. Corbeil*, [1991] 2 S.C.R. 830, 64 C.C.C. (3d) 272 (4:1).

It is unnecessary to show that the accused participated in the day-to-day running of the premises where he is shown to be the directing mind of the corporation which owned the premises, participated in the management, received the proceeds and was aware of the activities being carried on: *R. v. Woszczyna; R. v. Soucy* (1983), 6 C.C.C. (3d) 221 (Ont. C.A.).

Even where the accused uses her own residence by herself for the purposes of prostitution she may be convicted under this section: *R. v. Worthington* (1972), 10 C.C.C. (2d) 311 (Ont. C.A.).

The Crown must establish an element of control over the care and regular management of the place which harboured the acts of indecency. Willful blindness on the part of the owner or delegation of responsibility are insufficient: *R. v. Kouri, supra.*

Prostitution is not limited to conventional sexual activities and includes lewd acts for payment for the sexual gratification of customers. In this case, sado-masochistic acts were lewd activities in that although they involved pain and humiliation, this did not detract from their sexuality nor the sexual gratification obtained by the clients: *R. v. Bedford* (2000), 143 C.C.C. (3d) 311 (Ont. C.A.), leave to appeal to S.C.C. refused 147 C.C.C. (3d) vi.

Indecency is not inherent in the offence of prostitution. In this case, even though there was no physical contact, the fact that dancers stimulated the customer by engaging in various sexual acts while the customers masturbated was sufficient to constitute prostitution: *R. v. St-Onge* (2001), 155 C.C.C. (3d) 517 (Que. C.A.), leave to appeal to S.C.C. refused [2002] 1 S.C.R. x, 160 C.C.C. (3d) vi.

And, in *R. v. Ni* (2002), 158 O.A.C. 230 (C.A.), the court held that the charge under this section could be made out on the basis of acts of prostitution consisting of acts of masturbation by employees of a massage parlour upon customers. It was unnecessary for the Crown to prove that the conduct also amounted to acts of indecency.

Found in (subsec. (2)(b)) – The offence of being found in a common bawdy-house is not a lesser offence included in the charge of keeping a common bawdy-house: *R. v. Labelle*, [1957] Que. Q.B. 81 (C.A.).

The offence under subsec. (2)(b) requires that the accused was found in the common bawdy house and it was not sufficient that the accused "was present". Mere proof of presence on the premises in question at some earlier time is not sufficient, the accused must have been perceived there or seen by someone. On the other hand, evidence that the accused was seen entering and leaving was sufficient to prove the offence, his presence in the bawdy house not being the object of subsequent admission but being discovered by the contemporaneous observation or inspection by the police: *R. v. Lemieux* (1991), 70 C.C.C. (3d) 434 (Que. C.A.).

Permitting (subsec. (2)(c)) – Where the accused knowingly allowed the premises to be used as a place to which men and women resorted for the purpose of illicit sexual intercourse then a conviction will be sustained even though there was no evidence that the women were charging money for their services or that the couples resorting to the premises were unmarried: *R. v. Turkiewich* (1962), 133 C.C.C. 301 (Man. C.A.).

A charge of being an occupier unlawfully permitting premises to be used as a common bawdy-house was held to be a lesser offence included in the charge of keeping a common bawdy-house: *R. v. Lafreniere*, [1965] 1 C.C.C. 31 (Ont. H.C.J.).

The words "or otherwise having charge or control" qualify the earlier words in the subsection and make it clear that the section is not directed at an owner or landlord, *per se*, but rather at such persons as being the ones having charge or control of the premises. Even where the landlord has power to acquire the charge or control of the premises by immediate termination of the lease, still, once he leased the premises, it was the tenant who had charge or control. The section is directed at a landlord who has actual charge or control in the sense that he has the right to intervene forthwith and whose failure to do so can be considered the granting of permission: *R. v. Wong* (1977), 33 C.C.C. (2d) 6 (Alta. S.C. App. Div.).

TRANSPORTING PERSON TO BAWDY-HOUSE.

211. Every one who knowingly takes, transports, directs, or offers to take, transport or direct, any other person to a common bawdy-house is guilty of an offence punishable on summary conviction. R.S., c. C-34, s. 194.

CROSS-REFERENCES

The term "common bawdy-house" is defined in s. 197.

The trial of this offence is conducted by a summary conviction court pursuant to Part XXVII. The punishment for the offence is as set out in s. 787 and the limitation period is set out in s. 786(2). Release pending trial is determined by s. 515, although the accused is eligible for release by a peace officer under s. 496, 497 or by the officer in charge under s. 498. Other offences in relation to bawdy-houses are found in s. 210. Offences in relation to prostitution are found in ss. 212 and 213.

As to production of records containing personal information of the complainant or a witness, see ss. 278.1 to 278.9.

Section 486(1) and (2) provide that the judge may make an order excluding all or any members of the public where such order is in the interest of public morals, the maintenance of order or the proper administration of justice, or is necessary to prevent injury to international relations or national defence or national security. The proper administration of justice includes safeguarding the interests of witnesses under the age of 18 years. Section 486.1 sets out the circumstances in which the judge shall or may order a support person to be present and close to a witness while the witness testifies. Where the witness is under the age of 18 years or has a mental or physical disability, the order is to be made upon request unless the judge is of the opinion that the order would interfere with the proper administration of justice. In the case of other witnesses, the order is to be made if necessary to obtain a full and candid account from the witness of the matters complained of. The application for this order may be made during the proceedings or before they begin to the judge who is to preside at the proceedings.

Similarly, s. 486.2 sets out the circumstances in which the judge shall or may order a witness to testify outside the courtroom or behind a screen or other device that would not allow the witness to see the accused. Where the witness is under the age of 18 years or may have difficulty communicating the evidence by reason of a mental or physical disability, the judge shall make the order unless the judge is of the opinion that the order would interfere with the proper administration of justice. In all other cases, the order may be made if the judge is of the opinion that the order is necessary to obtain a full and candid account from the witness of the acts complained of. Similarly, s. 486.3 provides that, on application by the prosecutor or a witness under the age of 18 years, the accused shall not personally cross-examine the witness unless the judge is of the opinion that the proper administration of justice requires the accused to personally conduct the cross-examination. In other cases, the judge may make an order that the accused not personally cross-examine the witness if the judge is of the opinion that the order is necessary to obtain a full and candid account from the witness of the acts complained of. The judge will appoint counsel to conduct the cross-examination.

Under s. 486.4, the judge may make an order directing that the identity of the complainant or a witness not be disclosed in any publication, broadcast or transmitted in any way. The order is mandatory where the complainant or a witness under the age of 18 years or the prosecutor applies for the order. Section 486.5 also gives the judge a discretion respecting non-publication orders in proceedings under these provisions in other circumstances.

SYNOPSIS

This section makes it a summary conviction offence to *transport a person to a common bawdy-house*. The actions encompassed by the section are broadly defined as including taking, transporting, directing or offering to do any of these things. The *mens rea* for the offence is that the action be done *knowingly*, namely, that the accused knew that the place was a common bawdy-house.

[Heading repealed, 2014, c. 25, s. 13.]

212. [Repealed, 2014, c. 25, s. 13.]

Offences in Relation to Offering, Providing or Obtaining Sexual Services for Consideration
2014, c. 25, s. 14.

STOPPING OR IMPEDING TRAFFIC / Communicating to provide sexual services for consideration / Definition of "public place".

213. (1) Everyone is guilty of an offence punishable on summary conviction who, in a public place or in any place open to public view, for the purpose of offering, providing or obtaining sexual services for consideration,

(a) stops or attempts to stop any motor vehicle, or

(b) impedes the free flow of pedestrian or vehicular traffic or ingress to or egress from premises adjacent to that place.

(c) [Repealed, 2014, c. 25, s. 15(2).]

(1.1) Everyone is guilty of an offence punishable on summary conviction who communicates with any person — for the purpose of offering or providing sexual services for consideration — in a public place, or in any place open to public view, that is or is next to a school ground, playground or daycare centre.

(2) In this section, "public place" includes any place to which the public have access as of right or by invitation, express or implied, and any motor vehicle located in a public place or in any place open to public view. 1972, c. 13, s. 15; R.S.C. 1985, c. 50 (1st Supp.), s. 1; 2014, c. 25, s. 15.

CROSS-REFERENCES

"Place" is defined in s. 197. "Motor vehicle" is defined in s. 2.

Other offences relating to sexual services are found in ss. 286.1, 286.2, 286.3 and 286.4.

The trial of this offence is conducted by a summary conviction court pursuant to Part XXVII. The punishment for the offence is as set out in s. 787 and the limitation period is set out in s. 786(2). Release pending trial is determined by s. 515, although the accused is eligible for release by a peace officer under s. 496, 497 or by the officer in charge under s. 498. Other offences in relation to prostitution are found in ss. 211 and 212. Offences in relation to bawdy-houses are found in ss. 210 and 211.

As to production of records containing personal information of the complainant or a witness, see ss. 278.1 to 278.9.

Section 486(2.1) provides that, where an accused is charged with this offence and the complainant is, at the time of the trial or preliminary inquiry, under the age of 18 years or may have difficulty communicating the evidence by reason of a mental or physical disability, the judge may order that the complainant testify outside the courtroom or behind a screen where such procedure is necessary to obtain a full and candid account of the acts complained of. Section 715.1 provides that, in proceedings under subsec. (2) or (3), a videotape, made within a reasonable time after the alleged offence, in which the complainant describes the acts complained of, is admissible in evidence if the complainant adopts its contents. Similarly, s. 715.2 provides that, in proceedings under this section in which the complainant or another witness may have difficulty communicating the evidence by reason of a mental or physical disability, a videotape made within a reasonable time after the alleged offence, in which the complainant or witness describes the acts complained of, is admissible in evidence if the complainant or witness adopts its contents.

SYNOPSIS

This section makes it an offence to do any of the prohibited acts (described in subsec. (1)(*a*) to (*c*)) if accompanied by the intention of offering, providing or obtaining sexual services for consideration. This summary conviction offence applies to the acts described below only if they are done in a *public place* (as defined by s. 213(2)) or a place open to public view.

Section 213(1)(*a*) applies to the act of either stopping a motor vehicle or attempting to do so for the prohibited purpose.

Section 213(1)(*b*) prohibits impeding either pedestrian or motor vehicle traffic, or impeding others from going in or out of any premises adjacent to a public place, or one open to the public for the purposes described above.

Section 213(1.1) creates an offence of communicating near schools, etc. for the purpose of offering or providing sexual services. Section 213(2) clarifies what counts as a public place for purposes of this section.

Part VIII / OFFENCES AGAINST THE PERSON AND REPUTATION

Interpretation

DEFINITIONS / "abandon" or "expose" / "aircraft" / "child" / "form of marriage" / "guardian" / "operate" / "vessel".

214. In this Part

"abandon" or "expose" includes

    (*a*) **a wilful omission to take charge of a child by a person who is under a legal duty to do so, and**

    (*b*) **dealing with a child in a manner that is likely to leave that child exposed to risk without protection;**

"aircraft" does not include a machine designed to derive support in the atmosphere primarily from reactions against the earth's surface of air expelled from the machine;

"child" [*Repealed*, 2002, c. 13, s. 9.]

"form of marriage" includes a ceremony of marriage that is recognized as valid

    (*a*) **by the law of the place where it was celebrated, or** (*b*) by the law of the place where an accused is tried, notwithstanding that it is not recognized as valid by the law of the place where it was celebrated;

"guardian" includes a person who has in law or in fact the custody or control of a child.
"operate"

(*a*) means, in respect of a motor vehicle, to drive the vehicle,

(*b*) means, in respect of railway equipment, to participate in the direct control of its motion, whether

(i) as a member of the crew of the equipment,

(ii) as a person who, by remote control, acts in lieu of such crew, or

(iii) as other than a member or person described in subparagraphs (i) and (ii), and

(*c*) includes, in respect of a vessel or an aircraft, to navigate the vessel or aircraft;

"vessel" includes a machine designed to derive support in the atmosphere primarily from reactions against the earth's surface of air expelled from the machine. R.S., c. C-34, s. 196; R.S.C. 1985, c. 27 (1st Supp.), s. 33; c. 32 (4th Supp.), s. 56.

CROSS-REFERENCES

In addition to the definitions in this section, see s. 2 and notes to that section. The terms "motor vehicle" and "railway equipment" are defined in s. 2. The term "wilfully" does not have a fixed meaning and must take its meaning from the context. Generally speaking, however, it connotes an intention to bring about a proscribed consequence. See: *R. v. Buzzanga and Durocher* (1979), 49 C.C.C. (2d) 369 (Ont. C.A.). Most of the legal duties referred to in the definition of "abandon" or "expose" may be found in ss. 215 to 217. Age is determined by reference to s. 30 of the *Interpretation Act*, R.S.C. 1985, c. I-21.

ANNOTATIONS

"abandon or expose" – A relative who undertakes to babysit young children is under a legal duty to take the same care of the children as their parents are at law required to do: *R. v. Reedy (No. 2)* (1981), 60 C.C.C. (2d) 104 (Ont. Dist. Ct.).

Duties Tending to Preservation of Life

DUTY OF PERSONS TO PROVIDE NECESSARIES / Offence / Punishment / Presumptions.

215. (1) Every one is under a legal duty

(*a*) as a parent, foster parent, guardian or head of a family, to provide necessaries of life for a child under the age of sixteen years;

(*b*) to provide necessaries of life to their spouse or common-law partner; and

(*c*) to provide necessaries of life to a person under his charge if that person

(i) is unable, by reason of detention, age, illness, mental disorder or other cause, to withdraw himself from that charge, and

(ii) is unable to provide himself with necessaries of life.

(2) Every one commits an offence who, being under a legal duty within the meaning of subsection (1), fails without lawful excuse, the proof of which lies upon him, to perform that duty, if

(*a*) with respect to a duty imposed by paragraph (1)(*a*) or (*b*),

(i) the person to whom the duty is owed is in destitute or necessitous circumstances, or

(ii) the failure to perform the duty endangers the life of the person to whom the duty is owed, or causes or is likely to cause the health of that person to be endangered permanently; or

(b) **with respect to a duty imposed by paragraph (1)(c), the failure to perform the duty endangers the life of the person to whom the duty is owed or causes or is likely to cause the health of that person to be injured permanently.**

(3) **Every one who commits an offence under subsection (2)**

    (a) **is guilty of an indictable offence and liable to imprisonment for a term not exceeding five years; or**

    (b) **is guilty of an offence punishable on summary conviction and liable to imprisonment for a term not exceeding eighteen months.**

(4) **For the purpose of proceedings under this section,**

    (a) **[*Repealed*, 2000, c. 12, s. 93(2).];**

    (b) **evidence that a person has in any way recognized a child as being his child is, in the absence of any evidence to the contrary, proof that the child is his child;**

    (c) **evidence that a person has failed for a period of one month to make provision for the maintenance of any child of theirs under the age of sixteen years is, in the absence of any evidence to the contrary, proof that the person has failed without lawful excuse to provide necessaries of life for the child; and**

    (d) **the fact that a spouse or common-law partner or child is receiving or has received necessaries of life from another person who is not under a legal duty to provide them is not a defence. R.S., c. C-34, s. 197; 1974-75-76, c. 66, s. 8; 1991, c. 43, s. 9; 2000, c. 12, ss. 93, 95(a); 2005, c. 32, s. 11.**

CROSS-REFERENCES

The terms "child" and "guardian" are defined in s. 214. The terms "mental disorder" and "common-law partner" are defined in s. 2. Omission to perform the duty imposed by subsec. (1) may, in some circumstances, amount to criminal negligence as defined in s. 219 and, if conduct results in death or bodily harm, will amount to an offence under ss. 220 and 221 respectively. Criminal negligence causing death is also a form of culpable homicide for the purposes of ss. 222 to 237. The related offence of abandoning a child is in s. 218. Neglecting to obtain assistance in child birth is an offence under s. 242. The accused's spouse is a competent and compellable witness at the instance of the Crown by virtue of s. 4(2).

Where the prosecution elects to proceed by indictment on this offence then the accused may elect his mode of trial pursuant to s. 536(2). Where the prosecution elects to proceed by way of summary conviction then the trial of this offence is conducted by a summary conviction court pursuant to Part XXVII. The punishment for the offence is then as set out in s. 787 and the limitation period is set out in s. 786(2). In either case, release pending trial is determined by s. 515, although the accused is eligible for release by a peace officer under s. 496, 497 or by the officer in charge under s. 498.

Section 718.01 provides that, in imposing a sentence for an offence involving the abuse of a person under the age of 18 years, the court shall give primary consideration to the objectives of denunciation and deterrence. Further, under s. 718.2, evidence that the offender, in committing the offence, abused a person under the age of 18 years is an aggravating circumstance.

SYNOPSIS

This section creates an offence for *failing to provide the necessaries of life* and contains a number of *rebuttable presumptions which facilitate proof of certain elements of the offence.*

Section 215(1) establishes three classes of relationships in which one party has a legal duty to provide the necessaries of life to the other party: (a) a parent, foster parent, guardian or head of a family must provide the necessaries of life to a child under the age of 16; (b) a married person must provide for his spouse; and (c) a person who has charge of another must provide the necessaries of life to that person if for one of the specified reasons that person is unable to withdraw from the charge and is unable to provide himself with the necessaries of life.

Section 215(2) states that failure to carry out the legal duty specified in subsec. (1) constitutes an offence. The first element of this offence is that the accused failed, without lawful excuse, to fulfil a duty imposed by subsec. (1) if the additional conditions in either s. 215(2)(a) or (b) are established. The onus of establishing a lawful excuse is on the accused and, as with all such burdens placed on the accused, it has been attacked as an alleged violation of ss. 7 and 11(d) of the Charter.

Section 215(2)(a) applies to cases in which the legal duty owed by the accused arises as a result of s. 215(1)(a) or (b) (basically parents and spouses). Under s. 215(2)(a), the offence will be made out if the person to whom the duty is owed is either *destitute or in necessitous circumstances* or if the result of the failure to fulfil the duty *endangers the life* of the person to whom the duty is owed or *causes or is likely to cause* permanent endangerment to the health of that person. Section 215(2)(b) applies if the duty upon the accused arose from s. 215(1)(c) (a person under the charge of the accused if certain circumstances pertain). The failure to fulfil that duty makes out the offence, if the result is that the *life* of the person to whom the duty is owed is *endangered* or it is *likely to cause the health* of that person to be *injured permanently*.

Subsection (3) provides that the offence created may be prosecuted by way of summary conviction procedure or by indictment. Where the Crown proceeds by way of indictment, the maximum sentence is five years and where the Crown proceeds by summary conviction, the maximum sentence is 18 months.

Section 215(4)(b) to (c) set out *rebuttable evidentiary presumptions* that evidence of the things specified is *proof* of certain elements of the offence *unless* there is *any evidence to the contrary*. Section 215(4)(d) limits what constitutes a defence to the charge of failing to provide the necessaries of life. It provides that it is not a defence that some one else, who is not under a legal duty to do so, provided a spouse or child the necessaries of life.

ANNOTATIONS

"Necessaries of life" – The words "necessaries of life" mean such necessaries as tend to preserve life, and not necessaries in their ordinary legal sense and may include medical aid: *R. v. Brooks* (1902), 5 C.C.C. 372 (B.C.S.C.).

Failure to provide medical treatment can amount to "necessitous circumstances" and can therefore lead to liability under either of subparas. (2)(a)(i) or (ii): *R. v. J. (S.)* (2015), 320 C.C.C. (3d) 524 (Ont. C.A.), leave to appeal to S.C.C. refused 2015 CarswellOnt 10364.

Lawful excuse – The accused's inability to support his wife may constitute a lawful excuse: *R. v. Yuman* (1910), 17 C.C.C. 474, 22 O.L.R. 500 (C.A.).

It is not a lawful excuse for a parent who, knowing that a child is in need of medical assistance, refused to obtain such assistance because to do so would be contrary to a tenet of his own particular faith. The guarantee to freedom of conscience and religion in s. 2(a) of the *Charter of Rights and Freedoms* does not affect that issue: *R. v. Tutton and Tutton* (1985), 18 C.C.C. (3d) 328, 44 C.R. (3d) 193, 14 C.R.R. 314 (Ont. C.A.), affd [1989] 1 S.C.R. 1392, 48 C.C.C. (3d) 129, 69 C.R. (3d) 289 (6:0).

Where an accused is charged with manslaughter in an indictment so worded as to make the offence under this subsection an included offence, it must be made clear to the jury that the issue of lawful excuse and the onus on the accused on that issue is not applicable on the manslaughter charge: *R. v. Tutton and Tutton, supra*.

Placing the persuasive burden of establishing lawful excuse upon the accused violates s. 11(d) of the Charter and does not constitute a reasonable limit pursuant to s. 1 of the Charter. Accordingly, the words "the proof of which lies upon him" are of no force and effect: *R. v. Curtis* (1998), 123 C.C.C. (3d) 178, 14 C.R. (5th) 328 (Ont. C.A.). See also *R. v. Scott* (1996), 110 C.C.C. (3d) 473, 1 C.R. (5th) 385 (Sask. Q.B.).

Mens rea – This offence imposes liability on an objective basis. On a charge contrary to subsec. (2)(a)(ii), the Crown must prove a marked departure from the conduct of a reasonably prudent parent in circumstances where it was objectively foreseeable that the failure to provide the necessaries of life would lead to a risk of danger to the life, or a risk of permanent endangerment to the health, of the child: *R. v. Naglik*, [1993] 3 S.C.R. 122, 83 C.C.C. (3d) 526, 23 C.R. (4th) 335.

In a series of cases, the Supreme Court of Canada had occasion to explore the fault element in cases of so-called "penal negligence" apparently as distinguished from criminal negligence. Failure to provide necessaries would be one of these offences. In *R. v. Creighton*, [1993] 3 S.C.R. 3, 83 C.C.C. (3d) 346, 23 C.R. (4th) 189, McLachlin J., writing for a majority of the court, suggested the following approach to proof of such offences. The first question is whether the *actus reus* is established. This requires that the negligence constitute a marked departure from the standards of a reasonable person in all the circumstances of the case. The next question is whether the *mens rea* is established. Normally the *mens rea* for objective foresight of risk of harm is inferred from the facts. The standard is that of the reasonable person in the circumstances of the accused. The normal inference that a person who committed a manifestly dangerous act failed to direct their mind to the risk and the need to take care may be negated by evidence raising a reasonable doubt as to lack of capacity to appreciate the risk. Short of incapacity, personal factors are not relevant whether those factors might indicate, for example, either a lack of experience or a special experience. Also see: *R. v. Naglik*, *supra*.

Under subsec. (2)(*a*)(ii), the Crown must prove that the failure to obtain medical attention would likely put the child at risk of permanent harm: *R. v. Barry* (2004), 187 C.C.C. (3d) 176, 23 C.R. (6th) 385 (Nfld. & Lab. C.A.).

There are differences between criminal negligence and failing to provide the necessaries of life. Criminal negligence requires conduct that constitutes a marked and substantial departure from what a reasonably prudent person would do under the circumstances. Failing to provide the necessaries of life requires proof only that the conduct constitutes a marked departure from the standard of care expected of a reasonably prudent person in the circumstances. Criminal negligence requires proof that the accused showed a wanton or reckless disregard for the life or safety of another, whereas failure to provide the necessaries of life requires proof that the accused's failure endangered the life of the person to whom he or she owed a duty, or that the accused caused, or was likely to cause, the health of that person to be endangered permanently. Finally, criminal negligence is the more serious of the two offences: *R. v. F. (J.)*, [2008] 3 S.C.R. 215, 236 C.C.C. (3d) 421.

"Under his charge" – This phrase imposed a duty where one person was under the other's charge, was unable to withdraw from that charge and was unable to provide himself or herself with the necessaries of life which include food, shelter, care, medical attention necessary to sustain life and protection from harm. "Charge" connoted the duty or responsibility of taking care of a person or thing and included the exercise of an element of control by one person and a dependency on the part of the other. Factors to be considered are the relative positions of the parties and their ability to understand and appreciate their circumstances and whether the accused had explicitly assumed responsibility for the other such as by obtaining a power of attorney for personal care. The offence is made out where there is a marked departure from the conduct of a reasonably prudent person having the charge of another in circumstances where it was reasonably foreseeable that failure to provide necessaries of life would risk danger to life or permanent endangerment of the health of the person under the charge of the accused. In this case, the accused's elderly and ill father was properly found to be under his charge having regard to the fact that the victim was dependent, had a familial relationship with the accused, the accused was fully aware of his father's need of the necessaries of life, the accused controlled the victim's living conditions and kept him in an unsafe environment, the accused had control over the victim's personal care, the accused chose not to make decisions such as contacting community services and the fact that the victim was incapable of withdrawing from the accused's charge having regard to his age and mental illness: *R. v. Peterson* (2005), 201 C.C.C. (3d) 220, 34 C.R. (6th) 120, 203 O.A.C. 364 (C.A.), leave to appeal to S.C.C. refused 204 C.C.C. (3d) vi.

DUTY OF PERSONS UNDERTAKING ACTS DANGEROUS TO LIFE.

216. Every one who undertakes to administer surgical or medical treatment to another person or to do any other lawful act that may endanger the life of another person is, except in cases of necessity, under a legal duty to have and to use reasonable knowledge, skill and care in so doing. R.S., c. C-34, s. 198.

CROSS-REFERENCES

Omission to perform the duty imposed by this section may, in some circumstances, amount to criminal negligence as defined in s. 219 and, if conduct results in death or bodily harm, will amount to an offence under ss. 220 and 221 respectively. Criminal negligence causing death is also a form of culpable homicide for the purposes of ss. 222 to 237. Also note s. 217 respecting the duty of persons undertaking acts. Section 45 protects a person from criminal responsibility for performing surgical operations in certain circumstances.

SYNOPSIS

This section creates a *legal duty* upon those who undertake *lawful* acts that may endanger the life of another to have and to *use reasonable knowledge, skill and care* in so doing. Section 216 specifically addresses those administering surgical or medical treatment, but also extends to anyone who does any other *lawful* act *that may endanger the life of another person*. This section explicitly *excludes* those cases in which the act was performed out of *necessity*.

ANNOTATIONS

Whether or not the accused, who were acting as midwives at a home birth, were administering medical treatment within the meaning of this section their conduct did constitute "any other lawful act that may endanger the life of another person" and they were therefore under a legal duty to have and use reasonable knowledge, skill and care and were to be held to the standard of a competent childbirth attendant notwithstanding their lack of formal training as midwives: *R. v. Sullivan* (1986), 31 C.C.C. (3d) 62, 55 C.R. (3d) 48 (B.C. Co. Ct.). [Appeal to Court of Appeal dismissed on other grounds (1988), 43 C.C.C. (3d) 65, 65 C.R. (3d) 256, 31 B.C.L.R. (2d) 145, further appeal to S.C.C. allowed on other grounds [1991] 1 S.C.R. 489, 63 C.C.C. (3d) 97, 3 C.R. (4th) 277.]

This section imposed a legal duty on the accused, who knew he was infected with the AIDS virus, to not donate blood to the Red Cross and breach of this duty may found a conviction for common nuisance under s. 180: *R. v. Thornton*, [1993] 2 S.C.R. 445, 82 C.C.C. (3d) 530, 21 C.R. (4th) 215 (9:0).

DUTY OF PERSONS UNDERTAKING ACTS.

217. Every one who undertakes to do an act is under a legal duty to do it if an omission to do the act is or may be dangerous to life. R.S., c. C-34, s. 199.

CROSS-REFERENCES

Omission to perform the duty imposed by this section may, in some circumstances, amount to criminal negligence as defined in s. 219 and, if conduct results in death or bodily harm, will amount to an offence under ss. 220 and 221 respectively. Criminal negligence causing death is also a form of culpable homicide for the purposes of ss. 222 to 237.

SYNOPSIS

Section 217 imposes a *legal duty* upon any one who undertakes to do an act if omitting to do it *is or may be dangerous to life*.

ANNOTATIONS

An "undertaking" must generally be something in the nature of a commitment upon which reliance is reasonably placed. The mere expression of words indicating a willingness to do an act cannot trigger a legal duty: *R. v. Browne* (1997), 116 C.C.C. (3d) 183, 33 O.R. (3d) 775, 100 O.A.C. 152 (C.A.), leave to appeal to S.C.C. refused 118 C.C.C. (3d) vi, 110 O.A.C. 200*n*, 225 N.R. 396*n*.

DUTY OF PERSONS DIRECTING WORK.

217.1 Every one who undertakes, or has the authority, to direct how another person does work or performs a task is under a legal duty to take reasonable steps to prevent bodily harm to that person, or any other person, arising from that work or task. 2003, c. 21, s. 3.

CROSS-REFERENCES

"Bodily harm", "every one" and "person" are defined in s. 2. Omission to perform the duty imposed by this section may, in some circumstances, amount to criminal negligence as defined in s. 219 and, if conduct results in death or bodily harm, will amount to an offence under ss. 220 and 221 respectively. Criminal negligence causing death is also a form of culpable homicide for the purposes of ss. 222 to 237. The liability of an organization for offences of negligence is set out in s. 22.1 and for offences requiring proof of fault, other than negligence, is set out in s. 22.2. Also note s. 217 respecting the duty of persons undertaking acts. Section 45 protects a person from criminal responsibility for performing surgical operations in certain circumstances.

SYNOPSIS

This section codifies a legal duty on everyone who undertakes or has authority to direct how others work or perform a task, to take reasonable steps to prevent bodily harm to the person performing the work or task, and to any other person.

ABANDONING CHILD.

218. Every one who unlawfully abandons or exposes a child who is under the age of ten years, so that its life is or is likely to be endangered or its health is or is likely to be permanently injured,

    (a) is guilty of an indictable offence and liable to imprisonment for a term not exceeding five years; or

    (b) is guilty of an offence punishable on summary conviction and liable to imprisonment for a term not exceeding eighteen months. R.S., c. C-34, s. 200; 2005, c. 32, s. 12.

CROSS-REFERENCES

The terms "child", "abandon" and "expose" are defined in s. 214. Age is determined by reference to s. 30 of the *Interpretation Act*, R.S.C. 1985, c. I-21. The related offence of failing to provide necessaries is found in s. 215. Neglecting to obtain assistance in child birth is an offence under s. 242.

The accused's spouse is a competent and compellable witness at the instance of the Crown by virtue of s. 4(2).

The accused has an election as to mode of trial pursuant to s. 536(2). Release pending trial is determined by s. 515, although the accused is eligible for release by the officer in charge under s. 498.

Section 718.01 provides that, in imposing a sentence for an offence involving the abuse of a person under the age of 18 years, the court shall give primary consideration to the objectives of denunciation and deterrence. Further, under s. 718.2, evidence that the offender, in committing the offence, abused a person under the age of 18 years is an aggravating circumstance.

SYNOPSIS

This section creates the hybrid offence of abandoning or exposing a child under 10 years of age so that the child's life is or is likely to be endangered or the health of the child is or is likely to be permanently injured. Since the abandonment or exposure must be unlawful, it would seem that the accused must intend to expose or abandon the child.

ANNOTATIONS

This provision requires proof of subjective *mens rea*: *R. v. H. (A.D.)*, [2013] 2 S.C.R. 269, 295 C.C.C. (3d) 376.

While the Crown, to prove this offence, must prove not only that the child was abandoned but that, *inter alia*, its life was likely to be endangered, the offence was made out where the accused abandoned her child in a motor vehicle for an indefinite period of time in an environment which posed a threat to its life due to the cold temperatures and risk of abduction. It was no excuse that the accused intended to return several hours later at a time, when according to expert evidence, the child would still be alive. It is the act of endangering that constitutes the offence: *R. v. Holzer* (1988), 63 C.R. (3d) 301 (Alta. Q.B.).

Criminal Negligence

CRIMINAL NEGLIGENCE / Definition of "duty".

219. (1) Every one is criminally negligent who
  (*a*) in doing anything, or
  (*b*) in omitting to do anything that it is his duty to do,
shows wanton or reckless disregard for the lives or safety of other persons.

(2) For the purposes of this section, "duty" means a duty imposed by law. R.S., c. C-34, s. 202.

CROSS-REFERENCES

The offences of criminal negligence causing death and causing bodily harm are set out in ss. 220 and 221 respectively. Criminal negligence is also a form of culpable homicide for the purposes of s. 222. Duties imposed under sections of the *Criminal Code* include the following: s. 33, duty to disperse rioters; s. 79, duty of care re explosives; s. 86, duty of care re firearms; s. 215, duty to provide necessaries; s. 216, duty of person undertaking acts dangerous to life; s. 217, duty of persons undertaking acts; s. 217.1, duty of persons directing work; s. 263(1) and (2), duty to safeguard opening in ice and excavations.

Related offences where the conduct results only in damage to property or animals are found in Part XI. Liability of an organization for an offence requiring proof of negligence is set out in s. 22.1.

SYNOPSIS

Section 219 defines the term *criminal negligence*.

Criminal negligence can arise from either acts or omissions, if the accused was under a *legal duty* to do the omitted act. If the act or omission shows a *wanton or reckless disregard for the lives or safety of other persons*, this makes out criminal negligence. Despite the reference to "other persons" the offence *need only* result in potential harm to *one* other person.

ANNOTATIONS

Meaning of criminal negligence – The mere breach of a duty imposed by a provincial statute does not *per se* constitute criminal negligence: *R. v. Titchner* (1961), 131 C.C.C. 64, 29 D.L.R. (2d) 1 (Ont. C.A.), but it is proper for the judge to refer the jury to the legislation which governs the particular activity in which the accused is engaged: *R. v. Leblanc*, [1977] 1 S.C.R. 339, 29 C.C.C. (2d) 97, 68 D.L.R. (3d) 243 (6:3).

Criminal negligence does not require proof of intention or deliberation, indifference being sufficient. Thus, the accused may be convicted on proof of driving amounting to a marked and substantial departure from the standard of a reasonable driver in circumstances where the accused either recognized and ran an obvious and serious risk to the lives and safety of others or, alternatively, gave no thought to that risk: *R. v. Sharp* (1984), 12 C.C.C. (3d) 428, 39 C.R. (3d) 367, 26 M.V.R. 279 (Ont. C.A.).

In two cases *R. v. Waite*, [1989] 1 S.C.R. 1436, 48 C.C.C. (3d) 1, 69 C.R. (3d) 323, and *R. v. Tutton*, [1989] 1 S.C.R. 1392, 48 C.C.C. (3d) 129, 69 C.R. (3d) 289, the Supreme Court considered the *mens rea* of the criminal negligence offence as it applied to acts of commission [*Waite*, operation of a motor vehicle] and omission [*Tutton*, failure of parents to provide medical treatment to a child]. In each case there were three judgments and no clear consensus emerged as to the requisite *mens rea*. On two points, there was agreement as follows: (1) There is no distinction between acts of commission or omission in determining the requisite *mens rea*; (2) It is an error to direct the jury that the Crown must prove elements of deliberateness and wilfulness. The court divided equally however on whether the *mens rea* required was subjective or objective. Three members of the court (McIntyre, Lamer and L'Heureux-Dubé JJ.) were of the view that an objective standard was to be applied. Thus, proof of conduct which reveals a marked and significant departure from the standard which could be expected of a reasonably prudent person in the circumstances will justify a conviction. The decision must be made, however, on a consideration of the facts existing at the time and in relation to the accused's perception of those facts. Thus, an honest and reasonably held belief in the existence of certain facts may be a relevant consideration in assessing the reasonableness of the accused's conduct. Further, McIntyre J., writing for himself and L'Heureux-Dubé J., adopted the reasons for judgment of Cory J.A. in the Ontario Court of Appeal in *R. v. Waite* (1986), 28 C.C.C. (3d) 326, 52 C.R. (3d) 355, 41 M.V.R. 119. This would appear to represent approval of that court's principle of fault as it applies to this offence, especially in the driving context. The clearest explanation of this principle may be found in *R. v. Sharp, supra*, where the Court of Appeal held that, while the jury may find the required fault in the nature of the accused's driving which amounts to a marked and substantial departure from the standard of a reasonable driver in the circumstances, the accused may be acquitted if there is an explanation which arises from the evidence that would account for the deviant conduct in a manner which would negative the element of fault, such as a cause resulting from circumstances beyond the accused's control, for example, a sudden mechanical malfunction. Lamer J. in his concurring reasons in both cases, while accepting the objective standard, was of the view that, in applying this, a generous allowance must be made for factors which are particular to the accused, such as youth, mental development, education. [*Quaere* whether such a generous allowance applies in the case of licensed activity such as driving.]

Wilson J. writing for herself, Dickson C.J.C. and Le Dain J., while explicitly adopting the fault notion as explained in *R. v. Sharp, supra*, in the motor vehicle context, would also require proof of some minimal blameworthy state of mind described as advertence to the risk or wilful blindness to the risk. In the driving context, however, where risks to lives and safety of others is constant and obvious, the accused's claim that he or she gave no thought to the risk or has simply a negative state of mind would, in most cases, amount to the culpable positive mental state of wilful blindness to the prohibited risk. More generally it was explained [*Tutton, supra*, at p. 154 C.C.C.]:

> "Conduct which shows a wanton or reckless disregard for the lives and safety of others will by its nature constitute *prima facie* evidence of the mental element, and in the absence of some evidence that casts doubt on the normal degree of mental awareness, proof of the act and reference to what a reasonable person in the circumstances must have realized will lead to a conclusion that the accused was aware of the risk or wilfully blind to the risk."

In the subsequent cases of *R. v. Nelson* (1990), 54 C.C.C. (3d) 285, 75 C.R. (3d) 70 , 21 M.V.R. (2d) 245 (Ont. C.A.), and *R. v. Cabral* (1990), 54 C.C.C. (3d) 317 , 21 M.V.R. (2d) 252 (Ont. C.A.), held that, until the Supreme Court of Canada holds otherwise, it is still open to that court to follow its decisions in *R. v. Sharp, supra*, and in *R. v. Waite* (1986), 28 C.C.C. (3d) 326, and apply the objective test as enunciated in those decisions. Further, the court noted that in the context of a charge of criminal negligence involving the operation of a motor vehicle, in most cases, as a practical matter, there will be very little difference between the limited subjective approach of Wilson J. and the objective approach in *R. v. Sharp, supra*, and in *R. v. Waite* (1986), 28 C.C.C. (3d) 326.

In *R. v. Anderson*, [1990] 1 S.C.R. 265, 53 C.C.C. (3d) 481, 75 C.R. (3d) 50 (7:0), the court returned to the question of criminal negligence in the context of a driving case. Sopinka J. for the court, while not attempting to resolve the objective/subjective issue, pointed out that fundamental to either approach is a finding that the conduct of the accused constituted a marked departure from the norm. He also pointed out that, as the risk created increases, the objective and subjective approaches begin to converge, since the easier it is to conclude that both a reasonably prudent person would have foreseen the consequences [the objective approach] and that the particular accused must have foreseen the consequences [the subjective approach]. In this case, it was unnecessary to resolve the issue because the trial judge had a reasonable doubt whether the conduct of the accused in driving in an impaired condition and failing to stop at a red light was a marked departure from the norm. That being the case, a conclusion that the accused had a wanton or reckless disregard for the lives and safety of others could not be drawn on either a subjective or objective basis.

The *mens rea* for a party to this offence requires the aider to do something with intent to assist conduct that is criminally negligent and to know sufficient details of the assisted conduct to render that conduct criminally negligent. Thus, the conduct that the aider knows he is assisting must constitute a marked and substantial departure from what is reasonable in the circumstances. It is not necessary that the aider know the law, nor that he appreciate the legal consequences of the conduct being assisted. The aider will have aided the commission of the offence if he or she intentionally assists conduct which constitutes the offence and knows the principal intends to commit it. In those circumstances, the aider did something "for the purpose of" assisting the commission of the offence. In addition, it is not necessary that the aider have subjective foresight of the consequence of the criminally negligent act he or she is assisting. It is sufficient to show that a reasonable person, in all the circumstances, would have appreciated a consequence — bodily harm that is not trivial or transient — would result. An individual who was the "flagman" in a street race could be held liable as a party as it was open to conclude that the race, as the accused anticipated it, was a marked and substantial departure from what was reasonable in the circumstances, and the bodily harm was a foreseeable consequence of the street race: *R. v. R. (M.)* (2011), 275 C.C.C. (3d) 45 (Ont. C.A.).

Death caused by dangerous driving and death caused by criminal negligence involve different degrees of moral blameworthiness. Further, proof of the offence under this section requires establishing a reckless disregard, rather than a marked departure from the standard of reasonable conduct, which is all that is required for dangerous driving: *R. v. Fortier* (1998), 127 C.C.C. (3d) 217 (Que. C.A.).

Fault is determined by considering whether the conduct constitutes a marked departure from that expected of a reasonable person in the circumstances. While the fault requirement applies uniformly to both acts and omissions, there may be situations in which a failure to act where there is a duty to do so will not fall below the standard, whereas actions which actually create a risk will fall below the standard: *R. v. Canhoto* (1999), 140 C.C.C. (3d) 321, 29 C.R. (5th) 170 (Ont. C.A.).

Reasonable foreseeability of harm is relevant in the analysis of legal causation in negligence based offences. Where conduct is inherently dangerous and carries with it a reasonable foreseeable risk of immediate and substantial harm, the test for legal causation will have been met. Independent voluntary human intervention in the events started by an accused may break the chain of causation: *R. v. Shilon* (2006), 240 C.C.C. (3d) 401 (Ont. C.A.), leave to appeal to S.C.C. refused [2007] 2 S.C.R. vi.

A finding of criminal negligence first requires the trial judge to find that there was a marked and substantial departure from the standard of care of a reasonable person in both the physical and mental elements of the offence. In this case, the trial judge erred in concluding that, because the accused realized there was a risk of injury to the deceased, he was wanton or reckless without making specific consideration of whether the accused's physical act was a marked departure from the norm: *R. v. L. (J.)* (2006), 204 C.C.C. (3d) 324, 206 O.A.C. 205 (C.A.).

In determining whether the conduct of the accused, a 16-year-old boy, constituted criminal negligence the standard to be used is that of a sane and sober 16-year-old. The question then was whether or not the conduct amounted to a marked and substantial departure from that standard. In this case the accused lightly pushed his friend at the top of a staircase who then fell to his death. While such conduct constituted negligence it involved only minimal force and momentary inadvertence and was not sufficient to amount to a marked and substantial departure from the standard of a reasonable person: *R. v. Barron* (1985), 23 C.C.C. (3d) 544, 48 C.R. (2d) 334 (Ont. C.A.).

Evidence that the accused suffered from mental retardation was relevant to determining whether he possessed the capacity to understand and appreciate the risks entailed by his conduct and could therefore be held to be criminally negligent: *R. v. Ubhi* (1994), 27 C.R. (4th) 332, 1 M.V.R. (3d) 161 (B.C.C.A.), leave to appeal to S.C.C. refused 31 C.R. (4th) 405, 5 M.V.R. (3d) 249n.

A "duty imposed by law" may be a duty arising by virtue of either statute or common law: *R. v. Coyne* (1958), 124 C.C.C. 176, 31 C.R. 335 (N.B.C.A.).

A parent is under a legal duty at common law to take reasonable steps to protect his child from illegal violence used by the other parent towards the child which the parent foresees or ought to foresee. Such a parent is criminally liable for failing to discharge that duty in circumstances which show a wanton or reckless disregard for the child's safety, where the failure to discharge the legal duty has contributed to the death of the child or resulted in bodily harm to the child: *R. v. Popen* (1981), 60 C.C.C. (2d) 232 (Ont. C.A.).

Criminal negligence requires conduct that constitutes a marked and substantial departure from what a reasonably prudent person would do under the circumstances. Failing to provide the necessaries of life requires proof only that the conduct constitutes a marked departure from the standard of care expected of a reasonably prudent person in the circumstances. Criminal negligence requires proof that the accused showed a wanton or reckless disregard for the life or safety of another, whereas failure to provide the necessaries of life requires proof that the accused's failure endangered the life of the person to whom he or she owed a duty, or that the accused caused, or was likely to cause, the health of that person to be endangered permanently. Finally, criminal negligence is the more serious of the two offences. Where criminal negligence and a failure to provide the necessaries of life are both alleged, the jury should first determine whether the accused had a duty to protect the victim and failed in that duty. If the offence of failing to provide the necessaries of life is established, the jury should then determine whether this constituted a wanton or reckless disregard for the life or safety of the victim so as to constitute criminal negligence: *R. v. F. (J.)*, [2008] 3 S.C.R. 215, 236 C.C.C. (3d) 421.

Constitutional considerations – Section 7 of the *Charter of Rights and Freedoms* does not require proof of subjective foresight for a conviction for criminal negligence: *R. v. Nelson*, *supra*.

CAUSING DEATH BY CRIMINAL NEGLIGENCE.

220. Every person who by criminal negligence causes death to another person is guilty of an indictable offence and liable

(*a*) **where a firearm is used in the commission of the offence, to imprisonment for life and to a minimum punishment of imprisonment for a term of four years; and**

(*b*) **in any other case, to imprisonment for life. R.S., c. C-34, s. 203; 1995, c. 39, s. 141.**

CROSS-REFERENCES

Criminal negligence is defined in s. 219. "Firearm" and "person" are defined in s. 2. Pursuant to s. 255.1, where the offence was committed by means of a motor vehicle, vessel or aircraft, evidence that the accused's blood alcohol level exceeded .160 at the time when the offence was committed is deemed to be an aggravating factor on sentencing. See s. 259 re driving prohibition orders. Note s. 732.1(3)(*g*.1) and (*g*.2), which allow for terms of probation that the offender attend for curative treatment in relation to the consumption of alcohol and drugs and participate in an alcohol ignition interlock device program. For liability of an organization for an offence requiring proof of negligence, see s. 22.1.

Section 249.2 creates the offence of causing death by criminal negligence while street racing (defined in s. 2). The penalty for that offence, as in this section, is a maximum of life imprisonment.

ANNOTATIONS

The word "person" should be interpreted in the same manner as "human being" as defined for the homicide provisions by s. 223. Thus for this section to apply the child must have been completely extruded from its mother's body and be born alive. Where the child dies while it is in the birth canal it is not at that time a "person" and the offence under this section could not be committed: *R. v. Sullivan*, [1991] 1 S.C.R. 489, 63 C.C.C. (3d) 97.

Evidence of the type of driving by the accused immediately after the accident is admissible as part of the *res gestae* and also for consideration on the issue of his wanton and reckless disregard prior to and at the time of the accident: *R. v. Balcerczyk*, [1957] 3 S.C.R. 20, 117 C.C.C. 71 (4:1).

For conviction the Crown must prove the breaching of an obligation imposed by law with a wanton or reckless disregard for the lives or safety of others and, to assist in the proof of *mens rea*, may lead evidence of previous similar conduct: *R. v. Leblanc*, [1977] 1 S.C.R. 339, 29 C.C.C. (2d) 97 (6:3).

A trial judge is not obliged to use the phrase "obvious and serious risk to others" in charging the jury. The phrase "a wanton or reckless disregard for the lives or safety of others", drawn from the language of s. 219, was adequate: *R. v. Kerr* (2013), 305 C.C.C. (3d) 127 (B.C.C.A.).

The test for causation for homicide is whether the acts of the accused were a significant contributing cause to the death: *R. v. Nette*, [2001] 3 S.C.R. 488, 158 C.C.C. (3d) 486.

Foreseeability of the risk of death is not a factor which the jury should consider on the question of whether the accused's conduct amounts to criminal negligence: *R. v. Pinske* (1988), 6 M.V.R. (2d) 19, 30 B.C.L.R. (2d) 114 (C.A.), affd [1989] 2 S.C.R. 979, 100 N.R. 399 (7:0).

The minimum sentence does not violate s. 12 of the Charter. The minimum sentence may, however, be reduced by considering the time spent in pre-trial custody: *R. v. Morrisey*, [2000] 2 S.C.R. 90, 148 C.C.C. (3d) 1.

CAUSING BODILY HARM BY CRIMINAL NEGLIGENCE.

221. Every one who by criminal negligence causes bodily harm to another person is guilty of an indictable offence and liable to imprisonment for a term not exceeding ten years. R.S., c. C-34, s. 204.

CROSS-REFERENCES

Criminal negligence is defined in s. 219. "Bodily harm" and "every one" are defined in s. 2. For liability of an organization for an offence requiring proof of negligence, see s. 22.1.

As to included offences, see s. 662(5).

The accused's spouse is a competent and compellable witness at the instance of the Crown by virtue of s. 4(4) where the victim is under the age of 14 years. Age is determined by reference to s. 30 of the *Interpretation Act*, R.S.C. 1985, c. I-21.

The accused has an election as to mode of trial pursuant to s. 536(2). Release pending trial is determined by s. 515. An accused convicted of this offence may, pursuant to s. 259, be ordered prohibited from operating a motor vehicle, vessel, aircraft or railway equipment for any period not exceeding ten years where the offence under this section was committed by means of a motor vehicle, vessel, aircraft or railway equipment. The procedure respecting the making of that order of prohibition is found in s. 260. It may be that, in some circumstances, the accused will also be liable to the mandatory prohibition order respecting firearms, ammunition and explosives by virtue of s. 109. With respect to causation see notes under ss. 220, 249 and 255.

Pursuant to s. 255.1, where the offence was committed by means of a motor vehicle, vessel or aircraft, evidence that the accused's blood alcohol level exceeded .160 at the time when the offence was committed is deemed to be an aggravating factor on sentencing. See s. 259 re driving prohibition orders. Note s. 732.1(3)(*g*.1) and (*g*.2), which allow for terms of probation that the offender attend for curative treatment in relation to the consumption of alcohol and drugs and participate in an alcohol ignition interlock device program.

Section 249.3 creates the offence of causing bodily harm by criminal negligence while street racing (defined in s. 2). The penalty for that offence is a maximum of 14 years.

Homicide

HOMICIDE / Kinds of homicide / Non culpable homicide / Culpable homicide / Idem / Exception.

222. (1) A person commits homicide when, directly or indirectly, by any means, he causes the death of a human being.

(2) Homicide is culpable or not culpable.

(3) Homicide that is not culpable is not an offence.

(4) Culpable homicide is murder or manslaughter or infanticide.

(5) A person commits culpable homicide when he causes the death of a human being,
    (*a*) by means of an unlawful act,
    (*b*) by criminal negligence,
    (*c*) by causing that human being, by threats or fear of violence or by deception, to do anything that causes his death, or
    (*d*) by wilfully frightening that human being, in the case of a child or sick person.

(6) Notwithstanding anything in this section, a person does not commit homicide within the meaning of this Act by reason only that he causes the death of a human being by procuring, by false evidence, the conviction and death of that human being by sentence of the law. R.S., c. C-34, s. 205.

CROSS-REFERENCES

The scheme of the homicide provisions is that this section defines culpable homicide and then other provisions determine whether culpable homicide is murder, manslaughter or infanticide. The distinction is largely, although not exclusively, dependent on the intent accompanying the conduct which resulted in death. Murder is defined in ss. 229 and 230. The punishment for murder is set out in s. 235. Infanticide is defined in s. 233. The punishment for infanticide is set out in s. 237. Manslaughter is defined in ss. 232, 234 and 263. The punishment for manslaughter is set out in s. 236.

As to causation, see ss. 223(2) and 224 to 227. As to definition of "human being" see s. 233.

Criminal negligence is defined in s. 219 and criminal negligence causing death is also a separate offence under s. 220. For liability of an organization for an offence requiring proof of negligence, see s. 22.1.

SYNOPSIS

This section spells out *what constitutes homicide* and sets out the *distinction between culpable and non-culpable homicide.*

Section 222(1) states that *homicide* is committed when a person *causes the death*, directly or indirectly, of another person. Homicide may be either culpable or not, and non-culpable homicide is not an offence. Subsection (6) provides a clarification by excluding from the ambit of homicide procuring the death of another by false evidence which leads to that person's conviction and the imposition of the death penalty.

Subsection (4) exhaustively *defines culpable homicide as being murder, manslaughter or infanticide.* Subsection (5) deals with the ways in which culpable homicide may be committed such as by an unlawful act (s. 222(5)(*a*)) or by criminal negligence (s. 222(5)(*b*)).

ANNOTATIONS

Causation – Where an issue of causation arises the jury in deciding the question is not limited to considering the testimony of expert witnesses but may also consider the evidence of lay witnesses who witnessed the assault alleged by the Crown to have been the cause of death. Causation as a question of fact is for the jury not the experts. Further, where it is established that the assault by the accused was at least a contributing cause of death, outside the *de minimis* range, then causation as a matter of law has been established. The accused must take his victim as he finds him and it is no defence to a charge of manslaughter that death was unexpected and the physical reactions of the victim to the assault unforseen or that death ordinarily would not result from the unlawful act: *R. v. Smithers*, [1978] 1 S.C.R. 506, 34 C.C.C. (2d) 427 (9:0).

Causation has both a factual and legal component. Factual causation is concerned with an inquiry about how the victim died in a medical, mechanical or physical sense. Legal causation is concerned with whether the person should be held responsible in law for the death. While causation is distinct from *mens rea*, the proper standard of causation expresses an element of fault that is sufficient to base responsibility. When an unlawful act is combined with the requisite mental element for the offence charged, causation is generally not an issue. The applicable standard for causation in relation to manslaughter is a contributing cause outside the *de minimis* range. For first degree murder during the commission of another offense, the causation must be a substantial and integral part of the killing. This causation requirement refers to the increased degree of moral culpability that is required before an accused can be found guilty of first degree murder. In charging the jury, there is a need to distinguish between the terms used to describe the relevant standard of causation and the terminology used to express it. Latin expressions and formulations that are negative should not be used. It is preferable to explain the standard of causation in terms of phrases such as "significant contributing cause" rather than "not a trivial cause" or "not insignificant": *R. v. Nette*, [2001] 3 S.C.R. 488, 158 C.C.C. (3d) 486.

The test for the time of death is whether any of the victim's vital organs including the heart continue to operate. The criminal law does not recognize brain death or cessation of brain function as the legal standard of determining when death occurs: *R. v. Green* (1988), 43 C.C.C. (3d) 413 (B.C.S.C.).

Intervening cause cases constitute a unique category of case such that the trial judge is obliged to give the jury a clear and specific instruction with respect to the intervening events. The jury must understand their obligation to consider whether or not any independent, intervening and therefore exculpatory factors occurred after the accused's act, thereby severing the link in the chain of events leading to the victim's death: *R. v. Reid* (2003), 180 C.C.C. (3d) 151, 18 C.R. (6th) 282 (N.S.C.A.).

Even in cases where it is alleged that an intervening act has interrupted the chain of legal causation, the causation test remains whether the dangerous and unlawful acts of the accused are a significant contributing cause of the victim's death. An intervening act that is reasonably foreseeable will usually not break or rupture the chain of causation so as to relieve the offender of legal responsibility for the unintended result. The time to assess reasonable foreseeability is at the time of the initial unlawful act, rather than at the time of the intervening act. It is the general nature of the intervening acts and the accompanying risk of harm, not the precise details, that need to be reasonably foreseeable. If they are, then the accused's actions may remain a significant contributing cause of death: *R. v. Maybin*, [2012] 2 S.C.R. 30, 283 C.C.C. (3d) 275.

Where the entire episode involving a series of unlawful acts is one continuing transaction then it is not open to the accused to rely upon the defence of honest but mistaken belief on the basis that at the time of the final act which actually resulted in the death of the victim the accused believed the victim to be already dead: *R. v. Frizzell* (1993), 81 C.C.C. (3d) 463, 22 C.R. (4th) 400 (B.C.C.A.).

The common law definition of causation requiring proof that the unlawful act was at least a contributing cause of death outside the *de minimis* range complies with the principles of fundamental justice as guaranteed by s. 7 of the Charter. When combined with the requisite fault element for manslaughter by an unlawful act, being commission of an unlawful dangerous act, in circumstances where a reasonable person would have foreseen the risk of bodily harm which is neither trivial nor transitory, there is no risk that a person who is morally innocent will be convicted for consequences that should not be attributed to him: *R. v. Cribbin* (1994), 89 C.C.C. (3d) 67, 28 C.R. (4th) 137 (Ont. C.A.).

Homicide by "unlawful act" – The *mens rea* of unlawful act manslaughter under subsec. (5)(*a*) is, in addition to the *mens rea* of the underlying offence, objective foreseeability of the risk of bodily harm which is neither trivial nor transitory: *R. v. Creighton*, [1993] 3 S.C.R. 3, 83 C.C.C. (3d) 346.

The unlawful act must also be objectively dangerous, that is, likely to injure another person: *R. v. DeSousa*, [1992] 2 S.C.R. 944, 76 C.C.C. (3d) 124; *R. v. Creighton, supra.*

Where the Crown relies on subsec. (5)(*a*), the unlawful act must be identified and the trial judge must determine whether the *actus reus* and *mens rea* of that offence have been proven beyond a reasonable doubt, and whether objective foreseeability of bodily harm was neither transitory nor trivial. It is insufficient to simply conclude that that the accused's conduct was dangerous without identifying the underlying unlawful act: *R. v. T. (K.)* (2005), 199 C.C.C. (3d) 551, 31 C.R. (6th) 187 (Man. C.A.), leave to appeal to S.C.C. quashed (improperly brought pursuant to s. 40 of the *Supreme Court Act*) [2006] 1 S.C.R. xiii, 205 C.C.C. (3d) vi, leave to appeal to S.C.C. refused [2006] 1 S.C.R. xiii, 208 C.C.C. (3d) vi.

Where the defence of self-defence is made out then the act done in self-defence is not unlawful, the homicide is not culpable and the accused must be acquitted: *R. v. Baker* (1988), 45 C.C.C. (3d) 368 (B.C.C.A.).

The unlawful act can be a breach of a federal or provincial statute as long as it is not an offence or absolute liability (or otherwise constitutionally deficient) and provided it is objectively dangerous. Here, the accused bar owners may have breached the provincial *Liquor Licence Act* by allowing someone to become intoxicated on their premises, but the act was not objectively dangerous. Therefore, the fact that the impaired person later caused a fatal car crash could not make the accused guilty of unlawful act manslaughter: *R. v. Sztejnmiler* (2013), 299 C.C.C. (3d) 456 (Ont. C.J.).

Homicide by criminal negligence – See notes under ss. 219 and 220.

WHEN CHILD BECOMES HUMAN BEING / Killing child.

223. (1) A child becomes a human being within the meaning of this Act when it has completely proceeded, in a living state, from the body of its mother whether or not

(*a*) **it has breathed,**

(*b*) **it has an independent circulation, or**

(*c*) **the navel string is severed.**

(2) A person commits homicide when he causes injury to a child before or during its birth as a result of which the child dies after becoming a human being. R.S., c. C-34, s. 206.

CROSS-REFERENCES

Culpable homicide is defined in s. 222 and see cross-references under that section respecting murder, manslaughter and infanticide. The effect of this section is that killing of a child who has become a human being can amount to homicide or also found the offence of criminal negligence causing death under s. 220. Where the child's death is caused in the act of birth before it becomes a human being then the accused commits the offence under s. 238. Neglecting to obtain assistance in child-birth is an offence under s. 242 and concealing the body of a child an offence under s. 243. Other causation provisions are found in ss. 224 to 226 and 228.

SYNOPSIS

This section establishes the point at which a *child becomes a human being* for the purpose of determining if a homicide has been committed.

Section 223(1) defines that a child is a human being if it has completely proceeded from its mother in a *living state*, even if it has not done one of the things listed in s. 223(1)(*a*) to (*c*). Subsection (2) provides that homicide is committed if a child dies after meeting the definition of human being, in subsec. (1) even if the cause of death was injuries sustained by the child before or during its birth.

ANNOTATIONS

A person who attacks an obviously pregnant woman with intent to harm her is guilty of at least manslaughter if the foetus being subsequently born alive dies from injury or disease caused by the attack: *R. v. Prince* (1988), 44 C.C.C. (3d) 510, [1989] 1 W.W.R. 80 (Man. C.A.).

DEATH THAT MIGHT HAVE BEEN PREVENTED.

224. Where a person, by an act or omission, does any thing that results in the death of a human being, he causes the death of that human being notwithstanding that death from that cause might have been prevented by resorting to proper means. R.S., c. C-34, s. 207.

CROSS-REFERENCES

Culpable homicide is defined in s. 222 and see cross-references under that section respecting murder, manslaughter and infanticide. Other causation provisions are found in ss. 223(2) and 225 to 228. "Human being" is defined in s. 223(1). This provision would also apply to the offences of criminal negligence causing death under s. 220, dangerous driving causing death under s. 249(4) and impaired operation causing death under s. 255(3).

SYNOPSIS

Section 224 deals with the issue of a *death which might have been prevented*, which arises as a question of causation in relation to homicide cases.

This section provides that a person commits homicide if that person does anything which results in the death of another person, even if proper treatment could have prevented death from that cause. The person may have caused the death by act or omission. This satisfies the first requirement of all homicides: proof that the person caused the death of another person (see s. 222(1)).

DEATH FROM TREATMENT OF INJURY.

225. Where a person causes to a human being a bodily injury that is of itself of a dangerous nature and from which death results, he causes the death of that human being notwithstanding that the immediate cause of death is proper or improper treatment that is applied in good faith. R.S., c. C-34, s. 208.

CROSS-REFERENCES

Culpable homicide is defined in s. 222 and see cross-references under that section respecting murder, manslaughter and infanticide. Other causation provisions are found in ss. 223(2), 224, 226 and 228. "Human being" is defined in s. 223(1). This provision would also apply to the offences of criminal negligence causing death under s. 220, dangerous driving causing death under s. 249(4) and impaired operation causing death under s. 255(3). The term "bodily injury" is not defined in this section. Some assistance may, however, be obtained from the definition of "bodily harm" in s. 2.

SYNOPSIS

Section 225 deals with one aspect of the issue of causation in homicide cases, namely, the effect of the *immediate cause of death being treatment* applied after the accused *caused a dangerous injury* to the deceased. The section provides that, if the *treatment was given in good faith*, it is irrelevant whether it was proper or not. The key is whether the *injury, caused by the accused* to the deceased, was of a *dangerous nature and that death resulted from it*. Thus, causation will be supplied by this section so long as the act of the accused causing injury was an operative factor, even if it was only one of the causes of the death.

ANNOTATIONS

In *R. v. Kitching and Adams* (1976), 32 C.C.C. (2d) 159, [1976] 6 W.W.R. 697 (Man. C.A.), the defence raised was that the cause of death was the act of doctors who, having detected no sign of brain activity, removed the deceased's kidneys and then disconnected the deceased from the mechanical devices which were used to keep his heart and other organs functioning. Matas J.A., for four of the judges, held that the jury had been adequately instructed on the effects of ss. 207 to 209 [now ss. 224 to 226]. O'Sullivan J.A., in a concurring opinion pointed out that those sections extend liability in certain cases and do not affect the principle that it is not necessary to prove that a criminal is the sole cause of his crime and that even if it could be shown that the actions of the doctors constituted an operative cause of death, still, that would not exonerate the accused unless the evidence left a reasonable doubt that the accused's actions also constituted an operative cause of the deceased's death.

A similar result was reached in *R. v. Malcherek; R. v. Steel* (1981), 73 Cr. App. R. 173 (C.A.).

In *R. v. Torbiak and Gillis* (1978), 40 C.C.C. (2d) 193 (Ont. C.A.), the court held that there could be no doubt that the cause of death in law was a gunshot wound to the groin inflicted by one of the accused although the doctors, because of the elderly victim's age decided to follow a conservative course of non-interventional treatment following the shooting until three weeks later the victim's condition deteriorated and he died on the operating table.

ACCELERATION OF DEATH.

226. Where a person causes to a human being a bodily injury that results in death, he causes the death of that human being notwithstanding that the effect of the bodily injury is only to accelerate his death from a disease or disorder arising from some other cause. R.S., c. C-34, s. 209.

CROSS-REFERENCES

Culpable homicide is defined in s. 222 and see cross-references under that section respecting murder, manslaughter and infanticide. Other causation provisions are found in ss. 223(2), 224, 225 and 228. "Human being" is defined in s. 223(1). This provision would also apply to the offences of criminal negligence causing death under s. 220, dangerous driving causing death under s. 249(4) and impaired operation causing death under s. 255(3). The term "bodily injury" is not defined in this section. Some assistance may, however, be obtained from the definition of "bodily harm" in s. 2.

SYNOPSIS

Section 226 deals with the legal effect of actions which *accelerate the death* of another person.

This section states that when a person causes bodily injury to another person which results in death, that person causes the death of the deceased, even if the only effect of the injury was to hasten the unavoidable death of that person.

227. [*Repealed*, 1999, c. 5, s. 9(1).]

Note: 1999, c. 5, s. 9(2) reads as follows:

(2) Subsection (1) [that is, 1999, c. 5, s. 9(1)] applies in respect of an offence referred to in section 227 of the Act if the last event by means of which a person caused or contributed to the cause of death occurs after the coming into force of that subsection or occurred not more than one year and a day before its coming into force.

KILLING BY INFLUENCE ON THE MIND.

228. No person commits culpable homicide where he causes the death of a human being
    (a) **by any influence on the mind alone, or**
    (b) **by any disorder or disease resulting from influence on the mind alone,**
but this section does not apply where a person causes the death of a child or sick person by wilfully frightening him. R.S., c. C-34, s. 211.

CROSS-REFERENCES

Culpable homicide is defined in s. 222 and see cross-references under that section respecting murder, manslaughter and infanticide. Other causation provisions are found in ss. 223(2), 224, 225, 226 and 228. "Human being" is defined in s. 223(1). The proviso in this section respecting death caused to a child or sick person relates back to s. 222(5)(*d*). Similarly, it would seem that, if the conduct fell within s. 222(5)(*c*) it would not likely come within the term "by any influence on the *mind alone*" in para. (*a*).

SYNOPSIS

This section excludes certain acts, which can be referred to as *killing by influence of the mind*, from what would otherwise constitute culpable homicide.

The acts excluded are causing the death of a human being as means of influence of the mind or as a consequence of any disorder or disease resulting from such influence. However, it does not exclude such acts if the person *wilfully frightens* a sick person or child and thereby causes the death. This exception is a corollary of s. 222(5)(*d*) which makes such conduct culpable homicide.

ANNOTATIONS

This section was applied and the accused's conviction for manslaughter quashed where the evidence indicated that the deceased died from acute heart failure precipitated by the fear and emotional stress of a break-in by the accused and an ensuing struggle. There was no evidence that either the physical exertion of the struggle or an assault during the struggle was a contributing factor to the victim's death. The victim did have a pre-existing heart condition: *R. v. Powder* (1981), 29 C.R. (3d) 183 (Alta. C.A.), leave to appeal to S.C.C. refused *loc. cit.*

Murder, Manslaughter and Infanticide

MURDER.

229. Culpable homicide is murder

  (*a*) where the person who causes the death of a human being
   (i) means to cause his death, or
   (ii) means to cause him bodily harm that he knows is likely to cause his death, and is reckless whether death ensues or not;

  (*b*) where a person, meaning to cause death to a human being or meaning to cause him bodily harm that he knows is likely to cause his death, and being reckless whether death ensues or not, by accident or mistake causes death to another human being, notwithstanding that he does not mean to cause death or bodily harm to that human being; or

  (*c*) where a person, for an unlawful object, does anything that he knows or ought to know is likely to cause death, and thereby causes death to a human being, notwithstanding that he desires to effect his object without causing death or bodily harm to any human being. R.S., c. C-34, s. 212.

CROSS-REFERENCES

Culpable homicide is defined in s. 222. Culpable homicide is also defined as murder in the circumstances set out in s. 230. Murder is classified as first or second degree murder under s. 231. The punishment for murder is, pursuant to s. 235, a minimum of life imprisonment. Eligibility for parole for a person convicted of murder is determined by ss. 742 to 747. [Respecting parole eligibility, see further cross-references under s. 235.] A person convicted of murder will also be liable to the mandatory prohibition order respecting certain weapons, ammunition and explosives by virtue of s. 109. As to included offences, see s. 662. For special provision respecting the plea of *autrefois*, see s. 610(2) to (4).

Pursuant to s. 582, no person may be convicted of first degree murder unless he is specifically charged with that offence in the indictment. Under s. 589, no count that charges an offence other than murder shall be joined in an indictment to a count that charges murder.

The offence of attempted murder is set out in s. 239, accessory after the fact to murder in s. 240 and conspiracy to commit murder in s. 465(1)(*a*).

This offence may be the basis for an application for an authorization to intercept private communications by reason of s. 183 or a warrant to conduct video surveillance under s. 487.01(5), and falls within the definition of "enterprise crime offence" in s. 462.3 for the purposes of Part XII.2.

Section 7(3) enacts special jurisdictional rules for commission of this offence outside Canada when the offence is in relation to an internationally protected person or property referred to in s. 431 [official premises, etc.].

The accused's spouse is a competent and compellable witness at the instance of the Crown by virtue of s. 4(4) where the victim is under the age of 14 years. Age is determined by reference to s. 30 of the *Interpretation Act*, R.S.C. 1985, c. I-21.

Section 17 limits the availability of the statutory defence of compulsion by threats. As to other defences see: s. 16, insanity; s. 25, use of force in enforcement of law; s. 27, use of force to prevent commission of certain offences; ss. 34 to 37, self defence and defence of person under accused's protection; ss. 38 to 41, defence of property; s. 44, use of force by master of vessel; s. 232, provocation. As to notes respecting the necessity defence, see s. 8.

Trial of murder is by the superior court of criminal jurisdiction (defined in s. 2) by virtue of ss. 468 and 469. By virtue of s. 522, only a judge of the superior court of criminal jurisdiction may release an accused charged with this offence.

SYNOPSIS

This section defines *culpable homicide* as murder in three circumstances.

Section 229(*a*)(i) provides the simplest definition, namely intentionally causing the death of a human being by s. 229(*a*)(ii), death caused by a person, who *means to cause bodily harm* that he *knows is likely to cause death* and is reckless whether death ensues or not, is also culpable homicide. The key elements of the mental element in this offence is the intention to cause the requisite degree of bodily harm, coupled with the necessary recklessness as to its effect.

Section 229(*b*) deals with the situation in which an *unintended victim is killed* as a result of accused's acts. The requisite *mental element described in s. 229(a)* must be proven in this paragraph, except that it is satisfied by proof *in relation to the intended victim.* If the mental element as well as the fact that the accused caused the death of the unintended victim are proven, then the fact that the death of that person is caused by accident or mistake is irrelevant and the acts will still render the accused guilty of culpable homicide. The paragraph specifically states that it is culpable homicide, even if the accused did not intend to cause death or inflict any bodily harm upon the person who was killed.

Section 229(*c*) deals with homicides which occur while a person commits another unlawful object. If a person does anything for an *unlawful object* that he *knows or ought to know* is *likely to cause death* and death results from this act, it is culpable homicide. The fact that the accused wanted to carry out the purpose without any death or bodily injury to anyone is legally irrelevant for the purposes of this paragraph. The unlawful object desired by the accused must be some additional object beyond the very act which resulted in the death.

ANNOTATIONS

Proof of intent – Notwithstanding that the accused's primary defence is self-defence where there is also evidence of alcohol consumption and provocation the jury should be directed to consider the cumulative effect of that evidence in determining whether the requisite intent is made out: *R. v. Desveaux* (1986), 26 C.C.C. (3d) 88 (Ont. C.A.); *R. v. Clow* (1985), 44 C.R. (3d) 228 (Ont. C.A.). Similarly, *R. v. Nealy* (1986), 30 C.C.C. (3d) 460 (Ont. C.A.), where there was evidence of alcohol consumption, provocation, anger and fear. However, intense anger alone is insufficient to reduce murder to manslaughter: *R. v. Parent*, [2001] 1 S.C.R. 761, 154 C.C.C. (3d) 1. See also *R. v. Walle* (2007), 230 C.C.C. (3d) 181 (Alta. C.A.).

The purpose of a "rolled-up" instruction on intent is to ensure that the jurors do not compartmentalize evidence that may be relevant to more than one of these issues. It brings together the evidence relevant to stand-alone defences such as intoxication and provocation with evidence related to proof of the basic fault requirement for murder, and invites the jury to consider the cumulative impact of several items of evidence in its decision about the accused's state of mind: *R. v. Flores* (2011), 269 C.C.C. (3d) 194 (Ont. C.A.).

The trial judge erroneously distinguished between intoxication and intention in instructing the jury on intent separately from the defence of intoxication. Furthermore, the trial judge made no reference to the evidence of intoxication in instructing the jury on the common sense inference: *R. v. Carriere* (2001), 159 C.C.C. (3d) 51 (Ont. C.A.).

Where the trial judge has clearly directed the jury as to the requirement of proof of intent there is no requirement for a "residual direction" as to the effect of self-defence and provocation. The judge could, however, give such a direction having regard to the equities and needs of a particular case: *R. v. Ferber* (1987), 36 C.C.C. (3d) 157 (Alta. C.A.), leave to appeal to S.C.C. refused *loc. cit.* To a similar effect, see *R. v. Smith* (1990), 53 C.C.C. (3d) 97 (N.S.C.A.).

Willful blindness can substitute for actual knowledge whenever knowledge is a component of *mens rea*. The doctrine of willful blindness imputes knowledge to an accused whose suspicion is aroused to the point where he or she sees the need for further inquiries but deliberately chooses not to make those inquiries. This is distinct from recklessness and involves no departure from the subjective inquiry into the accused's state of mind. Willful blindness is not simply a failure to inquire but deliberate ignorance: *R. v. Briscoe*, [2010] 1 S.C.R. 411, 253 C.C.C. (3d) 140.

Paragraph *(a)*(ii) represents only a slight relaxation of the *mens rea* for murder and requires proof of a subjective intent to cause bodily harm and subjective knowledge that the bodily harm is of such a nature that it is likely to result in death. Further, this *mens rea* must be concurrent with the impugned act. However, it is not always necessary for the guilty act and the intent to be completely concurrent or that the requisite *mens rea* persist throughout the entire commission of the wrongful act. If death results from a series of wrongful acts that are part of a single transaction, then it must be established that the requisite intent coincided at some point with the wrongful acts: *R. v. Cooper*, [1993] 1 S.C.R. 146, 78 C.C.C. (3d) 289.

The variation in the degree of culpability as between the fault elements in subparas. *(a)*(i) and *(a)*(ii) is too slight to warrant distinction. The requirement in subpara. *(a)*(ii) that the fatal assault be carried out in a reckless way by heedlessly proceeding with the deadly assault, knowing the obvious risks, adds nothing to the vital element of the intent to cause bodily harm that the killer knows is likely to cause death and yet persists in the assault. Anyone who causes bodily harm that knows is likely to cause death must, in those circumstances, have a deliberate disregard for the fatal consequences that he knows are likely to happen and accordingly, be reckless: *R. v. Cooper*, [1993] 1 S.C.R. 146, 78 C.C.C. (3d) 289; *R. v. Moo* (2009), 247 C.C.C. (3d) 34 (Ont. C.A.), leave to appeal to S.C.C. refused [2010] 2 S.C.R. viii, 255 C.C.C. (3d) vi.

The trial judge erred in charging the jury that the mental element was satisfied if they found that the accused had an "attitude of recklessness": *R. v. Dempsey* (2002), 165 C.C.C. (3d) 440 (B.C.C.A.).

In the case of a genuine suicide pact, the surviving party should have a defence to murder. This defence will only be available when the parties are in such a mental state that they have formed a common and irrevocable intent to commit suicide together simultaneously and by the same act where the risk of death is identical and equal for both: *R. v. Gagnon* (1993), 84 C.C.C. (3d) 143 (Que. C.A.).

Under para. *(c)*, the unlawful object must be different from the assault that gives rise to the charge of murder. The act that causes death need not be unlawful, although it will almost invariably be a dangerous act and unlawful. The test for causation is the same as under s. 222(5) as described in *R. v. Smithers*, [1978] 1 S.C.R. 506, 34 C.C.C. (2d) 427, noted under that section. While the unlawful object does not have to include an intent or object to assault or kill the deceased, it must be an object or conduct that would constitute a serious crime which is an indictable offence requiring *mens rea*. The second *mens rea* requirement is proof of subjective foresight of death. In the context of an unintentional death, the subjective foresight element does not require that an accused foresee the precise situation or all of the events that resulted in death. It is sufficient if the accused has the subjective foresight that the acts done for the unlawful object are likely to cause death and those acts are sufficiently linked to the death to have caused the death within the meaning of the section: *R. v. Meiler* (1999), 136 C.C.C. (3d) 11 (Ont. C.A.).

Intoxication defence *[Also see notes under s. 33.1]* – The rules in *D.P.P. v. Beard* (1920), 14 Cr. App. R. 159 (H.L.), violate ss. 7 and 11(*d*) of the Charter because they limit the defence of intoxication to the capacity of an accused to form the specific intent. Before a trial judge charges a jury on the issue of intoxication, the judge must be satisfied that the effect of the intoxication was such that its effect might have impaired the accused's foresight of consequences sufficient to raise a reasonable doubt. Once this threshold test is met, the judge must make clear to the jury that the issue is whether the Crown has satisfied them beyond a reasonable doubt that the accused had the requisite intent. In most circumstances, a one-step charge which omits any reference to "capacity" or "capability" and focuses the jury on the question of "intent in fact" is appropriate. Consequently, the jury must consider whether the accused possessed the requisite specific intent having regard to the evidence of intoxication, along with all of the other evidence in the case. In certain cases, however, in light of the facts of the case and/or the admission of expert evidence, a two-step charge may be appropriate. In this case, the jury is charged both with regard to the capacity to form the requisite intent and with regard to the need to determine in all of the circumstances whether the requisite intent was in fact formed by the accused. In these circumstances, the jury might be instructed that their overall duty is to determine whether or not the accused possessed the requisite intent for the crime. If, on the basis of the expert evidence, the jury is left with a reasonable doubt as to whether, as a result of the consumption of the alcohol, the accused had the capacity to form the requisite intent then that ends the inquiry and the accused must be acquitted of the offence and consideration must then be given to any included lesser offences. If the jury is not left with a reasonable doubt as a result of the expert evidence as to the capacity to form the intent then they must consider and take into account all the surrounding circumstances and the evidence pertaining to those circumstances in determining whether or not the accused possessed the requisite intent for the offence. Furthermore, the presumption that a person intends the natural consequences of their act refers only to a common-sense and logical inference that the jury can but is not compelled to make. Where there is some evidence of intoxication, the trial judge must link the instructions on intoxication with the instruction on the common-sense inference so that the jury is specifically instructed that evidence of intoxication can rebut the inference: *R. v. Robinson*, [1996] 1 S.C.R. 683, 105 C.C.C. (3d) 97. See also *R. v. McMaster*, [1996] 1 S.C.R. 740, 105 C.C.C. (3d) 193; *R. v. Lemky*, [1996] 1 S.C.R. 757, 105 C.C.C. (3d) 137; *R. v. Seymour*, [1996] 2 S.C.R. 252, 106 C.C.C. (3d) 520.

The trial judge need not explicitly link the effect of intoxication to the ability to foresee the consequences. A functional approach should be taken to the issue of linking of foreseeability and intoxication: *R. v. Daley*, [2007] 3 S.C.R. 523, 226 C.C.C. (3d) 1.

The distinction between conduct of a deceased relevant to an accused's state of mind and conduct that may qualify as provocation under s. 232 is especially important where there is evidence of intoxication. To qualify as provocation under s. 232, the jury must be satisfied that the conduct was sufficient to deprive an ordinary person of self-control. In making that assessment, the jury does not take into consideration the alcohol consumption of the particular accused. However, potentially provocative conduct that fails the ordinary person test and, therefore, cannot qualify as provocation under s. 232, must still be considered by a jury in assessing whether an accused lacked the necessary intent due to intoxication: *R. v. Bouchard* (2013), 305 C.C.C. (3d) 240 (Ont. C.A.), affd [2014] 3 S.C.R. 283, 316 C.C.C. (3d) 85.

It is essential in a case where the Crown relies upon the intent described in para. (*a*)(ii) that the jury receive an explanation of the essential difference between that intent and the intent in para. (*a*)(i), namely, that the former requires foresight of the likely consequences of the acts which cause bodily harm combined with recklessness as to that consequence: *R. v. Korzepa* (1991), 64 C.C.C. (3d) 489 (B.C.C.A.).

It was held in *R. v. Young*, [1981] 2 S.C.R. 39, 59 C.C.C. (2d) 305 (5:4), that where the only defence relied upon was drunkenness and the accused's acts were such as, in the normal course of events, to give rise to a probability of serious injury that would likely cause death, then in the absence of any indication that the accused lacked the normal intent which accompanies such acts the inference to be drawn from the facts, absent drunkenness, was that the accused intended to cause bodily harm which he knew was likely to cause death and was reckless as to whether death ensued or not. It did not constitute fatal non-direction for the trial judge not to direct the jury that manslaughter was an available verdict if apart from drunkenness the jury had a reasonable doubt as to the accused's intent.

A psychiatrist may give opinion evidence that an accused lacked capacity to form the intent required for murder, provided that there is a proper basis for such opinion. Thus, the psychiatrist may not express an opinion that the accused as a normal person did not have the capacity to form the required intent, based on his conclusion that the personality of the accused is such that he could not have had the intent requisite for murder in committing a crime of such brutality as was involved in the particular case. Such an opinion does not involve the application of knowledge within the expertise of the psychiatrist. On the other hand, an opinion that, for example, the accused had an organic amnesia as the result of the consumption of alcohol is within the expertise of a psychiatrist: *R. v. Gowland* (1978), 45 C.C.C. (2d) 303 (Ont. C.A.).

Included offences – Attempted murder is an included offence to murder: *R. v. Sarrazin*, [2011] 3 S.C.R. 505, 276 C.C.C. (3d) 210.

Liability of party – The accused's liability as a party to a killing cannot be determined simply by application of a principle that the accused was party to some single ongoing transaction. In the case of an accused who aids or abets in the killing of another, the requisite intent that the aider or abettor must have to warrant conviction for murder must be the same as that of the principal offender. The aider or abettor must intend that he or the perpetrator cause bodily harm of a kind likely to result in death and be reckless whether death ensues or not. If the intent of the aiding party is insufficient to support a conviction for murder, then the party may still be convicted of manslaughter if the unlawful act which was aided or abetted is one he knows is likely to cause some harm short of death: *R. v. Kirkness*, [1990] 3 S.C.R. 74, 60 C.C.C. (3d) 9 (5:2).

Transferred intent [para. (*b*)] – Even where the provisions of this paragraph apply the Crown must prove a concurrence of *mens rea* and *actus reus*; that at the time of the act, which killed the deceased, the accused had the specified intent with respect to the proposed victim: *R. v. Droste* (1979), 49 C.C.C. (2d) 52, 18 C.R. (3d) 64 (Ont. C.A.).

The doctrine of transferred intent has no application where an accused mistakenly kills someone else while attempting to kill himself. The harm caused and the harm intended must be of the same legal kind and accordingly, the *mens rea* for suicide and murder cannot be equated: *R. v. Fontaine* (2002), 168 C.C.C. (3d) 263, 7 C.R. (6th) 139 (Man. C.A.), affd 199 C.C.C. (3d) 349, 31 C.R. (6th) 273 (Man. C.A.). *Contra*: *R. v. Brown* (1983), 4 C.C.C. (3d) 571 (Ont. H.C.J.).

Homicide in course of effecting unlawful purpose [para. (*c*)] – Liability for murder cannot be based on any *mens rea* less than subjective foresight of death and, accordingly, that part of para. (*c*) allowing for a conviction upon proof that the accused ought to have known that death was likely to result is unconstitutional: *R. v. Martineau*, [1990] 2 S.C.R. 633, 58 C.C.C. (3d) 353 (5:2). See also *R. v. Haché* (2007), 227 C.C.C. (3d) 162 (N.B.C.A.).

This provision does not violate s. 7 of the Charter. Subsection (*c*) requires the subjective foresight of death together with the intent to pursue an unlawful object which is itself an indictable offence requiring full *mens rea*. The elements of the offence are as follows: (a) the accused must pursue an unlawful object other than to cause the death of the victim or bodily harm to the victim knowing that death is likely; (b) the unlawful object must itself be an indictable offence requiring *mens rea*; (c) in furtherance of the unlawful object, the accused must intentionally commit a dangerous act; (d) the dangerous act must be distinct from the unlawful object only in the sense that the unlawful object must be something other than the likelihood of death, which is the harm that is foreseen as a consequence of the dangerous act; (e) the dangerous act must be a specific act or series of acts that, in fact, result in death, although the dangerous act need not itself constitute an offence; and (f) when the dangerous act is committed, the accused must have subjective knowledge that death is likely to result. It is insufficient to prove the intention to carry out the unlawful object. The Crown must also establish an additional component of *mens rea* — the intent to commit the dangerous act knowing that it is likely to cause death. Vague realization that death is possible will not be sufficient. Similarly, if the dangerous act was done as a reaction and out of panic, this may suggest that the required subjective foresight of death was not present. "Likely" requires more than an awareness of risk or a possibility or chance of death. What is necessary is subjective knowledge that death is likely, which must be present at some point during the acts committed by the accused that caused the death: *R. v. Shand* (2011), 266 C.C.C. (3d) 137 (Ont. C.A.), leave to appeal to S.C.C. refused (2012), 295 O.A.C. 398n.

Inferring actual knowledge from the "common sense inference" risks substituting a constitutionally impermissible mental or fault element for subjective foresight. In the absence of any direct evidence on the foresight or knowledge issue, it can only be proven beyond a reasonable doubt if the only rational inference available on the evidence is that the accused knew the dangerous act was likely to cause someone's death: *R. v. Roks* (2011), 274 C.C.C. (3d) 1 (Ont. C.A.), additional reasons (2011), 284 C.C.C. (3d) 510 (Ont. C.A.).

MURDER IN COMMISSION OF OFFENCES.

230. Culpable homicide is murder where a person causes the death of a human being while committing or attempting to commit high treason or treason or an offence mentioned in section 52 (sabotage), 75 (piratical acts), 76 (hijacking an aircraft), 144 or subsection 145(1) or sections 146 to 148 (escape or rescue from prison or lawful custody), section 270 (assaulting a peace officer), section 271 (sexual assault), 272 (sexual assault with a weapon, threats to a third party or causing bodily harm), 273 (aggravated sexual assault), 279 (kidnapping and forcible confinement), 279.1 (hostage taking), 343 (robbery), 348 (breaking and entering) or 433 or 434 (arson), whether or not the person means to cause death to any human being and whether or not he knows that death is likely to be caused to any human being, if

(a) he means to cause bodily harm for the purpose of

(i) facilitating the commission of the offence, or

(ii) facilitating his flight after committing or attempting to commit the offence, and the death ensues from the bodily harm;

(b) he administers a stupefying or overpowering thing for a purpose mentioned in paragraph (a), and the death ensues therefrom; or

(c) he wilfully stops, by any means, the breath of a human being for a purpose mentioned in paragraph (a), and the death ensues therefrom. R.S., c. C-34, s. 213; 1974-75-76, c. 93, s. 13, c. 105, s. 29; 1980-81-82-83, c. 125, s. 15; R.S.C. 1985, c. 27 (1st Supp.), s. 40(2); 1991, c. 4, s. 1.

(d) [Repealed, 1991, c. 4, s. 1.]

CROSS-REFERENCES

Note that s. 3 provides that the descriptions in parenthesis after the section number are inserted for convenience of reference only and are no part of the provision.

Culpable homicide is defined in s. 222. Culpable homicide is also defined as murder in the circumstances set out in s. 229. Murder is classified as first or second degree murder under s. 231. The punishment for murder is, pursuant to s. 235, a minimum of life imprisonment.

ANNOTATIONS

Constitutional considerations – In two cases, *R. v. Vaillancourt*, [1987] 2 S.C.R. 636, 39 C.C.C. (3d) 118, and *R. v. Martineau*, [1990] 2 S.C.R. 633, 58 C.C.C. (3d) 353, the Supreme Court has considered the constitutionality of the provisions of this section. In the latter case, a majority of the court held that liability for murder cannot be based on any *mens rea* less than subjective foresight of death and that, accordingly, all of this section is unconstitutional.

In the subsequent case of *R. v. Sit*, [1991] 3 S.C.R. 124, 66 C.C.C. (3d) 449, the court confirmed the scope of its earlier decisions and, in particular, held that para. (*c*) is of no force and effect.

CLASSIFICATION OF MURDER / Planned and deliberate murder / Contracted murder / Murder of peace officer, etc. / Hijacking, sexual assault or kidnapping / Criminal harassment / Murder — terrorist activity / Murder — criminal organization / Intimidation / Second degree murder.

231. (1) Murder is first degree murder or second degree murder.

(2) Murder is first degree murder when it is planned and deliberate.

(3) Without limiting the generality of subsection (2), murder is planned and deliberate when it is committed pursuant to an arrangement under which money or anything of value passes or is intended to pass from one person to another, or is promised by one person to another, as consideration for that other's causing or assisting in causing the death of anyone or counselling another person to do any act causing or assisting in causing that death.

(4) Irrespective of whether a murder is planned and deliberate on the part of any person, murder is first degree murder when the victim is

    (*a*) a police officer, police constable, constable, sheriff, deputy sheriff, sheriff's officer or other person employed for the preservation and maintenance of the public peace, acting in the course of his duties;

    (*b*) a warden, deputy warden, instructor, keeper, jailer, guard or other officer or a permanent employee of a prison, acting in the course of his duties; or

    (*c*) a person working in a prison with the permission of the prison authorities and acting in the course of his work therein.

(5) Irrespective of whether a murder is planned and deliberate on the part of any person, murder is first degree murder in respect of a person when the death is caused by that person while committing or attempting to commit an offence under one of the following sections:

    (*a*) section 76 (hijacking an aircraft);

    (*b*) section 271 (sexual assault);

    (*c*) section 272 (sexual assault with a weapon, threats to a third party or causing bodily harm);

    (*d*) section 273 (aggravated sexual assault);

    (*e*) section 279 (kidnapping and forcible confinement); or

    (*f*) section 279.1 (hostage taking).

(6) [*Repealed*, R.S.C. 1985, c. 27 (1st Supp.), s. 35.]

(6) Irrespective of whether a murder is planned and deliberate on the part of any person, murder is first degree murder when the death is caused by that person while committing or attempting to commit an offence under section 264 and the person committing that offence intended to cause the person murdered to fear for the safety of the person murdered or the safety of anyone known to the person murdered.

(6.01) Irrespective of whether a murder is planned and deliberate on the part of a person, murder is first degree murder when the death is caused by that person while committing or attempting to commit an indictable offence under this or any other Act of Parliament if the act or omission constituting the offence also constitutes a terrorist activity.

(6.1) Irrespective of whether a murder is planned and deliberate on the part of a person, murder is first degree murder when

    (*a*) the death is caused by that person for the benefit of, at the direction of or in association with a criminal organization; or

    (*b*) the death is caused by that person while committing or attempting to commit an indictable offence under this or any other Act of Parliament for the benefit of, at the direction of or in association with a criminal organization.

(6.2) Irrespective of whether a murder is planned and deliberate on the part of a person, murder is first degree murder when the death is caused by that person while committing or attempting to commit an offence under section 423.1.

(7) All murder that is not first degree murder is second degree murder. R.S., c. C-34, s. 214; R.S. c. C-35, s. 4; 1973-74, c. 38, s. 2; 1974-75-76, c. 105, s. 4; 1980-81-82-83, c. 125, s. 16; R.S.C. 1985, c. 27 (1st Supp.), ss. 7(2)(*b*), 35, 40(2); 1997, c. 16, s. 3; 1997, c. 23, s. 8; 2001, c. 32, s. 9(2); 2001, c. 41, s. 9; 2009, c. 22, s. 5.

CROSS-REFERENCES

Note that s. 3 provides that the descriptions in parenthesis after the section number are inserted for convenience of reference only and are no part of the provision.

Murder is defined in ss. 229 and 230. The terms "prison", "criminal organization" and "terrorist activity" are defined in s. 2. The punishment for murder is, pursuant to s. 235, a minimum of life imprisonment. Eligibility for parole for a person convicted of murder is determined by ss. 745 to 746.1. [Respecting parole eligibility, see further cross-references under s. 235.] However, note that under s. 745, a person convicted of second degree murder must be sentenced to life imprisonment without eligibility for parole for 25 years where he has previously been convicted of murder, however described. A person convicted of murder will also be liable to the mandatory prohibition order respecting firearms, ammunition and explosives by virtue of s. 100(1). As to included offences, see s. 662. With respect to other notes concerning procedure and evidence, see CROSS-REFERENCES under ss. 229 and 230.

SYNOPSIS

This section *classifies* convictions for *murder* into first and second degree murder for the purpose of setting a parole eligibility date.

The effect of subsecs. (1) and (7) is that a murder which does not come within subsections (2) to (6.2) is second degree murder.

Subsection (2) states that murder is *first degree* murder when it is *planned and deliberate*. Subsection (3) deems conduct described in the subsection, which may be generally referred to as *contract killings*, to be planned and deliberate, and therefore, by definition, first degree murder.

The following subsections deem murders of specified victims (subsec. (4)) or while committing or attempting to commit specified offences (subsecs. (5) to (6.2)) to be first degree murder. The phrase "while committing" only requires proof that the underlying offence and the death were part of the same transaction, not that they occurred at the same moment. However, the death must have been caused "by that person". As to the meaning of that phrase, see the annotations in this section under the heading "**Liability of party**".

ANNOTATIONS

Subsection (2) [Planning and Deliberation] / *Meaning of planning and deliberation* – This subsection brings back the concept of "planned and deliberate" which was formerly part of the definition of capital murder. Some of the following cases were decided under the former capital murder sections.

The word "deliberate" means "considered, not impulsive" and as used in the subsection cannot have simply the meaning "intentional" because it is only if the accused's act was intentional that he can be guilty of murder. The subsection is creating an additional element. Psychiatric evidence that at the critical moment the accused was suffering from a depressive psychosis resulting in impairment of his ability to decide even inconsequential things would have a direct bearing on the issue of whether the act was deliberate and the trial judge's failure to adequately deal with this evidence in his charge to the jury necessitated a new trial: *R. v. More*, [1963] S.C.R. 522, [1963] 3 C.C.C. 289 (5:2).

In *R. v. Mitchell*, [1964] S.C.R. 471, [1965] 1 C.C.C. 155, the court was unanimous (7:0) on the manner in which a trial judge should instruct a jury to determine whether a murder, which they have found to have been committed by the accused, was "planned and deliberate". After referring to *R. v. More, supra*, and *R. v. McMartin*, [1964] S.C.R. 484, [1965] 1 C.C.C. 142, Spence J., wrote at p. 162 C.C.C.:

> I am of the opinion that the judgments in these two cases have as their *ratio decidendi* the principle that in determining whether the accused committed the crime of capital murder in that it was "planned and deliberate on the part of such person" the jury should have available and should be directed to consider all the circumstances including not only the evidence of the accused's actions but of his condition, his state of mind as affected by either real or imagined insults and provoking actions of the victim and by the accused's consumption of alcohol.

In *R. v. Widdifield* (1961), 6 Crim. L.Q. 152 (Ont. H.C.J.), Gale J. charged the jury in part as follows:

I think that in the Code "planned" is to be assigned, I think, its natural meaning of a calculated scheme or design which has been carefully thought out, and the nature and consequences of which have been considered and weighed. But that does not mean, of course, to say that the plan need be a complicated one. It may be a very simple one, and the simpler it is perhaps the easier it is to formulate.

The important element, it seems to me, so far as time is concerned, is the time involved in developing the plan, not the time between the development of the plan and the doing of the act. One can carefully prepare a plan and immediately it is prepared set out to do the planned act, or, alternatively, you can wait an appreciable time to do it once it has been formed.

As far as the word "deliberate" is concerned, I think that the Code means that it should also carry its natural meaning of "considered," "not impulsive," "slow in deciding," "cautious," implying that the accused must take time to weigh the advantages and disadvantages of his intended action. That is what, as it seems to me, "deliberate" means.

The direction in *R. v. Widdifield, supra,* as to the definition of "planned" was approved in *R. v. Reynolds* (1978), 44 C.C.C. (2d) 129, 22 O.R. (2d) 353 (C.A.).

Planning in this context requires evidence that the killing was the result of a scheme or design previously formulated. A murder committed on a sudden impulse and without prior consideration would not meet this test: *R. v. Smith* (1979), 51 C.C.C. (2d) 381, 1 Sask. R. 213 (C.A.).

The deliberation required under this subsection must occur before the act of murder commences: *R. v. Ruptash* (1982), 68 C.C.C. (2d) 182 (Alta. C.A.).

Intoxication – In *R. v. Reynolds* (1978), 44 C.C.C. (2d) 129, 22 O.R. (2d) 353 (C.A.), it was held that evidence of intoxication was not limited to the question of the accused's ability to plan and deliberate and that it would be open to the jury to find that the accused acted impulsively without deliberation due to the consumption of alcohol and other circumstances even though he was *able* to plan and deliberate.

In *R. v. Wallen*, [1990] 1 S.C.R. 827, 54 C.C.C. (3d) 383 (3:2), all members of the court agreed that the trial judge must direct the jury to consider the issue of intoxication as it applies to planning and deliberation separately from the issue of intoxication as a defence to murder. However, the court divided on whether it is mandatory in all cases for the trial judge to make it clear that a lesser degree of intoxication may suffice to negative planning and deliberation than to negative the intent to kill. In any event, all members of the court agreed that such a direction will be helpful to the jury.

Mental disorder – The existence of a mental disorder is not incompatible with the commission of a planned and deliberate murder. In particular, the word "deliberate" has not imported a requirement that the accused's previous determination to kill the victim must have been the result of normal thinking or must have been rationally motived: *R. v. Kirkby* (1985), 21 C.C.C. (3d) 31, 47 C.R. (3d) 97 (Ont. C.A.).

Liability of party – An accused sought to be made liable for first degree murder as an aider or abettor must be shown to have intended to aid a planned and deliberate murder: *R. v. Peters and Eldridge* (1985), 23 C.C.C. (3d) 171 (B.C.C.A.).

Application to murder defined in ss. 229 and 230 – This section does not create a separate substantive offence of first degree murder, but rather constitutes a characterization, for sentencing purposes, of the substantive offence of murder in ss. 229 and 230. A murder is first degree murder within the meaning of this subsection if there is planning and deliberation in relation to the specific *mens rea* of the applicable section, which in the case of a murder described by s. 229(*b*) is the intent to cause the death to one person although by accident or mistake, another is killed. While there may be certain mental states specified in ss. 229 and 230 which are incompatible with planning and deliberation, the *mens rea* of s. 229(*b*) is not one of them: *R. v. Droste*, [1984] 1 S.C.R. 208, 10 C.C.C. (3d) 404 (7:0).

However, the mental state described in s. 229(*a*)(ii) is not incompatible with planning and deliberation. There can be no doubt that a person can plan and deliberate to cause terrible bodily harm that he knows is likely to result in death. Nothing is added to the aspect of planning and deliberation by the requirement under s. 229(*a*)(ii) that the fatal assault be carried out in a reckless manner: *R. v. Nygaard*, [1989] 2 S.C.R. 1074, 51 C.C.C. (3d) 417.

Subsection (4) [Murder of police officer, etc.] / *Mens rea* – In a case decided under the former s. 202A(2) it was held that knowledge by the accused that the person killed was a police officer or other person employed for the preservation and maintenance of public peace is requisite for a conviction under that section: *R. v. Shand* (1971), 3 C.C.C. (2d) 8 (Man. C.A.).

It was held in *R. v. Collins* (1989), 48 C.C.C. (3d) 343 (Ont. C.A.), that for the offence to constitute first degree murder pursuant to this subsection, the Crown must prove that the deceased was a person who falls within the designation of the occupations set forth in that subsection acting in the course of his duties to the knowledge of the accused or with recklessness on his part as to whether or not the deceased was such a person so acting.

"Acting in the course of his duties" – Evidence that the victim was a member of a police detachment and performing regular police duties, was assigned to a police cruiser and was in uniform when his body was discovered and that he made a radio transmission shortly before his death was, in the absence of evidence to the contrary, sufficient to discharge the evidentiary burden on the Crown to prove that the deceased was acting in the course of his duties, notwithstanding the lack of any evidence as to exactly what the officer was doing at the time of his death: *R. v. Fitzgerald and Schoenberger* (1982), 70 C.C.C. (2d) 87 (Ont. C.A.).

The term "acting in the course of his duty" while wider than the phrase "engaged in the execution of his duty" will generally encompass the whole time-span of a police officer's tour of duty and would include any activity related to the performance of a duty or to the ability of the officer to perform his duty, including for example having lunch or receiving medical attention during a tour of duty: *R. v. Prevost* (1988), 42 C.C.C. (3d) 314 (Ont. C.A.), leave to appeal to S.C.C. refused [1989] 1 S.C.R. xii.

Constitutional considerations – The classification of murder of a police officer as first degree murder thus mandating a life sentence without eligibility for parole for 25 years does not offend the *Charter of Rights and Freedoms*, ss. 7, 9, 12 and 15: *R. v. Bowen* (1990), 59 C.C.C. (3d) 515 (Alta. C.A.); *R. v. Lefebvre* (1989), 71 C.R. (3d) 213 (Que. C.A.).

Subsection (5) / *Unlawful confinement* – In *R. v. Pritchard*, [2008] 3 S.C.R. 195, 236 C.C.C. (3d) 301, the Supreme Court of Canada reconciled conflicting appellate case law in respect of the requisite temporal and causal connection between the enumerated offence and any ancillary offence. While proof of robbery does not by itself trigger subsec. (5), proof of robbery does not bar or alter its application either. The phrase "while committing or attempting to commit" requires the killing to be closely connected, temporally and causally, with an enumerated offence. Although every robbery involves an element of violence or threatened violence, the level of violence does not always occasion confinement of the significant duration required to satisfy s. 279(2). Not all robberies involve domination of the victim and accordingly, not all robbery-murders will satisfy subsec. (5)(*e*). Even a confinement which satisfies s. 279(2) will not trigger this provision if it is consumed in the very act of killing. As set out in *R. v. Kimberley* (2001), 157 C.C.C. (3d) 129 (Ont. C.A.), in order to trigger this provision, the confinement and the murder must constitute distinct criminal acts. Where the jury is satisfied that there was confinement not limited to what was "integral to" the particular act of killing disclosed by the evidence, the Crown has established a distinct criminal act under s. 279(2). If the jury is satisfied that the murder was committed in the course of that confinement, such that the series of events may be characterized as a "single transaction", then the requirements of subsec. (5)(*e*) are met. The fact that the accused confined the victim for the purpose of committing a non-enumerated offence does not alter the operation of subsec. (5)(e). Second degree murder will be elevated to first degree murder whether the murder and the predicate offence, such as unlawful confinement, are linked together both causally and temporally in circumstances that make the entire course of conduct a single transaction. The temporal-causal connection is established where the unlawful confinement creates a "continuing illegal domination of the victim" that provides the accused with a position of power which he or she chooses to exploit to murder the victim. If these factors are established, the fact that, along the way other offences, such as robbery, are committed, is not a bar to the application of subsec. (5).

The predicate offence under subsec. (5) need not precede the mortal wound so long as the act of killing and the predicate offence, while distinct offences, remain part of the same transaction: *R. v. Mullings* (2014), 319 C.C.C. (3d) 1 (Ont. C.A.), leave to appeal to S.C.C. refused 2015 CarswellOnt 18931.

There is no basis for directing the jury that the unlawful confinement had ceased and thus that this subsection did not apply where the accused, having held the deceased and her relatives at gunpoint for a substantial period of time, shot his wife a short time after she indicated that she intended to leave: *R. v. Francella*, [1990] 2 S.C.R. 1420, 60 C.C.C. (3d) 96n (5:0), affg 46 C.C.C. (3d) 93 (Ont. C.A.).

This provision applies even if the victim of the murder and the victim of the enumerated offence are not the same. The purpose of the provision is to punish murders committed in connection with crimes of domination more severely. The provision is restricted to its appropriate context by the requirement that there must be a close temporal and causal connection between the murder and the enumerated offence: *R. v. Russell*, [2001] 2 S.C.R. 804, 157 C.C.C. (3d) 1.

Murder is treated as an exceptionally serious crime and elevated to first degree under this provision because the murder is committed by someone already abusing his or her power by illegally dominating another person, or because it is committed by someone who chooses to exploit his or her position of dominance and power to the point of murder. In this case, the accused did not illegally dominate the deceased where the victim had consented to having the accused pull a belt around the victim's neck while engaged in sexual activity. While consent to the tightening of the belt could not exclude the accused's responsibility for the victim's death, that fact could not retroactively make the confinement forcible: *R. v. McIlwaine* (1996), 111 C.C.C. (3d) 426 (Que. C.A.).

It was not an error for the jury to find that the victim was unlawfully confined within the meaning of this section where she had locked herself in the bathroom and the accused had broken the door down in order to attack her: *R. v. Johnstone* (2014), 313 C.C.C. (3d) 34 (Ont. C.A.).

This section is subservient to s. 229; it classifies for sentencing purposes the offences in that section as either first or second degree murder. Thus, an accused charged with second degree murder may be convicted of that offence even though the facts would support a conviction of first degree murder, as where death ensues as a result of the use of a weapon in the course of an unlawful confinement: *R. v. Farrant*, [1983] 1 S.C.R. 124, 4 C.C.C. (3d) 354 (5:2).

Subsection (6) / Murder in the course of criminal harassment – Just as a single act can amount to criminal harassment under s. 264, so too can the added mental element in subsec. (6) be inferred from a single act: *R. v. Smith* (2014), 308 C.C.C. (3d) 254 (Ont. C.A.).

Liability of party – The words "when the death is caused by that person" limit the application of this subsection and a person could not be convicted of first degree murder under this subsection when his liability for murder depended solely on the combined operation of ss. 21(2) and 230. The court noted that those words had been omitted from the French version of the *Criminal Code* but adopted the approach that the provision being a penal one the accused was entitled to rely on the interpretation which was most favourable to him, in this case the English version of s. 231(5): *R. v. Woods and Gruener* (1980), 57 C.C.C. (2d) 220 (Ont. C.A.).

The phrase, "when death is caused by that person" is broad enough to include a person who assists in the murder where that person is a substantial cause of the death. The Crown must establish that the accused has committed an act or series of acts which are of such a nature that they must be regarded as a substantial and integral cause of the death. The accused must play a very active, usually physical, role in the killing. In addition, the Crown must show that there was no intervening act of another which resulted in the accused no longer being substantially connected to the death of the victim and that the underlying offence and the murder were a part of the same transaction: *R. v. Harbottle*, [1993] 3 S.C.R. 306, 84 C.C.C. (3d) 1.

Thus, s. 21(2) cannot be a source of criminal liability for first-degree murder under this subsection: *R. v. Michaud* (2000), 144 C.C.C. (3d) 62 (N.B.C.A.).

"While committing" – There need not be an exact coincidence between the act causing death and the acts constituting the underlying offence. It is sufficient if they form part of one continuous sequence of events forming a single transaction: *R. v. Paré*, [1987] 2 S.C.R. 618, 38 C.C.C. (3d) 97 (7:0).

It was not necessary for the Crown to prove the exact time of death and that the sexual assault occurred prior to death provided it was shown that the sexual assault and the death were part of a continuous sequence of events: *R. v. Ganton* (1992), 77 C.C.C. (3d) 259 (Sask. C.A.).

In determining whether the sexual assault and murder are inextricably linked, it must be determined whether the temporal and causal connections between the murder and the sexual assault are so close together so as to form a continuous single transaction: *R. v. Muchikekwanape* (2002), 166 C.C.C. (3d) 144 (Man. C.A.).

This subsection does not apply where the murder was committed after the completion of the underlying offence even if to facilitate flight after commission of that offence: *R. v. Sargent* (1983), 5 C.C.C. (3d) 429 (Sask. C.A.).

Constitutional considerations – The combined effect of subsec. (5) and s. 745(*a*), requiring that a person, convicted of first degree murder where the murder is committed while comitting one of the offences specified in subsec. (5), must be sentenced to life imprisonment without eligibility for parole for 25 years, does not infringe ss. 7, 9 and 12 of the Charter: *R. v. Luxton*, [1990] 2 S.C.R. 711, 58 C.C.C. (3d) 449 (7:0); *R. v. Arkell*, [1990] 2 S.C.R. 695, 59 C.C.C. (3d) 65 (7:0).

MURDER REDUCED TO MANSLAUGHTER / What is provocation / Questions of fact / Death during illegal arrest.

232. (1) Culpable homicide that otherwise would be murder may be reduced to manslaughter if the person who committed it did so in the heat of passion caused by sudden provocation.

(2) Conduct of the victim that would constitute an indictable offence under this Act that is punishable by five or more years of imprisonment and that is of such a nature as to be sufficient to deprive an ordinary person of the power of self-control is provocation for the purposes of this section, if the accused acted on it on the sudden and before there was time for their passion to cool.

(3) For the purposes of this section, the questions

(*a*) whether the conduct of the victim amounted to provocation under subsection (2), and

(*b*) whether the accused was deprived of the power of self-control by the provocation that he alleges he received,

are questions of fact, but no one shall be deemed to have given provocation to another by doing anything that he had a legal right to do, or by doing anything that the accused incited him to do in order to provide the accused with an excuse for causing death or bodily harm to any human being.

(4) Culpable homicide that otherwise would be murder is not necessarily manslaughter by reason only that it was committed by a person who was being arrested illegally, but the fact that the illegality of the arrest was known to the accused may be evidence of provocation for the purpose of this section. R.S., c. C-34, s. 215; 2015, c. 29, s. 7.

CROSS-REFERENCES

Culpable homicide is defined in s. 222. Murder is defined by ss. 229 and 230. The punishment for manslaughter is set out in s. 236. It is not unusual for the excuse of provocation to be raised in circumstances where the accused also relies on the defence of intoxication [thus see notes under ss. 33.1 and 229]; use of force to prevent commission of certain offences [thus see s. 27]; self defence and defence of property [thus see ss. 34 to 42].

A person convicted of manslaughter may be subject to a dangerous offender application under Part XXIV.

SYNOPSIS

Section 232 sets out some of the circumstances under which *murder will be reduced to manslaughter*.

The first three subsections spell out the defence of *provocation*. Before subsec. (1) becomes relevant, it must be shown that the culpable homicide would *otherwise have been murder*. Despite the use of the word "may" in the section, murder will be reduced to manslaughter if the murder was committed as a result of provocation. Provocation occurs if the person who committed the act did so in the *heat of passion caused by sudden provocation*.

Pursuant to subsec. (2), the act which provokes the accused must be conduct that would constitute an indictable offence that is punishable by five or more years' imprisonment. It further requires a mix of subjective and objective factors in determining if that conduct constituted provocation. The *objective aspect* of the test is whether the wrongful act or insult is of such a nature as to be sufficient to deprive an ordinary man of self-control. Even in this aspect of the test, there appears to be some element of subjectivity as the ordinary person may include some of the general characteristics of the accused such as sex, race or age. The *subjective aspect* of the test is that the accused *did act on the provocation* and did so *before* there was *time for his passion to cool*. In this second part of the test, the background, temperament, idiosyncrasies or drunkenness of the accused may be considered. The requirement of suddenness must apply both to the provocation and to the accused's reaction to it.

Subsection (3) states that the issues of whether a particular wrongful act or insult amounted to provocation and whether the accused was deprived of his self-control as a result of the provocation are *questions of fact*. This means that the jury will ultimately determine these issues, although the judge will first consider, as a question of law, whether there is *any evidence* which could amount to provocation. The subsection makes it clear that if a person does anything which he has a legal right to do or which he does as a result of incitement by the accused to do for the purpose of providing the accused with an excuse to cause the person death or bodily harm, this does not amount to provocation. One example of a person who has a legal right to do something which might otherwise constitute provocation is a person who is justified in using force against the accused in self-defence.

Subsection (4) deals with the effect of an illegal arrest as it relates to provocation in this section. The fact that a person was arrested illegally does not necessarily reduce what would otherwise be murder to manslaughter. It also provides that an unlawful arrest of a person may constitute provocation if that person was aware of the illegality of the arrest.

ANNOTATIONS

Note: The cases annotated below should be relied upon with caution. They were decided before amendments in 2015 which specified that the defence of provocation only applies where the conduct of the victim constitutes an indictable offence punishable by five or more years in prison. Previously, subsec. (2) stated that the conduct of the victim need merely be a "wrongful act or insult".

Sufficiency of evidence to raise defence – In *R. v. Squire*, [1977] 2 S.C.R. 13, 29 C.C.C. (2d) 497, the accused's counsel at trial for non-capital murder relied only on the defence of drunkenness. On appeal against the conviction the defence of provocation was successfully raised. On further appeal by the Crown it was held (9:0) that a trial judge is under no duty to invite a jury to consider defences of which there is no evidence or which cannot reasonably be inferred from the evidence and where, as here, it can be said that no jury acting judicially on the evidence at trial could find a wrongful act or insult sufficient to deprive an ordinary person of self-control, the trial judge was not in error in not charging the jury on the defence of provocation.

An accused, who at the time of the offence had and kept the initiative in a situation where the acts of the deceased, whether they were insults or physical acts, were predictable, cannot avail himself of the defence of "sudden" provocation within the meaning of this section: *R. v. Louison* (1975), 26 C.C.C. (2d) 266, [1975] 6 W.W.R. 289 (Sask. C.A.), affd [1979] 1 S.C.R. 100, 51 C.C.C. (2d) 479n (9:0).

The words of the victim terminating her relationship with the accused cannot amount to a wrongful act or insult within this section: *R. v. Young* (1993), 78 C.C.C. (3d) 538, 117 N.S.R. (2d) 166 (C.A.), leave to appeal to S.C.C. refused 81 C.C.C. (3d) vi.

Nature of objective test of "ordinary person" – Provocation under this section is subject to a dual test. One must first consider the effect on an ordinary person of the particular wrongful act or insult relied on. This constitutes an objective test. If this first test is satisfied then the subjective test is to determine whether the accused acted actually upon the provocation, on the sudden and before there was time for his passion to cool. While the character, background, temperament, idiosyncracies, or the drunkenness of the accused are matters to be considered in the second test they are excluded from consideration in the first test: *R. v. Wright*, [1969] S.C.R. 335, [1969] 3 C.C.C. 258 (5:0); *R. v. Taylor*, [1947] S.C.R. 462, 89 C.C.C. 209; *R. v. Olbey*, [1980] 1 S.C.R. 1008, 50 C.C.C. (2d) 257 (6:1).

In relation to the objective element of the test, it is proper to consider the background of the relationship between the deceased and accused, including earlier insults which culminated in the final provocative actions or words. The "ordinary person" must be of the same age and sex, and share with the accused such other factors as would give the act or insult in question a special significance, and must have experienced the same series of acts or insults as those experienced by the accused. The defence may be available even if the insults might induce a desire for revenge so long as immediately before the last insult, the accused did not intend to kill: *R. v. Thibert*, [1996] 1 S.C.R. 37, 104 C.C.C. (3d) 1 (3:2).

The "ordinary person" standard is informed by contemporary norms of behaviour, including fundamental values such as the commitment to equality provided for in the Charter. The accused must have a justifiable sense of being wronged. The proper approach is one that takes into account some, but not all, of the individual characteristics of the accused. Personal circumstances may be relevant to determining whether the accused was in fact provoked (the subjective element), but they do not shift the ordinary person standard to suit the individual accused. There is an important distinction between contextualizing the objective standard, which is necessary and proper, and individualizing it, which would only serve to defeat its purpose: *R. v. Tran*, [2010] 3 S.C.R. 350, 261 C.C.C. (3d) 435.

A trier of fact is not required to consider the defences of provocation and intoxication together, or to take into account the accused's degree of intoxication when deciding whether an ordinary person would have lost self-control in response to the deceased's insult: *R. v. Sheehan* (2010), 264 C.C.C. (3d) 520 (N.B.C.A.).

The "ordinary person" test merely requires consideration of whether the ordinary person would have lost the power of self-control not whether the ordinary person would have done what the accused did: *R. v. Carpenter* (1993), 83 C.C.C. (3d) 193, 14 O.R. (3d) 641 (C.A.).

It was held in *R. v. Hill*, [1986] 1 S.C.R. 313, 25 C.C.C. (3d) 322 (6:3), that the ordinary or reasonable person under the objective test has a normal temperament and level of self-control and is not exceptionally excitable, pugnacious or in a state of drunkenness. Further, particular characteristics that are not peculiar or idiosyncratic can be ascribed to an ordinary person without subverting the logic of the objective test. However, the jury need not be instructed that the ordinary person is, for example, someone of the same age, sex or race as the accused, since the jury will naturally as a matter of good sense ascribe to the ordinary person any general characteristics relevant to the provocation in question. For example, if the provocation is a racial slur, the jury will think of an ordinary person with the racial background that forms the substance of the insult. Features such as sex, age or race do not detract from a person's characterization as ordinary.

The accused advanced provocation on the basis that his deceased wife's behaviour was contrary to the Sikh community values and brought shame to the accused. The trial judge was entitled to conclude that, although there was a reasonable doubt on the subjective element of provocation, the Crown had proven the objective requirement beyond a reasonable doubt. The trial judge could conclude that, even taking into account the accused's cultural background, an ordinary person would not have lost his power of self-control: *R. v. Nahar* (2004), 181 C.C.C. (3d) 449, 20 C.R. (6th) 30 (B.C.C.A.).

It was held that there is no air of reality to the proposition that an ordinary person in the accused's circumstances would be deprived of self-control when scolded about her level of education by her sister-in-law: *R. v. Mayuran*, [2012] 2 S.C.R. 162, 284 C.C.C. (3d) 1.

The application of the air of reality test assumes that the version of events in an accused's confession is true. However, an air of reality cannot spring from bare, unsupported assertions by the accused not reasonably borne out by the evidence. Here, there was no air of reality to the accused's assertion that he "snapped" after the victim, who had been extorting him for some time, threatened to continue the extortion. The subjective element of provocation was therefore lacking: *R. v. Pappas*, [2013] 3 S.C.R. 452, 302 C.C.C. (3d) 295.

Charge to jury / *Also see notes on "nature of objective test" above* – It had been held in a series of cases, *R. v. Daniels* (1983), 7 C.C.C. (3d) 542, 47 A.R. 149 (C.A.); *R. v. Conway* (1985), 17 C.C.C. (3d) 481 (Ont. C.A.); *R. v. Desveaux* (1986), 26 C.C.C. (3d) 88, 51 C.R. (3d) 173 (Ont. C.A.), that the jury must consider in relation to the objective test the same external pressures of insult by acts or words as were on the accused. Thus, the application of the objective test is not limited to the events which immediately triggered the attack by the accused, but also includes all of the events which put pressure on the accused and may have coloured and given meaning to the final triggering act or insult. These cases were decided prior to *R. v. Hill, supra*, but were not explicitly overruled. However, to the extent that these decisions like *R. v. Hill*, in the Ontario Court of Appeal (1982), 2 C.C.C. (3d) 394, 32 C.R. (3d) 88, reflect a mandatory requirement as to the component of the trial judge's charge, they should be read with care bearing in mind the admonishment from the Supreme Court majority in *R. v. Hill* that although a direction as to the particular relevant attributes of the "ordinary person" may be helpful in clarifying the application of the ordinary person standard it is neither wise nor necessary to make this a mandatory component of all jury charges on provocation and that whenever possible the court "should retain simplicity in charges to the jury and have confidence that the words of the *Criminal Code* will provide sufficient guidance to the jury". Again, it must be pointed out that the court was there only specifically considering the necessity of a mandatory direction concerning the age and sex of the "ordinary person".

The word "wrongful" only modifies "act" and not insult since an insult is always wrongful. However a reference to a "wrongful insult" while an error in English usage is not an error of law: *R. v. Murdock* (1978), 40 C.C.C. (2d) 97, [1978] 3 W.W.R. 313 (Man. C.A.).

It is misdirection to tell the jury that provocation operates to negate the intent for murder. Provocation may reduce murder to manslaughter even if the accused had the intention to kill: *R. v. Oickle* (1984), 11 C.C.C. (3d) 180, 61 N.S.R. (2d) 239 (S.C. App. Div.).

It was an error for the trial judge to refer to the accused's size and athletic ability and the difference in size between the accused and the victim when instructing the jury on the "ordinary person" component of the defence. Having been invited to draw these comparisons, the jury may have thought that the reasonableness or even justifiability of the accused's response to the provocative acts was a relevant consideration in the application of the ordinary person test. However, unlike some defences, provocation does not measure the conduct of the accused against standards of reasonableness or proportionality: *R. v. Hill* (2015), 330 C.C.C. (3d) 1 (Ont. C.A.).

Intense anger alone is insufficient to reduce murder to manslaughter. While anger can play a role in reducing murder to manslaughter in connection with the defence under this section, anger is not a stand-alone defence. Thus, the trial judge erred in directing the jury to the effect that they could find the accused guilty of manslaughter, on the basis of the anger felt by the accused, even if they concluded that the conditions set out in this section were not met: *R. v. Parent*, [2001] 1 S.C.R. 761, 154 C.C.C. (3d) 1.

Although subsec. (1) uses the word "may" the jury does not have a discretion to return a verdict of manslaughter where provocation is made out. Accordingly, it should be made clear to the jury that if they find there is provocation or if they have a reasonable doubt in that regard then the only verdict for what otherwise might be murder is manslaughter: *R. v. Leblanc* (1985), 22 C.C.C. (3d) 126 (Ont. C.A.).

Mistake of fact and transferred intent – If an accused, acting under such provocation as would reduce murder to manslaughter, shoots at one person with the intention of killing him, but accidentally kills a third person, the intention extenuated by provocation is transferred from the intended victim to the actual victim and the accused is guilty of manslaughter: *R. v. Droste (No. 2)* (1981), 63 C.C.C. (2d) 418, 34 O.R. (2d) 588 (C.A.), affd on other grounds [1984] 1 S.C.R. 208, 10 C.C.C. (3d) 404 (7:0).

Similarly, mistake of fact is relevant to the objective test, if any ordinary person would also have misinterpreted the facts which confronted the accused: *R. v. Hansford* (1987), 33 C.C.C. (3d) 74, 55 C.R. (3d) 347 (Alta. C.A.), leave to appeal to S.C.C. refused 79 A.R. 239.

Application to attempted murder – Provocation is not a defence to a charge of attempted murder so as to reduce the offence to one of attempted manslaughter. However, there may be cases where the conduct of the victim amounting to provocation produced in the accused a state of excitement, anger or disturbance as a result of which he might not contemplate the consequences of his acts and might not, in fact, intend to bring about those consequences: *R. v. Campbell* (1977), 38 C.C.C. (2d) 6, 17 O.R. (2d) 673 (C.A.).

Self-induced provocation [subsec. (3)] – The phrase "legal right" in subsec. (3) means a right which is sanctioned by law as distinct from something which a person may do without incurring legal liability. The defence of provocation is open to someone who is "insulted", and the words or act put forward as provocation need not be words or acts which are specifically prohibited by the law: *R. v. Thibert*, [1996] 1 S.C.R. 37, 104 C.C.C. (3d) 1 (3:2).

In considering whether a deceased was within his legal rights his action cannot be considered in isolation and in cases of "self-induced" provocation it is only where the actions by the deceased go to extreme lengths in the circumstances that such actions can form the basis of the defence of provocation. Where the only possible interpretation of the events was that the provocative act was self-induced in circumstances in which the deceased had the legal right to use as much force as necessary to attempt to effect his escape or protect his life, then subsec. (3)(*b*) applied: *R. v. Louison* (1975), 26 C.C.C. (2d) 266, [1975] 6 W.W.R. 289 (Sask. C.A.), affd [1979] 1 S.C.R. 100, 51 C.C.C. (2d) 479n (9:0).

Self-induced provocation is not a special category of the defence attracting special principles, but rather describes a particular application of the general principles that govern the defence of provocation. There is no absolute rule that a person who instigates a confrontation cannot rely on the defence of provocation. However, the fact that the victim's response to the accused's confrontational conduct fell within a range of reasonably predictable reactions may suggest that an ordinary person would not have lost self-control: *R. v. Cairney*, [2013] 3 S.C.R. 420, 302 C.C.C. (3d) 1.

Constitutional considerations – The fact that provocation operates as a defence only where the act or insult relied upon as provocation meets a threshold test that an ordinary person would have been deprived of self-control does not infringe the principles of fundamental justice as guaranteed by s. 7 of the Charter. This section does not impose liability where subjective fault does not exist but reduces the liability even when that fault does exist: *R. v. Cameron* (1992), 71 C.C.C. (3d) 272, 7 O.R. (3d) 545 (C.A.).

INFANTICIDE.

233. A female person commits infanticide when by a wilful act or omission she causes the death of her newly-born child, if at the time of the act or omission she is not fully recovered from the effects of giving birth to the child and by reason thereof or of the effect of lactation consequent on the birth of the child her mind is then disturbed. R.S., c. C-34, s. 216.

CROSS-REFERENCES

The term "newly-born child" is defined in s. 2. When a child becomes a human being is defined by s. 223(1). The punishment for infanticide is set out in s. 237. Related offences are as follows: s. 238, killing unborn child in act of birth; s. 242, neglect to obtain assistance in child-birth; s. 243, concealing body of child; s. 215, failing to provide necessaries; s. 218, abandoning child. Under s. 223(2) a person commits homicide when she causes injury to a child before or during its birth as a result of which the child dies after becoming a human being. As to other provisions respecting causation, see ss. 224 to 226.

As to included offences, see s. 662(4) which makes the offence under s. 243 an included offence. Reference should also be made to s. 663 which provides for conviction of infanticide although some of the elements of this offence are not made out.

For special provision respecting the plea of *autrefois*, see s. 610(2) and (4).

The accused's spouse is a competent and compellable witness at the instance of the Crown by virtue of s. 4(4).

SYNOPSIS

Section 233 defines what constitutes *infanticide*. It is one of four offences in Part VIII of the *Criminal Code* which deal with infants as victims of offences (also see ss. 238, 242 and 243).

The principal in this offence is the *mother* of a newly-born child. The *actus reus* occurs when the new mother, by *wilful act or omission*, causes the death of the newly-born child. The offence must occur at a time when the woman has *not fully recovered* from the effects of *giving birth and*, as a result of either those effects or lactation following the birth, her *mind* is *disturbed*. The child must have been born alive for this section to apply. Unlike murder and manslaughter (the other forms of culpable homicide), infanticide does not have either a minimum or maximum sentence of life imprisonment.

ANNOTATIONS

In *R. v. Borowiec*, [2016] 4 W.W.R. 1, the Supreme Court held that infanticide applies where (1) a mother, by a wilful act or omission, kills her newborn child and, (2) at the time of the act or omission, the mother's mind is "disturbed" either because she is not fully recovered from the effects of giving birth or by reason of the effect of lactation. The word "disturbed" is not a legal or medical term of art but should be applied in its grammatical and ordinary sense. The disturbance need not constitute a defined mental or psychological condition or a mental illness, and there is no requirement to prove that the act or omission was caused by the disturbance. However, the disturbance must be present at the time of the act or omission that caused the child's death, and it must occur at a time when the accused is not fully recovered from the effects of giving birth or of lactation. The disturbance is part of the *actus reus* of infanticide; the *mens rea* is the same as for manslaughter.

There is no reverse onus on the accused to prove the applicability of the defence of infanticide on the balance of probabilities: *R. v. Effert* (2009), 244 C.C.C. (3d) 510 (Alta. Q.B.).

Infanticide is both a discrete indictable offence and a partial defence to murder. To prove infanticide, the Crown must establish the *mens rea* associated with the unlawful act that caused the child's death and objective foreseeability of the risk of bodily harm to the child from that assault. It is the unique *actus reus* of infanticide that distinguishes it from murder and manslaughter. The presence of the *mens rea* for murder, while not negating the partial defence of infanticide, is not a condition precedent to the existence of that partial defence: *R. v. B. (L.)* (2011), 270 C.C.C. (3d) 208 (Ont. C.A.), leave to appeal to S.C.C. refused (2011), 291 O.A.C. 398*n*.

If there is an air of reality to the defence of infanticide and the Crown proves that the accused committed a culpable homicide, the jury should be told to consider infanticide first. If the Crown fails to negate at least one of the elements of infanticide beyond a reasonable doubt, the jury should be instructed to return a verdict of not guilty of murder, but guilty of infanticide: *R. v. B. (L.), supra.*

MANSLAUGHTER.

234. Culpable homicide that is not murder or infanticide is manslaughter. R.S., c. C-34, s. 217.

CROSS-REFERENCES

Murder is defined in ss. 229 and 230. Infanticide is defined in s. 233. As to included offences, see s. 662. As to special provisions respecting the plea of *autrefois*, see s. 610(2) to (4). The punishment for manslaughter is set out in s. 236. As to limits on intoxification defence, see s. 33.1.

SYNOPSIS

This section provides that all culpable homicide which is not murder (s. 229 or 230) or infanticide (s. 233) is manslaughter. Thus, manslaughter is defined both by specific provisions which reduce murder to manslaughter (see s. 232) and by declaring the residual category of acts amounting to culpable homicide to be manslaughter. Drunkenness, which is defined by common law principles and is not dealt with in the *Criminal Code*, also reduces murder to manslaughter. The mental element varies depending on what principle operates to reduce a culpable homicide to manslaughter. Thus, the intention ranges from the intention to do an unlawful act (s. 222(5)(*a*)) to the intention to kill which is mitigated by the presence of provocation (s. 232).

ANNOTATIONS

Intent – Once the jury has found that the homicide was culpable it must decide the accused's intent, and if at that stage there is a reasonable doubt that he intended to commit murder they should then consider the offence of manslaughter: *R. v. Kuzmack*, [1955] S.C.R. 292, 111 C.C.C. 1 (8:1).

Unlike the crime of murder which requires proof of a special intent to commit that offence, manslaughter only requires a general intent: *R. v. Mack* (1975), 22 C.C.C. (2d) 257, 29 C.R.N.S. 270 (Alta. S.C. App. Div.) (5:0).

Where there is evidence of mental illness or disorder at the time of the murder it would be prudent for the judge to instruct the jury that it would be open for them to find that although the accused was not at the time insane, he did not have the mental capacity to form the specific intent to commit murder, but had the general intent to warrant a conviction for manslaughter: *R. v. Baltzer* (1974), 27 C.C.C. (2d) 118 (N.S.S.C. App. Div.); *R. v. Hilton*

(1977), 34 C.C.C. (2d) 206 (Ont. C.A.); *R. v. Browning* (1976) 34 C.C.C. (2d) 200 (Ont. C.A.); *R. v. Lechasseur* (1977), 38 C.C.C. (2d) 319 (Que. C.A.).

Unlawful act manslaughter – The *mens rea* of unlawful act manslaughter under subsec. (5)(*a*) is, in addition to the *mens rea* of the underlying offence, objective foreseeability of the risk of bodily harm which is neither trivial nor transitory. In applying this objective test personal characteristics not directly relevant to an element of the offence such as experience, education and psychological defences serve as a defence only when there is an incapacity to appreciate the risk involved in the conduct. Likewise, the standard is not raised because the particular accused may have special experience or training. On the other hand, the particular activity may impose a higher *de facto* standard than others: *R. v. Creighton*, [1993] 3 S.C.R. 3, 83 C.C.C. (3d) 346.

The unlawful act must also be objectively dangerous, that is, likely to injure another person: *R. v. DeSousa*, [1992] 2 S.C.R. 944, 76 C.C.C. (3d) 124; *R. v. Creighton*, *supra*.

Party to manslaughter – An accused who lacks the necessary *mens rea* for murder may be convicted of manslaughter by aiding or abetting another in the offence of murder pursuant to s. 21(1), where a reasonable person in all the circumstances would have appreciated that bodily harm was the foreseeable consequence of the dangerous act which was being undertaken. Further, if the accused party did not foresee the probability of murder by the principal offender but a reasonable person in all the circumstances would have foreseen at least a risk of harm to another as a result of carrying out the common intention, the party could be found guilty of manslaughter pursuant to s. 21(2). Liability for manslaughter under s. 21(2) does not depend upon proof that a reasonable person would have foreseen the risk of death: *R. v. Jackson*, [1993] 4 S.C.R. 573, 86 C.C.C. (3d) 385.

Manslaughter by criminal negligence / *Also see notes under ss. 219 and 220* – On a trial for murder the verdicts left to the jury were murder, manslaughter due to intoxication and not guilty due to accident. On the accused's appeal from conviction for murder it was argued that the trial judge should have left with the jury the verdict of manslaughter as a result of criminal negligence. The court held however that such a theory was based on speculation, that there was no evidence to support criminal negligence as distinct from accident and, accordingly, the defence was not entitled to have this theory placed before the jury: *R. v. Charbonneau*, [1977] 2 S.C.R. 805, 33 C.C.C. (2d) 469 (8:1).

Constitutional considerations – Manslaughter is not one of those offences which because of its gravity or the stigma attached to it requires proof of a minimum *mens rea* of foreseeability of death to comply with s. 7 of the Charter. Thus, the offence of unlawful act manslaughter as interpreted by the courts and requiring only objective foreseeability of the risk of bodily harm does not violate s. 7. Thus, the so-called "thin skull" rule which renders offenders liable for the unforeseen consequences of their dangerous acts as well does not violate s. 7: *R. v. Creighton*, *supra*.

PUNISHMENT FOR MURDER / Minimum punishment.

235. (1) Every one who commits first degree murder or second degree murder is guilty of an indictable offence and shall be sentenced to imprisonment for life.

(2) For the purposes of Part XXIII, the sentence of imprisonment for life prescribed by this section is a minimum punishment. R.S., c. C-34, s. 218; 1973-74, c. 38, s. 3; 1974-75-76, c. 105, s. 5.

CROSS-REFERENCES
Murder is defined in ss. 229 and 230 and classified as first or second degree murder by s. 231. The determination of parole ineligibility is made in accordance with ss. 745 to 746.1. That scheme as applied to adults may, however, be briefly summarized as follows. A person convicted of first degree murder is liable to imprisonment for life without eligibility for parole for 25 years [s. 745],

but may apply for judicial review of the period of ineligibility after 15 years [s. 745.6]. A person convicted of second degree murder is liable to imprisonment for life without eligibility for parole for a period between 10 and 25 years [s. 745]. This period is set by the trial judge under s. 745.4 after taking the recommendation, if any, from the jury [where the case has been tried by a jury] pursuant to s. 745.2. Note, however, that where an accused is convicted of second degree murder, the period of parole ineligibility must be set at 25 years where the accused was previously convicted of murder however described under the *Criminal Code* [s. 745] [Note s. 664 which prohibits reference in the indictment to the previous conviction. However, s. 665 which requires service of notice of intention to seek greater punishment does not apply.] Again, the accused may apply for judicial review of the period of ineligibility after 15 years where the period set under s. 745.4 exceeds 15 years [s. 745.6]. A person convicted of murder will also be liable to the mandatory prohibition order respecting firearms, ammunition and explosives by virtue of s. 109. Pursuant to s. 745.5, where the accused was under 18 years of age at the time of the offence but has been transferred to the ordinary courts then the period of parole ineligibility may be between five and ten years whether the accused is convicted of first or second degree murder.

Section 17 limits the availability of the statutory defence of compulsion by threats. As to other notes respecting defences to murder, see ss. 229 and 230. As to included offences, see s. 662.

This offence may be the basis for an application for an authorization to intercept private communications by reason of s. 183 or a warrant to conduct video surveillance by reason of s. 487.01(5), and falls within the definition of "enterprise crime offence" in s. 462.3 for the purposes of Part XII.2.

Section 7(3) enacts special jurisdictional rules for commission of this offence outside Canada when the offence is in relation to an internationally protected person or property referred to in s. 431 [official premises, etc.]. A threat to commit an offence under this section against an internationally protected person (defined in s. 2) is an offence under s. 424.

Special provision respecting the plea of *autrefois* see s. 610(2) to (4).

Pursuant to s. 582, no person may be convicted of first degree murder unless he is specifically charged with that offence in the indictment. Under s. 589, no count that charges an offence other than murder shall be joined in an indictment to a count that charges murder.

Trial of murder is by the superior court of criminal jurisdiction (defined in s. 2) by virtue of ss. 468 and 469. By virtue of s. 522, only a judge of the superior court of criminal jurisdiction may release an accused charged with this offence.

The accused's spouse is a competent and compellable witness at the instance of the Crown by virtue of s. 4(4) where the victim is under the age of 14 years. Age is determined by reference to s. 30 of the *Interpretation Act*, R.S.C. 1985, c. I-21.

MANSLAUGHTER.

236. Every person who commits manslaughter is guilty of an indictable offence and liable

  (*a*) **where a firearm is used in the commission of the offence, to imprisonment for life and to a minimum punishment of imprisonment for a term of four years; and**

  (*b*) **in any other case, to imprisonment for life. R.S., c. C-34, s. 219; 1995, c. 39, s. 142.**

CROSS-REFERENCES

Manslaughter is defined by ss. 232, 234 and 263(3).

Section 7(3) enacts special jurisdictional rules for commission of this offence outside Canada when the offence is in relation to an internationally protected person or property referred to in s. 432 [official premises, etc.]. Firearm is defined in s. 2.

As to included offences see s. 662(5). For special provision respecting the plea of *autrefois*, see s. 610(2) to (4).

The accused's spouse is a competent and compellable witness at the instance of the Crown by virtue of s. 4(4) where the victim is under the age of 14 years. Age is determined by reference to s. 30 of the *Interpretation Act*, R.S.C. 1985, c. I-21.

The accused has an election as to mode of trial pursuant to s. 536(2). Release pending trial is determined by s. 515. An accused convicted of this offence may, pursuant to s. 259, be ordered prohibited from operating a motor vehicle, vessel, aircraft or railway equipment for during any period that the court considers proper, where the offence under this section was committed by means of a motor vehicle, vessel, aircraft or railway equipment. The procedure respecting the making of that order of prohibition is found in s. 260. In some circumstances, the accused will also be liable to the mandatory prohibition order respecting weapons, ammunition and explosives by virtue of s. 109. Where the offence was committed by means of a motor vehicle, vessel, aircraft or railway equipment, evidence that the accused's blood alcohol level exceeded .16 at the time of the offence is deemed an aggravating factor, for purposes of sentencing, under s. 255.1.

SYNOPSIS

Section 236 provides that the *maximum sentence* upon conviction for *manslaughter* is *life imprisonment*. This is to be contrasted to the punishment for murder for which the minimum sentence is life, and for which there are restrictions in the *Criminal Code* regarding eligibility for parole. There is no minimum sentence for manslaughter except where a firearm is used in the commission of the offence. In such a case, the minimum punishment is four years' imprisonment.

ANNOTATIONS

This provision does not violate s. 12 of the Charter: *R. v. Ferguson*, [2008] 1 S.C.R. 96, 228 C.C.C. (3d) 385.

PUNISHMENT FOR INFANTICIDE.

237. Every female person who commits infanticide is guilty of an indictable offence and liable to imprisonment for a term not exceeding five years. R.S., c. C-34, s. 220.

CROSS-REFERENCES

Infanticide is defined in ss. 233 and 663.

The accused has an election as to mode of trial pursuant to s. 536(2). Release pending trial is determined by s. 515. In some circumstances, the accused will also be liable to the discretionary prohibition order respecting firearms, ammunition and explosives by virtue of s. 110.

The accused's spouse is a competent and compellable witness at the instance of the Crown by virtue of s. 4(4). For other notes concerning the offence of infanticide, see s. 233.

SYNOPSIS

Section 237 sets out the *punishment for infanticide* (see s. 233). There is *no minimum* sentence for this offence. The maximum sentence upon conviction is five years.

ANNOTATIONS

Where the expert evidence indicated that the accused was seriously mentally ill at the time of the offence (even raising doubts as to her liability for this offence) the court on appeal against a prison sentence allowed the appeal and substituted a conditional discharge. The principle of deterrence simply had no application in the circumstances, the only real consideration being rehabilitation: *R. v. Szola* (1977), 33 C.C.C. (2d) 572 (Ont. C.A.).

KILLING UNBORN CHILD IN ACT OF BIRTH / Saving.

238. (1) Every one who causes the death, in the act of birth, of any child that has not become a human being, in such a manner that, if the child were a human being, he would be guilty of murder, is guilty of an indictable offence and liable to imprisonment for life.

(2) This section does not apply to a person who, by means that, in good faith, he considers necessary to preserve the life of the mother of a child, causes the death of that child. R.S., c. C-34, s. 221.

CROSS-REFERENCES

As to when a child becomes a human being, see s. 223(1). The accused has an election as to mode of trial pursuant to s. 536(2). Release pending trial is determined by s. 515. Murder is defined in ss. 229 and 230. The offence of infanticide is defined in s. 233. Related offences are as follows: s. 243, neglect to obtain assistance in child-birth; s. 243, concealing body of child; s. 215, failing to provide necessaries; s. 218, abandoning child.

SYNOPSIS

This section creates the indictable offence of *killing an unborn child in the act of birth*. This offence applies in circumstances where the death was caused in such a way that, had the child become a human being (see s. 223), the crime would have been murder. The maximum sentence upon conviction is imprisonment for life.

Section 238(2) provides an exception to liability for such acts dealing with cases in which the act, resulting in the death of the unborn child, was done to save the life of the mother. The person doing the act must consider *in good faith* that such act was necessary for that purpose.

ATTEMPT TO COMMIT MURDER / Subsequent offences / Sequence of convictions only.

239. (1) Every person who attempts by any means to commit murder is guilty of an indictable offence and liable

    (a) if a restricted firearm or prohibited firearm is used in the commission of the offence or if any firearm is used in the commission of the offence and the offence is committed for the benefit of, at the direction of, or in association with, a criminal organization, to imprisonment for life and to a minimum punishment of imprisonment for a term of

        (i) in the case of a first offence, five years, and

        (ii) in the case of a second or subsequent offence, seven years;

    (a.1) in any other case where a firearm is used in the commission of the offence, to imprisonment for life and to a minimum punishment of imprisonment for a term of four years; and

    (b) in any other case, to imprisonment for life.

(2) In determining, for the purpose of paragraph (1)(*a*), whether a convicted person has committed a second or subsequent offence, if the person was earlier convicted of any of the following offences, that offence is to be considered as an earlier offence:

    (a) an offence under this section;

    (b) an offence under subsection 85(1) or (2) or section 244 or 244.2; or

    (c) an offence under section 220, 236, 272 or 273, subsection 279(1) or section 279.1, 344 or 346 if a firearm was used in the commission of the offence.

However, an earlier offence shall not be taken into account if 10 years have elapsed between the day on which the person was convicted of the earlier offence and the day on which the person was convicted of the offence for which sentence is being imposed, not taking into account any time in custody.

(3) For the purposes of subsection (2), the only question to be considered is the sequence of convictions and no consideration shall be given to the sequence of commission of offences or whether any offence occurred before or after any conviction. R.S., c. C-34, s. 222; 1995, c. 39, s. 143; 2008, c. 6, s. 16; 2009, c. 22, s. 6.

CROSS-REFERENCES

Attempt is defined in s. 24. "Firearm" is defined in s. 2. "Criminal organization" is defined in ss. 2 and 467.1(1). "Restricted firearm" and "prohibited firearm" are defined in s. 84.

Section 17 limits the availability of the statutory defence of compulsion by threats. Under s. 662(2), an accused may be convicted of "attempted second degree murder" on an indictment charging first degree murder. Presumably, where the indictment charges second degree murder then the accused can be convicted of attempted second degree murder by virtue of s. 662(1)(*b*). Under s. 661, where an attempt is charged but the evidence proves commission of the full offence, the accused may be convicted of the attempt.

The accused's spouse is a competent and compellable witness at the instance of the Crown by virtue of s. 4(4) where the victim is under the age of 14 years. Age is determined by reference to s. 30 of the *Interpretation Act*, R.S.C. 1985, c. I-21.

The accused has an election as to mode of trial pursuant to s. 536(2). Release pending trial is determined by s. 515. A person convicted of attempted murder will be liable to the mandatory prohibition order respecting weapons, ammunition and explosives by virtue of s. 109. While s. 239 is not listed in s. 183 as an "offence" for the purposes of obtaining an authorization to intercept private communications, an authorization may be obtained in respect of an attempt to commit any of the offences listed in s. 183 and "235 (murder)" is listed in s. 183. Similarly, while s. 239 is not listed in s. 462.3 as an "enterprise crime offence" for the purposes of Part XII.1, "section 235 (punishment for murder)" is listed in s. 462.3 and para. (*c*) of the definition of enterprise crime offence provides that an attempt to commit any of the listed offences is as well an enterprise crime offence. A person convicted of attempted murder may be subject to a dangerous offender application under Part XXIV.

SYNOPSIS

This section makes it an indictable offence to attempt to commit murder. This part of the section is redundant as s. 24(1) would create such an offence. The key aspect of this section provides the maximum and minimum punishments. This is a departure from the general rule expressed in s. 463(*a*) that a person is liable to a sentence of 14 years upon conviction for attempting to commit an offence which would be punishable by life imprisonment upon completion of the full offence. The mental element for this offence is the intention to kill.

The sentencing regime operates as follows. In all cases, the maximum punishment is life imprisonment. Under subsec. (1)(*a*), where a restricted firearm or prohibited firearm is used or if any firearm is used where the offence is committed for the benefit of, at the direction of, or in association with a criminal organization, the minimum punishment for a first offence is five years, and seven years for a second or subsequent offence. The rules for determining second and subsequent offences are set out in subsecs. (2) and (3). Thus, certain earlier convictions for related offences, such as certain firearm offences or other offences involving use of a firearm, are deemed to be earlier offences. However, an earlier offence is not to be taken into account if 10 years have elapsed (not counting time spent in custody). Subsection (3) reverses the common law rule and provides that, in determining whether an offence is an earlier offence, the only question is whether the conviction was registered earlier; the sequence of commission of the offences is not relevant. Under subsec. (1)(*a*.1), in any other case in which a firearm is used, the minimum punishment is four years. Where no firearm is used there is no minimum, pursuant to subsec. (1)(*b*).

ANNOTATIONS

Intent – A conviction for attempted murder requires proof of the specific intent to kill. No lesser *mens rea* will suffice, and in particular a conviction under this section may not be based on the lesser intents described in s. 229(*a*)(ii) or s. 230: *R. v. Ancio*, [1984] 1 S.C.R. 225, 10 C.C.C. (3d) 385 (7:1).

The common law doctrine of transferred intent does not apply to attempted murder although it clearly applies to murder. Inchoate crimes such as attempted murder do not require a result of harm as part of the *actus reus*. The *actus reus* is complete upon the first act beyond preparation. Section 229(*b*) makes the accused liable for murder if innocent bystanders died from their injuries, but it does not speak to the application of transferred intent principles to attempted murder. Where both the *mens rea* and *actus reus* of an attempted are established, an accused is liable for an inchoate crime in relation to the intended victim, and might also be subject to punishment in connection with an unintended victim in accordance with his moral culpability and the injury caused: *R. v. Gordon* (2009), 241 C.C.C. (3d) 388 (Ont. C.A.), leave to appeal to S.C.C. refused 243 C.C.C. (3d) vi.

Neither excessive force in self-defence nor provocation are defences to this charge so as to reduce the offence to one of attempted manslaughter. However, the conduct of the victim may be a relevant piece of evidence on the question of whether the accused had the requisite intent to kill if the provocation by the victim produced in the accused a state of anger, excitement or disturbance to the extent that he did not contemplate the consequences of his act and did not intend those consequences: *R. v. Campbell* (1977), 38 C.C.C. (2d) 6, 17 O.R. (2d) 673 (C.A.).

To make out the offence under this section the Crown must prove that the accused, having the specific intent to cause the death of a human being, did anything for the purpose of carrying out that intent, by any means. The Crown need not prove that the accused had the specific intent to murder each of the victims, specified in the indictment, by name in a case where the accused intending to kill an occupant of a tavern returned to the tavern and opened fire on the area in which a number of patrons were standing: *R. v. Marshall* (1986), 25 C.C.C. (3d) 151 (N.S.C.A.).

Liability of party – A party cannot be convicted of this offence based on the objective foreseeability under s. 21(2). Accordingly, the words "ought to have known" in s. 21(2) are inoperative where liability is sought to be imposed on a party for the offence in this section: *R. v. Logan*, [1990] 2 S.C.R. 731, 58 C.C.C. (3d) 391.

Included offences – An indictment charging attempted murder *simpliciter* only includes the offence of attempting to unlawfully cause bodily harm: *R. v. Simpson (No. 2)* (1981), 58 C.C.C. (2d) 122, 20 C.R. (3d) 36 (Ont. C.A.); *R. v. Colburne* (1991), 66 C.C.C. (3d) 235 (Que. C.A.).

ACCESSORY AFTER FACT TO MURDER.

240. Every one who is an accessory after the fact to murder is guilty of an indictable offence and liable to imprisonment for life. R.S., c. C-34, s. 223.

CROSS-REFERENCES

The definition of accessory after the fact is in s. 23. Sections 23.1 and 592 deal with the trial of and charging of the accessory although the principal has not or cannot be convicted. Murder is defined in ss. 229 and 230.

Trial of accessory after the fact to murder is by the superior court of criminal jurisdiction (defined in s. 2) by virtue of ss. 468 and 469. By virtue of s. 522, only a judge of the superior court of criminal jurisdiction may release an accused charged with this offence. A person convicted of this offence may be liable to the mandatory prohibition order respecting firearms, ammunition and explosives by virtue of s. 109.

While s. 240 is not listed in s. 183 as an "offence" for the purposes of obtaining an authorization to intercept private communications, an authorization may be obtained for being an accessory after the fact in relation to any of the offences listed in s. 183 and "235 (murder)" is listed in s. 183. Similarly, while s. 240 is not listed in s. 462.3 as an "enterprise crime offence" for the purposes of Part XII.1, "section 235 (punishment for murder)" is listed in s. 462.3 and s. 462.3(*c*) provides that being an accessory after the fact in relation to any of the offences listed in the section is as well an enterprise crime offence.

The accused's spouse is a competent and compellable witness at the instance of the Crown by virtue of s. 4(4) where the victim is under the age of 14 years. Age is determined by reference to s. 30 of the *Interpretation Act*, R.S.C. 1985, c. I-21.

SYNOPSIS

This section provides that it is an indictable offence to be an *accessory after the fact* to the commission of a *murder*. This aspect of the section is redundant in light of s. 23 of the *Criminal Code*. The important aspect of the section is one which places the *maximum sentence*, upon conviction, at *life imprisonment*. This is an exception to the general rule as stated in s. 463(*a*) that the punishment for being an accessory after the fact is punishable by 14 years, if the sentence, to which the principal accused is subject, is life imprisonment. For a description of what constitutes being an accessory after the fact, see s. 23.

ANNOTATIONS

The offence of being an accessory after the fact to manslaughter under s. 463(*a*) is a lesser and included offence to that of being an accessory after the fact to murder: *R. v. Webber* (1995), 102 C.C.C. (3d) 248, 106 W.A.C. 161 (B.C.C.A.).

Suicide

COUNSELLING OR AIDING SUICIDE.

241. Every one who
    (*a*) **counsels a person to commit suicide, or**
    (*b*) **aids or abets a person to commit suicide,**
whether suicide ensues or not, is guilty of an indictable offence and liable to imprisonment for a term not exceeding fourteen years. R.S., c. C-34, s. 224; R.S.C. 1985, c. 27 (1st Supp.), s. 7(3).

CROSS-REFERENCES

"Counsel" is defined in s. 22(3). Note that s. 14 provides that no person is entitled to consent to have death inflicted on him and such consent does not affect the criminal responsibility of any person, by whom death may be inflicted, on the person, by whom consent is given. While s. 14 would seem to make a person who aids suicide guilty of culpable homicide, including first degree murder, apparently the predecessor to this offence was inserted in the 1892 Code expressly to avoid the problem that, at common law, suicide was murder and thus, a person who aided suicide was guilty of murder and liable to the death penalty. [See excerpt from Report of the Imperial Commissioners, respecting the English Draft Code of 1878, quoted in *Martin's Criminal Code, 1955* at p. 397.] and in *London Life Insurance Co. v. Lang Shirt Co.'s Trustee*, [1929] S.C.R. 117, [1929] 1 D.L.R. 328, it was held that a successful suicide was not a "homicide" within what is now s. 222.

    The accused has an election as to mode of trial pursuant to s. 536(2). Release pending trial is determined by s. 515.

SYNOPSIS

This section makes it an indictable offence to *counsel the act of suicide or to assist* in such an act. At one time, attempting suicide was an offence, but this section has been repealed so that the person who attempts to commit suicide does not commit an offence: only the person who counsels or assists is guilty of a crime. The offence is made out, regardless of whether the suicide ensues. A person convicted of this offence is liable to imprisonment for a period of not more than 14 years.

ANNOTATIONS

On a charge of aiding suicide, the Crown must prove an intent to aid suicide and drunkenness is a defence to the charge: *R. v. Loomes* (unreported January 6, 1975, Ont. C.A.).

    In *Carter v. Canada (Attorney General)*, [2015] 1 S.C.R. 331, 320 C.C.C. (3d) 1, the court revisited its earlier 5:4 holding in *Rodriguez v. British Columbia (Attorney General)*,

CR. CODE

[1993] 3 S.C.R. 519, 85 C.C.C. (3d) 15, and struck down the prohibition on physician-assisted suicide. The court held that, insofar as the law prohibits physician-assisted dying for competent adults who seek such assistance as a result of a grievous and irremediable medical condition that causes enduring and intolerable suffering, it is unconstitutionally overbroad in violation of s. 7.

In the case of a genuine suicide pact, the surviving party should have a defence to murder. This defence will only be available when the parties are in such a mental state that they have formed a common and irrevocable intent to commit suicide together simultaneously and by the same act where the risk of death is identical and equal for both. The survivor may, however, be liable to be convicted of the offence under this section: *R. v. Gagnon* (1993), 84 C.C.C. (3d) 143 (Que. C.A.).

Neglect in Child-birth and Concealing Dead Body

NEGLECT TO OBTAIN ASSISTANCE IN CHILD-BIRTH.

242. A female person who, being pregnant and about to be delivered, with intent that the child shall not live or with intent to conceal the birth of the child, fails to make provision for reasonable assistance in respect of her delivery is, if the child is permanently injured as a result thereof or dies immediately before, during or in a short time after birth, as a result thereof, guilty of an indictable offence and liable to imprisonment for a term not exceeding five years. R.S., c. C-34, s. 226.

CROSS-REFERENCES

Related offences are infanticide, defined in s. 237, killing unborn child in act of birth in s. 238 and concealing body of child in s. 243. See s. 223(2) as to when causing death to child during or before birth amounts to homicide.

The accused has an election as to mode of trial pursuant to s. 536(2). Release pending trial is determined by s. 515, although the accused is eligible for release by the officer in charge under s. 498.

A person convicted of this offence may be liable to the mandatory prohibition order respecting firearms, ammunition and explosives by virtue of s. 109.

SYNOPSIS

Section 242 makes it an indictable offence to *neglect to obtain help in child-birth* if the act or omission is done with the requisite intent, and the consequences to the child are as specified in the section. The *pregnant woman is liable as a principal* if she is about to give birth and fails to make provision for reasonable assistance for the delivery. This liability only attaches if the woman fails to get assistance *with the intention that the child should not live or to conceal the birth* and certain results follow. The *consequences* which must be proven are that the *child dies* immediately before, during or in a short time after the birth or is permanently injured *as result of the woman's failure to obtain assistance*. The maximum sentence on conviction for this offence is five years' imprisonment.

ANNOTATIONS

The death or injury must be a direct result of deliberate failure to obtain reasonable assistance at birth: *R. v. Bryan* (1959), 123 C.C.C. 160, [1959] O.W.N. 103 (C.A.) (2:1).

CONCEALING BODY OF CHILD.

243. Every one who in any manner disposes of the dead body of a child, with intent to conceal the fact that its mother has been delivered of it, whether the child died before, during or after birth, is guilty of an indictable offence and liable to imprisonment for a term not exceeding two years. R.S., c. C-34, s. 227.

CROSS-REFERENCES

By virtue of s. 662(4), this offence is an included offence where a count charges murder of a child or charges infanticide.

The accused has an election as to mode of trial pursuant to s. 536(2). Release pending trial is determined by s. 515, although the accused is eligible for release by the officer in charge under s. 498.

Related offences are infanticide, defined in s. 237, killing unborn child in act of birth in s. 238 and neglecting to obtain assistance in child birth in s. 243.

ANNOTATIONS

For the purposes of this section, a fetus becomes a child when it has reached a stage in its development when, but for some external event or other circumstances, it would likely have been born alive. This standard provides sufficient precision to comply with the s. 7 principle of fundamental justice that criminal laws must not be vague: *R. v. Levkovic*, [2013] 2 S.C.R. 204, 296 C.C.C. (3d) 457.

Bodily Harm and Acts and Omissions Causing Danger to the Person

DISCHARGING FIREARM WITH INTENT / Punishment / Subsequent offences / Sequence of convictions only.

244. (1) Every person commits an offence who discharges a firearm at a person with intent to wound, maim or disfigure, to endanger the life of or to prevent the arrest or detention of any person — whether or not that person is the one at whom the firearm is discharged.

(2) Every person who commits an offence under subsection (1) is guilty of an indictable offence and liable

   (a) if a restricted firearm or prohibited firearm is used in the commission of the offence or if the offence is committed for the benefit of, at the direction of, or in association with, a criminal organization, to imprisonment for a term not exceeding 14 years and to a minimum punishment of imprisonment for a term of

   (i) in the case of a first offence, five years, and

   (ii) in the case of a second or subsequent offence, seven years; and

   (b) in any other case, to imprisonment for a term not exceeding 14 years and to a minimum punishment of imprisonment for a term of four years.

(3) In determining, for the purpose of paragraph (2)(a), whether a convicted person has committed a second or subsequent offence, if the person was earlier convicted of any of the following offences, that offence is to be considered as an earlier offence:

   (a) an offence under this section;

   (b) an offence under subsection 85(1) or (2) or section 244.2; or

   (c) an offence under section 220, 236, 239, 272 or 273, subsection 279(1) or section 279.1, 344 or 346 if a firearm was used in the commission of the offence.

However, an earlier offence shall not be taken into account if 10 years have elapsed between the day on which the person was convicted of the earlier offence and the day on which the person was convicted of the offence for which sentence is being imposed, not taking into account any time in custody.

(4) For the purposes of subsection (3), the only question to be considered is the sequence of convictions and no consideration shall be given to the sequence of commission of offences or whether any offence occurred before or after any conviction. R.S., c. C-34, s. 228; 1980-81-82-83, c. 125, s. 17; 1995, c. 39, s. 144; 2008, c. 6, s. 17; 2009, c. 22, s. 7.

CROSS-REFERENCES

"Firearm" is defined in s. 2. "Criminal organization" is defined in ss. 2 and 467.1(1). "Restricted firearm" and "prohibited firearm" are defined in s. 84. Related offences are as follows: s. 239, attempted murder; s. 129, resisting arrest; s. 270(1)(*b*) assault with intent to resist arrest; s. 267, assault causing bodily harm and assault with a weapon; s. 268, aggravated assault; s. 269, unlawfully causing bodily harm; s. 272, sexual assault with a weapon and sexual assault causing bodily harm; s. 273, aggravated sexual assault; and s. 244.2, discharging firearm into a place. An authorization to intercept private communications may be obtained in relation to this offence.

The accused has an election as to mode of trial pursuant to s. 536(2). Release pending trial is determined by s. 515.

A person convicted of this offence may be liable to the mandatory prohibition order respecting weapons, ammunition and explosives by virtue of s. 109. A person convicted of this offence may be subject to a dangerous offender application under Part XXIV. This offence is also a primary designated offence under s. 487.04.

SYNOPSIS

This section makes it an indictable offence to discharge a firearm with one of the intentions specified in the section. The doing of any of the aforementioned acts with any of the intentions set out in paras. (*a*) to (*c*), namely, wounding, maiming or disfiguring any person, endangering the life of anyone or preventing the arrest of a person, makes out the offence. The offence is made out even if the person referred to in paras. (*a*) or (*b*) is not the person who was, in fact, fired at.

The sentencing regime operates as follows. In all cases, the maximum punishment is 14 years. Under subsec. (2)(*a*), where a restricted firearm or prohibited firearm is used or if any firearm is used where the offence is committed for the benefit of, at the direction of, or in association with a criminal organization, the minimum punishment for a first offence is five years, and seven years for a second or subsequent offence. The rules for determining second and subsequent offences are set out in subsecs. (3) and (4). Thus, certain earlier convictions for related offences, such as certain firearm offences or other offences involving use of a firearm, are deemed to be earlier offences. However, an earlier offence is not to be taken into account if 10 years have elapsed (not counting time spent in custody). Subsection (4) reverses the common law rule and provides that, in determining whether an offence is an earlier offence, the only question is whether the conviction was registered earlier; the sequence of commission of the offences is not relevant. Under subsec. (2)(*b*), in any other case, the minimum punishment is four years.

ANNOTATIONS

In *R. v. Schultz* (1962), 133 C.C.C. 174, 38 C.R. 76 (Alta. S.C. App. Div.), the court considered various definitions of the word "maim" all to the effect that the person is maimed when he is rendered less able to fight. In that case it was held that the breaking of a man's leg is a sufficiently serious injury to amount to a maiming.

In *R. v. Innes and Brotchie* (1972), 7 C.C.C. (2d) 544 (B.C.C.A.), Robertson J.A. considered various definitions of the words "wound, maim or disfigure" including that "maim" means to render the victim less able to defend himself and "disfigure" denotes more than a temporary marring of the figure or appearance of a person.

An acquittal on a charge of attempted murder and a conviction on a charge of discharging a firearm with intent to endanger life are not inconsistent verdicts as the intent to endanger life is different from the intent to murder: *R. v. Boomhower* (1974), 20 C.C.C. (2d) 89, 27 C.R.N.S. 188 (Ont. C.A.).

Assault as defined by s. 265(1)(*b*) is an included offence of this offence: *R. v. Colburne* (1991), 66 C.C.C. (3d) 235, [1991] R.J.Q. 1199 (C.A.).

Proof of an actual arrest pursuant to subsec. (*c*), whether in progress or intended, is not part of the *actus reus* of the offence: *R. v. Jackson* (2002), 163 C.C.C. (3d) 451, 58 O.R. (3d) 593 (C.A.).

The four-year minimum sentence prescribed for the offence under para. (b) does not infringe the guarantee to protection against cruel and unusual punishment under s. 12 of the *Canadian Charter of Rights and Freedoms*: *R. v. Roberts* (1998), 125 C.C.C. (3d) 471, 199 N.B.R. (2d) 387 (C.A.).

CAUSING BODILY HARM WITH INTENT — AIR GUN OR PISTOL.

244.1 Every person who, with intent
>   (a) **to wound, maim or disfigure any person,**
>   (b) **to endanger the life of any person, or**
>   (c) **to prevent the arrest or detention of any person,**

discharges an air or compressed gas gun or pistol at any person, whether or not that person is the person mentioned in paragraph (a), (b) or (c), is guilty of an indictable offence and liable to imprisonment for a term not exceeding fourteen years. 1995, c. 39, s. 144.

CROSS-REFERENCES

The comparable offence where a firearm is used is found in s. 244. The accused has an election as to mode of trial pursuant to s. 536(2). Release pending trial is determined by s. 515. A person convicted of this offence may be liable to the weapons prohibition under s. 109.

SYNOPSIS

This section makes it an indictable offence to discharge an air gun or pistol at any person with one of the intentions specified in the section. The offence is made out even if the person referred to in paras. (a) or (b) is not the person who was in fact fired at. The maximum punishment to which the offender is liable upon conviction is 14 years.

DISCHARGING FIREARM — RECKLESSNESS / Definition of "place" / Punishment / Subsequent offences / Sequence of convictions only.

244.2 (1) Every person commits an offence
>   (a) **who intentionally discharges a firearm into or at a place, knowing that or being reckless as to whether another person is present in the place; or**
>   (b) **who intentionally discharges a firearm while being reckless as to the life or safety of another person.**

(2) For the purpose of paragraph (1)(a), "place" means any building or structure — or part of one — or any motor vehicle, vessel, aircraft, railway vehicle, container or trailer.

(3) Every person who commits an offence under subsection (1) is guilty of an indictable offence and
>   (a) **if a restricted firearm or prohibited firearm is used in the commission of the offence or if the offence is committed for the benefit of, at the direction of or in association with a criminal organization, is liable to imprisonment for a term of not more than 14 years and to a minimum punishment of imprisonment for a term of**
>>   (i) **five years, in the case of a first offence, and**
>>   (ii) **seven years, in the case of a second or subsequent offence; and**
>   (b) **in any other case, is liable to imprisonment for a term of not more than 14 years and to a minimum punishment of imprisonment for a term of four years.**

(4) In determining, for the purpose of paragraph (3)(a), whether a convicted person has committed a second or subsequent offence, if the person was earlier convicted of any of the following offences, that offence is to be considered as an earlier offence:
>   (a) **an offence under this section;**
>   (b) **an offence under subsection 85(1) or (2) or section 244; or**

(c) an offence under section 220, 236, 239, 272 or 273, subsection 279(1) or section 279.1, 344 or 346 if a firearm was used in the commission of the offence. However, an earlier offence shall not be taken into account if 10 years have elapsed between the day on which the person was convicted of the earlier offence and the day on which the person was convicted of the offence for which sentence is being imposed, not taking into account any time in custody.

(5) For the purpose of subsection (4), the only question to be considered is the sequence of convictions and no consideration shall be given to the sequence of commission of offences or whether any offence occurred before or after any conviction. 2009; c. 22, s. 8.

CROSS-REFERENCES

"Firearm" and "criminal organization" are defined in s. 2. Pursuant to s. 2.1, "restricted firearm" and "prohibited firearm" have the same meaning as in s. 84. For related offences, see the note under s. 244. An authorization to intercept private communications may be obtained in relation to this offence. This offence is a primary designated offence for the purposes of the DNA Forensic Analysis provisions.

SYNOPSIS

This section creates an offence similar to the offence under s. 244. Under s. 244, the accused must discharge the firearm at a person. This offence merely requires that the accused discharged a firearm intentionally into or at a place knowing that, or being reckless whether, another person was present (subsec. (1)(a)), or intentionally discharging a firearm while being reckless as to the life or safety of another person. "Place" is defined in subsec. (2).

The sentencing regime operates as follows. In all cases, the maximum punishment is 14 years. However, where the accused used a restricted or prohibited firearm or the offence was committed for the benefit of, at the direction of, or in association with, a criminal organization there is a minimum punishment of five years for a first offence and seven years for second and subsequent offences. Subsections (4) and (5) set out the rules for whether a person has committed a second or subsequent offence. Note in particular that, if the accused has been out of custody for 10 years since the earlier offence, that offence will not be taken into account. Note also that subsec. (5) reverses the common law rule and it is simply the order of convictions that is considered, not the sequence in which the underlying offences were committed.

ADMINISTERING NOXIOUS THING.

245. Every one who administers or causes to be administered to any person or causes any person to take poison or any other destructive or noxious thing is guilty of an indictable offence and liable

    (a) to imprisonment for a term not exceeding fourteen years, if he intends thereby to endanger the life of or to cause bodily harm to that person; or

    (b) to imprisonment for a term not exceeding two years, if he intends thereby to aggrieve or annoy that person. R.S., c. C-34, s. 229.

CROSS-REFERENCES

The term "bodily harm" is defined in s. 2.

The offence of supplying a noxious thing intended to procure a miscarriage is found in s. 288.

The accused has an election as to mode of trial pursuant to s. 536(2). Release pending trial is determined by s. 515, although the accused is eligible for release by the officer in charge under s. 498 where charged with the offence under para. (b).

A person convicted of the offence under para. (a) may be liable to the mandatory prohibition order respecting weapons, ammunition and explosives by virtue of s. 109 and a person found guilty of the offence under para. (*b*) liable to the discretionary prohibition order under s. 110. A person convicted of the offence under para. (*a*) may be subject to a dangerous offender application under Part XXIV.

SYNOPSIS

Section 245 makes it an indictable *offence to administer a noxious thing*. The *actus reus* of the offence consists of administering, causing to be administered or causing to be taken a noxious thing, poison or destructive thing. To be guilty of an offence under this section, it must be proven that the accused intended to do the physical acts described. However, for sentencing purposes, a distinction is made between different intentions. If the accused intended that, by doing any of the acts described, he would endanger the life of another or cause that person bodily harm, the maximum sentence is 14 years. If the accused does any of the acts to aggrieve or annoy that person, the maximum sentence is two years.

ANNOTATIONS

The *mens rea* required by this section is proof that the accused intended a consequence defined in the section. A "noxious thing" is any substance which in the light of all the circumstances attendant upon its administration is capable of effecting or, in the normal course of events, will effect one of the defined consequences. Even an innocuous substance may in some circumstances come within the section. The Crown need not prove that the accused knew the substance was noxious, although this would be relevant in establishing intent, but only that the substance was in fact noxious: *R. v. Burkholder* (1977), 34 C.C.C. (2d) 214, [1977] 1 W.W.R. 627 (Alta. S.C. App. Div.).

Administration does not require that the accused intend that the noxious substance be taken internally: *R. v. Clark* (2008), 234 C.C.C. (3d) 12 (Alta. C.A.).

OVERCOMING RESISTANCE TO COMMISSION OF OFFENCE.

246. Every one who, with intent to enable or assist himself or another person to commit an indictable offence,

- (*a*) **attempts, by any means, to choke, suffocate or strangle another person, or by any means calculated to choke, suffocate or strangle, attempts to render another person insensible, unconscious or incapable of resistance, or**
- (*b*) **administers or causes to be administered to any person, or attempts to administer to any person, or causes or attempts to cause any person to take a stupefying or overpowering drug, matter or thing,**

is guilty of an indictable offence and liable to imprisonment for life. R.S., c. C-34, s. 230; 1972, c. 13, s. 70.

CROSS-REFERENCES

An "indictable offence" will include a hybrid offence, punishable on indictment or on summary conviction: *Interpretation Act*, R.S.C. 1985, c. I-21, s. 34(1)(*a*).

Note that where death is caused in the commission of certain offences by means similar to those referred to in this section then the accused will be liable to be convicted of murder under s. 230(*b*) or (*c*) [constructive murder]. The related offence of administering a noxious thing is found in s. 245.

The accused has an election as to mode of trial pursuant to s. 536(2). Release pending trial is determined by s. 515. A person convicted of this offence will be liable to the mandatory prohibition order respecting firearms, ammunition and explosives by virtue of s. 109. A person convicted of this offence may be subject to a dangerous offender application under Part XXIV.

SYNOPSIS

This section makes it an indictable offence for any person to *overcome resistance for the purpose of committing an indictable offence* or to do so to assist another person. The offence is made out by proving that the accused did any of the acts described in paras. (*a*) or (*b*) for this purpose. The maximum sentence upon conviction is life imprisonment.

TRAPS LIKELY TO CAUSE BODILY HARM / Bodily harm / Offence-related place / Offence-related place — bodily harm / Death.

247. (1) Every one is guilty of an indictable offence and is liable to imprisonment for a term not exceeding five years, who with intent to cause death or bodily harm to a person, whether ascertained or not,

> (*a*) sets or places a trap, device or other thing that is likely to cause death or bodily harm to a person; or
>
> (*b*) being in occupation or possession of a place, knowingly permits such a trap, device or other thing to remain in that place.

(2) Every one who commits an offence under subsection (1) and thereby causes bodily harm to any other person is guilty of an indictable offence and liable to imprisonment for a term not exceeding ten years.

(3) Every one who commits an offence under subsection (1), in a place kept or used for the purpose of committing another indictable offence, is guilty of an indictable offence and is liable to a term of imprisonment not exceeding ten years.

(4) Every one who commits an offence under subsection (1), in a place kept or used for the purpose of committing another indictable offence, and thereby causes bodily harm to a person is guilty of an indictable offence and liable to a term of imprisonment not exceeding fourteen years.

(5) Every one who commits an offence under subsection (1) and thereby causes the death of any other person is guilty of an indictable offence and liable to imprisonment for life. R.S., c. C-34, s. 231; 2004, c. 12, s. 6.

CROSS-REFERENCES

The term "property" is defined in s. 2. The term "bodily harm" is not defined in this section. Some assistance may, however, be obtained from the definition of "bodily harm" in s. 2.

The accused has an election as to mode of trial pursuant to s. 536(2). Release pending trial is determined by s. 515, although the accused is eligible for release by the officer in charge under s. 498. A person found guilty of this offence may be liable to the discretionary prohibition order respecting weapons, ammunition and explosives by virtue of s. 109, depending on the circumstances in which the offence was committed.

The related offences of criminal negligence causing death and causing bodily harm are found in ss. 220 and 221, respectively. The offences of failing to guard an opening in the ice and failing to guard excavations are found in s. 263.

SYNOPSIS

This section makes it an indictable offence to set or permit traps and other similar devices which are likely to cause death or bodily harm to any person.

The physical acts that make up the offence under subsec. (1) are setting, placing a trap, device or other thing that is likely to cause death or bodily harm to any person or being in occupation or possession of the place where such traps have been set or placed. The requisite intent is to cause death or bodily harm. Where the accused is merely in occupation or possession of the place, the prosecution must also proved that he or she knowingly permitted the trap to remain in the place. The simple offence carries a five-year maximum term of imprisonment.

Where the commission of the offence causes bodily harm, the maximum penalty is ten years and life if death is caused. Where the place is also kept or used for the purpose of committing another indictable offence such as producing marihuana, the maximum penalty is ten years and fourteen years if as a result of commission of the offence under subsec. (1) bodily harm is caused to a person.

INTERFERING WITH TRANSPORTATION FACILITIES.

248. Every one who, with intent to endanger the safety of any person, places anything on or does anything to any property that is used for or in connection with the transportation of persons or goods by land, water or air that is likely to cause death or bodily harm to persons is guilty of an indictable offence and liable to imprisonment for life. R.S., c. C-34, s. 232.

CROSS-REFERENCES

The term "bodily harm" is not defined in this section. Some assistance may, however, be obtained from the definition of "bodily harm" in s. 2. Related offences are as follows: ss. 76 to 78, offences involving aircraft; ss. 80 to 82, offences involving explosives; ss. 220 to 222, criminal negligence; s. 247, setting trap with intent; ss. 430 to 436, damage to property.

The accused has an election as to mode of trial pursuant to s. 536(2). Release pending trial is determined by s. 515. A person convicted of this offence may be liable to the mandatory prohibition order respecting firearms, ammunition and explosives by virtue of s. 109, depending on the circumstances in which the offence was committed.

SYNOPSIS

Section 248 creates the indictable offence of *interfering with transportation facilities* with the *intention of endangering the safety* of any *person*. The physical acts outlined in the section are placing anything on, or doing anything to property used in connection with transporting people or goods by land, water or air. In addition to proof of the physical act and the intention, it must be established that the act is likely to cause death or bodily harm. The maximum sentence for this offence is life imprisonment.

Motor Vehicles, Vessels and Aircraft

DANGEROUS OPERATION OF MOTOR VEHICLES, VESSELS AND AIRCRAFT / Punishment / Dangerous operation causing bodily harm / Dangerous operation causing death.

249. (1) Every one commits an offence who operates
- **(a) a motor vehicle in a manner that is dangerous to the public, having regard to all the circumstances, including the nature, condition and use of the place at which the motor vehicle is being operated and the amount of traffic that at the time is or might reasonably be expected to be at that place;**
- **(b) a vessel or any water skis, surf-board, water sled or other towed object on or over any of the internal waters of Canada or the territorial sea of Canada, in a manner that is dangerous to the public, having regard to all the circumstances, including the nature and condition of those waters or sea and the use that at the time is or might reasonably be expected to be made of those waters or sea;**
- **(c) an aircraft in a manner that is dangerous to the public, having regard to all the circumstances, including the nature and condition of that aircraft or the place or air space in or through which the aircraft is operated; or**
- **(d) railway equipment in a manner that is dangerous to the public, having regard to all the circumstances, including the nature and condition of the equipment or the place in or through which the equipment is operated.**

(2) Every one who commits an offence under subsection (1)
  (a) is guilty of an indictable offence and liable to imprisonment for a term not exceeding five years; or
  (b) is guilty of an offence punishable on summary conviction.

(3) Every one who commits an offence under subsection (1) and thereby causes bodily harm to any other person is guilty of an indictable offence and liable to imprisonment for a term not exceeding ten years.

(4) Every one who commits an offence under subsection (1) and thereby causes the death of any other person is guilty of an indictable offence and liable to imprisonment for a term not exceeding fourteen years. R.S.C. 1985, c. 27 (1st Supp.), s. 36; c. 32 (4th Supp.), s. 57; 1994, c. 44, s. 11.

CROSS-REFERENCES

The terms "motor vehicle" and "railway equipment" are defined in s. 2. The terms "aircraft", "vessel" and "operates" are defined in s. 214. The term "bodily harm" is defined in s. 2.

With respect to the offence in subsec. (4) and the issue of causation, see ss. 224 to 226. For special jurisdictional rules relating to offences committed on the water or on aircraft in the course of a flight see s. 476. Also see s. 477 respecting offences committed on the territorial sea or on internal waters [defined in s. 3 of the *Territorial Sea and Fishing Zones Act*, R.S.C. 1985, c. T-8]. Section 662(5) makes the offences under this section included offences where the count charges an offence of criminal negligence causing death [s. 220], criminal negligence causing bodily harm [s. 221] or manslaughter [s. 236] arising out of the operation of a vehicle or navigation of a vessel or aircraft. The related offences of impaired driving causing death and bodily harm are found in s. 255. The offence of failing to stop at the scene of an accident is found in s. 252. Where the accused not only commits the offence under subsec. (3) or (4), but at the time was being pursued by a peace officer operating a motor vehicle and in order to evade the officer fails without reasonable excuse to stop the vehicle as soon as possible, the accused commits an offence under s. 249.1(3) and is liable to the penalties set out in s. 249.1(4).

Where the prosecution elects to proceed by indictment on the offence in subsec. (2), dangerous operation, *simpliciter*, then the accused may elect his mode of trial pursuant to s. 536(2). Where the prosecution elects to proceed by way of summary conviction then the trial of this offence is conducted by a summary conviction court pursuant to Part XXVII. The punishment for the offence is then as set out in s. 787 and the limitation period is set out in s. 786(2). In either case, release pending trial is determined by s. 515, although the accused is eligible for release by a peace officer under s. 496, 497 or by the officer in charge under s. 498. The accused has an election as to mode of trial of the offences in subsecs. (3) and (4) pursuant to s. 536(2). Release pending trial is determined by s. 515.

An accused found guilty of these offences may, pursuant to s. 259, be ordered prohibited from operating a motor vehicle, vessel, aircraft or railway equipment, as the case may be, where the offence under this section was committed by means of a motor vehicle, vessel, aircraft or railway equipment. The length of the prohibition order is as follows: offence under subsec. (2), during any period not exceeding 3 years plus any period to which the offender is sentenced to imprisonment; offence under either subsec. (3) or (4), during any period not exceeding 10 years. The procedure respecting the making of the order of prohibition is found in s. 260. Evidence that the accused's blood alcohol level exceeded .16 at the time of the offence is deemed an aggravating factor, for purposes of sentencing, under s. 255.1.

Section 249.4 creates the offence of dangerous operation of a motor vehicle while street racing (defined in s. 2). That section provides for greater penalties where bodily harm or death is caused while street racing.

SYNOPSIS

Section 249 makes it an offence to operate motor vehicles, vessels or aircraft in a dangerous manner and provides for punishment upon conviction for these offences.

Section 249(1)(*a*) makes it an offence to *operate a motor vehicle* in a manner that is *dangerous*. To determine if the driving is dangerous, the paragraph indicates that one must *consider all of the circumstances* such as the nature, condition and the use of the place as well as the amount of traffic that is or might reasonably be expected to be present. In addition, it is essential that there be *danger to the public* who either were *present or who might have been expected to be present*. A passenger in the car is part of the public. The mental element for the offence requires proof of an intention to operate the vehicle in a way which, objectively viewed, constitutes a departure from the standard of care expected of a prudent driver in the circumstances.

Section 249(1)(*b*) creates a parallel offence in relation to the *dangerous operation of a vessel* or water skis, surf board, water sled or other towed object. The offence may be committed in the internal waters of Canada or on its territorial seas. Section 249(1)(*c*) creates a parallel offence in relation to the dangerous operation of an aircraft. Finally, s. 249(1)(*d*) sets out the similar offence of dangerous operation of railway equipment.

Subsection (2) provides that the aforementioned offences may be tried by way of summary conviction procedure or by way of indictment. In the latter case, the maximum sentence is five years' imprisonment.

Subsections (3) and (4) create more *aggravated* indictable offences which occur when a *particular consequence* flows from the commission of any of the offences described in subsec. (1). Subsection (3) applies if the acts described in subsec. (1) *result in bodily harm* to another person and it provides for a maximum sentence not exceeding 10 years. Subsection (4) creates the offence of doing one of the acts described in subsec. (1), when this *causes the death* of another person. A person convicted pursuant to subsec. (4) is liable to up to 14 years' imprisonment. In both subsecs. (3) and (4), there must be a *link proven between the accused's acts and the result*. Though it is not yet clearly defined how strong a link need be proven, the accused's act must at least be a cause of the consequences.

ANNOTATIONS

Elements of offence of dangerous operation – In *R. v. Peda*, [1969] S.C.R. 905, [1969] 4 C.C.C. 245, Judson J. (Fauteaux, Abbott, Martland and Ritchie JJ., concurring), held that subsec. (1)(*a*) contains its own definition of dangerous driving, and a court is not required to charge the jury other than in terms of the subsection itself.

In considering whether the manner of driving endangered the public, it was an error for the trial judge to simply consider the absence of other traffic in the course of a high speed police chase. The passenger in the accused's car and the officer in the police cruiser were included in the public contemplated by this section: *R. v. Edlund* (1990), 23 M.V.R. (2d) 37, 104 A.R. 354 (C.A.).

It is unnecessary for the Crown to prove that the lives or safety of others were actually endangered. The offence is proved where the Crown establishes that the driving complained of was dangerous to the public, that is, either the public actually present at the time of the offence or the public which might reasonably have been expected to be in the particular vicinity at the time: *R. v. Mueller* (1975), 29 C.C.C. (2d) 243, 32 C.R.N.S. 188 (Ont. C.A.).

The appropriate *mens rea* for this offence is based on a modified objective test. As a general rule, personal factors need not be taken into account and the accused may be convicted if it is proven that, viewed objectively, the accused was driving in a manner that was dangerous to the public, having regard to all of the circumstances. In making this assessment, the court should be satisfied that the conduct amounted to a *marked departure* from the standard of care that a reasonable person would observe in the accused's situation. An explanation, such as the sudden onset of an unexpected illness would negative liability if a reasonable person in the position of the accused would not have been aware of the risk: *R. v. Hundal*, [1993] 1 S.C.R. 867, 79 C.C.C. (3d) 97.

In *R. v. Beatty*, [2008] 1 S.C.R. 49, 228 C.C.C. (3d) 225, the Supreme Court of Canada fully considered the requisite *mens rea* and *actus reus*. The modified objective test requires a marked departure from the civil norm in the circumstances of the case. A mere departure from the standard expected of a reasonably prudent person will meet the threshold for civil negligence but will not be sufficient for penal negligence. The distinction between a mere departure and a marked departure is a question of degree. The *actus reus* requires proof beyond a reasonable doubt that, viewed objectively, the accused was driving in a manner that was dangerous to the public, having regard to all of the circumstances, including the nature, condition and use of the place at which the motor vehicle is being operated and the amount of traffic that, at the time, is or might reasonably be expected to be at that place. It is the manner in which the vehicle was operated that is at issue, not the consequence of the driving. While the consequence may assist in assessing the risk involved, it does not answer the question of whether or not the vehicle was operated in a manner dangerous to the public.

The *mens rea* requires the trier of fact to be satisfied on the basis of all of the evidence, including evidence, if any, about the accused's actual state of mind, that the conduct amounted to a marked departure from the standard of care that a reasonable person would observe in the accused's circumstances. If the trier of fact is convinced beyond a reasonable doubt that the objectively dangerous conduct constitutes a marked departure from the norm, the trier of fact must consider evidence, if any, about the actual state of mind of the accused to determine whether it raises a reasonable doubt about whether a reasonable person in the accused's position would have been aware of the risk created by this conduct. Subjective *mens rea* of intentionally creating a danger for other users of the highway will always constitute a marked departure from the standard expected of a reasonably prudent driver. Subjective *mens rea*, however, is not necessary. A lack of care must be serious enough to merit punishment. If an explanation is offered by the accused, then, in order to convict, the trier of fact must be satisfied that a reasonable person in similar circumstances ought to have been aware of the risk and of the danger involved in the conduct manifested by the accused. The objective *mens rea* is based on the premise that a reasonable person in the accused's position would have been aware of the risks arising from the conduct. The objective test must be modified to give the accused the benefit of any reasonable doubt about whether the reasonable person would have appreciated the risk or could and would have done something to avoid creating the danger. In addition, a reasonably held mistake of fact may provide a complete defence if, based on the accused's reasonable perception of the facts, the conduct measured up to the requisite standard of care. The modified objective test must be applied in the context of the events surrounding the incident. Personal attributes such as age, experience and education are not relevant. The reasonable person, however, must be put in the circumstances that the accused found himself in when the events occurred in order to assess the reasonableness of the conduct. See also *R. v. Roy* (2012), 281 C.C.C. (3d) 433 (S.C.C.), where in snowy and foggy conditions the accused had pulled onto a highway into the path of an oncoming tractor trailer, resulting in the death of his passenger. The accused had no memory of the collision. The accused's decision to pull onto the highway was consistent with a simple misjudgment and could not reasonably support an inference of a marked departure.

Under certain circumstances, excessive speed alone may be sufficient to constitute dangerous driving: *R. v. Richards* (2003), 174 C.C.C. (3d) 154, 169 O.A.C. 339 (C.A.).

A sleeping driver is not driving of their own volition and acts committed while in an automatic state of mind cannot form the *actus reus* of this offence. The elements of the offence are made out, however, where the driver embarked on driving in circumstances in which he knew or ought to have known that there was a real risk that he would fall asleep at the wheel: *R. v. Jiang* (2007), 220 C.C.C. (3d) 55, 48 C.R. (6th) 49 (B.C.C.A.).

A trier of fact is not precluded by issue estoppel from taking into consideration the consumption of alcohol by an accused in determining guilty on dangerous driving causing bodily harm, where the accused is acquitted of impaired driving in circumstances that arise from the same incident: *R. v. Settle* (2010), 261 C.C.C. (3d) 45 (B.C.C.A.).

Constitutional considerations – The offence created by subsec. (1)(*a*) is not unconstitutionally vague in violation of s. 7 of the *Charter of Rights and Freedoms*: *R. v. Demeyer* (1986), 27 C.C.C. (3d) 575, 40 M.V.R. 231 (Alta. C.A.).

Imposing liability for this offence on the basis of a modified objective test for fault does not infringe s. 7 of the Charter: *R. v. Hundal, supra.*

Causation (subsecs. (3) and (4)) – It was held in relation to the offence of criminal negligence causing death that the element of causation is satisfied if the evidence shows that the criminally negligent conduct of the accused meets the test in *R. v. Smithers*, [1978] 1 S.C.R. 506, 34 C.C.C. (2d) 427, being at least a contributing cause of death outside the *de minimis* range. It is misdirection to instruct the jury that the conduct must be shown to be a substantial cause: *R. v. Pinske* (1988), 30 B.C.L.R. (2d) 114, 6 M.V.R. (2d) 19 (B.C.C.A.), affd [1989] 2 S.C.R. 979, 100 N.R. 399. The *Smithers* test has been adopted for prosecutions under this section and the similar offences of impaired driving causing bodily harm or death under s. 255(2) and (3): *R. v. Larocque* (1988), 5 M.V.R. (2d) 221 (Ont. C.A.); *R. v. Halkett* (1988), 73 Sask. R. 241, 11 M.V.R. (2d) 109 (C.A.); *R. v. Singhal* (1988), 5 M.V.R. (2d) 173 (B.C.C.A.); *R. v. Arsenault* (1992), 16 C.R. (4th) 301, 104 Nfld. & P.E.I.R. 29 (P.E.I.C.A.); *R. v. Colby* (1989), 52 C.C.C. (3d) 321, 100 A.R. 142 (C.A.), and *R. v. Ewart* (1989), 53 C.C.C. (3d) 153, 100 A.R. 118 (C.A.), leave to appeal to S.C.C. refused 109 A.R. 320*n*. The court seems to have adopted a somewhat stricter test for causation in *R. v. F. (D.)* (1989), 52 C.C.C. (3d) 357, 73 C.R. (3d) 391 (C.A.).

In considering whether the *Smithers* test has been made out, reference should also now be made to *R. v. Nette*, [2001] 3 S.C.R. 488, 158 C.C.C. (3d) 486, where a majority of the court explained that causing death outside the *de minimis* range means that the acts of the accused were a significant contributing cause to the death.

FLIGHT / Punishment / Flight causing bodily harm or death / Punishment.

249.1 (1) Every one commits an offence who, operating a motor vehicle while being pursued by a peace officer operating a motor vehicle, fails, without reasonable excuse and in order to evade the peace officer, to stop the vehicle as soon as is reasonable in the circumstances.

(2) Every one who commits an offence under subsection (1)

> **(*a*) is guilty of an indictable offence and liable to imprisonment for a term not exceeding five years; or**

> **(*b*) is guilty of an offence punishable on summary conviction.**

(3) Every one commits an offence who causes bodily harm to or the death of another person by operating a motor vehicle in a manner described in paragraph 249(1)(*a*), if the person operating the motor vehicle was being pursued by a peace officer operating a motor vehicle and failed, without reasonable excuse and in order to evade the police officer, to stop the vehicle as soon as is reasonable in the circumstances.

(4) Every person who commits an offence under subsection (3)

> **(*a*) if bodily harm was caused, is guilty of an indictable offence and liable to imprisonment for a term not exceeding 14 years; and**

> **(*b*) if death was caused, is guilty of an indictable offence and liable to imprisonment for life. 2000, c. 2, s. 1.**

CROSS-REFERENCES

The terms "motor vehicle", "peace officer" and "bodily harm" are defined in s. 2. The term "operates" is defined in s. 214.

With respect to causation and death, see ss. 224 to 226. Section 662(5) makes the offences under this section included offences where the count charges an offence of criminal negligence causing death [s. 220], criminal negligence causing bodily harm [s. 221] or manslaughter [s. 236] arising out of the operation of a vehicle or navigation of a vessel or aircraft. The related offences of impaired driving causing death and bodily harm are found in s. 255. The offence of failing to stop at the scene of an accident is found in s. 252. The offence of dangerous operation is found in s. 249. The related offence of obstructing a peace office is found in s. 129.

Where the prosecution elects to proceed by indictment on the offence in subsec. (1), dangerous operation, the accused may elect his mode of trial pursuant to s. 536(2). Where the prosecution elects to proceed by way of summary conviction then the trial of this offence is conducted by a summary conviction court pursuant to Part XXVII. The punishment for the offence is then as set out in s. 787 and the limitation period is set out in s. 786(2). In either case, release pending trial is determined by s. 515, although the accused is eligible for release by a peace officer under ss. 496, 497 or by the officer in charge under s. 498. The accused has an election as to mode of trial of the offences in subsecs. (3). Release pending trial is determined by s. 515.

An accused found guilty of these offences may, pursuant to s. 259, be ordered prohibited from operating a motor vehicle. The length of the prohibition order is as follows: offence under subsec. (1), during any period not exceeding 3 years; offence under subsec. (4)(*a*), during any period not exceeding 10 years; offence under subsec. (4)(*b*), during any period that the court considers proper. The procedure respecting the making of the order of prohibition is found in s. 260. Evidence that the accused's blood alcohol level exceeded .16 at the time of the offence is deemed an aggravating factor, for purposes of sentencing, under s. 255.1.

SYNOPSIS

This section creates three offences of increasing gravity for motorists attempting to evade the police. The gravamen of each offence is failing without reasonable excuse to stop the motor vehicle as soon as is reasonable in the circumstances while being pursued by a peace officer. The offence requires proof of an intention (in order to) to evade the police officer. The flight offence *simpliciter* is a hybrid offence under subsec. (1).

Subsection (3) in effect creates an aggravated form of dangerous operation. Where the motorist not only engages in the conduct prohibited by subsec. (1), but operates the vehicle in a dangerous manner as described in s. 249 and causes death or bodily harm to another person, the motorist is liable to imprisonment for 14 years (where bodily harm caused) and life (where death caused).

CAUSING DEATH BY CRIMINAL NEGLIGENCE (STREET RACING).

249.2 Everyone who by criminal negligence causes death to another person while street racing is guilty of an indictable offence and liable to imprisonment for life. 2006, c. 14, s. 2.

CROSS-REFERENCES

The term "street-racing" is defined in s. 2. Criminal negligence is defined in s. 219. The general offence of criminal negligence causing death is set out in s. 220. The related offences of causing bodily harm by criminal negligence (street racing) and dangerous operation of a motor vehicle while street racing are set out in ss. 249.3 and 249.4 respectively. The driving prohibition for this offence is provided for in s. 259(3.3) and (3.4).

CAUSING BODILY HARM BY CRIMINAL NEGLIGENCE (STREET RACING).

249.3 Everyone who by criminal negligence causes bodily harm to another person while street racing is guilty of an indictable offence and liable to imprisonment for a term not exceeding fourteen years. 2006, c. 14, s. 2.

CROSS-REFERENCES

The term "street-racing" is defined in s. 2. Criminal negligence is defined in s. 219. The general offence of criminal negligence causing bodily harm is set out in s. 221. The related offences of causing death by criminal negligence (street racing) and dangerous operation of a motor vehicle while street racing are set out in ss. 249.2 and 249.4 respectively. The driving prohibition for this offence is provided for in s. 259(3.2) and (3.4).

DANGEROUS OPERATION OF MOTOR VEHICLE WHILE STREET RACING / Punishment / Dangerous operation causing bodily harm / Dangerous operation causing death.

249.4 (1) Everyone commits an offence who, while street racing, operates a motor vehicle in a manner described in paragraph 249(1)(*a*).

(2) Everyone who commits an offence under subsection (1)

    (*a*) **is guilty of an indictable offence and liable to imprisonment for a term not exceeding five years; or**

    (*b*) **is guilty of an offence punishable on summary conviction.**

(3) Everyone who commits an offence under subsection (1) and thereby causes bodily harm to another person is guilty of an indictable offence and liable to imprisonment for a term not exceeding fourteen years.

(4) Everyone who commits an offence under subsection (1) and thereby causes the death of another person is guilty of an indictable offence and liable to imprisonment for life. 2006, c. 14, s. 2.

CROSS-REFERENCES

The terms "motor vehicle" and "street-racing" are defined in s. 2. The general offence of dangerous operation of a motor vehicle is defined in s. 249. The related offences of causing death by criminal negligence (street racing) and causing bodily harm by criminal negligence while street racing are set out in ss. 249.2 and 249.3 respectively. The driving prohibition for this offence is provided for in s. 259(3.1) to (3.4).

SYNOPSIS

This section creates the offence of dangerous operation of a motor vehicle while street racing. Street racing is defined in s. 2 as operating a motor vehicle in a race with at least one other vehicle on a street, road, highway or other public place. The offence, however, depends upon, not only proof of street racing, but doing so in a manner that constitutes dangerous operation of a motor vehicle as defined in s. 249. Thus, in effect, this section creates enhanced penalties for dangerous operation where the accused is engaged in street racing. While the penalty for the basic offence is the same under this section as under s. 249(2), where the offence causes bodily harm or death, the penalties are higher under this section than under s. 249(3) and (4).

FAILURE TO KEEP WATCH ON PERSON TOWED / Towing of person after dark.

250. (1) Every one who operates a vessel while towing a person on any water skis, surfboard, water sled or other object, when there is not on board such vessel another responsible person keeping watch on the person being towed, is guilty of an offence punishable on summary conviction.

(2) Every one who operates a vessel while towing a person on any water skis, surfboard, water sled or other object during the period from one hour after sunset to sunrise is guilty of an offence punishable on summary conviction. R.S.C. 1985, c. 27 (1st Supp.), s. 36.

CROSS-REFERENCES

The term "vessel" is defined in s. 214. For special jurisdictional rules relating to offences committed on the water see s. 476. Also see s. 477 respecting offences committed on the territorial sea or on internal waters [defined in s. 3 of the *Territorial Sea and Fishing Zones Act*, R.S.C. 1985, c. T-8].

    The trial of these offences is conducted by a summary convictions court pursuant to Part XXVII. The punishment for the offence is then as set out in s. 787 and the limitation period is set out in s.

786(2). Release pending trial is determined by s. 515, although the accused is eligible for release by a peace officer under s. 496, 497 or by the officer in charge under s. 498. An accused convicted of this offence may, pursuant to s. 259, be ordered prohibited from operating a vessel during any period not exceeding 3 years. The procedure respecting the making of that order of prohibition is found in s. 260.

SYNOPSIS

A person who operates a vessel while towing another person on water skis, surf-board, water sled or other object is guilty of a summary conviction offence: (1) if there is not another responsible person watching the person being towed; or (2) if the towing takes place during the period from one hour after sunset to sunrise.

ANNOTATIONS

Subsection (1) does not apply to an accused being towed behind a remote controlled water-skiing device. While such device is a "vessel" within the meaning of the section, the provision contemplates that "every one" is a person who is actually on board the vessel: *R. v. Gatt* (1992), 72 C.C.C. (3d) 146 (B.C.S.C.).

UNSEAWORTHY VESSEL AND UNSAFE AIRCRAFT / Defences / Consent of Attorney General.

251. (1) Every one who knowingly

> (*a*) **sends or being the master takes a vessel that is registered or licensed, or for which an identification number has been issued, pursuant to any Act of Parliament and that is unseaworthy**
>> (i) **on a voyage from a place in Canada to any other place in or out of Canada, or**
>> (ii) **on a voyage from a place on the inland waters of the United States to a place in Canada,**
> (*b*) **sends an aircraft on a flight or operates an aircraft that is not fit and safe for flight, or**
> (*c*) **sends for operation or operates railway equipment that is not fit and safe for operation**

and thereby endangers the life of any person, is guilty of an indictable offence and liable to imprisonment for a term not exceeding five years.

(2) An accused shall not be convicted of an offence under this section where the accused establishes that,

> (*a*) **in the case of an offence under paragraph (1)(*a*),**
>> (i) **the accused used all reasonable means to ensure that the vessel was seaworthy, or**
>> (ii) **to send or take the vessel while it was unseaworthy was, under the circumstances, reasonable and justifiable;**
> (*b*) **in the case of an offence under paragraph (1)(*b*),**
>> (i) **the accused used all reasonable means to ensure that the aircraft was fit and safe for flight, or**
>> (ii) **to send or operate the aircraft while it was not fit and safe for flight was, under the circumstances, reasonable and justifiable; and**
> (*c*) **in the case of an offence under paragraph (1)(*c*),**
>> (i) **the accused used all reasonable means to ensure that the railway equipment was fit and safe for operation, or**
>> (ii) **to send the railway equipment for operation or to operate it while it was not fit and safe for operation was, under the circumstances, reasonable and justifiable.**

(3) No proceedings shall be instituted under this section in respect of a vessel or aircraft, or in respect of railway equipment sent for operation or operated on a line of railway that is within the legislative authority of Parliament, without the consent in writing of the Attorney General of Canada. R.S.C. 1985, c. 27 (1st Supp.), s. 36; c. 32 (4th Supp.), s. 58.

CROSS-REFERENCES

The terms "aircraft", "vessel" and "operates" are defined in s. 214. The term "railway equipment" is defined in s. 2. Section 583(*h*) provides that a count in an indictment is not insufficient by reason only that it does not state that the required consent has been obtained. [For notes on consent see s. 583.] The accused has an election as to mode of trial pursuant to s. 536(2). Release pending trial is determined by s. 515, although the accused is eligible for release by the officer in charge under s. 498.

An accused convicted of this offence may, pursuant to s. 259, be ordered prohibited from operating a motor vehicle, vessel, aircraft or railway equipment, as the case may be, during any period not exceeding 3 years. The procedure respecting the making of that order of prohibition is found in s. 260.

SYNOPSIS

This section makes it an indictable offence to endanger the life of any person by knowingly sending or taking a licensed or registered vessel that is unseaworthy on a voyage from a place in Canada to another place in or out of Canada or from a place on the inland waters of the United States to a place in Canada. Similarly, it is an indictable offence to endanger the life of any person by sending or operating an unfit or unsafe aircraft on a flight or by sending or operating railway equipment that is not fit and safe for operation. The maximum penalty for this offence is a term of imprisonment of five years. Subsection (2) provides that no criminal liability will attach to an accused person who establishes that he/she used all reasonable means to ensure that the vessel was seaworthy or that the aircraft or railway equipment was fit and safe. Furthermore, if an accused can establish that the operation of the unseaworthy vessel, or the unfit or unsafe aircraft or railway equipment was, under the circumstances, reasonable and justifiable, he/she cannot be convicted of this offence. The written consent of the Attorney General of Canada is necessary before any proceedings are instituted under this section.

FAILURE TO STOP AT SCENE OF ACCIDENT / Punishment / Offence involving bodily harm / Offence involving bodily harm or death / Evidence.

252. (1) Every person commits an offence who has the care, charge or control of a vehicle, vessel or aircraft that is involved in an accident with
   (*a*) another person,
   (*b*) a vehicle, vessel or aircraft, or
   (*c*) in the case of a vehicle, cattle in the charge of another person,
and with intent to escape civil or criminal liability fails to stop the vehicle, vessel or, if possible, the aircraft, give his or her name and address and, where any person has been injured or appears to require assistance, offer assistance.

(1.1) Every person who commits an offence under subsection (1) in a case not referred to in subsection (1.2) or (1.3) is guilty of an indictable offence and liable to imprisonment for a term not exceeding five years or is guilty of an offence punishable on summary conviction.

(1.2) Every person who commits an offence under subsection (1) knowing that bodily harm has been caused to another person involved in the accident is guilty of an indictable offence and liable to imprisonment for a term not exceeding ten years.

(1.3) Every person who commits an offence under subsection (1) is guilty of an indictable offence and liable to imprisonment for life if
  (*a*) the person knows that another person involved in the accident is dead; or
  (*b*) the person knows that bodily harm has been caused to another person involved in the accident and is reckless as to whether the death of the other person results from that bodily harm, and the death of that other person so results.

(2) In proceedings under subsection (1), evidence that an accused failed to stop his vehicle, vessel or, where possible, his aircraft, as the case may be, offer assistance where any person has been injured or appears to require assistance and give his name and address is, in the absence of evidence to the contrary, proof of an intent to escape civil or criminal liability. R.S.C. 1985, c. 27 (1st Supp.), s. 36; 1994, c. 44, s. 12; 1999, c. 32, s. 1.

CROSS-REFERENCES

The term "vehicle" is not defined, although "motor vehicle" is defined in s. 2. The terms "aircraft" and "vessel" are defined in s. 214.

Where the prosecution elects to proceed by indictment on the offence in subsec. (1) then the accused may elect his mode of trial pursuant to s. 536(2). Where the prosecution elects to proceed by way of summary conviction on the offence contrary to subsec. (1.1) then the trial of this offence is conducted by a summary conviction court pursuant to Part XXVII. The punishment for the offence is then as set out in s. 787 and the limitation period is set out in s. 786(2). In either case, release pending trial is determined by s. 515, although the accused is eligible for release by a peace officer under s. 496, 497 or by the officer in charge under s. 498. Where the offence involved the operation of a motor vehicle, vessel, aircraft or railway equipment then an accused found guilty of this offence may, pursuant to s. 259, be ordered prohibited from operating a motor vehicle, vessel, aircraft or railway equipment, as the case may be, during any period not exceeding 3 years. The procedure respecting the making of that order of prohibition is found in s. 260. Related offences: s. 249, dangerous operation; ss. 253 and 255, impaired operation and "over 80"; s. 254, failing to comply with screening device or breathalyzer demand; ss. 220 and 221, criminal negligence causing death or bodily harm.

The penalties for this offence were increased by S.C. 1999, c. 32. The transitional provisions of that Act provide that the lesser penalty or punishment applies in respect of any offence that was committed before the coming into force of the Act. Pursuant to s. 255.1, evidence that the accused's blood alcohol level exceeded .160 at the time when the offence was committed is deemed to be an aggravating factor on sentencing. Note s. 732.1(3)(*g*.1) and (*g*.2), which allow for terms of probation that the offender attend for curative treatment in relation to the consumption of alcohol and drugs and participate in an alcohol ignition interlock device program.

SYNOPSIS

This section makes it an offence, for any person who has the care, charge or control of a vehicle, vessel or aircraft that is involved in an accident with another person, vehicle, vessel or aircraft, to fail to stop at the scene of the accident in order to avoid civil or criminal liability. The person who is involved in the accident must give his name and address and, if there are injuries, offer assistance. By subsec. (2), uncontroverted evidence of his failure to do so is proof of an intent to escape civil or criminal liability. The offence contrary to subsec. (1.1) is hybrid and punishable on indictment by a maximum term of imprisonment of five years. Where the accused fails to stop knowing that bodily harm has been caused to another person, the offence is indictable and punishable by 10 years' imprisonment. Where the accused knows that another person is dead or knows that bodily harm has been caused and is reckless as to whether the death of the other person resulted from the bodily harm, the maximum punishment is life imprisonment.

ANNOTATIONS

Elements of offence generally – The offence is made out when it is established that the defendant failed to perform any one of the three statutory duties set out in the information. Furthermore, naming the defendant as the driver in the charge is within the designation of one who has care and control of the vehicle: *R. v. Steere* (1972), 6 C.C.C. (2d) 403, 19 C.R.N.S. 115 (B.C.C.A.).

Contemporaneous knowledge of the accident by the accused is an element of this offence which the Crown must prove. It is not sufficient that the accused "should have known" of the accident: *R. v. Slessor*, [1970] 2 C.C.C. 247, 7 C.R.N.S. 379 (Ont. C.A.); *R. v. Faulkner (No. 2)* (1977), 37 C.C.C. (2d) 217 (N.S. Co. Ct.).

In *R. v. Slessor, supra,* the majority divided on the liability of a passenger under this subsection. Gale C.J.O., held that a passenger in the vehicle, including the owner, who is asleep or otherwise unconscious at the time of an accident cannot be convicted of this offence unless, after the automobile has in fact been stopped in compliance with the section, the owner, upon regaining consciousness causes it to be driven off before the other requisites of the section are met. Further, *per* Gale C.J.O., apart from joint ventures, only one person in the car would have care, charge or control and if that person is the passenger he must have a degree of exercisable or exercised control over the actual driver. His Lordship would leave open the question whether the subsection is directed solely to the person who has care, charge or control at the moment of impact. Laskin J.A., held that the subsection could not apply to a person who did not have care, charge or control at the time the car was involved in the accident. Schroeder J.A., dissenting, held that if both the driver and the owner/passenger had care and control at the relevant time both could be liable for failing to comply with the subsection.

The court in *R. v. Shea* (1982), 17 M.V.R. 40, 37 Nfld. & P.E.I.R. 457 (Nfld. C.A.), considered that the law was correctly stated by Gale C.J.O. in *R. v. Slessor, supra,* and affirmed the acquittal of the owner of the vehicle because of the trial judge's finding that he only took over driving of the car some distance, albeit a short distance, from the accident scene.

Civil or criminal liability – The "civil or criminal liability" contemplated by this offence relates to liability which could arise from the accident not to some liability which the accused may have incurred prior to the accident, such as the risk of being arrested for a robbery: *R. v. Fournier* (1979), 8 C.R. (3d) 248 (Que. C.A.). Or the risk of being arrested on outstanding warrants for unpaid fines: *R. v. Hofer* (1982), 2 C.C.C. (3d) 236, 18 M.V.R. 230 (Sask. C.A.). Similarly, *R. v. MacLean* (1982), 40 Nfld. & P.E.I.R. 275, 18 M.V.R. 275 (P.E.I.S.C.), risk of being charged for driving while suspended. *Contra: R. v. Benson* (1987), 50 M.V.R. 131 (Ont. Dist. Ct.).

"Accident" – A deliberate act of mischief by the accused in relation to property, here lining up his car behind the car of another and then deliberately pushing it into a wall is not an "accident" within the meaning of this section: *R. v. O'Brien* (1987), 39 C.C.C. (3d) 528, 67 Nfld. & P.E.I.R. 68 (Nfld. S.C.T.D.).

The obligation to stop at the scene of an accident does not depend on the existence of damage or injury: *R. v. Chase* (2006), 209 C.C.C. (3d) 43 (B.C.C.A.).

This section does not apply where the accident involves the accused's car and a pole. The reference in subsec. (1)(*b*) is to another vehicle: *R. v. Vellow* (1990), 27 M.V.R. (2d) 59 (Ont. Ct. (Prov. Div.)).

Subsection (1)(*a*) – "Another person" includes a passenger in a single vehicle accident: *R. v. McColl* (2008), 235 C.C.C. (3d) 319, 60 C.R. (6th) 78 (Alta. C.A.).

Admissibility of statement – The existence of the statutory duty under this subsection does not dispense with the onus upon the Crown to establish that any statement made was not otherwise involuntary: *R. v. Fex* (1973), 14 C.C.C. (2d) 188, 23 C.R.N.S. 368 (Ont. C.A.), and *R. v. Cleavely* (1966), 49 C.R. 326, 57 W.W.R. 301 (Sask. Q.B.). *Contra: R. v. Smith*

(1973), 15 C.C.C. (2d) 113, 25 C.R.N.S. 246 (Alta. C.A.). Also see *R. v. White*, [1999] 2 S.C.R. 417, 135 C.C.C. (3d) 257, noted under s. 7 of the *Canadian Charter of Rights and Freedoms*.

Presumption of intent [subsec. (2)] – This subsection is to be read disjunctively and thus the presumption applies where the accused fails to perform any of the three duties imposed on him: *R. v. Roche*, [1983] 1 S.C.R. 491, 3 C.C.C. (3d) 193 (7:0).

As to the meaning of the phrase "in the absence of any evidence to the contrary", see *R. v. Proudlock*, [1979] 1 S.C.R. 525, 43 C.C.C. (2d) 321, noted under s. 348, *infra*.

Evidence which is not rejected by the trier of fact and which tends to show that the accused may not have had the requisite intent is evidence to the contrary. Evidence of drunkenness may constitute evidence to the contrary: *R. v. Nolet (Charette)* (1980), 4 M.V.R. 265 (Ont. C.A.).

Evidence that the accused, prior to walking away from the scene of the accident, was under the influence of alcohol and unresponsive to questions was capable of being evidence to the contrary and thus rebut the presumption: *R. v. Adler* (1981), 59 C.C.C. (2d) 517, [1981] 4 W.W.R. 379 (Sask. C.A.).

Constitutional considerations – This subsection is not an unconstitutional infringement on the guarantee to the presumption of innocence in s. 11(*d*) of the *Canadian Charter of Rights and Freedoms*: *R. v. T.* (1985), 18 C.C.C. (3d) 125, 43 C.R. (3d) 307 (N.S. S.C. App. Div.); *R. v. Gosselin* (1988), 45 C.C.C. (3d) 568, 9 M.V.R. (2d) 290 (Ont. C.A.).

OPERATING WHILE IMPAIRED / For greater certainty.

253. (1) Every one commits an offence who operates a motor vehicle or vessel or operates or assists in the operation of an aircraft or of railway equipment or has the care or control of a motor vehicle, vessel, aircraft or railway equipment, whether it is in motion or not,

    (*a*) **while the person's ability to operate the vehicle, vessel, aircraft or railway equipment is impaired by alcohol or a drug; or**

    (*b*) **having consumed alcohol in such a quantity that the concentration in the person's blood exceeds eighty milligrams of alcohol in one hundred millilitres of blood.**

(2) For greater certainty, the reference to impairment by alcohol or a drug in paragraph (1)(*a*) includes impairment by a combination of alcohol and a drug. R.S.C. 1985, c. 27 (1st Supp.), s. 36; c. 32 (4th Supp.), s. 59; 2008, c. 6, s. 18.

CROSS-REFERENCES

The terms "motor vehicle" and "railway equipment" are defined in s. 2. The terms "aircraft", "vessel" and "operate" are defined in s. 214. The presumption respecting "care or control" is found in s. 258(1)(*a*). Procedure for making a breathalyzer or approved screening device [A.L.E.R.T.] demand is found in s. 254 and for obtaining a warrant to obtain blood samples in s. 256. The adverse inference respecting the impaired offence for failing to comply with a demand under s. 254 is found in s. 258(3). The presumptions respecting the accused's blood alcohol level arising from analysis of a breath sample or blood sample are found in s. 258(1)(*c*), (*d*), (*d*.01) and (*d*.1). Procedure for admission of certificates of an analyst, qualified technician and medical practitioner is in s. 258(1)(*e*) to (*i*) and (6) and (7).

The punishment for these offences is set out in s. 255. Evidence that the accused's blood alcohol level exceeded .16 at the time of the offence is deemed to be an aggravating factor, for purposes of sentencing, under s. 255.1. Where the prosecution elects to proceed by indictment on this offence then the accused may elect his mode of trial pursuant to s. 536(2). Where the prosecution elects to proceed by way of summary conviction then the trial of this offence is conducted by a summary conviction court pursuant to Part XXVII. In either case, release pending trial is determined by s. 515, although the accused is eligible for release by a peace officer under s. 496, 497 or by the officer in charge under s. 498. Where the accused is charged with impaired operation causing death or causing bodily harm under s. 255(2) or (3) then he has an election as to mode of trial pursuant to s. 536(2) and release pending trial is determined by s. 515. An accused found guilty of this offence is subject to an order prohibiting him from operating a motor vehicle, vessel, aircraft or railway equipment, as the case may be. The length of the order is as follows: for a first offence, during a period of not more than three years and not less than one year; for a second offence, during a period of not more than five years and not less than two years; for each subsequent offence, during a period of not less than three years plus any period to which the offender is sentenced to imprisonment. For prohibition order where the accused is convicted of the offence of impaired causing bodily harm or causing death, see notes under s. 255. The procedure respecting the making of that order of prohibition is found in s. 260.

SYNOPSIS

This section makes it an offence for a person to operate a motor vehicle or vessel, operate or assist in the operation of an aircraft or railway equipment or have the care or control of a motor vehicle, vessel, aircraft or railway equipment, if that peron's ability to do so is impaired by alcohol or a drug or if that person has a concentration of alcohol in the blood exceeding eighty milligrams of alcohol in one hundred millilitres of blood. The fact that the motor vehicle, vessel, aircraft or railway equipment is not in motion is not a defence. Subsection (2) makes it clear that impairment can arise from a combination of alcohol and a drug.

ANNOTATIONS

Proof of care or control / *Also see notes under s. 258(1)(a)* – An intention to drive is not an element of the care or control offence. Care or control may be exercised without such intent where the accused performs some act or series of acts involving the use of the car, its fittings or equipment, whereby the vehicle may unintentionally be set in motion creating the danger this section is designed to prevent: *R. v. Ford*, [1982] 1 S.C.R. 231, 65 C.C.C. (2d) 392 (7:2).

"Care or control" signifies: (1) an intentional course of conduct associated with a motor vehicle; (2) by a person whose ability to drive is impaired, or whose blood alcohol level exceeds the legal limit; (3) in circumstances that create a realistic risk of danger to persons or property. The risk of danger must be realistic and not just theoretically possible. Parliament's objective in enacting this provision was to prevent the risk of danger to public safety that normally arises from the mere combination of alcohol and automobile. Conduct that presents no such risk falls outside the intended reach of the offence. Here, the judge did not err in acquitting an accused who fell asleep in his truck with the engine running while waiting for a taxi: *R. v. Boudreault*, [2012] 3 S.C.R. 157, 290 C.C.C. (3d) 222.

To convict the accused of the care or control offence, it is not necessary to establish some overt action on the part of the accused to indicate that he was involved with the vehicle in a way as to cause danger to the public. Where the accused had the immediate capacity and means of operating the vehicle, there existed the risk that he would put it in motion and become a danger to the public, even though at the time he was found by the police he was asleep in the front seat of the vehicle: *R. v. Diotte* (1991), 64 C.C.C. (3d) 209 (N.B.C.A.). See also *R. v. Rousseau* (1997), 121 C.C.C. (3d) 571 (Que. C.A.).

The intent to drive or the presence of danger is an essential element of the offence. If the person's interaction with the vehicle did not pose an immediate or potential risk of harm or risk to public safety, a conviction cannot be made out: *R. v. Mallery* (2008), 231 C.C.C. (3d) 203, 59 C.R. (6th) 209 (N.B.C.A.).

A course of conduct associated with the vehicle that would involve the risk of putting the vehicle in motion can constitute care and control. Accordingly, care and control was established where the accused was asleep in the driver's seat with the keys on the floor of the vehicle: *R. v. Pilon* (1998), 131 C.C.C. (3d) 236, 115 O.A.C. 324 (C.A.).

The mere fact that an individual is a custodian of a vehicle does not alone constitute care and control. There must be a risk of danger that the car might be put in motion or of other danger. Where there is no risk that the vehicle will unintentionally be set in motion or any other risk, care and control is not established: *R. v. Decker* (2002), 162 C.C.C. (3d) 503, 2 C.R. (6th) 352 (Nfld. C.A.), leave to appeal to S.C.C. refused [2004] 4 S.C.R. vi, 231 Nfld. & P.E.I.R. 355*n*.

Motor vehicle – The decision of the Supreme Court of Canada in *R. v. Saunders*, [1967] 3 C.C.C. 278, 1 C.R.N.S. 249, that the definition of a motor vehicle in s. 2 contemplates a kind of vehicle, not whether a vehicle is actually operable or effectively functionable, now renders irrelevant all the previous decisions on when a motor vehicle is a motor vehicle in spite of internal or external conditions causing malfunctioning or immobilization of the vehicle.

An automobile which is out of gas is still a motor vehicle for the purposes of this section: *R. v. Lloyd*, [1988] 4 W.W.R. 423, 6 M.V.R. (2d) 240 (Sask. C.A.).

On this issue, also see the note by J. Watson, "Proving the Actus Reus of Motor Vehicle Crimes: What is a Motor Vehicle?", 21 M.V.R. (2d) 93.

Operation of vessel – In *R. v. Wade* (1975), 23 C.C.C. (2d) 572 (N.S. Co. Ct.), it was considered that a dragger immobilized by its fishing nets being entangled around other vessels' mooring cables was not then navigated or operated by its captain.

However, a person "operates" a vessel which is merely drifting with its engine turned off: *R. v. Ernst* (1979), 50 C.C.C. (2d) 320, 34 N.S.R. (2d) 318 (C.A.).

Proof of impairment (para. (*a*)) – The *Criminal Code* does not prescribe any special test for determining impairment such as a "marked departure" from normal behaviour. If the evidence of impairment establishes any degree of impairment ranging from slight to great, the offence is made out: *R. v. Stellato* (1993), 78 C.C.C. (3d) 380, 18 C.R. (4th) 127 (Ont. C.A.), affd [1994] 2 S.C.R. 478*n*, 90 C.C.C. (3d) 160*n*.

It cannot be assumed, however, that, where a person's functional ability is affected in some respects by the consumption of alcohol, his ability to drive is also automatically impaired. Where the proof of impairment consists of observations of conduct, in most cases, if the conduct is a slight departure from normal conduct, it would be unsafe to conclude beyond a reasonable doubt that the ability to drive was impaired by alcohol: *R. v. Andrews* (1996), 104 C.C.C. (3d) 392, 110 W.A.C. 182 (Alta. C.A.), leave to appeal to S.C.C. refused 106 C.C.C. (3d) vi, 135 W.A.C. 79*n*.

An accused may be convicted of this offence although his impaired condition is due partly to fatigue and partly to the consumption of alcohol: *R. v. Pelletier* (1989), 51 C.C.C. (3d) 161 (Sask. Q.B.).

On a charge of impaired driving the trial judge was entitled to take the certificate of analysis into account as part of the whole case and as evidence that prior to being stopped the accused most likely had consumed alcohol. In so doing the judge was not drawing on any technical or special knowledge: *R. v. Dinelle* (1986), 44 M.V.R. 109 (N.S.C.A.).

The word "drug" includes not only drugs in the medicinal sense, but any substance consumed which will bring about the impairment contemplated by this section. In particular the word includes the ingredient in glue which produces a "high" from glue sniffing and which may impair a person's ability to drive: *R. v. Marionchuk* (1978), 42 C.C.C. (2d) 573, 4 C.R. (3d) 178 (Sask. C.A.).

Admissibility of opinion evidence of impairment – A qualified breathalyzer technician is not, without further credentials, capable of relating the defendant's reading to his ability to operate a motor vehicle: *R. v. Edson* (1976), 30 C.C.C. (2d) 470, [1976] 3 W.W.R. 695 (B.C. Co. Ct.).

A layman or police officer may give his opinion based on his own observations as to whether or not the accused's ability to drive was impaired. However, a police officer's opinion is entitled to no special regard: *R. v. Graat*, [1982] 2 S.C.R. 819, 2 C.C.C. (3d) 365 (7:0).

R. v. Graat, supra, was applied in *R. v. Polturak* (1988), 9 M.V.R. (2d) 89, 90 A.R. 158 (C.A.), upholding the admission of the opinion of police officers with experience in narcotics control that the accused's ability to drive was impaired by drugs or drugs and alcohol.

Mens rea of impairment offence – In *R. v. King,* [1962] S.C.R. 746, 133 C.C.C. 1, an appeal by the Crown, affirming 129 C.C.C. 391, 34 C.R. 264, the question before the court was whether *mens rea* relating to both the act of driving and to the state of being impaired by alcohol or a drug is an essential ingredient of the offence of impaired driving. Ritchie J. (Martland J., concurring), decided that neither necessary implication nor express language disclosed any intention of Parliament to rule out *mens rea* as an essential ingredient of this offence but was of the opinion that (at p. 19 C.C.C.):

> . . . that element need not necessarily be present in relation both to the act of driving and to the state of being impaired in order to make the offence complete. That is to say, that a man who becomes impaired as the result of taking a drug on medical advice without knowing its effect cannot escape liability if he became aware of his impaired condition before he started to drive his car just as a man who did not appreciate his impaired condition when he started to drive cannot escape liability on the ground that his lack of appreciation was brought about by voluntary consumption of liquor or drug.

The *mens rea* for the care or control offence is the intent to assume care or control after the voluntary consumption of alcohol or a drug and the *actus reus* is the act of assumption of care or control when the voluntary consumption of alcohol or a drug has impaired the ability to drive: *R. v. Toews,* [1985] 2 S.C.R. 119, 21 C.C.C. (3d) 24 (7:0).

Thus, the necessary *mens rea* was established where the accused voluntarily consumed a sedative drug which he knew might impair his ability to drive even if the accused as a result of previous experience believed the drug would not take effect until he completed driving: *R. v. Murray* (1985), 22 C.C.C. (3d) 502, 36 M.V.R. 12 (Ont. C.A.). In addition, the intent to become voluntarily intoxicated includes recklessness where the accused was aware that impairment could result, but persisted despite the risk: *R. v. Mavin* (1997), 119 C.C.C. (3d) 38, 154 Nfld. & P.E.I.R. 242 (Nfld. C.A.).

Drunkenness is no defence to the charge of impaired care or control under para. (*a*). The only mental element involved in the offence is voluntary intoxication: *R. v. Penno,* [1990] 2 S.C.R. 865, 59 C.C.C. (3d) 344 (7:0).

Even where the accused is in a state of automatism or "near automatism" brought about by the consumption of intoxicants, it would seem that this is no defence to the charge: *R. v. Honish* (1991), 68 C.C.C. (3d) 329 (Alta. C.A.).

Mens rea of "over 80" offence [para. (*b*)] – The requirement and the actual proof of *mens rea* are two different matters. This offence requires *mens rea,* but once there is established driving with an excessive amount of alcohol in his system the defendant then faces the rebuttable presumption of *mens rea* which may be negated by defence evidence. A mistaken belief by the accused, based on an inaccurate chart as to the progressive absorption of alcohol into the blood, that his blood-alcohol would not exceed .08 was held not to be a defence to this charge: *R. v. Penner* (1974), 16 C.C.C. (2d) 334, [1974] 3 W.W.R. 176 (Man. C.A.).

The requisite *mens rea* or fault for this offence is supplied by proof of the accused's voluntary consumption of alcohol. It is not necessary to prove that the accused either knew or was reckless to the fact that his blood-alcohol exceeded the legal limit: *R. v. MacCannell* (1980), 54 C.C.C. (2d) 188, 6 M.V.R. 19 (Ont. C.A.). Folld: *R. v. Lynch* (1982), 69 C.C.C. (2d) 88, 38 Nfld. & P.E.I.R. 267 (Nfld. C.A.): *R. v. Patterson* (1982), 69 C.C.C. (2d) 274, 15 M.V.R. 283 (N.S.C.A.).

Proof of "over 80" offence – Where the Crown is unable to rely on the presumption in s. 258(1)(*c*) the court cannot take judicial notice of the progressive absorption of alcohol into the blood to prove that a blood-alcohol reading which exceeded .08 at the time of the test exceeded .08 at the time of the offence: *R. v. Stevenson* (1972), 14 C.C.C. (2d) 412 (B.C.C.A.); *R. v. McBurney* (1974), 21 C.C.C. (2d) 207, [1975] 2 W.W.R. 448 (Man. C.A.);

R. v. Chandok (1973), 12 C.C.C. (2d) 500 (N.S. Co. Ct.); *R. v. Wolff* (1976), 31 C.C.C. (2d) 337 (Ont. H.C.J.). In the latter case it was also held that the evidence that the accused displayed obvious signs of impairment likewise did not prove the offence under this section, following *R. v. Coach* (1971), 4 C.C.C. (2d) 333, [1971] 3 O.R. 466 (H.C.J.). Similarly, *R. v. Robertson* (1979), 47 C.C.C. (2d) 159 (B.C.C.A.).

Where the *viva voce* evidence of the intoxilyzer technician was adduced instead of, or in addition to, the filing of the certificate, there was no need to rely on the presumption of accuracy. Accordingly, the trial judge did not err in considering the breathalyzer results when assessing the credibility of the defence: *R. v. Chow* (2010), 260 C.C.C. (3d) 289 (Ont. C.A.).

In *R. v. Perossa* (1974), 19 C.C.C. (2d) 553 (B.C.S.C.), a conviction for this offence was upheld despite the lack of expert evidence relating the results of analysis of a blood sample back to the time of the offence where there was evidence of erratic driving and a high degree of intoxication. In view of this other evidence the court distinguished *R. v. Stevenson, supra.*

When the toxicologist's opinion that the accused's blood-alcohol level exceeded 80 mg of alcohol at the time of driving was dependent on the assumption that the accused had not been drinking large quantities of alcohol immediately before being stopped, the Crown was required to prove the lack of such drinking by the accused. There was no burden on the accused to show that he had not been drinking immediately before being stopped nor was there a basis to create a presumption that in absence of evidence to the contrary, the accused is deemed not to have consumed large quantities of alcohol immediately before providing a breath sample. The trial judge was entitled, however, to consider the circumstantial evidence in determining whether the Crown had met the burden and could take into account the accused's failure to to testify about what would be an unusual drinking pattern: *R. v. Grosse* (1996), 107 C.C.C. (3d) 97, 91 O.A.C. 40 (C.A.), leave to appeal to S.C.C. refused 112 C.C.C. (3d) vi, 99 O.A.C. 239n.

In *R. v. Paszczenko; R. v. Lima* (2010), 81 C.R. (6th) 97 (Ont. C.A.), the Court of Appeal reiterated that the trier of fact is entitled to make a "common sense" inference of no "bolus drinking" where the accused has not pointed to anything in the evidence to suggest such an unusual drinking pattern. The court was also "inclined to the view" that courts are entitled to take judicial notice of the fact that (a) the majority of human beings eliminate alcohol in a range of 10-20 milligrams of alcohol per 100 millilitres of blood per hour, and (b) after rising relatively quickly during the first 30 minutes or so after the last drink, a person's BAC generally hits a plateau for a period of up to two hours, during which time the absorption rate and the elimination rate remain about equal and the BAC neither rises nor falls. See also: *R. v. Saul* (2015), 322 C.C.C. (3d) 356 (B.C.C.A.).

Pursuant to this section, breathalzyer results must be determined on the basis of milligrams of alcohol per 100 ml of blood and cannot be expressed as "grams percent": *R. v. Nyman* (1998), 131 C.C.C. (3d) 124, 113 O.A.C. 356 (C.A.).

In *R. v. Doell* (2007), 221 C.C.C. (3d) 336, the Saskatchewan Court of Appeal held that *R. v. Boucher* (2005), 202 C.C.C. (3d) 34 (S.C.C.), stood for the proposition that breath test results cannot be used to assess the credibility of a witness in the context of the inquiry into whether the accused has presented evidence to the contrary. It did not address, however, the question of whether those test results may be considered in determining if a .08 offence has been established. If evidence to the contrary is adduced and the presumption set aside, both breathalyzer and roadside test results may nonetheless be considered in determining whether an offence has been made out.

Included offences – The care or control offence is included in the offence of driving and thus an accused charged with the driving offence may be convicted of the care and control offence: *R. v. Drolet* (1988), 20 Q.A.C. 94, [1989] R.J.Q. 295 (C.A.), affd [1990] 2 S.C.R. 1107n. Where the charge is care or control evidence that the accused was in fact driving may be sufficient to sustain the conviction on the charge as laid: *R. v. Coultis* (1982), 66 C.C.C. (2d) 385, 29 C.R. (3d) 189 (Ont. C.A.); *R. v. Pielle* (1982), 18 M.V.R. 46 (B.C.S.C.).

However, where the Crown's case on a charge of care or control is based on evidence of the finding of the accused in the driver's seat, a conviction may not be entered on an admission by the accused that at some time prior to his arrest he had been driving the vehicle. The Crown is bound by the case it presents to the court and when it fails to prove that case, the accused having successfully rebutted the presumption in s. 258(1)(*a*), it cannot ask for a conviction of another offence disclosed by the accused's own evidence: *R. v. Pendleton* (1982), 1 C.C.C. (3d) 228 (Ont. C.A.).

In a case subsequent to the enactment of this section it has been held that para. (*b*) creates two separate offences, of operating and have care and control, of equal gravity and the care or control offence is not included in the operating offence: *R. v. Pitcher* (1988), 70 Nfld. & P.E.I.R. 96 (Nfld. C.A.).

Where the trial judge finds that although the accused has consumed alcohol he has a reasonable doubt as to her impairment and thus acquits on the charge contrary to para. (*a*), he may still convict on the charge under para. (*b*). In such circumstances the doctrine of issue estoppel has no application so as to bar a conviction on the latter offence: *R. v. Casson* (1976), 30 C.C.C. (2d) 506 (Alta. C.A.).

Multiple convictions – A motorist cannot be convicted of both offences under this section occurring at one time: *R. v. Houchen* (1976), 31 C.C.C. (2d) 274 (B.C.C.A.) (2:1); *R. v. Boivin* (1976), 34 C.C.C. (2d) 203 (Que. C.A.).

A motorist may not choose which of the over-80 or ability-impaired charges he will plead guilty to; the court will first dispose of the charge on which the Crown seeks a conviction: *R. v. Butler* (1975), 27 C.C.C. (2d) 26 (B.C. Prov. Ct.).

A 24-hour driving suspension imposed under provincial legislation does not bar a conviction under this section although the suspension and the charge under this section arose out of the same incident: *R. v. Art* (1987), 39 C.C.C. (3d) 563 (B.C.C.A.).

Charging offence – In *R. v. Hawryluk,* [1967] 3 C.C.C. 356 (Sask. C.A.), an information that followed the wording of the statute, "while his ability to drive a motor vehicle was impaired by alcohol or a drug, did unlawfully drive a motor vehicle", was held to be valid as it only charged one of the two alternative offences of driving while impaired or having the care or control of a motor vehicle while impaired, and as each offence may be committed in more than one way it is proper to set out both factors, "by alcohol or drug", in the charge.

DEFINITIONS / "analyst" / "approved container" / "approved instrument" / "approved screening device" / "evaluating officer" / "qualified medical practitioner" / "qualified technician" / Testing for presence of alcohol or a drug / Video recording / Samples of breath or blood / Evaluation / Video recording / Testing for presence of alcohol / Samples of bodily substances / Condition / Failure or refusal to comply with demand / Only one determination of guilt.

254. (1) In this section and sections 254.1 to 258.1,

"analyst" means a person designated by the Attorney General as an analyst for the purposes of section 258;

"approved container" means

> **(*a*) in respect of breath samples, a container of a kind that is designed to receive a sample of the breath of a person for analysis and is approved as suitable for the purposes of section 258 by order of the Attorney General of Canada, and**

> **(*b*) in respect of blood samples, a container of a kind that is designed to receive a sample of the blood of a person for analysis and is approved as suitable for the purposes of section 258 by order of the Attorney General of Canada;**

REGULATIONS: ORDER APPROVING BLOOD SAMPLE CONTAINERS
Approved Containers

1. The following containers, being containers of a kind that is designed to receive a sample of blood of a person for analysis, are hereby approved as suitable, in respect of blood samples, for the purposes of section 258 of the *Criminal Code*:

(a) Vacutainer® XF947;

(b) BD Vacutainer TM 367001;

(c) Vacutainer® 367001;

(d) Tri-Tech Inc. TUG10;

(e) BD Vacutainer® REF 367001; and

(f) TRITECHFORENSICS TUG10.

Repeal

2. The Approved Blood Sample Container Order is repealed.

Coming into force

3. This Order comes into force on the day on which it is registered. **SOR/2005-37; SOR/2010-64, s. 1; SOR/2012-60, s. 1.**

"approved instrument" means an instrument of a kind that is designed to receive and make an analysis of a sample of the breath of a person in order to measure the concentration of alcohol in the blood of that person and is approved as suitable for the purposes of section 258 by order of the Attorney General of Canada;

REGULATIONS: APPROVED BREATH ANALYSIS INSTRUMENTS ORDER

Approved Instruments

2. The following instruments, each being an instrument of a kind that is designed to receive and make an analysis of a sample of the breath of a person in order to measure the concentration of alcohol in the blood of that person, are hereby approved as suitable for the purposes of section 258 of the *Criminal Code*:

(a) [*Repealed*, SOR/2012-237, s. 1(1).]

(b) [*Repealed*, SOR/2012-237, s. 1(1).]

(c) [*Repealed*, SOR/2012-237, s. 1(1).]

(d) [*Repealed*, SOR/2013-107, s. 1(1).]

(e) [*Repealed*, SOR/2013-107, s. 1(1).]

(f) [*Repealed*, SOR/2013-107, s. 1(1).]

(g) [*Repealed*, SOR/2013-107, s. 1(1).]

(h) Intoxilyzer® 5000C;

(i) [*Repealed*, SOR/2012-237, s. 1(2).]

(j) [*Repealed*, SOR/2013-107, s. 1(2).]

(k) BAC Datamaster C;

(l) Alco-Sensor IV-RBT IV;

(m) [*Repealed*, SOR/2013-107, s. 1(3).]

(n) Alco-Sensor IV/RBT IV-K;

(o) Alcotest 7110 MKIII Dual C;

(p) Intoxilyzer® 8000 C;

(q) DataMaster DMT-C; and

(r) Intox EC/IR II.

SI/85-201, *Can. Gaz. Part II*, 27/11/85, p. 4692; SI/92-105, *Can. Gaz. Part II*, 17/6/92, p. 2577; SI/92-167, *Can. Gaz. Part II*, 23/9/92, p. 3807; SI/93-61, *Can. Gaz., Part II*, 5/5/93, p. 2198; SI/93-175, *Can. Gaz., Part II*, 8/9/93, p. 3714; SOR/94-422, *Can. Gaz., Part II*, 15/6/94, p. 2451; SOR/94-572, *Can. Gaz., Part II*, 7/9/94, p. 3132; SOR/95-312, *Can. Gaz., Part II*, 12/7/95, p. 1885; SOR/2000-200, *Can. Gaz., Part II*, s. 1; SOR/2002-99, *Can. Gaz., Part II*, s. 1; SOR/2007-197, s. 1; SOR/2008-106, s. 1; SOR/2009-205, s. 1; SOR/2012-237, s. 1; SOR/2013-107, s. 1.

"approved screening device" means a device of a kind that is designed to ascertain the presence of alcohol in the blood of a person and that is approved for the purposes of this section by order of the Attorney General of Canada;

REGULATIONS: APPROVED SCREENING DEVICES ORDER
Approved Screening Devices

2. The following devices, each being a device of a kind that is designed to ascertain the presence of alcohol in the blood of a person, are hereby approved for the purposes of section 254 of the *Criminal Code*:

(a)   Alcolmeter S-L2;

(b)   Alco-Sûr;

(c)   Alcotest® 7410 PA3;

(d)   Alcotest® 7410 GLC;

(e)   Alco-Sensor IV DWF;

(f)   Alco-Sensor IV PWF;

(g)   Intoxilyzer 400D;

(h)   Alco-Sensor FST; and

(i)   Dräger Alcotest 6810.

SI/85-200, *Can. Gaz. Part II*, 27/11/85, p. 4691; SI/88-136, *Can. Gaz. Part II*, 28/9/88, p. 4074; SOR/93-263, *Can. Gaz., Part II*, 2/6/93, p. 2403; SOR/94-193, *Can. Gaz., Part II*, 9/3/94, p. 1232; SOR/94-423, *Can. Gaz., Part II*, 15/6/94, p. 2453; SOR/96-81, *Can. Gaz., Part II*, 24/1/96, p. 609; SOR/97-116, *Can. Gaz., Part II*, 53/97, p. 649; SOR/2009-239, s. 1; SOR/2011-313, s. 1; SOR/2012-61, s. 1.

"evaluating officer" means a peace officer who is qualified under the regulations to conduct evaluations under subsection (3.1);

"qualified medical practitioner" means a person duly qualified by provincial law to practise medicine;

"qualified technician" means,

(a)   in respect of breath samples, a person designated by the Attorney General as being qualified to operate an approved instrument, and

(b)   in respect of blood samples, any person or person of a class of persons designated by the Attorney General as being qualified to take samples of blood for the purposes of this section and sections 256 and 258.

(2) If a peace officer has reasonable grounds to suspect that a person has alcohol or a drug in their body and that the person has, within the preceding three hours, operated a motor vehicle or vessel, operated or assisted in the operation of an aircraft or railway equipment or had the care or control of a motor vehicle, a vessel, an aircraft or railway equipment, whether it was in motion or not, the peace officer may, by demand, require the person to comply with paragraph (a), in the case of a drug, or with either or both of paragraphs (a) and (b), in the case of alcohol:

(a)   to perform forthwith physical coordination tests prescribed by regulation to enable the peace officer to determine whether a demand may be made under subsection (3) or (3.1) and, if necessary, to accompany the peace officer for that purpose; and

(b)   to provide forthwith a sample of breath that, in the peace officer's opinion, will enable a proper analysis to be made by means of an approved screening device and, if necessary, to accompany the peace officer for that purpose.

(2.1) For greater certainty, a peace officer may make a video recording of a performance of the physical coordination tests referred to in paragraph (2)(a).

(3) If a peace officer has reasonable grounds to believe that a person is committing, or at any time within the preceding three hours has committed, an offence under section 253 as a result of the consumption of alcohol, the peace officer may, by demand made as soon as practicable, require the person

   (*a*) to provide, as soon as practicable,

      (i) samples of breath that, in a qualified technician's opinion, will enable a proper analysis to be made to determine the concentration, if any, of alcohol in the person's blood, or

      (ii) if the peace officer has reasonable grounds to believe that, because of their physical condition, the person may be incapable of providing a sample of breath or it would be impracticable to obtain a sample of breath, samples of blood that, in the opinion of the qualified medical practitioner or qualified technician taking the samples, will enable a proper analysis to be made to determine the concentration, if any, of alcohol in the person's blood; and

   (*b*) if necessary, to accompany the peace officer for that purpose.

(3.1) If a peace officer has reasonable grounds to believe that a person is committing, or at any time within the preceding three hours has committed, an offence under paragraph 253(1)(*a*) as a result of the consumption of a drug or of a combination of alcohol and a drug, the peace officer may, by demand made as soon as practicable, require the person to submit, as soon as practicable, to an evaluation conducted by an evaluating officer to determine whether the person's ability to operate a motor vehicle, a vessel, an aircraft or railway equipment is impaired by a drug or by a combination of alcohol and a drug, and to accompany the peace officer for that purpose.

(3.2) For greater certainty, a peace officer may make a video recording of an evaluation referred to in subsection (3.1).

(3.3) If the evaluating officer has reasonable grounds to suspect that the person has alcohol in their body and if a demand was not made under paragraph (2)(*b*) or subsection (3), the evaluating officer may, by demand made as soon as practicable, require the person to provide, as soon as practicable, a sample of breath that, in the evaluating officer's opinion, will enable a proper analysis to be made by means of an approved instrument.

(3.4) If, on completion of the evaluation, the evaluating officer has reasonable grounds to believe, based on the evaluation, that the person's ability to operate a motor vehicle, a vessel, an aircraft or railway equipment is impaired by a drug or by a combination of alcohol and a drug, the evaluating officer may, by demand made as soon as practicable, require the person to provide, as soon as practicable,

   (*a*) a sample of either oral fluid or urine that, in the evaluating officer's opinion, will enable a proper analysis to be made to determine whether the person has a drug in their body; or

   (*b*) samples of blood that, in the opinion of the qualified medical practitioner or qualified technician taking the samples, will enable a proper analysis to be made to determine whether the person has a drug in their body.

(4) Samples of blood may be taken from a person under subsection (3) or (3.4) only by or under the direction of a qualified medical practitioner who is satisfied that taking the samples would not endanger the person's life or health.

(5) Everyone commits an offence who, without reasonable excuse, fails or refuses to comply with a demand made under this section.

(6) A person who is convicted of an offence under subsection (5) for a failure or refusal to comply with a demand may not be convicted of another offence under that subsection in respect of the same transaction. R.S.C. 1985, c. 27 (1st Supp.), s. 36; c. 1 (4th Supp.), s. 14; c. 32 (4th Supp.), s. 60; 1999, c. 32, s. 2; 2008, c. 6, s. 19.

CROSS-REFERENCES

The terms "peace officer", "motor vehicle" and "railway equipment" are defined in s. 2. The terms "aircraft", "vessel" and "operates" are defined in s. 214. The procedure for obtaining a warrant to obtain blood samples is set out in s. 256. The adverse inference respecting the impaired offence for failing to comply with a demand under this section is found in s. 258(3). The presumptions respecting the accused's blood alcohol level arising from analysis of a breath sample or blood sample are found in s. 258(1)(c), (d) and (d.1). Procedure for admission of certificates of an analyst, qualified technician and medical practitioner is set out in s. 258(1)(e) to (i) and (6) and (7). Note s. 258(4) which provides for summary application to a judge within 3 months of the date the blood sample was taken for an order releasing one of the samples for the purpose of testing by the defence.

The punishment for this offence is set out in s. 255. Under s. 255(2.2) and (3.2), an accused who is convicted of the offence under s. 254(5) and knew or ought to have known that operation of the vehicle caused an accident resulting in bodily harm or death, as the case may be, is liable to the same penalty as if the offender were convicted of impaired operation causing bodily harm or death, i.e. 10 years of life imprisonment, as the case may be. Where the prosecution elects to proceed by indictment on this offence then the accused may elect his mode of trial pursuant to s. 536(2). Where the prosecution elects to proceed by way of summary conviction then the trial of this offence is conducted by a summary conviction court pursuant to Part XXVII. In either case, release pending trial is determined by s. 515, although the accused is eligible for release by a peace officer under s. 496, 497 or by the officer in charge under s. 498. An accused found guilty of this offence is subject to an order prohibiting him from operating a motor vehicle, vessel, aircraft or railway equipment, as the case may be, where the accused was operating or had the care or control of a motor vehicle, vessel, aircraft or railway equipment or was assisting in the operation of an aircraft or of railway equipment at the time the offence was committed or within the two hours preceding that time. The length of the order is as follows: for a first offence, during a period of not more than three years and not less than three months; for a second offence, during a period of not more than three years and not less than six months; for each subsequent offence, during a period of not more than three years and not less than one year. The procedure respecting the making of that order of prohibition is found in s. 260. Pursuant to s. 255.1, evidence that the accused's blood alcohol level exceeded .160 at the time when the offence was committed is deemed to be an aggravating factor on sentencing. Note s. 732.1(3)(g.1) and (g.2), which allow for imposition of terms of probation that the offender attend for curative treatment in relation to the consumption of alcohol and drugs and participate in an alcohol ignition interlock device program.

Related offences: s. 249, dangerous operation; s. 252, failing to stop at scene of accident; ss. 253 and 255, impaired operation and "over 80"; ss. 220 and 221, criminal negligence causing death or bodily harm.

Section 257 protects the medical practitioner and qualified technician from criminal and civil liability when proceeding under this section. Section 258.1 enacts provisions to protect the privacy of the accused by prohibiting unauthorized use of bodily samples taken under this section and unauthorized disclosure of the results of physical coordination tests.

SYNOPSIS

Subsection (1) defines certain terms relating to demands for breath and blood and samples of other bodily substances. Subsection 254(2) provides that a peace officer may make a demand requiring a person to take part in certain investigatory tests if the officer has reasonable grounds to suspect that the person has alcohol or a drug in their body and that the person operated or had care or control of a motor vehicle, vessel, aircraft or railway equipment within the preceding three hours. If the suspicion relates to a drug, the officer may demand that the person perform physical coordination tests prescribed by regulations made under s. 254.1. If the suspicion relates to alcohol, the officer may demand that the person perform the coordination tests and/or supply a breath sample in an approved screening device. A peace officer may make a video recording of the physical coordination tests.

Under subsec. (3), if the peace officer has reasonable grounds to believe that a person is or has, during the preceding three hours, committed an offence under s. 253 by reason of the consumption of alcohol, the peace officer may make a demand of that person for breath samples (the breathalyzer or intoxilyzer demand). When the peace officer has reasonable grounds to believe that the physical condition of the person is such that he or she may not be capable of providing the breath sample or that it would be impractical to do so, a demand may be made that blood samples be taken by or under the supervision of a qualified physician as long as the physician is satisfied that this procedure would not endanger the life of the person (blood demand).

Subsection (3.1) sets up a system for detecting impairment by drugs or a combination of drugs and alcohol. If the peace officer has reasonable grounds to believe that a person is or has, during the preceding three hours, committed an offence under s. 253(1)(*a*) (impaired operation or care or control) by reason of the consumption of drugs or drugs and alcohol, the peace officer may make a demand that the person submit to an evaluation by an evaluating officer. If the evaluating officer has reasonable grounds to suspect that the person has alcohol in their body, the officer may make a demand for breath samples (subsec. (3.3)). If the evaluating officer has reasonable grounds to believe that the person's ability to operate is impaired by drugs or a combination of drugs and alcohol, the evaluating officer may make a demand that the person provide (a) oral fluid or urine, or (b) samples of blood.

Samples of blood may only be taken by or under the direction of a qualified medical practitioner who is satisfied that taking the samples would not endanger the person's life or health (subsec. (4)).

It is an offence to refuse to comply with a peace officer's demand under this section, pursuant to subsec. (5). Pursuant to subsec. (6), an accused can only be convicted of one offence under this section arising out of the same transaction.

ANNOTATIONS

Editor's Note: While some of the decisions noted below were decided under the predecessor legislation, they were felt to be relevant to these provisions. Also note, that some of these cases arose at a time when the demand under subsec. (3) had to be based on a belief that the accused committed the offence under s. 253 within the preceding two hours, not three hours, as is now provided for in that subsection; and when the demand under subsec. (2) be operating or having care or control at the time of the demand, not within the preceeding three hours.

Subsection (1) / Validity of designation of technician – Designation as a qualified technician by the Deputy Attorney General is valid: *R. v. Bourassa* (1972), 6 C.C.C. (2d) 414, 21 C.R.N.S. 355 (B.C.S.C.).

The designation in Ontario of a person as a qualified technician by the provincial Solicitor General is valid by virtue of the combined operation of this subsection and s. 2 which defines "Attorney General" in part as the Attorney General or Solicitor General of the province: *R. v. Wilkes; R. v. Foshay* (1979), 48 C.C.C. (2d) 362, 2 M.V.R. 289 (Ont. C.A.), leave to appeal to S.C.C. refused March 17, 1980.

A police officer designated as a qualified technician under the former s. 237 but who was not redesignated under this section, when many other technicians were, was not a qualified technician within the meaning of this section. Section 44(*a*) of the *Interpretation Act*, R.S.C. 1985, c. I-21, providing that a person acting under a former enactment shall continue to act, as if appointed under the new enactment, until another is appointed in his stead, could not apply in view of the designation under this section of other technicians: *R. v. Schemenauer* (1987), 34 C.C.C. (3d) 573, 58 Sask. R. 244 (C.A.).

In *R. v. Novis* (1987), 36 C.C.C. (3d) 275, 50 M.V.R. 1 (Ont. C.A.), s. 44 of the *Interpretation Act* was applied to find that the officer's original designation under former s. 237 was valid until his new designation became effective. There was, however, no evidence that another officer had been appointed in his stead.

By virtue of s. 7 of the *Interpretation Act*, R.S.C. 1985, c. I-21, a designation is valid although made prior to proclamation of this section. The effect of s. 7 is that the designation takes effect when the new provision is proclaimed in force: *R. v. Janes* (1987), 40 C.C.C. (3d) 209, 7 M.V.R. (2d) 41 (N.S.C.A.).

The flaw in the designation of an officer which referred to him as a "qualified technician" when in fact he was qualified to take only breath samples and not blood samples did not affect the admissibility of his certificate in relation to analysis of breath samples: *R. v. MacDonald* (1986), 65 Nfld. & P.E.I.R. 72, 46 M.V.R. 76 (P.E.I.S.C.), affd 39 C.C.C. (3d) 189, 7 M.V.R. (2d) 128, 67 Nfld. & P.E.I.R. 1 (C.A.). Similarly: *R. v. Janes, supra.*

Proof of designation of technician – If the designation by the Attorney General of a breathalyzer officer as a "qualified technician" is sought to be proved by Gazette the publication must be before the court; otherwise the officer's own evidence of his appointment being made and gazetted is, in the absence of evidence to the contrary, sufficient: *R. v. Leavitt* (1971), 5 C.C.C. (2d) 141, 16 C.R.N.S. 304 (Alta. S.C.).

Judicial notice must be taken of a designation made by the Attorney General and duly gazetted: *R. v. Betts* (1977), 34 C.C.C. (2d) 562, 16 N.B.R. (2d) 317 (S.C.).

The qualified technician's *viva voce* evidence that he had been so qualified by the Attorney General and his appointment had been gazetted establishes a rebuttable presumption of his position. In addition judicial notice may be taken that the Borkenstein breathalyzer is an approved instrument: *R. v. Leblanc* (1972), 7 C.C.C. (2d) 525, 4 N.S.R. (2d) 29 (C.A.).

Production of an original letter of appointment purportedly signed by the Attorney General is proof in the absence of any evidence to the contrary that the breathalyzer operator was a qualified technician: *R. v. Baskier* (1971), 4 C.C.C. (2d) 552, 17 C.R.N.S. 26 (Sask. C.A.).

Testimony by the breathalyzer operator that he was a qualified technician and production by him of a letter from the Attorney General to that effect is sufficient proof in the absence of evidence to the contrary that he is a qualified technician. The designation need not be proved by production of the provincial Gazette containing the designation: *R. v. Gettle* (1977), 34 C.C.C. (2d) 569 (B.C.C.A.).

The accused does not satisfy the evidential burden upon him to adduce evidence tending to negative the presumption of due appointment of the technician, which is raised by the Crown showing that the officer had acted in the requisite capacity, merely by cross-examination of the officer directed to show that the officer was unsure who had signed the letter notifying him of his appointment: *R. v. Adams* (1986), 30 C.C.C. (3d) 469, 51 Sask. R. 161 (C.A.).

The statement in the technician's signed certificate as to his designation as a qualified technician by the Attorney General is evidence of his official character: *R. v. Evanson* (1973), 11 C.C.C. (2d) 275, [1973] 4 W.W.R. 137 (Man. C.A.); *R. v. Novis* (1987), 36 C.C.C. (3d) 275, 50 M.V.R. 1 (Ont. C.A.).

Approved instrument – It was held considering a technician's certificate issued pursuant to the former s. 237 that a statement in the technician's certificate that the breath sample was received into a "Borkenstein Breathalyzer, an approved instrument pursuant to section 237(6)" is sufficient proof that the instrument was approved even though the particular model number of the Borkenstein Breathalyzer was not specified in the certificate: *R. v. Gorman* (1976), 32 C.C.C. (2d) 222, 15 N.B.R. (2d) 289 (C.A.); *R. v. Gilbert* (1976), 31 C.C.C. (2d) 251 (Ont. C.A.); *R. v. Pedrotti* (1976), 30 C.C.C. (2d) 575n (B.C.S.C.); *R. v. Gregorwich* (1975), 27 C.C.C. (2d) 267, [1975] W.W.D. 170 (C.A.). *Contra: R. v. Foley* (1975), 25 C.C.C. (2d) 514 (Sask. Q.B.).

A breathalyzer Model 900A is an approved instrument notwithstanding that the instrument has been modified to eliminate the instrument's susceptibility to radio frequency interference. Minor alterations to improve an instrument's efficiency do not alter the kind of instrument approved. It is only evidence of a modification to the instrument which goes to the issue of the kind, nature or character of the breathalyzer that should create a reasonable doubt as to whether the particular breathalyzer remains in a class of approved instruments: *R. v. Bebbington* (1988), 43 C.C.C. (3d) 456, 8 M.V.R. (2d) 151 (Ont. C.A.).

There is no requirement to adduce expert evidence regarding the reliability of or the manner in which the "Beckman CX-7" analyzes blood. It is sufficient if the expert operating the machine testified that it was capable of making the required measurements or producing the required data and that the machine was in good working order and was properly used: *R. v. Delorey* (2004), 188 C.C.C. (3d) 372, 226 N.S.R. (2d) 59 (N.S.C.A.).

Subsection (2) [Approved screening device demand] / Proof of reasonable suspicion – There is no requirement that the officer apprehending the motorist administer the test. A second officer attending the scene subsequently, who forms the requisite belief, may make the demand and administer the test: *R. v. Telford* (1979), 50 C.C.C. (2d) 322 (Alta. C.A.). See also *R. v. Padavattan* (2007), 223 C.C.C. (3d) 221, 45 C.R. (6th) 405 (Ont. S.C.J.).

However, the officer who makes the demand must also formulate the opinion as to the adequacy of the sample provided by the motorist: *R. v. Shea* (1979), 49 C.C.C. (2d) 497, 3 M.V.R. 134 (P.E.I.S.C.).

Reasonable suspicion can be achieved either by the officer's personal knowledge and observation or the communicated observations of others or a combination of both. It is not necessary for an officer to independently investigate and verify the grounds for reasonable suspicion conveyed to him as long as he subjectively believes them: *R. v. Nahorniak* (2010), 256 C.C.C. (3d) 147 (Sask. C.A.).

The test for making the demand is consumption of alcohol alone, and not its amount or behavioural consequence: *R. v. Gilroy* (1987), 3 M.V.R. (2d) 123, 79 A.R. 318 (C.A.), leave to appeal to S.C.C. refused 87 N.R. 236*n*, 85 A.R. 160*n*. Furthermore, the police officer only needs reasonable suspicion that the person operating the vehicle has alcohol in their body and need not believe that the accused has committed any offence: *R. v. Lindsay* (1999), 134 C.C.C. (3d) 159, 40 M.V.R. (3d) 225 (Ont. C.A.), or was operating or had care and control of the motor vehicle: *R. v. MacPherson* (2000), 150 C.C.C. (3d) 540, 140 O.A.C. 53 (C.A.). Similarly, *R. v. Butchko* (2004), 192 C.C.C. (3d) 552, [2005] 11 W.W.R. 95 (Sask. C.A.).

There is no requirement for the Crown to prove that the screening device was an approved device before relying on the results of the test to show that the police had reasonable grounds to make a breathalyzer demand: *R. v. Jacob* (2013), 296 C.C.C. (3d) 1 (Man. C.A.).

Breath sample to be provided "forthwith" – The term "forthwith" suggests that the breath sample is to be provided immediately. Thus, a demand made by a police officer, who is without the device and requires half an hour for the device to arrive, does not satisfy the conditions of this subsection. Since the demand was invalid, the accused was under no obligation to comply with it and his failure to comply could not constitute an offence: *R. v. Grant*, [1991] 3 S.C.R. 139, 67 C.C.C. (3d) 268.

In *R. v. Wilson* (1999), 41 M.V.R. (3d) 1 (B.C.C.A.), the court held that the Crown need not prove in every case that an approved screening device is in the possession of the police or immediately available. The mere absence of evidence that an approved screening device was immediately available is not enough to raise any doubt about the validity of the demand where it was made and immediately refused.

The demand did not comply with this subsection where the officer did not have the screening device with him and had to take the accused to the detachment. A total of 14 minutes elapsed between the making of the demand and the time when the device was ready. For the sample to be provided "forthwith" it must be provided immediately, meaning very shortly after the accused has been requested to accompany the officer for the purpose of providing the sample, usually at the side of the road or in the immediate vicinity: *R. v. Cote* (1992), 70 C.C.C. (3d) 280, 6 O.R. (3d) 667 (C.A.).

"Forthwith" means immediately or without delay. This provision requires that both the demand and the provision of the sample be made forthwith. In this case, the accused had refused to provide a roadside breath sample but, approximately one hour later at the police station, after speaking to counsel, he decided to do so. The second demand made more than one hour later at the police station was not lawful as it was not made forthwith. As the legitimacy of the breathalyzer demand was based on the legitimacy of the ASD demand, the breathalyzer demand was similarly unlawful: *R. v. Woods*, [2005] 2 S.C.R. 205, 197 C.C.C. (3d) 353.

In unusual circumstances, "forthwith" may be given a more flexible interpretation than its ordinary meaning strictly suggests. However, "forthwith" is not limited to circumstances in which there is sufficient delay such that a realistic opportunity to consult counsel was available but not provided. In considering the immediacy requirement, the court should consider the following: (i) the analysis must be contextual; (ii) the demand must be made by the police officer promptly once he or she forms the reasonable suspicion that the driver has alcohol in his or her body. The immediate requirement commences at the stage of reasonable suspicion; (iii) "forthwith" connotes a prompt demand and an immediate response, although in unusual circumstances a more flexible interpretation may be given. In the end, the time from the formation of reasonable suspicion to the making of the demand to the detainee's response to the demand by refusing or providing a sample must be no more than is reasonably necessary to enable the officer to discharge his or her duty as contemplated by subsec. (2); (iv) the immediacy requirement must take into account all the circumstances including a reasonably necessary delay where breath tests cannot immediately be performed because an ASD is not immediately available, or where a short delay is needed to ensure an accurate result of an immediate ASD test or where a short delay is required due to articulated and legitimate safety concerns. These are delays that are no more than are reasonably necessary to enable the officer to properly discharge his or her duty. Any delay not so justified exceeds the immediacy requirement; (v) one of the circumstances for consideration is whether the police could realistically have fulfilled their obligation to implement the detainee's s. 10(*b*) rights before requiring the sample. If so, the "forthwith" criterion is not met: *R. v. Quansah* (2012), 286 C.C.C. (3d) 307 (Ont. C.A.).

Where there is evidence that the officer knew that the suspect had recently consumed alcohol and expert evidence shows that the subsequent screening test would be unreliable due to the presence of alcohol in the mouth, and the officer knows that the resultant test will provide inaccurate results, the fact that the suspect failed the test could not itself provide the requisite reasonable and probable grounds to make a demand under subsec. (3). However, the officer is not required to wait 15 minutes on each occasion that the officer makes the demand. It is only where the officer had reason to believe that, without waiting, the test may be inaccurate, that the officer needs to delay the administration of the test. Where the particular screening device used has been approved under the statutory scheme, the officer is entitled to rely on its accuracy unless there is credible evidence to the contrary: *R. v. Bernshaw*, [1995] 1 S.C.R. 254, 95 C.C.C. (3d) 193.

The officer is entitled to delay taking the sample where there are grounds to believe that the delay is necessary to obtain accurate results, as where the suspect has recently consumed alcohol: *R. v. Dewald; R. v. Pierman* (1994), 92 C.C.C. (3d) 160, 19 O.R. (3d) 704 (C.A.), affd (*R. v. Dewald*) [1996] 1 S.C.R. 68, 103 C.C.C. (3d) 382.

The mere possibility that alcohol has been consumed within the 15 or 20-minute period prior to the administration of the tests does not preclude an officer from relying on the screening device. Where an officer honestly and reasonably concludes that he cannot form an opinion as to whether alcohol has been consumed within the preceding 15 or 20 minutes, he is entitled to rely on the screening device and administer the test without delay: *R. v. Einarson* (2004), 183 C.C.C. (3d) 19, 21 C.R. (6th) 185 (Ont. C.A.).

The approved screening device does not have to be warmed up and tested as operational before a demand is made: *R. v. Danychuk* (2004), 183 C.C.C. (3d) 337, 70 O.R. (3d) 215 (C.A.).

There is a relationship between the practicability of providing samples and the test for impracticability of obtaining a breath sample. The decision in respect of these issues must be made at about the same time and in light of the circumstances that exist at that time. In considering impracticability, the police officer must also consider the time period that might be required to pass before it would be practical to obtain a breath sample rather than a blood sample: *R. v. Salmon* (1999), 141 C.C.C. (3d) 207 (B.C.C.A.), leave to appeal to S.C.C. refused 150 C.C.C. (3d) vi.

Although the officer did not have the device when he stopped the accused, it was brought to him in less than five minutes at which time the demand was made. This was a valid demand and therefore there was no need to inform the accused of his rights under s. 10(*b*) of the Charter: *R. v. Misasi* (1993), 79 C.C.C. (3d) 339, 12 O.R. (3d) 232 (C.A.). Similarly: *R. v. Higgins* (1994), 88 C.C.C. (3d) 232, [1994] 3 W.W.R. 305 (Man. C.A.).

The fact that the device was not on the person of the police officer or in his police vehicle when the demand was made or that he did not know the time frame for the arrival of the device does not necessarily take the demand outside subsec. (2). The determination of whether the test has been administered forthwith is not a question of the number of seconds which have elapsed from the time the demand was made to the time the test was administered but rather is a question of the circumstances of the case. It would seem that if the time between the demand and the administering of the test is more than 30 minutes then in most situations the demand would be invalid, but if there are no more than 30 minutes between the demand and administering of the test the court must examine the circumstances: *R. v. Payne* (1994), 91 C.C.C. (3d) 144, 121 Nfld. & P.E.I.R. 137 (Nfld. C.A.).

In *R. v. Megahy* (2008), 233 C.C.C. (3d) 142, however, the Alberta Court of Appeal held that a delayed demand due to the failure of the officer to have a roadside device available when he was specifically tasked to conduct roadside stops was not forthwith. In particular, the demand was not made until the accused had walked four minutes to the location of the device.

There is no statutory requirement that the word "forthwith" be used when making the demand and its omission does not render the demand invalid. The demand need not be in any particular form provided that it is made clear to the driver that a sample must be provided forthwith. This can be accomplished through words or conduct, including the tenor of the officer's discussion with the accused: *R. v. Torsney* (2007), 217 C.C.C. (3d) 571 (Ont. C.A.), leave to appeal to S.C.C. refused [2007] 2 S.C.R. viii, 218 C.C.C. (3d) vi.

Similarly, in *R. v. Neitsch* (2007), 224 C.C.C. (3d) 91, 412 A.R. 200, the Alberta Court of Appeal concluded that there is no need for the officer to use the word "forthwith" in order for the demand to be valid. In determining whether the demand was made "forthwith", all of the contextual circumstances must be considered, not solely the initial conversation between the officer and the accused. In this case, the accused had been stopped, a demand was made, he was immediately taken to a nearby machine, and he did comply, all of which occurred within five minutes. All of the evidence was relevant to conclude that immediacy had been conveyed to the accused.

Validity of stop / random stops, R.I.D.E., etc. – The random stopping of a motor vehicle as part of a well-publicized program to reduce impaired driving such as the R.I.D.E. program is authorized at common law and therefore does not affect the validity of a demand made under this subsection once the officer forms the requisite suspicions: *R. v. Dedman*, [1985] 2 S.C.R. 2, 20 C.C.C. (3d) 97 (4:3).

The random stopping of a motorist for the purposes of a spot check procedure, even if of relatively brief duration, results in a detention within the meaning of s. 9 of the *Charter of Rights and Freedoms* and such detention is arbitrary in violation of s. 9 where, although the stop is done pursuant to statutory [provincial] authority and for lawful purposes there are no criteria for the selection of the drivers to be stopped and subjected to the spot check procedure. However, the authorization of such stops by the provincial legislation is a reasonable limit within the meaning of s. 1 of the Charter, having regard to the importance of highway safety and the role to be played in relation to it by a random stop authority for the purpose of increasing both the detection and the perceived risk of detection of motor vehicle offences, many of which cannot be detected by mere observation of driving. Finally, the demand by the police officer that the motorist surrender his driver's licence and proof of insurance for inspection as required by the provincial legislation does not infringe the motorist's right to be secure against unreasonable search and seizure as guaranteed by s. 8 of the Charter: *R. v. Hufsky*, [1988] 1 S.C.R. 621, 40 C.C.C. (3d) 398 (7:0).

It was held that, although there was no comparable legislation in Saskatchewan to the Ontario legislation considered in *R. v. Hufsky, supra*, the common law power to stop vehicles in the course of a checkpoint programme also constituted a reasonable limit on the right guaranteed by s. 9 of the Charter. Thus, evidence obtained as to the accused's blood-alcohol level following such a stop is admissible: *R. v. Burke* (1988), 45 C.C.C. (3d) 434 (Sask. C.A.).

Further, even purely random stops, not part of an organized programme such as the R.I.D.E. program, but permitted by provincial legislation and *semble* common law, are a reasonable limit on the s. 9 Charter rights where the stop is for a legal reason, such as to check the driver's licence and insurance, the driver's sobriety or the mechanical fitness of the vehicle: *R. v. Ladouceur*, [1990] 1 S.C.R. 1257, 56 C.C.C. (3d) 22; *R. v. Wilson*, [1990] 1 S.C.R. 1291, 56 C.C.C. (3d) 142. However, in *R. v. Griffin* (1996), 111 C.C.C. (3d) 490, 146 Nfld. & P.E.I.R. 142 (Nfld. C.A.), leave to appeal to S.C.C. refused 113 C.C.C. (3d) vi, 149 Nfld. & P.E.I.R. 270*n*, the Court of Appeal concluded that a roving random stop amounted to an arbitrary detention as it was neither authorized by the *Criminal Code* nor by provincial legislation. The provincial legislation which requires a driver to produce a vehicle license on request by a police officer does not expressly confer a power on the police to stop vehicles and, accordingly, such a random stop power could not be inferred merely as a result of the existence of a statutory duty on a motorist to carry and produce documents and maintain the vehicle properly. Furthermore, the statutory power to direct traffic could not be relied upon to conduct a random stop program.

Right to counsel under s. 10(*b*) of Charter – It was held that a motorist required to supply a breath sample under the predecessor to this subsection is detained within the meaning of s. 10(*b*) of the Charter, but it is a reasonable limitation on the right to retain and instruct counsel as guaranteed by that provision that the motorist supply the breath sample without being entitled to consult counsel: *R. v. Thomsen*, [1988] 1 S.C.R. 640, 40 C.C.C. (3d) 411.

Even where there is a delay to ensure that the officer can obtain a proper sample, as where the officer knows that the suspect has just recently consumed alcohol, the suspect is not entitled to his or her rights under s. 10(*b*) of the Charter: *R. v. Bernshaw*, [1995] 1 S.C.R. 254, 95 C.C.C. (3d) 193.

Where the demand is invalid, it could not constitute a reasonable limit. Accordingly, since the accused was detained, he should have been informed of his rights under s. 10(*b*): *R. v. Grant*, [1991] 3 S.C.R. 139, 67 C.C.C. (3d) 268.

Where the demand was made but the police officer had to wait for the device to arrive some 16 minutes later, the demand was not made forthwith. Accordingly, the police were required to provide the accused with a realistic opportunity to consult with counsel during the time between the issuance of the demand and the arrival of the screening device. The officer had to take reasonable steps to facilitate the accused's access to counsel having regard to the availability of a cell phone or pay phones in the vicinity: *R. v. George* (2004), 187 C.C.C. (3d) 289 (Ont. C.A.).

A "realistic opportunity to consult with counsel" cannot be equated with the mere chance to place a call to a lawyer. The central question was whether, in all of the circumstances, there was a realistic opportunity to the accused, in the space of six or seven minutes, to contact, seek and receive advice from counsel. In this case, denying the accused the opportunity to use a cell phone to call counsel in the early morning hours did not infringe any rights, as there was no realistic possibility that the accused would have been able to locate his counsel at this time: *R. v. Torsney* (2007), 217 C.C.C. (3d) 571 (Ont. C.A.), leave to appeal to S.C.C. refused [2007] 2 S.C.R. viii, 218 C.C.C. (3d) vi.

Note: Some of the cases noted below were decided before the enactment of subsec. (2)(*a*).

Right to counsel / *Sobriety tests other than screening device demand* – A motorist detained and requested to perform physical sobriety tests and answer questions about prior alcohol consumption does not have the right to consult counsel or be informed of that right under s. 10(*b*) of the *Canadian Charter of Rights and Freedoms*. Although there is no express statutory limit on the right to counsel, these measures fall within the scope of reasonable police authority conferred by necessary implication from the operational requirements of the governing provincial and federal legislative provisions — namely the right to stop vehicles under provincial highway traffic legislation and in the police duty to enforce this section and constitute a reasonable limit on the s. 10(*b*) rights: *R. v. Elias; R. v. Orbanski*, [2005] 2 S.C.R. 3, 196 C.C.C. (3d) 481. [Now see s. 254(2)(*a*).]

In *R. v. Milne* (1996), 107 C.C.C. (3d) 118 (Ont. C.A.), leave to appeal to S.C.C. refused 110 C.C.C. (3d) vi, the court concluded that the use of evidence obtained through roadside co-ordination tests is limited to determining whether to make a demand under this section. The right to counsel is not impaired as little as possible if the compelled and self-created incriminatory evidence gathered at the roadside, and before the accused has been informed of the right to counsel, could be used for trial purposes. Admission at trial of the co-ordination test results to prove impairment on a charge of impaired driving would render the trial unfair. See also *R. v. Oldham* (1996), 109 C.C.C. (3d) 392 (N.B.C.A.); and *R. v. Roy* (1997), 117 C.C.C. (3d) 243 (Que. C.A.). Similarly, see *R. v. Sundquist* (2000), 145 C.C.C. (3d) 145 (Sask. C.A.).

As noted above, in *R. v. Elias; R. v. Orbanski, supra*, the court held that a motorist requested to perform physical sobriety tests and answer questions about prior alcohol consumption does not have the right to consult counsel or be informed of that right under s. 10(*b*) of the *Canadian Charter of Rights and Freedoms*. In holding that this was a reasonable limit on the s. 10(*b*) rights, the court noted that the Crown conceded that evidence obtained as a result of the motorist's participation without the right to counsel can only be used as an investigative tool and cannot be used as direct evidence to incriminate the driver. The court thus appears to have approved this line of cases.

Similarly, statements given at the roadside are generally inadmissible on a charge of refusing to provide a breath sample under s. 254(5). The admission of any roadside utterances as part of the Crown's case is forbidden, other than on the basis of establishing grounds for the demand or the *actus reus* of the offence: *R. v. Rivera* (2011), 270 C.C.C. (3d) 469 (Ont. C.A.), leave to appeal to S.C.C. refused (2011), 291 O.A.C. 398*n*.

Where an accused is directed to exit the vehicle and answer questions about his alcohol consumption, the officer's observations about how the accused behaves after exiting the car are admissible only to establish grounds for the breathalyzer demand and not to incriminate the accused on an impaired driving charge: *R. v. Visser* (2013), 300 C.C.C. (3d) 388 (B.C.C.A.).

A request by an officer to "blow in his face" was a permissible sobriety test: *R. v. Weintz* (2008), 233 C.C.C. (3d) 365 (B.C.C.A.), leave to appeal to S.C.C. refused 235 C.C.C. (3d) vi.

Provincial legislation which authorizes the police to require a driver to stop for the purpose of determining whether there is sufficient evidence to justify making either an approved screening device demand or a breathalyzer demand constitutes a reasonable limit on the right to counsel. In addition, the right to silence was not infringed as a result of brief police questioning. In the absence of the right to counsel, the right to make an informed choice as to whether to speak to the police requires only that the police not engage in conduct that effectively and unfairly deprives the detainee of the right to choose whether to speak to the police: *R. v. Smith, supra*; *R. v. Housley* (1996), 105 C.C.C. (3d) 83 (Ont. C.A.), leave to appeal to S.C.C. refused 108 C.C.C. (3d) vi.

Effect of other Charter of Rights guarantees – Failure to show the accused the results of the test with the roadside screening device does not constitute a violation of the *Canadian Charter of Rights and Freedoms*: *R. v. Tanner* (1986), 41 M.V.R. 92 (N.S.C.A.).

Section 8 of the Charter does not impose an obligation on the police in all cases to inform a person of the right to refuse to provide a blood or saliva sample: *R. v. Blackstock* (1997), 10 C.R. (5th) 385 (Ont. C.A.).

This subsection does not violate the guarantee to fundamental justice under s. 7 of the Charter despite the lack of criteria in the legislation for determining when the peace officer might reasonably suspect there is alcohol in the person's body. Nor does it authorize an unreasonable search and seizure in violation of s. 8 of the Charter: *R. v. Broadhurst* (1985), 24 C.C.C. (3d) 27, 38 M.V.R. 35 (Ont. H.C.J.); *R. v. Dawson* (1986), 28 C.C.C. (3d) 46 (Alta. Q.B.). *Contra*: *R. v. Ward* (1989), 50 C.C.C. (3d) 376 (P.E.I.S.C.).

Subsection (3)(*a*)(i) [Breath demand] / *Grounds for demand* – Where the accused challenges the admissibility of the breath tet results on the basis of a violation of s. 8 of the Charter, the onus is on the Crown to prove that the officer had reasonable and probable grounds to make the demand because the Crown seeks to rely on breath samples obtained as a result of a warrantless search. There is both a subjective and objective component to establishing reasonable and probable grounds. In this case, the officer's subjective believe was supported objectively by the accused's erratic driving pattern and the various indicia of impairment upon arrest: *R. v. Shepherd* (2009), 245 C.C.C. (3d) 137 (S.C.C.).

The reasonable and probable grounds do not have to be based upon the actual operation of a vehicle as the officer's observations of the motorist's condition may disclose the grounds to give him the necessary belief: *R. v. Conway* (1974), 16 C.C.C. (2d) 233 (P.E.I.S.C.). Further, such grounds may be based on information supplied by third parties, not necessarily fellow police officers, and the officer may testify as to the contents of the conversations which caused him to make the demand: *R. v. Strongquill* (1978), 43 C.C.C. (2d) 232 (Sask. C.A.).

The motorist's failure to pass the test with the roadside screening device pursuant to subsec. (2), itself constitutes grounds for the demand under this section. There is no requirement that the device be proved to have been operating properly: *R. v. Arthurs* (1981), 63 C.C.C. (2d) 572 (Sask. C.A.); *R. v. Beaudette* (1981), 61 C.C.C. (2d) 61 (Man. Co. Ct.); *R. v. Hurley* (1980), 29 Nfld. & P.E.I.R. 263, 9 M.V.R. 46 (Nfld. C.A.); *R. v. Yurechuk*, [1983] 1 W.W.R. 460 (Alta. C.A.); *R. v. Denney* (1985), 34 M.V.R. 111 (N.S. S.C. App. Div.); or even that it is an approved instrument: *R. v. Seymour* (1986), 75 N.S.R. (2d) 174, 45 M.V.R. 132 (S.C. App. Div.).

If the accused does not challenge the admissibility of the results of the Intoxilizer/ Breathalyzer analysis on the basis that Charter rights were violated, the Crown is not required to establish that the officer had reasonable and probable grounds to make the demand. Reasonable and probable grounds involve an objective and subjective test. Where the grounds depend upon a "fail" from an approved screening device, the Crown must prove that the officer reasonably believed that he or she was using an approved device. In the absence of credible evidence to the contrary, the officer's testimony that he or she made a demand with an approved screening device is sufficient evidence that the officer had the requisite belief and it is not necessary for the officer to provide the particular model number or otherwise identify the device: *R. v. Gundy* (2008), 231 C.C.C. (3d) 26 (Ont. C.A.).

The fact that the screening device was one day past its scheduled recalibration date did not automatically make it unreasonable for the officer to rely on the device's "fail" reading to make a breath demand: *R. v. Biccum* (2012), 286 C.C.C. (3d) 536 (Alta. C.A.).

Validity of demand – A peace officer is only vested with the authority to make a demand in the territorial jurisdiction in which his appointment is effective: *R. v. Soucy* (1975), 23 C.C.C. (2d) 561, 11 N.B.R. (2d) 75 (S.C. App. Div.); *R. v. Arsenault* (1980), 55 C.C.C. (2d) 38, 31 N.B.R. (2d) 365 (C.A.).

Even though a demand for blood samples has been made and complied with, if thereafter it became practicable to make a demand under this paragraph for breath samples, then such demand may properly be made and the results of analysis of the breath samples is admissible: *R. v. Hiltz* (1988), 82 N.S.R. (2d) 387 (C.A.).

Form of demand – It is unnecessary that the demand be in any particular form provided it is made clear to the accused that he has to give a sample of his breath: *R. v. Nicholson* (1970), 8 C.C.C. (2d) 170, 27 C.R.N.S. 346 (N.S.S.C. App. Div.); *R. v. Flegel* (1972), 7 C.C.C. (2d) 55 (Sask. C.A.).

The demand under this subsection must be unequivocal and should not leave the accused with any doubt that he must comply, and that it is not a mere request or invitation: *R. v. Boucher* (1986), 73 N.B.R. (2d) 113 (Q.B.).

A demand that the accused supply "a sample" of his breath is a sufficient demand under this subsection despite the fact that the subsection refers to "such samples": *R. v. Rentoul* (1977), 37 C.C.C. (2d) 78 (Alta. S.C.T.D.).

Offence committed within preceding two hours [Note: This section now provides that the officer must form the belief that within the preceeding three hours the accused committed the offence.] – For a demand to be valid, the officer making the demand must form a belief within two hours of the time that he believes that an offence under s. 253 was committed. It is not necessary, however, that the demand be made within the two hour period or that the tests be performed within two hours: *R. v. Deruelle*, [1992] 2 S.C.R. 663, 75 C.C.C. (3d) 118.

Demand to be made "as soon as practicable" – "As soon as practicable" means within a reasonably prompt time, not "as soon as possible". In this case, a 59-minute delay while the officer satisfied himself that the accused had received medical treatment was appropriate: *R. v. Squires* (2002), 166 C.C.C. (3d) 65 (Ont. C.A.).

The failure to make a demand as soon as practicable does not render the evidence inadmissible, although it may afford the accused an argument pursuant to the Charter: *R. v. Forsythe* (2009), 250 C.C.C. (3d) 90 (Man. C.A.), leave to appeal to S.C.C. refused 254 C.C.C. (3d) vi.

Constitutionality of provision – In a lengthy judgment which considered many of the provisions of the *Canadian Bill of Rights* it was held that the compulsory breath test did not offend the Bill and in particular did not offend the provisions with respect to self-crimination, due process and protection of the law: *R. v. Curr*, [1972] S.C.R. 889, 7 C.C.C. (2d) 181 (9:0).

Similarly, these provisions do not offend the *Charter of Rights and Freedoms*: *R. v. Altseimer* (1982), 1 C.C.C. (3d) 7 (Ont. C.A.); *R. v. Gaff* (1984), 15 C.C.C. (3d) 126 (Sask. C.A.), leave to appeal to S.C.C. refused C.C.C. *loc. cit.*

Although this section gives the officer the right to detain the motorist for the purpose of complying with the demand, it is open to the officer to arrest the motorist pursuant to s. 495 and such arrest will not violate the accused's rights against arbitrary detention or imprisonment under s. 9 of the *Charter of Rights and Freedoms* where it was not unreasonable to prevent a repetition or continuation of the offence: *R. v. Cayer* (1988), 66 C.R. (3d) 30, 6 M.V.R. (2d) 1 (Ont. C.A.), or for the accused's own safety: *R. v. Faulkner* (1988), 9 M.V.R. (2d) 137 (B.C.C.A.). Similarly: *R. v. Baker* (1988), 9 M.V.R. (2d) 165 (N.S.C.A.).

As to other cases respecting the effect of a police officer or police department policy to arrest all impaired drivers prior to having them comply with the demand under this subsection and whether an arrest in such circumstances violates s. 9 of the *Charter of Rights and Freedoms*, see notes under s. 495, *infra*.

Right to counsel under s. 10(*b*) of Charter / generally – In *R. v. Therens*, [1985] 1 S.C.R. 613, 18 C.C.C. (3d) 481 (6:2), the court considered whether a motorist to whom a demand under this subsection is made is under detention within the meaning of s. 10(*b*) of the *Canadian Charter of Rights and Freedoms*. Estey J. (Beetz, Chouinard and Wilson JJ. concurring) held that, when the police officers administered the breathalyzer test, the motorist, who was not under arrest, was detained and accordingly prior to his complying with the demand, the police were required to inform him of his right to counsel. Le Dain J. (Dickson C.J.C., McIntyre and Lamer JJ. concurring on this issue) held that the motorist was under detention when the demand was made under this section to accompany the police officer and submit to a breathalyzer test. He was, accordingly, entitled at the time of his detention to be informed of his right to instruct counsel without delay.

The scope of available legal advice in this context is necessarily limited, but it is improper to speculate about the nature of the advice that a detainee would have received and whether the evidence would have been obtained had the right not been infringed. The burden is on the Crown to show that the accused would not have acted any differently had his s. 10(*b*) rights been fully respected and that, accordingly, the evidence would have been obtained irrespective of the breach. One of the purposes of s. 10(*b*) is to provide detainees with an opportunity to make informed choices about their legal rights and obligations. This opportunity is no less significant when breathalyzer charges are involved: *R. v. Bartle*, [1994] 3 S.C.R. 173, 92 C.C.C. (3d) 289; *R. v. Pozniak*, [1994] 3 S.C.R. 310, 92 C.C.C. (3d) 472.

Once it was proved that the accused had been informed of his right to counsel and indicated he understood his rights, there was no obligation on the Crown to establish that he waived the right to consult counsel merely because he had not sought legal advice: *R. v. Shannon* (1987), 34 C.C.C. (3d) 525 (N.W.T.C.A.). Also see: *R. v. Elgie* (1987), 35 C.C.C. (3d) 332, 48 M.V.R. 103 (B.C.C.A.), leave to appeal to S.C.C. refused 82 N.R. 185*n*. Similarly, see *R. v. Baig*, [1987] 2 S.C.R. 537, 37 C.C.C. (3d) 181 (7:0).

In *R. v. Stein* (1989), 14 M.V.R. (2d) 229 (B.C.C.A.), the court adopted the test approved by the Supreme Court of Canada in *R. v. Baig*, [1987] 2 S.C.R. 537, 37 C.C.C. (3d) 181, that absent proof of circumstances indicating that the accused did not understand his right to counsel when he was informed of it, the onus was on the accused to prove that he asked for the right but it was denied or he was denied any opportunity to even ask for it.

There is no burden on the Crown to establish that the accused was advised of his rights under s. 10 of the Charter, rather it is for the accused to put any alleged infringement in issue: *R. v. Roach* (1985), 23 C.C.C. (3d) 262 (Alta. C.A.).

At least where the relevant information can be obtained from the accused motorist, s. 10(*b*) of the Charter does not require that the officer answer counsel's questions before counsel speaks to the accused: *R. v. Fitzsimmons* (2006), 216 C.C.C. (3d) 141 (Ont. C.A.), leave to appeal to S.C.C. refused [2007] 1 S.C.R. ix, 217 C.C.C. (3d) vi.

Right to counsel / duty to inform – The duty imposed upon the police under s. 10(*b*) of the *Canadian Charter of Rights and Freedoms* is to inform the accused of his rights at a time when he was capable of understanding them and not to require the accused to provide potentially incriminating evidence prior to affording the accused a reasonable opportunity to make a reasoned choice to retain legal counsel. Thus the accused's rights under s. 10(*b*) were infringed where the police proceeded with the test under this paragraph at a time that the accused was so drunk that he could not understand what had been said to him: *R. v. Mohl* (1987), 34 C.C.C. (3d) 435 (Sask. C.A.), reversed on other grounds [see note below]; *R. v. D. (P.A.)*, [1987] 6 W.W.R. 175, 58 Sask. R. 48 (C.A.), or where as a result of a concussion he was incapable of understanding his right to counsel: *R. v. McAvena* (1987), 34 C.C.C. (3d) 461 (Sask. C.A.). **Note:** an appeal by the Crown was allowed in the case of *R. v. Mohl*, [1989] 1 S.C.R. 1389, 47 C.C.C. (3d) 575 (9:0), the court holding that, assuming there had been a violation of s. 10(*b*), to admit the evidence of the results of the breathalyzer test would not bring the administration of justice into disrepute within the meaning of s. 24(2) of the Charter. The court adopted the reasons of Sirois J. in the summary conviction appeal court.

The accused's right to be informed of his right to counsel under s. 10(*b*) was infringed where the information was given in English but the accused, to the knowledge of the officer, was French-speaking. The accused testified that he did not understand his right to counsel. Special circumstances existed requiring the officer to reasonably ascertain that the accused's rights were understood by him: *R. v. Vanstaceghem* (1987), 36 C.C.C. (3d) 142 (Ont. C.A.).

The accused's right to counsel is infringed where police inform him that he has the right to retain and instruct counsel without delay and then instruct him that he has the right to make only one telephone call, a statement with the detainee believes to be correct, and he thereupon makes one call which proves to be abortive and which he believes exhausts his right to further endeavour to contact counsel: *R. v. Pavel, supra.*

The accused, having been informed of his right to counsel in relation to the offence of dangerous driving for which he was arrested, need not again be informed of his rights under s. 10(*b*) of the *Charter of Rights and Freedoms* 10 minutes later, prior to the making of a breathalyzer demand under this paragraph: *R. v. MacDonald* (1986), 25 C.C.C. (3d) 572, 40 M.V.R. 46 (N.S.C.A.).

The officer, having advised the accused of his rights under s. 10(*b*) of the *Canadian Charter of Rights and Freedoms* before requiring that he comply with the demand to provide samples for analysis in the screening device, need not repeat the rights prior to requiring compliance with the breathalyzer demand: *R. v. Schechtel* (1985), 32 M.V.R. 316 (Sask. Q.B.).

The two preceding cases should now be read in light of the decision of the Supreme Court of Canada in *R. v. Black*, [1989] 2 S.C.R. 138, 50 C.C.C. (3d) 1 (5:0), where the court held that s. 10(*b*) of the Charter must be considered in light of s. 10(*a*) which requires the police to inform the detainee of the reason for the detention. A detainee can exercise her s. 10(*b*) rights in a meaningful way only if she knows the extent of her jeopardy and thus, the accused's rights under s. 10(*b*) were violated where she was initially arrested on a charge of attempted murder and not reinformed of her rights when the victim died and she was charged with first degree murder. The two charges were "significantly different".

However, in *R. v. Schmautz*, [1990] 1 S.C.R. 398, 53 C.C.C. (3d) 556, it was held that the accused's rights under s. 10(*b*) were not infringed in the following circumstances. The police informed the accused of his right to retain and instruct counsel and gave him the usual police caution after informing him that they were investigating an accident. The accused was not detained at that time. After several questions, the officers made a breathalyzer demand and the accused refused. While the accused was detained when the demand was made there was no requirement that he again be informed of his rights under s. 10(*b*). While there must be a close factual connection or linkage relating the warning to the detention and the reason therefor, here, by giving the accused both the police and Charter warnings at the outset of the short interview, the police alerted the accused that he was suspected and was being investigated in relation to a serious offence. The situation that arose with the breathalyzer demand was directly connected to the investigation. This was not a case where another more serious offence was suddenly being investigated because of changed circumstances external to the encounter. In this case, the demand arose directly and immediately out of the inquiry; it was part of a single incident at which the accused was fully made aware of his rights.

The accused having been informed of his rights under s. 10(*b*) of the Charter at the scene of an accident, following the making of a blood demand, he need not again be informed of his rights at the hospital, although the demand itself was repeated at that time: *R. v. Scott* (1991), 30 M.V.R. (2d) 42, 104 N.S.R. (2d) 112 (C.A.).

In *R. v. Brydges*, [1990] 1 S.C.R. 190, 53 C.C.C. (3d) 330 (7:0), a majority of the court, for the first time, laid down the rule that the police, as a matter of routine, must, as part of the duty to inform the accused of his right to counsel under s. 10(*b*), inform him of the availability of legal aid and duty counsel. The court left open the further question as to the effect this new caution will have on what constitutes due diligence, on the part of the accused, in the exercise of the right to counsel. The court noted, however, that the right to consult counsel of choice upon arrest or detention may now have to be considered, having regard to the immediate availability of duty counsel in most jurisdictions.

The detainee is entitled under the information component of s. 10(*b*) of the Charter to be advised of whatever system for free and immediate, preliminary legal advice exists in the jurisdiction at the time of detention and how such advice can be accessed: *R. v. Pozniak*, [1994] 3 S.C.R. 310, 92 C.C.C. (3d) 472.

The police officer complied with the informational component of the right to counsel when he indicated that the detainee could speak to a lawyer "now" during a roadside stop. The use of this phrase was not misleading and the officer was not required to advise the detainee that this contact would occur at the police station: *R. v. Devries* (2009), 244 C.C.C. (3d) 354 (Ont. C.A.).

Right to consult counsel in private – The right to privacy is inherent in the right to counsel as guaranteed by s. 10(*b*). The accused does not waive that right merely by acquiescing to conditions imposed by the police officer: *R. v. Lepage* (1986), 32 C.C.C. (3d) 171 (N.S.C.A.); *R. v. Rudolph* (1986), 32 C.C.C. (3d) 179 (Alta. Q.B.); *R. v. Young* (1987), 38 C.C.C. (3d) 452 (N.B.C.A.); *R. v. McKane* (1987), 35 C.C.C. (3d) 481 (Ont. C.A.).

The test to determine whether the right to privacy has been violated is whether it was more probable than not that the police did or could overhear the accused's conversation with counsel. The test is objective and requires a determination as to whether there was a real or substantial possibility that the police could have overheard the accused's conversation with counsel: *R. v. O'Donnell* (2004), 185 C.C.C. (3d) 367 (N.B.C.A.).

The right to privacy inherent in s. 10(*b*) of the Charter is the right to consult counsel and does not necessarily start with the attempt to reach a lawyer: *R. v. Standish* (1988), 41 C.C.C. (3d) 340, 5 M.V.R. (2d) 239 (B.C.C.A.).

The private communication to which the detainee is entitled is not restricted to a communication with his lawyer and includes communication with any person to whom the detainee wishes to speak in the process of exercising his rights under s. 10(*b*) of the Charter: *R. v. McNeilly* (1988), 10 M.V.R. (2d) 142 (Y.T.S.C.).

Where the circumstances surrounding the giving of information to an accused with respect to his rights under s. 10(*b*) of the Charter are such as to lead the accused to reasonably believe that he does not have the right to retain and instruct counsel in private or will not be given such right, and where such circumstances are known or ought to be known to the officer and the officer knows or ought to know the effect that such circumstances may reasonably have on the accused, there is a duty on the officer to explain to the accused that he has such right to privacy and that it will be given to him. Again, the failure to give such explanation constitutes a violation of s. 10(*b*): *R. v. Jackson* (1993), 86 C.C.C. (3d) 233 (Ont. C.A.).

Opportunity to consult counsel – Section 10(*b*) does not create a constitutional obligation on governments to ensure that free and immediate, preliminary legal advice is available to all detainees: *R. v. Matheson*, [1994] 3 S.C.R. 328, 92 C.C.C. (3d) 434. Nevertheless, where a detainee has indicated a desire to exercise his right to counsel, the state is required to provide him with a reasonable opportunity to do so. During this period, state agents must refrain from eliciting incriminating evidence from the detainee until he has had a reasonable opportunity to reach counsel. The police are obliged to "hold off" from attempting to elicit criminatory evidence from the detainee until he has had a reasonable opportunity to reach counsel. While there may be compelling and urgent circumstances in which despite a detainee's being unable to contact a lawyer due to the unavailability of duty counsel, police will not be required to hold off in requiring the detainee to comply with a breathalyzer demand, as the existence of the two-hour evidentiary presumption available to the Crown under s. 258(1)(*c*)(ii) does not by itself constitute such a compelling or urgent circumstance. Urgency is not created by a mere investigatory and evidentiary expediency in circumstances where duty counsel is unavailable to detainees who have asserted their desire to contact a lawyer and have been duly diligent in exercising their rights: *R. v. Prosper*, [1994] 3 S.C.R. 236, 92 C.C.C. (3d) 353.

Police officers making an arrest in a potentially volatile situation may be justified in denying the detainee the right then and there to call counsel in order to prevent any new factors from entering the situation. Once the police are clearly in control of the situation, however, they must afford the accused an opportunity to contact counsel in private: *R. v. Taylor* (1990), 54 C.C.C. (3d) 152 (N.S.C.A.).

Where the accused has been properly informed and provided with a reasonable opportunity to consult with counsel, there is no positive duty on police officers to inquire of the detainee whether he was successful in making contact with counsel before continuing the investigation. The accused's impairment does not relieve him of the duty to be reasonably diligent in exercising the right to counsel: *R. v. Maloney* (1995), 147 N.S.R. (2d) 139 (C.A.).

The refusal of the police to permit the accused's lawyer into the breathalyzer room to observe the administering of the test does not constitute a denial of the right to counsel as guaranteed by s. 10(*b*) of the Charter: *R. v. Atchison* (1991), 68 C.C.C. (3d) 241 (B.C.S.C.).

The right to consult in privacy, while requiring that the consultation be out of hearing of other persons, need not be out of sight of other persons: *R. v. Walkington* (1974), 17 C.C.C. (2d) 553 (Sask. C.A.); *R. v. Doherty* (1974), 16 C.C.C. (2d) 494 (N.S.C.A.); *R. v. Holmes* (1982), 2 C.C.C. (3d) 471 (Ont. C.A.).

That an enclosed glass booth in the police station may not be absolutely soundproof does not establish that a conversation carried on within it between the accused and his lawyer can be overheard. The test to be applied in determining whether the accused's right to consult in private has been complied with is whether the accused was afforded such privacy as would permit a discussion without fear of being overheard: *R. v. Miller* (1990), 87 Nfld. & P.E.I.R. 55 (Nfld. C.A.).

Subsection (3)(*a*)(ii) [blood demand] [Note: The period is now three hours.] – For a demand to be valid under this paragraph, the officer making the demand must have formed a belief within two hours of the time that he believes that an offence under s. 253 was committed. It is not necessary, however, that the demand be made within the two hour period or that the tests be performed within two hours: *R. v. Deruelle*, [1992] 2 S.C.R. 663, 75 C.C.C. (3d) 118, 15 C.R. (4th) 215. Nor is it necessary that the officer have formed a belief before the expiration of the two hour period that one of the preconditions within subpara. (i) or (ii) existed. Thus, a demand will be valid under this paragraph where, having formed the belief that the accused committed an offence under s. 253 within the preceding two hours, the officer first makes a demand for breath samples but later finds it to be impossible or impracticable to obtain a breath sample and therefore then makes a demand for blood samples, even if this latter demand is made after expiration of the two hour period: *R. v. Pavel, supra*; *R. v. Gale* (1991), 13 W.C.B. (2d) 408 (Nfld. C.A.).

It is the officer making the demand who must have formed the belief as to the commission of the offence within the two hour period. Where, initially, a breath demand was made which could not be complied with, a subsequent blood demand by another officer was invalid where this latter officer had no belief that the offence under s. 253 had been committed within the preceding two hours: *R. v. Pavel, supra*.

A demand for a blood sample was properly made where the motorist, although willing to take a breathalyzer test, had sustained a head injury, was receiving treatment in a hospital and the officer was concerned that the two hour limit would expire before the treatment was completed. The words "any physical condition of the person" give the officer a wide discretion to determine the practicability or capability of the motorist to provide a breath sample: *R. v. Wytiuk* (1989), 17 M.V.R. (2d) 18 (Man. Q.B.).

A demand made under this paragraph must make reference to the conditions set out in subsec. (4), namely that the samples of blood may only be taken by demand if the samples are taken by or under the direction of a qualified medical practitioner and the practitioner is satisfied that the taking of those samples will not endanger the life or health of the person: *R. v. Green*, [1992] 1 S.C.R. 614, 70 C.C.C. (3d) 285. On the other hand, the officer need not obtain the prior approval of the medical practitioner before making the demand: *R. v. Green* (1990), 60 C.C.C. (3d) 362, 25 M.V.R. (2d) 281 (N.S.C.A.).

Where the police have failed to comply with the requirements of *R. v. Green, supra*, the taking of the sample contravenes ss. 7 and 8 even if the accused would have complied with the demand in the absence of medical assurances. Where, however, the accused complies despite the lack of medical assurances, the admission of the blood samples will rarely bring the "administration of justice into disrepute": *R. v. Knox*, [1996] 3 S.C.R. 199, 109 C.C.C. (3d) 481.

An accused, who has been involved in a motor vehicle accident and taken to the hospital because of his serious injuries, is detained within the meaning of s. 10(*b*) of the Charter when a demand is made by a police officer under this paragraph that he consent to the taking of blood samples. While any actual physical restraint arose from his injuries, there was a detention from the psychological compulsion of the demand: *R. v. Harder* (1989), 49 C.C.C. (3d) 565, 14 M.V.R. (2d) 205 (B.C.C.A.).

A motorist, confined to hospital as a result of injuries received in the motor vehicle accident under investigation, is not detained when the officer merely asks some questions at the beginning of the investigation. He is only detained when the demand for a blood sample was made and it was only then that he was entitled to be informed of his rights under s. 10(*b*) of the Charter: *R. v. Kay* (1990), 53 C.C.C. (3d) 500 (B.C.C.A.).

The nature of the charge is irrelevant to the validity of the demand. The accused need not be advised of the specific offence for which he is being detained and is only entitled to be told that he was being detained for the purpose of effecting compliance with this section: *R. v. Nagy* (1997), 115 C.C.C. (3d) 473 (Ont. C.A.).

The demand under this paragraph need not be made in the presence of the qualified medical practitioner. Further, the word "impracticable" in subpara. (ii) does not mean impossible and connotes a degree of reason and involves some regard for practice: *R. v. Pearce* (1988), 56 Man. R. (2d) 77, 13 M.V.R. (2d) 116 (Q.B.).

The Crown is not required to prove the consent of the accused to the giving of a blood sample: *R. v. Knox, supra.*

Subsection (3.1) [drug evaluation demand] – A drug recognition expert's evaluation under this subsection is not solely a precondition to the making of a bodily fluid demand, but is admissible at trial without the need for a *voir dire* where it is established that the witness is certified as specified in the regulations. It is for the court to decide what weight to give the opinion evidence in a given case: *R. v. Bingley* (2015), 325 C.C.C. (3d) 525 (Ont. C.A.), leave to appeal to S.C.C. allowed 2016 CarswellOnt 1276.

Subsection (5) [Failure to comply with A.L.E.R.T. demand under subsec. (2)] – The Crown is not required to prove that the device which would have been used, had there been no refusal, was an approved device: *R. v. Reimer* (1980), 54 C.C.C. (2d) 127, 4 M.V.R. 270 (Sask. Q.B.). *R. v. Lemieux* (1990), 24 M.V.R. (2d) 157, 41 O.A.C. 326 (C.A.); *R. v. McCauley* (1997), 161 N.S.R. (2d) 154, 28 M.V.R. (3d) 257 (C.A.).

The criminalization of the refusal to comply with the demand under subsec. (2) does not infringe s. 7 of the *Canadian Charter of Rights and Freedoms* and is a reasonable limit on the rights under s. 10(*b*): *R. v. Thompson* (2001), 151 C.C.C. (3d) 339 (Ont. C.A.).

Subsection (5) [Failure to comply with breath demand] / Elements of offence – This subsection creates the single offence of non-compliance which may be committed either by failure or refusal, and it is immaterial whether or not a breathalyzer machine was available at the time of the demand: *R. v. Kitchemonia* (1973), 12 C.C.C. (2d) 225 (Sask. C.A.). See also: *R. v. Gesner* (1979), 46 C.C.C. (2d) 252 (N.B.C.A.).

Where the accused refused to blow into an approved screening device, it is not a defence to the offence under this subsection that the accused offered to provide a breath sample at a machine at the police station: *R. v. Wilson* (1996), 125 W.A.C. 223, 18 M.V.R. (3d) 298 (B.C.C.A.).

Similarly, the offence may be committed by either refusing to accompany the officer or refusing to supply breath samples and the Crown need only show the offence of refusing to comply with the demand was committed in either one of these modes even though both modes are set out in the information. The additional averment in the information is mere surplusage: *R. v. MacNeil* (1978), 41 C.C.C. (2d) 46 (Ont. C.A.); *B.C. (Attorney General) (Re)*, [1980] 3 W.W.R. 193 (B.C.S.C.).

The word "refuses" is fully comprised within the word "fails" and thus a verbal refusal to take the test will support a conviction on an information charging that the accused failed to comply: *R. v. Gesner* (1979), 46 C.C.C. (2d) 252 (N.B.C.A.).

As the combined effect of this section and s. 258(1) has been held to require that at least two samples be taken, an accused who refuses to give more than one sample may be convicted of the offence under this subsection and it is no defence to such a charge that the technician considered the first sample satisfactory: *R. v. Faulkner (No. 2)* (1977), 37 C.C.C. (2d) 217 (N.S. Co. Ct.); *R. v. Hatt* (1978), 41 C.C.C. (2d) 442 (N.B.C.A.); *R. v. Quiring* (1979), 46 C.C.C. (2d) 51 (B.C.C.A.); *R. v. Boswell* (1978), 44 C.C.C. (2d) 356 (P.E.I.S.C.); *R. v. Hazzard* (1978), 51 C.C.C. (2d) 344 (N.W.T.C.A.); *R. v. Giroux, supra.*

Statements made to a police officer at the roadside subsequent to an accident pursuant to a statutory requirement are compelled statements. Following *R. v. Powers* (2006), 213 C.C.C. (3d) 351 (B.C.C.A.), the court held that statutorily compelled statements were not admissible for any purpose, including establishing grounds for making either the approved screening device demand, or the breath demand: *R. v. Soules* (2011), 273 C.C.C. (3d) 496 (Ont. C.A.), leave to appeal to S.C.C. refused (2011), 294 O.A.C. 399n.

As to the *mens rea* of the refusal offence, the case law is divided. One view is that the Crown must prove that the accused intentionally refused or failed to provide a suitable sample: *R. v. Lewko* (2002), 169 C.C.C. (3d) 359 (Sask. C.A.); *R. v. Sullivan*, [2001] O.J. No. 2799 (C.J.); *R. v. Soucy* (2014), 316 C.C.C. (3d) 153 (Ont. C.J.); *R. v. Greenshields* (2014), 111 W.C.B. (2d) 674, [2014] O.J. No. 475 (C.J.). The other view is that the accused need only have knowledge or awareness of the prohibited act; the accused's intention to produce the prohibited consequence is relevant only to whether there was a "reasonable excuse": *R. v. Porter* (2012), 103 W.C.B. (2d) 246, [2012] O.J. No. 2841 (S.C.J.); *R. v. Pletsas* (2014), 112 W.C.B. (2d) 111, [2014] O.J. No. 1136 (S.C.J.); *R. v. Singh* (2013), 55 M.V.R. (6th) 39 (Ont. S.C.J.).

Charging offence – An information which, although it omits the words "without reasonable excuse", is otherwise in the words of the section and sets out the proper section number of the offence, is not defective: *R. v. Cote*, [1978] 1 S.C.R. 8, 33 C.C.C. (2d) 353 (8:0).

Change of mind – An offer by an accused to provide a breath sample after consulting his counsel is not a defence to this charge where the accused made two clear and unconditional refusals without giving any reason for refusing: *R. v. McGauley* (1974), 16 C.C.C. (2d) 419 (B.C.C.A.). Similarly, in *R. v. McKeen* (2001), 151 C.C.C. (3d) 449 (N.S.C.A.), leave to appeal to S.C.C. refused 154 C.C.C. (3d) vi, the court held that despite the accused's change of mind at the detachment, the offence of refusal to provide a breath sample was complete where the accused repeatedly refused to invoke the right to counsel at the roadside. Once the right to consult with counsel had been waived, there was no duty on the police to provide an opportunity for the accused to consult with counsel and not to elicit a response to the breathalyzer demand. The fact that the police subsequently asked the accused at the detachment if he wished to consult with counsel did not revive a right which the accused had previously refused to exercise.

But compare *R. v. Jumaga*, [1977] 1 S.C.R. 486, 29 C.C.C. (2d) 269, where it was held on the facts that a first refusal really constituted a request to consult counsel and it was so treated by the police and was therefore itself not sufficient to sustain the charge.

A definitive refusal can only be established once the accused, who is seeking access to counsel's advice, has received it at the police station and has then refused, or confirmed an earlier refusal, to provide a sample. Here, the accused had failed a roadside screening test, been arrested, and indicated that he wanted to speak to counsel. Subsequently, he said that he did not want to accompany the police to provide a breath sample and was arrested for refusal, then released from the scene. The trial judge erred in convicting him, because in the circumstances there was no final or definitive refusal: *R. v. Mandryk* (2012), 291 C.C.C. (3d) 182 (Ont. S.C.J.).

The requirement that the accused "comply" with the demand must be read as requiring compliance within a reasonable time, not necessarily forthwith. Where the accused initially refused to accompany the technician but later, within the two-hour period, offered to comply after consultation with a lawyer, the charge was not made out: *R. v. Brotton* (1983), 24 M.V.R. 76, 28 Sask. R. 78 (C.A.).

In determining whether an accused, who initially refused and later changed his mind, is guilty of this offence, the court ought not to minutely dissect a single conversation or take a single sentence out of context. It would seem that whether there has been a refusal depends on consideration of all the circumstances of each individual case, including the time elapsed and whether it can be said that the accused's offer to take the test was severable from his earlier words to the contrary: *R. v. Cunningham* (1989), 49 C.C.C. (3d) 521 (Alta. C.A.).

Where the original refusal was not unequivocal and was closely followed by an offer to provide a sample then the offence is not made out: *R. v. Sagh* (1981), 62 C.C.C. (2d) 299 (Alta. Q.B.).

Where, however, the accused unequivocally refuses and only changes his mind 15 minutes later, at which time the technician advised him that it was too late, the charge was made out. The two events were sufficiently separate as to constitute different transactions: *R. v. Butt* (1983), 23 M.V.R. 273, 44 Nfld. & P.E.I.R. 297 (Nfld. C.A.).

Proof of offence – The words of refusal need not be proved voluntary and therefore there is no necessity to hold a *voir dire* to determine the voluntariness of such utterance: *R. v. Gallaher* (1977), 37 C.C.C. (2d) 191 (B.C. Co. Ct.); *R. v. Stapleton* (1982), 66 C.C.C. (2d) 231 (Ont. C.A.); *R. v. Zerebeski* (1982), 66 C.C.C. (2d) 284 (Sask. Q.B.).

It is a question of fact whether or not the accused blew adequately or whether there is some other explanation for the accused's failure to provide adequate sample, namely, that the breathalyzer was not operating properly. The Crown is not as a matter of law required to prove that the breathalyzer was in working order: *R. v. Leveque* (1985), 22 C.C.C. (3d) 559, 37 M.V.R. 166 (B.C.C.A.).

Similarly, in *R. v. Fillier* (1995), 15 M.V.R. (3d) 272, 132 Nfld. & P.E.I.R. 339 (Nfld. S.C.), the court held that there is no requirement that the Crown adduce evidence as to the training and/or experience of the peace officer in the operation of the screening device for the officer's opinion to be received in respect of the failure to provide a suitable sample.

On a charge of refusal, there is no requirement that the police officer have a reasonable belief that he or she could administer the demand at the time it is made. Neither is there a requirement for the Crown to prove that an ASD would have been available within the "forthwith" period. Because the offence is complete upon the refusal, the police officer's ability to actually take the sample in accordance with the demand is not relevant to culpability: *R. v. Degiorgio* (2011), 275 C.C.C. (3d) 1 (Ont. C.A.).

Violation of right to counsel generally – Where the accused immediately refuses after the demand was made and before he was given his rights under s. 10(*b*) of the Charter, he should be informed of his right to counsel, that he was not bound by his earlier answers and that it was open to the accused to change his mind and consult counsel if he so wished: *R. v. MacIsaac* (1988), 72 Nfld. & P.E.I.R. 220, 9 M.V.R. (2d) 239 (P.E.I.S.C.).

However, compare *R. v. Cote* (1988), 8 M.V.R. (2d) 256, 87 N.B.R. (2d) 190 (C.A.), where it was held that while the accused's refusal was not irrevocable in such circumstances, evidence of the refusal was properly admitted where the accused was advised of her right to counsel, subsequently was given an opportunity to speak to a lawyer and never made a request to take the test. The court was divided on whether, since the original refusal is not irrevocable, the accused should be given another demand.

Where the act of refusal occurred after the time when the accused should have been informed of his right to counsel under s. 10(*b*) of the *Canadian Charter of Rights and Freedoms*, that is, immediately upon the making of the demand, the accused's rights under s. 10(*b*) have been infringed and the evidence of the refusal must be excluded under s. 24(2). It must be assumed that had the accused consulted counsel he would have complied with the demand: *R. v. Phillips; R. v. Reid* (1986), 26 C.C.C. (3d) 60 (Alta. C.A.).

R. v. Brownridge, [1972] S.C.R. 926, 7 C.C.C. (2d) 417 (6:3), decided the issue whether or not the fact that the police would not allow a suspected impaired motorist to contact his lawyer for advice after their demand for his breath sample was a "reasonable excuse" for his refusal to comply. In the first majority judgment, *per* Ritchie J. (Fauteux C.J.C., Martland

and Spence JJ., concurring), it was held that as there was a genuine reason for the motorist to seek legal advice it would run contrary to s. 2(*c*)(ii) (the right of a detained person to instruct counsel without delay) of the Bill of Rights to hold that the withholding of that right from him was incapable of constituting a reasonable excuse for him to provide a breath sample. In the second majority judgment Laskin J. (Hall J., concurring), held that s. 2 of the Bill of Rights enjoins a construction upon former s. 235 that would infringe any right recognized under the Bill of Rights and if efforts to reach counsel expend the time beyond the two-hour-limitation period primacy must be given the protection accorded by the Bill of Rights over the statutory rule of evidence under s. 258(1)(*c*)(ii). Moreover, denial of right to counsel does not constitute a "reasonable excuse" rather this right exists independently of those words and its denial vitiates a conviction for this offence. Pigeon J. (Abbott and Judson JJ., concurring) dissenting, was of the opinion that regardless of whether or not the suspected motorist was under arrest the denial of his request for counsel was not to be a reasonable excuse for him to refuse to provide his breath sample.

Although replacing the criminal offence of refusal with the presumption that failure or refusal to provide a roadside breath sample would constitute grounds for a breathalyzer demand would be less intrusive, it would undermine the effectiveness of roadside screening programs. Any infringement of ss. 7 or 10(*b*) of the Charter constitute a reasonable limit under s. 1: *R. v. Thompson* (2001), 151 C.C.C. (3d) 339 (Ont. C.A.).

Where a demand is made under subsec. (3) and the accused is not advised of his rights under s. 10(*b*) of the *Canadian Charter of Rights and Freedoms* then he has a reasonable excuse for refusing to comply with the demand: *R. v. Mackinnon* (1985), 21 C.C.C. (3d) 264 (P.E.I.C.A.).

Denial of the right to counsel is not a reasonable excuse for refusing to comply with the demand. Where, however, the accused proves that his right to counsel was violated then he would be entitled to an exclusion of evidence of the refusal if the accused can prove that to admit evidence would bring the administration of justice into disrepute within the meaning of s. 24(2) of the Charter. Since the onus is on the accused to establish the violation on a balance of probabilities, merely raising a reasonable doubt as to whether his right to counsel had been violated would not be sufficient: *R. v. Williams* (1992), 78 C.C.C. (3d) 72 (Ont. C.A.).

The accused's rights were violated when he was charged with refusal despite repeated unsuccessful attempts to reach a lawyer. The accused refused to comply with the demand until he spoke to a lawyer. He had been diligent in asserting his right and there was no urgency, the demand having been made only 45 minutes after he was arrested: *R. v. Dunnett* (1990), 62 C.C.C. (3d) 14 (N.B.C.A.), leave to appeal to S.C.C. refused 62 C.C.C. (3d) vi.

The refusal of the police to first await the motorist's lawyer's attendance before administering the breathalyzer test following a consultation on the telephone is not a reasonable excuse for the motorist to refuse to take the test: *R. v. Bond* (1973), 14 C.C.C. (2d) 497 (N.S.C.A.); *R. v. Kavanagh* (1981), 62 C.C.C. (2d) 518 (B.C.S.C.); *R. v. Giroux* (1981), 63 C.C.C. (2d) 555 (Que. C.A.), leave to appeal to S.C.C. refused C.C.C. *loc. cit.*

Where the accused was informed of his right to counsel and given a reasonable opportunity to consult, his inability to speak to his lawyer, which he did not communicate to the police, did not constitute a reasonable excuse for refusing to comply with the demand. Without any request on the part of the accused for more time to consult counsel, the police were entitled to conclude that the accused had refused without reasonable excuse: *R. v. Ferron* (1989), 49 C.C.C. (3d) 432, 16 M.V.R. (2d) 15 (B.C.C.A.).

Where the accused unsuccessfully attempted to contact two lawyers and then indicated that he no longer wished to consult with counsel and would not provide a breath sample, the officer was required to inform the accused again of the right to a reasonable opportunity to contact counsel as well as the fact that the police officer would not renew the demand for a breath sample during that time: *R. v. Russell* (2000), 150 C.C.C. (3d) 243 (N.B.C.A.).

Inability to consult in private – As indicated in the cases noted under s. 254(3), *supra*, it has been held that under s. 10(*b*) of the Charter, the right to consult with counsel in private is inherent in the right and there need not be any request for privacy. Nevertheless, it was held in *R. v. Young* (1987), 38 C.C.C. (3d) 452 (N.B.C.A.), that having regard to all the circumstances the trial judge did not err in refusing to exclude under s. 24(2) of the Charter the evidence of the accused's refusal notwithstanding the violation of s. 10(*b*) by reason of the failure of the police officer to move out of earshot. The court did not consider whether the breach of s. 10(*b*) provided the accused with a reasonable excuse. Also see: *R. v. Dempsey* (1987), 77 N.S.R. (2d) 284, 46 M.V.R. 179 (C.A.).

The right to consult with counsel includes the right to do so in privacy. The failure of the police to comply with a request for privacy constitutes a denial of the right to counsel and therefore a reasonable excuse to refuse to comply with the demand: *R. v. Penner* (1973), 12 C.C.C. (2d) 468, 22 C.R.N.S. 35 (Man. C.A.).

Reasonable excuse / burden of proof – By virtue of s. 794(2), an accused who asserts a "reasonable excuse" for failing or refusing to comply with a breathalyzer demand bears the burden of proving the factual foundation for that excuse on a balance of probabilities: *R. v. Goleski* (2014), 307 C.C.C. (3d) 1 (B.C.C.A.), affd [2015] 1 S.C.R. 399, 320 C.C.C. (3d) 433

Reasonable excuse / legal advice – An accused's statement that "My lawyer advised me not to take the test" in response to the making of a breathalyzer demand was a refusal within this subsection: *R. v. Hurley* (1980), 29 Nfld. & P.E.I.R. 263, 9 M.V.R. 46 (Nfld. C.A.).

The police officer's refusal to permit the accused's lawyer to verify the results of the first breathalyzer test does not constitute a reasonable excuse, nor does the accused's mistaken belief, based on the advice of the lawyer, that it would constitute a reasonable excuse: *R. v. Giroux* (1981), 63 C.C.C. (2d) 555 (Que. C.A.), leave to appeal to S.C.C. refused C.C.C. *loc. cit.*.

A motorist's mistaken belief, based on an erroneous judgment of a provincial court judge, that a police officer had no right to make the demand is not a reasonable excuse: *R. v. MacIntyre* (1983), 24 M.V.R. 67 (Ont. C.A.).

Reasonable excuse / grounds for demand – It is not a "reasonable excuse" for refusing to provide a breath sample that the accused is subsequently acquitted of the charge under former s. 234 [now s. 253], where the demand for the breath sample was lawfully made and the offence under this subsection is otherwise established. "Reasonable excuse" refers to matters which stand outside of the requirements which must be met (*i.e.*, those under subsec. (3)(*a*)) before a charge can be supported under this subsection: *R. v. Taraschuk*, [1977] 1 S.C.R. 385, 25 C.C.C. (2d) 108 (9:0). Note, this case overrules: *R. v. Canstone* (1971), 3 C.C.C. (2d) 539 (B.C.S.C.), and *R. v. Mitchell* (1973), 11 C.C.C. (2d) 12 (B.C.S.C.).

While it is a defence to a charge under this subsection that the officer did not have reasonable and probable grounds to believe that the accused had committed an offence under former s. 234 [now s. 253]: *R. v. MacDonald* (1974), 22 C.C.C. (2d) 350 (N.S.C.A.), to sustain the charge there need not be direct evidence from the officer that he had such a belief. Rather, the existence of the necessary belief can be inferred by the court: *R. v. Fraelic* (1977), 36 C.C.C. (2d) 473 (N.S. Co. Ct.); *R. v. Blanchette* (1978), 41 C.C.C. (2d) 205 (Alta. Dist. Ct.).

Reasonable excuse / offer of blood sample – An offer to provide a blood sample in lieu of a breath sample is not a reasonable excuse for refusing to comply with the demand under subsec. (3)(*a*): *R. v. Wall* (1974), 19 C.C.C. (2d) 146, [1974] 5 W.W.R. 634 (Sask. C.A.); *R. v. Weir* (1993), 79 C.C.C. (3d) 538 (N.S.C.A.); *R. v. Richardson* (1993), 80 C.C.C. (3d) 287 (Ont. C.A.); *R. v. Taylor* (1993), 39 W.A.C. 201, 43 M.V.R. (2d) 240 (B.C.C.A.).

Where, however, the accused's offer to supply a blood sample is taken up and it is not made clear to him that this is not a suitable alternative to complying with the demand the accused had a reasonable excuse to refuse: *Saskatchewan (Attorney General) v. Chrun*, [1973] 5 W.W.R. 611 (Sask. Dist. Ct.); *R. v. Larkin* (1979), 27 Nfld. & P.E.I.R. 284, 4 M.V.R. 149 (P.E.I.S.C.).

While evidence of sobriety cannot provide the basis for a "reasonable excuse", it can be relevant evidence of *mens rea*. In this case, the accused claimed that he tried to produce a breath sample but was unable; he offered to provide a blood sample instead. He then went on his own accord and had a blood test which demonstrated that he was, in fact, sober. The trial judge erred in refusing to consider this evidence because it properly bolstered the credibility of the accused's claim that, knowing himself to be sober, he genuinely tried to provide a breath sample: *R. v. Sceviour* (2010), 258 C.C.C. (3d) 196 (Nfld. & Lab. C.A.)).

Reasonable excuse / impairment – Establishing that the defendant's mind was so affected by alcohol or a drug that he could not grasp the demand at all would constitute a reasonable excuse for non-compliance: *R. v. Laybolt* (1974), 17 C.C.C. (2d) 16, 6 Nfld. & P.E.I.R. 85 (P.E.I.S.C.). *Contra: R. v. Warnica* (1980), 56 C.C.C. (2d) 100 (N.S.C.A.), where it was held that once it was shown that the accused appeared to understand the demand a rebuttable presumption arose that he intended the natural consequences of his own conduct which however may *not* be rebutted by testimony from the accused that he was too drunk to understand the demand. Further, lack of understanding is not a reasonable excuse.

Reasonable excuse / physical disability – In *R. v. Nadeau* (1974), 19 C.C.C. (2d) 199 (N.B.C.A.), Hughes C.J.N.B. expressed the view that "the "reasonable excuse' envisaged must be some circumstance which renders compliance with the demand either extremely difficult or likely to involve a substantial risk to the health of the person on whom the demand has been made".

The physical inability of the accused to take the test is a reasonable excuse within this subsection notwithstanding the inability is the result of the voluntary consumption of alcohol: *R. v. Henderson* (1976), 34 C.C.C. (2d) 40 (Ont. Co. Ct.).

The defence of reasonable excuse should not be confined to matters in the mind of the accused, to the exclusion of dangerous conditions not fully known or recognized by the accused. The defence should include rare situations where there is a reason at the time not to make the demand or to require compliance under threat of prosecution, but that reason is not fully known, either to the investigating officer or to the suspect. There is a reasonable excuse where both police and the accused have been seriously misled by mistaken medical diagnosis on a matter so fundamental to the interests of both. In this case, even though the accused was unaware of the exact nature of his injury, he did know that he was injured, perhaps seriously, and consequently, on the advice of counsel, he refused to comply with the police request until he was examined by a physician whom he knew and trusted. The accused had been examined briefly by a physician who advised the police that the accused was fit to comply with the demand. In fact, the accused had a very serious spinal injury and had he complied with the demand, he might well have become paralyzed. The fact that the accused was unaware of the specific danger to which he was exposed was no basis for a conclusion that he was not fearful for his safety and not justified in accepting the advice of his lawyer: *R. v. Moser* (1992), 71 C.C.C. (3d) 165 (Ont. C.A.).

Reasonable excuse / generally – The accused's belief that the results of the breathalyzer test would be inaccurate is not a reasonable excuse to refuse to comply with the demand. The accused must rely on the safeguard in s. 258(1)(*c*) which permits "evidence to the contrary" to rebut the presumption, which arises from the results of the breathalyzer test, taken pursuant to a demand under subsec. (3) that the blood alcohol reading from the breathalyzer is the same as at the time of the offence: *R. v. Campbell* (1978), 40 C.C.C. (2d) 570 (Alta. C.A.) (2:1). Similarily, *R. v. Roy* (1979), 11 C.R. (3d) 178 (Que. C.A.); *R. v. Dunn* (1980), 8 M.V.R. 198 (B.C.C.A.).

Thus the accused's fear that, because he was on medication, the results would be inaccurate is not a reasonable excuse for refusing to comply with the demand: *R. v. Frohwerk* (1979), 48 C.C.C. (2d) 214 (Man. C.A.).

Anxiety caused by accurate information supplied at the accused's request by the police officer as to the penalty for a second conviction for a drinking and driving offence (including information that a jail term would also result for a conviction under this subsection) is not a reasonable excuse: *R. v. Broda* (1983), 21 M.V.R. 85, 22 Sask. R. 239 (C.A.).

An extremely helpful review of the various factors which could constitute a "reasonable excuse" is found in the decision of the court in *R. v. Phinney* (1979), 49 C.C.C. (2d) 81 (N.S.C.A.), where the majority of the court concluded that the accused's honest belief based on reasonable grounds that the particular breathalyzer machine might not be functioning properly was a reasonable excuse to refuse to comply with the demand. The court emphasized, however, that this fear must be based on objective evidence.

Where the accused was to be taken 100 miles away for the breathalyzer test where he would be effectively stranded with no way to get home and no place to stay it was held that he had a reasonable excuse as contemplated by this subsection: *R. v. Iron* (1977), 35 C.C.C. (2d) 279 (Sask. Q.B.).

A possible financial loss for the accused if he were required to leave his vehicle and accompany the officer is not a reasonable excuse. In this case the accused claimed that he needed to remain with his truck to clean up the spilled cargo of fish otherwise there was risk that the cargo would be condemned resulting in a substantial financial loss: *R. v. Gidney* (1987), 7 M.V.R. (2d) 90, 81 N.S.R. (2d) 404 (C.A.).

Grounds of compassion, in this case the accused's desire to go to the hospital when he learned that his nephew who was at the hospital was in serious condition, do not constitute grounds for refusing to comply with the demand: *R. v. Heim* (1989), 98 N.S.R. (2d) 447, 13 M.V.R. (2d) 301 (C.A.).

A genuine religious belief is not an excuse for refusal to provide a breath sample: *R. v. Chomokowski* (1973), 11 C.C.C. (2d) 562, [1973] 5 W.W.R.184 (Man. C.A.).

The accused had a reasonable excuse for refusing to comply with the demand because of her concern about sanitation when the officer gave her an unwrapped mouthpiece: *R. v. Pittendreigh* (1994), 83 W.A.C. 169, 162 A.R. 169 (C.A.).

A reasonably held belief of a threat of unfairness or illegality by the police would support a reasonable excuse: *R. v. Dawson* (1996), 140 Nfld. & P.E.I.R. 176, 21 M.V.R. (3d) 299 (Nfld. C.A.).

Right to production – Failure to provide the accused with the mouthpiece he used in his attempt to blow into the breathalyzer did not violate the accused's rights under s. 7. It was highly improbable that a broken mouthpiece would not have been detected by even a brief inspection: *R. v. Mayer* (1989), 16 M.V.R. (2d) 174 (B.C. Co. Ct.).

Multiple convictions – The offences under this section and under s. 253(*a*) constitute separate and distinct acts or delicts and therefore the accused may be convicted of both offences though they arise out of one incident: *R. v. Schilbe* (1976), 30 C.C.C. (2d) 113 (Ont. C.A.).

REGULATIONS / Incorporated material / Incorporated material is not a regulation.

254.1 (1) The Governor in Council may make regulations
   (*a*) **respecting the qualifications and training of evaluating officers;**
   (*b*) **prescribing the physical coordination tests to be conducted under paragraph 254(2)(*a*); and**
   (*c*) **prescribing the tests to be conducted and procedures to be followed during an evaluation under subsection 254(3.1).**

(2) A regulation may incorporate any material by reference either as it exists on a specified date or as amended from time to time.

(3) For greater certainty, material does not become a regulation for the purposes of the *Statutory Instruments Act* because it is incorporated by reference. 2008, c. 6, s. 20.

PUNISHMENT / Impaired driving causing bodily harm / Blood alcohol level over legal limit — bodily harm / Failure or refusal to provide sample — bodily harm / Impaired driving causing death / Blood alcohol level over legal limit — death / Failure or refusal to provide sample — death / Interpretation / Previous convictions / Conditional discharge.

255. (1) Every one who commits an offence under section 253 or 254 is guilty of an indictable offence or an offence punishable on summary conviction and is liable,

    (*a*) whether the offence is prosecuted by indictment or punishable on summary conviction, to the following minimum punishment, namely,

        (i) for a first offence, to a fine of not less than $1,000,

        (ii) for a second offence, to imprisonment for not less than 30 days, and

        (iii) for each subsequent offence, to imprisonment for not less than 120 days;

    (*b*) where the offence is prosecuted by indictment, to imprisonment for a term not exceeding five years; and

    (*c*) if the offence is punishable on summary conviction, to imprisonment for a term of not more than 18 months.

(2) Everyone who commits an offence under paragraph 253(1)(*a*) and causes bodily harm to another person as a result is guilty of an indictable offence and liable to imprisonment for a term of not more than 10 years.

(2.1) Everyone who, while committing an offence under paragraph 253(1)(*b*), causes an accident resulting in bodily harm to another person is guilty of an indictable offence and liable to imprisonment for a term of not more than 10 years.

(2.2) Everyone who commits an offence under subsection 254(5) and, at the time of committing the offence, knows or ought to know that their operation of the motor vehicle, vessel, aircraft or railway equipment, their assistance in the operation of the aircraft or railway equipment or their care or control of the motor vehicle, vessel, aircraft or railway equipment caused an accident resulting in bodily harm to another person is guilty of an indictable offence and liable to imprisonment for a term of not more than 10 years.

(3) Everyone who commits an offence under paragraph 253(1)(*a*) and causes the death of another person as a result is guilty of an indictable offence and liable to imprisonment for life.

(3.1) Everyone who, while committing an offence under paragraph 253(1)(*b*), causes an accident resulting in the death of another person is guilty of an indictable offence and liable to imprisonment for life.

(3.2) Everyone who commits an offence under subsection 254(5) and, at the time of committing the offence, knows or ought to know that their operation of the motor vehicle, vessel, aircraft or railway equipment, their assistance in the operation of the aircraft or railway equipment or their care or control of the motor vehicle, vessel, aircraft or railway equipment caused an accident resulting in the death of another person, or in bodily harm to another person whose death ensues, is guilty of an indictable offence and liable to imprisonment for life.

(3.3) For greater certainty, everyone who is liable to the punishment described in any of subsections (2) to (3.2) is also liable to the minimum punishment described in paragraph (1)(*a*).

(4) A person who is convicted of an offence committed under section 253 or subsection 254(5) is, for the purposes of this Act, deemed to be convicted for a second or subsequent offence, as the case may be, if they have previously been convicted of

    (*a*) an offence committed under either of those provisions;

    (*b*) an offence under subsection (2) or (3); or

(c) **an offence under section 250, 251, 252, 253, 259 or 260 or subsection 258(4) of this Act as this Act read immediately before the coming into force of this subsection.**

(5) Notwithstanding subsection 730(1), a court may, instead of convicting a person of an offence committed under section 253, after hearing medical or other evidence, if it considers that the person is in need of curative treatment in relation to his consumption of alcohol or drugs and that it would not be contrary to the public interest, by order direct that the person be discharged under section 730 on the conditions prescribed in a probation order, including a condition respecting the person's attendance for curative treatment in relation to that consumption of alcohol or drugs. R.S.C. 1985, c. 27 (1st Supp.), s. 36; 1995, c. 22, s. 18; 1999, c. 32, s. 3; 2000, c. 25, s. 2; 2008, c. 6, s. 21; c. 18, s. 7.

Note: Subsection (5) has been proclaimed in force December 4, 1985 in New Brunswick, Manitoba, Prince Edward Island, Alberta, Saskatchewan, Yukon Territory, and Northwest Territories, proclaimed in force January 1, 1988 in Nova Scotia; and is to come into force on proclamation in the remaining provinces.

CROSS-REFERENCES

Mode of trial – Where the prosecution elects to proceed by indictment on the offences in subsec. (1) then the accused may elect his mode of trial pursuant to s. 536(2). Where the prosecution elects to proceed by way of summary conviction then the trial of the offence is conducted by a summary conviction court pursuant to Part XXVII. In either case, release pending trial is determined by s. 515, although the accused is eligible for release by a peace officer under s. 496, 497 or by the officer in charge under s. 498. Where the accused is charged with an offence under subsec. (2) or (3) then he has an election as to mode of trial pursuant to s. 536(2) and release pending trial is determined by s. 515.

Causation – With respect to the offence in subsec. (3) and the issue of causation, see ss. 224 to 226. As to case law, in addition to the notes under this section, see the notes under s. 249. The term "bodily harm" is defined s. 2.

Punishment – The maximum fine for the offences in subsec. (1), where the prosecution proceeds by way of summary conviction, is $2000 as set out in s. 787 and the limitation period is set out in s. 786(2). There is no limit on the fine where the prosecution proceeds by way of indictment. Where the prosecution seeks the higher penalty prescribed by para. (a)(ii) or (iii), it must comply with the provisions of s. 727. Section 667 provides one method of proof of the prior conviction. No reference to the prior conviction may be made in the information by virtue of s. 664. Note the extended definition of the meaning of previous convictions in subsec. (4). The wording of para. (4)(c) is somewhat confusing because the numbers refer to the section numbers of R.S.C. 1985 immediately prior to the *Criminal Law Amendment Act*, 1985, c. 19, proclaimed in force on December 4, 1985. For convenience, the following sets out a description of the offence referred to and in square brackets, the R.S.C. 1985 number as used in this subsection followed by the R.S.C. 1970 section number: impaired driving and care or control of motor vehicle [250/234]; refusing to comply with roadside screening device demand [251/234.1]; refusing to comply with breathalyzer demand [252/235]; "over 80" re motor vehicles [253/236]; refusal to comply with breath demand re operation of vessel [259/240.1]; "over 80" re vessels [260/240.2]; and impaired operation of vessel [258(4)/240(4)]. By reason of the change in the minimum term from 3 months to 90 days, a person sentenced to the minimum term of 90 days under para. (a)(iii) may be ordered to serve the sentence on an intermittent basis pursuant to s. 732. By reason of s. 730, since subsec. (1) prescribes a minimum punishment, a discharge is not available in relation to the offence under s. 254 nor for the offence under s. 253 in provinces where subsec. (5) has not been proclaimed in force.

An accused convicted of the offence under subsec. (2) or (3) may, pursuant to s. 259, be ordered prohibited from operating a motor vehicle, vessel, aircraft or railway equipment, as the case may be, for life if convicted of the offence under subsec. (3) and during any period not exceeding 10 years for the offence under subsec. (2). The prohibition order for the offence under subsec. (1) is mandatory by virtue of s. 259(1). The length of the order is as follows: for a first offence, during a period of not more than three years and not less than one year; for a second offence, during a period of not more than five years and not less than two years; for each subsequent offence, during a period of not less than three years plus any period to which the offender is sentenced to imprisonment. The procedure respecting the making of that order of prohibition is found in s. 260.

Pursuant to s. 255.1, evidence that the accused's blood alcohol level exceeded .160 at the time when the offence was committed is deemed to be an aggravating factor on sentencing. Note s. 732.1(3)(*g*.1) and (*g*.2), which allow for imposition of terms of probation that the offender attend for curative treatment in relation to the consumption of alcohol and drugs and participate in an alcohol ignition interlock device program.

SYNOPSIS

When a person is convicted of the basic offence under ss. 253 or 254, that person is liable to a maximum term of imprisonment of five years if prosecuted by indictment, and 18 months if prosecuted summarily. The minimum punishment upon a conviction for a first offence under ss. 253 or 254 is a fine of $1000; for a second offence, imprisonment for not less than 30 days; and for each subsequent offence, imprisonment for not less than 120 days, whether or not the offence is prosecuted summarily or by indictment. A person convicted of an offence under s. 253(1)(*a*) (impaired) who has caused either bodily harm or death to another person, is guilty of an indictable offence and is subject to a maximum term of imprisonment — in the case of bodily harm, for 10 years: and in the case of death, for life. A person who is convicted of an offence under s. 253(1)(*b*) (over "80") and causes an accident resulting in bodily harm to another or death is guilty of an indictable offence and is subject to a maximum term of imprisonment — in the case of bodily harm, for 10 years, and in the case of death, for life. Note that it does not appear that there needs to be a causal connection between the blood-alcohol level and the causing of the accident.

Subsections (2.2) and (3.2) enact the same penalties (*i.e.* 10 years or life) where the person is convicted of a refusal offence under s. 254(5) and knew or ought to have known that the operation of the vehicle, vessel, aircraft or railway equipment caused an accident resulting in bodily harm or death as the case may be.

Subsection (3.1) clarifies that the minimum punishments set out in subsec. (1)(*a*) also apply to the offences described in subsecs. (2) and (3). Thus, for example, a conditional sentence would not be available for second or subsequent offences.

A conviction under ss. 253 or 254(5) will be considered a second or subsequent offence, if a person has previously been convicted of an offence under any of these provisions, subsecs. (2) or (3) of this section, or ss. 250, 251, 252, 253, 259, or 260, or the former s. 258(4). Where it is proclaimed in force, subsec. (5) gives discretion to discharge the person, charged with a s. 253 offence, on the conditions set out in a probation order (which must include a requirement that the person seek treatment), provided there is evidence that a person has an alcohol or drug problem and a finding that it would not be contrary to the public interest to discharge him, notwithstanding that the person would otherwise not be eligible for discharge under s. 736(1) because the offence carries a minimum penalty.

ANNOTATIONS

Sentencing under subsec. (1) generally – It was open to the trial court to adopt a series of detailed guidelines for the imposition of penalties in drinking and driving offences, provided that the guidelines are used in conjunction with the appropriate principles and factors as they apply to the situation before the judge in the particular case: *R. v. Stephens* (1989), 51 C.C.C. (3d) 557, 21 M.V.R. (2d) 153 (P.E.I.C.A.).

In *R. v. Bradshaw*, [1976] 1 S.C.R. 162, 21 C.C.C. (2d) 69 (8:0), decided prior to the enactment of subsec. (5), it was held that a minimum fine is a minimum punishment within the meaning of s. 662.1 [now s. 736] and therefore a discharge is not available.

Second or subsequent offence [subsec. (1)(a)(ii) and (iii)] – The increased penalty for a "second" or "subsequent" offence does not apply where the offence is committed prior to the conviction for the offence relied upon as a prior offence even if committed after this prior offence: *R. v. Negridge* (1980), 54 C.C.C. (2d) 304 (Ont. C.A.); *R. v. Rahko* (1983), 29 M.V.R. 37 (B.C.C.A.). Similarly where the accused is convicted on the same day of impaired driving and refusing to comply with a breathalyzer demand arising out of the same transaction he has only one prior conviction for the purposes of penalty and is to be sentenced on the basis of para. (a)(ii) rather than para. (a)(iii): *R. v. Skolnick* (1981), 59 C.C.C. (2d) 286 (Ont. C.A.), affd [1982] 2 S.C.R. 47, 68 C.C.C. (2d) 385 (9:0).

Two prior convictions which are entered at the same time but arise out of separate incidents are properly considered a single prior conviction: *R. v. Robertson* (1998), 124 C.C.C. (3d) 558, 162 Nfld. & P.E.I.R. 163 (Nfld. C.A.), leave to appeal to S.C.C. refused 129 C.C.C. (3d) vi.

A curative discharge is not a conviction for the purpose of subsec. (1): *R. v. Conn* (2004), 190 C.C.C. (3d) 313, 190 Man. R. (2d) 172 (C.A.).

In deciding whether to seek an increased penalty, the Crown must exercise its discretion in a way that is consistent with the principles of fundamental justice. While a trial judge can review the prosecutor's exercise of discretion to determine whether it offends s. 7 of the Charter, this does not involve an assessment of the reasonableness of the prosecutor's decision but rather a consideration of whether the Crown's decision is arbitrary; undermines the integrity of the administration of justice; renders the sentencing proceedings fundamentally unfair; or if it results in a limit on the accused's liberty that is grossly disproportionate to the state interest in proving the notice: *R. v. Gill*, 2012 ONCA 607.

Consistent with *Gladue* and *Ipeelee*, the Crown must consider the accused's aboriginal status in determining whether to request a mandatory minimum sentence of imprisonment: *R. v. Anderson* (2013), 295 C.C.C. (3d) 262 (N.L.C.A.), leave to appeal to S.C.C. allowed [2013] S.C.C.A. No. 85.

Note: These cases were decided before the minimum punishment was increased to 120 days.

Constitutionality of minimum punishment – The mandatory jail term prescribed by para. (a) does not offend the fundamental justice guarantee in s. 7 of the *Charter of Rights and Freedoms*: *R. v. Tardif* (1983), 9 C.C.C. (3d) 223 (Sask. C.A.), nor s. 15 of the Charter: *R. v. Aucoin* (1987), 79 N.S.R. (2d) 32, 48 M.V.R. 154 (S.C. App. Div.).

The minimum punishment of 90 days prescribed by subsec. (1)(a)(iii) does not violate the guarantee to protection against imposition of cruel and unusual punishment under s. 12 of the Charter: *R. v. Parsons* (1988), 40 C.C.C. (3d) 128, 68 Nfld. & P.E.I.R. 206 (Nfld. S.C.T.D.).

The minimum jail sentence for repeat offenders will not ordinarily violate ss. 7 and 12 of the Charter and thus subsec. (1)(a)(ii) is not unconstitutional. However, in a particular case, as where there is a very significant time gap between the first and second offences, the minimum punishment may be grossly disproportionate in which case the accused may be entitled to a constitutional exemption under s. 24(1) of the Charter: *R. v. Kumar* (1993), 85 C.C.C. (3d) 417 (B.C.C.A.). However, now see *R. v. Ferguson*, [2008] 1 S.C.R. 96, 228 C.C.C. (3d) 385.

Causation (subsecs. (2) and (3)) – It was held in relation to the offence of criminal negligence causing death that the element of causation is satisfied if the evidence shows that the criminally negligent conduct of the accused meets the test in *R. v. Smithers*, [1978] 1 S.C.R. 506, 34 C.C.C. (2d) 427 (a manslaughter case noted under s. 222) being at least a contributing cause of death outside the *de minimis* range. It is misdirection to instruct the jury that the conduct must be shown to be a substantial cause: *R. v. Pinske* (1988), 30 B.C.L.R. (2d) 114, 6 M.V.R. (2d) 19 (B.C.C.A.), affd [1989] 2 S.C.R. 979. The *Smithers* test has been adopted for prosecutions under this section and the similar offences of dangerous driving causing bodily harm or death under s. 249(3) and (4): *R. v. Larocque* (1988), 5 M.V.R. (2d) 221 (Ont. C.A.); *R. v. Halkett* (1988), 73 Sask. R. 241, 11 M.V.R. (2d) 109 (C.A.); *R. v. Singhal* (1988), 5 M.V.R. (2d) 173 (B.C.C.A.); *R. v. Arsenault* (1992), 16 C.R.

(4th) 301, 104 Nfld. & P.E.I.R. 29 (P.E.I.C.A.); *R. v. Colby* (1989), 52 C.C.C. (3d) 321 (Alta. C.A.), and *R. v. Ewart* (1989), 53 C.C.C. (3d) 153 (Alta. C.A.), leave to appeal to S.C.C. refused 109 A.R. 320*n*. The court seems to have adopted a somewhat stricter test for causation in *R. v. F. (D.)* (1989), 52 C.C.C. (3d) 357 (Alta. C.A.).

In considering whether the *Smithers* test has been made out, reference should also now be made to *R. v. Nette*, [2001] 3 S.C.R. 488, 158 C.C.C. (3d) 486, where a majority of the court explained that causing death outside the *de minimis* range means that the acts of the accused were a significant contributing cause to the death.

Evidence of impairment *per se* is not sufficient to satisfy the test of causation even when coupled with expert opinion evidence as to the physiology of alcohol, an opinion, however, which was expressed in terms of averages and statistical probabilities and couched in qualifying language: *R. v. Fisher* (1992), 13 C.R. (4th) 222, 36 M.V.R. (2d) 6 (B.C.C.A.).

While it is sufficient to prove that the accused's impairment contributed in the smallest degree to the death, mere evidence that the accused's ability to drive was impaired is insufficient to establish causation. The Crown must prove unusual conduct on the part of the accused or that the accused's state of intoxication could have contributed in more than a minor way to the victim's death. The absence of an explanation from the accused can also lead to an adverse inference that his intoxication contributed to the victim's death: *R. v. Laprise* (1996), 113 C.C.C. (3d) 87 (Que. C.A.).

Where there is evidence to support a conviction beyond the fact of the accident, and no evidence to suggest a reason for the accident other than impairment, it is not an error for the trial judge to take account of the circumstances of the accident to establish both impairment and causation: *R. v. Rhyason* (2006), 214 C.C.C. (3d) 337 (Alta. C.A.), affd [2007] 3 S.C.R. 108, 221 C.C.C. (3d) 1.

Definition of "accident" (subsec. (3.1)) – A purposive rather than literalist reading must be given. Thus, there was no "accident" within the meaning of subsec. (3.1) where the deceased had jumped on the hood of the car and struck the windshield with a baseball bat, then fallen to the ground and struck his head when the accused applied the brakes to try to get him off the hood. The deceased's conduct was deliberate and criminal, so any "accident" was not caused by the accused's driving: *R. v. Jagoe* (2012), 302 C.C.C. (3d) 454 (N.B.C.A.).

Rule precluding multiple convictions [*Kienapple rule*] – Where the act of the accused, which amounts to dangerous driving, is operating her motor vehicle while her ability to do so was substantially impaired by alcohol, the rule precluding multiple convictions enunciated in *R. v. Kienapple*, [1975] 1 S.C.R. 725, 15 C.C.C. (2d) 524, applies and the accused cannot be convicted of this offence and the offence under s. 249(4). Since a conviction for the offence under this subsection more accurately describes the *delict*, the conviction should be entered on that charge and the charge under s. 249(4) stayed: *R. v. Colby* (1989), 52 C.C.C. (3d) 321 (Alta. C.A.).

The rule precluding multiple convictions does not prevent the conviction of the accused for the offence under subsec. (2) and the offence of criminal negligence causing bodily harm, although the injuries underlying both offences were to the same victim. The evidence disclosed facts concerning both the accused's manner of driving and, as well, her capacity to drive. The act of impaired operation did not encompass the manner of driving which, in this case, formed a part of the sequence of actions which constituted criminal negligence: *R. v. Andrew* (1990), 57 C.C.C. (3d) 301 (B.C.C.A.).

Discharge for curative treatment [subsec. (5)] / Constitutional considerations – While the validity of the selective proclamation of this subsection has been attacked as a violation of the equality rights in s. 15 of the *Canadian Charter of Rights and Freedoms*, most courts have held either that there is no violation or that the courts have no power to, in effect, proclaim this provision in force: *R. v. Killen* (1985), 24 C.C.C. (3d) 40 (N.S.C.A.); *R. v. Ellsworth* (1988), 46 C.C.C. (3d) 442 (Que. C.A.); *R. v. Van Vliet* (1988), 45 C.C.C. (3d) 481 (B.C.C.A.). Moreover, in *R. v. Turpin*, [1989] 1 S.C.R. 1296, 48 C.C.C. (3d) 8 (6:0), the court doubted the correctness of the decision of the Ontario Court of Appeal in *R. v.*

Hamilton; R. v. Asselin; R. v. McCullagh (1986), 30 C.C.C. (3d) 257, where that court had found a violation of s. 15 and in effect proclaimed this subsection to be in effect. Thus in *R. v. Alton* (1989), 53 C.C.C. (3d) 252 (Ont. C.A.), the court reversed the decision in *R. v. Hamilton, supra*, and held that this subsection is not available to an accused in Ontario.

However, in *R. v. Daybutch* (2015), 325 C.C.C. (3d) 568 (Ont. C.J.), the court held that the unavailability of a curative discharge for Aboriginal offenders in Ontario as a result of the province's policy not to proclaim it in force was discriminatory and violated the offender's s. 15 Charter right.

Circumstances where discharge should be granted – Where this subsection has been proclaimed in force, the court is entitled to assume that adequate facilities will be provided for curative treatment. Before invoking this subsection the court must be satisfied on a balance of probabilities that the accused is in need of curative treatment and that a discharge would not be contrary to the public interest. However, notwithstanding the accused has a lengthy record for *Criminal Code* driving offences this subsection may be resorted to where evidence adduced shows that the appropriate treatment for the accused's addiction is available and that the accused is now well-motivated and has a good chance of overcoming his alcoholism: *R. v. Beaulieu* (1980), 53 C.C.C. 342, 7 M.V.R. 9 (N.W.T.S.C.).

In considering whether a curative discharge would be contrary to the public interest, the court should consider, among other things, the circumstances of the offence and whether the accused was involved in an accident causing death, bodily harm or significant property damage; the *bona fides* of the accused; the accused's criminal record as it relates to alcohol-related driving offences; whether the accused was subject to a driving prohibition at the time of the offence; whether the accused had received the benefit of a prior curative discharge and what, if anything, the accused had done to facilitate his rehabilitation under the prior discharge: *R. v. Storr* (1995), 102 W.A.C. 65, 174 A.R. 65 (C.A.).

It will not always be contrary to the public interest to grant a discharge under this subsection to a recidivist. In some cases public protection may well be best served by effective measures to reduce the risk of repetition of the offence through rehabilitation of the offender. On the other hand it would be contrary to the public interest to grant a discharge if there was a real risk of repetition of the offence: *R. v. Wallner* (1988), 44 C.C.C. (3d) 358 (Alta. C.A.).

It was improper for the trial judge to adjourn the sentencing of the accused for a lengthy period of time presumably to determine whether he was an appropriate candidate for a discharge for curative treatment by seeing whether he would stop drinking. If the evidence was not sufficient at the time of the application for the discharge, then the judge should have invited the accused to call medical or other evidence: *R. v. Kidder* (1992), 127 A.R. 136, 38 M.V.R. (2d) 98 (C.A.).

In determining whether to grant a discharge, regard must be had to the circumstances and gravity of the offence, the motive of the offender to rehabilitate, the alcohol-related criminal record, whether there was a driving prohibition at the time and whether a previous curative discharge had been granted: *R. v. Soosay* (2001), 160 C.C.C. (3d) 437 (Alta. C.A.).

"Other evidence" must be evidence which is similar in quality and kind to medical evidence including evidence from other professionals who are able to provide information on treatment and rehabilitation. Accordingly, evidence of the accused and a youth justice committee worker was insufficient to support a discharge: *R. v. Soosay, supra*.

AGGRAVATING CIRCUMSTANCES FOR SENTENCING PURPOSES.

255.1 Without limiting the generality of section 718.2, where a court imposes a sentence for an offence committed under this Act by means of a motor vehicle, vessel or aircraft or of railway equipment, evidence that the concentration of alcohol in the blood of the offender at the time when the offence was committed exceeded one hundred and sixty milligrams of alcohol in one hundred millilitres of blood shall be deemed to be

aggravating circumstances relating to the offence that the court shall consider under paragraph 718.2(*a*). 1999, c. 32, s. 4.

CROSS-REFERENCES

"Motor vehicle" is defined in s. 2. "Aircraft" and "vessel" are defined in s. 214. Section 258(1)(*c*) and (*d*) assist the prosecution in establishing the accused's blood alcohol level at the time of the offence. Those provisions, however, only apply to proceedings for offences under s. 255. There are a number of other offences to which this section might have application. See in particular ss. 220 and 221 [criminal negligence], s. 252 [failing to stop], and s. 259 [operating a motor vehicle, vessel or aircraft while disqualified]. For notes on sentencing for driving offences, see s. 718.2.

SYNOPSIS

The effect of this section is that if the offence was committed by means of a motor vehicle, vessel or aircraft, evidence that the accused's blood alcohol level exceeded .160 at the time when the offence was committed is deemed to be an aggravating factor on sentencing. This section must be read with s. 718.2, which sets out other statutory aggravating factors.

WARRANTS TO OBTAIN BLOOD SAMPLES / Form / Information on oath / Duration of warrant / Copy or facsimile to person.

256. (1) Subject to subsection (2), if a justice is satisfied, on an information on oath in Form 1 or on an information on oath submitted to the justice under section 487.1 by telephone or other means of telecommunication, that there are reasonable grounds to believe that

(*a*) a person has, within the preceding four hours, committed, as a result of the consumption of alcohol or a drug, an offence under section 253 and the person was involved in an accident resulting in the death of another person or in bodily harm to himself or herself or to any other person, and

(*b*) a qualified medical practitioner is of the opinion that

(i) by reason of any physical or mental condition of the person that resulted from the consumption of alcohol or a drug, the accident or any other occurrence related to or resulting from the accident, the person is unable to consent to the taking of samples of his or her blood, and

(ii) the taking of samples of blood from the person would not endanger the life or health of the person,

the justice may issue a warrant authorizing a peace officer to require a qualified medical practitioner to take, or to cause to be taken by a qualified technician under the direction of the qualified medical practitioner, the samples of the blood of the person that in the opinion of the person taking the samples are necessary to enable a proper analysis to be made in order to determine the concentration, if any, of alcohol or drugs in the person's blood.

(2) A warrant issued pursuant to subsection (1) may be in Form 5 or 5.1 varied to suit the case.

(3) Notwithstanding paragraphs 487.1(4)(*b*) and (*c*), an information on oath submitted by telephone or other means of telecommunication for the purposes of this section shall include, instead of the statements referred to in those paragraphs, a statement setting out the offence alleged to have been committed and identifying the person from whom blood samples are to be taken.

(4) Samples of blood may be taken from a person pursuant to a warrant issued pursuant to subsection (1) only during such time as a qualified medical practitioner is satisfied that the conditions referred to in subparagraphs (1)(*b*)(i) and (ii) continue to exist in respect of that person.

(5) When a warrant issued under subsection (1) is executed, the peace officer shall, as soon as practicable, give a copy of it — or, in the case of a warrant issued by telephone or other means of telecommunication, a facsimile — to the person from whom the blood samples are taken. R.S.C. 1985, c. 27 (1st Supp.), s. 36; 1992, c. 1, s. 58; 1994, c. 44, s. 13; 2000, c. 25, s. 3; 2008, c. 6, s. 22.

CROSS-REFERENCES

The terms "peace officer" and "justice" are defined in s. 2 and the terms "qualified medical practitioner" and "qualified technician" in s. 254. The reference to s. 487.1 is to the telewarrant procedure set out in that section. The term "bodily harm" is defined in s. 2.

The normal procedure for obtaining blood samples by demand is set out in s. 254. Section 257 protects the medical practitioner and qualified technician from criminal and civil liability when proceeding under this section. Section 258.1 enacts provisions to protect the privacy of the accused by prohibiting unauthorized use of bodily samples taken under this section.

The presumption respecting the accused's blood alcohol level arising from analysis of a blood sample is found in s. 258(1)(d). Procedure for admission of certificates of an analyst, qualified technician and medical practitioner is set out in s. 258(1)(e) to (i) and (6) and (7). Note s. 258(4) which provides for summary application to a judge, within 3 months of the date the blood sample was taken, for an order releasing one of the samples for the purpose of testing by the defence.

Section 489.1 [which incorrectly refers to s. 258 rather than this section] requires that the peace officer make a report to a justice as soon as practicable following execution of the warrant.

SYNOPSIS

This section authorizes a justice who has reasonable grounds to believe: (a) that a person has committed an offence under s. 253 within the preceding four hours; (b) that the person has been involved in an accident resulting in bodily harm to himself or anyone else or death to another person; (c) that a physician is of the opinion that the person is physically or mentally unable to consent to the taking of blood samples; and (d) that the physician is also of the opinion that the taking of the blood samples would not endanger the life or health of the person, to issue a warrant authorizing a peace officer to require a physician to take or to supervise the taking of sufficient blood from the person to allow analysis for the concentration of alcohol or drugs. The information to obtain the warrant must be in Form 1 or, if obtained by telephone or other means of telecommunication, pursuant to s. 487.1, modified to contain a statement setting out the alleged offence and the identity of the person from whom blood samples are to be taken. The warrant may be in Form 5 or 5.1, varied to suit the case. The warrant may only be executed if the physician continues to be satisfied that the condition of the person precludes consent and that the person's health will not be endangered. If blood is taken pursuant to the warrant, the peace officer must give a copy or a facsimile of the warrant (as soon as practicable) to the person from whom the samples are obtained.

ANNOTATIONS

Constitutional considerations – The non-consensual taking of a blood sample from an unconscious motorist without a warrant and without any statutory authority is a serious intrusion into the person's privacy and this violation of s. 8 of the Charter warrants exclusion of the evidence obtained: *R. v. Pohoretsky*, [1987] 1 S.C.R. 945, 33 C.C.C. (3d) 398 (7:0). [**Note:** This case arose prior to the statutory amendments providing for the taking of blood samples in certain cases.] Similarly: *R. v. Tomaso* (1989), 70 C.R. (3d) 152, 33 O.A.C. 106 (C.A.).

To a similar effect, see *R. v. Dyment*, [1988] 2 S.C.R. 417, 45 C.C.C. (3d) 244 (5:0), where a blood sample originally taken from the accused for medical reasons was turned over to a police officer. The physician held the blood sample subject to a duty to respect the patient's privacy and this was sufficient to qualify the police officer's taking of the sample as a seizure. The officer had no warrant to seize the sample and the Crown adduced no evidence to justify a warrantless seizure. The seizure was unlawful and unreasonable under s. 8 of the Charter and the results of the analysis of the sample were inadmissible pursuant to s. 24(2) of the Charter.

Similarly, *R. v. Dersch*, [1993] 3 S.C.R. 768, 85 C.C.C. (3d) 1, where it was held that the accused's rights were violated when the police, without consent or a warrant, obtained confidential information from the physician as to the results of a blood alcohol test. The accused had repeatedly refused to provide a blood sample and the sample was only obtained, for medical purposes, when the accused was unconscious. Also, *R. v. Colarusso*, [1994] 1 S.C.R. 20, 87 C.C.C. (3d) 193, where it was held that the accused's rights under s. 8 of the Charter were violated when the results of analysis of blood samples originally obtained by the coroner for his purposes were appropriated for use in a criminal prosecution.

There was no violation of the Charter where the officer merely asked hospital personnel to not destroy a blood sample taken for medical purposes until the officer could obtain a warrant. The hospital staff were not agents of the state and the subsequent seizure pursuant to the warrant was valid: *R. v. Lunn* (1990), 61 C.C.C. (3d) 193, 26 M.V.R. (2d) 209 (B.C.C.A.).

It was proper for the police officer to take control of one of several blood samples taken by hospital personnel for medical purposes to preserve its continuity until a search warrant could be obtained. Such action did not violate s. 8 of the Charter where the officer had reasonable and probable grounds to protect the blood sample: *R. v. Katsigiorgis* (1987), 39 C.C.C. (3d) 256, 62 O.R. (2d) 441 (C.A.).

Procedural requirements – The failure of the officer to file the written report as required by s. 487.1(9) did not invalidate the warrant nor render inadmissible the results of analysis of a blood sample taken pursuant to the warrant: *R. v. Skin* (1988), 13 M.V.R. (2d) 130 (B.C. Co. Ct.).

NO OFFENCE COMMITTED / No criminal or civil liability.

257. (1) No qualified medical practitioner or qualified technician is guilty of an offence only by reason of his refusal to take a sample of blood from a person for the purposes of section 254 or 256 and no qualified medical practitioner is guilty of an offence only by reason of his refusal to cause to be taken by a qualified technician under his direction a sample of blood from a person for those purposes.

(2) No qualified medical practitioner by whom or under whose direction a sample of blood is taken from a person under subsection 254(3) or (3.4) or section 256, and no qualified technician acting under the direction of a qualified medical practitioner, incurs any criminal or civil liability for anything necessarily done with reasonable care and skill when taking the sample. R.S.C. 1985, c. 27 (1st Supp.), s. 36; 2008, c. 6, s. 23.

CROSS-REFERENCES

The terms "qualified medical practitioner" and "qualified technician" are defined in s. 254. As to protection of persons enforcing the law generally, see s. 25.

SYNOPSIS

This section makes it clear that neither a physician nor a qualified technician will be guilty of a criminal offence for refusing to take, or for causing to be taken, a blood sample from a person pursuant to s. 254 or s. 256. Similarly, no physician or qualified technician, acting under the directions of a physician, will incur criminal or civil liability for anything necessarily done with reasonable care and skill in taking the blood sample.

PROCEEDINGS UNDER SECTION 255 / Evidence of failure to give sample / Evidence of failure to comply with demand / Release of sample for analysis / Testing of blood for concentration of a drug / Attendance and right to cross-examine / Notice of intention to produce certificate.

258. (1) In any proceedings under subsection 255(1) in respect of an offence committed under section 253 or subsection 254(5) or in any proceedings under any of subsections 255(2) to (3.2),

(*a*) where it is proved that the accused occupied the seat or position ordinarily occupied by a person who operates a motor vehicle, vessel or aircraft or any railway equipment or who assists in the operation of an aircraft or of railway equipment, the accused shall be deemed to have had the care or control of the vehicle, vessel, aircraft or railway equipment, as the case may be, unless the accused establishes that the accused did not occupy that seat or position for the purpose of setting the vehicle, vessel, aircraft or railway equipment in motion or assisting in the operation of the aircraft or railway equipment, as the case may be;

(*b*) the result of an analysis of a sample of the accused's breath, blood, urine or other bodily substance — other than a sample taken under subsection 254(3), (3.3) or (3.4) — may be admitted in evidence even if the accused was not warned before they gave the sample that they need not give the sample or that the result of the analysis of the sample might be used in evidence;

(*c*) where samples of the breath of the accused have been taken pursuant to a demand made under subsection 254(3), if

   (i) [*Repealed* before coming into force R.S.C., c. 27 (1st Supp.), s. 36]

   (ii) each sample was taken as soon as practicable after the time when the offence was alleged to have been committed and, in the case of the first sample, not later than two hours after that time, with an interval of at least fifteen minutes between the times when the samples were taken,

   (iii) each sample was received from the accused directly into an approved container or into an approved instrument operated by a qualified technician, and

   (iv) an analysis of each sample was made by means of an approved instrument operated by a qualified technician,

   evidence of the results of the analyses so made is conclusive proof that the concentration of alcohol in the accused's blood both at the time when the analyses were made and at the time when the offence was alleged to have been committed was, if the results of the analyses are the same, the concentration determined by the analyses and, if the results of the analyses are different, the lowest of the concentrations determined by the analyses, in the absence of evidence tending to show all of the following three things — that the approved instrument was malfunctioning or was operated improperly, that the malfunction or improper operation resulted in the determination that the concentration of alcohol in the accused's blood exceeded 80 mg of alcohol in 100 mL of blood, and that the concentration of alcohol in the accused's blood would not in fact have exceeded 80 mg of alcohol in 100 mL of blood at the time when the offence was alleged to have been committed;

(*d*) if a sample of the accused's blood has been taken under subsection 254(3) or section 256 or with the accused's consent and if

   (i) at the time the sample was taken, the person taking the sample took an additional sample of the blood of the accused and one of the samples was retained to permit an analysis of it to be made by or on behalf of the accused and, in the case where the accused makes a request within six months from the taking of the samples, one of the samples was ordered to be released under subsection (4),

     (ii) both samples referred to in subparagraph (i) were taken as soon as practicable and in any event not later than two hours after the time when the offence was alleged to have been committed,

    (iii) both samples referred to in subparagraph (i) were taken by a qualified medical practitioner or a qualified technician under the direction of a qualified medical practitioner,

    (iv) both samples referred to in subparagraph (i) were received from the accused directly into, or placed directly into, approved containers that were subsequently sealed, and

    (v) an analysis was made by an analyst of at least one of the samples,

    evidence of the result of the analysis is conclusive proof that the concentration of alcohol in the accused's blood both at the time when the samples were taken and at the time when the offence was alleged to have been committed was the concentration determined by the analysis or, if more than one sample was analyzed and the results of the analyses are the same, the concentration determined by the analyses and, if the results of the analyses are different, the lowest of the concentrations determined by the analyses, in the absence of evidence tending to show all of the following three things — that the analysis was performed improperly, that the improper performance resulted in the determination that the concentration of alcohol in the accused's blood exceeded 80 mg of alcohol in 100 mL of blood, and that the concentration of alcohol in the accused's blood would not in fact have exceeded 80 mg of alcohol in 100 mL of blood at the time when the offence was alleged to have been committed;

(*d*.01) for greater certainty, evidence tending to show that an approved instrument was malfunctioning or was operated improperly, or that an analysis of a sample of the accused's blood was performed improperly, does not include evidence of

    (i) the amount of alcohol that the accused consumed,

    (ii) the rate at which the alcohol that the accused consumed would have been absorbed and eliminated by the accused's body, or

    (iii) a calculation based on that evidence of what the concentration of alcohol in the accused's blood would have been at the time when the offence was alleged to have been committed;

(*d*.1) if samples of the accused's breath or a sample of the accused's blood have been taken as described in paragraph (*c*) or (*d*) under the conditions described in that paragraph and the results of the analyses show a concentration of alcohol in blood exceeding 80 mg of alcohol in 100 mL of blood, evidence of the results of the analyses is proof that the concentration of alcohol in the accused's blood at the time when the offence was alleged to have been committed exceeded 80 mg of alcohol in 100 mL of blood, in the absence of evidence tending to show that the accused's consumption of alcohol was consistent with both

    (i) a concentration of alcohol in the accused's blood that did not exceed 80 mg of alcohol in 100 mL of blood at the time when the offence was alleged to have been committed, and

    (ii) the concentration of alcohol in the accused's blood as determined under paragraph (*c*) or (*d*), as the case may be, at the time when the sample or samples were taken;

(*e*) a certificate of an analyst stating that the analyst has made an analysis of a sample of the blood, urine, breath or other bodily substance of the accused and stating the result of that analysis is evidence of the facts alleged in the certificate without proof of the signature or the official character of the person appearing to have signed the certificate;

(*f*) a certificate of an analyst stating that the analyst has made an analysis of a sample of an alcohol standard that is identified in the certificate and intended for use with an approved instrument and that the sample of the standard analyzed by the analyst was found to be suitable for use with an approved instrument, is evidence that the alcohol standard so identified is suitable for use with an approved instrument without proof of the signature or the official character of the person appearing to have signed the certificate;

(f.1) the document printed out from an approved instrument and signed by a qualified technician who certifies it to be the printout produced by the approved instrument when it made the analysis of a sample of the accused's breath is evidence of the facts alleged in the document without proof of the signature or official character of the person appearing to have signed it;

(g) where samples of the breath of the accused have been taken pursuant to a demand made under subsection 254(3), a certificate of a qualified technician stating

    (i) that the analysis of each of the samples has been made by means of an approved instrument operated by the technician and ascertained by the technician to be in proper working order by means of an alcohol standard, identified in the certificate, that is suitable for use with an approved instrument,

    (ii) the results of the analyses so made, and

    (iii) if the samples were taken by the technician,

        (A) [Repealed without coming into force, 2008, c. 20, s. 3.]

        (B) the time when and place where each sample and any specimen described in clause (A) was taken, and

        (C) that each sample was received from the accused directly into an approved container or into an approved instrument operated by the technician,

is evidence of the facts alleged in the certificate without proof of the signature or the official character of the person appearing to have signed the certificate;

(h) if a sample of the accused's blood has been taken under subsection 254(3) or (3.4) or section 256 or with the accused's consent,

    (i) a certificate of a qualified medical practitioner stating that

        (A) they took the sample and before the sample was taken they were of the opinion that taking it would not endanger the accused's life or health and, in the case of a demand made under section 256, that by reason of any physical or mental condition of the accused that resulted from the consumption of alcohol or a drug, the accident or any other occurrence related to or resulting from the accident, the accused was unable to consent to the taking of the sample,

        (B) at the time the sample was taken, an additional sample of the blood of the accused was taken to permit analysis of one of the samples to be made by or on behalf of the accused,

        (C) the time when and place where both samples referred to in clause (B) were taken, and

        (D) both samples referred to in clause (B) were received from the accused directly into, or placed directly into, approved containers that were subsequently sealed and that are identified in the certificate,

    (ii) a certificate of a qualified medical practitioner stating that the medical practitioner caused the sample to be taken by a qualified technician under his direction and that before the sample was taken the qualified medical practitioner was of the opinion referred to in clause (i)(A), or

    (iii) a certificate of a qualified technician stating that the technician took the sample and the facts referred to in clauses (i)(B) to (D)

is evidence of the facts alleged in the certificate without proof of the signature or official character of the person appearing to have signed the certificate; and

(i) a certificate of an analyst stating that the analyst has made an analysis of a sample of the blood of the accused that was contained in a sealed approved container identified in the certificate, the date on which and place where the sample was analyzed and the result of that analysis is evidence of the facts alleged in the certificate without proof of the signature or official character of the person appearing to have signed it.

Transitional provision

Note: R.S.C. 1985, c. 27 (1st Supp.), s. 204, proclaimed in force December 4, 1985, provides as follows:

204. Paragraphs 258(1)(*f*) and (*g*) of the *Criminal Code*, as they read immediately before the coming into force of the amendments to those paragraphs, as enacted by section 36 of this Act, continue to apply to any proceedings in respect of which a certificate referred to in those paragraphs was issued prior to the coming into force of the amendments to those paragraphs.

(2) Unless a person is required to give a sample of a bodily substance under paragraph 254(2)(*b*) or subsection 254(3), (3.3) or (3.4), evidence that they failed or refused to give a sample for analysis for the purposes of this section or that a sample was not taken is not admissible and the failure, refusal or fact that a sample was not taken shall not be the subject of comment by any person in the proceedings.

(3) In any proceedings under subsection 255(1) in respect of an offence committed under paragraph 253(1)(*a*) or in any proceedings under subsection 255(2) or (3), evidence that the accused, without reasonable excuse, failed or refused to comply with a demand made under section 254 is admissible and the court may draw an inference adverse to the accused from that evidence.

(4) If, at the time a sample of an accused's blood is taken, an additional sample is taken and retained, a judge of a superior court of criminal jurisdiction or a court of criminal jurisdiction shall, on the summary application of the accused made within six months after the day on which the samples were taken, order the release of one of the samples for the purpose of examination or analysis, subject to any terms that appear to be necessary or desirable to ensure that the sample is safeguarded and preserved for use in any proceedings in respect of which it was taken.

(5) A sample of an accused's blood taken under subsection 254(3) or section 256 or with the accused's consent for the purpose of analysis to determine the concentration, if any, of alcohol in the blood may be tested to determine the concentration, if any, of a drug in the blood.

(6) A party against whom a certificate described in paragraph (1)(*e*), (*f*), (*f*.1), (*g*), (*h*) or (*i*) is produced may, with leave of the court, require the attendance of the qualified medical practitioner, analyst or qualified technician, as the case may be, for the purposes of cross-examination.

(7) No certificate shall be received in evidence pursuant to paragraph (1)(*e*), (*f*), (*g*), (*h*) or (*i*) unless the party intending to produce it has, before the trial, given to the other party reasonable notice of his intention and a copy of the certificate. R.S.C. 1985, c. 27 (1st Supp.), s. 36; c. 32 (4th Supp.), s. 61; 1994, c. 44, s. 14; 1997, c. 18, s. 10; 2008, c. 6, s. 24.

CROSS-REFERENCES

The terms "peace officer", "motor vehicle", "railway equipment", "superior court of criminal jurisdiction" and "court of criminal jurisdiction" are defined in s. 2. The terms "aircraft", "vessel" and "operates" are defined in s. 214. The terms "analyst", "approved container", "approved instrument", "qualified medical practitioner" and "qualified technician" are defined in s. 254. The offence of impaired operation is defined in ss. 253 and 255, of "over 80" in s. 253 and refusing to comply with a breath or blood demand in s. 254.

Section 25(1) of the *Interpretation Act*, R.S.C. 1985, c. I-21 provides that "Where an enactment provides that a document is evidence of a fact without anything in the context to indicate that the document is conclusive evidence, then, in any judicial proceedings, the document is admissible in evidence and the fact is deemed to be established in the absence of any evidence to the contrary."

As to proof of service by affidavit, see s. 4(6).

Section 258.1 enacts provisions to protect the privacy of the accused by prohibiting unauthorized use of bodily samples taken under ss. 254 or 256 and unauthorized disclosure of the results of physical coordination tests.

SYNOPSIS

This section provides that, where the prosecution establishes in proceedings under s. 255(1) with respect to an offence under ss. 253, 254(5) or 255(2) to (3.2) that the accused was sitting in the operator's seat of the vehicle, the accused is deemed to have care or control of that vehicle. This presumption can be overturned if the accused is able to establish that the purpose of occupying that seat was not for setting the vehicle in motion.

In addition, the result of an analysis of a breath or blood sample along with samples of urine or other bodily substances, may be admitted in evidence even if there was no warning prior to the taking of the sample that the accused need not consent to the procedure, nor that the result might be used in evidence. No person is required, however, to give a sample of urine or other bodily substance except as required under s. 254 and evidence of a failure or refusal to give such a sample is not admissible at trial, nor may it be made the subject of comment. When the technical requirements described in s. 258(1)(c), (d) and (d.1) are met, the evidence of the results of analysis is, in the absence of evidence to the contrary, proof of the concentration of alcohol in the accused's blood at the time of the offence and proof, where applicable, that the concentration of alcohol in blood exceeded 80 mg alcohol in 100 ml of blood. If more than one sample is analyzed and the results are different, the evidence of the lowest of the concentrations will be used in the proceedings.

To rebut the presumption in para. (c) (the presumption of identity for breath samples), the accused must show that the approved instrument was malfunctioning or was operated improperly, that the malfunction or improper operation resulted in the determination that the concentration of alcohol in the accused's blood exceeded 80 mg of alcohol in 100 mL of blood, and that the concentration of alcohol in the accused's blood would not, in fact, have exceeded 80 mg of alcohol in 100 mL of blood at the time when the offence was alleged to have been committed. Under para. (d.01), the presumption cannot be defeated by evidence of the amount of alcohol consumed, the rate of absorption or elimination of alcohol or a calculation based on what the concentration of alcohol in the accused's blood would have been at the time when the offence was alleged to have been committed. Further, under para. (d.1), where the analysis shows a concentration exceeding .08, the presumption of identity applies in the absence of evidence tending to show that the accused's consumption of alcohol was consistent with both (i) a concentration of alcohol in the accused's blood that did not exceed 80 mg of alcohol in 100 mL of blood at the time when the offence was alleged to have been committed, and (ii) the concentration of alcohol in the accused's blood as determined under para. (c) or (d), as the case may be, at the time when the sample or samples were taken.

The conditions for rebutting the presumption in para. (d) (the presumption of identity for blood samples) are almost identical except that the accused must show, not that the instrument was malfunctioning or operated improperly, but that the analysis was performed improperly, that the improper performance resulted in the determination that the concentration of alcohol in the accused's blood exceeded 80 mg of alcohol in 100 mL of blood, and that the concentration of alcohol in the accused's blood would not, in fact, have exceeded 80 mg of alcohol in 100 mL of blood at the time when the offence was alleged to have been committed. Paragraph (d.1) also applies to an attempt to rebut the para. (d) presumption.

It would seem that these provisions, which came into force on May 1, 2008, attempt to reverse a long line of cases that allowed the accused to rebut the presumption of identity by adducing expert evidence that, based on the defence testimony as to the amount of alcohol consumed, the blood-alcohol would not have exceeded .08. That kind of evidence would not seem to be sufficient since *inter alia* the evidence would not show that the machine was malfunctioning or that the analysis was performed improperly. It should be pointed out that, even before these provisions came into force on May 1, 2008, the value of this kind of evidence was placed in doubt by the decision of the Supreme Court of Canada in *R. v. Gibson*, 2008 SCC 16. In view of these amendments, the notes of decisions concerning this kind of expert evidence have been removed. If readers require information on these decisions they should refer to the 2008 edition of *Martin's Annual Criminal Code*.

Subsection (1)(*e*), (*f*), (*g*), (*h*) and (*i*) provide that the certificates of analysts, medical practitioners and qualified technicians are themselves evidence of the facts set out therein without the need to prove the signature or the official character of the person signing the certificate. The presumptions of accuracy enacted by these provisions can be rebutted by evidence to the contrary as provided for in s. 25(1) of the *Interpretation Act*, R.S.C. 1985, c. I-21. The party intending to produce the certificate as evidence must, prior to trial, give the other party reasonable notice of his intention, along with a copy of the certificate. An accused person may, with leave of the court, require the attendance for cross-examination of the medical practitioner, analyst or technician who signed the certificate.

Under subsec. (4), if an additional sample of blood was taken, the accused may apply to a judge of a superior court or court of criminal jurisdiction within six months of the date upon which the blood samples were taken for an order for the release of one of the samples for analysis. In proceedings under s. 255(1) in respect of an offence committed under s. 253(1)(*a*), or in proceedings under s. 255(2) or (3), evidence of failure by the accused to comply with a demand made under s. 254 is admissible. The court may draw an inference adverse to the accused from such evidence. Under subsec. (5), a blood sample taken for analysis of alcohol concentration may also be tested for the presence of drugs.

ANNOTATIONS

General – The amendments to subsec. (1) do not apply retrospectively to offences committed before July 2, 2009: *R. v. Dineley*, [2012] 3 S.C.R. 272, 290 C.C.C. (3d) 190.

Presumption of care or control [subsec. (1)(*a*)] – Proof of indecision on the part of the accused is not sufficient to rebut the presumption in subsec. (1)(*a*). While it may be that the accused need not establish on a balance of probabilities that he had a settled purpose at the time of initially occupying the driver's seat other than that of setting the vehicle in motion, he must nevertheless prove on a balance of probabilities that he did not occupy that seat for the purpose of putting the vehicle in motion: *R. v. George* (1994), 90 C.C.C. (3d) 502, 120 Nfld. & P.E.I.R. 237 (Nfld. C.A.).

The fact that the accused is able to rebut the presumption in this paragraph does not entitle him to an acquittal where the Crown is able to establish that he had care or control without reliance on the presumption. This paragraph does not import into the care or control offence an intent to drive and the accused may be convicted of that offence where although he does not have an intent to drive he performs some act or series of acts involving the use of a car, its fittings or equipment, whereby the vehicle may unintentionally be set in motion: *R. v. Ford*, [1982] 1 S.C.R. 231, 65 C.C.C. (2d) 392 (7:2).

The Crown does not have to make a formal election before it can rely on the presumption in this paragraph: *R. v. Journeaux* (1992), 38 M.V.R. (2d) 323 (Ont. C.A.).

The Crown was not entitled to rely on the presumption in this paragraph where the accused was lying across the seat with his head on the passenger side and his legs were encased in a sleeping-bag under the steering wheel. It could not be said that he was occupying the seat ordinarily occupied by the driver. It was further held that the Crown had not otherwise made out care or control. Acts of care or control, short of driving, are acts which involve some use of the vehicle or its fittings, or some course of conduct associated with the vehicle which would involve the risk of putting the vehicle in motion so that it could become dangerous, and in this case the accused was asleep in the sleeping-bag: *R. v. Toews*, [1985] 2 S.C.R. 119, 21 C.C.C. (3d) 24 (7:0).

Constitutionality of care or control presumption – It has been held that the predecessor to this paragraph, although it required the accused to prove on a balance of probabilities that he did not enter the vehicle with the intention of setting it in motion, is a reasonable limit on the guarantee to the presumption of innocence in s. 11(*d*) of the *Canadian Charter of Rights and Freedoms* and is therefore valid: *R. v. Whyte*, [1988] 2 S.C.R. 3, 42 C.C.C. (3d) 97 (6:0).

Right to production – In *R. v. Duke*, [1972] S.C.R. 917, 7 C.C.C. (2d) 474, it was held (9:0) that because Parliament specifically proclaimed the predecessor to this section in force, in the manner that it did, the failure of the Crown to provide the suspected driver with a sample of his breath did not deprive him of his right to a fair hearing.

Failure of the officer to show the accused the reading on the breathalyzer did not deprive the accused of a fair trial. The officer had been willing to do so but, by the time the request was made, the reading had been erased: *R. v. Cabanela* (1989), 25 M.V.R. (2d) 161 (Ont. C.A.).

The accused's rights under ss. 7 and 11(*d*) of the Charter were infringed when his polite request to view the breathalyzer gauge at the time the tests were being administered was refused. Viewing the readings would have assisted the accused in making full answer and defence and would not have interfered in the administration of the tests: *R. v. Selig* (1991), 4 C.R. (4th) 20, 27 M.V.R. (2d) 166 (N.S.C.A.). *Contra*: *R. v. Gillis* (1994), 91 C.C.C. (3d) 575, 149 A.R. 395 (C.A.).

Also see Lucas, D.M. "Production of Breathalyzer Material", (1989), 1 J.M.V.L. 103.

On this issue, also see the note by C. Finley, "Production Requests: The Crown's Duty to Provide", 21 M.V.R. (2d) 65.

Applicability of presumption (para. (1)(e)) – The Crown may rely on the presumption in this paragraph not only where it proceeds by way of certificate under subsec. (1)(*g*) but where the technician gives *viva voce* evidence: *R. v. Lightfoot*, [1981] 1 S.C.R. 566, 59 C.C.C. (2d) 414 (9:0).

When the Crown proceeds by way of *viva voce* evidence of the qualified technician and seeks to rely on the presumption in this paragraph, it need only meet the requirements of this subsection and therefore, *inter alia*, the provisions of subsec. (1)(*f*) have no application: *R. v. Walters* (1975), 26 C.C.C. (2d) 56, 11 N.S.R. (2d) 443 (App. Div.).

Where the Crown is unable to rely on the presumption in this paragraph it may still prove the offence by adducing expert evidence as to the progressive absorption of alcohol into the bloodstream in order to relate the readings in the certificate back to the time of the offence: *R. v. Bozek* (1977), 34 C.C.C. (2d) 457 (Sask. Dist. Ct.); *R. v. Burnison* (1979), 70 C.C.C. (2d) 38 (Ont. C.A.).

When proceeding by way of *viva voce* evidence from the breathalyzer technician rather than by certificate there is no requirement of proof as to the suitability of the substance or solution before the Crown may rely on the presumption in this subsection: *R. v. Lightfoot*, *supra*.

Requirement of two samples – The words "each sample" must be interpreted in conjunction with s. 254(3) meaning each sample which in the opinion of the qualified technician is necessary to enable a proper analysis to be made. It would not include for example, a breath sample a portion of which escapes due to a malfunction in the machine and which in the opinion of the technician will not give a proper analysis: *R. v. Perrier* (1984), 15 C.C.C. (3d) 506, 29 M.V.R. 92 (Ont. C.A.).

Despite the use of the superlative "lowest" the Crown may still rely on the presumption where only two samples were taken. It is not necessary that three or more samples be taken: *R. v. Schultz* (1977), 38 C.C.C. (2d) 39 (Ont. H.C.J.).

It was held in *R. v. Norman* (1978), 40 C.C.C. (2d) 27, [1978] 3 W.W.R. 542 (Alta. C.A.), that considering the certificate as a whole the fact that the certificate referred to the results of analysis of "one of the said samples" and "another of the said samples" did not leave open as a reasonable conclusion that a third sample was taken the results of which were not given in the certificate. In the absence of anything to suggest to the contrary "another" is to be read in the sense of "the other". Folld: *R. v. Grace* (1979), 47 C.C.C. (2d) 301 (N.S.C.A.).

Similarly, the fact that the printed form of the certificate has spaces for the results of three breath tests, only two of which were filled out does not give rise to an inference that a third sample was taken but that the results were not recorded: *R. v. Dempsey* (1979), 45 C.C.C. (2d) 267 (N.B.C.A.).

Similarly, the mere fact that the accused blew into the breathalyzer three times is not evidence that more than two "samples" were taken: *R. v. Mangialaio* (1984), 15 C.C.C. (3d) 331, 29 M.V.R. 244 (B.C.C.A.).

Where only one breath sample was obtained, although the Crown may not rely on the technician's certificate or the presumption in this section, it may still secure a conviction under s. 253(*b*) by proceeding by *viva voce* expert evidence where the technician is able to testify that the one sample was suitable: *R. v. Jones* (1976), 33 C.C.C. (2d) 50, 16 N.B.R. (2d) 32 (C.A.).

Requirement samples received directly into approved instrument [para. (*c*)(iii)] – Evidence from the technician, merely that samples were received into a "breathalyzer instrument" is not proof that the samples were received directly into an approved instrument as required by subpara. (iii): *R. v. Alatyppo* (1983), 4 C.C.C. (3d) 514, 20 M.V.R. 39 (Ont. C.A.).

The court may take judicial notice of the workings of the Borkenstein Breathalyzer, or at least refer to standard textbooks on the subject, and so take note of the fact that the only way to introduce the breath sample is by blowing directly into a tube attached to the machine. Thus, evidence that the breath sample was "introduced" is proof that it was received "directly" into the breathalyzer: *R. v. Walters* (1975), 26 C.C.C. (2d) 56, 11 N.S.R. (2d) 443 (C.A.).

Time element / interval of 15 minutes between samples – It was held by Seaton J.A., in *R. v. Perry* (1978), 41 C.C.C. (2d) 182, 33 N.R. at p. 108 (C.A.), that there was no basis for extending the provisions of s. 25(2) of the *Interpretation Act*, R.S.C. 1970, c. I-23, to minutes and thus breath tests taken at 3:00 a.m. and 3:15 a.m. complied with the requirement that the breath samples be taken "at least 15 minutes" apart. This holding, which was contrary to the conclusion reached by several other provincial appellate courts, was apparently upheld by the Supreme Court of Canada which dismissed the appeal by the accused on June 11, 1980, [1980] 1 S.C.R. 1104, 51 C.C.C. (2d) 576*n*, N.R. *loc. cit.* p. 106, in brief reasons to the effect that the court was in agreement with the reasons of Taggart J.A. Taggart J.A. concurred in the reasons of Seaton J.A., but in addition relied on a finding of fact by the trial judge that the actual time between the tests was 15 complete minutes.

In *R. v. Taylor* (1983), 7 C.C.C. (3d) 293, 22 M.V.R. 295 (Ont. C.A.), leave to appeal to S.C.C. refused C.C.C. *loc. cit.*, the court considered the judgments in *R. v. Perry, supra,* and the majority of the court concluded that while a bare 15 minutes is sufficient for compliance, that interval is the interval of time from the point when everything necessary to complete the taking of the first sample has been done and the point when the first act is done to commence the taking of the second sample. The requirement will not be met by a certificate which merely states that the samples were taken at, for example, 3:00 a.m. and 3:17 a.m. since such a certificate is open to the conclusion that the taking of the samples commenced at those two times and without additional information as to the length of time needed to finish taking the first sample, the trial judge would not be able to determine the interval between them. Folld: *R. v. Dawson* (1984), 12 C.C.C. (3d) 152, 47 Nfld. & P.E.I.R. 295 (P.E.I.S.C. *in banco*); not followed: *R. v. Kornak* (1984), 12 C.C.C. (3d) 182, 30 Alta. L.R. (2d) 193 (C.A.); *R. v. Moore* (1984), 13 C.C.C. (3d) 281, 28 M.V.R. 23 (B.C.C.A.); *R. v. Scott* (1984), 36 Sask. R. 216 (C.A.); *R. v. DeCoste* (1984), 15 C.C.C. (3d) 289, 65 N.S.R. (2d) 61 (S.C. App. Div.); *R. v. Hepditch* (1989), 47 C.C.C. (3d) 286, 13 M.V.R. (2d) 101, 75 Nfld. & P.E.I.R. 201 (Nfld. C.A.).

In a subsequent case, *R. v. Hayes* (1985), 19 C.C.C. (3d) 569, 32 M.V.R. 126 (Ont. C.A.), the court held that for the purpose of this paragraph the sample is taken once the accused's breath sample is inside the breathalyzer and in computing the time interval it is not necessary to take into account the period of time for the machine to analyze and indicate the results of each sample. Similarly, *R. v. Daly* (1985), 32 M.V.R. 213 (Ont. C.A.); *R. v. Atkinson* (1986), 42 M.V.R. 78 (N.S.C.A.); *R. v. Arsenault* (1986), 43 M.V.R. 287 (P.E.I.S.C.).

The requirement that the samples were taken at least 15 minutes apart applies to samples of which in the opinion of the technician a proper analysis can be made. Thus, where a "sample" is taken but not analyzed because the machine was not properly hooked up, the technician need not wait 15 minutes to take a proper sample: *R. v. Weselowski* (1984), 11 C.C.C. (3d) 574 (B.C.C.A.); *R. v. Denton* (1985), 32 M.V.R. 250 (Sask. Q.B.).

Time element / as soon as practicable and within two hours – A breath sample was taken "as soon as practicable" where it was taken one hour after the accused's arrival at the police station where the delay was due to the necessity of repairing the breathalyzer: *R. v. Finlayson* (1974), 21 C.C.C. (2d) 511, [1975] W.W.D. 57 (Sask. C.A.).

The test for determining whether or not breath samples were taken as soon as practicable is whether they were taken within a reasonably prompt time under the circumstances. The court must take into account both subjective and objective factors, including whether the police officer involved acted reasonably: *R. v. Van Der Veen* (1988), 44 C.C.C. (3d) 38, 89 A.R. 4 (C.A.); *R. v. Vanderbruggen* (2006), 206 C.C.C. (3d) 489, 208 O.A.C. 379 (C.A.).

The phrase "as soon as practicable" must be applied with reason having regard to the whole chain of events and bearing in mind that the *Criminal Code* permits an outside limit of two hours from the time of the offence to the taking of the first test. There is no requirement that the Crown provide a detailed explanation of what occurred during every minute that the accused is in custody: *R. v. Vanderbruggen, supra.*

The approach articulated in *Vanderbruggen, supra,* also applies to delay *between* the taking of the first and second samples: *R. v. Singh* (2014), 310 C.C.C. (3d) 285 (Ont. C.A.).

The phrase "as soon as practicable" does not require that the tests be taken at the very earliest moment. In the circumstances a 20-minute delay while the accused was kept under observation was permissible: *R. v. Mudry; R. v. Coverly* (1979), 50 C.C.C. (2d) 518 (Alta. C.A.). Folld: *R. v. Carter* (1980), 55 C.C.C. (2d) 405, 8 M.V.R. 108 (B.C.C.A.); *R. v. Ashby* (1980), 57 C.C.C. (2d) 348 (Ont. C.A.); *R. v. Cander* (1981), 59 C.C.C. (2d) 490, 28 B.C.L.R. 376 (C.A.), leave to appeal to S.C.C. refused 38 N.R. 450*n*. Similarly: *R. v. Phillips* (1988), 42 C.C.C. (3d) 150, 64 C.R. (3d) 154 (Ont. C.A.).

Similarly, a 21-minute delay between the time of the arrival at the police station and the time of the first test is not evidence that the tests were not taken as soon as practicable. The requirement that the tests be taken as soon as practicable must be applied with reason. There is no need to explain every incident which occurred from the time of the offence to the time the samples were taken unless the trial judge is not satisfied on the evidence before him that the samples were taken as soon as practicable: *R. v. Carter* (1981), 59 C.C.C. (2d) 450, 10 M.V.R. 187 (Sask. C.A.). Folld: *R. v. Cambrin* (1982), 1 C.C.C. (3d) 59, [1983] 2 W.W.R. 250 (B.C.C.A.).

The critical issue in each case, where it is alleged that the tests were not taken as soon as practicable, is whether the conduct of the police was reasonable, having regard to all the circumstances. The act of the arresting officer in commencing the preparation of the alcohol influence report for a period of nine minutes before turning the accused over to the breathalyzer technician, was not an unreasonable procedure: *R. v. Payne* (1990), 56 C.C.C. (3d) 548, 23 M.V.R. (2d) 37 (Ont. C.A.).

Although the officer has grounds to make an immediate demand under s. 254(3), the fact that he first makes a demand under s. 254(2) does not prevent the samples subsequently obtained pursuant to the s. 254(3) demand from being obtained as soon as practicable: *R. v. Jensen* (1982), 2 C.C.C. (3d) 11, 18 M.V.R. 52 (N.S.C.A.).

Judicial notice – It was held in *R. v. Dickson* (1973), 5 N.S.R. (2d) 240 (C.A.), that the trial Judge erred in taking judicial notice of the tolerance for error in the Borkenstein Breathalyzer.

And, it was held to be an error for the judge to base his decision in part on a breathalyzer manual which he obtained from the police and which was not properly introduced into evidence: *R. v. Robertson* (1979), 47 C.C.C. (2d) 159 (B.C.C.A.).

Note: Some of the cases noted below were decided prior to the significant amendments to this section in subsec. (1)(*c*), (*d*), (*d*.01) and (*d*.1).

Evidence to the contrary / generally – As to the meaning generally of the words "any evidence to the contrary" see *R. v. Proudlock*, [1979] 1 S.C.R. 525, 43 C.C.C. (2d) 321, noted under s. 348, *infra.*

"Evidence to the contrary" must be evidence which tends to establish that the proportion of alcohol in the accused's blood at the time of the offence was not the same as indicated by the approved instrument. No evidence is "evidence to the contrary" when its only effect is to demonstrate in general terms the possible uncertainty of the elements of the legislative scheme established by these provisions or the inherent fallibility of the instruments which are approved under statutory authority. Thus, for example, evidence that the particular type of Borkenstein Breathalyzer is subject to a possible margin of error is not evidence to the contrary: *R. v. Moreau*, [1979] 1 S.C.R. 261, 42 C.C.C. (2d) 525 (5:4).

Evidence that is disbelieved, such as testimony from the accused as to the amount he had to drink, cannot form the basis for an expert's opinion so as to constitute evidence to the contrary. Further, the absence of symptoms other than the smell of alcohol, while relevant to a charge of impaired driving, is a neutral factor and is not evidence to the contrary: *R. v. Boucher* (2005), 202 C.C.C. (3d) 34, 33 C.R. (6th) 32 (S.C.C.).

The prohibition against using breathalyzer readings in assessing credibility applies only to cases in which the accused challenges the presumption of accuracy because, in such circumstances, it would be circular to use readings as proof of their own accuracy. However, where defence counsel only challenges the presumption of identity, the consideration of breathalyzer readings does not raise the spectre of circular reasoning. They are part of the body of evidence which the trial judge has to consider in deciding whether there was a reasonable doubt: *R. v. Kernighan* (2010), 257 C.C.C. (3d) 12 (Ont. C.A.).

In *R. v. Kozun* (1981), 64 C.C.C. (2d) 62, 12 M.V.R. 285 (Sask. C.A.), it was held that the fact that a third test was taken, the results of which were not disclosed in the certificate did not constitute evidence to the contrary.

Rounding down or truncating the breathalyzer reading to the second digit does not produce a false result nor constitute evidence to the contrary: *R. v. Hanson* (1989), 75 C.R. (3d) 110, 18 M.V.R. (2d) 172 (Ont. C.A.); *R. v. Goosen* (1985), 34 Man. R. (2d) 242, 35 M.V.R. 145 (Q.B.).

Evidence that the accused failed a roadside screening test may not be used to discredit evidence capable of constituting "evidence to the contrary" as to do so would render the trial unfair: *R. v. Coutts* (1999), 136 C.C.C. (3d) 225, 25 C.R. (5th) 362 (Ont. C.A.). Also see *R. v. Milne* (1996), 107 C.C.C. (3d) 118, 48 C.R. (4th) 182 (Ont. C.A.), leave to appeal to S.C.C. refused 110 C.C.C. (3d) vi, 97 O.A.C. 159*n*, noted under s. 254, *supra.*

Contra: *R. v. Fox* (2003), 178 C.C.C. (3d) 223, 14 C.R. (6th) 116 (Sask. C.A.), and *R. v. Beston* (2006), 214 C.C.C. (3d) 509, 289 Sask. R. 165 (C.A.), where it was held that the results of the approved screening device test cannot be used to incriminate the accused but can be used to test the credibility of the accused giving evidence to the contrary in order to rebut the presumption of accuracy of a certificate of a breath test.

Results of a breathalyzer test without reliance on the statutory presumptions may be considered as part of the totality of evidence to discredit evidence to the contrary: *R. v. Bernard* (1999), 140 C.C.C. (3d) 412, 20 M.V.R. (4th) 98 (Que. C.A.).

Similarly, *R. v. Suttie* (2004), 188 C.C.C. (3d) 167, 24 C.R. (6th) 3 (Ont. C.A.), held that where the accused challenges the accuracy of the blood alcohol readings in the certificate by calling evidence tending to show that his or her blood alcohol level at the time of testing must have been below .08, subsec. (1)(*g*) permits the court to consider the certificate as some evidence of the facts contained in it in determining whether to accept or reject the accused's "evidence to the contrary".

The proper interpretation of subsec. (1)(*c*)(iii) is that the breath sample from the accused must be received into an approved instrument either from an approved container if one is used or, if not, directly into the approved instrument itself: *R. v. Mulroney* (2009), 248 C.C.C. (3d) 311 (Ont. C.A.).

Evidence to the contrary/constitutional considerations – In *R. c. St-Onge Lamoureux*, [2012] 3 S.C.R. 187, 294 C.C.C. (3d) 42, the court considered a constitutional challenge to the new restrictions on "evidence to the contrary". It held (5:2) that, while ss. 258(1)(*c*), 258(1)(*d*.01) and 258(1)(*d*.1) do not infringe ss. 7 and 11(*c*) of Charter, they do infringe s. 11(*d*). Sections 258(1)(*d*.01) and 258(1)(*d*.1) are justified under s. 1, but s. 258(1)(*c*) is only justified once two restrictions on the defence are severed. Section 258(1)(*c*)(iv) contains three separate and cumulative new requirements that the accused must satisfy to rebut the presumptions of accuracy and identity: (1) there must be evidence that the instrument was malfunctioning or was operated improperly; (2) there must be evidence tending to show that the malfunction or improper operation of the instrument resulted in a reading according to which the blood alcohol level of the accused exceeded .08; and (3) there must be evidence that the accused's blood alcohol level would not, in fact, have exceeded .08 at the time of the alleged offence. While (1) is demonstrably justified under s. 1, both (2) and (3) constitute serious infringements of the right to be presumed innocent that cannot be justified in a democratic society. The court therefore read down s. 258(1)(*c*)(iv) to exclude these two requirements.

Subsection (1)(*d*) [Special considerations re blood samples] Subparagraph (i) requires that the accused have notice within the three-month period [now six-month] that he is charged with an impaired driving offence, that the Crown has had a sample of the accused's blood analysed and that a second sample was taken and is available to permit an analysis of it by him or on his behalf. If the accused is given notice within this three-month [now six-month] period and then does not exercise his right to request production then, absent special circumstances, this would foreclose any complaints that the prosecution was later unable to produce the sample by reason of its destruction following the expiry of the three-month period. The most appropriate and convenient way to notify the accused of the existence of the second sample is by service of the certificate of the qualified technician or certificate of the qualified medical practitioner as the case may be. This does not mean that notice by other means cannot be given so long as it is to the same effect and it is proved in accordance with the criminal standard that the accused was made aware in a timely fashion. The accused must receive the information with enough time to apply for an order releasing the sample for analysis under subsec. (4). However, where the accused has been given proper notice of the availability of the second sample then the fact that he did not apply for its release for testing would not effect the availability of the presumption: *R. v. Egger*, [1993] 2 S.C.R. 451, 82 C.C.C. (3d) 193. However, the failure to give notice of the existence of the second sample merely precludes the Crown from relying on the presumption. The Crown is entitled to present *viva voce* evidence from an analyst and physician as to the blood-alcohol content: *R. v. Ross* (1996), 108 C.C.C. (3d) 168, 152 N.S.R. (2d) 62 (C.A.).

The "offence" referred to in para. (*d*)(ii) means not only the offence specified in the information but also any other offence properly included therein: *R. v. Cyr* (1983), 25 M.V.R. 62, 60 N.S.R. (2d) 159 (C.A.).

Where the Crown does not rely on the provisions of the *Criminal Code* respecting the obtaining of blood samples and proof of the blood alcohol level pursuant to this section, but rather relies on an analysis made at the hospital, the evidence of the hospital technologists as to the results of the analysis performed by the hospital equipment is admissible, notwithstanding that the technologists were unable to give evidence as to the capability or reliability of the equipment nor as to the accuracy of the results of the analyses. It is not necessary for evidence to be given to explain precisely how the machine operates, it being sufficient that the expert operating the machine establishes that the machine is capable of making the required measurements or producing the required data, that the machine was in good working order at the relevant times, and that it was properly used: *R. v. Redmond* (1990), 54 C.C.C. (3d) 273, 37 O.A.C. 133 (C.A.). *Contra: R. v. Bird* (1989), 71 C.R. (3d) 52, 76 Sask. R. 275 (C.A.).

The fact that the blood samples, taken from the accused for hospital purposes, were destroyed before the accused could apply for release of a sample for independent testing did not result in violation of the accused's rights under s. 7, although the Crown relied upon the analysis performed at the hospital to prove the accused's blood alcohol level. The Crown was not seeking to rely on the presumption in this paragraph and thus there was no reason for requiring that a blood sample should have been preserved for analysis: *R. v. Redmond, supra.*

Subsection (1)(d.1) ("straddle" evidence) – In *R. v. Gibson*, [2008] 1 S.C.R. 397, 230 C.C.C. (3d) 97, the Supreme Court held that expert evidence of alcohol elimination rates in the general population and "straddle" evidence can be relevant and are therefore not inherently inadmissible for the purpose of rebutting the presumption in subsec. (1)(d.1). However, because of variation between individuals, the probative value of evidence based on rates in the general population will often be so low that it will fail to raise a reasonable doubt that the accused had a blood alcohol content exceeding 80 mg. Expert evidence of the elimination rate of the accused as established by a test is potentially more probative of the blood alcohol content he or she had while driving than evidence based on elimination rates in the general population. However, because an individual's elimination rate varies over time based on a number of factors, the probative value of evidence based on the elimination rate of the accused will logically depend on the number of variables controlled for in the elimination rate test. Evidence of the elimination rate of the accused at the time of the offence would be more likely to rebut the presumption in subsec. (1)(d.1) than mere evidence of the elimination rate of the accused under testing conditions. In *R. v. Ibanescu*, [2013] 2 S.C.R. 400, 303 C.C.C. (3d) 1, the court confirmed that the reasons of LeBel J. in *Gibson*, summarized above, reflect the governing law.

Subsection (1)(e) [certificate of analyst] – It is not necessary for the certificate to name the defendant but it must identify the bodily substance in such a way so that that substance may be linked to the defendant by other evidence: *R. v. Larson* (1971), 3 C.C.C. (2d) 537, 15 C.R.N.S. 398 (Alta. C.A.).

Subsection (1)(f) [certificate of analyst re alcohol standard] – A rubber stamp facsimile of the analyst's signature is not the equivalent of his signature: *R. v. Faber* (1972), 9 C.C.C. (2d) 353, [1972] 6 W.W.R. 629 (B.C.S.C.).

This subsection is merely evidentiary providing the Crown with the means by which to rebut any evidence that the substance or solution was unsuitable: *R. v. Ware* (1975), 30 C.R.N.S. 308 (Ont. C.A.).

Subsection (1)(g) [qualified technician's certificate] / Identification of suitable alcohol standard – There is no requirement of proof by means of a separate certificate from an analyst under subsec. (1)(f) that the testing standard was suitable. Absent evidence to the contrary, the technician is the judge of the suitability of the standard and the technician's statement as to the suitability of the alcohol standard is sufficient. Further, unless there is some evidence that the certificate under s. 258(1)(g) is not reliable, there is no duty on the Crown to produce at or before trial a certificate under subsec. (1)(f) or to disclose that the standard used was suitable: *R. v. Squires* (1994), 87 C.C.C. (3d) 430, 114 Nfld. & P.E.I.R. 157 (Nfld. C.A.). Similarly, the technician's testimony that he had ascertained that the breathalyzer was in proper working order by means of alcohol standard was sufficient even though the operator testified that he did not personally examine the analyst's certificate accompanying ampoules of the standard alcohol solution: *R. v. Harding* (1994), 88 C.C.C. (3d) 97, 17 O.R. (3d) 462 (C.A.).

Other prerequisites to admissibility – The "place" is adequately identified for the purposes of para. (*g*)(iii)(B) where the municipality in which the tests were administered is set out in the certificate: *R. v. Padula* (1981), 59 C.C.C. (2d) 572, 10 M.V.R. 201 (Ont. C.A.).

The certificate is inadmissible when only one breath sample was taken nor *semble* may the Crown rely on the presumption in subsec. (1)(*c*) when only one sample was taken: *R. v. Noble*, [1978] 1 S.C.R. 632, 37 C.C.C. (2d) 193 (9:0).

The necessary nexus between the certificate and the charge may be inferred from circumstantial evidence based on the arresting officer's testimony as to the times of the tests and the identity of the technician and the contents of the notice of intention with the certificate of analysis attached thereto. In any event, it would seem that in determining the evidentiary link and the certificate's admissibility, the judge may refer to the contents of the certificate itself: *R. v. Andraishek* (1988), 9 M.V.R. (2d) 121 (Alta. C.A.). Similarly, *R. v. Walsh* (1980), 53 C.C.C. (2d) 568, 6 M.V.R. 125 (Ont. C.A.).

The only conditions precedent to the admissibility of the technician's certificate are that samples of breath be taken and that they be taken pursuant to a demand under s. 254. There is no further requirement that there be *viva voce* evidence from the technician that suitable samples had been taken by him: *R. v. Hall* (1981), 57 C.C.C. (2d) 305, 26 A.R. 313 (C.A.).

It is not necessary for the Crown to prove by extrinsic evidence that two or more samples were taken. While the Crown, to have the benefit of this paragraph, must establish a link between the breathalyzer demand and the test which resulted in the analysis, that link is established by proof that the test dealt with in the certificate was made pursuant to the demand: *R. v. Schlegel* (1985), 22 C.C.C. (3d) 436 (B.C.C.A.), leave to appeal to S.C.C. refused 66 N.R. 79*n*.

Paragraph (*g*)(iii)(B) does not require that the certificate record the time when the taking of the first sample commenced, where the certificate did set out the time when the taking of the first sample was complete and when the taking of the second sample commenced: *R. v. Eggen* (1988), 42 C.C.C. (3d) 94, 66 Sask. R. 124 (C.A.); *R. v. Hogg* (1990), 25 M.V.R. (2d) 1 (Ont. C.A.).

Forms vary from province to province and the issue is not compliance with a prescribed form but rather whether the requirements of subsec. (1)(*c*)(ii) are met given the particular certificate at issue. The requirements of this provision are satisfied without the necessity of stating the start and end times of when the accused began and finished providing a breath sample: *R. v. Gunn* (2010), 253 C.C.C. (3d) 1, 74 C.R. (6th) 241 (Sask. C.A.).

There is no requirement that the exact offences be stated in the notice: *R. v. Gazica* (2002), 168 C.C.C. (3d) 446, 317 A.R. 219 (C.A.).

Errors in certificate – Even though it seems obvious that there is only a minor typographical error an inaccurate certificate must be rejected: *R. v. Gosby* (1974), 26 C.R.N.S. 161, 8 N.S.R. (2d) 183 (C.A.). See also: *R. v. Michel* (2011), 276 C.C.C. (3d) 526 (Sask. Q.B.).

It was held, however, in *R. v. Bykowski* (1980), 54 C.C.C. (2d) 398, 23 A.R. 426 (C.A.) (2:1), that what was obviously a typographical error in the certificate the dates of the two samples being given as March "1978" and March "1979" could be "corrected" by evidence of a person other than a qualified technician, such as evidence from the arresting officer that all events occurred in March, 1979.

Effect of absence of grounds for making demand – While absence of reasonable and probable grounds for belief of impairment [or *semble* as result of the recent amendments, belief that the offence under s. 253(*b*) was committed] may afford a defence to a charge under s. 254(5) it does not render inadmissible certificate evidence of a qualified technician on a charge under s. 255: *R. v. Rilling*, [1976] 2 S.C.R. 183, 24 C.C.C. (2d) 81, 31 C.R.N.S. 142 (5:3). [However, consider now the impact of ss. 8 and 24(2) of the *Charter of Rights and Freedoms*.]

The amendment to [now] s. 254 to authorize a demand not only for an alleged breach of the impaired offence but also the "over 80" offence has not changed the effect of *R. v. Rilling*, *supra*, and thus, subject to the possible effect of the *Charter of Rights and*

Freedoms, the law remains that the certificate is admissible although the Crown fails to prove that the officer had the requisite reasonable and probable grounds: *R. v. Linttell* (1991), 64 C.C.C. (3d) 507 (Alta. C.A.).

The question of whether or not the decision in *R. v. Rilling, supra*, can still represent the law in light of the Charter, and especially the guarantee to protection against unreasonable search and seizure in s. 8, has been considered by a number of courts. For example, the following courts have held that *Rilling* is no longer the law: *R. v. Bajkov* (1988), 8 M.V.R. (2d) 213 (B.C.S.C.); *R. v. Wilson* (1985), 42 Sask. R. 181, 22 C.R.R. 32, 37 M.V.R. 203 (Q.B.); *R. v. Dennehy* (1986), 26 C.C.C. (3d) 339 (Y. Terr. Ct.), while the following courts have continued to apply *Rilling*; *R. v. Kiskotagan* (1986), 49 Sask. R. 10, 41 M.V.R. 161 (Q.B.); In *R. v. Marshall* (1989), 91 N.S.R. (2d) 211, 13 M.V.R. (2d) 251 (C.A.), the issue was left open because no application had been made at trial pursuant to s. 24 of the Charter. On the other hand, in *R. v. Wason* (1987), 35 C.R.R. 285, 7 M.V.R. (2d) 88 (Ont. C.A.), the court, without referring to *Rilling*, excluded evidence obtained as a result of a breathalyzer demand because the officer had no reasonable and probable grounds for making the demand which had been based on an improper approved screening device demand under s. 254(2).

In *R. v. Alex* (2015), 328 C.C.C. (3d) 448 (B.C.C.A.), leave to appeal to S.C.C. allowed 2016 CarswellBC 720, the court concluded that *Rilling, supra*, remains good law because it has never been reversed by the Supreme Court.

In *R. v. Charette* (2009), 243 C.C.C. (3d) 480, the Ontario Court of Appeal held that *R. v. Rilling, supra*, applies with equal force to s. 258(1)(*g*). For the purposes of s. 258(1)(*g*), where an accused is charged with driving "over 80", the Crown need not concern itself with proving the existence of reasonable and probable grounds under s. 254(3) unless the accused brings a Charter application challenging the admissibility of the test results.

It was held in *R. v. Dwernychuk* (1992), 77 C.C.C. (3d) 385, 135 A.R. 31, 42 M.V.R. (2d) 237 (C.A.), leave to appeal to S.C.C. refused 79 C.C.C. (3d) vi, 14 C.R.R. (2d) 192*n*, 151 N.R. 400*n*, that until the Supreme Court of Canada reconsiders *R. v. Rilling, supra*, the lower courts are bound by that decision and thus the lack of reasonable and probable grounds does not affect the admissibility of the certificate.

The absence of reasonable and probable grounds to make the demand will not necessarily result in a violation of the guarantee against arbitrary detention under s. 9 of the *Charter of Rights and Freedoms*, so as to require a determination whether the evidence of the certificate should be excluded under s. 24(2) of the Charter: *R. v. Moore* (1988), 45 C.C.C. (3d) 410, 9 M.V.R. (2d) 190 (N.S.C.A.).

Evidentiary effect of certificate – Section 25(1) of the *Interpretation Act*, R.S.C. 1985, c. I-21, applies to this paragraph and has the effect that the facts set out in the certificate are deemed to be established "in the absence of any evidence to the contrary". Evidence to the contrary would include evidence raising a reasonable doubt that the results of the analyses set out in the certificate correctly state the blood alcohol level at the time of those analyses: *R. v. Stewart* (1983), 8 C.C.C. (3d) 368, [1984] 1 W.W.R. 385 (B.C.C.A.).

Where the accused has adduced evidence to the contrary challenging the accuracy of the blood-alcohol readings, the trial judge may consider the certificate as some evidence of the facts contained in it in determining whether to accept or reject the evidence to the contrary. It will be in the rarest of cases, however, that the certificate alone is a sufficient basis to reject otherwise credible defence evidence to the contrary: *R. v. Suttie* (2004), 188 C.C.C. (3d) 167 (Ont. C.A.).

Subsection (1)(*h*) [certificate re blood samples] – The results of analysis of blood samples, taken for medical purposes and performed on hospital equipment, were inadmissible without some evidence from a qualified person that the machines used were capable of performing the function in question and that, if operated properly, would produce an accurate and reliable result. In the absence of such evidence, the results of the analyses produced by the machines lack any evidentiary value. It was precisely to avoid these problems of proof that this provision and s. 254 were enacted. Where the Crown is unable to rely on these provisions then it must prove its case in the usual way: *R. v. Bird* (1989), 71 C.R. (3d) 52, 76 Sask. R. 275 (C.A.).

The certificate of the qualified technician (a registered nurse) was not inadmissible although the technician failed to indicate what class of persons she fell into by marking one of the alternatives on the certificate. The omission was not substantially prejudicial to the accused since the technician signed the certificate and included the initials "R.N." In addition, the certificate of the qualified medical practitioner referred to the samples having been taken by a "qualified technician": *R. v. Fedun* (1993), 50 M.V.R. (2d) 286, 114 Sask. R. 127 (Q.B.).

Subsection (2) [No legal compulsion to provide samples] – Since this subsection is for the protection of the defence it is not improper for defence counsel to cross-examine to show that the accused's refusal to take a breathalyzer test reflected an attitude which would make it unlikely that her inculpatory statement was given voluntarily: *R. v. Lapinsky*, [1966] 3 C.C.C. 97 (B.C.S.C.).

In *R. v. Brager*, [1965] 4 C.C.C. 251 (B.C.C.A.), the court held that if defence counsel had elicited the fact that no physical sobriety tests were made then Crown counsel would be entitled to re-examine to disclose the reasons for that omission, not to prove guilt, but to alleviate any inference that such tests were not made because they would not support the charge.

Subsection (3) [Adverse inference from refusal to comply with demand] – Where the accused was acquitted of the charge under s. 254(5) and no appeal was taken the Crown is bound to accept the correctness of the verdict and may not rely on the adverse inference in this subsection on the accused's appeal from his conviction of the offence under s. 253: *R. v. Zink* (1977), 38 C.C.C. (2d) 97 (Alta. C.A.).

On the other hand the fact that the Crown by reliance on this subsection secures a conviction for the offence under s. 253(*a*) is not a bar to a conviction for the offence contrary to s. 254(5): *R. v. Mazurek* (1978), 41 C.C.C. (2d) 353 (Alta. Dist. Ct.).

Where the acquittal on the s. 254 charge is not the result of a finding that the accused did not comply with the demand but rather due to the "technicality" that the Crown failed to prove that the demand was made by the officer named in the information then this subsection may be invoked: *R. v. Fredrek* (1979), 17 A.R. 613, 5 M.V.R. 1 (C.A.); *R. v. Ranger* (1983), 26 M.V.R. 83 (B.C.C.A.).

The adverse inference arises merely upon proof that the accused refused without reasonable excuse to comply with the demand. There need not be proof also that the refusal was due to the accused's fear that the results would show that he was impaired: *R. v. Garneau* (1982), 66 C.C.C. (2d) 90 (Alta. Q.B.).

The adverse inference provided for by this subsection does not offend the guarantee to the presumption of innocence in s. 11(*d*) of the Charter: *R. v. Mackenzie* (1983), 6 C.C.C. (3d) 86 (Alta. Q.B.); *R. v. Van Den Elzen* (1983), 10 C.C.C. (3d) 532 (B.C.C.A.).

Subsection (4) [Application for order releasing sample] – See notes under heading: "Special considerations re blood samples" under subsec. (1)(*c*), (*d*) above.

Subsection (6) [Attendance of technician, etc.] – The analyst or qualified technician testifying under this subsection is a witness for the Crown and his evidence in chief would be the statements in his certificate: *R. v. Latter* (1971) 2 C.C.C. (2d) 453 (N.S.C.A.).

This subsection is neither pre-emptive nor exclusive and it is open to the accused to apply to a justice of the peace for a subpoena pursuant to s. 698 to compel the attendance of the analyst although the analyst would then be the accused's witness. In determining whether or not to issue the subpoena however, the same test should be applied by the justice of the peace as must be met under this subsection: *R. v. Forsythe* (1980), 54 C.C.C. (2d) 44 (Alta. Q.B.).

Leave to call the technician should not be given unless there is an indication in the evidence, or an affidavit or in the submissions or undertakings by counsel, of a material irregularity in the testing procedure followed by the technician which, if substantiated, could provide a legal basis for doubting the accuracy of the certificate. Further, it should be apparent that the evidence sought is within the peculiar knowledge of the technician *qua* technician and not evidence which, for example, could be given by any other officer present at the relevant time: *R. v. Davis* (1983), 4 C.C.C. (3d) 53 (Alta. C.A.).

Subsection (7) [Notice of intention to introduce certificate] / Reasonable notice / form and content of notice – The notice does not have to be in writing, but it must be exact for the specific offence proceeded upon. Accordingly notice given for use of a certificate for a s. 253(*a*) offence is of no avail upon the withdrawal of that charge and the proceeding upon a s. 253(*b*) offence: *R. v. Hannan* (1970), 1 C.C.C. (2d) 447 (Sask. Q.B.).

Written notice which is clear and unambiguous is not nullified by the fact that at the time the police officer serves it, he tells the accused the certificate would be used "if necessary": *R. v. Good, Schmidt and Winnipeg; R. v. Neubert* (1983), 6 C.C.C. (3d) 105 (Alta. C.A.).

It is not enough for an accused to point to an error in a notice and then allege that, by reason of the error alone, there is ambiguity or confusion which results in the notice not being reasonable. The bald generalization of ambiguity or confusion must be brought down to concrete terms, based on the facts of the case, to show a particular ambiguity or confusion which relates to the reasonableness of the notice. Thus, an accused charged with the offence under s. 253(*b*) was given reasonable notice, although the notice he was given referred to that charge as well as a charge under s. 253(*a*). The accused at all times knew he was facing a charge under s. 253(*b*) and that he had been given a notice which said that the Crown intended to tender the certificate in evidence at the trial on that charge. There was nothing confusing or ambiguous in this information and the superfluous reference to s. 253(*a*) could in no way have altered the impact of what was undoubtedly a straightforward statement: *R. v. McCullagh* (1990), 53 C.C.C. (3d) 130 (Ont. C.A.).

The Crown is required to prove compliance with the requirements of subsec. (7) on a balance of probabilities, not beyond a reasonable doubt: *R. v. Redford* (2014), 319 C.C.C. (3d) 170 (Alta. C.A.).

Section 4(6)(*a*) and (*b*) of the *Criminal Code* provides an alternative way of proving service and notice for the purpose of this section: *R. v. Veinot* (2010), 265 C.C.C. (3d) 193 (N.S.S.C.).

A printed notice of intention in which, through an apparent typographical error, the wrong section number was checked off, was not invalid and it was open to the trial judge to find that the accused was given reasonable notice: *R. v. Brebner* (1989), 49 C.C.C. (3d) 97 (Ont. C.A.).

This provision has no application where the Crown proceeds by way of *viva voce* evidence of the qualified technician rather than relying on his certificate: *R. v. Walters* (1975), 26 C.C.C. (2d) 56 (N.S.S.C. App. Div.).

Reasonable notice / time of service – For the purposes of this subsection the trial commences with the taking of the evidence and accordingly service of a notice after plea was taken about one month earlier was held to be sufficient: *R. v. Vereschagin* (1972), 10 C.C.C. (2d) 529 (B.C.S.C.).

A certificate of intention to use the resulting certificate of analysis was served upon the defendant a few minutes after he completed his breathalyzer test even though the information against him was not laid until two days later. It was held that since the primary purpose of service was to notify him of the use at trial of the certificate, there would not be any prejudice to him not knowing at the time of service whether he would be charged under the ability impaired or in excess of 80 mg. of alcohol section of the Code: *R. v. Goerz* (1971), 5 C.C.C. (2d) 92 (Alta. C.A.). Folld: *R. v. MacIsaac* (1972), 9 C.C.C. (2d) 46 (N.B.C.A.); *R. v. Ratto; R. v. Gillis; R. v. McMullin* (1972), 9 C.C.C. (2d) 63 (N.S.C.A.); *R. v. Faber* (1972), 8 C.C.C. (2d) 10 (B.C.C.A.); *R. v. Ledoux* (1972), 7 C.C.C. (2d) 18 (Sask. C.A.); and *R. v. Evanson* (1973), 11 C.C.C. (2d) 275 (Man. C.A.).

The notice of intention and the certificate may be served on the accused prior to the laying of an information and the certificate may be used on the trial of even a third information, where the first and second informations were quashed prior to plea, without service of a new notice, at least where the Crown has proceeded promptly in laying the new information: *R. v. Nykiforuk* (1981), 60 C.C.C. (2d) 128 (Alta. C.A.), leave to appeal to S.C.C. refused 33 A.R. 467*n*.

Similarly, *R. v. Koback* (1986), 43 M.V.R. 272 (Sask. C.A.), where the Crown withdrew one information charging the care or control offence and promptly relaid another information charging the driving offence.

Similarly, on a re-trial ordered after a successful appeal, the Crown may rely on the original notice of intention: *R. v. Nickerson* (1984), 27 M.V.R. 124, 64 N.S.R. (2d) 164 (S.C. App. Div.).

In the absence of evidence of the date of service, even though defence counsel did not object, the court is not entitled to infer that the defendant had been given both reasonable notice of the Crown's intention and a copy of the certificate: *R. v. Tunke* (1975), 25 C.C.C. (2d) 518 (Alta. S.C.).

Reasonable notice / capacity to understand – In *R. v. Hamm*, [1977] 2 S.C.R. 85, 28 C.C.C. (2d) 257 (6:3), the court held that the presumption that a person understood what was going on when he was served with the notice under this section was not rebutted merely by the high blood-alcohol reading set out in the certificate of the results of a breathalyzer test performed at the time since the effect of the consumption of alcohol varies among individuals. The trial judge therefore erred in finding that because of the high reading the accused was so intoxicated at the time of service as to be incapable of being served with reasonable notice. The majority accordingly did not consider the propriety of effecting service on a person in an even more intoxicated state. Spence J., dissenting, took a different view of the facts and would have upheld the trial judge's finding of fact of lack of reasonable notice. His Lordship also held that notice under this subsection could not validly be given until an information was laid for it is only then that there is an "accused".

The presumption that the accused understood the notice and certificate which were in English was not rebutted merely by evidence that the demand and other conversation between the accused and the police was in French: *R. v. Saulnier (No. 2)* (1980), 53 C.C.C. (2d) 237, 38 NS.R. (2d) 538 (C.A.).

The rebuttable presumption that the accused understood the notice was applied where the accused was hard of hearing: *R. v. Bender* (1980), 3 Sask. R. 277, 6 M.V.R. 44 (C.A.).

Service on persons other than accused – Service of the certificate and the notice of intention on a law student appearing to fix a date is sufficient compliance with this subsection just as service on the accused's counsel would constitute sufficient compliance: *R. v. Meyer* (1973), 29 C.C.C. (2d) 165 (B.C.C.A.).

Similarly, service on a lawyer who acknowledges that he acts for the accused is compliance with this subsection: *R. v. Monty* (1981), 65 C.C.C. (2d) 54, [1982] 1 W.W.R. 283 (Alta. Q.B.).

Proof of service – A certificate of an analysis is a document within the meaning of s. 4(6) and therefore proof of service may be by way of affidavit: *R. v. Spreen* (1987), 40 C.C.C. (3d) 190, 82 A.R. 318, 8 M.V.R. (2d) 148 (C.A.).

Copy of certificate – The copy of the certificate, served along with the notice of intention to produce the original at trial, does not have to be signed as a duplicate original, but is sufficient if it is a true copy in all essential particulars and conveys to the defendant all of the required information: *R. v. Glass* (1973), 12 C.C.C. (2d) 450, [1973] 5 W.W.R. 761 (Sask. C.A.).

Evidence that the copy of the certificate was prepared using a preassembled form containing carbon paper is *prima facie* proof that the copy given to the accused was a copy of the certificate and there is no requirement that the copy and the certificate have been specifically compared: *R. v. Bergstrom* (1982), 65 C.C.C. (2d) 351, [1982] 2 W.W.R. 95 (Man. C.A.). Also see: *R. v. Pederson* (1973), 15 C.C.C. (2d) 323, [1974] 1 W.W.R. 481

(B.C.S.C.); *R. v. Morgan* (1995), 104 C.C.C. (3d) 342, 136 Nfld. & P.E.I.R. 205 (Nfld. C.A.).

Proof that a copy has been served is *prima facie* evidence of its accuracy unless there is an issue raised that the copy is not a true counterpart of the original. It is not a requirement that the police officer serving the copy observe the certificate being typed or compare the copy with the original: *R. v. Mavin* (1997), 119 C.C.C. (3d) 38, 154 Nfld. & P.E.I.R. 242 (Nfld. C.A.).

The service on the accused of the top of three copies of the certificate, the lower two of which are carbon copies, complies with the requirement in this subsection that the accused be served with a "copy" of the certificate: *R. v. Walsh* (1980), 53 C.C.C. (2d) 568, 6 M.V.R. 125 (Ont. C.A.).

UNAUTHORIZED USE OF BODILY SUBSTANCE / Unauthorized use or disclosure of results / Exception / Exception / Offence.

258.1 (1) Subject to subsections 258(4) and (5) and subsection (3), no person shall use a bodily substance taken under paragraph 254(2)(*b*), subsection 254(3), (3.3) or (3.4) or section 256 or with the consent of the person from whom it was taken after a request by a peace officer or medical samples that are provided by consent and subsequently seized under a warrant, except for the purpose of an analysis that is referred to in that provision or for which the consent is given.

(2) Subject to subsections (3) and (4), no person shall use, disclose or allow the disclosure of the results of physical coordination tests under paragraph 254(2)(*a*), the results of an evaluation under subsection 254(3.1), the results of the analysis of a bodily substance taken under paragraph 254(2)(b), subsection 254(3), (3.3) or (3.4) or section 256 or with the consent of the person from whom it was taken after a request by a peace officer, or the results of the analysis of medical samples that are provided by consent and subsequently seized under a warrant, except

    (*a*) in the course of an investigation of, or in a proceeding for, an offence under any of sections 220, 221, 236 and 249 to 255, an offence under Part I of the *Aeronautics Act*, or an offence under the *Railway Safety Act* in respect of a contravention of a rule or regulation made under that Act respecting the use of alcohol or a drug; or

    (*b*) for the purpose of the administration or enforcement of the law of a province.

(3) Subsections (1) and (2) do not apply to persons who for medical purposes use samples or use or disclose the results of tests, taken for medical purposes, that are subsequently seized under a warrant.

(4) The results of physical coordination tests, an evaluation or an analysis referred to in subsection (2) may be disclosed to the person to whom they relate, and may be disclosed to any other person if the results are made anonymous and the disclosure is made for statistical or other research purposes.

(5) Every person who contravenes subsection (1) or (2) is guilty of an offence punishable on summary conviction. 2008, c. 6, s. 25.

CROSS-REFERENCES

"Peace officer" is defined in s. 2.

SYNOPSIS

This section enacts safeguards to prevent the unauthorized use of bodily substances that have been seized as part of the drinking and driving regime set out in ss. 254 and 256. Subsection (1) makes it an offence to use these substances other than for authorized purposes, namely for the analysis referred to in the provision authorizing the seizure, or pursuant to an order by a court under s. 258(4), to test for drugs under s. 258(5) or for medical purposes in accordance with subsec. (3) of this section. Subsection (3) creates a similar offence for unauthorized disclosure of the results of physical coordination tests, the results of analysis of bodily substances and medical samples seized under warrant. Under subsec. (4), the results of tests and analysis may be disclosed to the person to whom they relate. The offences in subsecs. (2) and (3) are summary conviction offences.

MANDATORY ORDER OF PROHIBITION / Alcohol ignition interlock device program / Minimum absolute prohibition period / Discretionary order of prohibition / Consecutive prohibition periods / Saving / Mandatory order of prohibition — street racing / Mandatory order of prohibition — bodily harm / Mandatory order of prohibition — death / Mandatory life prohibition / Operation while disqualified / Definition of "disqualification".

259. (1) When an offender is convicted of an offence committed under section 253 or 254 or this section or discharged under section 730 of an offence committed under section 253 and, at the time the offence was committed or, in the case of an offence committed under section 254, within the three hours preceding that time, was operating or had the care or control of a motor vehicle, vessel or aircraft or of railway equipment or was assisting in the operation of an aircraft or of railway equipment, the court that sentences the offender shall, in addition to any other punishment that may be imposed for that offence, make an order prohibiting the offender from operating a motor vehicle on any street, road, highway or other public place, or from operating a vessel or an aircraft or railway equipment, as the case may be,

    (*a*) **for a first offence, during a period of not more than three years plus any period to which the offender is sentenced to imprisonment, and not less than one year;**

    (*b*) **for a second offence, during a period of not more than five years plus any period to which the offender is sentenced to imprisonment, and not less than two years; and**

    (*c*) **for each subsequent offence, during a period of not less than three years plus any period to which the offender is sentenced to imprisonment.**

(1.1) If the offender is registered in an alcohol ignition interlock device program established under the law of the province in which the offender resides and complies with the conditions of the program, the offender may, subject to subsection (1.2), operate a motor vehicle equipped with an alcohol ignition interlock device during the prohibition period, unless the court orders otherwise.

(1.2) An offender who is registered in a program referred to in subsection (1.1) may not operate a motor vehicle equipped with an alcohol ignition interlock device until

    (*a*) **the expiry of a period of**

      (i) **for a first offence, 3 months after the day on which sentence is imposed,**

      (ii) **for a second offence, 6 months after the day on which sentence is imposed, and**

      (iii) **for each subsequent offence, 12 months after the day on which sentence is imposed; or**

    (*b*) **the expiry of any period that may be fixed by order of the court that is greater than a period referred to in paragraph (*a*).**

(2) If an offender is convicted or discharged under section 730 of an offence under section 220, 221, 236, 249, 249.1, 250, 251 or 252 or any of subsections 255(2) to (3.2) committed by means of a motor vehicle, a vessel, an aircraft or railway equipment, the court that sentences the offender may, in addition to any other punishment that may be imposed for that offence, make an order prohibiting the offender from operating a motor vehicle on any street, road, highway or other public place, or from operating a vessel, an aircraft or railway equipment, as the case may be,

    (*a*) **during any period that the court considers proper, if the offender is sentenced to imprisonment for life in respect of that offence;**

    (*a*.1) during any period that the court considers proper, plus any period to which the offender is sentenced to imprisonment, if the offender is liable to imprisonment for life in respect of that offence and if the sentence imposed is other than imprisonment for life;

    (*b*) during any period not exceeding ten years plus any period to which the offender is sentenced to imprisonment, if the offender is liable to imprisonment for more than five years but less than life in respect of that offence; and

    (*c*) during any period not exceeding three years plus any period to which the offender is sentenced to imprisonment, in any other case.

(2.1) The court may, when it makes an order under this section prohibiting the operation of a motor vehicle, a vessel, an aircraft or railway equipment, as the case may be, order that the time served under that order be served consecutively to the time served under any other order made under this section that prohibits the operation of the same means of transport and that is in force.

(3) No order made under subsection (1) or (2) shall operate to prevent any person from acting as master, mate or engineer of a vessel that is required to carry officers holding certificates as master, mate or engineer.

(3.1) When an offender is convicted or discharged under section 730 of an offence committed under subsection 249.4(1), the court that sentences the offender shall, in addition to any other punishment that may be imposed for that offence, make an order prohibiting the offender from operating a motor vehicle on any street, road, highway or other public place

    (*a*) for a first offence, during a period of not more than three years plus any period to which the offender is sentenced to imprisonment, and not less than one year;

    (*b*) for a second offence, during a period of not more than five years plus any period to which the offender is sentenced to imprisonment, and not less than two years; and

    (*c*) for each subsequent offence, during a period of not less than three years plus any period to which the offender is sentenced to imprisonment.

(3.2) When an offender is convicted or discharged under section 730 of an offence committed under section 249.3 or subsection 249.4(3), the court that sentences the offender shall, in addition to any other punishment that may be imposed for that offence, make an order prohibiting the offender from operating a motor vehicle on any street, road, highway or other public place

    (*a*) for a first offence, during a period of not more than ten years plus any period to which the offender is sentenced to imprisonment, and not less than one year;

    (*b*) for a second offence, during a period of not more than ten years plus any period to which the offender is sentenced to imprisonment, and not less than two years; and

    (*c*) or each subsequent offence, during a period of not less than three years plus any period to which the offender is sentenced to imprisonment.

(3.3) When an offender is convicted or discharged under section 730 of a first offence committed under section 249.2 or subsection 249.4(4), the court that sentences the offender shall, in addition to any other punishment that may be imposed for that offence, make an order prohibiting the offender from operating a motor vehicle on any street, road, highway or other public place

    (*a*) for an offence under section 249.2, during a period of not less than one year plus any period to which the offender is sentenced to imprisonment; and

    (*b*) for an offence under subsection 249.4(4), during a period of not more than ten years plus any period to which the offender is sentenced to imprisonment, and not less than one year.

(3.4) When an offender is convicted or discharged under section 730 of an offence committed under section 249.2 or 249.3 or subsection 249.4(3) or (4), the offender has previously been convicted or discharged under section 730 of one of those offences and at least one of the convictions or discharges is under section 249.2 or subsection 249.4(4), the court that sentences the offender shall make an order prohibiting the offender from operating a motor vehicle on any street, road, highway or other public place for life.

(4) Every offender who operates a motor vehicle, vessel or aircraft or any railway equipment in Canada while disqualified from doing so, other than an offender who is registered in an alcohol ignition interlock device program established under the law of the province in which the offender resides and who complies with the conditions of the program,

> (a) is guilty of an indictable offence and liable to imprisonment for a term not exceeding five years; or
>
> (b) is guilty of an offence punishable on summary conviction.

(5) For the purposes of this section, "disqualification" means

> (a) a prohibition from operating a motor vehicle, vessel or aircraft or any railway equipment ordered pursuant to any of subsections (1), (2) and (3.1) to (3.4); or
>
> (b) a disqualification or any other form of legal restriction of the right or privilege to operate a motor vehicle, vessel or aircraft imposed
>
> > (i) in the case of a motor vehicle, under the law of a province, or
> >
> > (ii) in the case of a vessel or an aircraft, under an Act of Parliament,

in respect of a conviction or discharge under section 730 of any offence referred to in any of subsections (1), (2) and (3.1) to (3.4). R.S.C. 1985, c. 27 (1st Supp.), s. 36; c. 32 (4th Supp.), s. 62; 1995, c. 22, ss. 10, 18; 1997, c. 18, s. 11; 1999, c. 32, s. 5; 2000, c. 2, s. 2; 2001, c. 37, s. 1; 2006, c. 14, ss. 3(2) and 3(3); 2008, c. 6, s. 26; c. 18, s. 8.

CROSS-REFERENCES

The terms "highway", "motor vehicle" and "railway equipment" are defined in s. 2. The terms "aircraft", "vessel" and "operate" are defined in s. 214. Where the prosecution seeks the longer prohibition order prescribed by para. (1)(b) or (c), it probably must comply with the provisions of s. 665. Section 667 provides one method of proof of the prior conviction. No reference to the prior conviction may be made in the information by virtue of s. 664. Procedure for making the prohibition order is set out in s. 260(1) to (3). Provision respecting a means of proof of notice of the disqualification and proof of the disqualification is set out in s. 260(4) to (7). Section 261 provides for an order staying the prohibition order pending appeal against a conviction or discharge. An order under this section is within the definition of "sentence" in ss. 673 and 785 for the purposes of appeals in proceedings by indictment and summary conviction respectively.

Where the Crown elects to proceed by indictment on the offence described in subsec. (4), the accused has an election as to mode of trial. Where the Crown elects to proceed by way of summary conviction for the offence under subsec. (4) then the trial is conducted by a summary conviction court pursuant to Part XXVII. The punishment for the summary conviction offence is as set out in s. 787 and the limitation period is set out in s. 786(2). The accused is also liable to imposition of a prohibition order under this section for a period not exceeding three years. For all offences under this section, release pending trial is determined by s. 515, although the accused is eligible for release by a peace officer under ss. 496 and 497, or by the officer in charge under s. 498.

Pursuant to s. 255.1, evidence that the accused's blood alcohol level exceeded .160 at the time when the offence was committed is deemed to be an aggravating factor on sentencing.

The maximum punishment for this offence and the length of the prohibition periods were increased by S.C. 1999, c. 32. The transitional provisions of that Act provide that the lesser penalty or punishment applies in respect of any offence that was committed before the coming into force of the Act.

Note s. 732.1(3)(g.1) and (g.2), which allow for terms of probation that the offender attend for curative treatment in relation to the consumption of alcohol and drugs and participate in an alcohol ignition interlock device program.

SYNOPSIS

This section describes the circumstances under which a judge is required to impose an order prohibiting an offender from operating a motor vehicle, vessel, aircraft or railway equipment. If an offender is convicted of an offence under ss. 253, 254 or this section, discharged of an offence under s. 253, and had at the time of the offence, or in the case of an offence under s. 254, three hours preceding that time, care or control of or was operating a motor vehicle, a vessel, an aircraft or railway equipment, the judge must impose a prohibition order. Such an order will last for a period of not more than three years and not less than one year for a first offence, not more than five years and not less than two years for a second offence, and not less than three years for each subsequent offence, plus any period to which the offender is sentenced to imprisonment. An exception is made in subsecs. (1.1) to (1.2) where the province in which the offender resides has established an alcohol ignition interlock device program, in which case the offender may operate a vehicle equipped with the device while registered in and complying with the conditions of the program, unless the court orders otherwise. The authorization has no effect until expiry of at least three months for a first offence, at least six months for a second offence, at least 12 months for a subsequent offence, or any period that may be fixed by order of the court that is greater than these minimums. If an offender is convicted or discharged of an offence under ss. 220, 221, 236, 249, 250, 251, 252 and 255(2) to (3.2), the judge may make an order prohibiting the offender from operating the motor vehicle, vessel, aircraft or railway equipment for any period that the court considers appropriate if the offender is liable to a maximum sentence of life imprisonment. If the offender is liable to a sentence greater than five years but less than life imprisonment, the prohibition order may last for a period of up to ten years plus any period to which the offender is sentenced to imprisonment. In any other case, the maximum length of the order is three years plus any period to which the offender is sentenced to imprisonment. Subsection (2.1) permits the court to make a prohibition order imposed under this section consecutive to other prohibition orders made under this section. Subsections (3.1) to (3.4) create enhanced prohibitions where the accused has been convicted or discharged of one of the street racing offences created by ss. 249.2 to 249.4. The principal difference is the creation of minimum prohibitions for the various street racing offences. The minimum and maximum penalties vary depending upon the number of prior convictions for the offence and whether the offender was convicted of an aggravated form of the offence because bodily harm or death was caused. This section also holds that no order under subsec. (1) or (2) shall prevent a person from acting as master, mate or engineer or a vessel required to carry such qualified individuals. Any person who is convicted of operating a motor vehicle, vessel, aircraft or railway equipment in Canada while disqualified is guilty of a hybrid offence punishable upon indictment to a maximum term of imprisonment of five years. If is an offence under the *Criminal Code* to drive while disqualified, even if the disqualification was made pursuant to a provincial statute or federal legislation other than the *Criminal Code*, provided that the disqualification arose from a conviction for an offence referred to in subsec. (1) or (2).

ANNOTATIONS

Principles in making prohibition order – The order made under subsec. (1) is an aspect of the sentence and the duty on the judge is to determine what is a fit period of prohibition applying proper sentencing principles. It is not proper to simply impose a one-year prohibition because the accused, an out-of-province resident, would not otherwise be suspended from driving for the one year prescribed by provincial legislation: *R. v. Goulding* (1987), 40 C.C.C. (3d) 244, 7 M.V.R. (2d) 188 (N.S.C.A.).

There is no power to provide for exceptions from the prohibition order to, for example, permit the accused to drive for the purposes of employment: *R. v. Girard* (1993), 79 C.C.C. (3d) 174, 132 N.B.R. (2d) 87 (C.A.).

Elements of offence – The offence under former s. 238(3) was held to be a true criminal offence requiring proof of *mens rea*. Further, the existence of a provincial licence suspension was a question of fact and ignorance of that fact is a defence to this charge, notwithstanding the suspension arises automatically by operation of a provincial law as a consequence of a conviction for a *Criminal Code* motor vehicle offence: *R. v. Prue; R. v. Baril*, [1979] 2 S.C.R. 547, 46 C.C.C. (2d) 257 (4:3).

An accused whose licence is suspended by virtue of provincial legislation should be convicted of the criminal offence only where he is driving in circumstances in which a licence is required by provincial legislation: *R. v. Mansour*, [1979] 2 S.C.R. 916, 47 C.C.C. (3d) 129 (9:0).

Both under the provincial legislation and the *Criminal Code*, upon conviction for the offences specified in the Registrar's certificate, the accused is to be informed by the court that he is disqualified from driving and under the provincial legislation where the accused is a resident of the province, the convicting judge is to secure the driver's licence, if any, from the accused. As well, under the provincial legislation, the accused would not be entitled to reinstatement of his licence so long as he was disqualified from driving. In the circumstances, the doctrine of regularity applies with the result that the only reasonable presumption was that the accused was notified of his disqualification. Accordingly, the Registrar's certificate together with the application of the doctrine of regularity was sufficient to constitute *prima facie* proof of the *mens rea* for the offence of driving while disqualified, that is proof that the accused knew he was disqualified from driving: *R. v. Larsen* (1992), 71 C.C.C. (3d) 335 (Sask. C.A.). [Also see notes under s. 260.] In certain circumstances, however, the presumption of regularity, together with the certificate of disqualification, is insufficient to establish *mens rea* where by the combined operation of s. 259(2) and the provincial statute it was possible that the offender was subject to a disqualification from driving without notification: *R. v. Miskiman*, [1997] 8 W.W.R. 280, 140 W.A.C. 256 (Sask. C.A.).

A prohibition order indicating that everyone who operated a motor vehicle while disqualified is "upon conviction, guilty of an offence and is liable to a term of custody and supervision" failed to comply with s. 260(1)(c) of the *Criminal Code*, in that it did not bring home to the individual the specifics of this provision. In particular, it must be clear that the individual could be found guilty of an indictable offence and imprisoned for up to five years or found guilty of an offence punishable on summary conviction: *R. v. Molina* (2008), 231 C.C.C. (3d) 193 (Ont. C.A.).

Knowledge of the prohibition order is an essential element. In this case, knowledge was not proven having regard to the fact that although the accused was subject to a three-year driving prohibition, he believed that the prohibition was over after one year subsequent to taking a driving test and receiving an apprentice driving license: *R. v. Lariviere* (2000), 38 C.R. (5th) 130, 15 M.V.R. (4th) 304 (Que. C.A.), quashed [2001] 3 S.C.R. 1013, 160 C.C.C. (3d) 129.

The onus of proving registration in and compliance with an ignition interlock program is on the accused, pursuant to s. 794(2) of the Code: *R. v. Whatmore* (2011), 281 C.C.C. (3d) 95 (Alta. Prov. Ct.).

Procedure – In order to obtain the greater driving prohibition mandated by subsec. (1)(c) the prosecution must give notice as required by s. 665: *R. v. Keldsen* (1987), 1 W.C.B. (2d) 75 (B.C.S.C.).

Constitutional considerations – It was held in *R. v. Boggs*, [1981] 1 S.C.R. 49, 58 C.C.C. (2d) 7 (7:0), that the predecessor to this subsection (s. 238(3)) was unconstitutional because it had the effect of attaching penal consequences to a breach of an order made under a provincial statute although the provincial order of disqualification did not arise out of a conviction for a criminal offence. This particular problem would seem to have been remedied by the limited definition of "disqualification" in subsec. (5).

This section does not violate the equality rights guaranteed by s. 15 of the Charter even though a person may be disqualified by reason of subsec. (5)(b) pursuant to a suspension imposed by provincial legislation and the length of suspension varies from province to province: *R. v. Buchanan* (1989), 46 C.C.C. (3d) 468, 88 N.S.R. (2d) 320 (C.A.).

PROCEEDINGS ON MAKING OF PROHIBITION ORDER / Endorsement by offender / Validity of order not affected / Onus / Certificate admissible in evidence / Notice to accused / Definition of "registrar of motor vehicles".

260. (1) If a court makes a prohibition order under section 259 in relation to an offender, it shall cause

    (*a*) the order to be read by or to the offender;

    (*b*) a copy of the order to be given to the offender; and

    (*c*) the offender to be informed of subsection 259(4).

(2) After subsection (1) has been complied with in relation to an offender who is bound by an order referred to in that subsection, the offender shall endorse the order, acknowledging receipt of a copy thereof and that the order has been explained to him.

(3) The failure of an offender to endorse an order pursuant to subsection (2) does not affect the validity of the order.

(4) In the absence of evidence to the contrary, where it is proved that a disqualification referred to in paragraph 259(5)(*b*) has been imposed on a person and that notice of the disqualification has been mailed by registered or certified mail to that person, that person shall, after five days following the mailing of the notice, be deemed to have received the notice and to have knowledge of the disqualification, of the date of its commencement and of its duration.

(5) In proceedings under section 259, a certificate setting out with reasonable particularity that a person is disqualified from

    (*a*) driving a motor vehicle in a province, purporting to be signed by the registrar of motor vehicles for that province, or

    (*b*) operating a vessel or aircraft, purporting to be signed by the Minister of Transport or any person authorized by the Minister of Transport for that purpose

is evidence of the facts alleged therein without proof of the signature or official character of the person by whom it purports to be signed.

(6) Subsection (5) does not apply in any proceedings unless at least seven days notice in writing is given to the accused that it is intended to tender the certificate in evidence.

(7) In subsection (5), "registrar of motor vehicles" includes the deputy of that registrar and any other person or body, by whatever name or title designated, that from time to time performs the duties of superintending the registration of motor vehicles in the province. R.S.C. 1985, c. 27 (1st Supp.), s. 36; 2006, c. 14, s. 4.

CROSS-REFERENCES

The term "offender" is defined in s. 2. The term "motor vehicle" is defined in s. 2. The terms "aircraft", "vessel" and "operate" are defined in s. 214. Procedure for stay of the prohibition order pending appeal is set out in s. 261.

With respect to the notice prescribed by subsec. (6), note s. 27(1) of the *Interpretation Act*, R.S.C. 1985, c. I-21, which provides that, where there is reference to "at least" a number of days between two events, in calculating that number of days, the days on which the events happened are excluded.

Section 25(1) of the *Interpretation Act* provides that "Where an enactment provides that a document is evidence of a fact without anything in the context to indicate that the document is conclusive evidence, then, in any judicial proceedings, the document is admissible in evidence and the fact is deemed to be established in the absence of any evidence to the contrary."

SYNOPSIS

This section sets out the steps that a court must take in imposing a prohibition order under s. 259(1) and (2). The court must ensure that the order is read by or to the offender, that a copy is given to the offender, and that the offender is informed of the criminal consequences of disobeying the order. After these steps are taken, the offender must endorse the order and acknowledge both receipt of it and the fact that the order has been explained. The order will be valid even if the offender fails to endorse it.

Where it is proved that a notice of disqualification as defined in s. 259 has been mailed by registered or certified mail to an offender, in the absence of evidence to the contrary, after five days of the mailing of the notice, the offender is deemed to have received it and to have knowledge of the disqualification, the date of its commencement and its duration. A certificate describing in reasonably particular terms that a person has been disqualified from driving a motor vehicle or operating a vessel or aircraft is evidence of the facts without further proof. The accused must be given at least seven days' notice in writing that the certificate will be used in evidence.

ANNOTATIONS

Note: Some of the decisions noted below, although decided under the predecessor legislation, were felt to be relevant to these provisions.

Procedure in making order [subsec. (1)] – While the judge may delegate to an appropriate official of the court compliance with this subsection, the duties cannot be delegated to the agent of the accused who appeared on his behalf and entered the plea of guilty: *R. v. Materi* (1987), 35 C.C.C. (3d) 273, 56 Sask. R. 37 (C.A.).

An accused cannot be convicted of the offence contrary to s. 259(4) in the absence of proof of compliance with this subsection, even where there is proof that the accused was aware of the prohibition order: *R. v. Kean* (1989), 22 M.V.R. (2d) 279, 80 Nfld. & P.E.I.R. 159 (Nfld. Prov. Ct.).

A prohibition order indicating that everyone who operated a motor vehicle while disqualified is "upon conviction, guilty of an offence and is liable to a term of custody and supervision" failed to comply with subsec. (1)(c) of the *Criminal Code*, in that it did not bring home the specifics of this provision and in particular, that they could be found guilty of an indictable offence and imprisoned for up to five years or found guilty of an offence punishable on summary conviction: *R. v. Molina* (2008), 231 C.C.C. (3d) 193 (Ont. C.A.).

Proof of knowledge of disqualification [subsec. (4)] – It was held in relation to former s. 238, which did not contain a provision respecting proof of knowledge, that nevertheless with the establishment of the accused's licence suspension the Crown is entitled to rely on the presumption that a man intends the natural consequences of his act in order to prove the necessary *mens rea* and if, in order to make his suspension order effective, the registrar was required to give notice of his suspension to the accused there is no obligation on the Crown to prove that such notice had been served on the accused prior to his driving as, in the absence of evidence to the contrary, the presumption that all acts required by law have been taken will apply: *R. v. Heisler*, [1967] 1 C.C.C. 97, 49 C.R. 297 (N.S.S.C.).

Similarly, it was held that once the Crown proves that the accused drove while disqualified it makes out a *prima facie* case notwithstanding there is no direct evidence that the accused knew of the suspension. The accused then runs the risk of being convicted unless he discharges the evidential burden of introducing evidence of lack of knowledge although if at the end of the case there is a reasonable doubt with respect to any element of the offence, including such knowledge, he is entitled to be acquitted: *R. v. Lock* (1974), 18 C.C.C. (2d) 477, 4 O.R. (2d) 178 (C.A.).

This provision is simply one method through which the Crown may prove *mens rea*: *R. v. Gale* (1995), 168 A.R. 212, 16 M.V.R. (3d) 33 (Q.B.).

The presumption of regularity applies to this provision but can be rebutted by evidence to the contrary arising from the Crown's case or led by the defence. Accordingly, where a record relied upon by the Crown to prove *mens rea* is defective on its face, evidence to the contrary arises from the Crown's case and the Crown is required to lead evidence to prove compliance with this provision beyond a reasonable doubt. Where no evidence to the contrary arises, the accused must rebut the *prima facie* case of knowledge: *R. v. Guilbault* (2010), 251 C.C.C. (3d) 563, 287 N.S.R. (2d) 305 (S.C.), affd 268 C.C.C. (3d) 48 (N.S.C.A.).

Sufficiency of certificate under subsec. (5) – It was held in relation to former s. 238(4), which was worded similarly to this subsection, that the certificate is not admissible to prove additionally that notice of suspension had been given to the accused: *R. v. Lock* (1974), 18 C.C.C. (2d) 477, 4 O.R. (2d) 178 (C.A.). *Quaere*, whether the same result would be reached now, in light of subsec. (4).

A notice which complied with the provisions of this subsection but went on to name the wrong date of the offence was held to be valid. This latter piece of information was not essential to the giving of notice and did not vitiate the effectiveness of the notice given: *R. v. Spezzano* (1976), 32 C.C.C. (2d) 303 (Ont. C.A.).

A typographical error will not render the certificate inadmissible provided that the identity of the accused, the period of suspension and the fact of prohibition are clear: *R. v. Alexis* (1999), 181 D.L.R. (4th) 719, 48 M.V.R. (3d) 1 (B.C.C.A.).

A stamped impression of the registrar's signature on the certificate is sufficient: *R. v. Layton* (1978), 40 C.C.C. (2d) 457, [1978] 4 W.W.R. 633 (B.C.S.C.).

However, a form which is pre-printed with the registrar's signature on it and then filled out later and which is never seen by the registrar does not comply: *R. v. Zwicker* (1979), 49 C.C.C. (2d) 340, 37 N.S.R. (2d) 622 (Mag. Ct.), affd (1980), 53 C.C.C. (2d) 239, 38 N.S.R. (2d) 361 (C.A.).

Sufficiency of notice under subsec. (6) – Service of the notice of intention in the period between the accused's first appearance and his trial is permissible, provided the notice is given to the accused seven days before the trial date: *R. v. Heisler*, [1967] 1 C.C.C. 97, 49 C.R. 297 (N.S.S.C.).

The Crown may not resort to provincial legislation which permits the admissibility of documents in the possession of the Registrar without notice: *R. v. Delyon* (1979), 47 C.C.C. (2d) 173 (Ont. Prov. Ct.), aprvd *R. v. Morrison* (1980), 53 C.C.C. (2d) 478 (Ont. H.C.J.). See also: *R. v. Albright*, [1987] 2 S.C.R. 383, 37 C.C.C. (3d) 105, noted under s. 645.

Other means of proof of disqualification – A certified copy of an order of driving prohibition, signed by a justice of the peace for the clerk of the court and bearing the seal of the provincial court, although not admissible under subsec. (5) because the notice required by this subsection was not given, is admissible at common law. At common law, judicial documents could be proved by production of the original record or an exemplification under the seal of the court, without notice: *R. v. Tatomir* (1989), 51 C.C.C. (3d) 321, [1990] 1 W.W.R. 470 (Alta. C.A.).

It was held in *R. v. Gramik* (1988), 9 M.V.R. (2d) 141 (Alta. Q.B.), that an order of a driving prohibition made by a court is admissible under the common law public documents exception to the hearsay rule.

However, it was held in *R. v. Kuzma* (1988), 5 M.V.R. (2d) 232, 66 Sask. R. 153 (C.A.), that a certified copy of the order of driving prohibition was not properly tendered under s. 667 since on its face it was a copy of an order by a clerk of the court and not a certified copy of an order made pursuant to s. 259. The court left open whether if there were a certified copy of a court order of prohibition this would be a certificate within the meaning of s. 667.

STAY OF ORDER PENDING APPEAL / Appeals to Supreme Court of Canada / Effect of conditions.

261. (1) Subject to subsection (1.1), if an appeal is taken against a conviction or discharge under section 730 for an offence committed under any of sections 220, 221, 236, 249 to 255 and 259, a judge of the court being appealed to may direct that any

prohibition order under section 259 arising out of the conviction or discharge shall, on any conditions that the judge or court imposes, be stayed pending the final disposition of the appeal or until otherwise ordered by that court.

(1.1) In the case of an appeal to the Supreme Court of Canada, the direction referred to in subsection (1) may be made only by a judge of the court being appealed from and not by a judge of the Supreme Court of Canada.

(2) If conditions are imposed under a direction made under subsection (1) or (1.1) that a prohibition order be stayed, the direction shall not operate to decrease the period of prohibition provided in the order. R.S.C. 1985, c. 27, (1st Supp.), s. 36; 1994, c. 44, ss. 15 and 103; 1995, c. 22, s. 10; 1997, c. 18, ss. 12, 141; 2006, c. 14, s. 5; 2008, c. 6, s. 27.

CROSS-REFERENCES

An order under this section is itself within the definition of "sentence" in ss. 673 and 785 for the purposes of appeals in proceedings by indictment and summary conviction respectively.

SYNOPSIS

This section empowers a judge of the court to which an appeal is taken against conviction or discharge under s. 730 for an offence committed under ss. 220, 221, 236, 249 to 255 or 259, to direct a stay of any prohibition order until the appeal is disposed of, or the court orders otherwise. In staying the order, the judge may impose conditions, but the inclusion of such conditions does not decrease the period of the prohibition. An application to stay a prohibition order pending an appeal to the Supreme Court of Canada is also made to a judge of the court of appeal, not a judge of the Supreme Court of Canada.

ANNOTATIONS

The burden is on the appellant to show that a stay of the order should be granted. The appellant must show that the appeal is not frivolous, that continuation of the driving prohibition pending appeal is not necessary in the public interest, and that to grant the stay would not detrimentally affect the confidence of the public in the effective enforcement and administration of criminal law: *R. v. Jay and MacLean* (1987), 66 Nfld. & P.E.I.R. 84, 50 M.V.R. 137 (P.E.I.S.C.).

The standard of frivolousness has two different aspects: (1) whether the appeal is brought for a motivation different than having success in the appeal, and (2) the appeal has little chance of success. In addition, the court must consider the hardship on the appellant and the protection of the public: *R. v. McPherson* (1999), 140 C.C.C. (3d) 316 (B.C.C.A.).

The Court of Appeal does not have jurisdiction to stay a driving prohibition pending an appeal to the Supreme Court of Canada: *R. v. Reed* (1997), 120 C.C.C. (3d) 556 (B.C.C.A.).

IMPEDING ATTEMPT TO SAVE LIFE.

262. Every one who
- (*a*) **prevents or impedes or attempts to prevent or impede any person who is attempting to save his own life, or**
- (*b*) **without reasonable cause prevents or impedes or attempts to prevent or impede any person who is attempting to save the life of another person,**

is guilty of an indictable offence and liable to imprisonment for a term not exceeding ten years. R.S., c. C-34, s. 241.

CROSS-REFERENCES

The accused has an election as to mode of trial pursuant to s. 536(2). Release pending trial is determined by s. 515.

SYNOPSIS

This section sets out the criminal consequences for preventing or impeding, or attempting to prevent or impede, any person who is attempting to save his own life or that of another person. Where the circumstances involve a person attempting to save the life of another person, an accused under this section has the defence of reasonable excuse. The offence is indictable and punishable upon conviction to a maximum term of imprisonment of ten years.

DUTY TO SAFEGUARD OPENING IN ICE / Excavation on land / Offences.

263. (1) Every one who makes or causes to be made an opening in ice that is open to or frequented by the public is under a legal duty to guard it in a manner that is adequate to prevent persons from falling in by accident and is adequate to warn them that the opening exists.

(2) Every one who leaves an excavation on land that he owns or of which he has charge or supervision is under a legal duty to guard it in a manner that is adequate to prevent persons from falling in by accident and is adequate to warn them that the excavation exists.

(3) Every one who fails to perform a duty imposed by subsection (1) or (2) is guilty of
  (*a*) manslaughter, if the death of any person results therefrom;
  (*b*) an offence under section 269, if bodily harm to any person results therefrom; or
  (*c*) an offence punishable on summary conviction. R.S., c. C-34, s. 242; 1980-81-82-83, c. 125, s. 18.

CROSS-REFERENCES

The offence of manslaughter is punishable pursuant to s. 236. An accused charged with manslaughter has an election as to mode of trial pursuant to s. 536(2) and release pending trial is determined under s. 515.

The offence under s. 269, referred to in subsec. (3)(*b*), is the offence of unlawfully causing bodily harm. "Bodily harm" is defined in s. 2. An accused, charged with the offence under s. 269, has an election as to mode of trial pursuant to s. 536(2) and release pending trial is determined under s. 515.

For the offence under subsec. (3)(*c*), the trial is conducted by a summary conviction court pursuant to Part XXVII. The punishment for the summary conviction offence is as set out in s. 787 [although, note that the maximum fine for a corporation is determined by s. 735(1)(*b*)] and the limitation period is set out in s. 786(2).

Related offences: ss. 219 to 221, criminal negligence; s. 247, setting traps with intent.

SYNOPSIS

This section sets out the legal requirements incumbent upon anyone who makes a hole in ice that is, or could be used by the public, or who leaves an excavation on land that he owns or supervises. A person who fails to guard such openings in the land or the ice in such manner as to prevent other persons from falling in, and to adequately warn them of the opening, is guilty of a criminal offence punishable on summary conviction.

If a person dies as a result of the failure to comply with this section, the offender will be guilty, upon conviction, of manslaughter. If a person suffers bodily harm, the offender, upon conviction, will be subject to the terms of s. 269.

ANNOTATIONS

This section sets up a statutory duty which if breached will lead to a conviction for manslaughter even in circumstances which would not amount to criminal negligence as defined by s. 219: *R. v. Aldergrove Competition Motorcycle Association and Levy* (1982), 69 C.C.C. (2d) 183 (B.C. Co. Ct.), affd 5 C.C.C. (3d) 114 (B.C.C.A.).

264. [*Repealed* (old provision), R.S.C. 1985, c. 27 (1st Supp.), s. 37.]

CRIMINAL HARASSMENT / Prohibited conduct / Punishment / Factors to be considered / Reasons.

264. (1) No person shall, without lawful authority and knowing that another person is harassed or recklessly as to whether the other person is harassed, engage in conduct referred to in subsection (2) that causes that other person reasonably, in all the circumstances, to fear for their safety or the safety of anyone known to them.

(2) The conduct mentioned in subsection (1) consists of

- (*a*) repeatedly following from place to place the other person or anyone known to them;
- (*b*) repeatedly communicating with, either directly or indirectly, the other person or anyone known to them;
- (*c*) besetting or watching the dwelling-house, or place where the other person, or anyone known to them, resides, works, carries on business or happens to be; or
- (*d*) engaging in threatening conduct directed at the other person or any member of their family.

(3) Every person who contravenes this section is guilty of

- (*a*) an indictable offence and is liable to imprisonment for a term not exceeding ten years; or
- (*b*) an offence punishable on summary conviction.

(4) Where a person is convicted of an offence under this section, the court imposing the sentence on the person shall consider as an aggravating factor that, at the time the offence was committed, the person contravened

- (*a*) the terms or conditions of an order made pursuant to section 161 or a recognizance entered into pursuant to section 810, 810.1 or 810.2; or
- (*b*) the terms or conditions of any other order or recognizance made or entered into under the common law or a provision of this or any other Act of Parliament or of a province that is similar in effect to an order or recognizance referred to in paragraph (*a*).

(5) Where the court is satisfied of the existence of an aggravating factor referred to in subsection (4), but decides not to give effect to it for sentencing purposes, the court shall give reasons for its decision. 1993, c. 45, s. 2; 1997, c. 16. s. 4; 1997, c. 17, s. 9; 2002, c. 13, s. 10.

CROSS-REFERENCES

Other related offences are: s. 177, trespassing by night; s. 264.1, uttering threats; s. 372, indecent and harassing telephone calls; s. 423, intimidation; s. 430, mischief. In addition, ss. 810 and 810.1 authorize a provincial court judge to require the defendant to enter into a recognizance and comply with conditions. A person convicted of this offence must have imposed a weapon, ammunition and explosives prohibition under s. 109. Other statutory aggravating factors for the purposes of sentencing are set out in s. 718.2(*a*). While this section requires the court to give reasons in certain circumstances, s. 726.2 requires the court to give reasons for sentence in every case.

Section 486(1) and (2) provide that the judge may make an order excluding all or any members of the public where such order is in the interest of public morals, the maintenance of order or the proper administration of justice, or is necessary to prevent injury to international relations or national defence or national security. The proper administration of justice includes safeguarding the interests of witnesses under the age of 18 years. Section 486.1 sets out the circumstances in which the judge shall or may order a support person to be present and close to a witness while the witness testifies. Where the witness is under the age of 18 years or has a mental or physical disability, the order is to be made upon request unless the judge is of the opinion that the order would interfere with the proper administration of justice. In the case of other witnesses, the order is to be made if necessary to obtain a full and candid account from the witness of the matters complained of. The application for this order may be made during the proceedings or before they begin to the judge who is to preside at the proceedings.

Similarly, s. 486.2 sets out the circumstances in which the judge shall or may order a witness to testify outside the courtroom or behind a screen or other device that would not allow the witness to see the accused. Where the witness is under the age of 18 years or may have difficulty communicating the evidence by reason of a mental or physical disability, the judge shall make the order unless the judge is of the opinion that the order would interfere with the proper administration of justice. In all other cases, the order may be made if the judge is of the opinion that the order is necessary to obtain a full and candid account from the witness of the acts complained of. Similarly, s. 486.3(4) provides that, on application by the prosecutor or the victim (defined in s. 2), the accused shall not personally cross-examine the witness unless the judge is of the opinion that the proper administration of justice requires the accused to personally conduct the cross-examination. The judge will appoint counsel to conduct the cross-examination.

Under s. 486.5, the judge may make an order directing that the identity of the victim or a witness not be disclosed in any publication, broadcast or transmitted in any way if the judge is satisfied that the order is necessary for the proper administration of justice.

Section 715.1 provides that, in proceedings against the accused in which the victim or other witness was under the age of 18 years at the time the offence is alleged to have been committed, a video recording made within a reasonable time after the alleged offence, in which the victim or witness describes the acts complained of, is admissible in evidence if the victim or witness, while testifying, adopts its contents, unless the judge is of the opinion that the admission of the video recoding would interfere with the proper administration of justice. Section 715.2 provides for a similar procedure where the victim or another witness may have difficulty communicating the evidence by reason of a mental or physical disability.

SYNOPSIS

This section creates the Crown option offence of criminal harassment. It is an offence to engage in harassing conduct as defined in subsec. (2). Knowing that the person is harassed [or being reckless in that respect] causes the other person to reasonably fear for their safety or the safety of anyone known to them. Subsection (4) deems the contravention of certain types of court orders in the commission of the offence to be aggravating factors for the purpose of sentencing. Where the court is satisfied that one of these factors exist, but decides not to give effect to it, the court must give reasons for its decisions.

ANNOTATIONS

The *mens rea* required for this offence is that the accused knew that his conduct caused the complainant to be harassed or that he was aware of such a risk and was reckless or willfully blind as to whether or not the person was harassed. Accordingly, honest mistake is a defence to this offence. Furthermore, this provision does not violate s. 7 of the Charter as foresight of the prohibited consequence of causing actual fear is not required in order to hold the accused responsible for the results of the unlawful activity. It must be established that: (1) the accused has engaged in conduct set out in s. 264(2)(*a*), (*b*), (*c*) or (*d*); (2) the complainant was harassed; (3) the accused who engaged in such conduct knew that the complainant was harassed or was reckless or willfully blind as to whether the complainant was harassed; (4) the conduct caused the complainant to fear for his or her safety or the safety of anyone known to the person; and (5) the complainants fear in all of the circumstances was reasonable: *R. v. Sillipp* (1997), 120 C.C.C. (3d) 384, 11 C.R. (5th) 71 (Alta. C.A.), leave to appeal to S.C.C. refused 123 C.C.C. (3d) vi. Folld: *R. v. Krushel* (2000), 142 C.C.C. (3d) 1, 31 C.R. (5th) 295 (Ont. C.A.), leave to appeal to S.C.C. refused [2004] 4 S.C.R. vi *sub nom. R. v. Grey*, 169 C.C.C. (3d) vi, 180 O.A.C. 199*n*.

Nor does this section constitute an unconstitutional violation of s. 2(*b*) of the *Canadian Charter of Rights and Freedoms*: *R. v. Krushel, supra*. See also *R. v. Davis* (2000), 224 W.A.C. 99, 148 Man. R. (2d) 99 (C.A.).

A single incident can constitute threatening conduct: *R. v. Kosikar* (1999), 138 C.C.C. (3d) 217, 178 D.L.R. (4th) 238 (Ont. C.A.), leave to appeal to S.C.C. refused 142 C.C.C. (3d) vi, 183 D.L.R. (4th) viii; *R. v. Hawkins* (2006), 215 C.C.C. (3d) 419 (B.C.C.A.).

Harassment is proven if as a consequence of the prohibited act, the complainant was in a state of being harassed or felt harassed in the sense of feeling tormented, troubled, worried continually or chronically plagued, bedeviled and badgered. *R. v. Kosikar, supra.*

Even though conduct occurred over a relatively short period of time and there was no prior contact, the requisite elements of the offence were met where it was highly threatening and persistent. In this case, the accused had jumped out from the bushes and blocked the path of a stranger jogging in a residential neighbourhood at night. He then chased the complainant to a house and stared at her while she waited for someone to answer the door: *R. v. K. (K.)* (2009), 241 C.C.C. (3d) 284 (Ont. C.A.), supp. reasons 244 C.C.C. (3d) 124 (Ont. C.A.), leave to appeal to S.C.C. refused 243 C.C.C. (3d) vi. See also *R. v. O'Connor* (2008), 234 O.A.C. 135 (C.A.), leave to appeal to S.C.C. refused [2008] 3 S.C.R. ix.

The words "tormented, troubled, worried continually or chronically, plagued, bedeviled and badgered" are not cumulative and are individually synonymous with the word "harrassed". Accordingly, establishing any of these factors can constitute harrassment: *R. v. Kordrostami* (2000), 143 C.C.C. (3d) 488, 47 O.R. (3d) 788 (C.A.).

Harassment should not be given a restrictive definition and includes "requests, solicitations, incitements" that have the effect of bothering someone because of their continuity or repetition: *R. v. Lamontagne* (1998), 129 C.C.C. (3d) 181 (Que. C.A.).

In considering whether repeated communications constitute criminal harassment, regard must be had to both the content and the repetitious nature of the calls, together with the context in which the calls were made: *R. v. Scuby* (2004), 181 C.C.C. (3d) 97, 20 C.R. (6th) 127 (B.C.C.A.).

"Watching" in para. (*c*) requires continuous observation for a particular purpose. Merely looking and smiling at someone, standing alone, is not sufficient to constitute "watching". The term must be construed with reference to the relationship between "watching" and "besetting": *R. v. Eltom* (2010), 258 C.C.C. (3d) 224 (Ont. S.C.J.).

Conduct can be repeated only if it occurs on two occasions. The trier of fact must consider the conduct that was the subject matter of the charge against the background of the relationship and the history between the complainant and the accused. In this case, where the accused had been previously convicted of threatening the complainant, two letters sent 18 months apart could constitute "repeated" communication: *R. v. Ohenhen* (2005), 200 C.C.C. (3d) 309, 33 C.R. (6th) 391 (Ont. C.A.).

An objective standard must apply in determining whether threatening conduct in subsec. (2)(*d*) amounts to intimidation designed to instill a sense of fear in the recipient: *R. v. George* (2002), 162 C.C.C. (3d) 337, 268 W.A.C. 29 (Y.T.C.A.).

Evidence of prior incidents of discreditable conduct may be admissible to provide context to assess the effect of the incident on the complainant and whether the accused knew that the conduct would cause the complainant to be fearful or that the accused was reckless as to whether the complainant would be fearful: *R. v. D. (D.)* (2005), 203 C.C.C. (3d) 6, 204 O.A.C. 55 (C.A.).

Assaults

UTTERING THREATS / Punishment / Idem.

264.1 (1) Every one commits an offence who, in any manner, knowingly utters, conveys or causes any person to receive a threat

    (*a*) **to cause death or bodily harm to any person;**

    (*b*) **to burn, destroy or damage real or personal property; or**

    (*c*) **to kill, poison or injure an animal or bird that is the property of any person.**

(2) Every one who commits an offence under paragraph (1)(*a*) is guilty of

(*a*) **an indictable offence and liable to imprisonment for a term not exceeding five years; or**

(*b*) **an offence punishable on summary conviction and liable to imprisonment for a term not exceeding eighteen months.**

(3) Every one who commits an offence under paragraph (1)(*b*) or (*c*)

(*a*) **is guilty of an indictable offence and liable to imprisonment for a term not exceeding two years; or**

(*b*) **is guilty of an offence punishable on summary conviction. R.S.C. 1985, c. 27 (1st Supp.), s. 38; 1994, c. 44, s. 16.**

CROSS-REFERENCES

The terms "bodily harm" and "property" are defined in s. 2. The term "person" is defined in s. 35 of the *Interpretation Act*, R.S.C. 1985, c. I-21.

This offence may be the basis for an application for an authorization to intercept private communications by reason of s. 183.

Where the threat is in relation to the use of nuclear material see s. 7(3.4).

An alternative to this offence is the procedure for requiring the offender to enter into a recognizance to keep the peace, either at common law or pursuant to s. 810. Related offences: s. 346, extortion; s. 423, intimidation; s. 423.1 intimidation of a justice system participant; s. 424, threat to commit offence against internationally protected person; ss. 430 to 432, damage to property; ss. 433 to 436, arson and other fires; ss. 444 to 447, offences in relation to animals.

SYNOPSIS

This section describes the kinds of threats that will attract criminal consequences. Any person who utters, conveys or causes another person to receive a threat of death, or serious bodily harm, is guilty of an indictable offence and liable to imprisonment for a maximum term of five years, or a summary conviction offence. If a person threatens to burn, damage or destroy another person's real or personal property or to kill, poison or injure an animal or bird belonging to another person, he is guilty of an indictable offence, with a maximum term of imprisonment of two years, or of a summary conviction offence.

ANNOTATIONS

Meaning of threat – A "conditional" threat, that if the police officer did not leave he would be shot, comes within the ordinary meaning of "threat" and can constitute an offence under this section. In this case the court adopted a dictionary definition of threat as "a denunciation to a person of ill to befall him; esp. a declaration of hostile determination or of loss, pain, punishment, or damage to be inflicted in retribution for or conditionally upon some course; a menace": *R. v. Ross* (1986), 26 C.C.C. (3d) 413, 50 C.R. (3d) 391 (Ont. C.A.).

Serious bodily harm in subsec. (1)(*a*) means any hurt or injury, whether physical or psychological, that interferes in a substantial way with the physical or psychological integrity, health or well-being of the complainant. The issue to be determined is whether looked at objectively in the context of all the words written and having regard to the person to whom they were directed, would the questioned words convey a threat of serious bodily harm to a reasonable person? A threat to rape is capable of constituting a threat to cause serious bodily harm: *R. v. McCraw*, [1991] 3 S.C.R. 72, 66 C.C.C. (3d) 517 (7:0).

Elements of offence generally – Aside from cases where the words might have a secondary, innocent meaning as between the parties it is immaterial whether the "victim" appreciated he was being threatened. The Crown is only required to prove the accused uttered the threat by one of the means specified: *R. v. Carons* (1978), 42 C.C.C. (2d) 19 (Alta. C.A.).

The *actus reus* will be made out if a reasonable person aware of the circumstances in which the words were uttered would have perceived them to be a threat of death or bodily harm. The Crown need not prove that the intended recipient of the threat was made aware of it, or if aware of it, that he or she was intimidated by it or took it seriously. Nor must the words be directed toward a specific person; a threat against an ascertained group of people is sufficient. The *mens rea* is made out if the accused intended the words uttered or conveyed to intimidate or to be taken seriously. It is not necessary to prove an intent that the words be conveyed to the subject of the threat or that the accused intended to carry out the threat: *R. v. McRae*, [2013] 3 S.C.R. 931, 307 C.C.C. (3d) 291.

In determining whether or not the accused's statements were a threat, the words are to be viewed objectively in the context or circumstances in which they were spoken, the issue being whether they would convey a threat of serious bodily harm to a reasonable person. The *mens rea* of the offence is that the words to be spoken or written as a threat to cause death or serious bodily harm; that is, they were meant to intimidate or to be taken seriously. Words spoken in jest or in such a manner that they could not be taken seriously could not lead a reasonable person to conclude that the words conveyed a threat. There is no requirement that the intended victim of the threat be aware of the threat: *R. v. Clemente*, [1994] 2 S.C.R. 758, 91 C.C.C. (3d) 1.

In considering whether a poem constituted a threat, regard must be had to a reasonable person's consideration of all of the relevant circumstances: *R. v. Batista* (2008), 238 C.C.C. (3d) 97 (Ont. C.A.).

In *R. v. Leblanc*, [1989] 1 S.C.R. 1583, 50 C.C.C. (3d) 192*n* (7:0), the court overturned the decision of the New Brunswick Court of Appeal, 44 C.C.C. (3d) 18, 66 C.R. (3d) 134, and restored the accused's conviction for the offence under this section, holding that the jury had been properly directed. The issue in the case was the *mens rea* of the offence and the trial judge, in directing the jury, had distinguished between a threat innocently made which was no offence and a threat which was an actual menace.

The fact that the victim of the offence was unknown at the time the threat was made did not preclude a conviction for the offence under this section. A threat to cause the death of a member of an ascertained group of persons contravenes this section: *R. v. Rémy* (1993), 82 C.C.C. (3d) 176, [1993] R.J.Q. 1383 (C.A.).

"Repeatedly" means conduct that is repeated on more than one occasion: *R. v. Ryback* (1996), 105 C.C.C. (3d) 240, 47 C.R. (4th) 108 (B.C.C.A.), leave to appeal to S.C.C. refused 107 C.C.C. (3d) vi.

Pre-charge conduct of the accused is relevant to whether the complainant's fear of the accused was reasonable, as well as to the accused's intent in knowing or being reckless as to whether conduct harassed the complainant: *R. v. Ryback, supra.*

ASSAULT / Application / Consent / Accused's belief as to consent.

265. **(1) A person commits an assault when**

    (*a*) **without the consent of another person, he applies force intentionally to that other person, directly or indirectly;**

    (*b*) **he attempts or threatens, by an act or a gesture, to apply force to another person, if he has, or causes that other person to believe upon reasonable grounds that he has, present ability to effect his purpose; or**

    (*c*) **while openly wearing or carrying a weapon or an imitation thereof, he accosts or impedes another person or begs.**

(2) This section applies to all forms of assault, including sexual assault, sexual assault with a weapon, threats to a third party or causing bodily harm and aggravated sexual assault.

(3) For the purposes of this section, no consent is obtained where the complainant submits or does not resist by reason of

    (*a*) **the application of force to the complainant or to a person other than the complainant;**

    (*b*) **threats or fear of the application of force to the complainant or to a person other than the complainant;**

    (*c*) **fraud; or**
    (*d*) **the exercise of authority.**

(4) Where an accused alleges that he believed that the complainant consented to the conduct that is the subject-matter of the charge, a judge, if satisfied that there is sufficient evidence and that, if believed by the jury, the evidence would constitute a defence, shall instruct the jury, when reviewing all the evidence relating to the determination of the honesty of the accused's belief, to consider the presence or absence of reasonable grounds for that belief. R.S., c. C-34, s. 244; 1974-75-76, c. 93, s. 21; 1980-81-82-83, c. 125, s. 19.

CROSS-REFERENCES

The terms "complainant" and "weapon" are defined in s. 2. The offences described in subsec. (2) may be found as follows: s. 266, punishment for assault *simpliciter* [formerly common assault]; s. 267, assault with weapon and assault causing bodily harm; s. 268, aggravated assault; s. 270, assault police; s. 271, sexual assault; s. 272, sexual assault with weapon, threats to a third party and causing bodily harm; s. 273, aggravated sexual assault.

As to defences see: s. 16, insanity; s. 17, compulsion by threats; s. 25, use of force in enforcement of law; s. 27, use of force to prevent commission of certain offences; s. 33.1 intoxication; ss. 34 to 37, self defence and defence of person under accused's protection; ss. 38 to 41, defence of property; s. 43, use of force by way of correction; s. 44, use of force by master of vessel.

As to notes respecting the intoxication and necessity defences see s. 8. These latter defences, especially intoxication are of limited application since most of the assault offences are general intent offences.

Section 273.1 defines consent for the sexual offences in ss. 271, 272 and 273 and, in particular, defines circumstances additional to those set out in s. 265(3) in which no consent is obtained. For the same group of offences, s. 273.2 sets out circumstances where belief in consent is not a defence. For additional notes concerning the defence of honest belief in consent, see the notes following s. 273.2.

As to mode of trial and punishment, see the cross-references under particular assault offence.

SYNOPSIS

This section describes what an assault is, when an assault is aggravated, and the extent to which *consent* can be used as a defence to a charge of assault. A person who directly or indirectly applies force *intentionally* to another person, or who attempts or threatens to do so, has committed an assault. If a person stops another person while openly wearing a weapon or an imitation weapon, he is also guilty of assault. All forms of assault, including sexual assault are covered by this section, but now see also s. 273.1. Consent may constitute a defence to a charge of assault but it cannot be invoked if the victim submits because force has been applied to, or is threatened to be applied to, the victim or another person. Furthermore, the defence of consent will not apply if a person has submitted as a result of fraud or the exercise of authority by the accused.

Section 265(4) requires that the jury in a case in which the defence of consent is raised, and which would be effective if accepted, be instructed by the judge to consider whether the accused had reasonable grounds for an honest belief that there was consent.

ANNOTATIONS

Elements of offence other than consent – Where the application of force is the result of carelessness, as in *R. v. Starratt* (1971), 5 C.C.C. (2d) 32, [1972] 1 O.R. 227 (C.A.), or through a reflex action as in *R. v. Wolfe* (1974), 20 C.C.C. (2d) 382 (Ont. C.A.), the essential element of intent is lacking and the accused must be acquitted.

An accused may commit an assault although he exerts no degree of strength or power when touching the victim: *R. v. Burden* (1981), 64 C.C.C. (2d) 68, 25 C.R. (3d) 283 (B.C.C.A.).

In *R. v. Byrne*, [1968] 3 C.C.C. 179, 3 C.R.N.S. 190 (B.C.C.A.), it was held that words alone unaccompanied by any gesture do not constitute the act of assault.

Whether or not there has been an assault as defined by subsec. (1)(*b*) depends on the facts of a particular case. Thus, where the accused school teacher, by acts and gestures, directed his pupils to perform various sexual acts upon him, the trier of fact could find that there were not mere invitations but threats to apply force, coupled with a present ability to effect that purpose and thus an assault, or, as here, a sexual assault: *R. v. Cadden* (1989), 48 C.C.C. (3d) 122, 70 C.R. (3d) 340 (B.C.C.A.).

An assault is committed when a person threatens to apply force and has the ability to do so: *R. v. Horncastle* (1972), 8 C.C.C. (2d) 253, 19 C.R.N.S. 362 (N.B.C.A.).

An assault is committed within the meaning of subsec. (1)(*b*) where the accused fires a gun at someone who was within range, even if the shot missed and the victim had no idea that he was being shot at: *R. v. Melaragni* (1992), 75 C.C.C. (3d) 546 (Ont. Ct. (Gen. Div.)).

Meaning of consent – To be effective the consent to the assault must be freely given with appreciation of all the risks and not merely submission to an apparently inevitable situation: *R. v. Stanley* (1977), 36 C.C.C. (2d) 216, [1977] 4 W.W.R. 578 (B.C.C.A.).

In *R. v. Cey* (1989), 48 C.C.C. (3d) 480, [1989] 5 W.W.R. 169 (Sask. C.A.), the court had to consider the scope of consent as a result of a charge of assault causing bodily harm, arising out of events in the course of an amateur hockey game. By agreeing to play the game, a hockey player consents to some forms of intentional bodily contact and to the risk of injury therefrom. Those forms of bodily contact sanctioned by the rules are the clearest examples but, as well, even those forms denounced by the rules, but falling within the accepted standards by which the game is played, may also come within the scope of the implied consent. While ordinarily, consent, being a state of mind, is a wholly subjective matter to be determined accordingly, when it comes to implied consent in the context of a team sport such as hockey, the scope of the implied consent must be determined by reference to objective criteria, at least in respect of those forms of conduct covered by the initial general consent. In determining the scope of the implied consent, the court will have regard to the conditions under which the game is played and the risk and degree of injury. Some forms of bodily contact carry with them such a high risk of injury and such a distinct probability of serious harm as to go beyond what, in fact, the players commonly consent to or what, in law, they are capable of consenting to.

In determining the scope of implied consent, the court must employ objective criteria and have regard to a number of factors, including the setting of the game, the extent of the force employed, the degree of risk of injury, the probabilities of serious harm and whether or not the rules of the game contemplate contact. Contact which evinces a deliberate purpose to inflict injury will generally be held to be outside of the immunity provided by implied consent in sporting events, but this does not mean that the prosecution must in all cases prove such deliberate purpose. Conversely, the fact that the rules do not allow for bodily contact is not itself determinative, especially where the ideal of non-contact is frequently breached in a spirited hockey game: *R. v. Leclerc* (1991), 67 C.C.C. (3d) 563, 7 C.R. (4th) 282 (Ont. C.A.).

In *R. v. M. (M.L.)*, [1994] 2 S.C.R. 3*n*, 89 C.C.C. (3d) 96*n*, it was held that the court of appeal erred in holding that the 16-year-old complainant, who was the accused's step-daughter, had to have offered some minimal word or gesture of objection in order for there to be proof that she did not consent and erred in holding that lack of resistance could be equated with consent.

Consensual fights – The common law limits on consent imposed for policy reasons apply to assaults as defined by this section and, thus, consent is vitiated where adults intentionally apply force causing serious hurt or non-trivial bodily harm to each other in the course of a fist fight or brawl. These limits do not, however, affect the validity or effectiveness of freely given consent to participate in rough sporting activities, so long as the intentional application of force to which one consents is within the customary norms and rules of the game. This limitation on consent would also not apply to medical treatment or appropriate surgical intervention nor would it necessarily nullify consent between stuntmen engaged in the creation of a socially valuable cultural product. Finally, these limits do not apply to ordinary school yard scuffles between children who immaturely seek to resolve differences through fighting: *R. v. Jobidon*, [1991] 2 S.C.R. 714, 66 C.C.C. (3d) 454 (7:0).

Serious bodily harm must be both intended and caused for consent to be vitiated: *R. v. Paice*, [2005] 1 S.C.R. 339, 195 C.C.C. (3d) 97.

Where the accused did not intend to cause bodily harm, consent is available as a defence if bodily harm is inadvertently caused: *R. v. Zhao* (2013), 297 C.C.C. (3d) 533 (Ont. C.A.).

In view of the 16-year-old offender's intention to cause serious harm to the complainant who was of the same age, the nature of the force applied, and the serious consequences of those actions, the complainant's consent could not nullify the offender's culpability on a charge of assault causing bodily harm notwithstanding the young age of both the accused and the complainant. The offender's actions were more than socially useless, they were dangerous and intended to be dangerous. It was unnecessary to decide in this case whether the consent could operate as a defence where a young person engages in a consensual fight, not intending to cause serious harm: *R. v. W. (G.)* (1994), 90 C.C.C. (3d) 139, 30 C.R. (4th) 393 (Ont. C.A.).

However, where the 15-year-old offender did not intend to cause the victim more than trivial bodily harm, the consent was not vitiated notwithstanding that more serious harm may have been caused: *R. v. B. (T.B.)* (1994), 93 C.C.C. (3d) 191, 34 C.R. (4th) 241 (P.E.I.C.A.).

Similarly, where the 16-year-old offender did not intend to cause the victim harm and only minor bodily harm resulted, the offender's honest belief that the victim consented to the fight was a defence: *R. v. M. (S.)* (1995), 97 C.C.C. (3d) 281, 39 C.R. (4th) 60 (Ont. C.A.).

Mistaken belief in consent [subsec. (4)] – This subsection which is consistent with the common law applicable to all defences does not infringe either s. 11(*d*) or (*f*) of the Charter. The accused who seeks to rely upon the defence of mistaken belief only bears a tactical evidentiary burden: *R. v. Osolin*, [1993] 4 S.C.R. 595, 86 C.C.C. (3d) 481. [Also see s. 273.2.]

As to when there is an air of reality of a defence, see note of *R. v. Cinous*, [2002] 2 S.C.R. 3, 162 C.C.C. (3d) 129, under s. 273.2.

Consent obtained by threats or fear of use of force [subsec. (3)(*b*)] – The threats referred to in this paragraph are threats of the application of force. A threat made by the accused to expose certain pictures of the complainant was not the type of threat contemplated. As the conduct did not otherwise fall within this subsection, which is exhaustive of the circumstances vitiating consent, then no assault was committed: *R. v. Guerrero* (1988), 64 C.R. (3d) 65 (Ont. C.A.).

Consent obtained by fraud [subsec. (3)(*c*)] – An accused who knows that he is HIV-positive and fails to disclose that fact has obtained consent by a type of fraud that may vitiate consent to sexual intercourse within the meaning of subsec. (3)(*c*). In addition to fraud that relates to the nature and quality of the act, fraud is made out by dishonest action or behaviour including non-disclosure that results in deprivation. Deprivation in this context means that the dishonest act (either falsehoods or failure to disclose) had the effect of exposing the complainant to a significant risk of serious bodily harm. In addition, the Crown must prove that the complainant would have refused to engage in unprotected sex with the accused if she had been advised that he was HIV-positive: *R. v. Cuerrier*, [1998] 2 S.C.R. 371, 127 C.C.C. (3d) 1. See also *R. v. Williams*, [2003] 2 S.C.R. 134, 176 C.C.C. (3d) 449.

The *Cuerrier* requirement of "significant risk of serious bodily harm" should be read as requiring disclosure of HIV status if there is a realistic possibility of transmission of HIV. If there is no realistic possibility of transmission of HIV, failure to disclose that one has HIV will not constitute fraud vitiating consent to sexual relations under subsec. (3)(*c*). A realistic possibility of transmission is negated if: (i) the accused's viral load at the time of sexual relations was low and (ii) condom protection was used. This general proposition does not preclude the common law from adapting to future advances in treatment and to circumstances where risk factors other than those considered in this case are at play: *R. v. Mabior*, [2012] 2 S.C.R. 584, 290 C.C.C. (3d) 32.

Where a complainant has chosen not to become pregnant, deceptions that expose her to an increased risk of becoming pregnant may constitute a sufficiently serious deprivation to vitiate consent under subsec. (3)(*c*). This application of "fraud" is consistent with Charter values of equality and autonomy, while recognizing that not every deception that induces consent should be criminalized. Here, where the accused had surreptitiously poked holes in the condom, there was no consent by reason of fraud: *R. v. Hutchinson*, [2014] S.C.J. No. 19.

Consent obtained by exercise of authority [subsec. (3)(*d*)] – Exercise of authority in this paragraph is not limited to relationships where there is a right to issue orders and to enforce obedience. Consent in the context of sexual relationships implies a reasonably informed choice, freely exercised. No such choice has been exercised where a person engages in sexual activity if, because of her mental state, she is incapable of understanding the sexual nature of the act or of realizing that she may choose to decline participation. Where there is a significant power imbalance between the accused and the complainant, this can have an effect on the apparent consent. It would be open to the court to find that there was no consent by reason of the overwhelming imbalance of power in the relationship between the accused psychiatrist and the particular patients: *R. v. Saint-Laurent* (1994), 90 C.C.C. (3d) 291, [1994] R.J.Q. 69 (C.A.), leave to appeal to S.C.C. refused 66 Q.A.C. 160*n*, 175 N.R. 240*n*.

An accused stands in a position of authority over a complainant if the accused can coerce the complainant into consent by virtue of their relationship. The existence of a position of authority does not mean that any sexual activity between the accused and the complainant is non-consensual. The Crown must also prove beyond a reasonable doubt that the accused secured the complainant's apparent consent to the sexual activity which is the subject matter of the charge by the exercise of that coercive authority over the complainant: *R. v. Geddes* (2015), 322 C.C.C. (3d) 414 (Ont. C.A.). See also *R. v. Matheson* (1999), 134 C.C.C. (3d) 289 (Ont. C.A.).

ASSAULT.

266. Every one who commits an assault is guilty of

    (*a*) **an indictable offence and liable to imprisonment for a term not exceeding five years; or**

    (*b*) **an offence punishable on summary conviction. R.S., c. C-34, s. 245; 1972, c. 13, s. 21; 1974-75-76, c. 93, s. 22; 1980-81-82-83, c. 125, s. 19.**

CROSS-REFERENCES

Assault is defined in s. 265. For cases respecting consent, especially assaults in course of a "consensual fight", see notes under s. 265. Where the prosecution elects to proceed by indictment on this offence, then the accused may elect his mode of trial pursuant to s. 536(2). Where the prosecution elects to proceed by way of summary conviction, then the trial of this offence is conducted by a summary conviction court pursuant to Part XXVII. The punishment for the offence is then as set out in s. 787 and the limitation period is set out in s. 786(2). In either case, release pending trial is determined by s. 515, although the accused is eligible for release by a peace officer under ss. 496, 497 or by the officer in charge under s. 498.

A person, found guilty of the offence in this section, will be liable to the discretionary prohibition order prescribed by s. 110, for possession of weapons, ammunition and explosives.

Section 7(3) enacts special jurisdictional rules for commission of this offence outside Canada when the offence is in relation to an internationally protected person or property referred to in s. 431 (official premises, etc.). A threat to commit an offence under this section against an internationally protected person (defined in s. 2) is an offence under s. 424. Section 33.1 limits the availability of the drunkenness defence.

The accused's spouse is a competent and compellable witness at the instance of the Crown by virtue of s. 4(4) of the *Canada Evidence Act*, R.S.C. 1985, c. C-5, where the complainant is under the age of 14 years. Age is determined by reference to s. 30 of the *Interpretation Act*, R.S.C. 1985, c. I-21.

Section 486(1) and (2) provide that the judge may make an order excluding all or any members of the public where such order is in the interest of public morals, the maintenance of order or the proper administration of justice, or is necessary to prevent injury to international relations or national defence or national security. The proper administration of justice includes safeguarding the interests of witnesses under the age of 18 years. Section 486.1 sets out the circumstances in which the judge shall or may order a support person to be present and close to a witness while the witness testifies. Where the witness is under the age of 18 years or has a mental or physical disability, the order is to be made upon request unless the judge is of the opinion that the order would interfere with the proper administration of justice. In the case of other witnesses, the order is to be made if necessary to obtain a full and candid account from the witness of the matters complained of. The application for this order may be made during the proceedings or before they begin to the judge who is to preside at the proceedings.

Similarly, s. 486.2 sets out the circumstances in which the judge shall or may order a witness to testify outside the courtroom or behind a screen or other device that would not allow the witness to see the accused. Where the witness is under the age of 18 years or may have difficulty communicating the evidence by reason of a mental or physical disability, the judge shall make the order unless the judge is of the opinion that the order would interfere with the proper administration of justice. In all other cases, the order may be made if the judge is of the opinion that the order is necessary to obtain a full and candid account from the witness of the acts complained of. Similarly, s. 486.3 provides that, on application by the prosecutor or a witness under the age of 18 years, the accused shall not personally cross-examine the witness unless the judge is of the opinion that the proper administration of justice requires the accused to personally conduct the cross-examination. In other cases, the judge may make an order that the accused not personally cross-examine the witness if the judge is of the opinion that the order is necessary to obtain a full and candid account from the witness of the acts complained of. The judge will appoint counsel to conduct the cross-examination.

Under s. 486.4, the judge may make an order directing that the identity of the complainant or a witness not be disclosed in any publication, broadcast or transmitted in any way. The order is mandatory where the complainant or a witness under the age of 18 years or the prosecutor applies for the order. Section 486.5 also gives the judge a discretion respecting non-publication orders in proceedings under these provisions in other circumstances.

Section 659 abrogates any rule requiring a warning about convicting the accused on the evidence of a child.

Section 715.1 provides that, in proceedings against the accused in which the victim (defined in s. 2) or other witness was under the age of 18 years at the time the offence is alleged to have been committed, a video recording made within a reasonable time after the alleged offence, in which the victim or witness describes the acts complained of, is admissible in evidence if the victim or witness, while testifying, adopts its contents, unless the judge is of the opinion that the admission of the video recoding would interfere with the proper administration of justice. Section 715.2 provides for a similar procedure where the victim or another witness may have difficulty communicating the evidence by reason of a mental or physical disability. Under s. 4(2) of the *Canada Evidence Act*, the spouse of an accused charged with this offence is a compellable witness at the instance of the prosecution. Sections 16 and 16.1 of the *Canada Evidence Act* deal with the competency of witnesses under the age of 14 years.

The offence in this section is a primary designated offence for the purpose of making a forensic DNA data bank order under s. 487.051.

ANNOTATIONS

The conduct of the accused in pushing the complainant aside in order to leave his office, even if it amounted to an assault, was of such a trifling nature that the maxim *de minimis non curat lex* applied, and the accused was acquitted: *R. v. Lepage* (1989), 74 C.R. (3d) 368 (Sask. Q.B.).

The double jeopardy guarantee in s. 11(*h*) of the Charter is not a bar to the trial of an officer for an offence under this section notwithstanding his previous conviction for a major service offence under the *Royal Canadian Mounted Police Act*, R.S.C. 1970, c. R-9, as a result of that assault: *R. v. Wigglesworth*, [1987] 2 S.C.R. 541, 37 C.C.C. (3d) 385, 60 C.R. (3d) 193 (6:1). Also see *R. v. Shubley*, [1990] 1 S.C.R. 3, 52 C.C.C. (3d) 481, 65 D.L.R. (4th) 193 (3:2), noted under s. 267.

ASSAULT WITH A WEAPON OR CAUSING BODILY HARM.

267. Every one who, in committing an assault,
>   **(*a*) carries, uses or threatens to use a weapon or an imitation thereof, or**
>   **(*b*) causes bodily harm to the complainant,**
is guilty of an indictable offence and liable to imprisonment for a term not exceeding ten years or an offence punishable on summary conviction and liable to imprisonment for a term not exceeding eighteen months. 1980-81-82-83, c. 125, s. 19; 1994, c. 44, s. 17.

CROSS-REFERENCES

The terms "bodily harm", "complainant" and "weapon" are defined in s. 2. Assault is defined in s. 265. Limits on availability of drunkenness defence, see s. 33.1.

For cases respecting consent, especially assaults in the course of a "consensual fight", see notes under s. 265.

This offence may be the basis for an application for an authorization to intercept private communications by reason of s. 183.

Section 7(3) enacts special jurisdictional rules for commission of this offence outside Canada when the offence is in relation to an internationally protected person or property referred to in s. 431 (official premises, etc.).

The accused's spouse is a competent and compellable witness at the instance of the Crown by virtue of s. 4(4) of the *Canada Evidence Act*, where the complainant is under the age of 14 years. Age is determined by reference to s. 30 of the *Interpretation Act*, R.S.C. 1985, c. I-21.

Where the Crown elects to proceed by indictment, the accused may elect the mode of trial pursuant to s. 536(2). Release pending trial is determined by s. 515. A person, found guilty of the offence in this section, will be liable to the mandatory prohibition order in s. 109 for possession of certain weapons, ammunition and explosives where the Crown proceeds by indictment. Otherwise, the accused may be subject to an order under s. 110. A person found guilty of this offence may be subject to a dangerous offender application under Part XXIV.

Where the acts described in this section also involve a sexual assault, see s. 272. Using a firearm in commission of an indictable offence is an offence under s. 85. Unlawfully causing bodily harm is an offence under s. 269.

Section 486(1) and (2) provide that the judge may make an order excluding all or any members of the public where such order is in the interest of public morals, the maintenance of order or the proper administration of justice, or is necessary to prevent injury to international relations or national defence or national security. The proper administration of justice includes safeguarding the interests of witnesses under the age of 18 years. Section 486.1 sets out the circumstances in which the judge shall or may order a support person to be present and close to a witness while the witness testifies. Where the witness is under the age of 18 years or has a mental or physical disability, the order is to be made upon request unless the judge is of the opinion that the order would interfere with the proper administration of justice. In the case of other witnesses, the order is to be made if necessary to obtain a full and candid account from the witness of the matters complained of. The application for this order may be made during the proceedings or before they begin to the judge who is to preside at the proceedings.

Similarly, s. 486.2 sets out the circumstances in which the judge shall or may order a witness to testify outside the courtroom or behind a screen or other device that would not allow the witness to see the accused. Where the witness is under the age of 18 years or may have difficulty communicating the evidence by reason of a mental or physical disability, the judge shall make the order unless the judge is of the opinion that the order would interfere with the proper administration of justice. In all other cases, the order may be made if the judge is of the opinion that the order is necessary to obtain a full and candid account from the witness of the acts complained of. Similarly, s. 486.3 provides that, on application by the prosecutor or a witness under the age of 18 years, the accused shall not personally cross-examine the witness unless the judge is of the opinion that the proper administration of justice requires the accused to personally conduct the cross-examination. In other cases, the judge may make an order that the accused not personally cross-examine the witness if the judge is of the opinion that the order is necessary to obtain a full and candid account from the witness of the acts complained of. The judge will appoint counsel to conduct the cross-examination.

Under s. 486.4, the judge may make an order directing that the identity of the complainant or a witness not be disclosed in any publication, broadcast or transmitted in any way. The order is mandatory where the complainant or a witness under the age of 18 years or the prosecutor applies for the order. Section 486.5 also gives the judge a discretion respecting non-publication orders in proceedings under these provisions in other circumstances.

Section 659 abrogates any rule requiring a warning about convicting the accused on the evidence of a child.

Section 715.1 provides that, in proceedings against the accused in which the victim (defined in s. 2) or other witness was under the age of 18 years at the time the offence is alleged to have been committed, a video recording made within a reasonable time after the alleged offence, in which the victim or witness describes the acts complained of, is admissible in evidence if the victim or witness, while testifying, adopts its contents, unless the judge is of the opinion that the admission of the video recoding would interfere with the proper administration of justice. Section 715.2 provides for a similar procedure where the victim or another witness may have difficulty communicating the evidence by reason of a mental or physical disability. Under s. 4(2) of the *Canada Evidence Act*, the spouse of an accused charged with this offence is a compellable witness at the instance of the prosecution. Sections 16 and 16.1 of the *Canada Evidence Act* deal with the competency of witnesses under the age of 14 years.

The offence in this section is a primary designated offence for the purpose of making a forensic DNA data bank order under s. 487.051.

SYNOPSIS

This section specifies that a person who commits an assault while using or carrying a weapon or an imitation weapon, or who causes any hurt or injury that is not transient or trifling in nature and interferes with the complainant's health or comfort, is guilty of an indictable offence and liable to imprisonment for a maximum term of 10 years.

ANNOTATIONS

Assault with weapon [para. (*a*)] – The offence under subsec. (1)(*a*) of this section or s. 272(*a*) [now s. 272(1)(*a*)] may be committed although the accused did not in fact have possession of the weapon at the time of the threat: *R. v. Kelly* (1983), 37 C.R. (3d) 190 (B.C. Co. Ct.).

Provided the instrument used by the accused in the course of the assault falls within the definition of weapon, then this offence is made out. It is not necessary to show that the weapon also caused injuries to the complainant: *R. v. Richard* (1992), 72 C.C.C. (3d) 349, 110 N.S.R. (2d) 345 (C.A.).

The term "weapon" is not limited to inanimate objects and can include a dog which the accused ordered to attack the complainant: *R. v. McLeod* (1993), 84 C.C.C. (3d) 336 (Y.T.C.A.).

A blade used by a father in a misguided attempt to circumcise his four-year-old son was a "weapon" notwithstanding that the accused did not attempt to harm the child. What prevents a normal surgical operation from constituting an offence in s. 45 is reasonable care and skill: *R. v. W. (D.J.)* (2011), 282 C.C.C. (3d) 352 (B.C.C.A.), affd (2012), 294 C.C.C. (3d) 480 (S.C.C.).

Assault causing bodily harm – Reasonable foreseeability that harm will occur as a result of the assault is not a necessary element of this offence: *R. v. Brooks, infra*. Similarly, *R. v. Swenson* (1994), 91 C.C.C. (3d) 541, [1994] 9 W.W.R. 124, 74 W.A.C. 106 (Sask. C.A.).

Where the evidence fails to show whether the bruising caused by the accused's acts was more than merely transient or trifling in nature the element of "bodily harm" as defined in subsec. (2) is not made out: *R. v. Dupperon* (1984), 16 C.C.C. (3d) 453, 43 C.R. (3d) 70, [1985] 2 W.W.R. 369 (Sask. C.A.).

In *R. v. Dixon* (1988), 42 C.C.C. (3d) 318, 64 C.R. (3d) 372, [1988] 5 W.W.R. 577 (Yukon Terr. C.A.), only Esson J.A. discussed at length the definition of bodily harm in subsec. (2) and considered that the words "transient or trifling in nature" import a very short period of time and an injury of a very minor degree which results in a very minor degree of distress.

Bodily harm need not meet a standard of interfering in a grave or substantial way with the physical integrity or well-being of the complainant. A functional impairment is not necessary. Interference with comfort is sufficient to constitute bodily harm if it is more than trifling and transient: *R. v. Moquin* (2010), 253 C.C.C. (3d) 96, 73 C.R. (6th) 310 (Man. C.A.).

As to the consent defence, also see cases noted under s. 265(1), *supra*.

Constitutional considerations – The offence created by subsec. (1)(*b*) does not violate the principles of fundamental justice as guaranteed by s. 7 of the Charter although there is no requirement of objective foreseeability that the consequences of the assault would be bodily harm: *R. v. Brooks* (1988), 41 C.C.C. (3d) 157, 64 C.R. (3d) 322 (B.C.C.A.).

Section 11(*h*) of the *Charter of Rights and Freedoms* (the double jeopardy provision) does not prevent the trial of an accused for an offence of assault causing bodily harm arising out of an assault by the accused, an inmate of a provincial correctional institution, on a fellow inmate, notwithstanding that the accused had previously been punished for the same conduct by the authorities within the institution. These prison disciplinary proceedings did not result in the accused being punished for an "offence" within the meaning of s. 11(*h*): *R. v. Shubley*, [1990] 1 S.C.R. 3, 52 C.C.C. (3d) 481, 65 D.L.R. (4th) 193 (3:2).

AGGRAVATED ASSAULT / Punishment / Excision / Consent.

268. (1) Every one commits an aggravated assault who wounds, maims, disfigures or endangers the life of the complainant.

(2) Every one who commits an aggravated assault is guilty of an indictable offence and liable to imprisonment for a term not exceeding fourteen years.

(3) For greater certainty, in this section, "wounds" or "maims" includes to excise, infibulate or mutilate, in whole or in part, the labia majora, labia minora or clitoris of a person, except where

(*a*) a surgical procedure is performed, by a person duly qualified by provincial law to practise medicine, for the benefit of the physical health of the person or for the purpose of that person having normal reproductive functions or normal sexual appearance or function; or

(*b*) the person is at least eighteen years of age and there is no resulting bodily harm.

(4) For the purposes of this section and section 265, no consent to the excision, infibulation or mutilation, in whole or in part, of the labia majora, labia minora or

clitoris of a person is valid, except in the cases described in paragraphs (3)(*a*) and (*b*). 1980-81-82-83, c. 125, s. 19; 1997, c. 16, s. 5.

CROSS-REFERENCES

The term "complainant" is defined in s. 2. Assault is defined in s. 265.

This offence may be the basis for an application for an authorization to intercept private communications by reason of s. 183.

Section 7(3) enacts special jurisdictional rules for commission of this offence outside Canada when the offence is in relation to an internationally protected person or property referred to in s. 431 (official premises, etc.).

The accused's spouse is a competent and compellable witness at the instance of the Crown by virtue of s. 4(4) of the *Canada Evidence Act*, R.S.C. 1985, c. C-5, where the complainant is under the age of 14 years. Age is determined by reference to s. 30 of the *Interpretation Act*, R.S.C. 1985, c. I-21.

The accused may elect his mode of trial pursuant to s. 536(2). Release pending trial is determined by s. 515. A person, found guilty of the offence in this section, will be liable to the mandatory prohibition order in s. 109 for possession of certain weapons, ammunition and explosives. A person found guilty of this offence may be subject to a dangerous offender application under Part XXIV.

Where the acts described in this section also involve a sexual assault, see s. 273.

Limits on the availability of drunkenness defence, see s. 33.1.

Section 486(1) and (2) provide that the judge may make an order excluding all or any members of the public where such order is in the interest of public morals, the maintenance of order or the proper administration of justice, or is necessary to prevent injury to international relations or national defence or national security. The proper administration of justice includes safeguarding the interests of witnesses under the age of 18 years. Section 486.1 sets out the circumstances in which the judge shall or may order a support person to be present and close to a witness while the witness testifies. Where the witness is under the age of 18 years or has a mental or physical disability, the order is to be made upon request unless the judge is of the opinion that the order would interfere with the proper administration of justice. In the case of other witnesses, the order is to be made if necessary to obtain a full and candid account from the witness of the matters complained of. The application for this order may be made during the proceedings or before they begin to the judge who is to preside at the proceedings.

Similarly, s. 486.2 sets out the circumstances in which the judge shall or may order a witness to testify outside the courtroom or behind a screen or other device that would not allow the witness to see the accused. Where the witness is under the age of 18 years or may have difficulty communicating the evidence by reason of a mental or physical disability, the judge shall make the order unless the judge is of the opinion that the order would interfere with the proper administration of justice. In all other cases, the order may be made if the judge is of the opinion that the order is necessary to obtain a full and candid account from the witness of the acts complained of. Similarly, s. 486.3 provides that, on application by the prosecutor or a witness under the age of 18 years, the accused shall not personally cross-examine the witness unless the judge is of the opinion that the proper administration of justice requires the accused to personally conduct the cross-examination. In other cases, the judge may make an order that the accused not personally cross-examine the witness if the judge is of the opinion that the order is necessary to obtain a full and candid account from the witness of the acts complained of. The judge will appoint counsel to conduct the cross-examination.

Under s. 486.4, the judge may make an order directing that the identity of the complainant or a witness not be disclosed in any publication, broadcast or transmitted in any way. The order is mandatory where the complainant or a witness under the age of 18 years or the prosecutor applies for the order. Section 486.5 also gives the judge a discretion respecting non-publication orders in proceedings under these provisions in other circumstances.

Section 659 abrogates any rule requiring a warning about convicting the accused on the evidence of a child.

Section 715.1 provides that, in proceedings against the accused in which the victim (defined in s. 2) or other witness was under the age of 18 years at the time the offence is alleged to have been committed, a video recording made within a reasonable time after the alleged offence, in which the victim or witness describes the acts complained of, is admissible in evidence if the victim or witness, while testifying, adopts its contents, unless the judge is of the opinion that the admission of the video recording would interfere with the proper administration of justice. Section 715.2 provides for a similar procedure where the victim or another witness may have difficulty communicating the evidence by reason of a mental or physical disability. Under s. 4(2) of the *Canada Evidence Act*, the spouse of an accused charged with this offence is a compellable witness at the instance of the prosecution. Sections 16 and 16.1 of the *Canada Evidence Act* deal with the competency of witnesses under the age of 14 years.

The offence in this section is a primary designated offence for the purpose of making a forensic DNA data bank order under s. 487.051.

SYNOPSIS

This section describes what constitutes an aggravated assault and sets out the punishment for such an assault. When a person wounds, maims, disfigures or endangers the life of a complainant that person is guilty of aggravated assault and is liable to a maximum term of imprisonment of 14 years.

ANNOTATIONS

The element of wounding requires a breaking of the skin but is satisfied by proof that the blows of the accused led to a perforation of the victim's ear-drum: *R. v. Littletent* (1985), 17 C.C.C. (3d) 520 (Alta. C.A.).

While endangerment of life does not require proof of bodily harm, the conduct must endanger the complainant's life and not merely have the potential to endanger life. Accordingly, where the accused made stabbing motions towards the victim's chest but did not injure the victim, the requisite endangerment of life was not proven: *R. v. De Freitas* (1999), 132 C.C.C. (3d) 333 (Man. C.A.).

Consent is no defence to this offence where the injuries were caused by use of a weapon such as a knife: *R. v. Carriere* (1987), 35 C.C.C. (3d) 276 (Alta. C.A.).

This section creates a form of assault offence and the offence of assault causing bodily harm in s. 267(*b*) is an included offence: *R. v. Lucas* (1987), 34 C.C.C. (3d) 28 (Que. C.A.). See also *R. v. Soluk* (2001), 157 C.C.C. (3d) 473 (B.C.C.A.).

The *mens rea* of this offence is objective foresight of bodily harm and does not require proof of an intent to maim, wound or disfigure: *R. v. Godin*, [1994] 2 S.C.R. 484, 89 C.C.C. (3d) 574*n*.

The Crown need not show that an accused alleged to be a party to the offence pursuant to s. 21(1)(*b*) had any greater *mens rea* than the actual perpetrator and, in particular, need not show an objective foresight of the specific wounds resulting from the assault: *R. v. Cuadra* (1998), 125 C.C.C. (3d) 289 (B.C.C.A.). Similarly, where the accused is alleged to be a party under s. 21(2): *R. v. Vang* (1999), 132 C.C.C. (3d) 32 (Ont. C.A.), leave to appeal to S.C.C. refused 137 C.C.C. (3d) vi.

The offence under this section is made out where the accused endangered the life of the complainant and intentionally applied force without the complainant's consent. The first element is made out where the accused, who was HIV-positive, had unprotected sexual intercourse with the complainant. It was unnecessary to establish that the complainant was in fact infected with the virus. The lack of consent is made out where the accused failed to disclose that he was HIV-positive thus vitiating consent by fraud: *R. v. Cuerrier*, [1998] 2 S.C.R. 371, 127 C.C.C. (3d) 1.

The *mens rea* for aggravated assault is the *mens rea* for assault plus objective foresight of the risk of bodily harm. Part of the *actus reus* is the endangerment of the victim's life. The *mens rea* and the *actus reus* must coincide. Where during his relationship with the victim, the accused had learned that he was HIV positive and continued to have unprotected intercourse

CR. CODE

without disclosing it to the victim, the offence of aggravated assault was not made out. It could not be shown that sexual activity after learning of his infected status harmed the victim or even exposed her to a significant risk of harm because, at that point, she was possibly already infected with HIV. While prior to the test, there was endangerment but no criminal intent, after the test, there was criminal intent but no proof of endangerment. In the circumstances, the accused was properly convicted of attempted aggravated assault: *R. v. Williams* (2003), 176 C.C.C. (3d) 449 (S.C.C.).

The *Cuerrier* requirement of "significant risk of serious bodily harm" should be read as requiring disclosure of HIV status if there is a realistic possibility of transmission of HIV. If there is no realistic possibility of transmission of HIV, failure to disclose that one has HIV will not constitute fraud vitiating consent to sexual relations. A realistic possibility of transmission is negated if: (i) the accused's viral load at the time of sexual relations was low and (ii) condom protection was used. This general proposition does not preclude the common law from adapting to future advances in treatment and to circumstances where risk factors other than those considered in this case are at play: *R. v. Mabior*, [2012] 2 S.C.R. 584, 290 C.C.C. (3d) 32.

Following an arrest for an unrelated offence, the accused proclaimed that he was HIV positive and proceeded to spit in the face of an officer. Though there was no evidence of a realistic possibility of transmission, the proper verdict on the evidence was guilty of attempted aggravated assault given the accused's clear intent to transmit HIV by spitting: *R. v. Bear* (2013), 304 C.C.C. (3d) 185 (Man. C.A.).

UNLAWFULLY CAUSING BODILY HARM.

269. Every one who unlawfully causes bodily harm to any person is guilty of

    (a) an indictable offence and liable to imprisonment for a term not exceeding ten years; or

    (b) an offence punishable on summary conviction and liable to imprisonment for a term not exceeding eighteen months. 1980-81-82-83, c. 125, s. 19; 1994, c. 44, s. 18.

CROSS-REFERENCES
"Bodily harm" is defined in s. 2.

This offence may be the basis for an application for an authorization to intercept private communications by reason of s. 183.

Section 7(3) enacts special jurisdictional rules for commission of this offence outside Canada when the offence is in relation to an internationally protected person or property referred to in s. 431 (official premises, etc.).

The accused's spouse is a competent and compellable witness at the instance of the Crown by virtue of s. 4(4) of the *Canada Evidence Act*, R.S.C. 1985, c. C-5, where the complainant is under the age of 14 years. Age is determined by reference to s. 30 of the *Interpretation Act*, R.S.C. 1985, c. I-21.

The accused may elect the mode of trial pursuant to s. 536(2) where the Crown proceeds by indictment. Release pending trial is determined by s. 515. A person found guilty of the offence in para. (*a*) will be liable to the mandatory prohibition order in s. 109 for possession of certain weapons, ammunition and explosives in such a case. Otherwise, the accused may be subject to an order under s. 110. A person found guilty of this offence may be subject to a dangerous offender application under Part XXIV.

The offence of assault causing bodily harm is found in s. 267(*b*). Limits on the availability of drunkenness defence, see s. 33.1.

ANNOTATIONS

The term "unlawfully" in this section refers only to provincial or federal offences and would not include any underlying offence of absolute liability. As well, the unlawful act must be at least objectively dangerous, an act that a reasonable person would inevitably realize would subject another person to the risk of bodily harm. This bodily harm must be more than merely trivial or transitory in nature and will, in most cases, involve an act of violence done deliberately to another person. So interpreted, this section does not violate s. 7 of the Charter, even though neither an intention to cause bodily harm nor subjective foresight of bodily harm is an element of the offence: *R. v. DeSousa*, [1992] 2 S.C.R. 944, 76 C.C.C. (3d) 124 (5:0).

An accused may be convicted of the offence under this section although the bodily harm was caused by an assault and a charge under s. 267(*b*) could have been laid: *R. v. Glowacki* (1984), 16 C.C.C. (3d) 574 (B.C.C.A.).

Consent is no defence to the charge under this section. However the accused's good faith belief as to the effectiveness of the treatment that he as a "healer" was providing the victim was evidence which could negative the *mens rea* of the offence. The fact that the treatment was not authorized by provincial legislation regulating treatment of illness did not fully determine the accused's guilt for this offence even though the treatment caused bodily harm: *R. v. Daigle* (1987), 39 C.C.C. (3d) 542, [1987] R.J.Q. 2374 (C.A.).

Although this offence is one of general intent and thus voluntary intoxication is no defence, an attempt to unlawfully cause bodily harm is an offence of specific intent and intoxication is a defence: *R. v. Colburne* (1991), 66 C.C.C. (3d) 235, [1991] R.J.Q. 1199 (C.A.).

While the *mens rea* requires proof of objective foreseeability of the risk of bodily harm generally, there is no requirement that the specific type of harm occasioned be objectively foreseeable: *R. v. Dewey* (1999), 132 C.C.C. (3d) 348, 21 C.R. (5th) 232 (Alta. C.A.).

AGGRAVAGING CIRCUMSTANCE — ASSAULT AGAINST A PUBLIC TRANSIT OPERATOR / Definitions.

269.01 (1) When a court imposes a sentence for an offence referred to in paragraph 264.1(1)(*a*) or any of sections 266 to 269, it shall consider as an aggravating circumstance the fact that the victim of the offence was, at the time of the commission of the offence, a public transit operator engaged in the performance of his or her duty.

(2) The following definitions apply in this section.

"public transit operator" means an individual who operates a vehicle used in the provision of passenger transportation services to the public, and includes an individual who operates a school bus.

"vehicle" includes a bus, paratransit vehicle, licensed taxi cab, train, subway, tram and ferry. 2015, c. 1, s. 1.

CROSS-REFERENCES

For other deemed aggravating factors on sentencing, see s. 718.2.

SYNOPSIS

This section provides that, when a person is convicted of an assault or threatening offence, it is deemed to be an aggravating factor that the victim was a public transit operator engaged in the performance of his or her duties. It must be read with s. 718.2, which sets out other statutory aggravating factors.

TORTURE / definitions / "official" / "torture" / no defence / evidence.

269.1 (1) Every official, or every person acting at the instigation of or with the consent or acquiescence of an official, who inflicts torture on any other person is guilty of an indictable offence and liable to imprisonment for a term not exceeding fourteen years.

(2) For the purposes of this section,
"official" means
    (*a*) **a peace officer,**

(b) a public officer,

(c) a member of the Canadian Forces, or

(d) any person who may exercise powers, pursuant to a law in force in a foreign state, that would, in Canada, be exercised by a person referred to in paragraph (a), (b), or (c),

whether the person exercises powers in Canada or outside Canada;

"torture" means any act or omission by which severe pain or suffering, whether physical or mental, is intentionally inflicted on a person

(a) for a purpose including

(i) obtaining from the person or from a third person information or a statement,

(ii) punishing the person for an act that the person or a third person has committed or is suspected of having committed, and

(iii) intimidating or coercing the person or a third person, or

(b) for any reason based on discrimination of any kind,

but does not include any act or omission arising only from, inherent in or incidental to lawful sanctions.

(3) It is no defence to a charge under this section that the accused was ordered by a superior or a public authority to perform the act or omission that forms the subject-matter of the charge or that the act or omission is alleged to have been justified by exceptional circumstances, including a state of war, a threat of war, internal political instability or any other public emergency.

(4) In any proceedings over which Parliament has jurisdiction, any statement obtained as a result of the commission of an offence under this section is inadmissible in evidence, except as evidence that the statement was so obtained. R.S.C. 1985, c. 10 (3rd Supp.), s. 2.

CROSS-REFERENCES

The terms "peace officer", "public officer", "Canadian Forces" are defined in s. 2.

Section 7(3.7) enacts special jurisdictional rules where commission of this offence was outside Canada.

The accused may elect his mode of trial pursuant to s. 536(2). Release pending trial is determined by s. 515. A person, found guilty of the offence in this section, will be liable to the mandatory prohibition order in s. 109 for possession of certain weapons, ammunition and explosives. A person found guilty of this offence may be subject to a dangerous offender application under Part XXIV.

In light of subsec. (3), the scope of the defence of obedience to de facto law in s. 15 is uncertain.

SYNOPSIS

This section makes it an offence for any person, either acting in an official capacity or acting at the instigation or acquiescence of an official, to inflict torture on another person. This is an indictable offence punishable by a maximum term of imprisonment of 14 years. The section contains complete definitions of the terms "official" and "torture". A person accused of an offence under this section may not escape criminal liability as a result of the fact that he was following the orders of a superior or a public authority, or that exceptional circumstances justified the action.

The contents of any statement obtained as a result of the commission of an offence under this section is inadmissible in evidence in any proceedings over which Parliament has jurisdiction.

ASSAULTING A PEACE OFFICER / Punishment.

270. (1) Every one commits an offence who

> (*a*) assaults a public officer or peace officer engaged in the execution of his duty or a person acting in aid of such an officer;
>
> (*b*) assaults a person with intent to resist or prevent the lawful arrest or detention of himself or another person; or
>
> (*c*) assaults a person
>
> > (i) who is engaged in the lawful execution of a process against lands or goods or in making a lawful distress or seizure, or
> >
> > (ii) with intent to rescue anything taken under lawful process, distress or seizure.
>
> (2) Every one who commits an offence under subsection (1) is guilty of
>
> (*a*) an indictable offence and liable to imprisonment for a term not exceeding five years; or
>
> (*b*) an offence punishable on summary conviction. R.S., c. C-34, s. 246; 1972, c. 13, s. 22; 1980-81-82-83, c. 125, s. 19.

CROSS-REFERENCES

The terms "peace officer" and "public officer" are defined in s. 2. It is an offence to disarm a peace officer under s. 270.1. Assault is defined in s. 265. Where the accused in committing this offence carries, uses or threatens to use a weapon or an imitation of one, or causes bodily harm to the complainant, they commit the separate offence under s. 270.01 and are subject to the more severe penalties set out in that section. Where the accused in committing this offence wounds, maims, disfigures or endangers the life of the complainant, they commit the offence under s. 270.02 and are liable to a term of imprisonment of 14 years. Section 718.02 provides that, in imposing sentence for this offence, the court is to give primary consideration to the objectives of denunciation and deterrence.

This offence may be the basis for a conviction for constructive murder under s. 230 and murder of a peace officer, acting in the course of his duties, is first degree murder under s. 231(4).

Where the prosecution elects to proceed by indictment on this offence, then the accused may elect his mode of trial pursuant to s. 536(2). Where the prosecution elects to proceed by way of summary conviction, then the trial of this offence is conducted by a summary conviction court pursuant to Part XXVII.

The punishment for the offence is then as set out in s. 787 and the limitation period is set out in s. 786(2). In either case, release pending trial is determined by s. 515, although the accused is eligible for release by a peace officer under s. 496, 497 or by the officer in charge under s. 498.

A person, found guilty of the offence in this section, will be liable to the discretionary prohibition order prescribed by s. 110 for possession of certain weapons, ammunition and explosives.

The related offence of obstructing a peace officer in the execution of his duty is set out in s. 129. Misconduct by a peace officer in executing process is an offence under s. 128. Section 29 imposes certain duties on anyone executing a process. The use of force in enforcement of the law is principally dealt with under s. 25 and see notes under that section. Sections 494 and 495 deal specifically with warrantless arrest powers. Additional duties are imposed under other provisions of the Code, especially in Parts I and II respecting breach of the peace and more serious disorders. Personating a peace officer is an offence under s. 130.

SYNOPSIS

This section describes the offence of assaulting a peace officer. Any person who assaults a public officer or peace officer engaged in the execution of his duty, or a person assisting such an officer, or who assaults a person with intent to resist or prevent a lawful arrest, or who assaults a person engaged in the lawful execution of a process against lands or goods is guilty of an offence under this section. An offence under this section is punishable on summary conviction, or, on indictment, to a term of imprisonment not exceeding five years.

ANNOTATIONS

"Engaged in the execution of his duty" [subsec. (1)(a)] – Taking the facts as found by the trial Judge, regardless as to whether or not the police officer was a trespasser on private property when he was engaged in investigating a possible unlawful entry into the building, he was at the time in the execution of his duty and since he was not unlawfully interfering with either the liberty or the property of the respondent, who assaulted him while being questioned, an offence was proven under this subsection: *R. v. Stenning*, [1970] S.C.R. 631, [1970] 3 C.C.C. 145.

In *R. v. Bushman*, [1968] 4 C.C.C. 17 (B.C.C.A.), it was held (2:1) that where the accused failed to give police officers investigating a hit and run offence reasonable opportunity to depart from his residence's vestibule, it cannot be said that he properly revoked the implied leave and licence to attend at a convenient outer door to converse with him, and accordingly his striking an officer amounted to assaulting a policeman.

The police officer was not in the execution of her duty when she entered the accused's trailer for the purpose of investigating an allegation of assault as there was no common law or statutory foundation which would justify the entry without consent: *R. v. Plamondon* (1997), 121 C.C.C. (3d) 314 (B.C.C.A.).

Validity of arrest – An officer is in execution of his duty where he is empowered to make a warrantless arrest by s. 495(1)(a), although the arrest is effected by entry on to private premises without the consent of the occupier, provided the officer has reasonable and probable grounds for the belief that the person sought is within the premises and proper announcement was made before entry: *R. v. Landry*, [1986] 1 S.C.R. 145, 25 C.C.C. (3d) 1 (8:1).

In *R. v. Cottam and Cottam*, [1970] 1 C.C.C. 117 (B.C.C.A.), it was held that to determine whether the officers in apprehending the accused were engaged in the execution of their duty a jury should be instructed (a) as to circumstances in which the arrest would be lawful and (b), if the arrest was unlawful, whether the officers had thereby so far exceeded their duty and authority as to be no longer in the execution of their duty.

An arrest is a submission to restraint on one's freedom and physical force is not an essential ingredient of that act. Where on the facts it was found that the accused was not told by the officer that he was under arrest or the reason for his arrest, when it was feasible to do so, he cannot be convicted of assaulting the officer under this section: *R. v. Acker*, [1970] 4 C.C.C. 269 (N.S.S.C. App. Div.).

A police officer arresting an accused pursuant to an outstanding warrant, but without possession of the warrant, fully discharges his duty under s. 29 by telling the person that the reason for the arrest is the existence of the warrant, he need not obtain the warrant, or ascertain its contents in order to tell the accused. An arrest in such circumstances is therefore lawful and a conviction under this subsection will lie where the accused assaults the officer: *R. v. Gamracy*, [1974] S.C.R. 640, 12 C.C.C. (2d) 209 (3:2).

Note: Also see notes under s. 129 and s. 495.

ASSAULTING PEACE OFFICER WITH WEAPON OR CAUSING BODILY HARM / Punishment.

270.01 (1) Everyone commits an offence who, in committing an assault referred to in section 270,

    (*a*) carries, uses or threatens to use a weapon or an imitation of one; or

    (*b*) causes bodily harm to the complainant.

(2) Everyone who commits an offence under subsection (1) is guilty of

    (*a*) an indictable offence and liable to imprisonment for a term of not more than 10 years; or

    (*b*) an offence punishable on summary conviction and liable to imprisonment for a term of not more than 18 months. 2009, c. 22, s. 9.

CROSS-REFERENCES

"Weapon", "bodily harm" and "complainant" are defined in s. 2. This offence is a primary designated offence for the purposes of the DNA Forensic Analysis provisions. For additional CROSS-REFERENCES, see s. 270. Section 718.02 provides that, in imposing sentence for this offence, the court is to give primary consideration to the objectives of denunciation and deterrence.

AGGRAVATED ASSAULT OF PEACE OFFICER.

270.02 Everyone who, in committing an assault referred to in section 270, wounds, maims, disfigures or endangers the life of the complainant is guilty of an indictable offence and liable to imprisonment for a term of not more than 14 years. 2009, c. 22, s. 9.

CROSS-REFERENCES

"Complainant" is defined in s. 2. This offence is a primary designated offence for the purposes of the DNA Forensic Analysis provisions. For additional CROSS-REFERENCES, see s. 270. For the meaning of the terms "wounds", "maims", "disfigures" or "endangers the life", see the notes under s. 268, which creates the related offence of aggravated assault. Section 718.02 provides that, in imposing sentence for this offence, the court is to give primary consideration to the objectives of denunciation and deterrence.

SENTENCES TO BE SERVED CONSECUTIVELY.

270.03 A sentence imposed on a person for an offence under subsection 270(1) or 270.01(1) or section 270.02 committed against a law enforcement officer, as defined in subsection 445.01(4), shall be served consecutively to any other punishment imposed on the person for an offence arising out of the same event or series of events. 2015, c. 34, s. 2.

DISARMING A PEACE OFFICER / Definition of "weapon" / Punishment.

270.1 (1) Every one commits an offence who, without the consent of a peace officer, takes or attempts to take a weapon that is in the possession of the peace officer when the peace officer is engaged in the execution of his or her duty.

(2) For the purpose of subsection (1), "weapon" means any thing that is designed to be used to cause injury or death to, or to temporarily incapacitate, a person.

(3) Every one who commits an offence under subsection (1) is guilty of

> **(a) an indictable offence and liable to imprisonment for a term of not more than five years; or**
>
> **(b) an offence punishable on summary conviction and liable to imprisonment for a term of not more than eighteen months. 2002, c. 13, s. 11.**

CROSS-REFERENCES

"Peace officer" is defined in s. 2. Section 270 creates the offence of assaulting a peace officer in the execution of his duty. See notes under that section for the meaning of the phrase "engaged in the execution of his or her duty". Obstructing a peace officer in the execution of his duty is an offence under s. 129.

SYNOPSIS

This section creates the hybrid offence of disarming a peace officer. It is an offence to take or attempt to take a weapon from the officer's possession when the officer is engaged in the execution of his or her duty. "Weapon" is defined in subsec. (2).

SEXUAL ASSAULT.

271. Everyone who commits a sexual assault is guilty of
> (*a*) an indictable offence and is liable to imprisonment for a term of not more than 10 years or, if the complainant is under the age of 16 years, to imprisonment for a term of not more than 14 years and to a minimum punishment of imprisonment for a term of one year; or
> (*b*) an offence punishable on summary conviction and is liable to imprisonment for a term of not more than 18 months or, if the complainant is under the age of 16 years, to imprisonment for a term of not more than two years less a day and to a minimum punishment of imprisonment for a term of six months. 1980-81-82-83, c. 125, c. 19; R.S.C. 1985, c. 19 (3rd Supp.), s. 10; 1994, c. 44, s. 19; 2012, c. 1, s. 25; 2015, c. 23, s. 14.

CROSS-REFERENCES

While assault is defined in s. 265 as, in effect, a touching without the consent of the complainant, s. 273.1 gives a specific definition of consent for the purpose of the offence in this section. Section 265(4) deals with the defence of mistaken belief in consent generally but again, s. 273.2 deals specifically with that defence in the context of this offence. A spouse may be charged with this offence (s. 278). Section 17 limits the availability of the statutory defence of compulsion by threats. Section 33.1 limits the availability of the intoxication defence.

Section 150.1(1) and (2) set out the circumstances in which consent is a defence where the complainant is under 14 years of age. Age is determined by s. 30 of the *Interpretation Act*, R.S.C. 1985, c. I-21. Section 658 provides a means of proving the age of a child. Section 150.1(4) provides a limited defence of mistake as to the age of the complainant.

A person found guilty of the offence in this section, may, depending on the circumstances, be liable to either the mandatory prohibition order in s. 109 or to the discretionary prohibition order prescribed by s. 110 for possession of certain weapons, ammunition and explosives. Where the accused is found guilty of this offence in respect of a person who is under 16 years of age, the court has the discretion to impose an order of prohibition under s. 161 prohibiting the accused from attending certain public areas and facilities or taking certain employment which will bring him into contact with persons under 16 years of age or using a computer system for the purpose of communicating with a person under the age of 16 years. This offence may be the basis for an application for an authorization to intercept private communications by reason of s. 183, or a video surveillance warrant under s. 487.01. This offence may be the basis for a conviction for first degree murder under s. 231(5) and also for a finding that the accused is a dangerous offender under Part XXIV. Section 7(3) enacts special jurisdictional rules for commission of this offence outside Canada, when the offence is in relation to an internationally protected person or property referred to in s. 431 (official premises, etc.).

The offences in this section and ss. 272 and 273 are primary designated offences for the purpose of making a forensic DNA data bank order under s. 487.051. Under s. 490.012, on application by the prosecutor, where an offender is convicted of these offences, the judge shall make an order requiring the offender to comply with the *Sex Offender Information Registration Act*, S.C. 2004, c. 10.

Other sexual offences are found in ss. 151 to 160 and 170 to 174. Section 171.1 makes it an offence to transmit, make available, distribute or sell sexually explicit material to a person who is, or who the accused believes is under the age of 16 years for the purpose of facilitating the commission of the offence created by this section or ss. 272 and 273. Section 172.1 makes it an offence to communicate by means of telecommunication with a person who is or who the accused believes is under the age of 16 years for the purpose of facilitating the commission of the offence under this section or ss. 272 and 273. Section 172.2 makes it an offence to agree with a person or make an arrangement with a person by means of telecommunication to commit an offence under this section or ss. 272 and 273 with a person who is or who the accused believes is under the age of 16 years.

Special evidentiary and procedural provisions – Section 274 specifically provides that no corroboration is required for a conviction for this offence and the offences in ss. 272 and 273 and the judge shall not instruct the jury that it is unsafe to find the accused guilty in the absence of corroboration. Section 275 provides that the rule relating to evidence of recent complaint is abrogated respecting this section. While assault is defined in s. 265 as, in effect, a touching without the consent of the complainant, s. 273.1 gives a specific definition of consent for the purpose of the offence in this section. Section 265(4) deals with the defence of mistaken belief in consent generally but again, s. 273.2 deals specifically with that defence in the context of this offence. Section 277 provides that evidence of sexual reputation is inadmissible in proceedings under this section. Production of records containing personal information of the complainant or a witness for use by the accused at the trial is governed by ss. 278.1 to 278.9. Section 486(1) and (2) provide that the judge may make an order excluding all or any members of the public where such order is in the interest of public morals, the maintenance of order or the proper administration of justice, or is necessary to prevent injury to international relations or national defence or national security. The proper administration of justice includes safeguarding the interests of witnesses under the age of 18 years. Where the accused is charged with an offence under this section and the application by the accused or the prosecutor for the exclusion order is dismissed, the judge shall state the reason for not making the order. Section 486.1 sets out the circumstances in which the judge shall or may order a support person to be present and close to a witness while the witness testifies. Where the witness is under the age of 18 years or has a mental or physical disability, the order is to be made upon request unless the judge is of the opinion that the order would interfere with the proper administration of justice. In the case of other witnesses, the order is to be made if necessary to obtain a full and candid account from the witness of the matters complained of. The application for this order may be made during the proceedings or before they begin to the judge who is to preside at the proceedings.

Similarly, s. 486.2 sets out the circumstances in which the judge shall or may order a witness to testify outside the courtroom or behind a screen or other device that would not allow the witness to see the accused. Where the witness is under the age of 18 years or may have difficulty communicating the evidence by reason of a mental or physical disability, the judge shall make the order unless the judge is of the opinion that the order would interfere with the proper administration of justice. In all other cases, the order may be made if the judge is of the opinion that the order is necessary to obtain a full and candid account from the witness of the acts complained of. Similarly, s. 486.3 provides that, on application by the prosecutor or a witness under the age of 18 years, the accused shall not personally cross-examine the witness unless the judge is of the opinion that the proper administration of justice requires the accused to personally conduct the cross-examination. In other cases, the judge may make an order that the accused not personally cross-examine the witness if the judge is of the opinion that the order is necessary to obtain a full and candid account from the witness of the acts complained of. The judge will appoint counsel to conduct the cross-examination.

Under s. 486.4, the judge may make an order directing that the identity of the complainant or a witness not be disclosed in any publication, broadcast or transmitted in any way. The order is mandatory where the complainant or a witness under the age of 18 years or the prosecutor applies for the order. Section 486.5 also gives the judge a discretion respecting non-publication orders in proceedings under these provisions in other circumstances.

Section 659 abrogates any rule requiring a warning about convicting the accused on the evidence of a child.

Section 715.1 provides that, in proceedings against the accused in which the victim (defined in s. 2) or other witness was under the age of 18 years at the time the offence is alleged to have been committed, a video recording made within a reasonable time after the alleged offence, in which the victim or witness describes the acts complained of, is admissible in evidence if the victim or witness, while testifying, adopts its contents, unless the judge is of the opinion that the admission of the video recoding would interfere with the proper administration of justice. Section 715.2 provides for a similar procedure where the victim or another witness may have difficulty communicating the evidence by reason of a mental or physical disability. Under s. 4(2) of the *Canada Evidence Act*, the spouse of an accused charged with this offence is a compellable witness at the instance of the prosecution. Sections 16 and 16.1 of the *Canada Evidence Act* deal with the competency of witnesses under the age of 14 years.

ANNOTATIONS

Meaning of "sexual assault" – Sexual assault is an assault, within any one of the definitions of that concept in s. 265(1), which is committed in circumstances of a sexual nature such that the sexual integrity of the victim is violated. The test to be applied in determining whether the impugned conduct has the requisite sexual nature is an objective one: whether viewed in the light of all the circumstances the sexual or carnal context of the assault is visible to a reasonable observer. The part of the body touched, the nature of the contact, the situation in which it occurred, the words and gestures accompanying the act, and all other circumstances surrounding the conduct, including threats, which may or may not be accompanied by force, will be relevant. The intent or purpose of the person committing the act, to the extent that this may appear from the evidence, may also be a factor in considering whether the conduct is sexual. If the motive of the accused is sexual gratification, to the extent that this may appear from the evidence it may be a factor in determining whether the conduct is sexual. The existence of such a motive is, however, merely one of many factors to be considered: *R. v. Chase*, [1987] 2 S.C.R. 293, 37 C.C.C. (3d) 97 (6:0).

The offence of sexual assault is one of general intent so that the issue is whether, notwithstanding the absence of a proven sexual intent, the touching was committed in circumstances of a sexual nature: *R. v. S. (P.L.)*, [1991] 1 S.C.R. 909, 64 C.C.C. (3d) 193.

The importance of the accused's purpose as a factor in determining whether or not there has been a sexual assault will vary depending on the circumstances. In this case, where the conduct involved "skylarking" which had been part of the regular life of the family for many years without any sexual connotations, the jury, in order to convict, would have to find that the impugned conduct had changed, from being incidental to the romping or "skylarking" but without sexual connotation, to acts with sexual intent. In such a case, the accused's purpose or motivation would be very relevant: *R. v. J. (C.)* (1990), 58 C.C.C. (3d) 167 (Nfld. C.A.).

Sexual assault does not require proof of sexuality or sexual gratification which are merely factors. The conduct of the accused in grabbing his young child's genitals as a form of "discipline" was an aggressive act of domination which violated the sexual integrity of the child which could be found to be a sexual assault: *R. v. V. (K.B.)* (1992), 71 C.C.C. (3d) 65 (Ont. C.A.), affd [1993] 2 S.C.R. 857, 82 C.C.C. (3d) 382. Therefore, the requisite *mens rea* was established where the accused had touched the complainants's breasts and testicles without hostility in the context of joking as a reasonable person would perceive the sexual context of the touchings: *R. v. Bernier* (1997), 119 C.C.C. (3d) 467 (Que. C.A.), affd [1998] 1 S.C.R. 975, 124 C.C.C. (3d) 383.

A fraudulent gynecological exam constituted a sexual assault even though the accused, posing as a medical doctor, was in a consensual sexual relationship with the victim at the time: *R. v. Mastronardi* (2014), 313 C.C.C. (3d) 295 (B.C.C.A.).

Abuse of process – The burden is on the accused to establish the facts which he alleges amount to an abuse of process. Even lengthy delay in the laying of charges alleging sexual assault by a person in *loco parentis* will not of itself amount to an abuse of process nor necessarily lead to an unfair trial. An allegation by the accused that his right to make full answer and defence has been prejudiced by delay, as a result of the death of potential defence witnesses, is to be determined at trial and not by way of a pre-trial motion to stay proceedings: *R. v. D. (E.)* (1990), 57 C.C.C. (3d) 151 (Ont. C.A.). To a similar effect, see: *R. v. G. (W.G.)* (1990), 58 C.C.C. (3d) 263 (Nfld. C.A.).

For further notes on abuse of process, see the annotations following s. 579.

SEXUAL ASSAULT WITH A WEAPON, THREATS TO A THIRD PARTY OR CAUSING BODILY HARM / Punishment / Subsequent offences / Sequence of convictions only.

272. (1) Every person commits an offence who, in committing a sexual assault,

    (*a*)   carries, uses or threatens to use a weapon or an imitation of a weapon;

    (*b*)   threatens to cause bodily harm to a person other than the complainant;

    (*c*)   causes bodily harm to the complainant; or

    (*d*)   is a party to the offence with any other person.

(2) Every person who commits an offence under subsection (1) is guilty of an indictable offence and liable

    (*a*)   if a restricted firearm or prohibited firearm is used in the commission of the offence or if any firearm is used in the commission of the offence and the offence is committed for the benefit of, at the direction of, or in association with, a criminal organization, to imprisonment for a term not exceeding 14 years and to a minimum punishment of imprisonment for a term of

        (i)   in the case of a first offence, five years, and

        (ii)   in the case of a second or subsequent offence, seven years;

    (*a*.1)   in any other case where a firearm is used in the commission of the offence, to imprisonment for a term not exceeding 14 years and to a minimum punishment of imprisonment for a term of four years;

    (*a*.2)   if the complainant is under the age of 16 years, to imprisonment for life and to a minimum punishment of imprisonment for a term of five years; and

    (*b*)   in any other case, to imprisonment for a term not exceeding fourteen years.

(3) In determining, for the purpose of paragraph (2)(*a*), whether a convicted person has committed a second or subsequent offence, if the person was earlier convicted of any of the following offences, that offence is to be considered as an earlier offence:

    (*a*)   an offence under this section;

    (*b*)   an offence under subsection 85(1) or (2) or section 244 or 244.2; or

    (*c*)   an offence under section 220, 236, 239 or 273, subsection 279(1) or section 279.1, 344 or 346 if a firearm was used in the commission of the offence.

However, an earlier offence shall not be taken into account if 10 years have elapsed between the day on which the person was convicted of the earlier offence and the day on which the person was convicted of the offence for which sentence is being imposed, not taking into account any time in custody.

(4) For the purposes of subsection (3), the only question to be considered is the sequence of convictions and no consideration shall be given to the sequence of commission of offences or whether any offence occurred before or after any conviction. 1980-81-82-83, c. 125, s. 19; 1995, c. 39, s. 145; 2008, c. 6, s. 28; 2009, c. 22, s. 10; 2012, c. 1, s. 26; 2015, c. 23, s. 15.

CROSS-REFERENCES

"Criminal organization" is defined in ss. 2 and 476.1. Pursuant to s. 2.1, "restricted firearm" and "prohibited firearm" are defined in s. 84. A person found guilty of the offence in this section will be liable to the mandatory prohibition order in s. 109 for possession of certain weapons, ammunition and explosives. For other cross-references, see CROSS-REFERENCES under s. 271.

SYNOPSIS

This section provides that any person who, in committing a sexual assault, carries, uses or threatens to use a weapon or imitation, who threatens to cause bodily harm to a person other than the complainant, who causes bodily harm to the complainant, or who is party to the offence, is guilty of an indictable offence. The maximum punishment for the offence is life imprisonment if the complainant is under the age of 16 years, or 14 years' imprisonment if the complainant is 16 or older. Where a restricted or prohibited firearm is used or the offence was committed for the benefit of, at the direction of, or in association with, a criminal organization, the offender is liable to a minimum punishment of at least five years' imprisonment for a first offence and seven years for a second or subsequent offence. The rules for determining whether the offender has committed a second or subsequent offence are set out in subsecs. (3) and (4) and, for example, provide that a prior offence includes not only convictions under this section, but other specified offences involving use of a firearm. However, an earlier offence is not to be taken into account if 10 years have elapsed from the conviction of the earlier offence, not counting time in custody. Subsection (4) reverses the common law rule and provides that the court only takes into account the sequence of convictions, not the order in which the offences were committed. In any other case where a firearm is used, the offender is liable to a minimum term of imprisonment of four years. Where no firearm is used, there is no minimum punishment, unless the complainant is under the age of 14 years, in which case the offender is liable to a minimum punishment of five years.

ANNOTATIONS

If an object is used in inflicting injury, be it physical or psychological, in the commission of a sexual assault, it is not necessary that the injury amount to bodily harm to trigger the application of para. (1)(*a*): *R. v. Lamy* (1993), 80 C.C.C. (3d) 558 (Man. C.A.).

The offence under [now] para. (*a*) does not require proof that the accused was actually in possession of a weapon. The offence is complete if the complainant believes, on reasonable grounds, that the accused had the present ability to affect his purpose: *R. v. Worobec* (1991), 63 C.C.C. (3d) 412 (B.C.C.A.).

The offence described by para. (*c*) is a general intent offence for which drunkenness due to voluntary consumption of alcohol is no defence: *R. v. Bernard* (1985), 18 C.C.C. (3d) 574 (Ont. C.A.). [Also see s. 33.1.]

Bodily harm as used in para. (*c*) can include psychological harm: *R. v. Mathieu* (1996), 111 C.C.C. (3d) 291, 187 A.R. 351 (C.A.), leave to appeal to S.C.C. refused 114 C.C.C. (3d) vi.

An object constitutes a "weapon" where it contributed to the harm caused to the victim. The object does not have to be designed or intended to injure in order to qualify as a weapon. Injury is not synonymous with "bodily harm" and includes any object used in inflicting psychological or physical injury: *R. v. Lamy*, [2002] 1 S.C.R. 860, 162 C.C.C. (3d) 353.

Consent is not vitiated in all circumstances of sexual assault causing bodily harm, but only where bodily harm was intended and in fact caused. Where the accused did not intend to cause bodily harm, consent is available as a defence if bodily harm is inadvertently caused: *R. v. Zhao* (2013), 297 C.C.C. (3d) 533 (Ont. C.A.).

AGGRAVATED SEXUAL ASSAULT / Punishment / Subsequent offences / Sequence of convictions only.

273. (1) Every one commits an aggravated sexual assault who, in committing a sexual assault, wounds, maims, disfigures or endangers the life of the complainant.

(2) Every person who commits an aggravated sexual assault is guilty of an indictable offence and liable
- (*a*) if a restricted firearm or prohibited firearm is used in the commission of the offence or if any firearm is used in the commission of the offence and the offence is committed for the benefit of, at the direction of, or in association with, a criminal organization, to imprisonment for life and to a minimum punishment of imprisonment for a term of
  - (i) in the case of a first offence, five years, and
  - (ii) in the case of a second or subsequent offence, seven years;
- (*a*.1) in any other case where a firearm is used in the commission of the offence, to imprisonment for life and to a minimum punishment of imprisonment for a term of four years;
- (*a*.2) if the complainant is under the age of 16 years, to imprisonment for life and to a minimum punishment of imprisonment for a term of five years; and
- (*b*) in any other case, to imprisonment for life.

(3) In determining, for the purpose of paragraph (2)(*a*), whether a convicted person has committed a second or subsequent offence, if the person was earlier convicted of any of the following offences, that offence is to be considered as an earlier offence:

    (*a*) an offence under this section;

    (*b*) an offence under subsection 85(1) or (2) or section 244 or 244.2; or

    (*c*) an offence under section 220, 236, 239 or 272, subsection 279(1) or section 279.1, 344 or 346 if a firearm was used in the commission of the offence.

However, an earlier offence shall not be taken into account if 10 years have elapsed between the day on which the person was convicted of the earlier offence and the day on which the person was convicted of the offence for which sentence is being imposed, not taking into account any time in custody.

(4) For the purposes of subsection (3), the only question to be considered is the sequence of convictions and no consideration shall be given to the sequence of commission of offences or whether any offence occurred before or after any conviction. 1980-81-82-83, c. 125, s. 19; 1995, c. 39, s. 146; 2008, c. 6, s. 29; 2009, c. 22, s. 11; 2012, c. 1, s. 27.

CROSS-REFERENCES

"Criminal organization" is defined in ss. 2 and 476.1. Pursuant to s. 2.1, "restricted firearm" and "prohibited firearm" are defined in s. 84. A person found guilty of the offence in this section will be liable to the mandatory prohibition order in s. 109 for possession of certain weapons, ammunition and explosives. For other cross-references, see CROSS-REFERENCES under s. 271.

SYNOPSIS

If a person wounds, maims, disfigures or endangers the life of a complainant during the commission of a sexual assault, that person is guilty of the indictable offence of aggravated sexual assault and liable to imprisonment for life. The section also enacts minimum punishments. Where a restricted or prohibited firearm is used or the offence was committed for the benefit of, at the direction of, or in association with, a criminal organization, the offender is liable to a minimum punishment of at least five years' imprisonment for a first offence and seven years for a second or subsequent offence. The rules for determining whether the offender has committed a second or subsequent offence are set out in subsecs. (3) and (4) and, for example, provide that a prior offence includes not only convictions under this section but other specified offences involving firearms. However, an earlier offence is not to be taken into account if 10 years have elapsed from the conviction of the earlier offence, not counting time in custody. Subsection (4) reverses the common law rule and provides that the court only takes into account the sequence of convictions, not the order in which the offences were committed. In any other case where a firearm is used, the offender is liable to a minimum term of imprisonment of four years. Where no firearm is used, there is no minimum punishment, unless the victim was under the age 16 years, in which case the minimum punishment is five years.

MEANING OF "CONSENT" / Where no consent obtained / Subsection (2) not limiting.

273.1 (1) Subject to subsection (2) and subsection 265(3), "consent" means, for the purposes of sections 271, 272 and 273, the voluntary agreement of the complainant to engage in the sexual activity in question.

(2) No consent is obtained, for the purposes of sections 271, 272 and 273, where

    (*a*) the agreement is expressed by the words or conduct of a person other than the complainant;

    (*b*) the complainant is incapable of consenting to the activity;

    (*c*) the accused induces the complainant to engage in the activity by abusing a position of trust, power or authority;

    (*d*) the complainant expresses, by words or conduct, a lack of agreement to engage in the activity; or (*e*) **the complainant, having consented to engage in sexual activity, expresses, by words or conduct, a lack of agreement to continue to engage in the activity.**

(3) Nothing in subsection (2) shall be construed as limiting the circumstance in which no consent is obtained. 1992, c. 38, s. 1.

CROSS-REFERENCES

The term "complainant" is defined in s. 2. Section 265(3) sets out additional circumstances in which no valid consent is given as where, for example, the consent is obtained by fraud or the exercise of authority. As to mistaken belief in consent as a defence, see s. 265(4) which sets out the minimum evidentiary requirement and the mandatory jury direction. Section 273.2 sets out circumstances where belief in consent is no defence.

SYNOPSIS

This section supplements the definition of consent in s. 265 which defines assault for all of the assault offences including sexual assault. The definition in this section applies only to the sexual assault offences. Subsection (1) provides a general definition which focuses on the voluntary agreement by the complainant. Subsection (2) then sets out a number of circumstances where the apparent agreement by the complainant cannot amount to consent. Subsection (2) makes a number of points: agreement cannot be based on the words or conduct of someone other than the complainant and there is no agreement where the complainant is incapable of giving consent [although incapacity is not defined], agreement is the result of abuse of a position of trust, power or authority, the complainant expresses lack of consent or the complainant, having initially consented, expresses a change of mind. This subsection is in addition to the circumstances set out in s. 265(3) where there is no consent to an assault generally.

ANNOTATIONS

There is no defence of implied consent to sexual assault. The absence of consent is subjective and must be determined by reference to the complainant's subjective internal state of mind towards the touching at the time it occurred. The complainant's statement that she did not consent is a matter of credibility to be weighed in light of all of the evidence including any ambiguous conduct. If the trier of fact accepts the complainant's testimony that she did not consent, no matter how strongly conduct may contradict her claim, the absence of consent is established. The trier of fact need only consider s. 265(3) if the complainant has chosen to participate in sexual activity or her ambiguous conduct or submission has given rise to doubt regarding the absence of consent. There is no consent where the complainant consents because she honestly believes that she will otherwise suffer physical violence. While the plausibility of the alleged fear and any overt expressions of it are relevant in assessing the complainant's credibility that she consented out of fear, the approach is subjective: *R. v. Ewanchuk*, [1999] 1 S.C.R. 330, 131 C.C.C. (3d) 481.

However, the Ontario Court of Appeal has subsequently held that consent is not vitiated in all circumstances of sexual assault causing bodily harm, but only where bodily harm was intended and in fact caused. The reasoning in *Welch* should be restricted to circumstances of sadomasochistic sex. Where the accused did not intend to cause bodily harm, consent is available as a defence if bodily harm is inadvertently caused: *R. v. Zhao* (2013), 297 C.C.C. (3d) 533 (Ont. C.A.).

Capacity is a factual issue to be decided by the jury and there is no mandatory requirement for expert testimony in assessing a special needs complainant's capacity to consent: *R. v. A. (A.)* (2001), 155 C.C.C. (3d) 279, 43 C.R. (5th) 272 (Ont. C.A.).

Subsection (2)(*d*) is not void for vagueness so as to constitute a breach of s. 7 of the *Canadian Charter of Rights and Freedoms: R. v. Darrach* (1998), 122 C.C.C. (3d) 225, 13 C.R. (5th) 283 *sub nom. R. v. D. (A.S.)* (Ont. C.A.), leave to appeal to S.C.C. granted 124 C.C.C. (3d) vi, 52 C.R.R. (2d) 188*n*.

A person cannot consent in advance to sexual activity expected to occur while unconscious. The definition of consent requires ongoing, conscious consent throughout the sexual activity in question: *R. v. A. (J.),* [2011] 2 S.C.R. 440, 271 C.C.C. (3d) 1 (5:4).

The 15-year-old complainant could not be said to have given a valid consent where she consented under the influence of a drug given to her by the accused. The complainant was at first unaware that the drug had been put in her drink and testified that thereafter she felt "out of control": *R. v. Daigle* (1998), 127 C.C.C. (3d) 130 (Que. C.A.), affd [1998] 1 S.C.R. 1220n, 127 C.C.C. (3d) 129. [Note: This case was decided before the age of consent was raised to 16 years; see s. 150.1.] Also see *R. v. Bernier* (1997), 119 C.C.C. (3d) 467, [1997] R.J.Q. 2404 (C.A.), affd [1998] 1 S.C.R. 975, 124 C.C.C. (3d) 383, a case involving acts, committed prior to this section coming into force, by a nurse's aid against patients who were mentally handicapped persons.

Where the complainant denied having freely consented to the sexual activity and the accused admitted to extorting her to have sex by threatening to expose her nude photos, the complainant cannot be said to have freely consented within the meaning of subsec. (1): *R. v. Stender* (2004), 188 C.C.C. (3d) 514, 24 C.R. (6th) 91 (C.A.), affd [2005] 1 S.C.R. 914, 201 C.C.C. (3d) 319.

A drug dealer may be in a position of power pursuant to subsec. (2)(*c*) in relation to an addicted client if the supplying of drugs created a relationship of dependency that could be exploited by the accused: *R. v. Hogg* (2000), 148 C.C.C. (3d) 86, 136 O.A.C. 91 (C.A.), revd (unreported, May 1, 2002, Court File No. C38095, Ont. C.A.).

The misrepresentation of an undercover police officer's occupation did not constitute fraud so as to vitiate the accused's consent in circumstances in which the accused invited the police officer to touch him to prove that he was not a police officer: *R. v. P. (N.M.)* (2000), 146 C.C.C. (3d) 167, 33 C.R. (5th) 113 (N.S.C.A.), motion for leave to intervene adjourned 149 C.C.C. (3d) 446 (S.C.C.), leave to appeal to S.C.C. refused 193 D.L.R. (4th) vi.

Voluntary agreement to the "sexual activity in question" in subsec. (1) means that the complainant must subjectively agree to the specific physical act itself, its sexual nature and the specific identity of the partner. The "sexual activity in question" does not include conditions or qualities of the physical act, such as birth control measures or the presence of sexually transmitted diseases. Here, the "sexual activity in question" was sexual intercourse and the complainant voluntarily agreed to it, notwithstanding the fact that her partner had furtively poked holes in the condom. However, where the complainant has chosen not to become pregnant, deceptions that expose her to an increased risk of becoming pregnant may constitute a sufficiently serious deprivation to vitiate consent via fraud under s. 265(3)(*c*): *R. v. Hutchinson,* [2014] 1 S.C.R. 346, 308 C.C.C. (3d) 413.

WHERE BELIEF IN CONSENT NOT A DEFENCE.

273.2 It is not a defence to a charge under section 271, 272 or 273 that the accused believed that the complainant consented to the activity that forms the subject-matter of the charge, where

   (*a*) **the accused's belief arose from the accused's**

      (i) **self-induced intoxication, or**

      (ii) **recklessness or wilful blindness; or**

   (*b*) **the accused did not take reasonable steps, in the circumstances known to the accused at the time, to ascertain that the complainant was consenting. 1992, c. 38, s. 1.**

CROSS-REFERENCES

The term "complainant" is defined in s. 2. Sections 265 and 273.1 set out circumstances in which no valid consent in fact is given. As to mistaken belief in consent as a defence see s. 265(4) which sets out the minimum evidentiary requirement and the mandatory jury direction. Also see s. 150.1 re mistake as to age.

SYNOPSIS

This section attempts to clarify the circumstances in which the common law defence of mistaken belief in consent is a defence to a charge of sexual assault. Paragraph (*a*)(i) is consistent with the common law rule that self-induced intoxication is no defence to sexual assault and para. (*a*)(ii) reflects the decision of the Supreme Court of Canada in *R. v. Sansregret, infra.* Paragraph (*b*) is something of a departure from the common law in that it introduces a partly objective standard in determining whether the accused's belief was honestly held. Note, however, that it is reasonable steps in the circumstances known to the accused. In this respect, the defence is not unlike other sections of the Code, such as self-defence under s. 34, which impose an objective and subjective standard.

ANNOTATIONS

The defence of honest but mistaken belief does not impose any burden of proof on the accused and may arise on any evidence including the Crown's case-in-chief. Honest but mistaken belief can be raised if it is established that the accused believed that the complainant affirmatively communicated consent through her words or actions. A belief that silence, passivity or ambiguous conduct constitutes consent provides no defence. An accused also cannot rely upon his purported belief that the complainant's expressed lack of agreement to sexual touching constituted an invitation to more persistent or aggressive contact. Once the complainant has expressed an unwillingness to engage in sexual contact, the accused must make certain that she has truly changed her mind before proceeding with any further intimacies. The accused cannot rely on the mere lapse of time, the complainant's silence or equivocal conduct to indicate that there has been a change of heart and that the consent now exists nor can he engage in further sexual touching to "test the waters". In this case, the complainant had clearly said no to any further contact. There was no evidence of anything that occurred between the communication of non-consent and the subsequent sexual touching which would lead the accused to honestly have believed that there was consent: *R. v. Ewanchuk*, [1999] 1 S.C.R. 330, 131 C.C.C. (3d) 481.

In *R. v. Cinous*, [2002] 2 S.C.R. 3, 162 C.C.C. (3d) 129, the court considered at length the test for when there is an air of reality requiring that a defence be left to the jury. While the court did not consider this section or s. 265(4), since the issue arose in the context of self-defence to a murder charge, the comments may be of assistance. While a trial judge has a duty to put to the jury any defence for which there is an air of reality, the judge also has a duty not to put defences for which there is no air of reality. A defence possesses an air of reality if a properly instructed jury acting reasonably could acquit the accused on the basis of the defence. In applying the air of reality test, a trial judge considers the totality of the evidence, and assumes the evidence relied upon by the accused to be true. The evidential foundation can be indicated by evidence emanating from the examination-in-chief or cross-examination of the accused, of defence witnesses, or of Crown witnesses. It can also rest upon the factual circumstances of the case or from any other evidential source on the record. There is no requirement that the evidence be adduced by the accused or that the accused's evidence be corroborated by other evidence. The trial judge does not make determinations about the credibility of witnesses, weigh the evidence, make findings of fact, or draw determinate factual inferences. Nor is the air of reality test intended to assess whether the defence is likely, unlikely, somewhat likely, or very likely to succeed at the end of the day. The question for the trial judge is whether the evidence discloses a real issue to be decided by the jury, and not how the jury should ultimately decide the issue. A single air of reality test applies to all defences. The question remains whether there is (1) evidence (2) upon which a properly instructed jury acting reasonably could acquit if it believed the evidence to be true. The second part of this question can be rendered by asking whether the evidence put forth is reasonably capable of supporting the inferences required to acquit the accused. This is the current state of the law, uniformly applicable to all defences. There is no special test for sexual offences.

The air of reality test applies to affirmative defences such as self-defence, but it is never the function of the trial judge in a jury trial to assess the evidence and make a determination that the Crown has proven one or more of the essential elements of the offence and direct the jury accordingly. It does not matter how obvious the judge may believe the answer to be or that the judge may be of the view that any other conclusion would be perverse. The trial judge may give an opinion on the matter but never a direction: *R. v. Gunning*, [2005] 1 S.C.R. 627, 196 C.C.C. (3d) 123.

While this section does not require in all cases that the accused first determine "unequivocally" that the complainant was consenting, there may be circumstances where nothing short of an unequivocal indication of consent from the complainant, at the time of the alleged offence, will suffice to meet the threshold test. In general, para. (*b*) creates a proportionate relationship between what will be required in the way of reasonable steps by the accused and the circumstances known to the accused at the time: *R. v. G. (R.)* (1994), 38 C.R. (4th) 123, 87 W.A.C. 254 (B.C.C.A.).

Assuming that sexual assault is an offence requiring proof of subjective *mens rea* to meet minimum constitutional standards, this section meets that requirement. The accused is not under an obligation to determine all relevant circumstances — the issue is what the accused actually knew, not what he or she ought to have known. Further, the accused is not required to have taken all reasonable steps. Finally, while this section and s. 265(4) may have the effect of placing a tactical or evidential burden on an accused to adduce some evidence capable of raising a reasonable doubt, this does not infringe the accused's right not to be compelled to be a witness. Accordingly, this section does not infringe ss. 7 and 11(*c*) of the *Canadian Charter of Rights and Freedoms: R. v. Darrach* (1998), 122 C.C.C. (3d) 225 (Ont. C.A.), affd on other grounds [2000] 2 S.C.R. 443, 148 C.C.C. (3d) 97.

Where the defences of consent and honest but mistaken belief in consent are raised, it must be determined whether it is proven beyond a reasonable doubt that sexual activity took place which, if there was no consent, constituted a sexual assault, whether it occurred without the consent of the victim and, if it occurred without the victim's consent, whether the defendant did not have an honest but mistaken belief in consent. It is only when the trial judge has reached the third step that this section is considered: *R. v. Butler* (1998), 13 C.R. (5th) 372 (Ont. C.A.).

This provision applies to offences of sexual assault only and did not apply to a charge of forcible confinement: *R. v. Niedermier* (2005), 193 C.C.C. (3d) 199 (B.C.C.A.), leave to appeal to S.C.C. refused 196 C.C.C. (3d) vi.

The following case arose prior to the enactment of this section.

The fact that the stories of the accused and the complainant are diametrically opposed is but one factor in determining whether or not there is an air of reality to the defence. If it is not realistically possible for a properly instructed jury, acting judiciously, to splice together some of each person's evidence with respect to the encounter, and settle upon a reasonably coherent set of facts, supported by the evidence, that is capable of sustaining a defence of mistaken belief in consent then the issue really is purely one of credibility, of consent or no consent, and the defence of mistaken belief in consent should not be put to the jury. When the complainant and the accused give similar versions of the facts, and the only material contradiction is in their interpretation of what happened, the defence of honest but mistaken belief in consent should generally be put to the jury, except in cases where the accused's conduct demonstrates recklessness or wilful blindness to the absence of consent. There is no requirement that the accused explicitly testify that he mistakenly believed that the complainant was consenting. Consent is a mental state experienced only by the complainant and thus an assertion by the accused that the complainant consented must mean that he in fact believed that she was consenting. The real question will be whether that belief was on honest one: *R. v. Park*, [1995] 2 S.C.R. 836, 99 C.C.C. (3d) 1. Also see: *R. v. Livermore*, [1995] 4 S.C.R. 123, 102 C.C.C. (3d) 212; *R. v. Esau*, [1997] 2 S.C.R. 777, 116 C.C.C. (3d) 289.

REMOVAL OF CHILD FROM CANADA / Punishment.

273.3 (1) No person shall do anything for the purpose of removing from Canada a person who is ordinarily resident in Canada and who is

    (*a*) under the age of 16 years, with the intention that an act be committed outside Canada that if it were committed in Canada would be an offence against section 151 or 152 or subsection 160(3) or 173(2) in respect of that person;

    (*b*) 16 years of age or more but under the age of eighteen years, with the intention that an act be committed outside Canada that if it were committed in Canada would be an offence against section 153 in respect of that person; or

    (*c*) under the age of eighteen years, with the intention that an act be committed outside Canada that if it were committed in Canada would be an offence against section 155 or 159, subsection 160(2) or section 170, 171, 267, 268, 269, 271, 272 or 273 in respect of that person; or

    (*d*) under the age of 18 years, with the intention that an act be committed outside Canada that, if it were committed in Canada, would be an offence against section 293.1 in respect of that person or under the age of 16 years, with the intention that an act be committed outside Canada that, if it were committed in Canada, would be an offence against section 293.2 in respect of that person.

(2) Every person who contravenes this section is guilty of

    (*a*) an indictable offence and is liable to imprisonment for a term not exceeding five years; or

    (*b*) an offence punishable on summary conviction. 1993, c. 45, s. 3; 1997, c. 18, s. 13; 2008, c. 6, s. 54(*i*); 2015, c. 29, s. 8.

SYNOPSIS

This section makes it an offence to do anything for the purpose of removing certain classes of persons from Canada who are ordinarily resident in Canada. It must be shown that the person to be removed from Canada is under a specified age and that the accused's intention was that an act be committed which would constitute one of the specified sexual offences if committed in Canada.

CORROBORATION NOT REQUIRED.

274. If an accused is charged with an offence under section 151, 152, 153, 153.1, 155, 159, 160, 170, 171, 172, 173, 271, 272, 273, 286.1, 286.2 or 286.3, no corroboration is required for a conviction and the judge shall not instruct the jury that it is unsafe to find the accused guilty in the absence of corroboration. 1980-81-82-83, c. 125, s. 19; R.S.C. 1985, c. 19 (3rd Supp.), s. 11; 2002, c. 13, s. 12; 2014, c. 25, s. 16.

CROSS-REFERENCES

As to other evidentiary and procedural provisions respecting the offences listed in this section, see the cross-references in relation to those provisions and the notes under s. 150.1.

SYNOPSIS

This section states that in the trial of an offence under ss. 151, 152, 153, 155, 159, 160, 170, 171, 172, 173, 271, 272, 273, 286.1, 286.2 or 286.3, *corroboration* is not required for a conviction and the judge shall not instruct the jury that it is unsafe to find the accused guilty in the absence of corroboration. The section is designed to ensure that, with the repeal of the statutory corroboration requirement, the courts do not revert to the common law position requiring corroboration of a sexual complainant's evidence. [See *R. v. Camp* (1977), 36 C.C.C. (2d) 511 (Ont. C.A.).] Also see s. 659 abrogating any mandatory rule as to the danger of acting on the evidence of children.

ANNOTATIONS

Notwithstanding this section, the trial judge still has a discretion when reviewing the facts with a jury to discuss with them the weight they might see fit to attach to the unsupported evidence of the complainant: *R. v. Saulnier* (1989), 48 C.C.C. (3d) 301 (N.S.C.A.).

There is no common law rule of practice which requires a judge to charge the jury as to the danger of acting on the uncorroborated evidence of the complainant on a charge of gross indecency under former s. 157 of the *Criminal Code*, R.S.C. 1970, c. C-34. The trial judge does, however, have a discretion to give the jury an instruction with respect to the weight of the unsupported testimony of the complainant: *R. v. Stymiest* (1993), 79 C.C.C. (3d) 408 (B.C.C.A.).

No corroboration is required in respect of the offence of incest (s. 155) for a charge laid in 2002, although the offence allegedly occurred in 1982, at a time when corroboration was required: *R. v. D. (A.)* (2005), 193 C.C.C. (3d) 314 (Sask. C.A.).

RULES RESPECTING RECENT COMPLAINT ABROGATED.

275. The rules relating to evidence of recent complaint are hereby abrogated with respect to offences under sections 151, 152, 153, 153.1, 155 and 159, subsections 160(2) and (3) and sections 170, 171, 172, 173, 271, 272 and 273. 1980-81-82-83, c. 125, s. 19; R.S.C. 1985, c. 19 (3rd Supp.), s. 11; 2002, c. 13, s. 12.

CROSS-REFERENCES

The "recent complaint" rule abrogated by this section was the rule, developed at common law, which permitted the prosecution to elicit from the complainant or other person a complaint of a sexual assault made at the first reasonable opportunity. The complaint was admitted, not for its truth, but, to show consistency and rebut the adverse inference, which the trier of fact would otherwise be invited to draw, that the victim's allegation was untrue. The rule was an exception to the rule at common law, that a witness's testimony in chief may not be buttressed by the party calling the witness by proving that she has made a prior consistent statement. The recent complaint rule was often criticized because of the anachronistic assumptions underlying it (see *R. v. Timm*, [1981] 2 S.C.R. 315, 59 C.C.C. (2d) 396) and was finally abolished by this provision. However, a form of this rule has now been revived in the case of youthful complainants by the provisions of s. 715.1 which permits the admission of a videotape of a complaint in some circumstances.

As to other evidentiary and procedural provisions respecting the offences listed in this section, see the cross-references in relation to those provisions and the notes under s. 150.1.

ANNOTATIONS

The effect of this section is that the Crown during its case in chief may not adduce evidence of recent complaints. However, since there was never a prohibition against the accused attempting to exploit the lack of a recent complaint, and since only the right of the Crown to lead the evidence in chief has been negated by this section, the defence can elect to cross-examine on this issue. In addition, prior consistent statements may be admissible as part of the Crown's case in chief if they fall within one of the other existing exceptions to the rule against prior consistent statements such as to rebut an allegation of recent fabrication, as part of the *res gestae*, or as narrative. If the Crown is relying upon recent fabrication as the basis for admissibility of prior consistent statements, it must wait until the defence has clearly opened the door by making an opening statement, or through cross-examination of the complainant or other Crown witnesses or by the allegation of fabrication becoming implicit from the defence conduct of the case. The *res gestae* exception is limited to cases where the words spoken are so interrelated to the fact in issue that they become part of the fact itself. The statements by children who have allegedly been sexually assaulted may properly be admitted as part of the narrative in the sense that the statement advances the story from offence to prosecution or explains why so little was done to terminate the abuse or bring the perpetrator to justice. It is part of the narrative of a complainant's testimony when she recounts the assaults, how they came to be terminated, and how the matter came to the attention of the police. This part of the narrative provides chronological cohesion and eliminates gaps which would divert the mind of the listener from the central issue. It may be supportive of the central allegation in the sense of creating a logical framework for its presentation but it cannot be used and the jury must be warned of this as confirmation of the truthfulness of the sworn allegations: *R. v. F. (J.E.)* (1993), 85 C.C.C. (3d) 457 (Ont. C.A.).

In determining whether there has been an allegation of recent fabrication so as to permit evidence of a complaint to be given as an exception to this provision, it is not sufficient to merely look at defence counsel's statements expressly disclaiming any such allegation. If having regard to the manner in which the complainant has been cross-examined, with defence counsel having elicited some but not all of the complainant's statements after the offence, so that the jury would wrongly infer that the complainant made no complaint on an earlier occasion, then the Crown must be permitted to correct the erroneous impression by re-examination and the adducing of other evidence. The accused cannot have an automatic unlimited power to choose among the complainant's various statements: *R. v. N. (L.)* (1989), 52 C.C.C. (3d) 1 (N.W.T.C.A.).

This section does not prevent evidence being given as to the fact of a complaint where such evidence is a necessary part of the narrative to understand an admission made by the accused when confronted with the complaint: *R. v. George* (1985), 23 C.C.C. (3d) 42 (B.C.C.A.).

If the full purpose underlying Parliament's abrogation of this rule is to be achieved, evidence of when a complaint was first made, why it was not made at the first available opportunity if that was the case, and what it was that precipitated the complaint eventually made, must be receivable as part of the narrative, in order to ensure that the jury has all of the evidence of the complainant's conduct necessary to enable the jury to draw the right inference with respect to her credibility. The prior complaint, admissible under the narrative exception to the rule against prior consistent statements, is not, however, admissible to gauge the consistency and thus the credibility of the complainant's evidence at trial. Accordingly, unless it is necessary to provide the context for some other circumstance relevant to the jury's consideration, the actual content of the prior complaint has no relevance and is inadmissible: *R. v. Ay* (1994), 93 C.C.C. (3d) 456 (B.C.C.A.).

For other cases approving the narrative exception see *R. v. Foster* (1995), 128 Sask. R. 292, 85 W.A.C. 292 (C.A.), leave to appeal to S.C.C. refused 152 Sask. R. 316*n* and *R. v. B. (O.)* (1995), 103 C.C.C. (3d) 531 (N.S.C.A.).

Where the Crown adduces prior complaint evidence that is part of the narrative, the trial judge will be required to provide a limiting instruction to the jury to the effect that such evidence is to be used only to assess the complainant's credibility and not for the truth of its contents. The defence should also be able to explore the issue of the timing of a complaint because it relates to the issue of the complainant's credibility. The trier of fact may, but need not, draw an adverse inference against the complainant's credibility by the reason of the lack of recent complaint: *R. v. Henrich* (1996), 108 C.C.C. (3d) 97 (Ont. C.A.).

In *R. v. D. (D.)*, [2000] 2 S.C.R. 275, 148 C.C.C. (3d) 41, the Supreme Court of Canada held that expert evidence regarding delayed disclosure was inadmissible as the expert's evidence was simply a statement of the law that the failure to make a timely complaint must not be the subject of a presumptive adverse inference against the complainant. Where there is an issue of delayed disclosure, the trial judge should instruct the jury that there is no inviolable rule relating to how people who are the victims of trauma like a sexual assault will behave. Some will make an immediate complaint, some will delay disclosure and some will not ever disclose the abuse. The reasons for delay are many and may include embarrassment, fear, guilt or a lack of understanding and knowledge. In assessing credibility, the timing of the complaint is simply one circumstance to consider the context of the case. Delayed disclosure, standing alone, will never give rise to an adverse inference against the credibility of the complainant.

Where evidence of failure to complain is adduced, the jury should be warned against the stereotype that a wronged woman will always complain. The jury must decide whether the complainant's conduct after the incident is consistent with her story by considering the complainant's state of mind at the time, the age and level of maturity of the complainant, the complainant's sense of confidence and composure and the relationship between the accused and the complainant: *R. v. M. (T.E.)* (1996), 110 C.C.C. (3d) 179 (Alta. C.A.), leave to appeal to S.C.C. refused 114 C.C.C. (3d) vi.

The child victims' complaints to their parents were admissible where the defence contended that the children's sworn testimony was inconsistent in vital respects with their prior statements and was the result of their parents' coaching or the product of suggestions made to them by their parents, and was not based on the children's antecedent memory of the event. The prior complaints became admissible under the common law exception to admission of prior consistent statements: *R. v. Owens* (1986), 33 C.C.C. (3d) 275 (Ont. C.A.).

In *R. v. B. (D.C.)* (1994), 91 C.C.C. (3d) 357 (Man. C.A.), the court held that the judge-made rule against prior consistent statements should no longer apply to the evidence of a child's complaint of sexual abuse.

EVIDENCE OF COMPLAINANT'S SEXUAL ACTIVITY / Idem / Factors that judge must consider.

276. (1) In proceedings in respect of an offence under section 151, 152, 153, 153.1, 155 or 159, subsection 160(2) or (3) or section 170, 171, 172, 173, 271, 272 or 273, evidence that the complainant has engaged in sexual activity, whether with the accused or with any other person, is not admissible to support an inference that, by reason of the sexual nature of that activity, the complainant

(a) **is more likely to have consented to the sexual activity that forms the subject-matter of the charge; or**

(b) **is less worthy of belief.**

(2) In proceedings in respect of an offence referred to in subsection (1), no evidence shall be adduced by or on behalf of the accused that the complainant has engaged in sexual activity other than the sexual activity that forms the subject-matter of the charge, whether with the accused or with any other person, unless the judge, provincial court judge or justice determines, in accordance with the procedures set out in sections 276.1 and 276.2, that the evidence

(a) **is of specific instances of sexual activity;**

(b) **is relevant to an issue at trial; and**

(c) **has significant probative value that is not substantially outweighed by the danger of prejudice to the proper administration of justice.**

(3) In determining whether evidence is admissible under subsection (2), the judge, provincial court judge or justice shall take into account

(a) **the interests of justice, including the right of the accused to make a full answer and defence;**

(b) **society's interest in encouraging the reporting of sexual assault offences;**

(c) **whether there is a reasonable prospect that the evidence will assist in arriving at a just determination in the case;**

(d) **the need to remove from the fact-finding process any discriminatory belief or bias;**

(e) **the risk that the evidence may unduly arouse sentiments of prejudice, sympathy or hostility in the jury;**

(f) **the potential prejudice to the complainant's personal dignity and right of privacy;**

(g) **the right of the complainant and of every individual to personal security and to the full protection and benefit of the law; and** (*h*) **any other factor that the judge, provincial court judge or justice considers relevant. 1980-81-82-83, c. 125, s. 19; R.S.C. 1985, c. 19 (3rd Supp.), s. 12; c. 27 (1st Supp.), s. 203; 1992, c. 38, s. 2; 2002, c. 13, s. 13.**

CROSS-REFERENCES

The terms "complainant", "justice" and "provincal court judge" are defined in s. 2.

As to other evidentiary and procedural provisions respecting the offences listed in this section, see the cross-references in relation to those provisions and the notes under s. 150.1 However, note in particular the companion provision in s. 277 respecting evidence of sexual reputation.

As to the procedure for determining the admissibility of sexual conduct evidence, see ss. 276.1 and 276.2. Section 276.3 limits the publications of the proceedings. Section 276.4 requires the judge to instruct the jury as to the proper use of sexual conduct evidence and s. 276.5 makes the determination of admissibility a question of law, thus giving the Attorney General a right of appeal.

SYNOPSIS

This section was enacted following the decision of the Supreme Court of Canada in *R. v. Seaboyer, infra.* Unlike the predecessor provision which was found to violate s. 7 of the Charter, this section does not attempt to delineate all the circumstances in which sexual conduct activity would be admissible. Rather, subsec. (1) sets out the *purpose* for which the evidence is not admissible, *i.e.*, the evidence is not admissible for the now discredited purposes of merely showing the complainant is more likely to have consented or is less worthly of belief. In this sense, the section is structured in a way similar to s. 277 which was found in the same case to be constitutional. Subsection (2) codifies the test enunciated in *Seaboyer* that defence evidence which is probative of an issue in the case can only be excluded if the prejudicial effect of that evidence substantially outweighs the probative value. The requirement that the evidence relate to specific instances of sexual activity excludes the use of more general character evidence. It is unclear as to the extent that this section could apply to expert psychiatric or psychological evidence of disposition. Subsection (3) attempts to identify a non-exhaustive list of factors to assist the judge in determining the prejudicial effect of the evidence as weighed against its probative value. Of the various factors, perhaps those in paras. (*c*) to (*e*) will prove to be most significant as they relate directly to the probative value and prejudicial effect of evidence as traditionally understood, *i.e.* whether the evidence will be misused by the trier of fact. In making this determination, the judge will bear in mind the mandatory requirement in s. 276.4 that the jury be instructed as to the proper use of the evidence. The other factors listed in subsec. (3) reflect the decision by Parliament that certain evidence may be excluded despite its apparent probative value because of policy considerations not strictly related to the potential improper use of the evidence by the trier of fact. The weight to be attached to these broader policy issues will be somewhat more difficult to quantify in the particular case.

ANNOTATIONS

Constitutional considerations – This provision, including the procedural requirements, does not violate ss. 7 or 11(*d*) of the Charter: *R. v. Darrach*, [2000] 2 S.C.R. 443, 148 C.C.C. (3d) 97.

Application – This provision applies to all sexual activity whether with the accused or with someone else and also applies to non-consensual as well as consensual sexual activity: *R. v. Darrach, supra.*

Where this provision is used to substantiate a claim of honest but mistaken belief in consent, the accused must provide some evidence of what he believed at the time of the alleged assault in the context of the *voir dire* pursuant to s. 276.1: *R. v. Darrach, supra.*

Evidence of a sexual relationship between the accused and the complainant proximate in time to the alleged offences might well support a defence of honest but mistaken belief in consent in some circumstances. However, such evidence should not have been admitted where the accused's defence to one count was consent, not mistaken belief in consent, and with respect to the other three counts a denial that the incidents ever occurred: *R. v. Dickson* (1993), 81 C.C.C. (3d) 224 (Y.T.C.A.), affd [1994] 1 S.C.R. 153, 86 C.C.C. (3d) 576*n*.

Where evidence of prior sexual activity between the parties is offered in support of the defence of honest but mistaken belief in consent, it must be tested on a case-by-case basis having regard to all circumstances, including, but not limited to: the viability of the defence itself; the nature and extent of the prior sexual activity as compared to the sexual activity forming the subject-matter of the charge; the time frame separating the incidents; and the nature of the relationship between the parties: *R. v. Harris* (1997), 118 C.C.C. (3d) 498 (Ont. C.A.).

"Sexual activity" includes a prior conviction for communicating for the purposes of prostitution: *R. v. Drakes* (1998), 122 C.C.C. (3d) 498 (B.C.C.A.).

While the admissibility of evidence that the complainant was a virgin prior to the alleged assault by the accused is not covered either by this section or s. 277, the jury must be warned against the improper use of such evidence and in particular that the fact the complainant was a virgin does not mean that she was of better character and therefore more truthful: *R. v. Brothers* (1995), 99 C.C.C. (3d) 64 (Alta. C.A.).

Where the Crown adduced evidence from the complainant that she terminated her relationship with the accused prior to the alleged assault because she had a sexual preference for women with the apparent intention of asking the jury to draw the inference that the complainant was not the type of person to consent to intercourse with the male accused, then the defence should have been permitted to adduce evidence that the complainant, two days before the alleged assault, had sexual intercourse with a man. Such evidence would have been admissible according to the guidelines set out in *R. v. Seaboyer, supra; R. v. Morden* (1991), 69 C.C.C. (3d) 123 (B.C.C.A.).

The trial judge did not err in refusing to permit defence counsel to cross-examine the complainant (his step-daughter) as to whether she had lied in telling a police-officer that she had been sexually assaulted by persons other than the accused. There was no indication that the complainant's evidence on this collateral matter might be false. The evidence was of tenuous relevancy but had a significant potential to mislead the jury: *R. v. W. (B.A.)*, [1992] 3 S.C.R. 811.

The trial judge did not err in curtailing cross-examination of the complainant concerning an allegation she made about another man, nor did he err in refusing the defence permission to call this man who would deny the allegation and testify that he had been charged with sexually assaulting the victim and had been acquitted. The only legal basis which would justify this cross-examination would be to lay the foundation for a pattern of fabrication by the complainant of similar allegations of sexual assault against other men. This should not be encouraged unless the defence is in a position to establish that the complainant has recanted her earlier accusations or that they are demonstrably false. The cross-examination was on a collateral matter being in the nature of an attack on the general character of the complainant: *R. v. Riley* (1992), 11 O.R. (3d) 151 (C.A.).

The trial judge did not err in refusing to permit cross-examination of the complainant about allegations of sexual abuse by her biological father made at the same time she claimed abuse by the accused, her uncle. The complainant made it clear in her evidence at the preliminary inquiry that the sexual activity with her father ceased before the accused began abusing her. The accused did not intend to call the biological father to confirm or refute her allegations against him. The proposed evidence was not relevant to the accused's denial that the sexual activity took place or to the identity of the perpetrators: *R. v. T. (M.)* (2012), 289 C.C.C. (3d) 115 (Ont. C.A.).

This section and the procedure set out in ss. 276.1 and 276.2 have no application to evidence tending to show that the complainant has fabricated stories of sexual activity in which she has admittedly never engaged. However, the trial judge must nevertheless determine whether the proposed evidence is sufficiently probative to warrant its admission: *R. v. Gauthier* (1995), 100 C.C.C. (3d) 563 (B.C.C.A.).

Where evidence of sexual conduct between the accused and the complainant after the alleged offence became relevant because of testimony given by the complainant in examination-in-chief, the trial judge should have permitted defence counsel to cross-examine the complainant on that conduct, notwithstanding an earlier pre-trial ruling to exclude the evidence: *R. v. Potvin* (1998), 124 C.C.C. (3d) 568 (Que. C.A.).

The trial judge erred in precluding cross-examination of the complainant on her statement to the police, wherein she admitted to having engaged in consensual sexual intercourse with the accused three days before the alleged assault and stated that was the reason for visiting the accused on the date of the alleged assault. At trial, the complainant denied visiting the accused on the date of the alleged assault with the intention of having sex with him. Ordinarily, nothing would prevent defence counsel from cross-examining the complainant on such a material inconsistency. The fact that the material inconsistency was inextricably linked in the police questioning to the earlier consensual sexual contact between the complainant and the accused should not prevent the cross-examination. Where the defence of honest but mistaken belief is not realistically advanced by the accused at trial, then evidence of prior, unrelated sexual activity between the complainant and the accused will seldom be relevant to an issue at trial. However, the circumstances of this case were exceptional, as the only reason the unrelated prior sexual activity was at all implicated was because it was directly referred to by the police while posing a question which did bear on the sexual activity forming the subject matter of the charge. It would be unfair for an accused to be denied access to evidence which is otherwise admissible and relevant to his defence if the prejudice related to admitting that evidence is uniquely attributable to the authorities' conduct: *R. v. Crosby*, [1995] 2 S.C.R. 912, 98 C.C.C. (3d) 225.

The trial judge erred in precluding the accused from cross-examining the complainant in relation to prior complaints of sexual assault regarding other persons. The questions were relevant to credibility in that they established the improbability of assaults involving virtually identical comments and actions by a number of alleged assailants in different circumstances over the years: *R. v. Anstey* (2002), 162 C.C.C. (3d) 567 (Nfld. C.A.).

This section applies to evidence of specific sexual activity, not sexual inactivity. Therefore, the defence was permitted to cross-examine the complainant on her purported prior statement to the accused that she had not had sex in six months: *R. v. Antonelli* (2011), 280 C.C.C. (3d) 96 (Ont. S.C.J.).

Subsection (2) – In considering the inadmissibility of the evidence under this subsection, the trial judge must consider the factors set out in subsec. (3). "Significant probative value" requires that the evidence not be so trifling as to be incapable, in the context of all the evidence, of raising a reasonable doubt. It is not necessary for the accused to demonstrate strong and compelling reasons for the admission of the evidence. Furthermore, the use of the word "substantially" raises the standard for exclusion once the accused has shown it to have significant probative value: *R. v. Darrach, supra.*

APPLICATION FOR HEARING / Form and content of application / Jury and public excluded / Judge may decide to hold hearing.

276.1 (1) Application may be made to the judge, provincial court judge or justice by or on behalf of the accused for a hearing under section 276.2 to determine whether evidence is admissible under subsection 276(2).

(2) An application referred to in subsection (1) must be made in writing and set out
  (a) detailed particulars of the evidence that the accused seeks to adduce, and
  (b) the relevance of that evidence to an issue at trial,

and a copy of the application must be given to the prosecutor and to the clerk of the court.

(3) The judge, provincial court judge or justice shall consider the application with the jury and the public excluded.

(4) Where the judge, provincial court judge or justice is satisfied

    (a) that the application was made in accordance with subsection (2),

    (b) that a copy of the application was given to the prosecutor and to the clerk of the court at least seven days previously, or such shorter interval as the judge, provincial court judge or justice may allow where the interests of justice so require, and

    (c) that the evidence sought to be adduced is capable of being admissible under subsection 276(2),

the judge, provincial court judge or justice shall grant the application and hold a hearing under section 276.2 to determine whether the evidence is admissible under subsection 276(2). 1992, c. 38, s. 2.

CROSS-REFERENCES

The term's "complainant", "justice", "provincial court judge" and "clerk of the court" are defined in s. 2. The term "prosecutor" is defined in s. 2 and s. 785. As to the procedure for determining the admissibility of sexual conduct evidence, see s. 276.2. Section 276.3 limits the publication of the proceedings. Section 276.4 requires the judge to instruct the jury as to the proper use of sexual conduct evidence and s. 276.5 makes the determination of admissibility a question of law thus giving the Attorney General a right of appeal.

SYNOPSIS

This section sets out the first step of the procedure for making an application to adduce evidence of the sexual conduct of the complainant, other than the sexual activity which forms the subject matter of the charge. This section requires a written application setting out the particulars of the evidence sought to be adduced by the accused and the relevance of that evidence. The application to admit the evidence is actually a two-stage proceeding. Under this section, the judge determines whether the formal requirements have been met such as the written application and notice [seven days unless otherwise ordered] and whether the evidence is capable of being admissible. If these requirements are met, then the accused is entitled to an evidentiary hearing, conducted in accordance with s. 276.2, to determine whether the evidence should be admitted. The test for admissibility is set out in s. 276(2). The hearing under this section is held *in camera* and in the absence of the jury.

ANNOTATIONS

Constitutional considerations – The requirement in subsec. (2)(*a*) that the accused supply detailed particulars does not infringe the rights guaranteed by ss. 7 and 11(*c*) of the *Canadian Charter of Rights and Freedoms*: *R. v. Darrach*, [2000] 2 S.C.R. 443, 148 C.C.C. (3d) 97, 36 C.R. (5th) 223.

Evidentiary requirements – While the trial judge may allow an information and belief affidavit at the first stage of presenting detailed particulars of the evidence, it must be a personal affidavit of a person who has relevant information and who can personally testify as to its truth. The Crown's cross-examination must be limited to what is necessary to determine whether the proposed evidence is admissible. Furthermore, the accused's testimony on the *voir dire* is protected pursuant to s. 13 of the *Canadian Charter of Rights and Freedoms* and can only be used at trial to impugn his credibility and not establish his culpability: *R. v. Darrach, supra.*

    The inquiry under this section entails only a facial consideration of the matter and a tentative decision as to whether the evidence appears capable of being admissible. Any doubts that might exist at this stage are better left to be resolved at the evidentiary hearing under s. 276.2. The courts must be cautious in applying limits on the right of an accused to cross-examine and adduce evidence and so, unless the evidence clearly appears to be incapable of being admissible, having regard for the criteria set out in s. 276(2) and the *indicia* in s. 276(3), the judge should proceed to the evidentiary hearing stage: *R. v. Ecker* (1995), 96 C.C.C. (3d) 161, 37 C.R. (4th) 51, 85 W.A.C. 161 (Sask. C.A.).

Having excluded the accused's statements due to a Charter violation, the trial judge did not err under this section in refusing to admit the accused's statements during the course of a *voir dire*, although in the result, the accused was required to testify on the *voir dire*: *R. v. Mathieu* (1996), 111 C.C.C. (3d) 291, 127 W.A.C. 351, 187 A.R. 351 (C.A.), leave to appeal to S.C.C. refused 114 C.C.C. (3d) vi.

A preliminary inquiry judge has jurisdiction to hear and decide an application under this section: *R. v. Alibhai* (1998), 123 C.C.C. (3d) 556 (Ont. Ct. (Gen. Div.)). *Contra: R. v. T. (W.S.)* (1997), 33 W.C.B. (2d) 212 (B.C.S.C.).

JURY AND PUBLIC EXCLUDED / Complainant not compellable / Judge's determination and reasons / Record of reasons.

276.2 (1) At a hearing to determine whether evidence is admissible under subsection 276(2), the jury and the public shall be excluded.

(2) The complainant is not a compellable witness at the hearing.

(3) At the conclusion of the hearing, the judge, provincial court judge or justice shall determine whether the evidence, or any part thereof, is admissible under subsection 276(2) and shall provide reasons for that determination, and

> (*a*) **where not all of the evidence is to be admitted, the reasons must state the part of the evidence that is to be admitted;**
>
> (*b*) **the reasons must state the factors referred to in subsection 276(3) that affected the determination; and**
>
> (*c*) **where all or any part of the evidence is to be admitted, the reasons must state the manner in which that evidence is expected to be relevant to an issue at trial.**

(4) The reasons provided under subsection (3) shall be entered in the record of the proceedings or, where the proceedings are not recorded, shall be provided in writing; 1992, c. 38, s. 2.

CROSS-REFERENCES

The terms "complainant", "justice", and "provincial court judge" are defined in s. 2. As to the procedure for determining whether or not the accused is entitled to the evidentiary hearing prescribed by this section, see s. 276.1. Section 276.3 limits the publication of the proceedings. Section 276.4 requires the judge to instruct the jury as to the proper use of sexual conduct evidence and s. 276.5 makes the determination of admissibility a question of law, thus giving the Attorney General a right of appeal.

SYNOPSIS

This section sets out the final step in the procedure for making an application to adduce evidence of the sexual conduct of the complainant, other than the sexual activity which forms the subject matter of the charge. If the prerequisites set out in s. 276.1 have been met, then the accused becomes entitled to an evidentiary hearing, conducted in accordance with this section, to attempt to show that the evidence sought to be adduced meets the test for admissibility as set out in s. 276(2). The hearing under this section is held *in camera* and in the absence of the jury. Moreover, the complainant is not a compellable witness at the hearing. This section requires the court to provide reasons for the decision and to specify what parts of the evidence are to be admitted.

ANNOTATIONS

The non-compellability of the complainant does not violate the accused's right to make full answer and defence pursuant to ss. 7 and 11(*d*) of the *Canadian Charter of Rights and Freedoms*: *R. v. Darrach*, [2000] 2 S.C.R. 443, 148 C.C.C. (3d) 97, 36 C.R. (5th) 223.

PUBLICATION PROHIBITED / Offence.

276.3 (1) No person shall publish in any document, or broadcast or transmit in any way, any of the following:

- (*a*) **the contents of an application made under section 276.1;**
- (*b*) **any evidence taken, the information given and the representations made at an application under section 276.1 or at a hearing under section 276.2;**
- (*c*) **the decision of a judge or justice under subsection 276.1(4), unless the judge or justice, after taking into account the complainant's right of privacy and the interests of justice, orders that the decision may be published, broadcast or transmitted; and**
- (*d*) **the determination made and the reasons provided under section 276.2, unless**
  - (i) **that determination is that evidence is admissible, or**
  - (ii) **the judge or justice, after taking into account the complainant's right of privacy and the interests of justice, orders that the determination and reasons may be published, broadcast or transmitted.**

(2) Every person who contravenes subsection (1) is guilty of an offence punishable on summary conviction; 1992, c. 38, s. 2; 2005, c. 32, s. 13.

CROSS-REFERENCES

The terms "complainant", "justice", and "provincial court judge" are defined is s. 2. Procedure for summary conviction offences is found in Part XXVII which sets out the maximum penalties and the time limitation. Whether or not proceedings may be published under this section, publishers should bear in mind the provisions of s. 648 restricting publication of proceedings in the absence of the jury.

SYNOPSIS

This section makes it an offence to publish in any document or broadcast or transmit in any way certain aspects of the hearings held under ss. 276.1 and 276.2, which are held *in camera* and in the absence of the jury, to determine the admissibility of sexual activity evidence as permitted by s. 276. This section prohibits publication, broadcast or transmission of the application and the proceedings under ss. 276.1 and 276.2 and of the court's decisions under s. 276.1, unless otherwise ordered by the judge. As well, the decision under s. 276.2 cannot be published, broadcasted or transmitted unless it is determined that the evidence is admissible or the court otherwise orders.

JUDGE TO INSTRUCT JURY RE USE OF EVIDENCE.

276.4 Where evidence is admitted at trial pursuant to a determination made under section 276.2, the judge shall instruct the jury as to the uses that the jury may and may not make of that evidence; 1992, c. 38, s. 2.

CROSS-REFERENCES

The procedure for determining whether evidence is admissible under s. 276 is set out in ss. 276.1 and 276.2.

ANNOTATIONS

Cross-examination of the complainant on allegedly deviant and aberrant sexual behaviour, to support a defence by the accused psychologist that his acts were legitimate therapy, had a great potential for undue prejudice and the trial judge erred in failing to direct the jury as to the limited use of that evidence: *R. v. Fiqia* (1993), 87 C.C.C. (3d) 377, 145 A.R. 254, 55 W.A.C. 254 (C.A.). [**Note**: this case was tried prior to the enactment of this section.]

Where evidence of a prior sexual act has been admitted, even if it was not admitted under s. 276 on the basis that the act was non-consensual, it is incumbent on the trial judge to instruct the jury as to the proper and limited use of the evidence and, where necessary, that the evidence was not to be used for some other, improper, purpose that was suggested in the course of defence counsel's jury address: *R. v. Bell* (1998), 126 C.C.C. (3d) 94 (N.W.T.C.A.).

APPEAL.

276.5 For the purposes of sections 675 and 676, a determination made under section 276.2 shall be deemed to be a question of law. 1992, c. 38, s. 2.

CROSS-REFERENCES

Sections 675 and 676 govern rights of appeal by the accused and the Attorney General respectively. The main importance of this section lies in the fact that the decision to admit sexual activity evidence being a question of law is appealable by the Crown should the accused be acquitted.

REPUTATION EVIDENCE.

277. In proceedings in respect of an offence under section 151, 152, 153, 153.1, 155 or 159, subsection 160(2) or (3) or section 170, 171, 172, 173, 271, 272 or 273, evidence of sexual reputation, whether general or specific, is not admissible for the purpose of challenging or supporting the credibility of the complainant. 1980-81-82-83, c. 125, s. 19; R.S.C. 1985, c. 19 (3rd Supp.), s. 13; 2002, c. 13, s. 14.

CROSS-REFERENCES

The term "complainant" is defined in s. 2. As to other evidentiary and procedural provisions respecting the offences listed in this section, see the cross-references in relation to those provisions and the notes under s. 150.1. However, note in particular the companion provisions in s. 276 respecting evidence of sexual conduct with persons other than the accused.

SYNOPSIS

This section states that evidence of sexual reputation is not admissible to challenge or support the credibility of the complainant in proceedings under ss. 151, 152, 153, 155, 159, 170, 171, 172, 173, 271, 272, 273, or s. 160(2) or (3). It, in effect, reverses the common law rule that evidence of a reputation for sexual promiscuity was relevant to the complainant's credibility.

ANNOTATIONS

This section is not unconstitutional by reason of ss. 7 and 11(*d*) of the Charter: *R. v. Seaboyer*, [1991] 2 S.C.R. 577, 66 C.C.C. (3d) 321, 7 C.R. (4th) 117 (7:2).

SPOUSE MAY BE CHARGED.

278. A husband or wife may be charged with an offence under section 271, 272 or 273 in respect of his or her spouse, whether or not the spouses were living together at the time

the activity that forms the subject-matter of the charge occurred. 1980-81-82-83, c. 125, s. 19.

CROSS-REFERENCES

As to other evidentiary and procedural provisions respecting the offences listed in this section, see the cross-references in relation to those provisions and the notes under s. 150.1.

SYNOPSIS

This section specifies that a person may be charged with the offences of sexual assault, sexual assault with a weapon or causing bodily harm, or aggravated sexual assault against his or her spouse, whether or not they were living together at the time of the alleged offence. This reverses the common law rule that a husband could not be guilty of rape committed, by himself, upon his lawful wife, on the basis that, by virtue of the marriage contract, she was deemed to have irrevocably consented to intercourse.

Editor's Note: PERSONAL INFORMATION RECORDS

The following ss. 278.1 to 278.91 were enacted in response to the decision of the Supreme Court of Canada in *R. v. O'Connor*, [1995] 4 S.C.R. 411, 103 C.C.C. (3d) 1, 44 C.R. (4th) 1, which mandated the disclosure of therapeutic records in the possession of the Crown and set out a common law procedure for production and disclosure of records in the possession of third parties. *O'Connor* and related cases are noted under s. 650.

These provisions are triggered by an application by the accused charged with any of the sexual offences, enumerated in s. 278.2, for disclosure or production of records as defined in s. 278.1. That section contains a wide definition to include any record that contains personal information for which there is a reasonable expectation of privacy. Certain types of documents are listed and, as well, the definition includes documents protected under provincial or other federal legislation. Hospital records would be an obvious example of such documents. The only exception is a record created by a person responsible for the investigation or prosecution of the offence. Further, the procedure set out in these sections applies even to records in the possession of the Crown, thus expressly overruling a part of the holding in *O'Connor*, unless the complainant or the person to whom the records relate expressly waives the application of these sections. The Crown's disclosure obligation with respect to such records is limited to notifying the accused that they are in the possession of the prosecution, but without disclosing the their contents.

Sections 278.3 to 278.7 envisage a careful multi-staged procedure. Under s. 278.3, the accused first makes a written application for production to the trial judge identifying the record, the person in control of the record and the grounds for seeking production. Section 278.3(3) identifies the two purposes for which a record may be produced, *i.e.*, that it is relevant to an issue at trial or to the competence of a witness. A key provision is subsec. (4), which deems certain assertions that, on their own, are not to be sufficient to provide grounds for production of the record. The application must be served on the prosecutor, the person in control of the record and the complainant or witness to whom the records relate. At the same time, the accused must serve a subpoena in Form 16.1 on the person having control of the record. This form of subpoena notifies the person that the record need not be disclosed to any other party nor brought to court until a judge has made an order for their production. A judge presiding at a preliminary inquiry has no jurisdiction to order production of records under these sections.

The next stage in the process requires the judge to conduct an in camera hearing in accordance with s. 278.4 to determine whether to require production of the records to the judge for review. The person in control of the records and the complainant or witness, as the case may be, have standing to make submissions at this hearing. No order for costs may be made against any such person in respect of their participation in the hearing. The basis upon which the judge may decide to require production of the records is set out in s. 278.5. It would seem clear that the judge is to make this determination without necessarily reviewing the documents, on the basis of submissions. It may be that the parties are entitled to call evidence on this hearing, but the person in control of the records, the complainant or the witness to whom the records relate, are not compellable witnesses. Before ordering that the records be produced, the judge must be satisfied that the application is in accordance with s. 278.3, that the accused has established that the record is likely to be relevant to an issue at trial or to the competence of a witness and that production is necessary in the interests of justice. Section 278.5(2) sets out the test the judge must apply. In general terms, the judge is required to consider the accused's right to make full answer and defence as well as the privacy and equality rights of the person to whom the records relate. The judge is also directed in mandatory terms to consider a number of listed factors that focus not only on the probative value of the evidence and the privacy interests of any person, but broader societal concerns such as the interest in encouraging complainants to obtain treatment. Section 278.8 requires the judge to give reason for the decision.

The third stage in the procedure is set out in s. 278.6. If the judge decides that the record should be produced to the judge, the judge must then decide whether to disclose the record to the accused. This determination will ordinarily be made by the judge in private in the absence of the parties. However, the judge may hold an in camera hearing if it will assist in making the determination. The person to whom the records relate or the person in control of the records is not a compellable witness at this hearing. This may pose a difficulty for the judge if, for example, the need for the hearing is the difficulty in deciphering or understanding the documents. The test for determining whether to order disclosure is set out in s. 278.7(1) and (2) and involves application of the same factors that the judge applied under s. 278.5. Section 278.8 requires the judge to give reason for the decision.

The final stage in the procedure is set out in s. 278.7(3) to (6), which applies where the judge decides that a record or part of a record should be produced to the accused. Subsection (3) permits the judge to impose conditions on the disclosure. For example, the judge may require that the record be edited, that copies of the record not be made and that it be examined only at the court offices. The judge will also order a copy of the record be disclosed to the prosecutor unless the judge determines that it is not in the interests of justice to do so. Production of the record is made subject to the condition that it not be used in any other proceeding. If the judge decides not to order production of the record, a copy is to be kept in a sealed packet pending any appeal proceedings.

A decision whether or not to order production of the record to the judge under s. 278.5 or to the accused under s. 278.7 is deemed to be a question of law for the purposes of appeal by the accused or the Crown under s. 675 or s. 676.

It is a summary conviction offence under s. 278.9 to publish, broadcast or transmit in any way the contents of the application or any of the proceedings at the in camera hearings. Moreover, it is also an offence to publish, broadcast or transmit in any way the judge's reasons unless the judge orders that the determination may be published taking into account the interests of justice and privacy interests. The penalty for this offence is as prescribed in s. 787. The limitation period for instituting proceedings for this offence is six months pursuant to s. 786(2).

DEFINITION OF "RECORD".

278.1 For the purposes of sections 278.2 to 278.9, "record" means any form of record that contains personal information for which there is a reasonable expectation of privacy and includes, without limiting the generality of the foregoing, medical, psychiatric, therapeutic, counselling, education, employment, child welfare, adoption and social services records, personal journals and diaries, and records containing personal information the production or disclosure of which is protected by any other Act of Parliament or a provincial legislature, but does not include records made by persons responsible for the investigation or prosecution of the offence. 1997, c. 30, s. 1.

ANNOTATIONS

The definition of "record" is not overly broad and applies only to documents that truly raise a legally recognized privacy interest: *R. v. Mills*, [1999] 3 S.C.R. 668, 139 C.C.C. (3d) 321.

The definition only applies to records in which the complainant or witness has a reasonable expectation of privacy. However, absent evidence from the accused to the contrary, a trial judge is entitled to assume that a reasonable expectation of privacy attaches to any of the records falling within the enumerated categories and that, accordingly, the accused must comply with the provisions in order to gain access to the records. The fact that the accused was present for some of the complainant's counselling sessions and may have been privy to some of the disclosures by the complainant and the advice from the counsellor did not undermine her reasonable expectation of privacy: *R. v. Clifford* (2001), 163 C.C.C. (3d) 3 (Ont. C.A.).

Police occurrence reports prepared in the investigation of previous incidents involving a complainant or witness other than the offence being prosecuted count as "records" and are subject to the *Mills* regime. Given the sensitive nature of the information frequently contained in such police occurrence reports, and the impact that their disclosure can have on the privacy interests of complainants and witnesses, there will generally be a reasonable expectation of privacy in such reports. Further, the exemption for investigatory and prosecutorial records does not exempt such reports from the *Mills* regime: *R. v. Quesnelle*, [2014] 2 S.C.R. 390, 312 C.C.C. (3d) 187.

This provision had no application where the defence sought to call a witness, who worked in the complainant's home with the child protection agency, to testify about the complainant's reputation for truthfulness: *R. v. P-P. (S.H.)* (2003), 176 C.C.C. (3d) 281, 215 N.S.R. (2d) 66 (C.A.).

The court file number of another prosecution involving the same complainant was not a "record" within the meaning of this section and should be disclosed. This information would allow the accused to obtain publicly available information associated with the court file and potentially pursue an application for further material under the statutory regime: *R. v. Shaugnessy* (2012), 288 C.C.C. (3d) 195 (Alta. Q.B.).

Occurrence reports pertaining to prior complaints of sexual assault made by the same complainant against others are not "records" for the purposes of s. 278.2. When the complainant spoke to police, she was not doing so in the context of a trust-like, confidential or therapeutic relationship, nor was she contemplating withholding that information from the state. She could not reasonably expect that it would remain private: *R. v. Quesnelle, supra.*

PRODUCTION OF RECORD TO ACCUSED / Application of provisions / Duty of prosecutor to give notice.

278.2 (1) Except in accordance with sections 278.3 to 278.91, no record relating to a complainant or a witness shall be produced to an accused in any proceedings in respect of any of the following offences or in any proceedings in respect of two or more offences at least one of which is any of the following offences:

(*a*) an offence under section 151, 152, 153, 153.1, 155, 159, 160, 170, 171, 172, 173, 210, 211, 213, 271, 272, 273, 279.01, 279.011, 279.02, 279.03, 286.1, 286.2 or 286.3, or

(*b*) any offence under this Act, as it read from time to time before the day on which this paragraph comes into force, if the conduct alleged would be an offence referred to in paragraph (*a*) if it occurred on or after that day.

(*c*) [*Repealed*, 2014, c. 25, s. 17(3).]

(2) Section 278.1, this section and sections 278.3 to 278.91 apply where a record is in the possession or control of any person, including the prosecutor in the proceedings, unless, in the case of a record in the possession or control of the prosecutor, the complainant or witness to whom the record relates has expressly waived the application of those sections.

(3) In the case of a record in respect of which this section applies that is in the possession or control of the prosecutor, the prosecutor shall notify the accused that the record is in the prosecutor's possession but, in doing so, the prosecutor shall not disclose the record's contents. 1997, c. 30, s. 1; 1998, c. 9, s. 3; 2014, c. 25, ss. 17, 48(5); 2015, c. 13, s. 5(2).

ANNOTATIONS

Constitutional considerations – Sections 278.1 to 278.91 do not violate ss. 7, 8, 11(*d*) or 15 of the Charter: *R. v. Mills*, [1999] 3 S.C.R. 668, 139 C.C.C. (3d) 321, 28 C.R. (5th) 207.

General – Neither these provisions nor the principles set out in *R. v. O'Connor*, [1995] 4 S.C.R. 411, 103 C.C.C. (3d) 1, 44 C.R. (4th) 1, have any application to the use of the complainant's diary which was in the defence's possession and had not been wrongfully taken. The balancing tests set out with respect to third party records have no application with respect to the scope of cross-examination. The issue was whether the complainant's privacy interest substantially outweighed the accused's right to test the complainant's memory by cross-examination on the absence of entries in the diary recording abuse: *R. v. Shearing*, [2002] 3 S.C.R. 33, 165 C.C.C. (3d) 225, 2 C.R. (4th) 213.

Where the accused was charged with historical sexual assaults under the former s. 246.1 (now s. 271), the third-party records regime under ss. 278.1 to 278.9, and not the common law regime, applied. As the enactment was purely procedural, the presumption of retroactive application was engaged: *R. v. Gibson* (2010), 264 C.C.C. (3d) 121 (Ont. S.C.J.).

APPLICATION FOR PRODUCTION / No application in other proceedings / Form and content of application / Insufficient grounds / Service of application and subpoena / Service on other persons.

278.3 (1) An accused who seeks production of a record referred to in subsection 278.2(1) must make an application to the judge before whom the accused is to be, or is being, tried.

(2) For greater certainty, an application under subsection (1) may not be made to a judge or justice presiding at any other proceedings, including a preliminary inquiry.

(3) An application must be made in writing and set out

  (*a*) **particulars identifying the record that the accused seeks to have produced and the name of the person who has possession or control of the record; and**

  (*b*) **the grounds on which the accused relies to establish that the record is likely relevant to an issue at trial or to the competence of a witness to testify.**

(4) Any one or more of the following assertions by the accused are not sufficient on their own to establish that the record is likely relevant to an issue at trial or to the competence of a witness to testify:

  (*a*) **that the record exists;**

  (*b*) **that the record relates to medical or psychiatric treatment, therapy or counselling that the complainant or witness has received or is receiving;**

  (*c*) **that the record relates to the incident that is the subject-matter of the proceedings;**

  (*d*) **that the record may disclose a prior inconsistent statement of the complainant or witness;**

  (*e*) **that the record may relate to the credibility of the complainant or witness;**

  (*f*) **that the record may relate to the reliability of the testimony of the complainant or witness merely because the complainant or witness has received or is receiving psychiatric treatment, therapy or counselling;**

  (*g*) **that the record may reveal allegations of sexual abuse of the complainant by a person other than the accused;**

(*h*) that the record relates to the sexual activity of the complainant with any person, including the accused;

(*i*) that the record relates to the presence or absence of a recent complaint;

(*j*) that the record relates to the complainant's sexual reputation; or

(*k*) that the record was made close in time to a complaint or to the activity that forms the subject-matter of the charge against the accused.

(5) The accused shall serve the application on the prosecutor, on the person who has possession or control of the record, on the complainant or witness, as the case may be, and on any other person to whom, to the knowledge of the accused, the record relates, at least 14 days before the hearing referred to in subsection 278.4(1) or any shorter interval that the judge may allow in the interests of justice. The accused shall also serve a subpoena issued under Part XXII in Form 16.1 on the person who has possession or control of the record at the same time as the application is served.

(6) The judge may at any time order that the application be served on any person to whom the judge considers the record may relate. 1997, c. 30, s. 1; 2015, c. 13, s. 6.

ANNOTATIONS

Subsection (4) – This provision does not prevent an accused from relying on the enumerated factors but rather prevents reliance on bare assertions of the listed matters where there is no other evidence and the bare assertion stands on its own. With the exception of "recent complaint", the accused may rely on the listed assertions where there is an evidentiary or informational foundation to suggest that they may be related to likely relevance. The evidentiary threshold the accused must meet is to point to case-specific evidence or information to show that the record in issue is likely relevant to an issue at trial or the competence of a witness to testify. The issue of likely relevance, however, is a matter for the trial judge's discretion: *R. v. Mills*, [1999] 3 S.C.R. 668, 139 C.C.C. (3d) 321.

Where the records contain statements made by a complainant on matters potentially relevant to credibility, the likely relevance threshold will be met if there is some basis for concluding that the statements have some potential to provide some added information not already available to the defence or have some potential impeachment value. For example, material differences between the initial statement and preliminary inquiry testimony coupled with the fact that the complainant spoke to a therapist about the matters between these two events is sufficient to satisfy likely relevance: *R. v. Batte* (2000), 145 C.C.C. (3d) 449.

The mere assertion that the complainant had written about the accused in her diary was insufficient to meet the likely relevance test: *R. v. L. (D.W.)* (2001), 156 C.C.C. (3d) 152 (N.S.C.A.).

HEARING *IN CAMERA* / Persons who may appear at hearing / Right to counsel / Costs.

278.4 (1) The judge shall hold a hearing *in camera* to determine whether to order the person who has possession or control of the record to produce it to the court for review by the judge.

(2) The person who has possession or control of the record, the complainant or witness, as the case may be, and any other person to whom the record relates may appear and make submissions at the hearing, but they are not compellable as witnesses at the hearing.

(2.1) The judge shall, as soon as feasible, inform any person referred to in subsection (2) who participates in the hearing of their right to be represented by counsel.

(3) No order for costs may be made against a person referred to in subsection (2) in respect of their participation in the hearing. 1997, c. 30, s. 1; 2015, c. 13, s. 7.

JUDGE MAY ORDER PRODUCTION OF RECORD FOR REVIEW / Factors to be considered.

278.5 (1) The judge may order the person who has possession or control of the record to produce the record or part of the record to the court for review by the judge if, after the hearing referred to in subsection 278.4(1), the judge is satisfied that

    (*a*) the application was made in accordance with subsections 278.3(2) to (6);

    (*b*) the accused has established that the record is likely relevant to an issue at trial or to the competence of a witness to testify; and

    (*c*) the production of the record is necessary in the interests of justice.

(2) In determining whether to order the production of the record or part of the record for review pursuant to subsection (1), the judge shall consider the salutary and deleterious effects of the determination on the accused's right to make a full answer and defence and on the right to privacy, personal security and equality of the complainant or witness, as the case may be, and of any other person to whom the record relates. In particular, the judge shall take the following factors into account:

    (*a*) the extent to which the record is necessary for the accused to make a full answer and defence;

    (*b*) the probative value of the record;

    (*c*) the nature and extent of the reasonable expectation of privacy with respect to the record;

    (*d*) whether production of the record is based on a discriminatory belief or bias;

    (*e*) the potential prejudice to the personal dignity and right to privacy of any person to whom the record relates;

    (*f*) society's interest in encouraging the reporting of sexual offences;

    (*g*) society's interest in encouraging the obtaining of treatment by complainants of sexual offences; and

    (*h*) the effect of the determination on the integrity of the trial process. 1997, c. 30, s. 1; 2015, c. 13, s. 8.

ANNOTATIONS

The requirement that production be "necessary in the interests of justice" at this stage refers to whether production to the judge is necessary in the interests of justice. The first factor in subsec. (2) requires the judge to consider the accused's right to make full answer and defence. If the judge concludes that it is necessary to examine the documents in order to determine whether they should be produced to enable the accused to make full answer and defence, then production to the judge is "necessary in the interests of justice". If the record is "likely relevant" and after considering the factors set out in subsec. (2), the judge is uncertain about whether production is necessary to make full answer and defence, the judge should also rule in favour of inspecting the documents. This provision does not require that the judge engage in a conclusive evaluation of each of the factors, but rather requires the judge to take these factors into account to the extent possible at this early stage of the proceedings in deciding whether to order the production of documents for inspection by the court. While the enumerated factors are relevant, the trial judge is free to make whatever order is necessary in the interests of justice. A sufficient evidentiary basis to support production to the court can be established through Crown disclosure, defence witnesses, the cross-examination of Crown witnesses at the preliminary inquiry and the trial, expert evidence, as well as the nature of the records in question: *R. v. Mills*, [1999] 3 S.C.R. 668, 139 C.C.C. (3d) 321.

In considering the application of the test under this section, the trial judge might well find that there is a somewhat reduced expectation of privacy in respect of records relating to counselling sessions where the accused was present. On the other hand, because the accused was present at the session, he should be in a position to provide specific details of the information sought: *R. v. Clifford* (2001), 163 C.C.C. (3d) 3 (Ont. C.A.).

REVIEW OF RECORD BY JUDGE / Hearing *in camera* / Provision re hearing.

278.6 (1) Where the judge has ordered the production of the record or part of the record for review, the judge shall review it in the absence of the parties in order to determine whether the record or part of the record should be produced to the accused.

(2) The judge may hold a hearing *in camera* if the judge considers that it will assist in making the determination.

(3) Subsections 278.4(2) to (3) apply in the case of a hearing under subsection (2). 1997, c. 30, s. 1; 2015, c. 13, s. 9.

JUDGE MAY ORDER PRODUCTION OF RECORD TO ACCUSED / Factors to be considered / Conditions on production / Copy to prosecutor / Record not to be used in other proceedings / Retention of record by court.

278.7 (1) Where the judge is satisfied that the record or part of the record is likely relevant to an issue at trial or to the competence of a witness to testify and its production is necessary in the interests of justice, the judge may order that the record or part of the record that is likely relevant be produced to the accused, subject to any conditions that may be imposed pursuant to subsection (3).

(2) In determining whether to order the production of the record or part of the record to the accused, the judge shall consider the salutary and deleterious effects of the determination on the accused's right to make a full answer and defence and on the right to privacy, personal security and equality of the complainant or witness, as the case may be, and of any other person to whom the record relates and, in particular, shall take the factors specified in paragraphs 278.5(2)(*a*) to (*h*) into account.

(3) If the judge orders the production of the record or part of the record to the accused, the judge may impose conditions on the production to protect the interests of justice and, to the greatest extent possible, the privacy, personal security and equality interests of the complainant or witness, as the case may be, and of any other person to whom the record relates, including, for example, the following conditions:
- (*a*) that the record be edited as directed by the judge;
- (*b*) that a copy of the record, rather than the original, be produced;
- (*c*) that the accused and counsel for the accused not disclose the contents of the record to any other person, except with the approval of the court;
- (*d*) that the record be viewed only at the offices of the court;
- (*e*) that no copies of the record be made or that restrictions be imposed on the number of copies of the record that may be made; and
- (*f*) that information regarding any person named in the record, such as their address, telephone number and place of employ ment, be severed from the record.

(4) Where the judge orders the production of the record or part of the record to the accused, the judge shall direct that a copy of the record or part of the record be provided to the prosecutor, unless the judge determines that it is not in the interests of justice to do so.

(5) The record or part of the record that is produced to the accused pursuant to an order under subsection (1) shall not be used in any other proceedings.

(6) Where the judge refuses to order the production of the record or part of the record to the accused, the record or part of the record shall, unless a court orders otherwise, be kept in a sealed package by the court until the later of the expiration of the time for any appeal and the completion of any appeal in the proceedings against the accused, whereupon the record or part of the record shall be returned to the person lawfully entitled to possession or control of it. 1997, c. 30, s. 1; 2015, c. 13, s. 10.

ANNOTATIONS

In considering whether to order production to the accused, the trial judge must again consider the factors set out in s. 278.5(2). The trial judge is not required to rule conclusively on each of the enumerated factors, nor are they required to determine whether factors relating to the privacy and equality of the complainant or witness outweigh factors relating to the accused's right to make full answer and defence. The societal interest factors in s. 278.5(2)(*f*) and (*g*) are not given controlling weight in the determination regarding production. In considering s. 278.5(2)(*h*), the trial judge is required to consider, along with the other enumerated factors, whether the search for truth would be advanced by the production of the records in question or whether the material would introduce discriminatory biases and beliefs into the fact-finding process: *R. v. Mills*, [1999] 3 S.C.R. 668, 139 C.C.C. (3d) 321.

Having granted production of the complainant's psychiatric records, the trial judge erred in relying on the *R. v. O'Connor*, [1995] 4 S.C.R. 411, 103 C.C.C. (3d) 1, procedure in determining the scope of cross-examination. Once production is granted, the propriety of cross-examination is to be determined based on the application of fundamental rules of evidence: *R. v. Pontbriand* (2004), 189 C.C.C. (3d) 30 (Que. C.A.), leave to appeal to S.C.C. refused [2005] 1 S.C.R. xiv. Similarly, in *R. v. C. (T.)* (2004), 189 C.C.C. (3d) 473 (Ont. C.A.), leave to appeal to S.C.C. refused [2005] 2 S.C.R. xi, 198 C.C.C. (3d) vi, the Ontario Court of Appeal held that the third party record provisions govern production, not admissibility or use, and therefore were not applicable to a social worker's report that was lawfully in the possession of the accused. Nonetheless, the trial judge was entitled to exclude the report on the basis that the prejudicial effect of the report substantially outweighed its probative value having regard to the distortion of the fact-finding process and the therapeutic relationship.

REASONS FOR DECISION / Record of reasons.

278.8 (1) The judge shall provide reasons for ordering or refusing to order the production of the record or part of the record pursuant to subsection 278.5(1) or 278.7(1).

(2) The reasons referred to in subsection (1) shall be entered in the record of the proceedings or, where the proceedings are not recorded, shall be provided in writing. 1997, c. 30, s. 1.

PUBLICATION PROHIBITED / Offence.

278.9 (1) No person shall publish in any document, or broadcast or transmit in any way, any of the following:

    (*a*) the contents of an application made under section 278.3;

    (*b*) any evidence taken, information given or submissions made at a hearing under subsection 278.4(1) or 278.6(2); or

    (*c*) the determination of the judge pursuant to subsection 278.5(1) or 278.7(1) and the reasons provided pursuant to section 278.8, unless the judge, after taking into account the interests of justice and the right to privacy of the person to whom the record relates, orders that the determination may be published.

(2) Every person who contravenes subsection (1) is guilty of an offence punishable on summary conviction. 1997, c. 30, s. 1; 2005, c. 32, s. 14.

APPEAL.

278.91 For the purposes of sections 675 and 676, a determination to make or refuse to make an order pursuant to subsection 278.5(1) or 278.7(1) is deemed to be a question of law. 1997, c. 30, s. 1.

Kidnapping, Trafficking in Persons, Hostage Taking and Abduction

2005, c. 43, s. 2.

KIDNAPPING / Punishment / Subsequent offences / Factors to consider / Sequence of convictions only / Forcible confinement / Non-resistance.

279. (1) Every person commits an offence who kidnaps a person with intent
  (a) to cause the person to be confined or imprisoned against the person's will;
  (b) to cause the person to be unlawfully sent or transported out of Canada against the person's will; or
  (c) to hold the person for ransom or to service against the person's will.

(1.1) Every person who commits an offence under subsection (1) is guilty of an indictable offence and liable
  (a) if a restricted firearm or prohibited firearm is used in the commission of the offence or if any firearm is used in the commission of the offence and the offence is committed for the benefit of, at the direction of, or in association with, a criminal organization, to imprisonment for life and to a minimum punishment of imprisonment for a term of
    (i) in the case of a first offence, five years, and
    (ii) in the case of a second or subsequent offence, seven years;
  (a.1) in any other case where a firearm is used in the commission of the offence, to imprisonment for life and to a minimum punishment of imprisonment for a term of four years;
  (a.2) if the person referred to in paragraph (1)(a), (b) or (c) is under 16 years of age, to imprisonment for life and, unless the person who commits the offence is a parent, guardian or person having the lawful care or charge of the person referred to in that paragraph, to a minimum punishment of imprisonment for a term of five years; and
  (b) in any other case, to imprisonment for life.

(1.2) In determining, for the purpose of paragraph (1.1)(a), whether a convicted person has committed a second or subsequent offence, if the person was earlier convicted of any of the following offences, that offence is to be considered as an earlier offence:
  (a) an offence under subsection (1);
  (b) an offence under subsection 85(1) or (2) or section 244 or 244.2; or
  (c) an offence under section 220, 236, 239, 272, 273, 279.1, 344 or 346 if a firearm was used in the commission of the offence.
However, an earlier offence shall not be taken into account if 10 years have elapsed between the day on which the person was convicted of the earlier offence and the day on which the person was convicted of the offence for which sentence is being imposed, not taking into account any time in custody.

(1.21) In imposing a sentence under paragraph (1.1)(a.2), the court shall take into account the age and vulnerability of the victim.

(1.3) For the purposes of subsection (1.2), the only question to be considered is the sequence of convictions and no consideration shall be given to the sequence of commission of offences or whether any offence occurred before or after any conviction.

(2) Every one who, without lawful authority, confines, imprisons or forcibly seizes another person is guilty of
  (a) an indictable offence and liable to imprisonment for a term not exceeding ten years; or
  (b) an offence punishable on summary conviction and liable to imprisonment for a term not exceeding eighteen months.

(3) In proceedings under this section, the fact that the person in relation to whom the offence is alleged to have been committed did not resist is not a defence unless the accused proves that the failure to resist was not caused by threats, duress, force or exhibition of force. R.S., c. C-34, s. 247; R.S.C. 1985, c. 27 (1st Supp.), s. 39; 1995, c. 39, s. 147; 1997, c. 18, s. 14; 2008, c. 6, s. 30; 2009, c. 22, s. 12; 2013, c. 32, s. 1.

CROSS-REFERENCES

"Victim" is defined in s. 2. Section 279.04 defines when a person exploits another person for the purpose of this section. Section 279.02 makes it an offence to receive a financial or other material benefit from the commission of the offence under this section. Under s. 279.03, it is an offence to withhold or destroy travel or identity documents for the purpose of committing the offence under this section.

The related offence of trafficking in persons under the age of 18 years is set out in s. 279.011. The two offences are virtually identical except that the s. 279.011 offence includes minimum punishments. The offences, referred to in this section, of kidnapping, aggravated assault and aggravated sexual assault are found in ss. 279, 268 and 273 respectively. Also see s. 212, which creates various offences relating to procuring persons for the purpose of prostitution, whether in or out of Canada.

Section 17 limits the availability of the statutory defence of compulsion by threats to the offence of "forcible abduction". However, forcible abduction has been held not to include kidnapping: *R. v. Robins* (1982), 66 C.C.C. (2d) 550 (Que. C.A.). This offence may be the basis for an application for an authorization to intercept private communications by reason of s. 183.

Section 486 provides that the judge may exclude members of the public from the courtroom where it is in the interests of the proper administration of justice, which includes ensuring that witnesses under the age of 18 years are safeguarded in all proceedings. If the prosecutor or the accused applies for an order excluding the public at proceedings for an offence under this section and the judge fails to make the order, the judge is required to give reasons for that decision. Under s. 486.4, where an accused is charged with the offence under this section, the judge may make an order directing that any information that could identify the complainant or a witness not be published, broadcast or transmitted in any way. The judge is to inform the complainant or any witness under the age of 18 years of the right to make an application under s. 486.4.

This offence is a primary designated offence for the DNA provisions and a designated offence for the sex offender information provisions of Part XV and is a designated offence for the dangerous offender and long-term offender provisions in Part XXIV.

SYNOPSIS

This section describes the offences of kidnapping and forcible confinement, the punishment for these offences, and the defence of non-resistance. Any person who kidnaps another person against his will, with intent to confine him, to cause him to be sent out of Canada, or to hold him for ransom or to service, is guilty of an indictable offence and liable to life imprisonment. The section also enacts minimum punishments for the kidnapping offence. Under para. (1.1)(*a*.2), if the victim was under 16 years of age, the accused is subject to a minimum punishment of five years' imprisonment, unless the accused is a parent, guardian or person having the lawful care or charge of the victim. In any event, in imposing sentence under this paragraph, the court shall take into consideration the age and vulnerability of the victim. Where a restricted or prohibited firearm is used or the offence was committed for the benefit of, at the direction of, or in association with, a criminal organization, the offender is liable to a minimum punishment of at least five years' imprisonment for a first offence and seven years for a second or subsequent offence. The rules for determining whether the offender has committed a second or subsequent offence are set out in subsecs. (2.1) and (2.2) and, for example, provide that a prior offence includes not only convictions under this subsection, but other specified offences involving firearms. However, an earlier offence is not to be taken into account if 10 years have elapsed from the conviction of the earlier offence, not counting time in custody. Subsection (2.2) reverses the common law rule and provides that the court only takes into account the sequence of convictions, not the order in which the offences were committed. In any other case where a firearm is used, the offender is liable to a minimum term of imprisonment of four years. Where no firearm is used, there is no minimum punishment. Anyone who confines, imprisons or forcibly seizes another person without lawful authority is guilty of an indictable offence punishable by a maximum term of imprisonment of 10 years where the Crown proceeds by indictment, and 18 months where the Crown proceeds by summary conviction. Evidence of the fact that the victim did not resist does not constitute a defence unless the accused proves that such failure to resist was not caused by threats, duress or force.

ANNOTATIONS

Kidnapping [subsec. (1)] – To constitute kidnapping there must be a movement or taking of the person from one place to another and not simply the placing of the person in the area of confinement. Where an accused binds the victim who originally voluntarily entered his truck, places her in the back of the truck and continues on his trip until he can find a suitable place to sexually assault her the offence is made out: *R. v. Oakley* (1977), 36 C.C.C. (2d) 436 (Alta. C.A.).

In *R. v. Elder* (1978), 40 C.C.C. (2d) 122 (Sask. Dist. Ct.), the accused was acquitted of the offences under both subsecs. (1) and (2) where during a hostage-taking incident at a prison while he assisted in moving the hostage from one area to another his only purpose was to remove him from danger. The accused's purpose negatived the element of *mens rea* for both offences.

False statements by the accused which induced his victim to willingly enter into his custody constitutes kidnapping: *R. v. Brown* (1972), 8 C.C.C. (2d) 13 (Ont. C.A.).

Similarly, *R. v. Metcalfe* (1983), 10 C.C.C. (3d) 114 (B.C.C.A.), where it was held that "kidnap" includes to take and carry away a person against his will by unlawful force or by fraud. Leave to appeal to S.C.C. was refused April 2, 1984.

The *mens rea* of the offence under subsec. (1)(*b*) does not require proof that the accused knew that transportation of the victim out of Canada was unlawful: *R. v. Kear* (1989), 51 C.C.C. (3d) 574 (Ont. C.A.).

The powers which the accused, who were acting for an American bail bondsman, had to arrest a fugitive did not extend outside the United States and could not give them authority to violate Canadian sovereignty. Accordingly, the accused, in seizing the fugitive in Canada, were acting unlawfully and were properly convicted of the offence under subsec. (1)(*b*): *R. v. Kear, supra*.

Kidnapping is a "continuing" offence, which begins with the taking of the victim and ends only when the victim is released or consents to the detention. Therefore, the accused was guilty as a party to kidnapping where he did not participate in the initial taking, but aided and abetted the victim's subsequent confinement and forced movements between locations: *R. v. Hernandez* (2011), 270 C.C.C. (3d) 546, *sub nom. R. v. Vu* (B.C.C.A.).

Kidnapping is a "continuing" offence which begins with the taking of the victim and ends only when the victim is released or consents to the detention. It is an aggravated form of unlawful confinement — aggravated by the additional element of movement, which increases the risk of harm to the victim by isolating him or her from a place where detection and rescue are more likely. Because kidnapping is a continuing offence, a person who chooses to participate in the victim's confinement — after having learned that the victim has been kidnapped — may be held responsible for the offence of kidnapping under s. 21(1): *R. v. Vu*, [2012] 2 S.C.R. 411, affg 270 C.C.C. (3d) 546 *sub nom. R. v. Hernandez* (B.C.C.A.).

Minimum sentence [subsec. (1.1)] – Credit for time spent in pre-trial custody may reduce the sentence to be imposed below the minimum prescribed by this subsection: *R. v. Mills* (1999), 133 C.C.C. (3d) 451 (B.C.C.A.).

Unlawful confinement [subsec. (2)] – The offence under this subsection does not require proof of total physical restraint of the victim: *R. v. Gratton* (1985), 18 C.C.C. (3d) 462 (Ont. C.A.), leave to appeal to S.C.C. refused [1985] 1 S.C.R. viii.

Forcible confinement deprives the individual of liberty to move from point to point while kidnapping consists of taking control of a person and carrying them away from one point to another. While kidnapping entails forcible confinement, forcible confinement can occur without kidnapping: *R. v. Tremblay* (1997), 117 C.C.C. (3d) 86 (Que. C.A.).

Constitutional considerations [subsec. (3)] – The reverse onus provision created by this subsection is of no force and effect being inconsistent with the guarantee to the presumption of innocence in s. 11(*d*) of the Charter: *R. v. Gough* (1985), 18 C.C.C. (3d) 453 (Ont. C.A.); *R. v. Grift* (1986), 28 C.C.C. (3d) 120 (Alta. Q.B.); *R. v. Pete* (1998), 131 C.C.C. (3d) 233 (B.C.C.A.).

TRAFFICKING IN PERSONS / Consent.

279.01 (1) Every person who recruits, transports, transfers, receives, holds, conceals or harbours a person, or exercises control, direction or influence over the movements of a person, for the purpose of exploiting them or facilitating their exploitation is guilty of an indictable offence and liable

> (*a*) **to imprisonment for life and to a minimum punishment of imprisonment for a term of five years if they kidnap, commit an aggravated assault or aggravated sexual assault against, or cause death to, the victim during the commission of the offence; or**
>
> (*b*) **to imprisonment for a term of not more than 14 years and to a minimum punishment of imprisonment for a term of four years in any other case.**

(2) No consent to the activity that forms the subject-matter of a charge under subsection (1) is valid. 2005, c. 43, s. 3; 2014, c. 25, s. 18; 2014, c. 25, s. 18.

Note: Section 279.01 amended by enacting subsec. (3), 2015, c. 16, s. 1 (to come into force by order of the Governor in Council):

Presumption

(3) For the purposes of subsections (1) and 279.011(1), evidence that a person who is not exploited lives with or is habitually in the company of a person who is exploited is, in the absence of evidence to the contrary, proof that the person exercises control, direction or influence over the movements of that person for the purpose of exploiting them or facilitating their exploitation.

CROSS-REFERENCES

"Victim" is defined in s. 2. Section 279.04 defines when a person exploits another person for the purpose of this section. Section 279.02 makes it an offence to receive a financial or other material benefit from the commission of the offence under this section. Under s. 279.03, it is an offence to withhold or destroy travel or identity documents for the purpose of committing the offence under this section.

The related offence of kidnapping is set out in s. 279. The offences of aggravated assault and aggravated sexual assault are found in ss. 268 and 273 respectively. The offence of trafficking of a person when the victim is under the age of 18 years is set out at s. 279.011.

Section 17 limits the availability of the statutory defence of compulsion by threats to the offence of "forcible abduction". However, forcible abduction has been held not to include kidnapping: *R. v. Robins* (1982), 66 C.C.C. (2d) 550 (Que. C.A.). This offence may be the basis for an application for an authorization to intercept private communications by reason of s. 183.

Section 486 provides that the judge may exclude members of the public from the courtroom where it is in the interests of the proper administration of justice, which includes ensuring that witnesses under the age of 18 years are safeguarded in all proceedings. If the prosecutor or the accused applies for an order excluding the public at proceedings for an offence under this section and the judge fails to make the order, the judge is required to give reasons for that decision. Under s. 486.4, where an accused is charged with the offence under this section, the judge may make an order directing that any information that could identify the complainant or a witness not be published, broadcast or transmitted in any way. The judge is to inform the complainant or any witness under the age of 18 years of the right to make any application under s. 486.4.

SYNOPSIS

This section creates the offence of trafficking in persons. It is an offence to recruit, transport or deal with persons in any other methods specified in the section for the purpose of exploiting them or facilitating their exploitation. Exploitation is defined in s. 279.04 and, broadly speaking, envisages two circumstances. One circumstance is where the victim is forced to provide services or labour because they fear for their safety or the safety of someone they know. The other form of exploitation is using deception or coercion to have an organ or tissue removed. The exploited person's consent is no defence to the charge by virtue of subsec. (2). Subsection (3) creates a presumption that subsec. (1) is met if, in the absence of evidence to the contrary, the accused, who is not exploited, lives or is habitually in the company of a person who is exploited. The penalty depends upon whether the accused commits other offences while committing this offence. If the accused kidnaps or commits an aggravated assault or aggravated sexual assault or causes death to the victim during the commission of the offence, the accused is liable to imprisonment for life. Otherwise the accused is liable to imprisonment for 14 years.

TRAFFICKING OF A PERSON UNDER THE AGE OF EIGHTEEN YEARS / Consent.

279.011 (1) Every person who recruits, transports, transfers, receives, holds, conceals or harbours a person under the age of eighteen years, or exercises control, direction or influence over the movements of a person under the age of eighteen years, for the purpose of exploiting them or facilitating their exploitation is guilty of an indictable offence and liable

(a) **to imprisonment for life and to a minimum punishment of imprisonment for a term of six years if they kidnap, commit an aggravated assault or aggravated sexual assault against, or cause death to, the victim during the commission of the offence; or**

(b) **to imprisonment for a term of not more than fourteen years and to a minimum punishment of imprisonment for a term of five years, in any other case.**

(2) No consent to the activity that forms the subject-matter of a charge under subsection (1) is valid. 2010, c. 3, s. 2.

CROSS-REFERENCES

"Victim" is defined in s. 2. Section 279.04 defines when a person exploits another person for the purpose of this section. Section 279.02 makes it an offence to receive a financial or other material benefit from the commission of the offence under this section. Under s. 279.03, it is an offence to withhold or destroy travel or identity documents for the purpose of committing the offence under this section.

The related offence of trafficking in persons is set out in s. 279.01, kidnapping is set out in s. 279. The presumption created by s. 279.01(3) applies to s. 279.011(1). The offences of aggravated assault and aggravated sexual assault are found in ss. 268 and 273 respectively. Also see s. 212, which creates various offences relating to procuring persons for the purpose of prostitution, including persons under the age of 18 years, whether in or out of Canada.

Section 17 limits the availability of the statutory defence of compulsion by threats to the offence of "forcible abduction". However, forcible abduction has been held not to include kidnapping: *R. v. Robins* (1982), 66 C.C.C. (2d) 550 (Que. C.A.). This offence may be the basis for an application for an authorization to intercept private communications by reason of s. 183.

Section 486 provides that the judge may exclude members of the public from the courtroom where it is in the interests of the proper administration of justice, which includes ensuring that witnesses under the age of 18 years are safeguarded in all proceedings. If the prosecutor or the accused applies for an order excluding the public at proceedings for an offence under this section and the judge fails to make the order, the judge is required to give reasons for that decision. Under s. 486.4, where an accused is charged with the offence under this section, the judge may make an order directing that any information that could identify the complainant or a witness not be published, broadcast or transmitted in any way. The judge is to inform the complainant or any witness under the age of 18 years of the right to make an application under s. 486.4.

This offence is a primary designated offence for the DNA provisions and a designated offence for the sex offender information provisions of Part XV and is a designated offence for the dangerous offender and long-term offender provisions in Part XXIV.

SYNOPSIS

This section creates the offence of trafficking in persons under the age of 18 years. It is an offence to recruit, transport or deal with persons under the age of 18 years in any other methods specified in the section for the purpose of exploiting them or facilitating their exploitation. Exploitation is defined in s. 279.04 and, broadly speaking, envisages two circumstances. One circumstance is where the victim is forced to provide services or labour because they fear for their safety or the safety of someone they know. The other form of exploitation is using deception or coercion to have an organ or tissue removed. The exploited person's consent is no defence to the charge by virtue of subsec. (2). Section 279.01(3) creates a presumption that s. 279.011(1) is met if, in the absence of evidence to the contrary, the accused, who is not exploited, lives or is habitually in the company of a person who is exploited. The penalty depends upon whether the accused commits other offences while committing this offence. If the accused kidnaps or commits an aggravated assault or aggravated sexual assault or causes death to the victim during the commission of the offence, the accused is liable to imprisonment for life and to a minimum term of imprisonment of six years. Otherwise the accused is liable to imprisonment for 14 years and to a minimum punishment of five years.

ANNOTATIONS

The fault element of this offence focuses on an accused's purpose in exercising control, direction or influence over the movements of a person in the proscribed age group. No exploitation need actually occur or be facilitated by the accused's conduct for an accused to be convicted of human trafficking: *R. v. A. (A.)* (2015), 327 C.C.C. (3d) 377 (Ont. C.A.); *R. c. Urizar* (2013), 99 C.R. (6th) 370 (C.A. Que.).

MATERIAL BENEFIT — TRAFFICKING / Material benefit — trafficking of person under 18 years.

279.02 (1) Everyone who receives a financial or other material benefit, knowing that it is obtained by or derived directly or indirectly from the commission of an offence under subsection 279.01(1), is guilty of an indictable offence and liable to imprisonment for a term of not more than 10 years.

(2) Everyone who receives a financial or other material benefit, knowing that it is obtained by or derived directly or indirectly from the commission of an offence under subsection 279.011(1), is guilty of an indictable offence and liable to imprisonment for a term of not more than 14 years and to a minimum punishment of imprisonment for a term of two years. 2005, c. 43, s. 3; 2010, c. 3, s. 3; 2014, c. 25, s. 19.

CROSS-REFERENCES

Sections 279.01 and 279.011, referred to in this section, create the offences of trafficking in persons and trafficking in persons under the age of 18 years respectively. Section 279.03 makes it an offence to withhold or destroy documents for the purpose of committing the s. 279.01 offence. Under s. 486.4, where an accused is charged with the offence under this section, the judge may make an order directing that any information that could identify the complainant or a witness not be published, broadcast or transmitted in any way. The judge is to inform the complainant or any witness under the age of 18 years of the right to make any application under s. 486.4.

SYNOPSIS

This section complements the offences in ss. 279.01 and 279.011 by making it an offence to receive a financial or other material benefit, knowing that it results from the commission of the offences under those sections.

WITHHOLDING OR DESTROYING DOCUMENTS — TRAFFICKING / Withholding or destroying documents — trafficking of person under 18 years.

279.03 (1) Everyone who, for the purpose of committing or facilitating an offence under subsection 279.01(1), conceals, removes, withholds or destroys any travel document that belongs to another person or any document that establishes or purports to establish another person's identity or immigration status — whether or not the document is of Canadian origin or is authentic — is guilty of an indictable offence and liable to imprisonment for a term of not more than five years.

(2) Everyone who, for the purpose of committing or facilitating an offence under subsection 279.011(1), conceals, removes, withholds or destroys any travel document that belongs to another person or any document that establishes or purports to establish another person's identity or immigration status — whether or not the document is of Canadian origin or is authentic — is guilty of an indictable offence and liable to imprisonment for a term of not more than 10 years and to a minimum punishment of imprisonment for a term of one year. 2005, c. 43, s. 3; 2010, c. 3, s. 3; 2014, c. 25, s. 19.

CROSS-REFERENCES

Sections 279.01 and 279.011 create the offences of trafficking in persons and trafficking in persons under the age of 18 years respectively.

Section 486 provides that the judge may exclude members of the public from the courtroom where it is in the interests of the proper administration of justice, which includes ensuring that witnesses under the age of 18 years are safeguarded in all proceedings. If the prosecutor or the accused applies for an order excluding the public at proceedings for an offence under this section and the judge fails to make the order, the judge is required to give reasons for that decision. Under s. 486.4, the judge may make an order protecting the identity of the complainant or witness in proceedings for an offence under this section.

SYNOPSIS

This section complements the trafficking in persons offences in ss. 279.01 and 279.011 by making it an offence to conceal or otherwise deal with travel or identity documents of another person for the purpose of committing those offences. The offence is committed whether or not the documents are of Canadian origin or authentic.

EXPLOITATION / Factors / Organ or tissue removal.

279.04 (1) For the purposes of sections 279.01 to 279.03, a person exploits another person if they cause them to provide, or offer to provide, labour or a service by engaging in conduct that, in all the circumstances, could reasonably be expected to cause the other person to believe that their safety or the safety of a person known to them would be threatened if they failed to provide, or offer to provide, the labour or service.

(2) In determining whether an accused exploits another person under subsection (1), the Court may consider, among other factors, whether the accused
- (*a*) **used or threatened to use force or another form of coercion;**
- (*b*) **used deception; or**
- (*c*) **abused a position of trust, power or authority.**

(3) For the purposes of sections 279.01 to 279.03, a person exploits another person if they cause them, by means of deception or the use or threat of force or of any other form of coercion, to have an organ or tissue removed. 2005, c. 43, s. 3; 2012, c. 15, s. 2.

CROSS-REFERENCES

Section 279.01 creates the offence of trafficking in persons. Section 279.04 defines when a person exploits another person for the purpose of this section. Section 279.02 makes it an offence to receive a financial or other material benefit from the commission of the offence under this section. Section 279.03 makes it an offence to withhold or destroy documents for the purpose of committing the s. 279.01 offence. Under s. 486.4, where an accused is charged with the offence under this section, the judge may make an order directing that any information that could identify the complainant or a witness not be published, broadcast or transmitted in any way. The judge is to inform the complainant or any witness under the age of 18 years of the right to make any application under s. 486.4.

SYNOPSIS

This section defines when a person exploits another for the purposes of the offences in ss. 279.01 to 279.03. The section is of greatest importance for applying s. 279.01, which makes it an offence to deal with persons in the ways set out in the section for the purpose of exploiting them or facilitating their exploitation. Exploitation is made out where, in effect, the accused causes the victim to provide labour or services by making the victim fear for their safety (or the safety of a person known to them). Subsection (2) provides factors to consider in determining whether exploitation has been proved. Subsection (3) specifies that exploitation has occurred where organ or tissue removal is brought about by threats or deception.

ANNOTATIONS

One person exploits another if they cause that other person to provide labour by doing something that, in all the circumstances, could reasonably be expected to cause the other person to believe that their safety or the safety of a person known to them would be threatened if they failed to provide the labour. The expectation of the specific belief engendered by the accused's conduct must be reasonable, thus introducing an objective element. The person's safety need not actually be threatened. In addition, the term "safety" is not limited to the state of being protected from physical harm, but also extends to psychological harm: *R. v. A. (A.)* (2015), 327 C.C.C. (3d) 377 (Ont. C.A.).

Note: Section 279.05 enacted, to come after s. 279.04, 2015, c. 16, s. 3 (to come into force by order of the Governor in Council):

Sentences to be served consecutively

279.05 A sentence imposed on a person for an offence under sections 279.01 to 279.03 shall be served consecutively to any other punishment imposed on the person for an offence arising out of the same event or series of events and to any other sentence to which the person is subject at the time the sentence is imposed on the person for an offence under any of those sections.

HOSTAGE TAKING / Punishment / Subsequent offences / Sequence of convictions only / Non-resistance.

279.1 (1) Everyone takes a person hostage who — with intent to induce any person, other than the hostage, or any group of persons or any state or international or intergovernmental organization to commit or cause to be committed any act or omission as a condition, whether express or implied, of the release of the hostage —

    (*a*) confines, imprisons, forcibly seizes or detains that person; and

    (*b*) in any manner utters, conveys or causes any person to receive a threat that the death of, or bodily harm to, the hostage will be caused or that the confinement, imprisonment or detention of the hostage will be continued.

(2) Every person who takes a person hostage is guilty of an indictable offence and liable

    (*a*) if a restricted firearm or prohibited firearm is used in the commission of the offence or if any firearm is used in the commission of the offence and the offence is committed for the benefit of, at the direction of, or in association with, a criminal organization, to imprisonment for life and to a minimum punishment of imprisonment for a term of

        (i) in the case of a first offence, five years, and

        (ii) in the case of a second or subsequent offence, seven years;

    (*a*.1) in any other case where a firearm is used in the commission of the offence, to imprisonment for life and to a minimum punishment of imprisonment for a term of four years; and

    (*b*) in any other case, to imprisonment for life.

(2.1) In determining, for the purpose of paragraph (2)(*a*), whether a convicted person has committed a second or subsequent offence, if the person was earlier convicted of any of the following offences, that offence is to be considered as an earlier offence:

    (*a*) an offence under this section;

    (*b*) an offence under subsection 85(1) or (2) or section 244 or 244.2; or

    (*c*) an offence under section 220, 236, 239, 272 or 273, subsection 279(1) or section 344 or 346 if a firearm was used in the commission of the offence.

However, an earlier offence shall not be taken into account if 10 years have elapsed between the day on which the person was convicted of the earlier offence and the day on which the person was convicted of the offence for which sentence is being imposed, not taking into account any time in custody.

(2.2) For the purposes of subsection (2.1), the only question to be considered is the sequence of convictions and no consideration shall be given to the sequence of commission of offences or whether any offence occurred before or after any conviction.

(3) Subsection 279(3) applies to proceedings under this section as if the offence under this section were an offence under section 279. R.S.C. 1985, c. 27 (1st Supp.), s. 40(1); 1995, c. 39, s. 148; 2008, c. 6, s. 31; 2009, c. 22, s. 13.

CROSS-REFERENCES

Section 17 limits the availability of the statutory defence of compulsion by threats to the offence of hostage taking. Firearm is defined in s. 2. Pursuant to s. 2.1, "restricted firearm" and "prohibited firearm" are defined in s. 84.

This offence may be the basis for an application for an authorization to intercept private communications by reason of s. 183 and for warrant to conduct video surveillance by reason of s. 487.01(5). This offence may be the basis for a conviction for constructive murder under s. 230 and first degree murder under s. 231(5). Section 7(3) and (3.1) enacts special jurisdictional rules where this offence is committed outside Canada. A threat to commit an offence under this section against an internationally protected person (defined in s. 2) is an offence under s. 424.

The accused may elect his mode of trial pursuant to s. 536(2). Release pending trial is determined by s. 515. A person found guilty of the offence in this section will be liable to the mandatory prohibition order in s. 109 for possession of certain weapons, ammunition and explosives. A person found guilty of this offence may be subject to a dangerous offender application under Part XXIV.

Uttering threats is an offence under s. 264.1. The related offences of kidnapping and unlawful confinement are found in s. 279.

SYNOPSIS

This section describes the offence of hostage-taking. Any one commits this offence when he unlawfully confines a person and threatens that the safety of that person will be compromised or that his detention will continue if another person or group of persons, including states or international governments, does not comply with the offender's demands. Anyone convicted of an offence under this section is guilty of an indictable offence and liable to a maximum term of life imprisonment and to a minimum punishment of four years if a firearm is used in the commission of the offence. The *defence* of non-resistance applies in the same circumstances as are set out in s. 279(3).

ABDUCTION OF PERSON UNDER SIXTEEN / Definition of "guardian".

280. (1) Every one who, without lawful authority, takes or causes to be taken an unmarried person under the age of sixteen years out of the possession of and against the will of the parent or guardian of that person or of any other person who has the lawful care or charge of that person is guilty of an indictable offence and liable to imprisonment for a term not exceeding five years.

(2) In this section and sections 281 to 283, "guardian" includes any person who has in law or in fact the custody or control of another person. R.S., c. C-34, s. 249; 1980-81-82-83, c. 125, s. 20.

CROSS-REFERENCES

Section 17 limits the availability of the statutory defence of compulsion by threats.

Section 7(3) enacts special jurisdictional rules for commission of this offence outside Canada when the offence is in relation to an internationally protected person. This offence may be the basis for an application to intercept private communications by reason of s. 183 and for a warrant to conduct video surveillance by reason of s. 487.01(5).

The accused may elect his mode of trial pursuant to s. 536(2). Release pending trial is determined by s. 515, although the accused is eligible for release by the officer in charge under s. 498.

The accused's spouse is a competent and compellable witness at the instance of the Crown by virtue of s. 4(2). Age is determined by s. 30 of the *Interpretation Act*, R.S.C. 1985, c. I-21. Section 658 provides a means of proving the age of a child.

Related offences: s. 279, kidnapping and unlawful confinement; s. 279.1, hostage taking; s. 281, abduction of child under 14 years of age; s. 282, abduction of child under 14 years of age in contravention of custody order; s. 283, abduction of child under 14 years of age where no custody order with intent to deprive parent, etc., of possession of child. Section 171.1 makes it an offence to transmit, make available, distribute or sell sexually explicit material to a person who is, or who the accused believes is under the age of 16 years for purpose of facilitating the commission of the offence created by this section. Section 172.1 makes it an offence to communicate by means of telecommunication with a person who is or who the accused believes is under the age of 16 years for the purpose of facilitating the commission of the offence under this section. Section 172.2 makes it an offence to agree with a person or make an arrangement with a person by means of telecommunication to commit an offence under this section with a person who is or who the accused believes is under the age of 16 years.

Defences: s. 285, where court satisfied that taking, etc., was necessary to protect young person from imminent harm; s. 286, *no* defence that young person consented to or suggested any conduct of the accused. As to mistake defence generally, see notes under ss. 19 and 150.1.

SYNOPSIS

This section makes it an offence for anyone to cause to be taken, without lawful authority, any unmarried person under the age of 16 from the possession of the parent, the guardian, or any other person who has the lawful care or charge of that person. This taking must occur without the consent of the parent, guardian or other responsible person. A person convicted under this section is guilty of an indictable offence and liable to a maximum term of imprisonment of five years.

ANNOTATIONS

The phrase "takes or causes to be taken" requires some participation by the accused in the removal of the girl either through physical involvement or inducement or enticement. The mere fact that the girl is aware she can find refuge with the accused does not constitute any inducement on his part: *R. v. Johnson* (1977), 37 C.C.C. (2d) 352 (Sask. Dist. Ct.).

Proof of the taking away does not require any element of persuasion and even if the girls involved took a very active, if not leading part, in what occurred a conviction will follow if it is proved that the taking was against the will of the parent: *R. v. Langevin and LaPensee* (1962), 133 C.C.C. 257, 38 C.R. 421 (Ont. C.A.). In this case the dicta by Lebel J.A., in *R. v. Bebee* (1958), 120 C.C.C. 310 (Ont. C.A.), that persuasion by the accused was a necessary element of the offence, was disapproved.

Possession includes physical possession as well as the right of a parent to exercise his or her right of control over the child. The Crown need not demonstrate some element of coercion or control over the child. Furthermore, consent is no defence pursuant to s. 286 of the *Criminal Code* such that a runaway child cannot extinguish the right of a parent or guardian to exercise parental control: *R. v. Vokey* (2005), 202 C.C.C. (3d) 236 (B.C.C.A.). See also *R. v. Flick* (2005), 202 C.C.C. (3d) 244, 34 C.R. (6th) 174 (B.C.C.A.).

ABDUCTION OF PERSON UNDER FOURTEEN.

281. Every one who, not being the parent, guardian or person having the lawful care or charge of a person under the age of fourteen years, unlawfully takes, entices away, conceals, detains, receives or harbours that person with intent to deprive a parent or guardian, or any other person who has the lawful care or charge of that person, of the possession of that person is guilty of an indictable offence and liable to imprisonment for a term not exceeding ten years. R.S., c. C-34, s. 250; 1980-81-82-83, c. 125, s. 20.

CROSS-REFERENCES

The term "guardian" is defined in s. 280(2).

Section 17 limits the availability of the statutory defence of compulsion by threats. Section 7(3) enacts special jurisdictional rules for commission of this offence outside Canada when the offence is in relation to an internationally protected person. This offence may be the basis for a warrant to intercept private communications by reason of s. 183 and for a warrant to conduct video surveillance by reason of s. 487.01(5).

The accused may elect his mode of trial pursuant to s. 536(2). Release pending trial is determined by s. 515.

The accused's spouse is a competent and compellable witness at the instance of the Crown by virtue of s. 4(2). Age is determined by s. 30 of the *Interpretation Act*, R.S.C. 1985, c. I-21. Section 658 provides a means of proving the age of a child.

Related offences: s. 279, kidnapping and unlawful confinement; s. 279.1, hostage taking; s. 280, abduction of person under 16 years of age against will of parent; s. 282, abduction of child under 14 years of age in contravention of custody order; s. 283, abduction of child under 14 years of age where no custody order with intent to deprive parent, etc., of possession of child.

Defences: s. 284, where the accused establishes that the taking away, etc., was with the consent of the parent, guardian or other person having the lawful possession, care or charge of the young person; s. 285, where court satisfied that taking, etc., was necessary to protect young person from imminent harm; s. 286 *no* defence that young person consented to or suggested any conduct of the accused. As to mistake defence generally, see notes under ss. 19 and 150.1.

Where the accused is found guilty of this offence in respect of a person who is under 14 years of age, the court has the discretion to impose an order of prohibition under s. 161 prohibiting the accused from attending certain public areas and facilities or taking certain employment which will bring him into contact with persons under 14 years of age or using a computer system for the purpose of communicating with a person under the age of 14 years.

SYNOPSIS

This section describes the offence of abduction of a person under the age of 14 years. Anyone other than the parent, guardian or person lawfully in charge of a person under 14, who takes, entices away, conceals, detains, receives or harbours such a person, with the intention of depriving a parent, guardian or person in charge of possession of the person under 14, commits this offence. The offence is indictable, and punishable by imprisonment not exceeding 10 years.

ANNOTATIONS

It was held under the predecessor to this section that the word "detains" was to be given its dictionary meaning of "withhold". Thus the gravamen of the offence was not merely the keeping or confinement of the child but the intentional withholding of the child from the accused's wife, who had lawful custody of the child, which had the effect of depriving her of her custodial rights. Thus, in Ontario, where the child had lived with its mother, the courts had jurisdiction to try an offence of detaining, although the child was taken and held by the accused in another province: *R. v. Bigelow* (1982), 69 C.C.C. (2d) 204, 37 O.R. (2d) 304 (C.A.), leave to appeal to S.C.C. refused C.C.C. *loc. cit.*

The word "unlawfully" in the English version of this section is surplusage and does not require proof of commission of some additional unlawful act in the taking of the child. The term "possession" is not limited to circumstances in which the parent or guardian is actually in physical control of the child at the time of the taking. The concept of deprivation of possession relates to the ability of a parent to exercise his right of control over the child. Although proof of the intent required by this section can be met by the intentional and purposeful deprivation of the parent's control over the child, the *mens rea* of the offence can also be proven by the mere fact of the deprivation of possession of the child through a taking as long as the trier of fact can infer that the accused knew or foresaw that his actions would be certain or substantially certain to result in the parents being deprived of the ability to exercise control over the child: *R. v. Chartrand*, [1994] 2 S.C.R. 864, 91 C.C.C. (3d) 396, 31 C.R. (4th) 1.

ABDUCTION IN CONTRAVENTION OF CUSTODY ORDER / Where no belief in validity of custody order.

282. (1) Every one who, being the parent, guardian or person having the lawful care or charge of a person under the age of fourteen years, takes, entices away, conceals, detains, receives or harbours that person, in contravention of the custody provisions of a custody order in relation to that person made by a court anywhere in Canada, with intent to deprive a parent or guardian, or any other person who has the lawful care or charge of that person, of the possession of that person is guilty of

> **(*a*) an indictable offence and liable to imprisonment for a term not exceeding ten years; or**
>
> **(*b*) an offence punishable on summary conviction.**

(2) Where a count charges an offence under subsection (1) and the offence is not proven only because the accused did not believe that there was a valid custody order but the evidence does prove an offence under section 283, the accused may be convicted of an offence under section 283. 1980-81-82-83, c. 125, s. 20; 1993, c. 45, s. 4.

CROSS-REFERENCES

The term "guardian" is defined in s. 280(2).

Section 17 limits the availability of the statutory defence of compulsion by threats. Section 7(3) enacts special jurisdictional rules for commission of this offence outside Canada when the offence is in relation to an internationally protected person. This offence may be the basis for an authorization to intercept private communications by reason of s. 183 and for a warrant to conduct video surveillance by reason of s. 487.01(5).

The accused's spouse is a competent and compellable witness at the instance of the Crown by virtue of s. 4(2). Age is determined by s. 30 of the *Interpretation Act*, R.S.C. 1985, c. I-21. Section 658 provides a means of proving the age of a child.

Where the prosecution elects to proceed by indictment on this offence then the accused may elect his mode of trial pursuant to s. 536(2). Where the prosecution elects to proceed by way of summary conviction then the trial of this offence is conducted by a summary conviction court pursuant to Part XXVII. The punishment for the offence is then as set out in s. 787 and the limitation period is set out in s. 786(2). In either case, release pending trial is determined by s. 515, although the accused is eligible for release by a peace officer under s. 496, 497 or by the officer in charge under s. 498.

Related offences: s. 279, kidnapping and unlawful confinement; s. 279.1, hostage taking; s. 280, abduction of person under 16 years of age against will of parent; s. 281, abduction of child under 14 years of age by person other than parent, guardian or person having lawful care of child; s. 283, abduction of child under 14 years of age where no custody order with intent to deprive parent, etc., of possession of child.

Defences: s. 284, where the accused establishes that the taking away, etc., was with the consent of the parent, guardian or other person having the lawful possession, care or charge of the young person; s. 285, where court satisfied that taking, etc., was necessary to protect young person from imminent harm; s. 286, *no* defence that young person consented to or suggested any conduct of the accused. As to mistake defence generally, see notes under ss. 19 and 150.1.

SYNOPSIS

Subsection (1) describes the offence of abduction of a person under the age of 14 years in contravention of a custody order. Anyone who is the parent, guardian or person lawfully in charge of a person under 14 who takes, entices away, conceals, detains, receives or harbours that person in violation of a custody order of a Canadian court, with the intention of depriving another parent, guardian or person in charge of possession of the person under 14, commits this offence. The offence may be prosecuted by indictment or summarily, and is punishable on indictment by imprisonment not exceeding 10 years.

Where the accused would otherwise be found not guilty only because he or she did not believe there was a valid custody order in existence then by virtue of subsec. (2) the accused may be convicted of the offence under s. 283, if that offence is made out.

ANNOTATIONS

The words "lawful care or charge" do not modify the word "parent" and the parent may therefore be convicted of the offence under this section although at the time of the taking he did not have lawful care or charge of the child: *R. v. Van Herk* (1984), 12 C.C.C. (3d) 359, 40 C.R. (3d) 264 (Alta. C.A.).

The *mens rea* of the offence under this section is proof that the accused intended to deprive the person with lawful care of the child, of the possession of the child, and with an intent to do so in contravention of a valid and subsisting court order. A mistaken belief as to the legal effect of a custody order is a defence to this charge. Such a mistake although a mistake of law is an error as to the legal effect of civil law and therefore a defence. However, the fact that the accused knew the terms of the custody order and acted in contravention of its terms would, in most cases, be sufficient to persuade the trier of fact that she intended to do so. *Quaere*, whether the mistaken belief as to the legal effect of the order must be based on reasonable grounds: *R. v. Ilczyszyn* (1988), 45 C.C.C. (3d) 91 (Ont. C.A.).

In the subsequent case of *R. v. Hammerbeck* (1991), 68 C.C.C. (3d) 161 (B.C.C.A.), that court held that an honest belief by the accused that he was not bound by the terms of the custody order was a defence and that the mistake need not be based on reasonable grounds.

The term "detain" in this section means "withhold" and thus the mere fact that a parent keeps a child longer than the prescribed access period would not necessarily constitute a withholding and thus a detention of the child. Further, to prove the requisite intent for the offence, there must be proof that the act was done for the express purpose of depriving the other parent of possession of the child. Mere recklessness would not suffice. There must be an intention to somehow put the child beyond the reach of the other parent's custody or control. An intention not to assist or co-operate in the regaining of physical control of the child by the other parent cannot be equated with the intention to deprive that parent of possession of the child: *R. v. McDougall* (1990), 62 C.C.C. (3d) 174, 3 C.R. (4th) 112 (Ont. C.A.).

A clause in a custody order, providing that neither parent may remove any of the children without consent of the other party or a court order, was a "custody provision" of the custody order within the meaning of this section. Further, although, by virtue of the order, the accused's wife did not have a right to custody of the child, the right of access given to her by the court order involved transfer of the lawful care or charge of the child to the mother for the duration of the access. While the order was not one contemplating joint custody, what is granted by such an "access" order is more than merely a right to visit while the child is in the possession, care or charge of the other parent. It involves transfer of the child from the possession, care or charge of the custodial parent, here the accused, to that of the non-custodial parent. If prevented from the exercise of the right to lawful care or charge of the child during these access periods, then the person entitled to such access is denied possession of the child for that period within the meaning of this section: *R. v. Petropoulos* (1990), 59 C.C.C. (3d) 393, 29 R.F.L. (3d) 289 (B.C.C.A.).

Where the order made under the *Divorce Act*, R.S.C. 1985, c. 3 (2nd Supp.), while providing for rights of access for the accused spouse, made no provision for custody of the child then the Territorial legislation making the spouses joint guardians applied and the accused could not be convicted of the offence under this section. While the order was a custody order, it did not contain "custody provisions": *R. v. Gustaw* (1991), 65 C.C.C. (3d) 296 (N.W.T.S.C.).

Every custody order is subject to variation and particularly where the order is only an interim custody order, police officers before attempting to arrest a parent for abduction in contravention of such an order should take reasonable steps and make such inquiries as are appropriate and possible to ensure that the order accurately reflects the true legal relationship between the parties: *R. v. McCoy* (1984), 17 C.C.C. (3d) 114 (Ont. Prov. Ct.).

Breach of an access order is insufficient to establish the requisite intent. An essential element of the offence was whether the accused had the intent to deprive the mother of possession of the child. In this case, the accused's uncontradicted evidence was that he kept the child in the United States only temporarily because he had been requested to keep the child available pending a child protective services investigation: *R. v. Muirhead* (2008), 230 C.C.C. (3d) 236 (P.E.I.C.A.).

ABDUCTION / Consent required.

283. (1) Every one who, being the parent, guardian or person having the lawful care or charge of a person under the age of fourteen years, takes, entices away, conceals, detains, receives or harbours that person, whether or not there is a custody order in relation to that person made by a court anywhere in Canada, with intent to deprive a parent or guardian, or any other person who has the lawful care or charge of that person, of the possession of that person, is guilty of

  (a) an indictable offence and is liable to imprisonment for a term not exceeding ten years; or

  (b) an offence punishable on summary conviction.

(2) No proceedings may be commenced under subsection (1) without the consent of the Attorney General or counsel instructed by him for that purpose. 1980-81-82-83, c. 125, s. 20; 1993, c. 45, s. 5.

CROSS-REFERENCES

The term "guardian" is defined in s. 280(2). "Attorney General" is defined in s. 2. Section 583(*h*) provides that a count in an indictment is not insufficient by reason only that it does not state that the required consent has been obtained (as to notes concerning sufficiency of consent, see s. 583).

Section 17 limits the availability of the statutory defence of compulsion by threats. Section 7(3) enacts special jurisdictional rules for commission of this offence outside Canada when the offence is in relation to an internationally protected person. This offence may be the basis of an application for an authorization to intercept private communications by reason of s. 183 and for a warrant to conduct video surveillance by reason of s. 487.01(5).

The accused's spouse is a competent and compellable witness at the instance of the Crown by virtue of s. 4(2). Age is determined by s. 30 of the *Interpretation Act*, R.S.C. 1985, c. I-21. Section 658 provides a means of proving the age of a child.

Where the prosecution elects to proceed by indictment on this offence then the accused may elect his mode of trial pursuant to s. 536(2). Where the prosecution elects to proceed by way of summary conviction then the trial of this offence is conducted by a summary conviction court pursuant to Part XXVII. The punishment for the offence is then as set out in s. 787 and the limitation period is set out in s. 786(2). In either case, release pending trial is determined by s. 515, although the accused is eligible for release by a peace officer under s. 496, 497 or by the officer in charge under s. 498.

Related offences: s. 279, kidnapping and unlawful confinement; s. 279.1, hostage taking; s. 280, abduction of person under 16 years of age against will of parent; s. 281, abduction of child under 14 years of age by person other than parent, guardian or person having lawful care of child; s. 282, abduction of child under 14 years of age in contravention of custody order with intent to deprive parent, etc., of possession of child.

Defences: s. 284, where the accused establishes that the taking away, etc., was with the consent of the parent, guardian or other person having the lawful possession, care or charge of the young person; s. 285, where court satisfied that taking, etc., was necessary to protect young person from imminent harm; s. 286, *no* defence that young person consented to or suggested any conduct of the accused. As to mistake defence generally, see notes under ss. 19 and 150.1.

SYNOPSIS

This section describes the offence of abduction by a parent, guardian or person lawfully in charge of a person under 14 years of age whether or not there is a custody order of a Canadian court in existence. In such circumstances, the offence is committed if the person under 14 is taken, enticed away, concealed, detained, received or harboured with the intention of depriving another parent, guardian or person lawfully in charge, of possession of the person under 14. The offence may be prosecuted by indictment or summarily, but only with the consent of an Attorney General, or counsel instructed by him. The offence is punishable, on indictment, by imprisonment not exceeding 10 years.

ANNOTATIONS

"Taking" occurs where the accused causes the child to come or go with him and in the process, excludes the authority of another person who has lawful care or charge of the child. Nothing in this provision requires the deprived parent, guardian or other person to actually have had possession of the child at the moment of the offence. To "deprive" a person of something means, among other things, to keep that person from that which he or she would otherwise have. "Possession" is not limited to circumstances in which the deprived parent is actually in physical control of the child at the time of the taking but extends to the ability to exercise control over the child. The intent to deprive of possession will exist whenever the taker knows or foresees that his or her actions would be certain or substantially certain to result in the parent being deprived of the ability to exercise control over the child. The *actus reus* of the offence requires nothing more than preventing a parent, guardian or other person having lawful care of charge of the child from exercising control over that child. Status as the custodial parent or the other parent's status as an access parent does not constitute a defence to this provision: *R. v. Dawson*, [1996] 3 S.C.R. 783, 111 C.C.C. (3d) 1.

While provincial legislation may define "parent" it is not clear whether such definition could apply or whether the common law definition applies. At common law "parent" is *prima facie* confined to the lawful mother and father and exceptionally includes the father of a child born out of wedlock: *R. v. Levesque* (1984), 15 C.C.C. (3d) 413 (N.S. Co. Ct.).

DEFENCE.

284. No one shall be found guilty of an offence under sections 281 to 283 if he establishes that the taking, enticing away, concealing, detaining, receiving or harbouring of any young person was done with the consent of the parent, guardian or other person having the lawful possession, care or charge of that young person. 1980-81-82-83, c. 125, s. 20.

CROSS-REFERENCES
The term "guardian" is defined in s. 280(2). The term "young person" is not defined but presumably was intended to refer to the child under the age of fourteen years referred to in ss. 281 to 283.

SYNOPSIS
This section provides a defence of consent to the abduction offences found in ss. 281 to 283. The consent must be given by the parent, guardian or other person in charge of a person under 14 who has lawful possession, care, or charge of that person. Consent of a young person provides no defence, by virtue of s. 286.

The consent must come from the person whom the accused intended to deprive of possesion of the child not from the accused himself. Therefore, the accused who was the parent who had lawful possession of the child at the time of the alleged offence could not rely on his own consent as a defence to the offence under s. 283: *R. v. Dawson*, [1996] 3 S.C.R. 783, 111 C.C.C. (3d) 1.

DEFENCE.

285. No one shall be found guilty of an offence under sections 280 to 283 if the court is satisfied that the taking, enticing away, concealing, detaining, receiving or harbouring of any young person was necessary to protect the young person from danger of imminent harm or if the person charged with the offence was escaping from danger of imminent harm. 1980-81-82-83, c. 125, s. 20; 1993, c. 45, s. 6.

CROSS-REFERENCES
The term "young person" is not defined but presumably was intended to refer to the child under the age of fourteen years or sixteen years, as the case may be, referred to in ss. 280 to 283.

SYNOPSIS
This section provides a defence of necessity to the abduction offences found in ss. 280 to 283. For the defence to succeed, the court must be satisfied that the taking or other conduct in relation to a young person prohibited by ss. 280 to 283 was necessary to protect the young person from danger of imminent harm or if the accused was escaping from danger or imminent harm.

ANNOTATIONS

In considering whether there is an air of reality to the defence of necessity, there must be some evidence that: (1) from the accused's point of view, using the modified objective standard, there was a danger of imminent harm to the children; (2) from the accused's point of view, using the modified objective standard, there were no reasonable legal alternatives to taking the children in breach of the custody order, and (3) viewed objectively, the harm to the children by taking them in contravention of the custody order was proportional to the potential harm to the children that was being avoided. The accused's honest belief that the trial judge in a family law matter would deprive her of all access to her children thereby causing them harm did not constitute imminent harm. There was no emergent situation and the accused had other legal avenues in which to address the issue: *R. v. VandenElsen* (2003), 177 C.C.C. (3d) 332, 230 D.L.R. (4th) 640, 175 O.A.C. 71 (C.A.).

An honest but mistaken belief that the child is in danger of imminent harm is a defence, provided that the taking of the child was necessary, in an objective sense, based on the circumstances as the accused honestly believed them to be. In considering the defence, the jury should be instructed to consider other remedial steps which might have been taken and to consider the reasonableness of the accused's mistaken belief: *R. v. Adams* (1993), 79 C.C.C. (3d) 193, 19 C.R. (4th) 277, 12 O.R. (3d) 248 (C.A.).

Where the accused invokes this provision on the basis that they were "escaping from the danger of imminent harm", there must be a connection between the taking of the child and the non-custodial parent's escape from the danger of imminent harm. In this case, even if the accused thought that he was in danger, he did not have to take his child in order to escape the harm: *R. v. Mendez* (1997), 113 C.C.C. (3d) 304, 320 O.R. (3d) 67 (C.A.), leave to appeal to S.C.C. refused 121 C.C.C. (3d) vi.

NO DEFENCE.

286. In proceedings in respect of an offence under sections 280 to 283, it is not a defence to any charge that a young person consented to or suggested any conduct of the accused. 1980-81-82-83, c. 125, s. 20.

CROSS-REFERENCES

The term "young person" is not defined but presumably was intended to refer to the child under the age of fourteen years or sixteen years, as the case may be, referred to in ss. 280 to 283.

SYNOPSIS

This section clarifies the fact that although a defence of consent by a person in charge of a young person exists with respect to ss. 281 to 283 (see s. 284), the consent or suggestion of *a young person* cannot provide a defence to abduction under any of ss. 280 to 283. They might, however, be relevant to establish necessity under s. 285.

Commodification of Sexual Activity   2014, c. 25, s. 20.

OBTAINING SEXUAL SERVICES FOR CONSIDERATION / Obtaining sexual services for person under 18 years / Subsequent offences / Sequence of convictions only / Definitions of "place" and "public place"

286.1 (1) Everyone who, in any place, obtains for consideration, or communicates with anyone for the purpose of obtaining for consideration, the sexual services of a person is guilty of

(*a*) an indictable offence and liable to imprisonment for a term of not more than five years and a minimum punishment of,

(i) in the case where the offence is committed in a public place, or in any place open to public view, that is or is next to a park or the grounds of a school or

religious institution or that is or is next to any other place where persons under the age of 18 can reasonably be expected to be present,

    (A) for a first offence, a fine of $2,000, and

    (B) for each subsequent offence, a fine of $4,000, or

  (ii) in any other case,

    (A) for a first offence, a fine of $1,000, and

    (B) for each subsequent offence, a fine of $2,000; or

 (*b*) an offence punishable on summary conviction and liable to imprisonment for a term of not more than 18 months and a minimum punishment of,

  (i) in the case referred to in subparagraph (*a*)(i),

    (A) for a first offence, a fine of $1,000, and

    (B) for each subsequent offence, a fine of $2,000, or

  (ii) in any other case,

    (A) for a first offence, a fine of $500, and

    (B) for each subsequent offence, a fine of $1,000.

(2) Everyone who, in any place, obtains for consideration, or communicates with anyone for the purpose of obtaining for consideration, the sexual services of a person under the age of 18 years is guilty of an indictable offence and liable to imprisonment for a term of not more than 10 years and to a minimum punishment of imprisonment for a term of

 (*a*) for a first offence, six months; and

 (*b*) for each subsequent offence, one year.

(3) In determining, for the purpose of subsection (2), whether a convicted person has committed a subsequent offence, if the person was earlier convicted of any of the following offences, that offence is to be considered as an earlier offence:

 (*a*) an offence under that subsection; or

 (*b*) an offence under subsection 212(4) of this Act, as it read from time to time before the day on which this subsection comes into force.

(4) In determining, for the purposes of this section, whether a convicted person has committed a subsequent offence, the only question to be considered is the sequence of convictions and no consideration shall be given to the sequence of commission of offences, whether any offence occurred before or after any conviction or whether offences were prosecuted by indictment or by way of summary conviction proceedings.

(5) For the purposes of this section, "place" and "public place" have the same meaning as in subsection 197(1). 2014, c. 25, s. 20.

CROSS-REFERENCES

"Place" and "public place" are defined in s. 197.

    Other offences relating to sexual services are found in ss. 213, 286.2, 286.3 and 286.4.

    Certain immunities to a charge on this provision are provided by s. 286.5.

    Where the prosecution elects to proceed by indictment on this offence, then the accused may elect his mode of trial pursuant to s. 536(2). Where the prosecution elects to proceed by way of summary conviction, then the trial of this offence is conducted by a summary conviction court pursuant to Part XXVII. The punishment for the offence is then set out in s. 787 and the limitation period is set out in s. 786(2). In either case, release pending trial is determined by s. 515, although the accused is eligible for release by a peace officer under ss. 496 or 497, or by the officer in charge under s. 498.

    This offence may be the basis for an application for an authorization to intercept private communications by reason of s. 183, or a video surveillance warrant under s. 487.01(5).

    As to production of records containing personal information of the complainant or a witness, see ss. 278.1 to 278.9.

    Section 486(1) and (2) provide that the judge may make an order excluding all or any members of the public where such order is in the interest of public morals, the maintenance of order or the proper administration of justice, or is necessary to prevent injury to international relations or national defence or national security. The proper administration of justice includes safeguarding the interests of witnesses under the age of 18 years.

Section 486.1 sets out the circumstances in which the judge shall or may order a support person to be present and close to a witness while the witness testifies. Where the witness is under the age of 18 years or had a mental or physical disability, the order is to be made upon request unless the judge is of the opinion that the order would interfere with the proper administration of justice. In the case of other witnesses, the order is to be made if necessary to obtain a full and candid account from the witness of the matters complained of. The application for this order may be made during the proceedings or before they begin to the judge who is to preside at the proceedings.

Similarly, s. 486.2 sets out the circumstances in which the judge shall or may order a witness to testify outside the courtroom or behind a screen or other device that would not allow the witness to see the accused. Where the witness is under the age of 18 years or may have difficulty communicating the evidence by reason of mental or physical disability, the judge shall make the order unless the judge is of the opinion that the order would interfere with the proper administration of justice. In all other cases, the order may be made if the judge is of the opinion that the order is necessary to obtain a full and candid account from the witness of the acts complained of.

Section 486.3 provides that, on application by the prosecutor or a witness under the age of 18 years, the accused shall not personally cross-examine the witness unless the judge is of the opinion that the proper administration of justice requires the accused to personally conduct the cross-examination. In other cases, the judge may make an order that the accused not personally cross-examine the witness if the judge is of the opinion that the order is necessary to obtain a full and candid account from the witness of the acts complained of. The judge will appoint counsel to conduct the cross-examination.

Under s. 486.4, the judge may make an order directing that the identity of a witness not be disclosed in any publication, broadcast or transmitted in any way. The order is mandatory where the complainant or a witness is under the age of 18 years or the prosecutor applies for the order. Section 486.5 also gives the judge a discretion respecting non-publication orders.

Section 718.01 provides that, in imposing a sentence for an offence involving the abuse of a person under the age of 18 years, the court shall give primary consideration to the objectives of denunciation and deterrence. Further, under s. 718.2, evidence that the offender, in committing the offence, abused a person under the age of 18 years is an aggravating circumstance.

The offence in subsec. (1) is a secondary designated offence for the purpose of making a forensic DNA data bank order under s. 487.051. The offence in subsec. (2) is a primary designated offence.

Pursuant to s. 490.012, where an offender is convicted of the offence under subsec. (2), the judge shall make an order requiring the offender to comply with the *Sex Offender Information Registration Act*, S.C. 2004, c. 10. Where an offender is convicted under subsec. (1), such an order shall be made on application of the prosecutor if certain circumstances are present.

If a person is found guilty of the offence in subsec. (2) in respect of a person who is under 16 years of age, the court may impose an order of prohibition under s. 161 prohibiting the accused from attending certain public areas and facilities or taking certain employment that will bring him into contact with persons under the age of 16 years.

Section 171.1 makes it an offence to transmit, make available, distribute or sell sexually explicit material to a person who is, or who the accused believes is under the age of 18 years for the purpose of facilitating the commission of an offence under subsec. (2).

Section 172.2 makes it an offence to agree with a person or make an arrangement with a person by means of telecommunication to commit an offence under subsec. (2) with a person who is or who the accused believes is under the age of 18 years.

SYNOPSIS

Sections 286.1 to 286.5 represent Parliament's response to the Supreme Court's decision in *Canada (Attorney General) v. Bedford* , [2013] 3 S.C.R. 1101, 303 C.C.C. (3d) 146, which struck down a number of prostitution-related prohibitions. In general, with certain exceptions, they enact an "asymmetrical" model which criminalizes the purchasing of sexual services but not the selling.

Section 286.1 creates offences related to obtaining sexual services for consideration, or communicating with anyone for that purpose.

Subsection (1) creates the basic offences, which may be prosecuted summarily or by indictment, and which stipulate escalating minimum penalties for subsequent offences.

Subsection (2) creates an aggravated form of the same offence with a minimum sentence of imprisonment, which is committed where the person providing the sexual services is under the age of 18.

Subsection (3) provides that a previous conviction for the equivalent offence under the former s. 212(4) counts as a prior conviction for the purposes of subsec. (2).

Subsection (4) places strictures on how the court determines whether a conviction counts as a "subsequent offence". Only the sequence of convictions is to be considered.

MATERIAL BENEFIT FROM SEXUAL SERVICES / Material benefit from sexual services provided by person under 18 years / Presumption / Exception / No exception / Aggravating factor

286.2 (1) Everyone who receives a financial or other material benefit, knowing that it is obtained by or derived directly or indirectly from the commission of an offence under subsection 286.1(1), is guilty of an indictable offence and liable to imprisonment for a term of not more than 10 years.

(2) Everyone who receives a financial or other material benefit, knowing that it is obtained by or derived directly or indirectly from the commission of an offence under subsection 286.1(2), is guilty of an indictable offence and liable to imprisonment for a term of not more than 14 years and to a minimum punishment of imprisonment for a term of two years.

(3) For the purposes of subsections (1) and (2), evidence that a person lives with or is habitually in the company of a person who offers or provides sexual services for consideration is, in the absence of evidence to the contrary, proof that the person received a financial or other material benefit from those services.

(4) Subject to subsection (5), subsections (1) and (2) do not apply to a person who receives the benefit

    (a) in the context of a legitimate living arrangement with the person from whose sexual services the benefit is derived;

    (b) as a result of a legal or moral obligation of the person from whose sexual services the benefit is derived;

    (c) in consideration for a service or good that they offer, on the same terms and conditions, to the general public; or

    (d) in consideration for a service or good that they do not offer to the general public but that they offered or provided to the person from whose sexual services the benefit is derived, if they did not counsel or encourage that person to provide sexual services and the benefit is proportionate to the value of the service or good.

(5) Subsection (4) does not apply to a person who commits an offence under subsection (1) or (2) if that person

    (a) used, threatened to use or attempted to use violence, intimidation or coercion in relation to the person from whose sexual services the benefit is derived;

    (b) abused a position of trust, power or authority in relation to the person from whose sexual services the benefit is derived;

    (c) provided a drug, alcohol or any other intoxicating substance to the person from whose sexual services the benefit is derived for the purpose of aiding or abetting that person to offer or provide sexual services for consideration;

(*d*) **engaged in conduct, in relation to any person, that would constitute an offence under section 286.3; or**

(*e*) **received the benefit in the context of a commercial enterprise that offers sexual services for consideration.**

(6) If a person is convicted of an offence under this section, the court that imposes the sentence shall consider as an aggravating factor the fact that that person received the benefit in the context of a commercial enterprise that offers sexual services for consideration. 2014, c. 25, s. 20.

CROSS-REFERENCES

Other offences relating to sexual services are found in ss. 213, 286.1, 286.3 and 286.4.

Certain immunities to a charge on this provision are provided by s. 286.5.

This offence may be the basis for an application for an authorization to intercept private communications by reason of s. 183, or a video surveillance warrant under s. 487.01(5).

The accused may elect his mode of trial pursuant to s. 536(2).

For special procedures in respect of vulnerable witnesses, see cross-references under s. 286.1.

Section 718.01 provides that, in imposing a sentence for an offence involving the abuse of a person under the age of 18 years, the court shall give primary consideration to the objectives of denunciation and deterrence. Further, under s. 718.2, evidence that the offender, in committing the offence, abused a person under the age of 18 years is an aggravating circumstance.

This offence is a primary designated offence for the purpose of making a forensic DNA data bank order under s. 487.051.

Pursuant to s. 490.012, where an offender is convicted of the offence under subsec. (2), the judge shall make an order requiring the offender to comply with the *Sex Offender Information Registration Act*, S.C. 2004, c. 10. Where an offender is convicted under subsec. (1), such an order shall be made on application of the prosecutor if certain circumstances are present.

If a person is found guilty of the offence in subsec. (2) in respect of a person who is under 16 years of age, the court may impose an order of prohibition under s. 161 prohibiting the accused from attending certain public areas and facilities or taking certain employment that will bring him into contact with persons under the age of 16 years.

Section 171.1 makes it an offence to transmit, make available, distribute or sell sexually explicit material to a person who is, or who the accused believes is under the age of 18 years for the purpose of facilitating the commission of an offence under subsec. (2).

Section 172.2 makes it an offence to agree with a person or make an arrangement with a person by means of telecommunication to commit an offence under subsec. (2) with a person who is or who the accused believes is under the age of 18 years.

SYNOPSIS

This provision creates the indictable offence of receiving a material benefit from sexual services. In essence, it replaces the former s. 212(1)(*j*) — living on the avails of prostitution — which the Supreme Court struck down in *Canada (Attorney General) v. Bedford* , [2013] 3 S.C.R. 1101, 303 C.C.C. (3d) 146. The court held that the former law captured a number of non-exploitative relationships which were not connected to the law's purpose, and also that its negative effect on the security and safety of prostitutes was grossly disproportionate to its objective of protecting prostitutes from harm. This provision attempts to remedy those problems by way of a number of exceptions to liability in subsec. (4).

Subsection (1) sets out the basic offence, while subsec. (2) creates an aggravated form of the offence with a minimum sentence of imprisonment where the sexual services in question are provided by someone under the age of 18.

Subsection (3) creates an evidentiary presumption that a person who lives with (or is habitually in the company of) someone who provides sexual services is committing the offence.

Subsection (4) creates exceptions to liability, apparently targeting the kind of non-exploitative relationships that concerned the court in *Bedford, supra.*

Subsection (5) in turn creates a number of exceptions to the exceptions in subsec. (4).

Finally, subsec. (6) stipulates that committing this offence in the context of a commercial enterprise is to be considered an aggravating factor on sentence.

PROCURING / Procuring — person under 18 years

286.3 (1) Everyone who procures a person to offer or provide sexual services for consideration or, for the purpose of facilitating an offence under subsection 286.1(1), recruits, holds, conceals or harbours a person who offers or provides sexual services for consideration, or exercises control, direction or influence over the movements of that person, is guilty of an indictable offence and liable to imprisonment for a term of not more than 14 years.

(2) Everyone who procures a person under the age of 18 years to offer or provide sexual services for consideration or, for the purpose of facilitating an offence under subsection 286.1(2), recruits, holds, conceals or harbours a person under the age of 18 who offers or provides sexual services for consideration, or exercises control, direction or influence over the movements of that person, is guilty of an indictable offence and liable to imprisonment for a term of not more than 14 years and to a minimum punishment of imprisonment for a term of five years. 2014, c. 25, s. 20.

CROSS-REFERENCES

Other offences relating to sexual services are found in ss. 213, 286.1, 286.2 and 286.4.

Certain immunities to a charge on this provision are provided by s. 286.5.

This offence may be the basis for an application for an authorization to intercept private communications by reason of s. 183, or a video surveillance warrant under s. 487.01(5).

The accused may elect his mode of trial pursuant to s. 536(2).

For special procedures in respect of vulnerable witnesses, see cross-references under s. 286.1.

Section 718.01 provides that, in imposing a sentence for an offence involving the abuse of a person under the age of 18 years, the court shall give primary consideration to the objectives of denunciation and deterrence. Further, under s. 718.2, evidence that the offender, in committing the offence, abused a person under the age of 18 years is an aggravating circumstance.

This offence is a primary designated offence for the purpose of making a forensic DNA data bank order under s. 487.051.

Pursuant to s. 490.012, where an offender is convicted of the offence under subsec. (2), the judge shall make an order requiring the offender to comply with the *Sex Offender Information Registration Act*, S.C. 2004, c. 10. Where an offender is convicted under subsec. (1), such an order shall be made on application of the prosecutor if certain circumstances are present.

If a person is found guilty of the offence in subsec. (2) in respect of a person who is under 16 years of age, the court may impose an order of prohibition under s. 161 prohibiting the accused from attending certain public areas and facilities or taking certain employment that will bring him into contact with persons under the age of 16 years.

Section 171.1 makes it an offence to transmit, make available, distribute or sell sexually explicit material to a person who is, or who the accused believes is under the age of 18 years for the purpose of facilitating the commission of an offence under subsec. (2).

Section 172.2 makes it an offence to agree with a person or make an arrangement with a person by means of telecommunication to commit an offence under subsec. (2) with a person who is or who the accused believes is under the age of 18 years.

SYNOPSIS

This provision creates the indictable offence of procuring a person to provide sexual services. It is similar in many respects to the "receiving material benefits" offence under s. 286.2, but requires a more active degree of involvement.

Subsection (1) sets out the basic offence, while subsec. (2) creates an aggravated form of the offence with a minimum sentence of imprisonment where the sexual services in question are provided by someone under the age of 18.

ADVERTISING SEXUAL SERVICES.

286.4 Everyone who knowingly advertises an offer to provide sexual services for consideration is guilty of

    (*a*) **an indictable offence and liable to imprisonment for a term of not more than five years; or**

    (*b*) **an offence punishable on summary conviction and liable to imprisonment for a term of not more than 18 months. 2014, c. 25, s. 20.**

CROSS-REFERENCES

"Advertisement of sexual services" is defined in s. 164(8) for the purposes of that section.

Other offences relating to sexual services are found in ss. 213, 286.1, 286.2 and 286.3.

Certain immunities to a charge on this provision are provided by s. 286.5.

This offence may be the basis for an application for an authorization to intercept private communications by reason of s. 183, or a video surveillance warrant under s. 487.01(5).

Section 164 enacts an alternative procedure, *in rem* proceedings, for the seizure, forfeiture and restoration of advertisements for sexual services. Where an order has been made under s. 164, no proceedings may be taken under this section except with the consent of the Attorney General.

Section 164.1 sets out an *in rem* procedure for removal of advertisements for sexual services from computer systems.

Section 164.2 provides that a court that convicts a person of an offence under this section may order that any thing, other than real property, be forfeited to the Crown if the court is satisfied that the thing was used in the commission of the offence and is the property of the offender, another person who was a party to the offence, or a person who acquired the thing from such a person in circumstances giving rise to a reasonable inference that it was transferred to avoid a forfeiture order.

Where the prosecution elects to proceed by indictment on this offence then the accused may elect his mode of trial pursuant to s. 536(2). Where the prosecution elects to proceed by way of summary conviction then the trial of this offence is conducted by a summary conviction court pursuant to Part XXVII. In either case, release pending trial is determined by s. 515, although the accused is eligible for release by a peace officer under ss. 496 or 497, or by the officer in charge under s. 498.

For special procedures in respect of vulnerable witnesses, see cross-references under s. 286.1.

SYNOPSIS

This provision creates the offence of advertising sexual services.

In s. 164(8), "advertisement of sexual services" is defined to mean "any material — including a photographic, film, video, audio or other recording, made by any means, a visual representation or any written material — that is used to advertise sexual services contrary to section 286.4".

IMMUNITY — MATERIAL BENEFIT AND ADVERTISING / Immunity — aiding, abetting, etc.

286.5 (1) No person shall be prosecuted for

    (*a*) **an offence under section 286.2 if the benefit is derived from the provision of their own sexual services; or**

    (*b*) **an offence under section 286.4 in relation to the advertisement of their own sexual services.**

(2) No person shall be prosecuted for aiding, abetting, conspiring or attempting to commit an offence under any of sections 286.1 to 286.4 or being an accessory after the fact or counselling a person to be a party to such an offence, if the offence relates to the offering or provision of their own sexual services. 2014, c. 25, s. 20.

CROSS-REFERENCES

Sections 286.1 to 286.4 set out the offences to which this immunity-granting provision relates.

SYNOPSIS

This provision creates certain immunities to the offences in ss. 286.1 to 286.4, apparently meant to address some of the constitutional defects in the previous prostitution-related provisions identified by the court in *Canada (Attorney General) v. Bedford*, [2013] 3 S.C.R. 1101, 303 C.C.C. (3d) 146. Because the new regime is meant primarily to criminalize the buyers rather than the sellers of sexual services, this provision closes off avenues of principal and accessorial liability under which sex workers could otherwise face conviction. In particular, it provides that a person cannot be criminally liable for advertising or obtaining a material benefit from the person's own sexual services, nor can a person be guilty as a party to any of the offences where the sexual services in question are the person's own.

Abortion

PROCURING MISCARRIAGE / Woman procuring her own miscarriage / Definition of "means" / Exceptions / Information requirement / Definitions / "accredited hospital" / "approved hospital" / "board" / "Minister of Health" / "qualified medical practitioner" / "therapeutic abortion committee" / Requirement of consent not affected.

287. (1) Every one who, with intent to procure the miscarriage of a female person, whether or not she is pregnant, uses any means for the purpose of carrying out his intention is guilty of an indictable offence and liable to imprisonment for life.

(2) Every female person who, being pregnant, with intent to procure her own miscarriage, uses any means or permits any means to be used for the purpose of carrying out her intention is guilty of an indictable offence and liable to imprisonment for a term not exceeding two years.

(3) In this section, "means" includes
    (a) the administration of a drug or other noxious thing;
    (b) the use of an instrument; and
    (c) manipulation of any kind.

(4) Subsections (1) and (2) do not apply to
    (a) a qualified medical practitioner, other than a member of a therapeutic abortion committee for any hospital, who in good faith uses in an accredited or approved hospital any means for the purpose of carrying out his intention to procure the miscarriage of a female person, or
    (b) a female person who, being pregnant, permits a qualified medical practitioner to use in an accredited or approved hospital any means for the purpose of carrying out her intention to procure her own miscarriage,

if, before the use of those means, the therapeutic abortion committee for that accredited or approved hospital, by a majority of the members of the committee and at a meeting of the committee at which the case of the female person has been reviewed,
    (c) has by certificate in writing stated that in its opinion the continuation of the pregnancy of the female person would or would be likely to endanger her life or health, and
    (d) has caused a copy of such certificate to be given to the qualified medical practitioner.

(5) The Minister of Health of a province may by order

   (*a*) require a therapeutic abortion committee for any hospital in that province, or any member thereof, to furnish him with a copy of any certificate described in paragraph (4)(*c*) issued by that committee, together with such other information relating to the circumstances surrounding the issue of that certificate as he may require, or

   (*b*) require a medical practitioner who, in that province, has procured the miscarriage of any female person named in a certificate described in paragraph (4)(*c*), to furnish him with a copy of that certificate, together with such other information relating to the procuring of the miscarriage as he may require.

(6) For the purposes of subsections (4) and (5) and this subsection,

"accredited hospital" means a hospital accredited by the Canadian Council on Hospital Accreditation in which diagnostic services and medical, surgical and obstetrical treatment are provided;

"approved hospital" means a hospital in a province approved for the purposes of this section by the Minister of Health of that province;

"board" means the board of governors, management or directors, or the trustees, commission or other person or group of persons having the control and management of an accredited or approved hospital;

"Minister of Health" means

   (*a*) in the Provinces of Ontario, Quebec, New Brunswick, Manitoba, Prince Edward Island and Newfoundland and Labrador, the Minister of Health,

   (*b*) in the Provinces of Nova Scotia and Saskatchewan, the Minister of Public Health, and

   (*c*) in the Province of British Columbia, the Minister of Health Services and Hospital Insurance,

   (*d*) in the Province of Alberta, the Minister of Hospitals and Medical Care,

   (*e*) in Yukon, the Northwest Territories and Nunavut, the Minister of Health;

"qualified medical practitioner" means a person entitled to engage in the practice of medicine under the laws of the province in which the hospital referred to in subsection (4) is situated;

"therapeutic abortion committee" for any hospital means a committee, comprised of not less than three members each of whom is a qualified medical practitioner, appointed by the board of that hospital for the purpose of considering and determining questions relating to terminations of pregnancy within that hospital.

(7) Nothing in subsection (4) shall be construed as making unnecessary the obtaining of any authorization or consent that is or may be required, otherwise than under this Act, before any means are used for the purpose of carrying out an intention to procure the miscarriage of a female person. R.S., c. C-34, s. 251; 1974-75-76, c. 93, s. 22.1; 1993, Sch. III, s. 30; 1996, c. 8, s. 32(1)(*d*); 2002, c. 7, s. 141; 2015, c. 3, s. 48.

CROSS-REFERENCES

The related offence of supplying noxious things, etc., for purpose of procuring a miscarriage is found in s. 288.

ANNOTATIONS

This section is of no force and effect by reason of its violation of s. 7 of the Charter: *R. v. Morgentaler, Smoling and Scott*, [1988] 1 S.C.R. 30, 37 C.C.C. (3d) 449, 62 C.R. (3d) 1 (5:2).

   Provincial legislation, whose central purpose and dominant characteristic was the restriction of abortion as a socially undesirable practice which should be suppressed or punished, is *ultra vires* the province. The prohibition of the performance of abortions in certain circumstances with penal consequences is traditionally regarded as a part of the criminal law. The legislation in this case was designed to prevent the defendant from opening free-standing abortion clinics within the province: *R. v. Morgentaler*, [1993] 3 S.C.R. 463, 85 C.C.C. (3d) 118, 25 C.R. (4th) 179.

There are no substantive rights under the Quebec *Charter of Human Rights and Freedoms*, R.S.Q. 1977, c. C-12, nor the *Civil Code of Lower Canada*, upon which an injunction could be founded to restrain a woman from having an abortion. Similarly, the common law did not recognize any right in the foetus until born alive. Additionally, a father's interest in a foetus cannot support a right to veto a woman's decision in respect of that foetus, including the decision to have an abortion. Accordingly, the courts of Quebec were not entitled to grant an injunction to the father to restrain the mother from having an abortion: *Tremblay v. Daigle*, [1989] 2 S.C.R. 530, 62 D.L.R. (4th) 634, 102 N.R. 81 (9:0).

SUPPLYING NOXIOUS THINGS.

288. Every one who unlawfully supplies or procures a drug or other noxious thing or an instrument or thing, knowing that it is intended to be used or employed to procure the miscarriage of a female person, whether or not she is pregnant, is guilty of an indictable offence and liable to imprisonment for a term not exceeding two years. R.S., c. C-34, s. 252.

CROSS-REFERENCES

The accused may elect his mode of trial pursuant to s. 536(2). Release pending trial is determined by s. 515, although the accused is eligible for release by the officer in charge under s. 498. The actual offence of procuring a miscarriage (abortion) is found in s. 287. However, as noted thereunder, s. 287 has been held to be unconstitutional.

SYNOPSIS

This section describes the indictable offence of supplying or procuring a drug or instrument which is to be used to cause the miscarriage of a female person. The accused must know that the item referred to above is intended to be employed to cause a miscarriage. The female need not be pregnant for the offence to be committed. Punishment upon conviction on indictment is a maximum jail term of two years.

ANNOTATIONS

In determining whether the accused knew that the drug he supplied was intended to be used to procure a miscarriage, it was irrelevant that the abortifacient was supplied to an unidentified policewoman who had no intention of using it: *R. v. Irwin*, [1968] S.C.R. 462, [1968] 4 C.C.C. 119, 3 C.R.N.S. 377.

Venereal Diseases

289. [*Repealed*, R.S.C. 1985, c. 27 (1st Supp.), s. 41.]

Offences Against Conjugal Rights

BIGAMY / Matters of defence / Incompetency no defence / Validity presumed / Act or omission by accused.

290. (1) Every one commits bigamy who
   (a) in Canada,
      (i) being married, goes through a form of marriage with another person,

      (ii) **knowing that another person is married, goes through a form of marriage with that person, or**

     (iii) **on the same day or simultaneously, goes through a form of marriage with more than one person; or**

  (*b*) **being a Canadian citizen resident in Canada leaves Canada with intent to do anything mentioned in subparagraphs (*a*)(i) to (iii) and, pursuant thereto, does outside Canada anything mentioned in those subparagraphs in circumstances mentioned therein.**

(2) No person commits bigamy by going through a form of marriage if

  (*a*) **that person in good faith and on reasonable grounds believes that his spouse is dead,**

  (*b*) **the spouse of that person has been continuously absent from him for seven years immediately preceding the time when he goes through the form of marriage, unless he knew that his spouse was alive at any time during those seven years,**

  (*c*) **that person has been divorced from the bond of the first marriage, or**

  (*d*) **the former marriage has been declared void by a court of competent jurisdiction.**

(3) Where a person is alleged to have committed bigamy, it is not a defence that the parties would, if unmarried, have been incompetent to contract marriage under the law of the place where the offence is alleged to have been committed.

(4) Every marriage or form of marriage shall, for the purpose of this section, be deemed to be valid unless the accused establishes that it was invalid.

(5) No act or omission on the part of an accused who is charged with bigamy invalidates a marriage or form of marriage that is otherwise valid. R.S., c. C-34, s. 254.

CROSS-REFERENCES

"Form of marriage" is defined in s. 214.

   The punishment for bigamy is found in s. 291(1). The accused may elect his mode of trial pursuant to s. 536(2). Release pending trial is determined by s. 515, although the accused is eligible for release by the officer in charge under s. 498.

   The accused's spouse is a competent and compellable witness at the instance of the Crown by virtue of s. 4(2). Section 291(2) provides for a means of proof of the marriage by way of certificate. Section 25(1) of the *Interpretation Act*, R.S.C. 1985, c. I-21, provides that "Where an enactment provides that a document is evidence of a fact without anything in the context to indicate that the document is conclusive evidence, then, in any judicial proceedings, the document is admissible in evidence and the fact is deemed to be established in the absence of any evidence to the contrary".

   The related offence of polygamy is found in s. 293 and of solemnizing a marriage in contravention of the laws of the province in s. 295.

SYNOPSIS

This section describes the offence of bigamy. Every one commits this offence who, in Canada goes through a form of marriage with a person while already married to another person, who goes through a form of marriage with another person knowing that person to be married to someone else, or who goes through a form of marriage with more than one other person simultaneously. If a resident Canadian citizen leaves Canada to do any of the things described above, that person also commits the offence of bigamy. These general prohibitions do not apply if the person in *good faith* and on *reasonable grounds* believes that his spouse is dead, if the person has been divorced from the spouse, if the spouse of the person has been absent for seven years without interruption and nothing has been heard of the spouse during that time, or if the former marriage has been declared void by a court of competent jurisdiction. A person charged under this section cannot use as a defence the fact that there would be a legal impediment to the original marriage in the place where the offence is alleged to have been committed. Unless the accused establishes otherwise, there is a presumption in this section that all forms of marriage are valid and no act or omission of the accused may be set up as invalidating the marriage.

ANNOTATIONS

All that is necessary is to prove that the ceremony was one known to and recognized by the law as capable of producing a valid marriage, and accordingly independent circumstances, such as the lack of a marriage licence, which might otherwise create a legal disability, are irrelevant: *R. v. Howard*, [1966] 3 C.C.C. 91, 54 W.W.R. 484 (B.C. Co. Ct.).

It has been held in a number of cases that a *bona fide* but mistaken belief that the first marriage had been dissolved through divorce was no defence to a charge under this section: *R. v. Bleiler* (1912), 19 C.C.C. 249, 1 D.L.R. 787 (Alta. S.C.); *R. v. Morgan* (1942), 78 C.C.C. 129, [1942] 4 D.L.R. 321 (N.S.S.C.); *R. v. Brinkley* (1907), 12 C.C.C. 454, 14 O.L.R. 434 (C.A.); *R. v. Queneau* (1949), 95 C.C.C. 187, 8 C.R. 235 (Que. C.A.). These cases are in accord with what was the leading English case of *R. v. Wheat and Stocks* (1921), 15 Cr. App. R. 134. In the later case of *R. v. King* (1963), 48 Cr. App. R. 17, *R. v. Wheat and Stocks* was distinguished and explained as being limited to the case where the accused's belief is that the first marriage was dissolved as a result of a divorce. In *R. v. King*, the court held that a belief that the first marriage was invalid would be a defence although the defence was rejected on the facts of the case. Interestingly, the accused's belief that the first marriage was invalid was due to his mistaken belief that he had not been validly divorced from an even earlier marriage. *R. v. Wheat and Stocks* was finally overruled by the Court of Appeal in *R. v. Gould* (1968), 52 Cr. App. R. 152, where it was held that a belief that the former marriage had been dissolved is a defence to the charge. It was held in *Gould* that the belief must be an honest one based on reasonable grounds.

The defence was accepted in *R. v. Woolridge* (1979), 49 C.C.C. (2d) 300 (Sask. Prov. Ct.), where the trial judge held that an honest *and* reasonable belief that the previous marriage had been dissolved by divorce was a defence to the charge under this section applying *R. v. Haugen* (1923), 41 C.C.C. 132, [1923] 2 W.W.R. 709 (Sask. C.A.), where it was held that an honest and reasonable belief that the accused's first marriage was a nullity because his first wife was still validly married was a defence.

It is submitted that such a defence is properly recognized and that a mistaken belief that the previous marriage had been dissolved by divorce should be a defence if the belief is honestly held. While some cases have foundered on the issue of whether the accused's mistake is one of fact or law, it is submitted that applying the decision of the Supreme Court of Canada in *R. v. Prue; R. v. Baril*, [1979] 2 S.C.R. 547, 46 C.C.C. (2d) 257, 8 C.R. (3d) 68 (a case under former s. 238(3)) this kind of mistake should be recognized as a mistake of fact. Finally, it is submitted that it is sufficient if the belief is honestly held and need not be based on reasonable grounds, applying *R. v. Rees*, [1956] S.C.R. 640, 115 C.C.C. 1, 24 C.R. 1; *D.P.P. v. Morgan* (1975), 61 Cr. App. R. 136 (H.L.); and *R. v. Pappajohn*, [1980] 2 S.C.R. 120, 52 C.C.C. (2d) 481, 111 D.L.R. (3d) 1.

PUNISHMENT / Certificate of marriage.

291. (1) Every one who commits bigamy is guilty of an indictable offence and liable to imprisonment for a term not exceeding five years.

(2) For the purposes of this section a certificate of marriage issued under the authority of law is evidence of the marriage or form of marriage to which it relates without proof of the signature or official character of the person by whom it purports to be signed. R.S., c. C-34, s. 255.

CROSS-REFERENCES

"Form of marriage" is defined in s. 214.

The offence of bigamy is defined in s. 290. The accused may elect his mode of trial pursuant to s. 536(2). Release pending trial is determined by s. 515, although the accused is eligible for release by the officer in charge under s. 498.

The accused's spouse is a competent and compellable witness at the instance of the Crown by virtue of s. 4(2).

With respect to subsec. (2), note than s. 25(1) of the *Interpretation Act*, R.S.C. 1985, c. I-21, provides that "Where an enactment provides that a document is evidence of a fact without anything in the context to indicate that the document is conclusive evidence, then, in any judicial proceedings, the document is admissible in evidence and the fact is deemed to be established in the absence of any evidence to the contrary".

For notes respecting mistake generally, see notes under s. 19.

The related offence of polygamy is found in s. 293 and of solemnizing a marriage in contravention of the laws of the province in s. 295.

SYNOPSIS

This section sets out the punishment for bigamy and facilitates the proof of a prior marriage. A person convicted of bigamy is guilty of an indictable offence and liable to a maximum term of imprisonment of five years. It is not necessary to prove the signature or official character of a person signing a marriage certificate for it to be admissible as evidence of a lawful prior marriage.

PROCURING FEIGNED MARRIAGE / Corroboration.

292. (1) Every person who procures or knowingly aids in procuring a feigned marriage between himself and another person is guilty of an indictable offence and liable to imprisonment for a term not exceeding five years.

(2) No person shall be convicted of an offence under this section on the evidence of only one witness unless the evidence of that witness is corroborated in a material particular by evidence that implicates the accused. R.S., c. C-34, s. 256; 1980-81-82-83, c. 125, s. 21.

CROSS-REFERENCES

"Form of marriage" is defined in s. 214.

The accused's spouse is a competent and compellable witness at the instance of the Crown by virtue of s. 4(2).

The accused may elect his mode of trial pursuant to s. 536(2). Release pending trial is determined by s. 515, although the accused is eligible for release by the officer in charge under s. 498.

The related offence of pretending to solemnize a marriage is found in s. 294 and of solemnizing a marriage in contravention of the laws of the province in s. 295.

SYNOPSIS

This section imposes criminal liability upon any person, *male* or *female*, who procures or *knowingly* aids in procuring a feigned marriage between that person and another person. The offence is indictable and the maximum sentence is a term of five years of imprisonment. No person can be convicted of an offence under this section on the *uncorroborated evidence* of one witness.

ANNOTATIONS

In *R. v. B. (G.)*, [1990] 2 S.C.R. 3, 56 C.C.C. (3d) 161 (5:0), the court considered the effect of, now repealed, s. 586 which provided that no person shall be convicted on the unsworn evidence of a child, "unless the evidence of the child is corroborated in a material particular by evidence that implicates the accused". The wording is thus almost identical to subsec. (2) of this section. It was there held that the requirement that the corroborating evidence implicate the accused requires only that the evidence confirm in some material particular the story of the witness giving the evidence which required corroboration. The confirming evidence need not also itself implicate the accused.

POLYGAMY / Evidence in case of polygamy.

293. (1) Every one who

(*a*) **practises or enters into or in any manner agrees or consents to practise or enter into**

(i) **any form of polygamy, or**

(ii) **any kind of conjugal union with more than one person at the same time,**

whether or not it is by law recognized as a binding form of marriage; or

(*b*) **celebrates, assists or is a party to a rite, ceremony, contract or consent that purports to sanction a relationship mentioned in subparagraph (*a*)(i) or (ii),**

is guilty of an indictable offence and liable to imprisonment for a term not exceeding five years.

(2) Where an accused is charged with an offence under this section, no averment or proof of the method by which the alleged relationship was entered into, agreed to or consented to is necessary in the indictment or upon the trial of the accused, nor is it necessary on the trial to prove that the persons who are alleged to have entered into the relationship had or intended to have sexual intercourse. R.S., c. C-34, s. 257.

CROSS-REFERENCES

"Form of marriage" is defined in s. 214.

The accused's spouse is a competent and compellable witness at the instance of the Crown by virtue of s. 4(2).

The accused may elect his mode of trial pursuant to s. 536(2). Release pending trial is determined by s. 515, although the accused is eligible for release by the officer in charge under s. 498.

The related offence of bigamy is found in s. 291 and of solemnizing a marriage in contravention of the laws of the province in s. 295.

SYNOPSIS

This section makes it a criminal offence to agree, consent to or practise any form of polygamy or conjugal union with more than one person at the same time. It also imposes criminal liability on anyone who celebrates, assists or is party to a rite, ceremony, contract or consent that sanctions a relationship described above. The offence is indictable with a maximum term of imprisonment of five years. Subsection (2) states that it is not necessary to include in the indictment or to prove at trial the method by which the relationship was entered into, agreed to or consented to, nor is it necessary to establish at trial that the parties had, or intended to have, sexual intercourse.

ANNOTATIONS

In *Reference re: Criminal Code (Can), s. 293* (2011), 279 C.C.C. (3d) 1, the British Columbia Supreme Court held that this provision is constitutionally valid, but should be read down to exclude the criminalization of persons under 18 who enter into a prohibited marriage. Though the offence triggers a breach of s. 2(*a*) in respect of religious minorities who avow a commitment to plural marriage, it is demonstrably justified under s. 1 because of the social and individual harms associated with polygamy.

The words "any kind of conjugal union" in subsec. (1)(*a*)(ii) predicate some form of union under the guise of marriage and were not intended to apply to adultery even where one or both of the persons are married at the time they are living together: *R. v. Tolhurst, R. v. Wright* (1937), 68 C.C.C. 319 (Ont. C.A.).

FORCED MARRIAGE.

293.1 Everyone who celebrates, aids or participates in a marriage rite or ceremony knowing that one of the persons being married is marrying against their will is guilty of an indictable offence and liable to imprisonment for a term not exceeding five years. 2015, c. 29, s. 9.

CROSS-REFERENCES
The terms "marriage rite" and "marriage ceremony" are not defined.

SYNOPSIS
This section makes it an offence to celebrate, aid or participate in a marriage rite or ceremony where one of the persons being married is being forced to do so. The offence is indictable and punishable by up to five years' imprisonment.

MARRIAGE UNDER AGE OF 16 YEARS.

293.2 Everyone who celebrates, aids or participates in a marriage rite or ceremony knowing that one of the persons being married is under the age of 16 years is guilty of an indictable offence and liable to imprisonment for a term not exceeding five years. 2015, c. 29, s. 9.

CROSS-REFERENCES
The terms "marriage rite" and "marriage ceremony" are not defined.

SYNOPSIS
This section makes it an offence to celebrate, aid or participate in a marriage rite or ceremony where one of the persons being married is under the age of 16, regardless of whether that person is doing so voluntarily. The offence is indictable and punishable by up to five years' imprisonment.

Unlawful Solemnization of Marriage

PRETENDING TO SOLEMNIZE MARRIAGE.

294. Every one who
(*a*) **solemnizes or pretends to solemnize a marriage without lawful authority, the proof of which lies on him, or**
(*b*) **procures a person to solemnize a marriage knowing that he is not lawfully authorized to solemnize the marriage,**
is guilty of an indictable offence and liable to imprisonment for a term not exceeding two years. R.S., c. C-34, s. 258.

CROSS-REFERENCES
"Form of marriage" is defined in s. 214.

The accused's spouse is a competent and compellable witness at the instance of the Crown by virtue of s. 4(2).

The accused may elect his mode of trial pursuant to s. 536(2). Release pending trial is determined by s. 515, although the accused is eligible for release by the officer in charge under s. 498.

The related offence of procuring a feigned marriage is found in s. 292.

SYNOPSIS

This section prohibits any person who does not have the lawful authority to do so from solemnizing or pretending to solemnize a marriage. It also prohibits any person from knowingly procuring an unqualified person to solemnize a marriage. A person charged with an offence under this section must prove that he is, in fact, lawfully entitled to solemnize a marriage — a requirement that has potential Charter implications.

A person convicted under this section is guilty of an indictable offence and liable to a maximum term of imprisonment of two years.

MARRIAGE CONTRARY TO LAW.

295. Everyone who, being lawfully authorized to solemnize marriage, knowingly solemnizes a marriage in contravention of federal law or the laws of the province in which the marriage is solemnized is guilty of an indictable offence and liable to imprisonment for a term not exceeding two years. R.S., c. C-34, s. 259; 2015, c. 29, s. 10.

CROSS-REFERENCES

"Form of marriage" is defined in s. 214.

The accused may elect his mode of trial pursuant to s. 536(2). Release pending trial is determined by s. 515, although the accused is eligible for release by the officer in charge under s. 498.

The related offence of bigamy is found in s. 291, of polygamy in s. 293, of forced marriage in s. 293.1, and of marriage under the age of 16 years in s. 293.2.

SYNOPSIS

This section imposes criminal liability on any person who is lawfully authorized to solemnize a marriage, but who *knowingly* solemnizes a marriage which contravenes either federal law or the law of the province where the marriage takes place. The offence is indictable and the maximum term of imprisonment is two years.

Blasphemous Libel

OFFENCE / Question of fact / Saving.

296. (1) Every one who publishes a blasphemous libel is guilty of an indictable offence and liable to imprisonment for a term not exceeding two years.

(2) It is a question of fact whether or not any matter that is published is a blasphemous libel.

(3) No person shall be convicted of an offence under this section for expressing in good faith and in decent language, or attempting to establish by argument used in good faith and conveyed in decent language, an opinion upon a religious subject. R.S., c. C-34, s. 260.

CROSS-REFERENCES

The term "publishes" is not defined in this section, but it may be that the definition in s. 299 applies in part to this section as well as to the defamatory libel offence.

The accused may elect his mode of trial pursuant to s. 536(2). Release pending trial is determined by s. 515, although the accused is eligible for release by the officer in charge under s. 498.

Section 584(1) provides that no count for publishing a blasphemous libel is insufficient by reason only that it does not set out the words that are alleged to be libellous. However, under s. 587(1)(*e*), particulars may be ordered further describing any writing or words that are the subject of the charge. Under s. 584(2), a count for publishing a libel may charge that the published matter was written in a sense that, by innuendo, made the publication thereof criminal and may specify that sense without any introductory assertion to show how the matter was written in that sense. Under s. 584(3), it is sufficient to prove that the matter was libellous, with or without innuendo.

Seditious libel is dealt with in ss. 59 to 61, defamatory libel in ss. 297 to 317 and hate propaganda in ss. 318 to 320. Publishing false news is an offence under s. 181.

SYNOPSIS

This section imposes criminal liability on anyone who publishes a blasphemous libel. The offence is indictable and carries a maximum punishment of two years' imprisonment. The determination of whether or not published material constitutes a blasphemous libel is a question of fact, but the term "blasphemous libel" is not defined in the section. Subsection (3) attempts to deal with the issue of freedom of speech by specifying that no person will be convicted of this offence if that person expresses an opinion or establishes an argument in good faith and in decent language on a religious topic. This rather archaic section, if used, would, in all likelihood, be challenged under the Charter.

Defamatory Libel

DEFINITION OF "NEWSPAPER".

297. In sections 303, 304 and 308, "newspaper" means any paper, magazine or periodical containing public news, intelligence or reports of events, or any remarks or observations thereon, printed for sale and published periodically or in parts or numbers, at intervals not exceeding thirty-one days between the publication of any two such papers, parts or numbers, and any paper, magazine or periodical printed in order to be dispersed and made public, weekly or more often, or at intervals not exceeding thirty-one days, that contains advertisements, exclusively or principally. R.S., c. C-34, s. 261.

CROSS-REFERENCES

The calculation of days is dealt with in s. 27 of the *Interpretation Act*, R.S.C. 1985, c. I-21.

SYNOPSIS

This section defines the term "newspaper" for the purpose of ss. 303, 304 and 308. Whether a publication is a newspaper depends on the frequency of publication and subject matter.

DEFINITION / Mode of expression.

298. (1) A defamatory libel is matter published, without lawful justification or excuse, that is likely to injure the reputation of any person by exposing him to hatred, contempt or ridicule, or that is designed to insult the person of or concerning whom it is published.

(2) A defamatory libel may be expressed directly or by insinuation or irony
    (a) in words legibly marked upon any substance; or
    (b) by any object signifying a defamatory libel otherwise than by words. R.S., c. C-34, s. 262.

CROSS-REFERENCES

Publishing a libel is defined in s. 299.

The punishment for publishing a defamatory libel known to be false is a maximum of five years under s. 300. The punishment for publishing a defamatory libel is a maximum of two years under s. 301. The punishment for extortion by libel is a maximum of five years under s. 302. For all these offences, the accused may elect his mode of trial pursuant to s. 536(2). Release pending trial is determined by s. 515, although the accused is eligible for release by the officer in charge under s. 498.

Liability of the proprietor of a newspaper is dealt with in s. 303. Various defences or excuses for publishing a defamatory libel are set out in ss. 304 to 316. Section 317 provides for a special verdict in the case of defamatory libel. Section 584(1) provides that no count for publishing a defamatory libel is insufficient by reason only that it does not set out the words that are alleged to be libellous. However, under s. 587(1)(*e*), particulars may be ordered further describing any writing or words that are the subject of the charge. Under s. 584(2), a count for publishing a libel may charge that the published matter was written in a sense that, by innuendo, made the publication thereof criminal and may specify that sense without any introductory assertion to show how the matter was written in that sense. Under s. 584(3), it is sufficient to prove that the matter was libellous, with or without innuendo. The plea of justification in cases of defamatory libel is dealt with in ss. 607(2), 611 and 612. Under s. 612(3), where the accused is convicted, the court may consider, in pronouncing sentence, whether the offence was aggravated or mitigated by the plea. Under s. 637, a private prosecutor has no right to stand jurors aside. Sections 728 and 729 make special provision for costs in cases of defamatory libel.

Seditious libel is dealt with in ss. 59 to 61, blasphemous libel in s. 296 and hate propaganda in ss. 318 to 320. Publishing false news is an offence under s. 181.

SYNOPSIS

This section defines defamatory libel and specifies that it may be expressed directly or by insinuation or irony in words legibly marked or through an object otherwise than by words. A defamatory libel is a matter published that is likely to injure the reputation of any person by exposing that person to hatred, contempt, ridicule or insult. Furthermore, a defamatory libel must be published *without lawful justification*.

ANNOTATIONS

This section is not so vague as to infringe s. 7 of the *Canadian Charter of Rights and Freedoms*. While this section infringes the guarantee to freedom of expression in s. 2(*b*) of the Charter, properly interpreted it is valid as a reasonable limit under s. 1 of the Charter. In particular, when regard is had to the French version of this section, it is apparent that the phrase "designed to insult" in subsec. (1) requires proof of a grave insult: *R. v. Lucas*, [1998] 1 S.C.R. 439, 123 C.C.C. (3d) 97.

PUBLISHING.

299. A person publishes a libel when he
  (*a*) **exhibits it in public;**
  (*b*) **causes it to be read or seen; or**
  (*c*) **shows or delivers it, or causes it to be shown or delivered, with intent that it should be read or seen by the person whom it defames or by any other person.**
  R.S., c. C-34, s. 263.

CROSS-REFERENCES

Defamatory libel is defined in s. 298.

SYNOPSIS

This section defines the term "publishing" as it relates to libel. The section holds that a person publishes a libel when that person exhibits it in public, causes it to be read or viewed, or causes it to be shown or delivered *with the intent* that it should be read or seen by any other person.

ANNOTATIONS

This section is not so vague as to infringe s. 7 of *Canadian Charter of Rights and Freedoms*. While this section infringes the guarantee to freedom of expression in s. 2(*b*) of the Charter, it is valid as a reasonable limit under s. 1 of the Charter, except for that part of para. (*c*) that makes it an offence, although the intent is only to show it to the person defamed. Accordingly, the words "by the person whom it defames or" should be severed from para. (*c*). The phrase "any other person" will not pertain to the situation where only the person defamed is shown the defamatory libel: *R. v. Lucas*, [1998] 1 S.C.R. 439, 123 C.C.C. (3d) 97.

PUNISHMENT OF LIBEL KNOWN TO BE FALSE.

300. Every one who publishes a defamatory libel that he knows is false is guilty of an indictable offence and liable to imprisonment for a term not exceeding five years. R.S., c. C-34, s. 264.

CROSS-REFERENCES

Defamatory libel is defined in s. 298 and see cross-references under that section concerning related offences, special procedural provisions and defences or excuses. Publishing is defined in s. 299. As to vicarious liability of a newspaper proprietor, see s. 303.

The accused may elect his mode of trial pursuant to s. 536(2). Release pending trial is determined by s. 515, although the accused is eligible for release by the officer in charge under s. 498.

SYNOPSIS

This section imposes criminal liability upon any person who publishes, as defined in s. 299, a defamatory libel, as defined in s. 298. The Crown must prove that the accused intended to defame the victim. Any person convicted under this section is guilty of an indictable offence with a maximum term of imprisonment of five years.

ANNOTATIONS

This section is not so vague as to infringe s. 7 of the *Canadian Charter of Rights and Freedoms*. While this section infringes the guarantee to freedom of expression in s. 2(*b*) of the Charter, properly interpreted, it is valid as a reasonable limit under s. 1 of the Charter. It would be contrary to constitutional principles to interpret this section as requiring anything less than a subjective intent to defame. Accordingly, the Crown can only make out the offence if it proves beyond a reasonable doubt that the accused intended to defame the victim: *R. v. Lucas*, [1998] 1 S.C.R. 439, 123 C.C.C. (3d) 97.

PUNISHMENT FOR DEFAMATORY LIBEL.

301. Every one who publishes a defamatory libel is guilty of an indictable offence and liable to imprisonment for a term not exceeding two years. R.S., c. C-34, s. 265.

CROSS-REFERENCES

Defamatory libel is defined in s. 298 and see cross-references under that section concerning related offences, special procedural provisions and defences or excuses. Publishing is defined in s. 299. As to vicarious liability of a newspaper proprietor, see s. 303.

The accused may elect his mode of trial pursuant to s. 536(2). Release pending trial is determined by s. 515, although the accused is eligible for release by the officer in charge under s. 498.

SYNOPSIS

This section provides that a person who is convicted of publishing a defamatory libel is guilty of an indictable offence, with a maximum term of imprisonment of two years. The difference between this section and s. 300 is that there is no requirement in this section that the libel be false.

ANNOTATIONS

This section was held to be of no force and effect as violating s. 2 of the *Canadian Charter of Rights and Freedoms* and not constituting a reasonable limit under s. 1: *R. v. Prior* (2008), 231 C.C.C. (3d) 12 (Nfld. & Lab. S.C.T.D.); *R. v. Gill* (1996), 29 O.R. (3d) 250 (Gen. Div.); and *R. v. Lucas* (1995), 129 Sask. R. 53 (Q.B.). [**Note:** There was no appeal from the finding in *R. v. Lucas* that this section is unconstitutional. The decision of the Supreme Court of Canada with respect to the constitutionality of s. 300 in *Lucas* is noted above, under that section.]

EXTORTION BY LIBEL / Idem / Punishment.

302. (1) Every one commits an offence who, with intent
    (*a*) **to extort money from any person, or**
    (*b*) **to induce a person to confer on or procure for another person an appointment or office of profit or trust,**
publishes or threatens to publish or offers to abstain from publishing or to prevent the publication of a defamatory libel.

(2) Every one commits an offence who, as the result of the refusal of any person to permit money to be extorted or to confer or procure an appointment or office of profit or trust, publishes or threatens to publish a defamatory libel.

(3) Every one who commits an offence under this section is guilty of an indictable offence and liable to imprisonment for a term not exceeding five years. R.S., c. C-34, s. 266.

CROSS-REFERENCES

Defamatory libel is defined in s. 298 and see cross-references under that section concerning related offences, special procedural provisions and defences or excuses. Publishing is defined in s. 299. The accused may elect his mode of trial pursuant to s. 536(2). Release pending trial is determined by s. 515, although the accused is eligible for release by the officer in charge under s. 498.

The general extortion offence is found in s. 346.

SYNOPSIS

This section describes the offence of extortion by libel. It states that anyone who, *with intent*, publishes, threatens to publish, or offers to refrain from or prevent the publication of a defamatory libel in order to extort money from a person or to induce that person to confer an appointment or office of profit or trust upon another person, commits an offence. An offence under this section is also committed if, as a result of a person's refusal to do any of the things described in subsec. (1), anyone threatens to publish, or in fact publishes a defamatory libel. The offences set out in this section are indictable and carry a maximum term of imprisonment of five years.

PROPRIETOR OF NEWSPAPER PRESUMED RESPONSIBLE / General authority to manager when negligence / Selling newspapers.

303. (1) The proprietor of a newspaper shall be deemed to publish defamatory matter that is inserted and published therein, unless he proves that the defamatory matter was inserted in the newspaper without his knowledge and without negligence on his part.

(2) Where the proprietor of a newspaper gives to a person general authority to manage or conduct the newspaper as editor or otherwise, the insertion by that person of defamatory matter in the newspaper shall, for the purposes of subsection (1), be deemed not to be negligence on the part of the proprietor unless it is proved that

> (*a*) he intended the general authority to include authority to insert defamatory matter in the newspaper; or
>
> (*b*) he continued to confer general authority after he knew that it had been exercised by the insertion of defamatory matter in the newspaper.

(3) No person shall be deemed to publish a defamatory libel by reason only that he sells a number or part of a newspaper that contains a defamatory libel, unless he knows that the number or part contains defamatory matter or that defamatory matter is habitually contained in the newspaper. R.S., c. C-34, s. 267.

CROSS-REFERENCES

The term "newspaper" is defined in s. 303. Defamatory libel is defined in s. 298 and see cross-references under that section concerning related offences, special procedural provisions and defences or excuses. Publishing is defined in s. 299. The liability of a party generally is set out in ss. 21 and 22.

SYNOPSIS

This section sets out the conditions under which a proprietor or vendor of a newspaper, as that term is defined in s. 297, is *deemed to publish defamatory matter*. The proprietor of a newspaper must prove that any *defamatory matter* in his newspaper was inserted *without* his *knowledge* and *without negligence* on his part or else he is deemed to have published it. If the proprietor has given authority to another person as manager or editor of the newspaper and that person has inserted *defamatory matter* in the newspaper, no negligence will be ascribed to the proprietor unless the prosecution proves that he intended to give the manager or editor the authority to insert *defamatory matter* in the newspaper, or allowed the manager or editor to continue to exercise general authority after the *defamatory matter* had been inserted in the newspaper. Subsection (3) states that a vendor of newspapers containing a *defamatory libel* will not be deemed to have published that *defamatory libel* unless the vendor *knows* that such material is, in fact, contained in the newspaper or that the newspaper habitually carries it.

SELLING BOOK CONTAINING DEFAMATORY LIBEL / Sale by servant.

304. (1) No person shall be deemed to publish a defamatory libel by reason only that he sells a book, magazine, pamphlet or other thing, other than a newspaper that contains a defamatory matter if, at the time of the sale, he does not know that it contains the defamatory matter.

(2) Where a servant, in the course of his employment, sells a book, magazine, pamphlet or other thing, other than a newspaper, the employer shall be deemed not to publish any defamatory matter contained therein unless it is proved that the employer authorized the sale knowing that

> (*a*) defamatory matter was contained therein; or
>
> (*b*) defamatory matter was habitually contained therein, in the case of a periodical. R.S., c. C-34, s. 268.

CROSS-REFERENCES

The term "newspaper" is defined in s. 303. Defamatory libel is defined in s. 298 and see cross-references under that section concerning related offences, special procedural provisions and other defences or excuses. Publishing is defined in s. 299. As to vicarious liability of a newspaper proprietor, see s. 303.

SYNOPSIS

This section sets out the circumstances in which a person who sells a book, pamphlet or publication other than a newspaper that contains *defamatory matter* is not deemed to have published a *defamatory libel*. The seller of the item mentioned in subsec. (1) is not deemed to have published a *defamatory libel* if, at the time of sale, he did not know that the item contained *defamatory matter*. Similarly, where an employee sells an item containing *defamatory matter*, the employer will not be deemed to have published that *defamatory matter* unless the prosecution proves that the employer knew the matter was contained in the item or, in the case of a periodical, that the item habitually contained such *defamatory matter*.

PUBLISHING PROCEEDINGS OF COURTS OF JUSTICE.

305. No person shall be deemed to publish a defamatory libel by reason only that he publishes defamatory matter

    (*a*) **in a proceeding held before or under the authority of a court exercising judicial authority; or**

    (*b*) **in an inquiry made under the authority of an Act or by order of Her Majesty, or under the authority of a public department or a department of the government of a province. R.S., c. C-34, s. 269.**

CROSS-REFERENCES

The term "newspaper" is defined in s. 303. Defamatory libel is defined in s. 298 and see cross-references under that section concerning related offences, special procedural provisions and other defences or excuses. Publishing is defined in s. 299. As to vicarious liability of a newspaper proprietor, see s. 303.

Note s. 166 which makes it an offence to publish certain judicial proceedings calculated to injure public morals or respecting marriage, judicial separation or restitution of conjugal rights.

SYNOPSIS

This section describes a general exemption from the provisions that apply to publishing *defamatory libel* for those persons who publish *defamatory matter* in a court proceeding or an authorized inquiry.

PARLIAMENTARY PAPERS.

306. No person shall be deemed to publish a defamatory libel by reason only that he

    (*a*) **publishes to the Senate or House of Commons or to a legislature of a province, defamatory matter contained in a petition to the Senate or House of Commons or to the legislature of a province, as the case may be;**

    (*b*) **publishes by order or under the authority of the Senate or House of Commons or of a legislature of a province, a paper containing defamatory matter; or**

    (*c*) **publishes, in good faith and without ill-will to the person defamed, an extract from or abstract of a petition or paper mentioned in paragraph (*a*) or (*b*). R.S., c. C-34, s. 270.**

CROSS-REFERENCES

Defamatory libel is defined in s. 298 and see cross-references under that section concerning related offences, special procedural provisions and other defences or excuses. Publishing is defined in s. 299. As to vicarious liability of a newspaper proprietor, see s. 303. Section 307 creates the related defence of publication of fair reports of parliamentary, legislative or judicial proceedings. Section 316 contains provision for proof that the matter alleged to be defamatory was published by order or under the authority of Parliament or of the legislature.

SYNOPSIS

This section, like s. 305, describes a general exemption from the provisions that apply to publishing a *defamatory libel* for those persons who publish *defamatory matter* contained in a petition to the Senate, House of Commons, or legislature of a province, who publish under the authority of these bodies a paper containing *defamatory matter*, or who publish, *in good faith* and without *ill-will* to the person defamed, an extract from or abstract of the documents referred to above.

FAIR REPORTS OF PARLIAMENTARY OR JUDICIAL PROCEEDINGS / Divorce proceedings an exception.

307. (1) No person shall be deemed to publish a defamatory libel by reason only that he publishes in good faith, for the information of the public, a fair report of the proceedings of the Senate or House of Commons or the legislature of a province, or a committee thereof, or of the public proceedings before a court exercising judicial authority, or publishes, in good faith, any fair comment on any such proceedings.

(2) This section does not apply to a person who publishes a report of evidence taken or offered in any proceeding before the Senate or House of Commons or any committee thereof, on a petition or bill relating to any matter of marriage or divorce, if the report is published without authority from or leave of the House in which the proceeding is held or is contrary to any rule, order or practice of that House. R.S., c. C-34, s. 271.

CROSS-REFERENCES

Defamatory libel is defined in s. 298 and see cross-references under that section concerning related offences, special procedural provisions and other defences or excuses. Publishing is defined in s. 299. As to vicarious liability of a newspaper proprietor, see s. 303. Section 306 creates the related defence of publication of parliamentary or legislative papers. Section 316 contains provision for proof that the matter alleged to be defamatory was published by order or under the authority of Parliament or of the legislature.

With reference to subsec. (2) of this section, note that s. 166 makes it an offence to publish certain judicial proceedings calculated to injure public morals or respecting marriage, judicial separation or restitution of conjugal rights.

SYNOPSIS

This section, like ss. 305 and 306, establishes an exemption from the provisions that apply to publishing a *defamatory libel* to a person who publishes *in good faith* or *for public information*, a fair report of, or fair comment on the proceedings of the Senate, House of Commons, provincial legislature, a committee of any of these bodies, or court matters that are open to the public. This exemption does not apply in relation to publication of evidence or a petition or bill relating to a matter of marriage or divorce in proceedings before the Senate, the House of Commons, or any committee thereof if the person who publishes the material does so without the authority of the appropriate House or the publication is contrary to any rule, order or practice of that House.

FAIR REPORT OF PUBLIC MEETING.

308. No person shall be deemed to publish a defamatory libel by reason only that he publishes in good faith, in a newspaper, a fair report of the proceedings of any public meeting if

(a) the meeting is lawfully convened for a lawful purpose and is open to the public;
(b) the report is fair and accurate;
(c) the publication of the matter complained of is for the public benefit; and

(*d*) **he does not refuse to publish in a conspicuous place in the newspaper a reasonable explanation or contradiction by the person defamed in respect of the defamatory matter. R.S., c. C-34, s. 272.**

CROSS-REFERENCES

The term "newspaper" is defined in s. 303. Defamatory libel is defined in s. 298 and see cross-references under that section concerning related offences, special procedural provisions and other defences or excuses. Publishing is defined in s. 299. As to vicarious liability of a newspaper proprietor, see s. 303. The general defence of publication for the public benefit is set out in s. 309.

SYNOPSIS

This section provides an exemption for any person who publishes defamatory libel when that person publishes in a newspaper, in *good faith*, a *fair report* of what occurred at a public meeting. The person who publishes the report may only resort to this exemption if the meeting is *lawfully convened* for a *lawful purpose* and is open to the public, the report is *fair* and *accurate*, the publication of the material complained of is for the *benefit of the public*, and the person agrees to publish, in a conspicuous place in the newspaper, any explanation or contradiction of the offending material by the person defamed. This section applies to publication of defamatory matter in newspapers only.

PUBLIC BENEFIT.

309. No person shall be deemed to publish a defamatory libel by reason only that he publishes defamatory matter that, on reasonable grounds, he believes is true, and that is relevant to any subject of public interest, the public discussion of which is for the public benefit. R.S., c. C-34, s. 273.

CROSS-REFERENCES

Defamatory libel is defined in s. 298 and see cross-references under that section concerning related offences, special procedural provisions and other defences or excuses. Note however, in particular, that the plea of justification in cases of defamatory libel is dealt with in ss. 607(2), 611 and 612. Under s. 612(3), where the accused is convicted, the court may consider, in pronouncing sentence, whether the offence was aggravated or mitigated by the plea. Publishing is defined in s. 299. As to vicarious liability of a newspaper proprietor, see s. 303. The special defence of publication for the public benefit in a newspaper is set out in s. 308.

SYNOPSIS

This section provides a more general exemption than the one found in s. 308 in that it applies to any publication, not just newspapers. So long as the person who publishes the defamatory matter believes, on *reasonable grounds*, that the material is true, relevant to a subject of public interest and that it is in the public interest to discuss it, the exemption in this section applies.

FAIR COMMENT ON PUBLIC PERSON OR WORK OF ART.

310. No person shall be deemed to publish a defamatory libel by reason only that he publishes fair comments

 (*a*) **on the public conduct of a person who takes part in public affairs; or**

 (*b*) **on a published book or other literary production, or on any composition or work of art or performance publicly exhibited, or on any other communication made to the public on any subject, if the comments are confined to criticism thereof. R.S., c. C-34, s. 274.**

CROSS-REFERENCES

Defamatory libel is defined in s. 298 and see cross-references under that section concerning related offences, special procedural provisions and other defences or excuses. Publishing is defined in s. 299. As to vicarious liability of a newspaper proprietor, see s. 303.

SYNOPSIS

This section provides that a person will not be deemed to have published a defamatory libel by reason of the fact that he makes *fair comment* about the *public* conduct of a person who participates in *public* affairs. Similarly, a person who makes *fair comment* in the form of criticism of any published book, literary production, publicly exhibited composition, work of art, performance or other communication, may avail himself of this section. This section allows for fair comment on public matters only.

WHEN TRUTH A DEFENCE.

311. No person shall be deemed to publish a defamatory libel where he proves that the publication of the defamatory matter in the manner in which it was published was for the public benefit at the time when it was published and that the matter itself was true. R.S., c. C-34, s. 275.

CROSS-REFERENCES

Defamatory libel is defined in s. 298 and see cross-references under that section concerning related offences, special procedural provisions and other defences or excuses. Note however, in particular, that the plea of justification in cases of defamatory libel is dealt with in ss. 607(2), 611 and 612. Under s. 612(3), where the accused is convicted, the court may consider, in pronouncing sentence, whether the offence was aggravated or mitigated by the plea. Publishing is defined in s. 299. As to vicarious liability of a newspaper proprietor, see s. 303. The related defence of publication for the public benefit is set out in ss. 308 and 309.

SYNOPSIS

This section, like s. 309, provides an exemption from criminal liability under s. 300 for any person who publishes defamatory matter that was true and the publication of which, both in manner and time, was for the public benefit. This section, unlike s. 309, however, requires the person charged under s. 300 to prove both of these elements.

PUBLICATION INVITED OR NECESSARY.

312. No person shall be deemed to publish a defamatory libel by reason only that he publishes defamatory matter

     (a) on the invitation or challenge of the person in respect of whom it is published, or

     (b) that it is necessary to publish in order to refute defamatory matter published in respect of him by another person,

if he believes that the defamatory matter is true and it is relevant to the invitation, challenge or necessary refutation, as the case may be, and does not in any respect exceed what is reasonably sufficient in the circumstances. R.S., c. C-34, s. 276.

CROSS-REFERENCES

Defamatory libel is defined in s. 298 and see cross-references under that section concerning related offences, special procedural provisions and other defences or excuses. Note however, in particular, that the plea of justification in cases of defamatory libel is dealt with in ss. 311, 607(2), 611 and 612. Under s. 612(3), where the accused is convicted, the court may consider, in pronouncing sentence, whether the offence was aggravated or mitigated by the plea. Publishing is defined in

s. 299. As to vicarious liability of a newspaper proprietor, see s. 303. The related defence of publication for the public benefit is set out in ss. 308 and 309.

SYNOPSIS

This section provides an exemption to an offence under s. 300 for any person who publishes defamatory matter upon the invitation or challenge of the person to whom the matter is relevant, or which is necessary to refute defamatory matter published by another person in respect of himself. In order to qualify for this exemption, the person using it must believe that the defamatory matter is true, relevant to the invitation, challenge or refutation, and does not go beyond what could be considered to be reasonably sufficient in the circumstances.

ANSWERS TO INQUIRIES.

313. No person shall be deemed to publish a defamatory libel by reason only that he publishes, in answer to inquiries made to him, defamatory matter relating to a subject-matter in respect of which the person by whom or on whose behalf the inquiries are made has an interest in knowing the truth or who, on reasonable grounds, the person who publishes the defamatory matter believes has such an interest, if

> (*a*) **the matter is published, in good faith, for the purpose of giving information in answer to the inquiries;**
> (*b*) **the person who publishes the defamatory matter believes that it is true;**
> (*c*) **the defamatory matter is relevant to the inquiries; and**
> (*d*) **the defamatory matter does not in any respect exceed what is reasonably sufficient in the circumstances. R.S., c. C-34, s. 277.**

CROSS-REFERENCES

Defamatory libel is defined in s. 298 and see cross-references under that section concerning related offences, special procedural provisions and other defences or excuses. Note however, in particular, that the plea of justification in cases of defamatory libel is dealt with in ss. 311, 607(2), 611 and 612. Under s. 612(3), where the accused is convicted, the court may consider, in pronouncing sentence, whether the offence was aggravated or mitigated by the plea. Publishing is defined in s. 299. As to vicarious liability of a newspaper proprietor, see s. 303.

SYNOPSIS

If a person publishes defamatory matter in response to inquiries made by another person who has, or is believed to have, an interest in knowing the truth, that person, subject to certain restrictions, will not be guilty of an offence under s. 300. This excuse applies if the person who publishes the defamatory matter believes that it is true, if the defamatory matter is relevant to the inquiries and does not exceed what is *reasonably sufficient* in the circumstances, and if the defamatory matter is published in *good faith* for the purpose of responding to the inquiries.

GIVING INFORMATION TO PERSON INTERESTED.

314. No person shall be deemed to publish a defamatory libel by reason only that he publishes to another person defamatory matter for the purpose of giving information to that person with respect to a subject-matter in which the person to whom the information is given has, or is believed on reasonable grounds by the person who gives it to have, an interest in knowing the truth with respect to that subject-matter if

> (*a*) **the conduct of the person who gives the information is reasonable in the circumstances;**
> (*b*) **the defamatory matter is relevant to the subject-matter; and**

(*c*) the defamatory matter is true, or if it is not true, is made without ill-will toward the person who is defamed and is made in the belief, on reasonable grounds, that it is true. R.S., c. C-34, s. 278.

CROSS-REFERENCES

Defamatory libel is defined in s. 298 and see cross-references under that section concerning related offences, special procedural provisions and other defences or excuses. Note however, in particular, that the plea of justification in cases of defamatory libel is dealt with in ss. 311, 607(2), 611 and 612. Under s. 612(3), where the accused is convicted, the court may consider, in pronouncing sentence, whether the offence was aggravated or mitigated by the plea. Publishing is defined in s. 299. As to vicarious liability of a newspaper proprietor, see s. 303.

SYNOPSIS

This section, like s. 313, provides an exemption from criminal liability under s. 300 to a person who publishes defamatory matter to another person whom the person *believes*, on *reasonable grounds*, has an interest in knowing the truth. This section applies only if the conduct of the person who gives out this matter is *reasonable*, if the defamatory matter is relevant to the subject, and if the defamatory matter is true or, if not true, if the person who gives the defamatory matter does so *without ill-will* and *believes*, on *reasonable grounds*, that the matter is true.

PUBLICATION IN GOOD FAITH FOR REDRESS OF WRONG.

315. No person shall be deemed to publish a defamatory libel by reason only that he publishes defamatory matter in good faith for the purpose of seeking remedy or redress for a private or public wrong or grievance from a person who has, or who on reasonable grounds he believes has, the right or is under an obligation to remedy or redress the wrong or grievance, if

(*a*) **he believes that the defamatory matter is true;**

(*b*) **the defamatory matter is relevant to the remedy or redress that is sought; and**

(*c*) **the defamatory matter does not in any respect exceed what is reasonably sufficient in the circumstances. R.S., c. C-34, s. 279.**

CROSS-REFERENCES

Defamatory libel is defined in s. 298 and see cross-references under that section concerning related offences, special procedural provisions and other defences or excuses. Note however, in particular, that the plea of justification in cases of defamatory libel is dealt with in ss. 311, 607(2), 611 and 612. Under s. 612(3), where the accused is convicted, the court may consider, in pronouncing sentence, whether the offence was aggravated or mitigated by the plea. Publishing is defined in s. 299. As to vicarious liability of a newspaper proprietor, see s. 303.

SYNOPSIS

A person will not be criminally liable under s. 300 only by reason of the fact that he publishes defamatory matter in *good faith* for the purpose of seeking a redress for a private or public wrong from another person whom he *believes*, on *reasonable grounds*, to be obliged to remedy that wrong or grievance. This section requires that the person who publishes the defamatory matter believes that this material is true, that it is relevant to the remedy being sought, and that it does not exceed what is reasonably sufficient in the circumstances.

PROVING PUBLICATION BY ORDER OF LEGISLATURE / Directing verdict / Certificate of order.

316. (1) An accused who is alleged to have published a defamatory libel may, at any stage of the proceedings, adduce evidence to prove that the matter that is alleged to be

defamatory was contained in a paper published by order or under the authority of the Senate or House of Commons or a legislature of a province.

(2) Where at any stage in proceedings referred to in subsection (1) the court, judge, justice or provincial court judge is satisfied that the matter alleged to be defamatory was contained in a paper published by order or under the authority of the Senate or House of Commons or a legislature of a province, he shall direct a verdict of not guilty to be entered and shall discharge the accused.

(3) For the purposes of this section, a certificate under the hand of the Speaker or clerk of the Senate or House of Commons or a legislature of a province to the effect that the matter that is alleged to be defamatory was contained in a paper published by order or under the authority of the Senate, House of Commons or legislature of a province, as the case may be, is conclusive evidence thereof. R.S., c. C-34, s. 280.

CROSS-REFERENCES

Defamatory libel is defined in s. 298 and see cross-references under that section concerning related offences, special procedural provisions and other defences or excuses. This section relates back to the defence set out in s. 307.

SYNOPSIS

This section provides a means by which a person, charged under s. 300, may prove that the matter alleged to be defamatory, was contained in a paper published by order or under the authority of the Senate or House of Commons or provincial legislature. (See s. 306(*b*).) The accused may raise s. 306(*b*) at any stage of the proceedings and, if the court is satisfied that the section applies, he shall direct a verdict of not guilty and discharge the accused. A certificate of the Speaker or clerk of the Senate, House of Commons or provincial legislature, to the effect that the matter alleged to be defamatory was contained in a paper published by order or under the authority of any of the bodies specified in s. 306(*b*), is conclusive evidence of facts contained in that certificate.

Verdicts

VERDICTS IN CASES OF DEFAMATORY LIBEL.

317. Where, on the trial of an indictment for publishing a defamatory libel, a plea of not guilty is pleaded, the jury that is sworn to try the issue may give a general verdict of guilty or not guilty on the whole matter put in issue on the indictment, and shall not be required or directed by the judge to find the defendant guilty merely on proof of publication by the defendant of the alleged defamatory libel, and of the sense ascribed thereto in the indictment, but the judge may, in his discretion, give a direction or opinion to the jury on the matter in issue as in other criminal proceedings, and the jury may, on the issue, find a special verdict. R.S., c. C-34, s. 281.

CROSS-REFERENCES

Defamatory libel is defined in s. 298 and see cross-references under that section concerning related offences, special procedural provisions and other defences or excuses. Note however, in particular, that the plea of justification in cases of defamatory libel is dealt with in ss. 311, 607(2), 611 and 612. Under s. 612(3), where the accused is convicted, the court may consider, in pronouncing sentence, whether the offence was aggravated or mitigated by the plea. Section 584(1) provides that no count for publishing a defamatory libel is insufficient by reason only that it does not set out the words that are alleged to be libellous. However, under s. 587(1)(*e*), particulars may be ordered further describing any writing or words that are the subject of the charge. Under s. 584(2), a count for publishing a libel may charge that the published matter was written in a sense that, by innuendo, made the publication thereof criminal and may specify that sense without any introductory assertion to show how the matter was written in that sense. Under s. 584(3), it is sufficient to prove that the matter was libellous, with or without innuendo.

SYNOPSIS

This section describes the kinds of verdicts that may flow from the trial on an indictment for publishing a defamatory libel. When the accused pleads not guilty to such an indictment, the jury may give a general verdict of guilty or not guilty on the whole matter. The judge is not empowered to direct the jury to find the accused guilty merely on the basis of proof of publication of the defamatory libel. The jury may, if the judge has exercised his discretion to give an opinion or direction to the jury on the matter in issue, find a special verdict.

Hate Propaganda

ADVOCATING GENOCIDE / Definition of "genocide" / Consent / Definition of "identifiable group".

318. (1) Every one who advocates or promotes genocide is guilty of an indictable offence and liable to imprisonment for a term not exceeding five years.

(2) In this section, "genocide" means any of the following acts committed with intent to destroy in whole or in part any identifiable group, namely,
   (*a*) killing members of the group; or
   (*b*) deliberately inflicting on the group conditions of life calculated to bring about its physical destruction.

(3) No proceeding for an offence under this section shall be instituted without the consent of the Attorney General.

(4) In this section, "identifiable group" means any section of the public distinguished by colour, race, religion, national or ethnic origin, age, sex, sexual orientation, or mental or physical disability. R.S., c. 11 (1st Supp.), s. 1; 2004, c. 14, s. 1; 2014, c. 31, s. 12.

CROSS-REFERENCES

"Attorney General" is defined in s. 2. Section 583(*h*) provides that a count in an indictment is not insufficient by reason only that it does not state that the required consent has been obtained. [As to notes concerning sufficiency of consent, see s. 583.]

The accused may elect his mode of trial pursuant to s. 536(2). Release pending trial is determined by s. 515, although the accused is eligible for release by the officer in charge under s. 498.

This offence may be the basis for an application for an authorization to intercept private communications by reason of s. 183.

Procedure for an *in rem* proceeding against hate propaganda, which includes material advocating genocide, is set out in s. 320. The offences in relation to inciting hatred and hate propaganda are set out in s. 319. The offence of publishing false news is in s. 181. The offence of defamatory libel is dealt with in ss. 297 to 317.

SYNOPSIS

This section describes the offence of advocating or promoting genocide. Genocide is defined as the act of killing members of an identifiable group or of deliberately inflicting conditions on an identifiable group calculated to bring about the destruction of that group, in whole or in part. An identifiable group is defined as any section of the public distinguished by colour, race, religion, national or ethnic origin, age, sex, sexual orientation, or mental or physical disability. The offence is indictable, and may be prosecuted only with the consent of an Attorney General and is punishable by imprisonment not exceeding five years.

CR. CODE

ANNOTATIONS

In *Mugesera v. Canada (Minister of Citizenship and Immigration)*, [2005] 2 S.C.R. 100, 197 C.C.C. (3d) 233, 30 C.R. (6th) 39, the Supreme Court of Canada held that this provision does not require proof that genocide had in fact occurred. The act of incitement has to be direct and public. The guilty mind required is an intent to directly prompt or provoke another to commit genocide. In this case, the applicant's public speech contained a deliberate call for the murder of Tutsis, which was sufficient to make a finding that he had attempted to incite citizens to act against one another. This finding and the fact that the applicant was aware of ethnic massacres that were taking place was sufficient to make out the necessary *mens rea*.

PUBLIC INCITEMENT OF HATRED / Wilful promotion of hatred / Defences / Forfeiture / Exemption from seizure of communication facilities / Consent / Definitions / "communicating" / "identifiable group" / "public place" / "statements".

319. (1) Every one who, by communicating statements in any public place, incites hatred against any identifiable group where such incitement is likely to lead to a breach of the peace is guilty of

    (a) an indictable offence and is liable to imprisonment for a term not exceeding two years; or

    (b) an offence punishable on summary conviction.

(2) Every one who, by communicating statements, other than in private conversation, wilfully promotes hatred against any identifiable group is guilty of

    (a) an indictable offence and is liable to imprisonment for a term not exceeding two years; or

    (b) an offence punishable on summary conviction.

(3) No person shall be convicted of an offence under subsection (2)

    (a) if he establishes that the statements communicated were true;

    (b) if, in good faith, the person expressed or attempted to establish by an argument an opinion on a religious subject or an opinion based on a belief in a religious text;

    (c) if the statements were relevant to any subject of public interest, the discussion of which was for the public benefit, and if on reasonable grounds he believed them to be true; or

    (d) if, in good faith, he intended to point out, for the purpose of removal, matters producing or tending to produce feelings of hatred toward an identifiable group in Canada.

(4) Where a person is convicted of an offence under section 318 or subsection (1) or (2) of this section, anything by means of or in relation to which the offence was committed, on such conviction, may, in addition to any other punishment imposed, be ordered by the presiding provincial court judge or judge to be forfeited to Her Majesty in right of the province in which that person is convicted, for disposal as the Attorney General may direct.

(5) Subsections 199(6) and (7) apply with such modifications as the circumstances require to section 318 or subsection (1) or (2) of this section.

(6) No proceeding for an offence under subsection (2) shall be instituted without the consent of the Attorney General.

(7) In this section,

"communicating" includes communicating by telephone, broadcasting or other audible or visible means;

"identifiable group" has the same meaning as in section 318;

"public place" includes any place to which the public have access as of right or by invitation, express or implied;

"statements" includes words spoken or written or recorded electronically or electro-magnetically or otherwise, and gestures, signs or other visible representations. R.S., c. 11 (1st Supp.), s. 1; 2004, c. 14, s. 2.

CROSS-REFERENCES

"Attorney General" is defined in s. 2. Section 583(*h*) provides that a count in an indictment is not insufficient by reason only that it does not state that the required consent has been obtained. [As to notes concerning sufficiency of consent, see s. 583.]

Where the prosecution elects to proceed by indictment on either of these offences then the accused may elect his mode of trial pursuant to s. 536(2). Where the prosecution elects to proceed by way of summary conviction then the trial of this offence is conducted by a summary conviction court pursuant to Part XXVII. The punishment for the offence is then as set out in s. 787 and the limitation period is set out in s. 786(2). In either case, release pending trial is determined by s. 515, although the accused is eligible for release by a peace officer under s. 496, 497 or by the officer in charge under s. 498.

Procedure for an *in rem* proceeding against hate propaganda is set out in s. 320. The offence of advocating genocide is in s. 318. The offence of publishing false news is in s. 181. The offence of defamatory libel is dealt with in ss. 297 to 317.

SYNOPSIS

This section creates two offences involving the inciting or promoting of hatred against an identifiable group.

In subsec. (1), the offence is committed if such hatred is incited by the communication, in a public place, of words likely to lead to a breach of the peace.

In subsec. (2) the offence is committed only by the *wilful* promotion of hatred against an identifiable group through the communication of statements other than in private conversation.

Subsection (3) creates defences to the offence where it is established that the statements are true, that they amount to the good faith expression of an opinion on a religious subject or an opinion based on a belief in a religious text, that they are reasonably believed to be true and are published with respect to a matter of public interest and to the public good, or that they are published in a good faith effort to identify hate engendering matters in order to have them removed. The wording seems to place the onus of establishing only the first of these four defences on the accused.

Both offences created in this section may be prosecuted by indictment or summarily, and are punishable, on indictment, to a term of imprisonment not exceeding two years. The offence in subsec. (2) may only be prosecuted with the consent of an Attorney General.

Subsections (4) and (5) specify that where a person is convicted of offences under this section or s. 318, the means of communication by which the offence is committed may be forfeited to the Crown, with the exception of communication facilities and equipment as described in s. 199(6) and (7).

Subsection (7) defines "communicating" to include audible or visible means, defines "identifiable group" as in s. 318, defines "public place" to include places in which the public has access by right or by express or implied invitation, and defines "statement" to include spoken, written or recorded words, and gestures, signs, or other visible representation.

ANNOTATIONS

Subsections (1) and (2) – "Wilful" in this subsection means with the intention of promoting hatred and does not include recklessness. The offence would therefore be made out only if the accused had as their conscious purpose the promotion of hatred against the identifiable group or if they foresaw that the promotion of hatred against that group was certain or morally certain to result and communicated the statements as a means of achieving some other purpose: *R. v. Buzzanga and Durocher* (1979), 49 C.C.C. (2d) 369, 101 D.L.R. (3d) 488 (Ont. C.A.).

This definition of the term "wilful" was approved by the Supreme Court of Canada in *R. v. Keegstra*, [1990] 3 S.C.R. 397, 61 C.C.C. (3d) 1. In that case, the court also considered the meaning to be attached to the other elements of the offence. The term "promotes" indicates active support or instigation. The term "hatred" connotes emotion of an intense and extreme nature that is clearly associated with vilification and detestation. It is an emotion that, if exercised against members of an identifiable group, implies that those individuals are to be despised, scorned, denied respect and made subject to ill-treatment on the basis of group affiliation.

"Promotes" means actively supports or instigates and requires more than mere encouragement. "Hatred" connotes emotions of an intense and extreme nature that is clearly associated with vilification and detestation. Only the most intense forms of dislike fall within the ambit of this offence. This offence does not require proof that the communication caused actual hatred. In determining whether the communication expressed hatred, the court must look at the understanding of a reasonable person in context. Although this requires the trier of fact to engage in a subjective interpretation of the communicated message to determine whether "hatred" was what the speaker intended to promote, it is insufficient that the message be offensive or that the trier of fact dislike the statements. The analysis must focus on the speech's audience and on its social and historical context. The speech is to be considered objectively having regard to the circumstances in which the speech was given, the manner and tone used and the persons to whom the message was addressed. In considering the *mens rea*, subsec. (1) requires something less than the intentional promotion of hatred while subsec. (2) requires the accused to have had, as a conscious purpose, the promotion of hatred against the identifiable group, or foresight that the promotion of hatred against that group was certain to result and nevertheless communicated the statements. In many instances, the *mens rea* will flow from the establishment of the elements of the criminal act of the offence: *Mugesera v. Canada (Minister of Citizenship and Immigration)*, [2005] 2 S.C.R. 100, 197 C.C.C. (3d) 233.

It constitutes misdirection to instruct the jury that if they found that the accused in his actions was aware that there was a danger that his conduct would cause the promotion of hatred against an identifiable group and knowing this he chose to persist in his conduct then the jury could make a finding of wilfullness. At most, the jury should be instructed that they may consider the risks known to the accused: *R. v. Keegstra* (1991), 63 C.C.C. (3d) 110, [1991] 4 W.W.R. 136 (Alta. C.A.).

"Willfully" includes willful blindness: *R. v. Harding* (2001), 40 C.R. (5th) 119, 52 O.R. (3d) 714 (S.C.J.), affd 160 C.C.C. (3d) 225, 48 C.R. (5th) 1 (Ont. C.A.), leave to appeal to S.C.C. refused [2003] 3 S.C.R. viii, 167 C.C.C. (3d) vi.

Although this subsection infringes freedom of expression, as guaranteed by s. 2(*b*) of the Charter, it constitutes a reasonable limit on that right and is therefore valid legislation: *R. v. Keegstra, supra.*

In *R. v. Krymowski*, [2005] 1 S.C.R. 101, 193 C.C.C. (3d) 129, the Crown particularized the identifiable group as being "Roma". The evidence showed that the accused referred to "gypsies" as the object of their hatred. To make out the offence, however, there was no need to prove any interchangeability between the specific hateful terms employed and the name by which the target group was identified in the information. The relevant questions to be asked were whether the Crown had proved beyond a reasonable doubt that the accused made some or all of the statements alleged in the information and whether the statements made, as a matter of fact, promoted hatred of the Roma. Moreover, dictionary definitions presented to the trial judge showed that "gypsy" can refer to an ethnic group properly known as "Roma", "Rom", or "Romany". The trial judge could therefore have taken judicial notice of that fact and then considered it, together with the rest of the evidence, to determine whether there was proof beyond a reasonable doubt that the accused did in fact intend to target Roma.

Subsection (3)(a) – Reversing the burden of proof to the defence that the statements were true as provided for in this paragraph while infringing the guarantee to the presumption of innocence in s. 11(*d*) of the Charter is a reasonable limit and therefore valid: *R. v. Keegstra*, *supra.* See also *R. v. Keegstra*, [1996] 1 S.C.R. 458, 105 C.C.C. (3d) 19, 39 Alta. L.R. (3d) 305.

Subsection (3)(d) – It would seem that this defence was simply provided out of an abundance of caution since it would be rare that a person could successfully invoke this exemption where it was shown that he *wilfully* promoted hatred: *R. v. Buzzanga and Durocher, supra.*

WARRANT OF SEIZURE / Summons to occupier / Owner and author may appear / Order of forfeiture / Disposal of matter / Appeal / Consent / Definitions / "court" / "genocide" / "hate propaganda" / "judge".

320. (1) A judge who is satisfied by information on oath that there are reasonable grounds for believing that any publication, copies of which are kept for sale or distribution in premises within the jurisdiction of the court, is hate propaganda, shall issue a warrant under his hand authorizing seizure of the copies.

(2) Within seven days of the issue of the warrant under subsection (1), the judge shall issue a summons to the occupier of the premises requiring him to appear before the court and show cause why the matter seized should not be forfeited to Her Majesty.

(3) The owner and the author of the matter seized under subsection (1) and alleged to be hate propaganda may appear and be represented in the proceedings in order to oppose the making of an order for the forfeiture of the matter.

(4) If the court is satisfied that the publication referred to in subsection (1) is hate propaganda, it shall make an order declaring the matter forfeited to Her Majesty in right of the province in which the proceedings take place, for disposal as the Attorney General may direct.

(5) If the court is not satisfied that the publication referred to in subsection (1) is hate propaganda, it shall order that the matter be restored to the person from whom it was seized forthwith after the time for final appeal has expired.

(6) An appeal lies from an order made under subsection (4) or (5) by any person who appeared in the proceedings
  (*a*) on any ground of appeal that involves a question of law alone,
  (*b*) on any ground of appeal that involves a question of fact alone, or
  (*c*) on any ground of appeal that involves a question of mixed law and fact,
as if it were an appeal against conviction or against a judgment or verdict of acquittal, as the case may be, on a question of law alone under Part XXI, and sections 673 to 696 apply with such modifications as the circumstances require.

(7) No proceeding under this section shall be instituted without the consent of the Attorney General.

(8) In this section,
"court" means
  (*a*) in the Province of Quebec, the Court of Quebec,
  (*a*.1) in the Province of Ontario, the Superior Court of Justice,
  (*b*) in the Provinces of New Brunswick, Manitoba, Saskatchewan and Alberta, the Court of Queen's Bench,
  (*c*) in the Province of Newfoundland and Labrador, the Supreme Court, Trial Division,
  (*c*.1) [*Repealed.* 1992, c. 51, s. 36.]
  (*d*) in the Provinces of Nova Scotia, British Columbia and Prince Edward Island, in Yukon and in the Northwest Territories, the Supreme Court, and
  (*e*) in Nunavut, the Nunavut Court of Justice;

"genocide" has the same meaning as in section 318;

"hate propaganda" means any writing, sign or visible representation that advocates or promotes genocide or the communication of which by any person would constitute an offence under section 319;

"judge" means a judge of a court. R.S., c. 11 (1st Supp.), s. 1; 1974-75, c. 48, s. 25; 1978-79, c. 11, s. 10; R.S.C. 1985, c. 27 (2nd Supp.), s. 10; c. 40 (4th Supp.), s. 2; 1990, c. 16, s. 4; 1990, c. 17, s. 11; 1992, c. 1, s. 58; 1993, c. 28, Sch. III, s. 31 (repealed 1999, c. 3, s. 12); 1998, c. 30, s. 14(*d*); 1999, c. 3, ss. 12, 29; 2002, c. 7, s. 142; 2015, c. 3, s. 49.

CROSS-REFERENCES

The procedure in this section resembles the *in rem* procedure for obscene publications in s. 164 and thus see notes under that section respecting procedure. The procedure for obtaining a normal search warrant to obtain evidence of commission of an offence is set out in ss. 487 and 487.1. The procedure for shutting down a hate-propaganda site on the internet is set out in s. 320.1.

SYNOPSIS

This section authorizes a judge of a court as defined in subsec. (8), with the consent of an Attorney General, to issue a warrant to seize copies of any publication where *reasonable grounds* exist *for believing* that the subject publication is hate propaganda and that copies are kept for sale or distribution in premises located within the court's jurisdiction. Hate propaganda means writings, signs or representations that advocate or promote genocide or which would constitute the incitement or promotion of hatred against an identifiable group contrary to s. 319. Subsection (2) requires the judge to issue a summons to the occupier of the premises that have been searched within seven days of the issuance of the warrant, requiring him to show cause why the seized copies should not be forfeited. The owner and author of the publication may appear and oppose forfeiture. Subsections (4) to (6) describe the procedure for forfeiture, restoration and appeal.

ANNOTATIONS

A warrant may be issued under the general search warrant provision, s. 487, although the investigation relates to hate literature offences: *R. v. Keegstra* (1984), 19 C.C.C. (3d) 254 (Alta. Q.B.), revd on other grounds 43 C.C.C. (3d) 150, 65 C.R. (3d) 289 (C.A.).

WARRANT OF SEIZURE / Notice to person who posted the material / Person who posted the material may appear / Non-appearance / Order / Destruction of copy / Return of material / Other provisions to apply / When order takes effect.

320.1 (1) If a judge is satisfied by information on oath that there are reasonable grounds to believe that there is material that is hate propaganda within the meaning of subsection 320(8) or computer data within the meaning of subsection 342.1(2) that makes hate propaganda available, that is stored on and made available to the public through a computer system within the meaning of subsection 342.1(2) that is within the jurisdiction of the court, the judge may order the custodian of the computer system to

    (*a*) **give an electronic copy of the material to the court;**

    (*b*) **ensure that the material is no longer stored on and made available through the computer system; and**

    (*c*) **provide the information necessary to identify and locate the person who posted the material.**

(2) Within a reasonable time after receiving the information referred to in paragraph (1)(*c*), the judge shall cause notice to be given to the person who posted the material, giving that person the opportunity to appear and be represented before the court and show cause why the material should not be deleted. If the person cannot be identified or located or does not reside in Canada, the judge may order the custodian of the

computer system to post the text of the notice at the location where the material was previously stored and made available, until the time set for the appearance.

(3) The person who posted the material may appear and be represented in the proceedings in order to oppose the making of an order under subsection (5).

(4) If the person who posted the material does not appear for the proceedings, the court may proceed *ex parte* to hear and determine the proceedings in the absence of the person as fully and effectually as if the person had appeared.

(5) If the court is satisfied, on a balance of probabilities, that the material is available to the public and is hate propaganda within the meaning of subsection 320(8) or computer data within the meaning of subsection 342.1(2) that makes hate propaganda available, it may order the custodian of the computer system to delete the material.

(6) When the court makes the order for the deletion of the material, it may order the destruction of the electronic copy in the court's possession.

(7) If the court is not satisfied that the material is available to the public and is hate propaganda within the meaning of subsection 320(8) or computer data within the meaning of subsection 342.1(2) that makes hate propaganda available, the court shall order that the electronic copy be returned to the custodian and terminate the order under paragraph (1)(*b*).

(8) Subsections 320(6) to (8) apply, with any modifications that the circumstances require, to this section.

(9) No order made under subsections (5) to (7) takes effect until the time for final appeal has expired. 2001, c. 41, s. 10; 2014, c. 31, s. 13.

CROSS-REFERENCES

"Judge" and "court" are defined in s. 320(8). No proceedings under this section shall be instituted without consent of the Attorney General in view of the combined operation of subsec. (8) and s. 320(7). Appeal rights are governed by s. 320(6).

SYNOPSIS

This section provides a procedure for shutting down sites on the Internet that contain material falling within the definition of hate propaganda. The procedure commences with an order made by a judge (defined in s. 320(8)) upon the judge being satisfied by information on oath of the matters set out in subsec. (1). Proceedings under this section cannot be instituted, however, without the consent of the Attorney General, in view of the combined operation of subsec. (8) and s. 320(7). Under the order, the custodian of the computer system must give an electronic copy to the court, ensure that the material is no longer stored on and made available through the computer system and provide information to identify and locate the person who posted the material. The judge must then cause notice to be given to the person who posted the material in accordance with subsec. (2). The person is then given an opportunity to show cause why the material should not be deleted from the computer system. If the person does not appear, the court may proceed *ex parte*. If the court is satisfied that the material is available to the public and is hate propaganda or data that makes hate propaganda available, the court may order the custodian of the computer system to delete the material (subsec. (5)) and destroy the electronic copy (subsec. (6)). If the court is not so satisfied, the electronic copy of the material is returned to the custodian and the order under subsec. (1) is terminated (subsec. (7)). Appeal rights are as provided for in s. 320. No order made under subsec. (5) to (7) takes effect until the time for final appeal has expired.

ANNOTATIONS

See *Citron v. Zundel* (2002), 41 C.H.R.R. D/274, a case concerning the Internet decided under s. 13 of the *Canadian Human Rights Act,* which proscribes telephonic communication of hate messages as a discriminatory practice if there is repeated communication of "any matter that is likely to expose a person or persons to hatred or contempt by reason of the fact that that person or those persons are identifiable on the basis of a prohibited ground of discrimination."

Part IX / OFFENCES AGAINST RIGHTS OF PROPERTY

Interpretation

DEFINITIONS / "break" / "credit card" / "document" / "exchequer bill" / "exchequer bill paper" / "false document" / "revenue paper".

321. In this Part

"break" means

(*a*) to break any part, internal or external, or

(*b*) to open any thing that is used or intended to be used to close or to cover an internal or external opening;

"Credit card" means any card, plate, coupon book or other device issued or otherwise distributed for the purpose of being used

(*a*) on presentation to obtain, on credit, money, goods, services or any other thing of value, or

(*b*) in an automated teller machine, a remote service unit or a similar automated banking device to obtain any of the services offered through the machine, unit or device;

"document" means any paper, parchment or other material on which is recorded or marked anything that is capable of being read or understood by a person, computer system or other device, and includes a credit card, but does not include trade-marks on articles of commerce or inscriptions on stone or metal or other like material;

"exchequer bill" means a bank-note, bond, note, debenture or security that is issued or guaranteed by Her Majesty under the authority of Parliament or the legislature of a province;

"exchequer bill paper" means paper that is used to manufacture exchequer bills;

"false document" means a document

(*a*) the whole or a material part of which purports to be made by or on behalf of a person

(i) who did not make it or authorize it to be made, or

(ii) who did not in fact exist,

(*b*) that is made by or on behalf of the person who purports to make it but is false in some material particular,

(*c*) that is made in the name of an existing person, by him or under his authority, with a fraudulent intention that it should pass as being made by a person, real or fictitious, other than the person who makes it or under whose authority it is made;

"revenue paper" means paper that is used to make stamps, licences or permits for any purpose connected with the public revenue. R.S., c. C-34, s. 282; R.S.C. 1985, c. 27 (1st Supp.), s. 42.

CROSS-REFERENCES

In addition to the definitions in this section, see s. 2 and notes to that section.

SYNOPSIS

This section contains definitions for a number of key terms that are employed throughout Part IX of the *Criminal Code* entitled "Offences Against Rights of Property".

ANNOTATIONS

False document – It is sufficient that the accused knows that the document purports to be a genuine document issued by an entity such as the government or other official authority that did not make the document or is non-existent. There is no requirement that there be an existing authentic document and a false document that so closely resembled the original as to raise a inference that it purported to be a copy of the authentic document: *R. v. Sommani* (2007), 218 C.C.C. (3d) 168, 46 C.R. (6th) 308 (B.C.C.A.), leave to appeal to S.C.C. refused 379 N.R. 394*n*.

Theft

THEFT / Time when theft completed / Secrecy / Purpose of taking / Wild living creature.

322. (1) Every one commits theft who fraudulently and without colour of right takes, or fraudulently and without colour of right converts to his use or to the use of another person, anything whether animate or inanimate, with intent,

> (*a*) **to deprive, temporarily or absolutely, the owner of it, or a person who has a special property or interest in it, of the thing or of his property or interest in it;**
>
> (*b*) **to pledge it or deposit it as security;**
>
> (*c*) **to part with it under a condition with respect to its return that the person who parts with it may be unable to perform; or**
>
> (*d*) **to deal with it in such a manner that it cannot be restored in the condition in which it was at the time it was taken or converted.**

(2) A person commits theft when, with intent to steal anything, he moves it or causes it to move or to be moved, or begins to cause it to become movable.

(3) A taking or conversion of anything may be fraudulent notwithstanding that it is effected without secrecy or attempt at concealment.

(4) For the purposes of this Act, the question whether anything that is converted is taken for the purpose of conversion, or whether it is, at the time it is converted, in the lawful possession of the person who converts it is not material.

(5) For the purposes of this section, a person who has a wild living creature in captivity shall be deemed to have a special property or interest in it while it is in captivity and after it has escaped from captivity. R.S., c. C-34, s. 283.

CROSS-REFERENCES

The punishment for theft is set out in s. 334 and therefore see that section for cross-references respecting mode of trial and release pending trial as well as special procedural provisions. For notes on the defence of mistake generally, see notes under s. 19. Section 323 deals with special property or interest in the case of oyster beds. Also, note s. 588 which deems certain persons to have a property interest in property of which they have the management, control or custody. Section 583(*b*) deals with sufficiency of an indictment which fails to name the person who owns or has a special property or interest in property mentioned in the count. Sections 324 to 333 define other means by which theft may be committed. Offences resembling theft are set out in ss. 335 to 342. The related offence of false pretences is dealt with in ss. 361 to 363. Fraudulently obtaining food and lodging is an offence under s. 364. The general offence of fraud is contained in s. 380. The offence of secret commissions is set out in s. 426. The offence of possession of goods obtained by commission of an indictable offence is set out in ss. 354 and 355. The break and enter offences are dealt with in ss. 348 to 352. Robbery is dealt with in ss. 343 and 344. For notes on doctrine of recent possession, see s. 354.

SYNOPSIS

This section describes the offence of theft.

Subsection (1) states that a person commits theft when the person takes or converts anything with the intent to deprive the owner or person who has special property in it, to deposit it as security, to part with it under conditions that make its return dubious, or to deal with it in a manner that makes it impossible to return it in the condition it was in when it was taken. The person who commits theft as defined above must deal *fraudulently* and *without colour of right* with the subject matter of the charge. Subsection (3) states that a taking or conversion of a thing may be fraudulent even if it is done without secrecy or attempt at concealment. The section further sets out that a person who moves or causes a thing to be moved, or begins to make the thing moveable, with the *intent to steal* that thing, commits the offence of theft. Under subsection (4), the question of whether a converted item was taken for the purpose of conversion, or whether it is lawfully in the possession of the person who converted it is not material to an offence under this section. Finally, subsection (4) establishes that a person who has kept a wild living creature in captivity is deemed to have a special property or interest in the creature when it is in captivity and after it has escaped.

ANNOTATIONS

Special property or interest [also see s. 328] – The special property or interest must be in the very thing alleged to have been stolen. The interest a person may have in protecting himself against loss or damage resulting from the use of a forged document by and in the possession of another is neither property nor special property nor interest in the forged document. Further, the property or the special property or interest must exist at the time at which the theft, either by taking or conversion, is committed: *R. v. Smith*, [1962] S.C.R. 215, 131 C.C.C. 403, 36 C.R. 384.

In *R. v. Ben Smith; R. v. Harry Smith*, [1963] 1 C.C.C. 68, 38 C.R. 378 (Ont. C.A.), convictions for theft were upheld where the accused, who were directors of a company, without the knowledge of the other directors and without any authority from the company used the company's money to purchase certain shares which they then pledged with a bank to cover a personal overdraft. It was immaterial that the accused honestly intended, with reasonable prospects, to redeem the shares and pay back the company or that they in fact did so to the eventual profit of the company or that the accused were trustees for the company. On the facts the accused had temporarily deprived the company of a special property or interest in the shares, which includes the equitable interest of a *cestui que trust*.

A holder of a conditional sale agreement has an interest in his goods which are in the possession of the conditional buyer: *R. v. Maroney*, [1975] 2 S.C.R. 306, 18 C.C.C. (2d) 257, 27 C.R.N.S. 185 (5:0).

Notwithstanding that it is being illegally held, a narcotic may be the subject of a theft as defined in this section, the person with *de facto* ownership of the narcotic having a special property or interest in it: *R. v. Grasser* (1981), 64 C.C.C. (2d) 520, 50 N.S.R. (2d) 230 (S.C. App. Div.).

"Anything" – In *R. v. Scallen* (1974), 15 C.C.C. (2d) 441 (B.C.C.A.), it was held that the word "anything" in this section was wide enough to include a bank credit and that "anything" need not be something tangible or material.

Similarly, in *R. v. Hardy* (1980), 57 C.C.C. (2d) 73 (B.C.C.A.), a conviction for theft of "money" from his employer was upheld where the accused caused cheques to be made out to himself as additional salary, caused other cheques to be issued to cover repairs to his own cars and home, and instructed the company bookkeeper to offset a supplier's invoice for supplies or services delivered to the accused against the supplier's indebtedness of the company. The majority of the court were of the view that these various money credits with the employer's banker and with its customers which the accused diverted to himself or to his benefit were "anything" within the meaning of this section. Lambert J.A. although concurring in the result was of the view that dealings whereby the employer's accounts receivable were set-off were not within the indictment, a trade account receivable not properly being described as "money".

To come within the term "anything" in this section, the thing which is taken, whether tangible or intangible, must be of a nature such that it can be the subject of a proprietary right and the property must be capable of being taken or converted in a manner that results in the deprivation of the victim. Confidential information per se, rather than a list or other tangible object containing confidential information does not fall within this definition. Confidential information does not qualify as property for the purposes of this section and except in very unusual circumstances is not of a nature such that it can be taken or converted: *R. v. Stewart*, [1988] 1 S.C.R. 963, 41 C.C.C. (3d) 481, 63 C.R. (3d) 305 (6:0).

A promissory note falls within the definition of property in s. 2 and is thus "anything" capable of being stolen within the meaning of this section: *R. v. Cinq-Mars* (1989), 51 C.C.C. (3d) 248 (Que. C.A.).

Proof of ownership – In *R. v. Little and Wolski*, [1976] 1 S.C.R. 20, 19 C.C.C. (2d) 385, 52 D.L.R. (3d) 1 (5:0), an appeal from conviction for theft was dismissed where although the owner of the goods allegedly stolen was named in the indictment as "Westwood Jewellers Limited" the only evidence was that the goods were stolen from "Westwood Jewellers" which was owned and managed by one of the witnesses. The court divided on the effect of this apparent failure to prove ownership in the entity named in the indictment. de Grandpré J., for the majority held that if the owner of the object allegedly stolen is mentioned in the indictment and if his ownership is not proven and there are no other circumstances to indicate to the accused the true nature of the charge, an acquittal should be entered. However, when, as in the present case there cannot be any possibility for the accused to fail to identify the transaction about which they are charged, there is no reason to discharge the accused for the sole reason that the owner mentioned in the indictment has not been mentioned in the evidence. Dickson J., for himself and Beetz J., while agreeing that the conviction was proper, held that except in exceptional circumstances as where the theft can be inferred from the suspicious circumstances of the accused's possession, an allegation of ownership is not mere surplusage. However, the identity of the owner is sufficiently established in instances in which the owner is named in the indictment when, (i) the evidence adduced by the Crown reasonably identifies the owner with the person named in the indictment as owner, and (ii) it is clear that failure to prove the identity of the owner with greater precision has not misled or prejudiced the accused in preparation or presentation of his defence. In this case both (i) and (ii) were met and therefore the conviction was proper.

Conversion – In *R. v. Konken* (1971), 3 C.C.C. (2d) 348 (B.C.C.A.), the accused was acquitted of theft through conversion of a water pump. The majority held that the accused's explanation for retaining the pump, after overhearing conversation which might have led him to believe the pump was not abandoned as he thought, was reasonable and therefore the Crown had failed to prove that the accused had fraudulently and without colour of right converted the pump. Nemetz J.A., agreed that the accused should be acquitted and went on to hold that where a person retains goods innocently taken the essential element to support a conversion is that the knowledge subsequently acquired by the person must be of an unequivocal and unambiguous nature. In this case no knowledge of ownership was brought home to the accused.

Intent to deprive owner – In *R. v. O'Mahoney*, [1966] 2 C.C.C. 264 (B.C.C.A.), the accused was personally responsible for any shortages in accounts. Some shortages he made up by switching funds from one account to the other, but the ultimate deficiency he always made up from his own pocket. It was held that he did not have an intent to steal as set out in s. 322(1).

"Fraudulently" including "prank" defence – In *R. v. Ben Smith; R. v. Harry Smith, supra*, with respect to the issue of fraudulent intent the Court stated as follows (at p. 83 C.C.C.): "In *Stephen's History of the Criminal Law*, 1883, vol. II, pp. 121-2 two essential elements of fraudulent intent are stated to be "deceit or an intention to deceive or in some cases mere secrecy; and, secondly, either actual injury or possible injury or an intent to expose some person either to actual injury or to a risk of possible injury by means of that deceit or secrecy'. In vol. III of the same work the learned author adds to these two essential elements a possible third element, really implicit in the first one, which is that the conduct must not only be wrongful but intentionally and knowingly wrongful."

In *R. v. Kerr*, [1965] 4 C.C.C. 37 (Man. C.A.), the accused openly took a large ashtray "as a prank", intending to return it. It was held that there was no *animus furandi* as is required by the Code. The "prank" defence was rejected in *R. v. Heminger and Hornigold*, [1969] 3 C.C.C. 201 (Man. C.A.), the court distinguishing *Kerr* on the facts. In this case the accused had taken a chair from a beer parlour.

In *R. v. Bogner* (1975), 33 C.R.N.S. 349 (2:1) (Que. C.A.), the court appears to have rejected the concept of a "prank" defence. The majority held that a general dishonest state of mind in addition to the intent to do the acts constituting the *actus reus* was not required.

In *R. v. Théroux*, [1993] 2 S.C.R. 5, 79 C.C.C. (3d) 449, the court considered the *mens rea* of fraud under s. 380 of the *Criminal Code*. In that context, the court held that "an act of deceit which is made carelessly without any expectation of consequences, as for example, an innocent prank or a statement made in debate which is not intended to be acted upon, would not amount to fraud because the accused would have no knowledge that the prank would put the property of those who heard it at risk." It is unclear whether this would have any application to the question of prank under this section.

The element of fraud cannot be inferred merely from the accused's failure to return goods which were given to him by the owner, although the time set for the return of the goods has expired: *Washington (State) v. Johnson*, [1988] 1 S.C.R. 327, 40 C.C.C. (3d) 546 (4:3).

Colour of right – The term "colour of right" denotes an honest belief in a state of facts that, if true, would at law justify or excuse the act done. An accused bears the onus of showing that there is an "air of reality" to the asserted defence — *i.e.*, whether there is some evidence upon which a trier of fact, properly instructed and acting reasonably, could be left in a state of reasonable doubt about colour of right: *R. v. Simpson*, [2015] 2 S.C.R. 827, 327 C.C.C. (3d) 360.

In *R. v. DeMarco* (1973), 13 C.C.C. (2d) 369 (Ont. C.A.), it was held that an honestly asserted proprietary or possessory claim constitutes a colour of right notwithstanding it is unfounded in law or fact. Further, an absence of fraudulent intent may exist apart from a colour of right as conduct to be fraudulent must be dishonest and morally wrong. Also see *R. v. Howson*, [1966] 3 C.C.C. 348 (Ont. C.A.).

It was held in *R. v. Pace*, [1965] 3 C.C.C. 55 (N.S.C.A.), that theft may still be committed though the object is of no use or value to the owner. The court considered that a belief that the owner would consent to the taking if asked might constitute a colour of right defence but such a defence is not made out where the accused's belief is merely that no one would object to the taking.

The accused did not act under a colour of right where he obtained and then destroyed a promissory note evidencing his indebtedness to the complainant, because he believed that he was the victim of a fraud and feared losing his money. It was apparent that the accused was acting merely on the basis of a moral right in order to avoid having to exercise his legal rights through the court. A moral right cannot of itself found a colour of right: *R. v. Cinq-Mars* (1989), 51 C.C.C. (3d) 248 (Que. C.A.).

On a charge of theft involving alleged misappropriation by a real estate broker, of money held in his trust account, the issue on the availability of the defence of colour of right was not what the jury thought the accused's rights were in relation to the account but whether the accused had an honest belief he had a right to the money: *R. v. Lilly*, [1983] 1 S.C.R. 794, 5 C.C.C. (3d) 1 (7:0).

An honest belief in a moral as opposed to a legal right cannot constitute a colour of right defence. However, a belief in a moral right may negative a fraudulent intent: *R. v. Hemmerly* (1976), 30 C.C.C. (2d) 141 (Ont. C.A.).

Colour of right refers to a situation where there is an assertion of a proprietary or possessory right to the thing that is the subject of the alleged theft. Colour of right can either be a mistake concerning the facts or an honest mistaken belief in a civil claim to the thing. In the latter case, the issue is not whether the civil claim was well founded but rather whether the accused honestly believed he had such a claim: *R. v. Dorosh* (2004), 183 C.C.C. (3d) 224 (Sask. C.A.).

Passing of property – In determining whether property passed so that the offence, if any, could not constitute theft, the focus should be on the knowledge of the accused rather than the knowledge of the victim. Where a transferor mistakenly transfers property to a recipient, and the recipient knows of the mistake, property does not pass for the purpose of the criminal law if the law of property creates a right of recovery, no matter whether the original transfer is said to be void or voidable. If the recipient then converts the property to his own use, fraudulently and without colour of right, and with intent to deprive the transferor of the property, then he is guilty of theft: *R. v. Milne*, [1992] 1 S.C.R. 697, 70 C.C.C. (3d) 481 (5:0).

Where the accused received goods because the victim was induced to deliver them through the accused's fraud in providing a cheque which the accused knew would be dishonoured, then no title in the goods passed to the accused and he could be convicted of conversion. The civil law, such as the provincial *Sale of Goods Act*, had no application, provided that, as here, the victim had a right to recover the goods. It would be open to find an act of conversion when the accused took delivery and asserted ownership and control or later when he effected sales to third parties: *R. v. Smith* (1992), 77 C.C.C. (3d) 182 (Ont. C.A.), affd [1993] 3 S.C.R. 635, 84 C.C.C. (3d) 160*n* (5:0).

Included offence – On a charge of theft, possession of property obtained by crime is a lesser included offence pursuant to s. 662(1): *R. v. Francis* (2011), 279 C.C.C. (3d) 541 (Ont. S.C.J.).

OYSTERS / Oyster bed.

323. (1) Where oysters and oyster brood are in oyster beds, layings or fisheries that are the property of any person and are sufficiently marked out or known as the property of that person, that person shall be deemed to have a special property or interest in them.

(2) An indictment is sufficient if it describes an oyster bed, laying or fishery by name or in any other way, without stating that it is situated in a particular territorial division. R.S., c. C-34, s. 284.

CROSS-REFERENCES

The general offence of theft is set out in s. 322 and see cross-references under that section respecting related offences. The punishment for theft is set out in s. 334 and therefore see that section for cross-references respecting mode of trial and release pending trial as well as special procedural provisions. Also, note s. 588 which deems certain persons to have a property interest in property of which they have the management, control or custody. Section 583(*b*) deals with sufficiency of an indictment which fails to name the person who owns or has a special property or interest in property mentioned in the count. Sections 324 to 333 define other means by which theft may be committed. Offences resembling theft are set out in ss. 335 to 342.

SYNOPSIS

This section bestows a special property interest in oysters and oyster brood contained in an oyster bed upon a person who owns the oysters and who has marked out or let it be known that they belong to him. An indictment charging on offence under this section does not require that the oyster bed be described as being situated in a particular territorial division so long as it is described by name or in some other way.

THEFT BY BAILEE OF THINGS UNDER SEIZURE.

324. Every one who is a bailee of anything that is under lawful seizure by a peace officer or public officer in the execution of the duties of his office, and who is obliged by law or agreement to produce and deliver it to that officer or to another person entitled thereto at a certain time and place, or on demand, steals it if he does not produce and deliver it in accordance with his obligation, but he does not steal it if his failure to produce and deliver it is not the result of a wilful act or omission by him. R.S., c. C-34, s. 285.

CROSS-REFERENCES

The term "steal" is defined in s. 2 as committing theft. The general offence of theft is defined in s. 322. The terms "peace officer" and "public officer" are defined in s. 2. The punishment for theft is set out in s. 334 and therefore see that section for cross-references respecting mode of trial and release pending trial as well as special procedural provisions. Also, note s. 588 which deems certain persons to have a property interest in property of which they have the management, control or custody. Section 583(*b*) deals with sufficiency of an indictment which fails to name the person who owns or has a special property or interest in property mentioned in the count. Sections 325 to 333 define other means by which theft may be committed. Offences resembling theft are set out in ss. 335 to 342. See, in particular, criminal breach of trust under s. 336 and public servant refusing to deliver property under s. 337. The offence of secret commission by an agent is set out in s. 426. See cross-references under s. 322 respecting other related offences.

SYNOPSIS

This section describes the offence of theft by a bailee of things under seizure. When a person is the bailee of any item that has been lawfully seized by a peace officer or a public officer and is obliged by law or agreement to produce that item to a specific person at a certain time and place, or on demand, he is deemed by this section to have stolen the item if he does not deliver it in accordance with his obligation. This section only applies if his failure to deliver the item is the result of a wilful act or omission on his part.

ANNOTATIONS

It is a necessary element of the offence under this section that the goods were lawfully seized. Where there is no evidence that the bailiff had ascertained that the goods which he purported to seize were on the premises at the time there was no valid seizure. An undertaking signed by the accused acknowledging the seizure and agreeing to hold the goods as a bailee could not be taken as an admission that the goods were on the premises if in fact they were not. Moreover whatever the civil consequences of signing the undertaking, in the absence of evidence that the accused read the undertaking it could not be taken as an admission in criminal proceedings: *R. v. Vroom* (1975), 23 C.C.C. (2d) 345, 58 D.L.R. (3d) 565 (Alta. S.C. App. Div.) (2:1).

AGENT PLEDGING GOODS, WHEN NOT THEFT.

325. A factor or an agent does not commit theft by pledging or giving a lien on goods or documents of title to goods that are entrusted to him for the purpose of sale or for any other purpose, if the pledge or lien is for an amount that does not exceed the sum of
- **(*a*) the amount due to him from his principal at the time the goods or documents are pledged or the lien is given; and**
- **(*b*) the amount of any bill of exchange that he has accepted for or on account of his principal. R.S., c. C-34, s. 286.**

CROSS-REFERENCES

The general offence of theft is defined in s. 322. The punishment for theft is set out in s. 334 and therefore see that section for cross-references respecting mode of trial and release pending trial as well as special procedural provisions. As to meaning of "bill of exchange", see *Bills of Exchange Act*, R.S.C. 1985, c. B-4. Sections 324, 326 and 328 to 333 define other means by which theft may be committed. Offences resembling theft are set out in ss. 335 to 342. See cross-references under s. 322 respecting other related offences.

SYNOPSIS

This section sets out the circumstances in which an agent *does not* commit the offence of theft when dealing with goods entrusted to him for the purpose of sale or otherwise. An agent who pledges or gives a lien on goods is not guilty of theft if the pledge or lien is for an amount that does not exceed the sum of the amount due to him from his principal or the amount of any bill of exchange that he has accepted for or on account of his principal.

THEFT OF TELECOMMUNICATION SERVICE / Definition of "telecommunication".

326. (1) Every one commits theft who fraudulently, maliciously, or without colour of right,

    (a) abstracts, consumes or uses electricity or gas or causes it to be wasted or diverted; or

    (b) uses any telecommunication facility or obtains any telecommunication service.
    R.S., c. C-34, s. 287; 1974-75-76, c. 93, s. 23; 2014, c. 31, s. 14(2).

(2) [*Repealed.* 2014, c. 31, s. 14(2).]

CROSS-REFERENCES

The term "radio" is defined in s. 35 of the *Interpretation Act*, R.S.C. 1985, c. I-21. The general offence of theft is defined in s. 322. The punishment for theft is set out in s. 334 and therefore see that section for cross-references respecting mode of trial and release pending trial as well as special procedural provisions. Section 327(2) provides for an order of forfeiture of an instrument or device in relation to which an offence under para. (1)(*b*) was committed. Sections 328 to 333 define other means by which theft may be committed. Offences resembling theft are set out in ss. 335 to 342. The related offence of possession of a device for unlawfully obtaining a telecommunication facility or service is in s. 327 and unauthorized use of a computer service in s. 342.1. See cross-references under s. 322 respecting other related offences. Part VI deals with interception of private communications and note, in particular, the offence in s. 191 of possession of a device designed for surreptitious interception of private communications.

SYNOPSIS

This section describes the offence of theft of electricity or gas, and also theft of a telecommunication service. Any person who *fraudulently, maliciously*, or *without colour of right*, abstracts, consumes, uses, diverts or wastes electricity or gas, or who uses any telecommunication facility or obtains any telecommunication services is guilty of theft.

ANNOTATIONS

The word "fraudulently" does not mean that the Crown must prove that the accused deceived the utility company into willingly providing the service; the expression only connotes an intentional and deliberate taking of service that was not his to obtain: *R. v. Brais* (1972), 7 C.C.C. (2d) 301 (B.C.C.A.).

A charge of fraudulently using a telecommunication wire requires that the accused acted intentionally and deliberately with knowledge that the service was not the accused's to obtain. Where the accused added several extension phones to the one properly installed by the telephone company the evidence failed to prove the element of knowledge that the incoming wire was not made available to him for use as he did and he was acquitted: *R. v. Renz* (1974), 18 C.C.C. (2d) 492 (B.C.C.A.).

The unauthorized use of the programmes and other information stored in a university computer did not involve use of a telecommunication facility within the meaning of this section notwithstanding access was gained to the computer through a remote terminal. This section is aimed at theft of information from a facility through which it is channelled; and a computer system is not a facility constructed to serve a telecommunication function as defined in subsec. (2) but is rather a data processing facility: *R. v. McLaughlin*, [1980] 2 S.C.R. 331, 53 C.C.C. (2d) 417 (5:0). [**Note:** now see s. 342.1, *infra*.]

The offence under para. (*b*) is not made out where the accused having innocently obtained the pay-TV signal continued to watch the signal without paying the cable company: *R. v. Miller and Miller* (1984), 12 C.C.C. (3d) 466 (Alta. C.A.).

POSSESSION ETC., OF DEVICE TO OBTAIN TELECOMMUNICATION FACILITY OR TELECOMMUNICATION SERVICE / Forfeiture / Limitation / Definition of "device".

327. (1) Everyone who, without lawful excuse, makes, possesses, sells, offers for sale, imports, obtains for use, distributes or makes available a device that is designed or adapted primarily to use a telecommunication facility or obtain a telecommunication service without payment of a lawful charge, under circumstances that give rise to a reasonable inference that the device has been used or is or was intended to be used for that purpose, is

> (*a*) **guilty of an indictable offence and liable to imprisonment for a term of not more than two years; or**
>
> (*b*) **guilty of an offence punishable on summary conviction.**

(2) If a person is convicted of an offence under subsection (1) or paragraph 326(1)(*b*), in addition to any punishment that is imposed, any device in relation to which the offence was committed or the possession of which constituted the offence may be ordered forfeited to Her Majesty and may be disposed of as the Attorney General directs.

(3) No order for forfeiture is to be made in respect of telecommunication facilities or equipment by means of which an offence under subsection (1) is committed if they are owned by a person engaged in providing a telecommunication service to the public or form part of such a person's telecommunication service or system and that person is not a party to the offence.

(4) In this section, "device" includes

> (*a*) **a component of a device; and**
>
> (*b*) **a computer program within the meaning of subsection 342.1(2). 1974-75-76, c. 93, s. 24; 2014, c. 31, s. 15.**

CROSS-REFERENCES

Possession is defined in s. 4(3). A party to an offence is defined in ss. 21 and 22. The related offence of theft of a telecommunication service is in s. 326. See cross-references under s. 322 respecting other related offences. See similar offences in relation to instruments for forging or falsifying credit cards (s. 342.01) and for unlawfully obtaining computer services (s. 342.2). Part VI deals with interception of private communications and note, in particular, the offence in s. 191 of possession of a device designed for surreptitious interception of private communications.

Where the Crown proceeds by indictment, the accused may elect the mode of trial pursuant to s. 536(2). Release pending trial is determined by s. 515, although the accused is eligible for release by the officer in charge under s. 498. This offence may be the basis of an application for an authorization to intercept private communications by reason of s. 183 and for a warrant to conduct video surveillance by reason of s. 487.01(5).

SYNOPSIS

This section makes it an offence for a person to manufacture, possess, sell or offer for sale, or distribute any device or component which is primarily useful in the activity described in s. 326(1)(*b*), *i.e.*, theft of a telecommunication service. The section specifies that no criminal liability will be found where the accused has a lawful excuse for possession of the described device. The section puts the onus of establishing the lawful excuse upon the accused and may thereby give rise to a challenge under s. 11(*d*) of the Charter. Subsections (2) and (3) deal with the issue of forfeiture of the device described above upon conviction, but such forfeiture will not be imposed in respect of a telephone, telegraph or other communications equipment which is owned by a person in the business of providing a telecommunications service to the public who was not a party to the offence.

ANNOTATIONS

A device used to descramble pay-TV signals is a device the design of which renders it primarily useful for obtaining the use of a telecommunication service within the meaning of this section although the pay-TV service is carried on the same cable as the regular television service which the accused legitimately receives: *R. v. Lefave* (1984), 15 C.C.C. (3d) 287 (Ont. Gen. Sess. Peace).

The possession offence under this section does not require proof that the accused intended to use the device himself and would cover circumstances where the accused is in possession for storage purposes under circumstances which give rise to a reasonable inference that he knows that the intended use of the device is to be by other persons who will eventually receive them for the purposes of obtaining the telecommunications service without payment of lawful charges: *R. v. Fulop* (1988), 46 C.C.C. (3d) 427 (Ont. C.A.), affd 63 C.C.C. (3d) 288*n* (S.C.C.).

A computer program on a computer disc by which the accused could make long-distance telephone calls without charge constitutes an instrument or device within the meaning of this section: *R. v. Duck* (1985), 21 C.C.C. (3d) 529 (Ont. Dist. Ct.).

THEFT BY OR FROM PERSON HAVING SPECIAL PROPERTY OR INTEREST.

328. A person may be convicted of theft notwithstanding that anything that is alleged to have been stolen was stolen

    (*a*) **by the owner of it from a person who has a special property or interest in it;**

    (*b*) **by a person who has a special property or interest in it from the owner of it;**

    (*c*) **by a lessee of it from his reversioner;**

    (*d*) **by one of several joint owners, tenants in common or partners of or in it from the other persons who have an interest in it; or**

    (*e*) **by the representatives of an organization from the organization. R.S., c. C-34, s. 288; 2003, c. 21, s. 4.**

CROSS-REFERENCES

The terms "organization", "representative" and "steal" are defined in s. 2 as committing theft. The general offence of theft is defined in s. 322. The punishment for theft is set out in s. 334 and therefore see that section for cross-references respecting mode of trial and release pending trial as well as special procedural provisions. Also, note s. 588 which deems certain persons to have a property interest in property of which they have the management, control or custody. Section 583(*b*) deals with sufficiency of an indictment which fails to name the person who owns or has a special property or interest in property mentioned in the count. Sections 324, 326 and 330 to 333 define other means by which theft may be committed. Offences resembling theft are set out in ss. 335 to 342. See cross-references under s. 322 respecting other related offences.

SYNOPSIS

This section describes the circumstances in which the offence of theft may be committed by the owner of an item or a person who has a special property or interest in it. The following are situations in which the offence will have been committed: (a) when an item is taken by the owner from a person who has a special property or interest in it; (b) when a person who has a special property or interest in an item steals it from the owner; (c) when an item is stolen by a lessee from the person to whom it reverts; (d) when one of several joint owners, tenants in common or partners of or in an item, takes it from the others; and (e) when the representatives of an organization steal from that organization.

ANNOTATIONS

In *R. v. Ben Smith; R. v. Harry Smith*, [1963] 1 C.C.C. 68 (Ont. C.A.), it was held that a special property or interest included the equitable interest of a *cestui que trust*. In this case the accused had converted the shares of a company for their own personal use. See s. 322.

A neighbour taking care of a dwelling-house in the absence of the owner, at the owner's request, has a special property or interest in the house and the moveable property in it: *R. v. Rodrigue* (1987), 61 C.R. (3d) 381 (Que. C.A.).

329. [*Repealed*, 2000, c. 12, s. 94.]

THEFT BY PERSON REQUIRED TO ACCOUNT / Effect of entry in account.

330. (1) Every one commits theft who, having received anything from any person on terms that require him to account for or pay it or the proceeds of it or a part of the proceeds to that person or another person, fraudulently fails to account for or pay it or the proceeds of it or the part of the proceeds of it accordingly.

(2) Where subsection (1) otherwise applies, but one of the terms is that the thing received or the proceeds or part of the proceeds of it shall be an item in a debtor and creditor account between the person who receives the thing and the person to whom he is to account for or to pay it, and that the latter shall rely only on the liability of the other as his debtor in respect thereof, a proper entry in that account of the thing received or the proceeds or part of the proceeds of it, as the case may be, is a sufficient accounting therefor, and no fraudulent conversion of the thing or the proceeds or part of the proceeds of it thereby accounted for shall be deemed to have taken place. R.S., c. C-34, s. 290.

CROSS-REFERENCES

As to limitation on restitution of property see s. 491.1(3). The general offence of theft is defined in s. 322. The punishment for theft is set out in s. 334 and therefore see that section for cross-references respecting mode of trial and release pending trial as well as special procedural provisions. Sections 324, 326, 328 and 331 to 333 define other means by which theft may be committed. Offences resembling theft are set out in ss. 335 to 342. See, in particular, criminal breach of trust under s. 336. The offence of secret commission by an agent is set out in s. 426. See cross-references under s. 322 respecting other related offences.

SYNOPSIS

This section describes a kind of theft which can be committed by a person who is required to account for, pay for or account for the proceeds of anything received from another person and *fraudulently* fails to do so. Subsection (2) creates an exception to this offence where a debtor-creditor account has been set up between two parties and a proper entry of the transaction is entered into that account.

ANNOTATIONS

Fraudulently – The element of fraud cannot be inferred merely from the accused's failure to return the goods within a reasonable time: *Washington (State) v. Johnson*, [1988] 1 S.C.R. 327, 40 C.C.C. (3d) 546 (4:3).

Terms requiring accused to account – In *R. v. Preston* (1958), 28 C.R. 51 (N.S.S.C., *in banco*), it was held (4:1) that the conviction failed upon lack of proof of the terms of accounting and fraudulent failure to account.

This section does not apply where the accused is required to return the specific article entrusted to him: *R. v. Kimbrough* (1918), 30 C.C.C. 56 (Alta. S.C. App. Div.).

An accused may be convicted of the offence described by this section where he failed to account for the proceeds of a cheque which he had been given while employed by a corporation, even if the improper dealings with the cheque may have arisen after the accused was fired by the corporation. The accused's obligation to account did not necessarily cease with his termination from the company: *R. v. Fischer* (1987), 31 C.C.C. (3d) 303 (Sask. C.A.).

Debtor and creditor account (subsec. (2)) – The saving provision of subsec. (2) does not apply where although the accused has a debtor and creditor relationship with persons to whom he is to pay the funds, it is no part of the terms on which the accused received the funds from a third party that the funds would be an item in a debtor and creditor account between the accused and the person to whom the funds were to be paid: *R. v. Lowden* (1981), 59 C.C.C. (2d) 1 (Alta. C.A.), affd on other grounds [1982] 2 S.C.R. 60, 68 C.C.C. (2d) 531 (9:0).

Charging offence – In *R. v. McKenzie*, [1972] S.C.R. 409, 4 C.C.C. (2d) 296, the accused was convicted on a charge that "unlawfully did commit theft of the sum of approximately sixteen dollars and fifty cents, the property of Dominic Louis Christian contrary to the form of the statute in such case made and provided", where as a taxi driver he failed to remit to the taxi's owner all the money due to him. On appeal by the Crown it was held (5:0), that the information was by virtue of s. 492(2)(*b*) [now s. 581(2)(*b*)] framed to declare the matter charged to be an indictable offence in the words of s. 280 [now s. 334] and was therefore sufficient and that the accused's failure to account to his employer was theft within this section.

THEFT BY PERSON HOLDING POWER OF ATTORNEY.

331. Every one commits theft who, being entrusted, whether solely or jointly with another person, with a power of attorney for the sale, mortgage, pledge or other disposition of real or personal property, fraudulently sells, mortgages, pledges or otherwise disposes of the property or any part of it, or fraudulently converts the proceeds of a sale, mortgage, pledge or other disposition of the property, or any part of the proceeds, to a purpose other than that for which he was entrusted by the power of attorney. R.S., c. C-34, s. 291.

CROSS-REFERENCES

The general offence of theft is defined in s. 322. The punishment for theft is set out in s. 334 and therefore see that section for cross-references respecting mode of trial and release pending trial as well as special procedural provisions. Sections 324, 326, 328, 330, 332 and 333 define other means by which theft may be committed. Offences resembling theft are set out in ss. 335 to 342. See, in particular, criminal breach of trust under s. 336. The offence of secret commission by an agent is set out in s. 426. See cross-references under s. 322 respecting other related offences.

As to limitation on restitution of property see, s. 491.1(3).

SYNOPSIS

This section sets out the offence of theft committed by a person who holds power of attorney. Any person entrusted solely or jointly with a power of attorney for the sale, mortgage, or other disposition of real or personal property, who *fraudulently* disposes of all or part of that property or *fraudulently* converts the proceeds of such disposition to a purpose other than that which the power of attorney specifies, commits the offence of theft.

MISAPPROPRIATION OF MONEY HELD UNDER DIRECTION / Effect of entry in account.

332. (1) Every one commits theft who, having received, either solely or jointly with another person, money or valuable security or a power of attorney for the sale of real or personal property, with a direction that the money or a part of it, or the proceeds or a part of the proceeds of the security or the property shall be applied to a purpose or paid to a person specified in the direction, fraudulently and contrary to the direction applies to any other purpose or pays to any other person the money or proceeds or any part of it.

(2) This section does not apply where a person who receives anything mentioned in subsection (1) and the person from whom he receives it deal with each other on such terms that all money paid to the former would, in the absence of any such direction, be properly treated as an item in a debtor and creditor account between them, unless the direction is in writing. R.S., c. C-34, s. 292.

CROSS-REFERENCES

The term "valuable security" is defined in s. 2 and its value determined by reference to s. 4(2). The general offence of theft is defined in s. 322. The punishment for theft is set out in s. 334 and therefore see that section for cross-references respecting mode of trial and release pending trial as well as special procedural provisions. Sections 324, 326, 328, 329 to 331 and 333 define other means by which theft may be committed. Offences resembling theft are set out in ss. 335 to 342. See, in particular, criminal breach of trust under s. 336. The offence of secret commission by an agent is set out in s. 426. See cross-references under s. 322 respecting other related offences.

   As to limitation on restitution of property see, s. 491.1(3).

SYNOPSIS

This section describes the offence of theft of money held under direction. Any person who, *fraudulently* and *contrary to a direction* that money or valuable security be applied or paid to a specific person, applies to another purpose or pays to another person, part or all of the money or proceeds, commits the offence of theft. Subsection (1) does not apply if a debtor-creditor account exists, unless the direction referred to in subsec. (1) is in writing.

ANNOTATIONS

Fraudulent requires an intentional misappropriation, without mistake. The dishonesty inherent in the offence lies in the intentional and unmistaken application of funds to an improper purpose. In this case, it was established that the accused was aware of receiving the money with a direction and applied it intentionally to another purpose contrary to that direction: *R. v. Skalbania*, [1997] 3 S.C.R. 1235, 120 C.C.C. (3d) 217.

   A conviction under this section was upheld where the accused, president of a brokerage house, received money for the purchase of a portion of a bond issue and on the date that the bonds were to be delivered was unable to effect delivery as the bonds were held by a bank and the accused lacked the funds to obtain delivery. The accused in the meantime had applied the money received for the purchase of the bonds to cover debts of his company. The offence under this section does not depend on the existence of a mandate. All that is required is a direction which in this case was the confirmation given by the accused confirming the sale and the date of delivery. The defence under subsec. (2) did not apply as by the terms of the agreement the accused was not to apply the funds to the credit of the victim's account generally but was to use the funds for a particular purpose, namely to pay for the bonds on the day they were issued. Finally, it was no defence to the charge that the accused was not required to keep the money *in specie*: *R. v. Legare*, [1978] 1 S.C.R. 275, 36 C.C.C. (2d) 463 (4:3).

The existence of a debtor and creditor relationship in the absence of a direction is a question of fact to be decided by the jury: *R. v. Finlay*, [1968] 2 C.C.C. 157 (Y.T.C.A.).

Where the only evidence of a direction is the expectation on the part of the person who gave the money to the accused then the offence under this section is not made out. However, expectations known to the accused as a result of express instructions are directions and there need not also be instructions as to what not to do with the money. Thus, an accused travel agent was properly convicted where money was paid to him by his clients for the express purpose of purchasing airline tickets for a particular trip on a regular carrier and the accused accepted the money for the purpose of satisfying those expectations and then dealt with the money so as to defeat that purpose: *R. v. Lowden*, [1982] 2 S.C.R. 60, 68 C.C.C. (2d) 531 (9:0).

TAKING ORE FOR SCIENTIFIC PURPOSE.

333. No person commits theft by reason only that he takes, for the purpose of exploration or scientific investigation, a specimen of ore or mineral from land that is not enclosed and is not occupied or worked as a mine, quarry or digging. R.S., c. C-34, s. 293.

CROSS-REFERENCES

The general offence of theft is defined in s. 322. The punishment for theft is set out in s. 334. For offences in relation to minerals and mines, see ss. 394 to 396.

SYNOPSIS

This section creates an exception to the offence of theft where a person takes, for the purpose of exploration or scientific investigation, a specimen of ore or mineral from land that is neither enclosed nor is being worked as a mine or quarry.

MOTOR VEHICLE THEFT / Subsequent offences.

333.1 (1) Everyone who commits theft is, if the property stolen is a motor vehicle, guilty of an offence and liable

(*a*) **on proceedings by way of indictment, to imprisonment for a term of not more than 10 years, and to a minimum punishment of imprisonment for a term of six months in the case of a third or subsequent offence under this subsection; or**

(*b*) **on summary conviction, to imprisonment for a term of not more than 18 months.**

(2) For the purpose of determining whether a convicted person has committed a third or subsequent offence, an offence for which the person was previously convicted is considered to be an earlier offence whether it was prosecuted by indictment or by way of summary conviction proceedings. 2010, c. 14, s. 3.

CROSS-REFERENCES

"Motor vehicle" is defined in s. 2. The offence of theft is defined in s. 322 and the punishment for the general offence of theft is set out in s. 334. The summary conviction offence of "joy-riding" is set out in s. 335. Also see s. 353 for offences with respect to automobile master keys, s. 353.1, offence of tampering with vehicle identification numbers, and s. 354(2), the presumption of knowing possession of stolen goods from possession of a vehicle or part with an obliterated vehicle identification number.

SYNOPSIS

This section simply creates elevated penalties for theft of automobiles. While the general theft offence in s. 334 would also apply to theft of motor vehicles, this section creates a different penalty structure which, *inter alia*, does not depend upon the value of the vehicle as would be the case under s. 334. In addition, this section creates a minimum penalty of six months' imprisonment for a third or subsequent offence under this section.

PUNISHMENT FOR THEFT.

334. Except where otherwise provided by law, every one who commits theft
  (*a*) is guilty of an indictable offence and liable to imprisonment for a term not exceeding ten years, where the property stolen is a testamentary instrument or the value of what is stolen exceeds five thousand dollars; or
  (*b*) is guilty
    (i) of an indictable offence and is liable to imprisonment for a term not exceeding two years, or
    (ii) of an offence punishable on summary conviction,

where the value of what is stolen does not exceed five thousand dollars. R.S., c. C-34, s. 294; 1972, c. 13, s. 23; 1974-75-76, c. 93, s. 25; R.S.C. 1985, c. 27 (1st Supp.), s. 43; 1994, c. 44, s. 20.

CROSS-REFERENCES

This section applies to theft as defined in ss. 322, 324, 326, 328 and 330 to 332. The terms "property" and "testamentary instrument" are defined in s. 2.

This offence may be the basis for an application for an authorization to intercept private communications by reason of s. 183 or for a warrant to conduct video surveillance by reason of s. 487.01(5). Theft is an enterprise crime offence for the purposes of Part XII.2.

As to admission of photographic evidence of property, see s. 491.2. For proof by way of affidavit of ownership, lawful possession, value, and that the person was deprived of property by fraud or otherwise without the person's lawful consent, see s. 657.1.

Where the offence, although committed outside Canada, is in relation to the use of nuclear material, see s. 7(3.4).

The offence in para. (*a*) is an indictable offence for which the accused may elect his mode of trial under s. 536(2). Where the prosecution elects to proceed by indictment for the offence under para. (*b*) then, by virtue of s. 553, it is an offence over which a provincial court judge has absolute jurisdiction and does not depend on the consent of the accused. That is, the accused does not have an election as to mode of trial, although the provincial court judge may, by virtue of s. 555(1), elect to continue the proceedings as a preliminary inquiry, in which case, the accused is deemed to have elected trial by judge and jury pursuant to s. 565(1)(*a*). As well, under s. 555(2), where, in the course of the trial, evidence establishes that the subject-matter of the offence is a testamentary instrument or that its value exceeds $5,000 then the provincial court judge shall put the accused to his election under s. 536(2). Where the prosecution elects to proceed by way of summary conviction then the proceedings are conducted by a summary conviction court pursuant to Part XXVII. The punishment is then as set out in s. 787 and the limitation period is set out in s. 786(2). For the offence under para. (*b*), release pending trial is determined by s. 515, although the accused is eligible for release by a peace officer under s. 496, 497 or by the officer in charge under s. 498. The value of a valuable security is determined in accordance with s. 4(2) and of a postal card or stamp in accordance with s. 4(1).

Section 588 deems certain persons to have a property interest in property of which they have the management, control or custody. By virtue of s. 583(*b*), an indictment which otherwise complies with s. 581 is not insufficient by reason that it fails to name the person who owns or has a special property or interest in property mentioned in the count. Offences resembling theft are set out in ss. 335 to 342. The related offence of false pretences is dealt with in ss. 361 to 363. Fraudulently obtaining food and lodging is an offence under s. 364. The general offence of fraud is contained in

s. 380. The offence of secret commission is set out in s. 426. The offence of possession of goods obtained by commission of an indictable offence is set out in ss. 354 and 355. The break and enter offences are dealt with in ss. 348 to 352. Robbery is dealt with in ss. 343 and 344. Under s. 357, it is an offence to bring into or have in Canada anything that the accused has obtained outside Canada by an act that, if it had been committed in Canada, would have been the offence of theft.

SYNOPSIS

This section sets out the punishment for the offence of theft as described in the preceding sections. Where the value of the property stolen is greater than $5,000 or it is a testamentary instrument, the offence of theft is indictable and a person convicted of the offence faces a maximum term of 10 years' imprisonment. In other cases, the offence is either indictable, with a maximum of two years of imprisonment, or summary. This section only applies if there is no other specific provision for punishment in law [for example, theft of a credit card under s. 342 which contains its own punishment section].

Offences Resembling Theft

TAKING MOTOR VEHICLE OR VESSEL OR FOUND THEREIN WITHOUT CONSENT / Exception / Definition of "vessel".

335. (1) Subject to subsection (1.1), every one who, without the consent of the owner, takes a motor vehicle or vessel with intent to drive, use, navigate or operate it or cause it to be driven, used, navigated or operated, or is an occupant of a motor vehicle or vessel knowing that it was taken without the consent of the owner, is guilty of an offence punishable on summary conviction.

(1.1) Subsection (1) does not apply to an occupant of a motor vehicle or vessel who, on becoming aware that it was taken without the consent of the owner, attempted to leave the motor vehicle or vessel, to the extent that it was feasible to do so, or actually left the motor vehicle or vessel.

(2) For the purposes of subsection (1), "vessel" has the meaning assigned by section 214. R.S., c. C-34, s. 296; 1972, c. 13, s. 23; R.S.C. 1985, c. 1 (4th Supp.), s. 15; 1997, c. 18, s. 15.

CROSS-REFERENCES

The term "motor vehicle" is defined in s. 2.

Trial of this offence is conducted by a summary conviction court pursuant to Part XXVII. The punishment is set out in s. 787 and the limitation period is set out in s. 786(2). Release pending trial is determined by s. 515, although the accused is eligible for release by a peace officer under ss. 496, 497 or by the officer in charge under s. 498.

The related offence of theft is defined in s. 322 and punished in accordance with s. 334. While the offence under this section is not specifically made an included offence of theft under s. 334, under s. 606(4), the accused may be permitted to plead guilty to this offence with the consent of the prosecutor.

SYNOPSIS

This section describes the offence of taking a motor vehicle or vessel, as defined in s. 214, with the intent to drive, operate, use or navigate it, or cause it to be driven, operated, used or navigated. The taking of the motor vehicle or vessel must be accomplished *without the owner's consent*. It is also an offence to be an occupant knowing it was taken without the consent of the owner. The offence is punishable on summary conviction. No offence is committed by the occupant if the occupant attempted to leave, to the extent feasible, upon becoming aware of the unlawful taking.

ANNOTATIONS

The offence under this section is not an included offence of theft under s. 334. The two offences are separate and in certain fact situations the accused may be prosecuted under either section at the option of the Crown. In particular an intent by the accused to return the vehicle does not preclude his conviction for theft: *R. v. LaFrance*, [1975] 2 S.C.R. 201, 13 C.C.C. (2d) 289 (6:3).

The offence of "occupant joyriding" created by this section does not violate ss. 7 or 11(*d*) of the *Canadian Charter of Rights and Freedoms*: *R. v. H. (P.)* (2000), 143 C.C.C. (3d) 223, 129 O.A.C. 299 (C.A.).

Section 794(2), which places the burden on the defendant to prove an exception, exemption, proviso, excuse or qualification prescribed by law, does not apply to the defence set out in subsec. (1.1): *R. v. H. (P.), supra*.

CRIMINAL BREACH OF TRUST.

336. Every one who, being a trustee of anything for the use or benefit, whether in whole or in part, of another person, or for a public or charitable purpose, converts, with intent to defraud and in contravention of his trust, that thing or any part of it to a use that is not authorized by the trust is guilty of an indictable offence and liable to imprisonment for a term not exceeding fourteen years. R.S., c. C-34, s. 296.

CROSS-REFERENCES

The term "trustee" is defined in s. 2.

Related offences: s. 122, breach of trust by official (defined in s. 118); s. 426, secret commission; s. 331, theft by person holding power of attorney; s. 322, conversion; s. 332, theft by person holding money, etc., under direction; s. 380, fraud.

Pursuant to s. 583, an indictment, which otherwise complies with s. 581, is not insufficient by reason (*b*), that it does not name the person who owns the property or (*c*), that it charges an intent to defraud without naming the person whom it was intended to defraud.

The accused may elect his mode of trial pursuant to s. 536(2). Release pending trial is determined by s. 515.

SYNOPSIS

This section describes the offence of criminal breach of trust. Any person who acts as a trustee and who, *with intent to defraud* and *in contravention of his trust*, converts the object of the trust, or any part of it, to a use not authorized by the trust, commits an indictable offence and is liable to a maximum term of imprisonment of 14 years.

ANNOTATIONS

The intent to defraud in this section is a limited intent directed to the trust duties: *R. v. Petricia* (1974), 17 C.C.C. (2d) 27, [1974] 4 W.W.R. 425 (B.C.C.A.).

Having charged the individual accused with the offence under this section in that "being a trustee of funds" he converted those funds to an unauthorized use, the Crown was required to prove that the accused was a trustee and it was not sufficient to prove he was party to an offence committed by the actual trustee, a corporate entity: *R. v. Rosen*, [1985] 1 S.C.R. 83, 16 C.C.C. (3d) 481 (7:0).

PUBLIC SERVANT REFUSING TO DELIVER PROPERTY.

337. Every one who, being or having been employed in the service of Her Majesty in right of Canada or a province, or in the service of a municipality, and entrusted by virtue of that employment with the receipt, custody, management or control of anything, refuses or fails to deliver it to a person who is authorized to demand it and

does demand it, is guilty of an indictable offence and liable to imprisonment for a term not exceeding fourteen years. R.S., c. C-34, s. 297.

CROSS-REFERENCES

Related offences: s. 122, breach of trust by official (defined in s. 118); s. 426, secret commission; s. 322, conversion; s. 331, theft by person holding power of attorney; s. 332, theft by person holding money, etc., under direction; s. 380, fraud; s. 399, false return by public officer.

The accused may elect his mode of trial pursuant to s. 536(2). Release pending trial is determined by s. 515.

SYNOPSIS

This section describes an offence which can only be committed by a public servant in the employ of the federal government or a provincial or municipal government. If such a public servant is entrusted in the course of employment with the custody, management or control of anything and *refuses* or *fails to deliver* it upon the *demand* of a *person authorized to make a demand*, that public servant commits an indictable offence under this section and is liable to imprisonment for a term not exceeding 14 years.

ANNOTATIONS

The history of this provision suggests that it was enacted to prevent theft by public employees of the monies, documents, or other chattel they possessed by virtue of their employment. It is not applicable where a complainant is simply seeking information and not return or possession of a thing or document. Thus, a person who is authorized to demand "anything" is a person in authority vis-à-vis the employee in the employee/employer relationship. To hold a government employee criminally accountable to anyone who requests "anything" from that employee would amount to an absurdity: *Ambrosi v. British Columbia (Attorney General)* (2014), 311 C.C.C. (3d) 264 (B.C.C.A.), leave to appeal to S.C.C. refused 2014 CarswellBC 3523.

FRAUDULENTLY TAKING CATTLE OR DEFACING BRAND / Punishment for theft of cattle / Evidence of property in cattle / Presumption from possession.

338. (1) Every one who, without the consent of the owner,
  (*a*) fraudulently takes, holds, keeps in his possession, conceals, receives, appropriates, purchases or sells cattle that are found astray, or
  (*b*) fraudulently, in whole or in part,
      (i) obliterates, alters or defaces a brand or mark on cattle, or
      (ii) makes a false or counterfeit brand or mark on cattle,
is guilty of an indictable offence and liable to imprisonment for a term not exceeding five years.

(2) Every one who commits theft of cattle is guilty of an indictable offence and liable to imprisonment for a term not exceeding ten years.

(3) In any proceedings under this Act, evidence that cattle are marked with a brand or mark that is recorded or registered in accordance with any Act is, in the absence of any evidence to the contrary, proof that the cattle are owned by the registered owner of that brand or mark.

(4) Where an accused is charged with an offence under subsection (1) or (2), the burden of proving that the cattle came lawfully into the possession of the accused or his employee or into the possession of another person on behalf of the accused is on the accused, if the accused is not the registered owner of the brand or mark with which the cattle are marked, unless it appears that possession of the cattle by an employee of the accused or by another person on behalf of the accused was without the knowledge and

authority, sanction or approval of the accused. R.S., c. C-34, s. 298; 1974-75-76, c. 93, s. 26.

CROSS-REFERENCES

The term "cattle" is defined in s. 2. Possession is defined by s. 4(3). The general theft offence is defined in s. 322 and the general offence of possession of goods obtained by crime in s. 354. Other offences in relation to cattle are in s. 444. Under s. 357, it is an offence to bring into or have in Canada anything that the accused has obtained outside Canada by an act that, if it had been committed in Canada, would have been the offence of theft.

Pursuant to s. 583(*b*), an indictment, which otherwise complies with s. 581, is not insufficient by reason that it does not name the person who owns the property.

The accused may elect his mode of trial pursuant to s. 536(2). Release pending trial is determined by s. 515, although the accused is eligible for release by the officer in charge pursuant to s. 498 for the offence under subsec. (1).

SYNOPSIS

This section sets up a code to govern the offence of stealing cattle, the punishment for this offence and some evidence and procedural provisions. Subsection (1) states that any person who, without the consent of the owner, *fraudulently* takes, keeps in his possession, holds, conceals, receives, appropriates, purchases or sells stray cattle is guilty of an indictable offence and liable to a maximum term of imprisonment of five years. Subsection (1) applies the same punishment to any person who *fraudulently* obliterates, alters or defaces a brand or mark, in whole or in part, on cattle, or who makes a false or counterfeit brand or mark on cattle. Subsection (2) describes the punishment for the more serious offence of cattle theft. This offence is also indictable but carries a maximum term of imprisonment of 10 years. Subsection (3) states that, in any proceedings under the *Criminal Code*, evidence that cattle are marked with a brand or mark registered in accordance with any Act is proof, in the absence of evidence to the contrary, that the cattle are owned by the registered owner of that brand. Subsection (4) puts the burden upon a person charged under subsec. (1) or (2) of proving that the cattle came lawfully into his possession or constructive possession, if that person is not the registered owner of the brand with which the cattle are marked. The accused will not bear the burden of proof under subsec. (4), if it appears that the possession of the cattle by an employee or other person on his behalf, was without the knowledge and authority, sanction or approval of the accused.

ANNOTATIONS

A charge under this section was dismissed where, although the circumstances were suspicious and established negligence on the part of the accused in that he failed to make any attempt to verify the identity of the cattle and make those inspections which a reasonably prudent rancher would make, still the Crown had not established the requisite *mens rea*. This case was interesting in that expert evidence was adduced as to the behaviour of cows in "mothering up" to their own calves in order to establish that certain calves were not the offspring of the accused's own cattle: *R. v. Galpin* (1977), 34 C.C.C. (2d) 545 (B.C. Prov. Ct.).

TAKING POSSESSION ETC., OF DRIFT TIMBER / Dealer in second-hand goods / Search for timber unlawfully detained / Evidence of property in timber / Presumption from possession / Definitions / "coastal waters of Canada" / "lumber" / "lumbering equipment".

339. (1) Every one is guilty of an indictable offence and liable to imprisonment for a term not exceeding five years who, without the consent of the owner,

(*a*) fraudulently takes, holds, keeps in his possession, conceals, receives, appropriates, purchases or sells,

(b) removes, alters, obliterates or defaces a mark or number on, or

(c) refuses to deliver up to the owner or to the person in charge thereof on behalf of the owner or to a person authorized by the owner to receive it,

any lumber or lumbering equipment that is found adrift, cast ashore or lying on or embedded in the bed or bottom, or on the bank or beach, of a river, stream or lake in Canada, or in the harbours or any of the coastal waters of Canada.

(2) Every one who, being a dealer in second-hand goods of any kind, trades or traffics in or has in his possession for sale or traffic any lumbering equipment that is marked with the mark, brand, registered timber mark, name or initials of a person, without the written consent of that person, is guilty of an offence punishable on summary conviction.

(3) A peace officer who suspects, on reasonable grounds, that any lumber owned by any person and bearing the registered timber mark of that person is kept or detained in or on any place without the knowledge or consent of that person, may enter into or on that place to ascertain whether or not it is detained there without the knowledge or consent of that person.

(4) Where any lumber or lumbering equipment is marked with a timber mark or a boom chain brand registered under any Act, the mark or brand is, in proceedings under subsection (1), and, in the absence of any evidence to the contrary, proof that it is the property of the registered owner of the mark or brand.

(5) Where an accused or his servants or agents are in possession of lumber or lumbering equipment marked with the mark, brand, registered timber mark, name or initials of another person, the burden of proving that it came lawfully into his possession or into possession of his servants or agents is, in proceedings under subsection (1), on the accused.

(6) In this section,

"coastal waters of Canada" includes all of Queen Charlotte Sound, all of the Strait of Georgia and the Canadian waters of the Strait of Juan de Fuca;

"lumber" means timber, mast, spar, shingle bolt, sawlog or lumber of any description;

"lumbering equipment" includes a boom chain, chain, line and shackle. R.S., c. C-34, s. 299.

CROSS-REFERENCES

Possession is defined by s. 4(3). The term "peace officer" is defined in s. 2. The power given a peace officer under subsec. (3) would seem to be a search within the meaning of s. 8 of the Charter of Rights and Freedoms and therefore see notes under that section.

Pursuant to s. 583(b), an indictment, which otherwise complies with s. 581, is not insufficient by reason that it does not name the person who owns the property.

The accused may elect his mode of trial pursuant to s. 536(2) for the offence under subsec. (1) and release pending trial is determined by s. 515, although the accused is eligible for release by the officer in charge pursuant to s. 498. Trial of the offence described by subsec. (2) is conducted by a summary conviction court pursuant to Part XXVII. The punishment is as set out in s. 787 [although note the maximum fine for a corporation is as set out in s. 735] and the limitation period is set out in s. 786(2). Release pending trial is determined by s. 515, although the accused is eligible for release by a peace officer under s. 496, 497 or by the officer in charge under s. 498.

SYNOPSIS

This section sets out a number of provisions that deal with offences in relation to certain specified kinds of lumber and lumbering equipment. Subsection (1)(a) states that any person who, *without the consent of the owner, fraudulently* takes, holds, keeps in his possession, appropriates, purchases or sells any lumber or lumbering equipment found adrift or embedded in the shore, bottom or bed of any river, stream or lake in Canada, or in the harbours of coastal waters of Canada commits an indictable offence with a maximum term of imprisonment of five years. Subsection (1)(*b*) and (*c*) apply the same punishment to any person who, *without the consent of the owner*, removes, alters, obliterates or defaces a mark or number, or who refuses to deliver to the owner or person authorized to receive it, any lumber found in the places described above. It is to be noted that subsec. (1)(*a*) specifies that the acts described therein be committed *fraudulently* whereas subsec. (1)(*b*) and (*c*) do not have the same requirement. Subsection (2) makes it a summary conviction offence for a second-hand dealer to trade, or have in his possession to sell, lumbering equipment that is marked with the name or initials of a person or with a name, brand or registered timber mark, unless the dealer has the *written consent* of that person. Subsection (3) empowers a peace officer, who has *reasonable grounds to suspect* that lumber owned by another person is being kept or detained in any place without the owner's knowledge or consent, to enter that place to ascertain whether or not his suspicions are founded. This section, which permits entry into a place without a warrant, may be found to offend s. 8 of the Charter. Any lumber or lumbering equipment marked with a registered timber mark or boom chain brand is presumed to be the property of the registered owner of the mark or brand in proceedings under subsec. (1), unless there is evidence to the contrary. Subsection (5) places on a person charged under subsec. (1) the burden of proving that lumber or lumbering equipment marked with a brand mark, registered timber mark, name or initials of another person, that is in the possession of the accused came to be so possessed lawfully.

DESTROYING DOCUMENTS OF TITLE.

340. Every one who, for a fraudulent purpose, destroys, cancels, conceals or obliterates
   (*a*) **a document of title to goods or lands,**
   (*b*) **a valuable security or testamentary instrument, or**
   (*c*) **a judicial or official document,**
is guilty of an indictable offence and liable to imprisonment for a term not exceeding ten years. R.S., c. C-34, s. 300.

CROSS-REFERENCES

The terms "document of title to goods", "document of title to lands", "valuable security" and "testamentary instrument" are defined in s. 2. The value of a valuable security is determined in accordance with s. 4(2).

   The accused may elect his mode of trial pursuant to s. 536(2). Release pending trial is determined by s. 515.

SYNOPSIS

This section describes the offence of destroying, cancelling, concealing or obliterating a document of title to lands or goods, a valuable security or testamentary instrument, or a judicial or official document. The action must be done with a *fraudulent purpose*. The offence is indictable and carries a maximum term of imprisonment of 10 years.

FRAUDULENT CONCEALMENT.

341. Every one who, for a fraudulent purpose, takes, obtains, removes or conceals anything is guilty of an indictable offence and liable to imprisonment for a term not exceeding two years. R.S., c. C-34, s. 301.

CROSS-REFERENCES

The accused may elect his mode of trial pursuant to s. 536(2). Release pending trial is determined by s. 515, although the accused is eligible for release by the officer in charge pursuant to s. 498. The related offences of fraudulent concealment of title documents are in ss. 340 and 385.

Where the offence, although committed outside Canada, is in relation to the use of nuclear material, see s. 7(3.4).

SYNOPSIS

This section describes the offence of fraudulent concealment. Any person who, *for a fraudulent purpose*, takes, removes or conceals *anything* commits the offence. The offence is indictable and carries a maximum term of two years' imprisonment.

THEFT, FORGERY, ETC., OF CREDIT CARD / Jurisdiction / Unauthorized use of credit card data / Definitions.

342. (1) Every person who

   (*a*) steals a credit card,

   (*b*) forges or falsifies a credit card,

   (*c*) possesses, uses or traffics in a credit card or a forged or falsified credit card, knowing that it was obtained, made or altered

      (i) by the commission in Canada of an offence, or

      (ii) by an act or omission anywhere that, if it had occurred in Canada, would have constituted an offence, or

   (*d*) uses a credit card knowing that it has been revoked or cancelled,

is guilty of

   (*e*) an indictable offence and is liable to imprisonment for a term not exceeding ten years, or

   (*f*) an offence punishable on summary conviction.

(2) An accused who is charged with an offence under subsection (1) may be tried and punished by any court having jurisdiction to try that offence in the place where the offence is alleged to have been committed or in the place where the accused is found, is arrested or is in custody, but where the place where the accused is found, is arrested or is in custody is outside the province in which the offence is alleged to have been committed, no proceedings in respect of that offence shall be commenced in that place without the consent of the Attorney General of that province.

(3) [*Repealed* (old provision), R.S.C. 1985, c. 27 (1st Supp.), s. 44.]

(3) Every person who, fraudulently and without colour of right, possesses, uses, traffics in or permits another person to use credit card data, including personal authentication information, whether or not the data is authentic, that would enable a person to use a credit card or to obtain the services that are provided by the issuer of a credit card to credit card holders is guilty of

   (*a*) an indictable offence and is liable to imprisonment for a term not exceeding ten years; or

   (*b*) an offence punishable on summary conviction.

(4) In this section,

"personal authentication information" means a personal identification number or any other password or information that a credit card holder creates or adopts to be used to authenticate his or her identity in relation to the credit card;

"traffic" means, in relation to a credit card or credit card data, to sell, export from or import into Canada, distribute or deal with in any other way. 1974-75-76, c. 93, s. 27; R.S.C. 1985, c. 27 (1st Supp.), s. 44; 1997, c. 18, s. 16; 2009, c. 28, s. 4.

CROSS-REFERENCES

The term "credit card" is defined in s. 321. The term "steal" is defined in s. 2 as theft. Possession is defined by s. 4(3), however, s. 358 defines circumstances in which possession is complete. "Attorney General" is defined in s. 2. Section 583(*h*) provides that a count in an indictment is not insufficient by reason only that it does not state that the required consent has been obtained. [As to notes concerning sufficiency of consent, see s. 583.] Section 359 enacts a special evidentiary rule. Under s. 359, evidence that stolen property was found in the accused's possession in the previous 12 months is admissible to prove knowledge that the property that forms the subject-matter of the proceedings was stolen property. For the section to be invoked, notice must be given to the accused. Under s. 657.2 evidence that anyone was found guilty of theft of the property is proof that the property was stolen.

The general theft offence is defined by s. 322; the general offence of possession of goods obtained by crime by s. 354; the general forgery and uttering offences by ss. 366 to 368. Obtaining credit by fraud or by false pretences is an offence under s. 362. Bringing into Canada anything obtained outside Canada by an act that, if committed in Canada, would have been an offence under this section if committed in Canada, is an offence under s. 357. Section 342.01 creates offences respecting instruments adapted or intended for use in forging or falsifying credit cards. Section 56.1 creates offences in relation to the unlawful possession, sale and transfer of identity documents.

It would seem that where the prosecution elects to proceed by indictment then the accused may elect his mode of trial pursuant to s. 536(2). However, s. 553(*a*) provides that a provincial court judge has absolute jurisdiction to try an accused charged with "theft" where the value of the subject-matter of the offence does not exceed $5000 and, therefore, query whether the offence described by para. (1)(*a*) is governed by s. 553(*a*). Where the prosecution elects to proceed by way of summary conviction then the trial of the offence is conducted by a summary conviction court pursuant to Part XXVII. The punishment is as set out in s. 787 and the limitation period is set out in s. 786(2). Release pending trial in any case is determined by s. 515, although the accused is eligible for release by a peace officer under s. 496, 497 or by the officer in charge under s. 498. This offence may be the basis of an application for authorization to intercept private communications by reason of s. 183 and for a warrant to conduct video surveillance by reason of s. 487.01(5).

SYNOPSIS

This section deals with offences in relation to a credit card. Subsection (1) makes it a hybrid offence, with a maximum term of imprisonment of ten years upon conviction for the indictable offence, to steal, forge or falsify a credit card, or to use a credit card which the accused knows has been revoked or cancelled. Subsection (1) further states that any person who has in his possession, uses or traffics in any way with a credit card which that person *knows* was obtained anywhere by an action which, in Canada, is or would be an offence, commits an offence. Subsection (2) provides that the trial of an offence under subsec. (1) may be held either where the offence is alleged to have been committed or anywhere the accused is found, arrested or in custody. If the accused is found, arrested or in custody outside the province where the offence under subsec. (1) is alleged to have been committed, *the consent of the Attorney General* of that province is required before a trial may be commenced. Subsection (3) creates offences in relation to fraudulent possession, use, trafficking in (defined in subsec. (4)), or permitting another person to use credit card data, including personal authentication information (defined in subsec. (4)).

ANNOTATIONS

Where the information is drafted to come within subsec. (1)(*c*)(ii) but specifies that the credit card was obtained by an "offence" that if it had occurred in Canada would have constituted an offence then the Crown having particularized the act or omission as an "offence" must prove that it was an offence known to the law of the place where it allegedly took place. This would require proof of the foreign law: *R. v. Ingram* (1978), 43 C.C.C. (2d) 211 (Ont. Prov. Ct.).

It was held in *R. v. Colman,* [1981] 3 W.W.R. 572, 29 A.R. 170 (Q.B.), that inasmuch as subsec. (1)(*c*) in the French version creates only one offence an accused charged with possession of the credit card may successfully plead *autrefois acquit* based on a prior acquittal on an information charging that she unlawfully did "use or deal" with the credit card. Since the French version was more favourable to the accused it was that version which must be adopted. Cavanagh J. noted that the Yukon Territory Court of Appeal came to a contrary conclusion in *R. v. McKay* (1978), 39 C.C.C. (2d) 101, 3 C.R. (3d) 1, but without any reference to the French version of this subsection.

A credit card was "obtained by" commission of an indictable offence where it was originally simply found by the accused but he subsequently formed the intention to convert the card to his own use: *R. v. Costello* (1982), 1 C.C.C. (3d) 403, [1983] 1 W.W.R. 666 (B.C.C.A.). Folld: *R. v. Zurowski* (1983), 5 C.C.C. (3d) 285, 33 C.R. (3d) 93 (Alta. C.A.); *R. v. Elias* (1986), 33 C.C.C. (3d) 476 (Que. C.A.), affd [1989] 1 S.C.R. 423, 46 C.C.C. (3d) 447 (5:0).

The offence under subsec. (3) is committed even where the credit card in question has been blocked and could not have been used successfully: *R. v. Tuduce* (2014), 314 C.C.C. (3d) 429 (Ont. C.A.), leave to appeal to S.C.C. refused 2015 CarswellOnt 18924. *Contra*: *R. v. Jahanrakhshan* (2011), 96 W.C.B. (2d) 158, [2011] B.C.J. No. 1657 (S.C.), affirmed (2013), 296 C.C.C. (3d) 553 (B.C.C.A.), additional reasons (2013), 301 C.C.C. (3d) 334 (B.C.C.A.), affirmed (2013), 582 W.A.C. 69 (B.C.C.A.).

INSTRUMENTS FOR COPYING CREDIT CARD DATA OR FORGING OR FALSIFYING CREDIT CARDS / Forfeiture / Limitation.

342.01 (1) Every person is guilty of an indictable offence and liable to imprisonment for a term of not more than 10 years, or is guilty of an offence punishable on summary conviction, who, without lawful justification or excuse, makes, repairs, buys, sells, exports from Canada, imports into Canada or possesses any instrument, device, apparatus, material or thing that they know has been used or know is adapted or intended for use

> (*a*) **in the copying of credit card data for use in the commission of an offence under subsection 342(3); or**
>
> (*b*) **in the forging or falsifying of credit cards.**

(2) Where a person is convicted of an offence under subsection (1), any instrument, device, apparatus, material or thing in relation to which the offence was committed or the possession of which constituted the offence may, in addition to any other punishment that may be imposed, be ordered forfeited to Her Majesty, whereupon it may be disposed of as the Attorney General directs.

(3) No order of forfeiture may be made under subsection (2) in respect of any thing that is the property of a person who was not a party to the offence under subsection (1). 1997, c. 18, s. 17; 2009, c. 28, s. 5.

CROSS-REFERENCES

"Attorney General" is defined in s. 2. Section 327 creates a similar offence in relation to instruments used for unlawfully obtaining telecommunication facilities. Section 342.2 creates a similar offence in relation to instruments used for obtaining unauthorized use of computers. As to the meaning of "reasonable inference", reference might be made to cases noted under s. 351.

SYNOPSIS

This section creates a Crown-option offence to complement the offence under s. 342 by making it an offence to make, possess, repair, buy, sell, export or import any instrument, device, material, apparatus or thing, that the person knows has been used or is adapted or intended for use in copying of credit card data for use in committing the offence under s. 342(3), or forging or falsifying credit cards. Upon conviction, the device, instrument etc. may be forfeited to the Crown, except if the matter was not the property of a person party to the offence.

UNAUTHORIZED USE OF COMPUTER / Definitions / "computer password" / "computer program" / "computer service" / "computer system" / "data" / "electro-magnetic, acoustic, mechanical or other device" / "function" / "intercept" / "traffic".

342.1 (1) Everyone is guilty of an indictable offence and liable to imprisonment for a term of not more than 10 years, or is guilty of an offence punishable on summary conviction who, fraudulently and without colour of right,

(*a*) obtains, directly or indirectly, any computer service;

(*b*) by means of an electro-magnetic, acoustic, mechanical or other device, intercepts or causes to be intercepted, directly or indirectly, any function of a computer system;

(*c*) uses or causes to be used, directly or indirectly, a computer system with intent to commit an offence under paragraph (*a*) or (*b*) or under section 430 in relation to computer data or a computer system; or

(*d*) uses, possesses, traffics in or permits another person to have access to a computer password that would enable a person to commit an offence under paragraph (*a*), (*b*) or (*c*).

(2) In this section,

"computer data" means representations, including signs, signals or symbols, that are in a form suitable for processing in a computer system;

"computer password" means any computer data by which a computer service or computer system is capable of being obtained or used;

"computer program" means computer data representing instructions or statements that, when executed in a computer system, causes the computer system to perform a function;

"computer service" includes data processing and the storage or retrieval of computer data;

"computer system" means a device that, or a group of interconnected or related devices one or more of which,

(*a*) contains computer programs or other computer data, and

(*b*) by means of computer programs,

(i) performs logic and control, and

(ii) may perform any other function;

"data" [*Repealed*. 2014, c. 31, s. 16(2).]

"electro-magnetic, acoustic, mechanical or other device" means any device or apparatus that is used or is capable of being used to intercept any function of a computer system, but does not include a hearing aid used to correct subnormal hearing of the user to not better than normal hearing;

"function" includes logic, control, arithmetic, deletion, storage and retrieval and communication or telecommunication to, from or within a computer system;

"intercept" includes listen to or record a function of a computer system, or acquire the substance, meaning or purport thereof.

"traffic" means, in respect of a computer password, to sell, export from or import into Canada, distribute or deal with in any other way. R.S.C. 1985, c. 27 (1st Supp.), s. 45; 1997, c. 18, s. 18; 2014, c. 31, s. 16.

CROSS-REFERENCES

The term "telecommunication" is defined in s. 35 of the *Interpretation Act*, R.S.C. 1985, c. I-21. As to notes respecting the term "colour of right", see notes under s. 322. This offence may be the basis of an application to intercept private communications by reason of s. 183 or for a warrant to conduct video surveillance by reason of s. 487.01(5).

Related offences: s. 184, unlawful interception of private communications; s. 326, theft of telecommunication service; s. 327, possession of device to unlawfully obtain telecommunication facility or service; s. 342.2, possession or sale of instruments for committing an offence under this section; s. 430(1.1), mischief in relation to data.

The accused may elect the mode of trial pursuant to s. 536(2) where the prosecution elects to proceed by way of indictment. Where the prosecution elects to proceed by way of summary conviction then the trial is conducted by a summary conviction court pursuant to Part XXVII. The punishment is as set out in s. 787 [although note the maximum fine for a corporation is as set out in s. 735] and the limitation period is set out in s. 786(2). Release pending trial is determined by s. 515, although the accused is eligible for release by a peace officer under s. 496, 497 or by the officer in charge under s. 498.

SYNOPSIS

This section makes it a hybrid offence for a person *fraudulently* or *without colour of right* to obtain, directly or indirectly, any computer service, or to intercept or cause to be intercepted, directly or indirectly, any function of a computer service by means of any device. It further states that it is an offence to use or cause to be used, directly or indirectly, a computer system *with intent* to commit either of the offences described above or an offence under s. 430, or to use, possess, traffic in or permit access to a computer password enabling a person to commit the offence in this section. Subsection (2) contains an extensive set of definitions of terms relevant to this offence. The maximum term of imprisonment upon conviction for the indictable offence described in this section is ten years.

ANNOTATIONS

"Computer system" includes text messaging via cellular telephones: *R. v. Woodward* (2011), 276 C.C.C. (3d) 86 (Ont. C.A.).

However, in *R. v. Cockell* (2013), 299 C.C.C. (3d) 221 (Alta. C.A.), leave to appeal to S.C.C. refused [2013] 3 S.C.R. x, the court held that the trial judge had erred by deeming the accused's Blackberry to be a "computer system" within the meaning of subsec. (2) in the absence of any expert evidence on this point.

POSSESSION OF DEVICE TO OBTAIN UNAUTHORIZED USE OF COMPUTER SYSTEM OR TO COMMIT MISCHIEF / Forfeiture / Limitation / Definition of "device".

342.2 (1) Everyone who, without lawful excuse, makes, possesses, sells, offers for sale, imports, obtains for use, distributes or makes available a device that is designed or adapted primarily to commit an offence under section 342.1 or 430, under circumstances that give rise to a reasonable inference that the device has been used or is or was intended to be used to commit such an offence, is

   (a) guilty of an indictable offence and liable to imprisonment for a term of not more than two years; or

   (b) guilty of an offence punishable on summary conviction.

(2) If a person is convicted of an offence under subsection (1), in addition to any punishment that is imposed, any device in relation to which the offence was committed or the possession of which constituted the offence may be ordered forfeited to Her Majesty and may be disposed of as the Attorney General directs.

(3) No order of forfeiture may be made under subsection (2) in respect of any thing that is the property of a person who was not a party to the offence under subsection (1).

(4) In this section, "device" includes

   (a) a component of a device; and

   (b) a computer program within the meaning of subsection 342.1(2). 1997, c. 18, s. 19; 2014, c. 31, s. 17.

CROSS-REFERENCES

"Attorney General" is defined in s. 2. Section 327 creates a similar offence in relation to instruments used for unlawfully obtaining telecommunication facilities. Section 342.01 creates a similar offence in relation to instruments used for forging or falsifying credit cards. As to the meaning of "reasonable inference", reference might be made to cases noted under s. 351. This offence may be the basis of an application to intercept private communications by reason of s. 183 or for a warrant to conduct video surveillance by reason of s. 487.01(5).

SYNOPSIS

This section creates a Crown-option offence to complement the offence under s. 342.1 by making it an offence to make, possess, sell, offer for sale or distribute any instrument, device or component thereof, the design of which renders it primarily useful for committing the offence under that section or under s. 430. The Crown must also prove that the person had the device under circumstances giving rise to a reasonable inference that the device, instrument or component was used or intended for use to commit the s. 342.1 or s. 430 offence. Upon conviction the device, instrument or component may be forfeited to the Crown, except if the matter was not the property of a person party to the offence.

Robbery and Extortion

ROBBERY.

343. Every one commits robbery who
- (*a*) **steals, and for the purpose of extorting whatever is stolen or to prevent or overcome resistance to the stealing, uses violence or threats of violence to a person or property;**
- (*b*) **steals from any person and, at the time he steals or immediately before or immediately thereafter, wounds, beats, strikes or uses any personal violence to that person;**
- (*c*) **assaults any person with intent to steal from him; or**
- (*d*) **steals from any person while armed with an offensive weapon or imitation thereof. R.S., c. C-34, s. 302.**

CROSS-REFERENCES

The terms "offensive weapon" and "property" are defined in s. 2. The term "steal" is defined in s. 2 as committing theft. Theft is defined in ss. 322 to 333, but principally in s. 322. Assault is defined in s. 265. The punishment for robbery is set out in s. 344.

Section 17 limits the availability of the statutory defence of compulsion by threats to the offence of "robbery". As to admission of photographic evidence of property, see s. 491.2. Under s. 583, an indictment, which otherwise complies with s. 581, is not insufficient by reason only that (*a*), it does not name the person injured or intended to be injured; (*b*), it does not name the person who owns or has a special property or interest in the property mentioned in the count, however, see s. 587 as to when particulars may be ordered. Also note s. 588 which deems certain persons to have a property interest in property of which they have the management, control or custody. This offence has often posed problems respecting included offences. Thus, see notes under s. 662.

This offence may be the basis for an application for an authorization to intercept private communications by reason of s. 183 or a warrant to conduct video surveillance by reason of s. 487.01(5). Robbery is an enterprise crime offence for the purposes of Part XII.2.

Where the offence, although committed outside Canada, is in relation to the use of nuclear material, see s. 7(3.4).

The accused may elect his mode of trial pursuant to s. 536(2). Release pending trial is determined by s. 515. A person convicted of the offence in this section will be liable to the mandatory prohibition order in s. 109 for possession of certain weapons, ammunition and explosives.

Related offences: s. 85, using firearm during commission or attempted commission of indictable offence; s. 244, discharging firearm with intent to wound; s. 264.1, uttering threats; s. 266, assault; s. 267, assault with a weapon or causing bodily harm; s. 268, aggravated assault; s. 272, sexual assault with a weapon; s. 273, aggravated sexual assault; s. 279, kidnapping and unlawful confinement; s. 345, stopping mail with intent to rob; s. 346, extortion; s. 348, break and enter; s. 351(2), disguised with intent. Section 98.1 creates a robbery offence where the object of the theft is a firearm.

Pursuant to s. 348.1, if a person is convicted of this offence in relation to a dwelling-house, it is an aggravating factor in sentencing that the dwelling-house was occupied at the time and the offender knew or was reckless as to whether the dwelling-house was occupied and used violence or threats of violence to a person or property.

SYNOPSIS

This section describes the offence of robbery. Every person who *steals* and uses violence or threats of violence to another person or property in order to overcome resistance to the stealing or to extort whatever is stolen, commits the form of robbery set out in para. (*a*). Everyone who *steals* from any person and, during the course of the stealing, or *immediately* before or after, wounds, beats or uses any personal violence to that person commits the form of robbery set out in para. (*b*). A person who assaults another person *with the intent to steal* from him commits the offence of robbery described in para. (*c*). Finally, everyone who *steals* from any person while armed, with an offensive weapon or an imitation thereof, commits the offence of robbery described in para. (*d*). It is to be noted that paras. (*a*), (*b*) and (*d*) require proof of the act of stealing as one of the elements of the offence. Paragraph (*c*) requires proof only of an intent to steal as an essential element.

ANNOTATIONS

Use of violence or threats of violence (para. (*a*)) – Assault, for which only a general intent is required, may be a lesser and included offence in the charge of unlawfully and by violence stealing, which also requires proof of the specific intent to carry out that purpose: *R. v. George*, [1960] S.C.R. 871, 128 C.C.C. 289 (4:1).

The offence under this paragraph is not made out in a "purse snatching" case where the accused simply snatches the purse before the victim could offer any resistance and he uses no other violence to the victim: *R. v. Picard* (1976), 39 C.C.C. (2d) 57 (Que. Sess. Ct.).

However, where the victim's arms are held to prevent resistance while the money is taken, then the offence is made out: *R. v. Trudel* (1984), 12 C.C.C. (3d) 342 (Que. C.A.).

Paragraph (*a*) requires the violence to be before or contemporaneous with the theft. In this case, the accused got into an altercation with a security guard in the parking lot after committing the theft in the store. As the theft was complete once the accused had left the store, a conviction for robbery could not be made out: *R. v. Newell* (2007), 217 C.C.C. (3d) 483, 263 Nfld. & P.E.I.R. 67 (Nfld. & Lab. C.A.). See also *R. v. Jean* (2012), 293 C.C.C. (3d) 66 (B.C.C.A.), leave to appeal to S.C.C. refused 2013 CarswellBC 1314 (S.C.C.); *R. v. McKay* (2014), 305 C.C.C. (3d) 409 (Sask. C.A.).

In *R. v. Katrensky* (1975), 24 C.C.C. (2d) 350, [1975] 5 W.W.R. 732 (B.C. Prov. Ct.), the accused was convicted of robbery as defined in this section where he merely handed the bank teller a note stating "empty your till". It was held that to constitute a threat of violence the Crown must prove that the victim felt threatened and that she had reasonable and probable grounds for her fear. In this case while there may not have been any immediate fear of violence, the implied threat of violence if the request was not carried out was sufficient to constitute the act of the accused robbery.

Threats of violence within the meaning of this paragraph would include any demonstration from which physical injury to the victim may be reasonably apprehended: *R. v. Sayers and McCoy* (1983), 8 C.C.C. (3d) 572 (Ont. C.A.).

A threat of violence is characterized by conduct which reflects an intent to have recourse to violence in order to carry out the theft or to prevent resistance to the theft. A threat may be expressed or implicit and made by means of words, writings or actions. There is no requirement that the accused be armed or utter words such as "This is a hold up". The question is whether the actions and words of the accused, in light of the context and circumstances in which they took place, could reasonably create a feeling of apprehension on the part of the victims: *R. v. Pelletier* (1992), 71 C.C.C. (3d) 438 (Que. C.A.).

Once a threat is established, there is no additional requirement of some minimum level of violence: *R. v. Lecky* (2001), 157 C.C.C. (3d) 351 (Ont. C.A.).

Stealing and using violence (para. (b)) – In order to avoid an interpretation repetitious to para. (a), this paragraph should be regarded as setting out what one might call constructive robbery occurring with theft and a proximate application of violence *R. v. Lieberman*, [1970] 5 C.C.C. 300, 11 C.R.N.S. 168 (Ont. C.A.) (2:1). It is not necessary that the violence be used to accomplish or further the theft. The purpose for which the personal violence is used is immaterial provided it accompanies the act of stealing or immediately precedes it or follows it: *R. v. Downer* (1978), 40 C.C.C. (2d) 532 (Ont. C.A.).

The "violence" contemplated by this paragraph requires proof of more than a mere assault. Thus the mere nudging of the victim to steal her purse is not sufficient: *R. v. Lew* (1978), 40 C.C.C. (2d) 140 (Ont. C.A.). Similarly: *R. v. Oakley* (1986), 24 C.C.C. (3d) 351 (Ont. C.A.).

In determining whether the conduct amounted to the use of threats or violence, a trier of fact may apply a partly subjective and partly objective test. In this case, the accused had given a note to the teller and indicated through gestures and grunts that he wanted money. Given the teller's evidence that the accused's hand was in his pocket throughout and that she assumed that he had a weapon in his pocket, the offence was made out: *R. v. Bourassa* (2004), 189 C.C.C. (3d) 438 (N.S.C.A.).

Assault with intent to steal (para. (c)) – A charge that the accused "did commit robbery [of the victim] of approximately $15" particularizes a completed stealing and where the Crown fails to prove that any money was stolen the Crown cannot rely on the definition of robbery in this paragraph to make out the offence. The accused may, however, be convicted of attempted robbery: *R. v. Bob* (1980), 54 C.C.C. (2d) 169 (B.C.C.A.).

Stealing while armed (para. (d)) – To be "armed" means to be equipped with or possessed of an instrument: *R. v. Sloan* (1974), 19 C.C.C. (2d) 190 (B.C.C.A.).

A charge of robbery was dismissed where the accused was charged that he "simulated with his fist that he was armed". It was held that this paragraph requires that the accused be armed with a weapon or an imitation thereof and no part of the body can resemble an offensive weapon: *R. v. Gouchie* (1976), 33 C.C.C. (2d) 120 (Que. Sess. Peace).

The offence under this paragraph does not require that the accused intended to use the weapon or that the victim be frightened or intimidated by its presence: *Tremblay v. Quebec (Attorney General)* (1984), 43 C.R. (3d) 92 (Que. C.A.).

Mens rea generally – An honest belief that a debt was due from the victim to himself will vitiate the element of theft in a robbery charge against the accused: *R. v. Carroll* (1975), 27 C.C.C. (2d) 276 (Ont. C.A.).

Included offences – This section creates only one offence, namely robbery, which may be committed in any of the different ways described. On a charge of stealing while armed, under para. (d) while theft is an included offence, assault is not as the mere fact of being armed does not necessarily involve an assault. Where the Crown alleges in the indictment the particular means by which the robbery was committed, as here, "did steal . . . while armed with an imitation of an offensive weapon" it is required to prove every essential averment of the charge and could not require the trial judge instruct the jury to consider whether robbery was committed in one of the other ways described in the section: *R. v. Johnson* (1977), 35 C.C.C. (2d) 439 (B.C.C.A.).

It is an error for the trial judge to instruct the jury that "simple robbery" is an included offence to "armed robbery". Notwithstanding that the trial judge erroneously left robbery with the jury and the indictment included the words "use a firearm, to wit: a sawed-off shotgun", the accused was still properly convicted. The words "sawed-off shotgun" did not particularize an element of the offence but rather put the accused on notice that he faced the minimum sentence for robbery where a firearm is used: *R. v. Manley* (2011), 269 C.C.C. (3d) 40 (Ont. C.A.).

The fact that robbery may be committed in ways which do not include an assault does not alter the fact that robbery as described in this section does include the offence of assault. It is sufficient that an offence such as assault is included in the enactment creating the principal offence, it need not be necessarily included. Thus common assault was an included offence although the indictment merely alleged that the accused "unlawfully did commit robbery of [the victim] of a quantity of cigarettes and approximately $4.00 in cash": *R. v. Luckett*, [1980] 1 S.C.R. 1140, 50 C.C.C. (2d) 489 (7:0).

The accused may be convicted of assault causing bodily harm on an indictment charging robbery *simpliciter*. The inclusion of the word "wounds" in the definition of robbery in para. (*b*) makes assault causing bodily harm an included offence: *R. v. Horsefall* (1990), 61 C.C.C. (3d) 245 (B.C.C.A.).

An indictment which charges robbery under para. (*c*) includes attempted theft so that the accused may be convicted of that offence where the evidence establishes a theft but no assault:*R. v. Boisvert* (1991), 68 C.C.C. (3d) 478 (Que. C.A.).

Property which may be subject-matter of offence – A narcotic may be the subject of a robbery notwithstanding it constitutes an offence for the victim to be in possession of it: *R. v. Janzic* (1982), 1 C.C.C. (3d) 246 (Ont. C.A.), leave to appeal to S.C.C. refused 46 N.R. 90*n*.

ROBBERY / Subsequent offences / Sequence of convictions only.

344. (1) Every person who commits robbery is guilty of an indictable offence and liable
  (*a*) if a restricted firearm or prohibited firearm is used in the commission of the offence or if any firearm is used in the commission of the offence and the offence is committed for the benefit of, at the direction of, or in association with, a criminal organization, to imprisonment for life and to a minimum punishment of imprisonment for a term of
      (i) in the case of a first offence, five years, and
      (ii) in the case of a second or subsequent offence, seven years;
  (*a*.1) in any other case where a firearm is used in the commission of the offence, to imprisonment for life and to a minimum punishment of imprisonment for a term of four years; and
  (*b*) in any other case, to imprisonment for life.

(2) In determining, for the purpose of paragraph (1)(*a*), whether a convicted person has committed a second or subsequent offence, if the person was earlier convicted of any of the following offences, that offence is to be considered as an earlier offence:
  (*a*) an offence under this section;
  (*b*) an offence under subsection 85(1) or (2) or section 244 or 244.2; or
  (*c*) an offence under section 220, 236, 239, 272 or 273, subsection 279(1) or section 279.1 or 346 if a firearm was used in the commission of the offence.
However, an earlier offence shall not be taken into account if 10 years have elapsed between the day on which the person was convicted of the earlier offence and the day on which the person was convicted of the offence for which sentence is being imposed, not taking into account any time in custody.

(3) For the purposes of subsection (2), the only question to be considered is the sequence of convictions and no consideration shall be given to the sequence of commission of offences or whether any offence occurred before or after any conviction. R.S., c. C-34, s. 303; 1972, c. 13, s. 70; 1995, c. 39, s. 149; 2008, c. 6, s. 32; 2009, c. 22, s. 14.

CROSS-REFERENCES

Robbery is defined in s. 343. "Firearm" is defined in s. 2. "Criminal organization" is defined in ss. 2 and 476.1. Pursuant to s. 2.1, "restricted firearm" and "prohibited firearm" are defined in s. 84.

As to admission of photographic evidence of property see, s. 491.2.

Section 17 limits the availability of the statutory defence of compulsion by threats to the offence of "robbery". Under s. 583, an indictment, which otherwise complies with s. 581, is not insufficient by reason only that (*a*), it does not name the person injured or intended to be injured; (*b*), it does not name the person who owns or has a special property or interest in the property mentioned in the count, however, see s. 587 as to when particulars may be ordered. Also note s. 588 which deems certain persons to have a property interest in property of which they have the management, control or custody. This offence has often posed problems respecting included offences. Thus, see notes under s. 662.

This offence may be the basis for an application for an authorization to intercept private communications by reason of s. 183 or a warrant to conduct video surveillance by reason of s. 487.01(5). Robbery is an enterprise crime offence for the purposes of Part XII.2.

The accused may elect his mode of trial pursuant to s. 536(2). Release pending trial is determined by s. 515. A person convicted of the offence in this section will be liable to the mandatory prohibition order in s. 109 for possession of certain weapons, ammunition and explosives.

Related offences: s. 85, using firearm during commission or attempted commission of indictable offence; s. 244, discharging firearm with intent to wound; s. 264.1, uttering threats; s. 266, assault; s. 267, assault with a weapon or causing bodily harm; s. 268, aggravated assault; s. 272, sexual assault with a weapon; s. 273, aggravated sexual assault; s. 279, kidnapping and unlawful confinement; s. 345, stopping mail with intent to rob; s. 346, extortion; s. 348, break and enter; s. 351(2), disguised with intent. Section 98.1 creates a robbery offence where the object of the theft is a firearm.

SYNOPSIS

This section sets out the penalties for the robbery offences described in s. 343. The maximum punishment is life imprisonment. The section also enacts minimum punishments. Where a restricted or prohibited firearm is used or the offence was committed for the benefit of, at the direction of, or in association with, a criminal organization, the offender is liable to a minimum punishment of at least five years' imprisonment for a first offence and seven years for a second or subsequent offence. The rules for determining whether the offender has committed a second or subsequent offence are set out in subsecs. (2) and (3) and, for example, provide that a prior offence includes not only convictions under this section, but other specified offences involving firearms. However, an earlier offence is not to be taken into account if 10 years have elapsed from the conviction of the earlier offence, not counting time in custody. Subsection (4) reverses the common law rule and provides that the court only takes into account the sequence of convictions, not the order in which the offences were committed. In any other case where a firearm is used, the offender is liable to a minimum term of imprisonment of four years. Where no firearm is used, there is no minimum punishment.

ANNOTATIONS

Note: These cases were decided before the increase in the minimum punishment as now set out in subsec. (1)(*a*).

Prior to the enactment of para. (*a*) it was held where the underlying offence is robbery, the minimum penalty prescribed for the offence contrary to s. 85 [using a firearm in the commission of an indictable offence] did not infringe s. 12 of the Charter although it could result in the imposition of a number of consecutive sentences for offences arising out of the same series of events: *R. v. Brown*, [1994] 3 S.C.R. 749, 93 C.C.C. (3d) 97.

The minimum punishment of four years set out in former para. (*a*) does not violate s. 12 of the Charter: *R. v. Lapierre* (1998), 123 C.C.C. (3d) 332, 15 C.R. (5th) 283 (Que. C.A.); *R. v. Wust* (1998), 125 C.C.C. (3d) 43, 17 C.R. (5th) 45 *sub nom. R. v. W. (L.W.)* (B.C.C.A.), revd on other grounds [2000] 1 S.C.R. 455, 143 C.C.C. (3d) 129; *R. v. McDonald* (1998), 127 C.C.C. (3d) 57, 17 C.R. (5th) 1 (Ont. C.A.).

The court may deduct the time spent in pre-sentence custody pursuant to s. 719(3) even if the resulting sentence is less than the four-year minimum. There is no mechanical formula for crediting pre-sentencing custody. While approximately two months' credit for each month spent in pre-sentence custody is entirely appropriate to reflect the harshness of pre-trial custody, a different rationale could also be applied depending on the circumstances of the detention. Accordingly, the amount of credit given for pre-trial custody should be left to the discretion of the sentencing judge: *R. v. Wust*, [2000] 1 S.C.R. 455, 143 C.C.C. (3d) 129. See also *R. v. Arrance*, [2000] 1 S.C.R. 488, 143 C.C.C. (3d) 154, and *R. v. Arthurs*, [2000] 1 S.C.R. 481, 143 C.C.C. (3d) 149.

It was held that former s. 85 could be resorted to only where there is a conviction for the underlying offence and the use of the firearm was in the actual commission or attempted commission of the underlying offence. Thus, the accused could not be convicted of using a firearm while a party to a robbery where, although a firearm was used to compel a third person to commit the robbery, this third person did not actually use the firearm to commit the robbery: *R. v. Ingraham* (1991), 66 C.C.C. (3d) 27, 46 O.A.C. 216 (C.A.).

STOPPING MAIL WITH INTENT.

345. Every one who stops a mail conveyance with intent to rob or search it is guilty of an indictable offence and liable to imprisonment for life. R.S., c. C-34, s. 304.

CROSS-REFERENCES

Robbery is defined in s. 343. The term "mail conveyance" is defined in s. 2 of the *Canada Post Corporation Act*, R.S.C. 1985, c. C-10, as meaning "any physical, electronic, optical or other means used to transmit the mail". That section also contains the definition of "mail".

Section 476(*e*) contains a special provision for territorial jurisdiction where an offence is committed in respect of a mail in the course of door-to-door delivery.

The related offence of theft from the mail is in s. 356. Using a firearm during commission or attempted commission of an indictable offence is an offence under s. 85. Disguised with intent is an offence under s. 351(2).

The accused may elect his mode of trial pursuant to s. 536(2). Release pending trial is determined by s. 515. A person convicted of the offence in this section may be liable to the mandatory prohibition order in s. 109 for possession of certain weapons, ammunition and explosives.

SYNOPSIS

This section describes the offence of stopping a mail conveyance with *the intent to rob or search* it. The offence is punishable by way of indictment and carries a maximum term of life imprisonment and a minimum punishment of four years where a firearm is used in the commission of the offence.

EXTORTION / Punishment / Subsequent offences / Sequence of convictions only / Saving.

346. (1) Every one commits extortion who, without reasonable justification or excuse and with intent to obtain anything, by threats, accusations, menaces or violence induces or attempts to induce any person, whether or not he is the person threatened, accused or menaced or to whom violence is shown, to do anything or cause anything to be done.

(1.1) Every person who commits extortion is guilty of an indictable offence and liable

(*a*) if a restricted firearm or prohibited firearm is used in the commission of the offence or if any firearm is used in the commission of the offence and the offence is committed for the benefit of, at the direction of, or in association with, a criminal organization, to imprisonment for life and to a minimum punishment of imprisonment for a term of

(i) in the case of a first offence, five years, and

(ii) in the case of a second or subsequent offence, seven years;

(*a*.1) in any other case where a firearm is used in the commission of the offence, to imprisonment for life and to a minimum punishment of imprisonment for a term of four years; and

(*b*) in any other case, to imprisonment for life.

(1.2) In determining, for the purpose of paragraph (1.1)(*a*), whether a convicted person has committed a second or subsequent offence, if the person was earlier convicted of any of the following offences, that offence is to be considered as an earlier offence:

(*a*) an offence under this section;

(*b*) an offence under subsection 85(1) or (2) or section 244 or 244.2; or

(*c*) an offence under section 220, 236, 239, 272 or 273, subsection 279(1) or section 279.1 or 344 if a firearm was used in the commission of the offence.

However, an earlier offence shall not be taken into account if 10 years have elapsed between the day on which the person was convicted of the earlier offence and the day on which the person was convicted of the offence for which sentence is being imposed, not taking into account any time in custody.

(1.3) For the purposes of subsection (1.2), the only question to be considered is the sequence of convictions and no consideration shall be given to the sequence of commission of offences or whether any offence occurred before or after any conviction.

(2) A threat to institute civil proceedings is not a threat for the purposes of this section. R.S., c. C-34, s. 305; R.S.C. 1985, c. 27 (1st Suppl.), s. 46; 1995, c. 39, s. 150; 2008, c. 6, s. 33; 2009, c. 22, s. 15.

CROSS-REFERENCES

This offence may be the basis for an application for an authorization to intercept private communications by reason of s. 183 or a warrant to conduct video surveillance by reason of s. 487.01(5). Extortion is an enterprise crime offence for the purposes of Part XII.2.

Where the offence, although committed outside Canada, is in relation to the use of nuclear material, see s. 7(3.4). Firearm is defined in s. 2. "Criminal organization" is defined in ss. 2 and 476.1. Pursuant to s. 2.1, "restricted firearm" and "prohibited firearm" are defined in s. 84.

Related offences: s. 85, using firearm during commission or attempted commission of indictable offence; s. 244, discharging firearm with intent to wound; s. 264.1, uttering threats; s. 266, assault; s. 267, assault with a weapon or causing bodily harm; s. 268, aggravated assault; s. 279, kidnapping and unlawful confinement; s. 343, robbery; s. 347, criminal interest rate; s. 302, extortion by libel.

The accused may elect his mode of trial pursuant to s. 536(2). Release pending trial is determined by s. 515. A person convicted of the offence in this section may be liable to the mandatory prohibition order in s. 109 for possession of certain weapons, ammunition and explosives. Pursuant to s. 486(3), the judge or justice may make an order banning publication of the identity of the complainant or witness and any information that could disclose the identity of the complainant or witness.

Pursuant to s. 348.1, if a person is convicted of the offence under this section in relation to a dwelling-house, it is an aggravating factor in sentencing that the dwelling-house was occupied at the time and the offender knew or was reckless as to whether the dwelling-house was occupied and used violence or threats of violence to a person or property.

Under s. 486.4, where an accused is charged with the offence under this section, the judge may make an order directing that any information that could identify the complainant or a witness not be published, broadcast or transmitted in any way. The judge is to inform the complainant or any witness under the age of 18 years of the right to make any application under s. 486.4. Under s. 486.6, it is an offence to violate the order made.

SYNOPSIS

This section describes the offence of extortion. Any person who, *without reasonable justification* or excuse and *with intent to obtain anything*, induces or attempts to induce another person by means of threats, accusations, menaces or violence, to do anything or cause anything to be done, commits the offence of extortion. The person threatened or menaced does not necessarily have to be the person from whom the accused is expecting action. This is an indictable offence with a maximum term of life imprisonment. The section also enacts minimum punishments. Where a restricted or prohibited firearm is used or the offence was committed for the benefit of, at the direction of, or in association with, a criminal organization, the offender is liable to a minimum punishment of at least five years' imprisonment for a first offence and seven years for a second or subsequent offence. The rules for determining whether the offender has committed a second or subsequent offence are set out in subsecs. (1.2) and (1.3) and, for example, provide that a prior offence includes not only convictions under this section, but other specified offences involving use of a firearm. However, an earlier offence is not to be taken into account if 10 years have elapsed from the conviction of the earlier offence, not counting time in custody. Subsection (1.3) reverses the common law rule and provides that the court only takes into account the sequence of convictions, not the order in which the offences were committed. In any other case where a firearm is used, the offender is liable to a minimum term of imprisonment of four years. Where no firearm is used, there is no minimum punishment.

Subsection (2) clarifies that a threat to institute civil proceedings is not a threat for the purposes of this section.

ANNOTATIONS

"Anything" – The purpose of the provision is to protect against interference with freedom of choice. The word "anything" should be given a wide, unrestricted application and can include extorting sexual favours: *R. v. Davis*, [1999] 3 S.C.R. 759, 139 C.C.C. (3d) 193.

Threats or menaces – A "threat" to come within this section does not necessarily connote a menace of ill to be personally inflicted by the threatener. Thus a false statement by the accused that if the victim does not do a certain thing he will be dealt with by a third person of known violent propensities or associations will constitute this offence: *R. v. Swartz* (1977), 37 C.C.C. (2d) 409 (Ont. C.A.), affd without reference to the point [1979] 2 S.C.R. 256, 45 C.C.C. (2d) 1, *sub nom. R. v. Cotroni; R. v. Papalia.*

A veiled reference may constitute a threat if it is sufficient, in light of all the circumstances, to convey to the complainant the consequences which he or she fears or would prefer to avoid. Whether such words amount to a threat must be considered contextually, including in light of the shared knowledge of the complainant and accused: *R. v. Barros*, [2011] 3 S.C.R. 368, 273 C.C.C. (3d) 129.

There is no requirement that the threats or menaces be shown to be of such a nature as to deprive the victim of the free and voluntary exercise of his will: *R. v. Syrmalis; R. v. Laurie* (1981), 63 C.C.C. (2d) 452 (Que. C.A.).

The offence is made out even if the victim does not capitulate to the accused's wishes: *R. v. Noel* (2001), 156 C.C.C. (3d) 169, 46 C.R. (5th) 189 (N.B.C.A.).

An approach by a lawyer to a lawyer acting for another party to have certain criminal charges dropped in exchange for a sum of money, if made without threats, accusations, menaces or violence does not constitute an offence under this section: *R. v. Rousseau*, [1985] 2 S.C.R. 38, 21 C.C.C. (3d) 1.

Subsection (1) is broadly worded to criminalize threats of any kind made with an attempt to induce any person to do anything, if those threats are made with the intention of obtaining anything. A legal justification must be reasonable and the burden is on the Crown to demonstrate beyond a reasonable doubt the absence of any reasonable excuse or justification. In this case, a threat to have the complainant fired if she did not repay money owed to the accused's wife constituted a threat within this provision as the threat to have the complainant fired was unlawful: *R. v. Alexander* (2005), 206 C.C.C. (3d) 233, 32 C.R. (6th) 159 (Ont. C.A.), leave to appeal to S.C.C. refused 352 N.R. 197*n*.

Reasonable justification of excuse – In *R. v. Natarelli and Volpe*, [1967] S.C.R. 539, [1968] 1 C.C.C. 154, 1 C.R.N.S. 302, it was held that in determining whether there could be reasonable justification or excuse for making the demand or using threats, the accused's entire course of conduct, and not one isolated item thereof, must be considered; and once it is proved that the accused made threats to cause death or bodily injury with intent to obtain consideration, then they are guilty regardless of whether they honestly believed that they did have or whether they actually had a right to the consideration demanded.

On a charge contrary to this section, arising out of seizure of certain property, evidence was admissible as to what the accused had been told by a bailiff to whom he had spoken. This information was not admissible for its truth, but was admissible to show the accused's state of mind and the honesty of his belief and whether he had reasonable justification or excuse for his actions: *R. v. Toth* (1989), 8 W.C.B. (2d) 255 (Ont. C.A.).

Criminal Interest Rate

CRIMINAL INTEREST RATE / Definitions / "credit advanced" / "criminal rate" / "insurance charge" / "interest" / "official fee" / "overdraft charge" / "required deposit balance" / Presumption / Proof of effective annual rate / Notice / Cross-examination with leave / Consent required for proceedings / Application.

347. (1) Despite any other Act of Parliament, every one who enters into an agreement or arrangement to receive interest at a criminal rate, or receives a payment or partial payment of interest at a criminal rate, is

    (*a*) **guilty of an indictable offence and liable to imprisonment for a term not exceeding five years; or**

    (*b*) **guilty of an offence punishable on summary conviction and liable to a fine not exceeding $25,000 or to imprisonment for a term not exceeding six months or to both.**

(2) In this section,

"credit advanced" means the aggregate of the money and the monetary value of any goods, services or benefits actually advanced or to be advanced under an agreement or arrangement minus the aggregate of any required deposit balance and any fee, fine, penalty, commission and other similar charge or expense directly or indirectly incurred under the original or any collateral agreement or arrangement;

"criminal rate" means an effective annual rate of interest calculated in accordance with generally accepted actuarial practices and principles that exceeds sixty per cent on the credit advanced under an agreement or arrangement;

"insurance charge" means the cost of insuring the risk assumed by the person who advances or is to advance credit under an agreement or arrangement, where the face amount of the insurance does not exceed the credit advanced;

"interest" means the aggregate of all charges and expenses, whether in the form of a fee, fine, penalty, commission or other similar charge or expense or in any other form, paid or payable for the advancing of credit under an agreement or arrangement, by or on behalf of the person to whom the credit is or is to be advanced, irrespective of the

person to whom any such charges and expenses are or are to be paid or payable, but does not include any repayment of credit advanced or any insurance charge, official fee, overdraft charge, required deposit balance or, in the case of a mortgage transaction, any amount required to be paid on account of property taxes;

"official fee" means a fee required by law to be paid to any governmental authority in connection with perfecting any security under an agreement or arrangement for the advancing of credit;

"overdraft charge" means a charge not exceeding five dollars for the creation of or increase in an overdraft, imposed by a credit union or caisse populaire the membership of which is wholly or substantially comprised of natural persons or a deposit taking institution the deposits in which are insured, in whole or in part, by the Canada Deposit Insurance Corporation or guaranteed, in whole or in part, by the Quebec Deposit Insurance Board;

"required deposit balance" means a fixed or an ascertainable amount of the money actually advanced or to be advanced under an agreement or arrangement that is required, as a condition of the agreement or arrangement, to be deposited or invested by or on behalf of the person to whom the advance is or is to be made and that may be available, in the event of his defaulting in any payment, to or for the benefit of the person who advances or is to advance the money.

(3) Where a person receives a payment or partial payment of interest at a criminal rate, he shall, in the absence of evidence to the contrary, be deemed to have knowledge of the nature of the payment and that it was received at a criminal rate.

(4) In any proceedings under this section, a certificate of a Fellow of the Canadian Institute of Actuaries stating that he has calculated the effective annual rate of interest on any credit advanced under an agreement or arrangement and setting out the calculations and the information on which they are based is, in the absence of evidence to the contrary, proof of the effective annual rate without proof of the signature or official character of the person appearing to have signed the certificate.

(5) A certificate referred to in subsection (4) shall not be received in evidence unless the party intending to produce it has given to the accused or defendant reasonable notice of that intention together with a copy of the certificate.

(6) An accused or a defendant against whom a certificate referred to in subsection (4) is produced may, with leave of the court, require the attendance of the actuary for the purposes of cross-examination.

(7) No proceedings shall be commenced under this section without the consent of the Attorney General.

(8) This section does not apply to any transaction to which the *Tax Rebate Discounting Act* applies. 1980-81-82-83, c. 43, s. 9; 2007, c. 9, s. 1.

CROSS-REFERENCES

"Attorney General" is defined in s. 2. Section 583(*h*) provides that a count in an indictment is not insufficient by reason only that it does not state that the required consent has been obtained. [As to notes concerning sufficiency of consent, see s. 583.] This offence may be the basis for an application for an authorization to intercept private communications by reason of s. 183 and an enterprise crime offence within the meaning of s. 462.3.

Where the prosecution elects to proceed by indictment on this offence then the accused may elect his mode of trial pursuant to s. 536(2). Where the prosecution elects to proceed by way of summary conviction then the trial of this offence is conducted by a summary conviction court pursuant to Part XXVII.

The limitation period is set out in s. 786(2). In either case, release pending trial is determined by s. 515, although the accused is eligible for release by a peace officer under s. 496, 497 or by the officer in charge under s. 498.

The related offence of extortion is found in s. 346. Under s. 486.4, where an accused is charged with the offence under this section, the judge may make an order directing that any information that could identify the complainant or a witness not be published, broadcast or transmitted in any way. The judge is to inform the complainant or any witness under the age of 18 years of the right to make any application under s. 486.4. Under s. 486.6, it is an offence to violate the order made.

Pursuant to s. 347.1, this section does not apply to certain payday loans by persons other than financial institutions where the loan is for $1500 or less, for a term of 62 days or less, and the lender is in a designated province and is licensed or authorized by the laws of the province. Payday loan is defined in s. 347.1 as "an advancement of money in exchange for a post-dated cheque, a pre-authorized debit or a future payment of a similar nature but not for any guarantee, suretyship, overdraft protection or security on property and not through a margin loan, pawnbroking, a line of credit or a credit card".

SYNOPSIS

This section describes the offence of charging a criminal interest rate. The offence is committed by anyone who enters into an agreement or arrangement to receive interest at a criminal rate, or who actually receives a payment or partial payment of interest at a criminal rate. The term "criminal rate" means an effective annual rate that exceeds 60 per cent on the credit advanced, calculated according to accepted actuarial principles and practices. The term "interest" means the aggregate of all charges and expenses, in any form, but with certain listed and defined exceptions, paid or payable for the advancing of credit. The offence may be tried by indictment, with a maximum penalty of five years, or by summary conviction, with a maximum penalty of a fine of $25,000 and imprisonment for six months, but only with the consent of an Attorney General. Subsection (3) creates a presumption, in the absence of evidence to the contrary, that a person receiving payment or partial payment of interest at a criminal rate does so *knowingly*. Subsections (4) and (5) permit, for the purposes of this section, proof of a rate of interest by a certificate of a fellow of the Canadian Institute of Actuaries, provided that the accused is given reasonable notice and a copy of the certificate. Subsection (6) permits the court to require the attendance of the actuary for cross-examination. The section applies, notwithstanding any other federal enactment, but does not apply to transactions governed by the *Tax Rebate Discounting Act*.

ANNOTATIONS

"Interest" – The term "interest" in this section is broadly defined and included in a "facility fee" which the borrower agreed to pay to obtain the loan: *William E. Thomson Associates Inc. v. Carpenter* (1989), 61 D.L.R. (4th) 1, 69 O.R. (2d) 545 (C.A.), leave to appeal to S.C.C. refused 65 D.L.R. (4th) viii, 71 O.R. (2d) x.

The stipulation that the borrower was to pay a share of the anticipated profit from a real estate deal was a condition of the borrower receiving the loan and fell within the all-inclusive definition of "interest": *677950 Ontario Ltd. v. Artell Developments Ltd.* (1992), 75 C.C.C. (3d) 343, 93 D.L.R. (4th) 334 (Ont. C.A.), affd [1993] 2 S.C.R. 443, 82 C.C.C. (3d) 192*n*, *sub nom. Horvat v. Artell Developments Ltd.*

A late payment penalty on a utility bill is capable of constituting interest within the meaning of this section: *Garland v. Consumers' Gas Co.*, [1998] 3 S.C.R. 112, 129 C.C.C. (3d) 97.

"Credit advanced" – In *Garland v. Consumers' Gas Co., supra*, the court had to consider a late payment penalty that the utility company imposed on accounts not paid by the due date. Merely because a particular charge constitutes a penalty, does not bring it within the meaning of "interest". The issue is whether that penalty constitutes, in substance, a cost incurred by customers to receive credit, which in turn depended on whether the relationship between the customer and the company involved any advancement of credit within this section. The definition of "credit advanced" includes a deferral of payment for goods, services or benefits. There must be a specified amount owing, and that amount must actually be due in the absence of an arrangement permitting later payment. In this case, the company provides goods and services to its customers for which a specified amount of money is payable each month on a certain date. The deferral of that payment past the due date constitutes credit advanced under an agreement or arrangement which in effect permits the two payment options: paying by the due date, which costs nothing, and a longer-term option, which involves an additional charge. Also see *Garland v. Consumers' Gas Co.*, [2004] 1 S.C.R. 629, 237 D.L.R. (4th) 385, as to customers' remedy for violation of this section.

Elements of the offence – The *mens rea* of this offence is proof that the accused voluntarily entered into a loan agreement providing for receipt by him of a criminal rate of interest. The Crown is not also required to prove that the accused knew that charging a rate above 60% was unlawful: *William E. Thomson Associates Inc. v. Carpenter* (1989), 61 D.L.R. (4th) 1, 69 O.R. (2d) 545 (C.A.), leave to appeal to S.C.C. refused 65 D.L.R. (4th) viii, 71 O.R. (2d) x.

In considering whether a fee or charge constituted interest within the meaning of this provision, the court must determine whether it was for the advancing of credit and whether the credit was being advanced pursuant to an agreement or arrangement. Charging a satellite subscriber for the cost of collecting an overdue account was a recovery of a disbursement rather than a cost for advancing credit and, accordingly, did not constitute interest: *De Wolf v. Bell ExpressVu Inc.* (2009), 247 C.C.C. (3d) 258, 311 D.L.R. (4th) 68 (Ont. C.A.), leave to appeal to S.C.C. refused 251 C.C.C. (3d) vii.

The offence under subsec. (1)(*a*) is to be narrowly construed. Whether an agreement or arrangement for credit violates this paragraph is determined as of the time the transaction is entered into. If the agreement permits but does not require the payment of interest at a criminal rate then there is no violation of subsec. (1)(*a*). However, subsec. (1)(*b*) is to be broadly construed and whether an interest payment violates this paragraph is determined as of the time the payment is received. The effective annual rate for the purposes of subsec. (1)(*b*) is calculated over the period during which credit is actually outstanding. There is no violation of that paragraph where the payment of interest at a criminal rate arises from a voluntary act of the debtor and not compelled by the lender or the occurrence of a determining event set out in the agreement: *Degelder Construction Co. v. Dancorp Developments Ltd.*, [1998] 3 S.C.R. 90, 129 C.C.C. (3d) 129.

Defences – It is no defence that the borrowers were willing to participate in the agreement and that the accused was not engaged in swindling or other trickery. It would, however, be a defence if in certain circumstances the accused had made an honest mistake as to the terms of the agreement: *R. v. McRobb* (1984), 20 C.C.C. (3d) 493 (Ont. Co. Ct.), vard 32 C.C.C. (3d) 479*n* (Ont. C.A.).

Admissibility of evidence – Although the Crown has proceeded by way of summary conviction, so that the six-month limitation period applies, evidence of payments made by the victims of the offence prior to this period is relevant and admissible to establish the effective annual rate of interest: *R. v. Duzan* (1993), 79 C.C.C. (3d) 552, 32 W.A.C. 295 (Sask. C.A.).

Effect on validity of contract – It was held in *William E. Thomson Associates Inc. v. Carpenter* (1989), 61 D.L.R. (4th) 1, 69 O.R. (2d) 545 (C.A.), leave to appeal to S.C.C. refused 65 D.L.R. (4th) viii, 71 O.R. (2d) x, a civil action, that the unlawfulness of the transaction did not render the entire loan agreement void. The illegal part of the agreement could be severed and the borrower required to repay the principal.

Constitutional considerations – This section is *intra vires* Parliament: *677950 Ontario Ltd. v. Artell Developments Ltd., supra.*

DEFINITIONS / "interest" / "payday loan" / Non-application / Designation of province / Revocation.

347.1 (1) The following definitions apply in subsection (2).

"interest" has the same meaning as in subsection 347(2).

"payday loan" means an advancement of money in exchange for a post-dated cheque, a pre-authorized debit or a future payment of a similar nature but not for any guarantee, suretyship, overdraft protection or security on property and not through a margin loan, pawnbroking, a line of credit or a credit card.

(2) Section 347 and section 2 of the *Interest Act* do not apply to a person, other than a financial institution within the meaning of paragraphs (*a*) to (*d*) of the definition "financial institution" in section 2 of the *Bank Act*, in respect of a payday loan agreement entered into by the person to receive interest, or in respect of interest received by that person under the agreement, if

(*a*) the amount of money advanced under the agreement is $1,500 or less and the term of the agreement is 62 days or less;

(*b*) the person is licensed or otherwise specifically authorized under the laws of a province to enter into the agreement; and

(*c*) the province is designated under subsection (3).

(3) The Governor in Council shall, by order and at the request of the lieutenant governor in council of a province, designate the province for the purposes of this section if the province has legislative measures that protect recipients of payday loans and that provide for limits on the total cost of borrowing under the agreements.

(4) The Governor in Council shall, by order, revoke the designation made under subsection (3) if requested to do so by the lieutenant governor in council of the province or if the legislative measures described in that subsection are no longer in force in that province. 2007, c. 9, s. 2.

CROSS-REFERENCES
The criminal interest rate offence is defined in s. 347.

SYNOPSIS
This section exempts certain types of so-called payday loans from the criminal interest rate offence in s. 347 and the similar offence in s. 2 of the *Interest Act*, R.S.C. 1985, c. I-15. Payday loans are defined in subsec. (1) and are, in effect, short-term loans made by persons other than financial institutions as defined in the *Bank Act*, S.C. 1991, c. 46. The exemption applies only if the conditions in subsec. (2) are met, that the loan is for $1500 or less, for a term of 62 days or less, and made by a lender that is licensed or specifically authorized by the laws of the province, and the province is designated by the Governor in Council in accordance with subsec. (3). Subsection (4) provides for the revocation of the designation.

Breaking and Entering

BREAKING AND ENTERING WITH INTENT, COMMITTING OFFENCE OR BREAKING OUT / Presumptions / Definition of "place".

348. (1) Every one who

(*a*) breaks and enters a place with intent to commit an indictable offence therein,

(*b*) breaks and enters a place and commits an indictable offence therein, or

(*c*) breaks out of a place after

(i) committing an indictable offence therein, or

(ii) entering the place with intent to commit an indictable offence therein,

is guilty

(*d*) if the offence is committed in relation to a dwelling-house, of an indictable offence and liable to imprisonment for life, and (*e*) if the offence is committed in relation to a place other than a dwelling-house, of an indictable offence and liable to imprisonment for a term not exceeding ten years or of an offence punishable on summary conviction.

(2) For the purposes of proceedings under this section, evidence that an accused

(*a*) broke and entered a place or attempted to break and enter a place is, in the absence of evidence to the contrary, proof that he broke and entered the place or attempted to do so, as the case may be, with intent to commit an indictable offence therein; or

(*b*) broke out of a place is, in the absence of any evidence to the contrary, proof that he broke out after

(i) committing an indictable offence therein, or

(ii) entering with intent to commit an indictable offence therein.

(3) For the purposes of this section and section 351, "place" means

(*a*) a dwelling-house;

(*b*) a building or structure or any part thereof, other than a dwelling-house;

(*c*) a railway vehicle, a vessel, an aircraft or a trailer; or

(*d*) a pen or an enclosure in which fur-bearing animals are kept in captivity for breeding or commercial purposes. R.S., c. C-34, s. 306; 1972, c. 13, s. 24; R.S.C. 1985, c. 27 (1st Supp.), s. 47; 1997, c. 18, s. 20.

CROSS-REFERENCES

The term "dwelling house" is defined in s. 2. The term "break" is defined in s. 321. "Enter" is defined in s. 350(*a*) and s. 350(*b*) deems a person to have broken and entered in circumstances defined therein. An indictable offence includes a Crown-option offence, which may be prosecuted by indictment, by virtue of s. 34(1) of the *Interpretation Act*, R.S.C. 1985, c. I-21.

As to admission of photographic evidence of property, see s. 491.2. For proof by way of affidavit of ownership, lawful possession, value, and that the person was deprived of property by fraud or otherwise without the person's lawful consent, see s. 657.1.

Section 662(6) provides that a person, charged with the offence under subsec. (1)(*b*), may be convicted of the offence under subsec. (1)(*a*) where the evidence does not prove the former offence but does prove the latter. Under s. 583, an indictment, which otherwise complies with s. 581, is not insufficient by reason only that (*a*) it does not name the person injured or intended to be injured; (*b*) it does not name the person who owns or has a special property or interest in the property mentioned in the count, however, see s. 587 as to when particulars may be ordered. Also note s. 588 which deems certain persons to have a property interest in property of which they have the management, control or custody.

This offence may be the basis for an application for an authorization to intercept private communications by reason of s. 183 or a warrant to conduct video surveillance under s. 487.01(5).

The accused may elect the mode of trial pursuant to s. 536(2) unless the Crown proceeds by way of summary conviction where the offence does not relate to a dwelling-house. Release pending trial is determined by s. 515. A person convicted of the offence in this section may be liable to the mandatory prohibition order in s. 109 for possession of certain weapons, ammunition and explosives.

The offence of forcible entry is in s. 72 and trespassing by night in s. 177. Being unlawfully in a dwelling house is an offence under s. 349. Possession of break-in instruments is an offence under s. 351(1). Defence of property is dealt with in ss. 38 to 42. Section 494 gives the owner of property or person in possession and persons authorized by them a power to arrest, without warrant, a person found committing a criminal offence on or in relation to that property. The offence which is most often alleged to be the indictable offence intended to be committed is theft under s. 334. Section 98 creates offences similar to the offences in this section where the object of the break and enter is a firearm. The only important distinction between the two provisions is that the s. 98 offence carries a maximum punishment of life imprisonment whether or not the place is a dwelling-house.

Pursuant to s. 348.1, if a person is convicted of the offence under this section in relation to a dwelling-house, it is an aggravating factor in sentencing that the dwelling-house was occupied at the time and the offender knew or was reckless as to whether the dwelling-house was occupied and used violence or threats of violence to a person or property.

SYNOPSIS

This section describes the offence of breaking and entering. The offence is committed by anyone: (a) who breaks and enters a place *with intent to commit an indictable offence* therein; (b) who breaks and enters a place and actually commits an indictable offence; or (c) breaks out of a place after committing an indictable offence, or after having entered intending to commit an indictable offence. The offence is indictable, with a maximum punishment of life imprisonment if the place is a dwelling house. For a non-dwelling-house the offence is a hybrid, the maximum punishment being 10 years by indictment and 6 months if the Crown elects to proceed summarily. The meaning of "place", for the purpose of this section, is defined by subsec. (3). Subsection (2) creates two presumptions. Where a person breaks and enters a place or attempts to do so, those acts are proof, in the absence of evidence to the contrary, that the person had the intent to commit an indictable offence therein. Similarly, where a person breaks out of a place, that act is proof that he committed, or entered with intent to commit, an indictable offence therein.

ANNOTATIONS

Intoxication defence – In *R. v. Gawel*, [1984] 6 W.W.R. 672*n* (Sask. C.A.), varg [1984] 5 W.W.R. 608, 40 C.R. (3d) 93 (Q.B.), on a charge of break and enter and committing assault, the accused was convicted of assault only, the evidence showing that the accused, who was in a highly intoxicated state, mistakenly believed he was in his own house when he assaulted the occupant.

Presumption of intent [subsec. (2)] – Once a *prima facie* case is made out using this presumption the accused need only raise a reasonable doubt, which he may do by adducing evidence of an explanation that may reasonably be true. However, an explanation that is disbelieved does not constitute "any evidence to the contrary" as it is no evidence. The evidence upon which the accused relies must at least raise a reasonable doubt as to his guilt, and if it does not meet this test then the *prima facie* case remains: *R. v. Proudlock*, [1979] 1 S.C.R. 525, 43 C.C.C. (2d) 321. [**Note:** Since this decision the *Criminal Code* has been amended to delete the word "any" from the phrase "in the absence of any evidence to the contrary". However, the majority judgment in *R. v. Proudlock* indicates that there is no basis for a distinction depending on the presence of the word "any"; the phrases "evidence to the contrary" and "any evidence to the contrary" both being the converse of "no evidence to the contrary".]

When there is any evidence to the contrary, in the sense of evidence tending to negative the existence of the necessary intent, the onus is then upon the Crown to prove the existence of the necessary intent beyond a reasonable doubt. Evidence of the accused's condition due to the consumption of alcohol and drugs which caused him to act in an irrational manner was evidence to the contrary in that it tended to negative an intent to commit an indictable offence: *R. v. Campbell* (1974), 17 C.C.C. (2d) 320 (Ont. C.A.).

Evidence that the accused is of good character is not of itself "evidence to the contrary": *R. v. Khan* (1982), 66 C.C.C. (2d) 32 (Ont. C.A.).

The presumption in this subsection is not available where the indictment specifies the particular indictable offence such as theft or mischief: *R. v. Khan, supra.*

Doctrine of recent possession / *Also see notes under s. 354* – Upon proof of unexplained possession of recently stolen goods the trier of fact may, but must not, draw an inference of guilt of not only the possession offence but an offence such as break and enter committed in obtaining the goods: *R. v. Kowlyk*, [1988] 2 S.C.R. 59, 43 C.C.C. (3d) 1 (4:1).

"Place" – The definition of "place" in subsec. (4)(*b*) contemplates a type of structure within which human beings function and not, for example, a glass show-case on the exterior wall of a building which gives no access to any part of the building: *R. v. Desjatnik* (1981), 64 C.C.C. (2d) 408 (Que. Ct. Sess. of Peace).

On the other hand a small boutique in a shopping mall which is a permanent structure closed in on all sides at night is a "place" notwithstanding it has no roof: *R. v. McKerness* (1983), 4 C.C.C. (3d) 233, 33 C.R. (3d) 71 (Que. Ct. Sess. Peace).

An oil bulk plant compound enclosed by a permanent fence in which are situated fuel storage tanks, an office and warehouse is a structure and hence a "place" within the meaning of this section: *R. v. Thibault* (1982), 66 C.C.C. (2d) 422 (N.S.C.A.).

Similarly, an area containing an office building surrounded by a 10 foot high fence is a place: *R. v. Fajtl* (1986), 53 C.R. (3d) 396 (B.C.C.A.).

A yard does not constitute a "place". "Structure" can include empty spaces that are enclosed but does not apply to open, unenclosed spaces: *R. v. Ausland* (2010), 251 C.C.C. (3d) 207 (Alta. C.A.).

Included offences – Possession of stolen goods contrary to s. 322 is included in a charge of break, enter and theft: *R. v. L'Hirondelle* (1992), 72 C.C.C. (3d) 254 (Alta. C.A.). *Contra: R. v. Rivet* (1975), 29 C.R.N.S. 301 (Ont. C.A.).

Being unlawfully in a dwelling house pursuant to s. 349 is an included offence under s. 349(1)(*a*). In addition, s. 348(1)(*a*) is an included offence under s. 348(1)(*b*): *R. v. Liang* (2008), 240 C.C.C. (3d) 197 (Alta. C.A.).

Constitutional considerations – While subsec. (2)(*b*) infringes the presumption of innocence in s. 11(*d*) of the Charter, it constitutes a reasonable limit within the meaning of s. 1 of the Charter and is therefore valid: *R. v. Slavens* (1991), 64 C.C.C. (3d) 29 (B.C.C.A.).

AGGRAVATING CIRCUMSTANCE — HOME INVASION.

348.1 If a person is convicted of an offence under section 98 or 98.1, subsection 279(2) or section 343, 346 or 348 in relation to a dwelling-house, the court imposing the sentence on the person shall consider as an aggravating circumstance the fact that the dwelling-house was occupied at the time of the commission of the offence and that the person, in committing the offence,

    (*a*) **knew that or was reckless as to whether the dwelling-house was occupied; and**

    (*b*) **used violence or threats of violence to a person or property. 2002, c. 13, s. 15; 2008, c. 6, s. 34.**

CROSS-REFERENCES

The terms "dwelling-house" and "property" are defined in s. 2. For other deemed aggravating circumstances on sentencing, see s. 718.2.

ANNOTATIONS

"Home invasion" in this section is not synonymous with "home invasion robbery". The essential elements of a home invasion are: (i) occupancy of a dwelling-house at the time one of the listed crimes was committed; (ii) knowledge or recklessness on the part of the offender as to whether the dwelling-house was occupied; and (iii) actual or threatened use of violence to persons or property: *R. v. C. (D.J.)* (2009), 245 C.C.C. (3d) 258 (Sask. C.A.).

Where the assailants showed up at the victim's house, pulled him outside the front door and assaulted him there, this aggravating circumstance still applied even though the assault was not strictly speaking in the "home": *R. v. Ginnish* (2014), 306 C.C.C. (3d) 118 (N.B.C.A.).

CR. CODE

BEING UNLAWFULLY IN DWELLING-HOUSE / Presumption.

349. (1) Every person who, without lawful excuse, the proof of which lies on that person, enters or is in a dwelling-house with intent to commit an indictable offence in it is guilty of an indictable offence and liable to imprisonment for a term not exceeding ten years or of an offence punishable on summary conviction.

(2) For the purposes of proceedings under this section, evidence that an accused, without lawful excuse, entered or was in a dwelling-house is, in the absence of any evidence to the contrary, proof that he entered or was in the dwelling-house with intent to commit an indictable offence therein. R.S., c. C-34, s. 307; 1997, c. 18, s. 21.

CROSS-REFERENCES

The term "dwelling house" is defined in s. 2. "Enter" is defined in s. 350(*a*). The offence which is most often alleged to be the indictable offence intended to be committed is theft under s. 334.

The accused may elect his mode of trial pursuant to s. 536(2) unless the Crown elects to proceed by way of summary conviction. Release pending trial is determined by s. 515. A person convicted of the offence in this section may, depending on the circumstances, be liable to the mandatory prohibition order in s. 109 for possession of certain weapons, ammunition and explosives or the discretionary order in s. 110 where the Crown proceeds summarily.

The offence of forcible entry is in s. 72 and trespassing by night in s. 177. Being unlawfully in a dwelling house is an offence under s. 349. Possession of break-in instruments is an offence under s. 351(1). Defence of property is dealt with in ss. 38 to 42. Section 494 gives the owner of property or person in possession and persons authorized by them a power to arrest, without warrant, a person found committing a criminal offence on or in relation to that property.

SYNOPSIS

This section describes the offence of being unlawfully in a dwelling house. Anyone who enters or is in a dwelling house, with intent to commit an indictable offence therein, commits the offence. A person is not guilty if he has a lawful excuse for entering or being present in the dwelling house, but the onus is on that person to so establish, on a balance of probabilities. It is important to note that the accused need not have entered with the requisite intent, provided that he formulates that intent while present in the dwelling house. Subsection (2) provides that evidence of entry or presence in a dwelling house without lawful excuse, in the absence of evidence to the contrary, is proof of the existence of the requisite intent.

ANNOTATIONS

"dwelling house" – A motel unit is a dwelling house: *R. v. Henderson*, [1975] 1 W.W.R. 360 (B.C. Prov. Ct.).

Presumption of intent (subsec. (2)) – Prior to the amendment of this subsection which replaced the words "*prima facie* evidence" with the words "in the absence of any evidence to the contrary, proof" it was held that even where the Crown could rely on the presumption because of proof of an unlawful entry there was no onus on the accused to provide a reasonable and logical explanation for his presence in the premises since the evidence, while not establishing a lawful excuse for the accused's presence, might well create a reasonable doubt as to his intent to commit an indictable offence therein which is a vital element in the commission of the offence: *R. v. Austin*, [1969] 1 C.C.C. 97, 4 C.R.N.S. 388 (S.C.C.) (3:2). In *R. v. Proudlock*, [1979] 1 S.C.R. 525, 43 C.C.C. (2d) 321, Pigeon J., whose judgment was concurred in by five members of the court, was of the view that the change in the wording had not affected the meaning which should be attributed to the presumption. In particular an explanation which is not believed does not constitute "any evidence to the contrary".

Evidence of drunkenness which discloses that the accused did not have the necessary specific intent is evidence to the contrary neutralizing the statutory presumption: *R. v. Johnnie* (1975), 23 C.C.C. (2d) 68, 30 C.R.N.S. 202 (B.C.C.A.).

Evidence to the contrary is evidence in either the prosecution or the defence case which is not disbelieved by the trier of fact and which gives rise to a reasonable doubt with respect to the existence of the intent to commit an indictable offence on the part of the accused: *R. v. Nagy* (1988), 45 C.C.C. (3d) 350, 30 O.A.C. 12 (C.A.).

Included offences – The offence of mischief as described in s. 430(1)(*d*) is an included offence: *R. v. E. (S.)* (1993), 80 C.C.C. (3d) 502, [1993] N.W.T.R. 97 (C.A.). *Contra*: *R. v. Drake* (1974), 16 C.C.C. (2d) 505, 8 N.S.R. (2d) 454 (C.A.); *R. v. Beyo* (2000), 144 C.C.C. (3d) 15, 47 O.R. (3d) 712 (C.A.), leave to appeal to S.C.C. refused 147 C.C.C. (3d) vi.

Constitutional considerations – It was held in *R. v. Nagy* (1988), 45 C.C.C. (3d) 350, 30 O.A.C. 12 (C.A.), that this subsection creates a mandatory presumption so that if the prosecution proves entry or presence in a dwelling-house without lawful excuse the trier of fact must, not may, convict in the absence of any evidence to the contrary and therefore this subsection offends the presumption of innocence guarantee in s. 11(*d*) of the Charter. However, it constitutes a reasonable limit within the meaning of s. 1 of the Charter and therefore the subsection is valid.

ENTRANCE.

350. For the purposes of sections 348 and 349,
   (*a*) a person enters as soon as any part of his body or any part of an instrument that he uses is within any thing that is being entered; and
   (*b*) a person shall be deemed to have broken and entered if
      (i) he obtained entrance by a threat or artifice or by collusion with a person within, or
      (ii) he entered without lawful justification or excuse, the proof of which lies upon him, by a permanent or temporary opening. R.S., c. C-34, s. 308.

CROSS-REFERENCES
The term "break" is defined in s. 321.

SYNOPSIS

For the purposes of s. 348 and 349, entry occurs as soon as any part of the body of, or an instrument used by, a person is within anything being entered. A person is deemed to have broken and entered if entry is obtained, by threat, artifice or collusion with a person inside, or through a permanent or temporary opening, without lawful justification. The onus is on the accused to establish that justification.

ANNOTATIONS

Entry by artifice, etc. (para. (*b*)(i)) – By artifice is by a manoeuvre or stratagem such as sneaking into premises behind someone making a lawful entry: *R. v. Leger* (1976), 31 C.C.C. (2d) 413 (Ont. C.A.).

Entry without lawful justification or excuse (para. (*b*)(ii)) – The words "by a permanent or temporary opening" are clear and should be given their ordinary meaning and embrace an entry not only through the further opening of a temporary opening, but any entry through any temporary opening. Thus entry by the accused through a doorway in a partly constructed house which was open, as the door had not yet been installed, comes within this provision: *R. v. Johnson*, [1977] 2 S.C.R. 646, 34 C.C.C. (2d) 12 (9:0).

In determining whether there was lawful justification or excuse, the time to be considered is the time of the entry. Thus, this paragraph did not apply to an accused who was licenced to enter a store as were other members of the public during normal business hours, notwithstanding he harboured an intent to remain in the store until after closing and then steal a quantity of goods: *R. v. Farbridge* (1984), 15 C.C.C. (3d) 521, [1985] 2 W.W.R. 56 (Alta. C.A.).

Constitutional considerations – The phrase "the proof of which lies upon him" in para. (*b*)(ii) is unconstitutional as violating s. 11(*d*) of the Charter. However, with that phrase eliminated this paragraph is valid: *R. v. Singh* (1987), 41 C.C.C. (3d) 278, 61 C.R. (3d) 353 (Alta. C.A.).

While para. (*b*)(ii) infringes the presumption of innocence as guaranteed by s. 11(*d*) of the *Canadian Charter of Rights and Freedoms*, it constitutes a reasonable limit and is therefore valid: *R. v. K. (T.B.)* (1998), 49 C.R.R. (2d) 328 (Ont. C.A.), leave to appeal to S.C.C. refused 55 C.R.R. (2d) 374*n*.

POSSESSION OF BREAK-IN INSTRUMENT / Disguise with intent.

351. (1) Every one who, without lawful excuse, the proof of which lies on them, has in their possession any instrument suitable for the purpose of breaking into any place, motor vehicle, vault or safe under circumstances that give rise to a reasonable inference that the instrument has been used or is or was intended to be used for such a purpose,

> **(*a*) is guilty of an indictable offence and liable to imprisonment for a term not exceeding ten years; or**
>
> **(*b*) is guilty of an offence punishable on summary conviction.**

(2) Every one who, with intent to commit an indictable offence, has his face masked or coloured or is otherwise disguised is guilty of an indictable offence and liable to imprisonment for a term not exceeding ten years. R.S., c. C-34, s. 309; 1972, c. 13, s. 25; R.S.C. 1985, c. 27 (1st Supp.), s. 48; 2008, c. 18, s. 9.

CROSS-REFERENCES

The term "motor vehicle" is defined in s. 2. The term "place" is defined in s. 351. Possession is defined in s. 4(3). An indictable offence include a Crown-option offence, which may be prosecuted by indictment, by virtue of s. 34(1) of the *Interpretation Act*, R.S.C. 1985, c. I-21.

The accused may elect his mode of trial pursuant to s. 536(2). Release pending trial is determined by s. 515.

Related offences: s. 85, using firearm during commission or attempted commission of indictable offence; s. 343, robbery; s. 348, break and enter; s. 349, unlawfully in dwelling house; s. 352, breaking into coin-operated device; s. 353, selling, etc., automobile master key.

SYNOPSIS

This section describes two offences — that of being in possession of a break-in instrument and that of being disguised with intent to commit an indictable offence. Subsection (1) makes it clear that the person accused of this offence may escape criminal liability, if he can establish a *lawful excuse* for possessing the instrument described above. Subsection (2) makes it an indictable offence, with a maximum term of imprisonment of 10 years, for a person to mask, colour or otherwise disguise his face with intent to commit an indictable offence.

ANNOTATIONS

Meaning of instrument (subsec. (1)) – Nitric acid, sulphuric acid, bicarbonate of soda and various implements, being proved sufficient to make nitroglycerine, were held to be an "instrument" within this section: *R. v. Benischek*, [1963] 3 C.C.C. 286, 39 C.R. 285 (Ont. C.A.).

Liability of party – In *R. v. Zanini*, [1967 S.C.R. 715, [1968] 2 C.C.C. 1 (5:0), the accused and his companions were charged with breaking and entering and committing theft in a dwelling-house and possession of house-breaking instruments. The two companions pleaded guilty to the former charge and the latter charge was withdrawn as against them. The accused was acquitted of the former charge as the stolen money could not be identified by the owner, but by application of s. 21(2) of the Code was convicted of the latter charge. The accused's appeal was dismissed, it being held that the fact that the possession charge was withdrawn against the two active principals did not affect the right of the Crown to proceed against the accused, as there is no requirement in s. 21(2) that the active participants must be convicted of possession; and it was open to the jury to find, as it did, that the accused knew or ought to have known that one of his confederates, for the purpose of effecting their common design of breaking and entering the dwelling-house at least would, of necessity, be in possession of house-breaking instruments.

Reasonable inference of intended use of instrument (subsec. (1)) – The phrase "a reasonable inference", in a criminal statute, requires proof beyond a reasonable doubt. Accordingly, the burden on the Crown to prove every element of the offence beyond a reasonable doubt requires proof beyond a reasonable doubt of (a) possession by the accused of the instruments specified in the indictment; (b) the suitability of the instruments for the prohibited purpose; and (c) and intention to use the instruments for the prohibited purpose. In the result, the phrase "without lawful excuse, the proof of which lies on him" added to a predecessor to this subsection to make available to the accused the defence of innocent purpose is now superfluous and was presumably kept in the provision, with subsequent amendments, out of an abundance of caution. The phrase does not encompass excuses or justifications that would exist if those words were omitted from the section and thus general common law excuses such as duress or authorization by law need not be proved by the accused on a balance of probabilities. In the result, this provision does not offend the guarantee to the presumption of innocence in s. 11(d) of the *Charter of Rights and Freedoms*: *R. v. Holmes*, [1988] 1 S.C.R. 914, 41 C.C.C. (3d) 497 (5:0).

It was not necessary for the Crown to establish a nexus between the accused's possession of instruments and a "target" vehicle where it was alleged that the tools were used for breaking into and theft of automobiles. The absence of a nexus in time and place between the possession of instruments and a particular automobile is, however, a significant factor in determining whether it is appropriate to draw an inference of intent to use instruments for the prohibited purpose: *R. v. K. (S.)* (1995), 103 C.C.C. (3d) 572, 108 W.A.C. 311 (B.C.C.A.).

Where an exculpatory explanation is given by an accused contemporaneously with his arrest, it is admissible at the instance of the accused without a determination as to whether there was an opportunity for concoction: *R. v. Crossley* (1997), 117 C.C.C. (3d) 533, 154 W.A.C. 61 (B.C.C.A.).

Masked with intent (subsec. (2)) – The Crown must prove the intention to commit one or more specific indictable offences: *R. v. Shay* (1976), 32 C.C.C. (2d) 13 (Ont. C.A.).

POSSESSION OF INSTRUMENTS FOR BREAKING INTO COIN-OPERATED OR CURRENCY EXCHANGE DEVICES.

352. Every one who, without lawful excuse, the proof of which lies on him, has in his possession any instrument suitable for breaking into a coin-operated device or a currency exchange device, under circumstances that give rise to a reasonable inference that the instrument has been used or is or was intended to be used for breaking into a coin-operated device or a currency exchange device, is guilty of an indictable offence and liable to imprisonment for a term not exceeding two years. R.S., c. C-34, s. 310; 1972, c. 13, s. 26; 1974-75-76, c. 93, s. 28.

CROSS-REFERENCES

Possession is defined in s. 4(3).

The accused may elect his mode of trial pursuant to s. 536(2). Release pending trial is determined by s. 515, although the accused is eligible for release by the officer in charge pursuant to s. 498.

The related offence of possession of break-in instruments is in s. 351 and of selling, etc., automobile master key in s. 353.

SYNOPSIS

This section describes the offence of possession of any instrument for breaking into coin-operated or currency exchange devices in circumstances which give rise to a *reasonable inference* that the instrument has been used, or is or was intended to be used for such a purpose. This section, like s. 351, puts the onus of proof on the accused to establish that such possession was *with lawful excuse*. This is an indictable offence with a maximum term of two years' imprisonment.

ANNOTATIONS

An instrument is "suitable" within the meaning of this section provided any reasonable person would assume or believe that it was capable, adequate or suitable for the purpose notwithstanding there is evidence that in fact the instruments could not break into the device: *R. v. Garland* (1978), 41 C.C.C. (2d) 346, 3 C.R. (3d) 206 (Nfld. Dist. Ct.).

Expert evidence merely to the effect that the instrument was suitable for picking locks is not evidence that it was within the specific category of instruments suitable for breaking into a coin-operated device: *R. v. Mackie* (1978), 43 C.C.C. (2d) 269, 4 C.R. (3d) 263 (Ont. H.C.J.).

A conviction for theft of the coins from a coin-operated device is a bar to a conviction under this section arising out of the same circumstances in view of the rule in *R. v. Kienapple*, [1975] 1 S.C.R. 729, 15 C.C.C. (2d) 524, where there is no evidence that the key had been used prior to the theft and the accused was arrested immediately after the theft so that there was no evidence from which an inference could be drawn of any intended future use of it: *R. v. Stanziale* (1979), 47 C.C.C. (2d) 348, 9 C.R. (3d) 281 (Ont. C.A.).

SELLING, ETC., AUTOMOBILE MASTER KEY / Exception / Terms and conditions of licence / Fees / Record to be kept / Failure to comply with subsection (3) / Definitions / "automobile master key" / "licence".

353. (1) Every one who

    (a) sells, offers for sale or advertises in a province an automobile master key otherwise than under the authority of a licence issued by the Attorney General of that province, or

    (b) purchases or has in his possession in a province an automobile master key otherwise than under the authority of a licence issued by the Attorney General of that province,

is guilty of an indictable offence and liable to imprisonment for a term not exceeding two years.

(1.1) A police officer specially authorized by the chief of the police force to possess an automobile master key is not guilty of an offence under subsection (1) by reason only that the police officer possesses an automobile master key for the purposes of the execution of the police officer's duties.

(2) A licence issued by the Attorney General of a province as described in paragraph (1)(a) or (b) may contain such terms and conditions relating to the sale, offering for sale, advertising, purchasing, having in possession or use of an automobile master key as the Attorney General of that province may prescribe.

(2.1) The Attorney General of a province may prescribe fees for the issue or renewal of licences as described in paragraph (1)(a) or (b).

(3) Every one who sells an automobile master key

(*a*) **shall keep a record of the transaction showing the name and address of the purchaser and particulars of the licence issued to the purchaser as described in paragraph (1)(*b*); and**

(*b*) **shall produce the record for inspection at the request of a peace officer.**

(4) Every one who fails to comply with subsection (3) is guilty of an offence punishable on summary conviction.

(5) The definitions in this subsection apply in this section.

"automobile master key" includes a key, pick, rocker key or other instrument designed or adapted to operate the ignition or other switches or locks of a series of motor vehicles.

"licence" includes any authorization.R.S., c. C-34, s. 311; 1997, c. 18, s. 22.

CROSS-REFERENCES

The terms "Attorney General" and "motor vehicle" are defined in s. 2. Possession is defined in s. 4(3). The accused may elect his mode of trial for the offence in subsec. (1), pursuant to s. 536(2). Release pending trial is determined by s. 515, although the accused is eligible for release by the officer in charge pursuant to s. 498. The offence under subsec. (4) is tried by a summary conviction court under Part XXVII. The punishment is as set out in s. 787 [although see s. 735(1)(*b*) respecting maximum fine for corporation] and the limitation period is set out in s. 786(2). Release pending trial is determined by s. 515, although the accused is eligible for release by a peace officer under s. 496, 497 or by the officer in charge under s. 498.

Related offences: s. 351, possession of break-in instruments; s. 352, possession of instruments for breaking into coin-operated devices; s. 334, theft; s. 335, joy-riding; s. 96, possession of weapons obtained by crime.

SYNOPSIS

This section creates several offences in relation to "automobile master key" (defined in subsec. (5)).

Subsection (1) describes the offence of selling, offering for sale, advertising in a province, purchasing, or possessing in a province an automobile master key *otherwise than under the authority* of *a licence* issued by the Attorney General of the province. That offence is indictable and carries a maximum term of two years' imprisonment. Subsection (2) states that a licence issued by the Attorney General of a province may contain such terms and conditions relating to the sale, offering for sale, advertising, purchasing or possession of an automobile master key as the Attorney General of that province may prescribe. Subsection (3) requires that any person who sells an automobile master key keep a record of the transaction, showing the name, address and particulars of the licence referred to in subsec. (1) of the purchaser. Subsection (3) further requires the vendor of the master key to produce the record at the request of a peace officer. A failure to comply with either of the requirements described in subsection (3) gives rise to a summary conviction offence. Subsection (1.1) creates an exemption for a police officer authorized by the chief of police to be in possession of an automobile master key for the purpose of the execution of the officer's duties.

ANNOTATIONS

This section contemplates a device which may be the subject of commerce, the sale and possession of which is lawful only under licence. A coat hanger although so fashioned as to be capable of lifting the latch on locked vehicles does not fall within the meaning of "automobile master key": *R. v. Young* (1983), 3 C.C.C. (3d) 395 (Ont. C.A.).

TAMPERING WITH VEHICLE IDENTIFICATION NUMBER / Definition of "vehicle identification number" / Exception / Punishment.

353.1 (1) Every person commits an offence who, without lawful excuse, wholly or partially alters, removes or obliterates a vehicle identification number on a motor vehicle.

(2) For the purpose of this section, "vehicle identification number" means any number or other mark placed on a motor vehicle for the purpose of distinguishing it from other similar motor vehicles.

(3) Despite subsection (1), it is not an offence to wholly or partially alter, remove or obliterate a vehicle identification number on a motor vehicle during regular maintenance or any repair or other work done on the vehicle for a legitimate purpose, including a modification of the vehicle.

(4) Every person who commits an offence under subsection (1)

    (*a*) is guilty of an indictable offence and liable to imprisonment for a term of not more than five years; or

    (*b*) is guilty of an offence punishable on summary conviction. 2010, c. 14, s. 4.

CROSS-REFERENCES

"Motor vehicle" is defined in s. 2. Section 354(2) creates a presumption of knowing possession of stolen goods from possession of a vehicle or part with an obliterated vehicle identification number. Section 333.1 creates an offence of theft of an automobile.

SYNOPSIS

This section creates the Crown-option offence of tampering, in any of the ways set out in subsec. (2), with vehicle identification numbers on a motor vehicle. There is a saving provision in subsec. (3) for alteration of the number during regular maintenance.

Possession and Trafficking 2010, c. 14, s. 5.

POSSESSION OF PROPERTY OBTAINED BY CRIME / Obliterated vehicle identification number / Definition of "vehicle identification number" / Exception.

354. (1) Every one commits an offence who has in his possession any property or thing or any proceeds of any property or thing knowing that all or part of the property or thing or of the proceeds was obtained by or derived directly or indirectly from

    (*a*) the commission in Canada of an offence punishable by indictment; or

    (*b*) an act or omission anywhere that, if it had occurred in Canada, would have constituted an offence punishable by indictment.

(2) In proceedings in respect of an offence under subsection (1), evidence that a person has in his possession a motor vehicle the vehicle identification number of which has been wholly or partially removed or obliterated or a part of a motor vehicle being a part bearing a vehicle identification number that has been wholly or partially removed or obliterated is, in the absence of any evidence to the contrary, proof that the motor vehicle or part, as the case may be, was obtained, and that such person had the motor vehicle or part, as the case may be, in his possession knowing that it was obtained,

    (*a*) by the commission in Canada of an offence punishable by indictment; or

    (*b*) by an act or omission anywhere that, if it had occurred in Canada, would have constituted an offence punishable by indictment.

(3) For the purposes of subsection (2), "vehicle identification number" means any number or other mark placed on a motor vehicle for the purpose of distinguishing the motor vehicle from other similar motor vehicles.

(4) A peace officer or a person acting under the direction of a peace officer is not guilty of an offence under this section by reason only that the peace officer or person possesses property or a thing or the proceeds of property or a thing mentioned in subsection (1) for the purposes of an investigation or otherwise in the execution of the peace officer's duties. R.S., c. C-34, s. 312; 1972, c. 13, s. 27; 1974-75-76, c. 93, s. 29; 1997, c. 18, s. 23.

CROSS-REFERENCES

The terms "motor vehicle", "peace officer" and "property" are defined in s. 2. Possession is defined in s. 4(3), however, s. 358 defines circumstances in which possession is complete. An indictable offence includes Crown-option offences which may be prosecuted by indictment, by virtue of s. 34(1) of the *Interpretation Act*, R.S.C. 1985, c. I-21.

The punishment for this offence is set out in s. 355 and see notes under that section respecting mode of trial and release pending trial. The offence which is most often alleged to be the indictable offence by which the goods were obtained is theft under s. 334. Other related offences are: s. 333.1, theft of automobile; s. 342, theft, etc., of credit card; s. 343, robbery; s. 346, extortion; s. 348, break and enter; s. 349, unlawfully in dwelling house; s. 351, possession of break-in instruments; s. 352, possession of instruments for breaking into coin-operated devices; s. 353.1, tampering with vehicle identification number; s. 362, obtaining by false pretences; s. 380, fraud; s. 355.2, trafficking in property obtained by crime; s. 355.3, prohibition on importing or exporting stolen property; s. 355.4, possession of property obtained by crime for the purpose of trafficking.

By virtue of s. 583(*b*), an indictment which otherwise complies with s. 581 is not insufficient by reason that it fails to name the person who owns or has a special property or interest in property mentioned in the count. Also note s. 588 which deems certain persons to have a property interest in property of which they have the management, control or custody. Sections 359 and 360 enact special evidentiary rules. Under s. 359, evidence that stolen property was found in the accused's possession in the previous 12 months is admissible to prove knowledge that the property which forms the subject-matter of the proceedings was stolen property. Under s. 360, evidence may be given that the accused was convicted in the previous 5 years of theft or an offence under this section, to prove that knowledge that the property which forms the subject-matter of the proceedings was unlawfully obtained. Note that, for both sections, notice must be given to the accused.

As to admission of photographic evidence of property, see s. 491.2. For proof by way of affidavit of ownership, lawful possession, value, and that the person was deprived of property by fraud or otherwise without the person's lawful consent, see s. 657.1. Under s. 657.2, evidence that any person was convicted or discharged for the theft of the property is proof that the property was stolen.

This offence may be the basis for an application for an authorization to intercept private communications by reason of s. 183 or a warrant to conduct video surveillance pursuant to s. 487.01(5). In some circumstances, the offence under this section will constitute an enterprise crime offence for the purposes of Part XII.2 [see s. 462.3, definition of enterprise crime offence para. (*b*)].

Bringing into Canada anything obtained outside Canada by an act that, if committed in Canada, would have been an offence under this section if committed in Canada is an offence under s. 357. Possession of mail, etc., obtained by theft is an offence under s. 356(1)(*b*).

The equivalent offence in the *Controlled Drugs and Substances Act* is s. 8.

SYNOPSIS

This section describes the offence of possession of property obtained by crime. Subsection (1) states that if a person has in his possession any property or the proceeds of any property, knowing that such property or proceeds were obtained or derived directly or indirectly from the commission in Canada of an indictable offence or an act or omission in any location which would in Canada constitute an indictable offence, that person is guilty of an offence. Subsection (2) states that evidence that the vehicle identification number of a motor vehicle, or a part of a motor vehicle, has been wholly or partially obliterated or removed is, absent evidence to the contrary, proof that *the item was obtained* and that the person in possession of it *knew that it was obtained* by the commission of an indictable offence. No offence is committed if a peace officer or a person acting under the direction of a peace officer has possession for the purpose of an investigation or in the execution of the officer's duties.

ANNOTATIONS

Doctrine of recent possession – A review of the elements of the "doctrine" of recent possession is found in *R. v. Kowlyk*, [1988] 2 S.C.R. 59, 43 C.C.C. (3d) 1 (4:1). Those elements, as set out in that case and distilled from the various decisions as approved in *Kowlyk*, may be summarized as follows:

1. No adverse inference may be drawn against an accused from the fact of possession alone unless it were recent: *R. v. Graham*, [1974] S.C.R. 59, 7 C.C.C. (2d) 93 (7:0);
2. If a pre-trial explanation of such possession were given by the accused, and if it possessed that degree of contemporaneity with the possession making evidence of it admissible, no adverse inference could be drawn on the basis of recent possession alone if the explanation were one which could reasonably be true: *R. v. Graham, supra*;
3. In the absence of such explanation, recent possession alone is quite sufficient to raise a factual inference of theft;
4. Where the accused does not testify, a jury instruction as to the inference arising from unexplained possession does not constitute a "comment" within the meaning of s. 4(6): *R. v. Newton*, [1977] 1 S.C.R. 399, 28 C.C.C. (2d) 286 (9:0);
5. Where an explanation which could reasonably be true is given for the possession, then no inference of guilt on the basis of recent possession alone may be drawn, even if the trier of fact is not satisfied as to the truth of the explanation and thus, to obtain a conviction in the face of such an explanation, it must establish by other evidence the guilt of the accused beyond a reasonable doubt;
6. The unexplained possession of stolen goods, standing alone, will also warrant an inference of guilt of breaking and entering and theft of those goods;
7. Upon proof of the unexplained possession of recently stolen goods, the trier of fact may – but not must – draw an inference of guilt of theft or of offences incidental thereto;
8. Where the circumstances are such that a question could arise as to whether the accused was a thief or merely a possessor, it will be for the trier of fact, upon a consideration of all the circumstances, to decide which, if either, inference should be drawn.

In the subsequent case of *R. v. Wiseman* (1989), 52 C.C.C. (3d) 160, 93 N.S.R. (2d) 306 (C.A.), the court interpreted *Kowlyk* as also standing for the proposition that, in charging the jury, the trial judge should avoid the use of the phrase "doctrine of recent possession". The court stated that what is really involved is an inference from unexplained possession of recently stolen goods. The court seems to have been concerned that use of a term such as "doctrine" implies some mandatory rule of law, rather than application of a common sense inference.

Although the doctrine is stated in terms of the inference applying in the absence of any reasonable explanation, there is no burden on the Crown to prove that no explanation was given prior to trial or that such explanation, if given, could not reasonably be true: *R. v. Graham, supra*. It would seem, however, that where an explanation was given to the police, then defence counsel can adduce it through the police: *R. v. Newton, supra*, per Dickson J. The exact basis for its admissibility is unclear, although the suggestion from *R. v. Graham, supra*, is that if made contemporaneously with the finding in possession, it is admissible as part of the *res gestae*. In that case, it was held that a statement made a few hours later was not admissible at the instance of the defence. In *R. v. Graham* and other cases such as *R. v. Ungaro*, [1950] S.C.R. 430, 96 C.C.C. 245, it was pointed out that where the accused gives a statement to the police, but also testifies, it is the explanation under oath which, if reasonably true, negatives the inference of guilty knowledge.

The trier of fact need not *believe* the explanation, it is enough that it raises a reasonable doubt: *R. v. L'Heureux*, [1985] 2 S.C.R. 159, 21 C.C.C. (3d) 574 (7:0). However, an explanation which is disbelieved cannot constitute a reasonable explanation: *R. v. Proudlock*, [1979] 1 S.C.R. 525, 43 C.C.C. (2d) 321.

Since no adverse inference may be drawn from the accused's failure to give an explanation for his possession of stolen goods upon his arrest and after he has been informed of his right to remain silent, then it would seem that evidence of silence at that time is irrelevant and should not be admitted. Where evidence has been admitted of silence at the time of arrest and following the caution, it is clearly misdirection to tell the jury that, in assessing the accused's explanation given on the witness stand, they may consider that an explanation given at once is more convincing than one given at some later time. Rather, the jury should be told that, while an explanation given before arrest or not too long after the arrest is more convincing than one given at some later time, they must not take into account that the accused, upon being arrested and warned, said nothing and they should be directed that he had the right to say nothing and to consult a lawyer: *R. v. Machado* (1989), 50 C.C.C. (3d) 133, 71 C.R. (3d) 158 (B.C.C.A.).

Where it was the theory of the Crown that the accused was the actual thief and the Crown did not rely on the doctrine of recent possession the trial Judge is not in error in failing to direct the jury on the doctrine: *R. v. Hewson*, [1978] 2 S.C.R. 111, 42 C.C.C. (2d) 507 (5:4).

In *R. v. Saieva*, [1982] 1 S.C.R. 897, 68 C.C.C. (2d) 97 (7:0), the court in considering whether possession was sufficiently "recent" to entitle reliance on the doctrine of recent possession approved the statement in *R. v. Killam* (1973), 12 C.C.C. (2d) 114, [1973] 5 W.W.R. 3 (B.C.C.A.), that the criteria to be used are the nature of the object "its rareness, the readiness in which it can, and is likely to, pass from hand to hand, the ease of its identification and the likelihood of transferability".

Proof of offence – This offence is an offence of dishonesty and requires proof of blameworthy conduct. The accused, having only become aware that the goods were stolen, panicked and drove them away from his premises. He was not guilty of this offence although he failed to inform the police. His conduct was inconsistent with any intention to retain or deal with the goods: *R. v. York* (2005), 193 C.C.C. (3d) 331 (B.C.C.A.).

Wilful blindness – To engage the doctrine of willful blindness, there must be a real suspicion in the mind of the accused that is ignored. Where an accused makes a single inquiry, willful blindness can still be found if the accused has real suspicions after the inquiry but did not make any further inquiry: *R. v. Lagace* (2003), 181 C.C.C. (3d) 12, 178 O.A.C. 391 (C.A.).

Proof that goods obtained by crime – An admission by the accused is admissible for its truth, even if the admission itself contains hearsay, provided that the accused indicates a belief in the acceptance of the truth of the hearsay statement. If, however, the accused merely reports a hearsay statement without either adopting it or indicating a belief in its truth then the statement is not admissible for the truth of its contents. Thus, out of court statements by an accused, charged with the offence under this section, that he did not know the origin of the goods but his friend had stolen the goods and he knew they were "hot", made in circumstances indicating he believed the statements were true, were admissible not only to prove guilty knowledge but that, in fact, the goods were stolen: *R. v. Streu*, [1989] 1 S.C.R. 1521, 48 C.C.C. (3d) 321 (5:0).

While the *mens rea* requirement is satisfied by actual knowledge or willful blindness, mere recklessness is insufficient: *R. v. Vinokurov* (2001), 156 C.C.C. (3d) 300, 44 C.R. (5th) 369 (Alta. C.A.).

Where the indictable offence is specified in the indictment as "theft" it is misdirection to instruct the jury that the offence is proven if the goods were obtained by fraud: *R. v. Beaudet* (1977), 34 C.C.C. (2d) 150 (Ont. C.A.).

Although it is alleged that the goods were obtained by the commission "in Canada" of an indictable offence the Crown is not required to prove whether the crime was committed in

Canada as long as it is, or would have been if committed in Canada, an indictable offence: *R. v. Elliott* (1984), 15 C.C.C. (3d) 195, [1985] 1 W.W.R. 97 (Alta. C.A.).

Meaning of "obtained by" – The words "obtained by", apply only where the indictable offence was committed in respect of the thing obtained. Thus where the owner willingly parts with the goods as part of a scheme to defraud his own insurance company by falsely reporting that the goods were stolen the goods have not been obtained by the commission of an indictable offence. They have however been "indirectly derived" from the commission of a crime within the meaning of this subsection: *R. v. Geauvreau* (1979), 51 C.C.C. (2d) 75 (Ont. C.A.), affd [1982] 1 S.C.R. 485, 66 C.C.C. (2d) 375 (9:0).

Goods were not, however, obtained by or derived directly or indirectly from commission of the offence of fraud where the goods were sold to the accused by the owner even if, to the knowledge of the accused, the owner had attempted to defraud his insurance company by arranging for a fake break and enter in which these goods were "stolen". In those circumstances the goods were not the proceeds of crime: *R. v. Epp* (1988), 42 C.C.C. (3d) 572, 68 Sask. R. 49 (C.A.).

Goods which the accused originally found were "obtained by" the commission of an indictable offence where she subsequently fraudulently converted them to her own use and then retained them in her possession: *R. v. Hayes* (1985), 20 C.C.C. (3d) 385, 46 C.R. (3d) 393 (Ont. C.A.).

Charging offence – Where a count named the property's owner with some imprecision, but still furnished the accused with reasonable information to identify the alleged owner, there was no error fatal to conviction: *R. v. Emmons* (1970), 1 C.C.C. (2d) 468, 13 C.R.N.S. 310 (Alta. S.C. App. Div.).

A charge of possession of stolen clothes the property of a person or persons unknown was held to be valid on the ground that for either theft or possession the Crown need only prove ownership in some person or persons other than the accused: *R. v. McDowell,* [1970] 5 C.C.C. 374, 18 C.R.N.S. 193 (Ont. C.A.), affd [1971] S.C.R. vi, 18 C.R.N.S. 195*n*.

A count alleging possession of property without alleging the owner or without even in the alternative alleging ownership in a person or persons unknown is valid: *R. v. Halliday* (1975), 25 C.C.C. (2d) 131, 12 N.S.R. (2d) 1 (S.C. App. Div.).

Where the indictment spells out the particulars of the actual commission of the offence punishable by indictment, from which the property originated, it is not necessary for the Crown to prove knowledge of those particulars on the part of the accused: *R. v. Gowing and Johnson* (1970), 2 C.C.C. (2d) 105, 12 C.R.N.S. 139 (Alta. C.A.).

Rule precluding multiple convictions – The majority theory (6:1) in *R. v. Cote*, [1975] 1 S.C.R. 303, 18 C.C.C. (2d) 321, 26 C.R.N.S. 26 (6:1), that in law there is no bar to a convicted thief, who is subsequently found with the very stolen articles, being convicted of unlawful possession should be carefully considered in view of the difficulty of establishing when the thief had consummated his theft and when the offence of his unlawful possession of the same property commenced. Although there is a division of opinion the weight of the previous authorities seems to be in favour of the proposition that where possession and theft are proximate the thief cannot also be convicted of illegal possession of the same articles: *R. v. Fergusson*, [1962] S.C.R. 229, 132 C.C.C. 112; *R. v. Siggins* (1960), 127 C.C.C. 409, 32 C.R. 306 (Ont. C.A.); *R. v. Varkonyi*, [1964] 1 C.C.C. 311, 42 W.W.R. 507 (Man. C.A.); *R. v. Pryce*, [1967] 3 C.C.C. 13, 50 C.R. 80 (B.C.C.A.); and *R. v. Hunt*, [1968] 4 C.C.C. 366, 4 C.R.N.S. 386 (N.S. Co. Ct.). *Contra, R. v. MacQuarrie*, [1964] 3 C.C.C. 261, 43 C.R. 97 (P.E.I.S.C.), *per* MacGuigan J., dissenting, and *R. v. McKay*, [1968] 4 C.C.C. 355, 4 C.R.N.S. 380 (N.W.T.T.C.).

Presumption for removal of V.I.N. number [subsec. (2)] – The presumption does not operate to provide proof of the type of indictable offence specified in the indictment by which the vehicle left the hands of its rightful possessor: *R. v. Leslie* (1975), 23 C.C.C. (2d) 343 (Ont. C.A.).

The presumption in this subsection may be rebutted by evidence that merely raises a reasonable doubt and is not rejected by the trier of fact: *R. v. Boyle, infra; R. v. Hill* (1983), 4 C.C.C. (3d) 519 (Ont. C.A.).

The term "obliterate" in this subsection includes the destruction of the integrity of the original vehicle identification number by altering some of the numbers and letters comprising it to produce a new and spurious vehicle identification number: *R. v. Hodgkins* (1985), 19 C.C.C. (3d) 109 (Ont. C.A.).

"Motor vehicle" includes agricultural implements: *R. v. Petrisor*, [1998] 3 W.W.R. 516, 160 Sask. R. 126 (Q.B.).

Constitutional considerations – Application of the doctrine of recent possession does not offend the guarantees in s. 11(*c*) and (*d*) of the *Charter of Rights and Freedoms*: *R. v. Russell* (1983), 4 C.C.C. (3d) 460, 32 C.R. (3d) 307 (N.S.C.A.).

Subsection (2) creates two presumptions: that the vehicle was obtained by commission of an indictable offence and that the accused had guilty knowledge. However, only the first is constitutionally valid. The presumption of guilty knowledge is arbitrary and contravenes the guarantee to the presumption of innocence in s. 11(*d*) of the *Charter of Rights and Freedoms*. Accordingly, while the Crown may rely on this subsection to prove that the vehicle was unlawfully obtained, guilty knowledge must be proved by inferences from other circumstances such as the unexplained possession of recently stolen goods: *R. v. Boyle* (1983), 5 C.C.C. (3d) 193, 35 C.R. (3d) 34 (Ont. C.A.).

PUNISHMENT.

355. Every one who commits an offence under section 354

    (*a*) **is guilty of an indictable offence and liable to imprisonment for a term not exceeding ten years, where the subject-matter of the offence is a testamentary instrument or the value of the subject-matter of the offence exceeds five thousand dollars; or**

    (*b*) **is guilty**

        (i) **of an indictable offence and liable to imprisonment for a term not exceeding two years, or**

        (ii) **of an offence punishable on summary conviction,**

where the value of the subject-matter of the offence does not exceed five thousand dollars. R.S., c. C-34, s. 313; 1972, c. 13, s. 28; 1974-75-76, c. 93, s. 30; R.S.C. 1985, c. 27 (1st Supp.), s. 49; 1994, c. 44, s. 21.

CROSS-REFERENCES

The offence in para. (*a*) is an indictable offence for which the accused may elect his mode of trial under s. 536(2). Release pending trial is determined under s. 515. Where the prosecution elects to proceed by indictment for the offence under para. (*b*) then, by virtue of s. 553, it is an offence over which a provincial court judge has absolute jurisdiction and does not depend on the consent of the accused. That is, the accused does not have an election as to mode of trial, although the provincial court judge may, by virtue of s. 555(1), elect to continue the proceedings as a preliminary inquiry, in which case, the accused is deemed to have elected trial by judge and jury pursuant to s. 565(1)(*a*). As well, under s. 555(2), where, in the course of the trial, evidence establishes that the subject-matter of the offence is a testamentary instrument or that its value exceeds $5,000 then the provincial court judge shall put the accused to his election under s. 536(2). Where the prosecution elects to proceed by way of summary conviction then the proceedings are conducted by a summary conviction court pursuant to Part XXVII. The punishment is then as set out in s. 787 and the limitation period is set out in s. 786(2). For the offence under para. (*b*), release pending trial is determined by s. 515, although the accused is eligible for release by a peace officer under s. 496, 497 or by the officer in charge under s. 498. The value of a valuable security (defined in s. 2) is determined in accordance with s. 4(2) and of a postal card or stamp in accordance with s. 4(1). The term "testamentary instrument" is defined in s. 2.

SYNOPSIS

This section sets out the punishment for an offence under s. 354. Paragraph (*a*) states that when the subject-matter of the offence is a testamentary instrument or when the value of the subject-matter of the offence exceeds $5,000, the offence is indictable with a maximum term of 10 years' imprisonment. Paragraph (*b*) states that when the value of the subject-matter of the offence does not exceed $5,000, it is a Crown election offence with a maximum term of imprisonment of two years on indictment.

ANNOTATIONS

An item's retail value *prima facie* establishes its value: *R. v. Belanger* (1972), 6 C.C.C. (2d) 210 (B.C.C.A.).

On a charge of possession of stolen property the value is not an essential ingredient of the offence but rather goes only to jurisdiction and sentence. Where the charge alleged the offence under para. (*a*) but there was no evidence to show that the value was in excess of that amount the court would be justified in entering a conviction under para. (*b*) provided there was evidence that the property was of some value: *R. v. Gillis* (1977), 35 C.C.C. (2d) 418 (N.S.C.A.).

DEFINITION OF "TRAFFIC".

355.1 For the purposes of sections 355.2 and 355.4, "traffic" means to sell, give, transfer, transport, export from Canada, import into Canada, send, deliver or deal with in any other way, or to offer to do any of those acts. 2010, c. 14, s. 6.

CROSS-REFERENCES

The offence of possession of property obtained by crime is set out in s. 354. The penalty for that offence is in s. 355. Section 357 makes it an offence to have possession of property obtained by crime outside of Canada. Section 355.2 creates the offence of trafficking in property obtained by crime or in the proceeds of such property. Section 355.3 prohibits the importing or exporting of property or proceeds obtained by an offence. Section 355.4 creates the offence of possession for the purpose of trafficking. The penalties for the offences in ss. 355.2 and 355.4 are set out in s. 355.5. The related offence of bringing stolen goods into Canada is found in s. 357. The offence which is most often alleged to be the indictable offence by which the goods were obtained is theft under s. 334. The specific offence of theft of a motor vehicle is set out in s. 333.1. Other related offences are: s. 342, theft, etc., of credit card; s. 343, robbery; s. 346, extortion; s. 348, break and enter; s. 349, unlawfully in dwelling house; s. 351, possession of break-in instruments; s. 352, possession of instruments for breaking into coin-operated devices; s. 362, obtaining by false pretences; s. 380, fraud.

Section 491.2 provides for use of photographic evidence to prove the offences under ss. 355.2 and 355.4. The offences under ss. 355.2 and 355.4 are offences for which the Attorney General may apply for a disclosure order under s. 462.48 of information from the Commissioner of Revenue.

TRAFFICKING IN PROPERTY OBTAINED BY CRIME.

355.2 Everyone commits an offence who traffics in any property or thing or any proceeds of any property or thing knowing that all or part of the property, thing or proceeds was obtained by or derived directly or indirectly from

(a) the commission in Canada of an offence punishable by indictment; or

(b) an act or omission anywhere that, if it had occurred in Canada, would have constituted an offence punishable by indictment. 2010, c. 14, s. 6.

CROSS-REFERENCES

"Traffic" is defined in s. 355.1. The punishment for this offence is set out in s. 355.5. Possession of property obtained by crime for the purpose of trafficking is an offence under s. 355.4. Section

355.3 prohibits the importing or exporting of property or proceeds obtained by an offence. As to admission of photographic evidence of property, see s. 491.2. For proof by way of affidavit of ownership, lawful possession, value, and that the person was deprived of property by fraud or otherwise without the person's lawful consent, see s. 657.1. For other Cross-References as to related offences, see s. 355.1.

IN REM PROHIBITION.

355.3 The importation into Canada or exportation from Canada of any property or thing or any proceeds of any property or thing is prohibited if all or part of the property, thing or proceeds was obtained by or derived directly or indirectly from
> *(a)* **the commission in Canada of an offence punishable by indictment; or**
> *(b)* **an act or omission anywhere that, if it had occurred in Canada, would have constituted an offence punishable by indictment. 2010, c. 14, s. 6.**

CROSS-REFERENCES
Section 355.2 creates the offence of trafficking in property obtained by crime or in the proceeds of such property. Section 355.4 creates the offence of possession for the purpose of trafficking. The penalties for the offences in ss. 355.2 and 355.4 are set out in s. 355.5. The offence of bringing stolen goods into Canada is found in s. 357. For other Cross-References as to related offences, see s. 355.1.

SYNOPSIS
This section does not itself create an offence, but rather prohibits importation into Canada or exportation from Canada of any property or thing or any proceeds of any property or thing if all or part of the property, thing or proceeds was obtained by or derived from the commission in Canada of an offence punishable by indictment, which would include Crown-option offences, or an act or omission that, if it had occurred in Canada, would have constituted an offence punishable by indictment. It would appear that this section was enacted to assist officers of the Canada Border Services Agency in investigating the illegal export or import of property obtained by crime.

POSSESSION OF PROPERTY OBTAINED BY CRIME — TRAFFICKING.

355.4 Everyone commits an offence who has in their possession, for the purpose of trafficking, any property or thing or any proceeds of any property or thing knowing that all or part of the property, thing or proceeds was obtained by or derived directly or indirectly from
> *(a)* **the commission in Canada of an offence punishable by indictment; or**
> *(b)* **an act or omission anywhere that, if it had occurred in Canada, would have constituted an offence punishable by indictment. 2010, c. 14, s. 6.**

CROSS-REFERENCES
"Property" is defined in s. 2. Possession is defined in s. 4(3); however, s. 358 defines circumstances in which possession is complete. "Traffic" is defined in s. 355.1. The punishment for this offence is set out in s. 355.5. Trafficking in property obtained by crime is an offence under s. 355.2. Section 355.3 prohibits the importing or exporting of property or proceeds obtained by an offence. By virtue of s. 583(*b*), an indictment which otherwise complies with s. 581 is not insufficient by reason that it fails to name the person who owns or has a special property or interest in property mentioned in the count. Also note s. 588 which deems certain persons to have a property interest in property of which they have the management, control or custody. Under s. 593, any number of persons may be charged in the same indictment with an offence under this section, notwithstanding that the property was in possession at different times or the person by whom the property was obtained is not indicted or is not in custody or is not amendable to justice. As to

admission of photographic evidence of property, see s. 491.2. For proof by way of affidavit of ownership, lawful possession, value, and that the person was deprived of property by fraud or otherwise without the person's lawful consent, see s. 657.1. For other Cross-References as to related offences, see s. 355.1.

PUNISHMENT.

355.5 Everyone who commits an offence under section 355.2 or 355.4

    (*a*) **is, if the value of the subject matter of the offence is more than $5,000, guilty of an indictable offence and liable to imprisonment for a term of not more than 14 years; or**

    (*b*) **is, if the value of the subject matter of the offence is not more than $5,000,**

        (i) **guilty of an indictable offence and liable to imprisonment for a term of not more than five years, or**

        (ii) **guilty of an offence punishable on summary conviction. 2010, c. 14, s. 6.**

CROSS-REFERENCES
See Cross-References under s. 355.1.

THEFT FROM MAIL / Allegation of value not necessary / Punishment.

356. (1) Everyone commits an offence who

    (*a*) **steals**

        (i) **anything sent by post, after it is deposited at a post office and before it is delivered, or after it is delivered but before it is in the possession of the addressee or of a person who may reasonably be considered to be authorized by the addressee to receive mail,**

        (ii) **a bag, sack or other container or covering in which mail is conveyed, whether or not it contains mail, or**

        (iii) **a key suited to a lock adopted for use by the Canada Post Corporation;**

    (*a*.1) **with intent to commit an offence under paragraph (*a*), makes, possesses or uses a copy of a key suited to a lock adopted for use by the Canada Post Corporation, or a key suited to obtaining access to a receptacle or device provided for the receipt of mail;**

    (*b*) **has in their possession anything that they know has been used to commit an offence under paragraph (*a*) or (*a*.1) or anything in respect of which they know that such an offence has been committed; or**

    (*c*) **fraudulently redirects, or causes to be redirected, anything sent by post.**

(2) In proceedings for an offence under this section it is not necessary to allege in the indictment or to prove on the trial that anything in respect of which the offence was committed had any value.

(3) Everyone who commits an offence under subsection (1)

    (*a*) **is guilty of an indictable offence and liable to imprisonment for a term of not more than 10 years; or**

    (*b*) **is guilty of an offence punishable on summary conviction. R.S., c. C-34, s. 314; 1980-81-82-83, c. 54, s. 56; 2009, c. 28, s. 6.**

CROSS-REFERENCES
Possession is defined by s. 4(3), however, s. 358 defines circumstances in which possession is complete. The terms "mail", "post" and "post office" are defined in s. 2(1) of the *Canada Post Corporation Act*, R.S.C. 1985, c. C-10 and "delivery" in s. 2(2) of that Act.

This offence may be the basis for an application for an authorization to intercept private communications by reason of s. 183 or a warrant to conduct video surveillance under s. 487.01(5).

The accused may elect his mode of trial pursuant to s. 536(2). Release pending trial is determined by s. 515.

Section 476(*e*) contains a special provision for territorial jurisdiction where an offence is committed, in respect of a mail, in the course of door-to-door delivery.

The related offence of stopping mail with intent to rob or search is in s. 345.

For the offence under subsec. (1)(*b*), ss. 359 and 360 enact special evidentiary rules.

Under s. 359, evidence that stolen property was found in the accused's possession in the previous 12 months is admissible to prove knowledge that the property that forms the subject-matter of the proceedings was stolen property. Under s. 360, evidence may be given that the accused was convicted in the previous 5 years, of theft or an offence under s. 354, that to prove that knowledge that the property which forms the subject-matter of the proceedings was unlawfully obtained. Note that, for both sections, notice must be given to the accused.

SYNOPSIS

This section creates various offences in relation to theft from the mail. Paragraph (1)(*a*) describes the offence of stealing mail and covers anything sent by post until it is in the possession of the addressee or of the person who may reasonably be considered to be authorized by the addresses to receive mail; stealing a container or covering in which mail is conveyed; and stealing a key suited to a lock adopted for use by the Canada Post Corporation. It is an offence under para. (1)(*a*.1), with intent to create an offence under para. (1)(*a*), to make, possess or use a copy of a key suited to a lock adopted by Canada Post, or a key suited to obtaining access to a receptacle or device for receiving mail. The complementary offence of possession of anything known to have been used to commit an offence under paras. (1)(*a*) and (*a*.1) is found in para. (1)(*b*). And, fraudulently redirected mail is an offence under para. (1)(*c*). By virtue of subsec. (2), it is not necessary to prove that anything in respect of which the offence was committed was of any value.

ANNOTATIONS

By virtue of s. 588 a letter once it is deposited at the post office becomes the property of the Postmaster General: *R. v. Wendland* (1970), 1 C.C.C. (2d) 382 (Sask. C.A.).

By virtue of the definition of "delivery" in the *Post Office Act*, R.S.C. 1970, c. P-14 [now s. 2(2) of the *Canada Post Corporation Act*, R.S.C. 1985, c. C-10], mail in a lock box is already delivered: *R. v. Burgess* (1976), 33 C.C.C. (2d) 126 (B.C.C.A.).

Mail is not "delivered" until it is in a receptacle to which the addressee has access and may remove the mail: *R. v. Weaver, Warwick and Smurthwaite* (1980), 55 C.C.C. (2d) 564, 30 O.R. (2d) 361 (C.A.).

BRINGING INTO CANADA PROPERTY OBTAINED BY CRIME.

357. Every one who brings into or has in Canada anything that he has obtained outside Canada by an act that, if it had been committed in Canada, would have been the offence of theft or an offence under section 342 or 354, is guilty of an indictable offence and liable to a term of imprisonment not exceeding ten years. R.S., c. C-34, s. 315; R.S.C. 1985, c. 27 (1st Supp.), s. 50.

CROSS-REFERENCES

The offence of theft is described in ss. 322 to 334 and 338. The accused may elect his mode of trial pursuant to s. 536(2). Release pending trial is determined by s. 515.

SYNOPSIS

This section makes it an offence to import into Canada or to have possession of anything so imported that the accused obtained by an act that would have been the offence of theft or an offence under s. 342 (credit card offences) or 354 (possession of goods obtained by crime) if it had been committed in Canada. The offence is indictable and carries a maximum term of imprisonment of 10 years.

HAVING IN POSSESSION WHEN COMPLETE.

358. For the purposes of sections 342 and 354 and paragraph 356(1)(*b*), the offence of having in possession is complete when a person has, alone or jointly with another person, possession of or control over anything mentioned in those sections or when he aids in concealing or disposing of it, as the case may be. R.S., c. C-34, s. 316; R.S.C. 1985, c. 27 (1st Supp.), s. 50.

CROSS-REFERENCES

For the definition of possession generally, see s. 4(3).

SYNOPSIS

This section states that the offence of possession, for the purposes of ss. 342, 354 and 356(1)(*b*), is complete when a person has, alone or jointly with another person, possession of or control over anything mentioned in those sections. Similarly, the offence of possession is complete when the accused aids in concealing or disposing of anything referred to in those sections.

ANNOTATIONS

It was held in *R. v. MacPherson; R. v. Resnick*, [1964] 3 C.C.C. 170, 43 C.R. 272 (Ont. C.A.), that a person aiding in concealing or disposing of stolen goods is held to be in possession of these goods.

It was found in *R. v. Hanson; R. v. Klepeck*, [1966] 4 C.C.C. 86 (B.C.C.A.), that the intention of the accused to possess only a part of the whole is inconsistent with an intention to possess the whole.

EVIDENCE / Notice to accused.

359. (1) Where an accused is charged with an offence under section 342 or 354 or paragraph 356(1)(*b*), evidence is admissible at any stage of the proceedings to show that property other than the property that is the subject-matter of the proceedings
    (*a*) was found in the possession of the accused, and
    (*b*) was stolen within twelve months before the proceedings were commenced,
and that evidence may be considered for the purpose of proving that the accused knew that the property that forms the subject-matter of the proceedings was stolen property.

(2) Subsection (1) does not apply unless
    (*a*) at least three days notice in writing is given to the accused that in the proceedings it is intended to prove that property other than the property that is the subject-matter of the proceedings was found in his possession; and
    (*b*) the notice sets out the nature or description of the property and describes the person from whom it is alleged to have been stolen. R.S., c. C-34, s. 317; R.S.C. 1985, c. 27 (1st Supp.), s. 51.

CROSS-REFERENCES

Possession is defined in s. 4(3). Under s. 27(1) of the *Interpretation Act*, R.S.C. 1985, c. I-21, in calculating "at least" a number of days between two events, the days on which the events happen are excluded.

SYNOPSIS

This section sets out evidentiary provisions which the prosecutor may rely upon in proceedings under ss. 342, 354 or 356(1)(b). Evidence that property, other than the property that is the subject-matter of the offence, was found in the possession of the accused and was stolen within the 12 months prior to the beginning of the proceedings, is admissible at any stage of the proceedings and may be considered for the purpose of proving that the accused knew that the property that forms the subject-matter of the offence was stolen property. Subsection (2) states that the prosecutor may only make use of subsec. (1) if written notice, at least three days prior to trial, is given to the accused. Subsection 2(b) further requires that the notice set out the nature or description of the property referred to in subsec. 2(a) and the person from whom the prosecutor alleges such property was stolen.

ANNOTATIONS

Compliance with subsec. (2) is not required where evidence of possession of another stolen article was offered only to identify the accused as the thief of both articles: *R. v. Boutilier* (1968), 4 C.R.N.S. 90 (N.S. Co. Ct.).

In *R. v. Hewitt* (1986), 32 C.C.C. (3d) 54, 55 C.R. (3d) 41 (Man. C.A.), the court considered the constitutionality of this section in view of s. 7 of the *Canadian Charter of Rights and Freedoms* and seems to have held that the section should be "read down" so as to apply only where the evidence of prior convictions would be relevant for a reason other than to show merely that the accused was of a bad disposition.

In *R. v. Guyett* (1989), 51 C.C.C. (3d) 368, 72 C.R. (3d) 383, 35 O.A.C. 135 (C.A.), the court also held that this section offends s. 7 of the Charter since, under it, evidence of bad character may be introduced, even if it shows nothing other than bad character. However, the court did not find it necessary to consider whether this section constitutes a reasonable limit within the meaning of s. 1 of the Charter, since the evidence, which had been admitted pursuant to this section, would have been admissible, in any event, under the common law rules of admissibility.

EVIDENCE OF PREVIOUS CONVICTION / Notice to accused.

360. (1) Where an accused is charged with an offence under section 354 or paragraph 356(1)(b) and evidence is adduced that the subject-matter of the proceedings was found in his possession, evidence that the accused was, within five years before the proceedings were commenced, convicted of an offence involving theft or an offence under section 354 is admissible at any stage of the proceedings and may be taken into consideration for the purpose of proving that the accused knew that the property that forms the subject-matter of the proceedings was unlawfully obtained.

(2) Subsection (1) does not apply unless at least three days notice in writing is given to the accused that in the proceedings it is intended to prove the previous conviction. R.S., c. C-34, s. 318.

CROSS-REFERENCES

Possession is defined in s. 4(3). Under s. 27(1) of the *Interpretation Act*, R.S.C. 1985, c. I-21, in calculating "at least" a number of days between two events, the days on which the events happen are excluded. Section 667 provides a means of proving prior convictions. Also note s. 666 which permits evidence of previous convictions to be introduced where the accused adduces evidence of his good character and s. 12 of the *Canada Evidence Act* which gives the judge a discretion to permit cross-examination of an accused on his prior criminal record.

SYNOPSIS

This section allows the prosecutor to introduce evidence, in proceedings under ss. 354 or 356(1)(b), that the accused has been convicted, within the five years prior to the commencement of these proceedings, of an offence involving theft or an offence under s. 354. Such evidence is admissible at any stage of the proceedings and may be considered for the purpose of proving that the accused knew that the property which forms the subject-matter of the offence in the proceedings was unlawfully obtained. Section 7 of the Charter may be raised in relation to this evidentiary provision. As in s. 359, the prosecutor must give the accused written notice, at least three days prior to the proceedings, that it is intended to prove the prior conviction.

ANNOTATIONS

The fact that the prior conviction was under appeal at the time of trial did not render it inadmissible pursuant to this section: *R. v. Hewson*, [1978] 2 S.C.R. 111 (5:4).

Where additional charges of break and enter and possession of housebreaking instruments are tried jointly with charges of possession and the Crown's emphasis is substantially on the break and enter aspect, evidence of previous convictions for theft or possession is not admissible: *R. v. Bowins, Doxtater and Stauffers* (1973), 24 C.R.N.S. 279 (Ont. Co. Ct.).

It would seem that to invoke this section the property which is the subject-matter of the proceedings must have been found in the accused's possession and it does not apply to the Crown's case that on some prior occasion the goods were in the accused's possession: *R. v. Alvey* (1971), 4 C.C.C. (2d) 174, [1971] 3 O.R. 527 (C.A.), referring to *R. v. Drage and Others* (1878), 14 Cox C.C. 85.

This provision offends s. 7 of the Charter and is of no force and effect: *R. v. Hudyma* (1988), 46 C.C.C. (3d) 88 (Ont. Dist. Ct.); *R. v. Wyatt* (1986), 32 C.R.R. 211 (Ont. Prov. Ct.). *Contra: R. v. Gallant* (1982), 70 C.C.C. (2d) 213, 38 O.R. (2d) 788, 2 C.R.R. 144 (Ont. Prov. Ct.).

False Pretences

FALSE PRETENCE / Exaggeration / Question of fact.

361. (1) A false pretence is a representation of a matter of fact either present or past, made by words or otherwise, that is known by the person who makes it to be false and that is made with a fraudulent intent to induce the person to whom it is made to act on it.

(2) Exaggerated commendation or depreciation of the quality of anything is not a false pretence unless it is carried to such an extent that it amounts to a fraudulent misrepresentation of fact.

(3) For the purposes of subsection (2) it is a question of fact whether commendation or depreciation amounts to a fraudulent misrepresentation of fact. R.S., c. C-34, s. 319.

CROSS-REFERENCES

The offences relating to false pretences are found in ss. 362 and 363. See the cross-references under those sections for mode of trial, release pending trial and special evidentiary provisions. The related offence of theft is defined in ss. 322 to 334, theft, etc., of credit card in s. 342 and fraud in s. 380.

SYNOPSIS

This section defines a false pretence as a representation of a matter of fact made in any fashion that is *known by the person who makes it* to be false *and* that is made with a *fraudulent intent* to induce the person to whom it is made to act on it. Both of the mental elements described above must be present in order to fall within the definition of a false pretence. Subsection (2) states that an exaggeration or depreciation of the quality of anything does not amount to a false pretence unless it amounts to a *fraudulent misrepresentation of fact*. Whether or not the exaggeration or depreciation described in subsec. (2) is a fraudulent misrepresentation is a question of fact.

ANNOTATIONS

A false representation amounting to a mere promise or profession of intention is not a false pretence within this section unless such promise or profession of intention necessarily and irresistibly involves a representation of an existing fact. Thus a false promise to pay for goods in the future is not within this section: *R. v. Reid* (1940), 74 C.C.C. 156, [1940] 4 D.L.R. 25 (B.C.C.A.). [Note however that where the means of payment is a cheque, Parliament has enacted a special rule set out in s. 362(4).]

FALSE PRETENCE OR FALSE STATEMENT / Punishment / Idem / Presumption from cheque issued without funds / Definition of "cheque".

362. (1) Every one commits an offence who

   (*a*) by a false pretence, whether directly or through the medium of a contract obtained by a false pretence, obtains anything in respect of which the offence of theft may be committed or causes it to be delivered to another person;

   (*b*) obtains credit by a false pretence or by fraud;

   (*c*) knowingly makes or causes to be made, directly or indirectly, a false statement in writing with intent that it should be relied on, with respect to the financial condition or means or ability to pay of himself or herself or any person or organization that he or she is interested in or that he or she acts for, for the purpose of procuring, in any form whatever, whether for his or her benefit or the benefit of that person or organization,

      (i) the delivery of personal property,

      (ii) the payment of money,

      (iii) the making of a loan,

      (iv) the grant or extension of credit,

      (v) the discount of an account receivable, or

      (vi) the making, accepting, discounting or endorsing of a bill of exchange, cheque, draft, or promissory note; or

   (*d*) knowing that a false statement in writing has been made with respect to the financial condition or means or ability to pay of himself or herself or another person or organization that he or she is interested in or that he or she acts for, procures on the faith of that statement, whether for his or her benefit or for the benefit of that person or organization, anything mentioned in subparagraphs (*c*)(i) to (vi).

(2) Every one who commits an offence under paragraph (1)(*a*)

   (*a*) is guilty of an indictable offence and liable to a term of imprisonment not exceeding ten years, where the property obtained is a testamentary instrument or the value of what is obtained exceeds five thousand dollars; or

   (*b*) is guilty

      (i) of an indictable offence and liable to imprisonment for a term not exceeding two years, or

      (ii) of an offence punishable on summary conviction,

   where the value of what is obtained does not exceed five thousand dollars.

(3) Every one who commits an offence under paragraph (1)(*b*), (*c*) or (*d*) is guilty of an indictable offence and liable to imprisonment for a term not exceeding ten years.

(4) Where, in proceedings under paragraph (1)(*a*), it is shown that anything was obtained by the accused by means of a cheque that, when presented for payment within a reasonable time, was dishonoured on the ground that no funds or insufficient funds were on deposit to the credit of the accused in the bank or other institution on which the cheque was drawn, it shall be presumed to have been obtained by a false pretence,

unless the court is satisfied by evidence that when the accused issued the cheque he believed on reasonable grounds that it would be honoured if presented for payment within a reasonable time after it was issued.

(5) In this section, "cheque" includes, in addition to its ordinary meaning, a bill of exchange drawn on any institution that makes it a business practice to honour bills of exchange or any particular kind thereof drawn on it by depositors. R.S., c. C-34, s. 320; 1972, c. 13, s. 29; 1974-75-76, c. 93, s. 31; R.S.C. 1985, c. 27 (1st Supp.), s. 52; 1994, c. 44, s. 22; 2003, c. 21, s. 5.

CROSS-REFERENCES

A false pretence is defined in s. 361. "Organization" and "person" are defined in s. 2.

As to admission of photographic evidence of property, see s. 491.2. For proof by way of affidavit of ownership, lawful possession, value, and that the person was deprived of property by fraud or otherwise without the person's lawful consent, see s. 657.1. By virtue of s. 583(*b*), an indictment which otherwise complies with s. 581 is not insufficient by reason only that (*b*), it fails to name the person who owns or has a special property or interest in property mentioned in the count or (*c*), it charges an intent to defraud without naming or describing the person whom it was intended to defraud. Also note s. 588 which deems certain persons to have a property interest in property of which they have the management, control or custody. Under s. 586, no count alleging false pretences or fraud is insufficient by reason only that it does not set out in detail the nature of the false pretences or fraud. However, under s. 587(1)(*b*), the court may order particulars of any false pretence or fraud that is alleged.

For the meaning of "bill of exchange", see *Bills of Exchange Act*, R.S.C. 1985, c. B-4.

Where the offence under subsec. (1)(*a*), although committed outside Canada, is in relation to the use of nuclear material, see s. 7(3.4).

The offence in para. (2)(*a*) is a pure indictable offence for which the accused may elect his mode of trial under s. 536(2). Where the prosecution elects to proceed by indictment for the offence under para. 2(*b*) then, by virtue of s. 553, it is an offence over which a provincial court judge has absolute jurisdiction and does not depend on the consent of the accused. That is, the accused does not have an election as to mode of trial, although the provincial court judge may, by virtue of s. 555(1), elect to continue the proceedings as a preliminary inquiry, in which case, the accused is deemed to have elected trial by judge and jury pursuant to s. 565(1)(*a*). As well, under s. 555(2), where, in the course of the trial, evidence establishes that the subject-matter of the offence is a testamentary instrument or that its value exceeds $5,000 then the provincial court judge shall put the accused to his election under s. 536(2). Where the prosecution elects to proceed by way of summary conviction then the proceedings are conducted by a summary conviction court pursuant to Part XXVII. The punishment is then as set out in s. 787 and the limitation period is set out in s. 786(2). For the offences under subsec. (2), release pending trial is determined by s. 515, although in case of the offence under subsec. (2)(*b*) the accused is eligible for release by a peace officer under s. 496, 497 or by the officer in charge under s. 498. The value of a valuable security (defined in s. 2) is determined in accordance with s. 4(2) and of a postal card or stamp in accordance with s. 4(1). The term "testamentary instrument" is defined in s. 2.

For the offences punished under subsec. (3), the accused may elect his mode of trial under s. 536(2) and release pending trial is governed by s. 515.

SYNOPSIS

This section describes the offence of false pretences and the punishment for the offence. Subsection (1) states that any person who, by a false pretence or fraud, obtains credit, or who *knowingly makes a false statement in writing*, intending it to be relied upon, with respect to his own financial state, or that of any entity in which he has an interest, in order to procure any of the benefits listed in subsec. (1)(*c*), is guilty of an offence. Subsection (1) further states that every one commits an offence who *knows that a false written statement* about his own financial state or that of any entity in which he has an interest has been made and, on the basis of that statement, procures anything mentioned in subsec. (1)(c). Finally, an offence under this section is committed when a person, by false pretence, directly or indirectly as described in subsec. (1)(a), obtains anything for himself or another person in respect of which the offence of theft may be committed. The form of the offence described in subsec. (1)(a) is indictable, with a maximum term of 10 years' imprisonment when the property obtained is a testamentary instrument, or its value exceeds $5,000. Where the value does not exceed $5,000, the offence is hybrid with a maximum term of imprisonment of two years on indictment. The forms of the offence described in subsec. (1)(b), (c) and (d) are all punishable by indictment only, with a maximum term of 10 years' imprisonment. Subsection (4) enacts a presumption that in proceedings under subsec. (1)(a) where the goods have been obtained by an N.S.F. cheque, it shall be presumed that those goods have been obtained by false pretences unless the court is satisfied that the accused *believed on reasonable grounds* that the cheque would be honoured when he wrote it. Subsection (5) gives a wide definition to the term "cheque" for the purposes of this section.

ANNOTATIONS

Whether property must pass – The word "obtains" does not mean that the goods must wholly or entirely pass to the accused; the passing of their possession and a property interest, *e.g.,* an insurable interest, in them is sufficient for conviction: *R. v. Hemingway*, [1955] S.C.R. 712, 112 C.C.C. 321, 22 C.R. 275.

Subsequently the view was expressed (2:1) that the acquiring of mere possession would satisfy the requirements of the offence of obtaining anything by a false pretence: *R. v. Campbell,* [1968] 1 C.C.C. 104, 1 C.R.N.S. 325 (B.C.C.A.).

A very useful review of the conflicting authorities on the issue whether or not, for the establishment of this offence, in addition to bare possession some aspect of ownership must also pass is found in *R. v. Vallillee* (1974), 15 C.C.C. (2d) 409, 24 C.R.N.S. 319 (Ont. C.A.).

Proof of offence of obtaining by false pretences [subsec. (1)(a)] – Where on appeal the court finds that a lesser amount than that set out in the indictment was proved to have been obtained it may amend the conviction accordingly and dismiss the appeal: *R. v. Lake*, [1969] S.C.R. 49, [1969] 2 C.C.C. 224 (5:0).

Where the victim made his own thorough investigation, not relying on the representations by the accused, a conviction under this section cannot be sustained: *R. v. Thornton* (1926), 46 C.C.C. 249, 37 B.C.L.R. 344 (C.A.).

Obtaining credit by fraud or false pretences [subsec. (1)(b)] – The credit obtained does not have to be that of the accused; it is sufficient for conviction if he obtained goods by falsely charging them to his employer's account. Furthermore, it is no defence for the accused to argue successfully that he could have been convicted under subsec. (1)(a) of obtaining by a false pretence: *R. v. Dvornek* (1962), 132 C.C.C. 231, 37 C.R. 344 (B.C.C.A.).

A loan of money secured by a property mortgage amounts to the obtaining of credit. Furthermore, there is a presumption that where money was obtained by a false pretence, *prima facie,* there is an intent to defraud. Even where the victim makes its own investigation, if the false representation by the accused is the operative inducement in the obtaining of the credit the offence is made out: *R. v. Dyke and Dyke* (1976), 33 C.C.C. (2d) 556, 37 C.R.N.S. 379 (Nfld. Dist. Ct.).

False statement respecting financial condition [subsec. (1)(c)] – It was held prior to the recent amendment to subpara. (iv), which added the word "grant", that the phrase "extension of credit" means granting or according credit and therefore does not include conduct by the accused which merely serves to keep open an existing line of credit: *R. v. Cohen* (1984), 15 C.C.C. (3d) 231 (Que. C.A.).

Presumption from N.S.F. cheque [subsec. (4)] – Where the case against the accused was that he obtained goods by a cheque drawn against a non-existent bank account it is not necessary, once the Crown has satisfactorily proven the non-existence of the account, to prove the presentment and dishonouring of the cheque: *R. v. Morphett* (1970), 1 C.C.C. (2d) 98, 13 C.R.N.S. 270 (B.C.C.A.).

More than a reasonable doubt is required to rebut the presumption which may be satisfied by evidence whether or not it flows from the accused: *R. v. Druckman* (1974), 31 C.R.N.S. 177 (Ont. Co. Ct.).

The accused's explanation is to be judged using a subjective test and a real belief that funds would be available even though considered objectively the belief was unreasonable will lead to an acquittal: *R. v. Lane* (1978), 42 C.C.C. (2d) 375 (Ont. Prov. Ct.).

This subsection is of no force and effect by reason of its violation of the guarantee to the presumption of innocence in s. 11(*d*) of the *Charter of Rights and Freedoms*: *R. v. Driscoll* (1987), 38 C.C.C. (3d) 28, 60 C.R. (3d) 88, [1987] 6 W.W.R. 748 (Alta. C.A.); *R. v. Ferguson* (1992), 70 C.C.C. (3d) 330, 12 C.R. (4th) 198 (P.E.I.S.C.). *Contra: R. v. Bunka* (1984), 12 C.C.C. (3d) 437, [1984] 4 W.W.R. 252, 32 Sask. R. 271 (Q.B.).

OBTAINING EXECUTION OF VALUABLE SECURITY BY FRAUD.

363. Every one who, with intent to defraud or injure another person, by a false pretence causes or induces any person

(*a*) **to execute, make, accept, endorse or destroy the whole or any part of a valuable security, or**

(*b*) **to write, impress or affix a name or seal on any paper or parchment in order that it may afterwards be made or converted into or used or dealt with as a valuable security,**

is guilty of an indictable offence and liable to imprisonment for a term not exceeding five years. R.S., c. C-34, s. 321.

CROSS-REFERENCES

The term "valuable security" is defined in s. 2 and its value determined in accordance with s. 4(2).

By virtue of s. 583, an indictment which otherwise complies with s. 581 is not insufficient by reason only that (*b*), it fails to name the person who owns or has a special property or interest in property mentioned in the count or (*c*), it charges an intent to defraud without naming or describing the person whom it was intended to defraud. Also note s. 588 which deems certain persons to have a property interest in property of which they have the management, control or custody. Under s. 586, no count alleging false pretences or fraud is insufficient by reason only that it does not set out in detail the nature of the false pretences or fraud. However, under s. 587(1)(*b*), the court may order particulars of any false pretence or fraud that is alleged.

The accused may elect his mode of trial pursuant to s. 536(2). Release pending trial is determined by s. 515, although the accused is eligible for release by the officer in charge pursuant to s. 498.

SYNOPSIS

This section describes the indictable offence of obtaining the execution of a valuable security by means of a false pretence. The accused must have *the intent to defraud or injure* another person. The maximum term of imprisonment upon conviction for this offence is five years.

FRAUDULENTLY OBTAINING FOOD, BEVERAGE OR ACCOMMODATION / Presumption / Definition of "cheque".

364. (1) Every one who fraudulently obtains food, a beverage or accommodation at any place that is in the business of providing those things is guilty of an offence punishable on summary conviction

(2) In proceedings under this section, evidence that the accused obtained food, a beverage or accommodation at a place that is in the business of providing those things and did not pay for it and

    (*a*) made a false or fictitious show or pretence of having baggage,

    (*b*) had any false or pretended baggage,

    (*c*) surreptitiously removed or attempted to remove his baggage or any material part of it,

    (*d*) absconded or surreptitiously left the premises,

    (*e*) knowingly made a false statement to obtain credit or time for payment, or

    (*f*) offered a worthless cheque, draft or security in payment for the food, beverage or accommodation,

is, in the absence of any evidence to the contrary, proof of fraud.

(3) In this section, "cheque" includes, in addition to its ordinary meaning, a bill of exchange drawn on any institution that makes it a business practice to honour bills of exchange or any particular kind thereof drawn on it by depositors. R.S., c. C-34, s. 322; 1994, c. 44, s. 23.

CROSS-REFERENCES

The terms "food", "beverage" and "accommodation" are not defined in this section. However, reference might be made to the definition of "food" in the *Food and Drugs Act*, s. 2. While there is no definition of "fraudulently" which is universally applicable, generally speaking, it refers to conduct which is dishonest and morally wrong: *R. v. DeMarco* (1973), 13 C.C.C. (2d) 369 (Ont. C.A.).

This offence resembles the offence of obtaining by false pretences and thus, see notes under s. 361 respecting related offences. Trial of this offence is conducted by a summary conviction court pursuant to Part XXVII. The punishment is as set out in s. 787 and the limitation period is set out in s. 786(2). Release pending trial is determined by s. 515, although the accused is eligible for release by a peace officer under s. 496, 497 or by the officer if charge under s. 498.

SYNOPSIS

This section describes the summary conviction offence of fraudulently obtaining food, beverage or accommodation at a place that is in the business of providing those things. Subsection (2) sets out a number of fact situations which, in conjunction with evidence that an accused obtained any of the accommodations described in subsec. (1) without paying, will constitute proof of the fraud, in the absence of evidence to the contrary.

PRETENDING TO PRACTISE WITCHCRAFT, ETC.

365. Every one who fraudulently

    (*a*) pretends to exercise or to use any kind of witchcraft, sorcery, enchantment or conjuration,

    (*b*) undertakes, for a consideration, to tell fortunes, or

    (*c*) pretends from his skill in or knowledge of an occult or crafty science to discover where or in what manner anything that is supposed to have been stolen or lost may be found,

is guilty of an offence punishable on summary conviction. R.S., c. C-34, s. 323.

CROSS-REFERENCES

While there is no definition of "fraudulently" which is universally applicable, generally speaking, it refers to conduct which is dishonest and morally wrong: *R. v. DeMarco* (1973), 13 C.C.C. (2d) 369 (Ont. C.A.).

This offence resembles the offence of obtaining by false pretences and thus, see notes under s. 361 respecting related offences. Trial of this offence is conducted by a summary conviction court pursuant to Part XXVII. The punishment is as set out in s. 787 and the limitation period is set out in s. 786(2). Release pending trial is determined by s. 515, although the accused is eligible for release by a peace officer under s. 496, 497 or by the officer in charge under s. 498.

SYNOPSIS

This section sets out the offence of *fraudulently* pretending to practise witchcraft, sorcery, enchantment or conjuration, of telling fortunes for money, and of pretending to discover, through the use of the occult, the location of a lost or stolen article or the manner in which it may be found. This is a summary conviction offence.

ANNOTATIONS

The mere telling of a fortune is not *per se* illegal, as the Crown must also prove an intent to delude or defraud: *R. v. Dazenbrook* (1975), 23 C.C.C. (2d) 252 (Ont. Prov. Ct.).

The trial judge could properly find the offence under para. (*b*) was made out upon evidence that the accused, who was given $10, represented she could predict events from reading lines on the customer's hands and that she was an expert and had taken special courses in Europe: *R. v. Corbeil* (1981), 65 C.C.C. (2d) 570 (Que. C.A.).

The offence under para. (*b*) of this section does not require proof that in fact the predictions were false, or that the accused expressly stated that she had a power to predict the future: *R. v. Labrosse* (1984), 17 C.C.C. (3d) 283 (Que. C.A.). On further appeal to the Supreme Court of Canada, [1987] 1 S.C.R. 310, 33 C.C.C. (3d) 220, 39 D.L.R. (4th) 639, the court left open the question whether it was a defence that the accused honestly believed that she could predict the future, in view of the trial judge's express finding that he disbelieved the accused when she made that assertion.

Forgery and Offences Resembling Forgery

FORGERY / Making false document / When forgery complete / Forgery complete though document incomplete / Exception.

366. (1) Every one commits forgery who makes a false document, knowing it to be false, with intent

> (*a*) **that it should in any way be used or acted on as genuine, to the prejudice of any one whether within Canada or not; or**
>
> (*b*) **that a person should be induced, by the belief that it is genuine, to do or to refrain from doing anything, whether within Canada or not.**

(2) Making a false document includes

> (*a*) **altering a genuine document in any material part;**
>
> (*b*) **making a material addition to a genuine document or adding to it a false date, attestation, seal or other thing that is material; or**
>
> (*c*) **making a material alteration in a genuine document by erasure, obliteration, removal or in any other way.**

(3) Forgery is complete as soon as a document is made with the knowledge and intent referred to in subsection (1), notwithstanding that the person who makes it does not intend that any particular person should use or act on it as genuine or be induced, by the belief that it is genuine, to do or refrain from doing anything.

(4) Forgery is complete notwithstanding that the false document is incomplete or does not purport to be a document that is binding in law, if it is such as to indicate that it was intended to be acted on as genuine.

(5) No person commits forgery by reason only that the person, in good faith, makes a false document at the request of a police force, the Canadian Forces or a department or agency of the federal government or of a provincial government. R.S., c. C-34, s. 324; 2009, c. 28, s. 7.

CROSS-REFERENCES

The terms "document" and "false document" are defined in s. 321.

The punishment for forgery is set out in s. 367 and for uttering a forged document in s. 368. For either offence, the accused may elect the mode of trial pursuant to s. 536(2) unless the Crown proceeds by way of summary conviction. Release pending trial is determined by s. 515.

Forgery and uttering offences may be the basis for an application for an authorization to intercept private communications by reason of s. 183 and a warrant to conduct video surveillance under s. 487.01(5), and are enterprise crime offences for the purposes of Part XII.2. Offences resembling forgery and uttering, but referring to specific types of documents, are in the following sections: s. 369, exchequer bill paper, public seals, etc.; s. 370, counterfeit government proclamation; ss. 371, 372, false telegram, etc.; s. 374, drawing document without authority; s. 375, obtaining by forged document; s. 376, counterfeiting stamp, mark, etc.; s. 377, defacing official documents; s. 378, offences in relation to registers; ss. 397 to 402, falsification of books and documents in relation to contracts and trade; ss. 406 to 414, forgery of trade-marks and trade descriptions; ss. 416 to 421, offences in relation to public stores; Part XII, offences in relation to currency, counterfeiting, etc. For forgery of credit card, see ss. 342, 342.01.

Also see s. 56.1, offences in relation to identity documents; s. 368.1, offences in relation to instruments for use in committing forgery; and s. 402.1, identity theft.

By virtue of s. 368.2, a public officer does not commit this offence where the acts were for the sole purpose of establishing or maintaining a covert identity for use in the course of the public officer's duties or employment.

SYNOPSIS

This section describes the offence of forgery. Every person who makes a false document, *knowing it to be false, with the intent* that it should be used as genuine to the prejudice of another person, or that another person should be induced, believing the document to be genuine, to do or refrain from doing anything, commits the offence of forgery. The action contemplated or the person to be induced may be inside or outside Canada. Subsection (2) defines the term "making a false document" in the context of altering a genuine document. Subsection (3) states that a forgery is complete as soon as the document is made with the intent and knowledge referred to in subsection (1), whether or not the accused intends a specific person to act on it. Subsection (4) further states that the offence of forgery is complete even if the false document is incomplete or of no binding legal effect so long as it can be demonstrated that it was intended to be acted upon as genuine.

ANNOTATIONS

Meaning of false document – The provisions of this subsection do not exclude the definition of "false document" in s. 321. Thus an accused may be convicted of forgery where he makes a "false document" as that phrase is defined in s. 321. Specifically, the accused makes a "false document" where he prepares a document which is false in some material particular. A document which is false in reference to the very purpose for which it was created is clearly one which is false in a material particular. Thus the act of the accused in preparing inventory sheets which contained false information as to the very matter which they purported to certify and so were false in a number of material particulars comes within this section: *R. v. Gaysek*, [1971] S.C.R. 888, 2 C.C.C. (2d) 545 (3:2).

It is not necessarily the case that a document which merely contains a lie falls within the definition of a false document. However, a document which is false in reference to the very purpose for which it was created is one that is false in a material particular within the meaning of s. 321 and therefore capable of founding a conviction under this section: *R. v. Ogilvie* (1993), 81 C.C.C. (3d) 125, [1993] R.J.Q. 453 (C.A.).

It is open to the trier of fact to find a document to be a false document where it is a photocopy which purports to be a true copy of the state of a particular instrument at the time of its reproduction. In this case the accused photocopied parts of two documents so that it appeared that what had been copied was a certified cheque: *R. v. Sebo* (1988), 42 C.C.C. (3d) 536, 64 C.R. (3d) 388 (Alta. C.A.), leave to appeal to S.C.C. refused 93 A.R. 240n.

Similarly: *R. v. Nuosci* (1991), 69 C.C.C. (3d) 64, 10 C.R. (3d) 332 (C.A.), leave to appeal to S.C.C. refused 71 C.C.C. (3d) vii, 56 O.A.C. 159*n*.

In *R. v. Paquette*, [1975] 2 S.C.R. 168, 45 C.C.C. (2d) 575 (7:0), the court in reversing the accused notary's acquittal on a charge of uttering approved the dissenting reasons of Montgomery J.A., in the Quebec Court of Appeal, 42 C.C.C. (2d) 57, who had held that in adding a false attestation to an affidavit the accused made a false document within the meaning of this subsection notwithstanding he was unaware that the entire document was a forgery. The accused had attested to the signature of one of the purported witnesses although he had not seen the "witness" sign the document.

Authorized signings are excluded from the ambit of this offence, even where the document fails on its face to specifically indicate that the actual signatory is acting as a proxy of another. Such documents may be misleading as a result, but they do not have the property of falsity inherent in forgery: *R. v. Foley* (1994), 90 C.C.C. (3d) 390, 30 C.R. (4th) 238 (Nfld. C.A.).

The Crown must establish that the document is false and that it was false in relation to the very purpose for which it was created: *R. v. Benson* (2012), 294 C.C.C. (3d) 109 (Man. C.A.).

Offences involving cheques – The accused was convicted of forgery where he endorsed the signature of the payee of a cheque. As the cheque was made out to the payee the payee could be the only endorser. When the accused signed the payee's name as endorser he did it to the prejudice of the payee and the offence was made out. Moreover, it was no defence that the payor had authorized the accused to deal with the cheque in that manner since such authorization could not come from the payor: *R. v. Cowan*, [1962] S.C.R. 476, 132 C.C.C. 352 (3:2).

A forged endorsement on an otherwise valid cheque converts the cheque into a false document: *R. v. Elkin* (1978), 42 C.C.C. (2d) 185, [1978] 5 W.W.R. 547 (B.C.C.A.); *R. v. Jones,* [1970] 4 C.C.C. 284, 11 C.R.N.S. 219 (Ont. C.A.); *R. v. Keshane* (1974), 20 C.C.C. (2d) 542, 27 C.R.N.S. 331 (Sask. C.A.).

The figures on a cheque are a material part: *R. v. O'Hearn,* [1964] 3 C.C.C. 296, 44 C.R. 48 (B.C.C.A.).

PUNISHMENT FOR FORGERY.

367. Every one who commits forgery
   (*a*) **is guilty of an indictable offence and liable to imprisonment for a term not exceeding ten years; or**
   (*b*) **is guilty of an offence punishable on summary conviction. R.S.C., c. C-34, s. 325; 1994, c. 44, s. 24; 1997, c. 18, s. 24.**

CROSS-REFERENCES

Forgery is defined in s. 366. This offence may be the basis for an application for an authorization to intercept private communications by reason of s. 183. Forgery is an enterprise crime offence for the purposes of Part XII.2.

The accused may elect the mode of trial pursuant to s. 536(2) unless the Crown proceeds by way of summary conviction. Release pending trial is determined by s. 515. For related offences, see cross-references under s. 366. The offence of uttering is defined in s. 368.

By virtue of s. 368.2, a public officer does not commit this offence where the acts were for the sole purpose of establishing or maintaining a covert identity for use in the course of the public officer's duties or employment.

SYNOPSIS

This section states that forgery is a hybrid offence with a maximum term of imprisonment of 10 years, where the Crown proceeds by indictment, and six months if the Crown proceeds by summary conviction pursuant to s. 787.

USE, TRAFFICKING OR POSSESSION OF FORGED DOCUMENT / Punishment / Wherever forged.

368. (1) Everyone commits an offence who, knowing or believing that a document is forged,

   (*a*) uses, deals with or acts on it as if it were genuine;

   (*b*) causes or attempts to cause any person to use, deal with or act on it as if it were genuine;

   (*c*) transfers, sells or offers to sell it or makes it available, to any person, knowing that or being reckless as to whether an offence will be committed under paragraph (*a*) or (*b*); or

   (*d*) possesses it with intent to commit an offence under any of paragraphs (*a*) to (*c*).

(1.1) Everyone who commits an offence under subsection (1)

   (*a*) is guilty of an indictable offence and liable to imprisonment for a term of not more than 10 years; or

   (*b*) is guilty of an offence punishable on summary conviction.

(2) For the purposes of proceedings under this section, the place where a document was forged is not material. R.S., c. C-34, s. 326; 1997, c. 18, s. 25; 2009, c. 28, s. 8.

CROSS-REFERENCES

The term "document" is defined in s. 321. The offence of forgery is defined in s. 366 and punished under s. 367.

This offence may be the basis for an application for an authorization to intercept private communications by reason of s. 183. Uttering a forged document is an enterprise crime offence for the purposes of Part XII.2. The accused may elect the mode of trial pursuant to s. 536(2) unless the Crown proceeds by way of summary conviction. Release pending trial is determined by s. 515.

Offences resembling forgery and uttering but referring to specific types of documents are in the following sections: s. 369, exchequer bill paper, public seals, etc.; s. 370, counterfeit government proclamation; ss. 371, 372, false telegram, etc.; s. 374, drawing document without authority; s. 375, obtaining by forged document; s. 376, counterfeiting stamp, mark, etc.; s. 377, defacing official documents; s. 378, offences in relation to registers; ss. 397 to 402, falsification of books and documents in relation to contracts and trade; ss. 406 to 414, forgery of trade-marks and trade descriptions; ss. 416 to 421, offences in relation to public stores; Part XII, offences in relation to currency, counterfeiting, etc.

Also see s. 56.1, offences in relation to identity documents; s. 368.1, offences in relation to instruments for use in committing forgery; and s. 402.1, identity theft.

By virtue of s. 368.2, a public officer does not commit this offence where the acts were for the sole purpose of establishing or maintaining a covert identity for use in the course of the public officer's duties or employment.

SYNOPSIS

This section replaces the offence of uttering forged documents. Paragraphs (1)(*a*) and (*b*) correspond to the old uttering offence in that they make it an offence to use, deal with, or act upon a document known or believed to be forged, or cause or attempt to cause any person to deal with or act on a document as if it were genuine. The new offences are found in paras. (1)(*c*) and (*d*) and make it an offence to transfer, sell, offer to sell or to make available a document to any person knowing that or being reckless as to whether an offence under para. (1)(*a*) or (*b*) was committed, and possession of a document within intent to commit an offence under any of paras. (1)(*a*), (*b*) or (*c*). The place where the document was forged is not material for the purposes of the offences under this section.

ANNOTATIONS

The requirement of corroboration only applies to the offence of forgery, not to the offence of uttering: *R. v. Susimaki,* [1968] 3 C.C.C. 381, 3 C.R.N.S. 281 (B.C.C.A.).

A forgery within the meaning of s. 366 must exist before an offence under this section can be committed. It is not sufficient that the document was a "false document" as defined by s. 321 if the document was not made with one of the intents specified in s. 366(1): *R. v. Hawrish* (1986), 32 C.C.C. (3d) 446, 52 Sask. R. 248 (C.A.). *Contra: R. v. Lapointe* (1984), 12 C.C.C. (3d) 238 (Que. C.A.), where it was held, relying in part on *R. v. Keshane* (1974), 20 C.C.C. (2d) 542, [1975] 1 W.W.R. 294 (Sask. C.A.), leave to appeal to S.C.C. refused C.C.C. *loc. cit.,* [1974] S.C.R. ix, now overruled on this point, that while on a charge under subsec. (1)(*b*) the Crown must establish that the accused intended that the other person use the document as genuine or that he was reckless in that respect, what need not be shown is the intent described in s. 366 with which the document was forged. And it was held in *R. v. Sebo* (1988), 42 C.C.C. (3d) 536, 64 C.R. (3d) 388 (Alta. C.A.), that an intention to defraud is not an element of the offence under this section. Rather, the intent required is the intent to deceive, such an interpretation is consistent with the forgery offence defined by s. 366(1)(*b*) which as well does not require proof of an intent to defraud.

The fact that the accused ought to have known that certain facts existed does not by itself form a basis for the application of the doctrine of wilful blindness: *R. v. Currie* (1975), 24 C.C.C. (2d) 292 (Ont. C.A.) (2:1).

Acts of the accused in preparing fictitious bills for fees which were to be used if necessary to cover the payment of a benefit to a bank manager, did not constitute uttering where the bills were never used and never seen either by the bank or the revenue authorities: *R. v. Valois,* [1986] 1 S.C.R. 278, 25 C.C.C. (3d) 97 (7:0).

FORGERY.

368.1 Everyone is guilty of an indictable offence and liable to imprisonment for a term of not more than 14 years, or is guilty of an offence punishable on summary conviction, who, without lawful authority or excuse, makes, repairs, buys, sells, exports from Canada, imports into Canada or possesses any instrument, device, apparatus, material or thing that they know has been used or know is adapted or intended for use by any person to commit forgery. 2009, c. 28, s. 9.

CROSS-REFERENCES

The related offences of forgery are found in ss. 366 and 367; trafficking or possession of forged documents in s. 368; and unlawful possession of exchequer bill paper, revenue paper or paper to make bank notes in s. 369. For further related offences, see the CROSS-REFERENCES under s. 366. By virtue of s. 368.2, a public officer does not commit this offence where the acts were for the sole purpose of establishing or maintaining a covert identity for use in the course of the public officer's duties or employment.

PUBLIC OFFICERS ACTING IN THE COURSE OF THEIR DUTIES OR EMPLOYMENT.

368.2 No public officer, as defined in subsection 25.1(1), is guilty of an offence under any of sections 366 to 368.1 if the acts alleged to constitute the offence were committed by the public officer for the sole purpose of establishing or maintaining a covert identity for use in the course of the public officer's duties or employment. 2009, c. 28, s. 9.

CROSS-REFERENCES

The similar defence providing immunity for public officers from what might otherwise be considered criminal conduct is set out in great detail in ss. 25.1 to 25.4.

EXCHEQUER BILL PAPER, PUBLIC SEALS, ETC.

369. Everyone is guilty of an indictable offence and liable to imprisonment for a term of not more than 14 years who, without lawful authority or excuse,

    (a) **makes, uses or possesses**

        (i) **any exchequer bill paper, revenue paper or paper that is used to make bank-notes, or**

        (ii) **any paper that is intended to resemble paper mentioned in subparagraph (i); or**

    (b) **makes, reproduces or uses a public seal of Canada or of a province, or the seal of a public body or authority in Canada or of a court of law. R.S., c. C-34, s. 327; 2009, c. 28, s. 9.**

CROSS-REFERENCES

The terms "exchequer bill", "exchequer bill paper", and "revenue paper" are defined in s. 321. The terms "bank-note" and "writing" are defined in s. 2. "Writing" is also defined in s. 35 of the *Interpretation Act*, R.S.C. 1985, c. I-21.

This offence resembles the offences of forgery and using, trafficking and possession of forged documents under ss. 366 to 368. Other related offences are as follows: s. 56.1, offences in relation to identity documents; s. 368.1, offences in relation to instruments for use in committing forgery; s. 370, counterfeit government proclamation; ss. 371, 372, false telegram, etc.; s. 374, drawing document without authority; s. 375, obtaining by forged document; s. 376, counterfeiting stamp, mark, etc.; s. 377, defacing official documents; s. 378, offences in relation to registers; ss. 397 to 402, falsification of books and documents in relation to contracts and trade; ss. 402.1 to 403, identity theft and fraud; ss. 406 to 414, forgery of trade-marks and trade descriptions; ss. 416 to 421, offences in relation to public stores; Part XII, offences in relation to currency, counterfeiting, etc.

SYNOPSIS

Paragraph *(a)* of this section describes the indictable offence of making use of or possessing exchequer bill paper, revenue bill paper, paper used to make bank notes, or any paper that is intended to look like those papers, without lawful authority or excuse. It further describes the offence of making, disposing of, or knowingly possessing any item that is intended to be used to commit forgery, and the offence of making or using a public seal of Canada, a province, a public body or a court of law. The maximum term of imprisonment for this offence is 14 years.

ANNOTATIONS

The word "other" in para. *(b)* relates back only to the word "instrument", which is used as meaning a written document. Thus there is no common category into which "plate, die, machinery and instrument" fall to warrant the *ejusdem generis* interpretation rule, so cheques and an unemployment insurance card found on the accused were held to be unlawful items: *R. v. Evans* (1962), 132 C.C.C. 271, 37 C.R. 341 (B.C.C.A.).

In *R. v. Griffiths* (1969), 7 C.R.N.S. 196 (Que. Q.B., App. Side), it was held that proof of mere possession of an unendorsed forged cheque, in the absence of proof that the cheque was intended to be used to commit forgery, is not an offence. Furthermore Rivard J., refused to follow *R. v. Evans, supra.*

Having regard to the definition of revenue paper in s. 321 as paper used to make stamps, licences or permits, the offence is not made out where the accused is in possession of a false birth certificate. The definition contemplates present possession of paper for the future purpose of making or manufacturing certain government documents. It was not intended to apply to completed documents: *R. v. Hagerman* (1988), 46 C.C.C. (3d) 432 (B.C. Co. Ct.).

The term "adapted" in para. *(b)* means "suitable for": *R. v. Mac*, [2002] 1 S.C.R. 856, 163 C.C.C. (3d) 1.

COUNTERFEIT PROCLAMATION, ETC.

370. Every one who knowingly

(a) prints a proclamation, order, regulation or appointment, or notice thereof, and causes it falsely to purport to have been printed by the Queen's Printer for Canada or the Queen's Printer for a province, or

(b) tenders in evidence a copy of any proclamation, order, regulation or appointment that falsely purports to have been printed by the Queen's Printer for Canada or the Queen's Printer for a province,

is guilty of an indictable offence and liable to imprisonment for a term not exceeding five years. R.S., c. C-34, s. 328.

CROSS-REFERENCES

The accused may elect his mode of trial pursuant to s. 536(2). Release pending trial is determined by s. 515, although the accused is eligible for release by the officer in charge under s. 498.

This offence resembles the offences of forgery and uttering under ss. 367 and 368. Other related offences are as follows: s. 369, exchequer bill paper, public seals, etc.; ss. 371, 372, false telegram, etc.; s. 374, drawing document without authority; s. 375, obtaining by forged document; s. 376, counterfeiting stamp, mark, etc.; s. 377, defacing official documents; s. 378, offences in relation to registers; ss. 397 to 402, falsification of books and documents in relation to contracts and trade; ss. 406 to 414, forgery of trade-marks and trade descriptions; ss. 416 to 421, offences in relation to public stores; Part XII, offences in relation to currency, counterfeiting, etc. With respect to the offence in para. (b), also see s. 131, perjury and s. 237, fabricating evidence.

SYNOPSIS

This section describes two offences relating to the counterfeiting of official documents. Everyone who *knowingly* prints a proclamation, order, regulation, or appointment, or a notice of such document, and causes it falsely to purport to have been printed by a federal or provincial Queen's Printer, commits the offence, as does anyone knowingly tendering a copy of such a document (with the exception of notices) in evidence. The offence is indictable, and is punishable by imprisonment for up to five years.

MESSAGE IN FALSE NAME.

371. Everyone who, with intent to defraud, causes a message to be sent as if it were sent under the authority of another person, knowing that it is not sent under that authority and with intent that it should be acted on as if it were, is guilty of an indictable offence and liable to imprisonment for a term of not more than five years. R.S., c. C-34, s. 329; 2014, c. 31, s. 18.

CROSS-REFERENCES

The accused may elect his mode of trial pursuant to s. 536(2). Release pending trial is determined by s. 515, although the accused is eligible for release by the officer in charge under s. 498.

This offence resembles the offences of forgery and uttering under ss. 367 and 368. Other related offences are as follows: s. 369, exchequer bill paper, public seals, etc.; s. 370, counterfeit government proclamation; s. 374, drawing document without authority; s. 375, obtaining by forged document; s. 376, counterfeiting stamp, mark, etc.; s. 377, defacing official documents; s. 378, offences in relation to registers; ss. 397 to 402, falsification of books and documents in relation to contracts and trade; ss. 406 to 414, forgery of trade-marks and trade descriptions; ss. 416 to 421, offences in relation to public stores; Part XII, offences in relation to currency, counterfeiting, etc. With respect to the offence in para. (b), also see s. 131, perjury and s. 237, fabricating evidence.

Also see related offences: s. 181, publishing false news; s. 372, conveying false information, indecent and harassing telephone calls.

SYNOPSIS

This section describes the offence of sending messages in a false name. Everyone causing a message to be sent or delivered purportedly by the authority of a person *known* not to have authorized it, intending that it be acted upon as if authorized by that person, and *intending to defraud*, commits the offence. The offence is indictable with a maximum punishment of five years' imprisonment.

FALSE INFORMATION / Indecent communications / Harassing communications / Punishment.

372. (1) Everyone commits an offence who, with intent to injure or alarm a person, conveys information that they know is false, or causes such information to be conveyed by letter or any means of telecommunication.

(2) Everyone commits an offence who, with intent to alarm or annoy a person, makes an indecent communication to that person or to any other person by a means of telecommunication.

(3) Everyone commits an offence who, without lawful excuse and with intent to harass a person, repeatedly communicates, or causes repeated communications to be made, with them by a means of telecommunication.

(4) Everyone who commits an offence under this section is

    (a) **guilty of an indictable offence and liable to imprisonment for a term of not more than two years; or**

    (b) **guilty of an offence punishable on summary conviction. R.S., c. C-34, s. 330; 2014, c. 31, s. 18.**

CROSS-REFERENCES

Section 4(8) provides that, if an offence contains an element of communication, it is deemed to include telecommunication.

On the definition of "indecent", see the notes under s. 163.

The accused may elect his mode of trial pursuant to s. 536(2) for the offence described in subsec. (1) and release pending trial is determined by s. 515, although the accused is eligible for release by the officer in charge under s. 498. It may be that, in some circumstances, the accused found guilty of this offence would be liable to the discretionary order prohibiting possession of firearms, ammunition or explosives.

Trial of the offences described by subsecs. (2) and (3) is conducted by a summary conviction court pursuant to Part XXVII. The punishment is as set out in s. 787 and the limitation period is set out in s. 786(2). Release pending trial is determined by s. 515, although the accused is eligible for release by a peace officer under s. 496, 497 or by the officer in charge under s. 498.

An alternative to this offence is the procedure for requiring the offender to enter into a recognizance to keep the peace either at common law or pursuant to s. 810. Other related offences: s. 175, causing disturbance; s. 264, criminal harassment; s. 264.1, uttering threats; s. 346, extortion; s. 423, intimidation and watching and besetting; s. 424, threat to commit offence against internationally protected person; s. 371, sending false telegram, etc., with intent to defraud.

SYNOPSIS

This section creates hybrid offences of conveying false information, and making indecent or harassing communications. Subsection (1) provides that anyone who *knowingly* conveys false information with intent to injure or alarm creates an offence. Subsection (2) creates an offence of making an indecent communication with intent to alarm or annoy. Subsection (3) prohibits harassing communications, provided they are made repeatedly and with intent to harass.

ANNOTATIONS

Subsection (2) – This subsection applies, although the calls were made to an answering machine. The accused was aware that the calls were being recorded and would be heard by the victim at a later time: *R. v. Manicke* (1993), 81 C.C.C. (3d) 255, 109 Sask. R. 126 (C.A.).

Subsection (3) – The victim of an offence under this subsection must be the recipient of the harassing telephone calls. Thus, the accused was acquitted where he made repeated calls intending to harass his wife, but the calls were intercepted by a friend: *R. v. Wood* (1983), 8 C.C.C. (3d) 217 (Ont. Prov. Ct.).

The term "harass" in this subsection is synonymous with annoy and could include conduct of the accused in repeatedly telephoning a person and simply hanging up when the call was answered: *R. v. Sabine* (1990), 57 C.C.C. (3d) 209, 78 C.R. (3d) 34 (N.B.Q.B.).

373. [*Repealed*, R.S.C. 1985, c. 27 (1st Supp.), s. 53.]

DRAWING DOCUMENT WITHOUT AUTHORITY, ETC.

374. Every one who

    (*a*) **with intent to defraud and without lawful authority makes, executes, draws, signs, accepts or endorses a document in the name or on the account of another person by procuration or otherwise, or**

    (*b*) **makes use of or utters a document knowing that it has been made, executed, signed, accepted or endorsed with intent to defraud and without lawful authority, in the name or on the account of another person, by procuration or otherwise,**

is guilty of an indictable offence and liable to imprisonment for a term not exceeding fourteen years. R.S., c. C-34, s. 332.

CROSS-REFERENCES

The term "document" is defined in s. 321.

The accused may elect his mode of trial pursuant to s. 536(2). Release pending trial is determined by s. 515.

This offence resembles the offences of forgery and uttering under ss. 367 and 368. Other related offences are as follows: s. 369, exchequer bill paper, public seals, etc.; s. 370, counterfeit government proclamation; ss. 371, 372, false telegram, etc.; s. 375, obtaining by forged document; s. 376, counterfeiting stamp, mark, etc.; s. 377, defacing official documents; s. 378, offences in relation to registers; ss. 397 to 402, falsification of books and documents in relation to contracts and trade; ss. 406 to 414, forgery of trade-marks and trade descriptions; ss. 416 to 421, offences in relation to public stores; Part XII, offences in relation to currency, counterfeiting, etc.

SYNOPSIS

This section describes the offence of drawing or using a document without authority. Anyone who makes, executes, draws, signs, accepts or endorses a document in the name of or on behalf of another person without lawful authority, and with an intention to defraud, or who knowingly makes use of, or utters such a document, commits an indictable offence. The maximum term of punishment is 14 years' imprisonment.

OBTAINING, ETC., BY INSTRUMENT BASED ON FORGED DOCUMENT.

375. Every one who demands, receives or obtains anything, or causes or procures anything to be delivered or paid to any person under, on, or by virtue of any instrument issued under the authority of law, knowing that it is based on a forged document, is guilty of an indictable offence and liable to imprisonment for a term not exceeding fourteen years. R.S., c. C-34, s. 333.

CROSS-REFERENCES

The term "document" is defined in s. 321.

The accused may elect his mode of trial pursuant to s. 536(2). Release pending trial is determined by s. 515.

This offence resembles the offences of forgery and uttering under ss. 367 and 368. Other related offences are as follows: s. 369, exchequer bill paper, public seals, etc.; s. 370, counterfeit government proclamation; ss. 371, 372, false telegram, etc.; s. 374, drawing document without authority; s. 376, counterfeiting stamp, mark, etc.; s. 377, defacing official documents; s. 378, offences in relation to registers; ss. 397 to 402, falsification of books and documents in relation to contracts and trade; ss. 406 to 414, forgery of trade-marks and trade descriptions; ss. 416 to 421, offences in relation to public stores; Part XII, offences in relation to currency, counterfeiting, etc.

SYNOPSIS

This section creates the offence of using an instrument based on a forged document. Anyone who demands, receives or obtains anything, or causes anything to be delivered or paid, by virtue of an instrument issued under legal authority, but knowing that it is based on a forged document, commits an indictable offence. The maximum term or punishment is 14 years.

COUNTERFEITING STAMP, ETC. / Counterfeiting mark / Definitions / "mark" / "stamp".

376. (1) Every one who

  (*a*) **fraudulently uses, mutilates, affixes, removes or counterfeits a stamp or part thereof,**

  (*b*) **knowingly and without lawful excuse, the proof of which lies on him, has in his possession**

   (i) **a counterfeit stamp or a stamp that has been fraudulently mutilated, or**

   (ii) **anything bearing a stamp of which a part has been fraudulently erased, removed or concealed, or**

  (*c*) **without lawful excuse, the proof of which lies on him, makes or knowingly has in his possession a die or instrument that is capable of making the impression of a stamp or part thereof,**

is guilty of an indictable offence and liable to imprisonment for a term not exceeding fourteen years.

(2) Every one who, without lawful authority,

  (*a*) **makes a mark,**

  (*b*) **sells, or exposes for sale, or has in his possession a counterfeit mark,**

  (*c*) **affixes a mark to anything that is required by law to be marked, branded, sealed or wrapped other than the thing to which the mark was originally affixed or was intended to be affixed, or**

  (*d*) **affixes a counterfeit mark to anything that is required by law to be marked, branded, sealed or wrapped,**

is guilty of an indictable offence and liable to imprisonment for a term not exceeding fourteen years.

(3) In this section

"mark" means a mark, brand, seal, wrapper or design used by or on behalf of

  (*a*) **the government of Canada or of a province,**

  (*b*) **the government of a state other than Canada, or**

  (*c*) **a department, board, commission or agent established by a government mentioned in paragraph (*a*) or (*b*) in connection with the service or business of that government;**

"stamp" means an impressed or adhesive stamp used for the purpose of revenue by the government of Canada or a province or by the government of a state other than Canada. R.S., c. C-34, s. 334.

CROSS-REFERENCES

Possession is defined in s. 4(3). While there is no definition of "fraudulently" which is universally applicable, generally speaking, it refers to conduct which is dishonest and morally wrong: *R. v. DeMarco* (1973), 13 C.C.C. (2d) 369 (Ont. C.A.).

The accused may elect his mode of trial pursuant to s. 536(2). Release pending trial is determined by s. 515.

This offence resembles the offences of forgery and uttering under ss. 367 and 368. Other related offences are as follows: s. 369, exchequer bill paper, public seals, etc.; s. 370, counterfeit government proclamation; s. 374, drawing document without authority; ss. 397 to 402, falsification of books and documents in relation to contracts and trade; ss. 406 to 414, forgery of trade-marks and trade descriptions; ss. 416 to 421, offences in relation to public stores; Part XII, offences in relation to currency, counterfeiting, etc.

SYNOPSIS

This section describes the offences of counterfeiting a stamp or a mark. *Stamp* and *mark* are both defined in subsec. (3), and are limited to government uses. Subsection (1) provides that an indictable offence is committed where anyone counterfeits a stamp or part of a stamp, fraudulently deals with a stamp or part of a stamp in a variety of ways, possesses a counterfeit or fraudulently mutilated stamp, or something bearing a stamp of which part has been fraudulently erased, removed or concealed, or makes or knowingly possesses a die or instrument capable of making the impression of a stamp or part thereof. In the case of the possession offences and the offence of making a die or instrument, the accused will not be convicted if he can establish that the act in question was done with a lawful excuse. Subsection (2) provides that an indictable offence is committed where anyone, without lawful authority, makes a mark, sells or exposes for sale a counterfeit mark, affixes a mark originally affixed, or intended to be affixed, to one thing to something else legally requiring a mark, or affixes a counterfeit mark to something requiring a mark. The maximum term of punishment for both offences is 14 years' imprisonment.

ANNOTATIONS

The *actus reus* of subsec. (1)(a) is established by proof that the use of the stamp is objectively impressed with a fraudulent element: *R. v. Lemay* (1999), 144 C.C.C. (3d) 74, [2000] R.J.Q. 406 (C.A.).

DAMAGING DOCUMENTS / Definition of "election document".

377. (1) Every one who unlawfully

    (a) **destroys, defaces or injures a register, or any part of a register, of births, baptisms, marriages, deaths or burials that is required or authorized by law to be kept in Canada, or a copy or any part of a copy of such a register that is required by law to be transmitted to a registrar or other officer,**

    (b) **inserts or causes to be inserted in a register or copy referred to in paragraph *(a)* an entry, that he knows is false, of any matter relating to a birth, baptism, marriage, death or burial, or erases any material part from that register or copy,**

    (c) **destroys, damages or obliterates an election document or causes an election document to be destroyed, damaged or obliterated, or**

    (d) **makes or causes to be made an erasure, alteration or interlineation in or on an election document,**

is guilty of an indictable offence and liable to imprisonment for a term not exceeding five years.

(2) In this section, "election document" means any document or writing issued under the authority of an Act of Parliament or the legislature of a province with respect to an election held pursuant to the authority of that Act. R.S., c. C-34, s. 335.

CROSS-REFERENCES

The term "document" is defined in s. 321.

The accused may elect his mode of trial pursuant to s. 536(2). Release pending trial is determined by s. 515, although the accused is eligible for release by the officer in charge under s. 498.

This offence resembles the offences of forgery and uttering under ss. 367 and 368. Other related offences are as follows: s. 369, exchequer bill paper, public seals, etc.; s. 370, counterfeit government proclamation; s. 374, drawing document without authority; s. 375, obtaining by instrument issued under authority of law knowing it is based on a forged document; s. 376, counterfeiting stamp, mark, etc.; s. 377, defacing official documents.

SYNOPSIS

This section describes the offence of damaging or interfering with certain registers and election documents. Paragraph (1)(*a*) prohibits a person from destroying, defacing or injuring a register or part of a register of births, baptisms, marriages, deaths or burials lawfully required or authorized to be kept, or a copy or partial copy lawfully required to be transmitted. Subsection (1)(*b*) prohibits false insertions or erasures in such a register or copy. Subsection (1)(*c*) prohibits a person from damaging or obliterating an election document, or causing such an act to be done. Subsection (1)(*d*) proscribes erasures, alterations or interlineations in election documents. An election document is defined in subsec. (2), and relates only to elections authorized by federal or provincial enactments. This offence is indictable and carries a maximum term of five years' imprisonment.

OFFENCES IN RELATION TO REGISTERS.

378. Every one who
  (*a*) being authorized or required by law to make or issue a certified copy of, extract from or certificate in respect of a register, record or document, knowingly makes or issues a false certified copy, extract or certificate,
  (*b*) not being authorized or required by law to make or issue a certified copy of, extract from or certificate in respect of a register, record or document, fraudulently makes or issues a copy, extract or certificate that purports to be certified as authorized or required by law, or
  (*c*) being authorized or required by law to make a certificate or declaration concerning any particular required for the purpose of making entries in a register, record or document, knowingly and falsely makes the certificate or declaration,
is guilty of an indictable offence and liable to imprisonment for a term not exceeding five years. R.S., c. C-34, s. 336.

CROSS-REFERENCES

The term "document" is defined in s. 321. The term "register" is not defined but probably refers to the registers described in s. 377.

The accused may elect his mode of trial pursuant to s. 536(2). Release pending trial is determined by s. 515, although the accused is eligible for release by the officer in charge under s. 498.

This offence resembles the offences of forgery and uttering under ss. 367 and 368. Other related offences are as follows: s. 369, exchequer bill paper, public seals, etc.; s. 370, counterfeit government proclamation; s. 374, drawing document without authority; s. 375, obtaining by instrument issued under authority of law knowing it is based on a forged document; s. 376, counterfeiting stamp, mark, etc.; s. 377, defacing official documents.

SYNOPSIS

This section describes the offence of issuing false or unauthorized certifications. Paragraph (*a*) prohibits persons legally required or authorized to issue certified copies of, extracts from, or certificates in respect of a register, record or document, from knowingly doing so falsely. Paragraph (*b*) prohibits other persons from *fraudulently issuing* such documents if they purport to be certified as legally required or authorized. Paragraph (*c*) prohibits persons legally authorized or required to make certificates or declarations concerning any particular required for making entries in such register, record or document from *knowingly* doing so falsely. In each case, the offence is indictable, with a maximum term of punishment of five years' imprisonment.

Part X / FRAUDULENT TRANSACTIONS RELATING TO CONTRACTS AND TRADE

Interpretation

DEFINITIONS / "goods" / "trading stamps".

379. In this Part,

"goods" means anything that is the subject of trade or commerce;

"trading stamps" includes any form of cash receipt, receipt, coupon, premium ticket or other device, designed or intended to be given to the purchaser of goods by the vendor thereof or on his behalf, and to represent a discount on the price of the goods or a premium to the purchaser thereof

> **(*a*) that may be redeemed**
> > **(i) by any person other than the vendor, the person from whom the vendor purchased the goods or the manufacturer of the goods,**
> > **(ii) by the vendor, the person from whom the vendor purchased the goods or the manufacturer of the goods in cash or in goods that are not his property in whole or in part, or**
> > **(iii) by the vendor elsewhere than in the premises where the goods are purchased, or**
> **(*b*) that does not show on its face the place where it is delivered and the merchantable value thereof, or**
> **(*c*) that may not be redeemed on demand at any time,**

but an offer, endorsed by the manufacturer upon a wrapper or container in which goods are sold, of a premium or reward for the return of that wrapper or container to the manufacturer is not a trading stamp. R.S., c. C-34, s. 337.

CROSS-REFERENCES

In addition to the definitions in this section, see s. 2 and notes to that section.

SYNOPSIS

This section provides a definition of the term *goods* and *trading stamps* for the purpose of Part X, which concerns fraudulent transactions relating to contracts and trade.

ANNOTATIONS

"Trading stamps" – The definition of "trading stamps" in this section is exhaustive notwithstanding the use of the word "includes": *R. v. Loblaw Groceterias Co. (Man.) Ltd.; R. v. Thomson (Niagara IGA Grocery)*, [1961] S.C.R. 138, 129 C.C.C. 223 (5:0).

Fraud

FRAUD / Minimum punishment / Affecting public market.

380. (1) Every one who, by deceit, falsehood or other fraudulent means, whether or not it is a false pretence within the meaning of this Act, defrauds the public or any person, whether ascertained or not, of any property, money or valuable security or any service,

  (*a*) is guilty of an indictable offence and liable to a term of imprisonment not exceeding fourteen years, where the subject-matter of the offence is a testamentary instrument or the value of the subject-matter of the offence exceeds five thousand dollars; or

  (*b*) is guilty

    (i) of an indictable offence and liable to imprisonment for a term not exceeding two years, or

    (ii) of an offence punishable on summary conviction,

  where the value of the subject-matter of the offence does not exceed five thousand dollars.

(1.1) When a person is prosecuted on indictment and convicted of one or more offences referred to in subsection (1), the court that imposes the sentence shall impose a minimum punishment of imprisonment for a term of two years if the total value of the subject-matter of the offences exceeds one million dollars.

(2) Every one who, by deceit, falsehood or other fraudulent means, whether or not it is a false pretence within the meaning of this Act, with intent to defraud, affects the public market price of stocks, shares, merchandise or anything that is offered for sale to the public is guilty of an indictable offence and liable to imprisonment for a term not exceeding fourteen years. R.S., c. C-34, s. 338; 1974-75-76, c. 93, s. 32; R.S.C. 1985, c. 27 (1st Supp.), s. 54; 1994, c. 44, s. 25; 1997, c. 18, s. 26; 2004, c. 3, s. 2; 2011, c. 6, s. 2.

CROSS-REFERENCES

The terms "every one", "person", "property" and "valuable security" are defined in s. 2.

As to admission of photographic evidence of property, see s. 491.2. For proof by way of affidavit of ownership, lawful possession, value, and that the person was deprived of property by fraud or otherwise without the person's lawful consent, see s. 657.1.

By virtue of s. 583, an indictment which otherwise complies with s. 581 is not insufficient by reason only that: para. (*b*), it fails to name the person who owns or has a special property or interest in property mentioned in the count or para. (*c*), it charges an intent to defraud without naming or describing the person whom it was intended to defraud. Also note s. 588 which deems certain persons to have a property interest in property of which they have the management, control or custody. Under s. 586, no count alleging fraud is insufficient by reason only that it does not set out in detail the nature of the fraud. However, under s. 587(1)(*b*) the court may order particulars of any fraud that is alleged.

This offence may be the basis for an application for an authorization to intercept private communications by reason of s. 183 and a warrant to conduct video surveillance under s. 487.01(5). Fraud is an enterprise crime offence for the purposes of Part XII.2.

Where the offence, although committed outside Canada, is in relation to the use of nuclear material, see s. 7(3.4).

The offence in para. (1)(*a*) is an indictable offence for which the accused may elect the mode of trial under s. 536(2) and release pending trial is determined in accordance with s. 515. Where the prosecution elects to proceed by indictment for the offence under subsec. (1)(*b*) then, by virtue of s. 553, it is an offence over which a provincial court judge has absolute jurisdiction and does not depend on the consent of the accused. That is, the accused does not have an election as to mode of trial, although the provincial court judge may, by virtue of s. 555(1), elect to continue the proceedings as a preliminary inquiry, in which case the accused is deemed to have elected trial by judge and jury pursuant to s. 565(1)(*a*). As well, under s. 555(2), where, in the course of the trial, evidence establishes that the subject-matter of the offence is a testamentary instrument or that its value exceeds $5,000 then the provincial court judge shall put the accused to his election under s. 536(2). Where the prosecution elects to proceed by way of summary conviction then the proceedings are conducted by a summary conviction court pursuant to Part XXVII. The punishment is then as set out in s. 787 and the limitation period is set out in s. 786(2). For the offence under para. (*b*), release pending trial is determined by s. 515, although the accused is eligible for release by a peace officer under s. 496, 497 or by the officer in charge under s. 498. The value of a valuable security is determined in accordance with s. 4(2) and of a postal card or stamp in accordance with s. 4(1). The term "testamentary instrument" is defined in s. 2.

For the offence under subsec. (2), the accused may elect his mode of trial under s. 536(2) and release pending trial is determined in accordance with s. 515.

The related offence of theft is generally described in s. 322 and false pretences in s. 362. Other offences relating to trading in securities, etc., are in ss. 382 to 384 and include "wash trading" (s. 382) and insider trading (s. 382.1) and in s. 400 (false prospectus). Section 380.1 provides that, in sentencing an offender for this offence, the court shall consider as aggravating circumstances the magnitude, complexity, duration or degree of planning of the fraud; that the offence adversely affected or had the potential to adversely affect the stability of the Canadian economy or financial system or any financial market in Canada or investor confidence in such markets; the offence involved a large number of victims; the offence had a significant impact on the victims given their personal circumstances such as age, health and financial situation; in committing the offence, the offender took advantage of the high regard in which the offender was held in the community; the offender did not comply with a licensing requirement or professional standard; and that the offender concealed or destroyed records. As well, the offender's employment, employment skills, or status or reputation in the community are not to be considered as mitigating factors if those circumstances were relevant to, contributed to, or were used in the commission of the offence. Section 380.1(3) requires the sentencing court to state the aggravating and mitigating circumstances that it took into account. Section 380.2 provides for the making of a prohibition order, prohibiting the offender from being involved in any capacity that involves authority over the property of another person. Section 380.3 directs the court to consider making a restitution order under ss. 738 or 739. Section 380.4 allows the court to consider a community impact statement.

Sections 487.012 to 487.017 provide procedures for the making of production orders that would require persons to produce documents, data or information to police officers or public officers designated in the order.

SYNOPSIS

This section describes the offences of defrauding the public, or any person, of property, money, valuable security or any service, and of affecting the public market price of stocks, shares, merchandise or anything offered for sale to the public. The activities described above must be accomplished by deceit, falsehood or other fraudulent means, whether or not they constitute false pretences within the meaning of the *Criminal Code*. The accused must have the intent to defraud to attract criminal liability for affecting the market price of stocks, shares, or publicly offered merchandise and this form of the offence is punishable on indictment by a maximum term of 14 years' imprisonment. The more general offence of defrauding the public is indictable, with a maximum punishment of 14 years, when the subject-matter of the offence is a testamentary instrument or has a value greater than $5,000. In other circumstances, this form of the offence is hybrid, with a maximum punishment on indictment of two years. Where the Crown proceeds by indictment and the value of the subject matter of the offences exceeds one million dollars, the offender is subject to a minimum sentence of two years' imprisonment.

ANNOTATIONS

Meaning of defrauds generally – The classic definition of fraud is found in the judgment of Buckley J., in *London & Globe Finance Corp. Ltd. (Re)*, [1903] 1 Ch. 728 at pp. 732-3: "To defraud is to deprive by deceit: it is by deceit to induce a man to act to his injury. More tersely it may be put, that to deceive is by falsehood to induce a state of mind; to defraud is by deceit to induce a course of action."

It was held, however, in *Scott v. Metropolitan Police Commissioner* (1974), 60 Cr. App. R. 124 (H.L.), that this definition is not exhaustive and that to "defraud" ordinarily means: "to deprive a person dishonestly of something which is his or of something to which he is or would or might but for the perpetration of the fraud, be entitled."

In *R. v. Renard* (1974), 17 C.C.C. (2d) 355 (Ont. C.A.), the court held that, a victim may be defrauded by being deprived of something and he may be deprived of something either by being fraudulently induced to part with it or by having that to which he is entitled fraudulently diverted or withheld from him.

An accused's acts in procuring a third person to put him in a position to take money to which the complainant would be otherwise entitled constitutes fraud: *R. v. Kribbs*, [1968] 1 C.C.C. 345, [1967] 2 O.R. 539 (C.A.).

A charge of fraud is valid against the principle shareholder who fraudulently depletes the assets of his *alter ego*, a limited company: *R. v. Marquardt* (1972), 6 C.C.C. (2d) 372, 18 C.R.N.S. 162 (B.C.C.A.).

Meaning of falsehood – It is a falsehood for a person to promise to pay cash for the purchase of an item without any intention of honouring the promise: *R. v. Stanley* (1957), 119 C.C.C. 220, 26 C.R. 180 (B.C.C.A.).

Meaning of "other fraudulent means" generally – In *R. v. Cox and Paton*, [1963] S.C.R. 500, [1963] 2 C.C.C. 148 (5:0), although no exhaustive definition of "other fraudulent means" was given it was held that if all the directors of a company were to join together to purchase a worthless asset with company funds in order to enrich themselves then even "supposing it could be said that the directors being the "mind of the company' and well knowing the true facts, the company was not deceived . . . it is clear that . . . the directors would have defrauded the company, if not by deceit or falsehood, by "other fraudulent means' ".

In *R. v. Olan, Hudson and Hartnett*, [1978] 2 S.C.R. 1175, 41 C.C.C. (2d) 145 (9:0), the court considered the application of *R. v. Cox and Paton, supra,* in a situation where the accused had caused a company over which they had control to divest its holdings in "blue chip" securities and to purchase shares in a company whose major asset was a debt owed to it by a company controlled by two of the accused. It was held that where it is alleged a corporation was defrauded by its directors' deception of the corporation is not an essential element of the offence, the words "other fraudulent means" include not only means which are in the nature of a falsehood or deceit but also all other means which can properly be stigmatized as dishonest. Further, while no exhaustive definition of "defraud" was attempted the Crown at least must prove dishonesty and deprivation. The element of deprivation is satisfied on proof of detriment, prejudice, or risk of prejudice to the economic interest of the victims. The issue in this case was whether the use of the victim's assets in this manner was in furtherance of a *bona fide* business interest of the victim or was it expended in advancing the personal interests of the accused and whether the victim suffered deprivation as a result. The court disagreed with the Ontario Court of Appeal view that there was no evidence of fraud and ordered a new trial. It was not necessary for the Crown to prove the new investment was worthless or negligible.

At least where the Crown relies on "other fraudulent means" rather than deceit or falsehood there need not be some form of relationship or nexus between the accused and the victim. Thus, the infringement of copyright by "counterfeiting" of video tapes may constitute fraud, whether or not it would also amount to theft, notwithstanding there is no relationship between the accused and the victim, the holder of the copyright or distribution rights to the tapes: *R. v. Kirkwood* (1983), 5 C.C.C. (3d) 393, 35 C.R. (3d) 97 (Ont. C.A.), relying on *Scott v. Metropolitan Police Commissioner, supra.* Folld: *R. v. Fitzpatrick* (1984), 11 C.C.C. (3d) 46 (B.C.C.A.).

Other fraudulent means includes mere omission where, through silence, an individual hides from the other person a fundamental and essential information. The silence or omission must be such that it would mislead a reasonable person: *R. v. Emond* (1997), 117 C.C.C. (3d) 275 (Que. C.A.), leave to appeal to S.C.C. refused 117 C.C.C. (3d) vi.

In considering whether the acts of the accused can properly be stigmatized as dishonest, the standard to be applied is that of a reasonable person. It connotes an underhanded design which has the effect, or which engenders the risk, of depriving others of what is theirs. The dishonesty lies in the wrongful use of something in which another person has an interest, in such a manner that this other's interest is extinguished or put at risk. The use is wrongful in this sense if it constitutes conduct which reasonable decent persons would consider dishonest and unscrupulous: *R. v. Zlatic*, [1993] 2 S.C.R. 29, 79 C.C.C. (3d) 466.

The requisite *mens rea* cannot be inferred from a finding that an accused's conduct was objectively dishonest when the *actus reus* is based on "other fraudulent means". Dishonesty with respect to the *actus reus* is to be measured against the objective standard of what a reasonable person would consider to be dishonest without regard for what the accused actually knew: *R. v. Wolsey* (2008), 233 C.C.C. (3d) 205 (B.C.C.A.).

Risk of deprivation – Where the "owner" of certain confidential information had no intention of dealing with it in a commercial way it could not be said that a person who obtains that information has committed fraud, since there was no risk of economic loss amounting to deprivation: *R. v. Stewart*, [1988] 1 S.C.R. 963, 41 C.C.C. (3d) 481 (6:0).

While there need not be actual economic loss there must be an actual risk of prejudice and where the victim named in the indictment merely acted as a conduit in the transactions so that there was no actual risk of prejudice to her economic interests the charge was not made out: *R. v. Campbell and Kotler*, [1986] 2 S.C.R. 376, 29 C.C.C. (3d) 97 (5:0).

In *R. v. Knowles* (1979), 51 C.C.C. (2d) 237 (Ont. C.A.), the court found the requisite dishonest deprivation where the victim was induced to make a loan which it would not have made had it known the true state of affairs, namely that the true borrower was an officer of a company which was a subsidiary of the victim. The deceit practised by the accused placed the accused in a conflict of interest and thus imperilled the victim's economic interests notwithstanding the loan was secured and used for the purpose for which it was advanced.

Economic loss does not have to be proven by the Crown and fraud is complete when money is paid for corporate shares to which the accused falsely ascribed certain attributes: *R. v. Knelson and Baran* (1962), 133 C.C.C. 210, 38 C.R. 181 (B.C.C.A.).

Mens rea – The *mens rea* of fraud is established by proof of subjective knowledge of the prohibited act, and subjective knowledge that the act could have as a consequence deprivation, in the sense of causing another to lose their pecuniary interest in certain property or in placing that interest at risk. There is no requirement that the accused subjectively appreciate the dishonesty of his acts: *R. v. Théroux*, [1993] 2 S.C.R. 5, 79 C.C.C. (3d) 449; *R. v. Zlatic, supra.*

An accused's honest belief that he was entitled to the property in question is a mistake of law and does not negate the *mens rea* of fraud. While lack of "colour of right" is an element of theft and therefore provides a defence, it does not provide a defence to a charge of fraud: *R. v. Kingsbury* (2012), 297 C.C.C. (3d) 255 (B.C.C.A.).

Expectation of subsequent validation – Where pursuant to the suggestion of his superior, who approved but would not authorize a salary increase, the accused submitted fictitious expense accounts to the Quebec government, it was held (4:3) that such a direction was not a valid defence to a charge of defrauding the public in general and the Government of the

Province of Quebec in particular, and that the accused's expectation that such a practice would ultimately be validated was also not a proper defence in law: *R. v. Lemire*, [1965] S.C.R. 174, [1965] 4 C.C.C. 11.

Proof of charge as particularized – Proprietorships are not in and of themselves persons capable of being defrauded but are merely the registered names under which persons capable of being defrauded do business. Where the prosecution alleges in an indictment that the victim is a proprietorship then it in effect has particularized as the victim the person who used the propriertorship to carry on business and that it was in the operation of that proprietorship that he was defrauded and not otherwise: *R. v. Campbell and Kotler*, [1986] 2 S.C.R. 376, 29 C.C.C. (3d) 97 (5:0). [However, now see definition of "person" in s. 2, which includes an organization, which in turn includes a partnership.]

On a charge under this section it is not necessary for the Crown to prove the accused actually obtained the property which was the subject of the charge, only that the victim was deprived of the property as a result of the accused's dishonest acts: *R. v. Huggett* (1978), 42 C.C.C. (2d) 198 (Ont. C.A.).

A charge of conspiracy or attempt to commit fraud may be made out although the victim is unascertained. Further, the victim need not be particularized in the indictment: *R. v. Vezina; R. v. Cote*, [1986] 1 S.C.R. 2, 23 C.C.C. (3d) 481 (7:0).

An indictment alleging that certain individuals were defrauded of "$2,500", rather than a sum of money, is sufficient to support a conviction although the evidence showed the individuals were induced by deceit, falsehood or other fraudulent means merely to part with a cheque in that amount drawn, moreover, on the bank accounts of corporations of which they were principal owners or co-owners: *R. v. Scheel* (1978), 42 C.C.C. (2d) 31, 3 C.R. (3d) 359 (Ont. C.A.).

Meaning of "property" [Also see "Risk of deprivation", *supra*] – The word "property" does not mean ownership, but is only descriptive of the thing of which one is defrauded and the offence is completed once there is a passing over of possession under deceitful circumstances: *R. v. Vallillee* (1974), 15 C.C.C. (2d) 409, 24 C.R.N.S. 319 (Ont. C.A.).

Other notes – Although the acts of the accused may also constitute a breach of provincial welfare legislation it is open to the Crown to proceed under this section: *R. v. Gladu* (1986), 29 C.C.C. (3d) 186 (Ont. C.A.); *R. v. Gallant* (1987), 34 C.C.C. (3d) 190, 64 Nfld. & P.E.I.R. 89 (P.E.I.C.A.). *R. v. Rouse* (1988), 39 C.C.C. (3d) 115, 85 A.R. 60 (C.A.).

Affecting public market [subsec. (2)] – In one of the few cases decided under this subsection a conviction was upheld where the accused was one of several persons involved in operating a "box". While ostensibly set up to maintain orderly marketing in shares the two companies involved in the "box" were in fact used to give the illusion of arms length transactions in the trading of the shares and gave the impression that the shares were continually rising in value: *R. v. McNaughton* (1976), 43 C.C.C. (2d) 293, 33 C.R.N.S. 279 (Que. C.A.).

SENTENCING — AGGRAVATING CIRCUMSTANCES / Aggravating circumstance — value of the fraud / Non-mitigating factors / Record of proceedings.

380.1 (1) Without limiting the generality of section 718.2, where a court imposes a sentence for an offence referred to in section 380, 382, 382.1 or 400, it shall consider the following as aggravating circumstances:

    (a) the magnitude, complexity, duration or degree of planning of the fraud committed was significant;

    (b) the offence adversely affected, or had the potential to adversely affect, the stability of the Canadian economy or financial system or any financial market in Canada or investor confidence in such a financial market;

    (c) the offence involved a large number of victims;

    (c.1) the offence had a significant impact on the victims given their personal circumstances including their age, health and financial situation;

(*d*) **in committing the offence, the offender took advantage of the high regard in which the offender was held in the community;**

(*e*) **the offender did not comply with a licensing requirement, or professional standard, that is normally applicable to the activity or conduct that forms the subject-matter of the offence; and**

(*f*) **the offender concealed or destroyed records related to the fraud or to the disbursement of the proceeds of the fraud.**

(1.1) Without limiting the generality of section 718.2, when a court imposes a sentence for an offence referred to in section 382, 382.1 or 400, it shall also consider as an aggravating circumstance the fact that the value of the fraud committed exceeded one million dollars.

(2) When a court imposes a sentence for an offence referred to in section 380, 382, 382.1 or 400, it shall not consider as mitigating circumstances the offender's employment, employment skills or status or reputation in the community if those circumstances were relevant to, contributed to, or were used in the commission of the offence.

(3) The court shall cause to be stated in the record the aggravating and mitigating circumstances it took into account when determining the sentence. 2004, c. 3, s. 2; 2011, c. 6, s. 3.

CROSS-REFERENCES

Section 380 describes the general offence of defrauding the public or any person and stock fraud. Section 382 creates the offence of fraudulent manipulation of stock exchange transactions. Section 382.1 creates offences of insider trading. Section 400 creates offences in relation to making a false prospectus.

Section 718.2 sets out other principles of sentencing including other deemed aggravating circumstances, such as para. (*a*)(iii), that the offender abused a position of trust or authority in relation to the victim. Section 380.2 provides for the making of a prohibition order, prohibiting the offender from being involved in any capacity that involves authority over the property of another person. Section 380.3 directs the court to consider making a restitution order under ss. 738 or 739. Section 380.4 allows the court to consider a community impact statement.

SYNOPSIS

This section deals with principles of sentencing specific to the various fraud offences created by ss. 380, 382, 382.1 and 400. Subsection (1) sets out various aggravating circumstances that the court is to take into account. Subsection (1.1) sets out the additional aggravating circumstances that the value of the fraud exceeded one million dollars for the offences in ss. 382, 382.1 and 400. Section 380(1.1) already takes that circumstance into account for the offence committed under s. 380 by creating a minimum punishment of two years' imprisonment where the value of the fraud exceeds one million dollars. Subsection (3) requires the sentencing court to set out the aggravating and mitigating circumstances that were taken into account.

PROHIBITION ORDER / Duration / Court may vary order / Offence.

380.2 (1) When an offender is convicted, or is discharged on the conditions prescribed in a probation order under section 730, of an offence referred to in subsection 380(1), the court that sentences or discharges the offender, in addition to any other punishment that may be imposed for that offence or any other condition prescribed in the order of discharge, may make, subject to the conditions or exemptions that the court directs, an order prohibiting the offender from seeking, obtaining or continuing any employment, or becoming or being a volunteer in any capacity, that involves having authority over the real property, money or valuable security of another person.

(2) The prohibition may be for any period that the court considers appropriate, including any period to which the offender is sentenced to imprisonment.

(3) A court that makes an order of prohibition or, if the court is for any reason unable to act, another court of equivalent jurisdiction in the same province, may, on application of the offender or the prosecutor, require the offender to appear before it at any time and, after hearing the parties, that court may vary the conditions prescribed in the order if, in the opinion of the court, the variation is desirable because of changed circumstances.

(4) Every person who is bound by an order of prohibition and who does not comply with the order is guilty of

    (*a*) an indictable offence and is liable to imprisonment for a term not exceeding two years; or

    (*b*) an offence punishable on summary conviction. **2011, c. 6, s. 4.**

CROSS-REFERENCES

Section 380(1) describes the general offence of defrauding the public or any person. Section 380.1 provides that, in sentencing an offender for the offence under s. 380, the court shall consider as aggravating circumstances the magnitude, complexity, duration or degree of planning of the fraud; that the offence adversely affected or had the potential to adversely affect the stability of the Canadian economy or financial system or any financial market in Canada or investor confidence in such markets; the offence involved a large number of victims; the offence had a significant impact on the victims given their personal circumstances such as age, health and financial situation; in committing the offence, the offender took advantage of the high regard in which the offender was held in the community; the offender did not comply with a licensing requirement or professional standard; and that the offender concealed or destroyed records. As well, the offender's employment, employment skills, or status or reputation in the community are not to be considered as mitigating factors if those circumstances were relevant to, contributed to, or were used in the commission of the offence. Section 380.1(3) requires the sentencing court to state the aggravating and mitigating circumstances that it took into account. Section 380.3 directs the court to consider making a restitution order under ss. 738 or 739. Section 380.4 allows the court to consider a community impact statement.

SYNOPSIS

This section gives the court the power to impose a prohibition order where the offender is convicted of the general fraud offence described in s. 380(1). The order prohibits the offender from any involvement (employment or volunteering) in authority over the property of another. The court can impose conditions or exemptions as part of the prohibition order and can be for any period the court considers appropriate. Failure to comply with the order is a Crown-option offence.

380.3 [*Repealed*, **2015, c. 13, s. 11.**]

380.4 [*Repealed*, **2015, c. 13, s. 11.**]

USING MAILS TO DEFRAUD.

381. Every one who makes use of the mails for the purpose of transmitting or delivering letters or circulars concerning schemes devised or intended to deceive or defraud the public, or for the purpose of obtaining money under false pretences, is guilty of an indictable offence and liable to imprisonment for a term not exceeding two years. **R.S., c. C-34, s. 339.**

CR. CODE

CROSS-REFERENCES

The term "mail" is defined in s. 2 of the *Canada Post Corporation Act*, R.S.C. 1985, c. C-10. By virtue of s. 583, an indictment, which otherwise complies with s. 581, is not insufficient by reason only that: para. (*c*), it charges an intent to defraud without naming or describing the person whom it was intended to defraud. Under s. 586, no count alleging false pretences or fraud is insufficient by reason only that it does not set out in detail the nature of the false pretences or fraud. However, under s. 587(1)(*b*), the court may order particulars of any false pretence or fraud that is alleged.

This offence may be the basis for an application for an authorization to intercept private communications by reason of s. 183 and a warrant to conduct video surveillance under s. 487.01(5).

The accused may elect his mode of trial pursuant to s. 536(2). Release pending trial is determined by s. 515, although the accused is eligible for release by the officer in charge pursuant to s. 498.

The related offence of fraud is described in s. 380 and of circulating a false prospectus in s. 400.

SYNOPSIS

This section makes it an offence to use the mails to deliver letters or circulars that either describe schemes intended to deceive the public, or that are to be used for the purpose of obtaining money under false pretences. This is an indictable offence with a maximum term of two years' imprisonment.

FRAUDULENT MANIPULATION OF STOCK EXCHANGE TRANSACTIONS.

382. Every one who, through the facility of a stock exchange, curb market or other market, with intent to create a false or misleading appearance of active public trading in a security or with intent to create a false or misleading appearance with respect to the market price of a security,

  (*a*) **effects a transaction in the security that involves no change in the beneficial ownership thereof,**

  (*b*) **enters an order for the purchase of the security, knowing that an order of substantially the same size at substantially the same time and at substantially the same price for the sale of the security has been or will be entered by or for the same or different persons, or**

  (*c*) **enters an order for the sale of the security, knowing that an order of substantially the same size at substantially the same time and at substantially the same price for the purchase of the security has been or will be entered by or for the same or different persons,**

is guilty of an indictable offence and liable to imprisonment for a term not exceeding ten years. R.S., c. C-34, s. 340; 2004, c. 3, s. 4.

CROSS-REFERENCES

This offence may be the basis for an application for an authorization to intercept private communications by reason of s. 183 and is an enterprise crime offence for the purposes of Part XII.2. The accused may elect his mode of trial pursuant to s. 536(2). Release pending trial is determined by s. 515, although the accused is eligible for release by the officer in charge pursuant to s. 498.

The related offence of fraud is described in s. 380, of insider trading and tipping in s. 382.1 and of circulating a false prospectus in s. 400.

Section 380.1 provides that, in sentencing an offender for the offence under this section, the court shall consider as aggravating circumstances the magnitude, complexity, duration or degree of planning of the fraud; that the offence adversely affected or had the potential to adversely affect the stability of the Canadian economy or financial system or any financial market in Canada or investor confidence in such markets; the offence involved a large number of victims; the offence had a significant impact on the victims given their personal circumstances such as age, health and financial situation; in committing the offence, the offender took advantage of the high regard in which the offender was held in the community; the offender did not comply with a licensing requirement or professional standard; and that the offender concealed or destroyed records. As well, the offender's employment, employment skills, or status or reputation in the community are not to be considered as mitigating factors if those circumstances were relevant to, contributed to, or were used in the commission of the offence. Section 380.1(2) requires the court to consider as an aggravating circumstance that the value of the fraud committed exceeded one million dollars. Section 380.1(3) requires the sentencing court to state the aggravating and mitigating circumstances that it took into account.

Sections 487.012 to 487.017 provide procedures for the making of production orders that would require persons to produce documents, data or information to police officers or public officers designated in the order.

SYNOPSIS

This section sets out the offence of manipulation of transactions on a stock exchange, curb market or other market and is colloquially known as "wash-trading". Every person who uses one of these institutions with *intent to create a false or misleading appearance* with respect to the market price, or activity of a security, and who engages in any of the activities specified in paras. (*a*), (*b*) or (*c*), commits an indictable offence and is liable to a maximum term of 10 years' imprisonment. Paragraph (*a*) describes a transaction in a security that involves no change in the *beneficial ownership*. Paragraphs (*b*) and (*c*) describe the entering of an order for the sale or purchase of a security, *knowing* that a substantially matching or counter balancing purchase or sale order has been, or will be entered on behalf of the same or different persons.

ANNOTATIONS

The section requires an "intent to create a false or misleading appearance of active public interest", and if the purpose is merely to stabilize the market price in the accused's own interest, an offence has not been committed: *R. v. Jay*, [1966] 1 C.C.C. 70 (Ont. C.A.).

For the offence of knowingly entering a cross-order the Crown need not prove that the cross-trade involved either fictitious persons or persons involved with the accused in a fraudulent conspiracy, since the purpose of this section is to prevent fraudulent misuse of the facilities of a market for profit: *R. v. MacMillan*, [1969] 2 C.C.C. 289, 66 D.L.R. (2d) 680 (Ont. C.A.).

The words "or other market" in this section include an "over-the-counter" market: *R. v. Bluestein* (1982), 70 C.C.C. (2d) 336, 36 C.R. (3d) 46, 142 D.L.R. (3d) 71 (Que. C.A.).

PROHIBITED INSIDER TRADING / Tipping / Saving / Definition of "inside information".

382.1 (1) A person is guilty of an indictable offence and liable to imprisonment for a term not exceeding ten years who, directly or indirectly, buys or sells a security, knowingly using inside information that they

  (*a*) **possess by virtue of being a shareholder of the issuer of that security;**

  (*b*) **possess by virtue of, or obtained in the course of, their business or professional relationship with that issuer;**

  (*c*) **possess by virtue of, or obtained in the course of, a proposed takeover or reorganization of, or amalgamation, merger or similar business combination with, that issuer;**

  (*d*) **possess by virtue of, or obtained in the course of, their employment, office, duties or occupation with that issuer or with a person referred to in paragraphs (*a*) to (*c*); or**

  (*e*) **obtained from a person who possesses or obtained the information in a manner referred to in paragraphs (*a*) to (*d*).**

(2) Except when necessary in the course of business, a person who knowingly conveys inside information that they possess or obtained in a manner referred to in subsection **(1)** to another person, knowing that there is a risk that the person will use the information to buy or sell, directly or indirectly, a security to which the information relates, or that they may convey the information to another person who may buy or sell such a security, is guilty of

    (*a*) an indictable offence and liable to imprisonment for a term not exceeding five years; or

    (*b*) an offence punishable on summary conviction.

(3) For greater certainty, an act is not an offence under this section if it is authorized or required, or is not prohibited, by any federal or provincial Act or regulation applicable to it.

(4) In this section, "inside information" means information relating to or affecting the issuer of a security or a security that they have issued, or are about to issue, that

    (*a*) has not been generally disclosed; and

    (*b*) could reasonably be expected to significantly affect the market price or value of a security of the issuer. 2004, c. 3, s. 5.

CROSS-REFERENCES

Other offences relating to trading in securities, etc., include fraud (s. 380), "wash trading" (s. 382) and false prospectus (s. 400).

Section 380.1 provides that, in sentencing an offender for the offence under this section, the court shall consider as aggravating circumstances the magnitude, complexity, duration or degree of planning of the fraud; that the offence adversely affected or had the potential to adversely affect the stability of the Canadian economy or financial system or any financial market in Canada or investor confidence in such markets; the offence involved a large number of victims; the offence had a significant impact on the victims given their personal circumstances such as age, health and financial situation; in committing the offence, the offender took advantage of the high regard in which the offender was held in the community; the offender did not comply with a licensing requirement or professional standard; and that the offender concealed or destroyed records. As well, the offender's employment, employment skills, or status or reputation in the community are not to be considered as mitigating factors if those circumstances were relevant to, contributed to, or were used in the commission of the offence. Section 380.1(2) requires the court to consider as an aggravating circumstance that the value of the fraud committed exceeded one million dollars. Section 380.1(3) requires the sentencing court to state the aggravating and mitigating circumstances that it took into account.

Sections 487.012 to 487.017 provide procedures for the making of production orders that would require persons to produce documents, data or information to police officers or public officers designated in the order.

SYNOPSIS

This section creates the offence of insider trading. Provincial statutes create offences or provide a civil remedy for some forms of insider trading. This section recognizes the provincial interest by providing in subsec. (3) that an act is not an offence under this section if it is authorized or required, or is not prohibited, by any other federal or provincial Act or regulation. The section creates two types of offences: insider trading where the insider uses the information for his or her own benefit by buying or selling securities, and tipping where the insider provides the information to another person to use for their benefit. Subsection (1) defines the insider trading offence and provides that the offender is liable to a maximum term of imprisonment of 10 years. The essence of that offence is directly or indirectly buying or selling a security knowingly using inside information that the person has acquired in any of the ways set out in paras. (*a*) to (*e*), for example by virtue of being a shareholder or because of a professional relationship with the security issuer. Subsection (2) defines the tipping offence where the person knowingly conveys to another inside information that they possess or obtained in a manner referred to in subsec. (1), knowing that there is a risk that the other person will use the information themselves to buy or sell, directly or indirectly, a security to which the information relates or convey the information to another person who will buy or sell such security. The tipping offence is a hybrid offence and on indictment is punishable by a maximum of five years' imprisonment.

Subsection (4) defines inside information as information that has not generally been disclosed and could reasonably be expected to "significantly" affect the market price or value of a security.

GAMING IN STOCKS OR MERCHANDISE / Onus.

383. (1) Every one is guilty of an indictable offence and liable to imprisonment for a term not exceeding five years who, with intent to make gain or profit by the rise or fall in price of the stock of an incorporated or unincorporated company or undertaking, whether in or outside Canada, or of any goods, wares or merchandise,

   (*a*) **makes or signs, or authorizes to be made or signed, any contract or agreement, oral or written, purporting to be for the purchase or sale of shares of stock or goods, wares or merchandise, without the *bona fide* intention of acquiring the shares, goods, wares or merchandise or of selling them, as the case may be, or**

   (*b*) **makes or signs, or authorizes to be made or signed, any contract or agreement, oral or written, purporting to be for the sale or purchase of shares of stock or goods, wares or merchandise in respect of which no delivery of the thing sold or purchased is made or received, and without the *bona fide* intention of making or receiving delivery thereof, as the case may be,**

but this section does not apply where a broker, on behalf of a purchaser, receives delivery, notwithstanding that the broker retains or pledges what is delivered as security for the advance of the purchase money or any part thereof.

(2) Where, in proceedings under this section, it is established that the accused made or signed a contract or agreement for the sale or purchase of shares of stock or goods, wares or merchandise, or acted, aided or abetted in the making or signing thereof, the burden of proof of a *bona fide* intention to acquire or to sell the shares, goods, wares or merchandise or to deliver or to receive delivery thereof, as the case may be, lies on the accused. R.S., C. C-34, s. 341.

CROSS-REFERENCES

The term "goods" is defined in s. 379.

The accused may elect his mode of trial pursuant to s. 536(2). Release pending trial is determined by s. 515, although the accused is eligible for release by the officer in charge pursuant to s. 498.

The related offence of fraud is described in s. 380, of wash-trading in s. 382, of a broker reducing stock by selling for his own account in s. 384 and of circulating a false prospectus in s. 400.

SYNOPSIS

This section describes the indictable offence of dealing in stocks or merchandise *with the intention of profiting* by the variation in the price of those goods but *without* the *bona fide intention of acquiring, selling,* or *making* or *receiving delivery* of the goods. Subsection (1) exempts brokers from this offence in certain circumstances. Subsection (2) states that when it has been established that the accused has made or signed an agreement for the sale or purchase of stocks or merchandise, or acted, aided and abetted in such a transaction, the burden of proof to establish the *bona fide* intention described in subsec. (1), lies on the accused. The maximum term of imprisonment upon conviction is five years.

BROKER REDUCING STOCK BY SELLING FOR HIS OWN ACCOUNT.

384. Every one is guilty of an indictable offence and liable to imprisonment for a term not exceeding five years who, being an individual, or a member or an employee of a partnership, or a director, an officer or an employee of a corporation, where he or the partnership or corporation is employed as a broker by any customer to buy and carry on margin any shares of an incorporated or unincorporated company or undertaking, whether in or out of Canada, thereafter sells or causes to be sold shares of the company or undertaking for any account in which

    (*a*) he or his firm or a partner thereof, or

    (*b*) the corporation or a director thereof,

has a direct or indirect interest, if the effect of the sale is, otherwise than unintentionally, to reduce the amount of those shares in the hands of the broker or under his control in the ordinary course of business below the amount of those shares that the broker should be carrying for all customers. R.S., c. C-34, s. 342.

CROSS-REFERENCES

The accused may elect his mode of trial pursuant to s. 536(2). Release pending trial is determined by s. 515, although the accused is eligible for release by the officer in charge pursuant to s. 498.

    The related offence of fraud is described in s. 380, of wash-trading in s. 382, of gaming in stocks or merchandise in s. 383 and of circulating a false prospectus in s. 400.

SYNOPSIS

This section describes an indictable offence in which a broker sells shares that have been bought and carried on margin for any account in which the broker, his firm, partner, corporation or corporate director has direct or indirect interest. The effect of the sale must be to reduce *intentionally* the amount of those shares in the hands or under the control of the broker below the amount of those shares that the broker should be carrying for all customers. The maximum term of imprisonment for this offence is five years.

FRAUDULENT CONCEALMENT OF TITLE DOCUMENTS / Consent required.

385. (1) Every one who, being a vendor or mortgagor of property or of a chose in action or being a solicitor for or agent of a vendor or mortgagor of property or a chose in action, is served with a written demand for an abstract of title by or on behalf of the purchaser or mortgagee before the completion of the purchase or mortgage, and who

    (*a*) with intent to defraud and for the purpose of inducing the purchaser or mortgagee to accept the title offered or produced to him, conceals from him any settlement, deed, will or other instrument material to the title, or any encumbrance on the title, or

    (*b*) falsifies any pedigree on which the title depends,

is guilty of an indictable offence and liable to imprisonment for a term not exceeding two years.

(2) No proceedings shall be instituted under this section without the consent of the Attorney General. R.S., c. C-34, s. 343.

CROSS-REFERENCES

"Property" and "Attorney General" are defined in s. 2. Section 583(*h*) provides that a count in an indictment is not insufficient by reason only that it does not state that the required consent has been obtained. [As to notes concerning sufficiency of consent, see s. 583.]

    Other offences relating to registers are found ss. 377 and 378 and the offence of fraudulent registration of title is in s. 386 and of fraudulent sale of real property in s. 387. By virtue of s. 583, an indictment which otherwise complies with s. 581 is not insufficient by reason only that: para. (*b*), it fails to name the person who owns or has a special property or interest in property mentioned in the count or para. (*c*), it charges an intent to defraud without naming or describing the person whom it was intended to defraud. Also note s. 588 which deems certain persons to have a property interest in property of which they have the management, control or custody. Under s. 586, no count alleging fraud is insufficient by reason only that it does not set out in detail the nature of the fraud. However, under s. 587(1)(*b*), the court may order particulars of any fraud that is alleged.

The accused may elect his mode of trial pursuant to s. 536(2). Release pending trial is determined by s. 515, although the accused is eligible for release by the officer in charge pursuant to s. 498.

SYNOPSIS

This section describes the indictable offence of concealing any settlement, deed, will or other instrument material to title, concealing any encumbrance on the title (subsec. (1)(*a*)), or falsifying any pedigree on which the title depends (subsec. (1)(*b*)). The accused must be a vendor or mortgagor of property or a chose in action or a solicitor or agent for the vendor or mortgagor, and must have been served with a written demand for an abstract of title by or on behalf of the purchaser or mortgagee prior to the completion of the purchase or mortgage. In proceedings under subsec. (1)(*a*), the accused must both intend to defraud and to induce the purchaser or mortgagee to accept the title offered. Subsection (2) requires the consent of the Attorney General for the institution of proceedings under this section. The maximum term of imprisonment for this offence is two years.

FRAUDULENT REGISTRATION OF TITLE.

386. Every one who, as principal or agent, in a proceeding to register title to real property, or in a transaction relating to real property that is or is proposed to be registered, knowingly and with intent to deceive,

> **(*a*) makes a material false statement or representation,**
> **(*b*) suppresses or conceals from a judge or registrar, or any person employed by or assisting the registrar, any material document, fact, matter or information, or**
> **(*c*) is privy to anything mentioned in paragraph (*a*) or (*b*),**

is guilty of an indictable offence and liable to imprisonment for a term not exceeding five years. R.S., c. C-34, s. 344.

CROSS-REFERENCES

The accused may elect his mode of trial pursuant to s. 536(2). Release pending trial is determined by s. 515, although the accused is eligible for release by the officer in charge pursuant to s. 498.

Related offences: s. 380, fraud; s. 385, fraudulent concealment of title document; s. 387, fraudulent sale of real property.

SYNOPSIS

This section describes the indictable offence of knowingly, and with intent to deceive, making a *material false* statement or representation, of suppressing or concealing from a judge, a registrar, or any person assisting the registrar, any *material* document, fact, matter or information, or of being privy to any of these activities, in a proceeding to register title to real property. The accused must be either the principal or agent in the real estate transaction. The maximum term of imprisonment upon conviction is five years.

FRAUDULENT SALE OF REAL PROPERTY.

387. Every one who, knowing of an unregistered prior sale or of an existing unregistered grant, mortgage, hypothec, privilege or encumbrance of or on real property, fraudulently sells the property or any part thereof is guilty of an indictable

offence and liable to imprisonment for a term not exceeding two years. R.S., c. C-34, s. 345.

CROSS-REFERENCES

While there is no definition of "fraudulently" which is universally applicable, generally speaking, it refers to conduct which is dishonest and morally wrong: *R. v. DeMarco* (1973), 13 C.C.C. (2d) 369 (Ont. C.A.).

The accused may elect his mode of trial pursuant to s. 536(2). Release pending trial is determined by s. 515, although the accused is eligible for release by the officer in charge pursuant to s. 498.

Related offences: s. 380, fraud; s. 385, fraudulent concealment of title documents; s. 386, fraudulent registration of title.

SYNOPSIS

This section describes the fraudulent sale of real estate. Any person who fraudulently sells property, either in whole or in part, knowing of the existence of an unregistered prior sale or an existing unregistered grant, mortgage or other encumbrance on real property, is guilty of an indictable offence and liable to a maximum term of two years' imprisonment.

MISLEADING RECEIPT.

388. Every one who wilfully

    (*a*) **with intent to mislead, injure or defraud any person, whether or not that person is known to him, gives to a person anything in writing that purports to be a receipt for or an acknowledgment of property that has been delivered to or received by him, before the property referred to in the purported receipt or acknowledgment has been delivered to or received by him, or**

    (*b*) **accepts, transmits or uses a purported receipt or acknowledgment to which paragraph (*a*) applies,**

is guilty of an indictable offence and liable to imprisonment for a term not exceeding two years. R.S., c. C-34, s. 346.

CROSS-REFERENCES

The terms "person" and "property" are defined in s. 2.

Note that s. 391 provides that where an offence is committed under this section by a person who acts in the name of a corporation, firm or partnership, no person other than the person who does the act by means of which the offence is committed or who is secretly privy to it is guilty of the offence.

The accused may elect his mode of trial pursuant to s. 536(2). Release pending trial is determined by s. 515, although the accused is eligible for release by the officer in charge pursuant to s. 498.

SYNOPSIS

This section describes the offence of dealing with a misleading receipt. Every person who *wilfully*, with *intent to mislead, injure,* or *defraud* another person, gives to any person anything in writing that purports to be a receipt for property prior to the delivery of that property is guilty of an offence. Any person who *wilfully* accepts, transmits or uses a receipt as described above is also guilty of an offence. The offence is indictable and carries a maximum term of two years' imprisonment.

FRAUDULENT DISPOSAL OF GOODS ON WHICH MONEY ADVANCED / Saving.

389. (1) Every one who

(*a*) having shipped or delivered to the keeper of a warehouse or to a factor, an agent or a carrier, anything on which the consignee thereof has advanced money or has given valuable security, thereafter, with intent to deceive, defraud or injure the consignee, disposes of it in a manner that is different from and inconsistent with any agreement that has been made in that behalf between him and the consignee, or

(*b*) knowingly and wilfully aids or assists any person to make a disposition of anything to which paragraph (*a*) applies for the purpose of deceiving, defrauding or injuring the consignee,

is guilty of an indictable offence and liable to imprisonment for a term not exceeding two years.

(2) No person is guilty of an offence under this section where, before disposing of anything in a manner that is different from and inconsistent with any agreement that has been made in that behalf between him and the consignee, he pays or tenders to the consignee the full amount of money or valuable security that the consignee has advanced. R.S., c. C-34, s. 347.

CROSS-REFERENCES

The term "valuable security" is defined in s. 2.

By virtue of s. 583, an indictment which otherwise complies with s. 581 is not insufficient by reason only that: para. (*b*), it fails to name the person who owns or has a special property or interest in property mentioned in the count or para. (*c*), it charges an intent to defraud without naming or describing the person whom it was intended to defraud. Also note s. 588 which deems certain persons to have a property interest in property of which they have the management, control or custody. Under s. 586, no count alleging fraud is insufficient by reason only that it does not set out in detail the nature of the fraud. However, under s. 587(1)(*b*), the court may order particulars of any fraud that is alleged.

Note that s. 391 provides that where an offence is committed under this section by a person who acts in the name of a corporation, firm or partnership, no person other than the person who does the act by means of which the offence is committed or who is secretly privy to it is guilty of the offence.

The accused may elect his mode of trial pursuant to s. 536(2). Release pending trial is determined by s. 515, although the accused is eligible for release by the officer in charge pursuant to s. 498.

SYNOPSIS

This section describes the offence of fraudulently disposing of goods that have been shipped or delivered to the keeper of a warehouse or to a factor, an agent or a carrier. Every person who has shipped to one of the above-named individuals goods upon which the consignee has advanced money, and who, *with intent to defraud* or *injure* the consignee, disposes of the goods in a fashion that is inconsistent with any agreement made between himself and the consignee, is guilty of an indictable offence and liable to a maximum term of two years' imprisonment. A person who *knowingly* and *wilfully* aids or assists another person to commit the offence described above *for the purpose of deceiving, defrauding or injuring* the consignee, is also guilty of the offence and subject to the same punishment. Subsection (2) provides a defence to the charge where a person pays back the full amount of money advanced by the consignee *prior* to disposing of anything in a fashion that contravenes their agreement.

FRAUDULENT RECEIPTS UNDER *BANK ACT.*

390. Every one is guilty of an indictable offence and liable to imprisonment for a term not exceeding two years who

(*a*) **wilfully makes a false statement in any receipt, certificate or acknowledgment for anything that may be used for a purpose mentioned in the *Bank Act*; or**
(*b*) **wilfully,**
    (i) **after giving to another person,**
    (ii) **after a person employed by him has, to his knowledge, given to another person, or**
    (iii) **after obtaining and endorsing or assigning to another person,**
    any receipt, certificate or acknowledgment for anything that may be used for a purpose mentioned in the *Bank Act*, without the consent in writing of the holder or endorsee or the production and delivery of the receipt, certificate or acknowledgment, alienates or parts with, or does not deliver to the holder or owner the property mentioned in the receipt, certificate or acknowledgment. R.S., c. C-34, s. 348.

CROSS-REFERENCES

The terms "every one", "person" and "property" are defined in s. 2.

Note that s. 391 provides that where an offence is committed under this section by a person who acts in the name of a corporation, firm or partnership, no person other than the person who does the act by means of which the offence is committed or who is secretly privy to it is guilty of the offence.

The accused may elect his mode of trial pursuant to s. 536(2). Release pending trial is determined by s. 515, although the accused is eligible for release by the officer in charge pursuant to s. 498.

SYNOPSIS

This section describes the offence of *fraudulently* dealing in receipts made for a purpose mentioned in the *Bank Act*. Paragraph (*a*) states that any person who *wilfully* makes a false statement in a receipt or other similar document that may be used for a purpose mentioned in the *Bank Act* commits an indictable offence and is liable to a maximum term of imprisonment of two years. Paragraph (*b*) also makes it an offence punishable on the same terms for a person to *wilfully* dispose of or fail to deliver the relevant property to a person to whom the accused has given or endorsed over a *Bank Act* receipt mentioning that property. The accused can raise the defence of written consent by the holder or endorsee of the receipt, or produce and deliver the receipt.

ANNOTATIONS

The words "receipt, certificate or acknowledgment for anything that may be used for a purpose mentioned in the *Bank Act*" have the same meaning in both paras. (*a*) and (*b*) and refer to documents which are evidence of title to property and which may be transferred by endorsement or delivery: *R. v. Dubois* (1979), 45 C.C.C. (2d) 531 (Ont. C.A.).

---

391. [*Repealed*, 2003, c. 21, s. 6.]

DISPOSAL OF PROPERTY TO DEFRAUD CREDITORS.

392. Every one who,
    (*a*) **with intent to defraud his creditors,**
        (i) **makes or causes to be made a gift, conveyance, assignment, sale, transfer or delivery of his property, or**
        (ii) **removes, conceals or disposes of any of his property, or**
    (*b*) **with intent that any one should defraud his creditors, receives any property by means of or in relation to which an offence has been committed under paragraph (*a*),**

is guilty of an indictable offence and liable to imprisonment for a term not exceeding two years. R.S., c. C-34, s. 350.

CROSS-REFERENCES

The term "property" is defined in s. 2.

By virtue of s. 583, an indictment which otherwise complies with s. 581 is not insufficient by reason only that: para. (*b*), it fails to name the person who owns or has a special property or interest in property mentioned in the count or para. (*c*), it charges an intent to defraud without naming or describing the person whom it was intended to defraud. Also note s. 588 which deems certain persons to have a property interest in property of which they have the management, control or custody.

Reference should also be made to the offences created by the *Bankruptcy Act* [now *Bankruptcy and Insolvency Act*], R.S.C. 1985, c. B-2.

The accused may elect his mode of trial pursuant to s. 536(2). Release pending trial is determined by s. 515, although the accused is eligible for release by the officer in charge pursuant to s. 498.

SYNOPSIS

This section describes the offence of disposing of property in order to defraud creditors. Every person who makes a gift, assignment or transfer of his property, or who conceals or disposes of it *with the intent to defraud his creditors* commits an indictable offence under para. (*a*). Similarly, a person who receives any property that has been dealt with in a fashion described in para. (*a*) *with the intent that anyone should defraud his creditors* is guilty of an indictable offence and liable to the same punishment of a maximum term of two years' imprisonment.

ANNOTATIONS

The giving of a third mortgage comes within the meaning of the words "makes an assignment" in this section: *R. v. Ehresman* (1980), 58 C.C.C. (2d) 574, 121 D.L.R. (3d) 505 (B.C.C.A.).

The word "conceals" in para. (*a*)(ii) is used in its primary sense of a positive act of secreting. Thus, the mere failure of a bankrupt to disclose the existence of property to the trustee and Official Receiver, as required by the *Bankruptcy Act*, R.S.C. 1970, c. B-3, does not constitute an offence under para. (*a*)(ii): *R. v. Goulis* (1981), 60 C.C.C. (2d) 347, 20 C.R. (3d) 360 (Ont. C.A.).

FRAUD IN RELATION TO FARES, ETC. / Idem / Fraudulently obtaining transportation.

393. (1) Every one whose duty it is to collect a fare, toll, ticket or admission who wilfully

    (*a*) **fails to collect it,**

    (*b*) **collects less than the proper amount payable in respect thereof, or**

    (*c*) **accepts any valuable consideration for failing to collect it or for collecting less than the proper amount payable in respect thereof,**

is guilty of an indictable offence and liable to imprisonment for a term not exceeding two years.

(2) Every one who gives or offers to a person whose duty it is to collect a fare, toll, ticket or admission fee any valuable consideration

    (*a*) **for failing to collect it, or**

    (*b*) **for collecting an amount less than the amount payable in respect thereof,**

is guilty of an indictable offence and liable to imprisonment for a term not exceeding two years.

(3) Every one who, by any false pretence or fraud, unlawfully obtains transportation by land, water or air is guilty of an offence punishable on summary conviction. R.S., c. C-34, s. 351.

CROSS-REFERENCES

By virtue of s. 583, an indictment which otherwise complies with s. 581 is not sufficient by reason only that: para. (*b*), it fails to name the person who owns or has a special property or interest in property mentioned in the count or para. (*c*), it charges an intent to defraud without naming or describing the person whom it was intended to defraud. Under s. 586, no count alleging false pretences or fraud is insufficient by reason only that it does not set out in detail the nature of the false pretences or fraud. However, under s. 587(1)(*b*), the court may order particulars of any false pretence or fraud that is alleged.

The offences in subsecs. (1) and (2) are indictable offences, but, by virtue of s. 553(*c*)(viii), are offences over which a provincial court judge has absolute jurisdiction and does not depend on the consent of the accused. That is, the accused does not have an election as to mode of trial, although the provincial court judge may, by virtue of s. 555(1), elect to continue the proceedings as a preliminary inquiry, in which case, the accused is deemed to have elected trial by judge and jury pursuant to s. 565(1)(*a*). The trial of the offence in subsec. (3) is conducted by a summary conviction court pursuant to Part XXVII. The punishment for the offence in subsec. (3) is as set out in s. 787 and the limitation period is set out in s. 786(2). For all offences under this section, release pending trial is determined by s. 515, although the accused is eligible for release by a peace officer under s. 496, 497 or by the officer in charge under s. 498.

Also see s. 454 which creates the offence of producing, etc., or possession of slugs to be fraudulently used in substitution for coins or tokens of value.

SYNOPSIS

This section describes the offence of fraud in relation to fares. Subsection (1) states that any person who *has a duty to collect* a fare, toll, ticket or admission and who *wilfully* fails to collect it, collects less than the full amount, or accepts valuable consideration for failing to collect, or collecting less than the proper amount, is guilty of an indictable offence and liable to a term of imprisonment not exceeding two years. Subsection (2) makes it an offence to give or offer to a person whose duty it is to collect a fare, toll, ticket or admission any valuable consideration for failing to collect the amount payable. This offence is indictable and carries a maximum term of imprisonment of two years. Subsection (3) describes the summary conviction offence of unlawfully obtaining transportation by any false pretence or fraud.

FRAUD IN RELATION TO VALUABLE MINERALS / Sale of valuable minerals / Purchase of valuable minerals / Presumption / Offence / Forfeiture / Exception.

394. (1) No person who is the holder of a lease or licence issued under an Act relating to the mining of valuable minerals, or by the owner of land that is supposed to contain valuable minerals, shall

    (*a*) by a fraudulent device or contrivance, defraud or attempt to defraud any person of

        (i) any valuable minerals obtained under or reserved by the lease or licence, or

        (ii) any money or valuable interest or thing payable in respect of valuable minerals obtained or rights reserved by the lease or licence; or

    (*b*) fraudulently conceal or make a false statement with respect to the amount of valuable minerals obtained under the lease or licence.

(2) No person, other than the owner or the owner's agent or someone otherwise acting under lawful authority, shall sell any valuable mineral that is unrefined, partly refined, uncut or otherwise unprocessed.

(3) No person shall buy any valuable mineral that is unrefined, partly refined, uncut or otherwise unprocessed from anyone who the person has reason to believe is not the owner or the owner's agent or someone otherwise acting under lawful authority.

(4) In any proceeding in relation to subsection (2) or (3), in the absence of evidence raising a reasonable doubt to the contrary, it is presumed that

(*a*) in the case of a sale, the seller is not the owner of the valuable mineral or the owner's agent or someone otherwise acting under lawful authority; and

(*b*) in the case of a purchase, the purchaser, when buying the valuable mineral, had reason to believe that the seller was not the owner of the mineral or the owner's agent or someone otherwise acting under lawful authority.

(5) A person who contravenes subsection (1), (2) or (3) is guilty of an indictable offence and liable to imprisonment for a term of not more than five years.

(6) If a person is convicted of an offence under this section, the court may order anything by means of or in relation to which the offence was committed, on such conviction, to be forfeited to Her Majesty.

(7) Subsection (6) does not apply to real property other than real property built or significantly modified for the purpose of facilitating the commission of an offence under this section. R.S., c. C-34, s. 352; R.S.C. 1985, c. 27 (1st Supp.), s. 186; 1999, c. 5, s. 10.

CROSS-REFERENCES

"Valuable mineral" is defined in s. 2. Section 394.1 makes it an offence to possess any unprocessed mineral that has been stolen or dealt with contrary to this section. A justice may issue a search warrant to search for any valuable mineral that is deposited contrary to this Act or any other Act of Parliament, under s. 395. Offences in relation to mines are set out in s. 396. Section 656 creates a presumption of theft or unlawful possession in any proceeding in relation to theft or possession of a valuable mineral that is unrefined, partly refined, uncut or otherwise unprocessed by any person actively engaged in or on a mine.

SYNOPSIS

This section creates a number of offences that in general deal with fraud in relation to valuable minerals (as defined in s. 2). Subsection (1) creates fraud offences for persons holding a lease or licence relating to mining of valuable minerals or persons owning land purporting to contain valuable minerals. Subsection (2) prohibits the sale of unrefined, partly refined, uncut or otherwise unprocessed valuable minerals except by the owner, the owner's agent or a person acting under lawful authority. Under subsec. (4)(*a*), the seller is presumed not to be the owner, the owner's agent or a person acting under lawful authority in the absence of evidence raising a reasonable doubt. Subsection (3) makes it an offence to buy such material from anyone other than a person the accused has reason to believe is not the owner, the owner's agent or a person acting under lawful authority. Subsection (4)(*b*) creates a presumption that the purchaser knew the seller was not the owner, the owner's agent or a person acting under lawful authority, in the absence of evidence raising a reasonable doubt. The offences under this section are indictable and punishable by not more than five years' imprisonment. Under subsec. (6), anything by means of or in relation to which the offence was committed may be forfeited to the Crown. That subsection, however, does not apply to real property, unless the real property has been built or significantly modified for the purpose of facilitating commission of an offence under this section.

POSSESSION OF STOLEN OR FRAUDULENTLY OBTAINED VALUABLE MINERALS / Evidence / Offence / Forfeiture / Exception.

394.1 (1) No person shall possess any valuable mineral that is unrefined, partly refined, uncut or otherwise unprocessed that has been stolen or dealt with contrary to section 394.

(2) Reasonable grounds to believe that the valuable mineral has been stolen or dealt with contrary to section 394 are, in the absence of evidence raising a reasonable doubt to the contrary, proof that the valuable mineral has been stolen or dealt with contrary to section 394.

(3) A person who contravenes subsection (1) is guilty of an indictable offence and liable to imprisonment for a term of not more than five years.

(4) If a person is convicted of an offence under this section, the court may, on that conviction, order that anything by means of or in relation to which the offence was committed be forfeited to Her Majesty.

(5) Subsection (4) does not apply to real property, other than real property built or significantly modified for the purpose of facilitating the commission of an offence under subsection (3). 1999, c. 5, s. 10.

CROSS-REFERENCES

"Valuable mineral" is defined in s. 2. Section 394 creates fraud offences for persons holding a lease or licence relating to mining of valuable minerals or persons owning land purporting to contain valuable minerals and prohibits the unauthorized sale or purchase of unrefined, partly refined, uncut or otherwise unprocessed valuable minerals. A justice may issue a search warrant to search for any valuable mineral that is deposited contrary to this Act or any other Act of Parliament, under s. 395. Offences in relation to mines are set out in s. 396. Section 656 creates a presumption of theft or unlawful possession in any proceeding in relation to theft or possession of a valuable mineral that is unrefined, partly refined, uncut or otherwise unprocessed by any person actively engaged in or on a mine.

SYNOPSIS

This section creates offences that complement the offences under s. 394 by making it an offence to possess unrefined, partly refined, uncut or otherwise unprocessed valuable minerals that have been dealt with contrary to s. 394 or have been stolen. Subsection (2) creates a presumption that the valuable mineral was stolen or dealt with contrary to s. 394, in the absence of evidence raising a reasonable doubt, if there are reasonable grounds to believe that the valuable mineral has been stolen or dealt with contrary to s. 394. The offences under this section are indictable and punishable by not more than five years' imprisonment. Under subsec. (4), anything by means of or in relation to which the offence was committed may be forfeited to the Crown. That subsection, however, does not apply to real property, unless the real property has been built or significantly modified for the purpose of facilitating commission of an offence under this section.

SEARCH FOR VALUABLE MINERALS / Power to seize / Appeal.

395. (1) If an information in writing is laid under oath before a justice by a peace officer or by a public officer who has been appointed or designated to administer or enforce a federal or provincial law and whose duties include the enforcement of this Act or any other Act of Parliament and the justice is satisfied that there are reasonable grounds to believe that, contrary to this Act or any other Act of Parliament, any valuable mineral is deposited in a place or held by a person, the justice may issue a warrant authorizing a peace officer or a public officer, if the public officer is named in it, to search any of the places or persons mentioned in the information.

(2) Where, on search, anything mentioned in subsection (1) is found, it shall be seized and carried before the justice who shall order

    (*a*) that it be detained for the purposes of an inquiry or a trial; or

    (*b*) if it is not detained for the purposes of an inquiry or a trial,

        (i) that it be restored to the owner, or

(ii) **that it be forfeited to Her Majesty in right of the province in which the proceedings take place if the owner cannot be ascertained.**

(3) An appeal lies from an order made under paragraph (2)(*b*) in the manner in which an appeal lies in summary conviction proceedings under Part XXVII and the provisions of that Part relating to appeals apply to appeals under this subsection. R.S., c. C-34, s. 353; 1999, c. 5, s. 11.

CROSS-REFERENCES

The term "justice", "peace officer", "public officer" and "valuable mineral" are defined in s. 2.

SYNOPSIS

This section sets out a scheme for obtaining a warrant to search for valuable minerals. Subsection (1) requires that an information in writing and under oath be laid before a justice by a peace officer or public officer. The information must state that the valuable mineral is unlawfully held by a person or deposited in a place. The justice may issue a warrant to search any of the places or persons in the information. Subsection (2) provides that anything found as a result of a search conducted under subsec. (1) must be seized and carried before the justice who shall order that it be detained for inquiry or trial, or that it be restored to the owner, or forfeited to Her Majesty in right of the province in which the proceedings took place if the owner cannot be ascertained. Subsection (3) provides a right of appeal from any order that the items seized be given to the owner or Her Majesty.

OFFENCES IN RELATION TO MINES / Presumption.

396. (1) Every one who
(*a*) **adds anything to or removes anything from any existing or prospective mine, mining claim or oil well with a fraudulent intent to affect the result of an assay, a test or a valuation that has been made or is to be made with respect to the mine, mining claim or oil well, or**
(*b*) **adds anything to, removes anything from or tampers with a sample or material that has been taken or is being or is about to be taken from any existing or prospective mine, mining claim or oil well for the purpose of being assayed, tested or otherwise valued, with a fraudulent intent to affect the result of the assay, test or valuation,**
is guilty of an indictable offence and liable to imprisonment for a term not exceeding ten years.

(2) For the purposes of proceedings under subsection (1), evidence that
(*a*) **something has been added to or removed from anything to which subsection (1) applies, or**
(*b*) **anything to which subsection (1) applies has been tampered with,**
is, in the absence of any evidence to the contrary, proof of a fraudulent intent to affect the result of an assay, a test or a valuation. R.S., c. C-34, s. 354.

CROSS-REFERENCES

The accused may elect his mode of trial pursuant to s. 536(2). Release pending trial is determined by s. 515.

Other offences relating to mines are found in ss. 394 and 394.1.

Section 395 provides for the issuance of a search warrant to search for valuable minerals alleged to be unlawfully deposited or held contrary to law.

See s. 333 for defence on charge of theft where ore is taken for exploration or scientific investigation.

SYNOPSIS

This section describes two offences in relation to mines. Both offences relate to specified activities that would affect the result of a test or valuation of a mine, a mining claim or an oil well. Both offences also require that the accused have the *fraudulent intent* to affect the results of the test. These offences are indictable and carry a maximum term of 10 years' imprisonment. Subsection (2) creates a presumption that the prosecution may rely on to prove, in the absence of evidence to the contrary, the fraudulent intent required under subsec. (1). Evidence of the addition to, the removal from, or the tampering with anything to which subsec. (1) applies proves the criminal intent required for conviction under this section.

Falsification of Books and Documents

BOOKS AND DOCUMENTS / Privy.

397. (1) Every one who, with intent to defraud,

  (a) destroys, mutilates, alters, falsifies, or makes a false entry in, or

  (b) omits a material particular from, or alters a material particular in,

a book, paper, writing, valuable security or document is guilty of an indictable offence and liable to imprisonment for a term not exceeding five years.

(2) Every one who, with intent to defraud his creditors, is privy to the commission of an offence under subsection (1) is guilty of an indictable offence and liable to imprisonment for a term not exceeding five years. R.S., c. C-34, s. 355.

CROSS-REFERENCES

The terms "valuable security" and "writing" are defined in s. 2. The term "document" is not defined for this Part but reference might be made to the definition in s. 321 for Part IX. By virtue of s. 583, an indictment which otherwise complies with s. 581 is not insufficient by reason only that: para. (*c*), it charges an intent to defraud without naming or describing the person whom it was intended to defraud. Under s. 586, no count alleging fraud is insufficient by reason only that it does not set out in detail the nature of the fraud. However, under s. 587(1)(*b*), the court may order particulars of any fraud that is alleged.

  The accused may elect his mode of trial pursuant to s. 536(2). Release pending trial is determined by s. 515, although the accused is eligible for release by the officer in charge pursuant to s. 498.

  This offence resembles the forgery and uttering offences and therefore see cross-references under ss. 266 to 268. Also see s. 392, disposal of property with intent to defraud creditors.

SYNOPSIS

This section describes the offence of destroying, mutilating, altering, falsifying, or omitting or altering a material particular in a book, paper, writing, valuable security or document. The accused must engage in the above-described activity with the *intent to defraud.* This is an indictable offence with a maximum term of five years' imprisonment. Subsection (2) states that every person who, *with the intent to defraud* his creditors, is privy to the offence described above is also guilty of an indictable offence which carries a maximum term of five years' imprisonment.

FALSIFYING EMPLOYMENT RECORD.

398. Every one who, with intent to deceive, falsifies an employment record by any means, including the punching of a time clock, is guilty of an offence punishable on summary conviction. R.S., c. C-34, s. 356.

CROSS-REFERENCES

Trial of this offence is conducted by a summary conviction court pursuant to Part XXVII.

The punishment is as set out in s. 787 and the limitation period is set out in s. 786(2).

Release pending trial is determined by s. 515, although the accused is eligible for release by a peace officer under s. 496, 497 or by the officer in charge under s. 498.

SYNOPSIS

This section describes the offence of falsifying an employment record. It states that every person who, *with the intent to deceive*, falsifies an employment record *by any means*, including the punching of a time clock, is guilty of a summary conviction offence.

FALSE RETURN BY PUBLIC OFFICER.

399. Every one who, being entrusted with the receipt, custody or management of any part of the public revenues, knowingly furnishes a false statement or return of

> (*a*) **any sum of money collected by him or entrusted to his care, or**
>
> (*b*) **any balance of money in his hands or under his control,**

is guilty of an indictable offence and liable to imprisonment for a term not exceeding five years. R.S., c. C-34, s. 357.

CROSS-REFERENCES

The accused may elect his mode of trial pursuant to s. 536(2). Release pending trial is determined by s. 515, although the accused is eligible for release by the officer in charge pursuant to s. 498.

Related offences: s. 122, breach of trust by public officer; s. 336, criminal breach of trust; s. 337, public servant refusing to deliver property.

SYNOPSIS

This section describes the offence of making a false return by a public officer. The offence is committed where a person entrusted with public revenues *knowingly* furnishes a false statement of any sum or balance of money entrusted to or controlled by him. The offence is indictable, with a maximum punishment of five years' imprisonment.

FALSE PROSPECTUS, ETC. / Definition of "company".

400. (1) Every one who makes, circulates or publishes a prospectus, a statement or an account, whether written or oral, that he knows is false in a material particular, with intent

> (*a*) **to induce persons, whether ascertained or not, to become shareholders or partners in a company,**
>
> (*b*) **to deceive or defraud the members, shareholders or creditors, whether ascertained or not, of a company, or**
>
> (*c*) **to induce any person to**
>
>> (i) **entrust or advance anything to a company, or**
>>
>> (ii) **enter into any security for the benefit of a company,**

is guilty of an indictable offence and liable to imprisonment for a term not exceeding ten years.

(2) In this section, "company" means a syndicate, body corporate or company, whether existing or proposed to be created. R.S., c. C-34, s. 358; 1994, c. 44, s. 26.

CROSS-REFERENCES

The term "person" is defined in s. 2.

By virtue of s. 583, an indictment which otherwise complies with s. 581 is not insufficient by reason only that: para. (*c*), it charges an intent to defraud without naming or describing the person whom it was intended to defraud. Under s. 586, no count alleging fraud is insufficient by reason only that it does not set out in detail the nature of the fraud. However, under s. 587(1)(b), the court may order particulars of any fraud that is alleged.

Other offences relating to trading in securities, etc., are in ss. 380(2) and 382 to 384.

The accused may elect his mode of trial pursuant to s. 536(2). Release pending trial is determined by s. 515.

Section 380.1 provides that, in sentencing an offender for the offence under this section, the court shall consider as aggravating circumstances the magnitude, complexity, duration or degree of planning of the fraud; that the offence adversely affected or had the potential to adversely affect the stability of the Canadian economy or financial system or any financial market in Canada or investor confidence in such markets; the offence involved a large number of victims; the offence had a significant impact on the victims given their personal circumstances such as age, health and financial situation; in committing the offence, the offender took advantage of the high regard in which the offender was held in the community; the offender did not comply with a licensing requirement or professional standard; and that the offender concealed or destroyed records. As well, the offender's employment, employment skills, or status or reputation in the community are not to be considered as mitigating factors if those circumstances were relevant to, contributed to, or were used in the commission of the offence. Section 380.1(2) requires the court to consider as an aggravating circumstance that the value of the fraud committed exceeded one million dollars. Section 380.1(3) requires the sentencing court to state the aggravating and mitigating circumstances that it took into account.

Sections 487.012 to 487.017 provide procedures for the making of production orders that would require persons to provide documents or data.

SYNOPSIS

This section describes offences in relation to a false prospectus. Anyone who makes, circulates or publishes a prospectus, statement or account, whether written or oral, which he knows is false in a material particular, commits an indictable offence, if his purpose in so doing is one of those listed in subsec. (1)(a) to (d). Those purposes are: to induce anyone to become a shareholder or partner in a company; to deceive or defraud members, shareholders or creditors of a company; to induce anyone to entrust or advance anything to a company; or to enter into any security for the benefit of a company. The maximum punishment for this offence is imprisonment for 10 years.

ANNOTATIONS

The falsity, which need not amount to a false pretence, may be found in a statement of purposes, which the author never had any intention of carrying out. Furthermore, for a para. (c) offence, a count is not duplicitous merely because it expresses the alternative modes of carrying out the offence by making, circulating or publishing a false prospectus, and the phrase "any person" includes all unascertained persons of the class of people to whom it was intended to give the prospectus at the time of its preparation: *R. v. Cox and Paton,* [1963] S.C.R. 500, [1963] 2 C.C.C. 148, 40 C.R. 52 (5:0).

A material omission may render a statement false: *R. v. Colucci,* [1965] 4 C.C.C. 56, 46 C.R. 256 (Ont. C.A.).

Where the defence is that the false material particular was a mistaken belief as to the correctness of that particular the jury must determine whether the belief was an honest one which negatived the guilty knowledge required to be proven by the Crown: *R. v. Davidson* (1971), 3 C.C.C. (2d) 509, [1971] 4 W.W.R. 731 (B.C.C.A.) (2:1).

The intent to defraud is not an element of the para. (a) offence which only requires falsity in a material particular, the accused's knowledge of it, and an overt act with the intent to induce members of the public to become shareholders: *R. v. Scallen* (1974), 15 C.C.C. (2d) 441 (B.C.C.A.).

OBTAINING CARRIAGE BY FALSE BILLING / Forfeiture.

401. (1) Every one who, by means of a false or misleading representation, knowingly obtains or attempts to obtain the carriage of anything by any person into a country, province, district or other place, whether or not within Canada, where the importation or transportation of it is, in the circumstances of the case, unlawful is guilty of an offence punishable on summary conviction.

(2) Where a person is convicted of an offence under subsection (1), anything by means of or in relation to which the offence was committed, on such conviction, in addition to any punishment that is imposed, is forfeited to Her Majesty and shall be disposed of as the court may direct. R.S., c. C-34, s. 359.

CROSS-REFERENCES

Trial of this offence is conducted by a summary conviction court pursuant to Part XXVII.

The punishment is as set out in s. 787 and the limitation period is set out in s. 786(2).

Release pending trial is determined by s. 515, although the accused is eligible for release by a peace officer under s. 496, 497 or by the officer in charge under s. 498.

Section 414 provides for a presumption as to the port of shipment where an offence relates to imported goods.

The similar offence of fraudulently obtaining food and lodging is in s. 364 and fraud in relation to fares, etc., is in s. 393.

SYNOPSIS

This section describes the offence of obtaining carriage by false billing. Anyone *knowingly* obtaining or attempting to obtain the unlawful carriage or importation of anything to any place within or outside Canada by means of a false or misleading representation, commits a summary conviction offence. Upon conviction, anything by means of, or in relation to which the offence is committed is forfeited to the Crown, to be disposed of as the court directs.

TRADER FAILING TO KEEP ACCOUNTS / Saving.

402. (1) Every one who, being a trader or in business,
    (a) is indebted in an amount exceeding one thousand dollars,
    (b) is unable to pay his creditors in full, and
    (c) has not kept books of account that, in the ordinary course of the trade or business in which he is engaged, are necessary to exhibit or explain his transactions,
is guilty of an indictable offence and liable to imprisonment for a term not exceeding two years.

(2) No person shall be convicted of an offence under this section
    (a) where, to the satisfaction of the court or judge, he
        (i) accounts for his losses, and
        (ii) shows that his failure to keep books was not intended to defraud his creditors; or
    (b) where his failure to keep books occurred at a time more than five years prior to the day on which he was unable to pay his creditors in full. R.S., c. C-34, s. 360.

CROSS-REFERENCES

Related offences respecting defrauding creditors and keeping books of account are found in ss. 392 and 397. The general offence of fraud is defined in s. 380. Also see the offence of theft by failing to account defined in s. 330.

The accused may elect his mode of trial pursuant to s. 536(2). Release pending trial is determined by s. 515, although the accused is eligible for release by the officer in charge pursuant to s. 498.

SYNOPSIS

This section describes the offence of failing to keep accounts. Any trader or person in business who owes more than $1,000, cannot pay his creditors in full, and has not kept ordinary books of account, commits an indictable offence, with a maximum punishment of two years' imprisonment. Subsection (2) creates a defence where the accused can account for his losses and show that his failure to keep books was not fraudulent, or where his failure occurred more than five years prior to his inability to pay his creditors.

Identity Theft and Identity Fraud

DEFINITION OF "IDENTITY INFORMATION".

402.1 For the purposes of sections 402.2 and 403, "identity information" means any information — including biological or physiological information — of a type that is commonly used alone or in combination with other information to identify or purport to identify an individual, including a fingerprint, voice print, retina image, iris image, DNA profile, name, address, date of birth, written signature, electronic signature, digital signature, user name, credit card number, debit card number, financial institution account number, passport number, Social Insurance Number, health insurance number, driver's licence number or password. 2009, c. 28, s. 10.

IDENTITY THEFT / Trafficking in identity information / Clarification / Jurisdiction / Punishment.

402.2 (1) Everyone commits an offence who knowingly obtains or possesses another person's identity information in circumstances giving rise to a reasonable inference that the information is intended to be used to commit an indictable offence that includes fraud, deceit or falsehood as an element of the offence.

(2) Everyone commits an offence who transmits, makes available, distributes, sells or offers for sale another person's identity information, or has it in their possession for any of those purposes, knowing that or being reckless as to whether the information will be used to commit an indictable offence that includes fraud, deceit or falsehood as an element of the offence.

(3) For the purposes of subsections (1) and (2), an indictable offence referred to in either of those subsections includes an offence under any of the following sections:
> (*a*) section 57 (forgery of or uttering forged passport);
> (*b*) section 58 (fraudulent use of certificate of citizenship);
> (*c*) section 130 (personating peace officer);
> (*d*) section 131 (perjury);
> (*e*) section 342 (theft, forgery, etc., of credit card);
> (*f*) section 362 (false pretence or false statement);
> (*g*) section 366 (forgery);
> (*h*) section 368 (use, trafficking or possession of forged document);
> (*i*) section 380 (fraud); and
> (*j*) section 403 (identity fraud).

(4) An accused who is charged with an offence under subsection (1) or (2) may be tried and punished by any court having jurisdiction to try that offence in the place where the offence is alleged to have been committed or in the place where the accused is found, is arrested or is in custody. However, no proceeding in respect of the offence shall be commenced in a province without the consent of the Attorney General of that province if the offence is alleged to have been committed outside that province.

(5) Everyone who commits an offence under subsection (1) or (2) (*a*) **is guilty of an indictable offence and liable to imprisonment for a term of not more than five years; or**

    (*b*) **is guilty of an offence punishable on summary conviction. 2009, c. 28, s. 10.**

CROSS-REFERENCES

"Attorney General" is defined in s. 2. "Identity information" is defined in s. 402.1. Section 403 creates the related offence of identity fraud. Section 56.1 creates the offence of procuring, making, possessing or transferring identity documents. Other related offences are: s. 57, offences in relation to passports; s. 130, personating a peace officer; s. 340, destroying identity documents; s. 342, unauthorized use of credit cards; s. 342.01, possession of instrument for copying credit cards; s. 362, obtaining by false pretences; s. 367, forgery; s. 368, use and trafficking in a forged document; s. 368.1, possession of instruments for purpose of committing forgery; s. 374, drawing a false document; s. 380, fraud; s. 403, identity fraud; s. 404, personation at an examination.

SYNOPSIS

This section, part of Bill S-4, a comprehensive scheme for dealing with identity theft and related offences, defines various forms of identity theft. Subsection (1) makes it an offence to knowingly obtain or possess another person's identity information under circumstances giving rise to a reasonable inference that the information is intended to be used to commit an indictable offence that includes fraud, deceit, or falsehood as an element of the offence. Subsection (2) in effect creates an offence of trafficking in identity information. Subsection (3) includes a non-exhaustive list of offences for the purposes of subsecs. (1) and (2). Subsection (4) creates a special rule for the place of trial of the offences in this section. The offence may be tried in the place where the offence is alleged to be committed or the place where the accused is found, arrested, or is in custody. However, where the offence was committed in another province, the consent of the Attorney General of the province where the offence is to be tried is required.

IDENTITY FRAUD / Clarification / Punishment.

403. (1) Everyone commits an offence who fraudulently personates another person, living or dead,

    (*a*) **with intent to gain advantage for themselves or another person;**

    (*b*) **with intent to obtain any property or an interest in any property;**

    (*c*) **with intent to cause disadvantage to the person being personated or another person; or**

    (*d*) **with intent to avoid arrest or prosecution or to obstruct, pervert or defeat the course of justice.**

(2) For the purposes of subsection (1), personating a person includes pretending to be the person or using the person's identity information — whether by itself or in combination with identity information pertaining to any person — as if it pertains to the person using it.

(3) Everyone who commits an offence under subsection (1)

    (*a*) **is guilty of an indictable offence and liable to imprisonment for a term of not more than 10 years; or**

    (*b*) **is guilty of an offence punishable on summary conviction. R.S., c. C-34, s. 361; 1994, c. 44, s. 27; 2009, c. 28, s. 10.**

CROSS-REFERENCES

"Identity information" is defined in s. 402.1. The related offence of identity theft is found in s. 402.2. Attempting to obstruct justice is also an offence under s. 139 and the general offence of fraud is found in s. 380. For other related offences, see notes under s. 402.1.

SYNOPSIS

This section, part of Bill S-4, a comprehensive scheme for dealing with identity theft and related offences, defines various forms of identity fraud, in general the fraudulent personation of another person, living or dead, to gain an advantage (paras. (1)(*a*) and (*b*)); to cause a disadvantage to another (para. (1)(*c*)); or with the intent to avoid arrest or prosecution or obstruct the course of justice (para. (1)(*d*)). Subsection (2) clarifies that personating a person includes pretending to be the person or using the person's identity information (a term defined in s. 402.1) as if it pertained to the person using it.

ANNOTATIONS

The word "advantage" in para. (*a*) is to be given its ordinary meaning and includes that which advances or serves or which gives profit and is thus not restricted to a pecuniary or economic advantage. Thus a personation to avoid arrest comes within this section: *R. v. Rozon* (1974), 28 C.R.N.S. 232 (Que. C.A.).

An impersonation in Canada to United States immigration authorities in order to obtain clearance to board an aircraft bound for the United States comes within this section. The offence is completely committed in Canada. Further, "advantage" is not confined to an economic or proprietary advantage and would include such a clearance. It does not matter that the ultimate effect of commission of the offence would be breach of the laws of a friendly country: *R. v. Hetsberger* (1980), 51 C.C.C. (2d) 257 (Ont. C.A.).

The word "person" in this section refers to a human being and does not include a fictitious person: *R. v. Northrup* (1982), 1 C.C.C. (3d) 210, 41 N.B.R. (2d) 610 (C.A.).

PERSONATION AT EXAMINATION.

404. Every one who falsely, with intent to gain advantage for himself or some other person, personates a candidate at a competitive or qualifying examination held under the authority of law or in connection with a university, college or school or who knowingly avails himself of the results of such personation is guilty of an offence punishable on summary conviction. R.S., c. C-34, s. 362.

CROSS-REFERENCES

Trial of this offence is conducted by a summary conviction court pursuant to Part XXVII.

The punishment is as set out in s. 787 and the limitation period is set out in s. 786(2).

Release pending trial is determined by s. 515, although the accused is eligible for release by a peace officer under s. 496, 497 or by the officer in charge under s. 498.

Related offences: s. 130, personating a peace officer; s. 140, public mischief; s. 403, personation with intent; s. 405, acknowledging instrument, including recognizance of bail, in false name.

As to meaning of "advantage", consider cases noted under s. 403.

SYNOPSIS

This section describes the offence of personation at an examination. Anyone who falsely personates a candidate at an examination held under the authority of law or in connection with a school in order to gain an advantage for anyone, or who makes use of the results of such personation, commits a summary conviction offence.

ACKNOWLEDGING INSTRUMENT IN FALSE NAME.

405. Every one who, without lawful authority or excuse, the proof of which lies on him, acknowledges, in the name of another person before a court or a judge or other person authorized to receive the acknowledgment, a recognizance of bail, a confession of judgment, a consent to judgment or a judgment, deed or other instrument, is guilty of an indictable offence and liable to imprisonment for a term not exceeding five years. R.S., c. C-34, s. 363.

CROSS-REFERENCES

The accused may elect his mode of trial pursuant to s. 536(2). Release pending trial is determined by s. 515, although the accused is eligible for release by the officer in charge pursuant to s. 498.

Related offences: s. 130, personating a peace officer; s. 403, personation with intent; s. 404, personation at examination.

SYNOPSIS

This section describes the offence of acknowledging an instrument in a false name. The offence is committed where a person acknowledges before a court or other authorized person any of a variety of legal documents in the name of another person. A defence is available where the accused can establish that he committed the act with lawful authority or excuse. The offence is indictable, and punishable by a maximum term of five years' imprisonment.

ANNOTATIONS

To make out the offence under this section where the recognizance purports to be issued by an officer in charge pursuant to s. 503(2), other than the officer for the time being in command of the police force responsible for the lock-up or other place where the accused is taken after arrest, the Crown must prove that the accused acknowledged the recognizance in a name other than his own, that he acknowledged it before a person who is an officer in charge of the lock-up or place at the time the accused was taken to that place to be detained in custody and that the officer in charge is a peace officer who has been designated for the purpose of Part XVI by the officer for the time being in command of the police force responsible for the lock-up or other place to which the accused was taken after arrest: *R. v. Gendron* (1985), 22 C.C.C. (3d) 312 (Ont. C.A.).

Forgery of Trade-marks and Trade Descriptions

FORGING TRADE-MARK.

406. For the purposes of this Part, every one forges a trade-mark who
>   **(a) without the consent of the proprietor of the trade-mark, makes or reproduces in any manner that trade-mark or a mark so nearly resembling it as to be calculated to deceive; or**
>   **(b) falsifies, in any manner, a genuine trade-mark. R.S., c. C-34, s. 364.**

CROSS-REFERENCES

The term trade-mark is defined in s. 2 of the *Trade-marks Act*, R.S.C. 1985, c. T-13. The offences created in this Part relating to trade-marks and trade-names are found in ss. 407 to 411 and punished pursuant to s. 412. Some of those offences resemble the general fraud offence which is defined in s. 380 and forgery as defined in ss. 366 to 368.

SYNOPSIS

This section defines the offence of forgery of a trade mark for the purposes of Part X of the Code, respecting fraudulent transactions. A person forges a trade mark where he makes or reproduces the mark, or a mark so nearly resembling it as to be calculated to deceive, without the consent of the proprietor, or where he falsifies a genuine mark in any manner.

OFFENCE.

407. Every one commits an offence who, with intent to deceive or defraud the public or any person, whether ascertained or not, forges a trade-mark. R.S., c. C-34, s. 365.

CROSS-REFERENCES

The term "person" is defined in s. 2. The term trade-mark is defined in s. 2 of the *Trade-marks Act*, R.S.C. 1985, c. T-13.

Forging a trade-mark is defined in s. 406. By virtue of s. 583, an indictment which otherwise complies with s. 581 is not insufficient by reason only that: para. (*c*), it charges an intent to defraud without naming or describing the person whom it was intended to defraud. Under s. 586, no count alleging fraud is insufficient by reason only that it does not set out in detail the nature of the fraud. However, under s. 587(1)(*b*), the court may order particulars of any fraud that is alleged.

The punishment for this offence is set out in s. 412 and therefore see notes under that section with respect to mode of trial and release pending trial. Section 412(2) also provides for forfeiture of anything by means of or in relation to which a person commits an offence under this section.

This offence resembles the general forgery offence and therefore see ss. 366 to 368.

SYNOPSIS

This section creates the offence of forging a trade mark. The offence is committed where the acts described in s. 406 are done with the intention to deceive or defraud any person or the public.

PASSING OFF.

408. Every one commits an offence who, with intent to deceive or defraud the public or any person, whether ascertained or not,

(*a*) **passes off other wares or services as and for those ordered or required; or**

(*b*) **makes use, in association with wares or services, of any description that is false in a material respect regarding**

(i) **the kind, quality, quantity or composition,**

(ii) **the geographical origin, or**

(iii) **the mode of the manufacture, production or performance**

of those wares or services. R.S., c. C-34, s. 366.

CROSS-REFERENCES

The term "person" is defined in s. 2.

By virtue of s. 583, an indictment which otherwise complies with s. 581 is not insufficient by reason only that: para. (*c*), it charges an intent to defraud without naming or describing the person whom it was intended to defraud. Under s. 586, no count alleging fraud is insufficient by reason only that it does not set out in detail the nature of the fraud. However, under s. 587(1)(*b*), the court may order particulars of any fraud that is alleged.

The punishment for this offence is set out in s. 412 and therefore see notes under that section with respect to mode of trial and release pending trial. Section 412(2) also provides for forfeiture of anything by means of or in relation to which a person commits an offence under this section.

Reference should also be made to the *Trade-marks Act*, R.S.C. 1985, c. T-13.

SYNOPSIS

This section describes the offence of "passing off". This offence is committed where a person, with the intention of deceiving any person or the public, passes off wares or services as being those actually ordered or required, or uses a description which is false in any of the material particulars enumerated in para. (*b*) in association with those wares or services.

INSTRUMENTS FOR FORGING TRADE-MARK / Saving.

409. (1) Every one commits an offence who makes, has in his possession or disposes of a die, block, machine or other instrument, designed or intended to be used in forging a trade-mark.

(2) No person shall be convicted of an offence under this section where he proves that he acted in good faith in the ordinary course of his business or employment. R.S., c. C-34, s. 367.

CROSS-REFERENCES

The term trade-mark is defined in the *Trade-marks Act*, R.S.C. 1985, c. T-13. Forging a trade-mark is defined in s. 406. Possession is defined in s. 4(3). The punishment for this offence is set out in s. 412 and therefore see notes under that section with respect to mode of trial and release pending trial. Section 412(2) also provides for forfeiture of anything by means of or in relation to which a person commits an offence under this section.

SYNOPSIS

This section creates the offence of dealing with instruments for forging a trade mark. The offence is committed where any person makes, possesses or disposes of an instrument designed or intended to be used in forging a trade mark. A defence exists where the accused establishes that he acted in *good faith* in the ordinary course of his business or employment.

ANNOTATIONS

While the Crown need not show that the trade-mark was or is registered it must prove it to be a trade-mark as defined by the *Trade Marks Act*: *R. v. Strong Cobb Arner of Canada Ltd.* (1973), 15 C.C.C. (2d) 288, 2 O.R. (2d) 220 (H.C.J.), affd 16 C.C.C. (2d) 150, 2 O.R. (2d) 692 (C.A.).

OTHER OFFENCES IN RELATION TO TRADE-MARKS.

410. Every one commits an offence who, with intent to deceive or defraud,
- **(a) defaces, conceals or removes a trade-mark or the name of another person from anything without the consent of that other person; or**
- **(b) being a manufacturer, dealer, trader or bottler, fills any bottle or siphon that bears the trade-mark or name of another person, without the consent of that other person, with a beverage, milk, by-product of milk or other liquid commodity for the purpose of sale or traffic. R.S., c. C-34, s. 368.**

CROSS-REFERENCES

The term trade-mark is defined in s. 2 of the *Trade-marks Act*, R.S.C. 1985, c. T-13. The term "person" is defined in s. 2. By virtue of s. 583, an indictment which otherwise complies with s. 581 is not insufficient by reason only that: para. (*c*), it charges an intent to defraud without naming or describing the person whom it was intended to defraud. Under s. 586, no count alleging fraud is insufficient by reason only that it does not set out in detail the nature of the fraud. However, under s. 587(1)(*b*), the court may order particulars of any fraud that is alleged.

The punishment for this offence is set out in s. 412 and therefore see notes under that section with respect to mode of trial and release pending trial. Section 412(2) also provides for forfeiture of anything by means of or in relation to which a person commits an offence under this section.

SYNOPSIS

This section creates additional offences in relation to trade marks. Paragraph (*a*) provides that an offence is committed where any person defaces, conceals or removes a trade mark or the name of another person from anything without consent, and with the intention to deceive or defraud. Paragraph (*b*) provides that an offence is committed where a manufacturer, dealer, trader or bottler for the purpose of sale or traffic, fills a bottle or siphon bearing a trade mark, or the name of a person, with any liquid commodity without consent, and with the intention to deceive or defraud.

USED GOODS SOLD WITHOUT DISCLOSURE.

411. Every one commits an offence who sells, exposes or has in his possession for sale, or advertises for sale, goods that have been used, reconditioned or remade and that bear the trade-mark or the trade-name of another person, without making full disclosure that the goods have been reconditioned, rebuilt or remade for sale and that they are not then in the condition in which they were originally made or produced. R.S., c. C-34, s. 369.

CROSS-REFERENCES
The terms "trade-mark" and "trade-name" are defined in s. 2 of the *Trade-marks Act*, R.S.C. 1985, c. T-13. The term "goods" is defined in s. 379. Possession is defined in s. 4(3). The term "person" is defined in s. 2.

The punishment for this offence is set out in s. 412 and therefore see notes under that section with respect to mode of trial and release pending trial. Section 412(2) also provides for forfeiture of anything by means of or in relation to which a person commits an offence under this section.

SYNOPSIS
This section describes the offence of selling used goods without appropriate disclosure. The offence is committed where a person sells, exposes for sale, possesses for sale or advertises goods bearing a trade mark or trade name of another person without disclosing that the goods were used, reconditioned or remade for sale.

PUNISHMENT / Forfeiture.

412. (1) Every one who commits an offence under section 407, 408, 409, 410 or 411 is guilty of

(a) an indictable offence and liable to imprisonment for a term not exceeding two years; or

(b) an offence punishable on summary conviction.

(2) Anything by means of or in relation to which a person commits an offence under section 407, 408, 409, 410 or 411 is, unless the court otherwise orders, forfeited on the conviction of that person for that offence. R.S., c. C-34, s. 370.

CROSS-REFERENCES
Where the prosecution elects to proceed by indictment for these offences then the accused may elect his mode of trial under s. 536(2). Where the prosecution elects to proceed by way of summary conviction then the proceedings are conducted by a summary conviction court pursuant to Part XXVII. The punishment is then as set out in s. 787 [although see s. 735(1)(b) where the accused is a corporation] and the limitation period is set out in s. 786(2).

Release pending trial for the offences is determined under s. 515, although the accused is eligible for release by a peace officer under s. 496, 497 or by the officer in charge under s. 498.

SYNOPSIS
This section provides that the offences described in ss. 407 to 411 may be prosecuted by indictment, with a maximum punishment of imprisonment for two years, or by summary conviction. Anything by means of or in relation to which any of these offences is committed is forfeited upon conviction, unless the court orders otherwise.

FALSELY CLAIMING ROYAL WARRANT.

413. Every one who falsely represents that goods are made by a person holding a royal warrant, or for the service of Her Majesty, a member of the Royal Family or a public

department is guilty of an offence punishable on summary conviction. R.S., c. C-34, s. 371.

CROSS-REFERENCES

"Her Majesty" is defined in s. 35 of the *Interpretation Act*, R.S.C. 1985, c. I-21. The term "public department" is defined in s. 2. The term "goods" is defined in s. 379.

Trial of this offence is conducted by a summary conviction court pursuant to Part XXVII.

The punishment is as set out in s. 787 [although see s. 735(1)(*b*) where the accused is a corporation] and the limitation period is set out in s. 786(2).

Release pending trial is determined by s. 515, although the accused is eligible for release by a peace officer under s. 496, 497 or by the officer in charge under s. 498.

SYNOPSIS

This section describes the offence of falsely claiming a royal warrant. The offence is committed where a person *falsely claims* that goods are made by a person holding a royal warrant, or for the service of Her Majesty, a member of the Royal Family, or a public department. The offence may be prosecuted by summary conviction.

PRESUMPTION FROM PORT OF SHIPMENT.

414. Where, in proceedings under this Part, the alleged offence relates to imported goods, evidence that the goods were shipped to Canada from a place outside Canada is, in the absence of any evidence to the contrary, proof that the goods were made or produced in the country from which they were shipped. R.S., c. C-34, s. 372.

CROSS-REFERENCES

The term "goods" is defined in s. 379.

SYNOPSIS

This section creates a presumption concerning the origin of goods in proceedings under Part X. Evidence that goods were shipped into Canada from another country is proof that the goods were produced in that country, in the absence of evidence to the contrary.

Wreck

OFFENCES IN RELATION TO WRECK.

415. Every one who
  (*a*) **secretes wreck, defaces or obliterates the marks on wreck or uses any means to disguise or conceal the fact that anything is wreck, or in any manner conceals the character of wreck, from a person who is entitled to inquire into the wreck,**
  (*b*) **receives wreck, knowing that it is wreck, from a person other than the owner thereof or a receiver of wreck, and does not within forty-eight hours thereafter inform the receiver of wreck thereof,**
  (*c*) **offers wreck for sale or otherwise deals with it, knowing that it is wreck, and not having a lawful authority to sell or deal with it,**
  (*d*) **keeps wreck in his possession knowing that it is wreck, without lawful authority to keep it, for any time longer than the time reasonably necessary to deliver it to the receiver of wreck, or**
  (*e*) **boards, against the will of the master, a vessel that is wrecked, stranded or in distress unless he is a receiver of wreck or a person acting under orders of a receiver of wreck,**

is guilty of

 (f) **an indictable offence and liable to imprisonment for a term not exceeding two years, or**

 (g) **an offence punishable on summary conviction. R.S., c. C-34, s. 373.**

CROSS-REFERENCES

The term "wreck" is defined in s. 2. The term "master" is defined in s. 2 of the *Canada Shipping Act*, R.S.C. 1985, c. S-9. The term "receiver of wreck" refers to a person appointed under s. 423 of the *Canada Shipping Act*, R.S.C. 1985, c. S-9 or a person acting under s. 424 of that Act. The *Canada Shipping Act* contains additional offences respecting wreck. In addition, s. 439(2) of that Act enacts a presumption applicable in "any indictment or prosecution of an accused for receiving, secreting or disguising any wreck, for having the possession thereof, for selling or dealing therewith or for defacing or obliterating marks thereon" and s. 439(3) permits evidence to be adduced of a prior conviction "on any indictment or prosecution of an accused for receiving, secreting, defacing, possessing, selling, dealing with or concealing the character of any wreck." The wide terms in which these provisions are cast would appear to make them applicable (assuming their constitutionality) to a prosecution under this section.

Where the prosecution elects to proceed by indictment then the accused may elect his mode of trial under s. 536(2). Where the prosecution elects to proceed by way of summary conviction then the proceedings are conducted by a summary conviction court pursuant to Part XXVII. The punishment is then as set out in s. 787 [although see s. 735(1)(b) where the accused is a corporation] and the limitation period is set out in s. 786(2). Release pending trial is determined under s. 515, although the accused is eligible for release by a peace officer under s. 496, 497 or by the officer in charge under s. 498.

Also see s. 438 which makes it an offence to interfere with the saving of a wrecked vessel.

SYNOPSIS

This section describes a series of offences in relation to wreck. "Wreck" is defined in s. 2 and includes the cargo, stores and parts of a vessel which are separated from it, and the property of persons who belong to, are on board or have left a wrecked vessel. An offence is committed where anyone secretes, disguises or conceals the character of wreck, *knowingly* receives wreck from a person other than the owner or a receiver of wreck without informing the receiver within 48 hours, *knowingly* deals with wreck without lawful authority, *knowingly* keeps wreck in possession without lawful authority longer than the time reasonably necessary to deliver it to the receiver; or, not being a receiver of wreck or a person acting under a receiver's orders, boards a wrecked, stranded or distressed vessel against the will of the master. The offence may be prosecuted by indictment or summarily. The maximum term of punishment on indictment is two years.

Public Stores

DISTINGUISHING MARK ON PUBLIC STORES.

416. The Governor in Council may, by notice to be published in the *Canada Gazette*, prescribe distinguishing marks that are appropriated for use on public stores to denote the property of Her Majesty therein, whether the stores belong to Her Majesty in right of Canada or to Her Majesty in any other right. R.S., c. C-34, s. 374.

CROSS-REFERENCES

The term "Her Majesty" is defined in s. 35 of the *Interpretation Act*, R.S.C. 1985, c. I-21. The terms "property" and "public stores" are defined in s. 2.

SYNOPSIS

This section authorizes the Governor in Council to prescribe distinguishing marks for use on public stores to denote that the stores belong to Her Majesty.

APPLYING OR REMOVING MARKS WITHOUT AUTHORITY / Unlawful transactions in public stores / Definition of "distinguishing mark".

417. (1) Every one who,

    (*a*) without lawful authority, the proof of which lies on him, applies a distinguishing mark to anything, or

    (*b*) with intent to conceal the property of Her Majesty in public stores, removes, destroys or obliterates, in whole or in part, a distinguishing mark,

is guilty of an indictable offence and liable to imprisonment for a term not exceeding two years.

(2) Every one who, without lawful authority, the proof of which lies on him, receives, possesses, keeps, sells or delivers public stores that he knows bear a distinguishing mark is guilty of

    (*a*) an indictable offence and liable to imprisonment for a term not exceeding two years; or

    (*b*) an offence punishable on summary conviction.

(3) For the purposes of this section, "distinguishing mark" means a distinguishing mark that is appropriated for use on public stores pursuant to section 416. R.S., c. C-34, s. 375.

CROSS-REFERENCES

The term "Her Majesty" is defined in s. 35 of the *Interpretation Act*, R.S.C. 1985, c. I-21. The terms "property" and "public stores" are defined in s. 2. Possession is defined in s. 4(3). Under s. 421(1), evidence that a person was at any time performing duties in the Canadian Forces [defined in s. 2] is, in the absence of evidence to the contrary, proof that his enrolment in the Canadian Forces prior to that time was regular. Under s. 421(2), an accused charged with the offence under subsec. (2) is presumed to have known that the stores bore a distinguishing mark if he was at the time of the offence in the service or employment of Her Majesty or was a dealer in marine stores or in old metals.

The accused may elect his mode of trial for the offence under subsec. (1) pursuant to s. 536(2). Release pending trial is determined by s. 515, although the accused is eligible for release by the officer in charge pursuant to s. 498. Where the prosecution elects to proceed by indictment for the offence under subsec. (2) then the accused may elect his mode of trial under s. 536(2). Where the prosecution elects to proceed by way of summary conviction then the proceedings are conducted by a summary conviction court pursuant to Part XXVII. The punishment is then as set out in s. 787 [although see s. 735(1)(*b*) where the accused is a corporation] and the limitation period is set out in s. 786(2). Release pending trial for the offence under subsec. (2) is determined under s. 515, although the accused is eligible for release by a peace officer under s. 496, 497 or by the officer in charge under s. 498.

Related offences concerning public stores are in ss. 418 and 420.

SYNOPSIS

This section describes offences with respect to distinguishing marks prescribed pursuant to s. 416. An offence is committed contrary to subsec. (1) where anyone applies a distinguishing mark *without lawful authority*, the onus of proof of which lies on him, or removes, destroys or obliterates a distinguishing mark in whole or in part, with intent to conceal Her Majesty's ownership. The offence is indictable, with a maximum term of imprisonment of two years. An offence is committed contrary to subsec. (2) where anyone knowingly receives, possesses, keeps, sells, or delivers public stores bearing a distinguishing mark *without lawful authority*, the proof of which lies on the accused. This offence may be prosecuted by indictment, with a maximum term of two years' imprisonment, or by summary conviction.

SELLING DEFECTIVE STORES TO HER MAJESTY / Offences by representatives.

418. (1) Every one who knowingly sells or delivers defective stores to Her Majesty or commits fraud in connection with the sale, lease or delivery of stores to Her Majesty or the manufacture of stores for Her Majesty is guilty of an indictable offence and liable to imprisonment for a term not exceeding fourteen years.

(2) Every one who, being a representative of an organization that commits, by fraud, an offence under subsection (1),

   (*a*) knowingly takes part in the fraud, or

   (*b*) knows or has reason to suspect that the fraud is being committed or has been or is about it be committed and does not inform the responsible government, or a department thereof, of Her Majesty,

is guilty of an indictable offence and liable to imprisonment for a term not exceeding fourteen years. R.S., c. C-34, s. 376; 2003, c. 21, s. 6.1.

CROSS-REFERENCES

The terms "organization", "every one" and "representative" are defined in s. 2. The term "Her Majesty" is defined in s. 35 of the *Interpretation Act*, R.S.C. 1985, c. I-21.

   Under s. 421(1), evidence that a person was at any time performing duties in the Canadian Forces (defined in s. 2) is, in the absence of evidence to the contrary, proof that his enrolment in the Canadian Forces prior to that time was regular.

   The accused may elect his mode of trial for the offence under subsec. (1) pursuant to s. 536(2). Release pending trial is determined by s. 515.

   Related offences concerning public stores are in ss. 417 and 420.

SYNOPSIS

This section describes the offence of selling defective stores to Her Majesty. An indictable offence is committed where a person *knowingly* sells or delivers defective stores to Her Majesty, or commits fraud in connection with the sale, lease, or delivery of stores to, or manufacture of stores for Her Majesty. The maximum term of imprisonment is 14 years. Subsection (2) provides that an officer, director, employee or agent of a corporation committing this offence by fraud is also guilty of an indictable offence with a maximum term of imprisonment of 14 years if he *knowingly* participates in the fraud, or *knows* or *has reason to suspect* that the fraud has been, is being or is about to be committed and fails to inform the responsible government department.

UNLAWFUL USE OF MILITARY UNIFORMS OR CERTIFICATES.

419. Every one who without lawful authority, the proof of which lies on him,

   (*a*) wears a uniform of the Canadian Forces or any other naval, army or air force or a uniform that is so similar to the uniform of any of those forces that it is likely to be mistaken therefor,

   (*b*) wears a distinctive mark relating to wounds received or service performed in war, or a military medal, ribbon, badge, chevron or any decoration or order that is awarded for war services, or any imitation thereof, or any mark or device or thing that is likely to be mistaken for any such mark, medal, ribbon, badge, chevron, decoration or order,

   (*c*) has in his possession a certificate of discharge, certificate of release, statement of service or identity card from the Canadian Forces or any other naval, army or air force that has not been issued to and does not belong to him, or

      (*d*) **has in his possession a commission or warrant or a certificate of discharge, certificate of release, statement of service or identity card, issued to an officer or person in or who has been in the Canadian Forces or any other naval, army or air force, that contains any alteration that is not verified by the initials of the officer who issued it, or by the initials of some officer thereto lawfully authorized,**

is guilty of an offence punishable on summary conviction. R.S., c. C-34, s. 377.

CROSS-REFERENCES

Under s. 421(1), evidence that a person was at any time performing duties in the Canadian Forces (defined in s. 2) is, in the absence of evidence to the contrary, proof that his enrolment in the Canadian Forces prior to that time was regular.

    Trial of this offence is conducted by a summary conviction court pursuant to Part XXVII. The punishment is as set out in s. 787 and the limitation period is set out in s. 786(2). Release pending trial is determined by s. 515, although the accused is eligible for release by a peace officer under s. 496, 497 or by the officer in charge under s. 498.

    The offence of personation with intent is found in s. 403 and of personating a police officer in s. 130.

SYNOPSIS

This section describes the offence of unlawful use of military uniforms or certificates or imitations thereof. The wearing or, in certain cases, possession of a wide variety of military apparel, marks, certificates, commissions and warrants without lawful authority, the proof of which lies on the accused, is a summary conviction offence.

MILITARY STORES / Exception.

420. (1) Every one who buys, receives or detains from a member of the Canadian Forces or a deserter or an absentee without leave therefrom any military stores that are owned by Her Majesty or for which the member, deserter or absentee without leave is accountable to Her Majesty is guilty of

      (*a*) **an indictable offence and liable to imprisonment for a term not exceeding five years; or**

      (*b*) **an offence punishable on summary conviction.**

(2) No person shall be convicted of an offence under this section where he establishes that he did not know and had no reason to suspect that the military stores in respect of which the offence was committed were owned by Her Majesty or were military stores for which the member, deserter or absentee without leave was accountable to Her Majesty. R.S., c. C-34, s. 378.

CROSS-REFERENCES

The term "military" is defined in s. 2.

    Under s. 421(1), evidence that a person was at any time performing duties in the Canadian Forces (defined in s. 2) is, in the absence of evidence to the contrary, proof that his enrolment in the Canadian Forces prior to that time was regular.

    Where the prosecution elects to proceed by indictment then the accused may elect his mode of trial under s. 536(2). Where the prosecution elects to proceed by way of summary conviction then the proceedings are conducted by a summary conviction court pursuant to Part XXVII. The punishment is then as set out in s. 787 [although see s. 735(1)(*b*) where the accused is a corporation] and the limitation period is set out in s. 786(2). Release pending trial is determined under s. 515, although the accused is eligible for release by a peace officer under ss. 496, 497 or by the officer in charge under s. 498.

    Related offences concerning public stores are in ss. 417 and 418.

Other offences relating to deserters are in ss. 54 and 62.

SYNOPSIS

This section describes the offence of unauthorized use of military stores. An offence is committed where a person buys, receives or detains military stores of Her Majesty from a member of the Canadian Forces, a deserter or an absentee without leave of the forces. The offence may be prosecuted by indictment, with a maximum term of imprisonment of five years, or by summary conviction. Subsection (2) creates a defence where the accused establishes that he did not know and had no reason to suspect that the stores were owned by Her Majesty.

EVIDENCE OF ENLISTMENT / Presumption when accused a dealer in stores.

421. (1) In proceedings under sections 417 to 420, evidence that a person was at any time performing duties in the Canadian Forces is, in the absence of any evidence to the contrary, proof that his enrolment in the Canadian Forces prior to that time was regular.

(2) An accused who is charged with an offence under subsection 417(2) shall be presumed to have known that the stores in respect of which the offence is alleged to have been committed bore a distinguishing mark within the meaning of that subsection at the time the offence is alleged to have been committed if he was, at that time, in the service or employment of Her Majesty or was a dealer in marine stores or in old metals. R.S., c. C-34, s. 379.

CROSS-REFERENCES

The term "Canadian Forces" is defined in s. 2. The term "Her Majesty" is defined in s. 35 of the *Interpretation Act*, R.S.C. 1985, c. I-21.

SYNOPSIS

This section creates certain presumptions relating to ss. 417 to 420. By virtue of subsec. (1), in proceedings under ss. 417 to 420, evidence that a person performed duties in the armed forces is proof of his earlier regular enrolment in the absence of evidence to the contrary. By virtue of subsec. (2), if the accused was in the service or employment of Her Majesty, or was a dealer in marine stores or old metals at the time he is alleged to have committed an offence contrary to s. 417(2), he is presumed to know that the stores in question bore a distinguishing mark at the time.

Breach of Contract, Intimidation and Discrimination Against Trade Unionists

---

CRIMINAL BREACH OF CONTRACT / Saving / Consent required.

422. (1) Every one who wilfully breaks a contract, knowing or having reasonable cause to believe that the probable consequences of doing so, whether alone or in combination with others, will be

> *(a)* **to endanger human life,**
> *(b)* **to cause serious bodily injury,**
> *(c)* **to expose valuable property, real or personal, to destruction or serious injury,**
> *(d)* **to deprive the inhabitants of a city or place, or part thereof, wholly or to a great extent, of their supply of light, power, gas or water, or**
> *(e)* **to delay or prevent the running of any locomotive engine, tender, freight or passenger train or car, on a railway that is a common carrier,**

is guilty of

    (f) an indictable offence and liable to imprisonment for a term not exceeding five years, or

    (g) an offence punishable on summary conviction.

(2) No person wilfully breaks a contract within the meaning of subsection (1) by reason only that

    (a) being the employee of an employer, he stops work as a result of the failure of his employer and himself to agree on any matter relating to his employment, or,

    (b) being a member of an organization of employees formed for the purpose of regulating relations between employers and employees, he stops work as a result of the failure of the employer and a bargaining agent acting on behalf of the organization to agree upon any matter relating to the employment of members of the organization,

if, before the stoppage of work occurs, all steps provided by law with respect to the settlement of industrial disputes are taken and any provision for the final settlement of differences, without stoppage of work, contained in or by law deemed to be contained in a collective agreement is complied with and effect given thereto.

(3) No proceedings shall be instituted under this section without the consent of the Attorney General. R.S., c. C-34, s. 380.

CROSS-REFERENCES

"Attorney General" is defined in s. 2. Section 583(h) provides that a count in an indictment is not insufficient by reason only that it does not state that the required consent has been obtained. [As to notes concerning sufficiency of consent, see s. 583.]

    Where the prosecution elects to proceed by indictment then the accused may elect his mode of trial under s. 536(2). Where the prosecution elects to proceed by way of summary conviction then the proceedings are conducted by a summary conviction court pursuant to Part XXVII. The punishment is then as set out in s. 787 [although see s. 719(b) where the accused is a corporation] and the limitation period is set out in s. 786(2). Release pending trial is determined under s. 515, although the accused is eligible for release by a peace officer under ss. 496, 497 or by the officer in charge under s. 498.

    Also see s. 466 which creates the offence of conspiracy in restraint of trade.

SYNOPSIS

This section describes the offence of criminal breach of contract. The offence is committed where a person *wilfully* breaches a contract, *knowing* or *having reasonable cause to believe* that the consequences will endanger life, cause serious bodily injury, expose valuable property to destruction or serious injury, deprive people wholly or substantially of light, power, gas, or water, or delay or prevent the running of a common carrier railway. These consequences may flow from a breach by the accused or by the accused in combination with others. The offence may be prosecuted by indictment, with a maximum term of punishment of five years' imprisonment, or by summary conviction. Subsection (2) provides that a contract is not broken within the meaning of this section where an employee lawfully stops work because matters relating to his employment are not agreed upon, or where he stops work as part of a lawful work stoppage by a union. Proceedings under this section may only be instituted with the consent of an Attorney General.

INTIMIDATION / Exception.

423. (1) Every one is guilty of an indictable offence and liable to imprisonment for a term of not more than five years or is guilty of an offence punishable on summary conviction who, wrongfully and without lawful authority, for the purpose of compelling another person to abstain from doing anything that he or she has a lawful right to do, or to do anything that he or she has a lawful right to abstain from doing,

(*a*) uses violence or threats of violence to that person or his or her spouse or common-law partner or children, or injures his or her property;

(*b*) intimidates or attempts to intimidate that person or a relative of that person by threats that, in Canada or elsewhere, violence or other injury will be done to or punishment inflicted on him or her or a relative of his or hers, or that the property of any of them will be damaged;

(*c*) persistently follows that person;

(*d*) hides any tools, clothes or other property owned or used by that person, or deprives him or her of them or hinders him or her in the use of them;

(*e*) with one or more other persons, follows that person, in a disorderly manner, on a highway;

(*f*) besets or watches the place where that person resides, works, carries on business or happens to be; or

(*g*) blocks or obstructs a highway.

(2) A person who attends at or near or approaches a dwelling-house or place, for the purpose only of obtaining or communicating information, does not watch or beset within the meaning of this section. R.S., c. C-34, s. 381; 1980-81-82-83, c. 125, s. 22; 2000, c. 12, s. 95(*b*); 2001, c. 32, s. 10.

CROSS-REFERENCES

Where the offence, although committed outside Canada, is in relation to a demand for nuclear material, see s. 7(3.4). "Common-law partner" and "dwelling-house" are defined in s. 2.

Trial of this offence is conducted by a summary conviction court pursuant to Part XXVII. The punishment is as set out in s. 787 and the limitation period is set out in s. 786(2). Release pending trial is determined by s. 515, although the accused is eligible for release by a peace officer under ss. 496, 497 or by the officer in charge under s. 498. In some circumstances, the accused found guilty of this offence would be liable to the discretionary order prohibiting possession of firearms, ammunition or explosives.

An alternative to this offence is the procedure for requiring the offender to enter into a recognizance to keep the peace either at common law or pursuant to s. 810. Other related offences: s. 175, causing disturbance; s. 264, criminal harassment; s. 264.1, uttering threats; s. 346, extortion; s. 424, threat to commit offence against internationally protected person; s. 371, sending false telegram, etc., with intent to defraud; s. 372, conveying false messages, harassing or indecent telephone calls.

SYNOPSIS

This section describes the offence of intimidation. The offence is committed where a person intending to compel someone to abstain from doing something he has a right to do, or to do something that he has the right to abstain from doing, *wrongfully* and *without authority*: uses violence or threats of violence against the person or his spouse or children; injures his property; intimidates or attempts to intimidate the person or a relative by threats of violence or injury to property; persistently follows the person; hides or deprives the person of the use of his property; with another or others follows the person in a disorderly manner on a highway; watches or besets the residence, work place or other place where the person happens to be; or blocks a highway. The offence may be prosecuted by summary conviction or indictment. By virtue of s. (2), where a person approaches a place for the sole purpose of obtaining or communicating information, he does not watch or beset within the meaning of this section.

ANNOTATIONS

A picket line, staffed by non-employees, advocating a collective bargaining agreement was held to be just as effective an interference with contractual relations as any other restraint might be and on the facts was held to involve the proposition that the defendants were in breach of subsec. (1)(*f*): *Smith Bros. Construction Co. v. Jones* (1955), 113 C.C.C. 16 (Ont. H.C.J.).

This section is not confined to industrial disputes and trade-union activity: *R. v. Basaraba* (1975), 24 C.C.C. (2d) 296 (Man. C.A.).

A road in a company town owned by the company but which the public have a *de facto* right to use constitutes a "highway" for the purposes of subsec. (1)(*g*): *R. v. Stockley* (1977), 36 C.C.C. (2d) 387 (Nfld. C.A.).

INTIMIDATION OF A JUSTICE SYSTEM PARTICIPANT OR A JOURNALIST / Prohibited conduct / Punishment.

423.1 (1) No person shall, without lawful authority, engage in any conduct with the intent to provoke a state of fear in

    (*a*) **a group of persons or the general public in order to impede the administration of criminal justice;**

    (*b*) **a justice system participant in order to impede him or her in the performance of his or her duties; or**

    (*c*) **a journalist in order to impede him or her in the transmission to the public of information in relation to a criminal organization.**

(2) [*Repealed*, 2015, c. 13, s. 12(2).]

(3) Every person who contravenes this section is guilty of an indictable offence and is liable to imprisonment for a term of not more than fourteen years. 2001, c. 32, s. 11; 2015, c. 13, s. 12.

CROSS-REFERENCES

"Justice system participant" is defined in s. 2. "Criminal organization" is defined in ss. 2 and 467.1(1). An alternative to this offence is the procedure for requiring the offender to enter into a recognizance to keep the peace either at common law or pursuant to s. 810. Other related offences: s. 175, causing disturbance; s. 264, criminal harassment; s. 346, extortion; s. 371, sending false telegram etc. with intent to defraud; s. 372, conveying false messages, harassing or indecent telephone calls; s. 423 intimidation and watching and besetting; s. 424, threat to commit offence against internationally protected person.

Section 486.5 sets out a procedure that allows a victim, witness, the prosecutor or a justice system participant to apply for an order prohibiting publication, broadcast or transmission in any way of information that would identify the person.

Section 718.02 provides that, in imposing sentence for the offence created by para. (1)(*b*), the court is to give primary consideration to the objectives of denunciation and deterrence.

SYNOPSIS

This section describes a form of intimidation directed to interference with the administration of justice and at journalists investigating criminal organizations. It is an offence to engage in the conduct set out in subsec. (2) without lawful excuse with intent to provoke a state of fear in (a) a group of persons or the public to impede the administration of justice; (b) justice system participants to impede them in their performance of their duties; or (c) journalists to impede them in transmission to the public of information in relation to a criminal organization. Subsection (2) sets out the kinds of prohibited conduct. This is an indictable offence with a maximum penalty of 14 years.

This section requires the Crown to prove a specific intent to impede a justice system participant in the exercise of his or her duties: *R. v. Armstrong* (2012), 288 C.C.C. (3d) 282 (B.C.C.A.), leave to appeal to S.C.C. refused 2013 CarswellBC 761.

THREAT AGAINST INTERNATIONALLY PROTECTED PERSON.

424. Every one who threatens to commit an offence under section 235, 236, 266, 267, 268, 269, 269.1, 271, 272, 273, 279 or 279.1 against an internationally protected person or who threatens to commit an offence under section 431 is guilty of an indictable offence and liable to imprisonment for a term of not more than five years. 1974-75-76, c. 93, s. 33; R.S.C. 1985, c. 27 (1st Supp.), s. 55; 2001, c. 41, s. 11.

CROSS-REFERENCES

The term "internationally protected person" is defined in s. 2. Section 7(10) provides for admissibility of a certificate from the Minister of Foreign Affairs stating any fact relevant to the question of whether any person is a person who is entitled, pursuant to international law, to special protection from any attack on his person, freedom or dignity.

This offence may be the basis for an application for an authorization to intercept private communications by reason of s. 183 and a warrant to conduct video surveillance under s. 487.01(5).

Section 7(3) enacts special jurisdictional rules for commission of this offence outside Canada when the offence is in relation to an internationally protected person or property referred to in s. 431 [official premises, etc.]. The related offence for United Nations personnel or associated personnel is in s. 424.1.

The accused may elect his mode of trial pursuant to s. 536(2). Release pending trial is determined by s. 515, although the accused is eligible for release by the officer in charge pursuant to s. 498. In some circumstances, the accused found guilty of this offence would be liable to the discretionary order prohibiting possession of firearms, ammunition or explosives.

SYNOPSIS

This section describes the offence of threatening to commit an offence against an internationally protected person. A person charged under this section must have threatened to commit one of the listed offences and the threats must be directed against an internationally protected person. A person who threatens to commit the offence under s. 431 of attacking the premises, residence or transport of an internationally protected person is also guilty of an offence under this section. This offence is indictable and carries a maximum term of five years' imprisonment.

THREAT AGAINST UNITED NATIONS OR ASSOCIATED PERSONNEL.

424.1 Every one who, with intent to compel any person, group of persons, state or any international or intergovernmental organization to do or refrain from doing any act, threatens to commit an offence under section 235, 236, 266, 267, 268, 269, 269.1, 271, 272, 273, 279 or 279.1 against a member of United Nations personnel or associated personnel or threatens to commit an offence under section 431.1 is guilty of an indictable offence and liable to imprisonment for a term of not more than ten years. 2001, c. 41, s. 11.

CROSS-REFERENCES

The terms "associated personnel" and "United Nations personnel" are defined in s. 2. This offence may be the basis for an application for an authorization to intercept private communications by reason of s. 183 and a warrant to conduct video surveillance under s. 487.01(5). Section 7(3.71) enacts special jurisdictional rules for commission of this offence outside Canada when the offence is in relation to United Nations personnel or associated personnel or property referred to in s. 431.1 [official premises, etc.]. The certificate of the Minister of Foreign Affairs is proof of facts relevant to the question of whether any person is a member of United Nations personnel or a member of associated personnel under s. 7(10).

SYNOPSIS

This section describes the offence of threatening to commit an offence against United Nations personnel or personnel associated with the United Nations. A person charged under this section must have threatened to commit one of the listed offences, and the threats must be directed against United Nations personnel or associated personnel with the intent to compel any person, group, state or international or intergovernmental organization to do or refrain from doing any act. A person who threatens to commit the offence under s. 431.1 of attacking the premises, residence or transport of a member of United Nations personnel or associated personnel is also guilty of an offence under this section. This offence is indictable and carries a maximum term of 10 years' imprisonment.

OFFENCES BY EMPLOYERS.

425. Every one who, being an employer or the agent of an employer, wrongfully and without lawful authority

    (*a*) **refuses to employ or dismisses from his employment any person for the reason only that the person is a member of a lawful trade union or of a lawful association or combination of workmen or employees formed for the purpose of advancing, in a lawful manner, their interests and organized for their protection in the regulation of wages and conditions of work,**

    (*b*) **seeks by intimidation, threat of loss of position or employment, or by causing actual loss of position or employment, or by threatening or imposing any pecuniary penalty, to compel workmen or employees to abstain from belonging to a trade union, association or combination to which they have a lawful right to belong, or**

    (*c*) **conspires, combines, agrees or arranges with any other employer or his agent to do anything mentioned in paragraph (*a*) or (*b*),**

is guilty of an offence punishable on summary conviction. R.S., c. C-34, s. 382.

CROSS-REFERENCES

Trial of this offence is conducted by a summary conviction court pursuant to Part XXVII. The punishment is as set out in s. 787 and the limitation period is set out in s. 786(2). Release pending trial is determined by s. 515, although the accused is eligible for release by a peace officer under s. 496, 497 or by the officer in charge under s. 498.

    The related offence of intimidation is found in s. 423. With respect to the offence in para. (*c*), see the saving provisions with respect to refusing to work and trade combinations in s. 467.

SYNOPSIS

This section describes several offences relating to labour disputes with which an employer can be charged. Any person who is either an employer or an agent of an employer and who *wrongfully and without lawful authority* refuses to hire or continue the employment of another person because he is a member of a *lawful* trade union or association, or who, employing the methods described in para. (*b*), attempts to keep his employees from joining a union or association to which they have a lawful right to belong is guilty of a summary conviction offence. Paragraph (*c*) imposes liability to summary conviction upon any person who *conspires, combines, agrees* or *arranges* with the employer or his agent to do any of the things described above.

ANNOTATIONS

Paragraph (*a*) – The "reason only" means the primary reason, the *causa causans,* the reason behind the act in question, and may be inferred from the attitudes or decisions not expressly outlined in detail: *R. ex rel. Perreault v. Alex Pelletier And Sons Ltd.* (1960), 33 C.R. 84 (Que. Mag. Ct.).

A charge under this subsection was dismissed where police officers, called by the employer, removed employees from the employer's premises but without instructions to do so from the employer. There was held to be no dismissal either directly or indirectly by the employer: *R. v. J. Alepin Freres Ltee*, [1965] S.C.R. 359, [1965] 3 C.C.C. 1.

Paragraph (b) – The offence of seeking to compel workmen or employees to abstain from belonging to a trade union is the prohibited activity expressed in two methods which may both be incorporated into one charge: *R. v. Hickey, ex p. Hebb Motors Ltd.*, [1965] 2 C.C.C. 170 (N.S.S.C.).

THREATS AND RETALIATION AGAINST EMPLOYEES / Punishment.

425.1 (1) No employer or person acting on behalf of an employer or in a position of authority in respect of an employee of the employer shall take a disciplinary measure against, demote, terminate or otherwise adversely affect the employment of such an employee, or threaten to do so,

 (*a*) with the intent to compel the employee to abstain from providing information to a person whose duties include the enforcement of federal or provincial law, respecting an offence that the employee believes has been or is being committed contrary to this or any other federal or provincial Act or regulation by the employer or an officer or employee of the employer or, if the employer is a corporation, by one or more of its directors; or

 (*b*) with the intent to retaliate against the employee because the employee has provided information referred to in paragraph (*a*) to a person whose duties include the enforcement of federal or provincial law.

(2) Any one who contravenes subsection (1) is guilty of

 (*a*) an indictable offence and liable to imprisonment for a term not exceeding five years; or

 (*b*) an offence punishable on summary conviction. 2004, c. 3, s. 6.

CROSS-REFERENCES
Sections 487.012 to 487.017 provide procedures for the making of production orders that would require persons to provide documents or data.

SYNOPSIS
This section creates a form of whistle-blower protection. The section makes it an offence for an employer or anyone acting on behalf of an employer to take or threaten to take disciplinary or other measures such as termination against an employee with the intent to compel the employee not to provide information to persons whose duties include enforcement of federal or provincial law respecting an offence that the employee believes has been or is being committed by the employer, an officer or employee of the employer or directors of a corporation. The section also makes it an offence for such persons to retaliate against the employee for having taken any of these steps. The offence created is a hybrid offence and the maximum penalty is five years if the Crown proceeds by indictment.

Secret Commissions

SECRET COMMISSIONS / Privity to offence / Punishment / Definition of "agent" and "principal".

426. (1) Every one commits an offence who

 (*a*) directly or indirectly, corruptly gives, offers or agrees to give or offer to an agent or to anyone for the benefit of the agent — or, being an agent, directly or indirectly, corruptly demands, accepts or offers or agrees to accept from any person, for themselves or another person — any reward, advantage or benefit of any kind as consideration for doing or not doing, or for having done or not done, any act relating to the affairs or business of the agent's principal, or for showing or not showing favour or disfavour to any person with relation to the affairs or business of the agent's principal; or

(*b*) with intent to deceive a principal, gives to an agent of that principal, or, being an agent, uses with intent to deceive his principal, a receipt, an account, or other writing

    (i) in which the principal has an interest,

    (ii) that contains any statement that is false or erroneous or defective in any material particular, and

    (iii) that is intended to mislead the principal.

(2) Every one commits an offence who is knowingly privy to the commission of an offence under subsection (1).

(3) A person who commits an offence under this section is guilty of an indictable offence and liable to imprisonment for a term not exceeding five years.

(4) In this section "agent" includes an employee, and "principal" includes an employer. R.S., c. C-34, s. 383; R.S.C. 1985, c. 27 (1st Supp.), s. 56; 2007, c. 13, s. 7.

CROSS-REFERENCES

This offence may be the basis for an application for an authorization to intercept private communications by reason of s. 183 and is an enterprise crime offence for the purposes of Part XII.2.

    The accused may elect his mode of trial pursuant to s. 536(2). Release pending trial is determined by s. 515, although the accused is eligible for release by a peace officer under s. 496, 497 or by the officer in charge under s. 498.

    This offence is often charged with the offence of fraud defined in s. 380. Other forms of breach of trust are as follows: s. 122, breach of trust by public officer; s. 330, theft by person required to account; s. 331, theft by person holding power of attorney; s. 332, theft of money held under direction; s. 336, criminal breach of trust; s. 384, broker selling for his own account.

SYNOPSIS

This section describes the offence of giving secret commissions. Subsection (1)(*a*) states that a person who directly or indirectly *corruptly* gives, offers or agrees to give or offer to an agent, or who, being an agent, *corruptly* demands, accepts or offers or agrees to accept any reward, advantage or benefit of any kind in return for doing or not doing an act, or for showing favour or disfavour to another person, in relation to the business of his principal, commits this indictable offence. Subsection (1)(*b*) describes another form of this offence which involves the giving to an agent or the using by an agent of a *receipt, account*, or *other writing* in which the principal has an interest and in which a false, erroneous or defective statement, intended to mislead the principal, is contained. In order to be convicted of an offence under subsec. (1)(*b*), the accused must have *the intent to deceive* a principal. Subsection (2) makes it an offence for a person to be *knowingly privy* to an offence under subsec. (1). The maximum term of imprisonment for offences under this section is five years.

ANNOTATIONS

Elements of offence – Where the person charged with the offence under subsec. (1)(*a*)(ii) is the agent, then the Crown must establish as elements of the *actus reus* the existence of an agency relationship; the accepting by an agent of a benefit as consideration for doing or forbearing to do any act in relation to the affairs of the agent's principals; and the failure by the agent to make adequate and timely disclosure of the source, amount and nature of the benefit. The requisite *mens rea* is proof that the agent was aware of the agency relationship;

that the agent knowingly accepted the benefit as consideration for an act to be undertaken in relation to the affairs of the principal; and that the agent was aware of the extent of the disclosure to the principal or lack thereof. If the accused was aware that some disclosure was made, then it will be for the court to determine whether in all the circumstances of the particular case it was in fact adequate and timely. The term "corruptly" means secretly or without requisite disclosure. There is no requirement of any corrupt bargain. Thus, it is possible to convict the agent who has accepted or taken a reward despite the innocence of the giver of the reward or benefit. The non-disclosure will be established if the Crown demonstrates that adequate and timely disclosure of the source, amount and nature of the benefit has not been made by the agent to the principal. A general and vague disclosure that the agent is receiving commissions will not meet the objective of the section. The agent must disclose the nature of the benefit which is being received, the amount of that benefit calculated to the best of the agent's ability and the source of the benefit. It may not be possible for the agent to be exact as to the amount of commission which will be received and it will, therefore, be sufficient if a reasonable effort is made to alert the principal as to the approximate amount and source of commission to be received. The disclosure must be timely in the sense that the principal must be aware of the benefit as soon as possible. The disclosure must be made at the point when the reward may influence the agent in relation to the principal's affairs and it is essential then that the agent clearly disclose to the principal as promptly as possible the source and amount or approximate amount of the benefit: *R. v. Kelly*, [1992] 2 S.C.R. 170, 73 C.C.C. (3d) 385, 14 C.R. (4th) 181; *R. v. Arnold*, [1992] 2 S.C.R. 208, 73 C.C.C. (3d) 31, 113 N.S.R. (2d) 271.

The evil to which this section is directed is secret transactions with an agent concerning the affairs of his principal, and it is no defence that the accused believed that he had a right to have a certain thing done by the agent's principal: *R. v. Brown* (1956), 116 C.C.C. 287, 24 C.R. 404 (Ont. C.A.) (2:1).

Meaning of "agent" – While the offence, contrary to subsec. (1)(*a*)(i), requires proof that the person who was offered the secret commission was in fact an agent, the agent need not have a specific principal at the time of the prohibited offer, nor need the agent intend to carry out the purpose for which the offer was made: *R. v. Wile* (1990), 58 C.C.C. (3d) 85, 79 C.R. (3d) 32, 74 O.R. (2d) 289 (C.A.).

The mere giving of advice with respect to investments does not establish an agency relationship: *R. v. Arnold* (1994), 88 C.C.C. (3d) 92, 129 N.S.R. (2d) 356 (C.A.).

Trading Stamps

ISSUING TRADING STAMPS / Giving to purchaser of goods.

427. (1) Every one who, by himself or his employee or agent, directly or indirectly issues, gives, sells or otherwise disposes of, or offers to issue, give, sell or otherwise dispose of trading stamps to a merchant or dealer in goods for use in his business is guilty of an offence punishable on summary conviction.

(2) Every one who, being a merchant or dealer in goods, by himself or his employee or agent, directly or indirectly gives or in any way disposes of, or offers to give or in any way dispose of, trading stamps to a person who purchases goods from him is guilty of an offence punishable on summary conviction. R.S., c. C-34, s. 384.

CROSS-REFERENCES

The terms "goods" and "trading stamps" are defined in s. 379.

Trial of these offences is conducted by a summary conviction court pursuant to Part XXVII. The punishment is as set out in s. 787 [although see s. 719(*b*) where the accused is a corporation] and the limitation period is set out in s. 786(2). Release pending trial is determined by s. 515, although the accused is eligible for release by a peace officer under s. 496, 497 or by the officer in charge under s. 498.

Also see lottery offences in s. 207.

SYNOPSIS

This section makes it a summary conviction offence to give, sell or issue, or to offer to give, sell or issue trading stamps to a *merchant or dealer in goods* for use in his business. Subsection (2) further makes it an offence for a merchant or dealer in goods to distribute trading stamps to purchasers.

ANNOTATIONS

The vendor's right to substitute an equal or better premium than the one claimed by the customer upon redemption of coupons did not make the arrangement a trading stamp scheme: *R. v. Kleckner*, [1963] 1 C.C.C. 64, 39 C.R. 77 (Sask. C.A.).

To be trading stamps the Crown must prove that the stamps were intended to represent a discount on the price of goods, and accordingly bonus coupons given only to cash as opposed to credit customers based on the amount paid are not trading stamps: *R. v. Lloyd H. Alford & Son Ltd.*, [1965] 3 C.C.C. 70, 45 C.R. 279 (Ont. H.C.J.).

Part XI / WILFUL AND FORBIDDEN ACTS IN RESPECT OF CERTAIN PROPERTY

Interpretation

DEFINITION OF "PROPERTY"

428. In this Part, "property" means real or personal corporeal property. R.S., c. C-34, s. 385.

CROSS-REFERENCES

In addition to the definition of this section, see s. 2 and notes to that section. For definition of "wilfully", see s. 429.

SYNOPSIS

This section defines the term "property" for the purposes of Part XI of the Code. The definition is more restricted than the one found in s. 2 of the Code and encompasses real or personal corporeal property.

WILFULLY CAUSING EVENT TO OCCUR / Colour of right / Interest.

429. (1) Every one who causes the occurrence of an event by doing an act or by omitting to do an act that it is his duty to do, knowing that the act or omission will probably cause the occurrence of the event and being reckless whether the event occurs or not, shall be deemed, for the purposes of this Part, wilfully to have caused the occurrence of the event.

(2) No person shall be convicted of an offence under sections 430 to 446 where he proves that he acted with legal justification or excuse and with colour of right.

(3) Where it is an offence to destroy or to damage anything,

    (a) the fact that a person has a partial interest in what is destroyed or damaged does not prevent him from being guilty of the offence if he caused the destruction or damage; and

(*b*) **the fact that a person has a total interest in what is destroyed or damaged does not prevent him from being guilty of the offence if he caused the destruction or damage with intent to defraud. R.S., c. C-34, s. 386.**

CROSS-REFERENCES

For other notes on the meaning of "colour of right", see s. 322 and with respect to mistake generally, see s. 19. With respect to subsec. (3)(*b*), note that where the accused is charged with an offence under s. 433 or 434, then s. 435 enacts a presumption of intent to defraud where the accused is the holder of or is named as the beneficiary under a policy of fire insurance relating to the property, and where intent to defraud is material.

SYNOPSIS

This section contains three provisions relevant to Part XI of the Code. Subsection (1) states that any person who does something (or fails to do something which it is his or her duty to do) knowing that this action or inaction will *probably cause* the occurrence of an event and who is *reckless* as to the outcome of his action, is deemed, for the purposes of this Part of the Code, to have wilfully caused the occurrence of the event. Subsection (2) makes it clear that no person who proves that he acted with *legal justification or excuse* and *with colour of right* shall be convicted of an offence under ss. 430 to 446. Subsection (3)(*a*) provides that where it is an offence to destroy or damage anything, a person who causes damage or destruction can be found guilty, notwithstanding the fact that he has a partial interest in that thing. Subsection (3)(*a*) states that a person who has a total interest in the damaged property can be found guilty of an offence if he caused the damage or destruction *with the intent to defraud*.

ANNOTATIONS

Application of definition of "wilfully" [subsec. (1)] – In view of this extended definition of "wilfully" an information containing an allegation of unlawfully damaging property is valid: *R. v. Rese,* [1968] 1 C.C.C. 363, 2 C.R.N.S. 99 (Ont. C.A.).

Legal justification or excuse and colour of right [subsec. (2)] – To come within this exception the accused must show that he believed in a state of facts which, if it actually existed, would constitute a legal justification or excuse: *R. v. Ninos and Walker,* [1964] 1 C.C.C. 326, 48 M.P.R. 383 (N.S.S.C. *in Banco*).

Where the accused shot and killed a dog which he had accidentally wounded in an attempt to frighten it off his land which he had turned into a wildlife refuge it was held that the first shot was justified as it was not done with the intent to wound or kill the dog and that the second shot, which was done for humanitarian reasons to put the dog out of its misery, was also justified. The accused's honest belief (proved to be wrong at trial) that the dog could not be saved provided him with a colour of right. The court left open the question whether the intentional shooting of dogs to protect wildlife would itself constitute a lawful justification or excuse: *R. v. Comber* (1975), 28 C.C.C. (2d) 444 (Ont. Co. Ct.).

The defence of colour of right is based on the accused's subjective, honest belief that at the time of the offence, he had a color of right. The color of right defence is an honest belief in a state of facts or civil law that, if it existed, would negate the *mens rea* of the offence. While the belief does not have to be reasonable, the reasonableness of the belief is a factor in determining if there is an honest belief. It is not sufficient, however, that the accused have a moral belief in a colour of right. Colour of right includes errors of fact and law and is not limited to areas of law respecting proprietary or possessory rights. In this case, however, the defence of color of right did not apply where it was based on the accused's ignorance of the jurisdiction of the *Criminal Code*: *R. v. Watson* (1999), 137 C.C.C. (3d) 422, 27 C.R. (5th) 139 (Nfld. C.A.).

The word "and" in this subsection should be read as "or" so it is sufficient if the accused establishes that he acted either with legal justification or excuse, or with a colour of right. Colour of right means an honest belief in a state of fact which, if it existed, would be a legal justification or excuse: *R. v. Creaghan* (1982), 1 C.C.C. (3d) 449, 31 C.R. (3d) 277 (Ont. C.A.).

It would seem that placing the onus on the accused to prove the legal justification or excuse is unconstitutional as violating s. 11(*d*) of the Charter: *R. v. Gamey* (1993), 80 C.C.C. (3d) 117, 85 Man. R. (2d) 41 (C.A.).

Destruction or damage to person's own property [subsec. (3)] – Where a trustee's interest is only a bare legal title the trustee does not have any sufficient interest in the property to remove the application of this paragraph: *R. v. Griffith*, [1987] 2 W.W.R. 564 (Man. Q.B.).

Mischief

MISCHIEF / Mischief in relation to computer data / Punishment / Punishment / Idem / Mischief relating to religious property / Mischief relating to war memorials / Mischief in relation to cultural property / Mischief in relation to computer data / Offence / Saving / Idem / Definition of "computer data".

430. (1) Every one commits mischief who wilfully
  (*a*) **destroys or damages property;**
  (*b*) **renders property dangerous, useless, inoperative or ineffective;**
  (*c*) **obstructs, interrupts or interferes with the lawful use, enjoyment or operation of property; or**
  (*d*) **obstructs, interrupts or interferes with any person in the lawful use, enjoyment or operation of property.**

(1.1) Everyone commits mischief who wilfully
  (*a*) **destroys or alters computer data;**
  (*b*) **renders computer data meaningless, useless or ineffective;**
  (*c*) **obstructs, interrupts or interferes with the lawful use of computer data; or**
  (*d*) **obstructs, interrupts or interferes with a person in the lawful use of computer data or denies access to computer data to a person who is entitled to access to it.**

(2) Every one who commits mischief that causes actual danger to life is guilty of an indictable offence and liable to imprisonment for life.

(3) Every one who commits mischief in relation to property that is a testamentary instrument or the value of which exceeds five thousand dollars
  (*a*) **is guilty of an indictable offence and liable to imprisonment for a term not exceeding ten years; or**
  (*b*) **is guilty of an offence punishable on summary conviction.**

(4) Every one who commits mischief in relation to property, other than property described in subsection (3),
  (*a*) **is guilty of an indictable offence and liable to imprisonment for a term not exceeding two years; or**
  (*b*) **is guilty of an offence punishable on summary conviction.**

(4.1) Every one who commits mischief in relation to property that is a building, structure or part thereof that is primarily used for religious worship, including a church, mosque, synagogue or temple, or an object associated with religious worship located in or on the grounds of such a building or structure, or a cemetery, if the commission of the mischief is motivated by bias, prejudice or hate based on religion, race, colour or national or ethnic origin,
  (*a*) **is guilty of an indictable offence and liable to imprisonment for a term not exceeding ten years; or**
  (*b*) **is guilty of an offence punishable on summary conviction and liable to imprisonment for a term not exceeding eighteen months.**

(4.11) Everyone who commits mischief in relation to property that is a building, structure or part thereof that primarily serves as a monument to honour persons who were killed or died as a consequence of a war, including a war memorial or cenotaph, or an object associated with honouring or remembering those persons that is located in or on the grounds of such a building or structure, or a cemetery is guilty of an indictable offence or an offence punishable on summary conviction and is liable,

> (*a*) whether the offence is prosecuted by indictment or punishable on summary conviction, to the following minimum punishment, namely,
>> (i) for a first offence, to a fine of not less than $1,000,
>> (ii) for a second offence, to imprisonment for not less than 14 days, and
>> (iii) for each subsequent offence, to imprisonment for not less than 30 days;
>
> (*b*) if the offence is prosecuted by indictment, to imprisonment for a term not exceeding 10 years; and
>
> (*c*) if the offence is punishable on summary conviction, to imprisonment for a term not exceeding 18 months.

(4.2) Every one who commits mischief in relation to cultural property as defined in Article 1 of the Convention for the Protection of Cultural Property in the Event of Armed Conflict, done at The Hague on May 14, 1954, as set out in the schedule to the *Cultural Property Export and Import Act*,

> (*a*) is guilty of an indictable offence and liable to imprisonment for a term not exceeding ten years; or
>
> (*b*) is guilty of an offence punishable on summary conviction.

(5) Everyone who commits mischief in relation to computer data

> (*a*) is guilty of an indictable offence and liable to imprisonment for a term not exceeding ten years; or
>
> (*b*) is guilty of an offence punishable on summary conviction.

(5.1) Everyone who wilfully does an act or wilfully omits to do an act that it is their duty to do, if that act or omission is likely to constitute mischief causing actual danger to life, or to constitute mischief in relation to property or computer data,

> (*a*) is guilty of an indictable offence and liable to imprisonment for a term not exceeding five years; or
>
> (*b*) is guilty of an offence punishable on summary conviction.

(6) No person commits mischief within the meaning of this section by reason only that

> (*a*) he stops work as a result of the failure of his employer and himself to agree on any matter relating to his employment; or
>
> (*b*) he stops work as a result of the failure of his employer and a bargaining agent acting on his behalf to agree on any matter relating to his employment; or
>
> (*c*) he stops work as a result of his taking part in a combination of workmen or employees for their own reasonable protection as workmen or employees.

(7) No person commits mischief within the meaning of this section by reason only that he attends at or near or approaches a dwelling-house or place for the purpose only of obtaining or communicating information.

(8) In this section, "computer data" has the same meaning as in subsection 342.1(2). R.S., c. C-34, s. 387; 1972, c. 13, s. 30; R.S.C. 1985, c. 27 (1st Supp.), s. 57; 1994, c. 44, s. 28; 2001, c. 41, s. 12; 2005, c. 40, s. 3; 2014, c. 9, s. 1; 2014, c. 31, s. 19.

CROSS-REFERENCES

The term "property" is defined in s. 428. The term "wilfully" is defined in s. 429(1). The defence of legal justification or excuse and colour of right is set out in s. 429(2). Where the accused has an interest in the thing destroyed, see s. 429(3). This offence may be the basis of an application for an authorization to intercept private communications pursuant to s. 183 or for a warrant to conduct video surveillance by reason of s. 487.01(5).

The definition of "cultural property" referred to in subsec. (4.2) is as follows:

For the purposes of the present Convention, the term "cultural property" shall cover, irrespective of origin or ownership:

(*a*) movable or immovable property of great importance to the cultural heritage of every people, such as monuments of architecture, art or history, whether religious or secular; archaeological sites; groups of buildings which, as a whole, are of historical or artistic interest; works of art; manuscripts, books and other objects of artistic, historical or archaeological interest; as well as scientific collections and important collections of books or archives or of reproductions of the property defined above;

(*b*) buildings whose main and effective purpose is to preserve or exhibit the movable cultural property defined in subparagraph (*a*) such as museums, large libraries and depositories of archives, and refuges intended to shelter, in the event of armed conflict, the movable cultural property defined in subparagraph (*a*);

(*c*) centres containing a large amount of cultural property as defined in subparagraphs (*a*) and (*b*), to be known as "centres containing monuments".

The offence in subsec. (2) is an indictable offence for which the accused may elect his mode of trial under s. 536(2). Release pending trial is determined under s. 515. Where the prosecution elects to proceed by indictment for the offence under subsecs. (3) to (5.1) the accused may elect the mode of trial under s. 536(2). Release pending trial is determined under s. 515, although the accused is eligible for release by a peace officer under s. 496, 497 or by the officer in charge under s. 498. Where the prosecution elects to proceed by way of summary conviction then the proceedings are conducted by a summary conviction court pursuant to Part XXVII. The punishment is then as set out in s. 787 and the limitation period is set out in s. 786(2). Where the prosecution elects to proceed by indictment for the offence under subsec. (4) then, by virtue of s. 553(*a*)(v), it is an offence over which a provincial court judge has absolute jurisdiction and does not depend on the consent of the accused. That is, the accused does not have an election as to mode of trial, although the provincial court judge may, by virtue of s. 555(1), elect to continue the proceedings as a preliminary inquiry, in which case, the accused is deemed to have elected trial by judge and jury pursuant to s. 565(1)(*a*). As well, under s. 555(2), where, in the course of the trial, evidence establishes that the subject-matter of the offence is a testamentary instrument or that its value exceeds $5,000 then the provincial court judge shall put the accused to his election under s. 536(2). Where the prosecution elects to proceed by way of summary conviction then the proceedings are conducted by a summary conviction court pursuant to Part XXVII. The punishment is then as set out in s. 787 and the limitation period is set out in s. 786(2). Release pending trial is determined by s. 515, although the accused is eligible for release by a peace officer under s. 496, 497 or by the officer in charge under s. 498. The value of a valuable security is determined in accordance with s. 4(2) and of a postal card or stamp in accordance with s. 4(1). The term "testamentary instrument" is defined in s. 2. Where the prosecution elects to proceed by indictment for the offence under subsec. (5) or (5.1) then the accused may elect his mode of trial under s. 536(2). Where the prosecution elects to proceed by way of summary conviction then the proceedings are conducted by a summary conviction court pursuant to Part XXVII. The punishment is then as set out in s. 787 and the limitation period is set out in s. 786(2). Release pending trial for the offences in subsec. (5) or (5.1) is determined under s. 515, although the accused is eligible for release by a peace officer under s. 496, 497 or by the officer in charge under s. 498.

Using a computer facility with intent to commit an offence under this section is an offence under s. 342.1(1)(*c*). The offence of public mischief [*i.e.*, misleading a peace officer] is in s. 140. Under s. 718.2(*a*)(i) evidence that the offence was motivated by bias, prejudice or hate based on certain grounds such as religion is an aggravating factor on sentencing.

SYNOPSIS

This section describes the offence of mischief in its various forms. It also sets out the punishment that will be applied after a finding of guilt under this section. Every person who *wilfully* does any of the things listed in subsec. (1) or (1.1) commits the offence of mischief. The punishment for this offence, depending on the circumstances of the case, can be life imprisonment. The penalty depends on the nature of the conduct or the property involved, such as religious property under subsec. (4.1), or cultural property under subsec. (4.2). Subsections (6) and (7) provide exemptions from the offence of mischief for the specific actions described therein. Subsection (6) would appear to apply to a situation involving a labour dispute.

ANNOTATIONS

Mischief to property [subsec. (1)] – The gravamen of this offence is the commission of mischief and an information that sets out the alternative modes in para. (*c*) is not duplicitous: *R. v. Hibbs* (1973), 10 C.C.C. (2d) 513 (Alta. S.C.).

This subsection defines one offence of mischief which has been classified for sentencing purposes by application of subsecs. (2), (3) or (4): *R. v. Lebrun* (1988), 65 C.R. (3d) 280 (Que. C.A.).

The offence under para. (*a*) of this subsection is a general intent offence for which intoxication as a result of voluntary consumption of alcohol or drugs is not a defence: *R. v. Schmidtke* (1985), 19 C.C.C. (3d) 390 (Ont. C.A.).

The offence in para. (*a*) requires proof that the property was rendered less suited for its intended purpose or that at least temporarily the usefulness or the value of the property was impaired. Putting a poster on a lamp-post did not impair the use or value of the property and could not amount to the offence: *R. v. Quickfall* (1993), 78 C.C.C. (3d) 563 (Que. C.A.), leave to appeal to S.C.C. refused 83 C.C.C. (3d) vi. To similar effect, see *R. v. Jeffers* (2012), 280 C.C.C. (3d) 54 (Ont. C.A.).

A person who as part of a labour dispute forms part of a human barricade so as to block access to the premises, in violation of an injunction limiting the number of picketers, may be found guilty of the offence under para. (*c*) either as a principal or a party though he neither says nor does anything other than stand shoulder to shoulder with other persons: *R. v. Mammolita* (1983), 9 C.C.C. (3d) 85 (Ont. C.A.).

However, members of a trade union lawfully on strike may picket an employer's place of business with the purpose of bringing economic pressure to bear on that employer and subsec. (1)(*c*) should not be interpreted so as to make this lawful activity an offence. The offence requires proof of some physical act on the part of the accused which operates as, or has the effect of causing, some sort of obstruction, interruption, or interference with the use or enjoyment or potential use or enjoyment of the property that goes beyond the mere communication of information through picketing. The fact that persons may be persuaded voluntarily not to do business with the owner or that the employer's attention is diverted from his business to deal with the actions of the accused is simply the inevitable consequence of the give and take of the economic pressures that are necessarily incidental to any labour dispute: *R. v. Dooling* (1994), 94 C.C.C. (3d) 525 (Nfld. S.C.).

Enjoyment of property as used in subsec. (1)(*c*) refers to "use" or "pleasure". Conduct of the accused in having a loud party, thus interfering with his neighbour's ability to sleep, can constitute interference with possessory rights so as to amount to an offence under subsec. (1)(*c*): *R. v. W. (T.)* (1993), 21 W.C.B. (2d) 194 (B.C.S.C.). Similarly, in *R. v. Maddeaux* (1997), 115 C.C.C. (3d) 122 (Ont. C.A.), leave to appeal to S.C.C. refused 118 C.C.C. (3d) vi, the court held that "use, enjoyment or operation" are to be read *ejusdem generis*. "Use" and "enjoyment" include presence for purposes of cooking, eating, cleaning, resting, sleeping, listening to the radio or watching television. "Operation" would normally apply to a commercial, institutional or industrial enterprise.

In *R. v. Nicol* (2002), 170 C.C.C. (3d) 59 (Man. C.A.), the court held that "enjoyment" is not limited to proprietary rights and includes taking pleasure from the use of the property.

The term "any person" in para. (*d*) includes employees or invitees and is not limited to the owner or leaseholder: *R. v. Biggin* (1980), 55 C.C.C. (2d) 408 (Ont. C.A.).

In *R. v. Drapeau* (1995), 96 C.C.C. (3d) 554 (Que. C.A.), a majority of the court held that the accused could not be convicted of the offence under subsec. (1)(*d*) based on his conduct in watching or staring at his neighbours and by making objectionable noises. Beauregard J.A. held that there was a doubt that the accused intended to interfere with the complainants' enjoyment of their land. Fish J.A. held that the term "enjoyment" must be restricted to the entitlement or exercise of a right in relation to property. It could not apply to conduct which merely diminishes the pleasure derived from a property by its owner. Chamberland J.A. dissenting would have upheld the accused's conviction on the basis that "enjoyment" should include the satisfaction which the property can provide to the owner.

Actual danger to life [subsec. (2)] – The actual danger to life must be the direct result of a deliberate act of mischief and not just merely incidental thereto: *R. v. Nairn* (1955), 112 C.C.C. 272 (Nfld. S.C.).

There is no requirement that the actual danger to life be caused by the damage as opposed to the act which caused the damage: *R. v. Humphrey* (1986), 21 O.A.C. 36 (C.A.).

Punishment [subsecs. (3) and (4)] – Other than a testamentary instrument it is the value of the property damaged not the amount of the damage which determines whether the charge lies under this subsection or subsec. (4). Accordingly the information should allege either the value of the property or make reference to subsec. (3) or (4): *R. v. Sargent and Hinds* (1986), 55 C.R. (3d) 78 (Ont. Prov. Ct.).

An information which merely fails to allege the value of the property still discloses an offence known to law and is capable of amendment to allege the value of the property: *R. v. Fediash* (1988), 44 C.C.C. (3d) 233 (Sask. Q.B.).

Subsection (5.1) – The *mens rea* for this offence is objective. Accordingly, the *mens rea* was made out where the accused lit a bag of chips on fire, a reasonable person would perceive that the resultant damage to property was a likely consequence: *R. v. D. (S.D.)* (2002), 164 C.C.C. (3d) 1 (Nfld. & Lab. C.A.).

Saving [subsec. (7)] – This subsection does not provide a defence to a person who trespasses on private property in order to communicate his message: *R. v. Waters* (1990), 54 C.C.C. (3d) 40 (Sask. Q.B.).

The accused's conduct in parking his truck near his property line and placing a sign on his truck directed at his neighbours fell within subsec. (7). The acts constituted no more than communication of a message and posed no danger to anyone or to the complainant's property, notwithstanding the fact that the message negatively affected the complainant's ability to sell their property: *R. v. Tremblay* (2010), 256 C.C.C. (3d) 389 (Ont. C.A.).

ATTACK ON PREMISES, RESIDENCE OR TRANSPORT OF INTERNATIONALLY PROTECTED PERSON.

431. Every one who commits a violent attack on the official premises, private accommodation or means of transport of an internationally protected person that is likely to endanger the life or liberty of such a person is guilty of an indictable offence and liable to imprisonment for a term of not more than fourteen years. 1974-75-76, c. 93, s. 34; R.S.C. 1985, c. 27 (1st Supp.), s. 58; 2001, c. 41, s. 13.

CROSS-REFERENCES

The term "internationally protected person" is defined in s. 2. Section 7(10) provides for admissibility of a certificate from the Secretary of State for External Affairs stating any fact relevant to the question of whether any person is a person who is entitled, pursuant to international law, to special protection from any attack on his person, freedom or dignity.

This offence may be the basis for an application for an authorization to intercept private communications by reason of s. 183 and for a warrant to conduct video surveillance by reason of s. 487.01(5).

Section 7(3) enacts special jurisdictional rules for commission of this offence outside Canada when the offence is in relation to an internationally protected person or property referred to in this section. A threat to commit an offence under this section is an offence under s. 424.

The accused may elect the mode of trial pursuant to s. 536(2). Release pending trial is determined by s. 515. A person convicted of the offence in this section may be liable to the mandatory prohibition order in s. 109 for possession of weapons, ammunition and explosives.

SYNOPSIS

This section describes the offence of attacking the official premises, private accommodation or means of transport of an internationally protected person. The attack must be likely to endanger the life or liberty of such a protected person. The offence is indictable and carries a maximum term of 14 years. This offence is related to s. 424.

ATTACK ON PREMISES, ACCOMMODATION OR TRANSPORT OF UNITED NATIONS OR ASSOCIATED PERSONNEL.

431.1 Every one who commits a violent attack on the official premises, private accommodation or means of transport of a member of United Nations personnel or associated personnel that is likely to endanger the life or liberty of such a person is guilty of an indictable offence and liable to imprisonment for a term of not more than fourteen years. 2001, c. 41, s. 13.

CROSS-REFERENCES

The terms "associated personnel" and "United Nations personnel" are defined in s. 2. This offence may be the basis for an application for an authorization to intercept private communications by reason of s. 183 and a warrant to conduct video surveillance under s. 487.01(5). Section 7(3) enacts special jurisdictional rules for commission of this offence outside Canada. A threat to commit an offence under this section is an offence under s. 424.1. The certificate of the Minister of Foreign Affairs is proof of facts relevant to the question of whether any person is a member of United Nations personnel or a member of associated personnel under s. 7(10).

SYNOPSIS

This section describes the offence of violently attacking the official premises, private accommodation or means of transport of a member of United Nations personnel or personnel associated with the United Nations. The attack must be likely to endanger the life or liberty of such a person. The offence is indictable and carries a maximum term of 14 years. This offence is related to s. 424.1.

DEFINITIONS / Explosive or other lethal device / Armed forces.

431.2 (1) The following definitions apply in this section.

"explosive or other lethal device" means

    (*a*) an explosive or incendiary weapon or device that is designed to cause, or is capable of causing, death, serious bodily injury or substantial material damage; or

    (*b*) a weapon or device that is designed to cause, or is capable of causing, death, serious bodily injury or substantial material damage through the release, dissemination or impact of toxic chemicals, biological agents or toxins or similar substances, or radiation or radioactive material.

"infrastructure facility" means a publicly or privately owned facility that provides or distributes services for the benefit of the public, including services relating to water, sewage, energy, fuel and communications.

809

"military forces of a state" means the armed forces that a state organizes, trains and equips in accordance with the law of the state for the primary purpose of national defence or national security, and every person acting in support of those armed forces who is under their formal command, control and responsibility.

"place of public use" means those parts of land, a building, street, waterway or other location that are accessible or open to members of the public, whether on a continuous, periodic or occasional basis, and includes any commercial, business, cultural, historical, educational, religious, governmental, entertainment, recreational or other place that is accessible or open to the public on such a basis.

"public transportation system" means a publicly or privately owned facility, conveyance or other thing that is used in connection with publicly available services for the transportation of persons or cargo.

(2) Every one who delivers, places, discharges or detonates an explosive or other lethal device to, into, in or against a place of public use, a government or public facility, a public transportation system or an infrastructure facility, either with intent to cause death or serious bodily injury or with intent to cause extensive destruction of such a place, system or facility that results in or is likely to result in major economic loss, is guilty of an indictable offence and liable to imprisonment for life.

(3) For greater certainty, subsection (2) does not apply to an act or omission that is committed during an armed conflict and that, at the time and in the place of its commission, is in accordance with customary international law or conventional international law applicable to the conflict, or to activities undertaken by military forces of a state in the exercise of their official duties, to the extent that those activities are governed by other rules of international law. 2001, c. 41, s. 13.

CROSS-REFERENCES

The other offences concerning explosives are found in ss. 79 to 82. Section 7(3.72) enacts special jurisdictional rules for commission of this offence outside Canada. This offence may be the basis for an application for an authorization to intercept private communications by reason of s. 183 and a warrant to conduct video surveillance under s. 487.01(5). "Government or public facility" is defined in s. 2.

SYNOPSIS

Although many of the acts covered by this section would also be covered by the general explosive offences especially under s. 81, this creates a specific offence for delivering, placing, discharging or detonating explosives or other lethal devices in public places, or government or public facilities, or public transportation systems or infrastructure facilities. The acts must be done with the intent to cause death, serious bodily harm or extensive destruction of such place or facility resulting in or likely to result in major economic loss. The maximum penalty for the offence is life imprisonment. There is a saving provision in subsec. (3) for acts carried out in times of war or by military forces of a state.

432. [*Repealed*, R.S.C. 1985, c. 27 (1st Supp.), s. 58 (old provision).]

UNAUTHORIZED RECORDING OF A MOVIE / Unauthorized recording for purpose of sale, etc. / Forfeiture / Forfeiture — limitation.

432. (1) A person who, without the consent of the theatre manager, records in a movie theatre a performance of a cinematographic work within the meaning of section 2 of the *Copyright Act* or its soundtrack
   (*a*) is guilty of an indictable offence and liable to imprisonment for a term of not more than two years; or
   (*b*) is guilty of an offence punishable on summary conviction.

(2) A person who, without the consent of the theatre manager, records in a movie theatre a performance of a cinematographic work within the meaning of section 2 of the *Copyright Act* or its soundtrack for the purpose of the sale, rental or other commercial distribution of a copy of the cinematographic work

    (a) is guilty of an indictable offence and liable to imprisonment for a term of not more than five years; or

    (b) is guilty of an offence punishable on summary conviction.

(3) In addition to any punishment that is imposed on a person who is convicted of an offence under this section, the court may order that anything that is used in the commission of the offence be forfeited to Her Majesty in right of the province in which the proceedings are taken. Anything that is forfeited may be disposed of as the Attorney General directs.

(4) No order may be made under subsection (3) in respect of anything that is the property of a person who is not a party to the offence. 2007, c. 28, s. 1.

CROSS-REFERENCES

"Attorney General" is defined in s. 2. Parties to offences are defined in ss. 21 to 22.2. This offence complements the offence under s. 42 of the *Copyright Act*, R.S.C. 1985, c. C-42, which makes it an offence to record for commercial purposes *e.g.* for sale or rental or distribution of copyright works. This section relies on the definitions in the *Copyright Act* for "cinematographic work" and "performance", which are as follows:

"cinematographic work" includes any work expressed by any process analogous to cinematography, whether or not accompanied by a soundtrack;

"performance" means any acoustic or visual representation of a work, performer's performance, sound recording or communication signal, including a representation made by means of any mechanical instrument, radio receiving set or television receiving set;

SYNOPSIS

This section creates two offences. Subsection (1) simply makes it an offence to record a performance in a movie theatre without the manager's consent. The Crown need not prove that the person had a commercial purpose. Subsection (2) overlaps with the offence under the *Copyright Act* and similarly makes it an offence to record without the consent of the theatre manager for purposes of sale, rental or other commercial distribution. Subsection (3) permits the sentencing court to order forfeiture of the equipment used in the commission of the offence. However, by virtue of subsec. (4), no order for forfeiture may be made in respect of anything that is the property of a person who is not a party to the offence.

Arson and Other Fires

ARSON / Disregard for human life.

433. Every person who intentionally or recklessly causes damage by fire or explosion to property, whether or not that person owns the property, is guilty of an indictable offence and liable to imprisonment for life where

    (a) the person knows that or is reckless with respect to whether the property is inhabited or occupied; or

    (b) the fire or explosion causes bodily harm to another person. R.S., c. C-34, s. 389; 1990, c. 15, s. 1.

CROSS-REFERENCES

The term "bodily harm" is defined in s. 2. The term "property" is defined in s. 428. The term "recklessly" is not defined, but reference might be made to *R. v. Sansregret*, [1985] 1 S.C.R. 570,

18 C.C.C. (3d) 223, where recklessness was defined as being found "in the attitude of one who, aware that there is danger that his conduct could bring about the result prohibited by the criminal law, nevertheless persists, despite the risk. It is, in other words, the conduct of one who sees the risk and who takes the chance." The defence of legal justification or excuse and colour of right is set out in s. 429(2).

This offence may be the basis for an application for an authorization to intercept private communications by reason of s. 183 and a warrant to conduct video surveillance under s. 487.01. Arson is an enterprise crime offence for the purposes of Part XII.2.

Section 17 limits the availability of the statutory defence of compulsion by threats to the offence of "arson".

The accused may elect this mode of trial pursuant to s. 536(2). Release pending trial is determined by s. 515.

Related offences: s. 81, using explosives; s. 434, intentionally or recklessly causing damage by fire or explosion to property not wholly owned by accused; s. 434.1, intentionally or recklessly causing damage by fire or explosion to property wholly owned by accused; s. 435, causing damage by fire or explosion with intent to defraud; s. 436, causing fire or explosion through negligence; s. 436.1, possession of incendiary material.

SYNOPSIS

The section creates the offence of *intentionally* or *recklessly* causing *damage to property* by fire or explosion. It must be shown either that: (1) the accused knew, or was reckless as to whether or not the property was inhabited or occupied; or (2) bodily harm to another person resulted from the fire or explosion. It is irrelevant whether or not the accused owns the property. This is an indictable offence carrying a maximum sentence of life imprisonment.

ANNOTATIONS

The offence contrary to s. 434 is not included in the offence of arson as described in this section. The offence of mischief under s. 430 is, however, an included offence: *R. v. Pascal* (1994), 90 C.C.C. (3d) 575 (Man. C.A.).

Recklessness requires proof that the accused actually knew that damage by fire to the property specified was the probable consequence of the proposed action and the accused proceeded with the conduct in the face of the risk. In this case, proof of the intentional burning of a bag of chips, without knowledge of the probable consequence that the building would burn, was insufficient to establish the requisite *mens rea*: *R. v. D. (S.D.)* (2002), 164 C.C.C. (3d) 1 (Nfld. & Lab. C.A.).

ARSON / Damage to property.

434. Every person who intentionally or recklessly causes damage by fire or explosion to property that is not wholly owned by that person is guilty of an indictable offence and liable to imprisonment for a term not exceeding fourteen years. R.S., c. C-34, s. 390; 1990, c. 15, s. 1.

CROSS-REFERENCES

The term "property" is defined in s. 428. The term "recklessly" is not defined but reference might be made to *R. v. Sansregret*, [1985] 1 S.C.R. 570, 18 C.C.C. (3d) 223, where recklessness was defined as being found "in the attitude of one who, aware that there is danger that his conduct could bring about the result prohibited by the criminal law, nevertheless persists, despite the risk. It is, in other words, the conduct of one who sees the risk and who takes the chance." The defence of legal justification or excuse and colour of right is set out in s. 429(2).

This offence may be the basis for a conviction for constructive murder under s. 230.

Section 17 limits the availability of the statutory defence of compulsion by threats to the offence of "arson".

The accused may elect his mode of trial under s. 536(2). Release pending trial is determined under s. 515.

Related offences: s. 81, using explosives; s. 433, intentionally or recklessly causing damage by fire or explosion to property where bodily harm is caused or where person knows property is occupied; s. 434.1, intentionally or recklessly causing damage by fire or explosion to property wholly owned by accused; s. 435, causing damage by fire or explosion with intent to defraud; s. 436, causing fire or explosion through negligence; s. 436.1, possession of incendiary material.

SYNOPSIS

The section creates the offence of willfully or recklessly causing damage by fire or explosion to property that the accused does not wholly own. This is an indictable offence carrying a maximum sentence of 14 years.

ANNOTATIONS

This is a general intent offence for which intoxication falling short of automatism is not available as a defence. The *actus reus* is the damaging of property by fire. The mental element is the intentional or reckless performance of the illegal act. No additional knowledge or purpose is needed. In assessing the issue of intent, the trier of fact must consider all of the surrounding circumstances. The manner in which the fire started is likely to be an important consideration. Ultimately, the question is whether it can be inferred that the accused intended to damage someone else's property or was reckless whether damage ensued or not: *R. v. Tatton*, [2015] 2 S.C.R. 574, 323 C.C.C. (3d) 166.

The term "damage" does not require proof that the property was diminished in value by the fire. Damage may include physical harm to the property: *R. v. V. (M.)* (1998), 123 C.C.C. (3d) 138 (Ont. C.A.).

Recklessness requires proof that the accused actually knew that damage by fire to the property specified was the probable consequence of the proposed action and the accused proceeded with the conduct in the face of the risk. In this case, proof of intentional burning of a bag of chips, without knowledge of the probable consequence that the building would burn, was insufficient to establish the requisite *mens rea*: *R. v. D. (S.D.)* (2002), 164 C.C.C. (3d) 1 (Nfld. & Lab. C.A.).

ARSON / Own property.

434.1 Every person who intentionally or recklessly causes damage by fire or explosion to property that is owned, in whole or in part, by that person is guilty of an indictable offence and liable to imprisonment for a term not exceeding fourteen years, where the fire or explosion seriously threatens the health, safety or property of another person. 1990, c. 15, s. 1.

CROSS-REFERENCES

The term "property" is defined in s. 428. The term "recklessly" is not defined but reference might be made to *R. v. Sansregret*, [1985] 1 S.C.R. 570, 18 C.C.C. (3d) 223, where recklessness was defined as being found "in the attitude of one who, aware that there is danger that his conduct could bring about the result prohibited by the criminal law, nevertheless persists, despite the risk. It is, in other words, the conduct of one who sees the risk and who takes the chance." The defence of legal justification or excuse and colour of right is set out in s. 429(2).

Section 17 limits the availability of the statutory defence of compulsion by threats to the offence of "arson".

The accused may elect his mode of trial under s. 536(2). Release pending trial is determined under s. 515.

Related offences: s. 81, using explosives; s. 433, intentionally or recklessly causing damage by fire or explosion to property where bodily harm is caused or where person knows property is occupied; s. 434, intentionally or recklessly causing damage by fire or explosion to property not wholly owned by accused; s. 435, causing damage by fire or explosion with intent to defraud; s. 436, causing fire or explosion through negligence; s. 436.1, possession of incendiary material.

SYNOPSIS

The section creates the offence of willfully or recklessly causing damage by fire or explosion to property owned, in whole or in part, by the accused, where the fire or explosion *seriously threatens* the health, safety or property of *another person*. This is an indictable offence carrying a maximum sentence of 14 years.

ARSON FOR FRAUDULENT PURPOSE / Holder or beneficiary of fire insurance policy.

435. (1) Every person who, with intent to defraud any other person, causes damage by fire or explosion to property, whether or not that person owns, in whole or in part, the property, is guilty of an indictable offence and liable to imprisonment for a term not exceeding ten years.

(2) Where a person is charged with an offence under subsection (1), the fact that the person was the holder of or was named as a beneficiary under a policy of fire insurance relating to the property in respect of which the offence is alleged to have been committed is a fact from which intent to defraud may be inferred by the court. R.S., c. C-34, s. 391; 1990, c. 15, s. 1.

CROSS-REFERENCES

The term "property" is defined in s. 428. Section 17 limits the availability of the statutory defence of compulsion by threats to the offence of "arson". The accused may elect his mode of trial under s. 536(2). Release pending trial is determined under s. 515.

Related offences: s. 81, using explosives; s. 433, intentionally or recklessly causing damage by fire or explosion to property where bodily harm is caused or where person knows property is occupied; s. 434, intentionally or recklessly causing damage by fire or explosion to property not wholly owned by accused; s. 434.1, intentionally or recklessly causing damage by fire or explosion to property wholly owned by accused; s. 436, causing fire or explosion through negligence; s. 436.1, possession of incendiary material.

SYNOPSIS

The section creates the offence of causing damage to property by fire or explosion with the *intent to defraud* another person. It is irrelevent whether or not the accused owns the property, in whole or in part. By subsec. (2), a court may *infer intention* to defraud from the fact that the accused is the holder of, or named beneficiary under, a policy of fire insurance in respect of damaged property. This is an indictable offence carrying a maximum sentence of 10 years.

ANNOTATIONS

Application of inference – It was held in relation to former s. 435 that the presumption did not apply where the accused were insured only in respect to loss of personal property within the burned premises: *R. v. Drouin and Drouin*, [1973] S.C.R. 747, 10 C.C.C. (2d) 381.

ARSON BY NEGLIGENCE / Non-compliance with prevention laws.

436. (1) Every person who owns, in whole or in part, or controls property is guilty of an indictable offence and liable to imprisonment for a term not exceeding five years where, as a result of a marked departure from the standard of care that a reasonably prudent person would use to prevent or control the spread of fires or to prevent explosions, that person is a cause of a fire or explosion in that property that causes bodily harm to another person or damage to property.

(2) Where a person is charged with an offence under subsection (1), the fact that the person has failed to comply with any law respecting the prevention or control of fires or explosions in the property is a fact from which a marked departure from the standard of care referred to in that subsection may be inferred by the court. R.S., c. C-34, s. 392; 1990, c. 15, s. 1.

CROSS-REFERENCES

The term "bodily harm" is defined in s. 2. The term "property" is defined in s. 428. The defence of legal justification or excuse and colour of right is set out in s. 429(2). The standard of liability in this section resembles the test adopted for the criminal negligence offences in ss. 220 and 221. Thus, see notes under those sections and s. 219.

Section 17 limits the availability of the statutory defence of compulsion by threats to the offence of "arson".

The accused may elect his mode of trial pursuant to s. 536(2). Release pending trial is determined by s. 515.

Related offences; s. 81, using explosives; s. 434, intentionally or recklessly causing damage by fire or explosion to property not wholly owned by accused; s. 434.1, intentionally or recklessly causing damage by fire or explosion to property wholly owned by accused; s. 435, causing damage by fire or explosion with intent to defraud; s. 436.1, possession of incendiary material.

SYNOPSIS

The section creates the offence of being a cause of any fire or explosion in a *property owned, in whole or in part, or controlled* by the accused where: (1) a marked departure from the standard of care that a reasonably prudent person would use, to prevent or control the spread of fires or to prevent explosions, is shown to be the cause of the fire or explosion; and (2) the fire or explosion resulted in bodily harm to another person, or damage to property. By subsec. (2), a court may *infer marked departure* from the subsec. (1) standard of care, from the fact that the accused has *failed to comply* with any law respecting the prevention or control of fires or explosions in the property. This is an indictable offence carrying a maximum sentence of five years.

ANNOTATIONS

This provision imposes a duty to prevent or control the spread of fires and thus an accused may be convicted under this section even if the fire may have originally been caused by an agency other than that of the accused. The section does, however, require proof of a causal connection between the accused's breach of duty, the resulting spread of the fire, and the injury or damage: *R. v. Harricharan* (1995), 98 C.C.C. (3d) 145, 23 O.R. (3d) 233 (C.A.).

POSSESSION OF INCENDIARY MATERIAL.

436.1 Every person who possesses any incendiary material, incendiary device or explosive substance for the purpose of committing an offence under any of sections 433 to 436 is guilty of an indictable offence and liable to imprisonment for a term not exceeding five years. 1990, c. 15, s. 1.

CROSS-REFERENCES

Possession is defined in s. 4(3). For definition of "explosive substance", see s. 2. The accused may elect his mode of trial pursuant to s. 536(2). Release pending trial is determined by s. 515.

Related offences: s. 81, using explosives; s. 82, possession of explosive substance without lawful excuse; s. 434, intentionally or recklessly causing damage by fire or explosion to property not wholly owned by accused; s. 434.1, intentionally or recklessly causing damage by fire or explosion to property wholly owned by accused; s. 435, causing damage by fire or explosion with intent to defraud; s. 436, causing fire or explosion through negligence.

SYNOPSIS

The section creates the offence of *possessing* any incendiary material or device, or explosive substance for the purpose of committing a ss. 433 to 436 offence. This is an indictable offence carrying a maximum term of five years.

Other Interference with Property

FALSE ALARM OF FIRE.

437. Every one who wilfully, without reasonable cause, by outcry, ringing bells, using a fire alarm, telephone or telegraph, or in any other manner, makes or circulates or causes to be made or circulated an alarm of fire is guilty of

   (*a*) **an indictable offence and liable to imprisonment for a term not exceeding two years; or**

   (*b*) **an offence punishable on summary conviction. R.S., c. C-34, s. 393; 1972, c. 13, s. 31.**

CROSS-REFERENCES

The term "wilfully" is defined in s. 429(1). The defence of legal justification or excuse and colour of right is set out in s. 429(2).

Where the prosecution elects to proceed by indictment on this offence then the accused may elect his mode of trial pursuant to s. 536(2). Where the prosecution elects to proceed by way of summary conviction then the trial of this offence is conducted by a summary conviction court pursuant to Part XXVII. The limitation period is set out in s. 786(2). In either case, release pending trial is determined by s. 515, although the accused is eligible for release by a peace officer under ss. 496, 497 or by the officer in charge under s. 498.

SYNOPSIS

This section describes the offence of raising a false alarm of fire. Every person who *wilfully* and *without reasonable cause* makes or circulates, or causes to be made or circulated, an alarm of fire is guilty of an offence punishable on summary conviction or by indictment. A person convicted of the indictable offence is liable to a maximum term of two years' imprisonment.

INTERFERING WITH SAVING OF WRECKED VESSEL / Interfering with saving of wreck.

438. (1) Every one who wilfully prevents or impedes, or who wilfully endeavours to prevent or impede,

   (*a*) **the saving of a vessel that is wrecked, stranded, abandoned or in distress, or**

   (*b*) **a person who attempts to save a vessel that is wrecked, stranded, abandoned or in distress,**

is guilty of an indictable offence and liable to imprisonment for a term not exceeding five years.

(2) Every one who wilfully prevents or impedes or wilfully endeavours to prevent or impede the saving of wreck is guilty of an offence punishable on summary conviction. R.S., c. C-34, s. 394.

CROSS-REFERENCES

The term "wreck" is defined in s. 2. The term "wilfully" is defined in s. 429(1). The defence of legal justification or excuse and colour of right is set out in s. 429(2).

For the offence under subsec. (1), the accused may elect his mode of trial under s. 536(2). Release pending trial is determined under s. 515, although the accused is eligible for release by the officer in charge under s. 498.

Trial of the offence under subsec. (2) is conducted by a summary conviction court pursuant to Part XXVII. The punishment is as set out in s. 787 and the limitation period is set out in s. 786(2). Release pending trial is determined by s. 515, although the accused is eligible for release by a peace officer under s. 496, 497 or by the officer in charge under s. 498. Other offences in relation to wreck are in s. 415 and see cross-references under that section.

SYNOPSIS

This section describes the offence of interfering with the saving of a wrecked vessel. Any person who *wilfully* prevents or impedes, or who *wilfully* endeavours to prevent or impede the saving of a vessel that is wrecked, stranded, abandoned or in distress is guilty of an indictable offence and liable to a maximum term of five years. Subsection (2) makes it a summary conviction offence to *wilfully* prevent or impede the saving of wreck.

INTERFERING WITH MARINE SIGNAL, ETC. / Idem.

439. (1) Every one who makes fast a vessel or boat to a signal, buoy or other sea-mark that is used for purposes of navigation is guilty of an offence punishable on summary conviction.

(2) Every one who wilfully alters, removes or conceals a signal, buoy or other sea-mark that is used for purposes of navigation is guilty of an indictable offence and liable to imprisonment for a term not exceeding ten years. R.S., c. C-34, s. 395.

CROSS-REFERENCES

The term "wilfully" is defined in s. 429(1). The defence of legal justification or excuse and colour of right is set out in s. 429(2).

Trial of the offence under subsec. (1) is conducted by a summary conviction court pursuant to Part XXVII. The punishment is as set out in s. 787 and the limitation period is set out in s. 786(2). Release pending trial is determined by s. 515, although the accused is eligible for release by a peace officer under s. 496, 497 or by the officer in charge under s. 498.

For the offence under subsec. (2), the accused may elect his mode of trial under s. 536(2). Release pending trial is determined under s. 515.

The more serious offence of destroying or causing serious damage to or interfering with the operation of any maritime navigational facility where the act is likely to endanger the safe navigation of a ship or the safety of a fixed platform is found in s. 78.1(2)(*c*).

SYNOPSIS

This section describes the offence of interfering with a marine signal. The summary conviction offence is committed by fastening a boat or vessel to a sea-mark used for navigation. A person who *wilfully* alters, removes or conceals a sea-mark that is used for navigation is guilty of the indictable form of the offence and is liable upon conviction to a maximum term of 10 years' imprisonment.

REMOVING NATURAL BAR WITHOUT PERMISSION.

440. Every one who wilfully and without the written permission of the Minister of Transport, the burden of proof of which lies on the accused, removes any stone, wood, earth or other material that forms a natural bar necessary to the existence of a public harbour, or that forms a natural protection to such a bar, is guilty of an indictable offence and liable to imprisonment for a term not exceeding two years. R.S., c. C-34, s. 396.

CROSS-REFERENCES

The term "wilfully" is defined in s. 429(1). The defence of legal justification or excuse and colour of right is set out in s. 429(2).

The accused may elect his mode of trial under s. 536(2). Release pending trial is determined under s. 515 although the accused is eligible for release by the officer in charge under s. 498.

SYNOPSIS

This section describes the indictable offence of removing any material that forms, or is protection to a natural bar necessary to the existence of a public harbour. The accused must act *wilfully* and *without the written permission* of the Minister of Transport, the proof of which lies upon him.

OCCUPANT INJURING BUILDING.

441. Every one who, wilfully and to the prejudice of a mortgagee or owner, pulls down, demolishes or removes, all or any part of a dwelling-house or other building of which he is in possession or occupation, or severs from the freehold any fixture fixed therein or thereto, is guilty of an indictable offence and liable to imprisonment for a term not exceeding five years. R.S., c. C-34, s. 397.

CROSS-REFERENCES

The term "wilfully" is defined in s. 429(1). The term "dwelling-house" is defined in s. 2. The defence of legal justification or excuse and colour of right is set out in s. 429(2). Where the accused has an interest in the thing destroyed see s. 429(3). The accused may elect his mode of trial under s. 536(2). Release pending trial is determined under s. 515 although the accused is eligible for release by the officer in charge under s. 498.

SYNOPSIS

In this section, an occupant of a dwelling-house or other building commits an indictable offence if he *wilfully* and *to the prejudice* of a mortgagee or owner demolishes or removes any part of the building or severs from the freehold any fixture. The maximum term of imprisonment upon conviction is five years.

ANNOTATIONS

The offence under this section is complete when any of the specified acts, done with the requisite intent, negatively affect the security interest of the mortgagee. The interest of the mortgagee may still be inchoate before any steps have been taken by the mortgagee to realize on its security: *R. v. Lundgard* (1991), 63 C.C.C. (3d) 368, [1991] 4 W.W.R. 259 (Alta. C.A.).

INTERFERING WITH BOUNDARY LINES.

442. Every one who wilfully pulls down, defaces, alters or removes anything planted or set up as the boundary line or part of the boundary line of land is guilty of an offence punishable on summary conviction. R.S., c. C-34, s. 398.

CROSS-REFERENCES

The term "wilfully" is defined in s. 429(1). The defence of legal justification or excuse and colour of right is set out in s. 429(2).

The related offence of interfering with boundary marks is in s. 443.

Trial of this offence is conducted by a summary conviction court pursuant to Part XXVII. The punishment is as set out in s. 787 and the limitation period is set out in s. 786(2). Release pending trial is determined by s. 515 although the accused is eligible for release by a peace officer under ss. 496, 497, or by the officer in charge under s. 498.

SYNOPSIS

This section describes the summary conviction offence of interfering with a boundary line. A person who *wilfully* defaces, alters or removes anything that forms a part of a boundary line is guilty of an offence under this section.

INTERFERING WITH INTERNATIONAL BOUNDARY MARKS, ETC. / Saving provision.

443. (1) Every one who wilfully pulls down, defaces, alters or removes

    (*a*) a boundary mark lawfully placed to mark any international, provincial, county or municipal boundary, or

    (*b*) a boundary mark lawfully placed by a land surveyor to mark a limit, boundary or angle of a concession, range, lot or parcel of land,

is guilty of an indictable offence and liable to imprisonment for a term not exceeding five years.

(2) A land surveyor does not commit an offence under subsection (1) where, in his operations as a land surveyor,

    (*a*) he takes up, when necessary, a boundary mark mentioned in paragraph (1)(*b*) and carefully replaces it as it was before he took it up; or

    (*b*) he takes up a boundary mark mentioned in paragraph (1)(*b*) in the course of surveying for a highway or other work that, when completed, will make it impossible or impracticable for that boundary mark to occupy its original position, and he establishes a permanent record of the original position sufficient to permit such position to be ascertained. R.S., c. C-34, s. 399.

CROSS-REFERENCES

The term "wilfully" is defined in s. 429(1). The terms "county" and "province" are defined in s. 35 of the *Interpretation Act*, R.S.C. 1985, c. I-21. The defence of legal justification or excuse and colour of right is set out in s. 429(2). Section 476 enacts special rules of territorial jurisdiction where an offence is committed on the boundary between territorial divisions.

The accused may elect his mode of trial under s. 536(2). Release pending trial is determined under s. 515 although the accused is eligible for release by the officer in charge under s. 498.

The related summary conviction offence of interfering with boundary lines is in s. 442.

SYNOPSIS

This section describes the offence of interfering with international and other boundary marks. Any person who *wilfully* defaces, alters or removes a boundary mark lawfully placed to mark an international, provincial, county or municipal boundary, or a boundary mark lawfully placed by a land surveyor, is guilty of an indictable offence and subject to a maximum term of five years' imprisonment. Subsection (2) describes specific circumstances in which a land surveyor who takes up boundary marks is not criminally liable under this section.

Cattle and Other Animals

INJURING OR ENDANGERING CATTLE / Punishment.

444. (1) Every one commits an offence who willfully

    (*a*) kills, maims, wounds, poisons or injures cattle; or

    (*b*) places poison in such a position that it may easily be consumed by cattle.

(2) Every one who commits an offence under subsection (1) is guilty of

    (*a*) an indictable offence and liable to imprisonment for a term of not more than five years; or (*b*) **an offence punishable on summary conviction and liable to a fine not exceeding ten thousand dollars or to imprisonment for a term of not more than eighteen months or to both. R.S., c. C-34, s. 400; 2008, c. 12, s. 1.**

CROSS-REFERENCES
The term "wilfully" is defined in s. 429(1). The term "cattle" is defined in s. 2. The defence of legal justification or excuse and colour of right is set out in s. 429(2).

The related offence of injuring animals other than cattle is in s. 445. Other offences in relation to animals are set out in ss. 446 and 447.

In addition to any other sentence, the court may make an order under s. 447.1(1)(*a*) prohibiting the accused from owning, having the custody or control of or residing in the same premises as an animal or a bird during any period that the court considers appropriate but, in the case of a second or subsequent offence, for a minimum of five years. Further, under s. 447.1(1)(*b*), the court may order that the accused pay reasonable costs to a person or an organization that has taken care of an animal or a bird as a result of the commission of the offence, provided the costs are readily ascertainable.

SYNOPSIS
This section describes the offence of injuring or endangering cattle. Any person who *wilfully* kills, maims, wounds, injures, or poisons cattle, or places poison in a position that might allow it to be *easily* consumed by cattle commits an indictable offence.

ANNOTATIONS
"Heifer" is included in the word "cattle": *R. v. Allen* (1974), 17 C.C.C. (2d) 549, 8 N.B.R. (2d) 131 (S.C. App. Div.).

This section covers the killing of stray cattle not shown to have been owned by anyone: *R. v. Brown* (1984), 11 C.C.C. (3d) 191 (B.C.C.A.).

The expanded definition of "wilfully" in s. 429(1) applies to this offence and "wilfully" in this section is not simply limited to an "evil intent": *R. v. Dupont* (1976), 22 N.R. at p. 519 (Alta. S.C. App. Div.), affd [1978] 1 S.C.R. 1017, 11 A.R. 148.

INJURING OR ENDANGERING OTHER ANIMALS / Punishment.

445. (1) Every one commits an offence who, wilfully and without lawful excuse,
(*a*) **kills, maims, wounds, poisons or injures dogs, birds or animals that are not cattle and are kept for a lawful purpose; or**
(*b*) **places poison in such a position that it may easily be consumed by dogs, birds or animals that are not cattle and are kept for a lawful purpose.**

(2) Every one who commits an offence under subsection (1) is guilty of
(*a*) **an indictable offence and liable to imprisonment for a term of not more than five years; or**
(*b*) **an offence punishable on summary conviction and liable to a fine not exceeding ten thousand dollars or to imprisonment for a term of not more than eighteen months or to both. R.S., c. C-34, s. 401, 2008, c. 12, s. 1.**

CROSS-REFERENCES
The term "wilfully" is defined in s. 429(1). The term "cattle" is defined in s. 2. The defence of legal justification or excuse and colour of right is set out in s. 429(2).

The related offence of injuring cattle is in s. 444. Other offences in relation to animals are set out in ss. 445.1 and 447.

In addition to any other sentence, the court may make an order under s. 447.1(1)(*a*) prohibiting the accused from owning, having the custody or control of or residing in the same premises as an animal or a bird during any period that the court considers appropriate but, in the case of a second or subsequent offence, for a minimum of five years. Further, under s. 447.1(1)(*b*), the court may order that the accused pay reasonable costs to a person or an organization that has taken care of an animal or a bird as a result of the commission of the offence, provided the costs are readily ascertainable.

SYNOPSIS

This section describes the offence of injuring or endangering animals other than cattle. Any person who *wilfully and without lawful excuse* kills, maims, wounds, injures or poisons dogs, birds or animals other than cattle that are kept for a lawful purpose or who places poison in a position that it might be easily consumed by those creatures, is guilty of a summary conviction offence.

ANNOTATIONS

These provisions are designed to protect domesticated or domestic animals and do not apply to stray animals, the words "kept for a lawful purpose" contemplating a keeper of the animal and a measure of control exercised by that person: *R. v. Deschamps* (1978), 43 C.C.C. (2d) 45 (Ont. Prov. Ct.).

Once the dog that the defendant believed had been worrying his sheep had left the scene and was no longer a danger he had no justification for wounding it: *R. v. Etherington,* [1963] 2 C.C.C. 230 (Ont. Mag. Ct.).

An accused would have a defence to a charge under this section involving the injury to a police service dog where the use of the dog in the circumstances constituted excessive use of force: *R. v. Barr* (1982), 1 C.C.C. (3d) 47 (Alta. Prov. Ct.).

KILLING OR INJURING CERTAIN ANIMALS / Punishment / Sentences to be served consecutively / Definitions.

445.01 (1) Every one commits an offence who, wilfully and without lawful excuse, kills, maims, wounds, poisons or injures a law enforcement animal while it is aiding a law enforcement officer in carrying out that officer's duties, a military animal while it is aiding a member of the Canadian Forces in carrying out that member's duties or a service animal.

(2) Every one who commits an offence under subsection (1) is guilty of

> **(*a*) an indictable offence and liable to imprisonment for a term of not more than five years and, if a law enforcement animal is killed in the commission of the offence, to a minimum punishment of imprisonment for a term of six months; or**

> **(*b*) an offence punishable on summary conviction and liable to a fine of not more than $10,000 or to imprisonment for a term of not more than 18 months or to both.**

(3) A sentence imposed on a person for an offence under subsection (1) committed against a law enforcement animal shall be served consecutively to any other punishment imposed on the person for an offence arising out of the same event or series of events.

(4) The following definitions apply in this section.

"law enforcement animal" means a dog or horse that is trained to aid a law enforcement officer in carrying out that officer's duties.

"law enforcement officer" means a police officer, a police constable or any person referred to in paragraph (*b*), (*c.1*), (*d*), (*d.1*), (*e*) or (*g*) of the definition "peace officer" in section 2.

"military animal" means an animal that is trained to aid a member of the Canadian Forces in carrying out that member's duties.

"service animal" means an animal that is required by a person with a disability for assistance and is certified, in writing, as having been trained by a professional service animal institution to assist a person with a disability. 2015, c. 34, s. 3.

CROSS-REFERENCES

The term "wilfully" is defined in s. 429(1). The defence of legal justification or excuse and colour of right is set out in s. 429(2). Section 718.03 provides that, when imposing a sentence for an offence under s. 445.01(1), the primary considerations are denunciation and deterrence.

SYNOPSIS

This section creates the hybrid offence of injuring or endangering law enforcement or military animals that are assisting officers or members in their duties, or service animals.

Cruelty to Animals

CAUSING UNNECESSARY SUFFERING / Punishment / Failure to exercise reasonable care as evidence / Presence at baiting as evidence.

445.1 (1) Every one commits an offence who

- (*a*) wilfully causes or, being the owner, wilfully permits to be caused unnecessary pain, suffering or injury to an animal or a bird;
- (*b*) in any manner encourages, aids or assists at the fighting or baiting of animals or birds;
- (*c*) wilfully, without reasonable excuse, administers a poisonous or an injurious drug or substance to a domestic animal or bird or an animal or a bird wild by nature that is kept in captivity or, being the owner of such an animal or a bird, wilfully permits a poisonous or an injurious drug or substance to be administered to it;
- (*d*) promotes, arranges, conducts, assists in, receives money for or takes part in any meeting, competition, exhibition, pastime, practice, display or event at or in the course of which captive birds are liberated by hand, trap, contrivance or any other means for the purpose of being shot when they are liberated; or
- (*e*) being the owner, occupier or person in charge of any premises, permits the premises or any part thereof to be used for a purpose mentioned in paragraph (*d*).

(2) Every one who commits an offence under subsection (1) is guilty of

- (*a*) an indictable offence and liable to imprisonment for a term of not more than five years; or
- (*b*) an offence punishable on summary conviction and liable to a fine not exceeding ten thousand dollars or to imprisonment for a term of not more than eighteen months or to both.

(3) For the purposes of proceedings under paragraph (1)(*a*), evidence that a person failed to exercise reasonable care or supervision of an animal or a bird thereby causing it pain, suffering or injury is, in the absence of any evidence to the contrary, proof that the pain, suffering or injury was caused or was permitted to be caused wilfully, as the case may be.

(4) For the purpose of proceedings under paragraph (1)(*b*), evidence that an accused was present at the fighting or baiting of animals or birds is, in the absence of any evidence to the contrary, proof that he or she encouraged, aided or assisted at the fighting or baiting. 2008, c. 12, s. 1.

CROSS-REFERENCES

"Wilfully" is defined in s. 429(1). Sections 444 and 445 create offences dealing with killing or endangering animals. Section 446 creates offences relating to the damaging or injuring of animals and birds while they are being driven or conveyed, or abandoning animals and birds. In addition to any other sentence, the court may make an order under s. 447.1(1)(*a*) prohibiting the accused from owning, having the custody or control of or residing in the same premises as an animal or a bird during any period that the court considers appropriate but, in the case of a second or subsequent offence, for a minimum of five years. Further, under s. 447.1(1)(*b*), the court may order that the accused pay reasonable costs to a person or an organization that has taken care of an animal or a bird as a result of the commission of the offence, provided the costs are readily ascertainable.

SYNOPSIS

This section is one of three dealing with cruelty to animals. Subsection (1) sets out a number of ways in which the offence is committed, including causing unnecessary cruelty, encouraging fighting or baiting animals or birds, administering poison or injurious drugs without reasonable excuse, and promoting meetings and similar pastimes where captive birds are liberated for the purpose of being shot. Subsections (3) and (4) create presumptions to aid in the prosecution of the offences.

ANNOTATIONS

Note: Some of the cases noted below were decided before the recent amendments but were thought to still be of assistance.

Subsection (1)(*a*) – "Unnecessary" in this context means that man in the pursuit of his legitimate purposes is obliged not to inflict pain, suffering or injury which is not inevitable taking into account the purpose sought and the circumstances of the particular case. Thus while euthanasia of stray animals is itself justified, where the method used by the accused causes pain and suffering which was not inevitable in view of alternative economically feasible methods available, the accused should be convicted: *R. v. Menard* (1978), 43 C.C.C. (2d) 458 (Que. C.A.).

Determining whether there is an absence of reasonable care or supervision is an objective exercise. In the absence of any evidence to the contrary, evidence that a person failed to exercise reasonable care is proof of wilfulness for the purposes of subsec. (1)(*a*). Where there is evidence to the contrary, the Crown must prove willful conduct and s. 429(1), which engages the subjective element of recklessness, applies: *R. v. Gerling*, [2016] B.C.J. No. 264 (C.A.).

Subsection (1)(*b*) – In *Pitts v. Miller* (1874), L.R. 9, Q.B. 380 (Q.B.), Cockburn C.J. considered baiting in terms of an animal either tied to a stake or unable to escape, and Quain J. relied upon dictionary definitions of attacking with violence or harassing with the help of others.

Subsection (1)(*d*) – The mischief sought to be prevented in this paragraph is cruelty to birds by their sudden release for the purpose of being shot at: *R. v. Prefontaine* (1973), 26 C.R.N.S. 367 (Que. C.A.).

CAUSING DAMAGE OR INJURY / Punishment / Failure to exercise reasonable care as evidence.

446. (1) Every one commits an offence who

    (*a*) **by wilful neglect causes damage or injury to animals or birds while they are being driven or conveyed; or**

    (*b*) **being the owner or the person having the custody or control of a domestic animal or a bird or an animal or a bird wild by nature that is in captivity,** abandons it in distress or wilfully neglects or fails to provide suitable and adequate food, water, shelter and care for it.

(2) Every one who commits an offence under subsection (1) is guilty of

    (a) an indictable offence and liable to imprisonment for a term of not more than two years; or

    (b) an offence punishable on summary conviction and liable to a fine not exceeding five thousand dollars or to imprisonment for a term of not more than six months or to both.

(3) For the purposes of proceedings under paragraph (1)(*a*), evidence that a person failed to exercise reasonable care or supervision of an animal or a bird thereby causing it damage or injury is, in the absence of any evidence to the contrary, proof that the damage or injury was caused by willful neglect. R.S., c. C-34, s. 402; 1974-75-76, c. 93, s. 35; 2008, c. 12, s. 1.

CROSS-REFERENCES

"Wilfully" is defined in s. 429(1). Sections 444 and 445 create offences dealing with killing or endangering animals. Section 445 creates offences relating to the causing of unnecessary suffering to animals or birds. In addition to any other sentence, the court may make an order under s. 447.1(1)(*a*) prohibiting the accused from owning, having the custody or control of or residing in the same premises as an animal or a bird during any period that the court considers appropriate but, in the case of a second or subsequent offence, for a minimum of five years. Further, under s. 447.1(1)(*b*), the court may order that the accused pay reasonable costs to a person or an organization that has taken care of an animal or a bird as a result of the commission of the offence, provided the costs are readily ascertainable.

SYNOPSIS

This section creates offences in the nature of wilful neglect of animals and birds in (a) the conveying of them, and (b) the abandoning of them. Subsection (3) creates a presumption to assist in the prosecution of the offence under subsec. (1)(*a*) arising out of the failure to exercise reasonable care or supervision.

KEEPING COCKPIT / Punishment / Confiscation.

447. (1) Every one commits an offence who builds, makes, maintains or keeps a cockpit on premises that he or she owns or occupies, or allows a cockpit to be built, made, maintained or kept on such premises.

(2) Every one who commits an offence under subsection (1) is guilty of

    (a) an indictable offence and liable to imprisonment for a term of not more than five years; or

    (b) an offence punishable on summary conviction and liable to a fine not exceeding ten thousand dollars or to imprisonment for a term of not more than eighteen months or to both.

(3) A peace officer who finds cocks in a cockpit or on premises where a cockpit is located shall seize them and take them before a justice who shall order them to be destroyed. R.S., c. C-34, s. 403; 2008, c. 12, s. 1.

CROSS-REFERENCES

The term "peace officer" is defined in s. 2. This offence applies to a person who may be described as the keeper of the cockpit. The offence, if any, committed by another person is described in s. 445.1(1)(*d*).

   In addition to any other sentence, the court may make an order under s. 447.1(1)(*a*) prohibiting the accused from owning, having the custody or control of or residing in the same premises as an animal or a bird during any period that the court considers appropriate but, in the case of a second or subsequent offence, for a minimum of five years. Further, under s. 447.1(1)(*b*), the court may order that the accused pay reasonable costs to a person or an organization that has taken care of an animal or a bird as a result of the commission of the offence, provided the costs are readily ascertainable.

SYNOPSIS

This section makes it an offence for a person to build or maintain, or to allow to be built or maintained, a cockpit on premises which that person owns or occupies. Subsection (3) empowers a peace officer who finds cocks in a cockpit, or on premises where there is a cockpit, to seize the birds and take them before a justice, who must order them destroyed.

ORDER OF PROHIBITION OR RESTITUTION / Breach of order / Application.

447.1 (1) The court may, in addition to any other sentence that it may impose under subsection 444(2), 445(2), 445.1(2), 446(2) or 447(2),

    (*a*) **make an order prohibiting the accused from owning, having the custody or control of or residing in the same premises as an animal or a bird during any period that the court considers appropriate but, in the case of a second or subsequent offence, for a minimum of five years; and**

    (*b*) **on application of the Attorney General or on its own motion, order that the accused pay to a person or an organization that has taken care of an animal or a bird as a result of the commission of the offence the reasonable costs that the person or organization incurred in respect of the animal or bird, if the costs are readily ascertainable.**

(2) Every one who contravenes an order made under paragraph (1)(*a*) is guilty of an offence punishable on summary conviction.

(3) Sections 740 to 741.2 apply, with any modifications that the circumstances require, to orders made under paragraph (1)(*b*). 2008, c. 12, s. 1.

CROSS-REFERENCES
"Attorney General" is defined in s. 2.

SYNOPSIS

This section provides for making a prohibition order for persons convicted of the offences relating to mistreatment of animals and birds. In addition, under subsec. (2), the sentencing court may require the offender to pay the reasonable costs of the person or organization that has had to care for the animals or birds as a result of the commission of the offence by the offender, provided the costs are readily ascertainable.

Part XII / OFFENCES RELATING TO CURRENCY

Interpretation

DEFINITIONS / "counterfeit money" / "counterfeit token of value" / "current" / "utter".

448. In this Part,

"counterfeit money" includes

    (*a*) **a false coin or false paper money that resembles or is apparently intended to resemble or pass for a current coin or current paper money,**

    (*b*) **a forged bank-note or forged blank bank-note, whether complete or incomplete,**

(c) a genuine coin or genuine paper money that is prepared or altered to resemble or pass for a current coin or current paper money of a higher denomination,

(d) a current coin from which the milling is removed by filing or cutting the edges and on which new milling is made to restore its appearance,

(e) a coin cased with gold, silver, or nickel, as the case may be, that is intended to resemble or pass for a current gold, silver or nickel coin, and

(f) a coin or a piece of metal or mixed metals that is washed or coloured by any means with a wash or material capable of producing the appearance of gold, silver or nickel and that is intended to resemble or pass for a current gold, silver or nickel coin;

"counterfeit token of value" means a counterfeit excise stamp, postage stamp or other evidence of value, by whatever technical, trivial or deceptive designation it may be described, and includes genuine coin or paper money that has no value as money;

"current" means lawfully current in Canada or elsewhere by virtue of a law, proclamation or regulation in force in Canada or elsewhere as the case may be;

"utter" includes sell, pay, tender and put off. R.S., c. C-34, s. 406.

CROSS-REFERENCES

In addition to the definitions in this section, see s. 2 and notes to that section. The term "bank-note" is defined in s. 2. Section 461(2) provides for admission of a certificate of an examiner of counterfeit money as proof that any money, coin or bank-note is counterfeit or genuine, as the case may be, and is or is not, as the case may be, current in Canada or elsewhere. Section 462 provides that counterfeit money, counterfeit tokens of value and anything used or intended to be used to make counterfeit money or tokens of value belong to Her Majesty. Section 462(2) gives a peace officer power to seize and detain these items.

SYNOPSIS

This section contains definitions of the terms "counterfeit money", "counterfeit token of value", "current" and "utter" for the purpose of Part XII of the *Criminal Code*.

ANNOTATIONS

A forged Government of Canada cheque does not constitute "counterfeit money" as defined in this provision: *R. v. Kirkness* (2004), 191 C.C.C. (3d) 17 (Man. C.A.).

Making

MAKING.

449. Every one who makes or begins to make counterfeit money is guilty of an indictable offence and liable to imprisonment for a term not exceeding fourteen years. R.S., c. C-34, s. 407.

CROSS-REFERENCES

The term "counterfeit money" is defined in s. 448. Section 461(1) enacts a conclusive presumption as to when the offence is complete. Section 461(2) provides for admission of a certificate of an examiner of counterfeit money as proof that any money, coin or bank-note is counterfeit or genuine and is or is not, as the case may be, current in Canada or elsewhere.

This offence may be the basis for an application for an authorization to intercept private communications by reason of s. 183 and is an enterprise crime offence for the purposes of Part XII.2.

The accused may elect his mode of trial under s. 536(2). Release pending trial is determined under s. 515. Section 462 provides that counterfeit money and anything used or intended to be used to make counterfeit money belong to Her Majesty. Section 462(2) gives a peace officer power to seize and detain these items.

Possession

POSSESSION, ETC., OF COUNTERFEIT MONEY.

450. Every one who, without lawful justification or excuse, the proof of which lies on him,

    (*a*) **buys, receives or offers to buy or receive,**

    (*b*) **has in his custody or possession, or**

    (*c*) **introduces into Canada,**

counterfeit money is guilty of an indictable offence and liable to imprisonment for a term not exceeding fourteen years. R.S., c. C-34, s. 408.

CROSS-REFERENCES

Possession is defined in s. 4(3). The term "counterfeit money" is defined in s. 448. Section 461(1) enacts a conclusive presumption as to when the offence is complete. Section 461(2) provides for admission of a certificate of an examiner of counterfeit money as proof that any money, coin or bank-note is counterfeit or genuine and is or is not, as the case may be, current in Canada or elsewhere.

This offence may be the basis for an application for an authorization to intercept private communications by reason of s. 183 and is an enterprise crime offence for the purposes of Part XII.2.

The accused may elect his mode of trial under s. 536(2). Release pending trial is determined under s. 515. Section 462 provides that counterfeit money and anything used or intended to be used to make counterfeit money belong to Her Majesty. Section 462(2) gives a peace officer power to seize and detain these items.

SYNOPSIS

This section describes the indictable offence of buying, receiving, offering to buy or receive, possessing or bringing into Canada counterfeit money. A person who is charged under this section and who has dealt with counterfeit money in a fashion described above, bears the onus of proving that he had *lawful justification or excuse* for his actions. The maximum term of imprisonment upon conviction is 14 years.

ANNOTATIONS

In *R. v. Robinson*, [1974] S.C.R. 573, 10 C.C.C. (2d) 505, it was held *per* Ritchie J. (Abbott, Judson, Spence and Laskin JJ., concurring), that it was no defence that the accused was in possession of counterfeit U.S. 1941/42 dimes (the genuine coins, because of some imperfections upon minting, having a numismatic value of between $100 and $800 each) for the purpose of sale as a numismatic curiosity and not for circulation as legal tender. The coins' primary characteristic was that they were intended to resemble a current coin within the definition of s. 448 of the Code. On the question of lawful justification or excuse upon the accused Laskin J., agreed with Ritchie J., on the merits that there was no evidence to support such a finding, but held that if evidence of a want of intention by the accused to use the counterfeit coins as currency had been led then the accused could be said to have discharged the shifting burden cast upon him by the section.

The offence under para. (*b*) does not require proof of an intention to use the money as currency: *R. v. Duane* (1984), 12 C.C.C. (3d) 368, 57 A.R. 227 (C.A.), affd [1985] 2 S.C.R. 612, 22 C.C.C. (3d) 448*n* (7:0).

It is not necessary as a foundation to the opinion of the Crown's expert witness as to the bank-note being counterfeit that he first prove the authenticity of the bank-note copied: *R. v. Gagnon* (1975), 31 C.R.N.S. 332 (Ont. Co. Ct.).

Proof that the accused knew of the counterfeit nature of the bills is an essential element of the "possession" required for the offence and the burden of proof is on the Crown to prove such knowledge beyond a reasonable doubt; lack of such knowledge is not a matter of "lawful excuse" which the accused has to prove. It is only after the Crown has proved possession, including knowledge of the counterfeit nature of the money, that the issue of lawful justification or excuse, arises: *R. v. Santeramo* (1976), 32 C.C.C. (2d) 35, 36 C.R.N.S. 1 (Ont. C.A.). Folld: *R. v. Freng* (1993), 86 C.C.C. (3d) 91 (B.C.C.A.).

The accused's knowledge may be inferred from the quality of the counterfeit bill: *R. v. Mak* (2000), 46 W.C.B. (2d) 581 (B.C.C.A.).

HAVING CLIPPINGS, ETC.

451. Every one who, without lawful justification or excuse, the proof of which lies on him, has in his custody or possession

    (*a*) **gold or silver filings or clippings,**

    (*b*) **gold or silver bullion, or**

    (*c*) **gold or silver in dust, solution or otherwise,**

produced or obtained by impairing, diminishing or lightening a current gold or silver coin, knowing that it has been so produced or obtained, is guilty of an indictable offence and liable to imprisonment for a term not exceeding five years. R.S., c. C-34, s. 409.

CROSS-REFERENCES

Possession is defined in s. 4(3). The term "current" is defined in s. 448. Section 461(2) provides for admission of a certificate of an examiner of counterfeit money as proof that any coin is or is not, as the case may be, current in Canada or elsewhere.

The accused may elect his mode of trial under s. 536(2). Release pending trial is determined under s. 515, although the accused is eligible for release by the officer in charge under s. 498.

The related offence of clipping or uttering clipped coin is in s. 455.

SYNOPSIS

This section describes the offence of possessing gold or silver filings, clippings, bullion or dust in any form, which has been produced by diminishing a *current* gold or silver coin. The prosecution must prove that the accused *knew* that the gold or silver was produced or obtained in the fashion described above. As in s. 450, the accused must prove *lawful justification or excuse* for the knowing possession of the items set out in this section. This is an indictable offence with a maximum term of five years' imprisonment.

Uttering

UTTERING, ETC., COUNTERFEIT MONEY

452. Every one who, without lawful justification or excuse, the proof of which lies on him,

    (*a*) **utters or offers to utter counterfeit money or uses counterfeit money as if it were genuine, or**

    (*b*) **exports, sends or takes counterfeit money out of Canada,**

is guilty of an indictable offence and liable to imprisonment for a term not exceeding fourteen years. R.S., c. C-34, s. 410.

CROSS-REFERENCES

The terms "counterfeit money" and "utter" are defined in s. 448. Section 461(1) enacts a conclusive presumption as to when the offence is complete. Section 461(2) provides for admission of a certificate of an examiner of counterfeit money as proof that any money, coin or bank-note is counterfeit or genuine and is or is not, as the case may be, current in Canada or elsewhere.

This offence may be the basis for an application for an authorization to intercept private communications by reason of s. 183 and is an enterprise crime offence for the purposes of Part XII.2.

The accused may elect his mode of trial under s. 536(2). Release pending trial is determined under s. 515. Section 462 provides that counterfeit money and anything used or intended to be used to make counterfeit money belong to Her Majesty. Section 462(2) gives a peace officer power to seize and detain these items.

The related offence of uttering coin that is not current is in s. 453.

SYNOPSIS
This section describes the offences of uttering or offering to utter counterfeit money, or using it as though it were genuine, and of exporting counterfeit money out of Canada. This is an indictable offence with a maximum term of 14 years' imprisonment.

ANNOTATIONS
Uttering counterfeit money includes the sale of counterfeit money as counterfeit to be put into circulation as currency notwithstanding the immediate purchaser is not deceived as to the genuineness of the money: *R. v. Kelly and Lauzon* (1979), 48 C.C.C. (2d) 560 (Ont. C.A.).

UTTERING COIN.
453. Every one who, with intent to defraud, knowingly utters
　　(*a*) **a coin that is not current, or**
　　(*b*) **a piece of metal or mixed metals that resembles in size, figure or colour a current coin for which it is uttered,**
is guilty of an indictable offence and liable to imprisonment for a term not exceeding two years. R.S., c. C-34, s. 411.

CROSS-REFERENCES
Possession is defined in s. 4(3). The terms "current" and "utter" are defined in s. 448. Section 461(2) provides for admission of a certificate of an examiner of counterfeit money as proof that any coin is or is not, as the case may be, current in Canada or elsewhere. By virtue of s. 583, an indictment which otherwise complies with s. 581 is not insufficient by reason only that: para. (*c*), it charges an intent to defraud without naming or describing the person whom it was intended to defraud.

The accused may elect his mode of trial under s. 536(2). Release pending trial is determined under s. 515, although the accused is eligible for release by the officer in charge under s. 498.

SYNOPSIS
This section describes the offence of *knowingly* uttering a coin that is not current, or a piece of metal that resembles a current coin in size, figure or colour. A person charged under this section must have an *intent to defraud* to be convicted. The offence is indictable and carries a maximum term of two years' imprisonment.

SLUGS AND TOKENS.
454. Every one who without lawful excuse, the proof of which lies on him,
　　(*a*) **manufactures, produces or sells, or**
　　(*b*) **has in his possession**

anything that is intended to be fraudulently used in substitution for a coin or token of value that any coin or token-operated device is designed to receive is guilty of an offence punishable on summary conviction. R.S., c. C-34, s. 412; 1972, c. 13, s. 32.

CROSS-REFERENCES

Possession is defined in s. 4(3). While there is no definition of "fraudulently" which is universally applicable, generally speaking, it refers to conduct which is dishonest and morally wrong: *R. v. DeMarco* (1973), 13 C.C.C. (2d) 369 (Ont. C.A.). This offence supplements the offence of fraudulently obtaining transportation in s. 393(3). Note also the offence of possession of instruments for breaking into coin-operated devices in s. 352. Trial of this offence is conducted by a summary conviction court pursuant to Part XXVII. The punishment is as set out in s. 787 and the limitation period is set out in s. 786(2). Release pending trial is determined by s. 515, although the accused is eligible for release by a peace officer under s. 496, 497 or by the officer in charge under s. 498.

SYNOPSIS

This section describes the summary conviction offence of manufacturing, producing, selling or possessing slugs or tokens. A person charged under this section must have the *intent* that these items be fraudulently used in substitution for a coin or a valuable token in a coin or token-operated device. Like ss. 450 and 451, the accused bears the onus of proving that the possession of these slugs and tokens for the purposes described in the section was with *lawful excuse*.

ANNOTATIONS

For the offence of possession the accused must be aware of the article's potential fraudulent use: *R. v. Kolot* (1975), 27 C.C.C. (2d) 79 (B.C. Co. Ct.).

Subway fare boxes monitored by operators who may scrutinize tickets and refuse entry do not constitute "token-operated devices". Furthermore, a subway ticket is not a token of value that a "token-operated device is designed to receive": *R. v. Aeso* (1996), 105 C.C.C. (3d) 283 (Ont. Ct. (Prov. Div.)).

Defacing or Impairing

CLIPPING AND UTTERING CLIPPED COIN.

455. Every one who
(*a*) **impairs, diminishes or lightens a current gold or silver coin with intent that it should pass for a current gold or silver coin, or**
(*b*) **utters a coin knowing that it has been impaired, diminished or lightened contrary to paragraph (*a*),**
is guilty of an indictable offence and liable to imprisonment for a term not exceeding fourteen years. R.S., c. C-34, s. 413.

CROSS-REFERENCES

The terms "current" and "utter" are defined in s. 448. Section 461(2) provides for admission of a certificate of an examiner of counterfeit money as proof that any coin is or is not, as the case may be, current in Canada or elsewhere.

The accused may elect his mode of trial under s. 536(2). Release pending trial is determined under s. 515.

The related offence of possession of clippings or filings is in s. 451.

SYNOPSIS

This section describes the offences of diminishing, impairing or lightening a current gold or silver coin *with intent* that it should pass for a current gold or silver coin, and of uttering a coin, knowing that it has been so diminished, impaired or lightened. These are indictable offences with a maximum of 14 years' imprisonment.

DEFACING CURRENT COINS.

456. Every one who
  (*a*) **defaces a current coin, or**
  (*b*) **utters a current coin that has been defaced,**
is guilty of an offence punishable on summary conviction. R.S., c. C-34, s. 414.

CROSS-REFERENCES

The terms "current" and "utter" are defined in s. 448. Section 461(2) provides for admission of a certificate of an examiner of counterfeit money as proof that any coin is or is not, as the case may be, current in Canada or elsewhere.

  Trial of this offence is conducted by a summary conviction court pursuant to Part XXVII. The punishment is as set out in s. 787 and the limitation period is set out in s. 786(2). Release pending trial is determined by s. 515, although the accused is eligible for release by a peace officer under ss. 496, 497 or by the officer in charge under s. 498.

LIKENESS OF BANK-NOTES / Exception / Offence / Defence.

457. (1) No person shall make, publish, print, execute, issue, distribute or circulate, including by electronic or computer-assisted means, anything in the likeness of
  (*a*) **a current bank-note; or**
  (*b*) **an obligation or a security of a government or bank.**

(2) Subsection (1) does not apply to
  (*a*) **the Bank of Canada or its employees when they are carrying out their duties;**
  (*b*) **the Royal Canadian Mounted Police or its members or employees when they are carrying out their duties; or**
  (*c*) **any person acting under a contract or licence from the Bank of Canada or Royal Canadian Mounted Police.**

(3) A person who contravenes subsection (1) is guilty of an offence punishable on summary conviction.

(4) No person shall be convicted of an offence under subsection (3) in relation to the printed likeness of a Canadian bank-note if it is established that the length or width of the likeness is less than three-fourths or greater than one-and-one-half times the length or width, as the case may be, of the bank-note and
  (*a*) **the likeness is in black-and-white only; or**
  (*b*) **the likeness of the bank-note appears on only one side of the likeness. R.S., c. C-34, s. 415; 1999, c. 5, s. 12.**

CROSS-REFERENCES

The term "current" is defined in s. 448. "Bank-note" is defined in s. 2. "Bank" is defined in s. 35 of the *Interpretation Act*, R.S.C. 1985, c. I-21. Section 461(2) provides for admission of a certificate of an examiner of counterfeit money as proof that any money or bank-note is or is not, as the case may be, current in Canada or elsewhere.

  Trial of these offences is conducted by a summary conviction court pursuant to Part XXVII. The punishment is as set out in s. 787 [although see s. 719(*b*) where the accused is a corporation] and the limitation period is set out in s. 786(2). Release pending trial is determined by s. 515, although the accused is eligible for release by a peace officer under s. 496, 497 or by the officer in charge under s. 498.

SYNOPSIS

This section describes the offence of making, issuing, publishing, printing, distributing, executing or circulating anything that has a *likeness* to or the *appearance* of a current banknote or any obligation or security of a government or a bank. The offence is punishable by summary conviction. The section stipulates that no person shall be convicted of an offence in relation to a printed likeness if the provisions set out in subsec. (4) are met. There is also exemption for employees of the Bank of Canada and the Royal Canadian Mounted Police or any person acting under contract or licence to the Bank or the R.C.M.P. when carrying out their duties.

ANNOTATIONS

It was held under the predecessor legislation that the act of importing and distributing goods, with the likeness or appearance of current bank-notes, to wholesalers and retailers comes within the prohibition against publishing: *R. v. Giftcraft Ltd.* (1984), 13 C.C.C. (3d) 192 (Ont. H.C.J.).

Instruments or Materials

MAKING, HAVING OR DEALING IN INSTRUMENTS FOR COUNTERFEITING.

458. Every one who, without lawful justification or excuse, the proof of which lies on him,

  (a) makes or repairs,

  (b) begins or proceeds to make or repair,

  (c) buys or sells, or

  (d) has in his custody or possession,

any machine, engine, tool, instrument, material or thing that he knows has been used or that he knows is adapted and intended for use in making counterfeit money or counterfeit tokens of value is guilty of an indictable offence and liable to imprisonment for a term not exceeding fourteen years. R.S., c. C-34, s. 416.

CROSS-REFERENCES

The terms "counterfeit money" and "counterfeit tokens of value" are defined in s. 448. Possession is defined in s. 4(3). Section 461(2) provides for admission of a certificate of an examiner of counterfeit money as proof that any money, coin or bank-note is counterfeit or genuine, as the case may be, and is or is not, as the case may be, current in Canada or elsewhere. Section 461(1) enacts a conclusive presumption as to when the offence is complete. Section 462 provides that counterfeit money, counterfeit tokens of value and anything used or intended to be used to make counterfeit money or tokens of value belong to Her Majesty. Section 462(2) gives a peace officer power to seize and detain these items. The accused may elect his mode of trial under s. 536(2). Release pending trial is determined under s. 515.

SYNOPSIS

This section describes the offence of possessing, making or repairing, beginning to make or repair, or buying or selling any instrument, material or thing that has been used or is intended to be used to make counterfeit money or valuable tokens. The prosecution must establish that the accused *knows* the use to which these items have been or are intended to be put. The section requires the accused to establish lawful justification or excuse for the acts described in paras. (a) to (d) and may thus be challenged under s. 11(d) of the Charter. The offence is indictable and carries a maximum term of 14 years' imprisonment.

CONVEYING INSTRUMENTS FOR COINING OUT OF MINT.

459. Every one who, without lawful justification or excuse, the proof of which lies on him, knowingly conveys out of any of Her Majesty's mints in Canada,

> (*a*) **any machine, engine, tool, instrument, material or thing used or employed in connection with the manufacture of coins,**
>
> (*b*) **a useful part of anything mentioned in paragraph (*a*), or**
>
> (*c*) **coin, bullion, metal or a mixture of metals,**

is guilty of an indictable offence and liable to imprisonment for a term not exceeding fourteen years. R.S., c. C-34, s. 417.

CROSS-REFERENCES

The accused may elect his mode of trial under s. 536(2). Release pending trial is determined under s. 515.

SYNOPSIS

This section describes the offence of conveying certain items out of any of Her Majesty's mints in Canada. The accused person must establish lawful justification or excuse for any of the actions described in the section — a provision which could be challenged under the Charter. Any person who *knowingly* conveys out of the mint any machine, engine, tool, instrument, material or thing used in connection with the manufacture of coins, a useful part of any of these items, or coin, bullion, metal, or a mixture of metals, commits this indictable offence and is liable to a maximum term of 14 years' imprisonment.

Advertising and Trafficking in Counterfeit Money or Counterfeit Tokens of Value

ADVERTISING AND DEALING IN COUNTERFEIT MONEY, ETC. / Fraudulent use of money genuine but valueless.

460. (1) Every one who

> (*a*) **by an advertisement or any other writing, offers to sell, procure or dispose of counterfeit money or counterfeit tokens of value or to give information with respect to the manner in which or the means by which counterfeit money or counterfeit tokens of value may be sold, procured or disposed of, or**
>
> (*b*) **purchases, obtains, negotiates or otherwise deals with counterfeit tokens of value, or offers to negotiate with a view to purchasing or obtaining them,**

is guilty of an indictable offence and liable to imprisonment for a term not exceeding five years.

(2) No person shall be convicted of an offence under subsection (1) in respect of genuine coin or genuine paper money that has no value as money unless, at the time when the offence is alleged to have been committed, he knew that the coin or paper money had no value as money and he had a fraudulent intent in his dealings with or with respect to the coin or paper money. R.S., c. C-34, s. 418.

CROSS-REFERENCES

The terms "counterfeit money" and "counterfeit tokens of value" are defined in s. 448. The term "writing" is defined in s. 2. Section 461(2) provides for admission of a certificate of an examiner of counterfeit money as proof that any money, coin or bank-note is counterfeit or genuine, as the case may be, and is or is not, as the case may be, current in Canada or elsewhere. Section 461(1) enacts a conclusive presumption as to when the offence is complete. Section 462 provides that counterfeit money, counterfeit tokens of value and anything used or intended to be used to make counterfeit money or tokens of value belong to Her Majesty. Section 462(2) gives a peace officer power to seize and detain these items. The accused may elect his mode of trial under s. 536(2). Release pending trial is determined under s. 515, although the accused is eligible for release by the officer in charge under s. 498.

SYNOPSIS

This section describes the offence of dealing in counterfeit money or counterfeit tokens.

Subsection (1)(*a*) provides that any person who, by advertisement or other writing offers to sell, obtain or dispose of counterfeit items, or to give information on how to sell, obtain or dispose of such things is guilty of an offence.

Subsection (1)(*b*) similarly makes it an offence to purchase, obtain, negotiate or offer to negotiate the purchase of such counterfeit items.

Subsection (2) provides that a person who deals in genuine coin or paper money that has no value is not guilty of an offence under subsec. (1), unless he *knew* that the items had no value and he had a *fraudulent* intent in his dealings. The offence is indictable and carries a maximum term of five years' imprisonment.

Special Provisions as to Proof

WHEN COUNTERFEIT COMPLETE / Certificate of examiner of counterfeit / Cross-examination and notice.

461. (1) Every offence relating to counterfeit money or counterfeit tokens of value shall be deemed to be complete notwithstanding that the money or tokens of value in respect of which the proceedings are taken are not finished or perfected or do not copy exactly the money or tokens of value that they are apparently intended to resemble or for which they are apparently intended to pass.

(2) In any proceedings under this Part, a certificate signed by a person designated as an examiner of counterfeit by the Minister of Public Safety and Emergency Preparedness, stating that any coin, paper money or bank-note described therein is counterfeit money or that any coin, paper money or bank-note described therein is genuine and is or is not, as the case may be, current in Canada or elsewhere, is evidence of the statements contained in the certificate without proof of the signature or official character of the person appearing to have signed the certificate.

(3) Subsections 258(6) and (7) apply, with such modifications as the circumstances require, in respect of a certificate described in subsection (2). R.S., c. C-34, s. 419; 1992, c. 1, s. 58; 2005, c. 10, s. 34(1)(*f*)(xi).

CROSS-REFERENCES

The terms "counterfeit money", "counterfeit tokens of value" and "current" are defined in s. 448. The term "bank-note" is defined in s. 2.

With respect to subsec. (2), note that s. 25(1) of the *Interpretation Act*, R.S.C. 1985, c. I-21, provides that "where an enactment provides that a document is evidence of a fact without anything in the context to indicate that the document is conclusive evidence, then, in any judicial proceedings, the document is admissible in evidence and the fact is deemed to be established in the absence of any evidence to the contrary".

With respect to subsec. (3), s. 258(6) and (7) require that the party intending to introduce the certificate give reasonable notice of his intention and a copy of the certificate and give the judge power to order that the examiner be produced for the purposes of cross-examination.

SYNOPSIS

This section sets out certain special provisions in relation to proving offences relating to counterfeiting.

Subsection (1) provides that counterfeiting offences are complete, even if the counterfeit money or tokens are not finished, perfected or are not exact copies of the genuine articles.

Subsection (2) provides that any certificate signed by a person designated by the Solicitor General of Canada as an examiner of counterfeit is evidence of the statements relating to the genuineness or currency of the money without proof of the signature or official character of the person appearing to have signed the certificate.

ANNOTATIONS

On a charge contrary to s. 450(*b*) the Crown may establish a *prima facie* case by having a police officer testify that he has been employed as an examiner of counterfeit bills and that having compared the bills with genuine bills he was of the opinion that they were counterfeit and that if they had been genuine, they would be lawfully current. It is not necessary that the Crown produce a certificate signed by a person designated as an examiner of counterfeit by the Solicitor General of Canada nor that it lead some documentary evidence or call some official from the Bank of Canada who was in a position to make reference to the proper law or proper proclamation or regulation pursuant to this section: *R. v. MacIntosh* (1971), 5 C.C.C. (2d) 239, 16 C.R.N.S. 119 (Ont. C.A.).

Similarly a member of the R.C.M.P. designated as an examiner of counterfeit by the Solicitor-General of Canada may give a *viva voce* opinion based on his training and experience that certain bills are not genuine and were intended to resemble paper money which was current legal tender in the United States: *R. v. Serratore* (1980), 53 C.C.C. (2d) 106 (Ont. C.A.).

Forfeiture

OWNERSHIP / Seizure.

462. (1) Counterfeit money, counterfeit tokens of value and anything that is used or is intended to be used to make counterfeit money or counterfeit tokens of value belong to Her Majesty.

(2) A peace officer may seize and detain
  (*a*) counterfeit money,
  (*b*) counterfeit tokens of value, and
  (*c*) machines, engines, tools, instruments, materials or things that have been used or that have been adapted and are intended for use in making counterfeit money or counterfeit tokens of value,

and anything seized shall be sent to the Minister of Finance to be disposed of or dealt with as he may direct, but anything that is required as evidence in any proceedings shall not be sent to the Minister until it is no longer required in those proceedings. R.S., c. C-34, s. 420.

CROSS-REFERENCES

The terms "counterfeit money" and "counterfeit tokens of value" are defined in s. 448. "Her Majesty" is defined in s. 35 of the *Interpretation Act*, R.S.C. 1985, c. I-21. The normal search warrant provisions are found in ss. 487 and 487.1.

SYNOPSIS

This section describes a procedure for seizing counterfeit money, tokens of value and instruments designed or adapted for use in counterfeiting.

Subsection (2) states that a peace officer may seize and detain any of these items and shall send them to the Minister of Finance for disposal unless they are needed as evidence in any proceedings.

Subsection (1) makes it clear that any of the items described in this section belong to Her Majesty.

This section creates a power to seize, without warrant, which might attract scrutiny under s. 8 of the Charter.

Part XII.1 / INSTRUMENTS AND LITERATURE FOR ILLICIT DRUG USE

Interpretation

"CONSUME" / "Illicit drug" / "Illicit drug use" / "Instrument for illicit drug use" / "Literature for illicit drug use" / "Sell".

462.1 In this Part,
"consume" includes inhale, inject into the human body, masticate and smoke;

"illicit drug" means a controlled substance or precursor the import, export, production, sale or possession of which is prohibited or restricted pursuant to the *Controlled Drugs and Substances Act*;

"illicit drug use" means the importation, exportation, production, sale or possession of a controlled substance or precursor contrary to the *Controlled Drugs and Substances Act* or a regulation made under that Act;

"instrument for illicit drug use" means anything designed primarily or intended under the circumstances for consuming or to facilitate the consumption of an illicit drug, but does not include a "device" as that term is defined in section 2 of the *Food and Drugs Act*;

"literature for illicit drug use" means any printed matter or video describing or depicting, and designed primarily or intended under the circumstances to promote, encourage or advocate the production, preparation or consumption of illicit drugs;

"sell" includes offer for sale, expose for sale, have in possession for sale and distribute, whether or not the distribution is made for consideration. R.S.C. 1985, c. 50 (4th Supp.), s. 1; 1996, c. 19, s. 67.

CROSS-REFERENCES
In addition to the definitions of this section, see s. 2 and notes to that section.

SYNOPSIS
This section provides definitions of the terms relevant to the offence described in Part XII.1 of the Code.

ANNOTATIONS
The prohibition in this Part in relation to "literature for illicit drug use" violates s. 2(*b*) of the Charter and is of no force and effect. Accordingly, the definition of "literature for illicit drug use" must be severed from the section: *Iorfida v. MacIntyre* (1994), 93 C.C.C. (3d) 395, 21 O.R. (3d) 186 (Gen. Div.).

Offence

OFFENCE.

462.2 Every one who knowingly imports into Canada, exports from Canada, manufactures, promotes or sells instruments or literature for illicit drug use is guilty of an offence and is liable on summary conviction

(*a*) for a first offence, to a fine not exceeding one hundred thousand dollars or to imprisonment for a term not exceeding six months or to both; or

(*b*) for a second or subsequent offence, to a fine not exceeding three hundred thousand dollars or to imprisonment for a term not exceeding one year or to both. R.S.C. 1985, c. 50 (4th Supp.), s. 1.

CROSS-REFERENCES

The terms "illicit drug use", "sell", "literature for illicit drug use", and "instrument for illicit drug use" are defined in s. 462.1.

The trial of this offence is conducted by a summary conviction court pursuant to Part XXVII. The limitation period is set out in s. 786(2). Release pending trial is determined by s. 515, although the accused is eligible for release by a peace officer under s. 496, 497 or by the officer in charge under s. 498.

Where the prosecution seeks the higher penalty prescribed by para. (*b*), it must comply with the provisions of s. 665. Section 667 provides one method of proof of the prior conviction. No reference to the prior conviction may be made in the information by virtue of s. 664.

SYNOPSIS

This section describes the offence of *knowingly* importing into Canada, exporting from Canada, manufacturing, promoting, or selling instruments or literature for *illicit* drug use. The offence is a summary one, punishable on a first conviction by a maximum fine of $100,000 and/or a term of imprisonment not exceeding six months. For every offence following a first conviction, the punishment increases to a maximum fine of $300,000 and/or a term of imprisonment not exceeding one year.

ANNOTATIONS

The prohibition in this section in relation to literature for illicit drug use violates s. 2(*b*) of the Charter and is of no force and effect. Accordingly, the words "or literature" must be severed from the section: *Iorfida v. MacIntyre* (1994), 93 C.C.C. (3d) 395, 21 O.R. (3d) 186 (Gen. Div.).

This provision is neither vague nor overbroad contrary to s. 7 of the Charter: *R. v. Spindloe* (2001), 154 C.C.C. (3d) 8, 42 C.R. (5th) 58 (Sask. C.A.).

Part XII.2 / PROCEEDS OF CRIME

Interpretation

DEFINITIONS / "designated drug offence" / "designated offence" / "enterprise crime offence" / "judge" / "proceeds of crime" / Regulations / Powers of Attorney General of Canada / Powers of Attorney General of a province.

462.3 (1) In this Part,

"designated drug offence" [*Repealed*, 1996, c. 19, s. 68(1).]

"designated offence" means

    (*a*) any offence that may be prosecuted as an indictable offence under this or any other Act of Parliament, other than an indictable offence prescribed by regulation, or

    (*b*) a conspiracy or an attempt to commit, being an accessory after the fact in relation to, or any counselling in relation to, an offence referred to in paragraph (*a*);

"designated substance offence" [*Repealed*, 2001, c. 32, s. 12(3).]

"enterprise crime offence" [*Repealed*, 2001, c. 32, s. 12(2).]

Note: Definition "enterprise crime offence" amended 2001, c. 27, s. 246; however definition repealed by 2001, c. 32, s. 12(2).

"judge" means a judge as defined in section 552 or a judge of a superior court of criminal jurisdiction;

"proceeds of crime" means any property, benefit or advantage, within or outside Canada, obtained or derived directly or indirectly as a result of

    (*a*) the commission in Canada of a designated offence, or

    (*b*) an act or omission anywhere that, if it had occurred in Canada, would have constituted a designated offence.

(2) The Governor in Council may make regulations prescribing indictable offences that are excluded from the definition "designated offence" in subsection (1).

(3) Despite the definition "Attorney General" in section 2, the Attorney General of Canada may

    (*a*) exercise all the powers and perform all the duties and functions assigned to the Attorney General by or under this Act in respect of a designated offence if the alleged offence arises out of conduct that in whole or in part is in relation to an alleged contravention of an Act of Parliament or a regulation made under such an Act, other than this Act or a regulation made under this Act; and

    (*b*) conduct proceedings and exercise all the powers and perform all the duties and functions assigned to the Attorney General by or under this Act in respect of

        (i) an offence referred to in section 354, 355.2, 355.4 or 462.31, if the alleged offence arises out of conduct that in whole or in part is in relation to an alleged contravention of an Act of Parliament, other than this Act, or a regulation made under such an Act, and

        (ii) an offence under subsection 462.33(11) if the restraint order was made on application of the Attorney General of Canada.

(4) Subsection (3) does not affect the authority of the Attorney General of a province to conduct proceedings in respect of a designated offence or to exercise any of the powers or perform any of the duties and functions assigned to the Attorney General by or under this Act. R.S.C. 1985, c. 42 (4th Supp.), s. 2; 1993, c. 25, s. 95; 1993, c. 37, s. 32; 1993, c. 46, s. 5; 1994, c. 44, s. 29; 1995, c. 39, s. 151; 1996, c. 19, ss. 68, 70(*a*); 1997, c. 18, s. 27; 1997, c. 23, s. 9; 1998, c. 34, ss. 9, 11; 1999, c. 5, s. 52; 2001, c. 32, s. 12; 2001, c. 41, ss. 14, 33; 2005, c. 44, s. 1; 2010, c. 14, s. 7.

CROSS-REFERENCES

The scope of what is considered an attempt is set out in s. 24 of the *Criminal Code*. The meaning of being an accessory after the offence is found in s. 23. Section 22 determines the meaning of counselling. The effect of the recent amendment to this section is that all indictable offences under the *Criminal Code* or other federal statutes are designated offences for the purpose of this Part, unless they are prescribed by regulations. Comparable provisions relating to drugs are found in ss. 14 to 27 of the *Controlled Drugs and Substances Act*.

SYNOPSIS

This section provides definitions for the proceeds of crime provisions of the *Criminal Code*.

The term "proceeds of crime" is also defined, and encompasses any property, benefit or advantage within or outside Canada, obtained or derived directly or indirectly as a result of an enterprise crime or designated drug offence or conduct that would have constituted such an offence if it had occurred in Canada.

ANNOTATIONS

The ability to impose a fine in lieu of forfeiture pursuant to subsec. (3) is discretionary and, unlike the sentencing provisions in s. 734(2), the judge may, but need not, consider the means of the accused to pay. The amount of the fine must be equal to the value of the property and not a lesser amount: *R. v. Neves* (2005), 202 C.C.C. (3d) 375, 32 C.R. (6th) 266 (Man. C.A.).

Offence

LAUNDERING PROCEEDS OF CRIME / Punishment / Exception.

462.31 (1) Every one commits an offence who uses, transfers the possession of, sends or delivers to any person or place, transports, transmits, alters, disposes of or otherwise deals with, in any manner and by any means, any property or any proceeds of any property with intent to conceal or convert that property or those proceeds, knowing or believing that all or a part of that property or of those proceeds was obtained or derived directly or indirectly as a result of

> (*a*) **the commission in Canada of a designated offence; or**
>
> (*b*) **an act or omission anywhere that, if it had occurred in Canada, would have constituted a designated offence.**

(2) Every one who commits an offence under subsection (1)

> (*a*) **is guilty of an indictable offence and is liable to imprisonment for a term not exceeding ten years; or**
>
> (*b*) **is guilty of an offence punishable on summary conviction.**

(3) A peace officer or a person acting under the direction of a peace officer is not guilty of an offence under subsection (1) if the peace officer or person does any of the things mentioned in that subsection for the purposes of an investigation or otherwise in the execution of the peace officer's duties. R.S.C. 1985, c. 42 (4th Supp.), s. 2; 1996, c. 19, s. 70; 1997, c. 18, s. 28; 2001, c. 32, s. 13.

CROSS-REFERENCES

The meaning of "property" and "person" are contained in s. 2.

The term "designated offence" is defined in s. 462.3. Section 4(3) sets out what being in "possession" means in this Act.

This offence has been added to the list of offences in relation to which, according to s. 183, an authorization for interception of private communications may be obtained or a warrant to conduct video surveillance may be obtained by reason of s. 487.01(5).

If the accused is prosecuted by indictment under s. 462.31(2)(*a*), the accused has a right to make an election under s. 536(2). If tried by summary conviction, Part XXVII will govern the procedure and s. 787(1) sets out the maximum punishment upon conviction as six months imprisonment or a $2,000 fine, or both [except in the case of a corporation, see s. 719(*b*)].

SYNOPSIS

This section describes the offence of laundering the proceeds of crime. The offence is committed when a person deals with any property, or any proceeds of property, in any manner and by any means, with the intent to conceal or convert it, knowing or believing that the property or proceeds were, in whole or in part, obtained or derived directly or indirectly as a result of the conduct described in the definition of the term "proceeds of crime".

The offence may be prosecuted by indictment, with a maximum punishment of imprisonment for 10 years, or by summary conviction.

By virtue of subsec. (3), no offence is committed by a peace officer or a person acting under the direction of a peace officer if the acts are done for the purpose of an investigation or otherwise in the execution of the officer's duties.

ANNOTATIONS

"Transfer of possession" is the act of a person who has control or possession of the object and then tries to pass it on to another. This provision applies only to the party originally having control of the property, not the recipient of the property. The act of purchasing the merchandise is not the equivalent of transferring its possession. A recipient of the property would be guilty of possession of property obtained by crime pursuant to s. 354 of the *Criminal Code*: *R. v. Daoust*, [2004] 1 S.C.R. 217, 180 C.C.C. (3d) 449, 18 C.R. (6th) 57.

The *mens rea* requires proof of an intent to conceal or convert property or proceeds of property and knowledge or belief that the property or proceeds were derived from a designated offence. "Convert" must be given its ordinary meaning and does not include an intent to disguise or conceal: *R. v. Daoust, supra.*

Search, Seizure and Detention of Proceeds of Crime

SPECIAL SEARCH WARRANT / Procedure / Execution of warrant / Execution in another province / Detention and record of property seized / Return of proceeds / Notice / Undertaking by Attorney General.

462.32 (1) Subject to subsection (3), if a judge, on application of the Attorney General, is satisfied by information on oath in Form 1 that there are reasonable grounds to believe that there is in any building, receptacle or place, within the province in which the judge has jurisdiction or any other province, any property in respect of which an order of forfeiture may be made under subsection 462.37(1) or (2.01) or 462.38(2), in respect of a designated offence alleged to have been committed within the province in which the judge has jurisdiction, the judge may issue a warrant authorizing a person named in the warrant or a peace officer to search the building, receptacle or place for that property and to seize that property and any other property in respect of which that person or peace officer believes, on reasonable grounds, that an order of forfeiture may be made under that subsection.

(2) An application for a warrant under subsection (1) may be made *ex parte*, shall be made in writing and shall include a statement as to whether any previous applications have been made under subsection (1) with respect to the property that is the subject of the application.

(2.1) Subject to subsection (2.2), a warrant issued pursuant to subsection (1) may be executed anywhere in Canada.

(2.2) Where a warrant is issued under subsection (1) in one province but it may be reasonably expected that it is to be executed in another province and the execution of the warrant would require entry into or on the property of any person in the other province, a judge in the other province may, on *ex parte* application, confirm the warrant, and when the warrant is so confirmed it shall have full force and effect in that other province as though it had originally been issued in that province.

(3) Subsections 487(2) to (4) and section 488 apply, with such modifications as the circumstances require, to a warrant issued under this section.

(4) Every person who executes a warrant issued by a judge under this section shall

(*a*) detain or cause to be detained the property seized, taking reasonable care to ensure that the property is preserved so that it may be dealt with in accordance with the law;

(*b*) as soon as practicable after the execution of the warrant but within a period not exceeding seven days thereafter, prepare a report in Form 5.3, identifying the property seized and the location where the property is being detained and cause the report to be filed with the clerk of the court; and

(*c*) cause a copy of the report to be provided, on request, to the person from whom the property was seized and to any other person who, in the opinion of the judge, appears to have a valid interest in the property.

(4.1) Subject to this or any other Act of Parliament, a peace officer who has seized anything under a warrant issued by a judge under this section may, with the written consent of the Attorney General, on being issued a receipt for it, return the thing seized to the person lawfully entitled to its possession, if

(*a*) the peace officer is satisfied that there is no dispute as to who is lawfully entitled to possession of the thing seized;

(*b*) the peace officer is satisfied that the continued detention of the thing seized is not required for the purpose of forfeiture; and

(*c*) the thing seized is returned before a report is filed with the clerk of the court under paragraph (4)(*b*).

(5) Before issuing a warrant under this section in relation to any property, a judge may require notice to be given to and may hear any person who, in the opinion of the judge, appears to have a valid interest in the property unless the judge is of the opinion that giving such notice before the issuance of the warrant would result in the disappearance, dissipation or reduction in value of the property or otherwise affect the property so that all or a part thereof could not be seized pursuant to the warrant.

(6) Before issuing a warrant under this section, a judge shall require the Attorney General to give such undertakings as the judge considers appropriate with respect to the payment of damages or costs, or both, in relation to the issuance and execution of the warrant. R.S.C. 1985, c. 42 (4th Supp.), s. 2; 1997, c. 18, s. 29; 2001, c. 32, s. 14; 2005, c. 44, s. 3.

CROSS-REFERENCES

The terms "property", "peace officer", "clerk of the court" and "person" are defined in s. 2. "Judge" and "Attorney General" are defined in ss. 2 and 462.3(3), (4).

Sections 487 to 489 deal with search warrants generally, and telewarrants are dealt with in s. 487.1. Form 5.3 has been created to report of what property is seized under a search warrant authorized by this section. Section 462.35 provides that the order detaining property seized under such warrants automatically expires after six months unless the Attorney General brings an application to extend the order within that time. In addition, any person with an interest in the property seized under this type of warrant may apply under s. 462.34 to examine the property or to have the property returned.

Section 462.34 provides that if a warrant is issued under this section and the accused is later committed to trial for a designated offence (as defined in s. 462.3) a copy of the report of what was seized shall be forwarded to the clerk of the court in which the accused is ordered to stand trial.

Property seized pursuant to a warrant issued under section may be managed in accordance with an order made under s. 462.331.

SYNOPSIS

This section provides for special search warrants with respect to property which falls into the category of proceeds of crime and which is subject to forfeiture under this Part.

An application for such a search warrant must be brought in writing, by an Attorney General, to a judge as defined in s. 462.3. It may be made *ex parte* and must include a statement as to whether any previous applications have been made in respect of the same property.

Where information on oath in Form 1 satisfies the judge that such property is in a building, receptacle or place, the judge may issue a warrant authorizing a named person or a peace officer to search for that property in that place, and to seize it and any other property which the person believes, on reasonable grounds, falls within this provision.

The warrant may be executed anywhere in Canada but if it is to be executed in another province and execution would require entry into or on the property of any person, it must first be confirmed by a judge in the other province.

The backing and time of execution provisions in ss. 487 and 488 apply to these special warrants.

Subsection (4) requires that a person executing a warrant under this section must detain and preserve the property seized and prepare a report within seven days of seizure which shall be given to the court, the person from whom the seizure was made and any other person whom the issuing judge decides has an apparent valid interest in the property. Subsection (4.1) sets out the circumstances in which the peace officer may, with the consent of the Attorney General, return the items seized before the report is filed.

Subsection (5) provides that, prior to issuing a warrant, a judge may require that notice be given to and may hear any person who, in the judge's opinion, appears to have a valid interest in the property, unless he believes that notice would result in disappearance, dissipation or reduction in value of the property, or otherwise affect the property so that all or part of it could not be seized.

Subsection (6) compels a judge, before issuing a warrant, to require the Attorney General to give such undertaking as the judge considers appropriate with respect to the payment of damages or costs in relation to the warrant.

ANNOTATIONS

The court may set aside an *ex parte* order made under this section where the court that made the order was misled because of the failure of the Crown to disclose material evidence: *R. v. Derksen* (1998), 126 C.C.C. (3d) 554, 169 Sask. R. 251 (Q.B.), affd 140 C.C.C. (3d) 184, [2000] 1 W.W.R. 609 (Sask. C.A.), leave to appeal to S.C.C. refused 142 C.C.C. (3d) vi, 203 Sask. R. 89n.

APPLICATION FOR RESTRAINT ORDER / Procedure / Restraint order / Appointment of Minister of Public Works and Government Services / Property outside Canada / Notice / Order in writing / Undertakings by Attorney General / Service of order / Registration of order / Continues in force / Offence.

462.33 (1) The Attorney General may make an application in accordance with subsection (2) for a restraint order under subsection (3) in respect of any property.

(2) An application made under subsection (1) for a restraint order under subsection (3) in respect of any property may be made *ex parte* and shall be made in writing to a judge and be accompanied by an affidavit sworn on the information and belief of the Attorney General or any other person deposing to the following matters, namely,

(*a*) the offence or matter under investigation;

(*b*) the person who is believed to be in possession of the property;

(*c*) the grounds for the belief that an order of forfeiture may be made under subsection 462.37(1) or (2.01) or 462.38(2) in respect of the property;

(*d*) a description of the property; and

(*e*) whether any previous applications have been made under this section with respect to the property.

(3) A judge who hears an application for a restraint order made under subsection (1) may — if the judge is satisfied that there are reasonable grounds to believe that there exists, within the province in which the judge has jurisdiction or any other province, any property in respect of which an order of forfeiture may be made under subsection 462.37(1) or (2.01) or 462.38(2), in respect of a designated offence alleged to have been committed within the province in which the judge has jurisdiction — make an order prohibiting any person from disposing of, or otherwise dealing with any interest in, the property specified in the order otherwise than in the manner that may be specified in the order.

(3.01) Subsections 462.32(2.1) and (2.2) apply, with such modifications as the circumstances require, in respect of a restraint order.

(3.1) A restraint order may be issued under this section in respect of property situated outside Canada, with any modifications that the circumstances require.

(4) An order made by a judge under subsection (3) may be subject to such reasonable conditions as the judge thinks fit.

(5) Before making an order under subsection (3) in relation to any property, a judge may require notice to be given to and may hear any person who, in the opinion of the judge, appears to have a valid interest in the property unless the judge is of the opinion that giving such notice before making the order would result in the disappearance, dissipation or reduction in value of the property or otherwise affect the property so that all or a part thereof could not be subject to an order of forfeiture under subsection 462.37(1) or (2.01) or 462.38(2).

(6) An order made under subsection (3) shall be made in writing.

(7) Before making an order under subsection (3), a judge shall require the Attorney General to give such undertakings as the judge considers appropriate with respect to the payment of damages or costs, or both, in relation to

    (*a*) the making of an order in respect of property situated within or outside Canada; and

    (*b*) the execution of an order in respect of property situated within Canada.

(8) A copy of an order made by a judge under subsection (3) shall be served on the person to whom the order is addressed in such manner as the judge directs or as may be prescribed by rules of court.

(9) A copy of an order made under subsection (3), shall be registered against any property in accordance with the laws of the province in which the property is situated.

(10) An order made under subsection (3) remains in effect until

    (*a*) it is revoked or varied under subsection 462.34(4) or revoked under paragraph 462.43(*a*);

    (*b*) it ceases to be in force under section 462.35; or

    (*c*) an order of forfeiture or restoration of the property is made under subsection 462.37(1) or (2.01), 462.38(2) or 462.41(3) or any other provision of this or any other Act of Parliament.

(11) Any person on whom an order made under subsection (3) is served in accordance with this section and who, while the order is in force, acts in contravention of or fails to comply with the order is guilty of an indictable offence or an offence punishable on summary conviction. R.S.C. 1985, c. 42 (4th Supp.), s. 2; 1993, c. 37, s. 21; 1996, c. 16, s. 60(1)(d); 1997, c. 18, s. 30; 2001, c. 32, s. 15; 2005, c. 44, s. 4.

CROSS-REFERENCES

The terms "property" and "person" are defined in s. 2. "Judge" and "designated offence" are defined in s. 462.3. "Attorney General" is defined in ss. 2 and 462.3(3), (4). Section 4(3) sets out when a person is in possession. Section 482 gives courts the power to make their own rules of court.

The offence created by 462.33(11) is one for which an application to intercept private communications may be made under s. 183. As there is no specified punishment if the prosecution is by way of indictment, s. 730 provides that the maximum period of imprisonment upon conviction is five years. In addition, an accused prosecuted by indictment would have a right to make an election under s. 536(2). If tried by summary conviction, Part XXVII will govern the procedure, and s. 787(1) sets out the maximum punishment upon conviction as six months imprisonment or a $2,000 fine, or both.

Section 462.35 provides for the automatic expiry of a restraint order made under this section after six months unless the Attorney General has, within that time, successfully applied for an extension of the order.

Section 462.36 provides that if the court makes a restraint order and the accused is later committed to trial for a designated offence (as defined in s. 462.3) a copy of the restraint order shall be forwarded to the clerk of the court in which the accused is ordered to stand trial.

If notice is given under subsec. (8), the court may use s. 462.4(b) to set aside any conveyance or transfer of property relating to the property subject to the restraint order unless the transaction was made for valuable consideration to a purchaser acting in good faith and without notice of the order.

Section 462.43 provides for the residual disposal of property seized under a restraint order.

As to restraint orders in relation to "offence-related property" under the *Controlled Drugs and Substances Act*, see s. 14 of that Act.

Property restrained pursuant to a restraint order made under this section on application of the Attorney General may be managed in accordance with an order made under s. 462.331.

SYNOPSIS

This section provides for the issuance of restraint orders with respect to property which falls into the definition of "proceeds of crime" and is subject to forfeiture under this part.

An application for such an order must be made in writing by an Attorney General to a judge as defined in s. 462.3. It may be made *ex parte* and shall be accompanied by an affidavit sworn on information or belief. The affidavit must identify the offence in question; the person believed to be in possession of the property; the grounds for the belief that the property is subject to forfeiture, and its description and a statement whether any previous application had been made with respect to the property.

If the judge is satisfied that reasonable grounds exist to believe that the property is subject to forfeiture, the judge may make an order in writing prohibiting any dealing with or disposing of any interest in the property. The judge may also impose such reasonable conditions as the judge thinks fit. Before making a restraint order, the judge may require notice be given to and may hear any person who in the judge's opinion appears to have a valid interest in the property unless he believes that giving such notice would result in the disappearance, dissipation or reduction in value of the property, or otherwise affect the property so that all or part of it could not be subject to an order of forfeiture. An order is valid throughout Canada, but if it is to be executed in another province and execution would require entry into or on the property of any person, it must first be confirmed by a judge in the other province.

Subsection (7) requires the judge, before making an order, to require the Attorney General to give such undertakings as the judge considers appropriate with respect to the payment of damages or costs in relation to the warrant.

A copy of an order must be served on the person to whom it is addressed, and a copy shall be registered in accordance with provincial law.

An order remains in effect until its revocation, variation or automatic expiry, or until an order of forfeiture or restoration is made.

Subsection (11) creates an offence triable by indictment or on summary conviction for contravening or failing to comply with a restraint order which has been served as required. As no punishment is specially provided for this offence, the indictable offence is punishable by imprisonment for a term not exceeding five years [s. 743], and the summary conviction offence is punishable by up to six months and a $2000 fine [s. 787].

ANNOTATIONS

An order made under this section is a seizure within the meaning of s. 8 of the *Canadian Charter of Rights and Freedoms*. However, the owner's rights under s. 8 were not violated because an agent of a provincial regulatory authority conducting an audit of the owner's business for compliance with provincial statutes passed on to the police information later used in a criminal investigation. The owner was required to keep the information under the provincial legislation and must have known that the legislation was not private in relation to the government. Transmitting information to the police, to initiate an investigation into the irregularities that had been observed, was connected with performance of the agent's duties and that information could be used by the police to support an application for an order under this section: *Quebec (Attorney General) v. Laroche*, [2002] 3 S.C.R. 708, 169 C.C.C. (3d) 97, 6 C.R. (6th) 272. [Also see note of this case under s. 462.34, *infra*.]

Offence-related property extends the proceeds of sale of offence-related property: *Scotia Mortgage Corp. v. Leung* (2007), 221 C.C.C. (3d) 505 (B.C.C.A.), leave to appeal to S.C.C. refused 223 C.C.C. (3d) vi.

While subsec. (3) refers to a forfeiture order under, *inter alia* s. 462.37(1), that necessarily includes an order that could be made on the basis of s. 462.37(2) because, although the evidence does not establish that the designated offence was committed in relation to property, the sentencing court is nevertheless satisfied beyond a reasonable doubt that the property is proceeds of crime: *Quebec (Attorney General) v. Laroche, supra.*

MANAGEMENT ORDER / Appointment of Minister of Public Works and Government Services / Power to manage / Application for destruction order / Notice / Manner of giving notice / Order / When management order ceases to have effect / Application to vary conditions.

462.331 (1) With respect to property seized under section 462.32 or restrained under section 462.33, other than a controlled substance within the meaning of the *Controlled Drugs and Substances Act*, on application of the Attorney General or of any other person with the written consent of the Attorney General, where a judge is of the opinion that the circumstances so require, the judge may

>   (*a*) appoint a person to take control of and to manage or otherwise deal with all or part of the property in accordance with the directions of the judge; and

>   (*b*) require any person having possession of that property to give possession of the property to the person appointed under paragraph (*a*).

(2) When the Attorney General of Canada so requests, a judge appointing a person under subsection (1) shall appoint the Minister of Public Works and Government Services.

(3) The power to manage or otherwise deal with property under subsection (1) includes

>   (*a*) in the case of perishable or rapidly depreciating property, the power to make an interlocutory sale of that property; and

>   (*b*) in the case of property that has little or no value, the power to destroy that property.

(4) Before a person appointed to manage property destroys property that has little or no value, he or she shall apply to a court for a destruction order.

(5) Before making a destruction order in relation to any property, a court shall require notice in accordance with subsection (6) to be given to, and may hear, any person who, in the opinion of the court, appears to have a valid interest in the property.

(6) A notice shall

>   (*a*) be given or served in the manner that the court directs or that may be specified in the rules of the court; and

>   (*b*) be of any duration that the court considers reasonable or that may be specified in the rules of the court.

(7) A court may order that the property be destroyed if it is satisfied that the property has little or no value, whether financial or other.

(8) A management order ceases to have effect when the property that is the subject of the management order is returned in accordance with the law to an applicant or forfeited to Her Majesty.

(9) The Attorney General may at any time apply to the judge to cancel or vary any condition to which a management order is subject but may not apply to vary an appointment made under subsection (2). 2001, c. 32, s. 16.

CROSS-REFERENCES

"Property" is defined in s. 2. "Judge" is defined in s. 462.3. "Attorney General" is defined in ss. 2 and 462.3(3), (4).

SYNOPSIS

This section allows the Attorney General or a person with the written consent of the Attorney General to apply to a judge for a management order in relation to property seized in accordance with a warrant issued under s. 462.32 or restrained under an order made under s. 462.33. The power to make the order includes the power to sell perishable or rapidly depreciating property and, if authorized by a destruction order, to destroy property of little or no value. Notice is to be given to persons with a valid interest in the property before a destruction order is made. A management order expires when it is returned or ordered forfeited. The Attorney General may apply to cancel or vary any conditions of the management order.

APPLICATION FOR REVIEW OF SPECIAL WARRANTS AND RESTRAINT ORDERS / Notice to Attorney General / Terms of examination order / Order of restoration of property or revocation or variation of order / Hearing / Expenses / Taxing legal fees / Conditions to be satisfied / Saving provision / Form of recognizance.

462.34 (1) Any person who has an interest in property that was seized under a warrant issued pursuant to section 462.32 or in respect of which a restraint order was made under subsection 462.33(3) may, at any time, apply to a judge
  (*a*) for an order under subsection (4); or
  (*b*) for permission to examine the property.

(2) Where an application is made under paragraph (1)(*a*),
  (*a*) the application shall not, without the consent of the Attorney General, be heard by a judge unless the applicant has given to the Attorney General at least two clear days notice in writing of the application; and
  (*b*) the judge may require notice of the application to be given to and may hear any person who, in the opinion of the judge, appears to have a valid interest in the property.

(3) A judge may, on an application made to the judge under paragraph (1)(*b*), order that the applicant be permitted to examine property subject to such terms as appear to the judge to be necessary or desirable to ensure that the property is safeguarded and preserved for any purpose for which it may subsequently be required.

(4) On an application made to a judge under paragraph (1)(*a*) in respect of any property and after hearing the applicant and the Attorney General and any other person to whom notice was given pursuant to paragraph (2)(*b*), the judge may order that the property or a part thereof be returned to the applicant or, in the case of a restraint order made under subsection 462.33(3), revoke the order, vary the order to exclude the property or any interest in the property or part thereof from the application of the order or make the order subject to such reasonable conditions as the judge thinks fit, (*a*) if the applicant enters into a recognizance before the judge, with or without sureties, in such amount and with such conditions, if any, as the judge directs and, where the judge considers it appropriate, deposits with the judge such sum of money or other valuable security as the judge directs;

   (*b*) if the conditions referred to in subsection (6) are satisfied; or

   (*c*) for the purpose of

      (i) meeting the reasonable living expenses of the person who was in possession of the property at the time the warrant was executed or the order was made or any person who, in the opinion of the judge, has a valid interest in the property and of the dependants of that person,

      (ii) meeting the reasonable business and legal expenses of a person referred to in subparagraph (i), or

      (iii) permitting the use of the property in order to enter into a recognizance under Part XVI,

if the judge is satisfied that the applicant has no other assets or means available for the purposes set out in this paragraph and that no other person appears to be the lawful owner of or lawfully entitled to possession of the property.

(5) For the purpose of determining the reasonableness of legal expenses referred to in subparagraph (4)(*c*)(ii), a judge shall hold an in camera hearing, without the presence of the Attorney General, and shall take into account the legal aid tariff of the province.

(5.1) For the purpose of determining the reasonableness of expenses referred to in paragraph (4)(*c*), the Attorney General may

   (*a*) at the hearing of the application, make representations as to what would constitute the reasonableness of the expenses, other than legal expenses; and

   (*b*) before or after the hearing of the application held in camera pursuant to subsection (5), make representations as to what would constitute reasonable legal expenses referred to in subparagraph (4)(*c*)(ii).

(5.2) The judge who made an order under paragraph (4)(*c*) may, and on the application of the Attorney General shall, tax the legal fees forming part of the legal expenses referred to in subparagraph (4)(*c*)(ii) and, in so doing, shall take into account

   (*a*) the value of property in respect of which an order of forfeiture may be made;

   (*b*) the complexity of the proceedings giving rise to those legal expenses;

   (*c*) the importance of the issues involved in those proceedings;

   (*d*) the duration of any hearings held in respect of those proceedings;

   (*e*) whether any stage of those proceedings was improper or vexatious;

   (*f*) any representations made by the Attorney General; and

   (*g*) any other relevant matter.

(6) An order under paragraph (4)(*b*) in respect of property may be made by a judge if the judge is satisfied

   (*a*) where the application is made by

      (i) a person charged with a designated offence, or

      (ii) any person who acquired title to or a right of possession of that property from a person referred to in subparagraph (i) under circumstances that give rise to a reasonable inference that the title or right was transferred from that person for the purpose of avoiding the forfeiture of the property, that a warrant should not have been issued pursuant to section 462.32 or a restraint order under subsection 462.33(3) should not have been made in respect of that property, or

   (*b*) in any other case, that the applicant is the lawful owner of or lawfully entitled to possession of the property and appears innocent of any complicity in a designated offence or of any collusion in relation to such an offence, and that no other person appears to be the lawful owner of or lawfully entitled to possession of the property, and that the property will no longer be required for the purpose of any investigation or as evidence in any proceeding.

(7) Sections 354, 355.2 and 355.4 do not apply to a person who comes into possession of any property that, by virtue of an order made under paragraph (4)(c), was returned to any person after having been seized or was excluded from the application of a restraint order made under subsection 462.33(3).

(8) A recognizance entered into pursuant to paragraph (4)(a) may be in Form 32. R.S.C. 1985, c. 42 (4th Supp.), s. 2; 1996, c. 19, ss. 69 and 70; 1997, c. 18, ss. 31, 140; 2001, c. 32, s. 17; 2010, c. 14, s. 8.

CROSS-REFERENCES

The terms "property" and "person" are defined in s. 2. "Judge" and "designated offence" are defined in s. 462.3. "Attorney General" is defined in ss. 2 and 462.3(3), (4). Pursuant to s. 462.341, certain parts of this section may apply to moneys seized under this Act or the *Controlled Drugs and Substances Act*.

If the Attorney General is required to return documents as part of a successful application under this section, copies can be made, pursuant to s. 462.46, of such documents before they are returned, and may be used as evidence as if they were the originals. Section 462.45 provides that an order returning property pursuant to s. 462.34(4) is suspended if an appeal from such an order or an application for restoration is made.

SYNOPSIS

This section provides for an application to a judge, as defined in s. 462.3, for an order returning property seized under s. 462.32, revoking a restraint order made under s. 462.34, or permitting the examination of seized or restrained property on such terms as the judge may require. Two clear days' notice must be given the Attorney General, unless the judge requires notice to be given to and hearing accorded to other interested parties.

The judge may also exclude property from the warrant or order if: the warrant or order should not have been issued with respect to that property; the property belongs to an innocent third party and the property is not required for evidence; the property is required for reasonable living, business or legal expenses (if the applicant has no other assets or means); or the applicant enters into a recognizance. The judge who made the order respecting release of funds to meet reasonable legal expenses shall tax those fees on application by the Attorney General.

Possession of property returned or excluded pursuant to this section is not an offence.

ANNOTATIONS

Standard of review – The review of a special warrant or restraint order which is designed to prevent the depletion of illegal property requires a different approach than that used in reviewing wiretap authorizations. The reviewing judge must determine whether the same decision would have been made, not merely whether there was a sufficient basis for the decision. In so doing, the judge must consider any evidence presented by the applicant to rebut or undermine the justifications for the authorization. Even if the judge concludes that the authorization should not have been granted, the Crown may request that the property remain under restraint if it is still required for a criminal investigation or as evidence in other cases. In addition, the rule against collateral attack is also relaxed to accommodate challenges to the underlying general search warrant while reviewing a special warrant or restraint order. *Quebec (Attorney General) v. Laroche*, [2002] 3 S.C.R. 708, 169 C.C.C. (3d) 97, 6 C.R. (6th) 272.

This provision does not violate ss. 7, 10(b), 11(c) or 11(d) of the Charter: *R. v. Trang* (2001), 161 C.C.C. (3d) 210, 300 A.R. 112, 88 C.R.R. (2d) 134 (Q.B.).

CR. CODE

Legal expenses – The application to vary the order must be made by the client, not the lawyer. On the hearing of the application, the client, who is still facing charges, cannot be examined as to the source of his assets. Further, the client should not be required to answer any questions which may assist the Crown to prosecute him on further charges in other proceedings. Once the accused has established that the variation is required to meet legal expenses, the judge will hold an *in camera* hearing in the absence of Crown counsel to determine the amount which should be released from the restraint order: *R. v. Morra* (1992), 77 C.C.C. (3d) 380, 17 C.R. (4th) 325, 11 C.R.R. (2d) 379 (Ont. Ct. (Gen. Div.)).

Before succeeding on an application to access funds under this section, the accused must first attempt to avail himself of legal aid funding: *R. v. Cheng* (2011), 284 C.C.C. (3d) 240 (Ont. S.C.J.). *Contra*: *R. v. Bedi*, [2003] O.J. No. 5825 (S.C.J.).

There is no right of appeal to the Court of Appeal from the dismissal of an application under subsec. (4)(*c*)(ii). The only avenue of appeal is pursuant to s. 40 of the *Supreme Court Act*, R.S.C. 1985, c. S-26: *R. v. Martin* (2011), 266 C.C.C. (3d) 262 (Nfld. & Lab. C.A.).

[Now also see subsecs. (5.1)(*b*) and (5.2).]

APPLICATION OF PROPERTY RESTITUTION PROVISIONS.

462.341 Subsection 462.34(2), paragraph 462.34(4)(*c*) and subsections 462.34(5), (5.1) and (5.2) apply, with any modifications that the circumstances require, to a person who has an interest in money or bank-notes that are seized under this Act or the *Controlled Drugs and Substances Act* and in respect of which proceedings may be taken under subsection 462.37(1) or (2.01) or 462.38(2). 1997, c. 18, ss. 32, 140; 1999, c. 5, s. 14; 2005, c. 44, s. 5.

EXPIRATION OF SPECIAL WARRANTS AND RESTRAINT ORDERS/Where proceedings instituted/Where application made.

462.35 (1) Subject to this section, where property has been seized under a warrant issued pursuant to section 462.32 or a restraint order has been made under section 462.33 in relation to property, the property may be detained or the order may continue in force, as the case may be, for a period not exceeding six months from the seizure or the making of the order, as the case may be.

(2) The property may continue to be detained, or the order may continue in force, for a period that exceeds six months if proceedings are instituted in respect of which the thing detained may be forfeited.

(3) The property may continue to be detained or the order may continue in force for a period or periods that exceed six months if the continuation is, on application made by the Attorney General, ordered by a judge, where the judge is satisfied that the property is required, after the expiration of the period or periods, for the purpose of section 462.37 or 462.38 or any other provision of this or any other Act of Parliament respecting forfeiture or for the purpose of any investigation or as evidence in any proceeding. R.S.C. 1985, c. 42 (4th Supp.), s. 2; 1997, c. 18, s. 33.

CROSS-REFERENCES

The term "property" is defined in s. 2. "Judge" is defined in s. 462.3. "Attorney General" is defined in ss. 2 and 462.3(3), (4).

If a successful application is not made by the Attorney General to extend the length of a restraint order or a search warrant issued under s. 462.32, the property seized will be disposed of under s. 462.32 or 462.43. If the Attorney General is required to return documents under this section, copies can be made, pursuant to s. 462.46, of such documents before they are returned, and may be used as evidence as if they were the originals.

Unlike most of the provisions in this Part, there is no right of appeal from a decision under this section.

SYNOPSIS

This section provides for the automatic expiry of warrants and restraint orders after six months, unless forfeiture proceedings are instituted; or a judge is satisfied by the Attorney General that the property may be required after the expiration of that period for the purpose of ss. 462.37, 462.38, any other provision of the Code, or any other federal Act respecting forfeiture, or for the purpose of any investigation or as evidence in any proceeding, extends the time. This section also pertains to property seized or restrained under ss. 462.32 and 462.33.

ANNOTATIONS

Even where the Crown complies with the provisions of this section, a judge has a discretion to refuse to order the continuing detention of the goods. The order was refused where the Crown had misled the judge who granted the initial *ex parte* order under s. 462.32 by failing to disclose that prior to the seizure of the goods an agreement had been reached between Crown counsel and counsel for the owner that would allow the owner to remain in possession of the goods: *R. v. Derksen* (1998), 126 C.C.C. (3d) 554 (Sask. Q.B.), affd 140 C.C.C. (3d) 184 (Sask. C.A.), leave to appeal to S.C.C. refused 142 C.C.C. (3d) vi.

FORWARDING TO CLERK WHERE ACCUSED TO STAND TRIAL.

462.36 Where a judge issues a warrant under section 462.32 or makes a restraint order under section 462.33 in respect of any property, the clerk of the court shall, when an accused is ordered to stand trial for a designated offence, cause to be forwarded to the clerk of the court to which the accused has been ordered to stand trial a copy of the report filed pursuant to paragraph 462.32(4)(b) or of the restraint order in respect of the property. R.S.C. 1985, c. 42 (4th Supp.), s. 2; 2001, c. 32, s. 18.

CROSS-REFERENCES

The terms "property" and "clerk of the court" are defined in s. 2. "Judge" and "designated offence" are defined in s. 462.3.

SYNOPSIS

This section provides for the transmission to the clerk of the court, to which an accused has been ordered to stand trial for a designated offence, of a copy of the report filed under s. 462.32(4)(b), or the restraint order under s. 462.33, with respect to the seized or restrained property.

Forfeiture of Proceeds of Crime

ORDER OF FORFEITURE OF PROPERTY ON CONVICTION / Proceeds of crime derived from other offences / Order of forfeiture — particular circumstances / Offences / Offender may establish that property is not proceeds of crime / Pattern of criminal activity / Conditions — pattern of criminal activity / Application under subsection (1) not prevented / Exception / Property outside Canada / Fine instead of forfeiture / Imprisonment in default of payment of fine / Fine option program not available to offender.

462.37 (1) Subject to this section and sections 462.39 to 462.41, where an offender is convicted, or discharged under section 730, of a designated offence and the court imposing sentence on the offender, on application of the Attorney General, is satisfied, on a balance of probabilities, that any property is proceeds of crime and that the designated offence was committed in relation to that property, the court shall order that

the property be forfeited to Her Majesty to be disposed of as the Attorney General directs or otherwise dealt with in accordance with the law.

(2) Where the evidence does not establish to the satisfaction of the court that the designated offence of which the offender is convicted, or discharged under section 730, was committed in relation to property in respect of which an order of forfeiture would otherwise be made under subsection (1) but the court is satisfied, beyond a reasonable doubt, that that property is proceeds of crime, the court may make an order of forfeiture under subsection (1) in relation to that property.

(2.01) A court imposing sentence on an offender convicted of an offence described in subsection (2.02) shall, on application of the Attorney General and subject to this section and sections 462.4 and 462.41, order that any property of the offender that is identified by the Attorney General in the application be forfeited to Her Majesty to be disposed of as the Attorney General directs or otherwise dealt with in accordance with the law if the court is satisfied, on a balance of probabilities, that

(*a*) within 10 years before the proceedings were commenced in respect of the offence for which the offender is being sentenced, the offender engaged in a pattern of criminal activity for the purpose of directly or indirectly receiving a material benefit, including a financial benefit; or

(*b*) the income of the offender from sources unrelated to designated offences cannot reasonably account for the value of all the property of the offender.

(2.02) The offences are the following:

(*a*) a criminal organization offence punishable by five or more years of imprisonment; and

(*b*) an offence under section 5, 6 or 7 of the *Controlled Drugs and Substances Act* — or a conspiracy or an attempt to commit, being an accessory after the fact in relation to, or any counselling in relation to an offence under those sections — prosecuted by indictment.

Note: Subsection 462.37(2.02) amended by striking out "and" at the end of para. (*a*), by adding "and" at the end of para. (*b*), and by enacting para. (*c*), 2015, c. 16, s. 4 (to come into force by order of the Governor in Council):

(*c*) an offence under any of sections 279.01 to 279.03.

(2.03) A court shall not make an order of forfeiture under subsection (2.01) in respect of any property that the offender establishes, on a balance of probabilities, is not proceeds of crime.

(2.04) In determining whether the offender has engaged in a pattern of criminal activity described in paragraph (2.01)(*a*), the court shall consider

(*a*) the circumstances of the offence for which the offender is being sentenced;

(*b*) any act or omission — other than an act or omission that constitutes the offence for which the offender is being sentenced — that the court is satisfied, on a balance of probabilities, was committed by the offender and constitutes an offence punishable by indictment under any Act of Parliament;

(*c*) any act or omission that the court is satisfied, on a balance of probabilities, was committed by the offender and is an offence in the place where it was committed and, if committed in Canada, would constitute an offence punishable by indictment under any Act of Parliament; and

(*d*) any other factor that the court considers relevant.

(2.05) A court shall not determine that an offender has engaged in a pattern of criminal activity unless the court is satisfied, on a balance of probabilities, that the offender committed, within the period referred to in paragraph (2.01)(*a*),

(*a*) acts or omissions — other than an act or omission that constitutes the offence for which the offender is being sentenced — that constitute at least two serious offences or one criminal organization offence;

(b) acts or omissions that are offences in the place where they were committed and, if committed in Canada, would constitute at least two serious offences or one criminal organization offence; or

(c) an act or omission described in paragraph (a) that constitutes a serious offence and an act or omission described in paragraph (b) that, if committed in Canada, would constitute a serious offence.

(2.06) Nothing in subsection (2.01) shall be interpreted as preventing the Attorney General from making an application under subsection (1) in respect of any property.

(2.07) A court may, if it considers it in the interests of justice, decline to make an order of forfeiture against any property that would otherwise be subject to forfeiture under subsection (2.01). The court shall give reasons for its decision.

(2.1) An order may be issued under this section in respect of property situated outside Canada, with any modifications that the circumstances require.

(3) If a court is satisfied that an order of forfeiture under subsection (1) or (2.01) should be made in respect of any property of an offender but that the property or any part of or interest in the property cannot be made subject to an order, the court may, instead of ordering the property or any part of or interest in the property to be forfeited, order the offender to pay a fine in an amount equal to the value of the property or the part of or interest in the property. In particular, a court may order the offender to pay a fine if the property or any part of or interest in the property

(a) cannot, on the exercise of due diligence, be located;

(b) has been transferred to a third party;

(c) is located outside Canada;

(d) has been substantially diminished in value or rendered worthless; or

(e) has been commingled with other property that cannot be divided without difficulty.

(4) Where a court orders an offender to pay a fine pursuant to subsection (3), the court shall

(a) impose, in default of payment of that fine, a term of imprisonment

(i) not exceeding six months, where the amount of the fine does not exceed ten thousand dollars,

(ii) of not less than six months and not exceeding twelve months, where the amount of the fine exceeds ten thousand dollars but does not exceed twenty thousand dollars,

(iii) of not less than twelve months and not exceeding eighteen months, where the amount of the fine exceeds twenty thousand dollars but does not exceed fifty thousand dollars,

(iv) of not less than eighteen months and not exceeding two years, where the amount of the fine exceeds fifty thousand dollars but does not exceed one hundred thousand dollars,

(v) of not less than two years and not exceeding three years, where the amount of the fine exceeds one hundred thousand dollars but does not exceed two hundred and fifty thousand dollars,

(vi) of not less than three years and not exceeding five years, where the amount of the fine exceeds two hundred and fifty thousand dollars but does not exceed one million dollars, or

(vii) of not less than five years and not exceeding ten years, where the amount of the fine exceeds one million dollars; and

(b) direct that the term of imprisonment imposed pursuant to paragraph (a) be served consecutively to any other term of imprisonment imposed on the offender or that the offender is then serving.

(5) Section 736 does not apply to an offender against whom a fine is imposed pursuant to subsection (3). R.S.C. 1985, c. 42 (4th Supp.), s. 2; 1995, c. 22, s. 10; 2001, c. 32, s. 19; 2005, c. 44, s. 6.

CROSS-REFERENCES

The terms "criminal organization offence", "serious offence", and "property" are defined in s. 2. The terms "designated offence" and "proceeds of crime" are defined in s. 462.3. "Attorney General" is defined in ss. 2 and 462.3(3), (4). The order may be executed in another province in accordance with s. 462.371.

Section 462.39 provides for an inference to be drawn that the property was obtained as a result of an "enterprise crime offence" if the conditions of that section are satisfied. Section 462.41 requires that notice be given to any person who may have a valid interest in the property before an order is made for the forfeiture of the property. In addition, before any property is forfeited under this section, the court may set aside any improper conveyances, using its powers under s. 462.4. Section 462.42 allows persons with a valid interest in the property which is to be forfeited to apply to have their interest declared not affected by any forfeiture, and to either retrieve the portion of the property in which they have an interest or an equivalent sum of money. Section 462.43 provides for the disposal of any residual property remaining after all persons with a valid interest have had their claims determined. If documents are returned under s. 462.37, the Attorney General has the right to make copies before returning the documents and to use them as evidence as if they were originals, pursuant to s. 462.46.

Section 673, which defines "sentence" for the purpose of indictable offences, includes an order under this section so that s. 683 permits an appeal to the appropriate appellate court. Section 462.45 provides that a forfeiture order is not to be carried out for 30 days and is stayed if it is under appeal, an application is made for restoration of the property or there are any proceedings in which the right to seize the property is questioned.

As to forfeiture of proceeds from a designated substance offence, see s. 23 of the *Controlled Drugs and Substances Act*.

Reference should also be made to the *Seized Property Management Act*, S.C. 1993, c. 37 [found in *Martin's Related Criminal Statutes*], where property is forfeited to Her Majesty and disposed of, or where a fine is imposed pursuant to this section.

SYNOPSIS

This section deals with the forfeiture of proceeds of crime after an accused person has been convicted of a designated offence.

Subsection (1) provides for an order, for the forfeiture of property, by the judge imposing sentence when a person is found guilty of the designated offence. If the Attorney General satisfies the judge, on a balance of probabilities, that any property is the proceeds of crime, and that the designated offence that was the subject of the trial was committed in relation to such property, the judge shall order its forfeiture.

Subsection (2) provides that, where in the proceedings described in subsec. (1), the connection between the offence and the property is not established, but the judge is satisfied beyond a reasonable doubt that the property is proceeds of crime, the judge may order its forfeiture.

Subsection (2.1) gives the judge extraterritorial jurisdiction in the sense that an order may be made under this section even where the property is outside Canada.

Subsections (2.01) to (2.07) provide an expanded jurisdiction to order forfeiture of property that is not directly connected to the crime for which the accused has been convicted, where the accused has been convicted of a criminal organization offence or an offence or a conspiracy, attempt or accessory after the fact to an offence under ss. 5 to 7 of the *Controlled Drugs and Substances Act*. Under subsec. (2.01), the forfeiture order may be made in relation to any property identified in an application by the Attorney General, where the court is satisfied on a balance of probabilities that, within the 10 years before the proceedings were commenced, the offender was engaged in a pattern of criminal activity for the purpose of directly or indirectly receiving a material benefit, or the offender's income from non-designated offences cannot reasonably account for the offender's wealth. However, under subsec. (2.03), the court shall not make a forfeiture order if the offender establishes on a balance of probabilities that the property identified in the application is not proceeds of crime. Subsection (2.04) sets out the circumstances the judge is to consider in determining whether the offender engaged in a pattern of criminal activity. Among other things, this subsection allows the judge to take into account other offences that have been shown to have likely been committed by the offender. However, under subsec. (2.05), the court shall not find that the offender engaged in a pattern of criminal activity unless the court is satisfied that, within the 10-year period referred to in subsec. (2.01), the offender probably committed certain offences; namely one criminal organization offence or two serious offences (terms defined in s. 2), or similar offences committed outside of Canada as specified in paras. (b) and (c). Further, under subsec. (2.07), the judge may decline to make the order but must give reasons for not doing so.

Where an order should be made under subsec. (1) or (2.01), but the property cannot be found after the exercise of due diligence, it has been transferred, it is outside Canada, or it has been diminished or commingled, the court may, instead of ordering forfeiture, impose a fine of equal value to such property on the offender.

Subsection (4) provides a sliding scale for consecutive imprisonment in lieu of payment of the fine.

ANNOTATIONS

The trial judge at the time of sentencing erred in refusing to make an order under subsec. (1) with respect to certain monies seized from the accused at the time of his arrest, in part because the judge believed that the monies had been given the accused by his mother. The entitlement claims of other persons to the proceeds are not to be dealt with in conjunction with a sentence hearing but rather pursuant to s. 462.42 after the order of forfeiture has been made: *R. v. Pawlyk* (1991), 65 C.C.C. (3d) 63 (Man. C.A.).

The forfeiture order is part of the sentence and, once the order has been made, the trial judge is *functus*. Thus, the judge had no jurisdiction to subsequently vacate a portion of the order on the application of the mortgagee: *R. v. Sterling* (1992), 71 C.C.C. (3d) 222 (B.C.S.C.). *Contra: Wilson v. Canada* (1993), 86 C.C.C. (3d) 464 (Ont. C.A.), where it was held that third party claims can be considered at the sentence hearing in view of s. 462.41.

The burden on the applicant seeking the return of property is less onerous at the forfeiture stage as opposed to the restraint order stage, in that the applicant need only show that he or she appears innocent of any complicity or collusion with respect to the offences regarding which the forfeiture order is sought: *Antillas Communication inc. v. La Reine* (2007), 232 C.C.C. (3d) 553 (Que. C.A.).

A valid security interest can attach to funds subsequently found to constitute proceeds of crime. In such circumstances, a corporation's interest is voidable but not void *ab initio*. Accordingly, in this case, although the bank had a valid security interest in moneys in an account pursuant to a security agreement, it was not appropriate in the circumstances to exercise the court's discretion in favour of the bank in respect of funds which were identifiable proceeds of crime that should be returned to the victims. The portion of the funds in the account which were not identifiable proceeds of crime were not properly the subject of a forfeiture order and should be returned to the bank: *R. v. Canadian Imperial Bank of Commerce* (2000), 151 C.C.C. (3d) 439 (Ont. C.A.).

It was not appropriate to impose a fine under subsec. (3) where the proceeds had been used by the accused to enter into a recognizance and then for lawyer fees. If the Crown had moved to seize the funds, they would have been available for these purposes in any event by an application under s. 462.34: *R. v. Gagnon* (1993), 80 C.C.C. (3d) 508 (Alta. Q.B.).

A provincial court judge acting as a trial judge has the jurisdiction to order the forfeiture of property under this section: *R. v. Rosenblum* (1998), 130 C.C.C. (3d) 481 (B.C.C.A.).

The fact that property is registered in the name of a third party does not create a discretion to impose a fine in lieu of forfeiture where the criteria of subsec. (1) have been met: *R. v. Rosenblum, infra.*

In view of the provisions of subsecs. (3) and (4) a lawyer, representing the accused, who has taken an assignment of seized funds is in a potential conflict of interest. If the court makes an order in favour of the lawyer then the accused is liable to have a fine (and jail in default) imposed in the equivalent amount. On the other hand, it would be inappropriate for the lawyer to wait until after sentencing and then make a claim under s. 462.42 in an effort to circumvent the scheme of the legislation: *R. v. Wilson, supra.*

While the judge has a discretion whether or not to impose a fine and as to the determination of the value of the property, the fine must equal the value of the property. The offender's ability to pay is not a factor reducing the amount of the fine and is not a factor to be considered in whether to impose a fine. However, the ability to pay may be taken into consideration in determining the time limit for payment of the fine: *R. v. Lavigne*, [2006] 1 S.C.R. 392, 206 C.C.C. (3d) 449.

An order for a fine in lieu of forfeiture can be made only where the offender has possession or control of the property in question or at least had possession of the property at some point. This conclusion flows from the use of the phrase "any property of an offender" in subsec. (3) and the definition of "property" in s. 2: *R. v. Dwyer* (2013), 296 C.C.C. (3d) 193 (Ont. C.A.), additional reasons 2013 ONCA 306.

DEFINITION OF "ORDER" / Execution / Filing of order from another province / Attorney General of Canada / Effect of registered order / Notice / Application of section 462.42 / Application under section 462.42 to be made in one province / Finding in one court binding

462.371 (1) In this section, "order" means an order made under section 462.37 or 462.38.

(2) An order may be executed anywhere in Canada.

(3) Where the Attorney General of a province in which property that is the subject of an order made in another province is situated receives a certified copy of the order and files it with the superior court of criminal jurisdiction of the province in which the property is situated, the order shall be entered as a judgment of that court.

(4) Where the Attorney General of Canada receives a certified copy of an order made in a province in respect of property situated in another province and files the order with the superior court of criminal jurisdiction of the province in which the property is situated, the order shall be entered as a judgment of that court.

(5) An order has, from the date it is filed in a court of a province under subsection (3) or (4), the same effect as if it had been an order originally made by that court.

(6) Where an order has been filed in a court under subsection (3) or (4), it shall not be executed before notice in accordance with subsection 462.41(2) is given to every person who, in the opinion of the court, appears to have a valid interest in the property.

(7) Section 462.42 applies, with such modifications as the circumstances require, in respect of a person who claims an interest in property that is the subject of an order filed under subsection (3) or (4).

(8) No person may make an application under section section 462.42 in relation to property that is the subject of an order filed under subsection (3) or (4) if that person has previously made an application in respect of the same property in another province.

(9) The finding by a court of a province in relation to property that is the subject of an order filed under subsection (3) or (4) as to whether or not an applicant referred to in subsection 462.42(4) is affected by the forfeiture referred to in that subsection or declaring the nature and extent of the interest of the applicant under that subsection is

binding on the superior court of criminal jurisdiction of the province where the order is entered as a judgment. 1997, c. 18, s. 34.

CROSS-REFERENCES

"Property" and "superior court of criminal jurisdiction" are defined in s. 2. "Attorney General" is defined in ss. 2 and 462.3(3), (4).

SYNOPSIS

This section sets out the procedure for executing forfeiture orders made under ss. 462.37 and 462.38 where the property is situated in another province. Upon receiving the order the Attorney General causes the order to be filed in the superior court of criminal jurisdiction and the order is then entered as a judgment of that court. However, the order cannot be executed until notice has been given in accordance with s. 462.41(2). A person affected by the order may then apply to the superior court in accordance with s. 462.42, provided that the person has not made an application in respect of the same property in another province. An order under s. 462.42 as to whether an applicant is affected by the forfeiture or declaring the nature and extent of the interest is binding on the superior court.

APPLICATION FOR FORFEITURE / Order of forfeiture of property / Property outside Canada / Person deemed absconded.

462.38 (1) Where an information has been laid in respect of a designated offence, the Attorney General may make an application to a judge for an order of forfeiture under subsection (2) in respect of any property.

(2) Subject to sections 462.39 to 462.41, where an application is made to a judge under subsection (1), the judge shall, if the judge is satisfied that

    (*a*) **any property is, beyond a reasonable doubt, proceeds of crime,**

    (*b*) **proceedings in respect of a designated offence committed in relation to that property were commenced, and**

    (*c*) **the accused charged with the offence referred to in paragraph (*b*) has died or absconded,**

order that the property be forfeited to Her Majesty to be disposed of as the Attorney General directs or otherwise dealt with in accordance with the law.

(2.1) An order may be issued under this section in respect of property situated outside Canada, with any modifications that the circumstances require.

(3) For the purposes of this section, a person shall be deemed to have absconded in connection with a designated offence if

    (*a*) **an information has been laid alleging the commission of the offence by the person,**

    (*b*) **a warrant for the arrest of the person or a summons in respect of an organization has been issued in relation to that information, and**

    (*c*) **reasonable attempts to arrest the person pursuant to the warrant or to serve the summons have been unsuccessful during the period of six months commencing on the day the warrant or summons was issued, or, in the case of a person who is not or never was in Canada, the person cannot be brought within that period to the jurisdiction in which the warrant or summons was issued,**

and the person shall be deemed to have so absconded on the last day of that period of six months. R.S.C. 1985, c. 42 (4th Supp.), s. 2; 1997, c. 18, s. 35(2); 2001, c. 32, s. 20; 2003, c. 21, s. 7.

CROSS-REFERENCES

The terms "organization", "property" and "person" are defined in s. 2. The terms "judge", "proceeds of crime" and "designated offence" are defined in s. 462.3. "Attorney General" is defined in ss. 2 and 462.3(3), (4). The order is executed in accordance with s. 462.371.

Section 462.39 provides for an inference to be drawn that the property was obtained as a result of a "designated offence" if the conditions of that section are satisfied. Section 462.41 requires that notice be given to any person who may have a valid interest in the property before an order is made for the forfeiture of the property. In addition, before any property is forfeited under this section, the court may set aside any improper conveyances using its powers under s. 462.4. Section 462.42 allows persons with a valid interest in the property which is to be forfeited to apply to have their interest declared not affected by any forfeiture, and to either retrieve the portion of the property in which they have an interest or an equivalent sum of money. Section 462.43 provides for the disposal of any residual property remaining after all persons with a valid interest have had their claims determined. If documents are returned under s. 462.37, the Attorney General has the right to make copies before returning the documents and to use them as evidence as if they were originals, pursuant to s. 462.46.

Section 462.44 provides for a right of appeal from a forfeiture order. Section 462.45 provides that a forfeiture order is not to be carried out for 30 days and is stayed if it is under appeal, an application is made for restoration of the property or there are any proceedings in which the right to seize the property is questioned.

Similar provisions relating to a designated substance offence are found in s. 17 of the *Controlled Drugs and Substances Act.*

Reference should also be made to the *Seized Property Management Act*, S.C. 1993, c. 37, where property is forfeited to Her Majesty under this section.

SYNOPSIS

This section provides for an *in rem* forfeiture hearing for proceeds of crime in certain circumstances. The Attorney General may apply for such a hearing if an information has been laid in respect of a designated offence. On such an application, the judge shall order forfeiture if the Attorney General establishes that the property is, *beyond reasonable doubt*, proceeds of crime, that related enterprise crime proceedings were commenced, and that the accused has died or absconded.

Subsection (3) deems a person to have absconded if an information has been laid, a warrant issued, and reasonable attempts to arrest have been unsuccessful during the six-month period after the issuance of the warrant.

ANNOTATIONS

In establishing that any seized property is beyond a reasonable doubt the "proceeds of crime", there is no burden on the Crown to prove that the funds seized were the proceeds of any specific illegal transaction such as sale of narcotics. Thus, the fact that the funds or other property are proceeds of crime may be established by circumstantial evidence. The hearing under s. 462.38 is in its nature between a criminal trial proper where the strict rules of evidence apply and a sentence hearing. Thus, while it must be proved beyond a reasonable doubt that the property was the proceeds of crime, the fact that proceedings in respect of an enterprise crime offence had been commenced and that the accused absconded need only be proved on a balance of probabilities. Similarly, bearing in mind the standard of proof beyond a reasonable doubt as to the source of the funds sought to be forefeited, the general rule that all relevant evidence is admissible applies and the effect of exclusionary rules of evidence is to be left to the judge hearing the application. This includes the weight, if any, to be accorded to hearsay evidence, bearing in mind its reliability and the explanation for not making better evidence available: *R. v. Clymore* (1992), 74 C.C.C. (3d) 217 (B.C.S.C.).

Where the prerequisites set out in subsec. (3) have been met so that the accused is deemed to have absconded, the requirement in subsec. (1)(*c*) has been made out even if, in the course of the proceedings, the accused's whereabouts become known. Thus, in this case, the accused had still absconded for the purpose of the Crown's application, even if during the course of the proceedings his whereabouts were discovered as a result of his arrest by American authorities while apparently attempting to import drugs into that country. There was no requirement that the Crown attempt to extradite the accused before the end of the proceedings under this section. His status as an absconding accused continues for the purpose of this section: *R. v. Clymore, supra.* [Now see also subsec. (3)(*c*).]

Although the proceedings under this section lead only to the forfeiture of property, it would be open to the accused to rely on s. 8 of the Charter and to argue for exclusion of the funds seized, on the basis that his right to protection against unreasonable search and seizure was violated: *R. v. Clymore, supra.*

Property is not limited to physical property and can apply to an interest in property. The property does not have to be in existence at the time that the charges are laid providing that the property is proceeds of crime from the charge period. Property can appreciate or be converted to substitute property after the charge period but still constitute proceeds of crime: *R. v. Stone Estate* (2001), 155 C.C.C. (3d) 168, 42 C.R. (5th) 339 (N.S.C.A.).

INFERENCE.

462.39 For the purpose of subsection 462.37(1) or 462.38(2), the court may infer that property was obtained or derived as a result of the commission of a designated offence where evidence establishes that the value, after the commission of that offence, of all the property of the person alleged to have committed the offence exceeds the value of all the property of that person before the commission of that offence and the court is satisfied that the income of that person from sources unrelated to designated offences committed by that person cannot reasonably account for such an increase in value. R.S.C. 1985, c. 42 (4th Supp.), s. 2; 1996, c. 19, s. 70; 2001, c. 32, s. 21.

CROSS-REFERENCES

The terms "property" and "person" are defined in s. 2. The term "designated offence" is defined in s. 462.3. This section is incorporated into the *Controlled Drugs and Substances Act.* See s. 23 of that Act.

SYNOPSIS

This section provides that the court may infer in forfeiture hearings under this Part that property was obtained or derived from an enterprise crime offence where it is established that the value of all of a person's property after the commission of such an offence exceeds the previous value, and that unrelated legitimate income cannot reasonably account for the increase.

VOIDABLE TRANSFERS.

462.4 A court may,

(*a*) **prior to ordering property to be forfeited under subsection 462.37(1) or (2.01) or 462.38(2), and**

(*b*) **in the case of property in respect of which a restraint order was made under section 462.33, where the order was served in accordance with subsection 462.33(8), set aside any conveyance or transfer of the property that occurred after the seizure of the property or the service of the order under section 462.33, unless the conveyance or transfer was for valuable consideration to a person acting in good faith. R.S. 1985, c. 42 (4th Supp.) s. 2; 1997, c. 18, s. 36; 2005, c. 44, s. 7.**

CROSS-REFERENCES

The term "property" is defined in s. 2. This property could have been seized by a warrant issued under s. 462.32.

This section is incorporated into the *Controlled Drugs and Substances Act* by s. 23 of that Act.

SYNOPSIS

This section provides that, prior to ordering forfeiture, a court may void any transfers of seized or restrained property. The court is authorized to so order in the case of restrained property if the order was served and unless the transfer was made for valuable consideration to a person acting in good faith.

NOTICE / Service, duration and contents of notice / Order of restoration of property.

462.41 (1) Before making an order under subsection 462.37(1) or (2.01) or 462.38(2) in relation to any property, a court shall require notice in accordance with subsection (2) to be given to and may hear any person who, in the opinion of the court, appears to have a valid interest in the property.

(2) A notice given under subsection (1) shall

    (a) be given or served in such manner as the court directs or as may be prescribed by the rules of the court;

    (b) be of such duration as the court considers reasonable or as may be prescribed by the rules of the court; and

    (c) set out the designated offence charged and a description of the property.

(3) Where a court is satisfied that any person, other than

    (a) a person who is charged with, or was convicted of, a designated offence, or

    (b) a person who acquired title to or a right of possession of that property from a person referred to in paragraph (a) under circumstances that give rise to a reasonable inference that the title or right was transferred for the purpose of avoiding the forfeiture of the property,

is the lawful owner or is lawfully entitled to possession of any property or any part thereof that would otherwise be forfeited pursuant to subsection 462.37(1) or (2.01) or 462.38(2) and that the person appears innocent of any complicity in an offence referred to in paragraph (a) or of any collusion in relation to such an offence, the court may order that the property or part thereof be returned to that person. R.S.C. 1985, c. 42 (4th Supp.), s. 2; 1996, c. 19, s. 70; 1997, c. 18, ss. 37, 140; 2001, c. 32, s. 22; 2005, c. 44, s. 8.

CROSS-REFERENCES

The terms "property" and "person" are defined in s. 2. The term "designated offence" is defined in s. 462.3. The powers of a court to make rules is stated in s. 482.

Persons who receive notice under this section and seek to prevent their property from being forfeited can apply under s. 462.42 for relief from forfeiture.

A right of appeal from an order under subsec. (3) is provided by s. 462.44 and the order is stayed pursuant to s. 462.45. If a proceeding is brought, under which the restoration of the property under s. 462.41(3) is challenged, s. 462.45 will stay the restoration pending the completion of the further proceedings to determine the validity of the restoration order.

If documents are ordered returned under s. 462.41(3), the Attorney General has the right to make copies before returning the documents and to use them as evidence as if they were originals, pursuant to s. 462.46.

This section is incorporated into the *Controlled Drugs and Substances Act* by s. 23 of that Act.

SYNOPSIS

This section provides for notice to and the hearing of interested parties before forfeiture is ordered, and for the return of property to such persons if they are innocent of complicity.

Before making a forfeiture order, whether after a conviction or in an *in rem* proceeding, a court must require notice to be given in accordance with subsec. (2) to any person whom the court believes has a valid interest in the property in question, and may hear such person.

Where the court is satisfied that a person is the lawful owner of, or is entitled to possession of, all or part of the property in question, and appears innocent of complicity of collusion in a designated offence, the court may order it returned to that person, unless that person was charged with or convicted of a designated offence, or derived his or her interest in the property from such persons, in circumstances giving rise to a reasonable inference that the transfer was made to avoid forfeiture.

ANNOTATIONS

This section provides for both notice to interested third parties and an opportunity for them to be heard on the application. They need not apply under s. 462.42 after forfeiture has been made for an order that their property is not forfeited: *R. v. Sankar* (2010), 270 C.C.C. (3d) 410 (Ont. S.C.J.).

Where the process under this section makes otherwise forfeitable property not subject to forfeiture, the judge may impose a fine equivalent pursuant to s. 462.37: *Wilson v. Canada* (1993), 86 C.C.C. (3d) 464, 25 C.R. (4th) 239 (Ont. C.A.).

Forfeited funds can be released for the purpose of paying legal fees to counsel and the Legal Aid Plan: *R. v. Thomas* (2001), 153 C.C.C. (3d) 94 (Ont. C.A.).

A deceased's estate can have a valid interest in seized properties even if the interest did not exist at the time of the seizure. In this case, the judge had the jurisdiction to order a partial return of seized monies in order to pay for the estate's reasonable legal costs in responding to the Crown's forfeiture application: *Beaulieu Estate v. Canada* (2001), 165 C.C.C. (3d) 563, 214 D.L.R. (4th) 663, 243 N.B.R. (2d) 338 *sub nom. R. v. Beaulieu Estate* (C.A.).

APPLICATION BY PERSON CLAIMING INTEREST FOR RELIEF FROM FORFEITURE / Fixing day for hearing / Notice / Order declaring interest not subject to forfeiture / Appeal from order under subsection (4) / Return of property.

462.42 (1) Any person who claims an interest in property that is forfeited to Her Majesty under subsection 462.37(1) or (2.01) or 462.38(2) may, within thirty days after the forfeiture, apply by notice in writing to a judge for an order under subsection (4) unless the person is

    (*a*) a person who is charged with, or was convicted of, a designated offence that resulted in the forfeiture; or

    (*b*) a person who acquired title to or a right of possession of the property from a person referred to in paragraph (*a*) under circumstances that give rise to a reasonable inference that the title or right was transferred from that person for the purpose of avoiding the forfeiture of the property.

(2) The judge to whom an application is made under subsection (1) shall fix a day not less than thirty days after the date of filing of the application for the hearing thereof.

(3) An applicant shall serve a notice of the application made under subsection (1) and of the hearing thereof on the Attorney General at least fifteen days before the day fixed for the hearing.

(4) Where, on the hearing of an application made under subsection (1), the judge is satisfied that the applicant is not a person referred to in paragraph (1)(*a*) or (*b*) and appears innocent of any complicity in any designated offence that resulted in the forfeiture or of any collusion in relation to any such offence, the judge may make an order declaring that the interest of the applicant is not affected by the forfeiture and declaring the nature and extent of the interest.

(5) An applicant or the Attorney General may appeal to the court of appeal from an order under subsection (4) and the provisions of Part XXI with respect to procedure on appeals apply, with such modifications as the circumstances require, to appeals under this subsection.

(6) The Attorney General shall, on application made to the Attorney General by any person who has obtained an order under subsection (4) and where the periods with respect to the taking of appeals from that order have expired and any appeal from that order taken under subsection (5) has been determined,

    (*a*) direct that the property or the part thereof to which the interest of the applicant relates be returned to the applicant; or

    (*b*) direct that an amount equal to the value of the interest of the applicant, as declared in the order, be paid to the applicant. R.S.C. 1985, c. 42 (4th Supp.), s. 2; 1996, c. 19, s. 70; 1997, c. 18, ss. 38, 140; 2001, c. 32, s. 23; 2005, c. 44, s. 9.

CROSS-REFERENCES

The terms "property" and "person" are defined in s. 2. The terms "judge" and "designated offence" are defined in s. 462.3. "Attorney General" is defined in ss. 2 and 462.3(3), (4).

    This section is incorporated into the *Controlled Drugs and Substances Act* by s. 23 of that Act.

SYNOPSIS

This section provides for written applications by innocent third parties for relief from forfeiture under this part within 30 days after such forfeiture is ordered.

    Such application may be brought by any person who claims an interest in forfeited property, other than a person described in subsec. (1)(*a*) or (*b*), that is, a person who was charged with or convicted of a designated offence in relation to the property, or a person who acquired his interest from such person, in circumstances giving rise to a reasonable inference that the transfer was made to avoid forfeiture.

    A judge to whom such application is made shall fix a hearing date not less than 30 days after the application is filed. The Attorney General is entitled to at least 15 days notice of the hearing.

    The judge hearing the application may make an order declaring the nature and extent of the applicant's interest, and also declaring that it is not affected by the forfeiture, if he is satisfied that the applicant was not a person described in subsec. (1)(*a*) or (*b*) and that he appears innocent of complicity or collusion in the offence that resulted in the forfeiture.

    Appeals are available from orders under this section to the Court of Appeal.

    Upon the application of a person who has obtained an order under this section, if the appeal period has expired and any appeal has been determined, the Attorney General is required to direct the return of the property or the repayment of its value as declared in the order to the applicant.

ANNOTATIONS

An application under this provision is more properly made to a superior court judge since that judge is not subject to the jurisdictional limitations of a kind that might hamper the inquiry of a provincial court judge: *R. v. Rosenblum* (1998), 130 C.C.C. (3d) 481, 167 D.L.R. (4th) 639 (B.C.C.A.).

    Even where the applicant has met the conditions in this section, the judge has a discretion to refuse to make a declaration in favour of the applicant. In exercising the discretion, the judge must consider whether the innocent third party should suffer so that the goal of divesting the accused of his proceeds of crime can be achieved: *R. v. Wilson* (1993), 86 C.C.C. (3d) 464, 25 C.R. (4th) 239 (Ont. C.A.).

    In *R. v. Wilson, supra*, the accused and his wife had assigned their interest in seized funds to their lawyers for the payment of legal fees. At the time of sentencing, an order was made forfeiting those funds pursuant to s. 462.37. Once that order was made, any interest that the accused and his wife had in the funds was extinguished as was the interest that the lawyers had. Accordingly, they had no assertable interest in the funds within the meaning of this section.

The victim of an offence who had served a garnishee summons upon a company holding funds owed to the accused, before the Attorney General applied for forfeiture of those funds, was entitled to an order declaring an interest in those funds; *R. v. Tatarchuk*, [1993] 1 W.W.R. 349, 4 Alta. L.R. (3d) 300 (Q.B.).

An ordinary creditor does not have an enforceable interest in any particular asset of the debtor and in principle does not enjoy a right of recourse in relation to the asset. Accordingly, ordinary creditors do not have a valid interest in the proceeds of an enterprise crime offence committed by the debtor as contemplated by subsec. (4) of this provision: *Lumen Inc. v. Canada (Attorney General)* (1997), 119 C.C.C. (3d) 91, 10 C.R. (5th) 246 (Que. C.A.), leave to appeal to S.C.C. refused 119 C.C.C. (3d) vi, 152 D.L.R. (4th) vi. However, where the interest in the property goes beyond that of an unsecured creditor, a claim may be brought. In *R. v. 1431633 Ontario Inc.* (2010), 250 C.C.C. (3d) 354 (Ont. S.C.J.), the court recognized the right of a creditor that had erroneously failed to perfect a construction lien as a result of counsel's error.

An interest in a property may be acquired where a third party creditor registered a mortgage after a restraint order had been made but before the order of forfeiture. The applicant must establish an absence of complicity or collusion in the enterprise crime offence on a balance of probabilities in order to obtain an interest in the property: *Villeneuve v. Canada* (1999), 140 C.C.C. (3d) 564 (Que. C.A.).

This section provides a mechanism by which third parties who claim an interest in property forfeited under s. 462.37 may apply to a judge for relief from the forfeiture order made at the sentencing stage of the trial. Where the applicant under this section establishes a valid claim, the forfeiture order is not rescinded. Rather, the Attorney General is required, pursuant to subsec. (6), to either return the property to the applicant or remit to the applicant an amount equal to the value of the applicant's interest: *R. v. 170888 Canada Ltee* (1999), 135 C.C.C. (3d) 367, 174 D.L.R. (4th) 340 (Que. C.A.).

In an unusual case, it was held that a corporation could bring an application under this section for an order under subsec. (4) in respect of a shareholder's loan, which had been declared forfeited under s. 462.37 as proceeds of crime at the shareholder's sentence hearing, although the corporation denied having received the loan. Even though it claimed that the loan was never received, the corporation had a sufficient interest in that forfeited property to seek relief under this section: *R. v. 170888 Canada Ltee., supra.*

RESIDUAL DISPOSAL OF PROPERTY SEIZED OR DEALT WITH PURSUANT TO SPECIAL WARRANTS OR RESTRAINT ORDERS / Property outside Canada.

462.43 (1) Where property has been seized under a warrant issued pursuant to section 462.32, a restraint order has been made under section 462.33 in relation to any property or a recognizance has been entered into pursuant to paragraph 462.34(4)(*a*) in relation to any property and a judge, on application made to the judge by the Attorney General or any person having an interest in the property or on the judge's own motion, after notice given to the Attorney General and any other person having an interest in the property, is satisfied that the property will no longer be required for the purpose of section 462.37, 462.38 or any other provision of this or any other Act of Parliament respecting forfeiture or for the purpose of any investigation or as evidence in any proceeding, the judge

    (*a*) in the case of a restraint order, shall revoke the order;

    (*b*) in the case of a recognizance, shall cancel the recognizance; and

    (*c*) in the case of property seized under a warrant issued pursuant to section 462.32 or property under the control of a person appointed pursuant to paragraph 462.331(1)(*a*),

(i) if possession of it by the person from whom it was taken is lawful, shall order that it be returned to that person,

(ii) if possession of it by the person from whom it was taken is unlawful and the lawful owner or person who is lawfully entitled to its possession is known, shall order that it be returned to the lawful owner or the person who is lawfully entitled to its possession, or

(iii) if possession of it by the person from whom it was taken is unlawful and the lawful owner or person who is lawfully entitled to its possession is not known, may order that it be forfeited to Her Majesty, to be disposed of as the Attorney General directs, or otherwise dealt with in accordance with the law.

(2) An order may be issued under this section in respect of property situated outside Canada, with any modifications that the circumstances require. R.S.C. 1985, c. 42 (4th Supp.), s. 2; 2001, c. 32, s. 24; 2004, c. 12, s. 7.

CROSS-REFERENCES

The terms "property" and "person" are defined in s. 2. "Attorney General" is defined in ss. 2 and 462.3(3), (4). "Judge" is defined in s. 462.3.

If documents are returned under s. 462.43, the Attorney General has the right to make copies before returning the documents and to use them as evidence as if they were originals, pursuant to s. 462.46.

Section 462.44 provides a right of appeal from a decision made under this section. Section 462.45 provides that a forfeiture order is not to be carried out for 30 days and is stayed if it is under appeal, an application is made for restoration of the property or there are any proceedings in which the right to seize the property is questioned.

Reference should also be made to the *Seized Property Management Act*, S.C. 1993, c. 37 [found in *Martin's Related Criminal Statutes*], where property is forfeited to Her Majesty under this section.

SYNOPSIS

This section provides for the revocation of restraint orders, the cancellation of any recognizances, and the return of seized property (or its forfeiture where the owner is not known), on application by the Attorney General or an interested party, where the property is no longer required for the purposes of this Part, or of any Act of Parliament, or for any investigation or as evidence.

ANNOTATIONS

Standard of review – The review of a special warrant or restraint order, which is designed to prevent the depletion of illegal property, requires a different approach than that used in reviewing wiretap authorizations. The reviewing judge must determine whether the same decision would have been made, not merely whether there was a sufficient basis for the decision. In so doing, the judge must consider any evidence presented by the applicant to rebut or undermine the justifications for the authorization. Even if the judge concludes that the authorization should not have been granted, the Crown may request that the property remain under restraint if it is still required for a criminal investigation or as evidence in other cases. In addition, the rule against collateral attack is also relaxed to accommodate challenges to the underlying general search warrant while reviewing a special warrant or restraint order. *Quebec (Attorney General) v. Laroche*, [2002] 3 S.C.R. 708, 169 C.C.C. (3d) 97.

APPEALS FROM CERTAIN ORDERS

462.44 Any person who considers that they are aggrieved by an order made under subsection 462.38(2) or 462.41(3) or section 462.43 may appeal from the order as if the order were an appeal against conviction or against a judgment or verdict of acquittal, as the case may be, under Part XXI, and that Part applies, with such modifications as the circumstances require, to such an appeal. R.S.C. 1985, c. 42 (4th Supp.), s. 2; 1997, c. 18, s. 39.

CROSS-REFERENCES

The term "person" is defined in s. 2.

Section 462.45 provides that any order for forfeiture or restoration is stayed if an appeal is brought.

Section 462.44 does not refer to orders made pursuant to s. 462.37 as they come within the definition of "sentence" under s. 673 (applicable to indictable offences), and s. 689(1) provides for the stay of such orders pending the appeal.

Section 462.42 provides an avenue for those not implicated in the "designated offence" to seek relief from a forfeiture order.

This section is incorporated into the *Controlled Drugs and Substances Act* by s. 23 of that Act.

SYNOPSIS

This section provides for appeals from *in rem* forfeiture decisions, and decisions under s. 462.43, as if they were appeals from convictions or acquittal in proceedings by indictment.

SUSPENSION OF FORFEITURE PENDING APPEAL.

462.45 Despite anything in this Part, the operation of an order of forfeiture or restoration of property under subsection 462.34(4), 462.37(1) or (2.01), 462.38(2) or 462.41(3) or section 462.43 is suspended pending

   (a) any application made in respect of the property under any of those provisions or any other provision of this or any other Act of Parliament that provides for the restoration or forfeiture of such property,

   (b) any appeal taken from an order of forfeiture or restoration in respect of the property, or

   (c) any other proceeding in which the right of seizure of the property is questioned, and property shall not be disposed of within thirty days after an order of forfeiture is made under any of those provisions. R.S.C. 1985, c. 42 (4th Supp.), s. 2; 2005, c. 44, s. 10.

CROSS-REFERENCES

The term "property" is defined in s. 2. Section 490(12), which also deals with the return, forfeiture and disposition of seized property, contains a similar provision requiring a 30 day stay of all such orders, in addition to stays pending any appeals or similar challenges to the order made under that section. If the order appealed from is made under s. 462.37(1), s. 689(1) stays the operation of the order if it was made in relation to an indictable offence and an appeal is launched against the order. This section is incorporated into the *Controlled Drugs and Substances Act* by s. 23 of that Act.

SYNOPSIS

This section provides for the automatic suspension of forfeiture or restoration orders pending applications or appeals under this Part, or other proceedings in which the right of seizure is questioned. In addition, it also stipulates that property may not be disposed of 30 days after being ordered forfeit.

COPIES OF DOCUMENTS RETURNED OR FORFEITED / Probative force.

462.46 (1) If any document is returned or ordered to be returned, forfeited or otherwise dealt with under subsection 462.34(3) or (4), 462.37(1) or (2.01), 462.38(2) or 462.41(3) or section 462.43, the Attorney General may, before returning the document or complying with the order, cause a copy of the document to be made and retained.

(2) Every copy made under subsection (1) shall, if certified as a true copy by the Attorney General, be admissible in evidence and, in the absence of evidence to the contrary, shall have the same probative force as the original document would have had if it had been proved in the ordinary way. R.S.C. 1985, c. 42 (4th Supp.), s. 2; 2005, c. 44, s. 11.

CROSS-REFERENCES

The term "Attorney General" is defined in s. 2.

This provision is quite similar to the power given under s. 490(13) and (14) to use photocopies of documents returned to their owner although those provisions require the Attorney General to certify that the copies are true before they may be admitted as if they were original documents.

This section is incorporated into the *Controlled Drugs and Substances Act* by s. 23 of that Act.

SYNOPSIS

This section permits the Attorney General to make and retain copies of documents returned or ordered to be returned, forfeited or otherwise dealt with under this Part. Such copies, if certified by the Attorney General, are admissible in evidence, and have the same probative force as the original, in the absence of evidence to the contrary.

Disclosure Provisions

NO CIVIL OR CRIMINAL LIABILITY INCURRED BY INFORMANTS.

462.47 For greater certainty but subject to section 241 of the *Income Tax Act*, a person is justified in disclosing to a peace officer or the Attorney General any facts on the basis of which that person reasonably suspects that any property is proceeds of crime or that any person has committed or is about to commit a designated offence. R.S.C. 1985, c. 42 (4th Supp.), s. 2; 1996, c. 19, s. 70; 2001, c. 32, s. 25.

CROSS-REFERENCES

The terms "property", "peace officer" and "person" are defined in s. 2. The terms "proceeds of crime" and "designated offence" are defined in s. 462.3. "Attorney General" is defined in ss. 2 and 462.3(3), (4). For protection of "whistle blowers", see s. 425.1.

SYNOPSIS

This section clarifies that, subject to s. 241 of the *Income Tax Act*, a person may disclose to a peace officer or the Attorney General information resulting in a reasonable suspicion that property is proceeds of crime, or that a person has committed or is about to commit an enterprise crime or designated drug offence.

DEFINITION OF "DESIGNATED SUBSTANCE OFFENCE" / Disclosure of income tax information / Application / Order for disclosure of information / Service of order / Extension of period for compliance with order / Objection to disclosure of information / Determination of objection / Judge may examine information / Limitation period / Appeal to Federal Court of Appeal / Limitation period for appeal / Special rules for hearings / *Ex parte* representations / Copies / Further disclosure / Form / Definitions of "police officer".

462.48 (1) In this section, "designated substance offence" means (*a*) an offence under Part I of the *Controlled Drugs and Substances Act*, except subsection 4(1) of that Act; or

    (*b*) a conspiracy or an attempt to commit, being an accessory after the fact in relation to, or any counselling in relation to, an offence referred to in paragraph (*a*).

(1.1) The Attorney General may make an application in accordance with subsection (2) for an order for disclosure of information under subsection (3), for the purposes of an investigation in relation to

    (*a*) a designated substance offence;

    (*b*) an offence against section 354, 355.2, 355.4 or 462.31 if the offence is alleged to have been committed in relation to any property, thing or proceeds obtained or derived directly or indirectly as a result of

        (i) the commission in Canada of a designated substance offence, or

        (ii) an act or omission anywhere that, if it had occurred in Canada, would have constituted a designated substance offence;

    (*c*) an offence against section 467.11, 467.111, 467.12 or 467.13 or a conspiracy or an attempt to commit, or being an accessory after the fact in relation to, such an offence; or

    (*d*) a terrorism offence.

(2) An application under subsection (1.1) shall be made *ex parte* in writing to a judge and be accompanied by an affidavit sworn on the information and belief of the Attorney General or a person specially designated by the Attorney General for that purpose deposing to the following matters, namely,

    (*a*) the offence or matter under investigation;

    (*b*) the person in relation to whom the information or documents referred to in paragraph (*c*) are required;

    (*c*) the type of information or book, record, writing, return or other document obtained by or on behalf of the Minister of National Revenue for the purposes of the *Income Tax Act* to which access is sought or that is proposed to be examined or communicated; and

    (*d*) the facts relied on to justify the belief, on reasonable grounds, that the person referred to in paragraph (*b*) has committed or benefited from the commission of any of the offences referred to in subsection (1.1) and that the information or documents referred to in paragraph (*c*) are likely to be of substantial value, whether alone or together with other material, to the investigation for the purposes of which the application is made.

(3) Where the judge to whom an application under subsection (1.1) is made is satisfied

    (*a*) of the matters referred to in paragraph (2)(*d*), and

    (*b*) that there are reasonable grounds for believing that it is in the public interest to allow access to the information or documents to which the application relates, having regard to the benefit likely to accrue to the investigation if the access is obtained,

the judge may, subject to any conditions that the judge considers advisable in the public interest, order the Commissioner of Revenue or any person specially designated in writing by the Commissioner for the purposes of this section

    (*c*) to allow a police officer named in the order access to all such information and documents and to examine them, or

    (*d*) where the judge considers it necessary in the circumstances, to produce all such information and documents to the police officer and allow the police officer to remove the information and documents from the possession of that person,

within such period as the judge may specify after the expiration of seven clear days following the service of the order pursuant to subsection (4).

(4) A copy of an order made by a judge under subsection (3) shall be served on the person to whom the order is addressed in such manner as the judge directs or as may be prescribed by rules of court.

(5) A judge who makes an order under subsection (3) may, on application of the Minister of National Revenue, extend the period within which the order is to be complied with.

(6) The Minister of National Revenue or any person specially designated in writing by that Minister for the purposes of this section may object to the disclosure of any information or document in respect of which an order under subsection (3) has been made by certifying orally or in writing that the information or document should not be disclosed on the ground that

   (a) the Minister of National Revenue is prohibited from disclosing the information or document by any bilateral or international treaty, convention or other agreement respecting taxation to which the Government of Canada is a signatory;

   (b) a privilege is attached by law to the information or document;

   (c) the information or document has been placed in a sealed package pursuant to law or an order of a court of competent jurisdiction; or

   (d) disclosure of the information or document would not, for any other reason, be in the public interest.

(7) Where an objection to the disclosure of information or a document is made under subsection (6), the objection may be determined, on application, in accordance with subsection (8), by the Chief Justice of the Federal Court, or by such other judge of that court as the Chief Justice may designate to hear such applications.

(8) A judge who is to determine an objection pursuant to subsection (7) may, if the judge considers it necessary to determine the objection, examine the information or document in relation to which the objection is made and shall grant the objection and order that disclosure of the information or document be refused where the judge is satisfied of any of the grounds mentioned in subsection (6).

(9) An application under subsection (7) shall be made within ten days after the objection is made or within such greater or lesser period as the Chief Justice of the Federal Court, or such other judge of that court as the Chief Justice may designate to hear such applications, considers appropriate.

(10) An appeal lies from a determination under subsection (7) to the Federal Court of Appeal.

(11) An appeal under subsection (10) shall be brought within ten days from the date of the determination appealed from or within such further time as the Federal Court of Appeal considers appropriate in the circumstances.

(12) An application under subsection (7) or an appeal brought in respect of that application shall

   (a) be heard in camera; and

   (b) on the request of the person objecting to the disclosure of information, be heard and determined in the National Capital Region described in the schedule to the *National Capital Act*.

(13) During the hearing of an application under subsection (7) or an appeal brought in respect of that application, the person who made the objection in respect of which the application was made or the appeal was brought shall, on the request of that person, be given the opportunity to make representations *ex parte*.

(14) When any information or document is examined or provided under subsection (3), the person by whom it is examined or to whom it is provided or any officer of the Canada Revenue Agency may make, or cause to be made, one or more copies of it, and

any copy purporting to be certified by the Minister of National Revenue or an authorized person to be a copy made under this subsection is evidence of the nature and content of the original information or document and has the same probative force as the original information or document would have had if it had been proved in the ordinary way.

(15) No person to whom information or documents have been disclosed or provided pursuant to this subsection or pursuant to an order made under subsection (3) shall further disclose the information or documents except for the purposes of the investigation in relation to which the order was made.

(16) An order made under subsection (3) may be in Form 47.

(17) In this section, "police officer" means any officer, constable or other person employed for the preservation and maintenance of the public peace. R.S.C. 1985, c. 42 (4th Supp.), s. 2; 1994, c. 13, s. 7; 1996, c. 19, s. 70; 1997, c. 23, s. 10; 1999, c. 17, s. 120; 2001, c. 32, s. 26; 2001, c. 41, s. 133(11); 2005, c. 38, ss. 138(e), 140(b); 2010, c. 14, s. 9; 2013, c. 9, s. 15; 2014, c. 17, s. 7.

CROSS-REFERENCES

The term "property" is defined in s. 2. The term "judge" is defined in s. 462.3. "Attorney General" is defined in ss. 2 and 462.3(3), (4). Section 46 of the *Federal Courts Act* gives that court the power to make rules of court. The meaning of "clear days" (see s. 462.3) is to be determined by referring to s. 27(1) of the *Interpretation Act*.

This section is incorporated into the *Controlled Drugs and Substances Act* by s. 23 of that Act.

SYNOPSIS

This section authorizes *ex parte* applications in writing by an Attorney General to a judge for an order that the Commissioner of Customs and Revenue, or designate, allow access to a peace officer, or produce information and documents.

The Attorney General must depose by affidavit sworn on his information and belief, or that of his designate, that the information is sought for the purpose of an investigation in relation to a designated substance offence (or certain related offences) or an offence under ss. 467.11 to 467.13 (and related offences). The Attorney General must also identify the person in relation to whom the information or documents are required, as well as the type of information sought, and set out the facts relied upon to justify the *belief on reasonable grounds* that the person has committed or benefited from the offence. Finally, the Attorney General must state that the information or documents are likely to be of substantial value.

In determining whether to grant the order the judge shall consider the facts attested to in the affidavit, the public interest and the likely benefit to the investigation.

Where an order is issued, it may be subject to such terms as the judge considers advisable in the public interest. The order shall also set out the period of its validity (commencing seven days after service), and shall provide for service in some manner on the person to whom it is addressed.

The section further provides for objection by the Minister of National Revenue or his/her designate to the disclosure of information and for extension of time to comply, and for certain appeals.

Where information or documents are examined or provided, they may be copied. Copies certified by the Minister of National Revenue may be used in evidence. No person to whom information or documents have been disclosed or provided can make further disclosure except for the purpose of the particular investigation.

Specific Rules of Forfeiture

SPECIFIC FORFEITURE PROVISIONS UNAFFECTED BY THIS PART / Priority for restitution to victims of crime.

462.49 (1) This Part does not affect the operation of any other provision of this or any other Act of Parliament respecting the forfeiture of property.

(2) The property of an offender may be used to satisfy the operation of a provision of this or any other Act of Parliament respecting the forfeiture of property only to the extent that is is not required to satisfy the operation of any other provision of this or any other Act of Parliament respecting the restitution or compensation of persons affected by the commission of offences. R.S.C. 1985, c. 42 (4th Supp.), s. 2.

CROSS-REFERENCES

The term "property" is defined in s. 2. Provisions regarding restitution of property are to be found in s. 491.1 and those regarding compensation to victims of crime are in ss. 725, 726 and 727 to 727.9.

This section is incorporated into the *Controlled Drugs and Substances Act* by s. 23 of that Act.

SYNOPSIS

This section clarifies that this Part does not affect the operation of other forfeiture provisions in the Code or in any other Act of Parliament. It also provides that the property of an offender may be used to satisfy such other forfeiture provisions only to the extent not required to satisfy orders for restitution or compensation of victims of crime made pursuant to federal enactment.

Regulations

REGULATIONS.

462.5 The Attorney General may make regulations governing the manner of disposing of or otherwise dealing with, in accordance with the law, property forfeited under this Part. R.S.C. 1985, c. 42 (4th Supp.), s. 2.

CROSS-REFERENCES

The term "property" is defined in s. 2. "Attorney General" is defined in ss. 2 and 462.3(3), (4).

This section is incorporated into the *Controlled Drugs and Substances Act*.

SYNOPSIS

This section provides for the making of regulations governing the disposition of forfeited property.

Part XIII / ATTEMPTS – CONSPIRACIES – ACCESSORIES

ATTEMPTS, ACCESSORIES.

463. Except where otherwise expressly provided by law, the following provisions apply in respect of persons who attempt to commit or are accessories after the fact to the commission of offences:

> **(a) every one who attempts to commit or is an accessory after the fact to the commission of an indictable offence for which, on conviction, an accused is liable to be sentenced to imprisonment for life is guilty of an indictable offence and liable to imprisonment for a term not exceeding fourteen years;**

(*b*) every one who attempts to commit or is an accessory after the fact to the commission of an indictable offence for which, on conviction, an accused is liable to imprisonment for fourteen years or less is guilty of an indictable offence and liable to imprisonment for a term that is one-half of the longest term to which a person who is guilty of that offence is liable;

(*c*) every one who attempts to commit or is an accessory after the fact to the commission of an offence punishable on summary conviction is guilty of an offence punishable on summary conviction; and

(*d*) every one who attempts to commit or is an accessory after the fact to the commission of an offence for which the offender may be prosecuted by indictment or for which he is punishable on summary conviction

    (i) is guilty of an indictable offence and liable to imprisonment for a term not exceeding a term that is one-half of the longest term to which a person who is guilty of that offence is liable, or

    (ii) is guilty of an offence punishable on summary conviction. R.S., c. C-34, s. 421; R.S.C. 1985, c. 27 (1st Supp.), s. 59; 1998, c. 35, s. 120.

CROSS-REFERENCES

Attempt is defined in s. 24. Accessory after the fact is defined in s. 23. Also see s. 23.1.

The offence of attempted murder is punishable under s. 239, of accessory after the fact to murder under s. 240. As to mode of trial for these offences, see the cross-references under those sections. Note that where the substantive offence, for example theft of goods of a value not exceeding $1,000, is within the absolute jurisdiction of a provincial court judge by virtue of s. 553, then an attempt to commit or being an accessory after the fact to the commission of the offence is, by virtue of s. 553(*b*), also within the absolute jurisdiction of the provincial court judge. For notes concerning the operation of that section as it applies to the particular offence, see the cross-references under the section creating the substantive offence.

Similarly, for other offences, the rights of election and mode of trial generally follow the substantive offence and therefore see notes under the section creating the substantive offence. Note however that attempted murder, unlike murder, is not within the exclusive jurisdiction of the superior court under s. 469.

See s. 7 enacting territorial jurisdictional rules respecting offences committed on aircraft, offences in relation to nuclear material, attempt to commit or being an accessory after the fact to the offence in s. 269.1 (torture), war crimes and crimes against humanity.

Under s. 586, no count that alleges an attempt by fraudulent means is insufficient by reason only that it does not set out in detail the nature of the fraudulent means. Section 587(1) however gives the court power to order that further particulars be provided of the alleged attempt by fraudulent means.

SYNOPSIS

This section sets out a general scheme of punishment for attempting to commit, or being an accessory after the fact, to the commission of all offences which are not otherwise expressly dealt with by law.

Paragraph (*a*) provides that a person who attempts to commit or is an accessory after the fact to the commission of an indictable offence which carries a maximum punishment of life imprisonment, is guilty of an indictable offence and liable to a term of imprisonment not exceeding 14 years.

Paragraph (*b*) provides that a person who attempts to commit, or is an accessory after the fact to the commission of an indictable offence which carries a maximum term of 14 years' imprisonment or less, is guilty of an indictable offence and liable to imprisonment for a term not exceeding one-half the maximum punishment set out for the actual commission of that offence.

Paragraph (*c*) provides that any person who attempts to commit, or is an accessory after the fact to the commission of a summary conviction offence is also guilty of a summary conviction offence.

Paragraph (*d*) states that any person who attempts to commit, or is an accessory after the fact to the commission of a hybrid offence is guilty of an indictable offence and liable to a term of imprisonment that is half the maximum provided for the actual commission of the offence, or is guilty of a summary conviction offence.

COUNSELLING OFFENCE THAT IS NOT COMMITTED.

464. Except where otherwise expressly provided by law, the following provisions apply in respect of persons who counsel other persons to commit offences, namely,

- (*a*) **every one who counsels another person to commit an indictable offence is, if the offence is not committed, guilty of an indictable offence and liable to the same punishment to which a person who attempts to commit that offence is liable; and**

- (*b*) **every one who counsels another person to commit an offence punishable on summary conviction is, if the offence is not committed, guilty of an offence punishable on summary conviction. R.S., c. C-34, s. 422; R.S.C. 1985, c. 27 (1st Supp.), s. 60.**

CROSS-REFERENCES

"Counsel" is defined in s. 22(3). The liability of a person who counsels commission of an offence and an offence is committed is defined in s. 22(1) and (2). Punishment for attempt to commit an offence is set out in s. 463 with the exception of attempted murder (s. 239) and thus see cross-references under s. 463. Note that where the substantive offence, for example theft of goods of a value not exceeding $1000, is within the absolute jurisdiction of a provincial court judge by virtue of s. 553, then counselling the offence is by virtue of s. 553(*b*) also within the absolute jurisdiction of the provincial court judge. Presumably, that provision would also apply to counselling an offence listed in s. 553 which is not committed. For counselling all other indictable offences which are not committed, the accused would have an election as to mode of trial under s. 536(2). For the offence in para. (*b*), the trial of the offence is conducted by a summary conviction court pursuant to Part XXVII. The limitation period is set out in s. 786(2).

See s. 7 enacting special territorial jurisdictional rules respecting offences committed on aircraft, offences in relation to nuclear material, counselling the offence in s. 269.1 (torture), war crimes and crimes against humanity.

SYNOPSIS

This section makes it an offence to counsel another person to commit an offence, where that offence is not committed.

Paragraph (*a*) states that every one who counsels another person to commit an indictable offence, provided that the offence is not committed, is him/herself guilty of an indictable offence and liable to the same punishment as would be imposed for an attempt to commit that offence.

Paragraph (*b*) likewise makes it a summary conviction offence to counsel another person to commit an offence punishable on summary conviction, given that the offence is not committed.

ANNOTATIONS

The accused was properly convicted of procuring the death of his wife where he accepted the offer of an undercover police officer posing as a contract killer and agreed to pay the officer for the killing. Further, although the officer had no intention of carrying out the plan and the accused's acts had no influence on the officer's conduct or state of mind, the accused was properly convicted of the full offence under this section rather than merely an attempt: *R. v.*

Glubisz (1979), 47 C.C.C. (2d) 232, 9 C.R. (3d) 300 (B.C.C.A.). Similarly, *R. v. Walia (No. 1)* (1975), 9 C.R. (3d) 293 (B.C.C.A.).

A person may be convicted of this offence although the person counselled would only be a party to the offence if it were committed: *R. v. Meikle* (1983), 9 C.C.C. (3d) 91 (Ont. H.C.J.).

"Procure" means to instigate, persuade or solicit. The offence is complete when the solicitation or incitement occurs even though it is immediately rejected by the person solicited and it is no defence to the charge that the accused subsequently renounces the criminal purpose: *R. v. Gonzague* (1983), 4 C.C.C. (3d) 505, 34 C.R. (3d) 169 (Ont. C.A.).

In *R. v. Hamilton*, [2005] 2 S.C.R. 432, 198 C.C.C. (3d) 1, the court considered the application of this section in the context of e-mails advertising software that would enable purchasers to generate credit card numbers that could be used to illegally obtain funds. The *actus reus* for counselling requires proof that the materials or statements made or transmitted actively induce or advocate, and do not merely describe, the commission of an offence. The *mens rea* requires proof, either of an intention that the offence counselled be committed, or knowingly counselling the commission of the offence while aware of the unjustified risk that the offence counselled was in fact likely to be committed as a result of the accused's conduct. The fact that the accused's motive was mercenary did not negative the *mens rea*.

Where the accused was charged with counseling murder for distributing a poster appearing to invite the killing of a local politician, the Crown had to prove that a reasonable person viewing the poster objectively would take it as an invitation to kill, and that the accused knowingly counseled the murder while aware of the unjustified risk that murder was likely to be committed: *R. v. Jeffers* (2012), 280 C.C.C. (3d) 54 (Ont. C.A.).

CONSPIRACY / Conspiracy to commit offences / Idem / Jurisdiction / Appearance of accused at trial / Where previously tried outside Canada.

465. (1) Except where otherwise expressly provided by law, the following provisions apply in respect of conspiracy:

- (*a*) every one who conspires with any one to commit murder or to cause another person to be murdered, whether in Canada or not, is guilty of an indictable offence and liable to a maximum term of imprisonment for life;

- (*b*) every one who conspires with any one to prosecute a person for an alleged offence, knowing that he did not commit that offence, is guilty of an indictable offence and liable

  - (i) to imprisonment for a term not exceeding ten years, if the alleged offence is one for which, on conviction, that person would be liable to be sentenced to imprisonment for life or for a term not exceeding fourteen years, or

  - (ii) to imprisonment for a term not exceeding five years, if the alleged offence is one for which, on conviction, that person would be liable to imprisonment for less than fourteen years; and

- (*c*) every one who conspires with any one to commit an indictable offence not provided for in paragraph (*a*) or (*b*) is guilty of an indictable offence and liable to the same punishment as that to which an accused who is guilty of that offence would, on conviction, be liable; and

- (*d*) every one who conspires with any one to commit an offence punishable on summary conviction is guilty of an offence punishable on summary conviction.

(2) [*Repealed*, R.S.C. 1985, c. 27 (1st Supp.), s. 61(3).]

(3) Every one who, while in Canada, conspires with any one to do anything referred to in subsection (1) in a place outside Canada that is an offence under the laws of that place shall be deemed to have conspired to do that thing in Canada.

(4) Every one who, while in a place outside Canada, conspires with any one to do anything referred to in subsection (1) in Canada shall be deemed to have conspired in Canada to do that thing.

(5) Where a person is alleged to have conspired to do anything that is an offence by virtue of subsection (3) or (4), proceedings in respect of that offence may, whether or not that person is in Canada, be commenced in any territorial division in Canada, and the accused may be tried and punished in respect of that offence in the same manner as if the offence had been committed in that territorial division.

(6) For greater certainty, the provisions of this Act relating to
    (*a*) requirements that an accused appear at and be present during proceedings, and
    (*b*) the exceptions to those requirements,
apply to proceedings commenced in any territorial division pursuant to subsection (5).

(7) Where a person is alleged to have conspired to do anything that is an offence by virtue of subsection (3) or (4) and that person has been tried and dealt with outside Canada in respect of the offence in such a manner that, if the person had been tried and dealt with in Canada, he would be able to plead *autrefois acquit, autrefois convict* or pardon, the person shall be deemed to have been so tried and dealt with in Canada. R.S., c. C-34, s. 423; 1974-75-76, c. 93, s. 36; 1980-81-82-83, c. 125, s. 23; R.S.C. 1985, c. 27 (1st Supp.), s. 61; 1998, c. 35, s. 121.

CROSS-REFERENCES

Trial of the offence of conspiracy to commit the offences listed in s. 469(*a*), namely: s. 47, treason; s. 49, alarming Her Majesty; s. 51, intimidating Parliament or a legislature; s. 53, inciting to mutiny; s. 61, seditious offences; s. 74, piracy; s. 75, piratical acts; s. 235, murder, is by the superior court of criminal jurisdiction (defined in s. 2) by virtue of ss. 468 and 469. By virtue of s. 522, only a judge of the superior court of criminal jurisdiction may release an accused charged with any of those offences. For the offence described in subsec. (1)(*b*), the accused has his election as to mode of trial pursuant to s. 536(2) and release is determined by s. 515, although the accused is eligible for release by the officer in charge pursuant to s. 498 for the offence described in para. (*b*)(ii). For conspiracy to commit all other indictable offences, including the indictable offences within the absolute jurisdiction of a provincial court judge under s. 553, the accused has his election as to mode of trial under s. 536(2). Release pending trial is determined by s. 515, although the accused is eligible for release by the officer in charge pursuant to s. 498 where the substantive offence is punishable by five years imprisonment or less.

For conspiracy to commit a summary conviction offence (para. (*d*)) then the proceedings are conducted by a summary conviction court pursuant to Part XXVII. The punishment is then as set out in s. 787 [although see s. 719(*b*) where the accused is a corporation] and the limitation period is set out in s. 786(2). Release pending trial is determined under s. 515, although the accused is eligible for release by a peace officer under s. 496, 497 or by the officer in charge under s. 498.

In addition to the special jurisdictional rules in subsecs. (3) to (6), see s. 7 respecting offences committed on aircraft, offences in relation to nuclear material, conspiracy to commit the offence in s. 269.1 (torture), war crimes and crimes against humanity.

The procedure respecting the pleas of *autrefois* is found in ss. 607 to 610.

Under s. 586, no count that alleges a conspiracy by fraudulent means is insufficient by reason only that it does not set out in detail the nature of the fraudulent means. Section 587(1), however, gives the court power to order that further particulars be provided of the alleged conspiracy by fraudulent means.

See s. 467, a saving provision in respect of refusing to work and trade combinations.

As to offences relating to the activities of "criminal organizations" see ss. 467.1 and 467.2.

SYNOPSIS

This section sets out various offences of conspiracy and provides for punishment upon conviction for each of these offences.

Subsection (1) states that the provisions contained therein apply except where otherwise expressly provided by law.

Subsection (1)(*a*) provides that any person who conspires with another person to commit murder anywhere is guilty of an indictable offence and liable to a maximum term of life imprisonment.

Subsection (1)(*b*) sets out the punishments applied to a person who is guilty of conspiring to prosecute another person for an alleged offence, *knowing* that that person did not commit the offence.

Subsection (1)(*c*) and (*d*) described the offences of conspiracy to commit either an indictable or a summary conviction offence and the punishment upon conviction for these offences.

Subsection (3) states that any person who, while in Canada, conspires to do anything described in subsec. (1) in a place outside Canada that is against the law in that place is deemed to have committed the conspiracy in Canada.

Subsection (4) provides that a person who conspires to do anything referred to in subsec. (1) in Canada while outside Canada is deemed to have committed the offence of conspiracy in Canada.

Subsection (5) states that proceedings against any person under subsecs. (3) or (4) may be commenced anywhere in Canada and that the accused may be tried and punished in the same manner as if the offence had been committed in that location.

Subsection (6) clarifies that, subject to certain exceptions the accused must appear and be present during proceedings commenced under subsec. (5).

Subsection (7) states that if a person has been tried and dealt with outside Canada in relation to offences under subsecs. (3) and (4), in such a manner that would, in Canada, give rise to the pleas of *autrefois acquit, autrefois convict*, or pardon, the person shall be deemed to have been so tried and dealt with in Canada.

ANNOTATIONS

Meaning of conspiracy – The essential elements of a conspiracy are an agreement by two or more persons to commit a criminal offence, or to achieve a lawful object by commission of a criminal offence; an intention by two or more persons to agree, and an intention to put this common design into effect. It is not necessary that there be proof of any overt act in furtherance of the conspiracy, to complete the crime. Where there are alleged to be only two conspirators and one of them had no intention of carrying out the common design, then there is no proof of a conspiracy: *R. v. O'Brien*, [1954] S.C.R. 666, 110 C.C.C. 1 (3:2).

Impossibility is not a defence to a charge of conspiracy, except that conspiracy to commit an imaginary crime cannot give rise to criminal liability: *United States of America v. Dynar*, [1997] 2 S.C.R. 462, 115 C.C.C. (3d) 481, 8 C.R. (5th) 79.

On the trial of a charge contrary to subsec. (1)(*c*) of conspiracy to commit a specified indictable offence the Crown must establish an intention by the accused to enter into an agreement to commit that offence. Mere recklessness with respect to the subject of the agreement is not sufficient where the evidence indicates that a number of courses of actions were being considered only some of which were illegal: *R. v. Lessard* (1982), 10 C.C.C. (3d) 61 (Que. C.A.).

Aiding and abetting pursuant to a common intent and design in the commission of a substantive offence is not necessarily the same thing as conspiring to commit the same offence, and accordingly an acquittal of the conspiracy is not inconsistent with a conviction on the substantive count: *R. v. Koury*, [1964] S.C.R. 212, [1964] 2 C.C.C. 97 (6:3).

It was held in *R. v. Cotroni; R. v. Papalia*, [1979] 2 S.C.R. 256, 45 C.C.C. (2d) 1 (7:0), that to have a conspiracy it was essential that there be an agreement between the co-conspirators, and that there must be a common purpose of a single enterprise. In this case although there was in the most general terms an adventure with a common object, namely to possess certain extorted funds, there was no general agreement, rather, two competing and mutually exclusive objects: the agreement of one group of conspirators being to relieve the others of the extorted funds. There were therefore two separate conspiracies revealed by the evidence and since only one took place in Ontario, the venue of the trial, it was to be assumed that it was this conspiracy which was embraced by the indictment.

The *actus reus* is proven where there is a formation of an agreement, tacit or express, between two or more individuals, to act together in pursuit of a mutual criminal objective. There must be a common goal borne out of a meeting of the minds whereby each agrees to act together with the other to achieve a common goal. A conspiracy is not established merely by proof of knowledge of the existence of a scheme to commit a crime or by the doing of acts in furtherance of that scheme. Neither knowledge nor participation in a criminal scheme can be equated with the *actus reus* necessary to prove conspiracy. Absent a true consensus to achieve a mutual criminal objective, conspiracy does not criminalize joint conduct that falls short of an attempt to commit the substantive crime: *R. v. Alexander* (2005), 206 C.C.C. (3d) 233 (Ont. C.A.), leave to appeal to S.C.C. refused 352 N.R. 197*n*. See also *R. v. Cebulak* (1988), 46 C.C.C. (3d) 437 (Ont. H.C.J.).

Liability as a party to a conspiracy is limited to cases where the accused aids or abets the initial formation of the agreement, or aids or abets a new member to join a pre-existing agreement. Aiding or abetting the furtherance of the unlawful object does not establish aiding or abetting the principal with any element of the offence of conspiracy, and thus cannot ground party liability for conspiracy. However, where a person, with knowledge of a conspiracy, does or omits to do something for the purpose of furthering the unlawful object, with the knowledge and consent of one or more of the existing conspirators, this provides powerful circumstantial evidence from which membership in the conspiracy can be inferred: *R. v. F. (J.)*, [2013] 1 S.C.R. 565, 293 C.C.C. (3d) 377. See also: *R. v. Trieu* (2008), 429 A.R. 200 (C.A.). The broader approach to party liability proposed in *R. v. McNamara (No. 1)* (1981), 56 C.C.C. (2d) 193 (Ont. C.A.), affd [1985] 1 S.C.R. 662, *sub nom. Canadian Dredge & Dock Co. v. R.*, 19 C.C.C. (3d) 1, must now be read in light of *R. v. F. (J.)*, *supra*.

Where the accused is alleged to have joined a pre-existing conspiracy, it is insufficient to merely prove that the accused had knowledge of an unlawful plan. It must be established that the accused adopted the plan as his own and consented to participate in achieving it. Mere recklessness as to the object of the agreement cannot establish conspiracy: *R. v. Lamontagne* (1999), 142 C.C.C. (3d) 561 (Que. C.A.).

Conspiracy between spouses – A husband and wife cannot be found guilty of conspiring together: *R. v. Kowbel*, [1954] S.C.R. 498, 110 C.C.C. 47 (4:1).

Effect of acquittal of co-conspirator or where co-conspirator cannot be convicted – Where two alleged co-conspirators are tried separately the acquittal of one does not necessarily invalidate the conviction of the other. Moreover, where the evidence against one of two conspirators is substantially stronger the better course is to direct separate trials, particularly when a damaging statement admissible only against the one is to be tendered by the Crown. Of course when substantially the same evidence is admissible against jointly-tried conspirators as a matter of logic (although not any imperative rule of law) both should be either convicted or acquitted: *R. v. Guimond*, [1979] 1 S.C.R. 960, 44 C.C.C. (2d) 481 (7:2).

Moreover, even where one of the two parties to the agreement cannot, as a matter of law, be convicted of the conspiracy, such as the prostitute on a charge of conspiracy to live on the avails of her prostitution, the other person may be convicted of conspiracy: *R. v. Murphy and Bieneck* (1981), 60 C.C.C. (2d) 1 (Alta. C.A.).

Proof of conspiracy alleged – Although the gravamen of the offence of conspiracy to import narcotics is the agreement to import narcotics rather than a particular narcotic, where the Crown has chosen to particularize the narcotic, in this case heroin, the Crown was required to prove that offence and not some other conspiracy. To allow the Crown to prove some other offence characterized by different particulars would be to undermine the purpose of providing particulars: that purpose is to permit the accused to be reasonably informed of the transaction alleged against him, thus giving him the possibility of a full defence and a fair trial. In this case, it was not appropriate to amend the indictment on appeal to remove reference to the term "heroin". No such amendment was sought at trial and the trial had proceeded originally on the basis that the Crown must prove a conspiracy relating to heroin and, on this basis, one of the accused took the stand and testified that he was only involved in a conspiracy relating to cocaine. It would be unfair and prejudicial to the accused after that course of events to permit an amendment fundamentally and retroactively changing the nature of what the Crown must prove: *R. v. Saunders*, [1990] 1 S.C.R. 1020, 56 C.C.C. (3d) 220.

Conspiracy having more than one object – A single conspiracy may have more than one illegal object, and it is proper to allege in one count a conspiracy to commit several crimes. If the Crown proves a conspiracy to do any of the prohibited acts alleged in the indictment as the objects of the conspiracy then that is sufficient to support a conviction. In fact, where there is but one agreement and not separate agreements as to the different unlawful objects there can be only one conviction. On the other hand, where the prosecution proves only that some of those accused had conspired with one of their number for their own purposes no common purpose such as that alleged has been established. However, where the evidence establishes the conspiracy alleged against two or more accused or against one accused and an unknown person, where the indictment alleges that the accused conspired together with persons unknown, it is immaterial that the evidence also discloses another wider conspiracy to which the accused or some of them were also parties: *R. v. Paterson, Ackworth and Kovach* (1985), 18 C.C.C. (3d) 137 (Ont. C.A.), affd [1987] 2 S.C.R. 291, 39 C.C.C. (3d) 575 (7:0).

Indictments charging conspiracy may raise problems as to whether a conspiracy count has charged the accused with two or more conspiracies, which raises an issue of duplicity. In the alternative, the count may charge only one conspiracy but the proof at trial may demonstrate that there was more than one conspiracy. In the latter case, the issue is whether the Crown has proved the conspiracy charged despite the evidence of a second conspiracy. In determining this issue, the court will have regard to the wording of the indictment and may also look to the opening of the Crown. In order to find that a specific conspiracy lies within the scope of the indictment, it is sufficient if the evidence adduced demonstrates that the conspiracy proven included some of the accused; established that it occurred at some time within the time frame alleged in the indictment; and had as its object the type of crime alleged: *R. v. Douglas*, [1991] 1 S.C.R. 301, 63 C.C.C. (3d) 29 (5:0).

Multiple convictions ["Kienapple rule"] – The doctrine in *R. v. Kienapple*, [1975] 1 S.C.R. 729, 15 C.C.C. (2d) 524, 26 C.R.N.S. 1, which precludes multiple convictions for the same delict does not prevent a conviction for conspiracy and for a substantive offence which also formed some of the evidence relied upon by the Crown in proof of the conspiracy: *R. v. Sheppe*, [1980] 2 S.C.R. 22, 51 C.C.C. (2d) 481 (7:0).

Conspiracy and attempt – Attempting to conspire to commit a substantive offence is not a crime in Canadian law: *R. v. Déry*, [2006] 2 S.C.R. 669, 213 C.C.C. (3d) 289.

Conspiracy to commit the offence contrary to s. 139(2) of attempting to obstruct justice is an offence known to law: *R. v. May* (1984), 13 C.C.C. (3d) 257 (Ont. C.A.), leave to appeal to S.C.C. refused [1984] 2 S.C.R. vii, 56 N.R. 239*n*.

Effect of withdrawal from conspiracy – It is no defence that an accused having agreed to carry out the unlawful act with the intention to carry out the common design later withdraws from the conspiracy, since the offence is already complete: *R. v. O'Brien, supra*.

Co-conspirator's exception to hearsay rule – The case of *R. v. Baron and Wertman* (1976), 31 C.C.C. (2d) 525, 73 D.L.R. (3d) 213 (Ont. C.A.), contains a detailed review of the law of evidence which permits evidence of the acts and declarations of one conspirator done in furtherance of the conspiracy to be admitted against other co-conspirators. Martin J.A., for the court, suggests that the following procedure be followed:

1. At the end of the whole case the trial judge must decide as a matter of law, whether there is any admissible evidence against an accused from his own acts and declarations, that he is a participant in the conspiracy charged.
2. If there is no evidence directly admissible against an accused connecting him with the conspiracy the trial judge must direct the jury to acquit that accused.
3. If the trial judge concludes that there is some evidence admissible directly against an accused that he was a party to the conspiracy, he will instruct the jury that they must first find from evidence admissible directly against an accused (that is by evidence other than the acts and declarations of alleged co-conspirators) that he was a party to the conspiracy charged. The trial judge will then instruct the jury that if they find from such evidence that the accused was a party to the conspiracy the acts and declarations of alleged co-conspirators in furtherance of the conspiracy may be used as evidence against him . . .
4. As a general rule, it would be desirable for the trial judge to *then* refer the jury to the principal evidence admissible *directly* against each accused from which they may find that such accused was a party to the conspiracy but the jury should be instructed that it is for them to say if the evidence has this effect.
5. Finally, he must instruct the jury that on the whole of the evidence they must be satisfied beyond a reasonable doubt that the accused was a member of the conspiracy.

In *R. v. Filiault and Kane* (1981), 63 C.C.C. (2d) 321 (Ont. C.A.), affd [1984] 1 S.C.R. 389, 15 C.C.C. (3d) 352*n* (7:0), it was held that in determining whether the condition in rule (1), *supra*, was met the trial judge is entitled to view the accused's own acts and declarations against the picture provided by the acts of the alleged co-conspirators. The judge is not required to view the accused's acts and declarations in isolation, divorced from the context in which they occurred.

Hearsay evidence is inadmissible on the initial determination whether the alleged conspiracy or alleged common design existed: *R. v. Jamieson* (1989), 48 C.C.C. (3d) 287, 90 N.S.R. (2d) 164 (C.A.).

In *R. v. Sutton* (1999), 140 C.C.C. (3d) 336, 222 N.B.R. (2d) 78 (C.A.), affd [2000] 2 S.C.R. 595, 148 C.C.C. (3d) 513, 38 C.R. (5th) 39, the court held that all hearsay evidence that meets the necessity and reliability criteria may be considered at the first step of determining whether the existence of a conspiracy has been proven.

The co-conspirators exception to the hearsay rule as applied in *R. v. Carter, infra*, meets the requirements of necessity and reliability and remains a valid exception to the hearsay rule. Such evidence is therefore admissible in all but the most exceptional cases: *R. v. Mapara*, [2005] 1 S.C.R. 358, 195 C.C.C. (3d) 225, 28 C.R. (6th) 1.

In charging the jury on the applicability of the co-conspirator's exception to the hearsay rule the trial judge should instruct them to consider whether on all the evidence they are satisfied beyond a reasonable doubt that the conspiracy charged in the indictment existed. If they conclude that a conspiracy as alleged did exist, they must then review the evidence and decide whether, on the basis of the evidence directly received against the accused, a probability is raised that he was a member of the conspiracy. If this conclusion is reached, they then become entitled to apply the hearsay exception and consider evidence of the acts and declarations performed and made by the co-conspirators in furtherance of the objects of the conspiracy as evidence against the accused on the issue of his guilt. They should be told, however, that the ultimate determination of guilt is for them alone and that the mere fact that they have found sufficient evidence directly admissible against the accused to enable them to consider his participation in the conspiracy probable, and to apply the hearsay exception, does not make a conviction automatic: *R. v. Carter*, [1982] 1 S.C.R. 938, 67 C.C.C. (2d) 568, 31 C.R. (3d) 97 (5:0).

On the difficult issue of applying the co-conspirator's exception to a two-person conspiracy, see *R. v. Bogiatzis* (2010), 285 C.C.C. (3d) 437 (Ont. C.A.).

In *R. v. Puddicombe* (2013), 299 C.C.C. (3d) 534 (Ont. C.A.), leave to appeal to S.C.C. refused 2014 CarswellOnt 2577, a five-judge panel re-affirmed the position in *Bogiatzis, supra,* that the *Carter* approach applies to a two-person conspiracy.

Conspiracy to commit offence outside Canada (subsec. (3)) – In *R. v. Gunn,* [1982] 1 S.C.R. 522, 66 C.C.C. (2d) 294, 27 C.R. (3d) 120, the Supreme Court of Canada, having allowed the accused's appeal from the decision of the Manitoba Court of Appeal (1980), 54 C.C.C. (2d) 163, 4 Man. R. (2d) 269 *sub nom. R. v. Apaya and Gunn* on other grounds, did not find it necessary to give any direction in detail as to how the charge of conspiracy involving breach of foreign criminal law as envisaged by this subsection should be framed. However, it was held that the statutory fiction of a conspiracy in Canada in violation of foreign law can only become operative if a breach of the foreign law is charged.

And in *R. v. Baldini and Gullekson* (1984), 39 C.R. (3d) 43, 31 Alta. L.R. (2d) 69 (C.A.), the court considered that the charge should also make specific reference to subsec. (3).

Although the accused had agreed to supply narcotics to an undercover police officer in the United States, there was a substantial link between the offence alleged and Canada. Thus, *inter alia,* the accused were in Canada for the negotiations with the officer and when the agreement was finally made. Accordingly, there was no need for the Crown to charge the accused under subsec. (3), but could rely on the general conspiracy provisions in subsec. (1)(*c*): *R. v. Douglas* (1989), 51 C.C.C. (3d) 129, 72 C.R. (3d) 309 (Ont. C.A.).

The accused could properly be convicted of conspiracy to traffic in narcotics without reference to subsec. (3) where the evidence showed that they agreed in Canada to sell or offered to sell narcotics to a third person, even if the deal was to be completed in the United States. Under the *Narcotic Control Act,* a simple offer to sell can constitute trafficking and the absence of delivery of the drug or receipt of the proceeds in Canada is not relevant: *R. v. Rowbotham; R. v. Roblin* (1992), 76 C.C.C. (3d) 542, 60 O.A.C. 75 (C.A.), affd [1993] 4 S.C.R. 834, 85 C.C.C. (3d) 575*n*, 69 O.A.C. 267, supplementary reasons [1994] 2 S.C.R. 463, 90 C.C.C. (3d) 449, 30 C.R. (4th) 141.

Conspiracy outside Canada to commit offence in Canada (subsec. (4)) – Where the indictment alleges that the conspiracy actually took place in Canada it is not open to the Crown to rely on the provisions of subsec. (4) to prove all the components of the charge. If the agreement took place wholly outside Canada the indictment must so allege: *R. v. Dass* (1979), 47 C.C.C. (2d) 194, 8 C.R. (3d) 224 (Man. C.A.), leave to appeal to S.C.C. refused 30 N.R. 609*n*, 4 Man. R. (2d) 86*n*.

Territorial jurisdiction (subsec. (5)) – An offence is "an offence by virtue of subsection . . . (4)" although it could also be tried in Canada, albeit in another province, at common law. Subsection (4) is not restricted to cases which would not have been offences against Canadian law before the passage of that provision: *R. v. Lai and Lau* (1985), 24 C.C.C. (3d) 237 (B.C.C.A.).

CONSPIRACY IN RESTRAINT OF TRADE / Trade union, exception.

466. (1) A conspiracy in restraint of trade is an agreement between two or more persons to do or to procure to be done any unlawful act in restraint of trade.

(2) The purposes of a trade union are not, by reason only that they are in restraint of trade, unlawful within the meaning of subsection (1). R.S., c. C-34, s. 424.

CROSS-REFERENCES

Conspiracy in restraint of trade is a common law offence. As this section does not create an offence and with the repeal of s. 465(2) (common law conspiracy), it is entirely possible that the offence of conspiracy in restraint of trade can no longer be charged nor punished and that resort must be had to the substantive offences in other parts of the Code such as ss. 422 to 425 or to the offences under Part VI of the *Competition Act,* R.S.C. 1985, c. C-34.

SYNOPSIS

This section provides a definition of conspiracy in restraint of trade.

Subsection (1) states that such a conspiracy is an agreement between two or more persons to do, or arrange to have done, any *unlawful act* in restraint of trade.

Subsection (2) specifically provides that a trade union does not commit an offence under this section only by reason of the fact that its purposes are in restraint of trade.

SAVING / Definition of "trade combination".

467. (1) No person shall be convicted of the offence of conspiracy by reason only that he
  (*a*) **refuses to work with a workman or for an employer; or**
  (*b*) **does any act or causes any act to be done for the purpose of a trade combination, unless that act is an offence expressly punishable by law.**

(2) In this section, "trade combination" means any combination between masters or workmen or other persons for the purpose of regulating or altering the relations between masters or workmen, or the conduct of a master or workman in or in respect of his business, employment or contract of employment or service. R.S., c. C-34, s. 425.

CROSS-REFERENCES

These provisions would appear to apply to any conspiracy offence, not just those punishable under s. 465. Thus see, for example, s. 425(*c*).

SYNOPSIS

This section provides an exception to the general offence of conspiracy.

Subsection (1) states that no person shall be convicted of conspiracy *by reason only* that he refuses to work with a workman or for an employer, or that he does any *lawful act* for the purpose of trade combination.

Subsection (2) defines the term "trade combination" for the purposes of subsec. (1).

DEFINITIONS / "Criminal organization" / "Serious offence" / Facilitation / Commission of offence / Regulations.

467.1 (1) The following definitions apply in this Act.

"criminal organization" means a group, however organized, that
  (*a*) **is composed of three or more persons in or outside Canada; and**
  (*b*) **has as one of its main purposes or main activities the facilitation or commission of one or more serious offences that, if committed, would likely result in the direct or indirect receipt of a material benefit, including a financial benefit, by the group or by any of the persons who constitute the group.**
It does not include a group of persons that forms randomly for the immediate commission of a single offence.

"serious offence" means an indictable offence under this or any other Act of Parliament for which the maximum punishment is imprisonment for five years or more, or another offence that is prescribed by regulation.

(2) For the purposes of this section, section 467.11 and 467.111, facilitation of an offence does not require knowledge of a particular offence the commission of which is facilitated, or that an offence actually be committed.

(3) In this section and in sections 467.11 to 467.13, committing an offence means being a party to it or counselling any person to be a party to it.

(4) The Governor in Council may make regulations prescribing offences that are included in the definition "serious offence" in subsection (1). 1997, c. 23, s. 11; 2001, c. 32, s. 27; 2014, c. 17, s. 8.

ANNOTATIONS

The definition of "criminal organization" does not violate ss. 2(*d*) or 7 of the Charter: *R. v. Terezakis* (2007), 223 C.C.C. (3d) 344, 51 C.R. (6th) 165 (B.C.C.A.), leave to appeal to S.C.C. refused 226 C.C.C. (3d) vi.

"Criminal organization" was neither vague nor overbroad and, accordingly, did not violate s. 7 of the Charter: *R. v. Lindsay* (2009), 245 C.C.C. (3d) 301 (Ont. C.A.).

By insisting that criminal groups be "organized", Parliament has made plain that some form of structure and degree of continuity are required to engage the organized crime provisions. However, courts must not limit the scope of the provisions to the stereotypical model of organized crime: *R. v. Venneri*, [2012] 2 S.C.R. 211, 286 C.C.C. (3d) 1.

In order to prove that commission of serious offences is one of the "main purposes or main activities", the Crown is not required to lead evidence comparing the legal and illegal components of the business on a quantitative basis: *R. v. Beauchamp* (2015), 326 C.C.C. (3d) 280 (Ont. C.A.).

PARTICIPATION IN ACTIVITIES OF CRIMINAL ORGANIZATION / Prosecution / Factors.

467.11 (1) Every person who, for the purpose of enhancing the ability of a criminal organization to facilitate or commit an indictable offence under this or any other Act of Parliament, knowingly, by act or omission, participates in or contributes to any activity of the criminal organization is guilty of an indictable offence and liable to imprisonment for a term not exceeding five years.

(2) In a prosecution for an offence under subsection (1), it is not necessary for the prosecutor to prove that

> (*a*) **the criminal organization actually facilitated or committed an indictable offence;**
> (*b*) **the participation or contribution of the accused actually enhanced the ability of the criminal organization to facilitate or commit an indictable offence;**
> (*c*) **the accused knew the specific nature of any indictable offence that may have been facilitated or committed by the criminal organization; or**
> (*d*) **the accused knew the identity of any of the persons who constitute the criminal organization.**

(3) In determining whether an accused participates in or contributes to any activity of a criminal organization, the Court may consider, among other factors, whether the accused

> (*a*) **uses a name, word, symbol or other representation that identifies, or is associated with, the criminal organization;**
> (*b*) **frequently associates with any of the persons who constitute the criminal organization;**
> (*c*) **receives any benefit from the criminal organization; or**
> (*d*) **repeatedly engages in activities at the instruction of any of the persons who constitute the criminal organization. 2001, c. 32, s. 27.**

CROSS-REFERENCES

"Criminal organization" is defined in s. 467.1. Under s. 467.1(2) "facilitation of an offence" does not require knowledge of a particular offence, the commission of which is facilitated, or that an offence actually be committed. Further "committing an offence" means being a party to it or counselling any person to be a party to it. Related offences include: possession of explosives for the benefit of a criminal organization [s. 82(2)] and first degree murder where death is caused while committing the using explosive offence in s. 81 for the benefit of a criminal organization [s. 231(6.1)]. A wiretap authorization may be obtained in relation to this offence. It is also an enterprise crime offence for the purpose of Part XII.2. Evidence that an offence was committed for the benefit of a criminal organization is a deemed aggravating factor for the purposes of

CR. CODE

sentencing pursuant to s. 718.2. A person who fears that another person will commit a criminal organization offence may lay an information seeking to have the person enter into a recognizance pursuant to s. 810.01. The authority of the Attorney General of Canada to conduct proceedings in respect of this offence is set out in s. 467.2. The sentence for this offence is to be served consecutively to any other punishment imposed on the person for an offence arising out of the same event or series of events and to any other sentence that the person is subject. As to parole ineligibility, see s. 743.6. Sections 490.1 to 490.81 set out a scheme for the forfeiture of "offence-related property" (defined in s. 2). Special protections for victims or witnesses in proceedings against an accused for this offence are set out in s. 486.

SYNOPSIS

This section creates the least serious of the criminal organization offences, making it an offence to participate in or contribute to any activity of the criminal organization for the purpose of enhancing the ability of a criminal organization to facilitate or commit an indictable offence. Subsection (2) sets out a series of things the prosecution need not prove in order to make out the offence. Subsection (3) sets out certain types of evidence that the court may consider in determining whether the offence has been made out.

ANNOTATIONS

This provision does not violate s. 7 of the Charter: *R. v. Lindsay* (2009), 245 C.C.C. (3d) 301 (Ont. C.A.), leave to appeal to S.C.C. refused March 4, 2010. See also *R. v. Pereira* (2008), 247 C.C.C. (3d) 311 (B.C.S.C.), holding that these provisions also did not violate s. 2(*d*) of the Charter.

RECRUITMENT OF MEMBERS BY A CRIMINAL ORGANIZATION.

467.111 Every person who, for the purpose of enhancing the ability of a criminal organization to facilitate or commit an indictable offence under this Act or any other Act of Parliament, recruits, solicits, encourages, coerces or invites a person to join the criminal organization, is guilty of an indictable offence and liable,
- **(*a*) in the case where the person recruited, solicited, encouraged or invited is under 18 years of age, to imprisonment for a term not exceeding five years, and to a minimum punishment of imprisonment for a term of six months; and**
- **(*b*) in any other case, to imprisonment for a term not exceeding five years. 2014, c. 17, s. 9.**

COMMISSION OF OFFENCE FOR CRIMINAL ORGANIZATION / Prosecution.

467.12 (1) Every person who commits an indictable offence under this or any other Act of Parliament for the benefit of, at the direction of, or in association with, a criminal organization is guilty of an indictable offence and liable to imprisonment for a term not exceeding fourteen years.

(2) In a prosecution for an offence under subsection (1), it is not necessary for the prosecutor to prove that the accused knew the identity of any of the persons who constitute the criminal organization. 2001, c. 32, s. 27.

CROSS-REFERENCES

"Criminal organization" is defined in s. 467.1. Related offences include: possession of explosives for the benefit of a criminal organization [s. 82(2)] and first degree murder where death is caused while committing the using explosive offence in s. 81 for the benefit of a criminal organization [s. 231(6.1)]. A wiretap authorization may be obtained in relation to this offence. It is also an enterprise crime offence for the purpose of Part XII.2. A person who fears that another person will commit a criminal organization offence may lay an information seeking to have the person enter into a recognizance pursuant to s. 810.01. The authority of the Attorney General of Canada to conduct proceedings in respect of a criminal organization offence is set out in s. 467.2. Pursuant to s. 467.14, the sentence for this offence is to be served consecutively to any other punishment imposed on the person for an offence arising out of the same event or series of events and to any other sentence that the person is subject. Evidence that an offence was committed for the benefit of a criminal organization is a deemed aggravating factor for the purposes of sentencing pursuant to s. 718.2. As to parole ineligibility, see s. 743.6. Sections 490.1 to 490.81 set out a scheme for the forfeiture of "offence-related property" (defined in s. 2).

Special protections for victims or witnesses in proceedings against an accused for this offence are set out in s. 486.

SYNOPSIS

This section creates one of the three special criminal organization offences, making it an offence to commit an indictable offence for the benefit of, at the direction of, or in association with a criminal organization. Under subsec. (2) it is not necessary to prove that the accused knew the identity of any of the persons constituting the criminal organization.

ANNOTATIONS

This provision was neither vague nor overbroad contrary to s. 7 of the Charter: *R. v. Lindsay* (2009), 245 C.C.C. (3d) 301 (Ont. C.A.), leave to appeal to S.C.C. refused March 4, 2010. See also *R. v. Pereira* (2008), 247 C.C.C. (3d) 311 (B.C.S.C.), holding that these provisions also did not violate s. 2(*d*) of the Charter.

The phrase "in association with" captures offences that advance, at least to some degree, the interests of a criminal organization. It requires a connection between the predicate offence and the organization, as opposed to simply an association between the accused and the organization. The Crown must also demonstrate that an accused knowingly dealt with a criminal organization. The fact that the accused was not a member of the organization did not preclude a finding that he operated "in association with" the organization when he acted as its client and its supplier contrary: *R. v. Venneri*, [2012] 2 S.C.R. 211, 286 C.C.C. (3d) 1.

INSTRUCTING COMMISSION OF OFFENCE FOR CRIMINAL ORGANIZATION / Prosecution.

467.13 (1) Every person who is one of the persons who constitute a criminal organization and who knowingly instructs, directly or indirectly, any person to commit an offence under this or any other Act of Parliament for the benefit of, at the direction of, or in association with, the criminal organization is guilty of an indictable offence and liable to imprisonment for life.

(2) In a prosecution for an offence under subsection (1), it is not necessary for the prosecutor to prove that
  (a) an offence other than the offence under subsection (1) was actually committed;
  (b) the accused instructed a particular person to commit an offence; or
  (c) the accused knew the identity of all of the persons who constitute the criminal organization. 2001, c. 32, s. 27.

CROSS-REFERENCES

"Criminal organization" is defined in s. 467.1. Related offences include: possession of explosives for the benefit of a criminal organization [s. 82(2)] and first degree murder where death is caused while committing the using explosive offence in s. 81 for the benefit of a criminal organization [s. 231(6.1)]. A wiretap authorization may be obtained in relation to this offence. It is also an enterprise crime offence for the purpose of Part XII.2. A person who fears that another person will commit a criminal organization offence may lay an information seeking to have the person enter into a recognizance pursuant to s. 810.01. The authority of the Attorney General of Canada to conduct proceedings in respect of a criminal organization offence is set out in s. 467.2. Pursuant to

s. 467.14, the sentence for this offence is to be served consecutively to any other punishment imposed on the person for an offence arising out of the same event or series of events and to any other sentence that the person is subject. Evidence that an offence was committed for the benefit of a criminal organization is a deemed aggravating factor for the purposes of sentencing pursuant to s. 718.2. As to parole ineligibility, see s. 743.6. Sections 490.1 to 490.81 set out a scheme for the forfeiture of "offence-related property" (defined in s. 2).

Special protections for victims or witnesses in proceedings against an accused for this offence are set out in s. 486.

SYNOPSIS

This section creates the most serious offence apparently aimed at the leaders of the criminal organization, making it an offence for a member of the organization to knowingly instruct any person to commit an offence for the benefit of, at the direction of, or in association with a criminal organization. Under subsec. (2), it is not necessary to prove that the offence was actually committed, that the accused instructed a particular person or that the accused knew the identity of all of the persons constituting the criminal organization.

ANNOTATIONS

This provision does not violate ss. 2(d) or 7 of the Charter: *R. v. Terezakis* (2007), 223 C.C.C. (3d) 344, 51 C.R. (6th) 165 (B.C.C.A.), leave to appeal to S.C.C. refused 226 C.C.C. (3d) vi.

"Knowingly" applies to all elements of the *actus reus*, which requires proof of being a member of a criminal organization and instructing the commission of an offence linked to a criminal organization. The *mens rea* requires proof of membership in a group, however organized; knowledge that a main purpose or activity of the group is the facilitation or commission of serious crime; knowledge that the crime likely would result in a direct or indirect benefit to the group or any person in the group; and, as a member of the group, knowingly instructing another to commit a crime for the benefit of the group, at its direction or in association with the group. An accused's assertion that he did not share the main criminal purpose or subscribe to the main criminal activity of the group has relevance to the conviction to be determined on a case by case basis. There is no doubt, however, that the citizen knows the zone of risk and the implications of being part of such a group and instructing others to commit crimes for the benefit of, at the direction of, or in association with the group. In addition, the Crown is not required to prove that the accused had authority in, or was the leader of, the criminal organization: *R. v. Terezakis, supra.*

SENTENCES TO BE SERVED CONSECUTIVELY.

467.14 A sentence imposed on a person for an offence under section 467.11, 467.111, 467.12 or 467.13 shall be served consecutively to any other punishment imposed on the person for an offence arising out of the same event or series of events and to any other sentence to which the person is subject at the time the sentence is imposed on the person for an offence under any of those sections. 2001, c. 32, s. 27; 2014, c. 17, s. 10.

POWERS OF ATTORNEY GENERAL OF CANADA / Powers of the Attorney General of a province.

467.2 (1) Notwithstanding the definition of "Attorney General" in section 2, the Attorney General of Canada may conduct proceedings in respect of

> (a) **an offence under section 467.11 or 467.111; or**
> (b) **another criminal organization offence where the alleged offence arises out of conduct that in whole or in part is in relation to an alleged contravention of an Act of Parliament or a regulation made under such an Act, other than this Act or a regulation made under this Act.**

For those purposes, the Attorney General of Canada may exercise all the powers and perform all the duties and functions assigned to the Attorney General by or under this Act.

(2) Subsection (1) does not affect the authority of the Attorney General of a province to conduct proceedings in respect of an offence referred to in section 467.11, 467.111, 467.12 or 467.13 or to exercise any of the powers or perform any of the duties and functions assigned to the Attorney General by or under this Act. 1997, c. 23, s. 11; 2001, c. 32, s. 28; 2014, c. 17, s. 11.

CROSS-REFERENCES

"Criminal organization offence" is defined in s. 2.

Part XIV / JURISDICTION

General

SUPERIOR COURT OF CRIMINAL JURISDICTION.

468. Every superior court of criminal jurisdiction has jurisdiction to try any indictable offence. R.S., c. C-34, s. 426.

CROSS-REFERENCES

The term "superior court of criminal jurisdiction" is defined in s. 2.

Note on mode of trial – The scheme of the *Criminal Code* is to classify offences as purely indictable (*e.g.*, robbery, s. 344), purely summary (*e.g.*, soliciting, s. 213) or hybrid, *i.e.*, the prosecution may elect whether to proceed by way of summary conviction or by indictment (*e.g.*, assault, s. 266). The effect of s. 468 is that the superior court of criminal jurisdiction may try any purely indictable offence or any hybrid offence where the prosecution elects to proceed by way of indictment. Other courts of criminal jurisdiction (defined in s. 2) may, however, try indictable offences except those offences listed in s. 469 (*e.g.*, murder, s. 235). The offences listed in s. 469 may only be tried by the superior court of criminal jurisdiction with a jury subject to a re-election in conformity with s. 473. Indictable offences not listed in s. 469 fall into two categories. For the majority of the indictable offences not listed in s. 469, the accused may elect the mode of trial as set out in s. 536(2) and, within limits, may change that election (see, *e.g.*, s. 561). While the Attorney General is given a narrow discretion to override this election and require a jury trial under s. 568 in the circumstances defined therein and, in addition, a provincial court judge has a discretion to override or not record an accused's election for trial by provincial court judge and hold a preliminary inquiry (see, for example, ss. 555 and 567), the thrust of the provisions is to give the accused the right to determine the manner of trial. The other group of offences are those offences listed in s. 553 (*e.g.*, keeping common bawdy house, s. 210(1)) that fall within the absolute jurisdiction of a provincial court judge, meaning that the accused does not have a normal election as to the mode of trial under s. 536(2). Nevertheless, the other courts with jurisdiction to try indictable offences have jurisdiction to try the offences listed in s. 553, if the provincial court judge elects not to try the offence and requires that the case proceed by way of preliminary inquiry pursuant to s. 555(1), or in the course of the trial it is disclosed that, in fact, the offence is not one over which the provincial court judge has absolute jurisdiction, in which case, the accused must then be put to his election under s. 536(2). [For example, a charge of theft of goods of a value not exceeding $5,000 where the evidence discloses that the value of the goods exceeds $5,000.]

For all summary conviction offences, meaning purely summary conviction or hybrid offences, where the prosecution elects to proceed by way of summary conviction, only the summary conviction court (defined in s. 785) may try the accused. The procedure for trial of summary conviction offences generally resembles trial of an indictable offence by a provincial court judge but that procedure, including special rights of appeal, is set out in Part XXVII.

ANNOTATIONS

A superior court of criminal jurisdiction has the right to try those offences within the absolute jurisdiction of a provincial court judge: *R. v. Holliday* (1973), 12 C.C.C. (2d) 56, [1973] 5 W.W.R. 363 (Alta. S.C. App. Div.).

COURT OF CRIMINAL JURISDICTION / Accessories / Corrupting justice / Attempts / Conspiracy.

469. Every court of criminal jurisdiction has jurisdiction to try an indictable offence other than

    (*a*) **an offence under any of the following sections:**

        (i) **section 47 (treason),**

       (ii) **section 49 (alarming Her Majesty),**

      (iii) **section 51 (intimidating Parliament or a legislature),**

      (iv) **section 53 (inciting to mutiny),**

       (v) **section 61 (seditious offences),**

      (vi) **section 74 (piracy),**

     (vii) **section 75 (piratical acts), or**

    (viii) **section 235 (murder);**

    (*b*) **the offence of being an accessory after the fact to high treason or treason or murder;**

    (*c*) **an offence under section 119 (bribery) by the holder of a judicial office;**

  (*c*.1) **an offence under any of sections 4 to 7 of the *Crimes Against Humanity and War Crimes Act*;**

    (*d*) **the offence of attempting to commit any offence mentioned in subparagraphs (*a*)(i) to (vii); or**

    (*e*) **the offence of conspiring to commit any offence mentioned in paragraph (*a*). R.S., c. C-34, s. 427; 1972, c. 13, s. 33; 1974-75-76, c. 93, s. 37, c. 105, s. 29; R.S.C. 1985, c. 27 (1st Supp.), s. 62; 2000, c. 24, s. 44.**

CROSS-REFERENCES

Note that s. 3 provides that the descriptions in parenthesis after the section number are inserted for convenience of reference only and are no part of the provision.

The term "court of criminal jurisdiction" is defined in s. 2. Only the superior court of criminal jurisdiction has jurisdiction to try the offences listed in this section. As well, only a judge of the superior court of criminal jurisdiction may release an accused pending trial for these offences, by virtue of s. 522. The ordinary mode of trial for these offences is by virtue of the combined effect of ss. 468 and 471, by way of jury. However, provision is made for re-election for trial by judge alone under s. 473.

As to mode of trial generally, see the note under s. 468.

ANNOTATIONS

Neither the superior court of criminal jurisdiction nor the court of criminal jurisdiction have jurisdiction to try a summary conviction offence *ab initio*: *R. v. Rahim* (1977), 36 C.C.C. (2d) 533 (Ont. Co. Ct.).

JURISDICTION OVER PERSON.

470. Subject to this Act, every superior court of criminal jurisdiction and every court of criminal jurisdiction that has power to try an indictable offence is competent to try an accused for that offence

    (*a*) **if the accused is found, is arrested or is in custody within the territorial jurisdiction of the court; or**

    (*b*) **if the accused has been ordered to be tried by**

      (i) **that court, or**

      (ii) **any other court, the jurisdiction of which has by lawful authority been transferred to that court. R.S., c. C-34, s. 428; R.S.C. 1985, c. 27 (1st Supp.), s. 101(3).**

CROSS-REFERENCES

The terms "superior court of criminal jurisdiction" and "court of criminal jurisdiction" are defined in s. 2. The effect of this section is to overcome the common law rule that a criminal court's jurisdiction to try the accused was strictly local and subject to a statutory exception, *e.g.*, for offences committed at sea, the court had no jurisdiction to try an accused for an offence committed in some other country. In the circumstances set out in this section, the court can try the accused, although the offence was not committed within the territorial division (defined in s. 2), provided that the accused is found, arrested or is in custody within the territorial jurisdiction (defined by provincial legislation) of the court or has been ordered to be tried by that court, *e.g.*, by an order for change of venue under s. 599. [Note that this section deals only with territorial jurisdiction over the person of the accused, some other section must be resorted to to ensure that the information or indictment is also before the court, *e.g.*, as in s. 599(4) where an order for a change of venue is made. An alternative is by laying the information under s. 504.]

    In addition to this section, a court may also acquire territorial jurisdiction over an accused by reason of special statutory provisions such as those found in s. 7, s. 465(5), or ss. 477 to 481. Sections 478 and 479 are especially useful in providing that offences committed in a number of different divisions or provinces may, with consent of the Crown, be transferred to the jurisdiction where the accused is for guilty pleas. Further, s. 476 attempts to resolve difficult issues of territorial jurisdiction where an offence is committed near the border of a territorial division, such as on a bridge between two divisions.

    As to mode of trial, see the note under s. 468.

SYNOPSIS

This section provides that every superior court of criminal jurisdiction and every court of criminal jurisdiction that has power to try an indictable offence is also *competent to try* a person for that offence: (a) if the person is physically found within the territorial jurisdiction of the court; or (b) if the person has been ordered to be tried by that court, or any other court, the jurisdiction of which has been *lawfully* transferred to that court.

ANNOTATIONS

Where proceedings were properly commenced under permissible territorial jurisdiction of a justice and the accused was committed for trial to a particular court of criminal jurisdiction that court has jurisdiction to hear and determine the charges even though the offence was committed in another territorial division within the same province: *R. v. McMorris and Francis* (1971), 4 C.C.C. (2d) 268, [1971] 3 O.R. 748 (Co. Ct.).

    Where an accused appears and enters a plea the court before which he appears has jurisdiction by virtue of para. (*a*) in that the accused is "in custody within the territorial jurisdiction of the Court" notwithstanding the offence was not committed in that territorial division. Alternatively, if an objection is taken to the court's jurisdiction and the objection is overruled then the accused has been "ordered to be tried by that Court" within the meaning of para. (*b*)(i) and the court by virtue of that section has jurisdiction: *R. v. Rice, ex p. Katz and Lavitch*, [1968] 3 C.C.C. 85, 63 W.W.R. 64 (Man. C.A.).

    At common law the accused has a *prima facie* right to be tried in the county in which the offence was committed and this rule, in the absence of a court-ordered change of venue, continues except as modified by this section. However, the words "is in custody within the territorial jurisdiction of the court" do not give the court of one county jurisdiction where the accused, arrested in another county where the offence was committed, is merely brought to the former county in custody and then released on bail. If this section were to apply in such circumstances then it would be open to the Crown to select the venue of the trial by simply arranging to have an accused held in custody in the jurisdiction of its choice: *R. v. Sarazin and Sarazin* (1978), 39 C.C.C. (2d) 131, 3 C.R. (3d) 97 (P.E.I.S.C.).

Where an indictment had been preferred and the accused had appeared in Superior Court and waived arraignment, the court had jurisdiction over the application from release for custody pursuant to this provision. Neither s. 485(2) or (3) operated to deprive the Superior Court of jurisdiction over the accused: *R. v. Holowaychuk* (2009), 244 C.C.C. (3d) 352 (Ont. C.A.).

TRIAL BY JURY COMPULSORY.

471. Except where otherwise expressly provided by law, every accused who is charged with an indictable offence shall be tried by a court composed of a judge and jury. R.S., c. C-34, s. 429.

CROSS-REFERENCES

The Code has, of course, enacted a number of exceptions to the rule set out in this section, generally, but not always conditional on the accused's consent to some other form of trial. As to mode of trial generally, see the note under s. 468. Also see notes under s. 11(*f*) of the Charter concerning the constitutional right to a jury trial.

---

472. [*Repealed*, R.S.C. 1985, c. 27 (1st Supp.), s. 63.]

TRIAL WITHOUT JURY / Joinder of other offences / Withdrawal of consent.

473. (1) Notwithstanding anything in this Act, an accused charged with an offence listed in section 469 may, with the consent of the accused and the Attorney General, be tried without a jury by a judge of a superior court of criminal jurisdiction.

(1.1) Where the consent of the accused and the Attorney General is given in accordance with subsection (1), the judge of the superior court of criminal jurisdiction may order that any offence be tried by that judge in conjunction with the offence listed in section 469.

(2) Notwithstanding anything in this Act, where the consent of an accused and the Attorney General is given in accordance with subsection (1), that consent shall not be withdrawn unless both the accused and the Attorney General agree to the withdrawal. R.S., c. C-34, s. 430; R.S.C. 1985, c. 27 (1st Supp.), s. 63; 1994, c. 44, s. 30.

CROSS-REFERENCES

The terms "Attorney General" and "superior court of criminal jurisdiction" are defined in s. 2. Also see the note as to mode of trial under s. 468.

SYNOPSIS

This section describes the circumstances in which a person charged with an offence listed in s. 469 may have a trial without a jury. If the accused and the Attorney General consent, a s. 469 offence may be tried by judge of a superior court of criminal jurisdiction without a jury. Consent given under this section cannot be withdrawn unless both the accused and the Attorney General agree to the withdrawal.

ANNOTATIONS

Where an accused who is represented by counsel consents under this section to be tried on a charge of murder by a judge alone there is no duty on the judge to inquire into the accused's understanding of his choice. Specifically no such duty arises merely because the accused is only 16 years of age: *R. v. Davis (No. 2)* (1977), 35 C.C.C. (2d) 464, [1977] 4 W.W.R. 47 (Alta. S.C. App. Div.).

A Crown Attorney, as agent of the Attorney General, may consent to the re-election under this section. On the other hand, no re-election is required where the jury has not been empanelled and the accused merely intends to plead guilty to the offence charged or an included offence: *R. v. Luis* (1989), 50 C.C.C. (3d) 398 (Ont. H.C.J.).

It was held in *R. v. Turpin*, [1989] 1 S.C.R. 1296, 48 C.C.C. (3d) 8 (6:0), that s. 11(*f*) of the Charter confers no constitutional right to be tried by a judge without a jury. The purpose of s. 11(*f*) is to give an accused the right to a jury trial and to ensure that if a jury trial is not of benefit to the accused, the accused may waive the constitutional right to a jury trial. However, where the *Criminal Code* requires a jury trial then s. 11(*f*) gives the accused no right to elect another mode of trial.

The prosecutor's refusal to consent must be motivated by a desire to achieve fundamental fairness and not by the desire to obtain a tactical or strategic advantage. In this case, the refusal of the Crown to consent was improper and was motivated in part by a consideration of the identity of the assigned trial judge. Accordingly, the consent of the Crown was dispensed with: *R. v. Bird* (1996), 107 C.C.C. (3d) 186, 39 Alta. L.R. (3d) 128 (Q.B.). See also *R. v. McGregor* (1999), 134 C.C.C. (3d) 570, 22 C.R. (5th) 233 (Ont. C.A.).

The accused relied on the defence of intoxication and led evidence from a psychologist of the difficulty juries experience in applying the intoxication instructions. However, this evidence was of limited weight since it was unrelated to the particular circumstances of this case. The accused was not entitled to a constitutional remedy dispensing with the Crown's consent to trial by judge alone: *R. v. Jensen* (2005), 195 C.C.C. (3d) 14, 27 C.R. (6th) 240 (Ont. C.A.).

There is no requirement that the Crown provide reasons for refusing to consent and the failure to provide reasons for such a refusal is not a basis for judicial intervention. The exercise of prosecutorial discretion must be arbitrary, capricious or motivated by improper considerations to constitute an abuse of process: *R. v. Ng* (2003), 173 C.C.C. (3d) 349, 12 C.R. (6th) 1 (Alta. C.A.), leave to appeal to S.C.C. refused 183 C.C.C. (3d) vi.

ADJOURNMENT WHEN NO JURY SUMMONED / Adjournment on instruction of judge.

474. (1) Where the competent authority has determined that a panel of jurors is not to be summoned for a term or sittings of the court for the trial of criminal cases in any territorial division, the clerk of the court may, on the day of the opening of the term or sittings, if a judge is not present to preside over the court, adjourn the court and the business of the court to a subsequent day. R.S., c. C-34, s. 431.

(2) A clerk of the court for the trial of criminal cases in any territorial division may, at any time, on the instructions of the presiding judge or another judge of the court, adjourn the court and the business of the court to a subsequent day. R.S., c. C-34, s. 431; 1994, c. 44, s. 31.

CROSS-REFERENCES

The terms "territorial division" and "clerk of the court" are defined in s. 2. See s. 763 respecting the accused's recognizance remaining in force.

SYNOPSIS

This section empowers the clerk of the court, where no judge is present at the opening of the term, to adjourn court proceedings to a subsequent day if the competent authority has determined that a panel of jurors is not to be summoned for a term or sittings of the court. It also provides in subsec. (2) that, on instructions of a judge, the clerk may, at any time, adjourn the court.

ACCUSED ABSCONDING DURING TRIAL / Adverse inference / Accused not entitled to re-opening / Counsel for accused may continue to act.

475. (1) Notwithstanding any other provision of this Act, where an accused, whether or not he is charged jointly with another, absconds during the course of his trial,

    (*a*) **he shall be deemed to have waived his right to be present at his trial, and**

    (*b*) **the court may**

        (i) **continue the trial and proceed to a judgment or verdict and, if it finds the accused guilty, impose a sentence on him in his absence, or**

        (ii) **if a warrant in Form 7 is issued for the arrest of the accused, adjourn the trial to await his appearance,**

but where the trial is adjourned pursuant to subparagraph (*b*)(ii), the court may, at any time, continue the trial if it is satisfied that it is no longer in the interests of justice to await the appearance of the accused.

(2) Where a court continues a trial pursuant to subsection (1), it may draw an inference adverse to the accused from the fact that he has absconded.

(3) Where an accused reappears at his trial that is continuing pursuant to subsection (1), he is not entitled to have any part of the proceedings that was conducted in his absence re-opened unless the court is satisfied that because of exceptional circumstances it is in the interests of justice to re-open the proceedings.

(4) Where an accused has absconded during the course of his trial and the court continues the trial, counsel for the accused is not thereby deprived of any authority he may have to continue to act for the accused in the proceedings. 1974-75-76, c. 93, s. 39.

CROSS-REFERENCES

The term "counsel" is defined in s. 2. A similar provision respecting an accused who absconds in the course of his preliminary inquiry is found in s. 544 and in the course of his summary conviction trial in s. 803(2). As well, an accused who fails to appear for his trial or remain at his trial may lose his right to trial by jury by virtue of s. 598.

Section 650 provides for other circumstances in which an accused may be absent from the trial.

SYNOPSIS

This section deals with the situation where an accused person absconds *during the course* of a trial.

Subsection (1) provides that an absconding accused, whether or not he is charged jointly with another, is deemed to have waived his right to be present at his trial. Subsection (1)(*b*) also provides that the court may continue the trial to its conclusion and impose a sentence on the absconding accused, or issue an arrest warrant and adjourn the trial until the accused appears. If the court adjourns the trial under subsec. (1)(*b*), that court may at any time continue the trial if it is satisfied that it is no longer in the interests of justice to await the appearance of the accused.

Subsection (2) allows the court to draw an adverse inference from the fact that the accused has absconded.

Subsection (3) provides that when an accused reappears at a trial that has continued in his absence, he is not entitled to have any portion of the proceedings conducted when he was not present reopened unless he establishes that because of exceptional circumstances, it is in the best interests of justice to re-open such proceedings.

Subsection (4) states that counsel for an absconding accused has the authority to continue to act for the accused during the proceedings.

ANNOTATIONS

Meaning of absconds – The word "absconds" in this section means more than mere failure to appear and imports a requirement that the accused has voluntarily absented himself from his trial for the purpose of impeding or frustrating the trial, or with the intention of avoiding its consequences. The necessary intent can however be inferred from proof that the accused deliberately absented himself. Upon proof that the accused absconded, the trial may proceed although defence counsel has been permitted to withdraw: *R. v. Garofoli* (1988), 41 C.C.C. (3d) 97, 64 C.R. (3d) 193 (Ont. C.A.), affd on this point [1990] 2 S.C.R. 1421, 60 C.C.C. (3d) 161. See also *R. v. Taylor* (2010), 252 C.C.C. (3d) 197 (B.C.C.A.).

Procedure – Once the accused absconds, he has waived his right to be present as required by s. 650 and even after he has been apprehended the trial may continue in his absence until it was reasonably practicable to return him to court: *R. v. Tzimopoulos* (1986), 29 C.C.C. (3d) 304, 54 C.R. (3d) 1 (Ont. C.A.), leave to appeal to S.C.C. refused [1987] 1 S.C.R. xv, 54 C.R. (3d) xxviii.

It is for the trial judge to determine whether or not the accused has absconded and in directing the jury as to the adverse inference as permitted by subsec. (2) the judge need not leave it to the jury to first determine whether the accused absconded: *R. v. Tzimopoulos, supra.*

Notwithstanding subsec. (4) in most cases it would be unfair to require defence counsel to continue to represent an accused who has absconded. This subsection does not confer any authority on counsel to continue to act, nor does it interfere with or restrict counsel's right, in accordance with professional standards, to cease to act for the accused: *R. v. Garofoli* (1988), 41 C.C.C. (3d) 97, 64 C.R. (3d) 193 (Ont. C.A.), revd on other grounds [1990] 2 S.C.R. 1421, 60 C.C.C. (3d) 161, 80 C.R. (3d) 317.

Constitutional considerations – This provision does not offend the guarantee to fundamental justice in s. 7 of the *Canadian Charter of Rights and Freedoms*: *R. v. Czuczman* (1986), 26 C.C.C. (3d) 43, 49 C.R. (3d) 385, 27 D.L.R. (4th) 694 (Ont. C.A.), nor the right to a fair trial under s. 11(*d*): *R. v. Tzimopoulos* (1986), 29 C.C.C. (3d) 304, 54 C.R. (3d) 1 (Ont. C.A.).

Special Jurisdiction

SPECIAL JURISDICTIONS.
476. For the purposes of this Act,
   (*a*) where an offence is committed in or on any water or on a bridge between two or more territorial divisions, the offence shall be deemed to have been committed in any of the territorial divisions;
   (*b*) where an offence is committed on the boundary of two or more territorial divisions or within five hundred metres of any such boundary, or the offence was commenced within one territorial division and completed within another, the offence shall be deemed to have been committed in any of the territorial divisions;
   (*c*) where an offence is committed in or on a vehicle employed in a journey, or on board a vessel employed on a navigable river, canal or inland water, the offence shall be deemed to have been committed in any territorial division through which the vehicle or vessel passed in the course of the journey or voyage on which the offence was committed, and where the center or other part of the road, or navigable river, canal or inland water on which the vehicle or vessel passed in the course of the journey or voyage is the boundary of two or more territorial divisions, the offence shall be deemed to have been committed in any of the territorial divisions;
   (*d*) where an offence is committed in an aircraft in the course of a flight of that aircraft, it shall be deemed to have been committed
        (i) in the territorial division in which the flight commenced,
        (ii) in any territorial division over which the aircraft passed in the course of the flight, or

CR. CODE

(iii) **in the territorial division in which the flight ended; and**

(*e*) **where an offence is committed in respect of the mail in the course of its door-to-door delivery, the offence shall be deemed to have been committed in any territorial division through which the mail was carried on that delivery. R.S., c. C-34, s. 432; R.S.C. 1985, c. 27 (1st Supp.), s. 186; 1992, c. 1, s. 58.**

CROSS-REFERENCES

The term "territorial division" is defined in s. 2. The term "mail" is defined in s. 2 of the *Canada Post Corporation Act*, R.S.C. 1985, c. C-10. For other notes respecting territorial jurisdiction, see cross-references under ss. 6, 7 and 470.

SYNOPSIS

This section clarifies territorial jurisdiction in a number of unusual or special sets of circumstances.

ANNOTATIONS

Offences committed in more than one division [para. (*b*)] – Jurisdiction in inferior courts must be established like any essential ingredient of an offence and is not presumed, as in the case of superior courts, so where the Crown in a questionable boundary case failed strictly to prove jurisdiction over the accused by a county magistrate an acquittal was ordered: *R. v. O'Blenis,* [1965] 2 C.C.C. 165, (N.B.S.C. App. Div.).

In *R. v. Bigelow* (1982), 69 C.C.C. (2d) 204, 37 O.R. (2d) 304 (C.A.), the court in holding that the effect of this paragraph was to establish a broad basis for jurisdiction over interprovincial offences reviewed the case law as to its application and drew the following conclusions: (i) this paragraph conferred jurisdiction over crimes involving continuity of operation extending over more than one province in any province where a component of the offence took place; (ii) the courts in one province have assumed jurisdiction where an overt act referrable to or in furtherance of a criminal plan extending beyond that province was committed in the province; and (iii) where the act of the accused in one province generates effects in another this paragraph confers jurisdiction on the courts of the second province.

A province may try an offence which is completed partly in that province and partly in another province or territory. Consequently, sexual assaults which occurred for several years in several provinces could be prosecuted in any of the provinces in which an assault was committed: *R. v. L. (D.A.)* (1996), 107 C.C.C. (3d) 178, 125 W.A.C. 65 (B.C.C.A.).

Offences committed on vehicle or vessel [para. (*c*)] – The word "deemed" in this paragraph means "deemed conclusively". Thus even where evidence is led that the offence actually took place in a particular territorial division, not the division named in the indictment, as long as the vehicle passed through the territorial division named in the indictment in the course of the journey in which the offence was committed, the offence is proved: *R. v. Moore and Grazier* (1970), 1 C.C.C. (2d) 521, [1971] 1 W.W.R. 656 (B.C.C.A.).

This provision does not have application where none of the constituent elements of the offence occurred in Canada. In this case, although the offence involved Canadians in a Canadian vehicle in the United States, there was no significant link between Canada and the formulation, initiation or commission of the offence: *R. v. B. (O.)* (1997), 116 C.C.C. (3d) 189, 99 O.A.C. 313 (C.A.).

WORDS AND EXPRESSIONS / Saving.

477. (1) In sections 477.1 to 477.4, "ship" includes any description of vessel, boat or craft designed, used or capable of being used solely or partly for marine navigation, without regard to method or lack of propulsion.

(2) Nothing in sections 477.1 to 477.4 limits the operation of any other Act of Parliament or the jurisdiction that a court may exercise apart from those sections. 1990, c. 44, s. 15; 1996, c. 31, s. 67.

OFFENCES IN, ABOVE OR BEYOND CONTINENTAL SHELF.

477.1 Every person who commits an act or omission that, if it occurred in Canada, would be an offence under a federal law, within the meaning of section 2 of the *Oceans Act*, is deemed to have committed that act or omission in Canada if it is an act or omission

    (*a*) in the exclusive economic zone of Canada that

        (i) is committed by a person who is in the exclusive economic zone of Canada in connection with exploring or exploiting, conserving or managing the natural resources, whether living or non-living, of the exclusive economic zone of Canada, and

        (ii) is committed by or in relation to a person who is a Canadian citizen or a permanent resident within the meaning of subsection 2(1) of the *Immigration and Refugee Protection Act*.

    (*b*) that is committed in a place in or above the continental shelf of Canada and that is an offence in that place by virtue of section 20 of the *Oceans Act*;

    (*c*) that is committed outside Canada on board or by means of a ship registered or licensed, or for which an identification number has been issued, pursuant to any Act of Parliament:

    (*d*) that is committed outside Canada in the course of hot pursuit; or

    (*e*) that is committed outside the territory of any state by a Canadian citizen. 1990, c. 44, s. 15; 1996, c. 31, s. 68; 2001, c. 27, s. 247.

CROSS-REFERENCES

The term "ship" is defined in s. 477. Section 2 of the *Oceans Act*, S.C. 1996, c. 31, defines "federal law" as follows:

> "federal laws" includes Acts of Parliament, regulations as defined in section 2 of the *Interpretation Act* and any other rules of law within the jurisdiction of Parliament, but does not include ordinances within the meaning of the *Northwest Territories Act* or the *Yukon Act* or, after section 3 of the *Nunavut Act* comes into force, laws made by the Legislature for Nunavut or continued by section 29 of that Act;

Section 20 of the *Oceans Act* provides:

> 20(1) Subject to any regulations made pursuant to paragraph 26(1)(*j*) or (*k*), federal laws apply
>
>   (*a*) on or under any marine installation or structure from the time it is attached or anchored to the continental shelf of Canada in connection with the exploration of that shelf or the exploitation of its mineral or other non-living resources until the marine installation or structure is removed from the waters above the continental shelf of Canada;
>
>   (*b*) on or under any artificial island constructed, erected or placed on the continental shelf of Canada; and
>
>   (*c*) within such safety zone surrounding any marine installation or structure or artificial island referred to in paragraph (*a*) or (*b*) as is determined by or pursuant to the regulations.
>
> (2) For the purposes of subsection (1), federal laws shall be applied
>
>   (*a*) as if the places referred to in that subsection formed part of the territory of Canada;
>
>   (*b*) notwithstanding that by their terms their application is limited to Canada; and
>
>   (*c*) in a manner that is consistent with the rights and freedoms of other states under international law and, in particular, with the rights and freedoms of other states in relation to navigation and overflight.

Pursuant to s. 477.2, the consent of the Attorney General of Canada is required to continue indictable proceedings if the accused is not a Canadian citizen and the offence is alleged to have been committed on board any ship registered outside Canada. The consent of the Attorney General of Canada is also required to continue proceedings where the courts only have jurisdiction by virtue of para. (*a*) or (*b*) if the accused is not a Canadian citizen and the offence is alleged to have been committed on board any ship registered outside Canada. Finally, the consent of the Attorney General of Canada is also required if the courts have jurisdiction by virtue of para. (*d*) or (*e*). The consent must be obtained not later than eight days after the proceedings are commenced. Section 477.3 gives the same powers of arrest, entry, search or seizure as may be exercise d in Canada in respect of an act or omission referred to in this section in the circumstances set out in that section. However, where the offence is alleged to have been committed on board a ship registered outside Canada, the powers shall not be exercised outside Canada without the consent of the Attorney General of Canada. A judge or justice also has the same powers to authorize an arrest, search or other investigative measure in the circumstances set out in s. 477.3(2). Section 477.4 provides for proof of certain matters by certificate issued under s. 23(1) of the *Oceans Act*.

Reference should also be made to s. 7 which sets out other circumstances in which Canadian courts have jurisdiction over offences not actually committed on Canadian territory.

SYNOPSIS

This section gives Canadian courts jurisdiction over offenders by deeming certain acts or omissions to have been committed in Canada although they were committed outside the territory of Canada.

ANNOTATIONS

In *R. v. Macooh*, [1993] 2 S.C.R. 802, 82 C.C.C. (3d) 481, 22 C.R. (4th) 70, the court adopted the definition of "hot pursuit" suggested by R.E. Salhany in *Canadian Criminal Procedure*, 5th ed. (Aurora, Ontario: Canada Law Book Inc., 1989), p. 44: "Generally, the essence of fresh pursuit is that it must be continuous pursuit conducted with reasonable diligence, so that pursuit and capture along with the commission of the offence may be considered as forming part of a single transaction."

CONSENT OF ATTORNEY GENERAL / Exception / Consent of Attorney General / Idem / Consent to be filed.

477.2 (1) No proceedings in respect of an offence committed in or on the territorial sea of Canada shall be continued unless the consent of the Attorney General of Canada is obtained not later than eight days after the proceedings are commenced, if the accused is not a Canadian citizen and the offence is alleged to have been committed on board any ship registered outside Canada.

(1.1) Subsection (1) does not apply to proceedings by way of summary conviction.

(2) No proceedings in respect of which courts have jurisdiction by virtue only of paragraph 477.1(*a*) or (*b*) shall be continued unless the consent of the Attorney General of Canada is obtained not later than eight days after the proceedings are commenced, if the accused is not a Canadian citizen and the offence is alleged to have been committed on board any ship registered outside Canada.

(3) No proceedings in respect of which courts have jurisdiction by virtue only of paragraph 477.1(*d*) or (*e*) shall be continued unless the consent of the Attorney General of Canada is obtained not later than eight days after the proceedings are commenced.

(4) The consent of the Attorney General required by subsection (1), (2) or (3) must be filed with the clerk of the court in which the proceedings have been instituted. 1990, c. 44, s. 15; 1994, c. 44, s. 32; 1996, c. 31, s. 69.

ANNOTATIONS

Note: Some of the following cases were decided prior to the re-enactment of this section but were considered of assistance in interpreting this section.

Where consent required – Consent is required where the offence is a hybrid offence for such offence is deemed to be indictable by s. 34(1) of the *Interpretation Act*, R.S.C. 1985, c. I-21: *R. v. Gallagher* (1981), 62 C.C.C. (2d) 3 (B.C. Co. Ct.).

There must at least be some evidence in the case to indicate that the accused is not a Canadian citizen before the Crown must prove that the accused was a Canadian citizen and that the consent of the Attorney General was not required: *R. v. Erickson* (1989), 49 C.C.C. (3d) 33, 14 M.V.R. (2d) 122 (B.C.C.A.), leave to appeal to S.C.C. refused 50 C.C.C. (3d) vi, 104 N.R. 109n.

Proof of consent – Failure to obtain the necessary consent will result in a conviction being quashed: *R. v. Ford; R. v. Gilkey* (1956), 115 C.C.C. 113, 18 W.W.R. 563 (B.C.C.A.).

The decision to consent under this section is not an administrative decision which can be delegated to an official such as the Assistant Deputy Attorney General: *R. v. Sunila* (1987), 35 C.C.C. (3d) 289, 78 N.S.R. (2d) 24 (S.C. App. Div.).

A consent given by the Deputy Attorney General is valid in view of the provision of s. 24(2)(*c*) of the *Interpretation Act*, R.S.C. 1985, c. I-21. Further, a consent referring to a charge of "murder" was sufficient to permit trial of the accused on a charge of first degree murder, there being nothing to indicate that the consent was restricted to a charge of second degree murder: *R. v. Frisbee* (1989), 48 C.C.C. (3d) 386 (B.C.C.A.) , leave to appeal to S.C.C. refused 50 C.C.C. (3d) vi.

An objection to the validity of the form of consent cannot be raised for the first time near the conclusion of the trial just prior to the charge to the jury: *R. v. Sunila* (1987), 35 C.C.C. (3d) 289, 78 N.S.R. (2d) 24 (S.C. App. Div.).

EXERCISING POWERS OF ARREST, ENTRY, ETC. / Arrest, search, seizure, etc. / Limitation.

477.3 (1) Every power of arrest, entry, search or seizure or other power that could be exercised in Canada in respect of an act or omission referred to in section 477.1 may be exercised, in the circumstances referred to in that section.

> (*a*) **at the place or on board the ship or marine installation or structure, within the meaning of section 2 of the *Oceans Act*, where the act or omission occurred; or**
>
> (*b*) **where hot pursuit has been commenced, at any place on the seas, other than a place that is part of the territorial sea of any other state.**

(2) A justice or judge in any territorial division in Canada has jurisdiction to authorize an arrest, entry, search or seizure or an investigation or other ancillary matter related to an offence

> (*a*) **committed in or on the territorial sea of Canada or any area of the sea that forms part of the internal waters of Canada, or**
>
> (*b*) **referred to in section 477.1 in the same manner as if the offence had been committed in that territorial division.**

(3) Where an act or omission that is an offence by virtue only of section 477.1 is alleged to have been committed on board any ship registered outside Canada, the powers referred to in subsection (1) shall not be exercised outside Canada with respect to that act or omission without the consent of the Attorney General of Canada. 1990, c. 44, s. 15; 1996, c. 31, s. 70.

CROSS-REFERENCES

"Justice" is defined in s. 2. For other cross-references respecting jurisdiction for offences committed outside Canada, see the notes following s. 477.1. For references to powers of search, entry and arrest generally see notes following ss. 487, 529 and 495, respectively.

SYNOPSIS

This section sets out the powers of arrest, search, seizure and entry that may be exercised in relation to offences mentioned in s. 477.1. Note that pursuant to subsec. (3), where the offence is alleged to have been committed on board any ship registered outside Canada, the powers of arrest, search, seizure and entry shall not be exercised outside Canada without the consent of the Attorney General of Canada.

ANNOTATIONS

In *R. v. Macooh*, [1993] 2 S.C.R. 802, 82 C.C.C. (3d) 481, 22 C.R. (4th) 70, the court adopted the definition of "hot pursuit" suggested by R.E. Salhany in *Canadian Criminal Procedure*, 5th ed. (Aurora, Ontario: Canada Law Book Inc., 1989), p. 44: "Generally, the essence of fresh pursuit is that it must be continuous pursuit conducted with reasonable diligence, so that pursuit and capture along with the commission of the offence may be considered as forming part of a single transaction."

TERRITORIAL DIVISION FOR PROSECUTION / Evidence / Certificate cannot be compelled.

477.4 (1) [*Repealed, 1996, c. 31, s. 71.*]

(2) [*Repealed, 1996, c. 31, s. 71.*]

(3) In proceedings in respect of an offence,

    (a) a certificate referred to in subsection 23(1) of the *Oceans Act*, or

    (b) a certificate issued by or under the authority of the Minister of Foreign Affairs containing a statement that any geographical location specified in the certificate was, at any time material to the proceedings, in an area of a fishing zone of Canada that is not within the internal waters of Canada or the territorial sea of Canada or outside the territory of any state,

is conclusive proof of the truth of the statement without proof of the signature or official character of the person appearing to have issued the certificate.

(4) A certificate referred to in subsection (3) is admissible in evidence in proceedings referred to in that subsection but its production cannot be compelled. 1990, c. 44, s. 15; 1995, c. 5, s. 25; 1996, c. 31, s. 71.

CROSS-REFERENCES

Section 23(1) of the *Oceans Act*, S.C. 1996, c. 31, provides as follows:

> 23(1) In any legal or other proceedings, a certificate issued by or under the authority of the Minister of Foreign Affairs containing a statement that any geographic location specified in the certificate was, at any time material to the proceedings,
>
>   (a) in the internal waters of Canada,
>
>   (b) in the territorial sea of Canada,
>
>   (c) in the contiguous zone of Canada,
>
>   (d) in the exclusive economic zone of Canada, or
>
>   (e) or above the continental shelf of Canada
>
> is conclusive proof of the truth of the statement without proof of the signature or official character of the person appearing to have issued the certificate.

For other cross-references respecting jurisdiction over offences committed outside Canada, see the notes following s. 477.1.

OFFENCE COMMITTED ENTIRELY IN ONE PROVINCE / Exception / Idem / Where accused committed to stand trial / Definition of "newspaper".

478. (1) Subject to this Act, a court in a province shall not try an offence committed entirely in another province.

(2) Every proprietor, publisher, editor or other person charged with the publication of a defamatory libel in a newspaper or with conspiracy to publish a defamatory libel in a newspaper shall be dealt with, indicted, tried and punished in the province where he resides or in which the newspaper is printed.

(3) An accused who is charged with an offence that is alleged to have been committed in Canada outside the province in which the accused is, may, if the offence is not an offence mentioned in section 469 and

    (a) in the case of proceedings instituted at the instance of the Government of Canada and conducted by or on behalf of that Government, if the Attorney General of Canada consents, or

    (b) in any other case, if the Attorney General of the province where the offence is alleged to have been committed consents,

appear before a court or judge that would have had jurisdiction to try that offence if it had been committed in the province where the accused is, and where the accused consents to plead guilty and pleads guilty to that offence, the court or judge shall determine the accused to be guilty of the offence and impose the punishment warranted by law, but where the accused does not consent to plead guilty and does not plead guilty, the accused shall, if the accused was in custody prior to appearance, be returned to custody and shall be dealt with according to law.

(4) Notwithstanding that an accused described in subsection (3) has been ordered to stand trial or that an indictment has been preferred against the accused in respect of the offence to which he desires to plead guilty, the accused shall be deemed simply to stand charged of that offence without a preliminary inquiry having been conducted or an indictment having been preferred with respect thereto.

(5) In this section, "newspaper" has the same meaning as in section 297. R.S., c. C-34, s. 434; 1974-75-76, c. 93, s. 40; R.S.C. 1985, c. 27 (1st Supp.), ss. 64, 101(3); 1994, c. 44, s. 33.

CROSS-REFERENCES

The term "province" is defined in s. 35 of the *Interpretation Act*, R.S.C. 1985, c. I-21. "Attorney General" is defined in s. 2. Section 583(*h*) provides that a count in an indictment is not insufficient by reason only that it does not state that the required consent has been obtained. [As to notes concerning sufficiency of consent, see s. 583.] Defamatory libel is dealt with under ss. 297 to 317. A related provision for transfer of charges between territorial divisions within the same province is in s. 479. Respecting transfer of probation orders between provinces, see s. 739. For other notes respecting territorial jurisdiction, see cross-references under ss. 6, 7 and 470.

SYNOPSIS

This section deals with offences committed within the jurisdiction of one province.

Subsection (1) provides that subject to exceptions found within the Code, a court in one province shall not try an offence entirely committed in another province.

Subsection (2) states that any person charged with the offence of publishing, or conspiring to publish, a defamatory libel in a newspaper must deal with in the province where he resides or where the newspaper is printed.

Subsection (3) provides that any person charged with an offence, other than an offence listed in s. 469, that is alleged to have been committed outside the province in which that person is, may plead guilty before a court having jurisdiction over the offence in that province and be sentenced in that location. The appropriate Attorney General must consent to this procedure.

Subsection (4) makes it clear that an accused person pleading guilty under subsec. (3), whether or not he has been ordered to stand trial, or an indictment has been preferred against him in the province where the offence was committed, shall be deemed to stand charged of that offence in the province in which the plea is entered without a preliminary inquiry having been held or an indictment preferred.

Subsection (5) gives the term "newspaper" the same meaning as is found in s. 297.

ANNOTATIONS

Subsection (1) – In determining jurisdiction it is questionable whether civil law should be employed to locate the *actus reus,* particularly where the offence is of a continuing character that might occur in more than one jurisdiction: *R. v. Trudel, ex p. Horbas and Myhaluk,* [1969] 3 C.C.C. 95, 5 C.R.N.S. 342 *sub nom. R. v. Horbas and Myhaluk* (Man. C.A.).

Subsection (3) – The authorities of one province did not notify the accused of an indictable offence warrant that they held for him while he was being tried, convicted and then serving his sentence in another province for other offences committed there. Upon appeal against the sentence finally imposed upon him when he was brought back for trial some years later the appellate court indicated its disapproval of this procedure by substantially reducing the sentence: *R. v. Parisien* (1971), 3 C.C.C. (2d) 433, [1971] 4 W.W.R. 81 (B.C.C.A.).

If the accused can show that the exercise of the discretion by the Attorney General to refuse to consent to the transfer is arbitrary, then the accused would be entitled to a remedy under s. 24 of the Charter on the basis that there has been an infringement of s. 7 of the Charter. However, if reasonable grounds exist for the exercise of the discretion one way or another and there has been a fair consideration as to whether, or in what way, the discretion should be exercised, the ultimate decision cannot be said to be arbitrary. In this case, Crown counsel provided the accused with a letter setting out several valid reasons for refusing to consent to the transfer including that, as a general rule, the accused should be sentenced in the community where the offence occurred in order for the deterrent affect of that sentence; disposition of the offence in the jurisdiction where it arose will most likely ensure the application of local provincial sentencing standards for like defences; and the more serious the offence the more appropriate it is to dispose of the case where the offence occurred: *R. v. Fleming* (1992), 72 C.C.C. (3d) 133 (Man. Q.B.).

OFFENCE OUTSTANDING IN SAME PROVINCE.

479. Where an accused is charged with an offence that is alleged to have been committed in the province in which he is, he may, if the offence is not an offence mentioned in section 469, and

    (a) in the case of proceedings instituted at the instance of the Government of Canada and conducted by or on behalf of that Government, the Attorney General of Canada consents, or

    (b) in any other case, the Attorney General of the province where the offence is alleged to have been committed consents,

appear before a court or judge that would have had jurisdiction to try that offence if it had been committed in the place where the accused is, and where the accused consents to plead guilty and pleads guilty to that offence, the court or judge shall determine the accused to be guilty of the offence and impose the punishment warranted by law, but where the accused does not consent to plead guilty and does not plead guilty, the accused shall, if the accused was in custody prior to his appearance, be returned to custody and shall be dealt with according to law. R.S., c. C-34, s. 435; 1974-75-76, c. 93, s. 41; R.S.C. 1985, c. 27 (1st Supp.), s. 65; 1994, c. 44, s. 34.

CROSS-REFERENCES

"Attorney General" is defined in s. 2. Section 583(*h*) provides that a count in an indictment is not insufficient by reason only that it does not state that the required consent has been obtained. [As to notes concerning sufficiency of consent, see s. 583.] For a related provision for transfer of charges between provinces, see s. 478. For other notes respecting territorial jurisdiction, see cross-references under ss. 6, 7 and 470. Change of venue for trial within the province but in another territorial division is governed by s. 599.

SYNOPSIS

This section allows an accused person to plead guilty to an offence, other than the one listed in s. 469, before a court or a judge within the province where the offence was committed but not within the territorial division of that province having jurisdiction over the offender. The appropriate Attorney General must consent to this procedure and the accused must, in fact, plead guilty to the offence.

OFFENCE IN UNORGANIZED TERRITORY / New territorial division.

480. (1) Where an offence is committed in an unorganized tract of country in any province or on a lake, river or other water therein, not included in a territorial division or in a provisional judicial district, proceedings in respect thereof may be commenced and an accused may be charged, tried and punished in respect thereof within any territorial division or provisional judicial district of the province in the same manner as if the offence had been committed within that territorial division or provisional judicial district.

(2) Where a provisional judicial district or a new territorial division is constituted in an unorganized tract referred to in subsection (1), the jurisdiction conferred by that subsection continues until appropriate provision is made by law for the administration of criminal justice within the provisional judicial district or new territorial division. R.S., c. C-34, s. 436.

CROSS-REFERENCES

The term "territorial division" is defined in s. 2. The term "province" is defined in s. 35 of the *Interpretation Act*, R.S.C. 1985, c. I-21. Also see s. 481 and for other notes respecting territorial jurisdiction, see cross-references under ss. 6, 7 and 470.

SYNOPSIS

This section clarifies jurisdiction in situations where an offence is committed in an unorganized tract in any province that is not included in a territorial division or provisional judicial district.

Subsection (1) states that the trial of an offence committed in such a location may take place in any territorial division or provisional judicial district in that province.

Subsection (2) provides that when a provincial judicial district or new territorial division is constituted in an unorganized tract, subsec. (1) will continue to apply until provision for the administration of justice within that division or district is made.

OFFENCE NOT IN A PROVINCE.

481. Where an offence is committed in a part of Canada not in a province, proceedings in respect thereof may be commenced and the accused may be charged, tried and punished within any territorial division in any province in the same manner as if that offence had been committed in that territorial division. R.S., c. C-34, s. 437.

CROSS-REFERENCES

The term "territorial division" is defined in s. 2. The term "province" is defined in s. 35 of the *Interpretation Act*, R.S.C. 1985, c. I-21. Also see s. 480 and for other notes respecting territorial jurisdiction, see cross-references under ss. 6, 7 and 470.

SYNOPSIS

This section provides that an accused who commits an offence in a part of Canada which is not a province may be tried and punished within any territorial division in any province of Canada.

OFFENCE IN CANADIAN WATERS.

481.1 Where an offence is committed in or on the territorial sea of Canada or any area of the sea that forms part of the internal waters of Canada, proceedings in respect thereof may, whether or not the accused is in Canada, be commenced and an accused may be charged, tried and punished within any territorial division in Canada in the same manner as if the offence had been committed in that territorial division. 1996, c. 31, s. 72.

CROSS-REFERENCES

The definition of territorial sea is in the *Territorial Sea and Fishing Zones Act*, R.S.C. 1985, T-8. "Attorney General" is defined in s. 2. See s. 477.2 as to when the consent of the Attorney General is required. Section 583(*h*) provides that a count in an indictment is not insufficient by reason only that it does not state that the required consent has been obtained. [As to other notes concerning sufficiency of consent, see s. 583.] The term "Canadian ship" is defined in s. 2 of the *Canada Shipping Act*, R.S.C. 1985, c. S-9. For definition of Canadian citizen, see *Citizenship Act*, R.S.C. 1985, c. C-29. For other notes respecting territorial jurisdiction, see cross-references under ss. 6, 7 and 470.

SYNOPSIS

This section states that where an offence is committed by any person on Canadian seas or waters off the Canadian coast, whether or not such offence was committed on a Canadian ship, the offence is within the jurisdiction of Canadian law. The offence will be tried in the same manner as it had been committed in that territorial jurisdiction.

ANNOTATIONS

This section gives Canadian courts jurisdiction to try offences committed on the territorial sea of Canada, although neither the accused nor the victim are Canadian citizens and the offence was committed on a foreign ship. This section is not limited to offences having extraterritorial effect such as piracy: *R. v. Frisbee* (1989), 48 C.C.C. (3d) 386 (B.C.C.A.), leave to appeal to S.C.C. refused 50 C.C.C. (3d) vi.

OFFENCE OUTSIDE CANADA.

481.2 Subject to this or any other Act of Parliament, where an act or omission is committed outside Canada and the act or omission is an offence when committed outside Canada under this or any other Act of Parliament, proceedings in respect of the offence may, whether or not the accused is in Canada, be commenced, and an accused may be charged, tried and punished within any territorial division in Canada in the same manner as if the offence had been committed in that territorial division. 1996, c. 31, s. 72; 2008, c. 18, s. 10.

CROSS-REFERENCES

A number of provisions of this Act and other federal legislation provide that an act or omission committed outside Canada is an offence in Canada. Many of the provisions are found in s. 7, which contains a provision similar to this in s. 7(5). Similarly, see s. 481.1 for offences committed on the territorial sea or the internal waters of Canada. Where this section applies, the provisions of the *Criminal Code* for the requirement of the appearance of the accused at proceedings apply, pursuant to s. 481.3.

APPEARANCE OF ACCUSED AT TRIAL.

481.3 For greater certainty, the provisions of this Act relating to

   (*a*) **the requirement of the appearance of an accused at proceedings, and**

   (*b*) **the exceptions to that requirement**

apply to proceedings commenced in any territorial division pursuant to section 481, 481.1 or 481.2. 1996, c. 31, s. 72.

Rules of Court

POWER TO MAKE RULES / Idem / Purpose of rules / Publication / Regulations to secure uniformity.

482. (1) Every superior court of criminal jurisdiction and every court of appeal may make rules of court not inconsistent with this or any other Act of Parliament, and any rules so made apply to any prosecution, proceeding, action or appeal, as the case may be, within the jurisdiction of that court, instituted in relation to any matter of a criminal nature or arising from or incidental to any such prosecution, proceeding, action or appeal.

(2) The following courts may, subject to the approval of the lieutenant governor in council of the relevant province, make rules of court not inconsistent with this Act or any other Act of Parliament that are applicable to any prosecution, proceeding, including a preliminary inquiry or proceedings within the meaning of Part XXVII, action or appeal, as the case may be, within the jurisdiction of that court, instituted in relation to any matter of a criminal nature or arising from or incidental to the prosecution, proceeding, action or appeal:

   (*a*) **every court of criminal jurisdiction for a province;**

   (*b*) **every appeal court within the meaning of section 812 that is not a court referred to in subsection (1);**

   (*c*) **the Ontario Court of Justice;**

   (*d*) **the Court of Quebec and every municipal court in the Province of Quebec;**

   (*e*) **the Provincial Court of Nova Scotia;**

   (*f*) **the Provincial Court of New Brunswick;**

   (*g*) **the Provincial Court of Manitoba;**

   (*h*) **the Provincial Court of British Columbia;**

   (*i*) **the Provincial Court of Prince Edward Island;**

   (*j*) **the Provincial Court of Saskatchewan;**

   (*k*) **the Provincial Court of Alberta;**

   (*l*) **the Provincial Court of Newfoundland and Labrador;**

   (*m*) **the Territorial Court of Yukon;**

   (*n*) **the Territorial Court of the Northwest Territories; and**

   (*o*) **the Nunavut Court of Justice.**

(3) Rules under subsection (1) or (2) may be made

   (*a*) **generally to regulate the duties of the officers of the court and any other matter considered expedient to attain the ends of justice and carry into effect the provisions of the law;**

CR. CODE

(b) to regulate the sittings of the court or any division thereof, or of any judge of the court sitting in chambers, except in so far as they are regulated by law;

(c) to regulate the pleading, practice and procedure in criminal matters, including pre-hearing conferences held under section 625.1, proceedings with respect to judicial interim release and preliminary inquiries and, in the case of rules under subsection (1), proceedings with respect to mandamus, certiorari, habeas corpus, prohibition and procedendo and proceedings on an appeal under section 830; and

(d) to carry out the provisions of this Act relating to appeals from conviction, acquittal or sentence and, without restricting the generality of this paragraph,

   (i) for furnishing necessary forms and instructions in relation to notices of appeal or applications for leave to appeal to officials or other persons requiring or demanding them,

   (ii) for ensuring the accuracy of notes taken at a trial and the verification of any copy or transcript,

   (iii) for keeping writings, exhibits or other things connected with the proceedings on the trial,

   (iv) for securing the safe custody of property during the period in which the operation of an order with respect to that property is suspended under subsection 689(1), and

   (v) for providing that the Attorney General and counsel who acted for the Attorney General at the trial be supplied with certified copies of writings, exhibits and things connected with the proceedings that are required for the purposes of their duties.

(4) Rules of court that are made under the authority of this section shall be published in the *Canada Gazette*.

(5) Notwithstanding anything in this section, the Governor in Council may make such provision as he considers proper to secure uniformity in the rules of court in criminal matters, and all uniform rules made under the authority of this subsection prevail and have effect as if enacted by this Act. R.S., c. C-34, s. 438; 1974-75-76, c. 93, s. 42; R.S.C. 1985, c. 27 (1st Supp.), s. 66; 1994, c. 44, s. 35; 2002, c. 13, s. 17; 2015, c. 3, s. 50.

CROSS-REFERENCES
The terms "Attorney General", "superior court of criminal jurisdiction", "court of appeal", "court of criminal jurisdiction" and "writing" are defined in s. 2. Section 745.5 makes separate provision for making of rules of procedure on applications for review of parole ineligibility of a person convicted of murder.

Where rules made under this section provide that the accused need not appear personally, by virtue of s. 485, jurisdiction over the person is not lost. Section 482.1 gives the courts mentioned in this section the power to make case management rules.

SYNOPSIS
Subsection (1) provides that every superior court of criminal jurisdiction and every court of appeal may make rules of court in relation to any criminal proceedings or matters incidental to a prosecution arising before it.

Subsection (2) states that every court of criminal jurisdiction for a province, every appeal court within the meaning of s. 812 that is not a court referred to in subsec. (1) and the trial courts that are not the superior court of justice, such as the provincial court, may, with the approval of the Lieutenant Governor in Council of the province, make similar rules that are applicable to any prosecution, proceeding, including a preliminary inquiry or summary conviction proceedings, action or appeal, as the case may be, within the jurisdiction of that court, instituted in relation to any matter of a criminal nature or arising from or incidental to the prosecution, proceeding, action or appeal. The rules made under both subsecs. (1) and (2) may not be inconsistent with the Code or any other Act of Parliament.

Subsection (3) sets out the matters which such rules may regulate and subsec. (4) requires publication of the rules in the Canada Gazette. Subsection (5) empowers the Governor in Council to ensure uniformity of the rules of court in criminal matters and any uniform rules made under this subsection prevail.

ANNOTATIONS

In *R. v. Jacobs*, [1971] S.C.R. 92, 2 C.C.C. (2d) 26, the Que. C.A. had, on March 24, 1969, dismissed the accused's appeal when his counsel failed to appear to argue the appeal. Subsequently, on April 18, 1969, the court rescinded its order, and from that order the Crown appealed. It was held (5:0) that both of the Appeal Court orders, neither of which dealt with the merits of the accused's appeal, were made in the exercise of its discretionary power relating to practice concerning the proper administration of justice in criminal matters.

While subsec. (3)(*c*) does not authorize the making of rules which would permit the court to award costs on an application for *habeas corpus,* in a criminal matter the Superior Court has the power to award costs by virtue of its inherent jurisdiction to control proceedings, to penalize abuses and to maintain its authority. However, the power to award costs arises only in circumstances similar to a contempt of court, such as misconduct or dishonesty by a party, or a serious interference with the administration of justice: *Quebec (Attorney General) v. Cronier* (1981), 63 C.C.C. (2d) 437 (Que. C.A.).

Similarly, while the Superior Court has an inherent jurisdiction to award costs against the inferior court, the power is to be used sparingly and only where the circumstances were akin to a contempt of court or reveal malice or bad faith thereby creating a flagrant injustice. Moreover, before the order is made the judge of the inferior court is entitled to notice and an opportunity to be heard on the question of costs: *Mayrand v. Cronier* (1981), 63 C.C.C. (2d) 561 (Que. C.A.).

POWER TO MAKE RULES RESPECTING CASE MANAGEMENT / Compliance with directions / Summons or warrant / Provisions to apply / Approval of lieutenant governor in council / Subsections 482(4) and (5) to apply.

482.1 (1) A court referred to in subsection 482(1) or (2) may make rules for case management, including rules

  (*a*) **for the determination of any matter that would assist the court in effective and efficient case management;**

  (*b*) **permitting personnel of the court to deal with administrative matters relating to proceedings out of court if the accused is represented by counsel; and**

  (*c*) **establishing case management schedules.**

(2) The parties to a case shall comply with any direction made in accordance with a rule made under subsection (1).

(3) If rules are made under subsection (1), a court, justice or judge may issue a summons or warrant to compel the presence of the accused at case management proceedings.

(4) Section 512 and subsection 524(1) apply, with any modifications that the circumstances require, to the issuance of a summons or a warrant under subsection (3).

(5) Rules made under this section by a court referred to in subsection 482(2) must be approved by the lieutenant governor in council of the relevant province in order to come into force.

(6) Subsections 482(4) and (5) apply, with any modifications that the circumstances require, to rules made under subsection (1). 2002, c. 13, s. 18.

CROSS-REFERENCES

The general power to make rules is set out in s. 482. By virtue of s. 485, where rules made under this section provide that the accused need not appear personally, jurisdiction over the person is not lost.

SYNOPSIS

This section gives all trial and appellate courts the powers to make case management rules in respect of proceedings in those courts. Importantly, the court is given the power to make rules delegating certain administrative tasks to court personnel, provided the accused is represented by counsel. The parties are required to comply with any directions made in accordance with the rules and the court may issue a summons or warrant to ensure the attendance of the accused at a case management conference. Where the rules are not made by the Court of Appeal or a superior court of criminal jurisdiction, they must be approved by the lieutenant governor in council in order to come into force. The rules must be published in the Canada Gazette and the Governor in Council must make such provisions as considered necessary to ensure uniformity of the rules of court in criminal matters and any uniform rules prevail.

Part XV / SPECIAL PROCEDURE AND POWERS

General Powers of Certain Officials

OFFICIALS WITH POWERS OF TWO JUSTICES.

483. Every judge or provincial court judge authorized by the law of the province in which he is appointed to do anything that is required to be done by two or more justices may do alone anything that this Act or any other Act of Parliament authorizes two or more justices to do. R.S., c. C-34, s. 439.

CROSS-REFERENCES

The terms "provincial court judge" and "justice" are defined in s. 2.

SYNOPSIS

This section authorizes every judge or provincial court judge who is authorized by the law of a province to do anything required to be done by two or more justices to also act in the place of two or more justices when such a provision is found in the Code or any other Act of Parliament.

PRESERVING ORDER IN COURT.

484. Every judge or provincial court judge has the same power and authority to preserve order in a court over which he presides as may be exercised by the superior court of criminal jurisdiction of the province during the sittings thereof. R.S., c. C-34, s. 440.

CROSS-REFERENCES

The terms "provincial court judge", "justice" and "superior court of criminal jurisdiction" are defined in s. 2.

For notes on the common law power over contempt of court, see notes following ss. 9 and 10.

SYNOPSIS

This section gives to every judge or provincial court judge the same power as may be exercised by the superior court of criminal jurisdiction to preserve order during the sittings of courts over which they preside.

ANNOTATIONS

A provincial court judge has the power to punish for contempt on preliminary inquiry a person who refused to rise when the Court was called to order: *R. v. Hume, ex p. Hawkins,* [1966] 3 C.C.C. 43, 53 D.L.R. (2d) 453, 53 W.W.R. 406 *sub nom. Hawkins Habeas Corpus Application (Re)* (B.C.S.C.).

This section gives a provincial court judge presiding at a preliminary hearing power to convict for contempt in the face of the court where required to preserve order in the court. Thus, a counsel's refusal despite the judge's order to remove a tape recorder from the court room during a preliminary hearing could in certain circumstances amount to contempt: *R. v. Barker* (1980), 53 C.C.C. (2d) 322, [1980] 4 W.W.R. 202 (Alta. C.A.).

This section gives a provincial court judge power to cite for contempt an accused who appears for his trial in such an intoxicated condition that the trial is unable to proceed: *R. v. Heer* (1982), 68 C.C.C. (2d) 333, 38 B.C.L.R. 176 (S.C.).

Under this section one judge of the Alberta Provincial Court has no jurisdiction to try a contempt of court charge initiated by another judge as a result of conduct by the accused committed in the face of the court: *R. v. Doz,* [1987] 2 S.C.R. 463, 38 C.C.C. (3d) 479, 55 Alta. L.R. (2d) 289 (7:0).

The words "order in a court" do not embrace a refusal by a witness to testify and thus this section cannot be invoked to authorize a provincial court judge presiding at a preliminary hearing to punish such refusal as a contempt of court. The judge's only power in such circumstances is to use the procedure in s. 545: *R. v. Bubley* (1976), 32 C.C.C. (2d) 79, [1976] 6 W.W.R. 179 (Alta. S.C. App. Div.).

PROCEDURAL IRREGULARITIES / Where accused not present / Summons or warrant / Dismissal for want of prosecution / Adjournment and order / Part XVI to apply.

485. (1) Jurisdiction over an offence is not lost by reason of the failure of any court, judge, provincial court judge or justice to act in the exercise of that jurisdiction at any particular time, or by reason of a failure to comply with any of the provisions of this Act respecting adjournments or remands.

(1.1) Jurisdiction over an accused is not lost by reason of the failure of the accused to appear personally, so long as subsection 515(2.2), paragraph 537(1)(j), (j.1) or (k), subsection 650(1.1) or (1.2), paragraph 650(2)(b) or 650.01(3)(a), subsection 683(2.1) or 688(2.1) or a rule of court made under section 482 or 482.1 applies.

(2) Where jurisdiction over an accused or a defendant is lost and has not been regained, a court, judge, provincial court judge or justice may, within three months after the loss of jurisdiction, issue a summons, or if it or he considers it necessary in the public interest, a warrant for the arrest of the accused or defendant.

(3) Where no summons or warrant is issued under subsection (2) within the period provided therein, the proceedings shall be deemed to be dismissed for want of prosecution and shall not be recommenced except in accordance with section 485.1.

(4) Where, in the opinion of the court, judge, provincial court judge or justice, an accused or a defendant who appears at a proceeding has been misled or prejudiced by reason of any matter referred to in subsection (1), the court, judge, provincial court judge or justice may adjourn the proceeding and may make such order as it or he considers appropriate.

(5) The provisions of Part XVI apply with such modifications as the circumstances require where a summons or warrant is issued under subsection (2). 1974-75-76, c. 93, s. 43; R.S.C. 1985, c. 27 (1st Supp.), s. 67; 1997, c. 18, s. 40; 2002, c. 13, s. 19.

CROSS-REFERENCES

The terms "provincial court judge" and "justice" are defined in s. 2.

Calculation of a period of months is determined in accordance with s. 28 of the *Interpretation Act*, R.S.C. 1985, c. I-21.

SYNOPSIS

This section deals with specific examples of procedural irregularities as they relate to jurisdiction over the offender and the offence.

Subsection (1) states that jurisdiction over an offence is not lost when the court fails to exercise jurisdiction at any particular time, or when it fails to comply with any of the provisions in the Code with respect to adjournments or remands.

Subsection (1.1) provides that jurisdiction over the person is not lost at the preliminary inquiry or the trial where the person was to appear by counsel or appear by video or similar system as permitted in the sections listed in the subsection or by a rule of court made under ss. 482 or 482.1.

Subsection (2) empowers a court to issue a summons or, if necessary in the public interest, a warrant for the arrest of an accused person within three months after jurisdiction over that person has been lost and has not been regained.

Subsection (3) states that if no summons or warrant is issued within the three-month period stipulated in subsec. (2), the proceedings shall be deemed dismissed for want of prosecution. Such proceedings cannot be reinstituted except in accordance with s. 485.1.

Subsection (4) empowers a court to adjourn a proceeding and make such order as is considered appropriate when it appears that an accused person has been misled or prejudiced by reason of any matter referred to in subsec. (1).

Subsection (5) provides that the provisions of Part XVI, which deal with compelling the appearance of an accused before a justice and interim release, apply with the necessary modifications when a summons or warrant is issued under subsec. (2).

ANNOTATIONS

This section was applied to cure a failure to comply with [former] s. 537(1)(a), the preliminary hearing having been adjourned for longer than eight days without the accused's consent. The court noted that *R. v. Doyle*, [1977] 1 S.C.R. 597, 29 C.C.C. (2d) 177, 68 D.L.R. (3d) 270, which held that adjourning a case for longer than eight days without the accused's consent resulted in a loss of jurisdiction over the person of the accused, was decided at a time when this section did not apply: *R. v. Ulrich* (1977), 38 C.C.C. (2d) 1, [1978] 1 W.W.R. 422 (Alta. S.C.T.D.).

It was held in *R. v. Krannenburg*, [1980] 1 S.C.R. 1053, 51 C.C.C. (2d) 205, 17 C.R. (3d) 357 (7:0), that the predecessor to this section could not cure a loss of jurisdiction which resulted when there was a proper adjournment to a fixed day but upon that day nothing happened. The court distinguished between a loss of jurisdiction "over the person" such as a remand in excess of eight days without consent, and a loss of jurisdiction "over the offence" when nothing is done on the return date of a proper adjournment. However, the recent amendment to this section with the addition of the reference to the failure to exercise jurisdiction at any particular time, may well cover the loss of jurisdiction dealt with in *R. v. Krannenburg*.

Where an accused did not appear, and nothing was done on the return date of an adjournment because the accused, on being remanded to a hospital for observation had been found unfit and not returned to court, the court regained jurisdiction over him on a subsequent appearance one month later. *R. v. Fogarty* (1988), 46 C.C.C. (3d) 289 (N.S.C.A.).

RECOMMENCEMENT WHERE DISMISSAL FOR WANT OF PROSECUTION.

485.1 Where an indictment in respect of a transaction is dismissed or deemed by any provision of this Act to be dismissed for want of prosecution, a new information shall not be laid and a new indictment shall not be preferred before any court in respect of the same transaction without

(*a*) **the personal consent in writing of the Attorney General or Deputy Attorney General, in any prosecution conducted by the Attorney General or in which the Attorney General intervenes; or**

(*b*) **the written order of a judge of that court, in any prosecution conducted by a prosecutor other than the Attorney General and in which the Attorney General does not intervene. R.S.C. 1985, c. 27 (1st Supp.), s. 67.**

CROSS-REFERENCES

The terms "indictment" and "prosecutor" are defined in s. 2. The latter term is also defined in s. 785 for summary conviction proceedings.

SYNOPSIS

This section sets out the circumstances under which a proceeding may be recommenced after it has been dismissed for want of prosecution. No new information can be laid, or indictment preferred, in this situation unless the personal written consent of the Attorney General or the Deputy Attorney General is obtained, or, in the case of a matter that is not prosecuted by the Attorney General and in which the Attorney General has not intervened, a judge of the relevant court issues a written order.

ANNOTATIONS

This section does not apply where the indictment is quashed by the trial judge for failing to comply with the sufficiency requirements of s. 581. Thus the Attorney General's consent is not required to lay a new information: *R. v. Richardson* (1987), 39 C.C.C. (3d) 262 (N.S.C.A.).

Although the charges which were initially dismissed for want of prosecution were laid by a private prosecutor, the Attorney General may consent to the laying of a new information by agents of the Crown: *R. v. Proctor & Gamble Inc.* (1993), 82 C.C.C. (3d) 477 (Alta. C.A.).

EXCLUSION OF PUBLIC / Application / Factors to be considered / Reasons to be stated / No adverse inference.

486. (1) Any proceedings against an accused shall be held in open court, but the presiding judge or justice may, on application of the prosecutor or a witness or on his or her own motion, order the exclusion of all or any members of the public from the court room for all or part of the proceedings, or order that the witness testify behind a screen or other device that would allow the witness not to be seen by members of the public, if the judge or justice is of the opinion that such an order is in the interest of public morals, the maintenance of order or the proper administration of justice or is necessary to prevent injury to international relations or national defence or national security.

(1.1) The application may be made, during the proceedings, to the presiding judge or justice or, before the proceedings begin, to the judge or justice who will preside at the proceedings or, if that judge or justice has not been determined, to any judge or justice having jurisdiction in the judicial district where the proceedings will take place.

(2) In determining whether the order is in the interest of the proper administration of justice, the judge or justice shall consider

(a) **society's interest in encouraging the reporting of offences and the participation of victims and witnesses in the criminal justice process;**

(b) **the safeguarding of the interests of witnesses under the age of 18 years in all proceedings;**

(c) **the ability of the witness to give a full and candid account of the acts complained of if the order were not made;**

(d) **whether the witness needs the order for their security or to protect them from intimidation or retaliation;**

(e) **the protection of justice system participants who are involved in the proceedings;**

(f) **whether effective alternatives to the making of the proposed order are available in the circumstances;**

(g) **the salutary and deleterious effects of the proposed order; and**

(h) **any other factor that the judge or justice considers relevant.**

(3) If an accused is charged with an offence under section 151, 152, 153, 153.1, 155 or 159, subsection 160(2) or (3) or section 163.1, 170, 171, 171.1, 172, 172.1, 172.2, 173, 271, 272, 273, 279.01, 279.011, 279.02, 279.03, 286.1, 286.2, 286.3 and the prosecutor or the accused applies for an order under subsection (1), the judge or justice shall, if no such order is made, state, by reference to the circumstances of the case, the reason for not making an order.

(4) No adverse inference may be drawn from the fact that an order is, or is not, made under this section. R.S., c. C-34, s. 442; 1974-75-76, c. 93, s. 44; 1980-81-82-83, c. 110, s. 74, c. 125, s. 25; R.S.C. 1985, c. 19 (3rd Supp.), s. 14; c. 23 (4th Supp.), s. 1; 1992, c. 21, s. 9; 1993, c. 45, s. 7; 1997, c. 16, s. 6; 1999, c. 25, s. 2; 2001, c. 32, s. 29; 2001, c. 41, s. 16, 34 and 133(13), (14); 2002, c. 13, s. 20; 2005, c. 32, s. 15; 2005, c. 43, ss. 4 and 8(3)(a); 2010, c. 3, s. 4; 2012, c. 1, s. 28; 2014, c. 25, s. 21; 2015, c. 13, s. 13; c. 20, s. 21.

CROSS-REFERENCES

The terms "justice" and "justice system participant" are defined in s. 2. Age is determined by reference to s. 30 of the *Interpretation Act*, R.S.C. 1985, c. I-21.

Section 486.1 provides for the making of an order to allow for a support person to be present and to be close to a witness while the witness testifies. Section 486.2 provides for taking testimony outside the courtroom or behind a screen so that the witness cannot see the accused. Section 486.3 provides for making of orders that the accused not personally cross-examine witnesses. Sections 486.4 and 486.5 provide for the making of non-publication orders.

SYNOPSIS

This section sets out the circumstances in which a judge may exclude the public from the courtroom.

Subsection (1) enacts the presumption that proceedings will be held in open court. If the judge or justice is of the opinion that, for any of the reasons set out therein, the public should be excluded from the courtroom, the judge or justice may make such an order. Subsection (1.1) governs when and to whom such an application may be made. One reason for exclusion is the proper administration of justice, which is defined in part in subsec. (2). Under subsec. (3), where the accused is charged with certain offences set out therein and the judge refuses to make the exclusion order, the judge shall state reasons for the refusal. Generally speaking, the offences referred to are the various sexual offences and the human trafficking offences. Finally, subsec. (4) prohibits any adverse inference being drawn from the making of (or refusal to make) such an order.

ANNOTATIONS

Note: The cases noted below were decided under the predecessor section.

Grounds for exclusion of public generally – The trial judge must exercise his or her discretion under subsec. (1) in conformity with the Charter. The trial judge must consider the following factors: (a) available options and whether there are any other reasonable and effective alternatives available; (b) whether the order is limited as much as possible, and (c) balance the objectives of the particular order and its probable effects against the importance of openness and the particular expression that will be limited in order to ensure that the positive and negative effects of the order are proportionate. The party making the application bears the burden of establishing that the rule of openness should be displaced by showing that the order is necessary to the proper administration of justice, that the order is as limited as possible and that the salutary effects of the order are proportionate to its deleterious effects. If the order sought is to protect a constitutional right, this factor must be considered in respect of proportionality. Where the facts are not in dispute, the statement of counsel is sufficient. However, if the facts are in dispute or there is insufficient evidence placed before the trial judge, the applicant should adduce evidence at the hearing held *in camera*: *Canadian Broadcasting Corp. v. New Brunswick (Attorney General)*, [1996] 3 S.C.R. 480, 110 C.C.C. (3d) 193.

On the trial of a drug charge, an application was made under the predecessor to this section to exclude the public while the accused testified, as she would be revealing the fact that she was a police informer. The application was refused and, on appeal, it was held there was no error in the refusal of the judge to exercise his power in this section. The reason put forward was not sufficient reason to exclude the public since it had already been revealed in open court that she was an informer and it could not be said that the disclosure that she intended to do it again added in any substantial way to whatever danger was alleged to attend her testifying in open court. It would, however, have been preferable for the trial judge to at least have listened *in camera* to defence counsel's reasons for seeking exclusion: *R. v. Douglas* (1977), 33 C.C.C. (2d) 395 (Ont. C.A.).

An order excluding the public may properly be made where the complainant in a sexual offence would otherwise be too nervous to give evidence. In such circumstances, the order is necessary for the proper administration of justice: *R. v. Lefebvre* (1984), 17 C.C.C. (3d) 277 (Que. C.A.).

A provincial court judge has no power under this section to order a newspaper reporter to be excluded from court so as to prevent the reporter from publishing the names of witnesses (in this case, the inmates of a bawdy-house). Such an order is a misuse of the section in attempting to prevent conduct that is not unlawful, interfering with freedom of the press, and it could not be justified on the basis of the proper administration of justice: *R. v. F.P. Publications (Western) Ltd.* (1979), 51 C.C.C. (2d) 110 (Man. C.A.) (4:1).

It was held in *R. v. Musitano* (1985), 24 C.C.C. (3d) 65 (Ont. C.A.), leave to appeal to S.C.C. refused 79 N.R. 79*n*, that the trial judge properly exercised his discretion in excluding the public in the interest of the proper administration of justice when conducting an inquiry in the course of the trial to determine the impartiality of several jurors.

Requirement of reasons in sexual offence cases [subsec. (3)] – The fact that the judge is required to give reasons does not enlarge the grounds, set out in subsec. (1), for excluding the public: *R. v. Brint* (1979), 45 C.C.C. (2d) 560 (Alta. S.C.).

Constitutional considerations – It was held that the predecessor to this section was a reasonable limit on the freedoms guaranteed by s. 2(*b*) of the Charter: *Canadian Broadcasting Corp. v. New Brunswick (Attorney General)*, [1996] 3 S.C.R. 480, 110 C.C.C. (3d) 193.

It has also been held that the section does not violate the rights of victims and their families as guaranteed by s. 7 of the *Canadian Charter of Rights and Freedoms*. In particular, the "public morals" exception to the open court rule is not vague or overly broad, nor is the provision procedurally defective, although the victim is not granted automatic standing. The fact that public access to child or coerced pornography will result in undue harm or violate the privacy interests of the victims or their families are matters properly coming within the ambit of the administration of justice branch of this subsection: *French Estate v. Ontario (Attorney General)* (1998), 122 C.C.C. (3d) 475 (Ont. C.A.), leave to appeal to S.C.C. refused 132 C.C.C. (3d) vi.

SUPPORT PERSON — WITNESSES UNDER 18 OR WHO HAVE A DISABILITY / Other witnesses / Application / Factors to be considered / Witness not to be a support person / No communication while testifying / No adverse inference.

486.1 (1) In any proceedings against an accused, the judge or justice shall, on application of the prosecutor in respect of a witness who is under the age of 18 years or who has a mental or physical disability, or on application of such a witness, order that a support person of the witness' choice be permitted to be present and to be close to the witness while the witness testifies, unless the judge or justice is of the opinion that the order would interfere with the proper administration of justice.

(2) In any proceedings against an accused, the judge or justice may, on application of the prosecutor in respect of a witness, or on application of a witness, order that a support person of the witness' choice be permitted to be present and to be close to the witness while the witness testifies if the judge or justice is of the opinion that the order would facilitate the giving of a full and candid account by the witness of the acts complained of or would otherwise be in the interest of the proper administration of justice.

(2.1) An application referred to in subsection (1) or (2) may be made, during the proceedings, to the presiding judge or justice or, before the proceedings begin, to the judge or justice who will preside at the proceedings or, if that judge or justice has not been determined, to any judge or justice having jurisdiction in the judicial district where the proceedings will take place.

(3) In determining whether to make an order under subsection (2), the judge or justice shall consider

   (a) the age of the witness;

   (b) the witness' mental or physical disabilities,if any;

   (c) the nature of the offence;

   (d) the nature of any relationship between the witness and the accused;

   (e) whether the witness needs the order for their security or to protect them from intimidation or retaliation;

   (f) society's interest in encouraging the reporting of offences and the participation of victims and witnesses in the criminal justice process; and

   (g) any other factor that the judge or justice considers relevant.

(4) The judge or justice shall not permit a witness to be a support person unless the judge or justice is of the opinion that doing so is necessary for the proper administration of justice.

(5) The judge or justice may order that the support person and the witness not communicate with each other while the witness testifies.

(6) No adverse inference may be drawn from the fact that an order is, or is not, made under this section. 2005, c. 32, s. 15; 2015, c. 13, s. 14.

CROSS-REFERENCES

"Justice" and "prosecutor" are defined in s. 2. Age is determined by reference to s. 30 of the *Interpretation Act*, R.S.C. 1985, c. I-21.

   Section 486 provides for the making of an order to exclude the public. Section 486.2 provides for taking testimony outside the courtroom or behind a screen so that the witness cannot see the accused. Section 486.3 provides for making of orders that the accused not personally cross-examine witnesses. Sections 486.4 and 486.5 provide for the making of non-publication orders.

SYNOPSIS

This section sets out the circumstances in which the judge or justice may make an order to permit a support person to be present and close to a witness while the witness testifies. The section envisages two sets of circumstances. Under subsec. (1), where the witness is under the age of 18 years or has a mental or physical disability, the order will be made where the prosecutor or the witness applies for it, unless the judge or justice is of the opinion that the order would interfere with the proper administration of justice. Under subsec. (2), in the case of all other witnesses, the order will only be made where the judge or justice is of the opinion that the order is necessary to obtain a full and candid account from the witness of the acts complained of. The application may be made during the proceedings or before they begin to the judge or justice who will preside at the proceedings (subsec. (2.1)). The factors to be considered in making the order under subsec. (2) are set out in subsec. (3). Ordinarily, another witness cannot be the support person except where it is necessary for the proper administration of justice (subsec. (4)). The judge or justice may order the witness and the support person not to communicate while the witness testifies (subsec. (5)). Under subsec. (6), no adverse inference may be drawn from the fact that an order is or is not made.

ANNOTATIONS

The complainant's mother was an appropriate support person, notwithstanding that she was a witness in the matter, given that, at the time that she acted as a support person, the mother had already testified and been fully cross-examined: *R. v. C. (D.)* (2008), 238 C.C.C. (3d) 16 (N.S.C.A.).

TESTIMONY OUTSIDE COURT ROOM — WITNESSES UNDER 18 OR WHO HAVE A DISABILITY / Other witnesses / Application / Factors to be considered / Same procedure for determination / Conditions of exclusion / No adverse inference.

486.2 (1) Despite section 650, in any proceedings against an accused, the judge or justice shall, on application of the prosecutor in respect of a witness who is under the age of 18 years or who is able to communicate evidence but may have difficulty doing so by reason of a mental or physical disability, or on application of such a witness, order that the witness testify outside the court room or behind a screen or other device that would allow the witness not to see the accused, unless the judge or justice is of the opinion that the order would interfere with the proper administration of justice.

(2) Despite section 650, in any proceedings against an accused, the judge or justice may, on application of the prosecutor in respect of a witness, or on application of a witness, order that the witness testify outside the court room or behind a screen or other device that would allow the witness not to see the accused if the judge or justice is of the opinion that the order would facilitate the giving of a full and candid account by the witness of the acts complained of or would otherwise be in the interest of the proper administration of justice.

(2.1) An application referred to in subsection (1) or (2) may be made, during the proceedings, to the presiding judge or justice or, before the proceedings begin, to the judge or justice who will preside at the proceedings or, if that judge or justice has not been determined, to any judge or justice having jurisdiction in the judicial district where the proceedings will take place.

(3) In determining whether to make an order under subsection (2), the judge or justice shall consider

    (*a*) **the age of the witness;**

    (*b*) **the witness' mental or physical disabilities, if any;**

    (*c*) **the nature of the offence;**

    (*d*) **the nature of any relationship between the witness and the accused;**

    (*e*) **whether the witness needs the order for their security or to protect them from intimidation or retaliation;**

(*f*) **whether the order is needed to protect the identity of a peace officer who has acted, is acting or will be acting in an undercover capacity, or of a person who has acted, is acting or will be acting covertly under the direction of a peace officer;**

(*f*.1) **whether the order is needed to protect the witness's identity if they have had, have or will have responsibilities relating to national security or intelligence;**

(*g*) **society's interest in encouraging the reporting of offences and the participation of victims and witnesses in the criminal justice process; and**

(*h*) **any other factor that the judge or justice considers relevant.**

(4) If the judge or justice is of the opinion that it is necessary for a witness to testify in order to determine whether an order under subsection (2) should be made in respect of that witness, the judge or justice shall order that the witness testify in accordance with that subsection.

(5) A witness shall not testify outside the court room in accordance with an order made under subsection (1) or (2) unless arrangements are made for the accused, the judge or justice and the jury to watch the testimony of the witness by means of closed-circuit television or otherwise and the accused is permitted to communicate with counsel while watching the testimony.

(6) No adverse inference may be drawn from the fact that an order is, or is not, made under subsection (1) or (2). 2005, c. 32, s. 15; 2014, c. 17, s. 12; 2015, c. 13, s. 15; 2015, c. 20, s. 38(2).

(7) [*Repealed*, 2015, c. 13, s. 15.]

(8) [*Repealed*, 2015, c. 13, s. 15.]

CROSS-REFERENCES

"Criminal organization", "justice", "prosecutor" and "terrorism offence" are defined in s. 2. Age is determined by reference to s. 30 of the *Interpretation Act*, R.S.C. 1985, c. I-21.

Section 486 provides for the making of an order to exclude the public. Section 486.1 provides for permitting a support person to be present while a witness testifies. Section 486.3 provides for making of orders that the accused not personally cross-examine witnesses. Sections 486.4 and 486.5 provide for the making of non-publication orders.

SYNOPSIS

This section sets out circumstances in which a witness may be permitted to testify outside the courtroom or behind a screen or device that would not allow the witness to see the accused. The section envisages three different situations. The first concerns witnesses who are under age of 18 years or may have difficulty communicating testimony because of a mental or physical disability. Where the witness or the prosecutor applies for the order, the judge is to make the order unless of the opinion that the order would interfere with the proper administration of justice.

The second situation is set out in subsec. (2) and concerns other witnesses. In that case, the order will be made only if the judge is of the opinion that it is necessary to obtain a full and candid account from the witness of the acts complained of. In making this determination, the judge takes into account the factors set out in s. 486.1(3) such as the nature of the offence and the relationship between the witness and the accused.

The third situation relates to a certain class of offences. These offences are listed in subsec. (5) and include various criminal organization offences, terrorism offences and national security offences listed in the *Security of Information Act*, R.S.C. 1985, c. O-5, such as communicating secret information to terrorist groups or foreign entities. The order is to be made under subsec. (4) permitting the witness to testify outside the courtroom if necessary to protect the safety of the witness, or outside the courtroom or behind a screen if the judge is of the opinion that the order is necessary to obtain a full and candid account from the witness.

If it is necessary to hear from the witness to decide whether an order should be made under subsec. (2) or (4), subsec. (6) provides that the witness may testify on that inquiry outside the courtroom or behind the screen as the case may be. A witness shall not testify outside the courtroom unless facilities are available to allow the accused, the judge and the jury to watch the testimony, and the accused has a means of communicating with counsel while watching the testimony. No adverse inference may be drawn from the fact that an order is or is not made.

ANNOTATIONS

Note: Some of these cases noted below were decided under the predecessor section and may be of greatest assistance in applying subsecs. (2) and (4).

When order should be made – It was held that the circumstances under which a judge may make an order under the predecessor to this section did not require that exceptional and inordinate stress be caused to the child. The trial judge has substantial latitude in deciding whether the use of the screen should be permitted and the evidence in support of the application need not take any particular form. In exercising the discretion under the section, the trial judge may consider evidence of the capabilities and demeanour of the child, the nature of the allegations and the circumstances of the case. It may well be that the trial judge may also consider the fact that the accused is unrepresented in determining whether or not to permit the use of the screen: *R. v. Levogiannis*, [1993] 4 S.C.R. 475, 85 C.C.C. (3d) 327 (9:0).

Before permitting the witness to testify outside of court, the trial judge may hold a *voir dire* to determine whether such an order is necessary to obtain a full and candid account. On that *voir dire*, however, the Crown may not ask witnesses who are not qualified as experts to give their opinion on that issue: *R. v. H. (B.C.)* (1990), 58 C.C.C. (3d) 16 (Man. C.A.). [Now see subsec. (6).]

It was held under the predecessor to this section that the trial judge is not empowered to form the requisite opinion that a screen is necessary unless there is an evidential base relating to the standard of necessity set out in this subsection. The necessary evidential base was lacking, where there was merely testimony from the complainant that she did not feel comfortable talking in front of a lot of people and the accused and that she would find it easier if people were excluded from the courtroom: *R. v. M. (P.)* (1990), 1 O.R. (3d) 341 (C.A.).

The court has the jurisdiction to make an order requiring the Attorney General to assume responsibility for the payment of the appointed lawyer's fees: *R. v. S. (B.)* (2007), 240 C.C.C. (3d) 375 (Que. C.A.).

Constitutional considerations – This provision does not violate ss. 7 or 11(*d*) of the Charter: *R. v. S. (J.)* (2008), 238 C.C.C. (3d) 522 (B.C.C.A.), affd 251 C.C.C. (3d) 1 (S.C.C.).

Procedure – Ordinarily, the trial judge should instruct the jury to the effect that the use of the screen is a procedure that is allowed in cases of this kind by reason of the youth of the witness and that, since it has nothing to do with the guilt or innocence of the accused, the jury must not draw any inference of any kind from its use, and, in particular, that no adverse inference should be drawn against the accused because of the screen: *R. v. Levogiannis*, *supra*. [Now see subsec. (8).]

The trial judge does not have independent discretion to determine which testimonial accommodation would be better in the circumstances, unless the requested testimonial accommodation would interfere with the proper administration of justice: *R. v. T. (S.B.)* (2008), 232 C.C.C. (3d) 115 (B.C.S.C.).

ACCUSED NOT TO CROSS-EXAMINE WITNESSES UNDER 18 / Accused not to cross-examine complainant — certain offences / Other witnesses / Factors to be considered / Application / No adverse inference.

486.3 (1) In any proceedings against an accused, the judge or justice shall, on application of the prosecutor in respect of a witness who is under the age of 18 years, or on application of such a witness, order that the accused not personally cross-examine the witness, unless the judge or justice is of the opinion that the proper administration of justice requires the accused to personally conduct the cross-examination. If such an order is made, the judge or justice shall appoint counsel to conduct the cross-examination.

(2) In any proceedings against an accused in respect of an offence under any of sections 264, 271, 272 and 273, the judge or justice shall, on application of the prosecutor in respect of a witness who is a victim, or on application of such a witness, order that the accused not personally cross-examine the witness, unless the judge or justice is of the opinion that the proper administration of justice requires the accused to personally conduct the cross-examination. If such an order is made, the judge or justice shall appoint counsel to conduct the cross-examination.

(3) In any proceedings against an accused, the judge or justice may, on application of the prosecutor in respect of a witness who is not entitled to make an application under subsection (1) or (2), or on application of such a witness, order that the accused not personally cross-examine the witness if the judge or justice is of the opinion that the order would allow the giving of a full and candid account from the witness of the acts complained of or would otherwise be in the interest of the proper administration of justice. If the order is made, the judge or justice shall appoint counsel to conduct the cross-examination.

(4) In determining whether to make an order under subsection (3), the judge or justice shall consider

  (*a*) the age of the witness;
  (*b*) the witness' mental or physical disabilities, if any;
  (*c*) the nature of the offence;
  (*d*) whether the witness needs the order for their security or to protect them from intimidation or retaliation;
  (*e*) the nature of any relationship between the witness and the accused;
  (*f*) society's interest in encouraging the reporting of offences and the participation of victims and witnesses in the criminal justice process; and
  (*g*) any other factor that the judge or justice considers relevant.

(4.1) An application referred to in any of subsections (1) to (3) may be made during the proceedings to the presiding judge or justice or, before the proceedings begin, to the judge or justice who will preside at the proceedings or, if that judge or justice has not been determined, to any judge or justice having jurisdiction in the judicial district where the proceedings will take place.

(5) No adverse inference may be drawn from the fact that counsel is, or is not, appointed under this section. 2005, c. 32, s. 15; 2015, c. 13, s. 16.

CROSS-REFERENCES

"Justice", "prosecutor" and "victim" are defined in s. 2. Age is determined by reference to s. 30 of the *Interpretation Act*, R.S.C. 1985, c. I-21.

Section 486 provides for the making of an order to exclude the public. Section 486.1 provides for permitting a support person to be present while a witness testifies. Section 486.2 provides for taking testimony outside the courtroom or behind a screen so that the witness cannot see the accused. Sections 486.4 and 486.5 provide for the making of non-publication orders.

SYNOPSIS

This section sets out circumstances in which the judge may order that the accused not personally cross-examine prosecution witnesses. Where the order is made, the judge appoints counsel to conduct the cross-examination. The section envisages three different situations. The first concerns witnesses who are under the age of 18 years. Where the witness or the prosecutor applies for the order, the judge is to make the order unless the judge is of the opinion that the proper administration of justice requires the accused to personally conduct the cross-examination.

The second situation is set out in subsec. (2) and concerns other witnesses. In that case, the order will be made only if the judge is of the opinion that it is necessary to obtain a full and candid account from the witness of the acts complained of. In making this determination, the judge takes into account the factors set out in s. 486.1(3), such as the nature of the offence and the relationship between the witness and the accused.

The third situation relates to an accused charged with the criminal harassment offence in s. 264. On application by the victim or the prosecutor, the accused shall not personally cross-examine the victim unless the judge is of the opinion that the proper administration of justice requires the accused to personally conduct the cross-examination.

Under subsec. (4.1), the application for an order under this section may be made during the proceedings or before they begin to the judge who will preside at the proceedings. No adverse inference may be drawn from the fact that an order is, or is not, made.

ANNOTATIONS

An evidentiary foundation must be laid before an order under this provision is made. At a minimum, there must be reliable, trustworthy evidence from sources with intimate knowledge of the individual witnesses so that the court could be satisfied, on the balance of probabilities, that a full and candid account could not have been achieved if the witnesses were cross-examined by the accused: *R. v. Tehrankari* (2008), 246 C.C.C. (3d) 70 (Ont. S.C.J.).

Where the accused's testimony made allegations against the complainants that had not been put to them in cross-examination by counsel appointed pursuant to subsec. (2), the trial judge erred by relying on the rule in *Browne v. Dunn* (1893), 6 R. 67 (U.K.H.L.), as a reason to reject the accused's evidence and convict him. It was not clear that the accused understood what he was required to do in relation to briefing appointed counsel about his anticipated testimony: *R. v. Wapass* (2014), 314 C.C.C. (3d) 561 (Sask. C.A.).

NON-DISCLOSURE OF WITNESS' IDENTITY / Hearing may be held / Factors to be considered / No adverse inference.

486.31 (1) In any proceedings against an accused, the judge or justice may, on application of the prosecutor in respect of a witness, or on application of a witness, make an order directing that any information that could identify the witness not be disclosed in the course of the proceedings if the judge or justice is of the opinion that the order is in the interest of the proper administration of justice.

(2) The judge or justice may hold a hearing to determine whether the order should be made, and the hearing may be in private.

(3) In determining whether to make the order, the judge or justice shall consider

    (a) the right to a fair and public hearing;

    (b) the nature of the offence;

    (c) whether the witness needs the order for their security or to protect them from intimidation or retaliation;

    (d) whether the order is needed to protect the security of anyone known to the witness;

    (e) whether the order is needed to protect the identity of a peace officer who has acted, is acting or will be acting in an undercover capacity, or of a person who

has acted, is acting or will be acting covertly under the direction of a peace officer;

(*e*.1) whether the order is needed to protect the witness's identity if they have had, have or will have responsibilities relating to national security or intelligence;

(*f*) society's interest in encouraging the reporting of offences and the participation of victims and witnesses in the criminal justice process;

(*g*) the importance of the witness' testimony to the case;

(*h*) whether effective alternatives to the making of the proposed order are available in the circumstances;

(*i*) the salutary and deleterious effects of the proposed order; and

(*j*) any other factor that the judge or justice considers relevant.

(4) No adverse inference may be drawn from the fact that an order is, or is not, made under this section. 2015, c. 13, s. 17; c. 20, s. 38(3).

CROSS-REFERENCES

"Justice" and "prosecutor" are defined in s. 2.

SYNOPSIS

This section allows the court, on application of the prosecutor or a witness, to make an order directing that any information that could identify the witness not be disclosed in the course of the proceedings when such an order is in the interest of the proper administration of justice. Subsection (2) provides that the hearing of such an application may be in private. Subsection (3) provides a list of mandatory considerations for the court to weigh in deciding whether to make an order. Subsection (4) prohibits any adverse inference being drawn from the making of (or refusal to make) such an order.

ORDER RESTRICTING PUBLICATION — SEXUAL OFFENCES / Mandatory order on application / Victim under 18 — other offences / Mandatory order on application / Child pornography / Limitation.

486.4 (1) Subject to subsection (2), the presiding judge or justice may make an order directing that any information that could identify the victim or a witness shall not be published in any document or broadcast or transmitted in any way, in proceedings in respect of

(*a*) any of the following offences:

(i) an offence under section 151, 152, 153, 153.1, 155, 159, 160, 162, 163.1, 170, 171, 171.1, 172, 172.1, 172.2, 173, 210, 211, 213, 271, 272, 273, 279.01, 279.011, 279.02, 279.03, 280, 281, 286.1, 286.2, 286.3, 346 or 347, or

(ii) any offence under this Act, as it read from time to time before the day on which this subparagraph comes into force, if the conduct alleged would be an offence referred to in subparagraph (i) if it occurred on or after that day; or

(iii) [*Repealed*, 2014, c. 25, s. 22(2).]

(*b*) two or more offences being dealt with in the same proceeding, at least one of which is an offence referred to in paragraph (*a*).

(2) In proceedings in respect of the offences referred to in paragraph (1)(*a*) or (*b*), the presiding judge or justice shall

(*a*) at the first reasonable opportunity, inform any witness under the age of eighteen years and the victim of the right to make an application for the order; and

(*b*) on application made by the victim, the prosecutor or any such witness, make the order.

(2.1) Subject to subsection (2.2), in proceedings in respect of an offence other than an offence referred to in subsection (1), if the victim is under the age of 18 years, the presiding judge or justice may make an order directing that any information that could identify the victim shall not be published in any document or broadcast or transmitted in any way.

(2.2) In proceedings in respect of an offence other than an offence referred to in subsection (1), if the victim is under the age of 18 years, the presiding judge or justice shall

    (*a*) as soon as feasible, inform the victim of their right to make an application for the order; and

    (*b*) on application of the victim or the prosecutor, make the order.

(3) In proceedings in respect of an offence under section 163.1, a judge or justice shall make an order directing that any information that could identify a witness who is under the age of eighteen years, or any person who is the subject of a representation, written material or a recording that constitutes child pornography within the meaning of that section, shall not be published in any document or broadcast or transmitted in any way.

(4) An order made under this section does not apply in respect of the disclosure of information in the course of the administration of justice when it is not the purpose of the disclosure to make the information known in the community. 2005, c. 32, s. 15; c. 43, s. 8(3)(*b*); 2010, c. 3, s. 5; 2012, c. 1, s. 29; 2014, c. 25, ss. 22, 48(6); 2015, c. 13, s. 18(1), (2), (4).

CROSS-REFERENCES

"Justice" and "prosecutor" are defined in s. 2. Age is determined by reference to s. 30 of the *Interpretation Act*, R.S.C. 1985, c. I-21.

Section 486 provides for the making of an order to exclude the public. Section 486.1 provides for permitting a support person to be present while a witness testifies. Section 486.2 provides for taking testimony outside the courtroom or behind a screen so that the witness cannot see the accused. Section 486.3 provides for making of orders that the accused not personally cross-examine witnesses. Section 486.5 provides for the making of non-publication orders not covered by this section. Failure to comply with an order made under this section is a summary conviction offence under s. 486.6.

SYNOPSIS

This section provides that when an accused is charged under any of the specified sections, the court may make an order directing that the identity of, or any information that would identify, the victim or another witness not be published, broadcasted or transmitted in any way. Generally speaking, the offences listed in subsec. (1) are sexual offences, but also included are the human trafficking offences (ss. 279.01 to 279.03) and offences such as extortion (s. 346) and charging a criminal interest rate (s. 347). Subsection (2) requires the presiding judge or justice to inform any witness under the age of 18 and the victim, at the first reasonable opportunity, of the right to make an application under subsec. (1). If such an application is made by the victim, the prosecutor, or a witness under the age of 18, the judge or justice must make the order.

Subsection (3) sets out a special rule in relation to the child pornography offence. The order is to be made for any witness who is under the age of 18 and any person who is the subject of a representation, written material or recording that constitutes child pornography.

Subsection (4) provides an exception for disclosure in the course of the administration of justice, where disclosure is not for the purpose of making the information known to the community.

ANNOTATIONS

Note: The cases noted below were decided under the predecessor section.

Procedure – It was held under a predecessor to this section that the order (which was mandatory upon application by the prosecutor) must be made, at the latest, at the time the complainant begins her testimony: *R. v. Calabrese* (1981), 64 C.C.C. (2d) 71 (Que. S.C.).

It was held considering the predecessor to this section that, where the complainant or the prosecutor wishes to obtain a more specific order prohibiting the naming of the accused or other persons or places on the ground that such information would disclose the identity of the complainant, evidence must be provided to support the application. The order cannot properly be made merely with the consent of the prosecutor and the complainant and without any supporting evidence. However, such evidence can be supplied either by *viva voce* evidence, affidavit or submissions of counsel, and the discretion of a judge to make a non-publication order beyond an order as to the name of the complainant is not restricted to a limited category of cases such as those of incest and other familial crimes. On the other hand, great weight should always be given by judges in the exercise of their discretion to the tradition of openness of the courts to the public and the constitutional guarantee of freedom of the media in s. 2(*b*) of the Charter: *R. v. Southam Inc.* (1989), 47 C.C.C. (3d) 21 (Ont. C.A.).

It was held that a court may not unilaterally revoke an order under this section. If, however, both the Crown and the complainant consent to a revocation of the order, then the circumstances which make the publication ban mandatory are no longer present, and, subject to any rights that the accused may have under subsec. (3), the trial judge can revoke the order: *R. v. Adams*, [1995] 4 S.C.R. 707, 103 C.C.C. (3d) 262.

A publication ban continues in effect during appellate proceedings: *R. v. K. (V.)* (1991), 68 C.C.C. (3d) 18 (B.C.C.A.).

Where a judge is *functus officio*, a judge of the superior court has inherent jurisdiction to vary or lift the ban on publication of the complainant's identity: *R. v. Ireland* (2005), 203 C.C.C. (3d) 443 (Ont. S.C.J.).

Constitutional considerations – While the predecessor to this section was held to infringe freedom of expression as guaranteed under s. 2(*b*) of the Charter it was also held to constitute a reasonable limit on that freedom and was valid: *Canadian Newspapers Co. v. Canada (Attorney General)*, [1988] 2 S.C.R. 122, 43 C.C.C. (3d) 24 (6:0). [Note: The court left open the question whether, in a proper case, the accused's right to a fair trial as guaranteed by s. 11(*d*) of the Charter would require that the complainant's name be published.]

Note: The following cases were decided prior to the amendment to these provisions and the inclusion of s. 486.5, which expand the statutory bases for non-publication orders.

Publication bans other than pursuant to statute – A trial judge has jurisdiction to prohibit the publication of the names of certain witnesses where the circumstances are sufficiently compelling, as where the witnesses are prison inmates who justifiably fear for their safety should their identity be disclosed: *R. v. McArthur* (1984), 13 C.C.C. (3d) 152 (Ont. H.C.J.). [These circumstances would likely now be covered by this section and s. 486.5.]

The superior court has an inherent jurisdiction to make an order prohibiting publication of the identity of the accused where such an order is necessary to protect a trial that is then being conducted before it. As well, the superior court has power under its inherent jurisdiction to render assistance to inferior courts to enable them to administer justice fully and effectively: *R. v. Unnamed Person* (1985), 22 C.C.C. (3d) 284 (Ont. C.A.).

To seek or challenge a ban on appeal, the Crown and the accused must follow the regular avenues of appeal available to them through the *Criminal Code*. For a third party, such as the media, who has been affected by the publication ban, where the ban has been imposed by a provincial court judge, then the third party may apply to the superior court by way of *certiorari* and may then follow the appellate routes prescribed in the *Criminal Code*. When the order has been made by a superior court judge, then the third party may apply for leave to appeal to the Supreme Court of Canada under s. 40 of the *Supreme Court Act*, R.S.C. 1985, c. S-26. The judge hearing the application for a ban has the discretion to direct that third parties, such as the media, be given notice in accordance with the provincial rules of criminal procedure and has the discretion to grant standing to interested third parties and determine what rights the third parties should have on the hearing of the application. A judge has the discretion at common law to impose a ban on publication to protect the fairness of the trial only where: (a) such a ban is necessary in order to prevent a real and substantial risk to the fairness of the trial, because reasonably available alternative measures will not prevent the risk; and (b) the salutary effects of the publication ban outweigh the deleterious: *Dagenais v. Canadian Broadcasting Corp.*, [1994] 3 S.C.R. 835, 94 C.C.C. (3d) 289.

The rights of an adult accused to equality as protected by s. 15 of the Charter are not infringed, notwithstanding that the judge may make an order prohibiting publication of the identity of the complainant or an accused young offender. Further, s. 7 of the Charter does not give the accused a right to privacy which may be enforced by a ban on publication of his identity: *R. v. D. (G.)* (1991), 63 C.C.C. (3d) 134 (Ont. C.A.), leave to appeal to S.C.C. refused 64 C.C.C. (3d) vi.

A trial judge, presiding at a retrial following the accused's successful appeal, has an inherent power to make an order prohibiting publication of aspects of the previous proceedings which could prejudice the jury hearing the retrial. Such an order does not violate the right to freedom of the press in s. 2(*b*) of the *Canadian Charter of Rights and Freedoms*: *R. v. Barrow* (1989), 48 C.C.C. (3d) 308, 91 N.S.R. (2d) 176 (S.C.T.D.).

ORDER RESTRICTING PUBLICATION — VICTIMS AND WITNESSES / Justice system participants / Offences / Limitation / Application and notice / Grounds / Hearing may be held / Factors to be considered / Conditions / Publication prohibited.

486.5 (1) Unless an order is made under section 486.4, on application of the prosecutor in respect of a victim or a witness, or on application of a victim or a witness, a judge or justice may make an order directing that any information that could identify the victim or witness shall not be published in any document or broadcast or transmitted in any way if the judge or justice is of the opinion that the order is in the interest of the proper administration of justice.

(2) On application of the prosecutor in respect of a justice system participant who is involved in proceedings in respect of an offence referred to in subsection (2.1), or on application of such a justice system participant, a judge or justice may make an order directing that any information that could identify the justice system participant shall not be published in any document or broadcast or transmitted in any way if the judge or justice is of the opinion that the order is in the interest of the proper administration of justice.

(2.1) The offences for the purposes of subsection (2) are

    (*a*) **an offence under section 423.1, 467.11, 467.111, 467.12 or 467.13, or a serious offence committed for the benefit of, at the direction of, or in association with, a criminal organization;**

    (*b*) **a terrorism offence;**

    (*c*) **an offence under subsection 16(1) or (2), 17(1), 19(1), 20(1) or 22(1) of the *Security of Information Act*; or**

    (*d*) **an offence under subsection 21(1) or section 23 of the *Security of Information Act* that is committed in relation to an offence referred to in paragraph (*c*).**

(3) An order made under this section does not apply in respect of the disclosure of information in the course of the administration of justice if it is not the purpose of the disclosure to make the information known in the community.

(4) An applicant for an order shall

    (*a*) apply in writing to the presiding judge or justice or, if the judge or justice has not been determined, to a judge of a superior court of criminal jurisdiction in the judicial district where the proceedings will take place; and

    (*b*) provide notice of the application to the prosecutor, the accused and any other person affected by the order that the judge or justice specifies.

(5) An applicant for an order shall set out the grounds on which the applicant relies to establish that the order is necessary for the proper administration of justice.

(6) The judge or justice may hold a hearing to determine whether an order should be made, and the hearing may be in private.

(7) In determining whether to make an order, the judge or justice shall consider

    (*a*) the right to a fair and public hearing;

    (*b*) whether there is a real and substantial risk that the victim, witness or justice system participant would suffer harm if their identity were disclosed;

    (*c*) whether the victim, witness or justice system participant needs the order for their security or to protect them from intimidation or retaliation;

    (*d*) society's interest in encouraging the reporting of offences and the participation of victims, witnesses and justice system participants in the criminal justice process;

    (*e*) whether effective alternatives are available to protect the identity of the victim, witness or justice system participant;

    (*f*) the salutary and deleterious effects of the proposed order;

    (*g*) the impact of the proposed order on the freedom of expression of those affected by it; and

    (*h*) any other factor that the judge or justice considers relevant.

(8) An order may be subject to any conditions that the judge or justice thinks fit.

(9) Unless the judge or justice refuses to make an order, no person shall publish in any document or broadcast or transmit in any way

    (*a*) the contents of an application;

    (*b*) any evidence taken, information given or submissions made at a hearing under subsection (6); or

    (*c*) any other information that could identify the person to whom the application relates as a victim, witness or justice system participant in the proceedings. 2005, c. 32, s. 15; 2015, c. 13, s. 19.

CROSS-REFERENCES

"Justice", "justice system participant", "prosecutor", "superior court of criminal jurisdiction" and "victim" are defined in s. 2.

    Section 486 provides for the making of an order to exclude the public. Section 486.1 provides for permitting a support person to be present while a witness testifies. Section 486.2 provides for taking testimony outside the courtroom or behind a screen so that the witness cannot see the accused. Section 486.3 provides for making of orders that the accused not personally cross-examine witnesses. Section 486.4 provides for the making of non-publication orders in relation to various enumerated offences such as the various sexual offences, child pornography, extortion and charging a criminal interest rate. Failure to comply with an order made under this section is a summary conviction offence under s. 486.6.

SYNOPSIS

This section creates a code of procedure for the prosecutor, a victim or a witness (subsec. (1)), or a justice system participant (subsec. (2)) to apply for a non-publication order. The basis for making the order is whether the judge is satisfied that the order is necessary for the proper administration of justice. Where the order is made, it applies to prohibit publication, broadcast or transmission in any way of any information that could identify the person.

Subsection (3) provides an exception for disclosure in the course of the administration of justice, where disclosure is not for the purpose of making the information known to the community.

Subsection (4) requires that the applicant apply in writing either to the presiding judge or, if a judge has not been determined, to a judge of the superior court of justice. The application must be on notice to the accused, prosecutor and any other person affected by the order as required by the judge and, pursuant to subsec. (5), must set out the grounds for the making of the order. The judge may hold a hearing, which may be *in camera*, to determine whether the order should be made The factors the judge must consider are set out in subsec. (7). The judge may include conditions in the order. Unless the judge refuses to make the order, the contents of the application, the proceedings at the hearing and any other information that would identify the person shall also not be published, broadcasted or transmitted in any way.

OFFENCE / Application of order.

486.6 (1) Every person who fails to comply with an order made under subsection 486.4(1), (2) or (3) or 486.5(1) or (2) is guilty of an offence punishable on summary conviction.

(2) For greater certainty, an order referred to in subsection (1) applies to prohibit, in relation to proceedings taken against any person who fails to comply with the order, the publication in any document or the broadcasting or transmission in any way of information that could identify a victim, witness or justice system participant whose identity is protected by the order. 2005, c. 32, s. 15.

CROSS-REFERENCES

"Victim" and "justice system participant" are defined in s. 2. Sections 486.4 and 486.5 provide for the making of orders prohibiting the publication, broadcasting or transmitting in any way of information that could identify the person named in the order.

SYNOPSIS

This section is complementary to ss. 486.4 and 486.5 and makes it a summary conviction offence to violate the orders made under those sections. The orders made under those sections also apply to protect the identity of the persons named in the orders in proceedings under this section.

ANNOTATIONS

It was held that a person could be cited for contempt of court in the superior court for violation of an order made under the predecessor to s. 486.4, notwithstanding the availability of the punishment under what is now this section: *Quebec (Procureur Général) v. Publications Photo-Police Inc.*, [1990] 1 S.C.R. 851 (7:0).

The accused journalist's conduct in writing and filing an article that identified the victim was sufficient to make out the *actus reus* of party liability under s. 21(1)(b) and (c) for the offence committed by the newspaper's publisher. However, whatever the fault element for the principal offender, party liability depended upon proof of intention to aid or abet the principal: *R. v. Helsdon* (2007), 216 C.C.C. (3d) 1 (Ont. C.A.).

SECURITY OF WITNESSES / Application / Factors to be considered / No adverse inference.

486.7 (1) In any proceedings against an accused, the presiding judge or justice may, on application of the prosecutor or a witness or on his or her own motion, make any order, other than one that may be made under any of sections 486 to 486.5, if the judge or justice is of the opinion that the order is necessary to protect the security of any witness and is otherwise in the interest of the proper administration of justice.

(2) The application may be made, during the proceedings, to the presiding judge or justice or, before the proceedings begin, to the judge or justice who will preside at the proceedings or, if that judge or justice has not been determined, to any judge or justice having jurisdiction in the judicial district where the proceedings will take place.

(3) In determining whether to make the order, the judge or justice shall consider

   (*a*) the age of the witness;

   (*b*) the witness's mental or physical disabilities, if any;

   (*c*) the right to a fair and public hearing;

   (*d*) the nature of the offence;

   (*e*) whether the witness needs the order to protect them from intimidation or retaliation;

   (*f*) whether the order is needed to protect the security of anyone known to the witness;

   (*g*) society's interest in encouraging the reporting of offences and the participation of victims and witnesses in the criminal justice process;

   (*h*) the importance of the witness's testimony to the case;

   (*i*) whether effective alternatives to the making of the proposed order are available in the circumstances;

   (*j*) the salutary and deleterious effects of the proposed order; and

   (*k*) any other factor that the judge or justice considers relevant.

(4) No adverse inference may be drawn from the fact that an order is, or is not, made under this section. 2015, c. 20, s. 22.

CROSS-REFERENCES

"Justice" and "prosecutor" are defined in s. 2.

SYNOPSIS

This section allows the court to make "any order" — other than those available under ss. 486 to 486.5 — to protect the security of a witness. For example, this may allow for the use of testimonial aids not contemplated by any of the foregoing sections. Subsection (2) governs the timing and venue of such an application, while subsec. (3) sets out a list of mandatory considerations for the court to weigh in deciding whether to make an order. Subsection (4) prohibits any adverse inference being drawn from the making of (or refusal to make) such an order.

INFORMATION FOR SEARCH WARRANT / Endorsement of search warrant / Operation of computer system and copying equipment / Duty of person in possession or control / Form / Effect of endorsement.

487. (1) A justice who is satisfied by information on oath in Form 1 that there are reasonable grounds to believe that there is in a building, receptacle or place

   (*a*) anything on or in respect of which any offence against this Act or any other Act of Parliament has been or is suspected to have been committed,

   (*b*) anything that there are reasonable grounds to believe will afford evidence with respect to the commission of an offence, or will reveal the whereabouts of a person who is believed to have committed an offence, against this Act or any other Act of Parliament,

   (*c*) anything that there are reasonable grounds to believe is intended to be used for the purpose of committing any offence against the person for which a person may be arrested without warrant, or

   (*c*.1) any offence-related property,

may at any time issue a warrant authorizing a peace officer or a public officer who has been appointed or designated to administer or enforce a federal or provincial law and whose duties include the enforcement of this Act or any other Act of Parliament and who is named in the warrant

    (*d*)   to search the building, receptacle or place for any such thing and to seize it, and

    (*e*)   subject to any other Act of Parliament, to, as soon as practicable, bring the thing seized before, or make a report in respect thereof to, the justice or some other justice for the same territorial division in accordance with section 489.1.

(2) If the building, receptacle or place is in another territorial division, the justice may issue the warrant with any modifications that the circumstances require, and it may be executed in the other territorial division after it has been endorsed, in Form 28, by a justice who has jurisdiction in that territorial division. The endorsement may be made on the original of the warrant or on a copy of the warrant transmitted by any means of telecommunication.

(2.1) A person authorized under this section to search a computer system in a building or place for data may

    (*a*)   use or cause to be used any computer system at the building or place to search any data contained in or available to the computer system;

    (*b*)   reproduce or cause to be reproduced any data in the form of a print-out or other intelligible output;

    (*c*)   seize the print-out or other output for examination or copying; and

    (*d*)   use or cause to be used any copying equipment at the place to make copies of the data.

(2.2) Every person who is in possession or control of any building or place in respect of which a search is carried out under this section shall, on presentation of the warrant, permit the person carrying out the search

    (*a*)   to use or cause to be used any computer system at the building or place in order to search any data contained in or available to the computer system for data that the person is authorized by this section to search for;

    (*b*)   to obtain a hard copy of the data and to seize it; and

    (*c*)   to use or cause to be used any copying equipment at the place to make copies of the data.

(3) A search warrant issued under this section may be in the form set out as Form 5 in Part XXVIII, varied to suit the case.

(4) An endorsement that is made in accordance with subsection (2) is sufficient authority to the peace officers or public officers to whom the warrant was originally directed, and to all peace officers within the jurisdiction of the justice by whom it is endorsed, to execute the warrant and to deal with the things seized in accordance with section 489.1 or as otherwise provided by law. R.S., c. C-34, s. 443; R.S.C. 1985, c. 27 (1st Supp.), s. 68; 1994, c. 44, s. 36; 1997, c. 18, s. 41; 1997, c. 23, s. 12; 1999, c. 5, s. 16; 2008, c. 18, s. 11.

CROSS-REFERENCES

The terms "justice", "offence-related property", "peace officer", "public officer" and "territorial division" are defined in s. 2. A definition of "data", albeit for that section, is provided in s. 342.1. Provision for granting of a telewarrant is made in s. 487.1. Section 487.11 allows a peace officer to search without a warrant in exigent circumstances. Restriction on publicity, see s. 487.2. A search warrant is executed in accordance with s. 488. If it is desired to execute the warrant at night, the grounds for doing so must be set out in the information. Execution of a warrant to search a lawyer's office is governed by s. 488.1. Section 489 provides for seizure of things not named in the warrant but which the person executing the warrant believes on reasonable grounds have been obtained by or have been used in the commission of an offence or may afford evidence. Section 489.1 sets out the procedure for restitution of goods to the lawful owner and s. 490 the procedure for detention of things which have been seized but not returned under s. 489.1. As to forfeiture of weapons and contraband, see ss. 491 and 491.1. Section 491.2 makes provision for use of photographic evidence in lieu of the actual property so that the property itself may be returned to the lawful owner. Other search or seizure powers: ss. 117.02 to 117.06, search and seizure re weapons; s. 164, *in rem* proceedings re obscene publications and crime comics; ss. 185 to 188, authorization to intercept private communications; ss. 254, 256 and 257, demand for breath and blood samples, warrant for blood sample; s. 199, disorderly house search warrant; s. 320, *in rem* proceedings re hate propaganda; s. 395, precious metals etc.; s. 462, seizure of counterfeit money, tokens and instruments for use in making counterfeit; s. 462.32, proceeds of crimes; s. 492, seizure of explosives. Also see s. 487.01 which allows for the obtaining of a "general" warrant in circumstances where a warrantless search or seizure would violate s. 8 of the Charter; s. 492.1, warrant to use tracking device; and s. 492.2, warrant to use telephone number recorder or obtain records of telephone calls.

Section 487.05 allows a provincial court judge to issue a warrant to seize bodily substances for forensic DNA analysis. For other cross-references respecting DNA analysis, see the summary immediately preceding s. 487.04. Section 487.091 provides that a justice may issue a warrant to obtain handprint, fingerprint, footprint, foot impression, teeth impression or other print or impression of the body or any part of the body.

Also see s. 487.11, which gives a peace officer or public officer appointed or designated to administer or enforce any federal or provincial law and whose duties also include the enforcement of the *Criminal Code* or any other Act of Parliament, a broad warrantless power of search and seizure in exigent circumstances. The officer may exercise the power to search and seizure in subsec. (1) without a warrant, provided that the conditions for granting a warrant exist but by reason of exigent circumstances it would be impracticable to obtain a warrant.

Note s. 31(1) of the *Interpretation Act*, R.S.C. 1985, c. I-21, which provides that where anything is required or authorized to be done by or before, *inter alia*, a justice of the peace it shall be done by or before one whose jurisdiction or powers extend to the place where the thing is to be done.

With respect to protection of persons executing warrants, see ss. 25 to 27. Also note s. 29(1) which imposes a duty on a person executing a warrant to have it with him, where it is feasible to do so, and produce it when requested.

Sections 487.012 and 487.013 provide alternatives to the search warrant procedure in this section by providing for an application for production orders.

Also see notes under s. 8 of the Charter.

SYNOPSIS

This section sets out the procedure that must be followed to obtain a search warrant.

Subsection (1) makes it clear that the justice must be *satisfied that there are reasonable grounds to believe* that the prescribed items will be found in a building, receptacle or place. The items being searched for may include anything in respect of which an offence against an Act of Parliament *has been*, or is *suspected* of *having been committed*, anything that there is *reasonable ground to believe* will afford evidence of an offence against an Act of Parliament, anything that will reveal the whereabouts of a person believed to have committed an offence, or anything that there are *reasonable grounds to believe* is intended to be used for the purpose of committing an offence against the person, for which a person may be arrested without a warrant. The justice may only be satisfied of the preceding if the information that comes before him is on oath and in Form 1.

The justice may issue a warrant authorizing a person named in that warrant, or a peace officer to search the building, receptacle or place for the specified items and to seize such items. The warrant will also require that the items seized be brought before a justice or that a report be made as soon as practicable.

Subsection (2) makes it clear that, if the building, receptacle or place in which the items sought are believed to be located is in another territorial division, the justice may issue the warrant in a form modified to fit the circumstances. This warrant must then be endorsed in Form 28, by a justice having jurisdiction, before it can be executed. This endorsement, which may be made on the original warrant or on a copy of the warrant transmitted by telecommunication, is sufficient authority to the person to whom the warrant was originally directed and to all peace officers within the new territorial division to execute the warrant. Once the warrant is endorsed, subsec. (4) provides that the warrant is authority for the officers to whom it was originally directed and officers in the jurisdiction of the justice to execute the warrant.

Subsections (2.1) and (2.2) provide for execution of the warrant in relation to data by using the computer system at the place to be searched.

ANNOTATIONS

Constitutional requirements generally – Where it is feasible to obtain prior authorization, such authorization, usually in the form of a warrant issued by a person able to act judicially and to assess the evidence as to whether the appropriate standard has been met in an entirely neutral and impartial manner, is a precondition for a valid search and seizure in conformity with s. 8 of the *Canadian Charter of Rights and Freedoms*. The person seeking to justify a warrantless search must rebut the presumption that such search is unreasonable in violation of s. 8: *Hunter v. Southam Inc.*, [1984] 2 S.C.R. 145, 14 C.C.C. (3d) 97 (8:0).

This section complies with s. 8 of the Charter: *R. v. Times Square Book Store* (1985), 21 C.C.C. (3d) 503, 48 C.R. (3d) 132 (Ont. C.A.).

Generally speaking, conformity to law is an essential component of reasonableness, although mere minor or technical defects in the warrant would not necessarily make an ensuing search or seizure unreasonable in violation of s. 8 of the Charter. However, a search or seizure conducted under a search warrant that is invalid in substance because it was issued upon information that did not set out facts upon which a justice acting judicially could be satisfied that there were grounds for issuing the warrant under subsec. (1)(*b*), or did not meet the minimum requirements of particularity respecting the things to be searched for, is unreasonable under s. 8: *R. v. Harris and Lighthouse Video Centres Ltd.* (1987), 35 C.C.C. (3d) 1, 57 C.R. (3d) 356 (Ont. C.A.), leave to appeal to S.C.C. refused [1986] 2 S.C.R. vii, 38 C.C.C. (3d) vi.

In considering the validity of a search warrant, facts obtained as a result of an unreasonable search must be excised. The court must then determine whether the warrant would have been issued without the improperly obtained facts: *R. v. Grant*, [1993] 3 S.C.R. 223, 84 C.C.C. (3d) 173 (9:0).

In *R. v. Tessling*, [2004] 3 S.C.R. 432, 189 C.C.C. (3d) 129, the Supreme Court of Canada held that the use of an infrared camera to obtain information about the patterns of heat distribution on the external surfaces of a house did not constitute a search within the meaning of s. 8 of the Charter. Information obtained via this technology cannot, by itself, constitute sufficient grounds to obtain a search warrant. The technology, at its current stage of development, was non-intrusive, did not "see" through the wall of a building and did not disclose a biographical core of information or reveal intimate details about the accused's lifestyle. Accordingly, there was no reasonable expectation of privacy in respect of this information.

Grounds for issuing warrant – Information supplied by a reliable informer, even though it is hearsay, may in some circumstances provide the necessary ground to justify granting of a search warrant. However, the mere statement by the informant that he was told by a reliable informer that a certain person is carrying on criminal activity or that contraband would be found at a certain place would be insufficient basis for granting a warrant. The underlying circumstances disclosed by the informer for his conclusion must be set out thus enabling the justice to satisfy himself that the requisite reasonable grounds exist: *R. v. Debot* (1986), 30 C.C.C. (3d) 207, 54 C.R. (3d) 120 (Ont. C.A.). A further appeal by the accused to the Supreme Court of Canada was dismissed [1989] 2 S.C.R. 1140, 52 C.C.C. (3d) 193 (5:0). The court agreed that the appropriate standard to establish reasonable grounds for a search is one of "reasonable probability" and, in making this determination, the court must have regard to the totality of the circumstances. The court also held that the suspect's criminal record and reputation could be taken into account provided that, *inter alia*, the reputation is related to the ostensible reasons for the search. Where the police rely on information from an informer, it is not necessary for the police to confirm each detail in the informer's tip, so long as the sequence of events actually observed conforms sufficiently to the anticipated pattern to remove the possibility of innocent coincidence. On the other hand, the level of verification required may be higher where the police rely on an informant whose credibility cannot be assessed or where fewer details are provided and the risk of innocent coincidence is greater.

Information from unnamed confidential sources was not a sufficient basis for issuing the warrant where there was no evidence to substantiate the veracity of the informers, no information as to how the informers acquired this knowledge and no independent evidence to support the story of the informers: *R. v. Berger* (1989), 48 C.C.C. (3d) 185, 74 Sask. R. 198 (C.A.).

Before granting the warrant the justice must be satisfied, *inter alia*, that the grounds stated for obtaining the warrant are current and that there is a nexus between the grounds for believing an offence has been committed and that evidence of the commission of the offence will be found on the premises to be searched: *R. v. Turcotte* (1987), 39 C.C.C. (3d) 193, [1982] 2 W.W.R. 97 (Sask. C.A.).

"Peace officer" includes a person appointed as a Special Provincial Constable under the *Police Act*, R.S.B.C. 1996, c. 367, with appointment restricted to "the performance of duties in respect to the mandate of the Ministry of Finance": *R. v. Semeniuk* (2007), 224 C.C.C. (3d) 71 (B.C.C.A.).

Things for which warrant may be obtained – A search warrant may authorize the removal and seizure of fixtures such as doors and windows: *R. v. Spitzer* (1984), 15 C.C.C. (3d) 98 (Sask. Q.B.). *Contra: R. v. Munn (No. 1)* (1938), 71 C.C.C. 139, [1938] 3 D.L.R. 772 (P.E.I.S.C.).

A search warrant is not available under this section to seize funds deposited in a savings account at a bank. A credit balance in a bank account is an intangible, merely proof that the bank has certain sums on deposit, and such funds are not segregated from the bank's other assets: *R. v. Banque Royale du Canada* (1985), 18 C.C.C. (3d) 98, 44 C.R. (3d) 387 (Que. C.A.), leave to appeal to S.C.C. refused C.C.C. *loc. cit.* [However, now see s. 462.33.]

The purpose of subsec. (1) is to allow the investigators to unearth and preserve as much relevant evidence as possible. They should therefore be able to locate, examine and preserve all the evidence relevant to events that may have given rise to criminal liability. Thus, this section is not limited to authorizing a search for evidence of the elements of the offence and may authorize a search for and seizure of evidence of negligence in the investigation of a strict liability offence going to a possible due diligence defence: *CanadianOxy Chemicals Ltd. v. Canada (Attorney General)*, [1999] 1 S.C.R. 743, 133 C.C.C. (3d) 426.

Seizure of hospital records – It was held in *R. v. French* (1977), 37 C.C.C. (2d) 201 (Ont. C.A.), affd on other grounds [1980] 1 S.C.R. 158, 47 C.C.C. (2d) 411, that in order to obtain hospital records the provincial legislation which brought those records into existence and safeguards their use must be complied with, even where the records are sought in criminal proceedings. Thus, see *R. v. Lyons* (1981), 64 C.C.C. (2d) 73 (Ont. H.C.J.), where an order was made within the terms of the provincial legislation. Also see *R. v. Coon* (1992), 74 C.C.C. (3d) 146 (Ont. Ct. (Gen. Div.)), noted under s. 698.

In *R. v. Waterford Hospital* (1983), 6 C.C.C. (3d) 481, 35 C.R. (3d) 348 (Nfld. C.A.), a search warrant to obtain hospital records made during a remand of the accused under s. 537(1)(c) was quashed, *inter alia*, because the Department of Justice could have applied under the provincial legislation to examine the records.

Where the applicable provincial legislation contained no code of procedure for obtaining medical records, a search warrant issued under this section was available to obtain the relevant records. The duty of confidentiality, which the hospital and staff owed to the accused, was not breached as the records were required to be released by law pursuant to the order of the justice: *R. v. Worth* (1989), 54 C.C.C. (3d) 215 (Ont. H.C.J.), affd 54 C.C.C. (3d) 223*n* (C.A.).

In *R. v. Serendip Physiotherapy Clinic* (2004), 189 C.C.C. (3d) 417, 25 C.R. (6th) 30, leave to appeal to S.C.C. refused [2005] 1 S.C.R. xv, 248 D.L.R. (4th) vii, the Ontario Court of Appeal held that there was no requirement that a search warrant for the seizure of physiotherapy records contain conditions protecting the patients' privacy. The search of a physiotherapy clinic did not risk the breach of an established class privilege and, accordingly, records seized from such a clinic were *prima facie* admissible.

Jurisdiction of justice – A justice of the peace appointed in and for the province has jurisdiction to issue a search warrant to be executed in one county although at the time the justice is sitting in another county, and such a warrant need not be endorsed pursuant to subsec. (2): *R. v. Haley* (1986), 27 C.C.C. (3d) 454, 51 C.R. (3d) 363 (Ont. C.A.). *Contra: R. v. Ciment Independant Inc., R. v. Ciment St-Laurent Inc.* (1985), 21 C.C.C. (3d) 429, 47 C.R. (3d) 83 (Que. C.A.).

A justice of the peace had jurisdiction to issue a search warrant to seize documents from a federal government department containing confidential information acquired under the *Old Age Security Act* (Can.) which was sought as evidence in relation to a fraud on provincial welfare authorities. The Act itself and the *Privacy Act* (Can.) created an exemption to the privilege and duty of non-disclosure in such circumstances. It was still open to the federal Minister to object to disclosure but this must be done under s. 37 of the *Canada Evidence Act*. On the other hand, in view of the confidential nature of the material sought, it would have been prudent for the justice of the peace to impose conditions and restrictions on the manner in which the warrant was executed: *Canada (Procureur General) v. Belanger* (1987), 42 C.C.C. (3d) 82, 61 C.R. (3d) 388 (Que. C.A.).

A provincial court judge has jurisdiction to issue the warrant on the same material where a justice of the peace refused to issue a warrant on the same material. A justice of the peace and provincial court judge have the same jurisdiction and the application before the provincial court judge is a *de novo* hearing. Furthermore, successive applications are not prohibited and do not constitute an abuse of process particularly where, as in this case, the officer had added paragraphs explaining that an application had been sought and rejected by the justice of the peace: *R. v. Duchcherer* (2006), 208 C.C.C. (3d) 201 (B.C.C.A.).

Search of persons / Search incident of arrest – Police officers have the power to search an accused as an incident to a lawful arrest and to seize anything in his possession or immediate surroundings to guarantee the safety of the police and the accused, prevent the accused's escape or provide evidence against him. The existence of reasonable and probable grounds to believe that the accused is in possession of weapons or evidence is not a prerequisite to the existence of the power to search, provided, however, that the search is for a valid objective and not unrelated to the objectives of the proper administration of justice. Proper objectives are to prevent the accused evading arrest and to collect evidence. Accordingly, a search done for weapons or other dangerous articles is necessary as an elementary precaution to preclude the possibility of their use against the police, the nearby public or the accused himself. A search is also proper to collect evidence that can be used in establishing the guilt of the accused. Further, the search must not be conducted in an abusive fashion and the use of physical or psychological constraint should be proportionate to the objectives sought and the other circumstances of the situation. A "frisk" or pat down search is a relatively non-intrusive procedure and, if done for valid reasons, is not a disproportionate interference with the freedom of persons lawfully arrested: *Cloutier v. Langlois*, [1990] 1 S.C.R. 158, 53 C.C.C. (3d) 257 (7:0). Also see *R. v. Caslake*, [1998] 1 S.C.R. 51, 121 C.C.C. (3d) 97.

Police have a limited power to detain for investigation where there are reasonable grounds to detain. The detention must be viewed as reasonably necessary on an objective view of the totality of the circumstances, informing the officer's suspicion that there is a clear nexus between the person to be detained and a recent or on-going criminal offence. The officer must have a reasonable suspicion that the particular individual is implicated in the criminal activity under investigation. The overall reasonableness of the decision to detain must further be assessed against all of the circumstances, most importantly the extent to which the interference with individual liberty is necessary to perform the officer's duty, the liberty interfered with, and the nature and extent of that interference. The power to detain cannot be exercised on the basis of a hunch, nor can it become a *de facto* arrest. Where the officer has lawfully detained the person for investigation, the officer may undertake a protective pat-down search where the officer believes on reasonable grounds that his or her safety or the safety of others is at risk. The search must be confined in scope to an intrusion reasonably designed to locate weapons. The detention and the pat-down search must be conducted in a reasonable manner: *R. v. Mann*, [2004] 3 S.C.R. 59, 185 C.C.C. (3d) 308.

Search and right to counsel – As a general rule, police proceeding to search are not obligated to suspend the search and give a person the opportunity to retain and instruct counsel, as, for example, when the search is of a home pursuant to a search warrant. Where a person is detained for a search, as in the case of a body search incident to arrest, then, immediately upon detention, the detainee has the right to be informed of the right to counsel under s. 10(*b*) of the *Charter of Rights and Freedoms*. However, the police are not obligated to suspend the search incident to arrest until the detainee has the opportunity to retain counsel. The police are, however, required to suspend the search where the lawfulness of the search is dependent on the detainee's consent or where the statute gives a person a right to seek review of the decision to search: *R. v. Debot*, [1989] 2 S.C.R. 1140, 52 C.C.C. (3d) 193.

Once the police have the situation clearly under control in the course of execution of a search warrant then they are required to afford an occupant of the premises, who has been arrested, an opportunity to exercise his rights under s. 10(*b*) of the Charter: *R. v. Strachan*, [1988] 2 S.C.R. 980, 46 C.C.C. (3d) 479 (7:0).

Execution of warrant [Also see notes under s. 488] – A police officer may have the assistance of persons, who are neither named in the warrant nor peace officers, provided that the police officer remains in control of and accountable for the search: *R. v. B. (J.E.)* (1989), 52 C.C.C. (3d) 224 (N.S.C.A.).

An officer executing a search warrant is required to have the warrant with her [see s. 29]. However, where the officer forgot to bring the warrant through inadvertence and the accused consented to the search commencing while the warrant was being brought to his home, then it was not shown that the search was unlawful: *R. v. B. (J.E.), supra.*

Where the police depart from the knock and announce principle, there is an onus on them to explain why they thought it was necessary to do so. The Crown must be able to lay an evidentiary framework to support the conclusion that the police had reasonable grounds to be concerned about the possibility of harm to themselves or occupants, or about the destruction of evidence. The greater the departure from the principle of announced entry, the heavier the onus. The evidence to justify such a departure must be judged by what was or should have reasonably been known to the police at the time. In addition, police must be allowed a certain amount of latitude in the manner in which they decide to enter premises and cannot be expected to measure in advance with nuanced precision the amount of force the situation will require. In this case, an unannounced, forced entry while masked was reasonable in all of the circumstances: *R. v. Cornell*, [2010] 2 S.C.R. 142, 258 C.C.C. (3d) 429.

A search is not presumptively unreasonable because the tactical team first entering did not have the warrant. The purpose of the provision is to allow the occupant to know why the search is being carried out, to allow an assessment of his or her legal position, and to know that there is a color of authority for the search making forcible resistance improper. This requirement is met if the warrant is in the possession of at least one member of the team executing the warrant: *R. v. Cornell, supra.*

Contents of warrant – The person whose premises are being searched is entitled to know from examination of the search warrant for what reason the search is taking place and the seizing officer must know in relation to what offence or circumstances the articles are to be seized. The failure, therefore, to describe the offence sufficiently in the search warrant is fatal to the validity of the warrant. A warrant merely setting out a conspiracy to defraud certain named companies "and other financial institutions" and not alleging the means of fraud nor what the victims were defrauded of was held to be defective and was quashed and the items seized ordered to be returned: *R. v. Alder* (1977), 37 C.C.C. (2d) 234, [1977] 5 W.W.R. 132 (Alta. S.C.T.D.).

In determining the degree of specificity required of things to be searched for, regard must be had to the nature of the offence alleged in the information to obtain the search warrant. In this case the court was required to consider the size and sophisticated nature of the target of the search as well as the continuing nature of the alleged offences and the lengthy period of time during which they were alleged to have been committed. Thus a warrant authorizing search and seizure of broad classes of documents was justified. Even where the informant did not allege the precise nexus between a thing to be searched for and an alleged offence, the justice of the peace who issued the warrant was entitled to draw reasonable inferences of such nexus from the allegations in the information. Where, by the very nature of the things to be searched for, it is not possible to describe them with precision or great particularity, it is inevitable that the executing officers will have to exercise some discretion in determining whether things found on the premises fall within the description of the things or classes of things described in the warrant: *R. v. Church of Scientology (No. 6)*; *R. v. Walsh* (1987), 31 C.C.C. (3d) 449 (C.A.).

The offence for which the items are sought need not be set out in the warrant with the same precision as would be required for an indictment, provided that the person in charge of the premises is reasonably informed from the warrant as to the nature of the offence and the object of the search: *R. v. PSI Mind Development Institute Ltd* (1977), 37 C.C.C. (2d) 263 (Ont. H.C.J.).

Religious privilege / freedom of religion – While it is not the function of the court to pass on the validity of religious beliefs sincerely held by any organization, the mere fact that an organization claims to be a religion does not bar the Crown or any other litigant from seeking the assistance of the courts in the determination of either criminal or civil wrong, including resort to the investigative tool of a search warrant: *R. v. Church of Scientology (No. 6)*; *R. v. Walsh, supra*.

There is no recognized class privilege accorded to the priest penitent relationship and so while s. 2(*a*) of the *Charter of Rights and Freedoms* may have enhanced the claim that communications made in the course of that relationship may have to be afforded privilege, its applicability must be determined on a case by case basis. The justice would have jurisdiction to issue a warrant to seize files which allegedly contained priest penitent communications where the information to obtain the warrant discloses a *prima facie* case of criminality and that no reasonable alternative source of obtaining the information was available: *R. v. Church of Scientology (No. 6)*; *R. v. Walsh, supra*.

The *Canadian Charter of Rights and Freedoms* does not require the application of a strict test such as the test of scrupulous exactitude in the assessment of the particularity of the search warrant, notwithstanding that the search allegedly involved intrusion into areas of protected freedoms such as freedom of religion: *R. v. Church of Scientology (No. 6)*; *R. v. Walsh, supra*.

Freedom of expression (media) – Even where the minimum requirements set out in this section have been met, the justice has a discretion whether or not to issue the warrant and, if so, whether to attach conditions to its execution. In the case of the media and in light of the guarantee to freedom of expression in s. 2(*b*) of the Charter, there must be a careful consideration as to whether the warrant should issue and also the conditions which might be imposed. Ordinarily, the information to obtain the warrant should disclose whether there are alternative sources from which the information may reasonably be obtained and if there is an alternative source, that it has been investigated and all reasonable efforts to obtain the information have been exhausted. If a search will impede the media from fulfilling its functions of news gatherer and disseminator, then a warrant should only be issued where a compelling state interest is demonstrated. The fact that the information sought has already been disseminated in whole or in part, to the public by the media will ordinarily favour the granting of the warrant: *Canadian Broadcasting Corp. v. New Brunswick (Attorney General)*, [1991] 3 S.C.R. 459, 67 C.C.C. (3d) 544 (6:1); *Canadian Broadcasting Corp. v. Lessard*, [1991] 3 S.C.R. 421, 67 C.C.C. (3d) 517 (6:1).

Obscene material [Also see notes under s. 164] – Where a search warrant is sought in relation to allegedly obscene magazines, it is not sufficient that the justice of the peace is satisfied that the items sought could be of assistance in establishing the commission of an offence. Rather, the justice must be satisfied on reasonable and probable grounds that the magazines to be seized are obscene and can be found at the specified premises. Further, the warrant should be reasonably specific when dealing with books and magazines since sexually explicit material, however distasteful it may be, so long as it is not obscene, is entitled to the same protection as other forms of expression. On the other hand, neither the material presented in support of the application for a warrant nor the warrant itself need specify the title of each magazine or book sought to be seized: *R. v. Times Square Book Store* (1985), 21 C.C.C. (3d) 503, 48 C.R. (3d) 132 (Ont. C.A.); *R. v. Comic Legends* (1987), 40 C.C.C. (3d) 203, 56 Alta. L.R. (2d) 170 (Q.B.).

Disclosure of identity of confidential informers – Where an accused seeks to attack the lawfulness and reasonableness of a search of his home on the basis that there were not sufficient grounds, in the information, for the issuance of the warrant then there should be reasonable disclosure made of the information which was used to obtain the search warrant, if it is needed and requested, despite the fact that it may disclose the identity of an informer. However, upon receipt of such a request, the trial judge should review the information with the object of deleting all references to the identity of the informer. The information so edited should then be made available to the accused. If, at the conclusion of the editing procedure, the Crown still believes that the informer would become known to the accused upon production of the information, then a decision would have to be made by the Crown. The informer might by this time be willing to consent to being identified. Alternatively, the informer's identity might have become so notorious in the community or become so well known to the accused that his identification would no longer be a significant issue. If the Crown is of the view that to produce the informer would be prejudicial to the administration of justice the Crown may elect not to proceed with the evidence or to proceed on the basis of a warrantless search. In those circumstances, the trial judge will have to consider the application of s. 24(2) of the Charter: *R. v. Hunter* (1987), 34 C.C.C. (3d) 14, 57 C.R. (3d) 1 (Ont. C.A.).

In *R. v. Collins* (1989), 48 C.C.C. (3d) 343, 69 C.R. (3d) 235 (Ont. C.A.), the court considered the related problem of disclosure of the identity of a confidential informer who is not named in the information to obtain the search warrant but whose information was the basis, at least in part, for obtaining the search warrant. It was held that the common law rules of evidence, which prohibit judicial disclosure of a police informer's identity by police officers who have learned the informer's identity in the course of their duties, were applicable. There is only one exception to this principle and that is where disclosure of the identity of the informer is necessary to demonstrate the innocence of the accused.

In *R. v. Leipert*, [1997] 1 S.C.R. 281, 112 C.C.C. (3d) 385, the court considered the problem of an information based upon a tip from an anonymous informer under a Crime Stoppers programme. Absent a basis for concluding that disclosure of the information that may reveal the identity of the informer is necessary to establish the innocence of the accused, the information remains privileged and cannot be produced, whether on a hearing into the reasonableness of the search or on the trial proper. Therefore anonymous tip sheets should not be edited with a view to disclosing them to the defence unless the accused's case falls within the innocence at stake exception. To do so runs the risk that the court will deprive the informer of the privilege that belongs to him or her absolutely, subject only to the innocence at stake exception. It also undermines the efficacy of programs such as Crime Stoppers that depend on guarantees of anonymity to those who volunteer information on crimes. When an accused seeks disclosure of privileged informer information on the basis of the exception, the accused must first show some basis to conclude that without the disclosure sought, his or her innocence is at stake. If such a basis is shown, the court may then review the information to determine whether, in fact, the information is necessary to prove the accused's innocence. If the court concludes that disclosure is necessary, the court should only reveal as much information as is essential to allow proof of innocence. Before disclosing the information to the accused, the Crown should be given the option of staying the proceedings. If the Crown chooses to proceed, disclosure of the information essential to establish innocence may be provided to the accused. If the accused cannot bring the case within the exception, the trial judge should permit the Crown to defend the warrant on the material in the information with the reference to the anonymous tip deleted.

Review of sufficiency of warrant / When review application should be brought – Where the sole purpose for attacking the validity of the search warrant issued by a justice of the peace is to lay a foundation for exclusion of evidence, obtained as a result of its execution, pursuant to ss. 8 and 24(2) of the *Charter of Rights and Freedoms*, then the issue should be determined at trial and not by way of an application to the superior court prior to trial. The rule against collateral attack of orders of a superior court does not extend to the orders of an inferior court: *R. v. Zevallos* (1987), 37 C.C.C. (3d) 79, 59 C.R. (3d) 153 (Ont. C.A.); *R. v. Williams* (1987), 38 C.C.C. (3d) 319, 17 B.C.L.R. (2d) 223 (Y.T.C.A.); *R. v. Jamieson* (1989), 48 C.C.C. (3d) 287, 90 N.S.R. (2d) 164 (C.A.); *R. v. Bailey* (1988), 87 N.S.R. (2d) 245, 39 C.R.R. 378 (C.A.). *Contra: R. v. Komadowski* (1986), 27 C.C.C. (3d) 319, [1986] 3 W.W.R. 657 (Man. C.A.), leave to appeal to S.C.C. refused C.C.C. *loc. cit.*, 44 Man. R. (2d) 79.

Scope of review – On an application to quash a search warrant the superior court judge may not substitute his opinion as to the sufficiency of the evidence. Rather he is limited to determining whether or not there is evidence upon which the justice acting judicially could determine that a warrant should be issued and whether the warrant contained sufficient particulars of the items to be seized so that it could not be said that the discretion of the officer was substituted for that of the justice as to the items to be seized: *R. v. Times Square Book Store, supra; Quebec (Attorney General) v. Mathieu* (1986), 50 C.R. (3d) 156 (Que. C.A.); *R. v. Turcotte*, [1988] 2 W.W.R. 97 (Sask. C.A.). The enactment of the *Canadian Charter of Rights and Freedoms* has not altered the scope of review which is limited to jurisdictional error: *R. v. Church of Scientology (No. 6); R. v. Walsh, supra.*

In determining the validity of an information or search warrant the court is not entitled to look at the results of the search: *Liberal Party of Quebec v. Mierzwinski* (1978), 46 C.C.C. (2d) 118 (Que. S.C.).

Procedure on review – Most of the recent cases on the procedure to review prior judicial authorization, including the threshold for permitting cross-examination of the affiant have taken place in the wiretap context. Accordingly, reference should be made to the cases noted under s. 186 and especially those noted under the headings "**Review of validity of authorization**" and "**Cross-examination of deponent of affidavit**". See in particular the notes of *R. v. Garofoli*, [1990] 2 S.C.R. 1421, 60 C.C.C. (3d) 161 and *R. v. Araujo*, [2000] 2 S.C.R. 992, 149 C.C.C. (3d) 449.

While in the result the court did not find it necessary to decide the point, some doubt was expressed as to whether a justice of the peace was a compellable witness to testify with respect to his mental processes in exercising the judicial function whether or not to grant a search warrant: *R. v. Moran* (1987), 36 C.C.C. (3d) 225, 21 O.A.C. 257 (C.A.), leave to appeal to S.C.C. refused [1988] 1 S.C.R. xi. [And now see: *MacKeigan v. Hickman*, [1989] 2 S.C.R. 796, 50 C.C.C. (3d) 449.]

Standing – In the absence of showing some possessory or proprietary interest either in the things seized or the premises, a third person has no standing to attempt to quash the search warrant even where the items seized relate to transactions by the applicant: *R. v. Model*

Power (1979), 21 C.R. (3d) at p. 196 (Ont. H.C.J.), affd C.R. *loc. cit.* p. 195 (C.A.), leave to appeal to S.C.C. refused C.R. *loc. cit.*, 32 N.R. 487*n*.

The accused had standing to challenge a search warrant executed at a property that he owned but did not reside in. The accused had the authority to regulate access to the property. While a non-resident might not have the same expectation of privacy as a resident, there was no evidence that the accused had given up possession or control to any other occupant: *R. v. Vi* (2008), 239 C.C.C. (3d) 57 (B.C.C.A.).

Severance of warrant – Where a search warrant is defective in part that part only may be severed: *R. v. Johnson & Franklin Wholesale Distributors Ltd.* (1971), 3 C.C.C. (2d) 484, 16 C.R.N.S. 107 (B.C.C.A.).

Although on an application to quash a search warrant the superior court has power to sever off bad parts of a warrant there is no authority to permit the court on a *certiorari* application to amend the warrant by, for example, narrowing the time period of the alleged offence to conform with the evidence disclosed in the information to obtain the warrant: *R. v. Dobney Holdings* (1985), 18 C.C.C. (3d) 238 (B.C.C.A.).

Return of items seized – Where the search warrant had a fatal defect it was wrong for the judge on *certiorari* to allow the Crown to decide which documents should be retained, and an order will be made directing that all documents and copies be returned to the applicant: *Bergeron v. Deschamps*, [1978] 1 S.C.R. 243, 33 C.C.C. (2d) 461 (9:0). The court without passing on the correctness of *R. v. Black* (1973), 13 C.C.C. (2d) 446, 24 C.R.N.S. 203 (B.C.S.C.), where it had been held that an order should go returning the seized goods provided they were not required as evidence, distinguished the case on the basis that in *R. v. Black* there was not the same fatal frailties as existed in this case. In *R. v. Black* the warrant was quashed because of failure of the person signing it to indicate he was a justice of the peace.

Even where charges have been laid and the items seized under the invalid warrant are required as evidence, the court, in quashing the warrant, has a discretion to order the items returned. This power existed prior to the *Charter of Rights and Freedoms* and exists as a remedy under s. 24(1): *R. v. Chapman* (1984), 12 C.C.C. (3d) 1, 9 D.L.R. (4th) 244 (Ont. C.A.).

In determining whether or not to make an order returning items seized after the warrant has been quashed the court will have regard to the conduct of the prosecuting authorities in relation to the search and seizure, the seriousness of the offence, the degree of potential cogency of the things seized in proving the charge, the nature of the defect in the warrant and the potential prejudice to the owner in being kept out of possession. In proper circumstances the court may give the authorities an opportunity to obtain a new warrant before ordering the return of the items seized: *R. v. Dobney Foundry Ltd. (No. 2)* (1985), 19 C.C.C. (3d) 465, [1985] 3 W.W.R. 626 (B.C.C.A.).

The court, having quashed the warrant, may in appropriate circumstances provide that the items are to be returned within a specified number of days unless the Crown obtains a fresh search warrant within that time: *R. v. Dobney Foundry Ltd. (No. 3)* (1986), 29 C.C.C. (3d) 285, [1987] 1 W.W.R. 281 (B.C.C.A.).

The Superior Court's inherent jurisdiction to order the return of items wrongfully seized under an invalid search warrant and which are not required as evidence also extends to items seized without a search warrant and which are wrongfully held by the police: *Butler and Butler v. Canada (Solicitor General)* (1981), 61 C.C.C. (2d) 512 (B.C.S.C.).

Application to other statutes – Although the former *Bankruptcy Act*, R.S.C. 1970, c. B-3, contained its own search and seizure provisions, the authorities could resort to this section to obtain evidence in relation to an offence under that Act. The addition of the words "or any other Act of Parliament" unambiguously show that every Act of Parliament could fall within the ambit of subsec. (1)(*a*) and (*b*): *R. v. Multiform Manufacturing Co.*, [1990] 2 S.C.R. 624, 58 C.C.C. (3d) 257 (7:0).

A search warrant may be obtained under this section to search for narcotics. In such a case, however, the authorities were not entitled to rely upon the broad powers in s. 12 of the [former] *Narcotic Control Act* for execution of the warrant: *R. v. Grant*, [1993] 3 S.C.R. 223, 84 C.C.C. (3d) 173.

INFORMATION FOR GENERAL WARRANT / Limitation / Search or seizure to be reasonable / Video surveillance / Other provisions to apply / Other provisions to apply / Telewarrant provisions to apply.

487.01 (1) A provincial court judge, a judge of a superior court of criminal jurisdiction or a judge as defined in section 552 may issue a warrant in writing authorizing a peace officer to, subject to this section, use any device or investigative technique or procedure or do any thing described in the warrant that would, if not authorized, constitute an unreasonable search or seizure in respect of a person or a person's property if

    (*a*) the judge is satisfied by information on oath in writing that there are reasonable grounds to believe that an offence against this or any other Act of Parliament has been or will be committed and that information concerning the offence will be obtained through the use of the technique, procedure or device or the doing of the thing;

    (*b*) the judge is satisfied that it is in the best interests of the administration of justice to issue the warrant; and

    (*c*) there is no other provision in this or any other Act of Parliament that would provide for a warrant, authorization or order permitting the technique, procedure or device to be used or the thing to be done.

(2) Nothing in subsection (1) shall be construed as to permit interference with the bodily integrity of any person.

(3) A warrant issued under subsection (1) shall contain such terms and conditions as the judge considers advisable to ensure that any search or seizure authorized by the warrant is reasonable in the circumstances.

(4) A warrant issued under subsection (1) that authorizes a peace officer to observe, by means of a television camera or other similar electronic device, any person who is engaged in activity in circumstances in which the person has a reasonable expectation of privacy shall contain such terms and conditions as the judge considers advisable to ensure that the privacy of the person or of any other person is respected as much as possible.

(5) The definition "offence" in section 183 and sections 183.1, 184.2, 184.3 and 185 to 188.2, subsection 189(5), and sections 190, 193 and 194 to 196 apply, with such modifications as the circumstances require, to a warrant referred to in subsection (4) as though references in those provisions to interceptions of private communications were read as references to observations by peace officers by means of television cameras or similar electronic devices of activities in circumstances in which persons had reasonable expectations of privacy.

(5.1) A warrant issued under subsection (1) that authorizes a peace officer to enter and search a place covertly shall require, as part of the terms and conditions referred to in subsection (3), that notice of the entry and search be given within any time after the execution of the warrant that the judge considers reasonable in the circumstances.

(5.2) Where the judge who issues a warrant under subsection (1) or any other judge having jurisdiction to issue such a warrant is, on the basis of an affidavit submitted in support of an application to vary the period within which the notice referred to in subsection (5.1) is to be given, is satisfied that the interests of justice warrant the granting of the application, the judge may grant an extension, or a subsequent extension, of the period, but no extension may exceed three years.

(6) Subsections 487(2) and (4) apply, with such modifications as the circumstances require, to a warrant issued under subsection (1).

(7) Where a peace officer believes that it would be impracticable to appear personally before a judge to make an application for a warrant under this section, a warrant may be issued under this section on an information submitted by telephone or other means of telecommunication and, for that purpose, section 487.1 applies, with such modifications as the circumstances require, to the warrant. 1993, c. 40, s. 15; 1997, c. 18, s. 42; 1997, c. 23, s. 13.

CROSS-REFERENCES

This section is part of a more or less comprehensive scheme relating to search and seizure. Interception of private communications are dealt with in Part VI. Use of telephone number recorders is regulated under s. 492.2 and use of tracking devices is regulated under s. 492.1. Section 487 deals with the granting of ordinary search warrants to seize tangible things. Provision is made in s. 487.02 for the making of an assistance order to require persons to co-operate in the carrying out of orders made under this section. As to warrants to obtain bodily substances for DNA analysis, see ss. 487.04 to 487.09, and for impression warrant, see s. 487.091.

The terms "peace officer", "provincial court judge" and "superior court judge" are defined in s. 2.

SYNOPSIS

This section allows for the obtaining of a warrant in circumstances where a warrantless search or seizure would violate s. 8 of the Charter. In effect, it fills a gap noted by various courts. For example, the Supreme Court had held in *R. v. Wong*, [1990] 3 S.C.R. 36, 60 C.C.C. (3d) 460, that warrantless surreptitious video surveillance by agents of the state in circumstances where the target has a reasonable expectation of privacy is a violation of s. 8 and yet no provision was made for obtaining a warrant or court authorization. A warrant for such surveillance could now be obtained under this section.

The warrant may be issued for any device or investigative technique or procedure or "any thing" except, pursuant to subsec. (2), anything which would interfere with the bodily integrity of any person. Subsection (3) permits the judge to impose appropriate conditions.

Subsection (5) makes special provision for video surveillance in circumstances where persons have a reasonable expectation of privacy. The effect of this subsection is that the authorization procedure under Part VI applies with the necessary modifications. In other words, a general warrant for this type of surveillance can only be obtained in the same circumstances as where an authorization to intercept private communications may be obtained. Thus, while a general warrant under subsec. (1) may be obtained in relation to any federal offence, a warrant in relation to video surveillance in circumstances where persons have a reasonable expectation of privacy can only be obtained for the offences listed in s. 183. To obtain the warrant, the police must meet the tests set out in Part VI rather than the test in subsec. (1) of this section. As well, the prohibition on disclosure of information from such surveillance in s. 193 is incorporated, as is notice of intention to introduce into evidence in s. 189(5), and the notice to targets provision in s. 196.

Subsection (4) requires the judge to impose conditions to protect the privacy of the targeted person and others in a case where the warrant is issued to authorize video surveillance in circumstances where persons have a reasonable expectation of privacy.

Subsection (5.1) and (5.2) deal with notice following a covert entry and search by a peace officer.

Subsection (6) makes applicable the provisions of s. 487 for "backing" the warrant if it is to be executed in another territorial division. Note that if the warrant is to be executed in another province and the investigative technique requires entry into private property or an assistance order under s. 487.02 then the warrant must be confirmed by a judge of the other province.

The warrant may be obtained by telephone etc. in accordance with subsec. (7).

ANNOTATIONS

Properly interpreted, this provision does not violate s. 8 of the Charter: *R. v. Lucas* (2014), 313 C.C.C. (3d) 159 (Ont. C.A.), leave to appeal to S.C.C. refused 2015 CarswellOnt 639.

A peace officer is not precluded from obtaining a general warrant solely because he has sufficient information to obtain a search warrant. A general warrant may be used with a view to gathering additional and possibly better evidence than that which could be seized immediately through the execution of a search warrant. Accordingly, the police were permitted to utilize the general warrant to covertly enter the premises where they detected evidence of a drug operation, and to subsequently use these observations as a basis to obtain a search warrant under s. 11 of the *Controlled Drugs and Substances Act*: *R. v. Brand* (2008), 229 C.C.C. (3d) 443 (B.C.C.A.).

A general warrant was validly issued under this section requiring employees of the Canada Post Corporation to photocopy the outside of envelopes and packages of mailable material after it was delivered to certain post office boxes. Compliance with the warrant would not require the employees to contravene the *Canada Post Corporation Act*: *Canada Post Corp. v. Canada (Attorney General)* (1995), 95 C.C.C. (3d) 568 (Ont. Ct. (Gen. Div.)).

An "anticipatory" search warrant for the re-seizure of items returned to the owner later the same day is authorized by this section: *R. v. Noseworthy* (1997), 116 C.C.C. (3d) 376, 33 O.R. (3d) 641 (C.A.).

In *R. v. Brooks* (2003), 178 C.C.C. (3d) 361, 15 C.R. (6th) 319 (Ont. C.A.), the court held that there should be explicit, clear and narrowly drawn pre-conditions to the issuance of a general warrant.

In *R. v. Brand* (2008), 229 C.C.C. (3d) 443, 56 C.R. (6th) 39, the British Columbia Court of Appeal held that a general warrant was properly utilized to allow for a covert entry to obtain information with a view to gathering additional and possibly better evidence than that which could be seized immediately through the execution of a search warrant.

This provision can authorize repeated covert entries and searches of private property. Covert entries constitute an "investigative technique or procedure". This provision is not limited to electronic devices to record and intercept communications. The focus of para. (*c*) was not on whether there were other investigative techniques that might accomplish the purported investigative purposes or goals of the police, but on the particular investigative technique or procedure that the police sought to utilize and whether it could be properly authorized by another provision. In this case, there was no other provision that could authorize repeated, covert entries and searches on private property over a two-month period. Further, the fact that some of the purposes of the investigation could have been obtained through the issuance of a traditional search warrant did not preclude reliance on this section: *R. v. Ha* (2009), 245 C.C.C. (3d) 546 (Ont. C.A.), leave to appeal to S.C.C. refused 247 C.C.C. (3d) vi.

Section 487.01(1)(*c*) should be broadly construed to ensure that the general warrant is not used to circumvent the more specific or rigorous pre-authorization requirements for warrants, such as those found in Part VI. A general warrant is not available to obtain an intercept of private communications, which includes text messages: *R. v. Telus Communication Co.*, [2013] 2 S.C.R. 3, 294 C.C.C. (3d) 498.

The validity of the warrant was not affected by the fact that the search warrant was signed before the information to obtain was sworn: *R. v. Ho* (2012), 293 C.C.C. (3d) 185 (Alta. C.A.).

A general warrant is not the proper form of authorization for the search of a computer. A regular search warrant under s. 487 is available: *R. v. Z. (K.)* (2014), 312 C.C.C. (3d) 346 (Alta. Q.B.).

DEFINITIONS.

487.011 The following definitions apply in this section and in sections 487.012 to 487.0199.

"computer data" has the same meaning as in subsection 342.1(2).

"data" means representations, including signs, signals or symbols, that are capable of being understood by an individual or processed by a computer system or other device.

"document" means a medium on which data is registered or marked.

"judge" means a judge of a superior court of criminal jurisdiction or a judge of the Court of Quebec.

"public officer" means a public officer who is appointed or designated to administer or enforce a federal or provincial law and whose duties include the enforcement of this Act or any other Act of Parliament.

"tracking data" means data that relates to the location of a transaction, individual or thing.

"transmission data" means data that
  (a) relates to the telecommunication functions of dialling, routing, addressing or signalling;
  (b) is transmitted to identify, activate or configure a device, including a computer program as defined in subsection 342.1(2), in order to establish or maintain access to a telecommunication service for the purpose of enabling a communication, or is generated during the creation, transmission or reception of a communication and identifies or purports to identify the type, direction, date, time, duration, size, origin, destination or termination of the communication; and
  (c) does not reveal the substance, meaning or purpose of the communication. 2004, c. 3, s. 7; 2014, c. 31, s. 20.

PRESERVATION DEMAND / Conditions for making demand / Limitation / Expiry and revocation of demand / Conditions in demand / No further demand.

487.012 (1) A peace officer or public officer may make a demand to a person in Form 5.001 requiring them to preserve computer data that is in their possession or control when the demand is made.

(2) The peace officer or public officer may make the demand only if they have reasonable grounds to suspect that
  (a) an offence has been or will be committed under this or any other Act of Parliament or has been committed under a law of a foreign state;
  (b) in the case of an offence committed under a law of a foreign state, an investigation is being conducted by a person or authority with responsibility in that state for the investigation of such offences; and
  (c) the computer data is in the person's possession or control and will assist in the investigation of the offence.

(3) A demand may not be made to a person who is under investigation for the offence referred to in paragraph (2)(a).

(4) A peace officer or public officer may revoke the demand by notice given to the person at any time. Unless the demand is revoked earlier, the demand expires
  (a) in the case of an offence that has been or will be committed under this or any other Act of Parliament, 21 days after the day on which it is made; and
  (b) in the case of an offence committed under a law of a foreign state, 90 days after the day on which it is made.

(5) The peace officer or public officer who makes the demand may impose any conditions in the demand that they consider appropriate - including conditions prohibiting the disclosure of its existence or some or all of its contents - and may revoke a condition at any time by notice given to the person.

(6) A peace officer or public officer may not make another demand requiring the person to preserve the same computer data in connection with the investigation. 2004, c. 3, s. 7; 2014, c. 31, s. 20.

(7) [*Repealed*, 2014, c. 31, s. 20.]

(8) [*Repealed*, 2014, c. 31, s. 20.]

CROSS-REFERENCES

"Computer data" is defined in ss. 487.011 and 342.1.

"Peace officer" is defined in s. 2, and "public officer" is defined in s. 487.011.

Section 487.013 provides for a preservation order in relation to computer data.

Section 487.014 provides for general production orders.

Sections 487.015 to 487.018 provide for other forms of production orders in relation to specified types of data.

Sections 487.019, 487.0191 and 487.0192 set out certain procedural requirements and options applicable to all preservation or production orders made under the foregoing provisions.

Section 487.0193 provides a procedure by which the target of a production order can seek to have the order varied or revoked.

Section 487.0194 governs the destruction of data following the expiration of a preservation demand or order.

Section 487.0195 clarifies that none of the foregoing provisions prevent a request for the voluntary preservation or production of data or documents.

Section 487.0196 provides that self-incrimination concerns do not excuse compliance with orders made under the foregoing provisions; however, immunity against subsequent incriminating use is provided.

Sections 487.0197 to 487.0199 create summary conviction offences for contravening preservation demands, preservation orders and production orders.

SYNOPSIS

This provision allows a peace officer or public officer to demand that a person preserve computer data in their possession. A demand may be made on the basis of a reasonable belief that an offence has been or will be committed under the *Criminal Code* or other Act of Parliament, or that an offence has been committed under a law of a foreign state provided an investigation is being carried out in the foreign state by someone with appropriate authority to do so. The demand must also be made on reasonable belief that the data in question will assist the investigation of the offence.

Subsection (3) provides that a demand cannot be made to the subject of the investigation.

Subsection (4) provides time periods for the expiry of the demand.

Subsection (5) allows the officer making the demand to stipulate appropriate conditions.

Subsection (6) prohibits subsequent demands for preservation of the same data.

PRESERVATION ORDER — COMPUTER DATA / Conditions for making order / Offence against law of foreign state / Form / Limitation / Expiry of order.

487.013 (1) On *ex parte* application made by a peace officer or public officer, a justice or judge may order a person to preserve computer data that is in their possession or control when they receive the order.

(2) Before making the order, the justice or judge must be satisfied by information on oath in Form 5.002

(*a*) that there are reasonable grounds to suspect that an offence has been or will be committed under this or any other Act of Parliament or has been committed under a law of a foreign state, that the computer data is in the person's possession or control and that it will assist in the investigation of the offence; and

(*b*) that a peace officer or public officer intends to apply or has applied for a warrant or an order in connection with the investigation to obtain a document that contains the computer data.

(3) If an offence has been committed under a law of a foreign state, the justice or judge must also be satisfied that a person or authority with responsibility in that state for the investigation of such offences is conducting the investigation.

(4) The order is to be in Form 5.003.

(5) A person who is under investigation for an offence referred to in paragraph (2)(*a*) may not be made subject to an order.

(6) Unless the order is revoked earlier, it expires 90 days after the day on which it is made. 2004, c. 3. s. 7; 2014, c. 31, s. 20.

CROSS-REFERENCES

"Computer data" is defined in ss. 487.011 and 342.1.

"Peace officer" is defined in s. 2, and "public officer" is defined in s. 487.011.

"Justice" is defined in s. 2 and "judge" is defined in s. 487.011.

For references to the other production and preservation order-related sections, see the cross-references under s. 487.012.

SYNOPSIS

This section provides for the making of a preservation order by a justice or judge in respect of computer data.

Pursuant to subsec. (2), the order may be made only where the justice or judge is satisfied on an *ex parte* application containing information on oath in writing that there are reasonable grounds to believe that an offence has been or will be committed under the *Criminal Code* or other Act of Parliament, or that an offence has been committed under a law of a foreign state; that the computer data is in the person's possession or control and that it will assist in the investigation of the offence; and that the officer intends to apply (or has applied) for a warrant or order to obtain the data.

Under subsec. (3), if a foreign offence is alleged to have been committed, the justice or judge must also be satisfied that it is being investigated by someone with appropriate authority in that jurisdiction.

Subsection (5) prohibits such an order from being made against a person under investigation for an offence.

GENERAL PRODUCTION ORDER / Conditions for making order / Form / Limitation.

487.014 (1) Subject to sections 487.015 to 487.018, on *ex parte* application made by a peace officer or public officer, a justice or judge may order a person to produce a document that is a copy of a document that is in their possession or control when they receive the order, or to prepare and produce a document containing data that is in their possession or control at that time.

(2) Before making the order, the justice or judge must be satisfied by information on oath in Form 5.004 that there are reasonable grounds to believe that

(*a*) an offence has been or will be committed under this or any other Act of Parliament; and

(*b*) the document or data is in the person's possession or control and will afford evidence respecting the commission of the offence.

(3) The order is to be in Form 5.005.

(4) A person who is under investigation for the offence referred to in subsection (2) may not be made subject to an order. 2004, c. 3, s. 7; 2014, c. 31, s. 20.

CROSS-REFERENCES

"Data" and "document" are defined in s. 487.011.

"Peace officer" is defined in s. 2, and "public officer" is defined in s. 487.011.

"Justice" is defined in s. 2 and "judge" is defined in s. 487.011.

For references to the other production and preservation order-related sections, see the cross-references under s. 487.012.

SYNOPSIS

This section provides for the making of a production order by a justice or judge against a person other than a person under investigation for an offence under the *Criminal Code* or other Act of Parliament. The order may require the person to produce a copy of a document in their possession or to prepare and produce a document containing data in their possession. The order may be made only where the justice or judge is satisfied on an *ex parte* application containing information on oath in writing that there are reasonable grounds to believe that an offence has been or will be committed, that the document or data will afford evidence of the offence, and that the document or data is in the person's possession or control.

ANNOTATIONS

A judge does not have power to make it a term or condition of a production order that the police compensate a third party for expenses incurred in complying with the order. Where the financial costs of compliance are unreasonable, the remedy lies in a full or partial exemption from the production order. In order to meet the threshold, the financial consequences must be so burdensome that it would be unreasonable in the circumstances to expect compliance. What is reasonable will be informed by a variety of factors including the breadth of the order being sought, the size and economic viability of the object of the order, and the extent of the order's financial impact on the party. Where the party is a repeated target of production orders, the cumulative impact of multiple orders may also be relevant: *Ontario v. Tele-Mobile Co.*, [2008] 1 S.C.R. 305, 229 C.C.C. (3d) 417.

The law regarding search warrants should also apply to production orders. Accordingly, the test for review of a production order is the same as the *Garofoli* test. Where the target of the production order is a media outlet, the reviewing judge must apply a somewhat modified *Garofoli* test. The media are entitled to particularly careful consideration because of the importance of their role in a democratic society. While this does not import any new or additional requirements for the issuance of a production order, the authorizing judge must consider all of the circumstances and conduct a balancing test in exercising his or her discretion having regard to the constitutional protection afforded by s. 2(*b*) of the Charter: *Canadian Broadcasting Corp. v. Manitoba (Attorney General)* (2009), 250 C.C.C. (3d) 61, [2010] 1 W.W.R. 389 (Man. C.A.).

A production order continues to compel the third party to release the information sought even if the period for compliance set out on the face of the order has expired: *R. v. Goulbourne* (2011), 267 C.C.C. (3d) 568 (Ont. S.C.J.).

The police were not entitled to use a production order to search the accused's safety deposit boxes and should have obtained a search warrant instead: *R. v. Huynh* (2012), 283 C.C.C. (3d) 189 (Alta. C.A.).

Police can obtain a production order for past text messages. An authorization under Part VI is only needed for the prospective interception of future text messages: *R. v. Belcourt* (2015), 322 C.C.C. (3d) 93 (B.C.C.A.); *R. v. Webster* (2015), 326 C.C.C. (3d) 228 (B.C.C.A.), leave to appeal to S.C.C. refused 2015 CarswellBC 3755; *R. v. Carty* (2014),

118 W.C.B. (2d) 362, [2014] O.J. No. 6081 (S.C.J.). *Contra: R. v. Croft* (2013), 304 C.C.C. (3d) 279 (Alta. Q.B.).

PRODUCTION ORDER TO TRACE SPECIFIED COMMUNICATION / Conditions for making order / Form / Service / Limitation / Report.

487.015 (1) On *ex parte* application made by a peace officer or public officer for the purpose of identifying a device or person involved in the transmission of a communication, a justice or judge may order a person to prepare and produce a document containing transmission data that is related to that purpose and that is, when they are served with the order, in their possession or control.

(2) Before making the order, the justice or judge must be satisfied by information on oath in Form 5.004 that there are reasonable grounds to suspect that

    (*a*) an offence has been or will be committed under this or any other Act of Parliament;

    (*b*) the identification of a device or person involved in the transmission of a communication will assist in the investigation of the offence; and

    (*c*) transmission data that is in the possession or control of one or more persons whose identity is unknown when the application is made will enable that identification.

(3) The order is to be in Form 5.006.

(4) A peace officer or public officer may serve the order on any person who was involved in the transmission of the communication and whose identity was unknown when the application was made

    (*a*) within 60 days after the day on which the order is made; or

    (*b*) within one year after the day on which the order is made, in the case of an offence under section 467.11, 467.12 or 467.13, an offence committed for the benefit of, at the direction of or in association with a criminal organization, or a terrorism offence.

(5) A person who is under investigation for the offence referred to in subsection (2) may not be made subject to an order.

(6) A peace officer or public officer named in the order must provide a written report to the justice or judge who made the order as soon as feasible after the person from whom the communication originated is identified or after the expiry of the period referred to in subsection (4), whichever occurs first. The report must state the name and address of each person on whom the order was served, and the date of service. 2004, c. 3, s. 7; 2014, c. 31, s. 20.

CROSS-REFERENCES

"Transmission data" and "document" are defined in s. 487.011.

"Peace officer" is defined in s. 2, and "public officer" is defined in s. 487.011.

"Justice" is defined in s. 2 and "judge" is defined in s. 487.011.

For references to the other production and preservation order-related sections, see the cross-references under s. 487.012.

SYNOPSIS

This section provides for the making of a production order to trace specified communications by a justice or judge against a person whose identity is unknown other than a person under investigation for an offence under the *Criminal Code* or other Act of Parliament. The order may require the person to produce a document containing transmission data that is related to that purpose and that is in their possession or control when they are served with the order. The order may be made only where the justice or judge is satisfied on an *ex parte* application containing information on oath in writing that there are reasonable grounds to suspect that an offence has been or will be committed, that the identification of a device or person involved in the transmission of a communication will assist in the investigation of the offence, and that transmission data that is in the possession or control of one or more unknown persons will enable the identification of the device or person involved in the offence.

Subsection (4) permits an officer to serve the order on any person involved in the transmission of the communication and whose identity was previously unknown at the time of the application. Service must be made within 60 days of the order, though it can be made up to one year after the order in the case of terrorism offences and offences in relation criminal organizations.

Subsection (6) sets out timelines for the making of a report to the justice or judge who made the order, with details of service.

PRODUCTION ORDER — TRANSMISSION DATA / Conditions for making order / Form / Limitation.

487.016 (1) On *ex parte* application made by a peace officer or public officer, a justice or judge may order a person to prepare and produce a document containing transmission data that is in their possession or control when they receive the order.

(2) Before making the order, the justice or judge must be satisfied by information on oath in Form 5.004 that there are reasonable grounds to suspect that

    (*a*) **an offence has been or will be committed under this or any other Act of Parliament; and**

    (*b*) **the transmission data is in the person's possession or control and will assist in the investigation of the offence.**

(3) The order is to be in Form 5.007.

(4) A person who is under investigation for the offence referred to in subsection (2) may not be made subject to an order. 2004, c. 3, s. 7; 2014, c. 31, s. 20.

CROSS-REFERENCES

"Transmission data" and "document" are defined in s. 487.011.

  "Peace officer" is defined in s. 2, and "public officer" is defined in s. 487.011.

  "Justice" is defined in s. 2 and "judge" is defined in s. 487.011.

  For references to the other production and preservation order-related sections, see the cross-references under s. 487.012.

SYNOPSIS

This section provides for the making of a more specific production order than the order under s. 487.014. Under this section, a justice or judge may require a person, other than a person under investigation for an offence under the *Criminal Code* or other Act of Parliament, to produce a document containing transmission data that is in their possession or control when they receive the order. The order may be made only where the justice or judge is satisfied on an *ex parte* application containing information on oath in writing that there are reasonable grounds to suspect that an offence has been or will be committed, that the transmission data will assist in the investigation of the offence, and that the transmission data is in the person's possession or control.

PRODUCTION ORDER — TRACKING DATA / Conditions for making order / Form / Limitation.

487.017 (1) On *ex parte* application made by a peace officer or public officer, a justice or judge may order a person to prepare and produce a document containing tracking data that is in their possession or control when they receive the order.

CR. CODE

(2) Before making the order, the justice or judge must be satisfied by information on oath in Form 5.004 that there are reasonable grounds to suspect that
  (a) an offence has been or will be committed under this or any other Act of Parliament; and
  (b) the tracking data is in the person's possession or control and will assist in the investigation of the offence.

(3) The order is to be in Form 5.007.

(4) A person who is under investigation for the offence referred to in subsection (2) may not be made subject to an order. 2004, c. 7, s. 7; 2014, c. 31, s. 20.

CROSS-REFERENCES
"Tracking data" and "document" are defined in s. 487.011.
  "Peace officer" is defined in s. 2, and "public officer" is defined in s. 487.011.
  "Justice" is defined in s. 2 and "judge" is defined in s. 487.011.
  For references to the other production and preservation order-related sections, see the cross-references under s. 487.012.

SYNOPSIS
This section provides for the making of a more specific production order than the order under s. 487.014. Under this section, a justice or judge may require a person, other than a person under investigation for an offence under the *Criminal Code* or other Act of Parliament, to produce a document containing tracking data that is in their possession or control when they receive the order. The order may be made only where the justice or judge is satisfied on an *ex parte* application containing information on oath in writing that there are reasonable grounds to suspect that an offence has been or will be committed, that the tracking data will assist in the investigation of the offence, and that the tracking data is in the person's possession or control.

PRODUCTION ORDER — FINANCIAL DATA / Identification of person / Conditions for making order / Form / Limitation.
487.018 (1) On *ex parte* application made by a peace officer or public officer, a justice or judge may order a financial institution, as defined in section 2 of the *Bank Act*, or a person or entity referred to in section 5 of the *Proceeds of Crime (Money Laundering) and Terrorist Financing Act*, to prepare and produce a document setting out the following data that is in their possession or control when they receive the order:
  (a) either the account number of a person named in the order or the name of a person whose account number is specified in the order;
  (b) the type of account;
  (c) the status of the account; and
  (d) the date on which it was opened or closed.

(2) For the purpose of confirming the identity of a person who is named or whose account number is specified in the order, the order may also require the institution, person or entity to prepare and produce a document setting out the following data that is in their possession or control:
  (a) the date of birth of a person who is named or whose account number is specified in the order;
  (b) that person's current address; and
  (c) any previous addresses of that person.

(3) Before making the order, the justice or judge must be satisfied by information on oath in Form 5.004 that there are reasonable grounds to suspect that
  (a) an offence has been or will be committed under this or any other Act of Parliament; and

(*b*) **the data is in the possession or control of the institution, person or entity and will assist in the investigation of the offence.**

(4) The order is to be in Form 5.008.

(5) A financial institution, person or entity that is under investigation for the offence referred to in subsection (3) may not be made subject to an order. 2014, c. 31, s. 20.

CROSS-REFERENCES

"Data" and "document" are defined in s. 487.011.

  "Peace officer" is defined in s. 2, and "public officer" is defined in s. 487.011.

  "Justice" is defined in s. 2 and "judge" is defined in s. 487.011.

  For references to the other production and preservation order-related sections, see the cross-references under s. 487.012.

SYNOPSIS

This section provides for the making of a more specific production order than the order under s. 487.014. Under this section, a justice or judge may require a financial institution or person or entity referred to in s. 5 of the *Proceeds of Crime (Money Laundering) and Terrorist Financing Act*, to produce account information about a person named in the order unless the institution, person or entity is under investigation for the offence that is under investigation. The order may also require the institution, person or entity to produce the person's date of birth, current address or previous address to confirm the identity of the person named in the order. The order may be made only where the justice or judge is satisfied on an *ex parte* application containing information on oath in writing that there are reasonable grounds to suspect that an offence against the *Criminal Code* or other federal legislation has been or is suspected to have been committed, that the information will assist in investigating the offence, and that the institution, person or entity has possession or control of the information.

CONDITIONS IN PRESERVATION AND PRODUCTION ORDERS / Effect of order / Power to revoke or vary order.

487.019 (1) An order made under any of sections 487.013 to 487.018 may contain any conditions that the justice or judge considers appropriate including, in the case of an order made under section 487.014, conditions to protect a privileged communication between a person who is qualified to give legal advice and their client.

(2) The order has effect throughout Canada and, for greater certainty, no endorsement is needed for the order to be effective in a territorial division that is not the one in which the order is made.

(3) On *ex parte* application made by a peace officer or public officer, the justice or judge who made the order — or a judge in the judicial district where the order was made — may, on the basis of an information on oath in Form 5.0081, revoke or vary the order. The peace officer or public officer must give notice of the revocation or variation to the person who is subject to the order as soon as feasible. 2014, c. 31, s. 20.

CROSS-REFERENCES

"Peace officer" is defined in s. 2, and "public officer" is defined in s. 487.011.

  "Justice" is defined in s. 2 and "judge" is defined in s. 487.011.

  For references to the other production and preservation order-related sections, see the cross-references under s. 487.012.

SYNOPSIS

This section provides certain procedural powers in relation to preservation and production orders under ss. 487.013 to 487.018. Subsection (2) provides that such orders have effect throughout Canada. Subsection (1) provides that the order may contain terms or conditions including terms and conditions to protect solicitor-client communications. Subsection (3) provides that, on an *ex parte* application made by a peace officer or public officer, the judge or justice who made the order, or a judge from the same judicial district, has the power to revoke or vary the order. Notice of the revocation or variation must be given to the person subject to the order as soon as feasible.

ORDER PROHIBITING DISCLOSURE / Conditions for making order / Form / Application to revoke or vary order.

487.0191 (1) On *ex parte* **application made by a peace officer or public officer, a justice or judge may make an order prohibiting a person from disclosing the existence or some or all of the contents of a preservation demand made under section 487.012 or a preservation or production order made under any of sections 487.013 to 487.018 during the period set out in the order.**

(2) Before making the order, the justice or judge must be satisfied by information on oath in Form 5.009 that there are reasonable grounds to believe that the disclosure during that period would jeopardize the conduct of the investigation of the offence to which the preservation demand or the preservation or production order relates.

(3) The order is to be in Form 5.0091.

(4) A peace officer or a public officer or a person, financial institution or entity that is subject to an order made under subsection (1) may apply in writing to the justice or judge who made the order — or to a judge in the judicial district where the order was made — to revoke or vary the order. 2014, c. 31, s. 20.

CROSS-REFERENCES

"Peace officer" is defined in s. 2, and "public officer" is defined in s. 487.011.

"Justice" is defined in s. 2 and "judge" is defined in s. 487.011.

For references to the other production and preservation order-related sections, see the cross-references under s. 487.012.

SYNOPSIS

Under this section, a judge or justice may make an order prohibiting the disclosure of the contents of a preservation demand under s. 487.012 or a preservation or production order under ss. 487.013 to 487.018 during the period of the order. The order may be made an *ex parte* application by a peace officer or public officer, containing information on oath in writing that there are reasonable grounds to believe that disclosure during the period would jeopardize the conduct of the investigation to which the demand or order under ss. 487.012 to 487.018 relates. Subsection (4) provides that a peace officer or public officer or a person, financial institution or entity that is subject to the non-disclosure order may apply in writing to have the order revoked or varied.

PARTICULARS — PRODUCTION ORDERS / Particulars — production order to trace specified communication / Form of production / Non-application / Probative force of copies / *Canada Evidence Act.*

487.0192 (1) An order made under any of sections 487.014 and 487.016 to 487.018 must require a person, financial institution or entity to produce the document to a peace officer or public officer named in the order within the time, at the place and in the form specified in the order.

(2) An order made under section 487.015 must require a person to produce the document to a peace officer or public officer named in the order as soon as feasible after they are served with the order at the place and in the form specified in the order.

(3) For greater certainty, an order under any of sections 487.014 to 487.018 may specify that a document may be produced on or through an electro-magnetic medium.

(4) For greater certainty, sections 489.1 and 490 do not apply to a document that is produced under an order under any of sections 487.014 to 487.018.

(5) Every copy of a document produced under section 487.014 is admissible in evidence in proceedings under this or any other Act of Parliament on proof by affidavit that it is a true copy and has the same probative force as the document would have if it were proved in the ordinary way.

(6) A document that is prepared for the purpose of production is considered to be original for the purposes of the *Canada Evidence Act*. 2014, c. 31, s. 20.

CROSS-REFERENCES
"Document" is defined in s. 487.011.
   "Peace officer" is defined in s. 2, and "public officer" is defined in s. 487.011.
   "Justice" is defined in s. 2 and "judge" is defined in s. 487.011.
   For references to the other production and preservation order-related sections, see the cross-references under s. 487.012.

SYNOPSIS
This section provides for particulars regarding production orders under ss. 487.014 to 487.018. Subsections (1) and (2) require that the order provide specifics as to the time, place and form of the required production. Such orders may specify that the document may be produced on or through an electro-magnetic medium. Subsection (4) provides that the procedural requirements under ss. 489.1 and 490 regarding the restitution of property, reports by a peace officer and the detention of things seized, do not apply to documents produced under production orders.
   The evidentiary provisions in subsecs. (5) and (6) provide that a document prepared for the purpose of production is considered to be an original under the *Canada Evidence Act*, and that copies of a document produced under the general production order provision in s. 487.014 are admissible in proceedings under the *Criminal Code* or other federal legislation on proof by affidavit that it is a true copy.

APPLICATION FOR REVIEW OF PRODUCTION ORDER / Notice required / No obligation to produce / Revocation or variation of order.

487.0193 (1) Before they are required by an order made under any of sections 487.014 to 487.018 to produce a document, a person, financial institution or entity may apply in writing to the justice or judge who made the order — or to a judge in the judicial district where the order was made — to revoke or vary the order.

(2) The person, institution or entity may make the application only if they give notice of their intention to do so to a peace officer or public officer named in the order within 30 days after the day on which the order is made.

(3) The person, institution or entity is not required to prepare or produce the document until a final decision is made with respect to the application.

(4) The justice or judge may revoke or vary the order if satisfied that
   (*a*) it is unreasonable in the circumstances to require the applicant to prepare or produce the document; or
   (*b*) production of the document would disclose information that is privileged or otherwise protected from disclosure by law. 2014, c. 31, s. 20.

CROSS-REFERENCES
"Document" is defined in s. 487.011.

"Peace officer" is defined in s. 2, and "public officer" is defined in s. 487.011.

"Justice" is defined in s. 2 and "judge" is defined in s. 487.011.

For references to the other production and preservation order-related sections, see the cross-references under s. 487.012.

SYNOPSIS

This section sets out the procedure by which the target of a production order under ss. 487.014 to 487.018 can, before producing a document, seek to have the order varied or revoked. An application in writing may be made to the justice or judge who made the order, or to a judge in the same judicial district. Notice of the application must be given to the peace officer or public officer named within the order within 30 days of the production order. The order may be revoked or varied if the justice or judge is satisfied that production is unreasonable in the circumstances or production would disclose information that is privileged or otherwise protected from disclosure by law.

DESTRUCTION OF PRESERVED COMPUTER DATA AND DOCUMENTS — PRESERVATION DEMAND / Destruction of preserved computer data and documents — preservation order / Destruction of preserved computer data and documents — production order / Destruction of preserved computer data and documents — warrant.

487.0194 (1) A person to whom a preservation demand is made under section 487.012 shall destroy the computer data that would not be retained in the ordinary course of business and any document that is prepared for the purpose of preserving computer data under that section as soon as feasible after the demand expires or is revoked, unless they are subject to an order made under any of sections 487.013 to 487.017 with respect to the computer data.

(2) A person who is subject to a preservation order made under section 487.013 shall destroy the computer data that would not be retained in the ordinary course of business and any document that is prepared for the purpose of preserving computer data under that section as soon as feasible after the order expires or is revoked, unless they are subject to a new preservation order or to a production order made under any of sections 487.014 to 487.017 with respect to the computer data.

(3) A person who is subject to a production order made under any of sections 487.014 to 487.017 with respect to computer data that they preserved under a preservation demand or order made under section 487.012 or 487.013 shall destroy the computer data that would not be retained in the ordinary course of business and any document that is prepared for the purpose of preserving computer data under that section as soon as feasible after the earlier of

    (*a*) the day on which the production order is revoked, and

    (*b*) the day on which a document that contains the computer data is produced under the production order.

(4) Despite subsections (1) to (3), a person who preserved computer data under a preservation demand or order made under section 487.012 or 487.013 shall destroy the computer data that would not be retained in the ordinary course of business and any document that is prepared for the purpose of preserving computer data under that section when a document that contains the computer data is obtained under a warrant. 2014, c. 31, s. 20.

CROSS-REFERENCES

"Computer data" is defined in ss. 487.011 and 342.1(2).

"Document" is defined in s. 487.011.

For references to the other production and preservation order-related sections, see the cross-references under s. 487.012.

Under s. 487.0199, it is a summary conviction offence to contravene this section without lawful excuse.

SYNOPSIS

This section governs the destruction of data following the expiration of a preservation demand or order under ss. 487.012 or 487.013. A person who receives a preservation demand or order is required, after the demand or order expires, or after the data has been given to the law enforcement agency under a production order or search warrant, to destroy the computer data that would not be retained in the ordinary course of business as soon as feasible.

FOR GREATER CERTAINTY / No civil or criminal liability.

487.0195 (1) For greater certainty, no preservation demand, preservation order or production order is necessary for a peace officer or public officer to ask a person to voluntarily preserve data that the person is not prohibited by law from preserving or to voluntarily provide a document to the officer that the person is not prohibited by law from disclosing.

(2) A person who preserves data or provides a document in those circumstances does not incur any criminal or civil liability for doing so. 2014, c. 31, s. 20.

CROSS-REFERENCES

"Data" and "document" are defined in s. 487.011.

"Peace officer" is defined in s. 2, and "public officer" is defined in s. 487.011.

"Justice" is defined in s. 2 and "judge" is defined in s. 487.011.

For references to the other production and preservation order-related sections, see the cross-references under s. 487.012.

SYNOPSIS

This section clarifies that none of the foregoing provisions on production demands, production orders or preservation orders prevent a request for the voluntary preservation or production of data or documents that a person is not prohibited by law from disclosing. No civil or criminal liability will be incurred for production or preservation of data in such circumstances.

SELF-INCRIMINATION.

487.0196 No one is excused from complying with an order made under any of sections 487.014 to 487.018 on the ground that the document that they are required to produce may tend to incriminate them or subject them to a proceeding or penalty. However, no document that an individual is required to prepare may be used or received in evidence against them in a criminal proceeding that is subsequently instituted against them, other than a prosecution for an offence under section 132, 136 or 137. 2014, c. 31, s. 20.

CROSS-REFERENCES

"Data" and "document" are defined in s. 487.011.

For references to the other production and preservation order-related sections, see the cross-references under s. 487.012.

Note that, under s. 487.0193, a person may apply for an variation or revocation of a production order on the basis that the order would require production of privileged information, documents or data or material that is otherwise protected by law.

Under s. 487.0198, it is an offence not to comply with a production order.

CR. CODE

SYNOPSIS

A person is not excused from complying with a production order on the grounds of self-incrimination. However, where an individual is required to prepare a document under ss. 487.014 to 487.018, that document cannot be used or received in evidence against the individual in any criminal proceedings subsequently instituted against the individual except for proceedings under s. 132 (perjury), s. 136 (giving contradictory evidence) or s. 137 (fabricating evidence).

OFFENCE — PRESERVATION DEMAND.

487.0197 A person who contravenes a preservation demand made under section 487.012 without lawful excuse is guilty of an offence punishable on summary conviction and is liable to a fine of not more than $5,000. 2014, c. 31, s. 20.

CROSS-REFERENCES

For references to the other production and preservation order-related sections, see the cross-references under s. 487.012.

OFFENCE — PRESERVATION OR PRODUCTION ORDER.

487.0198 A person, financial institution or entity that contravenes an order made under any of sections 487.013 to 487.018 without lawful excuse is guilty of an offence punishable on summary conviction and is liable to a fine of not more than $250,000 or to imprisonment for a term of not more than six months, or to both. 2014, c. 31, s. 20.

CROSS-REFERENCES

For references to the other production and preservation order-related sections, see the cross-references under s. 487.012.

Note that, under s. 487.0193, a person may apply for a variation or revocation of a production order on the basis that the order would require production of privileged information, documents or data, or material that is otherwise protected by law.

OFFENCE — DESTRUCTION OF PRESERVED DATA.

487.0199 A person who contravenes section 487.0194 without lawful excuse is guilty of an offence punishable on summary conviction. 2014, c. 31, s. 20.

CROSS-REFERENCES

For references to the other production and preservation order-related sections, see the cross-references under s. 487.012.

ASSISTANCE ORDER.

487.02 If an authorization is given under section 184.2, 184.3, 186 or 188 or a warrant is issued under this Act, the judge or justice who gives the authorization or issues the warrant may order a person to provide assistance, if the person's assistance may reasonably be considered to be required to give effect to the authorization or warrant. 1993, c. 40, s. 15; 1997, c. 18, s. 43; 2014, c. 31, s. 20.

CROSS-REFERENCES

Although violation of an order under this section is not specifically made an offence, presumably the failure to comply could be punished under s. 127.

SYNOPSIS

This section provides for the making of an order requiring persons to assist in the execution of various authorizations and warrants. For example, the assistance of the telephone company may be required to implement an authorization under s. 186 to intercept private communications.

ANNOTATIONS

An assistance order could be validly made under this section requiring employees of the Canada Post Corporation to photocopy the outside of envelopes and packages of mailable material after it was delivered to certain post office boxes and requiring the employees not to divulge the existence of the warrant and the order. *Canada Post Corp. v. Canada (Attorney General)* (1995), 95 C.C.C. (3d) 568 (Ont. Ct. (Gen. Div.)).

An assistance order was not required to effect an interception obtained in one province where the telephone company employees in the other province were prepared to assist the police by re-routing calls to equipment in the police interception room: *R. v. Pham* (1997), 122 C.C.C. (3d) 90 (B.C.C.A.), leave to appeal to S.C.C. refused 128 C.C.C. (3d) vi.

REVIEW / Report.

487.021 (1) Within seven years after the coming into force of this section, a comprehensive review of the provisions and operation of sections 487.011 to 487.02 shall be undertaken by such committee of the House of Commons as may be designated or established by the House for that purpose.

(2) The committee referred to in subsection (1) shall, within a year after a review is undertaken pursuant to that subsection or within such further time as the House may authorize, submit a report on the review to the Speaker of the House, including a statement of any changes the committee recommends. 2014, c. 31, s. 20.

CROSS-REFERENCES

Section 487.012 provides for a demand to preserve computer data.

Section 487.013 provides for a preservation order in relation to computer data.

Section 487.014 provides for general production orders.

Sections 487.015 to 487.018 provide for other forms of production orders in relation to specified types of data.

Sections 487.019, 487.0191 and 487.0192 set out certain procedural requirements and options applicable to all preservation or production orders made under the foregoing provisions.

Section 487.0193 provides a procedure by which the target of a production order can seek to have the order varied or revoked.

Section 487.0194 governs the destruction of data following the expiration of a preservation demand or order.

Section 487.0195 clarifies that none of the foregoing provisions prevent a request for the voluntary preservation or production of data or documents.

Section 487.0196 provides that self-incrimination concerns do not excuse compliance with orders made under the foregoing provisions; however, immunity against subsequent incriminating use is provided.

Sections 487.0197 to 487.0199 create summary conviction offences for contravening preservation demands, preservation orders and production orders.

Section 487.02 provides for an assistance order.

SYNOPSIS

This provision requires that a committee of the House of Commons undertake a comprehensive review of the provisions and operation of ss. 487.011 to 487.02 within seven years of the coming into force of this section, and the production of a report within a year after the review is undertaken.

EXECUTION IN ANOTHER PROVINCE / Endorsement.

487.03 (1) If a warrant is issued under section 487.01, 487.05 or 492.1 or subsection 492.2(1) in one province, a judge or justice, as the case may be, in another province may, on application, endorse the warrant if it may reasonably be expected that it is to be executed in the other province and that its execution would require entry into or on the property of any person, or would require that an order be made under section 487.02 with respect to any person, in that province.

(1.1) The endorsement may be made on the original of the warrant or on a copy of the warrant that is transmitted by any means of telecommunication and, once endorsed, the warrant has the same force in the other province as though it had originally been issued there. 1993, c. 40, s. 15; 1995, c. 27, s. 1; 2000, c. 10, s. 13; 2007, c. 22, s. 7; 2008, c. 18, s. 12.

(2) [*Repealed*, 2007, c. 22, s. 7.]

SYNOPSIS

Subsection (1) provides that a warrant may be confirmed where it is to be executed in another province. Such confirmation is in addition to the backing procedure set out in s. 487(2) [applicable to a general warrant issued under s. 487.01] and is required where it will be necessary to enter private premises or where an assistance order is made under s. 487.02.

Subsection (1.1) provides that the endorsement may be made on the original warrant or a copy of the warrant that is transmitted by any means of telecommunication.

Forensic DNA Analysis

DEFINITIONS / "Adult" / "Designated offence" / "DNA" / "Forensic DNA analysis" / "Primary designated offence" / "Provincial court judge" / "Secondary designated offence" / "Young Offenders Act" / "Young person".

487.04 In this section and in sections 487.05 to 487.0911,

"adult" has the meaning assigned by subsection 2(1) of the *Youth Criminal Justice Act*;

"designated offence" means a primary designated offence or a secondary designated offence;

"DNA" means deoxyribonucleic acid;

"forensic DNA analysis"

(*a*) **in relation to a bodily substance that is taken from a person in execution of a warrant under section 487.05, means forensic DNA analysis of the bodily substance and the comparison of the results of that analysis with the results of the analysis of the DNA in the bodily substance referred to in paragraph 487.05(1)(*b*), and includes any incidental tests associated with that analysis, and**

(*b*) **in relation to a bodily substance that is provided voluntarily in the course of an investigation of a designated offence or is taken from a person under an order made under section 487.051 or an authorization granted under section 487.055 or 487.091, or to a bodily substance referred to in paragraph 487.05(1)(*b*), means forensic DNA analysis of the bodily substance;**

"primary designated offence" means

(*a*) **an offence under any of the following provisions, namely,**

    (i) **subsection 7(4.1) (offence in relation to sexual offences against children),**

    (i.1) **section 151 (sexual interference),**

(i.2)   section 152 (invitation to sexual touching),

(i.3)   section 153 (sexual exploitation),

(i.4)   section 153.1 (sexual exploitation of person with disability),

(i.5)   section 155 (incest),

(i.6)   subsection 160(2) (compelling the commission of bestiality),

(i.7)   subsection 160(3) (bestiality in presence of or by a child),

(i.8)   section 163.1 (child pornography),

(i.9)   section 170 (parent or guardian procuring sexual activity),

(i.901)   section 171.1 (making sexually explicit material available to child),

(i.91)   section 172.1 (luring a child),

(i.911)   section 172.2 (agreement or arrangement — sexual offence against child),

(i.92)   subsection 173(2) (exposure),

(i.93)   [*Repealed*, 2014, c. 25, s. 23(1).]

(i.94)   [*Repealed*, 2014, c. 25, s. 23(1).]

(i.95)   [*Repealed*, 2014, c. 25, s. 23(1).]

(i.96)   [*Repealed*, 2014, c. 25, s. 23(1).]

(ii)   section 235 (murder),

(iii)   section 236 (manslaughter),

(iv)   section 239 (attempt to commit murder),

(v)   section 244 (discharging firearm with intent),

(vi)   section 244.1 (causing bodily harm with intent — air gun or pistol),

(vi.1)   section 244.2 (discharging firearm — recklessness),

(vii)   paragraph 245(a) (administering noxious thing with intent to endanger life or cause bodily harm),

(viii)   section 246 (overcoming resistance to commission of offence),

(ix)   section 267 (assault with a weapon or causing bodily harm),

(x)   section 268 (aggravated assault),

(xi)   section 269 (unlawfully causing bodily harm),

(xi.1)   section 270.01 (assaulting peace officer with weapon or causing bodily harm),

(xi.2)   section 270.02 (aggravated assault of peace officer),

(xi.3)   section 271 (sexual assault),

(xii)   section 272 (sexual assault with a weapon, threats to a third party or causing bodily harm),

(xiii)   section 273 (aggravated sexual assault),

(xiii.1)   subsection 273.3(2) (removal of a child from Canada),

(xiv)   section 279 (kidnapping),

(xiv.1)   section 279.011 (trafficking — person under 18 years),

(xiv.2)   subsection 279.02(2) (material benefit — trafficking of person under 18 years),

(xiv.3)   subsection 279.03(2) (withholding or destroying documents — trafficking of person under 18 years),

(xiv.4)   subsection 286.1(2) (obtaining sexual services for consideration from person under 18 years),

(xiv.5)   subsection 286.2(2) (material benefit from sexual services provided by person under 18 years),

(xiv.6)   subsection 286.3(2) (procuring — person under 18 years),

(xv)   section 344 (robbery), and

(xvi)   section 346 (extortion),

(*a*.1)   an offence under any of the following provisions, namely,

(i)   section 75 (piratical acts),

(i.01)   section 76 (hijacking),

(i.02)   section 77 (endangering safety of aircraft or airport),

(i.03)   section 78.1 (seizing control of ship or fixed platform), (i.04) subsection 81(1) (using explosives),

(i.041) section 82.3 (possession, etc., of nuclear material, radioactive material or device),

(i.042) section 82.4 (use or alteration of nuclear material, radioactive material or device),

(i.043) section 82.5 (commission of indictable offence to obtain nuclear material, etc.),

(i.044) section 82.6 (threats),

(i.05) section 83.18 (participation in activity of terrorist group),

(i.051) section 83.181 (leaving Canada to participate in activity of terrorist group),

(i.06) section 83.19 (facilitating terrorist activity),

(i.061) section 83.191 (leaving Canada to facilitate terrorist activity),

(i.07) section 83.2 (commission of offence for terrorist group),

(i.071) section 83.201 (leaving Canada to commit offence for terrorist group),

(i.072) section 83.202 (leaving Canada to commit offence that is terrorist activity),

(i.08) section 83.21 (instructing to carry out activity for terrorist group),

(i.09) section 83.22 (instructing to carry out terrorist activity),

(i.091) subsection 83.221(1) (advocating or promoting commission of terrorism offences),

(i.1) section 83.23 (harbouring or concealing),

(i.11) *[Repealed, 2010, c. 17, s. 3(4).]*

(ii) *[Repealed, 2010, c. 17, s. 3(4).]*

(iii) *[Repealed, 2010, c. 17, s. 3(4).]*

(iii.1) *[Repealed, 2010, c. 17, s. 3(4).]*

(iv) *[Repealed, 2014, c. 25, s. 23(3).]*

(iv.1) *[Repealed, 2010, c. 17, s. 3(4).]*

(iv.2) *[Repealed, 2010, c. 17, s. 3(4).]*

(iv.3) *[Repealed, 2010, c. 17, s. 3(4).]*

(iv.4) *[Repealed, 2010, c. 17, s. 3(4).]*

(iv.5) *[Repealed, 2010, c. 17, s. 3(4).]*

(v) *[Repealed, 2014, c. 25, s. 23(3).]*

(v.1) *[Repealed, 2010, c. 17, s. 3(4).]*

(v.2) *[Repealed, 2010, c. 17, s. 3(4).]*

(vi) section 233 (infanticide),

(vii) *[Repealed, 2010, c. 17, s. 3(5).]*

(vii.1) section 279.01 (trafficking in persons),

(vii.11) subsection 279.02(1) (material benefit — trafficking),

(vii.12) subsection 279.03(1) (withholding or destroying documents — trafficking),

(viii) section 279.1 (hostage taking),

(viii.1) subsection 286.2(1) (material benefit from sexual services),

(viii.2) subsection 286.3(1) (procuring),

(ix) paragraph 348(1)(*d*) (breaking and entering a dwelling-house),

(x) section 423.1 (intimidation of a justice system participant or journalist),

(xi) section 431 (attack on premises, residence or transport of internationally protected person),

(xii) section 431.1 (attack on premises, accommodation or transport of United Nations or associated personnel),

(xiii) subsection 431.2(2) (explosive or other lethal device),

(xiv) section 467.11 (participation in activities of criminal organization),

(xiv.1) section 467.111 (recruitment of members — criminal organization),

(xv) section 467.12 (commission of offence for criminal organization), and

(xvi) section 467.13 (instructing commission of offence for criminal organization),

(xvi.1) *[Repealed, 2005, c. 25, s. 1(4).]*

(xvii) [*Repealed*, 2005, c. 25, s. 1(4).]

(xviii) [*Repealed*, 2005, c. 25, s. 1(4).]

(xix) [*Repealed*, 2005, c. 25, s. 1(4).]

(xx) [*Repealed*, 2005, c. 25, s. 1(4).]

(*b*) an offence under any of the following provisions of the *Criminal Code*, chapter C-34 of the Revised Statutes of Canada, 1970, as they read from time to time before January 4, 1983, namely,

(i) section 144 (rape),

(i.1) section 145 (attempt to commit rape),

(ii) section 146 (sexual intercourse with female under fourteen and between fourteen and sixteen),

(iii) section 148 (sexual intercourse with feeble-minded, etc.),

(iv) section 149 (indecent assault on female),

(v) section 156 (indecent assault on male),

(vi) section 157 (acts of gross indecency), and

(vii) subsection 246(1) (assault with intent) if the intent is to commit an offence referred to in subparagraphs (i) to (vi),

(*c*) an offence under any of the following provisions of the *Criminal Code*, chapter C-34 of the Revised Statutes of Canada, 1970, as they read from time to time before January 1, 1988:

(i) subsection 146(1) (sexual intercourse with a female under age of 14),

(ii) subsection 146(2) (sexual intercourse with a female between ages of 14 and 16),

(iii) section 153 (sexual intercourse with step-daughter),

(iv) section 157 (gross indecency),

(v) section 166 (parent or guardian procuring defilement), and

(vi) section 167 (householder permitting defilement),

(*c*.01) an offence under any of the following provisions of the *Criminal Code*, chapter C-34 of the Revised Statutes of Canada, 1970, as enacted by section 19 of *An Act to amend the Criminal Code in relation to sexual offences and other offences against the person and to amend certain other Acts in relation thereto or in consequence thereof*, chapter 125 of the Statutes of Canada, 1980-81-82-83:

(i) section 246.1 (sexual assault),

(ii) section 246.2 (sexual assault with a weapon, threats to a third party or causing bodily harm), and

(iii) section 246.3 (aggravated sexual assault),

(*c*.02) an offence under any of the following provisions of this Act, as they read from time to time before the day on which this paragraph comes into force:

(i) paragraph 212(1)(i) (stupefying or overpowering for the purpose of sexual intercourse),

(ii) subsection 212(2) (living on the avails of prostitution of person under 18 years),

(iii) subsection 212(2.1) (aggravated offence in relation to living on the avails of prostitution of person under 18 years), and

(iv) subsection 212(4) (prostitution of person under 18 years),

(*c*.03) an offence under any of paragraphs 212(1)(*a*) to (*h*) (procuring) of this Act, as they read from time to time before the day on which this paragraph comes into force,

(*c*.1) an offence under any of the following provisions of the *Security of Information Act*, namely,

(i) section 6 (approaching, entering, etc., a prohibited place),

(ii) subsection 20(1) (threats or violence), and

(iii) subsection 21(1) (harbouring or concealing), and

(*d*) an attempt to commit or, other than for the purposes of subsection 487.05(1), a conspiracy to commit an offence referred to in any of paragraphs (*a*) to (*c*.03);

"provincial court judge", in relation to a young person, includes a youth court judge within the meaning of subsection 2(1) of the *Youth Criminal Justice Act*;

"secondary designated offence" means an offence, other than a primary designated offence, that is

(*a*) an offence under this Act that may be prosecuted by indictment — or, for section 487.051 to apply, is prosecuted by indictment — for which the maximum punishment is imprisonment for five years or more,

(*b*) an offence under any of the following provisions of the *Controlled Drugs and Substances Act* that may be prosecuted by indictment — or, for section 487.051 to apply, is prosecuted by indictment — for which the maximum punishment is imprisonment for five years or more

   (i) section 5 (trafficking in substance and possession for purpose of trafficking),

   (ii) section 6 (importing and exporting), and

   (iii) section 7 (production of substance),

(*c*) an offence under any of the following provisions of this Act:

   (i) section 145 (escape and being at large without excuse),

   (i.1) section 146 (permitting or assisting escape),

   (i.2) section 147 (rescue or permitting escape),

   (i.3) section 148 (assisting prisoner of war to escape),

   (i.4) and (ii) [*Repealed*, 2010, c. 17, s. 3(10).]

   (iii) subsection 173(1) (indecent acts),

   (iv) section 252 (failure to stop at scene of accident),

   (v) section 264 (criminal harassment),

   (vi) section 264.1 (uttering threats),

   (vii) section 266 (assault),

   (viii) section 270 (assaulting a peace officer),

   (viii.1) subsection 286.1(1) (obtaining sexual services for consideration),

   (ix) paragraph 348(1)(*e*) (breaking and entering a place other than a dwelling-house),

   (x) section 349 (being unlawfully in dwelling-house), and

   (xi) section 423 (intimidation),

(*d*) an offence under any of the following provisions of the *Criminal Code*, as they read from time to time before July 1, 1990:

   (i) section 433 (arson), and

   (ii) section 434 (setting fire to other substance), and

(*e*) an attempt to commit or, other than for the purposes of subsection 487.05(1), a conspiracy to commit

   (i) an offence referred to in paragraph (*a*) or (*b*) — which, for section 487.051 to apply, is prosecuted by indictment, or

   (ii) an offence referred to in paragraph (*c*) or (*d*);

"Young Offenders Act" means chapter Y-1 of the Revised Statutes of Canada, 1985.

"young person" has the meaning assigned by subsection 2(1) of the *Youth Criminal Justice Act* or subsection 2(1) of the *Young Offenders Act*, as the case may be. 1995, c. 27, s. 1; 1998, c. 37, s. 15; 2001, c. 41, s. 17; 2002, c. 1, s. 175; 2005, c. 25, s. 1; 2005, c. 43, ss. 5, 9(2); 2007, c. 22, ss. 2, 8; 2008, c. 6, s. 35, 63(2); 2009, c. 22, s. 16; 2010, c. 3, s. 6; 2010, c. 17, s. 3; 2012, c. 1, s. 30; 2013, c. 9, s. 16; 2013, c. 13, s. 8; 2014, c. 17, s. 13; 2014, c. 25, s. 23; 2015, c. 20, s. 23.

ANNOTATIONS

Although only kidnapping is specifically referenced in brackets in this provision, forcible confinement by reference to s. 279 is also a primary designated offence: *R. v. R. (J.J.)* (2004), 181 C.C.C. (3d) 7 (Ont. C.A.).

INFORMATION FOR WARRANT TO TAKE BODILY SUBSTANCES FOR DNA ANALYSIS / Criteria / Telewarrant.

487.05 (1) A provincial court judge who on *ex parte* application made in Form 5.01 is satisfied by information on oath that there are reasonable grounds to believe

(*a*) **that a designated offence has been committed,**

(*b*) **that a bodily substance has been found or obtained**

   (i) **at the place where the offence was committed,**

   (ii) **on or within the body of the victim of the offence,**

   (iii) **on anything worn or carried by the victim at the time when the offence was committed, or**

   (iv) **on or within the body of any person or thing or at any place associated with the commission of the offence,**

(*c*) **that a person was a party to the offence, and**

(*d*) **that forensic DNA analysis of a bodily substance from the person will provide evidence about whether the bodily substance referred to in paragraph (*b*) was from that person**

and who is satisfied that it is in the best interests of the administration of justice to do so may issue a warrant in Form 5.02 authorizing the taking, from that person, for the purpose of forensic DNA analysis, of any number of samples of one or more bodily substances that is reasonably required for that purpose, by means of the investigative procedures described in subsection 487.06(1).

(2) In considering whether to issue the warrant, the provincial court judge shall have regard to all relevant matters, including

(*a*) **the nature of the designated offence and the circumstances of its commission; and**

(*b*) **whether there is**

   (i) **a peace officer who is able, by virtue of training or experience, to take samples of bodily substances from the person, by means of the investigative procedures described in subsection 487.06(1), or**

   (ii) **another person who is able, by virtue of training or experience, to take, under the direction of a peace officer, samples of bodily substances from the person, by means of those investigative procedures.**

(3) Where a peace officer believes that it would be impracticable to appear personally before a judge to make an application for a warrant under this section, a warrant may be issued under this section on an information submitted by telephone or other means of telecommunication and, for that purpose, section 487.1 applies, with such modifications as the circumstances require, to the warrant. 1995, c. 27, s. 1; 1997, c. 18, s. 44; 1998, c. 37, s. 16.

CROSS-REFERENCES

The terms "provincial court judge", "designated offence", "DNA", and "forensic DNA analysis" are defined in s. 487.04. "Peace officer" is defined in s. 2. Under s. 487.057, the peace officer who is authorized to take or cause to be taken the samples of bodily substances is to make a report to the provincial court judge after the samples have been taken. Section 487.058 protects the peace officer or person acting under the direction of a peace officer from civil liability. Section 487.06(1) sets out those "bodily substances" that may be seized pursuant to a warrant issued under this section. Section 487.06(2) requires the judge to include appropriate terms and conditions. Section 487.07 sets out the special requirements with respect to execution of a warrant obtained under this section. Section 487.08 limits the use of evidence obtained as a result of the execution of a warrant obtained under this section. Section 487.09 contains special directions respecting destruction of bodily substances obtained under the warrant. Section 487.092 provides that a justice may issue a warrant to obtain handprint, fingerprint, footprint, foot impression, teeth impression or other print or impression of the body or any part of the body. Other provisions respecting search warrants include s. 487 [warrant to search for evidence and contraband] and s. 487.01 ["general warrant"]. Under s. 487.3, the judge may make a sealing order.

SYNOPSIS

This section permits a provincial court judge to issue a warrant for the taking of bodily samples for forensic DNA analysis. The judge may issue the warrant where there are reasonable grounds to believe that a designated offence (defined in s. 487.04) has been committed; that a bodily substance has been found or obtained at the scene, on or in the victim or on anything worn or carried by the victim or on or within the body of any person or thing or at any place associated with the commission of the designated offence; the person was a party to the offence; and that forensic DNA analysis of the suspect's bodily substance will provide evidence, in effect, by a comparison of the suspect's DNA with the analysis of the substance associated with the crime. In considering whether to grant the warrant, the judge must consider the nature of the designated offence and the circumstances of its commission and whether there is a peace officer or other person with the necessary training who is able to take the bodily samples from the suspect. The warrant may be obtained through the telewarrant procedure in s. 487.1.

ANNOTATIONS

The DNA warrant provisions under this section and the companion provisions in ss. 487.04 and 487.06 to 487.09 do not violate s. 8 of the *Canadian Charter of Rights and Freedoms*. In particular, there is no need to import a "last resort" requirement. The sections already strike the appropriate balance between the public interest in effective law enforcement and the rights of individuals to control the release of personal information about themselves. Further, the principles of fundamental justice, like the principle against self-incrimination said to be implicated by this section, are more appropriately considered under s. 8. There is no need for a separate s. 7 analysis: *R. v. B. (S.A.)*, [2003] 2 S.C.R. 678, 178 C.C.C. (3d) 193.

Reference to *ex parte* proceedings in this section is not mandatory. Subsection (1) does not deprive a judge of the option of requiring a contested hearing in a suitable case. An issuing judge may find it advisable to require notice to ensure reasonableness and fairness in the circumstances. However, such a hearing is not constitutionally mandated because of the risk that the suspect would take steps to frustrate the proper execution of the warrant: *R. v. B. (S.A.)*, *supra*.

Although this section authorizes an *ex parte* hearing, the judge is not bound to proceed in that manner and could in a proper case require that the accused be served with the application, as where the accused is already in custody: *R. v. F. (S.)* (2000), 141 C.C.C. (3d) 225 (Ont. C.A.). See also *R. v. Feeney* (2001), 152 C.C.C. (3d) 390 (B.C.C.A.).

It was held, in a case where the evidence was seized prior to the enactment of this section, that the taking of hair samples and buccal swabs without prior judicial authorization could not be justified as a search incident to arrest and violated the accused's rights under ss. 7 and 8 of the Charter: *R. v. Stillman*, [1997] 1 S.C.R. 607, 113 C.C.C. (3d) 321.

Where the Crown seeks to adduce novel scientific evidence, the trial judge's function is limited to an overview of the evidence to be satisfied that it reflects a scientific theory or technique that has either gained acceptance in the scientific community or, if not accepted, is considered otherwise reliable in accordance with the methodology validating it. The trial judge is required to hear sufficient evidence to determine reliability as a preliminary matter. The trial judge must not pass judgment on the particular application of the methodology by the expert. That is a question of weight for the jury. In charging the jury as to the weight to be attached to DNA evidence, in addition to the usual instructions concerning expert evidence, the trial judge would be well advised to instruct the jury not to be overwhelmed by the aura of scientific infallibility associated with scientific evidence. The judge should tell the jurors to use their common sense in their assessment of all of the evidence on the DNA issue and determine if it is reliable and valid as a piece of circumstantial evidence: *R. v. Terceira* (1998), 123 C.C.C. (3d) 1 (Ont. C.A.), affd [1999] 3 S.C.R. 866, 142 C.C.C. (3d) 95.

ORDER — PRIMARY DESIGNATED OFFENCES / Order — primary designated offences / Order — persons found not criminally responsible and secondary designated offences / Order to offender

487.051 (1) The court shall make an order in Form 5.03 authorizing the taking of the number of samples of bodily substances that is reasonably required for the purpose of forensic DNA analysis from a person who is convicted, discharged under section 730 or found guilty under the *Youth Criminal Justice Act* or the *Young Offenders Act*, of an offence committed at any time, including before June 30, 2000, if that offence is a primary designated offence within the meaning of paragraphs (*a*) and (*c.02*) of the definition "primary designated offence" in section 487.04 when the person is sentenced or discharged.

(2) The court shall make such an order in Form 5.03 in relation to a person who is convicted, discharged under section 730 or found guilty under the *Youth Criminal Justice Act* or the *Young Offenders Act*, of an offence committed at any time, including before June 30, 2000, if that offence is a primary designated offence within the meaning of any of paragraphs (*a.1*) to (*c.01*) and (*c.03*) to (*d*) of the definition "primary designated offence" in section 487.04 when the person is sentenced or discharged. However, the court is not required to make the order if it is satisfied that the person has established that the impact of such an order on their privacy and security of the person would be grossly disproportionate to the public interest in the protection of society and the proper administration of justice, to be achieved through the early detection, arrest and conviction of offenders.

(3) The court may, on application by the prosecutor and if it is satisfied that it is in the best interests of the administration of justice to do so, make such an order in Form 5.04 in relation to

> **(*a*) a person who is found not criminally responsible on account of mental disorder for an offence committed at any time, including before June 30, 2000, if that offence is a designated offence when the finding is made; or**
>
> **(*b*) a person who is convicted, discharged under section 730 or found guilty under the *Youth Criminal Justice Act* or the *Young Offenders Act*, of an offence committed at any time, including before June 30, 2000, if that offence is a secondary designated offence when the person is sentenced or discharged.**

In deciding whether to make the order, the court shall consider the person's criminal record, whether they were previously found not criminally responsible on account of mental disorder for a designated offence, the nature of the offence, the circumstances surrounding its commission and the impact such an order would have on the person's privacy and security of the person and shall give reasons for its decision.

(4) When the court makes an order authorizing the taking of samples of bodily substances, it may make an order in Form 5.041 to require the person to report at the place, day and time set out in the order and submit to the taking of the samples. 1998, c. 37, s. 17; 2002, c. 1, s. 176; 2005, c. 25, s. 3; 2007, c. 22, s. 9; 2014, c. 25, s. 24.

CROSS-REFERENCES

The terms "designated offence", "primary designated offence", "secondary designated offence", "DNA", "forensic DNA analysis", and "young person" are defined in s. 487.04. Section 487.05 allows for the issuance of a warrant to obtain bodily samples for forensic DNA analysis in the course of an investigation.

SYNOPSIS

This section and ss. 487.052 to 487.091 create the scheme for collecting bodily substances from offenders for forensic DNA analysis and storage of the results in the national DNA data bank established under the *DNA Identification Act*, S.C. 1998, c. 37. The foundation provisions are: this section, which gives the court that finds the adult or young offender guilty or not criminally responsible of certain offences the power to authorize the taking of the bodily substances, including the power in respect of offenders convicted of certain offences committed before June 30, 2000 when s. 5(1) of the *DNA Identification Act* came into force, and which directs the Solicitor General of Canada, for criminal identification purposes, to establish a national DNA data bank, consisting of a crime scene index and a convicted offenders index, to be maintained by the Commissioner of the R.C.M.P.; and s. 487.055, which gives a provincial court judge, on *ex parte* application, the power to authorize the taking of bodily substances for forensic DNA analysis from certain offenders who had previously been convicted of certain serious offences and are still serving sentence. These sections and the related provisions for implementing the scheme are summarized below.

Under this section, the nature of the power to order the taking of bodily substances for forensic DNA analysis depends on the offence of which the person was found guilty.

The order shall be made if the person was convicted of a primary designated offence as defined in paras. (*a*) and (*c*.02) of the definition of primary designated offence in s. 487.04, such as aggravated sexual assault whether or not the offence was committed before June 30, 2000. For primary designated offences defined in paras. (*a*.1) to (*d*) of the definition of primary designated offences, such as sexual assault, the order is also to be made, whether or not the offence was committed before June 30, 2000, but subject to the discretion described in subsec. (2), where the impact on a person's privacy and security of the person is grossly disproportionate to the public interest in the protection of society and the proper administration of justice, to be achieved through the early detection, arrest and conviction of offenders.

The order may be made if the person was found not criminally responsible on account of mental disorder for a primary or secondary designated offence committed at any time or convicted or found guilty of a secondary designated offence (also defined in s. 487.04), whether or not committed before June 30, 2000, and the court is satisfied that it is in the best interests of justice. In deciding whether to make the order, the court is directed under subsec. (3) to consider the offender's record, whether the person was previously found not criminally responsible on account of mental disorder, the nature of the offence, the circumstances surrounding its commission and the impact on the offender's privacy and security of the person. The court is required to give reasons for the decision.

The order is to be made at the time of disposition or, if the court did not consider the matter at that time, it shall within 90 days set a date for a hearing to do so, pursuant to s. 487.053.

Pursuant to s. 487.054, the decision of the court under s. 487.051 may be appealed by the offender or the prosecutor as the case may be. Section 487.056 sets out when the order is to be executed and allows for the issuing of a warrant if the person fails to appear as required.

Section 487.055 deals with persons who were convicted prior to these provisions coming into force. It allows for an *ex parte* application to a provincial court judge for authorization to take bodily substances for the purpose of forensic DNA analysis from persons (a) declared to be dangerous offenders; (b) dangerous offenders or dangerous sexual offenders under the former legislation; (c) convicted of murder; (c.1) convicted of attempted murder, or conspiracy to commit murder or to cause another person to be murdered and, on the date of the application, is serving a sentence of imprisonment for that offence; (d) convicted of a sexual offence and, on the date of the application, is serving a sentence of imprisonment for that offence; or (e) convicted of manslaughter and, on the date of the application, is serving a sentence of imprisonment for that offence. "Sexual offence" for this purpose is defined in s. 487.055(3). The application must be accompanied by a certificate under s. 667(1)(*a*) as proof of the finding or conviction as the case may be. In deciding whether to grant the authorization, the judge is to consider, under s. 487.055(3.1), the offender's criminal record, the nature of the offence and the circumstances surrounding its commission, and the impact on the offender's privacy and security of the person and is to give reasons for the decision. Although the application under subsec. (1) may be made *ex parte*, the section contemplates that the offender may be given notice. If so, and the person wishes to attend, subsec. (3.01) provides for attendance by closed-circuit television or similar means. If the offender is on conditional release, a summons may issue directing the offender to attend at the specified time and place for the purpose of submitting to the taking of the samples (subsecs. (3.11) and (4)). The summons is to be accompanied by a copy of the authorization and is to be served by a peace officer in the manner directed by subsec. (5). If the offender does not report as required, a justice of the peace may issue a warrant for the person's arrest pursuant to subsec. (8). Section 487.0551 allows for the issuing of a warrant to a person who fails to appear in accordance with an order or warrant made under these provisions. And, s. 487.0552 makes it an offence to fail, without reasonable excuse, to comply with an order or summons as the case may be.

Section 487.091 provides that, if a DNA profile could not be derived from the bodily substances obtained in execution of an order made under s. 487.051 or an authorization under s. 487.055, an *ex parte* application may be made to a provincial court judge for authorization to take further samples. The application must state the reasons why the DNA profile could not be derived. Section 487.055(5) and (6) apply, with the necessary modifications, so as to obtain the samples from a person who is not in custody. Thus, a summons may be issued to require the offender to attend for the taking of the samples and, if necessary, a justice of the peace may issue a warrant for that purpose.

Section 487.056 sets out when and where the sample is to be taken, depending upon the provision under which the order was made. Under s. 487.056(6), the samples of bodily substances are to be taken by a peace officer, or another person acting under the direction of a peace officer who is able by virtue of training or experience to take the samples. The peace officer is then required under s. 487.057 to make a written report as soon as is feasible after the samples have been taken. The report is to be filed with the court that made the order, or the provincial court judge who granted the authorization, as the case may be, and include the time and date that the samples were taken and a description of the bodily substances that were taken. The peace officer and the person acting under the officer's direction are protected from civil and criminal liability under s. 487.058 for anything necessarily done with reasonable care and skill in the taking of the samples in execution of the order or authorization. Section 487.06(1) sets out the means by which the bodily substances may be taken, namely, plucking of hairs, taking of buccal swabs or the taking of blood by a shallow pricking of the skin. Section 487.06(2) directs the court or provincial court judge to include terms or conditions that the judge or court considers advisable to ensure that the taking of the samples is reasonable in the circumstances. Under s. 487.06(3) the peace officer may also take fingerprints from the persons for the purpose of the *DNA Identification Act*. (Section 5(5)(*b*) of that Act provides that the profile in the convicted offenders index of the DNA data bank shall contain information as to the identity of the person from whose bodily substance the profile was derived.) Before taking the samples, the peace officer is, pursuant to s. 487.071, to verify that the DNA data bank does not already contain the person's DNA profile and, if it is already in the convicted offenders' index, the bodily sample is not to be taken. Before taking the sample the officer is to inform the offender of the matters set forth in s. 487.07(1), such as the means by which the samples will be taken, the purpose of taking the samples, and the contents of the authorization or order. Under subsec. (2), the offender may be detained for the purpose of taking the substances for a reasonable period and may be required to accompany the peace officer for that purpose. The peace officer is also to take reasonable steps to ensure the person's privacy while the samples are being taken. There are special provisions in s. 487.07(4) and (5) in the case of young persons.

The bodily samples and a copy of the order or authorization are to be transmitted to the Commissioner of the R.C.M.P. for entry into the convicted offenders index of the national DNA data bank (s. 487.071(3)). (Under s. 10(1) of the *DNA Identification Act*, the Commissioner shall safely and securely store, for the purpose of forensic DNA analysis, the portions of the samples of the bodily substances that the Commissioner considers appropriate and, without delay, destroy any remaining portions. Under subsec. (2), forensic DNA analysis of stored bodily substances may be performed if the Commissioner is of the opinion that the analysis is justified because significant technological advances have been made since the time when a DNA profile of the person who provided the bodily substances, or from whom they were taken, was last derived.) Section 487.08(1.1) limits the use of bodily substances taken pursuant to an order or authorization to use for forensic DNA analysis or to transmit any unused portions to the Commissioner. Contravention of these provisions is a Crown-option offence pursuant to s. 487.08(4).

Section 487.09 provides for the destruction of bodily substances or removal of electronic records in certain circumstances, as where the person has been finally acquitted of the designated offence. However, subsec. (2) provides that a provincial court judge may order that the bodily substances or results of the analyses not be destroyed if they might reasonably be required in an investigation or prosecution. Under subsec. (3), bodily substances that were provided voluntarily are to be destroyed and the results of the analysis destroyed where it is determined that the profile did not match the substance found at the place referred to in s. 487.05(1)(*b*), for example the scene of the offence. Section 487.091 allows a provincial court judge to make an *ex parte* order authorizing the taking of additional samples where, among other things, it was not possible to obtain a DNA profile from the original samples.

ANNOTATIONS

Note: Some of the cases cited below were decided prior to the amendments to this section.

The risk of re-offence is not a prerequisite to the making of an order: *R. v. Durham* (2007), 221 C.C.C. (3d) 304 (B.C.C.A.).

Strictly speaking there is no burden on either Crown or defence under [now] subsec. (3)(*b*). However, as the party seeking the order, the Crown bears an evidential burden to produce sufficient information to raise the issue. The trial judge must then be satisfied after weighing and balancing all the relevant considerations that the order should be made: *R. v. Hendry* (2001), 161 C.C.C. (3d) 275, 48 C.R. (5th) 310 (Ont. C.A.).

In cases falling under [now] subsec. (3)(*b*), the trial judge is to make the order sought if satisfied that it is in the best interests of the administration of justice to do so. The court is instructed to consider the offender's criminal record, the nature of the offence and the circumstances surrounding its commission, and the impact on the person's privacy and security of the person. Given an adult offender's diminished expectation of privacy following conviction, the minimal intrusion into the security of the person in the ordinary case and the important interests served by the DNA data bank, it will usually be in the best interests of the administration of justice for the judge to make the order: *R. v. Hendry supra.*

An order may be grossly disproportionate if the circumstances of the particular offender or the offence or risk of breach of privacy or security of the person varied markedly from the usual cases contemplated by the scheme. The order should be refused only if the imposition of terms and conditions of the authorizing order would not adequately restore the appropriate balance. In balancing law enforcement objectives with the person's privacy interests, regard should be had to the offender's criminal record, the nature of the offence and the specific risk of misuse or of particular dangers to the health of the offender: *R. v. Jordan* (2002), 162 C.C.C. (3d) 385, 1 C.R. (6th) 141 (N.S.C.A.).

For the purposes of [now] subsec. (2)(*b*), criminal record includes a youth court record: *R. v. S. (O.S.)* (2002), 168 C.C.C. (3d) 360, 317 A.R. 163 (C.A.).

Although the public interest is presumed to outweigh privacy interests in the case of primary designated offences, in [now] subsec. (2), that subsection recognizes that this is a rebuttable presumption. In balancing the privacy interest against the public interest, regard should be had to the criminal record of the offender, the nature of the offence, the circumstances surrounding its commission and the impact on the offender's privacy and security of the person. The offender must establish that the public interest is clearly and substantially outweighed by the individual's privacy and security interests. The purposes and principles set out in the *Youth Criminal Justice Act*, S.C. 2002, c. 1, should be considering in determining whether an order should be granted: *R. v. C. (R.W.)* (2005), 201 C.C.C. (3d) 321, 32 C.R. (6th) 201 (S.C.C.).

The words "best interests of the administration of justice" do not import a requirement that the order can only be made where there are reasonable and probable grounds to believe that a further offence will be committed where the offender's DNA will be of assistance in proving the case. The application of the provision requires a balancing between the competing rights of society and the interests of the accused. The state's interest is not simply detection of crime, but includes deterrence of potential repeat offenders, promotion of safety of the community, detecting the work of a serial offender, assistance in solving "cold crimes", streamlining investigations and assisting the innocent by early exclusion from investigative suspicion: *R. v. Briggs* (2001), 157 C.C.C. (3d) 38, 45 C.R. (5th) 99 (Ont. C.A.), leave to appeal to S.C.C. refused [2002] 2 S.C.R. v, 162 C.C.C. (3d) vi.

The judge may consider offences committed by the offender both before and after the commission of the designated offence. The existence of DNA at the scene of the offence is not necessarily a relevant consideration: *R. v. Briggs, supra*.

It was held, considering the predecessor to this section, that the Court of Appeal is not "the court" within the meaning of this section. Although the Court of Appeal had substituted a conviction for second degree murder, it did not become the "convicting" court for the purpose of this section: *R. v. Bellegarde* (2003), 181 C.C.C. (3d) 69, [2004] 5 W.W.R. 459 (Sask. C.A.).

It was held that the predecessor to this section allowing for taking of samples from a person convicted before June 30, 2000 did not offend ss. 7, 9 or 11(*i*) of the Charter: *R. v. Murrins* (2002), 162 C.C.C. (3d) 412, 1 C.R. (6th) 166 (N.S.C.A.). See also *R. v. Ku* (2002), 169 C.C.C. (3d) 535, 7 C.R. (6th) 241 (B.C.C.A.), leave to appeal to S.C.C. refused [2003] 3 S.C.R. vii, 178 C.C.C. (3d) vi.

This section does not offend ss. 7 or 8 of the Charter in its application to young offenders: *R. v. S. (C.)* (2011), 269 C.C.C. (3d) 431 (Ont. C.A.).

487.052 [*Repealed*, 2005, c. 25, s. 4; 2007, c. 22, s. 3.]

TIMING OF ORDER / Hearing.

487.053 (1) The court may make an order under section 487.051 authorizing the taking of samples of bodily substances when it imposes a sentence on a person, finds the person not criminally responsible on account of mental disorder or directs that they be discharged under section 730.

(2) If the court does not consider the matter at that time, it

   (a) shall, within 90 days after the day on which it imposes the sentence, makes the finding or directs that the person be discharged, set a date for a hearing to do so;

   (b) retains jurisdiction over the matter; and

   (c) may require the person to appear by closed-circuit television or any other means that allows the court and the person to engage in simultaneous visual and oral communication, as long as the person is given the opportunity to communicate privately with counsel if they are represented by counsel. 1998, c. 37, s. 17; 2000, c. 10, s. 14; 2005, c. 25, s. 4; 2007, c. 22, s. 3.

SYNOPSIS

For a synopsis of this and the related sections, see the synopsis under s. 487.051.

APPEAL.

487.054 The offender or the prosecutor may appeal from a decision of the court under any of subsections 487.051(1) to (3). 1998, c. 37, s. 17; 2007, c. 22, s. 10.

CROSS-REFERENCES

See cross-references under s. 487.051.

SYNOPSIS

For a synopsis of this and the related sections, see the synopsis under s. 487.051. For a synopsis of the provisions for DNA warrants, see the editor's note preceding s. 487.04.

ANNOTATIONS

The appeal route follows the scheme in the *Criminal Code* generally. That is, in indictable proceedings the appeal from the making or refusal to make the order lies to the Court of Appeal and in summary conviction proceedings the appeal is taken in accordance with Part XXVII of the *Criminal Code*. The appeal court has the power to make the order that should have been made by the trial court: *R. v. Hendry* (2001), 161 C.C.C. (3d) 275, 48 C.R. (5th) 310 (Ont. C.A.). See also *R. v. R. (B.)* (2011), 274 C.C.C. (3d) 490 (Nfld. & Lab. C.A.).

There is no jurisdiction to stay a DNA order pending an appeal from conviction: *R. v. Zurowski* (2003), 175 C.C.C. (3d) 494, [2003] 9 W.W.R. 400 (Alta. C.A.), motion to quash dismissed 183 C.C.C. (3d) 448 (S.C.C.). *Contra R. v. Briggs* (2001), 53 O.R. (3d) 124 (C.A.), leave to appeal to S.C.C. refused 154 O.A.C. 198n.

A DNA order is a discretionary decision that is entitled to deference on appeal: *R. v. Briggs* (2001), 157 C.C.C. (3d) 38, 45 C.R. (5th) 99 (Ont. C.A.), leave to appeal to S.C.C. refused 162 C.C.C. (3d) vi, 91 C.R.R. (2d) 187n.

In cases under [now] s. 487.051(2) and (3), absent an error in principle, failure to consider a relevant factor, or an overemphasis of the appropriate factors, a court of appeal should only intervene to vary a decision to either make or refuse to make a DNA data bank order if the decision was clearly unreasonable: *R. v. Hendry, supra.*

OFFENDERS SERVING SENTENCES / Certificate / Definition of "sexual offence" / Manner of appearance / Criteria / Order / Summons / Service on individual.

487.055 (1) A provincial court judge may, on *ex parte* application made in Form 5.05, authorize in Form 5.06 the taking, for the purpose of forensic DNA analysis, of any number of samples of bodily substances that is reasonably required for that purpose, by means of the investigative procedures described in subsection 487.06(1), from a person who, before June 30, 2000,

    (a) **had been declared a dangerous offender under Part XXIV;**

    (b) **had been declared a dangerous offender or a dangerous sexual offender under Part XXI of the *Criminal Code*, being chapter C-34 of the Revised Statutes of Canada, 1970, as it read from time to time before January 1, 1988;**

    (c) **had been convicted of murder;**

  (c.1) **had been convicted of attempted murder or conspiracy to commit murder or to cause another person to be murdered and, on the date of the application, is serving a sentence of imprisonment for that offence;**

    (d) **had been convicted of a sexual offence within the meaning of subsection (3) and, on the date of the application, is serving a sentence of imprisonment for that offence; or** (*e*) had been convicted of manslaughter and, on the date of the application, is serving a sentence of imprisonment for that offence.

(2) The application shall be accompanied by a certificate referred to in paragraph 667(1)(*a*) that establishes that the person is a person referred to in subsection (1). The certificate may be received in evidence without giving the notice referred to in subsection 667(4).

(3) For the purposes of subsection (1), "sexual offence" means

    (*a*) an offence under any of the following provisions, namely,

        (i) section 151 (sexual interference),

        (ii) section 152 (invitation to sexual touching),

        (iii) section 153 (sexual exploitation),

        (iv) section 155 (incest),

        (v) subsection 212(4) (offence in relation to juvenile prostitution),

        (vi) section 271 (sexual assault),

        (vii) section 272 (sexual assault with a weapon, threats to a third party or causing bodily harm), and

        (viii) section 273 (aggravated sexual assault);

  (*a*.1) an offence under subsection 348(1) if the indictable offence referred to in that subsection is a sexual offence within the meaning of paragraph (*a*), (*b*), (*c*) or (*d*);

    (*b*) an offence under any of the following provisions of the *Criminal Code*, chapter C-34 of the Revised Statutes of Canada, 1970, as they read from time to time before January 4, 1983, namely,

        (i) section 144 (rape),

        (ii) section 146 (sexual intercourse with female under fourteen or between fourteen and sixteen),

        (iii) section 148 (sexual intercourse with feeble-minded, etc.),

        (iv) section 149 (indecent assault on female),

        (v) section 156 (indecent assault on male), or

        (vi) section 157 (acts of gross indecency);

    (*c*) an offence under paragraph 153(1)(*a*) (sexual intercourse with step-daughter, etc.) of the *Criminal Code*, chapter C-34 of the Revised Statutes of Canada, 1970, as it read from time to time before January 1, 1988; and

    (*d*) an attempt to commit an offence referred to in any of paragraphs (*a*) to (*c*).

(3.01) The court may require a person who is given notice of an application under subsection (1) and who wishes to appear at the hearing to appear by closed-circuit television or any other means that allows the court and the person to engage in simultaneous visual and oral communication, as long as the person is given the opportunity to communicate privately with counsel if they are represented by counsel.

(3.1) In deciding whether to grant an authorization under subsection (1), the court shall consider the person's criminal record, the nature of the offence and the circumstances surrounding its commission and the impact such an authorization would have on the privacy and security of the person and shall give reasons for its decision.

(3.11) If the court authorizes the taking of samples of bodily substances from a person who is on conditional release and who has appeared at the hearing, it shall make an order in Form 5.041 to require the person to report at the place, day and time set out in the order and submit to the taking of the samples.

(4) However, if a person who is on conditional release has not appeared at the hearing, a summons in Form 5.061 setting out the information referred to in paragraphs 487.07(1)(*b*) to (*d*) shall be directed to them requiring them to report at the place, day and time set out in the summons and submit to the taking of the samples.

(5) The summons shall be accompanied by a copy of the authorization referred to in subsection (1) and be served by a peace officer who shall either deliver it personally to the person to whom it is directed or, if that person cannot conveniently be found, leave it for the person at their latest or usual place of residence with any person found there who appears to be at least sixteen years of age. 1998, c. 37, s. 17; 2000, c. 10, s. 15; 2005, c. 25, s. 5; 2007, c. 22, s. 11; 2008, c. 18, s. 13.

(6) [*Repealed*, 2008, c. 18, s. 13.]

(7) to (10) [*Repealed*, 2007, c. 22, s. 11(4).]

CROSS-REFERENCES

"Prosecutor" and "peace officer" are defined in s. 2. "Forensic DNA analysis" and "provincial court judge" are defined in s. 487.04. Also, see cross-references under s. 487.051.

SYNOPSIS

For a synopsis of this and the related sections, see the synopsis under s. 487.051.

ANNOTATIONS

It was held that the predecessor to this section, which also permitted an *ex parte* application, is clear and unambiguous and there is no requirement that the judge consider giving notice to the offender. Further, the section does not infringe either ss. 7 or 8 of the *Charter of Rights and Freedoms* and, since the taking of DNA samples is not a punishment, the retroactive application of the provision does not infringe ss. 11(*h*) or 11(*i*) of the Charter: *R. v. Rodgers* (2006), 207 C.C.C. (3d) 225, 37 C.R. (6th) 1 (S.C.C.).

Although there is no appeal from an order under this section, the decision of the judge is reviewable on *certiorari*: *R. v. Rodgers, supra*.

FAILURE TO APPEAR / Execution of warrant.

487.0551 (1) If a person fails to appear at the place, day and time set out in an order made under subsection 487.051(4) or 487.055(3.11) or in a summons referred to in subsection 487.055(4) or 487.091(3), a justice of the peace may issue a warrant for their arrest in Form 5.062 to allow samples of bodily substances to be taken.

(2) The warrant may be executed anywhere in Canada by a peace officer who has jurisdiction in that place or over the person. The warrant remains in force until it is executed. 2007, c. 22, s. 12.

CROSS-REFERENCES

"Peace officer" is defined in s. 2.

SYNOPSIS

For a synopsis of this and the related sections, see the synopsis under s. 487.051.

FAILURE TO COMPLY WITH ORDER OR SUMMONS / For greater certainty

487.0552 (1) Every person who, without reasonable excuse, fails to comply with an order made under subsection 487.051(4) or 487.055(3.11) of this Act or under subsection 196.14(4) or 196.24(4) of the *National Defence Act*, or with a summons referred to in subsection 487.055(4) or 487.091(3) of this Act, is guilty of

  (*a*) an indictable offence and liable to imprisonment for a term of not more than two years; or

  (*b*) an offence punishable on summary conviction.

(2) For greater certainty, a lawful command that prevents a person from complying with an order or summons is a reasonable excuse if, at the time, the person is subject to the Code of Service Discipline within the meaning of subsection 2(1) of the *National Defence Act*. 2007, c. 22, s. 12.

SYNOPSIS

For a synopsis of this and the related sections, see the synopsis under s. 487.051.

WHEN COLLECTION TO TAKE PLACE / When collection to take place / When collection to take place / Appeal / Collection of samples / Who collects samples.

487.056 (1) Samples of bodily substances shall be taken as authorized under section 487.051

    (a) **at the place, day and time set out in an order made under subsection 487.051(4) or as soon as feasible afterwards; or**

    (b) **in any other case, on the day on which the order authorizing the taking of the samples is made or as soon as feasible afterwards.**

(2) Samples of bodily substances shall be taken as authorized under section 487.055 or 487.091

    (a) **at the place, day and time set out in an order made under subsection 487.055(3.11) or a summons referred to in subsection 487.055(4) or 487.091(3) or as soon as feasible afterwards; or**

    (b) **in any other case, as soon as feasible after the authorization is granted.**

(3) If a person fails to appear as required by an order made under subsection 487.051(4) or 487.055(3.11) or a summons referred to in subsection 487.055(4) or 487.091(3), samples of bodily substances shall be taken

    (a) **when the person is arrested under a warrant issued under subsection 487.0551(1) or as soon as feasible afterwards; or**

    (b) **as soon as feasible after the person appears at the place set out in the order or summons if no warrant is issued.**

(4) Subsections (1) to (3) apply even if the order or authorization to take the samples of bodily substances is appealed.

(5) A peace officer who is authorized under section 487.051, 487.055 or 487.091 to take samples of bodily substances may cause the samples to be taken in any place in Canada in which the person who is subject to the order or authorization is located.

(6) The samples shall be taken by a peace officer who has jurisdiction over the person or in the place in which the samples are taken — or a person acting under their direction — who is able, by virtue of training or experience, to take them. 1998, c. 37, s. 17; 2000, c. 10, s. 16; 2002, c. 1, s. 179; 2005, c. 25, s. 6; 2007, c. 22, s. 13.

CROSS-REFERENCES

"Peace officer" is defined in s. 2. Under s. 487.057, after taking the samples, the peace officer is to make a written report. Section 487.058 protects the peace officer and the person acting under the officer's direction from civil and criminal liability. Also, see cross-references under s. 487.051.

SYNOPSIS

For a synopsis of this and the related sections, see the synopsis under s. 487.051.

ANNOTATIONS

There is no jurisdiction to stay a DNA order pending an appeal from conviction: *R. v. Zurowski* (2003), 175 C.C.C. (3d) 494, [2003] 9 W.W.R. 400 (Alta. C.A.), motion to quash dismissed February 9, 2004, Court File No. 30074, S.C.C. *Contra R. v. Briggs* (2001), 53

O.R. (3d) 124, 142 O.A.C. 41 (C.A.), leave to appeal to S.C.C. refused 154 O.A.C. 198*n*. See also *R. v. Gibson* (2011), 277 C.C.C. (3d) 247 (B.C.S.C.), holding that subsec. (4) does not remove a superior court's inherent jurisdiction to grant a stay of a DNA order pending a conviction appeal.

REPORT OF PEACE OFFICER / Contents of report / Copy of report.

487.057 (1) A peace officer who takes samples of bodily substances from a person or who causes a person who is not a peace officer to take samples under their direction shall, as soon as feasible after the samples are taken, make a written report in Form 5.07 and cause the report to be filed with

    (*a*) the provincial court judge who issued the warrant under section 487.05 or granted the authorization under section 487.055 or 487.091 or another judge of that provincial court; or

    (*b*) the court that made the order under section 487.051.

(2) The report shall include

    (*a*) a statement of the time and date the samples were taken; and

    (*b*) a description of the bodily substances that were taken.

(3) A peace officer who takes the samples or causes the samples to be taken under their direction at the request of another peace officer shall send a copy of the report to the other peace officer unless that other peace officer had jurisdiction to take the samples. 1998, c. 37, s. 17; 2000, c. 10, s. 17; 2007, c. 22, s. 14.

CROSS-REFERENCES

"Peace officer" is defined in s. 2. Also, see cross-references under s. 487.051.

SYNOPSIS

For a synopsis of this and the related sections with respect to taking of samples from persons found guilty of certain offences, see the synopsis under s. 487.051.

NO CRIMINAL OR CIVIL LIABILITY.

487.058 No peace officer, and no person acting under a peace officer's direction, incurs any criminal or civil liability for anything necessarily done with reasonable care and skill in the taking of samples of bodily substances from a person under a warrant issued under section 487.05, an order made under section 487.051 or an authorization granted under section 487.055 or 487.091. 1998, c. 37, s. 17; 2000; c. 10, s. 18; 2007, c. 22, s. 15.

CROSS-REFERENCES

"Peace officer" is defined in s. 2. For other cross-references see ss. 487.05 and 487.051.

SYNOPSIS

For a synopsis of this and the related sections with respect to taking of samples for forensic DNA analysis from persons found guilty of certain offences, see the synopsis under s. 487.051.

INVESTIGATIVE PROCEDURES / Terms and conditions / Fingerprints.

487.06 (1) A peace officer or a person acting under a peace officer's direction is authorized by a warrant issued under section 487.05, an order made under section 487.051 or an authorization granted under section 487.055 or 487.091 to take samples of bodily substances by any of the following means:

    (*a*) the plucking of individual hairs from the person, including the root sheath;

   (*b*) the taking of buccal swabs by swabbing the lips, tongue and inside cheeks of the mouth to collect epithelial cells; or

   (*c*) the taking of blood by pricking the skin surface with a sterile lancet.

(2) The warrant, order or authorization shall include any terms and conditions that the provincial court judge or court, as the case may be, considers advisable to ensure that the taking of the samples authorized by the warrant, order or authorization is reasonable in the circumstances.

(3) A peace officer who is authorized to take samples of bodily substances from a person by an order made under section 487.051 or an authorization granted under section 487.055 or 487.091, or a person acting under their direction, may take fingerprints from the person for the purpose of the *DNA Identification Act*. 1995, c. 27, s. 1; 1998, c. 37, s. 18; 2000, c. 10, s. 19; 2007, c. 22, s. 16.

CROSS-REFERENCES

The term "provincial court judge" is defined in s. 487.04. "Peace officer" is defined in s. 2. Section 487.05 sets out the circumstances in which a provincial court judge may issue a warrant to seize the bodily substances referred to in this section for forensic DNA analysis. Section 487.07 sets out the special requirements with respect to execution of a warrant obtained under this section. Section 487.08 limits the use of evidence obtained as a result of the execution of a warrant obtained under this section. Section 487.09 contains special directions respecting destruction of bodily substances obtained under the warrant. Section 487.091 provides that a justice may issue a warrant to obtain handprint, fingerprint, footprint, foot impression, teeth impression or other print or impression of the body or any part of the body. Other provisions respecting search warrants include s. 487 [warrant to search for evidence and contraband] and s. 487.01 ["general warrant"]. For other cross-references respecting search warrants, see notes following s. 487. For other cross-references with respect to taking of samples from persons found guilty of certain offences, see the cross-references under s. 487.051.

SYNOPSIS

For a synopsis of this and the related sections with respect to taking of samples for forensic DNA analysis from persons found guilty of certain offences, see the synopsis under s. 487.051.

ANNOTATIONS

This provision does not violate s. 7 of the Charter: *R. v. Ku* (2002), 169 C.C.C. (3d) 535, 7 C.R. (6th) 241 (B.C.C.A.), leave to appeal to S.C.C. refused 178 C.C.C. (3d) vi. See also *R. v. F. (S.)* (2000), 141 C.C.C. (3d) 225, 32 C.R. (5th) 79 (Ont. C.A.), which upheld the constitutional validity of the predecessor to this section.

DUTY TO INFORM / Detention of person / Respect of privacy / Execution of warrant against young person / Waiver of rights of young person.

487.07 (1) Before taking samples of bodily substances from a person, or causing samples to be taken under their direction, in execution of a warrant issued under section 487.05 or an order made under section 487.051 or under an authorization granted under section 487.055 or 487.091, a peace officer shall inform the person of

   (*a*) the contents of the warrant, order or authorization;

   (*b*) the nature of the investigative procedures by means of which the samples are to be taken;

   (*c*) the purpose of taking the samples;

   (*d*) the authority of the peace officer and any other person under the direction of the peace officer to use as much force as is necessary for the purpose of taking the samples; and

(*d*.1) [*Repealed*, 2000, c. 10, s. 20(2).]
  (*e*) in the case of samples of bodily substances taken in execution of a warrant,
     (i) the possibility that the results of forensic DNA analysis may be used in evidence, and
     (ii) if the sample is taken from a young person, the rights of the young person under subsection (4).

(2) A person from whom samples of bodily substances are to be taken may
  (*a*) be detained for that purpose for a period that is reasonable in the circumstances; and
  (*b*) be required to accompany a peace officer for that purpose.

(3) A peace officer who takes samples of bodily substances from a person, or a person who takes such samples under the direction of a peace officer, shall ensure that the person's privacy is respected in a manner that is reasonable in the circumstances.

(4) A young person against whom a warrant is executed has, in addition to any other rights arising from his or her detention under the warrant,
  (*a*) the right to a reasonable opportunity to consult with, and
  (*b*) the right to have the warrant executed in the presence of
counsel and a parent or, in the absence of a parent, an adult relative or, in the absence of a parent and an adult relative, any other appropriate adult chosen by the young person.

(5) A young person may waive his or her rights under subsection (4) but any such waiver
  (*a*) must be recorded on audio tape or video tape or otherwise; or
  (*b*) must be made in writing and contain a statement signed by the young person that he or she has been informed of the right being waived. 1995, c. 27, ss. 1 and 3; 1998, c. 37, s. 19; 2000, c. 10, s. 20; 2007, c. 22, s. 17.

CROSS-REFERENCES

The terms "young person", "adult", "DNA" and "forensic DNA analysis" are defined in s. 487.04. "Peace officer" is defined in s. 2. Section 487.05 sets out the circumstances in which a provincial court judge may issue a warrant to seize bodily substances for forensic DNA analysis. Section 487.06(1) sets out those "bodily substances" that may be seized pursuant to a warrant issued under s. 487.05. Section 487.06(2) requires the judge to include appropriate terms and conditions. Section 487.08 limits the use of evidence obtained as a result of the execution of a warrant obtained under this section. Section 487.09 contains special directions respecting destruction of bodily substances obtained under the warrant. Section 487.091 provides that a justice may issue a warrant to obtain handprint, fingerprint, footprint, foot impression, teeth impression o r other print or impression of the body or any part of the body. A warrant is executed in accordance with s. 29. Where a person is detained, the peace officer must comply with the provisions of s. 10 of the Charter, subject to reasonable limitations as permitted by s. 1 of the Charter. For protection of persons executing warrants, see ss. 25 to 28.

   Other provisions respecting search warrants include s. 487 [warrant to search for evidence and contraband] and s. 487.01 ["general warrant"]. For other cross-references respecting search warrants, see notes following s. 487. Also, see cross-references under s. 487.051.

SYNOPSIS

For a synopsis of this and the related sections with respect to taking of samples for forensic DNA analysis from persons found guilty of certain offences, see the synopsis under s. 487.051.

VERIFICATION / DNA profile in data bank / DNA profile not in data bank.

487.071 (1) Before taking samples of bodily substances from a person under an order made under section 487.051 or an authorization granted under section 487.055 or 487.091, a peace officer, or a person acting under their direction, shall verify whether the convicted offenders index of the national DNA data bank, established under the *DNA Identification Act*, contains the person's DNA profile.

(2) If the person's DNA profile is in the convicted offenders index of the national DNA data bank, the peace officer or person acting under their direction shall not take any bodily substances from the person but shall
- (*a*) confirm in writing on the order or authorization that he or she has been advised that the person's DNA profile is in the DNA data bank; and
- (*b*) transmit a copy of the order or authorization containing that confirmation and any other information prescribed by regulations made under the *DNA Identification Act* to the Commissioner of the Royal Canadian Mounted Police.

(3) If the person's DNA profile is not in the convicted offenders index of the national DNA data bank, the peace officer or person acting under their direction shall execute the order or authorization and transmit to the Commissioner of the Royal Canadian Mounted Police
- (*a*) any bodily substances taken; and
- (*b*) a copy of the order or authorization and any other information prescribed by regulations made under the *DNA Identification Act*. 1998, c. 37, s. 20; 2000, c. 10, s. 21; 2005, c. 25, s. 8; 2007, c. 22, s. 18.

CROSS-REFERENCES

"Forensic DNA analysis" is defined in s. 487.04. Section 5(1) of the *DNA Identification Act* directs the Solicitor General of Canada, for criminal identification purposes, to establish a national DNA data bank, consisting of a crime scene index and a convicted offenders index, to be maintained by the Commissioner of the R.C.M.P.

SYNOPSIS

For a synopsis of this and the related sections with respect to taking of samples from persons found guilty of certain offences, see the synopsis under s. 487.051.

USE OF BODILY SUBSTANCES — WARRANT / Use of bodily substances — order, authorization / Use of results — warrant / Offence / Offence.

487.08 (1) No person shall use bodily substances that are taken in execution of a warrant under section 487.05 or under section 196.12 of the *National Defence Act* except to use them for the purpose of forensic DNA analysis in the course of an investigation of a designated offence.

(1.1) No person shall use bodily substances that are taken in execution of an order made under section 487.051 of this Act or section 196.14 of the *National Defence Act*, or under an authorization granted under section 487.055 or 487.091 of this Act or section 196.24 of the *National Defence Act*, except to transmit them to the Commissioner of the Royal Canadian Mounted Police for the purpose of forensic DNA analysis in accordance with the *DNA Identification Act*.

(2) No person shall use the results of forensic DNA analysis of bodily substances that are taken in execution of a warrant under section 487.05 or under section 196.12 of the *National Defence Act* except
- (*a*) in the course of an investigation of the designated offence or any other designated offence in respect of which a warrant was issued or a bodily substance was found in the circumstances described in paragraph 487.05(1)(*b*) or in paragraph 196.12(1)(*b*) of the *National Defence Act*; or

(*b*) **in any proceeding for such an offence.**

(2.1) [*Repealed*, 2005, c. 25, s. 9(2).]

(3) Every person who contravenes subsection (1) or (2) is guilty of an offence punishable on summary conviction.

(4) Every person who contravenes subsection (1.1)

(*a*) **is guilty of an indictable offence and liable to imprisonment for a term not exceeding two years; or**

(*b*) **is guilty of an offence punishable on summary conviction and liable to a fine not exceeding $2,000 or to imprisonment for a term not exceeding six months, or to both.** 1995, c. 27, s. 1; 1998, c. 37, s. 21; 2000, c. 10, s. 22; 2005, c. 25, s. 9; 2007, c. 22, s. 19.

CROSS-REFERENCES

The terms "designated offence", "DNA", and "forensic DNA analysis" are defined in s. 487.04. Section 487.05 sets out the circumstances in which a provincial court judge may issue a warrant to seize bodily substances for forensic DNA analysis. Section 487.06(1) sets out those "bodily substances" that may be seized pursuant to a warrant issued under this section. Section 487.06(2) requires the judge to include appropriate terms and conditions. Section 487.07 sets out the special requirements with respect to execution of a warrant obtained under that section. Section 487.09 contains special directions respecting destruction of bodily substances obtained under the warrant. Section 487.091 provides that a justice may issue a warrant to obtain handprint, fingerprint, footprint, foot impression, teeth impression or other print or impression of the body or any part of the body. Other provisions respecting search warrants include s. 487 [warrant to search for evidence and contraband] and s. 487.01 ["general warrant"]. For other cross-references respecting search warrants, see notes following s. 487. For other cross-references with respect to taking of samples from persons found guilty of certain offences, see the cross-references under s. 487.051.

The limitation period for a summary conviction offence is six months as specified in s. 786(2). The maximum penalty for a summary conviction offence is set out in s. 687.

SYNOPSIS

For a synopsis of this and the related sections with respect to taking of samples for forensic DNA analysis from persons found guilty of certain offences, see the synopsis under s. 487.051.

DESTRUCTION OF BODILY SUBSTANCES, etc. — WARRANT / Exception / Destruction of bodily substances, etc., voluntarily given.

487.09 (1) Subject to subsection (2), bodily substances that are taken from a person in execution of a warrant under section 487.05 and the results of forensic DNA analysis shall be destroyed or, in the case of results in electronic form, access to those results shall be permanently removed, without delay after

(*a*) **the results of that analysis establish that the bodily substance referred to in paragraph 487.05(1)(*b*) was not from that person;**

(*b*) **the person is finally acquitted of the designated offence and any other offence in respect of the same transaction; or**

(*c*) **the expiration of one year after**

(i) **the person is discharged after a preliminary inquiry into the designated offence or any other offence in respect of the same transaction,**

(ii) **the dismissal, for any reason other than acquittal, or the withdrawal of any information charging the person with the designated offence or any other offence in respect of the same transaction, or**

>   (iii) any proceeding against the person for the offence or any other offence in respect of the same transaction is stayed under section 579 or under that section as applied by section 572 or 795,

unless during that year a new information is laid or an indictment is preferred charging the person with the designated offence or any other offence in respect of the same transaction or the proceeding is recommenced.

(2) A provincial court judge may order that the bodily substances that are taken from a person and the results of forensic DNA analysis not be destroyed during any period that the provincial court judge considers appropriate if the provincial court judge is satisfied that the bodily substances or results might reasonably be required in an investigation or prosecution of the person for another designated offence or of another person for the designated offence or any other offence in respect of the same transaction.

(3) Bodily substances that are provided voluntarily by a person and the results of forensic DNA analysis shall be destroyed or, in the case of results in electronic form, access to those results shall be permanently removed, without delay after the results of that analysis establish that the bodily substance referred to in paragraph 487.05(1)(b) was not from that person. 1995, c. 27, s. 1; 1998, c. 37, s. 22.

CROSS-REFERENCES

The terms "provincial court judge", "designated offence", "DNA" and "forensic DNA analysis" are defined in s. 487.04. The term "indictment" which includes an "information" is defined in s. 2. Section 487.05 sets out the circumstances in which a provincial court judge may issue a warrant to seize bodily substances for forensic DNA analysis. Section 487.06(1) sets out those "bodily substances" that may be seized pursuant to a warrant issued under that section. Section 487.06(2) requires the judge to include appropriate terms and conditions. Section 487.07 sets out the special requirements with respect to execution of a warrant obtained under this section. Section 487.08 limits the use of evidence obtained as a result of the execution of a warrant obtained under this section. Section 487.091 provides that a justice may issue a warrant to obtain hand print, fingerprint, footprint, foot impression, teeth impression or other print or impression of the body or any part of the body. Other provisions respecting search warrants include s. 487 [warrant to search for evidence and contraband] and s. 487.01 ["general warrant"]. For other cross-references respecting search warrants, see notes following s. 487. Section 579, referred to in subsec. (1), gives the Attorney General or counsel instructed by the Attorney General for that purpose the power to direct a stay of proceedings. Those proceedings may be recommenced, without laying a new information or preferring a new indictment, within one year of the entering of the stay.

COLLECTION OF ADDITIONAL BODILY SUBSTANCES / Reasons / Persons not in custody.

487.091 (1) A provincial court judge may, on *ex parte* application made in Form 5.08, authorize in Form 5.09 the taking from a person, for the purpose of forensic DNA analysis, of any number of additional samples of bodily substances that is reasonably required for that purpose, by means of the investigative procedures described in subsection 487.06(1), if

>   (a) a DNA profile cannot be derived from the bodily substances that were taken from that person under an order made under section 487.051 or an authorization granted under section 487.055; or
>
>   (b) the information or bodily substances required by regulations made under the *DNA Identification Act* were not transmitted in accordance with the requirements of the regulations or were lost.

(2) The application shall state the reasons why a DNA profile cannot be derived from the bodily substances or why the information or bodily substances were not transmitted in accordance with the regulations or were lost.

(3) If the court authorizes the taking of samples of bodily substances from a person who is not in custody, a summons in Form 5.061 setting out the information referred to in paragraphs 487.07(1)(*b*) to (*d*) shall be directed to the person requiring them to report at the place, day and time set out in the summons and submit to the taking of the samples. Subsections 487.055(5) and (6) apply, with any modifications that the circumstances require. 1998, c. 37, s. 23; 2000, c. 10, s. 23; 2005, c. 25, s. 10; 2007, c. 22, s. 20.

CROSS-REFERENCES

"Provincial court judge" is defined in ss. 2 and 487.04. "Forensic DNA analysis" is defined in s. 487.04. "DNA profile" is defined in s. 2 of the *DNA Identification Act* as "the results of forensic DNA analysis of a bodily substance". Also, see cross-references under s. 487.051.

SYNOPSIS

For a synopsis of this and the related sections with respect to taking of samples for forensic DNA analysis from persons found guilty of certain offences, see the synopsis under s. 487.051.

REVIEW BY ATTORNEY GENERAL / Clerical error / Substantive defect / No defect.

487.0911 (1) On receipt of a notice from the Commissioner of the Royal Canadian Mounted Police under subsection 5.2(1) of the *DNA Identification Act* that an order made under section 487.051 or an authorization granted under section 487.091 appears to be defective, the Attorney General shall review the order or authorization and the court record.

(2) If the Attorney General is of the opinion that the defect is due to a clerical error, the Attorney General shall

    (*a*) apply, *ex parte*, to the judge who made the order or authorization, or to a judge of the same court, to have it corrected; and

    (*b*) transmit a copy of the corrected order or authorization, if any, to the Commissioner.

(3) If the Attorney General is of the opinion that the offence referred to in the order or authorization is not a designated offence, the Attorney General shall inform the Commissioner of that opinion.

(4) If the Attorney General is of the opinion that the offence referred to in the order or authorization is a designated offence, the Attorney General shall transmit that opinion, with written reasons, to the Commissioner. 2005, c. 25, s. 11; 2007, c. 22, s. 21.

INFORMATION FOR IMPRESSION WARRANT / Search or seizure to be reasonable / Provisions to apply / Telewarrant

487.092 (1) A justice may issue a warrant in writing authorizing a peace officer to do any thing, or cause any thing to be done under the direction of the peace officer, described in the warrant in order to obtain any handprint, fingerprint, footprint, foot impression, teeth impression or other print or impression of the body or any part of the body in respect of a person if the justice is satisfied

    (*a*) by information on oath in writing that there are reasonable grounds to believe that an offence against this or any other Act of Parliament has been committed and that information concerning the offence will be obtained by the print or impression; and

    (*b*) that it is in the best interests of the administration of justice to issue the warrant.

(2) A warrant issued under subsection (1) shall contain such terms and conditions as the justice considers advisable to ensure that any search or seizure authorized by the warrant is reasonable in the circumstances.

(3) Subsections 487(2) and (4) apply, with such modifications as the circumstances require, to a warrant issued under subsection (1).

(4) Where a peace officer believes that it would be impracticable to appear personally before a justice to make an application for a warrant under this section, a warrant may be issued under this section on an information submitted by telephone or other means of telecommunication and, for that purpose, section 487.1 applies, with such modifications as the circumstances require, to the warrant. 1997, c. 18, s. 45; 1998, c. 37, s. 23.

CROSS-REFERENCES
The terms "justice" and "peace officer" are defined in s. 2. Section 487.05 sets out the circumstances in which a provincial court judge may issue a warrant to seize bodily substances for forensic DNA analysis. Other provisions respecting search warrants include s. 487 [warrant to search for evidence and contraband] and s. 487.01 ["general warrant"]. For other cross-references respecting search warrants, see notes following s. 487. A warrant is executed in accordance with s. 29. Where a person is detained, the peace officer must comply with the provisions of s. 10 of the Charter, subject to reasonable limitations as permitted by s. 1 of the Charter. For protection of persons executing warrants, see ss. 25 to 28.

SYNOPSIS
This section provides that a justice may issue a warrant authorizing the taking of impressions of the body or any part of the body, including teeth impressions, handprints, footprints and foot impressions. The justice must be satisfied that there are reasonable grounds to believe that an offence under the *Criminal Code* or another Act of Parliament has been committed, that information concerning the offence will be obtained and that it is in the best interests of the administration of justice to issue the warrant. The justice shall include such terms and conditions as considered advisable. Where it is not practicable for the peace officer to appear in person before the justice, the officer may apply for a telewarrant in accordance with the procedures set out in s. 487.1. Section 487(2) to (4) allows the justice to issue a warrant to be executed in another territorial division. A justice having jurisdiction in that territorial division must, however, endorse the warrant.

ANNOTATIONS
It was held, prior to the enactment of this section, that the taking of dental impressions without prior judicial authorization could not be justified as a search incident to arrest and violated the accused's rights under ss. 7 and 8 of the *Canadian Charter of Rights and Freedoms: R. v. Stillman*, [1997] 1 S.C.R. 607, 113 C.C.C. (3d) 321.

Other Provisions Respecting Search Warrants, Preservation Orders and Production Orders
2014, c. 31, s. 21.

TELEWARRANTS / Information submitted by telephone / Information submitted by other means of telecommunication / Administration of oath / Alternative to oath / Contents of information / Issuing warrant / Formalities respecting warrant and facsimiles / Issuance of warrant where telecommunication produces writing / Providing facsimile / Affixing facsimile / Report of peace officer / Bringing before justice / Proof of authorization / Duplicates and facsimiles acceptable.

487.1 (1) Where a peace officer believes that an indictable offence has been committed and that it would be impracticable to appear personally before a justice to make application for a warrant in accordance with section 256 or 487, the peace officer may submit an information on oath by telephone or other means of telecommunication to a justice designated for the purpose by the chief judge of the provincial court having jurisdiction in the matter.

(2) An information submitted by telephone or other means of telecommunication, other than a means of telecommunication that produces a writing, shall be on oath and shall be recorded verbatim by the justice, who shall, as soon as practicable, cause to be filed, with the clerk of the court for the territorial division in which the warrant is intended for execution, the record or a transcription of it, certified by the justice as to time, date and contents.

(2.1) The justice who receives an information submitted by a means of telecommunication that produces a writing shall, as soon as practicable, cause to be filed, with the clerk of the court for the territorial division in which the warrant is intended for execution, the information certified by the justice as to time and date of receipt.

(3) For the purposes of subsection (2), an oath may be administered by telephone or other means of telecommunication.

(3.1) A peace officer who uses a means of telecommunication referred to in subsection (2.1) may, instead of swearing an oath, make a statement in writing stating that all matters contained in the information are true to his or her knowledge and belief and such a statement is deemed to be a statement made under oath.

(4) An information submitted by telephone or other means of telecommunication shall include

    (a) a statement of the circumstances that make it impracticable for the peace officer to appear personally before a justice;

    (b) a statement of the indictable offence alleged, the place or premises to be searched and the items alleged to be liable to seizure;

    (c) a statement of the peace officer's grounds for believing that items liable to seizure in respect of the offence alleged will be found in the place of premises to be searched; and

    (d) a statement as to any prior application for a warrant under this section or any other search warrant, in respect of the same matter, of which the peace officer has knowledge.

(5) A justice referred to in subsection (1) who is satisfied that an information submitted by telephone or other means of telecommunication

    (a) is in respect of an indictable offence and conforms to the requirements of subsection (4),

    (b) discloses reasonable grounds for dispensing with an information presented personally and in writing, and

    (c) discloses reasonable grounds, in accordance with subsection 256(1) or paragraph 487(1)(a), (b) or (c), as the case may be, for the issuance of a warrant in respect of an indictable offence,

may issue a warrant to a peace officer conferring the same authority respecting search and seizure as may be conferred by a warrant issued by a justice before whom the peace officer appears personally pursuant to subsection 256(1) or 487(1), as the case may be, and may require that the warrant be executed within such time period as the justice may order.

(6) Where a justice issues a warrant by telephone or other means of telecommunication, other than a means of telecommunication that produces a writing,

    (a) the justice shall complete and sign the warrant in Form 5.1, noting on its face the time, date and place of issuance;

(b) the peace officer, on the direction of the justice, shall complete, in duplicate, a facsimile of the warrant in Form 5.1, noting on its face the name of the issuing justice and the time, date and place of issuance; and

(c) the justice shall, as soon as practicable after the warrant has been issued, cause the warrant to be filed with the clerk of the court for the territorial division in which the warrant is intended for execution.

(6.1) Where a justice issues a warrant by a means of telecommunication that produces a writing,

(a) the justice shall complete and sign the warrant in Form 5.1, noting on its face the time, date and place of issuance;

(b) the justice shall transmit the warrant by the means of telecommunication to the peace officer who submitted the information and the copy of the warrant received by the peace officer is deemed to be a facsimile within the meaning of paragraph (6)(b);

(c) the peace officer shall procure another facsimile of the warrant; and

(d) the justice shall, as soon as practicable after the warrant has been issued, cause the warrant to be filed with the clerk of the court for the territorial division in which the warrant is intended for execution.

(7) A peace officer who executes a warrant issued by telephone or other means of telecommunication, other than a warrant issued pursuant to subsection 256(1), shall, before entering the place or premises to be searched or as soon as practicable thereafter, give a facsimile of the warrant to any person present and ostensibly in control of the place or premises.

(8) A peace officer who, in any unoccupied place or premises, executes a warrant issued by telephone or other means of telecommunication, other than a warrant issued pursuant to subsection 256(1), shall, on entering the place or premises or as soon as practicable thereafter, cause a facsimile of the warrant to be suitably affixed in a prominent place within the place or premises.

(9) A peace officer to whom a warrant is issued by telephone or other means of telecommunication shall file a written report with the clerk of the court for the territorial division in which the warrant was intended for execution as soon as practicable but within a period not exceeding seven days after the warrant has been executed, which report shall include

(a) a statement of the time and date the warrant was executed or, if the warrant was not executed, a statement of the reasons why it was not executed;

(b) a statement of the things, if any, that were seized pursuant to the warrant and the location where they are being held; and

(c) a statement of the things, if any, that were seized in addition to the things mentioned in the warrant and the location where they are being held, together with a statement of the peace officer's grounds for believing that those additional things had been obtained by, or used in, the commission of an offence.

(10) The clerk of the court shall, as soon as practicable, cause the report, together with the information and the warrant to which it pertains, to be brought before a justice to be dealt with, in respect of the things seized referred to in the report, in the same manner as if the things were seized pursuant to a warrant issued, on an information presented personally by a peace officer, by that justice or another justice for the same territorial division.

(11) In any proceeding in which it is material for a court to be satisfied that a search or seizure was authorized by a warrant issued by telephone or other means of telecommunication, the absence of the information or warrant, signed by the justice and carrying on its face a notation of the time, date and place of issuance, is, in the

absence of evidence to the contrary, proof that the search or seizure was not authorized by a warrant issued by telephone or other means of telecommunication.

(12) A duplicate or a facsimile of an information or a warrant has the same probative force as the original for the purposes of subsection (11). R.S.C. 1985, c. 27 (1st Supp.), s. 69; 1992, c. 1, ss. 58, 59; 1994, c. 44, s. 37.

CROSS-REFERENCES

The terms "clerk of the court", "justice", "peace officer" and "territorial division" are defined in s. 2. The term "telecommunication" is defined in s. 35(1) of the *Interpretation Act*, R.S.C. 1985, c. I-21. The usual provision for granting of a warrant is in s. 487 and note that, unlike s. 487, this section is restricted to cases involving allegations of commission of an indictable offence, which would, however, include a hybrid offence by virtue of s. 34(1)(*a*) of the *Interpretation Act*, R.S.C. 1985, c. I-21. Restriction on publicity, see s. 487.2. A search warrant is executed in accordance with s. 488. Execution of a warrant to search a lawyer's office is governed by s. 488.1. Section 489 provides for seizure of things not named in the warrant but which the person executing the warrant believes on reasonable grounds have been obtained by or have been used in the commission of an offence. Section 489.1 sets out the procedure for restitution of goods to the lawful owner and s. 490 sets out the procedure for detention of things which have been seized but not returned under s. 489.1. As to forfeiture of weapons and contraband, see ss. 491 and 491.1. Section 491.2 makes provision for use of photographic evidence in lieu of the actual property so that the property itself may be returned to the lawful owner. For notes on other search or seizure powers, see s. 487. Power to obtain a telewarrant to enter a dwelling-house to effect an arrest is found in s. 529.5, and to obtain a telewarrant to obtain bodily impressions is found in s. 487.092(4).

Note s. 31(1) of the *Interpretation Act*, R.S.C. 1985, c. I-21 which provides that where anything is required or authorized to be done by or before, *inter alia*, a justice of the peace, it shall be done by or before one whose jurisdiction or powers extend to the place where the thing is to be done.

Also see notes under s. 8 of the Charter.

SYNOPSIS

This section sets out the requirements that must be met when a peace officer wishes to obtain a telewarrant.

Subsection (1) requires that the peace officer believe that an indictable offence has been committed and it is impracticable to appear personally before the justice to apply for the warrant. Under such circumstances, the peace officer may submit his sworn information by telephone or other means of telecommunication to a justice. This justice must have been designated for this purpose by the chief judge of the provincial court.

Subsection (2) states that the information referred to in subsec. (1) must be on oath, recorded verbatim by the justice, and filed with the clerk of the court having territorial jurisdiction as soon as practicable. The justice must certify the record of this information as to time, date and contents.

Subsections (2.1), (3.1) and (6.1) allow for receiving the information by use of a "fax" machine.

Subsection (4) sets out the requirements for an information or oath submitted by telephone or other means of telecommunication. Where the justice is satisfied that the requirements described in subsec. (5) have been met, that justice may issue a warrant to the peace officer authorizing the same powers as were found in ss. 256(1) or 487(1). The justice may also require that the warrant be executed within a specific time period.

Subsection (6) sets out specific obligations upon the justice and the peace officer who are involved in the application for telewarrants.

Subsection (7) requires that a peace officer who executes a telewarrant (other than a warrant under subsec. 256(1)) must give a facsimile of the warrant to any person present and apparently in control of the premises before entering. If the premises are unoccupied and the telewarrant does not relate to subsec. 256(1), the peace officer must affix the facsimile in a prominent place upon entering the premises or as soon as practicable thereafter.

Subsection (9) requires a peace officer who has executed a telewarrant to file a written report with the clerk of the court for the territorial jurisdiction in which the warrant was executed within seven days of the execution of the warrant. The report must include the things set out in paras. (*a*) to (*c*) in subsec. (9).

Subsection (10) makes it clear that the clerk of the court must place before a justice the report referred to in subsec. (9) along with the information and the warrant. There is no difference in the treatment of these items and that of similar documents produced upon personal applications for warrants.

Subsection (11) states that in any proceeding challenging a search authorized by telewarrant, the absence of a transcribed and certified information on oath or warrant is, unless there is evidence to the contrary, proof that the search and seizure was not authorized by a warrant.

ANNOTATIONS

The term "facsimile" in subsec. (6)(*b*) means a reasonable copy, being one without significant and misleading errors. Since the two documents are prepared in two different locations by two different persons, there will inevitably be differences, but if they are not significant nor misleading and could not have prejudiced the accused, then the statutory requirement has been fulfilled. Further, the failure of the officer to file the written report as required by subsec. (9) did not invalidate the warrant nor render inadmissible the results of analysis of a blood sample taken pursuant to the warrant: *R. v. Skin* (1988), 13 M.V.R. (2d) 130 (B.C. Co. Ct.).

WHERE WARRANT NOT NECESSARY.

487.11 A peace officer, or a public officer who has been appointed or designated to administer or enforce any federal or provincial law and whose duties include the enforcement of this or any other Act of Parliament, may, in the course of his or her duties, exercise any of the powers described in subsection 487(1) or 492.1(1) without a warrant if the conditions for obtaining a warrant exist but by reason of exigent circumstances it would be impracticable to obtain a warrant. 1997, c. 18, s. 46.

CROSS-REFERENCES

The terms "peace officer" and "public officer" are defined s. 2. Several other sections of the Code give a peace officer a warrantless search or seizure power, usually in exigent circumstances, including s. 101, weapons, and s. 529.3, entry of dwelling-house to effect arrest. Also see s. 11(7) of *Controlled Drugs and Substances Act* which gives a warrantless search and seizure power in exigent circumstances in relation to offences under that Act. The term "exigent circumstances" is not defined, but some assistance may be obtained from the definition of that phrase as contained in s. 529.3(2).

SYNOPSIS

This provision gives a peace officer or public officer appointed or designated to administer or enforce any federal or provincial law and whose duties also include the enforcement of the *Criminal Code* or any other Act of Parliament, a broad warrantless power of search and seizure in exigent circumstances. The officer may exercise the power to search and seizure granted by the two sections referred to without a warrant, provided that the conditions for granting a warrant exist, but by reason of exigent circumstances it would be impracticable to obtain a warrant. Section 487 is the normal search warrant power and allows a justice to issue a warrant to search for and seize in any "building receptacle or place" contraband [subsec. (1)(*a*)], evidence [subsec. (1)(*b*)], anything that is reasonably believed is intended for use for the purpose of committing an offence against the person for which a person may be arrested without warrant [subsec. (1)(*c*)], and offence-related property [subsec. (1)(*d*)]. Section 492.1 allows a justice to issue a warrant to install and monitor a tracking device. Reference must be made to ss. 487 and 492.1 to determine the grounds that the officer must have to obtain the warrant and hence to exercise the same powers without a warrant under this section in exigent circumstances. Section 489(2) gives the officer power to seize without warrant anything that the officer believes on reasonable grounds has been obtained by the commission of an offence, has been used in the commission of an offence or will afford evidence in respect of any offence under the *Criminal Code* or other federal statute, provided that the officer is lawfully present in the place pursuant to a warrant or in the execution of duties.

ANNOTATIONS

It would appear that this section was enacted partly in response to the decision of the Supreme Court of Canada in *R. v. Silveira*, [1995] 2 S.C.R. 297, 97 C.C.C. (3d) 450. The majority judgment in that case cast considerable doubt on the existence of a common law power to search and seize, especially a dwelling-house, in exigent circumstances as where the entry was required to prevent the destruction of evidence. In determining the meaning of "exigent circumstances", some assistance may be obtained by reference to the concurring opinion of L'Heureux-Dubé J. who would have recognized a common law power of warrantless search and seizure in exigent circumstances.

In the course of executing a warrant at the residence, the police conducted a safety check in the outbuildings where a grow operation was located. When a warrant has been issued to search one place or premises, the police, in the course of the execution of the warrant, have the authority at common law to inspect and enter other places or premises on that property to the extent reasonably necessary to protect themselves and others. Such action cannot be taken as a matter of course or on the basis of generalized, non-specific concerns. Before acting, they must have a reasonable basis for believing that there is a possibility that their immediate safety or the safety of others is at risk. While safety concerns can trigger a statutory exigent circumstances exception to a warrant requirement, such concerns will not always satisfy those exceptions. Those concerns must make obtaining a warrant impracticable: *R. v. Chuhaniuk* (2010), 261 C.C.C. (3d) 486 (B.C.C.A.).

RESTRICTION ON PUBLICATION.

487.2 If a search warrant is issued under section 487 or 487.1 or a search is made under such a warrant, every one who publishes in any document, or broadcasts or transmits in any way, any information with respect to

    (*a*) **the location of the place searched or to be searched, or**

    (*b*) **the identity of any person who is or appears to occupy or be in possession or control of that place or who is suspected of being involved in any offence in relation to which the warrant was issued,**

without the consent of every person referred to in paragraph (*b*) is, unless a charge has been laid in respect of any offence in relation to which the warrant was issued, guilty of an offence punishable on summary conviction.

(2) [*Repealed*, 2005, c. 32, s. 16(2).] R.S.C. 1985, c. 27 (1st Supp.), s. 69; 2005, c. 32, s. 16.

SYNOPSIS

This section applies certain restrictions on publication, broadcast or transmission in any way of certain information in relation to search warrants. It is a summary conviction offence to publish the location of the place searched or to be searched, or the identity of any person who appears to occupy, possess or control that place, or who is suspected of being involved in any offence relating to the warrant. Such information may be published if the consent of all of the persons described above has been obtained or if a charge in respect of any offence in relation to which the warrant was issued has been laid.

ANNOTATIONS

It has now been held that this section is of no force and effect in view of the unreasonable restrictions it places on freedom of expression as guaranteed by s. 2(*b*) of the *Charter of Rights and Freedoms*: *Canadian Newspapers Co. v. Canada (Attorney General)* (1986), 28 C.C.C. (3d) 379 (Man. Q.B.); *Canadian Newspapers Co. v. Canada (Attorney General)* (1986), 29 C.C.C. (3d) 109 (Ont. H.C.J.); *Girard (informant) v. Ouellet* (2001), 153 C.C.C. (3d) 217, 43 C.R. (5th) 161 *sub nom. Thibault v. Demers* (Que. C.A.), leave to appeal to S.C.C. refused 157 C.C.C. (3d) vi.

ORDER DENYING ACCESS TO INFORMATION / Reasons / Procedure / Application for variance of order.

487.3 (1) On application made at the time an application is made for a warrant under this or any other Act of Parliament, an order under any of sections 487.013 to 487.018 or an authorization under section 529 or 529.4, or at a later time, a justice, a judge of a superior court of criminal jurisdiction or a judge of the Court of Quebec may make an order prohibiting access to, and the disclosure of, any information relating to the warrant, order or authorization on the ground that

    (a) the ends of justice would be subverted by the disclosure for one of the reasons referred to in subsection (2) or the information might be used for an improper purpose; and

    (b) the reason referred to in paragraph (a) outweighs in importance the access to the information.

(2) For the purposes of paragraph (1)(a), an order may be made under subsection (1) on the ground that the ends of justice would be subverted by the disclosure

    (a) if disclosure of the information would

        (i) compromise the identity of a confidential informant,

        (ii) compromise the nature and extent of an ongoing investigation

        (iii) endanger a person engaged in particular intelligence-gathering techniques and thereby prejudice future investigations in which similar techniques would be used, or

        (iv) prejudice the interests of an innocent person; and

    (b) for any other sufficient reason

(3) Where an order is made under subsection (1), all documents relating to the application shall, subject to any terms and conditions that the justice or judge considers desirable in the circumstances, including, without limiting the generality of the foregoing, any term or condition concerning the duration of the prohibition, partial disclosure of a document, deletion of any information or the occurrence of a condition, be placed in a packet and sealed by the justice or judge immediately on determination of the application, and that packet shall be kept in the custody of the court in a place to which the public has no access or in any other place that the justice or judge may authorize and shall not be dealt with except in accordance with the terms and conditions specified in the order or as varied under subsection (4).

(4) An application to terminate the order or vary any of its terms and conditions may be made to the justice or judge who made the order or a judge of the court before which any proceedings arising out of the investigation in relation to which the warrant or production order was obtained may be held. 1997, c. 23, s. 14; 1997, c. 39, s. 1; 2004, c. 3, s. 8; 2014, c. 31, s. 22.

CROSS-REFERENCES

The term "justice" is defined in s. 2. For other cross-references with respect to search warrants, see s. 487.

SYNOPSIS

This section gives a judge or justice the power to make an order denying access to and the disclosure of any information relating to a warrant, a preservation or production order, or an authorization to enter a dwelling house under ss. 529 or 529.4. The application for such an order is to be made at the time of the issuing of the warrant or authorization. The order may be made only where the ends of justice would be subverted by disclosure or the information might be used for an improper purpose and the justice or judge is satisfied that these grounds outweigh the importance of access to the information. While the phrase "ends of justice would be subverted" is defined in subsec. (2), and refers to matter such as disclosure compromising the identity of a confidential informer, the phrase also includes "for any other sufficient reason". Where the order is made, all documents relating to the application are to be sealed, subject to any terms and conditions that the justice or judge considers desirable in the circumstances pursuant to subsec. (3). The wording of this subsection contemplates that the justice or judge may order the sealing of parts of the information or may allow access to some of the information on certain terms. For example, it would seem to be open to the judge to allow access to the material but prohibit publication for some period of time. Under subsec. (4), an application may be made to the justice or judge who made the order or to a judge of the court before which any proceedings arising out of the investigation may be held to terminate the order or vary any of its terms and conditions.

ANNOTATIONS

Note: Some of the following cases were decided prior to the enactment of this section but may be useful in interpreting its provisions.

Where a search warrant is executed and nothing is found then the public has no right to see either the warrant or the information. Where, however, the search warrant has been executed, and objects found as a result of the search are brought before a justice pursuant to s. 490, then any member of the public is entitled to inspect the warrant and the information upon which it has been issued pursuant to this section, unless it is established that the ends of justice would be subverted by disclosure or that the judicial documents might be used for an improper purpose. Finally, the public has no right to attend the hearing at which application is made for the issuance of a search warrant. That hearing may be held *in camera*: *Nova Scotia (Attorney General)*, [1982] 1 S.C.R. 175, 65 C.C.C. (2d) 129, 26 C.R. (3d) 193 (5:4).

This discretion must be judicially exercised with regard for the right of the accused to a fair trial and the guarantee of freedom of the press. The phrase "for any other sufficient reason" includes a serious threat to the fairness of the accused's trial. In this case, the publication of allegations including information from an accomplice prior to trial would have undermined the accused's right to a fair trial. Where an order of a provincial court judge imposing or refusing a publication ban would imperil the right to a fair trial, the accused who has elected to be tried by a judge and jury is entitled to challenge the order by way of *certiorari*: *R. v. Flahiff* (1998), 123 C.C.C. (3d) 79, 17 C.R. (5th) 94 (Que. C.A.).

In *Toronto Star Newspapers Ltd. v. Ontario*, [2005] 2 S.C.R. 188, 197 C.C.C. (3d) 1, 29 C.R. (6th) 251, the Supreme Court of Canada held that a sealing order should be made only when necessary to prevent serious risk to the proper administration of justice because reasonably alternative measures would not prevent the risk and the salutary effects of a publication ban outweighed the deleterious effects. This test is applied to all discretionary court orders that limit freedom of expression and freedom of the press in relation to legal proceedings. The test should not be applied mechanistically but with regard to the circumstances in which a sealing order was sought. It is not enough to rely on the general proposition that pre-trial publication of the details of a police investigation risks the tainting of statements taken from potential witnesses. See also *Ottawa Citizen Group Inc. v. Canada (Attorney General)* (2005), 197 C.C.C. (3d) 514, 31 C.R. (6th) 144, 255 D.L.R. (4th) 149 (Ont. C.A.), supp. reasons 197 C.C.C. (3d) 514 at p. 532, 255 D.L.R. (4th) 149 at p. 167, 75 O.R. (3d) 607 (C.A.).

This provision applies to the *Extradition Act: United States of America v. M. (D.J.)* (2001), 156 C.C.C. (3d) 276 (Ont. S.C.J.), leave to appeal to S.C.C. refused 158 C.C.C. (3d) vi.

Although nothing is seized during the search the accused who was the object of the investigation, as an interested party, is entitled to inspect the information, the warrant and the related documentation: *R. v. Jany* (1983), 9 C.C.C. (3d) 349 (B.C.S.C.).

The media were not entitled to access to portions of the information to obtain a search warrant which included references to intercepted communications: *National Post Co. v. Ontario* (2003), 176 C.C.C. (3d) 432 (Ont. S.C.J.), leave to appeal to S.C.C. refused 197 O.A.C. 200n.

An application to the Superior Court to gain access to documents relating to execution of a search warrant is premature while an application is pending in the provincial court to have the documents sealed: *Henderson v. Jolicouer* (1983), 9 C.C.C. (3d) 79 (Ont. H.C.J.).

When charges are not laid, the judge making the sealing order is not the only judge capable of varying the order: *Phillips v. Vancouver Sun* (2004), 182 C.C.C. (3d) 483, 19 C.R. (6th) 55, 238 D.L.R. (4th) 167 (B.C.C.A.).

EXECUTION OF SEARCH WARRANT.

488. A warrant issued under section 487 or 487.1 shall be executed by day, unless
- (*a*) **the justice is satisfied that there are reasonable grounds for it to be executed by night;**
- (*b*) **the reasonable grounds are included in the information; and**
- (*c*) **the warrant authorizes that it be executed by night. R.S., c. C-34, s. 444; R.S.C. 1985, c. 27, (1st. Supp.), s. 70; 1997, c. 18, s. 47.**

CROSS-REFERENCES

The terms "justice", "day" and "night" are defined in s. 2. With respect to protection of persons executing warrants, see ss. 25 to 27. Also note s. 29(1) which imposes a duty on a person executing a warrant to have it with him, where it is feasible to do so, and produce it when requested.

SYNOPSIS

This section states that a warrant issued pursuant to ss. 487 or 487.1 must be executed by day unless the justice, by the warrant, authorizes its execution by night. The grounds for execution at night must be set out in the authorization.

ANNOTATIONS

The execution of a search warrant at night is justified only in exceptional circumstances. A search warrant executed at night without justification constitutes a serious Charter violation: *R. v. Sutherland* (2000), 150 C.C.C. (3d) 231, 39 C.R. (5th) 310 (C.A.).

The fact that the affiant knew no one would be home when the warrant was executed was highly relevant and the reviewing judge was correct to hold that this reduced the degree to which privacy interests would be affected by a night search: *R. v. R. (L.V.)* (2014), 316 C.C.C. (3d) 120 (B.C.C.A.), leave to appeal to S.C.C. refused 2015 CarswellBC 554.

Once the warrant has expired with the completion of the search the officers' right to be on the premises is terminated and they become trespassers if they remain on, or return to the premises: *R. v. Moran* (1987), 36 C.C.C. (3d) 225 (Ont. C.A.).

In appropriate circumstances a search warrant may be issued for an extended period of time and its execution delayed for the purpose of apprehending a suspect who is at the premises only at certain times: *R. v. Coull and Dawe* (1986), 33 C.C.C. (3d) 186 (B.C.C.A.).

Where there is a risk of loss or destruction of evidence so that rapid action is required or where there is a real threat of violent behaviour whether directed at the police or third parties then the police may be justified in using special procedures in executing the warrant.

However, the consideration of the possibility of violence must be carefully limited and should not amount to a *carte blanche* for the police to ignore completely all restrictions on police behaviour. The greater the departure from the standards of behaviour required by the comnmon law and the *Charter of Rights and Freedoms*, then the heavier the onus on the police to show why they thought it necessary to use force in the execution of the warrant: *R. v. Genest*, [1989] 1 S.C.R. 59, 45 C.C.C. (3d) 385, 67 C.R. (3d) 224 (7:0).

This provision does not apply to a telewarrant issued under s. 11(2) of the *Controlled Drugs and Substances Act*: *R. v. Dueck* (2005), 200 C.C.C. (3d) 378 (B.C.C.A.).

DEFINITIONS / "custodian" / "document" / "judge" / "lawyer" / "officer" / Examination or seizure of certain documents where privilege claimed / Application to judge / Disposition of application / Privilege continues / Order to custodian to deliver / Application to another judge / Prohibition / Authority to make copies / Hearing in private / Exception.

488.1 (1) In this section,

"custodian" means a person in whose custody a package is placed pursuant to subsection (2);

"document", for the purposes of this section, has the same meaning as in section 321;

"judge" means a judge of a superior court of criminal jurisdiction of the province where the seizure was made;

"lawyer" means, in the Province of Quebec, an advocate, lawyer or notary and, in any other province, a barrister or solicitor;

"officer" means a peace officer or public officer.

(2) Where an officer acting under the authority of this or any other Act of Parliament is about to examine, copy or seize a document in the possession of a lawyer who claims that a named client of his has a solicitor-client privilege in respect of that document, the officer shall, without examining or making copies of the document,

    (*a*) **seize the document and place it in a package and suitably seal and identify the package; and**

    (*b*) **place the package in the custody of the sheriff of the district or county in which the seizure was made or, if there is agreement in writing that a specified person act as custodian, in the custody of that person.**

(3) Where a document has been seized and placed in custody under subsection (2), the Attorney General or the client or the lawyer on behalf of the client, may

    (*a*) **within fourteen days from the day the document was so placed in custody, apply, on two days notice of motion to all other persons entitled to make application, to a judge for an order**

        (i) **appointing a place and a day, not later than twenty-one days after the date of the order, for the determination of the question whether the document should be disclosed, and**

        (ii) **requiring the custodian to produce the document to the judge at that time and place;**

    (*b*) **serve a copy of the order on all other persons entitled to make application and on the custodian within six days of the date on which it was made; and**

    (*c*) **if he has proceeded as authorized by paragraph (*b*), apply, at the appointed time and place, for an order determining the question.**

(4) On an application under paragraph (3)(*c*), the judge

    (*a*) **may, if the judge considers it necessary to determine the question whether the document should be disclosed, inspect the document;**

    (*b*) **where the judge is of the opinion that it would materially assist him in deciding whether or not the document is privileged, may allow the Attorney General to inspect the document;**

    (*c*) shall allow the Attorney General and the person who objects to the disclosure of the document to make representations; and

    (*d*) shall determine the question summarily and,

        (i) if the judge is of the opinion that the document should not be disclosed, ensure that it is repackaged and resealed and order the custodian to deliver the document to the lawyer who claimed the solicitor-client privilege or to the client, or

        (ii) if the judge is of the opinion that the document should be disclosed, order the custodian to deliver the document to the officer who seized the document or some other person designated by the Attorney General, subject to such restrictions or conditions as the judge deems appropriate,

    and shall, at the same time, deliver concise reasons for the determination in which the nature of the document is described without divulging the details thereof.

(5) Where the judge determines pursuant to paragraph (4)(*d*) that a solicitor-client privilege exists in respect of a document, whether or not the judge has, pursuant to paragraph (4)(*b*), allowed the Attorney General to inspect the document, the document remains privileged and inadmissible as evidence unless the client consents to its admission in evidence or the privilege is otherwise lost.

(6) Where a document has been seized and placed in custody under subsection (2) and a judge, on the application of the Attorney General, is satisfied that no application has been made under paragraph (3)(*a*) or that following such an application no further application has been made under paragraph (3)(*c*), the judge shall order the custodian to deliver the document to the officer who seized the document or to some other person designated by the Attorney General.

(7) Where the judge to whom an application has been made under paragraph (3)(*c*) cannot act or continue to act under this section for any reason, subsequent applications under that paragraph may be made to another judge.

(8) No officer shall examine, make copies of or seize any document without affording a reasonable opportunity for a claim of solicitor-client privilege to be made under subsection (2).

(9) At any time while a document is in the custody of a custodian under this section, a judge may, on an *ex parte* application of a person claiming a solicitor-client privilege under this section, authorize that person to examine the document or make a copy of it in the presence of the custodian or the judge, but any such authorization shall contain provisions to ensure that the document is repackaged and that the package is resealed without alteration or damage.

(10) An application under paragraph (3)(*c*) shall be heard in private.

(11) This section does not apply in circumstances where a claim of solicitor-client privilege may be made under the *Income Tax Act* or under the *Proceeds of Crime (Money Laundering) and Terrorist Financing Act*. R.S.C. 1985, c. 27 (1st Supp.), s. 71; 2000, c. 17, s. 89; 2001, c. 41, s. 80.

CROSS-REFERENCES

The terms "peace officer", "public officer", "superior court of criminal jurisdiction" and "Attorney General" are defined in s. 2. With respect to protection of persons executing warrants, see ss. 25 to 27. Also note s. 29(1) which imposes a duty on a person executing a warrant to have it with him, where it is feasible to do so, and produce it when requested.

    For notes on other search powers see s. 487.

SYNOPSIS

This section sets out a procedure for determining a claim of solicitor-client privilege in relation to documents in the possession of a lawyer.

Subsection (2) states that where a peace officer or public officer is about to examine, copy or seize a document in the possession of a lawyer who makes a claim of solicitor-client privilege, that officer must place the document in a sealed and identified package and place the package in the custody of the sheriff of the relevant district or county or another person who, by written agreement, is empowered to act as custodian.

When documents have been dealt with in accordance with subsec. (1), the Attorney General, the client or the lawyer on behalf of the client may apply within 14 days and upon two days' notice to all other parties, to a judge for an order that would deal with the documents. The judge may make an order that a date and place for the determination of the issue of privilege be set within not more than 21 days. The judge may also order that the custodian produce the documents to the judge on the date and at the location fixed for determining the issue. Paragraph (*b*) provides for service of the order on all parties while para. (*c*) authorizes the application for an order determining the issue.

Subsection (4) describes the procedure on an application for an order determining the issue.

Subsection (5) provides that when the judge decides that a document is privileged, it will remain inadmissible as evidence unless the client consents to its admission, or the privilege is otherwise lost. This is so even if the document has been inspected by the Attorney General.

Subsection (6) states that upon determination that no claim of privilege is being pursued the custodian must deliver it to the Attorney General, a designate or the seizing officer.

Subsection (7) authorizes another judge to hear applications under subsec. (3)(*c*) where the original judge cannot act or continue to act.

Subsection (8) makes it clear that the authorized officer must give a reasonable opportunity for a claim of solicitor-client privilege to be made before seizing or copying documents. A person claiming privilege may make an *ex parte* application to a judge to examine or make copies of documents that are in the custody of a custodian. Any such order must contain provisions to ensure that no damage or alteration to the documents occurs during an examination of this sort. Furthermore, the documents may only be examined under this subsection in the presence of the custodian or judge.

Subsection (10) provides that an application under subsec. (3)(*c*) shall be heard in private.

Subsection (11) specifically exempts any claim of solicitor-client privilege in relation to proceedings under the *Income Tax Act* or the *Proceeds of Crime (Money Laundering) Act* from this section.

ANNOTATIONS

Constitutional Considerations: This provision violates s. 8 of the Charter and accordingly, is of no force and effect: *Lavallee, Rackel & Heintz v. Canada (Attorney General); White, Ottenheimer & Baker v. Canada (Attorney General); R. v. Fink*, [2002], 3 S.C.R. 209, 167 C.C.C. (3d) 1, 3 C.R. (6th) 209.

Search of Law Offices: In *Lavallee, Rackel & Heintz v. Canada (Attorney General)*, *supra*, the Supreme Court of Canada struck down this section and set out the following procedure for the search of law offices in the absence of new legislation. No search warrant can issue for documents that are known to be protected by solicitor-client privilege. A search warrant for a law office can only issue if there is no reasonable alternative to the search. Documents must be sealed unless the warrant specifically authorizes the immediate examination, copying and seizure of an identified document. Counsel and the client should be contacted at the time that the warrant is executed. Failing that, a representative of the Bar should supervise the sealing and seizure of documents. The police officer must advise the justice of the efforts made to contact privilege holders and they must be given a reasonable opportunity to assert privilege. If notification of privilege holders is not possible, then a lawyer appointed by the Law Society or court should examine the documents and determine whether a claim of privilege should be made. At such a hearing, the Attorney General is not entitled to inspect the documents beforehand.

The principle of minimization must be reflected in the wording of the authorization and affidavits in support of the authorization: *Maranda v. Richer*, [2003] 3 S.C.R. 193, 178 C.C.C. (3d) 321, 15 C.R. (6th) 1 *sub nom. Maranda v. Quebec (Juge de la Cour du Quebec)*.

"Law office" should be broadly interpreted to include "any place where privileged documents may reasonably be expected to be located" including a lawyer's home, a lawyer's office in multi-disciplinary business premises, the offices of in-house counsel for a business, and storage facilities where lawyers store their files. The word "document" should also be interpreted expansively as set out in s. 321 of the *Criminal Code*: *Festing v. Canada (Attorney General)* (2003), 172 C.C.C. (3d) 321, 223 D.L.R. (4th) 448, [2003] 5 W.W.R. 53 (B.C.C.A.).

Similarly, privilege was found to be engaged where the order was directed, not at a law office, but at the use of cellular and landline phone equipment belonging to the lawyer that was suspected of being used by the client. The process from *Lavallee, supra*, should have been followed: *R. v. B. (A.)* (2014), 307 C.C.C. (3d) 514 (N.L.C.A.).

Solicitor-client Privilege: Prior to the enactment of this section, the Supreme Court of Canada in *Descoteaux v. Mierzwinski*, [1982] 1 S.C.R. 860, 70 C.C.C. (2d) 385, 28 C.R. (3d) 289 (7:0), considered at length the relationship between solicitor-client privilege and the execution of a search warrant at a solicitor's office. The holding by the court may be summarized as follows: Although solicitor-client privilege was originally a rule of evidence, it is not necessary to wait for the trial or preliminary inquiry at which the communication is to be adduced in evidence before raising its confidentiality. The confidentiality of communications between solicitor and client may be raised in any circumstance where such communications are likely to be disclosed without the client's consent. A justice of the peace must be more demanding before authorizing the search of a lawyer's office or one of his files and, where necessary, should set out special procedures for the execution of the warrant in order to limit to what is absolutely inevitable the breach of confidentiality. Further, where the documents sought would in fact be inadmissible in evidence by reason of the solicitor-client privilege then the justice of the peace would have no jurisdiction to authorize the search pursuant to s. 443(1)(*b*) [now s. 487(1)(*b*)] of this section. In any case where the justice of the peace has the necessary jurisdiction to authorize the search because, for example, the documents, while originally subject to solicitor-client privilege, have lost that privilege as they would fall within an exception to the rule, nevertheless, the search should be limited to what is absolutely necessary in order to seize the things for which the search was authorized. Moreover, a justice of the peace has a discretion to refuse a warrant even where the conditions set out in this section have been met. Thus, where the search would interfere with rights as fundamental as freedom of the press or a solicitor's client's right to confidentiality, a justice of the peace may and should refuse to issue the warrant unless there is material to show (*a*) whether a reasonable alternative source of obtaining the information is or is not available, and (*b*) if available, that reasonable steps have been taken to obtain it from that alternative source. Where what is sought is evidence, then even where the justice of the peace is satisfied that there is such evidence on the premises of the lawyer, he should only allow a lawyer's office to be searched if, in addition, he is satisfied that there is no reasonable alternative to a search.

Billing information, including fees and disbursements, fall within the purview of solicitor-client privilege: *Maranda v. Richer, supra*.

No appeal lies from the determination under this section by the superior court judge as to whether the documents should be disclosed despite the claim of solicitor client privilege: *R. v. King* (1992), 74 C.C.C. (3d) 191 (P.E.I.C.A.). See also *R. v. Wilder* (1996), 110 C.C.C. (3d) 186, 130 W.A.C. 17 (B.C.C.A.).

SEIZURE OF THINGS NOT SPECIFIED / Seizure without warrant

489. (1) Every person who executes a warrant may seize, in addition to the things mentioned in the warrant, any thing that the person believes on reasonable grounds

> (*a*) **has been obtained by the commission of an offence against this or any other Act of Parliament;**
>
> (*b*) **has been used in the commission of an offence against this or any other Act of Parliament; or**
>
> (*c*) **will afford evidence in respect of an offence against this or any other Act of Parliament.**

(2) Every peace officer, and every public officer who has been appointed or designated to administer or enforce any federal or provincial law and whose duties include the enforcement of this or any other Act of Parliament, who is lawfully present in a place pursuant to a warrant or otherwise in the execution of duties may, without a warrant, seize any thing that the officer believes on reasonable grounds

> (*a*) **has been obtained by the commission of an offence against this or any other Act of Parliament;**
>
> (*b*) **has been used in the commission of an offence against this or any other Act of Parliament; or**
>
> (*c*) **will afford evidence in respect of an offence against this or any other Act of Parliament. R.S. c. C-34, s. 445; R.S.C 1985, c. 27 (1st. Supp.), s. 72; c. 42 (4th Supp.), s. 3; 1993, 40, s. 16; 1997, c. 18, s. 48.**

CROSS-REFERENCES

For other notes on search powers, see s. 487. With respect to protection of persons executing warrants, see ss. 25 to 27. Also note s. 29(1) which imposes a duty on a person executing a warrant to have it with him, where it is feasible to do so, and produce it when requested.

SYNOPSIS

Subsection (1) authorizes the seizure of items not specified in a warrant. Where a person executing such a warrant *believes on reasonable grounds* that a thing, not mentioned in the warrant, has been obtained by, or has been used in the commission of an offence or will afford evidence, the officer may seize that thing.

Subsection (2) allows seizure of such items where the officer is lawfully present pursuant to a warrant or otherwise in the execution of duties.

ANNOTATIONS

This is a self-contained provision, separate from the plain view doctrine. Thus, it does not require the police to meet all of the requirements of that common law doctrine: *R. v. B. (E.)* (2011), 269 C.C.C. (3d) 227 (Ont. C.A.), leave to appeal to S.C.C. refused (2012), 295 O.A.C. 398*n*; *R. v. Frieburg* (2013), 299 C.C.C. (3d) 254 (Man. C.A.), leave to appeal to S.C.C. refused 2013 CarswellMan 603; *R. v. T. (R.M.J.)* (2014), 311 C.C.C. (3d) 185 (Man. C.A.).

RESTITUTION OF PROPERTY OR REPORT BY PEACE OFFICER / Idem / Form.

489.1 (1) Subject to this or any other Act of Parliament, where a peace officer has seized anything under a warrant issued under this Act or under section 487.11 or 489 or otherwise in the execution of duties under this or any other Act of Parliament, the peace officer shall, as soon as is practicable,

> (*a*) **where the peace officer is satisfied,**
>
> > (i) **that there is no dispute as to who is lawfully entitled to possession of the thing seized, and**

      (ii) that the continued detention of the thing seized is not required for the purposes of any investigation or a preliminary inquiry, trial or other proceeding,

return the thing seized, on being issued a receipt therefor, to the person lawfully entitled to its possession and report to the justice who issued the warrant or some other justice for the same territorial division or, if no warrant was issued, a justice having jurisdiction in respect of the matter, that he has done so; or

(*b*) where the peace officer is not satisfied as described in subparagraphs (*a*)(i) and (ii),

      (i) bring the thing seized before the justice referred to in paragraph (*a*), or

      (ii) report to the justice that he has seized the thing and is detaining it or causing it to be detained

to be dealt with by the justice in accordance with subsection 490(1).

(2) Subject to this or any other Act of Parliament, where a person, other than a peace officer, has seized anything under a warrant issued under this Act or under section 487.11 or 489 or otherwise in the execution of duties under this or any other Act of Parliament, that person shall, as soon as is practicable,

(*a*) **bring the thing seized before the justice who issued the warrant or some other justice for the same territorial division or, if no warrant was issued, before a justice having jurisdiction in respect of the matter, or**

(*a*) **report to the justice referred to in paragraph (*a*) that he has seized the thing and is detaining it or causing it to be detained,**

to be dealt with by the justice in accordance with subsection 490(1).

(3) A report to a justice under this section shall be in the form set out as Form 5.2 in Part XXVIII, varied to suit the case and shall include, in the case of a report in respect of a warrant issued by telephone or other means of telecommunication, the statements referred to in subsection 487.1(9). R.S.C. 1985, c. 27 (1st Supp.), s. 72; 1993, c. 40, s. 17; 1997, c. 18, s. 49.

CROSS-REFERENCES

The terms "justice", "peace officer" and "territorial division" are defined in s. 2.

  In the case of property which is not returned to the person lawfully entitled to its possession, then the provisions of s. 490 must be complied with respecting continued detention. Under s. 491.2, before any property that would otherwise be required to be used in evidence under proceedings for offences under ss. 334, 344, 348, 354, 362 or 380 is returned or otherwise dealt with under this section, a peace officer or other person under the direction of a peace officer may take and retain a photograph for use in evidence. With respect to restitution or forfeiture of contraband, see ss. 491, 491.1 and 492.

  Note that the reference in this section to "section 258" is obviously in error. The reference should be to s. 256.

  This section also applies to material produced to a peace officer or public officer in accordance with a production order under s. 487.012.

SYNOPSIS

This section deals with the disposition of property that has been seized by a peace officer either under a warrant issued pursuant to ss. 258, 487, 487.01 or 487.1, or without warrant under ss. 487.11 or 489, or otherwise as a result of the execution of the peace officer's duties under any Act of Parliament.

  Subsection (1)(*a*) provides that where the peace officer is satisfied that lawful possession is not in issue and the continued detention of the thing seized is not required for the purposes of any investigation or court proceedings, the peace officer shall, as soon as practicable, return the item seized to the person lawfully entitled to it. The peace officer must obtain a receipt for the returned item and make a report to a justice having jurisdiction.

Subsection (1)(*b*) states that where the peace officer is not satisfied as required in para. (*a*), he must bring the item seized to a justice having jurisdiction *or* report to the justice that the thing has been seized and is detained. The justice must then deal with the item in accordance with s. 490(1).

Subsection (2) provides a scheme for the disposition of items seized by a person other than a peace officer either under a warrant or without warrant under ss. 487.11 or 489 or otherwise in the execution of that person's duties under any Act of Parliament. That person is required, as soon as practicable, to bring the items seized before a justice having jurisdiction or make a report to such a justice indicating that the item has been seized and is detained.

Any report made under this section must be in accordance with Form 5.2 in Part XXVIII, varied to suit the case. When a report is made in respect of a telewarrant, it must include the statements referred to in s. 487.1(9).

ANNOTATIONS
This section applies to a warrantless search and seizure as an incident to a lawful arrest for an offence under the *Criminal Code*: *R. v. Backhouse* (2005), 194 C.C.C. (3d) 1 (Ont. C.A.).

An officer's failure to comply with subsec. (1) violated s. 8 of the Charter, because an individual retains a residual, post-taking reasonable expectation of privacy in items lawfully seized: *R. v. Garcia-Machado* (2015), 327 C.C.C. (3d) 215 (Ont. C.A.).

DETENTION OF THINGS SEIZED / Further detention / Idem / Detention without application where consent / When accused ordered to stand trial / Where continued detention no longer required / Idem / Application for order of return / Exception / Disposal of things seized / Exception / Application by lawful owner / Order / Detention pending appeal, etc. / Copies of documents returned / Probative force / Access to things seized / Conditions / Appeal / Waiver of notice.

490. (1) Subject to this or any other Act of Parliament, where, pursuant to paragraph 489.1(1)(*b*) or subsection 489.1(2), anything that has been seized is brought before a justice or a report in respect of anything seized is made to a justice, the justice shall,

   (*a*) **where the lawful owner or person who is lawfully entitled to possession of the thing seized is known, order it to be returned to that owner or person, unless the prosecutor, or the peace officer or other person having custody of the thing seized, satisfies the justice that the detention of the thing seized is required for the purposes of any investigation or a preliminary inquiry, trial or other proceeding; or**

   (*b*) **where the prosecutor, or the peace officer or other person having custody of the thing seized, satisfies the justice that the thing seized should be detained for a reason set out in paragraph (*a*), detain the thing seized or order that it be detained, taking reasonable care to ensure that it is preserved until the conclusion of any investigation or until it is required to be produced for the purposes of a preliminary inquiry, trial or other proceeding.**

(2) Nothing shall be detained under the authority of paragraph (1)(*b*) for a period of more than three months after the day of the seizure, or any longer period that ends when an application made under paragraph (*a*) is decided, unless

   (*a*) **a justice, on the making of a summary application to him after three clear days' notice thereof to the person from whom the thing detained was seized, is satisfied that, having regard to the nature of the investigation, its further detention for a specified period is warranted and the justice so orders; or**

   (*b*) **proceedings are instituted in which the thing detained may be required.**

(3) More than one order for further detention may be made under paragraph (2)(*a*) but the cumulative period of detention shall not exceed one year from the day of the seizure,

or any longer period that ends when an application made under paragraph (*a*) is decided, unless

  (*a*) a judge of a superior court of criminal jurisdiction or a judge as defined in section 552, on the making of a summary application to him after three clear days notice thereof to the person from whom the thing detained was seized, is satisfied, having regard to the complex nature of the investigation, that the further detention of the thing seized is warranted for a specified period and subject to such other conditions as the judge considers just, and he so orders; or

  (*b*) proceedings are instituted in which the thing detained may be required.

(3.1) A thing may be detained under paragraph (1)(*b*) for any period, whether or not an application for an order under subsection (2) or (3) is made, if the lawful owner or person who is lawfully entitled to possession of the thing seized consents in writing to its detention for that period.

(4) When an accused has been ordered to stand trial, the justice shall forward anything detained pursuant to subsections (1) to (3) to the clerk of the court to which the accused has been ordered to stand trial to be detained by the clerk of the court and disposed of as the court directs.

(5) Where at any time before the expiration of the periods of detention provided for or ordered under subsections (1) to (3) in respect of anything seized, the prosecutor, or the peace officer or other person having custody of the thing seized, determines that the continued detention of the thing seized is no longer required for any purpose mentioned in subsection (1) or (4), the prosecutor, peace officer or other person shall apply to

  (*a*) a judge of a superior court of criminal jurisdiction or a judge as defined in section 552, where a judge ordered its detention under subsection (3), or

  (*b*) a justice, in any other case,

who shall, after affording the person from whom the thing was seized or the person who claims to be the lawful owner thereof or person entitled to its possession, if known, an opportunity to establish that he is lawfully entitled to the possession thereof, make an order in respect of the property under subsection (9).

(6) Where the periods of detention provided for or ordered under subsections (1) to (3) in respect of anything seized have expired and proceedings have not been instituted in which the thing detained may be required, the prosecutor, peace officer or other person shall apply to a judge or justice referred to in paragraph 5(*a*) or (*b*) in the circumstances set out in that paragraph, for an order in respect of the property under subsection (9) or (9.1).

(7) A person from whom anything has been seized may, after the expiration of the periods of detention provided for or ordered under subsections (1) to (3) and on three clear days notice to the Attorney General, apply summarily to

  (*a*) a judge of a superior court of criminal jurisdiction or a judge as defined in section 552, where a judge ordered the detention of the thing seized under subsection (3), or

  (*b*) a justice, in any other case,

for an order under paragraph (9)(*c*) that the thing seized be returned to the applicant.

(8) A judge of a superior court of criminal jurisdiction or a judge as defined in section 552, where a judge ordered the detention of the thing seized under subsection (3), or a justice, in any other case, may allow an application to be made under subsection (7) prior to the expiration of the periods referred to therein where he is satisfied that hardship will result unless the application is so allowed.

(9) Subject to this or any other Act of Parliament, if

  (*a*) a judge referred to in subsection (7), where a judge ordered the detention of anything seized under subsection (3), or

  (*b*) a justice, in any other case,

is satisfied that the periods of detention provided for or ordered under subsections (1) to (3) in respect of anything seized have expired and proceedings have not been instituted in which the thing detained may be required or, where those periods have not expired, that the continued detention of the thing seized will not be required for any purpose mentioned in subsection (1) or (4), he shall

    (*c*) if possession of it by the person from whom it was seized is lawful, order it to be returned to that person; or

    (*d*) if possession of it by the person from whom it was seized is unlawful and the lawful owner or person who is lawfully entitled to its possession is known, order it to be returned to the lawful owner or to the person who is lawfully entitled to its possession,

and may, if possession of it by the person from whom it was seized is unlawful, or if it was seized when it was not in the possession of any person, and the lawful owner or person who is lawfully entitled to its possession is not known, order it to be forfeited to Her Majesty, to be disposed of as the Attorney General directs, or otherwise dealt with in accordance with the law.

(9.1) Notwithstanding subsection (9), a judge or justice referred to in paragraph (9)(*a*) or (*b*) may, if the periods of detention provided for or ordered under subsections (1) to (3) in respect of a thing seized have expired but proceedings have not been instituted in which the thing may be required, order that the thing continue to be detained for such period as the judge or justice considers necessary if the judge or justice is satisfied

    (*a*) that the continued detention of the thing might reasonably be required for a purpose mentioned in subsection (1) or (4); and

    (*b*) that it is in the interests of justice to do so.

(10) Subject to this or any other Act of Parliament, a person, other than a person who may make an application under subsection (7), who claims to be the lawful owner or person lawfully entitled to possession of anything seized and brought before or reported to a justice under section 489.1 may, at any time, on three clear days notice to the Attorney General and the person from whom the thing was seized, apply summarily to

    (*a*) a judge referred to in subsection (7), where a judge ordered the detention of the thing seized under subsection (3), or

    (*b*) a justice, in any other case,

for an order that the thing detained be returned to the applicant.

(11) Subject to this or any other Act of Parliament, on an application under subsection (10), where a judge or justice is satisfied that

    (*a*) the applicant is the lawful owner or lawfully entitled to possession of the thing seized, and

    (*b*) the periods of detention provided for or ordered under subsections (1) to (3) in respect of the thing seized have expired and proceedings have not been instituted in which the thing detained may be required or, where such periods have not expired, that the continued detention of the thing seized will not be required for any purpose mentioned in subsection (1) or (4),

the judge or justice shall order that

    (*c*) the thing seized be returned to the applicant; or

    (*d*) except as otherwise provided by law, where, pursuant to subsection (9), the thing seized was forfeited, sold or otherwise dealt with in such a manner that it cannot be returned to the applicant, the applicant be paid the proceeds of sale or the value of the thing seized.

(12) Notwithstanding anything in this section, nothing shall be returned, forfeited or disposed of under this section pending any application made, or appeal taken, thereunder in respect of the thing or proceeding in which the right of seizure thereof is questioned or within thirty days after an order in respect of the thing is made under this section.

(13) The Attorney General, the prosecutor or the peace officer or other person having custody of a document seized may, before bringing it before a justice or complying with an order that the document be returned, forfeited or otherwise dealt with under subsection (1), (9) or (11), make or cause to be made, and may retain, a copy of the document.

(14) Every copy made under subsection (13) that is certified as a true copy by the Attorney General, the person who made the copy or the person in whose presence the copy was made is admissible in evidence and, in the absence of evidence to the contrary, has the same probative force as the original document would have if it had been proved in the ordinary way.

(15) Where anything is detained pursuant to subsections (1) to (3.1), a judge of a superior court of criminal jurisdiction, a judge as defined in section 552 or a provincial court judge may, on summary application on behalf of a person who has an interest in what is detained, after three clear days notice to the Attorney General, order that the person by or on whose behalf the application is made be permitted to examine anything so detained.

(16) An order that is made under subsection (15) shall be made on such terms as appear to the judge to be necessary or desirable to ensure that anything in respect of which the order is made is safeguarded and preserved for any purpose for which it may subsequently be required.

(17) A person who feels aggrieved by an order made under subsection (8), (9), (9.1) or (11) may appeal from the order

    (*a*) to the court of appeal as defined in section 673 if the order was made by a judge of a superior court of criminal jurisdiction, in which case sections 678 to 689 apply with any modifications that the circumstances require; or

    (*b*) to the appeal court as defined in section 812 in any other case, in which case sections 813 to 828 apply with any modifications that the circumstances require.

(18) Any person to whom three days notice must be given under paragraph (2)(*a*) or (3)(*a*) or subsection (7), (10) or (15) may agree that the application for which the notice is given be made before the expiration of the three days. R.S., c. C-34, s. 446; R.S.C. 1985, c. 27 (1st Supp.), s. 73; 1994, c. 44, s. 38; 1997, c. 18, s. 50; 2008, c. 18, s. 14.

CROSS-REFERENCES

The terms "Attorney General", "superior court of criminal jurisdiction", "justice", "peace officer" and "prosecutor" are defined in s. 2. Calculation of a period of months is determined in accordance with s. 28 of the *Interpretation Act*, R.S.C. 1985, c. I-21. As to calculation of "clear days" notice, see s. 27(1) of the *Interpretation Act*.

Under s. 491.2, before any property that would otherwise be required to be used in evidence under proceedings for offences under ss. 334, 344, 348, 354, 362 or 380 is forfeited or otherwise dealt with under this section, a peace officer or other person under the direction of a peace officer may take and retain a photograph for use in evidence. With respect to restitution or forfeiture of contraband, see ss. 491, 491.1 and 492. Section 490.1 (as enacted by 1997, c. 18, s. 51, see **note** before s. 490.1) provides a procedure for dealing with perishable goods. Sections 490.2 to 490.9 deal with forfeiture of "offence-related property".

An application for a management order under the *Seized Property Management Act*, S.C. 1993, c. 37, may be made at the same time as an application under this section. Where property that was subject to a management order has been forfeited under subsec. (9), the proceeds may be shared in accordance with the *Seized Property Management Act*.

This section also applies to material produced to a peace officer or public officer in accordance with a production order under s. 487.012.

SYNOPSIS

This section provides a comprehensive scheme that governs procedure when seized items are brought before a justice or a report is made and further detention of these items is requested.

Subsection (1) stipulates that the justice must return the goods to the lawfully entitled owner, if such information is available, unless the prosecutor satisfies the justice that their detention is required for the purposes of any investigation or proceedings. When the prosecutor satisfies this burden, the justice must order the detention of the seized items, taking care to ensure their preservation until the conclusion of the investigation or until they are required for further proceedings.

Subsection (2) makes it clear that any order under subsec. (1) must have a maximum life of three months from the day of the seizure unless the justice is satisfied upon a summary application that further detention for a specified period is required or that proceedings have been initiated which may require the detained items. Three clear days' notice to the person from whom the items were seized is necessary before such an application may be made.

However, subsec. (9.1) now allows a judge or justice to make an order for the further detention of the property even if the detention orders previously made have expired.

Subsection (3) states that more than one order under subsec. (2) may be made but that the cumulative period of detention cannot exceed one year from the date of seizure except in two circumstances. If an application on three days' notice is brought before a judge of a superior court of criminal jurisdiction or a judge as defined in s. 552, and that judge is satisfied that further detention is required due to the complex nature of the investigation, an order may be made detaining the seized items for a specified period, subject to such conditions as the judge may impose. If proceedings have been instituted in which the thing detained may be required, the cumulative period of detention may exceed one year. No order is required where the owner consents in writing to the detention under subsec. (3.1).

Subsection (4) provides that when an accused person has been ordered to stand trial, the justice shall forward the detained items to the clerk of the court having jurisdiction. The clerk will then detain the items and dispose of them as the court directs.

Subsection (5) states that when a prosecutor determines that the detained items are no longer required for the purposes described in subsec. (1) or (4), an application to the appropriate judge or justice shall be made. The judge or justice must give any person claiming to be the lawful owner of the items an opportunity to establish this claim. An order with respect to the items will be made in accordance with subsec. (9).

Subsection (6) provides for an application by the prosecutor for an order under subsec. (9) where the period of detention has expired and proceedings have not been instituted.

Subsection (7) likewise allows a person from whom anything has been seized to make an application, on three days' notice to the Attorney General, for the return of those items after the expiration of the period of detention. A judge or a justice may allow an application under subsec. (7) to be made prior to the expiration of the ordered period of detention where he has been satisfied that hardship will result if such an application is not allowed.

Subsection (9) states that if a judge or a justice is satisfied that the detention period has expired or that the continued detention of seized goods will not be required for any of the purposes referred to in the section, he shall order those goods returned to their lawful owner. If the lawful owner cannot be determined, the judge or justice may order the seized goods to be forfeited to Her Majesty, to be disposed of as directed by the Attorney General or in accordance with law. An order under subsec. (9) is subject to the other provisions in the Code or any other Act of Parliament. Pursuant to s. 490.9(2), where an order is made under s. 490(9)(c), and the property involved is offence-related property, the judge may require the applicant to enter into a recognizance.

Subsection (10) sets out the requirements for an application for the return of detained goods by a person, other than the person from whom these items were seized, who claims to be the lawful owner. The judge or justice who hears this application shall, if the requirements of subsec. (1) are met, order the return of the seized items to the applicant, or where those items have been sold and cannot be returned to the applicant, order the proceeds of such sale to be paid to the applicant.

Subsection (12) states that nothing shall be returned, forfeited or disposed of under this section pending any application or appeal of the seizure or within 30 days after an order is made.

Subsections (13) and (14) grant to the Attorney General, the prosecutor, peace officer or custodian of the documents the right to make copies of documents ordered to be returned or forfeited and if such copies are certified as true copies by the Attorney General, they are admissible in evidence with the same probative force, absent evidence to the contrary, as the original document.

Subsection (15) makes provision for an application by a person who has interest in seized property to examine the detained items. Such an examination must be regulated according to subsec. (16) in such a way as to safeguard and preserve the detained items.

Subsection (17) sets out the rights of appeal for any person who is not content with an order made under subsecs. (8), (9), (9.1) or (11).

Subsection (18) allows for an expedited hearing on consent.

ANNOTATIONS

Subsection (1) – The initial detention order made under this subsection is not an extension of the initial judicial process authorizing a search warrant and ss. 7 and 8 of the Charter of Rights and Freedoms are not applicable. Accordingly, the hearing may be held *ex parte* without notice to the owner of the goods. This is the case under the former legislation: *R. v. Church of Scientology (No. 6)*; *R. v. Walsh* (1987), 31 C.C.C. (3d) 449 (Ont. C.A.), and the present legislation: *R. v. Barnable P.C.J.* (1986), 27 C.C.C. (3d) 565 (Nfld. S.C.T.D.).

Where articles have been brought before the justice pursuant to s. 489.1 having been seized in the execution of a warrant, the justice must determine whether or not the article falls within the description contained in the warrant of things which may be searched for and seized and whether it is protentially relevant to the offence set out in the warrant. On the other hand, there is no requirement in the provisions that the justice give reasons for making the detention order under this subsection and until the contrary is shown, a superior court is not entitled to infer that the justice did not decide the issues that were confided to him for determination: *Famous Players Ltd. v. Director of Investigation and Research* (1986), 29 C.C.C. (3d) 251, 11 C.P.R. (3d) 161 (Ont. H.C.J.); *Radok v. Joubert* (1988), 44 C.C.C. (3d) 317 (B.C.S.C.).

Whether the court is proceeding under this subsection or subsec. (9), the person from whom the money was seized need only show that he was in lawful possession of the money. Upon such proof, the applicant's right to possession is presumed and the onus is then on the Crown to prove beyond a reasonable doubt that applicant is not lawfully entitled to the money by, for example, proof that the possession is tainted: *R. v. Mac* (1995), 97 C.C.C. (3d) 115, 80 O.A.C. 26 (C.A.).

Subsection (2) – The amendment to this subsection would appear to give statutory recognition to the holding in *R. v. Papalia* (1987), 38 C.C.C. (3d) 37 (B.C.S.C.), that it is sufficient that the application for further detention is made within three months and that there is no requirement that the detention order itself be made within three months. As well, Parliament has now added subsec. (9.1) to allow for an order of continued detention even though the detention order has expired.

A justice has no jurisdiction to make an order requiring the police to make photocopies of the detained documents. Jurisdiction to deal with the items seized after their further detention has been authorized is given to a judge, as under subsec. (15): *Filion v. Savard* (1988), 42 C.C.C. (3d) 182 (Que. C.A.).

Where the items seized have been held by the police, but under seal pending the determination of an application in the superior court to quash the warrant, then the owner is not entitled to the return of the items although no extension was obtained after expiration of the original three-month detention order. In the circumstances, the owner must be taken to have acquiesced to the continued detention, and the terms of subsec. (2) would not appear to contemplate a case where the reason for the delay is an application by the owner testing the validity of the seizure: *Société Radio-Canada v. Québec (Procureur-Général)* (1992), 78 C.C.C. (3d) 175, [1993] R.J.Q. 15 (C.A.), leave to appeal to S.C.C. refused 89 C.C.C. (3d) vi, 57 Q.A.C. 29*n*.

This subsection deals only with extending the time of detention beyond three months and does not give the judge jurisdiction to order the return of items allegedly improperly seized. The legal vehicle for the return of goods unlawfully taken or held is the civil action of replevin or an application under the *Charter of Rights and Freedoms* in the superior court: *R. v. Raponi*, [2004] 3 S.C.R. 35, 185 C.C.C. (3d) 338, 21 C.R. (6th) 197.

No appeal lies from an order made under subsec. (2): *R. v. Raponi, supra*.

Subsection (3) – An investigation is not "complex" within the meaning of this subsection merely because a large volume of documents were seized and a larger number of suspects have been identified than was initially thought to be the case. Had the authorities dedicated greater resources to the case, the investigation could have been completed within one year: *Moyer (Re)* (1994), 95 C.C.C. (3d) 174 (Ont. Ct. (Gen. Div.)).

The onus is on the Crown to establish the complexity of the investigation and the need for further detention of the items seized. In assessing the complexity of the investigation, the court may consider what work is yet to be done, the estimated time for completion, and whether the work should reasonably have been done earlier. In absence of evidence that a full year is required, it should not be granted automatically: *Canada Revenue Agency v. Okoroafor* (2010), 259 C.C.C. (3d) 87 (Ont. S.C.J.).

Subsection (7) – Where, prior to an application for return of moneys seized from the accused, the police have returned the moneys to the insurers of the victims of a robbbery which the accused were suspected of having committed (although the charge was stayed), then the judge should decline to make an order either under this section or pursuant to the superior court's inherent jurisdiction. In such circumstances the conflicting claims are most appropriately resolved by the civil courts: *R. v. Taylor* (1986), 31 C.C.C. (3d) 21 (B.C.S.C.).

A longer detention can only be permitted having regard to the complexity of the investigation but not the complexity of the potential charges or the number of hours required to review the material seized. The onus is on the applicant to establish the complexity of the investigation and the need for further detention. A non-complex investigation that investigators have had insufficient time to complete does not warrant a further detention order. A complex investigation is one that has many varied interrelated parts, patterns, or elements and consequently is hard to understand fully. Some factors that may be considered in determining whether the investigation is complex are: the number of police services and/or government departments involved; the involvement of foreign government; the investigation requires the assistance of lawyers, accountants, computer technicians and/or other professionals to decipher the documents or for other purposes; the investigation requires the cooperation of police services other than the applicant in Canada or elsewhere; the investigation requires witnesses to be interviewed outside Canada; the investigation covers an extensive timeframe or geographical area; there is a confusing paper trail; the offences were committed in more than one jurisdiction by more than one person or with nominees; complicated and time-consuming net worth calculations are required; it is a paper case; the investigative agency has no control over the timely responses of third parties; or documents require translation or transcripts of intercepted private communications must be prepared: *Canada Revenue Agency v. Okoroafor* (2010), 259 C.C.C. (3d) 87 (Ont. S.C.J.).

Subsection (9) – The Crown may seek an order of forfeiture under this subsection of moneys alleged to be the proceeds of crime. It is not restricted to the procedure set out in Part XII.2. Further, a conviction is not a condition precedent to an order under this subsection: *British Columbia (Attorney General) v. Forseth* (1995), 99 C.C.C. (3d) 296 (B.C.C.A.), leave to appeal to S.C.C. refused 104 C.C.C. (3d) vi.

Given that the Crown bears the burden of proof beyond a reasonable doubt, this provision requires adherence to the strict rules of evidence such as the exclusion of hearsay: *R. v. West* (2005), 199 C.C.C. (3d) 449 (Ont. C.A.). See also *Canada (Attorney General) v. Acero* (2006), 210 C.C.C. (3d) 549 (B.C.S.C.).

This subsection does not permit the judge to return items seized on the basis that the seizure was unlawful. The legal vehicle for the return of goods unlawfully taken or held is the civil action of replevin or an application under the *Charter of Rights and Freedoms* in the superior court: *R. v. Raponi*, [2004] 3 S.C.R. 35, 185 C.C.C. (3d) 338.

While s. 8 of the Charter has application to a forfeiture hearing, the same considerations did not apply with the same force as when an individual's liberty is at stake: *R. v. Daley* (2001), 156 C.C.C. (3d) 225 (Alta. C.A.).

An order under subsec. (9) cannot defeat a civil claim against the very property ordered returned: *Lin v. Ontario (Attorney General)* (2008), 240 C.C.C. (3d) 541 (Ont. S.C.J.).

Where the provincial court had made an order pursuant to subsec. (9)(c) for the return of property and the Crown had not appealed, the Crown's application for a preservation order in respect of that property under the Ontario *Civil Remedies Act* was held to be an impermissible collateral attack: *Ontario (Attorney General) v. $787,940 in Canadian Currency (In Rem)* (2014), 312 C.C.C. (3d) 150 (Ont. S.C.J.), additional reasons (2014), 243 A.C.W.S. (3d) 299, [2014] O.J. No. 2989 (S.C.J.).

Subsection (15) – It was held in relation to the predecessor to this subsection that there is no appeal from a decision made under this subsection: *R. v. Stewart*, [1970] 3 C.C.C. 428 (Sask. C.A.).

It was held that the word "examine" in the predecessor to this subsection includes making copies. Accordingly, a judge may order that the applicant be permitted to visually examine and make copies of documents under seizure: *R. v. Sutherland* (1977), 38 C.C.C. (2d) 252 (Ont. Co. Ct.). *Contra: R. v. Labrador Tool Supply Ltd.* (1982), 3 C.C.C. (3d) 269 (Nfld. S.C.T.D.).

Subsection (17) – An appeal lies to the court of appeal with leave pursuant to s. 839(1) from a decision under this subsection: *R. v. Church of Scientology of Toronto* (1991), 63 C.C.C. (3d) 328 (Ont. C.A.).

The Attorney General may appeal an order made under this section returning goods to the person from whom they were seized: *British Columbia (Attorney General) v. Forseth*, *supra*.

If the accused had the right to make an application under subsecs. (8) or (9), then he has the right to appeal the dismissal of the motion pursuant to subsec. (17) whether or not the order is interlocutory in nature: *R. v. Scott* (2015), 322 C.C.C. (3d) 448 (Man. C.A.).

PERISHABLE THINGS.

490.01 Where any thing seized pursuant to this Act is perishable or likely to depreciate rapidly, the person who seized the thing or any other person having custody of the thing

   (*a*) may return it to its lawful owner or the person who is lawfully entitled to possession of it; or

   (*b*) where, on *ex parte* application to a justice, the justice so authorizes, may

      (i) dispose of it and give the proceeds of disposition to the lawful owner of the thing seized, if the lawful owner was not a party to an offence in relation to the thing or, if the identity of that lawful owner cannot be reasonably ascertained, the proceeds of disposition are forfeited to Her Majesty, or

      (ii) destroy it. 1997, c. 18, s. 51; 1999, c. 5, s. 17.

SYNOPSIS

This section operates as an exception to the rules set out in s. 490 respecting the detention of things seized under the *Criminal Code*. Goods that are perishable or likely to rapidly depreciate may immediately be returned to their lawful owner or the person lawfully entitled to possession. Alternatively, an application may be made without notice to a justice for authorization to dispose of the goods, with the proceeds to be given to the lawful owner, or the justice may authorize destruction of the goods.

SEX OFFENDER INFORMATION

Interpretation

DEFINITIONS / Interpretation.

490.011 (1) The following definitions apply in this section and in sections 490.012 to 490.032.

"crime of a sexual nature" means a crime referred to in subsection 3(2) of the *Sex Offender Information Registration Act*.

"database" has the same meaning as in subsection 3(1) of the *Sex Offender Information Registration Act*.

"designated offence" means

    (*a*) an offence under any of the following provisions:

        (i) subsection 7(4.1) (offence in relation to sexual offences against children),

        (ii) section 151 (sexual interference),

        (iii) section 152 (invitation to sexual touching),

        (iv) section 153 (sexual exploitation),

        (v) section 153.1 (sexual exploitation of person with disability),

        (vi) section 155 (incest),

      (vi.1) subsection 160(2) (compelling the commission of bestiality),

        (vii) subsection 160(3) (bestiality in presence of or by a child),

       (viii) section 163.1 (child pornography),

        (ix) section 170 (parent or guardian procuring sexual activity),

      (ix.1) section 171.1 (making sexually explicit material available to child),

        (x) section 172.1 (luring a child),

       (x.1) section 172.2 (agreement or arrangement — sexual offence against child),

        (xi) subsection 173(2) (exposure),

       (xii) [*Repealed*, 2014, c. 25, s. 25(1).]

      (xiii) [*Repealed*, 2014, c. 25, s. 25(1).]

      (xiv) [*Repealed*, 2014, c. 25, s. 25(1).]

       (xv) [*Repealed*, 2014, c. 25, s. 25(1).]

      (xvi) section 271 (sexual assault),

      (xvii) section 272 (sexual assault with a weapon, threats to a third party or causing bodily harm),

     (xviii) paragraph 273(2)(*a*) (aggravated sexual assault — use of a restricted firearm or prohibited firearm or any firearm in connection with criminal organization),

    (xviii.1) paragraph 273(2)(*a*.1) (aggravated sexual assault — use of a firearm),

      (xix) paragraph 273(2)(*b*) (aggravated sexual assault),

      (xx) subsection 273.3(2) (removal of a child from Canada),

      (xxi) section 279.011 (trafficking — person under 18 years),

     (xxii) subsection 279.02(2) (material benefit — trafficking of person under 18 years),

    (xxiii) subsection 279.03(2) (withholding or destroying documents — trafficking of person under 18 years),

    (xxiv) subsection 286.1(2) (obtaining sexual services for consideration from person under 18 years),

(xxv) subsection 286.2(2) (material benefit from sexual services provided by person under 18 years), and

(xxvi) subsection 286.3(2) (procuring — person under 18 years);

(b) an offence under any of the following provisions:

(i) section 162 (voyeurism),

(i.1) subsection 173(1) (indecent acts),

(ii) section 177 (trespassing at night),

(iii) section 230 (murder in commission of offences),

(iii.1) section 231 (murder),

(iv) section 234 (manslaughter),

(v) paragraph 246(b) (overcoming resistance to commission of offence),

(vi) section 264 (criminal harassment),

(vii) section 279 (kidnapping),

(vii.1) section 279.01 (trafficking in persons),

(vii.11) subsection 279.02(1) (material benefit — trafficking),

(vii.12) subsection 279.03(1) (withholding or destroying documents — trafficking),

(viii) section 280 (abduction of a person under age of sixteen),

(ix) section 281 (abduction of a person under age of fourteen),

(ix.1) subsection 286.1(1) (obtaining sexual services for consideration),

(ix.2) subsection 286.2(1) (material benefit from sexual services),

(ix.3) subsection 286.3(1) (procuring),

(x) paragraph 348(1)(d) (breaking and entering a dwelling house with intent to commit an indictable offence),

(xi) paragraph 348(1)(d) (breaking and entering a dwelling house and committing an indictable offence),

(xii) paragraph 348(1)(e) (breaking and entering a place other than a dwelling house with intent to commit an indictable offence), and

(xiii) paragraph 348(1)(e) (breaking and entering a place other than a dwelling house and committing an indictable offence);

(c) an offence under any of the following provisions of the *Criminal Code*, chapter C-34 of the Revised Statutes of Canada, 1970, as they read from time to time before January 4, 1983:

(i) section 144 (rape),

(ii) section 145 (attempt to commit rape),

(iii) section 149 (indecent assault on female),

(iv) section 156 (indecent assault on male), and

(v) subsection 246(1) (assault with intent) if the intent is to commit an offence referred to in any of subparagraphs (i) to (iv);

(c.1) an offence under any of the following provisions of the *Criminal Code*, chapter C-34 of the Revised Statutes of Canada, 1970, as enacted by section 19 of *An Act to amend the Criminal Code in relation to sexual offences and other offences against the person and to amend certain other Acts in relation thereto or in consequence thereof*, chapter 125 of the Statutes of Canada, 1980-81-82-83:

(i) section 246.1 (sexual assault),

(ii) section 246.2 (sexual assault with a weapon, threats to a third party or causing bodily harm), and

(iii) section 246.3 (aggravated sexual assault);

(d) an offence under any of the following provisions of the *Criminal Code*, chapter C-34 of the Revised Statutes of Canada, 1970, as they read from time to time before January 1, 1988:

(i) subsection 146(1) (sexual intercourse with a female under age of fourteen),

(ii) subsection 146(2) (sexual intercourse with a female between ages of fourteen and sixteen),

(iii) section 153 (sexual intercourse with step-daughter),

(iv) section 157 (gross indecency),
(v) section 166 (parent or guardian procuring defilement), and
(vi) section 167 (householder permitting defilement);

(*d*.1) an offence under any of the following provisions of this Act, as they read from time to time before the day on which this paragraph comes into force:
(i) paragraph 212(1)(i) (stupefying or overpowering for the purpose of sexual intercourse),
(ii) subsection 212(2) (living on the avails of prostitution of person under 18 years),
(iii) subsection 212(2.1) (aggravated offence in relation to living on the avails of prostitution of person under 18 years), and
(iv) subsection 212(4) (prostitution of person under 18 years);

(*e*) an attempt or conspiracy to commit an offence referred to in any of paragraphs (*a*), (*c*), (*c*.1), (*d*) and (*d*.1); or

(*f*) an attempt or conspiracy to commit an offence referred to in paragraph (*b*).

"Ontario Act" means *Christopher's Law (Sex Offender Registry), 2000,* S.O. 2000, c. 1.

"pardon" means a conditional pardon granted under Her Majesty's royal prerogative of mercy or under section 748 that has not been revoked.

"record suspension" means a record suspension, as defined in subsection 2(1) of the *Criminal Records Act,* that has not been revoked or ceased to have effect.

"registration centre" has the same meaning as in subsection 3(1) of the *Sex Offender Information Registration Act.*

"Review Board" means the Review Board established or designated for a province under subsection 672.38(1).

"verdict of not criminally responsible on account of mental disorder" means a verdict of not criminally responsible on account of mental disorder within the meaning of subsection 672.1(1) or a finding of not responsible on account of mental disorder within the meaning of subsection 2(1) of the *National Defence Act,* as the case may be.

(2) For the purpose of this section and sections 490.012 to 490.032, a person who is convicted of, or found not criminally responsible on account of mental disorder for, a designated offence does not include a young person

(*a*) within the meaning of subsection 2(1) of the *Youth Criminal Justice Act* unless they are given an adult sentence within the meaning of that subsection for the offence; or

(*b*) within the meaning of subsection 2(1) of the *Young Offenders Act,* chapter Y-1 of the Revised Statutes of Canada, 1985, unless they are convicted of the offence in ordinary court within the meaning of that subsection. 2004, c. 10, s. 20; 2005, c. 43, s. 6; 2007, c. 5, s. 11; 2008, c. 6, s. 36; 2010, c. 3, s. 7; 2010, c. 17, s. 4; 2012, c. 1, s. 141(2) and (3); 2012, c. 1, s. 31; 2014, c. 25, s. 25.

CROSS-REFERENCES

Sections 490.011 to 490.032 were enacted by the *Sex Offender Information Registration Act,* S.C. 2004, c. 10. Section 3(2) of that Act (referred to in the definition of "crime of a sexual nature") provides as follows:

(2) For the purposes of this Act, a crime is of a sexual nature if it consists of one or more acts that
(*a*) are either sexual in nature or committed with the intent to commit an act or acts that are sexual in nature; and
(*b*) constitute an offence.

Section 18 of that Act provides that the lieutenant governor in council of a province may designate places or classes of places in the province as registration centres, and the area of the province served by each registration centre.

Section 5(*b*) of the *Criminal Records Act*, R.S.C. 1985, c. C-47, provides that the legal restrictions imposed by ss. 490.012 and 490.019 continue, notwithstanding that the individual has been granted a pardon under that Act.

ANNOTATIONS

The provisions of the *Sex Offender Information Registration Act*, S.C. 2004, c. 10, and these provisions were intended to be retrospective in application and to apply to any convicted offender sentenced after the coming into force of the legislation for an offence that is a designated offence. Further, registration is not a "punishment" so as to trigger the offender's right under s. 11(*i*) of the *Charter of Rights and Freedoms* to the benefit of lesser punishment where the punishment has varied between the time of the commission and the time of sentencing: *R. v. Cross* (2006), 205 C.C.C. (3d) 289 (N.S.C.A.), leave to appeal to S.C.C. refused [2006] 2 S.C.R. vi, 210 C.C.C. (3d) vi; *R. v. Rouschop*, [2005] O.J. No. 1336 (C.J.); *R. v. G. (M.)* (2005), 132 C.R.R. (2d) 289 (B.C.S.C.). Similarly, see *R. v. Dyck* (2005), 203 C.C.C. (3d) 365 (Ont. S.C.J.), holding that registration under *Christopher's Law (Sex Offender Registry), 2000*, S.O. 2000, c. 1, is not punishment for the purpose of s. 11(*i*). [Note: also now see *R. v. Rodgers* (2006), 207 C.C.C. (3d) 225 (S.C.C.), considering the retroactive application of the DNA data bank provision, s. 487.055.]

Christopher's Law (Sex Offender Registry), 2000, S.O. 2000, c. 1 (the "Ontario Act"), is valid legislation. It is *intra vires* the province, does not violate ss. 7 and 12 of the *Canadian Charter of Rights and Freedoms* and has not been rendered inoperative by enactment of the *Criminal Code* provisions and the *Sex Offender Information Registration Act: R. v. Dyck*, *supra*.

Order to Comply with the *Sex Offender Information Registration Act*

2007, c. 5, s. 12.

ORDER / Order — if intent established / Order — if previous offence established / Failure to make order.

490.012 (1) When a court imposes a sentence on a person for an offence referred to in paragraph (*a*), (*c*), (*c.1*), (*d*), (*d.1*) or (*e*) of the definition "designated offence" in subsection 490.011(1) or renders a verdict of not criminally responsible on account of mental disorder for such an offence, it shall make an order in Form 52 requiring the person to comply with the *Sex Offender Information Registration Act* for the applicable period specified in section 490.013.

(2) When a court imposes a sentence on a person for an offence referred to in paragraph (*b*) or (*f*) of the definition "designated offence" in subsection 490.011(1), it shall, on application of the prosecutor, make an order in Form 52 requiring the person to comply with the *Sex Offender Information Registration Act* for the applicable period specified in section 490.013 if the prosecutor establishes beyond a reasonable doubt that the person committed the offence with the intent to commit an offence referred to in paragraph (*a*), (*c*), (*c.1*), (*d*), (*d.1*) or (*e*) of that definition.

(3) When a court imposes a sentence on a person for a designated offence in connection with which an order may be made under subsection (1) or (2) or renders a verdict of not criminally responsible on account of mental disorder for such an offence, it shall, on application of the prosecutor, make an order in Form 52 requiring the person to comply with the *Sex Offender Information Registration Act* for the applicable period specified in section 490.013 if the prosecutor establishes that

   (*a*) **the person was, before or after the coming into force of this paragraph, previously convicted of, or found not criminally responsible on account of mental disorder for, an offence referred to in paragraph (*a*), (*c*), (*c.1*), (*d*), (*d.1*) or (*e*) of the definition "designated offence" in subsection 490.011(1) or in** paragraph (*a*) or (*c*) of the definition "designated offence" in section 227 of the *National Defence Act*;

(*b*) the person was not served with a notice under section 490.021 or 490.02903 or under section 227.08 of the *National Defence Act* in connection with that offence; and

(*c*) no order was made under subsection (1) or under subsection 227.01(1) of the *National Defence Act* in connection with that offence.

(4) If the court does not consider the matter under subsection (1) or (3) at that time, the court

(*a*) shall, within 90 days after the day on which it imposes the sentence or renders the verdict, set a date for a hearing to do so;

(*b*) retains jurisdiction over the matter; and

(*c*) may require the person to appear by closed-circuit television or any other means that allows the court and the person to engage in simultaneous visual and oral communication, as long as the person is given the opportunity to communicate privately with counsel if they are represented by counsel. 2004, c. 10, s. 20; 2007, c. 5, s. 13; 2010, c. 17, s. 5; 2014, c. 25, s. 26.

CROSS-REFERENCES

This section must be read with the *Sex Offender Information Registration Act*, S.C. 2004, c. 10. That Act sets out the reporting requirements of a person subject to an order under this section. That Act may be found in *Martin's Related Criminal Statutes*.

The duration of the order made under this section is determined by s. 490.013. If the order was made under subsec. (1) or (2) of this section, it ends 10 years after it was made if the offence was a summary conviction offence or punishable by two or five years. If the maximum penalty for the offence is 10 or 14 years, the order ends 20 years after it was made. However, if the order was made under s. 490.012(1) and the person was convicted of, or found not criminally responsible on account of mental disorder for more than one offence referred to in paras. (*a*), (*c*), (*c*.1), (*d*) or (*e*) of the definition of designated offence in s. 490.011(1) then the order applies for life. The order is also a lifetime order if the maximum penalty for the offence was life imprisonment or the person was already under an obligation under ss. 490.019 or 490.02901 or s. 227.06 of the *National Defence Act*, R.S.C. 1985, c. N-5, or s. 36.1 of the *International Transfer of Offenders Act*, S.C. 2004, c. 21. The Attorney General or minister of justice, as the case may be, may serve notice to comply with the registration requirements in accordance with s. 490.02 where on the day this Act came into force (December 15, 2004) the person was still serving sentence for or had not received an absolute discharge under Part XX.1 from an offence listed in paras. (*a*), (*c*), (*d*) or (*e*) of the definition of designated offence in s. 490.011(1), or the person was already listed in the sex offender registry established under the Ontario Act for such an offence and the person was a resident of Ontario at any time between April 23, 2001 and December 15, 2004.

The prosecutor or a person who is subject to an order under subsec. (2) of this section may appeal on any ground of law or mixed law and fact under s. 490.014. Under s. 490.015, the person may apply for a termination order. That section sets out the dates when an application may first be made for a termination order. The circumstances in which the termination may be made are set out in s. 490.016. Section 490.017 sets out the appeal provisions in relation to a termination order application. Section 490.018 sets out the requirements placed on a court that makes an order under this section. Section 490.03 sets out the circumstances in which information in the sex offender database may be disclosed. Section 490.031 creates the offence for failing to comply with an order under this section.

Sections 490.02901 to 490.02911 establish a similar scheme for registration under the *Sex Offender Information Registration Act* for persons who arrive in Canada and have been convicted or found not criminally responsible for offences outside of Canada that are equivalent to the definition of designated offence as defined in s. 490.011(1). Sections 490.02912 to 490.02915 deal with applications for termination of registration orders made under s. 36.1 of the *International Transfer of Offenders Act*.

Section 5(*b*) of the *Criminal Records Act*, R.S.C. 1985, c. C-47, provides that the legal restriction imposed by this section continues, notwithstanding that the individual has been granted a pardon under that Act. The person may, however, apply for a termination order at that point.

Sections 227 to 227.21 of the *National Defence Act* contain the analogous provisions in relation to court martial proceedings.

Under s. 487.051, persons convicted or found not criminally responsible of primary designated offences as defined in s. 487.04 are subject to orders for taking of bodily samples to allow for forensic DNA analysis. The court has a discretion to make such an order for persons convicted of secondary designated offences.

SYNOPSIS

This section provides that a court may make an order requiring the offender to comply with the requirements of the *Sex Offender Information Registration Act*, S.C. 2004, c. 10. The order is mandatory for the offences listed in subsec. (1) and is mandatory upon application of the prosecutor in the circumstances set out in subsecs. (2) and (3). The order is to be made when the offender is sentenced or the court renders a verdict of not criminally responsible on account of mental disorder. However, under subsec. (4), the court retains jurisdiction to make an order and is to do so by setting a date within 90 days of the sentence or the verdict. The court may require the person to appear by close-circuit television or other means. The court must give reasons for its decision.

This section contemplates three different circumstances in which the order will be made. Where the offence is listed in paras. (*a*), (*c*), (*c*.1), (*d*), (*d*.1) or (*e*) of the definition of designated offence in s. 490.011(1), no further finding is required. Those offences are the various sexual offences under the present Code or predecessor provisions (subsec. (1)). Where the offence is one listed in paras. (*b*) or (*f*), the court must make a further finding that the offence, such as trespassing by night (s. 177), was committed with the intent to commit one of the offences referred in paras. (*a*), (*c*), (*c*.1), (*d*), (*d*.1) or (*e*). The burden is on the prosecution to establish this intent beyond a reasonable doubt (subsec. (2)). Finally, where the offence falls within the definition of a designated offence under any of paras. (*a*) to (*f*), the order will be made where the offender was previously convicted of or found criminally responsible on account of mental disorder for an offence listed in paras. (*a*), (*c*), (*c*.1), (*d*), (*d*.1) or (*e*) of the definition of designated offence (subsec. (3)).

ANNOTATIONS

There is no right to appeal an order pursuant to subsec. (1) as it is not a sentence within the meaning of s. 673 of the Code: *R. v. Chisholm* (2012), 292 C.C.C. (3d) 132 (N.B.C.A.). See also *R. v. W. (J.J.)* (2012), 292 C.C.C. (3d) 292 (N.S.C.A.).

It was held under the predecessor to this section that, in a case where the application for registration must be initiated by the prosecutor and the issue was first raised by the sentencing judge and not pursued by the prosecutor, the judge did not err in failing to make the order: *R. v. R. (B.E.)* (2005), 32 C.R. (6th) 151 (B.C.C.A.).

The sentencing judge has no discretion to make the reporting period less than required by the applicable *Criminal Code* provisions: *R. v. R. (R.J.)* (2005), 252 Nfld. & P.E.I.R. 166 (Nfld. & Lab. C.A.).

This provision has no application where the accused receives an absolute or conditional discharge: *R. v. Jayswal* (2011), 266 C.C.C. (3d) 388 (Ont. C.J.).

Where the court imposed a 20-year SOIRA order in circumstances in which a lifetime order was mandatory, the court did not fail to "consider the matter" within the meaning of subsec. (4). As a result, the court was *functus officio* and dismissed the Crown's application to correct the defective order: *R. v. B. (C.D.)* (2013), 306 C.C.C. (3d) 369 (B.C.S.C.). *Contra*: *R. v. Merrick* (2013), 108 W.C.B. (2d) 821, [2013] O.J. No. 3965 (C.J.).

DATE ORDER BEGINS / Duration of order / Duration of order / Duration of order / Duration of order / Duration of order.

490.013 (1) An order made under section 490.012 begins on the day on which it is made.

(2) An order made under subsection 490.012(1) or (2)

    (*a*) ends 10 years after it was made if the offence in connection with which it was made was prosecuted summarily or if the maximum term of imprisonment for the offence is two or five years;

    (*b*) ends 20 years after it was made if the maximum term of imprisonment for the offence is 10 or 14 years; and

    (*c*) applies for life if the maximum term of imprisonment for the offence is life.

(2.1) An order made under subsection 490.012(1) applies for life if the person is convicted of, or found not criminally responsible on account of mental disorder for, more than one offence referred to in paragraph (*a*), (*c*), (*c*.1), (*d*), (*d*.1) or (*e*) of the definition "designated offence" in subsection 490.011(1).

(3) An order made under subsection 490.012(1) or (2) applies for life if the person is, or was at any time, subject to an obligation under section 490.019 or 490.02901, under section 227.06 of the *National Defence Act* or under section 36.1 of the *International Transfer of Offenders Act*.

(4) An order made under subsection 490.012(1) or (2) applies for life if the person is, or was at any time, subject to an order made previously under section 490.012 of this Act or section 227.01 of the *National Defence Act*.

(5) An order made under subsection 490.012(3) applies for life. 2004, c. 10, s. 20; 2007, c. 5, s. 14; 2010, c. 17, s. 6; 2014, c. 25, s. 27.

CROSS-REFERENCES

"Prosecutor" is defined in s. 2. For other cross-references, see s. 490.012.

SYNOPSIS

This section sets out the duration of the order to comply with registration requirements that is made under s. 490.012. If the order was made under subsec. (1) or (2) of s. 490.012, it ends 10 years after it was made if the offence was a summary conviction offence or punishable by two or five years. If the maximum penalty for the offence is 10 or 14 years, the order ends 20 years after it was made. If the maximum punishment was life or the order was made under s. 490.012(3), the order applies for life. The order is also a lifetime order if the person was convicted or found not criminally responsible for more than one offence referred to in paras. (*a*), (*c*), (*c*.1), (*d*), (*d*.1) or (*e*) of the definition of designated offence, or the offender was under an obligation under ss. 490.019 or 490.02901. The Attorney General or minister of justice, as the case may be, may serve notice to comply with the registration requirements in accordance with s. 490.02 where on the day this Act came into force (December 15, 2004) the person was still serving sentence for or had not received an absolute discharge under Part XX.1 from an offence listed in paras. (*a*), (*c*), (*d*), (*d*.1) or (*e*) of the definition of designated offence in s. 490.011, or the person was already listed in the sex offender registry established under the Ontario Act for such an offence and the person was a resident of Ontario at any time between April 23, 2001 and December 15, 2004. Finally, the order is for life if the person is or at any time was subject to an order made previously under either s. 490.012(1) or (2).

ANNOTATIONS

Under subsec. (2.1), an offender will be subject to a lifetime SOIRA order if convicted of multiple designated offences, even if he is sentenced for those offences simultaneously: *R. v. Burns* (2012), 285 C.C.C. (3d) 328 (Sask. C.A.).

APPEAL.

490.014 The prosecutor, or a person who is subject to an order under subsection 490.012(2), may appeal from a decision of the court under that subsection on any ground of appeal that raises a question of law or of mixed law and fact. The appeal court may dismiss the appeal, or allow it and order a new hearing, quash the order or make an order that may be made under that subsection. 2004, c. 10, s. 20; 2010, c. 17, s. 7.

CROSS-REFERENCES

"Prosecutor" is defined in s. 2. Section 490.018 imposes on the appeal court the same obligations as a trial court where the appeal court makes an order under s. 490.012. For other cross-references, see s. 490.012.

SYNOPSIS

This section gives the prosecutor or the person against whom an order was made under s. 490.012(2) a right of appeal on a question of law or mixed law and fact. The appeal court may dismiss the appeal, or allow the appeal and order a new hearing, quash the order or make an order that may be made under s. 490.012(2).

ANNOTATIONS

Section 487.054 provides for appeals in relation to making of DNA orders. Like this section, it does not specify the appeal court. In *R. v. Hendry* (2001), 161 C.C.C. (3d) 275, 48 C.R. (5th) 310 (Ont. C.A.), the court held that the appeal route follows the scheme in the *Criminal Code* generally. That is, in indictable proceedings, the appeal from the making or refusal to make the order lies to the Court of Appeal and, in summary conviction proceedings, the appeal is taken in accordance with Part XXVII of the *Criminal Code*.

There is no right of appeal from an order made under s. 490.012(1): *R. v. Chisholm* (2012), 292 C.C.C. (3d) 132 (N.B.C.A.); *R. v. W. (J.J.)* (2012), 292 C.C.C. (3d) 292 (N.S.C.A.); *R. v. Whiting* (2013), 304 C.C.C. (3d) 342 (Sask. C.A.); *R. v. R. (L.V.)*, [2016] B.C.J. No. 342 (C.A.).

APPLICATION FOR TERMINATION ORDER / Multiple orders / Pardon or record suspension / Scope of application / Re-application / Jurisdiction.

490.015 (1) A person who is subject to an order may apply for a termination order
  - **(a) if five years have elapsed since the order was made, in the case of an order referred to in paragraph 490.013(2)(a);**
  - **(b) if 10 years have elapsed since the order was made, in the case of an order referred to in paragraph 490.013(2)(b); or**
  - **(c) if 20 years have elapsed since the order was made, in the case of an order referred to in paragraph 490.013(2)(c) or subsection 490.013(2.1), (3) or (5).**

(2) A person who is subject to more than one order made under section 490.012 of this Act, or under that section and section 227.01 of the *National Defence Act*, may apply for a termination order if 20 years have elapsed since the most recent order was made.

(3) Despite subsections (1) and (2), a person may apply for a termination order once they receive a pardon or once a record suspension is ordered.

(4) The application shall be in relation to every order that is in effect. If a person is subject to an obligation under section 490.019 or 490.02901, under section 227.06 of the *National Defence Act* or under section 36.1 of the *International Transfer of Offenders Act*, the application shall also be in relation to that obligation.

(5) A person whose application is refused may re-apply if five years have elapsed since they made the previous application. They may also re-apply once they receive a pardon

or once a record suspension is ordered. However, they may not re-apply under this subsection if an order is made with respect to them under section 490.012 of this Act or section 227.01 of the *National Defence Act* after the previous application was made.

(6) The application shall be made to

    (*a*) a superior court of criminal jurisdiction if

        (i) one or more of the orders to which it relates were made by such a court under section 490.012, or

        (ii) one or more of the orders to which it relates were made under section 227.01 of the *National Defence Act* and the Chief Military Judge does not have jurisdiction to receive the application under subsection 227.03(6) of that Act; or

    (*b*) a court of criminal jurisdiction, in any other case in which the application relates to one or more orders made under section 490.012. 2004, c. 10, s. 20; 2007, c. 5, s. 15; 2010, c. 17, s. 8; 2012, c. 1, s. 142.

CROSS-REFERENCES

"Superior court of criminal jurisdiction" and "court of criminal jurisdiction" are defined in s. 2. "Pardon" and "record suspension" are defined in s. 490.011. For other cross-references, see s. 490.012. Section 490.026 provides for an application to terminate an order made under s. 490.019. Section 490.02908 provides for an application to terminate an obligation to comply with the *Sex Offender Information Registration Act*, S.C. 2004, c. 10, in relation to convictions or findings made outside Canada. It would appear that, in light of subsec. (3) of this section, a person subject to an order under s. 490.012 and an obligation under ss. 490.019 or 490.02901 makes an application under this section to terminate both.

SYNOPSIS

This section provides for the person who is subject to an order to comply with registration requirements made under s. 490.012 to apply for a termination order. The time for making the application depends on the duration of the order. If it was a 10-year order, the person may apply after five years. If the order was for 20 years, the person may apply after 10 years. If the order was for life, the person may apply after 20 years. Or, the person may apply on or after the day on which they receive a pardon or record suspension. If the person is subject to multiple orders, the order must be in relation to all of the orders and the application can only be made after 20 years or on or after the day on which the person receives a pardon or record suspension. Pursuant to subsec. (3), a person who is subject to an obligation under ss. 490.019 or 490.02901 must include an application to terminate that obligation as well. Where the person's application was unsuccessful, they may not reapply for five years, but if, in the meantime, a new s. 490.012 order was made, they may not reapply. The application is made to a court of criminal jurisdiction unless the original order was made by a superior court of criminal jurisdiction, in which case the application must be made to that court.

TERMINATION ORDER / Reasons for decision / Requirements relating to notice.

490.016 (1) The court shall make a termination order if it is satisfied that the person has established that the impact on them of continuing an order or an obligation, including on their privacy or liberty, would be grossly disproportionate to the public interest in protecting society through the effective prevention or investigation of crimes of a sexual nature, to be achieved by the registration of information relating to sex offenders under the *Sex Offender Information Registration Act*.

(2) The court shall give reasons for its decision.

(3) If the court makes a termination order, it shall cause the Commissioner of the Royal Canadian Mounted Police and the Attorney General of the province, or the minister of

justice of the territory, to be notified of the decision. 2004, c. 10, s. 20; 2007, c. 15, s. 16; 2010, c. 17, s. 9.

CROSS-REFERENCES

The time for making an application for a termination order is set out in s. 490.015. Section 490.017 provides for an appeal from a decision under this section. For other cross-references, see s. 490.012.

SYNOPSIS

This section sets out the circumstances when a court may terminate an order. The test is similar to the test set out in s. 490.012(4) for when the court may refuse to initially make the order. The applicant must establish that the impact of continuing the order or orders, and any obligation, to which the application relates, including on their privacy or liberty, would be grossly disproportionate to the public interest in the protection of society through the effective prevention or investigation of crimes of a sexual nature, to be achieved by the registration of information relating to sex offenders. The court must give reasons for the decision.

ANNOTATIONS

Note: the following cases were decided under s. 490.012(4) which, at that time, gave a judge a discretion to refuse to initially make an order requiring compliance with the *Sex Offender Information Registration Act*, S.C. 2004, c. 10. That discretion has now been removed. Notes of the following decisions have been included because s. 490.012(4) was worded similarly to the present s. 490.016(1), although the latter now specifically refers to the importance of protecting society through prevention of crimes of a sexual nature, whereas former s. 490.012(4) only referred to investigation of such crimes.

The standard of "grossly disproportionate" is very high. While registration will have some impact on the offender's privacy, this must be balanced against the purpose of the legislation and its confidentiality requirements. The purpose of registration is not to identify sex offenders to the community but, in accordance with this section, to help police services investigate crimes of a sexual nature by requiring the registration of certain information relating to sex offenders. The provisions of the *Sex Offender Information Registration Act* indicate an intention to keep information collected confidential and for use only by those with a legitimate reason in keeping with the purposes of investigation of crime and protection of society: *R. v. Casaway* (2005), 64 W.C.B. (2d) 610 (N.W.T.S.C.). Similarly, *R. v. Clarke* (2005), 197 C.C.C. (3d) 443 (N.S.S.C.), affd 208 C.C.C. (3d) 243 (N.S.C.A.), and *R. v. S. (L.)* (2005), 78 W.C.B. (2d) 378 (B.C. Prov. Ct.).

The impact to be assessed is the impact of the registration requirements on the offender's current and prospective circumstances. This includes a consideration of the impact of registration on the offender's privacy and liberty interests. The evidence upon which the convicted offender may rely to invoke and satisfy the exception may emerge from the trial or sentencing proceedings. Relevant factors include the nature of the offence, the risk to re-offend, the offender's criminal record and other matters personal to the offender's circumstances. The registration is not limited, however, to likely recidivism and the diminished risk of recidivism is not a basis to enhance the impact on the offender or dilute the public interest in registration: *R. v. Debidin* (2008), 241 C.C.C. (3d) 152 (Ont. C.A.).

The focus on the inquiry must be on the offender's present and possible future circumstances and not on the offence itself. In considering whether the order would be grossly disproportionate, the court must assess the impact of the order on the offender, including the impact on his privacy and liberty interests, and determine whether that impact is grossly disproportionate to the public interest. Factors that may be considered include unique individual circumstances such as a personal handicap, which would require the offender to obtain assistance to report, intangible effects such as stigma, undermining rehabilitation and reintegration in the community, and whether the order might result in police harassment. Absent disproportional impact, the length of the reporting obligation alone does not constitute gross disproportionality: *R. v. Redhead* (2006), 206 C.C.C. (3d) 315 (Alta. C.A.), leave to appeal to S.C.C. refused [2006] 2 S.C.R. x, 210 C.C.C. (3d) vi.

APPEAL / Requirements relating to notice.

490.017 (1) The prosecutor or the person who applied for a termination order may appeal from a decision made under subsection 490.016(1) on any ground of appeal that raises a question of law or of mixed law and fact. The appeal court may dismiss the appeal, or allow it and order a new hearing, quash the termination order or make an order that may be made under that subsection.

(2) If the appeal court makes an order that may be made under subsection 490.016(1), it shall cause the Commissioner of the Royal Canadian Mounted Police and the Attorney General of the province, or the minister of justice of the territory, in which the application for the order was made to be notified of the decision. 2004, c. 10, s. 20; 2007, c. 5, s. 17; 2010, c. 17, s. 10.

CROSS-REFERENCES

"Prosecutor" is defined in s. 2. For other cross-references, see s. 490.012.

SYNOPSIS

This section gives the prosecutor or the person who applied for a termination order a right of appeal on a question of law or mixed law and fact. The appeal court may dismiss the appeal, or allow the appeal and order a new hearing, quash the termination order or make an order that may be made under s. 490.016(1).

ANNOTATIONS

Section 487.054 provides for appeals in relation to making of DNA orders. Like this section, it does not specify the appeal court. In *R. v. Hendry* (2001), 161 C.C.C. (3d) 275, 48 C.R. (5th) 310 (Ont. C.A.), the court held that the appeal route follows the scheme in the *Criminal Code* generally. That is, in indictable proceedings, the appeal from the making or refusal to make the order lies to the Court of Appeal and, in summary conviction proceedings, the appeal is taken in accordance with Part XXVII of the *Criminal Code*.

REQUIREMENTS RELATING TO NOTICE / Endorsement / Notice on disposition by Review Board / Notice before release.

490.018 (1) When a court or appeal court makes an order under section 490.012, it shall cause

- (*a*) **the order to be read by or to the person who is subject to it;**
- (*b*) **a copy of the order to be given to that person;**
- (*c*) **that person to be informed of sections 4 to 7.1 of the *Sex Offender Information Registration Act*, sections 490.031 and 490.0311 of this Act and section 119.1 of the *National Defence Act*; and**
- (*d*) **a copy of the order to be sent to**
  - (i) **the Review Board that is responsible for making a disposition with respect to that person, if applicable,**
  - (ii) **the person in charge of the place in which that person is to serve the custodial portion of a sentence or is to be detained in custody as part of a disposition under Part XX.1, if applicable,**
  - (iii) **the police service whose member charged that person with the offence in connection with which the order is made, and**
  - (iv) **the Commissioner of the Royal Canadian Mounted Police.**

(2) After paragraphs (1)(*a*) to (*c*) have been complied with, the person who is subject to the order shall endorse the order.

(3) A Review Board shall cause a copy of the order to be given to the person who is subject to it when it directs

    (*a*)   **under paragraph 672.54(*a*), that the person be discharged absolutely; or**

    (*b*)   **under paragraph 672.54(*b*), that the person be discharged subject to conditions, unless the conditions restrict the person's liberty in a manner and to an extent that prevent them from complying with sections 4, 4.1, 4.3 and 6 of the *Sex Offender Information Registration Act*.**

(4) The person in charge of the place in which the person is serving the custodial portion of a sentence, or is detained in custody, before their release or discharge shall give the person a copy of the order not earlier than 10 days before their release or discharge. 2004, c. 10, s. 20; 2007, c. 5, s. 18; 2010, c. 17, s. 11.

CROSS-REFERENCES

"Review Board" is defined in s. 490.011. For other cross-references, see s. 490.012.

Section 119.1 of the *National Defence Act* provides as follows:

> 119.1 Every person who, without reasonable excuse, fails to comply with an order made under section 227.01 of this Act or section 490.012 of the *Criminal Code*, or with an obligation under section 227.06 of this Act or section 490.019 of the *Criminal Code*, is guilty of an offence and on conviction is liable to imprisonment for less than two years or to less punishment.

SYNOPSIS

This section sets out the notice requirements where a court makes an order to comply with registration requirements under the *Sex Offender Information Registration Act*, S.C. 2004, c. 10. Sections 4 to 7 of that Act set out the obligations of the person for reporting to a registration centre and providing information. A copy of the order is to be sent to the place where the person is detained, the Review Board, if applicable, and the police service that charged the offender. The offender is required to endorse the order. This section also places notice obligations on the Review Board. The person in charge of the place where the offender is serving sentence or is detained is required to give the person a copy of the order not earlier than 10 days before the offender's release or discharge.

Notice and Obligation to Comply with the *Sex Offender Information Registration Act* — Convictions Before December 15, 2004

2010, c. 17, s. 12.

OBLIGATION TO COMPLY.

490.019 A person who is served with a notice in Form 53 shall comply with the *Sex Offender Information Registration Act* for the applicable period specified in section 490.022 unless a court makes an exemption order under subsection 490.023(2). 2004, c. 10, s. 20.

CROSS-REFERENCES

Section 4(2) of the *Sex Offender Information Registration Act*, S.C. 2004, c. 10, provides as follows:

> (2) A person who is subject to an obligation under section 490.019 or 490.02901 of the *Criminal Code*, section 227.06 of the *National Defence Act* or section 36.1 of the *International Transfer of Offenders Act* shall report to a registration centre referred to in section 7.1

    (*a*) if they are not in custody on the day on which they become subject to the obligation, within seven days — or, if they are required to report to a registration centre designated under the *National Defence Act*, within 15 days — after that day; and

    (*b*) in any other case, within seven days — or, if they are required to report to a registration centre designated under the *National Defence Act*, within 15 days — after

        (i) they receive an absolute or conditional discharge under Part XX.1 of the *Criminal Code*,

        (i.1) they receive an absolute or conditional discharge or are released from custody under Division 7 of Part III of the *National Defence Act*,

        (i.2) an imprisonment or a detention to which they are sentenced is suspended under section 215 or 216 of the *National Defence Act*,

        (ii) they are released from custody pending the determination of an appeal, or

        (iii) they are released from custody after serving the custodial portion of a sentence.

Section 5(*b*) of the *Criminal Records Act*, R.S.C. 1985, c. C-47, provides that the legal restriction imposed by this section continues, notwithstanding that the individual has been granted a pardon under that Act.

Section 490.02 sets out the persons who may be served with a notice. Under s. 490.021, the notice must be served within one year after the day on which the *Sex Offender Information Registration Act* came into force (December 15, 2004). That section sets out the manner of service. Section 490.022 sets out the date that the obligation to comply begins and ends. Section 490.023 allows the person to apply to a court for an exemption order. Section 490.024 provides for an appeal from the refusal to make an exemption order or by the Attorney General from the making of the exemption order. Section 490.025 provides for notice to the person that they have not been granted an exemption order. Under s. 490.026, the person may apply for a termination order under s. 490.027. Section 490.028 deals with the case where the offender is eligible to apply for an exemption order and a termination order. Section 490.029 allows for appeals in relation to termination orders. Section 490.03 deals with disclosure of the material in the database. Section 490.031 creates an offence for failing to comply with an obligation as required by this section. The similar scheme for offenders who have been convicted or found not criminally responsible in relation to offences committed outside Canada is set out in ss. 490.02901 to 490.02911.

SYNOPSIS

This section creates the obligation to comply with the *Sex Offender Information Registration Act*, S.C. 2004, c. 10, for persons who fall within s. 490.02 and have been served with a notice, and the court has not made an exemption order.

ANNOTATIONS

These provisions do not violate ss. 7 or 11 of the Charter: *C. (P.S.) v. British Columbia (Attorney General)* (2007), 222 C.C.C. (3d) 230 (B.C.S.C.); *R. v. B. (C.L.)* (2007), 225 C.C.C. (3d) 237, [2007] 12 W.W.R. 120 (Alta. Q.B.).

    The retrospective application of the SOIRA provisions does not offend s. 7 of the Charter: *R. v. Warren* (2010), 254 C.C.C. (3d) 264 (Alta. C.A.).

PERSONS WHO MAY BE SERVED / Exception.

490.02 (1) The Attorney General of a province or minister of justice of a territory may serve a person with a notice only if the person was convicted of, or found not criminally responsible on account of mental disorder for, an offence referred to in paragraph (*a*), (*c*), (*c*.1), (*d*) or (*e*) of the definition "designated offence" in subsection 490.011(1) and

    (*a*) on the day on which the *Sex Offender Information Registration Act* comes into force, they are subject to a sentence for, or have not received an absolute discharge under Part XX.1 from, the offence; or

    (*b*) in any other case,

        (i) their name appears in connection with the offence, immediately before the *Sex Offender Information Registration Act* comes into force, in the sex offender registry established under the Ontario Act, and

      (ii) **they either were a resident of Ontario at any time between April 23, 2001 and the day on which the *Sex Offender Information Registration Act* comes into force or committed the offence in Ontario.**

(2) **A notice shall not be served on a person**

    (*a*) **if they have been finally acquitted of, or have received a free pardon granted under Her Majesty's royal prerogative of mercy or under section 748 for, every offence in connection with which a notice may be served on them under section 490.021 of this Act or section 227.08 of the *National Defence Act*;**

    (*b*) **if an application has been made for an order under subsection 490.012(3) of this Act or subsection 227.01(3) of the *National Defence Act* in relation to any offence in connection with which a notice may be served on them under section 490.021 of this Act or section 227.08 of the *National Defence Act*; or**

    (*c*) **who is referred to in paragraph (1)(*b*) if they have provided proof of a pardon in accordance with subsection 9(1) of the Ontario Act. 2004, c. 10, s. 20; 2007, c. 5, s. 20.**

CROSS-REFERENCES

"Attorney General" is defined in s. 2. Section 490.021 provides that the notice must be served within one year of the day the *Sex Offender Information Registration Act*, S.C. 2004, c. 10, came into force (December 15, 2004) and sets out the manner of service. Section 490.022 sets out the date that the obligation to comply begins and its duration. Section 490.023 allows the person to apply to a court for an exemption order. Section 490.024 provides for an appeal from the refusal to make an exemption order or by the Attorney General from the making of the exemption order. Section 490.025 provides for notice to the person that they have not been granted an exemption order. Under s. 490.026, the person may apply for a termination order under s. 490.027. Section 490.028 deals with the case where the offender is eligible to apply for an exemption order and a termination order. Section 490.029 allows for appeals in relation to termination orders. Section 490.03 deals with disclosure of the material in the database. Section 490.031 creates an offence for failing to comply with an obligation as required by s. 490.019.

SYNOPSIS

This section deals with cases where the offender is not before a court and therefore not liable to an order made under s. 490.012. Presumably, it was intended to deal with offenders who were dealt with before the *Sex Offender Information Registration Act*, S.C. 2004, c. 10, came into force on December 15, 2004. It sets out two circumstances where a person may be served with a notice to comply with the *Sex Offender Information Registration Act*. The first is where the person was convicted or found not criminally responsible for one of the sexual offences listed in the definition of designated offences in s. 490.011(1)(*a*), (*c*), (*d*) or (*e*) and was still under sentence or had not received an absolute discharge on the day the Act came into force. The second circumstance is where the person's name appears in connection with the offence on the sex offender registry created by the Ontario Act and the person was a resident of Ontario between April 23, 2001 and December 15, 2004. However, the notice shall not be served if the person has received a free pardon, has already been served with a notice under s. 490.012 or, in the case of a person in the Ontario registry, they have provided proof of a pardon in accordance with the Ontario Act. Section 490.012(5) and (6) set out the manner of proof of service.

ANNOTATIONS

The provisions of the *Sex Offender Information Registration Act*, S.C. 2004, c. 10, and these provisions were intended to be retrospective in application and to apply to any convicted offender sentenced after the coming into force of the legislation for an offence that is a designated offence. Further, registration is not a "punishment" so as to trigger the offender's right under s. 11(*i*) of the *Charter of Rights and Freedoms* to the benefit of lesser punishment where the punishment has varied between the time of the commission and the time of sentencing: *R. v. Cross* (2006), 205 C.C.C. (3d) 289, 37 C.R. (6th) 81 (N.S.C.A.), leave to appeal to S.C.C. refused [2006] 2 S.C.R. (3d) vi, 210 C.C.C. (3d) vi; *R. v. C. (S.S.)* (2008), 234 C.C.C. (3d) 365, 59 C.R. (6th) 237 (B.C.C.A.). See also *R. v. B. (C.L.)* (2010), 253 C.C.C. (3d) 486, 477 A.R. 365 (C.A.). Similarly, see *R. v. Dyck* (2005), 203 C.C.C. (3d) 365, 35 C.R. (6th) 56 (Ont. S.C.J.), holding that registration under *Christopher's Law (Sex Offender Registry), 2000*, S.O. 2000, c. 1, is not punishment for the purpose of s. 11(*i*). [Note: also now see *R. v. Rodgers* (2006), 207 C.C.C. (3d) 225, 37 C.R. (6th) 1 (S.C.C.), considering the retroactive application of the DNA data bank provision, s. 487.055.]

Christopher's Law (Sex Offender Registry), 2000, S.O. 2000, c. 1 (the "Ontario Act"), is valid legislation. It is *intra vires* the province, does not violate ss. 7 and 12 of the *Canadian Charter of Rights and Freedoms* and has not been rendered inoperative by enactment of this Act and the related *Criminal Code* provisions: *R. v. Dyck, supra.*

Someone who is subject to a firearms prohibition under s. 109 is "subject to a sentence" within the meaning of subsec. (1)(*a*): *T. (R.A.) v. British Columbia (Attorney General)* (2011), 277 C.C.C. (3d) 334 (B.C.C.A.).

PERIOD FOR AND METHOD OF SERVICE / Exception / Exception / Exception / Proof of Service / Requirements relating to notice.

490.021 (1) The notice shall be personally served within one year after the day on which the *Sex Offender Information Registration Act* comes into force.

(2) If a person referred to in paragraph 490.02(1)(*a*) is unlawfully at large or is in breach of any terms of their sentence or discharge, or of any conditions set under this Act or under Part III of the *National Defence Act*, that relate to residence, the notice may be served by registered mail at their last known address.

(3) If a person referred to in paragraph 490.02(1)(*b*) is not in compliance with section 3 of the Ontario Act on the day on which the *Sex Offender Information Registration Act* comes into force, the notice may be served by registered mail at their last known address.

(4) If a person referred to in paragraph 490.02(1)(*b*) is in compliance with section 3 and subsection 7(2) of the Ontario Act on the day on which the *Sex Offender Information Registration Act* comes into force but fails to comply with subsection 3(1) or 7(2) of the Ontario Act within one year after that day, the notice shall be served within one year after the day on which they failed to comply and may be served by registered mail at their last known address.

(5) An affidavit of the person who served the notice, sworn before a commissioner or other person authorized to take affidavits, is evidence of the service and the notice if it sets out that
> **(*a*) the person who served the notice has charge of the appropriate records and has knowledge of the facts in the particular case;**
> **(*b*) the notice was personally served on, or mailed to, the person to whom it was directed on a named day; and**
> **(*c*) the person who served the notice identifies a true copy of the notice as an exhibit attached to the affidavit.**

(6) The person who served the notice shall, without delay, send a copy of the affidavit and the notice to the Attorney General of the province, or the minister of justice of the territory, in which the person was served. 2004, c. 10, s. 20; 2007, c. 5, s. 21(2).

CROSS-REFERENCES
"Attorney General" is defined in s. 2. "Pardon" is defined in s. 490.011. Section 490.02 sets out the persons who may be served with a notice to comply with the obligations under s. 490.019. Section 490.022 sets out the date that the obligation to comply begins and its duration. Section 490.023

allows the person to apply to a court for an exemption order. Section 490.024 provides for an appeal from the refusal to make an exemption order or by the Attorney General from the making of the exemption order. Section 490.025 provides for notice to the person that they have not been granted an exemption order. Under s. 490.026, the person may apply for a termination order under s. 490.027. Section 490.028 deals with the case where the offender is eligible to apply for an exemption order and a termination order. Section 490.029 allows for appeals in relation to termination orders. Section 490.03 deals with disclosure of the material in the database. Section 490.031 creates an offence for failing to comply with an obligation as required by s. 490.019.

SYNOPSIS

The notice to comply with the *Sex Offender Information Registration Act*, S.C. 2004, c. 10, must be served within one year after the day on which the Act came into force (December 15, 2004). The notice must be served personally unless the person is unlawfully at large or in breach of the terms of the sentence or discharge or in breach of s. 3 of the Ontario Act, which sets out the times for the offender to report to the police force, in which case service may be effected by registered mail at the last known address. Subsections (5) and (6) provide for proof of service.

DATE OBLIGATION BEGINS / Date obligation ends / Duration of obligation.

490.022 (1) The obligation under section 490.019 begins

    (*a*) **either one year after the day on which the person is served with the notice or when an exemption order is refused under subsection 490.023(2), whichever is later; or**

    (*b*) **when an exemption order is quashed.**

(2) The obligation ends on the earliest of

    (*a*) **the day on which an exemption order is made on an appeal from a decision made under subsection 490.023(2),**

    (*b*) **the day on which the obligation of a person referred to in paragraph 490.02(1)(*b*) to comply with section 3 of the Ontario Act ends under paragraph 7(1)(*a*) of that Act, or**

    (*c*) **the day on which a person referred to in paragraph 490.02(1)(*b*) provides satisfactory proof of a pardon or record suspension to a person who collects information, as defined in subsection 3(1) of the *Sex Offender Information Registration Act*, at a registration centre.**

(3) If none of paragraphs (2)(*a*) to (*c*) applies earlier, the obligation

    (*a*) **ends 10 years after the person was sentenced, or found not criminally responsible on account of mental disorder, for the offence listed in the notice if the offence was prosecuted summarily or if the maximum term of imprisonment for the offence is two or five years;**

    (*b*) **ends 20 years after the person was sentenced, or found not criminally responsible on account of mental disorder, for the offence listed in the notice if the maximum term of imprisonment for the offence is 10 or 14 years;**

    (*c*) **applies for life if the maximum term of imprisonment for the offence listed in the notice is life; or**

    (*d*) **applies for life if, at any time, the person was convicted of, or found not criminally responsible on account of mental disorder for, more than one offence that is referred to in paragraph (*a*), (*c*), (*c*.1), (*d*) or (*e*) of the definition "designated offence" in subsection 490.011(1) of this Act or in paragraph (*a*) or (*c*) of the definition "designated offence" in section 227 of the *National Defence Act* and if more than one of those offences is listed in the notice. 2004, c. 10, s. 20; 2007, c. 5, s. 22; 2012, c. 1, s. 143.**

CROSS-REFERENCES

"Ontario Act", "pardon" and "record suspension" are defined in s. 490.011. Section 490.02 sets out the persons who may be served with a notice to comply with the obligations under s. 490.019. Section 490.023 allows the person to apply to a court for an exemption order. Section 490.024 provides for an appeal from the refusal to make an exemption order or by the Attorney General from the making of the exemption order. Section 490.025 provides for notice to the person that they have not been granted an exemption order. Under s. 490.026, the person may apply for a termination order under s. 490.027. Section 490.028 deals with the case where the offender is eligible to apply for an exemption order and a termination order. Section 490.029 allows for appeals in relation to termination orders. Section 490.03 deals with disclosure of the material in the database. Section 490.031 creates an offence for failing to comply with an obligation as required by s. 490.019.

SYNOPSIS

This section sets out the length of the obligation to comply with the relevant provisions of the *Sex Offender Information Registration Act*, S.C. 2004, c. 10, in accordance with s. 490.019. The obligation begins one year after the date of service with the notice of the obligation or when a court decides not to make an exemption order, whichever is later, or when an exemption order is quashed. The obligation ends when an exemption order is made, when the obligation of a person who is registered under the Ontario Act ends, or the person provides proof of a pardon or record suspension. Subsection (3) sets out the duration of the obligation to comply.

APPLICATION FOR EXEMPTION ORDER / Jurisdiction / Exemption order / Reasons for decision / Removal of information from database.

490.023 (1) A person who is not subject to an order under section 490.012 of this Act or section 227.01 of the *National Defence Act* may apply for an order exempting them from the obligation within one year after they are served with a notice under section 490.021 of this Act or section 227.08 of the *National Defence Act*.

(1.1) The application shall be made to a court of criminal jurisdiction if

(a) it relates to an obligation under section 490.019 of this Act; or

(b) it relates to an obligation under section 227.06 of the *National Defence Act* and the Chief Military Judge does not have jurisdiction to receive the application under subsection 227.1(2) of that Act.

(2) The court shall make an exemption order if it is satisfied that the person has established that the impact of the obligation on them, including on their privacy or liberty, would be grossly disproportionate to the public interest in protecting society through the effective prevention or investigation of crimes of a sexual nature, to be achieved by the registration of information relating to sex offenders under the *Sex Offender Information Registration Act*.

(3) The court shall give reasons for its decision.

(4) If the court makes an exemption order, it shall also make an order requiring the Royal Canadian Mounted Police to permanently remove from the database all information that relates to the person that was registered in the database on receipt of the copy of the notice. 2004, c. 10, s. 20; 2007, c. 5, s. 23; 2010, c. 17, s. 13.

CROSS-REFERENCES

"Court of criminal jurisdiction" is defined in s. 2. "Database" is defined in s. 490.011. Section 490.02 sets out the persons who may be served with a notice to comply with the obligations under s. 490.019. Section 490.022 sets out the date that the obligation to comply begins and its duration. Section 490.024 provides for an appeal from the refusal to make an exemption order or by the Attorney General from the making of the exemption order. Section 490.025 provides for notice to the person that they have not been granted an exemption order. Under s. 490.026, the person may apply for a termination order under s. 490.027. Section 490.028 deals with the case where the offender is eligible to apply for an exemption order and a termination order. Section 490.029 allows for appeals in relation to termination orders. Section 490.03 deals with disclosure of the material in the database. Section 490.031 creates an offence for failing to comply with an obligation as required by s. 490.019.

SYNOPSIS

This section provides that a person may apply for an order exempting them from complying with an obligation under s. 490.019. The application must be brought within one year from the date they were served with the notice of the obligation. Subsection (2) sets out the test the court is to apply in deciding whether to make the order. The court is required to give reasons for the decision. If the court makes the exemption order, they are also required to remove all information from the database relating to the person.

ANNOTATIONS

The court has no power to make a partial exemption order, such as an order relieving the offender from complying with the temporarily absent reporting conditions in s. 6 of the *Sex Offender Information Registration Act*. The fact that there is no such power may be taken into account in considering the impact the order would have on the applicant's ability to seek more remunerative employment in the long distance trucking industry. In considering whether to make an exemption order, it is open to the court to consider the broader public interest including the public interest in rehabilitation, which might be impaired by the reporting requirements: *R. v. W. (G.E.)* (2006), 396 A.R. 149 (Q.B.).

There is no jurisdiction to alter the duration of the order: *R. v. R. (M.J.)* (2007), 224 C.C.C. (3d) 80, 257 N.S.R. (2d) 120 (C.A.).

APPEAL / Removal of information from database.

490.024 (1) The Attorney General or the person who applied for an exemption order may appeal from a decision of the court under subsection 490.023(2) on any ground of appeal that raises a question of law or of mixed law and fact. The appeal court may dismiss the appeal, or allow it and order a new hearing, quash the exemption order or make an order that may be made under that subsection.

(2) If the appeal court makes an exemption order, it shall also make an order requiring the Royal Canadian Mounted Police to permanently remove from the database all information that relates to the person that was registered in the database on receipt of the copy of the notice. 2004, c. 10, s. 20; 2010, c. 17, s. 14.

CROSS-REFERENCES

"Attorney General" is defined in s. 2. Section 490.02 sets out the persons who may be served with a notice to comply with the obligations under s. 490.019. Section 490.022 sets out the date that the obligation to comply begins and its duration. Section 490.023 allows the person to apply to a court for an exemption order. Section 490.025 provides for notice to the person that they have not been granted an exemption order. Under s. 490.026, the person may apply for a termination order under s. 490.027. Section 490.028 deals with the case where the offender is eligible to apply for an exemption order and a termination order. Section 490.029 allows for appeals in relation to termination orders. Section 490.03 deals with disclosure of the material in the database. Section 490.031 creates an offence for failing to comply with an obligation as required by s. 490.019.

SYNOPSIS

This section creates a right of appeal in the Attorney General or the person who applied for the exemption. The appeal is limited to questions of law or mixed law and fact.

ANNOTATIONS

Section 487.054 provides for appeals in relation to making of DNA orders. Like this section, it does not specify the appeal court. In *R. v. Hendry* (2001), 161 C.C.C. (3d) 275, 48 C.R. (5th) 310 (Ont. C.A.), the court held that the appeal route follows the scheme in the *Criminal Code* generally. That is, in indictable proceedings, the appeal from the making or refusal to make the order lies to the Court of Appeal and, in summary conviction proceedings, the appeal is taken in accordance with Part XXVII of the *Criminal Code*.

REQUIREMENTS RELATING TO NOTICE.

490.025 If a court refuses to make an exemption order or an appeal court dismisses an appeal from such a decision or quashes an exemption order, it shall cause the Commissioner of the Royal Canadian Mounted Police and the Attorney General of the province, or the minister of justice of the territory, in which the application for the order was made to be notified of the decision and shall cause the person who applied for the order to be informed of sections 4 to 7.1 of the *Sex Offender Information Registration Act*, sections 490.031 and 490.0311 of this Act and section 119.1 of the *National Defence Act*. 2004, c. 10, s. 20; 2007, c. 5, s. 24; 2010, c. 17, s. 15.

CROSS-REFERENCES

Section 490.02 sets out the persons who may be served with a notice to comply with the obligations under s. 490.019. Section 490.022 sets out the date that the obligation to comply begins and its duration. Section 490.023 allows the person to apply to a court for an exemption order. Section 490.024 provides for an appeal from the refusal to make an exemption order or by the Attorney General from the making of the exemption order. Under s. 490.026, the person may apply for a termination order under s. 490.027. Section 490.028 deals with the case where the offender is eligible to apply for an exemption order and a termination order. Section 490.029 allows for appeals in relation to termination orders. Section 490.03 deals with disclosure of the material in the database. Section 490.031 creates an offence for failing to comply with an obligation as required by s. 490.019.

SYNOPSIS

This section provides the mechanism to ensure that the person who has been unsuccessful either at first instance or on appeal in an application for an exemption order is notified of the result and of their obligation to therefore comply with the relevant provisions of the *Sex Offender Information Registration Act*, S.C. 2004, c. 10, and that it is an offence under s. 490.031 not to comply.

APPLICATION FOR TERMINATION ORDER / Time for application / More than one offence / Pardon or record suspension / Re-application / Jurisdiction.

490.026 (1) A person who is subject to an obligation under section 490.019 may apply for a termination order unless they are also subject to an obligation under section 490.02901, under section 227.06 of the *National Defence Act* or under section 36.1 of the *International Transfer of Offenders Act* — or an order under section 490.012 or under section 227.01 of the *National Defence Act* — that began later.

(2) A person may apply for a termination order if the following period has elapsed since they were sentenced, or found not criminally responsible on account of mental disorder, for an offence referred to in paragraph (*a*), (*c*), (*c*.1), (*d*) or (*e*) of the definition "designated offence" in subsection 490.011(1) of this Act or in paragraph (*a*) or (*c*) of the definition "designated offence" in section 227 of the *National Defence Act*:

    (*a*) five years if the offence was prosecuted summarily or if the maximum term of imprisonment for the offence is two or five years;

    (*b*) **10 years if the maximum term of imprisonment for the offence is 10 or 14 years; or**

    (*c*) **20 years if the maximum term of imprisonment for the offence is life.**

(3) If more than one offence is listed in the notice served under section 490.021, the person may apply for a termination order if 20 years have elapsed since they were sentenced, or found not criminally responsible on account of mental disorder, for the most recent offence referred to in paragraph (*a*), (*c*), (*c*.1), (*d*) or (*e*) of the definition "designated offence" in subsection 490.011(1) of this Act or in paragraph (*a*) or (*c*) of the definition "designated offence" in section 227 of the *National Defence Act*.

(4) Despite subsections (2) and (3), a person may apply for a termination order once they receive a pardon or once a record suspension is ordered.

(5) A person whose application is refused may apply again if five years have elapsed since they made the previous application. They may also apply again once they receive a pardon or once a record suspension is ordered. However, they may not apply again if, after the previous application was made, they become subject to an obligation under section 490.02901, under section 227.06 of the *National Defence Act* or under section 36.1 of the *International Transfer of Offenders Act* or to an order under section 490.012 or under section 227.01 of the *National Defence Act*.

(6) The application shall be made to a court of criminal jurisdiction if

    (*a*) **it relates to an obligation under section 490.019 of this Act; or**

    (*b*) **it relates to an obligation under section 227.06 of the *National Defence Act* and the Chief Military Judge does not have jurisdiction to receive the application under subsection 227.12(6) of that Act. 2004, c. 10, s. 20; 2007, c. 5, s. 24; 2010, c. 17, s. 16; 2012, c. 1, s. 144.**

CROSS-REFERENCES

"Court of criminal jurisdiction" is defined in s. 2. "Pardon" and "record suspension" are defined in s. 490.011. Section 490.02 sets out the persons who may be served with a notice to comply with the obligations under s. 490.019. Section 490.022 sets out the date that the obligation to comply begins and its duration. Section 490.023 allows the person to apply to a court for an exemption order. Section 490.024 provides for an appeal from the refusal to make an exemption order or by the Attorney General from the making of the exemption order. Section 490.025 provides for notice to the person that they have not been granted an exemption order. The termination order is made under s. 490.027. Section 490.028 deals with the case where the offender is eligible to apply for an exemption order and a termination order. Section 490.029 allows for appeals in relation to termination orders. Section 490.03 deals with disclosure of the material in the database. Section 490.031 creates an offence for failing to comply with an obligation as required by s. 490.019. Pursuant to s. 490.015(3), a person who is subject to an obligation under s. 490.019 and has applied for a termination order under s. 490.015 must include an application to terminate the obligation as well.

SYNOPSIS

This section sets out the circumstances in which the person may apply for an order terminating the obligation under s. 490.019. The person cannot be subject to an order under s. 490.012. (If they are, they must apply under s. 490.015 to terminate the order and the obligation.) Subsection (2) sets out the times when the application may be made. Where the person has committed more than one offence, they can only apply to terminate the obligation after 20 years from the date when they were sentenced or found not criminally responsible, pursuant to subsec. (3). The person may reapply after five years from the date of the application or if they have received a pardon or record suspension, unless in the interim they became subject to an obligation under s. 490.02901 for offences committed outside Canada or obligations or orders made under certain provisions of the *National Defence Act*, R.S.C. 1985, c. N-5, or the *International Transfer of Offenders Act*, S.C. 2004, c. 21.

TERMINATION ORDER / Reasons for decision / Requirements relating to notice.

490.027 (1) The court shall make an order terminating the obligation if it is satisfied that the person has established that the impact on them of continuing the obligation, including on their privacy or liberty, would be grossly disproportionate to the public interest in protecting society through the effective prevention or investigation of crimes of a sexual nature, to be achieved by the registration of information relating to sex offenders under the *Sex Offender Information Registration Act*.

(2) The court shall give reasons for its decision.

(3) If the court makes a termination order, it shall cause the Commissioner of the Royal Canadian Mounted Police and the Attorney General of the province, or the minister of justice of the territory, to be notified of the decision. 2004, c. 10, s. 20; 2007, c. 5, s. 25; 2010, c. 17, s. 17.

CROSS-REFERENCES

"Crime of a sexual nature" is defined in s. 490.011. Section 490.02 sets out the persons who may be served with a notice to comply with the obligations under s. 490.019. Section 490.022 sets out the date that the obligation to comply begins and its duration. Section 490.023 allows the person to apply to a court for an exemption order. Section 490.024 provides for an appeal from the refusal to make an exemption order or by the Attorney General from the making of the exemption order. Section 490.025 provides for notice to the person that they have not been granted an exemption order. Under s. 490.026, the person may apply for a termination order under this section. Section 490.028 deals with the case where the offender is eligible to apply for an exemption order and a termination order. Section 490.029 allows for appeals in relation to termination orders. Section 490.03 deals with disclosure of the material in the database. Section 490.031 creates an offence for failing to comply with an obligation as required by s. 490.019.

SYNOPSIS

This section sets out the circumstances in which the court may make an order terminating the obligation. The test is whether the impact of continuing the obligation would be grossly disproportionate to the public interest in the protection of society through the effective prevention or investigation of crimes of a sexual nature to be achieved through registration.

ANNOTATIONS

Note: The following cases were decided under s. 490.012(4) which, at that time, gave a judge a discretion to refuse to initially make an order requiring compliance with the *Sex Offender Information Registration Act*, S.C. 2004, c. 10. That discretion has now been removed. Notes of the following decisions have been included because s. 490.012(4) was worded similarly to the present s. 490.027(1), although the latter now specifically refers to the importance of protecting society through prevention of crimes of a sexual nature, whereas former s. 490.012(4) only referred to investigation of such crimes.

The standard of "grossly disproportionate" is very high. While registration will have some impact on the offender's privacy, this must be balanced against the purpose of the legislation and its confidentiality requirements. The purpose of registration is not to identify sex offenders to the community but, in accordance with this section, to help police services investigate crimes of a sexual nature by requiring the registration of certain information relating to sex offenders. The provisions of the *Sex Offender Information Registration Act* indicate an intention to keep information collected confidential and for use only by those with a legitimate reason in keeping with the purposes of investigation of crime and protection of society: *R. v. Casaway* (2005), 64 W.C.B. (2d) 610 (N.W.T.S.C.). Similarly, *R. v. Clarke*

(2005), 197 C.C.C. (3d) 443 (N.S.S.C.), affd 208 C.C.C. (3d) 243 (N.S.C.A.), and *R. v. S. (L.)* (2005), 78 W.C.B. (2d) 378 (B.C. Prov. Ct.).

The impact to be assessed is the impact of the registration requirements on the offender's current and prospective circumstances. This includes a consideration of the impact of registration on the offender's privacy and liberty interests. The evidence upon which the convicted offender may rely to invoke and satisfy the exception may emerge from the trial or sentencing proceedings. Relevant factors include the nature of the offence, the risk to re-offend, the offender's criminal record and other matters personal to the offender's circumstances. The registration is not limited, however, to likely recidivism and the diminished risk of recidivism is not a basis to enhance the impact on the offender or dilute the public interest in registration: *R. v. Debidin* (2008), 241 C.C.C. (3d) 152 (Ont. C.A.).

The focus on the inquiry must be on the offender's present and possible future circumstances and not on the offence itself. In considering whether the order would be grossly disproportionate, the court must assess the impact of the order on the offender, including the impact on his privacy and liberty interests, and determine whether that impact is grossly disproportionate to the public interest. Factors that may be considered include unique individual circumstances such as a personal handicap, which would require the offender to obtain assistance to report, intangible effects such as stigma, undermining rehabilitation and reintegration in the community, and whether the order might result in police harassment. Absent disproportional impact, the length of the reporting obligation alone does not constitute gross disproportionality: *R. v. Redhead* (2006), 206 C.C.C. (3d) 315 (Alta. C.A.), leave to appeal to S.C.C. refused [2006] 2 S.C.R. x, 210 C.C.C. (3d) vi.

DEEMED APPLICATION.

490.028 If a person is eligible to apply for both an exemption order under section 490.023 and a termination order under section 490.026 within one year after they are served with a notice under section 490.021 of this Act or section 227.08 of the *National Defence Act*, an application within that period for one order is deemed to be an application for both. 2004, c. 10, s. 20; 2007, c. 5, s. 26.

CROSS-REFERENCES

Section 490.02 sets out the persons who may be served with a notice to comply with the obligations under s. 490.019. Section 490.022 sets out the date that the obligation to comply begins and its duration. Section 490.023 allows the person to apply to a court for an exemption order. Section 490.024 provides for an appeal from the refusal to make an exemption order or by the Attorney General from the making of the exemption order. Section 490.025 provides for notice to the person that they have not been granted an exemption order. Under s. 490.026, the person may apply for a termination order under s. 490.027. Section 490.029 allows for appeals in relation to termination orders. Section 490.03 deals with disclosure of the material in the database. Section 490.031 creates an offence for failing to comply with an obligation as required by s. 490.019.

SYNOPSIS

It would seem that this section is designed to avoid duplication of applications. Thus, a person who is eligible for an exemption order and a termination order within one year after they were served with a notice of an obligation to comply with the provisions of the *Sex Offender Registration Act*, S.C. 2004, c. 10, is deemed to have applied for both orders.

APPEAL / Requirements relating to notice.

490.029 (1) The Attorney General or the person who applied for a termination order may appeal from a decision of the court made under subsection 490.027(1) on any ground of appeal that raises a question of law or of mixed law and fact. The appeal court may dismiss the appeal, or allow it and order a new hearing, quash the termination order or make an order that may be made under that subsection.

(2) If the appeal court makes an order that may be made under subsection 490.027(1), it shall cause the Commissioner of the Royal Canadian Mounted Police and the Attorney General of the province, or the minister of justice of the territory, in which the application for the order was made to be notified of the decision. 2004, c. 10, s. 20; 2007, c. 5, s. 26; 2010, c. 17, s. 18.

CROSS-REFERENCES

Section 490.02 sets out the persons who may be served with a notice to comply with the obligations under s. 490.019. Section 490.022 sets out the date that the obligation to comply begins and its duration. Section 490.023 allows the person to apply to a court for an exemption order. Section 490.024 provides for an appeal from the refusal to make an exemption order or by the Attorney General from the making of the exemption order. Section 490.025 provides for notice to the person that they have not been granted an exemption order. Under s. 490.026, the person may apply for a termination order under s. 490.027. Section 490.028 deals with the case where the offender is eligible to apply for an exemption order and a termination order. Section 490.03 deals with disclosure of the material in the database. Section 490.031 creates an offence for failing to comply with an obligation as required by s. 490.019.

SYNOPSIS

This section creates a right of appeal in the Attorney General or the person who applied for a termination order. The appeal is limited to questions of law or mixed law and fact.

ANNOTATIONS

Section 487.054 provides for appeals in relation to making of DNA orders. Like this section, it does not specify the appeal court. In *R. v. Hendry* (2001), 161 C.C.C. (3d) 275, 48 C.R. (5th) 310 (Ont. C.A.), the court held that the appeal route follows the scheme in the *Criminal Code* generally. That is, in indictable proceedings, the appeal from the making or refusal to make the order lies to the Court of Appeal and, in summary conviction proceedings, the appeal is taken in accordance with Part XXVII of the *Criminal Code*.

Notice and Obligation to Comply with the *Sex Offender Information Registration Act* — Convictions Outside Canada

OBLIGATION.

490.02901 A person who is served with a notice in Form 54 shall comply with the *Sex Offender Information Registration Act* for the applicable period specified in section 490.02904 unless a court makes an exemption order under subsection 490.02905(2). 2010, c. 17, s. 19.

CROSS-REFERENCES

Sections 490.02901 to 490.02911 establish a scheme requiring registration under the *Sex Offender Information Registration Act*, S.C. 2004, c. 10, for offences committed outside Canada. The scheme is, in many ways, similar to the scheme obliging persons who were convicted of offences before the Act came into force to register. Thus, see Cross-References under s. 490.019. The basic scheme for making an order against a person convicted or found not criminally responsible of a designated offence in Canada is set out in ss. 490.012 to 490.018.

This section sets out the basic obligation to comply with the Act for a person convicted or found not criminal responsible on account of mental disorder of an offence outside Canada that is, in the opinion of the Attorney General or minister of justice, equivalent to an offence referred to in para. (*a*) of the definition of designated offence in s. 490.011(1). Section 4(2) of the *Sex Offender Information Registration Act*, provides as follows:

(2) A person who is subject to an obligation under section 490.019 or 490.02901 of the *Criminal Code*, section 227.06 of the *National Defence Act* or section 36.1 of the *International Transfer of Offenders Act* shall report to a registration centre referred to in section 7.1

    (*a*)   if they are not in custody on the day on which they become subject to the obligation, within seven days — or, if they are required to report to a registration centre designated under the *National Defence Act*, within 15 days — after that day; and

    (*b*)   in any other case, within seven days — or, if they are required to report to a registration centre designated under the *National Defence Act*, within 15 days — after

        (i)   they receive an absolute or conditional discharge under Part XX.1 of the *Criminal Code*,

        (i.1) they receive an absolute or conditional discharge or are released from custody under Division 7 of Part III of the *National Defence Act*,

        (i.2) an imprisonment or a detention to which they are sentenced is suspended under section 215 or 216 of the *National Defence Act*,

        (ii) they are released from custody pending the determination of an appeal, or

        (iii) they are released from custody after serving the custodial portion of a sentence.

Failure to comply with the obligation is an offence under s. 490.031. Section 490.02902 sets out the persons who may be served with the obligation. In short, it is persons convicted of or found not criminally responsible on account of mental disorder for an offence outside Canada that is, in the opinion of the Attorney General or minister of justice, equivalent to an offence referred to in para. (*a*) of the definition of designated offence in s. 490.011(1). Section 490.02903 sets out the notice requirements for complying with the obligation. Section 490.02904 sets out the time frame for the length of the reporting obligations. The person may apply for an order exempting them from an obligation to register under the Act within one year after they are served. Section 490.02905 sets out the circumstances under which a court is to make an exemption order. Section 490.02906(1) provides a right of appeal by the Attorney General or the person who applied for the exemption. Sections 490.02906(2) and 490.02907 set out the consequences of an appeal. Section 490.02908 gives a person subject to an obligation the right to apply for a termination order. That section sets out when the person may apply for the termination order. Section 490.02909 sets out the test the court is to apply in deciding whether to make the order. An appeal from the decision under s. 490.02909 is taken in accordance with s. 490.0291. Section 490.02911 places an obligation on a person who was convicted or found not criminally responsible of an equivalent offence to advise the police within seven days after they arrive in Canada of their name and other identifying information. The failure to comply with the obligation under that section is an offence under s. 490.0312.

SYNOPSIS

This section sets out the obligation of a person, who has been convicted or found not criminally responsible of the equivalent of designated offence, and is served with a notice to comply with the *Sex Offender Information Registration Act*. The person must comply unless a court makes an exemption order under s. 490.02905(2).

PERSONS WHO MAY BE SERVED / Exception.

490.02902 (1) The Attorney General of a province, or the minister of justice of a territory, may serve a person with a notice in Form 54 only if the person arrived in Canada after the coming into force of this subsection and they were convicted of or found not criminally responsible on account of mental disorder for an offence outside Canada — other than a service offence as defined in subsection 2(1) of the *National Defence Act* — that is, in the opinion of the Attorney General or minister of justice, equivalent to an offence referred to in paragraph (*a*) of the definition "designated offence" in subsection 490.011(1).

(2) The notice shall not be served on a person who has been acquitted of every offence in connection with which a notice may be served on them under section 490.02903. 2010, c. 17, s. 19.

CROSS-REFERENCES

"Attorney General" is defined in s. 2. For other Cross-References, see s. 490.02901.

SYNOPSIS

This section sets out which persons, convicted or found not criminal responsible of offences outside Canada, may be served with an obligation to comply with the *Sex Offender Information Registration Act*, S.C. 2004, c. 10. A person may be served with the notice only if they entered Canada after this section came into force on April 15, 2011 and the person has been convicted or found not criminally responsible of the equivalent of a designated offence, in the opinion of the Attorney General of the province or the minister of justice of the territory.

PERIOD FOR AND METHOD OF SERVICE / Proof of service / Requirements relating to notice.

490.02903 (1) A notice in Form 54 shall be personally served.

(2) An affidavit of the person who served the notice, sworn before a commissioner or other person authorized to take affidavits, is evidence of the service and the notice if it sets out that

  (*a*) **the person who served the notice has charge of the appropriate records and has knowledge of the facts in the particular case;**

  (*b*) **the notice was personally served on the person to whom it was directed on a named day; and**

  (*c*) **the person who served the notice identifies a true copy of the notice as an exhibit attached to the affidavit.**

(3) The person who served the notice shall, without delay, send a copy of the affidavit and the notice to the Attorney General of the province, or the minister of justice of the territory, in which the person was served. 2010, c. 17, s. 19.

CROSS-REFERENCES

"Attorney General" is defined in s. 2. For other Cross-References, see s. 490.02901.

SYNOPSIS

This section sets out the notice requirements for compliance with the *Sex Offender Information Registration Act*, S.C. 2004, c. 10, for persons, convicted or found not criminally responsible, of offences outside Canada of the equivalent of a designated offence. There must be personal service in accordance with subsec. (1). Subsection (2) provides for an affidavit of service, which is to be sent to the Attorney General of the province or minister of justice pursuant to subsec. (3).

WHEN OBLIGATION BEGINS / When obligation ends / Duration of obligation.

490.02904 (1) The obligation under section 490.02901 begins on the day on which the person is served with the notice.

(2) The obligation ends on the day on which an exemption order is made.

(3) If subsection (2) does not apply, the obligation

  (*a*) **ends 10 years after the person was sentenced or found not criminally responsible on account of mental disorder if the maximum term of imprisonment provided for in Canadian law for the equivalent offence is two or five years;**

  (*b*) **ends 20 years after the person was sentenced or found not criminally responsible on account of mental disorder if the maximum term of** imprisonment provided for in Canadian law for the equivalent offence is 10 or 14 years;

(c) applies for life if the maximum term of imprisonment provided for in Canadian law for the equivalent offence is life; or

(d) applies for life if, before or after the coming into force of this paragraph, the person was convicted of, or found not criminally responsible on account of mental disorder for, more than one offence referred to in paragraph (a), (c), (c.1), (d), (d.1) or (e) of the definition "designated offence" in subsection 490.011(1) or referred to in paragraph (a) or (c) of the definition "designated offence" in section 227 of the *National Defence Act* and if more than one of those offences is listed in the notice. 2010, c. 17, s. 19; 2014, c. 25, s. 28.

CROSS-REFERENCES
For Cross-References, see s. 490.02901.

SYNOPSIS
This section sets out the length of the obligation for compliance with the *Sex Offender Information Registration Act*, S.C. 2004, c. 10, for persons convicted or found not criminally responsible of offences outside Canada of the equivalent of a designated offence. The obligation to comply begins on the day the person is served with the notice and ends when an exemption order is made, or if no exemption order is made, after expiration of the times set out in subsec. (3): 10 years after the person was sentenced or found not criminally responsible if the maximum penalty for the equivalent Canadian offence is imprisonment for two or five years; 20 years after the person was sentenced or found not criminally responsible if the maximum penalty for the equivalent Canadian offence is imprisonment for 10 or 14 years; life if the maximum term for the equivalent Canadian offence is life imprisonment; and life if the person was convicted or found not criminally responsible for more than one offence referred to in paras. (a), (c), (d), (d.1) or (e) of the definition of designated offence in s. 490.011(1) or similar offences in the *National Defence Act*, R.S.C. 1985, c. N-5.

APPLICATION FOR EXEMPTION ORDER / Exemption order / Reasons for decision / Removal of information from database / Notification.

490.02905 (1) A person who is served with a notice in Form 54 under section 490.02903 may apply to a court of criminal jurisdiction for an order exempting them from the obligation within one year after they are served.

(2) The court

(a) shall make an exemption order if it is satisfied that the person has established that

(i) they were not convicted of or found not criminally responsible on account of mental disorder for or were acquitted of the offence in question, or

(ii) the offence in question is not equivalent to an offence referred to in paragraph (a) of the definition "designated offence" in subsection 490.011(1); and

(b) shall order that the notice be corrected if it is satisfied that the offence in question is not equivalent to the offence referred to in the notice but is equivalent to another offence referred to in paragraph (a) of the definition "designated offence" in subsection 490.011(1).

(3) The court shall give reasons for its decision.

(4) If the court makes an exemption order, it shall also make an order requiring the Royal Canadian Mounted Police to permanently remove from the database all information that relates to the person that was registered in the database on receipt of the copy of the notice.

(5) If the court makes an order referred to in paragraph (2)(b), it shall cause the Commissioner of the Royal Canadian Mounted Police and the Attorney General of the province, or the minister of justice of the territory, in which the application for the order was made to be notified of the decision. 2010, c. 17, s. 19.

CROSS-REFERENCES

An appeal from a decision under this section is provided for in s. 490.02906. For other Cross-References, see s. 490.02901.

SYNOPSIS

This section sets out the process for an offender, who has been served with a s. 490.02903 notice, to apply for an exemption from the registration requirements under the *Sex Offender Information Registration Act*, S.C. 2004, c. 10, in relation to offences committed outside Canada. The application must be made within one year after the person was served with the notice. Subsection (2) sets out two grounds for the exemption order, namely: the person was not convicted or not found criminally responsible or acquitted of the offence, or the offence is not an equivalent of a designated offence as defined in s. 490.011(1). Alternatively, the court may correct the notice if the person was convicted of an equivalent offence, although not the one named in the notice. The court is required to give reasons for its decision. Subsections (3) and (4) set out the process for either removing the person's information from the database or correcting the record.

APPEAL / Removal of information from database.

490.02906 (1) The Attorney General or the person who applied for an exemption order may appeal from a decision under subsection 490.02905(2) on any ground of appeal that raises a question of law or of mixed law and fact. The appeal court may

    (a) **dismiss the appeal;**

    (b) **allow the appeal and order a new hearing;**

    (c) **quash the exemption order; or**

    (d) **make an order that may be made under that subsection.**

(2) If an appeal court makes an exemption order, it shall also make an order requiring the Royal Canadian Mounted Police to permanently remove from the database all information that relates to the person that was registered in the database on receipt of the copy of the notice. 2010, c. 17, s. 19.

CROSS-REFERENCES

"Attorney General" is defined in s. 2. For other Cross-References, see s. 490.02901.

SYNOPSIS

This section provides for an appeal from an order granting or refusing an exemption order in relation to an obligation to comply with the *Sex Offender Information Registration Act*, S.C. 2004, c. 10, in relation to offences committed outside Canada. The person or the Attorney General may appeal on any ground of law or mixed law and fact. The appellate court may dismiss the appeal, allow the appeal and order a new hearing, quash the exemption order or make any order, such as an exemption order or an order correcting the notice, that the court at first instance could have made. If the court makes an exemption order it must also make an order requiring the R.C.M.P. to permanently remove all information from the database. Section 490.02907 sets out the requirements for notifying the police and the Attorney General or minister of justice, if the appeal court quashes the exemption order.

REQUIREMENTS RELATING TO NOTICE.

490.02907 If an appeal court quashes an exemption order, it shall cause the Commissioner of the Royal Canadian Mounted Police and the Attorney General of the province, or the minister of justice of the territory, in which the application for the order was made to be notified of the decision and shall cause the person who applied for the order to be informed of sections 4 to 7.1 of the *Sex Offender Information Registration Act*, sections 490.031 and 490.0311 of this Act and section 119.1 of the *National Defence Act*. 2010, c. 17, s. 19.

CROSS-REFERENCES

"Attorney General" is defined in s. 2. If the court makes an exemption order, the process for notifying the R.C.M.P. is set out in s. 490.02906(2). For other Cross-References, see s. 490.02901.

APPLICATION FOR TERMINATION ORDER / Time for application — one offence / Time for application — more than one offence / Re-application.

490.02908 (1) A person who is subject to an obligation under section 490.02901 may apply to a court of criminal jurisdiction for a termination order unless they are also subject to another obligation under that section — or to an obligation under section 490.019, under section 227.06 of the *National Defence Act* or under section 36.1 of the *International Transfer of Offenders Act* or an order under section 490.012 or under section 227.01 of the *National Defence Act* — that began later.

(2) The person may apply for a termination order if the following period has elapsed since the sentence was imposed or the verdict of not criminally responsible on account of mental disorder was rendered:

> (a) five years if the maximum term of imprisonment provided for in Canadian law for the equivalent offence is two or five years;

> (b) 10 years if the maximum term of imprisonment provided for in Canadian law for the equivalent offence is 10 or 14 years; or

> (c) 20 years if the maximum term of imprisonment provided for in Canadian law for the equivalent offence is life.

(3) If more than one offence is listed in the notice served under section 490.02903, the person may apply for a termination order if 20 years have elapsed since the sentence was imposed, or the verdict of not criminally responsible on account of mental disorder was rendered, for the most recent offence.

(4) A person whose application is refused may apply again if five years have elapsed since the application was made. 2010, c. 17, s. 19.

CROSS-REFERENCES

If the person is subject to other obligations or orders to comply with the *Sex Offender Information Registration Act*, S.C. 2004, c. 10, in addition to an obligation for offences committed outside Canada, the application for a termination order must be made under s. 490.015. "Court of criminal jurisdiction" is defined in s. 2. The test for making a termination order is set out in s. 490.02909. An appeal from an order made under s. 490.02909 is provided for in s. 490.0291. For other Cross-References, see s. 490.02901.

SYNOPSIS

This section allows a person, subject only to an obligation under s. 490.02901 to comply with the provisions of the *Sex Offender Information Registration Act* for offences committed outside Canada, to terminate the obligation. When the person may apply depends upon the nature of the equivalent Canadian offence. The person may apply five years after the person was sentenced or found not criminally responsible if the maximum penalty for the equivalent Canadian offence is imprisonment for two or five years; 10 years after the person was sentenced or found not criminally responsible if the maximum penalty for the equivalent Canadian offence is imprisonment for 10 or 14 years; 20 years if the maximum term for the equivalent Canadian offence is life imprisonment or if more than one offence is listed in the notice. A person whose application is refused may apply again in five years.

TERMINATION ORDER / Reasons for decision / Requirements relating to notice.

490.02909 (1) The court shall make an order terminating the obligation if it is satisfied that the person has established that the impact on them of continuing the obligation, including on their privacy or liberty, would be grossly disproportionate to the public interest in protecting society through the effective prevention or investigation of crimes of a sexual nature to be achieved by the registration of information relating to sex offenders under the *Sex Offender Information Registration Act*.

(2) The court shall give reasons for its decision.

(3) If the court makes a termination order, it shall cause the Commissioner of the Royal Canadian Mounted Police and the Attorney General of the province, or the minister of justice of the territory, to be notified of the decision. 2010, c. 17, s. 19.

CROSS-REFERENCES

If the person is subject to other obligations or orders to comply with the *Sex Offender Information Registration Act*, S.C. 2004, c. 10, in addition to an obligation for offences committed outside Canada, the application for a termination order must be made under s. 490.015. An appeal from an order made under this section is provided for in s. 490.0291. The test for making a termination order under this section is similar to the test for making similar orders under s. 490.015. Accordingly, see Cross-References and Annotations under that section. For other Cross-References, see s. 490.02901.

SYNOPSIS

This section sets out the test for making an order terminating obligations under the *Sex Offender Information Registration Act* in relation to offences committed outside Canada. The test is set out in subsec. (1). The court is required to give reasons for the decision. If the termination order is made, the court is required to notify the Commissioner of the R.C.M.P. accordingly.

APPEAL / Requirements relating to notice.

490.0291 (1) The Attorney General or the person who applied for a termination order may appeal from a decision under subsection 490.02909(1) on any ground of appeal that raises a question of law or of mixed law and fact. The appeal court may dismiss the appeal, allow the appeal and order a new hearing, quash the termination order or make an order that may be made under that subsection.

(2) If the appeal court makes an order that may be made under subsection 490.02909(1), it shall cause the Commissioner of the Royal Canadian Mounted Police and the Attorney General of the province, or the minister of justice of the territory, in which the application for the order was made to be notified of the decision. 2010, c. 17, s. 19.

CROSS-REFERENCES

"Attorney General" is defined in s. 2. The basis for an appeal under this section is similar to the appeal from similar orders made under s. 490.017. Accordingly, see Cross-References and Annotations under that section. For other Cross-References, see s. 490.02901.

SYNOPSIS

This section sets out the grounds of appeal for a decision made on an application for an order terminating obligations to comply with the *Sex Offender Information Registration Act*, S.C. 2004, c. 10, in relation to offences committed outside Canada. The applicant and the Attorney General may appeal on any ground of law or mixed law and fact. The appeal court may dismiss the appeal, allow the appeal and order a new hearing, quash the termination order or make a termination order. If the termination order is made, the court is required to notify the Commissioner of the R.C.M.P. accordingly.

OBLIGATION TO ADVISE POLICE SERVICE / Change in address / Information to be provided to Attorney General / Obligation ends.

490.02911 (1) A person who was convicted of or found not criminally responsible on account of mental disorder for an offence outside Canada shall, if the offence is equivalent to one referred to in paragraph (*a*) of the definition "designated offence" in subsection 490.011(1), advise a police service within seven days after the day on which they arrive in Canada of that fact and of their name, date of birth, gender and address. They are not required to so advise the police service again unless they are later convicted of or found not criminally responsible on account of mental disorder for another such offence.

(2) The person shall, if they are in Canada, advise a police service of a change in address within seven days after the day on which the change is made.

(3) The police service shall cause the Attorney General of the province, or the minister of justice of the territory, in which it is located to be provided with the information.

(4) A person's obligation under subsection (2) ends when they are served under section 490.02902 or, if it is earlier, one year after the day on which they advise the police service under subsection (1). 2010, c. 17, s. 19.

CROSS-REFERENCES

"Attorney General" is defined in s. 2. The failure to comply with the obligation under this section is an offence under s. 490.0312. For other Cross-References, see s. 490.02901.

SYNOPSIS

This section places an obligation on persons, who were convicted of or found not criminally responsible on account of mental disorder for offences committed outside Canada that are the equivalent to offences referred to in para. (*a*) of the definition "designated offence" in s. 490.011(1), to advise the police service within seven days after the day on which they arrive in Canada of that fact and of their name, date of birth, gender and address. The police will then notify the Attorney General of the province or the minister of justice of the territory, presumably so that they can consider whether to serve a notice under s. 490.02901. The person must also notify the police service of any change of address within seven days of the change. The obligation to notify the police of change of address ends once they are served with the notice to comply with provisions of the *Sex Offender Information Registration Act*, S.C. 2004, c. 10, or one year after they originally advised the police service.

International Transfer of Offenders Act

APPLICATION FOR TERMINATION ORDER / Time for application — one offence / More than one offence / Re-application.

490.02912 (1) A person who is subject to an obligation under section 36.1 of the *International Transfer of Offenders Act* may apply to a court of criminal jurisdiction for a termination order unless they are also subject to an obligation under section 490.019

or 490.02901 or under section 227.06 of the *National Defence Act* — or to an order under section 490.012 or under section 227.01 of the *National Defence Act* — that began later.

(2) The person may apply for a termination order if the following period has elapsed since the sentence was imposed or the verdict of not criminally responsible on account of mental disorder was rendered:

    (*a*) five years if the maximum term of imprisonment provided for in Canadian law for the equivalent offence is two or five years;

    (*b*) 10 years if the maximum term of imprisonment provided for in Canadian law for the equivalent offence is 10 or 14 years; or

    (*c*) 20 years if the maximum term of imprisonment provided for in Canadian law for the equivalent offence is life.

(3) If more than one offence is listed in the copy of the Form 1 that was delivered under subparagraph 8(4)(*a*)(ii) of the *International Transfer of Offenders Act*, the person may apply for a termination order if 20 years have elapsed since the sentence was imposed, or the verdict of not criminally responsible on account of mental disorder was rendered, for the most recent offence.

(4) A person whose application is refused may apply again if five years have elapsed since the application was made. 2010, c. 17, s. 19.

CROSS-REFERENCES

This section and ss. 490.02913 to 490.02914 establish a procedure for an offender subject to an obligation to comply with the *Sex Offender Information Registration Act*, S.C. 2004, c. 10, under s. 36.1 of the *International Transfer of Offenders Act*, S.C. 2004, c. 21, to terminate that obligation. The obligation to comply begins on the day of the person's transfer. Section 4(2) of the *Sex Offender Information Registration Act*, provides as follows:

    (2) A person who is subject to an obligation under section 490.019 or 490.02901 of the *Criminal Code*, section 227.06 of the *National Defence Act* or section 36.1 of the *International Transfer of Offenders Act* shall report to a registration centre referred to in section 7.1

        (*a*) if they are not in custody on the day on which they become subject to the obligation, within seven days — or, if they are required to report to a registration centre designated under the *National Defence Act*, within 15 days — after that day; and

        (*b*) in any other case, within seven days — or, if they are required to report to a registration centre designated under the *National Defence Act*, within 15 days — after

           (i) they receive an absolute or conditional discharge under Part XX.1 of the *Criminal Code*,

          (i.1) they receive an absolute or conditional discharge or are released from custody under Division 7 of Part III of the *National Defence Act*,

          (i.2) an imprisonment or a detention to which they are sentenced is suspended under section 215 or 216 of the *National Defence Act*,

          (ii) they are released from custody pending the determination of an appeal, or

          (iii) they are released from custody after serving the custodial portion of a sentence.

Section 8(4) of the *International Transfer of Offenders Act* provides as follows:

(4) The Minister

    (*a*) shall inform a Canadian offender, in writing, as to how their foreign sentence is to be served in Canada and, in the case of an offender who is required to comply with the *Sex Offender Information Registration Act*,

        (i) inform them, in writing, of that obligation and of sections 4 to 7.1 of that Act and sections 490.031 and 490.0311 of the *Criminal Code*, and

        (ii) on the day of the transfer at the earliest, deliver a copy of Form 1 of the schedule to

           (A) the offender,

           (B) the Attorney General of the province, or the minister of justice of the territory, in which the person is to be detained in custody, and

           (C) the person in charge of the place in which the person is to be detained in custody; and

Section 36.2 of the *International Transfer of Offenders Act* provides for the point at which the obligation terminates and the duration of the obligation to comply. The process for terminating the obligation is similar to that established under ss. 490.015 to 490.017; thus, see Cross-References under those sections. If the person is subject to other obligations or orders to comply with the *Sex Offender Information Registration Act*, the application for a termination order must be made under s. 490.015. The test for making the termination order is set out in s. 490.02913. An appeal from an order made under this section is provided for in s. 490.02904. Failure to comply with the s. 36.1 obligation is an offence under s. 490.031.

SYNOPSIS

This section allows a person, subject only to an obligation under s. 36.1 of the *International Transfer of Offenders Act* to comply with the provisions of the *Sex Offender Information Registration Act*, to terminate the obligation. When the person may apply depends upon the nature of the equivalent Canadian offence. The person may apply five years after the person was sentenced or found not criminally responsible if the maximum penalty for the equivalent Canadian offence is imprisonment for two or five years; 10 years after the person was sentenced or found not criminally responsible if the maximum penalty for the equivalent Canadian offence is imprisonment for 10 or 14 years; 20 years if the maximum term for the equivalent Canadian offence is life imprisonment or if more than one offence is listed in the Form 1 that was delivered to the person under s. 8(4) of the *International Transfer of Offenders Act*. A person whose application is refused may apply again in five years.

TERMINATION ORDER / Reasons for decision / Requirements relating to notice.

490.02913 (1) The court shall make an order terminating the obligation if it is satisfied that the person has established that the impact on them of continuing the obligation, including on their privacy or liberty, would be grossly disproportionate to the public interest in protecting society through the effective prevention or investigation of crimes of a sexual nature to be achieved by the registration of information relating to sex offenders under the *Sex Offender Information Registration Act*.

(2) The court shall give reasons for its decision.

(3) If the court makes a termination order, it shall cause the Commissioner of the Royal Canadian Mounted Police and the Attorney General of the province, or the minister of justice of the territory, to be notified of the decision. 2010, c. 17, s. 19.

CROSS-REFERENCES

If the person is subject to other obligations or orders to comply with the *Sex Offender Information Registration Act*, S.C. 2004, c. 10, in addition to an obligation under s. 36.1 of the *International Transfer of Offenders Act*, S.C. 2004, c. 21, the application for a termination order must be made under s. 490.015. An appeal from an order made under this section is provided for in s. 490.02914. The test for making a termination order under this section is similar to the test for making similar orders under s. 490.015. Accordingly, see Cross-References and Annotations under that section. For other Cross-References, see s. 490.02912.

SYNOPSIS

This section sets out the test for making an order terminating obligations under the *Sex Offender Information Registration Act* as a result of s. 36.1 of the *International Transfer of Offenders Act*. The test is set out in subsec. (1). The court is required to give reasons for the decision. If the termination order is made, the court is required to notify the Commissioner of the R.C.M.P. accordingly.

APPEAL / Requirements relating to notice.

490.02914 (1) The Attorney General or the person who applied for a termination order may appeal from a decision under subsection 490.02913(1) on any ground of appeal that raises a question of law or of mixed law and fact. The appeal court may dismiss the appeal, allow the appeal and order a new hearing, quash the termination order or make an order that may be made under that subsection.

(2) If the appeal court makes an order that may be made under subsection 490.02913(1), it shall cause the Commissioner of the Royal Canadian Mounted Police and the Attorney General of the province, or the minister of justice of the territory, in which the application for the order was made to be notified of the decision. 2010, c. 17, s. 19.

CROSS-REFERENCES

"Attorney General" is defined in s. 2. The basis for an appeal under this section is similar to the appeal for similar orders made under s. 490.017. Accordingly, see Cross-References and Annotations under that section. For other Cross-References, see s. 490.02912.

SYNOPSIS

This section sets out the grounds of appeal for a decision made on an application for an order terminating obligations to comply with the *Sex Offender Information Registration Act*, S.C. 2004, c. 10, in relation to s. 36.1 of the *International Transfer of Offenders Act*, S.C. 2004, c. 21. The applicant and the Attorney General may appeal on any ground of law or mixed law and fact. The appeal court may dismiss the appeal, allow the appeal and order a new hearing, quash the termination order or make a termination order. If the termination order is made, the court is required to notify the Commissioner of the R.C.M.P. accordingly.

NOTICE BEFORE RELEASE / Notice on disposition by Review Board.

490.02915 (1) The person in charge of the place in which a person who is subject to an obligation under section 36.1 of the *International Transfer of Offenders Act* is serving the custodial portion of a sentence, or is detained in custody before their release or discharge, shall give the person a copy of the Form 1 referred to in subsection 490.02912(3) not earlier than 10 days before their release or discharge.

(2) A Review Board shall cause a copy of the Form 1 to be given to the person when it directs
  (*a*) under paragraph 672.54(*a*), that the person be discharged absolutely; or
  (*b*) under paragraph 672.54(*b*), that the person be discharged subject to conditions unless the conditions restrict the person's liberty in a manner and to an extent that prevent them from complying with sections 4, 4.1, 4.3 and 6 of the *Sex Offender Information Registration Act*. 2010, c. 17, s. 19.

CROSS-REFERENCES

See Cross-References under s. 490.02912.

SYNOPSIS

This section sets out an administrative procedure to ensure that, when persons transferred to Canada under the *International Transfer of Offenders Act*, S.C. 2004, c. 21, are released from custody, they are aware of their obligations to report in accordance with s. 36.1 of that Act and the *Sex Offender Information Registration Act*, S.C. 2004, c. 10.

Disclosure of Information

DISCLOSURE BY COMMISSIONER / Disclosure in connection with proceedings / Disclosure in proceedings.

490.03 (1) The Commissioner of the Royal Canadian Mounted Police or a person authorized by the Commissioner shall, on request, disclose information that is registered in the database or the fact that such information is registered in the database

   (*a*) **to the prosecutor if the disclosure is necessary for the purpose of a proceeding under section 490.012; or**

   (*b*) **to the Attorney General if the disclosure is necessary for the purpose of a proceeding under subsection 490.016(1), 490.023(2), 490.027(1), 490.02905(2), 490.02909(1) or 490.02913(1) or for the purpose of an appeal from a decision made in any of those proceedings or in a proceeding under subsection 490.012(2).**

(2) The Commissioner or that person shall, on request, disclose to the prosecutor or Attorney General the information that is registered in the database relating to a person if the person discloses, in connection with a proceeding or appeal other than one referred to in subsection (1), the fact that information relating to them is registered in the database.

(3) The prosecutor or the Attorney General may, if the information is relevant to the proceeding, appeal or any subsequent appeal, disclose it to the presiding court. 2004, c. 10, s. 20; 2007, c. 5, s. 27; 2010, c. 17, s. 20.

CROSS-REFERENCES

"Attorney General" and "prosecutor" are defined in s. 2. "Database" and "crime of a sexual nature" are defined in s. 490.011. Section 490.02 sets out the persons who may be served with a notice to comply with the obligations under s. 490.019. Section 490.022 sets out the date that the obligation to comply begins and its duration. Section 490.023 allows the person to apply to a court for an exemption order. Section 490.024 provides for an appeal from the refusal to make an exemption order or by the Attorney General from the making of the exemption order. Section 490.025 provides for notice to the person that they have not been granted an exemption order. Under s. 490.026, the person may apply for a termination order under s. 490.027. Section 490.028 deals with the case where the offender is eligible to apply for an exemption order and a termination order. Section 490.029 allows for appeals in relation to termination orders. Section 490.031 creates an offence for failing to comply with an obligation as required by s. 490.019.

SYNOPSIS

This section sets out the circumstances in which information in the sex offender database may be disclosed. There are, in effect, four circumstances in which information may be disclosed. At the request of the Attorney General or the prosecutor, information may be disclosed under subsec. (1) for proceedings in relation to the making or terminating an order or obligation or granting an exemption or appeals in such proceeding, or under subsec. (2) where the person him or herself disclose information. Under subsec. (3), the Attorney General or the prosecutor may disclose information to a court in connection with such proceedings. Finally, under subsec. (4), information may be disclosed to a judge or justice on an application for a search warrant in connection with an investigation of a crime that there are reasonable grounds to suspect is of a sexual nature.

Offences

OFFENCE / Reasonable excuse / Proof of certain facts by certificate / Attendance and cross-examination / Notice of intention to produce.

490.031 (1) Every person who, without reasonable excuse, fails to comply with an order made under section 490.012 or under section 227.01 of the *National Defence Act* or with an obligation under section 490.019 or 490.02901, under section 227.06 of the *National Defence Act* or under section 36.1 of the *International Transfer of Offenders Act* is guilty of an offence and liable

> (*a*) **on conviction on indictment, to a fine of not more than $10,000 or to imprisonment for a term of not more than two years, or to both; or**
>
> (*b*) **on summary conviction, to a fine of not more than $10,000 or to imprisonment for a term of not more than six months, or to both.**

(2) For greater certainty, a lawful command that prevents a person from complying with an order or obligation is a reasonable excuse if, at the time, the person is subject to the Code of Service Discipline within the meaning of subsection 2(1) of the *National Defence Act.*

(3) In proceedings under subsection (1), a certificate of a person referred to in paragraph 16(2)(*b*) of the *Sex Offender Information Registration Act* stating that the sex offender failed to report under section 4, 4.1, 4.2 or 4.3 — or provide information under section 5 or notify a person under subsection 6(1) — of that Act is evidence of the statements contained in it without proof of the signature or official character of the person appearing to have signed it.

Note: Subsection 490.031(3) replaced, 2015, c. 23, s. 30 (to come into force by order of the Governor in Council):

Proof of certain facts by certificate

(3) In proceedings under subsection (1), a certificate of a person referred to in paragraph 16(2)(*b*) of the *Sex Offender Information Registration Act* stating that the sex offender failed to report under section 4, 4.1, 4.2 or 4.3 — or provide information under section 5 or notify a person under subsection 6(1) or (1.01) — of that Act is evidence of the statements contained in it without proof of the signature or official character of the person appearing to have signed it.

(4) The sex offender named in the certificate may, with the leave of the court, require the attendance of the person who signed it for the purpose of cross-examination.

(5) A certificate is not to be received in evidence unless, before the commencement of the trial, the party who intends to produce it gives the sex offender a copy of it and reasonable notice of their intention to produce it. 2004, c. 10, s. 20; 2007, c. 5, s. 28; 2010, c. 17, s. 21.

CROSS-REFERENCES

Section 490.02 sets out the persons who may be served with a notice to comply with the obligations under s. 490.019. Section 490.022 sets out the date that the obligation to comply begins and its duration. Section 490.023 allows the person to apply to a court for an exemption order. Section 490.024 provides for an appeal from the refusal to make an exemption order or by the Attorney General from the making of the exemption order. Section 490.025 provides for notice to the person that they have not been granted an exemption order. Under s. 490.026, the person may apply for a termination order under s. 490.027. Section 490.028 deals with the case where the offender is eligible to apply for an exemption order and a termination order. Section 490.029 allows for appeals in relation to termination orders. Section 490.03 deals with disclosure of the material in the database. For Cross-References in relation to obligations imposed in relation to offences committed outside Canada or where the person has been transferred to Canada under the

International Transfer of Offenders Act, S.C. 2004, c. 21, see ss. 490.02901 and 490.02912 respectively.

SYNOPSIS

This section creates the offence for failing to comply with an order made by a court under s. 490.012 or an obligation under s. 490.019 or s. 490.02901. Subsection (3) provides for proof, by way of certificate, of the person's failure to comply with the *Sex Offender Information Registration Act*, S.C. 2004, c. 10. The prosecutor must give notice of the intention to produce the certificate and, under subsec. (4), the offender may seek leave of the court to require the attendance of the person who signed the certificate for purposes of cross-examination.

OFFENCE.

490.0311 Every person who knowingly provides false or misleading information under subsection 5(1) or 6(1) of the *Sex Offender Information Registration Act* is guilty of an offence and liable

Note: The portion of section 490.0311 before para. (*a*) replaced, 2015, c. 23, s. 31 (to come into force by order of the Governor in Council):

Offence

490.0311 Every person who knowingly provides false or misleading information under subsection 5(1) or 6(1) or (1.01) of the *Sex Offender Information Registration Act* is guilty of an offence and liable

(*a*) **on conviction on indictment, to a fine of not more than $10,000 or to imprisonment for a term of not more than two years, or to both; or**

(*b*) **on summary conviction, to a fine of not more than $10,000 or to imprisonment for a term of not more than six months, or to both. 2007, c. 5, s. 29; 2010, c. 17, s. 22.**

OFFENCE.

490.0312 Every person who, without reasonable excuse, fails to comply with an obligation under subsection 490.02911(1) or (2) is guilty of an offence punishable on summary conviction. 2010, c. 17, s. 23.

Regulations

REGULATIONS.

490.032 The Governor in Council may make regulations

(*a*) **requiring that additional information be contained in a notice under Form 53 or Form 54; and**

(*b*) **prescribing, for one or more provinces, the form and content of that information. 2004, c. 10, s. 20; 2010, c. 17, s. 24.**

Forfeiture of Offence-related Property

ORDER OF FORFEITURE OF PROPERTY ON CONVICTION / Property related to other offences / Property outside Canada / Appeal.

490.1 (1) Subject to sections 490.3 to 490.41, if a person is convicted of an indictable offence under this Act or the *Corruption of Foreign Public Officials Act* and, on application of the Attorney General, the court is satisfied, on a balance of probabilities,

that any property is offence-related property and that the offence was committed in relation to that property, the court shall

    (*a*) where the prosecution of the offence was commenced at the instance of the government of a province and conducted by or on behalf of that government, order that the property be forfeited to Her Majesty in right of that province and disposed of by the Attorney General or Solicitor General of that province in accordance with the law; and

    (*b*) in any other case, order that the property be forfeited to Her Majesty in right of Canada and disposed of by the member of the Queen's Privy Council for Canada that may be designated for the purpose of this paragraph in accordance with the law.

(1.1) [*Repealed*, 2001, c. 41, s. 130(7.1).]

(2) Subject to sections 490.3 to 490.41, if the evidence does not establish to the satisfaction of the court that the indictable offence under this Act or the *Corruption of Foreign Public Officials Act* of which a person has been convicted was committed in relation to property in respect of which an order of forfeiture would otherwise be made under subsection (1) but the court is satisfied, beyond a reasonable doubt, that the property is offence-related property, the court may make an order of forfeiture under subsection (1) in relation to that property.

(2.1) An order may be issued under this section in respect of property situated outside Canada, with any modifications that the circumstances require.

(3) A person who has been convicted of an indictable offence under this Act or the *Corruption of Foreign Public Officials Act*, or the Attorney General, may appeal to the court of appeal from an order or a failure to make an order under subsection (1) as if the appeal were an appeal against the sentence imposed on the person in respect of the offence. 1997, c. 23, s. 15; 2001, c. 32, s. 30(2); 2001, c. 41, s. 18, 130(7.1); 2007, c. 13, s. 8.

CROSS-REFERENCES

"Attorney General", "offence-related property" and "property" are defined in s. 2. A related scheme for forfeiture of proceeds of crime is set out in Part XII.2. An order made under subsec. (1) is, pursuant to s. 490.7, stayed pending appeal.

SYNOPSIS

Sections 490.1 to 490.9 set up a legislative scheme for dealing with property believed to be "offence-related property". The scheme is similar to the parallel scheme enacted in Part XII.2 for Proceeds of Crime. These provisions were enacted as part of a package of legislative measures to deal with criminal organizations but that connection has been removed in view of the broad definition of "offence-related property" in s. 2 being any property, within or outside Canada, by means of or in respect of which any indictable offence under the Code is committed, that is used in any manner in connection with the commission of any indictable offence or that is intended for use for the purpose of committing an indictable offence.

    This property may have been seized under one of the seizure powers in this Act or some other federal statute such as the *Controlled Drugs and Substances Act*. Alternatively, it may be under the control of the state as a result of an application for a restraint order under s. 490.8. The restraint order may be granted if the judge is satisfied that there are reasonable grounds to believe that the property is offence-related property and may be made in relation to property in or outside Canada. Failure to comply with a restraint order is a hybrid offence. As no punishment is specially provided for this offence, the indictable offence is punishable by imprisonment for a term not exceeding five years [s. 743] and the summary conviction offence is punishable by up to six months and a $2000 fine [s. 787]. Unlike the proceeds of crime restraint order obtained under s. 462.33, s. 490.8 does not expressly give the judge power to require that notice be given to persons having an interest in the property. Further, s.

490.8 does not mandate that the judge require the Attorney General to give undertakings with respect to the payment of damages or costs [compare s. 462.33(7)]. As well, no express provision is made for exempting from the restraint order, property required for living expenses or payment of legal fees [compare s. 462.34]. A judge may make an order for management of offence-related property subject to a restraint order or seized pursuant to a search warrant under s. 487, in accordance with s. 490.81. The judge may also make a destruction order where the property is of little or no value after notice to persons with a valid interest.

These sections envisage essentially two different procedures by which offence-related property will be forfeited to the Crown. Under s. 490.1, forfeiture is triggered upon the conviction of the person for an indictable offence. If the court is satisfied on a balance of probabilities that the offence was committed in relation to the offence-related property, it is ordered forfeited. If the court is not so satisfied but is satisfied beyond a reasonable doubt that the property was nevertheless offence-related property, the property may also be forfeited. An order made under s. 490.1 or the failure to make the order may be appealed as if it were a sentence appeal. Section 490.2 sets out an alternative *in rem* procedure because the accused who was charged with the criminal organization offence has died or absconded. The forfeiture order may only be made where the judge is satisfied beyond a reasonable doubt that the property is offence-related property. Any person aggrieved by an order made under s. 490.2 may appeal that order pursuant to s. 490.6 to the Court of Appeal as if the order were a conviction or acquittal as the case may be.

Section 490.3 gives the court an additional power, prior to making the forfeiture order, to set aside transactions that occurred after the seizure of the property or the making of a restraint order. The transaction will not be set aside if the person acquiring the property gave valuable consideration and was acting in good faith. Pursuant to s. 490.4, the judge shall require notice to be given to any person who appears to have a valid interest in the property and such a person has standing to oppose the forfeiture order. The judge may order the property returned to the lawful owner provided that person is not charged with a criminal organization offence and has not acquired property from a person charged with a criminal organization offence in circumstances giving rise to a reasonable inference that the transfer was made to avoid a forfeiture order. Special provision is made in s. 490.41, where the property is a dwelling-house, for notice to persons residing in the house.

Even where the property has been forfeited, s. 490.5 allows an application by innocent persons for an order that their interest in the property is not affected by the forfeiture. Where the application has been successful, the applicant applies to the Attorney General under s. 490.5(6) for the return of the property or an amount equal in value to the value of the interest of the applicant, as declared by the court. The applicant and the Attorney General may appeal an order made under s. 490.5 to the Court of Appeal.

Any of the orders made under ss. 490.1(1), 490.2(2) and 490.5(4) are stayed pending any appeal or any other proceedings relating to restoration or forfeiture of the property.

Section 490.9 makes ss. 489.1 and 490 applicable to any offence-related property subject to ss. 490.1 to 490.7. References should be made to the notes under those sections. Section 489.1 requires the seizing officer to return the property or take it before a justice to be dealt with under s. 490. Section 490 deals with the detention and restoration of goods that have been seized. The reference in s. 490.9(2) to an order under s. 490(9)(*c*) refers to an order returning goods to their lawful owner because the order detaining the goods has expired and proceedings have not been instituted in which the thing detained may be required. Where the property involved is offence-related property, the judge may require the applicant to enter into a recognizance.

Forfeiture does not form part of the sentencing proceedings. Accordingly, the normal rules of evidence apply and hearsay is inadmissible: *R. v. Faulkner* (2007), 222 C.C.C. (3d) 359 (N.B.C.A.).

APPLICATION FOR *IN REM* FORFEITURE / Order of forfeiture of property / Accused deemed absconded / Who may dispose of property / Property outside Canada / Definition of "judge".

490.2 (1) If an information has been laid in respect of an indictable offence under this Act or the *Corruption of Foreign Public Officials Act*, the Attorney General may make an application to a judge for an order of forfeiture under subsection (2).

(2) Subject to sections 490.3 to 490.41, the judge to whom an application is made under subsection (1) shall order that the property that is subject to the application be forfeited and disposed of in accordance with subsection (4) if the judge is satisfied

    (*a*)   beyond a reasonable doubt that the property is offence-related property;

    (*b*)   that proceedings in respect of an indictable offence under this Act or the *Corruption of Foreign Public Officials Act* in relation to the property were commenced; and

    (*c*)   that the accused charged with the offence has died or absconded.

(3) For the purpose of subsection (2), an accused is deemed to have absconded in connection with the indictable offence if

    (*a*)   an information has been laid alleging the commission of the offence by the accused,

    (*b*)   a warrant for the arrest of the accused has been issued in relation to that information, and

    (*c*)   reasonable attempts to arrest the accused under the warrant have been unsuccessful during a period of six months beginning on the day on which the warrant was issued,

and the accused is deemed to have so absconded on the last day of that six month period.

(4) For the purpose of subsection (2), the judge shall

    (*a*)   where the prosecution of the offence was commenced at the instance of the government of a province and conducted by or on behalf of that government, order that the property be forfeited to Her Majesty in right of that province and disposed of by the Attorney General or Solicitor General of that province in accordance with the law; and

    (*b*)   in any other case, order that the property be forfeited to Her Majesty in right of Canada and disposed of by the member of the Queen's Privy Council for Canada that may be designated for the purpose of this paragraph in accordance with the law.

(4.1) An order may be issued under this section in respect of property situated outside Canada, with any modifications that the circumstances require.

(5) In this section and sections 490.5 and 490.8, "judge" means a judge as defined in section 552 or a judge of a superior court of criminal jurisdiction. 1997, c. 23, s. 15; 2001, c. 32, s. 31; 2007, c. 13, s. 9.

CROSS-REFERENCES

"Attorney General", "offence-related property" and "property" are defined in s. 2. A related scheme for forfeiture of proceeds of crime is set out in Part XII.2. Any person aggrieved by an order made under subsec. (2) may appeal to the court of appeal pursuant to s. 490.6. The order is stayed pending the appeal, pursuant to s. 490.7.

SYNOPSIS

See synopsis under s. 490.1.

VOIDABLE TRANSFERS.

490.3 A court may, before ordering that offence-related property be forfeited under subsection 490.1(1) or 490.2(2), set aside any conveyance or transfer of the property that occurred after the seizure of the property, or the making of a restraint order in respect of the property, unless the conveyance or transfer was for valuable consideration to a person acting in good faith. 1997, c. 23, s. 15.

CROSS-REFERENCES

"Offence-related property" is defined in s. 2.

SYNOPSIS

See synopsis under s. 490.1.

NOTICE / Manner of giving notice / Order of restoration of property.

490.4 (1) Before making an order under subsection 490.1(1) or 490.2(2) in relation to any property, a court shall require notice in accordance with subsection (2) to be given to, and may hear, any person who, in the opinion of the court, appears to have a valid interest in the property.

(2) A notice given under subsection (1) shall

    (*a*) be given or served in the manner that the court directs or that may be specified in the rules of the court;

    (*b*) be of any duration that the court considers reasonable or that may be specified in the rules of the court; and

    (*c*) set out the offence charged and a description of the property.

(3) A court may order that all or part of the property that would otherwise be forfeited under subsection 490.1(1) or 490.2(2) be returned to a person — other than a person who was charged with an indictable offence under this Act or the *Corruption of Foreign Public Officials Act* or a person who acquired title to or a right of possession of the property from such a person under circumstances that give rise to a reasonable inference that the title or right was transferred for the purpose of avoiding the forfeiture of the property — if the court is satisfied that the person is the lawful owner or is lawfully entitled to possession of all or part of that property, and that the person appears innocent of any complicity in, or collusion in relation to, the offence. 1997, c. 23, s. 15; 2001, c. 32, s. 32; 2007, c. 13, s. 10.

CROSS-REFERENCES

"Property" is defined in s. 2.

SYNOPSIS

See synopsis under s. 490.1.

NOTICE / Manner of giving notice / Non-forfeiture of property / Factors in relation to dwelling-house.

490.41 (1) If all or part of offence-related property that would otherwise be forfeited under subsection 490.1(1) or 490.2(2) is a dwelling-house, before making an order of forfeiture, a court shall require that notice in accordance with subsection (2) be given to, and may hear, any person who resides in the dwelling-house and is a member of the immediate family of the person charged with or convicted of the indictable offence under this Act or the *Corruption of Foreign Public Officials Act* in relation to which the property would be forfeited.

(2) A notice shall

    (*a*) be given or served in the manner that the court directs or that may be specified in the rules of the court;

    (*b*) be of any duration that the court considers reasonable or that may be specified in the rules of the court; and

    (*c*) set out the offence charged and a description of the property.

(3) Subject to an order made under subsection 490.4(3), if a court is satisfied that the impact of an order of forfeiture made under subsection 490.1(1) or 490.2(2) would be disproportionate to the nature and gravity of the offence, the circumstances surrounding the commission of the offence and the criminal record, if any, of the person charged with or convicted of the offence, as the case may be, it may decide not to order the forfeiture of the property or part of the property and may revoke any restraint order made in respect of that property or part.

(4) Where all or part of the property that would otherwise be forfeited under subsection 490.1(1) or 490.2(2) is a dwelling-house, when making a decision under subsection (3), the court shall also consider

    (*a*) the impact of an order of forfeiture on any member of the immediate family of the person charged with or convicted of the offence, if the dwelling-house was the member's principal residence at the time the charge was laid and continues to be the member's principal residence; and

    (*b*) whether the member referred to in paragraph (*a*) appears innocent of any complicity in the offence or of any collusion in relation to the offence. 2001, c. 32, s. 33; 2007, c. 13, s. 11.

CROSS-REFERENCES

"Property" and "dwelling-house" are defined in s. 2.

SYNOPSIS

See synopsis under s. 490.1.

APPLICATION / Fixing day for hearing / Notice / Order declaring interest not affected by forfeiture / Appeal from order made under subsection (4) / Return of property.

490.5 (1) Where any offence-related property is forfeited to Her Majesty pursuant to an order made under subsection 490.1(1) or 490.2(2), any person who claims an interest in the property, other than

    (*a*) in the case of property forfeited pursuant to an order made under subsection 490.1(1), a person who was convicted of the indictable offence in relation to which the property was forfeited,

    (*b*) in the case of property forfeited pursuant to an order made under subsection 490.2(2), a person who was charged with the indictable offence in relation to which the property was forfeited, or

    (*c*) a person who acquired title to or a right of possession of the property from a person referred to in paragraph (*a*) or (*b*) under circumstances that give rise to a reasonable inference that the title or right was transferred from that person for the purpose of avoiding the forfeiture of the property,

may, within thirty days after the forfeiture, apply by notice in writing to a judge for an order under subsection (4).

(2) The judge to whom an application is made under subsection (1) shall fix a day not less than thirty days after the date of the filing of the application for the hearing of the application.

(3) An applicant shall serve a notice of the application made under subsection (1) and of the hearing of it on the Attorney General at least fifteen days before the day fixed for the hearing.

(4) Where, on the hearing of an application made under subsection (1), the judge is satisfied that the applicant

    (*a*) is not a person referred to in paragraph (1)(*a*), (*b*) or (*c*) and appears innocent of any complicity in any indictable offence that resulted in the forfeiture of the property or of any collusion in relation to such an offence, and

    (*b*) exercised all reasonable care to be satisfied that the property was not likely to have been used in connection with the commission of an unlawful act by the person who was permitted by the applicant to obtain possession of the property or from whom the applicant obtained possession or, where the applicant is a mortgagee or lienholder, by the mortgagor or lien-giver,

the judge may make an order declaring that the interest of the applicant is not affected by the forfeiture and declaring the nature and the extent or value of the interest.

(5) An applicant or the Attorney General may appeal to the court of appeal from an order made under subsection (4), and the provisions of Part XXI with respect to procedure on appeals apply, with any modifications that the circumstances require, in respect of appeals under this subsection.

(6) The Attorney General shall, on application made to the Attorney General by any person in respect of whom a judge has made an order under subsection (4), and where the periods with respect to the taking of appeals from that order have expired and any appeal from that order taken under subsection (5) has been determined, direct that

    (*a*) the property, or the part of it to which the interest of the applicant relates, be returned to the applicant; or

    (*b*) an amount equal to the value of the interest of the applicant, as declared in the order, be paid to the applicant. 1997, c. 23, s. 15; 2001, c. 32, s. 34.

CROSS-REFERENCES

"Attorney General", "offence-related property" and "property" are defined in s. 2. "Judge" is defined in s. 490.2(5). An order made under subsec. (4) is, pursuant to s. 490.7, stayed pending appeal.

SYNOPSIS

See synopsis under s. 490.1.

APPEALS FROM ORDERS UNDER SUBSECTION 490.2(2).

490.6 Any person who, in their opinion, is aggrieved by an order made under subsection 490.2(2) may appeal from the order as if the order were an appeal against conviction or against a judgment or verdict of acquittal, as the case may be, under Part XXI, and that Part applies, with any modifications that the circumstances require, in respect of such an appeal. 1997, c. 23, s. 15.

CROSS-REFERENCES

The order is stayed pending appeal, pursuant to s. 490.7.

SYNOPSIS

See synopsis under s. 490.1.

SUSPENSION OF ORDER PENDING APPEAL.

490.7 Notwithstanding anything in this Act, the operation of an order made in respect of property under subsection 490.1(1), 490.2(2) or 490.5(4) is suspended pending

CR. CODE

(*a*) any application made in respect of the property under any of those provisions or any other provision of this or any other Act of Parliament that provides for restoration or forfeiture of the property, or

(*b*) any appeal taken from an order of forfeiture or restoration in respect of the property,

and the property shall not be disposed of or otherwise dealt with until thirty days have expired after an order is made under any of those provisions. 1997, c. 23, s. 15.

SYNOPSIS
See synopsis under s. 490.1.

APPLICATION FOR RESTRAINT ORDER / Procedure / Restraint order / Property outside Canada / Conditions / Order in writing / Service of order / Registration of order / Order continues in force / Offence.

490.8 (1) The Attorney General may make an application in accordance with this section for a restraint order under this section in respect of any offence-related property.

(2) An application made under subsection (1) for a restraint order in respect of any offence-related property may be made *ex parte* and shall be made in writing to a judge and be accompanied by an affidavit sworn on the information and belief of the Attorney General or any other person deposing to the following matters:

(*a*) the indictable offence to which the offence-related property relates;

(*b*) the person who is believed to be in possession of the offence-related property; and

(*c*) a description of the offence-related property.

(3) Where an application for a restraint order is made to a judge under subsection (1), the judge may, if satisfied that there are reasonable grounds to believe that the property is offence-related property, make a restraint order prohibiting any person from disposing of, or otherwise dealing with any interest in, the offence-related property specified in the order otherwise than in the manner that may be specified in the order.

(3.1) A restraint order may be issued under this section in respect of property situated outside Canada, with any modifications that the circumstances require.

(4) A restraint order made by a judge under this section may be subject to any reasonable conditions that the judge thinks fit.

(5) A restraint order made under this section shall be made in writing.

(6) A copy of a restraint order made under this section shall be served on the person to whom the order is addressed in any manner that the judge making the order directs or in accordance with the rules of the court.

(7) A copy of a restraint order made under this section shall be registered against any property in accordance with the laws of the province in which the property is situated.

(8) A restraint order made under this section remains in effect until

(*a*) an order is made under subsection 490(9) or (11), 490.4(3) or 490.41(3) in relation to the property; or

(*b*) an order of forfeiture of the property is made under section 490 or subsection 490.1(1) or 490.2(2).

(9) Any person on whom a restraint order made under this section is served in accordance with this section and who, while the order is in force, acts in contravention of or fails to comply with the order is guilty of an indictable offence or an offence punishable on summary conviction. 1997, c. 23, s. 15; 2001, c. 32, s. 35.

"Attorney General", "offence-related property" and "property" are defined in s. 2. A related scheme for restraining disposition of proceeds of crime is set out in Part XII.2. "Judge" is defined in s. 490.2(5).

SYNOPSIS

See synopsis under s. 490.1.

MANAGEMENT ORDER / Appointment of Minister of Public Works and Government Services / Power to manage / Application for destruction order / Notice / Manner of giving notice / Order / When management order ceases to have effect / Application to vary conditions.

490.81 (1) With respect to offence-related property other than a controlled substance within the meaning of the *Controlled Drugs and Substances Act*, on application of the Attorney General or of any other person with the written consent of the Attorney General, a judge or justice in the case of offence-related property seized under section 487, or a judge in the case of offence-related property restrained under section 490.8, may, where he or she is of the opinion that the circumstances so require,

   (*a*) appoint a person to take control of and to manage or otherwise deal with all or part of the property in accordance with the directions of the judge or justice; and

   (*b*) require any person having possession of that property to give possession of the property to the person appointed under paragraph (*a*).

(2) When the Attorney General of Canada so requests, a judge or justice appointing a person under subsection (1) shall appoint the Minister of Public Works and Government Services.

(3) The power to manage or otherwise deal with property under subsection (1) includes

   (*a*) in the case of perishable or rapidly depreciating property, the power to make an interlocutory sale of that property; and

   (*b*) in the case of property that has little or no value, the power to destroy that property.

(4) Before a person appointed to manage property destroys property that has little or no value, he or she shall apply to a court for a destruction order.

(5) Before making a destruction order in relation to any property, a court shall require notice in accordance with subsection (6) to be given to, and may hear, any person who, in the opinion of the court, appears to have a valid interest in the property.

(6) A notice shall

   (*a*) be given or served in the manner that the court directs or that may be specified in the rules of the court; and

   (*b*) be of any duration that the court considers reasonable or that may be specified in the rules of the court.

(7) A court may order that the property be destroyed if it is satisfied that the property has little or no value, whether financial or other.

(8) A management order ceases to have effect when the property that is the subject of the management order is returned in accordance with the law to an applicant or forfeited to Her Majesty.

(9) The Attorney General may at any time apply to the judge or justice to cancel or vary any condition to which a management order is subject, but may not apply to vary an appointment made under subsection (2). 2001, c. 32, s. 36.

CROSS-REFERENCES

"Attorney General", "offence-related property" and "property" are defined in s. 2. A related scheme for management of proceeds of crime is set out in Part XII.2.

SYNOPSIS

See synopsis under s. 490.1.

SECTIONS 489.1 AND 490 APPLICABLE / Recognizance.

490.9 (1) Subject to sections 490.1 to 490.7, sections 489.1 and 490 apply, with any modifications that the circumstances require, to any offence-related property that is the subject of a restraint order made under section 490.8.

(2) Where, pursuant to subsection (1), an order is made under paragraph 490(9)(c) for the return of any offence-related property that is the subject of a restraint order under section 490.8, the judge or justice making the order may require the applicant for the order to enter into a recognizance before the judge or justice, with or without sureties, in any amount and with any conditions that the judge or justice directs and, where the judge or justice considers it appropriate, require the applicant to deposit with the judge or justice any sum of money or other valuable security that the judge or justice directs. 1997, c. 23, s. 15.

CROSS-REFERENCES

"Offence-related property" and "property" are defined in s. 2.

SYNOPSIS

See synopsis under s. 490.1.

FORFEITURE OF WEAPONS AND AMMUNITION / Return to lawful owner / Application of proceeds.

491. (1) Subject to subsection (2), where it is determined by a court that
  (a) a weapon, an imitation firearm, a prohibited device, any ammunition, any prohibited ammunition or an explosive substance was used in the commission of an offence and that thing has been seized and detained, or
  (b) that a person has committed an offence that involves, or the subject-matter of which is, a firearm, a cross-bow, a prohibited weapon, a restricted weapon, a prohibited device, ammunition, prohibited ammunition or an explosive substance and any such thing has been seized and detained,

the thing so seized and detained is forfeited to Her Majesty and shall be disposed of as the Attorney General directs.

(2) If the court by which a determination referred to in subsection (1) is made is satisfied that the lawful owner of any thing that is or may be forfeited to Her Majesty under subsection (1) was not a party to the offence and had no reasonable grounds to believe that the thing would or might be used in the commission of an offence, the court shall order that the thing be returned to that lawful owner, that the proceeds of any sale of the thing be paid to that lawful owner or, if the thing was destroyed, that an amount equal to the value of the thing be paid to the owner.

(3) Where any thing in respect of which this section applies is sold, the proceeds of the sale shall be paid to the Attorney General or, where an order is made under subsection (2), to the person who was, immediately prior to the sale, the lawful owner of the thing. 1972, c. 13, s. 37; 1991, c. 40, s. 30; 1995, c. 39, s. 152.

CROSS-REFERENCES

The terms "weapon", "firearm" and "Attorney General" are defined in s. 2. Liability of a person as a party to an offence is defined in ss. 21 and 22. For other provisions respecting forfeiture of contraband, see ss. 491.1 and 492. For special provision for search and seizure of weapons, see ss. 117.02 to 117.06.

Pursuant to s. 2.1, the terms "cross-bow", "prohibited weapon", "restricted weapon", "prohibited device", "ammunition", and "prohibited ammunition" have the same meaning as in s. 84(1).

SYNOPSIS

This section sets out a special code for dealing with forfeiture of weapons and ammunition and their subsequent disposal.

Subsection (1) provides that, where a court determines (a) that a weapon was used in the commission of an offence and it has been seized and detained, or (b) that a person has committed an offence involving, or the subject matter of which is, a firearm or other listed weapon or ammunition, that weapon or ammunition is forfeited and will be dealt with as the Attorney General directs. This determination is subject to the provisions of subsec. (2).

Subsection (2) provides that where the court determines that the lawful owner of the weapon or ammunition referred to in subsec. (1) was not a party to the offence and had no reason to believe that the weapon or ammunition would be so used, the court shall order the weapon returned to that person. Where the weapon or ammunition has been sold, the proceeds will be paid, either to the Attorney General, or the lawful owner described in subsec. (2). Subsection (3) deals with the proceeds of sale.

ANNOTATIONS

Due to the amendment to this provision, however, forfeiture is mandatory pursuant to subsec. (1)(b) where the item has not been used but is merely involved in the offence. Accordingly, where the accused was stopped and two loaded firearms were found in his vehicle, the items were properly forfeited under this provision: *R. v. Roberts* (2005), 199 C.C.C. (3d) 442 (Sask. Prov. Ct.).

A firearms forfeiture order made under this section is one of the consequences that forms part of the punishment, and is therefore appealable with leave under s. 675(1)(b): *R. v. Montague* (2014), 312 C.C.C. (3d) 1 (Ont. C.A.), leave to appeal to S.C.C. refused 2014 CarswellOnt 16354.

Forfeiture of a large firearms collection pursuant to this section does not constitute cruel and unusual punishment within the meaning of s. 12 of the Charter: *R. v. Montague, supra.*

The wording of subsec. (2) contemplates that lawful owners can apply for return of their seized property either before or after forfeiture is ordered: *R. v. Saunders* (2014), 317 C.C.C. (3d) 246 (N.L.C.A.).

ORDER FOR RESTITUTION OR FORFEITURE OF PROPERTY OBTAINED BY CRIME / Idem / When certain orders not to be made / By whom order executed.

491.1 (1) Where an accused or defendant is tried for an offence and the court determines that an offence has been committed, whether or not the accused has been convicted or discharged under section 730 of the offence, and at the time of the trial any property obtained by the commission of the offence

(*a*) **is before the court or has been detained so that it can be immediately dealt with, and**

(*b*) **will not be required as evidence in any other proceedings,**

section 490 does not apply in respect of the property and the court shall make an order under subsection (2) in respect of the property.

(2) In the circumstances referred to in subsection (1), the court shall order, in respect of any property,

(a) if the lawful owner or person lawfully entitled to possession of the property is known, that it be returned to that person; and

(b) if the lawful owner or person lawfully entitled to possession of the property is not known, that it be forfeited to Her Majesty, to be disposed of as the Attorney General directs or otherwise dealt with in accordance with the law.

(3) An order shall not be made under subsection (2)

(a) in the case of proceedings against a trustee, banker, merchant, attorney, factor, broker or other agent entrusted with the possession of goods or documents of title to goods, for an offence under section 330, 331, 332 or 336; or

(b) in respect of

(i) property to which a person acting in good faith and without notice has acquired lawful title for valuable consideration,

(ii) a valuable security that has been paid or discharged in good faith by a person who was liable to pay or discharge it,

(iii) a negotiable instrument that has, in good faith, been taken or received by transfer or delivery for valuable consideration by a person who had no notice and no reasonable cause to suspect that an offence had been committed, or

(iv) property in respect of which there is a dispute as to ownership or right of possession by claimants other than the accused or defendant.

(4) An order made under this section shall, on the direction of the court, be executed by the peace officers by whom the process of the court is ordinarily executed. R.S.C. 1985, c. 27 (1st Supp.), s. 74.

CROSS-REFERENCES

The terms "Attorney General", "valuable security", "document of title", "peace officer" and "property" are defined in s. 2.

Forfeiture of the proceeds of crime seized or subject to a restraint order pursuant to Part XII.2 is dealt with under the provisions of that Part. Forfeiture of "offence-related property" is dealt with in ss. 490.1 to 490.9.

SYNOPSIS

This section deals with the disposition of property which has been obtained by crime.

Subsection (1) describes the situation where, during the trial of an accused or defendant, the court determines that an offence has been committed and any property obtained by the commission of the offence is before the court or detained and will not be required as evidence in any other proceedings. Under such circumstances, s. 490 will not apply in respect of this property, but the court will make an order under subsec. (2) to dispose of it.

Subsection (2) states that the court shall order that the property be returned to the lawful owner, if such person is known. If the identity of the lawful owner is not known, the property will be ordered forfeit to Her Majesty, to be dealt with as the Attorney General directs or otherwise in accordance with the law.

Subsection (3) sets out the circumstances in which an order under subsec. (2) will not be made.

Subsection (4) provides that an order made under this section shall be executed, on the direction of the court, by such peace officers as normally execute process of the court.

ANNOTATIONS

It was held in *R. v. Kolstad* (1959), 123 C.C.C. 170, 30 C.R. 176 (Alta. C.A.), affd [1960] S.C.R. 110, 125 C.C.C. 254, that money paid by the accused for the purpose of bribery and filed as an exhibit at his trial should not be paid out to the accused, but rather held in court until further order.

This provision does not apply where the accused has been found not guilty. In such circumstances, the court has the jurisdiction to deal with an application for the return of seized funds as part of its inherent jurisdiction or under s. 24(1) of the Charter: *R. v. Perello* (2005), 207 C.C.C. (3d) 209 (Sask. Q.B.), affd 216 C.C.C. (3d) 327, 289 Sask. R. 214 (C.A.).

PHOTOGRAPHIC EVIDENCE / Certified photograph admissible in evidence / Statements made in certificate / Secondary evidence of peace officer / Notice of intention to produce certified photograph / Attendance for examination / Production of property in court / Definition of "photograph".

491.2 (1) Before any property that would otherwise be required to be produced for the purposes of a preliminary inquiry, trial or other proceeding in respect of an offence under section 334, 344, 348, 354, 355.2, 355.4, 362 or 380 is returned or ordered to be returned, forfeited or otherwise dealt with under section 489.1 or 490 or is otherwise returned, a peace officer or any person under the direction of a peace officer may take and retain a photograph of the property.

(2) Every photograph of property taken under subsection (1), accompanied by a certificate of a person containing the statements referred to in subsection (3), shall be admissible in evidence and, in the absence of evidence to the contrary, shall have the same probative force as the property would have had if it had been proved in the ordinary way.

(3) For the purposes of subsection (2), a certificate of a person stating that
  (*a*)   the person took the photograph under the authority of subsection (1),
  (*b*)   the person is a peace officer or took the photograph under the direction of a peace officer, and
  (*c*)   the photograph is a true photograph

shall be admissible in evidence and, in the absence of evidence to the contrary, is evidence of the statements contained in the certificate without proof of the signature of the person appearing to have signed the certificate.

(4) An affidavit or solemn declaration of a peace officer or other person stating that the person has seized property and detained it or caused it to be detained from the time that person took possession of the property until a photograph of the property was taken under subsection (1) and that the property was not altered in any manner before the photograph was taken shall be admissible in evidence and, in the absence of evidence to the contrary, is evidence of the statements contained in the affidavit or solemn declaration without proof of the signature or official character of the person appearing to have signed the affidavit or solemn declaration.

(5) Unless the court orders otherwise, no photograph, certificate, affidavit or solemn declaration shall be received in evidence at a trial or other proceeding pursuant to subsection (2), (3) or (4) unless the prosecutor has, before the trial or other proceeding, given to the accused a copy thereof and reasonable notice of intention to produce it in evidence.

(6) Notwithstanding subsection (3) or (4), the court may require the person who appears to have signed a certificate, an affidavit or a solemn declaration referred to in that subsection to appear before it for examination or cross-examination in respect of the issue of proof of any of the facts contained in the certificate, affidavit or solemn declaration.

(7) A court may order any property seized and returned pursuant to section 489.1 or 490 to be produced in court or made available for examination by all parties to a proceeding at a reasonable time and place, notwithstanding that a photograph of the property has been received in evidence pursuant to subsection (2), where the court is satisfied that the interests of justice so require and that it is possible and practicable to do so in the circumstances.

(8) In this section, "photograph" includes a still photograph, a photographic film or plate, a microphotographic film, a photostatic negative, an X-ray film, a motion picture and a videotape. R.S.C. 1985, c. 23 (4th Supp.), s. 2; 1992, c. 1, s. 58; 2010, c. 14, s. 10.

CROSS-REFERENCES

The terms "prosecutor", "peace officer" and "property" are defined in s. 2. "Prosecutor" is also defined in s. 785 for the purpose of summary conviction proceedings. Section 4(6) provides that service of any document may be proved by oral evidence or by way of affidavit.

SEIZURE OF EXPLOSIVES / Forfeiture / Application of proceeds.

492. (1) Every person who executes a warrant issued under section 487 or 487.1 may seize any explosive substance that he suspects is intended to be used for an unlawful purpose, and shall, as soon as possible, remove to a place of safety anything that he seizes by virtue of this section and detain it until he is ordered by a judge of a superior court to deliver it to some other person or an order is made pursuant to subsection (2).

(2) Where an accused is convicted of an offence in respect of anything seized by virtue of subsection (1), it is forfeited and shall be dealt with as the court that makes the conviction may direct.

(3) Where anything to which this section applies is sold, the proceeds of the sale shall be paid to the Attorney General. R.S., c. C-34, s. 447; R.S.C. 1985, c. 27 (1st Supp.), s. 70.

CROSS-REFERENCES

The terms "explosive substance" and "Attorney General" are defined in s. 2. For other provisions respecting forfeiture of contraband, see ss. 491 and 491.1.

SYNOPSIS

This section sets out special provisions for seizing and disposing of explosives.

Subsection (1) provides that a person who executes a warrant under s. 487 may seize any explosives which are suspected to be held for an unlawful purpose. Such person must, as soon as possible, put these explosives in a safe place and hold them there until ordered by a judge of a superior court to deliver them to another person, or in accordance with subsec. (2).

Subsection (2) states that where a person is convicted of an offence in relation to the seized explosives, such explosives are forfeited and will be dealt with in accordance with the direction of the court that imposed the conviction.

Subsection (3) ensures that the proceeds from the sale of any explosives seized under this section will be paid to the Attorney General.

WARRANT FOR TRACKING DEVICE — TRANSACTIONS AND THINGS / Warrant for tracking device — individuals / Scope of warrant / Conditions / Period of validity / Period of validity — organized crime and terrorism offence / Removal after expiry of warrant / Definitions.

492.1 (1) A justice or judge who is satisfied by information on oath that there are reasonable grounds to suspect that an offence has been or will be committed under this or any other Act of Parliament and that tracking the location of one or more transactions or the location or movement of a thing, including a vehicle, will assist in the investigation of the offence may issue a warrant authorizing a peace officer or a public officer to obtain that tracking data by means of a tracking device.

(2) A justice or judge who is satisfied by information on oath that there are reasonable grounds to believe that an offence has been or will be committed under this or any other Act of Parliament and that tracking an individual's movement by identifying the location of a thing that is usually carried or worn by the individual will assist in the

investigation of the offence may issue a warrant authorizing a peace officer or a public officer to obtain that tracking data by means of a tracking device.

(3) The warrant authorizes the peace officer or public officer, or a person acting under their direction, to install, activate, use, maintain, monitor and remove the tracking device, including covertly.

(4) A warrant may contain any conditions that the justice or judge considers appropriate, including conditions to protect a person's interests.

(5) Subject to subsection (6), a warrant is valid for the period specified in it as long as that period ends no more than 60 days after the day on which the warrant is issued.

(6) A warrant is valid for the period specified in it as long as that period ends no more than one year after the day on which the warrant is issued, if the warrant relates to

(a) an offence under any of sections 467.11 to 467.13;

(b) an offence committed for the benefit of, at the direction of, or in association with a criminal organization; or

(c) a terrorism offence.

(7) On *ex parte* application supported by an affidavit, the justice or judge who issued a warrant or another justice or judge who has jurisdiction to issue such warrants may authorize the covert removal of the tracking device after the expiry of the warrant under any conditions that the justice or judge considers advisable in the public interest. The authorization is valid for the period specified in it as long as that period is not more than 90 days.

(8) The following definitions apply in this section.

"data" means representations, including signs, signals or symbols, that are capable of being understood by an individual or processed by a computer system or other device.

"judge" means a judge of a superior court of criminal jurisdiction or a judge of the Court of Quebec.

"public officer" means a public officer who is appointed or designated to administer or enforce a federal or provincial law and whose duties include the enforcement of this or any other Act of Parliament.

"tracking data" means data that relates to the location of a transaction, individual or thing.

"tracking device" means a device, including a computer program within the meaning of subsection 342.1(2), that may be used to obtain or record tracking data or to transmit it by a means of telecommunication. 1993, c. 40, s. 18; 1999, c. 5, s. 18; 2014, c. 31, s. 23.

CROSS-REFERENCES

"Peace officer" and "justice" are defined in s. 2.

This section is part of a more or less comprehensive scheme relating to surreptitious electronic surveillance. Interception of private communications are dealt with in Part VI. Use of transmission data recorders under ss. 492.2 and 487.01 would cover the use of other electronic devices, authorizing the collection of telephonic data and internet communications. Provision is made in s. 487.02 for the making of an assistance order to require persons to co-operate in the carrying out of orders made under this section.

SYNOPSIS

This section provides for the granting of a warrant to authorize the use of "tracking devices", as defined in subsec. (8). Subsection (1) permits a justice or a judge to authorize the tracking of the movement of a *thing*, including a vehicle, if he or she is satisfied by information on oath, that there are reasonable grounds to suspect that an offence has been committed or will be committed, and that tracking the location of the thing will assist in the investigation of the offence. Subsection (2) relates to the authorization to track the movements of a *thing usually carried or worn by an individual*, and requires reasonable grounds to believe that an offence has been committed or will be committed, and that tracking the location of the thing will assist in the investigation of the offence.

Warrants issued under this section may contain any conditions that the justice or judge considers appropriate. They are valid for a specified period, which can be no longer than one year in relation to specific terrorism and criminal organization offences, and can be no longer than 60 days for all other offences. Under subsec. (7), the justice or judge may authorize the covert removal of the device after the expiration of the warrant.

WARRANT FOR TRANSMISSION DATA RECORDER / Scope of warrant / Limitation / Period of validity / Period of validity — organized crime or terrorism offence / Definitions.

492.2 (1) A justice or judge who is satisfied by information on oath that there are reasonable grounds to suspect that an offence has been or will be committed against this or any other Act of Parliament and that transmission data will assist in the investigation of the offence may issue a warrant authorizing a peace officer or a public officer to obtain the transmission data by means of a transmission data recorder.

(2) The warrant authorizes the peace officer or public officer, or a person acting under their direction, to install, activate, use, maintain, monitor and remove the transmission data recorder, including covertly.

(3) No warrant shall be issued under this section for the purpose of obtaining tracking data.

(4) Subject to subsection (5), a warrant is valid for the period specified in it as long as that period ends no more than 60 days after the day on which the warrant is issued.

(5) The warrant is valid for the period specified in it as long as that period ends no more than one year after the day on which the warrant is issued, if the warrant relates to

    (*a*) an offence under any of sections 467.11 to 467.13;

    (*b*) an offence committed for the benefit of, at the direction of, or in association with a criminal organization; or

    (*c*) a terrorism offence.

(6) The following definitions apply in this section.

"data" means representations, including signs, signals or symbols, that are capable of being understood by an individual or processed by a computer system or other device.

"judge" means a judge of a superior court of criminal jurisdiction or a judge of the Court of Quebec.

"public officer" means a public officer who is appointed or designated to administer or enforce a federal or provincial law and whose duties include the enforcement of this or any other Act of Parliament.

"transmission data" means data that

    (*a*) relates to the telecommunication functions of dialling, routing, addressing or signalling;

    (*b*) is transmitted to identify, activate or configure a device, including a computer program as defined in subsection 342.1(2), in order to establish or maintain access to a telecommunication service for the purpose of enabling a communication, or is generated during the creation, transmission or reception of a communication and identifies or purports to identify the type, direction, date, time, duration, size, origin, destination or termination of the communication; and

    (*c*) does not reveal the substance, meaning or purpose of the communication.

"transmission data recorder" means a device, including a computer program within the meaning of subsection 342.1(2), that may be used to obtain or record transmission data or to transmit it by a means of telecommunication. 1993, c. 40, s. 18; 1999, c. 5, s. 19; 2014, c. 31, s. 23.

CROSS-REFERENCES

The terms "justice" and "peace officer" are defined in s. 2. This section is part of a more or less comprehensive scheme relating to surreptitious electronic surveillance. Interception of private communications are dealt with in Part VI. Use of tracking devices as regulated under s. 492.1 and s. 487.01 would cover the use of other electronic devices such as video cameras. Provision is made in s. 487.02 for the making of an assistance order to require persons to co-operate in the carrying out of orders made under this section.

SYNOPSIS

This section provides for the granting of a warrant to authorize the covert use of a "transmission data recorder" to obtain "transmission data", as defined in subsec. (6). The justice or judge must be satisfied by information on oath that there are reasonable grounds to suspect that an offence has been or will be committed and that transmission data will assist in the investigation of the offence. Warrants issued under this section are valid for a specified period, which can be no longer than one year in relation to specific terrorism and criminal organization offences, and can be no longer than 60 days for all other offences.

Part XVI / COMPELLING APPEARANCE OF ACCUSED BEFORE A JUSTICE AND INTERIM RELEASE

Interpretation

DEFINITIONS / "accused" / "appearance notice" / "judge" / "officer in charge" / "promise to appear" / "recognizance" / "summons" / "undertaking" / "warrant".

493. In this Part,

"accused" includes

   (*a*) a person to whom a peace officer has issued an appearance notice under section 496, and

   (*b*) a person arrested for a criminal offence;

"appearance notice" means a notice in Form 9 issued by a peace officer;

"judge" means

   (*a*) in the Province of Ontario, a judge of the superior court of criminal jurisdiction of the Province,

   (*b*) in the Province of Quebec, a judge of the superior court of criminal jurisdiction of the province or three judges of the Court of Quebec,

   (*c*) [*Repealed*, 1992, c. 51, s. 37.]

   (*d*) in the Provinces of Nova Scotia, New Brunswick, Manitoba, British Columbia, Prince Edward Island, Saskatchewan, Alberta and Newfoundland and Labrador, a judge of the superior court of criminal jurisdiction of the Province,

   (*e*) in Yukon and the Northwest Territories, a judge of the Supreme Court, and

   (*f*) in Nunavut, a judge of the Nunavut Court of Justice;

"officer in charge" means the officer for the time being in command of the police force responsible for the lock-up or other place to which an accused is taken after arrest or a peace officer designated by him for the purposes of this Part who is in charge of that place at the time an accused is taken to that place to be detained in custody;

"promise to appear" means a promise in Form 10;

"recognizance", when used in relation to a recognizance entered into before an officer in charge, or other peace officer, means a recognizance in Form 11, and when used in relation to a recognizance entered into before a justice or judge, means a recognizance in Form 32;

"summons" means a summons in Form 6 issued by a justice or a judge;

"undertaking" means an undertaking in Form 11.1 or 12;

"warrant", when used in relation to a warrant for the arrest of a person, means a warrant in Form 7 and, when used in relation to a warrant for the committal of a person, means a warrant in Form 8. R.S., c. C-34, s. 448; R.S., c. 2 (2nd Supp.), s. 5; 1972, c. 17, s. 3; 1974-75-76, c. 48, s. 25(1); 1978-79, c. 11, s. 10; R.S.C. 1985, c. 11 (1st Supp.), s. 2; c. 27 (2nd Supp.), s. 10; c. 40 (4th Supp.), s. 2; 1990, c. 16, s. 5; 1990, c. 17, s. 12; 1992, c. 51, s. 37; 1993, c. 28, Sch. III, s. 32 (repealed 1999, c. 3, s. 12); 1994, c. 44, s. 39; 1999, c. 3, ss. 12, 30; 2002, c. 7, s. 143; 2015, c. 3, s. 51.

CROSS-REFERENCES

The terms "peace officer", "property", "justice", "superior court of criminal jurisdiction" and "Attorney General" are defined in s. 2. In addition to the definition in this section see s. 2 and notes to that section. Section 841 provides that forms varied to suit the case and forms to the like effect shall be deemed to be good, valid and sufficient in the circumstances for which, respectively, they are provided. Also note s. 849(3) requiring preprinted portions of forms to be printed in both official languages.

SYNOPSIS

This section contains definitions of key terms found in Part XVI of the *Criminal Code*. Part XVI provides a legislative scheme for compelling the appearance of an accused person before a justice and for judicial interim release.

ANNOTATIONS

"Officer in charge" – This definition contemplates a delegation of authority by the officer for the time being in command of the police force to a police officer who is at the time in charge of the place of detention. The officer in charge of such place does not have the powers conferred and imposed under this Part unless and until he has been designated for such purposes: *R. v. Gendron* (1985), 22 C.C.C. (3d) 312 (Ont. C.A.).

Arrest Without Warrant and Release from Custody

ARREST WITHOUT WARRANT BY ANY PERSON / Arrest by owner, etc. of property / Delivery to peace officer / For greater certainty.

494. (1) Any one may arrest without warrant
    (*a*) a person whom he finds committing an indictable offence; or
    (*b*) a person who, on reasonable grounds, he believes
        (i) has committed a criminal offence, and
        (ii) is escaping from and freshly pursued by persons who have lawful authority
           to arrest that person.

(2) The owner or a person in lawful possession of property, or a person authorized by the owner or by a person in lawful possession of property, may arrest a person without a warrant if they find them committing a criminal offence on or in relation to that property and
    (*a*) they make the arrest at that time; or

(*b*) **they make the arrest within a reasonable time after the offence is committed and they believe on reasonable grounds that it is not feasible in the circumstances for a peace officer to make the arrest.**

(3) Any one other than a peace officer who arrests a person without warrant shall forthwith deliver the person to a peace officer.

(4) For greater certainty, a person who is authorized to make an arrest under this section is a person who is authorized by law to do so for the purposes of section 25. R.S., c. C-34, s. 449; R.S., c. 2 (2nd Supp.), s. 5; 2012, c. 9, s. 3.

CROSS-REFERENCES

The term "peace officer" is defined in s. 2. Indictable offence includes a hybrid offence by virtue of s. 34(1)(*a*) of the *Interpretation Act*, R.S.C. 1985, c. I-21. See *R. v. Huff* (1979), 50 C.C.C. (2d) 324 (Alta. C.A.). With respect to protection of persons acting in the administration or enforcement of the law see ss. 25 to 27. Also note s. 29(2) which imposes a duty on a person making an arrest to give notice of the reason for the arrest. An additional power of arrest is given under s. 30 with respect to breach of the peace. The additional powers of arrest by peace officers are dealt with in ss. 31 and 495.

Section 529.3 gives a peace officer power to enter a dwelling-house to effect the arrest without a warrant in exigent circumstances. The officer may enter the dwelling-house without prior announcement in the circumstances set out in s. 529.4(3). Power to issue a warrant to arrest a person in a dwelling-house is set out in ss. 529 and 529.1.

SYNOPSIS

This section describes the power of any person, whether or not they are a peace officer, to arrest another person without a warrant.

Subsection (1) grants to every person the authority to arrest without warrant another person in two sets of circumstances. If a person is found committing an indictable offence, he may be arrested without a warrant by any other person. A person who is not a peace officer may also arrest without a warrant another person whom the individual making the arrest has reasonable grounds to believe has committed a criminal offence and has escaped from, and is being freshly pursued by persons with the lawful authority to make the arrest.

Subsection (2) states that anyone who is either the owner of, in lawful possession of, or has been authorized by the owner of the person in lawful possession of property, may arrest without a warrant a person whom they find committing a criminal offence in relation to or on that property provided they make the arrest at the time they find them committing the offence or within a reasonable time after the offence is committed, and they believe on reasonable grounds that it is not feasible in the circumstances for a peace officer to make the arrest.

Subsection (3) requires that any person, other than a peace officer, who arrests another person without a warrant, must deliver the arrested person forthwith to a peace officer.

Under subsec. (4), a person who makes a lawful arrest under this section is a person authorized by law to do so for purposes of s. 25. Section 25 authorizes the use of force to *inter alia* carry out an arrest.

ANNOTATIONS

Constitutional considerations – The arrest of a citizen by another private citizen is a governmental function to which the Charter applies and thus a search incident to that arrest must comply with s. 8 of the Charter: *R. v. Lerke* (1986), 24 C.C.C. (3d) 129, 49 C.R. (3d) 324, 25 D.L.R. (4th) 403 (Alta. C.A.). *Contra*: See *R. v. J. (A.M.)* (1999), 137 C.C.C. (3d) 213, 204 W.A.C. 238 (B.C.C.A.), in which the court held that a person other than a peace officer making a citizen's arrest is not required to give the accused the requisite Charter warnings.

Grounds for arrest (subsec. (1)) – A citizen must have reasonable grounds to believe that a person was apparently in the process of committing an indictable offence in his or her presence: *R. v. Abel* (2008), 229 C.C.C. (3d) 465 (B.C.C.A.).

Meaning of "forthwith" (subsec. (3)) – "Forthwith" does not mean instantly but merely as soon as is reasonably practicable under all the circumstances: *R. v. Cunningham* (1979), 49 C.C.C. (2d) 390 (Man. Co. Ct.).

ARREST WITHOUT WARRANT BY PEACE OFFICER / Limitation / Consequences of arrest without warrant.

495. (1) A peace officer may arrest without warrant

    (*a*) **a person who has committed an indictable offence or who, on reasonable grounds, he believes has committed or is about to commit an indictable offence;**

    (*b*) **a person whom he finds committing a criminal offence; or**

    (*c*) **a person in respect of whom he has reasonable grounds to believe that a warrant of arrest or committal, in any form set out in Part XXVIII in relation thereto, is in force within the territorial jurisdiction in which the person is found.**

(2) A peace officer shall not arrest a person without warrant for

    (*a*) **an indictable offence mentioned in section 553,**

    (*b*) **an offence for which the person may be prosecuted by indictment or for which he is punishable on summary conviction, or**

    (*c*) **an offence punishable on summary conviction,**

in any case where

    (*d*) **he believes on reasonable grounds that the public interest, having regard to all the circumstances including the need to**

        (i) **establish the identity of the person,**

        (ii) **secure or preserve evidence of or relating to the offence, or**

        (iii) **prevent the continuation or repetition of the offence or the commission of another offence,**

may be satisfied without so arresting the person, and

    (*e*) **he has no reasonable grounds to believe that, if he does not so arrest the person, the person will fail to attend court in order to be dealt with according to law.**

(3) Notwithstanding subsection (2), a peace officer acting under subsection (1) is deemed to be acting lawfully and in the execution of his duty for the purposes of

    (*a*) **any proceedings under this or any other Act of Parliament; and**

    (*b*) **any other proceedings, unless in any such proceedings it is alleged and established by the person making the allegation that the peace officer did not comply with the requirements of subsection (2). R.S., c. C-34, s. 450; R.S., c. 2 (2nd Supp.), s. 5; R.S.C. 1985, c. 27 (1st Supp.), s. 75.**

CROSS-REFERENCES

The term "peace officer" is defined in s. 2. Indictable offence includes a hybrid offence by virtue of s. 34(1)(*a*) of the *Interpretation Act*, R.S.C. 1985, c. I-21. See *R. v. Huff* (1979), 50 C.C.C. (2d) 324 (Alta. C.A.). With respect to protection of persons acting in the administration or enforcement of the law see ss. 25 to 27. Section 28 protects the peace officer in case of arrest of the wrong person when executing a warrant. Also note s. 29(1), which requires the person executing the warrant to have it with him where feasible and produce it upon request, and s. 29(2) which imposes a duty on a person making an arrest to give notice of the warrant under which he makes the arrest and the reason for the arrest. An additional power of arrest is given under s. 31 with respect to breach of the peace. Section 10 of the Charter, as well, imposes duties with respect to reason for arrest and right to counsel and see notes under that section. A peace officer of course also may exercise the powers of arrest given to a private citizen under ss. 30 and 494.

Section 529.3 gives a peace officer power to enter a dwelling-house to effect the arrest without a warrant in exigent circumstances. The officer may enter the dwelling-house without prior announcement in the circumstances set out in s. 529.4(3). Power to issue a warrant to arrest a person in a dwelling-house is set out in ss. 529 and 529.1.

Note the special procedure set out in s. 507.1 where a private prosecutor lays an information under s. 504 and seeks to have a summons or warrant issued.

Note on the scheme for pre-trial release – Where an officer does not arrest the person by virtue of s. 495(2) because the accused is alleged to have committed a hybrid offence, a summary conviction offence or an offence listed in s. 553 and there is not cause for arrest to, for example, establish identity, preserve evidence, prevent commission of an offence, or ensure attendance in court, then he shall issue an appearance notice under s. 496. Where the officer arrests the person but the person falls within the categories set out in s. 497(1) then he shall release him pursuant to s. 497 on an appearance notice (defined in s. 493), or with the intention of compelling his appearance by way of summons (defined in s. 493), once there is no cause for further detention. If the person is arrested and not released under s. 497 then he shall be released by the officer in charge (defined in s. 493) or another officer pursuant to s. 498 on a promise to appear or recognizance (defined in s. 493) once there is no cause for further detention. The officer may release not only for the offences described in s. 495(2) but for any offence punishable by imprisonment for five years or less. While the provisions of ss. 495(2), 497 and 498 are stated in mandatory terms, in effect requiring the accused's release unless there is cause to further detain him where he is charged with one of the specified offences, s. 503(2) gives the peace officer and officer in charge a discretion to release an accused charged with other offences (except an offence listed in s. 469) on a promise to appear or recognizance, if the officer is satisfied that the accused "should be released from custody conditionally". The contents of the appearance notice, promise to appear and recognizance are described in s. 501 and may also require that the accused attend at a time and place stated therein for the purposes of the *Identification of Criminals Act*, R.S.C. 1985, c. I-1. The officer may also require the accused to enter into an undertaking including terms in s. 503(2.1). The accused and the prosecutor can apply to replace this undertaking. Where the accused does not attend as required then a justice may issue a warrant for the accused's arrest pursuant to s. 502. In all cases where the accused is given process by the peace officer or officer in charge an information is to be laid before a justice as soon as practicable and, in any event, before the return date set out in the process pursuant to s. 505. The justice then will either confirm the process or cancel it pursuant to s. 508. Where the accused is not released by the peace officer or officer in charge then he must be taken before a justice pursuant to s. 503, usually within 24 hours. The justice will then deal with release pursuant to s. 515 unless the accused is charged with an offence listed in s. 469 such as murder. In the latter case the justice will order that the accused be detained in custody and the onus is upon the accused to bring an application under s. 522 to a judge of the superior court of criminal jurisdiction (defined in s. 2) for release pending trial. Section 503 also makes special provision for an accused who is arrested for an offence alleged to have been committed in another province.

Where the accused is not released on a form of process by a peace officer or officer in charge then an information will be laid before the justice pursuant to s. 504. Where the accused has not yet been arrested then the justice may issue a summons or warrant [both defined in s. 493] pursuant to s. 507. The contents of the summons is described in s. 509 and served in accordance with s. 509(2) and may also require that the accused attend at a time and place stated therein for the purposes of the *Identification of Criminals Act*. Where the accused does not attend as required then a justice may issue a warrant for the accused's arrest pursuant to s. 510. Once the person is arrested on a warrant then again he will be taken before a justice pursuant to s. 503, unless the warrant has been endorsed permitting the officer in charge to release under s. 499. The contents of the warrant are described in ss. 511 and 513. The warrant is executed pursuant to s. 513. The duties of a peace officer executing an arrest warrant are described in ss. 29 and 10 of the Charter. Further, under s. 512, notwithstanding that an accused has been released on a form of process by a peace officer or officer in charge, or a summons has been issued, a justice may issue a summons or warrant where he believes on reasonable and probable grounds that this action is necessary in the public interest. The information laid under s. 504 or s. 505 may be in Form 2 pursuant to s. 506.

Failure to attend court as required, comply with conditions in a recognizance or undertaking or attend for the purposes of the *Identification of Criminals Act* is an offence under s. 145. A warrant may issue under s. 512 where the accused fails to appear for court as required.

A warrant, summons, appearance notice, promise to appear, undertaking or recognizance may be issued, executed, given or entered into on a holiday by virtue of s. 20.

SYNOPSIS

This section specifies the powers of a peace officer to arrest without a warrant, and the limitations thereon.

Subsection (1) states that a peace officer may arrest without warrant any person whom he finds committing a criminal offence, any person whom he believes on reasonable grounds has committed or is about to commit an indictable offence, or any person whom he reasonably believes is the subject of a warrant of arrest or committal.

Subsection (2) limits the powers of arrest without warrant available to a peace officer. A peace officer shall not arrest a person without warrant for an indictable offence within the absolute jurisdiction of a provincial court judge, for a Crown election offence, or for a summary conviction offence, in any of the circumstances set out in subsec. 2(*d*) and (*e*). In other words, the peace officer should arrest without warrant persons committing the offences listed in paras. (*a*), (*b*) or (*c*) only where it is necessary to establish the identity of the person, to preserve evidence of the offence, to prevent the continuation of or repetition of the offence, or to secure the attendance of the accused in court.

Subsection (3) makes it clear that a peace officer, acting under subsec. (1), is deemed to be acting lawfully and in the execution of his duty for the purposes of any Act of Parliament, notwithstanding subsec. (2). This deeming provision also extends to any other proceedings, unless it is established that the peace officer did not comply with subsec. (2).

ANNOTATIONS

Meaning of "reasonable grounds" (subsec. (1)(*a*)) – For an arrest to be valid on the basis of reasonable and probable grounds, it is not sufficient for the police officer to subjectively believe that he has reasonable and probable grounds to make an arrest. Rather, it must also be shown that a reasonable person, standing in the shoes of the officer, would have believed that reasonable and probable grounds existed to make the arrest. However, the police need not go further and establish a *prima facie* case. An arrest which is lawfully made does not become unlawful simply because the police intend to continue their investigation after the arrest, nor does the arrest thereby constitute a violation of s. 9 of the Charter: *R. v. Storrey*, [1990] 1 S.C.R. 241, 53 C.C.C. (3d) 316 (7:0).

For a peace officer to have reasonable and probable grounds his belief in the person's guilt must take into account all the information available to him. He is entitled to disregard only what he has good reason for believing is not reliable: *Chartier v. Quebec (Attorney General)*, [1979] 2 S.C.R. 474, 48 C.C.C. (2d) 34.

Although the accused's arrest was based on the information of a third party civilian who was unknown to the police, the police were not required to obtain confirmation of the civilian's information in order to have reasonable and probable grounds to arrest the accused. The officer must conduct the inquiry which the circumstances reasonably permit to determine whether there are reasonable and probable grounds. In so doing, the officer must take into account all information available to him and is entitled to disregard only information which he has good reason to believe is unreliable. In this case, the third party witnessed the events, provided a specific and detailed complaint and made no claim to anonymity. Accordingly, the police were able to assess the third party's reliability and had no reason to discount his information: *R. v. Golub* (1997), 117 C.C.C. (3d) 193, 9 C.R. (5th) 98 (Ont. C.A.), leave to appeal to S.C.C. refused 128 C.C.C. (3d) vi.

Finds committing criminal offence (subsec. (1)(*b*)) – Where a peace officer makes an arrest under para. *(b)*, the validity of the arrest does not depend upon a subsequent conviction for the commission of that offence, but rather upon the circumstances which were apparent to the officer at the time: *R. v. Biron*, [1976] 2 S.C.R. 56, 23 C.C.C. (2d) 513 (5:3), and *R. v. Fuhr*, [1975] 4 W.W.R. 403 (Alta. S.C. App. Div.).

In *R. v. Stevens* (1976), 33 C.C.C. (2d) 429, 18 N.S.R. (2d) 96 (S.C. App. Div.), the court, considering *R. v. Biron, supra,* held that in order to arrest a person without a warrant for a summary conviction offence it is not sufficient for the arresting officer to show that he had reasonable and probable grounds to believe such offence had been, or was about to be, committed, rather he must go further and show that he found a situation in which a person was apparently committing an offence. Where the accused is acquitted on a charge of causing a disturbance on the basis that the accused was in a dwelling home at the time a charge of resisting an officer in the execution of his duty in attempting to arrest for that offence must also fail, the arrest being unlawful.

The police officer did not find the accused committing an offence where the police officer stopped the accused in his vehicle and smelled burning marihuana emanating from the vehicle. The officer did not see, hear or smell the accused committing the offence of possession of marihuana. Observation of recently smoked marihuana is not an observation of current possession of additional unsmoked marihuana, nor is it objectively reasonable to conclude that more, unsmoked marihuana is present: *R. v. Janvier* (2007), 227 C.C.C. (3d) 294 (Sask. C.A.).

However, the smell of raw (as opposed to burnt) marihuana detected by an experienced officer as emanating from a vehicle did amount to the observation that a crime (possession of marihuana) was being committed at that time. The possession of marihuana was not a past event and the officer did not need to infer that he could find more marihuana by conducting a search. Because the smell alone was sufficient to conclude that the subject was contemporaneously in possession of marihuana, the arrest was lawful under s. 495(1)(*b*): *R. v. Harding* (2010), 256 C.C.C. (3d) 284 (Alta. C.A.). See also *R. v. Loewen* (2010), 260 C.C.C. (3d) 296 (Alta. C.A.), affd on other grounds [2011] 2 S.C.R. 167, 273 C.C.C. (3d) 1, in which the court held that the smell of burned marihuana did not preclude the possibility of continuing possession of a controlled substance. The amount of cash seized during a valid pat-down search and the odour of burnt drugs constituted objective reasonable grounds.

Similarly, in *R. v. MacCannell* (2014), 314 C.C.C. (3d) 514 (B.C.C.A.), the court held that "odour alone" — whether burnt or fresh — *may* be sufficient to support an arrest under para. (1)(*b*), depending on the facts of the case.

Person for whom arrest warrant outstanding (subsec. (1)(*c*)) – It is not necessary that the peace officer ascertain the nature of the offence for which the warrant is outstanding: *R. v. Gamracy*, [1974] S.C.R. 640, 12 C.C.C. (2d) 209 (3:2).

Where it was clearly feasible for a police officer to possess the warrant his failure to do so vitiated any lawful arrest: *R. v. Richard* (1974), 27 C.R.N.S. 337 (Que. S.C.).

Right to enter premises to effect arrest – See notes following s. 529.3.

Search incident to arrest – Police officers have the power to search an accused as an incident to a lawful arrest and to seize anything in his possession or immediate surroundings to guarantee the safety of the police and the accused, prevent the accused's escape or provide evidence against him. The existence of reasonable and probable grounds to believe that the accused is in possession of weapons or evidence is not a prerequisite to the existence of the power to search, provided, however, that the search is for a valid objective and not unrelated to the objectives of the proper administration of justice. Accordingly, a search done for weapons or other dangerous articles is necessary as an elementary precaution to preclude the possibility of their use against the police, the nearby public or the accused himself. A search is also proper to collect evidence that can be used in establishing the guilt of the accused. Further, the search must not be conducted in an abusive fashion and the use of physical or psychological constraint should be proportionate to the objectives sought and the other circumstances of the situation. A "frisk" or pat down search is a relatively non-intrusive procedure and, if done for valid reasons, is not a disproportionate interference with the freedom of persons lawfully arrested: *Cloutier v. Langlois*, [1990] 1 S.C.R. 158, 53 C.C.C. (3d) 257 (7:0).

A strip search is the removal or rearrangement of some or all of the clothing of a person to permit a visual inspect of a person's private areas or undergarments. This is distinguishable from the less intrusive "frisk" or "pat down" searches, which do not involve the removal of clothing, and the more intrusive body cavity searches. Before a strip search may be justified as an incident to arrest, the arrest itself must be lawful and the search must be truly incident to the arrest in the sense that it must be related to the reasons for the arrest. The reasonableness of the search for evidence is governed by the need to preserve the evidence and to prevent its disposal by the detainee. Where only a strip search will expose the evidence, the risk of disposal must be realistically assessed. A search incident to arrest may also be focused on weapons. Usually, a pat down or frisk search will suffice for determining whether a person has a weapon on his person. Only if the frisk search reveals a possible weapon or if the particular circumstances of the case raise the risk that a weapon is concealed will a strip search be justified. The mere possibility that evidence or weapons are concealed on the body of the accused is not sufficient to justify a strip search. Strip searches cannot be carried out as a matter of routine policy. A strip search will always be unreasonable if carried out abusively. Merely because the police have reasonable and probable grounds to carry out an arrest does not confer authority on them to automatically carry out a strip search. Additional grounds pertaining to the purpose of the strip search are required. To meet the constitutional standard of reasonableness, the police must establish that they have reasonable and probable grounds for concluding that a strip search is necessary to discover weapons or evidence related to the reason for the arrest. Beyond this, the search must still be carried out in a reasonable manner.

Several factors should be considered in determining whether and, if so, how to conduct a strip search, such as, whether the search can be conducted at the police station, whether it can be done in a manner that ensures the health and safety of all involved, whether the search will be authorized by a police officer acting in a supervisory capacity, whether the search will be carried out by officers of the same gender as the accused and whether the search is carried out with minimum force. Strip searches should only be conducted in police stations unless exigent circumstances exist. Strip searches conducted in the field can only be justified where there is a demonstrated necessity and urgency to search for weapons and objects that could be used to threaten the safety of the accused, arresting officers or other individuals: *R. v. Golden*, [2001] 3 S.C.R. 679, 159 C.C.C. (3d) 449.

The warrantless search of a home incident to arrest is generally prohibited subject to exceptional circumstances where the law enforcement interest is so compelling that it overrides the individual's right to privacy within the home. The state interest upon arrest is the effective administration of justice, the various components of which include the need to secure the arrested person, protect those at the scene of the arrest and preserve evidence. The frustration of the effective enforcement of justice is the hallmark of exceptional circumstances. The risk of physical harm to those at the scene of the arrest constitutes exceptional circumstances justifying the warrantless entry and search of a residence. If the circumstances of an arrest give rise to a legitimate cause for concern with respect to the safety of those at the scene, reasonable steps to allay that concern may be taken. The nature of the apprehended risk, the potential consequences of not taking protective measures, the availability of alternative measures and the likelihood of the contemplated danger actually existing, must all be considered. The officers making this assessment must do so on the spot with no time for careful reflection: *R. v. Golub*, *supra*.

The common law power to search incident to arrest permits the search of cell phones and similar devices found on the suspect. Because the search of a cell phone has the potential to be a much more significant invasion of privacy than the typical search incident to arrest, four conditions must be met in order for the search to comply with s. 8. First, the arrest must be lawful. Second, the search must be truly incidental to the arrest. This requirement should be strictly applied to permit searches that must be done promptly upon arrest in order to effectively serve the law enforcement purposes. In this context, those purposes are protecting the police, the accused or the public; preserving evidence; and, if the investigation will be stymied or significantly hampered absent the ability to promptly conduct the search, discovering evidence. Third, the nature and the extent of the search must be tailored to its purpose. In practice, this will mean that only recently sent or drafted emails, texts, photos and the call log will, generally, be available, although other searches may, in some circumstances, be justified. Finally, the police must take detailed notes of what they have examined on the device and how they examined it. The notes should generally include the applications searched, the extent of the search, the time of the search, its purpose and its duration: *R. v. Fearon*, [2014] 3 S.C.R. 621, 318 C.C.C. (3d) 182 (4:3).

Right to counsel on arrest – Where a person is detained for a search, as in the case of a body search incident to arrest, then, immediately upon detention, the detainee has the right to be informed of the right to counsel under s. 10(*b*) of the Charter. However, the police are not obligated to suspend the search incident to arrest until the detainee has the opportunity to retain counsel. The police are, however, required to suspend the search where the lawfulness of the search is dependent on the detainee's consent or where the statute gives a person a right to seek review of the decision to search: *R. v. Debot*, [1989] 2 S.C.R. 1140, 52 C.C.C. (3d) 193.

Arrest to establish identity – It was held in *R. v. Moore*, [1979] 1 S.C.R. 195, 43 C.C.C. (2d) 83 (5:2), which arose out of an arrest for a summary conviction provincial traffic offence for which these provisions are applicable by virtue of the provincial *Summary Convictions Act*, that as a constable has no power to arrest an accused for a summary conviction offence by virtue of this subsection unless, *inter alia,* the arrest was necessary to establish the person's identity, a constable in requesting that the person whom he finds committing such an offence identify himself is in the execution of his duty and the accused's refusal to accede to the request constitutes the offence of obstructing police under s. 129.

Arrest and arbitrary detention under s. 9 of Charter [Also see meaning of "reasonable grounds", *supra***]** – In *R. v. Grant*, [2009] 2 S.C.R. 353, 245 C.C.C. (3d) 1, the Supreme Court of Canada held that an unlawful detention will necessarily be arbitrary within the meaning of s. 9 of the Charter. Earlier suggestions that an unlawful detention was not necessarily arbitrary (see *R. v. Duguay* (1985), 18 C.C.C. (3d) 289 (Ont. C.A.)) should not be followed. Mirroring the framework developed for assessing unreasonable searches and seizures under s. 8 of the Charter, it should now be understood that, for a detention to be non-arbitrary, it must be authorized by a law which is itself non-arbitrary. As with other rights, the s. 9 prohibition of arbitrary detention may be limited under s. 1 by such measures "prescribed by law as can be demonstrably justified in a free and democratic society": see *R. v. Hufsky*, [1988] 1 S.C.R. 621, 40 C.C.C. (3d) 398, and *R. v. Ladouceur*, [1990] 1 S.C.R. 1257, 56 C.C.C. (3d) 22.

The police advised the accused that he was being detained in relation to an investigation into the death of his daughter but he was formally arrested only subsequent to questioning at the police station. The initial detention of the accused was not arbitrary. The police officer put the accused under *de facto* arrest through the use of words that conveyed clearly to the accused that he was under arrest, the conduct of the officers and the accused's submission to police authority and this arrest was lawful as it was based on reasonable and probable grounds: *R. v. Latimer*, [1997] 1 S.C.R. 217, 112 C.C.C. (3d) 193.

Also see *R. v. Keeling* (1988), 10 M.V.R. (2d) 57 (B.C.C.A.), where the accused was arrested only after he had been detained as a consequence of the breathalyzer demand. In those circumstances, the imposition of the arrest, even if pursuant to the police officer's policy that he arrests all impaired drivers, was inconsequential. At all times, the accused was lawfully detained for a legitimate reason. To a similar effect is: *R. v. Sieben* (1989), 51 C.C.C. (3d) 343, 73 C.R. (3d) 33 (Alta. C.A.).

It was held in *R. v. Fosseneuve* (1995), 101 C.C.C. (3d) 61, 43 C.R. (4th) 260 (Man. Q.B.), that subsec. (2)(*d*) of this section is invalid to the extent that it permits an arrest without

CR. CODE

warrant for the offences mentioned therein, solely on the ground of the "public interest". However, it is valid to the extent that it permits the arrest in a public interest, limited to the needs to establish identity, secure evidence, and prevent the continuation or repetition of the offence or the commission of another offence.

Subsection (3) – Subsection (3) must be construed to mean that no reliance can be placed on a peace officer's failure to comply with subsec. (2) to support the argument that he was not acting in the execution of his duty in making an arrest: *R. v. Adams* (1972), 21 C.R.N.S. 257, [1973] 1 W.W.R. 371 (Sask.C.A.). Folld: *R. v. McKibbon* (1973), 12 C.C.C. (2d) 66 (B.C.C.A.); *R. v. Bunn* (1986), 29 C.C.C. (3d) 133 (Man. Q.B.).

This subsection had no application to charges of assault of police under s. 270 where there was no allegation of a failure to comply with subsec. (2) but, rather, it was alleged that the officers were not in execution of their duty because, when they attempted to arrest the accused at his home, they were trespassers and the arrest was illegal: *R. v. Delong* (1989), 47 C.C.C. (3d) 402, 69 C.R. (3d) 147 (Ont. C.A.).

ISSUE OF APPEARANCE NOTICE BY PEACE OFFICER.

496. Where, by virtue of subsection 495(2), a peace officer does not arrest a person, he may issue an appearance notice to the person if the offence is
- (*a*) **an indictable offence mentioned in section 553;**
- (*b*) **an offence for which the person may be prosecuted by indictment or for which he is punishable on summary conviction; or**
- (*c*) **an offence punishable on summary conviction. R.S., c. C-34, s. 451; R.S., c. 2 (2nd Supp.), s. 5.**

CROSS-REFERENCES
The term "peace officer" is defined in s. 2. The term "appearance notice" is defined in s. 493. An appearance notice may be issued or entered into on a holiday by virtue of s. 20. A warrant may issue under s. 512 where the accused fails to appear for court as required. For discussion of the pre-trial release provisions see the *Note on the scheme for pre-trial release* under s. 495.

SYNOPSIS

This section authorizes a peace officer to issue an appearance notice where the officer decides not to arrest a person on the basis of subsec. 495(2).

RELEASE FROM CUSTODY BY PEACE OFFICER / Exception / Where subsection (1) does not apply / Consequences of non-release.

497. (1) Subject to subsection (1.1), if a peace officer arrests a person without warrant for an offence described in paragraph 496(*a*), (*b*) or (*c*), the peace officer shall, as soon as practicable,
- (*a*) **release the person from custody with the intention of compelling their appearance by way of summons; or**
- (*b*) **issue an appearance notice to the person and then release them.**

(1.1) A peace officer shall not release a person under subsection (1) if the peace officer believes, on reasonable grounds,
- (*a*) **that it is necessary in the public interest that the person be detained in custody or that the matter of their release from custody be dealt with under another provision of this Part, having regard to all the circumstances including the need to**
  - (i) **establish the identity of the person,**
  - (ii) **secure or preserve evidence of or relating to the offence,**
  - (iii) **prevent the continuation or repetition of the offence or the commission of another offence, or**

(iv) **ensure the safety and security of any victim of or witness to the offence; or**

(b) **that if the person is released from custody, the person will fail to attend court in order to be dealt with according to law.**

(2) Subsection (1) does not apply in respect of a person who has been arrested without warrant by a peace officer for an offence described in subsection 503(3).

(3) A peace officer who has arrested a person without warrant for an offence described in subsection (1) and who does not release the person from custody as soon as practicable in the manner described in that subsection shall be deemed to be acting lawfully and in the execution of the peace officer's duty for the purposes of

(a) any proceedings under this or any other Act of Parliament; and

(b) any other proceedings, unless in any such proceedings it is alleged and established by the person making the allegation that the peace officer did not comply with the requirements of subsection (1). R.S., c. C-34, s. 452; R.S., c. 2 (2nd Supp.), s. 5; 1999, c. 25, s. 3.

CROSS-REFERENCES

The terms "peace officer" and "victim" are defined in s. 2. The terms "appearance notice" and "summons" are defined in s. 493. The contents of the appearance notice are set out in s. 501. An appearance notice may be issued or entered into on a holiday by virtue of s. 20. A warrant may issue under s. 512 where the accused fails to appear for court as required. For discussion of the pre-trial release provisions see the *Note on the scheme for pre-trial release* under s. 495.

SYNOPSIS

This section sets out the powers of a peace officer to release a person who has been arrested without a warrant.

Subsection (1) provides that where a peace officer arrests a person without a warrant for an offence set out in s. 496(a), the officer must, as soon as practicable, release the person from custody with the intention of issuing a summons. The peace officer may also decide to issue an appearance notice to the person and then release him. However, the officer shall not release the accused if the officer believes on reasonable grounds that the accused's detention is necessary in the public interest as defined in subsec. (1.1)(a) or because the accused will fail to attend court.

Subsection (2) makes it clear that the requirements of subsec. (1) do not apply where a person has been arrested without warrant by a peace officer for an indictable offence alleged to have been committed in Canada but in a different province.

Subsection (3) provides that a peace officer is deemed to be acting lawfully and in the execution of his or her duties even if he or she does not comply with subsec. (1) for the purposes set out in paras. (a) and (b), unless it is established that the provisions of subsec. (1) were not complied with.

ANNOTATIONS

The continued detention of a motorist, arrested for impaired driving, until he has sobered up is authorized by subsec. (1)(f) of this section and does not violate the guarantee against arbitrary detention in s. 9 of the *Charter of Rights and Freedoms*: *R. v. Williamson* (1986), 25 C.C.C. (3d) 139, 40 M.V.R. 15 (Alta. Q.B.). Similarly: *R. v. Pashovitz* (1987), 59 C.R. (3d) 396, 59 Sask. R. 165 (C.A.).

Where the alleged breach of the Charter does not give rise to a defence, did not lead to the obtaining of evidence and could not have had a bearing on the sentence, then it ought not to be the subject of inquiry at trial, as in this case where the alleged breach of s. 9 resulted from the continued detention of the motorist several hours after it was safe for him to go: *R. v. Cutforth*, (1987), 40 C.C.C. (3d) 253, 61 C.R. (3d) 187 (Alta. C.A.). However, compare *R. v. Davidson* (1988), 46 C.C.C. (3d) 403, 88 N.S.R. (2d) 271 (C.A.).

There was a sufficient temporal nexus to warrant the application of s. 24(2) of the *Charter of Rights and Freedoms* to permit exclusion of a notice of intention to produce a certificate of analysis in a drinking and driving case, where the notice was served following the period of arbitrary detention: *R. v. Weaver* (2005), 194 C.C.C. (3d) 350, 27 C.R. (6th) 397 (Alta. C.A.).

RELEASE FROM CUSTODY BY OFFICER IN CHARGE / Exception / Where subsection (1) does not apply / Consequences of non-release.

498. (1) Subject to subsection (1.1), if a person who has been arrested without warrant by a peace officer is taken into custody, or if a person who has been arrested without warrant and delivered to a peace officer under subsection 494(3) or placed in the custody of a peace officer under subsection 163.5(3) of the *Customs Act* is detained in custody under subsection 503(1) for an offence described in paragraph 496(*a*), (*b*) or (*c*), or any other offence that is punishable by imprisonment for five years or less, and has not been taken before a justice or released from custody under any other provision of this Part, the officer in charge or another peace officer shall, as soon as practicable,

    (*a*) release the person with the intention of compelling their appearance by way of summons;

    (*b*) release the person on their giving a promise to appear;

    (*c*) release the person on the person's entering into a recognizance before the officer in charge or another peace officer without sureties in an amount not exceeding $500 that the officer directs, but without deposit of money or other valuable security; or

    (*d*) if the person is not ordinarily resident in the province in which the person is in custody or does not ordinarily reside within 200 kilometres of the place in which the person is in custody, release the person on the person's entering into a recognizance before the officer in charge or another peace officer without sureties in an amount not exceeding $500 that the officer directs and, if the officer so directs, on depositing with the officer a sum of money or other valuable security not exceeding in amount or value $500, that the officer directs.

(1.1) The officer in charge or the peace officer shall not release a person under subsection (1) if the officer in charge or peace officer believes, on reasonable grounds,

    (*a*) that it is necessary in the public interest that the person be detained in custody or that the matter of their release from custody be dealt with under another provision of this Part, having regard to all the circumstances including the need to

        (i) establish the identity of the person,

        (ii) secure or preserve evidence of or relating to the offence,

        (iii) prevent the continuation or repetition of the offence or the commission of another offence, or

        (iv) ensure the safety and security of any victim of or witness to the offence; or

    (*b*) that, if the person is released from custody, the person will fail to attend court in order to be dealt with according to law.

(2) Subsection (1) does not apply in respect of a person who has been arrested without warrant by a peace officer for an offence described in subsection 503(3).

(3) An officer in charge or another peace officer who has the custody of a person taken into or detained in custody for an offence described in subsection (1) and who does not release the person from custody as soon as practicable in the manner described in that subsection shall be deemed to be acting lawfully and in the execution of the officer's duty for the purposes of

    (*a*) any proceedings under this or any other Act of Parliament; or

(b) **any other proceedings, unless in any such proceedings it is alleged and established by the person making the allegation that the officer in charge or other peace officer did not comply with the requirements of subsection (1). R.S., c. C-34, s. 453; R.S., c. 2 (2nd Supp.), s. 5; R.S.C. 1985, c. 27 (1st Supp.), s. 186; 1997, c. 18, s. 52; 1998, c. 7, s. 2; 1999, c. 25, ss. 4, 30.**

CROSS-REFERENCES

The terms "officer in charge", "recognizance", "summons" and "promise to appear" are defined in s. 493. The terms "peace officer", "valuable security", "justice" and "victim" are defined in s. 2. Money or other valuable security deposited with the officer in charge is to be delivered to a justice under s. 500. The contents of the promise to appear and recognizance are set out in s. 501. A promise to appear or recognizance may be issued, given or entered into on a holiday by virtue of s. 20. A warrant may issue under s. 512 where the accused fails to appear for court as required. For discussion of the pre-trial release provisions see the *Note on the scheme for pre-trial release* under s. 495.

SYNOPSIS

This section describes the powers of an officer in charge or another peace officer to effect the release of a person who has been arrested without warrant by a peace officer and who has been taken into custody or detained in custody under s. 503(1), for an offence described in s. 496(a), (b) or (c).

Subsection (1) provides that if the person has not been taken before a justice, or released from custody under any other provision in Part XVI, the officer must, subject to certain specified exceptions, release that person as soon as practicable with the intention of compelling their appearance by way of summons. If the officer does not release in that manner, the officer may release if the accused enters into some form of release as specified in para. (b), (c) or (d). Subsection (1.1) describes the circumstances in which the officer may decide not to release the person.

In accordance with subsec. (2), subsec. (1) does not apply where a person has been arrested without a warrant by a peace officer for an indictable offence alleged to have been committed in a different province.

Subsection (3) provides that an officer is deemed to be acting lawfully and in the execution of duty even if the officer does not release the person as soon as practicable and in accordance with subsec. (1) for the purposes described in subsec. (3)(a) or (b), unless it is established that the officer did not comply with the requirements of subsec. (1).

RELEASE FROM CUSTODY BY OFFICER IN CHARGE WHERE ARREST MADE WITH WARRANT / Additional conditions / Application to justice / Application by prosecutor.

499. (1) Where a person who has been arrested with a warrant by a peace officer is taken into custody for an offence other than one mentioned in section 522, the officer in charge may, if the warrant has been endorsed by a justice under subsection 507(6),

    (a) **release the person on the person's giving a promise to appear;**

    (b) **release the person on the person's entering into a recognizance before the officer in charge without sureties in the amount not exceeding five hundred dollars that the officer in charge directs, but without deposit of money or other valuable security; or**

    (c) **if the person is not ordinarily resident in the province in which the person is in custody or does not ordinarily reside within two hundred kilometres of the place in which the person is in custody, release the person on the person's entering into a recognizance before the officer in charge without sureties in the amount not exceeding five hundred dollars that the officer in charge directs and, if the officer in charge so directs, on depositing with the officer in charge** such sum of money or other valuable security not exceeding in amount or value five hundred dollars, as the officer in charge directs.

(2) In addition to the conditions for release set out in paragraphs (1)(*a*), (*b*) and (*c*), the officer in charge may also require the person to enter into an undertaking in Form 11.1 in which the person, in order to be released, undertakes to do one or more of the following things:

(*a*) to remain within a territorial jurisdiction specified in the undertaking;

(*b*) to notify a peace officer or another person mentioned in the undertaking of any change in his or her address, employment or occupation;

(*c*) to abstain from communicating, directly or indirectly, with any victim, witness or other person identified in the undertaking, or from going to a place specified in the undertaking, except in accordance with the conditions specified in the undertaking;

(*d*) to deposit the person's passport with the peace officer or other person mentioned in the undertaking,

(*e*) to abstain from possessing a firearm and to surrender any firearm in the possession of the person and any authorization, licence or registration certificate or other document enabling that person to acquire or possess a firearm;

(*f*) to report at the times specified in the undertaking to a peace officer or other person designated in the undertaking;

(*g*) to abstain from
 (i) the consumption of alcohol or other intoxicating substances, or
 (ii) the consumption of drugs except in accordance with a medical prescription; and

(*h*) to comply with any other condition specified in the undertaking that the officer in charge considers necessary to ensure the safety and security of any victim of or witness to the offence.

(3) A person who has entered into an undertaking under subsection (2) may, at any time before or at his or her appearance pursuant to a promise to appear or recognizance, apply to a justice for an order under subsection 515(1) to replace his or her undertaking, and section 515 applies, with such modifications as the circumstances require, to such a person.

(4) Where a person has entered into an undertaking under subsection (2), the prosecutor may

(*a*) at any time before the appearance of the person pursuant to a promise to appear or recognizance, after three days notice has been given to that person, or

(*b*) at the appearance,

apply to a justice for an order under subsection 515(2) to replace the undertaking, and section 515 applies, with such modifications as the circumstances require, to such a person. R.S., c. 2 (2nd Supp.), s. 5; R.S.C. 1985, c. 27 (1st Supp.), s. 186; 1994, c. 44, s. 40, 1997, c. 18, s. 53; 1999, c. 25, s. 5.

CROSS-REFERENCES

The terms "officer in charge", "recognizance" and "promise to appear" are defined in s. 493. The terms "peace officer", "valuable security", "justice" and "victim" are defined in s. 2. Money or other valuable security deposited with the officer in charge is to be delivered to a justice under s. 500. The contents of the promise to appear and recognizance are set out in s. 501. A warrant, summons, appearance notice, promise to appear, undertaking or recognizance may be issued, executed, given or entered into on a holiday by virtue of s. 20. A warrant may issue under s. 512 where the accused fails to appear for court as required. For discussion of the pre-trial release provisions see the *Note on the scheme for pre-trial release* under s. 495.

SYNOPSIS

This section describes the powers of an officer in charge to release a person from custody when that person has been arrested with a warrant.

The provisions of this section apply only if the warrant has been endorsed by a justice under s. 507(6) and the arrest for a non- s. 522 offence.

The officer in charge may order the release of such a person on a promise to appear or a recognizance in accordance with the terms set out in subsec. (1) and may also require the accused to enter into an undertaking including terms set out in subsec. (2). Either the accused or the prosecutor may apply to replace the undertaking.

MONEY OR OTHER VALUABLE SECURITY TO BE DEPOSITED WITH JUSTICE.

500. If a person has, under paragraph 498(1)(*d*) or 499(1)(*c*), deposited any sum of money or other valuable security with the officer in charge, the officer in charge shall, without delay after the deposit, cause the money or valuable security to be delivered to a justice for deposit with the justice. R.S., c. 2 (2nd Supp.), s. 5; 1999, c. 5, s. 20; c. 25, s. 6.

CROSS-REFERENCES

The term "officer in charge" is defined in s. 493. The terms "valuable security", "peace officer" and "justice" are defined in s. 2.

SYNOPSIS

This section requires the officer in charge who has received a deposit of money or valuable security from a person pursuant to s. 498(1)(*d*) or s. 499(1)(*c*) to ensure that such money or security is delivered forthwith to a justice for deposit.

CONTENTS OF APPEARANCE NOTICE, PROMISE TO APPEAR AND RECOGNIZANCE / Idem / Attendance for purposes of *Identification of Criminals Act* / Signature of accused.

501. (1) An appearance notice issued by a peace officer or a promise to appear given to, or a recognizance entered into before, an officer in charge or another peace officer shall

    (*a*) **set out the name of the accused;**

    (*b*) **set out the substance of the offence that the accused is alleged to have committed; and**

    (*c*) **require the accused to attend court at a time and place to be stated therein and to attend thereafter as required by the court in order to be dealt with according to law.**

(2) An appearance notice issued by a peace officer or a promise to appear given to, or a recognizance entered into before, an officer in charge or another peace officer shall set out the text of subsections 145(5) and (6) and section 502.

(3) An appearance notice issued by a peace officer or a promise to appear given to, or a recognizance entered into before, an officer in charge or another peace officer may require the accused to appear at a time and place stated in it for the purposes of the *Identification of Criminals Act*, where the accused is alleged to have committed an indictable offence and, in the case of an offence designated as a contravention under the *Contraventions Act*, within the meaning of the Act, has not made an election under section 50 of that Act.

(4) An accused shall be requested to sign in duplicate his appearance notice, promise to appear or recognizance and, whether or not he complies with that request, one of the duplicates shall be given to the accused, but if the accused fails or refuses to sign, the lack of his signature does not invalidate the appearance notice, promise to appear or recognizance, as the case may be. R.S., c. 2 (2nd Supp.), s. 5; R.S.C. 1985, c. 27 (1st Supp.), s. 76; 1992, c. 47, s. 69; 1994, c. 44, s. 41; 1996, c. 7, s. 38; 2008, c. 18, s. 15.

(5) [*Repealed*, 2008, c. 18, s. 15.]

CROSS-REFERENCES

The terms "officer in charge", "appearance notice", "recognizance" and "promise to appear" are defined in s. 493. The terms "valuable security", "peace officer" and "justice" are defined in s. 2. Where the accused does not attend as required for the purpose of the *Identification of Criminals Act*, R.S.C. 1985, c. I-1, then a justice may issue a warrant for the accused's arrest pursuant to s. 502. A warrant may issue under s. 512 where the accused fails to appear for court as required. For discussion of the pre-trial release provisions see the *Note on the scheme for pre-trial release* under s. 495.

SYNOPSIS

This section describes the required contents of an appearance notice, a promise to appear and a recognizance and deals with several related issues.

Subsection (1) states that an appearance notice, a promise to appear or a recognizance must set out the name of the accused, describe the substance of the offence alleged to have been committed, and require that the accused attend court at a time and place stated therein and attend thereafter as required by the court. These documents must also set out the text of ss. 145(5) and (6) and 502.

Subsection (3) provides that a promise to appear, and appearance notice or a recognizance may also require that the accused appear at the stated time and place for the purposes of the *Identification of Criminals Act*. This further requirement can be imposed only where the accused is alleged to have committed an indictable offence.

Subsection (4) requires that the accused be requested to sign in duplicate the appearance notice, the promise to appear or the recognizance. Even if the accused does not comply with this request, one of the duplicate copies must be given to him. If the accused fails, or refuses to sign, the lack of a signature does not invalidate the appearance notice, the promise to appear or the recognizance.

ANNOTATIONS

Subsection (1)(*b*) – An appearance notice that merely sets out for the substance of the offence a section and paragraph number without even identifying the statute does not meet the test of sufficiency: *R. v. Powers* (1973), 10 C.C.C. (2d) 395, 21 C.R.N.S. 116 (N.B.Q.B.).

Subsection (1)(*c*) – The officer in charge has no jurisdiction to designate another territorial jurisdiction other than the county in which the accused was arrested as the place he is to appear before a justice to answer to the charge: *R. v. Simons* (1976), 30 C.C.C. (2d) 162, 34 C.R.N.S. 273 (Ont. C.A.).

To attend court within the meaning of this paragraph involves making one's presence known to the presiding justice, and not simply being physically present in the courtroom: *R. v. Anderson* (1983), 9 C.C.C. (3d) 539, 37 C.R. (3d) 67 (Alta. C.A.).

Subsection (2) – The omission in a promise to appear to set out the complete text of s. 145(5) does not affect the court's jurisdiction to proceed with the trial where the accused appears, whether under protest or not: *R. v. Gougeon; R. v. Haesler; R. v. Gray* (1980), 55 C.C.C. (2d) 218 (Ont. C.A.), leave to appeal to S.C.C. refused 35 N.R. 83n.

Subsection (3) – The discretionary power to require an accused to attend for fingerprinting does not violate the principles of fundamental justice as guaranteed by s. 7 of the *Charter of Rights and Freedoms*: *R. v. Beare; R. v. Higgins*, [1988] 2 S.C.R. 387, 45 C.C.C. (3d) 57.

A Crown option offence is deemed to be indictable until Crown counsel elects otherwise and thus an accused can be compelled to attend for fingerprinting in relation to such offence as provided for in the *Identification of Criminals Act*, R.S.C. 1985, c. I-1. Moreover, it was open to the Crown to delay electing the mode of proceeding on a Crown option offence until the accused had complied with a condition in the appearance notice or promise to appear to attend for fingerprinting: *R. v. Abarca* (1980), 57 C.C.C. (2d) 410 (Ont. C.A.); *R. v. Lavoie* (1990), 58 C.C.C. (3d) 246 (Que. S.C.).

FAILURE TO APPEAR.

502. Where an accused who is required by an appearance notice or promise to appear or by a recognizance entered into before an officer in charge or another peace officer to appear at a time and place stated therein for the purposes of the *Identification of Criminals Act* does not appear at that time and place, a justice may, where the appearance notice, promise to appear or recognizance has been confirmed by a justice under section 508, issue a warrant for the arrest of the accused for the offence with which the accused is charged. R.S., c. 2 (2nd Supp.), s. 5; 1992, c. 47, s. 70; 1996, c. 7, s. 38; 1997, c. 18, s. 54.

CROSS-REFERENCES

The terms "officer in charge", "appearance notice", "recognizance" and "promise to appear" are defined in s. 493. The terms "justice" and "peace officer" are defined in s. 2. A warrant may issue under s. 512 where the accused fails to appear for court as required.

SYNOPSIS

This section describes the consequences of failing to appear for the purposes of the *Identification of Criminals Act* as required by a promise to appear, an appearance notice or a recognizance. Should the accused not appear at the time and place stipulated, a justice may issue a warrant for the arrest of the accused for the charged offence. The justice may only issue a warrant if the appearance notice, the promise to appear or the recognizance has been confirmed by a justice under s. 508.

ANNOTATIONS

Once the court has become *functus* with respect to the original charge because it has been disposed of completely, the justice has no power to issue a warrant under this section for failure of the accused to attend for fingerprinting as required by the appearance notice: *R. v. McHardy* (1980), 53 C.C.C. (2d) 91, [1980] 5 W.W.R. 1 (Sask. Q.B.).

Appearance of Accused Before Justice

TAKING BEFORE JUSTICE / Conditional release / Undertaking / Application by prosecutor / Application to justice / Remand to custody for return to jurisdiction where offence alleged to have been committed / Interim release / Release of person about to commit indictable offence / Consequences of non-release.

503. (1) A peace officer who arrests a person with or without warrant or to whom a person is delivered under subsection 494(3) or into whose custody a person is placed under subsection 163.5(3) of the *Customs Act* shall cause the person to be detained in custody and, in accordance with the following provisions, to be taken before a justice to be dealt with according to law:

> **(*a*) where a justice is available within a period of twenty-four hours after the person has been arrested by or delivered to the peace officer, the person shall be taken before a justice without unreasonable delay and in any event within that period, and**
>
> **(*b*) where a justice is not available within a period of twenty-four hours after the person has been arrested by or delivered to the peace officer, the person shall be taken before a justice as soon as possible,**

unless, at any time before the expiration of the time prescribed in paragraph (*a*) or (*b*) for taking the person before a justice,

    (*c*) the peace officer or officer in charge releases the person under any other provision of this Part, or

    (*d*) the peace officer or officer in charge is satisfied that the person should be released from custody, whether unconditionally under subsection (4) or otherwise conditionally or unconditionally, and so releases him.

(2) If a peace officer or an officer in charge is satisfied that a person described in subsection (1) should be released from custody conditionally, the officer may, unless the person is detained in custody for an offence mentioned in section 522, release that person on the person's giving a promise to appear or entering into a recognizance in accordance with paragraphs 498(1)(*b*) to (*d*) and subsection (2.1).

(2.1) In addition to the conditions referred to in subsection (2), the peace officer or officer in charge may, in order to release the person, require the person to enter into an undertaking in Form 11.1 in which the person undertakes to do one or more of the following things:

    (*a*) to remain within a territorial jurisdiction specified in the undertaking;

    (*b*) to notify the peace officer or another person mentioned in the undertaking of any change in his or her address, employment or occupation;

    (*c*) to abstain from communicating, directly or indirectly, with any victim, witness or other person identified in the undertaking, or from going to a place specified in the undertaking, except in accordance with the conditions specified in the undertaking;

    (*d*) to deposit the person's passport with the peace officer or other person mentioned in the undertaking,

    (*e*) to abstain from possessing a firearm and to surrender any firearm in the possession of the person and any authorization, licence or registration certificate or other document enabling that person to acquire or possess a firearm;

    (*f*) to report at the times specified in the undertaking to a peace officer or other person designated in the undertaking;

    (*g*) to abstain from

        (i) the consumption of alcohol or other intoxicating substances, or

        (ii) the consumption of drugs except in accordance with a medical prescription; or

    (*h*) to comply with any other condition specified in the undertaking that the peace officer or officer in charge considers necessary to ensure the safety and security of any victim of or witness to the offence.

(2.2) A person who has entered into an undertaking under subsection (2.1) may, at any time before or at his or her appearance pursuant to a promise to appear or recognizance, apply to a justice for an order under subsection 515(1) to replace his or her undertaking, and section 515 applies, with such modifications as the circumstances require, to such a person.

(2.3) Where a person has entered into an undertaking under subsection (2.1), the prosecutor may

    (*a*) at any time before the appearance of the person pursuant to a promise to appear or recognizance, after three days notice has been given to that person, or

    (*b*) at the appearance,

apply to a justice for an order under subsection 515(2) to replace the undertaking, and section 515 applies, with such modifications as the circumstances require, to such a person.

(3) Where a person has been arrested without warrant for an indictable offence alleged to have been committed in Canada outside the territorial division to where the arrest took place, the person shall, within the time prescribed in paragraph (1)(*a*) or (*b*), be taken before a justice within whose jurisdiction the person was arrested unless, where the offence was alleged to have been committed within the province in which the person was arrested, the person was taken before a justice within whose jurisdiction the offence was alleged to have been committed, and the justice within whose jurisdiction the person was arrested

    (*a*) if the justice is not satisfied that there are reasonable grounds to believe that the person arrested is the person alleged to have committed the offence, shall release that person; or

    (*b*) if the justice is satisfied that there are reasonable grounds to believe that the person arrested is the person alleged to have committed the offence, may

        (i) remand the person to the custody of a peace officer to await execution of a warrant for his or her arrest in accordance with section 528, but if no warrant is so executed within a period of six days after the time he or she is remanded to such custody, the person in whose custody he or she then is shall release him or her, or

        (ii) where the offence was alleged to have been committed within the province in which the person was arrested, order the person to be taken before a justice having jurisdiction with respect to the offence.

(3.1) Notwithstanding paragraph (3)(*b*), a justice may, with the consent of the prosecutor, order that the person referred to in subsection (3), pending the execution of a warrant for the arrest of that person, be released

    (*a*) unconditionally; or

    (*b*) on any of the following terms to which the prosecutor consents, namely,

        (i) giving an undertaking, including an undertaking to appear at a specified time before the court that has jurisdiction with respect to the indictable offence that the person is alleged to have committed, or

        (ii) entering into a recognizance described in any of paragraphs 515(2)(*a*) to (*e*) with such conditions described in subsection 515(4) as the justice considers desirable and to which the prosecutor consents.

(4) A peace officer or an officer in charge having the custody of a person who has been arrested without warrant as a person about to commit an indictable offence shall release that person unconditionally as soon as practicable after he is satisfied that the continued detention of that person in custody is no longer necessary in order to prevent the commission by him of an indictable offence.

(5) Notwithstanding subsection (4), a peace officer or an officer in charge having the custody of a person referred to in that subsection who does not release the person before the expiration of the time prescribed in paragraph (1)(*a*) or (*b*) for taking the person before the justice shall be deemed to be acting lawfully and in the execution of his duty for the purposes of

    (*a*) any proceedings under this or any other Act of Parliament; or

    (*b*) any other proceedings, unless in such proceedings it is alleged and established by the person making the allegation that the peace officer or officer in charge did not comply with the requirements of subsection (4). R.S., c. C-34, s. 454; R.S., c. 2 (2nd Supp.), s. 5; 1974-75-76, c. 93, s. 46; R.S.C. 1985, c. 27 (1st Supp.), s. 77; 1994, c. 44, s. 42; 1997, c. 18, s. 55; 1998, c. 7, s. 3; 1999, c. 25, s. 7.

CROSS-REFERENCES

The terms "officer in charge", "undertaking" and "recognizance" are defined in s. 493. The terms "peace officer", "prosecutor", "justice" and "victim" are defined in s. 2. For discussion of the pre-trial release provisions see the *Note on the scheme for pre-trial release* under s. 495.

CR. CODE

SYNOPSIS

This section describes the requirements placed on a peace officer to ensure that a person arrested with or without a warrant be brought before a justice to be dealt with according to law.

Subsection (1) provides that where a justice is available within 24 hours of a person's arrest or delivery to a peace officer, that person shall be taken before the justice without unreasonable delay and, in any event, within that period. If a justice is not available within a period of 24 hours, the person shall be taken before a justice as soon as possible. These requirements apply unless, prior to the expiration of time periods described above, the peace officer or officer in charge releases the person under any other provision in Part XVI, under s. 503(4), or otherwise, conditionally or unconditionally.

Subsection (2) provides that where a peace officer or officer in charge is satisfied that a person described in subsec. (1) should be released upon conditions, that officer may make such a release in accordance with s. 498(1)(b) to (d). In addition, the officer can require the accused to enter into an undertaking containing the conditions set out in subsec. (2.1). Note in particular that the officer may impose conditions necessary to ensure the safety and security of any victm or witness. Both the accused and the prosecutor may apply to a justice to replace the undertaking. Subsection (2) may not be resorted to if the person is being held in custody pursuant to s. 522.

Subsection (3) deals with the situation in which a person has been arrested, without a warrant, for an indictable offence alleged to have been committed outside the territorial division in which he has been apprehended. Such a person must be brought before a justice within the time periods described in subsec. (1)(a) or (b) above and the justice shall release that person if there are no reasonable grounds to believe that the person committed the offence. If the justice is satisfied that there are reasonable grounds to believe that the arrested person is the person alleged to have committed the offence, the justice may remand the person in the custody of the peace officer to await the execution of an arrest warrant pursuant to s. 528. If no warrant is executed within six days of this remand, the accused person must be released. If the offence was committed in the same province, the justice may order that the accused be taken before a justice having jurisdiction over the offence.

Subsection (3.1) provides that a justice may order the release of a person referred to in subsec. (3), with the consent of the prosecutor, pending the execution of the arrest warrant. Such a release may be unconditional or according to the terms set out in subsec. (3.1).

Subsection (4) provides that a peace officer or officer in charge having custody of a person who has been arrested without a warrant as a person about to commit an indictable offence shall release that person unconditionally as soon as practicable after the officer is satisfied that the continued detention of that person is no longer necessary to prevent the commission of an indictable offence.

Subsection (5) makes it clear that a peace officer having custody of a person referred to in subsec. (4) and who does not release that person within the time limits prescribed by subsec. (1)(a) and (b), is deemed to be acting lawfully and in the execution of his or her duty for the purposes specified in subsec. (5)(a) and (b), unless it is established that the officer did not comply with the requirements of subsec. (4).

ANNOTATIONS

An 18-hour delay, following the arrest of the accused before he was taken before a justice, so that a line-up could be arranged, did not infringe this section nor constitute a violation of s. 9 of the Charter: *R. v. Storrey*, [1990] 1 S.C.R. 241, 53 C.C.C. (3d) 316 (7:0).

The breach of this section resulting in the accused's detention for 36 hours before being brought before a justice constituted a violation of s. 9 of the Charter: *R. v. Charles* (1987), 36 C.C.C. (3d) 286, 59 C.R. (3d) 94 (Sask. C.A.). See, however, *R. v. Tam* (1995), 100 C.C.C. (3d) 196, 100 W.A.C. 40 (B.C.C.A.), in which a delay of over 24 hours rendered the detention "unlawful" contrary to this section but not "arbitrary" within the meaning of s. 9 of the Charter.

In *R. v. W. (E.)* (2002), 168 C.C.C. (3d) 38, 7 C.R. (6th) 343, the Manitoba Court of Appeal held that 24 hours merely establishes the outer limit of permissible detention. A detention of more than 6 hours was, in the circumstances, unlawful and constituted a violation of s. 9 of the Charter.

The actions of the police in purposely keeping the accused in custody beyond the statutory limit so that they could obtain an inculpatory statement constituted a breach of s. 9 of the *Canadian Charter of Rights and Freedoms*: *R. v. Mangat* (2006), 209 C.C.C. (3d) 225 (Ont. C.A.).

An accused arrested on the strength of Telex information of a warrant outstanding elsewhere in the province must be brought before a justice within 24 hours. The court which issued the warrant does not have exclusive jurisdiction to deal with the matter of the accused's release. If the Crown because of a lack of information is unable to proceed with the show cause hearing at that time the proper course is to apply for an adjournment for three days under s. 515 during which time the Crown can either transport the accused to the locale where the warrant was issued or obtain the necessary information: *R. v. Ragan* (1974), 21 C.C.C. (2d) 115, [1975] 2 W.W.R. 284 (B.C. Prov. Ct.).

The provisions of subsec. (3) are mandatory and require that the person arrested be personally brought before the justice for the identity hearing. On the hearing the onus is on the Crown. In calculating the six-day period in para. (*b*) neither the remand date nor the release date should be excluded. The remand order under para. (*b*) should provide for the accused's release unless a warrant is executed within that six-day period: *R. v. Marshall* (1984), 13 C.C.C. (3d) 73 (Ont. H.C.J.).

Information, Summons and Warrant

IN WHAT CASES JUSTICE MAY RECEIVE INFORMATION.

504. Any one who, on reasonable grounds, believes that a person has committed an indictable offence may lay an information in writing and under oath before a justice, and the justice shall receive the information, where it is alleged

> (*a*) **that the person has committed, anywhere, an indictable offence that may be tried in the province in which the justice resides, and that the person**
>> (i) **is or is believed to be, or**
>> (ii) **resides or is believed to reside,**
>> **within the territorial jurisdiction of the justice;**
> (*b*) **that the person, wherever he may be, has committed an indictable offence within the territorial jurisdiction of the justice;**
> (*c*) **that the person has, anywhere, unlawfully received property that was unlawfully obtained within the territorial jurisdiction of the justice; or**
> (*d*) **that the person has in his possession stolen property within the territorial jurisdiction of the justice. R.S., c. C-34, s. 455; R.S., c. 2 (2nd Supp.), s. 5.**

CROSS-REFERENCES

The terms "justice", "property" and "steal" are defined in s. 2. Indictable offence includes a hybrid offence by virtue of s. 34(1)(*a*) of the *Interpretation Act*, R.S.C. 1985, c. I-21. The determination as to whether process should issue is made in accordance with s. 507. Under s. 506 an information may be laid in Form 2. For discussion of the pre-trial release provisions see the *Note on the scheme for pre-trial release* under s. 495. The information may be laid by means of telecommunication in accordance with s. 508.1.

SYNOPSIS

This section describes the process by which any person may lay an information before a justice that another person has committed an indictable offence.

The information must be in writing and under oath. The justice must receive the information if it contains any of the allegations set out in paras. (*a*) to (*d*).

ANNOTATIONS

Constitutional considerations – This provision is *intra vires* Parliament, and provincial provisions such as those contained in the *Youth Protection Act, 1977* (Que.), c. 20, which attempt to prevent anyone from laying an information unless the person has consent of a government official are inoperative: *Quebec (Attorney General) v. Lechasseur*, [1981] 2 S.C.R. 253, 63 C.C.C. (2d) 301 (9:0).

In *Ellis v. Ontario* (2009), 244 C.C.C. (3d) 438, 67 C.R. (6th) 313 (Ont. C.A.), the court held that "territorial jurisdiction" refers to the entire province of Ontario and not to administrative regions created by the *Courts of Justice Act*, R.S.O. 1990, c. C.43. Territorial jurisdiction requires the justice of the peace to receive information. provided that there is a connection between the alleged offender and the justice's territorial jurisdiction.

Duty of justice – The act of receiving an information is ministerial rather than judicial: *R. v. Jean Talon Fashion Center Inc.* (1975), 22 C.C.C. (2d) 223, 56 D.L.R. (3d) 296 (Que. Q.B.).

When information laid – In *R. v. Southwick, ex p. Gilbert Steel Ltd.*, [1968] 1 C.C.C. 356, 2 C.R.N.S. 46 (Ont. C.A.), it was held that on the swearing of the written complaint the information is "laid" and becomes the commencement of criminal proceedings.

Separate informations outstanding – It does not affect the validity of either information to have two separate informations charging the same offence outstanding at the same time: *R. v. Policha, ex p. Hrischuk*, [1970] 5 C.C.C. 165, 11 C.R.N.S. 99 *sub nom. Hrischuk v. Clark and Policha.* (Sask. Q.B.).

Defects in jurat [Also see notes under s. 789] – The cases are divided as to the effect of the failure to indicate the date in the jurat upon which the information may be sworn. In *R. v. Bobcaygeon (Village)* (1974), 17 C.C.C. (2d) 236 (Ont. C.A.), the court left open whether such an omission was fatal to the validity of the information, but doubted whether the trial court's power to amend an information could extend to inserting the date in the jurat. The court upheld the refusal to issue *mandamus* in that case to require the judge to continue with the trial since by reason of the absence of the date when the information was sworn it did not disclose that it was sworn within the applicable limitation period. The defendant and the trial judge were entitled to know by perusing the information the components of the offence, the time and place of its commission and that the informant had laid the information within the prescribed time. The information, which failed to convey to them this information, was a nullity.

However, in *R. v. Government of Saskatchewan* (1982), 20 Sask. R. 213 (C.A.), the court refused to follow *R. v. Bobcaygeon (Village), supra*, and held that an information was not a nullity even though, by reason of the failure to complete the jurat, it was not clear whether the information was laid within the limitation period. The court held that whether or not the prosecution was commenced within the limitation period was a matter to be decided by the trial judge upon hearing evidence.

To a similar effect is *R. v. Dean* (1985), 17 C.C.C. (3d) 410 (Alta. Q.B.), where the validity of the information was upheld although the year that the information was sworn was missing from the jurat. In view of the five-year limitation period, there was no possibility that the information was laid outside the limitation period. *Contra: R. v. Platt; R. v. Cowan*, [1981] 4 W.W.R. 601, 9 Man. R. (2d) 75 (Q.B.).

And in *R. v. Akey* (1990), 11 W.C.B. (2d) 594 (Ont. Ct. (Gen. Div.)), it was held that the absence from the jurat, of the month in which the information was sworn, did not render the information invalid when it was apparent that the information, charging Crown option offences upon which the Crown elected to proceed by way of summary conviction, must have been sworn within six months of the offence.

Illegibility of justice's signature – The illegibility in the jurat of the signature of the justice of the peace who took the information does not render the information invalid where the identity of the person signing the information appears on the face of the information. Thus, in this case, below the illegible signature were the words "A justice of the peace in and for the Province of Ontario": *R. v. Kapoor* (1989), 52 C.C.C. (3d) 41 (Ont. H.C.J.).

Other defects – In *R. v. Zastawny* (1970), 10 C.R.N.S. 155, 72 W.W.R. 537 (Sask. Q.B.), an information that failed to state on its face the site of the offence was quashed as not disclosing an offence within the territorial jurisdiction of the Magistrate.

Omission of the informant's name and occupation from the place indicated in Form 2 does not invalidate the information: *R. v. Eddy* (1982), 69 C.C.C. (2d) 568 (B.C.S.C.).

TIME WITHIN WHICH INFORMATION TO BE LAID IN CERTAIN CASES.

505. Where
  (*a*) **an appearance notice has been issued to an accused under section 496, or**
  (*b*) **an accused has been released from custody under section 497 or 498,**
an information relating to the offence alleged to have been committed by the accused or relating to an included or other offence alleged to have been committed by him shall be laid before a justice as soon as practicable thereafter and in any event before the time stated in the appearance notice, promise to appear or recognizance issued to or given or entered into by the accused for his attendance in court. R.S., c. 2 (2nd Supp.), s. 5.

CROSS-REFERENCES
The term "justice" is defined in s. 2. The terms "appearance notice", "recognizance" and "promise to appear" are defined in s. 493. The determination as to whether process issued by the officer should be confirmed or cancelled is made in accordance with s. 508. Under s. 506 an information may be laid in Form 2. For discussion of the pre-trial release provisions see the *Note on the scheme for pre-trial release* under s. 495.

SYNOPSIS
This section sets out the time periods within which informations must be laid in specified cases.

The section requires that where an appearance notice has been issued under s. 496 or an accused has been released from custody under ss. 497 or 498, an information shall be laid before a justice as soon as practicable thereafter. The information must be laid, in any event, prior to the first appearance of the accused in court.

ANNOTATIONS
It was held in *R. v. Naylor* (1978), 42 C.C.C. (2d) 12 (Ont. C.A.), that this section sets out two time-limits both of which are mandatory, (1) that the information be laid as soon as practicable and (2) that it be laid before the time (meaning time of day) of the appearance in court. However, where there is a failure to comply with these time-limits while no charge of fail to appear under s. 145(5) will lie and the court has no power to issue a warrant under s. 512(2), if the accused does appear this is sufficient to give the court jurisdiction. The failure to follow the procedure in this section does not invalidate the information nor result in a loss of jurisdiction over the offence and the accused's appearance in court gives the court jurisdiction over the person. Folld: *R. v. Hrankowski* (1980), 54 C.C.C. (2d) 174, [1980] 5 W.W.R. 684 (Alta. C.A.), leave to appeal to S.C.C. refused C.C.C. *loc. cit.,* 26 A.R. 268*n*.

The court has jurisdiction even if the accused appears under protest to the court's jurisdiction: *R. v. Gougeon; R. v. Haesler; R. v. Gray* (1980), 55 C.C.C. (2d) 218 (Ont. C.A.), leave to appeal to S.C.C. refused 35 N.R. 83*n*.

Similarly, in *Alberta v. Sinopec Shanghai Engineering Co.* (2011), 286 C.C.C. (3d) 406 (Alta. C.A.), leave to appeal to S.C.C. refused (2012), 438 N.R. 391*n*, the court held that any attempt to appear conditionally to challenge the efficacy of service will be ineffective and result in attornment to the court's jurisdiction. This is to be distinguished from a challenge to the court's jurisdiction to try to the offence, in which case a conditional appearance is possible.

The manner in which the accused is brought before the court does not affect jurisdiction over the offence of the accused. Failure to comply with the time limitation in this section does not cause the provincial court to lose jurisdiction: *R. v. Black* (2010), 255 C.C.C. (3d) 62 (N.B.C.A.), leave to appeal to S.C.C. refused [2011] 1 S.C.R. vi, 261 C.C.C. (3d) iv.

The failure to follow the time requirements in para. (*b*) does not invalidate the information or result in a loss of jurisdiction over the offence. Where there has been a failure to comply, the court must determine whether the accused was prejudiced in the circumstances: *R. v. Markovic* (2005), 200 C.C.C. (3d) 449, 77 O.R. (3d) 752 (C.A.), leave to appeal to S.C.C. refused 204 C.C.C. (3d) vi.

Similarly a "conditional appearance" by counsel on the required date gives the court jurisdiction. The criminal law does not recognize "conditional" appearances: *R. v. Harnish* (1979), 49 C.C.C. (2d) 190 (N.S.S.C. App. Div.).

The laying of an information after the time stated in the appearance notice is only an administrative failure and while that information does not qualify as an information under this section it will qualify as an information under s. 507 so that the accused's appearance in court brings him within the court's jurisdiction: *R. v. Powers* (1973), 10 C.C.C. (2d) 395, 21 C.R.N.S. 116 (N.S.Q.B.). *Contra: R. v. Fleming* (1979), 47 C.C.C. (2d) 406 (B.C.S.C.).

The fact that an appearance notice has been given to the accused does not preclude the officer, because the return date on the notice is wrong, from subsequently invoking the procedure under s. 507 by going before a justice and laying an information and serving the accused with a summons: *R. v. Benteau* (1975), 24 C.C.C. (2d) 96 (Ont. H.C.J.).

FORM

506. An information laid under section 504 or 505 may be in Form 2. R.S., c. 2 (2nd Supp.), s. 5.

CROSS-REFERENCES

Note that s. 788(1) requires that Form 2 be used to initiate summary conviction proceedings. Section 841 provides that forms varied to suit the case and forms to the like effect shall be deemed to be good, valid and sufficient in the circumstances for which, respectively, they are provided. Also note s. 841(3) requiring preprinted portions of forms to be printed in both official languages.

ANNOTATIONS

The information may be laid in the name of the complainant alone: *R. v. Ostler, ex p. A.-G. B.C.*, [1966] 1 C.C.C. 249, 52 W.W.R. 483, *sub nom. R. v. Harvey*, and *R. v. Gyles, ex p. Mandelbaum*, [1969] 3 C.C.C. 119, 5 C.R.N.S. 307 *sub nom. Mandelbaum v. Denstedt* (Man. C.A.).

JUSTICE TO HEAR INFORMANT AND WITNESSES — PUBLIC PROSECUTIONS / Process compulsory / Procedure when witnesses attend / Summons to be issued except in certain cases / No process in blank / Endorsement of warrant by justice / Promise to appear or recognizance deemed to have been confirmed / Issue of summons or warrant.

507. (1) Subject to subsection 523(1.1), a justice who receives an information laid under section 504 by a peace officer, a public officer, the Attorney General or the Attorney General's agent, other than an information laid before the justice under section 505, shall, except if an accused has already been arrested with or without a warrant,

    (*a*) hear and consider, *ex parte*,

        (i) the allegations of the informant, and

      (ii) **the evidence of witnesses, where he considers it desirable or necessary to do so; and**

    (b) **where he considers that a case for so doing is made out, issue, in accordance with this section, either a summons or a warrant for the arrest of the accused to compel the accused to attend before him or some other justice for the same territorial division to answer to a charge of an offence.**

(2) No justice shall refuse to issue a summons or warrant by reason only that the alleged offence is one for which a person may be arrested without warrant.

(3) A justice who hears the evidence of a witness pursuant to subsection (1) shall

    (a) **take the evidence on oath; and**

    (b) **cause the evidence to be taken in accordance with section 540 in so far as that section is capable of being applied.**

(4) Where a justice considers that a case is made out for compelling an accused to attend before him to answer to a charge of an offence, he shall issue a summons to the accused unless the allegations of the informant or the evidence of any witness or witnesses taken in accordance with subsection (3) discloses reasonable grounds to believe that it is necessary in the public interest to issue a warrant for the arrest of the accused.

(5) A justice shall not sign a summons or warrant in blank.

(6) A justice who issues a warrant under this section or section 508 or 512 may, unless the offence is one mentioned in section 522, authorize the release of the accused pursuant to section 499 by making an endorsement on the warrant in Form 29.

(7) Where, pursuant to subsection (6), a justice authorizes the release of an accused pursuant to section 499, a promise to appear given by the accused or a recognizance entered into by the accused pursuant to that section shall be deemed, for the purposes of subsection 145(5), to have been confirmed by a justice under section 508.

(8) Where, on an appeal from or review of any decision or matter of jurisdiction, a new trial or hearing or a continuance or renewal of a trial or hearing is ordered, a justice may issue either a summons or a warrant for the arrest of the accused in order to compel the accused to attend at the new or continued or renewed trial or hearing. R.S., c. 2 (2nd Supp.), s. 5; 1972, c. 13, s. 35; R.S.C. 1985, c. 27 (1st Supp.), s. 78; 1994, c. 44, s. 43; 2002, c. 13, s. 21.

CROSS-REFERENCES

The terms "Attorney General", "justice", "peace officer" and "public officer" are defined in s. 2. With respect to oaths and solemn affirmations, see ss. 13 to 15 of the *Canada Evidence Act*, R.S.C. 1985, c. C-5. The terms "summons" and "warrant" are defined in s. 493. The contents of a summons and the means of service are set out in s. 509. The contents of a warrant are set out in ss. 511 and 513. It is executed in accordance with s. 514. A warrant or summons may be issued, executed, given or entered into on a holiday by virtue of s. 20. Where the information is laid under s. 505, then the process issued by the peace officer or officer in charge is confirmed or cancelled in accordance with s. 508. This section sets out the procedure where the information is laid in a public prosecution. Where the information is laid by a private prosecutor, the procedure set out in s. 507.1 is to be followed. For discussion of the pre-trial release provisions see the Note on the scheme for pre-trial release under s. 495.

Note s. 31(1) of the *Interpretation Act*, R.S.C. 1985, c. I-21, which provides that where anything is required or authorized to be done by or before, *inter alia*, a justice of the peace it shall be done by or before one whose jurisdiction or powers extend to the place where the thing is to be done.

Failure to attend court as required or attend for the purposes of the *Identification of Criminals Act* is an offence under s. 145. As well a warrant may issue under s. 510 for failure to attend for the purposes of the *Identification of Criminals Act*, R.S.C. 1985, c. I-1, as required in a summons.

A warrant may issue under s. 512 where the accused fails to appear for court as required or where a summons cannot be served because the accused is evading service.

Probative value of electronically transmitted copy of summons or warrant, see s. 708.1.

SYNOPSIS

This section sets out the procedure to be followed for issuing process where an information is laid under s. 504 in a public prosecution. Section 507.1 sets out the procedure to be followed for private prosecutions. Section 508 governs the procedure where process has been issued under s. 505, before the information has been laid.

Subsection (1) states that except where an accused has already been arrested, the justice shall hear and consider, *ex parte*, the allegations of the informant. Where the justice considers it desirable or necessary, he shall also hear the evidence of witnesses. Where the justice considers that a case for so doing has been established, he shall issue a summons or a warrant for the arrest of the accused. A justice may not refuse to issue a summons or a warrant only for the reason that the offence is one which permits arrest without a warrant.

Subsection (3) requires that any evidence heard pursuant to subsec. (1) must be taken on oath and in accordance with s. 540 to the extent that this is possible.

Subsection (4) provides that the justice may issue a summons to compel the attendance of the accused to answer a charge of an offence if a case for doing so is made out. The justice may issue a warrant for the arrest of the accused if there are reasonable grounds to believe that this is necessary in the public interest. The justice may not sign a warrant or a summons in blank.

Subsection (6) empowers the justice who issues a warrant under this section, s. 508 or 512, where the offence is one described in paras. (*a*) to (*d*), to authorize the release of the accused pursuant to s. 499 by endorsing the warrant. Where an accused is released under subsec. (6), the promise to appear or recognizance shall be deemed to have been confirmed under s. 508 for the purposes of s. 145(5).

Subsection (8) states that a justice may issue a summons or a warrant to compel the attendance of the accused where a new trial or hearing is ordered on appeal or review or a continuance of a trial is ordered.

ANNOTATIONS

Minimum requirements of information – Although the information may not comply with the requirements as to sufficiency in s. 581(3) such a defect does not render the information null and void *ab initio* and incapable of founding jurisdiction to compel the appearance of the accused before the court to answer the allegation that he committed an indictable offence: *R. v. Bahinipaty* (1983), 5 C.C.C. (3d) 439, 23 Sask. R. 36 (C.A.).

To be valid, an information cannot be laid against an unknown person but must be sworn against a named person or against a person who can be sufficiently described so as to be identifiable. As a precondition to the exercise of the power to hear and consider the evidence of witnesses under this section, the information must comply with ss. 504 and 581 and the name or sufficient description of the accused is an essential part of an information. The justice of the peace has no power to embark on an inquiry on an information which does not conform with the provisions of s. 581 in order to obtain sufficient information to take a proper information: *R. v. Buchbinder* (1985), 20 C.C.C. (3d) 481, 47 C.R. (3d) 135 (Ont. C.A.).

Duty to hold inquiry [subsec. (1)(*a*)] – The justice's failure to hold an inquiry as required by this section prior to issuing the summons does not affect the jurisdiction of the provincial court judge: *R. v. Pottle* (1979), 49 C.C.C. (2d) 113 (Nfld. C.A.); *R. v. Bachman*, [1979] 6 W.W.R. 468 (B.C.C.A.). It would seem that the law in Ontario is to the contrary: *R. v. Gougeon; R. v. Haesler; R. v. Gray* (1980), 55 C.C.C. (2d) 218 (Ont. C.A.), leave to appeal to S.C.C. refused 35 N.R. 83*n*.

Procedure in holding inquiry [subsec. (3)] – The inquiry under this section is to be held *in camera* and the accused has no right to attend and no right to notice. On the hearing Crown counsel may attend as counsel for the informant: *R. v. Whitmore* (1987), 41 C.C.C. (3d) 555 (Ont. H.C.J.), affd 51 C.C.C. (3d) 294 (Ont. C.A.), as to propriety of holding an *ex parte* hearing, and the attendance of Crown counsel.

While the requirement that the hearing be held *in camera* is an infringement on the guarantee to freedom of expression under s. 2(*b*) of the Charter, it represents a reasonable limit: *Southam Inc. v. Coulter* (1990), 60 C.C.C. (3d) 267, 75 O.R. (3d) 1, 40 O.A.C. 341 (C.A.).

A justice of the peace, although appointed by the Attorney General and as court administrator required to maintain a good working relationship with other components of the justice system, had the necessary independence and impartiality to carry out her duties under this section. Of importance in this respect is the oath that she must take to truly and faithfully execute her duties as a justice of the peace: *R. v. Isaac* (1989), 47 C.C.C. (3d) 353 (B.C.S.C.).

Nature of decision to issue process – In determining whether to issue a summons or a warrant a provincial court judge exercises his discretion and accordingly *mandamus* cannot lie against him: *R. v. Coughlan, ex p. Evans*, [1970] 3 C.C.C. 61, 8 C.R.N.S. 201 (Alta. S.C.). In any event the supervisory court may only order the inferior court to hear the matter again: *R. v. Jones, ex p. Cohen*, [1970] 2 C.C.C. 374 (B.C.S.C.).

A justice has jurisdiction to withdraw and annul his warrant where he issued it under a misconception of the facts: *R. v. Eckersley* (1972), 7 C.C.C. (2d) 314 (Que. Mun. Ct.).

If the justice's refusal to issue process was based on extraneous considerations, or if his discretion was not exercised judicially following a proper hearing, *mandamus* will lie: *R. v. Blythe* (1973), 13 C.C.C. (2d) 192 (B.C.S.C.); *R. v. Swan* (1979), 48 C.C.C. (2d) 501 (Ont. H.C.J.).

A justice acts judicially in determining whether or not he will issue a process requiring attendance in court. A refusal does not invalidate an information; the informant is entitled to re-apply before the same or another justice for process to be issued: *R. v. Allen* (1974), 20 C.C.C. (2d) 447 (Ont. C.A.).

Access to evidence taken on hearing – Although the justice presiding at a preliminary hearing has no power to order production of any statements given before a justice under this section, as a matter of fairness such statements should be made available to the accused notwithstanding the proceedings under this section are conducted *ex parte* and *in camera*. If the defence has these statements he may cross-examine the witness on them in the same manner as any other prior statement: *R. v. Cohen* (1976), 32 C.C.C. (2d) 446, 34 C.R.N.S. 362 *sub nom. Quebec (Attorney General) v. Cohen* (Que. C.A.). An appeal by the Crown to the S.C.C. was allowed 46 C.C.C. (2d) 473, 13 C.R. (3d) 36, the court holding that the decision of the justice refusing such cross-examination was not reviewable on *certiorari*. In the result the court did not consider the correctness of the justice's ruling.

The Crown is entitled to documentation and information relating to the *in camera* hearing: *R. v. Billingham* (1995), 26 O.R. (3d) 226 (Gen. Div.).

Right to proceed under this section where s. 501 or 505 not complied with – Where there has been non-compliance with the mandatory provisions of s. 505, it is open to the Crown to proceed by way of an information laid under s. 504 and the justice may issue either a summons or a warrant under this section in order to compel the accused's attendance unless it can be said that the subsequent proceedings constitute an abuse of process: *R. v. Riley* (1981), 60 C.C.C. (2d) 193 (Ont. C.A.).

Where the provisions of s. 505 have not been complied with, the information having been sworn after the return date in the appearance notice, a warrant or summons may issue under this section: *R. v. Gagné* (1989), 53 C.C.C. (3d) 89 (Que. C.A.). There is no necessity to cancel the appearance notice and in fact no jurisdiction to do so: *R. v. Tremblay* (1982), 68 C.C.C. (2d) 273, 28 C.R. (3d) 262 (B.C.C.A.).

A summons may also issue under this section although the appearance notice was invalid for failure to comply with s. 501(4) and the information laid under s. 505 was neither cancelled nor confirmed by the justice: *R. v. Thomson* (1984), 11 C.C.C. (3d) 435, 51 A.R. 273 (C.A.).

Until such time as the accused comes before a judge capable of taking his election and plea, the court has not assumed any jurisdiction in the matter and should any error be made in the method of summoning the accused to court then it may be corrected by the issuance of a new summons or warrant. It is only when the accused has appeared in court and made his election or plea that the court has become seized with jurisdiction which can be lost if nothing is done on a court date: *R. v. Macaskill* (1981), 58 C.C.C. (2d) 361, 45 N.S.R. (2d) 181 (S.C. App. Div.). Similarly, *R. v. Kennedy* (1983), 8 C.C.C. (3d) 322, [1983] 6 W.W.R. 673 (B.C.C.A.).

Other notes – The issuance of a summons by a justice of the peace other than the justice before whom the complaint was sworn is legal: *R. v. Southwick, ex p. Gilbert Steel Ltd.,* [1968] 1 C.C.C. 356, 2 C.R.N.S. 46 (Ont. C.A.).

REFERRAL WHEN PRIVATE PROSECUTION / Summons or warrant / Conditions for issuance / Appearance of Attorney General / Information deemed not to have been laid / Information deemed not to have been laid — proceedings commenced / New evidence required for new hearing / Subsections 507(2) to (8) to apply / Non-application — informations laid under sections 810 and 810.1 / Definition of "designated justice" / Meaning of "Attorney General".

507.1 (1) A justice who receives an information laid under section 504, other than an information referred to in subsection 507(1), shall refer it to a provincial court judge or, in Quebec, a judge of the Court of Quebec, or to a designated justice, to consider whether to compel the appearance of the accused on the information.

(2) A judge or designated justice to whom an information is referred under subsection (1) and who considers that a case for doing so is made out shall issue either a summons or warrant for the arrest of the accused to compel him or her to attend before a justice to answer to a charge of the offence charged in the information.

(3) The judge or designated justice may issue a summons or warrant only if he or she
  (a) has heard and considered the allegations of the informant and the evidence of witnesses;
  (b) is satisfied that the Attorney General has received a copy of the information;
  (c) is satisfied that the Attorney General has received reasonable notice of the hearing under paragraph (a); and
  (d) has given the Attorney General an opportunity to attend the hearing under paragraph (a) and to cross-examine and call witnesses and to present any relevant evidence at the hearing.

(4) The Attorney General may appear at the hearing held under paragraph (3)(a) without being deemed to intervene in the proceeding.

(5) If the judge or designated justice does not issue a summons or warrant under subsection (2), he or she shall endorse the information with a statement to that effect. Unless the informant, not later than six months after the endorsement, commences proceedings to compel the judge or designated justice to issue a summons or warrant, the information is deemed never to have been laid.

(6) If proceedings are commenced under subsection (5) and a summons or warrant is not issued as a result of those proceedings, the information is deemed never to have been laid.

(7) If a hearing in respect of an offence has been held under paragraph (3)(a) and the judge or designated justice has not issued a summons or a warrant, no other hearings may be held under that paragraph with respect to the offence or an included offence

unless there is new evidence in support of the allegation in respect of which the hearing is sought to be held.

(8) Subsections 507(2) to (8) apply to proceedings under this section.

(9) Subsections (1) to (8) do not apply in respect of an information laid under section 810 or 810.1.

(10) In this section, "designated justice" means a justice designated for the purpose by the chief judge of the provincial court having jurisdiction in the matter or, in Quebec, a justice designated by the chief judge of the Court of Quebec.

(11) In this section, "Attorney General" includes the Attorney General of Canada and his or her lawful deputy in respect of proceedings that could have been commenced at the instance of the Government of Canada and conducted by or on behalf of that Government. 2002, c. 13, s. 22; 2008, c. 18, s. 16.

CROSS-REFERENCES

The terms "Attorney General", "justice" and "provincial court judge" are defined in s. 2. The procedure for issuing process in public prosecutions is set out in s. 507. Section 579.01 permits the Attorney General to intervene in private prosecutions by calling witnesses and examining and cross-examining witnesses without actually taking over the prosecution.

The terms "summons" and "warrant" are defined in s. 493. The contents of a summons and the means of service are set out in s. 509. The contents of a warrant are set out in ss. 511 and 513. It is executed in accordance with s. 514. A warrant or summons may be issued, executed, given or entered into on a holiday by virtue of s. 20. Where the information is laid under s. 505 then the process issued by the peace officer or officer in charge is confirmed or cancelled in accordance with s. 508. For discussion of the pre-trial release provisions see the Note on the scheme for pre-trial release under s. 495.

Failure to attend court as required or attend for the purposes of the *Identification of Criminals Act* is an offence under s. 145. As well a warrant may issue under s. 510 for failure to attend for the purposes of the *Identification of Criminals Act*, R.S.C. 1985, c. I-1, as required in a summons. A warrant may issue under s. 512 where the accused fails to appear for court as required or where a summons cannot be served because the accused is evading service.

Probative value of electronically transmitted copy of summons or warrant, see s. 708.1.

SYNOPSIS

This section sets out the procedure to be followed before process is issued in a private prosecution, *i.e.* where the information is not laid by a police officer, public officer, the Attorney General or the Attorney General's agent, under s. 504. The section contains additional protections not found in the companion provision for public prosecutions under s. 507. (In accordance with subsec. (9) this section does not apply to the "peace bond" provisions in ss. 810 and 810.1.) The justice must refer the information to a provincial court judge or a judge of the Court of Quebec, as the case may be, or a designated justice of the peace. Before issuing process, whether a summons or a warrant, the judge or designated justice must hear the allegations of the informant and evidence, be satisfied that the Attorney General has received a copy of the information and reasonable notice of the hearing and given the Attorney General an opportunity to attend the hearing, cross-examine witnesses and present evidence. The Attorney General may participate in the proceedings without being deemed to have intervened in the prosecution, thus allowing the private prosecutor to continue the prosecution, should process be issued.

If the judge or designated judge does not issue process, no further hearings may be held unless there is new evidence to support the allegations. If a summons or warrant is not issued and no proceedings are instituted, e.g. through *mandamus*, to compel the judge or designated justice to issue process within six months or the proceedings are instituted but process is not issued as a result, the information is deemed never to have been laid.

The procedure for conducting the hearing under this section is set out in s. 507(2) to (8). Subsection (10) provides for the appointment of designated justices. Subsection (11) gives the Attorney General of Canada the same rights as the Attorney General of the province in respect of proceedings that could have been commenced at the instance of the Government of Canada and conducted by or on behalf of that government.

ANNOTATIONS

A Crown does not have the jurisdiction to withdraw an information before the pre-enquete hearing: *R. v. McHale* (2009), 251 C.C.C. (3d) 283 (Ont. S.C.J.), affd 256 C.C.C. (3d) 26 (Ont. C.A.), leave to appeal to S.C.C. refused 259 C.C.C. (3d) iv.

If the justice's refusal to issue process was based on extraneous considerations, or if his discretion was not exercised judicially following a proper hearing, *mandamus* will lie: *R. v. Blythe* (1973), 13 C.C.C. (2d) 192 (B.C.S.C.); *Swan (Re)* (1979), 48 C.C.C. (2d) 501 (Ont. H.C.J.).

Unlike s. 507(1)(*a*)(ii), s. 507.1(3)(*a*) appears to make the introduction of "evidence of witnesses" mandatory. Such a requirement serves as an important control over invocation of the criminal process by private informants: *R. v. Vasarhelyi* (2011), 272 C.C.C. (3d) 193 (Ont. C.A.), leave to appeal to S.C.C. refused (2012), 295 O.A.C. 400*n*.

For other annotations, see notes under s. 507.

JUSTICE TO HEAR INFORMANT AND WITNESSES / Procedure when witnesses attend.

508. (1) A justice who receives an information laid before him under section 505 shall

    (*a*) **hear and consider,** *ex parte,*

        (i) **the allegations of the informant, and**

        (ii) **the evidence of witnesses, where he considers it desirable or necessary to do so;**

    (*b*) **where he considers that a case for so doing is made out, whether the information relates to the offence alleged in the appearance notice, promise to appear or recognizance or to an included or other offence,**

        (i) **confirm the appearance notice, promise to appear or recognizance, as the case may be, and endorse the information accordingly, or**

        (ii) **cancel the appearance notice, promise to appear or recognizance, as the case may be, and issue, in accordance with section 507, either a summons or a warrant for the arrest of the accused to compel the accused to attend before him or some other justice for the same territorial division to answer to a charge of an offence and endorse on the summons or warrant that the appearance notice, promise to appear or recognizance, as the case may be, has been cancelled; and**

    (*c*) **where he considers that a case is not made out for the purposes of paragraph (*b*), cancel the appearance notice, promise to appear or recognizance, as the case may be, and cause the accused to be notified forthwith of such cancellation.**

(2) A justice who hears the evidence of a witness pursuant to subsection (1) shall

    (*a*) **take the evidence on oath; and**

    (*b*) **cause the evidence to be taken in accordance with section 540 in so far as that section is capable of being applied. R.S., c. 2 (2nd Supp.), s. 5; R.S.C. 1985, c. 27 (1st Supp.), s. 79.**

CROSS-REFERENCES

The term "justice" is defined in s. 2. With respect to oaths and solemn affirmations see ss. 13 to 15 of the *Canada Evidence Act*, R.S.C. 1985, c. C-5. The terms "appearance notice", "promise to appear" and "recognizance" are defined in s. 493. The contents of these forms of release are set out in s. 501. Under s. 512 even though the accused has been released on one of these forms of release the justice may issue a summons or warrant. Where the information is laid under s. 504 then the process is issued by the justice in accordance with s. 507. The information may be laid by a peace officer by telecommunication in accordance with s. 508.1. For discussion of the pre-trial release provisions see the *Note on the scheme for pre-trial release* under s. 495.

Note s. 31(1) of the *Interpretation Act*, R.S.C. 1985, c. I-21, which provides that where anything is required or authorized to be done by or before, *inter alia*, a justice of the peace it shall be done by or before one whose jurisdiction or powers extend to the place where the thing is to be done.

Failure to attend court as required or attend for the purposes of the *Identification of Criminals Act*, R.S.C. 1985, c. I-1, is an offence under s. 145.

SYNOPSIS

This section sets out the procedure that must be followed when a justice receives an information laid before him under s. 505.

Subsection (1) requires a justice in this situation to hear and consider, *ex parte*, the allegations of the informant and, where it is considered desirable or necessary, the evidence of witnesses. Where a case is made out, the justice shall confirm the appearance notice, the promise to appear or the recognizance and endorse the information accordingly. The justice may also cancel the appearance notice, the promise to appear, or the recognizance and compel the accused, by summons or warrant, to appear in order to answer to a charge of an offence. If the justice considers that a case is not made out for the purposes of para. (*b*), the justice may cancel the appearance notice, promise to appear or recognizance and order that the accused be notified of this cancellation.

Subsection (2) requires that a justice, who hears the evidence of a witness pursuant to subsec. (1), must take the evidence on oath and, in so far as is possible, in accordance with s. 540.

ANNOTATIONS

Failure to confirm the appearance notice has relevance only to any proceedings taken against the accused should he fail to attend court as required therein. Such failure does not void the information and once the accused appears there is no necessity that the appearance notice be confirmed: *R. v. Wetmore* (1976), 32 C.C.C. (2d) 347 (N.S. S.C. App. Div.); *R. v. Maximick* (1979), 48 C.C.C. (2d) 417 (B.C.C.A.); *R. v. McGinnis* (1979), 51 C.C.C. (2d) 301 (Alta. C.A.); *R. v. Romanchuk* (2011), 278 C.C.C. (3d) 92 (Sask. C.A.); *R. v. Duran* (2011), 285 C.C.C. (3d) 46 (Ont. S.C.J.); *R. v. Millar* (2012), 285 C.C.C. (3d) 208 (Ont. S.C.J.). *Contra: R. v. Harris* (1978), 39 C.C.C. (2d) 256 (Ont. Prov. Ct.), and *semble, R. v. Gougeon; R. v. Haesler; R. v. Gray* (1980), 55 C.C.C. (2d) 218 (Ont. C.A.), at least where timely objection is made.

Prior to confirming the appearance notice, the justice must be satisfied that the notice complies with provisions of the *Criminal Code* including the requirement that the accused was served with copy of the notice. Where the accused fails to appear as required, a judge may issue a summons or warrant without proof of service of the appearance notice: *R. v. DeMelo* (1994), 92 C.C.C. (3d) 52, 73 O.A.C. 371 (C.A.).

Where an accused challenges the sufficiency of the *ex parte* hearing required by subsec. (1), the presumption of regularity applies and the burden is on the accused to show on a balance of probabilities that the requisite hearing had not taken place. For there to be compliance with this subsection, there need not be a "formal" hearing, although it would be preferable for the justice of the peace to ask the informant to briefly divulge the factual basis of the charge: *R. v. Morton* (1992), 70 C.C.C. (3d) 244, 7 O.R. (3d) 625 (Gen. Div.), affd 83 C.C.C. (3d) 95*n* (C.A.).

A charge of failing to comply with a requirement that the accused attend for fingerprinting must be dismissed if the promise to appear is only confirmed after the date set out for attendance for fingerprinting: *R. v. Tulloch* (1987), 40 C.C.C. (3d) 90 (Ont. Prov. Ct.).

INFORMATION LAID OTHERWISE THAN IN PERSON / Alternative to oath.

508.1 (1) For the purposes of sections 504 to 508, a peace officer may lay an information by any means of telecommunication that produces a writing.

(2) A peace officer who uses a means of telecommunication referred to in subsection (1) shall, instead of swearing an oath, make a statement in writing stating that all matters contained in the information are true to the officer's knowledge and belief, and such a statement is deemed to be a statement made under oath. 1997, c. 18, s. 56.

ANNOTATIONS

An officer is entitled to use a fax machine to lay an information. Section 507(1)(*a*) does not require that another person read the faxed material out loud to the justice so that she could "hear" it: *R. v. Lupyrypa* (2011), 270 C.C.C. (3d) 571 (Alta. C.A.).

SUMMONS / Service on individual / Content of summons / Attendance for purposes of *Identification of Criminals Act*.

509. (1) A summons issued under this Part shall
  (*a*) be directed to the accused;
  (*b*) set out briefly the offence in respect of which the accused is charged; and
  (*c*) require the accused to attend court at a time and place to be stated therein and to attend thereafter as required by the court in order to be dealt with according to law.

(2) A summons shall be served by a peace officer who shall deliver it personally to the person to whom it is directed or, if that person cannot conveniently be found, shall leave it for him at his last or usual place of abode with some inmate thereof who appears to be at least sixteen years of age.

(3) [*Repealed*, 2008, c. 18, s. 17.]

(4) There shall be set out in every summons the text of subsection 145(4) and section 510.

(5) A summons may require the accused to appear at a time and place stated in it for the purposes of the *Identification of Criminals Act*, where the accused is alleged to have committed an indictable offence and, in the case of an offence designated as a contravention under the *Contraventions Act*, the Attorney General, within the meaning of that Act, has not made an election under section 50 of that Act. R.S., c. 2 (2nd Supp.), s. 5; R.S.C. 1985, c. 27 (1st Supp.), s. 80; 1992, c. 47, s. 71; 1996, c. 7, s. 38; 2008, c. 18, s. 17.

CROSS-REFERENCES

The term "peace officer" is defined in s. 2. Summons is defined in s. 493 as a summons in Form 6. Section 841 provides that forms varied to suit the case and forms to the like effect shall be deemed to be good, valid and sufficient in the circumstances for which, respectively, they are provided. A summons may be issued or given on a holiday by virtue of s. 20. For protection of person executing process see ss. 25 to 28. Service of a summons on a corporation, see s. 703.2.

Failure to attend court as required or attend for the purposes of the *Identification of Criminals Act*, R.S.C. 1985, c. I-1, is an offence under s. 145. As well a warrant may issue under s. 510 for failure to attend for the purposes of the *Identification of Criminals Act*. A warrant may issue under s. 512 where the accused fails to appear for court as required or where a summons cannot be served because the accused is evading service. A summons is effective throughout Canada (s. 703.1). Probative value of electronically transmitted copy, see s. 708.1.

SYNOPSIS

This section deals with the summons.

Subsection (1) requires that a summons issued under Part XVI be directed to the accused, set out the offence with which the accused is charged, and require the accused to attend in court at a time and place to be stated and thereafter as required by the court.

Subsection (2) states that a summons must be served by a peace officer for personal delivery upon the person to whom it is directed. If that person cannot be *conveniently* found, the peace officer must leave the summons at the person's latest or usual residence with a person who lives in the premises and who appears to be at least 16 years old.

Subsection (4) requires that the text of ss. 145(4) and 510 be set out in every summons.

Subsection (5) states that a summons may require the accused to appear at a stated time and place for the purposes of the *Identification of Criminals Act*, if the offence the accused is alleged to have committed is an indictable one.

ANNOTATIONS

There is no jurisdiction in a court to proceed *ex parte* against a defendant served with a summons outside Canada: *R. v. Shulman* (1975), 23 C.C.C. (2d) 242, 58 D.L.R. (3d) 586 (B.C.C.A.).

A justice has no power to issue a summons to an accused solely for the purpose of the *Identification of Criminals Act* and not in conjunction with procuring his attendance at court: *R. v. Michelsen* (1983), 4 C.C.C. (3d) 371, 33 C.R. (3d) 285 (Man. Q.B.).

Subsection (5) – The discretionary power to require an accused to attend for fingerprinting does not violate the principles of fundamental justice as guaranteed by s. 7 of the *Charter of Rights and Freedoms*: *R. v. Beare; R. v. Higgins*, [1988] 2 S.C.R. 387, 45 C.C.C. (3d) 57 (7:0).

FAILURE TO APPEAR.

510. Where an accused who is required by a summons to appear at a time and place stated in it for the purposes of the *Identification of Criminals Act* does not appear at that time and place and, in the case of an offence designated as a contravention under the *Contraventions Act*, the Attorney General, within the meaning of the Act, has not made an election under section 50 of that Act, a justice may issue a warrant for the arrest of the accused for the offence with which the accused is charged. R.S., c. 2 (2nd Supp.), s. 5; 1992, c. 47, s. 72; 1996, c. 7, s. 38.

CROSS-REFERENCES

The term "justice" is defined in s. 2. The terms "summons" and "warrant" are defined in s. 493. Failure to attend for the purposes of the *Identification of Criminals Act*, R.S.C. 1985, c. I-1, is an offence under s. 145. A warrant may also issue for failure to attend for the purposes of the *Identification of Criminals Act* as required in a promise-to-appear appearance notice or recognizance pursuant to s. 502. A warrant may issue under s. 512 where the accused fails to appear for court as required or where a summons cannot be served because the accused is evading service.

SYNOPSIS

This section deals with the failure to appear by an accused, who is required by summons to appear at a stated time and place for the *Identification of Criminals Act*. If the accused does not appear as required, the justice may issue a warrant for the arrest of the accused for the offence with which he is charged.

CONTENTS OF WARRANT TO ARREST / No return day / Discretion to postpone execution / Deemed execution of warrant.

511. (1) A warrant issued under this Part shall
   (*a*) name or describe the accused;

(*b*) set out briefly the offence in respect of which the accused is charged; and

(*c*) order that the accused be forthwith arrested and brought before the judge or justice who issued the warrant or before some other judge or justice having jurisdiction in the same territorial division, to be dealt with according to law.

(2) A warrant issued under this Part remains in force until it is executed and need not be made returnable at any particular time.

(3) Notwithstanding paragraph (1)(*c*), a judge or justice who issues a warrant may specify in the warrant the period before which the warrant shall not be executed, to allow the accused to appear voluntarily before a judge or justice having jurisdiction in the territorial division in which the warrant was issued.

(4) Where the accused appears voluntarily for the offence in respect of which the accused is charged, the warrant is deemed to be executed. R.S., c. C-34, s. 456; R.S., c. 2 (2nd Supp.), s. 5; R.S.C. 1985, c. 27 (1st Supp.), s. 81; 1997, c. 18, s. 57.

CROSS-REFERENCES

The term "justice" is defined in s. 2. Section 31(1) of the *Interpretation Act*, R.S.C. 1985, c. I-21, provides that where anything is required or authorized to be done by or before, *inter alia*, a justice of the peace it shall be done by or before one whose jurisdiction or powers extend to the place where the thing is to be done. The terms "accused" and "warrant" are defined in s. 493.

Formalities in a warrant are set out in s. 513. Under s. 20 a warrant may be executed on a holiday. A warrant is executed in accordance with ss. 29 and 514, and s. 10 of the Charter. For protection of person executing warrants and other process see ss. 25 to 28.

SYNOPSIS

This section sets out the necessary contents of a warrant to arrest issued under Part XVI.

Subsection (1) states that a warrant issued under Part XVI shall name or describe the accused, set out briefly the charge, and order the immediate arrest of the accused, who must then be brought before a judge or justice having jurisdiction, in order to be dealt with according to law.

Subsection (2) states that a warrant issued under Part XVI remains in force until it is executed. It is not necessary that it be made returnable at any specific time.

Subsection (3) allows the justice to require that the warrant be held for a specified time to allow the accused to appear voluntarily.

ANNOTATIONS

There is no jurisdiction for the Provincial Court Judges to seize themselves of release hearings by requiring that the accused be brought before the issuer of the warrant: *R. v. Davidson* (2004), 193 C.C.C. (3d) 63, 26 C.R. (6th) 264, 357 A.R. 353 (C.A.).

CERTAIN ACTIONS NOT TO PRECLUDE ISSUE OF WARRANT / Warrant in default of appearance.

512. (1) A justice may, where the justice has reasonable and probable grounds to believe that it is necessary in the public interest to issue a summons or a warrant for the arrest of the accused, issue a summons or warrant notwithstanding that

(*a*) an appearance notice or a promise to appear or a recognizance entered into before an officer in charge or another peace officer has been confirmed or cancelled under subsection 508(1);

(*b*) a summons has previously been issued under subsection 507(4); or

(*c*) the accused has been released unconditionally or with the intention of compelling his appearance by way of summons.

(2) **Where**

    (*a*) **service of a summons is proved and the accused fails to attend court in accordance with the summons,**

    (*b*) **an appearance notice or a promise to appear or a recognizance entered into before an officer in charge or another peace officer has been confirmed under subsection 508(1) and the accused fails to attend court in accordance therewith in order to be dealt with according to law, or**

    (*c*) **it appears that a summons cannot be served because the accused is evading service,**

a justice may issue a warrant for the arrest of the accused. R.S., c. 2 (2nd Supp.), s. 5; R.S.C. 1985, c. 27 (1st Supp.), s. 82; 1997, c. 18, s. 58.

CROSS-REFERENCES

The terms "justice" and "peace officer" are defined in s. 2. The terms "accused", "appearance notice", "officer in charge", "promise to appear", "summons", "warrant" and "recognizance" are defined in s. 493. As to contents of warrant see ss. 511 and 513. A warrant is executed in accordance with ss. 29 and 514, and s. 10 of the Charter. For protection of person executing warrants and other process see ss. 25 to 28.

SYNOPSIS

This section empowers a justice to issue a warrant in certain specific situations.

Subsection (1) states that a justice may issue a summons or a warrant for the arrest of an accused notwithstanding that an appearance notice, a promise to appear or a recognizance has been confirmed or cancelled under s. 508(1). A summons or warrant may also be issued by a justice under this subsection even if another summons has been issued under s. 507(4) or the accused has been released unconditionally or with the intention of compelling his appearance by way of summons. However, in all of these instances the justice must believe that it is in the public interest to issue the summons or warrant.

Subsection (2) provides that a justice may issue a warrant for the arrest of the accused where service of summons is proved and the accused fails to appear in court. The justice may also issue a warrant when an appearance notice, a promise to appear or a recognizance has been confirmed under s. 508(1) and the accused fails to appear in court, or when a summons cannot be served because the accused appears to be evading service.

ANNOTATIONS

Subsection (1) – An accused's release from custody because of non-compliance with s. 525 does not preclude a justice from issuing a warrant for his arrest again for the same offence: *Ex p. Chung* (1975), 26 C.C.C. (2d) 497, [1976] 1 W.W.R. 453 (B.C.C.A.).

This subsection gives a judge a residual power to issue a warrant where the accused after an initial appearance in court fails to appear, even if the initial appearance was pursuant to defective process such as a failure to comply with s. 505: *R. v. Gougeon; R. v. Haesler; R. v. Gray* (1980), 55 C.C.C. (2d) 218 (Ont. C.A.), leave to appeal to S.C.C. refused 35 N.R. 83*n*. Folld: *R. v. Siller* (1980), 59 C.C.C. (2d) 169 (B.C.C.A.).

Subsection (2) – There is no jurisdiction to issue a warrant simply to preserve jurisdiction where the accused is already in custody but has not been brought before the court: *R. v. Inverarity* (1984), 18 C.C.C. (3d) 74 (Sask. Q.B.). [**Note:** as to whether jurisdiction would be lost in such circumstances regard must be had to s. 485.]

However, to the contrary is *R. v. Hartmann* (1986), 30 C.C.C. (3d) 286 (Ont. H.C.J.), where it was held that a warrant could issue under this subsection, and possibly under subsec. (1), to preserve jurisdiction where the accused was not brought to court on a remand date. It is not a condition precedent to the issuance of a warrant under this subsection that its issuance be necessary in the public interest and resort to this subsection does not depend on the fact that the accused did not have a lawful excuse for failing to attend in court.

FORMALITIES OF WARRANT.

513. A warrant in accordance with this Part shall be directed to the peace officers within the territorial jurisdiction of the justice, judge or court by whom or by which it is issued. R.S., c. 2 (2nd Supp.), s. 5.

CROSS-REFERENCES
"Warrant" is defined in s. 493. The contents of the warrant are described in s. 511. Under s. 20 a warrant may be executed on a holiday. A warrant is executed in accordance with ss. 29 and 514, and s. 10 of the Charter. For protection of person executing warrants and other process see ss. 25 to 28.

SYNOPSIS
This section requires that a warrant issued under Part XVI be directed to the peace officers within the territorial jurisdiction of the issuing justice, judge or court.

EXECUTION OF WARRANT / By whom warrant may be executed.

514. (1) A warrant in accordance with this Part may be executed by arresting the accused

(a) **wherever he is found within the territorial jurisdiction of the justice, judge or court by whom or by which the warrant was issued; or**

(b) **wherever he is found in Canada, in the case of fresh pursuit.**

(2) A warrant in accordance with this Part may be executed by a person who is one of the peace officers to whom it is directed, whether or not the place in which the warrant is to be executed is within the territory for which the person is a peace officer. R.S., c. 2 (2nd Supp.), s. 5.

CROSS-REFERENCES
"Justice" and "peace officer" are defined in s. 2. "Warrant" is defined in s. 493. The contents of the warrant are described in ss. 511 and 513. Under s. 20 a warrant may be executed on a holiday. A warrant is executed in accordance with ss. 29 and 513, and s. 10 of the Charter. For protection of person executing warrants see ss. 25 to 28. Where the warrant cannot be executed in accordance with this section then an application may be made under s. 528 to a justice, in whose jurisdiction the accused is believed to be, who may endorse the warrant authorizing the arrest within his jurisdiction. As to effect of warrant from superior court in another province, see s. 703.

As to execution of a warrant where the accused is believed to be in a dwelling-house, see ss. 529 to 529.5.

SYNOPSIS
This section describes the execution of a warrant issued under Part XVI on the accused.

Subsection (1) states that a warrant may be executed by arresting the accused wherever he is found within the territorial jurisdiction of the issuing court. In the case of fresh pursuit, the warrant may be executed wherever the accused is found in Canada.

Subsection (2) provides that the warrant may be executed by one of the peace officers to whom it is directed, even if the place where the warrant is to be executed is not part of that peace officer's territory.

Judicial Interim Release

ORDER OF RELEASE / Release on undertaking with conditions, etc. / Power of justice to name sureties in order / Alternative to physical presence / Where consent required / Release on undertaking with conditions, etc. / Conditions authorized / Condition prohibiting possession of firearms, etc. / Surrender, etc. / Reasons / Additional conditions / Offences / Detention in custody / Order of detention / Reasons / Order of release / Idem / Sufficiency of record / Written reasons / Justification for detention in custody / Detention in custody for offence mentioned in s. 469 / Order re no communication / Consideration of victim's safety and security / Copy to victim.

515. (1) Subject to this section, where an accused who is charged with an offence other than an offence listed in section 469 is taken before a justice, the justice shall, unless a plea of guilty by the accused is accepted, order, in respect of that offence, that the accused be released on his giving an undertaking without conditions, unless the prosecutor, having been given a reasonable opportunity to do so, shows cause, in respect of that offence, why the detention of the accused in custody is justified or why an order under any other provision of this section should be made and where the justice makes an order under any other provision of this section, the order shall refer only to the particular offence for which the accused was taken before the justice.

(2) Where the justice does not make an order under subsection (1), he shall, unless the prosecutor shows cause why the detention of the accused is justified, order that the accused be released

  (a) on his giving an undertaking with such conditions as the justice directs;

  (b) on his entering into a recognizance before the justice, without sureties, in such amount and with such conditions, if any, as the justice directs but without deposit of money or other valuable security;

  (c) on his entering into a recognizance before the justice with sureties in such amount and with such conditions, if any, as the justice directs but without deposit of money or other valuable security;

  (d) with the consent of the prosecutor, on his entering into a recognizance before the justice, without sureties, in such amount and with such conditions, if any, as the justice directs and on his depositing with the justice such sum of money or other valuable security as the justice directs; or

  (e) if the accused is not ordinarily resident in the province in which the accused is in custody or does not ordinarily reside within two hundred kilometres of the place in which he is in custody, on his entering into a recognizance before the justice with or without sureties in such amount and with such conditions, if any, as the justice directs, and upon his depositing with the justice such sum of money or other valuable security as the justice directs.

(2.1) Where, pursuant to subsection (2) or any other provision of this Act, a justice, judge or court orders that an accused be released on his entering into a recognizance with sureties, the justice, judge or court may, in the order, name particular persons as sureties.

(2.2) Where, by this Act, the appearance of an accused is required for the purposes of judicial interim release, the appearance shall be by actual physical attendance of the accused but the justice may, subject to subsection (2.3), allow the accused to appear by means of any suitable telecommunication device, including telephone, that is satisfactory to the justice.

(2.3) The consent of the prosecutor and the accused is required for the purposes of an appearance if the evidence of a witness is to be taken at the appearance and the accused cannot appear by closed-circuit television or any other means that allow the court and the accused to engage in simultaneous visual and oral communication.

(3) The justice shall not make an order under any of paragraphs (2)(*b*) to (*e*) unless the prosecution shows cause why an order under the immediately preceding paragraph should not be made.

(4) The justice may direct as conditions under subsection (2) that the accused shall do any one or more of the following things as specified in the order:

(*a*) report at times to be stated in the order to a peace officer or other person designated in the order;

(*b*) remain within a territorial jurisdiction specified in the order;

(*c*) notify the peace officer or other person designated under paragraph (*a*) of any change in his address or his employment or occupation;

(*d*) abstain from communicating, directly or indirectly, with any victim, witness or other person identified in the order, or refrain from going to any place specified in the order, except in accordance with the conditions specified in the order that the justice considers necessary;

(*e*) where the accused is the holder of a passport, deposit his passport as specified in the order;

(*e*.1) comply with any other condition specified in the order that the justice considers necessary to ensure the safety and security of any victim of or witness to the offence; and

(*f*) comply with such other reasonable conditions specified in the order as the justice considers desirable.

(4.1) When making an order under subsection (2), in the case of an accused who is charged with

(*a*) an offence in the commission of which violence against a person was used, threatened or attempted,

(*a*.1) a terrorism offence,

(*b*) an offence under section 264 (criminal harassment),

(*b*.1) an offence under section 423.1 (intimidation of a justice system participant),

(*c*) an offence relating to the contravention of any of sections 5 to 7 of the *Controlled Drugs and Substances Act*,

(*d*) an offence that involves, or the subject-matter of which is, a firearm, a cross-bow, a prohibited weapon, a restricted weapon, a prohibited device, ammunition, prohibited ammunition or an explosive substance, or

(*e*) an offence under subsection 20(1) of the *Security of Information Act*, or an offence under subsection 21(1) or 22(1) or section 23 of that Act that is committed in relation to an offence under subsection 20(1) of that Act,

the justice shall add to the order a condition prohibiting the accused from possessing a firearm, cross-bow, prohibited weapon, restricted weapon, prohibited device, ammunition, prohibited ammunition or explosive substance, or all those things, until the accused is dealt with according to law unless the justice considers that such a condition is not required in the interests of the safety of the accused or the safety and security of a victim of the offence or of any other person.

(4.11) Where the justice adds a condition described in subsection (4.1) to an order made under subsection (2), the justice shall specify in the order the manner and method by which

(*a*) the things referred to in subsection (4.1) that are in the possession of the accused shall be surrendered, disposed of, detained, stored or dealt with; and

(*b*) the authorizations, licences and registration certificates held by the person shall be surrendered.

(4.12) Where the justice does not add a condition described in subsection (4.1) to an order made under subsection (2), the justice shall include in the record a statement of the reasons for not adding the condition.

(4.2) Before making an order under subsection (2), in the case of an accused who is charged with an offence referred to in subsection (4.3), the justice shall consider whether it is desirable, in the interests of the safety and security of any person, particularly a victim of or witness to the offence or a justice system participant, to include as a condition of the order

(a) that the accused abstain from communicating, directly or indirectly, with any victim, witness or other person identified in the order, or refrain from going to any place specified in the order; or

(b) that the accused comply with any other condition specified in the order that the justice considers necessary to ensure the safety and security of those persons.

(4.3) The offences for the purposes of subsection (4.2) are

(a) a terrorism offence;

(b) an offence described in section 264 or 423.1;

(c) an offence in the commission of which violence against a person was used, threatened or attempted; and

(d) an offence under subsection 20(1) of the *Security of Information Act*, or an offence under subsection 21(1) or 22(1) or section 23 of that Act that is committed in relation to an offence under subsection 20(1) of that Act.

(5) Where the prosecutor shows cause why the detention of the accused in custody is justified, the justice shall order that the accused be detained in custody until he is dealt with according to law and shall include in the record a statement of his reasons for making the order.

(6) Unless the accused, having been given a reasonable opportunity to do so, shows cause why the accused's detention in custody is not justified, the justice shall order, despite any provision of this section, that the accused be detained in custody until the accused is dealt with according to law, if the accused is charged

(a) with an indictable offence, other than an offence listed in section 469,

(i) that is alleged to have been committed while at large after being released in respect of another indictable offence pursuant to the provisions of this Part or section 679 or 680,

(ii) that is an offence under section 467.11, 467.111, 467.12 or 467.13, or a serious offence alleged to have been committed for the benefit of, at the direction of, or in association with, a criminal organization,

(iii) that is an offence under any of sections 83.02 to 83.04 and 83.18 to 83.23 or otherwise is alleged to be a terrorism offence,

(iv) an offence under subsection 16(1) or (2), 17(1), 19(1), 20(1) or 22(1) of the *Security of Information Act*,

(v) an offence under subsection 21(1) or 22(1) or section 23 of the *Security of Information Act* that is committed in relation to on offence referred to in subparagraph (iv),

(vi) that is an offence under section 99, 100 or 103,

(vii) that is an offence under section 244 or 244.2, or an offence under section 239, 272 or 273, subsection 279(1) or section 279.1, 344 or 346 that is alleged to have been committed with a firearm, or

(viii) that is alleged to involve, or whose subject-matter is alleged to be, a firearm, a cross-bow, a prohibited weapon, a restricted weapon, a prohibited device, any ammunition or prohibited ammunition or an explosive substance, and that is alleged to have been committed while the accused was under a prohibition order within the meaning of subsection 84(1);

(b) with an indictable offence, other than an offence listed in section 469 and is not ordinarily resident in Canada,

(c) with an offence under any of subsections 145(2) to (5) that is alleged to have been committed while he was at large after being released in respect of another offence pursuant to the provisions of this Part or section 679, 680 or 816, or (*d*) with having committed an offence punishable by imprisonment for life under any of sections 5 to 7 of the *Controlled Drugs and Substances Act* or the offence of conspiring to commit such an offence.

(6.1) If the justice orders that an accused to whom subsection (6) applies be released, the justice shall include in the record a statement of the justice's reasons for making the order.

(7) Where an accused to whom paragraph 6(*a*), (*c*) or (*d*) applies shows cause why the accused's detention in custody is not justified, the justice shall order that the accused be released on giving an undertaking or entering into a recognizance described in any of paragraphs (2)(*a*) to (*e*) with the conditions described in subsections (4) to (4.2) or, where the accused was at large on an undertaking or recognizance with conditions, the additional conditions described in subsections (4) to (4.2), that the justice considers desirable, unless the accused, having been given a reasonable opportunity to do so, shows cause why the conditions or additional conditions should not be imposed.

(8) Where an accused to whom paragraph (6)(*b*) applies shows cause why the accused's detention in custody is not justified, the justice shall order that the accused be released on giving an undertaking or entering into a recognizance described in any of paragraphs (2)(*a*) to (*e*) with the conditions, described in subsections (4) to (4.2), that the justice considers desirable.

(9) For the purposes of subsections (5) and (6), it is sufficient if a record is made of the reasons in accordance with the provisions of Part XVIII relating to the taking of evidence at preliminary inquiries.

(9.1) Despite subsection (9), if the justice orders that the accused be detained in custody primarily because of a previous conviction of the accused, the justice shall state that reason, in writing, in the record.

(10) For the purposes of this section, the detention of an accused in custody is justified only on one or more of the following grounds:
- (*a*) where the detention is necessary to ensure his or her attendance in court in order to be dealt with according to law;
- (*b*) where the detention is necessary for the protection or safety of the public, including any victim of or witness to the offence, or any person under the age of 18 years, having regard to all the circumstances including any substantial likelihood that the accused will, if released from custody, commit a criminal offence or interfere with the administration of justice; and
- (*c*) if the detention is necessary to maintain confidence in the administration of justice, having regard to all the circumstances, including
  - (i) the apparent strength of the prosecution's case,
  - (ii) the gravity of the offence,
  - (iii) the circumstances surrounding the commission of the offence, including whether a firearm was used, and
  - (iv) the fact that the accused is liable, on conviction, for a potentially lengthy term of imprisonment or, in the case of an offence that involves, or whose subject-matter is, a firearm, a minimum punishment of imprisonment for a term of three years or more.

(11) Where an accused who is charged with an offence mentioned in section 469 is taken before a justice, the justice shall order that the accused be detained in custody until he is dealt with according to law and shall issue a warrant in Form 8 for the committal of the accused.

(12) A justice who orders that an accused be detained in custody under this section may include in the order a direction that the accused abstain from communicating, directly or indirectly, with any victim, witness or other person identified in the order, except in

accordance with such conditions specified in the order as the justice considers necessary.

(13) A justice who makes an order under this section shall include in the record of the proceedings a statement that he or she considered the safety and security of every victim of the offence when making the order.

(14) If an order is made under this section, the justice shall, on request by a victim of the offence, cause a copy of the order to be given to the victim. R.S., c. C-34, s. 457; R.S., c. 2 (2nd Supp.), s. 5; 1974-75-76, c. 93, s. 47; R.S.C. 1985, c. 27 (1st Supp.), ss. 83, 186 (Sched. IV, item 7); 1991, c. 40, s. 31; 1993, c. 45, s. 8; 1994, c. 44, s. 44; 1995, c. 39, ss. 153, 188(*b*); 1996, c. 19, ss. 71, 93.3; 1997, c. 18, s. 59; c. 23, s. 16; 1999, c. 5, s. 21; c. 25, s. 8; 2001, c. 32, s. 37; c. 41, ss. 19, 133(15)-(17); 2008, c. 6, s. 37; 2009, c. 22, s. 17; c. 29, s. 2; 2010, c. 20, s. 1; 2012, c. 1, s. 32; 2014, c. 17, s. 14; 2015, c. 13, s. 20.

CROSS-REFERENCES

The terms "justice", "criminal organization", "terrorism offence", "justice system participant" and "victim" are defined in s. 2. The terms "recognizance" and "undertaking" are defined in s. 493. "Sureties" is defined in s. 35 of the *Interpretation Act*, R.S.C. 1985, c. I-21, as sufficient sureties and when those words are used one person is sufficient therefor, unless otherwise expressly required.

Pursuant to s. 2.1, the terms "cross-bow", "prohibited weapon", "restricted weapon", "prohibited device", "ammunition", and "prohibited ammunition" have the same meaning as in s. 84(1).

Where the justice stated in writing on the record, in accordance with subsec. (9.1) of this section, that the reason for detention was primarily because of a previous conviction, the sentencing judge may not give more than 1 for 1 credit for pre-sentence custody, pursuant to s. 719(3.1). The term "conviction" is not defined in this section, but presumably has the same meaning as "convicted of a criminal offence" in s. 518(1)(*c*).

Note on judicial interim release – Where the accused is not released by the arresting officer or the officer in charge (defined in s. 493) then s. 503 requires that he be taken before a justice (defined in s. 2) without unreasonable delay and within 24 hours where a justice is available. Upon being taken before a justice the accused is entitled to a bail hearing under s. 515 unless he is charged with an offence listed in s. 469, such as murder, or he pleads guilty. Following is a brief discussion of the procedure and the relationship between the various provisions as they apply to an accused charged with an offence other than an offence listed in s. 469. For the s. 469 offences see the note under s. 522.

The hearing under s. 515 is variously described in the case law as a judicial interim release hearing or "show cause" hearing because in most cases the onus is on the prosecution to show cause why the accused should not be released on an undertaking (defined in s. 493) without conditions. There are certain exceptions, listed in s. 515(6), where the onus is reversed and it is the accused who must show cause why he should not be detained. The justice must provide reasons in accordance with s. 515(6.1) if the justice nevertheless releases the accused. In either case cause for detention is set out in s. 515(10). Where the prosecutor shows cause why the accused should not be released on an unconditional undertaking then the onus is on the prosecutor to show why the accused should not be released on a form of release representing the least interference with the accused's liberty, from an undertaking with conditions to a recognizance (defined in s. 493), with or without sureties (defined in s. 35 of the *Interpretation Act*), and finally a detention order. These forms of release are described in s. 515(2) and the conditions which may be imposed are set out in s. 515(4), (4.1) and (4.3). Note that where a prohibition order is made under subsec. (4.1), pursuant to s. 113, the justice or judge may make an order authorizing a chief firearms officer or the Registrar to issue, in accordance with such terms and conditions as is considered appropriate, an authorization, a licence or a registration certificate, as the case may be, to the accused for sustenance or employment purposes. Under s. 114, the prohibition order may require the accused to surrender anything the possession of which is prohibited by the order and every authorization, licence and registration certificate relating to any such thing. Unless the prohibition order provides otherwise, everything the possession of which is prohibited by the order is forfeited to the Crown pursuant to s. 115, subject to the true owner making an application under s. 117. Under s. 116, every authorization, licence and registration certificate relating to anything the possession of which is prohibited by a prohibition order and issued to the accused is, on the commencement of the prohibition order, revoked, or amended, as the case may be, to the extent of the prohibitions in the order. In certain cases, described in s. 515(2)(*d*), and (*e*), the justice may also make an order requiring a cash deposit with or without sureties. Where the onus is on the prosecutor to show cause s. 515(5) requires the justice to give reasons for making a detention order. Where the onus is on the accused then s. 515(6) requires that the justice give reasons for making a release order. Even where the accused is detained for some other reason, *e.g.*, because he is serving sentence, he is entitled to a hearing under s. 515, however, if the justice makes a release order then by virtue of s. 519 the accused will still remain in custody until he is no longer required to be detained for some other reason. If the justice detains the accused "primarily" because of a previous conviction, subsec. (9.1) requires the justice to record that fact in writing (presumably on the information). The purpose of this record is that it limits the amount of credit that can be awarded for pre-sentence custody in accordance with s. 719(3.1).

Sections 516 to 518 set out the procedure to be followed on the bail hearing. Section 516 deals with adjournments and permits the justice to order the accused to abstain from communicating with witnesses or other named persons. Section 517 provides for a non-publication order. Section 518 sets out the kind of evidence which may be tendered on the hearing. The effect of s. 518 is to give a relatively wide latitude to the justice permitting him to receive and base his decision on evidence "considered credible or trustworthy". Thus the rules of evidence which would apply at a trial would not apply on the bail hearing. One limit on the receipt of evidence is the proviso in s. 518(1)(*b*), which prohibits questioning of the accused respecting the offence with which he is charged. The scope of this subsection is uncertain, there being some case law noted under s. 518 holding that, while the accused cannot be asked by the justice or the prosecutor about the offence, he is entitled to volunteer his testimony concerning the offence. Where a release order is made then s. 519 sets out the procedure for putting the order into effect and the circumstances in which the accused will be released.

The Code also sets out an elaborate system of review. Under s. 515.1 the undertaking or recognizance may be "varied" with consent of the prosecutor. Under s. 520 the accused may apply to a judge (defined in s. 493) to review a detention order or to review the terms upon which he was released. Section 521 gives a similar right of review to the prosecutor to review any release order made by a justice. It would also seem that orders made under ss. 520 or 521 can in turn be reviewed under those sections. The application is on notice to the prosecutor or accused as the case may be (ss. 520(2) and 521(2)). The procedure on the review hearing resembles the procedure on the original s. 515 hearing, except that the onus is on the applicant to show cause why the original order should be vacated (ss. 520(7) and 521(8)). The presence of the accused would not appear to be mandatory but the judge may make an order requiring the accused's presence which order may be enforced through issuance of a warrant (ss. 520(3), (5) and 521(3), (5)). Ordinarily, the judge will consider the transcript of proceedings sought to be reviewed but has power to consider other additional evidence or exhibits (ss. 520(7) and 521(8)). Adjournment of the proceeding is provided for in ss. 520(4) and 521(4).

Section 523(2) also provides for a more informal review process at various stages of the proceedings by a justice, a preliminary inquiry judge, a judge of the trial court, or the trial judge. Note, however, that the release or detention order can only be vacated under this subsection upon cause being shown and, in some circumstances, the review can only be undertaken where both the accused and the prosecutor consent. Section 524 enacts a procedure for dealing with cases where it is alleged that the accused has violated or is about to violate any form of release either issued by a peace officer or by a justice or has committed an indictable offence while on a form of release. That section gives a power to arrest with (subsec. (1)) or without warrant (subsec. (2)). Upon arrest under this section the accused will be taken before a justice and where it is shown that his arrest was justified (subsec. (8)) then the release order is cancelled and the accused ordered detained unless he can show cause why he should not be detained in custody. If the accused shows cause then s. 524(9) provides for the types of release order which may be made. Any order made under s.

524 may be reviewed under ss. 520 and 521 by the accused or the prosecutor as the case may be. The procedure on the s. 524 hearing is similar to the original show cause hearing (subsec. (12)). Finally, s. 525 sets out a procedure for an automatic review, by a judge, of the detention of any accused who is ordered detained either under s. 515, 521 or 524. The time when the review occurs depends on whether the accused is charged with an indictable offence (90 days) or a summary conviction offence (30 days). The scope of s. 525 remains subject to some uncertainty. In particular it is not clear whether the accused is entitled to a review where he has been ordered released but is unable to comply with the terms of the recognizance and it is unclear whether the section applies where the accused has previously unsuccessfully applied to a judge under s. 520. The procedure under the s. 525 hearing resembles the procedure under s. 515, except that notwithstanding where the onus originally lay the judge must be satisfied that the accused's continued detention is justified within the meaning of s. 515(10) (subsec. (4)). Subsections (5) to (7) describe a procedure for cancelling any release order made under s. 525, a procedure which resembles the s. 524 procedure. Aside from those subsections there would not appear to be any mechanism for reviewing a release order made under s. 525. Subsection (9) also requires the judge in any event to give directions for expediting the trial. A similar discretionary power is given to any justice or judge conducting a hearing under any of the other sections, pursuant to s. 526.

Barring a review under these provisions the effect of s. 523(1) is that the release or detention order remains in effect until verdict. Where the accused is found guilty then the release order remains in effect unless the judge orders that he be taken into custody pending sentence. Section 523(1.1) provides a procedure for the release order in respect of one information to apply to a new information charging the same offence, or an included offence.

Where the accused pleads guilty either prior to the show cause hearing under s. 515 or in the course of the hearing then, pursuant to s. 518(2), the justice may make an order provided for in s. 515 for his release pending sentence.

The procedure for enforcement of a recognizance is set out in Part XXV. That Part sets out the responsibilities of sureties (s. 764); procedure for rendering of accused by his sureties (ss. 766, 767 and 769); substitution of a new surety (s. 767.1), and the new release hearing where the accused is rendered into custody by his sureties (s. 769). That Part also sets out the procedure in case of default by the accused, including endorsing the fact of the default (s. 770); the hearing for estreat of the bail (s. 771); levying execution to enforce a writ of *fieri facias* where the recognizance is ordered forfeited (ss. 772 and 773).

There are special limitations on the making of interim release and detention orders where the court makes an assessment order under Part XX.1. See in particular ss. 672.16, 672.17 and 672.18.

ANNOTATIONS

Jurisdiction – A justice has continuing jurisdiction to hear an application for release under subsec. (1) regardless of the point in the proceedings. Jurisdiction is not lost merely because the accused has been committed for trial in the superior court and the charging document is no longer before the provincial court. However, where an accused is being tried in the superior court and no order in respect of bail or detention has been made, the superior court judge may exercise his or her inherent jurisdiction to entertain an initial bail application: *R. v. Mayen* (2014), 311 C.C.C. (3d) 225 (Man. Q.B.).

Burden of proof – The evidentiary burden upon the Crown at this early stage is upon the minimum standard, the balance of probability: *R. v. Julian* (1972), 20 C.R.N.S. 227 (N.S.S.C.).

Fixing amount of deposit – It was held in *R. v. Garrington* (1972), 9 C.C.C. (2d) 472 (Ont. H.C.J.), that it was wrong to fix the amount of the cash deposit as some portion of the amount still unrecovered (the accused were charged with a robbery of a large amount of money) or to fix the amount so high that it was effectively a detention order.

Subsection 2(*d*) which requires the consent of the prosecutor before a cash bail can be ordered violates s. 11(*e*) of the Charter and should be read down to exclude these words: *R. v. Saunders* (2001), 159 C.C.C. (3d) 558 (B.C.S.C.).

It was held in *R. v. Folkes* (2007), 228 C.C.C. (3d) 284 (Alta. Q.B.), addt'l reasons *loc. cit.* at p. 301, that the limitations in subsec. (2)(*e*) as to when a court may order sureties and a deposit violate s. 11(*e*) of the *Charter of Rights and Freedoms*. Accordingly, the phrase "if the accused is not ordinarily resident in the province in which the accused is in custody or does not ordinarily reside within two hundred kilometres of the place in which he is in custody", is to be read out of the provision.

Fixing amount of surety – Where the amount fixed for sureties is so high that in effect it amounts to a detention order it will be reduced accordingly: *R. v. Cichanski* (1976), 25 C.C.C. (2d) 84 (Ont. H.C.J.).

Naming sureties – The inclusion of subsec. (2.1) confers a permissive authority. The court is not required to name sureties and, because a prospective surety is not in court or is as yet unidentified, the court is often not in a position to in effect pre-approve a surety to be named in the order. It then falls to the justice exercising the compliance jurisdiction in s. 519 to approve, or not, the sureties before release can occur. There is no legal requirement that a surety be present in court and testify in order for judicial interim release to be considered. While there may be circumstances where the judge may wish to see a surety, a blanket requirement that all prospective sureties in every case must appear before the court at the show cause hearing amounts to an abuse of discretion: *R. v. Brooks* (2001), 153 C.C.C. (3d) 533 (Ont. S.C.J.); *R. v. Villota* (2002), 163 C.C.C. (3d) 507 (Ont. S.C.J.).

Reasonable conditions – To come within the meaning of the term "reasonable conditions", the particular term must be related to a purpose which would otherwise justify the accused's detention pending trial: *R. v. Keenan* (1979), 57 C.C.C. (2d) 267 (Que. C.A.).

The justice may validly impose a condition that the accused remain out of a certain part of the city where the term is designed to prevent the commission of further offences while the accused is on judicial interim release: *R. v. Bielefeld* (1981), 64 C.C.C. (2d) 216 (B.C.S.C.).

Effect of order to stand trial on lesser offence – Where an accused who has been ordered detained on a charge of robbery is committed for trial on the lesser offence of attempted robbery the original order remains in effect: *Ex p. Walker* (1974), 20 C.C.C. (2d) 539 (Ont. H.C.J.); *cf. R. v. Lafontaine* (1973), 13 C.C.C. (2d) 316 (Ont. H.C.J.), noted under s. 522.

Requirement of reasons – The requirement of reasons is directory only and the failure to give reasons does not affect the validity of the detention order: *R. v. Baker* (1973), 13 C.C.C. (2d) 340 (B.C.S.C.).

Adjournment – There is no need for a full hearing before a justice exercises discretion concerning the length of the remand: *R. v. F. (C.G.)* (2003), 181 C.C.C. (3d) 422 (N.S.C.A.).

Right to counsel – An unrepresented accused charged with an indictable offence may have the right to counsel at a bail hearing or bail review. The presiding judge has a duty to inquire whether the accused wishes to be represented by counsel. The determination must be made on a case-by-case basis having regard to the complexity of the proceedings and the seriousness of the charge: *R. v. Chan* (2000), 146 C.C.C. (3d) 494 (Alta. C.A.).

Reverse onus (subsec. (6)) – Notwithstanding an accused may fall within this subsection the basic philosophy of the interim release provisions is that prior to conviction all those persons who do not constitute a danger to public and who will show up for trial ought not to be detained in custody. Where as a result of this subsection the onus is on the accused the justice must still consider the two grounds set out in subsec. (10) in determining whether or not to release the accused. The justice does not have a residual discretion to refuse bail: *R. v. Quinn* (1977), 34 C.C.C. (2d) 473 (N.S. Co. Ct.); *Batson (Re)* (1977), 21 N.B.R. (2d) 275 (C.A.).

The reverse onus prescribed by subsec. (2)(*d*) does not violate ss. 7, 9 or 11(*e*) of the Charter. The onus which subsec. (2)(*d*) imposes is reasonable in the sense that it requires the accused to provide information which he is most capable of providing. The special rules combat the pre-trial recidivism and absconding problems which are characteristic of systematic drug trafficking which usually occurs in a highly sophisticated and lucrative commercial setting. While the provision also applies to the small or casual drug dealers, they will normally have no difficulty in justifying their release and obtaining bail: *R. v. Pearson*, [1992] 3 S.C.R. 665, 77 C.C.C. (3d) 124.

Similarly, the scopt of subsec. (6)(*a*) is sufficiently narrow to constitute just cause under s. 11(*e*) and is constitutional: *R. v. Morales*, [1992] 3 S.C.R. 711, 77 C.C.C. (3d) 91.

The determination of whether a person is ordinarily resident in Canada is a question of fact and status as a refugee claimant is but one factor bearing on this determination. Undue weight should not be given to refugee status as compared to landed immigrant or citizenship status. Absent special factors, such as an imminent appeal hearing where the individual has been advised success will be unlikely or the complete lack of any surrounding indicia of stability, a refugee claimant ought not to be automatically saddled with the reverse onus: *R. v. Oladipo* (2004), 191 C.C.C. (3d) 237 (Ont. S.C.J.).

Grounds for detention (subsec. (10)) – The public safety component or para. (*b*), namely where there is a substantial likelihood that the accused if released will interfere with the administration of justice or commit further crimes, constitutes just cause for the denial of bail within the meanings of s. 11(*e*) of the Charter: *R. v. Morales, supra*. In this case the court struck down the "public interest" ground under former subsec. (10)(*b*) as a basis for pre-trial detention because it authorized detention in terms which were vague and imprecise and thus authorizes a denial of bail without just cause. This component is thus unconstitutional and the words "in the public interest or" should be struck down: *R. v. Morales, supra*. This subsection has since been amended to delete "public interest" and add para. (*c*).

The constitutionality of the predecessor to para. (*c*) was considered in *R. v. Hall*, [2002] 3 S.C.R. 309, 167 C.C.C. (3d) 449. The court held that the words "on any other just cause being shown and, without restricting the generality of the foregoing", which have now been removed, violated ss. 7 and 11(*e*) of the Charter and were accordingly inoperative. The remainder of the former provision, however, was not unconstitutional. To allow an accused to be released in the face of a heinous crime and overwhelming evidence may erode the public's confidence in the administration of justice. In considering whether detention is necessary to maintain confidence in the administration of justice, the inquiry must focus on the reasonable community perception of the necessity of denying bail to maintain confidence in the administration of justice, judicially determined through the objective lens having regard to all the circumstances including the strength of the case, the gravity of the nature of the offence, the circumstances surrounding the offence and the potential for a lengthy term of imprisonment.

Even where there is very strong evidence against the accused this is merely one factor to be taken into account by the judge: *R. v. Perron* (1989), 51 C.C.C. (3d) 518 (Que. C.A.).

In *R. v. St-Cloud*, [2015] 2 S.C.R. 328, 321 C.C.C. (3d) 307, the court clarified that para. (*c*) is a distinct ground for detention, not a residual ground that applies only where the first two grounds in paras. (*a*) and (*b*) are not satisfied. It should not be interpreted narrowly or applied sparingly. Its application is not limited to exceptional circumstances, to unexplainable crimes, to the most heinous of crimes or to certain classes of offence. In applying this ground, the justice must first consider the four circumstances that are expressly referred to in para. (*c*), then consider any other relevant circumstances. At the end of this balancing exercise, the ultimate question is whether detention is necessary to maintain confidence in the administration of justice. The court must not order detention automatically even where the four listed circumstances support such a result. Some other circumstances that might be relevant are the personal circumstances of the accused (age, criminal record, physical or mental condition, and membership in a criminal organization), the status of the victim and the impact on society of a crime committed against that person, and the fact that the trial of the accused will be held at a much later date.

Cases dictating that para. (*c*) should be invoked rarely and in a narrow set of circumstances should now be read cautiously in light of *St-Cloud, supra*. See, *e.g.*: *R. v. B.*

(A.) (2006), 204 C.C.C. (3d) 490 (Ont. S.C.J.); *R. v. LaFramboise* (2005), 203 C.C.C. (3d) 492 (Ont. C.A. [In Chambers]).

No one factor in para. *(c)* is determinative. The factors should be analyzed together having regard to their combined effect. Where each of the four factors is assessed as having maximum force, a determination that refusal of bail is necessary to maintain public confidence in the administration of justice is expected: *R. v. Mordue* (2006), 223 C.C.C. (3d) 407 (Ont. C.A.).

No communication (subsec. 12) – A no-contact order only remains in effect while the accused is detained under s. 515. Accordingly, after the accused was found guilty and remanded into custody pending sentence, his detention was no longer pursuant to this provision and the original remand order containing the no-contact provision was no longer in effect: *R. v. Brown* (2000), 151 C.C.C. (3d) 85 (N.S.C.A.).

VARIATION OF UNDERTAKING OR RECOGNIZANCE.

515.1 An undertaking or recognizance pursuant to which the accused was released that has been entered into under section 499, 503 or 515 may, with the written consent of the prosecutor, be varied, and where so varied, is deemed to have been entered into pursuant to section 515. 1997, c. 18, s. 60.

ANNOTATIONS

The surety is released from his obligations if the conditions of release in the recognizance have been altered without the knowledge of the surety: *R. v. Millward* (1998), 128 C.C.C. (3d) 67 (Alta. Q.B.).

This provision allows for the amendment or variation of an existing release order without the necessity of vacating or cancelling the prior release order. Accordingly, the accused does not have to surrender into custody, the sureties do not need to reattend and a new order does not have to be signed. Where the original release was made by a judge, however, the variation must nonetheless be approved by the court. It is necessary that the surety have notice of the application and that evidence, such as an affidavit, be put before the court proving notice and confirming that the surety agrees to be bound by the new recognizance. It is also necessary to establish that the accused has knowledge that the variation has been allowed and that he is bound by the new order. This may be accomplished by requiring the applicant to sign a witnessed acknowledgment that he had read and received a copy of the order and agreed to be bound by its terms on a certified copy of the variation order: *R. v. Ford* (1998), 129 C.C.C. (3d) 189 (Ont. Ct. (Gen. Div.)).

REMAND IN CUSTODY.

516. (1) A justice may, before or at any time during the course of any proceedings under section 515, on application by the prosecutor or the accused, adjourn the proceedings and remand the accused to custody in prison by warrant in Form 19, but no adjournment shall be for more than three clear days except with the consent of the accused.

(2) A justice who remands an accused to custody under subsection (1) or subsection 515(11) may order that the accused abstain from communicating directly or indirectly, with any victim, witness or other person identified in the order, except in accordance with any conditions specified in the order that the justice considers necessary. R.S., c. 2 (2nd Supp.), s. 5; 1999, c. 5, s. 22; c. 25, s. 31(3).

CROSS-REFERENCES

The term "justice" is defined in s. 2. As to calculation of "clear days" see s. 27(1) of the *Interpretation Act*, R.S.C. 1985, c. I-21. For an overview of the application of this Part and the procedure respecting release pending trial see *Note on judicial interim release* under s. 515, or the

Note on judicial interim release under s. 522 where the accused is charged with an offence listed in s. 469.

SYNOPSIS

This section authorizes a justice at any time, either before or during a hearing under s. 515, to adjourn proceedings and remand the accused to custody in prison. Such a remand will be made in Form 19 and shall not be for a longer period than three clear days, unless the accused person consents. The remand may be made upon application by either the prosecutor or the accused. The justice may order the accused to abstain from communicating with witnesses or other persons named in the order.

ANNOTATIONS

Failure to comply with this section, *i.e.*, by failing to issue a warrant of committal, though it may render unlawful his detention during the period does not affect the court's jurisdiction over the accused or the offence: *R. v. Morrison* (1975), 29 C.C.C. (2d) 323 (B.C.S.C.).

The proceedings must be continued within the three clear days. Thus an adjournment on the 22nd day of the month to the 26th day of the month without the accused's consent does not comply with this section: *R. v. Khabra* (1978), 39 C.C.C. (2d) 475 (B.C.S.C.).

On a court-ordered remand in custody if gaol facilities are available the accused must be held there separate from police investigation holding-cells: *R. v. Precourt* (1976), 39 C.C.C. (2d) 311 (Ont. C.A.).

ORDER DIRECTING MATTERS NOT TO BE PUBLISHED FOR SPECIFIED PERIOD / Failure to comply / Definition of "newspaper".

517. (1) If the prosecutor or the accused intends to show cause under section 515, he or she shall so state to the justice and the justice may, and shall on application by the accused, before or at any time during the course of the proceedings under that section, make an order directing that the evidence taken, the information given or the representations made and the reasons, if any, given or to be given by the justice shall not be published in any document, or broadcast or transmitted in any way before such time as

    (a) if a preliminary inquiry is held, the accused in respect of whom the proceedings are held is discharged; or

    (b) if the accused in respect of whom the proceedings are held is tried or ordered to stand trial, the trial is ended.

(2) Every one who fails without lawful excuse, the proof of which lies on him, to comply with an order made under subsection (1) is guilty of an offence punishable on summary conviction.

(3) [*Repealed*, 2005, c. 32, s. 17(2).] R.S., c. 2 (2nd Supp.), s. 5; 1974-75-76, c. 93, s. 48; R.S.C. 1985, c. 27 (1st Supp.), s. 101(2)(a); 2005, c. 32, s. 17.

CROSS-REFERENCES

The terms "prosecutor" and "justice" are defined in s. 2. For an overview of the application of this Part and the procedure respecting release pending trial see *Note on judicial interim release* under s. 515, or the *Note on judicial interim release* under s. 522 where the accused is charged with an offence listed in s. 469.

Trial of the offence under subsec. (2) is conducted by a summary conviction court pursuant to Part XXVII. The punishment is as set out in s. 787 [except note the maximum fine provided for in s. 719 in the case of a corporation] and the limitation period is set out in s. 786(2).

SYNOPSIS

This section authorizes a justice dealing with a hearing under s. 515 to make an order directing that matters not be published for a specified period.

Subsection (1) provides that the justice shall, upon application by the accused during proceedings under s. 515, make an order that evidence, information, representations and reasons given, not be published, broadcast or transmitted in any way. Such an order may be made to last, if a preliminary hearing is held, until such time, if applicable, as the accused is discharged or, if the accused is committed for trial, until the trial ends. The justice may also make such an order on his or her own initiative.

Subsection (2) makes failure to comply with an order under this section a summary conviction offence. The accused must prove that such a failure to comply was with lawful excuse.

ANNOTATIONS

While this provision violates s. 2(b) of the Charter, it is saved under s. 1: *Toronto Star Newspapers Ltd. v. Canada*, [2010] 1 S.C.R. 721, 255 C.C.C. (3d) 473.

A judge has no power to prohibit publication of his decision granting or refusing release. He may only prohibit publication of his reasons for the decision: *R. v. Forget* (1982), 65 C.C.C. (2d) 373 (Ont. C.A.).

A judge has no power under this section to also order a ban on publication of the identity of the accused or on information which journalists have obtained from the police: *Southam Inc. v. Brassard* (1987), 38 C.C.C. (3d) 74 (Que. S.C.), where however it was pointed out that publication of material which would interfere in some manner with the course of justice would amount to contempt of court.

Subsection (1) is to be broadly interpreted to include even non-prejudicial information: *R. v. Daly* (2003), 178 C.C.C. (3d) 31 (B.C.S.C.), affd on other grounds 198 C.C.C. (3d) 185 (B.C.C.A.).

It was no defence that the reporter had obtained legal advice prior to the publication: *R. v. Daly, supra.*

This provision is applicable to proceedings under the *Extradition Act*: *United States of America v. Amhaz* (2001), 159 C.C.C. (3d) 570 (B.C.S.C.).

INQUIRIES TO BE MADE BY JUSTICE AND EVIDENCE / Release pending sentence.

518. (1) In any proceedings under section 515,

   (*a*) **the justice may, subject to paragraph (*b*), make such inquiries, on oath or otherwise, of and concerning the accused as he considers desirable;**

   (*b*) **the accused shall not be examined by the justice or any other person except counsel for the accused respecting the offence with which the accused is charged, and no inquiry shall be made of the accused respecting that offence by way of cross-examination unless the accused has testified respecting the offence;**

   (*c*) **the prosecutor may, in addition to any other relevant evidence, lead evidence**

      (i) **to prove that the accused has previously been convicted of a criminal offence,**

      (ii) **to prove that the accused has been charged with and is awaiting trial for another criminal offence,**

      (iii) **to prove that the accused has previously committed an offence under section 145, or**

      (iv) **to show the circumstances of the alleged offence, particularly as they relate to the probability of conviction of the accused;**

   (*d*) **the justice may take into consideration any relevant matters agreed on by the prosecutor and the accused or his counsel;**

    (*d*.1) **the justice may receive evidence obtained as a result of an interception of a private communication under and within the meaning of Part VI, in writing, orally or in the form of a recording and, for the purposes of this section, subsection 189(5) does not apply to that evidence;**

    (*d*.2) **the justice shall take into consideration any evidence submitted regarding the need to ensure the safety or security of any victim of or witness to an offence; and**

    (*e*) **the justice may receive and base his decision on evidence considered credible or trustworthy by him in the circumstances of each case.**

(2) Where, before or at any time during the course of any proceedings under section 515, the accused pleads guilty and that plea is accepted, the justice may make any order provided for in this Part for the release of the accused until the accused is sentenced. R.S., c. 2 (2nd Supp.), s. 5; 1974-75-76, c. 93, s. 49; R.S.C. 1985, c. 27 (1st Supp.), s. 84; 1994, c. 44, s. 45; 1999, c. 25, s. 9.

CROSS-REFERENCES

The terms "prosecutor", "justice" and "victim" are defined in s. 2. For an overview of the application of this Part and the procedure respecting release pending trial see *Note on judicial interim release* under s. 515, or the *Note on judicial interim release* under s. 522 where the accused is charged with an offence listed in s. 469.

SYNOPSIS

This section describes the kinds of inquiries that may be made and evidence that may be led in proceedings under s. 515.

While the justice is empowered to make such inquiries as he considers desirable, para. (*b*) makes it clear that the accused may not be cross-examined respecting the offence with which he has been charged unless the accused has testified in chief respecting the offence. The prosecutor may lead evidence on issues that are enumerated in para. (*c*) as well as on other relevant matters. The justice may consider any relevant information agreed to by the prosecutor and the accused or counsel for the accused.

Paragraph (*d*.1) states that the justice may receive evidence obtained as a result of an interception of private communications. Section 189(5), which deals with admission into evidence of intercepted communications, does not apply. Paragraph (*d*.2) requires the justice to take into consideration evidence concerning the need to ensure the safety or security of any victim or witness.

Subsection (2) allows a justice to make any order of release found in Part XVI when the accused pleads guilty and is remanded for sentence.

ANNOTATIONS

Examination of accused (subsec. (1)(*b*)) – This subsection does not preclude the Crown from tendering evidence as to the accused's extra-judicial statements and such statements to persons in authority are admissible without a *voir dire* to determine voluntariness: *R. v. Bouffard* (1979), 16 C.R. (3d) 373 (Que. S.C.).

A statement obtained from the accused during the hearing in violation of this paragraph is not admissible in subsequent court proceedings against the accused: *R. v. Deom* (1981), 64 C.C.C. (2d) 222 (B.C.S.C.). This is so even where the violation is initiated by the accused's own counsel in examination of the accused: *R. v. Paonessa and Paquette* (1982), 66 C.C.C. (2d) 300 (Ont. C.A.), affd on other grounds [1983] 1 S.C.R. 660, 3 C.C.C. (3d) 384 (5:0).

Matters agreed upon (subsec. (1)(*d*)) – The bail hearing may proceed on the basis of counsel's submissions including submissions challenging the accuracy and weight of factors asserted by the opposing party: *R. v. Courchene* (1999), 141 C.C.C. (3d) 431 (Man. Q.B.).

Meaning of "credible or trustworthy" (subsec. (1)(e)) – Credible and trustworthy evidence includes evidence ordinarily inadmissible at trial as long as the other party has fair opportunity to correct or contradict it: *R. v. Powers* (1972), 9 C.C.C. (2d) 533 (Ont. H.C.J.). Similarly *R. v. Woo* (1994), 90 C.C.C. (3d) 404 (B.C.S.C.).

While this paragraph entitles the justice to act on hearsay evidence considered trustworthy as well as direct evidence considered credible, it is not authority for Crown counsel simply reading a statement of the circumstances of the offence, a procedure which deprives the accused of his right to cross-examine: *R. v. Hajdu* (1984), 14 C.C.C. (3d) 563 (Ont. H.C.J.). Similarly, *R. v. Woo, supra; R. v. Courchene, supra.*

However, consider *R. v. Dhinsa* (1986), 30 C.C.C. (3d) 368 (B.C.S.C.), holding that both Crown and defence counsel may make statements as to the anticipated evidence. Where there is a controversy or contradiction, then affidavits may be tendered and relied upon and if affidavits will not suffice to resolve the conflict, then *viva voce* evidence could be called and cross-examination take place.

The attendance of sureties is not always required to effect the release of an accused ordered to be released on a recognizance with sureties. Counsel was permitted to file surety questionnaires completed by prospective sureties unable to attend court on the basis that the questionnaires were credible and trustworthy: *R. v. Brooks* (2001), 153 C.C.C. (3d) 533 (Ont. S.C.J.).

Right to make submissions – A show cause hearing is an adversarial proceeding and both sides including the prosecutor have a right to be heard. The court is not entitled to frustrate this right by predicting the Crown's submissions: *R. v. Villota* (2002), 163 C.C.C. (3d) 507, 3 C.R. (6th) 342 (Ont. S.C.J.).

RELEASE OF ACCUSED / Discharge from custody / Warrant for committal.

519. (1) Where a justice makes an order under subsection 515(1), (2), (7) or (8),

   (*a*) **if the accused thereupon complies with the order, the justice shall direct that the accused be released**

      (i) **forthwith, if the accused is not required to be detained in custody in respect of any other matter, or**

      (ii) **as soon thereafter as the accused is no longer required to be detained in custody in respect of any other matter; and**

   (*b*) **if the accused does not thereupon comply with the order, the justice who made the order or another justice having jurisdiction shall issue a warrant for the committal of the accused and may endorse thereon an authorization to the person having the custody of the accused to release the accused when the accused complies with the order**

      (i) **forthwith after the compliance, if the accused is not required to be detained in custody in respect of any other matter, or**

      (ii) **as soon thereafter as the accused is no longer required to be detained in custody in respect of any other matter**

   and if the justice so endorses the warrant, he shall attach to it a copy of the order.

(2) Where the accused complies with an order referred to in paragraph (1)(b) and is not required to be detained in custody in respect of any other matter, the justice who made the order or another justice having jurisdiction shall, unless the accused has been or will be released pursuant to an authorization referred to in that paragraph, issue an order for discharge in Form 39.

(3) Where the justice makes an order under subsection 515(5) or (6) for the detention of the accused, he shall issue a warrant for the committal of the accused. R.S., c. 2 (2nd Supp.), s. 5; 1974-75-76, c. 93, s. 50; R.S.C. 1985, c. 27 (1st Supp.), s. 85.

CROSS-REFERENCES

The term "justice" is defined in s. 2. "Warrant of committal" is defined in s. 493. Section 841 provides that forms varied to suit the case and forms to the like effect shall be deemed to be good, valid and sufficient in the circumstances for which, respectively, they are provided. For an overview of the application of this Part and the procedure respecting release pending trial see *Note on judicial interim release* under s. 515, or the *Note on judicial interim release* under s. 522 where the accused is charged with an offence listed in s. 469.

SYNOPSIS

This section deals with the release of the accused after a justice has made an order under s. 515(1), (2), (7) or (8).

Subsection (1) provides that where a justice makes a release order under s. 515, the accused shall be released if he complies with the order. Such release will be immediate if the accused is not required to be held in custody on another matter, or as soon as the accused is not required to be detained on another matter. If the accused does not comply with the order under s. 515, a justice having jurisdiction must issue a warrant for the accused's committal. In such a case, the justice may endorse on the warrant an authorization to release the accused when he complies with the order. The timing of this release will depend on the matters set out in para. (*b*)(i) and (ii).

Subsection (2) states that when the accused complies with an order referred to in subsec. (1)(*b*) and is not required to be detained in custody on another matter, the accused may also be released by way of an order for discharge in Form 39.

Subsection (3) states that a justice who has ordered the detention of the accused must issue a warrant of committal.

ANNOTATIONS

A judge has no power to make a "release" order permitting an accused serving a penitentiary sentence to be released on condition that he reside at the penitentiary except where entitled to be absent pursuant to passes granted by the Parole Board: *R. v. Arviv* (1987), 38 C.C.C. (3d) 283 (Ont. Dist. Ct.).

It is the duty of the justice or judge to determine the sufficiency of a proposed surety not the Crown Attorney: *R. v. Dewsbury* (1989), 50 C.C.C. (3d) 163 (Ont. H.C.J.).

REVIEW OF ORDER / Notice to prosecutor / Accused to be present / Adjournment of proceedings / Failure of accused to attend / Execution / Evidence and powers of judge on review / Limitation of further applications / Application of ss. 517, 518 and 519.

520. (1) If a justice, or a judge of the Nunavut Court of Justice, makes an order under subsection 515(2), (5), (6), (7), (8) or (12) or makes or vacates any order under paragraph 523(2)(*b*), the accused may, at any time before the trial of the charge, apply to a judge for a review of the order.

(2) An application under this section shall not, unless the prosecutor otherwise consents, be heard by a judge unless the accused has given to the prosecutor at least two clear days notice in writing of the application.

(3) If the judge so orders or the prosecutor or the accused or his counsel so requests, the accused shall be present at the hearing of an application under this section and, where the accused is in custody, the judge may order, in writing, the person having the custody of the accused to bring him before the court.

(4) A judge may, before or at any time during the hearing of an application under this section, on application by the prosecutor or the accused, adjourn the proceedings, but if the accused is in custody no adjournment shall be for more than three clear days except with the consent of the accused.

(5) Where an accused, other than an accused who is in custody, has been ordered by a judge to be present at the hearing of an application under this section and does not attend the hearing, the judge may issue a warrant for the arrest of the accused.

(6) A warrant issued under subsection (5) may be executed anywhere in Canada.

(7) On the hearing of an application under this section, the judge may consider

    (*a*) the transcript, if any, of the proceedings heard by the justice and by any judge who previously reviewed the order made by the justice,

    (*b*) the exhibits, if any, filed in the proceedings before the justice, and

    (*c*) such additional evidence or exhibits as may be tendered by the accused or the prosecutor,

and shall either

    (*d*) dismiss the application, or

    (*e*) if the accused shows cause, allow the application, vacate the order previously made by the justice and make any other order provided for in section 515 that he considers is warranted.

(8) Where an application under this section or section 521 has been heard, a further or other application under this section or section 521 shall not be made with respect to that same accused, except with leave of a judge, prior to the expiration of thirty days from the date of the decision of the judge who heard the previous application.

(9) The provisions of section 517, 518 and 519 apply with such modifications as the circumstances require in respect of an application under this section. R.S., c. 2 (2nd Supp.), s. 5; 1974-75-76, c. 93, s. 51; R.S.C. 1985, c. 27 (1st Supp.), s. 86; 1994, c. 44, s. 46; 1999, c. 3, s. 31.

CROSS-REFERENCES

The terms "prosecutor" and "justice" are defined in s. 2 and "judge" in s. 493. As to calculation of "at least two clear days" see s. 27 of the *Interpretation Act*, R.S.C. 1985, c. I-21. For an overview of the application of this Part and the procedure respecting release pending trial see *Note on judicial interim release* under s. 515, or the *Note on judicial interim release* under s. 522 where the accused is charged with an offence listed in s. 469. As to the Nunavut Courtof Justice, see the note under s. 536.1.

SYNOPSIS

This section sets out the procedure by which an accused may obtain a review of the order made by a justice under s. 515(2), (5), (6), (7), (8) or (12). The decision of a justice to vacate an order under s. 523(2)(*b*) may also be reviewed by the accused under this section.

Subsection (1) allows the accused to apply to a judge for a review of the order at any time prior to trial.

Unless the prosecutor consents, subsec. (2) requires that a review under this section be heard only if the accused has given to the prosecutor two clear days' notice.

If the prosecutor, the accused or his counsel requests, or the judge so orders, the accused shall be present at the hearing of an application under this section.

Subsection (3) provides that where the accused is in custody, the judge may order in writing the person having custody of the accused to bring him to court.

Subsection (4) authorizes a judge to adjourn the hearing of the application at the request of the prosecutor or the accused. Such application may be brought prior to or during the hearing. If the accused is in custody, no adjournment for more than three clear days will be granted unless the accused consents.

If an accused who is not in custody is ordered by a judge to be present at the hearing and does not attend, the judge is authorized by subsec. (5) to issue an arrest warrant. This warrant may be executed anywhere in Canada.

Subsection (7) lists in paras. (*a*), (*b*) and (*c*) the items that the judge hearing the application may consider. Subsection (7)(*d*) and (*e*) empower the judge to either dismiss the application or, if the accused shows cause, allow the application, vacate the earlier order and make any other order under s. 515 that is appropriate.

Subsection (8) makes it clear that the accused may make further applications under this section or s. 521 only after 30 days have expired since the previous application, unless the judge gives leave.

Subsection (9) states that the provisions of ss. 517, 518 and 519 will apply with necessary modifications in an application under this section.

ANNOTATIONS

Jurisdiction – While subsec. (1) only refers to review of an order by a "justice", the wording of this subsection indicates that the accused may apply for review of an order of a judge made either under this section or s. 521: *R. v. Gouveia* (1982), 1 C.C.C. (3d) 143 (Ont. H.C.J.); *R. v. Saracino* (1989), 47 C.C.C. (3d) 185 (Ont. H.C.J.). *Contra: R. v. Lahooti* (1978), 38 C.C.C. (2d) 481 (Ont. H.C.J.).

While a judge of the Manitoba Court of Appeal has jurisdiction to review a refusal to make an order for judicial interim release, in the absence of special circumstances the further application for review should be made to a judge of the Court of Queen's Bench: *R. v. Petrie*, [1985] 2 W.W.R. 128, 30 Man. R. (2d) 145 (C.A. in chambers); *R. v. Semenick*, [1985] 2 W.W.R. 132, 30 Man. R. (2d) 147 (C.A. in chambers). See also: *R. v. Durrani* (2008), 242 C.C.C. (3d) 103 (Ont. C.A.); *R. v. Parsons* (2010), 259 C.C.C. (3d) 347 (Nfld. & Lab. C.A.).

Where a superior court judge allows an application for review and vacates the bail order, the parties have no further right to apply to a superior court judge for a further review: *R. v. Smith* (2003), 171 C.C.C. (3d) 383 (Sask. C.A.).

Nature of review – In *R. v. St-Cloud*, [2015] 2 S.C.R. 328, 321 C.C.C. (3d) 307, the court comprehensively explained the review process set out in ss. 520 and 521. It held that these provisions do not confer an open-ended discretion on the reviewing judge to vary the initial decision concerning the detention or release of the accused. They establish not a *de novo* proceeding, but a hybrid remedy. The judge must determine whether it is appropriate to exercise his or her power of review. Exercising this power will be appropriate in only three situations: (1) where there is admissible new evidence if that evidence shows a material and relevant change in the circumstances of the case; (2) where the impugned decision contains an error of law; or (3) where the decision is clearly inappropriate. A decision may be clearly inappropriate if the justice gave excessive weight to one relevant factor or insufficient weight to another. However, the reviewing judge does not have the power to interfere with the initial decision simply because he or she would have weighed the relevant factors differently.

Procedure on review – Upon review the onus is upon the applicant to demonstrate an error in law or principle by the justice of the peace who made the order under review: *R. v. Horvat* (1972), 9 C.C.C. (2d) 1 (B.C.S.C.).

The order of a justice of the peace vacated in para. (*e*) is not rendered *void ab initio* so as to negative any charge laid for breaching it, but instead is terminated in favour of the substituted order: *R. v. Goldrick* (1974), 17 C.C.C. (2d) 74 (Ont. H.C.J.).

While the judge may hear additional evidence, the transcript of the proceedings before the justice should be filed with the court, otherwise it would be impossible to determine whether or not the justice was in error: *R. v. Hunter* (1973), 24 C.R.N.S. 197 (Ont. Co. Ct.).

However, a transcript is not always required, particularly where no *viva voce* evidence was heard before the justice, merely counsel's submissions, and to require the transcript might defeat the intent of this legislation which was to encourage expeditious disposition of bail matters: *R. v. Carrier, supra*.

It has been held, considering the predecessor to para. (*e*), that even where the accused demonstrates some error by the justice in the making of the initial detention order or the conduct of the hearing, the judge is not required to vacate the detention order and make a release order unless the accused shows why the detention order was not justified on the primary or secondary ground. On the review the Crown may rely on the evidence at the original hearing and may adduce additional evidence to justify the accused's continued detention: *R. v. English* (1983), 8 C.C.C. (3d) 487 (Ont. Co. Ct.); *R. v. Saswirsky* (1984), 17 C.C.C. (3d) 341 (Ont. H.C.J.).

Right to counsel – An unrepresented accused charged with an indictable offence may have the right to counsel at a bail hearing or bail review. The presiding judge has a duty to inquire whether the accused wishes to be represented by counsel. The determination must be made on a case-by-case basis having regard to the complexity of the proceedings and the seriousness of the charge: *R. v. Chan* (2000), 146 C.C.C. (3d) 494 (Alta. C.A.).

Subsection (7) [new evidence] – The four criteria from *R. v. Palmer* (1979), [1980] 1 S.C.R. 759, 50 C.C.C. (2d) 193, for the admission of fresh evidence on appeal are relevant to the determination of what constitutes admissible new evidence for the purposes of the review provided for in ss. 520 and 521. Given the generally expeditious nature of the interim release process and the risks of violating the rights of the accused, and since the release hearing takes place at the very start of criminal proceedings, a reviewing judge must be flexible in applying these four criteria: *R. v. St-Cloud*, [2015] 2 S.C.R. 328, 321 C.C.C. (3d) 307.

Subsection (8) – Leave should not be granted unless the decision of the reviewing judge was clearly wrong in law or there have been intervening events which require granting of leave in the interests of justice: *R. v. McCue, infra.* See also *R. v. MacIver* (1998), 157 W.A.C. 84, 131 Man. R. (2d) 84 (C.A.).

REVIEW OF ORDER / Notice to accused / Accused to be present / Adjournment of proceedings / Failure of accused to attend / Warrant for detention / Execution / Evidence and powers of judge on review / Limitation of further applications / Application of ss. 517, 518 and 519.

521. (1) If a justice, or a judge of the Nunavut Court of Justice, makes an order under subsection 515(1), (2), (7), (8) or (12) or makes or vacates any order under paragraph 523(2)(*b*), the prosecutor may, at any time before the trial of the charge, apply to a judge for a review of the order.

(2) An application under this section shall not be heard by a judge unless the prosecutor has given to the accused at least two clear days notice in writing of the application.

(3) If the judge so orders or the prosecutor or the accused or his counsel so requests, the accused shall be present at the hearing of an application under this section and, where the accused is in custody, the judge may order, in writing, the person having the custody of the accused to bring him before the court.

(4) A judge may, before or at any time during the hearing of an application under this section, on application of the prosecutor or the accused, adjourn the proceedings, but if the accused is in custody no adjournment shall be for more than three clear days except with the consent of the accused.

(5) Where an accused, other than an accused who is in custody, has been ordered by a judge to be present at the hearing of an application under this section and does not attend the hearing, the judge may issue a warrant for the arrest of the accused.

(6) Where, pursuant to paragraph (8)(*e*), the judge makes an order that the accused be detained in custody until he is dealt with according to law, he shall, if the accused is not in custody, issue a warrant for the committal of the accused.

(7) A warrant issued under subsection (5) or (6) may be executed anywhere in Canada.

(8) On the hearing of an application under this section, the judge may consider

(a) the transcript, if any, of the proceedings heard by the justice and by any judge who previously reviewed the order made by the justice,

(b) the exhibits, if any, filed in the proceedings before the justice, and

(c) such additional evidence or exhibits as may be tendered by the prosecutor or the accused,

and shall either

(d) dismiss the application, or

(e) if the prosecutor shows cause, allow the application, vacate the order previously made by the justice and make any other order provided for in section 515 that he considers to be warranted.

(9) Where an application under this section or section 520 has been heard, a further or other application under this section or section 520 shall not be made with respect to the same accused, except with leave of a judge, prior to the expiration of thirty days from the date of the decision of the judge who heard the previous application.

(10) The provisions of sections 517, 518 and 519 apply with such modifications as the circumstances require in respect of an application under this section. R.S., c. 2 (2nd Supp.), s. 5; 1974-75-76, c. 93, s. 52; R.S.C. 1985, c. 27 (1st Supp.), s. 87; 1994, c. 44, s. 47; 1999, c. 3, s. 32.

CROSS-REFERENCES

The terms "prosecutor" and "justice" are defined in s. 2 and "judge" in s. 493. As to calculation of "at least two clear days" see s. 27 of the *Interpretation Act*, R.S.C. 1985, c. I-21. For an overview of the application of this Part and the procedure respecting release pending trial see *Note on judicial interim release* under s. 515, or the *Note on judicial interim release* under s. 522 where the accused is charged with an offence listed in s. 469.

SYNOPSIS

This section is the companion to s. 520. It describes the procedure that the prosecutor must follow to review an order made by a justice under s. 515(1), (2), (7), (8) or (12) or vacated by a justice under s. 523(2)(b).

Subsection (2) requires that the prosecutor give the accused at least two clear days' notice in writing of the application.

Subsection (3) provides for the presence of the accused if the judge so orders or the prosecutor or the accused so requests. Where the accused is in custody, the judge may order in writing the person having custody of the accused to bring him to court.

Subsection (4) authorizes the judge to adjourn the proceedings at any time prior to or during the hearing upon application by the prosecutor or the accused. If the accused is in custody, no adjournment shall be longer than three days unless the accused consents.

Subsection (5) states that when an accused who is not in custody and who has been ordered by the judge to be present at the hearing of an application under this section, fails to attend, the judge may issue an arrest warrant.

If the judge makes an order under this section that the accused be detained in custody, he must issue a warrant of committal if the accused is not in custody. A warrant issued under this subsection or subsec. (5) may be executed anywhere in Canada.

Subsection (8) sets out items that a judge may consider in a hearing under this section. It also describes the dispositions available to the judge at the conclusion of the hearing.

Subsection (9), like s. 520(8), requires a waiting period of 30 days between applications under this section or s. 520, unless a judge gives leave.

Subsection (10) makes the provision of ss. 517, 518 and 519 applicable to a proceeding under this section with such modifications as circumstances require.

ANNOTATIONS

Note: see also the notes under s. 520, in particular concerning the Supreme Court's explanation of the bail review regime in *R. v. St-Cloud*, [2015] 2 S.C.R. 328, 321 C.C.C. (3d) 307.

In the absence of evidence of excess of jurisdiction or error in principle, a judge on review, even though he would not have come to the same decision as did the justice, should not alter it unless the prosecutor can show cause by additional evidence or by pointing to a demonstrable error: *R. v. La Chapelle and La Chapelle* (1974), 19 C.C.C. (2d) 70 (N.S.S.C.).

An application may be made under this section although the order sought to be reviewed is that of a judge under s. 520 rather than an order of a justice. However, except where there has been a substantial change in circumstances, the judge conducting the second review should not interfere with the existing order unless it is established that the judge conducting the first review made an error in principle in application of the relevant provisions which materially affected the outcome of the initial application: *R. v. Saracino* (1989), 47 C.C.C. (3d) 185 (Ont. H.C.J.).

The refusal to hear submissions by the Crown is a breach of natural justice and constitutes jurisdictional error: *R. v. Villota* (2002), 163 C.C.C. (3d) 507 (Ont. S.C.J.).

Where a superior court judge allows an application for review and vacates the bail order, the parties have no further right to apply to a superior court judge for a further review: *R. v. Smith* (2003), 171 C.C.C. (3d) 383 (Sask. C.A.).

INTERIM RELEASE BY JUDGE ONLY / Idem / Order re no communication / Release of accused / Order not reviewable except under s. 680 / Application of sections 517, 518 and 519 / Other offences.

522. (1) Where an accused is charged with an offence listed in section 469, no court, judge or justice, other than a judge of or a judge presiding in a superior court of criminal jurisdiction for the province in which the accused is so charged, may release the accused before or after the accused has been ordered to stand trial.

(2) Where an accused is charged with an offence listed in section 469, a judge of or a judge presiding in a superior court of criminal jurisdiction for the province in which the accused is charged shall order that the accused be detained in custody unless the accused, having been given a reasonable opportunity to do so, shows cause why his detention in custody is not justified within the meaning of subsection 515(10).

(2.1) A judge referred to in subsection (2) who orders that an accused be detained in custody under this section may include in the order a direction that the accused abstain from communicating, directly or indirectly, with any victim, witness or other person identified in the order except in accordance with such conditions specified in the order as the judge considers necessary.

(3) If the judge does not order that the accused be detained in custody under subsection (2), the judge may order that the accused be released on giving an undertaking or entering into a recognizance described in any of paragraphs 515(2)(*a*) to (*e*) with such conditions described in subsections 515(4), (4.1) and (4.2) as the judge considers desirable.

(4) An order made under this section is not subject to review, except as provided in section 680.

(5) The provisions of sections 517, 518 except subsection (2) thereof, and 519 apply with such modifications as the circumstances require in respect of an application for an order under subsection (2).

(6) Where an accused is charged with an offence mentioned in section 469 and with any other offence, a judge acting under this section may apply the provisions of this Part respecting judicial interim release to that other offence. R.S., c. 2 (2nd Supp.), s. 5; 1972,

c. 13, s. 36; 1974-75-76, c. 93, s. 53; R.S.C. 1985, c. 27 (1st Supp.), s. 88; 1991, c. 40, s. 32; 1994, c. 44, s. 48; 1999, c. 25, s. 10.

CROSS-REFERENCES

The terms "superior court of criminal jurisdiction" and "victim" are defined in s. 2. The terms "accused", "recognizance" and "undertaking" are defined in s. 493.

Note on judicial interim release – Where the accused is charged with an offence listed in s. 469 such as murder then he may not be released by a peace officer, officer in charge or justice. Section 503 requires that he be taken before a justice (defined in s. 2) without unreasonable delay and, in any event, within 24 hours, where a justice is available. The justice will then make a detention order (s. 515(11)). The onus is then on the accused to apply for a show cause hearing by making an application under s. 522 to a judge of the superior court of criminal jurisdiction (defined in s. 2). The procedure on the s. 522 hearing is similar to the show cause hearing under s. 515 except that the onus is on the accused in all cases to show why his detention is not justified for the reasons set out in s. 515(10). Where the accused shows cause then the judge may order the accused's release on an undertaking or recognizance on the same terms as may a justice acting under s. 515(2), (4) and (4.1) and thus see the discussion under s. 515.

Sections 517 and 518 set out the procedure to be followed on the bail hearing. Section 517 provides for a non-publication order. Section 518 sets out the kind of evidence which may be tendered on the hearing. The effect of s. 518 is to give a relatively wide latitude to the judge permitting him to receive and base his decision on evidence "considered credible or trustworthy". Thus the rules of evidence which would apply at a trial would not apply on the bail hearing. One limit on the receipt of evidence is the proviso in s. 518(1)(*b*) which prohibits questioning of the accused respecting the offence with which he is charged. The scope of this subsection is uncertain, there being some case law noted under s. 518 holding that while the accused cannot be asked by the judge or the prosecutor about the offence he is entitled to volunteer his testimony concerning it. The presence of the accused would not appear to be mandatory. Where a release order is made then s. 519 sets out the procedure for putting the order into effect and the circumstances in which the accused will be released.

The system for review of either a release or detention order is more restricted than is the case of an accused charged with a non-s. 469 offence. There is no *right* to a review. The only formal review mechanism is set out in s. 680 and requires an application to the Chief Justice or acting Chief Justice of the Court of Appeal for directions referring the case to the Court of Appeal (defined in ss. 2 and 673). Where the Chief Justice gives such directions then the Court of Appeal will hear the review application and may confirm the decision, vary the decision or substitute such other decision as, in its opinion, should have been made. Under s. 680(2) with the consent of the parties the review directed by the Chief Justice may be heard by a single judge rather than by three judges of the Court of Appeal.

Section 523(2) also provides for a more informal review process at various stages of the proceedings but only by a judge of the superior court of criminal jurisdiction. Note, however, that the release or detention order can only be vacated under this subsection upon cause being shown and in some circumstances the review can only be undertaken where both the accused and the prosecutor consent. Section 524 enacts a procedure for dealing with cases where it is alleged that the accused has violated or is about to violate the release order or has committed an indictable offence while on a form of release. That section gives a power to arrest with (subsec. (1)) or without warrant (subsec. (2)). Upon arrest under this section the accused will be taken before a justice who is required to remand the accused to appear before a judge of the superior court of criminal jurisdiction. Where it is shown that his arrest was justified (subsec. (4)) then the release order is cancelled by the judge. The accused is then ordered detained unless he can show cause why he should not be detained in custody. If the accused shows cause then s. 524(5) provides for the types of release order which may be made. Any order made under s. 524 may only be reviewed pursuant to s. 680. The procedure on the s. 524 hearing is similar to the original show cause hearing (subsec. (12)). There is some uncertainty as to the scope of s. 524 where the accused is arrested for an indictable offence while on a s. 522 release order. It would seem that the procedure to be followed is that unless the prosecutor elects to proceed under s. 524 the justice will have jurisdiction to proceed with a bail hearing in relation to the new non-s. 469 charge under s. 515. See *R. v. Yarema* (1989), 52 C.C.C. (3d) 242 (Ont. H.C.J.), noted under s. 524.

The automatic review procedure set out in s. 525 does not apply to an accused charged with a s. 469 offence. Section 526 however provides that the judge conducting a hearing under this Part may give directions for expediting the trial.

Barring a review under ss. 680, 523(2) or 524 then the effect of s. 523(1) is that the release order remains in effect until the trial is completed. Section 523(1.1) provides a procedure for the release order in respect of one information to apply to a new information charging the same offence or an included offence.

Under s. 522(6) where the accused is also charged with an offence not listed in s. 469 the judge to whom an application is made under s. 522 may also make an order for release or detention in respect of this other offence. Invoking subsec. (6) will avoid the necessity of multiple hearings in the case of an accused charged with an offence listed in s. 469 and some other offence.

The procedure for enforcement of a recognizance is set out in Part XXV. That Part sets out the responsibilities of sureties (s. 764); procedure for rendering of the accused by his sureties (ss. 766, 767, 769); substitution of a new surety (s. 767.1), and the new release hearing where the accused is rendered into custody by his sureties (s. 769). That Part also sets out the procedure in case of default by the accused, including endorsing the fact of the default (s. 770); the hearing for estreat of bail (s. 771), and levying execution to enforce a writ of *fieri facias* where the recognizance is ordered forfeited (ss. 772, 773).

There are special limitations on the making of interim release and detention orders where the court makes an assessment order under Part XX.1. See in particular ss. 672.16, 672.17 and 672.18.

ANNOTATIONS

Prior to the recent amendments to this section there was some uncertainty as to whether a detention or release order made under this section in relation to a murder charge lapsed when the accused was committed for trial on a charge of manslaughter (an offence not specified in s. 469). The following cases hold that in such circumstances there should be a new bail hearing before a justice or provincial court judge: *R. v. LaFontaine* (1973), 13 C.C.C. (2d) 316 (Ont. H.C.J.); *R. v. Manuel* (1981), 60 C.C.C. (2d) 97 (Ont. H.C.J.); *R. v. Favel* (1985), 19 C.C.C. (3d) 335 (Sask. Q.B.). To the contrary is *R. v. Degerness* (1980), 57 C.C.C. (2d) 534 (B.C.S.C.).

The Superior Court has the jurisdiction, notwithstanding s. 680 of the *Criminal Code*, to entertain successive applications for bail in respect of a murder charge where the correctness of the earlier decision is conceded, but it is alleged that there has been a material change in circumstances. The matter requires a *de novo* consideration of the request for release: *R. v. Saleh* (2007), 252 C.C.C. (3d) 521 (Ont. S.C.J.).

A detention order made on a charge of first degree murder does not lapse when the accused is committed for trial on a charge of second degree murder and is reviewable only pursuant to s. 680: *R. v. Archer* (1981), 59 C.C.C. (2d) 384 (Ont. C.A.). *Contra*, *R. v. Turner* (1999), 133 C.C.C. (3d) 180 (Nfld. C.A.), holding that the proper procedure is to reapply under this section in view of the change in circumstances.

The reverse onus in subsec. (2) does not offend the guarantee to reasonable bail pursuant to s. 11(*e*) of the Charter. The provision is only applicable in a narrow set of circumstances in that bail is denied only to those who cannot show cause why their detention is not justified: *R. v. Sanchez* (1999), 136 C.C.C. (3d) 31 (N.S.C.A.). See also *R. v. Bray* (1983), 2 C.C.C. (3d) 325 (Ont. C.A.), and *R. v. Dubois (No. 2)* (1983), 8 C.C.C. (3d) 344 (Que. S.C.), which upheld the constitutionality of the predecessor to this section.

The reverse onus requires the accused to establish that on a balance of probabilities his detention is not justified on either the primary or secondary ground. However, there is no burden on the accused to disprove the offence or his implication in it; the onus is on the Crown to adduce evidence of the accused's implication in the offence: *R. v. Bray, supra.*

Where the "substantial likelihood" of committing an offence or interfering with the administration of justice involves an assessment of the likelihood of dangerousness, the court must consider the following:

(1)   the nature of the offence;

(2)   the relevant circumstances of the offence which may put into issue events prior to and subsequent to the offence;

(3)   the likelihood of conviction, the degree of participation of the accused;

(4)   the relationship between the accused and the victim;

(5)   the profile of the accused which includes occupation, lifestyle, criminal record, family situation and mental state;

(6)   his conduct prior to the commission of the alleged offence, and

(7)   the danger which the interim release of the accused represents for the community specifically affected by the matter: *R. v. Rondeau* (1996), 108 C.C.C. (3d) 474, [1996] R.J.Q. 1155 (C.A.).

The overwhelming nature of the evidence of guilt and the probability of conviction are merely factors to be considered and are the determining factors in deciding whether the accused should be released pending trial. The accused is entitled to the benefit of the presumption of innocence and the judge should not decide the result of the trial: *R. v. Braun* (1994), 91 C.C.C. (3d) 237 (Sask. C.A.).

Subsection (4) of this section must be read with s. 523(2) which gives a judge of the trial court power to vacate any order previously made upon cause being shown. While resort must be had to the procedure under s. 680 where the allegation is that the original judge made an error, where it is submitted that there has been a change in circumstances the parties should resort to s. 523(2). Where the Crown's consent is required for the review powers to be exercised by a superior court judge, it would be expected that in cases of new circumstances the Crown would not unreasonably withhold its consent: *R. v. Patterson* (1985), 19 C.C.C. (3d) 149 (Alta. C.A.).

A superior court judge has the jurisdiction to vary an order made by the Court of Appeal, where the variation was based on a change in circumstances and the correctness of the original order was not in issue: *R. v. Klymchuk* (2007), 220 C.C.C. (3d) 439 (Ont. S.C.J.).

PERIOD FOR WHICH APPEARANCE NOTICE, ETC., CONTINUES IN FORCE / Where new information charging same offence / When direct indictment is preferred charging same offence / Order vacating previous order for release or detention / Provisions applicable to proceedings under subsection (2).

523. (1) Where an accused, in respect of an offence with which he is charged, has not been taken into custody or has been released from custody under or by virtue of any provision of this Part, the appearance notice, promise to appear, summons, undertaking or recognizance issued to, given or entered into by the accused continues in force, subject to its terms, and applies in respect of any new information charging the same offence or an included offence that was received after the appearance notice, promise to appear, summons, undertaking or recognizance was issued, given or entered into,

(*a*)   **where the accused was released from custody pursuant to an order of a judge made under subsection 522(3), until his trial is completed; or**

(*b*)   **in any other case,**

(i)   **until his trial is completed, and**

(ii)   **where the accused is, at his trial, determined to be guilty of the offence, until a sentence within the meaning of section 673 is imposed on the accused unless, at the time the accused is determined to be guilty, the court, judge or justice orders that the accused be taken into custody pending such sentence.**

(1.1) Where an accused, in respect of an offence with which he is charged, has not been taken into custody or is being detained or has been released from custody under or by

virtue of any provision of this Part and after the order for interim release or detention has been made, or the appearance notice, promise to appear, summons, undertaking or recognizance has been issued, given or entered into, a new information, charging the same offence or an included offence, is received, section 507 or 508, as the case may be, does not apply in respect of the new information and the order for interim release or detention of the accused and the appearance notice, promise to appear, summons, undertaking or recognizance, if any, applies in respect of the new information.

(1.2) When an accused, in respect of an offence with which the accused is charged, has not been taken into custody or is being detained or has been released from custody under or by virtue of any provision of this Part and after the order for interim release or detention has been made, or the appearance notice, promise to appear, summons, undertaking or recognizance has been issued, given or entered into, and an indictment is preferred under section 577 charging the same offence or an included offence, the order for interim release or detention of the accused and the appearance notice, promise to appear, summons, undertaking or recognizance, if any, applies in respect of the indictment.

(2) Despite subsections (1) to (1.2),

    (a) the court, judge or justice before whom an accused is being tried, at any time,

    (b) the justice, on completion of the preliminary inquiry in relation to an offence for which an accused is ordered to stand trial, other than an offence listed in section 469, or

    (c) with the consent of the prosecutor and the accused or, where the accused or the prosecutor applies to vacate an order that would otherwise apply pursuant to subsection (1.1), without such consent, at any time

        (i) where the accused is charged with an offence other than an offence listed in section 469, the justice by whom an order was made under this Part or any other justice,

        (ii) where the accused is charged with an offence listed in section 469, a judge of or a judge presiding in a superior court of criminal jurisdiction for the province, or

        (iii) the court, judge or justice before which or whom an accused is to be tried,

may, on cause being shown, vacate any order previously made under this Part for the interim release or detention of the accused and make any other order provided for in this Part for the detention or release of the accused until his trial is completed that the court, judge or justice considers to be warranted.

(3) The provisions of sections 517, 518 and 519 apply, with such modifications as the circumstances require, in respect of any proceedings under subsection (2), except that subsection 518(2) does not apply in respect of an accused who is charged with an offence listed in section 469. R.S., c. 2 (2nd Supp.), s. 5; 1974-75-76, c. 93, s. 54; R.S.C. 1985, c. 27 (1st Supp.), s. 89; 2011, c. 16, s. 2.

CROSS-REFERENCES

The term "justice" is defined in s. 2 and "accused", "appearance notice", "promise to appear", "undertaking", "recognizance" and "summons" in s. 493. An order under subsec. (2)(b) is reviewable pursuant to s. 520 or s. 521 by the accused or the prosecutor as the case may be. For an overview of the application of this Part and the procedure respecting release pending trial see *Note on judicial interim release* under s. 515, or the *Note on judicial interim release* under s. 522 where the accused is charged with an offence listed in s. 469.

SYNOPSIS

This section describes the periods of time for which various specified forms of release continue to be in force.

Subsection (1) provides that an appearance notice, promise to appear, summons, undertaking or recognizance remains in force until the completion of the accused's trial and, unless the judge orders the accused to be detained prior to the imposition of sentence, until the sentencing has been completed. For an accused charged with an offence listed under s. 469, the form of release remains valid until the completion of the trial. Subsection (1.1) provides that, when an accused is at liberty on a form of release and a new information charging the same or an included offence is received, the original form of release continues to apply. Under subsec. (1.2), a similar procedure applies where a direct indictment is preferred under s. 577.

Subsection (2) applies notwithstanding subsecs. (1) to (1.2), and authorizes any order previously made under Part XVI to be vacated and replaced with any other order provided for by this Part.

Subsection (3) states that ss. 517, 518 and 519 apply with such modifications as are necessary in respect of any proceedings under subsec. (2).

ANNOTATIONS

Subsection (1.1) – The Crown cannot proceed on a revised information in reliance upon process issued under s. 507 by a justice of the peace on a prior information. A provincial court judge has jurisdiction over the accused by virtue of the accused's appearance before him. It is not necessary for process to issue with respect to the relaid information in order for the provincial court judge to have jurisdiction over the offences: *R. v. McCarthy* (1998), 131 C.C.C. (3d) 102 (B.C.S.C.).

Subsection (2) – The mere fact that the accused has been ordered to stand trial is not sufficient cause to warrant the revocation of the accused's release order under para. (*a*) and the making of a detention order: *R. v. Braithwaite* (1980), 57 C.C.C. (2d) 351 (N.S.S.C. App. Div.).

Unless the accused was being tried by a superior court judge, there was no jurisdiction to vary a release order in the absence of the consent of the Crown, where the accused had been released on conditions by a superior court judge acting under s. 522. The appropriate venue to vary bail conditions in the absence of Crown consent was the Court of Appeal pursuant to s. 680: *R. v. Hardiman* (2003), 172 C.C.C. (3d) 211, 211 N.S.R. (2d) 358 (C.A.).

Subsection (2)(*a*) may only be invoked once the trial has actually commenced. This provision, therefore, did not authorize the judge seized of the trial to conduct a bail review one month prior to the scheduled trial date: *R. v. McCreery* (1996), 110 C.C.C. (3d) 561 (B.C.S.C.).

The justice may exercise his jurisdiction under para. (*b*) even where the release order was made by a judge on a review: *R. v. Wedow* (1981), 62 C.C.C. (2d) 381, 23 C.R. (3d) 187 (Alta. Q.B.).

A judge has the jurisdiction to issue an arrest warrant where the accused, previously appearing by counsel, did not subsequently attend court in person on a plea date. There is no requirement that the judge specifically order the accused to appear in person. Warrants should not be issued on arbitrary or capricious grounds or for any indirect motive not directed to compelling the accused's attendance where his presence is necessary: *R. v. Sidorov* (2001), 160 C.C.C. (3d) 122, 281 A.R. 357 (C.A.), leave to appeal to S.C.C. refused *loc. cit.* C.C.C. at p. vi.

A provincial court judge before whom an application is made to have an accused found to be a dangerous offender has jurisdiction under subsec. (2)(*a*) to release the accused pending the hearing: *R. v. Davidson* (1999), 140 C.C.C. (3d) 166 (B.C.S.C.).

No appeal lies to the Court of Appeal from an order made by a superior court of criminal jurisdiction pursuant to this section. Such an order can be reviewed only by the Supreme Court of Canada under s. 40(1) of the *Supreme Court Act*, R.S.C. 1985, c. S-26: *R. v. Bukmeier* (1996), 107 C.C.C. (3d) 272, 123 W.A.C. 312 (B.C.C.A.).

Arrest of Accused on Interim Release

ISSUE OF WARRANT FOR ARREST OF ACCUSED / Arrest of accused without warrant / Hearing / Retention of accused / Release of accused / Order not reviewable / Release of accused / Powers of justice after hearing / Release of accused / Reasons / Where justice to order that accused be released / Provisions applicable to proceedings under this section / Certain provisions applicable to order under this section.

524. (1) Where a justice is satisfied that there are reasonable and probable grounds to believe that an accused

(*a*) has contravened or is about to contravene any summons, appearance notice, promise to appear, undertaking or recognizance that was issued or given to him or entered into by him, or

(*b*) has committed an indictable offence after any summons, appearance notice, promise to appear, undertaking or recognizance was issued or given to him or entered into by him,

he may issue a warrant for the arrest of the accused.

(2) Notwithstanding anything in this Act, a peace officer who believes on reasonable grounds that an accused

(*a*) has contravened or is about to contravene any summons, appearance notice, promise to appear, undertaking or recognizance that was issued or given to him or entered into by him, or

(*b*) has committed an indictable offence after any summons, appearance notice, promise to appear, undertaking or recognizance was issued or given to him or entered into by him,

may arrest the accused without warrant.

(3) Where an accused who has been arrested with a warrant issued under subsection (1), or who has been arrested under subsection (2), is taken before a justice, the justice shall

(*a*) where the accused was released from custody pursuant to an order made under subsection 522(3) by a judge of the superior court of criminal jurisdiction of any province, order that the accused be taken before a judge of that court; or

(*b*) in any other case, hear the prosecutor and his witnesses, if any, and the accused and his witnesses, if any.

(4) Where an accused described in paragraph (3)(*a*) is taken before a judge and the judge finds

(*a*) that the accused has contravened or had been about to contravene his summons, appearance notice, promise to appear, undertaking or recognizance, or

(*b*) that there are reasonable grounds to believe that the accused has committed an indictable offence after any summons, appearance notice, promise to appear, undertaking or recognizance was issued or given to him or entered into by him,

he shall cancel the summons, appearance notice, promise to appear, undertaking or recognizance and order that the accused be detained in custody unless the accused, having been given a reasonable opportunity to do so, shows cause why his detention in custody is not justified within the meaning of subsection 515(10).

(5) Where the judge does not order that the accused be detained in custody pursuant to subsection (4), he may order that the accused be released upon his giving an undertaking or entering into a recognizance described in any of paragraphs 515(2)(*a*) to (*e*) with such conditions described in subsection 515(4) or, where the accused was at large on an undertaking or a recognizance with conditions, such additional conditions, described in subsection 515(4), as the judge considers desirable.

(6) Any order made under subsection (4) or (5) is not subject to review, except as provided in section 680.

(7) Where the judge does not make a finding under paragraph (4)(*a*) or (*b*), he shall order that the accused be released from custody.

(8) Where an accused described in subsection (3), other than an accused to whom paragraph (*a*) of that subsection applies, is taken before the justice and the justice finds

> (*a*) that the accused has contravened or had been about to contravene his summons, appearance notice, promise to appear, undertaking or recognizance, or
>
> (*b*) that there are reasonable grounds to believe that the accused has committed an indictable offence after any summons, appearance notice, promise to appear, undertaking or recognizance was issued or given to him or entered into by him,

he shall cancel the summons, appearance notice, promise to appear, undertaking or recognizance and order that the accused be detained in custody unless the accused, having been given a reasonable opportunity to do so, shows cause why his detention in custody is not justified within the meaning of subsection 515(10).

(9) Where the accused shows cause why his detention in custody is not justified within the meaning of subsection 515(10), the justice shall order that the accused be released upon his giving an undertaking or entering into a recognizance described in any of paragraphs 515(2)(*a*) to (*e*) with such conditions, described in subsection 515(4), as the justice considers desirable.

(10) Where the justice makes an order under subsection (9), he shall include in the record a statement of his reasons for making the order, and subsection 515(9) is applicable with such modifications as the circumstances require in respect thereof.

(11) Where the justice does not make a finding under paragraph (8)(*a*) or (*b*), he shall order that the accused be released from custody.

(12) The provisions of sections 517, 518 and 519 apply with such modifications as the circumstances require in respect of any proceedings under this section, except that subsection 518(2) does not apply in respect of an accused who is charged with an offence mentioned in section 522.

(13) Section 520 applies in respect of any order made under subsection (8) or (9) as though the order were an order made by a justice or a judge of the Nunavut Court of Justice under subsection 515(2) or (5), and section 521 applies in respect of any order made under subsection (9) as though the order were an order made by a justice or a judge of the Nunavut Court of Justice under subsection 515(2). R.S., c. C-34, s. 458; R.S., c. 2 (2nd Supp.), s. 5; 1974-75-76, c. 93, s. 55; 1999, c. 3, s. 33.

CROSS-REFERENCES

The term "justice" is defined in s. 2 and "accused", "appearance notice", "promise to appear", "undertaking", "recognizance" and "summons" in s. 493. Breach of the terms of a release order issued by a peace officer, officer in charge, justice or judge is an offence under s. 145. The procedure for enforcement of a recognizance is set out in Part XXV. That Part sets out the responsibilities of sureties (s. 764); procedure for rendering of the accused by his sureties (ss. 766, 767, 769); substitution of a new surety (s. 767.1); and the new release hearing where the accused is rendered into custody by his sureties (s. 769). That Part also sets out the procedure in case of default by the accused, including endorsing the fact of the default (s. 770); the hearing for estreat of the bail (s. 771); levying execution to enforce a writ of *fieri facias* where the recognizance is ordered forfeited (ss. 772, 773). For an overview of the application of this Part and the procedure respecting release pending trial see *Note on judicial interim release* under s. 515, or the *Note on judicial interim release* under s. 522 where the accused is charged with an offence listed in s. 469. As to the Nunavut Court of Justice, see the note under s. 536.1.

Where the accused was detaining prior to sentencing under subsec. (4) or (8), the sentencing judge may not give more than 1 for 1 credit for pre-sentence custody, pursuant to s. 719(3.1).

SYNOPSIS

This section sets out the procedure to be followed when a warrant for the arrest of an accused who is on interim release is sought.

Subsection (1) provides that where a justice is satisfied that there are reasonable grounds to believe that an accused person has contravened or is about to contravene his form of release or has committed an indictable offence after entering into a form of release, that justice may issue a warrant for the arrest of the accused.

Subsection (2) states that when a peace officer has reasonable grounds to believe that the accused has done any of the things listed above, the officer may arrest the accused without a warrant.

Subsection (3) requires the justice before whom an accused, apprehended under subsec. (1) or (2), is brought, to hear the prosecutor, the accused and any witness. If the accused was released in relation to an offence under s. 469, the justice must order that the accused be taken before a judge of the superior court of criminal jurisdiction.

Subsection (4) requires a judge of the superior court of criminal jurisdiction before whom an accused, charged with an offence under s. 469, appears pursuant to subsec. (3), to cancel the accused's form of release if that judge finds that the accused has done any of the things listed in subsec. (4)(*a*) and (*b*). The judge must order that the accused be detained in custody unless the accused, after being given a reasonable opportunity to do so, shows cause why such detention is not justified.

Subsection (5) allows the judge to release the accused, on conditions, if the judge considers this to be desirable. Any order made under subsec. (4) or (5) above can be reviewed only as provided for in s. 680. If the judge does not find that the accused has done the things described in subsec. (4)(*a*) and (*b*), he shall order the release of the accused.

Subsections (8), (9), (10) and (11) provide for a similar scheme to deal with an accused who has been taken into custody after release on charges relating to offences other than those listed in s. 469. In this situation, a justice is empowered to deal with the accused when that person is apprehended.

Subsection (12) provides that ss. 517, 518 and 519 apply, with any necessary modifications, to proceedings under this section except that s. 518(2) does not apply in respect of an accused charged with an offence under s. 469.

Subsection (13) provides that the review procedures described in ss. 520 and 521 apply to a judge under this section.

ANNOTATIONS

Subsection (1) – A justice may without the necessity of a specific charge in writing being laid before him issue a warrant for arrest pursuant to this section: *R. v. Fulton* (1972), 10 C.C.C. (2d) 120 (Sask. Q.B.).

In acting under this subsection the justice must act judicially. A provincial court judge who has himself been witness to the reasonable and probable grounds has no jurisdiction to issue the warrant or conduct the subsequent hearing under subsec. (3). Such a judge does not have the requisite measure of neutrality and detachment: *R. v. Kot* (1983), 10 C.C.C. (3d) 297 (Ont. H.C.J.). [**Note:** an appeal to the Ontario Court of Appeal was quashed the issue being moot: 11 C.C.C. (3d) 96*n* (Ont. C.A.).]

A judge has the jurisdiction to issue an arrest warrant where the accused, previously appearing by counsel, did not subsequently attend court in person on a plea date. There is no requirement that the judge specifically order the accused to appear in person. Warrants should not be issued on arbitrary or capricious grounds or for any indirect motive not directed to compelling the accused's attendance where his presence is necessary: *R. v. Sidorov* (2001), 160 C.C.C. (3d) 122 (Alta. C.A.), leave to appeal to S.C.C. refused *loc. cit.* C.C.C. at p. vi.

As it is not a term of an appearance notice that the accused keep the peace and be of good behaviour, a justice has no power to issue a warrant under this subsection based merely upon the fact that the accused is charged with subsequently committing a similar offence: *R. v. S.* (1986), 33 C.C.C. (3d) 383 (Sask. Q.B.).

Where the accused is released pursuant to an order of the Court of Appeal pending a new trial, a single judge of the court of appeal has jurisdiction to hear an application to revoke a release order: *R. v. Parsons* (1997), 124 C.C.C. (3d) 92 (Nfld. C.A.).

Subsection (3) – An application under this subsection to cancel the accused's recognizance is properly brought before a justice notwithstanding the release order was made by a judge on a review under s. 520: *R. v. Kinger* (1982), 65 C.C.C. (2d) 483 (Alta. C.A.).

Where an accused appears before a justice for alleged misconduct, either under subsec. (1) or (2), as a result of misconduct alleged to have occurred after release by a superior court judge pursuant to s. 522, the justice should first ascertain the basis of the accused's appearance. Where the only reason for the appearance is that the accused has been arrested for alleged misconduct then the justice must order that the accused appear before a superior court judge pursuant to subsec. (3)(*a*). If, however, in addition, charges have been laid under s. 145 for failing to comply with the release order or for commission of some other criminal offence then the prosecutor should indicate whether or not he proposes to proceed under this section. If the prosecutor elects to proceed under this section then again the justice should order that the accused appear before a superior court judge pursuant to subsec. (3)(*a*) before dealing with release on the new charges. Where, however, the prosecutor does not so elect then the justice has jurisdiction to deal with release of the accused on the new charges pursuant to s. 515: *R. v. Yarema* (1989), 52 C.C.C. (3d) 242 (Ont. H.C.J.), affd 64 C.C.C. (3d) 260 (Ont. C.A.).

This section and s. 515 are not mutually exclusive. Thus, even where a hearing has been held before a justice under s. 515 for offences committed while the accused was at large on a release order made by a superior court judge under s. 522, the Crown is not precluded from subsequently applying to the superior court under this section to review the original release order: *R. v. Yarema, supra.*

Where an accused has not only failed to comply with the conditions of the recognizance but has been charged with new offences then the justice has jurisdiction to hear an application for bail on the new charges as well as to cancel the previous release order: *R. v. Gabrielson* (1991), 62 C.C.C. (3d) 571 (Ont. Ct. (Gen. Div.)).

Subsection (8) – It was held in *R. v. Lafond* (1975), 25 C.C.C. (2d) 568 (Que. Sess. Peace), that where an accused who has previously been released is brought before the justice for a show cause hearing for an offence committed while released then even though the accused does not technically come within subsec. (3) the justice may exercise the jurisdiction under this subsection and cancel the previous form of release. Such a situation would arise where the accused was arrested under s. 495 and not as the result of a warrant issued under subsec. (1) or as a result of a police officer's belief under subsec. (2).

In determining whether the conditions of release have been violated any issue as to whether the conditions allegedly violated were ambiguous must be determined on the basis of where the original burden lay for interim release. Thus where the offence was one for which the original burden was on the accused to show cause why he should be released, for example, on a charge of conspiracy to traffic in narcotics, then any ambiguity in the terms must be resolved in favour of the Crown: *Ex p. Clarke (No. 2)* (1978), 42 C.C.C. (2d) 23 (Nfld. S.C.T.D.).

The court had jurisdiction to proceed under subsec. (8) notwithstanding that the accused had not formally been arrested pursuant to subsecs. (1) or (2). Because the accused had been lawfully arrested, was lawfully detained, and had repeatedly been given notice of the Crown's intention to seek revocation of her existing bail, an arrest specifically pursuant to subsecs. (1) or (2) was unnecessary: *R. v. Ramage* (2011), 273 C.C.C. (3d) 331 (Ont. S.C.J.).

Where the Crown has elected to proceed summarily in respect of the new offence(s) alleged to have been committed by the accused, there is no "indictable offence" within the meaning of subsec. (8)(*b*) and the court has no jurisdiction to proceed with a hearing under this section: *R. v. Webley* (2015), 325 C.C.C. (3d) 239 (Ont. S.C.J.).

Review of Detention Where Trial Delayed

TIME FOR APPLICATION TO JUDGE / Notice of hearing / Matters to be considered on hearing / Order / Warrant of judge for arrest / Arrest without warrant by peace officer / Hearing and order / Provisions applicable to proceedings / Directions for expediting trial.

525. (1) Where an accused who has been charged with an offence other than an offence listed in section 469 and who is not required to be detained in custody in respect of any other matter is being detained in custody pending his trial for that offence and the trial has not commenced

(*a*) **in the case of an indictable offence, within ninety days from**

  (i) **the day on which the accused was taken before a justice under section 503, or**

  (ii) **where an order that the accused be detained in custody has been made under section 521 or 524, or a decision has been made with respect to a review under section 520, the later of the day on which the accused was taken into custody under that order and the day of the decision, or**

(*b*) **in the case of an offence for which the accused is being prosecuted in proceedings by way of summary conviction, within thirty days from**

  (i) **the day on which the accused was taken before a justice under subsection 503(1), or**

  (ii) **where an order that the accused be detained in custody has been made under section 521 or 524, or a decision has been made with respect to a review under section 520, the later of the day on which the accused was taken into custody under that order and the day of the decision,**

the person having the custody of the accused shall, forthwith on the expiration of those ninety or thirty days, as the case may be, apply to a judge having jurisdiction in the place in which the accused is in custody to fix a date for a hearing to determine whether or not the accused should be released from custody.

(2) On receiving an application under subsection (1), the judge shall

(*a*) **fix a date for the hearing described in subsection (1) to be held in the jurisdiction**

  (i) **where the accused is in custody, or**

  (ii) **where the trial is to take place; and**

(*b*) **direct that notice of the hearing be given to such persons, including the prosecutor and the accused, and in such manner, as the judge may specify.**

(3) On the hearing described in subsection (1), the judge may, in deciding whether or not the accused should be released from custody, take into consideration whether the prosecutor or the accused has been responsible for any unreasonable delay in the trial of the charge.

(4) If, following the hearing described in subsection (1), the judge is not satisfied that the continued detention of the accused in custody is justified within the meaning of subsection 515(10), the judge shall order that the accused be released from custody pending the trial of the charge on his giving an undertaking or entering into a recognizance described in any of paragraphs 515(2)(*a*) to (*e*) with such conditions described in subsection 515(4) as the judge considers desirable.

(5) Where a judge having jurisdiction in the province where an order under subsection (4) for the release of an accused has been made is satisfied that there are reasonable grounds to believe that the accused

    (*a*) has contravened or is about to contravene the undertaking or recognizance upon which he has been released, or

    (*b*) has, after his release from custody on his undertaking or recognizance, committed an indictable offence,

he may issue a warrant for the arrest of the accused.

(6) Notwithstanding anything in this Act, a peace officer who believes on reasonable grounds that an accused who has been released from custody under subsection (4)

    (*a*) has contravened or is about to contravene the undertaking or recognizance on which he has been released, or

    (*b*) has, after his release from custody on his undertaking or recognizance, committed an indictable offence,

may arrest the accused without warrant and take him or cause him to be taken before a judge having jurisdiction in the province where the order for his release was made.

(7) A judge before whom an accused is taken pursuant to a warrant issued under subsection (5) or pursuant to subsection (6) may, where the accused shows cause why his detention in custody is not justified within the meaning of subsection 515(10), order that the accused be released on his giving an undertaking or entering into a recognizance described in any of paragraphs 515(2)(*a*) to (*e*) with such conditions, described in subsection 515(4), as the judge considers desirable.

(8) The provisions of sections 517, 518 and 519 apply with such modifications as the circumstances require in respect of any proceedings under this section.

(9) Where an accused is before a judge under any of the provisions of this section, the judge may give directions for expediting the trial of the accused. R.S., c. C-34, s. 459; R.S., c. 2 (2nd Supp.), s. 5; 1974-75-76, c. 93, s. 56; R.S.C. 1985, c. 27 (1st Supp.), s. 90; 1994, c. 44, s. 49; 1997, c. 18, s. 61.

CROSS-REFERENCES

The term "justice" is defined in s. 2 and "judge", "recognizance" and "undertaking" in s. 493. As to calculation of "within" a certain number of days see s. 27(5) of the *Interpretation Act*, R.S.C. 1985, c. I-21. For an overview of the application of this Part and the procedure respecting release pending trial see *Note on judicial interim release* under s. 515, or the *Note on judicial interim release* under s. 522 where the accused is charged with an offence listed in s. 469.

The accused of course has a constitutional right to trial within a reasonable time and thus see notes under s. 11(*b*) of the Charter.

SYNOPSIS

This section provides for a review of the detention of an accused person when that person's trial has been delayed. This review applies only to persons charged with offences other than those listed in s. 469.

Subsection (1) places an obligation on the person having custody of the accused to apply to the judge having jurisdiction to fix a date for a hearing to determine whether an accused should be released after the applicable time period has expired. The time periods vary according to the type of offence alleged to have been committed and the section under which the accused has been detained.

Subsection (2) requires a judge, upon receipt of the application under subsec. (1), to fix a date for the hearing, and to direct that notice be given to the prosecutor and the accused.

Subsection (3) authorizes the judge to consider whether the prosecutor or the accused has been responsible for any unreasonable delay in the trial of the charge.

Under subsec. (4), the judge must consider, following the hearing, whether the continued detention of the accused is justified on the primary or secondary grounds as outlined in s. 515(10). The judge may decide to release the accused under this section using any of the forms of release described in s. 515(2)(*a*) to (*e*) with such conditions described in s. 515(4) as are appropriate.

Subsections (5) and (6) authorize the arrest of an accused person who has been released under subsec. (4) with or without a warrant where there are grounds to believe that he has violated or is about to violate his undertaking or recognizance, or that he has committed an indictable offence subsequent to release.

Subsection (7) states that the onus is on the accused brought before a justice under subsec. (5) or (6) to show cause why detention is not justified. Section 515(10), (2) and (4) are applicable, depending on the circumstances. Sections 517, 518 and 519 are applicable with such modifications as circumstances require.

Subsection (9) gives the judge dealing with an accused under this section a discretion to give directions for expediting the trial.

ANNOTATIONS

Application of section – This section only applies where the accused is held on a detention order and not where he is being held by virtue of s. 519, *i.e.,* bail has been set but the accused is unable to meet the conditions for release: *Ex p. Srebot* (1975), 28 C.C.C. (2d) 160 (B.C.C.A.).

An accused in custody on a detention order and a warrant under s. 524 is entitled to a review under this section: *R. v. Ferreira* (1981), 58 C.C.C. (2d) 147 (B.C.C.A.).

Procedure – An application brought on a week later and then set for hearing is reasonable compliance with this section: *R. v. Kozak and Lewis* (1975), 32 C.R.N.S. 245, [1976] 1 W.W.R. 356 (B.C.S.C.).

Jurisdiction over the offence is not affected by the fact that due to inadvertence nothing was done on the date to which a review under this section was adjourned: *R. v. Gagliardi* (1981), 60 C.C.C. (2d) 267 (B.C.C.A.), leave to appeal to S.C.C. refused C.C.C. *loc. cit.*.

A youth court judge has jurisdiction to conduct the 90-day review pursuant to the *Youth Criminal Justice Act*: *R. v. O. (A.J.)* (2004), 185 C.C.C. (3d) 120 (Ont. S.C.J.).

Effect of failure to comply with section – It was held by the court in *Ex. p. Cordes* (1976), 31 C.C.C. (2d) 279 (Alta. S.C. App. Div.), that failure to comply with this section does not *ipso facto* vacate the previous detention order and render the accused's detention illegal entitling him to release on *habeas corpus*. On a *habeas corpus* application brought because of unreasonable delay the judge would have regard to the same considerations set out in this section. Where the section has not been complied with the appropriate remedy is *mandamus* to require compliance therewith.

To a similar effect is *R. v. Pomfret* (1990), 53 C.C.C. (3d) 56 (Man. C.A.), where the court also held that the failure to hold the review as required by this section did not, in the circumstances, result in arbitrary detention in violation of s. 9 of the Charter. The lapse of time was not of such an extent that the court could infer deliberateness or design on the part of the gaoler. Finally, refusing to release the accused on his application for *habeas corpus* did not violate s. 10(*c*) of the Charter. The *habeas corpus* application brought to the court's attention that the accused was entitled to a review under this section and resulted in him receiving that to which he was entitled under the law, namely a bail review hearing.

The reverse onus contained in s. 515(6) of the *Criminal Code* applies to a review under this provision and cannot be eliminated merely through a delay: *R. v. Thorsteinson* (2006), 238 C.C.C. (3d) 83 (Man. Q.B.).

The accused's detention does not become unlawful merely upon the expiration of the 90 days. The custodian is under a statutory obligation to seek the hearing required under this section as soon as practicable after the expiration of the 90-day period. Where an application for a hearing has been made by the custodian, the appropriate disposition of a claim to release on *habeas corpus* is to refer that claim to the judge conducting the hearing under this section. Where no application has been made, *habeas corpus* may lie to determine whether the lapse of time has tainted the legality of the detention. Alternatively, an accused may apply by way of *mandamus* to compel the director to comply: *Vukelich v. Vancouver Pre-Trial Centre, Director* (1993), 87 C.C.C. (3d) 32, 27 C.R. (4th) 15 (B.C.C.A.).

DIRECTIONS FOR EXPEDITING PROCEEDINGS.

526. Subject to subsection 525(9), a court, judge or justice before which or whom an accused appears pursuant to this Part may give directions for expediting any proceedings in respect of the accused. R.S., c. 2 (2nd Supp.), s. 5; R.S.C. 1985, c. 27 (1st Supp.), s. 91.

CROSS-REFERENCES

The term "justice" is defined in s. 2 and "accused" and "judge" in s. 493. The accused of course has a constitutional right to trial within a reasonable time and thus see notes under s. 11(*b*) of the Charter. For an overview of the application of this Part and the procedure respecting release pending trial see *Note on judicial interim release* under s. 515, or the *Note on judicial interim release* under s. 522 where the accused is charged with an offence listed in s. 469.

SYNOPSIS

This section authorizes a court, judge, or justice dealing with an accused under Part XVI of the Code to give directions for expediting any proceedings relating to the accused.

Procedure to Procure Attendance of a Prisoner

PROCURING ATTENDANCE / Provincial court judge's order / Conveyance of prisoner / Detention of prisoner required as witness / Detention in other cases / Application of sections respecting sentence / Transfer of prisoner / Conveyance of prisoner / Return.

527. (1) A judge of a superior court of criminal jurisdiction may order in writing that a person who is confined in a prison be brought before the court, judge, justice or provincial court judge before whom the prisoner is required to attend, from day to day as may be necessary, if

   (*a*)   **the applicant for the order sets out the facts of the case in an affidavit and produces the warrant, if any; and**

   (*b*)   **the judge is satisfied that the ends of justice require that an order be made.**

(2) A provincial court judge has the same powers for the purposes of subsection (1) or (7) as a judge has under that subsection where the person whose attendance is required is within the province in which the provincial court judge has jurisdiction.

(3) An order that is made under subsection (1) or (2) shall be addressed to the person who has custody of the prisoner, and on receipt thereof that person shall

   (*a*)   **deliver the prisoner to any person who is named in the order to receive him; or**

   (*b*)   **bring the prisoner before the court, judge, justice or provincial court judge, as the case may be, on payment of his reasonable charges in respect thereof.**

(4) Where a prisoner is required as a witness, the judge or provincial court judge shall direct, in the order, the manner in which the prisoner shall be kept in custody and returned to the prison from which he is brought.

(5) Where the appearance of a prisoner is required for the purposes of paragraph (1)(*a*) or (*b*), the judge or provincial court judge shall give appropriate directions in the order with respect to the manner in which the prisoner is

   (*a*)   **to be kept in custody, if he is ordered to stand trial; or** (*b*) to be returned, if he is discharged on a preliminary inquiry or if he is acquitted of the charge against him.

(6) Sections 718.3 and 743.1 apply where a prisoner to whom this section applies is convicted and sentenced to imprisonment by the court, judge, justice or provincial court judge.

(7) On application by the prosecutor, a judge of a superior court of criminal jurisdiction may, if a prisoner or a person in the custody of a peace officer consents in writing, order the transfer of the prisoner or other person to the custody of a peace officer named in the order for a period specified in the order, where the judge is satisfied that the transfer is required for the purpose of assisting a peace officer acting in the execution of his or her duties.

(8) An order under subsection (7) shall be addressed to the person who has custody of the prisoner and on receipt thereof that person shall deliver the prisoner to the peace officer who is named in the order to receive him.

(9) When the purposes of any order made under this section have been carried out, the prisoner shall be returned to the place where he was confined at the time the order was made. R.S., c. C-34, s. 460; R.S.C. 1985, c. 27 (1st Supp.), ss. 92, 101(2)(*b*); 1994, c. 44, s. 50; 1995, c. 22, s. 10; 1997, c. 18, s. 62.

CROSS-REFERENCES

"Provincial court judge", "superior court of criminal jurisdiction", "prosecutor", "justice", "prison", and "peace officer" are defined in s. 2. Section 672.85 gives the chairperson of the Criminal Code Review Board the power to order the attendance of the accused for a review hearing under s. 672.81.

SYNOPSIS

This section sets out the procedure to procure the attendance of a prisoner at his preliminary hearing, the trial of his charge, or to give evidence in criminal proceedings.

Subsection (1) states that when a prisoner's attendance is required, an application must be made to a judge of a superior court of criminal jurisdiction. The applicant must set out the facts of the case in an affidavit and produce any warrant to the judge. The judge may, if satisfied that the ends of justice require it, make a written order to bring the prisoner before the court.

Subsection (2) provides that a provincial court judge has the same powers as the judges described in subsecs. (1) and (7) except that the provincial court judge may only order the appearance of a prisoner being held in that province.

Subsection (3) describes the requirements of an order made under subsecs. (1) and (2).

Subsection (4) states that the judge or provincial court judge must direct the manner in which a prisoner, required to testify as a witness, shall be kept in custody and returned to prison.

Subsection (5) sets out the kinds of directions a judge or provincial court judge must include in an order compelling the attendance of a prisoner at his preliminary hearing or trial.

Subsection (7) authorizes a superior court judge (or a provincial court judge if the prisoner is in the judge's province) to order the transfer of a prisoner to a named peace officer for a specified period where such a transfer would assist the peace officer in the execution of his duties. The prisoner must consent in writing to this procedure. An order under subsec. (7) must be addressed to the person having custody of the prisoner and, upon receipt, that person must deliver the prisoner to the named peace officer.

Subsection (9) requires that the prisoner be returned to the place of confinement when the purposes of any order made under this section have been accomplished.

ANNOTATIONS

A witness brought to court pursuant to an order under this section may be compelled to testify notwithstanding he has not been served with a subpoena and there is no warrant issued under s. 698 outstanding: *R. v. Ayres* (1984), 15 C.C.C. (3d) 208 (Ont. C.A.).

The judge in making an order under this section in relation to an accused who is detained in another district has power under subsec. (5) to order that the accused be brought to the local gaol several days prior to the actual trial date to afford him a reasonable opportunity to properly prepare his defence: *Auclair v. Dube J.S.P. and R.* (1984), 39 C.R. (3d) 398 (Que. S.C.).

Although this section provides a convenient procedure for securing the attendance at court of persons confined in custody on other matters, it was open to a justice of the peace to resort to the provisions of s. 512 and issue a bench warrant for the arrest of an accused where the accused, detained on another matter, was not brought to court to set a date for his trial: *R. v. Hartmann* (1986), 30 C.C.C. (3d) 286 (Ont. H.C.J.).

Endorsement of Warrant

ENDORSING WARRANT / Copy of affidavit or warrant / Effect of endorsement.

528. (1) Where a warrant for the arrest or committal of an accused, in any form set out in Part XXVIII in relation thereto, cannot be executed in accordance with section 514 or 703, a justice within whose jurisdiction the accused is or is believed to be shall, on application and proof on oath or by affidavit of the signature of the justice who issued the warrant, authorize the arrest of the accused within his jurisdiction by making an endorsement, which may be in Form 28, on the warrant.

(1.1) A copy of an affidavit or warrant submitted by a means of telecommunication that produces a writing has the same probative force as the original for the purposes of subsection (1).

(2) An endorsement that is made upon a warrant pursuant to subsection (1) is sufficient authority to the peace officers to whom it was originally directed, and to all peace officers within the territorial jurisdiction of the justice by whom it is endorsed, to execute the warrant and to take the accused before the justice who issued the warrant or before any other justice for the same territorial division. R.S., c. C-34, s. 461; 1974-75-76, c. 93, s. 57; R.S.C. 1985, c. 27 (1st Supp.), s. 93; 1994, c. 44, s. 51.

CROSS-REFERENCES

"Justice" and "peace officer" are defined in s. 2. "Warrant" is defined in s. 493. Under s. 20, a warrant may be executed on a holiday. A warrant is executed in accordance with this section and s. 29 and s. 10 of the Charter. For protection of persons executing warrants see ss. 25 to 28.

SYNOPSIS

This section empowers a justice to authorize the arrest of an accused person who is believed to be in that justice's jurisdiction, when a warrant for arrest or committal cannot be executed in accordance with ss. 514 or 703. The justice being asked to authorize the arrest of the accused will endorse the warrant only upon proof on oath or by affidavit of the signature of the justice who issued the warrant. Under subsec. (1.1), a faxed copy has the same probative value as the original.

Subsection (2) states that an endorsement on the warrant pursuant to subsec. (1) is sufficient authority to the peace officers to whom it was originally directed, along with all peace officers within the territorial jurisdiction of the endorsing justice, to execute the warrant.

ANNOTATIONS

The trial judge correctly found that a warrant issued by a justice of the peace in Ontario was ineffective in Saskatchewan because it had never been endorsed by a justice in Saskatchewan in accordance with this section. However, the judge erred in finding the arrest illegal without considering whether it was a valid warrantless arrest for an indictable offence pursuant to s. 495(1): *R. v. Charles* (2012), 289 C.C.C. (3d) 170 (Sask. C.A.).

529. [*Repealed* (old provision, with heading), 1994, c. 44, s. 52.]

Powers to Enter Dwelling-houses to Carry out Arrests

INCLUDING AUTHORIZATION TO ENTER IN WARRANT OF ARREST / Execution

529. (1) A warrant to arrest or apprehend a person issued by a judge or justice under this or any other Act of Parliament may authorize a peace officer, subject to subsection (2), to enter a dwelling-house described in the warrant for the purpose of arresting or apprehending the person if the judge or justice is satisfied by information on oath in writing that there are reasonable grounds to believe that the person is or will be present in the dwelling-house.

(2) An authorization to enter a dwelling-house granted under subsection (1) is subject to the condition that the peace officer may not enter the dwelling-house unless the peace officer has, immediately before entering the dwelling-house, reasonable grounds to believe that the person to be arrested or apprehended is present in the dwelling-house. 1994, c. 44, s. 52; 1997, c. 39, s. 2.

CROSS-REFERENCES

"Justice", "dwelling-house" and "peace officer" are defined in s. 2. A warrant to arrest may be issued under various provisions of this Act. The most important provision is s. 507. Sections 511 and 512 set out the contents of the arrest warrant. Section 514 contains other provisions concerning execution of an arrest warrant. Under s. 20, a warrant may be executed on a holiday. A warrant is executed in accordance with ss. 29 and 10 of the Charter. For protection of persons executing warrants, see ss. 25 to 28. Section 528 deals with endorsing the warrant where it cannot be executed in accordance with s. 514. Section 529.1 permits a justice or judge to issue a warrant authorizing a peace officer to enter a dwelling-house for the purpose of arresting or apprehending a person, where a warrant is already in force anywhere in Canada or where grounds exist for a warrantless arrest. Section 529.2 requires the justice or judge to include terms and conditions in the warrant to ensure that the entry is reasonable in the circumstances. Section 529.3 allows for warrantless entry to effect an arrest in exigent circumstances. Section 529.4 sets out the circumstances in which a peace officer may enter without prior announcement. Section 529.5 permits application for a telewarrant where it is impracticable to appear personally before a judge or justice to obtain a warrant to enter a dwelling-house or the authorization to enter or enter without announcement under ss. 529 or 529.4. The provisions respecting issuance of a telewarrant are set out in s. 487.1.

Section 34.1 of the *Interpretation Act*, R.S.C. 1985, c. I-21, provides that any person who may issue a warrant to arrest or apprehend a person under any other Act of Parliament may also authorize entry into a dwelling-house to effect the arrest and without prior announcement.

For notes on warrantless search of the home, see annotations following s. 529.3. For notes with respect to prior announcement, see annotations following s. 529.4.

Section 489(2) gives the officer power to seize without warrant anything that the officer believes on reasonable grounds has been obtained by the commission of an offence, has been used in the commission of an offence or will afford evidence in respect of any offence under the *Criminal Code* or other federal statute, provided that the officer is lawfully present in the place pursuant to a warrant or in the execution of duties.

SYNOPSIS

This section allows a justice or judge to include in a warrant to arrest or apprehend, the power to authorize the peace officer to enter a dwelling-house for the purpose of effect the arrest or apprehension. This authorization is dependent upon the judge or justice being satisfied by information on oath in writing that there are reasonable grounds to believe that the person is or will be present. Nevertheless, the warrant mus t include a condition that the officer only enter the dwelling-house if the officer has, immediately before entering, reasonable grounds to believe the person is in the dwelling-house. This provision and the companion provisions in ss. 529.1 to 529.5 were apparently enacted in response to the decision of the Supreme Court of Canada in *R. v. Feeney*, noted below.

ANNOTATIONS

It was held in *R. v. Feeney*, [1997] 2 S.C.R. 13, 115 C.C.C. (3d) 129, that the common law right to make a warrantless arrest on private premises must now be adjusted to comport with Charter values. In general, the privacy interest in a dwelling-house now outweighs the interests of the police and warrantless arrests in dwelling-houses are prohibited. An arrest warrant alone is insufficient protection of a suspect's privacy rights. [**Note:** This case was decided prior to the enactment of this section and the companion provisions of ss. 529.1 to 529.5. This section and s. 529.1 now provide for judicial authorization of entry into a dwelling-house to effect an arrest. In addition, s. 529.2 now gives statutory authority for a warrantless entry in exigent circumstances.]

The warrant requirement to effect an arrest of the accused is not restricted to an accused's dwelling house. Accordingly, a warrant to enter a dwelling house was required where the accused was arrested in a laundry room of a rooming house shared with others: *R. v. Adams* (2001), 157 C.C.C. (3d) 220, 203 D.L.R. (4th) 290, 148 O.A.C. 253 (C.A.).

WARRANT TO ENTER DWELLING-HOUSE

529.1 A judge or justice may issue a warrant in Form 7.1 authorizing a peace officer to enter a dwelling-house described in the warrant for the purpose of arresting or apprehending a person identified or identifiable by the warrant if the judge or justice is satisfied by information on oath that there are reasonable grounds to believe that the person is or will be present in the dwelling-house and that

    (*a*) **a warrant referred to in this or any other Act of Parliament to arrest or apprehend the person is in force anywhere in Canada;**

    (*b*) **grounds exist to arrest the person without warrant under paragraph 495(1)(*a*) or (*b*) or section 672.91; or**

    (*c*) **grounds exist to arrest or apprehend without warrant the person under an Act of Parliament, other than this Act. 1997, c. 39, s. 2; 2002, c. 13, s. 23.**

CROSS-REFERENCES

"Justice", "dwelling-house" and "peace officer" are defined in s. 2. Section 495 sets out the circumstances in which a peace officer may make an arrest without warrant. A warrant to arrest may be issued under various provisions of this Act. The most important provision is s. 507. Sections 511 and 512 set out the contents of the arrest warrant. Section 514 contains other provisions concerning execution of an arrest warrant. Under s. 20, a warrant may be executed on a holiday. A warrant is executed in accordance with ss. 29 and 10 of the Charter. For protection of persons executing warrants, see ss. 25 to 28. Section 528 deals with endorsing the warrant where it cannot be executed in accordance with s. 514. Section 529 permits a justice or judge to include a term in an arrest warrant authorizing a peace officer to enter a dwelling-house for the purpose of arresting or apprehending a person. Section 529.2 requires the justice or judge to include terms and conditions in the warrant to ensure that the entry is reasonable in the circumstances. Section 529.3 allows for warrantless entry to effect an arrest in exigent circumstances. Section 529.4 sets out the circumstances in which a peace officer may enter without prior announcement. Section 529.5

permits application for a telewarrant where it is impracticable to appear personally before a judge or justice to obtain a warrant to enter a dwelling-house or the authorization to enter or enter without announcement under s. 529 or s. 529.4. The provisions respecting issuance of a telewarrant are set out in s. 487.1.

Section 34.1 of the *Interpretation Act*, R.S.C. 1985, c. I-21, provides that any person who may issue a warrant to arrest or apprehend a person under any other Act of Parliament may also authorize entry into a dwelling-house to effect the arrest and without prior announcement.

For notes on warrantless search of the home, see annotations following s. 529.3. For notes with respect to prior announcement, see annotations following s. 529.4.

Section 489(2) gives the officer power to seize without warrant anything that the officer believes on reasonable grounds has been obtained by the commission of an offence, has been used in the commission of an offence or will afford evidence in respect of any offence under the *Criminal Code* or other federal statute, provided that the officer is lawfully present in the place pursuant to a warrant or in the execution of duties.

SYNOPSIS

This section allows a justice or judge to issue a warrant to authorize the peace officer to enter a dwelling-house for the purpose of effecting the arrest or apprehension. This authorization is dependent upon the judge or justice being satisfied by information on oath in writing that there are reasonable grounds to believe that the person is or will be present and that an arrest warrant is in force anywhere in Canada or that grounds for a warrantless arrest exist. This provision and the companion provisions in ss. 529.1 to 529.5 were apparently enacted in response to the decision of the Supreme Court of Canada in *R. v. Feeney*, [1997] 2 S.C.R. 13, 115 C.C.C. (3d) 129, noted below.

ANNOTATIONS

It was held in *R. v. Feeney*, [1997] 2 S.C.R. 13, 115 C.C.C. (3d) 129, that the common law right to make a warrantless arrest on private premises must now be adjusted to comport with Charter values. In general, the privacy interest in a dwelling-house now outweighs the interests of the police and warrantless arrests in dwelling-houses are prohibited. An arrest warrant alone is insufficient protection of a suspect's privacy rights. [**Note:** This case was decided prior to the enactment of this section and the companion provisions of ss. 529 and 529.2 to 529.5. This section and s. 529 now provide for judicial authorization of entry into a dwelling-house to effect an arrest. In addition, s. 529.2 now gives statutory authority for a warrantless entry in exigent circumstances.]

REASONABLE TERMS AND CONDITIONS

529.2 Subject to section 529.4, the judge or justice shall include in a warrant referred to in section 529 or 529.1 any terms and conditions that the judge or justice considers advisable to ensure that the entry into the dwelling-house is reasonable in the circumstances. 1997, c. 39, s. 2.

CROSS-REFERENCES

"Justice" is defined in s. 2. A warrant to arrest may be issued under various provisions of this Act. The most important provision is s. 507. Sections 511 and 512 set out the contents of the arrest warrant. Section 514 contains other provisions concerning execution of an arrest warrant. Under s. 20, a warrant may be executed on a holiday. A warrant is executed in accordance with ss. 29 and 10 of the Charter. For protection of persons executing warrants, see ss. 25 to 28. Section 528 deals with endorsing the warrant where it cannot be executed in accordance with s. 514. Section 529 permits a justice or judge to include a term in an arrest warrant authorizing a peace officer to enter a dwelling-house for the purpose of arresting or apprehending a person. An authorization granted under s. 529 is subject to the condition that the peace officer may not enter the dwelling-house unless the officer has, immediately before entering the dwelling-house, reasonable grounds to believe that the person to be arrested is present in the dwelling-house. Section 529.1 permits a justice or judge to issue a warrant authorizing a peace officer to enter a dwelling-house for the purpose of arresting or apprehending a person, where a warrant is already in force anywhere in Canada or where there exists grounds for a warrantless arrest. Section 529.3 allows for warrantless entry to effect an arrest in exigent circumstances. Section 529.4 sets out the circumstances in which a peace officer may enter without prior announcement. Section 529.5 permits application for a telewarrant where it is impracticable to appear personally before a judge or justice to obtain a warrant to enter a dwelling-house or the authorization to enter or enter without announcement under s. 529 or s. 529.4. The provisions respecting issuance of a telewarrant are set out in s. 487.1.

Section 34.1 of the *Interpretation Act*, R.S.C. 1985, c. I-21, provides that any person who may issue a warrant to arrest or apprehend a person under any other Act of Parliament may also authorize entry into a dwelling-house to effect the arrest and without prior announcement.

For notes on warrantless search of the home, see annotations following s. 529.3. For notes with respect to prior announcement, see annotations following s. 529.4.

Section 489(2) gives the officer power to seize without warrant anything that the officer believes on reasonable grounds has been obtained by the commission of an offence, has been used in the commission of an offence or will afford evidence in respect of any offence under the *Criminal Code* or other federal statute, provided that the officer is lawfully present in the place pursuant to a warrant or in the execution of duties.

SYNOPSIS

This section requires the justice or judge to include terms and conditions in the warrant to ensure that the entry is reasonable in the circumstances.

AUTHORITY TO ENTER DWELLING WITHOUT WARRANT / Exigent circumstances

529.3 (1) Without limiting or restricting any power a peace officer may have to enter a dwelling-house under this or any other Act or law, the peace officer may enter the dwelling-house for the purpose of arresting or apprehending a person, without a warrant referred to in section 529 or 529.1 authorizing the entry, if the peace officer has reasonable grounds to believe that the person is present in the dwelling-house, and the conditions for obtaining a warrant under section 529.1 exist but by reason of exigent circumstances it would be impracticable to obtain a warrant.

(2) For the purposes of subsection (1), exigent circumstances include circumstances in which the peace officer

> **(a) has reasonable grounds to suspect that entry into the dwelling-house is necessary to prevent imminent bodily harm or death to any person; or**

> **(b) has reasonable grounds to believe that evidence relating to the commission of an indictable offence is present in the dwelling-house and that entry into the dwelling-house is necessary to prevent the imminent loss or imminent destruction of the evidence. 1997, c. 39, s. 2.**

CROSS-REFERENCES

"Peace officer" and "dwelling-house" are defined in s. 2. Section 495 is the most important provision setting out the circumstances in which a peace officer may make an arrest without warrant. A warrantless arrest must conform to the dictates of s. 10 of the Charter. A warrant to arrest may be issued under various provisions of this Act. The most important provision is s. 507. Sections 511 and 512 set out the contents of the arrest warrant. Section 514 contains other provisions concerning execution of an arrest warrant. Under s. 20, a warrant may be executed on a holiday. A warrant is executed in accordance with ss. 29 and 10 of the Charter. For protection of persons executing warrants, see ss. 25 to 28. Section 528 deals with endorsing the warrant where it cannot be executed in accordance with s. 514. Section 529 permits a justice or judge to include a term in an arrest warrant authorizing a peace officer to enter a dwelling-house for the purpose of arresting or apprehending a person. Section 529.1 permits a justice or judge to issue a warrant authorizing a peace officer to enter a dwelling-house for the purpose of arresting or apprehending a person, where a warrant is already in force anywhere in Canada or where grounds exist for a warrantless arrest. Section 529.2 requires the justice or judge to include terms and conditions in the warrant to ensure that the entry is reasonable in the circumstances. Section 529.4 sets out the circumstances in which a peace officer may enter without prior announcement. Section 529.5 permits application for a telewarrant where it is impracticable to appear personally before a judge or justice to obtain a warrant to enter a dwelling-house or the authorization to enter or enter without announcement under s. 529 or s. 529.4.

For notes with respect to prior announcement, see annotations following s. 529.4.

SYNOPSIS

This section provides statutory authority for a peace officer to enter a dwelling-house to effect an arrest although the officer does not have a warrant or specific authorization from a judicial official to enter. This section defines some of the circumstances in which the warrantless entry may be made. Subsection (2) defines certain exigent circumstances justifying the warrantless entry. They include where the officer has reasonable grounds to suspect that entry is necessary to prevent imminent bodily harm or death or where the officer has reasonable grounds to believe that entry is necessary to prevent the imminent loss or destruction of evidence. Note the different standard of belief depending on the reason for entry. This section is in addition to any other warrantless entry powers that may be given to an officer either by statute or common law. This provision and the companion provisions in ss. 529, 529.1, 529.2, 529.4 and 529.5 were apparently enacted in response to the decision of the Supreme Court of Canada in *R. v. Feeney*, [1997] 2 S.C.R. 13, 115 C.C.C. (3d) 129, noted below and under s. 529.

ANNOTATIONS

Note: Some of the following cases were decided prior to the enactment of this section.

In *R. v. Macooh*, [1993] 2 S.C.R. 802, 82 C.C.C. (3d) 481, the court held that the police have the power to enter private premises to effect an arrest where they are in hot pursuit and they have a warrant for an arrest or have the power to make an arrest without a warrant. It was also held that the power to enter private premises to make an arrest while in hot pursuit is not limited to an arrest for an indictable offence. Nor is it necessary that the offence had been committed in the presence of the police. The essence of hot or fresh pursuit is that it must be continuous pursuit conducted with reasonable diligence so that the pursuit and capture along with the commission of the offence may be considered as forming part of a single transaction.

In the subsequent case of *R. v. Feeney*, [1997] 2 S.C.R. 13, 115 C.C.C. (3d) 129, the court held that warrantless entry to effect an arrest was ordinarily inconsistent with s. 8 of the Charter. However, there may be exigent circumstances were warrantless entry is reasonable. At least one exception is where the officer is in hot pursuit as recognized in *R. v. Macooh*, *supra*.

The warrantless search of a home incident to arrest is generally prohibited subject to exceptional circumstances where the law enforcement interest is so compelling that it overrides the individual's right to privacy within the home. The risk of physical harm to those at the scene of the arrest constitutes exceptional circumstances justifying the warrantless entry and search of a residence. If the circumstances of an arrest give rise to a legitimate cause for concern with respect to the safety of those at the scene, reasonable steps to allay that concern may be taken. The nature of the apprehended risk, the potential consequences of not taking protective measures, the availability of alternative measures and the likelihood of the contemplated danger actually existing, must all be considered: *R. v. Golub* (1997), 117 C.C.C. (3d) 193 (Ont. C.A.), leave to appeal to S.C.C. refused 128 C.C.C. (3d) vi.

In *R. v. Godoy*, [1999] 1 S.C.R. 311, 131 C.C.C. (3d) 129, the Supreme Court of Canada held that forced entry into a dwelling house in response to a disconnected 911 call did not violate s. 8. The common law duty of police to preserve life is engaged whenever it may be inferred that the 911 caller may be in distress. In this case, the accused had refused entry to the police responding to the 911 call. The forced entry of the apartment to locate the caller and determine the reason for the call constituted a justifiable use of police powers. The police do not, however, have a further authority to search the premises or otherwise intrude on a resident's privacy or property. The court did not consider the applicability of the plain view doctrine in such circumstances.

Exigent circumstances include reasonable grounds to believe that entry was necessary to prevent the imminent loss or destruction of evidence: *R. v. Duong* (2002), 162 C.C.C. (3d) 242 (B.C.C.A.), leave to appeal to S.C.C. refused [2002] 3 S.C.R. vii, 167 C.C.C. (3d) vi.

"Any person" in subsec. (2)(*a*) includes the accused. In this case, therefore, the police were in lawful execution of their duty when entering the accused's home without a warrant, on the basis that he was suicidal and needed to be returned to hospital: *R. v. Phillips* (2006), 219 C.C.C. (3d) 252 (N.S.C.A.).

OMITTING ANNOUNCEMENT BEFORE ENTRY / Execution of authorization / Exception.

529.4 (1) A judge or justice who authorizes a peace officer to enter a dwelling-house under section 529 or 529.1, or any other judge or justice, may authorize the peace officer to enter the dwelling-house without prior announcement if the judge or justice is satisfied by information on oath that there are reasonable grounds to believe that prior announcement of the entry would

- **(*a*) expose the peace officer or any other person to imminent bodily harm or death; or**
- **(*b*) result in the imminent loss or imminent destruction of evidence relating to the commission of an indictable offence.**

(2) An authorization under this section is subject to the condition that the peace officer may not enter the dwelling-house without prior announcement despite being authorized to do so unless the peace officer has, immediately before entering the dwelling-house,

- **(*a*) reasonable grounds to suspect that prior announcement of the entry would expose the peace officer or any other person to imminent bodily harm or death; or**
- **(*b*) reasonable grounds to believe that prior announcement of the entry would result in the imminent loss or imminent destruction of evidence relating to the commission of an indictable offence.**

(3) A peace officer who enters a dwelling-house without a warrant under section 529.3 may not enter the dwelling-house without prior announcement unless the peace officer has, immediately before entering the dwelling-house,

- **(*a*) reasonable grounds to suspect that prior announcement of the entry would expose the peace officer or any other person to imminent bodily harm or death; or**
- **(*b*) reasonable grounds to believe that prior announcement of the entry would result in the imminent loss or imminent destruction of evidence relating to the commission of an indictable offence. R.S. 1985, c. 27 (1st Supp.), s. 203; 1997, c. 39, s. 2.**

CROSS-REFERENCES

"Justice", "dwelling-house" and "peace officer" are defined in s. 2. A warrant to arrest may be issued under various provisions of this Act. The most important provision is s. 507. Sections 511 and 512 set out the contents of the arrest warrant. Section 514 contains other provisions concerning execution of an arrest warrant. Under s. 20, a warrant may be executed on a holiday. A warrant is executed in accordance with ss. 29 and 10 of the Charter. For protection of persons executing warrants see, ss. 25 to 28. Section 528 deals with endorsing the warrant where the warrant cannot be executed in accordance with s. 514. Section 529 permits a justice or judge to include a term in an arrest warrant authorizing a peace officer to enter a dwelling-house for the purpose of arresting or apprehending a person. Section 529.1 permits a justice or judge to issue a warrant authorizing a peace officer to enter a dwelling-house for the purpose of arresting or apprehending a person, where a warrant is already in force anywhere in Canada or where grounds exist for a warrantless arrest. Section 529.2 requires the justice or judge to include terms and conditions in the warrant to ensure that the entry is reasonable in the circumstances. Section 529.3 allows for warrantless entry to effect an arrest in exigent circumstances. Section 529.5 permits application for a telewarrant where it is impracticable to appear personally before a judge or justice to obtain a warrant to enter a dwelling-house or the authorization to enter or enter without announcement under s. 529 or 529.4. The provisions respecting issuance of a telewarrant are set out in s. 487.1.

Section 34.1 of the *Interpretation Act*, R.S.C. 1985, c. I-21, provides that any person who may issue a warrant to arrest or apprehend a person under any other Act of Parliament may also authorize entry into a dwelling-house to effect the arrest and without prior announcement.

For notes on warrantless search of the home, see annotations following s. 529.3.

SYNOPSIS

This section sets out the circumstances in which a peace officer may enter a dwelling-house without prior announcement. The section contemplates two different circumstances. A judicial official when granting authorization to enter a dwelling-house may also authorize entry to effect an arrest without prior announcement. This authorization is dependent upon the judge or justice being satisfied by information on oath in writing that there are reasonable grounds to believe that prior announcement would expose the officer or another person to imminent bodily harm or death or result in the imminent loss or destruction of evidence relating to the commission of an indictable offence. Nevertheless, the warrant must include a condition that the officer only enter the dwelling-house if the officer has, immediately before entering, reasonable grounds to suspect that prior announcement would expose the officer or another person to imminent bodily harm or death or the officer has reasonable grounds to believe that prior announcement would result in the imminent loss or destruction of evidence relating to the commission of an indictable offence. The second circumstance contemplated by this section is where the officer is making a warrantless entry as authorized by s. 529.3 as a result of the exigent circumstances there set out. The officer may only enter the dwelling-house if the officer has, immediately before entering, reasonable grounds to suspect that prior announcement would expose the officer or another person to imminent bodily harm or death or the officer has reasonable grounds to believe that prior announcement would result in the imminent loss or destruction of evidence relating to the commission of an indictable offence. It would seem that, in enacting this section, Parliament did not necessarily intend to exclude other circumstances where, at common law and consistent with the Charter, entry without prior announcement is authorized. This provision and the companion provisions in ss. 529 to 529.2 and s. 529.5 were apparently enacted in response to the decision of the Supreme Court of Canada in *R. v. Feeney*, [1997] 2 S.C.R. 13, 115 C.C.C. (3d) 129, noted above under s. 529.

ANNOTATIONS

Note: the following cases were decided prior to the enactment of this section.

At common law, except in exigent circumstances, the requirements of prior announcement by police officers include giving notice of presence by knocking or ringing the doorbell, giving notice of authority by identifying themselves as law enforcement police officers and giving notice of purpose by stating a lawful reason for entry. Further, before forcing entry, police should, at a minimum, request admission and have admission denied: *R. v. Feeney*, [1997] 2 S.C.R. 13, 115 C.C.C. (3d) 129.

The requirement of prior announcement is not limited to a forcible entry and applies even where the officers enter private premises through an open door for the purpose of effecting an arrest, unless in the circumstances the open door can be construed as an invitation to enter: *R. v. Delong* (1989), 47 C.C.C. (3d) 402 (Ont. C.A.).

TELEWARRANT

529.5 If a peace officer believes that it would be impracticable in the circumstances to appear personally before a judge or justice to make an application for a warrant under section 529.1 or an authorization under section 529 or 529.4, the warrant or authorization may be issued on an information submitted by telephone or other means of telecommunication and, for that purpose, section 487.1 applies, with any modifications that the circumstances require, to the warrant or authorization. 1997, c. 39, s. 2.

CROSS-REFERENCES

"Justice" and "peace officer" are defined in s. 2. A warrant to arrest may be issued under various provisions of this Act. The most important provision is s. 507. Sections 511 and 512 set out the contents of the arrest warrant. Section 514 contains other provisions concerning execution of an arrest warrant. Under s. 20, a warrant may be executed on a holiday. A warrant is executed in accordance with ss. 29 and 10 of the Charter. For protection of persons executing warrants, see ss. 25 to 28. Section 528 deals with endorsing the warrant where the warrant cannot be executed in accordance with s. 514. Section 529 permits a justice or judge to include a term in an arrest warrant authorizing a peace officer to enter a dwelling-house for the purpose of arresting or apprehending a person. Section 529.1 permits a justice or judge to issue a warrant authorizing a peace officer to enter a dwelling-house for the purpose of arresting or apprehending a person, where a warrant is already in force anywhere in Canada or where grounds exist for a warrantless arrest. Section 529.2 requires the justice or judge to include terms and conditions in the warrant to ensure that the entry is reasonable in the circumstances. Section 529.3 allows for warrantless entry to effect an arrest in exigent circumstances. Section 529.4 sets out the circumstances in which a peace officer may enter without prior announcement. The provisions respecting issuance of a telewarrant are set out in s. 487.1.

Section 34.1 of the *Interpretation Act*, R.S.C. 1985, c. I-21, provides that any person who may issue a warrant to arrest or apprehend a person under any other Act of Parliament may also authorize entry into a dwelling-house to effect the arrest and without prior announcement.

SYNOPSIS

This section permits application for a telewarrant where it is impracticable to appear personally before a judge or justice to obtain a warrant to enter a dwelling-house or the authorization to enter or enter without announcement under s. 529 or s. 529.4.

Part XVII / LANGUAGE OF ACCUSED

LANGUAGE OF ACCUSED / Idem / Accused to be advised of right / Remand / Variation of order / Circumstances warranting order directing trial in both official languages.

530. (1) On application by an accused whose language is one of the official languages of Canada, made not later than

 (a) the time of the appearance of the accused at which his trial date is set, if

  (i)   he is accused of an offence mentioned in section 553 or punishable on summary conviction, or

  (ii) the accused is to be tried on an indictment preferred under section 577,

 (b) the time of the accused's election, if the accused elects under section 536 to be tried by a provincial court judge or under section 536.1 to be tried by a judge without a jury and without having a preliminary inquiry, or

    (*c*) the time when the accused is ordered to stand trial, if the accused

        (i) is charged with an offence listed in section **469**,

        (ii) has elected to be tried by a court composed of a judge or a judge and jury, or

        (iii) is deemed to have elected to be tried by a court composed of a judge and jury,

a justice of the peace, provincial court judge or judge of the Nunavut Court of Justice shall grant an order directing that the accused be tried before a justice of the peace, provincial court judge, judge or judge and jury, as the case may be, who speak the official language of Canada that is the language of the accused or, if the circumstances warrant, who speak both official languages of Canada.

(2) On application by an accused whose language is not one of the official languages of Canada, made not later than whichever of the times referred to in paragraphs (1)(*a*) to (*c*) is applicable, a justice of the peace or provincial court judge may grant an order directing that the accused be tried before a justice of the peace, provincial court judge, judge or judge and jury, as the case may be, who speak the official language of Canada in which the accused, in the opinion of the justice or provincial court judge, can best give testimony or, if the circumstances warrant, who speak both official languages of Canada.

(3) The justice of the peace or provincial court judge before whom an accused first appears shall ensure that they are advised of their right to apply for an order under subsection (1) or (2) and of the time before which such an application must be made.

(4) Where an accused fails to apply for an order under subsection (1) or (2) and the justice of the peace, provincial court judge or judge before whom the accused is to be tried, in this Part referred to as "the court", is satisfied that it is in the best interests of justice that the accused be tried before a justice of the peace, provincial court judge, judge or judge and jury who speak the official language of Canada that is the language of the accused or, if the language of the accused is not one of the official languages of Canada, the official language of Canada in which the accused, in the opinion of the court, can best give testimony, the court may, if it does not speak that language, by order remand the accused to be tried by a justice of the peace, provincial court judge, judge or judge and jury, as the case may be, who speak that language or, if the circumstances warrant, who speak both official languages of Canada.

(5) An order under this section that a trial be held in one of the official languages of Canada may, if the circumstances warrant, be varied by the court to require that it be held in both official languages of Canada, and vice versa.

(6) The facts that two or more accused who are to be tried together are each entitled to be tried before a justice of the peace, provincial court judge, judge or judge and jury who speak one of the official languages of Canada and that those official languages are different may constitute circumstances that warrant that an order be granted directing that they be tried before a justice of the peace, provincial court judge, judge or judge and jury who speak both official languages of Canada. 1977-78, c. 36, s. 1; R.S.C. 1985, c. 27 (1st Supp.), s. 94; 1999, c. 3, s. 34; 2008, c. 18, s. 18.

CROSS-REFERENCES

The terms "justice" and "provincial court judge" are defined in s. 2.

    The procedure respecting conduct of the proceedings is set out in s. 530.1. Change of venue where necessary to facilitate the trial where an order is made under this section is provided for in s. 531. This Part does not derogate from other rights which may be afforded by provincial legislation, by virtue of s. 532. Provision for making regulations to carry out the provisions of this Part is provided for in s. 533. Where an order is made under this section, s. 530.01 requires the public prosecutor, on application of the accused, to provide a copy of the information or indictment translated into the official language used by the accused. Under s. 530.2, if an order is made for a bilingual proceeding, the judicial officer may make an order setting out the circumstances in which the prosecutor, justice and judge may use each official language. The order shall, to the extent possible, respect the right of the accused to use their official language. Section 531 provides for a change of venue, other than in New Brunswick, if the order under this section cannot be conveniently complied with in the territorial division in which the offence would ordinarily be tried.

Also see s. 841(3) which requires that any preprinted portions of a form set out in Part XXVIII shall be printed in both official languages.

SYNOPSIS

This section sets out the procedure whereby an accused can elect to be tried before a court (including a jury) which speaks one *or both* official languages.

Subsection (1), which deals with an accused whose mother tongue is either French or English, provides that the application in this regard shall be made not later than the time a trial date is fixed where: (a) the offence is indictable, but within the absolute jurisdiction of a provincial court judge; (b) the offence is a summary conviction matter; (c) proceedings are commenced by way of a "direct" indictment (s. 577), or (d) the accused "elects" to be tried before a provincial court judge. In cases where there is a preliminary inquiry, the application need not be made until the accused has been ordered to stand trial.

Under subsec. (2) a similar application can be made by an accused whose mother tongue is not one of the two official languages but who is able to testify in one, or both, of them.

Subsection (3) imposes upon the justice of the peace or provincial court judge before whom the accused first appears an obligation to ensure that the accused is advised of his or her rights in this regard.

Even if no application is made by the accused under this provision, subsec. (4) empowers the trial court to make the necessary order if it is satisfied that to do so would be in the best interests of the administration of justice. If the justice of the peace or judge who makes the order does not speak the necessary language(s), he can remand the accused to appear before someone who does.

Subsection (5) provides that any order made under this provision for a trial in only one official language can, if circumstances warrant, be varied to encompass both languages and vice versa. Under subsec. (6), one basis for making such an order is that accused who are to be tried together speak different official languages.

ANNOTATIONS

Constitutional considerations – In the companion cases of *Manitoba (Attorney General) v. Forest*, [1979] 2 S.C.R. 1032, 49 C.C.C. (2d) 353 (7:0), and *Quebec (Attorney General) v. Blaikie; Quebec (Attorney General) v. Laurier*, [1979] 2 S.C.R. 1016, 49 C.C.C. (2d) 359 (7:0), provincial legislation in Manitoba and Quebec respectively making English in the former and French in the latter the official language of, *inter alia,* the courts was held *ultra vires* as being in conflict with the *Manitoba Act, 1870* (Can.), c. 3, as confirmed by the *British North America Act, 1871*, in the case of Manitoba and in conflict with s. 133 of the *British North America Act, 1867*, in the case of Quebec. In both those provinces use of either official language in the courts is an entrenched right.

Section 16(3) of the Charter does not have the effect of constitutionalizing this provision: *R. v. Schneider* (2004), 192 C.C.C. (3d) 1, 247 D.L.R. (4th) 693 (N.S.C.A.), leave to appeal to S.C.C. refused [2005] 2 S.C.R. xi, 198 C.C.C. (3d) vi.

Sections 530 and 530.1 are intended to ensure equal access to the courts by accused persons who speak either official language. Those sections must be given a large and liberal interpretation in order to achieve that objective: *R. v. Munkonda* (2015), 324 C.C.C. (3d) 9 (Ont. C.A.).

"language of the accused" – The term "language of the accused" in this section is either official language to which the accused has a sufficient connection. It does not have to be the dominant language. If the accused has sufficient knowledge of an official language to instruct counsel, he or she will be able to assert that language is his or her language, regardless of his or her ability to speak the official language: *R. v. Beaulac*, [1999] 1 S.C.R. 768, 134 C.C.C. (3d) 481.

Circumstances where order to be made – The combined effect of this section and s. 530.1 is to permit the ordering of a bilingual trial being a trial before a judge and jury who speak both official languages but in which both English and French are used interchangeably as the working languages, depending upon who is speaking and in what context, and interpretation and translation are available if needed. Thus, where different accused, who are alleged to have participated in a common enterprise or conspiracy seek to be tried in different official languages of choice, severance is not mandatory and it would be open to the judge to order a joint bilingual trial: *R. v. Sarrazin* (2005), 195 C.C.C. (3d) 257, 75 O.R. (3d) 485 (Ont. C.A.). Similarly: *R. v. Garcia* (1990), 58 C.C.C. (3d) 43 (Que. S.C.). [And now see subsec. (6) which confirms the appropriateness of a bilingual trial in such circumstances.]

Duty to advise unrepresented accused [subsec. (3)] – It is not necessary for unrepresented accused to identify themselves as French speaking or state a preference for French prior to the judge notifying them of the right to apply for a trial in either official language. This provision, however, did not constitute a Charter violation as ss. 16 and 19 of the Charter do not apply to provincial courts which are established by provincial legislation rather than Parliament: *R. v. MacKenzie* (2004), 181 C.C.C. (3d) 485, 221 N.S.R. (2d) 51 (C.A.), leave to appeal to S.C.C. refused 191 C.C.C. (3d) vi.

Subsection (4) – Where a new trial has been ordered, the application is made under subsec. (4), rather than subsec. (1), and thus the order is discretionary. There is, however, a strong presumption in favour of granting the order because of the similarity between that situation and the one contemplated by subsec. (1): *R. v. Beaulac*, [1999] 1 S.C.R. 768, 134 C.C.C. (3d) 481.

In the context of subsec. (4), the term "best interests of justice" requires that the foremost consideration be the reasons for the delay in making the application. The trial judge must then consider other factors including whether the accused is represented by counsel, the language in which the evidence is available, the language of witnesses, whether a jury has been empanelled, whether witnesses have already testified, whether they are still available, whether proceedings can continue in a different language, the fact that there may be co-accused (which would indicate the need for separate trials), the need for counsel for the accused or the Crown to change, and the language ability of the judge. However, neither trial fairness nor mere administrative inconvenience is a relevant factor. Generally, the best interests of justice will be served by accepting the application of the accused to be tried in his official language. It was an error to refuse the order solely because the accused was fluent in the majority language (in this case English): *R. v. Beaulac, supra*.

Procedure on trial – The accused having requested a trial of a drinking and driving offence to be in the French language, the trial judge did not err in refusing to admit into evidence a breathalyzer certificate which was only in the English language. The Crown had made no attempt at trial to have the certificate translated: *R. v. Boudreau* (1990), 59 C.C.C. (3d) 436, 25 M.V.R. (2d) 103 (N.B.C.A.).

While there may be circumstances in which a court before trial would order translation of a document to enable the accused to make full answer and defence and to have a fair trial, the mere fact that the accused has chosen to have his trial in the French language pursuant to s. 530 does not thereby entitle him to have disclosure from the Crown and police provided to him in the French language: *R. v. Rodrigue* (1994), 91 C.C.C. (3d) 455 (Y.T.S.C.), affd 95 C.C.C. (3d) 129, 26 C.R.R. (2d) 175 (Y.T.C.A.), leave to appeal to S.C.C. refused 99 C.C.C. (3d) vi, 112 W.A.C. 240*n*.

Once an order is made that a trial shall proceed solely in the official language of the accused, the trial should comply with the terms of the order. In this case, the accused was denied the benefit of a trial in French, as the trial judge and Crown continued to speak

English and simply provided the accused with a translator. The judge and prosecutor must communicate in the official language of the accused's choice so that the accused can understand the remarks of the judge and prosecutor in the original language spoken by them at trial: *R. v. Potvin* (2004), 186 C.C.C. (3d) 257, 69 O.R. (3d) 641 (C.A.).

The accused is not required to bring a formal application under this provision in order to have a trial in his official language of choice: *R. v. Dow* (2009), 245 C.C.C. (3d) 368 (Que. C.A.), leave to appeal to S.C.C. refused 245 C.C.C. (3d) vi.

Where one accused requested a trial in English and the other requested a trial in French, the trial judge did not err in ordering a bilingual trial with an interpretor in the circumstances: *R. v. Schneider* (2004), 188 C.C.C. (3d) 137, 226 N.S.R. (2d) 110 (C.A.), leave to appeal to S.C.C. refused 194 C.C.C. (3d) vi.

An order that a trial or preliminary inquiry be held before a judge or justice of the peace who speaks both official languages is an exception to the rule that an accused has an absolute right to a trial before a judge who speaks the official language of the accused. An order that a trial or preliminary inquiry be held before a bilingual judge will be made only "if the circumstances warrant". However, in the case of two or more accused who are to be tried together and who speak different official languages, the trial or preliminary inquiry is really a bilingual trial or preliminary inquiry, in the sense that there are accused who have the right to a trial in each of the two official languages and both rights operate within a single trial. In such cases, the accused retain their right to equal access to proceedings in their language notwithstanding the imposition of a bilingual proceeding, and the court and the prosecution must be bilingual and must not favour either of the official languages: *R. v. Munkonda*, 2015 ONCA 309.

The effect of an order for a bilingual trial or preliminary inquiry under s. 530 is that all court personnel whose presence is necessary to the proper conduct of the proceeding must be bilingual. To the extent that the presence of the court reporter is necessary for the proper conduct of the inquiry or the trial, the judge must ensure that the reporter is bilingual: *R. v. Mukonda, supra*.

TRANSLATION OF DOCUMENTS / Original version prevails.

530.01 (1) If an order is granted under section 530, a prosecutor — other than a private prosecutor — shall, on application by the accused,

    (*a*) **cause any portion of an information or indictment against the accused that is in an official language that is not that of the accused or that in which the accused can best give testimony to be translated into the other official language; and**

    (*b*) **provide the accused with a written copy of the translated text at the earliest possible time.**

(2) In the case of a discrepancy between the original version of a document and the translated text, the original version shall prevail. 2008, c. 18, s. 19.

SYNOPSIS
This section requires that a public prosecution provide translated copies of the indictment or information. If there is a discrepancy, the original prevails.

IF ORDER GRANTED.

530.1 If an order is granted under section 530,

    (*a*) **the accused and his counsel have the right to use either official language for all purposes during the preliminary inquiry and trial of the accused;**

    (*b*) **the accused and his counsel may use either official language in written pleadings or other documents used in any proceedings relating to the preliminary inquiry or trial of the accused;**

    (*c*) **any witness may give evidence in either official language during the preliminary inquiry or trial;**

(*c*.1) the presiding justice or judge may, if the circumstances warrant, authorize the prosecutor to examine or cross-examine a witness in the official language of the witness even though it is not that of the accused or that in which the accused can best give testimony;

(*d*) the accused has a right to have a justice presiding over the preliminary inquiry who speaks the official language of the accused or both official languages, as the case may be;

(*e*) the accused has a right to have a prosecutor — other than a private prosecutor — who speaks the official language of the accused or both official languages, as the case may be;

(*f*) the court shall make interpreters available to assist the accused, his counsel or any witness during the preliminary inquiry or trial;

(*g*) the record of proceedings during the preliminary inquiry or trial shall include

   (i) a transcript of everything that was said during those proceedings in the official language in which it was said,

  (ii) a transcript of any interpretation into the other official language of what was said, and

 (iii) any documentary evidence that was tendered during those proceedings in the official language in which it was tendered; and

(*h*) any trial judgment, including any reasons given therefor, issued in writing in either official language, shall be made available by the court in the official language that is the language of the accused. R.S.C. 1985, c. 31 (4th Supp.), s. 94; 2008, c. 18, s. 20.

CROSS-REFERENCES

The terms "justice" and "provincial court judge" are defined in s. 2.

Change of venue, where necessary to facilitate the trial where an order is made under s. 530, is provided for in s. 531. This Part does not derogate from other rights which may be afforded by provincial legislation, by virtue of s. 532. Provision for making regulations to carry out the provisions of this Part is provided for in s. 533.

Also see s. 841(3) which requires that any preprinted portions of a form set out in Part XXVIII shall be printed in both official languages.

Where an order is made under s. 530, s. 530.01 requires the public prosecutor, on application of the accused, to provide a copy of the information or indictment translated into the official language used by the accused. Under s. 530.2, if an order is made for a bilingual proceeding, the judicial officer may make an order setting out the circumstances in which the prosecutor, justice and judge may use each official language. The order shall, to the extent possible, respect the right of the accused to use their official language. Section 531 provides for a change of venue, other than in New Brunswick, if the order under s. 530 cannot be conveniently complied with in the territorial division in which the offence would ordinarily be tried.

SYNOPSIS

This section deals with the effect of an order made under s. 530. Where there is such an order, this section provides that: (a) the accused and defence counsel have the right to use either official language during the preliminary inquiry or trial; (b) the accused and defence counsel may use pleadings and documents in either official language during such proceedings; (c) any witness may give evidence in either official language; (c.1) the justice or judge may authorize the prosecutor to examine or cross-examine the witness, in the witness's official language; (d) the accused has the right to have a justice presiding over the preliminary inquiry who speaks the official language of the accused; (e) except in the case of private prosecutions, the accused has the right to a prosecutor who speaks the official language of the accused or is bilingual as the case may be; (f) interpreters shall be made available as required to the accused, defence counsel and witnesses during the preliminary inquiry or trial (this is also required by s. 14 of the *Canadian Charter of Rights and*

Freedoms); (g) the record of the proceedings will be in the official language which was spoken, and will contain any interpretation which was given in the other official language, documents will be in the official language in which they were tendered; and (h) any written reasons will be made available in the official language of the accused.

ANNOTATIONS

This section is valid and applicable in Quebec. Where an order is made under s. 530, this section imposes an obligation on the Attorney General to choose a Crown counsel who is capable and agrees to conduct the trial in the official language of the accused. If it happens that during the trial this Crown counsel feels unable to proceed with the case in the language of the accused, s. 133 of the *Constitution Act, 1867* permits the counsel in Quebec to speak in French or English as the case may be. However, in such circumstances the judge should adjourn the trial to permit the Attorney General to find a replacement ready to continue the case in the language of the accused: *R. v. Cross* (1998), 128 C.C.C. (3d) 161, 165 D.L.R. (4th) 288 (Que. C.A.), leave to appeal to S.C.C. granted 132 C.C.C. (3d) vi, 169 D.L.R. (4th) vi.

This section applies to a bilingual trial, *i.e.* where the trial is ordered to be before a trier or triers who speak both official languages: *R. v. Beaulac*, [1999] 1 S.C.R. 768, 134 C.C.C. (3d) 481.

All Crown prosecutors in a bilingual trial must be bilingual and capable of participating fully in the trial in both languages: *R. v. Munkonda* (2015), 324 C.C.C. (3d) 9 (Ont. C.A.).

The accused could not be said to have waived his rights where on two occasions the judge asked the accused if it was agreeable if he spoke with counsel about certain legal matters in French and the accused gave his consent: *R. v. Dow* (2009), 245 C.C.C. (3d) 368 (Que. C.A.), leave to appeal to S.C.C. refused 245 C.C.C. (3d) vi.

Where the accused had received an order under s. 530 that he be tried in French, the Crown's use of English during an adjournment application violated the accused's right under s. 530.1(*e*). However, the violation was relatively minor and did not warrant setting aside the conviction: *R. v. Bujold* (2011), 276 C.C.C. (3d) 442 (N.B.C.A.).

Section 530.1(*b*) gives the accused the right to use either official language in written pleadings or other documents at the preliminary inquiry and trial. The Crown is not given the same right and must provide the documents in the accused's language. The obligation to make judgments available in the official language of the accused as set out in para. (*h*) applies to all judgments, including interlocutory and oral judgments. A summary or synopsis is not sufficient: *R. v. Munkonda, supra.*

LANGUAGE USED IN PROCEEDING / Right of the accused.

530.2 (1) If an order is granted directing that an accused be tried before a justice of the peace, provincial court judge, judge or judge and jury who speak both official languages, the justice or judge presiding over a preliminary inquiry or trial may, at the start of the proceeding, make an order setting out the circumstances in which, and the extent to which, the prosecutor and the justice or judge may use each official language.

(2) Any order granted under this section shall, to the extent possible, respect the right of the accused to be tried in his or her official language. 2008, c. 18, s. 21.

CROSS-REFERENCES

See Cross-References under s. 530.

SYNOPSIS

This section gives the judge or justice presiding at a bilingual proceeding to make an order setting out the circumstances in which, and the extent to which, the prosecutor, justice or judge may use each official language. The order shall, to the extent possible, respect the right of the accused to be tried in their official language.

ANNOTATIONS

In a bilingual trial or preliminary inquiry, the language rights of each of the accused must be respected to the extent possible, and provided that it is reasonable. The equality of the two official languages is a governing principle that is particularly important in a bilingual trial or preliminary inquiry since both languages, English and French, have the same official status in the proceeding. This means, for example, that, if an accused or his or her counsel addresses the court or the prosecution in the language of that accused, the prosecution or the court should interact with that accused or his or her counsel in that language. The duty to deal with each accused in his or her own language is not diminished if the proceeding becomes a bilingual proceeding. The rights of the accused and the obligation of the state and the court to provide the service are not reduced or diminished by the fact that an accused understands and speaks the language of the majority: *R. v. Munkonda* (2015), 324 C.C.C. (3d) 9 (Ont. C.A.).

CHANGE OF VENUE.

531. Despite any other provision of this Act but subject to any regulations made under section 533, if an order made under section 530 cannot be conveniently complied with in the territorial division in which the offence would otherwise be tried, the court shall, except if that territorial division is in the Province of New Brunswick, order that the trial of the accused be held in another territorial division in the same province. 1977-78, c. 36, s. 1; R.S. 1985, c. 27 (1st Supp.), s. 203; 2008, c. 18, s. 21.

CROSS-REFERENCES

The terms "justice", "provincial court judge" and "territorial division" are defined in s. 2. Procedure for an order for a trial in the official language of the accused is in s. 530. The procedure respecting conduct of the proceedings is set out in s. 530.1. This Part does not derogate from other rights which may be afforded by provincial legislation, by virtue of s. 532. Provision for making regulations to carry out the provisions of this Part is provided for in s. 533.

Also see s. 841(3) which requires that any preprinted portions of a form set out in Part XXVIII shall be printed in both official languages.

Provision for change of venue in other circumstances is provided for in ss. 599 and 600.

SYNOPSIS

This section provides that, except in New Brunswick, subject to any regulations made pursuant to s. 533, the court must make an order changing the venue of the trial of an accused to another location within the province where an order has been made under s. 530, and that order cannot be conveniently complied with in the territorial division in which the offence would otherwise be tried.

It is expected that such orders will be made only in jury trials. In all other situations, court officials will be able to arrange for a justice of the peace or judge fluent in the required language(s) to travel to the area where proceedings would normally be held.

SAVING.

532. Nothing in this Part or the *Official Languages Act* derogates from or otherwise adversely affects any right afforded by a law of a province in force on the coming into force of this Part in that province or thereafter coming into force relating to the language of proceedings or testimony in criminal matters that is not inconsistent with this Part or that Act. 1977-78, c. 36, s. 1.

CROSS-REFERENCES

Procedure for an order for a trial in the official language of the accused is in s. 530.

The procedure respecting conduct of the proceedings is set out in s. 530.1. Change of venue where necessary to facilitate the trial where an order is made under s. 530 is provided for in s. 531. Provision for making regulations to carry out the provisions of this Part is provided for in s. 533.

Also see s. 841(3) which requires that any preprinted portions of a form set out in Part XXVIII shall be printed in both official languages.

ANNOTATIONS

As a result of pre-Confederation legislation still in force in Alberta an accused and his counsel have the right to use the French language for all purposes during his preliminary hearing and trial but the presiding judge or the jury need not be able to comprehend the French language without an interpreter: *R. v. Paquette* (1987), 38 C.C.C. (3d) 333, [1988] 1 W.W.R. 97 (Alta. C.A.). The same pre-Confederation legislation was also considered in Saskatchewan in *R. v. Mercure*, [1988] 1 S.C.R. 234, 39 C.C.C. (3d) 385 (6:2), in relation, however, to a trial of a provincial offence. It was there held that while the defendant was entitled to use French and to have his plea entered in French the defendant did not have the right to insist on a trial before a judge who understood that language without an interpreter.

REGULATIONS.

533. The Lieutenant Governor in Council of a province may make regulations generally for carrying into effect the purposes and provisions of this Part in the province and the Commissioner of Yukon, the Commissioner of the Northwest Territories and the Commissioner of Nunavut may make regulations generally for carrying into effect the purposes and provisions of this Part in Yukon, the Northwest Territories and Nunavut, respectively. 1977-78, c. 36, s. 1; 1993, c. 28, Sch. III, s. 33; 2002, c. 7, s. 144.

CROSS-REFERENCES

Procedure for an order for a trial in the official language of the accused is in s. 530. The procedure respecting conduct of the proceedings is set out in s. 530.1. This Part does not derogate from other rights which may be afforded by provincial legislation, by virtue of s. 532. Change of venue, where necessary to facilitate the trial where an order is made under s. 530, is provided for in s. 531.

Also see s. 841(3) which requires that any preprinted portions of a form set out in Part XXVIII shall be printed in both official languages.

534. [*Repealed*, 1997, c. 18, s. 63.]

Part XVIII / PROCEDURE ON PRELIMINARY INQUIRY

Jurisdiction

INQUIRY BY JUSTICE.

535. If an accused who is charged with an indictable offence is before a justice and a request has been made for a preliminary inquiry under subsection 536(4) or 536.1(3), the justice shall, in accordance with this Part, inquire into the charge and any other indictable offence, in respect of the same transaction, founded on the facts that are disclosed by the evidence taken in accordance with this Part. R.S., c. C-34, s. 463; R.S.C. 1985, c. 27 (1st Supp.), s. 96; 2002, c. 13, s. 24.

CROSS-REFERENCES

The term "justice" is defined in s. 2. As a matter of practice preliminary inquiries are usually conducted by provincial court judges. For further discussion re procedure on preliminary inquiries see *Note on procedure at preliminary inquiry* under s. 537.

SYNOPSIS

This provision confers general jurisdiction on a "justice" to deal with accused persons, in accordance with Part XVIII, who are charged with indictable offences.

Section 2 defines "justice" as including justices of the peace and provincial court judges. Local practice will determine which functions are carried out by a justice and which by a judge. For the most part, it is the provincial court judge who will deal with matters of bail and election, and preside over preliminary inquiries.

ANNOTATIONS

In *R. v. Mairs* (1961), 130 C.C.C. 361, 35 C.R. 265 (B.C.S.C.), it was held, following *R. v. Hughes* (1879), 4 Q.B.D. 614, and *R. v. Shaw* (1865), 10 Cox. C.C. 66, that process is not necessary to the jurisdiction of the justices to hear and adjudicate and that when a person is before justices who have jurisdiction to try the case they need not inquire how he came there but may try it.

If the justice is of the opinion that the charge does not reveal an offence known to law and is an absolute nullity, the accused is not "charged with an indictable offence" and the justice may discharge him without taking evidence: *R. v. Bolduc* (1980), 60 C.C.C. (2d) 357, 20 C.R. (3d) 372 (Que. C.A.), affd [1982] 1 S.C.R. 573, 68 C.C.C. (2d) 413 (7:0).

Aside from determining whether the charge in the information is valid on its face, the justice presiding at a preliminary inquiry has no jurisdiction to inquire into the validity of the allegation contained in the information itself, by embarking on an inquiry as to whether or not the informant had reasonable grounds for swearing the information: *R. v. Hislop* (1983), 7 C.C.C. (3d) 240, 36 C.R. (3d) 29 (Ont. C.A.), leave to appeal to S.C.C. refused November 7, 1983.

REMAND BY JUSTICE TO PROVINCIAL COURT JUDGE IN CERTAIN CASES / Election before justice in certain cases / Procedure where accused elects trial by provincial court judge / Request for preliminary inquiry / Endorsement on the information / Preliminary inquiry if two or more accused / When no request for preliminary inquiry / Jurisdiction.

536. (1) Where an accused is before a justice other than a provincial court judge charged with an offence over which a provincial court judge has absolute jurisdiction under section 553, the justice shall remand the accused to appear before a provincial court judge having jurisdiction in the territorial division in which the offence is alleged to have been committed.

(2) If an accused is before a justice charged with an indictable offence, other than an offence listed in section 469, and the offence is not one over which a provincial court judge has absolute jurisdiction under section 553, the justice shall, after the information has been read to the accused, put the accused to an election in the following words:

> **You have the option to elect to be tried by a provincial court judge without a jury and without having had a preliminary inquiry; or you may elect to be tried by a judge without a jury; or you may elect to be tried by a court composed of a judge and jury. If you do not elect now, you are deemed to have elected to be tried by a court composed of a judge and jury. If you elect to be tried by a judge without a jury or by a court composed of a judge and jury or if you are deemed to have elected to be tried by a court composed of a judge and jury, you will have a preliminary inquiry only if you or the prosecutor requests one. How do you elect to be tried?**

(3) Where an accused elects to be tried by a provincial court judge, the justice shall endorse on the information a record of the election and shall

  (*a*) where the justice is not a provincial court judge, remand the accused to appear and plead to the charge before a provincial court judge having jurisdiction in the territorial division in which the offence is alleged to have been committed; or

  (*b*) where the justice is a provincial court judge, call on the accused to plead to the charge and if the accused does not plead guilty, proceed with the trial or fix a time for the trial.

(4) If an accused elects to be tried by a judge without a jury or by a court composed of a judge and jury or does not elect when put to the election or is deemed under paragraph 565(1)(*b*) to have elected to be tried by a court composed of a judge and jury or is charged with an offence listed in section 469, the justice shall, subject to section 577, on the request of the accused or the prosecutor made at that time or within the period fixed by rules of court made under section 482 or 482.1 or, if there are no such rules, by the justice, hold a preliminary inquiry into the charge.

(4.1) If an accused elects to be tried by a judge without a jury or by a court composed of a judge and jury or does not elect when put to the election or is deemed under paragraph 565(1)(*b*) to have elected to be tried by a court composed of a judge and jury or is charged with an offence listed in section 469, the justice shall endorse on the information and, if the accused is in custody, on the warrant of remand, a statement showing

  (*a*) the nature of the election or deemed election of the accused or that the accused did not elect, as the case may be; and

  (*b*) whether the accused or the prosecutor has requested that a preliminary inquiry be held.

(4.2) If two or more persons are jointly charged in an information and one or more of them make a request for a preliminary inquiry under subsection (4), a preliminary inquiry must be held with respect to all of them.

(4.3) If no request for a preliminary inquiry is made under subsection (4), the justice shall fix the date for the trial or the date on which the accused must appear in the trial court to have the date fixed.

(5) Where a justice before whom a preliminary inquiry is being or is to be held has not commenced to take evidence, any justice having jurisdiction in the province where the offence with which the accused is charged is alleged to have been committed has jurisdiction for the purposes of subsection (4). R.S., c. C-34, s. 464; R.S.C. 1985, c. 27 (1st Supp.), s. 96; 2002, c. 13, s. 25; 2004, c. 12, s. 9.

CROSS-REFERENCES

The terms "justice", "provincial court judge" and "territorial division" are defined in s. 2. Territorial jurisdiction is generally dealt with in Part XIV. The pleas that the accused may enter are set out in ss. 606 to 613. Validity of an information is dealt with in ss. 580 to 601. The jurisdiction of the provincial court judge to try the accused is set out in Part XIX. Where the accused refuses to elect under this section then by virtue of s. 565(1)(c) the accused is deemed to have elected trial by judge and jury. The accused may, however, re-elect in accordance with s. 561. Where accused who are jointly charged fail to elect the same mode of trial, pursuant to s. 567, the justice may decline to record the elections and the accused are deemed to have elected trial by judge and jury under s. 565(1)(b). Where the accused or the prosecutor request a preliminary inquiry the party making the request is to identify the issues and the witnesses required under s. 536.3. The justice may hold a hearing under s. 536.4 to assist in managing the conduct of the hearing. Under s. 536.5 the parties may agree to limit the scope of the preliminary inquiry and the agreement is then filed with the court. An election or re-election by an accused in respect of mode of trial may be made in writing without the accused's attendance.